CRIMINAL PROCEDURE

West's Criminal Practice Series

THIRD EDITION

By

Wayne R. LaFave
David C. Baum Professor of Law Emeritus and
Center for Advanced Study Professor Emeritus,
University of Illinois

Jerold H. Israel
Ed Root Eminent Scholar in Trial Advocacy and Procedure,
University of Florida, Levin College of Law
and Alene and Allan F. Smith Professor of Law Emeritus,
University of Michigan

Nancy J. King
Lee S. and Charles A. Speir Professor of Law,
Vanderbilt University

and

Orin S. Kerr
Professor of Law, George Washington University

Volume 7
Sections 27.1 to End
Tables-Index

THOMSON

WEST

For Customer Assistance Call 1-800-328-4880

Mat #40612872

ISBN 978-0-314-97876-9

WESTLAW® ELECTRONIC RESEARCH GUIDE

WESTLAW, COMPUTER® ASSISTED LEGAL RESEARCH

Westlaw is part of the research system provided by West, a Thomson business. With Westlaw, you find the same quality and integrity that you have come to expect from West books. For the most current and comprehensive legal research, combine the strengths of West books and Westlaw.

Westlaw Adds to Your Library

Whether you wish to expand or update your research, Westlaw can help. For instance, Westlaw is the most current source for case law, including slip opinions and unreported decisions. In addition to case law, the online availability of statutes, statutory indexes, legislation, court rules and orders, administrative materials, looseleaf publications, texts, periodicals, news and business information makes Westlaw an important asset to any library. Check the online Westlaw Directory or the print Westlaw Database Directory for a list of available databases and services. The following is a brief description of some of the capabilities that Westlaw offers.

Natural Language Searching

You can search most Westlaw databases using WIN®, the revolutionary Natural Language search method. As an alternative to formulating a query using terms and connectors, WIN allows you to simply enter a description of your research issue in plain English:

> What is the government's obligation to warn military
> personnel of the danger of past exposure to radiation?

Westlaw then retrieves the set of documents that have the highest statistical likelihood of matching your description.

Retrieving a Specific Document

When you know the citation to a case or statute that is not in your library, use the Find service to retrieve the document on Westlaw. Access Find and type a citation like the following:

> 181 ne2d 520
> in st 27–1–12–1

Updating Your Research

You can use Westlaw to update your research in many ways:

- Retrieve cases citing a particular statute.
- Update a state or federal statute by accessing the Update service from the displayed statute using the Jump marker.
- Retrieve newly enacted legislation by searching in the appropriate legislative service database.
- Retrieve cases not yet reported by searching in case law databases.
- Read the latest U.S. Supreme Court opinions within an hour of their release.
- Update West digests by searching with topic and key numbers.

Determining Case History and Retrieving Cited Cases

KeyCite®, the new citation research service developed by West and made available through the Westlaw computer-assisted legal research service, integrates all the case law on Westlaw, giving you the power to

- trace the history of a case;
- retrieve a list of all cases on Westlaw that cite to a case; and
- track legal issues in a case.

Citing references from the extensive library of secondary sources on Westlaw, such as ALR® annotations and law review articles, are covered by KeyCite as well. You can use these citing references to find case discussions by legal experts.

In addition, KeyCite is completely integrated with West's Key Number System so that it provides the tools for navigating the case law databases on Westlaw. Only KeyCite combines the up-to-the-minute case-verification functions of an online citator service with the case-finding tools needed to find relevant case law.

Additional Information

For more detailed information or assistance, contact your Westlaw account representative or call 1–800–REF–ATTY (1–800–733–2889).

RELATED PRODUCTS FROM WEST

West's Criminal Practice Series

Search and Seizure, Fourth Edition
Wayne R. LaFave

Substantive Criminal Law, Second Edition
Wayne R. LaFave

Criminal Law Defenses
Paul H. Robinson

Criminal Procedure, Third Edition
Wayne R. LaFave, Jerold H. Israel, Nancy J. King and Orin S. Kerr

Federal Sentencing Law and Practice
Thomas W. Hutchison, Peter B. Hoffman, Deborah Young
and Sigmund G. Popko

**Federal Grand Jury: A Guide to Law and Practice,
Second Edition**
Susan W. Brenner and Lori E. Shaw

**Federal Practice and Procedure
Vols. 1, 2, 3 and 3A – Criminal**
Charles Alan Wright

**Federal Jury Practice and Instructions
Civil and Criminal**
Kevin F. O'Malley, Jay E. Grenig and William C. Lee

Federal Criminal Rules Handbook
Laurie L. Levenson

Federal Criminal Code and Rules Pamphlet

Federal Sentencing Guidelines Manual
United States Sentencing Commission

West's State Practice Series

West has the following specialized criminal practice and procedure volumes in the state practice series:

Arizona Criminal Procedure Forms

California Jury Instructions – Criminal

Colorado Jury Instructions – Criminal

Connecticut Criminal Jury Instructions

Illinois Criminal Practice and Procedure

Illinois Pattern Jury Instructions – Criminal

Indiana Criminal Procedure

Westlaw Criminal Justice Databases

Westlaw®

WIN®

WEST*Check*® and *WESTMATE*®

KeyCite®

West CD-ROM Libraries®
West Books, CD-ROM Libraries, Disk Products and Westlaw
The Ultimate Research System

———————

If you would like to inquire about these West publications or place an order, please call 1–800–344–5009.

West
610 Opperman Drive
Eagan, MN 55123

Visit West on the Internet:
http://west.thomson.com

Summary of Contents

Volume 1

PART I INTRODUCTION AND OVERVIEW

Chapter 1 An Overview of the Criminal Justice
Process... 1

Chapter 2 The Constitutionalization of Criminal
Procedure 515

Volume 2

PART II DETECTION AND INVESTIGATION OF CRIME

Chapter 3 Arrest, Search and Seizure 1

Chapter 4 Network Surveillance 445

Chapter 5 Police "Encouragement" and the Entrapment
Defense 553

Chapter 6 Interrogation and Confessions 601

Chapter 7 Identification Procedures 889

Volume 3

**PART II DETECTION AND INVESTIGATION OF CRIME
(CONTINUED)**

Chapter 8 Grand Jury Investigation 1

Chapter 9 Scope of the Exclusionary Rules 379

Chapter 10 Administration of the Exclusionary Rules .. 505

PART III THE COMMENCEMENT OF FORMAL PROCEEDINGS

Chapter 11 The Right to Counsel 565

Volume 4

PART III THE COMMENCEMENT OF FORMAL PROCEEDINGS (CONTINUED)

Chapter 12 Pretrial Release 1

Chapter 13 The Decision Whether to Prosecute 109

Chapter 14 The Preliminary Hearing 273

Chapter 15 Grand Jury Review 377

Chapter 16 The Location of the Prosecution 691

Volume 5

PART III THE COMMENCEMENT OF FORMAL PROCEEDINGS (CONTINUED)

Chapter 17 The Scope of the Prosecution: Joinder and Severance 1

Chapter 18 Speedy Trial and Other Prompt Disposition 105

PART IV THE ADVERSARY SYSTEM AND THE DETERMINATION OF GUILT AND INNOCENCE

Chapter 19 The Accusatory Pleading 205

Chapter 20 Pretrial Discovery 341

Chapter 21 Pleas of Guilty 519

Volume 6

PART IV THE ADVERSARY SYSTEM AND THE DETERMINATION OF GUILT AND INNOCENCE (CONTINUED)

Chapter 22 Trial by Jury and Impartial Judge 1

Chapter 23 Fair Trial and Free Press 191

Chapter 24 The Criminal Trial 299

Chapter 25 Double Jeopardy 573

Volume 7

PART V POST-CONVICTION REVIEW: APPEALS AND COLLATERAL REMEDIES

Summary of Contents by Section

Volume 1

PART I INTRODUCTION AND OVERVIEW

Chapter 1 An Overview of the Criminal Justice Process

§ 1.1 The subject under inquiry.................................... 3
§ 1.2 Considering state and federal criminal justice processes. 7
§ 1.3 Similarities and differences in the laws of fifty-two
      jurisdictions 80
§ 1.4 The agencies of administration and their organizational
      structures... 106
§ 1.5 The cornerstone objectives of the process 141
§ 1.6 Historical development of the process 245
§ 1.7 The laws regulating the process............................. 338
§ 1.8 Procedural subsets 398
§ 1.9 Deviance, discretion, and the limits of legal regulation .. 421
§ 1.10 Administrative policies and the local administrative
      setting... 457
§ 1.11 Criminal justice statistics................................... 505

**Chapter 2 The Constitutionalization of Criminal
Procedure**

§ 2.1 The elements of constitutionalization....................... 516
§ 2.2 The Fourteenth Amendment and the extension of the
      bill of rights guarantees to the states 534
§ 2.3 Total incorporation.. 538
§ 2.4 Fundamental fairness 570
§ 2.5 Selective incorporation 619
§ 2.6 Application of the selective incorporation doctrine........ 643
§ 2.7 The independent content of due process.................... 668
§ 2.8 The preference for expansive interpretations 723
§ 2.9 Guideposts for constitutional interpretation 747
§ 2.10 Applying interpretive guideposts: the case of the
      privilege against self-incrimination....................... 827
§ 2.11 The non-retroactivity doctrine 864
§ 2.12 The influence of federal constitutional rulings upon
      state constitutional law.................................... 883

Volume 2

PART II DETECTION AND INVESTIGATION OF CRIME

Chapter 3 Arrest, Search and Seizure
§ 3.1 The Fourth Amendment exclusionary rule and other remedies 3
§ 3.2 Protected areas and interests........................... 61
§ 3.3 Probable cause.. 105
§ 3.4 Search warrants.. 150
§ 3.5 Seizure and search of persons and personal effects 198
§ 3.6 Entry and search of premises.......................... 238
§ 3.7 Search and seizure of vehicles......................... 268
§ 3.8 Stop and frisk and similar lesser intrusions 300
§ 3.9 Inspections and regulatory searches 351
§ 3.10 Consent searches.. 405

Chapter 4 Network Surveillance
§ 4.1 Introduction 446
§ 4.2 Postal mail 446
§ 4.3 Telephone surveillance and the Fourth Amendment 451
§ 4.4 Internet communications and the Fourth Amendment 456
§ 4.5 Overview of statutory protections 464
§ 4.6 The Wiretap Act 467
§ 4.7 The Pen Register statute 521
§ 4.8 The Stored Communications Act........................ 529
§ 4.9 Foreign intelligence surveillance 544

Chapter 5 Police "Encouragement" and the Entrapment Defense
§ 5.1 Encouragement of crime and the defense of entrapment .. 553
§ 5.2 Subjective versus objective test for entrapment............ 561
§ 5.3 Procedural considerations re entrapment defense 578
§ 5.4 Other challenges to encouragement practices 587

Chapter 6 Interrogation and Confessions
§ 6.1 Introduction and overview confessions 602
§ 6.2 The "voluntariness" test.................................. 608
§ 6.3 The prompt appearance requirement....................... 648
§ 6.4 The right to counsel re interrogation 658
§ 6.5 The privilege against self-incrimination; *Miranda* 700
§ 6.6 *Miranda*: When interrogation is "custodial" 720
§ 6.7 *Miranda*: "Interrogation"................................. 752
§ 6.8 *Miranda*: Required warnings 794
§ 6.9 *Miranda*: Waiver of rights 813
§ 6.10 *Miranda*: Nature of offense, interrogator, and proceedings.. 870

Chapter 7 Identification Procedures
§ 7.1 Introduction to identification............................... 889
§ 7.2 The privilege against self-incrimination and identification... 895
§ 7.3 The right to counsel and to confrontation re

identification... 905
§ 7.4 Due process and identification: "The totality of the circumstances"... 929
§ 7.5 Additional possible safeguards re identification............. 968

Volume 3

PART II DETECTION AND INVESTIGATION OF CRIME (CONTINUED)

Chapter 8 Grand Jury Investigation

§ 8.1 The investigative grand jury................................. 3
§ 8.2 Historical development of the grand jury 10
§ 8.3 Investigative advantages of the grand jury 22
§ 8.4 The legal structure of the investigative grand jury 38
§ 8.5 Grand jury secrecy....................................... 64
§ 8.6 The right to every man's evidence 139
§ 8.7 Fourth Amendment challenges to subpoenas 151
§ 8.8 Challenges to misuse of the subpoena authority 177
§ 8.9 Grand jury inquiries based on illegally obtained evidence... 230
§ 8.10 Grand jury testimony and the privilege against self-incrimination 238
§ 8.11 Self-incrimination immunity and compelled testimony ... 269
§ 8.12 Self-incrimination and the compulsory production of documents 298
§ 8.13 Application of the act-of-production doctrine.............. 324
§ 8.14 The grand jury witness' right to counsel 366

Chapter 9 Scope of the Exclusionary Rules

§ 9.1 Standing: the "personal rights" approach.................... 379
§ 9.2 Standing: other possible bases 409
§ 9.3 "Fruit of the poisonous tree" theories 418
§ 9.4 Fruits of illegal arrests and searches 439
§ 9.5 Fruits of illegally obtained confessions..................... 466
§ 9.6 Permissible use of illegally obtained evidence at trial 485

Chapter 10 Administration of the Exclusionary Rules

§ 10.1 The pretrial motion to suppress 505
§ 10.2 Waiver or forfeiture of objection re suppression of evidence... 515
§ 10.3 Burden of proof at suppression hearing 523
§ 10.4 Standard of proof at suppression hearing................. 536
§ 10.5 The suppression hearing 542
§ 10.6 The suppression hearing ruling and its effect 554

PART III THE COMMENCEMENT OF FORMAL PROCEEDINGS

Chapter 11 The Right to Counsel

§ 11.1 The constitutional rights to retained and appointed counsel... 566
§ 11.2 Scope of the indigent's right to counsel and other assistance 608
§ 11.3 Waiver of the right to counsel............................ 678
§ 11.4 Choice of counsel.. 695
§ 11.5 The constitutional right to self-representation 731
§ 11.6 Counsel's control over defense strategy 770
§ 11.7 The right to effective assistance of counsel: guiding principles... 808
§ 11.8 Ineffective assistance claims based upon state interference and other extrinsic factors 840
§ 11.9 Ineffective assistance claims based upon attorney conflicts of interest..................................... 864
§ 11.10 Ineffective assistance claims based upon lawyer incompetence 940

Volume 4

PART III THE COMMENCEMENT OF FORMAL PROCEEDINGS (CONTINUED)

Chapter 12 Pretrial Release

§ 12.1 Pretrial release procedures 1
§ 12.2 Constitutionality of limits on pretrial freedom 26
§ 12.3 Constitutionality of mandating pretrial detention 41
§ 12.4 Special situations re release 79
§ 12.5 Alternatives to arrest...................................... 100

Chapter 13 The Decision Whether to Prosecute

§ 13.1 Nature of the decision whether to prosecute.............. 110
§ 13.2 Discretionary enforcement 120
§ 13.3 Challenges to and checks upon the decision not to prosecute 151
§ 13.4 Challenging the decision to prosecute: equal protection.. 168
§ 13.5 Other challenges to the decision to prosecute............. 198
§ 13.6 Challenges to the decision to forego or terminate diversion... 238
§ 13.7 Challenges to the charge selection 252

Chapter 14 The Preliminary Hearing

§ 14.1 Functions of the preliminary hearing...................... 273
§ 14.2 Defendant's right to a preliminary hearing 291
§ 14.3 The preliminary hearing bindover determination 317
§ 14.4 Preliminary hearing procedures............................ 340

Chapter 15 Grand Jury Review

§ 15.1 Defendant's right to prosecution by indictment 378
§ 15.2 The structure of grand jury screening 450
§ 15.3 The effectiveness of grand jury screening 498
§ 15.4 Indictment challenges based on grand jury composition
       deficiencies 514
§ 15.5 Indictment challenges based on evidentiary deficiencies . 563
§ 15.6 Indictment challenges based on misconduct: general
       principles 596
§ 15.7 Indictment challenges based on misconduct: common
       claims 646

Chapter 16 The Location of the Prosecution

§ 16.1 Venue: general principles 691
§ 16.2 Applying the crime-committed formula to establish
       venue 758
§ 16.3 Change of venue 804
§ 16.4 Jurisdiction 829

Volume 5

PART III THE COMMENCEMENT OF FORMAL PROCEEDINGS (CONTINUED)

Chapter 17 The Scope of the Prosecution: Joinder and Severance

§ 17.1 Joinder and severance of offenses 1
§ 17.2 Joinder and severance of defendants 17
§ 17.3 Joinder and severance: procedural considerations 48
§ 17.4 Failure to join related offenses 59

Chapter 18 Speedy Trial and Other Prompt Disposition

§ 18.1 The constitutional right to speedy trial 105
§ 18.2 The constitutional balancing test re speedy trial 116
§ 18.3 Statutes and court rules on speedy trial 132
§ 18.4 Speedy trial and the imprisoned defendant 162
§ 18.5 The right to other speedy disposition 184

PART IV THE ADVERSARY SYSTEM AND THE DETERMINATION OF GUILT AND INNOCENCE

Chapter 19 The Accusatory Pleading

§ 19.1 The liberalization of pleading requirements 206
§ 19.2 Pleading functions 222
§ 19.3 Basic pleading defects 247
§ 19.4 Bill of particulars 299
§ 19.5 Amendments of the pleading 308
§ 19.6 Variances and pleadings 328

Chapter 20 Pretrial Discovery

§ 20.1 The expansion of discovery 342
§ 20.2 The structure of discovery law 359

§ 20.3 Defense discovery 381
§ 20.4 Constitutional limitations upon pretrial discovery for
      the prosecution 440
§ 20.5 Prosecution discovery provisions 473
§ 20.6 Sanctions for discovery violations 492

Chapter 21 Pleas of Guilty
§ 21.1 The plea negotiation system 520
§ 21.2 Kept, broken, rejected and nonexistent bargains 559
§ 21.3 Plea negotiation responsibilities of the attorneys and
      judge 694
§ 21.4 Receiving the defendant's plea 788
§ 21.5 Challenge of guilty plea by defendant 860
§ 21.6 Effect of guilty plea 905

Volume 6

PART IV THE ADVERSARY SYSTEM AND THE DETERMINATION OF GUILT AND INNOCENCE (CONTINUED)

Chapter 22 Trial by Jury and Impartial Judge
§ 22.1 The right to jury trial 2
§ 22.2 Selection of prospective jurors 42
§ 22.3 Voir dire; challenges 71
§ 22.4 Challenging the judge 165
§ 22.5 Challenging the prosecutor 179

Chapter 23 Fair Trial and Free Press
§ 23.1 Preventing prejudicial publicity 191
§ 23.2 Overcoming prejudicial publicity 262
§ 23.3 Conduct of the trial 292

Chapter 24 The Criminal Trial
§ 24.1 The right to a public trial 300
§ 24.2 Presence of the defendant 309
§ 24.3 The defendant's right of access to evidence 339
§ 24.4 The presentation of evidence 405
§ 24.5 Defendant's rights to remain silent and to testify 423
§ 24.6 Trial court evaluation of the evidence 438
§ 24.7 The arguments of counsel 451
§ 24.8 Jury instructions 476
§ 24.9 Jury procedures 510
§ 24.10 Jury verdicts 543
§ 24.11 Post-verdict motions 559

Chapter 25 Double Jeopardy
§ 25.1 Dimensions of the guarantee 573
§ 25.2 Reprosecution following mistrial 606
§ 25.3 Reprosecution following acquittal or dismissal 627
§ 25.4 Reprosecution following conviction 640
§ 25.5 Reprosecution by a different sovereign 657

Chapter 26 Sentencing Procedures

§ 26.1 Legislative structuring of sentencing: sanctions 668
§ 26.2 Legislative structuring of sentencing: the allocation of
       sentencing authority 698
§ 26.3 The guidance of judicial sentencing discretion 718
§ 26.4 Due process: the framework for sentencing procedure .. 741
§ 26.5 Sentencing information 801
§ 26.6 Special sentences 817
§ 26.7 Resentencing: double jeopardy 834
§ 26.8 Resentencing: the prohibition against vindictiveness.... 849
§ 26.9 Probation conditions....................................... 860
§ 26.10 Revocation of probation 880

Volume 7

PART V POST-CONVICTION REVIEW: APPEALS AND COLLATERAL REMEDIES

Chapter 27 Appeals

§ 27.1 Constitutional protection of the defendant's right to
      appeal.. 2
§ 27.2 Defense appeals and the final judgment rule 7
§ 27.3 Prosecution appeals... 31
§ 27.4 Review by writ 46
§ 27.5 The scope of appellate review.............................. 61
§ 27.6 Harmless error on appeal 99

Chapter 28 Post Conviction Review: Collateral Remedies

§ 28.1 Current collateral remedies and historical antecedents. 138
§ 28.2 The statutory structure and habeas policy 144
§ 28.3 Claims cognizable in habeas............................ 164
§ 28.4 Claims in habeas foreclosed by state procedural
      defaults.. 189
§ 28.5 Claims in habeas foreclosed due to premature,
      successive, or delayed applications...................... 213
§ 28.6 Constitutional interpretation on habeas review.......... 241
§ 28.7 Fact-finding and evidentiary hearings in habeas 263
§ 28.8 Habeas review of capital cases under Chapter 154 of
      the 1996 Act 273
§ 28.9 Remedies for federal prisoners........................... 279
§ 28.10 Appeal of district court decisions in habeas 299
§ 28.11 State collateral remedies................................... 301
§ 28.12 Assistance of counsel in post-conviction proceedings 308

Table of Cases .... Table of Cases-1

Table of Law and Rules .... Tbl of L&R-1

Table of Secondary Authorities .... Tbl of Sec Auth-1

Index Index-1

Table of Contents

Volume 1

PART I INTRODUCTION AND OVERVIEW

Chapter 1   An Overview of the Criminal Justice Process

§ 1.1   The subject under inquiry.................................... 3
   § 1.1(a)   Coverage 3
   § 1.1(b)   Organization................................. 5
§ 1.2   Considering state and federal criminal justice processes. 7
   § 1.2(a)   The fifty-two jurisdictions.............................. 8
   § 1.2(b)   State authority............................... 10
   § 1.2(c)   Federal authority 12
   § 1.2(d)   Expansion of the federal criminal justice system ... 53
   § 1.2(e)   The continued dominance of the state systems...... 73
   § 1.2(f)   The special significance of the federal system 75
§ 1.3   Similarities and differences in the laws of fifty-two
      jurisdictions 80
   § 1.3(a)   Describing the laws of fifty-two jurisdictions........ 80
   § 1.3(b)   The limits of mandated uniformity................... 80
   § 1.3(c)   The tendency to individualize....................... 84
   § 1.3(d)   The tendency to emulate 89
   § 1.3(e)   State reliance on the federal model 92
   § 1.3(f)   State reliance on other models 97
   § 1.3(g)   Patterns in state laws 102
§ 1.4   The agencies of administration and their organizational
      structures... 106
   § 1.4(a)   The agencies of administration...................... 106
   § 1.4(b)   Localism and criminal justice administration 106
   § 1.4(c)   Fragmentation of enforcement agencies............. 112
   § 1.4(d)   Police agencies 118
   § 1.4(e)   Prosecution agencies................................. 122
   § 1.4(f)   Defense counsel 128
   § 1.4(g)   Magistrates 134
   § 1.4(h)   Trial courts of general jurisdiction................... 138
§ 1.5   The cornerstone objectives of the process 141
   § 1.5(a)   Implementing the enforcement of the substantive
         law 142
   § 1.5(b)   Discovery of the truth 166
   § 1.5(c)   Adversary adjudication.............................. 171
   § 1.5(d)   Accusatorial burdens 189
   § 1.5(e)   Minimizing erroneous convictions.................... 194
   § 1.5(f)   Minimizing the burdens of accusation and
         litigation... 205

§ 1.5(g)   Providing lay participation.............................. 207
§ 1.5(h)   Respecting the dignity of the individual.............. 211
§ 1.5(i)   Maintaining the appearance of fairness............. 215
§ 1.5(j)   Achieving equality in the application of the
               process... 217
§ 1.5(k)   Addressing the concerns of the victim 227
§ 1.6 Historical development of the process 245
§ 1.6(a)   Introduction 246
§ 1.6(b)   The colonial period 250
§ 1.6(c)   The post-revolutionary period 266
§ 1.6(d)   The core of nineteenth century........................ 277
§ 1.6(e)   The progressive era..................................... 301
§ 1.6(f)   The second quarter of the twentieth century........ 308
§ 1.6(g)   The era of liberal idealism............................ 318
§ 1.6(h)   The post-liberalism period 327
§ 1.6(i)   The future of reform.................................... 337
§ 1.7 The laws regulating the process............................ 338
§ 1.7(a)   Varied sources of legal regulation.................... 338
§ 1.7(b)   The federal constitution 339
§ 1.7(c)   Federal statutes.. 340
§ 1.7(d)   State constitutions 354
§ 1.7(e)   Statutes 355
§ 1.7(f)   General court rules 358
§ 1.7(g)   Local court rules 364
§ 1.7(h)   Common law rulings.................................... 366
§ 1.7(i)   Supervisory authority rulings 370
§ 1.7(j)   Internal administrative standards.................... 383
§ 1.7(k)   Local ordinances 397
§ 1.8 Procedural subsets.. 398
§ 1.8(a)   Lines of division for procedural requirements 398
§ 1.8(b)   Specified offense distinctions......................... 399
§ 1.8(c)   Misdemeanor/felony and related distinctions 401
§ 1.8(d)   Ordinance violations 406
§ 1.8(e)   Capital offenses.. 415
§ 1.8(f)   Agency variations and procedural distinctions...... 417
§ 1.8(g)   Magistrate courts not of record...................... 420
§ 1.9 Deviance, discretion, and the limits of legal regulation .. 421
§ 1.9(a)   Law vs. practice 421
§ 1.9(b)   Deviance... 425
§ 1.9(c)   The nature and range of discretion 436
§ 1.9(d)   The reasons for discretion............................ 444
§ 1.9(e)   The challenge to discretion........................... 450
§ 1.10 Administrative policies and the local administrative
     setting.. 457
§ 1.10(a)   Significance of administrative environment 457
§ 1.10(b)   Policy differences...................................... 463
§ 1.10(c)   Caseload pressures 466
§ 1.10(d)   Administrative interactions........................... 481
§ 1.10(e)   The influence of the local community............... 496
§ 1.11 Criminal justice statistics 505
§ 1.11(a)   Significance... 505

§ 1.11(b) National statistics 507
§ 1.11(c) State statistics 508
§ 1.11(d) Federal statistics.. 512
§ 1.11(e) Funded studies... 513

Chapter 2 The Constitutionalization of Criminal Procedure

§ 2.1 The elements of constitutionalization...................... 516
§ 2.2 The Fourteenth Amendment and the extension of the
       bill of rights guarantees to the states 534
§ 2.3 Total incorporation.. 538
   § 2.3(a) The rationale of total incorporation.................. 539
   § 2.3(b) Rejection by the court 562
§ 2.4 Fundamental fairness 570
   § 2.4(a) The rationale of fundamental fairness 572
   § 2.4(b) The original meaning of due process 577
   § 2.4(c) The pre-Fourteenth Amendment cases............... 593
   § 2.4(d) The establishment and initial application of the
             fundamental fairness doctrine: from
             reconstruction to the 1930s 601
   § 2.4(e) Application of fundamental fairness: from the mid-
             1930s to the early 1960s............................. 607
   § 2.4(f) Subjectivity and fundamental fairness 615
§ 2.5 Selective incorporation 619
   § 2.5(a) Fundamental fairness and selective incorporation:
             similarities and differences.......................... 619
   § 2.5(b) The rationale of selective incorporation 621
   § 2.5(c) Prior precedent and the "absorption" of individual
             guarantees 623
   § 2.5(d) Selective incorporation as a means of avoiding
             subjectivity... 626
   § 2.5(e) Facilitating state enforcement of due process
             standards... 628
   § 2.5(f) The legitimate interests of federalism................ 629
§ 2.6 Application of the selective incorporation doctrine........ 643
   § 2.6(a) The decisions of the sixties.......................... 643
   § 2.6(b) Guarantees not yet incorporated 648
   § 2.6(c) Acceptance of selective incorporation in the
             post-1960s 657
   § 2.6(d) Selective incorporation and the concerns of
             federalism.. 662
   § 2.6(e) The retention of due process methodology........... 667
§ 2.7 The independent content of due process.................... 668
   § 2.7(a) Regulation by procedural due process after
             selective incorporation 669
   § 2.7(b) The "limited" role of free-standing due process..... 676
   § 2.7(c) Due process methodology............................ 685
   § 2.7(d) Substantive due process............................. 713
§ 2.8 The preference for expansive interpretations.............. 723
   § 2.8(a) The nature of the preference......................... 723
   § 2.8(b) The shifting strength of the preference.............. 730

§ 2.8(c)   The reasons for the preference................... 738
§ 2.9 Guideposts for constitutional interpretation 747
    § 2.9(a)   The role of guideposts 748
    § 2.9(b)   Stare decisis 749
    § 2.9(c)   The text 761
    § 2.9(d)   The original understanding................. 764
    § 2.9(e)   Policy analysis 778
    § 2.9(f)   Priority for truth-finding................. 779
    § 2.9(g)   The appropriateness of administratively based per
               se rules 787
    § 2.9(h)   The appropriateness of prophylactic rules 803
    § 2.9(i)   Weighing the impact upon efficiency 821
§ 2.10 Applying interpretive guideposts: the case of the
       privilege against self-incrimination..................... 827
    § 2.10(a)   Range of self-incrimination issues 827
    § 2.10(b)   Basic privilege doctrines..................... 829
    § 2.10(c)   History of the privilege 840
    § 2.10(d)   Policies of the privilege 850
§ 2.11 The non-retroactivity doctrine....................... 864
    § 2.11(a)   The significance of retroactive application 864
    § 2.11(b)   The Linkletter rationale of non-retroactive
               application 868
    § 2.11(c)   Application of Linkletter 869
    § 2.11(d)   Rejecting Linkletter: convictions not yet final...... 875
    § 2.11(e)   Rejecting Linkletter: finalized convictions under
               the Teague standards 879
§ 2.12 The influence of federal constitutional rulings upon
       state constitutional law........................... 883
    § 2.12(a)   The "new federalism" movement.................. 884
    § 2.12(b)   The mirroring presumption: scope 903
    § 2.12(c)   The mirroring debate....................... 912
    § 2.12(d)   Judicial acceptance and rejection of mirroring 930
    § 2.12(e)   State specific factors....................... 934

Volume 2

PART II DETECTION AND INVESTIGATION OF CRIME

Chapter 3 Arrest, Search and Seizure

§ 3.1 The Fourth Amendment exclusionary rule and other remedies 3
    § 3.1(a) Origins of the exclusionary rule 4
    § 3.1(b) Purposes of the exclusionary rule 7
    § 3.1(c) The exclusionary rule under attack 9
    § 3.1(d) The significance of underlying motivation; more on the deterrence objective and inquiry into subjective matters 23
    § 3.1(e) Constitutional vs. other violations 30
    § 3.1(f) Application of exclusionary rule in criminal proceedings 33
    § 3.1(g) Application of exclusionary rule in non-criminal proceedings 38
    § 3.1(h) The exclusionary rule and "private" or nonpolice searches 42
    § 3.1(i) The exclusionary rule and searches by foreign police 48
    § 3.1(j) Challenge of jurisdiction............................. 50
    § 3.1(k) The "constitutional tort"............................ 53
    § 3.1(*l*) Criminal prosecution; disciplinary proceedings..... 57
    § 3.1(m) Expungement of arrest records 58
    § 3.1(n) Injunction 59
    § 3.1(o) Self-help.. 60
§ 3.2 Protected areas and interests................................ 61
    § 3.2(a) The *Katz* expectation of privacy test.................. 61
    § 3.2(b) Plain view, smell, hearing and touch; aiding the senses 66
    § 3.2(c) Residential premises 79
    § 3.2(d) "Open fields"... 85
    § 3.2(e) Business and commercial premises 87
    § 3.2(f) Vehicles 89
    § 3.2(g) Personal characteristics.............................. 92
    § 3.2(h) Abandoned effects..................................... 93
    § 3.2(i) "Mere evidence" in general and private papers in particular... 96
    § 3.2(j) Surveillance of relationships and movements 98
§ 3.3 Probable cause... 105
    § 3.3(a) General considerations 105
    § 3.3(b) Nature of probable cause............................ 109
    § 3.3(c) Information from an informant...................... 116
    § 3.3(d) Information from a victim or witness................ 131
    § 3.3(e) Information from or held by other police 136
    § 3.3(f) First-hand information 140
    § 3.3(g) Special problems in search cases..................... 145
§ 3.4 Search warrants... 150

§ 3.4(a)   When warrant may be utilized........................   150
§ 3.4(b)   The "neutral and detached magistrate"
               requirement...   157
§ 3.4(c)   Oath or affirmation; record   160
§ 3.4(d)   Probable cause: the facially-sufficient affidavit......   162
§ 3.4(e)   Particular description of place to be searched.......   165
§ 3.4(f)   Particular description of things to be seized.........   170
§ 3.4(g)   Time of execution   175
§ 3.4(h)   Entry without notice....................................   177
§ 3.4(i)   Detention and search of persons   183
§ 3.4(j)   Scope and intensity of the search....................   186
§ 3.4(k)   What may be seized   191
§ 3.4(*l*)   Miscellaneous requirements   196
§ 3.5   Seizure and search of persons and personal effects.......   198
§ 3.5(a)   Arrest...   199
§ 3.5(b)   Search of the person at scene of prior arrest........   213
§ 3.5(c)   Search of the person during post-arrest detention .   219
§ 3.5(d)   Other search of the person...........................   224
§ 3.5(e)   Seizure and search of containers and other
               personal effects.....................................   231
§ 3.6   Entry and search of premises...........................   238
§ 3.6(a)   Basis for entry to arrest..............................   238
§ 3.6(b)   Entry without notice to arrest.......................   245
§ 3.6(c)   Search before and incident to arrest.................   248
§ 3.6(d)   Search and exploration after arrest..................   250
§ 3.6(e)   Warrantless entry and search for evidence   253
§ 3.6(f)   Warrantless entry and search for other purposes ..   262
§ 3.6(g)   What may be seized...................................   265
§ 3.7   Search and seizure of vehicles...........................   268
§ 3.7(a)   Search incident to arrest.............................   268
§ 3.7(b)   Search and seizure to search for evidence   273
§ 3.7(c)   Search of containers and persons within.............   278
§ 3.7(d)   Seizure for other purposes............................   284
§ 3.7(e)   Search for other purposes.............................   289
§ 3.7(f)   Plain view, subterfuge and related matters   297
§ 3.8   Stop and frisk and similar lesser intrusions...............   300
§ 3.8(a)   Stop and frisk: Fourth Amendment theory   300
§ 3.8(b)   Dimensions of a permissible "stop"   303
§ 3.8(c)   Action short of a stop.................................   313
§ 3.8(d)   Grounds for a permissible "stop"......................   326
§ 3.8(e)   "Frisk" for weapons...................................   338
§ 3.8(f)   Roadblocks...   345
§ 3.8(g)   Detention at the police station for investigation ...   346
§ 3.8(h)   Brief seizure of objects   349
§ 3.9   Inspections and regulatory searches......................   351
§ 3.9(a)   General considerations.................................   351
§ 3.9(b)   Inspection of housing..................................   353
§ 3.9(c)   Inspection of businesses...............................   358
§ 3.9(d)   Welfare inspections....................................   364
§ 3.9(e)   Inspections at fire scenes   366
§ 3.9(f)   Border searches and related activities   368

§ 3.9(g) Vehicle use regulation............................ 375
§ 3.9(h) Airport searches................................. 380
§ 3.9(i) Searches directed at prisoners 384
§ 3.9(j) Searches directed at probationers and parolees..... 388
§ 3.9(k) Searches directed at students 395
§ 3.9(l) Searches directed at public employees 401
§ 3.10 Consent searches...................................... 405
§ 3.10(a) Nature of consent 405
§ 3.10(b) Factors bearing on validity of consent 410
§ 3.10(c) Consent by deception 418
§ 3.10(d) Third party consent: general considerations 422
§ 3.10(e) Common relationships in third party consent...... 431
§ 3.10(f) Scope of consent 439

Chapter 4 Network Surveillance

§ 4.1 Introduction.. 446
§ 4.2 Postal mail 446
§ 4.2(a) Access to postal mail and packages 446
§ 4.2(b) Detaining mail and packages 449
§ 4.2(c) Mail covers................................... 450
§ 4.3 Telephone surveillance and the Fourth Amendment........ 451
§ 4.3(a) Wiretapping and eavesdropping.................... 451
§ 4.3(b) Exceptions to the usual rule that telephone
          wiretapping and eavesdropping is a search....... 452
§ 4.3(c) Numbers "dialed" and text messages 454
§ 4.4 Internet communications and the Fourth Amendment 456
§ 4.4(a) Introduction.................................. 456
§ 4.4(b) Non-content information........................ 457
§ 4.4(c) Contents of communications 459
§ 4.4(d) The line between contents and non-content
          information 461
§ 4.4(e) Exceptions for Fourth Amendment protections in
          e-mail and internet communications 462
§ 4.5 Overview of statutory protections 464
§ 4.6 The Wiretap Act..................................... 467
§ 4.6(a) Wire, oral, and electronic communications.......... 468
§ 4.6(b) Interception................................... 473
§ 4.6(c) Overview of obtaining and executing wiretap
          orders 480
§ 4.6(d) Application procedure........................... 484
§ 4.6(e) Contents of application 485
§ 4.6(f) Review of application 493
§ 4.6(g) Contents of order............................... 494
§ 4.6(h) Minimization................................... 496
§ 4.6(i) Amendment and extension......................... 498
§ 4.6(j) Post-surveillance notice.......................... 500
§ 4.6(k) Sealing.. 501
§ 4.6(l) Statutory exceptions to liability 502
§ 4.6(m) Supression of evidence........................... 511
§ 4.6(n) Civil remedies 518
§ 4.6(o) Criminal penalties 520

§ 4.7 The Pen Register statute 521
    § 4.7(a)   Overview of the Pen Register statute................ 521
    § 4.7(b)   Application for a Pen Register order................. 523
    § 4.7(c)   Dialing routing, addressing, and signaling
                information 524
    § 4.7(d)   Exceptions to the Pen Register statute.............. 528
    § 4.7(e)   Remedies for violations............................. 529
§ 4.8 The Stored Communications Act............................ 529
    § 4.8(a)   Overview of the Stored Communications Act........ 530
    § 4.8(b)   Providers of electronic communication service and
                remote computing service 530
    § 4.8(c)   Rules for compelling non-content information....... 533
    § 4.8(d)   Rules for compelling content information............ 534
    § 4.8(e)   Rules for voluntary disclosure of information 539
    § 4.8(f)   Remedies for violations 543
§ 4.9 Foreign intelligence surveillance 544
    § 4.9(a)   The Fourth Amendment............................ 544
    § 4.9(b)   The Foreign Intelligence Surveillance Act 546

Chapter 5   Police "Encouragement" and the Entrapment Defense

§ 5.1 Encouragement of crime and the defense of entrapment .. 553
    § 5.1(a)   Encouragement of criminal activity................. 553
    § 5.1(b)   Entrapment defense as a limit...................... 554
    § 5.1(c)   Scope of the defense................................ 555
§ 5.2 Subjective versus objective test for entrapment............. 561
    § 5.2(a)   The subjective approach............................ 561
    § 5.2(b)   The objective approach 569
    § 5.2(c)   Objections to the subjective approach 574
    § 5.2(d)   Objections to the objective approach................ 576
§ 5.3 Procedural considerations re entrapment defense 578
    § 5.3(a)   Admissibility of evidence of defendant's past
                conduct... 578
    § 5.3(b)   Triable by court or jury............................ 581
    § 5.3(c)   Inconsistent defenses 583
    § 5.3(d)   Burden of proof.................................... 585
§ 5.4 Other challenges to encouragement practices 587
    § 5.4(a)   Contingent fee arrangements 587
    § 5.4(b)   Inducements to those not reasonably suspected 589
    § 5.4(c)   Government "overinvolvement" in a criminal
                enterprise.. 592

Chapter 6   Interrogation and Confessions

§ 6.1 Introduction and overview confessions 602
    § 6.1(a)   The need for confessions............................ 602
    § 6.1(b)   The extent of police abuse.......................... 604
    § 6.1(c)   The Supreme Court's response...................... 606
§ 6.2 The "voluntariness" test................................... 608
    § 6.2(a)   The common law rule............................... 608
    § 6.2(b)   Due process and the "complex of values"............ 610
    § 6.2(c)   Relevant factors in the "totality of circumstances". 616

§ 6.2(d)   Critique of the "voluntariness" test   646
§ 6.3   The prompt appearance requirement   648
  § 6.3(a)   The *McNabb-Mallory* rule   649
  § 6.3(b)   Reactions to the rule   652
  § 6.3(c)   Prompt appearance in the states   656
§ 6.4   The right to counsel re interrogation   658
  § 6.4(a)   Pre-*Massiah* developments   659
  § 6.4(b)   The *Massiah* case   661
  § 6.4(c)   The *Escobedo* case   663
  § 6.4(d)   The *Williams* case   666
  § 6.4(e)   When the right to counsel begins   668
  § 6.4(f)   Waiver of counsel   682
  § 6.4(g)   Infringement of the right   690
  § 6.4(h)   Critique of the right to counsel approach   697
  § 6.4(i)   The "repeal" of the *Massiah* rule   699
§ 6.5   The privilege against self-incrimination; *Miranda*   700
  § 6.5(a)   The privilege in the police station   700
  § 6.5(b)   The *Miranda* rules   703
  § 6.5(c)   The experience under *Miranda*   707
  § 6.5(d)   Critique of the *Miranda* approach   712
  § 6.5(e)   The "repeal" of *Miranda*   716
§ 6.6   *Miranda*: When interrogation is "custodial"   720
  § 6.6(a)   "Custody" vs. "focus"   720
  § 6.6(b)   Purpose of custody   723
  § 6.6(c)   Subjective vs. objective approach   726
  § 6.6(d)   Presence at station   732
  § 6.6(e)   Presence elsewhere   738
  § 6.6(f)   Other considerations   749
§ 6.7   *Miranda*: "Interrogation"   752
  § 6.7(a)   The "functional equivalent" test   752
  § 6.7(b)   Questioning   759
  § 6.7(c)   Other "words or actions"   781
  § 6.7(d)   "Volunteered" statements and follow-up
             questioning   790
§ 6.8   *Miranda*: Required warnings   794
  § 6.8(a)   Content   794
  § 6.8(b)   Time and frequency   802
  § 6.8(c)   Manner; proof   808
  § 6.8(d)   Additional admonitions   811
§ 6.9   *Miranda*: Waiver of rights   813
  § 6.9(a)   Express or implied   814
  § 6.9(b)   Competence of the defendant   816
  § 6.9(c)   Conduct of the police   825
  § 6.9(d)   Implied waiver   830
  § 6.9(e)   "Qualified" or limited waiver   832
  § 6.9(f)   Waiver after assertion of rights   836
  § 6.9(g)   Ambiguous, equivocal, limited and untimely
             assertions of rights   852
§ 6.10 *Miranda*: Nature of offense, interrogator, and
        proceedings   870
  § 6.10(a) Questioning about minor offense   870

§ 6.10(b)   Questioning by private citizen....................... 871
§ 6.10(c)   Questioning by non-police official 875
§ 6.10(d)   Questioning by foreign police....................... 880
§ 6.10(e)   Proceedings at which confession offered........... 882

Chapter 7 Identification Procedures

§ 7.1 Introduction to identification.............................. 889
§ 7.1(a)   The problem of misidentification 889
§ 7.1(b)   The causes of misidentification 891
§ 7.1(c)   The Supreme Court's response....................... 894
§ 7.2 The privilege against self-incrimination and
         identification.. 895
§ 7.2(a)   The *Schmerber* rule............................... 895
§ 7.2(b)   Application to identification procedures 897
§ 7.2(c)   Refusal to cooperate 900
§ 7.2(d)   Change in appearance............................... 902
§ 7.3 The right to counsel and to confrontation re
         identification.. 905
§ 7.3(a)   Procedures required................................ 905
§ 7.3(b)   Time of identification 908
§ 7.3(c)   Nature of identification procedure................... 914
§ 7.3(d)   Waiver or substitution of counsel 919
§ 7.3(e)   Role of counsel..................................... 922
§ 7.3(f)   Consequences of violation 926
§ 7.3(g)   The "repeal" of the right............................ 929
§ 7.4 Due process and identification: "The totality of the
         circumstances".. 929
§ 7.4(a)   Generally... 930
§ 7.4(b)   The "unnecessarily suggestive" element............. 931
§ 7.4(c)   The risk of misidentification element................ 939
§ 7.4(d)   Lineups... 944
§ 7.4(e)   Use of pictures 949
§ 7.4(f)   One-man showups 958
§ 7.4(g)   In-court identifications 963
§ 7.4(h)   The "repeal" of the right 967
§ 7.5 Additional possible safeguards re identification............. 968
§ 7.5(a)   Jury instructions 968
§ 7.5(b)   Expert testimony 971
§ 7.5(c)   Improved police procedures 975

Volume 3

PART II DETECTION AND INVESTIGATION OF CRIME (CONTINUED)

Chapter 8 Grand Jury Investigation

§ 8.1 The investigative grand jury...............................   3
§ 8.1(a)   Dual functions of the traditional grand jury   3
§ 8.1(b)   Special grand juries.................................   5
§ 8.1(c)   Alternative procedures..............................   7
§ 8.2 Historical development of the grand jury 10

§ 8.2(a)   English origins... 11
§ 8.2(b)   Developments in the United States 13
§ 8.2(c)   Relevance of history.................................... 17
§ 8.3 Investigative advantages of the grand jury 22
§ 8.3(a)   Subpoena authority and the contempt sanction 23
§ 8.3(b)   Subpoena ad testificandum 26
§ 8.3(c)   Subpoena duces tecum 28
§ 8.3(d)   Psychological pressure................................. 30
§ 8.3(e)   Immunity grants 30
§ 8.3(f)   Secrecy 31
§ 8.3(g)   Maintaining public confidence....................... 33
§ 8.3(h)   Grand jury reports.................................... 34
§ 8.4 The legal structure of the investigative grand jury 38
§ 8.4(a)   The representativeness of the grand jurors 39
§ 8.4(b)   Independent investigative authority 41
§ 8.4(c)   Judicial supervision................................... 58
§ 8.5 Grand jury secrecy....................................... 64
§ 8.5(a)   Underlying considerations 65
§ 8.5(b)   Statutory structure 68
§ 8.5(c)   Protected information 76
§ 8.5(d)   Disclosure by a witness 91
§ 8.5(e)   Disclosure to further criminal law enforcement..... 100
§ 8.5(f)   Disclosure pursuant to a challenge to grand jury
            proceedings...................................... 112
§ 8.5(g)   Disclosure to defendant pursuant to discovery
            rules 112
§ 8.5(h)   Disclosure to third parties 116
§ 8.5(i)   Remedies... 133
§ 8.6 The right to every man's evidence 139
§ 8.6(a)   The public's right and the grand jury............... 139
§ 8.6(b)   Privileges and other protections..................... 143
§ 8.7 Fourth Amendment challenges to subpoenas 151
§ 8.7(a)   Applicability of the Fourth Amendment to
            subpoenas for documents 152
§ 8.7(b)   The prohibition against overbreadth in
            documentary subpoenas........................... 161
§ 8.7(c)   Application of the Fourth Amendment to other
            subpoenas: *Dionisio* and *Mara* 168
§ 8.7(d)   Subpoenas for identification evidence................ 171
§ 8.7(e)   "Forthwith" subpoenas................................ 175
§ 8.8 Challenges to misuse of the subpoena authority 177
§ 8.8(a)   Improper subject of investigation 177
§ 8.8(b)   Relevancy objections.................................. 181
§ 8.8(c)   Oppressiveness objections............................ 190
§ 8.8(d)   "Chilling effect" objections 192
§ 8.8(e)   Use for civil discovery 213
§ 8.8(f)   Use for post-indictment criminal discovery.......... 219
§ 8.8(g)   Prosecution or police usurpation of the subpoena
            power 223
§ 8.8(h)   Harassment... 227
§ 8.8(i)   Structural objections 229

§ 8.9 Grand jury inquiries based on illegally obtained evidence 230
    § 8.9(a)   The *Calandra* rule 231
    § 8.9(b)   Illegal electronic surveillance 234
§ 8.10 Grand jury testimony and the privilege against self-incrimination 238
    § 8.10(a) The standard of potential incrimination 238
    § 8.10(b) Incrimination under the laws of another sovereign 247
    § 8.10(c) Compelling the target to appear 250
    § 8.10(d) Advice as to rights 258
    § 8.10(e) Waiver 266
    § 8.10(f)   Adverse consequences 268
§ 8.11 Self-incrimination immunity and compelled testimony ... 269
    § 8.11(a) Constitutionality 269
    § 8.11(b) Transactional vs. use/derivative-use immunity 274
    § 8.11(c) Applying the use/derivative-use prohibition 279
    § 8.11(d) Immunity procedures 289
    § 8.11(e) Informal grants of immunity 293
§ 8.12 Self-incrimination and the compulsory production of documents 298
    § 8.12(a) The *Boyd* "principle" 298
    § 8.12(b) The entity exception 301
    § 8.12(c) The required records exception 307
    § 8.12(d) The *Schmerber* rule 312
    § 8.12(e) Third-party production 314
    § 8.12(f)   Testimonial aspects of production 316
    § 8.12(g) The remnants of *Boyd* 320
§ 8.13 Application of the act-of-production doctrine 324
    § 8.13(a) Testimonial character and the foregone conclusion standard 324
    § 8.13(b) Potential incrimination 341
    § 8.13(c) Act-of-production immunity 349
    § 8.13(d) Claims by entity agents 356
    § 8.13(e) Non-documentary subpoenas 365
§ 8.14 The grand jury witness' right to counsel 366
    § 8.14(a) Constitutional requirements 366
    § 8.14(b) Counsel within the grand jury room 370
    § 8.14(c) Counsel in the anteroom 372
    § 8.14(d) Multiple representation 373

Chapter 9 Scope of the Exclusionary Rules

§ 9.1 Standing: the "personal rights" approach 379
    § 9.1(a)   "Personal rights" as to searches, confessions and identifications 380
    § 9.1(b)   Residential premises 386
    § 9.1(c)   Business premises 400
    § 9.1(d)   Vehicles 403
§ 9.2 Standing: other possible bases 409
    § 9.2(a)   "Automatic" standing 409
    § 9.2(b)   "Target" standing 412

§ 9.2(c) "Derivative" standing 414
§ 9.2(d) Abolition of standing 416
§ 9.3 "Fruit of the poisonous tree" theories 418
§ 9.3(a) Generally 418
§ 9.3(b) "But for" rejected 420
§ 9.3(c) "Attenuated connection" 421
§ 9.3(d) "Independent source" 425
§ 9.3(e) "Inevitable discovery" 428
§ 9.4 Fruits of illegal arrests and searches 439
§ 9.4(a) Confessions 439
§ 9.4(b) Searches 448
§ 9.4(c) Arrests 455
§ 9.4(d) Identification of person 455
§ 9.4(e) Testimony of witness 460
§ 9.4(f) New crime 464
§ 9.5 Fruits of illegally obtained confessions 466
§ 9.5(a) The confession as a "poisonous tree" 466
§ 9.5(b) Searches 472
§ 9.5(c) Confessions 477
§ 9.5(d) Testimony of witness 482
§ 9.5(e) New crime 484
§ 9.6 Permissible use of illegally obtained evidence at trial 485
§ 9.6(a) Impeachment 485
§ 9.6(b) Defense tactics which "open the door" 499
§ 9.6(c) Prosecution for perjury or other "new" offense 500

Chapter 10 Administration of the Exclusionary Rules

§ 10.1 The pretrial motion to suppress 505
§ 10.1(a) Contemporaneous objection or pretrial motion 506
§ 10.1(b) Form of the motion 508
§ 10.1(c) Pre-charge and post-trial motions distinguished .. 511
§ 10.2 Waiver or forfeiture of objection re suppression of
      evidence 515
§ 10.2(a) Failure to make timely objection 515
§ 10.2(b) Failure to renew objection 519
§ 10.2(c) Testimony by defendant 521
§ 10.2(d) Plea of guilty or nolo contendere 522
§ 10.3 Burden of proof at suppression hearing 523
§ 10.3(a) Generally 523
§ 10.3(b) Search and seizure 525
§ 10.3(c) Confessions 532
§ 10.3(d) Identification 533
§ 10.4 Standard of proof at suppression hearing 536
§ 10.4(a) Generally 536
§ 10.4(b) Confessions 536
§ 10.4(c) Search and seizure 539
§ 10.4(d) Identification 541
§ 10.5 The suppression hearing 542
§ 10.5(a) The trier of fact 542
§ 10.5(b) Presence of jury 545
§ 10.5(c) Testimony by defendant 547

§ 10.5(d)   Evidentiary rules... 549
§ 10.5(e)   Right of confrontation.................................. 550
§ 10.5(f)   Right of compulsory process........................ 552
§ 10.6 The suppression hearing ruling and its effect 554
§ 10.6(a)   Findings 554
§ 10.6(b)   Recommendations 556
§ 10.6(c)   Reconsideration at trial.............................. 558
§ 10.6(d)   Effect of ruling in other cases...................... 561

PART III THE COMMENCEMENT OF FORMAL PROCEEDINGS

Chapter 11 The Right to Counsel

§ 11.1 The constitutional rights to retained and appointed
         counsel.. 566
    § 11.1(a)   Sixth Amendment rights........................... 566
    § 11.1(b)   Due process rights................................ 578
    § 11.1(c)   Derivative rights to counsel 599
    § 11.1(d)   Equal protection and appointed counsel 600
§ 11.2 Scope of the indigent's right to counsel and other
         assistance 608
    § 11.2(a)   Right to appointed counsel: misdemeanor
                 prosecutions...................................... 608
    § 11.2(b)   Right to appointed counsel: stages of the
                 proceeding.. 620
    § 11.2(c)   The *Anders* rules 631
    § 11.2(d)   Transcripts 640
    § 11.2(e)   Assistance of experts............................ 644
    § 11.2(f)   The *Bounds* right of access 661
    § 11.2(g)   Indigency standards.............................. 667
    § 11.2(h)   Partial contribution and recoupment.............. 676
§ 11.3 Waiver of the right to counsel............................. 678
    § 11.3(a)   General requirements for waiver of counsel 678
    § 11.3(b)   Waiver of counsel at trial: the necessary advice
                 and inquiry...................................... 683
    § 11.3(c)   Forfeiture of the right to counsel................ 691
§ 11.4 Choice of counsel... 695
    § 11.4(a)   Judicial discretion in selecting appointed
                 counsel 695
    § 11.4(b)   Replacement of appointed counsel................. 700
    § 11.4(c)   Choice of retained counsel....................... 711
    § 11.4(d)   The pro se alternative........................... 727
§ 11.5 The constitutional right to self-representation............ 731
    § 11.5(a)   The *Faretta* ruling............................. 731
    § 11.5(b)   Notification 737
    § 11.5(c)   Requisite warnings and judicial inquiry 739
    § 11.5(d)   Grounds for denial............................... 752
    § 11.5(e)   Subsequent challenge to ineffective
                 representation 759
    § 11.5(f)   Standby counsel.................................. 760
    § 11.5(g)   Hybrid representation............................ 765

§ 11.6   Counsel's control over defense strategy 770
　§ 11.6(a)   "Strategic" vs. "personal" decisions 770
　§ 11.6(b)   Consultation..................................... 788
　§ 11.6(c)   Balancing of interests 796
　§ 11.6(d)   Prejudice....................................... 804
§ 11.7   The right to effective assistance of counsel: guiding
　　　　　principles.. 808
　§ 11.7(a)   The prerequisite of a constitutional right to
　　　　　　　counsel... 808
　§ 11.7(b)   Retained vs. appointed counsel.................... 815
　§ 11.7(c)   The adversary system touchstone.................. 816
　§ 11.7(d)   Per se vs. actual ineffectiveness................. 819
　§ 11.7(e)   Raising an ineffectiveness claim 826
§ 11.8   Ineffective assistance claims based upon state
　　　　　interference and other extrinsic factors 840
　§ 11.8(a)   Restrictions upon counsel's assistance............ 840
　§ 11.8(b)   State invasions of the lawyer-client relationship.. 845
　§ 11.8(c)   Conditions of representation..................... 854
§ 11.9   Ineffective assistance claims based upon attorney
　　　　　conflicts of interest 864
　§ 11.9(a)   The range of possible conflicts of interest.......... 865
　§ 11.9(b)   The trial court duty to inquire 877
　§ 11.9(c)   Waiver and disqualification 893
　§ 11.9(d)   Challenging convictions........................... 911
§ 11.10 Ineffective assistance claims based upon lawyer
　　　　　incompetence 940
　§ 11.10(a) Guiding considerations 940
　§ 11.10(b) The competency standard 948
　§ 11.10(c) Applying the reasonableness standard 955
　§ 11.10(d) The prejudice element 989

Volume 4

PART III THE COMMENCEMENT OF FORMAL PROCEEDINGS (CONTINUED)

Chapter 12 Pretrial Release

§ 12.1 Pretrial release procedures 1
　§ 12.1(a)   The Federal Bail Reform Act 2
　§ 12.1(b)   State practice generally........................... 8
　§ 12.1(c)   Counsel at bail hearing............................ 13
　§ 12.1(d)   Proof at bail hearing 15
　§ 12.1(e)   Defendant's statements............................ 17
　§ 12.1(f)   Victim's right to be heard 19
§ 12.2 Constitutionality of limits on pretrial freedom 26
　§ 12.2(a)   Amount of money bail.............................. 26
　§ 12.2(b)   Poverty and pretrial release....................... 32
　§ 12.2(c)   Opportunity to prepare a defense................... 37
　§ 12.2(d)   Nature of pretrial custody 39
§ 12.3 Constitutionality of mandating pretrial detention 41

§ 12.3(a)   Preventive detention in the federal system........   41
§ 12.3(b)   Preventive detention and the state constitutions .   47
§ 12.3(c)   The Eighth Amendment ambiguity.................   60
§ 12.3(d)   Other constitutional objections......................   64
§ 12.3(e)   Detention where serious offense charged   69
§ 12.3(f)   Detention upon individual finding of
               dangerousness.......................................   72
§ 12.3(g)   Detention for misconduct during release..........   76
§ 12.4 Special situations re release   79
§ 12.4(a)   Capital cases   80
§ 12.4(b)   Juvenile cases.......................................   87
§ 12.4(c)   During trial...   89
§ 12.4(d)   After conviction   90
§ 12.4(e)   During interlocutory appeal by prosecution   95
§ 12.4(f)   Probation or parole revocation   97
§ 12.4(g)   Material witnesses...................................   97
§ 12.5 Alternatives to arrest.......................................   100
§ 12.5(a)   Summons in lieu of arrest warrant.................   100
§ 12.5(b)   Citation in lieu of arrest without warrant.........   103

Chapter 13   The Decision Whether to Prosecute

§ 13.1 Nature of the decision whether to prosecute...............   110
§ 13.1(a)   In general..   110
§ 13.1(b)   Evidence sufficiency   116
§ 13.1(c)   Screening out cases..................................   117
§ 13.1(d)   Diversion..   118
§ 13.1(e)   Selection of the charge   119
§ 13.2 Discretionary enforcement   120
§ 13.2(a)   The prosecutor's discretion   120
§ 13.2(b)   Police discretion....................................   128
§ 13.2(c)   Jury and judge discretion............................   131
§ 13.2(d)   The "problem" of discretion.........................   138
§ 13.2(e)   Confining the prosecutor's discretion...............   140
§ 13.2(f)   Structuring the prosecutor's discretion.............   141
§ 13.2(g)   Checking the prosecutor's discretion   145
§ 13.2(h)   Mandating the prosecutor's discretion   149
§ 13.3 Challenges to and checks upon the decision not to
          prosecute   151
§ 13.3(a)   Mandamus   151
§ 13.3(b)   Private prosecution; qui tam actions................   154
§ 13.3(c)   Judicial approval of nolle prosequi   158
§ 13.3(d)   Grand jury   163
§ 13.3(e)   Attorney General....................................   164
§ 13.3(f)   Removal; special prosecutor.........................   165
§ 13.4 Challenging the decision to prosecute: equal protection ..   168
§ 13.4(a)   Discriminatory prosecution   168
§ 13.4(b)   Problems of proof   172
§ 13.4(c)   "Arbitrary classification"   181
§ 13.4(d)   "Intentional or purposeful"..........................   191
§ 13.4(e)   Nonprosecution of others............................   194
§ 13.5 Other challenges to the decision to prosecute.............   198

§ 13.5(a)   Vindictive prosecution............................... 199
§ 13.5(b)   Reneging on a promise............................ 206
§ 13.5(c)   Desuetude and lack of fair notice.................. 213
§ 13.5(d)   Federal relief from state prosecution: removal.... 216
§ 13.5(e)   Federal relief from state prosecution: injunction
             and declaratory judgment......................... 218
§ 13.5(f)   Federal relief from state prosecution: habeas
             corpus 221
§ 13.5(g)   Civil action against prosecutor.................... 221
§ 13.5(h)   Recoupment of litigation expenses................. 223
§ 13.6 Challenges to the decision to forego or terminate
       diversion... 238
§ 13.6(a)   The diversion process 238
§ 13.6(b)   Statutory standards for diversion.................. 240
§ 13.6(c)   Decision not to divert 242
§ 13.6(d)   Decision to terminate by prosecution.............. 248
§ 13.7 Challenges to the charge selection 252
§ 13.7(a)   Duplicative and overlapping statutes 253
§ 13.7(b)   Discriminatory charge selection................... 260
§ 13.7(c)   Vindictive charge selection 261
§ 13.7(d)   Reneging on a promise............................ 272

Chapter 14   The Preliminary Hearing

§ 14.1 Functions of the preliminary hearing................... 273
§ 14.1(a)   Screening 273
§ 14.1(b)   Discovery.. 279
§ 14.1(c)   Future impeachment 281
§ 14.1(d)   The perpetuation of testimony 283
§ 14.1(e)   Other functions 291
§ 14.2 Defendant's right to a preliminary hearing............. 291
§ 14.2(a)   The Federal Constitution 291
§ 14.2(b)   The federal practice 296
§ 14.2(c)   Indictment states 300
§ 14.2(d)   Information states 303
§ 14.2(e)   Waiver and demand 308
§ 14.2(f)   Time of hearing 311
§ 14.2(g)   Remedies.. 313
§ 14.3 The preliminary hearing bindover determination 317
§ 14.3(a)   The applicable standard 318
§ 14.3(b)   Assessment of credibility 329
§ 14.3(c)   Consequences of a dismissal...................... 331
§ 14.3(d)   Consequences of a bindover 336
§ 14.4 Preliminary hearing procedures......................... 340
§ 14.4(a)   Right to counsel................................. 340
§ 14.4(b)   Application of the rules of evidence.............. 341
§ 14.4(c)   The defendant's right of cross-examination........ 352
§ 14.4(d)   The right to present defense witnesses............ 357
§ 14.4(e)   Challenging procedural rulings 364

Chapter 15 Grand Jury Review

§ 15.1 Defendant's right to prosecution by indictment 378
  § 15.1(a) The Fifth Amendment right: history 378
  § 15.1(b) The Fifth Amendment right: scope 381
  § 15.1(c) Fourteenth Amendment due process 404
  § 15.1(d) Indictment jurisdictions.......................... 410
  § 15.1(e) Limited indictment jurisdictions 431
  § 15.1(f) Waiver in indictment and limited-indictment
             jurisdictions...................................... 433
  § 15.1(g) Information states 445
§ 15.2 The structure of grand jury screening 450
  § 15.2(a) Grand jury composition........................... 450
  § 15.2(b) Control over proof 452
  § 15.2(c) The prospective defendant's testimony.............. 461
  § 15.2(d) Evidentiary rules................................. 467
  § 15.2(e) Legal advice...................................... 476
  § 15.2(f) Quantum of proof................................. 481
  § 15.2(g) The indictment decision 482
  § 15.2(h) Resubmission 485
  § 15.2(i) Secrecy requirements 487
  § 15.2(j) Transcription..................................... 495
§ 15.3 The effectiveness of grand jury screening 498
  § 15.3(a) The ongoing debate............................... 498
  § 15.3(b) Statistics.. 506
  § 15.3(c) Screening variations.............................. 510
  § 15.3(d) Judicial responses 511
§ 15.4 Indictment challenges based on grand jury composition
       deficiencies 514
  § 15.4(a) Grand jury selection procedures.................... 514
  § 15.4(b) Objection procedures and timing 519
  § 15.4(c) Equal protection claims........................... 530
  § 15.4(d) The "fair cross-section requirement" 534
  § 15.4(e) Constitutional challenges to the selection of the
             foreperson.. 542
  § 15.4(f) Statutory violations 548
  § 15.4(g) Juror bias 549
  § 15.4(h) Preindictment publicity........................... 556
  § 15.4(i) Postconviction review 559
§ 15.5 Indictment challenges based on evidentiary deficiencies . 563
  § 15.5(a) The federal standard: the *Costello* rule............ 563
  § 15.5(b) The federal standard: the rise and demise of
             "misconduct exception" to *Costello*............... 574
  § 15.5(c) State standards 590
§ 15.6 Indictment challenges based on misconduct: general
       principles 596
  § 15.6(a) Prosecutorial misconduct 596
  § 15.6(b) The federal standard; the *Williams* limits 603
  § 15.6(c) Juror misconduct 612
  § 15.6(d) The prejudice requirement......................... 615
  § 15.6(e) The prejudice standard of *Bank of Nova Scotia* ... 621

§ 15.6(f)   Postconviction review 633
§ 15.6(g)   Establishing misconduct 644
§ 15.7 Indictment challenges based on misconduct: common
        claims.. 646
§ 15.7(a)   The range of objections 646
§ 15.7(b)   Prejudicial comments and information............. 648
§ 15.7(c)   The prosecutor's assumption of other roles........ 655
§ 15.7(d)   Violation of the defendant's witness-rights........ 658
§ 15.7(e)   Deception in presenting evidence................... 662
§ 15.7(f)   Failure to present known exculpatory evidence... 669
§ 15.7(g)   Erroneous legal advice............................ 680
§ 15.7(h)   Presence of unauthorized persons 684

Chapter 16   The Location of the Prosecution

§ 16.1 Venue: general principles................................ 691
§ 16.1(a)   Distinguishing venue from jurisdiction 692
§ 16.1(b)   Distinguishing vicinage 696
§ 16.1(c)   The "crime-committed" formula.................... 708
§ 16.1(d)   Multi-venue offenses 716
§ 16.1(e)   Special legislation 725
§ 16.1(f)   Joinder and venue............................... 736
§ 16.1(g)   Proof of venue.................................. 742
§ 16.1(h)   Waiver 753
§ 16.2 Applying the crime-committed formula to establish
        venue.. 758
§ 16.2(a)   Recurring questions 759
§ 16.2(b)   Constitutional policy 763
§ 16.2(c)   Literalism 770
§ 16.2(d)   Nature of the offense............................ 776
§ 16.2(e)   Substantial contacts............................ 779
§ 16.2(f)   Transportation offenses 789
§ 16.2(g)   Multiple participants........................... 793
§ 16.2(h)   Enterprise offenses 800
§ 16.3 Change of venue.. 804
§ 16.3(a)   Variations..................................... 804
§ 16.3(b)   "Fair trial" venue changes on defense motion 805
§ 16.3(c)   Convenience venue changes on defense motion ... 809
§ 16.3(d)   "Fair trial" venue changes on prosecution
             motion..................................... 814
§ 16.3(e)   Convenience venue changes on prosecution
             motion..................................... 818
§ 16.3(f)   Venue changes on the court's own motion 820
§ 16.3(g)   Selection of the transfer district 821
§ 16.4 Jurisdiction 829
§ 16.4(a)   The concept of jurisdiction...................... 830
§ 16.4(b)   Federal jurisdiction............................ 830
§ 16.4(c)   State jurisdiction 838
§ 16.4(d)   Proof and waiver............................... 858

Volume 5

PART III THE COMMENCEMENT OF FORMAL PROCEEDINGS (CONTINUED)

Chapter 17 The Scope of the Prosecution: Joinder and Severance

§ 17.1 Joinder and severance of offenses 1
  § 17.1(a) Joinder: related offenses 2
  § 17.1(b) Joinder: offenses of similar character 6
  § 17.1(c) Severance: separate defenses 9
  § 17.1(d) Severance: evidence of other crimes................. 11
  § 17.1(e) Severance: cumulation of evidence 14
  § 17.1(f) Severance as of right or as a more favored
             alternative.. 16
§ 17.2 Joinder and severance of defendants 17
  § 17.2(a) Joinder of defendants 18
  § 17.2(b) Severance: codefendant's confession incriminates. 22
  § 17.2(c) Severance: codefendant's testimony would
             exculpate 34
  § 17.2(d) Severance: conflicting defenses and strategies 38
  § 17.2(e) Severance: guilt by association..................... 43
  § 17.2(f) Severance: confusion of evidence.................... 46
  § 17.2(g) Severance as of right 48
§ 17.3 Joinder and severance: procedural considerations 48
  § 17.3(a) Court's authority to consolidate and sever......... 49
  § 17.3(b) Misjoinder 50
  § 17.3(c) Failure to prove joinder basis 53
  § 17.3(d) Waiver or forfeiture................................ 55
  § 17.3(e) Appellate review of prejudice claim................. 57
§ 17.4 Failure to join related offenses 59
  § 17.4(a) Collateral estoppel.................................. 59
  § 17.4(b) Double jeopardy: same offense....................... 79
  § 17.4(c) "Same transaction" joinder.......................... 97

Chapter 18 Speedy Trial and Other Prompt Disposition

§ 18.1 The constitutional right to speedy trial.................... 105
  § 18.1(a) Generally 105
  § 18.1(b) Interests involved.................................. 107
  § 18.1(c) When right attaches................................ 109
  § 18.1(d) Waiver or forfeiture of the right 114
  § 18.1(e) Remedy for violation............................... 115
§ 18.2 The constitutional balancing test re speedy trial.......... 116
  § 18.2(a) The *Barker* case.................................... 116
  § 18.2(b) The length of the delay............................. 118
  § 18.2(c) Reason for delay 121
  § 18.2(d) Defendant's responsibility to assert the right 127
  § 18.2(e) Prejudice... 128
§ 18.3 Statutes and court rules on speedy trial 132
  § 18.3(a) The need 133
  § 18.3(b) Federal Speedy Trial Act of 1974 133

§ 18.3(c)   State provisions 151
§ 18.4 Speedy trial and the imprisoned defendant 162
    § 18.4(a)   Constitutional right 162
    § 18.4(b)   Federal Speedy Trial Act of 1974 166
    § 18.4(c)   Interstate agreement on detainers 167
    § 18.4(d)   Uniform Mandatory Disposition of Detainers
               Act 182
§ 18.5 The right to other speedy disposition 184
    § 18.5(a)   Statutes of limitations................................ 184
    § 18.5(b)   Unconstitutional pre-accusation delays 194
    § 18.5(c)   Post-trial delays...................................... 199

PART IV THE ADVERSARY SYSTEM AND THE DETERMINATION OF GUILT AND INNOCENCE

Chapter 19 The Accusatory Pleading

§ 19.1 The liberalization of pleading requirements 206
    § 19.1(a)   Common law technicalities 206
    § 19.1(b)   Initial attempts at reform........................... 209
    § 19.1(c)   The short-form pleading movement................ 211
    § 19.1(d)   The more successful reforms 212
    § 19.1(e)   Recent reforms 222
§ 19.2 Pleading functions 222
    § 19.2(a)   Functional analysis 222
    § 19.2(b)   Double jeopardy protection.......................... 225
    § 19.2(c)   Providing notice 227
    § 19.2(d)   Facilitating judicial review.......................... 233
    § 19.2(e)   Providing a jurisdictional grounding 235
    § 19.2(f)   Safeguarding defendant's right to prosecution by
               indictment 243
§ 19.3 Basic pleading defects 247
    § 19.3(a)   Failure to allege essential elements 247
    § 19.3(b)   Factual specificity.................................... 276
    § 19.3(c)   Duplicity and multiplicity........................... 285
    § 19.3(d)   Defects in form 288
    § 19.3(e)   Late objections 289
§ 19.4 Bill of particulars 299
    § 19.4(a)   Nature of the bill 299
    § 19.4(b)   Standards for issuance................................ 301
§ 19.5 Amendments of the pleading 308
    § 19.5(a)   Varied uses.. 308
    § 19.5(b)   The prejudice/different-offense standard 309
    § 19.5(c)   The form/substance distinction...................... 319
    § 19.5(d)   The *Bain* rule 322
§ 19.6 Variances and pleadings 328
    § 19.6(a)   Challenging variances................................. 329
    § 19.6(b)   The *Berger* standard................................. 330
    § 19.6(c)   The constructive amendment limitation............ 333

Chapter 20 Pretrial Discovery

§ 20.1 The expansion of discovery.. 342
   § 20.1(a)   The break from the common law 342
   § 20.1(b)   The discovery debate 345
   § 20.1(c)   Outcome of the discovery debate.................... 354
   § 20.1(d)   The "two-way street" movement in discovery...... 357
§ 20.2 The structure of discovery law............................... 359
   § 20.2(a)   "Common law" jurisdictions 359
   § 20.2(b)   Court rules and statutes 360
   § 20.2(c)   The operation of discovery provisions 367
   § 20.2(d)   Other discovery vehicles 369
   § 20.2(e)   Depositions 374
§ 20.3 Defense discovery 381
   § 20.3(a)   Prosecution possession or control.................. 381
   § 20.3(b)   Written or recorded statements.................... 387
   § 20.3(c)   Defendant's statements 394
   § 20.3(d)   Codefendant's statements 399
   § 20.3(e)   Criminal records.................................... 401
   § 20.3(f)   Scientific reports.................................... 402
   § 20.3(g)   Documents and tangible objects 405
   § 20.3(h)   Witness lists.. 410
   § 20.3(i)   Witness statements................................. 415
   § 20.3(j)   The work product exemption 421
   § 20.3(k)   Police reports....................................... 429
   § 20.3(l)   Protective orders................................... 431
   § 20.3(m)   Constitutional overtones............................ 433
   § 20.3(n)   Exculpatory material provisions 439
§ 20.4 Constitutional limitations upon pretrial discovery for
      the prosecution.. 440
   § 20.4(a)   Due process... 440
   § 20.4(b)   Self-incrimination: non-testimonial disclosures ... 443
   § 20.4(c)   Self-incrimination: the testimonial disclosure 451
   § 20.4(d)   Self-incrimination: the acceleration doctrine 454
   § 20.4(e)   Self-incrimination: the special case of the
            insanity defense 461
   § 20.4(f)   Sixth Amendment limitations...................... 465
   § 20.4(g)   Conditional discovery............................... 469
§ 20.5 Prosecution discovery provisions 473
   § 20.5(a)   Variations in approach............................. 473
   § 20.5(b)   Alibi defense provisions............................ 476
   § 20.5(c)   Insanity and related defenses...................... 479
   § 20.5(d)   Identification of defenses 483
   § 20.5(e)   Witness lists.. 484
   § 20.5(f)   Witness statements................................. 485
   § 20.5(g)   Documents and tangible objects 488
   § 20.5(h)   Scientific reports.................................... 489
§ 20.6 Sanctions for discovery violations.......................... 492
   § 20.6(a)   Range.. 492
   § 20.6(b)   Prosecution violations 494
   § 20.6(c)   Defense violations................................... 509

Chapter 21 Pleas of Guilty

§ 21.1 The plea negotiation system 520
  § 21.1(a) Forms of plea bargaining 520
  § 21.1(b) Development of plea bargaining 522
  § 21.1(c) Administrative convenience 526
  § 21.1(d) Accurate and fair results 528
  § 21.1(e) The problem of disparity 531
  § 21.1(f) Other attributes and consequences 540
  § 21.1(g) Prohibiting plea bargaining 542
  § 21.1(h) Plea bargaining and the federal sentencing
             guidelines 546
§ 21.2 Kept, broken, rejected and nonexistent bargains 559
  § 21.2(a) Statutory inducements to plead guilty 559
  § 21.2(b) Inducements by the prosecutor 565
  § 21.2(c) Inducements by the judge 590
  § 21.2(d) The broken bargain 598
  § 21.2(e) Remedy for broken bargain 652
  § 21.2(f) The withdrawn offer 672
  § 21.2(g) The unrealized expectation 681
  § 21.2(h) Admission of statements made during
             bargaining 687
§ 21.3 Plea negotiation responsibilities of the attorneys and
       judge 694
  § 21.3(a) Right to counsel during plea bargaining 694
  § 21.3(b) Effective assistance by defense counsel 701
  § 21.3(c) The prosecutor's bargaining tactics 731
  § 21.3(d) Judicial involvement in negotiations 745
  § 21.3(e) Judicial evaluation of contemplated concessions ... 757
  § 21.3(f) Responsibilities to the victim 768
§ 21.4 Receiving the defendant's plea 788
  § 21.4(a) Arraignment; pleading alternatives 789
  § 21.4(b) Determining voluntariness of plea and
             competency of defendant to plead 799
  § 21.4(c) Determining understanding of charge 806
  § 21.4(d) Determining understanding of possible
             consequences 816
  § 21.4(e) Determining understanding of rights waived 831
  § 21.4(f) Determining factual basis of plea 835
  § 21.4(g) Acting on the plea bargain 851
§ 21.5 Challenge of guilty plea by defendant 860
  § 21.5(a) Withdrawal of plea 861
  § 21.5(b) Other challenges to plea 874
  § 21.5(c) Significance of noncompliance with plea-receiving
             procedures 876
  § 21.5(d) Significance of compliance with plea-receiving
             procedures 885
  § 21.5(e) Effect of withdrawn or overturned plea 892
  § 21.5(f) Admissibility of withdrawn or overturned plea
             and related statements 902
§ 21.6 Effect of guilty plea 905

§ 21.6(a)   Rights waived or forfeited by plea 905
§ 21.6(b)   Conditional pleas 922
§ 21.6(c)   Trial on stipulated facts.............................. 929

Volume 6

PART IV THE ADVERSARY SYSTEM AND THE DETERMINATION OF GUILT AND INNOCENCE (CONTINUED)

Chapter 22 Trial by Jury and Impartial Judge

§ 22.1 The right to jury trial......................................   2
  § 22.1(a)   Generally; applicable to the states   2
  § 22.1(b)   Petty offenses   8
  § 22.1(c)   Noncriminal trials.................................. 15
  § 22.1(d)   Size of jury 17
  § 22.1(e)   Unanimity... 20
  § 22.1(f)   Trial de novo 23
  § 22.1(g)   Jury nullification 24
  § 22.1(h)   Waiver of jury trial................................ 31
§ 22.2 Selection of prospective jurors............................ 42
  § 22.2(a)   Federal jury selection procedures 42
  § 22.2(b)   State jury selection procedures 46
  § 22.2(c)   Denial of equal protection.......................... 47
  § 22.2(d)   The "fair cross-section" requirement 52
  § 22.2(e)   Vicinage 68
  § 22.2(f)   Challenge to the array.............................. 70
§ 22.3 Voir dire; challenges...................................... 71
  § 22.3(a)   Nature of voir dire................................. 71
  § 22.3(b)   Prosecution and defense access to information.... 85
  § 22.3(c)   Challenges for cause................................ 98
  § 22.3(d)   Peremptory challenges 121
  § 22.3(e)   Alternate jurors 158
§ 22.4 Challenging the judge 165
  § 22.4(a)   Right to impartial judge 165
  § 22.4(b)   Challenge for cause................................. 168
  § 22.4(c)   Recusal by judge 169
  § 22.4(d)   Peremptory challenge 175
  § 22.4(e)   Substitution of judge 178
§ 22.5 Challenging the prosecutor 179
  § 22.5(a)   Challenge for cause................................. 179
  § 22.5(b)   Prior relationship with defendant 183
  § 22.5(c)   Prosecutor as witness 185
  § 22.5(d)   Imputed disqualification 187

Chapter 23 Fair Trial and Free Press

§ 23.1 Preventing prejudicial publicity 191
   § 23.1(a) The problem of prejudicial publicity 191
   § 23.1(b) Restricting public statements 194
   § 23.1(c) Restricting the media 224
   § 23.1(d) Closed proceedings: First Amendment right of
          access 232
   § 23.1(e) Closing proceedings and placing documents
          under seal: restricting the First Amendment
          right 252
§ 23.2 Overcoming prejudicial publicity 262
   § 23.2(a) Change of venue on a defense motion 262
   § 23.2(b) Change of venue without a defense motion 274
   § 23.2(c) Change of venire 276
   § 23.2(d) Continuance 276
   § 23.2(e) Severance 278
   § 23.2(f) Jury selection 278
   § 23.2(g) Admonishment or sequestration of the jury 290
   § 23.2(h) Excusal of jurors 292
§ 23.3 Conduct of the trial 292
   § 23.3(a) Media representatives in the courtroom 293
   § 23.3(b) Broadcast, video and photographic coverage 294

Chapter 24 The Criminal Trial

§ 24.1 The right to a public trial 300
   § 24.1(a) Nature of the right 300
   § 24.1(b) When closure justified 304
§ 24.2 Presence of the defendant 309
   § 24.2(a) Origins and scope of the right to be present 309
   § 24.2(b) Harmless error and waiver, generally 316
   § 24.2(c) The disorderly defendant: forfeiture by conduct... 319
   § 24.2(d) Forfeiture by voluntary absence 321
   § 24.2(e) Prejudicial circumstances of presence 325
   § 24.2(f) Video conferencing 334
   § 24.2(g) Presence and understanding—Competency and
          interpreters 337
§ 24.3 The defendant's right of access to evidence 339
   § 24.3(a) Constitutional grounding 339
   § 24.3(b) Due process duty to disclose evidence favorable to
          the accused 344
   § 24.3(c) Disclosure of witness statements—Jencks Act 370
   § 24.3(d) The duty to correct false evidence 376
   § 24.3(e) The government's obligation to preserve evidence. 382
   § 24.3(f) Defense use of subpoenas 389
   § 24.3(g) Assisting the defense in obtaining evidence 395
   § 24.3(h) Government interference with defense access 399
   § 24.3(i) Defense witness immunity 402
§ 24.4 The presentation of evidence 405
   § 24.4(a) Constitutional limitations on the rules of
          evidence 406
   § 24.4(b) Cross-examination 408

§ 24.4(c)   Forcing a claim of privilege by a witness 409
§ 24.4(d)   Sequestration of witnesses 414
§ 24.5 Defendant's rights to remain silent and to testify 423
§ 24.5(a)   Right not to take the stand......................... 424
§ 24.5(b)   Comment on defendant's silence..................... 428
§ 24.5(c)   Instruction on defendant's silence 432
§ 24.5(d)   The defendant's right to testify 434
§ 24.6 Trial court evaluation of the evidence.................... 438
§ 24.6(a)   Bench trials.. 438
§ 24.6(b)   Motions for directed acquittal 440
§ 24.6(c)   The sufficiency standard 446
§ 24.6(d)   New trial motion................................... 448
§ 24.6(e)   Summary and comment on the evidence........... 449
§ 24.7 The arguments of counsel 451
§ 24.7(a)   Opening statements................................ 451
§ 24.7(b)   Closing argument 454
§ 24.7(c)   Order of closing argument.......................... 457
§ 24.7(d)   The roles of the prosecutor and defense counsel... 457
§ 24.7(e)   Prohibited argument............................... 460
§ 24.7(f)   The invited response............................... 469
§ 24.7(g)   Objections 470
§ 24.7(h)   Due process 471
§ 24.7(i)   Standard of review 472
§ 24.8 Jury instructions... 476
§ 24.8(a)   Multiple stages for instructions.................... 476
§ 24.8(b)   Requests and objections to instructions............ 482
§ 24.8(c)   Content of instructions 485
§ 24.8(d)   Lesser-included offenses generally 487
§ 24.8(e)   Defining the lesser-included offense................ 489
§ 24.8(f)   Entitlements to lesser offense charges.............. 500
§ 24.9 Jury procedures.. 510
§ 24.9(a)   Sequestering the jury 510
§ 24.9(b)   Jury questions and note-taking 512
§ 24.9(c)   Items taken to the jury room....................... 515
§ 24.9(d)   The deadlocked jury 517
§ 24.9(e)   Polling the jury 522
§ 24.9(f)   Jury misconduct 525
§ 24.9(g)   Limitations on juror testimony about
                misconduct 537
§ 24.10 Jury verdicts 543
§ 24.10(a)   Special verdicts and special interrogatories...... 543
§ 24.10(b)   Inconsistent verdicts or findings.................. 548
§ 24.10(c)   Multi-theory verdicts 551
§ 24.10(d)   Partial verdicts................................... 558
§ 24.11 Post-verdict motions..................................... 559
§ 24.11(a)   Judgment of acquittal 559
§ 24.11(b)   New trial 559
§ 24.11(c)   Arrest of judgment................................ 560
§ 24.11(d)   Newly discovered evidence......................... 561

Chapter 25 Double Jeopardy

§ 25.1 Dimensions of the guarantee 573
    § 25.1(a) Introduction 574
    § 25.1(b) Policies and history..................................... 574
    § 25.1(c) Proceedings to which applicable 579
    § 25.1(d) When jeopardy attaches.............................. 587
    § 25.1(e) Termination of jeopardy............................. 602
    § 25.1(f) The "same offence"..................................... 604
    § 25.1(g) Reprosecutions: an overview....................... 605
§ 25.2 Reprosecution following mistrial 606
    § 25.2(a) With defendant's consent............................ 607
    § 25.2(b) The "goaded" mistrial motion 610
    § 25.2(c) The "manifest necessity" standard 613
    § 25.2(d) Manifest necessity and alternatives to a mistrial . 615
    § 25.2(e) Manifest necessity and trial court discretion....... 620
    § 25.2(f) Dismissals equivalent to mistrials 625
§ 25.3 Reprosecution following acquittal or dismissal 627
    § 25.3(a) Dismissals vs. acquittals............................. 627
    § 25.3(b) The jury acquittal..................................... 630
    § 25.3(c) Acquittal by the judge................................ 633
    § 25.3(d) Pre-jeopardy "acquittals"............................. 637
    § 25.3(e) Postconviction judgments of acquittal.............. 638
§ 25.4 Reprosecution following conviction......................... 640
    § 25.4(a) The general rule 640
    § 25.4(b) The evidence insufficiency exception 643
    § 25.4(c) The determination of sufficiency 649
    § 25.4(d) Conviction as implied acquittal 653
§ 25.5 Reprosecution by a different sovereign 657
    § 25.5(a) Federal prosecution after state...................... 657
    § 25.5(b) State prosecution after federal 661
    § 25.5(c) State-state and state-municipal..................... 663

Chapter 26 Sentencing Procedures

§ 26.1 Legislative structuring of sentencing: sanctions 668
    § 26.1(a) Structure and procedure............................. 668
    § 26.1(b) Capital punishment................................... 670
    § 26.1(c) Incarceration... 676
    § 26.1(d) Community release.................................... 681
    § 26.1(e) Intermediate sanctions 687
    § 26.1(f) Financial sanctions.................................... 695
§ 26.2 Legislative structuring of sentencing: the allocation of
        sentencing authority...................................... 698
    § 26.2(a) Judicial sentencing 698
    § 26.2(b) Jury sentencing 699
    § 26.2(c) Administrative agency decisions 705
§ 26.3 The guidance of judicial sentencing discretion 718
    § 26.3(a) Unguided discretion 718
    § 26.3(b) The challenge to unguided discretion.............. 719
    § 26.3(c) Mandatory minimum sentences..................... 721
    § 26.3(d) Presumptive sentencing.............................. 724
    § 26.3(e) Sentencing guidelines 725

§ 26.3(f)   Concurrent and consecutive sentences   730
§ 26.3(g)   Appellate review   735
§ 26.4 Due process: the framework for sentencing procedure ..   741
§ 26.4(a)   *Williams v. New York*   741
§ 26.4(b)   The range of relevant information.................   744
§ 26.4(c)   Consideration of the defendant's exercise of
            procedural rights................................   751
§ 26.4(d)   Notice...   756
§ 26.4(e)   The right to the assistance of counsel.............   764
§ 26.4(f)   Ensuring the reliability of sentencing
            information   767
§ 26.4(g)   The right to be heard: allocation and the right to
            offer rebuttal evidence..........................   775
§ 26.4(h)   Burden of proof   783
§ 26.4(i)   When sentencing factors are elements..............   787
§ 26.5 Sentencing information   801
§ 26.5(a)   Evidentiary standards   802
§ 26.5(b)   The presentence report...........................   806
§ 26.5(c)   Disclosure of the presentence report   809
§ 26.5(d)   Victim impact statement..........................   814
§ 26.6 Special sentences   817
§ 26.6(a)   Special sentences and special procedures   818
§ 26.6(b)   Recidivist statutes   818
§ 26.6(c)   Restitution......................................   824
§ 26.6(d)   Forfeiture   826
§ 26.6(e)   "Dangerous" offenders   831
§ 26.7 Resentencing: double jeopardy   834
§ 26.7(a)   Resentencing following reconviction...............   834
§ 26.7(b)   Resentencing and sentencing appeals...............   838
§ 26.7(c)   Resentencing by the trial judge...................   841
§ 26.7(d)   Sentencing based upon other criminal conduct ...   848
§ 26.8 Resentencing: the prohibition against vindictiveness....   849
§ 26.8(a)   Presumed vindictiveness: the *Pearce* ruling   849
§ 26.8(b)   Rebutting the *Pearce* presumption.................   851
§ 26.8(c)   Applying the *Pearce* presumption in other
            resentencing settings............................   854
§ 26.9 Probation conditions................................   860
§ 26.9(a)   General standards   860
§ 26.9(b)   Probation conditions and constitutional rights   863
§ 26.9(c)   Challenging conditions   878
§ 26.10 Revocation of probation   880
§ 26.10(a)   Basis for revocation   880
§ 26.10(b)   The revocation process..........................   883
§ 26.10(c)   Proof at revocation hearing   888
§ 26.10(d)   Decision on revocation and its consequences.....   896

Volume 7

PART V POST-CONVICTION REVIEW: APPEALS AND COLLATERAL REMEDIES

Chapter 27 Appeals
§ 27.1 Constitutional protection of the defendant's right to appeal...... 2
§ 27.1(a) No federal constitutional right...... 2
§ 27.1(b) Constitutional protection of the statutory right of appeal...... 5
§ 27.2 Defense appeals and the final judgment rule...... 7
§ 27.2(a) The statutory requirement of a final judgment.... 7
§ 27.2(b) Underlying policies and statutory exceptions...... 9
§ 27.2(c) Collateral orders...... 12
§ 27.2(d) Independent proceedings...... 24
§ 27.2(e) Grand jury proceedings...... 27
§ 27.3 Prosecution appeals...... 31
§ 27.3(a) Constitutional constraints...... 32
§ 27.3(b) The need for specific statutory authorization...... 34
§ 27.3(c) Pretrial rulings...... 37
§ 27.3(d) Post-jeopardy rulings...... 43
§ 27.4 Review by writ...... 46
§ 27.4(a) Extraordinary writs generally...... 47
§ 27.4(b) Prohibition and mandamus: traditional limits and modern extensions...... 47
§ 27.4(c) Defense petitions...... 50
§ 27.4(d) Prosecution applications...... 54
§ 27.4(e) Third-party applications...... 58
§ 27.4(f) Habeas corpus...... 60
§ 27.5 The scope of appellate review...... 61
§ 27.5(a) Mootness...... 61
§ 27.5(b) The concurrent sentence doctrine...... 71
§ 27.5(c) Waiver or forfeiture of the right to appeal...... 74
§ 27.5(d) Plain error...... 87
§ 27.5(e) Standard of review...... 94
§ 27.6 Harmless error on appeal...... 99
§ 27.6(a) Origins of harmless error review...... 99
§ 27.6(b) Harmless error review of nonconstitutional errors...... 102
§ 27.6(c) Application to constitutional violations...... 113
§ 27.6(d) Harmless error or automatic reversal...... 115
§ 27.6(e) Applying the reasonable doubt standard for constitutional errors...... 133

Chapter 28 Post Conviction Review: Collateral Remedies
§ 28.1 Current collateral remedies and historical antecedents. 138
§ 28.1(a) The nature of collateral remedies...... 138
§ 28.1(b) The common law writ of habeas corpus...... 140
§ 28.1(c) The common law writ of coram nobis...... 143
§ 28.2 The statutory structure and habeas policy...... 144

§ 28.2(a)   Constitutional right or legislative grace?   144
§ 28.2(b)   Statutory structure: from the 1867 Act to the
            1996 Act.   148
§ 28.2(c)   Balancing within the statutory framework   153
§ 28.2(d)   Competing models of habeas review   159
§ 28.3   Claims cognizable in habeas   164
§ 28.3(a)   Cognizable claimants: the custody requirement . . .   164
§ 28.3(b)   Cognizable claims   172
§ 28.3(c)   The exception for Fourth Amendment claims   179
§ 28.3(d)   The opportunity for full and fair litigation   183
§ 28.3(e)   "Bare innocence" claims   186
§ 28.4   Claims in habeas foreclosed by state procedural
         defaults   189
§ 28.4(a)   Claims "defaulted" in state court-the policy
            debate   189
§ 28.4(b)   Which defaults count: the "adequate and
            independent state ground" standard   192
§ 28.4(c)   Excusing default: state waiver of the procedural
            default defense   196
§ 28.4(d)   Excusing default: the "cause and prejudice"
            standard   198
§ 28.4(e)   Excusing default: the "miscarriage of justice"
            exception   208
§ 28.5   Claims in habeas foreclosed due to premature,
         successive, or delayed applications   213
§ 28.5(a)   Exhaustion of state remedies   213
§ 28.5(b)   Time limits for filing petitions   223
§ 28.5(c)   Successive petitions: claims previously advanced .   231
§ 28.5(d)   Successive petitions: new claims   234
§ 28.5(e)   Successive petitions: court of appeals
            certification   240
§ 28.6   Constitutional interpretation on habeas review   241
§ 28.6(a)   The changing role of federal habeas courts   241
§ 28.6(b)   *Teague*: limiting the retroactive application of
            new rules of procedure   242
§ 28.6(c)   Determining when a state conviction becomes
            final   245
§ 28.6(d)   The "new rule" concept   245
§ 28.6(e)   The *Teague* exceptions   249
§ 28.6(f)   Review of state court rulings under § 2254(d)   254
§ 28.6(g)   Harmless error on habeas review   259
§ 28.7   Fact-finding and evidentiary hearings in habeas   263
§ 28.7(a)   Presuming the correctness of state court
            determinations of fact   263
§ 28.7(b)   Distinguishing mixed determinations of law and
            fact from fact-finding   266
§ 28.7(c)   Obtaining evidentiary hearings   268
§ 28.7(d)   Discovery   272
§ 28.8   Habeas review of capital cases under Chapter 154 of
         the 1996 Act   273

§ 28.8(a)   Special standards for applicants from certain
            states 273
§ 28.8(b)   The opt-in requirements: electing the special
            standards... 278
§ 28.9 Remedies for federal prisoners 279
§ 28.9(a)   The range of remedies................................ 279
§ 28.9(b)   Limits on relief under § 2255 286
§ 28.9(c)   Nonconstitutional claims under § 2255 296
§ 28.10 Appeal of district court decisions in habeas 299
§ 28.11 State collateral remedies.................................. 301
§ 28.11(a) Supreme Court "encouragement" of state
            remedies 301
§ 28.11(b) Types of state remedies............................. 303
§ 28.12 Assistance of counsel in post-conviction proceedings 308
§ 28.12(a) Petitioner access to legal assistance-
            constitutional requirements 308
§ 28.12(b) Statutory entitlements to legal assistance 309

Table of Cases .... Table of Cases-1

Table of Laws and Rules .... Tbl of L&R-1

Table of Secondary Authorities .... Tbl of Sec Auth-1

Index Index-1

PART V

POST-CONVICTION REVIEW: APPEALS AND COLLATERAL REMEDIES

CHAPTER 27

APPEALS

§ 27.1 Constitutional protection of the defendant's right to appeal
  § 27.1(a)   No federal constitutional right
  § 27.1(b)   Constitutional protection of the statutory right of appeal
§ 27.2 Defense appeals and the final judgment rule
  § 27.2(a)   The statutory requirement of a final judgment
  § 27.2(b)   Underlying policies and statutory exceptions
  § 27.2(c)   Collateral orders
  § 27.2(d)   Independent proceedings
  § 27.2(e)   Grand jury proceedings
§ 27.3 Prosecution appeals
  § 27.3(a)   Constitutional constraints
  § 27.3(b)   The need for specific statutory authorization
  § 27.3(c)   Pretrial rulings
  § 27.3(d)   Post-jeopardy rulings
§ 27.4 Review by writ
  § 27.4(a)   Extraordinary writs generally
  § 27.4(b)   Prohibition and mandamus: traditional limits and modern extensions
  § 27.4(c)   Defense petitions
  § 27.4(d)   Prosecution applications
  § 27.4(e)   Third-party applications
  § 27.4(f)   Habeas corpus
§ 27.5 The scope of appellate review
  § 27.5(a)   Mootness
  § 27.5(b)   The concurrent sentence doctrine
  § 27.5(c)   Waiver or forfeiture of the right to appeal
  § 27.5(d)   Plain error
  § 27.5(e)   Standard of review
§ 27.6 Harmless error on appeal
  § 27.6(a)   Origins of harmless error review
  § 27.6(b)   Harmless error review of nonconstitutional errors
  § 27.6(c)   Application to constitutional violations
  § 27.6(d)   Harmless error or automatic reversal
  § 27.6(e)   Applying the reasonable doubt standard for constitutional errors

§ 27.1 Constitutional protection of the defendant's right to appeal

§ 27.1(a)   No federal constitutional right
§ 27.1(b)   Constitutional protection of the statutory right of appeal

§ 27.1(a) No federal constitutional right

Following dictum written over a century ago, the Supreme Court has consistently maintained that the due process guaranteed to the accused by the Constitution does not include access to appellate review of criminal convictions. In 1894, the Court in *McKane v. Durston*[1] upheld a state's denial of bail pending appeal, reasoning that the state had no constitutional obligation to provide appellate review at all. It stated:

> An appeal from a judgment of conviction is not a matter of absolute right, independently of [state] constitutional or statutory provisions allowing such appeal. A review by an appellate court of the final judgment in a criminal case, however grave the offense of which the accused is convicted, was not at common-law, and is not now, a necessary element of due process of law. It is wholly within the discretion of the state to allow or not to allow such a review.

McKane was written at a time in which appellate review had only recently been introduced into the federal judicial structure. Congress did not grant circuit courts the authority to review federal criminal convictions until 1879, and did not give the Supreme Court jurisdiction to entertain writs of error in federal criminal cases until 1889.[2] While the appellate review process in the state courts developed more quickly, it remained quite limited well into the mid-1800s.[3]

Today appellate review is a much more important element of

[Section 27.1(a)]

[1]McKane v. Durston, 153 U.S. 684, 14 S.Ct. 913, 38 L.Ed. 867 (1894).

[2]See, e.g., Abney v. United States, 431 U.S. 651, 97 S.Ct. 2034, 52 L.Ed.2d 651 (1977) (discussing the right of appeal in federal criminal cases).

[3]See L. Orfield, Criminal Appeals in America 215–16 (1939) (noting that although most of the former colonies set up appellate courts after the Revolution, there was no right to appeal in criminal cases in several states until the mid-or late 1800s). The number of cases heard by state appellate courts remained quite small into the 1900s. Id. at 225–26.

See also Martinez v. Court of Appeal of California, 528 U.S. 152, 120 S.Ct. 684, 145 L.Ed.2d 597 (2000) (finding no historical basis for a right to self-representation on appeal and stating, "Appeals of right in federal courts were nonexistent for the first century of our Nation, and appellate review of any sort was "rarely allowed." * * * The States, also, did not generally recognize an appeal as of right until Washington became the first to constitutionalize the right explicitly in 1889. There was similarly no right to appeal in criminal cases at common law, and appellate review of any sort was "limited" and "rarely used.""); id. (Scalia, J., concurring) ("a State could, as far as the federal Constitution is concerned, subject its trial-court determinations to no review whatever"). Compare Rossman, "Were There No Appeal": The History of

the criminal justice process than it was when *McKane* was decided. As discussed in the sections that follow, every state and the federal government provides some means of appellate review for defendants in criminal cases. In the federal system[4] and in most states, statutes (or state constitutional provisions) guarantee defendants in all felony cases a right to appellate review.[5] In a small number of states, review of felony convictions remains at the discretion of the state's highest court, but the defendant has at least the opportunity to gain appellate review.[6] In misdemeanor cases, defendants commonly have a right of review in the general trial court (in some states, by trial de novo) with subsequent discretionary appellate review.

The criminal appellate caseload in state and federal courts has

---

Review in American Criminal Courts, 81 J.Crim.L. & Criminology 518, 525–50 (1990) (noting the use of multi-judge tribunals at trial, trials de novo, writs of error, removal or referral of cases to higher courts for trial, new trial motions, and motions to arrest judgment and arguing that while review per se was not seen at the Founding as a fundamental right of all criminal defendants, the presence of multi-judge panels, including members of higher courts, together with this wide variety of review procedures, undercut the conclusion that the Due Process Clause allows the final determination of constitutional issues by an individual trial judge); Arkin, Rethinking the Constitutional Right to a Criminal Appeal, 39 UCLA L.Rev. 503, 524–33 (1992) (documenting review procedures in eighteenth and nineteenth centuries in federal and state courts and concluding that the "legal community expected the review of trial court decisions").

[4]A general right to appeal in federal criminal cases was first created in 1911. See 36 Stat. 1133 (1911). It was not until 1928 that the writ of error was abolished and all review was provided by appeal. See 45 Stat. 54, ch. 14 (1928). See also L. Orfield, Criminal Appeals in America 243–48 (1939) (reviewing history of criminal appeals in federal courts).

[5]State constitutional provisions include Ariz.Const.art.II, § 24;

Fla.Const.art.V, §§ 4 to 6; Ga.Cons.art. VI, § 5; Ill.Cons.art.VI., § 6; Ind.Const. art.VII, § 6; Ky.Const. § 115; La.Const. art. I, § 19; Deegan v. State, 711 N.W.2d 89 (Minn.2006) (finding a state constitutional right to one review of conviction). For a listing of each state's court structure and appellate jurisdiction, noting whether appellate review in criminal cases is mandatory or discretionary, and which appellate courts review guilty pleas, death penalty cases, and sentencing issues, see D. Rottman & S. Strickland, State Court Organization 2004 Table 22 (Aug. 2006, NCJ 212351). On the scope of appeal in guilty plea cases generally, see § 21.5(b) at notes 61–66; Neb.Const. art.I, § 23; N.M.Const.art.VI, § 2; Ohio Const.art.IV, § 3; Utah Const.art.I, § 12; Wash.Const.art.I, § 22.

[6]See, e.g., W.Va.CodeAnn. § 58-5-1 to § 58-5-9; Bundy v. Wilson, 815 F.2d 125 (1st Cir.1987) (summarizing the state rules and noting that New Hampshire does not guarantee appeal as of right). See also Halbert v. Michigan, 545 U.S. 605, 125 S.Ct. 2582, 162 L.Ed.2d 552 (2005) (finding that defendant seeking discretionary review of plea-based conviction, the only appeal allowed under state law, has the right to counsel). Several states provide appeal directly from the trial court to the state's highest court, particularly in cases involving constitutional questions, or the sentence of death.

continued to rise.[7] A sizable percentage of all criminal appeals result in reversal, with reversal rates ranging between approximately 4 and 13 percent.[8] In addition, players in the criminal justice system have come to expect that it is the appellate courts that will announce the rules that govern their behavior.[9]

The significance of appellate review in the contemporary criminal justice system[10] has led some commentators and judges to advocate a constitutional conclusion different from that expressed in *McKane*.[11] Although constitutional status for the right to appeal may seem unnecessary given the widespread statutory protection of the right to appeal, some have expressed apprehension that burgeoning appellate caseloads combined with political and fiscal pressures to cut back on procedural relief for convicted criminals will lead legislatures to erode existing appellate processes.[12] The Court, however, has yet to reconsider its position

---

[7]For example, during the first five years following the implementation of the federal sentencing guidelines, the rate at which federal criminal appeals were filed increased an average of 10% annually to nearly one of every four convictions in 1993. The rate declined through 1999, see www.o jp.usdoj.gov/bjs/pub/pdf/fca99.pdf, then picked up again. The number of appeals rose steadily through 2005. See www.uscourts.gov.judbus2006.

[8]See Arkin, Rethinking the Constitutional Right to a Criminal Appeal, 39 UCLA L.Rev. 503, 515–516 (1992) (collecting statistics on reversal rates as of 1992).

[9]Rossman, "Were There No Appeal": The History of Review in American Criminal Courts, 81 J.Crim.L. & Criminology 518, 519 (1990).

[10]See Shavell, The Appeals Process as a Means of Error Correction, 24 J.Legal Stud. 379 (1995).

[11]See, e.g., Jones v. Barnes, 463 U.S. 745, 103 S.Ct. 3308, 77 L.Ed.2d 987 (1983) (Justice Blackmun, concurring, Justices Brennan and Marshall, dissenting); Arkin, Rethinking the Constitutional Right to a Criminal Appeal, 39 UCLA L.Rev. 503 (1992); Rossman, "Were There No Appeal": The History of Review in American

Criminal Courts, 81 J.Crim.L. & Criminology 518 (1990); Dalton, Taking the Right to Appeal (More or Less) Seriously, 95 Yale L.J. 62 (1985); Hood, The Right of Appeal, 29 La.L.Rev. 498 (1969); Note, 91 Colum.L.Rev. 373 (1991). See also Meltzer, Harmless Error and Constitutional Remedies, 51 U.Chi.L.Rev. 1, 5–10 (1994) (collecting support for a constitutional right of appeal).

[12]See Arkin, Rethinking the Constitutional Right to a Criminal Appeal, 39 UCLA L.Rev. 503, 507–13 (1992). See also Cavallaro, Better Off Dead: Abatement, Innocence, and the Evolving Right to Appeal, 73 U.Colo. L.Rev. 943 (2003); Dalton, Taking the Right to Appeal (More or Less) Seriously, 95 Yale L.J. 62 (1985); Note, 91 Colum.L.Rev. 373 (1991); R. Stern, Appellate Practice in the United States (2d ed. 1988) §§ 2.1–2.8 (2d ed.1988) (collecting proposed and implemented methods of addressing appellate case loads); Sullivan, New Mexico's Summary Calendar for Disposition of Criminal Appeals: An Invitation for Inefficiency, Ineffectiveness and Injustice, 24 N.M.L.Rev. 27 (1994) (noting that some states, in order to cope with caseloads, have created intermediate or specialized criminal appellate courts, shifted decision-making authority, and adopted summary pro-

in *McKane*.[13]

§ 27.1(b) Constitutional protection of the statutory right of appeal

Various strands of constitutional doctrine protect the defendant's access to that appellate review which is provided under state law. Perhaps the most significant and certainly the most extensive line of cases in this regard are the equal protection decisions safeguarding indigents' access to appellate review. As noted in Chapter 11, *Griffin v. Illinois*[14] holds that once a state grants defendants a right of appeal, it cannot condition that right in a manner that violates the constitutional guarantee of equal protection.[15] The *Griffin* principle has been utilized primarily to ensure that the indigent defendant has equal access to the appellate process. Thus, the state is precluded from conditioning appellate review on an appellate transcript and then failing to provide a free transcript for an indigent appellant.[16] Similarly, to ensure the indigent defendant "meaningful access" to the appellate process, the state had to provide defendant with appointed counsel for his first appeal. *Douglas v. California*[17] and *Halbert v.*

---

cesses for considering appeals); Kelso, Special Report on California Appellate Justice, 45 Hastings L.J. 433, 445–47 (1994) (discussing option of eliminating appeal as of right in California).

[13]In Jones v. Barnes, 463 U.S. 745, 103 S.Ct. 3308, 77 L.Ed.2d 987 (1983), the majority pronounced simply, "There is, of course, no constitutional right to an appeal." The Court has continued to adhere to this view in subsequent opinions. For other affirmations of the conclusion in *McKane*, see Halbert v. Michigan, 545 U.S. 605, 125 S.Ct. 2582, 162 L.Ed.2d 552 (2005) ("The Federal Constitution imposes on the States no obligation to provide appellate review of criminal convictions."); Ross v. Moffitt, 417 U.S. 600, 94 S.Ct. 2437, 41 L.Ed.2d 341 (1974); Douglas v. California, 372 U.S. 353, 83 S.Ct. 814, 9 L.Ed.2d 811 (1963), discussed in § 11.1(d) at note 107; Pennsylvania v. Finley, 481 U.S. 551, 107 S.Ct. 1990, 95 L.Ed.2d 539 (1987) (reasoning that there is no right to counsel in discretionary appeal, given that "the State need not provide any appeal at all"); Goeke v. Branch, 514 U.S. 115, 115 S.Ct. 1275, 131

L.Ed.2d 152 (1995); Whitmore v. Arkansas, 495 U.S. 149, 110 S.Ct. 1717, 109 L.Ed.2d 135 (1990) (Marshall, J., dissenting); and Lewis v. Casey, 518 U.S. 343, 116 S.Ct. 2174, 135 L.Ed.2d 606 (1996) (Thomas, J., concurring).

[Section 27.1(b)]

[14]Griffin v. Illinois, 351 U.S. 12, 76 S.Ct. 585, 100 L.Ed. 891 (1956).

[15]See § 11.1(d), at notes 104–106.

[16]See § 11.2(d). See also Britt v. North Carolina, 404 U.S. 226, 92 S.Ct. 431, 30 L.Ed.2d 400 (1971) (state ordinarily required to provide an indigent defendant with a transcript of a prior mistrial in order to aid him in preparing for a second trial); State ex rel. Spirko v. Judges of Court of Appeals, 27 Ohio St.3d 13, 501 N.E.2d 625 (1986) (state constitution requires that capital defendants be provided complete transcript for appeal).

[17]Douglas v. California, 372 U.S. 353, 83 S.Ct. 814, 9 L.Ed.2d 811 (1963), discussed in § 11.1(d) at note 107.

Michigan,[18] held that *Anders v. California*[19] added to this protection by ensuring that appointed counsel could not withdraw from that obligation by mere assertion that the appeal would be frivolous.[20]

The constitutional guarantee of effective assistance of counsel on the first appeal granted of right under state law is not limited to appointed counsel. The Supreme Court has held that the Constitution guarantees to all defendants a right to be represented by counsel on such an appeal and to effective assistance by such counsel.[21] However, beyond that point, as on application for discretionary review, the defendant has no such guarantee.[22]

The due process prohibition against vindictiveness in sentencing also serves to safeguard the defendant's right of appeal under state law. In *North Carolina v. Pearce*,[23] discussed in § 26.8, the Court established a presumption of vindictiveness for cases in which a defendant, retried and reconvicted after a successful appeal, received a sentence higher than that imposed following his original trial. The Court in *Pearce* was unanimous in holding that due process was denied where a sentencing judge sought to punish a defendant for having taken an appeal by imposing a more severe sentence following reconviction. Justice Stewart's opinion for the Court noted that "a court is 'without right to put a price on an appeal.'" As in *Griffin*, though a state had no duty to establish avenues of appellate review, it could not subject those avenues, once established, to "unreasoned distinctions" that would deter a defendant's "free and unfettered" exercise of his right to challenge his conviction. While the scope of that presumption has been narrowed, the Court remains committed to the pro-

[18]Halbert v. Michigan, 545 U.S. 605, 125 S.Ct. 2582, 162 L.Ed.2d 552 (2005). See § 11.1(d) at note 117.

[19]Anders v. California, 386 U.S. 738, 87 S.Ct. 1396, 18 L.Ed.2d 493 (1967), discussed in § 11.2(c) at note 84.

[20]But see Smith v. Robbins, 528 U.S. 259, 120 S.Ct. 746, 145 L.Ed.2d 756 (2000), discussed in § 11.2(c) at note 103 (upholding state procedure less protective than that approved in Anders).

[21]See Evitts v. Lucey, 469 U.S. 387, 105 S.Ct. 830, 83 L.Ed.2d 821 (1985), discussed in § 11.1(b) at note 53 and in § 11.7(a) at note 7. See also Ohio Adult Parole Auth. v. Woodard, 523 U.S. 272, 118 S.Ct. 1244, 140 L.Ed.2d 387 (1998) (discussing basis

for Evitts).

[22]See Murray v. Giarratano, 492 U.S. 1, 109 S.Ct. 2765, 106 L.Ed.2d 1 (1989), discussed in § 11.7(a). Compare Blankenship v. Johnson, 118 F.3d 312, 317 (5th Cir.1997) (right to appointed counsel extends to discretionary review once review is granted at the state's request); Taveras v. Smith, 388 F.Supp.2d 256 (S.D.N.Y.2005) (no exception to the right to counsel on appeal for cases in which the threshold issue on appeal is the applicability of the fugitive disentitlement doctrine). The fugitive disentitlement doctrine is discussed in § 27.5 at notes 69–87.

[23]North Carolina v. Pearce, 395 U.S. 711, 89 S.Ct. 2072, 23 L.Ed.2d 656 (1969).

hibition against actual vindictiveness announced in *Pearce*.[24]

Although the defendant has been granted some sort of right to appeal his conviction in every jurisdiction, he is not guaranteed review of each and every trial court ruling. Appellate review typically is limited to claims that challenge trial court decisions which can be characterized as "final judgments" or that fit within an exception to the final judgment rule, claims that are not moot, and claims that are not expressly waived by agreement or forfeited by the defendant's failure to comply with procedural requirements. Moreover, even meritorious claims may not produce relief on appeal if the error reviewed is considered by the reviewing court to be "harmless." These and other limits on appellate relief are examined in the sections that follow.

§ 27.2 Defense appeals and the final judgment rule

§ 27.2(a)   The statutory requirement of a final judgment
§ 27.2(b)   Underlying policies and statutory exceptions
§ 27.2(c)   Collateral orders
§ 27.2(d)   Independent proceedings
§ 27.2(e)   Grand jury proceedings

§ 27.2(a) The statutory requirement of a final judgment

The statutory provisions that govern defense appeals uniformly reflect the view that piecemeal appellate review of litigation is generally inappropriate and therefore appeals ordinarily should be allowed only from a final judgment.[1] Special double jeopardy concerns guide the implementation of this policy in the context of prosecution appeals, which are discussed in § 27.3. This section considers the final judgment rule as it applies to appeals by defendants, potential defendants (e.g., grand jury targets), and third parties (e.g., witnesses).

In many jurisdictions defense appeals in criminal cases are governed by the same statutes that regulate civil appeals. The

---

[24]See § 26.8 (discussing cases following *Pearce*). See also § 26.7 (discussing constitutional regulation of resentencing after appeal under the Double Jeopardy Clause). The Due Process Clause also protects a defendant against an excessively long wait for an appellate court to decide his appeal. See § 18.5(c) at notes 77–84.

[Section 27.2(a)]

[1]The history of the final judgment rule in federal courts is re-

counted in 15A C. Wright, A. Miller, and E. Cooper, Federal Practice and Procedure § 3906 (2d ed.1992). The requirement of finality was well established in civil appeals prior to the recognition of a right to appeal in criminal cases. Id.

federal provision, 28 U.S.C.A. § 1291, is typical. It provides that the "courts of appeals * * * shall have jurisdiction of appeals from all final decisions of the district courts * * *."[2] Counterpart state statutes often refer to appeals from "final orders."[3] In those states with separate statutes governing defense appeals in criminal cases, the statutes commonly refer to a "final judgment of conviction."[4]

Notwithstanding such references to "convictions" or "adverse verdicts of guilt," the prevailing view is that an appealable final judgment does not come with conviction alone, but requires the imposition of a sentence for that conviction.[5] This is consistent with the view frequently expressed in civil cases that a judgment is final only "when it ends the litigation on the merits and leaves nothing for the court to do but execute the judgment."[6]

---

[2]The Judiciary Act of 1789 referred to appeals from "final decrees and judgments," but the 1891 provision creating the circuit courts provided for an appeal from a "final decision." That language was carried over in 28 U.S.C.A. § 1291. The federal courts have consistently held that the substitution of the word "decision" for the phrase "decrees and judgments" was not intended to change the law, and treat the phrases "final decision" and "final judgment" as interchangeable. See 15A C. Wright, A. Miller, and E. Cooper, Federal Practice and Procedure § 3906 (2d ed.1992).

[3]See, e.g., Minn.Stat.Ann. § 480A.06; Neb.Rev.Stat.Ann. § 25-1912.

[4]See, e.g., Ariz.Rev.Stat.Ann. § 13-4033; Mont.Code Ann. § 46-20-104; Utah R.Crim.P. 26(2)(a). These provisions sometimes list separately appeals from certain post-judgment rulings, such as the denial of a motion in arrest of judgment. See, e.g., Ariz.Rev.Stat.Ann.   § 13-4033; N.D.Century Code § 29-28-06.

[5]See, e.g., Berman v. United States, 302 U.S. 211, 58 S.Ct. 164, 82 L.Ed. 204 (1937) ("Final judgment in a criminal case means sentence. The sentence is the judgment."); Fort Wayne Books, Inc. v. Indiana, 489 U.S. 46, 54, 109 S.Ct. 916, 103 L.Ed.2d 34 (1989); Parr v. United States, 351 U.S.

513, 76 S.Ct. 912, 100 L.Ed. 1377 (1956) (no appeal allowed from order dismissing an indictment); Florida v. Thomas, 532 U.S. 774, 121 S.Ct. 1905, 150 L.Ed.2d 1 (2001) (applying final judgment rule in review of state case, noting cases in which Court had "treated state-court judgments as final for jurisdictional purposes although there were further proceedings to take place in the state court"); State v. Coleman, 202 Conn. 86, 519 A.2d 1201 (1987) Annot., 51 A.L.R.4th 939 (2002) (collecting state cases on appealability where the defendant's sentence is suspended or probated).

[6]Cunningham v. Hamilton County, 527 U.S. 198, 119 S.Ct. 1915, 144 L.Ed.2d 184 (1999) (order imposing sanctions on attorney not a final decision appealable under § 1291, even where attorney no longer represents a party in the case). Compare State v. Wright, 699 N.W.2d 782 (Minn.App. 2005) (after guilty plea, defendant asked for, presentence investigation report recommended, and judge imposed a "stay of adjudication" of defendant's conviction because he would lose his job if convicted of a felony; conditions of the stay included ordering that the defendant serve six months in jail, undergo a month of home monitoring with an alco-sensor, fines, and seven years of no arrests and abstaining from alcohol; this order was essentially a sentence, not a

§ 27.2(b) Underlying policies and statutory exceptions

The final judgment rule reflects a determination that, on balance, postponing an appeal until a final judgment is reached best protects the interests of the litigants in a fair and accessible process while conserving judicial resources.[7] Weighing against the final judgment rule is the possibility that not allowing an interlocutory appeal from a potentially erroneous pretrial[8] ruling may result in a final judgment reversed on appeal, causing the litigants to repeat the entire trial. Retrial brings additional expense and anxiety for the defendant and trial participants. It can also produce a final determination that is considerably different from what it might have been had the error been caught before the case was first tried, since delay can result in memory lapses, strategic advantages, and less effective impeachment of witnesses.

Yet the costs of permitting interlocutory appeals are thought to be greater. Awaiting a final judgment benefits litigants as a group even if it does occasionally require a particular litigant to undergo an unnecessary trial. Permitting either or both parties to postpone a trial with interlocutory appeals is likely to result in even greater delay in final adjudication than allowing appeals only from final judgment. Interlocutory review would be especially wasteful, it is argued, because most trial court rulings are correct and even those that are incorrect are unlikely, in the end, to taint the final judgment.[9] The end result of freely allowing interlocutory appeals would be a greater injustice to litigants overall than is occasioned by that small portion of cases in which trials must be repeated because appellate review was delayed until

---

pretrial order, and the state's appeal of this order is timely); Commonwealth v. Clark, 746 A.2d 1128 (Pa.2000) (where a sentencing court expressly or by implication indicates that no penalty is to be imposed after conviction, that action is a "sentence" which will support an appeal).

[Section 27.2(b)]

[7]The policies underlying the final judgment rule, as applied to both civil and criminal cases, have been explored at length by various commentators. See 15A C. Wright, A. Miller, and E. Cooper, Federal Practice and Procedure § 3907 (2d ed.1992) (collecting authorities and providing its own excellent analysis).

[8]We focus on interlocutory appeals from pretrial rulings due to the obvious impracticability of interlocutory appeals during trial. See 15A C. Wright, A. Miller, and E. Cooper, Federal Practice and Procedure § 3907 (2d ed.1992) ("it would be impossible to conduct a coherent trial if every evidential and procedural ruling could be subjected to immediate appellate scrutiny, even in a fanciful world in which appellate panels sat at the trial bench").

[9]Cf. 15A C. Wright, A. Miller, and E. Cooper, Federal Practice and Procedure § 3907 (2d ed.1992) (noting that the broad responsibility allocated to the trial judge and the corresponding limited function of appellate review "is the most fundamental foundation of the final judgment rule").

after final judgment was reached.[10] That injustice would be particularly likely when the adversaries had unequal resources and interests in securing or avoiding a prompt disposition of the case. The party interested in a prompt adjudication would be at the mercy of an opponent willing and able to delay litigation by appealing adverse pretrial rulings.

The advantages of the final judgment rule in securing efficient judicial administration are even more apparent. The rule provides savings for both trial and appellate courts. A major responsibility of the trial court is self-correction, and the delay of appellate review until final judgment permits the trial court to reassess its decisions in light of later trial developments. From the perspective of the appellate court, rulings also are better judged in light of the completed proceeding when more information is available with which to assess the impact of the error upon the outcome of the trial. Even errors that require a new trial are judged more efficiently since a single appeal may consider more than one error. Most significantly, the final judgment rule avoids appeals that become unnecessary as the case develops. Thus, pretrial rulings often become moot when the party adversely affected by the erroneous ruling ultimately gains a favorable jury verdict.

While all of the above considerations have relevance to both civil and criminal cases, the delay that can accompany interlocutory appeals is especially pernicious in the criminal justice process, where a speedy trial advances a "societal interest which exists separate from the interests of the accused."[11] In his frequently quoted opinion in *Cobbledick v. United States*,[12] Justice Frankfurter emphasized the dangers of delay in urging strict adherence to the final judgment rule in criminal cases. He noted:

> Since the right to a judgment from more than one court is a matter of grace and not a necessary ingredient of justice, Congress from the very beginning has, by forbidding piecemeal disposition on appeal of what for practical purposes is a single controversy, set itself against enfeebling judicial administration. Thereby is avoided the obstruction to just claims that would come from permitting the harassment and cost of a succession of separate appeals from the various rulings to which a litigation may give rise, from its initiation to entry of judgment. To be effective, judicial administration must not be leaden-footed. Its momentum would be arrested by permitting separate reviews of the component elements in a unified cause. These considerations of policy are especially compelling in

---

[10]See Note, 67 Iowa L.Rev. 1037, 1043 (1982) (arguing that disallowing interlocutory appeals is justified by the fact that adverse cost of a repeated trial is only infrequently experienced).

[11]See *Barker v. Wingo*, discussed

in § 18.1(b). See also DiBella v. United States, 369 U.S. 121, 82 S.Ct. 654, 7 L.Ed.2d 614 (1962).

[12]Cobbledick v. United States, 309 U.S. 323, 60 S.Ct. 540, 84 L.Ed. 783 (1940).

the administration of criminal justice.

* * * An accused is entitled to scrupulous observance of constitutional safeguards. But encouragement of delay is fatal to the vindication of the criminal law. Bearing the discomfiture and cost of a prosecution for crime even by an innocent person is one of the painful obligations of citizenship. The correctness of a trial court's rejection even of a constitutional claim made by the accused in the process of prosecution must await his conviction before its reconsideration by an appellate tribunal.

The viewpoint expressed in *Cobbledick* has dominated the federal statutory scheme for defense appeals in criminal cases. While Congress has adopted several statutory provisions allowing interlocutory appeals in civil cases,[13] only three federal statutes authorize interlocutory appeals in criminal cases. One is quite narrow and carefully limited to prosecution appeals;[14] a second provides both defense and prosecution with a right to appeal orders concerning pretrial release or detention,[15] and the third provides for expedited appellate review of specific alleged violations of the statutory rights of victims.[16]

A substantial number of states have much broader provisions permitting discretionary interlocutory appeals by defendants in criminal cases. Several have adopted provisions similar to 28 U.S.C.A. § 1291(b) that apply to criminal as well as civil cases, which require that the trial judge certify that immediate appeal is warranted.[17] Others simply provide for interlocutory appeal by leave of the appellate court, without requiring certification by the

---

[13]The most significant is 28 U.S.C.A. § 1292(b), which grants the courts of appeals discretionary jurisdiction to hear an interlocutory appeal on certification by the trial judge that the challenged order "involves a controlling question of law as to which there is a substantial ground for difference of opinion and that an immediate appeal from the order may materially advance the ultimate termination of the litigation." However, 28 U.S.C.A. § 1292(a)(1) applies to orders granting injunctions and is not by its terms limited to civil cases. United States v. Pace, 201 F.3d 1116 (9th Cir.2000) (§ 1292(b) certifications cannot confer interlocutory appellate jurisdiction in criminal prosecutions). It has been suggested that certain orders issued in a criminal case (e.g., a gag order) may constitute injunctions subject to appeal under this provision. See United States v. Harold

Ford, 830 F.2d 596 (6th Cir.1987).

[14]See 18 U.S.C.A. § 3731, discussed in § 27.3(b), (c).

[15]18 U.S.C.A. § 3154(c); see also § 12.1(a), discussing the Bail Reform Act. This provision provides only a partial legislative expansion of review already available under the final judgment rule. Even prior to the adoption of the Bail Reform Act, constitutional or statutory challenges to excessive bail had been held immediately appealable under the collateral order "exception" to the final judgment standard. See text at notes 24–25 infra, discussing *Stack v. Boyle*, which had allowed an immediate challenge to bail set in an excessive amount.

[16]See the Crime Victims Rights Act, 18 U.S.C.A. §§ 3771 et seq., discussed in § 27.4(e) at note 61.

[17]See, e.g., Ga.Code Ann. § 5-6-34(b); Tenn.R.App.P. 9(b).

trial judge. Such provisions often identify a series of factors to be considered by the appellate court in determining whether to grant review, such as whether immediate review will "clarify an issue of general importance in the administration of justice" or "protect the petitioner from substantial or irreparable injury."[18] Jurisdictions with such provisions have not rejected Justice Frankfurter's conclusion that defendants may be required, as one of the "painful obligations of citizenship," to "bear the discomfiture and cost" of an unnecessary trial. Rather, they have concluded that the final judgment rule should be subject to exception where the circumstances of the individual case convince the appellate court that the protection of the defendant's substantive rights or the conservation of judicial resources would be better served by interlocutory review.[19]

§ 27.2(c) Collateral orders

The final judgment rule has been subject to considerable judicial development in both criminal and civil cases. One major judicially recognized "exception"[20] to the final judgment rule is the collateral order doctrine, established in the civil case of *Cohen v. Beneficial Industrial Loan Corp.*[21] In that case, the defendant in a stockholder's derivative suit sought to appeal a district court's pretrial ruling refusing to direct the plaintiffs to post a security bond. The Supreme Court held that the ruling was appealable under 28 U.S.C.A. § 1291.[22] A final decision, the Court noted, did not necessarily have to terminate an action. Given a "practi-

---

[18]See, e.g., Alaska R.App.P. 402; Minn.R.Crim.P. 28.02(3); Utah R.Crim.P. 26 (2)(c); Wis.Stat.Ann. § 808.03(2); Mich.Comp.Laws Ann. § 770.3(2).

[19]See State v. McKim, 215 S.W.3d 781 (Tenn.2007) (defendant allowed to appeal pretrial ruling denying pretrial diversion under state appellate Rule 9, when the denial was based on the consideration of a clearly irrelevant factor, noting that the state criminal justice system will experience a net reduction in the duration and expense of litigation commenced upon the defendant's indictment if the state does not have to try him); State v. Webb, 160 Wis.2d 622, 467 N.W.2d 108 (1991); Note, 67 Iowa L.Rev. 1037 (1982).

[Section 27.2(c)]

[20]Although the collateral order doctrine is often described as an "ex-

ception" to the final judgment rule, it was initially advanced by the Court as no more than a "practical rather than technical" interpretation of the final judgment rule. See *Cohen v. Beneficial Industrial Loan Corp.*, infra note 21. But see Abney v. United States, 431 U.S. 651, 97 S.Ct. 2034, 52 L.Ed.2d 651 (1977), quoted following note 29 infra.

[21]Cohen v. Beneficial Industrial Loan Corp, 337 U.S. 541, 69 S.Ct. 1221, 93 L.Ed. 1528 (1949).

[22]See also 28 U.S.C.A. § 2072 (1988) (providing that the Supreme Court's rules "may define when a ruling of a district court is final for the purposes of appeal under section 1291 of this title").

cal rather than technical construction," the final judgment concept also encompassed certain orders collateral to the basic litigation. These were described as "that small class [of orders] which finally determine claims of right separable from, and collateral to, rights asserted in the action, too important to be denied review and too independent of the cause itself to require that appellate consideration be deferred until the whole case is adjudicated."

The required characteristics of decisions appealable as collateral orders were expressed in *Coopers & Lybrand v. Livesay*[23] as follows: "To come within the "small class" of decisions excepted from the final-judgment rule by Cohen, the order must conclusively determine the disputed question, resolve an important issue completely separate from the merits of the action, and be effectively unreviewable on appeal from a final judgment." The first of these three prerequisites demands that the trial court ruling not be "tentative, informal, or incomplete," but constitute a firm and final decision on the issue. If there is a reasonable prospect that the trial court might alter its rulings, immediate appellate intrusion clearly is not appropriate. As to the second prerequisite, it demands that the issue ruled upon not "affect, or * * * be affected by" any subsequent decision on the merits of the case. If the trial court ruling is not "independent of the cause" itself, determining rights "separable from and collateral to [those] rights asserted in the action," then review prior to the ultimate disposition constitutes a wasteful use of appellate resources. Depending upon the disposition of the case, permitting appeal will produce either an unnecessary review or a review that will only be repeated, possibly in a new light that would require the appellate court to withdraw from an earlier ruling. The second prerequisite also requires that the issue resolved by the trial court be not only independent but "important." Thus, in *Cohen* the Court noted that the trial court order there might not have been appealable if the only issue presented was one of the proper exercise of the trial court's discretion. Finally, the third prerequisite insists that interlocutory appeal be withheld if review on appeal following the final disposition would provide a satisfactory remedy. For example, in authorizing interlocutory review in *Cohen*, the Court noted that the petitioner's right to security for its costs would be lost, "probably irreparably," if review came only after the petitioner had won the case on the merits.

The Supreme Court first applied the collateral order doctrine to

---

[23]Coopers & Lybrand v. Livesay,   351 (1978).
437 U.S. 463, 98 S.Ct. 2454, 57 L.Ed.2d

a criminal case in *Stack v. Boyle*.[24] The defendants there were unable to make bail and sought habeas corpus relief after the trial court denied their motion to reduce bail. The Supreme Court concluded that the use of the habeas remedy was inappropriate since the defendants had an unexhausted remedy available in a direct appeal from the trial court's order. The Court said very little about why the bail ruling met the prerequisites of *Cohen*. It noted only that, as in *Cohen*, the rejected motion "did not merely invoke the discretion of the district court," as it "challenged the bail as violating statutory and constitutional standards."[25] In a concurring opinion, Justice Jackson, the author of *Cohen*, added a brief explanation. "An order fixing bail," he noted, "can be reviewed without halting the main trial—its issues are entirely independent of the issues to be tried—and unless it can be reviewed before sentence, it can never be reviewed at all."

Six years later, in a much more extensive discussion of the final judgment rule the Court in *Carroll v. United States*,[26] warned against extension of the *Cohen* rule to criminal cases and characterized those orders in criminal cases that fit within *Cohen* as "very few." For a substantial period thereafter, lower court and Supreme Court rulings treated *Stack* as an almost one-of-a-kind ruling. A broad range of pretrial rulings in criminal cases were held not to fall within the collateral order doctrine. Thus, defense appeals were not allowed as to orders denying motions to suppress evidence,[27] or orders denying or granting a transfer or change of venue.[28]

---

[24]Stack v. Boyle, 342 U.S. 1, 72 S.Ct. 1, 96 L.Ed. 3 (1951).

[25]Unlike the *Stack* decision, the present statute authorizing appellate review of pretrial release orders in federal court, 18 U.S.C.A. § 3154(c), is not so limited. See § 12.3(a) at note 28 discussing review of detention orders; 3A C. Wright, A. Miller, and E. Cooper, Federal Practice and Procedure § 772 (2d ed.1992). See also Pagan v. United States, 353 F.3d 1343 (11th Cir.2003) (a decision on whether to grant bond to a prisoner while the merits of his claim are being considered in a post-conviction relief proceeding is a final judgment).

[26]Carroll v. United States, 354 U.S. 394, 77 S.Ct. 1332, 1 L.Ed.2d 1442 (1957) (holding that the trial court's ruling granting the defendant's motion to suppress was not a "collat-eral order" and was not subject to interlocutory appeal by the government).

[27]DiBella v. United States, 369 U.S. 121, 82 S.Ct. 654, 7 L.Ed.2d 614 (1962).

[28]Parr v. United States, 351 U.S. 513, 76 S.Ct. 912, 100 L.Ed. 1377 (1956). In *Parr*, following the transfer of a criminal case to a different division over the objection of the government, the government secured a new indictment in a different district and obtained an order dismissing the original indictment. The defendant's appeal from that dismissal was rejected on the ground that the dismissal order would "merge" in any final judgment of conviction on the second indictment and could be effectively reviewed on appeal from such a conviction. See also Note, 68 Geo.L.J. 1163, 1178–80 (1978).

In *Abney v. United States*,[29] the Supreme Court added an additional ruling to the list of orders deemed collateral, but its opinion seemed to many to open the door to substantial further extensions of the *Cohen* doctrine. The Court there held appealable the denial of a pretrial defense motion seeking dismissal of an indictment on double jeopardy grounds. Chief Justice Burger's opinion for the Court concluded that the trial court's order met all the prerequisites for fitting within " 'the small class of cases' that *Cohen* has placed beyond the confines of the final-judgment rule." Initially, there had been a "fully consummated decision" of the trial court. The denial of the motion to dismiss had constituted a "complete, formal and * * * final rejection" of the defendant's double jeopardy claim. Secondly, the double jeopardy issue was "collateral to, and separable from, the principal issue at the accused's impending criminal trial, i.e., whether or not the accused is guilty of the offense charged." The defendant's challenge did not go to the "merits of the charge against him" nor did it relate to the evidence the government might use in proving its case. Finally, "the rights conferred upon the criminal accused by the Double Jeopardy Clause would be significantly undermined if appellate review of double jeopardy claims were postponed until after conviction and sentence." The function of the double jeopardy clause, the Court stressed, was not simply to insulate the defendant against being subjected to double punishment, but also to protect the defendant against being forced "to endure the personal strain, public embarrassment, and expense of a criminal trial more than once for the same offense." Reversal on appeal from a conviction following a second trial was too late to afford protection against "being twice put to trial for the same offense."[30] Admittedly, allowing review prior to trial might "encourage some defendants to engage in dilatory appeals," but that was a necessary cost of protecting the double jeopardy right. Moreover, that problem, the Court noted, could be "obviated by * * * summary procedures and calendars [designed] to weed out frivolous claims of former jeopardy."[31]

Unlike the claim in *Stack*, which would have been moot if

---

[29]Abney v. United States, 431 U.S. 651, 97 S.Ct. 2034, 52 L.Ed.2d 651 (1977).

[30]In Richardson v. United States, 468 U.S. 317, 104 S.Ct. 3081, 82 L.Ed.2d 242 (1984), the Court also held that the denial of a defendant's double jeopardy objection to a pending retrial was immediately appealable where defendant's claim rested on the contention that a directed verdict should have been granted in the first trial and a retrial therefore was precluded under the rationale of Burks v. United States, 437 U.S. 1, 98 S.Ct. 2141, 57 L.Ed.2d 1 (1978), discussed in § 25.4(b).

[31]Several lower courts have held that where the district court finds no "colorable foundation" for defendant's double jeopardy claim, it may proceed to trial on schedule, notwithstanding

reviewed following conviction, the claim in *Abney* was held for other reasons not to be adequately protected by review of conviction. Arguably, various other claims could fall in the same category. In *Helstoski v. Meanor*,[32] the Court found appealable an order denying a former Congressman's claim that the indictment against him violated the Speech or Debate Clause (which provides that "for any speech or debate," a Congressperson "shall not be questioned in any Place").[33] But in *United States v. MacDonald*[34] and *United States v. Hollywood Motor Car Company*,[35] the Court concluded that trial court orders rejecting speedy trial and vindictive prosecution claims prior to trial did not have the special qualities needed to fall under the "collateral order exception," which was to be construed "with the utmost strictness in criminal cases."

A critical factor distinguishing *Abney* and *Helstoski* on the one hand, and *MacDonald* and *Hollywood Motor Car* on the other, was the Court's characterization of the nature of the claim presented by defendant's pretrial motion. Helstoski held that the constitutional right of a Congressperson not to "be questioned" encompassed a protection against trial itself, not just conviction, and therefore was analogous to the double jeopardy claim presented in *Abney*. The claims presented in *Hollywood Motor Car* and *MacDonald*, the Court concluded, did not include the right not to be tried at all. The dissenters in *Hollywood Motor Car* argued that the constitutional prohibition against vindictive prosecution should encompass protection against the burdens of trial,

---

the defendant's filing of a notice of appeal; United States v. Lanci, 669 F.2d 391 (6th Cir.1982) (collecting cases); United States v. Wood, 950 F.2d 638 (10th Cir.1991). The district court is required to make written findings to support its determination that the double jeopardy appeal is frivolous. See United States v. Leppo, 634 F.2d 101 (3d Cir.1980); 15B C. Wright, A. Miller, and E. Cooper, Federal Practice and Procedure § 3918.5 (2d ed.1992). Compare Sherman v. State, 326 Ark. 153, 931 S.W.2d 417 (1996) (interlocutory appeal of order denying motion to dismiss based on double jeopardy does not require a "colorable foundation").

The right to appeal a double jeopardy claims does not carry with it a form of pendent jurisdiction which would permit review of other, supplementary claims raised in the same motion. See Abney v. United States, 431 U.S. 651, 97 S.Ct. 2034, 52 L.Ed.2d 651 (1977) (rejecting review of that portion of order denying motion to dismiss based on ground other than double jeopardy); People v. Schram, 283 Ill.App.3d 1056, 220 Ill.Dec. 225, 672 N.E.2d 1237 (1996) (same, interpreting state statute).

[32]Helstoski v. Meanor, 442 U.S. 500, 99 S.Ct. 2445, 61 L.Ed.2d 30 (1979).

[33]See also United States v. McDade, 28 F.3d 283 (3d Cir.1994) (allowing appeal of district court's denial of motion to dismiss under the Speech or Debate Clause).

[34]United States v. MacDonald, 435 U.S. 850, 98 S.Ct. 1547, 56 L.Ed.2d 18 (1978).

[35]United States v. Hollywood Motor Car Co., 458 U.S. 263, 102 S.Ct. 3081, 73 L.Ed.2d 754 (1982).

but the majority viewed the scope of the right quite differently. While earlier vindictive prosecution cases had spoken of a defendant's right "not to be hauled into court" by a prosecutor who added a more serious criminal charge in order to punish the defendant for his earlier exercise of a procedural right in connection with a lesser charge,[36] those cases had also recognized that the appropriate relief was simply the dismissal of the charge added vindictively. The defendant was never thought to be free of retrial on the original charge that was not tainted by vindictiveness. Hence, the petitioner's claim could not be characterized as presenting "a right not to be tried," but only as "a right whose remedy requires the dismissal of charges." As in the case of other challenges to the validity of a charge, such as a challenge to the constitutionality of the statute on which a charge is based, dismissal on an appeal following a conviction constituted an adequate remedy. Thus, what was at stake here was not a right, "the legal and practical value of which would be destroyed if it were not vindicated before trial." In *MacDonald*, a unanimous Court similarly characterized a defendant's speedy trial claim as not encompassing a "right not to be tried." Here, it was "the delay before trial, not the trial itself that offends the constitutional guarantee." Indeed, to present an appeal prior to trial would threaten many of the interests protected by the speedy trial clause.[37]

MacDonald also distinguished *Abney* on other grounds. The determination as to whether there had been a denial of a speedy trial was often dependent upon an assessment of the prejudice caused by the delay, which could best be considered "only after the relevant facts had been developed at trial." Hence, the pretrial denial of the defendant's motion could not be considered a "complete, formal, and final rejection" of that claim, and the prejudice element of the claim could not be viewed as separable from the trial on the merits. Also, unlike the double jeopardy claim presented in *Abney*, which required an initial showing of prior jeopardy, there was "nothing about * * * a speedy trial claim which inherently limits the availability of the claim." If a right to immediate appeal were recognized, "any defendant" could raise such a claim in anticipation of a dilatory pretrial appeal. Given this reasoning and the Court's insistence that the claim present a right "not to be tried," any door to immediate appeals left open in *Abney* would seem to have been tightly shut by *MacDonald*.

With one exception, further attempts to expand the "very few"

---

[36]See, e.g., Blackledge v. Perry, 417 U.S. 21, 94 S.Ct. 2098, 40 L.Ed.2d 628 (1974), discussed in § 13.5(a) at notes 2–3.

[37]See also the discussion of speedy trial rights in Chapter 18, and in Amar, Foreword: Sixth Amendment First Principles, 84 Geo.L.J. 641 (1996).

instances in which pretrial rulings come within *Cohen* have been rejected by the Court. In *Flanagan v. United States*,[38] for example, the Court rebuffed a defendant's attempt to appeal an order disqualifying defense counsel on conflict grounds under Federal Rule 44(c). The petitioners in *Flanagan* argued that appellate review upon conviction was an inadequate remedy because relief on appeal from a conviction would be available only upon a showing that the loss of preferred counsel resulted in some "specifically demonstrated prejudice to the defense." That would require an impossibly speculative judgment, the defendant argued, assuming that the replacement counsel had been competent. Responding to this contention, the Supreme Court noted that providing fully effective review would present no difficulty if the asserted right to counsel of one's choice were treated like the sixth amendment right to represent oneself, with a denial of the right requiring automatic reversal. However, that question need not be decided because, even if a showing of prejudice were required, as petitioner contended, the second condition of *Cohen*—"that the order be truly collateral"—was not satisfied. Assuming that a constitutional violation was tied to a finding of prejudice, a disqualification order could hardly be said to be "independent of the issues to be tried." The "effect of the disqualification on the defense, and hence whether the asserted right had been violated, cannot be fairly assessed until the substance of the prosecution's and defendant's case is known." In this respect, the petitioner's claim was analogous to the speedy trial claim presented in *MacDonald*.[39]

In *Midland Asphalt Corp. v. United States*,[40] the defendant had stronger grounds for arguing that his constitutional claim would be "effectively unreviewable on appeal from a conviction," but the Court held that the ruling below still failed to fall with the *Cohen* exception because the very quality that made it unreviewable on appeal also established that it was not truly collateral to a decision on the merits of the case. The trial court in *Midland Asphalt* had denied the defendant's motion to dismiss the indictment

---

[38]Flanagan v. United States, 465 U.S. 259, 104 S.Ct. 1051, 79 L.Ed.2d 288 (1984).

[39]Disqualification orders regarding government counsel may be appealable, however. See § 27.3(b) at note 16.

[40]Midland Asphalt Corp. v. United States, 489 U.S. 794, 109 S.Ct. 1494, 103 L.Ed.2d 879 (1989). For lower court cases, see, e.g., United States v. Hickey, 367 F.3d 888 (9th Cir.2004)

(denial of motion to dismiss based on allegation of insufficient evidence before the grand jury does not fit within the collateral order doctrine because, even if meritorious, the error would not rise to the level of a fundamental defect; cannot be said to be completely separate from the merits of the action, and is unlike cases in which an explicit statutory or constitutional guarantee prohibits trial, is reviewable following conviction).

based on an alleged violation of Rule 6(e). The Supreme Court reasoned that if, under *United States v. Mechanik*,[41] such a ruling would be considered harmless error after conviction due to the subsequent petit jury finding of guilt beyond a reasonable doubt, the trial court's denial did not "resolve an important issue completely separate from the merits of the action." Instead, the trial court's ruling would "involve considerations "enmeshed in the merits of the dispute" * * * [that] would * * * "be affected by" the decision on the merits." If, in the alternative, *Mechanik* allowed relief for some Rule 6(e) denials after conviction, the Court noted, then it was "obvious" that the ruling was not "effectively unreviewable on appeal."

The exception came in *Sell v. United States*.[42] The Court added to the short list of collateral orders subject to interlocutory appeal a trial court's decision to forcibly medicate a defendant into competency for trial. "By the time of trial," the Court reasoned, the defendant "will have undergone forced medication—the very harm that he seeks to avoid. He cannot undo that harm if he is acquitted. Indeed, if he is acquitted, there will be no appeal through which he might obtain review." This, combined with "the severity of the intrusion and corresponding importance of the constitutional issue, readily distinguish" the order authorizing forced medication from the examples given by the dissenting justices, concluded the Court. The orders that the dissenters warned would be appealable under the majority's rule included an order requiring a defendant to wear an electronic bracelet, an order prohibiting the defendant from wearing a "Black Power" t-shirt in front of the jury, and an order compelling testimony in violation of the Fifth Amendment. It is possible to read the majority's decision as expanding the collateral order exception to allow for the interlocutory appeal of any ruling unrelated to the merits that could be characterized as a constitutional violation independent of guilt or innocence, so long as there was an "intrusion" as "severe" as that threatened in *Sell*, and the harm could not be "undone" after acquittal. Violations of the right to a public trial would seem to meet the independence criterion, but might not be intrusive enough to qualify; while an unconstitutional order to don a stun belt during trial would appear to approximate the type of order that would fall within *Sell*'s rationale. The history

---

[41]United States v. Mechanik, 475 U.S. 66, 106 S. Ct. 938, 89 L. Ed. 2d 50 (1986), discussed in § 15.6(f) at note 172–202.

[42]Sell v. United States, 539 U.S. 166, 123 S.Ct. 2174, 156 L.Ed.2d 197 (2003). See also Cunningham v. Hamilton County, 527 U.S. 198, 119 S.Ct. 1915, 144 L.Ed.2d 184 (1999), where the Court held that an attorney may not immediately appeal an order to pay sanctions due to a discovery violation, noting that immediate appeal would undermine judicial discretion to structure sanctions and give rise to piecemeal appeals and delays.

of the exception, and the policy reasons for the rule against interlocutory appeals in criminal cases, support an even narrower
reading, limiting *Sell*'s rule to forced medication, uniquely harmful in its violation of autonomy and bodily integrity.[43]

Lower federal courts have added only a few pre-trial orders to
the list of those subject to appeal as collateral orders. Courts of
appeals will review orders committing defendants to the custody
of the Attorney General to determine competency to stand trial,[44]
and orders that require juvenile defendants to be tried as adults.[45]
In addition, while most courts have reasoned that agreements
not to prosecute resemble rulings concerning the enforcement of
grants to immunity, which are not appealable prior to judgment
and may be enforced on appeal following a final judgment,[46] at
least one court of appeals has allowed a defendant to appeal a
ruling denying dismissal due to the alleged violation of an agreement not to prosecute, on the theory that the defendant's claim
more closely resembles a claim of double jeopardy.[47] Also appealable is an order rejecting a claim by a federal judge that he can-

---

[43]For post-*Sell* decisions, see
United States v. Rivera-Guerrero, 377
F.3d 1064 (9th Cir.2004) (interlocutory
appeal of order authorizing involuntary medication, finding also that an
order authorizing involuntary medication is not among the pretrial matters
that can be fully delegated to the magistrate judge under § 636(b)(1)(A));
United States v. Bradley, 417 F.3d
1107 (10th Cir.2005) (district court
properly followed procedures for the
involuntary administration of antipsychotic medication to a non-dangerous
criminal defendant for the purpose of
rendering him competent to stand
trial, when defendant was not a candidate for civil commitment, and if found
guilty would have faced up to fifty
years in prison, so need for treatment
with antipsychotic drugs was sufficiently important to overcome interest in refusing it).

[44]United States v. Ferro, 321 F.3d
756 (8th Cir.2003) (order of district
court finding defendant incompetent
and committing defendant to custody
of attorney general is immediately appealable under the collateral order
exception to the final judgment rule; if
not allowed to appeal the order at this
time, defendant's right to avoid involuntary hospitalization will be lost);

United States v. Friedman, 366 F.3d
975 (9th Cir.2004) (same); United
States v. Deters, 143 F.3d 577 (10th
Cir.1998) (reasoning that the decision
is similar to the denial of bail and collecting cases). Compare State v.
O'Connell, 36 Conn.App. 135, 648 A.2d
168 (1994) (order to submit to competency exam may not be appealed).

[45]See United States v. J.J.K., 76
F.3d 870 (7th Cir.1996) (collecting
cases, and reasoning that the statutory "right not to be tried as an adult"
would be "irretrievably lost, the decision would be "effectively unreviewable," if a transferred juvenile were
forced to wait until after conviction in
adult court before appealing his transfer"); United States v. M.C.E., 232
F.3d 1252 (9th Cir.2000).

[46]See United States v. Crosby, 20
F.3d 480 (D.C.Cir.1994).

[47]See United States v. Romero,
967 F.2d 63 (2d Cir.1992). See also
Jackson v. State, 358 Md. 259, 747
A.2d 1199 (2000) (order appealable as
a collateral order, waiting until after
conviction would deny the defendant
the benefit of his bargain under which
state agreed to dismiss if DNA test
excluded defendant).

not be tried on criminal charges while holding office,[48] and orders upholding gag orders on trial participants.[49]

Far more pre-judgment rulings have been held by lower federal courts not to qualify for appellate review under the collateral order doctrine. They include orders granting or denying discovery,[50] orders denying or granting a transfer or change of venue,[51] orders denying motions to disqualify a judge,[52] orders dismissing an indictment without prejudice under the Speedy Trial Act,[53] orders denying motions to dismiss certain counts of a single indictment that the defendant had alleged would be subject him to multiple punishment,[54] orders denying motions for injunctive relief to prevent the use and disclosure of intercepted conversations,[55] orders to attorneys to serve as stand-by counsel,[56] orders denying motions to dismiss due to the expiration of the statute of limitations,[57] an order refusing to strike the government's notice that it

[48]United States v. Hastings, 681 F.2d 706 (11th Cir.1982).

[49]United States v. Brown, 218 F.3d 415 (5th Cir.2000) (reviewing denial of motion to vacate or modify gag order that prohibited attorneys, parties, or witnesses from discussing with "any public communications media" anything about the case "which could interfere with a fair trial," including statements "intended to influence public opinion regarding the merits of this case," with exceptions for matters of public record and matters such as assertions of innocence).

[50]See 15B C. Wright, A. Miller, and E. Cooper, Federal Practice and Procedure § 3918.3 (2d ed.1992) (collecting cases); 2 C. Wright, A. Miller, and E. Cooper, Federal Practice and Procedure § 261 (2d ed.1992).

[51]See, e.g., United States v. Blackwell, 900 F.2d 742 (4th Cir.1990); United States v. French, 787 F.2d 1381 (9th Cir.1986); United States v. Garber, 413 F.2d 284 (2d Cir.1969); discussing Parr v. United States, 351 U.S. 513, 76 S.Ct. 912, 100 L.Ed. 1377 (1956), discussed in note 27.

[52]United States v. Gregory, 656 F.2d 1132 (5th Cir.1981); United States v. Washington, 573 F.2d 1121 (9th Cir. 1978).

[53]See United States v. Tsosie, 966 F.2d 1357 (10th Cir.1992) (collecting cases).

[54]United States v. Ramirez-Burgos, 44 F.3d 17 (1st Cir.1995) (reasoning that such a claim, unlike an allegation of multiple prosecution, can be fully vindicated on appeal from a final judgment).

[55]United States v. Miller, 14 F.3d 761 (2d Cir.1994).

[56]United States v. Bertoli, 994 F.2d 1002 (3d Cir.1993) (order to provide stand-by counsel not appealable). Compare Harris v. State, 107 Md.App. 399 668 A.2d 938 (1995) (rejecting Bertoli), rev'd on other grounds, 344 Md. 497, 687 A.2d 970 (1997). See also In re Grand Jury Investigation, 182 F.3d 668 (9th Cir.1999) (district judge's order disqualifying an attorney from representing multiple witnesses in a grand jury investigation not immediately appealable).

[57]United States v. Garib-Bazain, 222 F.3d 17 (1st Cir.2000); United States v. Weiss, 7 F.3d 1088 (2d Cir.1993) (collecting cases). See also State v. Loyd, 269 Neb. 762, 696 N.W.2d 860 (2005) (order denying motion to discharge based on statute of limitations is not a final order).

will seek the death penalty,[58] and orders denying motions challenging indictments on various other grounds.[59]

The collateral order of doctrine of *Cohen* is applied in many states,[60] and several others apply doctrines that are roughly similar.[61] These jurisdictions generally reach the same results as the federal courts, and often follow closely the leading Supreme Court rulings.[62] Another group of states, however, does not recognize even the narrow exception to the final judgment concept recognized in *Cohen*.[63] In most of these jurisdictions, alternative routes are available to defendants for obtaining immediate review of the few orders that the federal courts would describe as collateral.[64] Some provide review through a discretionary inter-

[58]United States v. Robinson, 473 F.3d 487 (2d Cir.2007) (order is not effectively unreviewable on appeal from a final judgment).

[59]See, e.g., United States v. Luloff, 15 F.3d 763 (8th Cir.1994) (indictment allegedly tainted by immunized testimony); United States v. Pace, 201 F.3d 1116 (9th Cir.2000) (order rejecting claim that prosecution was barred by McCarran-Ferguson Act); United States v. Bendis, 681 F.2d 561 (9th Cir.1981) (grand jury irregularities). See also Jones v. United States, 669 A.2d 724 (D.C.App.1995) (order rejecting vagueness challenge not appealable).

[60]See, e.g., State v. Ontiveros, 82 Haw. 446, 923 P.2d 388 (1996); Jolley v. State, 282 Md. 353, 384 A.2d 91 (1978); Commonwealth v. Johnson, 550 Pa. 298, 705 A.2d 830 (1998).

[61]See, e.g., State v. Garcia, 233 Conn. 44, 658 A.2d 947 (1995) (finding appealable a trial court's order to medicate defendant involuntarily in order to restore him to competency, as the defendant's constitutionally protected liberty interest to be free from involuntary medication would be abrogated without review).

[62]See, e.g., Commonwealth v. Johnson, 550 Pa. 298, 705 A.2d 830 (1998) (following *Flanagan*, holding that order disqualifying counsel does not satisfy the collateral order exception); Gottlieb v. State, 697 A.2d 400 (Del.1997) (same); State ex rel. Keenan

v. Calabrese, 69 Ohio St.3d 176, 631 N.E.2d 119 (1994) (same); State v. Harrington, 705 A.2d 998 (R.I.1997) (following *Abney*); State v. Schlund, 249 Neb. 173, 542 N.W.2d 421 (1996) (same); State v. Lebroke, 589 A.2d 941 (Me.1991) (same); Pulley v. State, 287 Md. 406, 412 A.2d 1244 (1980) (same); State v. Lynch, 248 Neb. 234, 533 N.W.2d 905 (1995) (same); Stewart v. State, 282 Md. 557, 386 A.2d 1206 (1978) (following *MacDonald*); De La Beckwith v. State, 615 So.2d 1134 (Miss.1992) (following *MacDonald*). But see State v. Gibbs, 253 Neb. 241, 570 N.W.2d 326 (1997) (allowing appeal of trial court ruling rejecting speedy trial motion); State v. Harris, 104 P.3d 1250 (Utah 2004) (a defendant may file a petition for permission to appeal an interlocutory order denying a motion to dismiss on double jeopardy grounds).

[63]See, e.g., State v. Fisher, 2 Kan.App.2d 353, 579 P.2d 167 (1978); State v. Mestas, 93 N.M. 765, 605 P.2d 1164 (N.M.App.1980); State v. Forsyth, 587 P.2d 1387 (Utah 1978).

[64]See, e.g., Okeani v. Superior Court, 178 Ariz. 180, 871 P.2d 727 (Ariz.App.1993) (order denying defense motion to withdraw while not subject to interlocutory appeal is suitable for "special action review," citing Rodriguez v. State, 129 Ariz. 67, 628 P.2d 950 (1981)); Hamilton v. State, 320 Ark. 346, 896 S.W.2d 877 (1995) (approving interlocutory appeal of juvenile transfer rulings); In the Matter of

locutory appeal, for example, but this does not furnish defendants with the assurance of review that they would have with a right to appeal under the collateral order doctrine.

Some courts have questioned whether such an arrangement, insofar as it fails to grant a right to immediate appeal from a denial of a double jeopardy claim, is constitutionally acceptable. *Abney*, they note, stated that the protection afforded by the Double Jeopardy Clause "would be significantly undermined if appellate review of double jeopardy claims were postponed until after conviction." These courts therefore suggest that the state, as part of its constitutional obligation to effectively enforce the double jeopardy bar, must provide for an immediate appeal from the trial court's denial of a nonfrivolous double jeopardy objection.[65] *Abney*, however, is better interpreted as a case interpreting the federal statute governing appeals, not the scope of the constitutional prohibition against double jeopardy, so that its holding is not binding on state courts interpreting their own law.[66]

---

the Application of Berkowitz for a Writ of Habeas Corpus, 3 Kan.App.2d 726, 602 P.2d 99 (1979) (defendant in custody can use original habeas corpus proceeding to raise pretrial double jeopardy claim and appeal from denial of relief) Franklin v. Kearney, 814 So.2d 462 (Fla.App.2001) (order finding incompetent); State v. Apodaca, 123 N.M. 372, 940 P.2d 478 (App.1997) (defendant may use New Mexico's constitutional provision granting every aggrieved party right to one appeal to raise double jeopardy claims); State v. Jenich, 94 Wis.2d 74, 292 N.W.2d 348 (1980) (pretrial order denying motion to dismiss as double jeopardy grounds did not satisfy statutory test for finality and was appealable only by permission of court of appeals); State v. Ross, 166 Vt. 630, 699 A.2d 47 (1997) (granting petition for extraordinary relief due to "the importance of the issue," namely the validity of a order requiring the social services agency to disclose its confidential records to defense counsel).

[65] See, e.g., State v. Baranco, 77 Haw. 351, 884 P.2d 729 (1994) ("if a criminal defendant is to avoid exposure to double jeopardy and thereby enjoy the full protection of the Clause,

his double jeopardy challenge * * * must be reviewable before that subsequent exposure occurs"); McGuinness v. Commonwealth, 423 Mass. 1003, 667 N.E.2d 818 (1996); State v. Berberian, 122 R.I. 693, 411 A.2d 308 (1980); Ex parte Robinson, 641 S.W.2d 552 (Tex.Cr.App.1982).

[66] State v. Salzmann, 119 Or.App. 217, 850 P.2d 1122 (1993) (rejecting argument that *Abney* is constitutionally compelled and holding that a defendant has no right to appeal a trial judge's denial of a motion to dismiss on double jeopardy grounds, reasoning "*Abney* is merely a case of statutory construction of a federal statute and not one that establishes a constitutional mandate for interlocutory appeals throughout the several states"); Wenzel v. Enright, 68 Ohio St.3d 63, 623 N.E.2d 69 (1993) (no constitutional right to interlocutory appeal of such an order); State v. Murphy, 537 N.W.2d 492 (Minn.App.1995) (same); Jones v. State, 450 So.2d 186 (Ala.App.1984) (same); State v. Shoff, 118 N.C.App. 724, 456 S.E.2d 875 (1995) (order denying motion to dismiss on double jeopardy grounds not appealable). See also Tanigawa, The Application of the Collateral Order Doctrine to Criminal

§ 27.2(d) Independent proceedings

The collateral order doctrine permits an immediate appeal from orders that clearly are a part of the ongoing litigation. Certain proceedings, though related to an ongoing or contemplated litigation, may be viewed as sufficiently separate from that litigation so that an order terminating that proceeding is itself a final judgment and therefore appealable. The crucial question here, the Supreme Court has noted, is whether the proceeding is "independent * * * or merely a step in the trial of the criminal case."[67]

Perhaps the clearest illustration of an independent proceeding is the third-party challenge to an order issued in a criminal case. Consider, for example, a news organization's objection to a trial court ruling that portions of a trial will be closed to the public. If the defendant, rather than a news organization, had objected to the closure, the trial court's rejection of that objection would be part of the criminal case and its immediate appeal subject to the limitations of the *Cohen* doctrine. When a third party such as a news organization brings an action to vindicate its alleged right to be present at the proceedings, that action is deemed independent and the denial of its challenge is appealable by that party as a final judgment without applying the *Cohen* standards.[68] Similarly, while the denial of a defense motion to strike surplusage in an indictment would not be appealable by the defendant, an unindicted co-conspirator may appeal from an order rejecting his motion to strike his name from the indictment.[69] Another example of an independent order would be the denial of a third

---

Appeals in Hawaii, 19 U.Haw.L.Rev. 73 (1997).

[Section 27.2(d)]

[67]Cogen v. United States, 278 U.S. 221, 49 S.Ct. 118, 73 L.Ed. 275 (1929).

[68]See, e.g., In re the Matter of the New York Times Co., 828 F.2d 110 (2d Cir.1987) (media objection can be viewed as "separate civil case" rather than intervention in the criminal case, and even if viewed as part of criminal case, the rejection of that objection constitutes a collateral order since deferral of appellate ruling until after the case is tried "would effectively deny appellants much of the relief they seek, namely, prompt public disclosure"); Gannett Co. v. State, 565 A.2d 895 (Del.1989) (holding that order requiring jurors to be identified by number rather than by name was subject to review, as it "constituted a final decision * * * [of] a matter independent of the issues to be resolved in the criminal proceeding itself, [and] bound persons who were non-parties in the underlying criminal proceeding and had a substantial, continuing effect on important rights"). But see In re T.R., 52 Ohio St.3d 6, 556 N.E.2d 439 (1990) (restrictions on public access may only be challenged during the pendency of litigation through writ of prohibition); Commonwealth v. Sartin, 708 A.2d 121 (Pa.Sup.1998) (finding that order suppressing transcript of pretrial hearing does not meet the requirements of the collateral rule, newspaper may not appeal prior to final judgment).

[69]United States v. Briggs, 514 F.2d 794 (5th Cir.1975). See also

party's motion under Federal Rule 41(g) for the return of property illegally seized in an unlawful search.[70]

Where the party seeking to appeal is a defendant or a potential defendant who has sought relief that would have a direct bearing on the criminal trial, both federal and state courts are much less likely to find that the denial of such relief is subject to immediate appeal. The leading case on the application of the independent proceeding doctrine in this context is *DiBella v. United States*.[71] A unanimous Supreme Court there held nonappealable the denial of a defense motion to suppress that had been filed before the defendant was indicted but after he had been arrested. The Court, per Frankfurter, J., reasoned that the factors that led to the characterization of a post-indictment suppression ruling as an interlocutory order were equally applicable to a pre-indictment ruling. Because the disposition of the motion, whether made before or after indictment, would "necessarily determine the conduct of the [eventual] trial," the ruling was not "fairly severable from the context of a larger litigious process." Similarly, whether the suppression motion was filed before or after indictment, the same "practical reasons" existed for not granting immediate review. First, treating "such a disjointed ruling on the admissibility of a potential item of evidence as an independent proceeding, with full panoply of appeal and attendant stay, [would] entail serious disruption of the conduct of a criminal trial." Second, appellate intervention prior to trial would result in a "truncated presentation of the issue of admissibility because the legality of the search too often cannot truly be determined until the evidence at the trial has brought all circumstances to light."

Although holding that pre-indictment and post-indictment suppression motions would be treated alike for the purpose of appellate review, Justice Frankfurter held open the possibility that under some circumstances a precharge motion challenging an illegal search could be immediately appealable. After noting that a suppression motion must be viewed "as a step in the criminal case preliminary to the trial thereof" when the criminal process has reached the stage of an arrest or a filing of a complaint, he added: "Only if the motion is solely for return of property and is in no way tied to a criminal prosecution *in esse* against the mov-

---

United States v. Hubbard, 650 F.2d 293 (D.C.Cir.1980) (third-party objection to unsealing of its documents not disclosed during the trial itself).

[70]United States v. Hess, 982 F.2d 181 (6th Cir.1992) (distinguishing case in which defendant seeks return of property and suppression of evidence under Rule 41).

[71]DiBella v. United States, 369 U.S. 121, 82 S.Ct. 654, 7 L.Ed.2d 614 (1962).

ant can the proceedings be regarded as independent."[72]

In judging whether Rule 41 denials may be appealed under *DiBella*, lower courts have divided over exactly when a prosecution is "in esse" ("in being"). Specifically, they have disagreed about the significance of the initiation of a grand jury investigation. Noting that the *DiBella* opinion characterized a presentation before a grand jury as a "part of the federal prosecution," many courts hold that the prosecution is "in esse" whenever the movant is the target of a grand jury investigation.[73] Others maintain that a "prosecution" requires more than mere investigation.[74]

The critical issue dividing the lower courts in determining when a criminal prosecution in *"in esse"* is not so much the technical definition of the criminal prosecution as the appropriate balance between the petitioner's interest in gaining prompt return of his property and the potential disruption of the investigatory proceedings. In other contexts, the Supreme Court has viewed the grand jury investigation as entitled to substantial protection against the disruption of piecemeal appeals.[75] These rulings lend support to the lower court decisions holding that a criminal prosecution is *in esse* when the petitioner is the target of an ongoing

---

[72]See 15B C. Wright, A. Miller, and E. Cooper, Federal Practice and Procedure § 3918.4 (2d ed.1992). A 1972 amendment of Federal Rule 41(e), which governs the motion for return of unlawfully seized property, provided that a successful Rule 41(e) motion automatically results not only in the return of the property but also in a preclusion of its use at trial. Lower courts agreed that this amendment did not automatically bar a Rule 41(e) motion from being treated as a motion "solely for return of property" under the *DiBella* dictum. See, e.g., Standard Drywall Inc. v. United States, 668 F.2d 156 (2d Cir.1982). Congress amended Rule 41 again in 1989, adding the language, "If a motion for return of property is made or comes on for hearing * * * after an indictment or information is filed, it shall be treated also as a motion to suppress * * *." Some courts have interpreted this change to mean that now all 41(e) motions filed *prior* to indictment or information meet the *DiBella* standard. See In re the Matter of the Search of Kitty's East, 905 F.2d 1367 (10th Cir.1990) ("By amending the rule to

preclude suppression as a de facto result of returning the property, the Court has made every Rule 41(e) motion into one solely for the return of property." Others continue to examine whether such motions are "solely" for the return of property, or designed instead to suppress evidence. Rule 41(e) became Rule 41(g) in 2002.

[73]See, e.g., Standard Drywall Inc. v. United States, 668 F.2d 156 (2d Cir. 1982); United States v. Regional Consulting Services for Economic and Community Development, Inc., 766 F.2d 870 (4th Cir.1985); DeMassa v. Nunez, 747 F.2d 1283 (9th Cir.1984).

[74]Frisby v. United States, 79 F.3d 29 (6th Cir.1996) (because a motion was filed when "there is only a pending investigation, and no outstanding indictment or information," the motion is not tied to a "prosecution *in esse*"); In re Warrant Dated December 14, 1990 and Records Seized from 3273 Hubbard, Detroit, Michigan on December 17, 1990, 961 F.2d 1241 (6th Cir.1992).

[75]See § 27.2(e).

grand jury investigation. However, because the return of the petitioner's property need not disrupt the grand jury investigation, a petitioner should be entitled to appellate review despite this concern for disruption at least when he can show that the government's investigation would not be disturbed by the return of his property.[76]

§ 27.2(e) Grand jury proceedings

As suggested by the preceding subsection, application of both the independent proceeding and collateral order doctrines has proven especially troublesome in the analysis of court orders growing out of grand jury proceedings. Even though the absence of indictment makes each grand jury proceeding "party-less,"[77] courts have refused to treat all challenges by witnesses and others to grand jury orders as independent proceedings subject to appeal prior to resolution of the criminal case. In the leading case, *Cobbledick v. United States*,[78] the Supreme Court held that the denial of a witness's motion to quash a grand jury subpoena was not appealable. The Court distinguished the proceeding to enforce an administrative subpoena which is commonly regarded as an independent action for agency discovery, thereby rendering orders granting or quashing an agency subpoena final and appealable. The ongoing grand jury proceeding, *Cobbledick* noted, was instead part of the ongoing prosecution:

> The proceeding before a grand jury constitutes "a judicial inquiry" * * * of the most ancient lineage. The duration of its life, frequently short, is limited by statute. It is no less important to safeguard against undue interruption the inquiry instituted by a grand jury than to protect from delay the progress of the trial after an indictment has been found. * * * That a grand jury proceeding has no defined litigants and that none may emerge from it, is irrelevant to the issue.

The Court did recognize one avenue for appeal by a grand jury witness, however. In the context of a trial, the Court had held that the rejection of a witness's objection to a subpoena was not a final order. To gain appellate review, the witness had to refuse to

---

[76]See, e.g., United States v. Premises Known as 608 Taylor Ave., Apartment 302, Pittsburgh, Pa., 584 F.2d 1297 (3d Cir.1978) (appeal allowed where petitioner offered to allow federal authorities to photograph and otherwise preserve the evidentiary usefulness of seized currency).

For one state's treatment of the Rule 41 issue, see State v. Wetherbee, 177 Vt. 274, 866 A.2d 527 (2004) (defendant may appeal denial of Rule 41(e) action commenced after the termination of the criminal prosecution).

[Section 27.2(e)]

[77]See In re Grand Jury Investigation, 610 F.2d 202 (5th Cir.1980) (Kravitch, J., dissenting).

[78]Cobbledick v. United States, 309 U.S. 323, 60 S.Ct. 540, 84 L.Ed. 783 (1940).

comply and be held in contempt, which did produce a final order.[79] The same requirement, *Cobbledick* held, was applicable to the grand jury witness. If the witness "chooses to disobey and is held in contempt," an immediate appeal will be allowed. That appeal "may involve an interruption of * * * the investigation," but allowing it is essential to preserve the witness's rights. "[N]ot to allow this interruption," the Court reasoned, "would forever preclude review of the witness's claim, for his alternatives are to abandon the claim or languish in jail." Accordingly, once held in contempt, the "witness' situation becomes so severed from the main proceeding as to permit an appeal."

In addition, an exception to the contempt prerequisite exists when a subpoena duces tecum is directed at a person other than the appellant and the appellant cannot expect that person to risk contempt for the purpose of protecting the appellant's interest in the property or information subpoenaed. The exception was established in a case decided before *Cobbledick*, *Perlman v. United States*.[80] In *Perlman*, the clerk of a federal court was directed to produce before a grand jury documents that Perlman had deposited with the clerk in connection with a patent infringement suit. Claiming a continuing right to those documents, Perlman challenged the order directed to the clerk and subsequently appealed from the denial of that challenge. As later explained in *United States v. Ryan*,[81] Perlman's appeal was allowed without the witness (the clerk) meeting the contempt prerequisite of *Cobbledick* because the witness did not share Perlman's interest in challenging the order. Without immediate review, Perlman would have been "powerless to avert the mischief of the [challenged] order." In *Ryan*, the Court stressed that *Perlman* created only a narrow exception to a sound policy that, in the interest of limiting appeals that would disrupt "expedition in the administration of the criminal law," puts the objecting witness to the inhibiting cost of standing in contempt.[82]

Rather than restrict the *Perlman* exception to situations in

---

[79]See Alexander v. United States, 201 U.S. 117, 26 S.Ct. 356, 50 L.Ed. 686 (1906).

[80]Perlman v. United States, 247 U.S. 7, 38 S.Ct. 417, 62 L.Ed. 950 (1918).

[81]United States v. Ryan, 402 U.S. 530, 91 S.Ct. 1580, 29 L.Ed.2d 85 (1971).

[82]For commentary on the *Perlman* exception, see Comment, 49 U.Chi.L. Rev. 798 (1982).

Another exception to the con-

tempt requirement was recognized by the Court in United States v. Nixon, 418 U.S. 683, 94 S.Ct. 3090, 41 L.Ed.2d 1039 (1974). There the Court held that it was "peculiarly inappropriate" to require "a President of the United States to place himself in the posture of disobeying an order of a court merely to trigger the procedural mechanism for review." Courts have refused to extend this exception to public officials generally. See 15B C. Wright, A. Miller, and E. Cooper, Federal Practice and Procedure §§ 3914.23,

which the intervenor and witness are total strangers,[83] the lower courts have also applied that exception to a variety of situations in which the interests of the party subpoenaed do not coincide with those of the person objecting to the subpoena. For example, appeals have been allowed from orders denying an appellant's motion to quash subpoenas directing her treating physician to turn over her medical records,[84] an order upholding a subpoena to a grand jury target's supervisor,[85] an order denying a bank depositor's motion to quash a grand jury subpoena issued to his bank,[86] and an order denying a record custodian's motion to quash a subpoena issued to a corporation.[87] In addition, employers have been allowed to appeal orders denying their motions to quash grand jury subpoenas issued to employees,[88] and clients have been permitted to appeal orders denying their motions to quash subpoenas issued to their attorneys.[89] The latter two situations, however, have produced conflicting decisions among the lower courts. A minority of courts continue to insist that *Perlman* ordinarily should not apply, because lawyers can be expected to submit to contempt in order to preserve the right to appeal for

3918.3 (2d ed.1992) (collecting cases); Corporacion Insular de Seguros v. Garcia, 876 F.2d 254 (1st Cir.1989) (not applicable to aide of the President of the Puerto Rican Senate).

[83] An interested party seeking review in "stranger" subpoena cases may face another obstacle. Should the court issuing the order refuse to stay its order and the stranger/possessor then comply with the order, the availability of an appeal under *Perlman* may be worthless, as the delivery of the property may render the appeal moot. See In re Grand Jury Subpoena Dated June 5, 825 F.2d 231 (9th Cir.1987) (clerk of court disclosed documents to grand jury as directed and grand jury indicted; relief sought precluding submission to grand jury was moot).

[84] In re Grand Jury Proceedings, 867 F.2d 562 (9th Cir.1989) (finding that since psychiatrist and hospitals will produce the records rather than risk contempt, the *Perlman* exception applies), abrogated on other grounds, Jaffee v. Redmond, 518 U.S. 1, 116 S.Ct. 1923, 135 L.Ed.2d 337 (1996).

[85] In re Grand Jury Subpoenas Dated December 7 and 8, Issued to

Bob Stover, Chief of Albuquerque Police Dept. v. United States, 40 F.3d 1096 (10th Cir.1994) (where police chief informed officers that he intended to turn over the requested documents).

[86] Harris v. United States, 413 F.2d 316 (9th Cir.1969); National Commodity and Barter Assn. v. United States, 951 F.2d 1172 (10th Cir.1991).

[87] In re Two Grand Jury Subpoenae Duces Tecum, 769 F.2d 52 (2d Cir. 1985). See also In re Grand Jury, 111 F.3d 1066 (3d Cir.1997) (target allowed to appeal order denying his motion to quash a subpoena directing perpetrator of wiretap to turn over recordings to grand jury).

[88] In re Matter of Grand Jury Applicants, 619 F.2d 1022 (3d Cir. 1980); United States v. Doe, 455 F.2d 753 (1st Cir.1972) (senator could appeal denial of his motion to quash a grand jury subpoena issued to his legislative aide), vacated on other grounds, 408 U.S. 606, 92 S.Ct. 2614, 33 L.Ed.2d 583 (1972).

[89] In re Grand Jury Subpoenas, 123 F.3d 695 (1st Cir.1997) (reviewing cases); United States v. Davis, 1 F.3d 606 (7th Cir.1993); In the Matter of Klein, 776 F.2d 628 (7th Cir.1985).

their clients, as can employees for their employers.[90] Obviously, these decisions may be criticized as expecting unrealistic sacrifice from employee or counsel. Still, such expectations may be justified in some cases. An employee may have participated in the activities being investigated so that his personal interest in nondisclosure may be as great as that of his employer. Likewise, the client may have anticipated the subpoena and sought "to elevate the *Perlman* argument by transferring internally produced documents to an outside representative."[91] Most courts, however, find it "unduly optimistic to anticipate that all attorneys will accept contempt rather than compromise their clients' appeal."[92]

Where the challenge to ongoing grand jury proceedings does not relate to the appearance of a witness, the contempt alternative of *Cobbledick* may not be available. In such cases, courts focus on whether the petitioner (who is usually the target of the investigation) will have a subsequently available appellate remedy if an immediate appeal from his denied request for relief is not available.[93] Thus, if the target is objecting to the alleged use of the grand jury to develop evidence for a civil case, a court is likely to hold that an immediate appeal is not permissible since a

---

[90]See, e.g., In re Grand Jury Subpoena Dated January 30, 1986 to Bronx Democratic Party, 784 F.2d 116 (2d Cir.1986) (representative of political party must stand in contempt); In re Grand Jury Subpoena, 190 F.3d 375 (5th Cir.1999) (no immediate appeal for individual who protested order compelling production by his client-employer corporation, reasoning that although only corporation was under subpoena, both individual and corporation were targets of the grand jury investigation and corporation "can hardly be described as having "no independent interest in preserving [the documents'] confidentiality""); In re Grand Jury Subpoena Issued to Bailin, 51 F.3d 203 (9th Cir.1995) (subpoena to accountant); In re Grand Jury Proceedings Subpoena to Vargas, 723 F.2d 1461 (10th Cir.1983); In re Grand Jury Subpoena Served Upon Niren, 784 F.2d 939 (9th Cir.1986) (in-house counsel); In the Matter of a Rhode Island Grand Jury Subpoena, 414 Mass. 104, 605 N.E.2d 840 (1993); In the Matter of a Grand Jury Subpoena, 411 Mass. 489, 583 N.E.2d 241 (1992)

(appeal not available by corporation to protest subpoena directed to accounting firm).

[91]See In re Sealed Case, 655 F.2d 1298 (D.C.Cir.1981). But see In re Grand Jury Proceedings, 43 F.3d 966 (5th Cir.1994) (appeal by lawyers permitted without contempt finding).

[92]In re Grand Jury Subpoenas, 123 F.3d 695 (1st Cir.1997). In some states, review is commonly obtained by extraordinary writ rather than by appeal, but immediate review is available in most states through one route or another. See § 27.4, discussing review by writ.

[93]See Fraser v. United States, 834 F.2d 911 (11th Cir.1987) (when target of criminal investigation served with order directing that he submit to the Attorney General a copy of his opposition filed with a foreign government to the release of his foreign bank records, his appeal from the district court's refusal to vacate that order was "premature" as he had not "risk[ed] litigating his objections in contempt proceedings").

later objection (and appeal) is available if the government should seek to transfer any such evidence to a potential civil litigant or to use it in a civil proceeding.[94] Similarly, if the target claims that the grand jury proceeding is being tainted by misconduct, a court may hold that such an objection can be advanced when (and if) an indictment is issued and an appeal can then be taken when (and if) the target is convicted.[95] Some courts are less willing than others, however, to view such subsequent avenues of appeal as adequate. Thus, appeals have been allowed from rulings denying target-petitioner motions to preclude grand-jury gathering of evidence to be used in prosecuting a pending indictment,[96] and motions requesting an evidentiary hearing concerning the alleged resumption of prosecutorial misconduct that had led to the dismissal of a prior indictment.[97]

Once the grand jury investigation has ended, a petitioner seeking relief unrelated to an ongoing prosecution can more readily claim that his request involves an independent proceeding. Thus, an appeal can be taken from the grant or denial of a Rule 6(e) motion for disclosure of grand jury minutes for use in an unrelated proceeding.[98]

§ 27.3 Prosecution appeals

§ 27.3(a)   Constitutional constraints
§ 27.3(b)   The need for specific statutory authorization
§ 27.3(c)   Pretrial rulings

[94]See In re Grand Jury Subpoenas, April, 1978, at Baltimore, 581 F.2d 1103 (4th Cir.1978); In re April 1977 Grand Jury Subpoenas, 584 F.2d 1366 (6th Cir.1978).

[95]See In re Grand Jury Proceedings, 632 F.2d 1033 (3d Cir.1980); In re Grand Jury Subpoenas, April, 1978, at Baltimore, 581 F.2d 1103 (4th Cir. 1978); In re Grand Jury Subpoenas, 818 F.2d 330 (5th Cir.1987) (rejecting attempt to appeal judge's refusal to quash subpoenas after allegations that the prosecutor was misusing the grand jury process); In re April 1977 Grand Jury Subpoenas, 584 F.2d 1366 (6th Cir.1978); In re Grand Jury Subpoena, 119 F.3d 750 (9th Cir.1997) (trial court's refusal to hold a *Kastigar* hearing during grand jury investigation can be reviewed by the trial court after indictment, and by the court of appeals after conviction).

[96]United States v. Doe, 455 F.2d 1270 (1st Cir.1972); In re Grand Jury Proceedings, 814 F.2d 61 (1st Cir. 1987).

[97]In re November 1979 Grand Jury, 616 F.2d 1021 (7th Cir.1980).

[98]See, e.g., Douglas Oil Co. of California v. Petrol Stops Northwest, 441 U.S. 211, 99 S.Ct. 1667, 60 L.Ed.2d 156 (1979). See also In re Grand Jury Investigation, 55 F.3d 350 (8th Cir. 1995); United States v. Fischbach and Moore, Inc., 776 F.2d 839 (9th Cir. 1985). So too, a district court order providing for the transfer of the grand jury transcripts to a court in another district may be appealed. In re Grand Jury Proceedings at Chattanoogo, Tennessee, 649 F.2d 387 (6th Cir. 1981); In the Matter of Grand Jury Proceedings, Miller Brewing Co., 687 F.2d 1079 (7th Cir.1982).

§ 27.3(a) Constitutional constraints

Through much of the 19th century, most states denied the government an opportunity to appeal an acquittal through writ of error, and many states disallowed writs of error for the state in criminal cases altogether.[1] Government appeals of acquittals were considered a violation of the defendant's freedom from double jeopardy, a right originally guaranteed to most state defendants by state constitutional provisions and to federal defendants by the Fifth Amendment.[2] As discussed in more detail in Chapter 25, the Supreme Court's double jeopardy decisions have indeed barred government attempts to review acquittals, but the Court has also recognized that some government appeals do not violate the double jeopardy rights of criminal defendants. Pretrial dismissals, prior to the attachment of jeopardy, for example, may be appealed.[3] Post-trial rulings discharging a defendant following a guilty verdict are also reviewable, as reversal would require only the reinstatement of the guilty verdict.[4] Resentencing also does not involve retrial, allowing the government appeal of sentencing orders.[5] Even midtrial dismissals may be appealed when requested by the defense and not based on a

---

[Section 27.3(a)]

[1] See Report to the Attorney General on Double Jeopardy and Government Appeals of Acquittals, Office of Legal Policy, reprinted in 22 U.Mich.J.L.Ref. 831, 895, 879–880 (1989) (reviewing state practice in nineteenth century, noting that although four states "accorded some recognition to the state's right to file writs of error in criminal cases" no state "clearly established the right of the state to appeal an acquittal," also concluding that "prior to the incorporation of the double jeopardy clause, only two states authorized the government to appeal an acquittal on the basis of error").

[2] See Kepner v. United States, 195 U.S. 100, 24 S.Ct. 797, 49 L.Ed. 114 (1904) (following government appeal of bench acquittal by Philippine court, defendant was convicted by Philippine Supreme Court, then appealed to the United States Supreme Court, which reversed, rejecting argument by Justice Holmes that a crimi-

nal case remains one continuing jeopardy throughout the appellate and remand process, and finding instead that the Double Jeopardy Clause bars review of a verdict of acquittal); Fong Foo v. United States, 369 U.S. 141, 82 S.Ct. 671, 7 L.Ed.2d 629 (1962) (disallowing writ of mandamus from directed verdict of acquittal allegedly the product of judicial error of law); Sanabria v. United States, 437 U.S. 54, 98 S.Ct. 2170, 57 L.Ed.2d 43 (1978) (double jeopardy bars government appeal of midtrial dismissal based on an allegedly "egregiously erroneous" legal ruling).

[3] See Serfass v. United States, 420 U.S. 377, 95 S.Ct. 1055, 43 L.Ed.2d 265 (1975), discussed in § 25.3(d) at note 33.

[4] See United States v. Wilson, 420 U.S. 332, 95 S.Ct. 1013, 43 L.Ed.2d 232 (1975).

[5] See United States v. DiFrancesco, 449 U.S. 117, 101 S.Ct. 426, 66 L.Ed.2d 328 (1980) (upholding statute authorizing the United States

failure of proof of factual elements of the offense.[6] Nevertheless, double jeopardy continues to bar the government from appealing a variety of other rulings,[7] and statutes impose further restrictions on prosecution appeals, so that access to appellate relief remains asymmetric.

Some commentators have argued that one "by product" of this asymmetry is "pro-defendant bias in the development and application of legal standards."[8] Not only do defendant-appellants exert "one-way pressure" on appellate judges, trial judges may seek to avoid reversal by favoring the defendant. A competing view is that the limitations on government appeals may instead motivate judges to deliberately compensate for the absence of review by favoring the government, particularly since the harmless error doctrine operates to insulate many pro-prosecution rul-

[6] See United States v. Scott, 437 U.S. 82, 98 S.Ct. 2187, 57 L.Ed.2d 65 (1978), discussed in § 25.3(a).

[7] Double jeopardy limitations are more fully discussed in Chapter 25. See also Strazzella, The Relationship of Double Jeopardy to Prosecution Appeals, 73 Notre Dame L.Rev. 1 (1997). While it is sometimes said that double jeopardy "bars an appeal by the prosecution following a jury verdict of acquittal," see Arizona v. Manypenny, 451 U.S. 232, 101 S.Ct. 1657, 68 L.Ed.2d 58 (1981), that assertion overlooks what is sometimes termed the "moot appeal." If the government's victory on appeal would not permit a reprosecution (due to the double jeopardy prohibition), then the appeal presents "basically a moot issue" and ordinarily will not be allowed for that reason. In several jurisdictions in which justiciability is not limited by a "case or controversy" restriction, however, "moot" or "advisory appeals" from

to appeal from certain sentencing decisions). But see Bullington v. Missouri, 451 U.S. 430, 101 S.Ct. 1852, 68 L.Ed.2d 270 (1981) (resentencing in capital case limited by double jeopardy). These cases are discussed in § 26.7. See also Westen, The Three Faces of Double Jeopardy: Reflections on Government Appeals of Criminal Sentences, 78 Mich.L.Rev. 1001 (1980).

acquittals have been accepted as consistent with the double jeopardy prohibition. See, e.g., Kan.Stat.Ann. § 22-3602(b); Neb.Rev.Stat. §§ 29-2315.01 to 39-2315.02; State v. Mountjoy, 257 Kan. 163, 891 P.2d 376 (1995) (discussing purpose of allowing review); State v. Canelo, 139 N.H. 376, 653 A.2d 1097 (1995); State v. Shelton, 692 N.E.2d 947 (Ind.App.1998). Compare State v. Viers, 86 Nev. 385, 469 P.2d 53 (1970) (advisory appeal not allowed, as it presents no case or controversy under state constitution); Shaw, Prosecution Appeals Taken Midtrial and Following Acquittal: Changing the Trial and Review of Criminal Cases in Ohio, 22 Ohio N.U.L.Rev. 729 (1996) (discussing such "advisory" appeals in Ohio); Strazzella, supra, at 18–19 (collecting authority). In a moot appeal, the prosecution raises issues solely for the purpose of determining the law for future cases; the appellate court lacks authority to upset the judgment of acquittal. To ensure that the prosecution's appeal is contested, defense counsel is commonly paid by the state to argue the defense side. The discussion that follows excludes such moot appeals.

[8] Stith, The Risk of Legal Error in Criminal Cases: Some Consequences of the Asymmetry in the Right to Appeal, 57 U.Chi.L.Rev. 1, 7 (1990).

ings from reversal.[9] The actual effects of the constitutionally imposed asymmetry in appellate review on the behavior of judges may never be settled, but its influence on legislators is clear enough. Over the past several decades, legislatures have consistently expanded, rather than curtailed, the prosecutor's access to appellate review of trial court decisions.[10]

§ 27.3(b) The need for specific statutory authorization

Absent specific statutory authorization, the prosecution lacks the right to appeal an adverse ruling in a criminal case. The policy underlying that position was set forth by the Supreme Court's 1892 ruling in *United States v. Sanges*.[11] Congress had granted federal defendants the statutory right to apply for writs of error in criminal cases, but had not extended the same opportunity to the government. Consequently, the Court concluded, "the defendant, having been once put upon his trial and discharged by the court, is not to be again vexed for the same cause, unless the legislature, acting within its constitutional authority, has made express provision for a review of the judgment at the instance of the government."[12]

Soon thereafter, Congress adopted in 1907 a statute allowing

---

[9]Damaska, Evidentiary Barriers to Conviction and Two Models of Criminal Procedure: A Comparative Study, 121 U.Pa.L.Rev. 506, 522 (1973); Stith, The Risk of Legal Error in Criminal Cases: Some Consequences of the Asymmetry in the Right to Appeal, 57 U.Chi.L.Rev. 1, 42, 43–47 (1990) (acknowledging that trial judges may indeed "err for the government when ruling 'upon novel or difficult-to-categorize legal issues,'" in order to obtain authoritative delineation of the proper standard from the appellate courts; also noting that the harmless error doctrine, by reducing the risk of reversal, lessens the incentives for trial judges to shade their rulings for the defense). See also Khanna, Double Jeopardy's Asymmetric Appeal Rights: What Purpose Do They Serve, 82 B.U.L.Rev. 341 (2002), where the author argues that asymmetric appeal rights may actually increase the number of false convictions because the government, facing only one shot at conviction, has increased incentives to win at trial and may spend the resources to secure more "marginal" convictions than it would under a regime of symmetric rights to appeal.

[10]The Criminal Appeals Act, 18 U.S.C.A. § 3731, governing the appeal of orders in federal criminal cases, was amended to provide additional appellate review for prosecutors in 1970, for example. See note 19. Several states have expanded their government appeal provisions as well. See, e.g., Ariz.Rev.Stat.Ann.   § 13-4032; Ind.CodeAnn. 35-38-42; Mo.Stat.Ann. § 547.20; N.Y.Cons.Law § 450.20.

[Section 27.3(b)]

[11]United States v. Sanges, 144 U.S. 310, 12 S.Ct. 609, 36 L.Ed. 445 (1892).

[12]See also Arizona v. Manypenny, 451 U.S. 232, 101 S.Ct. 1657, 68 L.Ed.2d 58 (1981) (stating that both "prudential and constitutional interests contributed" to this rule, and noting that the "need to restrict appeals by the prosecutor reflected a prudential concern that individuals should be free from the harassment and vexation of unbounded litigation by the sovereign," citing state cases).

government appeals under specified circumstances.[13] The Supreme Court, consistent with *Sanges*, strictly limited such appeals to the letter of that provision. Government attempts to gain more expansive appellate review using the general appeals statute, 18 U.S.C.A. § 1291 (allowing for appeals from final decisions), were rejected by the Supreme Court in *Carroll v. United States*:[14]

> [A]ppeals by the Government in criminal cases are something unusual, exceptional, not favored. The history shows resistance of the Court to the opening of an appellate route for the Government until it was plainly provided by the Congress, and after that a close restriction of its uses to those authorized by the statute.

In *Arizona v. Manypenny*,[15] the Court reiterated this limitation and reviewed its basis, noting that the Court's "continuing refusal to assume that the United States possesses any inherent right to appeal" reflects the need "to check the Federal Government's possible misuse of its enormous prosecutorial powers." Requiring Congress "to speak with a clear voice when extending to the Executive a right to expand criminal prosecutions" through appeal places the responsibility for "such assertions of authority over citizens in the democratically elected Legislature where it belongs."[16]

The philosophy expressed in *Sanges*, *Carroll*, and *Manypenny*

---

[13]The Criminal Appeals Act of 1907, ch. 2564, 34 Stat. 1246 (1907) (codified as amended at 18 U.S.C.A. § 3731). For a history of the passage of the Act, see Note, 99 Yale L.J. 905 (1990).

[14]Carroll v. United States, 354 U.S. 394, 77 S.Ct. 1332, 1 L.Ed.2d 1442 (1957).

[15]Arizona v. Manypenny, 451 U.S. 232, 101 S.Ct. 1657, 68 L.Ed.2d 58 (1981).

[16]The Court went on to rule that the limitation on appeals by the United States under 28 U.S.C.A. § 1291 does not prevent a State from appealing under that provision an adverse judgment in a criminal proceeding removed to federal court (under 28 U.S.C.A. § 1442(a)(1)), if authority to seek such review is conferred by state law.

While the United States is thus prohibited from relying upon the general appeals statute (28 U.S.C.A. § 1291) and its accompanying "collateral order exception" for appellate authority, lower federal courts have nonetheless relied upon dictum in the *Carroll* decision noting that some orders "may be found to possess sufficient independence from the main course of the prosecution to warrant treatment as plenary orders, and thus be appealable [under § 1291]." The two illustrations mentioned were appeals of orders setting the amount of bail and orders suppressing or returning seized evidence have since been expressly authorized by Congress. See Bail Reform Act, 18 U.S.C.A. § 3154, and the amended Criminal Appeals Act, 18 U.S.C.A. § 3731, discussed at note 19.

Lower federal courts have termed this dictum in *Carroll* the "special circumstance exception," and have allowed the government to appeal as collateral orders under § 1291 orders assessing attorneys' fees and costs against federal prosecutors, and orders disqualifying government counsel, on the theory that the unique qualities of such orders avoid the prudential concerns supporting the

is repeated frequently in state[17] as well as federal decisions.[18] All of the states now have provisions allowing prosecution appeals from at least a limited class of orders in criminal cases. These provisions, like the Criminal Appeals Act governing federal criminal cases (18 U.S.C.A. § 3731),[19] typically list which interlocutory and final orders may be appealed by the prosecution. Whenever the statutory language refers to appeals from specific types of orders (e.g., an "order arresting judgment"), courts will insist

---

general limits on government appeals. See United States v. Horn, 29 F.3d 754 (1st Cir.1994) (collecting similar rulings); United States v. Vlahos, 33 F.3d 758 (7th Cir.1994) (government's appeal of order disqualifying government counsel permitted under § 1291 and the collateral order doctrine, collecting cases).

    Compare State v. Smith, 268 Ga. 75, 485 S.E.2d 491 (1997) (order disqualifying district attorney does not fall within the limited number of cases in which the State has the right to appeal); United States v. McVeigh, 106 F.3d 325 (10th Cir.1997) (rejecting attempt to employ § 1291 as authority for interlocutory appeal of witness sequestration order, distinguishing *Horn*). Given the availability of review by writ in such cases, see § 27.4, this "exception" to the general rule expressed in *Carroll* and *Manypenny* seems unwarranted.

[17]See, e.g., Exposito v. State, 891 So.2d 525 (Fla.2004) (the "State's right to appeal a post-trial order reducing the charge must be the product of express legislative authorization, not judicial extension of provisions authorizing State appeals in other circumstances"); State v. Manck, 385 Md.App. 581, 870 A.2d 196 (2005) (refusing to allow state to proceed by writ in seeking review of trial judge's order striking state's notice of intention to seek the penalty of death, noting "for this court to expand the State's right to appeal beyond the statutory limits would violate the separation of powers doctrine"); State v. Green, 367 Md. 61, 785 A.2d 1275 (2001) (prosecutors do not have a common-law right to appeal a sentence and are limited to the right to appeal provided by statute);

State v. Lewis, 188 W.Va. 85, 422 S.E.2d 807 (1992).

[18]See, e.g., United States v. Vlahos, 33 F.3d 758 (7th Cir.1994); United States v. Carrillo-Bernal, 58 F.3d 1490 (10th Cir.1995) (surveying in detail the historical evolution of the government's right to appeal in criminal cases).

[19]18 U.S.C.A. § 3731 provides:

    In a criminal case an appeal by the United States shall lie to a court of appeals from a decision, judgment, or order of a district court dismissing an indictment or information or granting a new trial after verdict or judgment as to any one or more counts, except that no appeal shall lie where the double jeopardy clause of the United States Constitution prohibits further prosecution.

    This provision has been read as intending "to remove all statutory barriers to Government appeals and to allow appeals whenever the Constitution would permit." See United States v. Wilson, 420 U.S. 332, 95 S.Ct. 1013, 43 L.Ed.2d 232 (1975). Section 3731 also contains a separate provision governing appeals from suppression orders (discussed infra), and a separate provision allowing an appeal from a district court order "granting the release of a person charged with or convicted of an offense, or denying a motion for revocation of, or modification of the conditions of, a decision or order granting release." For more on the 1970 amendments, see Note, 99 Yale L.J. 905, 909–911 (1990). The provisions of 18 U.S.C.A. § 3731 are also discussed in 15B C. Wright, A. Miller, and E. Cooper, Federal Practice and Procedure § 3919 (2d ed.1992).

that the ruling appealed fits squarely within the specified category. In many jurisdictions, these provisions narrow the government's right to appeal considerably, well beyond the limitations on appeal imposed by the final judgment rule and the Double Jeopardy Clause. The discussion of statutory limits on government appeals that follows is divided into two sections. The first addresses the appeal of rulings entered prior to the attachment of jeopardy; the second examines the appeal of orders entered after jeopardy has attached.

§ 27.3(c) Pretrial rulings

As noted above, provisions limiting appeals by the prosecution commonly authorize appeals from pretrial rulings that would be considered final judgments, as well as from other interlocutory orders.

Final Judgments. As to final judgments, some statutes refer broadly to appeals from all "final judgments,"[20] or (as in the federal provision) from all "dismissals of an indictment or information * * * as to one or more counts."[21] These provisions encompass dismissals based upon such grounds as the insufficiency of the accusatory pleading,[22] prior jeopardy,[23] denial of a speedy trial,[24] lack of sufficient evidence to support a bindover,[25] prosecutorial misconduct,[26] and the unconstitutionality of the underlying statute.[27] Other jurisdictions restrict the category of appealable final judgments to dismissals based on a deficiency in

---

[Section 27.3(c)]

[20]See, e.g., Wis.Stat.Ann. § 974.05(1)(a).

[21]See, e.g., 18 U.S.C.A. § 3731; Vt.Stat.Ann. tit. 13, § 7404(b); Ga.Code Ann. § 5 to 71(a)(1). Compare Kan.Stat. Ann. § 22-3602(b) (providing appeal as of right by State from order dismissing a complaint, information, or indictment); State v. Nelson, 263 Kan. 115, 946 P.2d 1355 (1997) (partial dismissal, leaving one count pending, was not subject to appeal).

[22]See, e.g., State v. Larabee, 69 Oh.St.3d 357, 632 N.E.2d 511 (1994); State v. Thomas, 34 Or.App. 187, 578 P.2d 452 (1978); State v. Jelliff, 251 N.W.2d 1 (N.D.1977).

[23]See, e.g., United States v. Terry, 131 F.3d 138 (4th Cir.1997); State v. Rice, 329 Ark. 219, 947 S.W.2d 3 (1997); State v. Woodruff, 676 So.2d 975 (Fla.1996). See also State v. Casaretto, 818 S.W.2d 313 (Mo.App.1991) (appeal of dismissal based on statute of limitations).

[24]See, e.g., State v. Lee, 132 Wash.2d 498, 939 P.2d 1223 (1997).

[25]See, e.g., People v. Williams, 226 Mich.App. 568, 576 N.W.2d 390 (1997). But see State v. Duffy, 559 N.W.2d 109 (Minn.App.1997) (appeals from such rulings not allowed).

[26]See, e.g., Sedgwick v. Superior Court, 584 F.2d 1044 (D.C.Cir.1978); People v. Marbly, 85 Ill.App.3d 935, 41 Ill.Dec. 223, 407 N.E.2d 721 (1980); State v. Edwards, 279 N.W.2d 9 (Iowa 1979).

[27]State v. Kimpel, 665 So.2d 990 (Ala.App.1995) (appeal of order holding statute unconstitutional).

the pleading itself.[28] A few states have even more restrictive provisions, providing a prosecution appeal as of right only from a ruling holding unconstitutional the statute forming the basis for the charges.[29] In addition, some states limit appeals to dismissals of felony indictments,[30] or, even more narrowly, to serious felonies.[31]

Interlocutory Pretrial Rulings Generally. The states also vary in their treatment of prosecution appeals from interlocutory pretrial rulings. As noted in § 27.2, with some exceptions, a defendant typically cannot appeal an adverse interlocutory order, but can gain review of the adverse pretrial ruling on appeal if he is convicted. The prosecution, however, is in a quite different position. If the government is not allowed an immediate appeal from an adverse interlocutory ruling, there will be no opportunity for later appellate review should the defendant be acquitted, since the double jeopardy prohibition then bars further prosecution.

This circumstance has led a few jurisdictions to provide the prosecution with the opportunity to appeal nearly any adverse pretrial interlocutory order.[32] Most jurisdictions, however, have stopped short of conferring such broad authority, considering the interests of the defendant and society in the swift resolution of criminal cases to be worthy of greater protection. After all, interlocutory appeals may interrupt a case and delay trial for months,[33] during which time proof may be lost and the defendant remain

---

[28]See, e.g., W.Va.Code § 58-5-30 (appeal allowed where an indictment held "bad or insufficient"); State ex rel. Forbes v. Canady, 197 W.Va. 37, 475 S.E.2d 37 (1996) (rejecting appeal of dismissal based on state's failure to join counts).

[29]See State v. James, 329 So.2d 713 (La.1976) (appeal as of right limited to cases in which a law has been declared unconstitutional, although noting that broader *discretionary* review is also available).

[30]City of Huntsville v. Shanes, 645 So.2d 339 (Ala.App.1994) (no authorization for pretrial appeal by state in misdemeanor case). See also Va.Code Ann. § 19.2-398 (appeals authorized only in felony cases); W.Va.Code Ann. § 58-5-30.

[31]Md.Code Cts. & Jud.Proc. § 12-302(c)(3)(i) (limiting appeals to certain cases involving violence or drugs).

[32]Alaska Stat. § 22.07.020(d)(2) (providing state right to appeal limited only by double jeopardy). See Colo.Rev. Stat.Ann. § 16-12-102(1) ("The prosecution may appeal any decision of the trial court in a criminal case upon any question of law * * *."). See also State v. Gray, 958 S.W.2d 302 (Ark.1997) (construing Ark.R.Cr.P. 3(c), allowing appeals when holding will set a precedent that is "important to the correct and uniform administration" of Arkansas criminal law).

[33]See Note, 60 B.U.L.Rev. 664, 675–79 (1980) (collecting cases). See also Commonwealth v. Gordon, 543 Pa. 513, 673 A.2d 866 (1996) (Cappy, J., dissenting). These periods of delay are occasionally treated as "excluded periods" under speedy trial statutes., e.g., 18 U.S.C.A. § 3161(h); Commonwealth v. Malinowski, 543 Pa. 350, 671 A.2d 674 (1996). Some statutes require that prosecution appeals

incarcerated.[34] A common approach is to allow the prosecution to appeal from only designated categories of pretrial interlocutory orders.[35]

Suppression Orders. The interlocutory order most frequently included in statutes authorizing appeal by the prosecution is the suppression order. An order suppressing evidence generally is held not to fall within a provision authorizing appeals from a "final judgment" or a "dismissal of an indictment" since it does not formally terminate the proceeding.[36] The federal government and most states have adopted legislation providing for review of suppression orders as a matter of right.[37]

Two grounds are advanced in support of allowing the prosecution to appeal from a trial court's decision to grant a defendant's motion to suppress evidence. One justification is the special need for appellate court rulings on legal issues relating to searches

---

be given docket priority, see, e.g., Haw.Rev.Stat.Ann. § 641-13(7), (8), but that policy is generally followed even without a statutory directive. The defendant's constitutional interest in a timely appellate process is discussed in § 18.5(c).

[34] For statutes governing release pending appeal, see, e.g., 18 U.S.C.A. § 3143(c); Minn.R.Crim.P. 28.04; S.D.Codified LawsAnn. § 23A-32-7. Several jurisdictions require that the defendant be released pending disposition of the appeal unless there are "compelling reasons for continued detention." Ill.S.Ct.R.art. 604(a)(3); Fla.Stat.Ann. § 924.071 (defendant shall be released unless the offense is nonbailable). See also 4 ABA Standards for Criminal Justice § 21-1.4(c) (2d ed.1980). Release during interlocutory appeal is also discussed in § 12.4. Some jurisdictions have chosen to discourage unwarranted prosecution appeals by imposing sanctions should the appeal be decided in defendant's favor. See, e.g., State v. Bertram, 80 Oh.St.3d 281, 685 N.E.2d 1239 (1997) (upon affirmance of an order suppressing state's evidence, the state is prohibited from prosecuting the defendant for the same offense absent a showing of newly discovered, and previously undiscoverable, evidence of guilt); McNeil v. State, 112 Md.App. 434, 685 A.2d 839 (1996) (same).

[35] E.g., State v. Quinn, 930 P.2d 267 (Utah 1996) (noting that Utah R.Crim.P. 26(3) allows the state to appeal from a pretrial order suppressing evidence when, upon a petition for review, the appellate court decides that the appeal would be in the interest of justice; or an order of the court granting a motion to withdraw a plea of guilty or no contest).

[36] See, e.g., McNeil v. State, 112 Md.App. 434, 685 A.2d 839 (1996); State v. Collins, 24 Ohio St.2d 107, 265 N.E.2d 261 (1970) (collecting cases). But see State v. Pease, 531 N.E.2d 1207 (Ind.App.1988) (where suppression order precludes prosecution use of its "principal items of evidence," it was "tantamount to a dismissal" and appeal could be brought under a court rule allowing appeals from "final judgments"). Even where the prosecution has little proof of guilt other than the evidence suppressed by the order, the prosecution and trial would proceed unless terminated by a *nolle prosequi* motion which ordinarily will not be appealable. See, e.g., State v. Tatum, 642 So.2d 523 (Ala.App. 1994).

[37] See, e.g., 18 U.S.C.A. § 3731; Ariz.Rev.Stat.Ann. § 13-4032; N.Y.Crim.Proc.Law § 450.20(8); Kan.Stat.Ann. § 22-3603; Tex.Ann. Crim.P.Code art. 44.01.

and seizures and interrogation. The law in this area is so uncertain, it has been argued, that law enforcement officers dissatisfied with the rulings of individual trial judges will persist in a challenged practice until they obtain a favorable decision from another trial judge, and perhaps a favorable ruling on appeal after a resulting conviction. The better rule, it is argued, is to give the prosecution the opportunity to gain immediate review of those trial court rulings that it considers questionable.[38] Perhaps for this reason, some state provisions authorizing the appeal of suppression orders by the government limit that authority to the appeal of orders relating to illegal practices by police in obtaining evidence.[39]

Other statutes, such as 18 U.S.C.A. § 3731, speak generally of orders "suppressing or excluding" evidence, and have been held applicable to a broad range of pretrial orders limiting the government's proof at trial.[40] Appealable rulings have included orders quashing witness subpoenas,[41] orders barring testimony due to defense claims of privilege and work-product protection,[42]

[38]See President's Comm'n on Law Enforcement and the Administration of Justice, Task Force Report: The Courts 47 (1967).

[39]See, e.g., State v. Pastorini, 226 Ga.App. 260, 486 S.E.2d 399 (Ga.1997) (order appealable when based in part on general rules of evidence and in part on non-compliance with *Miranda*); Berky v. State, 266 Ga. 28, 463 S.E.2d 891 (1995); State v. Carney, 219 Mont. 412, 714 P.2d 532 (1986); State v. Swope, 939 S.W.2d 491 (Mo.App.1997) (order excluding out of court statements of child victim as unreliable not appealable); People v. McCollins, 126 Ill.App.3d 1083, 82 Ill.Dec. 134, 468 N.E.2d 196 (1984) (in limine ruling that the state would not be allowed to use evidence of defendant's alleged refusal to submit to breath analysis not a suppression order subject to appeal); State v. Isaac, 696 So.2d 813 (Fla.App.1997) (order refusing to compel release of medical records not within Fla.R.App.Proc. 9, 140(c)). See also Commonwealth v. Rodgers, 21 Va.App. 745, 467 S.E.2d 813 (1996) (rejecting appeal of suppression order based on collateral estoppel, because state statute autho-

rized appeals of only orders based upon those provisions of the Constitution "prohibiting illegal searches and seizures and protecting rights against self-incrimination"). Compare State v. Medrano, 67 S.W.3d 892 (Tex.Cr.App. 2002) (appeal allowable for all suppression orders, regardless of whether evidence illegally obtained, overruling prior limitations as "unworkable").

[40]See, e.g., 10 Del.CodeAnn. tit. 10, § 9902(b); Haw. Rev.Stat.Ann. § 641-13; 15 Me.Rev.Stat.Ann. tit. 15, § 2115-A(1). See also State v. Newman, 235 Kan. 29, 680 P.2d 257 (1984) ("suppressing evidence" includes not only "constitutional suppression" but also rulings of a trial court which excludes state's evidence so as to substantially impair the state's ability to prosecute the case).

[41]E.g., In re Grand Jury Subpoena Duces Tecum, 112 F.3d 910 (8th Cir. 1997); In the Matter of Grand Jury Empanelled February 14, 1978, 597 F.2d 851 (3d Cir.1979).

[42]E.g., Commonwealth v. Noll, 443 Pa.Super. 602, 662 A.2d 1123 (1995).

orders striking the death penalty from an indictment,[43] and orders excluding testimony as a sanction for the prosecution's failure to comply with discovery rules.[44] The broader review extended to prosecutors under these statutes builds upon the second justification for allowing the prosecution to appeal suppression orders, namely the recognition that the practical effect of such an order is, in many cases, equivalent to dismissal. A ruling suppressing evidence often eliminates the heart of the prosecution's case. With the opportunity to appeal such rulings, even those that result from its own motions in limine, the prosecution may have the opportunity to gain appellate review of a wide range of orders that otherwise would be subsumed in an acquittal.[45]

---

[43]United States v. Acosta-Martinez, 252 F.3d 13 (1st Cir.2001).

[44]State v. Maass, 178 Wis.2d 63, 502 N.W.2d 913 (Wis.App.1993). See also United States v. Horwitz, 622 F.2d 1101 (2d Cir.1980) (appeal of order excluding testimony of immunized government witness because prosecutor refused to immunize defense witnesses was appealable); United States v. Kane, 646 F.2d 4 (1st Cir.1981) (collecting cases); People v. Phipps, 83 Ill.2d 87, 46 Ill.Dec. 164, 413 N.E.2d 1277 (1980) (order directing the prosecution to disclose psychiatric reports pertaining to its witnesses where the sanction for failing to disclose was the exclusion of the testimony of those witnesses).

[45]See United States v. Helstoski, 442 U.S. 477, 99 S.Ct. 2432, 61 L.Ed.2d 12 (1979). There, after the trial court indicated in its rejection of a motion to dismiss that the Speech or Debate Clause would bar prosecution reference to the legislative activities of the defendant (a former Congressman), the government sought a pretrial ruling on the admissibility of 23 categories of evidence. When the district court responded with an adverse ruling, the government obtained appellate review since that ruling was treated as one "excluding evidence" and the prosecution was able to file the necessary certification under 18 U.S.C.A. § 3731 based on the significance of the evidence. See notes 46–50 (discussing certification requirements).

Helstoski involved a ruling in response to a defense motion, but lower courts have also upheld appeals from orders resolving suppression issues first raised by the prosecution. United States v. Valencia, 826 F.2d 169 (2d Cir.1987); United States v. Layton, 720 F.2d 548 (9th Cir.1983). See also United States v. Fernandez, 231 F.3d 1240 (9th Cir.2000) (reviewing order precluding government from seeking death penalty, as a sanction for refusing discovery request, noting that "one who seeks to resist the production of desired information [must choose] between compliance with a trial court's order to produce prior to any review of that order, and resistance to that order with the concomitant possibility of an adjudication of contempt if his claims are rejected on appeal," and that here the government selected the latter option); United States v. Bolden, 353 F.3d 870 (10th Cir.2003) (order disqualifying entire United States Attorneys office was immediately appealable, raises a separation of powers concern that is separate from the underlying merits and was not at issue in Flanagan, and, although double jeopardy would not bar later review, appellate vindication cannot undo the invasion of executive authority); State v. Ratner, 948 So.2d 700 (Fla.2007) (order excluding excited utterance of victim to police officer was appealable by the state prior to trial, because it fell within rule authorizing interlocutory appeals and was certified as a question of great public im-

Consistent with this case-ending justification for review, a state may limit prosecution appeals to cases in which the suppressed evidence is shown to be critical to the prosecution's case.[46] Several states condition appeal on a prosecutor's certification that the suppression order will eliminate any "reasonable possibility" of a successful prosecution.[47] The federal statute and a number of state provisions, for example, require certification that "the appeal is not taken for the purpose of delay and that the [suppressed] evidence is a substantial part of the proof of the charge pending against the defendant."[48] In other jurisdictions, certification is not required, but the prosecution must otherwise establish that the trial court's ruling will have a substantial impact upon the outcome of the prosecution,[49] or is "in the best interests of justice."[50]

Other Interlocutory Orders. Many jurisdictions allowing prose-

---

portance).

[46]E.g., Pa.R.App.P. 311(d); Ill.Sup. Ct.R. art. IV, Rule 604(a)(1).

[47]See, e.g., N.Y.Crim.Proc.Law § 450.50 (prosecution must certify that suppression will render available evidence either insufficient as a matter of law or "so weak * * * that any reasonable possibility of prosecuting such charge to a conviction has been effectively destroyed"); Me.Rev.Stat. Ann. tit. 15, § 2115-A(1) ("reasonable likelihood of causing either serious impairment to or termination of the prosecution"). Other jurisdictions require that the trial judge find that the practical effect of suppression is to terminate the case. See, e.g., Wash.R. A.L.J. 2.2(c)(2).

[48]Colo.Rev.Stat.Ann. § 16-12-102(2); Vt.Stat.Ann. tit. 13, § 7403; N.D.Cent.Code § 29-28-07-(5). See also N.C.Gen.Stat.Ann. § 15A-0979 (evidence must be "essential to the case"). Jurisdictions are divided over whether the appellate court has the power to test the validity of the certification. Compare United States v. Bouthot, 878 F.2d 1506 (1st Cir.1989) (noting division as to appellate court authority to independently assess the "materiality" certification by reference to a standard that looks only to the relationship of the evidence to proof of an element of the offense, thereby precluding certification as to suppressed evidence that will be used only for impeachment); People v. MacCallum, 925 P.2d 758 (Colo.1996) (en banc) (denying appeal under Colo.R.App.P. 4.1(a) after undertaking independent review of the record and determining appeal unwarranted despite certification); State v. Schindele, 540 N.W.2d 139 (N.D.1995) (rejecting appeal after finding the suppressed evidence cumulative, and the statement in certification that evidence is substantial proof of a material fact unsupported by record); State v. Bertram, 80 Oh.St.3d 281, 685 N.E.2d 1239 (1997) (appellate court without authority to review prosecutor's certification that the suppression has destroyed any reasonable possibility of effective prosecution).

[49]See, e.g., People v. Drum, 194 Ill.2d 485, 252 Ill.Dec. 470, 743 N.E.2d 44 (2000); State v. Newman, 235 Kan. 29, 35, 680 P.2d 257, 262 (1984) (state must be prepared to make a showing that suppression order substantially impaired ability to prosecute).

[50]State v. Sayerwinnie, 157 P.3d 137 (Okla.Cr.App.2007) (interpreting this statutory language "to mean that the evidence suppressed forms a substantial part of the proof of a pending charge, and the state's ability to prosecute the case is substantially impaired or restricted absent the suppressed or excluded evidence").

cution appeals from pretrial interlocutory orders do not extend that authority beyond orders suppressing evidence.[51] Several jurisdictions, however, also authorize appeals from one or more additional categories of interlocutory rulings as specified by statute. Thus, the 1984 Bail Reform Act allows a prosecution appeal from a district court's pretrial release order.[52] State provisions may authorize the appeal of orders concerning change of venue,[53] the disclosure of witnesses,[54] or the defendant's capacity to be tried.[55]

Rather than designate particular categories of orders that a prosecutor may appeal as of right, some states limit the prosecution's ability to appeal using the standards that apply to defense requests for interlocutory review, or rely on the discretion of the court.[56] A handful grant a right to appeal if the interlocutory ruling will have a "reasonable likelihood of causing either serious impairment to or a termination of the prosecution."[57]

§ 27.3(d) Post-jeopardy rulings

Statutory provisions authorizing government appeals typically include one or more provisions applicable to rulings issued after jeopardy has attached. Most allow a prosecution appeal from "an

---

[51]E.g., State v. Hill, 314 S.C. 330, 444 S.E.2d 255 (1994) (state may not appeal bail order, only suppression orders).

[52]18 U.S.C.A. § 3145(c). See also §§ 12.1, 12.3 (discussing the federal pretrial release provision).

[53]See, e.g., Mont.Code Ann. § 46-20-103.

[54]See Haw. Rev.Stat.Ann. § 641-13(8).

[55]See Mo.Stat.Ann. § 547.200(1), (2). Compare State v. Bibb, 922 S.W.2d 798 (Mo.App.1996) (state may not appeal order allowing defense counsel to withdraw).

[56]See, e.g., Conn.Gen.Stat.Ann. §§ 54 to 96 (permitting appeals from decisions upon all questions of law, with the permission of the presiding judge); Mich.Comp.L.Ann. 770.12 (providing appeal by leave of all orders that are not appealable as of right); N.J.R.App.P. 2:3-1(b)(5); Ohio Rev.Code Ann. § 2945.67(a) (authorizing appeal of any decision of trial court except final verdict). See also Ga.Code Ann. § 5-7-2 (trial judge certification necessary); State v. McMillan, 43 Conn.App. 698, 685 A.2d 1138 (1996) (considering prosecutor's appeal of trial court's refusal to grant permission to appeal); State v. Wilen, 4 Neb.App. 132, 539 N.W.2d 650 (1995).

[57]Me.Rev.Stat.Ann. tit. 15, § 2115-A(1). See also State v. Zanter, 535 N.W.2d 624 (Minn.1995) (under Minn.R.Crim.P. 28.04, state may appeal any pretrial order "except for dismissal based on lack of probable cause or dismissal pursuant to statute"); Ohio.Rev.CodeAnn. § 2505.02-3 (allowing appeal of any "order that affects a substantial right * * * which in effect determines the action"); Vt.Stat.Ann. tit. 13, § 7403 (allowing appeal where effect of ruling "is to impede seriously, although not to foreclose completely, the continuation of the prosecution"); Ind.CodeAnn. § 35-38-4-2(6) (appeals allowed from "any interlocutory order" with trial court certification and appellate court finding of substantial injury, substantial question of law, or inadequate remedy after judgment).

order arresting judgment."[58] These provisions have not met significant opposition because (1) the order arresting judgment clearly constitutes a final judgment; (2) since the defendant has been found guilty prior to the issuance of the order, reversal on appeal does not require a new trial but simply an order reinstating the original verdict; and (3) the order arresting judgment commonly must be based on grounds that are unrelated to the factual innocence of the defendant (e.g., lack of jurisdiction).

While only the second factor cited above applies to the grant of a new trial following a conviction, the federal system and a substantial number of states now allow a prosecution appeal from a new trial order.[59] Such an appeal permits the prosecution to challenge underlying rulings that could not have been appealed if they had been made before or during trial. The new trial order might be based, for example, on a trial court's post-verdict determination that the trial had been marred by improper joinder or an erroneous charge to the jury. If the trial court had originally ruled in favor of the defendant on the same points, the end result would have been a mistrial (on the joinder issue) or perhaps an acquittal (depending upon the influence of the jury charge), and the prosecution would not have had the opportunity to appeal either ruling.

Statutory provisions that allow the prosecutor to appeal from the dismissal of an indictment or information may also provide a basis for a post-jeopardy appeal. Although some of these provisions refer specifically to dismissals prior to trial,[60] most do not contain that limitation.[61] Where the dismissal occurred after jeopardy attached, but before a verdict was reached, reprosecution

---

[Section 27.3(d)]

[58]See, e.g., Cal.Penal Code § 1238(a)(4); Fla.Stat.Ann. § 924.07(1)(c).

[59]18 U.S.C.A. § 3731; Cal.Penal Code § 1238(a)(3); State v. Matthews, 81 Oh.St.3d. 375, 691 N.E.2d 1041 (1998); Kan.Stat.Ann. § 22-3602(b) (authorizing prosecution appeals of orders granting new trials in cases of serious crime); Colo.Rev.Stat.Ann. § 16-12-102(1) ("any order of the trial court granting a new trial * * * shall be immediately appealable"); People v. Smith, 921 P.2d 80 (Colo.App.1996); State v. Boyd, 202 S.W.3d 393 (Tex.App.2006) (order entered after guilty verdict granting mistrial was functionally indistinguishable from order for new trial, Texas law allows the state to appeal new trial orders). But see State v. Walker, 887 P.2d 971 (Alaska App.1994) (orders granting new trials not appealable under expansive state appeal provision, as it is not a "final" order that would fall within the final judgment rule); State v. Thurmond, 195 Ga.App. 369, 393 S.E.2d 518 (1990) (same); State v. Rietveld, 151 Or.App. 318, 948 P.2d 758 (1997) (no appeal of new trial order); State v. Oren, 160 Vt. 245, 627 A.2d 337 (1993) (no appeal of order granting new trial).

[60]See, e.g., Or.Rev.Stat. § 157.020.

[61]See, e.g., 18 U.S.C.A. § 3731; Ariz.Rev.Stat.Ann. § 13-4032; Fla.Stat. Ann. § 924.07. See also State v. Wells, 78 Haw. 373, 894 P.2d 70 (1995) (reviewing dismissal of certain counts of

will be barred by the double jeopardy prohibition if the "dismissal" was in fact an "acquittal" or constituted the equivalent of a mistrial not justified by either "manifest necessity" or a defense request.[62] The federal statute and several state provisions expressly prohibit an appeal from a post-jeopardy "dismissal" where reprosecution would be barred by the Double Jeopardy Clause.[63] In other jurisdictions, statutes have been interpreted in light of that prohibition, and held not to allow an appeal where reprosecution is prohibited by the Constitution.

Because the provisions authorizing the government to appeal from suppression orders apply only to *pretrial* suppression rulings,[64] conceivably a defendant could cut off appellate review by delaying his motion to suppress until after jeopardy has attached. In the case of the typical suppression motion claiming the unconstitutional acquisition of evidence, however, statutes ordinarily require that such a motion be presented before trial.[65] Nevertheless, most jurisdictions allow the trial court at least limited discretion to entertain a defense motion to suppress made during trial,[66] and there will be cases in which the circumstances justify allowing an otherwise untimely motion (e.g., where defendant lacked a reasonable opportunity to present the motion before trial). To enable the government to defeat deliberate manipulation by the defense of the government's statutory right to appeal, some courts treat a defendant's successful mid-trial suppression motion as implicit consent to the granting of a mistrial, consent that would overcome any subsequent double jeopardy objection to

---

indictment for failure to state essential elements).

[62] See § 25.3(a).

[63] See, e.g., N.M.Stat.Ann. § 39-3-3. See also Strazzella, The Relationship of Double Jeopardy to Prosecution Appeals, 73 Notre Dame L.Rev. 1, 14 (1997) (collecting statutes).

[64] Many of the provisions refer specifically to orders issued before "the defendant had been put in jeopardy," or "prior to trial." See, e.g., 18 U.S.C.A. § 3731; Cal.Penal Code § 1238(a)(7). Even without such language, that limitation would be assumed, in the absence of a specific statutory direction to the contrary. See generally People v. Garofalo, 71 App.Div.2d 782, 419 N.Y.S.2d 784 (1979); State v. Glenn, 267 Ark. 501, 592 S.W.2d 116

(1980). On the obligation of the trial judge to rule before trial on a motion made before trial, see United States v. Barletta, 644 F.2d 50 (1st Cir.1981).

[65] See § 10.1(a).

[66] See § 10.2. Some jurisdictions grant the trial court authority to allow an untimely motion to suppress upon "cause shown." See, e.g., Fed.R.Crim.P. 12(e); Alaska R.Crim.P. 12(e). Others refer to specific excuses. See, e.g., Cal.Penal Code § 1538.5(h) ("opportunity for this motion did not exist or the defendant was not aware of the grounds for the motion"); Ariz.R. Crim.P. 16.1(c). Still others note that the court "in its discretion" may entertain the motion at trial. See, e.g., Del.Super.Ct.Crim.R. 12(c); Kan.Stat. Ann. § 3216(3).

reprosecution.[67]

Where a guilty verdict has been returned, but the judge rejects that verdict and enters an acquittal, double jeopardy again does not bar appellate review.[68] Appeal from such an order is not clearly authorized, however, by the usual provisions governing prosecution appeals. Accordingly, several states have adopted provisions specifically allowing appeals from acquittals entered by the trial court following a guilty verdict.[69] Finally, prosecutors in most jurisdictions are allowed to appeal sentences, as well.[70]

§ 27.4 Review by writ

§ 27.4(a)   Extraordinary writs generally

§ 27.4(b)   Prohibition and mandamus: traditional limits and modern extensions

§ 27.4(c)   Defense petitions

§ 27.4(d)   Prosecution applications

§ 27.4(e)   Third-party applications

§ 27.4(f)   Habeas corpus

---

[67]See Ill.Comp.Stat. Ann.ch. 725, ILCS § 5/114-12. See also People v. Flatt, 82 Ill.2d 250, 45 Ill.Dec. 158, 412 N.E.2d 509 (1980); United States v. Kington, 801 F.2d 733 (5th Cir.1986) (where motion was heard after jury was sworn, with defense waiving double jeopardy objection to mistrial should its motion prevail, government could appeal under 18 U.S.C.A. § 3731); United States v. Kington, 835 F.2d 106 (5th Cir.1988) (reaffirming the lack of a jeopardy bar). See also State v. Fraternal Order of Eagles Aerie 0337 Buckeye, 58 Ohio St.3d 166, 569 N.E.2d 478 (Ohio.1991) ("where a motion to suppress is made and granted after the commencement of trial, a trial court shall not proceed to enter a judgment of acquittal so as to defeat the state's right to appeal pursuant to Crim. R. 12(J)"); Note, 99 Yale L.J. 905 (1990). See also cases collected in § 25.3(a) at note 7. For a discussion of double jeopardy limits on reprosecution after mistrial, see § 25.2. Compare State v. Gaines, 770 So.2d 1221 (Fla.2000) (retrial after motion to suppress granted mid-trial barred by double jeopardy when motion not conditioned on acceptance of mistrial).

[68]See § 25.3(e).

[69]See, e.g., Ariz.Rev.Stat.Ann. § 13-4032(7); N.J.R.App.P. 2:3-1(b)(3).

Compare Exposito v. State, 891 So.2d 525 (Fla.2004) (holding that the "State's right to appeal a post-trial order reducing the charge must be the product of express legislative authorization, not judicial extension of provisions authorizing State appeals in other circumstances," with concurring justice urging legislature to amend the statute to allow appeal in this situation).

[70]See 18 U.S.C.A. § 3742; ABA Stds. for Criminal Justice; Sentencing § 18-8.3 (3d ed.1994) (allowing appeals by defense and prosecution). But compare People v. Bailey, 45 Cal.App.4th 926, 53 Cal.Rptr.2d 198 (1996) (no right to appeal from order granting probation).

§ 27.4(a) Extraordinary writs generally

Where a trial court's order is not appealable, the defense or prosecution may seek higher court review through an application for one of the "extraordinary" writs. These include the writ of habeas corpus, the writ of certiorari,[1] the writ of mandamus, and the writ of prohibition.

The writs of mandamus and prohibition (or a local law replacement for those writs)[2] provide an avenue for both prosecution and defense to obtain review of a broad range of rulings that are not appealable. Both sides may utilize the writs to gain review of interlocutory orders not otherwise subject to immediate review. Since the defense has a right to appeal from all final judgments, it has no need to look to the writs to obtain review of final orders. The prosecution, however, may be forced to turn to the writs where particular final orders, though they could be appealed consistent with double jeopardy, are not within the authorization of statute specifying decisions that may be appealed by the government.

The objections that may be presented through writ applications are often quite limited. The writs are always available to raise certain types of objections (e.g., lack of subject matter jurisdiction) and unavailable to raise others (e.g., error in a factual determination). Outside of these areas of consensus, there is significant variation from one jurisdiction to another.[3]

§ 27.4(b) Prohibition and mandamus: traditional limits and modern extensions

The writs of prohibition and mandamus traditionally were available only to control jurisdictional excesses. Prohibition was

---

[Section 27.4(a)]

[1] The common law writ of certiorari, although restricted in many jurisdictions to obtaining discretionary review of final judgments, is still used in some jurisdictions as a means of obtaining immediate review of trial court pretrial orders on grounds essentially similar to the writs of mandamus and prohibition. See, e.g., Childress v. Humphrey, 329 Ark. 504, 950 S.W.2d 220 (1997) (noting proper remedy to review bail determination is certiorari). For a detailed summary of the discretionary review of intermediate courts by state high courts, see Cope, Discretionary Review of the Decisions of Intermediate Appellate Courts: A Comparison of Florida's System with Those of the Other States and the Federal System, 45 Fla.L.Rev. 21 (1993).

[2] For example, separate writs of prohibition and mandamus were replaced in Michigan by a single "writ of superintending control," see People v. Burton, 429 Mich. 133, 413 N.W.2d 413 (1987); Mich.Ct.Rule 3.302 (describing writ of superintending control). In Arizona, they have been replaced by the "special action." See Ariz.R.P. Spec.Act. 1.

[3] For a listing of which appellate courts in each state have mandatory or discretionary jurisdiction to consider applications for extraordinary writs, see D. Rottman & S. Strickland, State Court Organization 2004 Table 22 (Aug. 2006, NCJ 212351).

used to confine a lower court to a lawful exercise of its prescribed jurisdiction and mandamus was used to compel it to exercise that jurisdiction.[4] When raising jurisdictional issues, the writs serve to protect the "interests of the judicial system as a whole" by correcting action or inaction contrary to the structural limits that control the system.[5] Other decisions employed the writs in cases properly before a court,[6] issuing the writ of mandamus to require a lower court to take action that it had no discretion to avoid (action commonly described as "ministerial" in nature), and the writ of prohibition to bar an order that the court lacked authority to issue under any set of circumstances.[7] Although some states continue to adhere to these traditional limits, a majority have moved substantially beyond them.

One special consideration has contributed to restrictions on access to the writs in criminal cases. As the Court explained in *Will v. United States*,[8] the "general policy against piecemeal appeals takes on added weight in criminal cases, where the defendant is entitled to a speedy resolution of the charges against him." In rejecting the government's attempt in *Will* to use the writ of mandamus to compel a district judge to vacate an order requiring the government to furnish a bill of particulars that encompassed items not then covered by the discovery rules, the Court found that the record before it did not support the government's allegation that the lower court's ruling reflected "a pattern of manifest noncompliance" with the Federal Rules.

In light of *Will*, some lower federal courts maintain that use of the writs in criminal cases must be very carefully limited to jurisdictional issues. Others find no bar in *Will* to the use of the writs to overturn pretrial interlocutory orders whenever the "district court's finding of fact and conclusions of law [are] in error" and could readily have an "immediate and continuing

---

[Section 27.4(b)]

[4] See Crick, The Final Judgment as a Basis for Appeal, 41 Yale L.J. 539, 554–56 (1932); Goldberg, The Extraordinary Writs and the Review of Inferior Court Judgments, 36 Cal.L. Rev. 558 (1948).

[5] See Note, 86 Harv.L.Rev. 595, 626 (1973). See, e.g., Ex parte State, 703 So.2d 333 (Ala.1997) (granting writ of mandamus directing court of civil appeals to rescind order directing the return of criminal defendant's property, since court had no jurisdiction over rulings arising out of criminal cases).

[6] See, e.g., De Beers Consol. Mines, Ltd. v. United States, 325 U.S. 212, 65 S.Ct. 1130, 89 L.Ed. 1566 (1945); State ex rel. Zeller v. Montgomery Circuit Court, 223 Ind. 476, 62 N.E.2d 149 (1945).

[7] See 16 C. Wright, A. Miller, and E. Cooper, Federal Practice and Procedure § 3933 (2d ed.1996) (describing the pre-1950s federal decisions that adhered to this view). See also Goldberg, The Extraordinary Writs and the Review of Inferior Court Judgments, 36 Cal.L.Rev. 558, 572 (1948).

[8] Will v. United States, 389 U.S. 90, 88 S.Ct. 269, 19 L.Ed.2d 305 (1967).

detrimental impact on the administration of criminal justice in the district."[9] Still other courts recognize considerable leeway in exercising the writs, but only when the defendant seeks relief.[10]

The division among the federal courts roughly parallels the division among state courts in their treatment of the writs in criminal cases. Some state courts view use of the writs in criminal cases as particularly pernicious and restrict review to cases that involve undisputable jurisdictional excesses.[11] Others take that position as to petitions brought by the government, but will consider a broad range of errors raised in petitions by defendants.[12] Still others will allow the prosecution as well as the defense to use the writs to challenge rulings that are acknowledged to be within the trial court's general authority but thought to merit immediate review. In some states, courts candidly acknowledge that the writs are available to correct, in an exceptional case, any ruling "so arbitrary and unreasonable" as to amount to an abuse of discretion.[13] Such an exceptional case is said by some courts to be presented where the appellate court must exercise its supervisory jurisdiction to ensure that there will be a prompt resolution of "important questions" which "are of a recurring nature."[14] In those jurisdictions taking this most expansive view of the writs, including the federal system, there is almost no error (except, possibly, for an erroneous factual determination) that is beyond their reach. As commentators have noted, in these jurisdictions, the question of whether the writ is

---

[9]United States v. Newman, 549 F.2d 240 (2d Cir.1977).

[10]See 16 C. Wright, A. Miller, and E. Cooper, Federal Practice and Procedure § 3936.1–3936.3 (2d ed.1996) (collecting cases).

[11]See, e.g., Bull v. Owens, 595 N.Y.S.2d 535, 191 App.Div.2d 692 (1993); In the matter of Graham v. O'Dwyer, 198 App.D.2d 505, 604 N.Y.S.2d 199 (1993); State ex rel. Jennings v. Nurre, 72 Ohio St.3d 596, 651 N.E.2d 1006 (1995). See also In re Petition of Wittrock, 649 A.2d 1053 (Del.1994) (writ also available to prevent proceedings from continuing in front of a judge who is biased).

[12]See, e.g., State v. Lewis, 188 W.Va. 85, 422 S.E.2d 807 (1992) (contrasting broad availability of writ to defendant with "only a few cases" extending writ to state).

[13]Easter v. McDonald, 903 S.W.2d 887 (Tex.App.1995); State ex rel. Kaneshiro v. Huddy, 82 Haw. 188, 921 P.2d 108 (1996) (granting mandamus vacating pretrial order excluding evidence for an alleged discovery violation, an order the court termed a "flagrant and manifest abuse of discretion," and collecting cases).

[14]Stockwell v. State, 98 Idaho 797, 573 P.2d 116 (1977). See also United States v. Horn, 29 F.3d 754 (1st Cir.1994) (writ review appropriate when issue is "novel, of great public importance, and likely to recur"); Demarce v. Willrich, 203 Ariz. 502, 56 P.3d 76 (Ariz.App. 2002) (accepting jurisdiction when statute precluded appeals from plea-bargained sentence, and issue was "purely a question of law" and "likely to arise again").

available is left largely to the discretion of the reviewing court.[15]

Prominent among the factors that courts consider in determining whether the writs should apply to non-jurisdictional claims is the availability of an alternative means of obtaining relief (e.g., through a subsequent appeal). Nevertheless, if the harm to the petitioner is unlikely to be remedied by a later appeal, if the issue presented is of great significance, or if there is a need to preclude recurring error, the appellate court may conclude that the advantages of immediate disposition outweigh the policies of finality.[16]

Even in those jurisdictions that reach a broad range of issues under the writs, courts continue to stress that the writs should be sparingly allowed.[17] This reluctance reflects both the apprehension that the writs could be used so frequently that their use would imperil the policies that limit the right of appeal, particularly the final judgment rule, and the concern that the writs not become a form of open-ended discretionary review for orders not appealable as of right.[18]

§ 27.4(c) Defense petitions

Certain types of defense claims will be subject to review by writ without question. Allegations that the lower court lacked jurisdiction over the proceeding are reviewable, as discussed above. Review by writ also has been available where the grand jury or prosecutor lacked authority to initiate prosecution of a particular

---

[15]Cooper, Extraordinary Writ Practice in Criminal Cases: Analogies for the Military Courts, 98 F.R.D. 593 (1983).

[16]See 16 C. Wright, A. Miller, and E. Cooper, Federal Practice and Procedure § 3936.1-3 (2d ed.1996) (reviewing cases). See, e.g., Powell v. Graham, 185 S.W.3d 624 (Ky.2006) (a writ of prohibition might be appropriate: (1) where the lower court is acting outside its jurisdiction and (2) where the lower court is acting erroneously but within its jurisdiction, and there exists no adequate remedy by appeal or otherwise and great injustice and irreparable injury will result if the petition is not granted; writ issued here to prevent trial court from ordering a mental examination of the defendant, when defendant had no adequate remedy by appeal because once he has been compelled to submit to the mental examination, any statements he has made cannot subsequently be unmade by an appellate court; suppression is an imperfect remedy, and the nature of the potential constitutional violation in this setting requires more than an after-the-fact, ad hoc appellate fix); State ex rel. Bailes v. Jolliffe, 208 W.Va. 481, 541 S.E.2d 571 (2000) (setting out five-factor test for issuing a writ of prohibition).

[17]See, e.g., Kerr v. United States Dist. Court, 426 U.S. 394, 96 S.Ct. 2119, 48 L.Ed.2d 725 (1976); United States v. Bertoli, 994 F.2d 1002 (3d Cir.1993); In re State, 139 N.H. 705, 661 A.2d 766 (1995).

[18]See, e.g., Schlagenhauf v. Holder, 379 U.S. 104, 85 S.Ct. 234, 13 L.Ed.2d 152 (1964) (writ "is not to be used as a substitute for appeal").

crime,[19] venue was improper,[20] or the lower court otherwise lacked authority to try the particular offense.[21]

Certain other claims, too, are thought to raise interests so urgently demanding immediate relief that the judicial system cannot rely upon appeal following a conviction. These are claims that, like jurisdictional challenges, address impending harm that goes beyond the hardship of a possibly needless or flawed trial.[22] Such claims include the alleged violation of the statutory or constitutional right to a speedy trial,[23] the denial of a potentially meritorious double jeopardy claim (when appeal is not available),[24] or allegations that the trial would be conducted by the

---

[Section 27.4(c)]

[19]See, e.g., State ex rel. Keene v. Jordan, 192 W.Va. 131, 451 S.E.2d 432 (1994); Griffin v. Santagata, 168 App.Div.2d 557, 562 N.Y.S.2d 778 (1990).

[20]See, e.g., State v. Webb, 323 Ark. 80, 913 S.W.2d 259 (1996).

[21]See, e.g., Ex parte Jackson, 614 So.2d 405 (Ala.1993) (indictment based on erroneous interpretation of statute); State ex rel. Koren v. Grogan, 68 Ohio St.3d 590, 629 N.E.2d 446 (1994) (statute divested court of jurisdiction); State ex rel. Starr v. Halbritter, 183 W.Va. 350, 395 S.E.2d 773 (1990) (void indictment).

[22]Courts frequently hold that there must be some "irreparable" injury to justify interlocutory review by writ and that there is no such injury when an individual is required to defend himself against a criminal charge. The concept of "irreparable harm" (i.e., harm not remediable on appeal from a conviction) is sometimes described as including harm beyond that suffered by the defendant, permitting writ challenges to defects that impose no particular burden on the defendant (e.g., jurisdictional defects). See Note, 86 Harv.L.Rev. 595, 626 (1973).

[23]See, e.g., Lively v. State, 326 Ark. 398, 930 S.W.2d 339 (1996) (granting writ of prohibition barring trial due to violation of state speedy trial provisions); Underwood v. Johnson, 651 So.2d 760 (Fla.App.

1995); State ex rel. Bishop v. Madison Circuit Court, 690 N.E.2d 1173 (Ind.1998) (issuing writ of mandamus ordering court to discharge defendant due to violation of state speedy trial provision); State ex rel. Riederer v. Mason, 810 S.W.2d 541 (Mo.App. 1991); Butts v. Heller, 69 Wash.App. 263, 848 P.2d 213 (1993). See also Gallimore v. State, 944 P.2d 939 (Okla.Cr. App.1997) (granting writ of mandamus directing dismissal of charges due to violation of the 120-day period specified by Interstate Agreement on Detainers Act). Compare Smith v. Gohmert, 962 S.W.2d 590 (Tex.Cr.App. 1998), in which the court reasoned that mandamus was not available to a petitioner seeking dismissal on speedy trial grounds because such a defendant has an "adequate remedy at law," namely, appeal from conviction. The writ ordinarily will not be available, however, where the defendant's speedy trial claim rests on a factual determination or a debatable legal issue. See, e.g., Brown v. State, 330 Ark. 239, 952 S.W.2d 673 (1997); Ordunez v. Bean, 579 S.W.2d 911 (Tex.Cr.App.1979).

[24]See, e.g., Rodriguez v. Burk, 637 So.2d 317 (Fla.Ct.App.1994) (writ of prohibition granted to bar retrial where retrial after mistrial would violate bar against double jeopardy); In re A.P., 636 So.2d 790 (Fla.App. 1994) (violation of double jeopardy); Grimes v. McAnulty, 957 S.W.2d 223 (Ky.1997) (noting writ of prohibition is appropriate when retrial after mistrial would violate Constitution, but denying writ in this case); Davis v. Brown,

wrong decisionmaker.[25] Similarly, where the defendant claims that compliance with an interlocutory order will force him to submit to a loss of privacy or privilege which would not be remedied by a subsequent ruling that the evidence should be excluded, the writ may be available on the ground that immediate relief is necessary to avoid irreparable harm.[26] Irreparable harm has also been the basis for the review of a variety of orders that if left standing could have resulted in the permanent loss of evidence.[27]

In some jurisdictions, defense access to the writs goes far beyond the above limitations. Appellate courts will consider on a writ application challenges directed at almost any pretrial ruling, provided the legal issue presented has some general significance.[28] Federal courts, despite frequent references to the limited use of

---

87 N.Y.2d 626, 641 N.Y.S.2d 819, 664 N.E.2d 884 (1996) (granting writ of prohibition barring retrial); State ex rel. Turner v. Frankel, 322 Ore. 363, 908 P.2d 293 (1995) (mandamus granted, directing judge to vacate mistrial and retrial order); Ex parte Gary, 895 S.W.2d 465 (Tex.App.1995) (noting pretrial writ of habeas corpus is the appropriate means to seek relief from alleged exposure to double jeopardy, but denying writ in this case).

[25]See, e.g., Donahue v. City of Sparks, 111 Nev. 1281, 903 P.2d 225 (1995) (affirming writ of certiorari vacating municipal court decision to grant jury trial on grounds that municipal court lacked discretion to order jury trial); State ex rel. Mace v. Circuit Court, 193 Wis.2d 208, 532 N.W.2d 720 (1995) (granting writ of prohibition directing trial judge to honor defendant's request for substitution of judge).

[26]See, e.g., Doe v. Connell, 179 App.Div.2d 196, 583 N.Y.S.2d 707 (1992) (granting writ of prohibition barring enforcement of trial court's orders compelling defendant in rape case to provide blood sample for HIV testing and disclose the results to the victim). Compare In re Dorsey, 710 A.2d 217 (Del.Super.1998) (denying defense petition for writ of prohibition to stay prosecution pending discovery disclosure by the state).

[27]See, e.g., Arnold v. Higa, 61 Haw. 203, 600 P.2d 1383 (1979) (writ would issue to correct clear error in failing to appoint investigator to assist the defense in contacting out-of-state witnesses; if defendant "is forced to wait for a reversal on appeal * * * these witnesses will be increasingly difficult to locate and their statements will be considerably less accurate"). See also State v. Turner, 550 N.W.2d 622 (Minn.1996) (writ of prohibition appropriate to restrain court from enforcing its order to quash trial subpoenas to newspaper personnel who were eyewitnesses); State ex rel. Storer Broadcasting Co. v. Gorenstein, 131 Wis.2d 342, 388 N.W.2d 633 (1986) (granting writ of prohibition barring trial court from conducting voir dire of selected jurors in sessions closed to the press and public).

[28]See, e.g., State v. Lewis, 188 W.Va. 85, 422 S.E.2d 807 (1992) (collecting cases granting writ applications including those alleging disqualification of the prosecutor, breach of a plea agreement, misconduct before the grand jury, and insufficiency of the indictment). See also Ex parte Duboise, 675 So.2d 420 (Ala.1996) (granting writ of mandamus directing case be tried without a jury, given defendant's right to a bench trial in misdemeanor cases, noting the following requirements of mandamus were met: (1) a clear legal right in the petitioner to the order sought; (2) an imperative duty on the respondent to perform, ac-

the writs, have granted defense petitions to review a broad range of lower court rulings that may have been in error but hardly dealt with matters beyond the authority of the district courts.[29]

Among the states adopting this generous view of the writs, California makes particularly extensive use of the writs in criminal cases. California courts have reviewed by writ pretrial orders denying defense motions to obtain broader pretrial discovery,[30] to change venue to a community less saturated by publicity,[31] to dismiss an indictment where the prosecutor failed to present exculpatory evidence to the grand jury,[32] to appoint a requested attorney as defense counsel,[33] to place defendant in a statutorily prescribed diversion program,[34] to substitute a trial judge,[35] and to exclude from consideration in a pending prosecution a prior conviction obtained without an effective waiver of counsel.[36] The

---

companied by a refusal to do so; (3) the lack of another adequate remedy; and (4) properly invoked jurisdiction of the court); Sandy v. Fifth Judicial Dist. Ct., 113 Nev. 435, 935 P.2d 1148 (1997) (mandamus available where the judge allegedly rejected plea agreement without authority); Webber v. District Court, 895 P.2d 728 (Okla. Crim.App.1995) (mandamus available to ensure timely rulings on defense discovery motions prior to trial); Annot., 92 A.L.R.2d 306 (1963) (collecting cases).

[29]See Cooper, Extraordinary Writ Practice in Criminal Cases: Analogies for the Military Courts, 98 F.R.D. 593, 607 (1983) (noting that writs have issued to review an order to appear in a lineup; denial of dismissal; revocation of bail; gag orders; refusal to hold a probable cause hearing; denial of jury trial; limitations on discovery; and refusal to permit out-state counsel to appear pro hac vice); 16 C. Wright, A. Miller, and E. Cooper, Federal Practice and Procedure § 3936.1 (2d ed.1996); In re Grand Jury Subpoenas, 581 F.2d 1103 (4th Cir.1978) (review of misuse of the grand jury process).

[30]See, e.g., Warrick v. Superior Court, 35 Cal.4th 1011, 29 Cal.Rptr.3d 2, 112 P.3d 2 (2005); City of Santa Cruz v. Municipal Court, 49 Cal.3d 74, 260 Cal.Rptr. 520, 776 P.2d 222 (1989).

[31]See, e.g., Odle v. Superior Court,

32 Cal.3d 932, 187 Cal.Rptr. 455, 654 P.2d 225 (1982); Frazier v. Superior Court, 5 Cal.3d 287, 95 Cal.Rptr. 798, 486 P.2d 694 (1971); Powell v. Superior Court, 232 Cal.App.3d 785, 283 Cal.Rptr. 777 (1991).

[32]Johnson v. Superior Court, 15 Cal.3d 248, 124 Cal.Rptr. 32, 539 P.2d 792 (1975). See also Cummiskey v. Superior Court, 3 Cal.4th 1018, 13 Cal.Rptr.2d 551, 839 P.2d 1059 (1992) (prosecutor misinstructed grand jury as to the burden of proof).

[33]See, e.g., Harris v. Superior Court, 19 Cal.3d 786, 140 Cal.Rptr. 318, 567 P.2d 750 (1977); Drumgo v. Superior Court, 8 Cal.3d 930, 106 Cal.Rptr. 631, 506 P.2d 1007 (1973); Alexander v. Superior Court, 22 Cal.App.4th 901, 27 Cal.Rptr.2d 732 (1994). See also Yorn v. Superior Court, 90 Cal.App.3d 669, 153 Cal.Rptr. 295 (1979) (disqualification of defense counsel).

[34]Parra v. Municipal Court, 83 Cal.App.3d 690, 148 Cal.Rptr. 203 (1978) (raising issue of statutory interpretation of widespread concern).

[35]Cal.Civ.Proc.Code § 170.3(a) (providing that exclusive remedy for violation of a party's right to peremptorily remove a judge is through a writ of mandate).

[36]Illingworth v. Municipal Court, 102 Cal.App.3d 19, 164 Cal.Rptr. 53 (1980).

"common thread" woven through these cases, the California Supreme Court has noted, is "the responsiveness of appellate tribunals when initiative is required to protect a defendant's fundamental right to a fair trial," recognizing that "the burden, expense and delay involved in a trial" may often render "an appeal from an eventual judgment an inadequate remedy."[37]

§ 27.4(d) Prosecution applications

Prosecutors have sought to use the extraordinary writs to gain appellate review of a wide variety of orders issued at various stages of the criminal process. Once a charge is brought, the prosecution may seek to obtain review of significant pretrial interlocutory orders. As discussed in § 27.3, apart from suppression rulings, such orders will not be appealable in many jurisdictions.[38] Where appeals of final judgments are limited to a particular class of orders (e.g., the granting of a motion to quash), the prosecutor may also look to the writs to gain review of a pretrial dismissal that does not fit within the appeals statute.[39] Finally, the writs may be used by prosecutors to gain review of unappealable rulings entered after a jury returns a guilty verdict. Thus, where the appeals statute refers only to appeals from post-conviction orders arresting a judgment or dismissing an indictment, challenges to the grant of a new trial or the entry of a judgment n.o.v. may be pursued through a writ application.[40]

Some courts hold that the writ will be available to the prosecution only when the lower court "acted in excess of its jurisdiction" by issuing an order that it had no authority to issue under any circumstances or by failing to issue an order that it had no discretion under any circumstances not to issue.[41] Other courts have held that the writ will issue to correct a gross abuse of discretion

---

[37]Maine v. Superior Court, 68 Cal.2d 375, 378, 66 Cal.Rptr. 724, 726, 438 P.2d 372, 374 (1968). See also Powell v. Superior Court, 232 Cal.App.3d 785, 283 Cal.Rptr. 777 (1991) (reviewing *Maine* and reaffirming defendant's right to pretrial writ review of important issues).

[Section 27.4(d)]

[38]See § 27.3(b).

[39]See, e.g., State ex rel. Hannah v. Seier, 654 S.W.2d 894 (Mo.1983). Ex parte Sullivan, 779 So.2d 1157 (Ala.2000) (state sought mandamus relief from a final order which the State was forbidden to appeal, held: mandamus not appropriate where state sought to appeal order of trial court dismissing case after finding no manifest necessity warranted its earlier declaration of mistrial due to unavailability of prosecution witness).

[40]See State ex rel. Hyder v. Superior Ct., 128 Ariz. 216, 624 P.2d 1264 (1981); State ex rel. Haas v. Schwabe, 276 Or. 853, 556 P.2d 1366 (1976); State ex rel. Forbes v. Canady, 197 W.Va. 37, 475 S.E.2d 37 (1996) (granting writ vacating order dismissing charges due to failure to join, noting state has no right to appeal dismissal unless indictment bad or insufficient).

[41]Even then, these courts may grant review only if the need for "review [by writ] outweighs the risk of harassment of the accused." People v.

where a significant prosecution interest is at stake.[42] Still other courts hold that the prosecution may use the writ to gain review of any ruling that raises a legal question of general significance.[43]

In part, the scope of review will depend upon the view of the appropriate role of the writs in general, without regard to the fact that the applicant is the prosecutor. But there are two concerns that may lead a court to apply more stringent standards to prosecution petitions than are applied to either civil cases or defense petitions in criminal cases. Courts frequently note the need to approach the prosecution's use of the writs with "an awareness * * * that a man is entitled to a speedy trial."[44] Courts also express concern that the writs not be used so as to undermine the limitations that the legislature has placed on the prosecution's right to appeal.[45] The significance of each of these concerns varies with the nature of the lower court ruling challenged by the

---

Superior Court, 235 Cal.App.3d 1261, 1267, 1 Cal.Rptr.2d 333, 336 (1991). See also State v. Pulaski County Circuit-Chancery Court, 316 Ark. 473, 872 S.W.2d 854 (1994) (prohibition not available to review order enjoining prosecutor from charging juveniles as adults because trial court was not wholly without jurisdiction to issue such an order); Morgenthau v. Marks, 177 App.Div.2d 131, 581 N.Y.S.2d 296 (1992) (prohibition not available to review order to suppress evidence where the order constitutes an error of law rather than an act in excess of the court's powers); State ex rel. Rusen v. Hill, 193 W.Va. 133, 454 S.E.2d 427 (1994) (noting State must prove that court abused its powers to obtain review by writ of an order dismissing an indictment). Compare State ex rel. Dally v. Elliston, 811 S.W.2d 371 (Mo.1991) (departure from the unusual application of prohibition is warranted in "peculiarly limited" situations where irreparable harm may result if some form of relief is not granted).

[42]State v. Sabalos, 178 Ariz. 420, 874 P.2d 977 (1994) (review by special action is appropriate when lower court abuses its discretion and the state has no remedy through appeal); State v. Thorup, 659 So.2d 1116 (Fla.App. 1995) (writ review appropriate where defendant's request for a non-jury trial was granted without the state's con-

sent because order not remediable on appeal); State ex rel. State v. Hill, 201 W.Va. 95, 491 S.E.2d 765 (1997) (issuing writ vacating erroneous dismissal based on prosecutor's failure to join offenses noting that state may seek writ of prohibition where trial court has exceeded or acted outside of jurisdiction, or has abused its power in such a flagrant manner as to deprive the prosecution of valid conviction); State v. Washington, 83 Wis.2d 808, 266 N.W.2d 597 (1978) (recognizing that a judge who improperly conducts a John Doe proceeding may be restrained by writ of prohibition for abuse of discretion).

[43]See, e.g., Sedlak v. Dick, 256 Kan. 779, 887 P.2d 1119 (1995) (noting mandamus action, though extraordinary, will be available if the issue is a matter of "great public importance and concern"); State ex rel. Stephan v. Finney, 251 Kan. 559, 836 P.2d 1169 (1992) (mandamus is appropriate to obtain an authoritative interpretation of the law for the guidance of public officials in important matters).

[44]See Will v. United States, 389 U.S. 90, 88 S.Ct. 269, 19 L.Ed.2d 305 (1967).

[45]State v. Manck, 385 Md.App. 581, 870 A.2d 196 (2005) (refusing to allow state to proceed by writ in seeking review of trial judge's order striking state's notice of intention to seek

prosecutor.

A prosecutor's application for a writ will not always threaten the defendant's interest in a speedy trial. Review by writ application of orders issued prior to indictment or during an investigation may delay the charging determination, but the person affected is hardly in the same position as a defendant awaiting trial.[46] Similarly, if the government challenges an order issued after the defendant was tried and found guilty, there is delay in the final disposition, but usually not in the presentation of evidence.[47] Delay generally causes far less judicial concern where the only consequence of the delay is, for example, a continued period of uncertainty as to what sentence will be imposed. Thus, when appellate review of a sentence is not available, the writs are regularly used by the prosecution to obtain review of sentences that are allegedly outside the trial court's sentencing authority under the facts of the case.[48]

By contrast, when review of a post-trial order will delay the presentation of evidence in a second trial, as is the case when a prosecutor seeks review of a new trial order, courts in jurisdictions that have otherwise barred the prosecutor from appealing such orders are not inclined to permit review by writ.[49]

The most serious threat to the defendant's speedy trial interest

the death penalty, noting "for this court to expand the State's right to appeal beyond the statutory limits would violate the separation of powers doctrine").

[46]Mandamus may also be sought by a state from federal court to obtain another state's compliance with the constitutional duty to extradite a fugitive. See, e.g., State ex rel. Governor v. Engler, 85 F.3d 1205 (6th Cir.1996). Cf. United States v. Weinstein, 511 F.2d 622 (2nd Cir.1975) (noting that review of challenge to pretrial disclosure order would not interfere with speedy trial interests of defendants who had long been fugitives and had not sought trial).

[47]See, e.g., State ex rel. Penn v. Norblad, 323 Or. 464, 918 P.2d 426 (1996) (granting writ of mandamus directing trial judge to vacate post-verdict order dismissing charges, noting that the convicted defendant remains free to file motion for new trial after judgment is entered).

[48]See, e.g., State v. Buckalew, 561

P.2d 289 (Alaska 1977); State v. Hamili, 87 Haw. 102, 952 P.2d 390 (1998) (as prosecutor cannot appeal from an order granting deferred acceptance of a no contest plea, writ issued, vacating illegal plea and remanding for resentencing); State v. Palmer, 270 Ind. 493, 386 N.E.2d 946 (1979); In re State, 139 N.H. 705, 661 A.2d 766 (1995); State ex rel. Moomau v. Hamilton, 184 W.Va. 251, 400 S.E.2d 259 (1990). See also Daley v. Hett, 113 Ill.2d 75, 99 Ill.Dec. 132, 495 N.E.2d 513 (1986) (reviewing, on application for a writ, judge's acceptance of defendant's waiver of a sentencing jury); Doering v. Fader, 316 Md. 351, 558 A.2d 733 (1989) (noting mandamus is appropriate to compel judge to preside at sentencing proceeding).

[49]Of course, a similar possibility is faced in providing for appellate review of pretrial dismissals since reversal will often result in a long delayed trial, but here the lower court's order is a final judgment. Courts stressing the need for extreme caution in allowing the prosecutor to

is presented by a government petition seeking review of an interlocutory pretrial ruling. Many courts insist that the writs here be used only to challenge a ruling that the trial court clearly had no authority to issue under any circumstances.[50] Some courts, however, are willing to make the defendant bear the burden of delay in order to benefit the system as a whole by correcting an erroneous application of a trial judge's authority, especially when the error could have a recurring impact within the jurisdiction.[51]

Federal courts generally limit the government's access to mandamus to "rare cases" in which the lower court's order falls outside the limits of judicial power and poses irreparable harm, but they have also recognized mandamus can be appropriate when an application presents an issue that is "novel, of great importance, and likely to recur."[52] Thus federal courts have extended review to an order assessing fees against the govern-

---

challenge a new trial order by writ emphasize both the broad range of discretion granted the trial judge and the need to avoid piecemeal appellate review. See, e.g., In re Petition for Writ of Prohibition, 312 Md. 280, 539 A.2d 664 (1988) (reviewing history of use of writ and denying relief by writ from new trial order). State v. Forte, 154 Vt. 46, 572 A.2d 941 (1990) (refusing to review new trial ruling absent clear abuse of discretion); State ex rel. Trump v. Hott, 187 W.Va. 749, 421 S.E.2d 500 (1992) (prohibition proceeding to prevent new trial must not offend double jeopardy or defendant's right to speedy trial).

[50]See, e.g., State v. Pulaski County Circuit Court, 327 Ark. 287, 938 S.W.2d 815 (1997) (without proper filing, court had no authority to reduce bond); State ex rel. Rusen v. Hill, 193 W.Va. 133, 454 S.E.2d 427 (1994).

[51]See, e.g., State ex rel. Romley v. Superior Court, 183 Ariz. 139, 901 P.2d 1169 (1995) (vacating order that vacated another judge's ruling allowing trial in absentia); People v. District Court, 953 P.2d 184 (Colo.1998) (writ issued vacating order allowing bench trial over the People's objection); People ex rel. Sandstrom v. District Court, 904 P.2d 874 (Colo.1995) (writ issued preventing enforcement of order to disclose identities of confidential informants); State v. Roberts, 686 So.2d 722 (Fla.App.1997) (granting petition for writ of certiorari filed by the state quashing trial court's order requiring disclosure of a confidential informant's identity); State ex rel. Kaneshiro v. Huddy, 82 Haw. 188, 921 P.2d 108 (1996) (mandamus vacating trial court's erroneous order excluding expert witness, finding the order a "flagrant and manifest abuse of discretion") (collecting cases); Newman v. Lance, 129 Idaho 98, 922 P.2d 395 (1996) (issuing writ of prohibition barring Attorney General from "asserting dominion and control" over county prosecution); State ex rel. Macy v. Owens, 934 P.2d 343 (Okla.Cr.App. 1997) (granting writ of prohibition barring trial judge from disqualifying county district attorney's office from prosecuting retrials); State v. Powers, 952 P.2d 997 (Okla.Cr.App.1997) (noting that for writ of prohibition, state must show court's exercise of power is not authorized by law and will result in injury for which there is no other adequate remedy, granting writ to bar district court from ordering prosecution in grand jury investigation to disclose target status to witnesses). Compare State v. Isaac, 696 So.2d 813 (Fla.App.1997) (reviewing, but denying, petition objecting to order suppressing evidence, otherwise not appealable).

[52]See United States v. Horn, 29 F.3d 754 (1st Cir.1994) (terming this

ment,[53] an order denying a motion to dismiss charges and appointing a special prosecutor,[54] an order not to execute an arrest warrant,[55] an order refusing to convene a grand jury,[56] an order denying the press access to jury lists,[57] a trial judge's decision to order a bench trial over the government's objection,[58] even an order adopting an erroneous jury instruction.[59]

§ 27.4(e) Third-party applications

On occasion, a party other than a defendant or prosecutor will seek review of a court ruling issued in a criminal case. When that ruling is not reviewable as an order resolving an independent proceeding or as a collateral order subject to direct appeal, a writ of mandamus or prohibition may be available. Because third parties often seek to protect interests that would be lost without immediate review, courts tend to be less reluctant to permit use of

---

type of case "advisory mandamus").

[53]*Horn,* 29 F.3d 754 (1st Cir. 1994) (collecting cases).

[54]In re United States, 345 F.3d 450 (7th Cir.2003) (when government sought to dismiss charge with prejudice and with consent of defendant, judge in refusing to dismiss and appointing special prosecutor was "playing U.S. Attorney," granting mandamus and ordering judge to grant motion to dismiss).

[55]United States v. Santtini, 963 F.2d 585 (3d Cir.1992).

[56]United States v. Christian, 660 F.2d 892 (3d Cir.1981).

[57]In re Globe Newspaper Co., 920 F.2d 88 (1st Cir.1990).

[58]United States v. United States District Court for Eastern Dist. of Cal., 464 F.3d 1065 (9th Cir.2006) ("the government has no other mechanism by which it can force the district court to try this case by jury," "any error following a bench trial would not be correctable on appeal" if acquittal resulted, and although the issue "is not one that arises often, * * * it is one on which we have not directly ruled and thus raises an important question of law.) For a similar state court ruling, see State ex rel. Long v. Justice Court, Lake County, 335 Mont. 219,

156 P.3d 5 (2007) (finding trial court erred in granting bench trial over state's objection, and concluding that review of that order upon the request of the state is appropriate for the exercise of supervisory control, an extraordinary remedy exercised when a court is proceeding under a mistake of law which, if uncorrected, would cause significant injustice and the remedy of appeal is adequate).

[59]United States v. Wexler, 31 F.3d 117 (3d Cir.1994). But compare In re Braxton, 258 F.3d 250 (4th Cir.2001) (denying mandamus petition by state seeking to block district court's order directing state to make evidence available for DNA testing, authorize funding for investigation of innocence claim, and order DNA testing, noting that the order may be reviewed on appeal from final judgment with no conceivable risk of harm to the state); United States v. McVeigh, 106 F.3d 325 (10th Cir.1997) (refusing to consider review by writ order denying victim-impact witnesses opportunity to attend proceedings, quoting that if "there is a serious need for appeals by the Government from [witness sequestration] orders, * * * it is the function of the Congress to decide whether to initiate a departure from the historical pattern of restricted appellate jurisdiction in criminal cases.").

the writs by third parties.[60]

Some jurisdictions have provided to victims of crime the statutory right to seek review of trial court rulings denying them procedural rights granted by statute. In the federal courts, the Crime Victims Rights Act places strict time limits on these proceedings.[61] No state victims' rights provisions may expressly provide for review mechanisms as well.[62]

[Section 27.4(e)]

[60]See, e.g., State v. Register, 308 S.C. 534, 419 S.E.2d 771 (1992) (granting petition for writ of supersedeas filed by girlfriend of defendant, vacating state order compelling her to furnish blood, saliva, and hair samples, absent compliance with guidelines for compelled bodily intrusions). See also In re T.R., 52 Ohio St.3d 6, 556 N.E.2d 439 (1990) (denying interlocutory appeal and suggesting that "members of the press" instead seek a writ of prohibition instead to challenge orders restricting access to pending litigation); Rendleman, Free Press-Fair Trial: Review of Silence Orders, 52 N.C.L.Rev. 127 (1973) (discussing the review of "gag orders"); Note, 65 Minn.L.Rev. 1110, 1114–16 (1981) (discussing media challenges to closure orders).

[61]See 18 U.S.C.A. § 3771(d), providing that if the district court denies the relief sought by the victim, the victim may seek a writ of mandamus, which must be decided expeditiously. The Act provides, however, that "In no case shall a failure to afford a right under this chapter provide grounds for a new trial. A victim may make a motion to re-open a plea or sentence only if-(A) the victim has asserted the right to be heard before or during the proceeding at issue and such right was denied; (B) the victim petitions the court of appeals for a writ of mandamus within 10 days; and (C) in the case of a plea, the accused has not pled to the highest offense charged." A writ of mandamus was entered under this section in Kenna v. United States District Court for the Central District of California, 435 F.3d 1011 (9th Cir.

2006). The court concluded that although it normally grants a writ "only when there is something truly extraordinary about the case," under the CVRA "we must issue the writ whenever we find the district court's order reflects an abuse of discretion."

The provisions of the new federal act authorizing the remedy of review by writ for victims in federal prosecutions are also discussed at § 21.3(f), § 25.1(d) at notes 55–74, and § 26.7(b) at note 21. See also State v. Casey, 44 P.3d 756 (Utah 2002), where the victim, who had been initially denied his right to be heard at the change of plea hearing in violation of state law, appealed to the state court of appeals, which in turn certified his appeal to the state supreme court. The state supreme court held that the victim was entitled to appellate review of the district court's rulings related to his right to be heard, but denied relief after finding that the violation of his right to be heard had been remedied when the trial judge gave him a chance to be heard at a reopened hearing.

[62]See Beloof, The Third Wave of Crime Victims' Rights: Standing, Remedy, and Review, 2005, B.Y.U.L. Rev. 255, 246 (2005) (collecting provisions from eight states that provide to victims access to appellate courts). But see Cooper v. District Court, 133 P.3d 692 (Alaska App.2006) ("many courts are prepared to recognize a crime victim's standing to sue for enforcement of the procedural rights granted by the victims' rights act—the rights to notice, to attend court proceedings, and to offer their views on certain decisions * * * but no court has endorsed the position * * * that the enactment of a victim's rights act gives crime

§ 27.4(f) Habeas corpus

Of the extraordinary writs, habeas corpus probably has the most limited utility as an alternative to appeal.[63] Since it serves to challenge illegal custody only,[64] the habeas writ is helpful to the defendant alone. Moreover, its focus on custody limits challenges to those orders that commence or continue custody. This limitation is sufficiently flexible, however, to encompass several common pretrial rulings that relate to a defendant's pretrial detention, including bail orders,[65] extradition orders,[66] bindovers

victims the right to participate as independent parties to a criminal prosecution or to otherwise challenge the substantive rulings of the trial court," collecting authority); Lamb v. Kontgias, 169 Md.App. 466, 901 A.2d 860 (2006) (victims denied notice of sentencing proceeding had no standing to appeal revised judgment).

[Section 27.4(f)]

[63]The habeas route to appellate court review ordinarily is indirect, as the application for the writ initially must be presented to the court of general jurisdiction in the district of detention. Jurisdictions are divided as to whether that trial court's ruling is then appealable, with those jurisdictions allowing the appeal treating the habeas proceeding as an independent proceeding. Compare In re Review of Habeas Corpus Proceedings, 313 Ark. 168, 852 S.W.2d 791 (1993) (appealable); In re Serrano, 10 Cal.4th 447, 41 Cal.Rptr.2d 695, 895 P.2d 936 (1995) (appealable); Commonwealth v. Bernhardt, 359 Pa.Super. 413, 519 A.2d 417 (1986); Gomm v. Cook, 754 P.2d 1226 (Utah App.1988); with Remington v. Montana Dept. Of Corrections and Human Servs., 255 Mont. 480, 844 P.2d 50 (1992) (not appealable) (overruled on other grounds by Orozco v. Day, 281 Mont. 341, 934 P.2d 1009 (1997)); Johnson v. Raftevold, 505 N.W.2d 110 (N.D.1993) (not appealable); Ex parte Bamburg, 890 S.W.2d 549 (Tex.App.1994); Ex parte Bamburg, 890 S.W.2d 549 (Tex. App.1994). In those jurisdictions that do not authorize the appeal of the denial of a habeas application, there

usually are other avenues for obtaining higher court review, although those tend to be discretionary. Johnson v. Raftevold, 505 N.W.2d 110 (N.D.1993) (Supreme Court has discretion to review under power of superintending control); State v. Jordan, 116 N.M. 76, 860 P.2d 206 (N.M.App.1993) (certiorari available); Coble v. Magone, 229 Mont. 45, 744 P.2d 1244 (1987) (certiorari available).

[64]See § 28.3(a).

[65]Alvarez v. Crowder, 645 So.2d 63 (Fla.App.1994); State ex rel. Pirman v. Money, 69 Ohio St.3d 591, 635 N.E.2d 26 (1994); State ex rel. Bennett v. Whyte, 163 W.Va. 522, 258 S.E.2d 123 (1979); Annot., 13 A.L.R.5th 118 (1993). But see People ex rel. Hardy v. Sielaff, 79 N.Y.2d 618, 584 N.Y.S.2d 742, 595 N.E.2d 817 (1992) (discretion of trial court in setting bail is beyond correction in habeas corpus).

[66]See, e.g., California v. Superior Court, 482 U.S. 400, 107 S.Ct. 2433, 96 L.Ed.2d 332 (1987) (limiting state's use of habeas corpus to block extradition under the Extradition Act); In re Extradition of Siegmund, 887 F.Supp. 1383 (D.Nev.1995) (listing federal cases); State ex rel. Coryell v. Gooden, 193 W.Va. 461, 457 S.E.2d 138 (1995); Jenkins v. Garrison, 265 Ga. 42, 453 S.E.2d 698 (1995); Kennon v. State, 248 Kan. 515, 809 P.2d 546 (1991); State ex rel. Sneed v. Long, 871 S.W.2d 148 (Tenn.1994); Johnson v. Manson, 196 Conn. 309, 493 A.2d 846 (1985); Galloway v. Josey, 507 So.2d 590 (Fla. 1987); In re Complaint in Habeas Corpus of Rowe, 67 Ohio St.2d 115, 423 N.E.2d 167 (1981); In re Everett,

after preliminary hearings,[67] and contempt adjudications,[68] provided those rulings are not directly appealable in the particular jurisdiction.[69] In some jurisdictions a defendant may seek a writ of habeas corpus to assert a double jeopardy claim that further prosecution is barred.[70]

Federal courts may also review habeas petitions filed under 28 U.S.C.A. § 2241 by state detainees awaiting trial who claim violation of their constitutional right to speedy trial and seek an order compelling the state to commence the proceedings,[71] or who claim a second trial would violate double jeopardy.[72] Habeas is most commonly employed as an avenue for post-conviction relief following direct review, as discussed in Chapter 28.

§ 27.5 The scope of appellate review

§ 27.5(a)   Mootness
§ 27.5(b)   The concurrent sentence doctrine
§ 27.5(c)   Waiver or forfeiture of the right to appeal
§ 27.5(d)   Plain error
§ 27.5(e)   Standard of review

§ 27.5(a) Mootness

An appellate court will not review a lower court decision, in either a civil or criminal case, where post-trial events have

---

139 Vt. 317, 427 A.2d 349 (1981).

[67]State v. Godfrey, 204 Ga.App. 58, 418 S.E.2d 383 (1992); Kammer v. State, 748 S.W.2d 844 (Mo.App.1988); Luna v. Russell, 70 Ohio St.3d 561, 639 N.E.2d 1168 (1994); Commonwealth v. Morman, 373 Pa.Super. 360, 541 A.2d 356 (1988).

[68]In re Jackson, 170 Cal.App.3d 773, 216 Cal.Rptr. 539 (1985); Roundtree v. Felton, 656 So.2d 584 (Fla.App. 1995); Wells v. State, 474 A.2d 846 (Me.1984); State ex rel. Nesser v. Pennoyer, 887 S.W.2d 394 (Mo.1994); Ex parte Bowers, 886 S.W.2d 346 (Tex. App.1994). See also Annot., 33 A.L.R.3d 589, §§ 14 to 16 (1970 & Supp.1997) (collecting cases).

[69]Where an appeal is available, a collateral attack via the habeas writ generally is not permitted. For more on petitions for habeas corpus relief,

see Chapter 28.

[70]See, e.g., Ex parte Masonheimer, 220 S.W.3d 494 (Tex.Cr.App. 2007).

[71]See, e.g., Braden v. 30th Judicial Circuit Court of Kentucky, 410 U.S. 484, 93 S.Ct. 1123, 35 L.Ed.2d 443 (1973); Atkins v. Michigan, 644 F.2d 543 (6th Cir.1981); Dickerson v. Louisiana, 816 F.2d 220 (5th Cir.1987) (explaining and distinguishing Braden and Atkins); United States v. Castor, 937 F.2d 293 (7th Cir.1991).

[72]Justices of Boston Mun. Court v. Lydon, 466 U.S. 294, 104 S.Ct. 1805, 80 L.Ed.2d 311 (1984); Laswell v. Frey, 45 F.3d 1011 (6th Cir.1995); Mannes v. Gillespie, 967 F.2d 1310 (9th Cir.1992). See also J. Liebman & R. Hertz, Federal Habeas Corpus Practice and Procedure § 5.2 (3d ed. 2005).

rendered the claim moot.[1] One such event is the death of the defendant. Should the defendant die pending discretionary or collateral review, courts typically will simply dismiss the petition and let the underlying judgment or ruling stand.[2] When a defendant dies pending direct review, however, most courts will set aside the conviction and dismiss the indictment or information.[3] Such abatement is premised on the theory that without it, the defendant would be deprived of his statutory right to review,[4] and that abatement prevents both recovery against the decedent's estate (if there is a fine) and the use of the conviction in civil liti-

---

[Section 27.5(a)]

[1]In federal courts, jurisdiction is limited by Article III of the Constitution to cases or controversies, see, e.g., Spencer v. Kemna, 523 U.S. 1, 118 S.Ct. 978, 140 L.Ed.2d 43 (1998). Some states do not confine the exercise of judicial power to actual cases or controversies, leaving the courts discretion to entertain cases that have become moot. See, e.g., State v. Gartland, 149 N.J. 456, 694 A.2d 564 (1997). On mootness as it relates to appeals generally, see 13A C. Wright, A. Miller, and E. Cooper, Federal Practice and Procedure § 3533 (2d ed. 1984).

[2]See Dove v. United States, 423 U.S. 325, 96 S.Ct. 579, 46 L.Ed.2d 531 (1976) (dismissing petition for certiorari following petitioner's death); Warden v. Palermo, 431 U.S. 911, 97 S.Ct. 2166, 53 L.Ed.2d 221 (1977) (dismissing petition, citing *Dove*); United States v. Green, 507 U.S. 545, 113 S.Ct. 1835, 123 L.Ed.2d 260 (1993); People v. Valdez, 911 P.2d 703 (Colo.App.1996) (dismissing post-conviction petition, noting that appropriate action had defendant died during direct appeal would have been abatement of the conviction); West v. United States, 659 A.2d 1260 (D.C.App. 1995) (dismissing petition for rehearing en banc, noting that "appellant has had his appeal of right fully considered and ruled upon by the court and no further appeal of right remains," so that "appellant's death does not warrant vacating the opinion and remanding the case for vacation of the conviction and abatement of the

proceedings"); Commonwealth v. De La Zerda, 416 Mass. 247, 619 N.E.2d 617 (1993); State v. Dalman, 520 N.W.2d 860 (N.D.1994). But see State v. Witkowski, 163 Wis.2d 985, 473 N.W.2d 512 (1991) (post-conviction claim not mooted by death). See also Note, 13 U.Mich.L.J.Ref. 143 (1979); Annot., 80 A.L.R.Fed. 446 (1998) (collecting federal cases); Annot., 80 A.L.R. 4th 189 (1998) (collecting state cases).

[3]See, e.g., United States v. Pogue, 19 F.3d 663 (D.C.Cir.1994); United States v. Davis, 953 F.2d 1482 (10th Cir.1992); United States v. Schumann, 861 F.2d 1234 (11th Cir.1988); People v. Valdez, 911 P.2d 703 (Colo.App. 1996); People v. Robinson, 187 Ill.2d 461, 719 N.E.2d 662 (Ill.1999); People v. Peters, 449 Mich. 515, 537 N.W.2d 160 (1995); Howell v. United States, 455 A.2d 1371 (D.C.App.1983) (en banc); United States v. Sheehan, 874 F.Supp. 31 (D.Mass.1994) (returning fine). But compare United States v. DeMichael, 461 F.3d 414 (3d Cir.2006) (abatement of fine only, because deceased appealed only his fine, not his conviction).

[4]At least one commentator has observed that this rationale for abatement is particularly incongruous when the Court continues to suggest that a defendant could be deprived of the right of appeal without violating the Constitution. Cavallaro, Better Off Dead: Abatement, Innocence, and the Evolving Right to Appeal, 73 U.Colo. L.Rev. 943 (2003) (noting this inconsistency, but arguing for constitutional recognition of the right to appeal).

gation against the estate.[5] Another justification is that punishment—the purpose of the criminal justice system—is not possible after the defendant dies.[6]

Heightened concern for the rights of victims, however, has led several courts to abandon the abatement rule for at least some aspects of the sentence, most commonly restitution orders. Stated one judge, if the "goal is to ward off potential harm to innocent people, it makes no sense to protect the heirs of criminal but not their victims."[7] At least three states have adopted an intermedi-

---

[5]See United States v. Parsons, 367 F.3d 409 (5th Cir.2004) (en banc) (terming this the "finality principle," that the state should not label one as guilty until he has exhausted his opportunity to appeal; abating restitution order, rejecting its earlier distinction allowing restitution orders to stand when compensatory rather than punitive, victim may seek compensation through civil actions); United States v. Moehlenkamp, 557 F.2d 126 (7th Cir.1977); United States v. Oberlin, 718 F.2d 894 (9th Cir.1983).

[6]See Surland v. State, 392 Md. 17, 895 A.2d 1034 (2006) (collecting authority that notes this rationale).

[7]State v. Devin, 142 P.3d 599 (Wash.2006). See also United States v. Christopher, 273 F.3d 294 (3d Cir.2001) (restitution order that is compensatory in nature does not abate upon the defendant's death, collecting conflicting authority); United States v. Koblan, 478 F.3d 1324 (11th Cir.2007) (abating restitution order, noting circuit split); State v. Wheat, 907 So.2d 461 (Ala.2005) (discussing recognition of crime victims under state law and holding "when a person convicted of a crime dies while an appeal is pending in the Court of Criminal Appeals and that court abates the appeal * * * by reason of the death of that person, the Court of Criminal of Appeals shall instruct the trial court to place in the record a notation stating the fact of the defendant's conviction removed the presumption of the defendant's innocence, but that the conviction was appealed and it was neither affirmed nor reversed on appeal because the de-

fendant died while the appeal of the conviction was pending and the appeal was dismissed"); State v. Korsen, 141 Idaho 445, 111 P.3d 130 (2005) ("by virtue of the substantial changes brought about by * * * the victims" rights provisions, we hold that a criminal conviction and any attendant order requiring payment of court costs and fees, restitution or other sums to the victim, or other similar charges, are not abated, but remain intact, in the event of a defendant's death following conviction and pending appeal"); People v. Peters, 449 Mich. 515, 537 N.W.2d 160 (1995) (collecting authority, noting that a majority of jurisdictions abate or dismiss sanctions that are primarily penal, and refusing to abate order of restitution to state, reasoning that "[e]rasing the order of restitution or even attempting to divine the portion of the order that the trial judge acknowledged he hoped would cause some "financial pain" is inconsistent with the Michigan Constitution and the Michigan Crime Victim's Rights Act"); People v. Ekinici, 191 Misc.2d 510, 743 N.Y.S.2d 651 (N.Y.Sup.2002) (rejecting abatement of fine and mandatory surcharge/victim assistance fees because a fine promotes general deterrence and the death of defendant does not effect this, also noting that estate must not profit from criminal activity); Cavallaro, Better Off Dead: Abatement, Innocence, and the Evolving Right to Appeal, 73 U.Colo.L.Rev. 943 (2003); Comment, 71 Temp.L.Rev. 347 (1998) (collecting authority for three different approaches to restitution orders: abating conviction while preserving resti-

ate position, requiring abatement under some conditions but not others. Reasoning that "it seems unreasonable automatically to * * * pretend the defendant was never indicted, tried, and found guilty," these courts will leave the criminal judgment in place unless the deceased's personal representative or the state moves for the substitution of another person for the deceased party, enabling the appeal to go ahead.[8]

Traditionally, a criminal appeal also was viewed as moot once the sentence imposed by the trial court was fully satisfied, that is, when the defendant had paid his fine and served the full period of imprisonment or probation. Although one jurisdiction still adheres to this view when a defendant has "voluntarily" served her sentence,[9] the fully-satisfied-sentence standard is no longer enforced.

Not Moot Because of Collateral Consequences. The most significant barrier to finding an appeal moot after a sentence has been served is known as the collateral consequences exception. A case is not moot, notwithstanding full satisfaction of the sentence, if the defendant is still subject to a collateral legal disability as a result of his conviction.[10]

---

tution order; abating restitution as well as conviction; or abating conviction while allowing a substitute party to appeal restitution order); Note, 73 Fordham L.Rev. 2711 (2005) (collecting conflicting authority concerning abatement of restitution orders); Note, 75 Fordham L.Rev. 2193 (2007) (collecting authority).

But see People v. Robinson, 187 Ill.2d 461, 241 Ill.Dec. 533, 719 N.E.2d 662 (1999) (ruling that the state's victim's rights amendment has no effect on the traditional abatement rule). Compare United States v. Lay, 456 F.Supp.2d 869 (S.D.Tx.2006) (conviction abated when defendant died before sentencing, distinguishing cases in which the defendant dies pending appeal).

[8]See Surland v. State, 392 Md. 17, 895 A.2d 1034 (2006) (reviewing the five separate approaches by state and federal courts and holding that when defendant dies before an appeal is decided, upon notice of the death of the appellant, a substituted party may be appointed by the defendant's estate who can elect whether to continue the appeal, if no substituted party comes forth within the time allotted to elect to continue the appeal, it will be dismissed for want of prosecution and the judgment will remain intact). See also State v. Timas, 82 Haw. 499, 923 P.2d 916 (Haw.App.1996); State v. Makaila, 79 Haw. 40, 897 P.2d 967 (1995) (collecting cases); Gollott v. State, 646 So.2d 1297 (Miss.1994); Note, 64 Miss.L.J. 819 (1995). For another intermediate position, see Note, 75 Fordham L.Rev. 2193, 2223–2227 (2007) (proposing a four-factor test to determine when a criminal conviction and sentence should be abated).

[9]See State v. Snowman, 698 A.2d 1057 (Me.1997); Lewis v. State, 747 A.2d 1191 (Me.2000) distinguishing *Snowman* as a case in which the defendant voluntarily completed sentence).

[10]The collateral consequences exception may also allow appellate review of a trial court decision even after a criminal charge has been dismissed. As the Court stated in Minnesota v. Dickerson, 508 U.S. 366, 113 S.Ct. 2130 124 L.Ed.2d 334 (1993),

In *Sibron v. New York*,[11] the Supreme Court adopted for the federal courts a liberal view of the collateral consequences exception. The Supreme Court in *Sibron* construed its earlier mootness opinions as having "abandoned all inquiry into the actual existence of specific collateral consequences and in effect presumed that they existed."[12] The "mere possibility" that there would be "adverse collateral legal consequences" was sufficient to keep a case "from ending 'ignominiously in the limbo of mootness.' " The Court added that, "without pausing to canvass the possibilities in detail," it was clear that *Sibron's* case met that "mere possibility" standard. New York statutes would allow *Sibron's* conviction to be used to impeach him if he should become a defendant in a future trial, and they required that the conviction be considered in sentencing should he be convicted of a future offense. Moreover, the fact that *Sibron* was already a multiple offender was not critical. Sentencing judges and trial juries might be willing to discount a certain number of prior transgressions. It was "impossible * * * to say at what point the number of convictions on a man's record renders his reputation irredeemable." So too, the Court could not "foretell what opportunities might present themselves in the future for the removal of [the] other convictions."

In holding that the mere possibility of collateral legal consequences forestalled a finding of mootness, the *Sibron* opinion stressed the need to face the reality of the broad range of legal disabilities that traditionally attach to a criminal conviction.[13] The Court also stressed the importance of adopting a mootness standard that was consistent with both the policies underlying "the constitutional rule against entertaining moot controversies" and the need for an efficient system of adjudication. There was nothing "abstract or feigned" about the appeal before it, and neither the defendant nor the prosecution had been "wanting in diligence or fervor in the litigation." Moreover, "the question of the validity of [Sibron's] criminal conviction" could arise in "many

---

where a certain type of dismissal was included in the calculation of a defendant's criminal history for federal sentencing, "reinstatement of the record of the charges" against the defendant "would carry collateral legal consequences" so that "a live controversy remains."

[11]Sibron v. New York, 392 U.S. 40, 88 S.Ct. 1889, 20 L.Ed.2d 917 (1968).

[12]See also Spencer v. Kemna, 523 U.S. 1, 118 S.Ct. 978, 140 L.Ed.2d 43 (1998), discussed infra note 16, tracing the treatment of collateral consequences doctrine in the Supreme Court and the abandonment of the Court's earlier "fastidious approach."

[13]For a state by state listing of which of the following consequences follow from a felony conviction and whether the rights lost are restorable under state law, see D. Rottman & S. Strickland, State Court Organization 2004 Table 47 (Aug. 2006, NCJ 212351).

[future] contexts," and it was "always preferable to litigate a matter when it is directly and principally in dispute, rather than in a proceeding where it is collateral to the central controversy." Reviewing the conviction on direct appeal would ensure that the dispute would be fully litigated when it was "fresh," and when additional facts could be gathered, if necessary, "without a substantial risk that witnesses will die or memories fade."

Building upon *Sibron*, most courts have taken the position that the possibility of adverse collateral consequences from a criminal conviction will be " 'presumed' as an 'obvious fact of life.' "[14] Even where a defendant's conviction is for a low-level misdemeanor, a careful search of state law is likely to turn up some provision through which the conviction could come back to haunt him. In those misdemeanor cases in which defendants have lost their appeals to a mootness finding, they apparently sought to rely on the consequences of future adverse treatment by private parties rather than disabilities that flowed from state or federal law.[15]

---

[14]Government of the Canal Zone v. Castillo, 568 F.2d 405 (5th Cir. 1978). See also United States v. Chavez-Palacios, 30 F.3d 1290 (10th Cir.1994) (explaining that since the enactment of the Sentencing Guidelines, anyone sentenced to more than 60 days is subject to an automatic increase of his criminal history score in future sentencing proceedings); United States v. Fadayini, 28 F.3d 1236 (D.C.Cir.1994) (remote possibility of increase in criminal history category in future sentencing sufficient); United States v. Page, 69 F.3d 482 (11th Cir.1995); People v. Jordan, 241 Ill.App.3d 464, 181 Ill.Dec. 553, 608 N.E.2d 626 (1993) (completion of felony sentence does not render the appeal of underlying conviction moot); State v. Jones, 516 N.W.2d 545 (Minn. 1994) (criminal record could affect a future sentence or defendant's ability to obtain future employment); State v. Patterson, 237 Neb. 198, 465 N.W.2d 743 (1991) (loss of right to vote and possible use as impeachment or sentence enhancement sufficient collateral consequences); Angle v. State, 113 Nev. 757, 942 P.2d 177 (1997) (possible effect on future sentences sufficient); People v. DeLeo, 185 App.Div.2d 374, 585 N.Y.S.2d 629 (1992) (possible

future impeachment or recidivist liability sufficient); State v. Key, 388 N.W.2d 866 (N.D.1986) (possibility of negative consequences sufficient); State v. Golston, 71 Ohio St.3d 224, 643 N.E.2d 109 (Ohio 1994) (collateral consequences of conviction "severe and obvious").

[15]Thus, in one case the court held moot an attorney's appeal from a criminal contempt order (resulting in a fully paid $50 fine) when the attorney's only claim of collateral consequences was the possible impact the conviction might have on "his future career for political office," his opportunities for a judgeship, and his ability to attract clients. Cancino v. Craven, 511 F.2d 1371 (9th Cir.1975) (also noting that petitioner had not sought a stay, and that case might have been decided differently if petitioner had chosen the alternative sentence of a day in jail). Consider also Arnold v. Panora, 593 F.2d 161 (1st Cir.1979) (where defendant challenged an automatic suspension of his driver's license, and that suspension had been revoked when he was subsequently acquitted in a trial de novo, concern that his insurance company would view suspension adversely was not an "adverse legal consequence," within the meaning of *Si-*

In *Spencer v. Kemna*,[16] the Court retreated somewhat from its earlier willingness to presume adverse consequences sufficient to defeat a claim of mootness. In *Spencer*, the Court refused to presume that a defendant who has served his sentence and challenges not his conviction, but rather the revocation of his parole, continues to suffer collateral consequences from the revocation sufficient to keep his habeas corpus proceeding alive after he was released from the confinement brought about by the revocation. The Court distinguished *Sibron*, first discounting the decision as one that developed prior to the tightening of the requirements for establishing standing under Article III, and second, observing that while "the presumption of significant collateral consequences is likely to comport with reality" when a defendant challenges a conviction, the same cannot be said when a defendant challenges the revocation of parole. The *Spencer* Court also drew upon reasoning in *Lane v. Williams*,[17] a case concluding that the presumption of adverse consequences will not apply when a defendant on habeas review challenges the penalty imposed for a parole violation. Just as adverse collateral consequences could not be presumed when a defendant challenged the penalty imposed for a parole or probation violation, the presumption was also inappropriate when the challenge went to the validity of the revocation itself. The appellant's predictions of harm from an unreviewed revocation proceeding were speculative, the Court in *Spencer* concluded, for the parole violation would be only one factor among many that would be considered by a parole board in any future parole decision, and even then would only become relevant if the defendant at some future date committed a crime and was returned to prison. The Court also went on to reject as speculative apprehensions that the revocation would be used to impeach the defendant, or introduced as substantive evidence, should the defendant appear in a future criminal proceeding. Moreover, the Court discounted possible employment or sentencing repercussions from the parole violation as "insufficient to keep the controversy alive." *Spencer* has compelled at least one lower court to question "whether the burden of establishing collateral consequences of a judgment other than a conviction can,

---

bron); State v. Eastman, 92 Conn.App. 261, 884 A.2d 442 (2005) (appeal dismissed as moot after defendants voluntarily paid fines because the defendants were unable to demonstrate a reasonable possibility of collateral consequences so as to overcome the mootness of their appeal when they were convicted only of violations and not of crimes, and will not have criminal histories resulting from their convictions); Newton v. State, 205 Ga.App. 762, 423 S.E.2d 707 (1992) (no adverse collateral consequences shown from speeding conviction).

[16]Spencer v. Kemna, 523 U.S.1, 118 S.Ct. 978, 140 L.Ed.2d 43 (1998).

[17]Lane v. Williams, 455 U.S. 624, 102 S.Ct. 1322, 71 L.Ed.2d 508 (1982).

after Spencer, ever be carried when * * * the only consequences of which the defendant is complaining are contingent upon his committing future crimes or future disciplinary violations."[18]

Not Moot when Issue Is "Capable of Repetition, Yet Evades Review." One other common exception exists under which courts will examine otherwise moot claims on appeal, regardless of whether it is the death of the defendant, the completion of sentence, or some other event that has rendered the claim moot. Courts regularly decide appeals, notwithstanding mootness, where the issue presented is "capable of repetition, yet evading review." In the federal courts, this doctrine applies only where "(1) the challenged action [is] in its duration too short to be fully litigated prior to cessation or expiration, and (2) there [is] a reasonable expectation that the same complaining party [will] be subject to the same action again."[19] In *Spencer*, for example, after holding that the defendant's challenge to his parole revocation did not qualify under the collateral consequences exception, the Court rejected review under the "capable-of-repetition" doctrine as well. The Court concluded that the defendant had not shown either "that the time between parole revocation and expiration of sentence is always so short as to evade review" or "a reasonable likelihood that he will once again be paroled and have that parole revoked."[20]

States do not necessarily insist on such an exacting showing, and may require only a likelihood that *other* litigants will confront the same issues, accompanied by some barrier to

---

[18]Diaz v. Duckworth, 143 F.3d 345 (7th Cir.1998) (noting that consequences that are within the power of the defendant to avoid are not relevant under *Spencer*, holding that "whatever is left of *Sibron*" is not enough to save habeas claim of petitioner, deported during the pendency of his appeal, who sought relief for allegedly unconstitutional prison discipline).

[19]Spencer v. Kemna, 523 U.S. 1, 118 S.Ct. 978, 140 L.Ed.2d 43 (1998) (quoting Lewis v. Continental Bank Corp., 494 U.S. 472, 110 S.Ct. 1249, 108 L.Ed.2d 400 (1990)). See also Weinstein v. Bradford, 423 U.S. 147, 96 S.Ct. 347, 46 L.Ed.2d 350 (1975).

[20]For other federal cases applying this exception, see In re Grand Jury Proceedings, 814 F.2d 61 (1st Cir.1987) (erroneous instruction in letter sent to grand jury witnesses); United States v. Preate, 91 F.3d 10 (3d Cir.1996) (order refusing to delay sentencing pending litigation concerning press access to sentencing documents); In re South Carolina Press, 946 F.2d 1037 (4th Cir.1991) (closure order); In re Associated Press, 162 F.3d 503 (7th Cir.1998) (closure order); United States v. Ellis, 90 F.3d 447 (11th Cir.1996) (reviewing order denying press access to transcript of *in camera* hearing on defendant's application for appointment of counsel). Compare In re Federal Grand Jury Proceedings, 938 F.2d 1578 (11th Cir.1991) (issue whether government could compel testimony from former attorney of defendant was moot, rejecting as speculative the argument that the issue may arise again, and collecting cases).

review.[21] Most states, however, also require that in order for a court to reach an otherwise moot, but recurring question, the question must be important, or of "broad public interest."[22] The issues that courts have addressed under this exception are quite varied, and include press access to court proceedings and documents,[23] the meaning or constitutionality of new statutes,[24] issues regarding release from custody prior to trial or pending appeal,[25] appellate procedure,[26] and a variety of sentencing issues.[27]

Not Moot When Stay of Sentence Was Refused. An additional exception to the rule that full satisfaction of sentence renders a defendant's appeal moot is of more limited impact but is worth mentioning. Where a court refuses to stay a defendant's sentence, and the defendant has no alternative but to immediately comply with the sentence, his appeal will be heard notwithstanding the fact that the sentence has been fully satisfied. This exception usually comes into play when the defendant is forced to make im-

[21]See, e.g., People v. Black, 915 P.2d 1257 (Colo.1996); West v. Commonwealth, 887 S.W.2d 338 (Ky.1994) (addressing alleged denial of the right to consult with an attorney during interrogation).

[22]See, e.g., Williams v. Superior Court, 46 Cal.App.4th 320, 53 Cal.Rptr.2d 832 (1996) (appointment of counsel); People v. McCoy, 9 Cal.App. 4th 1578, 12 Cal.Rptr.2d 476 (1992) (addressing appeal despite defendant's death); State v. Deptula, 34 Conn.App. 1, 639 A.2d 1049 (1994) (addressing limits of probation revocation); State v. Gartland, 149 N.J. 456, 694 A.2d 564 (1997) (reviewing claim of dead appellant concerning the scope of a spouse's duty to retreat when attacked by a spouse).

[23]See, e.g., In re Closure of Preliminary Exam, 200 Mich.App. 566, 505 N.W.2d 24 (1993) (closure of preliminary examination); People v. Palacio, 240 Ill.App.3d 1078, 180 Ill.Dec. 862, 607 N.E.2d 1375 (1993) (addressing propriety of post-trial subpoena to newspaper reporter); State v. Archuleta, 857 P.2d 234 (Utah 1993). But see Commonwealth v. Dorler, 403 Pa.Super. 150, 588 A.2d 525 (1991) (closure order will not evade review).

[24]Aime v. Commonwealth, 414 Mass. 667, 611 N.E.2d 204 (1993)

(interpreting new bail statute); State v. Kuhn, 74 Wash. App. 787, 875 P.2d 1225 (1994) (construing deferred prosecution statute); State v. J.D., 86 Wash.App. 501, 937 P.2d 630 (1997) (addressing constitutionality of youth curfew ordinance).

[25]See, e.g., Tyler v. United States, 705 A.2d 270 (D.C.App.1997) (right of defendant to present evidence at bail hearing); State v. Lipke, 186 Wis.2d 358, 521 N.W.2d 444 (1994) (propriety of requiring indigent to post bond as a condition of release pending appeal of misdemeanor).

[26]State v. Wilson, 138 N.M. 551, 123 P.3d 784 (N.M.App.2005) (appeal will not be considered moot, but raising issues capable of repetition so that defendants charged with DWI or domestic violence who are sentenced to no more than a year, but who contend they are entitled to appeal by a de novo trial will not be exposed to the danger of losing the right to a trial de novo, without appellate relief).

[27]See e.g., State v. Zimmer, 19 Kan.App.2d 617, 873 P.2d 1381 (1994) (propriety of commitment to state security hospital); People v. Briseno, 211 Mich.App. 11, 535 N.W.2d 559 (1995) (illegal sentence); State v. Avila, 192 Wis.2d 870, 532 N.W.2d 423 (1995) (failure to credit pretrial detention).

mediate payment of a fine,[28] but it can also arise where a short jail sentence is involved. Indeed, when the appeal reaches a second or third level appellate court, it may arise even in a case involving a fairly substantial sentence.[29] Thus, in *Sibron* where the defendant's six-month sentence had been completed before his appeal reached the United States Supreme Court, the Court rejected the state's contention of mootness on the ground that "there was no way for *Sibron* to bring his case here before his * * * sentence expired." The Court added that it would not allow the state, through a combination of "inevitable delays" in its court system and a statutory prohibition against bail pending appeal, to effectively "cut off federal review" of a criminal offense. This "estoppel analysis" has been criticized as "contradict[ing] the fundamental role of mootness as a constitutional limitation on the Supreme Court's case or controversy jurisdiction."[30] But it has been supported as "recogniz[ing] the importance of the principle that federal constitutional rights of personal liberty shall not be denied without the fullest opportunity for plenary federal judicial review."[31]

It is also worth noting that even though the discussion in this section is directed to mootness as it applies to defense appeals, under some circumstances a prosecution appeal also can become moot as well.[32] As discussed in § 27.3, just as some courts will entertain moot appeals of defendants raising particularly

---

[28]See, e.g., In re Contempt of Morris, 110 Ohio App.3d 475, 674 N.E.2d 761 (1996); State v. Freeman, 113 Or.App. 246, 831 P.2d 84 (1992); Cody v. State, 548 S.W.2d 401 (Tex. Cr.App.1977); In re F.E.F., 156 Vt. 503, 594 A.2d 897 (1991). Compare State v. Hamm, 807 S.W.2d 692 (Mo.App.1991) (appeal moot unless record reflects payment of fine made under protest, suggesting defendant must file an appeal bond to preserve appeal).

[29]See, e.g., State v. Harris, 109 Ohio App.3d 873, 673 N.E.2d 237 (1996) (appeal not moot where defendant completed six-month sentence after trial court refused to stay the execution of the sentence).

[30]See Note, 82 Harv.L.Rev. 63, 299 (1968).

[31]United States v. Frumento, 552 F.2d 534 (3d Cir.1977) (en banc).

[32]See United States v. Suleiman, 208 F.3d 32 (2d Cir.2000) (government appeal not mooted by defendant's completion of sentence and deportation); United States v. Under Seal, 757 F.2d 600 (4th Cir.1985) (government appeal from order preventing its use of knowledge wrongfully obtained in an ongoing grand jury investigation was mooted when grand jury investigation was terminated through issuance of indictments); State v. McCormick, 246 Neb. 890, 523 N.W.2d 697 (1994) (dismissing appeal as moot). Compare United States v. Diaz-Diaz, 135 F.3d 572 (8th Cir.1998) (deportation of defendant who has completed his sentence does not automatically moot government's appeal of a downward departure, as defendant might return to United States); United States v. Hunter, 692 A.2d 1370 (D.C.App. 1997) (government appeal of suppression order not moot despite order granting government's motion to dismiss, as government intended to seek a new indictment).

important issues of law, they will also entertain otherwise mooted claims of the state on appeal.[33]

§ 27.5(b) The concurrent sentence doctrine

Where a defendant receives concurrent sentences on each of several counts of an indictment, and the appellate court finds no error in the conviction on any one count carrying a sentence at least equal to a remaining challenged count, the validity of the conviction remaining on the count will not be reviewed in jurisdictions that continue to adhere to what is commonly termed the "concurrent sentence doctrine." Prior to the Supreme Court's decision in *Sibron*, this doctrine was often described as an application of traditional mootness principles. There was thought to be no "live controversy" as to the remaining counts since, once a count carrying an equal concurrent sentence was affirmed, reversal of the remaining counts would not reduce the length of the defendant's confinement.[34] In *Benton v. Maryland*,[35] the Supreme Court held that, in light of its *Sibron* ruling, the concurrent sentence doctrine could no longer be justified on mootness grounds. The defendant had an obvious interest in challenging each and every count on which he was convicted because separate collateral consequences could flow from each. It was possible, for example, that petitioner might find himself in a jurisdiction in which each of the counts was treated separately under a recidivist statute. Although "this possibility might well be a remote one, it is enough," the *Benton* opinion noted, "to give this case an adversary cast and make it justiciable."

While rejecting mootness as a grounding for the concurrent sentence doctrine, the *Benton* opinion left open the possibility that the doctrine might be justified as a "rule of judicial convenience," to be applied at the discretion of the appellate court. The Court later applied the doctrine in *Barnes v. United States*,[36] where it noted that while challenges to certain remaining counts were not moot, it would "decline as a discretionary matter" to rule on their validity.[37] In *Ray v. United States*,[38] however, the Court emphasized the limits of the discretion a court may exercise

---

[33]See § 27.3(a) at note 7 (collecting cases). See also State v. Dumars, 37 Kan.App.2d 600, 154 P.3d 1120 (2007) (noting the state's "interest in prosecuting a violation of the law and in redressing the victims of that violation, including members of society at large").

[Section 27.5(b)]

[34]See Emanuel, The Concurrent Sentence Doctrine Dies a Quiet Death—Or Are the Reports Greatly Exaggerated?, 16 Fla.St.U.L.Rev. 269, 270–278 (1988) (tracing the history of the doctrine prior to *Benton*).

[35]Benton v. Maryland, 395 U.S. 784, 89 S.Ct. 2056, 23 L.Ed.2d 707 (1969).

[36]Barnes v. United States, 412 U.S. 837, 93 S.Ct. 2357, 37 L.Ed.2d 380 (1973).

[37]See also Andresen v. Maryland,

in declining to address a defendant's challenge to a conviction for a count which carries a sentence concurrent to the sentence on another count. The Court held that because Ray was obligated to pay a $50 "special assessment" for each of count of conviction, the sentences were not truly concurrent, precluding application of the doctrine.[39]

Some lower federal courts have concluded that *Ray* essentially abolished the doctrine for direct review of federal convictions, since the count-by-count assessment is mandated by statute.[40] For at least one panel, the resulting duty to "grapple with some thorny issues to determine whether the $50 assessments stand" creates "grave doubt that public resources have been wisely deployed."[41] Other courts have opted to avoid reviewing such convictions simply by vacating them and returning the assessment,[42] a solution that objecting judges have asserted violates the separation of powers.[43] This approach may adequately protect the immediate interests of the executive branch, however, only when it is applied in cases in which the government anticipates that it will not rely on the conviction in the future, rather than upon the court's independent conclusion that the value of those conse-

---

427 U.S. 463, 96 S.Ct. 2737, 49 L.Ed.2d 627 (1976) (noting, but not applying, doctrine); Pinkus v. United States, 436 U.S. 293, 98 S.Ct. 1808, 56 L.Ed.2d 293 (1978) (finding doctrine inapplicable due to additional fine imposed for challenged conviction).

[38]Ray v. United States, 481 U.S. 736, 107 S.Ct. 2093, 95 L.Ed.2d 693 (1987) (per curiam).

[39]See also Rutledge v. United States, 517 U.S. 292, 116 S.Ct. 1241, 134 L.Ed.2d 419 (1996) (noting $50 assessment amounts to cumulative punishment).

[40]See, e.g., United States v. McKie, 112 F.3d 626 (3d Cir.1997) (doctrine "rarely invoked in federal court now because of the mandatory $50.00 assessment imposed on each federal count resulting in conviction"). See also United States v. Upton, 91 F.3d 677 (5th Cir.1996); United States v. Morehead, 959 F.2d 1489 (10th Cir. 1992); United States v. Hudacek, 24 F.3d 143 (11th Cir.1994).

Federal misdemeanor convictions are also accompanied by a separate $25.00 assessment. See 18 U.S.C.A. § 3013(a)(1)(A).

[41]United States v. Duff, 76 F.3d 122 (7th Cir.1996).

[42]United States v. Tolliver, 116 F.3d 120 (5th Cir.1997). See also United States v. Hooper, 432 F.2d 604 (D.C. Cir.1970); United States v. Dorsey, 865 F.2d 1275 (D.C.Cir.1989).

[43]In United States v. DeBright, 730 F.2d 1255 (9th Cir.1984), the Ninth Circuit, in criticizing the practice of vacating unreviewed sentences, faulted this option as (1) violating the principle of separation of powers, which gives "the executive primary responsibility for determining which violations of the law will be prosecuted," (2) failing to give sufficient weight to the government's and the public's interest in "retaining unreviewed convictions," and (3) presenting "substantial practical difficulties" in its implementation, particularly in holding open the possibility of postponed review. But see Emanuel, The Concurrent Sentence Doctrine Dies a Quiet Death—Or Are the Reports Greatly Exaggerated?, 16 Fla.St.U.L. Rev. 269, 270–278 (1988) (refuting the separation of powers objection).

quences to the government does not outweigh the court's interest in conserving its resources. Because the government might later decide it will rely on the conviction, some courts have suggested the government should be allowed to reinstate the vacated judgment at some later time if "necessary in the interests of justice."[44] At that point, the reinstated conviction would be subject to appellate review on motion of the defendant. Federal courts also continue to invoke the concurrent sentence doctrine in cases in which the defendant appeals only a sentence, as opposed to a conviction, as the defendant would remain responsible for the statutory assessment even if the sentence were vacated.[45]

Several state courts and one federal court of appeals have rejected the use of the concurrent sentence doctrine entirely, even as a rule of judicial convenience. The Ninth Circuit has concluded that whatever convenience is achieved through application of the concurrent sentence doctrine is dwarfed by the potential injury to the defendant. Drawing on *Sibron* and other mootness cases, it has reasoned that "an erroneous conviction may be prejudicial even if the error did not immediately lead to additional jail time," with consequences including sentences of incarceration for future convictions due to heightened criminal history scores, liability under recidivist statutes, stigma, and use of the conviction as impeachment.[46] State courts rejecting the doctrine have pointed to these concerns, as well as the possibility that an additional conviction could "act as an impediment" to clemency, pardon, more lenient conditions of imprisonment,[47] and professional licensing.[48] By contrast, those state courts that continue to apply the concurrent sentence doctrine stress its

---

[44]United States v. Niver, 689 F.2d 520 (5th Cir.1982).

[45]See, e.g., United States v. Pardo, 25 F.3d 1187 (3d Cir.1994); United States v. Hughes, 964 F.2d 536 (6th Cir.1992) ("because there is no likely collateral consequence to Hughes of being sentenced on both counts, we find no significant legal issue to compel our attention"); United States v. Olunloyo, 10 F.3d 578 (8th Cir.1993).

[46]United States v. Palomba, 31 F.3d 1456 (9th Cir.1994); United States v. Kincaid, 898 F.2d 110 (9th Cir. 1990); United States v. DeBright, 730 F.2d 1255 (9th Cir.1984) (en banc) (also noting that refusing to consider a properly raised appeal "impinges on the defendant's statutory right" to appeal each conviction).

[47]Williamson v. State, 669 A.2d 95 (Del.1995) (collecting federal and state cases applying and rejecting doctrine); Hughes v. State, 112 Nev. 84, 910 P.2d 254 (1996).

[48]State v. Reynolds, 819 S.W.2d 322 (Mo.1991) (overruling prior cases sanctioning the use of the concurrent sentencing doctrine, after reviewing federal and state cases, and concluding that "the judicial convenience actually served by the doctrine as practical is slight"). See also West v. Director of Department of Corrections, 639 S.E.2d 190 (Va.2007) ("Because acceptance of such a perspective would close the doors of our courts to many petitioners regardless of the merits of their claims, we decline to apply the 'concurrent sentencing doctrine' in Virginia," granting writ of habeas corpus even

value in preserving scarce judicial resources and in avoiding the unnecessary decision of potentially difficult legal questions.[49]

§ 27.5(c) Waiver or forfeiture of the right to appeal

Express Waiver of Right to Appeal. Some appeals are barred because the defendant expressly waives his right to appeal.[50] With increasing frequency, negotiated plea bargains include an express waiver of the right to appeal by the defendant. A defendant may agree to waive the right to appeal only his sentence, waive his right to appeal his conviction after trial in return for a favorable sentence recommendation,[51] or give up the right to appeal both conviction and sentence as part of a plea agreement.[52]

---

though petitioner serving concurrent sentences); State v. Fortner, 182 W.Va. 345, 387 S.E.2d 812 (1989) (direct appeal, rejecting doctrine); State ex rel. Blake v. Chafin, 183 W.Va. 269, 395 S.E.2d 513 (1990) (petition for writ of mandamus to decide post-conviction habeas petition, rejecting doctrine).

[49]Smith v. State, 51 Md.App. 408, 443 A.2d 985 (1982); State v. Edwards, 51 Wash.App. 763, 755 P.2d 821 (1988); Driskill v. State, 761 P.2d 980 (Wyo.1988) (dicta); Osborn v. State, 806 P.2d 259 (Wyo.1991) (dicta). See also Annot., 56 A.L.R.5th 385 (1998) (collecting state cases applying and rejecting collateral sentence doctrine); Emanuel, The Concurrent Sentence Doctrine Dies a Quiet Death—Or Are the Reports Greatly Exaggerated?, 16 Fla.St.U.L.Rev. 269, 270–278 (1988) (arguing that the doctrine is really a form of harmless error review).

[Section 27.5(c)]

[50]See, e.g., State v. Jimenez, 935 P.2d 920 (Ariz.App.1996) (defendant waives right to appeal any judgment or sentence entered pursuant to a plea agreement in a non-capital case). These express waivers are to be contrasted with the forfeiture of the right to appeal that results when a defendant flees, or fails to comply with procedural requirements for raising and preserving the issue, discussed below. As discussed in § 21.6(a), a defendant also forfeits the right to appeal most claims relating to the validity of his conviction when he

voluntarily pleads guilty. Conditional pleas allow a defendant to preserve an issue for appeal despite his guilty plea. See § 21.6(b); State v. Hodge, 118 N.M. 410, 882 P.2d 1 (1994) (collecting cases and sources discussing conditional pleas). Authority for conditional pleas in thirty jurisdictions is collected in Glenn v. Commonwealth, 633 S.E.2d 205, 48 Va.App. 556 (2006).

See also United States v. Calderon, 428 F.3d 928 (10th Cir.2005) (government has obligation to file a motion to enforce waiver or raise the waiver in its brief; it is not relieved of this duty just because the defendant's attorney acknowledged in an *Anders* brief that his client's plea agreement included a waiver of appeal). Compare Campusano v. United States, 442 F.3d 770 (2d Cir.2006) (failure to file notice of appeal and adequate *Anders* brief, even when the client waived appeal in his plea agreement, constitutes ineffective assistance, and the defendant will be entitled to direct appeal without any showing on collateral review that his appeal will likely have merit).

[51]See, e.g., Spann v. State, 704 N.W.2d 486 (Minn. 2005).

[52]See, e.g., United States v. Capaldi, 134 F.3d 307 (5th Cir.1998); United States v. Rosa, 123 F.3d 94 (2d Cir.1997). See also People v. Hidalgo, 91 N.Y.2d 733, 698 N.E.2d 46, 675 N.Y.S.2d 327 (1998) (finding waiver of rights to appeal unknown sentence valid, noting defendant was aware of sentencing options and agreed to abide by judge's discretion). See generally

The validity of these waivers has been tested in most jurisdictions.[53] A few state courts have refused to enforce them, on the grounds that they violate "public policy" by allowing prosecutors to insulate themselves from scrutiny.[54] Commentators also have challenged such waivers as impeding the appellate development of the law, enlisting courts as "accomplices to police violations and trial court errors, and undermining legislative efforts to regulate the discretion of trial judges."[55]

Most courts uphold appeal waivers, so long as the waiver is made voluntarily and with an understanding of the consequences.[56] These courts are persuaded that because other

---

The Appeal Waiver Controversy, 10 Fed.Sent.Rptr. 209–238 (1998) (collecting sources on appeal waivers); King, Priceless Process: Nonnegotiable Features of Criminal Litigation, 47 U.C.L.A. L.Rev. 113 (1999) (collecting authority). For an empirical look at appeal waivers in the federal system, as well as a discussion of the policy debate over appeal waivers and collected authority, see King & O'Neill, Appeal Waivers and the Future of Sentencing Policy, 55 Duke L.J. 209 (2005). Appeal waivers are also examined in § 21.2(b) at notes 76–90. The decision to waive appeal is defendant's not counsel's. See § 11.6(a) at note 23. See also § 11.2(c), regarding frivolous appeals.

[53]See Annot., 89 A.L.R.3d 864 (1998 & Supp.) (collecting cases); Calhoun, Waiver of the Right to Appeal, 23 Hastings Const.L.Q. 127 (1995); King & O'Neill, Appeal Waivers and the Future of Sentencing Policy, 55 Duke L.J. 209 (2005). See also State v. Patton, 37 Kan.App. 166, 150 P.3d 328 (2007) (enforcing written waiver of right of appeal exchanged for sentence reduction and dismissal of additional charges).

Fed.R.Crim.P.11 now provides that the court must include in its colloquy with the defendant "the terms of any provision in a plea agreement waiving the right to appeal or to collaterally attack the sentence."

[54]See Spann v. State, 704 N.W.2d 486 (Minn.2005) (invalidating agreement to waive appeal entered following defendant's conviction at trial, noting "there is no legitimate State interest in preserving an unjust conviction for the sake of the conviction alone," and concluding that the need to have trial proceedings reviewed for error outweighs a defendant's interest in accepting a particular benefit). Compare also People v. Butler, 43 Mich.App. 270, 204 N.W.2d 325 (1972); People v. Soto, 62 Mich.App. 370, 233 N.W.2d 545 (1975) with People v. Rodriguez, 192 Mich.App. 1, 480 N.W.2d 287 (1991) (disagreeing with Butler, finding "no affirmative public policy to be served in fostering appeals of prohibiting their waiver").

[55]Note, 65 Notre Dame L.Rev. 649, 664 (1990); Calhoun, Waiver of the Right to Appeal, 23 Hastings Const. L.Q. 127 (1995).

[56]See, e.g., United States v. Teeter, 257 F.3d 14 (1st Cir.2001) (holding that "given the general availability of waivers in criminal cases, the public policy gains to be reaped by allowing plea-agreement waivers of appellate rights, and the impressive body of precedent sanctioning such waivers," presentence waivers of appellate rights are enforceable, noting that blanket assurances of appellate rights at sentencing do not cancel such waivers, but finding that the waiver in the case before it was not enforceable due to the failure of the district court to comply with Rule 11(c)(6) and inquire specifically about the waiver); United States v. Fisher, 232 F.3d 301 (2d Cir.2000) (joining the Fifth, Seventh,

important constitutional rights of the defendant may be waived by plea agreement,[57] the right to appeal, which is not even guaranteed by the Constitution, but by statute, should also be subject to waiver.[58] In sustaining such waivers, courts also point to the importance of plea bargaining, the value of saving appellate resources, and the advantages gained by the defendant in entering the agreement.[59] Some courts impose more stringent requirements for ensuring that a defendant's waiver of appellate

Eighth, and Tenth Circuits in holding that an otherwise enforceable waiver of appellate rights is not rendered ineffective by a district judge's post-sentencing advice suggesting, or even stating, that the defendant may appeal); United States v. Brown, 232 F.3d 399 (4th Cir.2000); United States v. Melancon, 972 F.2d 566 (5th Cir. 1992); United States v. Woolley, 123 F.3d 627 (7th Cir.1997); People v. Panizzon, 13 Cal.4th 68, 51 Cal.Rptr.2d 851, 913 P.2d 1061 (1996); Cruzado v. State, 110 Nev. 745, 879 P.2d 1195 (1994) ("A knowing and voluntary waiver of the right to appeal made pursuant to a plea bargain is valid and enforceable."), overruled on other grounds, Lee v. State, 115 Nev. 207, 985 P.2d 164 (1999). But compare United States v. Raynor, 989 F.Supp. 43 (D.D.C.1997) (rejecting plea agreement by which defendant would waive a sentence that has yet to be imposed).

Compare also United States v. Buchanan, 59 F.3d 914 (9th Cir.1995) (statement from court concerning appellate rights at sentencing created reasonable expectation in defendant that he could appeal sentence, despite earlier waiver) with United States v. Berberich, 254 F.3d 721 (8th Cir.2001) (finding that any statement by the court at the sentencing hearing could not have affected defendant's earlier decision to plead guilty and waive his appellate rights).

[57] See United States v. Ruiz, 536 U.S. 622, 122 S.Ct. 2450, 153 L.Ed.2d 586 (2002) (noting "the Constitution, in respect to a defendant's awareness of relevant circumstances, does not require complete knowledge of the relevant circumstances, but permits a court to accept a guilty plea, with its accompanying waiver of various constitutional rights, despite various forms of misapprehension under which a defendant might labor"); United States v. Mezzanatto, 513 U.S. 196, 115 S.Ct. 797, 130 L.Ed.2d 697 (1995) (discussing waiver generally, and noting that the most fundamental protections afforded by the Constitution and statute are presumed to be waivable). See also State v. Patton, 150 P.3d 328 (Kan.App.2007) (appeal of erroneous sentence barred by waiver in plea agreement).

[58] See, e.g., State v. Murphy, 125 Idaho 456, 872 P.2d 719 (1994).

[59] E.g., United States v. Bownes, 405 F.3d 634 (7th Cir.2005) (upholding appeal waiver of valid *Booker* claim noting that had the defendant "insisted on an escape hatch that would have enabled him to appeal if the law changed in his favor after he was sentenced, the government would have been charier in its concessions"; a sentence based on constitutionally impermissible criteria, such as race, or a sentence in excess of the statutory maximum sentence for the defendant's crime, can be challenged on appeal even if the defendant executed a blanket waiver of his appeal rights); United States v. Elliott, 264 F.3d 1171 (10th Cir.2001) (waivers of rights to appeal can be useful bargaining chips for defendants and save time and resources). See also King & O'Neill, 55 Duke L.J. 209 (2005); Note, 111 Harv.L. Rev. 1116 (1998).

rights in a capital case is informed and voluntary.[60] Moreover, courts that otherwise honor waivers have noted that an appeal waiver cannot foreclose appellate review of allegations that the trial court relied on a constitutionally impermissible factor, such as race, in setting the defendant's sentence,[61] or that a sentence was imposed in violation of the plea bargain.[62] Courts that otherwise honor broad waivers of the right to appeal will also entertain claims on appeal that the defendant's waiver of appeal rights was entered into unknowingly, or without the effective assistance of counsel.[63]

---

[60]See, e.g., Wallace v. State, 893 P.2d 504 (Okla.Cr.App.1995) (requiring for the waiver to be valid that court determine the defendant has the capacity to understand the choice between life and death and to knowingly and intelligently waive any and all rights to appeal his sentence). Compare Comer v. Schriro, 463 F.3d 934 (9th Cir.2006) (Constitution bars a state from executing a capital defendant who wants to die but whose habeas appeal has not been reviewed, refusing to enforce waiver).

[61]United States v. Woolley, 123 F.3d 627 (7th Cir.1997).

[62]United States v. Michelsen, 141 F.3d 867 (8th Cir.1998). See also United States v. Castillo, 496 F.3d 947 (9th Cir.2007) (en banc) (court retains jurisdiction to hear appeal of pre-plea constitutional claim when defendant waived right to appeal in plea agreement, collecting cases).

[63]E.g., United States v. Teeter, 257 F.3d 14 (1st Cir.2001) (adopting miscarriage-of-justice standard for evaluating challenges to waivers of rights to appeal in plea agreements); United States v. Nelson, 277 F.3d 164 (2d Cir.2002) (a defendant cannot waive claim of deprivation of impartial jury when biased jury resulted from judge's erroneous failure to grant cause challenge to an actually biased juror, at least where it is not clear that the waiver is totally free and uncoerced and consideration given for consent is utterly free from taint); United States v. Hernandez, 242 F.3d 110 (2d Cir.2001) (plea agreement containing waiver of the right to appeal is not enforceable where the defendant claims that the plea agreement was entered into without effective assistance of counsel); United States v. Craig, 985 F.2d 175 (4th Cir.1993); United States v. Andis, 333 F.3d 886 (8th Cir.2003) (waiver will not be enforced if it will result in miscarriage of justice, defendant may appeal an illegal sentence despite waiver); United States v. Schuman, 127 F.3d 815 (9th Cir.1997) (Kozinski, C.J., concurring) (listing those certain issues that a defendant who waives his right to appeal will nevertheless be allowed to appeal); United States v. Hahn, 359 F.3d 1315 (10th Cir.2004) (court will not enforce waiver if it will result in a miscarriage of justice, as where the court relied on race; ineffective assistance of counsel in connection with the negotiation of the waiver; sentence exceeds statutory maximum; or waiver is otherwise unlawful and the error seriously affects the fairness, integrity or public reputation of judicial proceedings). For state authority, see State v. LaRue, 619 N.W.2d 395 (Iowa 2000) (distinguishing case before it as one involving claim of ineffective assistance that did not affect the plea); People v. Rodriguez, 192 Mich.App. 1, 480 N.W.2d 287 (1991); State v. Padilla, 132 N.M. 247, 46 P.3d 1247 (2002) (waiver of the right to presence during jury selection is possible, but there was insufficient proof that defendant's waiver was knowing and voluntary); People v. Lopez, 16 App.Div.3d 258, 791 N.Y.S.2d 111 (2005) (claim that DNA databank fee was enacted into

Lower courts have interpreted appeal waivers to bar a defendant from claiming on appeal that his sentence violates not only rules recognized at the time the plea was entered, but also rules recognized only after the plea was entered,[64] such as the Court's holding in *Blakely v. Washington* which took many by surprise.[65] In upholding as "knowing" the waiver of yet-to-be-recognized rights, courts often rely on the Supreme Court's holding in *Brady v. United States*.[66] *Brady* had entered a guilty plea in order to avoid the death penalty, a punishment that the kidnapping statute at the time authorized only for those who were convicted following a trial. After the Supreme Court announced in a different case that imposition of the death penalty under this statute was an unconstitutional penalty on the exercise of the right to trial, *Brady* challenged his prior guilty plea as unknowing and involuntary, because it had been based on the faulty assumption that he would be subject to the death penalty if he had been convicted after trial. The Court rejected *Brady's* claim. Three decades later in *United States v. Ruiz*,[67] the Court reiterated its rationale from *Brady*, stating that a court may "accept a guilty plea, with its ac-

---

law only after the time of defendant's offense survives defendant's waiver of his right to appeal because it "involves the substantive illegality of the sentence," but waiver bars excessive sentence claim).

The trend has been to enforce waivers of the right to the effective assistance of counsel, so long as the defendant is not claiming that substandard advice led to an unknowing or involuntary decision to sign the agreement containing the waiver. In other words, courts of appeals enforce agreements waiving ineffective assistance claims when the defendant alleges on appeal an ineffective assistance claim that pertains to events after the agreement has been signed or prior to the plea agreement stage. See King & O'Neill, 55 Duke L.J. 209 (2005) (collecting cases allowing waivers of claims of ineffective assistance). See also United States v. Monzon, 359 F.3d 110 (2d Cir.2004) (where defendant alleges ineffective assistance challenging her sentence but does not seek to set aside her plea, she does not claim that ineffective assistance led to her waiver); Davila v. United States, 258 F.3d 448 (6th Cir.2001) (claim of ineffective assistance is barred by

waiver as part of plea bargain of such claims, so long as the waiver was knowing, intelligent, and voluntary).

[64]See King & O'Neill, Appeal Waivers and the Future of Sentencing Policy, 55 Duke L.J. 209 (2005) (collecting authority finding that pre-*Blakely* and *Booker* waivers will bar defendants from challenging their sentences as violating *Blakely* or *Booker*); State v. Ermels, 125 Wash.App. 195, 104 P.3d 67 (2005) (pre-*Blakely* waiver bars *Blakely* claim).

[65]Blakely v. Washington, 542 U.S. 296, 124 S.Ct. 2531, 159 L.Ed.2d 403 (2004), is discussed at § 26.4(i) note 149.13.

[66]Brady v. United States, 397 U.S. 742, 90 S.Ct. 1463, 25 L.Ed.2d 747 (1970), and its companion case Parker v. North Carolina, 397 U.S. 790, 90 S.Ct. 1458, 25 L.Ed.2d 785 (1970), are discussed in § 21.2(a) at notes 6–9, and in § 21.2(b) at note 27–30.

[67]United States v. Ruiz, 536 U.S. 622, 122 S.Ct. 2450, 153 L.Ed.2d 586 (2002), also discussed in § 21.3(c) at notes 176–192.

companying waiver of various constitutional rights, despite various forms of misapprehensions under which a defendant might labor."[68]

Forfeiture of the Right to Appeal—The Fugitive Disentitlement Doctrine. The right to appeal may be relinquished by less deliberate means as well. As the Court explained in *Ortega-Rodriguez v. United States*,[69] "it has been settled for well over a century that an appellate court may dismiss the appeal of a defendant who is a fugitive from justice during the pendency of his appeal." This rule, aptly termed the "fugitive disentitlement doctrine," is followed in some form or another by state as well as federal courts.[70] While the federal courts and many states have developed the rule through case law, some states have adopted the doctrine through legislation or court rule.[71]

The Court has identified two justifications for dismissing the appeal of a fugitive defendant. Practically speaking, any judgment reached on appeal would be unenforceable against an absent appellant, rendering appellate review an uncertain, if not entirely futile, expenditure of judicial resources.[72] Thus, courts have readily dismissed appeals by prisoners who remain fugi-

---

[68]The extent to which courts must honor the waiver of unannounced rights was touched upon subsequently in an exchange between Justice Ginsburg and Justice Thomas in *Halbert v. Michigan*. Justice Ginsburg argued for the Court that by pleading nolo Halbert had not waived his right to appointed counsel, a right that had not yet been recognized for a defendant in Halbert's situation. Justice Thomas protested in dissent that the suggestion that an "unrecognized" right is nonwaiveable is "bound to wreak havoc." *Halbert* can be distinguished from the appeal waiver cases, however. Halbert's case involved the right to counsel on appeal, not the right to appeal itself, and he pleaded nolo without signing an express waiver clause. Halbert v. Michigan, 545 U.S. 605, 125 S.Ct. 2582, 162 L.Ed.2d 552 (2005), discussed in § 11.1(b) at note 65, and holding that the right to counsel extends to first appeal, even when discretionary.

[69]Ortega-Rodriguez v. United States, 507 U.S. 234, 113 S.Ct. 1199, 122 L.Ed.2d 581 (1993).

[70]See generally Note, 87 J.Crim.L. & Criminology 751 (1997).

[71]See, e.g., Tex.Crim.P.Code art. 44.09 (considered in Estelle v. Dorrough, 420 U.S. 534, 95 S.Ct. 1173, 43 L.Ed.2d 377 (1975), and superseded by Texas R.App.Proc 60(b)); State v. Troupe, 891 S.W.2d 808 (Mo.1995) (en banc) (tracing the history of the judicially adopted "escape rule" in Missouri); State v. Schneider, 126 Idaho 624, 888 P.2d 798 (1995) (adopting but declining to invoke doctrine); State v. LaFromboise, 542 N.W.2d 110 (N.D.1996) (declining to consider whether to adopt the "fugitive dismissal rule," collecting cases from other states).

[72]See Ortega-Rodriguez v. United States, 507 U.S. 234, 113 S.Ct. 1199, 122 L.Ed.2d 581 (1993) (noting that "it is 'clearly within our discretion to refuse to hear a criminal case in error unless the convicted party, suing out the writ, is where he can be made to respond to any judgment we may render,'" quoting Smith v. United States, 94 U.S. 97, 24 L.Ed. 32 (1876)). See also People v. Diaz, 7 N.Y.3d 831, 857 N.E.2d 47, 823 N.Y.S.2d 752 (2006) (dismissing appeal of defendant who

tives at the time that their claims are considered.[73]

In addition, dismissal serves "an important deterrent function" that discourages escape, encourages voluntary surrender, and advances "an interest in efficient, dignified appellate practice."[74] This additional justification explains the Court's decisions in *Allen v. Georgia*,[75] and *Estelle v. Dorrough*,[76] each upholding state rules providing for the dismissal of the appeals of prisoners who escape during the pendency of their appeal, but are recaptured.[77]

Deterrence, however, normally would not justify the sanction of dismissal for an appellant who escapes *prior* to filing his appeal, held the Court in *Ortega-Rodriguez*. Escape and recapture prior to invoking appellate jurisdiction, the Court concluded, does not interrupt proceedings in the court of appeals,[78] and flouts not the authority of the court of appeals, but only the authority of the

---

was involuntarily deported, citing this reason, but noting appeal will be reinstated upon defendant's return to custody).

[73]See, e.g., Smith v. United States, 94 U.S. 97, 24 L.Ed. 32 (1876); Bonahan v. Nebraska, 125 U.S. 692, 8 S.Ct. 1390, 31 L.Ed. 854 (1887); Molinaro v. New Jersey, 396 U.S. 365, 90 S.Ct. 498, 24 L.Ed.2d 586 (1970); State v. Smith, 312 Ore. 561, 822 P.2d 1193 (1992); State v. Dyer, 551 N.W.2d 320 (Iowa 1996).

United States v. Awadalla, 357 F.3d 243 (2d Cir.2004) (applying multifactor test, finding that appeal should be dismissed when appellant's whereabouts are unknown, appellant absconded after he initiated his appeal, and dismissal would preserve court resources and deter similarly situated appellants from fleeing from justice).

[74]Ortega-Rodriguez v. United States, 507 U.S. 234, 113 S.Ct. 1199, 122 L.Ed.2d 581 (1993). See also Luciano v. State, 906 S.W.2d 523 (Tex.Cr.App.1995) (applying Tex.R. App.Pro. 60(b) to uphold dismissal of a habeas appeal by prisoner who absconded from community corrections facility, noting "the dignity of an appellate court is maligned by an appellant who attempts to access the power of the judicial system to reverse a conviction, while at the same time treating with contemptuous disregard the authority of the judiciary to man-

date his incarceration").

A court has discretion to dismiss the appeal of a fugitive with or without prejudice to renewal of the appeal at a later time. United States v. Awadalla, 357 F.3d 243 (2d Cir.2004) (reviewing authority, and dismissing with prejudice after concluding that "any other course of action would dilute the sanction imposed for flouting the judicial process and reduce the deterrent effect of that sanction").

[75]Allen v. Georgia, 166 U.S. 138, 17 S.Ct. 525, 41 L.Ed. 949 (1897).

[76]Estelle v. Dorrough, 420 U.S. 534, 95 S.Ct. 1173, 43 L.Ed.2d 377 (1975).

[77]See, e.g., Bargo v. State, 364 Ark. 197, 217 S.W.3d 825 (2005) (refusing to reinstate appeal when defendant moved for reinstatement, collecting cases). But see State v. Tuttle, 713 P.2d 703 (Utah 1985) (holding that once a defendant is returned to custody, there is no justification for denying right to appeal); Estep v. State, 901 S.W.2d 491 (Tex.Cr.App.1995) (reinstating appeal of prisoner who was mistakenly released and did not voluntarily return within ten days, finding that his absence did not qualify as escape, and reviewing cases).

[78]The four dissenters in *Ortega-Rodriguez* were unpersuaded that a defendant who flees prior to filing his notice of appeal interferes with the appellate process to a lesser extent than

District Court. The District Court can tailor a response to deter such misconduct that is "more finely calibrated" than "the blunderbuss of dismissal" accessible to the court of appeals, the Supreme Court reasoned. Moreover, the Court feared that dismissal would be invoked inappropriately as a response to much less egregious misconduct prior to appeal.[79]

The Court left open "the possibility that some actions by a defendant, though they occur while his case is before the district court, might have an impact on the appellate process sufficient to warrant an appellate sanction," and went on to suggest that such a case might be presented if the delay caused by escape makes it difficult for the Government to locate witnesses and present evidence at retrial after a successful appeal, or made "meaningful appeal impossible."[80] Lower courts have also refused to find sufficient interference with the appellate process in cases involving lost evidence which the government was unable to prove would

---

the defendant who flees after filing, particularly when the prisoner's absence, like Oretga-Rodriguez's flight, forces the court to consider the fugitive's claims separately from those of his codefendants, "requiring duplication of precious appellate resources, and raising the specter of inconsistent judgments."

[79]"Such a rule" the court explained, "would sweep far too broadly, permitting for instance, this Court to dismiss a petition solely because the petitioner absconded for a day during district court proceedings, or even because the petitioner once violated a condition of parole or probation." The Court's final argument against dismissal for pre-appeal escape was that "[u]se of the dismissal sanction as, in practical effect, a second punishment for a defendant's flight is almost certain to produce the kind of disparity in sentencing that the Sentencing Reform Act of 1984 and the Sentencing Guidelines were intended to eliminate." One might, however, raise the same objection to the application of the fugitive disentitlement doctrine to prisoners who escape during the pendency of their appeals.

In Degen v. United States, 517 U.S. 820, 116 S.Ct. 1777, 135 L.Ed.2d 102 (1996), a unanimous Court refused to extend the doctrine to justify the entry of summary judgment against a forfeiture claimant who failed to appear in a related criminal prosecution, despite the "spectacle of a criminal defendant reposing in Switzerland, beyond the reach of our criminal courts, while at the same time mailing papers to the court in a related civil action and expecting them to be honored." The Court noted that even though the defendant's absence makes impracticable a stay of the civil proceeding pending the outcome of the criminal proceeding, the district court has means available to protect the Government's interests other than the "blunt instrument" of dismissal. See also Daccarett-Ghia v. Commissioner, 70 F.3d 621 (D.C.Cir.1995) (reinstating petition for redetermination of taxes after Tax Court dismissed the proceeding following petitioner's failure to appear in related criminal case).

[80]United States v. Smith, 419 F.3d 521 (6th Cir.2005) (before court could bar a defendant's appeal under the fugitive disentitlement doctrine due to a 12-year flight from justice, which the government alleged made it impossible to retry the case, a hearing would be necessary to determine whether the government would in fact be prejudiced by a retrial; here appeal rejected on merits, so no hearing ordered).

not have been destroyed absent the escape.[81]

Many states agree with the Court's rationale in *Ortega-Rodriguez*, and reject automatic dismissal of appeals filed by former fugitives,[82] reserving dismissal for cases in which the defendant's conduct significantly interferes with the appellate process.[83] Yet because the limits imposed in *Ortega-Rodriguez* were an exercise of the Court's supervisory powers over the federal courts and were not mandated by the Constitution,[84] state courts remain free to apply much more sweeping disentitlement rules, such as a rule dismissing a defendant's appeal when his escape merely delayed sentencing for a few months.[85]

[81]United States v. Delagarza-Villarreal, 141 F.3d 133 (5th Cir.1997). In refusing to dismiss the appeal, the Delagarza-Villarreal court also emphasized that because his codefendants did not appeal, the defendant's fugitive status did not require piecemeal review of joint claims, even though this argument did not seem determinative to the majority in *Ortega-Rodriguez*.

[82]See Commonwealth v. Huff, 540 Pa. 535, 658 A.2d 1340 (1995) (following *Ortega-Rodriguez*); In the Interest of J.J., 540 Pa. 274, 656 A.2d 1355 (1995) (approving of the rule in *Ortega-Rodriguez*, overruling precedent requiring dismissal whenever a defendant had been a fugitive at any time during the appellate process). Compare *Commonwealth v. Huff*, (Castille, J., dissenting) ("a defendant's escape or flight from justice acts as a per se forfeiture of the right of appeal regardless of when he chooses to flee the jurisdiction of the court").

[83]See, e.g., People v. Kang, 107 Cal.App.4th 43, 131 Cal.Rptr.2d 447 (Cal.App.2003) (defendant was not barred from pursuing new appeal when apprehended after fleeing during his first appeal, dismissing appeal might create "palpable injustice"); Griffis v. State, 759 So.2d 668 (Fla.2000) (appeal not dismissed when returned before filing); Bellows v. State, 110 Nev. 289, 871 P.2d 340 (1994) (dismissal appropriate when escape results in the loss of a trial transcript). Lower courts have also

declined to dismiss appeals when the prisoner who escapes during the pendency of his appeal remained at large only a few days. See United States v. Boyd, 958 F.2d 247 (8th Cir.1992); State v. Schneider, 126 Idaho 624, 888 P.2d 798 (1995) (noting that defendant's "status as a fugitive did not disrupt the appellate process," and that this was not a case in which "an escapee flagrantly refuses to obey a court order to return to custody, knowing quite well his recalcitrance will cost him an appeal," quoting United States v. Snow, 748 F.2d 928 (4th Cir. 1984)).

[84]See Goeke v. Branch, 514 U.S. 115, 115 S.Ct. 1275, 131 L.Ed.2d 152 (1995) (stating that *Ortega-Rodriguez* was based on the Court's supervisory powers, and quoting the dissenting opinion in that case, "There can be no argument that the fugitive dismissal rule * * * violates the Constitution because a convicted criminal has no constitutional right to an appeal.").

[85]See President v. State, 925 S.W.2d 866 (Mo.App.1996) (collecting cases). See also Bargo v. State, 364 Ark. 197, 217 S.W.3d 825 (2005) (refusing to reinstate appeal of absconder who returns); Hires v. State, 882 So.2d 225 (Miss.2004) (when defendant absconded in 1978 prior to sentencing and was captured and sentenced in 1985, court held that defendant's escape and absence for seven years so delayed the onset of appellate proceedings that the state, as a matter of law, would be prejudiced in locating and

If the forfeiture rule is not automatic, and the court of appeals must first determine whether to exercise discretion to dismiss an appeal, the state must afford the right of counsel to indigent defendants who contest the dismissal.[86] The doctrine is also employed to bar collateral review of criminal judgments.[87]

Forfeiture of the Right to Appeal—Issues Not Raised in the Trial Court. Perhaps no standard governing the scope of appellate review is more frequently applied than the rule that "an error not raised and preserved at trial will not be considered on appeal."[88] Even a constitutional right "may be forfeited in criminal as well as civil cases by the failure to make timely assertion of the right."[89] In the federal system, the principal rule is codified in Federal Rules 51 and 5, although preservation requirements are also stated elsewhere in statute, court rule, and judicial decision.[90] States have similar provisions.[91] The values underlying this rule were aptly summarized by the Oregon Court of

---

presenting evidence at a possible retrial; court dismissed appeal and collected cases for dismissing the appeals of defendants who had escaped before appeal had been filed or before sentencing had taken place).

[86]See Taveras v. Smith, 463 F.3d 141 (2d Cir.2006) (New York's rule is not mandatory, automatic, and permanent as in some other states, counsel required for returning fugitive).

[87]Compare Hanson v. Phillips, 442 F.3d 789 (2d Cir.2006) (although courts have the authority to dismiss a habeas appeal under the fugitive disentitlement doctrine even if the appellant is no longer a fugitive during the pendency of his appeal—collecting cases where habeas appeals were dismissed under the fugitive disentitlement doctrine—dismissal not justified in this case when, following denial of habeas petition in district court, petitioner became a fugitive for two months, was apprehended, prosecuted and sentenced for bail jumping, and the judgment will be enforceable against him; the state has not been prejudiced by the two-months absence) with Searle v. Juvenile Court for Williamson County, 188 S.W.3d 547 (Tenn.2006) (petitioner was a fugitive when she refused to appear and comply with orders of the court concerning her minor child, leading to the con-

tempt conviction and subsequent sentence, and the sentence she challenges on appeal is the same sentence she presently evades, as a fugitive, she is not entitled to a hearing on the merits of her habeas corpus petition).

[88]State v. Green, 49 Or.App. 949, 621 P.2d 67 (1980).

[89]Yakus v. United States, 321 U.S. 414, 444, 64 S.Ct. 660, 677, 88 L.Ed. 834 (1944). See, e.g., Martin v. State, 316 Ark. 715, 875 S.W.2d 81 (1994); State v. Ledbetter, 240 Conn. 317, 692 A.2d 713 (1997) (double jeopardy); Heavrin v. State, 675 N.E.2d 1075 (Ind.1996) (failure to challenge improper argument by prosecutor); State v. Ford, 306 Mont. 517, 39 P.3d 108 (2001) (*Batson* claim waived when counsel failed to raise objection until the jury was impaneled and the venire was dismissed). See also § 28.4 (discussing procedural default barring review of claims on collateral review).

[90]Fed.R.Crim.Pro. 51 requires that "a party, at the time the ruling or order of the [trial] court is made or sought, [to] make known to the court the action which that party desires the court to take or that party's objection to the action of the court and the grounds therefore." See also Fed.R. Evid. 103 (requiring evidentiary objections to be raised). Special requirements for raising particular objections

Appeals:

There are many rationales for the raise-or-waive rule:[92] that it is a necessary corollary of our adversary system in which issues are framed by the litigants and presented to a court; that fairness to all parties requires a litigant to advance his contentions at a time when there is an opportunity to respond to them factually, if his opponent chooses to; that the rule promotes efficient trial proceedings; that reversing for error not preserved permits the losing side to second-guess its tactical decisions after they do not produce the desired result; and that there is something unseemly about telling a lower court it was wrong when it never was presented with the opportunity to be right. The principal rationale, however, is judicial economy. There are two components to judicial economy: (1) if the losing side can obtain an appellate reversal because of error not objected to, the parties and public are put to the expense of retrial that could have been avoided had an objection been made; and (2) if an issue had been raised in the trial court, it could have been resolved there, and the parties and public would be spared the expense of an appeal.[93]

There is, of course, nothing in these rationales that requires that the "raise-or-waive" rule be absolute, and all jurisdictions recognize one or more situations in which issues not raised below will be considered on appeal. The plain error rule, discussed in the next subsection, is the most important of these "exceptions" to the raise-or-waive rule. Several other exceptions, discussed below, either do not cover as broad a range of objections, or are not as widely accepted, but they nevertheless have a fairly significant impact upon the scope of review in many jurisdictions.

It is a basic premise of the raise-or-waive rule that the defense will have adequate opportunity to present its objection before the

---

at the trial court level have been discussed in the sections of this treatise dealing with those objections. See, e.g., § 10.1(a) (suppression of illegally obtained evidence); § 15.4 (objections to the composition of the grand jury); § 19.2 (objections to pleadings); § 26.3(f) (objections to sentence).

[91]See, e.g., Ind.Trial Rule 51; Cal.Evid.Code § 353; Fla.Stat.Ann. § 924.051, Tex.Crim.P.Code Ann. art. 1.14. See also Commonwealth v. Freeman, 573 Pa. 532, 827 A.2d 385 (2003) (rejecting rule of "relaxed waiver" in capital cases holding that claims that were not properly raised and preserved in the trial court are waived and unreviewable, and may be pursued on state collateral review).

[92]The description of the rule as one of "waiver," rather than "forfei-ture" is unfortunate. "Waiver," suggests an "intentional relinquishment of a known right," while forfeiture may occur either inadvertently or intentionally. See, e.g., Wangerin, "Plain Error" and "Fundamental Fairness": Toward a Definition of Exceptions to the Rules of Procedural Default, 29 DePaul L.Rev. 753, 757–58 (1980). See also the discussions of waiver and forfeiture in §§ 10.2(a), 11.3(a) and (c), 21.6(a), 24.2(b), and 28.4(e). Most courts nevertheless speak of "waiver," although some refer to the rule as one of "forfeiture" or "default."

[93]State v. Applegate, 39 Or.App. 17, 591 P.2d 371 (1979). See also State v. Salmons, 203 W.Va. 561, 509 S.E.2d 842 (1998) (discussing rationale for rule).

trial court in compliance with the jurisdiction's procedural rules. Where that opportunity was not present, or was not likely to be exercised for some legitimate reason, the defendant's failure to raise his objection below is likely to be excused. The clearest case for considering an issue not raised in accordance with a particular procedural requirement occurs when that requirement fails to allow the defense a reasonable time within which to raise the issue.[94] In other situations the general timing requirements may be fair, but the defendant may be in a situation where the failure to comply was excusable. Thus, appellate courts may also consider objections not raised at trial where an intervening ruling established the grounds for the objection and counsel's failure to raise the issue was understandable in light of the controlling precedent at the time of trial.[95]

A lack of jurisdiction also is treated as a "venerable exception" to the raise-or-waive rule.[96] However, courts tend to utilize a narrower definition of a jurisdictional defect for this purpose than in other areas in which jurisdictional claims may be given separate treatment.[97] A challenge to subject matter jurisdiction clearly may be raised for the first time on appeal,[98] and many courts will also consider on a similar basis an allegation that the offense occurred outside the territorial jurisdiction of the state.[99] Courts generally are reluctant, however, to include within the jurisdictional category objections to other aspects of the proceedings.[100] For example, while several appellate courts allow a first-time challenge to the constitutionality of the statute on which the

---

[94]See, e.g., Reece v. Georgia, 350 U.S. 85, 76 S.Ct. 167, 100 L.Ed. 77 (1955), also noted in § 15.4(b) at note 81.

[95]For an extensive discussion of the appropriate scope of this exception to the raise-or-waive rule, and its relation to the plain error rule, see Judge Robinson's concurring opinion in United States v. Byers, 740 F.2d 1104 (D.C.Cir.1984).

[96]Peretz v. United States, 501 U.S. 923, 953, 111 S.Ct. 2661, 2678, 115 L.Ed.2d 808 (1991) (Scalia, J., dissenting). See, e.g., State v. Anonymous, 240 Conn. 708, 694 A.2d 766 (1997).

[97]See, e.g., the discussions of "jurisdictional" defects at §§ 27.4(b), 28.3(a), 21.6(a). Consider generally Westen, Forfeiture by Guilty Plea—A Reply, 76 Mich.L.Rev. 1308, 1330–34

(1978).

[98]See, e.g., Haskins v. State, 264 Ark. 454, 572 S.W.2d 411 (1978); Radford v. State, 360 So.2d 1303 (Fla. App.1978); State v. Pinckney, 306 N.W.2d 726 (Iowa 1981).

[99]See, e.g., State v. Williams, 23 Wash.App. 694, 598 P.2d 731 (1979).

[100]See, e.g., State v. Orosco, 113 N.M. 780, 833 P.2d 1146 (1992) (omission of element not "jurisdictional"). Thus, defects in the indictment process generally cannot be presented for the first time on appeal. See, e.g., United States v. Hubbard, 603 F.2d 137 (10th Cir.1979); United States v. McKneely, 69 F.3d 1067 (10th Cir. 1995). A similar approach is applied to defects in the presentation of an information. See, e.g., State v. Sheets, 291 N.W.2d 35 (Iowa 1980).

prosecution is based,[101] most hold that such an objection also is not jurisdictional and therefore cannot be raised unless it fits within some other exception to the raise-or-waive rule.[102] Similarly, most jurisdictions consider a double jeopardy claim as a defect that cannot be raised for the first time on appeal.[103] And, in *United States v. Cotton*,[104] the Court held that the failure to allege an element of the offense for which the defendant was sentenced was not jurisdictional error. The Court reasoned that even the failure to allege any federal offense at all did not deprive the court of jurisdiction.[105] If a federal defendant raises such an error for the first time on appeal, that error must be reviewed under Rule 52's plain-error standard, described below.[106]

In addition, claims of ineffective assistance of counsel typically are not expected to be raised at trial, or even on direct appeal when trial counsel continues to represent a defendant on appeal.[107] Instead, in most states and in the federal courts, a claim of ineffective assistance of counsel need not be raised until a post-conviction proceeding, after the completion of direct

---

[101]See, e.g., R.C. v. State, 760 P.2d 501 (Alaska 1988); State v. Andazola, 95 N.M. 430, 622 P.2d 1050 (N.M.App. 1981); State v. Shives, 601 S.W.2d 22 (Mo.App.1980).

[102]See, e.g., State v. Houston, 122 N.C.App. 648, 471 S.E.2d 127 (1996); Poe v. State, 389 So.2d 154 (Ala.Cr. App.1980).

[103]See, e.g., State v. Belcher, 51 Conn.App. 117, 721 A.2d 899 (1998); State v. Hightower, 661 A.2d 948 (R.I. 1995). But see Rolling v. State, 673 So.2d 812 (Ala.App.1995); Spencer v. State, 805 S.W.2d 677 (Mo.App.1990).

[104]United States v. Cotton, 535 U.S. 625, 122 S.Ct. 1781, 152 L.Ed.2d 860 (2002).

[105]The Court relied upon Lamar v. United States, 240 U.S. 60, 36 S.Ct. 255, 60 L.Ed. 526 (1916) ("a district court "has jurisdiction of all crimes cognizable under the authority of the United States * * * [and] [t]he objection that the indictment does not charge a crime against the United States goes only to the merits of the case""). See also § 19.3(e).

[106]The Court's rejection of automatic reversal for such errors under federal law is sure to affect case law in states which had, prior to *Cotton*, considered such errors grounds for relief without the showing required by plain-error review. See § 19.2 at note 83 and § 19.3 at note 26 (discussing *Cotton*). *Cotton* may undermine cases that have held that constructive amendment of an indictment, an error closely related to the failure to allege an essential element of the offense, requires reversal even when not raised by the defendant., e.g., United States v. Syme, 276 F.3d 131 (3d Cir.2002) (constructive amendments, which are per se reversible under harmless error review, are presumptively prejudicial under plain-error review). Compare United States v. Daniels, 252 F.3d 411 (5th Cir.2001) (applying plain-error standard, upholding conviction). See also § 19.6(c) at notes 46–51.

[107]See e.g. Stoia v. United States, 22 F.3d 766 (7th Cir.1994); Sharkey v. State, 672 N.E.2d 937 (Ind.App.1996). See also People v. Wilk, 124 Ill.2d 93, 529 N.E.2d 218 (1988) (ineffective assistance claims must be made in petition for post-conviction relief).

appeal.[108]

Finally, appellate courts in numerous states have noted their discretion to consider an issue on appeal, notwithstanding the lack of objection below, when appellate review of that issue would serve the "interest of judicial economy."[109] Thus, a court may consider an issue raised for the first time on appeal where there is a "strong possibility of reoccurrence" or the "issue is one of public policy or of broad * * * concern."[110] Ordinarily, failure to comply with the procedural requirements for raising claims at trial also will block collateral review of those claims, as discussed in § 28.4.

Related to the raise-or-waive rule is the common sense principle that a party introducing evidence cannot complain on appeal that the evidence was erroneously admitted. The Court in *Ohler v. United States*[111] rejected the defense argument that this principle should not apply when a testifying defendant seeks to "draw the sting" of his prior convictions by admitting them during direct examination before the prosecutor brings them out to impeach the defendant on cross. A defendant who does this, the Court concluded, forfeits his ability to appeal the trial court's denial of a previous motion in limine to exclude those prior convictions. Consequently, a federal defendant has a hard choice if he faces what he thinks is an erroneous ruling rejecting his efforts to bar the government from introducing prior convictions: preserve the right to appeal and not mention the evidence on direct, risking that the jury will conclude that the defendant was trying to conceal the conviction and is not to be believed; waive the right to appeal in the hopes of deflating the prosecution's impeachment efforts; or not testify at all. *Ohler* is contrary to precedent in some states, at least one of which has expressly rejected it, and continues to permit a defendant who "draws the sting" of a prior conviction by admitting it on direct to appeal the ruling allowing the conviction to be used for impeachment.[112]

§ 27.5(d) Plain error

All but a few jurisdictions recognize the authority of an appellate court to reverse on the basis of a plain error even though that error was not properly raised and preserved at the trial

---

[108]For more on the rational for this rule and a collection of authority, see § 11.7(e) at notes 75–109 and § 28.4(d) at note 58.

[109]Barnes v. State, 244 Ga. 302, 260 S.E.2d 40 (1979).

[110]State v. Junkin, 123 Ariz. 288, 599 P.2d 244 (1979).

[111]Ohler v. United States, 529 U.S. 753, 120 S.Ct. 1851, 146 L.Ed.2d 826 (2000).

[112]State v. Daly, 623 N.W.2d 799 (Iowa 2001). See also Ohler v. United States, 529 U.S. 753, 120 S.Ct. 1851, 146 L.Ed.2d 826 (2000) (Souter, J., dissenting) (collecting authority).

level.[113] The plain error exception is recognized in Federal Rule 52(b) and in similar provisions in most states. Others have adopted it as a common law exception to the raise-or-waive rule, based upon the appellate court's inherent authority to prevent a "miscarriage of justice."[114] The doctrine usually extends to all types of errors.[115] provided they are "plain errors or defects affecting substantial rights."[116] In federal courts, plain error review is

[Section 27.5(d)]

[113]For those rejecting plain error review, see State v. Sexton, 256 Kan. 344, 886 P.2d 811 (1994) (not allowing review for "plain error"); State v. Heath, 264 Kan. 557, 957 P.2d 449 (Kan.1998); State v. Escobedo, 573 N.W.2d 271 (Iowa App.1997) (same); Lamphere v. State, 348 N.W.2d 212 (Iowa 1984) (same).

See also People v. Miller, 113 P.3d 743 (Colo.2005) (overruling prior precedent applying harmless, not plain, error review to unpreserved constitutional claims, holding that harmless error review is reserved for those cases in which the defendant preserved his claim for review by raising a contemporaneous objection); State v. Rupert, 649 A.2d 1013 (R.I.1994) (although Rhode Island "does not recognize the plain-error rule," "an exception to the [state's] "raise or waive" rule does exist": "the error * * * must be more than harmless error, the record must be sufficient determination of the issue, the issue must be of constitutional dimension, and counsel's failure to raise the issue must be attributed to a novel rule of law that counsel could not reasonably have known during trial."). Compare also Commonwealth v. Freeman, 573 Pa. 532, 827 A.2d 385 (2003) (abandoning "relaxed waiver" rule for capital appeals, holding claims that were not properly raised and preserved in the trial court are waived and unreviewable on direct appeal, but may be pursued under the PCRA as claims sounding in counsel's ineffectiveness or, if applicable, a statutory exemption to the PCRA's waiver provision); Commonwealth v. Aponte, 579 Pa. 246, 855 A.2d 800 (2004) (court noted

failure to raise challenge to illegality of sentence under *Apprendi* did not waive claim on direct appeal, prompting concurring justices to protest that application of relaxed waiver rule to sentencing error was inconsistent with *Freeman*). For one collection of plain error statutes and cases in all states, see Blume & Wilkins, Death By Default: State Procedural Default Doctrine in Capital Cases, 50 S.Cal.L. Rev. 1 (1998).

[114]State v. Dexter, 954 S.W.2d 332 (Mo.1997) (collecting cases); State v. Mascarenas, 129 N.M. 230, 4 P.3d 1221 (2000) (appellate court may reverse for "fundamental error," which "exists "when guilt is so doubtful that it would shock the judicial conscience to allow the conviction to stand,"" and "must go to the foundation of the case or take from the defendant a right which was essential to his defense and which no court could or ought to permit him to waive"). See also Bell v. State, 443 So.2d 16 (Miss.1983); State v. Holden, 346 N.C. 404, 488 S.E.2d 514 (1997); Note, 84 J.Crim.L. & Criminology 1065 (1994).

[115]E.g., United States v. Vonn, 535 U.S. 55, 122 S.Ct. 1043, 152 L.Ed.2d 90 (2002) (express mention of harmless error but not plain error review in Rule 11 did not repeal by implication the application of Rule 52(b) to violations of Rule 11).

[116]Fed.R.Crim.Pr. 52(b). See also State v. Cullen, 86 Haw. 1, 946 P 2d 955 (1997); Tenn.R.Crim.Pro. 52(b); Stephens v. State, 911 So.2d 424 (Miss. 2005) (party seeking relief after failure to make a contemporaneous objection must show (i) an error at the trial level and (ii) such an error resulted in a manifest miscarriage of justice,

available to the government appealing a sentence, as well as to the defendant.[117] In some jurisdictions, however, the doctrine is restricted to a limited class of errors. Thus, one state limits review to unpreserved errors that are discoverable "by a mere inspection of the pleadings and proceedings * * * without inspection of the evidence."[118] Another includes only gross omissions from instructions in capital cases, errors by the trial judge to which defense counsel has no opportunity to object, and errors so serious as to warrant mistrial.[119] Several apply it only to the most flagrant constitutional violations.[120] As for those jurisdictions without such limitations, opinions have stressed that "no talismanic method exists for determining plain error," and each case must be examined on its own facts.[121]

In *United States v. Olano,*[122] and *Johnson v. United States,*[123] the Court developed a four-step analysis for determining whether an error is subject to review as "plain error" under Federal Rule

---

which exists where a defendant's substantive rights have been affected); State v. Kula, 252 Neb. 471, 562 N.W.2d 717 (1997) (error must result in damage to the integrity, reputation, or fairness of the judicial process); State v. DeGraff, 139 N.M. 211, 131 P.3d 61 (2006) (applying a standard of "fundamental error" which asks "whether there is a reasonable probability that the error was a significant factor in the jury's deliberations relative to the other evidence before them," finding no fundamental error when prosecutor commented on the defendant's silence); Gayler v. State, 957 P.2d 855 (Wyo. 1998).

[117]See, e.g., United States v. Gordon, 291 F.3d 181 (2d Cir.2002); United States v. Perkins, 108 F.3d 512 (4th Cir.1997).

[118]La.C.Cr.P. art 920(2). See also State v. Tabor, __ So.2d __, 2007 WL 1653113 (La.App.2007) (remanding for "patent" error in sentence).

[119]Green v. State, 362 Ark. 459, 209 S.W.3d 339 (2005) ("Arkansas does not recognize plain error, i.e., an error not brought to the attention of the trial court by objection, but nonetheless affecting substantial rights of the defendant," noting four exceptions were recognized in *Wicks*); Hale v. State, 343 Ark. 62, 31 S.W.3d 850 (2000) (*Kastigar* error not reviewable

due to failure to object in timely fashion in trial court); Wicks v. State, 270 Ark. 781, 606 S.W.2d 366 (1980) (noting four exceptions to bar on recognition of plain error). See also Paul v. State, 272 Ga. 845, 537 S.E.2d 58 (2000) (permitting plain error review in capital cases where trial judge expresses an opinion about guilt in violation of Ga.CodeAnn. § 17-8-57).

[120]See, e.g., Castor v. State, 365 So.2d 701 (Fla.1978) (error must amount to a denial of due process); People v. Hanson, 283 Mont. 316, 940 P.2d 1166 (1997) (may review errors, despite restrictive plain-error statute, that implicate fundamental constitutional rights); Nelson v. State, 274 Ind. 218, 409 N.E.2d 637 (1980); See also Note, 72 N.C.L.Rev. 1721 (1994) (reviewing application of plain error doctrine in North Carolina, and collecting cases in which the state's courts have rejected pleas to overturn criminal convictions based on the plain error rule).

[121]State v. Moore, 575 S.W.2d 253 (Mo.App.1978).

[122]United States v. Olano, 507 U.S. 725, 113 S.Ct. 1770, 123 L.Ed.2d 508 (1993).

[123]Johnson v. United States, 520 U.S. 461, 117 S.Ct. 1544, 137 L.Ed.2d 718 (1997).

52(b). As the Court summarized in *Johnson*, an appellate court can correct an error not raised at trial only if there is (1) error, (2) that is plain, (3) that "affects substantial rights," and (4) "seriously affects the fairness, integrity, or public reputation of judicial proceedings." Applying this analysis, the Court held that neither the *Olano* trial court's violation of Federal Rule 24(c), in allowing alternate jurors to be present during jury deliberations,[124] nor the failure to submit the question of materiality to the jury in a perjury prosecution in *Johnson*, qualified as "plain error" subject to correction under Rule 52.

Initially, the Court in *Olano* reasoned, for an error to be presented, the appellant must have "forfeited" his right to review of an error by the failure to make a timely assertion of right rather than "waived" his right to review that error.[125] Second, the error must be "plain," which "is synonymous with "clear," or equivalently "obvious." At a minimum," the Court explained, the error must be "clear under current law." *Johnson* added that clear errors will also include actions that violated rules established after trial but applied retroactively on direct review. In *Johnson*, the Court concluded that even though the trial court's action was not recognized as error by the Supreme Court until after *Johnson*'s trial,[126] "it is enough that an error be "plain" at the time of appellate consideration," at least in a case where "the law at the time of trial was settled and clearly contrary to the law at the time of appeal." Otherwise, defense counsel would "inevitably" make "a long and virtually useless laundry list of objections to rulings that were plainly supported by existing precedent."

The third requirement specified in *Olano* was that the error must "affec[t] substantial rights," in that the error "must have been prejudicial" in the sense of "affect[ing] the outcome" of the lower court proceedings. Here, however, in contrast to a harmless error inquiry,[127] "the defendant rather than the Government bears the burden of persuasion with respect to prejudice." In *Olano*, the Court concluded that the erroneous presence of alternate jurors during deliberations did not meet this requirement, noting that the defendants had not shown that the error had prejudiced them

---

[124]The Rule provides that "an alternate juror who does not replace a regular juror shall be discharged after the jury retires to consider its verdict."

[125]See notes 50–68 (discussing waiver). The Court noted in this connection: "Whether a particular right is waivable; whether the defendant must participate personally in the waiver; whether certain procedures are required for waiver; and whether the defendant's choice must be particularly informed or voluntary, all depend on the right at stake." See also § 11.6.

[126]See United States v. Gaudin, 515 U.S. 506, 115 S.Ct. 2310, 132 L.Ed.2d 444 (1995), decided after Johnson's trial, held that the materiality element of perjury must be submitted to the jury.

[127]See § 27.6(b).

and refusing to find that the error was "inherently prejudicial."[128]

Reasoning that the burden of establishing entitlement to relief for plain error "should not be too easy," the Court in *United States v. Dominguez Benitez*,[129] held that a defendant who seeks relief for plain error for a violation of Federal Rule 11 must show "a reasonable probability that, but for the error, he would not have entered the plea." This standard, the Court noted, "should not be confused with a requirement that a defendant prove by a preponderance of the evidence that but for error things would have been different."[130] In *Dominguez Benitez*, the judge had advised the defendant at his plea hearing that his plea agreement would not bind her in setting his sentence, but failed to warn him specifically, as Rule 11 mandates, that he could not withdraw his plea if she later rejected the sentencing recommendations in the agreement. The judge later rejected the sentencing reduction stipulated to in the agreement. On review, the Supreme Court stated that it was "hard to see here how the warning could have had an effect on the defendant's assessment of his strategic position," when the omitted warning was included in the agreement itself, evidence of guilt was strong, the defendant himself had made it clear earlier that he did not intend to go to trial and had not known about, much less relied upon, the sentencing reduc-

---

[128]In *Johnson*, the Court declined to decide whether an error that qualifies as a "structural error" evading harmless error review would automatically qualify as one "affecting substantial rights." Several federal courts have held that it does. United States v. Recio, 371 F.3d 1093 (9th Cir.2004) ("At least two other circuits have recognized that structural errors satisfy the third prong of the *Olano* test, [citing United States v. Vazquez, 271 F.3d 93, 100 (3d Cir.2001) and United States v. David, 83 F.3d 638, 646–47 (4th Cir.1996)]. "We now join these circuits and hold that a finding of structural error satisfies the third prong of the *Olano* test."). See also State v. Garrard, 170 Ohio App.3d 487, 867 N.E.2d 887 (Ohio App.2007) (finding that denial of closing argument was "structural error mandates a finding of 'per se prejudice.' " * * * * and affected appellant's "substantial rights," but declining relief nevertheless based on the fourth prong of the plain error test); The First Circuit has

stated the same in dicta. See U.S. v. Padilla, 415 F.3d 211 (1st Cir. 2005). See also U.S. v. Rodriguez, 406 F.3d 1261 (11th Cir.2005) (Carnes, J., concurring) ("So far as can be discovered, no court has ever actually held that an error is structural but fails to meet the fourth prong of the plain error test."); State v. Garrard, 170 Ohio App.3d 487, 867 N.E.2d 887 (Ohio App.2007) (finding that denial of closing argument was "structural error mandates a finding of 'per se prejudice.' " * * * * and affected appellant's "substantial rights," but declining relief nevertheless based on the fourth prong of the plain error test).

[129]United States v. Dominguez Benitez, 542 U.S. 74, 124 S.Ct. 2333, 159 L.Ed.2d 157 (2004).

[130]Justice Scalia concurred, stating that the standard should be a preponderance—more likely than not — rather than the "reasonable probability" standard of *Strickland* and *Bagley*.

tion at issue.[131]

Finally, the Court in *Olano* explained, Rule 52(b) is "permissive rather than mandatory," allowing rather than requiring correction when an error is found to be "plain" and "affecting substantial rights." In previous cases the Court had indicated that this discretion should be employed "in those circumstances in which a miscarriage of justice would otherwise result."[132] However, in contrast to the position taken in its habeas corpus jurisprudence,[133] this use of "miscarriage of justice" in plain-error cases was not meant to restrict plain-error review to only those errors that caused "the conviction or sentencing of an actually innocent defendant." An appellate court should, in addition, "correct a plain forfeited error affecting substantial rights if the error 'seriously affects the fairness, integrity, or public reputation of judicial proceedings.'" This determination, the Court later explained in *Johnson*, was to be made on an analysis of the facts of the individual case. In *Johnson*, the record showed that the error in question—failure to submit the element of materiality to the jury—did not seriously affect either the outcome, or the "fairness, integrity, or public reputation of judicial proceedings" because the evidence supporting materiality was "overwhelming." "Indeed," the Court ventured, "it would be the reversal of a conviction such as this which would have that effect." Despite the Court's representations in *Johnson*, it is not clear what showing other than innocence would warrant relief under Rule 52(b) when the defendant raises a challenge to a conviction.[134] The Court's

---

[131]The holding in *Dominguez Benitez* may be limited to violations of Rule 11 as opposed to more fundamental errors in the guilty plea process. The Court noted in dicta that it was not suggesting that a conviction based on a *Boykin* violation—where the record lacks evidence that the defendant knew of the rights he was waiving— "could be saved even by overwhelming evidence that the defendant would have pleaded guilty regardless." See § 21.4(e).

[132]See United States v. Frady, 456 U.S. 152, 102 S.Ct. 1584, 71 L.Ed.2d 816 (1982); United States v. Young, 470 U.S. 1, 105 S.Ct. 1038, 84 L.Ed.2d 1 (1985) (holding prosecutor's remarks did not constitute "plain error"). See also Annot., 84 L.Ed.2d 876 (1987) (collecting Supreme Court's application of Rule 52(b)).

[133]See § 28.4(g).

[134]Federal courts divided over the appropriate application of plain error review to claims of sentencing error after the decision United States v. Booker, 543 U.S. 220, 125 S.Ct. 738, 160 L.Ed.2d 621 (2005), discussed at § 26.4(i) at note 184. Reviewing sentences of defendants who have claimed their sentences violated the Sixth Amendment, or were imposed under the mistaken assumption that the guidelines were mandatory, some courts held that Rule 52 requires that defendants must offer some evidence that they would have received more favorable sentences under advisory guidelines. Others granted relief without demanding a showing of prejudice, rejecting as unrealistic the burden of producing evidence that a judge would have sentenced differently, when prior

unanimous decision in *United States v. Cotton*,[135] in which defendants objected on appeal to the government's failure to allege an element of the greater drug offense for which they were sentenced, illustrates how difficult this fourth step is to overcome if proof of guilt is strong. The *Cotton* Court refused to grant relief, noting the "overwhelming and uncontroverted evidence" that the defendants were guilty of the greater offense.

The Court has furnished one example of a rare case where unraised error requires relief despite the absence of a showing of prejudice. The Court in *Nguyen v. United States*[136] sidestepped the *Olano* analysis, and vacated, under the Court's supervisory powers, an appellate order upholding the convictions of two drug defendants, because the appellate panel included a non-Article III judge. The majority reasoned that neither the failure to object nor an express stipulation of the parties could create authority that Congress had withheld. Rejecting the dissenters' argument that under *Olano* no relief was required, the majority noted that allowing the judgment to stand would "call into serious question the integrity as well as the public reputation of judicial proceedings * * * for *no one* other than a properly constituted panel of Article III judges was empowered to exercise appellate jurisdiction in these cases."

Although many states follow the federal formula,[137] a few states shift the burden to the prosecution to prove lack of prejudice

---

to *Booker* judges had no reason to make comments on the record concerning their dissatisfaction with guidelines ranges or to speculate about the sentences they might impose without the guidelines. Still other courts adopted a third approach, granting a "limited remand" to defendants who establish *Booker* error, so that the trial court may indicate whether or not the defendant might have been sentenced differently under advisory guidelines. Compare U.S. v. Rodriguez, 406 F.3d 1261 (11th Cir.2005) (requiring defendant show prejudice), and United States v. Serrano-Beauvaix, 400 F.3d 50 (1st Cir.2005) (following *Rodriguez*), with United States v. Barnett, 398 F.3d 516 (6th Cir.2005) (following *Hughes*), with United States v. Crosby, 397 F.3d 103 (2d Cir.2005) (requiring remand but only for the limited purpose of asking the trial court to indicate whether a different sentence might have been entered) and United States v. Paladino, 401 F.3d 471 (7th

Cir.2005) (following *Crosby*).

[135]United States v. Cotton, 535 U.S. 625, 122 S.Ct. 1781, 152 L.Ed.2d 860 (2002).

[136]Nguyen v. United States, 539 U.S. 69, 123 S.Ct. 2130, 156 L.Ed.2d 64 (2003).

[137]Several states have adopted the four-part test of *Olano*. See Belisle v. State, — So.2d. —, 2007 WL 625025 (Ala.Cr.App.2007); Brown v. State, 729 A.2d 259 (Del. 1999); Rogers v. State, 247 Ga.App. 219, 543 S.E.2d 81 (2000); People v. Grant, 445 Mich. 535, 520 N.W.2d 123 (1994); State v. Reed, 737 N.W.2d 572, 2007 WL 2389774 (Minn. 2007); State v. Chew, 150 N.J. 30, 695 A.2d 1301 (N.J.1997); State v. Olander, 575 N.W.2d 658 (N.D.1998); State v. Barnes, 94 Ohio St.3d 21, 759 N.E.2d 1240 (2002); State v. Yoh, 180 Vt. 317, 910 A.2d 853 (2006). See also People v. Herron, 215 Ill.2d 167, 294 Ill.Dec. 55, 830 N.E.2d 467 (2005) ("the plain-error doctrine bypasses normal forfei-

rather than requiring the defendant to prove that the error may have affected the outcome,[138] or for specific errors require the state to carry the same burden on appeal that it would had the defendant made a timely objection.[139]

§ 27.5(e) Standard of review

Assuming review is not precluded by the doctrines examined in the preceding sections, a reviewing court must decide how much deference to accord the trial court's decision in order to determine whether or not that decision was erroneous. As in civil cases, different standards of review are used by appellate courts to examine different types of trial court decisions. The Supreme Court has summed up the law on this topic succinctly: "For purposes of standard of review, decisions by judges are traditionally divided into three categories, denominated questions of law (reviewable de novo), questions of fact (reviewable for clear error), and matters of discretion (reviewable for "abuse of discretion")."[140] This subsection discusses when and why the different standards of review will apply on direct appeal in a criminal case.[141]

For some issues on appeal, the standard of review will be dictated by statute. When not specified by statute, courts will

---

ture principles and allows a reviewing court to consider unpreserved error when either (1) the evidence is close, regardless of the seriousness of the error, or (2) the error is serious, regardless of the closeness of the evidence"); People v. Johnson, 208 Ill.2d 53, 281 Ill.Dec. 1, 803 N.E.2d 405 (2004) (under Illinois plain error rule, courts may review unpreserved error when "(1) the evidence in a criminal case is closely balanced or (2) the error is so fundamental and of such magnitude that the accused is denied the right to a fair trial and remedying the error is necessary to preserve the integrity of the judicial process"); State v. Mead, 105 S.W.3d 552 (Mo.App.2003) (appellant must demonstrate error so substantially violated his rights that manifest injustice would result if the error were left uncorrected); State v. Smith, 24 S.W.3d 274 (Tenn. 2000) (adopting five-factor test); State v. Cruz, 122 P.3d 543 (Utah 2005) (applying three-part test that "differs slightly" from the analysis in Utah); State v. Miller, 194 W.Va. 3, 459 S.E.2d 114 (1995). See also Becker, To Review or Not to Review: The Plain Truth About Illinois' Plain Error Rule, 37 Loyola U.Chi.L.Rev. 455 (2006).

[138]State v. King, 205 Wis.2d 81, 555 N.W.2d 189 (1996) (state must prove plain error is harmless).

[139]State v. Nichols, 111 Haw. 327, 141 P.3d 974 (2006) (holding the same standard of review is to be applied both in cases in which a timely objection to a jury instruction was made and those in which no timely objection was made, noting that the duty to properly instruct the jury lies with the court, finding the harmfulness of an erroneous instruction must be presumed).

[Section 27.5(e)]

[140]Pierce v. Underwood, 487 U.S. 552, 108 S.Ct. 2541, 101 L.Ed.2d 490 (1988).

[141]Standards of review in collateral proceedings are discussed in Chapter 28. For comprehensive treatment, see S. Childress & M. Davis, 2 Federal Standards of Review (1992 & Supp.1997).

choose the standard to apply.[142] In general, concerns of efficiency and accuracy will determine the standard applied. Deferential standards of review are used when the trial judge is likely to have more information or expertise than reviewing judges, or when uniform rules to guide trial courts are not essential. Although states clearly are free to adopt standards of direct review for federal constitutional issues that are more exacting than those adopted by federal courts,[143] because the standard of review (like the applicability of harmless error) is part and parcel of the federal right itself, a state court may be prohibited from adopting standards of review that are more deferential than the standards adopted by federal courts.

Abuse of discretion review. Some trial court decisions are considered erroneous only if the reviewing court determines that the trial court "abused its discretion." Abuse of discretion has been defined variously as "exceeding the bounds of reason or disregard of the rules or principles of law or practice,"[144] a decision "no reasonable person" could reach[145] or one that leaves the appellate court with a "definite and firm conviction that the district court committed a clear error of judgment."[146] This most lenient oversight is applied to decisions to admit or exclude evidence,[147] to rulings on motions for recusal,[148] substitution of counsel,[149] continuance,[150] severance,[151] discovery,[152] challenges for cause,[153] jury

---

[142]See State v. Thurman, 846 P.2d 1256 (Utah 1993) ("Unless constrained by a constitutional or statutory provision, we exercise our power to fashion standards of review that we think best allocate responsibility between appellate and trial courts in light of the particular determination under review.").

[143]See, e.g., Greene v. Georgia, 519 U.S. 145, 117 S.Ct. 578, 136 L.Ed.2d 507 (1996) (per curiam).

[144]State v. Adams, 76 Haw. 408, 879 P.2d 513 (1994).

[145]United States v. Hughes, 970 F.2d 227 (7th Cir.1992).

[146]In re Grand Jury Investigation, 974 F.2d 1068 (9th Cir.1992).

[147]See Old Chief v. United States, 519 U.S. 172, 117 S.Ct. 644, 136 L.Ed.2d 574 (1997); United States v. Abel, 469 U.S. 45, 105 S.Ct. 465, 83 L.Ed.2d 450 (1984); State v. Crea, 119 Idaho 352, 806 P.2d 445 (1991); State v. Most, 578 N.W.2d 250 (Iowa App.

1998). Some states use a slightly different formula, reviewing evidentiary rulings for "manifest error." See, e.g., Qualls v. State, 961 P.2d 765 (Nev. 1998).

[148]United States v. Franco, 163 F.3d 1359 (11th Cir.1998).

[149]State v. Langley, 314 Or. 247, 839 P.2d 692 (1992).

[150]State v. Oatman, 275 Mont. 139, 911 P.2d 213 (1996); State v. Thomson, 123 Wash.2d 877, 872 P.2d 1097 (1994).

[151]State v. Dent, 123 Wash.2d 467, 869 P.2d 392 (1994); United States v. Brown, 16 F.3d 423 (D.C.Cir.1994).

[152]E.g., Bracy v. Gramley, 520 U.S. 899, 117 S.Ct. 1793, 138 L.Ed.2d 97 (1997).

[153]Brown v. State, 913 S.W.2d 577 (Tex.Cr.App.1996). But compare Wainwright v. Witt, 469 U.S. 412, 105 S.Ct. 844, 83 L.Ed.2d 841 (1985) (applying clearly erroneous review for

instructions,[154] specific performance of plea agreements,[155] as well as motions for mistrial or new trial.[156]

Sentencing decisions in many jurisdictions are subject only to review for abuse of discretion.[157] In some states, sentences are evaluated under an even less exacting "shock-the-conscience" standard.[158] Death sentences are often provided more rigorous appellate review.[159]

Decisions reviewed for abuse of discretion share one or more common characteristics. They often depend upon the trial judge's first-hand observations of the litigants and the evidence, observations that cannot be replicated by reviewing judges who have ac-

---

findings "concerning the venireman's state of mind," which are factual findings "based upon determination of demeanor and credibility that are peculiarly within a trial judge's province" and are "entitled to deference * * * on direct review").

[154]United States v. Giraldi, 86 F.3d 1368 (5th Cir.1996) (a district court abuses its discretion in denying a requested instruction if: "(1) the requested instruction is substantively correct; (2) the requested instruction is not substantially covered in the charge given to the jury; and (3) the omission of the instruction would seriously impair the defendant's ability to present his defense"); United States v. Fawley, 137 F.3d 458 (7th Cir.1998) ("Because the trial court is in the best position to make decisions regarding jury guidance and evidentiary matters, the appellate court must give special deference to the rulings of the trial court."); State v. Blankenship, 198 W.Va. 290, 480 S.E.2d 178 (1996).

[155]United States v. Anthony, 93 F.3d 614 (9th Cir.1996). See also McCard v. State, 78 P.3d 1040, 1042–43 (Wyo.2003) ("[t]he findings of fact that led to denial of a motion to withdraw a guilty plea are subject to the clearly erroneous standard of review, while the decision to deny the motion is reversed only if it constituted an abuse of discretion," quoting 3 C. Wright, N. King & S. Klein, Federal Practice and Procedure: Criminal 2d § 538 (Supp.2003)).

[156]United States v. Ferguson, 246 F.3d 129 (2d Cir.2001) (applying abuse-of-discretion review to trial court's order granting new trial based on finding that verdict was against the great weight of the evidence, rejecting government argument that a less deferential review standard should apply for reviewing this type of new-trial order); United States v. Gabaldon, 91 F.3d 91 (10th Cir.1996) (mistrial); United States v. Boyd, 55 F.3d 239 (7th Cir.1995) (new trial); United States v. Rapanos, 115 F.3d 367 (6th Cir.1997) (new trial); State v. Menzies, 845 P.2d 220 (Utah 1992) (new trial).

[157]State v. Griffin, 83 Haw. 105, 924 P.2d 1211 (1996) (sentencing subject to abuse of discretion review). See also Rita v. United States, __U.S. __, 127 S.Ct. 2456, 168 L.Ed.2d 203 (2007) (an appellate court conducting reasonableness review of a federal sentence "merely asks whether the trial court abused its discretion").

[158]See, e.g., State v. Megargel, 143 N.J. 484, 673 A.2d 259 (1996) ("shock-the-conscience"); State v. Anderson, 546 N.W.2d 395 (S.D.1996) (same).

[159]Clemons v. Mississippi, 494 U.S. 738, 110 S.Ct. 1441, 108 L.Ed.2d 725, 749 (1990) (review of weighing of aggravating and mitigating factors de novo). For a collection of authority and an example of one state's decision to review each death sentence de novo, see Hoffmann, Protecting the Innocent: The Massachusetts Governor's Council Report, 95 J.Crim.L. & Criminology 561, 576–583 (2005).

cess only to the written record. Second, they often involve the judge's ability to control the trial proceedings. Third, decisions reviewed for abuse of discretion often address issues about which the trial judge has a greater understanding than an appellate judge. Finally, discretionary decisions tend to be context specific and resistant to general rules.[160]

Clearly erroneous review. Factual findings by trial judges may form the basis for relief on appeal if found to be "clearly erroneous." Judge Learned Hand once concluded that "it is idle to try and unpack the meaning of the phrase, "clearly erroneous.""[161] Nevertheless, other judges have tried, explaining that a finding of fact is clearly erroneous when a "court is left with a firm and definite conviction that a mistake has been committed."[162] The differences between this standard and the abuse of discretion standard are somewhat elusive, to say the least.[163] This type of review is common for decisions concerning the presence or absence of discriminatory intent,[164] the competency of a defendant,[165] the breach of plea agreements,[166] the intelligence and voluntariness of waivers,[167] and factual decisions underlying rulings on motions to suppress.[168]

Appeals of guilty verdicts by juries and guilty findings by judges based on insufficiency of evidence are evaluated by asking, "whether, after viewing the evidence in the light most favorable to the prosecution, any rational trier of fact could have found the essential elements beyond a reasonable doubt."[169] At least one state court applies a review standard with different phrasing, al-

---

[160]On abuse of discretion review in criminal cases, see generally S. Childress & M. Davis, 2 Federal Standards of Review § 11.01 (1992 & Supp. 1997).

[161]See United States v. Aluminum Co. of America, 148 F.2d 416 (2d Cir. 1945).

[162]United States v. United States Gypsum Co., 333 U.S. 364, 68 S.Ct. 525, 92 L.Ed. 746 (1948); State v. Hin Chow, 77 Hawaii 241, 883 P.2d 663 (1994).

[163]See, e.g., Comment, Hawaii Appellate Standards of Review Revisited, 18 Haw.L.Rev. 645, 652–53 (1996).

[164]See, e.g., United States v. James, 113 F.3d 721, 728 (7th Cir.1997) (holding that the clearly erroneous standard of review applies to the trial court's findings under *Batson*); Whitsey

v. State, 796 S.W.2d 707 (Tex.Cr.App. 1989) (same). See also State v. Quinn, 169 Wis.2d 620, 486 N.W.2d 542 (Wis.App.1992) (reviewing finding that prosecutor did not intend to provoke mistrial).

[165]Maggio v. Fulford, 462 U.S. 111, 103 S.Ct. 2261, 76 L.Ed.2d 794 (1983); Roberts v. Secretary of State, 334 Ark. 244, 973 S.W.2d 797 (1998).

[166]State v. Starcher, 195 W.Va. 185, 465 S.E.2d 185 (1995); St. James v. People, 948 P.2d 1028 (Colo.1997).

[167]Riggs v. Humphrey, 334 Ark. 231, 972 S.W.2d 946 (1998) (review of waiver of appeal).

[168]State v. Glaesman, 545 N.W.2d 178 (N.D.1996); State v. Anderson, 84 Haw. 462, 935 P.2d 1007 (1997).

[169]Jackson v. Virginia, 443 U.S. 307, 99 S.Ct. 2781, 61 L.Ed.2d 560 (1979); United States v. Harris, 491

though probably reaching similar results.[170]

De novo review. Although the trial judge's better vantage point for making factual assessments warrants greater deference to the fact-findings of a trial judge,[171] appellate judges are equally well situated to decide legal questions. Indeed, appellate courts may have more time to concentrate on the law and benefit from deliberation as a panel, which can reduce the risk of error.[172] Consequently, determinations of law by the trial court are reviewed *de novo* on direct appeal and no weight is given to the legal conclusions of the trial judge. De novo review also promotes uniformity and predictability.[173] This is especially important for "fluid concepts that take their substantive content from the particular contexts in which the standards are being assessed," such as probable cause or reasonable suspicion.[174] Questions reviewed in this manner include questions of statutory or constitutional interpretation[175] and questions concerning the scope of the attorney client privilege.[176]

Mixed questions of law and fact requiring the application of

F.3d 440 (D.C.Cir.2007); Hartman v. Bagley, 492 F.3d 347 (6th Cir.2007); United States v. Jones, 84 F.3d 1206 (9th Cir.1996). Compare Ex parte Mason, 711 So.2d 468 (Ala.1998) (sufficiency of evidence for jury's guilty verdict is reviewed by asking "whether the jury might reasonably find that the evidence excluded every reasonable hypothesis except that of guilt; not whether such evidence excludes every reasonable hypothesis, but whether a jury might reasonably so conclude"). See also § 24.6(b) at note 38 (discussing Jackson); S. Childress & M. Davis, 2 Federal Standards of Review § 9.01–9.04 (1992 & Supp. 1997). The decision of the trial judge to deny a motion for acquittal at the close of all the evidence will be reviewed with great deference as well. Courts will "consider the evidence in the light most favorable to the government, drawing 'all reasonable inferences and credibility choice made in support of the verdict.' " See § 24.11(a).

[170]Hale v. State, 343 Ark. 62, 31 S.W.3d 850 (2000) (reaffirming *Jones*); Jones v. State, 269 Ark. 119, 598 S.W.2d 748 (1980) (refusing to abandon standard requiring substantial evidence supporting jury's verdict in favor of *Jackson's* "rational-fact-finder"

test).

[171]See Anderson v. Bessemer City, 470 U.S. 564, 105 S.Ct. 1504, 84 L.Ed.2d 518 (1985).

[172]See Kelso, Special Report on California Appellate Justice: A Report on the California Appellate System, 45 Hastings L.J. 433, 468 (1994).

[173]See Ornelas v. United States, 517 U.S. 690, 116 S.Ct. 1657, 134 L.Ed.2d 911 (1996).

[174]Cooper Industries, Inc. v. Leatherman Tool Group, Inc., 532 U.S. 424, 121 S.Ct. 1678, 149 L.Ed.2d 674 (2001), quoting Ornelas v. United States, 517 U.S. 690, 116 S.Ct. 1657, 134 L.Ed.2d 911 (1996).

[175]See also United States v. Fonseca-Martinez, 36 F.3d 62 (9th Cir.1994) (reviewing availability of writ of audita querela under de novo standard).

[176]In re Grand Jury Subpoena 92-1(SJ), 31 F.3d 826 (9th Cir.1994) (reviewing de novo "whether an evidentiary showing is sufficient to allow in camera inspection" and noting that if the requisite evidentiary showing is made, the decision to allow inspection is reviewed by abuse of discretion).

legal principles to historical fact usually receive de novo review as well.[177] For example, whether or not there was probable cause to justify a warrantless search,[178] whether a defendant had received the notice required by due process,[179] was denied the effective assistance of counsel,[180] or whether a statute as applied to a defendant violates the First Amendment[181] are all questions reviewed de novo on appeal.[182]

§ 27.6 Harmless error on appeal

§ 27.6(a)   Origins of harmless error review
§ 27.6(b)   Harmless error review of nonconstitutional errors
§ 27.6(c)   Application to constitutional violations
§ 27.6(d)   Harmless error or automatic reversal
§ 27.6(e)   Applying the reasonable doubt standard for
             constitutional errors

§ 27.6(a) Origins of harmless error review

Harmless error review has been termed "the most far-reaching doctrinal change in American procedural jurisprudence since its inception."[1] Harmless error principles, it has been said, "may determine the outcome of more criminal appeals than any other doctrine."[2]Although not well established in the United States until the twentieth century, the practice of applying the concept of harmless error to the review of criminal cases had its roots in English jurisprudence. During the mid-1800s the English courts

---

[177]See e.g., Thompson v. Keohane, 516 U.S. 99, 116 S.Ct. 457, 133 L.Ed.2d 383 (1995); Pederson v. State, 692 N.W.2d 452 (Minn.2005) (because materiality issues under *Brady* combine issues of fact and law, the proper standard of review is de novo).

[178]Ornelas v. United States, 517 U.S. 690, 116 S.Ct. 1657, 134 L.Ed.2d 911 (1996); United States v. Khounsavanh, 113 F.3d 279 (1st Cir.1997); Connor v. State, 803 So.2d 598 (Fla.2001) (discussing review of rulings on suppression motions). See also State v. Thurman, 846 P.2d 1256 (Utah 1993) (adopting de novo review to determinations of the voluntariness of consent to fourth amendment purposes).

[179]United States v. Havier, 155 F.3d 1090 (9th Cir.1998).

[180]United States v. Blackwell, 127 F.3d 947 (10th Cir.1997); Oliver v. Wainwright, 782 F.2d 1521 (11th Cir. 1986); State v. Orr, 262 Kan. 312, 940 P.2d 42 (1997); State v. Madison, 163 Vt. 360, 658 A.2d 536 (1995).

[181]Farina v. United States, 622 A.2d 50 (D.C.App.1993).

[182]See also United States v. James, 257 F.3d 1173 (10th Cir.2001) (de novo review appropriate for reviewing an order granting or denying a motion for discovery based on selective prosecution).

[Section 27.6(a)]

[1]Childress & Davis, Federal Standards of Review § 7.01 (2d ed.1986).

[2]Solomon, Causing Constitutional Harm: How Tort Law Can Help Determine Harmless Error in Criminal Trials, 99 N.W.L.Rev 1053 (2005) (collecting authority).

adopted a rule of appellate review that became known as the Exchequer Rule.[3] Under that rule, a trial error as to the admission of evidence was presumed to have caused prejudice and therefore required a new trial. The presumption of prejudice was designed to ensure that the appellate court did not encroach upon the jury's fact-finding function by discounting the improperly admitted evidence and sustaining the conviction on the court's belief that the remaining evidence established guilt. The presumption of prejudice was stringently applied to even the most insignificant items of evidence, and a similar policy was extended to errors in jury instruction. As a result, retrials became so commonplace that English litigation "seemed to survive until the parties expired."[4] Parliament responded with the Judicature Act of 1873, which stated that the Court of Appeal was not to order a new trial on the basis of "the improper admission or rejection of evidence" or a "misdirection" of the jury "unless in the opinion of the Court of Appeal some substantial wrong or miscarriage has thereby been occasioned."[5] Exactly what constituted a "substantial wrong" or "miscarriage of justice" was left for judicial definition, but the courts were clearly directed to look to the actual impact of the error upon the outcome of the proceeding, and not simply to assume that every error in the admission of evidence or the charging of the jury was per se prejudicial.

Early American courts adopted the Exchequer Rule from English law, extending it to a wide range of trial errors. However, when the rule was subsequently rejected in England, American courts did not follow suit immediately. Retrials for seemingly insignificant errors mounted, and appellate courts were criticized as "impregnable citadels of technicality."[6] Reformers urged adoption of harmless error legislation. Their efforts began to bear fruit during the early 1900s when a substantial number of states adopted such legislation.[7] By the 1960s "all 50 states [had] harm-

---

[3]See R. Traynor, The Riddle of Harmless Error 6–10 (1970); 1 J. Wigmore, Evidence § 21 (3d ed.1940).

[4]Goldberg, Harmless Error: Constitutional Sneak Thief, 71 J.Crim.L. & Criminology 421, 422 (1980).

[5]See R. Traynor, The Riddle of Harmless Error 10–11 (1970), for a review of the English legislation.

[6]Kavanaugh, Improvement of Administration of Criminal Justice by Exercise of Judicial Power, 11 A.B.A.J. 217, 222 (1925).

[7]By the mid-1920s, 18 states had adopted harmless error legislation and "ten states had reached the same result by judicial action." Sunderland, The Problem of Appellate Review, 5 Tex.L.Rev. 126, 147 (1926). See also People v. Mateo, 453 Mich. 203, 551 N.W.2d 891 (1996) (tracing the history of harmless error legislation in Michigan); Simpson v. State, 876 P.2d 690 (Okla.Cr.App.1994) (same, for Oklahoma).

less error statutes or rules."[8]

Unlike the English harmless error legislation, the provisions authorizing harmless error review in the United States were not limited to specific types of errors. American courts had been criticized as much for their treatment of technical pleading errors as for reversals due to incorrect admission of insignificant evidence.[9] The federal statute, adopted in 1919, provided the model for much of the state legislation. It required a federal appellate court to "give judgment after an examination of the entire record before the court, without regard to technical errors, defects, or exceptions which do not affect the substantial rights of the parties."[10]

For decades, these statutes were applied only to claims of nonconstitutional error. In the 1960s, with the expansion of the constitutional regulation of the criminal process, appellate courts extended harmless error analysis to constitutional violations as well, a practice authorized by the United States Supreme Court in *Chapman v. California*.[11] Contemporary harmless error rules may differ, however, depending upon whether the procedural defect reviewed is one that violates constitutional command, or is an error under statute or common law. Accordingly, the discussion that follows begins with an examination of the appellate review of nonconstitutional error, then turns to the application of harmless error doctrine to constitutional violations.

---

[8]Chapman v. California, 386 U.S. 18, 87 S.Ct. 824, 17 L.Ed.2d 705 (1967), discussed infra note 64.

[9]See, e.g., Wigmore, Criminal Procedure: "Good" Reversals and "Bad" Reversals, 4 Ill.L.Rev. 352 (1909). Judge Harry Edwards recounts one notorious example "in which the court reversed a conviction for rape on the ground that the indictment described the charged offense as "against the peace and dignity of state," rather than "against the peace and dignity of *the* state, as the Missouri Constitution required." Edwards, To Err is Human, But Not Always Harmless: When Should Legal Error Be Tolerated?, 70 N.Y.U.L.Rev. 1167, 1174 (1995) (quoting State v. Campbell, 210 Mo. 202, 109 S.W. 706 (Mo.1908)).

[10]Act of Feb. 26, 1919, ch. 48, 40 Stat. 1181. See also 28 U.S.C.A. § 2111 and Fed.R.Crim.P. 52(a), both based on this provision. Although there had been a movement to limit the federal harmless error provision to civil cases, it was made applicable to "any case, civil or criminal." 40 Stat. 1181. See Goldberg, Harmless Error: Constitutional Sneak Thief, 71 J.Crim.L. & Criminology 421, 422 (1980). The earlier state provisions are collected in ALI, Code of Criminal Procedure 1302–04 (1931). Provisions modeled after Fed.R.Crim.P. 52(a) are found in most of these states with rules similar to the Federal Rules. See, e.g., Ohio R.Crim.P. 52(A); N.D.R. Crim.P. 52(a).

[11]Chapman v. California, 386 U.S. 18, 87 S.Ct. 824, 17 L.Ed.2d 705 (1967), discussed in § 27.6(c).

§ 27.6(b) Harmless error review of nonconstitutional errors

American appellate courts initially applied harmless error legislation differently to different types of rights. In judging the impact of an error on a matter such as jury selection, courts focused on whether the error had resulted in a "miscarriage of justice," that is, whether the error was technical in nature or deprived the defendant of the substance of what that right was designed to provide.[12] However, where the error related to the admission or evaluation of evidence, the reviewing court asked not whether the defendant had been denied the basic benefit of the evidentiary rule, but whether the error had produced a miscarriage of justice as measured by its likely impact upon the outcome of the proceeding. For example, if a trial judge erroneously admitted hearsay, the issue was not simply whether the particular violation of the hearsay rule was "technical" (e.g., where the court admitted a single hearsay statement that would have fit within a hearsay exception but for some minor detail); even if a substantial quantity of patently inadmissible hearsay evidence had been introduced, the court still had to decide whether that evidence had a sufficient bearing upon the total evidentiary picture to require a reversal.[13]

Building upon these earlier distinctions in review based on the type of right violated, some American courts reviewing nonconstitutional errors today continue to use two modes of analysis when applying harmless error statutes. The first, which considers the likely impact of the error on case outcome, is applied to trial errors that determine what evidence is presented to the jury, such as rulings on admissibility[14] and joinder.[15] It also is applied to erroneous pretrial rulings that have an impact upon the presentation of evidence, such as rulings on discovery,[16] and to actions of the judge and prosecutor that may have influenced the jury in its

---

[Section 27.6(b)]

[12]See, e.g., Reynolds v. Commonwealth, 133 Va. 760, 112 S.E. 707 (1922); Long v. State, 109 Ohio St. 77, 141 N.E. 691 (1923); People v. Moore, 64 Cal.App. 328, 221 P. 665 (1923). Even if the defendant was denied the substance of the right by the seating of an unqualified juror, if the defendant could have cured the error by exercise of an available peremptory challenge and failed to do so, the error was viewed as harmless. See, e.g., Hoyt v. United States, 273 F. 792 (2d Cir.1921).

[13]Walls v. State, 24 Ga.App. 697,

102 S.E. 43 (1920); Williams v. United States, 265 F. 625 (8th Cir.1920); People v. Pickens, 61 Cal.App. 405, 214 P. 1027 (1923).

[14]See, e.g., United States v. Ince, 21 F.3d 576 (4th Cir.1994); Note, 64 Cornell L.Rev. 538, 558–61 (1979). See also United States v. Bauer, 132 F.3d 504 (9th Cir.1997) (violation of attorney-client privilege).

[15]See, e.g., United States v. Lane, 474 U.S. 438, 106 S.Ct. 725, 88 L.Ed.2d 814 (1986), discussed at notes 24–26 infra.

[16]See, e.g., United States v. Ogbuehi, 18 F.3d 807 (9th Cir.1994)

evaluation of the evidence, such as erroneous jury instructions[17] or trial misconduct by the prosecutor.[18] Finally, this impact-on-outcome analysis is applied to violations of rules regulating plea bargaining and plea taking,[19] and to errors in sentencing.[20]

For rights that might loosely be described as concerned with the structure of the proceeding, courts have looked to a second analysis: whether the error was merely a technical violation or took from the defendant the substantive protection of the right. A violation of the substance of such a right automatically requires a new trial, so that the strength of the evidence supporting the conviction is irrelevant. Examples of this automatic-reversal analysis include decisions reviewing errors in jury selection[21] prosecu-

---

(Jencks Act violation); Commonwealth v. Donovan, 610 S.W.2d 601 (Ky.1980) (prosecution discovery).

[17] See, e.g., United States v. Simon, 995 F.2d 1236 (3d Cir.1993) (alibi instruction); Note, 64 Cornell L.Rev. 538, 553–54 (1979) (collecting cases). But see Commonwealth v. Karaffa, 551 Pa. 173, 709 A.2d 887 (1998) (holding that harmless error analysis cannot apply to the trial court's submission of written instructions to the jury, an action prohibited by state common law, ordering new trial).

[18] See, e.g., United States v. Zehrbach, 47 F.3d 1252 (3d Cir.1995) (finding harmless prosecutor's argument based on facts not in the record). See also United States v. Thompson, 76 F.3d 442 (2d Cir.1996) (improper encouragement of jurors to submit questions for witnesses was subject to harmless error review).

[19] See Fed.Cr.P.R. 11(h). See also Little v. Warden, 117 Nev. 845, 34 P.3d 540 (2001) (failure to advise defendant that the offense to which he is pleading guilty makes him ineligible for probation is harmless error if the record shows defendant was aware of this fact). Harmless error review of the plea proceeding is discussed in § 21.5(c).

[20] See, e.g., United States v. Gonzalez-Lerma, 71 F.3d 1537 (10th Cir.1995) (holding harmless a violation of 21 U.S.C.A. § 851(b), applying Rule 52(a), and collecting cases), over-

ruled on other grounds, United States v. Flowers, 441 F.3d 900 (10th Cir. 2006); United States v. Garcia, 78 F.3d 1457 (10th Cir.1996) (holding harmless judge's failure to comply with Federal Rule 32(c)(3)(A)).

[21] See § 22.2(f) (discussing challenges to the array). Lower courts have divided over the proper application of harmless error review to violations of the defendant's statutory right to exercise peremptory challenges. The better rule is that no substantial right is impaired so long as the jury that actually sits is impartial. This position is supported by United States v. Martinez-Salazar, 528 U.S. 304, 120 S.Ct. 774, 145 L.Ed.2d 792 (2000), where the Court failed to reach whether the failure to provide a full complement of peremptory challenges can be harmless, but noted that dicta from an earlier case suggesting that reversal is always required pre-dated the acceptance of harmless error review in the federal courts. See, e.g., People v. Bell, 473 Mich. 275, 702 N.W.2d 128 (Mich.2005) (erroneous deprivation of peremptory challenge would be reviewed under harmless error standard because the right to a peremptory challenge is of nonconstitutional dimension, distinguishing contrary authority); State v. Rivera, 108 Wash.App. 645, 32 P.3d 292 (2001) (deprivation of alternate-juror peremptory challenges can be harmless error). See also State v. Hickman, 205 Ariz. 192, 68 P.3d 418 (2003) (loss of pe-

tion by someone who was not a prosecutor,[22] and erroneous changes of venue.[23]

In the federal courts, however, all nonconstitutional, nonjurisdictional violations are reviewed under the harmless error standard of Federal Rule of Criminal Procedure 52(a), which governs the direct appeal of federal cases. For example, in *United States v. Lane*,[24] the Court stated that "Rule 52(a) admits of no broad exceptions to its applicability," rejecting "bright-line per se rules whether to conduct harmless error analysis."[25] The Court in *Lane* applied harmless error analysis to a misjoinder of parties in violation of Federal Rule 8(b). In dissent, Justice Stevens argued that such an error should not be subject to harmless error analysis for two reasons. First, Rule 8(b) implicates an "independent value besides reliability of outcome," namely "our deep abhorrence of the motion of "guilt by association." Second, the impact of the error upon the outcome "cannot be measured with precision." The

remptory challenge to cure wrongful denial of for cause challenge is no longer grounds for automatic reversal, reversing earlier precedent); State v. Lindell, 245 Wis.2d 689, 629 N.W.2d 223 (2001) (same); Pizzi & Hoffman, Jury Selection Errors on Appeal, 38 Am.Crim.L.Rev. 1391 (2001) (collecting state and federal authority on either side of the harmless error issue, criticizing *Martinez-Salazar*, and arguing that the deprivation of a peremptory challenge is harmless error).

Disagreement has also emerged over whether or not the denial of the right to allocution at sentencing can be harmless. See United States v. Adams, 252 F.3d 276 (3d Cir.2001) (denial of allocution subject to plain and harmless error review, reviewing and discussing conflicting authority); United States v. Cole, 27 F.3d 996 (4th Cir.1994) (not harmless if grounds exist upon which the court might have imposed a reduced sentence). See also United States v. Luepke, 495 F.3d 443 (7th Cir.2007) ("In our view, our colleagues in the Third and Fifth Circuits have determined correctly that, when there has been a violation of the right to allocute, a reviewing court should presume prejudice when there is any possibility that the defendant would have received a lesser sentence had the district court heard from him before imposing sentence. This ap-

proach acknowledges the immense practical difficulty facing a defendant who otherwise would have to attempt to prove that a violation affected a specific sentence; it also avoids our speculation about what the defendant might have said had the right been properly afforded him."; ordering resentencing, collecting conflicting authority).

[22]People v. Dunson, 316 Ill.App.3d 760, 250 Ill.Dec. 77, 737 N.E.2d 699 (2000) (unlicensed attorney, collecting authority); State v. Culbreath, 30 S.W.3d 309 (Tenn.2000).

[23]See, e.g., Stapleton v. State, 565 S.W.2d 532 (Tex.Cr.App.1978); Commonwealth v. Taylor, 259 Pa.Super. 484, 393 A.2d 929 (1978).

[24]United States v. Lane, 474 U.S. 438, 106 S.Ct. 725, 88 L.Ed.2d 814 (1986), also discussed in § 17.3(b).

[25]See also the opinion of Justice Brennan, concurring in part, stating, "Absent some contrary indication, then, it would seem logical to conclude that when Congress used the phrase "affect[s] the substantial rights of the parties" in the 1919 Act, Congress meant to require an inquiry into whether an error cast doubt on the verdict, not to create a class of rights as to which error was per se reversible."

majority, holding the traditional harmless error standard to be applicable, saw the Rule 8(b) restriction as directed at ensuring reliability by setting the scope of relevancy in the admission of evidence and saw the impact of its violation as no more difficult to measure than other evidentiary errors.[26]

In *United States v. Mechanik*,[27] the Court rejected defendant's claim that certain grand jury errors should be exempt from harmless error review under Rule 52(a). According to the Court, most grand jury error is *necessarily* harmless beyond a reasonable doubt if followed by an otherwise valid conviction. The Court explained that a subsequent guilty verdict renders harmless any error in failing to dismiss an indictment due to a violation of Federal Rule 6(d).[28] However, if the error during the grand jury process is raised in a motion to dismiss and considered by the trial court prior to trial, relief may be available, but only if the traditional standard for harmless error was satisfied. In explaining this pretrial application of harmless error review to grand jury error, the Court in *Bank of Nova Scotia v. United States*[29] emphasized that "a federal court may not invoke supervisory power to circumvent the harmless-error inquiry prescribed by" Rule 52(a). The Court noted, "federal courts have no more discretion to disregard the Rule's mandate than they do to disregard constitutional or statutory provisions."[30] Indeed, harmless error

---

[26]Responding to Justice Steven's independent-value argument, Justice Brennan, in a concurring opinion, noted that limitations under joinder "are based on recognition that the multiplication of charges or defendants may confuse the jury and lead to inferences of habitual criminality or guilt by association," and that those were concerns that related directly to the quality of the evidence before the jury. See also State v. Mason, 150 N.H. 53, 834 A.2d 339 (2003) (as a matter of first impression, misjoinder of criminal offenses for trial is subject to harmless error analysis, collecting authority following *Lane*).

[27]United States v. Mechanik, 475 U.S. 66, 106 S.Ct. 938, 89 L.Ed.2d 50 (1986) discussed in § 15.6(f) at notes 172–202.

[28]The Court stated that there was "no reason not to apply [Rule 52(a)] to "errors, defects, irregularities, or vari-

ances" occurring before a grand jury just as we have applied it to such error occurring during the criminal trial itself." *Mechanik* has been extended by lower courts to a variety of grand jury violations. See Note, 1988 Duke L.J. 1242 (reviewing cases assessing whether prosecutorial misconduct in the grand jury is harmless). See § 15.6(f) at notes 172–202.

[29]Bank of Nova Scotia v. United States, 487 U.S. 250, 108 S.Ct. 2369, 101 L.Ed.2d 228 (1988).

[30]See also Peguero v. United States, 526 U.S. 23, 119 S.Ct. 961, 143 L.Ed.2d 18 (1999) (observing, in the course of a decision requiring a showing of prejudice before granting habeas relief for the failure to inform a defendant of his right to appeal, that Rule 52(a) "prohibits federal courts from granting relief based on errors that 'do not affect substantial rights' ").

can be raised sua sponte.[31]

Despite these rulings, the Court has recognized at least one nonconstitutional error as grounds for automatic reversal, without regard to its impact on the outcome of the proceeding. In *Gomez v. United States*,[32] the Court considered a defense appeal based on a violation of the statute governing the duties of federal magistrates—a magistrate had supervised jury selection rather than a district court judge. The Court characterized the error as a violation of the right "to have all critical stages of a criminal trial conducted by a person with jurisdiction to preside." Equating this error to the defendant's constitutional right to an impartial adjudicator, the Court went on to hold that the violation was subject to automatic reversal.

The *Gomez* decision appears out of step with the language in *Lane* and *Nova Scotia* disapproving judicially created exceptions to Rule 52. Indeed, in interpreting a different subsection of Rule 52—the plain error provision in 52(b)—the Court in *Johnson v. United States*[33] rejected the petitioner's claim that the "error she complains of [failure to submit an essential element to the jury] is "structural"" and thus not subject to the restrictions in the Rule. The Court explained that Rule 52 "by its terms governs direct appeals from judgments of conviction in the federal system," and that creating an exception to it, even for the serious *constitutional* violation reviewed in *Johnson*, would be inappropriate and unauthorized. The same arguments certainly would support application of subsection (a) of Rule 52 to all nonconstitutional errors raised in federal cases on direct appeal. Alternatively, *Gomez* may reflect the Court's recognition that at least absent a clear statement from Congress to the contrary, errors which involve court action beyond the authority extended by Congress are essentially jurisdictional and must be corrected without regard to their impact on outcome.[34]

---

[31]United States v. Gonzalez-Flores, 418 F.3d 1093 (9th Cir.2005) (in extraordinary cases, federal courts of appeals may apply harmless error rule sua sponte, even when government does not raise it, after considering three factors: (1) the length and complexity of the record, (2) whether the harmlessness of an error is certain or debatable; and (3) the futility and costliness of reversal and further litigation; collecting authority).

[32]Gomez v. United States, 490 U.S. 858, 109 S.Ct. 2237, 104 L.Ed.2d 923 (1989).

[33]Johnson v. United States, 520 U.S. 461, 117 S.Ct. 1544, 137 L.Ed.2d 718 (1997), also discussed in § 27.5(d).

[34]See also Thomas v. Whitworth, 136 F.3d 756 (11th Cir.1998) (explaining that the harm from this type of error "flows not from the adequacy or inadequacy of the magistrate judge's handling of the jury selection process, but rather from the fact that Congress did not afford magistrate judges the power to preside over any aspect of the trial * * * without the express consent of the parties").

See also Young v. United States

In *Zedner v. United States*,[35] the Court found that Congress had impliedly repealed the application of Rule 52 to certain violations of the Speedy Trial Act. Congress provided in the Speedy Trial Act that relief shall be granted whenever a judge failed to make certain mandated findings on the record before granting an ends-of-justice continuance prior to trial. Applying harmless error review to this sort of error, the Court reasoned, would contradict the clear language of the Speedy Trial Act, as well as the "strategy" of "procedural strictness" Congress had pursued in enacting its provisions.

Once an appellate court concludes that an error is subject to harmless error review, the court must identify the proper standard for measuring the impact of the error on the outcome of the proceeding. Few areas of doctrinal development have been marked by greater twisting and turning than the development of standards for applying the harmless error rule. Its history has been described as one "of innovation and regression, of instability and uncertainty," that cannot be explained in terms of any "evolving progression of jurisprudential theories."[36]

For this reason alone, one cannot discard consideration of what may be described as the "correct result" test of harmless error, although it is doubtful that any court today continues to adhere to that standard. That test asks whether, in light of all of the admissible evidence (including any defense evidence improperly excluded), the jury's finding of guilt is clearly correct. The test rests on the premise that the defendant has not been harmed by the error if he should have been convicted in any event. Critics of

---

ex rel Vuitton et Fils S.A., 481 U.S. 787, 107 S.Ct. 2124, 95 L.Ed.2d 740 (1987), in which the Court divided over whether to treat as harmless a district court's decision to appoint as special prosecutor in a criminal contempt case the attorney for the party who had obtained the court order which the defendant had allegedly violated. Seven justices viewed that appointment as exceeding the district court's inherent authority to initiate contempt proceedings because the attorney appointed was not "disinterested." Of those seven, four argued that the violation was "fundamental and pervasive" and not subject to a traditional harmless error analysis that looked to the impact of the error upon the outcome of the proceedings. They maintained that automatic reversal was required because (1) "appointment of an interested prosecutor creates an appear-

ance of impropriety that diminishes faith in the fairness of the criminal justice system" and the "narrow focus of harmless-error analysis is not sensitive to this underlying concern"; and (2) "[d]etermining the effect of * * * [such an] appointment would be extremely difficult" since a "prosecution contains a myriad of occasions for the exercise of discretion, each of which goes to shape the record in a case, but few of which are part of the record." Three justices argued that a traditional harmless error analysis should apply.

[35]Zedner v. United States, 126 S.Ct. 1976, 164 L.Ed.2d 749 (2006), also discussed in § 18.3(b) at note 46.

[36]Saltzburg, The Harm of Harmless Error, 59 Va.L.Rev. 988, 998 (1973).

this formula contend that it converts the appellate court into the trier of fact and fails to recognize that the defendant has a right to a fair trial even when he is clearly guilty.[37]

The Supreme Court looked to both of those factors in rejecting a "correct result" standard in *Kotteakos v. United States*.[38] In the course of an extensive discussion of the harmless error guidelines to be applied by federal courts, Justice Rutledge noted:

> Some aids to right judgment may be stated more safely in negative than in affirmative form. Thus, it is not the appellate court's function to determine guilt or innocence. Nor is it to speculate upon probable reconviction and decide according to how the speculation comes out. Appellate judges cannot escape such impressions. But they may not make them sole criteria for reversal or affirmance. Those judgments are exclusively for the jury * * *. But this does not mean that the appellate court can escape altogether taking account of the outcome. To weigh the error's effect against the entire setting of the record without relation to the verdict or judgment would be almost to work in a vacuum. In criminal cases that outcome is conviction. This is different, or may be, from guilt in fact. It is guilt in law, established by the judgment of laymen. And the question is, not were they right in their judgment, regardless of the error or its effect upon the verdict. It is rather what effect the error had or reasonably may be taken to have had upon the jury's decision. The crucial thing is the impact of the thing done wrong in the minds of other men, not on one's own, in the total setting.

The Court in *Kotteakos* offered the following standard:

> If, when all is said and done, the conviction is sure that the error did not influence the jury, or had but very slight effect, the verdict and the judgment should stand, except perhaps where the departure is from a constitutional norm or a specific command of Congress.[39] But if one cannot say, with fair assurance, after pondering all that happened without stripping the erroneous action from the whole, that the judgment was not substantially swayed by the error, it is impossible to conclude that substantial rights were not affected.

While most federal courts have adhered closely to the language of *Kotteakos* in reviewing nonconstitutional error on direct appeal under Rule 52(a), several have offered somewhat different

---

[37] In dissents that had attracted considerable attention, Judge Frank had sharply criticized his Second Circuit brethren for adopting a harmless error standard that he characterized as follows: "If we, sitting on a reviewing court, believe, from merely reading the record, that a defendant is guilty, then we * * * hold that an error, in admitting evidence, even if it may seriously have prejudiced the jury against the defendant, is to be regarded as 'harmless.'" United States v. Rubenstein, 151 F.2d 915 (2d Cir.

1945). See also United States v. Antonelli Fireworks Co., 155 F.2d 631 (2d Cir.1946).

[38] Kotteakos v. United States, 328 U.S. 750, 66 S.Ct. 1239, 90 L.Ed. 1557 (1946).

[39] The error in *Kotteakos* was a violation of a common law right, but federal courts generally have found no reason to apply a different standard to violations of federal statutes or the Federal Rules. As for constitutional violations, see § 27.6(c).

descriptions of the federal harmless error test.[40] Many state courts have adopted the *Kotteakos* standard for reviewing violations of state statutes and rules.[41] Others use a variety of different phrases to describe the requisite likelihood that the error did not contribute to the verdict. Michigan has interpreted its harmless error statute to prohibit relief "unless "after an examination of the entire cause, it shall affirmatively appear" that it is more probable than not that the error was outcome determinative."[42] Courts have spoken of the lack of any "reasonable possibility" that the error might have contributed to the conviction,[43] or a "high probability" that the error did not contribute to the judgment.[44] To avoid converting such standards into a "correct result" test, states commonly stress that the appellate court's answer to the question of what would have happened without the error should not be based on the court's own satisfaction with the verdict or on whether the evidence was sufficient for the jury to have reached the same verdict. The issue, they note, is what the

---

[40]See, e.g., United States v. Simon, 995 F.2d 1236 (3d Cir.1993) (assessing whether it is "highly probable" that an alleged error did not contribute to a verdict); United States v. Hawkins, 905 F.2d 1489 (11th Cir.1990) (nonconstitutional errors "do not constitute grounds for reversal unless there is a reasonable likelihood that they affected the defendant's substantial rights"); United States v. Neuroth, 809 F.2d 339 (6th Cir.1987) (determining harmlessness by asking whether it is more probable than not, i.e., a preponderance of the evidence, that the error did not affect the verdict). See also 3A C. Wright, N. King & S. Klein, Federal Practice and Procedure, Criminal 3d, at § 854 (collecting cases).

[41]See, e.g., Simpson v. State, 876 P.2d 690 (Okla.Cr.App.1994) (adopting *Kotteakos* standard for review of nonconstitutional error).

[42]People v. Hawthorne, 474 Mich. 174, 713 N.W.2d 724 (2006) (failure to instruct on the defense of accident, a preserved, nonconstitutional error, the defendant has the burden of establishing that the error asserted resulted in a miscarriage of justice under a "more probable than not" standard); People v. Lukity, 460 Mich. 484, 596 N.W.2d 607 (1999).

[43]State v. Dinagen, 639 A.2d 1353 (R.I.1994) (nonconstitutional error is harmless if "it is not reasonably possible that such evidence would influence an average jury on the ultimate issue of guilt or innocence"). See also People v. Osband, 13 Cal.4th 622, 55 Cal.Rptr.2d 26, 919 P.2d 640 (1996) (an error will not be harmless if there is a "reasonable likelihood" that the result would have been different); State v. Urias, 609 P.2d 1326 (Utah 1980) (reasonable likelihood).

[44]State v. Shortsleeves, 580 A.2d 145 (Me.1990) (error is harmless "if it is highly probable that it did not affect the judgment"); Showker v. State, 146 Ga.App. 862, 247 S.E.2d 515 (1978). See also State v. Johnson, 664 So.2d 94 (La.1995) (asking "whether the verdict actually rendered was surely unattributable to the error"); State v. Merrill, 252 Neb. 736, 566 N.W.2d 742 (1997) ("the erroneous admission of evidence which is not cumulative may constitute harmless error beyond a reasonable doubt when the defendant's conviction is supported by overwhelming evidence which has been properly admitted or admitted without objection"); People v. Gooljar, 80 A.D.2d 860, 436 N.Y.S.2d 754 (1981).

jury actually would have done without the error.[45]

Some commentators and state courts have favored still another standard, one that resembles the analysis the United States Supreme Court has required for the review of constitutional errors. Initially adopted in a leading case by the Pennsylvania Supreme Court, this approach requires that the appellate court must be convinced "beyond a reasonable doubt" that there is no "reasonable possibility" that the error contributed to the verdict.[46] This standard is viewed as more stringent than *Kotteakos*, and it is supported as providing greater protection against a "lenient" application of the harmless error rule that would effectively undercut the force of procedural requirements.[47]

Several reasons have been advanced for preferring this test over the *Kotteakos* standard. First, a nonconstitutional evidentiary or procedural error can cause just as much prejudice to the defendant as constitutional error, and the prejudice that it causes can be just as hard to assess.[48] Second, the reasonable-doubt standard is already in "wide use," and applying it to all errors obviates "an unnecessary inquiry into whether the error is constitutionally based."[49] Some argue in addition that any lesser standard would be inconsistent with the constitutional requirement that guilt be determined under a reasonable-doubt standard.[50] Most state courts, however, view the trial-proof standard as a false analogy, no more applicable in testing the harmlessness of an error than in making the initial assessment as to whether the error occurred.

Courts have also sought, with varying success, to identify the

---

[45]Green v. State, 688 So.2d 301 (Fla.1996); People v. Crimmins, 36 N.Y.2d 230, 367 N.Y.S.2d 213, 326 N.E.2d 787 (1975); State v. Van Hooser, 266 Or. 19, 511 P.2d 359 (1973).

[46]Commonwealth v. Story, 476 Pa. 391, 383 A.2d 155 (1978).

[47]See, e.g., State v. Carter, 164 Vt. 545, 674 A.2d 1258 (1996) (adopting the beyond-a-reasonable-doubt standard for nonconstitutional error); State v. Vandebogart, 139 N.H. 145, 652 A.2d 671 (1994) (applying beyond-a-reasonable-doubt standard to erroneous admission of DNA evidence).

[48]See Dorsey v. State, 276 Md. 638, 350 A.2d 665 (Md.App.1976).

[49]State v. Carter, 164 Vt. 545, 674 A.2d 1258 (1996).

[50]See Commonwealth v. Story, 476 Pa. 391, 383 A.2d 155 (1978). Professor Saltzburg has observed (Saltzburg, The Harm of Harmless Error, 59 Va.L.Rev. 988, 992 (1973)):

It would make little sense to adopt the *Winship* standard, which is designed to prevent criminal convictions if there is even a reasonable doubt in the minds of jurors as to the guilt of the person charged, and then on appeal to emasculate that evidentiary standard when the trial court has violated evidentiary rules which might have influenced the jury by creating the requisite doubt. * * * If [what Justice Brennan described in *Winship* as] the "moral force" of the criminal law is not to be diluted on appeal, convictions must be reversed where the appellate court cannot arrive at a conclusion about the impact of an error on the jury verdict with the same degree of certainty demanded at the trial.

process for determining whether a particular error is so unlikely to have influenced the jury's judgment that it meets the applicable probability standard. Considerable attention has been given, for example, to the allocation of the burden of showing potential prejudice. In *Kotteakos*, the Supreme Court rejected the idea of uniformly placing the burden on either party. Any presumptions of prejudice, shifting the burden to one side or the other, should "aris[e] from the nature of the error and its "natural effect" for or against prejudice in the particular setting." Chief Justice Traynor of the California Supreme Court suggested that the entire issue of presumptions and burdens was largely meaningless in the harmless error context,[51]

Another significant issue is what weight should be assigned to overwhelming evidence of guilt in determining the impact of a trial error. Several possibilities have been suggested.[52] One approach that has not had a favorable reception in the courts is to look to the error almost in isolation. The critical question under this approach is whether the error is of a type likely to have influenced a reasonable juror. Where evidence was erroneously admitted, the court would focus on the extent to which that evidence was incriminating. Thus, evidence that improperly brought out a defendant's prior offense would be judged according to the damaging quality of that information. If the offense revealed was serious and roughly similar to that charged, the error clearly would not be harmless (in contrast, for example, to the revelation of an unrelated traffic offense). It would not matter that the other evidence overwhelmingly established guilt or even that another prior offense, similar in nature had been properly placed before the jury. Proponents of this approach argue that it affords protection against appellate court usurpation of the jury's function, precludes extensive reliance on the harmless error doctrine (and the resulting dilution of defendant's procedural rights), and serves to deter intentional misconduct by prosecutors who might otherwise rely on the strength of the evidence to shield their misconduct on appellate review. Appellate courts generally have not been receptive to these arguments, in part because they are viewed as imposing an artificial restriction on the task of assess-

---

[51]R. Traynor, The Riddle of Harmless Error 25–26 (1970). See also O'Neal v. McAninch, 513 U.S. 432, 115 S.Ct. 992, 130 L.Ed.2d 947 (1995), discussed at note [53] where the Court majority quoted with approval Justice Traynor's comments on the meaninglessness of allocating a "burden of proof" in this context.

[52]For an excellent analysis of this issue, examined in the context of harmless constitutional error, see Field, Assessing the Harmlessness of Federal Constitutional Error—A Process in Need of a Rationale, 125 U.Pa.L.Rev. 15 (1976). A leading judicial exploration of the issue is Justice Roberts opinion for the court in Commonwealth v. Story, 476 Pa. 391, 383 A.2d 155 (1978).

ing the impact of the error. As various courts have noted, one can hardly evaluate the impact of an error upon a jury decision without considering the totality of the case before the jury.[53]

Once it is agreed that the impact of an error must be measured in light of all of the evidence before the jury, it does not follow that an overwhelming prosecution case will inevitably render the error harmless. In *O'Neal v. McAninch*,[54] a case concerning the application of the *Kotteakos* standard on collateral review, the Court described the appropriate inquiry as whether the error "had substantial and injurious effect or influence in determining the jury's verdict," not whether, despite the error, the jury reached the right result.[55] One method of measuring that impact, and ensuring that the weight of the state's evidence does not become determinative, is to match the potential element of prejudice against the state's evidence. For example, to render harmless the erroneous admission of potentially prejudicial evidence, it would have to be shown that the government had properly introduced other, more persuasive evidence on the same point.[56] Most courts,[57] however, view a requirement that the prosecution's evidence independently establish the same fact as the inadmissible evidence as unduly restrictive. Even without a "perfect match," strong prosecution evidence may indicate that a particular error was most unlikely to have contributed to the jury's verdict. For example, erroneously admitted evidence may have

---

[53]See, e.g., Kotteakos v. United States, 328 U.S. 750, 66 S.Ct. 1239, 90 L.Ed. 1557 (1946); R. Traynor, The Riddle of Harmless Error 36 (1970).

[54]O'Neal v. McAninch, 513 U.S. 432, 115 S.Ct. 992, 130 L.Ed.2d 947 (1995).

[55]Lower courts, too, have stated that they will not allow overwhelming evidence of guilt to render the error harmless automatically, since to do so comes too close to returning to a "correct result" standard. See, e.g., Higginbotham v. State, 807 S.W.2d 732 (Tex. Cr.App.1991); State v. LaBranche, 118 N.H. 176, 385 A.2d 108 (1978); Commonwealth v. Story, 476 Pa. 391, 383 A.2d 155 (1978). See also Stacy & Dayton, Rethinking Harmless Constitutional Error, 88 Colum.L.Rev. 79, 82 (1988) (criticizing the "correct result" approach in the context of constitutional error).

[56]The application of such a "cumulative evidence test" is analyzed in Field, Assessing the Harmlessness of Federal Constitutional Error—A Process in Need of a Rationale, 125 U.Pa.L.Rev. 15. 37–54 (1976); Note, 64 Cornell L.Rev. 538, 562–63 (1979) (citing case supporting such a test).

[57]Montana has adopted a modified version of this approach. See State v. Van Kirk, 306 Mont. 215, 32 P.3d 735 (2001) (overruling prior precedent and finding "if there was no cumulative evidence presented as to a fact proving an element of the crime charged, then the error in admitting the tainted evidence which proved that element cannot be considered harmless"); State v. Baldwin, 318 Mont. 489, 81 P.3d 488 (2003) (the State must point to admissible evidence that proved the same facts as the tainted evidence and also demonstrate that the *quality* of the tainted evidence was such that there was no reasonable possibility that it might have contributed to the defendant's conviction).

been the only evidence casting doubt upon defendant's reputation for honesty, but it may nevertheless have been inconsequential in light of strong eyewitness testimony clearly establishing that the defendant had committed the crime.[58]

Many courts apply what may be described as a comparative analysis of the likely impact of the error and the overwhelming evidence. The question to be answered, they note, is "whether the properly admitted evidence of guilt is so overwhelming and the prejudicial effect of the error is so insignificant by comparison" that the court can say, with the requisite degree of certainty, that the error could not have contributed to the verdict.[59] As for some types of error, such as the erroneous admission or exclusion of evidence, overwhelming evidence of guilt will ordinarily lead to the conclusion that the error was harmless. It would take evidence of an extraordinary quality to conclude that its erroneous admission or exclusion may have contributed to the verdict where the government had before the jury other evidence that would clearly and positively establish guilt.[60]

§ 27.6(c) Application to constitutional violations

Prior to the 1960s, it was assumed that constitutional violations could never be regarded as harmless error. Aside from one ambiguous ruling at the turn of the century, a Supreme Court finding of constitutional error had always resulted in a reversal of the defendant's conviction.[61] Since the Court's opinions had never sought to analyze those reversals under a harmless error rule, both commentators and lower courts concluded that the rule simply did not apply to constitutional violations.[62] This assumption was called into question by the due process revolution of the

---

[58]Consider, e.g., Blackwell v. State, 34 Md.App. 547, 369 A.2d 153 (1977); United States v. Porter, 544 F.2d 936 (8th Cir.1976).

[59]Commonwealth v. Story, 476 Pa. 391, 383 A.2d 155 (1978). See also People v. Krueger, 466 Mich. 50, 643 N.W.2d 223 (2002) (error is presumed not to be a ground for reversal unless it affirmatively appears that, more likely than not, it was outcome determinative; an error is "outcome determinative" if it undermines the reliability of the verdict, focusing on the nature of the error in light of the weight and strength of the untainted evidence).

[60]On occasion, a series of errors in the admission of evidence may lead the court to conclude that the overall effect was prejudicial and therefore must have contributed to the judgment, notwithstanding a strong prosecution case. See United States v. Rivera, 900 F.2d 1462 (10th Cir.1990) (en banc) (discussing "cumulative error" review).

[Section 27.6(c)]

[61]The one possible exception was Motes v. United States, 178 U.S. 458, 20 S.Ct. 993, 44 L.Ed. 1150 (1900), but that case could also be read as resting on a waiver theory. See Saltzburg, The Harm of Harmless Error, 59 Va.L.Rev. 988, 1099–01 (1973).

[62]See Stacy & Dayton, Rethinking Harmless Constitutional Error, 88 Colum.L.Rev. 79, 83 (1988) (collecting sources). But see Note, 20 Stan.L.Rev. 83, 86 (1967) (collecting cases that had

1960s and its dramatic expansion of federal constitutional regulation of state procedures.[63]

In *Chapman v. California*,[64] the Court addressed the application of harmless error review to a clear violation of the Court's decision in *Griffin v. California* prohibiting comment on the defendant's failure to testify at trial.[65] The California Supreme Court, stressing the overwhelming evidence of guilt, had held the *Griffin* violation harmless under the California harmless error rule. Before the Supreme Court, the defendant contended that no constitutional error could be harmless, while the prosecution claimed that the state court could appropriately apply to a constitutional violation the same harmless error standard it applied to nonconstitutional errors. The Court majority rejected both arguments.

The *Chapman* majority held initially that federal rather than state law determined whether the harmless error rule applied to constitutional violations, and if so, whether a particular constitutional violation was harmless. "Whether a conviction for a crime should stand when a state had failed to accord federally constitutionally guaranteed rights" was as much a matter of constitutional law as the definition of the constitutional right itself.[66] The Court then turned to the question of whether the Constitution required automatic reversal as to all constitutional errors. It was true, the Court noted, that a rule of automatic reversal had been applied to certain constitutional errors in the past, but that did not mean constitutional errors could never be treated as harmless. A proper harmless error standard could appropriately be applied to some constitutional violations, including a violation of the *Griffin* ruling. However, that standard was not the harmless error rule applied by the California court, but rather a standard that required the appellate court to be convinced "beyond a reasonable doubt that the error complained of did not contribute to the verdict obtained."[67]

The *Chapman* opinion established a two-step analysis for an

---

applied harmless error rule to the use at trial of evidence obtained through an unconstitutional search).

[63]See Kitch, The Supreme Court's Code of Criminal Procedure: 1968–1969 Edition, 1969 S.Ct.Rev. 155, 194–200; F. Graham, The Self-Inflicted Wound 318–19 (1970). See also §§ 2.5 to 2.6.

[64]Chapman v. California, 386 U.S. 18, 87 S.Ct. 824, 17 L.Ed.2d 705 (1967).

[65]See § 24.4(b).

[66]Compare Meltzer, Harmless

Error and Constitutional Remedies, 61 U.Chi.L.Rev. 1 (1994) (arguing that Chapman is best viewed as a rule of constitutional common law, born of concern that state courts, if left free to apply their own harmless error standards, would dilute federal constitutional norms by too easily finding that constitutional errors were not prejudicial).

[67]Several state courts apply the higher "beyond-a-reasonable-doubt" standard to the review of violations of the state's constitution, although ap-

appellate court dealing with a constitutional error. First, the court must determine if the error falls in that category of violations subject to the harmless error rule or instead falls in that category of errors requiring automatic reversal. Second, if the harmless error rule is applicable, the court must determine the impact of the error in the case before it under the federal standard laid down in *Chapman*. These two determinations are analyzed in the subsections that follow.

§ 27.6(d) Harmless error or automatic reversal

The *Chapman* opinion focused primarily on responding to the contention that the harmless error rule should never apply to constitutional error. The Court found no basis in theory or past precedent for granting constitutional errors a blanket exemption from this rule of appellate review. It noted that the harmless error statutes, including the federal provision, did not on their face distinguish between federal constitutional errors and nonconstitutional errors. These statutes, the Court noted, served "a very useful purpose insofar as they block setting aside convictions for small errors or defects that have little, if any, likelihood of having changed the result of the trial." The Court was not prepared to conclude that there could not be "some constitutional errors which in the setting of a particular case are so unimportant and insignificant that they may, consistent with the Federal Constitution, be deemed harmless."

The *Chapman* opinion acknowledged that prior cases had indicated "that there are some constitutional rights so basic to a fair trial that their infraction can never be treated as harmless error." A footnote to this statement cited and described three illustrative cases: "*Payne v. Arkansas* (coerced confessions)[68]; *Gideon v. Wainwright* (right to counsel)[69]; [and] *Tumey v. Ohio* (impartial judge).[70]" The Court made no attempt to identify the characteristics that distinguished these constitutional errors from the *Griffin* violation before it. An improper comment on defendant's silence was the type of "trial error" as to which a harmless error analysis traditionally had been applied, and the Court apparently concluded that once it was decided that "some constitutional errors" could be deemed harmless, the *Griffin* violation clearly fell within that group. Only Justice Stewart disagreed with that

---

plying a more lenient standard to nonconstitutional error. See, e.g., State v. Oquendo, 223 Conn. 635, 613 A.2d 1300 (1992); Commonwealth v. Rios, 412 Mass. 208, 588 N.E.2d 6 (1992).

[Section 27.6(d)]

[68]Payne v. Arkansas, 356 U.S.
560, 78 S.Ct. 844, 2 L.Ed.2d 975 (1958). See § 6.2.

[69]Gideon v. Wainwright, 372 U.S. 335, 83 S.Ct. 792, 9 L.Ed.2d 799 (1963).

[70]Tumey v. Ohio, 273 U.S. 510, 47 S.Ct. 437, 71 L.Ed. 749 (1927). See § 21.4(a).

conclusion. He suggested that recognition of a harmless constitutional error should be limited narrowly to constitutional requirements, like the exclusionary rule, that involved a balancing of a deterrence objective against the exclusion of "relevant and reliable evidence."

The *Chapman* opinion was criticized for providing "little guidance on the matter of determining when an error automatically requires reversal and when it does not."[71] It was obvious that the Court's citation to three constitutional errors requiring automatic reversal was only by example and did not serve to exhaust the list of constitutional violations so treated. As Justice Stewart noted, past precedent had clearly indicated that certain other violations would also be placed in the automatic-reversal category. The *Chapman* opinion said only that "some constitutional errors," including a *Griffin* violation, could be deemed harmless. It did not clearly indicate whether "some" would be "most," "many," or only a "few." That determination awaited further development, but the logic of *Chapman* did exclude from the outset two very different types of constitutional violations.

The very nature of the harmless error inquiry made harmless error analysis irrelevant to one major group of constitutional violations. Where the constitutional error is one that requires the remedy of barring reprosecution, reversal is automatic upon concluding that there was such a violation. That is the case, for example, where defendant establishes a violation of his right to a speedy trial or the bar against double jeopardy.[72]

An additional group of violations were destined not to be analyzed under the *Chapman*'s harmless error test because they were harmful by definition, inherently incapable of meeting the rigorous *Chapman* prerequisite for finding an error to be harmless. *Chapman* insisted upon a judicial finding of lack of prejudicial impact "beyond a reasonable doubt." As a result, it would be wasted effort to look to *Chapman* where the constitutional violation is one of those that already requires—as an element of the violation—a finding of likely prejudicial impact. Typi-

---

[71]Note, 83 Harv.L.Rev. 814, 816 (1970).

[72]See, e.g., Strunk v. United States, 412 U.S. 434, 93 S.Ct. 2260, 37 L.Ed.2d 56 (1973), discussed at § 18.1(e). Even where the double jeopardy violation extended to only part of the charge, and therefore did not bar a retrial entirely, the Court has characterized the question as to whether to order a retrial on the nonjeopardy-barred charge as one relating to the fashioning of an appropriate remedy

for the jeopardy violation, and not as a harmless error question. See the discussion of *Morris v. Mathews* in § 25.4(b) and Price v. Georgia, 398 U.S. 323, 331, 90 S.Ct. 1757, 1762, 26 L.Ed.2d 300 (1970) in § 25.4(d). For criticism of the Court's decisions requiring automatic dismissal as a remedy for a violation of the sixth amendment right to a speedy trial, see Amar, Foreword: Sixth Amendment First Principles, 84 Geo.L.J. 641 (1996).

cally, those violations do not exist unless the challenged behavior presented a "reasonable probability" of having affected the outcome of the proceeding. Examples include a finding that counsel's representation was ineffective under the *Strickland* standard,[73] or that nondisclosed exculpatory evidence was material under the *Bagley* standard.[74] As the Court explained in *Kyles v. Whitley*,[75] "once a reviewing court applying *Bagley* has found constitutional error there is no need for further harmless error review." Indeed, one issue that has repeatedly divided the Court in the years since *Chapman* is whether particular conduct should be viewed as a constitutional violation in itself, with that violation then subject to the *Chapman* standard, or instead should be viewed as error only if the defendant can first establish a reasonable probability of that conduct having a prejudicial impact upon the outcome of the proceeding.[76]

Leaving aside those constitutional violations that bar reprosecution and those that already require a finding of probable impact upon outcome, the *Chapman* harmless error analysis still offered the potential of applying to a broad range of constitutional errors. In the years after *Chapman*, that potential was fully

---

[73]See § 11.10(d).

[74]See § 24.3(b).

[75]Kyles v. Whitley, 514 U.S. 419, 115 S.Ct. 1555, 131 L.Ed.2d 490 (1995). *Kyles* is also discussed in § 24.3(b).

[76]Consider in this regard United States v. Bagley, 473 U.S. 476, 103 S.Ct. 3164, 77 L.Ed.2d 785 (1983), discussed in § 24.3(b), and Delaware v. Van Arsdall, 475 U.S. 673, 106 S.Ct. 1431, 89 L.Ed.2d 674 (1986), and the debate about defining improper argument by the prosecution, summarized in § 24.7(h) and (i). In *Bagley*, the Court majority held that an element of the due process violation was a showing of "materiality," established by a reasonable probability that disclosure of the exculpatory evidence would have produced a different result. Justice Marshall, in dissent, argued that once it had been shown that the prosecutor failed to disclose favorable evidence, a constitutional violation was established and the prosecutor should then bear the burden of showing that the error was harmless under the *Chapman* standard. In *Van Arsdall*, the majority held that defendant's constitutional right of confrontation was violated by a state ruling prohibiting inquiry into a prosecution witness's bias, and a new trial was required unless the prosecution could establish that error to be harmless under the *Chapman* standard. Justice White, concurring in the judgment, argued that "it makes more sense to hold that no violation of the Confrontation Clause has occurred unless there is some likelihood that the outcome of the trial was affected."

This debate surfaced again in the context of a case in which the defendant was prohibited from presenting evidence in his defense in violation of the due process clause. In Fry v. Pliler, __ U.S. __, 127 S.Ct. 2321 (2007), the majority sidestepped the question of whether such error can ever be harmless, assuming for purposes of the case that if it is reviewed for harmlessness, the standard must be the more deferential standard reserved for habeas review. The dissenters argued, however, that this sort of constitutional error is by its nature, inherently prejudicial, so that it can never be "harmless," under any standard.

realized. *Chapman*'s harmless error standard has now been held by the Supreme Court to apply to each of the following constitutional violations: improper comment on the defendant's failure to testify;[77] admission of evidence obtained in violation of the Fourth Amendment;[78] admission of evidence obtained in violation of an accused's right to counsel;[79] admission at trial of an out-of-court statement of a non-testifying codefendant in violation of the Sixth Amendment's Confrontation Clause;[80] admission of evidence at the sentencing stage of a capital case in violation of the right to counsel;[81] erroneous use during trial of defendant's silence following *Miranda* warnings;[82] a restriction on a defendant's right to cross-examine in violation of the Sixth Amendment's Confrontation Clause;[83] denial of the right to be present during a trial proceeding;[84] shackling of defendant in front of jury in violation of

---

[77]See, e.g., *Chapman*; Anderson v. Nelson, 390 U.S. 523, 88 S.Ct. 1133, 20 L.Ed.2d 81 (1968).

[78]Chambers v. Maroney, 399 U.S. 42, 90 S.Ct. 1975, 26 L.Ed.2d 419 (1970); Bumper v. North Carolina, 391 U.S. 543, 88 S.Ct. 1788, 20 L.Ed.2d 797 (1968).

[79]United States v. Wade, 388 U.S. 218, 87 S.Ct. 1926, 18 L.Ed.2d 1149 (1967) (lineups); Milton v. Wainwright, 407 U.S. 371, 92 S.Ct. 2174, 33 L.Ed.2d 1 (1972) (statements). See also Moore v. Illinois, 434 U.S. 220, 98 S.Ct. 458, 54 L.Ed.2d 424 (1977) (remanding for harmless error review of error in introduction of evidence of pretrial identification made in violation of right to counsel).

[80]See, e.g., Schneble v. Florida, 405 U.S. 427, 92 S.Ct. 1056, 31 L.Ed.2d 340 (1972); Harrington v. California, 395 U.S. 250, 89 S.Ct. 1726, 23 L.Ed.2d 284 (1969), also discussed at notes 144–145.

[81]Satterwhite v. Texas, 486 U.S. 249, 108 S.Ct. 1792, 100 L.Ed.2d 284 (1988).

[82]Brecht v. Abrahamson, 507 U.S. 619, 113 S.Ct. 1710, 123 L.Ed.2d 353 (1993), also discussed in § 28.3(g).

[83]Lee v. Illinois, 476 U.S. 530, 106 S.Ct. 2056, 90 L.Ed.2d 514 (1986); Delaware v. Van Arsdall, 475 U.S. 673, 106 S.Ct. 1431, 89 L.Ed.2d 674 (1986). See also Coy v. Iowa, 487 U.S. 1012, 108 S.Ct. 2798, 101 L.Ed.2d 857 (1988) (denial of face-to-face-confrontation).

[84]Rushen v. Spain, 464 U.S. 114, 104 S.Ct. 453, 78 L.Ed.2d 267 (1983), discussed at note 121 and also in § 24.2(b). In that case the Court explained (somewhat elliptically) that violations of the right to be present, like violations of the right to counsel, are subject to harmless error analysis, "unless the deprivation, by its very nature, cannot be harmless," a comment it followed with a citation to *Gideon*. Accordingly, lower courts have attempted to distinguish between defendant absences that are subject to harmless error review and more significant exclusions that require reversal without inquiry into possible prejudice. Regularly assessed for harmlessness are various ex parte communications, like that between the judge and juror in *Rushen*, and other brief exclusions that can be linked to specific testimony. See Yarborough v. Keane, 101 F.3d 894 (2d Cir.1996) (absence from hearing on witness sequestration, noting witness's testimony "was of virtually no significance" so that it would have made no difference if the defendant had been successful in the hearing in disqualifying the witness from testifying); Campbell v. Rice, 408 F.3d 1166 (9th Cir.2005) (en banc) (declining to decide whether

due process,[85] denial of an indigent's right to appointed counsel at a preliminary hearing;[86] a jury instruction containing an unconstitutional rebuttable presumption;[87] a jury instruction containing an unconstitutional conclusive presumption;[88] an unconstitutionally overbroad jury instruction in a capital case;[89] the

---

defendant had right to attend in-chambers hearing concerning defense counsel's conflict of interest, finding not unreasonable the state court decision that any error was harmless); Rice v. Wood, 77 F.3d 1138 (9th Cir.1996) (absence at return of verdict of death in sentencing proceeding, collecting cases evaluating violations of the defendant's right to be present at the return of verdicts of conviction and sentence, and reviewing application of harmless error in general); Hegler v. Borg, 50 F.3d 1472 (9th Cir.1995) (readback of testimony); State v. Garcia-Contreras, 191 Ariz. 144, 953 P.2d 536 (1998); Oregon v. Wilson, 323 Ore. 498, 918 P.2d 826 (1996) (exclusion from preliminary instruction orienting potential jurors harmless); Massingill v. State, 8 S.W.3d 733 (Tex.Cr.App.1999) (denial of counsel after imposition of sentence and before the deadline for filing a motion for new trial is not structural error, conducting harmless error review). See also § 24.2(b). United States v. Toliver, 330 F.3d 607 (3d Cir.2003) (finding harmless error applies to violations of Rule 43).

But see State v. Bird, 308 Mont. 75, 43 P.3d 266 (2002) (defendant's exclusion from in-chambers individual voir dire proceedings was structural error and as such it undermined the integrity of the entire trial, failure to object was not waiver).

[85]Deck v. Missouri, 544 U.S. 622, 125 S.Ct. 2007, 161 L.Ed.2d 953 (2005) ("where a court, without adequate justification, orders the defendant to wear shackles that will be seen by the jury, the defendant need not demonstrate actual prejudice to make out a due process violation," instead the state must prove "beyond a reasonable doubt that the [shackling] error com-

plained of did not contribute to the verdict obtained"). See also Ruimveld v. Birkett, 404 F.3d 1006 (6th Cir.2005) (shackling could result in harmless error, but unjustified shackling here was not harmless); Wiseman v. State, __ S.W.3d __, 2006 WL 2773088 (Tex.App. 2006) (shackling not harmless when it was not clear from the record that the shackles were not heard or seen by the jury and did not constrain the defendant's ability to communicate with counsel).

[86]Coleman v. Alabama, 399 U.S. 1, 90 S.Ct. 1999, 26 L.Ed.2d 387 (1970).

[87]Rose v. Clark, 478 U.S. 570, 106 S.Ct. 3101, 92 L.Ed.2d 460 (1986) (harmless error applies to an unconstitutional shift in the burden of proof as to the element of malice even where the defendant contests intent; "[i]n many cases, the predicate facts conclusively establish intent, so that no rational jury could find that the defendant committed the relevant criminal act but did not intend to cause injury," thereby rendering the erroneous instruction "simply superfluous").

[88]Carella v. California, 491 U.S. 263, 109 S.Ct. 2419, 105 L.Ed.2d 218 (1989); Yates v. Evatt, 500 U.S. 391, 111 S.Ct. 1884, 114 L.Ed.2d 432 (1991).

[89]Pope v. Illinois, 481 U.S. 497, 107 S.Ct. 1918, 95 L.Ed.2d 439 (1987) (where state court in an obscenity prosecution unconstitutionally charged the jury to apply community standards in determining whether the distributed magazines lacked literary or artistic value, rather than to judge the "value factor" on an objective basis, the error would be harmless if the reviewing court could conclude that "no rational juror, if properly in-

submission of an invalid aggravating factor to the jury in a capital sentencing proceeding,[90] and the omission from the jury charge of an element of the offense.[91] In *Arizona v. Fulminante*,[92] the Court also overruled one of *Chapman*'s three illustrations of errors requiring automatic reversal, holding that harmless error analysis is applicable to the admission of a coerced confession.

This string of decisions has been supplemented by lower court rulings applying *Chapman* to many additional errors, such as the admission of evidence obtained in violation of *Miranda*[93] or *Edwards v. Arizona*,[94] a denial of the accused's right to testify,[95] various types of jury misconduct,[96] selective re-reading of testimony invading the province of the jury,[97] the failure to instruct the jury that it had to be unanimous as to every element,[98] the failure to instruct on a lesser included offense,[99] and

---

structed, could find value in the magazines").

[90]Stringer v. Black, 503 U.S. 222, 112 S.Ct. 1130, 117 L.Ed.2d 367 (1992).

[91]Neder v. United States, 527 U.S. 1, 119 S.Ct. 1827, 144 L.Ed.2d 35 (1999). See also California v. Roy, 519 U.S. 2, 117 S.Ct. 337, 136 L.Ed.2d 266 (1996) (holding that an error in the instruction that defines the crime—a failure to inform the jury that it had to find that defendant, convicted of aiding another's murder, had the "knowledge [and] intent or purpose of committing, encouraging, or facilitating" the confederate's crime—was "trial error," not the "structural" sort that defies analysis by harmless error standards).

[92]Arizona v. Fulminante, 499 U.S. 279, 111 S.Ct. 1246, 113 L.Ed.2d 302 (1991).

[93]See, e.g., Gorham v. Franzen, 760 F.2d 786 (7th Cir.1985); United States v. Packer, 730 F.2d 1151 (8th Cir.1984); Harryman v. Estelle, 616 F.2d 870 (5th Cir.1980).

[94]Correll v. Thompson, 63 F.3d 1279 (4th Cir.1995).

[95]Ortega v. O'Leary, 843 F.2d 258 (7th Cir.1988); Wright v. Estelle, 572 F.2d 1071 (5th Cir.1978) (en banc).

[96]See, e.g., United States v. Mackey, 114 F.3d 470 (4th Cir.1997)

(jurors performed research on evidence and summarized results for jurors who had gone home); Pyles v. Johnson, 136 F.3d 986 (5th Cir.1998) (unauthorized visit to crime scene, collecting cases); In re Carpenter, 9 Cal.4th 634, 889 P.2d 985, 38 Cal.Rptr.2d 665 (1995) (improper exposure to prejudicial information, collecting cases); Stokes v. State, 379 Md. 618, 843 A.2d 64 (Md.App.2004) (the presence of alternate jurors impairs the integrity of the jury trial, prejudice must be presumed, and is effectively unrebuttable except for cases in which the presence was fleeting). See also § 24.9 (discussing jury misconduct cases).

[97]United States v. Rivera-Santiago, 107 F.3d 960 (1st Cir.1997) (finding a reasonable possibility that the error influenced the jury). See also State v. Levy, 156 Wash.2d 709, 132 P.3d 1076 (2006) (en banc) (improper judicial comment on the evidence were not structural error requiring reversal without regard to prejudice, but instead will be presumed prejudicial unless the record affirmatively shows that no prejudice could have resulted).

[98]People v. Wolfe, 114 Cal.App. 4th 177, 7 Cal.Rptr.3d 483 (Cal.App. 2003) (failure to give a unanimity instruction was error but harmless beyond a reasonable doubt). See also United States v. Zabriskie, 415 F.3d 1139 (10th Cir.2005) (error in giving what amounts to an *Allen* instruction

the total denial of the opportunity to cross-examine a witness.[100]

In *Rose v. Clark*,[101] the Supreme Court, looking to the wide range of constitutional errors already held subject to the *Chapman* standard as of 1986, offered the following synopsis:

[W]hile there are some errors to which *Chapman* does not apply, they are the exception and not the rule. Accordingly, if the defendant had counsel and was tried by an impartial adjudicator, there is a strong presumption that any other errors that may have occurred are subject to harmless-error analysis.

The errors for which harmless error review has been rejected reach well beyond those violations that deprive the defendant of counsel or an impartial adjudicator. Indeed, following *Chapman*, the rule of automatic reversal has been held by the Court to apply to numerous violations in addition to the two categories discussed earlier in this section,[102] the denial of defendant's constitutional right to self-representation;[103] the denial of the right to select counsel of one's choice,[104] discrimination in the selection of the petit jury;[105] the improper exclusion of a juror because of his views on capital punishment;[106] racial discrimina-

---

to a juror the judge knows to be the holdout will be reviewed under harmless error, government failed to negate "any reasonable possibility that prejudice arose from the district court's ex parte communication with one of the jurors").

[99]State v. Allen, 69 S.W.3d 181 (Tenn.2002). But compare State v. Tomlin, 266 Conn. 608, 835 A.2d 12 (2003) (failure to instruct on lesser included offenses was not harmless. The mere fact that a defendant is convicted of the greater offense does not compel the conclusion that any failure to instruct the jury on a lesser included offense is harmless error).

[100]United States v. Mills, 138 F.3d 928 (11th Cir.1998).

[101]Rose v. Clark, 478 U.S. 570, 106 S.Ct. 3101, 92 L.Ed.2d 460 (1986).

[102]See text at notes 72–76 supra, discussing errors barring reprosecution and errors already including a finding of prejudice.

[103]McKaskle v. Wiggins, 465 U.S. 168, 104 S. Ct. 944, 79 L. Ed. 2d 122 (1984), discussed in § 11.5.

[104]United States v. Gonzalez-

Lopez, __ U.S. __, 126 S.Ct. 2557, 165 L.Ed.2d 409 (2006) ("A choice-of-counsel violation occurs *whenever* the defendant's choice is wrongfully denied" reasoning the right to counsel of choice is part of the "root meaning" of the Sixth Amendment and does not require a showing of prejudice, unlike the right to the effective assistance of counsel, which was derived instead from the larger purpose of the Sixth Amendment in ensuring a fair trial and does require a showing of prejudice), also discussed in 11.7(d) at note 54, and 11.4(b) at note 49.

[105]Batson v. Kentucky, 476 U.S. 79, 106 S.Ct. 1712, 90 L.Ed.2d 69 (1986) ("If the trial court decides that the facts establish, prima facie, purposeful discrimination and the prosecutor does not come forward with a neutral explanation for his action, our precedents require that petitioner's conviction be reversed."). But compare People v. Morris, 107 Cal.App.4th 402, 131 Cal.Rptr.2d 872 (2003) (defendant may not seek to overturn conviction on the basis of his own race discrimination against jurors).

[106]See Gray v. Mississippi, 481 U.S. 648, 107 S.Ct. 2045, 95 L.Ed.2d

tion in the selection of the grand jury;[107] the violation of the *Anders* standards governing the withdrawal of appointed appellate counsel;[108] the denial of consultation between defendant and his counsel during an overnight trial recess;[109] the denial of a defendant's right to a public trial;[110] an erroneous reasonable doubt instruction to the jury,[111] representation by counsel acting under an actual conflict of interest that adversely affects his performance;[112] and the failure of the trial court to make an appropriate inquiry into a possible conflict of interest under those special circumstances that constitutionally mandate such an inquiry.[113]

The justices continue to disagree about the appropriate analy-

---

622 (1987), discussed in § 22.3(c) at notes 148–151, and infra note 134.

[107]Rose v. Mitchell, 443 U.S. 545, 99 S.Ct. 2993, 61 L.Ed.2d 739 (1979); Vasquez v. Hillery, 474 U.S. 254, 106 S.Ct. 617, 88 L.Ed.2d 598 (1986). See also Ballard v. United States, 329 U.S. 187, 67 S.Ct. 261, 91 L.Ed. 181 (1946), characterized later by the Court as a case like *Vasquez,* in which "[t]he nature of the violation," the exclusion of women from the grand jury, "allowed a presumption that the defendant was prejudiced, and any inquiry into harmless error would have required unguarded speculation." Bank of Nova Scotia v. United States, 487 U.S. 250, 108 S.Ct. 2369, 101 L.Ed.2d 228 (1988). See, e.g., Rideau v. Whitley, 237 F.3d 472 (5th Cir.2000) (collecting authority and granting defendant habeas relief from conviction for murder, due to discrimination in the selection of grand jury, resulting in only one black juror on the grand jury that indicted him in 1961).

[108]Penson v. Ohio, 488 U.S. 75, 109 S.Ct. 346, 102 L.Ed.2d 300 (1988).

[109]Geders v. United States, 425 U.S. 80, 96 S.Ct. 1330, 47 L.Ed.2d 592 (1976).

[110]Waller v. Georgia, 467 U.S. 39, 104 S.Ct. 2210, 81 L.Ed.2d 31 (1984). By contrast, although the Court held in Waller v. Georgia, 467 U.S. 39, 104 S.Ct. 2210, 81 L.Ed.2d 31 (1984), that the denial of the right to a public trial was not subject to harmless error review, a variety of exclusions short of

total or sustained closure have been upheld as harmless. See, e.g., United States v. Huntley, 535 F.2d 1400 (5th Cir.1976) (failure to announce verdict publicly subject to harmless error); Brown v. Kuhlmann, 142 F.3d 529 (2d Cir.1998) (closure of courtroom during officer's testimony does not require reversal, collecting federal and conflicting New York cases). Compare Stacy & Dayton, Rethinking Harmless Constitutional Error, 88 Colum.L.Rev. 79, 113–114 (1988) (violations of the right to public trial should be exempt from harmless error review due to the indeterminate effect of the violation on the reliability of the process and the independent goals (other than truth-finding) that the right serves, namely, enabling a defendant to air complaints about the government and educating the public). See § 24.1(b).

[111]Sullivan v. Louisiana, 508 U.S. 275, 113 S.Ct. 2078, 124 L.Ed.2d 182 (1993), discussed in § 27.6(e).

[112]Cuyler v. Sullivan, 446 U.S. 335, 100 S.Ct. 1708, 64 L.Ed.2d 333 (1980); Burger v. Kemp, 483 U.S. 776, 107 S.Ct. 3114, 97 L.Ed.2d 638 (1987).

[113]Holloway v. Arkansas, 435 U.S. 475, 98 S.Ct. 1173, 55 L.Ed.2d 426 (1978). The Court has also reversed convictions without inquiry into harmlessness in order to remedy the constructive amendment of an indictment, see § 19.3, but these cases have been undermined by subsequent precedent. In United States v. Cotton, 535 U.S. 625, 122 S.Ct. 1781, 152 L.Ed.2d 860 (2002), the Court refused to exempt

sis for distinguishing between those errors that may be harmless and those that may not be harmless. In its 1991 opinion *Arizona v. Fulminante*, the majority characterized those errors placed within the automatic-reversal category as involving "structural defect[s] affecting the framework within which the trial proceeds, rather than simply an error in the trial process itself." Their nature was quite distinct, the Court noted, from those errors held subject to the *Chapman* harmless error standard. The latter group of violations were tied together by the "common thread" of "involv[ing] "trial error"—error which occurred during the presentation of the case to the jury and which may therefore be quantitatively assessed in the context of other evidence presented in order to determine whether its admission was harmless beyond a reasonable doubt." The Court later discounted the idea of a "rigid dichotomy" between structural and trial errors, preferring to refer to the difference as a "spectrum of constitutional errors,"[114] but it has also continued to cite to *Fulminante's* classification scheme as authoritative.[115] Exactly what sort of case involves an error affects the framework of the trial has divided the Court over the years.

One characteristic of violations requiring automatic reversal that is frequently mentioned by the Supreme Court is the "inherently indeterminate" impact of the violation upon the outcome of

---

this sort of error from plain error review and instead relied on uncontroverted evidence of guilt to uphold the conviction and sentence despite the absence of an essential element from the indictment. See § 27.5(c) at note 106. Although the Court in *Cotton* distinguished the case before it from the earlier cases in which defendants had objected in the trial court to indictment errors and received relief without regard to harmlessness, those earlier cases have been undermined by *Chapman's* subsequent application of harmless error review to constitutional error generally, the application of harmless error review to missing elements in jury instructions, see *Neder v. United States,* 527 U.S. 1, 119 S.Ct. 1827, 144 L.Ed.2d 35 (1999), and a number of decisions that have reduced the significance of the grand jury's screening function. See *United States v. Williams,* 504 U.S. 36, 112 S.Ct. 1735, 118 L.Ed.2d 352 (1992); *United States v. Mechanik,* 475 U.S. 66, 106 S.Ct. 938, 89 L.Ed.2d 50 (1986). Cf. *United States v. Stewart,* 306 F.3d 295

(6th Cir.2002) (after *Cotton,* failure to allege essential element is not structural error, but can be harmless beyond a reasonable doubt, reviewing authority).

See also § 19.6, at notes 46–51. The Court in its 2006 term agreed to review whether the omission of an element of a criminal offense from a federal indictment can constitute harmless error, but ultimately did not address the issue. *United States v. Resendiz-Ponce,* 127 S.Ct. 782, 166 L.Ed.2d 591 (2007).

[114]*Brecht v. Abrahamson,* 507 U.S. 619, 113 S.Ct. 1710, 123 L.Ed.2d 353 (1993).

[115]See *Johnson v. United States,* 520 U.S. 461, 117 S.Ct. 1544, 137 L.Ed.2d 718 (1997). The dual approach also resembles the traditional distinction that in the past has been used to divide nonconstitutional violations into errors that might be harmless and those that will always require reversal. See § 27.6(b).

the trial. Unlike most errors at trial, such errors do not relate to the introduction or evaluation of particular items of evidence. Of course, certain violations held subject to the *Chapman* standard, such as the failure to charge on the presumption of innocence, could also be said to have a pervasive effect. But the impact of that omission can be measured by reference to the other charges given and the verdict delivered. Thus, in *United States v. Gonzalez-Lopez*,[116] the Court explained that its conclusion that the denial of the right to counsel of one's choice was structural error rested "upon the difficulty of assessing the effect of the error." In *Sullivan v. Louisiana*,[117] the Court deemed "structural" and requiring automatic reversal a constitutional error in charging the jury on the reasonable doubt standard. The *Sullivan* Court initially identified the resulting constitutional violation as extending beyond the due process requirement that the state establish guilt beyond a reasonable doubt, and including also the "interrelated" sixth amendment right to a "jury verdict of guilty beyond a reasonable doubt." Because of the constitutionally deficient instruction, there simply had not been such a verdict, and therefore application of *Chapman* would be contrary to the basic logic of *Chapman*'s harmless error analysis. *Chapman* directs a reviewing court to determine the basis on which the jury rested its verdict, and to ask whether that verdict "was surely unattributable to the error." Here since there never was a jury verdict of guilty beyond a reasonable doubt, the "most an appellate court could conclude is that a jury surely would have found petitioner guilty beyond a reasonable doubt"—an inquiry *Chapman* prohibits.[118] The Court distinguished cases involving unconstitutional jury instructions relating to presumptions, reasoning that a court reviewing such error is able to assess the bearing of the presumption upon the jury's verdict by reference to the various findings the jury did make. "But the essential connection to a "beyond a reasonable doubt" factual finding cannot be made where the instructional error consists of a misdescription of the burden of proof which vitiates all the jury's findings."[119]

Sullivan's reasoning appeared to prohibit harmless error

---

[116]See United States v. Gonzalez-Lopez, __ U.S. __, 126 S.Ct. 2557, 165 L.Ed.2d 409 (2006) (the denial arose from barring the defendant from consult with one of his attorneys during trial, "It is impossible to know what different choices the rejected counsel would have made, and then to quantify the impact of those different choices on the outcome of the proceeding").

[117]Sullivan v. Louisiana, 508 U.S. 275, 113 S.Ct. 2078, 124 L.Ed.2d 182 (1993).

[118]See § 27.6(e) at note 152.

[119]Justice Scalia and Justice Ginsberg later argued in a concurring opinion in California v. Roy, 519 U.S. 2, 117 S.Ct. 337, 136 L.Ed.2d 266 (1996), that the rationale of *Sullivan* should also bar a reviewing court from holding harmless the failure to instruct on an element simply because

review of a judge's complete failure to submit an element to the jury, or at least limit harmless error review to cases in which the actual verdict delivered by the jury necessarily included a finding of guilt beyond a reasonable doubt on that element. In *Neder v. United States*,[120] the Court interpreted *Sullivan* differently. Neder had been convicted of several charges of fraud as well as filing a false tax return. The trial judge, in accordance with the Court of Appeals precedent at the time and over the objection of the defendant, did not include materiality as an element of these crimes in its charge to the jury. Following trial, a Supreme Court decision refuted the trial judge's assumption that the element of materiality for the tax offense was a question for the court, not the jury, raising in Neder's case the question whether the failure to instruct the jury on this element could be considered harmless. Reaching that question, the Supreme Court in *Neder* admitted that it would not be "illogical to extend the reasoning of *Sullivan*" to this case, but concluded that "settled precedent" closed that avenue. Five justices decided that the evidence of materiality was "overwhelming" and "uncontested," and therefore harmless, reasoning that "where an omitted element is supported by uncontroverted evidence, this approach reaches an appropriate balance between "society's interest in punishing the guilty [and] the method by which decisions of guilt are made." Assessments of the harmlessness of an omitted instruction, the Court reasoned, do not differ from assessments of the harmlessness of instructions that erroneously describe an element[121] or that involve an unconstitutional presumption[122]—all foreclose independent jury consideration of whether the facts proved establish beyond a reasonable doubt the element in question. By contrast, the Court continued, the error in *Sullivan* "vitiate[d] *all* of the jury's findings."

Justice Scalia, joined by Justices Souter and Ginsburg, dissented in *Neder*, arguing that harmless error review may be ap-

---

the court concludes that "given the evidence, no reasonable jury would have found otherwise." Rather, there must be an actual jury finding, which may be shown in one of two ways—the actual finding either "effectively embraces" a finding on the missing element, or it is "impossible" to have found what the verdict did without finding the missing point as well. See also United States v. Edmonds, 80 F.3d 810 (3d Cir.1996) (en banc) (failure to instruct jury to make unanimous findings on some issues was nevertheless subject to harmless error review because the jury made proper

unanimous findings of other facts which are "functionally equivalent").

[120]Neder v. United States, 527 U.S. 1, 119 S.Ct. 1827, 144 L.Ed.2d 35 (1999).

[121]See California v. Roy, 519 U.S. 2, 117 S.Ct. 337, 136 L.Ed.2d 266 (1996); Pope v. Illinois, 481 U.S. 497, 107 S.Ct. 1918, 95 L.Ed.2d 439 (1987).

[122]See Yates v. Evatt, 500 U.S. 391, 111 S.Ct. 1884, 114 L.Ed.2d 432 (1991); Carella v. California, 491 U.S. 263, 109 S.Ct. 2419, 105 L.Ed.2d 218 (1989).

plied "only when the jury *actually renders* a verdict—that is when
it has found the defendant guilty of all the elements of the crime."
For the dissenting justices, misdescribing or omitting an element
could only be harmless "if the elements of guilt that the jury *did*
find necessarily embraced the one omitted or misdescribed."[123]
The *Neder* majority considered this approach inconsistent with
precedent and burdensome, requiring a reviewing court in each
individual case to determine the seriousness of an omission or
misdescription. "Under our cases, a constitutional error is either
structural or it is not." As the dissent pointed out, however, the
structural/trial error distinction has been determined on a case-
by-case basis for some errors, and in any event, the burden "would
seem a small price to pay for keeping the appellate function consistent with the Sixth Amendment." In the words of the dissent,
under the Court's opinion "the remedy for the constitutional violation is a repetition of the same violation by a different judge."

The *Neder* majority also dismissed the prediction of the dissenting justices that the decision would undercut the prohibition
against directed verdicts of guilt in criminal cases, stating only
"Happily, our course of constitutional adjudication has not been
characterized by this 'in for a penny, in for a pound' approach."
Particularly considering that trial judges by omitting an element
from the jury's instruction can obtain the equivalent of a directed
verdict of guilt on that element, the Court's failure to offer a
substantive response to the dissenters' point left much to the
lower courts to resolve. The decision also did not address whether
harmless error review was appropriate when more than one element was omitted or misdescribed, or when a different kind of element, say mens rea, was omitted from the jury's instructions,
although the Court's categorical approach suggested that it was
not inclined to pursue such distinctions.[124]

The Court in *Washington v. Recuenco*,[125] soon held that the
denial of the Sixth Amendment right to have a jury, not a judge,

---

[123]Justice Stevens concurred spe-
cially with the judgment of the five-
Justice majority on this basis, finding
that the error was harmless because
the jury's verdict "necessarily included
a finding" that the omitted element
existed.

[124]Whether the failure to instruct
a jury on a required element in a
capital case is subject to harmless error review was at issue in Mitchell v.
Esparza, 540 U.S. 12, 124 S.Ct. 7, 157
L.Ed.2d 263 (2003). The Court did not
reach the merits of the question, but
did hold that a state court's conclusion

that harmless error was appropriate
in this context was not an unreasonable application of existing precedent.
"We cannot say that because the violation occurred in the context of a capital
sentencing proceeding that our precedent requires the opposite result.
Indeed, a number of our harmless-
error cases have involved capital defendants * * * and we left a question
similar to the one presented here open
in [Ring]."

[125]Washington v. Recuenco, __ U.S.
__, 126 S.Ct. 2546, 165 L.Ed.2d 466
(2006).

determine the existence of an aggravating sentencing factor was indistinguishable from the error in *Neder*, and was subject to harmless error analysis. The Court rejected Recuenco's characterization of his sentencing as essentially a directed verdict of guilt on an offense greater than the offense that had been charged and submitted to the jury in his case. Rather, the Court stated, the failure to submit a sentence enhancement to the jury, like failure to submit an element to the jury, is not structural error.[126] Lower courts also have not hesitated to find harmless incomplete jury instructions omitting other elements, at least when proof of the element was introduced and uncontested at trial.[127] Some lower courts, however, have rejected harmless error review when an el-

---

[126]Most lower courts had anticipated the holding in *Recuenco*, and had been applying harmless error review to violations of the right to a jury determination of maximum-enhancing sentencing facts since *Apprendi*. But see State v. Franklin, 184 N.J. 516, 878 A.2d 757 (2005) ("On appellate review, we cannot find that the State satisfied an element of an offense that was never presented to the jury * * * a jury, once properly charged, has the power to disregard even overwhelming proof of culpability and either acquit entirely or convict of a lesser-included offense.").

[127]People v. Geisendorfer, 991 P.2d 308, 312 (Colo.App.1999) (finding that failure to instruct jury that fear of serious bodily harm experienced by the victims must be "imminent" was harmless when no reasonable jury could have determined that the victims' fear was of anything other than imminent serious bodily harm); State v. Price, 61 Conn.App. 417, 767 A.2d 107 (2001); State v. Thompson, 143 Idaho 155, 139 P.3d 757 (Idaho App.2006) (omitting from the instructions the element that the defendant must have known the substance possessed was a controlled substance was harmless, when defendant did not present any evidence whereby the jury could find as it did that he had meth in his pockets and nevertheless, acquit on a reasonable doubt as to whether he realized that the substance was a controlled substance, there was no rational basis for a jury to doubt that

he knew the nature of the substance in his pocket); Clark v. State, 621 N.W.2d 576 (N.D.2001) (failure to charge element of firearm use harmless when defense at jury trial for manslaughter was self defense and there was no question defendant used a gun).

Compare United States v. Brown, 202 F.3d 691, 703 (4th Cir.2000) (error not harmless when defendant "genuinely contested" evidence); Keating v. Hood, 191 F.3d 1053, 1065 (9th Cir.1999) (instructions omitting the element of mens rea, and thus allowing defendant to be convicted of securities fraud as either a direct perpetrator or an aider and abettor, not harmless); People v. Peoples, 8 P.3d 577 (Colo.App.2000) (omitting from instructions element that dwelling was that of "another" in a trespass case was not harmless when defendant contested missing element "vigorously" at trial and presented conflicting witness testimony); Hopkins v. State, 759 N.E.2d 633 (Ind.2001) (failure to instruct jury on specific intent for accomplice liability for attempted murder was not harmless); People v. Duncan, 462 Mich. 47, 610 N.W.2d 551 (2000) (finding that omitting *all* of the elements of the offense can never be harmless error, distinguishing *Neder* in case where jury found defendant guilty of felony-firearm offense listed on verdict form but omitted from jury instructions, over dissenting opinion arguing that error was not plain error because the jury necessarily found that the defendant possessed a firearm

ement of the offense is omitted from the indictment or information, as opposed to being left out of the instructions to the jury.[128]

A second critical factor in determining the applicability of harmless error analysis is the impact of allowing harmless error review upon the function that the right is designed to achieve. Consider, for example, the withdrawal of appellate counsel without the procedures specified by *Anders*.[129] Here, a subsequent analysis could determine that the appeal truly was frivolous and that defendant was not hurt since counsel would have been allowed to withdraw after filing an *Anders* brief. But as the court noted in *Penson v. Ohio*,[130] applying *Chapman* to an *Anders* violation would leave the defendant without the very protection that *Anders* sought to provide when it barred withdrawal on counsel's bare assertion that the appeal was frivolous. In applying a harmless error analysis, *Penson* noted, the appellate court would be required to assess the potential merits of the defendant's appeal, finding the error harmless or not harmless according to its view as to whether a reversal on the merits would be required. To allow such an analysis would thereby "render * * * meaningless the protections afforded * * * by *Anders*." A similar consideration may help to explain the Court's decision in *Holloway v. Arkansas*[131] holding not subject to harmless error analysis a trial court's failure to inquire into a possible conflict of interest when the circumstances strongly suggest such a conflict exists. It might be possible in a post-conviction hearing to determine that, notwithstanding those circumstances, there was in fact no actual conflict and thus the lack of a hearing was not prejudicial. But the very premise of the constitutionally mandated inquiry was that post-conviction review was not adequate protection where such special circumstances existed. Though allowing a post-conviction harmless error inquiry would not go so far as to "render meaningless" *Holloway*'s inquiry requirement, it would certainly undermine a

---

during the commission of a felony when it found that he murdered the victims with a gun); State v. Warren, 9 Neb.App. 60, 608 N.W.2d 617 (2000) (instructions placing burden of proving self defense on defendant not harmless, applying Neder). See also Beem v. McKune, 278 F.3d 1108 (10th Cir.2002) (not harmless error when state court vacated rape sentence and conviction and substituted judgment and sentence for lesser (but not lesser-included) crime of aggravated incest, when defendant was never charged and convicted of aggravated incest, rejecting dissenters argument that

because all of the elements of aggravated incest were charged and proven in the rape charge, except the element of familial relationship, an element the defendants admit, the failure to charge and prove the crime of conviction was harmless error).

[128]See also note 113 supra; § 19.6 at notes 46–51.

[129]See § 11.2(c).

[130]Penson v. Ohio, 488 U.S. 75, 109 S.Ct. 346, 102 L.Ed.2d 300 (1988).

[131]Holloway v. Arkansas, 435 U.S. 475, 98 S.Ct. 1173, 55 L.Ed.2d 426 (1978). See also § 11.9(e).

basic premise of that requirement.

In some instances, constitutional violations have fallen in the automatic-reversal category because the right violated is not primarily concerned with ensuring reliable verdicts, but serves an entirely different function. The Court has also described this consideration as the "irrelevance of harmlessness" to the right at issue.[132] The Court relied on this rational to explain its refusal to apply *Chapman* to a denial of defendant's right to proceed pro se in *McKaskle v. Wiggins*.[133] That right, the Court noted, is designed to permit the defendant to control his own destiny, even though its exercise "usually increases the likelihood of a trial outcome unfavorable to the defendant"; accordingly, "its denial is not amenable to "harmless error" analysis." The broader function of the right violated may also explain, in part, the Court's refusal to apply a harmless-error analysis in the jury selection cases.[134] The functions of the rights to grand jury review and trial by jury extend beyond simply providing the defendant with a fact-finding process that is reliable (e.g., community participation). Indeed, the Court in its post-*Batson* decisions has characterized jury discrimination as impairing not the rights of defendants, but the

---

[132]See United States v. Gonzalez-Lopez, __ U.S. __, 126 S.Ct. 2557, 165 L.Ed.2d 409 (2006), discussed at note 116 supra.

[133]See § 11.5(a).

[134]The Court has required automatic reversal even where a single juror was excluded unconstitutionally and there was no suggestion of bias on the part of the jurors actually selected. See Gray v. Mississippi, 481 U.S. 648, 107 S.Ct. 2045, 95 L.Ed.2d 622 (1987), discussed in § 22.3(c) at notes 148–151. Although the *Gray* plurality cited an "integrity of the process" rationale in refusing to treat a *Witherspoon-Witt* violation as subject to a harmless error analysis, all of the opinions in that case recognized the special role of the jury, particularly in determining whether a capital sentence should be imposed. As discussed in § 22.3(c), the *Gray* Court rejected the state's contention that the exclusion of a single juror not unequivocally opposed to capital punishment constituted "an isolated incident without prejudicial effect" since the ultimate panel would still "fairly represent the community." In reaching this conclusion, the plurality opinion stressed that treatment of the exclusion as an isolated incident, not affecting the balance of the jury on the capital punishment issue, failed to take into account the possibility that the prosecution may have used its peremptory challenges to exclude other jurors with similar views. Justice Powell, the fifth member of the majority, saw no need to consider that possibility; the key was the possible impact that the single excluded juror might have had upon "the panel as a whole." The dissent, although arguing that the exclusion was harmless error in this case, did so on the ground that the composition of the jury would have been the same even if the juror had not been excluded for cause. The dissent maintained that it was certain that the prosecution, given the additional peremptory challenges to which it was entitled, would have excluded the juror on a peremptory challenge (a conclusion the majority rejected). See also State v. Anderson, 197 Ariz. 314, 4 P.3d 369 (2000) (*Witherspoon* error is structural error).

rights of potential jurors.[135]

Of course, the recognition that a constitutional right serves a function other than promoting the reliability of verdicts does not in itself place that error beyond the reach of *Chapman*. The self-incrimination privilege serves a variety of functions beyond the protection of the innocent,[136] yet *Chapman* itself applied the harmless error standard to an infringement of that right. Admittedly, those additional functions might be thought less significant in the context of the *Griffin* prohibition against adverse prosecutorial comment, but they certainly are at the core of prohibition against the admission of coerced confessions, which has also been held subject to the *Chapman* rule.[137] The key may be that unlike some of the other rights which, when violated warrant a rule of automatic reversal, the self-incrimination privilege, operates solely as a prohibition against the use of evidence. So too, while the Fourth Amendment serves privacy interests unrelated to fact-finding reliability, in applying *Chapman* to *Mapp* violations, the Court was concerned only with a bar against evidentiary use that serves basically a prophylactic function and does not itself preclude a violation of privacy. Not surprisingly in light of the other limitations imposed upon the *Mapp* exclusionary rule,[138] the Court concluded that a requirement of automatic reversal was not needed to satisfy that prophylactic function.

Closely linked to the idea that some errors require reversal in order to vindicate an interest other than verdict reliability are the Court's references to the need to protect the integrity of the judicial process. This "judicial integrity" rationale has been cited as an explanation for the requirements of automatic-reversal in both the jury selection cases and in *Tumey*, the paradigmatic example of a biased judge.

Finally the need for deterrence of error may play a role in the decision to require relief regardless of harm. Thus, the Court has noted "that racial discrimination in the selection of grand jurors is so pernicious, and other remedies so impractical, that the remedy of automatic reversal was necessary as a prophylactic means of deterring grand jury discrimination in the future."[139]

The lower federal courts and state courts have contributed as

---

[135]See § 22.3(d).

[136]See § 2.10(d).

[137]See Ogletree, *Arizona v. Fulminante*: The Harm of Applying Harmless Error to Coerced Confessions, 105 Harv.L.Rev. 152 (1991).

[138]See §§ 3.1, 9.1, 9.3, 9.4.

[139]United States v. Mechanik, 475 U.S. 66, 106 S.Ct. 938, 89 L.Ed.2d 50 (1986) (describing jury selection cases). See also Stacy & Dayton, Rethinking Harmless Constitutional Error, 88 Colum.L.Rev. 79, 95–98 (1988) (noting that "[t]he relatively mild deterrence flowing from the *Chapman* rule * * * may well be insufficient when there is a significant probability that any given error of a particular type will escape detection").

well to the Supreme Court's list of those constitutional errors requiring automatic reversal. "Structural errors" recognized by these courts include the violation of the due process right of self-representation on direct appeal,[140] racial discrimination in the use of peremptory challenges[141] and the denial of the defendant's right to an impartial jury under the Sixth Amendment.[142] A number of errors, however, continue to evade consensus. For

---

See also Kamin, Harmless Error and the Right/Remedies Split, 88 Va.L.Rev. 1 (2002) (arguing that harmless error blunts the effectiveness of changes in the law and will continue to do so unless reviewing courts first reach the merits of an issue before ruling on harmlessness and prosecutors are not able to benefit from the harmless error rule if they should have known that their conduct was error. Cf. Landes & Posner, Harmless Error, 30 J.Leg.Stud. 161 (2001) (finding in sample of more than 1,000 criminal defendants who appealed their convictions in the U.S. Courts of Appeals between 1996 and 1998, intentional prosecutor and judge errors are more likely to be found harmful and lead to reversal than are inadvertent errors, and prosecutor errors are more likely to be forgiven than judge errors, in part because judge errors are likely to have greater influence on jurors).

[140]See Myers v. Johnson, 76 F.3d 1330 (5th Cir.1996); Annot., 24 A.L.R. 4th 430 (1998).

[141]See, e.g., Dawson v. Delaware, 503 U.S. 159, 112 S.Ct. 1093, 117 L.Ed.2d 309 (1992) (Blackmun, J., concurring) (Batson error not subject to harmless error analysis); Tankleff v. Senkowski, 135 F.3d 235 (2d Cir.1998) (violation of Powers, collecting cases); United States v. McFerron, 163 F.3d 952, 956 (6th Cir.1998) (Batson error); Ford v. Norris, 67 F.3d 162 (8th Cir.1995) (violation of Swain).

[142]United States v. Iribe-Perez, 129 F.3d 1167 (10th Cir.1997) (requiring reversal when judge empanelled jurors who had heard from him that the defendant would plead guilty, noting that it "is not the function of this court to predict whether a properly constituted jury would have convicted the defendant"); Hughes v. United States, 689 A.2d 1206 (D.C.App.1997) (failure to strike biased juror was structural error); Mach v. Stewart, 137 F.3d 630 (9th Cir.1997) (alternative ground, holding that the seating of a biased juror and the trial judge's repeated elicitation of her statements that in her years of practice as with Child Protective Services that children do not lie about being sexually assaulted was structural error in prosecution of defendant for criminal sexual conduct with a minor); State v. LaMere, 298 Mont. 358, 2 P.3d 204 (2000) (telephone-summons procedure violated cross-section guarantee and was not subject to harmless error analysis).

See also United States v. Curbelo, 343 F.3d 273 (4th Cir.2003) (violation of Rule 23(b)-dismissal of twelfth juror prior to deliberations without the defendant's consent-is structural error and requires reversal without regard to prejudice, collecting authority); State v. Pare, 253 Conn. 611, 755 A.2d 180 (2000) (new trial ordered when defendant timely requested the judge to poll the jury, and the judge's failure to do so was error when jury had been dismissed from the courtroom but not discharged and remained in the jury room; also holding failure is not subject to harmless error, citing weight of authority; noting "we cannot know the results of polling the jury"); State v. Costello, 646 N.W.2d 204 (Minn.2002) (the practice of permitting jurors to become active participants in the solicitation of evidence by questioning witnesses compromises the impartiality of the jury and is not subject to a harmlessness analysis).

131

example, courts have divided over whether harmless error review can apply to the denial of counsel of choice,[143] or the failure to furnish certain capital defendants with the assistance of a competent psychiatrist, an entitlement established in *Ake v. Oklahoma*.[144] Some courts reason that this error "eliminates a basic tool of an adequate defense" and that measuring its effect would require "unguided speculation,"[145] while others have concluded that *Ake* error results in either the improper admission or the improper exclusion of evidence, both of which should be subject to harmless error analysis.[146] Divided, too, have been opinions concerning the effect of a judge's absence during trial.[147] Some courts require reversal, others treat all such lapses as harmless, while others apply an analysis similar to that found in the cases addressing the denial of the defendant's right to be present or right to consult counsel—treating a sustained gap as structural, but evaluating brief absences under the harmless error rule. An abuse of discretion by the trial judge in refusing to

---

[143]Compare United States v. Gonzalez-Lopez, 399 F.3d 924 (8th Cir.2005) (joining majority position requiring reversal, collecting authority) with Rodriguez v. Chandler, 382 F.3d 670 (7th Cir.2004) (adopting a middle-ground "adverse effect" standard) and United States v. Walters, 309 F.3d 589 (9th Cir.2002) (holding harmless error review applies to denial of counsel of choice at sentencing phase only because denial was not a complete denial of counsel of choice). See § 11.4 at notes 49–54.

[144]Ake v. Oklahoma, 470 U.S. 68, 105 S.Ct. 1087 84 L.Ed.2d 53 (1985).

[145]Federick v. State, 902 P.2d 1092 (Okla.Cr.App.1995) (error involved defendant's "only potential defense [and] affected the entire conduct of the trial from the beginning to the end. * * * This Court simply cannot look to the record and make an intelligent judgment about whether the evidence which may have been discovered would have affected the outcome of the trial."); Rey v. State, 897 S.W.2d 333 (Tex.Cr.App.1995) (noting that the Supreme Court in Ake reversed without conducting a harmlessness analysis, and noting "[w]e can conceive of few errors that are more structural in nature than one which eliminates a

basic tool of an adequate defense and in doing so dramatically affects the accuracy of the jury's determination").

[146]See White v. Johnson, 153 F.3d 197 (5th Cir.1998); Brewer v. Reynolds, 51 F.3d 1519 (10th Cir.1995); Tuggle v. Netherland, 79 F.3d 1386 (4th Cir.1996) (finding error harmless and likening error in admitting psychiatric testimony to Satterwhite v. Texas, 486 U.S. 249, 108 S.Ct. 1792, 100 L.Ed.2d 284 (1988), and error in denying assistance to Delaware v. Van Arsdall, 475 U.S. 673, 106 S.Ct. 1431, 89 L.Ed.2d 674 (1986)). See also Note, 87 J.Crim.L. & Criminology 786 (1997); Note, 81 Va.L.Rev. 521 (1995).

[147]Compare Riley v. Deeds, 56 F.3d 1117 (9th Cir.1995) (collecting cases, and holding that readback of victim's testimony held in judge's absence, with the judge's law clerk presiding, was structural error) with McIntyre v. State, 266 Ga. 7, 463 S.E.2d 476 (1995) (error in the substitution of judges is subject to harmless error analysis, collecting authority).

See also People v. Salyer, 80 P.3d 831 (Colo.App.2003) (when parties consent to judge's absence from courtroom during hours video was played, harmless error review appropriate, collecting authority).

allow substitute counsel mandates reversal in some courts, but not in others.[148] The failure to submit aggravating factors to a capital sentencing jury in violation of *Ring v. Arizona*,[149] is reviewed for harmless error by some courts, but not all.[150] State constitutional errors may be reviewed under separate standards.[151]

§ 27.6(e) Applying the reasonable doubt standard for constitutional errors

When the Court in *Chapman* sought to fashion a federal harmless error standard for constitutional errors, it stated:

'The question is whether there is a reasonable possibility that the evidence complained of might have contributed to the conviction.' * * * An error in admitting plainly relevant evidence which possibly influenced the jury adversely to a litigant cannot * * * be conceived of as harmless. Certainly error, constitutional error, in illegally admitting highly prejudicial evidence or comments, casts on someone other than the person prejudiced by it a burden to show that it was harmless. It is for that reason that the original common-law harmless error rule put the burden on the beneficiary of the error either to prove that there was no injury or to suffer a reversal of his erroneously obtained judgment.

The Court found "little, if any, difference" between this standard and "requiring the beneficiary of a constitutional error to prove beyond a reasonable doubt that the error complained of did not contribute to the verdict obtained."

The *Chapman* standard clearly rejected a "correct result" test, especially if the correct result was to be measured simply by sufficient evidence to sustain a conviction. The standard looked not

---

[148]Compare United States v. Allen, 895 F.2d 1577 (10th Cir.1990) (harmless error does not apply when a defendant has been denied the right to substitute counsel) with United States v. Zillges, 978 F.2d 369 (7th Cir.1992) (denial of motion for substitution of counsel will be upheld, despite an abuse of discretion, if error was harmless, that is, if it does not result in a violation of a defendant's right to the effective assistance of counsel).

[149]Ring v. Arizona, 536 U.S. 584, 122 S.Ct. 2428, 153 L.Ed.2d 556 (2002). See § 26.4(i) at notes 177–179. See also the discussion of Washington v. Recuenco, __ U.S. __, 126 S.Ct. 2546, 165 L.Ed.2d 466 (2006), at note 125 supra.

[150]See Woldt v. People, 64 P.3d 256 (Colo.2003) (collecting authority); State v. Ring, 204 Ariz. 534, 65 P.3d 915 (2003). See also United States v. Robinson, 367 F.3d 278 (5th Cir.2004) (failure to charge aggravating factors required for death eligibility under federal death penalty act was harmless error). But compare State v. Lovelace, 140 Idaho 73, 90 P.3d 298 (2004) (*Ring* error is not susceptible to harmless error analysis when factors are of a more subjective nature than guilt/innocence facts that can be objectively examined). See also supra note 125.

[151]See Ryan v. Palmateer, 108 P.3d 1127, 338 Or.278 (2005) (relying on state constitutional provision and rejecting the concept of "structural error" for the review of error in trial proceedings under Oregon law).

to the hypothetical question of whether the jury could have convicted without regard to the error, or whether the appellate court itself would have convicted without the error, but to the historical question whether the error had influenced the jury in reaching its verdict.[152] It required that the appellate court be convinced "beyond a reasonable doubt" that there was no "reasonable possibility" that the error contributed to the jury's verdict. The *Chapman* opinion did not clearly indicate, however, precisely what weight was to be given to the presence of overwhelming untainted evidence in making that judgment. The government's case in *Chapman* clearly was not overwhelming, and the Court had no reason to deal directly with the issue. In subsequent opinions, the Court has appeared to move back and forth between relying heavily upon the presence of proof of guilt in its harmless error analysis, and considering that proof as less central to the inquiry.

For example, in *Harrington v. California*,[153] a case evaluating the introduction of the confessions of two codefendants who did not take the stand,[154] Justice Douglas, speaking for the majority, concluded that the error was harmless in light of the remaining evidence. The confessions placed the defendant at the scene of the crime, but so did the defendant's own statements and several eye witnesses. Moreover, the third codefendant, who did take the stand, placed him at the scene with a gun in his hand. Justice Douglas stressed that the improperly admitted confessions of the codefendant was merely "cumulative" evidence. The Court in some later opinions relied primarily on the overwhelming evidence of guilt,[155] in others on the inability to say that the error did not influence or contribute to the verdict.[156]

In *Fulminante*, five justices appeared to return to an analysis

---

[Section 27.6(e)]

[152]See,, e.g., Leading Cases, 120 Harv.L.Rev. 125, 193 (2006) (characterizing the difference between the "influence on the jury" approach and the "guilt-based" approach to harmless error, and collecting sources).

[153]Harrington v. California, 395 U.S. 250, 89 S.Ct. 1726, 23 L.Ed.2d 284 (1969).

[154]See § 17.2(b).

[155]See United States v. Hasting, 461 U.S. 499, 103 S.Ct. 1974, 76 L.Ed.2d 96 (1983).

[156]Satterwhite v. Texas, 486 U.S. 249, 108 S.Ct. 1792, 100 L.Ed.2d 284 (1988) (noting that the inquiry is not whether legally admitted evidence was sufficient, but "whether the State has proved "beyond a reasonable doubt that the error complained of did not contribute to the verdict obtained""). See also Coy v. Iowa, 487 U.S. 1012, 108 S.Ct. 2798, 101 L.Ed.2d 857 (1988) (noting that an "assessment of harmlessness [of the denial of face-to-face confrontation] cannot include consideration of whether the witness' testimony would have been unchanged, or the jury's assessment unaltered, had there been confrontation; such an inquiry would obviously involve pure speculation, and harmlessness must therefore be determined on the basis of the remaining evidence"); Delaware v. Van Arsdall, 475 U.S. 673, 106 S.Ct.

that looked primarily to the influence on the conviction, rather than relying entirely on the weight of the evidence of guilt. In finding the admission of defendant's coerced confession was not harmless, Justice White wrote for the majority,[157] "[I]t must be determined whether the State has met its burden of demonstrating that the admission of the confession * * * did not contribute to Fulminante's conviction."[158] Read broadly, the Court's 1993 opinion in *Sullivan* also seemed to undercut any attempts to gauge the harmlessness or error simply by assessing the weight of the evidence of guilt. The appropriate analysis, the Court explained in that case, was not to ask whether a hypothetical jury would surely have convicted. "The Sixth Amendment," Justice Scalia wrote for the Court, "requires more than appellate speculation about a hypothetical jury's action, or else directed verdicts for the State would be sustainable on appeal; it requires an actual jury finding of guilty."

The Court in its most recent decisions has applied an analysis more like that used in *Harrington*. The Court in *Neder v. United States*[159] stated that "where a reviewing court concludes beyond a reasonable doubt that the omitted element was uncontested and supported by overwhelming evidence, such that the jury verdict would have been the same absent the error, the erroneous instruction is properly found to be harmless." The evidence in *Neder* "incontrovertibly establishe[d]" the omitted element of

---

1431, 89 L.Ed.2d 674 (1986) (noting that whether a denial of the right of cross examination is harmless "depends upon a host of factors," including "the importance of the witness's testimony in the prosecution's case, whether the testimony was cumulative, the presence or absence of evidence corroborating or contradicting the testimony of the witness on material points, the extent of cross-examination otherwise permitted, and, of course, the overall strength of the prosecution's case").

[157]*Fulminante* included separate majorities on three separate issues—the presence of a constitutional violation, the applicability of harmless error analysis to that violation, and the harmlessness of the error. Justice White's opinion concluding that the error was not harmless was joined by Justices Marshall, Blackmun, Stevens, and Kennedy.

[158]Arizona v. Fulminante, 499 U.S. 279, 111 S.Ct. 1246, 113 L.Ed.2d 302 (1991) opinion of White, J., at 296, writing for five Justices on the separate issue of whether the error was harmless. See also Justice Kennedy's concurring opinion, in which he argued that the court must "appreciate the indelible impact a full confession may have on the trier of fact."

[159]Neder v. United States, 527 U.S. 1, 119 S.Ct. 1827, 144 L.Ed.2d 35 (1999). See note 112.1. For additional debate about whether or not *Neder* modified the *Chapman* standard for harmlessness, see State v. Hale, 277 Wis.2d 593, 691 N.W.2d 637 (2005). The Court itself appears to refer to only one standard, see, e.g., *Mitchell v. Esparza*, cited in note 141.2, noting that a "constitutional error is harmless when" it appears "beyond a reasonable doubt that the error complained of did not contribute to the verdict obtained," quoting *Neder*, which in turn quotes *Chapman*.

materiality. Indeed, the Court observed that the evidence on this point was "so overwhelming" that Neder had never argued his statements could be found immaterial. The Court added that if, after "a thorough examination of the record," the reviewing court "cannot conclude beyond a reasonable doubt that the jury verdict would have been the same absent the error—for example, where the defendant contested the omitted element and raised evidence sufficient to support a contrary finding—it should not find the error harmless." Similarly, when the Court in *Washington v. Recuenco*[160] found harmless the judge's failure to submit a fact raising the maximum sentence to the jury, it again followed the approach of asking what the outcome would have been had the trial error not occurred, rather than assessing the effect of the error on the trial that took place, as in *Sullivan*.[161] In the end, as Judge Harry Edwards observed, no matter what the appropriate standard for reviewing error on appeal from a conviction, it may be "hard for a judge to discount a strong feeling that the defendant is guilty."[162]

---

[160]Washington v. Recuenco, __ U.S. __, 126 S.Ct. 2546, 165 L.Ed.2d 466 (2006).

[161]See Leading Cases, 120 Harv.L. Rev. 125, 199 (2006) (noting that even Justice Scalia, the author of *Sullivan*, joined the majority's application of the guilt-based or correct result approach in *Recuenco*).

[162]Edwards, To Err is Human, But Not Always Harmless: When Should Legal Error Be Tolerated?, 70 N.Y.U. L.Rev. 1167, 1174 (1995) (also concluding based on a judicial survey that the weight of the evidence of guilt has become "not just one factor playing into the harmless-error analysis, but rather the sole criterion by which harmlessness is gauged"). See also Comment, 82 Cal.L.Rev. 1335 (1994) (criticizing the overwhelming evidence approach to harmless error review of constitutional claims); Geabe, Spelling Guilt Out of A Record? Harmless-Error Review of Conclusive Mandatory Presumptions and Elemental Misdescriptions, 74 B.U.L.Rev. 819 (1994) (arguing that courts usurp "fact-finding functions that the Sixth Amendment entrusts to a jury," particularly when applying harmless error review to conclusive mandatory presumptions or the failure to instruct a jury on an element of a crime); Stacy & Dayton, Rethinking Harmless Constitutional Error, 88 Colum.L.Rev. 79, 82 (1988) ("courts do a remarkably poor job of evaluating the importance jurors attach to specific issues and evidence," judges are left to apply "their own perceptions," essentially replicating the "correct result" test rejected in theory by the Court).

CHAPTER 28

POST CONVICTION REVIEW: COLLATERAL REMEDIES

§ 28.1 Current collateral remedies and historical antecedents
  § 28.1(a) The nature of collateral remedies
  § 28.1(b) The common law writ of habeas corpus
  § 28.1(c) The common law writ of coram nobis
§ 28.2 The statutory structure and habeas policy
  § 28.2(a) Constitutional right or legislative grace?
  § 28.2(b) Statutory structure: from the 1867 Act to the 1996 Act
  § 28.2(c) Balancing within the statutory framework
  § 28.2(d) Competing models of habeas review
§ 28.3 Claims cognizable in habeas
  § 28.3(a) Cognizable claimants: the custody requirement
  § 28.3(b) Cognizable claims
  § 28.3(c) The exception for Fourth Amendment claims
  § 28.3(d) The opportunity for full and fair litigation
  § 28.3(e) "Bare innocence" claims
§ 28.4 Claims in habeas foreclosed by state procedural defaults
  § 28.4(a) Claims "defaulted" in state court-the policy debate
  § 28.4(b) Which defaults count: the "adequate and independent state ground" standard
  § 28.4(c) Excusing default: state waiver of the procedural default defense
  § 28.4(d) Excusing default: the "cause and prejudice" standard
  § 28.4(e) Excusing default: the "miscarriage of justice" exception
§ 28.5 Claims in habeas foreclosed due to premature, successive, or delayed applications
  § 28.5(a) Exhaustion of state remedies
  § 28.5(b) Time limits for filing petitions
  § 28.5(c) Successive petitions: claims previously advanced
  § 28.5(d) Successive petitions: new claims
  § 28.5(e) Successive petitions: court of appeals certification
§ 28.6 Constitutional interpretation on habeas review
  § 28.6(a) The changing role of federal habeas courts
  § 28.6(b) *Teague*: limiting the retroactive application of new rules of procedure
  § 28.6(c) Determining when a state conviction becomes final
  § 28.6(d) The "new rule" concept
  § 28.6(e) The *Teague* exceptions
  § 28.6(f) Review of state court rulings under § 2254(d)
  § 28.6(g) Harmless error on habeas review

§ 28.7 Fact-finding and evidentiary hearings in habeas
  § 28.7(a) Presuming the correctness of state court determinations of fact
  § 28.7(b) Distinguishing mixed determinations of law and fact from fact-finding
  § 28.7(c) Obtaining evidentiary hearings
  § 28.7(d) Discovery
§ 28.8 Habeas review of capital cases under Chapter 154 of the 1996 Act
  § 28.8(a) Special standards for applicants from certain states
  § 28.8(b) The opt-in requirements: electing the special standards
§ 28.9 Remedies for federal prisoners
  § 28.9(a) The range of remedies
  § 28.9(b) Limits on relief under § 2255
  § 28.9(c) Nonconstitutional claims under § 2255
§ 28.10 Appeal of district court decisions in habeas
§ 28.11 State collateral remedies
  § 28.11(a) Supreme Court "encouragement" of state remedies
  § 28.11(b) Types of state remedies
§ 28.12 Assistance of counsel in post-conviction proceedings
  § 28.12(a) Petitioner access to legal assistance-constitutional requirements
  § 28.12(b) Statutory entitlements to legal assistance

§ 28.1 Current collateral remedies and historical antecedents

  § 28.1(a) The nature of collateral remedies
  § 28.1(b) The common law writ of habeas corpus
  § 28.1(c) The common law writ of coram nobis

§ 28.1(a) The nature of collateral remedies

Every jurisdiction has one or more procedures through which defendants can present post-appeal challenges to their convictions on at least limited grounds.[1] In addition, through the federal writ of habeas corpus, a state defendant may challenge his state conviction on federal constitutional grounds in the federal courts.[2]

[Section 28.1(a)]

[1]See § 28.11 (discussing state remedies). If the issue to be raised on collateral attack could still be presented through direct appeal, the defendant may be required to pursue that possibility before utilizing a collateral remedy. See § 28.5(a). The discussion that follows assumes that an appeal either has been taken or is no longer available. It is in that sense that collateral remedies are also described here as "post-appeal" challenges.

[2]Particularly thorough is R. Hertz & J. Liebman, 1 Federal Habeas Corpus Practice and Procedure (5th ed. 2005) (also collecting post–AEDPA

The various state and federal procedures for presenting post-appeal challenges are commonly described as "collateral remedies." That description is not limited to separately filed suits challenging some aspect of a judgment in a criminal case, but means simply that the remedy "provide[s] an avenue for upsetting judgments [of conviction] that have become otherwise final."[3]

Most common collateral remedies today are derived from the common law writs of habeas corpus and coram nobis. The common law habeas proceeding was a separate civil action in which a petitioner challenged his continued detention by attacking the conviction on which his detention was based. Because the petitioner sought release from custody, the petition was filed in the court having jurisdiction over the official who held the petitioner in custody (e.g., the prison warden), rather than the court that had entered judgment of conviction. The writ of coram nobis directly attacked the conviction and was pursued in the court of conviction, but it also was commonly viewed as an independent civil action. Most of today's post-conviction proceedings are viewed as independent civil actions, but some are considered part of the original criminal case, similar to a post-appeal motion for a new trial.

Modern collateral remedies vary considerably in their scope. Some are available only to defendants who are held in custody, while others permit a challenge by any convicted defendant whose claims have not become moot. The narrowest allow challenges only to jurisdictional defects, while the broadest extend to constitutional violations and various nonconstitutional claims.

Following a brief review in this section of the common law writs of habeas corpus and coram nobis, this chapter focuses on the contemporary writ of habeas corpus provided by federal statute under 28 U.S.C.A. §§ 2241 and 2254. Federal habeas is the one collateral remedy available to all state prisoners. It also provides the doctrinal framework for the primary post-conviction remedy for federal prisoners challenging their convictions: the motion under 28 U.S.C.A. § 2255, discussed in § 28.9 of this

---

habeas scholarship at § 2.1, note 2). Another excellent, regularly updated source is C. Wright, A. Miller, E. Cooper & V. Amar, Federal Practice and Procedure: Jurisdiction 3d § 4261–4268 (2007). For one more concise overview, see L. Yackle, Federal Courts 485–587 (2d ed.2003).

[3]Mackey v. United States, 401 U.S. 667, 91 S.Ct. 1160, 28 L.Ed.2d 404 (1971). This chapter treats primarily challenges to the conviction and sentence. Habeas review is also available for certain administrative decisions affecting custody, such as the revocation of parole or good-time credit. See, e.g., Wilkinson v. Dotson, 544 U.S. 74, 125 S.Ct. 1242, 161 L.Ed.2d 253 (2005) (habeas corpus, not § 1983, is the appropriate remedy when a state prisoner requests present or future release, or where success would necessarily demonstrate the invalidity of confinement or its duration).

chapter. In addition, many states have modeled their own collateral remedies after the federal habeas writ.[4]

§ 28.1(b) The common law writ of habeas corpus

The common law writ of habeas corpus, simply defined, is a judicial order directing a person to have the body of another brought before a tribunal at a certain time and place.[5] The writ apparently takes its name from its directive, originally stated in Latin, that the court would "have the body."[6] Developed sometime before the thirteenth century, the writ was not an avenue for reviewing the custody of those who were convicted of crime. Instead, it started as a process by which a court compelled the attendance of parties whose presence would facilitate its proceedings. By the mid-fourteenth century it had taken the form of an independent proceeding to challenge illegal detention. By the sixteenth century habeas corpus was known as the Great Writ of Liberty—the alleged procedural underpinning of the guarantees of the Magna Carta—an effective remedy for imprisonment by the Crown without judicial authorization.[7]

The use of the writ to enforce the Magna Carta's guarantee of adherence to the "law of the land" (later described as "due process"[8]) was forcefully advocated in 1627 by leading counsel in *Darnel's Case*, where the writ was sought to gain release of five knights imprisoned for refusing to comply with the King's "forced loan" program.[9] The King's Bench apparently accepted counsels' contention that the writ could be used to enforce the Magna Carta's guarantee, but responded that it could not look beyond the Crown's return, which stated on its face that the detention was lawfully authorized. Dissatisfaction with this ruling eventually led to a 1641 Act that removed the power of the Crown to arrest without probable cause and granted to any arrested person immediate access by writ of habeas corpus to a judicial determination of the legality of his detention.[10] When procedural difficulties undermined the effectiveness of that Act, the Parliament

---

[4]See § 28.11.

[Section 28.1(b)]

[5]D. Meador, Habeas Corpus and Magna Carta 7 (1966).

[6]Id. See also Longsdorf, Habeas Corpus: A Protean Writ and Remedy, 8 F.R.D. 179, 182–84 (1948).

[7]See 3 W. Blackstone, Commentaries on the Laws of England 131–38 (4th ed.1770); A. Dicey, Law of the Constitution 214–16 (8th ed.1927); 9 W. Holdsworth, A History of English Law 115–19 (3d ed.1926).

[8]See Berger, Law of the Land Reconsidered, 74 Nw.U.L.Rev. 1 (1979).

[9]3 How.St.Tr. 1 (1627) (also known as the Case of the Five Knights). See Meador, Habeas Corpus and Magna Carta 7, 13–19 (1966); Chafee, The Most Important Right in the Constitution, 32 B.U.L.Rev. 143, 153–60 (1952).

[10]See W. Duker, A Constitutional History of Habeas Corpus 47–48 (1980). This Act is sometimes described as the Habeas Corpus Act of

responded with the celebrated Habeas Corpus Act of 1679.[11] The 1679 Act reinforced judicial authority to use the writ to release persons illegally detained by the Crown's sheriffs or officers, but specifically excluded from its coverage persons confined by courts as a result of criminal conviction.

Although it could be argued that the exclusion in the 1679 Act eliminated the authority of English courts to issue the writ on behalf of convicted persons,[12] it seems unlikely that Parliament intended to bar use of the writ in such cases, at least where the court of conviction lacked jurisdiction. In *Bushell's Case*,[13] decided in 1670, the writ had been used to order the release of a juror who had been held in contempt for refusing to return a guilty verdict as directed by the trial court. The ruling in *Bushell's Case* had attracted widespread attention (partly because the case arose out of a jury's refusal to convict William Penn and other Quakers charged with unlawful assembly[14]), and it is doubtful that a Parliament intent upon strengthening the writ would have deprived the courts of that precedent. Even assuming that the writ remained available to convicted persons, how far *Bushell's Case* extended the scope of habeas review as to convicted persons has been a matter of disagreement. Justice Brennan concluded in *Fay v. Noia*[15] that *Bushell's Case* established that the writ was available at common law to challenge imprisonment based on a conviction obtained in violation of due process. However, Justice Powell later suggested, based on the historical analysis of Professor Oaks, that Justice Brennan's reading of *Bushell's Case* was

---

1641. It also abolished the Star Chamber.

[11]31 Car. 2, c.2 (1679). For a discussion of the legislative history, see 9 W. Holdsworth, A History of English Law 119–22 (3d ed.1926); Forsythe, The Historical Origins of Broad Habeas Review Reconsidered, 70 Notre Dame L.Rev. 1079, 1095–1102 (1995) (discussing the 1679 Act as well as earlier history). The Act was designed to eliminate confusion as to which courts could issue the writ, which could empower certain judicial officers to issue the writs when courts were not in session, and which could establish procedures that would preclude evasionary tactics (e.g., the transfer of the prisoner to a different custodian).

[12]See Collings, Habeas Corpus for Convicts—Constitutional Right or Legislative Grace?, 40 Cal.L.Rev. 335, 337–38 (1952). See also Oaks, Legal History in the High Court—Habeas Corpus, 64 Mich.L.Rev. 401, 460–61 (1966).

[13]Bushell's Case, 124 Eng.Rep. 1006 (C.P.1670); 6 State Trials 999 (1670).

[14]See Rosenn, The Great Writ—A Reflection of Societal Change, 44 Ohio St.L.J. 308, 309 (1983).

[15]Fay v. Noia, 372 U.S. 391, 83 S.Ct. 822, 9 L.Ed.2d 837 (1963), also discussed in § 28.3(c). The reasoning and result in *Bushell's Case*, the Court argued, showed that the writ was available to respond to "judicial as well as executive restraints" that were "contrary to fundamental law."

far too broad.[16] Professor Oaks maintained that *Bushell's Case* did not expand the reach of the writ, but left convicted persons only with the traditional challenge to the jurisdiction of the convicting court. In both England and the colonies, he argued, the writ had "won its place as the most important safeguard of personal liberty," not as applied to convicted persons, but "when employed against the crown and its officers * * * to elicit the cause for an individual's imprisonment and to ensure that he was released admitted to bail, or promptly tried." In any event, as a remedy for persons detained upon a conviction, the writ historically had very limited utility.

English habeas corpus jurisprudence was transplanted into post-colonial America,[17] and a reference to the writ of habeas corpus was included in the text of Article I of the Federal Constitution. The Judiciary Act of 1789 granted federal courts limited habeas review,[18] and after the Civil War, Congress passed the Habeas Corpus Act of 1867, broadening significantly federal judicial authority to review state court judgments. For the first time federal courts were given the power to grant writs of habeas corpus when any person was held "in violation of the Constitution."[19] Despite the significant changes in the statute that have occurred since that era,[20] the history of the writ and its use in federal courts during the nineteenth century continue to inform the Court's application of the contemporary commands of Congress.[21]

---

[16]*Schneckloth v. Bustamonte*, discussed in § 28.3(c), citing with approval Oaks, Legal History in the High Court—Habeas Corpus, 64 Mich.L. Rev. 401, 461–68 (1966).

[17]See Oaks, Habeas Corpus in the States—1776–1865, 32 U.Chi.L.Rev. 243 (1965). The enlistment cases, arising from the faulty federal recruitment of soldiers during the War of 1812, applied the writ to federal prisoners. See, e.g., Commonwealth v. Cushing, 11 Mass. 67 (1814) (holding that a minor's enlistment contract was voidable at the minor's request). See also Arkin, The Ghost at the Banquet: Slavery, Federalism, and Habeas Corpus for State Prisoners, 70 Tul.L.Rev. 1, 14–22 (1995), for an extended examination of the enlistment cases.

[18]Arkin, The Ghost at the Banquet: Slavery, Federalism, and Habeas Corpus for State Prisoners, 70 Tul.L.Rev. 1, 7–10 (1995). See also Woolhandler, Demodeling Habeas, 45 Stan.L.Rev. 575 (1993).

[19]The Habeas Corpus Act of 1867, ch. 20, 14 Stat. 385. For an analysis of habeas corpus jurisprudence during Reconstruction, see Woolhandler, Demodeling Habeas, 45 Stan.L.Rev. 575, 569–629 (1993).

[20]See § 28.2(b).

[21]See, e.g., Felker v. Turpin, 518 U.S. 651, 656–63, 116 S.Ct. 2333, 2337–39, 135 L.Ed.2d 827 (1996); Steiker, Innocence and Federal Habeas, 41 UCLA L.Rev. 303, 309 (1993) (noting the "extensive historiography" surrounding federal habeas jurisprudence). See also Oaks, Habeas Corpus in the States—1776–1865, 32 U.Chi.L.Rev. 243, 245–46 (1965):

Although the federal constitution and statutes contain detailed provisions on habeas corpus, the leading

§ 28.1(c) The common law writ of coram nobis

The writ of coram nobis can be traced back to the sixteenth century, but it was viewed at common law as not nearly as important a writ as habeas corpus.[22] At the time of the development of the writ of coram nobis a trial court was not authorized to correct its own errors, and a higher court on writ of error could consider only alleged mistakes of law. Accordingly, there was no means available for correcting errors of fact. The writs of error quae coram nobis resident and quae coram vobis resident were developed to fill this gap. The former was issued to challenge a judgment of the King's Bench while the latter applied to judgments of the Court of Common Pleas.[23] Both forms of the writ extended to civil as well as criminal cases. The writ provided for review by the trial court. Its objective was "to bring to light errors of fact that the trial court could not have avoided—mistakes that, if known at the time of the trial, would have prevented entry of the judgment."[24] Thus, it allowed presentation of facts not apparent on the face of the record, such as the death or infancy of a party or an error of the clerk in recording the judgment. The writ could be used only where no other remedy was available and the defendant was "without negligence" in fail-

---

federal decisions have relied heavily on history and on the common law. Chief Justice Marshall set the precedent in an important early case by declaring that "for the meaning of the term *habeas corpus*, resort may unquestionably be had to the common law * * *." [Ex parte Bollman, discussed in § 28.2(a)]. A hundred and fifty-six years later history was still of such significance that the majority opinion in a leading habeas corpus case declared that the Court could not answer the question posed "without a preliminary inquiry into the historical development of the writ of habeas corpus."

But see Arkin, The Ghost at the Banquet: Slavery, Federalism, and Habeas Corpus for State Prisoners, 70 Tul.L.Rev. 12 (1995) (concluding that debate over habeas corpus must be adapted to the twentieth century).

The history of the writ has been the subject of a great deal of scholarly debate and criticism. In addition to the sources cited in prior footnotes, see Bator, Finality in Criminal Law and Federal Habeas Corpus for State Prisoners, 76 Harv.L.Rev. 441 (1963);

Freedman, Habeas Corpus: Rethinking the Great Writ of Liberty (2002); Peller, In Defense of Federal Habeas Corpus Relitigation, 16 Harv.C.R.-C.L. L.Rev. 579 (1982); Liebman, Apocalypse Next Time?: The Anachronistic Attack on Habeas Corpus/Direct Review Parity, 92 Colum.L.Rev. 1997 (1992).

[Section 28.1(c)]

[22] L. Yackle, Postconviction Remedies § 9 (1981 & Supp.2007); E. Frank, Coram Nobis 1–8 (1953).

[23] The writ of coram vobis, issued by a higher court, directed the Court of Common Pleas to hold the record "before you," while the writ of coram nobis directed at the King's Bench to keep the record "before us." E.g., L. Yackle, Postconviction Remedies § 9 (1981 & Supp.2007). For a brief review of the history of the writ of coram nobis, see Note, 58 Fordham L.Rev. 979, 981–85 (1990).

[24] L. Yackle, Postconviction Remedies § 8 (1981 & Supp.2007).

ing to alert the trial judge to the crucial fact.[25]

Although the common law writ of coram nobis was noted primarily for its use in civil cases, it came to have some significance in criminal cases during the 1800s. Coram nobis was used to challenge a conviction on the grounds that the defendant was an escaped slave (and therefore could not be confined against the wishes of his master), that defendant was insane at the time of trial, and the defendant had entered a guilty plea out of fear of mob violence.[26] Eventually, the writ of coram nobis was largely displaced by the motion for a new trial based on newly discovered evidence, and an expanded writ of habeas corpus. Moreover, with defendants more frequently represented by counsel, it became more difficult to contend that the defendant's failure to bring the factual error to the attention of the trial court was excusable. Accordingly, this common law writ has fallen into disuse, except in the very narrow circumstances summarized in § 28.9(a).

§ 28.2 The statutory structure and habeas policy
§ 28.2(a)   Constitutional right or legislative grace?
§ 28.2(b)   Statutory structure: from the 1867 Act to the 1996 Act
§ 28.2(c)   Balancing within the statutory framework
§ 28.2(d)   Competing models of habeas review

---

§ 28.2(a) Constitutional right or legislative grace?[1]
In a provision commonly known as the "Suspension Clause," Article I of the United States Constitution states: "[T]he Privilege of the Writ of Habeas Corpus shall not be suspended, unless when in Cases of Rebellion or Invasion the Public Safety may require it."[2] On its face, this provision suggests that federal courts have the inherent authority to issue the writ in the absence of a valid suspension.[3] Such a reading would establish, in effect, a constitutional right to habeas relief, at least to the extent such

---

[25]R. Popper, Post-conviction Remedies 51 (1978).

[26]See Ex parte Toney, 11 Mo. 661 (1848); Sanders v. State, 85 Ind. 318 (1882).

[Section 28.2(a)]

[1]This subtitle is taken from Collings, Habeas Corpus for Convicts—Constitutional Right or Legislative Grace?, 40 Cal.L.Rev. 335 (1952).

[2]U.S. Const. Art. I, § 9. cl. 2.

[3]See Steiker, Incorporating the Suspension Clause: Is There a Constitutional Right to Federal Habeas Corpus for State Prisoners?, 92 Mich.L. Rev. 862 (1994); Chafee, The Most Important Right in the Constitution, 32 B.U.L.Rev. 143 (1952). See also W. Duker, A Constitutional History of Habeas Corpus 126–80 (1980); Pascal, Habeas Corpus and the Constitution, 1970 Duke L.J. 605 (arguing that the clause directed the judiciary, "state as well as federal, to make the privilege routinely available").

relief was available at common law,[4] for persons held in custody. Professor Duker has argued that "the debates in the federal and state conventions, the location of the habeas clause [among restrictions upon congressional power], and the contemporary commentary" suggest that the Clause was designed only "to restrict congressional power to suspend state habeas for federal prisoners."[5] Insofar as issuance of the writ by federal courts was concerned, that was apparently a matter to be determined by Congress if and when it created inferior federal courts. Additional support for this view is found in the fact that the first Congress specifically authorized in the Judiciary Act of 1789 the issuance of the writ by the newly created federal courts, thereby suggesting that it did not believe that those courts had any inherent power under the habeas clause to issue the writ.[6]

Although the Court occasionally had suggested that the later 1867 provision making the federal writ available to state prisoners might have constitutional roots,[7] the Court did not find it necessary to consider whether the Suspension Clause guarantees that authority until Congress cut back significantly the availability of the writ in 1996.[8] The Court in *Felker v. Turpin*[9] unanimously rejected the contention that the Clause was violated by those provisions of the Antiterrorism and Effective Death

---

[4]As suggested by Chief Justice Burger, concurring in Swain v. Pressley, 430 U.S. 372, 97 S.Ct. 1224, 51 L.Ed.2d 411 (1977), the Clause, even assuming that it guarantees a federal writ of habeas corpus, may provide a right to the writ only as it existed when the Constitution was drafted.

[5]W. Duker, A Constitutional History of Habeas Corpus 126 (1980). At the time the Constitution was adopted, the habeas remedy was widely available in the state courts. It was assumed that the state courts could use the writ on behalf of federal prisoners, particularly if there were no federal courts. Indeed, even after inferior federal courts were created, the state courts commonly issued the writ on behalf of federal prisoners. Not until 1859 did the Supreme Court hold that practice to constitute an unauthorized infringement upon federal authority. See Ableman v. Booth, 62 U.S. (21 How.) 506, 16 L.Ed. 169 (1859).

[6]The authorization was contained in article 14 of the Judiciary Act of 1789, 1 Stat. 81 to 82 (1789).

[7]See, e.g., Fay v. Noia, 372 U.S. 391, 83 S.Ct. 822, 9 L.Ed.2d 837 (1963) (declining "to consider whether it was the Framers' understanding that congressional refusal to permit the federal courts to accord the writ its full common-law scope as we have described it might constitute an unconstitutional suspension of the privilege of the writ"); Jones v. Cunningham, 371 U.S. 236, 83 S.Ct. 373, 9 L.Ed.2d 285 (1963) (describing the pre-1996 habeas corpus statutes as "implement[ing] the constitutional command that the writ of habeas corpus be available").

[8]Chief Justice Marshall's opinion in Ex parte Bollman, 8 U.S. (4 Cranch) 75, 2 L.Ed. 554 (1807), the first major ruling on the 1789 habeas provision, suggested that a congressional refusal to authorize federal habeas corpus relief would be inconsistent with the assumption of the Framers, but would nevertheless be constitutionally acceptable. In Ex parte Dorr, 44 U.S. (3 How.) 103, 11 L.Ed. 514 (1845), the Court held that the 1789 provision provided relief for only federal prison-

Penalty Act of 1996 that sharply limit habeas relief for state petitioners filing successive petitions.[10] Chief Justice Rehnquist's opinion for the Court initially noted that "the writ of habeas corpus known to the Framers was quite different from that which exists today" as the writ at that time was available "only to prisoners confined under the authority of the United States, not under state authority" and "[t]he class of judicial actions reviewable by the writ was more restricted as well." It "was not until 1867 that Congress made the writ generally available * * * [to state prisoners,] [a]nd it was not until well into this century that this Court interpreted that provision to allow a final judgment of conviction in a state court to be collaterally attacked." The *Felker* Court assumed, however, for purposes of its decision, "that the Suspension Clause of the Constitution refers to the writ as it exists today, rather than as it existed in 1789." The Court had long recognized that "judgments about the proper scope of the writ are 'normally for Congress to make.'" In enacting new restrictions on the authority of federal courts to consider successive petitions, Congress dealt with an area of habeas law which the Court had previously described as the product of "a complex and evolving body of equitable principles informed and controlled by historical usage, statutory developments and judicial decisions." The new limitations were "well within the compass of this evolutionary process." Noting that the 1996 Act did not repeal the authority of the Supreme Court to entertain original habeas petitions filed under § 2241, the Court concluded that the limitations on successive petitions did "not amount to a suspension of the writ contrary to Article I, § 9."[11]

The extent to which the Suspension Clause prohibits limits on habeas review for those imprisoned by federal authorities has been the subject of considerably more litigation. When Congress limited habeas review of deportation orders in the late 1990s, and then again when the United States refused to release "enemy combatants" seized following the terrorist attacks of September 11, 2001, the Court has had the opportunity to address, albeit

---

ers. It wasn't until 1833 that Congress extended the federal habeas statute to a limited class of persons held in state custody, and it was not until 1867 that the statute was made applicable to state prisoners generally. See § 28.2(b). Throughout this period, there was no suggestion by the Court that this "gap" in the availability of the federal coverage posed any constitutional difficulties.

[9]Felker v. Turpin, 518 U.S. 651, 116 S.Ct. 2333, 135 L.Ed.2d 827 (1996).

[10]See § 28.5(c), (d) (discussing these provisions).

[11]For discussions of *Felker*, see Koehn, A Line in the Sand: The Supreme Court and the Writ of Habeas Corpus, 32 Tulsa L.J. 389 (1997); Tushnet, "The King of France with Forty Thousand Men": Felker v. Turpin and the Supreme Court's Deliberative Processes, 1996 Sup.Ct.Rev. 163; Note, 32 Harv.C.R.-C.L.L.Rev. 249 (1997).

obliquely, the Suspension Clause. A challenge to the 1996 statute limiting habeas review of deportation orders reached the Court in *INS v. St. Cyr.*[12] The Court invoked the principle of constitutional doubt to interpret the statute in a way that allowed habeas review of a question of law in connection with the detention of an alien, specifically whether certain discretionary relief was available for aliens whose convictions were obtained through plea agreements and who would have been eligible for that discretionary relief at the time of their plea. It reasoned that aliens subject to a federal removal order had access to the writ at common law in 1789, so "even assuming that the Suspension Clause protects only the writ as it existed in 1789," a "serious Suspension Clause issue would be presented if we were to accept the INS's submission that the 1996 statutes have withdrawn that power from federal judges and provided no adequate substitute for its exercise." The Court noted that historically it is in the context of reviewing the legality of executive detention that the writ's protections have been strongest.[13]

The use of the writ to challenge executive detention was again presented in *Hamdi v. Rumsfeld.*[14] There the Court addressed a petition under § 2241 filed by a United States citizen imprisoned within the borders of the United States as an alleged "enemy combatant." After finding that the writ had not been suspended, the Court went on to detail the procedures that must be provided in those circumstances. Justice Scalia, dissenting, stated his view that military exigency does not permit detention without criminal prosecution, and that only Congress can suspend the writ or

---

[12]INS v. St. Cyr, 533 U.S. 289, 121 S.Ct. 2271, 150 L.Ed.2d 347 (2001). The Court explained, "the absence of [another judicial forum], coupled with the lack of a clear, unambiguous, and express statement of congressional intent to preclude judicial consideration on habeas of such an important question of law, strongly counsels against adopting a construction [of AEDPA, the 1996 habeas statute] that would raise serious constitutional questions." The Court concluded that "habeas jurisdiction under § 2241" to hear questions of law concerning detention of aliens subject to removal orders "was not repealed by AEDPA and IIRIRA." See also Neuman, Habeas Corpus, Executive Detention, and the Removal of Aliens, 98 Colum.L.Rev. 961 (1998).

[13]In dissent, three justices reached the Suspension Clause issue and argued that the Clause only prohibits Congress from temporarily eliminating access to the writ for certain areas or classes of claimants, it does not prohibit permanent alteration of its content. Moreover, the dissenters argued, even if the Clause "guarantees some constitutional minimum of habeas relief, that minimum would assuredly not embrace the rarified right asserted here: the right to judicial compulsion of the exercise of Executive discretion * * * regarding a prisoner's release."

[14]Hamdi v. Rumsfeld, 542 U.S. 507, 124 S.Ct. 2633, 159 L.Ed.2d 578 (2004).

determine what constitutes a case of "rebellion or invasion."[15] In *Rasul v. Bush*,[16] the Court held that federal courts had jurisdiction to consider petitions filed under § 2241 by foreign nationals alleging that their detention at Guantanamo Bay Naval Base was in violation of federal law. These cases, evaluating the opportunities for those imprisoned by the United States government without criminal prosecution to challenge their detention in the federal courts, raise concerns central to the foundation of the common law writ centuries ago.[17] Nevertheless, because this chapter is primarily concerned with the procedures that allow those convicted of crime in state court to challenge their convictions and sentences in federal court, the discussion of the use of the writ for those imprisoned by the federal government without criminal prosecution must be left to other sources.[18]

§ 28.2(b) Statutory structure: from the 1867 Act to the 1996 Act

For over a century, the Habeas Corpus Act of 1867 provided the basic statutory framework for federal habeas relief for state prisoners. Although several key provisions have now been superseded by provisions of the 1996 Antiterrorism and Effective Death Penalty Act ("AEDPA"), an understanding of the earlier statute is an essential backdrop to litigation under the new provisions.

The 1867 Act provided federal habeas relief for any person "restrained of his or her liberty." This included state prisoners, who had been excluded under the 1789 Act. A federal court applying the writ to a person held in state custody was not to exam-

---

[15]In another case involving a United States citizen challenging his detention as a military combatant under § 2241, the Court concluded that he had filed his petition in the wrong court. Rumsfeld v. Padilla, 542 U.S. 426, 124 S.Ct. 2711, 159 L.Ed.2d 513 (2004).

[16]Rasul v. Bush, 542 U.S. 466, 124 S.Ct. 2686, 159 L.Ed.2d 548 (2004).

Hamdan v. Rumsfeld, __ U.S. __, 126 S.Ct. 2749, 165 L.Ed.2d 72 (2006) (finding Court had jurisdiction to consider habeas petition filed by Hamdan, a Yemeni national imprisoned in Guantanamo Bay, that challenged the authority of the military commission to try him).

[17]See, e.g., Hamdi v. Rumsfeld, 542 U.S. 507, 124 S.Ct. 2633, 159 L.Ed.2d 578 (2004) (Scalia, J., dissent-

ing) ("The very core of liberty secured by our Anglo-Saxon system of separated powers has been freedom from indefinite imprisonment at the will of the Executive"); Rumsfeld v. Padilla, 542 U.S. 426, 124 S.Ct. 2711, 159 L.Ed.2d 513 (2004) (Stevens, J., dissenting) (what is "[a]t stake * * * is nothing less than the essence of a free society").

[18]For additional commentary on executive detention, see, e.g., Fallon & Meltzer, Habeas Corpus Jurisdiction, Substantive Rights, and the War on Terror, 120 Harv.L.Rev. this topic was growing; Katyal & Tribe, Waging War, Deciding Guilt: Trying the Military Tribunals, 111 Yale L.J. 1259 (2002); Swanson, Enemy Combatants and the Writ of Habeas Corpus, 35 Ariz.St.L.J. 939 (2003).

ine the legality of the detention under state law. Relief could be granted from only those restraints imposed in violation of federal law—the Constitution, treaties, and statutes of the United States. The 1867 Act also changed habeas procedure by providing that petitioners could "deny any of the material facts set forth in the return" or allege additional facts. Thus, the habeas court was "empowered to conduct an inquiry into the facts underlying the detention and was no longer limited to bare legal review."[19]

The objectives of the Thirty-ninth Congress in adopting the Habeas Corpus Act of 1867 have been debated for years.[20] Of the several views advanced, two in particular attracted attention during the latter decades of the twentieth century as the Supreme Court and Congress reconsidered the appropriate scope of the habeas remedy. Professor Paul Bator argued for a narrow reading that assumed that the Act incorporated the "historical meaning and scope"[21] of the writ, including earlier cases that had applied the 1789 Act to federal prisoners and had limited habeas review to a determination of whether the convicting court had jurisdiction over the person and the subject matter.[22] Commentators adhering to this position have contended that this reading fully

---

[Section 28.2(b)]

[19]Rosenn, The Great Writ—A Reflection of Societal Change, 44 Ohio St.L.J. 337, 341 (1983). For one review of changes made by the 1867 Act and the legislative history of that Act, see Forsythe, The Historical Origins of Broad Federal Habeas Review Reconsidered, 70 Notre Dame L.Rev. 1079, 1101–17 (1995).

[20]Compare for example, the views expressed in the following articles: Bator, Finality in Criminal Law and Federal Habeas Corpus for State Prisoners, 76 Harv.L.Rev. 441 (1963); Forsythe, The Historical Origins of Broad Federal Habeas Review Reconsidered, 70 Notre Dame L.Rev. 1079 (1995); Liebman, Apocalypse Next Time?: The Anachronistic Attack on Habeas Corpus/Direct Review Parity, 92 Colum.L.Rev. 1997 (1992); Mayers, The Habeas Corpus Act of 1867: The Supreme Court as Legal Historian, 33 U.Chi.L.Rev. 31 (1965); McCord, Visions of Habeas, 1994 B.Y.U.L.Rev. 735 (1994); Peller, In Defense of Federal Habeas Corpus Relitigation, 16 Harv.Civ.Rts.-Civ.Lib. L.Rev. 579 (1982); Saltzburg, Habeas

Corpus: The Supreme Court and the Congress, 44 Ohio St.L.Rev. 367 (1983); Woolhandler, Demodeling Habeas, 45 Stan.L.Rev. 575 (1993).

[21]Bator, Finality in Criminal Law and Federal Habeas Corpus for State Prisoners, 76 Harv.L.Rev. 441, 475 (1963).

[22]A wider range of review, proponents of this narrow view argued, would have undercut the then existing limitations on appellate review of federal convictions. At the time, the federal prisoner did not have a right to direct appellate review of his conviction by the Supreme Court (although Supreme Court review was available to state defendants as to federal questions). Habeas challenges, on the other hand, were subject to Supreme Court review, and an expansive habeas challenge therefore would give the federal prisoner indirectly the appellate review denied him directly, without the previously accepted reconciliation based on the special quality of jurisdictional defects. Until 1889 federal criminal cases were reviewed by the Supreme Court only in the event of a division of opinion by the circuit court

satisfies the major concern of Congress in adopting the 1867 Act, which was that the states not be allowed to keep the newly freed slaves from exercising their rights by applying to them broadly phrased state laws that were contrary to the recently enacted Thirteenth Amendment and Civil Rights Act.[23] The Civil Rights Act of 1866 provided citizens "of every race or color" should be "subject to like punishment, pains and penalties and to none other." Detention pursuant to state statutes in violation of this command could be challenged under the writ, consistent with the earlier habeas rulings, because the unconstitutionality of the statute on which it was based deprived the state court of its jurisdiction.[24]

Proponents of a broader view of the 1867 Act also looked to the Reconstruction-era context in which the habeas statute was adopted.[25] They argued that Congress expected that the courts of the Southern states would be totally unreceptive to Reconstruction legislation and wanted to give the federal courts superin-

---

on a question of law. See 2 Stat. 156, 159 to 61 (Act of April 29, 1802); 25 Stat. 656 (Act of February 6, 1889). Moreover, the provision for review on a division in the circuit was rarely invoked because of the practice of single district judges holding circuit court. Thus, "there was, in practical effect, no appellate review." Stone v. Powell, 428 U.S. 465, 96 S.Ct. 3037, 49 L.Ed.2d 1067 (1976). In habeas cases, which were treated as civil, an appeal was available, as recognized in the 1867 Act. Subsequently, Congress, responding to possible judicial rejection of the Reconstruction Acts in the first habeas appeal to reach the Supreme Court under the 1867 Act, withdrew the Court's appellate jurisdiction under that Act. See Ex parte McCardle, 74 U.S. (7 Wall.) 506, 19 L.Ed. 264 (1869). That jurisdiction was not restored until 1885. See W. Duker, A Constitutional History of Habeas Corpus 194–199 (1980).

[23]See, e.g., Forsythe, The Historical Origins of Broad Federal Habeas Review Reconsidered, 70 Notre Dame L.Rev. 1079 (1995).

[24]Forsythe, The Historical Origins of Broad Federal Habeas Review Reconsidered, 70 Notre Dame L.Rev. 1079, 1101–1169 (1995) (arguing that the legislative history of the 1867 Act

and the 1885 jurisdiction act demonstrate no intent on the part of Congress to change the nature of the writ from one available for jurisdictional errors only, and that "the legal case for broad habeas review is a house of cards").

[25]See, e.g., Peller, In Defense of Federal Habeas Corpus Relitigation, 16 Harv.Civ.Rts.-Civ.Lib.L.Rev. 579 (1982); Saltzburg, Habeas Corpus: The Supreme Court and the Congress, 44 Ohio St.L.Rev. 367 (1983); Tushnet, Judicial Revision of the Habeas Corpus Statutes: A Note on *Schneckloth v. Bustamonte*, 1975 Wis.L.Rev. 484. The Act's provisions for determination of fact were said to reflect an intent to have the federal courts "try * * * the facts anew" insofar as they relate to federal rights. Fay v. Noia, 372 U.S. 391, 83 S.Ct. 822, 9 L.Ed.2d 837 (1963). But see Mayers, The Habeas Corpus Act of 1867: The Supreme Court as Legal Historian, 33 U.Chi.L. Rev. 31, 57 (1965) (suggesting that, at the time, the courts considered that factual examination to be limited to determining whether "there was an indictment, a trial, a conviction, a final judgment, a sentence, and process of execution and jurisdiction of such proceedings").

tending control to ensure that there would be full recognition of the federal rights in the 1866 Civil Rights Act and the Fourteenth Amendment.[26]

In the 1960s the Court adopted this broader interpretation of the Act's purpose in several expansive decisions, noting that the writ was capable of growth to meet "changed conceptions of the kind of criminal proceedings so fundamentally defective as to make imprisonment pursuant to them constitutionally intolerable."[27] But by the mid-1970s the tide had turned,[28] and the Court's interpretations of the habeas statute narrowed. Meanwhile, Congress offered little further direction, adding various provisions to the habeas statute, none of which modified the core statutory authorization set forth in the 1867 Act.[29] In 1976 habeas cases became subject to newly promulgated "Rules Governing 2254 Cases in the United States District Courts," supplementing the statutory provisions and intended to increase the efficiency of habeas proceedings.

Substantial change came in 1996, when Congress enacted the Antiterrorism and Effective Death Penalty Act (AEDPA), narrowing the basic provisions of the 1867 Act.[30] The Act was prompted in part by frustration over delays that accompanied habeas

---

[26]The Fourteenth Amendment was under consideration in the Congress at the same time that the Habeas Act was passed. Its Due Process and Equal Protection Clauses were designed in part to provide a constitutional foundation for the already enacted Civil Rights Act. See § 2.3(a).

[27]Fay v. Noia, 372 U.S. 391, 83 S.Ct. 822, 9 L.Ed.2d 837 (1963).

[28]See Schneckloth v. Bustamonte, 412 U.S. 218, 93 S.Ct. 2041, 36 L.Ed.2d 854 (1973), where Justice Powell, speaking for four members of the Court, characterized "Fay v. Noia's version of the writ's historic function" as resting upon a "revisionist view of history." Justice Powell relied on writings of Professors Bator and Oaks. See Bator, Finality in Criminal Law and Federal Habeas Corpus for State Prisoners, 76 Harv.L.Rev. 441 (1963), and Oaks, Legal History in the High Court—Habeas Corpus, 64 Mich.L. Rev.451 (1966). Schneckloth was followed by the 1976 ruling of Stone v. Powell, 428 U.S. 465, 96 S.Ct. 3037, 49 L.Ed.2d 1067 (1976), where Justice Powell, now speaking for a majority,

appeared again to reject the broader Noia interpretation.

[29]For example, in 1948, Congress codified the "state exhaustion" requirement, see § 28.5(a), and established a separate procedure—described as a motion to vacate a sentence—to replace the habeas writ for federal prisoners. That procedure, codified in 18 U.S.C.A. § 2255, similarly refers to "violation[s] of the Constitution or laws of the United States" (treaty violations falling within the latter category), although it also encompasses challenges to illegal sentences and to sentences issued by a court "without jurisdiction to impose such sentence." See § 28.9. Congress also specified in 1966 the conditions under which a federal court must provide an evidentiary hearing or honor a state court's factual finding. See § 28.7(a).

[30]Pub.L. 104-132, 110 Stat. 1217 (1996). See Yackle, A Primer on the New Habeas Corpus Statute, 44 Buff.L. Rev. 381 (1996). On the genesis of AEDPA, see also Liebman, An "Effective Death Penalty"? AEDPA and Error Detection in Capital Cases, 67 Brook.

review in capital cases, but modified the rules governing collateral relief in both capital and non-capital cases, for both state and federal prisoners. What follows below is a very brief outline of current statutory provisions governing the writ of habeas corpus for persons in state custody, provisions that will be examined in more detail in later sections of this chapter.

Unchanged by the 1996 amendments, 28 U.S.C.A. § 2241 contains the basic authorization of the federal courts to issue the writ. Subsection (c) sets forth the conditions under which the writ may "extend to a prisoner." Subsection (c)(3), with only a slight alteration of the language of the 1867 Act, provides that the writ may issue when the prisoner "is in custody in violation of the Constitution or laws or treaties of the United States." Section 2241 also provides authority for the Supreme Court to grant a petition filed originally with the High Court, although Rule 20.4(a) of the Supreme Court Rules limits such relief to "exceptional circumstances."

Section 2243, also unchanged, deals primarily with matters of procedure (e.g., the use of show cause orders and the timing of the hearings), but ends by noting that the habeas court, after concluding its hearing, shall "dispose of the matter as law and justice require." This provision has been cited by the Court as evidencing the "equitable nature" of the habeas remedy.[31]

Section 2244, completely revised in 1996 and entitled "Finality of Determinations," deals with second or successive petitions and time limits for filing. It sets forth circumstances under which a judge may refuse to consider a petition on the basis of the disposition of an earlier petition and includes a one-year limitations period during which a petitioner may apply for a writ of habeas

---

L.Rev. 411 (2001) (describing push for passage of bill after the Oklahoma City bombing).

[31] Fay v. Noia, 372 U.S. 391, 83 S.Ct. 822, 9 L.Ed.2d 837 (1963). Federal courts are not restricted to ordering immediate release from custody. See, e.g., Carafas v. LaVallee, 391 U.S. 234, 88 S.Ct. 1556, 20 L.Ed.2d 554 (1968), discussed in § 28.3(a) at notes 23–26; Hardcastle v. Horn, 368 F.3d 246 (3d Cir.2004) (after finding that state court unreasonably applied *Batson*, remanding to district court for hearing in order to provide state a chance to present justifications for challenged strikes, rather than requir-

ing retrial); Saterlee v. Wolfenburger, 453 F.3d 362 (6th Cir.2006) (collecting authority and holding a district court may order the expungement of the record of state conviction); Gentry v. Deuth, 456 F.3d 687 (6th Cir.2006) ("having correctly issued the writ, the choice of habeas remedy lies within the district court's sound discretion," here court did not abuse its discretion by nullifying the state conviction when the state decided, by its inaction, not to provide the petitioner with appropriate relief"). See generally R. Hertz & J. Liebman, 2 Federal Habeas Practice and Procedure § 33.4 (5th ed.2005).

corpus.[32]

Under § 2253, governing appeals, a prisoner has no absolute entitlement to appeal a district court's denial or dismissal of his petition, but must first seek and obtain a "certificate of appealability" from a circuit justice or judge, by demonstrating a "substantial showing of the denial of a constitutional right."[33]

Section 2254 deals specifically with applications "on behalf of a person in custody pursuant to the judgment of a state court."[34] Sections 2254(b) and (c) contain the requirement that a state prisoner exhaust state remedies before federal relief may be granted.[35] Rewritten § 2254(d), perhaps the most important section added by the 1996 Act, defines the circumstances under which a writ may be granted when the petitioner's claim was adjudicated on the merits in state court.[36] New § 2254(e) governs fact-finding and evidentiary hearings, and includes a presumption concerning state factfinding.[37]

Sections 2261 through 2266 impose special standards for considering habeas petitions filed by state prisoners sentenced to death in states which have met certain prerequisites.[38]

§ 28.2(c) Balancing within the statutory framework

Except where the language of the statute is quite specific, the Court generally has considered its task in interpreting the habeas statute as one of achieving the appropriate balance between the value of expansive habeas review and the costs of providing such review. The specific limitations on relief in the 1996 Act have restricted the circumstances under which the Court is free to balance such interests, and have tipped that balance distinctly in the direction of narrowing relief. Nevertheless, some room still remains for judicial policy analysis under the revised statute, which is far from a model of statutory drafting.[39]

The benefits of expansive collateral review for both state and

---

[32]The remaining provisions in §§ 2241 to 2252 deal with matters of pleading and procedure.

[33]This provision was addressed by the Court in Miller-El v. Cockrell, 537 U.S. 322, 123 S.Ct. 1029, 154 L.Ed.2d 931 (2003). See § 28.10.

[34]See, e.g., Medberry v. Crosby, 351 F.3d 1049 (11th Cir.2003) (tracing the history of the statutes establishing collateral relief, finding that § 2254 limits the remedies state prisoners would otherwise have under § 2241; § 2241 and § 2254 govern a single post-conviction remedy, with § 2254 requirements applying to petitions by

state prisoners, thus a state prisoner seeking post-conviction relief from a federal court may apply only for a writ of habeas corpus and are subject to the restrictions of § 2254).

[35]See § 28.5(a).

[36]See § 28.6(f).

[37]See § 28.7(a) and (c).

[38]See § 28.8.

[Section 28.2(c)]

[39]See, e.g., Justice Souter's oft-quoted comment in Lindh v. Murphy, 521 U.S. 320, 336, 117 S.Ct. 2059, 138 L.Ed.2d 481 (1997), "in a world of silk purses and pigs' ears, the Act is not a

federal prisoners were advocated most forcefully in the opinions of Justice Brennan.[40] Plenary review of constitutional claims on collateral attack, Justice Brennan maintained, is essential to fulfilling the historic function of habeas corpus—providing relief to persons detained in violation of their fundamental liberties.[41] An open-ended mechanism is needed, in particular, to consider claims that were not presented in the original proceeding that led to conviction, often through no fault of the defendant himself. "Conventional notions of finality of litigation," including concepts of res judicata, should "have no place where life or liberty is at stake and infringement of constitutional rights is alleged."[42]

In addition, expansive habeas review is supported by the institutional and political premises underlying the Fourteenth Amendment, as well as the 1867 Habeas Act, which give "federal courts the 'last say' with respect to question of federal law."[43] Federal habeas corpus rests, it is said, on "the proposition that persons convicted of crimes in state courts are entitled to at least one opportunity to litigate their federal claims in a federal forum."[44] Since the Supreme Court obviously lacks the resources necessary to review all but a small portion of the state cases in which direct review is sought, the lower federal courts must serve as its functional surrogate in providing federal review.[45] Only the federal habeas court can provide the evidentiary hearings often

---

silk purse of the art of statutory drafting."

[40] See, e.g., Justice Brennan's opinions for the Court in Fay v. Noia, 372 U.S. 391, 83 S.Ct. 822, 9 L.Ed.2d 837 (1963); Kaufman v. United States, 394 U.S. 217, 89 S.Ct. 1068, 22 L.Ed.2d 227 (1969); and Sanders v. United States, 373 U.S. 1, 83 S.Ct. 1068, 10 L.Ed.2d 148 (1963). See also Justice Brennan's dissents in Stone v. Powell, 428 U.S. 465, 96 S.Ct. 3037, 49 L.Ed.2d 1067 (1976); Wainwright v. Sykes, 433 U.S. 72, 97 S.Ct. 2497, 53 L.Ed.2d 594 (1977); and Engle v. Isaac, 456 U.S. 107, 102 S.Ct. 1558, 71 L.Ed.2d 783 (1982).

[41] Even as applied to federal convictions, where the defendant has had the advantage of a federal forum, "adequate protection of constitutional rights * * * requires the continuing availability of a mechanism for relief." Kaufman v. United States, 394 U.S. 217, 89 S.Ct. 1068, 22 L.Ed.2d 227 (1969).

[42] Sanders v. United States, 373 U.S. 1, 83 S.Ct. 1068, 10 L.Ed.2d 148 (1963). As Judge Lay noted in Lay, Modern Administrative Proposals for Federal Habeas, 21 DePaul L.Rev. 701, 709–10 (1972):

We would not send two astronauts to the moon without providing them with at least three or four back-up systems. Should we send literally thousands of men to prison with even less reserve? * * * [W]ith knowledge of our fallibility and a realization of past errors, we can hardly insure our confidence by creating an irrevocable end to the guilt determining process.

[43] Kaufman v. United States, 394 U.S. 217, 89 S.Ct. 1068, 22 L.Ed.2d 227 (1969). See also Rose v. Mitchell, 443 U.S. 545, 99 S.Ct. 2993, 61 L.Ed.2d 739 (1979).

[44] Kaufman, 394 U.S. at 225, 89 S.Ct. at 1073.

[45] This role of the federal habeas courts, it is argued, also provides greater uniformity in constitutional in-

needed to provide a complete review of the constitutional claims of state prisoners.

The demand for a federal forum, Justice Brennan noted, is not based on any doubts as to the personal integrity of state judges, but rather on the recognition of the institutional limitations under which state judges operate. "State judges popularly elected," he explained, "may have difficulty resisting popular pressures not experienced by federal judges given lifetime tenure designed to immunize them from such influences, and the federal habeas statutes reflect the congressional judgment that such detached federal review is a salutary safeguard * * *."[46]

The Court, however, has questioned the assumption that institutional factors render state judges less receptive to federal constitutional claims than federal judges. Justice O'Connor has noted, for example, that many states utilize merit selection systems that give state judges security against "majoritorian pressures" comparable to that provided by the life tenure afforded federal judges.[47] Without substantial evidence of concerted failure by state courts to abide by their obligations, the Court has not been prepared to assure that federal habeas courts must conduct de novo review of all federal claims notwithstanding adequate state procedures for considering those claims. As the Court stated in *Stone v. Powell*:

> Despite differences in institutional environment and the unsympathetic attitude to federal constitutional claims of some state judges in years past, we are unwilling to assume that there now exists a general lack of appropriate sensitivity to constitutional rights in the trial and appellate courts of the several States. * * * [T]here is "no intrinsic reason why the fact that a man is a federal judge should make him more competent, or conscientious, or learned with respect to the [consideration of claims] than his neighbor in the state courthouse."[48]

The cost of expansive federal habeas review of state cases was

---

terpretation. See sources cited in §28.2(d) at note 75.

[46]Stone v. Powell, 428 U.S. 465, 96 S.Ct. 3037, 49 L.Ed.2d 1067 (1976) (Brennan, J. dissenting). See also Cover and Aleinikoff, Dialectical Federalism: Habeas Corpus and the Court, 86 Yale L.J. 1035, 1050–52 (1979) (federal courts tend to reflect a "utopian perspective" while state courts tend to reflect a "pragmatic perspective"); Neuborne, The Myth of Parity, 90 Harv.L.Rev. 1105 (1977) (citing various differences in the "psychological attitudinal characteristics" of state and federal trial judges).

[47]O'Connor, Trends in the Relationship Between the Federal and State Courts From the Perspective of a State Court Judge, 22 Wm. & Mary L.Rev. 801, 812–15 (1981) (written prior to her appointment to the Supreme Court, but reflecting a viewpoint reiterated in her opinions, see, e.g., Engle v. Isaac, 456 U.S. 107, 102 S.Ct. 1558, 71 L.Ed.2d 783 (1982)).

[48]Stone v. Powell, 428 U.S. 465, 493, n. 35, 96 S.Ct. 3037, 49 L.Ed.2d 1067 (1976), quoting Bator, Finality in Criminal Law and Federal Habeas Corpus for State Prisoners, 76 Harv.L. Rev. 441, 509 (1963). See also Aldis-

raised by Justice Powell,[49] who stressed primarily three concerns. First was the concern that broad habeas review results in an unwise expenditure of scarce judicial resources. Second, he argued, systematic habeas review of state decisions is inconsistent with the "constitutional balance upon which the doctrine of federalism is founded."[50] A third concern was that plenary habeas review works against the important objective of achieving a rational point of finality in the criminal justice process.

On the first point, caseload statistics reflect the significant resources devoted to litigation in habeas cases. The federal courts each year rule upon nearly 20,000 habeas petitions filed by state prisoners. Approximately one in every fourteen civil cases filed in district court is a habeas case filed by a state prisoner.[51] Justice Powell in 1973, when the caseload was considerably smaller, argued that such a significant expenditure of the finite resources of the federal judiciary would be more wisely devoted to other portions of the federal docket, civil actions "which affect intimately the lives of greater numbers of people" and criminal trials and appeals.[52] Proponents of limits on habeas review argue that the failure to restrict the scope of habeas may work against even that small class of state prisoners for whom habeas review may be necessary to ensure a full and fair opportunity for litigation of their constitutional claim. Of the non-capital state habeas petitions filed in the early 1990s, for example, relief was granted in only a tiny proportion, less than 2%.[53] Among petitions filed ten years later, the rate of relief dropped to about 1/3 of 1%.[54] Justice Jackson, commenting upon a "progressive trivialization of

---

ert, Judicial Expansion of Federal Jurisdiction: A Federal Judge's Thoughts on Section 1983, Comity and the Federal Caseload, 1973 Law & Soc.Ord. 557, 559 ("present infatuation with federal courts as the preferred forum" reflects the misguided "influence of academia").

[49]See Schneckloth v. Bustamonte, 412 U.S. 218, 93 S.Ct. 2041, 36 L.Ed.2d 854 (1973) (concurring opinion); Stone v. Powell, 428 U.S. 465, 96 S.Ct. 3037, 49 L.Ed.2d 1067 (1976), Rose v. Mitchell, 443 U.S. 545, 99 S.Ct. 2993, 61 L.Ed.2d 739 (1979) (concurring opinion). See also Engle v. Isaac, 456 U.S. 107, 102 S.Ct. 1558, 71 L.Ed.2d 783 (1982) (opinion of O'Connor, J.); Snead v. Stringer, 454 U.S. 988, 102 S.Ct. 535, 70 L.Ed.2d 402 (1981) (Rehnquist, J., dissenting from a denial of certiorari).

[50]Schneckloth v. Bustamonte, 412 U.S. 218, 93 S.Ct. 2041, 36 L.Ed.2d 854 (1973) (concurring opinion).

[51]N. King, F. Cheesman & B. Ostrom, Habeas Litigation in U.S. District Courts (2007), available at htt p://www.ncjrs.gov/pdffiles1/nij/grants/219559.pdf.

[52]Schneckloth v. Bustamonte, 412 U.S. 218, 93 S.Ct. 2041, 36 L.Ed.2d 854 (1973) (Powell J., concurring).

[53]R. Hanson & J. Daley, Federal Habeas Corpus Review: Challenging State Court Criminal Convictions (1995). But see Israel, Criminal Procedure, The Burger Court, and the Legacy of the Warren Court, 75 Mich. L. Rev. 1319, 1407 (1977).

[54]N. King, F. Cheesman & B. Ostrom, Habeas Litigation in U.S. District Courts (2007), available at htt

the writ" that could "inundate the dockets of the lower courts," warned in 1953 that "he who must search a haystack for a needle is likely to end up with the attitude that the needle is not worth the search."[55]

Proponents of broad review have argued that the burden imposed upon the federal courts is exaggerated. Evidentiary hearings are held in only a tiny fraction of the petitions filed, for example.[56] Moreover, they argue, the burden imposed is justified by the importance of the quest. Thus, Justice Schaefer of Illinois, responding to Justice Jackson's comment, noted: "It is not a needle we are looking for in these stacks of papers, but the rights of a human being."[57] Collateral review has been particularly significant in death cases, where the percentage of successful petitions is much higher than in non-capital cases. One study of death sentences imposed in the United States between 1973 and 1995 reported that in 40% of the cases reviewed, federal habeas courts overturned the death sentence.[58] A study of cases filed after the 1996 amendments to the statute found the grant rate in capital cases in district courts to be less than 15%, still much higher than the grant rate in non–capital cases.[59]

Justice Powell further characterized expansive federal habeas review as "tend[ing] to undermine the values inherent in our federal system of government."[60] The primary protection of constitutional rights must come from a state judiciary that has a strong sense of responsibility for performing that function; Justice Powell warned that state courts may become "so frustrated with the extent of federal court intervention that they [will] simply abdicate in favor of the federal jurisdiction."[61]

Proponents of broad habeas review argue that these "federal-

---

p://www.ncjrs.gov/pdffiles1/nij/grants/219559.pdf.

[55]Brown v. Allen, 344 U.S. 443, 73 S.Ct. 397, 97 L.Ed. 469 (1953).

[56]N. King, F. Cheesman & B. Ostrom, Habeas Litigation in U.S. District Courts (2007), available at http://www.ncjrs.gov/pdffiles1/nij/grants/219559.pdf (evidentiary hearings were held in fewer than 1% of non-capital cases, and in about 10% of capital cases).

[57]Schaefer, Federalism and State Criminal Procedure, 70 Harv.L.Rev. 1, 25 (1956).

[58]J. Fagan, J. Liebman, V. West, A. Gelman, A. Kiss & G. Davies, Getting to Death: Fairness and Efficiency in the Processing and Conclusion of Death Penalty Cases after Furman, Final Technical Report, Dept. of Justice Doc. No. 203935, Award No. 2000-IJ-CX-0035 (Feb. 2004).

[59]N. King, F. Cheesman & B. Ostrom, Habeas Litigation in U.S. District Courts (2007), available at http://www.ncjrs.gov/pdffiles1/nij/grants/219559.pdf.

[60]Schneckloth v. Bustamonte, 412 U.S. 218, 93 S.Ct. 2041, 36 L.Ed.2d 854 (1973) (concurring opinion).

[61]Id. See also Calderon v. Thompson, 523 U.S. 538, 118 S.Ct. 1489, 140 L.Ed.2d 728 (1998) (holding that the court of appeals abused its discretion by deciding belatedly to reconsider its decision denying relief, citing respect for state courts and state

ism costs" of habeas review have largely dissipated. State courts have become accustomed to such review, they argue,[62] and any remaining state court resentment is due to a failure to understand that reversal of state court decisions occurs only rarely and usually only after review by a federal court of appeals.[63] Indeed, some have argued that federal habeas review has had a positive impact on federal-state relations, having encouraged a useful dialogue between federal and state courts.[64] Finally, proponents of broad habeas review have noted, even if friction is inevitable, an unjustly incarcerated prisoner should not have his liberty sacrificed on the altar of improving federal-state relations.[65]

The third cost of broad habeas review, Justice Powell maintained, is its detrimental impact upon those interests underlying the achievement in the criminal justice process of a definite point of finality. Deterrence depends upon the expectation that one violating the law will swiftly and certainly be subject to punishment, but the reopening of convictions through habeas corpus is said to cast doubt upon the judicial system's ability to achieve that objective.[66] Society can rightfully question, it is argued, whether broad habeas review does not invite defendants to postpone presentation of their claims to that point at which a successful petition cannot feasibly be followed by reprosecution. Justice Powell noted further that broad habeas review undercuts the need "at some point [for] the law * * * to convey to those in custody that a wrong has been committed, that consequent punishment has been imposed, that one should no longer look back with the view to resurrecting every imaginable basis for further litigation but rather should look forward to rehabilitation and to becoming a constructive citizen."[67] Expansive habeas review is also said to undercut society's need to reach a point of

---

government); O'Connor, Trends in the Relationship Between the Federal and State Courts From the Perspective of a State Court Judge, 22 Wm. & Mary L.Rev. 801, 156 (1981).

[62]See Remington, State Prisoner Access to Post-conviction Relief—A Lessening Role for Federal Courts; An Increasingly Important Role for State Courts, 44 Ohio St.L.J. 287, 289 (1983) ("In the 1970s the criticism by state judges subsided, and a much more harmonious relationship developed between state and federal judiciaries.").

[63]Olsen, Judicial Proposals to Limit The Jurisdictional Scope of Federal Post-Conviction Habeas Corpus Consideration of the Claims of

State Prisoners, 31 Buff.L.Rev. 301, 308 (1982).

[64]See Cover and Aleinikoff, Dialectical Federalism: Habeas Corpus and the Court, 86 Yale L.J. 1035 (1979).

[65]See Fay v. Noia, 372 U.S. 391, 83 S.Ct. 822, 9 L.Ed.2d 837 (1963); Chisum, In Defense of Modern Habeas Corpus for State Prisoners, 21 DePaul L.Rev. 682, 712–25 (1972).

[66]See, e.g., Calderon v. Thompson, 523 U.S. 538, 118 S.Ct. 1489, 140 L.Ed.2d 728 (1998) ("Finality is essential to both the retributive and deterrent functions of criminal law.").

[67]Schneckloth v. Bustamonte, 412 U.S. 218, 93 S.Ct. 2041, 36 L.Ed.2d

repose, where it can say that the system has gone far enough and one can now safely assume that "justice has been done."[68]

§ 28.2(d) Competing models of habeas review

Over the years, jurists and habeas scholars have offered a variety of approaches to balancing the costs and benefits of habeas review. Several distinct theories have emerged.[69]

Ensuring Responsible State Court Adjudication of Constitutional Rights: The "One Fair Chance" Model.[70] One of the narrowest models of habeas review is that which views the primary function of the writ as ensuring that the state judicial systems fulfill their obligation to apply in a responsible manner the prevailing constitutional doctrine. Such a model, supplemented by the traditional review of jurisdictional defects, furnished the foundation for the standards that governed habeas review for a good part of the first half of the twentieth century. Utilizing what was later described as a "due process" approach to habeas review, those standards looked to whether the state process had afforded the habeas petitioner an adequate opportunity to gain a fair determination of his constitutional claim. One of the primary champions of this approach was Professor Paul Bator, who argued that, as a general principle, federal court review was no more likely than state court review to guarantee a result "correct in an ultimate sense," and that adding federal review on top of state review therefore was simply a wasteful and unnecessary interference with the state criminal justice process, provided the defendant had available a meaningful review from the state system.[71] One lasting development in federal habeas doctrine has reflected this single fair chance model. In *Stone v. Powell*,[72] the Court barred federal habeas review of a Fourth Amendment claim provided state procedure had granted the defendant a "full and fair opportunity" for litigating that claim.

Vindicating Federal Constitutional Rights in a Federal Forum. The broadest model of habeas review was that espoused by

---

854 (1973) (Powell, J., concurring).

[68]Bator, Finality in Criminal Law and Federal Habeas Corpus for State Prisoners, 76 Harv.L.Rev. 441, 452 (1963). Proponents of expansive habeas review do not quarrel with the basic objectives of finality, but claim that the adverse impact of habeas review upon those objectives is grossly exaggerated.

[Section 28.2(d)]

[69]See also McCord, Visions of Habeas, 1994 B.Y.U.L.Rev. 735 (1994)

(analyzing eight separate models); Woolhandler, Demodeling Habeas, 45 Stan.L.Rev. 575 (1993).

[70]See McCord, Visions of Habeas, 1994 B.Y.U.L.Rev. 735, 769 (1994) (terming this approach the "one fair-chance vision" of habeas).

[71]Bator, Finality in Criminal Law and Federal Habeas Corpus for State Prisoners, 76 Harv.L.Rev. 441 (1963).

[72]Stone v. Powell, 428 U.S. 465, 96 S.Ct. 3037, 49 L.Ed.2d 1067 (1976), discussed in § 28.3(c).

159

Justice Brennan.[73] A defendant could be denied relief because he (or in some instances, his counsel) abused either the state process or the habeas process, but the habeas court also had discretion to grant relief notwithstanding such abuse. Comity generally required that the state be given an opportunity to rule on a constitutional claim before a federal court would review that claim, but only if the state court could provide that ruling expeditiously. Under this expansive interpretation of habeas review, the habeas court retained the authority to make its own findings of fact. Today, the model advocated by Justice Brennan has been rejected. Perhaps the only aspect remaining is the broad definition of custody advanced in the 1960s. Even before the 1996 amendments, the Court had already narrowed relief for defaulted claims, held that Fourth Amendment violations were not cognizable on habeas review, and limited the ability of habeas courts to strengthen constitutional protections using habeas review.[74] The 1996 amendments further limited access to federal evidentiary hearings, narrowed relief for claims raised in second petitions, barred late petitions, and required federal courts to defer to "reasonable" state court interpretations and applications of established federal law.

Surrogate Supreme Courts. Another model of federal habeas review considers the federal habeas courts as primarily quasi-appellate courts, serving as a replacement for a Supreme Court that can review only a small fraction of all petitions for certiorari presented to it by prisoners seeking review of state court judgments. This "surrogate" model was premised upon the importance of development and interpretation of federal constitutional guarantees by federal, not state, courts.[75] This model found its strongest support in decisions of the 1950s and 60s when the

---

[73]Professor Yackle has also advocated a broad model for federal habeas. He has urged that federal habeas review should give prisoners an opportunity to litigate claims in federal habeas court "that is roughly equivalent to the opportunity they would have had if they had been allowed to remove" to federal court. Yackle, The Habeas Hagioscope, 66 S.Cal.L.Rev. 2331, 2333 (1993).

[74]See § 28.4, discussing state procedural default, § 28.3(c), discussing Stone v. Powell, 428 U.S. 465, 96 S.Ct. 3037, 49 L.Ed.2d 1067 (1976), and § 28.6(b)-(e), discussing Teague v. Lane, 489 U.S. 288, 109 S.Ct. 1060, 103 L.Ed.2d 334 (1989).

[75]See Friedman, A Tale of Two Habeas, 73 Minn.L.Rev. 247 (1988) (arguing that the Supreme Court originally expanded the scope of federal habeas review because it could no longer review all of the constitutional claims arising from state criminal trials on direct review); Liebman, Apocalypse Next Time? The Anachronistic Attack on Habeas Corpus/Direct Review Parity, 92 Colum.L.Rev. 1997 (1992) (habeas has served as a substitute for appeal to the Supreme Court). See also Steiker, Restructuring Post-Conviction Review of Federal Constitutional Claims Raised by State Prisoners: Confronting the New Face of Excessive Proceduralism, 1998 U.Chi.L. Forum 315 (proposing right to habeas

Court was engaged in extending the federal constitutional guarantees in the Bill of Rights to state defendants.[76] It was significantly weakened by the Court in *Teague v. Lane*,[77] a decision that "took habeas courts out of the business of defining," or at least expanding, the rights of criminal defendants.[78] *Teague* barred the announcement or application of new rules of constitutional criminal procedure in habeas cases, except in a few narrow circumstances. The 1996 amendments narrowed those circumstances further still.[79] So circumscribed, habeas litigation is no longer a vehicle for developing federal constitutional criminal procedure. To the extent that habeas courts replace Supreme Court review in correcting state court decisions contrary to preexisting federal law, the surrogate model retains vitality.[80]

The "Fundamental Fairness" Model. Justice Stevens, in a series of opinions in the 1980s, advanced what has come to be known as the "fundamental fairness" model of habeas review. Justice Stevens' position was that "constitutional errors are not fungible," at least with respect to remedies.[81] Just as there are some errors that call for automatic reversal and some that call for reversal on appeal only if deemed not to have been harmless, there are some errors "important enough" to require reversal on direct appeal but not important enough to require the overturning of a conviction on collateral review, and some errors so significant that they should be recognized on habeas review under almost any circumstance. In this latter category, Justice Stevens placed "errors so fundamental that they infect the validity of the underlying judgment itself, or the integrity by which that judgment was obtained," such as a trial dominated by mob violence, the prosecutor's knowing use of perjured testimony, or the admission of a confession "extorted from the defendant by brutal methods." While Justice Stevens agreed courts must be cautious when

---

review in the federal courts of appeals for all state capital cases, with district courts involved only when factual record insufficient).

[76]E.g., Brown v. Allen, 344 U.S. 443, 73 S.Ct. 397, 97 L.Ed. 469 (1953).

[77]Teague v. Lane, 489 U.S. 288, 109 S.Ct. 1060, 103 L.Ed.2d 334 (1989), is discussed in §§ 28.6(b) through (e).

[78]Friedman, Habeas and Hubris, 45 Vand.L.Rev. 797, 820 (1992).

[79]See § 28.6(g).

[80]See Friedman, Habeas and Hubris, 45 Vand.L.Rev. 797 (1992). Professors Hertz and Liebman also

argue for habeas review as "a surrogate for Supreme Court review as of right." See R. Hertz & J. Liebman, 1 Federal Habeas Corpus Practice and Procedure § 2.4 (5th ed.2005). For another argument endorsing this appellate model and reviewing other theories for shaping, and in particular narrowing, habeas review, see Hoffstadt, How Congress Might Redesign A Leaner, Cleaner Writ of Habeas Corpus, 49 Duke L.J. 947 (2000).

[81]See Rose v. Lundy, 455 U.S. 509, 538, 102 S.Ct. 1198, 1213, 71 L.Ed.2d 379 (1982) (Stevens, J., dissenting).

considering claims that were not raised at trial (in part on the premise that the tardiness in their presentation suggests in itself their likely irrelevance), he was willing to push aside even weighty state interests in procedural regularity when a clear denial of fundamental fairness was presented. Although neither the Court majority nor Congress has accepted Justice Stevens' fundamental fairness doctrine, both adopted the basic premise that certain claims should prevail over limits that would otherwise bar habeas review.[82]

Protection of the "Innocent." In 1969 Justice Black, in a brief dissent from a majority ruling granting collateral relief based on a Fourth Amendment violation, noted: "I would always require that the convicted defendant raise the kind of constitutional claim that casts some shadow of a doubt on his guilt."[83] This comment was expanded upon in a highly influential article by Judge Henry Friendly, with the provocative title "Is Innocence Irrelevant?"[84] Judge Friendly argued that "with a few important exceptions," "convictions should be subject to collateral attack only when the prisoner supplements his constitutional plea with a colorable claim of innocence."[85] There were important distinctions in the manner in which Judge Friendly and Justice Black would have used habeas review as a safety net for the innocent. Justice Black focused on the general nature of the constitutional claim, asking whether its basic function is to protect the innocent by safeguarding the reliability of the guilt determining process. Judge Friendly, on the other hand, focused on actual factual innocence on a case-by-case basis. The defendant would have to show factual innocence that may have gone unrecognized due to a constitu-

---

[82]See, e.g., Teague v. Lane, 489 U.S. 288, 109 S.Ct. 1060, 103 L.Ed.2d 334 (1989) (Stevens, J., concurring). See also 28 U.S.C.A. §§ 2254(a)(2), § 2253(b)(2), and 2254(d)(2).

[83]Kaufman v. United States, 394 U.S. 217, 89 S.Ct. 1068, 22 L.Ed.2d 227 (1969) (Black, J., dissenting). For a discussion of the role that innocence has played in the Court's habeas decisions, see Steiker, Innocence and Federal Habeas, 41 UCLA L.Rev. 303 (1993). See also Hoffmann & Stuntz, Habeas After the Revolution, 1993 Sup.Ct.Rev. 65; Jeffries & Stuntz, Ineffective Assistance and Procedural Default in Federal Habeas Corpus, 57 U.Chi.L.Rev. 679 (1990) (advocating use of the innocence model).

[84]Friendly, Is Innocence Irrelevant? Collateral Attack on Criminal Judgments, 38 U.Chi.L.Rev. 142 (1970).

[85]Judge Friendly would create exceptions where (1) the original tribunal either lacked jurisdiction or provided a trial well outside the constitutional guarantees, (2) the constitutional claim was based on facts not contained in the record and only collateral attack would vindicate the claim, (3) there was no proper procedure for making a defense at trial or appeal, or (4) there had been a change in the governing law. Friendly, Is Innocence Irrelevant? Collateral Attack on Criminal Judgments, 38 U.Chi.L.Rev. 142, 160 (1970).

tional violation that affected the determination of guilt.[86] Habeas could be considered an important protection against wrongful convictions.

Both versions of habeas review as a safety net for the innocent have been incorporated into various aspects of habeas law. Whether or not a claim affects the reliability of a guilty verdict may be critical in determining whether a new constitutional rule will be applied retroactively,[87] or whether review will be available notwithstanding a procedural forfeiture that would otherwise bar review.[88] The Court's holding in *Stone v. Powell* that Fourth Amendment claims ordinarily are not cognizable on habeas review is also linked to the salience of innocence, since it is based in part on the recognition that such claims have no bearing on the reliability of a conviction.[89] Innocence has not, however, become the exclusive theme of habeas review. With one possible exception, see § 28.3(e), habeas review remains focused on whether a constitutional right was violated, not whether a petitioner is in fact innocent.

The Mixing of Models. Current law, as the above discussion indicates, does not exclusively follow any one model of habeas review. Rather, the 1996 Act and the doctrinal landscape against which it must be interpreted contain elements, sometimes inconsistent, of several different models. The law of habeas has been especially sensitive to changes in the composition of the Court. Because the Court has so often returned to concepts that appeared to have been rejected in an earlier period and used them as at least a springboard for reshaping habeas doctrine, special attention will be given in the sections that follow to where the law has been as well as to where it now stands.

---

[86]Friendly, Is Innocence Irrelevant? Collateral Attack on Criminal Judgments, 38 U.Chi.L.Rev. 142, 160 (1970). In 1973 Justice Powell lent support to both the Black and Friendly positions in arguing against granting habeas relief based on Fourth Amendment violations. Schneckloth v. Bustamonte, 412 U.S. 218, 93 S.Ct. 2041, 36 L.Ed.2d 854 (1973) (Powell, J., concurring). See also McCord, Visions of Habeas, 1994 B.Y.U.L.Rev. 735 (1994) arguing that Justice Powell was the leading proponent of the innocence rationale in recent decades); Hoffmann & Stuntz, Habeas After the Revolution, 1993 Sup.Ct.Rev. 65 (arguing

that petitioners who can show a reasonable probability of innocence deserve de novo federal review of their constitutional claims).

[87]See § 28.6(b) to (e).

[88]See § 28.4(e) (discussing procedural default); § 28.5(d) (discussing new claims in second or successive petitions). The role of innocence in habeas policy is particularly controversial in capital cases. See the discussion in § 1.5(e) at notes 237–246.

[89]See § 28.3(c), discussing Stone v. Powell, 428 U.S. 465, 96 S.Ct. 3037, 49 L.Ed.2d 1067 (1976).

§ 28.3 Claims cognizable in habeas

§ 28.3(a)   Cognizable claimants: the custody requirement
§ 28.3(b)   Cognizable claims
§ 28.3(c)   The exception for Fourth Amendment claims
§ 28.3(d)   The opportunity for full and fair litigation
§ 28.3(e)   "Bare innocence" claims

§ 28.3(a) Cognizable claimants: the custody requirement

The writ of habeas corpus is limited under §§ 2241 and 2254 to persons "in custody in violation of the Constitution or laws or treaties of the United States." The jurisdictional requirement of custody is explored in this subsection. Further limits on the types of claims that may form the basis for relief by writ of habeas corpus are discussed in the several subsections that follow.

History and Purpose of the Custody Requirement. Because the common law writ took the form of a directive to the jailer to bring forth his prisoner, the element of custody was long an inherent requirement of the writ's operation. The custody requirement gradually took on a substantive character as the writ came to be viewed as an "extraordinary remedy [directed to] the extraordinary restraints of custodial situations."[1] The federal habeas corpus statutes, from the 1789 Act to the current provisions, have all provided that the writ extend to a person "in custody."[2] Congress, however, has never sought to provide a legislative definition of that phrase. Not surprisingly, as the Court expanded the scope of the writ in its treatment of such matters as the range of cognizable claims during the 1960s, it also broadened the element of custody. Subsequent decisions have continued to interpret generously the custody prerequisite, despite markedly restrictive readings of other requirements for habeas relief. As the Court recently observed in *Duncan v. Walker*,[3] even state court orders other than criminal convictions may create "custody" within the meaning of the federal habeas statute, including an

---

[Section 28.3(a)]

[1] Note, 83 Harv.L.Rev. 1038, 1073 (1970). For detailed treatment of the custody requirement, see L. Yackle, Postconviction Remedies (1981 & Supp.2007); R. Hertz & J. Liebman, 1 Federal Habeas Corpus Practice and Procedure ch. 8 (5th ed.2005).

[2] Presently, custody is specified in 28 U.S.C.A. § 2241 (writ available to a person "in custody in violation" of the Constitution of federal law) and

28 U.S.C.A. § 2254(b)(1) (person "in custody pursuant to judgment of state court").

[3] Duncan v. Walker, 533 U.S. 167, 121 S.Ct. 2120, 150 L.Ed.2d 251 (2001) (citing Francois v. Henderson, 850 F.2d 231 (5th Cir.1988) (commitment to mental institution upon verdict of not guilty by reason of insanity) and Leonard v. Hammond, 804 F.2d 838 (4th Cir.1986) (civil contempt order for failure to pay child support)).

order of "civil commitment" or "civil contempt."[4] Indeed, "custody" may exist not only when a petitioner is incarcerated, but also when a petitioner suffers certain significant "present restraints."[5]

Custody Other Than Incarceration—Parole. The 1963 decision of *Jones v. Cunningham*[6] was the critical ruling extending the concept of "custody" beyond the restraints of actual incarceration. The Court there held, in an opinion by Justice Black, that a petitioner subject to typical conditions of parole was "in custody" for the purposes of § 2254. After noting that the statute "does not attempt to mark the boundaries of 'custody,'" Justice Black turned to the history and function of the writ. He noted that the writ had been used both in this country and in England in situations in which the applicant was not "in actual physical custody." The Supreme Court had "repeatedly held that habeas corpus is available to an alien seeking entry into the United States, although in those cases each alien was free to go anywhere else in the world." Habeas corpus had been used in the lower courts as an "appropriate vehicle" for questioning the legality of induction into the military service, and for resolving disputes relating to child custody. These developments and others led Justice Black to conclude:

> History, usage, and precedent can leave no doubt that, besides physical imprisonment, there are other restraints on a man's liberty, restraints not shared by the public generally, which have been thought sufficient in the English-speaking world to support the issuance of habeas corpus. * * *
>
> Of course, that writ always could and still can reach behind prison walls and iron bars. But it can do more. It is not now and never has been a static, narrow, formalistic remedy; its scope has grown to achieve its grand purpose—the protection of individuals against erosion of their rights to be free from wrongful restraints upon their liberty.

---

[4]For example, persons who are civilly committed as sexual predators are in "custody." Carty v. Nelson, 426 F.3d 1064 (9th Cir.2005). See also Dries, Sex Predators and Federal Habeas Corpus: Has the Great Writ Gone AWOL?, 39 Suffolk U.L.Rev. 673 (2006) (noting habeas case challenging confinement, and arguing that constitutional standard established for commitment of sex offenders is so vague that petitioners cannot show state courts apply it "unreasonably" in order to obtain relief under AEDPA). For a list of 24 "custodial statuses," see R. Hertz & J. Liebman, 1 Federal Habeas Practice and Procedure § 8.2d (5th ed.2005).

[5]See Maleng v. Cook, 490 U.S. 488, 109 S.Ct. 1923, 104 L.Ed.2d 540 (1989), discussed at note 14 (noting that the Court has "very liberally construed the 'in custody' requirement for purposes of federal habeas"); Rosenberg, The Federal Habeas Corpus Custody Decisions: Liberal Oasis or Conservative Prop?, 23 Am.J.Crim.L. 99 (1995). See also Annot., 176 A.L.R. Fed. 189 (2004) and (supp) (cataloguing custody case law).

[6]Jones v. Cunningham, 371 U.S. 236, 83 S.Ct. 373, 9 L.Ed.2d 285 (1963).

Turning to the restraints that had been imposed upon the petitioner in *Jones*, Justice Black concluded that they clearly were of a degree sufficient to justify use of the writ. Four aspects of petitioner's parole were cited. He was restricted in his lawful physical movement, unable to leave his community or change residence without special permission. He was subject to special regulations which restricted other aspects of his liberty, including the requirements that he obtain special permission before operating an automobile and that he report regularly to his parole officer. He was threatened with reincarceration for the duration of his original sentence for even the most insignificant violation of the parole regulations. Moreover, he could be ordered back to prison for violation of parole without a judicial hearing. The particular significance of each of these elements of restraint was not clear, but taken together they were "enough to invoke the help of The Great Writ."[7]

Custody Other Than Incarceration—Probation and Other Conditional Release. In *Hensley v. Municipal Court,*[8] *Jones* was held applicable to a habeas petitioner who was at large on his own recognizance pending execution of the sentence on his misdemeanor conviction. Due to an unusual combination of stays, the petitioner had been able to pursue his appeals within the state system and present his habeas application before starting to serve his one-year sentence. Petitioner continued to be bound by the conditions imposed during his pretrial release. He had agreed to "appear at all times and places" as ordered by the court, to waive extradition if he failed to appear and was apprehended outside the state, and to be subject to a court order at any time that could revoke his release. The state contended that these conditions were less restrictive than those imposed on the petitioner in *Jones*. The Court did not disagree. It held that, nevertheless, the petitioner was "in custody" within the meaning of the habeas statutes.

In his opinion for the Court in *Hensley*, Justice Brennan argued that habeas corpus is "an extraordinary remedy" which is aimed at "cases of special urgency" and leaves to more conventional remedies "cases in which restraints on liberty are neither severe nor immediate." The petitioner here clearly fell within the former rather than the latter category. He was subject to "restraints not shared by the public generally" (quoting *Jones*). Those restraints placed his freedom of movement "in the hands of judicial officers who may demand his presence at any time." This was surely no

---

[7]See also Mabry v. Johnson, 467 U.S. 504, 507 n. 3, 104 S.Ct. 2543, 81 L.Ed.2d 437 (1984) (petition not moot due to parole status).

[8]Hensley v. Municipal Court, 411 U.S. 345, 93 S.Ct. 1571, 36 L.Ed.2d 294 (1973).

lesser basis for employing the writ than had been recognized in prior cases, such as the ruling allowing its use by an unattached reserve officer to challenge his military status. The majority opinion also noted that in *Hensley*, the petitioner was dealing with future incarceration which was not speculative or remote, but certain and immediate if his habeas petition was denied. Indeed, the net effect of denying his use of the writ at this time would be no more than to postpone consideration of his application until he began to serve his sentence shortly thereafter.

Lower courts regularly find that the restraints attending probation are sufficient to establish custody.[9] Similar treatment is due the suspended sentence that poses a threat of future imprisonment if the petitioner fails to comply with a condition that does not restrict his freedom of movement.[10]

Custody Other Than Incarceration—Pretrial Release. The *Hensley* Court stressed that its ruling would not make the writ generally available to persons released on bail pending trial, noting simply that such petitioners "would still [have to] contend with the requirements of the exhaustion doctrine." In *Justices of Boston Municipal Court v. Lydon*,[11] however, the Court held that a person released on his own recognizance pending a trial de novo was in custody where the terms of the recognizance imposed restraints roughly similar to those found in *Hensley*, such that the petitioner was subject to restraints " 'not shared by the public generally.' "[12] The Court was not convinced by the arguments advanced by the three dissenting justices who sought to distin-

---

[9]See, e.g., Jackson v. Coalter, 337 F.3d 74 (1st Cir.2003) (probation counts as "custody"); Lee v. Stickman, 357 F.3d 338 (3d Cir.2004); Barry v. Bergen County Probation Dep't, 128 F.3d 152 (3d Cir.1997) (community service is "custody"); Barry v. Brower, 864 F.2d 294, 296 (3d Cir.1988) ("We can see no material difference between probation and parole in applying the 'in custody' requirement."); Dawson v. Scott, 50 F.3d 884 (11th Cir.1995) (supervised release is "custody"). See also Dow v. Circuit Court of the First Circuit, 995 F.2d 922 (9th Cir.1993) (sentence of fourteen hours of attendance at alcohol rehabilitation program was "custody").

[10]See, e.g., Sammons v. Rodgers, 785 F.2d 1343 (5th Cir.1986) (suspended sentence carrying a threat of future imprisonment qualifies as "custody").

[11]Justices of Boston Municipal Court v. Lydon, 466 U.S. 294, 104 S.Ct. 1805, 80 L.Ed.2d 311 (1984).

[12]The state recognizance statute imposed upon petitioner "an obligation to appear for trial" and "from time to time" as the court specified. Failure to appear without sufficient excuse constituted a criminal offense, and it could also result in the immediate imposition of the two-year sentence on the conviction from which he was seeking de novo review. The Court also noted that "the statute require[d] that he 'not depart without leave, and in the meantime * * * keep the peace and be of good behavior.' " These restraints, it concluded, were "not shared by the public generally," and though "not identical to those imposed on Hensley, * * * [also were] not sufficiently different to require a different result."

guish *Hensley*. They argued that *"Hensley* is best understood as interpreting 'custody' to include those cases where a criminal defendant, already convicted and sentenced, would be imprisoned without further state action had not the prison sentence been stayed by the federal [habeas] court." Here, if the trial de novo court found that defendant had defaulted on his recognizance, the sentence set by the first-tier court could be imposed, but the defendant would still have the opportunity to challenge his conviction on state appeal. The majority suggested that this was a factor relevant only to the exhaustion of state remedies, and here the petitioner had met the exhaustion requirement.[13]

Conditions Not Constituting Custody. Many disadvantages flowing from conviction do not constitute custody for purposes of habeas review, however. In *Maleng v. Cook*,[14] for example, the Court rejected the petitioner's contention that he remained in custody at the time he had filed his petition, notwithstanding the prior expiration of his sentence, because of the "possibility" that the conviction "will be used to enhance the sentences imposed for any subsequent crimes of which he is convicted." The Court responded that since almost all states have habitual offender statutes, acceptance of such a contention "would read the 'in custody' requirement out of the statute." Such a reading would also "be contrary to clear implication of the opinion in *Carafas v. LaVallee*," a case, discussed below, in which the Court assumed that such collateral consequences are not sufficient alone to establish custody. The Court nevertheless stated that the custody requirement might be met where there actually had been an enhanced sentence following a subsequent state conviction, and the state had filed a detainer to ensure petitioner's service of that enhanced sentence following his completion of a separate federal sentence.[15]

In addition to the mere possibility of a future enhanced sentence, other consequences deemed insufficient to establish custody include the payment of a fine (despite the possibility of physical restraint as a penalty for nonpayment),[16] an order of restitution,[17] the revocation of professional licenses,[18] the suspen-

---

[13]See § 28.5(a), discussing this requirement.

[14]Maleng v. Cook, 490 U.S. 488, 109 S.Ct. 1923, 104 L.Ed.2d 540 (1989).

[15]See also Annot., 176 A.L.R.Fed. 189 (2002) (and supp)(collecting cases).

[16]See, e.g., Lillios v. New Hampshire, 788 F.2d 60 (1st Cir.1986) (modest fine and suspension of driver's license insufficient); Barnickel v. United States, 113 F.3d 704 (7th Cir. 1997); Edmunds v. Won Bae Chang, 509 F.2d 39 (9th Cir.1975) ($25 fine insufficient to trigger custody).

[17]Obado v. State of New Jersey, 328 F.3d 716 (3d Cir.2003) (restitution order does not constitute custody).

sion of drivers licenses,[19] the prohibition against possessing firearms,[20] sex offender registration,[21] and the inability to hold public office.[22]

Continuing Jurisdiction if Petition Filed While in Custody. In *Carafas v. LaVallee,*[23] the petitioner filed his habeas application while still in prison, but he was unconditionally discharged (upon completion of his sentence) while the habeas court's denial of relief was on appeal. The state contended that appellate review was barred because the case was moot. Rejecting this claim, the Supreme Court noted that petitioner remained subject to various disabilities as a result of his conviction. He could not, for example, engage in certain businesses, hold public office, or serve as a juror. Under the collateral consequences doctrine of *Sibron v. New York,*[24] the case clearly was not moot. The unconditional release did present, however, a "substantial issue" as to whether the custody requirement of the federal habeas statutes was met. The answer to that issue, the Court noted, depended upon the import of the existence of custody at the time the petition was filed.

The *Carafas* opinion acknowledged that the usual relief granted in a habeas action was the release of the petitioner from custody, but concluded that the habeas court did not necessarily lose its jurisdiction when it could no longer provide such relief. Section 2243 permitted the court to "dispose of the matter as law and justice require" and § 2244(b) referred to a "release from custody or other remedy."[25] Thus, there was no suggestion in the statute itself that jurisdiction once gained was subsequently lost because the petitioner was no longer in custody. So long as the applicant was in custody when the writ was filed, the habeas court has jurisdiction, which it retains pending a final disposition of the case.[26] A contrary view, the Court noted, would "only aggravate the

---

[18]Lefkowitz v. Fair, 816 F.2d 17 (1st Cir.1987) (medical license); Ginsberg v. Abrams, 702 F.2d 48 (2d Cir.1984) (removal from bench, revocation of law and real-estate broker's licenses).

[19]Lillios v. New Hampshire, 788 F.2d 60 (1st Cir.1986); Harts v. Indiana, 732 F.2d 95 (7th Cir.1984) (suspension of driver's license did not establish custody).

[20]Harvey v. South Dakota, 526 F.2d 840 (8th Cir.1975).

[21]Williamson v. Gregoire, 151 F.3d 1180 (9th Cir.1998) (sex-offender registration requirement imposed following completion of sentence does not constitute custody despite "chill" placed on petitioner's movement and potential for prosecution if violated).

[22]Furey v. Hyland, 395 F.Supp. 1356 (D.N.J.1975).

[23]Carafas v. LaVallee, 391 U.S. 234, 88 S.Ct. 1556, 20 L.Ed.2d 554 (1968).

[24]Sibron v. New York, 392 U.S. 40, 88 S.Ct. 1889, 20 L.Ed.2d 917 (1968), discussed in § 27.5(a).

[25]This provision was removed by the 1996 amendments.

[26]As noted in Hanson v. Circuit Court, 591 F.2d 404 (7th Cir.1979),

hardships that may result from the 'intolerable delays in affording justice.'" A habeas petitioner "should not be thwarted * * * simply because the path of litigation has been so long * * * that he served his sentence."

Under the continuing jurisdiction analysis of *Carafas*, if custody exists at the time of the filing of the petition, the litigation can proceed so long as the case does not become moot. The *Carafas* discussion of mootness relied upon standards developed in cases assessing mootness on direct appellate review, most notably *Sibron v. New York*.[27] Lower courts accordingly have assumed that mootness is judged no differently in the habeas context than in the original proceedings, continue to follow *Sibron* in finding that a challenge to a state conviction is not moot when the conviction still carries "collateral consequences."[28] It is important to note that these collateral consequences would not be sufficient, on their own, to establish custody in a case where a petition had been filed after the petitioner had been released from incarceration.[29] When a petitioner who has served his sentence claims he is in custody in violation of federal law due to constitutional violations at his parole revocation proceeding, as opposed to alleging violations underlying the conviction itself, speculative collateral consequences that may result in the future due to the revocation, such as its potential consideration in a future parole decision should the petitioner be convicted of another offense and receive an indeterminate sentence, or its potential use as impeachment should the petitioner later testify as a witness, are not sufficient to defeat mootness.[30]

Challenging A Decision That Orders Future Custody. In 1968 the Court in *Peyton v. Rowe*[31] overruled its earlier decision *McNally v. Hill*,[32] which had held that a prisoner serving the first of two consecutive sentences could not use the writ to attack the second. *Peyton* concluded that neither the text nor history of the statute indicated that the writ was available only to secure immediate release. The petitioner facing a future sentence was, "practically speaking," in custody "under the aggregate of the consecutive

---

this position was no more than an application of the general rule that the jurisdiction of the federal court is determined at the time of the filing of the complaint.

[27]See § 27.5(a).

[28]E.g., Lee v. Stickman, 357 F.3d 338 (3d Cir.2004); Gentry v. Deuth, 456 F.3d 687 (6th Cir.2006); A.M. v. Butler, 360 F.3d 787 (7th Cir.2004) (when conviction would by statute increase petitioners potential punishment in the future, habeas claim is not moot).

[29]See Maleng v. Cook, 490 U.S. 488, 109 S.Ct. 1923, 104 L.Ed.2d 540 (1989).

[30]Spencer v. Kemna, 523 U.S. 1, 118 S.Ct. 978, 140 L.Ed.2d 43 (1998), discussed in § 27.5(a) at notes 16–18.

[31]Peyton v. Rowe, 391 U.S. 54, 88 S.Ct. 1549, 20 L.Ed.2d 426 (1968).

[32]McNally v. Hill, 293 U.S. 131, 55 S.Ct. 24, 79 L.Ed. 238 (1934).

sentences imposed on [him]." Postponing the habeas inquiry into the conviction underlying the second sentence undercut the accurate assessment of a petitioner's claim and a state's chances of convicting the prisoner at retrial. Moreover, requiring that a petitioner wait until he is serving the challenged sentence compels an ultimately successful petitioner to remain in custody illegally for at least some period of time while his habeas application is being processed.

Peyton's reasoning was soon extended to allow immediate habeas review where the sentence not yet served was imposed by a different sovereign, in *Braden v. 30th Judicial Circuit Court*.[33] There, an Alabama prisoner was subject to a detainer filed with his Alabama warden by Kentucky officials. The detainer was based on a pending felony charge in Kentucky. The petitioner contended that the Kentucky charge was barred by that state's failure to afford him a speedy trial. Explained the Court, "Since the Alabama warden acts here as the agent of the Commonwealth of Kentucky in holding the petitioner pursuant to the Kentucky detainer, we have no difficulty concluding that petitioner is in custody for purposes of 28 U.S.C.A. § 2241(c)(3)."[34] Courts have also allowed a federal prisoner to challenge a consecutive state sentence, where that sentence is certain to follow upon completion of the federal sentence.[35]

Garlotte v. Fordice[36] extended the rationale of *Peyton* to allow a petitioner to challenge a conviction underlying a sentence already served, when that petitioner is incarcerated under a consecutive sentence. The prisoner's efforts to exhaust in state court his challenge to one conviction, carrying a three-year sentence, outlasted the sentence for that conviction. The Court held that he was still "in custody" under that earlier sentence for purposes of

---

[33] Braden v. 30th Judicial Circuit Court, 410 U.S. 484, 93 S.Ct. 1123, 35 L.Ed.2d 443 (1973).

[34] Braden v. 30th Judicial Circuit Court, 410 U.S. 484, 93 S.Ct. 1123, 35 L.Ed.2d 443 (1973). See also Thompson v. Missouri Bd. of Parole, 929 F.2d 396 (8th Cir.1991); McDowell v. Chesney, 2004 WL 1376591 (D.Del.2004) (considering petitioner's request for writ under § 2241 when imprisoned in Pennsylvania, but seeking pre trial relief raising speedy trial claim on pending Delaware charges and a Delaware detainer, but rejecting claim as unexhausted in state courts).

[35] Frazier v. Wilkinson, 842 F.2d 42 (2d Cir.1988) (relying on policies noted in *Peyton*, but also distinguishing the parole violation situation, where insistence upon a detainer is needed to ensure that the parole state "will expend its resources" to insist upon service of the unexpired term). See also Rule 1(a)(2) of the Rules Governing Section 2254 Cases (referencing petitions filed by a "person in custody pursuant to a judgment of either a state or a federal writ, who makes an application for a determination that custody to which he may be subject in the future under a judgment of a state court will be in violation of the Constitution").

[36] Garlotte v. Fordice, 515 U.S. 39, 115 S.Ct. 1948, 132 L.Ed.2d 36 (1995).

his petition for habeas relief, when his date of release from his second sentence would advance if the first conviction was invalidated. The Court stated, "consecutive sentences should be treated as a continuous series," and explained that a prisoner "remains 'in custody' under all of his sentences until all are served." *Garlotte* was sentenced to consecutive sentences after a single trial. Lower courts have extended *Garlotte* to consecutive sentences imposed at different times by courts of different counties in the same state.[37] The case does not provide a means for a prisoner in the custody of the federal government to challenge a state conviction underlying that federal custody.[38]

§ 28.3(b) Cognizable claims

Petitioners "in custody" who seek habeas relief must also demonstrate that they are in custody in violation of federal law. The habeas remedy was not always this broad. According to the conventional view, for over a century, first under the 1789 Act and later under the 1867 Act, Supreme Court rulings limited federal habeas review for convicted prisoners to those claims that challenged the jurisdiction of the court of conviction.[39] Federal habeas review is no longer so limited but the Court's expansion

---

[37]DeFoy v. McCullough, 393 F.3d 439 (3d Cir.2005) (review available for petitioner's challenge to the denial of parole for a sentence he is no longer serving when petitioner is serving a sentence for another crime, at least when the sentence he is challenging delayed the start of the sentence he is serving, and relief may affect his release date); Foster v. Booher, 296 F.3d 947 (10th Cir.2002).

[38]Brown v. Warden, 315 F.3d 1268 (10th Cir.2003) (prisoner in federal custody cannot challenge prior state conviction under § 2254 when state sentence fully served); Contreras v. Schiltgen, 122 F.3d 30 (9th Cir.1997) (prisoner cannot challenge in § 2254 petition a state conviction underlying otherwise lawful INS custody). See also Lackawanna County District Attorney v. Coss, 532 U.S. 394, 121 S.Ct. 1567, 149 L.Ed.2d 608 (2001), discussed in § 28.3(b) at note 60, and in § 26.4(f) at note 100, holding that a state prisoner may not challenge a prior conviction that enhanced the sentence he currently serves, unless the prisoner can show that the prior conviction used to enhance his sen-

tence was obtained in violation of *Gideon*.

[Section 28.3(b)]

[39]See § 28.2(b) at notes 22–24. Compare, however, Peller, In Defense of Federal Habeas Corpus Relitigation, 16 Harv.Civ.Rts.-Civ.Lib.L.Rev. 579, 610–43 (1982) (offering a much broader reading of the earlier cases). In INS v. St. Cyr, 533 U.S. 289, 121 S.Ct. 2271, 150 L.Ed.2d 347 (2001), five Justices declared that:

In England prior to 1789, in the Colonies, and in this Nation during the formative years of our Government, the writ of habeas corpus was available to nonenemy aliens as well as to citizens," to challenge detention in civil and criminal cases, and "was not limited to challenges to the jurisdiction of the custodian, but encompassed detentions based on errors of law, including the erroneous application or interpretation of statutes. It was used to command the discharge of seamen who had a statutory exemption from impressment into the British Navy, to emancipate slaves, and to obtain the freedom of apprentices and asylum inmates. * * * [T]hose early cases contain no suggestion that habeas relief in cases involving executive detention was available

of the remedy from jurisdictional defects to constitutional claims remains important, both to states that are continuing to develop their own collateral remedies, and to those seeking an understanding of the historical basis for the contemporary statute.

That the earliest Supreme Court rulings looked to jurisdictional defects is not surprising in light of the history of the common law writ, and the long accepted principle that a judgment did not become "final" when it was "void" due to the trial court's lack of jurisdiction over either the subject matter or the person.[40] Consistent with this principle, the Supreme Court initially took a narrow view of what constituted a jurisdictional defect. In *Ex parte Watkins*,[41] the Court refused to review on habeas a federal prisoner's claim that his conviction was obtained on an indictment that failed to state a crime, finding that error on the part of a court of competent jurisdiction does not render detention "illegal" for purposes of habeas corpus.[42]

Beginning in 1873, in *Ex parte Lange*,[43] the Court initiated what has been described as "a long process of expansion of the concept of a lack of jurisdiction."[44] Lange contended that he had been twice sentenced for the same offense, in violation of the Fifth Amendment's Double Jeopardy Clause, when he had been resentenced to a term of imprisonment after having paid the fine originally imposed. Carefully disclaiming the use of habeas as a writ of error, the Supreme Court ordered Lange released from imprisonment because the lower court's jurisdiction terminated upon the satisfaction of the original sentence. The *Lange* ruling

---

only for constitutional error.

[40]See Bator, Finality in Criminal Law and Federal Habeas Corpus for State Prisoners, 76 Harv.L.Rev. 441, 460–62 (1963). A limitation of habeas review to jurisdictional defects may also have been influenced by the limitation upon the Supreme Court's appellate jurisdiction in criminal cases. See also Saltzburg, Habeas Corpus: The Supreme Court and the Congress, 44 Ohio St.L.J. 367, 370–71 (1983) ("whether the distinction between void and voidable judgments was logical, by drawing it the Court was able to respect Congress' decision not to give it general appellate jurisdiction while it used habeas corpus to assure that lower federal courts did not exceed their jurisdiction").

[41]Ex parte Watkins, 28 U.S. (3 Pet.) 193, 7 L.Ed. 650 (1830).

[42]Bator, Finality in Criminal Law and Federal Habeas Corpus for State Prisoners, 76 Harv.L.Rev. 441, 466 (1963).

[43]Ex parte Lange, 85 U.S. (18 Wall.) 163, 21 L.Ed. 872 (1873).

[44]Hart, Forward: The Time Chart of the Justices, 73 Harv.L.Rev. 84, 103–04 (1959). While *Lange* and the other post-Civil War decisions are commonly viewed as only having "soften[ed] the concept of jurisdiction," Note, 83 Harv.L.Rev. 1038, 1048 (1970), they were characterized by Justice Brennan in Fay v. Noia, 372 U.S. 391, 83 S.Ct. 822, 9 L.Ed.2d 837 (1963), discussed infra at note 56, as having "ma[de] plain that restraints contrary to our fundamental law, the Constitution, may be challenged on federal habeas corpus even though imposed pursuant to the conviction of a federal court of competent jurisdiction."

was extended in *Ex parte Wilson*[45] to a defendant who challenged his sentence on the ground that it imposed punishment for an "infamous" crime even though he had not been indicted by a grand jury as the Fifth Amendment required for all infamous offenses. Both *Lange* and *Wilson* stressed the trial court's lack of power to impose a sentence beyond its jurisdictional authority, rather than the constitutional character of the petitioners' claims. Accordingly, during the same period, when a federal prisoner sought habeas relief on the ground that he had been retried in violation of the Double Jeopardy Clause, the Court held that his claim was not cognizable on a habeas challenge since a trial court obviously had jurisdiction to determine whether a retrial was permissible.[46]

Ex parte Siebold,[47] decided in 1879, produced another doctrinal expansion of the concept of a jurisdictional defect. The Court held there that a prisoner could properly raise on habeas corpus the claim that the statute under which he was convicted violated the United States Constitution. If the petitioner was correct in his claim, the Court noted, then "the foundation of the whole proceeding" would be affected. The trial court's authority to try the petitioners "arose solely upon these laws," so if the "laws were unconstitutional and void," the trial court "acquired no jurisdiction of the causes."[48] *Moore v. Dempsey*,[49] decided in 1923, involved five black petitioners who protested they had been sentenced to death after a mob-dominated trial. The Court agreed that such a claim went to the "jurisdiction" of the trial court.[50] Where the "proceeding is a mask," the Court noted, with the "counsel, jury,

---

[45]Ex parte Wilson, 114 U.S. 417, 5 S.Ct. 935, 29 L.Ed. 89 (1885).

[46]In re Bigelow, 113 U.S. 328, 5 S.Ct. 542, 28 L.Ed. 1005 (1885). Other rulings of the same character are discussed in Bator, Finality in Criminal Law and Federal Habeas Corpus for State Prisoners, 76 Harv.L.Rev. 441, 468–71 (1963), where the author notes that the distinctions drawn by the Court were "not completely unintelligible" when viewed in "a historical context," but nevertheless difficult to justify on the basis of a "principled distinction."

[47]Ex parte Siebold, 100 U.S. 371, 25 L.Ed. 717 (1879).

[48]The Court held several years later that habeas review was available to remedy a sentence that was illegal because the two indictments under which petitioner was separately sentenced charged the same offense. See Nielsen, Petitioner, 131 U.S. 176, 9 S.Ct. 672, 33 L.Ed. 118 (1889); In re Snow, 120 U.S. 274, 7 S.Ct. 556, 30 L.Ed. 658 (1887).

[49]Moore v. Dempsey, 261 U.S. 86, 43 S.Ct. 265, 67 L.Ed. 543 (1923).

[50]See also Frank v. Magnum, 237 U.S. 309, 35 S.Ct. 582, 59 L.Ed. 969 (1915). Varying views as to the meaning of Frank and Moore are presented in the majority and dissenting opinions in Fay v. Noia, 372 U.S. 391, 83 S.Ct. 822, 9 L.Ed.2d 837 (1963), discussed in text at note 55, and in a series of articles collected in Olsen, Judicial Proposals to Limit the Jurisdictional Scope of Federal Post-Conviction Habeas Corpus Consideration of the Claims of State Prisoners, 31 Buffalo L.Rev. 301, 333

and judge * * * swept to the fatal end by an irresistible wave of public passion," the trial becomes "absolutely void."[51]

In *Johnson v. Zerbst*,[52] Justice Black's opinion for the Court expanded upon the "loss-of-jurisdiction" analysis of *Moore*. The petitioner in *Johnson*, a federal prisoner, claimed that his conviction had been obtained in violation of the Sixth Amendment because the trial judge had failed to provide him with appointed counsel. Justice Black concluded:

> Since the Sixth Amendment constitutionally entitles one charged with crime to the assistance of counsel, compliance with this constitutional mandate is an essential jurisdictional prerequisite to a federal court's authority to deprive an accused of his life or liberty. * * * A court's jurisdiction at the beginning of trial may be lost "in the course of the proceedings" [quoting Frank] due to failure to complete the court—as the Sixth Amendment requires—by providing counsel for an accused. * * * If this requirement of the Sixth Amendment is not complied with, the court no longer has jurisdiction to proceed.

Four years later the Court faced on habeas review a constitutional claim that it could not so readily characterize as undermining the structure of the proceeding and therefore causing the trial court to "lose jurisdiction." In *Waley v. Johnston*,[53] the petitioner claimed that his guilty plea had been coerced by an F.B.I. agent. The Court concluded that petitioner's claim was subject to habeas review:

> The facts relied on are dehors the record and their effect on the judgment was not open to consideration and review on appeal. In such circumstances the use of the writ in the federal courts to test the constitutional validity of a conviction for crime is not restricted to those cases where the judgment of conviction is void for want of jurisdiction of the trial court to render it. It extends also to those exceptional cases where the conviction has been in disregard of the constitutional rights of the accused, and where the writ is the only effective means of preserving his rights.

As various commentators have noted, *Waley* "finally dispensed with the fiction of 'jurisdiction,'" expanded beyond definable bounds in cases such as *Moore* and *Johnson*.[54] Over a decade after *Waley* put to rest the jurisdictional-defect limitation on habeas relief for claims requiring factual development, in *Brown v.*

(1982). Consider also Peller, In Defense of Federal Habeas Corpus Relitigation, 16 Harv.Civ.Rts.-Civ.Lib.L.Rev. 579, 644–49 (1982).

[51] *Moore*, 261 U.S. at 91.

[52] Johnson v. Zerbst, 304 U.S. 458, 58 S.Ct. 1019, 82 L.Ed. 1461 (1938).

[53] Waley v. Johnston, 316 U.S. 101, 62 S.Ct. 964, 86 L.Ed. 1302 (1942).

[54] Bator, Finality in Criminal Law and Federal Habeas Corpus for State Prisoners, 76 Harv.L.Rev. 441, 495 (1963).

Allen,[55] the Court made it plain that habeas review extends to all constitutional claims. Habeas courts should consider and render their own independent judgment on the merits of a petitioner's federal claims, held the Court, notwithstanding adjudication of the very same claim in state court. At issue in *Brown* was whether a federal habeas court could review the petitioner's claims of grand jury and trial jury discrimination and the admission of a coerced confession. The claims had been fully litigated and decided against the petitioner in the state courts. While the state court rulings were entitled to the same respect ordinarily given to opinions of a court of another jurisdiction, they did not preclude federal review of those claims on a habeas application. The habeas court could rely on the state court's findings of fact (unless there was a vital flaw in the latter's fact-finding procedures), but it was required to "exercise its own independent judgment" as to the legal consequences of those facts. The 1867 Act, the Court concluded, gave to federal courts the "final say" on federal claims. The habeas writ guaranteed federal review of the petitioner's federal claim, not simply a fair state consideration of the claim, for such consideration "may have misconceived a federal constitutional right."

In *Fay v. Noia*,[56] the Supreme Court reaffirmed and defended its *Brown* decision. Responding to criticism that *Brown* had departed unjustifiably from past precedent,[57] Justice Brennan's majority opinion traced the history of the writ from the common law through earlier Supreme Court decisions. He concluded that the writ had always been available "to remedy any kind of governmental restraint contrary to fundamental law" (as evidenced, in particular, by *Bushell's Case*[58]), and that this objective logically encompassed detention imposed pursuant to a conviction that had been obtained in violation of the defendant's constitutional rights. *Brown* accordingly had been consistent

---

[55]Brown v. Allen, 344 U.S. 443, 73 S.Ct. 397, 97 L.Ed. 469 (1953).

[56]Fay v. Noia, 372 U.S. 391, 83 S.Ct. 822, 9 L.Ed.2d 837 (1963).

[57]The constitutional violation alleged by petitioner *Noia* was the admission of a coerced confession. Since *Brown* had dealt with precisely that claim, the government acknowledged that the claim would have been cognizable if the issue had been properly raised in the state courts. Thus, the issue immediately presented in *Noia* was whether petitioner's claim had been lost by his failure to raise it on appeal. Both the majority and dissenting opinions thought it necessary, however, to reexamine the foundation of the *Brown* opinion before reaching that issue. Justice Brennan's opinion for the majority responded in particular to the historical analysis in Bator, Finality in Criminal Law and Federal Habeas Corpus for State Prisoners, 76 Harv.L.Rev. 441 (1963) (which viewed *Brown* as breaking new ground), while Justice Harlan's dissent relied heavily on that historical analysis. The Court's treatment of a petitioner's failure to fully litigate his claim in the state courts is discussed in § 28.4.

[58]See § 28.1, at note 13.

with the "historic office of The Great Writ," as well as the language of the federal habeas provisions, in holding that all constitutional claims were cognizable under the writ, without regard to their relationship to the trial court's jurisdiction or the full litigation of the claim in the state proceedings.

The scope of habeas review is no longer contingent upon whether the claimed defect deprived the trial court of its authority to proceed. However, the classification of error as jurisdictional or non-jurisdictional lives on in other contexts. In a series of cases determining what claims may be raised on habeas following a valid plea of guilty, the Court has invoked the jurisdictional defect distinction. Cognizable claims in this context have been limited to "incurable" defects that deprived the trial court of its authority to proceed notwithstanding the valid guilty plea (such as a double jeopardy violation that barred the prosecution under which the plea was taken).[59] In addition, the Court in *Lackawanna County District Attorney v. Coss*,[60] used the concept of "jurisdictional" defect to distinguish between claims that can and cannot be raised to challenge a prior conviction used to enhance a state sentence. The Court held that habeas relief is not available for a state prisoner who alleges that his state sentence was enhanced due to an invalid prior conviction, unless the prisoner can show that the prior conviction used to enhance his sentence was obtained in violation of *Gideon v. Wainwright*,[61] an error the Court has termed a "unique constitutional defect * * * ris[ing] to the level of a jurisdictional defect."

The habeas statute provides that a state prisoner may obtain relief on the ground that he is "in custody in violation of the Constitution or laws or treaties of the United States." State defendants are not often in a position to allege violations of federal statutes, and when they are, not all violations are cognizable. For example, prisoners may raise claims in habeas under the Interstate Agreement on Detainers, a compact between the states and the federal government. In *Reed v. Farley*,[62] the Court held that a violation of the time limitation in the IAD is not cognizable "when the defendant registered no objection to the trial date at the time it was set, and suffered no prejudice attributable to the delayed commencement." However, the Court declined to decide whether it would confront such a violation "if a

---

[59] See § 20.6(a). But see Westen, Forfeiture by Guilty Plea: A Reply, 76 Mich.L.Rev. 1308, 1334 (1978) ("for purposes of defining the claims that survive a guilty plea, the notion of jurisdictional error is either fallacious or useless").

[60] Lackawanna County District Attorney v. Coss, 532 U.S. 394, 121 S.Ct. 1567, 149 L.Ed.2d 608 (2001).

[61] See § 11.7.

[62] Reed v. Farley, 512 U.S. 339, 114 S.Ct. 2291, 129 L.Ed.2d 277 (1994).

state court, presented with a timely request to set a trial date within the IAD's 120-day period, nonetheless refused to comply * * *." Further, the Court, citing *Hill v. United States*,[63] stated in *Reed* that habeas review is available when the error qualifies as a "fundamental defect which inherently results in a complete miscarriage of justice." Lower courts, using this as the appropriate standard for federal habeas review of IAD violations, will deny relief when the defendant is unable to show that the delay or violation affected the petitioner's ability to get a fair trial or "caused a possibility that an innocent man was convicted and imprisoned."[64]

Although the Court has yet to decide whether the habeas statute permits review a claim that a state prisoner is held in violation of the Vienna Convention's consular access provisions,[65] lower courts have permitted petitioners to raise under § 2241 claims that removal orders violated the Convention Against Torture and Other Cruel, Inhuman or Degrading Treatment or Punishment.[66]

Habeas corpus may also be used to seek release from custody resulting from proceedings and decisions that occur well after conviction, such as parole or probation revocation, or denial of good time credits. The habeas remedy under § 2254 is not available to a petitioner who does not challenge the state court judgment forming the basis for his custody, but instead challenges the circumstances of his confinement. Prison condition claims are properly presented in an action under 42 U.S.C.A. § 1983.[67]

---

[63]Hill v. United States, 368 U.S. 424, 428, 82 S.Ct. 468, 7 L.Ed.2d 417 (1962), discussed in § 28.9(c) at note 78.

[64]Lara v. Johnson, 141 F.3d 239 (5th Cir.1998) (collecting authority).

[65]See Sanchez-Llamas v. Oregon, __ U.S. __, 126 S.Ct. 2669, 165 L.Ed.2d 557 (2006) (assuming without deciding that a violation of Article 36 is cognizable in habeas). See also Medellin v. Dretke, 544 U.S. 660, 125 S.Ct 2088, 161 L.Ed.2d 982 (2005) (stating a violation of the provisions may not be cognizable, noting that nonconstitutional claims must meet the 'fundamental defect' test announced in *Hill*).

[66]Cognizable claims do not include review of administrative fact findings or the exercise of discretion. See Cadet v. Bulger, 377 F.3d 1173 (11th Cir.2004) (finding no error in

district court's conclusion that Haitian prison conditions did not amount to treaty-prohibited torture, and declining to apply Eighth Amendment to deportation, which is a civil, rather than criminal procedure).

[67]See, e.g., Muhammad v. Close, 540 U.S. 749, 124 S.Ct. 1303, 158 L.Ed.2d 32 (2004) (per curiam).

In Wilkinson v. Dotson, 544 U.S. 74, 125 S.Ct. 1242, 161 L.Ed.2d 253 (2005), the Court explained the standard for assessing which sorts of prisoner claims are cognizable under § 1983 and which must be pursued in habeas corpus. Reviewing prior precedent, the Court declared that habeas corpus, not § 1983, is the appropriate remedy when a state prisoner requests present or future release, or where success would necessarily demonstrate the invalidity of confinement or its duration. The challenges to parole

§ 28.3(c) The exception for Fourth Amendment claims

It was not long after expanding the reach of federal habeas review to de novo consideration of non-jurisdictional constitutional claims before the Court carved out an exception. In *Stone v. Powell*,[68] the Court concluded that "where the State has provided an opportunity for full and fair litigation of a Fourth Amendment claim, the Constitution does not require that a state prisoner be granted federal habeas corpus relief on the ground that the evidence obtained in an unconstitutional search and seizure was introduced at his trial." Justice Powell's opinion for the Court in *Stone* was based on an earlier position he had taken in a concurring opinion in *Schneckloth v. Bustamonte*.[69] He had argued that a "nonguilt-related claim," such as the admission at trial of unconstitutionally seized evidence, should not be considered on collateral attack, provided "the petitioner was provided a fair opportunity to raise and have adjudicated the question in state courts." The exclusionary rule, Justice Powell noted, was not a "personal constitutional right," but a "judicially created means of effectuating rights secured by the Compare United States v. Wynn, 292 F.3d 226 (5th Cir.2002) (tolling is appropriate when the prisoner's attorney lied to the prisoner about having filed a petition); United States v. Martin, 408 F.3d 1089 (8th Cir.2005) (equitable tolling will be granted where petitioner's attorney failed to return forty phone calls by petitioner's wife, refused to return documents, lied about the petition being filed, told petitioner and his wife there was no filing deadline for 2255 motions, failed to attend appointments with petitioner's wife at his office, refused to take petitioner's phone calls); United States v. Schwartz, 274 F.3d 1220 (9th Cir.2001) (refusing to toll during time when government could have voided a petitioner's plea agreement due to her obligation to testify against her codefendants); Dunlap v. United States, 250 F.3d 1001 (6th Cir.2001) (refusing tolling for defendant who filed previous premature petitions, then missed the deadline on his third); Kahn v. United

---

procedures raised by the prisoners in *Dotson* did not meet this description and were properly brought to federal court as an action under § 1983.

In Hill v. McDonough, __ U.S. __, 126 S.Ct. 2096, 165 L.Ed.2d 44 (2006), the Court also held that a § 1983 action was the appropriate vehicle for a death row inmate to use to challenge the constitutionality of using lethal injection, and that such a challenge did not constitute a successive petition. Explained the Court, "Challenges to the lawfulness of con-finement or to particulars affecting its duration are the province of habeas corpus," while an "inmate's challenge to the circumstances of his confinement * * * may be brought under § 1983."

[Section 28.3(c)]

[68]Stone v. Powell, 428 U.S. 465, 96 S.Ct. 3037, 49 L.Ed.2d 1067 (1976).

[69]Schneckloth v. Bustamonte, 412 U.S. 218, 93 S.Ct. 2041, 36 L.Ed.2d 854 (1973).

States, 414 F.Supp.2d 210 (E.D.N.Y.2006) (federal judgment of conviction becomes final after ten days when no notice of appeal is filed, and petitioner's failure to understand this rule does not warrant equitable tolling) Fourth Amendment," which had a "primary function" of deterring police illegality. Accordingly, it "has never been interpreted to proscribe the introduction of illegally seized evidence in all proceedings against all persons." Thus, the Court had previously concluded, through the application of a "balancing process," that the exclusionary rule would not "prevent the use of illegally seized evidence in grand jury proceedings"[70] or "exclude such evidence from use for impeachment of a defendant."[71] Applying the same "balancing process" in *Stone*, it was clear that "the additional contribution, if any, of the consideration of search-and-seizure claims of state prisoners in collateral review is small in relation to the costs."

In reaching this cost-benefit conclusion, Justice Powell proceeded from the premise that the deterrent function of the exclusionary rule was served effectively by exclusion at trial and on direct appeal. There was no reason to assume that "any specific disincentive already created by the risk of exclusion * * * [in those proceedings] would be enhanced if there were the further risk that a conviction obtained in a state court and affirmed on direct review might be overturned in collateral proceedings often occurring years after the incarceration of the defendant." Petitioners argued that habeas review was essential because state courts might not enforce the Fourth Amendment as rigorously as federal courts, and the effectiveness of the exclusionary remedy as a deterrent therefore depended upon police awareness that "federal habeas might reveal flaws in a search or seizure that went undetected" in the state proceedings. For reasons noted previously,[72] the *Stone* opinion refused to accept such "a basic mistrust of state courts as fair and competent forums for adjudication of constitutional rights."

Turning to the other side of its cost-benefit ledger, the *Stone* opinion first noted that the application of the exclusionary rule necessarily "deflects the truthfinding process and often frees the guilty." While these costs were justified by the deterrence gained from applying the rule in the original proceedings, they could not be sustained by the marginal increase in deterrence that might be provided by the rule's application in a collateral proceeding. Moreover, "resort to habeas corpus, especially for purposes other

---

[70]Citing United States v. Calandra, 414 U.S. 338, 94 S.Ct. 613, 38 L.Ed.2d 561 (1974), discussed in §§ 3.1(f), 8.9(a).

[71]Citing Walder v. United States,

347 U.S. 62, 74 S.Ct. 354, 98 L.Ed. 503 (1954), discussed in § 9.6(a).

[72]See § 28.2(d) at note 71.

than to assure that no innocent person suffers an unconstitutional loss of liberties," entailed additional costs, including the consumption of scarce federal judicial resources, the delayed finality of criminal proceedings, and the frustration of good-faith state court efforts to fulfill their responsibilities to honor federal constitutional rights.

The Court has considered, and rejected, the possible extension of *Stone* to claims other than Fourth Amendment violations on four separate occasions. In *Jackson v. Virginia*,[73] the Court examined whether a federal habeas court, considering a due process challenge to the sufficiency of the evidence before the state trier of fact, had to look to the In re Winship standard of proof beyond a reasonable doubt,[74] or to a lesser standard, taken from a pre-*Winship* ruling, that would hold due process violated only when the record was "wholly devoid of any relevant evidence of a crucial element of the offense charged." The state argued that *Winship* review was unwarranted on habeas once the petitioner had received a "full and fair hearing" on his insufficient evidence claim in the state's appellate court. Responding to these contentions, the Court noted that the constitutional issue presented here was "far different" from that presented in *Stone*: "The question whether a defendant has been convicted upon inadequate evidence is central to the basic question of guilt or innocence."

In *Rose v. Mitchell*,[75] the Court again refused to extend *Stone*, this time to a constitutional claim that the justices agreed had no bearing on the reliability of the truth-finding process at trial. The habeas petitioner in *Mitchell* claimed that the foreman of the indicting grand jury had been selected on the basis of racial discrimination in violation of the Equal Protection Clause of the Fourteenth Amendment.[76] The defendant had been found guilty by a fairly drawn petit jury, following a fair trial, so the claim clearly did not involve the "protect[ion] of the innocent from incarceration." Nevertheless, the *Mitchell* majority offered several reasons for not extending *Stone* to bar habeas review of grand jury discrimination claims. Initially, the Court noted that while *Stone* assumed that state courts were as capable as federal courts in dealing with Fourth Amendment claims, the same could not be said of grand jury discrimination claims. Such a claim required the state bench to review its own conduct and procedures rather

---

[73]Jackson v. Virginia, 443 U.S. 307, 99 S.Ct. 2781, 61 L.Ed.2d 560 (1979).

[74]In re Winship, 397 U.S. 358, 90 S.Ct. 1068, 25 L.Ed.2d 368 (1970).

[75]Rose v. Mitchell, 443 U.S. 545, 99 S.Ct. 2993, 61 L.Ed.2d 739 (1979),

also discussed in § 15.4(e) at note 130.

[76]The Court assumed without deciding that racial discrimination in the selection of the foreman constituted an equal protection violation, but concluded that such discrimination had not been established. See § 15.4(e).

than the actions of police. In most cases, the trial court that initially rules on the claim will be the same court that has responsibility for the grand jury selection process. These differences, the Court noted, led it "to doubt that claims of [grand jury discrimination] in general will receive the type of full and fair hearings deemed essential to the holding of *Stone*." For similar reasons, it could not be said here, as it was said in *Stone*, that federal habeas review would have no significant "educative and deterrent effect." There was "strong reason to believe that federal review would indeed reveal flaws not appreciated by state judges perhaps too close to the day-to-day operation of the system." While *Stone* doubted that habeas rulings would have a substantial additional deterrent or educative impact with respect to the police, the responsible state officials here—the courts and their employees—were very likely to take note of the federal decisions and respond accordingly. Moreover, the "costs associated with quashing an indictment returned by an improperly constituted grand jury" were "significantly less than those associated with suppressing evidence." A prisoner who "is guilty in fact" is "less likely to go free" since the prosecution, after a reindictment, can retry the defendant on the same evidence. Finally, the "constitutional interests" that are vindicated in rectifying grand jury discrimination were characterized as "substantially more compelling than those at issue in *Stone*." Racial discrimination "strikes at the core concerns of the Fourteenth Amendment and at fundamental values of our society and our legal system." The "harm is not only to the accused," but "to society as a whole."

In *Kimmelman v. Morrison*,[77] the state contended that the reasoning of *Stone* barred habeas review of the petitioner's claim of ineffective assistance of counsel where counsel's incompetency lay solely in failing at trial to properly present an objection to the introduction of damaging evidence that had been seized in violation of the Fourth Amendment. Rejecting that argument, the Court held that an ineffective assistance claim is based on a separate constitutional right and therefore is cognizable even though the alleged incompetency consisted of counsel's mishandling of a Fourth Amendment objection. Habeas review served to vindicate the defendant's right to a fair trial within the structure of an adversary system, not merely the exclusionary rule.

Taken together, *Jackson*, *Kimmelman*, and *Mitchell* suggested that if *Stone* was to be extended to any other constitutional claim, the most likely candidate would be a prophylactic rule of comparatively recent vintage, aimed at controlling police behavior, and resulting in the exclusion of reliable evidence. However, in *Withrow*

---

[77]Kimmelman v. Morrison, 477　305 (1986).
U.S. 365, 106 S.Ct. 2574, 91 L.Ed.2d

v. Williams,[78] a closely divided Court refused to extend *Stone* to the one claim that seemingly had the best chance of being placed in this category—a violation of *Miranda*. Several features of *Miranda* violations, the majority reasoned, distinguished those violations from the *Mapp* violations considered in *Stone*. First, *Miranda*, "prophylactic though it may be, in protecting a defendant's Fifth Amendment privilege, * * * safeguards a fundamental trial right [of the individual]." Second, unlike *Mapp*'s exclusionary rule, *Miranda* did not serve only "some value necessarily divorced from the correct ascertainment of guilt." Rather, by "bracing against the possibility of unreliable statements in every instance of in-custody interrogation, *Miranda* serves to guard against the use of unreliable statements at trial." Finally, "eliminating [habeas] review of *Miranda* claims would not significantly benefit the federal courts in their exercise of habeas jurisdiction or advance the cause of federalism in any substantial way, * * * as it would not prevent a state prisoner from simply converting his barred *Miranda* claim into a due process [voluntariness] claim" that would still be cognizable on habeas review.

The 1996 amendments did not modify the effect of this line of decisions. Because § 2254(d), the section governing which claims litigated on the merits in state court may serve as grounds for relief, does not limit relief to claims related to reliability, or otherwise allude to the rule in *Stone*, it is possible to read the language of § 2254(d) as displacing *Stone*, so that claims for relief based on a state court's unreasonable interpretation of Fourth Amendment law would be cognizable under the new statute.[79] But given the thrust of the amendments in narrowing habeas relief, it is improbable that Congress intended this result, absent a more explicit legislative rejection of the then two-decade-old rule in *Stone*.[80]

§ 28.3(d) The opportunity for full and fair litigation

Consistent with its assumption that state courts would conscientiously enforce Fourth Amendment rights, the *Stone* Court was careful to point out that federal habeas review would

---

[78] Withrow v. Williams, 507 U.S. 680, 113 S.Ct. 1745, 123 L.Ed.2d 407 (1993).

[79] Indeed, this position had some adherents. See Carlson v. Ferguson, 9 F.Supp.2d 654 (S.D.W.Va.1998) (considering Fourth Amendment claim under § 2254(d)); Semeraro, Enforcing Fourth Amendment Rights Through Federal Habeas Corpus, 58 Rutgers L.Rev. 983 (2006).

[80] See, e.g., Sweet v. Delo, 125 F.3d 1144 (8th Cir.1997) (*Stone* still good law after 1996 amendments); Villafuerte v. Stewart, 111 F.3d 616 (9th Cir.1997) (per curiam) (same, dicta); Herrera v. Lemaster, 225 F.3d 1176 (10th Cir.2000) (stating court was "not persuaded * * * that by enacting AEDPA Congress intended to expand in any way a habeas petitioner's right to overturn a state court decision").

be available if the state had not provided the petitioner an "opportunity for full and fair litigation." This "exception" arguably is broader than what would be needed simply to serve *Stone*'s view of the deterrent function of the exclusionary rule. Certainly, if a state regularly fails to provide an adequate litigation opportunity, its enforcement of the exclusionary rule would not provide a substantial deterrent and habeas review would then provide more than a marginal increment in deterrence. The *Stone* exception, however, focuses on the individual case. Thus, the *Stone* majority apparently concluded that even though the exclusionary rule is a "judicially created" remedy rather than a "personal constitutional right," the defendant is entitled to at least one opportunity for a "full and fair consideration" of his claim.[81]

The *Stone* opinion offered little by way of definition of its full and fair opportunity standard. The Court referred at different points to "a fair and full opportunity to raise and have adjudicated the question," an opportunity for "full and fair consideration" of the claim, and an opportunity for "full and fair litigation * * * at trial and on direct review." Lower courts assessing the adequacy of state procedures typically apply a two-step inquiry asking (1) whether the state procedural mechanism is satisfactory in the abstract, and (2) whether there was a failure of the mechanism in the individual case.[82] Since the procedure for raising Fourth Amendment claims in state court usually is similar to the procedure in federal court, a finding of inadequacy is most likely to come under the second inquiry.[83] Thus, it was held that a petitioner did not receive a full and fair opportunity when his counsel was appointed one day before the expiration of the time period for presenting a suppression motion and in denying counsel's oral request for an extension the trial court applied an

---

[Section 28.3(d)]

[81]See also Halpern, Federal Habeas Corpus and the Mapp Exclusionary Rule After *Stone v. Powell*, 82 Colum.L.Rev. 1, 30–31 (1982); Seidman, Factual Guilt and the Burger Court: An Examination of Continuity and Change in Criminal Procedure, 80 Colum.L.Rev. 436, 455–59 (1980) (both discussing the theoretical foundation of the exception). The exception is discussed at length in Snyder, Habeas Corpus: Stoned But Not Dead, 19 Crim.L.Bull. 197 (1983), and various articles cited there.

[82]See, e.g., Boyd v. Mintz, 631 F.2d 247 (3d Cir.1980); Riley v. Gray, 674 F.2d 522 (6th Cir.1982); Cabrera

v. Hinsley, 324 F.3d 527 (7th Cir.2003) (noting that even if the state provides a mechanism under which to litigate a claim, *Stone* would not block habeas review if the mechanism was in some way a sham); Willett v. Lockhart, 37 F.3d 1265 (8th Cir.1994) (en banc) (reviewing authority).

[83]Counsel's failure to take advantage of an opportunity to litigate Fourth Amendment claims in state court will ordinarily bar review. See Turentine v. Miller, 80 F.3d 222 (7th Cir.1996). A breakdown in the state machinery will result in the state being held responsible for the default. See, e.g., Boyd v. Mintz, 631 F.2d 247 (3d Cir. 1980).

unwritten local rule mandating a written application.[84] Similarly, a petitioner was denied an adequate opportunity to present his claim where the state appellate court rejected the claim based on a recent decision which had not been raised by the state.[85]

An erroneous application of the Fourth Amendment, without more, does not constitute a denial of an opportunity for full and fair litigation. It is said to be "of no consequence whether the state courts employed an incorrect legal standard, misapplied the correct standard, or erred in finding the underlying facts."[86] Even the state appellate court in one of the cases before the Court in *Stone* apparently applied an incorrect legal standard.[87] Lower courts have also noted that if the *Stone* exception could be based on the misapplication of Fourth Amendment standards, "*Stone's* bar would become a nullity, since petitioners would routinely allege the necessary error."[88] Nevertheless, some courts have held that a state court's "willful refusal to apply the appropriate constitutional standard" or other "egregious error" would fall

---

[84]Boyd v. Mintz, 631 F.2d 247 (3d Cir.1980); see also Holloway v. Woodard, 655 F.Supp. 1245 (W.D.N.C. 1987) (although state rule requiring that suppression motion be accompanied by factual affidavit is legitimate on its face, reliance on that rule to reject motion on appeal—after the trial court had taken testimony and ruled on the merits, with the state's acquiescence, notwithstanding the lack of an affidavit—constituted a "procedural ambush").

[85]Riley v. Gray, 674 F.2d 522 (6th Cir.1982). See also United States ex rel. Bostick v. Peters, 3 F.3d 1023 (7th Cir.1993) (defendant denied opportunity for full and fair litigation of Fourth Amendment claim by unanticipated and unforeseeable application of a rule on appeal). A summary disposition of the claim by the appellate court is not inadequate, provided the state's procedure permitted more extensive review at the appellate court's discretion. See Tackno v. Blackburn, 571 F.2d 1383 (5th Cir.1978); Bradley v. Cowan, 561 F.2d 1213 (6th Cir.1977).

[86]Halpern, Federal Habeas Corpus and the Mapp Exclusionary Rule After *Stone v. Powell*, 82 Colum.L.Rev. 1,

17–18 (1982) (collecting cases). See also Marshall v. Hendricks, 307 F.3d 36 (3d Cir.2002) (no structural defect prevented full and fair litigation of petitioner's Fourth Amendment claims in state court, allegations that claims were decided incorrectly by state courts are insufficient to surmount the *Stone* bar); L. Yackle, Postconviction Remedies § 99 (1981 & Supp.2007).

[87]See Snyder, Habeas Corpus: Stoned But Not Dead, 19 Crim.L.Bull. 197, 204–05 (1983). A footnote in *Stone* noted that the Nebraska Supreme Court had found the challenged search warrant affidavit sufficient on its face but had also referred to additional information that had not been before the magistrate. The majority opinion added that the state's argument that it could "supplement the affidavit" with such additional information was "a contention that we have several times rejected and need not reach here again." See also Gilmore v. Marks, 799 F.2d 51 (3d Cir.1986).

[88]Halpern, Federal Habeas Corpus and the Mapp Exclusionary Rule After *Stone v. Powell*, 82 Colum.L.Rev. 1, 18 (1982) (collecting cases).

within the *Stone* exception.[89]

Where the state procedure provided defense counsel with a full opportunity, but counsel failed to take advantage of that opportunity, the habeas petitioner may have lost his Fourth Amendment claim, but he may pursue another avenue for obtaining relief—a claim of ineffective assistance of counsel. In *Kimmelman v. Morrison*,[90] as discussed earlier, the Supreme Court held that a claim of ineffective assistance of counsel is based on a separate constitutional right and therefore is cognizable even though the alleged deficiency in representation consisted primarily of counsel's mishandling of a Fourth Amendment objection.[91]

§ 28.3(e) "Bare innocence" claims

Until 1993, the Court had insisted that showing of factual innocence alone was not a basis for relief, as the writ was designed to ensure that state court processes comply with the Constitution, not to enlist federal courts to duplicate guilt-innocence determinations.[92] Indeed, nothing would seem to upset more the interests in finality and comity than the prospect of allowing a defendant, fairly convicted in state court upon constitutionally sufficient evidence,[93] to reopen his conviction with "new" evidence of innocence discovered years after trial, especially when the state provides its own review of such claims.[94] As the Court narrowed access to the writ in the 1970s and '80s, a showing of possible or probable innocence became a common ingredient of habeas relief, but only as a gateway to habeas review of a separate constitutional claim.[95] For example, a petitioner who could persuade a federal court that he may be innocent could overcome

---

[89]Gamble v. Oklahoma, 583 F.2d 1161 (10th Cir.1978); Turentine v. Miller, 80 F.3d 222 (7th Cir.1996).

[90]Kimmelman v. Morrison, 477 U.S. 365, 106 S.Ct. 2574, 91 L.Ed.2d 305 (1986), also discussed at note 77 supra and at § 11.10(c) at note 102. See also Jeffries & Stuntz, Ineffective Assistance and Procedural Default in Federal Habeas Corpus, 57 U.Chi.L. Rev. 679 (1990).

[91]E.g., Northrop v. Trippett, 265 F.3d 372 (6th Cir.2001) (state court unreasonably applied clearly established federal law in denying petitioner's ineffective assistance claim when counsel failed to argue that evidence from stop was inadmissible).

[Section 28.3(e)]

[92]See, e.g., Townsend v. Sain, 372 U.S. 293, 317, 83 S.Ct. 745, 759, 9 L.Ed.2d 770 (1963) (noting that newly discovered evidence must "bear upon the constitutionality of the applicant's detention; the existence merely of newly discovered evidence relevant to the guilt of a state prisoner is not a ground for relief on federal habeas corpus").

[93]See Jackson v. Virginia, 443 U.S. 307, 99 S.Ct. 2781, 61 L.Ed.2d 560 (1979).

[94]See Friedman, Failed Enterprise, 83 Cal.L.Rev. 485, 506–11 (1995) (discussing how bare innocence claims in habeas undermine the Court's agenda in promoting finality, federalism, and fairness).

[95]See generally § 28.2(d), discussing the doctrinal manifestations of the "innocence model."

a procedural default for which he could not show "cause and prejudice,"[96] or pursue in a second petition a claim he had failed to raise in his first petition.[97]

In 1993, in *Herrera v. Collins*,[98] the Court considered whether habeas relief was available for claims of "bare innocence," and if so, when such claims required relief. *Herrera* claimed that several new affidavits demonstrated that his brother had committed the crime for which he had been sentenced to die. State law required defendants to bring motions for new trial based on newly discovered evidence within thirty days of trial; *Herrera* had missed this deadline, so a state challenge to his conviction and sentence was unavailable. He argued in federal court that the execution of an innocent man would violate the Eighth and Fourteenth Amendments, although he alleged no constitutional violation during the state prosecution. Despite considerable ambiguity in their opinions, most of the justices seemed to agree that in extremely unusual circumstances, a claim of innocence, even one unaccompanied by a separate constitutional claim, could warrant federal habeas relief. Justice Rehnquist wrote: "We may assume, for the sake of argument in deciding this case, that in a capital case a truly persuasive demonstration of 'actual innocence' made after trial would render the execution of a defendant unconstitutional, and warrants federal habeas relief if there were no state avenue open to process such a claim." The showing required "would necessarily be extraordinarily high." While the Court's recognition of such a bare-innocence claim was only dicta, the Court has made the same assumption in later cases,[99] and many lower courts since *Herrera* have held that such claims are at least theoretically cognizable.[100] In *House v. Bell*,[101] the Court again declined to decide whether federal courts have authority to review a freestanding claim of innocence as a basis for invalidat-

---

[96]See § 28.4(e).

[97]See § 28.5(c) and (d).

[98]Herrera v. Collins, 506 U.S. 390, 113 S.Ct. 853, 122 L.Ed.2d 203 (1993), also discussed in § 26.2(c) at note 66.

[99]See Schlup v. Delo, 513 U.S. 298, 115 S.Ct. 851, 130 L.Ed.2d 808 (1995) ("If there were no question about the fairness of the criminal trial, a *Herrera*-type claim would have to fail unless the federal habeas court is itself convinced that those new facts unquestionably establish [the defendant's] innocence."); House v. Bell, __ U.S. __, 126 S.Ct. 2064, 165 L.Ed.2d 1 (2006).

[100]See Thomas et al., Is It Ever Too Late For Innocence?, 64 U.Pitt.L. Rev. 263 (2003), for one survey of lower court opinions applying *Herrera*. But compare LaFevers v. Gibson, 238 F.3d 1263 (10th Cir.2001) (finding that evidence did not show defendant was actually innocent of both the crime and the death penalty, and concluding that furthermore, "an assertion of actual innocence * * * does not, standing alone, support the granting of the writ of habeas corpus").

[101]House v. Bell, __ U.S. __, 126 S.Ct. 2064, 165 L.Ed.2d 1 (2006), also discussed in § 28.4(e) at note 77.

ing a state conviction or death sentence. Although House had managed to gather DNA and other forensic evidence that "cast considerable doubt on his guilt—doubt sufficient to satisfy [the] standard for obtaining federal review despite a state procedural default," his was "not a case of conclusive exoneration." His showing fell "short of the threshold implied in *Herrera*."

The chances that such a claim will ever succeed are extremely small, and the questions such a claim raises are numerous and daunting. The first issue is what type of showing of innocence is required. Because most lower courts have found claims of innocence unconvincing, they have avoided answering this question with more specificity than that offered by the justices who have stated only that the showing of innocence must be "truly persuasive" amounting to "conclusive exoneration." The tenor of the opinions in *Herrera* suggests that the Court had in mind a demonstration more stringent than one that would leave a fact-finder to believe the petitioner is "probably" innocent, perhaps requiring proof of innocence "beyond a reasonable doubt."[102]

A second question raised by the *Herrera* decision is the meaning of the Court's condition that there be "no state avenue open to process such a claim." If the provision of even the most limited, rarely exercised clemency relief is sufficient to preclude a claim of bare innocence in habeas court, then bare innocence claims are truly hypothetical.[103]

Third, the Court has yet to clarify who is eligible to raise a

---

[102]See, e.g., Carriger v. Stewart, 132 F.3d 463 (9th Cir.1997) (en banc) (petitioner must affirmatively prove that he is probably innocent, collecting commentary). *Herrera*'s standard has been debated at length in law reviews. E.g., Steiker, Innocence and Federal Habeas, 41 UCLA L.Rev. 303, 385 (1993) (advocating relief upon showing of innocence by a preponderance). It is not likely that inadmissible evidence, generally excluded due to its lack of reliability, such as polygraph results, the results of novel and experimental scientific procedures, or hearsay, would ever be sufficient to meet a petitioner's burden.

One author reports that since *Herrera* was decided, "petitioners have presented at least 173 bare-innocence claims squarely before federal courts." Note, 42 Am.Crim.L.Rev. 121 (2005). According to this author, only a handful of these cases (both capital and noncapital) were resolved in favor of the defendant: two defendants received either an evidentiary hearing or a remand; two others received an order for DNA testing. Five other petitioners received clemency, three of these from Governor Ryan of Illinois who in 2003 granted commutations to all death row defendants in Illinois at the end of his term.

[103]Steiker, Innocence and Federal Habeas, 41 UCLA L.Rev. 303, 385 (1993) (noting and collecting authority documenting the inadequacy of clemency procedures). See also Perry v. Norris, 879 F.Supp. 1503 (E.D.Ark. 1995) (terming this requirement "nothing more than a corollary to the exhaustion-of-remedies doctrine," and rejecting the position that a petitioner must seek clemency before raising a bare-innocence claim). See also Miller v. Comm'r of Correction, 242 Conn. 745, 700 A.2d 1108 (1997) (state relief

Herrera claim. The Court's opinion spoke of a showing of innocence that would make an execution unconstitutional, suggesting that the claim is open only to defendants sentenced to death. Yet if punishment of the factually innocent is what the Constitution forbids, limiting relief to capital defendants is difficult to justify. Also, with innocence of the offense as the focus, it also follows that the petitioner who concedes he committed the crime but disputes the factual allegations that make him eligible for the death penalty would be barred from raising a *Herrera* claim.[104]

§ 28.4 Claims in habeas foreclosed by state procedural defaults

§ 28.4(a)   Claims "defaulted" in state court-the policy debate
§ 28.4(b)   Which defaults count: the "adequate and independent state ground" standard
§ 28.4(c)   Excusing default: state waiver of the procedural default defense
§ 28.4(d)   Excusing default: the "cause and prejudice" standard
§ 28.4(e)   Excusing default: the "miscarriage of justice" exception

§ 28.4(a) Claims "defaulted" in state court-the policy debate

When a petitioner has failed to present his claim in the state proceedings in accordance with state procedural requirements, and the state courts have held that this lapse bars consideration

---

requires prisoner to establish no reasonable fact-finder would find guilt). Dozens of states have enacted statutes allowing for post-conviction DNA testing under some circumstances. See, e.g., Swedlow, Don't Believe Everything You Read: A Review of Modern "Post-Conviction" DNA Testing Statutes, 38 Cal.W.L.Rev. 255 (2002); § 24.11 notes [35–45].

[104]See, e.g., Noel v. Norris, 322 F.3d 500 (8th Cir.2003) (noting petitioner contests only the appropriateness of his death sentence, rejecting *Herrera* claim).

Courts have also refused to grant relief in the form of access to DNA testing to habeas petitioners claiming innocence alone. See, e.g., Harvey v. Horan, 278 F.3d 370 (4th Cir.2002) (holding that a defendant has no constitutional right to post-conviction DNA testing, and conclud-

ing that the defendant's request constituted a successive petition barred by the AEDPA). See also United States v. Quinones, 313 F.3d 49 (2d Cir.2002) (rejecting due process challenge to federal death penalty and concluding that there is no "right of an innocent person not to be deprived by execution of the opportunity to demonstrate his innocence"). But see Cherrix v. Braxton, 131 F.Supp.2d 756 (E.D.Va. 2001) (finding good cause for DNA testing); Kreimer & Rudovsky, Double Helix, Double Bind: Factual Innocence and Post-conviction DNA Testing, 151 U.Pa.L.Rev. 547 (2002) (arguing for a constitutional right to post-conviction access to DNA testing). See generally Alldredge, Federal Habeas Corpus and Post-conviction Claims of Actual Innocence Based on DNA Evidence, 56 S.M.U.L.Rev. 1005 (2003).

of the claim on its merits, the issue presented to the habeas court is under what conditions, if any, should that state procedural default also bar federal habeas review of the claim. In the absence of controlling language from Congress,[1] the rules for reviewing defaulted claims have been developed in a long line of decisions by the Supreme Court.

The decisions defining the scope of the affirmative defense of procedural default reflect deep differences among the justices over the significance of two sets of competing interests. On the one hand, the petitioner has an obvious interest in obtaining review of a federal constitutional claim at least once. The nation, too, has an interest in ensuring that constitutional commands are followed in state proceedings. On the other hand, there are many reasons to limit habeas review of defaulted claims.

First, the state has a stake in the finality of the judgments of its courts, and in the effective enforcement of its procedural rules.[2] Second is the risk that federal review will require initial fact-finding long after the critical event has passed.[3] Depending on the type of claim raised by the petitioner, delay may result in the loss to "society [of] the right to punish admitted offenders" since the "erosion of memory, and dispersion of witnesses * * * render retrial difficult, even impossible."[4]

Third, the Supreme Court has also expressed concern that habeas review not reward what has been described as "sandbag-

---

[Section 28.4(a)]

[1] The 1996 amendments specify the consequences of state procedural default in a particular class of capital cases. See § 28.8(a). The consequence of default in other cases, however, is not addressed by the amendments, nor was procedural default addressed by the statute prior to the 1996 amendments.

[2] Commentary on procedural default is plentiful. See, e.g., Jeffries & Stuntz, Ineffective Assistance and Procedural Default, 57 U.Chi.L.Rev. 679 (1990); R. Hertz & J. Liebman, 2 Federal Habeas Corpus Practice and Procedure ch. 26 (5th ed.2005); Meltzer, State Forfeitures of Federal Rights, 99 Harv.L.Rev. 1128 (1986). The issue has also been characterized as determining the impact of "an abortive state proceeding." See Reitz, Federal Habeas Corpus: Impact of An Abortive

State Proceeding, 74 Harv.L.Rev. 1315 (1961).

[3] See, e.g., Wainwright v. Sykes, 433 U.S. 72, 97 S.Ct. 2497, 53 L.Ed.2d 594 (1977).

[4] Engle v. Isaac, 456 U.S. 107, 102 S.Ct. 1558, 71 L.Ed.2d 783 (1982), discussed at note 41. When a claim was heard and decided at the trial level, and the default occurred through a failure to appeal, the federal habeas court can rely upon the state fact-finding just as it could if the claim had been considered by the state appellate court. Also, certain types of claims, such as a double jeopardy objection, may be readily resolved on the basis of the state court record even if they were not pressed at trial. While there may be reasons for barring review based on such procedural defaults, the problem of delayed fact-finding is not one of them.

ging" tactics by defense counsel.[5] If habeas review is available for claims not addressed in state court, there are arguably some situations in which counsel may prefer not to raise an issue at trial, holding it in reserve as a means of obtaining a new trial through the writ if the trial should result in a conviction.[6] Consider, for example, an objection to grand jury discrimination in a case in which the grand jury would almost certainly have indicted even if fairly composed. Raising the issue before trial will "only delay the inevitable date of prosecution,"[7] but holding the issue in reserve opens up the possibility of gaining, years later, a second trial through habeas review if the first results in a conviction. Of course, when the defaulted claim is one that if raised successfully would have absolutely barred prosecution (as in the case of a double jeopardy or speedy trial claim), there is no incentive to sandbag and any forfeiture would almost certainly be the result of inadvertence or negligence.[8] When a forfeiture is attributable to the ignorance or negligence of counsel, Justice Brennan argued that "closing the federal courthouse doors" is an "unnecessary and misdirected sanction."[9] Not only is "the potential loss of all valuable state remedies" a sufficient sanction, under this view, the defendant is not the person responsible for the default. In response, it has been argued that this objection is adequately met by allowing review in those cases in which the defendant can show that counsel's negligence in procedurally forfeiting a claim amounted to a violation of the Sixth Amendment under the stan-

---

[5]See, e.g., Wainwright v. Sykes, 433 U.S. 72, 97 S.Ct. 2497, 53 L.Ed.2d 594 (1977).

[6]Many commentators have questioned the legitimacy of assuming that such tactics are employed except in "rare instances," see, e.g., Note, 130 U.Pa.L.Rev. 981, 994–98 (1982), but the Supreme Court is not convinced. See, e.g., Wainwright v. Sykes, 433 U.S. 72, 97 S.Ct. 2497, 53 L.Ed.2d 594 (1977).

In a decision holding that a violation of the Vienna Convention is not exempt from state procedural default rules, the Court distinguished a decision by the International Court of Justice that had rejected the application of default rules to such violations. Explained Chief Justice Roberts, "Procedural default rules generally take on greater importance in an adversary system such as ours than in

the sort of magistrate-directed, inquisitorial legal system characteristic of many other countries." "In an inquisitorial system, the failure to raise a legal error can in part be attributed to the magistrate, and thus to the state itself. In our system, however, the responsibility for failing to raise an issue generally rests with the parties themselves." Sanchez-Llamas v. Oregon, __ U.S. __, 126 S.Ct. 2669, 165 L.Ed.2d 557 (2006). See also § 1.7.

[7]Tollett v. Henderson, 411 U.S. 258, 93 S.Ct. 1602, 36 L.Ed.2d 235 (1973).

[8]See also Teague, Federal Habeas Corpus and Ineffective Representation of Counsel: The Supreme Court Has Work To Do, 31 Stan.L.Rev. 1 (1978).

[9]Brennan, J., dissenting in Wainwright v. Sykes, 433 U.S. 72, 97 S.Ct. 2497, 53 L.Ed.2d 594 (1977).

dards of *Strickland*.[10]

A final concern repeatedly noted by the Court in its decisions addressing procedural default is that federal review after a state court's efforts to enforce its own procedural rules demonstrates a lack of respect for the state justice system. "Comity," it is argued, may require deference to such state decisions, in order to maintain the appropriate federal balance and prevent strained federal-state relations.

The Court's decisions balancing these interests follow the familiar pattern of expansion during the 1960s and gradual restriction in the 1970s and 1980s. The standards for reviewing defaulted claims, discussed in the sections that follow, have remained relatively stable since the late 1980s and were unchanged by the 1996 Act that fundamentally altered so many other aspects of the federal habeas review. The affirmative defense of procedural default continues to bar review of claims in a significant portion of habeas cases.[11]

§ 28.4(b) Which defaults count: the "adequate and independent state ground" standard

The present standards for determining which defaulted claims are reviewable in habeas proceedings and which are not are discussed in § 28.4(c) to (d). The different issue addressed in this subsection is when a federal court will recognize that there has been a default in state court, so that such standards will be applicable.

Prior to the 1963 decision of *Fay v. Noia*,[12] federal courts applied to state procedural defaults the same principle that would have been applied if the case had come to the Supreme Court on direct review from the state courts. The Court had long held that on direct review it would not reach the merits of an appellant's constitutional claim if the court below had relied upon an "adequate state ground."[13] If the state court ruling had been based on a state law, independent from the federal constitutional claim, then that ground would necessarily control the outcome of the

---

[10]Engle v. Isaac, 456 U.S. 107, 102 S.Ct. 1558, 71 L.Ed.2d 783 (1982), discussed at note 41. See also Jeffries & Stuntz, Ineffective Assistance and Procedural Default, 57 U.Chi.L.Rev. 679 (1990). Review of claims defaulted due to the ineffective assistance of counsel is discussed in § 28.4(d).

[11]An estimated 12% of non-capital habeas cases included claims denied for this reason, according to a recent study. N. King, F. Cheesman & B. Ostrom, Habeas Litigation in U.S.

District Courts (2007), available at htt p://www.ncjrs.gov/pdffiles1/nij/grants/ 219559.pdf.

[Section 28.4(b)]

[12]Fay v. Noia, 372 U.S. 391, 83 S.Ct. 822, 9 L.Ed.2d 837 (1963).

[13]The adequate state ground doctrine is explored in 16B C. Wright, A. Miller, and E. Cooper, Federal Practice and Procedure: Jurisdiction 2d §§ 4019 to 4028 (1996).

case. Even if the Court were to find that there had been a constitutional violation, it lacked authority to review the question of state law and the state court's ruling would therefore have to be affirmed. Although this analysis was developed initially in connection with state rulings based on substantive grounds, it soon was held applicable to rulings involving procedural grounds as well. Application of the same principle on habeas review was viewed as consistent with the role of the habeas court as a functional surrogate of the Supreme Court in providing a federal forum for federal claims. If a procedural default constituted an independent and adequate state ground, thereby barring *direct* review by the Supreme Court, it would also bar *habeas* review.

The Court eventually abandoned this principle as the sole measure of the propriety of federal review of a claim defaulted in state court, and allowed review, despite an adequate and independent state procedural ground for default, under certain circumstances. Nevertheless, the adequacy of the state's application of its procedural rule remains a threshold issue in any case in which procedural default is raised as a defense by the state. The Court explained *this* two-part analysis in *Dugger v. Adams*:[14] a procedural default will not bar habeas review if either (i) the state procedural rule had been applied so unevenly as not to constitute an adequate state ground or (ii) the default was excused under the cause and prejudice standard, described in § 28.4(c) through (e) below.

Although there is some authority to the contrary, most courts agree that the state bears the burden of persuasion on the issue of "adequacy" of the state ground.[15] A state ground is "adequate" only if it is applied evenhandedly by the state courts and serves a "legitimate state interest."[16] A state court may not manipulate its rules to evade federal rights, or exercise its discretion to discriminate against the presentation of such rights.[17] For example, a state procedural rule that was not firmly established at the time of a defendant's trial cannot be applied retroactively to bar as untimely a defendant's objection to jury selection. Such a rule is

---

[14]Dugger v. Adams, 489 U.S. 401, 109 S.Ct. 1211, 103 L.Ed.2d 435 (1989).

[15]See Bennett v. Mueller, 322 F.3d 573 (9th Cir.2003) (collecting authority).

[16]See Henry v. Mississippi, 379 U.S. 443, 85 S.Ct. 564, 13 L.Ed.2d 408 (1965). See also Sandalow, *Henry v. Mississippi* and the Adequate State Ground: Proposals for a Revised Doctrine, 1965 Sup.Ct.Rev. 187; Hill, The Inadequate State Ground, 65 Colum.L.Rev. 943 (1965); 16B C. Wright, A. Miller, and E. Cooper, Federal Practice and Procedure: Jurisdiction 2d § 4028 (1996).

[17]See 16A C. Wright, A. Miller, and E. Cooper, Federal Practice and Procedure: Jurisdiction 2d § 4026 (1996).

"inadequate to serve as an independent state ground."[18] A state procedural rule must be "regularly" and "consistently" applied by state courts to be considered an adequate ground for barring habeas review.[19] Inadequate, too, are state procedural rules that deny to petitioners "any meaningful review of [an] ineffective as-

---

[18]Ford v. Georgia, 498 U.S. 411, 111 S.Ct. 850, 112 L.Ed.2d 935 (1991). See also White v. Bowersox, 206 F.3d 776 (8th Cir.2000) (because the principles announced by the state court in his case were "neither readily ascertainable nor firmly established, the procedural default that ensued cannot be considered an adequate state ground to bar federal review"); Franklin v. Anderson, 434 F.3d 412 (6th Cir. 2006).

[19]See, e.g., Bronshtein v. Horn, 404 F.3d 700 (3d Cir.2005) (rule not consistently applied, no bar); Rosales v. Dretke, 444 F.3d 703 (5th Cir.2006) (because state court applied a more exacting standard for the objection necessary to preserve a *Batson* claim that it had in other cases where the defendants were in the same position as petitioner, state court's procedural bar was not adequate to preclude federal court review, rejecting the state's argument that petitioner should not receive a windfall on account of the prior errors of state courts in applying too lenient a standard, stating that the state court "is entitled to exercise whatever leniency or grace it wishes in establishing its procedural rules; our task is to determine whether [those rules] have been strictly and regularly applied"); Deitz v. Money, 391 F.3d 804 (6th Cir.2005) (state court's denial of leave to appeal under Rules 5(A) and 26(B) of the Ohio Rules of Appellate Procedure was not an adequate state ground because a rule that grants "such discretion to the courts is not 'firmly established and regularly followed' "; the fact that petitioner waited four years before raising claim of ineffective assistance does not matter because state courts have treated such delay inconsistently); Franklin v. Anderson, 434 F.3d 412 (6th Cir.2006) (divided opinion finding no default when rule applied to bar claim in state court went into effect the day after petitioner filed his motion, motion was timely under either new or old rule, and in any event Ohio courts were "erratic" and "fluctuating" in handling untimely motions in capital cases); Powell v. Lambert, 357 F.3d 871 (9th Cir.2004) (unpublished decisions applying the state's rule can be considered when assessing "adequacy" since it is state *practice* that must not be arbitrary, finding inconsistent application of Washington's rule requiring dismissal of mixed petitions, a rule that was announced four years after petitioner filed his petition, rendering it not adequate to bar federal review); Bentley v. Bock, 239 F.Supp.2d 686 (E.D.Mich. 2002) (finding contemporaneous objection rule was not "adequate" state bar because state courts frequently waived the rule when they perceived the issue raised to have significant constitutional import).

Compare Johnson v. Pinchack, 392 F.3d 551 (3d Cir.2004) (concluding that although there exist a few exceptional cases where the five-year limit under state law was not applied rigidly due to compelling circumstances, because the state enforces the limit in the vast majority of cases, and because the state courts have determined that petitioner's claim does not fit into the exceptional category of cases, the rule is an adequate state ground); Hedrick v. True, 443 F.3d 342 (4th Cir.2006) (state's rule barring the review of claims not raised in merits brief was consistently applied, and petitioner's belief that it was sufficient to include extensive discussion in an earlier pleading seeking review and not in the merits brief was not reasonable, *Brady* claim barred); Hicks v. Straub, 377 F.3d 538 (6th Cir.2004) (denial of leave to appeal under MCR 6.508(D) was an

sistance claim."[20]

In "rare circumstances," the Court has held, "exorbitant application of a generally sound rule renders the state ground inadequate to stop consideration of a federal question." One of those rare circumstances occurred in *Lee v. Kemna*,[21] where the alleged default was defense counsel's failure to comply with the requirement for a "written motion" for continuance when the defendant's alibi witnesses disappeared unexpectedly through no fault of the defendant, and the judge denying the defense's oral motion for continuance informed the defendant that he could not carry over the trial until the next day because he (the judge) had to be with his daughter at the hospital. The Court found the failure to comply with the state's rule did not bar federal review because 1) the judge's reason for denying the continuance could not have been countered by a perfect motion, 2) the application of the rule to the defendant's "predicament" was novel, indeed no one mentioned the rule until the state decided belatedly to raise it on appeal, and 3) the defendant "substantially complied" with the rule. Nothing would have been gained by requiring more exact adherence to the rule at trial.

In order for a state to rely on the defense of procedural default in a habeas action, not only must it show that the state court's reason for rejecting the petitioner's claim was "adequate," it must also show that the court's reason was "independent," that is, based on state, not federal law. A state court's decision is not "independent" if either 1) the " 'resolution of [a] state procedural law question depends on a federal constitutional ruling,' "[22] or 2) the state court decision actually rested on such a ruling.[23] There is no bar to habeas review unless the state court has "clearly and

---

adequate and independent state ground, because it was both firmly established and regularly followed at the time of the petitioner's appeal).

[20]Brecheen v. Reynolds, 41 F.3d 1343 (10th Cir.1994). See also English v. Cody, 146 F.3d 1257 (10th Cir. 1998); Hoffman v. Arave, 236 F.3d 523 (9th Cir.2001).

[21]Lee v. Kemna, 534 U.S. 362, 122 S.Ct. 877, 151 L.Ed.2d 820 (2002). The Court in *Lee* relied upon Osborne v. Ohio, 495 U.S. 103, 110 S.Ct. 1691, 109 L.Ed.2d 98 (1990) (no adequate state bar when nothing would have been gained by requiring defense lawyer to object a second time after the trial judge had overruled a motion to dismiss based on the same argument

just before trial).

[22]A state law ground is too interwoven if "the state has made application of the procedural bar depend on an antecedent ruling on federal law [such as] the determination of whether federal constitutional error has been committed." Ake v. Oklahoma, 470 U.S. 68, 105 S.Ct. 1087, 84 L.Ed.2d 53 (1985). Compare Bennett v. Mueller, 322 F.3d 573 (9th Cir.2003) (state ground independent) with Park v. California, 202 F.3d 1146 (9th Cir.2000) (no independent state ground when state court "necessarily made an antecedent ruling on federal law before applying" its rule).

[23]Stewart v. Smith, 536 U.S. 856, 122 S.Ct. 2578, 153 L.Ed.2d 762 (2002)

expressly" stated that its judgment rests on a state procedural rule.[24]

§ 28.4(c) Excusing default: state waiver of the procedural default defense

Where the state courts ignore a procedural default and reach the merits of a petitioner's claim, federal habeas review will not be precluded by that default.[25] If state courts are willing to ignore a procedural default, a federal court "implies no disrespect" in doing the same.[26]

Often a state court's ruling is ambiguous, and it is not clear from the decision whether the prisoner's federal claim was rejected because the state court found the claim wanting on the merits, or because the claim was not raised in accordance with state procedure. When a state court ruling discusses both state and federal reasons for rejecting a federal claim, habeas courts will presume that the state court ruling was based on the merits of the federal claim, excusing the procedural default, absent some indication to the contrary by the state court.[27] Where there has been "one reasoned state judgment rejecting a federal claim, later

---

(quoting Ake v. Oklahoma, 470 U.S. 68, 105 S.Ct. 1087, 84 L.Ed.2d 53 (1985), and concluding that the state court's determination that respondent waived his ineffective-assistance-of-counsel claim under Ariz.R.Crim.Pr. 32.2(a)(3) did not require an examination of the merits of that claim, and was independent of federal law).

[24]Harris v. Reed, 489 U.S. 255, 109 S.Ct. 1038, 103 L.Ed.2d 308 (1989). See also Fama v. Commissioner of Correctional Services, 235 F.3d 804 (2d Cir.2000) (holding that "when a state court uses language such as 'the defendant's remaining contentions are either unpreserved for appellate review or without merit,' the validity of the claim is preserved and is subject to federal review").

[Section 28.4(c)]

[25]This doctrine has been applied when the standard governing defaults was the standard of "cause and prejudice," see Ulster County Court v. Allen, 442 U.S. 140, 99 S.Ct. 2213, 60 L.Ed.2d 777 (1979); when it was the "deliberate bypass" standard, see Warden v. Hayden, 387 U.S. 294, 87 S.Ct. 1642, 18 L.Ed.2d 782 (1967); and when it

was the traditional "adequate state ground" standard, see Irvin v. Dowd, 359 U.S. 394, 79 S.Ct. 825, 3 L.Ed.2d 900 (1959).

[26]Ulster County Court v. Allen, 442 U.S. 140, 99 S.Ct. 2213, 60 L.Ed.2d 777 (1979).

[27]Harris v. Reed, 489 U.S. 255, 109 S.Ct. 1038, 103 L.Ed.2d 308 (1989); Michigan v. Long, 463 U.S. 1032, 103 S.Ct. 3469, 77 L.Ed.2d 1201 (1983); Caldwell v. Mississippi, 472 U.S. 320, 105 S.Ct. 2633, 86 L.Ed.2d 231 (1985). See also Coleman v. Thompson, 501 U.S. 722, 111 S.Ct. 2546, 115 L.Ed.2d 640 (1991) (holding that presumption did not apply where the prosecution on appeal had advanced a procedural forfeiture argument and the state court then issued a summary order dismissing the appeal, noting that it did so "upon consideration" of the prosecution's motion and the briefs filed by the parties— even though those briefs dealt with the merits as well as the procedural forfeiture); Ylst v. Nunnemaker, 501 U.S. 797, 111 S.Ct. 2590, 115 L.Ed.2d 706 (1991) (*Harris* predicate was not present where the "last reasoned opinion" imposed a procedural default and

unexplained orders upholding that judgment * * * [will be assumed to] rest upon the same ground."[28]

Where the state fails to raise procedural default as a defense to a petition in federal court, the defense is also waived, and the federal court may, but is not bound to raise the issue sua sponte.[29] No provision in AEDPA appears to have modified this rule,[30] and federal courts continue to exercise their discretion to raise the issue when the state has not.[31]

The state procedural default of a petitioner under a capital sentence challenging a judgment from a qualifying state appears not be subject to waiver by the state under Chapter 154 of

---

was then followed by formulary order that, unlike the order in *Coleman*, referred to a "denial" rather than a "dismissal" of defendant's petition for state collateral relief); Hunter v. Aispuro, 982 F.2d 344 (9th Cir.1992) (unexplained denial from California Supreme Court did not bar habeas review).

Compare Johnson v. Pinchack, 392 F.3d 551 (3d Cir.2004) (only if the decision of the last state court to which the petitioner presented his federal claims "fairly appears to rest primarily on federal law, or to be interwoven with the federal law * * * do we look at whether the state court clearly and expressly based its ruling on a state procedural ground; in this case there was a clear independent state basis, triggering default, despite the state court's reference to federal law as an alternative holding); Clinkscale v. Carter, 375 F.3d 430 (6th Cir.2004) (finding no such clear and express statement, reaching ineffective assistance claim, and granting relief); Loveland v. Hatcher, 231 F.3d 640 (9th Cir. 2000) (state bar explicit).

[28]Ylst v. Nunnemaker, 501 U.S. 797, 111 S.Ct. 2590, 115 L.Ed.2d 706 (1991).

[29]Trest v. Cain, 522 U.S. 87, 118 S.Ct. 478, 139 L.Ed.2d 444 (1997).

[30]The waiver of the requirement of exhaustion of claims in state court, by contrast, has been specifically addressed by Congress. See § 28.5(a).

[31]Oakes v. United States, 400 F.3d 92 (1st Cir.2005) (collecting and reviewing authority endorsing sua sponte invocation of procedural default defense by habeas court in actions under § 2254, and stating "preventing the facile use of a habeas petition as a substitute for a direct appeal can be best accomplished if district courts have the discretion to enforce the procedural default rule even though the government (federal or state) turns a blind eye"); Prieto v. Quarterman, 456 F.3d 511 (5th Cir. 2006) (raising procedural default sua sponte when neither party had notice the court would consider procedural bar as an issue); Howard v. Bouchard, 405 F.3d 459 (6th Cir.2005) (although appellate courts should not "embrace *sua sponte* raising of procedural default issues as a matter of course, it was appropriate here because the petitioner had notice procedural default would be an issue); McNair v. Campbell, 416 F.3d 1291 (11th Cir.2005) ("Because § 2254(b)(3) provides that the state can waive [a petitioner's] failure to properly exhaust his claim only by expressly doing so, it logically follows that the resulting procedural bar, which arises from and is dependent upon the failure to properly exhaust, can only be waived expressly"). Compare Hills v. Washington, 441 F.3d 1374 (11th Cir.2006) (state waived procedural bar defense when brief represented there was no procedural bar and sought resolution of the claim on the merits).

AEDPA.[32] Section 2264 provides that the court "shall only consider a claim or claims that have been raised and decided on the merits in the State courts," unless the exceptions apply. This mandatory language suggests that a federal court would be powerless to reach such a claim even when the state fails entirely to assert, or even affirmatively waives, the defense of procedural default in federal court. Moreover, if "raised" is construed as meaning "raised by the defendant" and not "raised by the state court," even a state court's decision to reach the merits of a defaulted claim would not excuse default.

§ 28.4(d) Excusing default: the "cause and prejudice" standard

For more than a decade before it settled on the current "cause-and-prejudice" test for determining which claims defaulted in state court could nevertheless receive review in federal courts, the Court applied an approach more favorable to petitioners known as the "deliberate bypass" standard. Established in *Fay v. Noia*,[33] the "deliberate bypass" standard permitted federal review of all claims defaulted in state court unless the failure to comply with state law was a "deliberate bypassing" of "the orderly procedure of the state courts." If an applicant "understandingly and knowingly forewent the privilege of seeking to vindicate his federal claims in the State courts, whether for strategic, tactical, or any other reasons that can fairly be described as the deliberate bypassing of state procedures, then it is open to the federal court on habeas to deny him all relief if the state courts refused to entertain his federal claims on the merits."[34]

Fay v. Noia was widely recognized as one of the more expansive decisions of the Warren Court,[35] but its protections were soon

---

[32]See § 28.8.

[Section 28.4(d)]

[33]Fay v. Noia, 372 U.S. 391, 83 S.Ct. 822, 9 L.Ed.2d 837 (1963).

[34]The Court explained that the "classic definition of waiver enunciated in Johnson v. Zerbst, 304 U.S. 458, 58 S.Ct. 1019, 82 L.Ed. 1461 (1938)—an intentional relinquishment or abandonment of a known right or privilege—furnishes the controlling standard" for determining what would constitute a deliberate bypass.

[35]See Gibbons, Waiver: Habeas Corpus Jurisdiction, 2 Seton Hall L.Rev. 291 (1971) (suggesting also that *Noia*'s expansion of habeas corpus jurisdiction may have contributed to the development of the doctrine of "harmless constitutional error"). *Noia*'s adoption of a deliberate bypass standard is credited also with having delayed the development of more stringent constitutional standards relating to the adequacy of counsel, since it permitted habeas courts to focus on the merits of petitioners' claims rather than the inadequacy of counsel in failing to present those claims in the state proceedings. See Teague, Federal Habeas Corpus and Ineffective Representation of Counsel: The Supreme Court Has Work To Do, 31 Stan.L.Rev. 1 (1978); Strazzella, Ineffective Assistance of

eroded. In *Henry v. Mississippi*[36] the Court indicated that the defendant's personal participation in the decision that led to the default was not required, at least as to those constitutional objections that could be controlled by counsel alone. *Murch v. Mottram*[37] added that a deliberate bypass by counsel did not require knowledge that the tactical maneuver would result in a procedural default under state law, provided counsel had "reasonable warning" that he ran that risk.[38] Then, in *Davis v. United States*,[39] the Court rejected the deliberate bypass standard for collateral review of constitutional claims by federal prisoners. The Court noted that if Davis' case had come before it on direct review, it would have been decided under Federal Rule 12(b). That Rule provided that the failure to raise before trial a defect such as the grand jury discrimination Davis alleged would "constitute a waiver, but the court for cause shown may grant relief from the waiver." The Court found it "inconceivable" that Congress, having foreclosed such a claim from review in the initial proceeding, meant to nonetheless allow it to be presented on collateral attack. Accordingly, the Rule 12(b) standard was held to govern the collateral review of claims by federal prisoners under § 2255 as well as review on appeal. A federal prisoner's defaulted claim would be considered only if he could show "cause" for and "prejudice" from his failure to object. *Francis v. Henderson*[40] extended the cause-and-prejudice test of Davis to a state prisoner seeking federal habeas review of grand jury discrimination. "Surely," the Court concluded, "considerations of comity and federalism require that * * * [habeas courts] give no less effect to the same clear interests when asked to overturn state convictions."

Conceivably, the Court could have preserved "deliberate bypass" as the standard for rejecting review of most defaulted claims, and limited the "cause-and-prejudice" test to grand jury discrimination claims, which, by their nature, arguably provide counsel some incentive to "sandbag."[41] In *Wainwright v. Sykes*,[42] however, the Court chose instead to expand the test to trial er-

Counsel Claims: New Uses, New Problems, 19 Ariz.L.Rev. 443 (1977).

[36]Henry v. Mississippi, 379 U.S. 443, 85 S.Ct. 564, 13 L.Ed.2d 408 (1965). See also § 11.6(a).

[37]Murch v. Mottram, 409 U.S. 41, 93 S.Ct. 71, 34 L.Ed.2d 194 (1972).

[38]Many lower courts were willing to find a deliberate bypass if any strategic reason could be hypothesized for failing to object. See Note, 31 La.L.Rev. 601, 607–08 (1971) (collecting cases). See also the cases cited by Justice Stevens in Wainwright v. Sykes, 433 U.S. 72, 97 S.Ct. 2497, 53 L.Ed.2d 594 (1977). These rulings may have suggested to the Supreme Court a need to reexamine the *Noia* standard.

[39]Davis v. United States, 411 U.S. 233, 93 S.Ct. 1577, 36 L.Ed.2d 216 (1973).

[40]Francis v. Henderson, 425 U.S. 536, 96 S.Ct. 1708, 48 L.Ed.2d 149 (1976).

[41]See § 28.4(a) at notes 5–10.

rors as well. The petitioner *Sykes* had sought habeas relief on the ground that his conviction had been based on a confession obtained without his full understanding of the *Miranda* warnings. The state's rules required at least a contemporaneous objection to the admission of illegally obtained evidence, and he had made no objection before or during the trial. Justice Rehnquist's opinion for the Court explained that the issue before the Court was "whether the rule of *Francis v. Henderson*, barring federal habeas review absent a showing of 'cause' and 'prejudice' attendant to a state procedural waiver [should] be applied to a waived objection to the admission of a confession at trial." The Court answered that question in the affirmative.

The *Sykes* opinion offered three reasons for preferring the *Francis* test over *Noia*'s deliberate bypass standard. First, the "contemporaneous-objection" rule applied in the state court deserved "greater respect" than the deliberate bypass standard would give it, because "it is employed by a coordinate jurisdiction within the federal system." The rule served many valid interests, including ensuring the development of a factual record when "the recollections of witnesses are freshest" (rather than "years later in a federal habeas proceeding"), allowing the judge "who observed the demeanor of the witnesses [at trial] to make the factual determinations," offering the opportunity for exclusion at a point where doing so will make "a major contribution to finality in a criminal litigation," and forcing the prosecution at a propitious time "to take a hard look at its hole card" (which might lead it to decide not to rely upon the challenged evidence).

Second, the Court expressed the view that the "rule of *Fay v. Noia*, broadly stated, may encourage 'sandbagging' on the part of defense lawyers, who may take their chances on a verdict of not guilty in a state trial court with the intent to raise their constitutional claims in a federal habeas court if their initial gamble does not pay off." Justice Brennan, in dissent, argued that the deliberate bypass standard barred exactly that tactical maneuver, but the majority apparently concluded that the potential looseness of that standard in application (and perhaps *Noia*'s recognition of district court discretion to ignore a bypass) offered a continuing incentive to sandbag.

Finally, the *Sykes* majority criticized the deliberate bypass rule for detracting from the appropriate role of the trial. The "failure of the federal habeas courts generally to require compliance with a contemporaneous-objection rule [would] tend to detract from the perception of the trial in a criminal case * * * as a decisive and portentous event." The "adoption of the *Francis* rule," on the

---

[42]Wainwright v. Sykes, 433 U.S. (1977).
72, 97 S.Ct. 2497, 53 L.Ed.2d 594

other hand, would have "the salutary effect of making the trial on the merits the 'main event,' so to speak, rather than a 'tryout on the road' for what will later be the determinative federal habeas hearing." Responding to the dissenters, the majority also stressed that the cause-and-prejudice test would still serve the basic function of habeas review, and "not prevent a federal habeas court from adjudicating for the first time the federal constitutional claim of a defendant who in the absence of such an adjudication will be the victim of a miscarriage of justice." This miscarriage of justice exception for petitioners who are unable to demonstrate cause and prejudice is discussed in subsection 28.4(e).

In *Engle v. Isaac*[43] and *United States v. Frady*,[44] the Court extended the cause-and-prejudice test to claims of faulty jury instructions, errors that unlike the *Miranda* violation alleged in *Sykes* clearly related to the reliability of the trial process. Writing for the majority in both cases, Justice O'Connor explained that the costs of the "liberal allowance" of habeas review—the degradation of the "prominence of the trial," the difficulties of retrials long after the event, and the impact upon the interests of the state—were escalated "when a trial default has barred a prisoner from obtaining adjudication of his constitutional claim in the state courts." These considerations "do not depend upon the type of claim raised by the prisoner."[45] Eventually, in *Coleman v. Thompson*,[46] the Court finally put *Noia* to rest, stating: "We now make it explicit: In all cases in which a state prisoner has defaulted his federal claims in state court pursuant to an independent and adequate state procedural rule, federal habeas

---

[43]Engle v. Isaac, 456 U.S. 107, 102 S.Ct. 1558, 71 L.Ed.2d 783 (1982).

[44]United States v. Frady, 456 U.S. 152, 102 S.Ct. 1584, 71 L.Ed.2d 816 (1982).

[45]The possibility of substituting a "plain error" standard for the *Francis* standard was considered in both *Isaac* and *Frady*, but the primary discussion was in the latter case. Relying on Federal Rule 52(b), which states that plain errors may be noticed by a court even if not brought to its attention by counsel, Frady argued that, as in *Davis*, the Federal Rule provision should be held applicable to collateral review. The Court responded that Rule 52(b) obviously was aimed at direct review. Application of the same standard was "out of place when a prisoner launches a collateral attack against a criminal conviction after society's legitimate

interest in the finality of the judgment has been perfected by the expiration of the time allowed for direct review or by the affirmance of the conviction on appeal." The petitioner here, for example, was seeking habeas "nineteen years after his crime." To adopt the same standard for collateral attack that was used on direct appeal would "accord no significance whatever to the existence of a final judgment perfected by appeal." It would be inconsistent with the "long and consistently affirmed [principle] that a collateral challenge may not do service for an appeal." See also § 27.5(d), discussing plain error review on appeal.

[46]Coleman v. Thompson, 501 U.S. 722, 111 S.Ct. 2546, 115 L.Ed.2d 640 (1991). Coleman's claim was lost when he filed his brief in state post conviction proceedings three days late.

review of the claim is barred unless the prisoner can demonstrate cause for the default and actual prejudice as a result of the alleged violation of federal law, or demonstrates that failure to consider the claims will result in a fundamental miscarriage of justice."

Establishing Cause. Petitioners typically attempt to establish "cause" for their failure to comply with state procedural rules in one of two ways: (1) by showing that the failure to raise an issue properly in state court was due to constitutionally ineffective assistance of counsel at trial or on direct appeal, or, (2) by showing that the failure was due to government interference. For a short time, the novelty of a constitutional claim was considered a third basis for excusing the failure to raise that claim in state court. A divided Court held in *Reed v. Ross*[47] that neither courts nor attorneys are likely to appreciate truly novel claims, and that "encouraging defense counsel to include any and all remotely plausible constitutional claims that could, some day, gain recognition" could be disruptive to orderly proceedings in state court. Subsequently, in *Teague v. Lane*,[48] the Court limited habeas review to claims based on the law as it stood when the defendant's conviction became final, except in rare circumstances.[49] These changes have gutted "novelty" as a viable option for state prisoners who seek to establish cause for their defaults. A petitioner cannot successfully argue that clearly established law supported his claim, while at the same time maintaining that his claim was "so novel that its legal basis [was] not reasonably available" to counsel in state proceedings.[50]

Ineffective assistance is the most commonly argued basis for establishing cause.[51] A defendant need not bear the cost of his counsel's error in failing to raise a claim properly in state court, provided that his attorney's failings amount to a violation of the

---

[47]Reed v. Ross, 468 U.S. 1, 104 S.Ct. 2901, 82 L.Ed.2d 1 (1984).

[48]Teague v. Lane, 489 U.S. 288, 109 S.Ct. 1060, 103 L.Ed.2d 334 (1989), discussed in § 28.6.

[49]This limitation was codified in the 1996 Act. See 28 U.S.C.A. § 2254(d), discussed in § 28.6(f).

[50]Novelty is still available as a means of establishing cause for federal prisoners who seek retroactive application of new rulings of substantive federal criminal law, since *Teague* does not bar retroactive application in these circumstances. See § 28.9(b).

[51]See, e.g., Ege v. Yukins, 485 F.3d 364 (6th Cir.2007) (cause for failure to raise in state court claim that admission of bitemark expert's unreliable evidence was "so extremely unfair that its admission violates fundamental concepts of justice," demonstrated by ineffective assistance of counsel). Cause and prejudice are rarely established, according to a recent study. N. King, F. Cheesman & B. Ostrom, Habeas Litigation in U.S. District Courts (2007), available at http://www.ncjrs.gov/pdffiles1/nij/grants/219559.pdf (finding that in less than 2% of cases court rejected default defense; default barred at least one claim in about 1 in 5 non-capital cases, and in about half of the capital cases.

right of effective assistance of counsel under the Sixth Amendment. As Justice O'Connor explained in *Coleman*:

> Attorney error that constitutes ineffective assistance of counsel is cause * * * not because * * * the error is so bad that "the lawyer ceases to be an agent of the petitioner." Rather, * * * "if the procedural default is the result of ineffective assistance of counsel, the Sixth Amendment itself requires that responsibility for the default be imputed to the State." In other words, it is not the gravity of the attorney's error that matters, but that it constitutes a violation of petitioner's right to counsel, so that the error must be seen as an external factor, i.e., "imputed to the State." * * * Where a petitioner defaults a claim as a result of the denial of the right to effective assistance of counsel, the State, which is responsible for the denial as a constitutional matter, must bear the cost of any resulting default and the harm to state interests that federal habeas review entails.

The "mere fact that counsel failed to recognize the factual or legal basis for a claim, or failed to raise the claim despite recognizing it, does not constitute cause for a procedural default."[52] "So long as defendant is represented by counsel whose performance is not constitutionally ineffective," the Court has concluded, "we discern no inequity in requiring him to bear the risk of attorney error that results in a procedural default."[53]

Even attorney incompetence equivalent to that required under *Strickland* will not be sufficient to establish cause if counsel's failures take place in a phase of the criminal process during which the defendant has no Sixth Amendment right to the effective assistance of counsel. In *Coleman*, defense counsel had failed to file a timely notice of appeal from a denial of a state habeas corpus petition. The Supreme Court concluded that because the defendant had no constitutional right to the assistance of counsel in such a collateral proceeding, the incompetency of his attorney could not give rise to a constitutional claim of ineffective assistance. Such incompetency, not amounting to a constitutional violation in itself, did not constitute cause. "[I]n those circumstances where the State has no responsibility to ensure that the petitioner was represented by competent counsel," Justice O'Connor explained, "it is the petitioner" not the state "who must bear the burden of a failure to follow state procedural rules."

Rather than pursue the underlying constitutional claim

---

[52]Murray v. Carrier, 477 U.S. 478, 106 S.Ct. 2639, 91 L.Ed.2d 397 (1986).

[53]*Carrier* noted, however, that the exhaustion requirement (see § 28.5(a)) "generally requires that a claim of ineffective assistance be presented to the state courts as an independent claim before it may be used to estab-lish cause for a procedural default." Also, the failure to raise the ineffectiveness claim in a previous state proceeding where represented by different counsel can itself constitute a procedural default. See infra text at notes 55–58.

forfeited by his attorney's failings, a petitioner may choose to seek relief on the basis of the Sixth Amendment violation itself. Competency of counsel for Sixth Amendment purposes generally looks to the overall performance of counsel. This will work to defendant's advantage where counsel's failures extend beyond the default on a single constitutional claim. Even where counsel's only error related to the default, "the right to effective assistance of counsel * * * may in a particular case be violated by even an isolated error of counsel if that error is sufficiently egregious and prejudicial." Moreover, if the defaulted claim involves a violation of rights under the Fourth Amendment, a petitioner will not receive habeas review at all unless he casts his claim as a denial of the Sixth Amendment right to the effective assistance of counsel.[54]

In *Edwards v. Carpenter*,[55] however, the Court emphasized that an ineffective-assistance-of-counsel claim asserted as cause for the procedural default of another claim may *itself* be barred by procedural default. After completing one round through state appellate and post-conviction procedure, *Carpenter* tried to re-open his state appeal and argue that his appellate counsel had been ineffective in failing to challenge the sufficiency of the evidence against him, but he was rebuffed by the state courts, who said that it was too late to challenge the effectiveness of his appellate counsel. In order to get beyond this state default in federal court, the Supreme Court explained, *Carpenter* would have to show cause for his failure to raise the ineffective assistance claim on time under state law.[56]

In most states, but not all, a claim of ineffective assistance of counsel need not be raised until a post-conviction proceeding, after a prisoner's direct appeal.[57] This means that in these states, a prisoner will not have defaulted his claim of ineffective assis-

---

[54]See Kimmelman v. Morrison, 477 U.S. 365, 106 S.Ct. 2574, 91 L.Ed.2d 305 (1986), discussed in § 28.3(c) at note 77.

[55]Edwards v. Carpenter, 529 U.S. 446, 120 S.Ct. 1587, 146 L.Ed.2d 518 (2000).

[56]See also Stewart v. LaGrand, 526 U.S. 115, 119 S.Ct. 1018, 143 L.Ed.2d 196 (1999) (finding petitioner's Eighth Amendment challenge to execution by lethal gas barred by procedural default, and finding petitioner's argument that his ineffective assistance of counsel claim suffices as cause was, itself, procedurally defaulted). Compare e.g., Reagan v. Norris, 279

F.3d 651 (8th Cir.2002) (cause for failure to bring claim of ineffective trial counsel was established by petitioner's demonstration that the assistance of his state appellate and post-trial counsel was constitutionally ineffective).

[57]E.g., State v. Herrman, 316 Mont. 198, 70 P.3d 738 (2003) (a petitioner should wait to raise claims of ineffective assistance of counsel until collateral review, collecting cases); Commonwealth v. Grant, 572 Pa. 48, 813 A.2d 726 (2002) (same).

Compare Keats v. State, 115 P.3d 1110 (Wyo.2005) (post-conviction claim of ineffective assistance of trial counsel must be raised on direct appeal first or it is waived, except, as in

tance if he raises it only after his appeal is complete. The Court approved of this approach for federal appeals in *Massaro v. United States*,[58] and held that a federal prisoner may reserve a claim of ineffective assistance of counsel until his application for relief under § 2255. Were defendants required to raise ineffectiveness claims on appeal, the Court explained, "trial counsel [would] be unwilling to help appellate counsel familiarize himself with a record for the purpose of understanding how it reflects trial counsel's own incompetence," and "[a]ppellate courts would waste time and resources attempting to address some claims that were meritless and other claims that, though colorable, would be handled more efficiently if addressed in the first instance" by the trial court. The trial court, the Court reasoned, is "the forum best suited to developing the facts necessary to determining the adequacy of representation during an entire trial. The court may take testimony from witnesses * * * and from the counsel alleged to have rendered the deficient performance." When presented in post-appeal collateral proceedings in the trial court, rather than on appeal, a claim of ineffective assistance "often will be ruled upon by the same * * * judge who presided at trial, [who] should have an advantageous perspective for determining the effectiveness of counsel's conduct and whether any deficiencies were prejudicial."

Other than a properly preserved claim of ineffective assistance of counsel, yet another circumstance that constitutes "cause" is a showing of " 'some interference by officials' that made compliance impracticable," explained the Court in *Murray v. Carrier*.[59] One such example, the Court suggested, was a case in which a warden had suppressed the prisoner's timely appeal papers. Another example arose in *Amadeo v. Zant*,[60] where the Court held that the state's concealment of a prosecutor's request to jury commis-

---

this case, when petitioner had same counsel at trial and appeal; claim of ineffective assistance of appellate counsel is reviewable only if a petitioner clearly shows on state post-conviction review that an unequivocal rule of law was transgressed at trial in a clear and obvious manner, and the alleged error had an adverse effect upon a substantial right; also, the simple failure to raise an issue on appeal, even meritorious, does not demonstrate ineffective assistance); Powers v. Lord, 462 F.Supp.2d 371 (W.D.N.Y. 2006) (under New York law, ineffective counsel claims involving matters outside the record, like the claim in

this case of failure to investigate and secure DNA testing, generally must be pursued in post-conviction proceedings, which can develop the evidentiary record; ineffective assistance claims demonstrable on the record are defaulted if not raised on appeal). See also the discussion in § 11.7(e) at note 103.

[58] Massaro v. United States, 538 U.S. 500, 123 S.Ct. 1690, 155 L.Ed.2d 714 (2003).

[59] Murray v. Carrier, 477 U.S. 478, 106 S.Ct. 2639, 91 L.Ed.2d 397 (1986).

[60] Amadeo v. Zant, 486 U.S. 214, 108 S.Ct. 1771, 100 L.Ed.2d 249

sioners to underrepresent African Americans and women would suffice as "cause" for defense counsel's failure to object to the composition of the jury at trial. *Strickler v. Greene*[61] provided an illustration of what is probably the most frequently alleged form of governmental interference with a defendant's ability to raise a claim. In *Strickler*, the petitioner had failed to raise his *Brady* claim in state court. The Court found that he had established cause for this failure "because (a) the prosecution withheld exculpatory evidence; (b) petitioner reasonably relied on the prosecution's open file policy as fulfilling the prosecution's duty to disclose such evidence; and (c) the Commonwealth confirmed petitioner's reliance on the open file policy by asserting during state habeas proceedings that the petitioner had already received 'everything known to the government.' " Although the Court declined to decide whether any one or two of these factors would be sufficient to constitute cause, lower courts have subsequently held that a showing that the government's concealment of exculpatory evidence, rendering the factual basis for a *Brady* claim unavailable to the defense, will constitute cause excusing the failure to raise that *Brady* claim on time in state court.[62] As the Court explained in *Banks v. Dretke*,[63] another case in which the government had lied when it assured the defense it had produced all *Brady* material and then maintained that the defense had not been diligent in uncovering its claim in state court, "Our decisions lend no support to the notion that defendants must scavenge for hints of undisclosed *Brady* material when the prosecution represents that all such material has been disclosed."

The state's interference must actually have impeded the defendant's efforts to comply with procedural rules in order to amount to cause. In *McCleskey v Zant*,[64] for example, the Court held that the prosecution's failure to disclose a recorded statement of an informant did not relieve the petitioner of the forfeiture that occurred when counsel failed to raise a Sixth Amendment challenge to the use of the informant's statement at trial,

---

(1988).

[61]Strickler v. Greene, 527 U.S. 263, 119 S.Ct. 1936, 144 L.Ed.2d 286 (1999), also discussed in § 24.3(b) at note 33.

[62]See also Graves v. Cockrell, 351 F.3d 156 (5th Cir.2003) (finding it debatable whether *Brady* claim was barred when state concealed witnesses statement that defendant was not involved but that witness's wife was involved; what the state did give the defendant was so vague that it may not have put defense counsel on notice sufficient to cause counsel to make an inquiry that would likely lead to full disclosure of witnesses statement).

[63]Banks v. Dretke, 540 U.S. 668, 124 S.Ct. 1256, 157 L.Ed.2d 1166 (2004), also discussed in § 24.3(b) at note 34.

[64]McCleskey v Zant, 499 U.S. 467, 111 S.Ct. 1454, 113 L.Ed.2d 517 (1991).

when the statement was not "critical" to the substance of petitioner's Sixth Amendment challenge, and the petitioner had sufficient information to raise the claim in any event. The Court described the question before it as "whether petitioner possessed, or by reasonable means could have obtained, a sufficient basis to allege a claim * * * and pursue the matter." It noted further that a petitioner's inability to obtain relevant evidence "fails to establish cause if other known or discoverable evidence could have supported the claim," and that the failure to assert the claim "will not be excused merely because evidence discovered later might also have supported or strengthened the claim."

Lower courts have refused to extend the state interference theory to excuse a default on the basis that counsel lacked financial resources to fully develop the facts needed to support a claim, noting that counsel should at least bring such difficulty to the attention of the trial court.[65] Courts have also rejected the contention that cause exists simply because the defendant was acting *pro se*.[66] The state's delay in providing a defendant with a transcript of trial proceedings also will not constitute cause for failing to raise a claim unless the petitioner was prevented from making the claim by that delay. This will not be the case when the factual and legal basis for the claim was apparent at the time of trial, or was known to the defendant prior to receiving the transcript.[67]

Assuming that "cause" is established, what type of showing will establish "actual prejudice"? In *Kyles v. Whitley*[68] and *Strickler v. Greene*,[69] the Court clarified that in order to establish prejudice under *Sykes*, a petitioner must demonstrate that had the constitutional claim been raised in accordance with state rules, there is a "reasonable probability that the result of the trial would have been different." A "reasonable probability" is described as a probability sufficient to "undermine confidence in the verdict." This produces consistency in cases where the defendant seeks to convert the procedural default into a Sixth Amendment claim of ineffective assistance of counsel, because the reasonable probability standard is also used to establish the prejudice required

---

[65]Hughes v. Idaho State Board of Corrections, 800 F.2d 905 (9th Cir. 1986); Smith v. Newsome, 876 F.2d 1461 (11th Cir.1989). See also Marcus, Federal Habeas Corpus After State Default: A Definition of Cause and Prejudice, 53 Fordham L.Rev. 663 (1985).

[66]E.g., Bannister v. Delo, 100 F.3d 610 (8th Cir.1996).

[67]See Glover v. Cain, 128 F.3d 900 (5th Cir.1997) (collecting conflicting authority).

[68]Kyles v. Whitley, 514 U.S. 419, 115 S.Ct. 1555, 131 L.Ed.2d 490 (1995), discussed in § 24.3(b).

[69]Strickler v. Greene, 527 U.S. 263, 119 S.Ct. 1936, 144 L.Ed.2d 286 (1999), discussed in § 24.3(b).

for such Sixth Amendment claims.[70]

§ 28.4(e) Excusing default: the "miscarriage of justice" exception

Justice O'Connor's opinion in *Engle v. Isaac*[71] stressed that "cause" and "prejudice" were not rigid concepts, but were based upon general principles of "comity and finality." "In appropriate cases," Justice O'Connor noted, "those principles must yield to the imperative of fundamentally unjust incarceration." An exception to the "cause-and-prejudice" requirement was also noted in *Sykes* when the Court stated that the standard developed there would not bar habeas relief for a victim of a "miscarriage of justice." The initial discussions of the scope of this exception to the cause-and-prejudice requirement came in *Murray v. Carrier*[72]

---

[70]See Jeffries & Stuntz, Ineffective Assistance and Procedural Default, 57 U.Chi.L.Rev. 679, 684–85 (1990). Establishing prejudice under either *Sykes* or Strickland has proven particularly controversial when the alleged default involves a claim that if raised properly, would have required relief without regard to prejudice, such as a claim under *Batson*. Compare Allen v. Lee, 366 F.3d 319 (4th Cir.2004) (en banc) (noting in dicta that defendant failed to raise *Batson* objective at trial so that "if there ever was a case of 'sandbagging,' this is it," preventing the state of fresh recollections of its jury selection strategy that would have accompanied a contemporaneous objection) with Davis v. Secretary for the Department of Corrections, 341 F.3d 1310 (11th Cir.2003) (when appellate counsel fails to raise *Batson* claim, prejudice requires a showing of some likelihood of a more favorable result on appeal; when trial counsel fails to raise *Batson* claim at trial, prejudice requires a showing of some likelihood of more favorable result at trial; when trial counsel fails to renew objection in order to preserve it for appeal, effect on appeal, not trial, is relevant and because *Batson* violations are not subject to harmless error review, there is a reasonable probability that defendant would have received appellate relief had counsel preserved the challenge) with Morales

v. Greiner, 273 F.Supp.2d 236 (E.D.N.Y.2003) (finding no merit to *Batson* claim, but noting that failing to raise it would not satisfy the prejudice prong of *Strickland* because the defendant "cannot possibly demonstrate that the replacement of one or two admittedly impartial jurors with one or two other equally impartial jurors would have a reasonable probability of altering the verdict."). See also In re Commitment of Taylor, 272 Wis.2d 642, 679 N.W.2d 893 (Wis.App.2004) (in order to establish ineffective assistance claim for failing to raise *Batson* challenge, petition must show that the results of the jury selection process would have been different, noting that defendant should not be required to show the outcome of the trial would have been different, rejecting presumptive prejudice); Wilcher v. State, 863 So.2d 719 (2003) (even if it is assumed that the four jurors excluded were black, defendant has not proven that he was prejudiced in any fashion by his attorney's decision not to assert a *Batson* challenge); § 11.10(d) at note 171 (collecting cases applying *Strickland* in this context).

[Section 28.4(e)]

[71]Engle v. Isaac, 456 U.S. 107, 102 S.Ct. 1558, 71 L.Ed.2d 783 (1982).

[72]Murray v. Carrier, 477 U.S. 478, 106 S.Ct. 2639, 91 L.Ed.2d 397 (1986).

and *Smith v. Murray*.[73] The Court in *Carrier* explained: "[I]n an extraordinary case, where a constitutional violation has probably resulted in the conviction of one who is actually innocent, a federal habeas court may grant the writ even in the absence of a showing of cause for the procedural default." With this exception, the "cause and prejudice test" established a "sound and workable means of channeling the discretion of federal habeas courts" in treating procedural defaults at the state level. All non-defaulted claims must be addressed by a habeas court before addressing the possibility that relief is available for a defaulted claim through the actual innocence exception.[74]

The exception's focus is on "actual" as distinct from "legal innocence." For example, the petitioner in *Smith* claimed that the state court had violated his self-incrimination privilege when it allowed into evidence at his capital sentencing hearing a psychiatrist's testimony recounting a damaging statement defendant had made during a psychiatric examination without being warned as to its possible use against him. For the purpose of determining whether there was an unjust incarceration, the key was whether admission of the defendant's statement to the psychiatrist had "pervert[ed] the jury's deliberations concerning the ultimate question whether *in fact* petitioner constituted a continuing threat to society." Since there was no suggestion that his statement was "false or in any way misleading," it had not adversely influenced the factual correctness of the jurors' verdict even though that verdict might have been otherwise if the statement had been excluded as constitutionally inadmissible.

Schlup v. Delo[75] clarified that in order to establish "actual innocence" sufficient to overcome the absence of cause or prejudice where the procedurally defaulted constitutional claim related to the determination of the petitioner's guilt, the habeas petitioner has to show that "it is more likely than not that no reasonable juror would have convicted him."[76] This standard, the Court concluded, struck an appropriate balance—"ensur[ing] that

---

[73]Smith v. Murray, 477 U.S. 527, 106 S.Ct. 2661, 91 L.Ed.2d 434 (1986).

[74]Dretke v. Haley, 541 U.S. 386, 124 S.Ct. 1847, 158 L.Ed.2d 659 (2004).

[75]Schlup v. Delo, 513 U.S. 298, 115 S.Ct. 851, 130 L.Ed.2d 808 (1995).

[76]The standard here is less demanding than the "extraordinarily high" standard suggested in Herrera v. Collins, 506 U.S. 390, 113 S.Ct. 853, 122 L.Ed.2d 203 (1993), discussed in § 28.3(e) at notes 98–104, applicable

where a habeas petitioner claims that newly discovered evidence establishes his actual innocence but does not claim any constitutional error occurred during his prosecution. See Griffin v. Johnson, 350 F.3d 956 (9th Cir.2003) (evidence used to establish actual innocence, to avoid procedural default of claim of ineffective assistance for failing to raise insanity defense, must not have been presented to the trial court, but need not be "newly discovered," that is, unknown to the defense at the time of plea or trial; here defendant's

petitioner's case is truly 'extraordinary,' while still providing a meaningful avenue by which to avoid a manifest injustice." In *House v. Bell*,[77] a majority of justices agreed that a death row petitioner's showing entitled him to pass through the *Schlup* "innocence gateway" and receive federal review of his defaulted claims of ineffective assistance of counsel and prosecutorial misconduct. The Court emphasized that in evaluating whether a petitioner has demonstrated that "more likely than not any reasonable juror would have reasonable doubt," a habeas court must consider all the evidence, "old and new, incriminating and exculpatory, without regard to whether it would necessarily be admitted [at trial]." The petitioner's "new reliable evidence" of innocence, included (1) forensic evidence indicating that blood from the victim found on petitioner's jeans was spilled on them from vials of blood taken from the victim at her autopsy; (2) DNA evidence demonstrating that the semen found on the victim's clothing was from her husband, not the petitioner; and (3) testimony by several witnesses describing a confession to the killing by the victim's husband, the indifferent reception one of these witnesses encountered when reporting the confession to authorities, a history of abuse of the victim by her husband, and an attempt by the husband to construct a false alibi. The Court found that "the central forensic proof connecting House to the crime * * * has been called into question, and House has put forward substantial evidence pointing to a different suspect. * * * [T]his is the rare case where—had the jury heard all the conflicting testimony—it is more likely than not that no reasonable juror viewing the record as a whole would lack reasonable doubt."

Interpreting the "miscarriage of justice" exception to provide an opportunity for reviewing only those claims of error that implicate actual innocence may prevent habeas review of defaulted claims of errors that would not affect the accuracy of a jury's verdict of guilt. Such claims include grand jury error preceding an otherwise valid conviction, a violation of the prohibition against double jeopardy, and a denial of a speedy or public trial.[78] Also excluded are claims based on the introduction of reliable evidence obtained in violation of a defendant's right to counsel or privilege against self-incrimination, claims that a petitioner's jury venire was selected in violation of the Sixth or Fourteenth Amendments, as well as claims of selective

---

evidence did not demonstrate that it is more likely than not that no reasonable juror would have voted to convict).

[77]House v. Bell, __ U.S. __, 126 S.Ct. 2064, 165 L.Ed.2d 1 (2006), also discussed in § 28.3(e) at note 21.

[78]See, e.g., Selsor v. Kaiser, 22 F.3d 1029 (10th Cir.1994) (no "miscarriage of justice" since double jeopardy claim would only show "legal innocence," not "factual innocence").

prosecution.[79] In other words, once defaulted in state court, claims unrelated to factual innocence do not receive the same hearing in federal court as claims that if valid would have raised the risk that a factually innocent person was convicted. The Court's willingness to restrict collateral review of such claims suggests that it has concluded that sufficient incentive to comply with these particular constitutional requirements is provided by litigation on behalf of those defendants who, while still in state court, manage to learn of and effectively raise such claims. As *Schlup* explained, "Explicitly tying the miscarriage of justice exception to innocence thus accommodates both the systemic interests in finality, comity, and conservation of judicial resources, and the overriding individual interest in doing justice in the 'extraordinary case.' "[80]

For a petitioner who is seeking relief from a conviction following a plea of guilty, actual innocence means "factual innocence," based on "any admissible evidence of petitioner's guilt even if that evidence was not presented during petitioner's plea colloquy," declared the Court in *Bousley v. United States*.[81] Furthermore, the Court added, in cases when there is "record evidence" that "the government has foregone more serious charges in the course of plea bargaining, petitioner's showing of actual innocence must also extend to those charges."[82] As Justice Scalia observed in his dissent in *Bousley*, the majority's approach raises a number of difficulties for application. First, by limiting the innocence inquiry to the consideration of "admissible" evidence, the Court departed from earlier decisions authorizing the consideration of illegally admitted, albeit reliable, evidence when assessing actual innocence.[83] Evidentiary hearings may be required to resolve the issue.[84] Second, the factual record to support a plea-based conviction is bound to be considerably less developed than a trial

---

[79]See, e.g., Clark v. Lewis, 1 F.3d 814 (9th Cir.1993) ("because the jury pool composition does not bear on Clark's actual innocence of the underlying crimes or the death penalty, we decline to reach the merits of this claim").

[80]*Schlup*, 513 U.S. at 321–22, 115 S.Ct. at 864–65.

[81]Bousley v. United States, 523 U.S. 614, 118 S.Ct. 1604, 140 L.Ed.2d 828 (1998).

[82]See, e.g., Simpson v. Matesanz, 175 F.3d 200 (1st Cir.1999).

[83]See, e.g., Calderon v. Thompson, 523 U.S. 538, 118 S.Ct. 1489, 140 L.Ed.2d 728 (1998). See also Hall v. Luebbers, 296 F.3d 685 (8th Cir.2002) (requiring admissible evidence).

[84]Consider United States v. Montano, 398 F.3d 1276 (11th Cir.2005) (remanding to district court with these instructions: "appellant bears the burden of establishing that, in light of all the evidence available to support the foregone charges, it is more likely than not that no reasonable juror would have convicted him; the Government must be permitted to introduce any admissible evidence of Appellant's guilt, whether or not that evidence was presented in the plea colloquy, or even would have been offered

transcript, consisting in many cases of only the prosecutor's proffer of factual basis for the charge. Third, the factual basis for bargained-away charges may not appear in the record at all.

As some lower courts have noted, the logic of *Bousley*, which prevents a petitioner from raising a defaulted challenge to a sentence he bargained for while escaping punishment for dismissed counts that he actually committed, should also require a defendant to establish factual innocence of dropped charges that were as serious as the challenged offense, not simply those that were "more serious."[85]

Sawyer v. Whitley[86] confirmed that the actual innocence exception to procedural default applies not only to a petitioner claiming to be innocent of the crime of conviction, but also to a petitioner sentenced to death claiming that an error in capital sentencing resulted in a death sentence when he was "actually innocent of the death penalty." In order to succeed, the Court stated, a petitioner making such a claim must "show by clear and convincing evidence that but for a constitutional error no reasonable juror would find the petitioner eligible for the death penalty."[87] The Court has so far declined to resolve a split in the courts over the application of the actual innocence exception to

---

before our decision today"); Peveler v. United States, 269 F.3d 693 (6th Cir.2001) (upholding magistrate's finding, adopted by district court, that defendant did not meet burden of proving by a preponderance his innocence of other charges, based on hearing held by magistrate at which government witness testified; and rejecting argument that magistrate erred in discrediting defendant's testimony at hearing and crediting the testimony of the government witness).

[85]Compare Lewis v. Peterson, 329 F.3d 934 (7th Cir.2003) (the logic of the *Bousley* opinion does not require that the charge that was dropped or forgone in the plea negotiations be more serious than the charge to which the petitioner pleaded guilty, it need only be as serious, for the petitioner would have gained little or nothing had the government and he realized that the charge to which he pleaded guilty was unsound. Had they realized this, they would have switched the plea to the sound charge, and as long as it was an equally serious charge, as it was here, the punishment would

probably have been the same, subject to our earlier acknowledgment that the government might drive a harder plea bargain if it had two good counts to brandish rather than just one) with United States v. Johnson, 260 F.3d 919 (8th Cir.2001) (government's showing of guilt on dismissed charge under same provision irrelevant under *Bousley*).

[86]Sawyer v. Whitley, 505 U.S. 333, 112 S.Ct. 2514, 120 L.Ed.2d 269 (1992).

[87]See also Dugger v. Adams, 489 U.S. 401, 109 S.Ct. 1211, 103 L.Ed.2d 435 (1989), rejecting the contention that "a fundamental miscarriage of justice results whenever * * * 'the very essence' of [the constitutional claim] * * * is that the accuracy of the sentencing determination is undermined." The *Dugger* majority noted: "Demonstrating that an error is by its nature the kind of error that might have affected the accuracy of a death sentence is far from demonstrating that a defendant probably is 'actually innocent' of the sentence he or she received." So too, the mere fact that

noncapital sentencing.[88]

§ 28.5 Claims in habeas foreclosed due to premature, successive, or delayed applications

§ 28.5(a)   Exhaustion of state remedies
§ 28.5(b)   Time limits for filing petitions
§ 28.5(c)   Successive petitions: claims previously advanced
§ 28.5(d)   Successive petitions: new claims
§ 28.5(e)   Successive petitions: court of appeals certification

---

§ 28.5(a) Exhaustion of state remedies

Overview and Origins. The "exhaustion doctrine," presently codified in § 2254, requires the petitioner to "exhaust" the available state remedies for his claim before seeking federal habeas relief.[1] This requirement, the Supreme Court has noted is "principally designed to protect the state courts' role in the enforcement of federal law and prevent the disruption of state judicial proceedings."[2]

Both the "equitable nature" of the doctrine and the consider-

---

the trial judge found an equal number of aggravating and mitigating circumstances established at petitioner's capital sentencing proceeding "was not sufficient to show that an alleged error in instructing the jury [conveying the false impression that sentencing responsibility rested elsewhere] * * * resulted in a fundamental miscarriage of justice."

[88]Dretke v. Haley, 541 U.S. 386, 124 S.Ct. 1847, 158 L.Ed.2d 659 (2004). Courts that have extended the exception to the non-capital sentencing context have reasoned that the "ultimate issue, the justice of the incarceration, is the same, there is no reason why the actual innocence exception should not apply to noncapital sentencing procedures." Spence v. Superintendent, Great Meadow Correctional Facility, 219 F.3d 162 (2d Cir.2000) (finding defendant was actually innocent of fact triggering his sentence). See also United States v. Mikalajunas, 186 F.3d 490 (4th Cir.1999) (actual innocence applies in non capital sentencing only in the context of eligibility for application of a career offender or other habitual offender guideline provision). Those

rejecting its application have countered that it would swallow the rule that more than prejudice is required to excuse procedural default. Embrey v. Hershberger, 131 F.3d 739 (8th Cir.1997) (en banc); Reid v Oklahoma, 101 F.3d 628 (10th Cir.1996).

[Section 28.5(a)]

[1]See Fay v. Noia, 372 U.S. 391, 83 S.Ct. 822, 9 L.Ed.2d 837 (1963). For detailed discussions of the exhaustion requirement, see R. Hertz & J. Liebman, 2 Federal Habeas Corpus Practice and Procedure ch. 23 (5th ed. 2005); L. Yackle, Postconviction Remedies § 52 (1981 & Supp.2007). Prior to AEDPA, an estimated 30–65% of claims and petitions were dismissed for failure to meet this requirement, after AEDPA, that percentage has dropped to under 15%. See N. King, F. Cheesman & B. Ostrom, Habeas Litigation in U.S. District Courts (2007), available at http://www.ncjrs.gov/pdffil es1/nij/grants/219559.pdf.

[2]Duncan v. Walker, 533 U.S. 167, 121 S.Ct. 2120, 150 L.Ed.2d 251 (2001) (citing O'Sullivan v. Boerckel, 526 U.S. 838, 119 S.Ct. 1728, 144 L.Ed.2d 1 (1999)).

213

ations underlying its exercise were set in place by the Court's seminal opinion in *Ex parte Royall*.[3] Decided in 1886, Royall was one of the first cases under the 1867 Habeas Act to reach the Supreme Court. The petitioner there, while awaiting trial in his state case, sought federal habeas relief on the ground that the pending state prosecution was based on an unconstitutional statute. Sustaining the lower court's denial of the writ, the Supreme Court noted:

> The [statute's] injunction to hear the case summarily, and thereupon "to dispose of the party as law and justice require" does not deprive the court of discretion as to the time and mode in which it will exert the powers conferred upon it. That discretion should be exercised in the light of the relations existing, under our system of government, between the judicial tribunals of the Union and of the States, and in recognition of the fact that the public good requires that those relations be not disturbed by unnecessary conflict between courts equally bound to guard and protect rights secured by the Constitution.

By 1944, the Court was able to announce as settled law that "ordinarily an application for habeas corpus by one detained under a state court judgment of conviction will be entertained * * * only after all state remedies available, including all appellate remedies in the state courts and in this Court by appeal or writ of certiorari have been exhausted."[4] This statement might have extended the doctrine somewhat in requiring the prisoner to seek review from the Supreme Court itself (a position later rejected[5]), but it otherwise clearly had support in a long line of cases.[6]

Congress soon incorporated the exhaustion requirement in the habeas statutes and the provision is carried forward today in § 2254(b)(1), which bars the writ unless "the applicant has exhausted the remedies available in the courts of the State, or * * * there is either an absence of available State corrective process or * * * circumstances exist that render such process ineffective to protect the rights of the applicant." Section 2254(c) also provides that an applicant may not be deemed to have exhausted his remedies "if he has a right under the law of the State to raise, by any available procedure, the question presented."

---

[3] Ex parte Royall, 117 U.S. 241, 6 S.Ct. 734, 29 L.Ed. 868 (1886).

[4] Ex parte Hawk, 321 U.S. 114, 64 S.Ct. 448, 88 L.Ed. 572 (1944).

[5] Darr v. Burford, 339 U.S. 200, 70 S.Ct. 587, 94 L.Ed. 761 (1950), held that the exhaustion requirement did extend to a petition for Supreme Court review, but that holding was overruled in Fay v. Noia, 372 U.S. 391, 83 S.Ct. 822, 9 L.Ed.2d 837 (1963). On the present law regarding how far in the state system a petitioner must first pursue his claim, see infra text at notes 36–39.

[6] See, e.g., the various cases cited in Ex parte Hawk, 321 U.S. 114, 64 S.Ct. 448, 88 L.Ed. 572 (1944).

The Supreme Court has assumed substantial leeway in determining the precise content of the exhaustion requirement.[7] The Court's approach has depended to a substantial extent on its view of the policies underlying the exhaustion requirement. These policies are close cousins to those that the Court has stressed in giving deference to state procedural defaults.[8] Justice O'Connor explained the objectives of the exhaustion rule in *Rose v. Lundy*:[9]

> The exhaustion doctrine is principally designed to protect the state courts' role in the enforcement of federal law and prevent disruption of state judicial proceedings. * * * Because "it would be unseemly in our dual system of government for a federal district court to upset a state court conviction without an opportunity to the state courts to correct a constitutional violation," federal courts apply the doctrine of comity, which "teaches that one court should defer action on causes properly within its jurisdiction until the courts of another sovereignty with concurrent powers, and already cognizant of the litigation, have had an opportunity to pass upon the matter." * * * A rigorously enforced total exhaustion rule will encourage state prisoners to seek full relief first from the state courts, thus giving those courts the first opportunity to review all claims of constitutional error. As the number of prisoners who exhaust all of their federal claims increases, state courts may become increasingly familiar with and hospitable toward federal constitutional issues. * * * Equally as important, federal claims that have been fully exhausted in state courts will more often be accompanied by a complete factual record to aid the federal courts in their review.

Some situations may require a petitioner to present the same claim more than once to the state's highest court. An intervening Supreme Court decision which casts petitioner's claim in a new light may require him to reapply for state relief if still available.[10] On the other hand, when the highest state court changes its own view of preexisting Supreme Court precedent, the petitioner need not return to the state courts, since the state's opportunity to reach the correct result when it first heard petitioner's case had

---

[7] See, e.g., Irvin v. Dowd, 359 U.S. 394, 79 S.Ct. 825, 3 L.Ed.2d 900 (1959); Fay v. Noia, 372 U.S. 391, 83 S.Ct. 822, 9 L.Ed.2d 837 (1963).

[8] See, e.g., Coleman v. Thompson, 501 U.S. 722, 111 S.Ct. 2546, 115 L.Ed.2d 640 (1991), and the majority opinion in Engle v. Isaac, 456 U.S. 107, 102 S.Ct. 1558, 71 L.Ed.2d 783 (1982), which was written by Justice O'Connor.

[9] Rose v. Lundy, 455 U.S. 509, 102 S.Ct. 1198, 71 L.Ed.2d 379 (1982), discussed infra at note 21.

[10] Picard v. Connor, 404 U.S. 270, 92 S.Ct. 509, 30 L.Ed.2d 438 (1971), discussed infra at note 27. In discussing whether the state had been given a fair opportunity to consider petitioner's claim, the Court put aside what it apparently viewed as easier cases of nonexhaustion. Cited among such examples was "a case in which an intervening change in federal law cast the legal issue in a fundamentally different light." The Court then added citations to two lower court cases that required the petitioner to return to the state courts in such a case.

not been altered.[11] Nor must a petitioner return to the state courts after later state decisions have invalidated the statute under which he was prosecuted.[12]

Exceptions to Exhaustion. The 1996 amendments added § 2254(b)(2), which provides: "An application for a writ of habeas corpus may be denied on the merits, notwithstanding the failure of the applicant to exhaust the remedies available in the courts of the State." This provision gives to habeas courts no greater authority to grant relief for unexhausted claims, but expressly authorizes them to deny relief by skipping the exhaustion analysis and rejecting a petitioner's claim on the merits.[13]

Section 2254(b) also notes that state exhaustion is not required where there is either "an absence of available state corrective process" or "circumstances * * * render such process ineffective to protect the rights of the applicant." A state remedy will be considered unavailable or ineffective under this provision two circumstances. First, if state law creates a procedural bar to the review of a petitioner's claim should he return to state court, the claim will be considered exhausted.[14] As one court put it, "Having avoided the Scylla of exhaustion, [the petitioner] must also steer by the Charybdis of procedural default before his petition can be heard on the merits."[15] For example, when a petitioner presented his claim to state courts for the first and only time in a procedural context in which its merits would not be considered unless "there are special and important reasons therefore," he has exhausted his claim in state courts, but he also has defaulted on his opportunity to obtain a state ruling on the merits and must show cause for and prejudice from such default.[16]

Second, futile or uncertain remedies constitute "ineffective" avenues under the statute and need not be exhausted.[17] As Justice Rutledge once noted, the exhaustion requirement does

---

[11]Roberts v. LaVallee, 389 U.S. 40, 88 S.Ct. 194, 19 L.Ed.2d 41 (1967).

[12]Francisco v. Gathright, 419 U.S. 59, 95 S.Ct. 257, 42 L.Ed.2d 226 (1974).

[13]Cassett v. Stewart, 406 F.3d 614 (9th Cir.2005) (district court's ability to deny relief under § 2254(b)(2) is limited to circumstances in which it is perfectly clear that the petitioner has no hope of prevailing, noting a "contrary rule would deprive state courts of the opportunity to address a colorable federal claim in the first instance and grant relief if they believe it is warranted").

[14]Woodford v. Ngo, ___ U.S. ___, 126 S.Ct. 2378, 165 L.Ed.2d 368 (2006) ("if state court remedies are no longer available because the prisoner failed to comply with the deadline for seeking state-court review or for taking an appeal, those remedies are technically exhausted").

[15]Moleterno v. Nelson, 114 F.3d 629 (7th Cir.1997).

[16]Castille v. Peoples, 489 U.S. 346, 109 S.Ct. 1056, 103 L.Ed.2d 380 (1989). On procedural default, see § 28.4.

[17]Duckworth v. Serrano, 454 U.S. 1, 102 S.Ct. 18, 70 L.Ed.2d 1 (1981)

not require that the habeas court accept a state "merry-go-round of habeas corpus, coram nobis, and writ of error."[18] A theoretical system of relief need not be pursued. A state remedy may be "ineffective" if there has been inordinate delay in the administration of that remedy.[19] Of course, the fault for the delay must rest with the state rather than the petitioner. Even then, the delay found to be inordinate is usually a full year or longer.[20]

Mixed Petitions. Prior to the passage of AEDPA, the Court in *Rose v. Lundy*[21] considered the question whether a federal habeas court had to dismiss a petition containing both exhausted and unexhausted claims or could instead simply rule on those claims that were unexhausted. The "policies underlying the statutory provision" requiring exhaustion, the Court concluded, required that the habeas court dismiss a mixed petition. This would leave the petitioner with the alternatives of either (1) returning to the state courts and exhausting all of his claims so they could then be presented together later in a single petition or (2) dropping his unexhausted claims and filing a new petition containing only the exhausted claims. Prior to the 1996 amendments, over half of all petitions dismissed were dismissed for failure to exhaust state remedies.[22]

With the addition of a strict statute of limitations in 1996, the Court revisited its earlier approach of requiring the petitioner to return to federal court with a single petition filed after exhausting claims from a mixed petition that had been dismissed without prejudice. As the Court observed in *Pliler v. Ford*,[23] requiring dismissal of "mixed petitions" could result in a loss of all claims,

---

("An exception is made [to the § 2254 exhaustion requirement] only if there is no opportunity to obtain redress in state court or if the corrective process is so clearly deficient as to render futile any effort to obtain relief."); Blackledge v. Perry, 417 U.S. 21, 94 S.Ct. 2098, 40 L.Ed.2d 628 (1974). See also R. Hertz & J. Liebman, 2 Federal Habeas Corpus Practice and Procedure § 23.4a (5th ed.2005) (listing examples of cases in which an exception to exhaustion requirement was recognized); 17B C. Wright, A. Miller, E. Cooper & V. Amar, Federal Practice and Procedure: Jurisdiction 3d § 4264.5 (2007); L. Yackle, Postconviction Remedies § 66 (1981 & Supp.2007).

[18]Marino v. Ragen, 332 U.S. 561, 68 S.Ct. 240, 92 L.Ed. 170 (1947) (concurring opinion).

[19]See, e.g., Sapienza v. Vincent, 534 F.2d 1007 (2d Cir.1976); Lee v. Stickman, 357 F.3d 338 (3d Cir.2004); Jackson v. Duckworth, 112 F.3d 878 (7th Cir.1997); Lowe v. Duckworth, 663 F.2d 42 (7th Cir.1981).

[20]Cases on delay are collected in 2 R. Hertz & J. Liebman, Federal Habeas Corpus Practice and Procedure § 23.4(a) at n. 22 (5th ed.2005); L. Yackle, Postconviction Remedies § 65 (1981 & Supp.2007).

[21]Rose v. Lundy, 455 U.S. 509, 102 S.Ct. 1198, 71 L.Ed.2d 379 (1982).

[22]R. Hanson & J. Daley, Federal Habeas Corpus Review: Challenging State Court Criminal Convictions 17 (1995).

[23]Pliler v. Ford, 542 U.S. 225, 124 S.Ct. 2441, 159 L.Ed.2d 338 (2004).

even those already exhausted, because the limitations period could expire during the time a petitioner returns to state court to exhaust his unexhausted claims. In *Rhines v. Weber*,[24] the Court held that a district court has discretion to stay a mixed petition holding the exhausted claims in abeyance while allowing a petitioner to present his unexhausted claims to the state court and then return to federal court for review of his perfected petition, without risking being time barred. This "stay and abeyance" procedure, however, is appropriate only when three conditions are met. First, the petitioner's claims must not be "plainly meritless." Second, the petitioner must have had good cause for failing to exhaust his claims in state court—there must be no indication that the petitioner engaged in intentionally dilatory litigation tactics.[25] Finally, the judge should "place reasonable time limits on the petitioner's trip to state court and back." If "employed too frequently," the Supreme Court warned, the procedure has the potential to undermine the goals of promoting finality and reducing delay in habeas litigation.

Providing a "Fair Opportunity"—Presenting the Claim to the State Courts. In order to provide the state with a fair opportunity to decide his claim, a petitioner must (1) present to the state courts a claim substantially equivalent to the claim he raises in his federal petition and (2) allow the state courts to complete their review of that claim. A petitioner does not "fairly present" his constitutional claim to a state court if that court must read beyond the petition, brief, or similar document in order to find

---

[24] Rhines v. Weber, 544 U.S. 269, 125 S.Ct. 1528, 161 L.Ed.2d 440 (2005). See also Day v. McDonough, 547 U.S. 198, 126 S.Ct. 1675, 1684 n.10, 164 L.Ed.2d 376 (2006).

[25] As for what might constitute good cause, consider Riner v. Crawford, 415 F.Supp.2d 1207 (D.Nev.2006) (collecting authority that good cause requires some "objective factor external to the defense" that made it impossible to bring the claim earlier in the state court proceedings, conflicting authority that does not require a showing of extreme and unusual events beyond the control of the defendant, and conflicting authority on whether alleged ineffective assistance counsel during post-conviction proceedings can constitute good cause for failure to exhaust claims; holding that the good cause standard applicable in consideration of a request for stay and abeyance of a federal habeas petition requires the petitioner to show that he was prevented from raising the claim, either by his own ignorance or confusion about the law or the status of his case, or by circumstances over which he had little or no control, such as the actions of counsel either in contravention of the petitioner's clearly expressed desire to raise the claim or when petitioner had no knowledge of the claim's existence); Carter v. Friel, 415 F.Supp.2d 1314 (D.Utah 2006) (applying *Rhines*, finding that inexperience and ineffectiveness of state post conviction counsel does not constitute good cause for failing to exhaust state remedies, collecting authority, "good cause" for stay and abeyance is the same "cause" required for procedural default; claims appear to be procedurally barred in state court and are therefore not potentially meritorious).

material, such as a lower court opinion in the case, that would alert it to the presence of a federal claim.[26] Nor is the exhaustion requirement met if the petitioner raises "one claim in the state courts and another in the federal courts," explained the Court in *Picard v. Connor*.[27] A petitioner must present to the state court "the substance" of his claim in a manner sufficient to give that court "a fair opportunity" to rule upon it.[28] *Picard* itself illustrates a situation in which there was so much variation between the theories advanced before the state and federal courts that the state court never had "a fair opportunity" to rule on the contention raised in the federal courts. That case involved a state practice under which the grand jury originally indicted a named individual and a fictitious "John Doe," with the true name of the alleged accomplice then added by amendment following his arrest. Before the state courts, petitioner argued that amendment of the indictment to substitute his name for John Doe violated his right to be prosecuted only upon an indictment actually issued by the grand jury. On habeas review, the federal court held for petitioner but relied on a different theory. The amendment of the indictment did not violate due process since the state had no constitutional obligation to proceed by indictment; but once having granted the protection of a grand jury indictment to defendants generally, the state had denied petitioner equal protection by utilizing the John Doe indictment. The Supreme Court held that while the same facts were before both state and federal courts, the state court could not be expected to consider the equal protection claim sua sponte, and it had not been raised in any fashion before the state courts. While a claim could be presented without citing "book and verse in the federal constitution," it could not be said that the original challenge in the state courts was the "substantial equivalent" of the unconstitutional discrimi-

---

[26]Baldwin v. Reese, 541 U.S. 27, 124 S.Ct. 1347, 158 L.Ed.2d 64 (2004). The Court in *Baldwin* declined to reach petitioner's contention that when state and federal standards for adjudicating a constitutional claim are identical, raising a state law claim in his state petition would "necessarily 'fairly present'" the corresponding federal claim.

[27]Picard v. Connor, 404 U.S. 270, 92 S.Ct. 509, 30 L.Ed.2d 438 (1971).

[28]See also Keeney v. Tamayo-Reyes, 504 U.S. 1, 112 S.Ct. 1715, 118 L.Ed.2d 318 (1992):

The purpose of exhaustion is not to create a procedural hurdle on the path to federal habeas court, but to channel claims into an appropriate forum, where meritorious claims may be vindicated and unfounded litigation obviated before resort to federal court. Comity concerns dictate that the requirement of exhaustion is not satisfied by the mere statement of a federal claim in state court. Just as the State must afford the petitioner a full and fair hearing on his federal claim, so must the petitioner afford the State a full and fair opportunity to address and resolve the claim on the merits.

nation claim.[29]

In *Anderson v. Harless*,[30] *Duncan v. Henry*,[31] and *Gray v. Netherland*,[32] the Court reached similar conclusions. When the petitioner in *Anderson* challenged in the state courts a jury charge on "malice," he characterized the charge as simply "erroneous" and cited a state case that referred only to a due process requirement that the jury instructions "properly explain" the law. This was not sufficient indication of the theory later advanced in the federal courts, that the charge created a mandatory presumption contrary to the prosecution's constitutional obligation to prove guilt beyond a reasonable doubt. In *Duncan*, the Court concluded that arguing a similar claim under state law does not satisfy the exhaustion requirement because the claim must be clearly identified as one made under federal law and the "mere similarity of claims is insufficient to exhaust."[33] So too, in *Gray*, the petitioner did not fairly present to the state courts his

---

[29]Justice Douglas, dissenting, argued that the petitioner had specified the practice under constitutional attack and his reference to due process was adequate since that clause could encompass invidious discrimination under Supreme Court precedent. Lower court cases applying the *Picard* ruling are collected in 17B C. Wright, A. Miller, E. Cooper & V. Amar, Federal Practice and Procedure: Jurisdiction 3d § 4264.3 (2007); L. Yackle, Postconviction Remedies § 60 (1981 & Supp.2007).

[30]Anderson v. Harless, 459 U.S. 4, 103 S.Ct. 276, 74 L.Ed.2d 3 (1982).

[31]Duncan v. Henry, 513 U.S. 364, 115 S.Ct. 887, 130 L.Ed.2d 865 (1995) (per curiam).

[32]Gray v. Netherland, 518 U.S. 152, 116 S.Ct. 2074, 135 L.Ed.2d 457 (1996).

[33]See also Keller v. Larkins, 251 F.3d 408 (3d Cir.2001) (not fairly presented when petitioner failed to cite to federal Constitution or to any cases resting on it, and did not give state courts fair notice that he was asserting federal constitutional claim). Lower courts have also held, however, that when the state and federal claims are identical, raising the state claim provides a "fair opportunity to pass upon and correct alleged violations of federal rights." See Jackson v. Edwards, 404 F.3d 612 (2d Cir.2005). See also Rose v. Palmateer, 395 F.3d 1108 (9th Cir.2005) (petitioner did not fairly present his claim that his confession and reenactment violated his rights under the Fifth Amendment "when he merely discussed it as one of several issues which were handled ineffectively by his trial and appellate counsel"); Castillo v. McFadden, 399 F.3d 993 (9th Cir.2005) (petitioner cannot raise state evidentiary claims, cite cases dealing with the admission of evidence, mention the words "fair trial" and then reasonably expect the Arizona Court of Appeals to understand he is raising a constitutional rather than an evidentiary issue); McNair v. Campbell, 416 F.3d 1291 (11th Cir.2005) (where nine-page petition in state court did not cite a single federal case and only mention of federal law was in a repetition of the concluding paragraph of his argument before the lower court where he had one federal district court case buried in a string cite, his references to federal law "are exactly the type of needles in the haystack that we have previously held are insufficient to satisfy the exhaustion requirement." Instead of citing any federal appellate case dealing with extraneous evidence, or even mentioning the presumption of prejudice that arises under federal

claim that the state misled him about evidence it intended to introduce, when he had referred in the state courts to a broad federal due process right and cited cases that forbid the use of secret testimony. The cases cited by petitioner in state court and those he later cited in federal court, the Court explained, "arise in widely differing contexts."[34]

Just as different legal claims will not suffice as a fair presentation to the state court, neither will factual claims significantly different than those advanced in federal court. Where a petitioner presents newly discovered evidence "such as to place the case in a significantly different and stronger evidentiary posture than it was when the state courts considered it," that the petitioner must first give the state courts an opportunity to consider the evidence.[35]

The second element of the state's fair opportunity to review a

---

law when jurors consider such evidence, he instead relied on state law to argue a state law claim under a state law standard).

[34]Consider also the position of three justices (O'Connor, Rehnquist, and Burger, C.J.) dissenting from the denial of certiorari in McKaskle v. Vela, 464 U.S. 1053, 104 S.Ct. 736, 79 L.Ed.2d 195 (1984), arguing that where defendant in state court claimed ineffectiveness of counsel due to certain alleged errors of counsel, the reliance upon different alleged errors in the habeas proceedings presents an unexhausted claim. Compare also Banks v. Dretke, 540 U.S. 668, 124 S.Ct. 1256, 157 L.Ed.2d 1166 (2004) (the parties disputed, but the Court declined to resolve, whether a petitioner who raises a *Brady* claim adequately raises a *Giglio* claim as well, or whether the claim under *Napue* or *Giglio* must be separately pleaded); Dorsey v. Kelly, 112 F.3d 50 (2d Cir.1997) (fairly presented); Purnell v. Missouri Department of Corrections, 753 F.2d 703 (8th Cir.1985) (surveying lower court cases speaking to the question of what degree of specificity is required in an appellate argument to put a state appellate court on notice as to defendant's constitutional argument); Moleterno v. Nelson, 114 F.3d 629 (7th Cir.1997) (no fair presentation of claim); Porter v. Gramley, 112

F.3d 1308 (7th Cir.1997) (fairly presented); Anderson v. Groose, 106 F.3d 242 (8th Cir.1997) (fairly presented).

[35]Demarest v. Price, 130 F.3d 922 (10th Cir.1997) (collecting authority). See also Graham v. Johnson, 94 F.3d 958 (5th Cir.1996) (significant additional evidence not presented to the state courts). The Fifth Circuit has decided a series of capital habeas cases in which the state has argued that the petitioner's claim of retardation under Atkins v. Virginia, 536 U.S. 304, 122 S.Ct. 2242, 153 L.Ed.2d 335 (2002), was not fairly presented to the state courts when the factual allegations advanced and proof submitted in federal habeas were more detailed than that presented to state courts. Compare Moore v. Quarterman, 454 F.3d 484 (5th Cir.2006) (not fairly presented by "conclusional allegation") with Morris v. Dretke, 413 F.3d 484 (5th Cir.2005) (fairly presented by "robust claim of mental retardation").

See also Vasquez v. Hillery, 474 U.S. 254, 106 S.Ct. 617, 88 L.Ed.2d 598 (1986), when the Court noted that the district court had not circumvented the exhaustion requirement in directing the parties to expand the record by presenting a statistical analysis of the possibility that chance would have accounted for exclusion of blacks from grand jury, as that did not fundamentally alter the claim presented to the

claim is permitting the state to complete its review. The Court held in *Brown v. Allen*[36] that a petitioner need only give the state system a single opportunity to rule on his claim, and that a petitioner need not pursue collateral remedies in state court in addition to direct appeal. Ordinarily that opportunity must be extended to the highest reaches of the state judiciary, usually the state supreme court.[37] In *O'Sullivan v. Boerckel*,[38] however, the Court held that although a petitioner is required to invoke "one full round of the State's established appellate review process," he need not invoke "extraordinary remedies when those remedies are alternatives to the standard review process and where the state courts have not provided relief through those remedies in the past." When the state's appellate process includes discretionary review by the state supreme court, a petitioner must pursue this remedy before seeking relief in federal court.[39]

Waiver of Exhaustion Requirement by the State. The 1996 amendments added § 2254(b)(3), which provides: "A State shall not be deemed to have waived the exhaustion requirement or be estopped from reliance upon the requirement unless the State, through counsel, expressly waives the requirement." This provision has limited the ability of a habeas court to dispense with the exhaustion requirement given a state's failure to raise the issue.[40]

---

state courts.

[36]Brown v. Allen, 344 U.S. 443, 73 S.Ct. 397, 97 L.Ed. 469 (1953).

[37]See, e.g., Pesina v. Johnson, 913 F.2d 53 (2d Cir.1990).

[38]O'Sullivan v. Boerckel, 526 U.S. 838, 119 S.Ct. 1728, 144 L.Ed.2d 1 (1999).

[39]The Court also recognized an exception when a State has provided that a remedy is "unavailable." See Swoopes v. Sublett, 196 F.3d 1008 (9th Cir.1999) (Arizona has declared that its "complete round" does not include discretionary review before the Arizona Supreme Court). Consider also Hills v. Washington, 441 F.3d 1374 (11th Cir.2006) (Carnes, J., concurring) (noting that in 2004 state of Georgia amended its certiorari review rule to read, "In appeals from criminal convictions, a litigant shall not be required to petition for rehearing and certiorari following an adverse decision of the Court of Appeals in order to be deemed to have exhausted all

available state remedies respecting a claim of error", and urging that the issues raised by "letting a state court decide the federal habeas effect of a petitioner bypassing an unchanged state procedure" be given the attention they deserve, "never before have federal courts delegated to state courts the authority to decide what federal habeas law will be"); DeFoy v. McCullough, 393 F.3d 439 (3d Cir.2005) (petitioner challenging decision of parole board in Pennsylvania need not apply for mandamus in state court in order to exhaust his claims).

[40]See Demarest v. Price, 130 F.3d 922 (10th Cir.1997) (holding that the state's failure to object to the testimony of certain witnesses was not a waiver of the exhaustion requirement). Prior to the 1996 Act, in Granberry v. Greer, 481 U.S. 129, 107 S.Ct. 1671, 95 L.Ed.2d 119 (1987), the Court had held that where a state raises nonexhaustion for the first time in federal court on appeal, the appellate court is neither required to dismiss for nonex-

§ 28.5(b) Time limits for filing petitions

Although a petition with unexhausted claims may be filed too early, a petition may also be filed too late. Prior to the 1996 amendments, the only time limitation imposed on the filing of a habeas petition was that flowing from the application of the doctrine of laches contained in Rule 9 of the Rules Governing Section 2254 Cases. Rule 9(a) provided that a petition may be dismissed if "the state has been prejudiced in its ability to respond to the petition by delay in filing unless the petitioner shows that it is based on grounds of which he could not have had knowledge by the exercise of reasonable diligence before the circumstances prejudicial to the state occurred." If the petition was not filed until many years after conviction, that was of no consequence, provided the state was unable to show that delay prejudiced its ability to respond to the petition.[41] Indeed, in *Lonchar v. Thomas*,[42] the Court held that a district court could not rely on general equitable principles—independent of those embodied in Rule 9(a)—to dismiss a death row inmate's first habeas petition on the ground that the inmate purposely delayed filing it.

The 1996 legislation included, for the first time, a specific time limitation for the filing of federal habeas petitions. This limitation has replaced the discretionary authority under Rule 9(a).[43] Section 2244(d) now provides a one-year period for filing a habeas petition. The limitation period begins to run on the date on which the judgment challenged became final by the "conclusion of direct review or the expiration of the time for seeking such review." This language has been construed as indicating the date on which direct review[44] is concluded in the Supreme Court or the expira-

---

haustion nor obligated to regard the state's omission as an absolute waiver.

[Section 28.5(b)]

[41]Prejudice has been construed narrowly, and does not include difficulties in retrying the defendant that result from the passage of time. See Vasquez v. Hillery, 474 U.S. 254, 106 S.Ct. 617, 88 L.Ed.2d 598 (1986); Rideau v. Whitley, 237 F.3d 472 (5th Cir.2000) (finding state failed to make a sufficient showing of prejudice in its ability to respond to the petition that was caused by the petitioner's delay, when petitioner filed a petition for habeas corpus relief in 1994, challenging indictment filed in 1961 on the basis of race discrimination in the selection of grand jurors); Clinton, Rule 9 of the

Federal Habeas Corpus Rules: A Case Study on the Need for Reform of The Rules Enabling Act, 63 Iowa L.Rev. 15 (1997).

[42]Lonchar v. Thomas, 517 U.S. 314, 116 S.Ct. 1293, 134 L.Ed.2d 440 (1996).

[43]Rule 9 of the Rules Governing Section 2254 Cases was amended to delete the previous language concerning late petitions in 2004, in light of the more rigid limitations adopted as part of AEDPA.

[44]Even in guilty plea cases the state may provide the functional equivalent of a direct appeal and call it something else. See Summers v. Schriro, 481 F.3d 710 (9th Cir.2007) (Rule 32 "of-right" proceeding in Ari-

tion of time for seeking such review.[45] In *Clay v. United States*,[46] the Court interpreted similar but not identical language in § 2255 to impose this standard for triggering the commencement of the one-year limitations period. Thus, the limitations period for both state and federal prisoners does not begin until the Court denies review or, if no petition for certiorari is filed, the time for seeking such review expires. If no direct appeal is taken, then the judgment becomes final and the limitation period begins to run at the end of the period during which an appeal could have been filed.[47]

The limitation period is tolled for any period during which a properly filed[48] collateral attack was pending before the state[49] courts. When a state has not defined the permissible period for

---

zona is a form of direct review for purposes of statute of limitations).

[45]E.g., Abela v. Martin, 348 F.3d 164 (6th Cir.2003); Robinson v. United States, 416 F.3d 645 (7th Cir.2005) (conviction becomes final when the Court denies certiorari, not upon the expiration of the 25-day period for rehearing that denial; nor is equitable tolling available for petitioner's mistaken understanding about the deadline for filing).

In a case involving resentencing, the commencement of the statute of limitations period will be delayed until the resentencing becomes final. Burton v. Stewart, __ U.S. __, 127 S.Ct. 793, 166 L.Ed.2d 628 (2007), also discussed in § 28.5(d) at notes 74–75; Ferreira v. Secretary, Dept. of Corrections, 494 F.3d 1286 (11th Cir. 2007).

[46]Clay v. United States, 537 U.S. 522, 123 S.Ct. 1072, 155 L.Ed.2d 88 (2003).

[47]See also Caldwell v. Dretke, 429 F.3d 521 (5th Cir.2006) (deferred adjudication is final judgment for purposes of statute of limitations, as is an order of straight probation, rejecting argument that limitations should begin once guilt is adjudicated and sentence imposed).

[48]The application for state postconviction relief must have been "delivered to, and accepted by the appropriate court officer for placement into the official record," and "its delivery and acceptance are in compliance with the applicable laws and rules

governing filings," such as "time limits" for delivery and filing fees; Artuz v. Bennett, 531 U.S. 4, 121 S.Ct. 361, 148 L.Ed.2d 213 (2000); Pace v. DiGuglielmo, 544 U.S. 408, 125 S.Ct. 1807, 161 L.Ed.2d 669 (2005) (a state post-conviction petition rejected by the state court as untimely is not "properly filed" within the meaning of § 2244(d)(2)); Carey v. Saffold, 536 U.S. 214, 122 S.Ct. 2134, 153 L.Ed.2d 260 (2002) (finding that so long as the state petition was filed in the state court within the time specified by state law, the federal limitations period did not run, noting that if a state would prefer that federal courts reach its prisoners' claims sooner, it need only change its own law).

See also Smith v. Walls, 276 F.3d 340 (7th Cir.2002) (limitations period tolled even if state application is later dismissed by state court as procedurally barred, so long as its delivery and acceptance are in compliance with applicable laws and rules); Carter v. Litscher, 275 F.3d 663 (7th Cir.2001) (properly filed state challenge will toll limitations period even if issues presented to the state tribunal differ from those presented in federal court); Dictado v. Ducharme, 244 F.3d 724 (9th Cir.2001); Tillema v. Long, 253 F.3d 494 (9th Cir.2001) (properly filed state challenge will toll limitations period even if issues presented to the state tribunal differ from those presented in federal court).

But see Tinker v. Hanks, 255 F.3d 444 (7th Cir.2001) (not tolled by application to state court for leave to

filing state collateral proceedings, as in California, federal courts must determine if the petitioner sought state remedies with reasonable diligence, so as to stop the limitations period from running. If the petitioner's delay in seeking state relief was unreasonable, tolling is not available. In *Evans v. Chavis*,[50] the Court held that the statute of limitations was not tolled during a delay of three years and one month that elapsed between a lower court's denial of state habeas petition and the filing of notice of appeal from that decision. The Court considered the petitioner's

file second petition); Malcom v. Payne, 281 F.3d 951 (9th Cir.2002) (not tolled during pendency of clemency application); Satterfield v. Johnson, 434 F.3d 185 (3d Cir.2006) (when petitioner filed his state post-conviction petition in the wrong court, his filing did not toll the statute of limitations); Sibley v. Culliver, 377 F.3d 1196 (11th Cir.2004) (no tolling allowed when document submitted to state court was not a legitimate filing; the Act requires more than simply mailing "nonsense" to a state court; even if this was a petition for relief it was mailed to the state supreme court instead of sent to the district court so was not "filed," supreme court did not transfer the filing most likely because the court did not recognize the Notice as being a petition for post-conviction relief).

[49]See Duncan v. Walker, 533 U.S. 167, 121 S.Ct. 2120, 150 L.Ed.2d 251 (2001) (interpreting § 2244(d) to allow tolling only for properly filed collateral attacks in state court, holding that an application for federal habeas review does not toll the limitations period, reasoning that this interpretation of the provision provides a powerful incentive to exhaust state remedies before turning to federal court, while at the same time limiting the harm to the interest in finality).

[50]Evans v. Chavis, __ U.S. __, 126 S.Ct. 846, 163 L.Ed.2d 684 (2006), discussing Carey v. Saffold, 536 U.S. 214, 122 S.Ct. 2134, 153 L.Ed.2d 260 (2002) (holding that a collateral attack is pending during the time between a lower state court's decision and the filing of a notice of appeal to a higher state court). See also Gaston v. Palmer,

447 F.3d 1165 (9th Cir.2006) (applying *Evans*, federal judges must determine for themselves whether the equivalent of a notice of appeal was filed within a reasonable time, and holding that petitioner in this case was not entitled to tolling due to delays in filing applications in state court); Culver v. Director of Corrections, 450 F.Supp.2d 1135 (C.D.Cal. 2006) (unreasonable delay when petitioner waited 97 days after the first state habeas petition was denied before filing his second state habeas petition in the Court of Appeal, and when he waited 71 days before filing his next state habeas petition in the California Supreme Court).

Several aspects of tolling for properly filed state collateral proceedings remain unresolved by the Court. See, e.g., Delhomme v. Ramirez, 340 F.3d 817 (9th Cir.2003) (tolling while first petition pending under state law continues and is not ended when petitioner files additional or overlapping state petitions); Cramer v. Secretary, Dept. of Corrections, 461 F.3d 1380 (11th Cir.2006) (finding, as a matter of first impression, claim is "pending" regardless of whether the inmate actually files the notice of appeal, and remains pending until the time to seek review expires); Walker v. Crosby, 341 F.3d 1240 (11th Cir.2003) (a single limitations period applies to the entire application, individual claims within an application cannot be reviewed separately for timeliness, limitations period must run from the "latest" of the several possible triggering dates collecting authority).

claims that hindrances on library access and lockdowns prevented him from filing his request for appeal sooner, but noted that no evidence refuted the state's showing that for a period of at least six months the petitioner had full access to the library without lockdowns. Because six months is far longer than the period of 30 to 60 days that most states provide for an appeal to the state supreme court, the delay in filing was unreasonable.

The period tolled for properly filed state collateral proceedings also does not include the time period during which a petition for certiorari is pending before the United States Supreme Court.[51] Accordingly, in order to avoid the statute of limitations bar, some petitioners will have to file their federal petitions before the Supreme Court has resolved an application for review of state court collateral proceedings.

Tolling is also provided by statute where: (1) state action in violation of the Constitution or other federal law impeded the timely filing of the habeas petition; (2) the petition relies on a constitutional right that was initially recognized by the Supreme Court after the date of finality and that also was held to be retroactive in application;[52] or (3) the petition relies on a constitutional claim as to which the factual predicate[53] could not have been

---

[51]Lawrence v. Florida, __ U.S. __, 127 S.Ct. 1079, 166 L.Ed.2d 924 (2007).

[52]In Tyler v. Cain, 533 U.S. 656, 121 S.Ct. 2478, 150 L.Ed.2d 632 (2001), discussed in § 28.5(e) at note 93, and § 28.6(e) at note 51, four justices in dissent noted that in order to avoid unfairness, § 2244(d)(1)(C) should be interpreted to permit the one-year period to run "from the time that the Court has 'made' the new rule retroactive, not from the time it initially recognized that new right." The majority did not address this issue.

[53]See Shannon v. Newland, 410 F.3d 1083 (9th Cir.2005) (although a state court order of vacatur can be the fact that begins the one-year period, a state-court decision establishing an abstract proposition of law arguably helpful to the petitioner's claim does not constitute the factual predicate for that claim).

For computation of the limitations period in cases challenging administrative decisions while incarcerated, see Dulworth v. Evans, 442 F.3d 1265 (10th Cir.2006) (addressing for the first time the question whether the one year statute of limitations applies to § 2241 petitions contesting administrative decisions, court joins the Second, Fourth, Fifth and Ninth Circuits and hold that the limitation period applies, and that it begins to run on the date on which the factual predicate of a petitioner's claim could have been discovered through the exercise of due diligence, which in this case was the date that the denial of the administrative appeal becomes final). Compare Cox v. McBride, 279 F.3d 492 (7th Cir.2002) (statute of limitations period does not apply to petitions contesting administrative decisions rather than state judgments); Kimbrell v. Cockrell, 311 F.3d 361 (5th Cir.2002) (limitations period begins on the date of the administrative decision, but is tolled while administrative appeals are pending).

discovered at the date of finality by the exercise of due diligence.[54] These exceptions resemble other provisions added elsewhere to the habeas statute by AEDPA.[55]

The Court in *Dodd v. United States*[56] interpreted strictly a similar provision in § 2255 governing exceptions to the one-year rule for federal prisoners, and held that although the statute provides that the one-year clock does not start ticking until the Court initially recognizes the new rule, the clock keeps running while a petitioner waits for the rule to be "held" to apply retroactively. If, after the Court initially recognizes the rule, twelve months pass before the rule is held to be retroactive, any claim under that new rule will be time-barred.

The harsh effects of this and other strict interpretations of the filing deadline have been tempered somewhat by lower court rulings.[57] Due to the "pro se petitioner's lack of control over the filing of documents," the petition will be deemed filed "at the moment [petitioner] delivers it to prison officials for mailing to the district court."[58] Lower courts have also interpreted the statute to allow for "equitable tolling" of the limitations period in extraordi-

---

[54]Wilson v. Beard, 426 F.3d 653 (3d Cir. 2005) (finding petitioner met § 2244(d)(1)(D)'s "due diligence" standard, where he heard about a videotape of his prosecutor admitting jury discrimination after an attorney called him about it two days after the tape received widespread attention on local newscasts; rejecting the state's argument that petitioner should have learned about it days earlier when news broadcasts took place, stating, "No person would reasonably expect that the local news would be a source of information relevant to his case, given that his conviction had occurred thirteen years ago and his final appeal had been rejected by the Supreme Court the previous year * * * absent some reasonable basis for concluding that the local news is likely to be a source of information at the particular time, due diligence does not require a prisoner * * * to monitor the news on a regular basis on the unlikely chance that he might learn something which would be useful to his case."); Ege v. Yukins, 485 F.3d 364 (6th Cir.2007) (factual predicate of due process claim concerning erroneous admission of bite-marks testimony was the discovery that neighboring county prosecu-

tor would not approve warrants where identity is based on the bite-mark expert's testimony because of its unreliability, rejecting dissenter's view that information was cumulative).

[55]See §§ 2244(b); 2254(e)(2); 2255. See also Note, 70 S.Cal.L.Rev. 1513, 1566–67 (1997) (discussing the alternative starting point for new rules).

[56]Dodd v. United States, 545 U.S. 353, 125 S.Ct. 2478, 162 L.Ed.2d 343 (2005).

[57]See Hill v. Braxton, 277 F.3d 701 (4th Cir.2002) (before dismissing what appears to be untimely petition, habeas court must warn the prisoner that absent a sufficient explanation, the case is subject to dismissal pursuant to the limitations period, unless it is indisputably clear from the materials presented that the petition's lateness cannot be salvaged by tolling or by exceptions that may delay the commencement of the one-year period).

[58]Burns v. Morton, 134 F.3d 109 (3d Cir.1998). See also Rule 3(d) of the Rules Governing § 2254 Cases (filing by inmate timely if deposited in prison mail system on or before the last day for filing). Compare Burger v. Scott, 317 F.3d 1133 (10th Cir.2003) (Be-

nary circumstances, despite the lack of any reference to such an exception in the statute itself.[59] Equitable tolling has yet to be

cause Oklahoma does not recognize the prisoner mailbox rule, it does not apply in determining whether a *state* court proceeding was "properly filed" for purposes of tolling the one-year statute of limitations).

[59]See, e.g., Miller v. New Jersey State Dept. of Corrections, 145 F.3d 616 (3d Cir.1998); Fahy v. Horn, 240 F.3d 239 (3d Cir.2001) (equitable tolling appropriate in capital case where state law issues involved in delayed filing were not settled at relevant time and rigid application of the statute of limitations would be unfair); Harris v. Hutchinson, 209 F.3d 325 (4th Cir. 2000); Prieto v. Quarterman, 456 F.3d 511 (5th Cir. 2006) (equitable tolling appropriate when petitioner relied to his detriment and in good faith on the district court's order extending the filing time, when that order was entered before the limitations period expired); Davis v. Johnson, 158 F.3d 806 (5th Cir.1998); In re Wilson, 442 F.3d 872 (5th Cir.2006) (allowing equitable tolling when state rule preventing petitioners from maintaining applications in both state and federal court at the same time prevented him from filing his Atkins claim, forcing him to file his successive petition in state court while his federal petition remained pending, anticipating the state petition would be dismissed, or he could have dismissed his federal petition and filed his successive petition in state court); Vroman v. Brigano, 346 F.3d 598 (6th Cir.2003) (applying five-factor test to determine whether to equitably toll statute of limitations); Mendoza v. Carey, 449 F.3d 1065 (9th Cir.2006) (extraordinary circumstances justifying equitable tolling could be established when prison law library lack's Spanish-language legal materials and the petitioner is unable to obtain translation assistance before the one-year deadline); Brambles v. Duncan, 330 F.3d 1197 (9th Cir.2003) (equitable tolling appropriate when petitioner

misled by court), amended 342 F.3d 898; Burger v. Scott, 317 F.3d 1133 (10th Cir.2003) (equitable tolling for four months documents were in possession of court but failed to affix stamp); Knight v. Schofield, 292 F.3d 709 (11th Cir.2002) (tolling due to clerk's sending of notice to wrong person).

But compare Johnson v. Hendricks, 314 F.3d 159 (3d Cir.2002) (counsel's erroneous advice about expiration of limitations period was not an extraordinary circumstance sufficient to warrant equitable tolling); Rouse v. Lee, 339 F.3d 238 (4th Cir.2003) (en banc) (rejecting as untimely the petition of death row prisoner filed one day late, when petitioner has not shown any extraordinary circumstances beyond his control that prevented him from complying with the statute of limitations); Felder v. Johnson, 204 F.3d 168 (5th Cir.2000); Modrowski v. Mote, 322 F.3d 965 (7th Cir.2003) (equitable tolling not warranted when late filing was due to attorney incapacity; attorney incapacity is equivalent to attorney negligence, which does not toll the period).

Brinson v. Vaughn, 398 F.3d 225 (3d Cir.2005) (courts are divided about what standard of appellate review should govern when a District Court applies the doctrine of equitable tolling in a habeas case, with some applying de novo, some abuse-of-discretion, some other standards, collecting authority and adopting de novo review, and upholding finding of equitable tolling when district court had erroneously dismissed a claim as unexhausted and "relegated Brinson to another round of state court litigation that was bound to fail").

See generally Bellamy, Playing for Time: The Need for Equitable Tolling of the Habeas Corpus Statute of Limitations, 32 Am.J.Crim.L. 1 (2004).

endorsed by the Supreme Court, although it has "assume[d] without deciding" that it is available. In *Lawrence v. Florida*,[60] the Court found that even assuming equitable tolling is allowed by the statute, errors in calculating deadlines by state-appointed post-conviction counsel do not amount to the showing of "extraordinary circumstances" necessary to support equitable tolling. Lower courts have approved of equitable tolling when a prisoner was transferred to a facility where there was no access to the federal habeas statute and there was no lack of diligence in pursuing their rights.[61] Some courts have suggested that the Constitution requires that courts recognize, in addition, an "actual innocence" exception to the statute of limitations.[62]

---

[60]Lawrence v. Florida, __ U.S. __, 127 S.Ct. 1079, 166 L.Ed.2d 924 (2007). See also Pace v. DiGugliemo, 544 U.S. 408, 125 S.Ct. 1807, 161 L.Ed.2d 669 (2005) (assuming without deciding that equitable tolling is available, holding that petitioner failed to establish the requisite diligence in pursuing his claim when he waited years, without any valid justification, to assert his claims). Consider also Duncan v. Walker, 533 U.S. 167, 121 S.Ct. 2120, 150 L.Ed.2d 251 (2001), where Justices Souter and Stevens expressed approval of the lower court's use of their equitable powers to toll the limitations period. Justice Souter suggested equitable tolling "could present a serious issue on facts different from those before us." Justice Stevens argued that nothing "in the text of legislative history of AEDPA, precludes a federal court from deeming the limitations period tolled for [a federal habeas] petition as a matter of equity." He reasoned that "federal courts may well conclude that Congress simply overlooked the class of petitioners whose timely filed habeas petitions remain pending in district court past the limitations period, only to be dismissed after the court belatedly realizes that one or more claims have not been exhausted."

[61]Roy v. Lampert, 465 F.3d 964 (9th Cir.2006). But compare Arthur v. Allen, 452 F.3d 1234 (11th Cir.2006) (a prisoner claiming deficiencies in the prison law library as a basis for equitable tolling must provide details of the specific actions taken toward filing the petition, when he found out about the deficiency, and demonstrate how the prison thwarted his efforts; this petitioner failed to make such a showing).

[62]See Whitley v. Senkowski, 317 F.3d 223 (2d Cir.2003) (noting that an actual innocence exception to the statute of limitations is an open question, and instructing district court on remand to determine, in order, "(1) Did [petitioner] pursue his actual innocence claim with reasonable diligence? (2) If [petitioner] did not pursue the claim with reasonable diligence, must an actual innocence claim be pursued with reasonable diligence in order to raise the issue of whether the United States Constitution requires an 'actual innocence' exception to the AEDPA statute of limitations? (3) If [petitioner] did pursue the claim with reasonable diligence or if reasonable diligence is unnecessary, does [petitioner] make a credible claim of actual innocence? (4) If [petitioner] does make a credible claim of actual innocence, does the United States Constitution require an 'actual innocence' exception to the AEDPA statute of limitations on federal habeas petitions?"); Souter v. Jones, 395 F.3d 577 (6th Cir.2005) (petitioner's case is "a rare and extraordinary case" where new evidence raises sufficient doubt about his guilt that statute of limitations should be tolled, collecting authority, and noting that an actual innocence exception to

A habeas action is filed once pleading that seeks affirmative relief on the merits is filed, and not a mere request for appointment of counsel.[63] Under some circumstances prisoners may amend their petitions and add certain claims after the statute of limitations has expired. In 2005, the Court held in *Mayle v. Felix*[64] that under Rule 15(b), the petitioner may amend the petition to add claims after the statute of limitations has expired, but those additional claims will not "relate back" if they are supported by facts that differ in time and type from those alleged in the original, timely filed petition. In *Felix*, the Court concluded that the claim the petitioner sought to add was not based on a single "transaction or occurrence" when in his original petition he alleged a Confrontation Clause violation concerning the admission of a prosecution witness' videotaped testimony, and his amendment alleged that the police used coercion to extract statements from him and that admitting those statements violated the Fifth Amendment. The Court rejected the argument that because both claims arose out of the same trial, they arose out of the "same core of operative facts."

The statute of limitations bar is not jurisdictional, but is an affirmative defense, which may be waived by the state. However, the trial court may accept an amended answer raising the limita-

---

the limitations provisions is consistent with the underlying principles of AEDPA and has not resulted in abuse and delay, and that refusal to recognize equitable tolling for a credible claim of actual innocence would be constitutionally problematic); O'Neal v. Lampert, 199 F.Supp.2d 1064 (D.Or. 2002) (finding that creating an actual-innocence exception to the habeas corpus statute of limitations is a logical extension of the well-established rule that a habeas corpus petitioner may circumvent a "procedural default" by proving his "actual innocence"). See also Comment, 90 Cal.L.Rev. 2101 (2002) (arguing for an actual innocence exception to the statute of limitations, criticizing the harsh effects of the one-year filing limit, collecting cases); Note, 27 N.Y.U.Rev.L. & Soc.Change 343 (2001–02).

But compare Araujo v. Chandler, 435 F.3d 678 (7th Cir.2005) (there is no exception to the statute of limitations for claims of innocence; in any event petitioner has made an insufficient showing to raise the inference

that he is actually innocent, noting that the Eighth Circuit has concluded innocence is relevant to tolling the statute of limitations but the petitioner must show reasonable diligence in discovering the facts underlying his claim, and that the sixth Circuit recognizes an exception to the statute of limitations for petitioners who can demonstrate that it is more likely than not that no reasonable juror would have found him guilty, collecting authority); Arthur v. Allen, 452 F.3d 1234 (11th Cir.2006) (declining to reach the issue of whether the Suspension Clause requires an innocence exception to the limitations period because the petitioner failed to make a sufficient showing of actual innocence).

[63] Woodford v. Garceau, 538 U.S. 202, 123 S.Ct. 1398, 155 L.Ed.2d 363 (2003).

[64] Mayle v. Felix, 545 U.S. 644, 125 S.Ct. 2562, 162 L.Ed.2d 582 (2005).

tions bar, or raise the limitations issue sua sponte.[65]

For states that qualify for the special habeas procedures for capital cases provided in §§ 2261 et seq., § 2263 imposes a shorter, 180-day time limitation. The time limitation under § 2263 runs from the "final state court affirmance of the conviction and sentence on direct review or the expiration of the time for seeking [such] review," but then is tolled during the pendency of a petition for certiorari filed with the Supreme Court and the pendency of an initial state collateral challenge. In addition, subsection (3) provides for a 30-day extension under special circumstances.[66]

§ 28.5(c) Successive petitions: claims previously advanced

Under the current statute, a habeas petitioner may raise any particular claim only once. This limitation is a significant departure from the common law rule that the doctrine of res judicata did not apply to the rulings of the habeas court. Denied relief by one judge, a prisoner could simply turn to another, seeking the same relief on the same grounds. Although numerous explanations have been offered, the earlier refusal to limit habeas applications through the doctrine of res judicata is most frequently attributed to the traditional absence of direct appellate review of writ denials.[67] Accordingly, in *Salinger v. Loisel*,[68] a 1924 ruling, the Supreme Court concluded that, with appellate review long available in the federal system, a habeas court could give the rejection of a previous application such weight as it deemed appropriate in light of factors such as the "fullness of the consideration" given to the prior application.

The demise of this flexible approach was gradual. When the habeas statutes were revised in 1948, § 2244 provided that no

---

[65]In a 5:4 decision, the Court held that unlike most affirmative defenses, the defense of statute of limitations in a habeas proceeding may, but need not, be considered by the court sua sponte, so long as the court accords the parties fair notice and an opportunity to present their positions. Day v. McDonough, __ U.S. __, 126 S.Ct. 1675, 164 L.Ed.2d 376 (2006). The Court suggested the same rule that applies to other "threshold constraints" on habeas review, including failure to exhaust, procedural default, and non-retroactivity, which can be considered sua sponte, should apply to the limitations period. See Granberry v. Greer, 481 U.S. 129 107 S.Ct. 1671, 95 L.Ed.2d 119 (1987) (exhaustion); Caspari v. Bohlen, 510 U.S. 383, 114 S.Ct. 948, 127 L.Ed.2d 236 (1994) (retroactivity). The Court did not go so far as to authorize the consideration of the statute of limitations defense if the state has made an affirmative decision to waive the defense.

[66]See § 28.8(a).

[Section 28.5(c)]

[67]See, e.g., R. Hertz & J. Liebman, 2 Federal Habeas Practice and Procedure § 28.2a (5th ed.2005); L. Yackle, Postconviction Remedies § 151 (1981 & Supp.2007).

[68]Salinger v. Loisel, 265 U.S. 224, 44 S.Ct. 519, 68 L.Ed. 989 (1924).

federal habeas court was "required to entertain an application" by a federal or state prisoner if "the legality of the [the applicant's] detention has been determined * * * on a prior application for a writ of habeas corpus and the petition presents no new ground not theretofore presented and determined, and the judge * * * is satisfied that the ends of justice will not be served by such inquiry." The benchmark ruling on the application of this early statute is *Sanders v. United States*.[69] The Court in *Sanders* considered the two-pronged question: What weight, if any, should be given to a prior disposition where the habeas petition presents (1) the same ground advanced in the prior application or (2) a ground not previously advanced? The Court's answer to the first question was the following standard: "Controlling weight may be given to denial of a prior application for federal habeas corpus or § 2255 relief only if (1) the same ground presented in the subsequent application was determined adversely to the applicant on the prior application, (2) the prior determination was on the merits, and (3) the ends of justice would not be served by reaching the merits of the subsequent application." The Court stressed that this standard determined only when a habeas court had discretion to give controlling weight to the prior adjudication. Even if the standard was met, the habeas court retained "the power" to give full consideration to a claim without regard to the prior habeas adjudication.

In 1966, Congress enacted former § 2244(b), essentially codifying the first two *Sanders* guidelines. It provided that a successive application "need not be entertained" unless the application alleges a "factual or other ground not adjudicated in the hearing of the earlier application."[70] In *Kuhlmann v. Wilson*,[71] seven justices agreed that under this provision, the "ends of justice" standard could still serve as an appropriate point of reference for determining when that discretion should be exercised to consider a claim previously decided on its merits, but as to the content of that standard, the justices disagreed. A plurality of four justices construed the "ends of justice" as limited to circumstances in which the prisoner's interest in relitigation outweighed the "countervailing interests served by * * * finality," and to those situations in which the prisoner retains the most "powerful and legitimate interest in obtaining release from custody." This is present, the plurality reasoned, "only where the petitioner supple-

---

[69] Sanders v. United States, 373 U.S. 1, 83 S.Ct. 1068, 10 L.Ed.2d 148 (1963).

[70] Ten years later Rule 9(b) of the Federal Rules Governing Section 2254 Cases was adopted, stating that such a petition "may be dismissed if it fails to allege new or different grounds for relief and the prior determination was on the merits."

[71] Kuhlmann v. Wilson, 477 U.S. 436, 106 S.Ct. 2616, 91 L.Ed.2d 364 (1986).

ments his constitutional claim with a colorable showing of factual innocence."

The 1996 Act replaced the provision interpreted in *Kuhlmann* with a new § 2244(b)(1), which simply states: "A claim presented in second or successive habeas corpus application under section 2254 that was presented in a prior application shall be dismissed." The new provision appears to impose an absolute bar to federal court review of previously raised claims. In particular, the statute removes the prior authority of federal courts to consider again a claim by a petitioner who could supplement his previously presented constitutional claim with a newly discovered evidence of "actual innocence."

A return trip to federal court with the same claim following a dismissal without prejudice for failure to exhaust is not "successive" under § 2244(b).[72] Nor is a petition successive when it challenges competency for execution and is filed when the claim is first ripe.[73] A challenge to new sentencing or administrative proceeding that had not taken place when the first petition was filed is also not successive.[74] Unripe claims regarding claims of error already raised in ongoing state proceedings must be

---

[72]See Stewart v. Martinez-Villareal, 523 U.S. 637, 118 S.Ct. 1618, 140 L.Ed.2d 849 (1998). See also Slack v. McDaniel, 529 U.S. 473, 120 S.Ct. 1595, 146 L.Ed.2d 542 (2000) ("A petition filed after a mixed petition has been dismissed under Rose v. Lundy, 455 U.S. 509, 102 S.Ct. 1198, 71 L.Ed.2d 379 (1982), discussed in § 28.5(a), at notes 9 and 21 before the district court adjudicated any claims is to be treated as 'any other first petition' and is not a second or successive petition."). The statute of limitations, however, may bar the return trip to federal court after exhaustion if too much time elapses. See also § 28.5(a) at notes 23–25, discussing the "stay and abeyance" response to this issue.

[73]See Panetti v. Quarterman, — U.S. —, 127 S.Ct. 2842, — L.Ed.2d — (2007) (holding petition alleging lack of competency for execution was not successive to earlier petition filed before competency claim was ripe, reasoning that any other interpretation of the statute would require unripe claims to be raised as a mere formality, to the benefit of no party, and would not advance the statutory goals

of finality, comity, and conservation of resources).

[74]In re Taylor, 171 F.3d 185 (4th Cir.1999) (petition challenging resentencing not successive to petition challenging first judgment); In re Cabey, 429 F.3d 93 (4th Cir.2005) (petition challenging parole proceedings is not successive to an earlier petition challenging conviction and sentence, collecting authority). But see Burton v. Stewart, — U.S. —, 127 S.Ct. 793, 166 L.Ed.2d 628 (2007) (per curiam), finding petition barred as successive when first petition did not include unripe claims concerning resentencing then on appeal in state court, distinguishing *Taylor* as a case involving a "new judgment intervening between the two habeas petitions." Compare also In re Williams, 444 F.3d 233 (4th Cir.2006) (if a habeas petitioner files an application for collateral relief that raises a denial of appeal claim and additional claims and the writ is granted on the denial of appeal claim, after the new appeal that results, any subsequent petition will be considered successive if (a) the district court ruled on the merits of the additional claims in the initial petition and (b) the petitioner

included in the first federal habeas petition, however, or lost.[75]

§ 28.5(d) Successive petitions: new claims

Prior to the 1996 amendments, a new claim in a successive petition was treated much like a claim that the petitioner failed to raise properly in state court. Even before the enactment of former § 2244 in 1966, the "abuse-of-the-writ doctrine" recognized that "the prisoner who on prior motion * * * has deliberately withheld a ground for relief need not be heard if he asserts that ground on a successive motion; his action is inequitable—an abuse of the remedy—and the court may in its discretion deny him a hearing."[76] In *Sanders*,[77] the Court furnished two illustrations of defense tactics that would constitute an abuse of the writ. The first was the prisoner who "withholds one of two grounds for federal collateral relief at the time of filing his first application in the hope of being granted two hearings rather than one." The second was the situation in which "the prisoner deliberately abandons one of his grounds at the first hearing." *Sanders* noted, however, that the federal habeas court always had "the duty" to "reach the merits" when the "ends of justice" so demand.

When Congress reframed the successive application provision in 1966, former § 2244 provided that the federal habeas court "need not entertain" a successive petition "unless the application alleges and is predicted on a factual or other ground not adjudicated on the hearing of the earlier application * * * and unless the court * * * is satisfied that the applicant has in the earlier application deliberately withheld the newly asserted ground or otherwise abused the writ." Rule 9(b) of the § 2254 Rules added that the habeas court may dismiss the application if it finds "the failure of the petitioner to assert those grounds [referring to "new and different grounds"] in a prior petition constituted an abuse of writ."

These provisions were interpreted by the Court in *McCleskey v. Zant*.[78] The Court rejected the earlier requirement that state show the petitioner deliberately withheld a claim. Instead, it

---

seeks to raise those claims again in the subsequent petition; the petitioner has a choice between deleting the improper, successive claims and proceeding only on those that were not ripe at the time of the first petition, or having the entire motion treated as a successive petition).

[75]Burton v. Stewart, __ U.S. __, 127 S.Ct. 793, 166 L.Ed.2d 628 (2007) (per curiam).

[Section 28.5(d)]

[76]See Wong Doo v. United States, 265 U.S. 239, 44 S.Ct. 524, 68 L.Ed. 999 (1924); Price v. Johnston, 334 U.S. 266, 68 S.Ct. 1049, 92 L.Ed. 1356 (1948).

[77]Sanders v. United States, 373 U.S. 1, 83 S.Ct. 1068, 10 L.Ed.2d 148 (1963).

[78]McCleskey v. Zant, 499 U.S. 467, 111 S.Ct. 1454, 113 L.Ed.2d 517

adopted the less generous "cause-and-prejudice" test, concluding that "determination of inexcusable neglect in the abuse of writ context" would be assessed by reference to the "same standard used to determine whether to excuse procedural defaults." That standard was appropriate, the Court reasoned, because "[t]he doctrines of procedural default and abuse of writ implicate nearly identical concerns flowing from the significant costs of federal habeas review."[79] In addition, *McClesky* held that a new claim would be considered, notwithstanding the absence of excuse under the cause and prejudice standard, where necessary to "correct a miscarriage of justice." This would require a "colorable showing of factual innocence," as set forth in *Kuhlmann*[80] and procedural default cases such as *Murray v. Carrier*,[81] and thereby would provide " 'an additional safeguard against compelling an innocent man to suffer an unconstitutional loss of liberty.' "

The 1996 Act replaced the § 2244(b) provision interpreted in *McCleskey* with a quite different provision on new claims. Presently § 2244(b)(2) directs that a second or successive application advancing a "claim" not presented in a prior application "shall be dismissed" unless one of two specified exceptions is found applicable.[82]

The first exception, contained in § 2244(b)(2)(A), allows for

---

(1991).

[79]Justice Marshall argued in dissent that the "strictness of the cause-and-prejudice test had been justified on the ground that the defendant's procedural default is akin to an independent and adequate state-law ground for the judgment of conviction," but here similar concerns of comity were not present. The dissent also argued that there was no need for a cause-and-prejudice test because "a habeas petitioner's own interest in liberty furnishes a powerful incentive to assert on his first petition all claims that the petitioner (or his counsel) believes have a reasonable prospect for success." However, the majority noted that "habeas corpus review may give litigants incentives to withhold claims for manipulative purposes and may establish disincentives to present claims when evidence is fresh." *McCleskey* was a capital case, and several justices in earlier cases had expressed concern about "a pattern that seems to be developing in capital cases of multiple review in which claims that could have

been presented years ago are brought forward—often in a piecemeal fashion—only after the execution date is set or becomes imminent." Woodard v. Hutchins, 464 U.S. 377, 104 S.Ct. 752, 78 L.Ed.2d 541 (1984) (Powell, J., concurring).

[80]Kuhlmann v. Wilson, 477 U.S. 436, 106 S.Ct. 2616, 91 L.Ed.2d 364 (1986), discussed in § 28.5(c) at note 71.

[81]Murray v. Carrier, 477 U.S. 478, 106 S.Ct. 2639, 91 L.Ed.2d 397 (1986), discussed in § 28.4(e) at note 72.

[82]For example, see Burton v. Stewart, __ U.S. __, 127 S.Ct. 793, 166 L.Ed.2d 628 (2007) (district court had no jurisdiction over second petition raising sentencing claim when petitioner litigated to conclusion on the merits various claims regarding his conviction, in his first petition, then brought a second petition with newly exhausted claims about his sentence).

For commentary on the treatment of successive claims under the AEDPA, see R. Hertz & J. Liebman, 2 Federal Habeas Corpus Practice and

review if the new claim relies on a new rule of constitutional law, previously unavailable, that the Supreme Court has made retroactively applicable on collateral review. This standard would appear to take its content from *Teague v. Lane*, discussed in § 28.6(c) to (e), which bars federal courts from granting relief to state prisoners based on rules of law that were not already dictated by precedent at the time the state judgment became final, unless the new rule is one that either 1) protects a class of conduct from criminal punishment or a class of persons from capital punishment or 2) relates to the accuracy of the conviction and constitutes a watershed ruling that alters the bedrock procedural elements essential to the fairness of the proceeding. Notably, unlike *Teague*, which allowed lower courts to determine for themselves when a new rule must be applied retroactively pending consideration of retroactivity by the Supreme Court, the changes to the habeas statute adopted in 1996 limit the consideration of claims in successive petitions to new rules rendered retroactive "by the Supreme Court." In *Tyler v. Cain*,[83] the Court interpreted this provision to require a petitioner who brings a second or successive petition to identify a Supreme Court holding that "necessarily dictate[s] retroactivity of the new rule." The Court explained that it is not sufficient to point to a Supreme Court decision that either 1) "establishes principles of retroactivity and leaves the application of those principles to lower courts," or 2) suggests in dictum that the new rule is retroactively applicable. The *Tyler* Court argued that this strict reading of the statute makes sense given the very short time period within which courts of appeals had to determine whether applications for relief are warranted, noting that it is unlikely that a court could make such a determination if it had to do more than simply rely on Supreme Court holdings. The Court also rejected the petitioner's claim that this interpretation would block relief entirely for petitioners seeking to raise a valid claim in a second petition, noting, "we do not have license to question" the decision of Congress to establish stringent procedural requirements for retroactive application of new rules. Supplying the fifth vote, Justice O'Connor concurred, and explained that "the Court * * * can be said to have 'made' a rule retroactive within the meaning of § 2244(b)(2)(A) only where the Court's holdings logically permit no other conclusion than that the rule is retroactive." Applying this exception, lower courts have permitted petitioners to bring

---

Procedure Ch. 28 (5th ed.2005); Stevenson, The Politics of Fear and Death: Successive Problems in Capital Federal Habeas Corpus Cases, 77 N.Y.U.L.

Rev. 699 (2002).

[83] Tyler v. Cain, 533 U.S. 656, 121 S.Ct. 2478, 150 L.Ed.2d 632 (2001).

successive petitions raising claims under *Atkins v. Virginia*,[84] barring the execution of the mentally retarded.[85]

The second exception, recognized in § 2244(b)(2)(B), allows for the review of certain claims based on newly discovered evidence. This exception has two requirements. The factual predicate for the new claim must be one that could not have been discovered previously through "due diligence." Second, the "facts underlying the claim, if proven and viewed in light of the evidence as a whole" must be "sufficient to establish by clear and convincing evidence that but for the constitutional error, no reasonable factfinder would have found the applicant guilty of the underlying offense." Section 2244(b)(2), then, is much narrower than the *Sykes/McClesky* formula that it superseded. *McClesky* allowed for review of a new claim with a showing of cause and prejudice, or actual innocence. Under the new provision, only one type of situation other than a retroactively applied rule, discussed earlier, counts as cause. Only when the petitioner can demonstrate that he was unable with due diligence to discover the factual predicate for his new claim will that claim be considered. This may encompass many cases of state interference that would have qualified as "cause" under the former standards (*Brady* violations and the like). But many petitioners who would have been able to establish "cause" under the old standard can no longer demonstrate under the new standard that the factual predicate for their claims was previously undiscoverable. For example, the incompetence of trial or appellate counsel in failing to discover, or recognize the significance of, certain facts, even if amounting to a denial of the right to the effective assistance of counsel, falls short of proof that the facts could not have been discovered by a duly diligent attorney and client.[86]

Addressing a similar requirement from another section of AEDPA in *Johnson v. United States*,[87] the Court considered a case where the applicant sought relief from his federal sentence

---

[84]Atkins v. Virginia, 536 U.S. 304, 122 S.Ct. 2242, 153 L.Ed.2d 335 (2002). *Atkins* is discussed in § 26.4(h) at note 155.

[85]E.g. Ochoa v. Sirmons, 485 F.3d 538 (10th Cir.2007) (collecting authority).

[86]See Woratzeck v. Stewart, 118 F.3d 648 (9th Cir.1997) (due diligence not established); In re Magwood, 113 F.3d 1544 (11th Cir.1997) (same). See also Crone v. Cockrell, 324 F.3d 833 (5th Cir.2003) (second petition barred when claim had arisen prior to the fil-

ing of his initial petition, but was unexhausted).

[87]Johnson v. United States, 544 U.S. 295, 125 S.Ct. 1571, 161 L.Ed.2d 542 (2005). See also Johnson v. Dretke, 442 F.3d 901 (5th Cir.2006) (when petitioner seeks to raise *Brady* claim and meet newly discovered evidence exception to bar of successive petitions, noting that a separate showing of due diligence under 2244(b)(2)(B) is required, and the petitioner may not rely solely upon the ultimate merits of the *Brady* claim in order to demonstrate due diligence).

under § 2255 based on a state court decision vacating one of the prior convictions on which that sentence was based. A "state-court vacatur" of a prior conviction is essentially a fact not previously discoverable, giving rise to a new one-year limitations period within which to file an application for relief under § 2255, the Court concluded. But the vacatur sets a new limitations period running "only if the petitioner has shown due diligence in seeking the order." Diligence can be shown by prompt action on the part of the petitioner as soon as he is in a position to realize that he has an interest in challenging the prior conviction, which the Court determined was the date that the federal judgment is entered. Likewise, for a petitioner who basis his § 2255 claim on the result of a DNA test, the one year limitations period begins to run from the date that the test result is "discovered," but only if the petitioner began the testing process with reasonable promptness once the DNA sample and testing technology became available. The majority was unmoved by the view of the four dissenting justices who argued that the statutory exception did not depend on the petitioner's diligence in commencing promptly the process of securing the vacatur, that the states are free to set their own diligence requirements, and that defense counsel should not be saddled with the additional burden of seeking collateral relief in state court during the critical time immediately after judgment and before appeal. In *Johnson*, the defendant waited three years after his federal judgment to attack his underlying state conviction, "prolonged inattention" that the Court held was not excused by Johnson's pro se status or procedural ignorance.

Limiting the scope of the § 2244(b)(2) exception for claims in successive petitions even further is the requirement that a petitioner must also show that "the facts underlying the claim, if proven and viewed in light of the evidence as a whole, would be sufficient to establish by clear and convincing evidence that, but for constitutional error, no reasonable fact-finder would have found the applicant guilty of the underlying offense." Several features of this innocence standard warrant notice. First, the clear and convincing showing required is very demanding. Second, the new provision permits relief only for petitioners who can show that no reasonable fact-finder would have found the petitioner guilty of "the underlying offense," conceivably prohibiting successive claims challenging only a sentence.[88] Third, the innocence test in § 2244(b)(2) also restricts the types of errors that

---

[88]See LaFevers v. Gibson, 238 F.3d 1263 (10th Cir.2001) (collecting conflicting authority). Consider also In re Lott, 424 F.3d 446 (6th Cir.2005) (assertion of actual innocence under 2244(b)(2)(B), specifically that the police invented the confession, does not constitute a waiver of the attorney-

may be reviewed under the exception to those that would affect a jury's assessment of guilt. Review of newly discovered errors that do not affect the fact-finder's assessment of guilt, such as jury discrimination or the introduction of evidence obtained in violation of the defendant's right to counsel, would presumably be barred. A claim based on newly discovered evidence that the petitioner's jury venire was selected in violation of the Sixth Amendment, or that the defendant was singled out for prosecution because of his race or gender, also would not qualify. Because a similar showing of effect on guilt—either "prejudice" or "actual innocence"—is required in order to obtain federal review of such a claim even in a first petition should the defendant fail to raise it in state court,[89] conceivably a state could completely escape scrutiny of such errors by successfully secreting the facts that would prove the violation until after the petitioner's first habeas petition is filed. As mentioned earlier in the discussion of the actual innocence exception to the cause-and-prejudice analysis for claims defaulted in state court,[90] this scheme seems to assume that sufficient incentive to comply with these innocence-neutral constitutional requirements would be provided by scrutiny of the claims of defendants who manage to discover and effectively raise such claims in state court.

To avoid the successive petition bar, petitioners will sometimes cast their applications for relief as filed under another Rule or statute. If a petitioner who has already filed a first petition under § 2254 subsequently files a Rule 60(b) motion for reconsideration of the district judge's order, that motion must be treated as a second application for relief if it presents a new claim, presents new evidence in support of a claim already litigated, or relies on a purported change in the law governing the prior claim. Any motion attacking the federal court's previous resolution of a claim on the merits advances a "claim." But a Rule 60(b) motion attacking "not the substance of the federal court's resolution of a claim on the merits, but some defect in the integrity of the federal ha-

---

client and work product privileges, although courts have found an implied waiver of privileges when the petitioner injects into the litigation an issue that requires testimony from his attorneys, such as his own counsel's ineffectiveness). Compare id. (Boggs, J., dissenting) ("For a petitioner to show he is entirely innocent, and that he is truly deserving of extraordinary relief, one would think he must be willing to test his innocence against literally all the evidence, including whatever is protected by privilege.").

[89] See § 28.4(d) and (e).

[90] See § 28.4(e). The Court has yet to decide of the restrictions on successive petitions in § 2244 apply as well to petitions filed originally in the Supreme Court under § 2241. See Felker v. Turpin, 518 U.S. 651, 116 S.Ct. 2333, 135 L.Ed.2d 827 (1996) (noting "whether or not we are bound by these restrictions they certainly inform our consideration of original habeas corpus petitions").

beas proceedings," such as fraud on the federal court, is properly considered under Rule 60(b). Announcing and applying this standard in *Gonzalez v. Crosby*, the Court considered a prisoner's allegation that the district court had misapplied the one-year statute of limitations in deciding not to reach the merits of a claim. This allegation, the Court reasoned, was the proper subject of a Rule 60 motion and should not be treated as a second application for relief.[91]

§ 28.5(e) Successive petitions: court of appeals certification

Another innovation of § 2244(b) is its subdivision (3), making the court of appeals the "gatekeeper" in applying the standards described above for second or successive petitions. Before filing a second or successive petition, the petitioner must seek from the court of appeals an order authorizing the district court to consider the second or successive petition. The statute states that a three-judge panel must rule on whether the "application makes a prima facie showing" that it will satisfy the standard for filing a second or successive petition, and make that ruling within 30 days. While courts of appeals are understandably reluctant to bind themselves to demanding (or even unrealistic) deadlines, an overly relaxed approach to the 30-day period may undercut Congressional efforts to streamline habeas proceedings.[92] The Court in *Tyler v. Cain*,[93] relied on this provision in concluding that courts of appeals in only 30 days cannot be expected to conduct an independent retroactivity analysis for every new rule raised in an application to file a successive petition, and need only determine if the Supreme Court has actually held that the particular new rule applies retroactively. *Tyler* suggests that the Court is inclined to

---

[91]Gonzalez v. Crosby, 545 U.S. 524, 125 S.Ct. 2641, 162 L.Ed.2d 480 (2005). When a petitioner makes a motion that includes both claims that should be treated as a second petition and claims that raise a defect in the habeas proceedings and this is properly considered under Rule 60(b), lower courts have divided over the proper approach. Some have instructed district courts to take an all or nothing approach and require a movant bringing such a "mixed" motion to seek authorization to file the entire motion as a successive petition, or else dismiss the successive claims and proceed on the true Rule 60(b) claims. In the Tenth Circuit, courts address the merits of the true Rule 60(b) allegations, then forward the succes-sive claims to the court of appeals for authorization to file them as a succes-sive petition. Spitznas v. Boone, 464 F.3d 1213 (10th Cir.2006) (collecting conflicting authority).

[Section 28.5(e)]

[92]See generally Ryan, Rush to Judgment: A Constitutional Analysis of Time Limits on Judicial Decisions, 77 B.U.L.Rev. 761 (1997) (noting that while "ignoring" the time limit would exhibit "too little respect for Congress's legitimate constitutional role in regulating court procedure," courts should treat "the time limit strictly as a command to prioritize" their workload).

[93]Tyler v. Cain, 533 U.S. 656, 121 S.Ct. 2478, 150 L.Ed.2d 632 (2001).

take Congress at its word and interpret the thirty-day limit literally.

The panel's decision granting or denying the application is "not appealable" and "shall not be the subject of a petition for rehearing or for a writ of certiorari."[94] Thus, if the application is denied, the petitioner cannot seek further judicial action, apart from an original petition to the Supreme Court.

§ 28.6 Constitutional interpretation on habeas review

§ 28.6(a)   The changing role of federal habeas courts
§ 28.6(b)   *Teague*: limiting the retroactive application of new rules of procedure
§ 28.6(c)   Determining when a state conviction becomes final
§ 28.6(d)   The "new rule" concept
§ 28.6(e)   The *Teague* exceptions
§ 28.6(f)   Review of state court rulings under § 2254(d)
§ 28.6(g)   Harmless error on habeas review

§ 28.6(a) The changing role of federal habeas courts

From the mid 1950s through the 1970s, federal courts exercised expansive habeas review of state court decisions. Both of the separate opinions for the Court in *Brown v. Allen*[1] had flatly rejected the contention that a state court's interpretation of the Constitution should be binding on the federal habeas court. *Brown* directed federal habeas courts to "independently apply the correct constitutional standards" to a petitioner's claim, "no matter how fair and completely the claim had been litigated in state courts." The function of the 1867 Habeas Act, characterized by Justice Frankfurter, was to give to federal courts the "final say" on the merits of a state prisoner's federal constitutional claim. In exercising de novo review of constitutional questions, the federal habeas court was to give the state court's adjudication no more "weight" than what "federal practice [commonly] gives to the conclusion of a court last resort of another jurisdiction on federal constitutional issues."

Almost forty years after *Brown*, the Court in *Teague v. Lane*[2] substantially altered the nature of that "final say" given to the federal habeas courts. *Teague* barred retroactive application of

---

[94]28 U.S.C.A. § 2244(b)(3)(E).

[Section 28.6(a)]

[1]Brown v. Allen, 344 U.S. 443, 73 S.Ct. 397, 97 L.Ed. 469 (1953), discussed in § 28.3(b) at note 55.

[2]Teague v. Lane, 489 U.S. 288, 109 S.Ct. 1060, 103 L.Ed.2d 334 (1989). *Teague* is also discussed in § 2.11(e) at notes 54–65. See also the debate on this point in Wright v. West, 505 U.S. 277, 112 S.Ct. 2482, 120 L.Ed.2d 225 (1992).

new rules of constitutional law to habeas petitions. The task of the federal habeas court was not to ask if a petitioner was in custody in violation of the Constitution, but to ask whether the state court's interpretation of federal law was a reasonable reading of the Supreme Court precedent prevailing at the point in time when the opportunity for direct review of the prisoner's conviction ended. The passage of the 1996 Act narrowed habeas review of state court decisions further still. Congress in § 2254(d) explicitly rejected de novo consideration of constitutional claims, and barred relief unless "the adjudication of the claim by the State court * * * resulted in a decision that was contrary to, or involved an unreasonable application of, clearly established Federal Law as determined by the Supreme Court of the United States * * *." This new standard for reviewing state court decisions limited relief in ways similar to *Teague*, but did not displace *Teague*. As the Court explained in *Horn v. Banks*,[3] "[T]he AEDPA and *Teague* inquiries are distinct * * *. [I]n addition to performing any analysis required by the AEDPA, a federal court considering a habeas petition must conduct a threshold *Teague* analysis when the issue is properly raised by the state." The meaning of § 2254(d) is discussed in subsection 28.6(f), below, following an analysis of *Teague* and its progeny in subsections 28.6(b) through 28.6(e).

§ 28.6(b) *Teague*: limiting the retroactive application of new rules of procedure

The habeas petitioner in *Teague* raised a constitutional objection to the prosecutor's use of peremptory challenges to exclude African Americans from his jury. While his habeas petition was working its way through the federal appellate process, the Supreme Court decided *Batson v. Kentucky*,[4] barring racial discrimination in the use of peremptory challenges. *Teague* argued that *Batson* sustained his constitutional claim. He further argued that even if *Batson* had come too late for him to take advantage of the *Batson* ruling itself, a similar prohibition should be incorporated into the Sixth Amendment right to a jury venire selected from a fair cross-section of the community, a right that had been recognized several years prior to his conviction.[5]

The issue addressed by the Court was whether a habeas petitioner could gain the benefit of a Supreme Court ruling that had come after the exhaustion of the direct appellate review of

---

[3]Horn v. Banks, 536 U.S. 266, 122 S.Ct. 2147, 153 L.Ed.2d 301 (2002) (per curiam).

[Section 28.6(b)]

[4]Batson v. Kentucky, 476 U.S.

79, 106 S.Ct. 1712, 90 L.Ed.2d 69 (1986), discussed in § 22.3(d) at note 187.

[5]See § 22.2(d).

his conviction and had clearly expanded constitutional protection beyond what previous precedent had required. A majority agreed that, subject to certain exceptions, a habeas petitioner's conviction should be reviewed by reference to the "law prevailing at the time [his] conviction became final."[6]

Justice O'Connor's plurality opinion derived this "law-at-the-time" principle from what was described as the "deterrence function" of the habeas writ. A central function of federal habeas review, it was argued, is ensuring that the state courts faithfully apply the prevailing "constitutional principles" as announced by the Supreme Court. Because the Supreme Court's docket limitations preclude its review of all but a small number of state court departures from prevailing constitutional principles, habeas review in the lower federal courts was needed to deter state courts from taking advantage of the likelihood that their departures from prevailing precedents would escape Supreme Court review. Federal habeas review was to "serve as a necessary incentive for trial and appellate judges * * * to conduct their proceedings in a manner consistent with established constitutional principles." Such a "deterrence function" requires only that the conviction be reviewed by reference to the law prevailing at the time of its final review in the state system. The state courts can hardly be required to have applied constitutional principles that did not yet exist. Hence, a federal habeas court, as a general principle, should not invalidate a conviction based upon a "new ruling" of constitutional law issued after state review had ended. The *Teague* plurality opinion recognized two exceptions to the "law-at-the-time" principle, which are discussed in subsection 28.6(e).

Unless the exceptions apply, a habeas petitioner could not obtain the benefit of either 1) a "new" Supreme Court ruling decided after his conviction became final,[7] or 2) a "new" expansion of the protection established by preexisting precedent (i.e., the Supreme Court rulings prevailing at the time the conviction

---

[6]The Court rejected the argument that an earlier standard used by the Court to determine retroactivity should govern habeas claims. See § 2.11(a)-(c) (discussing the *Linkletter-Stovall* standard for assessing retroactivity), and see § 2.11(e), discussing the differences between *Linkletter* and *Teague*.

[7]The "law-at-the-time" principle, while preventing relief based on "new" rules, does not always allow relief based on old rules. Petitioners may not take advantage of previously decided favorable decisions that have since been discredited. Thus, if the habeas court should find that the petitioner clearly should have prevailed on his claim on the basis of the law of the time, but the Supreme Court has subsequently adopted a new ruling that narrows constitutional protection and defeats that claim, relief will be denied on the ground that the petitioner is not now being held in custody in violation of the Constitution. See Lockhart v. Fretwell, 506 U.S. 364, 113 S.Ct. 838, 122 L.Ed.2d 180 (1993).

became final). As the Court stated later in *Stringer v. Black*,[8] "the interests in finality, predictability and comity underlying our new rule jurisprudence may be undermined [either] * * * by the invocation of a rule that was not dictated by precedent * * * [or by] the application of an old rule in a manner that was not dictated by precedent." Thus, the *Teague* Court concluded that a habeas court could neither apply retroactively the *Batson* decision, which came after the defendant's conviction had become final, nor itself establish a new ruling by reading a similar prohibition into a series of Sixth Amendment cases that had been decided before the defendant's conviction became final.

The Court has distilled the "*Teague* inquiry" into "three steps."[9] Each of those steps will be explored in the following subsections. First, the habeas court must determine the date on which the petitioner's conviction became final. Second, the habeas court must consider "whether 'a state court considering [the petitioner's] claim at the time his conviction became final would have felt compelled by existing precedent to conclude that the rule [he] seeks was required by the Constitution.' "[10] If not, then the rule is new, and as a third step the "court must determine whether the rule nonetheless falls within one of the two narrow exceptions to the *Teague* doctrine." The Supreme Court also applies the *Teague* analysis as a "threshold matter" before reaching the merits of a petitioner's claim.[11] However, because "the *Teague* inquiry requires a detailed analysis of federal constitutional law," and "[c]onstitutional issues are generally to be avoided," the Court has suggested that normally a habeas court should first consider other prerequisites for habeas review, such as whether the petitioner is "in custody" or whether the state judgment was based on an independent and adequate state ground,[12] before turning to the *Teague* analysis.[13] If the state does not argue the *Teague* bar, a federal court may, but need not conduct a *Teague* analysis.[14]

---

[8] Stringer v. Black, 503 U.S. 222, 112 S.Ct. 1130, 117 L.Ed.2d 367 (1992).

[9] O'Dell v. Netherland, 521 U.S. 151, 117 S.Ct. 1969, 138 L.Ed.2d 351 (1997).

[10] *O'dell* (quoting Lambrix v. Singletary, 520 U.S. 518, 117 S.Ct. 1517, 137 L.Ed.2d 771 (1997)).

[11] Horn v. Banks, 536 U.S. 266, 122 S.Ct. 2147, 153 L.Ed.2d 301 (2002). See also Campiti v. Matesanz, 333 F.3d 317 (1st Cir.2003) (collecting

authority on whether *Teague* must be applied before reaching other issues).

[12] Horn v. Banks, 536 U.S. 266, 122 S.Ct. 2147, 153 L.Ed.2d 301 (2002).

[13] Lambrix v. Singletary, 520 U.S. 518, 117 S.Ct. 1517, 137 L.Ed.2d 771 (1997).

[14] Bradshaw v. Stumpf, 545 U.S. 175, 125 S.Ct. 2398, 2405, 162 L.Ed.2d 143 (2005); Goeke v. Branch, 514 U.S. 115, 115 S.Ct. 1275, 131 L.Ed.2d 152 (1995) (per curiam).

§ 28.6(c) Determining when a state conviction becomes final

A petitioner's state conviction is final only after the time has expired for filing a petition for certiorari from the state judgment affirming the conviction, or after the Court has denied certiorari.[15] This point in time is arguably inconsistent with the deterrence rationale of *Teague*, since the opportunity of the state courts to evade federal law normally ends prior to the time defendant seeks certiorari review in the United States Supreme Court.[16] The assumption may be that if certiorari were sought, the Court could remand the case to the state court for reconsideration in light of its new rule, so that the state appellate court would have an opportunity to apply any new ruling handed down between the time of its decision and the Supreme Court's disposal of a petition for certiorari. Even where the defense failed to seek certiorari the defendant is likely to have had a chance to petition the state court for a rehearing prior to the exhaustion of the time period for filing for certiorari.[17]

§ 28.6(d) The "new rule" concept

The second step in applying *Teague* is to determine whether the rule on which the petitioner relies is a "new" rule of criminal procedure, given precedent at the time the conviction became final.[18] Speaking for a plurality in *Teague*, Justice O'Connor advanced a broad definition of a new ruling that was later

---

[Section 28.6(c)]

[15]See Sawyer v. Smith, 497 U.S. 227, 232, 110 S.Ct. 2822, 2826, 111 L.Ed.2d 193 (1990); Saffle v. Parks, 494 U.S. 484, 110 S.Ct. 1257, 108 L.Ed.2d 415 (1990).

[16]See Hoffman, The Supreme Court's New Vision of Federal Habeas Corpus for State Prisoners, 1989 Sup.Ct.Rev. 165.

[17]Some commentators have argued that placing finality at the denial of certiorari is appropriate in order to give the state prisoner "at least one opportunity for federal judicial declaration of a new rule following the state court's refusal to declare it." R. Hertz & J. Liebman, 2 Federal Habeas Corpus Practice and Procedure § 25.6 (5th ed.2005). Including the denial of certiorari in the formula creates difficult anomalies. See Arkin, The Prisoner's Dilemma: Life in the Lower Federal Courts After *Teague v. Lane*,

69 N.C.L.Rev. 371 (1991) (noting the Supreme Court's timing rule in *Teague* means that a person may be executed or not, depending upon the date on which his petition for certiorari is denied).

[Section 28.6(d)]

[18]The Court in Bousley v. United States, 523 U.S. 614, 118 S.Ct. 1604, 140 L.Ed.2d 828 (1998), discussed in § 21.4(c) at note 83, and in § 28.9(b) at note 36, explained that *Teague* bars only application of new rules of *procedure,* not interpretations of substantive law. "[D]ecisions of this Court holding that a substantive federal criminal statute does not reach certain conduct * * * necessarily carry a significant risk that a defendant stands convicted of 'an act that the law does not make criminal.' * * * Accordingly, it would be inconsistent with the doctrinal underpinnings of habeas review to preclude petitioner from relying" on such a decision in a proceeding under

extended to include applications of prior precedent that would not have been classified as new rulings under the Supreme Court's previous retroactivity decisions.[19] She acknowledged that it was "often difficult to determine when a case announces a new rule," and declined to "attempt to define the spectrum of what may or may not constitute a new rule" for retroactivity purposes. She added, however, that

> in general * * *, a case announces a new rule when it breaks new ground or imposes a new obligation on the States or the Federal Government. See e.g., *Rock v. Arkansas*,[20] (per se rule excluding all hypnotically refreshed testimony infringes impermissibly on a criminal defendant's right to testify on his behalf); *Ford v. Wainwright*,[21] (Eighth Amendment prohibits the execution of prisoners who are insane). To put it differently, a case announces a new rule if the result was not dictated by precedent existing at the time the defendant's conviction became final.

Because *Rock* and *Ford* were quite expansive interpretations of past precedents, as was the ruling petitioner sought to gain in *Teague*, it was far from clear as to how literally lower courts should read Justice O'Connor's reference to a result "not dictated" by precedent. In *Penry v. Lynaugh*,[22] the Court suggested that what was "dictated" should not be read too narrowly, and that it would include the application of the logic of the earlier precedent to an analogous situation. The case involved a petitioner's challenge that the Texas capital sentencing scheme unconstitutionally limited the jury's consideration of mitigating evidence. Justice O'Connor, speaking for the *Penry* majority, concluded that upholding petitioner's challenge did not demand a new rule as it "merely asked the State to fulfill the assurances upon which [the Court's prior precedent] was based" by applying a general

---

§ 2255."

[19]In earlier decisions applying the *Linkletter-Stovall* standard to assess the retroactive application of intervening Supreme Court decisions, the Court had held that considerably less expansion of earlier precedent than was called for by the petitioner in *Teague* had rendered those decisions new rulings. An intervening ruling deciding a true case of first impression in the Supreme Court was likely to be deemed a new ruling, even where it relied on concepts developed in earlier precedent. This was especially so if a former decision specifically had left open the issue decided in the intervening ruling, or if the intervening ruling overturned a widely accepted practice. On the other hand, there was not a new ruling when the intervening Supreme Court decisions had "simply applied a well-established constitutional principle to govern a case which [was] closely analogous to those which had been previously covered in the prior case law." Desist v. United States, 394 U.S. 244, 89 S.Ct. 1030, 22 L.Ed.2d 248 (1969) (Harlan, J., dissenting).

[20]Rock v. Arkansas, 483 U.S. 44, 107 S.Ct. 2704, 97 L.Ed. 37 (1987), discussed in § 24.5(d) at note 44.

[21]Ford v. Wainwright, 477 U.S. 399, 106 S.Ct. 2595, 91 L.Ed.2d 335 (1986).

[22]Penry v. Lynaugh, 492 U.S. 302, 109 S.Ct. 2934, 106 L.Ed.2d 256 (1989).

prohibition that was "clear" under earlier rulings. Again in *Stringer v. Black*,[23] the Court held that the rule of *Clemons v. Mississippi*,[24] which applied a rule concerning invalid aggravating factors in death sentencing to "weighing" states, also was not "new" under *Teague*. The majority noted: "The purpose of the new rule doctrine is to validate reasonable interpretations of existing precedents. Reasonableness in this, as in many other contexts, is an objective standard, and the ultimate decision * * * [must be] based on an objective reading of the relevant cases."

More frequently, however, the Court has found that the rule advanced by a petitioner is new, precluding habeas relief.[25] An abrupt break from past precedent, such as the Court's decision in *Crawford v. Washington*,[26] is perhaps the classic "new" rule.[27] But a decision need not overrule a prior decision in order to qualify as "new." In *Butler v. McKellar*,[28] for example, the Court rejected the petitioner's claim that the rule upon which he relied fell within the "logical compass" of an earlier precedent and as a result was not a new rule. There had been a significant difference among the lower courts as to whether the rule advanced by the petitioner followed from that precedent, and that division of authority in itself provided proof that the state court in rejecting the rule had adopted a position "susceptible to debate among reasonable minds."

Two closely divided decisions by the Court in 1997 illustrate that the "new rule" concept of *Teague* can be difficult to apply.[29] In *Lambrix v. Singletary*,[30] the majority characterized *Teague's* holding this way: It was not enough that the rule sought to be

---

[23]Stringer v. Black, 503 U.S. 222, 112 S.Ct. 1130, 117 L.Ed.2d 367 (1992).

[24]Clemons v. Mississippi, 494 U.S. 738, 110 S.Ct. 1441, 108 L.Ed.2d 725 (1990).

[25]See Saffle v. Parks, 494 U.S. 484, 110 S.Ct. 1257, 108 L.Ed.2d 415 (1990); Butler v. McKellar, 494 U.S. 407, 110 S.Ct. 1212, 108 L.Ed.2d 347 (1990); Sawyer v. Smith, 497 U.S. 227, 232, 110 S.Ct. 2822, 2826, 111 L.Ed.2d 193 (1990); Caspari v. Bohlen, 510 U.S. 383, 114 S.Ct. 948, 127 L.Ed.2d 236 (1994); Gilmore v. Taylor, 508 U.S. 333, 113 S.Ct. 2112, 124 L.Ed.2d 306 (1993); Goeke v. Branch, 514 U.S. 115, 115 S.Ct. 1275, 131 L.Ed.2d 152 (1995); Gray v. Netherland, 518 U.S. 152, 116 S.Ct. 2074, 135 L.Ed.2d 457 (1996).

[26]Crawford v. Washington, 541 U.S. 36 (2004) (overruling Ohio v. Roberts, 448 U.S. 56 (1980)).

[27]A unanimous Court so held in Whorton v. Bockting, __ U.S. __, 127 S.Ct. 1173, 167 L.Ed.2d 1 (2007).

[28]Butler v. McKellar, 494 U.S. 407, 110 S.Ct. 1212, 108 L.Ed.2d 347 (1990).

[29]Cf. Friedman, Failed Enterprise, 83 Cal.L.Rev. 485 (1995) (terming *Teague* a "disaster of judicial administration," and noting that the case "requires lawyers and judges to churn out countless pages arguing over something that has nothing to do with the merits, seems to have no precedential value from case to case, and is * * * nearly impenetrable anyway").

[30]Lambrix v. Singletary, 520 U.S. 518, 117 S.Ct. 1517, 137 L.Ed.2d 771

applied by the habeas petitioner was "a reasonable interpretation of prior law—perhaps even the most reasonable one"; *Teague* asks "whether no other interpretation was reasonable." Applying this standard, the majority detailed three "reasonable" approaches that would have suggested a rule other than the one the petitioner advanced, given the precedent at the time that his conviction became final. Four justices disagreed.

Similarly, in *O'Dell v. Netherland*,[31] the Court held that its decision in *Simmons v. South Carolina*,[32] which provided that a capital defendant should be permitted to inform his sentencing jury that he may be ineligible for parole, was a new rule for *Teague* purposes. The majority first reviewed the "complex" "legal landscape" present at the time the petitioner's conviction became final. One line of cases had protected the right of a capital defendant to introduce certain mitigating evidence at his sentencing hearing, specifically, evidence that he had behaved himself in prison and would not pose a danger if incarcerated. The majority found it significant that one of the cases relied upon by the petitioner "produced seven opinions, none for a majority of the Court," and noted that the holding of that case was that expressed by the justice who concurred on the narrowest grounds.[33] The majority also disavowed the statement by the Court in the *Simmons* case itself that its decision was "compelled" by another earlier case, noting that this characterization failed to demonstrate that *Simmons* was not new under *Teague*. A competing line of cases, the majority argued, established the "general proposition that the States retained the prerogative to determine how much (if at all) juries would be informed about the postsentencing legal regime." Thus, "a reasonable jurist * * * would not have felt compelled to adopt the rule later set out in *Simmons*" and could have "drawn a distinction between information about a defendant" and information concerning "postsentencing legal eventualities." The majority explained, "*Teague* asks state court judges to judge reasonably, not presciently." The four dissenters protested that "our decision in *Simmons* applied a fundamental principle that is as old as the adversary system itself, and that had been quite clearly articulated by the Court in two earlier opinions."

The Court in *Beard v. Banks*,[34] suggested that if the Supreme Court decision announcing the rule at issue is closely divided on

---

(1997).

[31]O'Dell v. Netherland, 521 U.S. 151, 117 S.Ct. 1969, 138 L.Ed.2d 351 (1997).

[32]Simmons v. South Carolina, 512 U.S. 154, 114 S.Ct. 2187, 129 L.Ed.2d

133 (1994).

[33]Citing Marks v. United States, 430 U.S. 188, 193, 97 S.Ct. 990, 993, 51 L.Ed.2d 260 (1977).

[34]Beard v. Banks, 542 U.S. 406, 124 S.Ct. 2504, 159 L.Ed.2d 494

the merits, the rule is not likely to apply retroactively. *Banks* held that the rule in *Mills v. Maryland*[35] was "new," because it "broke new ground" and was not "mandate[d]" by precedent. Pointing out that four justices dissented in *Mills*, at least one of whom protested that the decision was "stretching" precedent beyond proper bounds, the *Banks* majority concluded that "reasonable jurists differed" as to whether the rule the petitioner asked to be applied to him was "compel[led]" by existing precedent.[36]

A number of critics have accused the Court of using *Teague* analysis as an indirect method of expressing its views on the merits of a constitutional question advanced in a habeas petition that the Court has yet to address on point. A conclusion that a rule is "new" may be interpreted as tantamount to a finding that the Constitution does not include the rule, while a conclusion that a rule is not new signals the Court's approval of that interpretation of the Constitution on the merits.[37]

§ 28.6(e) The *Teague* exceptions

Two exceptions to the prohibition against applying new rules on habeas review were recognized in *Teague*. The justices relied upon arguments made by Justice Harlan in an earlier case that retroactive application should be permissible only as to two types of new rulings.

Rules Establishing Constitutionally Protected Conduct. In *Teague*, Justice O'Connor's plurality opinion and Justice Stevens' concurring opinion expressly approved of an exception for rulings that "place certain kinds of primary, private individual conduct beyond the power of the criminal law-making authority."[38] A prior example of such a rule was a holding that a statute creating an offense violated the self-incrimination privilege; all defendants previously convicted of that offense were entitled to the benefit of that new ruling.[39] Since *Teague*, the Court has reserved this exception for rules that either "decriminalize a class of conduct"

(2004).

[35]Mills v. Maryland, 486 U.S. 367, 108 S.Ct. 1860, 100 L.Ed.2d 384 (1988) (invalidating capital sentencing schemes requiring juries to disregard mitigating factors not found unanimously).

[36]Division among lower courts prior to the Court's resolution of the rule at issue is also taken as evidence that the rule is one that is "susceptible to debate among reasonable minds." Howard v. United States, 374 F.3d 1068 (11th Cir. 2004) (noting split among circuits prior to the Court's

holding in Alabama v. Shelton, 535 U.S. 654, 122 S.Ct. 1764, 152 L.Ed.2d 888 (2002), discussed in § 11.1(a)).

[37]See, e.g., Friedman, Failed Enterprise, 83 Cal.L.Rev. 485, 524–26 (1995). See also Meyer, "Nothing We Say Matters": *Teague* and New Rules, 61 U.Chi.L.Rev. 423, 459 (1994).

[Section 28.6(e)]

[38]Mackey v. United States, 401 U.S. 667, 91 S.Ct. 1160, 28 L.Ed.2d 404 (1971) (opinion of Harlan, J.).

[39]See United States v. United States Coin and Currency, 401 U.S. 715, 91 S.Ct. 1041, 28 L.Ed.2d 434

or "prohibit the imposition of capital punishment on a particular class of persons."[40] As a result, few rules have qualified.[41]

Rules of Fundamental Fairness Protecting Accuracy. The *Teague* plurality also argued that new rulings that implicate "fundamental fairness" by mandating procedures "central to an accurate determination of innocence or guilt" should be applied retroactively. This was consistent with a basic function of the habeas writ: "to assure that no man has been incarcerated under a procedure which creates an impermissibly large risk that the innocent will be convicted."[42] Speaking for the plurality, Justice O'Connor stated in *Teague* that procedures "central to an accurate determination of innocence or guilt" were best illustrated by what Justice Stevens had once described as the "classic" grounds for habeas review—the mob-dominated trial, the knowing use of perjured testimony, and conviction based on a confession "extorted from defendant by brutal methods."[43] The plurality opinion added that it seemed "unlikely that many such components of basic due process have yet to emerge."[44]

This second *Teague* exception is quite restrictive. As one judge concluded, examples of watershed rules are "hen's-teeth rare."[45] Holding out the Court's decision in *Gideon* as the "paradigmatic example of a watershed rule of criminal procedure,"[46] by 1996 the Court had "examined at least seven new rules of law against the second exception and found that none of them fits its narrow confines."[47] The Court in *Beard v. Banks*[48] summed up the application of the second *Teague* exception:

(1971) (retroactive application of ruling that invalidated, on Fifth Amendment grounds, a forfeiture proceeding for money possessed by one who failed to comply with the wagering tax law).

[40]Graham v. Collins, 506 U.S. 461, 477, 113 S.Ct. 892, 902, 122 L.Ed.2d 260 (1993) (quoting Saffle v. Parks, 494 U.S. 484, 110 S.Ct. 1257, 108 L.Ed.2d 415 (1990)).

[41]See Penry v. Lynaugh, 492 U.S. 302, 330, 109 S.Ct. 2934, 2952–53, 106 L.Ed.2d 256 (1989) (discussing rule barring execution of mentally ill defendant).

[42]Quoting Justice Harlan from Desist v. United States, 394 U.S. 244, 89 S.Ct. 1030, 22 L.Ed.2d 248 (1969).

[43]See § 28.2(d) at note 82.

[44]See § 2.4. Justices Stevens and Blackmun stated in *Teague* that they would retain this exception as described somewhat differently by Justice Harlan. Justice Harlan had described a second exception for decisions that establish a "watershed rule of criminal procedure," "implicit in the concept of ordered liberty." His formula did not necessarily include an innocence component, and referred to the basic "fundamental fairness" standard applied to define due process prior to the adoption of the selective incorporation doctrine.

[45]Sepulveda v. United States, 330 F.3d 55 (1st Cir.2003) (finding rule of *Apprendi* is not within exception for watershed rules).

[46]Gray v. Netherland, 518 U.S. 152, 116 S.Ct. 2074, 135 L.Ed.2d 457 (1996) (citing Saffle v. Parks, 494 U.S. 484, 110 S.Ct. 1257, 108 L.Ed.2d 415 (1990)).

[47]United States v. Swindall, 107 F.3d 831 (11th Cir.1997).

We have repeatedly emphasized the limited scope of the second *Teague* exception, explaining that " 'it is clearly meant to apply only to a small core of rules requiring observance of those procedures that . . . are implicit in the concept of ordered liberty.' " * * * And, because any qualifying rule "would be so central to an accurate determination of innocence or guilt [that it is] unlikely that many such components of basic due process have yet to emerge," * * *, it should come as no surprise that we have yet to find a new rule that falls under the second *Teague* exception. * * * In providing guidance as to what might fall within this exception, we have repeatedly referred to the rule of Gideon, and only to this rule.[49]

Some rulings fail the requirement that they affect the accuracy of a criminal judgment. Consider, for example, the new ruling advanced by the petitioner in *Teague*—an innovative reading of the Sixth Amendment's cross-section requirement that would have provided a *Batson*-like prohibition against racially discriminatory use of peremptory challenges. The cross-section guarantee is supported by a variety of significant values, but it "does not rest on the premise that every criminal trial, or any particular trial, is necessarily unfair because it is not conducted in accordance with what we determine to be the requirements of the Sixth Amendment." Though a *Batson*-type rule might promote accuracy in a systemic sense, it did not necessarily affect accuracy in any particular case, and it therefore fell outside of *Teague*'s second exception.

Other new rules fail the exception because they are not sufficiently fundamental, less "sweeping" than *Gideon*, which established an affirmative right to counsel in all felony cases. In *Sawyer v. Smith*,[50] the "new rule" in question was one prohibiting a prosecutorial closing argument which suggested that the ultimate responsibility for determining the appropriateness of the death penalty rested on the appellate court and thereby reduced the jury's sense of responsibility. This rule certainly was "aimed at improving the accuracy of the trial." It was not, however, a "watershed ruling" in this regard; it did not "alter our understanding of the bedrock procedural elements essential to the fairness of the proceeding." Rather it was a per se prohibition of a particular type of argument that served basically to supple-

---

[48]Beard v. Banks, 542 U.S. 406, 124 S.Ct. 2504, 159 L.Ed.2d 494 (2004).

[49]For a unique example of a *Gideon*-related rule that may fall within this exception, consider the Supreme Court's ruling in Alabama v. Shelton, 535 U.S. 654, 122 S.Ct. 1764, 152 L.Ed.2d 888 (2002), discussed in § 11.1(a). See Howard v. United States,

374 F.3d 1068 (11th Cir.2004) (noting that the Court has never found a rule that fits the second *Teague* exception, collecting authority, but concluding that the rule in *Shelton*, concerning the right to counsel, as an extension of *Gideon*, must be applied retroactively).

[50]See Sawyer v. Smith, 497 U.S. 227, 232, 110 S.Ct. 2822, 2826, 111 L.Ed.2d 193 (1990).

ment the traditional due process prohibition against closing arguments that "so infected the trial with unfairness" as to violate due process, and the lower court here had held that the prosecutor's argument had not violated that more basic standard.

In *Tyler v. Cain*[51] the Court explained in dicta that a decision holding that a rule falls within the second *Teague* exception is not the same as a decision holding that a rule is "structural error" not subject to harmless-error analysis. Classifying an error as structural does not necessarily alter our understanding of "[the] bedrock procedural elements" essential to the fairness of the proceeding. "On the contrary, the second *Teague* exception is reserved only for truly 'watershed' rules" and "[a]s we have recognized, it is unlikely that any of these watershed rules 'ha[s] yet to emerge.'"

The effects of the non-retroactivity principle are most stark in capital cases like Banks and the several cases cited there, where relief from a death sentence may turn on "an accident of timing." Consider, for example, *Schriro v. Summerlin*,[52] where the Court refused to find that the rule of *Ring v. Arizona*, entitling a defendant to a jury determination of facts that state law requires must be found before a death sentence may be imposed, fit within an exception to *Teague*. Summerlin had been sentenced to death, following a judicial finding of two facts that made him death-eligible—that he had been convicted before for a felony involving the use or threatened use of violence, and that he committed the offense in an especially heinous, cruel, or depraved manner. Summerlin sought relief from his death sentence, arguing that his sentence suffered from the same constitutional violation as Ring's, and that he deserved the same relief that Ring received. The majority rejected the dissenters' arguments that a jury finding beyond a reasonable doubt was central to an accurate determination that death is a legally appropriate punishment. Instead, the Court noted that "for every argument why juries are more accurate fact-finders, there is another why they are less accurate," and "when so many presumably reasonable minds continue to disagree over whether juries are better fact-finders *at all*, we cannot confidently say that judicial fact-finding *seriously* diminishes accuracy." Indeed, the Court reasoned, in its pre-*Teague* decision

---

[51]Tyler v. Cain, 533 U.S. 656, 121 S.Ct. 2478, 150 L.Ed.2d 632 (2001).

[52]Schriro v. Summerlin, 542 U.S. 348, 124 S.Ct. 2519, 159 L.Ed.2d 442 (2004). The Court has yet to decide whether the rule in Blakely v. Washington, 542 U.S. 296, 124 S.Ct. 2531, 159 L.Ed.2d 403 (2004), discussed in § 26.4(i) at note 183, applies retroactively. See Burton v. Stewart, __ U.S. __, 127 S.Ct. 793, 166 L.Ed.2d 628 (2007) (declining to reach question).

refusing retroactive application of *Duncan v. Louisiana*,[53] which first applied the Sixth Amendment's jury trial right to the states, the Court had stopped short of asserting " 'that every criminal trial—or any particular trial—held before a judge alone is unfair or that a defendant may never be as fairly treated by a judge as he would be by a jury.' " Rejecting the argument that judicial findings of the particular aggravator in Summerlin's case would be "impermissibly inaccurate," the majority noted that the fact to be found under state law was not "whether the offense is heinous, cruel, or depraved as *determined by community standards*." Nor was the majority persuaded that the exception should apply because the rule implicated only about 110 people on death row, posed a limited burden on the administration of justice, and the reliance interest on the part of state courts was less weighty. These arguments, it reasoned, were simply "irrelevant under *Teague*."

Other rules rejected by the Court as insufficiently fundamental include: a rule providing to capital defendants jury instructions concerning "mitigating evidence of youth, family background, and positive character traits;"[54] a rule barring jury instructions that do not warn the jury that it could not find the defendant guilty of murder without even considering voluntary manslaughter;[55] a rule prohibiting states from requiring capital sentencing juries to disregard mitigating factors not found unanimously;[56] a double jeopardy bar limiting successive noncapital sentencing proceedings;[57] and a rule that would have required notice of evidence to be used at sentencing.[58] None of these rules satisfied the two-pronged test requiring that the rule both "relate to the accuracy of the conviction" and "alter our understanding of the 'bedrock procedural elements' essential to the fundamental fairness of a proceeding."[59]

Lower courts have rejected arguments to bring within the

---

[53]Duncan v. Louisiana, 391 U.S. 145, 88 S.Ct. 1444, 20 L.Ed.2d 491 (1968).

[54]Graham v. Collins, 506 U.S. 461, 477, 113 S.Ct. 892, 902, 122 L.Ed.2d 260 (1993).

[55]Gilmore v. Taylor, 508 U.S. 333, 113 S.Ct. 2112, 124 L.Ed.2d 306 (1993).

[56]Beard v. Banks, 542 U.S. 406, 124 S.Ct. 2504, 159 L.Ed.2d 494 (2004), reasoning that "because '[a]ll of our Eighth Amendment jurisprudence concerning capital sentencing is directed toward the enhancement of reliability and accuracy in some sense,' the fact that a new rule removes some remote possibility of arbitrary infliction of the death sentence does not suffice to bring it within *Teague*'s second exception."

[57]Caspari v. Bohlen, 510 U.S. 383, 114 S.Ct. 948, 127 L.Ed.2d 236 (1994).

[58]Gray v. Netherland, 518 U.S. 152, 116 S.Ct. 2074, 135 L.Ed.2d 457 (1996).

[59]Sawyer v. Smith, 497 U.S. 227, 232, 110 S.Ct. 2822, 2826, 111 L.Ed.2d 193 (1990). See also O'Dell v. Netherland, 521 U.S. 151, 117 S.Ct. 1969, 138

second exception rules including that of *Ake v. Oklahoma*,[60] establishing the Sixth Amendment right to psychiatric assistance,[61] determination based on proof beyond a reasonable doubt of any fact that extends a defendant's sentence beyond the statutory maximum for the offense of which he was convicted, and the holding of *United States v. Gaudin*,[62] which entitles a defendant to a jury determination of the materiality element of the federal crime of false statement.[63]

§ 28.6(f) Review of state court rulings under § 2254(d)

Federal judges considering a petition for habeas relief from a state court decision on the merits do not review that decision de novo. Instead, § 2254(d) provides:

> An application for a writ of habeas corpus on behalf of a person in custody pursuant to the judgment of a State court shall not be granted with respect to any claim that was adjudicated on the merits in State court proceedings unless the adjudication of the claim—
>
> (1) resulted in a decision that was contrary to, or involved an unreasonable application of, clearly established Federal law, as determined by the Supreme Court of the United States; or
>
> (2) resulted in a decision that was based on an unreasonable determination of the facts in light of the evidence presented in the State court proceeding.

Section 2254(d)(2), governing the review of state determinations of fact, will be discussed in § 28.7. The first subsection of § 2254(d), governing the review of state determinations and applications of law, is discussed here.

Standards for Reviewing State Court Determinations and Applications of Law. Section 2254(d)(1) states that federal courts may grant habeas relief only when the state decision on the merits is "contrary to, or involved an unreasonable application of, clearly established Federal law as determined by the Supreme Court of the United States." Interpreting this provision in *(Terry)*

L.Ed.2d 351 (1997).

[60]Ake v. Oklahoma, 470 U.S. 68, 105 S.Ct. 1087, 84 L.Ed.2d 53 (1985), discussed in § 11.2(e).

[61]See Gretzler v. Stewart, 112 F.3d 992 (9th Cir.1997).

[62]United States v. Gaudin, 515 U.S. 506, 115 S.Ct. 2310, 132 L.Ed.2d 444 (1995).

[63]United States v. Mandanici, 205 F.3d 519 (2d Cir.2000) (*Gaudin*'s holding merely shifts the determination of materiality from the judge to the jury, and, unlike *Gideon*, affects only "a limited class" of cases); United States v. Shunk, 113 F.3d 31 (5th Cir.1997). See also Fryer v. United States, 243 F.3d 1004 (7th Cir.2001) (collecting authority that has concluded that the Court's decision in Old Chief v. United States, 519 U.S. 172, 177 S.Ct. 644, 136 L.Ed.2d 574 (1997), which held that evidence of prior felony convictions used to support a felony-firearm charge should not be heard by the jury where the defendant offers to stipulate to the existence of such convictions, does not fall within either exception).

Williams v. Taylor,[64] the Court held that under "the 'contrary to' clause, a federal habeas court may grant the writ if the state court arrives at a conclusion opposite to that reached by this Court on a question of law or if the state court decides a case differently than this Court has on a set of materially indistinguishable facts." The "unreasonable application" clause limits relief to cases in which "the state court identifies the correct governing legal principle from this court's decision but unreasonably applies that principle to the facts of the prisoner's case." The inquiry into reasonableness is objective, and does not turn on whether "one of the Nation's jurists has applied the relevant federal law in the same manner the state court did in the habeas petitioner's case." Furthermore, stated the Court, drawing upon the discussion in *Wright v. West*,[65] "an unreasonable application of federal law is different from an incorrect application of federal law." It is not enough that a state court decision applying federal law was erroneous, "that application must also be unreasonable."

Six justices in *Williams* agreed that the state court decision in that case was "both contrary to and involved an unreasonable application of this Court's clearly established precedent." First, the Virginia Supreme Court misinterpreted the Court's decision in *Strickland*,[66] erroneously assuming that a later decision of the Court had modified the test for prejudice to require more than "mere outcome determination." Second, because it failed to "consider the totality of the omitted mitigation evidence," the state court unreasonably applied *Strickland* to *Williams'* case when it found that the grossly deficient performance did not prejudice *Williams*.

The Court applied this analysis to two separate state-court rulings the next term in *Penry v. Johnson (Penry II)*.[67] First, the Court found objectively reasonable (as well as harmless, even if error) a Texas court's decision that *Estelle v. Smith*,[68] barring the government from introducing in a capital sentencing proceeding a psychiatrist's opinion regarding future dangerousness, did not prohibit admission into *Penry's* sentencing hearing of a psychiatric evaluation prepared for a competency hearing in an unrelated case prior to the charged offense. The Court noted many grounds

---

[Section 28.6(f)]

[64](Terry) Williams v. Taylor, 529 U.S. 362, 120 S.Ct. 1495, 146 L.Ed.2d 389 (2000).

[65]Wright v. West, 505 U.S. 277, 112 S.Ct. 2482, 120 L.Ed.2d 225 (1992).

[66]Strickland v. Washington, 466 U.S. 668, 104 S.Ct. 2052, 80 L.Ed.2d 674 (1984), discussed in § 11.7(c).

[67]Penry v. Johnson (Penry II), 532 U.S. 782, 121 S.Ct. 1910, 150 L.Ed.2d 9 (2001). The case had reached the Court before, in Penry v. Lynaugh, 492 U.S. 302, 109 S.Ct. 2934, 106 L.Ed.2d 256 (1989) (Penry I).

[68]Estelle v. Smith, 451 U.S. 454, 101 S.Ct. 1866, 68 L.Ed.2d 359 (1981).

on which the state court acted reasonably in distinguishing *Estelle*: *Penry*, unlike the defendant in *Estelle*, had placed his mental condition in issue; *Penry's* own counsel, albeit his former counsel, had requested the examination and psychiatrist, whereas the court in *Estelle* had ordered the examination and picked the doctor; the evidence was introduced during cross examination of *Penry's* expert witness, unlike in *Estelle* where the government introduced the predictions of dangerousness as part of its affirmative case for a death sentence; and finally, "in *Estelle*, the defendant was charged with a capital crime at the time of his competency exam, and it was thus clear that his future dangerousness would be a specific issue at sentencing," while *Penry* "had not yet murdered" the victim at the time of his interview. Second, a majority of justices in *Penry II* went on to find objectively unreasonable the state court's decision to uphold the death sentence despite a faulty instruction on mitigating evidence. The majority concluded that the state courts had not complied with the Court's earlier ruling in the same case, twelve years earlier, in *Penry I*, when it had vacated *Penry's* death sentence due to the same faulty instructions.

As in *Penry II*, later applications of the § 2254 standard by the Court have often been closely divided, and have produced very few general principles.[69] "[E]valuating whether a rule application was unreasonable requires considering the rule's specificity,"

---

[69]For additional illustrations of cases in which the Court has applied the § 2254(d) review standard, compare Wiggins v. Smith, 539 U.S. 510, 123 S.Ct. 2527, 156 L.Ed.2d 471 (2003) (state court unreasonably applied *Strickland*); and Rompilla v. Beard, 545 U.S. 374, 125 S.Ct. 2456, 162 L.Ed.2d 360 (2005) (state court's conclusion that defense counsel's efforts were constitutionally sufficient was objectively unreasonable); with Price v. Vincent, 538 U.S. 634, 123 S.Ct. 1848, 155 L.Ed.2d 877 (2003) (concluding that state court's application of prior precedent was not objectively unreasonable, noting "numerous other courts have refused to find double jeopardy violations under similar circumstances" and stating, "Even if we agreed * * * that the Double Jeopardy Clause should be read to prevent continued prosecution of a defendant" under the circumstances in this case, "it was at least reasonable for the state court to conclude otherwise."); Lockyer v. Andrade, 538 U.S. 63, 123 S.Ct. 1166, 155 L.Ed.2d 144 (2003) (finding, 5:4, that the state court's decision to reject an offender's Eighth Amendment challenge to his sentence of two consecutive 25-to-life terms for theft was an objectively reasonable application of clearly established law); Early v. Packer, 537 U.S. 3, 123 S.Ct. 362, 154 L.Ed.2d 263 (2002) ("Even if we agreed with the [court of appeals majority] that there was jury coercion here, it is at least reasonable to conclude that there was not, which means that the state court's determination to that effect must stand."); Bell v. Cone, 535 U.S. 685, 122 S.Ct. 1843, 152 L.Ed.2d 914 (2002) (petitioner "must do more than show that he would have satisfied *Strickland's* test if his claim were being analyzed in the first instance, * * * [r]ather he must show that the [state court] applied *Strickland* to the facts of his case in an objectively unreasonable manner"; concluding that the state court's decision was not an unreasonable applica-

explained the five-justice majority in *Yarborough v. Alvarado*.[70] "The more general the rule, the more leeway courts have in reaching outcomes in case by case determinations." The *Alvarado* majority found that the rule for when a suspect is in custody for purposes of *Miranda* was "general," and the state court's application of that rule—finding no custody and refusing to consider the suspect's age and inexperience—fit "within the matrix of our prior decisions."

A narrow holding, too, permits more freedom to state courts in distinguishing the decision as not controlling. Consider, for example, the Court's decision in *Carey v. Musladin*.[71] The Court found that a state court did not unreasonably apply clearly established law when, in a case involving prejudicial spectator conduct, the state court did not include in its analysis Supreme Court precedent regulating other prejudicial circumstances— requiring a defendant to wear prison clothes and seating four uniformed troopers behind the defendant at trial. Those holdings involved government-compelled practices, reasoned the majority, unlike the spectator practices at issue. "This Court has never addressed a claim that such private-actor courtroom conduct was so inherently prejudicial that it deprived a defendant of a fair trial." The broader view of precedent taken by justices who did not join the majority opinion would have reached courtroom circumstances apparent to the jury that create coercive, intimidating, or prejudicial conditions, including spectator conduct.

The Court has also rejected efforts to equate the § 2254 standard with "clear error," noting that "the gloss of clear error fails

---

tion of *Strickland*); Woodford v. Visciotti, 537 U.S. 19, 123 S.Ct. 357, 154 L.Ed.2d 279 (2002) (state court rejection of ineffective assistance claim in capital case was not objectively unreasonable); Rice v. Collins, 546 U.S. 333, 126 S.Ct. 969, 163 L.Ed.2d 824 (2006) (upholding as reasonable state court's application of *Batson* and *Purkett v. Elam*); Brown v. Payton, 544 U.S. 133, 125 S.Ct. 1432, 161 L.Ed.2d 334 (2005) (state court's conclusion that prosecutor's argument was not contrary to or an unreasonable application of constitutional law); Uttecht v. Brown, __ U.S. __, 127 S.Ct. 2218, 167 L.Ed.2d 1014 (2007) (finding that state court reasonably applied correct standard in reviewing trial judge's decision to exclude juror in death case).

See also Abdul-Kabir v. Quarterman, __ U.S. __, 127 S.Ct. 1654, 167 L.Ed.2d 585 (2007) (Texas Court of Criminal Appeals' decision was not reasonable when the trial judge ignored an entire line of cases establishing the importance of allowing juries to give meaningful effect to any mitigating evidence providing a basis for a sentence of life rather than death). But compare *Abdul-Kabir*, 127 S.Ct. at 1676 (Roberts, C.J. dissenting) (writing for four justices, Chief Justice Roberts argued that the "sharply divided, ebbing and flowing decisions in this area" did not create "clearly established" law, "but instead a dog's breakfast of divided, conflicting, and ever changing analysis").

[70] Yarborough v. Alvarado, 541 U.S. 652, 124 S.Ct. 2140, 158 L.Ed.2d 938 (2004).

[71] Carey v. Musladin, __ U.S. __, 127 S.Ct. 649, 166 L.Ed.2d 482 (2006).

to give proper deference to state courts by conflating error (even clear error) with reasonableness."[72]

*Clearly established * * * by the Supreme Court.* The language "clearly established Federal law, as determined by the Supreme Court of the United States" was interpreted in *Williams* as restricting "the source of clearly established law to this Court's jurisprudence." The provision refers to "the holdings, as opposed to the dicta, of this Court's decisions as of the time of the relevant state-court decision."[73] This standard differs from *Teague* in two ways. First, the date on which federal law must be assessed is different. After *Teague*, a petitioner could obtain relief from a state court decision only if that decision was not in accordance with federal law existing at the time when the defendant's ability to apply for review in the Supreme Court expired or when Supreme Court denied the defendant's petition for certiorari.[74] Under § 2254(d), the Court's decisions in place at the time of the relevant state decision govern. Second, § 2254(d) allows consideration only of the holdings of the Court, while *Teague* arguably permits consideration of even dicta.[75]

Adjudicated on the Merits. The deferential standard of review in Section 2254(d) applies only to claims "adjudicated on the merits" in state court. If a claim was rejected on procedural grounds rather than on the "merits," pre-1996 de novo standards of review are applied.[76] Lower courts have divided over whether summary decisions disposing of federal claims without comment

---

[72]Lockyer v. Andrade, 538 U.S. 63, 123 S.Ct. 1166, 155 L.Ed.2d 144 (2003) (finding, 5:4, that the state court's decision to reject an offender's Eighth Amendment challenge to his sentence of two consecutive 25-to-life terms for theft was an objectively reasonable application of clearly established law). For a proposal for a different standard for assessing reasonableness, one that turns on whether the state court's reasoning process was reasonable, see Semararo, A Reasoning-Process Review Model for Federal Habeas Corpus, 94 J.Crim.L. & Criminology 897 (2004).

[73]See also Lockyer v. Andrade, 538 U.S. 63, 123 S.Ct. 1166, 155 L.Ed.2d 144 (2003) (concluding that the only relevant "clearly established law" was the "gross disproportionality principle, the precise contours of which are unclear," and that because *Harmelin* and *Solem* specifically stated that

they did not overrule *Rummel*, it was "not contrary to our clearly established law for" the state court to "turn to *Rummel* in deciding whether a sentence is grossly disproportionate").

[74]See § 28.6(c) at notes 15–17.

[75]Williams v. Taylor, 529 U.S. 362, 412, 120 S.Ct. 1495, 146 L.Ed.2d 389 (2000).

[76]DiBenedetto v. Hall, 272 F.3d 1 (1st Cir.2001) ("If the state court has not decided the federal constitutional claim (even by reference to state court decisions dealing with federal constitutional issues), then we cannot say that the constitutional claim was 'adjudicated on the merits' within the meaning of § 2254 and therefore entitled to the deferential review prescribed in subsection 28.6(d)."); Fortini v. Murphy, 257 F.3d 39 (1st Cir.2001) ("We can hardly defer to the state court on an issue that the state court did not address."); Miranda v. Bennett,

should qualify as "on the merits" rulings triggering deferential review, with most granting terse denials the same deference as that given to rulings accompanied by reasoning.[77]

§ 28.6(g) Harmless error on habeas review

The Court has emphasized that habeas corpus is an "extraordinary remedy," appropriately limited to "those persons whom society has grievously wronged in light of modern concepts of justice."[78] In *Brecht v. Abramson*,[79] the Court held the beyond-a-reasonable-doubt harmless error standard was too stringent to

---

322 F.3d 171 (2d Cir.2003); Liegakos v. Cooke, 106 F.3d 1381 (7th Cir.1997) (under the new Act, when state court relied on procedural default rule to deny claim, federal court must review it "as if nothing had changed since 1987"); Robinson v. Crist, 278 F.3d 862 (8th Cir.2002) (suggesting that federal courts "likely should apply the pre-AEDPA standard of review" when state courts fail to adjudicate claims on the merits); Pirtle v. Morgan, 313 F.3d 1160 (9th Cir.2002); McGregor v. Gibson, 248 F.3d 946 (10th Cir.2001); Romine v. Head, 253 F.3d 1349 (11th Cir.2001) (applying de novo review because state court failed to apply federal law).

[77]Compare Jiminez v. Walker, 458 F.3d 130 (2d Cir.2006) (holding that the presumption designed in the context of the procedural default doctrine to determine whether a state court decision was on the merits or on a procedural ground is the appropriate method of determining whether the state court decision was on the merits for purposes of 2254(d) deference; state decision rejecting claim as either unpreserved or without merit qualifies as a holding on the merits under 2254(d); when applying 2254(d) to "silent state-court opinions, we review outcomes, not reasoning"); Fullwood v. Lee, 290 F.3d 663 (4th Cir.2002) (noting that if the petitioner has properly presented a claim to the state court but the state court has not adjudicated the claim on the merits, de novo standard of review applies; although state court specifically discussed only state evidentiary law in resolving this claim,

claim was adjudicated on the merits for purposes of § 2254); Wright v. Secretary, Dep't of Corr., 278 F.3d 1245 (11th Cir.2002) (a decision that does not rest on procedural grounds one is an adjudication on the merits regardless of the form in which it is expressed) with Howard v. Bouchard, 405 F.3d 459 (6th Cir.2005) (when the state court disposes of a constitutional claim but fails to articulate its analysis, habeas court must conduct an independent review of the record and applicable law to determine whether the state court decision is contrary to federal law, unreasonably applies clearly established law, or is based on an unreasonable determination of the facts in light of the evidence presented; this is not a full, de novo review of the claims, the review remains deferential); Himes v. Thompson, 336 F.3d 848 (9th Cir.2003) (independent review of record required when no reasoned decision provided). See also Dodson, Habeas Review of Perfunctory State Court Decisions on the Merits, 29 Am.J.Crim.L. 223 (2002); Note, 77 N.Y.U.L.Rev. 1442 (2002); Lee, Section 2254(d) of the Federal Habeas Statute: Is It Beyond Reason?, 56 Hastings L.J. 283 (2004) (collecting authority).

[Section 28.6(g)]

[78]Brecht v. Abrahamson, 507 U.S. 619, 113 S.Ct. 1710, 123 L.Ed.2d 353 (1993).

[79]Brecht v. Abrahamson, 507 U.S. 619, 113 S.Ct. 1710, 123 L.Ed.2d 353 (1993).

apply on habeas review.[80] It reasoned: "Overturning final and presumptively correct convictions on collateral review because the State cannot prove that an error is harmless under [*Chapman v. California*] undermines the States' interest in finality and infringes upon their sovereignty over criminal matters. Moreover, granting habeas relief merely because there is a 'reasonable possibility' that trial error contributed to the verdict [the Chapman standard] is at odds with the historic meaning of habeas corpus—to afford relief to those whom society has 'grievously wronged.' "

Concluding that the "imbalance of the costs and benefits of applying the *Chapman* harmless-error standard on collateral review counsels in favor of applying a less onerous standard on habeas review," the *Brecht* majority opted for application of the *Kotteakos* standard, which federal appellate courts have traditionally applied on direct review to non-constitutional errors.[81] "Under this standard," habeas petitioners "are not entitled to habeas relief based on trial error unless they can establish that it resulted in 'actual prejudice.' "[82] As the Court explained later in *Calderon v. Coleman*,[83] the standard "protects the State's sovereign interest in punishing offenders and its good-faith attempts to honor constitutional rights."

In *O'Neal v. McAninch*,[84] the Court majority rejected the government's contention that the habeas petitioner bore the "burden of establishing" that a constitutional error was "prejudicial" under the *Brecht-Kotteakos* harmless-error standard. The Court noted initially that characterizing the harmless error inquiry as one controlled by a "burden of proof" was misleading, for harmless-error analysis "does not involve a judge who shifts a

---

[80]This standard, established by Chapman v. California, 386 U.S. 18, 87 S.Ct. 824, 17 L.Ed.2d 705 (1967), is discussed in § 27.6(c)-(e).

[81]See § 27.6(b), at notes 38–39, discussing Kotteakos v. United States, 328 U.S. 750, 66 S.Ct. 1239, 90 L.Ed. 1557 (1946).

[82]Commentators have been critical of *Brecht*. See Blume & Garvey, Harmless Error in Federal Habeas Corpus After Brecht v. Abramson, 35 Wm. & Mary L.Rev. 163 (1993); Friedman, Failed Enterprise, 83 Cal.L.Rev. 485, 495–502 (1995); Gershman, The Gate is Open But the Door Is Locked—Habeas Corpus and Harmless Error, 51 Wash. & Lee L.Rev. 115, 116 (1994) (decrying the "unwarranted and un-

principled extension" of the policies of finality, federalism and judicial economy in the *Brecht* opinion); Liebman & Hertz, *Brecht v. Abrahamson:* Harmful Error in Habeas Corpus Law, 84 Crim.L. & Criminology 1109 (1994) (rejecting view that finality, comity, and federalism rationales justify "departure from over 200 years of direct appeal/habeas parity" in the standard of review); Note, 72 Wash.L. Rev. 567, 579 (1997) (attacking *Brecht* as "fundamentally unfair").

[83]Calderon v. Coleman, 525 U.S. 141, 119 S.Ct. 500, 142 L.Ed.2d 521 (1998).

[84]O'Neal v. McAninch, 513 U.S. 432, 115 S.Ct. 992, 130 L.Ed.2d 947 (1995).

'burden' to help control the presentation of evidence at trial, but rather involves judges who apply a legal standard (harmlessness) to a record that the presentation of evidence is no longer likely to affect."[85] According to the Court, a judge better puts the question as whether " 'I, the judge, think that the error substantially influenced the jury's decision?' " Imposing a burden on the petitioner could produce a misapplication of this standard where the record is so evenly balanced that a conscientious judge is in grave doubt as to harmlessness of an error. If the judge is left with a "grave doubt" that the error may have had a "substantial influence," then the "conviction cannot stand."[86]

There are at least two situations in which a habeas court need not apply the *Brecht* standard. First, in *Kyles v. Whitley*,[87] the Court explained that this standard is met whenever a petitioner establishes a constitutional violation that already requires a showing of prejudice. Thus no harmlessness analysis is required once a court determines that a petitioner has established a due process violation under *Brady* or *Strickland*, for example.[88]

---

[85]See § 27.6(b).

[86]See Fry v. Pliler, __ U.S. __, 127 S.Ct. 2321, 168 L.Ed.2d 16 (2007) (noting that although one of the issues the Court had agreed to review was whether the state or the petitioner bore the burden of persuasion on the question of prejudice under *Brecht*, *O'Neal* places the burden on the state, a point the state had conceded throughout). In California v. Roy, 519 U.S. 2, 117 S.Ct. 337, 136 L.Ed.2d 266 (1996), the Court rejected the lower court's application of a somewhat stricter standard to an error in instructing the jury concerning the required state of mind for a finding of guilt. The court of appeals had held that the error was harmless if "review of the facts found by the jury establishes that the jury necessarily found the omitted element." The Supreme Court concluded that this standard had to yield to the standard enunciated in *Brecht* due to the "special function" of habeas review. But compare Penry v. Johnson (Penry II), 532 U.S. 782, 121 S.Ct. 1910, 150 L.Ed.2d 9 (2001) (noting that petitioner Penry had to establish that the error had a "substantial and injurious effect or influence in determining the jury's

verdict" and concluding, "We think it unlikely that Penry could make such a showing.").

See also Solomon, Causing Constitutional Harm: How Tort Law Can Help Determine Harmless Error in Criminal Trials, 99 N.W.L.Rev 1053 (2005) (reporting results of study of "a sample of 263 published habeas opinions from the federal courts of appeals, decided from May 1993 through July 2004, in which the majority opinion directly addressed the issue of whether an alleged error was harmless or harmful, and urging courts to consider not simply evidence of guilt, but empirical research on how various type of evidence impact jurors, evidence of influence on the jury such as the length of deliberations, requests for read backs, and questions from jurors, and the relevance of the error to the competing narratives presented to the jury).

[87]Kyles v. Whitley, 514 U.S. 419, 115 S.Ct. 1555, 131 L.Ed.2d 490 (1995).

[88]But see Fry v. Pliler, __ U.S. __, 127 S.Ct. 2321, 168 L.Ed.2d 16 (2007) (holding *Brecht* applies to what it assumes (without deciding) is a violation of Chambers v. Mississippi, 410 U.S.

Second, *Brecht* spoke only to "trial type" errors, to which *Chapman* would otherwise apply. It did not reach the proper treatment of "structural errors" that would not be subject to harmless error analysis on direct review. Lower courts have assumed that structural errors, once proven, require relief on habeas review without a showing of harm or prejudice, just as they do on direct appeal. The Court in *Brecht* also mentioned that it need not decide whether "in an unusual case, a deliberate and especially egregious error of the trial type, or one that is combined with a pattern of prosecutorial misconduct, might so infect the integrity of the proceeding as to warrant * * * habeas relief" without the showing required under *Kotteakos*. Some lower courts have treated this language as specifying a "hybrid" of structural and trial error that would be subject to review under the *Chapman* standard.[89]

After the 1996 Act, some lower courts reasoned that when reviewing a case in which the state court explicitly conducted harmless error review of a constitutional error, federal courts must review whether or not the state court's decision was 'contrary to, or involved an unreasonable application of' *Chapman*.[90] But in *Fry v. Pliler*,[91] the Court held that *Brecht* is the appropriate standard whether or not the state appellate court recognized the error or reviewed it for harmlessness under *Chapman*. Each of the primary reasons for adopting the less onerous standard in *Brecht*—strengthening finality, respecting state sovereignty over criminal matters, preserving historic limitation of habeas to those "grievously wronged," and avoiding significant societal costs— applies with equal force whether or not the state court reaches the *Chapman* question, explained the Court.

284, 93 S.Ct. 1038, 35 L.Ed.2d 297 (1973)).

[89]See, e.g., Cupit v. Whitley, 28 F.3d 532 (5th Cir.1994) (recognizing hybrid cases that do not fit into other categories); Hardnett v. Marshall, 25 F.3d 875 (9th Cir.1994) (debating whether such error would be subject to harmless error review at all).

[90]Gutierrez v. McGinnis, 389 F.3d 300 (2d Cir.2004). See also Madrigal v. Bagley, 413 F.3d 548 (6th Cir.2005) (Ohio court's harmless error analysis was an unreasonable application of clearly established federal law, granting habeas relief). But see Inthavong v. Lamarque, 420 F.3d 1055 (9th Cir.2005) (court must perform both an AEDPA-based review of the state court's *Chapman* harmless-error analysis and a *Brecht* harmless-error review of the original error as a precondition to granting habeas relief).

[91]Fry v. Pliler, __ U.S. __, 127 S.Ct. 2321, 168 L.Ed.2d 16 (2007). See also Penry v. Johnson, 532 U.S. 782, 121 S.Ct. 1910, 150 L.Ed.2d 9 (2001) (applying *Brecht* to post-AEDPA habeas claims, when the state appellate court had not engaged in harmless error review in the first instance).

§ 28.7 Fact-finding and evidentiary hearings in habeas

§ 28.7(a)   Presuming the correctness of state court determinations
             of fact
§ 28.7(b)   Distinguishing mixed determinations of law and fact
             from fact-finding
§ 28.7(c)   Obtaining evidentiary hearings
§ 28.7(d)   Discovery

§ 28.7(a) Presuming the correctness of state court determinations of fact

The next sections address two issues: First, the standards the federal court will use to review factual findings by state courts; and second, the availability of evidentiary hearings or discovery to develop facts in federal court.

The Development of Current Standards. The present rules regarding both the review of state court fact finding and the provision of evidentiary hearings in federal habeas proceedings have evolved from a 1963 decision, *Townsend v. Sain.*[1] In *Townsend*, the Court addressed when a petitioner was entitled to an evidentiary hearing and concluded that a habeas court must hold an evidentiary hearing if the habeas applicant did not receive a "full and fair" evidentiary hearing in a state court, either at the time of trial or in a collateral proceeding. The Court listed several specific conditions that indicated when the state hearing was deficient. Former § 2254(d), enacted in 1966 to regulate fact-finding in habeas proceedings, appeared to track much of *Townsend*. Thirty years later, however, the 1996 amendments to the habeas statute substantially altered the treatment of state fact-finding in habeas proceedings. Because at least some of the prior doctrine that was developed under *Townsend* and former § 2254(d) may inform the meaning of the current provisions, and because prior practice continues to apply in proceedings under § 2255 for federal prisoners, a brief review is in order.

Former § 2254(d) provided that "a determination after a hearing on the merits of a factual dispute made by a state court of competent jurisdiction * * * evidenced by * * * reliable and adequate written indicia * * * shall be presumed to be correct," unless the habeas court finds that one of eight conditions are present. Those conditions are: (1) that the merits of the factual dispute were not resolved in the State court hearing; (2) that the fact-finding procedure employed by the State court was not adequate to afford a full and fair hearing; (3) that the material facts

---

[Section 28.7(a)]

[1] Townsend v. Sain, 372 U.S. 293, 83 S.Ct. 745, 9 L.Ed.2d 770 (1963).

were not adequately developed at the State court hearing; (4) that the State court lacked jurisdiction of the subject matter or over the person of the applicant in the State court proceeding; (5) that the applicant was an indigent and the State court, in deprivation of his constitutional right, failed to appoint counsel to represent him in the State court proceeding; (6) that the applicant did not receive a full, fair, and adequate hearing in the State court proceeding; or (7) that the applicant was otherwise denied due process of law in the State court proceeding; (8) or unless that part of the record of the State court proceeding in which the determination of such factual issue was made, pertinent to a determination of the sufficiency of the evidence to support such factual determination, is produced as provided for hereinafter, and the Federal court on a consideration of such part of the record as a whole concludes that such factual determination is not fairly supported by the record. Upon "due proof" of a state finding of fact not exempted by any of these conditions, stated the former statute, the "burden shall rest upon the applicant to establish by convincing evidence that the factual determination by the State court was erroneous."[2]

Review of Factfinding Under AEDPA. The Antiterrorism and Effective Death Penalty Act in 1996 carried forward the presumption that state court findings of fact are correct, but replaced former § 2254(d) with two provisions: § 2254(d)(2) and § 2254(e)(1). Section 2254(e)(1) provides that "a determination of a factual issue by a State court shall be presumed to be correct," with the petitioner having the "burden of rebutting the presumption of correctness by clear and convincing evidence." New § 2254(d)(2) provides that relief shall not be granted for any claim adjudicated on the merits in state court unless the state decision "was based on an unreasonable determination of the facts in light of the evi-

---

[2]See also LaVallee v. Delle Rose, 410 U.S. 690, 93 S.Ct. 1203, 35 L.Ed.2d 637 (1973) (evidentiary hearing was not warranted, as the state court's factual findings on voluntariness could be reconstructed readily from the state judge's decision, providing sufficient evidence of actual factual findings to bring the § 2254(d) presumption into play); Maggio v. Fulford, 462 U.S. 111, 103 S.Ct. 2261, 76 L.Ed.2d 794 (1983) (denying relief, finding that the lower federal court had "erroneously substituted its own judgment as to the credibility of witnesses for that of the Louisiana courts—a prerogative which 28 U.S.C.A. § 2254 does not allow"); Marshall v. Lonberger, 459 U.S. 422, 103 S.Ct. 843, 74 L.Ed.2d 646 (1983).

Consider also Patton v. Yount, 467 U.S. 1025, 104 S.Ct. 2885, 81 L.Ed.2d 847 (1984) (holding that the testimony of a prospective juror on voir dire provided "fair support" for the state court's factual determination that the juror would be impartial; deference had to be given to the state trial judge as the judge best situated to evaluate that testimony); Sumner v. Mata, 449 U.S. 539, 101 S.Ct. 764, 66 L.Ed.2d 722 (1981) (the presumption applied to a factual determination by a state appellate court just as it did to a factual determination by a state trial court).

dence presented in the state court proceeding." As the Court explained in *Miller-El v. Dretke*[3] a federal court must "presume the [state] court's factual findings to be sound unless [the petitioner] rebuts the 'presumption of correctness by clear and convincing evidence.' " *Miller-El* was a case in which the petitioner did just that. Referring to evidence before the state court "too powerful to conclude anything but discrimination" in violation of *Batson*, the Court found the state's conclusion "wrong to a clear and convincing degree * * * unreasonable as well as erroneous."

Although the 1996 Act no longer includes a "full and fair hearing" on the facts in state court as a prerequisite to federal court deference under §§ 2254(d)(2) or (e)(1), lower courts have concluded that the fact finding process afforded the defendant in state courts remains relevant in determining whether or not a petitioner has met his burden of demonstrating that the state finding was unreasonable.[4]

---

[3]Miller-El v. Dretke, 545 U.S. 231, 125 S.Ct. 2317, 162 L.Ed.2d 196 (2005), discussed in § 22.3(d) at note 241. The dissenters argued that the petitioner had presented to the habeas court evidence not presented to the state courts—jury questionnaires—and that review of the state's finding under § 2254(d) must be based only on evidence that was before the state court. The majority noted that the state had relied on the questionnaires in federal court, and that the record without them looked even more bleak for the state.

[4]E.g., Lambert v. Blackwell, 387 F.3d 210 (3d Cir.2004) (explaining that whether the state court afforded the defendant a "full and fair hearing" may well affect whether "a state court's factual determination was 'reasonable' in 'light of the evidence presented in the State court proceeding' or whether the petitioner has adequately rebutted a presumption that the state court's determination is correct. * * * In other words, the extent to which a state court provides a 'full and fair hearing' is no longer a threshold requirement before deference applies; but it might be a consideration while applying deference" under § 2254(d)(2) and (e)(1)).

The Ninth Circuit summarized its approach as follows: "First, challenges to purely factual questions resolved by the state court are reviewed under (d)(2); the question on review is whether an appellate panel, applying the normal standards of appellate review, could reasonably conclude that the finding is supported by the record. Second, fact-based challenges founded on evidence raised for the first time in federal court are reviewed under (e)(1); the question on review is whether the new evidence amounts to clear and convincing proof sufficient to overcome the presumption of correctness given the state court's factual findings * * *." James to Blodgett, 393 F.3d 943 (9th Cir.2004).

See also Weeks v. Snyder, 219 F.3d 245 (3d Cir.2000) (federal courts must provide the same presumption of correctness to implicit findings of fact that is accorded explicit findings of fact, concluding that state court implicitly found counsel had informed petitioner of the implications of cohort's failure to testify, a finding petitioner had failed to defeat by clear and convincing evidence); Valdez v. Cockrell, 274 F.3d 941 (5th Cir.2001) (full and fair hearing is not a precondition to according § 2254(e)(1)'s presumption of correctness to state ha-

Indeed, the fact-finding process used by the state court can itself violate constitutional command, so that the factual conclusions reached through that process do not warrant the deference state court factual findings would otherwise receive. In *Panetti v. Quarterman*,[5] the Court refused to defer to the state court's conclusion that a death row petitioner was competent to be executed because that conclusion had been reached "after failing to provide petitioner with "procedures mandated by the Constitution, including "an adequate means by which to submit expert psychiatric evidence in response to the evidence that had been solicited by the state court."

§ 28.7(b) Distinguishing mixed determinations of law and fact from fact-finding

The reach of the presumption of correctness contained new § 2254(e)(1) is, like of its predecessor, former § 2254(d), limited to pure questions of historical fact. State decisions applying law to facts are governed by § 2254(d)(1), discussed in § 28.6(g), limiting habeas relief to "unreasonable" applications by state courts. The distinction between a "factual" and a "mixed" determination is not always easy to apply. In the *Summer v. Mata* litigation, for example, the Court divided sharply divided over whether state court findings concerning the admission of a pretrial photo-identification were limited to historic fact. Ultimately, the Supreme Court held in *Mata II*[6] that the lower court had erred. The Court agreed that "the ultimate question as to the constitutionality of the pretrial identification procedures used in this case is a mixed question of law and fact" that is not governed by § 2254. But, the Court went on, "the questions of fact that underlie this ultimate conclusion," including whether the witnesses "had an opportunity to observe the crime or were too distracted; whether the witnesses gave a detailed, accurate description; and whether the witnesses were under pressure" were "questions of fact as to which the statutory presumption applies."

---

beas court findings of fact nor to applying § 2254(d)'s standards of review); Mendiola v. Schomig, 224 F.3d 589 (7th Cir.2000) (defendant must defeat presumption by clear and convincing evidence, also noting that § 2254(e) "omits any mention of a hearing. If a state court's finding rests on thin air, the petitioner will have little difficulty satisfying the standards for relief under § 2254. But if the state court's finding is supported by the record, even though not by a 'hearing on the merits of [the] factual issue,' then it is presumed to be correct."). But see

Saiz v. Ortiz, 392 F.3d 1166 (10th Cir.2004) (in reviewing state court fact-findings, "our concern is only whether the state court's result, not its rationale, is clearly contrary to or unreasonable under federal law").

[5]Panetti v. Quarterman, __ U.S. __, 127 S.Ct. 2842, __ L.Ed.2d __ (2007). The dissenters would have found the state court's determination presumptively correct.

[Section 28.7(b)]

[6]Sumner v. Mata, 455 U.S. 591, 102 S.Ct. 1303, 71 L.Ed.2d 480 (1982).

A series of Supreme Court rulings after *Mata*, each considering the appropriate treatment of state trial court rulings relating to juror prejudice, also applied the distinction between mixed findings and purely factual findings. In *Patton v. Yount*,[7] the Court held that the presumption of correctness did not apply to a state court's finding as to whether prejudicial publicity had made a fair trial impossible, but it did apply to a trial judge's finding, based on the juror's responses on voir dire, that the individual juror was not biased.[8] Similarly, *Rushen v. Spain*[9] held that the presumption of correctness was applicable to a finding that a juror's ex parte communication with the judge had no bearing on the juror's impartiality, and *Wainwright v. Witt*[10] applied the presumption to a finding that a prospective juror's opposition to capital punishment would substantially impair her ability to comply with the trial court's instructions.

Recognizing the sharp division within the Court, Justice O'Connor in *Miller v. Fenton*[11] sought to explain why the "appropriate methodology for distinguishing questions of fact from questions of law has been, to say the least, elusive." She there noted that the Court's "difficulty" may stem "from the practical truth that the decision to label an issue a 'question of law,' a 'question of fact' or a 'mixed question of law and fact' is sometimes as much a matter of allocation as it is of analysis. * * * At least in those instances in which Congress has not spoken and in which the issue falls somewhere between a pristine legal standard and a simple historical fact, the fact/law distinction at times has turned on a determination that, as a matter of the sound administration of justice, one judicial actor is better positioned than another to decide the issue in question." Justice O'Connor cited earlier cases that had held the "voluntariness" of a confession to be "a legal question requiring independent federal determination," and noted that "on rare occasions in years past the Court has justified independent federal or appellate review as a means of compensating for 'perceived shortcomings of the trier of fact by way of bias or some other factor.'" As an example of a setting in which allocation considerations led to the opposite conclusion, Justice O'Connor cited the prejudiced juror cases. Where, as in those cases, "the issue involves the credibility of witnesses and therefore turns largely on an evaluation of demeanor," the process of "applying law to fact" was appropriately left to the trial

---

[7]Patton v. Yount, 467 U.S. 1025, 104 S.Ct. 2885, 81 L.Ed.2d 847 (1984).

[8]Patton v. Yount, 467 U.S. 1025, 104 S.Ct. 2885, 81 L.Ed.2d 847 (1984).

[9]Rushen v. Spain, 464 U.S. 114, 104 S.Ct. 453, 78 L.Ed.2d 267 (1983).

[10]Wainwright v. Witt, 469 U.S. 412, 105 S.Ct. 844, 83 L.Ed.2d 841 (1985).

[11]Miller v. Fenton, 474 U.S. 104, 106 S.Ct. 445, 88 L.Ed.2d 405 (1985).

court.

The ruling in *Miller v. Fenton* itself reflected the broad range of factors that may enter into the characterization of a particular issue as one within or without the presumption of correctness. The Court there held that the voluntariness of a confession was a "legal inquiry requiring plenary federal review." "Subsidiary factual questions," such as whether a drug had certain properties or whether the police used certain interrogation tactics, are considered questions of fact alone, but not the "ultimate question whether, under the totality of the circumstances, the challenged confession was obtained in a *manner* compatible with the requirements of the Constitution." Voluntariness was held in *Miller* to be an issue beyond the presumption of correctness due to the combined influence of *stare decisis*, congressional intent, the "uniquely legal dimension" of the voluntariness determination, and "practical considerations" that favored "independent federal review" as necessary to "protec[t] the rights at stake."

Admitting again that it has found the characterization of a question as one of law or fact "sometimes slippery," the Court in *Thompson v. Keohane*,[12] reviewed its earlier decisions in the area held that a state court determination whether or not a defendant was "in custody" for *Miranda* purposes is a mixed question of law and fact that is not subject to the presumption of correctness under former § 2254(d). The question of custody turns on whether there was a "formal arrest or restraint on freedom of movement, of the degree associated with a formal arrest." As in *Miller*, the Court reasoned that assessments of credibility were not crucial to the proper assessment of this issue.[13]

§ 28.7(c) Obtaining evidentiary hearings

The decision to grant a hearing depends first upon whether the facts to be developed could have been developed in state court but were not because of the petitioner's lack of diligence. This situation is governed by the restrictions in § 2254(e)(2). The provision of an evidentiary hearing in all other cases is governed by case law. Each of these standards is examined below.

The Failure to Develop Facts in State Court. Prior to AEDPA, a petitioner who failed to develop facts in state court was entitled to an evidentiary hearing in federal court, but only by showing either 1) "cause" for and "prejudice" from his failure to develop

---

[12]Thompson v. Keohane, 516 U.S. 99, 116 S.Ct. 457, 133 L.Ed.2d 383 (1995).

[13]See also Williams v. Taylor, 529 U.S. 362, 120 S.Ct. 1495, (opinion of Stevens, J.) (terming efforts to distin- guish between questions of fact, questions of law, and "mixed questions," * * * generated some not insubstantial differences of opinion as to which issues of law fell into which category of question * * *.").

the facts adequately in state court or 2) actual innocence.[14] AEDPA restricted access to hearings in this situation even further. Section 2254(e)(2) states that the federal habeas court shall not hold an evidentiary hearing on a claim as to which there was "a failure to develop the factual basis" in state court proceedings, unless that claim rests on either (i) an intervening new rule held to apply retroactively, *or* (ii) a factual predicate not previously discoverable with due diligence, *and* the facts underlying the claim would be sufficient to "establish by clear and convincing evidence that but for the constitutional error, no reasonable fact-finder would have found the applicant guilty of the underlying offense."

This provision bars an evidentiary hearing only in cases in which the failure to develop the factual basis of a claim was due to some fault of the petitioner or his counsel. The opening clause of this provision—"failure to develop"—the Court concluded in *(Michael) Williams v. Taylor*,[15] requires "lack of diligence or some greater fault, attributable to the prisoner or to the prisoner's counsel." It does not apply if a claim had been "pursued with diligence but remained undeveloped in state court because, for instance, the prosecution concealed the facts." Diligence requires "a reasonable attempt, in light of the information available at the time, to investigate and pursue claims in state court," and that "the prisoner, at a minimum, seek an evidentiary hearing in state court in the manner prescribed by state law." A petitioner who has "neglected his rights" through lack of diligence will be unable to secure an evidentiary hearing unless "efforts to discover the facts would have been in vain, see § 2254(e)(2)(A)(ii), and there is a convincing claim of innocence, see § 2254(e)(2)(B) * * *."

Applying this provision, the Court found that *Williams* was diligent in his efforts to develop the facts supporting his juror bias and prosecutorial misconduct claims in state court, and that an evidentiary hearing was not barred by § 2254(e). The facts supporting juror bias were not revealed during state proceedings because the allegedly biased juror's answers to questions posed to her by the court and counsel during voir dire were misleading, and because the prosecutor had "completely forgotten" his earlier

---

[Section 28.7(c)]

[14]Keeney v. Tamayo-Reyes, 504 U.S. 1, 112 S.Ct. 1715, 118 L.Ed.2d 318 (1992). For a more recent application of the Keeney standard, see Banks v. Dretke, 540 U.S. 668, 124 S.Ct. 1256, 157 L.Ed.2d 1166 (2004) (a petitioner raising a *Brady* claim in a pre-AEDPA case, who shows the suppression of favorable evidence and prejudice from that suppression also demonstrates cause and prejudice for his failure to develop the facts supporting his claim in state court).

[15](Michael) Williams v. Taylor, 529 U.S. 420, 120 S.Ct. 1479, 146 L.Ed.2d 435 (2000).

representation of the juror in her divorce from the state's witness. "Counsel had no reason to believe" the juror had been married to the state's witness or been represented by the prosecutor.[16] The "standards of trial practice" did not require "counsel to check public records containing personal information pertaining to each and every juror."[17] Williams, however, had not been diligent, ruled the Court, in developing in state court the basis for his *Brady* claim. Petitioner's state habeas counsel had notice of the existence and materiality of the psychiatric report in question, but made no effort to find the report other than a making a general request for all psychological tests. "Given knowledge of the report's existence and potential importance, a diligent attorney would have done more."[18]

If a petitioner was not diligent in developing the factual basis for this claim, an evidentiary hearing on the claim is unavailable unless the stringent requirements of § 2254(e) are met. Under these requirements, a petitioner must make two showings. First, he must demonstrate that "the legal or factual basis of the claims did not exist at the time of the state court proceedings," either by showing that his claim was based on a "new rule of constitutional law" not available at the time of the earlier proceedings (§ 2254(e)(2)(A)(I)) or by showing that had he exercised due dili-

---

[16]The foreperson of the jury had fifteen years earlier divorced one of the state's witnesses—the officer who had investigated the crime scene and interrogated the state's lead witness. This juror also was represented in the divorce by the attorney serving as Williams's prosecutor. None of this was disclosed at trial, and was discovered only after the investigator helping to prepare Williams's federal habeas petition interviewed two other trial jurors who referred in passing to the juror by her married name, leading the investigator to check the County's marriage records.

[17]For additional examples of cases in which the lack of factual development in state court was not considered the petitioner's fault, see, e.g., Thomas v. Varner, 428 F.3d 491, 498 (3d Cir. 2005) (petitioner's request for evidentiary hearing in state court was denied, § 2254(e)(2) not applicable); Jaramillo v. Stewart, 340 F.3d 877 (9th Cir.2003) (petitioner's failure to discover the factual basis for his claim was the state's withholding of its in-

formation, so requirement did not apply; when undisclosed witness statement, if credible, and considered in light of all the evidence, demonstrated that defendant would have established his conduct was in self-defense and thus non-criminal, it is more likely than not that no reasonable juror would have convicted the defendant of the charged offenses, remanding for evidentiary hearing on *Brady* claim); Gonzalez v. Phillips, 147 F.Supp.2d 791 (E.D.Mich.2001) (petitioner acted with sufficient diligence in state court and was entitled to hearing on his claim that state should have provided translator when he had filed a motion in the state appellate court to remand to the trial court for an evidentiary hearing on his claims).

[18]Hawkins v. Mullin, 291 F.3d 658 (10th Cir.2002) (petitioner failed to develop diligently the factual basis of his ineffectiveness of counsel claim and was properly denied an evidentiary hearing; ineffectiveness claim also procedurally defaulted).

gence, "the factual predicate could not have been discovered" (§ 2254 (e)(2)(A)(ii)). Second, § 2254(e)(2)(B) requires a petitioner seeking to develop facts undeveloped in state court to show prejudice, that is, that the new facts, if proven, "would be sufficient to establish by clear and convincing evidence" that "no reasonable fact-finder would have found the [petitioner] guilty of the underlying offense" if the constitutional error had not occurred. This provision specifically codifies the Supreme Court's definition of actual innocence announced in *Sawyer v. Whitley*,[19] and the later limitation placed on that definition in the dissent in *Schlup v. Delo*.[20] The term "offense" in the phrase "but for the constitutional error, no reasonable fact-finder would have found the applicant guilty of the underlying offense," has troubled courts interpreting § 2254(e)(2)(B) in the same way that it has divided courts interpreting the same phrase in § 2244. If the term offense is interpreted literally, then the statute would seem to bar evidentiary hearings in cases of factual default in state court when a petitioner can show only "innocence of the death penalty," and not innocence of the underlying crime.[21]

Hearings in Other Cases. If not barred by § 2254(e), an evidentiary hearing may be ordered by the district court in the exercise of its discretion. In *Schriro v. Landrigan*,[22] the Court stated that in "deciding whether to grant an evidentiary hearing, a federal court must consider whether such a hearing could enable an applicant to prove the petition's factual allegations, which, if true, would entitle the applicant to federal habeas relief . . . [I]f the record refutes the applicant's factual allegations or otherwise precludes habeas relief, a district court is not required to hold an evidentiary hearing." In *Landrigan*, the Court found that because the petitioner would not have been entitled to relief even if all

---

[19]Sawyer v. Whitley, 505 U.S. 333, 112 S.Ct. 2514, 120 L.Ed. 2d 269 (1992), discussed in § 28.4(e), at note 86.

[20]Schlup v. Delo, 513 U.S. 298, 115 S.Ct. 851, 130 L.Ed.2d 808 (1995) (Rehnquist, C.J. dissenting) (requiring proof by clear and convincing evidence that no reasonable fact-finder would have found the petitioner guilty). *Schlup* is discussed in § 28.4(e), at note 75. Because it is unclear whether the lower burden of proof announced by the Supreme Court in *Schlup* was premised on the Due Process Clause or upon the former habeas corpus statute, at least one court has suggested that the clear and convincing standard in § 2254(e)(2)(B) is unconstitutional.

Lambert v. Blackwell, 962 F.Supp. 1521, 1527–28 (E.D.Pa.1997).

[21]See Wright v. Angelone, 151 F.3d 151 (4th Cir.1998); Greenawalt v. Stewart, 105 F.3d 1287 (9th Cir.1997); In re Medina, 109 F.3d 1556 (11th Cir. 1997). See also § 28.5(d) at note 88.

[22]Schriro v. Landrigan, __ U.S. __, 127 S.Ct. 1933, 167 L.Ed.2d 836 (2007). The Court stated "Prior to [AEDPA], the decision to grant an evidentiary hearing was generally left to the sound discretion of district courts. * * * That basic rule has not changed." (citing Townsend v. Sain, 372 U.S. 293, 83 S.Ct. 745, 9 L.Ed.2d 770 (1963) and Rule 8 of the Rules Governing Section 2254 Cases).

271

the facts he alleged were true, the district court did not abuse its discretion by denying the petitioner the opportunity to prove those facts at an evidentiary hearing.[23] Despite the discretion to order evidentiary hearings, district courts rarely hold them in non-capital cases, and most capital cases are resolved without hearings.[24]

§ 28.7(d) Discovery

Discovery in habeas proceedings is useful to allow the parties to prepare for a hearing, or, even if no hearing is granted, to develop facts needed for disposition.[25] Discovery is more limited than discovery in other civil proceedings in federal court. Rule 6 of the Rules Governing § 2254 Cases allows discovery under the Federal Rules of Civil Procedure if the judge finds "good cause" to authorize it.

Good cause is not established unless discovery would assist the court to resolve a factual dispute that, if resolved in petitioner's favor, would entitle him to relief.[26] In *Bracy v. Gramley*[27] the Court considered this Rule in the context of a case in which the petitioner had been sentenced to death by a judge who was later convicted of taking bribes from other defendants to fix their cases. The petitioner argued that the judge had convicted him and sentenced him to death in order to "cover up" for this illegal activity. The Court held that this was "good cause" for discovery since the allegations provided "reason to believe that the petitioner may, if the facts are fully developed, be able to demonstrate that he is * * * entitled to relief," and that it was "an abuse of discretion not to permit any discovery."[28]

---

[23]See also McCarver v. Lee, 221 F.3d 583 (4th Cir.2000) ("Even if [the petitioner's] claim is not precluded by § 2254(e)(2), that does not mean he is entitled to an evidentiary hearing—only that he may be."); McDonald v. Johnson, 139 F.3d 1056 (5th Cir.1998).

[24]N. King, F. Cheesman & B. Ostrom, Habeas Litigation in U.S. District Court (2007), available at htt p://www.ncjrs.gov/pdffiles1/nij/grants/219559.pdf.

[Section 28.7(d)]

[25]See generally R. Hertz & J. Liebman, 1 Federal Habeas Corpus Practice and Procedure ch.19 (5th ed. 2005).

[26]See Rector v. Johnson, 120 F.3d 551 (5th Cir.1997) (criticizing petition-

er's request as "fishing expedition"); Martinez v. Johnson, 104 F.3d 769 (5th Cir.1997) (denial of discovery request upheld, noting the requested documents were once furnished to the petitioner, and petitioner did not explain why he no longer had access to them); Williams v. Bagley, 380 F.3d 932 (6th Cir.2004); Hubanks v. Frank, 392 F.3d 926 (7th Cir.2004); Newton v. Kemna, 354 F.3d 776 (8th Cir.2004).

[27]Bracy v. Gramley, 520 U.S. 899, 117 S.Ct. 1793, 138 L.Ed.2d 97 (1997).

[28]See also Lonchar v. Thomas, 517 U.S. 314, 116 S.Ct. 1293, 134 L.Ed.2d 440 (1996) (district judges have discretion to grant or deny discovery under Rule 6); Drake v. Portuondo, 321 F.3d 338 (2d Cir.2003) (remanding for discovery concluding

§ 28.8 Habeas review of capital cases under Chapter 154 of the 1996 Act

§ 28.8(a)   Special standards for applicants from certain states
§ 28.8(b)   The opt-in requirements: electing the special standards

§ 28.8(a) Special standards for applicants from certain states

Responding to what it perceived as "acute problems of unnecessary delay and abuse in capital cases,"[1] Congress included in Title I of the Antiterrorism and Effective Death Penalty Act a new chapter 154 of 28 U.S.C.A., containing §§ 2261 to 2266. This chapter, titled "Special Habeas Corpus Procedures in Capital Cases" imposes special standards applicable to habeas petitions by state prisoners sentenced to death in states which have adopted a counsel appointment mechanism that meets the prerequisites specified in § 2261.

Chapter 154 tracks in large part a proposal advanced in 1989 by a Committee of the United States Judicial Conference chaired by retired Supreme Court Justice Lewis F. Powell, Jr., and commonly referred to as the "Powell Committee."[2] The Powell Committee endorsed the adoption of a series of procedural requirements designed to promote a promptly adjudicated "one-shot" federal habeas challenge in state capital cases. Application of these requirements was to be conditioned, however, on a state voluntarily establishing a program that provided to indigent capital defendants the assistance of adequate counsel in state post-conviction proceedings (the Supreme Court having held that the state had no constitutional obligation to provide appointed

good cause shown regarding government's culpability in connection with perjured testimony by expert witness); Lave v. Dretke, 416 F.3d 372 (5th Cir.2005) (no good cause when petitioner failed to indicate what specific information he anticipated, DNA testing would provide how it would be used to impeach state's witness's testimony); East v. Scott, 55 F.3d 996, 1001 (5th Cir.1995) ("While the district court generally has discretion to grant or deny discovery requests under Rule 6, a court's blanket denial of discovery is an abuse of discretion if discovery is 'indispensable to a fair, rounded, development of the material facts.' "); Green v. Artuz, 990 F.Supp. 267 (S.D.N.Y.1998) (generalized statements about the possible existence of material not good cause); Cherrix v. True, 177 F.Supp.2d 485 (E.D.Va. 2001) (granting leave to conduct limited deposition of police chief concerning items on a list of evidence prepared by the police in response to earlier court order).

Discovery orders are not available ex parte; discovery motions must be served on the opposing party. See In re Pruett, 133 F.3d 275 (4th Cir. 1997).

[Section 28.8(a)]

[1]H.Conf.Rept. 104-518, at 111 (1996).

[2]See Ad Hoc Committee on Federal Habeas Corpus in Capital Cases, Report on Habeas Corpus in Capital Cases, reprinted in 135 Cong.Rec. 24694 (1989).

counsel at this stage[3]). Once a state has established that it had such a program, federal habeas petitions by its death row inmates would be subject to a streamlined procedure that had three primary components.

First, the Committee recommended that habeas petitions should be filed within 180 days from the end of the (state proceedings,) but prisoners would receive an automatic stay of execution, allowing them the full period to prepare their petition. Second, the habeas court would be limited to consideration of constitutional claims properly presented in the state proceedings, excepting only those claims that had not been presented as a result of (1) state action that violated the Constitution, (2) the Supreme Court's subsequent recognition of a new right given retroactive application, or (3) a factual predicate that could not have been timely discovered through the exercise of due diligence. Third, the stay of execution would terminate after the resolution of the first federal habeas application and the federal courts would lack authority to grant a further stay, or to award relief on any subsequent petition, unless (1) the prisoner presented a constitutional claim not previously raised, (2) the failure to raise that claim previously was the product of one of the same three factors that would extend the time limitation, and (3) "the facts underlying the [new] claim would be sufficient, if proven, to undermine the court's confidence in the jury's determination of guilt on the offense or offenses for which the death penalty was imposed."[4] The Powell Committee reasoned that with competent counsel assisting the prisoner in the state post-conviction proceeding, ordinarily all possible constitutional contentions should have been presented in the state proceedings. Also, with counsel provided in capital cases in federal habeas proceedings,[5] the prisoner should be able to present all of his claims in a single habeas petition and do so in a fairly prompt fashion.

Section 2261, following the recommendation of the Powell Committee, conditions the application of the remainder of chapter 154 on the state's compliance with certain requirements regarding the provision of counsel in state post conviction proceedings. These requirements are discussed in § 28.9(b), below. Initially, § 2262 requires an automatic stay of execution upon request of the state prisoner, thereby insuring that the prisoner will be able to utilize the post-conviction procedures anticipated under chapter 154. The stay continues in effect until either (1) the

---

[3]See Murray v. Giarratano, 492 U.S. 1, 109 S.Ct. 2765, 106 L.Ed.2d 397 (1986), discussed in § 11.1.

[4]Ad Hoc Committee on Federal Habeas Corpus in Capital Cases,

Report on Habeas Corpus in Capital Cases, reprinted in 135 Cong.Rec. 24694 (1989).

[5]See 21 U.S.C.A. § 848(q)(4)(B), discussed also in § 28.12(b) at note 8.

prisoner waives in open court his right to seek federal habeas relief, (2) the period allowed for filing under § 2263 expires without a filing, (3) the prisoner files a petition but fails to make a substantial showing of a denial of federal claim, or (4) the prisoner files and relief is denied "in the district court or at any subsequent stage of review."

The time limitation for filing specified in § 2263, is the 180-day period urged by the Powell Committee, although Congress shortened the length of the extension allowed for extraordinary circumstances to 30 days. Section 2263 utilizes a starting point roughly parallel to that utilized for the general, one-year limitation imposed under § 2244(d), but § 2263 describes somewhat differently the period that is excluded due to pending proceedings. Section 2266 supplements the time limitation for filing by imposing a time limitation for judicial disposition once the petition is filed. The district court ordinarily must render a final ruling on the petition within 450 days of the filing, although here too, a 30-day extension is possible under special circumstances. If an appeal of the district court's ruling is taken to the Court of Appeals, that court must issue its ruling within 120 days after the final brief is filed.

Section 2264 limits the scope of the issues to be considered by the habeas court, here again following recommendation of the Powell Committee. As a general matter, the federal habeas court may consider only "claims that have been raised and decided on the merits" in state courts.[6] The Powell Committee recognized three exceptions to this principle, and § 2264 also includes those exceptions—instances in which the failure to raise the claim in the state courts was the result of (1) state action itself violating the Constitution, (2) a factual predicate that could not have been discovered through due diligence in time to present the claim in the state proceedings, and (3) the Supreme Court's subsequent recognition of a new federal right that is made "retroactively applicable." The Powell Committee recommended that a combination of one of these three circumstances and a factual showing that undermined confidence in the accuracy of the guilty verdict should also create an exception to its general rule limiting the prisoner to one habeas challenge. Such a limitation is not included in chapter 154, perhaps because the 1996 amendments also included a new § 2244(b), which imposes even more stringent limits on successive petitions that are applicable to all petitions by state prisoners. Also, a showing of probable innocence is a prerequisite for obtaining an evidentiary hearing under § 2254(e)(2).

As for claims not considered on their merits in state court, Sec-

---

[6]See § 28.4.

tion 2264(a) allows habeas review only when the "failure to raise the claim properly is—(1) the result of State action in violation of the Constitution or laws of the United States; (2) the result of the Supreme Court's recognition of a new Federal right that is made retroactively applicable; or (3) based on a factual predicate that could not have been discovered through the exercise of due diligence in time to present the claim for State or Federal post-conviction review." For those capital cases covered by this provision, it operates as the legislative replacement of the *Sykes* "cause and prejudice" standard and its "fundamental miscarriage of justice" exception.

The first exception recognized in § 2264(a)—where the "failure to raise the claim properly" was a "result of State action in violation of the Constitution or laws of the United States"—clearly includes much of the "government interference" that constitutes "cause" under the *Sykes* standard. In one respect it is narrower, as the cases discussing this type of cause have not suggested that the interference constituting "cause" must itself amount to a "violation of the Constitution or laws of the United States." Notably absent in § 2264(a) is any authority to consider a procedurally defaulted claim where the state court based that default on a ground that would not constitute "an adequate state ground" on direct review by the Supreme Court.[7] It seems unlikely, however, that Congress intended to withdraw such authority, which has never been controversial.[8] Eliminating in capital cases alone such a well-established and long-standing ground for reaching the merits of a claim notwithstanding a procedural default under state law would be unwarranted without more express direction from Congress.

The second exception recognized in § 2264(a)—where the "failure to raise the claim properly" was "the result of the Supreme Court's recognition of a new Federal right that is made retroactively applicable"—appears to incorporate the retroactivity doc-

---

[7]See § 28.4(b).

[8]The original version of what became § 2646(a)(1), the Powell Commission proposal, more readily encompassed review after such a state court ruling. It established a general restriction of habeas review to "claims actually presented and litigated in the state courts," subject to an exception where the "failure to raise or develop a claim in the state courts is * * * the result of state action in violation of the Constitution or laws of the United States." Ad Hoc Committee on Federal Habeas Corpus in Capital Cases, Report on Habeas Corpus in Capital Cases, reprinted in 135 Cong.Rec. 24694 (1989). The changes made by Congress do not appear to be aimed at narrowing the character of the state action that would fit within the exception. Compare § 2244(d)(1)(B) and § 2255, both dealing with the extension of the one-year time period for filing, and referring only to "state action in violation of the Constitution or laws of the United States" that created an "impediment" to filing.

trine of *Teague*,[9] and provide review for cases alleging violations of any "new rule" that is to be applied retroactively under the principles of that case. A "new rule" for this purpose is any rule "not dictated by precedent" at the time that the defendant failed to press the claim in the state courts. Under § 2264(a)'s second exception, it is sufficient that the failure to present the claim in the state court was the "result" of the Court's recognition of the new rule (i.e., that the new rule was not anticipated). There appears to be no requirement that counsel's failure to anticipate the new rule reflect the gross incompetence required for a Sixth Amendment violation. The exception remains sharply confined, however, by the Court's limitation of the retroactive application of new rulings on habeas corpus to two, narrowly construed categories of new rules (the so-called *Teague* exceptions).[10]

The third exception of § 2264(a) allows relief when the defaulted claim could not have be properly raised in the state court because its factual predicate could not have been earlier discovered through the exercise of due diligence. Ordinarily, where a constitutional claim is based on newly discovered evidence that could not have been previously discovered with the exercise of due diligence, state courts will allow that claim to be raised for the first time on a post-conviction challenge. However, as illustrated by the *Herrera* case,[11] some states require that motions based on newly discovered evidence be made within a fairly brief time period after conviction.[12] The third exception ensures that claims prevented by such time limits from being considered on the merits in the state courts will be considered by the federal habeas court in qualified capital cases.

Perhaps the most significant feature of § 2264(a) is its failure to specifically take into account the impact of the alleged constitutional violation that was procedurally defaulted. None of its three exceptions justifying consideration of a defaulted claim include an exception for a "miscarriage of justice." The absence of any "actual innocence" component is especially striking since Congress included an actual innocence exception to two other provisions elsewhere in the Act, both of which would otherwise bar relief in cases in which only a petitioner's liberty, not his life, may be at stake.[13] Thus, a petitioner sentenced to death from a qualifying state, who fails to raise his claim in state court, and

---

[9]Teague v. Lane, 489 U.S. 288, 109 S.Ct. 1060, 103 L.Ed.2d 334 (1989), discussed in § 28.6(c) to (e). See also § 28.5(d) at notes 83–85, discussing a similar exception for successive petitions.

[10]See § 28.6(e).

[11]Herrera v. Collins, 506 U.S. 390, 113 S.Ct. 853, 122 L.Ed.2d 203 (1983), discussed in § 28.3(e).

[12]See § 24.11 (discussing new trial motions).

[13]See § 2244(b)(2)(B) (allowing review of a new claim in a successive

cannot meet any of the exceptions in § 2264(a) (say, a petitioner whose attorney was less than diligent in uncovering the basis for his constitutional claim), may receive no relief in federal habeas, despite a showing of probable innocence.[14]

§ 28.8(b) The opt-in requirements: electing the special standards

In order to gain the benefit of the new standards outlined above, a state must adopt a "mechanism for the appointment, compensation, and payment of reasonable litigation expenses of competent counsel in State post-conviction proceedings brought by indigent prisoners whose capital sentences have been upheld on direct review." Recognizing that some states utilize a unitary appeal procedure in capital cases, which allows the defendant in a single proceeding to both appeal trial court rulings and raise issues that otherwise would be considered only in collateral attack, § 2265 also makes the chapter applicable to states which provide counsel that meet the standards of § 2261 in such a proceeding. Section 2261 insists that the state prescribe "standards of competency for the appointment of counsel," but itself imposes only one specific standard—that the counsel appointed not have been the trial or appellate counsel (or simply not the trial counsel in a state with a unitary review procedure), unless "the prisoner and counsel expressly request continued representation." The focus of § 2261 is on the general standards utilized in appointing counsel and in providing "reasonable litigation expenses."[15] As of this writing, only one state's program for the provision of counsel has been approved as meeting the standards specified in chapter 154, and then only in dicta.[16]

Congress amended the approval mechanism for qualifying

---

petition, discussed in § 28.5(d)), and § 2254(e)(2) (providing evidentiary hearing, discussed in § 28.7(b)). Of course, as with all claims, the habeas court will refuse to grant relief if the constitutional violation constitutes harmless error. See § 28.3(f).

[14]Such an individual may be able to pursue relief under § 2241, with an extraordinarily compelling demonstration of innocence. See § 28.3(e).

[Section 28.8(b)]

[15]Should the counsel provided under a satisfactory appointment mechanism turn out to be ineffective in the assistance rendered in the state post-conviction proceeding or in subsequent federal habeas proceedings, however, the incompetence of counsel at either stage "shall not be grounds for relief" under § 2254. This provision is identical to 28 U.S.C.A. § 2254(i).

[16]See Spears v. Stewart, 283 F.3d 992 (9th Cir.2002) (although Arizona's scheme for providing counsel to indigent prisoners in capital cases satisfies the "opt-in" provisions, the state "failed utterly" to comply with its own system in this case). For examples of decisions finding other state system's insufficient, see, e.g., Death Row Prisoners of Pennsylvania v. Ridge, 106 F.3d 35 (3d Cir.1997) (Pennsylvania); Scott v. Anderson, 958 F.Supp. 330 (N.D.Ohio 1997) (Ohio); Breard v. Netherland, 949 F.Supp. 1255 (E.D.Va. 1996) (Virginia); Baker v. Corcoran,

states in 2005.[17] The United States Attorney General is now authorized to determine whether a state has met the statutory standards, with review by the Court of Appeals for the D.C. Circuit.

§ 28.9 Remedies for federal prisoners
§ 28.9(a)   The range of remedies
§ 28.9(b)   Limits on relief under § 2255
§ 28.9(c)   Nonconstitutional claims under § 2255

§ 28.9(a) The range of remedies

Section 2255. First adopted in 1948, 28 U.S.C.A. § 2255 provides the major collateral remedy for challenging federal convictions. The statute authorizes a motion to vacate, set aside, or correct a sentence, filed in the sentencing court. That motion is available to a person "in custody" under the sentence of a federal court upon a claim that "the sentence was imposed in violation of the Constitution or laws of the United States, or that the court was without jurisdiction to impose such sentence, or that the sentence was in excess of the maximum authorized by law, or is otherwise subject to collateral attack." While this language might suggest that the motion serves only to challenge the sentence itself, the § 2255 provision governing the granting of relief indicates otherwise in noting that the court may "set the judgment aside and * * * discharge the prisoner." Read in light of this language and the legislative history of the provision, the term "sentence" has been regarded as a generic term including all of the proceedings leading up to the sentence.[1]

There was some initial confusion as to the precise nature of the motion, given the Reviser's Note to the 1948 Judicial Code which

---

220 F.3d 276 (4th Cir.2000); Ashmus v. Woodford, 202 F.3d 1160 (9th Cir.2000) (California does not qualify). See also Kappler, Small Favors: Chapter 154 of the Antiterrorism and Effective Death Penalty Act, the States, and the Right to Counsel, 90 J.Crim.L. & Criminology 469 (2000) (reviewing "opt-in" provisions and surveying case law); R. Hertz & J. Liebman, 1 Federal Habeas Corpus Practice and Procedure § 3.3a at n. 2 (5th ed.2005) (collecting cases); McCoy and Lichtenberg, Providing Effective Habeas Counsel for Indigents in Capital Cases, 21 Just.Syst.J. 81 (1999).

[17]See 28 U.S.C.A. § 2266(b)(1)(A).

[Section 28.9(a)]

[1]See Davis v. United States, 417 U.S. 333, 94 S.Ct. 2298, 41 L.Ed.2d 109 (1974), where the Court stated that "the statutory language is somewhat lacking in precision," but that the legislative history clearly established that § 2255 was to provide a remedy "identical in scope" to that previously provided under §§ 2254 and 2241, the habeas provisions. For a detailed treatment of relief under Section 2255, see C. Wright, N. King & S. Klein, Federal Practice and Procedure, Criminal §§ 591 to 602 (3d ed. 2004).

stated that § 2255 "restates, clarifies, and simplifies the procedure in the nature of the ancient writ of coram nobis." Like coram nobis, the motion was to be filed in the sentencing court, but the requirement of custody and the grounds of attack did not fit within the framework of that common law writ. In *United States v. Hayman*,[2] the Court stated that the § 2255 motion was the functional equivalent of the habeas writ, simply moved to a more convenient forum. It noted the new remedy was intended only to respond to venue difficulties created by the increasing number of petitions filed by federal prisoners. Since habeas petitions were filed in the district of the petitioner's detention, judges in districts containing major federal penal institutions "were required to handle an inordinate number of habeas actions far from the scene of the facts, the homes of the witnesses, and records of the sentencing courts." Section 2255, the Court noted, was enacted to meet this practical problem, not to restrict the scope of collateral attack. The Court described § 2255 as "provid[ing] in the sentencing court a remedy exactly commensurate with that which had previously been available by habeas corpus."[3] In light of the *Hayman* ruling, the § 2255 motion has displaced the writ of habeas corpus under § 2241 as the basic collateral remedy for persons confined pursuant to a federal criminal conviction.

Habeas Corpus Relief Under § 2241 for Federal Prisoners. The so-called "savings clause" in § 2255 prohibits review of applications under § 2241 filed by a prisoner "authorized to apply for relief" under § 2255 "unless it also appears that the remedy by motion is inadequate or ineffective to test the legality of his detention."[4] This phrase has been interpreted very strictly, so as to prevent prisoners from seeking habeas relief under § 2241 as an end run around congressional efforts to limit § 2255 relief under § 2241. For example, § 2241 is not open to an applicant who raises a claim otherwise appropriate under § 2255, but who is unable to secure § 2255 relief because he raises the claim in a successive application and the Court has not made retroactive

---

[2]United States v. Hayman, 342 U.S. 205, 72 S.Ct. 263, 96 L.Ed. 232 (1952).

[3]Subsequent cases have attributed to the motion the general qualities of a habeas writ. See, e.g., Heflin v. United States, 358 U.S. 415, 79 S.Ct. 451, 3 L.Ed.2d 407 (1959); Kaufman v. United States, 394 U.S. 217, 89 S.Ct. 1068, 22 L.Ed.2d 227 (1969); United States v. Timmreck, 441 U.S. 780, 99 S.Ct. 2085, 60 L.Ed.2d 634 (1979). See also Ferrara v. United

States, 372 F.Supp.2d 108 (D.Mass. 2005) (court has equitable power under § 2255 to devise a remedy for the violation of constitutional rights, including substituting a non-Guidelines sentence for the defendant, who had already served more time than he probably would have served had the government not violated *Brady*).

[4]See United States v. Hayman, 342 U.S. 205, 72 S.Ct. 263, 96 L.Ed. 232 (1952).

the rule on which he relies.[5]

By contrast, § 2255 relief is impossible—i.e., "inadequate or ineffective"—for an applicant who claims in a successive application under § 2255 that subsequent to his first petition the Court has held that what she did was not prohibited by federal law. Prisoners who fall within this narrow class of applicants, incarcerated for conduct that was never a criminal offense, have uniformly been allowed to pursue habeas relief.[6] As the Second Circuit Court of Appeals explained, habeas relief should be available, at the least, when the petitioner cannot use § 2255 and when the failure to allow for collateral review would raise "serious constitutional questions."[7]

Relief under § 2241 also remains available for certain aliens incarcerated by the Immigration and Naturalization Service,[8] for some incarcerated by the United States military,[9] and has also been extended to prisoners who challenge the manner in which his sentence is being executed, after exhausting federal adminis-

---

[5]United States ex rel Perez v. Warden, 286 F.3d 1059 (8th Cir.2002); Ivy v. Pontesso, 328 F.3d 1057 (9th Cir.2003) (as amended) (remedy under § 2255 is "inadequate or ineffective" only when the petitioner (1) claims he is factually of the crime of conviction and (2) has never had an "unobstructed procedural shot" at presenting this claim). See also Adams v. United States, 372 F.3d 132 (2d Cir.2004) (district court can treat the § 2241 petition as a second or successive § 2255 petition and refer the petition to court of appeals for certification, or if it is plain from the petition that the prisoner cannot demonstrate that a remedy under § 2255 would be inadequate or ineffective to test the legality of his detention, the district court may dismiss the § 2241 petition for lack of jurisdiction).

[6]E.g., In re Smith, 285 F.3d 6 (D.C.Cir.2002) (collecting authority); Reyes-Requena v. United States, 243 F.3d 893 (5th Cir.2001) (collecting authority and allowing § 2241 petition, distinguishing cases in which petitioner not allowed to pursue relief under § 2241 due to expiration of limitations on § 2255 motion or due to nonretroactivity of new rule of constitutional law). Compare Paulino v. United States, 352 F.3d 1056 (6th Cir.2003)

(Section 2241 permits relief, in lieu of relief under § 2255 only in those instances where the individual can make a showing of factual innocence, no showing here).

[7]Triestman v. United States, 124 F.3d 361 (2d Cir.1997) (finding that "serious Eighth Amendment and due process questions would arise" if the new § 2255 were construed to preclude "post-conviction relief for a claim of actual innocence that was based on the existing record and that could not have been effectively brought previously"). See also In re Dorsainvil, 119 F.3d 245 (3d Cir.1997); Garza v. Lappin, 253 F.3d 918 (7th Cir.2001) (court had jurisdiction in § 2241 petition despite former § 2255 application when petitioner's claim arose under treaty and could not have been advanced in § 2255 application). Compare Charles v. Chandler, 180 F.3d 753 (6th Cir.1999); Wofford v. Scott, 177 F.3d 1236 (11th Cir.1999).

[8]See § 28.2(a) at note 12. See also Zadvydas v. Davis, 533 U.S. 678, 121 S.Ct. 2491, 150 L.Ed.2d 653 (2001) (aliens detained indefinitely when efforts to deport them have failed).

[9]See enemy combatant cases discussed in § 28.2(a) at notes 14–18.

trative remedies.[10]

Coram Nobis. The writ of coram nobis also remains an avenue of relief for federal defendants under the All Writs Act, 28 U.S.C.A. § 1651.[11] The authority of federal courts to issue the writ of coram nobis, notwithstanding the adoption of § 2255, was established in *United States v. Morgan.*[12] The petitioner there sought to challenge his federal conviction on the ground that he had not been afforded his constitutional right to counsel before pleading guilty. After having fully served his federal sentence, he was convicted of a state offense and sentenced to an enhanced term as a second offender. Because he was no longer "in custody" on the federal offense, he sought to utilize the writ of coram nobis rather than § 2255. That writ traditionally had been available without regard to a custody requirement.[13] The government contended, however, that § 2255 had codified the remedy and restricted it to petitioners who were still in custody. The Supreme Court rejected that contention, noting that § 2255 had been enacted to meet practical difficulties relating to the use of the habeas writ by federal prisoners. Neither § 2255 nor Rule 60(b) of the Federal Rules of Civil Procedure foreclosed federal prisoners from seeking relief through a writ of coram nobis.

The Court's opinion in *Morgan* suggested three prerequisites to coram nobis relief. First, the writ is only an option if § 2255 or other relief is not available or adequate,[14] ruling out most claims by prisoners "in custody" who are able to seek relief under § 2255.[15] The writ of coram nobis remains useful, however, when the defendant is not "in custody."[16]

Second, the Court noted that coram nobis is available for "er-

---

[10]Carmona v. U.S. Bureau of Prisons, 243 F.3d 629 (2d Cir.2001).

[11]See generally 3 C. Wright, N. King & S. Klein, Federal Practice and Procedure § 592 (3d ed.2004). Coram nobis is not available in a federal court as a means of attack on a state criminal judgment. Obado v. State of New Jersey, 328 F.3d 716 (3d Cir.2003) (collecting authority).

[12]United States v. Morgan, 346 U.S. 502, 74 S.Ct. 247, 98 L.Ed. 248 (1954).

[13]See § 28.1(c).

[14]See United States v. Camacho-Bordes, 94 F.3d 1168 (8th Cir.1996); United States v. Brown, 117 F.3d 471 (11th Cir.1997); C. Wright, N. King & S. Klein, Federal Practice and Procedure, Criminal § 592 (3d ed.2004) (col-

lecting cases).

[15]See United States v. Kindle, 88 F.3d 535 (8th Cir.1996); United States v. Torres, 282 F.3d 1241 (10th Cir.2002) (a prisoner may not challenge a sentence or conviction for which he is currently in custody through a writ of *coram nobis*); United States v. Brown, 117 F.3d 471 (11th Cir.1997) (concluding that coram nobis relief was unavailable to prisoner in custody within the meaning of § 2255); United States v. Butler, 295 F.Supp.2d 816 (S.D.Oh. 2003) (petitioner released on personal recognizance bond prior to serving sentence was in custody, and therefore barred from seeking writ of coram nobis).

[16]Thus, the writ was used successfully by a petitioner who had fully served his sentence in attacking a

rors 'of the most fundamental character,'" and held that petitioner's Sixth Amendment claim was such a claim. The Court later explained in *Carlisle v. United States*[17] that the writ "was traditionally available only to bring before the court factual errors 'material to the validity and regularity of the legal proceeding itself,' such as the defendants being under age or having died before the verdict."[18]

Thus, the writ has been granted in cases where the applicant demonstrates that his conduct was not criminal under the law as later interpreted by the Court.[19] Third, drawing upon the Court's statement in *Morgan* that "sound reasons exist[ed] for [the petitioner's] failure to seek appropriate earlier relief," lower courts have insisted that petitioners seeking a writ of coram

---

conviction that actually had been sustained by the Supreme Court. In Korematsu v. United States, 584 F.Supp. 1406 (N.D.Cal.1984), the petitioner challenged his conviction for violating a World War II statute that made it a crime to violate a military order excluding persons of Japanese ancestry from areas specified by the military. The Supreme Court had rejected petitioner's challenge to his conviction in 1944, holding that the exclusion order constituted a valid exercise of military authority. The government, in the current action, asked that the conviction be vacated under its Rule 48(a) authority, maintaining that a nolle prosequi could be entered at any time. The district court instead relied on newly discovered information establishing "prosecutorial impropriety" and a "miscarriage of justice" in the original conviction. It cited a 1982 National Commission Report concluding that military necessity had not justified the exclusion order and various internal documents indicating that the government knowingly withheld information relevant to the military necessity issue from the courts that considered petitioner's original conviction.

[17]Carlisle v. United States, 517 U.S. 416, 116 S.Ct. 1460, 134 L.Ed.2d 613 (1996).

[18]*Carlisle*, (citing United States v. Mayer, 235 U.S. 55, 35 S.Ct. 16, 59 L.Ed. 129 (1914)). See also United States v. Sawyer, 239 F.3d 31 (1st Cir.2001) (reviewing authority, citing treatise, and finding no fundamental error when defendant challenged conviction based on subsequent construction of the statute of conviction by the Supreme Court); United States v. Stoneman, 870 F.2d 102 (3d Cir.1989) (error must go to jurisdiction of trial court, and writ not available to challenge conviction under theory of federal mail fraud statute later rejected by Supreme Court); United States v. Swindall, 107 F.3d 831 (11th Cir.1997) and supp) (concluding that "if *Teague* bars a petitioner's claim relying on a case decided after his conviction and sentence became final, then he has not suffered such compelling injustice that would deserve relief pursuant to a writ of error coram nobis"); Annot., 37 A.L.R.Fed. 499 (1997) (and supp) (collecting cases considering relief prior to serving sentence); Annot., 38 A.L.R. Fed. 617 (1997) (collecting cases considering relief after sentence has been served).

[19]E.g., United States v. Mandel, 862 F.2d 1067 (4th Cir.1988) (not guilty after *McNally*); United States v. Peters, 310 F.3d 709 (11th Cir.2002) (not guilty after *Cleveland*). See also DeCecco v. United States, 485 F.2d 372 (1st Cir.1973) (not guilty of tax crime found later by the Supreme Court to violate Fifth Amendment); Rewak v. United States, 512 F.2d 1184 (9th Cir.1975).

nobis must exercise "reasonable diligence" in seeking prompt relief.[20] This requirement is not as strict as the one-year limitations period for filing restricting relief for prisoners who are in custody and attack the constitutionality of their conviction or sentence, although many of those cases dismissed as untimely would have been untimely under either standard.[21] An additional requirement that has been adopted by most circuits is that an applicant must demonstrate "lingering civil disabilities" from a conviction.[22] Given this daunting array of prerequisites, the Court understandably concluded in *Carlisle* that " 'it is difficult to

---

[20]See United States v. Dyer, 136 F.3d 417 (5th Cir.1998) (quoting *Morgan*). Compare Foont v. United States, 93 F.3d 76 (2d Cir.1996) (claim of new evidence, without constitutional or jurisdictional error in the underlying proceeding, cannot support a coram nobis claim, nor constitute "sound reason" for failing to seek relief from 1990 conviction until 1995); United States v. Dos Santos, 979 F.Supp. 949 (E.D.N.Y.1997) ("The petitioner failed to avail itself of a direct appeal from his conviction and sentence, and he cannot recapture that lost opportunity by restoring to coram nobis," and noting that the defendant's decision to seek coram nobis relief "may be prompted by the need to avoid the limitation of the * * * AEDPA" which includes a statute of limitation that would bar relief under § 2255) with Blanton v. United States, 94 F.3d 227 (6th Cir.1996) (laches applies to coram nobis proceedings, but finding that three years was "not an unduly long delay; it was a reasonable amount of time for [petitioner] to obtain new counsel and file suit"); Nicks v. United States, 835 F.Supp. 151 (S.D.N.Y.1993) (petitioner's mental state was "sound reason" for failure to petition at an earlier time). See also Annot., 62 A.L.R.2d 432 (Supp.1997) (collecting cases addressing the effect of delay on the availability of coram nobis relief).

[21]In re Foont v. United States, 93 F.3d 76 (2d Cir.1996) (petitioner failed to demonstrate sufficient reasons for the five-year delay between plea and filing of petition); United States v. Darnell, 716 F.2d 479 (7th Cir.1983)

(20-year delay barred relief); Telink v. United States, 24 F.3d 42 (9th Cir.1994) (upholding dismissal of challenge filed in 1992, claiming 1988 decision in *McNally* undermined their 1986 convictions); Klein v. United States, 880 F.2d 250 (10th Cir.1989) (no due diligence when applicant had access to information from 1978 to 1985 and did nothing, and during that time two witnesses died); Weichert v. United States, 458 F.Supp.2d 57 (N.D.N.Y.2006) (no sound reasons for nineteen-year delay in filing); United States v. Dyer, 136 F.3d 417 (5th Cir.1998) (*McNally* challenge filed in 1996 was untimely).

But see United States v. Cariola, 323 F.2d 180 (3d Cir.1963) (coram nobis relief ordered despite 18-month delay in filing after learning that the conviction applicant thought was a misdemeanor was actually a felony); United States v. Kwan, 407 F.3d 1005 (9th Cir. 2005) (allowing 2001 action challenging 1996 bank fraud guilty plea due to ineffective assistance of counsel); Nicks v. United States, 835 F. Supp. 151 (S.D.N.Y.1993) (finding sound reasons for delay in challenging 1975 conviction in 1989).

[22]United States v. Dyer, 136 F.3d 417 (5th Cir.1998); Blanton v. United States, 94 F.3d 227 (6th Cir.1996) (collecting authority, noting that while the First, Second, Third, Fifth, Seventh, and Eighth Circuits all require ongoing collateral consequences, the Fourth and Ninth Circuits have "indicated that a coram nobis petitioner need not show that he is suffering from an ongoing civil disability"); United States v.

conceive of a situation in a federal criminal case today where [a writ of coram nobis] would be necessary or appropriate.' "[23] Moreover, the writ of coram nobis may also be limited to applicants who can get around the *Teague* bar on retroactive application of new rules of procedure.[24]

Audita Querela. The common law writ of *audita querela* remains available, at least hypothetically, to a defendant who raises a "legal objection" that is "not cognizable under existing federal post-conviction remedies"[25] and that "arises after the judgment."[26] Recently, this writ has been invoked by defendants facing deportation for past convictions, or whose § 2255 motions would be barred as successive. Courts considering such challenges, however, have agreed that equitable reasons alone, even of the most compelling nature, are insufficient to warrant relief by *audita querela.* Legal reasons for challenging a conviction are typically within the scope of either § 2255 or other remedies, so that *audita querela* is unavailable.[27] Interpreting *audita querela* as an unbounded equitable remedy would depart from the writ's common law constraints,[28] and, when the conviction challenged is a basis for deportation, may threaten the discretionary power of the executive to prosecute and pardon as well as the power of

---

Bush, 888 F.2d 1145 (7th Cir.1989) (coram nobis not available when only continuing consequence of conviction was inability to pursue professional career).

[23]See, e.g., United States v. Sawyer, 239 F.3d 31 (1st Cir.2001) (characterizing the three-part test as requiring 1) an explanation for failing to seek relief earlier; 2) continuing collateral consequences from conviction; and 3) an error was fundamental to the validity of the judgment, assuming without deciding that a writ of coram nobis is available to vacate a criminal conviction premised upon a fundamental error of law, but finding no fundamental legal error).

[24]United States v. Mandanici, 205 F.3d 519 (2d Cir.2000).

[25]United States v. Ayala, 894 F.2d 425 (D.C.Cir.1990) ("The teaching of *Morgan* is that federal courts may properly fill the interstices of the federal post-conviction remedial framework through remedies available at common law.").

[26]See United States v. Banda, 1 F.3d 354 (5th Cir.1993). See also 11 Wright & Miller, Federal Practice and Procedure § 2867 (1973) (writ permits defendant to obtain "relief against a judgment or execution because of some defense or discharge arising subsequent to the rendition of the judgment").

[27]Carrington v. United States, 470 F.3d 920 (9th Cir.2006); United States v. Holt, 417 F.3d 1172 (11th Cir.2005).

[28]E.g., United States v. Bravo-Diaz, 312 F.3d 995 (9th Cir.2002) (court had no jurisdiction to issue writ of *audita querela*); United States v. Torres, 282 F.3d 1241 (10th Cir.2002) (a writ of *audita querela* is not available to a petitioner when other remedies exist, such as a motion under § 2255, collecting authority, and noting differences between writs of audita querela and coram nobis).

Congress to set standards for deportation.[29]

§ 28.9(b) Limits on relief under § 2255

Many of the same limitations on a judge's authority to grant the writ under § 2254 also restrict relief under § 2255. There are important differences, however. As a policy matter, federalism concerns, which weigh heavily in the role of federal habeas review of state court action, should play no role in federal collateral review of another federal proceeding. Perhaps reflecting this difference, § 2255, as amended by the AEDPA, provides to federal prisoners somewhat more generous review than is provided to state prisoners by §§ 2244 and 2254.

Custody. Section 2255 imposes a custody requirement identical in scope to that applied under § 2254.[30] Thus, decisions discussed in § 28.3(a) are fully applicable to § 2255 cases.[31]

Cognizable Claims. The range of claims cognizable under § 2255 is broader than under § 2254, as it allows federal prisoners to raise claims based on federal statutory law as well as constitutional law. Such claims are discussed in the § 28.9(c), and are cognizable under § 2255 only when establishing a "fundamental defect." In *Kaufman v. United States*[32] the Supreme Court held that, as to constitutional claims, the two remedies should be construed to have equal scope. Justice Brennan, speaking for the Court, reasoned that § 2255, like the habeas writ for state prisoners, "rests * * * fundamentally upon a recognition that adequate protection of constitutional rights relating to the criminal trial process requires the continuing availability of a mechanism for relief." Following the demise of habeas review of Fourth Amendment claims, such claims were held non-cognizable under § 2255 as well.[33]

Retroactivity. Although the Court's decision in *Teague v. Lane*[34] to restrict habeas relief based upon "new" rules of criminal procedure was based in part upon concerns about comity and federal-

---

[29]See Doe v. Immigration and Naturalization Service, 120 F.3d 200 (9th Cir.1997) (collecting authority).

[Section 28.9(b)]

[30]See Heflin v. United States, 358 U.S. 415, 79 S.Ct. 451, 3 L.Ed.2d 407 (1959); United States v. Condit, 621 F.2d 1096 (10th Cir.1980).

[31]See, e.g., Custis v. United States, 511 U.S. 485, 114 S.Ct. 1732, 128 L.Ed.2d 517 (1994). See also United States v. Thiele, 314 F.3d 399 (9th Cir.2002) (Section 2255 not available to vacate restitution order, collecting

authority).

[32]Kaufman v. United States, 394 U.S. 217, 89 S.Ct. 1068, 22 L.Ed.2d 227 (1969).

[33]See Tisnado v. United States, 547 F.2d 452 (9th Cir.1976) (*Stone* applies in § 2255 proceedings); United States v. Cook, 997 F.2d 1312 (10th Cir.1993) (same, collecting authority); United States v. Ishmael, 343 F.3d 741 (5th Cir.2003) (following *Cook*).

[34]Teague v. Lane, 489 U.S. 288, 109 S.Ct. 1060, 103 L.Ed.2d 334 (1989).

state relations, the retroactivity analysis of *Teague* has also been extended to applications from federal prisoners for relief under § 2255.[35] The 1996 amendments also added two separate references in § 2255 to new rights "recognized by the Supreme Court and made retroactively applicable to cases on collateral review." These provisions, similar to those found in § 2244 and § 2254, suggest that Congress intended the same retroactivity rules to apply to the collateral review of both state and federal judgments, and did not consider those rules to be premised primarily upon federalism concerns.

Teague bars only those claims of error that are based upon new procedural rulings; claims based on new interpretations of substantive federal criminal law are not barred. Specifically, a court will review an applicant's claim under § 2255 that he is entitled to the benefit of a decision of the Supreme Court, handed down following his conviction, that the federal criminal statute under which he was convicted does not reach his conduct. For example, in *Bousley v. United States*,[36] a prisoner sought relief based on a decision of the Supreme Court holding that the crime he was charged with violating did not reach his conduct, claimed that he was misinformed about the elements of his offense, and as a result, pleaded guilty to a crime he did not commit. The Court rejected the application of *Teague* to this issue of "substance" rather than procedure, and concluded that "it would be inconsistent with the doctrinal underpinnings of habeas review to preclude petitioner from relying on our decision * * * in support of his claims that his guilty plea was constitutionally invalid."[37]

Procedural Default. Noting that the objectives of encouraging adherence to procedural requirements and making the trial the "main event" are equally important to the federal process, the Supreme Court has interpreted § 2255 to incorporate the principles governing procedural defaults by state petitioners.[38] Thus, a prisoner who has failed to raise his claim in conformity

---

[35]See, e.g., United States v. Sanchez-Cervantes, 282 F.3d 664 (9th Cir.2002) (collecting authority applying *Teague* to § 2255 applications).

[36]Bousley v. United States, 523 U.S. 614, 118 S.Ct. 1604, 140 L.Ed.2d 828 (1998).

[37]See also United States v. Montalvo, 331 F.3d 1052 (9th Cir.2003) (*Richardson* decision, requiring specific unanimity instruction, was a substantive rule, not governed by *Teague*, but error was harmless under

Brecht); United States v. Barajas-Diaz, 313 F.3d 1242 (10th Cir.2002) (noting every court of appeals that has considered the issue has held that *Richardson* announced a new rule of substantive law, and may be applied retrospectively despite *Teague*).

[38]See United States v. Frady, 456 U.S. 152, 102 S.Ct. 1584, 71 L.Ed.2d 816 (1982); Kaufman v. United States, 394 U.S. 217, 89 S.Ct. 1068, 22 L.Ed.2d 227 (1969). See also Daniels v. United States, 532 U.S. 374, 121 S.Ct. 1578, 149 L.Ed.2d 590 (2001) ("A defendant

with procedural rules at the trial or appeal stage will be unable to present that claim in a § 2255 motion, absent a showing of cause and prejudice, or, alternatively, a miscarriage of justice.[39] However, petitioners who fail to raise claims of ineffective assis-

---

may challenge a prior conviction as the product of a *Gideon* violation in a § 2255 motion, but generally only if he raised that claim at his federal sentencing proceeding," citing *Frady*); Campino v. United States, 968 F.2d 187 (2d Cir.1992) (noting that even though a collateral challenge to a federal conviction under § 2255 does not implicate federalism issues the interests of finality, accuracy, integrity of prior proceedings and judicial economy justify a district court's refusal to entertain a § 2255 action containing a procedurally barred claim, absent a showing of cause and prejudice); Carmona v. United States Bureau of Prisons, 243 F.3d 629 (2d Cir.2001) (same, original habeas action under § 2241).

[39]See § 28.4(d) and (e). Consider, for example, Bousley v. United States, 523 U.S. 614, 118 S.Ct. 1604, 140 L.Ed.2d 828 (1998). There the Court rejected the defendant's argument that the novelty of the of the decision on which his claim was based—a Supreme Court decision interpreting a federal crime to include an element contrary to the unanimous position of the lower courts—provided "cause" for his default. The Court concluded that the legal basis for Bousley's claim *was* reasonably available at the time (noting "the Federal Reporters were replete with cases involving" similar claims), so that novelty as cause was unavailable. As to the futility of raising such a claim at a time when the lower courts were rejecting such claims, the Court responded that "futility cannot constitute cause if it means simply that a claim was unacceptable to that particular court at that particular time." See also Simpson v. Matesanz, 175 F.3d 200 (1st Cir.1999) (*Bousley*'s rule may seem harsh, and reflects a further restriction on federal habeas, but a real claim

of actual innocence trumps this restriction); Brache v. United States, 165 F.3d 99 (1st Cir.1999); Murphy v. United States, 282 F.3d 940 (7th Cir.2002) (cause for not raising in trial court an objection to the failure to charge the jury on an element of the offense was not established simply because the law of the Circuit at the time did not require such an instruction and counsel did not anticipate the Supreme Court's later contrary ruling in *Neder*—"the fact that an argument was unacceptable at a particular time does not constitute cause for failing to raise it," citing *Bousley*); Lynn v. United States, 365 F.3d 1225 (11th Cir.2004) (when appeal dismissed under the fugitive disentitlement doctrine, traditional rules of procedural default and exhaustion apply, prisoner is not per se barred from pursuing § 2255 relief, although this prisoner's claims are barred, reviewing authority).

A related problem arose in Daniels v. United States, 532 U.S. 374, 121 S.Ct. 1578, 149 L.Ed.2d 590 (2001), where the court held that a petitioner may not challenge a federal sentence on the basis that it was enhanced due to a constitutionally flawed prior state conviction. "To be sure, the text of § 2255 is broad enough to cover a claim that an enhanced federal sentence violated due process. * * * But when such a due process claim is predicated on the consideration at sentencing of a fully expired prior conviction, we think that the goals of easy administration and finality have ample 'horsepower' to justify foreclosing relief under § 2255." The Court left open the possibility that "there may be rare cases in which no channel of review was actually available to a defendant with respect to a prior conviction, due to no fault of his own."

tance of counsel on direct appeal will not have defaulted those claims. Such claims may be raised for the first time in a § 2255 motion[40] although some courts of appeals will remand such claims to the district court for fact-finding when raised on direct appeal.[41] As in state habeas proceedings, the government waives the defense of procedural default by failing to raise it.[42] Lower courts have held nevertheless, that sua sponte invocation of procedural default is within the court's discretion.[43]

Exhaustion of Direct Appeal and Co-ordination with Other Post-Conviction Remedies. The exhaustion doctrine is grounded in part on federalism concerns and incorporated in § 2254,[44] but not repeated in § 2255. Nevertheless, the federal courts have developed an analogue to § 2254 exhaustion applicable to § 2255. Normally, the § 2255 motion is not available until direct review of the applicant's conviction is complete.[45]

Time Limit for Filing. The AEDPA added a one-year statute of

---

[40]See, e.g., Massaro v. United States, 538 U.S. 500, 123 S.Ct. 1690, 155 L.Ed.2d 714 (2003), discussed in § 28.4(d) at note 58.

[41]United States v. Rashad, 331 F.3d 908 (D.C.Cir.2003) (defendant is not required to raise an ineffective assistance claim on collateral review, remand practice "derives from the perceived unfairness of holding a defendant making a claim of ineffective assistance to the seven-day time limit in Rule 33; remand of the record in a case raising ineffective assistance as the sole issue is appropriate if the trial record does not conclusively show whether the defendant is entitled to relief, an approach consistent with *Massaro*); United States v. Doe, 365 F.3d 150 (2d Cir.2004) (although the Court in *Massaro* did not express a preference either for or against remanding for fact-finding where the claims have in fact been raised on direct appeal, and did not hold that ineffective assistance claims must be reserved for collateral review, judicial economy is best served by requiring the district court to await the defendant's Section 2255 motion before addressing his ineffectiveness claim. "The delay occasioned by his being unable to have his ineffectiveness claim decided immediately upon remand is unlikely to have a material impact on the promptness of its resolution." The *Massaro* Court also rejected the argument that remand was better than requiring defendant to raise his claim in a § 2255 motion because counsel would be available if the appeal were remanded, but not available for a collateral challenge).

[42]E.g., United States v. Rezin, 322 F.3d 443 (7th Cir.2003).

[43]See, e.g., United States v. Wiseman, 297 F.3d 975 (10th Cir.2002) (the decision to raise default sua sponte depends on various factors, including the interests of finality and judicial efficiency, declining to enforce procedural bar sua sponte); Oakes v. United States, 400 F.3d 92 (1st Cir.2005) (reviewing authority, and stating "preventing the facile use of a habeas petition as a substitute for a direct appeal can be best accomplished if district courts have the discretion to enforce the procedural default rule even though the government (federal or state) turns a blind eye"). For similar rulings regarding state petitions, see § 28.4(c) note 31.

[44]See § 28.5(a).

[45]See, e.g., United States v. Means, 133 F.3d 444 (6th Cir.1998) (detailing procedure for securing relief in court of appeals under § 2255).

limitation for § 2255 motions, which "shall run from the latest of—(1) the date on which the judgment of conviction becomes final;[46] (2) the date on which the impediment to making a motion created by governmental action in violation of the Constitution or laws of the United States is removed, if the movant was prevented from making a motion by such governmental action; (3) the date on which the right asserted was initially recognized by the Supreme Court, if that right has been newly recognized by the Supreme Court and made retroactively applicable to cases on collateral review; or (4) the date on which the facts supporting the claim or claims presented could have been discovered through the exercise of due diligence."

The second condition seems to encompass at least those forms of "state interference" that would constitute "cause" under *Sykes* and that also amount to a constitutional violation.[47] The third condition—like similar provisions in § 2244(b)(2)(A), § 2244(d)(1)(C), and § 2254(e)(2)(A)(i)—was addressed in *Dodd v. United States*[48], where the court held that although the statute provides that the one-year clock does not start ticking until the Court initially recognizes the new rule, the clock keeps running while a petitioner waits for the rule to be "held" to apply retroactively. If, after the Court initially recognizes the rule, twelve months pass before the rule is held to be retroactive, any claim under that new rule will be time-barred. The Court termed this interpretation "strict," but "not absurd," even though it will bar most new-rule petitioners from presenting their claims.

For the fourth condition, courts consider cases interpreting similar language elsewhere in the statute, such as the language in §§ 2254(e)(2)(A)(ii) and 2254(a)(3). For example, the Court in *Johnson v. United States*,[49] found that a defendant who waited three years after his federal judgment to attack his underlying

---

[46]A judgment of conviction becomes final when the time expires for filing a petition for certiorari contesting the appellate court's affirmation of the conviction. Clay v. United States, 537 U.S. 522, 123 S.Ct. 1072, 155 L.Ed.2d 88 (2003).

[47]See § 28.4(d) (discussing "cause" for procedurally defaulted claims).

[48]Dodd v. United States, 545 U.S. 353, 125 S.Ct. 2478, 162 L.Ed.2d 343 (2005). An order vacating a state court conviction is a "new fact" that can trigger a new limitations period for a § 2255 action seeking relief from a sentence enhanced by that prior conviction.

[49]See § 28.5(d), discussing Johnson v. United States, 544 U.S. 295, 125 S.Ct. 1571, 161 L.Ed.2d 542 (2005).

See also Dodd v. United States, 545 U.S. 353, 125 S.Ct. 2478, 162 L.Ed.2d 343 (2005) (applicant must file application seeking relief under new interpretation of substantive criminal law within one-year of the decision announcing that new interpretation); Weigand v. United States, 380 F.3d 890 (6th Cir.2004) (collecting authority); Howard v. United States, 374 F.3d 1068 (11th Cir.2004). Rivers v. United States, 416 F.3d 1319 (11th Cir.2005) (on remand after Johnson, holding that although state order

state conviction had not exercised due diligence in seeking relief.

In addition to these statutory tolling conditions, most courts of appeals have held that this provision should allow "equitable tolling."[50] This interpretation is at odds with the language of the provision, but, like so many other questions raised by the new Act, the availability of equitable tolling has yet to be addressed by the Court.[51]

When a petitioner seeks to amend a petition to add a claim under Federal Rule of Civil Procedure 15(a), after the one-year statute of limitations has run, the question arises whether or not that amendment is barred by the limitations period. Rule 15(c)(2)

---

vacating conviction was a "fact" under § 2255 paragraph 6(4), petitioner did not exercise due diligence when he waited four years after judgment was entered on his federal sentence to challenge his state conviction.

[50]Trenkler v. United States, 268 F.3d 16 (1st Cir.2001) (collecting authority from Second, Third, Fifth, Sixth, and Eleventh Circuits); Baldayaque v. United States, 338 F.3d 145 (2d Cir.2003) (although state prisoners are not entitled to counsel as of right in collateral proceedings, "an attorney's conduct, if it is sufficiently egregious, may constitute the sort of 'extraordinary circumstance' that would justify the application of equitable tolling"); United States v. Patterson, 211 F.3d 927 (5th Cir.2000) (collecting authority, and tolling limitations period, finding extraordinary circumstances present when petitioner misled by district court about filing deadlines); Sandvik v. United States, 177 F.3d 1269 (11th Cir.1999); United States v. Jackson-Bey, 302 F.Supp.2d 621 (E.D.Va.2004) (defendant entitled to equitable tolling in § 2255 action when the pleading may have been misplaced by the Clerk's office, given that defendant's own conduct did not lead to the inexplicable long lapse of time in this case, "it would be unconscionable to enforce the limitations period against the [defendant] and gross injustice would result" by doing so). Compare United States v. Wynn, 292 F.3d 226 (5th Cir.2002) (tolling is appropriate when the prisoner's attorney lied to the prisoner about hav-

ing filed a petition); United States v. Martin, 408 F.3d 1089 (8th Cir.2005) (equitable tolling will be granted where petitioner's attorney failed to return forty phone calls by petitioner's wife, refused to return documents, lied about the petition being filed, told petitioner and his wife there was no filing deadline for 2255 motions, failed to attend appointments with petitioner's wife at his office, refused to take petitioner's phone calls); United States v. Schwartz, 274 F.3d 1220 (9th Cir.2001) (refusing to toll during time when government could have voided a petitioner's plea agreement due to her obligation to testify against her codefendants); Dunlap v. United States, 250 F.3d 1001 (6th Cir.2001) (refusing tolling for defendant who filed previous premature petitions, then missed the deadline on his third); Kahn v. United States, 414 F.Supp.2d 210 (E.D.N.Y.2006) (federal judgment of conviction becomes final after ten days when no notice of appeal is filed, and petitioner's failure to understand this rule does not warrant equitable tolling).

[51]See United States v. Marcello, 212 F.3d 1005 (7th Cir.2000) (affirming dismissal of petition filed one day late, reasoning that "equitable tolling is granted sparingly" and that "[e]xtraordinary circumstances far beyond the litigant's control must have prevented timely filing," finding that defense counsel's loss of her father several weeks before the deadline was not such a circumstance).

provides for "relation back" of an amendment when "the claim or defense asserted in the amended pleading arose out of the conduct, transaction, or occurrence set forth or attempted to be set forth in the original pleading." The Court ruled in *Mayle v. Felix*[52] that in the context of a § 2254 petition, a petitioner may amend the petition to add claims after the statute of limitations has expired, but those additional claims will not "relate back" if they are supported by facts that differ in time and type from those alleged in the original, timely filed petition. In *Felix*, the Court concluded that the claim the petitioner sought to add was not based on a single "transaction or occurrence" when in his original petition he alleged a Confrontation Clause violation concerning the admission of a prosecution witness' videotaped testimony, and his amendment alleged that the police used coercion to extract statements from him and that admitting those statements violated the Fifth Amendment. The Court rejected the argument that because both claims arose out of the same trial, they arose out of the "same core of operative facts." The same rule presumably applies in proceedings seeking relief under § 2255.[53] As with petitions under § 2254, most lower courts have found that the statute of limitations may be raised by the court sua sponte.[54]

Successive Petitions. Under the 1996 Act a "second or successive motion" may not be filed unless first certified by the court of appeals[55] to contain either: "(1) newly discovered evidence that, if proven and viewed in light of the evidence as a whole, would be

---

[52]Mayle v. Felix, 545 U.S. 644, 125 S.Ct. 2562, 162 L.Ed.2d 582 (2005).

[53]United States v. Thomas, 221 F.3d 430, 436 (3d Cir.2000) (holding that Rule 15(c) applies to post-AEDPA § 2255 petitions); Mandacina v. United States, 328 F.3d 995 (8th Cir.2003); United States v. Espinoza-Saenz, 235 F.3d 501 (10th Cir.2000) (same as *Thomas*, collecting authority). See also United States v. Hicks, 283 F.3d 380 (D.C.Cir.2002) (holding that Rule 15(c) does not allow applicant to amend § 2255 application after statute of limitations has run in order to add entirely new legal theory (collecting authority, and noting that Rule does not allow amendment when new law makes old facts more significant); Mandacina v. United States, 328 F.3d 995 (8th Cir.2003) (applying relation back, finding that each alleged with-

holding of evidence represented a distinct act, such that the original motion does not provide fair notice of *Brady* claims not specifically asserted); Dean v. United States, 278 F.3d 1218 (11th Cir.2002).

[54]United States v. Bendolph, 409 F.3d 155 (3d Cir.2005) (collecting authority from "all of the courts of appeals that have considered the issue"). See Day v. McDonough, __ U.S. __, 126 S.Ct. 1675, 164 L.Ed.2d 376 (2006) (limitations period for § 2254 petitions may be raised sua sponte).

[55]Prisoners seeking review of a successive § 2255 application must first obtain permission from the court of appeals, just as successive § 2244 petitioners are required to seek authorization under § 2244(b)(3)(C). Reyes-Requena v. United States, 243 F.3d 893 (5th Cir.2001). Lower courts have held that the 30-day time period for

sufficient to establish by clear and convincing evidence that no reasonable fact-finder would have found the movant guilty of the offense;[56] or (2) a new rule of constitutional law, made retroactive to cases on collateral review by the Supreme Court that was previously unavailable." This provision replaces the "cause and prejudice" and "miscarriage of justice" standards previously applied to both old and new claims in second or successive petitions.

This standard for entertaining successive § 2255 motions by federal prisoners is more generous than the standard in § 2244(b) governing successive petitions by state prisoners. State petitioners basically have one shot at each claim, and are barred from raising a previously advanced claim in later petitions. As explained in § 28.5(c), state petitioners seeking to raise a claim they raised previously must instead argue that the claim is actually a new claim that falls within one of the narrow exceptions for review of new claims provided in § 2244(b)(2). By contrast, a slightly wider window of opportunity remains open to federal movants who seek to raise the same claim again. Applicants under § 2255 can secure review of previously raised claims if the claimed error is a violation of a new rule retroactively applied on collateral review or if the claim is based on newly discovered evidence and the movant can show that had the error not occurred no reasonable fact-finder would have found guilt.

Because the Act bars relief for those filing a second or successive petition except in narrow circumstances, the Court in *Castro v. United States*,[57] prohibited federal judges from recharacterizing a pro se litigant's motion styled as a motion under Rule 33, Rule 60(b), or as a petition for relief under § 2241, as a first motion under § 2255 against the wishes of the movant, unless the court (1) first informs the litigant of its intent to recharacterize, (2) warns the litigant that any subsequent § 2255 motion will be subject to the restrictions on "second or successive" motions, and (3) provides the litigant an opportunity to withdraw the motion or to amend it so that it contains all the § 2255 claims he believes

---

granting such applications may be expanded when necessary, similar to rulings concerning the gatekeeping provision for successive petitions by state prisoners. See, e.g., Gray-Bey v. United States, 201 F.3d 866 (7th Cir.2000) (collecting authority, arguing, "the alternative—uninformed and arbitrary grants or denials of applications—is unacceptable in a system that strives always to operate under the rule of law," and rejecting the argument of the dissenting opinion

that the court lacks authority to depart from 30-day command).

[56]For a narrow interpretation of the term "offense," see Hope v. United States, 108 F.3d 119 (7th Cir.1997) (concluding that the 1996 amendments prohibit relief when newly discovered evidence forms the basis of a challenge to the petitioner's sentence).

[57]Castro v. United States, 540 U.S. 375, 124 S.Ct. 786, 157 L.Ed.2d 778 (2004).

he has.[58]

If an applicant who has already filed a first application for relief under § 2255 subsequently files a Rule 60(b) motion, that motion must be treated as a second application for relief if it presents a new claim, presents new evidence in support of a claim already litigated, or relies on a purported change in the law governing the prior claim. Any motion attacking the federal court's previous resolution of a claim on the merits advances a "claim." But a Rule 60(b) motion attacking "not the substance of the federal court's resolution of a claim on the merits, but some defect in the integrity of the federal habeas proceedings," such as the allegation that the court misapplied the one-year statute of limitations in deciding not to reach the merits of a claim, should not be treated like an second application for relief.[59]

The bar on successive petitions does not apply to a prisoner who is resentenced after filing his first application for relief, and raises only claims that originated at resentencing in his second application.[60]

Fact-finding. Section 2255 and § 2254 treat fact-finding differently. The 1996 Act amended the fact-finding procedures for petitions under § 2254, but did not amend those for § 2255 motions. The standards governing the need for an evidentiary hearing under § 2255, then, presumably are unchanged from prior to AEDPA.[61] Application of those standards may be altered slightly by the fact that the § 2255 motion is usually heard by the judge who presided at trial.[62] In general, however, that judge's familiarity with the proceedings will not permit him to reject,

---

[58]See also Villanueva v. United States, 346 F.3d 55 (2d Cir.2003) (dispositions that count as "first" petitions for purposes of successive petition limitation include dismissals because the petitioner exceeded the statute of limitations, dismissals for procedural default, or dismissals under *Stone v. Powell*, but dismissals due to a failure to exhaust do not count as "first" petitions, in §§ 2255 and 2254 actions alike); United States v. Lloyd, 398 F.3d 978 (7th Cir.2005) ("Call it a motion for a new trial, arrest of judgment, mandamus, prohibition, coram nobis, coram vobis, audita querela, certiorari, capias, habeas corpus, ejectment, quare impedit, bill of review, writ of error, or an application for a Get-Out-of-Jail Card; the name makes no difference. It is substance that controls."); Johnson v. United States,

362 F.3d 636 (9th Cir.2004) (collecting conflicting authority and holding that a first petition challenging the attorney's failure to file a timely notice of appeal was "only to rescue his right to appeal," it was not a true collateral attack on the sentence, and did not render a later petition "successive").

[59]Gonzalez v. Crosby, 545 U.S. 524, 125 S.Ct. 2641, 162 L.Ed.2d 480 (2005).

[60]E.g. Lang v. United States, 474 F.3d 348 (6th Cir.2007) (collecting authority).

[61]See § 28.7 (discussing these standards); Rule 8 of the Rules Governing § 2255 Procedures.

[62]Rule 4(a) of the § 2255 Rules provides that the motion shall be presented "to the judge of the district court who presided at the movant's

without a hearing, a claim relying on factual allegations dehors the record.[63] Although the judge is permitted to draw upon "his personal knowledge or recollection,"[64] the information known to the judge will rarely be so clearly inconsistent with the petitioner's factual allegations that the Court can justify a summary dismissal (allowed under Rule 4 only if it "plainly appears" from the "prior proceedings" that the petitioner is not entitled to relief).[65]

Where the applicant's claim was considered by the trial court in the original proceeding, the § 2255 court is permitted to rely upon the factual findings made at that proceeding, provided the petitioner had been afforded what *Townsend v. Sain* described as a "full and fair" hearing.[66] In determining whether a full and fair hearing was provided, a court considering the § 2255 motion looks to all but one of the six criteria specified in *Townsend*.[67] The one exception is the third *Townsend* criterion, which requires an evidentiary hearing when the original hearing was "inadequate" due to faulty procedures. This standard is irrelevant to fact-finding at a federal criminal trial because "federal fact-finding procedures are by hypothesis adequate to assure the integrity of the underlying constitutional rights."[68]

Assuming that the *Townsend* standards do not require new fact-finding, the prior findings do not carry the presumption of correctness that applies to state court findings. However, when a

---

trial and sentenced him, or, if the judge who imposed sentence was not the trial judge, then it shall go to the judge who was in charge of that part of the proceeding being attacked by the movant." If that judge is unavailable, then another judge of the same district will hear the motion. The Advisory Committee Note cites as a major advantage of this assignment system that "the judge who is familiar with the facts and circumstances surrounding the trial * * * is not likely to be misled by false allegations as to what occurred," quoting Carvell v. United States, 173 F.2d 348 (4th Cir. 1949).

[63] See, e.g., Machibroda v. United States, 368 U.S. 487, 82 S.Ct. 510, 7 L.Ed.2d 473 (1962) (judge could not reject claim of unfulfilled prosecution promise by reference to his recollection that he had never received letters that the petitioner alleged to have sent to him); Fontaine v. United States, 411 U.S. 213, 93 S.Ct. 1461, 36 L.Ed.2d 169 (1973) (petitioner's statement, at

the time of the plea, that he waived counsel voluntarily, did not conclusively reject his § 2255 allegation that he was coerced by a combination of illness, physical abuse, and prolonged interrogation).

[64] Machibroda v. United States, 368 U.S. 487, 82 S.Ct. 510, 7 L.Ed.2d 473 (1962).

[65] The Rule 4 standard allows the judge to make his determination as to summary dismissal based on "the face of the motion," annexed exhibits, and "the prior proceeding." Section 2255 itself requires that the "motion and the files and the records of the case conclusively show the prisoner is entitled to no relief."

[66] Kaufman v. United States, 394 U.S. 217, 89 S.Ct. 1068, 22 L.Ed.2d 227 (1969).

[67] See § 28.7(a).

[68] Kaufman v. United States, 394 U.S. 217, 89 S.Ct. 1068, 22 L.Ed.2d 227 (1969).

§ 2255 judge has concluded that his own prior findings were the result of a full and fair hearing, it ordinarily does not require a statutory presumption to convince him to accept those findings without a hearing.

If additional fact-finding is required, counsel must be appointed if the petitioner is granted an evidentiary hearing or if counsel is necessary to use discovery effectively.[69] The court retains discretion as to the appointment of counsel under other circumstances.[70] The § 2255 Rules grant the court considerable flexibility in allowing the use of discovery and providing for expansion of the record short of a full evidentiary hearing.[71]

Waiver. A waiver of collateral attack rights under § 2255 is generally enforceable where the waiver is expressly stated in the defendant's plea agreement and where both the plea and the waiver were knowingly and voluntarily made. The same exceptions to the waiver of the right to appeal, if they arise, would be available to the waiver of the right to collateral attack.[72]

§ 28.9(c) Nonconstitutional claims under § 2255

Although § 2255 refers to persons held in custody in violation of the "Constitution *or laws* of the United States,"[73] the Court has long held that a nonconstitutional violation of federal law will justify the granting of relief only under "exceptional circumstances."[74] This position rests on both the traditional view of the habeas writ as an "exceptional remedy" and the language of § 2255. The provision in § 2255 directing the court to grant relief does not refer to all violations of federal law, but to relief granted where the sentence is "open to collateral attack." In determining whether a nonconstitutional claim fits within this

---

[69]See § 2255 Rule 6(a); United States v. Vasquez, 7 F.3d 81 (5th Cir. 1993).

[70]See, e.g., United States v. Ferri, 652 F.2d 325 (3d Cir.1981); Brown v. United States, 623 F.2d 54 (9th Cir. 1980). See also the new language added by the 1996 amendments: "Except as provided in section 408 of the Controlled Substances Act, in all proceedings brought under this section, and any subsequent proceedings on review, the court may appoint counsel, except as provided by a rule promulgated by the Supreme Court pursuant to statutory authority."

[71]See § 2255 Rules 6, 7. The same "good cause" requirement applies to discovery motion as is applied in § 2254 cases. See, e.g., United States

v. Webster, 392 F.3d 787 (5th Cir.2004) (no abuse of discretion to deny discovery when applicant failed to allege a single factual dispute, which, if resolved in his favor, would entitle him to relief.").

[72]United States v. Cockerham, 237 F.3d 1179 (10th Cir.2001) (collecting authority).

[Section 28.9(c)]

[73]A majority of claims are constitutional in nature—67% of § 2255 applications filed during 1995 challenged the constitutionality of the sentence. BJS, Prisoner Petitions in the Federal Courts, 1980–1996.

[74]Sunal v. Large, 332 U.S. 174, 67 S.Ct. 1588, 91 L.Ed. 1982 (1947).

language, the Supreme Court has looked to both the nature of the claim and the need for the § 2255 remedy to vindicate that claim.

United States v. Addonizio[75] provides a classic statement of the range of nonconstitutional errors cognizable under § 2255. Justice Stevens, speaking for the Court, noted: "[U]nless the claim alleges a lack of jurisdiction or constitutional error, the scope of collateral attack has remained far more limited." He continued, "The Court has held that an error of law does not provide a basis for collateral attack unless the claimed error constituted 'a fundamental defect which inherently results in a complete miscarriage of justice.' "[76]

Several Supreme Court decisions illustrate the application of this "fundamental defect" standard to nonconstitutional errors that are not jurisdictional in nature.[77] *Addonizio* held not cognizable a claim that a post-sentencing change in the policies of the Parole Commission had prolonged petitioner's imprisonment beyond the period intended by the trial judge, who had allegedly relied upon the preexisting parole policies in setting petitioner's sentence. Noting that the period of imprisonment was still within the range allowed by law, the Court held that the judge's alleged factual error in assuming that certain parole policies would apply was not a "fundamental defect." There was "no basis for enlarging the grounds for collateral attack to include claims based not on any objectively ascertainable error but on the frustration of the subjective intent of the sentencing judge." *Hill v. United States*[78] similarly held that, in the absence of any aggravating circumstances, the failure to comply with Rule 32(a) (providing a right of allocution) was not cognizable under § 2255. The Court noted that this was not a case where the trial court affirmatively denied the defendant an opportunity to speak, but simply one in which the sentencing judge failed to ask defendant, represented by counsel, whether he had anything to say. "[C]ollateral relief," the Court noted, "is not available when all that is shown is a failure to comply with the formal requirements of the Rule."

---

[75]United States v. Addonizio, 442 U.S. 178, 99 S.Ct. 2235, 60 L.Ed.2d 805 (1979).

[76]Quoting from Hill v. United States, 368 U.S. 424, 82 S.Ct. 468, 7 L.Ed.2d 417 (1962) (rejecting collateral relief for denial of allocution at sentencing).

[77]As to jurisdictional defects, see Bowen v. Johnston, 306 U.S. 19, 59

S.Ct. 442, 83 L.Ed. 455 (1939); United States v. Harper, 901 F.2d 471 (5th Cir.1990); Johnson v. United States, 805 F.2d 1284 (7th Cir.1986); Poor Thunder v. United States, 810 F.2d 817 (8th Cir.1987).

[78]Hill v. United States, 368 U.S. 424, 82 S.Ct. 468, 7 L.Ed.2d 417 (1962).

Relying on *Hill*, the Court in *United States v. Timmreck*[79] held that a "formal violation of Rule 11" also was not cognizable under § 2255. The trial court there had failed to inform the petitioner of a mandatory parole period in taking his guilty plea, but petitioner did not contend that he was actually unaware of the special parole term. The Court noted that the "concern with finality served by the limitation on collateral attack has special force with respect to convictions based on guilty pleas," but held open the possibility that § 2255 relief would be available "if a violation of Rule 11 occurred in the context of other aggravating circumstances." Both *Timmreck* and *Hill* led the Court to conclude in *Peguero v. United States*,[80] that § 2255 relief was not available to a federal defendant who was not informed of his right to appeal at sentencing in violation of Rule 32, when the defendant "had full knowledge of his right to appeal."

A federal prisoner's challenge to a conviction for an act that federal law does not make criminal is also cognizable under § 2255. For example in *Davis v. United States*,[81] the petitioner had been convicted of failing to report for induction into the military service. Under the applicable substantive law, the invalidity of the induction order would constitute a complete defense to the charge, but the trial judge rejected Davis' contention that his accelerated induction rendered his induction order invalid. While Davis' appeal was pending, the Supreme Court's decision in *Gutknecht v. United States*[82] struck down the accelerated induction of delinquent registrants. Davis claimed that *Gutknecht* governed his case, but the Court of Appeals disagreed and the Supreme Court denied certiorari. Davis turned to § 2255, and the Court granted relief. It explained:

> [P]etitioner's contention is that the decision in *Gutknecht v. United States*, * * * establishes that his induction order was invalid under the Selective Service Act and that he could not be lawfully convicted for failure to comply with that order. If this contention is well taken, then Davis' conviction and punishment are for an act that the law does not make criminal. There can be no room for doubt that such a circumstance "inherently results in a complete miscarriage of justice" and "present[s] exceptional circumstances" that justify collateral relief under § 2255.

Since *Davis*, federal prisoners have turned to § 2255 following decisions of the Supreme Court that have declared what was assumed to be criminal conduct to be otherwise. For example, after

---

[79]United States v. Timmreck, 441 U.S. 780, 99 S.Ct. 2085, 60 L.Ed.2d 634 (1979). See also § 20.5(c).

[80]Peguero v. United States, 526 U.S. 23, 119 S.Ct. 961, 143 L.Ed.2d 18 (1999).

[81]Davis v. United States, 417 U.S. 333, 94 S.Ct. 2298, 41 L.Ed.2d 109 (1974).

[82]Gutknecht v. United States, 396 U.S. 295, 90 S.Ct. 506, 24 L.Ed.2d 532 (1970).

the Court held in *Bailey v. United States*[83] 18 U.S.C.A. § 924(c)(1) required the government to show active employment of a firearm, § 2255 offered an avenue for federal prisoners incarcerated under the statute who had not actively employed a firearm to seek release.[84]

§ 28.10 Appeal of district court decisions in habeas

Under § 2253, there is no absolute entitlement to appeal a district court's denial of a petition under § 2254 or § 2255.[1] A prisoner must first seek and obtain a "certificate of appealability," by demonstrating a "substantial showing of the denial of a constitutional right." Both circuit and district judges have the authority to grant such certificates.[2] Although a similar requirement had been in place for state prisoners prior to the 1996 Act, the Act added this requirement for federal prisoners.

As the Court held in *Slack v. McDaniel*[3] and *Miller-El v.*

---

[83]Bailey v. United States, 516 U.S. 137, 116 S.Ct. 501, 133 L.Ed.2d 472 (1995).

[84]See Bousley v. United States, 523 U.S. 614, 118 S.Ct. 1604, 140 L.Ed.2d 828 (1998) (considering *Bailey* claim in § 2255 application, but remanding after finding no cause for failure to raise below).

[Section 28.10]

[1]See 28 U.S.C.A. § 2253 and Fed.R.App.Proc. 22. See also Gonzalez v. Secretary for Dept. of Corrections, 366 F.3d 1253 (11th Cir.2004) (certificate of appealability is required for the appeal of any denial of a Rule 60(b) motion for relief from a judgment in a § 2254 or § 2255 proceeding); Jackson v. Albany Appeal Bureau Unit, 442 F.3d 51 (2d Cir.2006) (§ 2253(c)(1)'s COA requirement applies to an appeal from an order denying a Rule 59(e) motion when the underlying judgment is a denial of a § 2254 petition).

Decisions of the district court other than those dismissing or denying a petition may be reviewable in unusual circumstances by extraordinary writ. See In re Lott, 424 F.3d 446 (6th Cir.2005) (writ of mandamus granted from order in habeas action authorizing discovery by government of material protected by the attorney client privilege, finding that the petitioner has no other readily available means of relief and the issue raised— whether an assertion of innocence constitutes a waiver of the privilege—is an issue of first impression in the federal courts). See also In re Parker, 49 F.3d 204 (6th Cir.1995) (mandamus proper method to review stay of execution where the order was effectively unreviewable on appeal and delay harmed the state's interests in finality and carrying out the law).

[2]See, e.g., United States v. Asrar, 116 F.3d 1268 (9th Cir.1997); Fed.R. App.P. 22(b)(1).

Judges have no power to extend the filing deadlines established by the Federal Rules, even if a petitioner is misled into filing late by the judge's mistake. See Bowles v. Russell, __ U.S. __, 127 S.Ct. 2360, 168 L.Ed.2d 96 (2007) (judge's mistaken extension beyond the 14-day period was void, appeal must be dismissed as untimely even if it was reasonable to rely on the judge's order, depriving the appellate court of jurisdiction).

[3]Slack v. McDaniel, 529 U.S. 473, 120 S.Ct. 1595, 146 L.Ed.2d 542

Cockrell,[4] a petitioner need only demonstrate that a ruling was "debatable," "that jurists of reason could disagree with the district court's resolution of his constitutional claims or that jurists could conclude the issues presented are adequate to deserve encouragement to proceed further." The Court explained in *Miller-El*, "We do not require petitioner to prove, before the issuance of a COA, that some jurists would grant the petition for habeas corpus. Indeed, a claim can be debatable even though every jurist of reason might agree, after the COA has been granted and the case has received full consideration, that the petitioner will not prevail." In reversing the decision of the Court of Appeals to deny the COA for the petitioner's *Batson* claim, the Supreme Court in *Miller-El* also noted that a defendant seeking a COA need not show by clear and convincing evidence, that the state court's factual findings were incorrect. Instead, "[o]nly after a COA is granted will a reviewing court determine whether the trial court's determination of the prosecutor's neutrality with respect to race was objectively unreasonable and has been rebutted by clear and convincing evidence to the contrary."

When the district court's decision denying or dismissing the petition is based on procedural grounds, a COA requires the petitioner to demonstrate both that the district court's resolution of the procedural issue is debatable and that it is debatable whether the petition states a valid constitutional claim.[5] An applicant denied a certificate of applicability may petition the Supreme Court for a writ of certiorari.[6] Should a certificate of applicability be granted, the applicant may not raise issues other than those specified in the certificate of applicability.[7]

(2000).

[4]Miller-El v. Cockrell, 537 U.S. 322, 123 S.Ct. 1029, 154 L.Ed.2d 931 (2003). See also Tennard v. Dretke, 542 U.S. 274, 124 S.Ct. 2562, 159 L.Ed.2d 384 (2004).

[5]See Banks v. Dretke, 540 U.S. 668, 124 S.Ct. 1256, 157 L.Ed.2d 1166 (2004) (reversing lower court's decision not to issue a certificate of appealability on petitioner *Brady*'s claim, finding it debatable whether Rule 15(b) permitted him to raise it); Slack v. McDaniel, 529 U.S. 473, 120 S.Ct. 1595, 146 L.Ed.2d 542 (2000) (COA should issue when district court denies a petition on procedural grounds without reaching the merits of petitioner's claim if the petitioner shows that

jurists of reason would find it debatable whether the petition states a valid claim of the denial of a constitutional right and that jurists of reason would find it debatable whether the district court was correct in its procedural ruling).

[6]Hohn v. United States, 524 U.S. 236, 118 S.Ct. 1969, 141 L.Ed.2d 242 (1998).

[7]E.g., Murray v. United States, 145 F.3d 1249 (11th Cir.1998) (collecting authority). Some courts have also permitted the party successful in the district court to file in the court of appeals a motion to vacate the COA prior to full briefing. See Buie v. McAdory, 322 F.3d 980 (7th Cir.2003) (holding that the court of appeals has jurisdic-

§ 28.11 State collateral remedies

§ 28.11(a)   Supreme Court "encouragement" of state remedies
§ 28.11(b)   Types of state remedies

§ 28.11(a) Supreme Court "encouragement" of state remedies

In *Young v. Ragen*,[1] in the course of determining whether a state's complex system of common law writs left petitioner with an effective and unexhausted state remedy, the Supreme Court spoke of the "requirement that prisoners be given some clearly defined method by which they may raise claims of denial of federal rights." Although this "requirement" clearly was a prerequisite to the application of the exhaustion doctrine, some commentators contended that it had a constitutional foundation. The state's obligation to enforce federal constitutional rights, it was argued, carried with it a duty to provide collateral remedies for raising at least those constitutional claims that could not reasonably be presented in the original trial and appeal.[2] In 1964, the Court granted certiorari in *Case v. Nebraska*[3] to consider just such a contention. The state there had held that an alleged denial of the assistance of counsel was not cognizable under state habeas corpus because it did not challenge the jurisdiction of the trial court.[4] After certiorari was granted, however, the state adopted a broad post-conviction remedy, and the Court remanded the case for reconsideration in light of that remedy. In a concurring opinion, Justice Brennan applauded the state's action. Adoption of effective state post-conviction procedures, he noted, would promote "state primacy" in the protection of federal constitutional rights. It would

> assure not only that meritorious claims would generally be vindicated without any need for federal court intervention, but that nonmeritorious claims would be fully ventilated, making easier the task of the federal judge if the state prisoner pursued his cause further. Greater finality would inevitably attach to state court determinations of federal constitutional questions, because further

---

tion to vacate an improperly granted COA in extreme cases to conserve judicial resources, noting conflicting position of another court, and collecting authority).

[Section 28.11(a)]

[1]Young v. Ragen, 337 U.S. 235, 69 S.Ct. 1073, 93 L.Ed. 1333 (1949).

[2]See Sandalow, Henry v. Mississippi and the Adequate State Ground: Proposals for a Revised Doctrine, 1965 Sup.Ct.Rev. 187 (analyzing and largely rejecting the arguments advanced in favor of such an obligation); L. Yackle, Postconviction Remedies §§ 4 to 5 (1981 & Supp.2007) (describing development of state remedies based on this perceived obligation).

[3]Case v. Nebraska, 381 U.S. 336, 85 S.Ct. 1486, 14 L.Ed.2d 422 (1965).

[4]Compare Johnson v. Zerbst, 304 U.S. 458, 58 S.Ct. 1019, 82 L.Ed. 1461 (1938), discussed in § 28.3(b) at note 52.

evidentiary hearings on federal habeas corpus would, if the conditions of *Townsend v. Sain* were met, prove unnecessary.[5]

As Professor Wilkes has observed, the states responded en masse to the urgings of Justice Brennan and others, and today "all of the various principal post-conviction remedies in the 50 states authorize the granting of relief from a conviction or sentence which is found to be unconstitutional on either federal or state constitutional grounds."[6]

At the same time that states have voluntarily adopted at least limited post-conviction remedies, the view that the Constitution required them to do so has been undermined by the Court's discussion of state obligations in more recent cases. In *United States v. MacCollum*,[7] a plurality of justices declared that neither the right to collaterally attack a conviction nor the right a appeal is guaranteed by the Due Process Clause. The Court has continued to maintain that there is no constitutional right to a direct appeal.[8] Denying a petitioner's claim that he was denied counsel for collateral proceedings, at least four justices have stated that states have no obligation to provide post-conviction relief, even in capital cases.[9] Although mandatory appellate review of a death sentence is not uncommon, even when the de-

---

[5]See also Note, 40 NYU L.Rev. 154, 161 (1965); Meador, Accommodating State Criminal Procedure and Federal Post Conviction Review, 50 A.B.A.J. 928 (1964). But compare Holman, Multiple Post-Trial Litigation in Criminal Cases, 19 DePaul L.Rev. 490 (1970) (suggestion of state Supreme Court Justice that the prisoner and the public might be in a "better position" if the states did not adopt such remedies so that collateral attacks would go "in the first instance directly to the federal system").

[6]See D. Wilkes, Federal and State Postconviction Remedies and Relief 216 (1983) ("[A]s late as the mid-1960's, when Case arose, state post-conviction relief machinery was woefully inadequate to protect the basic rights of criminal suspects. Only a few states had a modern post-conviction remedy, i.e., a remedy (1) providing relief on grounds of violations of constitutional and other basic rights generally, and (2) unhampered by obsolete, unjustified, and irksome obstacles to relief making it almost impossible, as a practical matter, ever to grant post-

conviction relief, regardless of how meritorious the claim."). See also R. Hertz & J. Liebman, 1 Federal Habeas Corpus Practice and Procedure §§ 6.1–7.2 (5th ed.2005); Steiker, Restructuring Post-Conviction Review of Federal Constitutional Claims Raised by State Prisoners: Confronting the New Face of Excessive Proceduralism, 1998 U.Chi.Leg.F. 315 ("Today, virtually all states conduct post-conviction review of federal constitutional claims precisely to define the record that the federal habeas court will ultimately review.").

[7]United States v. MacCollom, 426 U.S. 317, 96 S.Ct. 2086, 48 L.Ed.2d 666 (1976).

[8]See § 27.1(a) at note 13.

[9]See Murray v. Giarratano, 492 U.S. 1, 109 S.Ct. 2765, 106 L.Ed.2d 1 (1989) (plurality); Pennsylvania v. Finley, 481 U.S. 551, 107 S.Ct. 1990, 95 L.Ed.2d 539 (1987). See also Iovieno v. Commissioner of Correction, 242 Conn. 689, 699 A.2d 1003 (1997) (concluding the Constitution "does not require state to provide post-conviction remedies for persons convicted in state

fendant does not seek to appeal, mandatory post-conviction review in capital cases is rare.[10]

§ 28.11(b) Types of state remedies

Although all but a few states have adopted expanded collateral remedies, those remedies vary substantially in structure and scope. An exhaustive treatment of those variations must be left to sources devoted to the remedies in a particular jurisdiction.[11] The state remedies can be roughly surveyed, however, by dividing them into three groups: (1) habeas corpus provisions; (2) provisions adopting the Uniform Post-Conviction Procedure Act; and (3) provisions tracking § 2255. There will be, of course, some variation within each category, and several states have remedies that do not fit within any of these groups.

Habeas Statutes. About a dozen states utilize the writ of habeas corpus as their primary collateral remedy.[12] A few apparently limit the writ to challenges to the trial court's jurisdiction, but adopt a broad view of jurisdictional defects similar to that taken by the Supreme Court under rulings like *Johnson v. Zerbst.*[13] Others have held the writ roughly parallels the federal

---

courts so long as the states have provided some avenue of direct review of the conviction"); Reuscher v. State, 887 S.W.2d 588 (Mo.1994) (no constitutional right to a state post-conviction proceeding); State v. Victor, 242 Neb. 306, 494 N.W.2d 565 (1993) (same).

[10]See Pike v. State, 164 S.W.3d 257 (Tenn.2005) (noting that the only state to mandate post-conviction review of a death sentence over the objection of a competent death-sentenced inmate); State v. Martini, 144 N.J. 603, 677 A.2d 1106 (2006). For information on state collateral review of death sentences in the 1980s and 90s, see Flango & McKenna, Federal Habeas Corpus Review of State Court Convictions, 31 Cal.W.L. Rev. 237 (1995) (noting most denials are without explanation); J. Liebman, J. Fagan & V. West, A Broken System: Error Rates in Capital Cases, 1973–95 (2000) (finding that 6 of every 100 death sentences studied were turned back at the state post-conviction stage).

[Section 28.11(b)]

[11]See L. Yackle, Postconviction Remedies §§ 12–13 (1981 & Supp.2007)

for a survey of the state provisions and citations to helpful articles. See also See D. Wilkes, State Postconviction Remedies and Relief App. A (2001), for a similar survey.

[12]See D. Wilkes, State Postconviction Remedies and Relief App. A, 16 (2001).

[13]See, e.g., Cal.Penal Code §§ 1473 et seq.; Conn.Gen.Stat.Ann. §§ 52-466 et seq.; Haw.Rev.Stat.Ann. § 660; N.H.Rev.Stat.Ann. § 534; S.D.Codified Laws §§ 21 to 27; W.Va.Code Ann. §§ 53-4A-1 et seq.

See Deegan v. State, 711 N.W.2d 89 (Minn.2006) (although grounds for post-conviction relief are substantially limited once a direct appeal has been taken, where a post-conviction petitioner did not take a direct appeal from the conviction, but seeks review of a constitutional violation for the first time by post-conviction petition, he is entitled to "raise nearly the same breadth of claims" that could have been brought in a direct appeal).

remedy in its coverage of constitutional claims.[14] The federal decisions may also be followed as to the standard for assessing retroactivity,[15] whether an error was harmless,[16] or successive petitions.[17] Law in many states on the impact of a procedural default[18] resembles federal authority, although some states apparently adhere to the traditional rule that habeas my never be used to present a non-jurisdictional claim that could have been

---

[14]See, e.g., Jacobs v. Hopper, 238 Ga. 461, 233 S.E.2d 169 (1977) (following *Stone v. Powell*). See also People v. Haynes, 192 Ill.2d 437, 249 Ill.Dec. 779, 737 N.E.2d 169 (2000) (state post-conviction relief limited to substantial deprivations of federal or state constitutional rights in the proceedings that produced the challenged judgment; review permits inquiry into constitutional issues that have not been, and could not have been, adjudicated previously upon direct appeal). But compare Amrine v. Roper, 102 S.W.3d 541 (Mo.2003) (petitioner may obtain state habeas relief for clear and convincing showing of actual innocence that undermines confidence in the correctness of the judgment, even if there is no claim that the Constitution was violated at trial).

[15]People v. Gholston, 332 Ill.App.3d 179, 265 Ill.Dec. 509, 772 N.E.2d 880 (2002) (using *Teague* analysis to conclude that *Apprendi* will not apply retroactively on state post-conviction review); Daniels v. State, 561 N.E.2d 487 (Ind.1990); State v. Purnell, 161 N.J. 44, 735 A.2d 513 (1999); Page v. Palmateer, 336 Or. 379, 84 P.3d 133 (2004) (rule in *Apprendi* does not fit an exception for retroactive application). See also Easterwood v. State, 273 Kan. 361, 44 P.3d 1209 (2002) (refusing to apply retroactively new rule limiting scope of felony murder statute, although noting that change in substantive state crime not barred by *Teague* in state post-conviction proceedings); Hutton, Retroactivity in the States: The Impact of *Teague v. Lane* on State Post-conviction Remedies, 44 Ala.L. Rev. 421 (1993).

[16]See, e.g., Ex Parte Fierro, 934 S.W.2d 370 (Tex.Cr.App.1996) (citing *Brecht*, and requiring the applicant to prove harm by a preponderance of the evidence).

[17]See Ex parte Blue, __ S.W.3d __, 2007 WL 676194 (Tex.Cr.App.2007) (Tex.Code Crim.Proc. art. 11.071 Section 5(a)(1) prohibits consideration of the merits of a claim raised for the first time in a subsequent writ application unless the subsequent application shows that the claim could not have been raised in a previous writ "because the factual or legal basis for the claim was unavailable" at the time the applicant filed his previous writ or writs; but holding that death row inmate alleging constitutional ineligibility for execution (retardation) for the first time in a subsequent writ application will be allowed to proceed to the merits if he presents evidence of a sufficiently clear and convincing character that we could ultimately conclude that no rational fact-finder would fail to find he is in fact mentally retarded).

[18]See, e.g., Johnson v. Commissioner of Correction, 218 Conn. 403, 589 A.2d 1214 (1991); Cox v. Ballard, 259 Ga. 176, 377 S.E.2d 842 (1989); Clay v. Dormire, 37 S.W.3d 214 (Mo.2000) (following federal precedent in defining an exception to the bar on defaulted claims for cases of "manifest injustice"). Compare In re Harris, 5 Cal.4th 813, 21 Cal.Rptr.2d 373, 855 P.2d 391 (1993) ("Where an issue was available on direct appeal, * * * only where the claimed constitutional error is both clear and fundamental, and strikes at the heart of the trial process, is an opportunity for a third chance at judicial review * * * justified.").

presented on appeal,[19] and others have concluded that the concerns of comity and federalism that prompted the Court to adopt stringent limits on the review of defaulted or new claims "simply do not apply" in the state context.[20] In general, states utilizing the habeas remedy have adopted an expansive view of "custody" in line with Supreme Court decisions.[21]

---

[19]Fortner v. State, 825 So.2d 876 (Ala.App.2001) (defendant cannot raise in a successive petition for post-conviction relief his claim that the jury was not properly sworn, as this claim is not jurisdictional and was waived); Reuscher v. State, 887 S.W.2d 588 (Mo.1994) (state habeas corpus may not be used to challenge a final judgment after an individual's failure to pursue appellate and post-conviction remedies except to raise jurisdictional issues or in "circumstances so rare and exceptional that manifest injustice results"); Archer v. State, 851 S.W.2d 157 (Tenn.1993) (relief available "only if it appears upon the face of the judgment or the record of the proceedings * * * that a convicting court was without jurisdiction or authority to sentence a defendant").

[20]See, e.g., State v. Precise, 129 N.J. 451, 609 A.2d 1280 (1992), stating:

It would be a bitter irony indeed if our courts, in an attempt to accommodate the Supreme Court's retrenchment of federal habeas review, were artificially to elevate procedural rulings over substantive adjudications in post-conviction review, at a time when the Court's curtailment of habeas review forces state prisoners to rely increasingly on state post-conviction proceedings as their last resort for vindicating their state and federal constitutional rights. When appropriate, [state] procedural bars * * * may be asserted to preclude post-conviction relief, but their use should not be shaped or influenced in the slightest by the federal courts' restrictive standards for allowing or disallowing habeas review.

See also Cowell v. Leapley, 458 N.W.2d 514 (S.D.1990) (rejecting Teague's bar on the application of "new" rules, finding it "unduly nar-

row"); Smart v. Alaska, 146 P.3d 15 (Alaska.2006) (declining to follow Teague, collecting authority from over a dozen states that apply Teague rule and several that have rejected it). Compare also Lott v. State, 334 Mont. 270, 150 P.3d 337 (2006) (noting, in state where state habeas has been largely supplanted by state post-conviction remedy, prisoner who was barred by statute from seeking relief in state habeas from a sentence rendered facially invalid by decisions handed down after the expiration of the filing period for prisoner's state post-conviction proceeding will nevertheless be allowed to proceed in habeas in light of the state constitution's guarantee that the writ of habeas corpus shall never be suspended).

[21]See, e.g., Maggard v. State, 27 Kan.App.2d 1060, 11 P.3d 89 (2000); State v. Smith, 700 So.2d 493 (La.1997) (custody broadly defined); People v. Pack, 224 Ill.2d 144, 862 N.E.2d 938 (Ill.2007) (pursuant to the reasoning of Garlotte v. Fordice, discussed in § 28.3(a) holding that a prisoner serving consecutive sentences is "imprisoned" under any one of them for purposes of the post-conviction hearing act). Compare In re Azurin, 87 Cal.App. 4th 20, 104 Cal.Rptr.2d 284 (2001) (finding no custody for state habeas, applying federal precedent).

Compare Green v. Baldwin, 204 Or.App. 351, 129 P.3d 734 (2006) (appeal of dismissal of state post-conviction challenge to one of several decisions of the parole board to deny parole release was moot when petitioner was released on parole before appeal decided and there was no showing that a more favorable decision by the parole board would have resulted in any change in petitioner's present parole status).

Coram Nobis or "Post-Conviction" Statutes. A majority of states have adopted post-conviction processes somewhat resembling the writ or coram nobis. Approximately a dozen states adopted the Uniform Post-Conviction Act in one of its versions approved by the Commissioners on Uniform State Laws.[22] Several other states opted for roughly similar provisions.[23] In 1980, the Commissioners approved a revised Uniform Act,[24] tracking the ABA Standards,[25] which also has served as a model for state legislation.[26] Like the writ of coram nobis, the Uniform Act is not limited by a custody requirement and provides for a collateral attack to be filed in the court of conviction. That remedy encompasses a wide range of claims including: (1) all constitutional violations; (2) jurisdictional defects; (3) the presentation of material evidence, not previously heard, that justifies vacating the judgment "in the interest of justice"; and (4) any other objection recognized as a proper subject of collateral attack under any common law or statutory remedy recognized in the jurisdiction.[27] The 1980 revision adds a provision specifically recognizing a claim based upon a "significant change in substantive or procedural law" that is to be applied retroactively.[28]

Under the 1966 revision, the petitioner is barred only from raising otherwise cognizable claims that were "voluntarily and intelligently waived in prior proceedings," but is required to raise

---

[22]See 11A U.L.A. 274 (1997 Supp.). See, e.g., Idaho Code §§ 19-4901 to 19-4911; Iowa Code Ann. §§ 822.1 to 822.11; Minn.Stat.Ann. § 590.01 to 590.06; Okla.Stat.Ann. tit. 22, §§ 1080 to 1089; R.I.Gen.Laws §§ 10-9.1 to 10-9.1-91. Three states adopted the 1955 Act. See Md.Code Ann. art. 27, §§ 645A to 645J; Mont.Code Ann. §§ 46-21-101 to 46-21-203; Or.Rev.Stat.Ann. §§ 138. 510 to 138.680. See also Lott v. State, 150 P.3d 337, 334 Mont. 270 (2006) (tracing the history of collateral review in Montana and characterizing the Montana Post-Conviction Hearing Act enacted in 1967 as "an amalgam of the 1955 Uniform Post-Conviction Procedure Act and the Illinois Post-Conviction Hearing Act").

[23]See D. Wilkes, State Postconviction Remedies and Relief App. A (2001); Nev.Rev.Stat.Ann. §§ 177.315 et seq.

[24]See 11 U.L.A. 149 (1983 Supp.).

[25]4 ABA Standard for Criminal Justice §§ 21-1.1 et seq. (2d ed.1980 & Supp.1986).

[26]See N.D.Century Code §§ 29-32. 1-01 to 29-32.1-14 (adopting 1980 Act).

[27]1966 UPCPA § 1.

[28]1980 UPCPA § 1(a)(6). Clark v. State, 621 N.W.2d 576 (N.D.2001) (discussing this section and relying upon *Teague*).

See also Millemann, Collateral Remedies in Criminal Cases in Maryland: An Assessment, 64 Md.L.Rev. 968 (2005) (although the state's Uniform Post-conviction Procedure Act provides the primary remedy (detailed in this article), there are several additional avenues; noting the state has rejected the *Teague* rule; adopted a doctrine of procedural default more favorable to petitioners and has a three-year statute of limitations).

all grounds in his first application.[29] The court may, however, excuse such a default if there was "sufficient reason" for failing to raise the issue. The 1980 revision treats procedural defaults under a general "misuse-of-process" provision that allows the court to refuse to consider a claim that the petitioner "inexcusably failed to raise" in a prior proceeding.[30] Both versions permit the court to refuse to reconsider a claim previously litigated, although that authority is restricted by the new evidence and change of law provisions.[31] The 1980 revision also includes a special provision allowing the court to assess costs against a petitioner who has "misused the process" or filed a claim "so completely lacking in factual support or legal basis as to be frivolous."[32]

Several states have added to their original post-conviction acts a statute of limitations for filing.[33] Most also have time limitations on appeals from trial court rulings as well.[34]

---

[29]1966 UPCPA § 8. See State v. Escalona-Naranjo, 185 Wis.2d 168, 517 N.W.2d 157 (1994).

[30]1980 UPCPA § 12.

[31]See 1966 UPCPA § 8; 1980 UPCPA § 12(c).

[32]1980 UPCPA § 13.

[33]See, e.g., Mont.Code Ann. § 46-21-102(2) (1997) (one-year from conviction unless the claim alleges the discovery of new evidence). See also State v. Pope, 318 Mont. 383, 80 P.3d 1232 (Mont.2003) (jurisdictional bar to post-conviction review presented by statute of limitation can be overcome by either a showing that no reasonable juror would have found the defendant guilty for the defendant who claims that he is truly innocent, citing Herrera, or for the defendant who claims ineffective assistance, in light of newly discovered evidence, a showing that a juror acting reasonably would, more likely than not, find that the State did not prove he was guilty of the crime for which he was convicted, citing Schlup; petitioner here satisfied this latter burden in light of DNA report obtained post-trial).

[34]See Carey v. Saffold, 536 U.S. 214, 122 S.Ct. 2134, 153 L.Ed.2d 260 (2002):

In most States, relevant state law sets forth some version of the following collateral review procedures. First, the prisoner files a petition in a state court of first instance, typically a trial court. Second, a petitioner seeking to appeal from the trial court's judgment must file a notice of appeal within, say, 30 or 45 days after entry of the trial court's judgment. See, e.g., Ala. R.App.P. 4 (2001); Colo.App.R. 4(b)(1) (2001); Ky. Rule Crim. Proc. 12.04(3) (2002). Third, a petitioner seeking further review of an appellate court's judgment must file a further notice of appeal to the state supreme court (or seek that court's discretionary review) within a short period of time, say, 20 or 30 days, after entry of the court of appeals judgment. See, e.g., Ala. R. App.P. 5 (2001); Colo.Rev.Stat. § 13-4-108 (2001); Conn.R.App.P. 80-1 (2002); Ky. Rule Civ. Proc. 76.20(2)(b) (2002). * * * California's collateral review process functions very much like that of other States, but for the fact that its timeliness rule is indeterminate. Other States (with the exception of North Carolina, see Allen v. Mitchell, 276 F.3d 183, 186 (4th Cir.2001)), specify precise time limits, such as 30 or 45 days, within which an appeal must be taken, while California applies a general "reasonableness" standard.

§ 28.12 Assistance of counsel in post-conviction proceedings

§ 28.12(a)   Petitioner access to legal assistance-constitutional requirements

§ 28.12(b)   Statutory entitlements to legal assistance

§ 28.12(a) Petitioner access to legal assistance-constitutional requirements

As Justice Ginsburg has observed, "68% of the state prison population did not complete high school and many lack the most basic literacy skills. * * * [A]bout seven out of ten inmates fall in the lowest two out of five levels of literacy-marked by an inability to do such basic tasks as write a brief letter to explain an error on a credit card bill, use a bus schedule, or state in writing an argument made in a lengthy newspaper article * * * [A]n inmate so handicapped surely does not possess the skill necessary to pursue a competent pro se appeal."[1] The Supreme Court has concluded, however, that the Constitution does not guarantee the assistance of counsel for those seeking relief in state or federal collateral proceedings.[2] Even death row prisoners must make do on collateral review in state and federal court with what legal assistance legislatures choose to provide.[3]

The Constitution does, however, guarantee prisoners access to

---

[Section 28.12(a)]

[1]Kowalski v. Tesmer, 543 U.S. 125, 125 S.Ct. 564 160 L.Ed.2d 519 (2004) (Ginsburg, J., dissenting) (citing U.S. Dept. of Justice, BJS, Harlow, Education and Correctional Populations 1 (Jan.2003) and U.S. Dept of Ed., National Center for Education Statistics, Literacy Behind Prison Walls xviii, 10, 17 (Oct.1994) (NCES 1994-102), available at http:/nces.ed.g ov/pubs94/94102.pdf). See also Halbert v. Michigan, 545 U.S. 605, 125 S.Ct. 2582, 162 L.Ed.2d 552 (2005) (Ginsburg, J., writing for the Court).

[2]See Murray v. Giarratano, 492 U.S. 1, 109 S.Ct. 2765, 106 L.Ed.2d 1 (1989) (discussed in § 11.2(b)); Pennsylvania v. Finley, 481 U.S. 551, 107 S.Ct. 1990, 95 L.Ed.2d 539 (1987) (discussed in § 11.7(a)); Barbour v. Haley, 471 F.3d 1222 (11th Cir.2006) (Alabama's failure to provide death-sentenced inmates with counsel for post-conviction proceedings did not violate the Constitution). Distinguish-

ing the cases finding no right to appointed counsel for seeking discretionary review of appellate rulings or for seeking collateral relief, the Court held in Halbert v. Michigan, 545 U.S. 605, 125 S.Ct. 2582, 162 L.Ed.2d 552 (2005), that a state may not deny appointed counsel to defendants whose first-tier review is discretionary.

[3]For criticism of the Court's refusal to extend the right to counsel to collateral proceedings for death row prisoners, see Freedman, *Giarratano is a Scarecrow: The Right to Counsel in State Capital Post-conviction Proceedings*, 91 Cornell L.Rev. 1079 (2006) (arguing that Kennedy's concurring opinion in *Giarratano,* finding that Virginia's practice of staffing the prison system with institutional lawyers to assist in preparing petitions did not violate the Eighth Amendment, was controlling, and that Alabama's system is unconstitutional because has no system for providing prefiling assistance to capital prisoners in post-conviction proceedings).

the "tools" that "inmates need in order to attack their sentences, directly or collaterally, and in order to challenge the conditions of their confinement."[4] In first recognizing this limited right, the Supreme Court in *Bounds v. Smith*[5] urged the states to furnish paralegal assistants, law students, or full-time staff attorneys, rather than simply rely on prison libraries. Two decades later, striking down a federal court injunction which it termed "wildly intrusive," the Court explained in *Lewis v. Casey* that the right established in *Bounds* was limited to "the conferral of a capability—the capability of bringing contemplated challenges to sentences or conditions of confinement before the courts."[6]

§ 28.12(b) Statutory entitlements to legal assistance

Congress has enacted legislation providing for the appointment of counsel to assist indigents seeking collateral relief in federal court, including the Criminal Justice Act[7] and Rules 6 and 8 of the Rules Governing § 2254 and § 2255 proceedings. Those challenging capital sentences or convictions in federal court have a statutory right to the assistance of counsel,[8] as do those habeas petitioners, capital or non-capital, who are granted evidentiary

---

See also McConville, The Right to Effective Assistance of Capital Post-conviction Counsel: Constitutional Implications of Statutory Grants of Capital Counsel, 2003 Wis.L.Rev. 31 (2003) (reviewing state and federal statutory provision of counsel in post-conviction proceedings and arguing that when the government voluntary provides post-conviction assistance under statute, it is obligated to provide effective assistance).

[4]Lewis v. Casey, 518 U.S. 343, 355, 116 S.Ct. 2174, 2182, 135 L.Ed.2d 606 (1996).

[5]Bounds v. Smith, 430 U.S. 817, 97 S.Ct. 1491, 52 L.Ed.2d 72 (1977) (discussed in § 11.2(f)). See also Barbour v. Haley, 410 F.Supp.2d 1120 (M.D.Ala.2006) (rejecting claim of Sixth Amendment violation due to failure to ensure representation for death row inmates to prepare petitions, noting "such a conclusion would effectively nullify the Supreme Court's holding * * * that * * * there is no right to counsel in state collateral proceedings").

[6]Lewis v. Casey, 518 U.S. 343,

116 S.Ct. 2174, 135 L.Ed.2d 606 (1996). This guarantee, one court has held, bars the arbitrary withholding of access to library space or means of binding a pleading. Phillips v. Hust, 477 F.3d 1070 (9th Cir.2007).

[Section 28.12(b)]

[7]18 U.S.C.A. § 3006(a).

[8]See 18 U.S.C.A. § 3599 (2006) (formerly 18 U.S.C.A. § 848(9)(4)); McFarland v. Scott, 512 U.S. 849, 114 S.Ct. 2568, 129 L.Ed.2d 666 (1994) (interpreting the Anti-Drug Abuse Act of 1988, 21 U.S.C.A. § 848(q)(4)(B), which mandates the appointment of counsel for all indigent capital prisoners who seek post-conviction relief in federal court). But see Clark v. Johnson, 278 F.3d 459 (5th Cir.2002) (counsel appointed to represent a death row inmate in federal habeas corpus proceeding was not entitled to compensation and reimbursement for expenses incurred in connection with the inmate's state clemency proceeding); Hain v. Mullin, 436 F.3d 1168 (10th Cir.2006) (federal statute providing for counsel in federal habeas proceedings for petitioners seeking to vacate or set aside a death sentence

hearings.[9] Other indigent petitioners may be appointed counsel at the discretion of the trial court, whenever the court determines that "the interests of justice so require."[10] Rates at which these attorneys are paid are limited by statute and fees must be disclosed to the public. Only a tiny fraction of the prisoner petitions filed by prisoners serving non-capital cases are prepared with legal assistance.[11] In death cases, the statute provides not only for appointed counsel but also for the provision of "other services" which at least one court has interpreted to include DNA testing to establish actual innocence.[12]

State statutes may provide for the appointment of counsel for indigents seeking collateral relief in state court, as well.[13] The 1996 Act requires that states seeking expedited review of federal

---

also mandates representation for indigent death row inmates at state clemency proceedings, based on the plain language of the statute. Also noting "It is entirely plausible that Congress did not want condemned men and women to be abandoned by their counsel at the last moment and left to navigate the sometimes labyrinthine clemency process from their jail cells, relying on limited resources and little education in a final attempt at convincing the government to spare their lives."). See also § 11.2 at note 64.

[9]See Rule 8 of the § 2254 Rules. Rule 6 also authorizes the appointment of counsel if the court grants leave to employ discovery devices and counsel's participation is deemed "necessary for effective utilization of [such] procedures."

[10]18 U.S.C.A. § 3006A(a)(2)(B); Rule 8(c) of the Rules Governing § 2254 Cases; 28 U.S.C.A. § 2254(h). See also C. Wright, N. King and S. Klein, Federal Practice and Procedure, Criminal §§ 731 to 735 (3d ed.2004).

[11]See N. King, F. Cheesman & B. Ostrom, Habeas Litigation in U.S. District Courts (2007), available at http://www.ncjrs.gov/pdffiles1/nij/grants/219559.pdf (7% of non-capital petitioners had counsel); R. Hertz & J. Liebman, 1 Federal Habeas Corpus Practice and Procedure § 12.2 (5th ed.2005); Scalia, Prisoner Petitions in the Federal Courts, 1980-96 at 2 (Oct. 1997, NCJ 164615) (noting 81.6%; of

state habeas petitioners represented themselves); U.S. Dept. of Justice, Office of Justice Programs, Bureau of Justice Statistics, Federal Habeas Corpus Review: Challenging State Court Criminal Convictions 14 (1995, NCJ 155544) (93% of habeas petitioners were pro se).

[12]Cherrix v. Braxton, 131 F.Supp.2d 756 (E.D.Va.2001) (services of experts may be funded under 21 U.S.C.A. § 848 [now 18 U.S.C.A. § 3599] so long as the petitioner demonstrates they are "reasonably necessary," finding good cause established where petitioner asks for DNA evidence that could demonstrate a viable claim of actual innocence, and the habeas petitioner faces execution).

[13]See Gibson v. Turpin, 270 Ga. 855, 513 S.E.2d 186 (1999) (collecting state statutes providing counsel in death cases). Compare State v. Hall, 154 N.H. 180, 908 A.2d 766 (2006) (rejecting state constitutional right to counsel in post-conviction motion for a new trial, noting that frequently a single prisoner will attempt to collaterally attack a conviction several time and that requiring the State to appoint counsel in all such proceedings would impose a significant financial burden on the state).

State constitutional provisions regarding counsel may also establish rights to representation in collateral proceedings. See Deegan v. State, 711 N.W.2d 89 (Minn.2006) (finding a state constitutional right to one review of

habeas petitions by capital defendants under chapter 154 must first establish "a mechanism for the appointment, compensation, and payment of reasonable litigation expenses of competent counsel in State post-conviction proceedings" brought by indigent prisoners under capital sentences, and standards of competency for such counsel. Counsel for indigent capital defendants will thus be available in states that choose to take advantage of the favorable treatment offered to them in federal habeas cases by the 1996 Act.[14] Even when counsel is provided, however, the "ineffectiveness or incompetence of counsel during Federal or State collateral post-conviction proceedings shall not be a ground for relief" in a federal habeas corpus proceeding.[15]

---

his or her conviction, and that the state constitutional right to the assistance of counsel extends to one review of a criminal conviction, whether by direct appeal or a first review by post-conviction proceeding).

[14]See § 28.8.

[15]28 U.S.C.A. § 2254(i). This provision codifies Pennsylvania v. Finley, 481 U.S. 551, 107 S.Ct. 1990, 95 L.Ed. 2d 539 (1987), discussed in §§ 11.2(b) and 11.7(a), which held that incompetency of counsel on a collateral attack would not present a due process viola-

tion since there was no constitutional right to the assistance of counsel at that stage. Arguably, the provision's statement that incompetency shall not be "grounds for relief" goes beyond *Finley* and also codifies Coleman v. Thompson, 501 U.S. 722, 111 S.Ct. 2546, 115 L.Ed.2d 640 (1991), discussed in § 28.4(d), which held that incompetency at this stage also did not constitute "cause" excusing a procedural default because that incompetency is not a constitutional violation.

Table of Cases

A

A. v. District Court, 191 Colo. 10, 550 P.2d 315 (Colo.1976)—§§ 8.10(c) n.62, 65

Aaron, State v., 218 S.W.3d 501 (Mo.2007)—§ 14.1(d) n.66

Aaron v. State, 300 Ark. 13, 775 S.W.2d 894 (1989)—§ 10.2(c) n.30

Aaron v. State, 273 Ala. 337, 139 So.2d 309 (1961)—§ 7.2(b) n.16

Aaron, State ex rel. v. King, 199 W.Va. 533, 485 S.E.2d 702 (W.Va.1997)—§§ 26.5(c) n.43, 44

Abad, People v., 98 N.Y.2d 12, 744 N.Y.S.2d 353, 771 N.E.2d 235 (2002)—§ 3.8(d) n.182

Abad, United States v., 350 F.3d 793 (8th Cir.2003)—§§ 12.3(a) n.23, 24

Abanatha, United States v., 999 F.2d 1246 (8th Cir.1993)—§ 8.11(c) n.35

Abar, People v., 99 N.Y.2d 406, 757 N.Y.S.2d 219, 786 N.E.2d 1255 (2003)—§§ 11.9(a) n.24; 11.9(d) n.178

Abarca, United States v., 985 F.2d 1012 (9th Cir.1993)—§ 26.3(g) n.95

Abbamonte, People v., 43 N.Y.2d 74, 400 N.Y.S.2d 766, 371 N.E.2d 485 (1977)—§ 25.5(b) n.28

Abbas, United States v., 74 F.3d 506 (4th Cir.1996)—§§ 24.3(i) n.185, 190

Abbate v. United States, 359 U.S. 187, 79 S.Ct. 666, 3 L.Ed.2d 729 (1959)—§§ 1.2(c) n.11; 2.5(f) n.62; 25.5(a) n.2

Abbell, United States v., 271 F.3d 1286 (11th Cir.2001)—§§ 22.1(g) n.109, 110; 24.9(f) n.104

Abbell, United States v., 939 F.Supp. 860 (S.D.Fla.1996)—§§ 11.9(a) n.22; 11.9(c) n.117, 143

Abbott v. County Court of Fourteenth Judicial District, 886 P.2d 730 (Colo.1994)—§ 14.4(b) n.13

Abbott v. Laurie, 422 F.Supp. 976 (D.R.I.1976)—§ 12.4(d) n.85

Abbott, State v., 277 Kan. 161, 83 P.3d 794 (2004)—§ 3.3(c) n.132

Abbott v. State, 307 Ark. 278, 819 S.W.2d 694 (1991)—§ 3.5(a) n.65

Abbott v. United States, 871 A.2d 514 (D.C.App.2005)—§ 21.2(d) n.174

Abbott Laboratories, United States v., 505 F.2d 565 (4th Cir.1974)—§§ 16.3(d) n.51, 64; 16.3(g) n.120

ABC, Inc. v. Stewart, 360 F.3d 90 (2d Cir.2004)—§§ 23.1(e) n.221, 247; 24.1(b) n.17; 243

Abdi v. Georgia, 744 F.2d 1500 (11th Cir.1984)—§ 25.2(d) n.24

Abdo, State v., 518 N.W.2d 223 (S.D.1994)—§§ 10.3(d) n.72; 10.4(d) n.30, 32

Abdouch, State v., 230 Neb. 929, 434 N.W.2d 317 (1989)—§ 9.4(a) n.41

Abdul-Kabir v. Quarterman, _____ U.S. _____, 127 S.Ct. 1654, 167 L.Ed.2d 585 (2007)—§§ 26.1(b) n.21; 28.6(f) n.69

Abdulla, United States v., 294 F.3d 830 (7th Cir.2002)—§ 9.5(c) n.68

Abdullah, State v., 878 A.2d 746 (N.J.2005)—§ 26.4(i) n.189

Abdullah v. United States, 240 F.3d 683 (8th Cir.2001)—§ 11.5(g) n.124

Abdullah, United States v., 947 F.2d 306 (8th Cir.1991)—§§ 21.4(f) n.174, 178

Abdullahi, State v., 607 N.W.2d 561 (N.D.2000)—§ 21.4(d) n.134

Abel, United States v., 469 U.S. 45, 105 S.Ct. 465, 83 L.Ed.2d 450 (1984)—§ 27.5(e) n.147

Abel v. United States, 362 U.S. 217, 80 S.Ct. 683, 4 L.Ed.2d 668 (1960)— §§ 3.1(d) n.107; 3.2(h) n.202; 3.10(e) n.151; 9.1(b) n.52, 85

Abel, United States v., 155 F.Supp. 8 (E.D.N.Y.1957)—§ 3.1(d) n.108

Abela v. Martin, 380 F.3d 915 (6th Cir.2004)—§ 6.9(g) n.166

Abela v. Martin, 348 F.3d 164 (6th Cir.2003)—§ 28.5(b) n.45

Abell, United States v., 552 F.Supp. 316 (D.Me.1982)—§ 15.4(e) n.129

Abello-Silva, United States v., 948 F.2d 1168 (10th Cir.1991)—§ 23.2(a) n.20

Abels v. Kaiser, 913 F.2d 821 (10th Cir.1990)—§ 11.6(d) n.119

Ableman v. Booth, 62 U.S. (21 How.) 506, 16 L.Ed. 169 (1859)— § 28.2(a) n.5

A Blue in Color, 1993 Chevrolet, State v., 328 Mont. 10, 116 P.3d 800 (2005)—§ 2.12(b) n.106

Abney v. United States, 431 U.S. 651, 97 S.Ct. 2034, 52 L.Ed.2d 651 (1977)—§§ 27.1(a) n.2; 27.2(c) n.20, 29, 31

Abod, United States v., 770 F.2d 1293 (5th Cir.1985)—§ 21.4(f) n.214

Abou-Saada, United States v., 785 F.2d 1 (1st Cir.1986)—§ 4.6(e) n.97

Abraham v. County of Greenville, 237 F.3d 386 (4th Cir.2001)—§ 4.6(b) n.51

Abraham, State v., 338 N.C. 315, 451 S.E.2d 131 (1994)—§§ 19.5(c) n.57; 24.4(d) n.42

Abrahams, United States v., 453 F.Supp. 749 (D.Mass.1978)—§ 16.3(b) n.23

Abrahams, United States v., 466 F.Supp. 552 (1978)—§ 23.2(a) n.43

Abrahams, United States v., 575 F.2d 3 (1st Cir.1978)—§ 12.2(a) n.14

Abram v. State, 606 So.2d 1015 (Miss.1992)—§ 10.5(b) n.18

Abrams, Matter of, 62 N.Y.2d 183, 476 N.Y.S.2d 494, 465 N.E.2d 1 (1984)—§ 8.14(d) n.58

Abrams v. Barnett, 121 F.3d 1036 (7th Cir.1997)—§ 7.4(c) n.51

Abrams, United States v., 137 F.3d 704 (2d Cir.1998)—§§ 24.9(f) n.63, 85

Abrams, United States v., 539 F.Supp. 378 (S.D.N.Y.1982)—§§ 15.2(i) n.228; 19.2(f) n.91

Abreu, United States v., 202 F.3d 386 (1st Cir.2000)—§ 11.2(e) n.170

Abreu-Cabrera, United States v., 64 F.3d 67 (2d Cir.1995)—§ 26.7(c) n.35

Abruska v. State, 705 P.2d 1261 (Alaska App.1985)—§ 15.7(f) n.168

Abshire, United States v., 471 F.2d 116 (5th Cir.1972)—§ 17.1(a) n.11

Abuhamra, United States v., 389 F.3d 309 (2d Cir.2004)—§ 12.3(f) n.143

Abuhouran, United States v., 161 F.3d 206 (3d Cir.1998)—§ 21.2(d) n.264

Abu-Jamal, Commonwealth v., 553 Pa. 485, 720 A.2d 79 (1998)—§ 22.4(c) n.29

Abu-Jamal, Commonwealth v., 521 Pa. 188, 555 A.2d 846 (1989)— § 26.4(g) n.141

Abu Marzook, United States v., 412 F.Supp.2d 913 (N.D.Ill.2006)— § 24.1(b) n.29

Abushaar, United States v., 761 F.2d 954 (3d Cir.1985)—§ 26.9(b) n.74

Accardi, United States ex rel. v. Shaughnessey, 347 U.S. 260, 745 S.Ct. 499, 98 L.Ed. 681 (1954)—§ 1.7(j) n.229

Accetturo, United States v., 783 F.2d 382 (3d Cir.1986)—§§ 12.3(f) n.144, 146

Acen, Commonwealth v., 396 Mass. 472, 487 N.E.2d 189 (1986)— §§ 22.1(a) n.5; 22.2(d) n.87, 88

Acevedo, United States v., 891 F.2d 607 (7th Cir.1989)—§ 11.9(d) n.220

Acevedo-Ramos v. United States, 961 F.2d 305 (1st Cir.1992)—§§ 18.5(a) n.50; 21.6(a) n.19

Acevedo-Ramos, United States v., 755 F.2d 203 (1st Cir.1985)—§§ 12.1(d) n.50; 12.3(a) n.20; 12.3(f) n.144, 146

Acha v. United States, 910 F.2d 28 (1st Cir.1990)—§§ 18.1(c) n.36; 18.3(b) n.5

Achter, State v., 512 S.W.2d 894 (Mo.App.1974)—§§ 3.2(f) n.173; 3.7(f) n.142

Ackerman v. Houston, 45 Ariz. 293, 43 P.2d 194 (1935)—§ 13.3(a) n.14

Ackerman, State v., 499 N.W.2d 882 (N.D.1993)—§ 9.1(b) n.70

Ackies v. Purdy, 322 F.Supp. 38 (S.D.Fla.1970)—§ 12.2(a) n.8

Acme Markets, Inc., People v., 37 N.Y.2d 326, 372 N.Y.S.2d 590, 334 N.E.2d 555 (1975)—§§ 13.3(b) n.33; 13.4(c) n.113; 13.4(d) n.162

Acomb, People v., 94 A.D.2d 978, 464 N.Y.S.2d 103 (1983)—§ 16.3(b) n.15

Acosta, State v., 125 Ariz. 146, 608 P.2d 83 (App.1980)—§ 15.4(d) n.125

Acosta, United States v., 363 F.3d 1141 (11th Cir.2004)—§ 6.6(e) n.91

Acosta, United States v., 303 F.3d 78 (1st Cir.2002)—§ 26.5(a) n.8

Acosta, United States v., 965 F.2d 1248 (3d Cir.1992)—§ 3.2(d) n.157

Acosta-Martinez, United States v., 252 F.3d 13 (1st Cir.2001)—§ 27.3(c) n.43

Acremant, State v., 338 Or. 302, 108 P.3d 1139 (2005)—§ 6.9(g) n.166

Adair v. United States, 391 A.2d 288 (D.C.App.1978)—§ 16.4(d) n.128

Adames, United States v., 56 F.3d 737 (7th Cir.1995)—§ 3.1(c) n.79

Adamo, United States v., 742 F.2d 927 (6th Cir.1984)—§§ 9.1(b) n.80; 15.7(e) n.106

Adams, Ex parte, 768 S.W.2d 281 (Tex.Cr.App.1989)—§ 24.3(d) n.111

Adams v. Carroll, 875 F.2d 1441 (9th Cir.1989)—§§ 11.5(b) n.27, 29; 11.5(d) n.67, 68

Adams v. City of Battle Creek, 250 F.3d 980 (6th Cir.2001)—§§ 4.3(b) n.13; 4.6(b) n.39, 46, 50, 51; 4.6(n) n.247

Adams v. Illinois, 405 U.S. 278, 92 S.Ct. 916, 31 L.Ed.2d 202 (1972)—§§ 1.5(c) n.140; 2.11(c) n.32, 38; 20.1(b) n.28

Adams v. New York, 192 U.S. 585, 24 S.Ct. 372, 48 L.Ed. 575 (1904)—§ 3.1(a) n.4

Adams, People v., 316 Ill.App.3d 202, 249 Ill.Dec. 534, 736 N.E.2d 728 (2000)—§ 25.2(a) n.5

Adams, People v., 149 Ill.2d 331, 173 Ill.Dec. 600, 597 N.E.2d 574 (1992)—§ 3.5(d) n.144

Adams, People v., 57 N.Y.2d 1035, 457 N.Y.S.2d 783, 444 N.E.2d 33 (1982)—§ 21.4(f) n.197

Adams, People v., 53 N.Y.2d 241, 440 N.Y.S.2d 902, 423 N.E.2d 379 (1981)—§ 7.4(c) n.38

Adams, People v., 1 N.Y. 173 (1848)—§ 16.4(c) n.62

Adams v. Peterson, 968 F.2d 835 (9th Cir.1992)—§ 21.6(c) n.118

Adams v. State, 103 Haw. 214, 81 P.3d 394 (2003)—§ 18.5(a) n.50

Adams, State v., 554 N.W.2d 686 (Iowa 1996)—§ 14.2(g) n.106

Adams, State v., 193 W.Va. 277, 456 S.E.2d 4 (1995)—§§ 19.5(b) n.6, 25, 37

Adams, State v., 76 Haw. 408, 879 P.2d 513 (1994)—§ 27.5(e) n.144

Adams v. State, 264 Ga. 71, 440 S.E.2d 639 (1994)—§ 22.3(d) n.176

Adams, State v., 133 N.H. 818, 585 A.2d 853 (1991)—§ 24.3(f) n.141

Adams v. State, 707 S.W.2d 900 (Tex.Crim.App.1986)—§§ 19.2(c) n.38; 19.3(b) n.149

Adams, State v., 56 Or.App. 303, 641 P.2d 647 (1982)—§ 20.6(b) n.62

Adams v. State, 380 So.2d 421 (Fla.1980)—§§ 11.7(e) n.66, 67

Adams v. State, 577 S.W.2d 717 (Tex.Crim.App.1979)—§ 8.5(g) n.222

Adams v. State, 598 P.2d 503 (Alaska 1979)—§ 15.5(c) n.131

Adams v. State, 192 So.2d 762 (Fla.1966)—§ 24.7(e) n.63

Adams v. Sumner, 39 F.3d 933 (9th Cir.1994)—§ 4.6(l) n.187

Adams, United States v., 448 F.3d 492 (2d Cir.2006)—§ 21.4(f) n.192

Adams v. United States, 883 A.2d 76 (D.C.App.2005)—§ 7.4(c) n.49

Adams v. United States, 372 F.3d 132 (2d Cir.2004)—§ 28.9(a) n.5

Adams, United States v., 388 F.3d 708 (9th Cir.2004)—§ 13.4(e) n.169

Adams, United States v., 252 F.3d 276 (3d Cir.2001)—§ 27.6(b) n.21

Adams, United States v., 1 F.3d 1566 (11th Cir.1993)—§§ 6.6(e) n.95; 17.4(b) n.94

Adams, United States v., 914 F.2d 1404 (10th Cir.1990)—§ 24.5(c) n.39

Adams, United States v., 870 F.2d 1140 (6th Cir.1989)—§ 13.5(a) n.7

Adams, United States v., 759 F.2d 1099 (3d Cir.1985)—§§ 4.6(d) n.100; 4.6(e) n.97; 4.6(m) n.237

Adams, United States v., 778 F.2d 1117 (5th Cir.1985)—§ 19.6(c) n.40

Adams v. United States, 466 A.2d 439 (D.C.1983)—§ 3.8(d) n.160

Adams, United States v., 634 F.2d 830 (5th Cir.1981)—§ 21.2(c) n.102

Adams v. United States ex rel McCann, 317 U.S. 269, 63 S.Ct. 236, 87 L.Ed. 268 (1942)—§ 11.6(a) n.20

Adams v. Williams, 407 U.S. 143, 92 S.Ct. 1921, 32 L.Ed.2d 612 (1972)—§§ 3.8(a) n.4; 3.8(c) n.65; 3.8(d) n.120, 157; 3.8(e) n.190, 208

Adamson v. California, 332 U.S. 46, 67 S.Ct. 1672, 91 L.Ed. 1903 (1947)— §§ 2.3(a) n.4, 6, 7, 11, 19, 39, 51, 53, 56; 2.3(b) n.88; 2.4(a) n.14; 2.4(e) n.159; 2.4(f) n.181, 187; 2.5(c) n.17, 20; 2.5(f) n.53; 2.6(b) n.34; 2.7(c) n.107

Adamson v. Ricketts, 758 F.2d 441 (9th Cir.1985)—§ 21.5(e) n.137

Adamson, State v., 140 Ariz. 198, 680 P.2d 1259 (1984)—§ 24.5(b) n.24

Addington v. Texas, 441 U.S. 418, 99 S.Ct. 1804, 60 L.Ed.2d 323 (1979)—§ 26.10(c) n.47

Addonizio, In re, 53 N.J. 107, 248 A.2d 531 (1968)—§§ 8.6(a) n.8, 14; 8.7(a) n.2, 15

Addonizio, United States v., 442 U.S. 178, 99 S.Ct. 2235, 60 L.Ed.2d 805 (1979)—§ 28.9(c) n.75

Addonizio, United States v., 451 F.2d 49 (3d Cir.1971)—§§ 16.3(g) n.101, 103

Adedoyin, United States v., 369 F.3d 337 (3d Cir.2004)—§ 21.4(a) n.22

Adekunle, United States v., 2 F.3d 559 (5th Cir.1993)—§ 6.3(b) n.36

Adekunle, United States v., 980 F.2d 985 (5th Cir.1992)—§ 3.9(f) n.110

Adel, State v., 136 Wash.2d 629, 965 P.2d 1072 (1998)—§ 17.4(b) n.73

Aderholt, United States v., 87 F.3d 740 (5th Cir.1996)—§ 21.2(d) n.253

Adesida, United States v., 129 F.3d 846 (6th Cir.1997)—§§ 19.3(c) n.184, 189

A.D.G., People in Interest of, 895 P.2d 1067 (Colo.App.1994)—§ 6.10(e) n.76

Adkins v. Commonwealth, 96 S.W.3d 779 (Ky.2003)—§§ 6.10(b) n.14; 6.10(c) n.50, 51

Adkins, People v., 113 P.3d 788 (Colo.2005)—§ 6.9(g) n.166

Adkins, People v., 452 Mich. 702, 551 N.W.2d 108 (1996)—§§ 11.3(a) n.12; 11.5(c) n.32, 46, 47, 54; 11.5(d) n.67

Adkins, State v., 702 So.2d 1115 (La.App.1997)—§ 13.1(a) n.27

Adkins, State v., 170 W.Va. 46, 289 S.E.2d 720 (1982)—§ 19.6(a) n.2

Adkins, United States v., 429 F.3d 631 (6th Cir.2005)—§ 26.4(i) n.201

Adkins, United States v., 274 F.3d 444 (7th Cir.2001)—§ 19.3(a) n.88

Adkinson, United States v., 360 F.3d 1257 (11th Cir.2004)—§ 13.5(h) n.123

Adkinson, United States v., 247 F.3d 1289 (11th Cir.2001)—§ 13.5(h) n.178

Adkison, State v., 175 W.Va. 706, 338 S.E.2d 185 (1985)—§ 6.2(c) n.113

Adler, State v., 189 Ariz. 280, 942 P.2d 439 (1997)—§ 26.10(b) n.16

Administrative Subpoena John Doe (D.P.M.), In re, 253 F.3d 256 (6th Cir.2001)—§ 8.7(a) n.26

Advisory Opinion to the Senate, 108 R.I. 628, 278 A.2d 852 (1971)—§ 2.12(e) n.216

Aero Mayflower Transit Co., United States v., 831 F.2d 1142 (D.C.Cir.1987)—§ 8.5(c) n.87

Aetna Casualty & Surety Co. v. Niziolek, 395 Mass. 737, 481 N.E.2d 1356 (1985)—§ 21.4(a) n.20

Afflerbach, United States v., 754 F.2d 866 (10th Cir.1985)—§ 22.2(d) n.85

Africa v. Anderson, 542 F.Supp. 224 (E.D.Pa.1982)—§ 11.5(d) n.75

Afterbuffalo, State v., 308 Mont. 163, 40 P.3d 375 (2002)—§ 21.2(d) n.194

Agan, State v., 259 Ga. 541, 384 S.E.2d 863 (1989)—§§ 13.4(b) n.44, 46

A.G.D., State v., 178 N.J. 56, 835 A.2d 291 (2003)—§ 6.4(f) n.124

Age, State v., 38 Or.App. 501, 590 P.2d 759 (1979)—§ 26.9(b) n.72

Agent, State v., 443 N.W.2d 701 (Iowa 1989)—§ 5.2(b) n.29

Ager, People v., 928 P.2d 784 (Colo.App.1996)—§ 15.6(c) n.98

Agnello v. United States, 269 U.S. 20, 46 S.Ct. 4, 70 L.Ed. 145 (1925)—§§ 3.6(e) n.103; 9.6(a) n.1

Agnew, State v., 361 N.C. 333, 643 S.E.2d 581 (2007)—§ 21.4(f) n.177

Agosto, United States v., 675 F.2d 965 (8th Cir.1982)—§§ 11.9(a) n.8; 11.9(c) n.123

Agrabante, State v., 73 Haw. 179, 830 P.2d 492 (1992)—§§ 5.1(c) n.26; 5.4(c) n.44

Agron, United States ex rel. v. Herold, 426 F.2d 125 (2d Cir.1970)—§ 11.6(a) n.43

Aguiar, United States v., 825 F.2d 39 (4th Cir.1987)—§ 3.8(c) n.76

Aguilar v. State, 106 N.M. 798, 751 P.2d 178 (1988)—§ 6.2(c) n.169

Aguilar v. Texas, 378 U.S. 108, 84 S.Ct. 1509, 12 L.Ed.2d 723 (1964)—§§ 3.3(a) n.18, 19; 3.3(b) n.65; 3.3(c) n.77; 3.8(d) n.159

Aguilar, United States v., 384 F.3d 520 (8th Cir.2004)—§ 6.8(b) n.49

Aguilar, United States v., 883 F.2d 662 (9th Cir.1989)—§ 3.10(c) n.84

Aguilar, United States v., 756 F.2d 1418 (9th Cir.1985)—§ 19.3(c) n.185

Aguilar-Muniz, United States v., 156 F.3d 974 (9th Cir.1998)—§ 21.2(f) n.363

Aguilar-Ramos, People v., 86 P.3d 397 (Colo.2004)—§ 6.8(a) n.36

Aguilera, United States v., 654 F.2d 352 (5th Cir.1981)—§ 21.2(f) n.372

Aguirre v. State, 683 S.W.2d 502 (Tex.App.1984)—§ 24.9(f) n.81

Aguirre, United States v., 839 F.2d 854 (1st Cir.1988)—§ 9.1(d) n.124

Aguirre-Mata v. State, 125 S.W.3d 473 (Tex.Crim.App.2003)—§ 21.5(c) n.88

Agurs, United States v., 427 U.S. 97, 96 S.Ct. 2392, 49 L.Ed.2d 342 (1976)—§§ 11.10(d) n.158; 15.5(b) n.51; 15.7(e) n.117; 21.3(c) n.172; 24.3(b) n.18, 22, 43

Aguwa, United States v., 123 F.3d 418 (6th Cir.1997)—§ 11.7(e) n.63

Ahearn, Commonwealth v., 543 Pa. 174, 670 A.2d 133 (1996)—§ 13.3(c) n.36

Ahlo, State v., 79 Hawai'i 385, 903 P.2d 690 (1995)—§ 20.6(c) n.67

Ahmad, United States v., 53 F.R.D. 186 (M.D.Pa.1971)—§ 20.3(d) n.94

Ahmed, United States v., 980 F.2d 161 (2d Cir.1992)—§ 12.1(a) n.21

Ahn, United States v., 231 F.3d 26 (D.C.Cir.2000)—§ 21.2(d) n.157

A House and 1.37 Acres of Real Property, State v., 886 P.2d 534 (Utah 1994)—§ 2.6(b) n.42

Ah Sin v. Wittman, 198 U.S. 500, 25 S.Ct. 756, 49 L.Ed. 1142 (1905)—§ 13.4(b) n.75

Ahvakana v. State, 768 P.2d 631 (Alaska App.1989)—§ 24.11(d) n.23

Aichele, United States v., 941 F.2d 761 (9th Cir.1991)—§ 20.3(a) n.20

Aiello, United States v., 900 F.2d 528 (2d Cir.1990)—§ 11.9(d) n.223

Aikins, State v., 261 Kan. 346, 932 P.2d 408 (1997)—§ 24.3(b) n.69

Aime v. Commonwealth, 414 Mass. 667, 611 N.E.2d 204 (1993)—§§ 12.3(d) n.96, 111; 12.3(f) n.136; 27.5(a) n.24

Airdo, United States v., 380 F.2d 103 (7th Cir.1967)—§ 9.1(b) n.66

Aisenberg, United States v., 358 F.3d 1327 (11th Cir.2004)—§§ 13.5(h) n.123, 145

Aitken, United States v., 898 F.2d 104 (9th Cir.1990)—§ 12.3(a) n.20

Ajabu v. State, 693 N.E.2d 921 (Ind.1998)—§§ 6.9(c) n.63, 65

Ajayi, United States v., 935 F.Supp. 90 (D.R.I.1996)—§ 25.1(d) n.65

Ajiboye, United States v., 961 F.2d 892 (9th Cir.1992)—§ 24.9(d) n.43

Ajugwo, United States v., 82 F.3d 925 (9th Cir.1996)—§ 26.4(h) n.159

A Juvenile, Commonwealth v., 402 Mass. 275, 521 N.E.2d 1368 (1988)—§§ 6.6(b) n.15; 6.9(b) n.22; 6.10(c) n.49, 51

A Juvenile (No. 2), Commonwealth v., 411 Mass. 157, 580 N.E.2d 1014 (1991)—§ 3.2(f) n.182

Ake v. Oklahoma, 470 U.S. 68, 105 S.Ct. 1087, 84 L.Ed.2d 53 (1985)—§§ 1.5(e) n.207; 2.7(a) n.23; 2.7(c) n.128, 213, 218; 2.8(b) n.53; 11.1(d) n.110; 11.2(e) n.142, 199; 20.5(c) n.37; 22.3(b) n.94; 27.6(d) n.144; 28.4(b) n.22, 23; 28.6(e) n.60

Akin, United States v., 562 F.2d 459 (7th Cir.1977)—§ 3.10(e) n.151

Akindele, United States v., 84 F.3d 948 (7th Cir.1996)—§ 26.4(h) n.159

Akins v. State, 330 Ark. 228, 955 S.W.2d 483 (1997)—§ 11.5(d) n.71

Akins v. State, 691 So.2d 587 (Fla.1997)—§ 19.5(b) n.43

Akins, State v., 198 Wis.2d 495, 544 N.W.2d 392 (1996)—§ 14.3(d) n.89

Akins, United States v., 276 F.3d 1141 (9th Cir.2002)—§ 21.3(a) n.32

Akinsola, United States v., 105 F.3d 331 (7th Cir.1997)—§ 21.5(b) n.66

Akpan, United States v., 407 F.3d 360 (5th Cir.2005)—§ 24.9(f) n.62

Akram, United States v., 152 F.3d 698 (7th Cir.1998)—§ 24.10(b) n.26

Akrawi v. Jabe, 979 F.2d 418 (6th Cir.1992)—§ 24.4(d) n.62

Akrawi, United States v., 920 F.2d 418 (6th Cir.1990)—§ 3.6(d) n.99

Akridge, United States v., 346 F.3d 618 (6th Cir.2003)—§ 9.4(e) n.107

Akron, City of v. Akins, 15 Ohio App.2d 168, 239 N.E.2d 430 (1968)—§ 18.5(a) n.48

Akron, City of v. Sabol, 2 Ohio App.2d 109, 206 N.E.2d 575 (1965)—§ 1.8(d) n.70

Alabama, Ex parte State of, 588 So.2d 903 (Ala.1991)—§ 3.3(f) n.213

Alabama v. Bozeman, 533 U.S. 146, 121 S.Ct. 2079, 150 L.Ed.2d 188 (2001)—§§ 18.4(c) n.46, 69, 74

Alabama v. Shelton, 535 U.S. 654, 122 S.Ct. 1764, 152 L.Ed.2d 888 (2002)—§§ 2.9(i) n.279, 280; 11.2(a) n.22, 30; 26.1(d) n.68; 28.6(d) n.36; 28.6(e) n.49

Alabama v. Smith, 490 U.S. 794, 109 S.Ct. 2201, 104 L.Ed.2d 865 (1989)—§§ 2.9(b) n.25; 21.2(c) n.133; 21.5(e) n.139; 26.7(b) n.20; 26.8(c) n.26

Alabama v. White, 496 U.S. 325, 110 S.Ct. 2412, 110 L.Ed.2d 301 (1990)—§§ 3.3(c) n.137; 3.8(d) n.163

Alabama (In re Pace), Ex parte, 714 So.2d 332 (1997)—§ 15.4(e) n.141

Alameh, United States v., 341 F.3d 167 (2d Cir.2003)—§ 13.4(b) n.69

Alamillo, People v., 113 Cal.App.2d 617, 248 P.2d 421 (1952)—§ 5.3(b) n.16

Al Amin v. State, 278 Ga. 74, 597 S.E.2d 332 (2004)—§§ 6.7(b) n.72; 22.2(d) n.77, 94

Alamont, State v., 577 A.2d 665 (R.I.1990)—§ 3.4(i) n.175

Alanis v. State, 583 N.W.2d 573 (Minn.1998)—§§ 21.3(b) n.66; 21.4(d) n.134

Alanis, United States v., 265 F.3d 576 (7th Cir.2001)—§§ 13.4(e) n.169; 22.3(d) n.249

Alarik, United States v., 439 F.2d 1349 (8th Cir.1971)—§ 13.4(c) n.104

Alayon, State v., 459 N.W.2d 325 (Minn.1990)—§ 3.10(a) n.1

Albanese, United States v., 554 F.2d 543 (2d Cir.1977)—§ 26.9(b) n.50

Albarado, United States v., 495 F.2d 799 (2d Cir.1974)—§§ 3.2(b) n.53; 3.9(h) n.153

Albaugh v. State, 721 N.E.2d 1233 (Ind.1999)—§ 5.1(c) n.16

Al-Bayyinah, State v., 359 N.C. 741, 616 S.E.2d 500 (2005)—§ 6.7(b) n.85

Al-Bayyinah, State v., 356 N.C. 150, 567 S.E.2d 120 (2002)—§§ 7.4(e) n.86, 90

Albea, People v., 2 Ill.2d 317, 118 N.E.2d 277 (1954)—§ 9.4(e) n.109

Albee, State v., 61 N.H. 423, 60 AM.Rep. 325 (1881)—§ 16.1(c) n.127

Albernaz v. United States, 450 U.S. 333, 101 S.Ct. 1137, 67 L.Ed.2d 275 (1981)—§§ 17.4(b) n.90; 25.1(b) n.18

Alberts, United States v., 721 F.2d 636 (8th Cir.1983)—§ 9.1(b) n.95

Albertson v. Subversive Activities Control Board, 382 U.S. 70, 86 S.Ct. 194, 15 L.Ed.2d 165 (1965)—§§ 2.10(b) n.7; 8.10(a) n.22

Albrecht v. State, 737 N.E.2d 719 (Ind.2000)—§ 6.6(d) n.57

Albrecht v. United States, 273 U.S. 1, 47 S.Ct. 250, 71 L.Ed. 505 (1927)—§ 3.5(a) n.60

Albright v. Florida, 622 So.2d 1171 (Fla.App.1993)—§ 26.9(a) n.7

Albright v. Oliver, 510 U.S. 266, 114 S.Ct. 807, 127 L.Ed.2d 114 (1994)—§§ 2.1 n.2; 2.6(c) n.87; 2.7(d) n.240, 254; 14.2(a) n.9; 15.1(b) n.25; 15.5(b) n.49; 15.6(a) n.22; 15.7(e) n.96; 26.4(d) n.67

Albright, United States v., 388 F.2d 719 (4th Cir.1968)—§ 20.4(e) n.84

Albuquerque, City of v. One (1) 1984 White Chevy Ut., 132 N.M. 187, 46 P.3d 94 (2002)—§ 17.4(b) n.120

Alcalde v. State, 74 P.3d 1253 (Wyo.2003)—§ 22.3(e) n.272

Alcantar, United States v., 271 F.3d 731 (8th Cir.2001)—§ 17.2(b) n.40

Alcantra, United States v., 396 F.3d 189 (2d Cir.2005)—§§ 23.1(d) n.121; 24.1(a) n.13

Alcaraz-Arellano, United States v., 441 F.3d 1252 (10th Cir.2006)—§ 13.4(d) n.156

Alcocer v. Superior Court, 206 Cal.App.3d 951, 254 Cal.Rptr. 72 (1988)—§§ 11.9(c) n.109, 126, 130, 131

Alcorta v. Texas, 355 U.S. 28, 78 S.Ct. 103, 2 L.Ed.2d 9 (1957)—§ 24.3(d) n.106

Aldaco, United States v., 201 F.3d 979 (7th Cir.2000)—§§ 24.3(e) n.131, 135; 24.5(b) n.24

Alden, United States v., 776 F.2d 771 (8th Cir.1985)—§ 22.3(b) n.54

Alden, United States v., 767 F.2d 314 (7th Cir.1984)—§§ 11.2(e) n.159, 225, 227

Alderete, State v., 95 N.M. 691, 625 P.2d 1208 (App.1980)—§ 18.4(c) n.59

Alderman, State v., 70 Ohio App.3d 147, 590 N.E.2d 836 (1990)—§ 26.10(c) n.72

Alderman v. United States, 394 U.S. 165, 89 S.Ct. 961, 22 L.Ed.2d 176 (1969)—§§ 1.5(c) n.163; 2.9(f) n.135; 9.1(b) n.31, 50; 9.1(c) n.100; 9.2(b) n.12; 9.2(c) n.19; 9.2(d) n.37; 10.3(b) n.41

Alderson, State v., 260 Kan. 445, 922 P.2d 435 (1996)—§ 24.4(d) n.31

Alderwood Assocs. v. Washington Environmental Council, 96 Wash.2d 230, 635 P.2d 108 (1981)—§ 2.12(c) n.158

Aldridge, People v., 47 Mich.App. 639, 209 N.W.2d 796 (1973)—§ 22.3(b) n.89

Aldridge v. State, 232 Miss. 368, 99 So.2d 456 (1958)—§ 16.1(d) n.157

Aldus, State v., 1998 ME 2, 704 A.2d 386 (1998)—§ 6.10(e) n.82

Alegria, United States v., 192 F.3d 179 (1st Cir.1999)—§ 21.2(d) n.264

Alegria, United States v., 980 F.2d 830 (2d Cir.1992)—§§ 8.8(f) n.154, 156

Aleksey, State v., 343 S.C. 20, 538 S.E.2d 248 (2000)—§§ 6.9(f) n.102; 6.9(g) n.157

Aleman v. Judges of the Circuit Court, 138 F.3d 302 (7th Cir.1998)—§ 25.1(d) n.91

Aleman, United States v., 286 F.3d 86 (2d Cir.2002)—§ 13.5(b) n.48

Alen, State v., 616 So.2d 452 (Fla.1993)—§ 22.3(d) n.193

Alessio, United States v., 528 F.2d 1079 (9th Cir.1976)—§ 24.3(i) n.191

Alex, United States v., 788 F.Supp. 359 (N.D.Ill.1992)—§§ 11.9(c) n.105, 124, 136, 140

Alex, United States v., 791 F.Supp. 723 (N.D.Ill.1992)—§ 20.3(h) n.151

Alexander v. City of Anchorage, 490 P.2d 910 (Alaska 1971)—§§ 11.2(a) n.30, 34

Alexander v. Connecticut, 917 F.2d 747 (2d Cir.1990)—§§ 6.7(c) n.141, 142; 6.10(b) n.33

Alexander v. Connecticut, 876 F.2d 277 (2d Cir.1989)—§ 6.10(b) n.28

Alexander v. Louisiana, 405 U.S. 625, 92 S.Ct. 1221, 31 L.Ed.2d 536 (1972)—§§ 15.1(c) n.141; 15.4(c) n.87; 15.4(d) n.103; 22.2(c) n.37

Alexander, People v., 97 N.Y.2d 482, 743 N.Y.S.2d 45, 769 N.E.2d 802 (2002)—§§ 21.4(b) n.59; 21.5(a) n.43

Alexander, People v., 663 P.2d 1024 (Colo.1983)—§ 14.3(d) n.102

Alexander, State v., 359 N.C. 824, 616 S.E.2d 914 (2005)—§ 21.1(b) n.34

Alexander v. State, 273 Ga. 311, 540 S.E.2d 196 (2001)—§ 22.3(d) n.250

Alexander v. State, 270 Ga. 346, 509 S.E.2d 56 (1998)—§ 24.7(a) n.15

Alexander, State v., 214 Wis.2d 628, 571 N.W.2d 662 (1997)—§ 26.2(b) n.21

Alexander, State v., 620 So.2d 1166 (La.1993)—§ 22.3(c) n.125

Alexander, State v., 157 Vt. 60, 595 A.2d 282 (1991)—§ 9.4(f) n.118

Alexander, State v., 197 Conn. 180, 496 A.2d 486 (1985)—§ 6.10(b) n.13

Alexander, State v., 281 N.W.2d 349 (Minn.1979)—§ 8.13(a) n.24

Alexander, State v., 130 Vt. 54, 286 A.2d 262 (1971)—§ 8.1(c) n.32

Alexander v. Superior Court, 22 Cal.App.4th 901, 27 Cal.Rptr.2d 732 (1994)—§§ 11.4(a) n.15; 27.4(c) n.33

Alexander, United States v., 447 F.3d 1290 (10th Cir.2006)—§ 6.9(f) n.102

Alexander v. United States, 718 A.2d 137 (D.C.App.1998)—§ 9.6(a) n.47

Alexander v. United States, 509 U.S. 544, 113 S.Ct. 2766, 125 L.Ed.2d 441 (1993)—§ 26.6(d) n.74

Alexander, United States v., 869 F.2d 91 (2d Cir.1989)—§§ 21.2(d) n.235; 21.2(e) n.351

Alexander, United States v., 869 F.2d 808 (5th Cir.1989)—§§ 20.6(c) n.73, 74

Alexander, United States v., 860 F.2d 508 (2d Cir.1988)—§§ 8.5(e) n.182, 192; 8.5(h) n.248

Alexander, United States v., 789 F.2d 1046 (4th Cir.1986)—§ 15.5(a) n.4

Alexander, United States v., 743 F.2d 472 (7th Cir.1984)—§ 26.1(d) n.89

Alexander v. United States, 390 F.2d 101 (5th Cir.1968)—§ 3.10(c) n.92

Alexander v. United States, 362 F.2d 379 (9th Cir.1966)—§ 3.9(f) n.94

Alexander v. United States, 201 U.S. 117, 26 S.Ct. 356, 50 L.Ed. 686 (1906)—§ 27.2(e) n.79

Alfaro v. State, 478 N.E.2d 670 (Ind.1985)—§§ 6.7(d) n.143; 6.9(b) n.44

Alfinito, People v., 16 N.Y.2d 181, 264 N.Y.S.2d 243, 211 N.E.2d 644 (1965)—§ 10.6(a) n.3

Alfonsi, State v., 33 Wis.2d 469, 147 N.W.2d 550 (1967)—§ 16.3(f) n.94

Alfonso, United States v., 552 F.2d 605 (5th Cir.1977)—§ 4.6(j) n.164

Alford v. Haner, 333 F.3d 972 (9th Cir.2003)—§ 3.1(d) n.99

Alford v. Superior Court, 29 Cal.4th 1033, 130 Cal.Rptr.2d 672, 63 P.3d 228 (2003)—§ 20.3(g) n.126

Ali, State v., 233 Conn. 403, 660 A.2d 337 (1995)—§ 18.5(a) n.32

Ali, State v., 329 N.C. 394, 407 S.E.2d 183 (1991)—§§ 11.6(a) n.40, 65

Alidani v. Dooley, 365 F.3d 635 (8th Cir.2004)—§ 24.6(e) n.51

Aliotta, United States v., 199 F.3d 78 (2d Cir.1999)—§ 21.3(f) n.426

Al Jibori, United States v., 90 F.3d 22 (2d Cir.1996)—§§ 13.4(b) n.62, 69

Allah, State v., 170 N.J. 269, 787 A.2d 887 (2002)—§§ 11.10(c) n.116; 11.10(d) n.159, 181

Allain, United States v., 671 F.2d 248 (7th Cir.1982)—§ 24.3(b) n.63

Allan v. State, 118 Nev. 19, 38 P.3d 175 (2002)—§§ 6.2(c) n.183; 9.6(a) n.21

Allee, People v., 740 P.2d 1 (Colo.1987)—§§ 17.4(a) n.46, 65

Allegri, People v., 109 Ill.2d 309, 93 Ill.Dec. 781, 487 N.E.2d 606 (1985)—§ 26.10(a) n.5

Allen, In re, 127 N.H. 718, 506 A.2d 329 (1986)—§ 11.2(e) n.189

Allen v. Commonwealth, 901 S.W.2d 881 (Ky.Ct.App.1995)—§ 15.4(b) n.59

Allen, Commonwealth v., 395 Mass. 448, 480 N.E.2d 630 (1985)—§ 6.10(b) n.16

Allen, Commonwealth v., 280 Pa.Super. 599, 421 A.2d 1094 (1980)—§ 21.5(a) n.51

Allen v. Georgia, 166 U.S. 138, 17 S.Ct. 525, 41 L.Ed. 949 (1897)—§ 27.5(c) n.75

Allen v. Hadden, 57 F.3d 1529 (10th Cir.1995)—§§ 21.2(d) n.150, 213

Allen v. Illinois, 478 U.S. 364, 106 S.Ct. 2988, 92 L.Ed.2d 296 (1986)—§§ 2.10(b) n.26; 2.10(d) n.124, 125; 6.10(e) n.83; 25.1(c) n.37

Allen v. Lee, 366 F.3d 319 (4th Cir.2004)—§§ 22.3(d) n.214, 215; 28.4(d) n.70

Allen v. McCurry, 449 U.S. 90, 101 S.Ct. 411, 66 L.Ed.2d 308 (1980)—§ 3.1(k) n.263

Allen, People v., 86 N.Y.2d 599, 635 N.Y.S.2d 139, 658 N.E.2d 1012 (1995)—§ 21.6(a) n.68

Allen, People v., 201 Mich.App. 98, 505 N.W.2d 869 (1993)—§ 9.6(a) n.36

Allen, People v., 50 Cal.App.3d 896, 123 Cal.Rptr. 80 (1975)—§§ 3.8(e) n.187, 213

Allen, People v., 8 Ill.App.3d 176, 289 N.E.2d 467 (1972)—§ 19.5(c) n.53

Allen, People v., 410 Ill. 508, 103 N.E.2d 92 (1951)—§§ 8.7(a) n.20; 8.7(b) n.32, 48, 52

Allen, People v., 413 Ill. 69, 107 N.E.2d 826 (1952)—§§ 16.1(g) n.243, 271

Allen v. Rhay, 431 F.2d 1160 (9th Cir.1970)—§ 7.4(g) n.118

Allen v. Roe, 305 F.3d 1046 (9th Cir.2002)—§§ 6.7(b) n.81, 85

Allen, State v., 370 S.C. 88, 634 S.E.2d 653 (2006)—§ 26.9(b) n.50

Allen, State v., 150 N.H. 290, 837 A.2d 324 (2003)—§ 13.3(c) n.40

Allen, State v., 69 S.W.3d 181 (Tenn.2002)—§§ 24.8(e) n.70; 27.6(d) n.99

Allen v. State, 686 N.E.2d 760 (Ind.1997)—§§ 6.8(b) n.61; 6.9(g) n.177

Allen v. State, 662 So.2d 380 (Fla.App.1995)—§ 26.10(c) n.57

Allen v. State, 91 Md.App. 775, 605 A.2d 994 (1992)—§ 17.4(b) n.96

Allen, State v., 254 N.J.Super. 62, 603 A.2d 71 (1992)—§ 3.10(a) n.2

Allen, State v., 839 P.2d 291 (Utah 1992)—§ 10.4(b) n.11

Allen v. State, 821 P.2d 371 (Okl.Cr.1991)—§ 21.4(c) n.92

Allen, State v., 133 N.H. 306, 577 A.2d 801 (1990)—§§ 10.3(d) n.66, 72

Allen, State v., 800 S.W.2d 82 (Mo.App.1990)—§ 24.3(h) n.176

Allen, State v., 323 N.C. 208, 372 S.E.2d 855 (1988)—§ 6.9(f) n.135

Allen, State v., 205 Conn. 370, 533 A.2d 559 (1987)—§ 24.6(b) n.25

Allen, State v., 485 A.2d 953 (Me.1984)—§ 6.7(b) n.41

Allen, State v., 293 N.W.2d 16 (Iowa 1980)—§§ 16.1(g) n.235, 236, 264, 267, 270, 273; 16.1(h) n.303

Allen, State v., 12 Or.App. 455, 506 P.2d 528 (1973)—§ 26.9(b) n.51

Allen v. State, 474 S.W.2d 480 (Tex.Cr.App.1971)—§ 21.4(a) n.32

Allen v. Thomas, 161 F.3d 667 (11th Cir.1998)—§ 21.2(d) n.158

Allen, United States v., 434 F.3d 1166 (9th Cir.2006)—§ 21.2(d) n.174

Allen, United States v., 406 F.3d 940 (8th Cir.2005)—§§ 19.3(a) n.27, 88, 99, 100, 129; 19.6(c) n.50

Allen, United States v., 425 F.3d 1231 (9th Cir.2005)—§ 17.2(b) n.40

Allen, United States v., 247 F.3d 741 (8th Cir.2001)—§ 6.9(f) n.133

Allen, United States v., 235 F.3d 482 (10th Cir.2000)—§ 18.3(b) n.31

Allen, United States v., 755 A.2d 402 (D.C.App.2000)—§ 25.4(d) n.45

Allen, United States v., 106 F.3d 695 (6th Cir.1997)—§ 3.1(h) n.201

Allen, United States v., 75 F.3d 439 (8th Cir.1996)—§ 21.2(d) n.210

Allen, United States v., 895 F.2d 1577 (10th Cir.1990)—§§ 11.3(c) n.60, 61, 67; 11.4(c) n.55; 11.5(c) n.32, 49, 50, 52; 27.6(d) n.148

Allen, United States v., 675 F.2d 1373 (9th Cir.1980)—§ 3.2(b) n.58

Allen, United States v., 408 F.2d 1287 (D.C.Cir.1969)—§ 7.3(e) n.97

Allen v. United States, 390 F.2d 476 (D.C.Cir.1968)—§§ 6.6(d) n.56; 6.6(f) n.112

Allen v. United States, 202 F.2d 329 (D.C.Cir.1952)—§ 6.3(a) n.9

Allen v. United States, 164 U.S. 492, 17 S.Ct. 154, 41 L.Ed. 528 (1896)—§ 24.9(d) n.41

Allen v. Woodford, 395 F.3d 979 (9th Cir.2005)—§ 11.10(d) n.162

Allen-Brown, United States v., 243 F.3d 1293 (11th Cir.2001)—§ 22.3(d) n.208

Alley, State v., 841 A.2d 803 (Me.2004)—§§ 3.5(d) n.141; 6.9(f) n.145

Alley v. State, 704 P.2d 233 (Alaska App.1985)—§ 25.1(d) n.60

Alleyne, United States v., 454 F.Supp. 1164 (S.D.N.Y.1978)—§ 13.4(c) n.82

Allgood v. State, 309 Md. 58, 522 A.2d 917 (1987)—§ 21.5(f) n.163

Allie, State v., 147 Ariz. 320, 710 P.2d 430 (1985)—§ 26.4(g) n.115

Allies, State v., 186 Mont. 99, 606 P.2d 1043 (1979)—§ 6.2(c) n.104

Alligood v. State, 160 Ga.App. 785, 287 S.E.2d 125 (1982)—§ 26.10(c) n.49

Allinder v. Ohio, 808 F.2d 1180 (6th Cir.1987)—§§ 3.2(c) n.125; 3.2(d) n.152

Allison, State v., 427 A.2d 471 (Me.1981)—§ 19.1(d) n.66

Allison v. State, 62 Wis.2d 14, 214 N.W.2d 437 (1974)—§ 3.3(d) n.148

Allison, United States v., 619 F.2d 1254 (8th Cir.1980)—§ 8.7(e) n.93

Allison, United States v., 191 F.Supp. 443 (S.D.Cal.1960)—§ 19.3(e) n.245

Allred v. State, 622 So.2d 984 (Fla.1993)—§ 6.7(b) n.38

Allridge v. Scott, 41 F.3d 213 (5th Cir.1994)—§ 24.8(f) n.91

Alls, People v., 83 N.Y.2d 94, 608 N.Y.S.2d 139, 629 N.E.2d 1018 (1993)—§ 6.6(e) n.82

Allstate Ins.Co. v. McCarn, 466 Mich. 277, 645 N.W.2d 20 (2002)—§ 21.4(a) n.21

Allsup, United States v., 566 F.2d 68 (9th Cir.1977)—§ 22.3(c) n.131

Almada v. State, 994 P.2d 299 (Wyo.1999)—§§ 14.4(c) n.62; 20.2(c) n.45

Almeda, State v., 211 Conn. 441, 560 A.2d 389 (1989)—§ 18.5(a) n.37

Almeida v. State, 737 So.2d 520 (Fla.1999)—§ 6.9(g) n.166

Almeida-Sanchez v. United States, 413 U.S. 266, 93 S.Ct. 2535, 37 L.Ed.2d 596 (1973)—§§ 2.11(c) n.26; 3.9(f) n.111

Almendarez-Torres v. United States, 523 U.S. 224, 118 S.Ct. 1219, 140 L.Ed.2d 350 (1998)—§§ 26.4(i) n.165; 26.6(b) n.13

Almohandis, United States v., 307 F.Supp.2d 253 (2004)—§ 20.3(c) n.77

Almonacid v. United States, 476 F.3d 518 (7th Cir.2007)—§ 21.3(b) n.101

Almond, In the Petition of, 603 A.2d 1087 (R.I.1992)—§ 8.8(d) n.103

Almond, State v., 511 N.W.2d 572 (S.D.1994)—§§ 3.8(c) n.114; 10.4(c) n.23

Almonte, Commonwealth v., 444 Mass. 511, 829 N.E.2d 1094 (2005)—§ 6.9(g) n.157

Almonte, United States v., 952 F.2d 20 (1st Cir.1991)—§ 3.6(e) n.111

Al Mudarris, United States v., 695 F.2d 1182 (9th Cir.1983)—§§ 15.2(d) n.112; 15.5(b) n.63 to 66; 15.6(d) n.104, 129; 15.7(b) n.16

Al-Muqsit, United States v., 191 F.3d 928 (8th Cir.1999)—§ 6.9(g) n.153

Al Odah v. United States, 346 F.Supp.2d 1 (D.D.C.2004)—§ 11.8(b) n.44

Aloi, United States v., 449 F.Supp. 698 (E.D.N.Y.1977)—§ 15.7(d) n.80

Alonso, United States v., 740 F.2d 862 (11th Cir.1984)—§ 4.6(e) n.92

Alosa, State v., 137 N.H. 33, 623 A.2d 218 (1993)—§ 9.2(b) n.15

Alosa, United States v., 14 F.3d 693 (1st Cir.1994)—§ 24.5(a) n.16

Alred, United States v., 144 F.3d 1405 (11th Cir.1998)—§ 8.8(f) n.146

Al-Shahin, United States v., 474 F.3d 941 (7th Cir.2007)—§ 5.2(a) n.9

Alspach, State v., 554 N.W.2d 882 (Iowa 1996)—§ 26.4(e) n.79

Alspach, State v., 524 N.W.2d 665 (Iowa 1994)—§ 10.3(c) n.52

Alston, People v., 88 N.Y.2d 519, 647 N.Y.S.2d 142, 670 N.E.2d 426 (1996)—§ 22.3(d) n.180

Alston v. Redman, 34 F.3d 1237 (3d Cir.1994)—§§ 6.9(f) n.141; 6.9(g) n.199

Alston v. State, 723 So.2d 148 (Fla.1998)—§ 6.9(e) n.84

Alston, State v., 75 Haw. 517, 865 P.2d 157 (1994)—§ 24.8(e) n.76

Alston, State v., 256 Kan. 571, 887 P.2d 681 (1994)—§§ 23.1(c) n.101, 103, 112, 113

Alston, United States v., 491 F.Supp. 215 (D.D.C.1980)—§ 8.5(h) n.233

Alston, United States v., 311 F.Supp. 296 (D.D.C.1970)—§ 9.4(e) n.102

Al-Talib, United States v., 55 F.3d 923 (4th Cir.1995)—§ 5.2(a) n.5

Altamirano, United States v., 633 F.2d 147 (9th Cir.1980)—§§ 11.10(a) n.5, 13

Alter, United States v., 81 F.R.D. 524 (S.D.N.Y.1979)—§ 16.3(c) n.37

Alter, United States v., 482 F.2d 1016 (9th Cir.1973)—§§ 8.5(c) n.76; 10.3(b) n.34

Althoff v. State, 209 Ind. 42, 197 N.E. 896 (1935)—§§ 16.1(b) n.83, 91

Altizer, United States v., 477 F.2d 846 (5th Cir.1973)—§ 9.2(c) n.25

Altman, State v., 107 Ariz. 93, 482 P.2d 460 (1971)—§§ 14.4(c) n.53; 14.4(d) n.96

Altro, In re, 180 F.3d 372 (2d Cir.1999)—§ 21.2(d) n.148

Altum, State v., 262 Kan. 733, 941 P.2d 1348 (1997)—§ 6.2(c) n.107

Aluminum Co. of America, United States v., 148 F.2d 416 (2d Cir.1945)—§ 27.5(e) n.161

Alvarado v. Hickman, 316 F.3d 841 (9th Cir.2002)—§ 6.6(d) n.53

Alvarado v. State, 853 S.W.2d 17 (Tex.Cr.App.1993)—§§ 6.10(d) n.60, 62, 63

Alvarado, State v., 226 Neb. 195, 410 N.W.2d 118 (1987)—§ 22.3(d) n.250

Alvarado v. State, 486 P.2d 891 (Alaska 1971)—§ 22.2(d) n.71

Alvarado v. Superior Court of Los Angeles County, 23 Cal.4th 1121, 99 Cal.Rptr.2d 149, 5 P.3d 203 (2000)—§§ 20.3(l) n.227; 24.3(g) n.168

Alvarado, United States v., 440 F.3d 191 (4th Cir.2006)—§§ 6.4(e) n.69, 101

Alvarado v. United States, 497 U.S. 543, 110 S.Ct. 2995, 111 L.Ed.2d 439 (1990)—§ 22.3(d) n.251

Alvarado, United States v., 882 F.2d 645 (2d Cir.1989)—§ 6.2(c) n.106

Alvarez, In re, 351 F.Supp. 1089 (S.D.Cal.1972)—§ 8.5(d) n.142

Alvarez, Commonwealth v., 433 Mass. 93, 740 N.E.2d 610 (2000)—§§ 11.10(c) n.87, 126

Alvarez v. Crowder, 645 So.2d 63 (Fla.App.1994)—§ 27.4(f) n.65

Alvarez v. Gomez, 185 F.3d 995 (9th Cir.1999)—§ 6.9(g) n.162

Alvarez v. People, 653 P.2d 1127 (Colo.1982)—§ 24.9(f) n.68

Alvarez v. State, 827 So.2d 269 (Fla.App.2002)—§§ 24.1(a) n.5, 13

Alvarez v. State, 864 S.W.2d 64 (Tex.Cr.App.1993)—§ 25.2(f) n.49

Alvarez, State v., 145 Ariz. 370, 701 P.2d 1178 (1985)—§§ 7.4(d) n.77; 7.4(e) n.92

Alvarez, United States v., 812 F.2d 668 (11th Cir.1987)—§ 3.4(h) n.149

Alvarez, United States v., 519 F.2d 1036 (3d Cir.1975)—§ 20.5(c) n.54

Alvarez v. Wainwright, 522 F.2d 100 (5th Cir.1975)—§ 21.3(b) n.136

Alvarez-Del Prado, United States v., 222 F.3d 12 (1st Cir.2000)—§ 21.4(c) n.81

Alvarez-Gonzalez, United States v., 542 F.2d 226 (5th Cir.1976)—§ 3.9(f) n.117

Alvarez-Machain, United States v., 504 U.S. 655, 112 S.Ct. 2188, 119 L.Ed.2d 441 (1992)—§§ 3.1(j) n.241, 242

Alvarez-Moreno, United States v., 874 F.2d 1402 (11th Cir.1989)—§ 19.3(a) n.68

Alvarez-Sanchez, United States v., 511 U.S. 350, 114 S.Ct. 1599, 128 L.Ed.2d 319 (1994)—§§ 6.3(b) n.36, 41, 44

Alvarez-Sanchez, United States v., 975 F.2d 1396 (9th Cir.1992)—§§ 6.3(b) n.39, 42, 43

Alvarez-Tautimez, United States v., 160 F.3d 573 (9th Cir.1998)—§§ 21.5(a) n.9, 10

Alverez, United States v., 235 F.3d 1086 (8th Cir.2000)—§ 3.10(f) n.192

Alvernaz, In re, 2 Cal.4th 924, 8 Cal.Rptr.2d 713, 830 P.2d 747 (1992)—§§ 11.10(d) n.173, 175; 21.3(b) n.62, 102

Alvernaz v. Ratelle, 831 F.Supp. 790 (S.D.Cal.1993)—§ 11.10(d) n.175

Alvidres v. Superior Court, 12 Cal.App.3d 575, 90 Cal.Rptr. 682 (1970)—§§ 3.3(g) n.236, 240

Alvillar, United States v., 575 F.2d 1316 (10th Cir.1978)—§§ 8.9(b) n.27, 33

Al-Yousif, People v., 49 P.3d 1165 (Colo.2002)—§ 6.9(b) n.44

Al-Zubaidy, United States v., 283 F.3d 804 (6th Cir.2002)—§ 1.2(c) n.172

A.M. v. Butler, 360 F.3d 787 (7th Cir.2004)—§§ 6.2(c) n.163; 28.3(a) n.28

Amadeo v. State, 259 Ga. 469, 384 S.E.2d 181 (1989)—§§ 11.4(a) n.8, 12, 16

Amadeo v. Zant, 486 U.S. 214, 108 S.Ct. 1771, 100 L.Ed.2d 249 (1988)—§ 28.4(d) n.60

Amador-Galvan, United States v., 9 F.3d 1414 (9th Cir.1993)—§ 7.5(b) n.22

Amador-Leal, United States v., 276 F.3d 511 (9th Cir.2002)—§ 21.4(d) n.135

Amaechi v. West, 237 F.3d 356 (4th Cir.2001)—§ 3.5(b) n.80

Amalgamated Union, Local 224 v. Levine, 31 Misc.2d 416, 219 N.Y.S.2d 851 (Sup.Ct.1961)—§ 8.7(e) n.92

Aman v. State, 50 Ala.App. 262, 278 So.2d 380 (1972)—§ 14.4(e) n.135

Amano, United States v., 229 F.3d 801 (9th Cir.2000)—§ 6.8(a) n.36

Amaral, United States v., 488 F.2d 1148 (9th Cir.1973)—§ 7.5(b) n.30

Amarillo, State v., 198 Conn. 285, 503 A.2d 146 (1986)—§ 7.4(f) n.103

Amati v. City of Woodstock, 176 F.3d 952 (7th Cir.1999)—§ 4.6(n) n.247

Amaya, United States v., 509 F.2d 8 (5th Cir.1975)—§ 24.9(d) n.47

Amaya-Portillo, United States v., 423 F.3d 427 (4th Cir.2005)—§ 21.2(b) n.76

Amaya-Ruiz, State v., 166 Ariz. 152, 800 P.2d 1260 (1990)—§§ 6.2(c) n.125, 178; 6.9(g) n.154

Amaya-Ruiz v. Stewart, 121 F.3d 486 (10th Cir.1997)—§ 6.2(c) n.152

Amazon Industrial Chemical Corp., United States v., 55 F.2d 254 (D.Md.1931)—§ 8.5(a) n.8

Ambrose, United States v., 707 F.2d 1209 (11th Cir.1983)—§ 5.1(c) n.36

Ameling, United States v., 328 F.3d 443 (8th Cir.2003)—§§ 3.3(f) n.212; 9.1(d) n.120

Amendment of Rules of Civil and Criminal Procedure, Matter of, 128 Wis.2d 422, 383 N.W.2d 496 (1986)—§ 21.3(d) n.219

American Airlines, Inc., Privacy Litigation, In re, 370 F.Supp.2d 552 (N.D.Tex. 2005)—§ 4.8(b) n.16

American Bag & Paper Corp., United States v., 609 F.2d 1066 (3d Cir.1979)—§ 21.2(e) n.299

American Civil Liberties Union of Georgia v. Barnes, 168 F.3d 423 (11th Cir.1999)—§ 13.5(h) n.212

American Fork City v. Crosgrove, 701 P.2d 1069 (Utah 1985)—§§ 2.12(e) n.207 to 209, 212

American Historical Association, In re Petition of, 49 F.Supp.2d 274 (S.D.N.Y.1999)—§ 8.5(b) n.40

American Historical Association, In re Petition of, 62 F.Supp.2d 1100 (S.D.N.Y.1999)—§ 8.5(b) n.39

American Radiator & Standard Sanitary Corp., United States v., 45 F.R.D. 477 (W.D.Pa.1968)—§ 8.5(e) n.187

Amerigas Propane LP, Inc., State v., 146 N.H. 267, 769 A.2d 401 (2001)—§ 18.5(a) n.19

Amerson, State v., 129 Idaho 395, 925 P.2d 399 (Idaho Ct.App.1996)—§ 16.1(a) n.24

Ames v. New York State Division of Parole, 772 F.2d 13 (2d Cir.1985)—§§ 21.4(c) n.82; 21.4(f) n.207

Ames, State v., 222 Kan. 88, 563 P.2d 1034 (1977)—§ 3.4(l) n.242

Ames, State v., 90 Minn. 183, 96 N.W. 330 (Minn.1903)—§§ 15.4(b) n.23, 38

Amick, United States v., 439 F.2d 351 (7th Cir.1971)—§ 17.2(a) n.12

Amico, United States v., 416 F.3d 163 (2d Cir.2005)—§ 21.2(d) n.167

Amie v. State, 89 S.W.3d 670 (Tex.App.2002)—§ 16.3(b) n.12

Amiel v. United States, 209 F.3d 195 (2d Cir.2000)—§ 11.9(d) n.207

Amiker, United States v., 414 F.3d 606 (6th Cir.2005)—§ 21.2(a) n.7

Amin v. State, 774 P.2d 597 (Wyo.1989)—§§ 11.7(e) n.63, 75, 98

Amirault, Commonwealth v., 399 Mass. 617, 506 N.E.2d 129 (1987)—§ 22.3(c) n.135

Ammerman v. Hubbard Broadcasting, Inc., 89 N.M. 307, 551 P.2d 1354 (1976)—§ 1.7(f) n.90

Ammidown, United States v., 497 F.2d 615 (D.C.Cir.1973)—§§ 13.7(a) n.16; 21.3(e) n.274; 21.4(g) n.242

Amora, People v., 28 Cal.3d 88, 167 Cal.Rptr. 573, 615 P.2d 1361 (1980)—§ 20.6(a) n.7

Amores v. State, 816 S.W.2d 407 (Tex.Cr.App.1991)—§ 3.3(d) n.152

Amos v. United States, 255 U.S. 313, 41 S.Ct. 266, 65 L.Ed. 654 (1921)—§§ 3.2(a) n.8; 3.10(b) n.30

Amphy, State v., 259 La. 161, 249 So.2d 560 (1971)—§ 10.4(c) n.23

Amrine v. Roper, 102 S.W.3d 541 (Mo.2003)—§ 28.11(b) n.14

Amuso, United States ex rel. v. La-Vallee, 291 F.Supp. 383 (E.D.N.Y.1968)—§ 21.2(b) n.76

Anagnos, United States v., 853 F.2d 1 (1st Cir.1988)—§ 22.3(a) n.23

Analla, United States v., 975 F.2d 119 (4th Cir.1992)—§§ 3.8(c) n.75, 89; 3.10(b) n.43

Anastaplo, In re, 366 U.S. 82, 81 S.Ct. 978, 6 L.Ed.2d 135 (1961)—§ 2.5(f) n.72

Anaya v. Baker, 427 F.2d 73 (10th Cir.1970)—§ 11.2(g) n.265

Anaya v. Hansen, 781 F.2d 1 (1st Cir.1986)—§ 22.2(d) n.68

Anaya, State v., 456 A.2d 1255 (Me.1983)—§ 15.4(d) n.98

Anaya v. United States, 815 F.2d 1373 (10th Cir.1987)—§§ 8.5(c) n.85, 100

Ancona, State v., 270 Conn. 568, 854 A.2d 718 (2004)—§ 24.7(i) n.86

Andazola, State v., 95 N.M. 430, 622 P.2d 1050 (N.M.App.1981)—§ 27.5(c) n.101

Anderer, Ex parte, 61 S.W.3d 398 (Tex.Crim.App.2001)—§ 12.4(d) n.82

Anders v. California, 386 U.S. 738, 87 S.Ct. 1396, 18 L.Ed.2d 493 (1967)—§§ 2.6(d) n.104; 2.9(h) n.214, 221; 11.1(d) n.109; 11.2(c) n.84; 11.2(g) n.257; 11.6(a) n.11; 11.7(a) n.18; 27.1(b) n.19

Anders, State v., 596 So.2d 463 (Fla.App.1992)—§ 5.4(a) n.5

Andersen, State v., 232 Neb. 187, 440 N.W.2d 203 (1989)—§ 9.3(e) n.70

Andersen v. Thieret, 903 F.2d 526 (7th Cir.1990)—§ 6.7(d) n.153

Andersen Consulting LLP v. UOP, 991 F.Supp. 1041 (N.D. Ill. 1998)—§§ 4.8(d) n.31; 4.8(e) n.42, 43

Anderson, In re, 730 N.W.2d 570 (N.D. 2007)—§ 22.1(c) n.60

Anderson v. Bessemer City, 470 U.S. 564, 105 S.Ct. 1504, 84 L.Ed.2d 518 (1985)—§ 27.5(e) n.171

Anderson v. Calderon, 232 F.3d 1053 (9th Cir.2000)—§§ 3.5(a) n.50; 9.4(a) n.10

Anderson v. Charles, 447 U.S. 404, 100 S.Ct. 2180, 65 L.Ed.2d 222 (1980)—§ 9.6(a) n.37

Anderson v. Collins, 18 F.3d 1208 (5th Cir.1994)—§ 24.8(f) n.121

Anderson v. Commonwealth, 48 Va.App. 704, 634 S.E.2d 372 (2006)—§ 3.5(d) n.161

Anderson v. Commonwealth, 256 Va. 580, 507 S.E.2d 339 (1998)— § 21.2(b) n.68

Anderson v. Commonwealth, 349 S.W.2d 826 (Ky.App.1961)— § 16.1(g) n.242

Anderson v. Creighton, 483 U.S. 635, 107 S.Ct. 3034, 97 L.Ed.2d 523 (1987)—§ 3.1(k) n.274

Anderson v. Groose, 106 F.3d 242 (8th Cir.1997)—§ 28.5(a) n.34

Anderson v. Harless, 459 U.S. 4, 103 S.Ct. 276, 74 L.Ed.2d 3 (1982)— § 28.5(a) n.30

Anderson v. Leeke, 271 S.C. 435, 248 S.E.2d 120 (1978)—§ 24.3(b) n.62

Anderson v. Mullin, 327 F.3d 1148 (10th Cir.2003)—§ 25.4(b) n.22

Anderson v. Nelson, 390 U.S. 523, 88 S.Ct. 1133, 20 L.Ed.2d 81 (1968)— § 27.6(d) n.77

Anderson v. Norfolk & Western Railway, 349 F.Supp. 121 (W.D.Va.1972)—§ 13.3(b) n.31

Anderson v. North Carolina, 221 F.Supp. 930 (W.D.N.C.1963)— §§ 21.3(a) n.4, 15, 21, 36

Anderson, People v., 52 Cal.3d 453, 276 Cal.Rptr. 356, 801 P.2d 1107 (1990)—§ 22.3(e) n.279

Anderson, People v., 43 Cal.3d 1104, 240 Cal.Rptr. 585, 742 P.2d 1306 (1987)—§ 26.1(b) n.31

Anderson, People v., 398 Mich. 361, 247 N.W.2d 857 (1976)—§§ 11.4(c) n.81; 11.5(c) n.49; 11.5(d) n.71, 74

Anderson, People v., 389 Mich. 155, 205 N.W.2d 461 (1973)—§§ 7.3(c) n.47; 7.4(d) n.65

Anderson, People v., 6 Cal.3d 628, 100 Cal.Rptr. 152, 493 P.2d 880 (1972)—§ 12.4(a) n.11

Anderson, People v., 16 N.Y.2d 282, 266 N.Y.S.2d 110, 213 N.E.2d 445 (1965)—§ 10.5(e) n.57

Anderson v. Smith, 751 F.2d 96 (2d Cir.1984)—§§ 6.9(f) n.109, 114

Anderson v. State, 130 P.3d 273 (Okl.Cr.App.2006)—§ 26.2(b) n.17

Anderson v. State, 182 S.W.3d 914 (Tex.Crim.App.2006)—§ 21.4(d) n.138

Anderson, State v., 710 N.W.2d 392 (N.D.2006)—§ 6.7(b) n.75

Anderson, State v., 280 Wis.2d 104, 695 N.W.2d 731 (2005)—§§ 16.4(c) n.91, 93

Anderson, State v., 905 So.2d 111 (Fla.2005)—§ 26.3(g) n.88

Anderson, State v., 877 So.2d 336 (La.App. 2004)—§ 16.1(e) n.173

Anderson, State v., 138 Idaho 359, 63 P.3d 485 (2003)—§ 17.3(b) n.27

Anderson, State v., 79 S.W.3d 420 (Mo.2002)—§ 6.5(b) n.30

Anderson, State v., 249 Wis.2d 586, 638 N.W.2d 301 (2002)—§§ 22.1(h) n.133, 149

Anderson, State v., 355 N.C. 136, 558 S.E.2d 87 (2002)—§ 22.3(d) n.181

Anderson, State v., 197 Ariz. 314, 4 P.3d 369 (2000)—§§ 22.3(c) n.147, 158; 27.6(d) n.134

Anderson, State v., 258 Neb. 627, 605 N.W.2d 124 (2000)—§ 25.4(c) n.28

Anderson v. State, 342 S.C. 54, 535 S.E.2d 649 (2000)—§ 21.4(f) n.194

Anderson, State v., 604 N.W.2d 482 (S.D.2000)—§ 21.4(a) n.14

Anderson, State v., 608 N.W.2d 644 (S.D.2000)—§ 6.6(d) n.48

Anderson, State v., 219 Wis.2d 739, 580 N.W.2d 329 (1998)—§ 19.2(b) n.9

Anderson, State v., 583 N.W.2d 151 (S.D.1998)—§ 16.1(h) n.286

Anderson, State v., 84 Haw. 462, 935 P.2d 1007 (1997)—§ 27.5(e) n.168

Anderson, State v., 129 Idaho 763, 932 P.2d 886 (1997)—§ 21.6(b) n.96

Anderson, State v., 252 Neb. 675, 564 N.W.2d 581 (1997)—§ 24.9(f) n.85

Anderson, State v., 546 N.W.2d 395 (S.D.1996)—§§ 26.3(g) n.78; 27.5(e) n.158

Anderson, State v., 929 P.2d 1107 (Utah 1996)—§ 26.4(g) n.124

Anderson, State v., 937 S.W.2d 851 (Tenn.1996)—§§ 6.6(c) n.31, 34

Anderson v. State, 901 S.W.2d 946 (Tex.Cr.App.1995)—§ 26.4(b) n.17

Anderson, State v., 1 Neb.App. 914, 511 N.W.2d 174 (1993)—§ 24.10(c) n.40

Anderson, State v., 116 N.M. 599, 866 P.2d 327 (1993)—§ 21.2(h) n.423

Anderson, State v., 121 Wash.2d 852, 855 P.2d 671 (1993)—§ 18.4(c) n.40

Anderson v. State, 574 So.2d 87 (Fla.1991)—§§ 15.5(c) n.109, 112; 15.6(a) n.10, 18; 15.7(e) n.93, 99, 115, 116

Anderson v. State, 577 So.2d 390 (Miss.1991)—§ 18.1(d) n.48

Anderson, State v., 243 Kan. 677, 763 P.2d 597 (1988)—§ 22.1(h) n.138

Anderson, State v., 417 N.W.2d 403 (S.D.1988)—§ 21.6(a) n.57

Anderson v. State, 749 P.2d 369 (Alaska App.1988)—§ 15.4(g) n.178

Anderson, State v., 108 Wash.2d 188, 736 P.2d 661 (1987)—§ 26.1(b) n.27

Anderson, State v., 286 Ark. 58, 688 S.W.2d 947 (1985)—§ 3.4(c) n.36

Anderson, State v., 303 N.C. 185, 278 S.E.2d 238 (1981)—§ 20.6(b) n.16

Anderson, State v., 612 P.2d 778 (Utah 1980)—§§ 14.1(b) n.31; 14.3(a) n.30

Anderson, State v., 23 Wash.App. 445, 597 P.2d 417 (1979)—§ 21.2(b) n.41

Anderson, State v., 332 So.2d 452 (La.1976)—§ 6.6(e) n.62

Anderson v. State, 263 Ind. 583, 335 N.E.2d 225 (1975)—§§ 21.2(c) n.106, 108

Anderson v. State, 133 Ga.App. 45, 209 S.E.2d 665 (1974)—§ 3.2(d) n.149

Anderson v. State, 297 So.2d 871 (Fla.App.1974)—§ 20.4(b) n.32

Anderson, State v., 211 Kan. 148, 505 P.2d 691 (1973)—§ 7.3(b) n.29

Anderson, State v., 30 Ohio St.2d 66, 282 N.E.2d 568 (1972)—§ 22.3(a) n.4

Anderson v. State, 241 So.2d 390 (Fla.1970)—§ 20.3(f) n.109

Anderson v. State, 6 Md.App. 688, 253 A.2d 387 (1969)—§ 6.8(a) n.37

Anderson v. State, 218 Ind. 299, 32 N.E.2d 705 (1941)—§ 15.4(b) n.23

Anderson, State v., 191 Mo. 134, 90 S.W. 95 (1905)—§ 16.1(e) n.196

Anderson v. Terhune, 467 F.3d 1208 (9th Cir.2006)—§ 6.9(f) n.138

Anderson v. United States, 393 F.3d 749 (8th Cir.2005)—§ 11.10(c) n.110

Anderson, United States v., 280 F.3d 1121 (7th Cir.2002)—§ 19.3(a) n.101

Anderson, United States v., 289 F.3d 1321 (11th Cir.2002)—§ 19.3(a) n.89

Anderson, United States v., 160 F.3d 231 (5th Cir.1998)—§§ 22.4(c) n.28, 30

Anderson, United States v., 787 F.Supp. 537 (D.Md.1992)—§ 26.1(e) n.102

Anderson, United States v., 790 F.Supp. 231 (W.D.Wash.1992)—§ 11.9(c) n.116

Anderson, United States v., 981 F.2d 1560 (10th Cir.1992)—§§ 3.6(e) n.127; 10.3(b) n.15

Anderson, United States v., 923 F.2d 450 (6th Cir.1991)—§ 3.3(f) n.209

Anderson, United States v., 929 F.2d 96 (2d Cir.1991)—§§ 6.2(c) n.140, 161; 6.9(c) n.58

Anderson, United States v., 896 F.2d 1076 (7th Cir.1990)—§ 25.4(c) n.34

Anderson, United States v., 902 F.2d 1105 (2d Cir.1990)—§ 18.3(b) n.10

Anderson, United States v., 851 F.2d 384 (D.C.Cir.1988)—§ 3.1(c) n.74

Anderson, United States v., 859 F.2d 1171 (3d Cir.1988)—§ 3.10(e) n.167

Anderson, United States v., 778 F.2d 602 (10th Cir.1985)—§§ 8.5(e) n.174; 8.8(g) n.167; 8.11(e) n.100

Anderson, United States v., 739 F.2d 1254 (7th Cir.1984)—§ 7.5(a) n.5

Anderson, United States v., 709 F.2d 1305 (9th Cir.1983)—§ 19.3(c) n.197

Anderson, United States v., 552 F.2d 1296 (8th Cir.1977)—§ 3.2(c) n.127

Anderson, United States v., 567 F.2d 839 (8th Cir.1977)—§ 11.2(g) n.306

Anderson, United States v., 514 F.2d 583 (7th Cir.1975)—§§ 13.7(c) n.59; 21.5(e) n.123, 127

Anderson, United States v., 490 F.2d 785 (D.C.Cir.1974)—§§ 7.3(b) n.14; 7.4(f) n.104

Anderson, United States v., 368 F.Supp. 1253 (D.Md.1973)—§ 8.5(g) n.227

Anderson, United States v., 471 F.2d 201 (5th Cir.1973)—§§ 18.2(c) n.45, 47

Anderson, United States v., 453 F.2d 174 (9th Cir.1971)—§ 9.1(b) n.38

Anderson v. United States, 344 F.2d 792 (10th Cir.1965)—§ 10.3(b) n.44

Anderson v. United States, 318 U.S. 350, 63 S.Ct. 599, 87 L.Ed. 829 (1943)—§§ 6.3(a) n.24; 6.3(b) n.45

Anderson, United States v., 328 U.S. 699, 66 S.Ct. 1213, 90 L.Ed. 1529 (1946)—§ 16.2(c) n.47

Anderson, State ex rel. v. Haas, 43 Or.App. 169, 602 P.2d 346 (1979)—§§ 13.6(b) n.18; 13.6(c) n.46

Anderton, United States v., 752 F.2d 1005 (5th Cir.1985)—§ 18.4(b) n.26

Anderton, United States v., 629 F.2d 1044 (5th Cir.1980)—§ 5.1(c) n.37

Andis, United States v., 333 F.3d 886 (8th Cir.2003)—§ 27.5(c) n.63

Andrades, People v., 4 N.Y.2d 355, 795 N.Y.S.2d 497, 828 N.E.2d 599 (2005)—§ 11.10(b) n.44

Andrades, United States v., 169 F.3d 131 (2d Cir.1999)—§§ 21.4(d) n.114; 21.5(c) n.83

Andreano, United States v., 417 F.3d 967 (8th Cir.2005)—§ 21.2(b) n.76

Andrei, State v., 574 A.2d 295 (Me.1990)—§ 3.2(i) n.225

Andresen v. Maryland, 427 U.S. 463, 96 S.Ct. 2737, 49 L.Ed.2d 627 (1976)—§§ 2.10(d) n.108; 3.2(i) n.221; 3.4(a) n.3; 3.4(f) n.106; 3.4(j) n.202; 3.4(k) n.222; 8.7(a) n.6, 22; 8.12(f) n.57, 59; 8.12(g) n.77; 27.5(b) n.37

Andress, United States v., 943 F.2d 622 (6th Cir.1991)—§ 18.3(b) n.27

Andre W., People v., 44 N.Y.2d 179, 404 N.Y.S.2d 578, 375 N.E.2d 758 (1978)—§ 20.3(h) n.157

Andrews v. Ellsworth, 190 Mich. 157, 156 N.W. 115 (1916)—§ 16.1(e) n.191

Andrews, People v., 358 Ill.App.3d 744, 294 Ill.Dec. 543, 831 N.E.2d 66 (2005)—§ 25.2(e) n.38

Andrews, People v., 155 Ill.2d 286, 185 Ill.Dec. 499, 614 N.E.2d 1184 (1993)—§ 22.3(d) n.247

Andrews v. State, 40 P.3d 708 (Wyo.2002)—§ 3.5(e) n.178

Andrews v. State, 2002 WY 28, 40 P.3d 708 (Wyo.2002)—§ 3.2(h) n.207

Andrews, State v., 253 Conn. 497, 752 A.2d 49 (2000)—§ 21.4(d) n.119

Andrews, State v., 624 A.2d 1235 (Me.1993)—§ 21.5(c) n.88

Andrews, State v., 388 N.W.2d 723 (Minn.1986)—§ 6.8(b) n.55

Andrews v. State, 291 Md. 622, 436 A.2d 1315 (1981)—§ 7.2(d) n.54

Andrews v. State, 344 So.2d 533 (Ala.App.1977)—§ 19.2(a) n.6

Andrews, State v., 35 Or. 388, 58 P. 765 (1899)—§ 2.12(a) n.7

Andrews, United States v., 22 F.3d 1328 (5th Cir.1994)—§ 10.6(a) n.2

Andrews, United States v., 754 F.Supp. 1161 (N.D.Ill.1990)—§ 17.2(f) n.131

Andrews, United States v., 754 F.Supp. 1189 (N.D.Ill.1990)—§ 19.2(b) n.21

Andrews, United States v., 790 F.2d 803 (10th Cir.1986)—§§ 18.3(b) n.7, 53

Andrews, United States v., 746 F.2d 247 (5th Cir.1984)—§ 3.10(c) n.94

Andrews, United States v., 633 F.2d 449 (6th Cir.1980)—§ 13.7(c) n.58

Andrews v. Utah Board of Pardons, 836 P.2d 790 (Utah 1992)—§ 26.2(c) n.76

Andries, State v., 297 N.W.2d 124 (Minn.1980)—§ 3.4(c) n.41

Andrus, United States v., 483 F.3d 711 (10th Cir.2007)—§ 3.10(e) n.166

Andrus, United States v., 775 F.2d 825 (7th Cir.1985)—§ 17.2(c) n.90

Andujar, Commonwealth v., 7 Mass.App.Ct. 777, 390 N.E.2d 276 (1979)—§ 6.4(f) n.126

Anello, United States v., 765 F.2d 253 (1st Cir.1985)—§ 8.13(a) n.24

Angarano v. United States, 329 A.2d 453 (D.C.App.1974)—§ 11.7(e) n.67

Angel, State v., 132 N.M. 501, 51 P.3d 1155 (2002)—§§ 21.3(f) n.426; 25.1(d) n.66

Angelia D.B., Interest of, 211 Wis.2d 140, 564 N.W.2d 682 (1997)—§ 3.9(k) n.258

Angelos, United States v., 433 F.3d 738 (10th Cir.2006)—§ 3.4(k) n.228

Angelos, United States v., 345 F.Supp.2d 1227 (D.Utah 2004)—§ 26.3(c) n.20

Angevine, United States v., 281 F.3d 1130 (10th Cir.2002)—§ 3.9(l) n.269

Angiulo, Appeal of, 579 F.2d 104 (1st Cir.1978)—§ 8.10(c) n.67

Angiulo, Commonwealth v., 415 Mass. 502, 615 N.E.2d 155 (1993)—§§ 22.3(b) n.68, 70

Angiulo, United States v., 897 F.2d 1169 (1st Cir.1990)—§ 24.3(i) n.190

Angiulo, United States v., 847 F.2d 956 (1st Cir.1988)—§§ 4.6(h) n.147; 4.6(j) n.165; 4.6(m) n.236

Angiulo, United States v., 497 F.2d 440 (1st Cir.1974)—§§ 16.3(g) n.99, 103, 121

Angle v. State, 113 Nev. 757, 942 P.2d 177 (1997)—§ 27.5(a) n.14

Anglian, United States v., 784 F.2d 765 (6th Cir.1986)—§ 8.4(b) n.25

Anglin, State v., 751 A.2d 1007 (Me.2000)—§ 9.6(a) n.36

Anglin, United States v., 215 F.3d 1064 (9th Cir.2000)—§ 21.2(d) n.177

Angotti, United States v., 105 F.3d 539 (9th Cir.1997)—§§ 16.2(e) n.77, 84

Angulo, United States v., 4 F.3d 843 (9th Cir.1993)—§ 24.9(f) n.86

Angwin, United States v., 263 F.3d 979 (9th Cir.2001)—§ 17.2(d) n.95

Angwin, United States v., 271 F.3d 786 (9th Cir.2001)—§§ 17.2(b) n.60; 17.2(d) n.94

Annala, State v., 168 Wis.2d 453, 484 N.W.2d 138 (1992)—§§ 13.2(g) n.117, 119

Annerino, United States v., 495 F.2d 1159 (7th Cir.1974)—§ 18.2(c) n.50

Anobile v. Pelligrino, 284 F.3d 104 (2d Cir.2002)—§ 3.9(c) n.41

Anonymous v. Anonymous, 558 F.2d 677 (2d Cir.1977)—§ 4.6(b) n.47

Anonymous, State v., 240 Conn. 708, 694 A.2d 766 (1997)—§ 27.5(c) n.96

Anonymous, State v., 33 Conn.Sup. 716, 368 A.2d 609 (1977)—§ 19.4(a) n.1

Anson, State v., 282 Wis.2d 629, 698 N.W.2d 776 (2005)—§ 10.2(c) n.42

Anspach, State v., 627 N.W.2d 227 (Iowa 2001)—§ 13.7(a) n.5

Antar, United States v., 38 F.3d 1348 (3d Cir.1994)—§§ 23.1(d) n.172, 175, 178

Antelope, United States v., 395 F.3d 1128 (9th Cir.2005)—§§ 26.9(b) n.57, 71

Anthes, Commonwealth v., 71 Mass. (5 Gray) 185 (1855)—§ 1.6(d) n.236

Anthony, State v., 354 N.C. 372, 555 S.E.2d 557 (2001)—§§ 22.3(c) n.147; 22.5(d) n.34, 36

Anthony, State v., 257 Kan. 1003, 898 P.2d 1109 (1995)—§§ 11.4(c) n.73, 79, 80; 17.1(a) n.15

Anthony, United States v., 93 F.3d 614 (9th Cir.1996)—§§ 21.2(d) n.250; 27.5(e) n.155

Anthony F., In re, 293 Md. 146, 442 A.2d 975 (1982)—§ 3.10(d) n.124

Antobenedetto, Commonwealth v., 366 Mass. 51, 315 N.E.2d 530 (1974)— §§ 10.3(b) n.20, 48

Antommarchi, People v., 80 N.Y.2d 247, 590 N.Y.S.2d 33, 604 N.E.2d 95 (1992)—§ 24.2(a) n.5

Antone v. State, 382 So.2d 1205 (Fla.1980)—§ 24.3(d) n.111

Antone, United States v., 603 F.2d 566 (5th Cir.1979)—§ 24.3(d) n.111

Antonelli Fireworks Co., United States v., 155 F.2d 631 (2d Cir.1946)— §§ 3.10(e) n.177; 27.6(b) n.37

Antonino, United States v., 830 F.2d 798 (7th Cir.1987)—§ 18.5(b) n.64

Antonio, United States v., 705 F.2d 1483 (9th Cir.1983)—§ 18.3(b) n.53

Antonio-Antimo, People v., 29 P.3d 298 (Colo.2000)—§ 21.2(e) n.294

Antonio J. Sancetta, M.D., P.C., United States v., 788 F.2d 67 (2d Cir.1986)—§ 8.12(b) n.22

Antoon, United States v., 933 F.2d 200 (3d Cir.1991)—§ 4.6(l) n.200

Antwine, State v., 743 S.W.2d 51 (Mo.1987)—§ 22.3(d) n.240

Anzelmo, United States v., 319 F.Supp. 1106 (D.La.1970)—§§ 15.4(g) n.177; 15.4(h) n.188

A.P., In re, 636 So.2d 790 (Fla.App.1994)—§ 27.4(c) n.24

Apfelbaum, United States v., 445 U.S. 115, 100 S.Ct. 948, 63 L.Ed.2d 250 (1980)—§ 8.11(a) n.8

Apkins, Commonwealth v., 148 Ky. 207, 146 S.W. 431 (1912)— § 16.4(c) n.44

Apodaca v. Oregon, 406 U.S. 404, 92 S.Ct. 1628, 32 L.Ed.2d 184 (1972)—§§ 2.1 n.59; 2.5(f) n.78, 103; 2.6(c) n.78, 84; 22.1(e) n.81; 22.2(d) n.53

Apodaca v. People, 712 P.2d 467 (Colo.1985)—§ 24.5(d) n.51

Apodaca, State v., 123 N.M. 372, 940 P.2d 478 (App.1997)—§ 27.2(c) n.64

Apodaca v. State, 891 P.2d 83 (Wyo.1995)—§ 26.3(f) n.56

Aponte, Commonwealth v., 579 Pa. 246, 855 A.2d 800 (2004)—§ 27.5(d) n.113

Aponte, Commonwealth v., 391 Mass. 494, 462 N.E.2d 284 (1984)— § 15.4(d) n.101

Aponte-Suarez, United States v., 905 F.2d 483 (1st Cir.1990)—§ 22.2(a) n.8

Appel v. Horn, 250 F.3d 203 (3d Cir.2001)—§ 11.10(d) n.204

Apperson, United States v., 441 F.3d 1162 (10th Cir.2006)—§ 18.3(b) n.27

Apple, United States v., 915 F.2d 899 (4th Cir.1990)—§§ 8.9(b) n.30, 32

Appleby, State ex rel. v. Recht, 213 W.Va. 503, 583 S.E.2d 800 (W.Va.2002)—§ 21.4(d) n.112

Applegate, State v., 39 Or.App. 17, 591 P.2d 371 (1979)—§ 27.5(c) n.93

Appleton, Ex parte, 828 So.2d 894 (Ala.2001)—§ 7.4(f) n.95

Applewhite v. United States, 614 A.2d 888 (D.C.App.1992)—§ 26.10(c) n.81

Applying Mathews v. Eldridge, 424 U.S. 319, 96 S.Ct. 893, 47 L.Ed.2d 18 (1976)—§ 26.2(c) n.42

Appointment of Independent Counsel, Matter of Application for, 766 F.2d 70 (2d Cir.1985)—§ 8.4(b) n.110

Apprendi v. New Jersey, 530 U.S. 466, 120 S.Ct. 2348, 147 L.Ed.2d 435 (2000)—§§ 1.6(b) n.29; 2.8(a) n.24; 2.9(d) n.57, 66, 67; 19.2(e) n.62; 19.3(a) n.19, 81; 21.4(e) n.156;

22.1(a) n.21; 24.8(e) n.68; 26.4(h) n.159; 26.4(i) n.160, 168; 26.6(c) n.42

April 25, 1978 Grand Jury Subpoena Duces Tecum (Gruberg), In re, 453 F.Supp. 1225 (S.D.N.Y.1978)— §§ 8.8(e) n.124, 131, 137

April 1956 Term Grand Jury, In re, 239 F.2d 263 (7th Cir.1956)— §§ 8.4(c) n.111; 8.5(e) n.173

April 1977 Grand Jury Subpoenas, In re, 584 F.2d 1366 (6th Cir.1978)— §§ 27.2(e) n.94, 95

April 1977 Grand Jury Subpoenas, (General Motors Corp.), In re, 573 F.2d 936 (6th Cir.1978)— § 15.7(c) n.55

A Quantity of Copies of Books v. Kansas, 378 U.S. 205, 84 S.Ct. 1723, 12 L.Ed.2d 809 (1964)— § 3.4(a) n.5

Aquino-Chacon, United States v., 109 F.3d 936 (4th Cir.1997)— § 5.4(c) n.30

Arace Bros., State v., 230 N.J.Super. 22, 552 A.2d 628 (1989)— §§ 8.5(e) n.181; 8.5(h) n.276

Aragon v. State, 114 Idaho 758, 760 P.2d 1174 (1988)— § 24.5(d) n.58

Aragon, United States v., 962 F.2d 439 (5th Cir.1992)— § 23.2(h) n.126

Araiza, State v., 124 Idaho 82, 856 P.2d 872 (Idaho 1993)— §§ 20.3(b) n.38; 22.3(d) n.235

Araki, State v., 82 Hawai'i 474, 923 P.2d 891 (1996)— § 9.1(c) n.106

Aranda-Hernandez, United States v., 95 F.3d 977 (10th Cir.1996)— § 14.2(g) n.96

Arango, United States v., 912 F.2d 441 (10th Cir.1990)— § 10.3(b) n.31

Arango-Montoya, United States v., 61 F.3d 1331 (7th Cir.1995)— § 26.4(f) n.101

Araujo v. Chandler, 435 F.3d 678 (7th Cir.2005)— § 28.5(b) n.62

Araujo, United States v., 539 F.2d 287 (2d Cir.1976)— § 21.1(e) n.67

Arbelaez v. State, 626 So.2d 169 (Fla.1993)— § 6.6(f) n.100

Arbogast, State ex rel. v. Mohn, 164 W.Va. 6, 260 S.E.2d 820 (1979)— § 11.6(a) n.4

Arbuckle, People v., 22 Cal.3d 749, 150 Cal.Rptr. 778, 587 P.2d 220 (1978)— § 21.2(d) n.161

Arce, United States v., 997 F.2d 1123 (5th Cir.1993)— § 22.3(d) n.234

Archanian v. State, ___ Nev. ___, 145 P.3d 1008 (2006)— §§ 6.6(e) n.91; 6.7(b) n.72

Archer v. State, 851 S.W.2d 157 (Tenn.1993)— § 28.11(b) n.19

Archer, State v., 32 N.M. 319, 255 P. 396 (1927)— § 16.3(d) n.57

Archer v. State, 106 Ind. 426, 7 N.E. 225 (1886)— §§ 16.1(d) n.158; 16.2(a) n.6

Archer, United States v., 486 F.2d 670 (2d Cir.1973)— § 5.4(c) n.40

Archer, United States v., 355 F.Supp. 981 (S.D.N.Y.1972)— § 8.5(i) n.318

Archer v. United States, 393 F.2d 124 (5th Cir.1968)— § 6.6(f) n.108

Archer, United States v., 51 F.Supp. 708 (S.D.Cal.1943)— § 16.4(b) n.33

Archie, United States v., 452 F.2d 897 (3d Cir.1971)— § 17.3(a) n.11

Archuleta, In Matter of, 432 F.Supp. 583 (S.D.N.Y.1977)— §§ 8.5(i) n.308, 324; 8.8(i) n.195

Archuleta, Matter of, 561 F.2d 1059 (2d Cir.1977)— § 8.8(i) n.196

Archuleta v. Kerby, 864 F.2d 709 (10th Cir.1989)— § 7.4(c) n.51

Archuleta, State v., 857 P.2d 234 (Utah 1993)— § 27.5(a) n.23

Archuleta, State v., 112 N.M. 55, 811 P.2d 88 (1991)— § 25.3(e) n.39

Archuleta, State v., 82 N.M. 378, 482 P.2d 242 (1970)— § 6.10(b) n.22

Arcuri, United States v., 282 F.Supp. 347 (E.D.N.Y. 1968)— §§ 15.2(d) n.113; 15.5(b) n.70

Arditti, United States v., 955 F.2d 331 (5th Cir.1992)— §§ 5.4(b) n.18; 24.3(f) n.146, 150

Ardolino, State v., 697 A.2d 73 (Me.1997)—§ 19.3(a) n.62

Arellano-Gallegos, United States v., 351 F.3d 966 (9th Cir.2003)—§ 21.4(e) n.163

Arellano-Ochoa, United States v., 461 F.3d 1142 (9th Cir.2006)—§§ 3.2(c) n.105; 6.7(b) n.41

Arenal, United States v., 768 F.2d 263 (8th Cir.1985)—§ 3.4(e) n.68

Arenas-Ortiz, United States v., 339 F.3d 1066 (9th Cir.2003)—§ 13.4(b) n.69

A Residence Located at 218 3rd Street, United States v., 805 F.2d 256 (7th Cir.1986)—§ 8.8(g) n.166

Arevalo v. State, 943 S.W.2d 887 (Tex.Cr.App.1997)—§ 24.8(f) n.98

Argersinger v. Hamlin, 407 U.S. 25, 92 S.Ct. 2006, 32 L.Ed.2d 530 (1972)—§§ 1.11(a) n.2; 2.6(d) n.95; 11.1(a) n.24; 11.2(a) n.1, 8, 9

Argomaniz, United States v., 925 F.2d 1349 (11th Cir.1991)—§§ 8.13(b) n.56, 61, 62

Arguelles, State v., 63 P.3d 731 (Utah 2003)—§ 11.4(d) n.112

Arguello, People v., 772 P.2d 87 (Colo.1989)—§§ 11.4(d) n.116; 11.5(c) n.46

Arguello, State v., 655 N.W.2d 451 (S.D.2002)—§ 21.4(d) n.131

Arguello, State v., 502 N.W.2d 548 (S.D.1993)—§ 17.1(c) n.45

Arias v. Mutual Central Alarm Service, Inc., 202 F.3d 553 (2d Cir.2000)—§ 4.6(b) n.46

Arias, People v., 13 Cal.4th 92, 51 Cal.Rptr.2d 770, 913 P.2d 980 (1996)—§ 22.3(d) n.202

Arias, United States v., 678 F.2d 1202 (4th Cir.1982)—§ 11.9(b) n.98

Arizona v. Evans, 514 U.S. 1, 115 S.Ct. 1185, 131 L.Ed.2d 34 (1995)—§§ 3.1(b) n.24; 3.1(h) n.213; 3.9(h) n.165

Arizona v. Fulminante, 499 U.S. 279, 111 S.Ct. 1246, 113 L.Ed.2d 302 (1991)—§§ 1.5(b) n.69; 2.9(f) n.116; 6.2(b) n.27; 6.2(c) n.72, 93; 24.1(a) n.12; 27.6(d) n.92; 27.6(e) n.158

Arizona v. Hicks, 480 U.S. 321, 107 S.Ct. 1149, 94 L.Ed.2d 347 (1987)—§§ 3.1(c) n.29; 3.2(b) n.69; 3.4(j) n.201; 3.4(k) n.226; 3.6(g) n.161; 3.7(a) n.17

Arizona v. Manypenny, 451 U.S. 232, 101 S.Ct. 1657, 68 L.Ed.2d 58 (1981)—§§ 27.3(a) n.7; 27.3(b) n.12, 15

Arizona v. Mauro, 481 U.S. 520, 107 S.Ct. 1931, 95 L.Ed.2d 458 (1987)—§§ 6.7(a) n.27; 6.7(c) n.112

Arizona v. Roberson, 486 U.S. 675, 108 S.Ct. 2093, 100 L.Ed.2d 704 (1988)—§§ 2.9(b) n.43; 2.9(g) n.172, 176; 2.9(h) n.223, 227; 6.5(e) n.94; 6.9(f) n.124

Arizona v. Rumsey, 467 U.S. 203, 104 S.Ct. 2305, 81 L.Ed.2d 164 (1984)—§§ 2.9(b) n.16; 26.7(a) n.7

Arizona v. Washington, 434 U.S. 497, 98 S.Ct. 824, 54 L.Ed.2d 717 (1978)—§§ 1.10(a) n.17; 24.7(a) n.17; 24.7(d) n.34; 25.2(c) n.18; 25.2(d) n.23, 33; 25.2(e) n.36

Arizona v. Youngblood, 488 U.S. 51, 109 S.Ct. 333, 102 L.Ed.2d 281 (1988)—§§ 2.7(a) n.17; 24.3(a) n.1; 24.3(e) n.121

Arkansas v. Sanders, 442 U.S. 753, 99 S.Ct. 2586, 61 L.Ed.2d 235 (1979)—§§ 3.5(e) n.189, 203; 3.6(e) n.125; 3.7(c) n.41

Arkansas v. Sullivan, 532 U.S. 769, 121 S.Ct. 1876, 149 L.Ed.2d 994 (2001)—§§ 3.1(d) n.116, 120; 3.5(a) n.68

Arkebauer v. Kiley, 985 F.2d 1351 (7th Cir.1993)—§ 8.11(e) n.99

Arlotta v. Bradley Center, 349 F.3d 517 (7th Cir.2003)—§ 3.5(a) n.41

Arman, People v., 131 Ill.2d 115, 137 Ill.Dec. 5, 545 N.E.2d 658 (1989)— § 24.5(b) n.22

Armand, In re, 454 A.2d 1216 (R.I.1983)—§ 3.3(f) n.219

Armani, In re, 79 Misc.2d 231, 359 N.Y.S.2d 231 (Sup.1974)— § 15.2(e) n.137

Armantrout, United States v., 278 F.Supp. 517 (S.D.N.Y.1968)— § 20.3(b) n.46

Armco Steel Corp., United States v., 458 F.Supp. 784 (W.D.Mo.1978)— § 8.5(c) n.83

Armenakes v. State, 821 A.2d 239 (R.I.2003)—§ 21.4(f) n.213

Armenta, United States v., 69 F.3d 304 (9th Cir.1995)—§ 9.1(b) n.69

Armentrout, State v., 8 S.W.3d 99 (Mo.1999)—§ 22.3(a) n.6

Armer v. State, 326 Ark. 7, 929 S.W.2d 705 (1996)—§ 26.2(b) n.14

Armfield, State v., 214 Mont. 229, 693 P.2d 1226 (1984)—§ 7.3(c) n.50

Armienti v. United States, 313 F.3d 807 (2d Cir.2002)—§ 11.9(d) n.230

Armintrout v. People, 864 P.2d 576 (Colo.1993)—§§ 24.8(e) n.65; 26.3(f) n.54

Armocida, United States v., 515 F.2d 29 (3d Cir.1975)—§§ 4.6(e) n.77, 92

Armored Transport, Inc., United States v., 629 F.2d 1313 (9th Cir.1980)— §§ 15.1(b) n.26, 31, 35, 38

Armour Packing Co. v. United States, 209 U.S. 56, 28 S.Ct. 428, 52 L.Ed. 681 (1908)—§ 16.2(f) n.93

Arms, United States v., 392 F.2d 300 (6th Cir.1968)—§ 3.4(g) n.127

Armstead v. Scott, 37 F.3d 202 (5th Cir.1994)—§ 11.10(d) n.176

Armstrong v. Davis, 275 F.3d 849 (9th Cir.2001)—§ 26.2(c) n.43

Armstrong v. Dugger, 833 F.2d 1430 (11th Cir.1987)—§ 11.10(c) n.111

Armstrong v. Egeler, 563 F.2d 796 (6th Cir.1977)—§ 21.4(d) n.119

Armstrong v. Gammon, 195 F.3d 441 (8th Cir.1999)—§ 7.4(e) n.92

Armstrong, State v., 223 Wis.2d 331, 588 N.W.2d 606 (1999)—§ 6.6(b) n.15

Armstrong v. State, 573 So.2d 1329 (Miss.1990)—§§ 11.9(d) n.190, 232

Armstrong, State v., 46 Md.App. 641, 421 A.2d 98 (1980)—§ 18.3(c) n.109

Armstrong v. State, 294 Ala. 100, 312 So.2d 620 (1975)—§ 26.10(c) n.49

Armstrong, State v., 207 Kan. 681, 486 P.2d 1322 (1971)—§ 7.3(d) n.68

Armstrong v. State, 41 Tenn. 338, 1 Coldw. 338 (Tenn.1860)—§ 16.1(e) n.190

Armstrong, United States v., 187 F.3d 392 (4th Cir.1999)—§§ 3.1(f) n.158; 26.10(c) n.66

Armstrong, United States v., 517 U.S. 456, 116 S.Ct. 1480, 134 L.Ed.2d 687 (1996)—§§ 13.4(a) n.8, 16, 25; 13.4(b) n.38, 64, 78; 13.4(e) n.169; 20.3(g) n.128; 24.3(b) n.49

Armstrong, United States v., 16 F.3d 289 (8th Cir.1994)—§§ 3.5(e) n.185; 9.1(d) n.128

Armstrong, United States v., 781 F.2d 700 (9th Cir.1986)—§§ 8.3(a) n.6, 7

Armstrong v. United States, 367 F.2d 821 (7th Cir.1966)—§ 11.6(c) n.108

Arnett, In re, 804 F.2d 1200 (11th Cir.1986)—§ 8.11(e) n.110

Arnett v. Meade, 462 S.W.2d 940 (Ky.1971)—§ 8.3(a) n.10

Arnett v. State, 353 Ark. 165, 122 S.W.3d 484 (2003)—§ 6.7(b) n.66

Arnett v. State, 342 Ark. 66, 27 S.W.3d 721 (2000)—§ 6.3(c) n.53

Arnett, United States v., 628 F.2d 1162 (9th Cir.1979)—§§ 21.2(d) n.187, 189

Arnett, United States v., 342 F.Supp. 1255 (D.Mass.1970)—§§ 15.4(b) n.66; 22.2(d) n.86

Arnold v. Commonwealth, 17 Va.App. 313, 437 S.E.2d 235 (Va.App. 1993)—§ 9.1(d) n.122

Arnold v. Higa, 61 Haw. 203, 600 P.2d 1383 (1979)—§ 27.4(c) n.27

Arnold v. Panora, 593 F.2d 161 (1st Cir.1979)—§ 27.5(a) n.15

Arnold, People v., 96 N.Y.2d 358, 729 N.Y.S.2d 51, 753 N.E.2d 846 (2001)—§ 22.3(c) n.112

Arnold, People v., 186 Colo. 372, 527 P.2d 806 (1974)—§ 3.3(c) n.92

Arnold, People v., 66 Cal.2d 438, 58 Cal.Rptr. 115, 426 P.2d 515 (1967)—§§ 6.6(c) n.27; 6.6(f) n.111

Arnold, People v., 46 Mich. 268, 9 N.W. 406 (1881)—§ 16.1(d) n.137

Arnold v. Runnels, 421 F.3d 859 (9th Cir.2005)—§ 6.9(g) n.156

Arnold, State v., 280 Ga. 487, 629 S.E.2d 807 (2006)—§ 24.9(f) n.72

Arnold, State v., 816 So.2d 289 (La.2002)—§ 21.6(a) n.64

Arnold, State v., 421 A.2d 932 (Me.1980)—§ 14.1(a) n.3

Arnold, United States v., 113 F.3d 1146 (10th Cir.1997)—§ 18.3(b) n.27

Arnold, United States v., 117 F.3d 1308 (11th Cir.1997)—§ 24.3(b) n.49

Arnold, United States v., 773 F.2d 823 (7th Cir.1985)—§ 4.6(i) n.155

Arnsberg, State v., 27 Ariz.App. 205, 553 P.2d 238 (1976)—§ 10.2(d) n.49

Aronoff, United States v., 463 F.Supp. 454 (S.D.N.Y.1978)—§§ 16.3(c) n.35, 39 to 41

Arrant v. Wainwright, 468 F.2d 677 (5th Cir.1972)—§ 18.2(c) n.29

Arreola, People v., 7 Cal.4th 1144, 31 Cal.Rptr.2d 631, 875 P.2d 736 (1994)—§ 26.10(c) n.73

Arriaga, Commonwealth v., 438 Mass. 556, 781 N.E.2d 1253 (2003)—§§ 22.2(d) n.76, 77, 80

Arrington, State v., 311 N.C. 633, 319 S.E.2d 254 (1984)—§ 2.12(d) n.196

Arrington, United States v., 867 F.2d 122 (2d Cir.1989)—§ 11.9(c) n.120

Arrington v. United States, 382 A.2d 14 (D.C.1978)—§ 3.7(d) n.85

Arrington v. United States, 311 A.2d 838 (D.C.1973)—§ 3.3(f) n.193

Arriola v. State, 520 P.2d 690 (Okl.Crim.1973)—§ 7.4(d) n.71

Arroya, People v., 988 P.2d 1124 (Colo.1999)—§§ 6.9(f) n.111; 6.9(g) n.149, 161

Arroyo, State v., 796 P.2d 684 (Utah 1990)—§ 3.1(d) n.111

Arsenault, State v., 153 N.H. 413, 897 A.2d 988 (2006)—§ 21.4(c) n.92

A.R., State ex rel. v. C.R., 982 P.2d 73 (Utah 1999)—§ 3.1(g) n.174

Arthur, Ex parte, 711 So.2d 1097 (Ala.1997)—§§ 11.3(b) n.36; 11.5(g) n.112

Arthur v. Allen, 452 F.3d 1234 (11th Cir.2006)—§§ 28.5(b) n.61, 62

Arthur, People v., 22 N.Y.2d 325, 292 N.Y.S.2d 663, 239 N.E.2d 537 (1968)—§ 6.4(e) n.84

Arthur, State v., 390 So.2d 717 (Fla.1980)—§§ 12.4(a) n.5, 22

Arthur v. State, 264 Ind. 419, 345 N.E.2d 841 (1976)—§ 12.4(a) n.10

Arthur, United States v., 602 F.2d 660 (4th Cir.1979)—§ 26.9(b) n.39

Artieri, United States v., 491 F.2d 440 (2d Cir.1974)—§ 3.6(b) n.51

Artuz v. Bennett, 531 U.S. 4, 121 S.Ct. 361, 148 L.Ed.2d 213 (2000)—§ 28.5(b) n.48

Arvanitis, United States v., 902 F.2d 489 (7th Cir.1990)—§ 21.2(g) n.399

Arvizu, United States v., 534 U.S. 266, 122 S.Ct. 744, 151 L.Ed.2d 740 (2002)—§§ 3.8(d) n.122, 123; 3.9(f) n.115

A.S., Matter of, 614 A.2d 534 (D.C.1992)—§ 3.8(d) n.151

Asbury, People v., 173 Cal.App.3d 362, 218 Cal.Rptr. 902 (1985)—§ 24.10(a) n.15

Asch v. State, 62 P.3d 945 (Wyo.2003)—§§ 11.9(a) n.6, 30, 34; 11.9(b) n.97; 11.9(c) n.128

Aschan, State v., 366 N.W.2d 912 (Iowa 1985)—§ 13.6(d) n.56

Ascolillo, Commonwealth v., 405 Mass. 456, 541 N.E.2d 570 (1989)—§ 22.3(c) n.125

Asdrubal-Herrera, United States v., 470 F.Supp. 939 (N.D.Ill.1979)—§§ 15.2(g) n.156; 15.5(b) n.57

Ash v. Reilly, 431 F.3d 826 (D.C.Cir. 2005)—§ 26.10(c) n.71

Ash, State v., 94 Idaho 542, 493 P.2d 701 (1971)—§ 16.3(f) n.91

Ash, United States v., 413 U.S. 300, 93 S.Ct. 2568, 37 L.Ed.2d 619 (1973)—§§ 3.10(b) n.77; 7.3(c) n.40; 11.2(b) n.36

Ashba v. State, 816 N.E.2d 862 (Ind.App.2004)—§ 24.9(b) n.12

Ashburn, United States v., 38 F.3d 803 (5th Cir.1994)—§§ 21.1(h) n.233; 21.2(d) n.216

Ashby, State v., 245 So.2d 225 (Fla.1971)—§§ 21.4(a)   n.32; 21.6(b) n.111

Ashby, State v., 43 N.J. 273, 204 A.2d 1 (1964)—§ 8.11(e) n.98

Ashcraft v. State, 465 So.2d 1374 (Fla.App.1985)—§ 11.5(d) n.82

Ashcraft v. Tennessee, 322 U.S. 143, 64 S.Ct. 921, 88 L.Ed. 1192 (1944)—§§ 1.2(c) n.11; 2.5(f) n.47, 62; 2.9(g) n.169; 6.2(b) n.40; 6.2(c) n.60, 79, 88, 168

Ashcroft v. ACLU, 542 U.S. 656, 124 S.Ct. 2783, 159 L.Ed.2d 690 (2004)—§ 13.5(b) n.49

Ashe, State v., 745 P.2d 1255 (Utah 1987)—§ 3.1(d) n.95

Ashe v. Swenson, 397 U.S. 436, 90 S.Ct. 1189, 25 L.Ed.2d 469 (1970)—§§ 2.8(a) n.20; 2.9(d) n.76; 10.6(d) n.37; 17.4(a) n.1; 17.4(b) n.108; 17.4(c)   n.141; 21.2(d) n.230; 25.1(b) n.16

Ashenfelder, Commonwealth v., 413 Pa. 517, 198 A.2d 514 (1964)—§ 1.8(d) n.55

Asherman v. Meachum, 957 F.2d 978 (2d Cir.1992)—§ 26.10(c) n.60

Asherman, State v., 193 Conn. 695, 478 A.2d 227 (1984)—§ 7.2(b) n.19

Ashford, People v., 265 Cal.App.2d 673, 71 Cal.Rptr. 619 (1968)—§ 6.7(b) n.61

Ashimi, United States v., 932 F.2d 643 (7th Cir.1991)—§ 18.3(b) n.11

Ashimi, United States v., 725 F.Supp. 389 (N.D.Ill.1989)—§ 24.11(d) n.34

Ashland, City of v. Heck's Inc., 407 S.W.2d 421 (Ky.1966)—§ 13.4(a) n.10

Ashland Oil, Inc., United States v., 705 F.Supp. 270 (W.D.Pa.1989)—§§ 15.5(b) n.53, 79; 15.6(e) n.164; 15.7(e) n.101, 112

Ashland Oil, Inc., United States v., 457 F.Supp. 661 (W.D.Ky.1978)—§ 16.3(c) n.44

Ashley, State v., 161 Vt. 65, 632 A.2d 1368 (1993)—§ 12.1(b) n.32

Ashley v. State, 614 So.2d 486 (Fla.1993)—§§ 21.4(a)   n.23; 21.4(d) n.111

Ashley v. State, 261 Ga. 488, 405 S.E.2d 657 (1991)—§ 6.9(f) n.139

Ashley, United States v., 54 F.3d 311 (7th Cir.1995)—§ 22.2(d) n.56

Ashley, United States v., 876 F.2d 1069 (1st Cir.1989)—§§ 4.6(e) n.97, 101

Ashley Transfer & Storage Co., United States v., 858 F.2d 221 (4th Cir.1988)—§ 17.4(a) n.24

Ashman, In re, 608 N.W.2d 853 (Minn.2000)—§ 21.2(d) n.157

Ashman, Commonwealth ex rel. v. Banmiller, 391 Pa. 141, 137 A.2d 236 (1958)—§ 21.5(f) n.154

Ashmus v. Woodford, 202 F.3d 1160 (9th Cir.2000)—§ 28.8(b) n.16

Ashurst, United States v., 96 F.3d 1055 (7th Cir.1996)—§ 21.2(d) n.222

Askerooth, State v., 681 N.W.2d 353 (Minn.2004)—§ 2.12(b) n.111

Askew v. City of Chicago, 440 F.3d 894 (7th Cir.2006)—§ 3.3(d) n.151

Askew, United States v., 482 F.3d 532 (D.C.Cir.2007)—§§ 3.8(e) n.222; 7.4(f) n.96

Askew, United States v., 584 F.2d 960 (10th Cir.1978)—§ 18.4(a) n.20

Askew, State ex rel. v. Goldhart, 75 Ohio St.3d 608, 665 N.E.2d 200 (1996)—§ 15.2(f) n.148

Asrar, United States v., 116 F.3d 1268 (9th Cir.1997)—§ 28.10 n.2

Assenza, United States v., 337 F.Supp. 1057 (M.D.Fla.1972)—§ 14.2(g) n.99

Associated Press, In re, 162 F.3d 503 (7th Cir.1998)—§§ 23.1(d) n.180; 23.1(e) n.247, 261; 27.5(a) n.20

Associated Press v. Bell, 70 N.Y.2d 32, 517 N.Y.S.2d 444, 510 N.E.2d 313 (1987)—§§ 23.1(d) n.144; 23.1(e) n.230, 231, 247

Associated Press v. United States District Court, 705 F.2d 1143 (9th Cir.1983)—§ 23.1(d) n.172

Asta, People v., 337 Mich. 590, 60 N.W.2d 472 (1953)—§ 14.3(a) n.3

Astling, United States v., 733 F.2d 1446 (11th Cir.1984)—§ 17.2(b) n.47

Ataya, United States v., 864 F.2d 1324 (7th Cir.1988)—§ 21.2(d) n.244

Atkins v. Commonwealth, 260 Va. 375, 534 S.E.2d 312 (2000)—§ 22.3(d) n.249

Atkins, Commonwealth v., 233 Pa.Super. 202, 336 A.2d 368 (1975)—§§ 11.4(c) n.76, 82

Atkins v. Michigan, 644 F.2d 543 (6th Cir.1981)—§§ 12.3(d) n.105; 27.4(f) n.71

Atkins v. Virginia, 536 U.S. 304, 122 S.Ct. 2242, 153 L.Ed.2d 335 (2002)—§§ 2.7(c) n.157, 182, 183; 2.9(d) n.87; 26.1(b) n.34; 26.4(h) n.156; 28.5(a) n.35; 28.5(d) n.84

Atkinson v. State, 347 Ark. 336, 64 S.W.3d 259 (2002)—§ 24.8(f) n.98

Atkinson v. State, 778 A.2d 1058 (Del.2001)—§ 24.3(b) n.49

Atkinson, State v., 235 Conn. 748, 670 A.2d 276 (1996)—§ 6.6(d) n.50

Atkinson, United States v., 979 F.2d 1219 (7th Cir.1992)—§§ 21.2(d) n.157; 21.2(f) n.365

Atkinson, United States v., 450 F.2d 835 (5th Cir.1971)—§ 3.5(a) n.45

Atlantic Container Line, Limited, United States v., 511 F.Supp. 115 (D.D.C.1980)—§ 8.5(h) n.255

Atlas Lathing Corp., In re, 176 Misc. 959, 29 N.Y.S.2d 458 (Sup.Ct.1941)—§ 8.7(e) n.89

Atley v. Ault, 191 F.3d 865 (8th Cir.1999)—§ 11.9(b) n.90

Atley v. Ault, 21 F.Supp.2d 949 (S.D.Iowa 1998)—§§ 11.9(b) n.53, 85, 90; 11.9(c) n.149; 11.9(d) n.208

Attebury, People v., 463 Mich. 662, 624 N.W.2d 912 (2001)—§§ 6.7(b) n.76, 85

Atterberry, United States v., 144 F.3d 1299 (10th Cir.1998)—§ 21.2(b) n.79

Attorney A, People v., 861 P.2d 705 (Colo.1993)—§ 21.3(b) n.121

Attorney C, In the Matter of, 47 P.3d 1167 (Colo.2002)—§§ 1.7(j) n.241; 14.4(c) n.71

Attorney General v. Colleton, 387 Mass. 790, 444 N.E.2d 915 (1982)—§§ 2.12(e) n.218; 8.11(b) n.21

Attorney General v. Irish People, Inc., 684 F.2d 928 (D.C.Cir.1982)—§§ 13.4(b) n.60; 13.4(e) n.170

Attorney General v. Pelletier, 240 Mass. 264, 134 N.E. 407 (1922)—§ 15.7(b) n.41

Attorney General of New Jersey, Application of, 116 N.J.Super. 143, 281 A.2d 284 (1971)—§ 8.7(e) n.89

Atwater v. City of Lago Vista, 532 U.S. 318, 121 S.Ct. 1536, 149 L.Ed.2d 549 (2001)—§§ 1.5(j) n.334; 2.4(b) n.37; 2.8(c) n.66; 2.9(d) n.57, 61, 66, 90; 2.9(g) n.155, 163, 172; 3.5(a) n.19, 22, 67; 3.5(b) n.91;

3.5(d) n.138; 12.5(b) n.24, 37

Atwood v. Mapes, 325 F.Supp.2d 950 (N.D.Iowa 2004)—§ 24.9(f) n.85

Atwood, State v., 16 S.W.3d 192 (Tex.Cr.App.2000)—§ 26.7(a) n.13

Atwood, State v., 171 Ariz. 576, 832 P.2d 593 (1992)—§§ 3.10(b) n.66, 74; 24.6(c) n.40

Atwood v. Vilsack, 725 N.W.2d 641 (Iowa 2006)—§ 12.3(b) n.32

Aubin, State v., 622 A.2d 444 (R.I.1993)—§ 3.8(e) n.202

Aubrey v. State, 478 N.E.2d 70 (Ind.1985)—§ 11.9(a) n.20

Aubry v. Gadbois, 50 Cal.App.3d 470, 123 Cal.Rptr. 365 (1975)—§ 12.4(b) n.48

Aubuchont, State v., 147 N.H. 142, 784 A.2d 1170 (2001)—§§ 6.2(c) n.96; 6.9(g) n.200

Aucoin, State v., 756 S.W.2d 705 (Tenn.Crim.App.1988)—§ 11.2(e) n.148

Aucoin, United States v., 964 F.2d 1492 (5th Cir.1992)—§ 13.7(a) n.29

Aud v. State, 72 Md.App. 508, 531 A.2d 706 (1987)—§ 16.1(d) n.143

Audette, State v., 797 A.2d 742 (Me.2002)—§ 5.3(d) n.43

August 1993 Regular Grand Jury, In re, 854 F.Supp. 1392 (S.D.Ind.1993)—§§ 8.8(b) n.41; 8.8(c) n.43, 44

Auguste v. Ridge, 395 F.3d 123 (3d Cir.2005)—§ 1.7(c) n.18

Augustine v. Brewer, 821 F.2d 365 (7th Cir.1987)—§ 21.2(d) n.184

Auler, United States v., 539 F.2d 642 (7th Cir.1976)—§§ 4.6(l) n.184, 191

Aulet, United States v., 618 F.2d 182 (2d Cir.1980)—§ 11.7(e) n.83

Ault, State v., 150 Ariz. 459, 724 P.2d 545 (1986)—§§ 9.3(e) n.56, 68, 75

Aurilio, State v., 366 So.2d 71 (Fla.App.1978)—§ 1.7(c) n.10

Austin, Commonwealth v., 421 Mass. 357, 657 N.E.2d 458 (1995)—§ 7.4(f) n.103

Austin, People v., 185 Colo. 229, 523 P.2d 989 (1974)—§ 24.9(a) n.4

Austin, State v., 731 A.2d 678 (R.I.1999)—§§ 7.4(d) n.69; 18.2(c) n.53; 18.2(e) n.76

Austin, State v., 244 Conn. 226, 710 A.2d 732 (1998)—§§ 7.4(e) n.82; 7.4(f) n.103

Austin, State v., 165 Vt. 389, 685 A.2d 1076 (Vt.1996)—§§ 26.9(c) n.80, 90, 93; 26.10(c) n.73

Austin v. State, 327 Md. 375, 609 A.2d 728 (1992)—§§ 11.9(a) n.27; 11.9(d) n.179, 192, 202, 233

Austin, State v., 320 N.C. 276, 357 S.E.2d 641 (1987)—§ 9.1(b) n.42

Austin, State v., 195 Conn. 496, 488 A.2d 1250 (1985)—§ 7.4(e) n.90

Austin v. State, 468 N.E.2d 1027 (Ind.1984)—§ 21.4(d) n.103

Austin, United States v., 255 F.3d 593 (8th Cir.2001)—§ 21.2(d) n.148

Austin v. United States, 513 U.S. 5, 115 S.Ct. 380, 130 L.Ed.2d 219 (1994)—§§ 11.2(b) n.67; 11.2(c) n.111

Austin v. United States, 509 U.S. 602, 113 S.Ct. 2801, 125 L.Ed.2d 488 (1993)—§§ 2.6(b) n.40; 25.1(c) n.34, 35

Austin, United States v., 448 F.2d 399 (9th Cir.1971)—§ 6.6(d) n.45

Austin-Bagley, United States v., 31 F.2d 229 (2d Cir.1929)—§ 8.13(d) n.101

Automated Medical Laboratories, Inc., United States v., 770 F.2d 399 (4th Cir.1985)—§§ 18.5(b) n.65, 69

Autry, State v., 103 Nev. 552, 746 P.2d 637 (1987)—§ 18.5(b) n.65

Avalos, United States v., 541 F.2d 1100 (5th Cir.1976)—§ 18.2(e) n.75

Avants, United States v., 278 F.3d 510 (5th Cir.2002)—§ 6.4(e) n.101

Avcollie, State v., 188 Conn. 626, 453 A.2d 418 (1982)—§ 15.2(d) n.108

Avcollie, State v., 178 Conn. 450, 423 A.2d 118 (1979)—§ 24.6(b) n.16

Avellino, United States v., 136 F.3d 249 (2d Cir.1998)—§ 24.3(b) n.77

Averell, United States v., 296 F.Supp. 1004 (S.D.N.Y.1969)—§ 6.6(f) n.101

Aversa, State v., 197 Conn. 685, 501 A.2d 370 (1985)—§ 6.9(d) n.72

Avery v. Georgia, 345 U.S. 559, 73 S.Ct. 891, 97 L.Ed. 1244 (1953)—§ 22.2(c) n.29

Avery v. State, _____ Nev. _____, 129 P.3d 664 (2006)—§ 6.6(e) n.61

Avery, United States v., 621 F.2d 214 (5th Cir.1980)—§ 21.2(d) n.183

Avgoustov, State v., _____ Vt. _____, 907 A.2d 1185 (2006)—§ 12.3(e) n.123

Avila, People v., 38 Cal.4th 491, 43 Cal.Rptr.3d 1, 133 P.3d 1076 (Cal.2006)—§§ 22.3(d) n.178, 179

Avila, State v., 192 Wis.2d 870, 532 N.W.2d 423 (1995)—§ 27.5(a) n.27

Avila v. State, 856 S.W.2d 260 (Tex.App. 1993)—§ 10.5(b) n.18

Avila, State v., 127 Ariz. 21, 617 P.2d 1137 (1980)—§ 21.4(a) n.39

Avila-Gallegos v. Immigration and Naturalization Service, 525 F.2d 666 (2d Cir.1975)—§ 6.10(e) n.80

Aviles, United States v., 153 F.3d 931 (9th Cir.1998)—§ 18.3(b) n.26

Avilla, People v., 212 A.D.2d 800, 623 N.Y.S.2d 280 (App.Div.1995)—§§ 15.2(e) n.143; 15.7(g) n.211

Aviv, United States v., 923 F.Supp. 35 (S.D.N.Y.1996)—§ 13.5(a) n.6

Awadalla, United States v., 357 F.3d 243 (2d Cir.2004)—§§ 27.5(c) n.73, 74

Awadallah, United States v., 349 F.3d 42 (2d Cir.2003)—§§ 8.7(e) n.88; 12.4(g) n.103

Awadallah, United States v., 202 F.Supp.2d 82 (S.D.N.Y.2002)—§ 12.4(g) n.102

Ayala, People v., 23 Cal.4th 225, 96 Cal.Rptr.2d 682, 1 P.3d 3 (2000)—§§ 22.2(d) n.57, 66

Ayala, People v., 24 Cal.4th 243, 99 Cal.Rptr.2d 532, 6 P.3d 193 (2000)—§§ 22.3(d) n.229; 24.2(a) n.5

Ayala, People v., 770 P.2d 1265 (Colo.1989)—§§ 14.3(a) n.10; 14.3(c) n.63

Ayala v. Speckard, 131 F.3d 62 (2d Cir.1997)—§§ 24.1(b) n.17, 18, 29

Ayala v. State, 262 Ga. 704, 425 S.E.2d 282 (1993)—§ 12.1(d) n.57

Ayala, State v., 222 Conn. 331, 610 A.2d 1162 (1992)—§§ 12.3(b) n.69; 12.3(g) n.151

Ayala, United States v., 894 F.2d 425 (D.C.Cir.1990)—§ 28.9(a) n.25

Ayd, United States v., 25 F.3d 624 (8th Cir.1994)—§§ 21.2(f) n.383; 21.3(b) n.107

Ayer, State v., 150 N.H. 14, 834 A.2d 277 (2003)—§§ 11.5(a) n.11; 22.2(d) n.70; 22.4(c) n.24

Ayers, State v., 207 Or.App. 668, 143 P.3d 251 (2006)—§ 18.4(c) n.39

Ayers, United States v., 426 F.2d 524 (2d Cir.1970)—§ 7.3(d) n.69

Ayres, United States v., 46 F. 651 (D.S.D.1891)—§ 16.1(b) n.84

Azania, State v., 865 N.E.2d 994 (Ind.2007)—§ 18.5(c) n.75

Azizi v. State, 270 Ga. 709, 512 S.E.2d 622 (1999)—§ 7.4(b) n.29

Azurin, In re, 87 Cal.App.4th 20, 104 Cal.Rptr.2d 284 (2001)—§ 28.11(b) n.21

B

Babb, United States v., 807 F.2d 272 (1st Cir.1986)—§§ 8.10(d) n.90, 111

Babcock, People v., 244 Mich.App. 64, 624 N.W.2d 479 (2000)—§ 26.3(g) n.80

Babcock v. State, 473 S.W.2d 941 (Tex.Cr.App.1971)—§ 6.8(b) n.51

Baber, United States v., 161 F.3d 531 (8th Cir.1998)—§ 5.2(a) n.6

Babich, United States v., 785 F.2d 415 (3d Cir.1986)—§ 26.10(c) n.78

Baca v. State, 106 N.M. 338, 742 P.2d 1043 (1987)—§ 5.4(c) n.36

Bacall, United States v., 443 F.2d 1050 (9th Cir.1971)—§ 9.3(d) n.37

Bach, United States v., 310 F.3d 1063 (8th Cir.2002)—§§ 3.4(j) n.209; 4.4(c) n.12; 4.8(d) n.27

Bachner v. United States, 517 F.2d 589 (7th Cir.1975)—§ 21.2(e) n.285

Bacon, People v., 225 Ill.App.3d 795, 167 Ill.Dec. 337, 587 N.E.2d 606 (Ill.App.1992)—§ 26.10(d) n.93

Bacon, State v., 167 Vt. 88, 702 A.2d 116 (1997)—§ 26.5(c) n.59

Bacon v. United States, 449 F.2d 933 (9th Cir.1971)—§ 12.4(g) n.98

Badaracco, United States v., 954 F.2d 928 (3d Cir.1992)—§ 21.2(d) n.174

Bader, State v., 148 N.H. 265, 808 A.2d 12 (2002)—§ 22.4(a) n.12

Bader v. State, 344 Ark. 241, 40 S.W.3d 738 (2001)—§ 22.3(a) n.7

Badger v. Cardwell, 587 F.2d 968 (9th Cir.1978)—§ 24.2(c) n.35

Badger, Commonwealth v., 482 Pa. 240, 393 A.2d 642 (1978)—§ 11.10(a) n.12

Badger v. State, 637 N.E.2d 800 (Ind.1994)—§ 21.2(f) n.383

Badger, United States v., 983 F.2d 1443 (7th Cir.1993)—§§ 8.8(f) n.145, 151

Badger, United States v., 925 F.2d 101 (5th Cir.1991)—§§ 21.5(a) n.38, 40

Badgett, People v., 10 Cal.4th 330, 41 Cal.Rptr.2d 635, 895 P.2d 877 (1995)—§§ 9.1(a) n.22; 10.3(c) n.51

Badgett, State v., 200 Conn. 412, 512 A.2d 160 (1986)—§§ 3.7(a) n.13; 21.4(e) n.165

Badia, United States v., 827 F.2d 1458 (11th Cir.1987)—§ 4.9(b) n.8

Badoni, State v., 133 N.M. 257, 62 P.3d 348 (App.2003)—§§ 19.3(a) n.39, 42

Badura v. State, 832 P.2d 1390 (Wyo.1992)—§ 26.1(f) n.145

Bae v. Peters, 950 F.2d 469 (7th Cir.1991)—§§ 6.2(c) n.182; 19.2(c) n.26; 19.4(a) n.7

Baehler, State v., 604 N.W.2d 601 (Iowa 1999)—§ 17.4(b) n.138

Baez, Commonwealth v., 554 Pa. 66, 720 A.2d 711 (1998)—§§ 6.7(d) n.145; 22.2(d) n.80

Baez, United States v., 87 F.3d 805 (6th Cir.1996)—§ 21.4(f) n.178

Baggett v. State, 254 Ark. 553, 494 S.W.2d 717 (1973)—§ 9.1(b) n.53

Baggett, United States v., 901 F.2d 1546 (11th Cir.1990)—§ 21.5(e) n.119

Baggot, United States v., 463 U.S. 476, 103 S.Ct. 3164, 77 L.Ed.2d 785 (1983)—§§ 8.5(b) n.41; 8.5(h) n.238, 292

Bagley, People v., 338 Ill.App.3d 978, 273 Ill.Dec. 686, 789 N.E.2d 860 (2003)—§ 20.6(a) n.8

Bagley, United States v., 473 U.S. 667, 105 S.Ct. 3375, 87 L.Ed.2d 481 (1985)—§§ 2.7(a) n.25, 48; 2.7(b) n.73; 2.7(c) n.192, 203; 14.4(c) n.69; 20.2(d) n.80; 20.3(m) n.237; 21.3(c) n.172; 24.3(a) n.6; 24.3(b) n.16, 19, 24; 24.3(d) n.112, 115

Bagley, United States v., 772 F.2d 482 (9th Cir.1985)—§ 7.4(d) n.73

Bagley, United States v., 473 U.S. 476, 103 S.Ct. 3164, 77 L.Ed.2d 785 (1983)—§ 27.6(d) n.76

Baglioni v. Chief of Police, 421 Mass. 229, 656 N.E.2d 1223 (1995)—§ 13.3(c) n.36

Bagliore, United States v., 182 F.Supp. 714 (E.D.N.Y.1960)—§ 21.4(a) n.30

Bagnell, United States v., 679 F.2d 826 (11th Cir.1982)—§ 16.3(c) n.49

Bagster, United States v., 915 F.2d 607 (10th Cir.1990)—§ 18.3(b) n.5

Bahadar, United States v., 954 F.2d 821 (2d Cir.1992)—§ 24.3(i) n.189

Bailes, State ex rel. v. Jolliffe, 208 W.Va. 481, 541 S.E.2d 571 (2000)—§§ 25.2(e) n.39; 27.4(b) n.16

Bailey v. Commonwealth, 194 S.W.3d 296 (Ky.2006)—§§ 6.2(c) n.170, 183

Bailey v. Commonwealth, 259 Va. 723, 529 S.E.2d 570 (2000)—§ 6.6(d) n.57

Bailey, People v., 45 Cal.App.4th 926, 53 Cal.Rptr.2d 198 (1996)— § 27.3(d) n.70

Bailey, People v., 451 Mich. 657, 549 N.W.2d 325 (1996)—§ 24.8(f) n.98

Bailey, People v., 167 Ill.2d 210, 212 Ill.Dec. 608, 657 N.E.2d 953 (1995)—§ 12.3(b) n.58

Bailey, People v., 9 Cal.App.4th 1252, 12 Cal.Rptr.2d 339 (1992)— § 11.9(d) n.218

Bailey, People v., 42 Mich.App. 359, 202 N.W.2d 557 (1972)—§ 3.9(e) n.75

Bailey, State v., 677 N.W.2d 380 (Minn.2004)—§ 9.5(c) n.68

Bailey v. State, 763 N.E.2d 998 (Ind.2002)—§§ 6.2(c) n.181; 6.7(b) n.90; 6.9(b) n.38; 6.9(g) n.166

Bailey, State v., 546 N.W.2d 387 (S.D.1996)—§ 21.5(a) n.35

Bailey v. State, 885 S.W.2d 193 (Tex.App.1994)—§ 16.1(d) n.142

Bailey v. State, 327 Md. 689, 612 A.2d 288 (1992)—§ 26.10(a) n.3

Bailey, State v., 452 N.W.2d 181 (Iowa 1990)—§§ 3.1(d) n.98; 10.5(d) n.42

Bailey v. State, 65 Wis.2d 331, 222 N.W.2d 871 (1974)—§ 14.3(d) n.90

Bailey v. United States, 516 U.S. 137, 116 S.Ct. 501, 133 L.Ed.2d 472 (1995)—§§ 21.4(c) n.84; 21.5(e) n.142; 28.9(c) n.83

Bailey, United States v., 675 F.2d 1292 (D.C.Cir.1982)—§§ 11.3(b) n.33, 34; 11.5(c) n.52, 54

Bailey, United States v., 468 F.2d 652 (5th Cir.1972)—§ 6.8(c) n.70

Bailey, United States v., 332 F.Supp. 1351 (N.D.Ill.1971)—§ 8.2(c) n.42

Bailey, United States v., 447 F.2d 735 (5th Cir.1971)—§ 3.10(c) n.93

Bailey, United States v., 262 F.Supp. 331 (D.C.Kan.1967)—§ 20.3(d) n.94

Bailleaux, United States v., 685 F.2d 1105 (9th Cir.1982)—§ 20.3(b) n.59

Bailon-Santana, United States v., 429 F.3d 1258 (9th Cir.2005)— § 22.1(h) n.134

Bain, Ex parte, 121 U.S. 1, 7 S.Ct. 781, 30 L.Ed. 849 (1887)—§§ 15.1(a) n.7; 19.2(e) n.84; 19.2(f) n.89; 19.3(e) n.226; 19.5(d) n.67; 19.6(c) n.25

Bainbridge, State v., 117 Idaho 245, 787 P.2d 231 (1990)—§ 9.4(a) n.26

Baird, In re, 668 F.2d 432 (8th Cir.1982)—§ 8.10(b) n.45

Baird v. State, 263 Ga. 868, 440 S.E.2d 196 (1994)—§ 6.9(g) n.167

Baird, United States v., 218 F.3d 221 (3d Cir.2000)—§ 21.2(d) n.247

Baird, United States v., 109 F.3d 856 (3d Cir.1997)—§§ 21.1(h) n.233; 21.2(d) n.216

Baird, United States v., 414 F.2d 700 (2d Cir.1969)—§§ 20.4(e) n.83, 86

Baity v. Ciccone, 379 F.Supp. 552 (W.D.Mo.1974)—§ 18.4(c) n.49

Baity, Commonwealth v., 428 Pa. 306, 237 A.2d 172 (1968)—§ 6.2(c) n.128

Bajakajian, United States v., 524 U.S. 321, 118 S.Ct. 2028, 141 L.Ed.2d 314 (1998)—§ 26.6(d) n.75

Bajaras-Chavez, United States v., 358 F.3d 1263 (10th Cir.2004)— § 10.1(a) n.3

Baker v. Carr, 369 U.S. 186, 82 S.Ct. 691, 7 L.Ed.2d 663 (1962)— § 9.1(a) n.1

Baker v. City of Fairbanks, 471 P.2d 386 (Alaska 1970)—§ 2.12(e) n.212

Baker, Commonwealth v., 11 S.W.3d 585 (Ky.App.2000)—§§ 15.5(b) n.79; 15.5(c) n.112; 15.6(a) n.25, 44; 15.6(d) n.127; 15.7(e) n.99

Baker, Commonwealth v., 531 Pa. 541, 614 A.2d 663 (1992)—§ 7.3(e) n.100

Baker, Commonwealth v., 532 Pa. 121, 615 A.2d 23 (1992)—§ 3.4(d) n.58

Baker, Commonwealth v., 429 Pa. 209, 239 A.2d 201 (1968)—§ 11.2(c) n.98

Baker v. Corcoran, 220 F.3d 276 (4th Cir.2000)—§ 28.8(b) n.16

Baker, People v., 133 Misc.2d 31, 505 N.Y.S.2d 995 (Sup.Ct.1986)—§§ 19.5(b) n.23, 25

Baker, People v., 268 Cal.App.2d 254, 73 Cal.Rptr. 758 (1968)—§ 11.9(a) n.40

Baker v. State, 363 Ark. 339, 214 S.W.3d 239 (2005)—§ 6.9(g) n.167

Baker, State v., 103 S.W.3d 711 (Mo.2003)—§ 3.3(e) n.182

Baker v. State, 367 Md. 648, 790 A.2d 629 (2002)—§ 22.1(h) n.159

Baker, State v., 328 Or. 355, 976 P.2d 1132 (1999)—§§ 22.1(h) n.148; 24.6(a) n.7

Baker v. State, 956 S.W.2d 19 (Tex.Cr.App.1997)—§ 9.5(b) n.43

Baker, State v., 312 N.C. 34, 320 S.E.2d 670 (1984)—§ 16.3(b) n.25

Baker v. State, 449 N.E.2d 1085 (Ind.1983)—§ 3.8(g) n.242

Baker, State v., 2 Kan.App.2d 395, 580 P.2d 90 (1978)—§ 6.9(d) n.73

Baker v. State, 358 So.2d 401 (Miss.1978)—§ 21.5(d) n.101

Baker, United States v., 438 F.3d 749 (7th Cir.2006)—§ 5.4(c) n.30

Baker, United States v., 458 F.3d 513 (6th Cir.2006)—§ 10.1(a) n.3

Baker v. United States, 891 A.2d 208 (D.C.App.2006)—§ 13.7(a) n.5

Baker, United States v., 256 F.3d 855 (9th Cir.2001)—§ 9.3(a) n.6

Baker, United States v., 262 F.3d 124 (2d Cir.2001)—§ 24.9(f) n.75

Baker, United States v., 221 F.3d 438 (3d Cir.2000)—§ 9.1(d) n.128

Baker, United States v., 98 F.3d 330 (8th Cir.1996)—§ 22.2(e) n.105

Baker, United States v., 47 F.3d 691 (5th Cir.1995)—§ 3.8(e) n.197

Baker, United States v., 10 F.3d 1374 (9th Cir.1993)—§ 11.9(c) n.115

Baker, United States v., 894 F.2d 1144 (10th Cir.1990)—§ 3.1(c) n.63

Baker, United States v., 609 F.2d 134 (5th Cir.1980)—§§ 16.4(b) n.7, 19, 25

Baker v. United States, 401 F.2d 958 (D.C.Cir.1968)—§§ 17.1(c) n.45; 17.1(d) n.58; 17.3(b) n.22

Baker Brush Co., United States v., 197 F.Supp. 922 (S.D.N.Y.1961)—§ 19.4(b) n.37

Bakker, United States v., 925 F.2d 728 (4th Cir.1991)—§ 26.4(b) n.19

Bakoian, Commonwealth v., 412 Mass. 295, 588 N.E.2d 667 (1992)—§§ 3.3(c) n.138; 10.5(e) n.44

Bala, United States v., 236 F.3d 87 (2d Cir.2000)—§ 5.2(a) n.6

Balan, People v., 107 A.D.2d 811, 484 N.Y.S.2d 648 (1985)—§ 24.11(d) n.19

Balanza, State v., 93 Haw. 279, 1 P.3d 281 (2000)—§ 13.2(c) n.77

Baldasar v. Illinois, 446 U.S. 222, 100 S.Ct. 1585, 64 L.Ed.2d 169 (1980)—§§ 11.2(a) n.20; 21.6(a) n.80

Baldayaque v. United States, 338 F.3d 145 (2d Cir.2003)—§ 28.9(b) n.50

Baldic, State v., 131 N.H. 225, 551 A.2d 977 (1988)—§§ 3.3(d) n.167, 168, 178

Baldridge, People v., 19 Ill.2d 616, 169 N.E.2d 353 (1960)—§ 21.4(g) n.235

Baldwin v. Commonwealth, 314 Ky. 369, 235 S.W.2d 771 (1951)—§ 15.1(d) n.222

Baldwin v. Dep't of Motor Vehicles, 35 Cal.App.4th 1630, 42 Cal.Rptr.2d 422 (1995)—§ 17.4(b) n.124

Baldwin v. Maggio, 704 F.2d 1325 (5th Cir.1983)—§ 11.10(a) n.4

Baldwin v. New York, 399 U.S. 66, 90 S.Ct. 1886, 26 L.Ed.2d 437 (1970)—§§ 2.1 n.59; 2.5(f) n.83; 2.6(d) n.96; 2.9(i) n.271, 286; 22.1(b) n.31

Baldwin, People v., 199 Ill.2d 1, 262 Ill.Dec. 9, 764 N.E.2d 1126 (2002)—§ 24.8(e) n.72

Baldwin v. Reese, 541 U.S. 27, 124 S.Ct. 1347, 158 L.Ed.2d 64 (2004)—§ 28.5(a) n.26

Baldwin, State v., 318 Mont. 489, 81 P.3d 488 (2003)—§ 27.6(b) n.57

Baldwin, State v., 305 A.2d 555 (Me.1973)—§§ 16.1(a) n.17, 20; 16.1(e) n.190; 16.4(d) n.120, 133

Baldwin, United States v., 414 F.3d 791 (7th Cir.2005)—§ 18.5(a) n.50

Baldwin, United States v., 60 F.3d 363 (7th Cir.1995)—§§ 6.2(c) n.94, 106

Baldwin, United States v., 644 F.2d 381 (5th Cir.1981)—§ 3.10(d) n.116

Baldyga, United States v., 233 F.3d 674 (1st Cir.2000)—§ 3.4(j) n.214

Bales v. State, 829 P.2d 998 (Okla.Crim.App.1992)—§ 16.1(h) n.289

Balfa, State v., 506 So.2d 1369 (La.App.1987)—§ 11.2(e) n.211

Balicki, Commonwealth v., 436 Mass. 1, 762 N.E.2d 290 (2002)—§ 3.4(j) n.205

Balint, United States v., 201 F.3d 928 (7th Cir.2000)—§ 22.1(b) n.47

Ball, Ex parte, 106 Kan. 536, 188 P. 424 (1920)—§ 12.4(a) n.7

Ball, State v., 824 So.2d 1089 (La.2002)—§ 22.3(a) n.5

Ball v. State, 347 Md. 156, 699 A.2d 1170 (1997)—§§ 6.2(c) n.101, 152

Ball, State v., 34 N.M. 254, 280 P. 256 (1929)—§ 16.3(d) n.76

Ball v. United States, 429 A.2d 1353 (D.C.App.1981)—§ 24.8(e) n.86

Ball v. United States, 140 U.S. 118, 11 S.Ct. 761, 35 L.Ed. 377 (1891)—§ 26.4(g) n.135

Ball v. United States, 163 U.S. 662, 16 S.Ct. 1192, 41 L.Ed. 300 (1896)—§§ 25.1(d) n.80; 25.3(b) n.10; 25.4(a) n.1

Ballard v. Bengston, 702 F.2d 656 (7th Cir.1983)—§§ 19.2(c) n.26, 31

Ballard, People v., 206 Ill.2d 151, 276 Ill.Dec. 538, 794 N.E.2d 788 (2002)—§§ 6.3(c) n.50; 6.4(e) n.72

Ballard, State v., 617 N.W.2d 837 (S.D.2000)—§ 3.8(c) n.118

Ballard, State v., 747 So.2d 1077 (La.1999)—§ 22.3(c) n.125

Ballard, State v., 114 Idaho 799, 761 P.2d 1151 (1988)—§ 21.5(a) n.35

Ballard, State v., 65 Ill.App.3d 831, 22 Ill.Dec. 410, 382 N.E.2d 800 (1978)—§§ 19.1(d) n.66; 19.3(b) n.153

Ballard v. United States, 152 F.2d 941 (9th Cir.1945)—§ 24.7(d) n.31

Ballard v. United States, 329 U.S. 187, 67 S.Ct. 261, 91 L.Ed. 181 (1946)—§§ 1.7(i) n.159; 8.4(a) n.5; 15.4(d) n.126; 15.4(i) n.211; 22.2(d) n.46, 64; 27.6(d) n.107

Ballek, United States v., 170 F.3d 871 (9th Cir.1999)—§§ 22.1(b) n.43, 49

Ballenger, State v., 123 N.C.App. 179, 472 S.E.2d 572 (1996)—§ 17.4(b) n.138

Ballenger, State v., 322 S.C. 196, 470 S.E.2d 851 (1996)—§ 25.4(b) n.12

Ballew v. Georgia, 435 U.S. 223, 98 S.Ct. 1029, 55 L.Ed.2d 234 (1978)—§§ 2.6(c) n.82, 84; 22.1(d) n.75

Ballinger, State v., 99 N.M. 707, 663 P.2d 366 (N.M.App.1983)—§ 15.7(b) n.41

Balliro, Commonwealth v., 437 Mass. 163, 769 N.E.2d 1258 (2002)—§ 21.5(a) n.58

Balliro, Commonwealth v., 370 Mass. 585, 350 N.E.2d 702 (1976)—§ 21.2(b) n.53

Ballis, United States v., 28 F.3d 1399 (5th Cir.1994)—§ 21.2(e) n.352

Ballistrea, United States v., 101 F.3d 827 (2d Cir.1996)—§ 24.3(i) n.189

Bally v. Kemna, 65 F.3d 104 (8th Cir.1995)—§§ 21.3(f) n.426; 25.1(d) n.70; 25.4(d) n.46

Balough, United States v., 820 F.2d 1485 (9th Cir.1987)—§§ 11.3(b) n.34, 36; 11.5(c) n.32, 43

Balsam, State v., 130 Ariz. 452, 636 P.2d 1234 (1981)—§ 26.9(b) n.29

Balsam, United States v., 203 F.3d 72 (1st Cir.2000)—§ 18.3(b) n.43

Balsimo, Matter of, 68 F.3d 185 (7th Cir.1995)—§ 16.3(c) n.32

Balsys, United States v., 524 U.S. 666, 118 S.Ct. 2218, 141 L.Ed.2d 575 (1998)—§§ 2.10(b) n.4, 29; 2.10(c) n.88, 89; 2.10(d) n.105; 8.10(b) n.40, 44

Balsz v. State Dep't of Public Safety, 366 N.W.2d 492 (S.D.1985)—§ 6.10(e) n.81

Balter, United States v., 91 F.3d 427 (3d Cir.1996)—§ 1.7(j) n.262

Baltimore v. 1995 Corvette, 119 Md.App. 691, 706 A.2d 43 (1998)—§ 3.1(g) n.168

Baltimore, State v., 242 Neb. 562, 495 N.W.2d 921 (1993)—§ 9.1(b) n.76

Baltimore & Ohio Railroad, United States v., 538 F.Supp. 200 (D.D.C.1982)—§ 16.3(c) n.38

Baltimore & O.R. Co. v. Kepner, 314 U.S. 44, 62 S.Ct. 6, 86 L.Ed. 28 (1941)—§ 16.1(b) n.44

Baltimore City Department of Social Services v. Bouknight, 493 U.S. 549, 110 S.Ct. 900, 107 L.Ed.2d 992 (1990)—§§ 8.10(a); 8.10(a) n.30; 8.12(g) n.67; 8.13(e) n.117

Baltimore Sun Co. v. Goetz, 886 F.2d 60 (4th Cir.1989)—§§ 23.1(d) n.197, 201, 213

Baluyut v. Superior Court, 12 Cal.4th 826, 50 Cal.Rptr.2d 101, 911 P.2d 1 (1996)—§ 13.4(d) n.157

Balzac v. Porto Rico, 258 U.S. 298, 42 S.Ct. 342, 66 L.Ed. 627 (1922)—§ 1.2(a) n.2

Balzano, United States v., 916 F.2d 1273 (7th Cir.1990)—§ 11.9(d) n.223

Bamburg, Ex parte, 890 S.W.2d 549 (Tex.App.1994)—§ 27.4(f) n.63

Banch, People v., 80 N.Y.2d 610, 593 N.Y.S.2d 491, 608 N.E.2d 1069 (1992)—§ 20.3(j) n.202

Banda, United States v., 1 F.3d 354 (5th Cir.1993)—§ 28.9(a) n.26

Bandoni v. State, 715 A.2d 580 (R.I.1998)—§ 21.3(f) n.339

Bandy v. United States, 81 S.Ct. 197, 5 L.Ed.2d 218 (1960)—§ 12.2(b) n.20

Bane, State v., 57 S.W.3d 411 (Tenn.2001)—§ 24.4(d) n.50

Baney, Commonwealth v., 860 A.2d 127 (Pa.Super.2004)—§ 11.2(c) n.86

Bang v. State, 620 So.2d 106 (Ala.Cr.App.1993)—§ 24.8(f) n.96

Bangert, State v., 131 Wis.2d 246, 389 N.W.2d 12 (1986)—§§ 1.7(i) n.202, 206

Bango, Commonwealth v., 454 Pa.Super. 339, 685 A.2d 564 (1996)—§ 24.9(c) n.19

Bangs v. State, 338 Ark. 515, 998 S.W.2d 738 (1999)—§ 6.9(e) n.88

Bank Brussels Lambert v. Chase Manhattan Bank, 174 F.R.D. 306 (S.D.N.Y.1997)—§ 8.5(h) n.269

Bankhead, Ex parte, 625 So.2d 1146 (Ala.1993)—§ 22.3(d) n.245

Bank of Nova Scotia v. United States, 487 U.S. 250, 108 S.Ct. 2369, 101 L.Ed.2d 228 (1988)—§§ 1.7(i) n.184, 190; 8.4(c) n.136; 8.10(d) n.112; 8.11(e) n.100; 15.4(i) n.210; 15.5(b) n.59, 72, 76; 15.6(a) n.45; 15.6(b) n.66; 15.6(d) n.103, 114; 15.6(e) n.131, 151, 153; 15.7(a) n.4; 15.7(d) n.87; 15.7(e) n.97, 111; 15.7(h) n.244; 27.6(b) n.29; 27.6(d) n.107

Banks v. Dretke, 540 U.S. 668, 124 S.Ct. 1256, 157 L.Ed.2d 1166 (2004)—§§ 24.3(b) n.34; 28.4(d) n.63; 28.5(a) n.34; 28.7(c) n.14; 28.10 n.5

Banks, People v., 249 Mich.App. 247, 642 N.W.2d 351 (2002)—§ 24.2(e) n.58

Banks, State v., 260 Kan. 918, 927 P.2d 456 (1996)—§ 6.2(c) n.107

Banks, State v., 88 N.C.App. 737, 364 S.E.2d 452 (1988)—§ 9.1(b) n.55

Banks, State v., 322 N.C. 753, 370 S.E.2d 398 (1988)—§ 6.7(b) n.43

Banks, State v., 157 N.J.Super. 442, 384 A.2d 1164 (1978)—§ 3.1(f) n.154

Banks, United States v., 540 U.S. 31, 124 S.Ct. 521, 157 L.Ed.2d 343 (2003)—§ 3.4(h) n.152

Banks, United States v., 282 F.3d 699 (9th Cir.2002)—§ 6.9(g) n.167

Banks, United States v., 942 F.2d 1576 (11th Cir.1991)—§ 8.11(d) n.84

Banks v. United States, 414 F.2d 1150 (D.C.Cir.1969)—§ 12.1(c) n.45

Bankston, United States v., 182 F.3d 296 (5th Cir.1999)—§§ 4.6(e) n.97; 4.6(m) n.235

Bannister v. Delo, 100 F.3d 610 (8th Cir.1996)—§ 28.4(d) n.66

Bannister, People v., 18 Ill.App.3d 154, 309 N.E.2d 279 (1974)—§ 21.2(c) n.121

Bannister v. State, 726 S.W.2d 821 (Mo.App.1987)—§ 11.2(e) n.148

Banther v. State, 823 A.2d 467 (Del.2003)—§ 21.2(h) n.423

Banuelos-Rodriguez, United States v., 215 F.3d 969 (9th Cir.2000)—§§ 13.2(a) n.3; 21.3(e) n.298

Banville, People v., 523 N.Y.S.2d 844, 134 A.D.2d 116 (1988)—§ 15.1(f) n.279

Baptiste, United States v., 264 F.3d 578 (5th Cir.2001)—§ 19.3(a) n.88

Barajas v. State, 115 Nev. 440, 991 P.2d 474 (1999)—§§ 21.3(b) n.66; 21.4(d) n.134

Barajas-Diaz, United States v., 313 F.3d 1242 (10th Cir.2002)—§ 28.9(b) n.37

Baranco, State v., 77 Haw. 351, 884 P.2d 729 (1994)—§ 27.2(c) n.65

Baranek, United States v., 903 F.2d 1068 (6th Cir.1990)—§ 4.6(b) n.29

Barba-Reyes v. United States, 387 F.2d 91 (9th Cir.1967)—§ 11.10(c) n.115

Barber v. Page, 390 U.S. 719, 88 S.Ct. 1318, 20 L.Ed.2d 255 (1968)—§§ 2.11(c) n.25; 18.4(a) n.13

Barber v. Ponte, 772 F.2d 982 (1st Cir.1985)—§§ 22.2(d) n.67; 22.2(e) n.107

Barber, State v., 118 Wash.2d 335, 823 P.2d 1068 (1992)—§ 10.6(a) n.6

Barber, United States v., 119 F.3d 276 (4th Cir.1997)—§§ 21.1(h) n.233; 21.2(d) n.216

Barber, United States v., 80 F.3d 964 (4th Cir.1996)—§ 22.3(a) n.16

Barbera, United States v., 514 F.2d 294 (2d Cir.1975)—§ 3.8(d) n.181

Barbier v. Connolly, 113 U.S. 27, 5 S.Ct. 35, 28 L.Ed. 923 (1884)—§ 1.2(b) n.5

Barbosa, United States v., 271 F.3d 438 (3d Cir.2001)—§ 5.4(c) n.40

Barbour v. Haley, 410 F.Supp.2d 1120 (M.D.Ala.2006)—§§ 11.1(b) n.79, 83; 11.2(f) n.255; 28.12(a) n.5

Barbour v. Haley, 471 F.3d 1222 (11th Cir.2006)—§ 28.12(a) n.2

Barboza, Commonwealth v., 387 Mass. 105, 438 N.E.2d 1064 (1982)—§ 22.1(c) n.60

Barboza, State v., 115 N.J. 415, 558 A.2d 1303 (1989)—§§ 21.4(f) n.172, 186, 193

Barcenas v. State, 343 Ark. 181, 33 S.W.3d 136 (2000)—§ 6.8(a) n.36

Barclay v. Florida, 463 U.S. 939, 103 S.Ct. 3418, 77 L.Ed.2d 1134 (1983)—§§ 1.8(e) n.87; 26.4(b) n.14

Barczak, State v., 562 A.2d 140 (Me.1989)—§ 6.9(b) n.35

Barden v. Northern Pacific Railroad, 154 U.S. 288, 14 S.Ct. 1030, 38 L.Ed. 992 (1894)—§ 2.9(b) n.16

Barella, People v., 20 Cal.4th 261, 84 Cal.Rptr.2d 248, 975 P.2d 37 (1999)—§ 21.4(d) n.119

Barfield, State v., 298 N.C. 306, 259 S.E.2d 510 (1979)—§ 16.3(g) n.105

Bargain City U.S.A., Inc. v. Dilworth, 29 U.S.L. Week 2002 (Pa.C.P. 1960)—§ 13.2(b) n.42

Bargen, State v., 219 Neb. 416, 363 N.W.2d 393 (1985)—§§ 19.3(a) n.13; 21.6(a) n.25

Barger, United States v., 931 F.2d 359 (6th Cir.1991)—§§ 5.2(a) n.11, 16; 5.3(a) n.5; 5.4(c) n.39

Bargeron, Commonwealth v., 402 Mass. 589, 524 N.E.2d 829 (1988)— § 18.5(a) n.6

Bargo v. State, 364 Ark. 197, 217 S.W.3d 825 (2005)—§§ 27.5(c) n.77, 85

Barham, United States v., 595 F.2d 231 (5th Cir.1979)—§§ 24.3(d) n.107, 110

Bari, United States v., 750 F.2d 1169 (2d Cir.1984)—§§ 11.2(d)   n.131; 17.2(c) n.84

Barker, In re, 741 F.2d 250 (9th Cir.1984)—§ 8.5(h) n.300

Barker v. Fox, 160 W.Va. 749, 238 S.E.2d   235   (W.Va.1977)— § 15.2(a) n.1

Barker, People v., 180 Colo. 28, 501 P.2d 1041 (1972)—§ 17.3(d) n.55

Barker, State v., 809 N.E.2d 312 (Ind.2004)—§ 26.4(i) n.179

Barker, State v., 143 Wash.2d 915, 25 P.3d 423 (2001)—§ 3.5(a) n.25

Barker, State v., 227 Neb. 842, 420 N.W.2d 695 (1988)—§ 22.4(c) n.28

Barker v. State, 259 So.2d 200 (Fla.App.1972)—§ 21.2(e) n.307

Barker, United States v., 771 F.2d 1362 (9th Cir.1985)—§ 26.3(g) n.74

Barker, United States v., 735 F.2d 1280 (11th Cir.1984)—§ 22.3(e) n.279

Barker, United States v., 514 F.2d 208 (D.C.Cir.1975)—§§ 21.5(a) n.28, 33, 37, 40, 43

Barker v. Wingo, 407 U.S. 514, 92 S.Ct. 2182, 33 L.Ed.2d 101 (1972)— §§ 1.5(f) n.257; 2.6(e) n.112; 11.6(a) n.25; 18.1(b) n.10, 12, 16; 18.2(a) n.1; 18.3(c) n.62, 64; 18.4(a) n.8; 18.5(b) n.54, 70; 18.5(c) n.73

Barkley v. State, 724 A.2d 558 (Del.1999)—§ 21.4(d) n.128

Barkman v. Sanford, 162 F.2d 592 (5th Cir.1947)—§§ 15.1(f) n.273, 275

Barletta, United States v., 644 F.2d 50 (1st Cir.1981)—§ 27.3(d) n.64

Barlow, State v., 320 A.2d 895 (Me.1974)—§ 3.10(b) n.29

Barlow, United States v., 41 F.3d 935 (5th Cir.1994)—§ 6.9(f) n.144

Barnard, United States v., 490 F.2d 907 (9th Cir.1973)—§§ 16.2(g) n.129, 132

Barnard, United States ex rel. v. Lane, 819 F.2d 798 (7th Cir.1987)— § 11.10(c) n.88

Barner, United States v., 441 F.3d 1310 (11th Cir.2006)—§ 13.7(c) n.53

Barnes v. Commonwealth, 234 Va. 130, 360 S.E.2d 196 (1987)—§ 9.1(b) n.79

Barnes, Commonwealth v., 399 Mass. 385, 504 N.E.2d 624 (1987)— § 11.5(c) n.52

Barnes v. Glen Theatre, Inc. 501 U.S. 560, 111 S.Ct. 2456, 15 L.Ed.2d 504 (1991)—§ 1.2(b) n.5

Barnes v. Johnson, 160 F.3d 218 (5th Cir.1998)—§ 6.8(d) n.84

Barnes, State v., 278 Kan. 121, 92 P.3d 578 (2004)—§ 21.6(a) n.79

Barnes, State v., 94 Ohio St.3d 21, 759 N.E.2d 1240 (2002)—§ 27.5(d) n.137

Barnes v. State, 269 Ga. 345, 496 S.E.2d 674 (1998)—§§ 22.3(c) n.125; 22.3(d) n.247

Barnes, State v., 345 N.C. 184, 481 S.E.2d 44 (1997)—§ 23.2(f) n.89

Barnes, State v., 124 Idaho 379, 859 P.2d 1387 (1993)—§ 18.5(a) n.11

Barnes v. State, 489 N.W.2d 273 (Minn.App.1992)—§ 21.4(b) n.44

Barnes v. State, 577 So.2d 840 (Miss.1991)—§§ 11.10(c) n.71, 116

Barnes v. State, 244 Ga. 302, 260 S.E.2d 40 (1979)—§ 27.5(c) n.109

Barnes v. State, 375 So.2d 40 (Fla.App.1979)—§ 24.7(e) n.57

Barnes, State v., 220 Kan. 25, 551 P.2d 815 (1976)—§ 3.3(d) n.166

Barnes, United States v., 278 F.3d 644 (6th Cir.2002)—§ 21.2(d) n.143

Barnes, United States v., 195 F.3d 1027 (8th Cir.1999)—§ 3.4(h) n.162

Barnes, United States v., 159 F.3d 4 (1st Cir.1998)—§§ 18.3(b) n.23, 25, 36, 43

Barnes, United States v., 83 F.3d 934 (7th Cir.1996)—§ 21.1(h) n.209

Barnes, United States v., 47 F.3d 963 (8th Cir.1995)—§ 4.6(i) n.160

Barnes, United States v., 604 F.2d 121 (2d Cir.1979)—§ 22.3(a) n.7

Barnes v. United States, 412 U.S. 837, 93 S.Ct. 2357, 37 L.Ed.2d 380 (1973)—§ 27.5(b) n.36

Barnes, United States v., 432 F.2d 89 (9th Cir.1970)—§ 6.7(c) n.107

Barnett, Commonwealth v., 471 Pa. 34, 369 A.2d 1180 (1977)—§§ 9.4(a) n.14, 32

Barnett, People v., 17 Cal.4th 1044, 74 Cal.Rptr.2d 121, 954 P.2d 384 (1998)—§ 12.2(c) n.43

Barnett, State v., 147 N.H. 334, 789 A.2d 629 (2001)—§ 6.8(c) n.64

Barnett v. State, 336 Ark. 165, 984 S.W.2d 444 (1999)—§ 21.6(b) n.95

Barnett, State v., 980 S.W.2d 297 (Mo.1998)—§ 13.1(a) n.26

Barnett v. State, 853 P.2d 226 (Okl.Crim.App. 1993)—§ 10.5(b) n.18

Barnett, United States v., 398 F.3d 516 (6th Cir.2005)—§ 27.5(d) n.134

Barnett, United States v., 415 F.3d 690 (7th Cir.2005)—§§ 21.2(b) n.68; 26.9(b) n.61

Barnett, United States v., 989 F.2d 546 (1st Cir.1993)—§§ 3.10(b) n.36, 37, 74

Barnette, United States v., 390 F.3d 775 (4th Cir.2004)—§ 19.3(a) n.88

Barney, People v., 363 Ill.App.3d 590, 300 Ill.Dec. 408, 844 N.E.2d 80 (2006)—§ 24.2(e) n.66

Barnhardt, United States v., 93 F.3d 706 (10th Cir.1996)—§ 21.6(a) n.25

Barnickel v. United States, 113 F.3d 704 (7th Cir.1997)—§ 28.3(a) n.16

Barns v. State, 768 So.2d 529 (Fla.App.2000)—§ 12.3(b) n.44

Barnum, People v., 29 Cal.4th 1210, 64 P.3d 788, 131 Cal.Rptr.2d 499 (2003)—§§ 11.5(e) n.88; 24.5(a) n.6

Baron, United States v., 860 F.2d 911 (9th Cir.1988)—§ 3.8(b) n.49

Barone, State v., 147 N.J. 599, 689 A.2d 132 (1997)—§ 21.2(e) n.326

Barone, United States v., 968 F.2d 1378 (1st Cir.1992)—§§ 6.9(f) n.102, 111, 113

Barone, United States v., 83 F.R.D. 565 (S.D.Fla.1979)—§ 22.3(e) n.274

Barone, United States v., 584 F.2d 118 (6th Cir.1978)—§§ 15.5(b) n.66, 68

Barr, United States v., 605 F.Supp. 114 (S.D.N.Y. 1985)—§ 4.4(c) n.13

Barragan, People v., 32 Cal.4th 236, 9 Cal.Rptr.3d 76, 83 P.3d 480 (2004)—§ 26.7(a) n.13

Barragan, People v., 266 Ill.App.3d 961, 204 Ill.Dec. 311, 641 N.E.2d 535 (1993)—§ 10.4(b) n.10

Barragan, State v., 131 N.M. 281, 34 P.3d 1157 (N.M.App.2001)—§ 24.6(b) n.23

Barragan-Espinoza, United States v., 350 F.3d 978 (9th Cir.2003)—§ 21.4(d) n.104

Barraza, People v., 23 Cal.3d 675, 153 Cal.Rptr. 459, 591 P.2d 947 (1979)—§ 5.3(b) n.28

Barraza, United States v., 318 F.Supp.2d 1031 (S.D.Cal.2004)—§ 26.10(c) n.71

Barrera, State v., 130 N.M. 227, 22 P.3d 1177 (2001)—§ 6.9(g) n.166

Barrett v. Commonwealth, 268 Va. 170, 597 S.E.2d 104 (2004)—§ 13.7(c) n.62

Barrett v. Commonwealth, 262 Va. 823, 553 S.E.2d 731 (2001)—§ 22.3(c) n.102

Barrett, State v., 401 N.W.2d 184 (Iowa 1987)—§ 8.12(g) n.67

Barrett, United States v., 469 F.3d 1079 (10th Cir.2007)—§ 26.4(i) n.179

Barrett, United States v., 173 F.3d 682 (8th Cir.1999)—§ 21.2(d) n.258

Barrett, United States v., 111 F.3d 947 (D.C.Cir.1997)—§ 22.4(c) n.30

Barrett, United States v., 982 F.2d 193 (6th Cir.1992)—§§ 21.3(d) n.229, 238

Barrett, United States v., 870 F.2d 953 (3d Cir.1989)—§ 24.10(a) n.8

Barrett, United States v., 505 F.2d 1091 (7th Cir.1974)—§ 17.1(a) n.13

Barrilleaux, State v., 620 So.2d 1317 (La.1993)—§ 3.4(c) n.37

Barrington, United States v., 806 F.2d 529 (5th Cir.1986)—§ 10.6(d) n.48

Barrios-Gutierrez, United States v., 255 F.3d 1024 (9th Cir.2001)—§ 21.4(d) n.111

Barrios-Moriera, United States v., 872 F.2d 12 (2d Cir.1989)—§ 3.2(c) n.107

Barron v. Baltimore, 32 U.S. (7 Pet.) 243, 8 L.Ed. 672 (1833)—§§ 2.2 n.1; 2.3(a) n.42; 2.3(b) n.83

Barron, United States v., 172 F.3d 1153 (9th Cir.1999)—§§ 21.2(e) n.309; 21.5(e) n.151

Barron, United States v., 127 F.3d 890 (9th Cir.1997)—§§ 21.5(e) n.144, 146

Barrow v. State, 207 S.W.3d 377 (Tex.Cr.App.2006)—§ 26.4(i) n.189

Barrow, United States v., 363 F.2d 62 (3d Cir.1966)—§ 1.2(c) n.114

Barrows v. Jackson, 346 U.S. 249, 73 S.Ct. 1031, 97 L.Ed. 1586 (1953)—§ 9.1(a) n.2

Barrows, State v., 158 Vt. 445, 614 A.2d 377 (Vt.1992)—§ 1.7(h) n.134

Barry v. Bergen County Probation Dep't, 128 F.3d 152 (3d Cir.1997)—§ 28.3(a) n.9

Barry v. Brower, 864 F.2d 294 (3d Cir.1988)—§§ 11.2(g) n.273; 28.3(a) n.9

Barry v. Fowler, 902 F.2d 770 (9th Cir.1990)—§ 3.5(b) n.97

Barry v. Truax, 13 N.D. 131, 99 N.W. 769 (1904)—§§ 16.3(d) n.55, 56

Barry, United States v., 71 F.3d 1269 (7th Cir.1995)—§ 22.2(d) n.70

Barry, United States v., 938 F.2d 1327 (D.C.Cir.1991)—§ 26.5(c) n.51

Barry v. United States, 740 F.Supp. 888 (D.D.C.1990)—§ 8.5(i) n.324

Barry v. United States, 865 F.2d 1317 (D.C.Cir.1989)—§§ 8.5(i) n.304, 308, 309, 319, 320

Barsanti, United States v., 943 F.2d 428 (4th Cir.1991)—§ 16.2(e) n.76

Barte, United States v., 868 F.2d 773 (5th Cir.1989)—§ 9.5(b) n.42

Bartel, United States v., 19 F.3d 1105 (6th Cir.1994)—§§ 10.3(c) n.57; 15.7(d) n.66, 68

Barter, State v., 310 Ark. 94, 833 S.W.2d 372 (1992)—§ 3.8(e) n.194

Barth v. Commonwealth, 80 S.W.3d 390 (Ky.2001)—§§ 17.2(b) n.38, 62, 71

Barth, State v., 637 N.W.2d 369 (N.D.2001)—§ 22.3(d) n.182

Bartholomew, State v., 101 Or.App. 243, 789 P.2d 20 (1990)—§ 26.1(d) n.89

Bartkus v. Illinois, 359 U.S. 121, 79 S.Ct. 676, 3 L.Ed.2d 684 (1959)—§§ 2.3(a) n.58; 2.9(d) n.61; 25.5(b) n.19

Bartlett, Commonwealth v., 446 Pa. 392, 288 A.2d 796 (1972)—§ 6.8(b) n.39

Bartlett v. Hamwi, 626 So.2d 1040 (Fla.App.1993)—§§ 3.5(d) n.165 to 167, 175

Bartnicki v. Vopper, 532 U.S. 514, 121 S.Ct. 1753, 149 L.Ed.2d 787 (2001)—§ 4.6(n) n.246

Bartolomeo, People v., 53 N.Y.2d 225, 440 N.Y.S.2d 894, 423 N.E.2d 371 (1981)—§ 3.3(c) n.110

Barton, People v., 12 Cal.4th 186, 47 Cal.Rptr.2d 569, 906 P.2d 531 (1995)—§ 24.8(f) n.120

Barton, People v., 190 Ill.App.3d 701, 138 Ill.Dec. 36, 546 N.E.2d 1091 (1989)—§§ 15.6(a) n.18, 44; 15.7(e) n.127

Barton, State v., 108 Ohio St. 2d 402, 844 N.E.2d 307 (2006)—§ 19.2(e) n.55

Barton, State v., 625 N.W.2d 275 (S.D.2001)—§ 22.1(b) n.49

Barton, State v., 998 S.W.2d 19 (Mo.1999)—§§ 23.2(d) n.70; 23.2(f) n.92

Barton, State v., 936 S.W.2d 781 (Mo.1996)—§ 24.7(b) n.19

Barton, State v., 219 Conn. 529, 594 A.2d 917 (1991)—§ 2.12(d) n.195

Barton, State v., 93 Wash.2d 301, 609 P.2d 1353 (1980)—§ 21.4(d) n.112

Bartosh, State v., 336 Mont. 212, 154 P.3d 58 (2007)—§§ 21.2(d) n.167, 174

Bartram v. State, 280 Md. 616, 374 A.2d 1144 (1977)—§§ 15.2(d) n.108; 15.2(e) n.142

Bary v. United States, 248 F.2d 201 (10th Cir.1957)—§ 16.2(g) n.129

Basani, In re, 149 N.H. 259, 817 A.2d 957 (2003)—§ 13.4(c) n.80

Bascomb, United States v., 451 F.3d 1292 (11th Cir.2006)—§ 26.3(g) n.95

Basden v. State, 897 S.W.2d 319 (Tex.Cr.App.1993)—§ 26.3(f) n.64

Basham v. Commonwealth, 675 S.W.2d 376 (Ky.1984)—§ 2.12(c) n.175

Bashorun, United States v., 225 F.3d 9 (1st Cir.2000)—§§ 10.1(b) n.21; 21.6(b) n.93

Basile, State v., 942 S.W.2d 342 (Mo.1997)—§ 24.2(a) n.13

Basile, United States v., 109 F.3d 1304 (8th Cir.1997)—§§ 25.5(a) n.10, 11

Basilicato, People v., 64 N.Y.2d 103, 485 N.Y.S.2d 7, 474 N.E.2d 215 (1984)—§ 3.4(j) n.203

Basoff v. State, 208 Md. 643, 119 A.2d 917 (1956)—§ 7.1(c) n.25

Bass, United States v., 460 F.3d 830 (6th Cir.2006)—§§ 18.2(c) n.44; 18.3(b) n.26

Bass, United States v., 315 F.3d 561 (6th Cir.2002)—§ 3.6(c) n.69

Bass, United States v., 266 F.3d 532 (6th Cir.2001)—§ 13.4(b) n.68

Bass, United States v., 477 F.2d 723 (9th Cir.1973)—§ 11.2(e) n.227

Bass, United States v., 404 U.S. 336, 92 S.Ct. 515, 30 L.Ed.2d 488 (1971)—§§ 1.2(c) n.135, 139, 141, 181

Bassett, State v., 128 Wash.2d 612, 911 P.2d 385 (1996)—§§ 23.1(b) n.69, 71 to 73, 77, 80

Bassford, United States v., 812 F.2d 16 (1st Cir.1987)—§ 13.3(c) n.43

Bassin, People ex rel. v. Isreal, 31 Ill.App.3d 744, 335 N.E.2d 53 (1975)—§ 21.4(f) n.198

Bast v. United States, 542 F.2d 893 (4th Cir.1976)—§ 8.5(d) n.128

Bastarache, Commonwealth v., 382 Mass. 86, 414 N.E.2d 984 (1980)—§§ 15.4(d) n.98, 106, 125; 22.2(d) n.67

Baston, State v., 261 Kan. 100, 928 P.2d 79 (1996)—§ 6.2(c) n.103

Basurto, United States v., 497 F.2d 781 (9th Cir.1974)—§§ 15.5(b) n.48, 54; 15.7(e) n.93, 104, 116

Batashure, People v., 75 N.Y.2d 306, 552 N.Y.S.2d 896, 552 N.E.2d 144 (1990)—§ 15.7(g) n.221

Batchelder, United States v., 442 U.S. 114, 99 S.Ct. 2198, 60 L.Ed.2d 755 (1979)—§§ 13.4(a) n.8; 13.7(a) n.1; 13.7(b) n.30

Batchelder, United States v., 581 F.2d 626 (7th Cir.1978)—§ 13.7(a) n.4

Bates v. Ogata, 52 Haw. 573, 482 P.2d 153 (1971)—§§ 12.1(d) n.52; 12.4(a) n.37, 38

Bates, State v., 203 Or.App. 245, 125 P.3d 42 (2005)—§ 24.2(e) n.68

Bates, State v., 689 N.W.2d 479 (Iowa App.2004)—§ 18.4(c) n.39

Bates, State v., 804 S.W.2d 868 (Tenn.1991)—§ 23.2(a) n.47

Bates v. State, 64 Md.App. 279, 494 A.2d 976 (1985)—§ 9.1(d) n.128

Bates, United States v., 627 F.2d 349 (D.C.Cir.1980)—§§ 8.5(e) n.170; 8.5(h) n.303

Bath v. State, 951 S.W.2d 11 (Tex.App.1997)—§§ 2.6(b) n.69; 22.2(e) n.110

Batie v. State, 545 P.2d 797 (Okla.Crim.App.1976)—§§ 14.3(d) n.100; 14.4(b) n.36; 14.4(e) n.103

Batino, People v., 48 A.D.2d 619, 367 N.Y.S.2d 784 (1975)—§ 3.8(e) n.186

Batista, People v., 164 Misc.2d 632, 625 N.Y.S.2d 1008 (Sup.Ct.1995)—§ 15.7(f) n.180

Batiste, State v., 939 So.2d 1245 (La.2006)—§ 13.3(c) n.37

Batiste v. State, 888 S.W.2d 9 (Tex.Crim.App.1994)—§ 11.10(d) n.171

Batiste v. State, 785 S.W.2d 432 (Tex.App.1990)—§ 19.5(b) n.21

Batiste, United States v., 868 F.2d 1089 (9th Cir.1989)—§ 10.5(f) n.69

Batson v. Kentucky, 476 U.S. 79, 106 S.Ct. 1712, 90 L.Ed.2d 69 (1986)—§§ 2.8(b) n.53; 15.4(c) n.87; 15.4(e) n.128; 16.3(g) n.126; 22.3(d) n.187; 27.6(d) n.105; 28.6(b) n.4

Batson, State v., 73 Haw. 236, 831 P.2d 924 (1992)—§ 19.3(b) n.178

Batson, State v., 35 Or.App. 175, 580 P.2d 1066 (1978)—§§ 19.3(a) n.70; 19.3(b) n.147; 19.3(e) n.211, 254

Batson, State v., 339 Mo. 298, 96 S.W.2d 384 (1936)—§ 15.1(f) n.323

Battaglia, Matter of, 653 F.2d 419 (9th Cir.1981)—§ 8.3(b) n.13

Battenfield v. State, 953 P.2d 1123 (Okla.Crim.App.1998)—§ 22.3(d) n.216

Battie v. Estelle, 655 F.2d 692 (5th Cir.1981)—§ 20.4(e) n.86

Battista, People ex rel. v. Christian, 249 N.Y. 314, 164 N.E. 111 (1928)—§§ 15.1(f) n.276 to 278

Battle, Ex parte, 817 S.W.2d 81 (Tex.Cr.App.1991)—§ 21.3(b) n.71

Battle, United States v., 836 F.2d 1084 (8th Cir.1987)—§§ 22.3(d) n.212, 251

Battle, United States v., 510 F.2d 776 (D.C.Cir.1975)—§ 3.5(e) n.181

Battle, United States v., 467 F.2d 569 (5th Cir.1972)—§§ 21.2(d) n.147; 21.2(g) n.396

Batts, People v., 30 Cal.4th 660, 134 Cal.Rptr.2d 67, 68 P.3d 357 (2003)—§ 25.2(b) n.15

Batungbacal, State v., 81 Hawai'i 123, 913 P.2d 49 (1996)—§ 18.4(c) n.60

Baty, United States v., 980 F.2d 977 (5th Cir.1992)—§ 21.2(b) n.61

Batzer, State v., 448 N.W.2d 565 (Minn.App.1989)—§ 1.7(f) n.101

Bauberger, State v., 626 S.E.2d 700 (N.C.App.2006)—§ 24.9(f) n.68

Bauder v. State, 921 S.W.2d 696 (Tex.Cr.App.1996)—§ 25.2(b) n.15

Bauer, United States v., 132 F.3d 504 (9th Cir.1997)—§ 27.6(b) n.14

Bauer, United States v., 956 F.2d 693 (7th Cir.1992)—§§ 11.3(c) n.54, 56; 11.5(c) n.31

Baugh, People v., 19 Ill.App.3d 448, 311 N.E.2d 607 (1974)—§ 6.10(b) n.29

Baugh v. State, 801 N.E.2d 629 (Ind.2004)—§ 16.1(e) n.194

Baugus, United States v., 761 F.2d 506 (8th Cir.1985)—§ 17.4(a) n.38

Baum, United States v., 482 F.2d 1325 (2d Cir.1973)—§ 20.6(b) n.54

Baumann, State v., 125 Ariz. 404, 610 P.2d 38 (1980)—§ 15.6(d) n.105

Baumann v. United States, 692 F.2d 565 (9th Cir.1982)—§§ 6.4(e) n.107; 6.10(c) n.48; 6.10(e) n.67; 26.5(a) n.11

Baumgarten, United States v., 517 F.2d 1020 (8th Cir.1975)—§ 18.2(c) n.46

Baumruk, State v., 85 S.W.3d 644 (Mo.2002)—§ 23.2(a) n.32

Bautista, United States v., 145 F.3d 1140 (10th Cir.1998)—§§ 6.6(f) n.114; 6.9(f) n.144

Bautista, United States v., 23 F.3d 726 (2d Cir.1994)—§ 7.4(b) n.23

Bautista-Avila, United States v., 6 F.3d 1360 (9th Cir.1993)—§§ 6.2(c) n.100; 6.9(b) n.32

Baxter v. Palmigiano, 425 U.S. 308, 96 S.Ct. 1551, 47 L.Ed.2d 810 (1976)—§§ 1.5(b) n.76; 2.10(b) n.44, 47; 2.10(d) n.124, 131; 2.12(a) n.22; 6.10(e) n.73

Baxter, State v., 19 Conn.App. 304, 563 A.2d 721 (1989)—§§ 26.10(b) n.36, 39

Baxter v. State, 262 Ark. 303, 556 S.W.2d 428 (1977)—§ 3.4(l) n.242

Baxter v. United States, 640 A.2d 714 (D.C.App.1994)—§ 22.3(d) n.200

Baxter v. United States, 966 F.2d 387 (8th Cir.1992)—§§ 18.4(c) n.40, 73

Baxter, United States v., 889 F.2d 731 (6th Cir.1989)—§ 3.1(c) n.77

Baxter v. United States, 483 A.2d 1170 (D.C.App.1984)—§§ 13.6(d) n.53, 56

Bay, United States v., 820 F.2d 1511 (9th Cir.1987)—§ 24.8(a) n.23

Bay County Prosecutor v. Bay County District Judge, 109 Mich.App. 476, 311 N.W.2d 399 (1981)—§ 20.3(i) n.176

Bayer, United States v., 331 U.S. 532, 67 S.Ct. 1394, 91 L.Ed. 1654 (1947)—§ 9.5(c) n.62

Bayko, United States v., 774 F.2d 516 (1st Cir.1985)—§ 12.4(d) n.69

Bayless v. State, 326 Ark. 869, 935 S.W.2d 534 (1996)—§ 24.4(d) n.42

Bayless, United States v., 201 F.3d 116 (2d Cir.2000)—§ 22.4(c) n.29

Baylin, United States v., 696 F.2d 1030 (3d Cir.1982)—§ 21.2(d) n.183

Baylor, United States v., 97 F.3d 542 (D.C.Cir.1996)—§ 26.4(b) n.8

Baylson v. Disciplinary Board of the Supreme Court of Pennsylvania, 975 F.2d 102 (3d Cir.1992)—§§ 1.7(i) n.197; 8.8(d) n.102

Baynes, State v., 287 N.J.Super. 467, 671 A.2d 211 (1995)—§ 13.6(c) n.43

Baynor v. State, 355 Md. 726, 736 A.2d 325 (1999)—§ 6.2(d) n.202

Bays, State v., 87 Ohio St.3d 15, 716 N.E.2d 1126 (1999)—§§ 6.2(c) n.132; 22.1(h) n.132, 133

Bayside, Village of v. Bruner, 33 Wis.2d 533, 148 N.W.2d 5 (1967)— § 1.8(d) n.58

Baysinger, State v., 470 N.W.2d 840 (S.D.1991)—§ 3.5(a) n.36

Baze v. Commonwealth, 23 S.W.3d 619 (Ky.2000)—§§ 11.10(c) n.68; 11.10(d) n.171

Baze v. Parker, 371 F.3d 310 (6th Cir.2004)—§ 22.3(c) n.125

Bazemore, Commonwealth v., 531 Pa. 582, 614 A.2d 684 (1992)— §§ 14.1(d) n.64, 68

Bazemore v. State, 273 Ga. 160, 535 S.E.2d 760 (2000)—§ 21.5(c) n.91

Bazinet, State v., 372 A.2d 1036 (Me.1977)—§ 23.2(h) n.126

Bazzano, United States v., 712 F.2d 826 (3d Cir.1983)—§ 3.1(f) n.156

Bazzano, United States v., 570 F.2d 1120 (3d Cir.1977)—§ 8.5(e) n.187

BCCI Holdings (Luxembourg), United States v., 69 F.Supp.2d 36 (D.D.C.1999)—§ 26.6(d) n.48

BCCI Holdings (Luxembourg), S.A., United States v., 961 F.Supp. 287 (D.D.C.1997)—§ 26.6(d) n.72

Beachem, People v., 374 Ill.App.3d 145, 871 N.E.2d 805 (Ill.App.2007)— § 26.1(e) n.124

Beachman, People v., 98 Mich.App. 544, 296 N.W.2d 305 (1980)— § 3.2(c) n.107

Beachner Const. Co., United States v., 538 F.Supp. 718 (D.Kan.1982)— § 8.11(c) n.47

Beacon Journal Publishing Company, State ex rel. v. Bond, 98 Ohio St.3d 146, 781 N.E.2d 180 (2002)— §§ 23.1(d) n.192, 193

Beagen v. State, 705 A.2d 173 (R.I.1998)—§ 21.4(d) n.132

Beal, People v., 104 Mich.App. 159, 304 N.W.2d 513 (1981)—§ 26.5(c) n.52

Beal, State v., 614 S.W.2d 77 (Tenn.Cr.App.1981)—§ 15.4(e) n.128

Beal, United States v., 961 F.2d 1512 (10th Cir.1992)—§ 5.2(a) n.17

Beale, United States v., 921 F.2d 1412 (11th Cir.1991)—§§ 6.9(c) n.58, 59

Beam v. Paskett, 3 F.3d 1301 (9th Cir.1993)—§ 26.4(b) n.19

Beam, State v., 181 N.C. 597, 107 S.E. 429 (1921)—§ 16.4(c) n.52

Beamon, People v., 83 Mich.App. 121, 268 N.W.2d 310 (1978)—§ 18.4(c) n.51

Bean v. Calderon, 163 F.3d 1073 (9th Cir.1998)—§§ 11.10(c) n.74, 130; 17.1(d) n.52, 55, 57

Bean, People v., 46 Cal.3d 919, 251 Cal.Rptr. 467, 760 P.2d 996 (1988)—§ 17.1(d) n.52

Bean, People v., 109 Ill.2d 80, 92 Ill.Dec. 538, 485 N.E.2d 349 (1985)—§ 17.2(d) n.108

Bean, State v., 171 Vt. 290, 762 A.2d 1259 (Vt.2000)—§§ 11.5(d) n.72; 11.6(a) n.26

Bean, United States v., 564 F.2d 700 (5th Cir.1977)—§ 19.3(b) n.178

Beans v. Black, 757 F.2d 933 (8th Cir.1985)—§§ 21.3(b) n.53, 54, 112

Beard v. Banks, 542 U.S. 406, 124 S.Ct. 2504, 159 L.Ed.2d 494 (2004)—§§ 28.6(d) n.34; 28.6(e) n.48, 56

Beard, State v., 194 W.Va. 740, 461 S.E.2d 486 (1995)—§ 8.11(c) n.66

Beard, United States v., 41 F.3d 1486 (11th Cir.1995)—§ 18.4(b) n.24

Beard v. United States, 535 A.2d 1373 (D.C.App.1988)—§ 24.2(b) n.28

Bearden v. Georgia, 461 U.S. 660, 103 S.Ct. 2064, 76 L.Ed.2d 221 (1983)—§§ 12.2(b) n.27; 26.1(e) n.122; 26.1(f) n.142; 26.9(b) n.33; 26.10(a) n.3

Bearden, United States v., 265 F.3d 732 (8th Cir.2001)—§ 17.4(a) n.36

Bearden, United States v., 274 F.3d 1031 (6th Cir.2001)—§§ 21.4(a) n.31, 33, 37

Bearden, United States v., 659 F.2d 590 (5th Cir.1981)—§ 15.4(f) n.145

Bearden, United States v., 423 F.2d 805 (5th Cir.1970)—§ 19.4(b) n.14

Beardslee v. United States, 541 F.2d 705 (8th Cir.1976)—§§ 15.1(f) n.315, 321

Beardslee v. Woodford, 327 F.3d 799 (9th Cir.2003)—§ 9.3(c) n.27

Bearss, People v., 463 Mich. 623, 625 N.W.2d 10 (2001)—§ 25.4(b) n.22

Bear Sterns & Co. v. Wyler, 182 F.Supp.2d 679 (N.D.Ill.2002)—§ 8.13(b) n.62

Beasley, United States v., 102 F.3d 1440 (8th Cir.1996)—§ 13.2(g) n.126

Beasley v. United States, 512 A.2d 1007 (D.C.App.1986)—§ 6.2(c) n.107

Beasley v. United States, 491 F.2d 687 (6th Cir.1974)—§ 11.10(b) n.30

Beatrice Foods Co. v. United States, 312 F.2d 29 (8th Cir.1963)—§§ 15.2(i) n.219, 223, 227, 228

Beattie, People v., 80 N.Y.2d 840, 587 N.Y.S.2d 585, 600 N.E.2d 216 (1992)—§ 21.6(a) n.25

Beattie, United States v., 541 F.2d 329 (2d Cir.1976)—§ 8.13(a) n.17

Beatty v. State, 56 Md.App. 627, 468 A.2d 663 (1983)—§ 17.4(b) n.109

Beaty, People v., 351 Ill.App.3d 717, 286 Ill.Dec. 602, 814 N.E.2d 590 (2004)—§ 12.4(e) n.93

Beaty v. Stewart, 303 F.3d 975 (9th Cir.2002)—§§ 6.2(c) n.140; 6.4(g) n.154; 6.7(d) n.145

Beaty, United States v., 147 F.3d 522 (6th Cir.1998)—§ 17.4(b) n.138

Beauchesne, State v., 151 N.H. 803, 868 A.2d 972 (2005)—§§ 9.4(f) n.119; 10.2(a) n.2

Beauharnais v. Illinois, 343 U.S. 250, 72 S.Ct. 725, 96 L.Ed. 919 (1952)—§§ 2.3(a) n.58; 2.5(c) n.25

Beaulieu v. United States, 930 F.2d 805 (10th Cir.1991)—§ 11.7(e) n.82

Beaver v. State, 933 P.2d 1178 (Alaska App.1997)—§ 26.5(a) n.11

Beavers v. Haubert, 198 U.S. 77, 25 S.Ct. 573, 49 L.Ed. 950 (1905)— § 18.1(a) n.6

Beavers, People v., 393 Mich. 554, 227 N.W.2d 511 (1975)—§ 2.12(d) n.192

Beavers v. State, 998 P.2d 1040 (Alaska 2000)—§ 6.2(c) n.113

Beavers, State v., 364 So.2d 1004 (La.1978)—§ 24.10(a) n.8

Beazley v. Johnson, 242 F.3d 248 (5th Cir.2001)—§ 1.7(c) n.16

Becerra, State v., 66 Wash.App. 202, 831 P.2d 781 (1992)—§ 25.4(c) n.37

Becich, State v., 13 Or.App. 415, 509 P.2d 1232 (1973)—§ 3.1(h) n.192

Beck v. Alabama, 447 U.S. 625, 100 S.Ct. 2382, 65 L.Ed.2d 392 (1980)—§§ 1.8(e) n.95; 2.7(a) n.59; 2.7(b) n.90; 17.4(b) n.76; 18.5(a) n.43; 24.8(f) n.87, 89; 26.1(b) n.25

Beck v. Bowersox, 362 F.3d 1095 (8th Cir.2004)—§§ 6.4(e) n.69; 6.9(c) n.63

Beck v. Commonwealth, 253 Va. 373, 484 S.E.2d 898 (1997)—§ 26.5(d) n.65

Beck v. Ohio, 379 U.S. 89, 85 S.Ct. 223, 13 L.Ed.2d 142 (1964)—§§ 3.2(a) n.3; 3.3(a) n.13; 3.3(b) n.42, 44; 10.3(b) n.50

Beck, State v., 687 S.W.2d 155 (Mo.1985)—§ 6.4(e) n.69

Beck v. Texas Bd. Of Dental Examiners, 204 F.3d 629 (5th Cir.2000)— § 3.9(c) n.57

Beck, United States v., 418 F.3d 1008 (9th Cir.2005)—§ 7.4(e) n.86

Beck v. Washington, 369 U.S. 541, 82 S.Ct. 955, 8 L.Ed.2d 98 (1962)— §§ 2.6(b) n.33; 14.2(a) n.3; 15.1(c) n.141; 15.4(g) n.183

Becker, United States v., 36 F.3d 708 (7th Cir.1994)—§ 26.3(f) n.59

Becker, United States v., 995 F.2d 779 (7th Cir.1993)—§ 3.5(c) n.105

Becker, United States v., 929 F.2d 442 (9th Cir.1991)—§ 3.4(j) n.201

Becker, United States v., 585 F.2d 703 (4th Cir.1978)—§ 17.2(c) n.84

Beckford, United States v., 962 F.Supp. 780 (E.D.Va.1997)—§§ 20.3(m) n.255; 24.3(b) n.54, 66

Beckford, United States v., 966 F.Supp. 1415 (E.D.Va.1997)—§ 24.8(f) n.91

Beckham, United States v., 789 F.2d 401 (6th Cir.1986)—§ 23.1(d) n.180

Beckham v. Wainwright, 639 F.2d 262 (5th Cir.1981)—§ 21.3(b) n.58

Beckley, State v., 157 Vt. 446, 600 A.2d 294 (1991)—§§ 6.2(c) n.103, 105, 107

Beckmeyer, Village of v. Wheelan, 212 Ill.App.3d 287, 155 Ill.Dec. 514, 569 N.E.2d 1125 (1991)—§ 1.8(d) n.79

Beckstead, State v., _____ Utah _____, 140 P.3d 1288 (2006)— § 21.4(b) n.61

Beckwith v. United States, 425 U.S. 341, 96 S.Ct. 1612, 48 L.Ed.2d 1 (1976)—§§ 6.6(a) n.8; 6.6(e) n.60

Becnel, State v., 674 So.2d 959 (La.1996)—§ 26.9(c) n.79

Beddow, United States v., 957 F.2d 1330 (6th Cir.1992)—§ 16.2(e) n.84

Bedell v. State, 257 Ark. 895, 521 S.W.2d 200 (1975)—§ 3.2(d) n.146

Beecher v. Alabama, 389 U.S. 35, 88 S.Ct. 189, 19 L.Ed.2d 35 (1967)— §§ 6.2(c) n.69, 166; 9.5(c) n.64

Beech-Nut Nutrition Corp., United States v., 871 F.2d 1181 (2d Cir.1989)—§ 16.2(e) n.64

Beede, United States v., 974 F.2d 948 (8th Cir.1992)—§ 18.3(b) n.5

Beeler, United States v., 587 F.2d 340 (6th Cir.1978)—§§ 19.6(c) n.34, 38

Beem v. McKune, 278 F.3d 1108 (10th Cir.2002)—§ 27.6(d) n.127

Beer, State v., 177 Vt. 245, 864 A.2d 643 (2004)—§ 6.7(b) n.30

Beerbower, State v., 262 Kan. 248, 936 P.2d 248 (1997)—§ 25.1(d) n.51

Beery, United States v., 678 F.2d 856 (10th Cir.1982)—§ 15.7(d) n.78

Beeson, State v., 569 N.W.2d 107 (Iowa 1997)—§ 17.4(b) n.133

Beets v. Scott, 65 F.3d 1258 (5th Cir.1995)—§§ 11.9(a) n.15; 11.9(d) n.164, 213

Begins, State v., 147 Vt. 295, 514 A.2d 719 (1986)—§ 26.10(c) n.79

Behety, United States v., 32 F.3d 503 (11th Cir.1994)—§§ 3.1(i) n.229, 232

Behnke, State v., 203 Wis.2d 43, 553 N.W.2d 265 (1996)—§ 24.3(f) n.154

Bein, United States v., 214 F.3d 408 (3d Cir.2000)—§ 10.1(c) n.44

Bekowies, United States v., 432 F.2d 8 (9th Cir.1970)—§ 6.6(c) n.27

Beland, Commonwealth v., 436 Mass. 273, 764 N.E.2d 324 (2002)—§§ 6.4(e) n.87; 6.9(c) n.66

Beland, State v., 138 N.H. 735, 645 A.2d 79 (1994)—§ 6.2(c) n.140

Belanger, People v., 73 Mich.App. 438, 252 N.W.2d 472 (1977)—§ 21.4(a) n.33

Belanger, United States v., 936 F.2d 916 (7th Cir.1991)—§§ 11.5(c) n.32, 40

Belanus, State v., 144 Vt. 166, 475 A.2d 227 (1984)—§ 21.4(g) n.233

Belcher, State v., 51 Conn.App. 117, 721 A.2d 899 (1998)—§ 27.5(c) n.103

Belcher, State v., 317 So.2d 842 (Fla.App.1975)—§ 3.2(c) n.130

Belcher, United States v., 762 F.Supp. 666 (W.D.Va.1991)—§ 24.3(e) n.132

Belfry, State v., 431 N.W.2d 572 (Minn.App.1988)—§ 26.9(b) n.35

Belgard, State v., 830 P.2d 264 (Utah 1992)—§ 10.2(a) n.7

Belgarde, State v., 289 Mont. 287, 962 P.2d 571 (1998)—§ 6.7(d) n.145

Belge, People v., 83 Misc.2d 186, 372 N.Y.S.2d 798 (County Ct.1975)—§ 20.4(b) n.29

Belisle v. State, _____ So.2d. _____, 2007 WL 625025 (Ala.Cr.App.2007)—§ 27.5(d) n.137

Belk, United States v., 346 F.3d 305 (2d Cir.2003)—§ 26.2(b) n.21

Belken, State v., 633 N.W.2d 786 (Iowa 2001)—§§ 20.2(e) n.108; 20.6(b) n.21, 27

Bell v. Commonwealth, 264 Va. 172, 563 S.E.2d 695 (2002)—§ 9.1(d) n.133

Bell v. Cone, 535 U.S. 685, 122 S.Ct. 1843, 152 L.Ed.2d 914 (2002)—§§ 11.7(d) n.49; 11.10(c) n.138; 11.10(d) n.196; 28.6(f) n.69

Bell v. Duckworth, 861 F.2d 169 (7th Cir.1988)—§ 24.4(d) n.30

Bell v. Hill, 190 F.3d 1089 (9th Cir.1999)—§ 11.2(b) n.52

Bell v. Jarvis, 236 F.3d 149 (4th Cir.2000)—§ 24.1(b) n.24

Bell v. Ozmint, 332 F.3d 229 (4th Cir.2003)—§ 24.9(g) n.125

Bell, People v., 473 Mich. 275, 702 N.W.2d 128 (Mich.2005)—§§ 22.3(d) n.219; 27.6(b) n.21

Bell, People v., 49 Cal.3d 502, 262 Cal.Rptr. 1, 778 P.2d 129 (1989)—§ 22.2(d) n.76

Bell, People v., 152 Ill.App.3d 1007, 106 Ill.Dec. 59, 505 N.E.2d 365 (1987)—§ 11.10(c) n.98

Bell, People v., 74 Mich.App. 270, 253 N.W.2d 726 (1977)—§§ 20.2(a) n.2, 7; 24.3(g) n.161

Bell, People v., 53 Ill.2d 122, 290 N.E.2d 214 (1972)—§ 3.4(c) n.46

Bell v. Quintero, 535 U.S. 1109, 122 S.Ct. 2324, 153 L.Ed.2d 152 (2002)—§ 11.10(d) n.171

Bell, State v., 283 Conn. 748, 931 A.2d 198 (2007)—§ 26.4(i) n.197

Bell v. State, 280 Ga. 562, 629 S.E.2d 213 (2006)—§§ 6.6(d) n.57; 6.9(c) n.63

Bell, State v., 211 W.Va. 308, 565 S.E.2d 430 (2002)—§ 24.8(e) n.50

Bell, State v., 268 Kan. 764, 1 P.3d 325 (2000)—§§ 14.3(a) n.10; 14.4(d) n.98

Bell v. State, 751 So.2d 1035 (Miss.1999)—§ 21.2(e) n.321

Bell v. State, 725 So.2d 836 (Miss.1998)—§ 22.3(c) n.133

Bell, State v., 259 Kan. 131, 910 P.2d 205 (1996)—§§ 14.3(a) n.4, 7

Bell v. State, 678 So.2d 994 (Miss.1996)—§ 13.5(b) n.35

Bell, State v., 305 S.C. 11, 406 S.E.2d 165 (1991)—§§ 6.3(c) n.50; 22.3(c) n.151; 22.3(d) n.202

Bell, State v., 832 S.W.2d 583 (Tenn.Crim.App.1991)—§ 10.1(b) n.17

Bell, State v., 745 S.W.2d 858 (Tenn.1988)—§§ 6.9(e) n.86; 22.2(d) n.86

Bell, State v., 770 P.2d 100 (Utah 1988)—§ 24.10(a) n.16

Bell, State v., 446 So.2d 1191 (La.1984)—§ 9.6(a) n.51

Bell v. State, 443 So.2d 16 (Miss.1983)—§ 27.5(d) n.114

Bell, State v., 90 N.J. 163, 447 A.2d 525 (1982)—§§ 11.9(a) n.30, 31

Bell, State v., 60 Haw. 241, 589 P.2d 517 (1978)—§§ 15.2(b) n.50, 57; 15.7(f) n.135, 145, 152, 159, 168, 169, 180; 15.7(g) n.215, 216

Bell, State v., 315 So.2d 307 (La.1975)—§ 16.3(b) n.11

Bell, United States v., 740 A.2d 958 (D.C.App.1999)—§§ 6.3(a) n.15; 6.8(b) n.50

Bell, United States v., 113 F.3d 1345 (3d Cir.1997)—§ 13.4(c) n.98

Bell, United States v., 54 F.3d 502 (8th Cir.1995)—§ 3.1(e) n.129

Bell, United States v., 966 F.2d 914 (5th Cir.1992)—§ 21.6(a) n.57

Bell, United States v., 901 F.2d 574 (7th Cir.1990)—§ 11.5(c) n.54

Bell, United States v., 902 F.2d 563 (7th Cir.1990)—§§ 8.8(f) n.158, 159; 8.8(h) n.186; 8.11(b) n.32

Bell, United States v., 820 F.2d 980 (9th Cir.1987)—§ 12.4(d) n.64

Bell, United States v., 785 F.2d 640 (8th Cir.1986)—§ 26.10(c) n.74

Bell, United States v., 506 F.2d 207 (D.C.Cir.1974)—§ 21.3(c) n.156

Bell, United States v., 457 F.2d 1231 (5th Cir.1972)—§§ 3.3(d) n.156; 7.4(e) n.89

Bell, United States v., 464 F.2d 667 (2d Cir.1972)—§ 10.5(e) n.45

Bell v. Wolfish, 441 U.S. 520, 99 S.Ct. 1861, 60 L.Ed.2d 447 (1979)—§§ 1.5(d) n.193; 3.9(i) n.178; 12.2(a) n.16; 12.2(d) n.48; 12.3(d) n.92, 93; 12.4(b) n.54

Bellamy v. Cogdell, 974 F.2d 302 (2d Cir.1992)—§ 11.8(c) n.78

Bellamy v. Judges and Justices Authorized to Sit in the New York City Criminal Court and the New York State Supreme Court in New York County, 41 A.D.2d 196, 342 N.Y.S.2d 137 (1973)—§ 12.2(b) n.26

Bellamy, State v., 178 N.J. 127, 835 A.2d 1231 (2003)—§ 21.4(d) n.132

Bellanca v. New York State Liquor Authority, 54 N.Y.2d 228, 429 N.E.2d 765, 445 N.Y.S.2d 87 (1981)—§ 1.2(b) n.6

Bellanca, People v., 386 Mich. 708, 194 N.W.2d 863 (1972)—§ 8.4(c) n.130

Bellas v. Superior Court of Alameda County, 85 Cal.App.4th 636, 102 Cal.Rptr.2d 380 (2000)—§§ 23.1(d) n.193; 23.1(e) n.218, 247

Belle Terre, Village of v. Boraas, 416 U.S. 1, 94 S.Ct. 1536, 39 L.Ed.2d 797 (1974)—§ 13.5(e) n.100

Bellinger, People v., 269 N.Y. 265, 199 N.E. 213 (1935)—§§ 15.1(d) n.142, 212

Bellino, Commonwealth v., 320 Mass. 635, 71 N.E.2d 411 (1947)—§ 22.3(e) n.261

Bellino, State v., 557 A.2d 963 (Me.1989)—§ 18.4(c) n.47

Bellis v. United States, 417 U.S. 85, 94 S.Ct. 2179, 40 L.Ed.2d 678 (1974)—§§ 8.12(a) n.9; 8.12(b) n.19

Bellmyer, People v., 199 Ill.2d 529, 264 Ill.Dec. 687, 771 N.E.2d 391 (2002)—§§ 21.3(f) n.426; 25.1(d) n.52

Bellosi, United States v., 501 F.2d 833 (D.C.Cir.1974)—§ 4.6(e) n.110

Bellows v. State, 110 Nev. 289, 871 P.2d 340 (1994)—§ 27.5(c) n.83

Bellows v. State, 508 So.2d 1330 (Fla.App.1987)—§ 11.9(d) n.202

Bellucci, State v., 81 N.J. 531, 410 A.2d 666 (1980)—§ 2.12(b) n.111

Bellville v. Town of Northboro, 375 F.3d 25 (1st Cir.2004)—§ 3.4(j) n.208

Belmarez, State v., 254 Neb. 467, 577 N.W.2d 264 (1998)—§ 21.5(e) n.119

Belmontes v. Brown, 414 F.3d 1094 (9th Cir.2005)—§§ 13.4(b) n.70, 71

Belmontes, State v., 615 N.W.2d 634 (S.D.2000)—§ 3.1(c) n.77

Belmontes v. Woodford, 335 F.3d 1024 (9th Cir.2003)—§ 13.4(b) n.70

Belmontes v. Woodford, 350 F.3d 861 (9th Cir.2003)—§ 13.4(b) n.71

Belnavis, State v., 246 Kan. 309, 787 P.2d 1172 (1990)—§ 22.3(d) n.242

Belo Broadcasting Corp. v. Clark, 654 F.2d 423 (5th Cir.1981)—§§ 23.1(d) n.211; 23.1(e) n.248

Belt, State v., 505 N.W.2d 182 (Iowa 1993)—§ 25.4(b) n.23

Belt, United States v., 89 F.3d 710 (10th Cir.1996)—§ 21.2(d) n.177

Belton, State v., 318 N.C. 141, 347 S.E.2d 755 (1986)—§ 17.2(d) n.93

Beltran, United States v., 109 F.3d 365 (7th Cir.1997)—§ 26.4(g) n.131

Beltran-Felix, State v., 922 P.2d 30 (Utah App.1996)—§§ 24.4(d) n.30, 36, 54

Belvin v. State, 922 So.2d 1046 (Fla.App.2006)—§ 20.2(e) n.95

Belvin, United States v., 46 F. 381 (E.D.Va.1891)—§ 15.4(a) n.10

Belzer, United States v., 743 F.2d 1213 (7th Cir.1984)—§ 5.4(c) n.46

Bement v. State, 91 Idaho 388, 422 P.2d 55 (1966)—§ 11.3(a) n.12

Benavides, United States v., 596 F.2d 137 (5th Cir.1979)—§ 24.2(d) n.45

Benbo, State v., 174 Mont. 252, 570 P.2d 894 (1977)—§ 6.3(c) n.52

Benbow v. State, 614 So.2d 398 (Miss.1993)—§ 21.3(a) n.2

Benchimol, United States v., 471 U.S. 453, 105 S.Ct. 2103, 85 L.Ed.2d 462 (1985)—§ 21.2(d) n.168

Bencs, United States v., 28 F.3d 555 (6th Cir.1994)—§§ 20.3(m) n.243, 257

Bender, United States v., 221 F.3d 265 (1st Cir.2000)—§ 6.4(e) n.96

Bender, United States v., 5 F.3d 267 (7th Cir.1993)—§ 24.3(g) n.169

Bendis, United States v., 681 F.2d 561 (9th Cir.1981)—§ 27.2(c) n.59

Bendolph, United States v., 409 F.3d 155 (3d Cir.2005)—§ 28.9(b) n.54

Benedict, United States v., 95 F.3d 17 (8th Cir.1996)—§ 24.10(d) n.45

Benedict, United States v., 647 F.2d 928 (9th Cir.1981)—§ 3.1(i) n.232

Beneficial Finance Co., Commonwealth v., 360 Mass. 188, 275 N.E.2d 33 (1971)—§ 13.4(c) n.117

Benfield, State v., 264 N.C. 75, 140 S.E.2d 706 (1965)—§ 21.2(c) n.119

Benge v. State, 862 A.2d 385 (Del.2004)—§ 26.4(i) n.188

Bengivenga, United States v., 845 F.2d 593 (5th Cir.1988)—§ 6.6(e) n.91

Benham v. State, 637 N.E.2d 133 (Ind.1994)—§§ 16.1(a) n.2, 24

Benitez v. Dunevant, 198 Ariz. 90, 7 P.3d 99 (2000)—§ 22.1(b) n.57

Benitez, United States v., 741 F.2d 1312 (11th Cir.1984)—§ 16.4(b) n.34

Benitez-Arreguin, United States v., 973 F.2d 823 (10th Cir.1992)—§ 9.1(d) n.128

Benitz, United States v., 34 F.3d 1489 (9th Cir.1994)—§ 18.3(b) n.5

Benjamin, People v., 732 P.2d 1167 (Colo.1987)—§ 6.9(g) n.183

Benjamin, State v., 345 S.C. 470, 549 S.E.2d 258 (2001)—§§ 6.9(f) n.101, 106

Benjamin, State v., 417 N.W.2d 838 (N.D.1988)—§ 9.2(b) n.15

Benjamin, United States v., 138 F.3d 1069 (6th Cir.1998)—§ 21.2(d) n.255

Benjamin, United States v., 852 F.2d 413 (9th Cir.1988)—§ 8.10(c) n.68

Benjamin, United States v., 623 F.Supp. 1204 (D.D.C.1985)—§§ 16.3(c) n.34, 36, 41, 43, 46

Benlian, United States v., 63 F.3d 824 (9th Cir.1995)—§ 26.4(e) n.82

Benmuhar, United States v., 658 F.2d 14 (1st Cir.1981)—§ 22.2(d) n.88

Bennefield, State v., 567 A.2d 863 (Del.1989)—§ 24.7(d) n.29

Benner, State v., 64 Me. 267 (1874)— § 15.2(i) n.223

Bennet v. State, 371 S.C. 198, 638 S.E.2d 673 (2006)—§ 21.3(b) n.89

Bennett v. City of Grand Prairie, 883 F.2d 400 (5th Cir.1989)—§ 3.3(e) n.182

Bennett v. Kalamazoo Judge, 183 Mich. 200, 150 N.W. 141 (1914)— § 8.3(h) n.38

Bennett v. Mueller, 322 F.3d 573 (9th Cir.2003)—§§ 28.4(b) n.15, 22

Bennett, People v., 331 Ill.App.3d 198, 264 Ill.Dec. 829, 771 N.E.2d 533 (2002)—§ 24.6(b) n.23

Bennett, People v., 17 Cal.4th 373, 70 Cal.Rptr.2d 850, 949 P.2d 947 (1998)—§ 3.6(e) n.126

Bennett, People v., 154 Ill.App.3d 469, 107 Ill.Dec. 431, 507 N.E.2d 95 (1987)—§ 24.9(e) n.56

Bennett, People v., 116 Mich.App. 700, 323 N.W.2d 520 (1982)—§ 20.6(a) n.13

Bennett, People v., 58 Cal.App.3d 230, 129 Cal.Rptr. 679 (1976)—§ 6.8(b) n.53

Bennett, State v., 903 A.2d 853 (Me.2006)—§ 24.2(e) n.66

Bennett v. State, 933 So.2d 930 (Miss.2006)—§ 21.4(f) n.173

Bennett, State v., 633 So.2d 272 (La.App.1993)—§ 10.3(d) n.63

Bennett, State v., 798 S.W.2d 783 (Tenn.Cr.App.1990)—§ 13.3(b) n.20

Bennett, State v., 517 So.2d 1115 (La.App.1987)—§ 19.3(d) n.204

Bennett, State v., 454 So.2d 1165 (La.App.1984)—§ 23.2(a) n.13

Bennett v. State, 570 P.2d 345 (Okla.Cr.App.1977)—§ 14.3(a) n.23

Bennett, United States v., 332 F.3d 1094 (7th Cir.2003)—§ 21.2(b) n.57

Bennett, United States v., 291 F.3d 888 (6th Cir.2002)—§§ 21.4(f) n.176, 179

Bennett v. United States, 797 A.2d 1251 (D.C.App.2002)—§ 24.3(b) n.49

Bennett, United States v., 219 F.3d 1117 (9th Cir.2000)—§§ 4.6(e) n.97; 4.6(i) n.151; 4.6(m) n.237

Bennett v. United States, 726 A.2d 156 (D.C.App.1999)—§ 21.5(a) n.38

Bennett, United States v., 161 F.3d 171 (3d Cir.1998)—§ 21.1(h) n.199

Bennett, United States v., 75 F.3d 40 (1st Cir.1996)—§ 24.9(c) n.29

Bennett, United States v., 990 F.2d 998 (7th Cir.1993)—§ 21.2(d) n.198

Bennett, United States v., 729 F.2d 923 (2d Cir.1984)—§ 3.1(h) n.193

Bennett, United States v., 702 F.2d 833 (9th Cir.1983)—§ 15.2(i) n.217

Bennetto, People v., 10 Cal.3d 695, 111 Cal.Rptr. 699, 517 P.2d 1163 (1974)—§ 3.6(b) n.59

Bennett, State ex rel. v. Whyte, 163 W.Va. 522, 258 S.E.2d 123 (1979)—§ 27.4(f) n.65

Benniefield, People v., 88 Ill.App.3d 150, 43 Ill.Dec. 455, 410 N.E.2d 455 (1980)—§ 21.2(h) n.431

Bennis v. Michigan, 516 U.S. 442, 116 S.Ct. 994, 134 L.Ed.2d 68 (1996)— §§ 2.6(b) n.39; 2.7(d) n.233; 2.9(d) n.75

Benoit, State v., 173 Vt. 583, 795 A.2d 1188 (2002)—§ 6.7(a) n.3

Benoit, State v., 21 Kan.App.2d 184, 898 P.2d 653 (1995)—§ 6.10(c) n.51

Benoit, State v., 126 N.H. 6, 490 A.2d 295 (1985)—§§ 6.8(d) n.84; 6.9(b) n.20, 23

Benoit, State v., 83 Wis.2d 394, 265 N.W.2d 298 (1978)—§ 14.3(a) n.20

Benson v. United States, 146 U.S. 325, 13 S.Ct. 60, 36 L.Ed. 991 (1892)—§ 21.2(b) n.72

Benter, United States v., 457 F.2d 1174 (2d Cir.1972)—§ 24.7(i) n.93

Bentley v. Bock, 239 F.Supp.2d 686 (E.D.Mich.2002)—§ 28.4(b) n.19

Bentley v. State, 411 So.2d 1361 (Fla.App.1982)—§ 26.9(c) n.92

Bentley-Smith, United States v., 2 F.3d 1368 (5th Cir.1993)—§ 22.3(d) n.245

Benton v. Maryland, 395 U.S. 784, 89 S.Ct. 2056, 23 L.Ed.2d 707 (1969)—§§ 2.5(f) n.53; 2.6(a) n.6, 12, 13; 2.6(b) n.34; 25.1(b) n.15; 25.5(a) n.4; 27.5(b) n.35

Benton, United States v., 996 F.2d 642 (3d Cir.1993)—§ 6.7(c) n.133

Benton, United States v., 637 F.2d 1052 (5th Cir.1981)—§ 8.5(g) n.228

Bentvena, United States v., 319 F.2d 916 (2d Cir.1963)—§ 11.4(c) n.64

Bentvena, United States v., 288 F.2d 442 (2d Cir.1961)—§ 12.4(c) n.59

Bentz, United States v., 21 F.3d 37 (3d Cir.1994)—§ 21.6(b) n.92

Benz, United States v., 472 F.3d 657 (9th Cir.2006)—§ 21.4(d) n.102

Benz, United States v., 282 U.S. 304, 51 S.Ct. 113, 75 L.Ed. 354 (1931)—§ 26.7(c) n.25

Ben Zvi, United States v., 242 F.3d 89 (2d Cir.2001)—§ 18.5(a) n.37

Berardi, United States v., 675 F.2d 894 (7th Cir.1982)—§§ 19.3(c) n.185, 186, 190

Beraun-Panez, United States v., 812 F.2d 578 (9th Cir.1987)—§§ 6.6(c) n.42; 6.6(f) n.109, 111

Berberian, State v., 122 R.I. 693, 411 A.2d 308 (1980)—§ 27.2(c) n.65

Berberich, United States v., 254 F.3d 721 (8th Cir.2001)—§ 27.5(c) n.56

Berby, State v., 81 Wis.2d 677, 260 N.W.2d 798 (1978)—§§ 14.3(a) n.20; 14.3(c) n.63

Berg, People v., 92 N.Y.2d 701, 685 N.Y.S.2d 906, 708 N.E.2d 979 (1999)—§ 6.7(a) n.3

Berg v. State, 131 Idaho 517, 960 P.2d 738 (1998)—§ 21.2(d) n.223

Berg, State v., 236 Kan. 562, 694 P.2d 427 (1985)—§ 13.3(b) n.19

Berg, United States v., 178 F.3d 976 (8th Cir.1999)—§ 5.4(c) n.46

Berger v. California, 393 U.S. 314, 89 S.Ct. 540, 21 L.Ed.2d 508 (1969)—§ 2.11(c) n.25

Berger v. New York, 388 U.S. 41, 87 S.Ct. 1873, 18 L.Ed.2d 1040 (1967)—§§ 2.9(d) n.59; 3.1(d) n.92; 3.3(b) n.38; 3.4(g) n.132; 3.4(l) n.245; 4.3(a) n.2; 4.5 n.3; 4.6(h) n.145

Berger v. New York, 381 U.S. 41, 85 S.Ct. 1293, 14 L.Ed.2d 205 (1965)—§ 4.6(b) n.27

Berger, People v., 44 Cal.2d 459, 282 P.2d 509 (1955)—§§ 10.1(a) n.5, 6

Berger, State v., 590 N.W.2d 884 (N.D.1999)—§ 21.4(d) n.131

Berger, United States v., 473 F.3d 1080 (9th Cir.2007)—§§ 24.2(b) n.25; 24.9(d) n.48

Berger, United States v., 990 F.Supp. 1054 (C.D.Ill.1998)—§ 23.1(d) n.180

Berger, United States v., 976 F.Supp. 947 (N.D.Cal.1997)—§ 26.10(b) n.27

Berger v. United States, 295 U.S. 78, 55 S.Ct. 629, 79 L.Ed. 1314 (1935)—§§ 1.5(c) n.133; 2.7(c) n.203; 19.6(b) n.8; 19.6(c) n.27; 24.7(d) n.28

Bergeron, State v., 105 Wash.2d 1, 711 P.2d 1000 (1985)—§ 19.4(b) n.38

Bergeron ex rel. Perez v. O'Neil, 205 Ariz. 640, 74 P.3d 952 (Ariz.App.2003)—§§ 22.4(d) n.34, 45

Bergeson, United States v., 425 F.3d 1221 (9th Cir.2005)—§ 8.8(d) n.97

Bergfeld, United States v., 280 F.3d 486 (5th Cir.2002)—§§ 18.2(b) n.15; 18.2(e) n.71, 84

Bergin, State v., 214 Conn. 657, 574 A.2d 164 (1990)—§ 3.4(d) n.51

Bergman v. Lefkowitz, 569 F.2d 705 (2d Cir.1977)—§ 21.2(d) n.191

Bergman v. State, 874 P.2d 958 (Alaska App. 1994)—§ 4.2(a) n.9

Bergmann, State v., 633 N.W.2d 328 (Iowa 2001)—§ 3.2(b) n.70

Bergstrom, Commonwealth v., 402 Mass. 534, 524 N.E.2d 366 (1988)—§ 2.12(e) n.210

Bergstrom, State v., 196 W.Va. 656, 474 S.E.2d 586 (1996)—§ 22.1(f) n.95

Berheide, United States v., 421 F.3d 538 (7th Cir.2005)—§ 21.6(a) n.80

Berke, United States v., 930 F.2d 1219 (7th Cir.1991)—§ 3.8(c) n.82

Berkeley, City of v. Stringfellow, 783 S.W.2d 501 (Mo.App.1990)—§ 1.8(d) n.78

Berkemer v. McCarty, 468 U.S. 420, 104 S.Ct. 3138, 82 L.Ed.2d 317 (1984)—§§ 2.9(g) n.180; 6.6(c) n.28; 6.6(e) n.87; 6.10(a) n.9; 11.1(c) n.98

Berkey v. United States, 318 F.3d 768 (7th Cir.2003)—§ 21.3(b) n.44

Berkowitz, United States v., 927 F.2d 1376 (7th Cir.1991)—§ 3.6(a) n.35

Berkowitz, United States v., 662 F.2d 1127 (5th Cir.1981)—§§ 17.2(d) n.98, 109

Berkowitz for a Writ of Habeas Corpus, In the Matter of the Application of, 3 Kan.App.2d 726, 602 P.2d 99 (1979)—§ 27.2(c) n.64

Berky v. State, 266 Ga. 28, 463 S.E.2d 891 (1995)—§ 27.3(c) n.39

Berlin, State v., 133 Wash.2d 541, 947 P.2d 700 (1997)—§ 24.8(e) n.76

Berman v. United States, 302 U.S. 211, 58 S.Ct. 164, 82 L.Ed. 204 (1937)—§ 27.2(a) n.5

Bermea, United States v., 30 F.3d 1539 (5th Cir.1994)—§ 23.2(h) n.127

Bernades, State v., 71 Haw. 485, 795 P.2d 842 (1990)—§ 26.1(d) n.82

Bernal, State v., 140 N.M. 644, 146 P.3d 289 (2006)—§ 17.4(b) n.73

Bernal, United States v., 28 F.3d 630 (7th Cir.1994)—§ 3.8(d) n.154

Bernard, People v., 27 Cal.App.4th 458, 32 Cal.Rptr.2d 486 (1994)—§ 19.3(a) n.67

Bernard v. State, 248 Ind. 688, 230 N.E.2d 536 (1967)—§§ 20.2(a) n.2, 5, 10; 20.3(h) n.155

Bernard, United States v., 373 F.3d 339 (3d Cir.2004)—§§ 21.1(h) n.210; 21.2(e) n.321

Bernhardt, Commonwealth v., 359 Pa.Super. 413, 519 A.2d 417 (1986)—§ 27.4(f) n.63

Bernloehr, United States v., 833 F.2d 749 (8th Cir.1987)—§ 11.6(c) n.100

Berra v. United States, 351 U.S. 131, 76 S.Ct. 685, 100 L.Ed. 1013 (1956)—§ 24.8(f) n.97

Berrett, United States v., 513 F.2d 154 (1st Cir.1975)—§ 3.2(e) n.159

Berrier, People v., 362 Ill.App.3d 1153, 299 Ill.Dec. 385, 841 N.E.2d 1117 (2006)—§§ 24.6(b) n.22, 24

Berrigan, United States v., 482 F.2d 171 (3d Cir.1973)—§§ 13.4(a) n.10, 23; 13.4(b) n.39, 59

Berrio, In re, 145 Vt. 6, 481 A.2d 1057 (1984)—§ 21.4(g) n.233

Berrios, People v., 28 N.Y.2d 361, 321 N.Y.S.2d 884, 270 N.E.2d 709 (1971)—§§ 1.9(b) n.19, 27; 10.3(a) n.7

Berrios, United States v., 501 F.2d 1207 (2d Cir.1974)—§§ 13.4(a) n.15; 13.4(b) n.60, 62; 13.6(c) n.30

Berrios-Centeno, United States v., 250 F.3d 294 (5th Cir.2001)—§ 19.3(a) n.101

Berroa, United States v., 374 F.3d 1053 (11th Cir.2004)—§ 25.2(e) n.38

Berroa v. United States, 763 A.2d 93 (D.C.App.2000)—§ 22.1(b) n.55

Berry v. City of Cincinnati, 414 U.S. 29, 94 S.Ct. 193, 38 L.Ed.2d 187 (1973)—§ 2.11(c) n.25

Berry v. Funk, 146 F.3d 1003 (D.C.Cir.1998)—§ 4.6(b) n.46

Berry v. State, 93 P.3d 222 (Wyo.2004)—§§ 18.2(d) n.64; 18.2(e) n.76; 21.4(a) n.17

Berry v. State, 802 So.2d 1033 (Miss.2001)—§ 22.3(d) n.249

Berry v. State, 728 So.2d 568 (Miss.1999)—§ 22.3(d) n.242

Berry, State v., 223 Kan. 102, 573 P.2d 584 (1977)—§ 3.2(c) n.131

Berry v. State, 552 P.2d 87 (Okla.Crim.1976)—§ 11.5(e) n.88

Berry v. State, 10 Ga. 511 (1851)—§ 24.11(d) n.18

Berry, United States v., 90 F.3d 148 (6th Cir.1996)—§ 18.3(b) n.5

Berry, United States v., 670 F.2d 583 (5th Cir.1982)—§ 3.8(c) n.88

Berry v. United States, 412 F.2d 189 (3d Cir.1969)—§ 21.4(d) n.118

Berryhill, State v., 703 So.2d 250 (1997)—§§ 19.3(a) n.67, 70

Berryhill, United States v., 352 F.3d 315 (6th Cir.2003)—§ 9.1(b) n.47

Berryhill v. Zant, 858 F.2d 633 (11th Cir.1988)—§ 22.2(d) n.76

Berryman v. United States, 378 A.2d 1317 (D.C.App.1977)—§ 7.4(g) n.116

Berrysmith, State v., 87 Wash.App. 268, 944 P.2d 397 (1997)—§§ 24.2(a) n.21; 24.3(d) n.109

Berthold, Commonwealth v., 441 Mass. 183, 804 N.E.2d 355 (2004)—§§ 21.4(d) n.136, 137

Bertoli, United States v., 40 F.3d 1384 (3d Cir.1994)—§ 24.9(c) n.29

Bertoli, United States v., 994 F.2d 1002 (3d Cir.1993)—§§ 11.5(f) n.94; 27.2(c) n.56; 27.4(b) n.17

Bertolotti v. State, 476 So.2d 130 (Fla.1985)—§ 24.7(e) n.62

Bertram, State v., 80 Oh.St.3d 281, 685 N.E.2d 1239 (1997)—§§ 27.3(c) n.34, 48

Bertrand, United States v., 926 F.2d 838 (9th Cir.1991)—§ 3.3(e) n.189

Bervaldi, United States v., 226 F.3d 1256 (11th Cir.2000)—§§ 3.6(a) n.11, 12

Berzups, People v., 49 N.Y.2d 417, 426 N.Y.S.2d 253, 402 N.E.2d 1155 (1980)—§ 17.2(b) n.56

Bessenecker, State v., 404 N.W.2d 134 (Iowa 1987)—§§ 22.3(b) n.73, 88

Best v. United States, 651 A.2d 790 (D.C.App.1994)—§ 12.3(g) n.154

Best v. United States, 582 A.2d 966 (D.C.App.1990)—§ 10.1(b) n.24

Betances, State v., 265 Conn. 493, 828 A.2d 1248 (2003)—§ 6.7(b) n.90

Betancourt-Arretuche, United States v., 933 F.2d 89 (1st Cir.1991)—§§ 11.5(d) n.72; 11.5(f) n.102

Bethea, People v., 67 N.Y.2d 364, 502 N.Y.S.2d 713, 493 N.E.2d 937 (1986)—§§ 9.5(a) n.23; 9.5(c) n.66

Bethea, United States v., 483 F.2d 1024 (4th Cir.1973)—§§ 13.5(b) n.28; 13.6(d) n.51

Bethel, State v., 110 Ohio St.3d 416, 854 N.E.2d 150 (2006)—§§ 6.8(a) n.33; 13.7(c) n.59; 21.2(d) n.157, 158; 21.2(h) n.439

Bethel v. State, 162 Ark. 76, 257 S.W. 740 (1924)—§ 15.2(e) n.141

Betterley, State v., 191 Wis.2d 407, 529 N.W.2d 216 (1995)—§ 3.5(c) n.124

Bettlyoun v. State, 562 P.2d 862 (Okla.Crim.App.1977)—§§ 20.2(a) n.6; 20.3(i) n.169

Betts v. Brady, 316 U.S. 455, 62 S.Ct. 1252, 86 L.Ed. 1595 (1942)—§§ 1.5(c) n.110; 2.4(a) n.7, 15; 2.4(e) n.140, 157; 2.5(f) n.69; 2.6(b) n.34; 2.7(c) n.112; 6.4(a) n.4;

11.1(a) n.7, 10, 15, 16; 11.1(b) n.46

Betts v. Litscher, 241 F.3d 594 (7th Cir.2001)—§§ 11.2(c) n.106, 115

Betts, People v., 34 Cal.4th 1039, 23 Cal.Rptr.3d 138, 103 P.3d 883 (2005)—§§ 16.1(g) n.252; 16.4(c) n.93; 16.4(d) n.119

Beuke, State v., 38 Ohio St.3d 29, 526 N.E.2d 274 (1988)—§§ 2.6(b) n.58; 16.4(c) n.105

Beusch, United States v., 596 F.2d 871 (9th Cir.1979)—§ 3.4(k) n.219

Bevans, United States v., 16 U.S. [3 Wheat.] 336, 4 L.Ed. 404 (1818)—§§ 1.2(c) n.35, 41

Beverly, Ex parte, 497 So.2d 519 (Ala.1986)—§ 25.4(b) n.25

Beverly v. State, 349 Md. 106, 707 A.2d 91 (1998)—§§ 13.2(a) n.4; 21.2(e) n.313; 21.2(f) n.390

Beverly, State v., 224 Conn. 372, 618 A.2d 1335 (1993)—§§ 16.4(d) n.119, 122, 123

Beverly, United States v., 369 F.3d 516 (6th Cir.2004)—§ 7.4(f) n.106

Beverly, United States v., 913 F.2d 337 (7th Cir.1990)—§ 24.9(d) n.40

Beverly, United States v., 723 F.2d 11 (3d Cir.1983)—§§ 5.1(c) n.26, 36; 5.4(c) n.46

Beverly v. United States, 468 F.2d 732 (5th Cir.1972)—§§ 8.8(f) n.148, 151

Bevilacqua, People v., 45 N.Y.2d 508, 410 N.Y.S.2d 549, 382 N.E.2d 1326 (1978)—§ 6.9(g) n.175

Bevill v. State, 669 So.2d 14 (Miss.1996)—§ 21.4(d) n.103

Bevill v. State, 556 So.2d 699 (Miss.1990)—§ 24.7(a) n.8

Bevill v. State, 472 N.E.2d 1247 (Ind.1985)—§ 6.9(e) n.87

Beville v. Ednie, 74 F.3d 210 (10th Cir.1996)—§ 3.9(i) n.198

Bevis v. State, 614 N.E.2d 599 (Ind.App.1993)—§ 9.6(a) n.47

Bey v. Morton, 124 F.3d 524 (3d Cir.1997)—§ 6.4(g) n.154

Bey, People v., 21 Cal.App.4th 1623, 27 Cal.Rptr.2d 28 (1993)—§ 9.6(a) n.32

Bey, State v., 270 Kan. 544, 17 P.3d 322 (2001)—§ 21.2(b) n.57

Bey, State v., 129 N.J. 557, 610 A.2d 814 (1992)—§ 22.2(c) n.43

Bey, State v., 112 N.J. 45, 548 A.2d 846 (1988)—§ 6.9(g) n.149

Bey, State v., 112 N.J. 123, 548 A.2d 887 (1988)—§ 6.9(g) n.149

Beydoun, United States v., 469 F.3d 102 (5th Cir.2006)—§ 26.4(f) n.93

Bezanson-Perkins, United States v., 390 F.3d 34 (1st Cir.2004)—§ 6.9(c) n.58

Bhagwat v. State, 338 Md. 263, 658 A.2d 244 (1995)—§ 21.2(b) n.62

Biaggi, In re, 478 F.2d 489 (2d Cir.1973)—§§ 8.5(b) n.38; 8.5(d) n.136, 139

Biaggi, United States v., 909 F.2d 662 (2d Cir.1990)—§§ 22.2(c) n.43; 22.2(d) n.59

Biaggi, United States v., 680 F.Supp. 641 (S.D.N.Y.1988)—§ 15.4(d) n.124

Bianco, United States v., 998 F.2d 1112 (2d Cir.1993)—§§ 3.4(e) n.84; 4.6(e) n.80

Bibb, State v., 922 S.W.2d 798 (Mo.App.1996)—§ 27.3(c) n.55

Bible v. State, 162 S.W.3d 234 (Tex.Crim.App.2005)—§ 6.8(b) n.50

Bible, State v., 175 Ariz. 549, 858 P.2d 1152 (Ariz.1993)—§§ 22.3(a) n.43; 23.2(a) n.16, 21, 33; 23.2(f) n.89; 23.3(a) n.8

Bickham Lincoln-Mercury Inc. v. United States, 168 F.3d 790 (5th Cir.1999)—§ 21.2(d) n.206

Biddinger v. Commissioner of Police, 245 U.S. 128, 38 S.Ct. 41, 62 L.Ed. 193 (1917)—§ 24.8(f) n.104

Biddle, State v., 652 N.W.2d 191 (Iowa 2002)—§§ 21.2(a) n.15; 22.4(c) n.29

Bieber, People v., 100 N.Y.S.2d 821 (Mag.Ct.1950)—§ 14.3(b) n.54

Biedinger v. City of East Chicago, 129 Ind.App. 42, 154 N.E.2d 58 (1958)—§ 1.8(d) n.55

Bieganowski, United States v., 313 F.3d 264 (5th Cir.2002)—§ 19.6(c) n.46

Bielecki, People v., 41 Colo.App. 256, 588 P.2d 377 (1978)—§ 18.4(c) n.59

Bielicki v. Superior Court, 57 Cal.2d 602, 21 Cal.Rptr. 552, 371 P.2d 288 (1962)—§ 3.2(e) n.171

Biemel v. State, 71 Wis. 444, 37 N.W. 244 (1888)—§ 1.6(d) n.209

Bierd, United States v., 217 F.3d 15 (1st Cir.2000)—§ 21.3(d) n.218

Biernacki, State v., 237 Neb. 215, 465 N.W.2d 732 (1991)—§ 21.4(c) n.81

Bigby v. Cockrell, 340 F.3d 259 (5th Cir.2003)—§ 22.4(c) n.24

Bigelow, In re, 113 U.S. 328, 5 S.Ct. 542, 28 L.Ed. 1005 (1885)— § 28.3(b) n.46

Bigelow, People v., 37 Cal.3d 731, 209 Cal.Rptr. 328, 691 P.2d 994 (1984)—§ 11.5(f) n.102

Bigford v. Taylor, 834 F.2d 1213 (5th Cir.1988)—§ 3.3(b) n.67

Biggs, People v., 1 N.Y.3d 225, 771 N.Y.S.2d 49, 803 N.E.2d 370 (2003)—§ 25.3(c) n.30

Bigler, United States v., 810 F.2d 1317 (5th Cir.1987)—§§ 18.3(b) n.11, 21

Biglieri v. Washoe County Grand Jury Report, 95 Nev. 696, 601 P.2d 703 (1979)—§ 8.3(h) n.47

Big Medicine, United States v., 73 F.3d 994 (10th Cir.1995)—§ 21.2(d) n.210

Bilanzich, United States v., 771 F.2d 292 (7th Cir.1985)—§ 12.4(d) n.69

Bilbrey, United States v., 896 F.Supp. 1207 (M.D.Fla.1995)—§ 23.1(d) n.158

Bilick v. Dudley, 356 F.Supp. 945 (S.D.N.Y.1973)—§ 3.1(m) n.293

Bilida v. McCleod, 211 F.3d 166 (1st Cir.2000)—§ 3.1(h) n.201

Biller v. State, 618 So.2d 734 (Fla.1993)—§ 26.9(b) n.24

Billings v. People, 171 Colo. 236, 466 P.2d 474 (1970)—§ 6.9(d) n.75

Billings, State v., 348 N.C. 169, 500 S.E.2d 423 (1998)—§ 23.2(f) n.108

Billington, United States v., 844 F.2d 445 (7th Cir.1988)—§ 21.2(d) n.185

Billis v. State, 800 P.2d 401 (Wyo.1990)—§ 13.6(c) n.39

Billups, State v., 68 Ohio App.3d 248, 588 N.E.2d 208 (1990)—§ 20.4(c) n.48

Billups, United States v., 692 F.2d 320 (4th Cir.1982)—§§ 16.2(c) n.45, 46, 49; 16.2(e) n.70

Billy-Eko v. United States, 8 F.3d 111 (2d Cir.1993)—§ 11.7(e) n.91

Bilokur v. Commonwealth, 221 Va. 467, 270 S.E.2d 747 (1980)—§ 11.6(a) n.49

Bilsky, United States v., 664 F.2d 613 (6th Cir.1981)—§ 18.3(b) n.53

Binder, United States v., 794 F.2d 1195 (7th Cir.1986)—§§ 11.2(g) n.304, 306

Binegar v. Eighth Judicial District, 112 Nev. 544, 915 P.2d 889 (1996)— §§ 20.4(b) n.21; 20.4(c) n.51

Bingham, United States v., 769 F.Supp. 1039 (N.D.Ill.1991)—§§ 23.1(b) n.12, 67

Bingman, State v., 229 Mont. 101, 745 P.2d 342 (1987)—§ 17.1(a) n.15

Binion v. United States, 658 A.2d 187 (D.C.App.1995)—§ 21.5(a) n.2

Bin Laden, United States v., 132 F.Supp.2d 168 (S.D.N.Y.2001)— § 6.10(d) n.61

Bin Laden, United States v., 146 F.Supp.2d 373 (S.D.N.Y. 2001)— § 16.2(e) n.90

Bin Laden, United States v., 92 F.Supp.2d 225 (S.D.N.Y.2000)— §§ 19.4(b) n.23, 31, 34

Bins v. United States, 331 F.2d 390 (5th Cir.1964)—§ 19.3(c) n.187

Bionic Auto Parts and Sales, Inc. v. Fahner, 721 F.2d 1072 (7th Cir.1983)—§ 8.12(c) n.36

Birano, State v., 109 Haw. 314, 126 P.3d 357 (2006)—§ 24.2(b) n.25

Birbal, United States v., 113 F.3d 342 (2d Cir.1997)—§ 6.4(g) n.161

Birch, In re, 10 Cal.3d 314, 110 Cal.Rptr. 212, 515 P.2d 12 (1973)—§ 21.4(d) n.138

Bird, Commonwealth v., 979 S.W.2d 915 (Ky.1998)—§ 25.1(c) n.31

Bird, State v., 308 Mont. 75, 43 P.3d 266 (2002)—§§ 24.2(a) n.5; 24.2(b) n.27; 27.6(d) n.84

Bird, United States v., 287 F.3d 709 (8th Cir.2002)—§§ 6.4(e) n.76, 77

Bird Head, State v., 204 Neb. 807, 285 N.W.2d 698 (1979)—§ 13.4(c) n.82

Birdman, United States v., 602 F.2d 547 (3d Cir.1979)—§§ 8.5(e) n.172; 15.6(b) n.51; 15.7(b) n.10; 15.7(c) n.54, 56, 59, 60

Birdsall, State v., 23 Ari.App. 454, 533 P.2d 1191 (1975)—§§ 20.6(b) n.34, 35

Birdsong, People v., 958 P.2d 1124 (Colo.1998)—§§ 21.4(f) n.218, 220

Birdsong, United States v., 982 F.2d 481 (11th Cir.1993)—§ 26.2(b) n.21

Birdwell v. Skeen, 983 F.2d 1332 (5th Cir.1993)—§ 18.4(c) n.60

Birge, State v., 263 Neb. 77, 638 N.W.2d 529 (2002)—§§ 21.2(d) n.143, 179; 21.2(e) n.316; 21.5(b) n.64

Birkett, People ex rel. v. Bakalis, 196 Ill.2d 510, 256 Ill.Dec. 865, 752 N.E.2d 1107 (2001)—§ 20.2(d) n.75

Birks, People v., 19 Cal.4th 108, 77 Cal.Rptr.2d 848, 960 P.2d 1073 (1998)—§ 24.8(e) n.50

Birmingham News Co., Ex parte, 624 So.2d 1117 (Ala.Crim.App.1993)—§§ 23.1(d) n.147, 159, 169, 187

Birney, United States v., 686 F.2d 102 (2d Cir.1982)—§ 18.5(b) n.61

Birrell, United States v., 482 F.2d 890 (2d Cir.1973)—§ 11.2(b) n.53

Birrell, United States v., 421 F.2d 665 (9th Cir.1970)—§ 24.7(e) n.63

Bisaccia, State v., 45 N.J. 504, 213 A.2d 185 (1965)—§ 3.2(i) n.217

Bisbee v. State, 341 Ark. 508, 17 S.W.3d 477 (2000)—§ 6.2(c) n.115

Bishop v. Parratt, 509 F.Supp. 1140 (D.Neb.1981)—§ 11.9(b) n.53

Bishop v. State, 268 Ga. 286, 486 S.E.2d 887 (1997)—§ 6.9(b) n.36

Bishop, State v., 343 N.C. 518, 472 S.E.2d 842 (1996)—§ 24.7(e) n.72

Bishop v. State, 310 Ark. 479, 839 S.W.2d 6 (1992)—§§ 7.4(c) n.48; 7.4(e) n.90

Bishop, State v., 753 P.2d 439 (Utah 1988)—§ 22.3(d) n.202

Bishop, State v., 139 Ariz. 567, 679 P.2d 1054 (1984)—§ 21.6(a) n.78

Bishop, State v., 118 Ariz. 263, 576 P.2d 122 (1978)—§ 10.3(c) n.52

Bishop, United States v., 66 F.3d 569 (3d Cir.1995)—§ 1.2(c) n.147

Bishop, State ex rel. v. Madison Circuit Court, 690 N.E.2d 1173 (Ind.1998)—§ 27.4(c) n.23

Bisogni, People v., 4 Cal.3d 582, 94 Cal.Rptr. 164, 483 P.2d 780 (1971)—§ 9.1(a) n.28

Bisson, State v., 156 Wash.2d 507, 130 P.3d 820 (2006)—§§ 21.2(e) n.309; 21.5(e) n.153

Bisson, State v., 491 A.2d 544 (Me.1985)—§ 5.1(c) n.16

Biswell, United States v., 406 U.S. 311, 92 S.Ct. 1593, 32 L.Ed.2d 87 (1972)—§ 3.9(c) n.35

Bittaker v. Enomoto, 587 F.2d 400 (9th Cir.1978)—§ 11.5(a) n.8

Bittaker, People v., 48 Cal.3d 1046, 259 Cal.Rptr. 630, 774 P.2d 659 (1989)—§ 3.5(a) n.61

Bittaker v. Woodford, 331 F.3d 715 (9th Cir.2003)—§ 11.7(e) n.87

Bitter v. United States, 389 U.S. 15, 88 S.Ct. 6, 19 L.Ed.2d 15 (1967)—§ 12.4(c) n.57

Bitz, State v., 487 N.W.2d 533 (Minn.App.1992)—§§ 15.4(f) n.144; 15.6(d) n.120, 122

Bivens, People v., 43 Ill.App.3d 79, 1 Ill.Dec. 477, 356 N.E.2d 665 (1976)—§ 18.1(d) n.44

Bivens v. Six Unknown Named Agents, 403 U.S. 388, 91 S.Ct. 1999, 29 L.Ed.2d 619 (1971)—§§ 3.1(b) n.26; 3.1(c) n.33; 3.1(k) n.273

Bivins v. State, 735 N.E.2d 1116 (2000)—§ 11.10(c) n.127

Bivins v. State, 642 N.E.2d 928 (Ind.1994)—§ 26.5(d) n.74

Bixler, State v., 62 Md. 354 (1884)—§§ 15.1(b) n.73, 77

Bizarria, Commonwealth v., 31 Mass.App.Ct. 370, 578 N.E.2d 424 (1991)—§ 3.9(c) n.59

Bizzell, United States v., 19 F.3d 1524 (4th Cir.1994)—§ 3.7(d) n.72

Bjorkman, United States v., 270 F.3d 482 (7th Cir.2001)—§ 19.3(a) n.103

Black, In re, 47 F.2d 542 (2d Cir.1931)—§ 8.8(a) n.1

Black, People v., 35 Cal.4th 1238, 113 P.3d 534 (Cal.2005)—§ 26.4(i) n.191

Black, People v., 114 Cal.App.4th 830, 7 Cal.Rptr.3d 902 (2003)—§ 24.7(e) n.55

Black, People v., 915 P.2d 1257 (Colo.1996)—§ 27.5(a) n.21

Black, People v., 52 Ill.2d 544, 288 N.E.2d 376 (1972)—§ 10.3(b) n.44

Black v. Romano, 471 U.S. 606, 105 S.Ct. 2254, 85 L.Ed.2d 636 (1985)—§§ 26.1(d) n.73; 26.4(g) n.120; 26.10(b) n.11, 21, 33; 26.10(d) n.87

Black v. State, 21 P.3d 1047 (Okla.Cr.App.2001)—§§ 22.3(a) n.5; 22.3(b) n.86; 22.3(d) n.250

Black, State v., 242 Wis.2d 126, 624 N.W.2d 363 (2001)—§§ 21.4(f) n.173, 180

Black, State v., 153 N.J. 438, 710 A.2d 428 (1998)—§ 17.4(b) n.132

Black, State v., 506 N.W.2d 738 (S.D.1993)—§ 24.8(e) n.50

Black, State v., 328 N.C. 191, 400 S.E.2d 398 (N.C.1991)—§§ 24.9(e) n.51, 53

Black, State v., 66 Haw. 530, 668 P.2d 32 (1983)—§ 16.1(h) n.308

Black v. State, 645 S.W.2d 789 (Tex.Crim.App.1983)—§ 16.1(g) n.242

Black, State v., 385 So.2d 1372 (Fla.1980)—§ 19.1(d) n.67

Black v. State, 360 So.2d 142 (Fla.App.1978)—§ 19.1(d) n.67

Black, State v., 131 Or. 218, 282 P. 228 (1929)—§ 16.3(f) n.95

Black v. United States, 810 A.2d 410 (D.C.2002)—§ 3.8(d) n.135

Black, United States v., 125 F.3d 454 (7th Cir.1997)—§ 1.2(c) n.174

Black v. United States, 385 U.S. 26, 87 S.Ct. 190, 17 L.Ed.2d 26 (1966)—§ 11.8(b) n.25

Black Bear, United States v., 422 F.3d 658 (8th Cir.2005)—§§ 6.6(d) n.57; 6.8(b) n.49

Blackburn v. Alabama, 361 U.S. 199, 80 S.Ct. 274, 4 L.Ed.2d 242 (1960)—§§ 3.10(a) n.16; 6.2(b) n.33

Blackburn v. Foltz, 828 F.2d 1177 (6th Cir.1987)—§§ 11.10(c) n.70, 125

Blackburn, State v., 214 Wis.2d 372, 571 N.W.2d 695 (App.1997)—§ 18.4(c) n.53

Black Hills Institute v. Department of Justice, 967 F.2d 1237 (8th Cir.1992)—§ 10.1(c) n.38

Blackledge v. Allison, 431 U.S. 63, 97 S.Ct. 1621, 52 L.Ed.2d 136 (1977)—§§ 21.2(b) n.29; 21.5(d) n.97

Blackledge v. Perry, 417 U.S. 21, 94 S.Ct. 2098, 40 L.Ed.2d 628 (1974)—§§ 2.7(a) n.20, 61; 2.7(c) n.128; 2.9(h) n.221, 240; 13.5(a) n.2; 13.6(c) n.33; 13.7(c) n.35; 21.2(b) n.32; 21.2(c) n.129; 21.5(e) n.126; 21.6(a) n.11; 26.8(c) n.20; 27.2(c) n.36; 28.5(a) n.17

Blackmer, State v., 160 Vt. 451, 631 A.2d 1134 (Vt.1993)—§§ 12.3(e) n.123; 12.4(a) n.5, 22

Blackmer v. United States, 284 U.S. 421, 52 S.Ct. 252, 76 L.Ed. 375 (1932)—§ 16.4(b) n.26

Blackmon, Ex parte, 734 So.2d 995 (Ala.1999)—§ 21.5(d) n.101

Blackmon v. Johnson, 145 F.3d 205 (5th Cir.1998)—§ 6.4(g) n.161

Blackmon, State v., 78 S.W.3d 322 (Tenn.Crim.App.2001)—§§ 5.2(a) n.6; 5.4(c) n.38

Blackmon, State v., 984 S.W.2d 589 (Tenn.1998)—§ 17.4(b) n.120

Blackmon v. United States, 835 A.2d 1070 (D.C.2003)—§ 3.5(e) n.190

Blackmon, United States v., 273 F.3d 1204 (9th Cir.2001)—§ 4.6(e) n.93

Blackmon v. White, 825 F.2d 1263 (8th Cir.1987)—§ 24.8(e) n.55

Blackson v. United States, 897 A.2d 187 (D.C.App.2006)—§ 12.3(a) n.6

Blackwell, State v., 245 Ga.App. 135, 537 S.E.2d 457 (2000)—§ 24.3(e) n.136

Blackwell, State v., 120 Wash.2d 822, 845 P.2d 1017 (1993)—§ 13.2(c) n.60

Blackwell v. State, 34 Md.App. 547, 369 A.2d 153 (1977)—§ 27.6(b) n.58

Blackwell, United States v., 199 F.3d 623 (2d Cir.1999)—§§ 21.4(c) n.78; 21.5(c) n.83

Blackwell, United States v., 127 F.3d 947 (10th Cir.1997)—§ 27.5(e) n.180

Blackwell, United States v., 900 F.2d 742 (4th Cir.1990)—§ 27.2(c) n.51

Blackwell, United States v., 767 F.2d 1486 (11th Cir.1985)—§ 11.2(c) n.98

Blackwell, United States v., 694 F.2d 1325 (D.C.Cir.1982)—§ 24.3(h) n.176

Blair v. Armontrout, 916 F.2d 1310 (8th Cir.1990)—§§ 24.3(d) n.107; 24.7(e) n.74

Blair v. Armontrout, 626 F.Supp. 512 (W.D.Mo.1985)—§ 22.5(d) n.33

Blair, People v., 36 Cal.4th 686, 31 Cal.Rptr.3d 485, 115 P.3d 1145 (2005)—§ 24.8(f) n.118

Blair v. Pitchess, 5 Cal.3d 258, 96 Cal.Rptr. 42, 486 P.2d 1242 (1971)—§ 10.4(c) n.23

Blair v. United States, 250 U.S. 273, 39 S.Ct. 468, 63 L.Ed. 979 (1919)—§§ 8.2(c) n.31, 34; 8.4(c) n.113; 8.6(a) n.4, 9, 18 to 20; 8.8(a) n.4; 8.8(i) n.191; 15.1(d) n.173; 15.6(b) n.71

Blais, State v., 391 A.2d 1198 (Me.1978)—§§ 19.3(a) n.51, 52

Blaisdell v. Commonwealth, 372 Mass. 753, 364 N.E.2d 191 (1977)—§ 20.4(e) n.82

Blake v. Kemp, 758 F.2d 523 (11th Cir.1985)—§ 11.8(a) n.10

Blake v. State, 395 Md. 213, 909 A.2d 1020 (Md.App.2006)—§ 24.11(d) n.43

Blake v. State, 272 Ga.App. 402, 612 S.E.2d 589 (2005)—§ 26.6(d) n.75

Blake v. State, 381 Md. 218, 849 A.2d 410 (2004)—§§ 6.7(c) n.118; 6.9(f) n.133

Blake v. State, 814 So.2d 1163 (Fla.App.2002)—§ 26.9(b) n.78

Blake, State v., 642 So.2d 959 (Ala.1994)—§§ 12.2(a) n.11; 12.2(b) n.31

Blake, United States v., 415 F.3d 625 (7th Cir.2005)—§§ 13.4(a) n.11; 13.4(c) n.103

Blake, United States v., 881 F.2d 1070 (4th Cir.1989)—§ 3.10(f) n.196

Blake, United States v., 484 F.2d 50 (8th Cir.1973)—§ 3.6(e) n.110

Blake v. Wright, 179 F.3d 1003 (6th Cir.1999)—§ 4.6(n) n.258

Blakely v. Washington, 542 U.S. 296, 124 S.Ct. 2531, 159 L.Ed.2d 403 (2004)—§§ 2.8(a) n.24; 19.3(a) n.23; 22.1(a) n.22; 26.3(d) n.28; 26.4(i) n.183; 27.5(c) n.65; 28.6(e) n.52

Blakeney, State v., 352 N.C. 287, 531 S.E.2d 799 (2000)—§§ 13.2(a) n.5; 22.2(d) n.76; 24.2(a) n.14

Blakeney, United States v., 942 F.2d 1001 (6th Cir.1991)—§ 3.10(b) n.74

Blake, State ex rel. v. Chafin, 183 W.Va. 269, 395 S.E.2d 513 (1990)— § 27.5(b) n.48

Blake, State ex rel. v. Hatcher, 218 W.Va. 407, 624 S.E.2d 844 (2005)—§§ 11.9(c) n.110, 115

Blakey v. District Court, 232 Mont. 178, 755 P.2d 1380 (1988)—§ 18.4(c) n.32

Blakley, State v., 204 Ariz. 429, 65 P.3d 77 (2003)—§ 6.2(c) n.107

Blalark v. State, 112 Nev. 795, 918 P.2d 1314 (1996)—§ 21.2(b) n.76

Blalock v. United States, 844 F.2d 1546 (11th Cir.1988)—§§ 8.5(i) n.304, 308, 309, 324

Blalock, United States v., 449 F.Supp. 916 (N.D.Ga.1978)—§ 20.6(b) n.50

Blalock, United States v., 578 F.2d 245 (9th Cir.1978)—§§ 3.6(a) n.2, 30

Blanche, People v., 90 N.Y.2d 821, 660 N.Y.S.2d 375, 682 N.E.2d 976 (1997)—§ 7.4(b) n.19

Blanche, State v., 696 N.W.2d 351 (Minn.2005)—§§ 17.2(b) n.60, 71

Blanchett, People v., 33 Ill.2d 527, 212 N.E.2d 97 (1965)—§ 19.3(b) n.164

Blanco, United States v., 466 F.3d 916 (10th Cir.2006)—§ 21.1(h) n.213

Blanco, United States v., 844 F.2d 344 (6th Cir.1988)—§§ 9.1(d) n.127, 128

Blanco, United States v., 861 F.2d 773 (2d Cir.1988)—§ 18.2(c) n.49

Bland v. California Department of Corrections, 20 F.3d 1469 (9th Cir.1994)—§§ 11.4(b) n.20; 11.4(c) n.66, 67, 70, 75, 85, 88

Bland v. State, 803 P.2d 856 (Wyo.1990)—§ 6.7(c) n.133

Bland, State v., 337 N.W.2d 378 (Minn.1983)—§ 24.7(a) n.13

Blanding, State v., 69 Haw. 583, 752 P.2d 99 (1988)—§§ 6.6(a) n.12; 6.6(e) n.72

Blanding, United States v., 250 F.3d 858 (4th Cir.2001)—§ 22.3(d) n.247

Blaney v. State, 74 Md. 153, 21 A. 547 (1891)—§§ 8.4(b) n.46, 51, 68, 71

Blank v. State, 3 P.3d 359 (Alaska App.2000)—§ 3.2(g) n.195

Blank, State v., 131 Wash.2d 230, 930 P.2d 1213 (1997)—§ 26.1(f) n.139

Blankenship v. Estelle, 545 F.2d 510 (5th Cir.1977)—§ 24.3(d) n.110

Blankenship v. Johnson, 118 F.3d 312 (5th Cir.1997)—§ 27.1(b) n.22

Blankenship, State v., 198 W.Va. 290, 480 S.E.2d 178 (1996)—§ 27.5(e) n.154

Blankenship, State v., 757 S.W.2d 354 (Tenn.Crim.App.1988)—§ 3.8(b) n.16

Blankenship v. State, 673 S.W.2d 578 (Tex.Crim.App.1984)—§ 11.5(d) n.75

Blankenship, United States v., 923 F.2d 1110 (5th Cir.1991)—§ 11.7(e) n.83

Blanton v. City of North Las Vegas, 489 U.S. 538, 109 S.Ct. 1289, 103 L.Ed.2d 550 (1989)—§§ 2.6(c) n.84; 2.9(d) n.72; 22.1(b) n.40

Blanton v. State, 880 So.2d 798 (Fla.App.2004)—§ 20.2(e) n.95

Blanton v. United States, 94 F.3d 227 (6th Cir.1996)—§§ 28.9(a) n.20, 22

Blasco, United States v., 702 F.2d 1315 (11th Cir.1983)—§§ 24.4(d) n.37, 62

Blasius, People v., 435 Mich. 573, 459 N.W.2d 906 (1990)—§ 3.6(e) n.127

Blassingame, United States v., 197 F.3d 271 (7th Cir.1999)—§§ 5.2(a) n.9; 5.3(d) n.42

Blau v. State, 82 Miss. 514, 34 So. 153 (1903)—§ 15.7(b) n.36

Blaylock, United States v., 421 F.3d 758 (8th Cir.2005)—§ 22.3(d) n.201

Blaylock, United States v., 20 F.3d 1458 (9th Cir.1994)—§ 21.3(b) n.107

Blaze, United States v., 143 F.3d 585 (10th Cir.1998)—§ 9.1(d) n.127

Bledsoe, State v., 200 N.W.2d 529 (Iowa 1972)—§ 18.2(b) n.10

Blehm, People v., 983 P.2d 779 (Colo.1999)—§ 3.1(c) n.63

Blevins, State v., 40 N.M. 367, 60 P.2d 208 (1936)—§ 13.7(a) n.29

Blevins v. Tihonovich, 728 P.2d 732 (Colo.1986)—§ 14.4(d) n.92

Blevins, United States v., 593 F.2d 646 (5th Cir.1979)—§ 18.1(c) n.35

Blish, State v., 172 Vt. 265, 776 A.2d 380 (Vt.2001)—§ 21.4(f) n.174

Bliss, State v., 238 A.2d 848 (Del.1968)—§ 6.10(a) n.4

Bliss v. United States, 445 A.2d 625 (D.C.App.1982)—§ 6.9(g) n.158

Blissett v. Lefevre, 924 F.2d 434 (2d Cir.1991)—§§ 24.3(i) n.194, 195

Blitz, United States v., 533 F.2d 1329 (2d Cir.1976)—§ 15.5(b) n.65

Blizzard, State v., 278 Md. 556, 366 A.2d 1026 (1976)—§ 6.4(b) n.28

Block v. State, 41 Wis.2d 205, 163 N.W.2d 196 (1968)—§ 1.8(c) n.11

Block, United States v., 660 F.2d 1086 (5th Cir.1981)—§ 21.2(d) n.186

Blockburger v. United States, 284 U.S. 299, 52 S.Ct. 180, 76 L.Ed. 306 (1932)—§§ 6.4(e) n.100; 17.4(b) n.70

Blodgett, United States v., 35 Ga. 336, 30 F.Cas. 1157 (S.D.Ga.1867) (No. 18,312)—§ 15.4(b) n.23

Blok, United States v., 188 F.2d 1019 (D.C.Cir.1951)—§ 3.10(e) n.182

Blom, United States v., 242 F.3d 799 (8th Cir.2001)—§§ 23.2(a) n.15, 46

Blood, Commonwealth v., 400 Mass. 61, 507 N.E.2d 1029 (1987)—§ 2.12(d) n.196

Blood, State v., 70 R.I. 85, 37 A.2d 452 (1944)—§ 22.3(e) n.264

Bloodworth v. State, 233 Ga. 589, 212 S.E.2d 774 (1975)—§ 3.2(c) n.99

Blooflat, State v., 524 N.W.2d 482 (Minn.App.1994)—§§ 16.1(g) n.271; 16.1(h) n.292, 297, 304, 305

Bloom v. Illinois, 391 U.S. 194, 88 S.Ct. 1477, 20 L.Ed.2d 522 (1968)—§§ 1.7(i) n.165; 2.9(d) n.95; 8.5(b) n.61; 15.1(b) n.84; 22.1(b) n.35

Bloom, People v., 48 Cal.3d 1194, 259 Cal.Rptr. 669, 774 P.2d 698 (1989)—§ 11.5(d) n.84

Bloom, United States v., 865 F.2d 485 (2d Cir.1989)—§ 18.3(b) n.5

Bloom, United States v., 78 F.R.D. 591 (E.D.Pa.1977)—§ 16.3(c) n.32

Bloomfield, United States v., 40 F.3d 910 (8th Cir.1994)—§ 10.6(a) n.2

Bloomquist v. State, 914 P.2d 812 (Wyo.1996)—§ 26.4(g) n.125

Blotcher, United States v., 142 F.3d 728 (4th Cir.1998)—§ 22.3(d) n.250

Blouin, State v., 168 Vt. 119, 716 A.2d 826 (1998)—§§ 6.7(a) n.3; 6.7(b) n.41

Blouin, United States v., 666 F.2d 796 (2d Cir.1981)—§ 22.3(d) n.181

Blount, People v., 90 N.Y.2d 998, 665 N.Y.S.2d 626, 688 N.E.2d 500 (1997)—§ 13.4(c) n.98

Blouse, Commonwealth v., 531 Pa. 167, 611 A.2d 1177 (1992)—§ 3.9(g) n.125

Blow, State v., 157 Vt. 513, 602 A.2d 552 (1991)—§ 10.6(c) n.30

Blubaugh, State v., 904 P.2d 688 (Utah 1995)—§ 19.3(a) n.62

Blucher, United States v., 730 F.Supp. 428 (S.D.Fla.1990)—§ 24.11(d) n.36

Bludson, People v., 97 N.Y.2d 644, 736 N.Y.S.2d 289, 761 N.E.2d 1016 (2001)—§ 22.3(c) n.106

Bludworth v. Palm Beach Newspapers, Inc., 476 So.2d 775 (Fla.App.1985)—§ 23.1(b) n.21

Blue, Ex parte, _____ S.W.3d _____, 2007 WL 676194 (Tex.Cr.App.2007)—§ 28.11(b) n.17

Blue, State v., 225 Kan. 576, 592 P.2d 897 (1979)—§ 24.6(b) n.29

Blue v. State, 558 P.2d 636 (Alaska 1977)—§ 7.3(b) n.31

Blue, United States v., 384 U.S. 251, 86 S.Ct. 1416, 16 L.Ed.2d 510 (1966)—§§ 3.1(f) n.144; 15.5(a) n.5, 8; 15.5(b) n.100

Blum, State v., 560 N.W.2d 7 (Iowa 1997)—§ 21.2(c) n.124

Blume, People v., 443 Mich. 476, 505 N.W.2d 843 (1993)—§§ 16.4(c) n.57, 64

Blumler, State v., 458 N.W.2d 300 (N.D.1990)—§ 3.2(c) n.118

Blunt v. United States, 322 A.2d 579 (D.C.App.1974)—§§ 12.3(g) n.150, 160

Bluske, United States v., 969 F.2d 609 (8th Cir.1992)—§§ 11.9(a) n.7; 11.9(b) n.54

Bly, Commonwealth v., 448 Mass. 473, 862 N.E.2d 341 (2007)—§§ 6.6(d) n.46, 50

Blyden, United States v., 964 F.2d 1375 (3d Cir.1992)—§ 17.4(a) n.24

B.M.B., Matter of, 264 Kan. 417, 955 P.2d 1302 (1998)—§ 6.9(b) n.22

Boardman v. Estelle, 957 F.2d 1523 (9th Cir.1992)—§ 26.4(g) n.141

Boarman v. State, 509 N.E.2d 177 (Ind.1987)—§ 6.7(b) n.43

Boatner, United States v., 966 F.2d 1575 (11th Cir.1992)—§§ 21.1(h) n.220; 21.2(e) n.306

Boatwright, People v., 748 N.Y.S.2d 541, 297 A.D. 2d 603 (N.Y.A.D.2002)—§ 25.3(b) n.18

Boatwright, United States v., 822 F.2d 862 (9th Cir.1987)—§ 9.3(e) n.71

Boatwright, United States v., 425 F.Supp. 747 (E.D.Pa.1977)—§ 7.2(d) n.51

Bobadilla-Lopez, United States v., 954 F.2d 519 (9th Cir.1992)—§ 20.3(b) n.52

Bobisink, United States v., 415 F.Supp. 1334 (D.Mass.1976)—§ 3.2(j) n.250

Bobo v. Kolb, 969 F.2d 391 (7th Cir.1992)—§ 6.9(g) n.150

Bobo, State v., 814 S.W.2d 353 (Tenn.1991)—§§ 1.7(h) n.127; 22.3(e) n.279

Bobo, State v., 803 P.2d 1268 (Utah App.1990)—§§ 2.12(c) n.153; 2.12(d) n.192

Bockert, State v., 257 Kan. 488, 893 P.2d 832 (1995)—§§ 14.1(e) n.69; 14.3(a) n.12, 23, 25

Bock Leung Chew, People v., 142 Cal.App.2d 400, 298 P.2d 118 (1956)—§ 3.5(a) n.33

Boclair, People v., 129 Ill.2d 458, 136 Ill.Dec. 29, 544 N.E.2d 715 (1989)—§ 20.4(f) n.95

Boclair, People v., 119 Ill.2d 368, 116 Ill.Dec. 545, 519 N.E.2d 437 (1987)—§§ 20.5(f) n.81, 88

Bocra, United States v., 623 F.2d 281 (3d Cir.1980)—§ 5.4(c) n.46

Boczkowski, Commonwealth v., 577 Pa. 421, 846 A.2d 75 (2004)—§ 6.6(d) n.57

Boddie v. State, 875 So.2d 180 (Miss.2004)—§ 21.4(f) n.173

Bodley, State v., 394 So.2d 584 (La.1981)—§§ 3.10(e) n.164, 165

Bodner v. Superior Court, 42 Cal.App.4th 1801, 50 Cal.Rptr.2d 236 (1996)—§ 14.3(c) n.73

Bodtke, State v., 219 Neb. 504, 363 N.W.2d 917 (1985)—§§ 6.2(c) n.116; 6.10(b) n.16

Boeglin, State v., 105 N.M. 247, 731 P.2d 943 (1987)—§ 11.6(a) n.50

Boehm, People v., 270 Cal.App.2d 13, 75 Cal.Rptr. 590 (1969)—§ 15.4(g) n.161

Boehm v. State, 113 Nev. 910, 944 P.2d 269 (1997)—§ 6.7(c) n.141

Boehme, State v., 71 Wash.2d 621, 430 P.2d 527 (1967)—§ 20.5(a) n.1

Boerne, City of v. Flores, 521 U.S. 507, 117 S.Ct. 2157, 138 L.Ed.2d 624 (1997)—§ 6.5(e) n.89

Boettcher, People v., 69 N.Y.2d 174, 513 N.Y.S.2d 83, 505 N.E.2d 594 (1987)—§ 24.8(d) n.46

Boettcher, State v., 338 So.2d 1356 (La.1976)—§ 7.4(g) n.116

Boettcher, United States v., 164 F.Supp.2d 925 (E.D.Mich.2001)—§ 15.6(b) n.78

Boff, People v., 766 P.2d 646 (Colo.1988)—§ 3.5(e) n.190

Bogard, United States v., 846 F.2d 563 (9th Cir.1988)—§ 18.3(b) n.11

Bogdanoff, People v., 254 N.Y. 16, 171 N.E. 890 (1930)—§§ 19.1(a) n.11; 19.1(c) n.29, 30

Boggess, State v., 358 N.C. 676, 600 S.E.2d 453 (2004)—§ 6.9(g) n.166

Boggess v. State, 783 P.2d 1173 (Alaska App.1989)—§ 15.7(h) n.226

Boggs, People v., 255 Cal.App.2d 693, 63 Cal.Rptr. 430 (1967)—§ 17.2(b) n.69

Boggs v. State, 667 So.2d 765 (Fla.1996)—§ 23.2(f) n.90

Bogolowski, People v., 326 Ill. 253, 157 N.E. 181 (1927)—§ 8.11(e) n.100

Bogue v. Fennelly, 705 So.2d 575 (Fla.App.1997)—§ 18.4(c) n.39

Bohach v. City of Reno, 932 F.Supp. 1232 (D. Nev. 1996)—§ 4.6(b) n.25

Bohl, United States v., 25 F.3d 904 (10th Cir.1994)—§ 24.3(e) n.132

Bohle, United States v., 445 F.2d 54 (7th Cir.1971)—§ 16.1(h) n.305

Boire, State v., 124 N.H. 622, 474 A.2d 568 (1984)—§ 19.3(b) n.162

Bojorquez, State v., 111 Ariz. 549, 535 P.2d 6 (1975)—§§ 15.2(e) n.145; 15.7(b) n.14, 41

Boland, State v., 115 Wash.2d 571, 800 P.2d 1112 (1990)—§ 2.12(e) n.205

Bolden, People v., 197 Ill.2d 166, 258 Ill.Dec. 538, 756 N.E.2d 812 (2001)—§ 7.3(b) n.38

Bolden, State v., 639 So.2d 721 (La.1994)—§ 17.4(a) n.39

Bolden, United States v., 353 F.3d 870 (10th Cir.2003)—§§ 22.5(a) n.2; 27.3(c) n.45

Bolden, United States v., 92 F.3d 686 (8th Cir.1996)—§ 17.2(b) n.69

Bolden, United States v., 461 F.2d 998 (8th Cir.1972)—§ 6.10(b) n.19

Boldridge, State v., 274 Kan. 795, 57 P.3d 8 (2002)—§ 6.6(d) n.46

Bolds v. State, 195 Ga.App. 586, 394 S.E.2d 593 (1990)—§ 15.4(g) n.161

Bolen, State v., 270 Kan. 337, 13 P.3d 1270 (2000)—§ 13.3(c) n.40

Boles v. Foltz, 816 F.2d 1132 (6th Cir.1987)—§§ 6.4(f) n.136; 6.9(f) n.121

Boley, State v., 279 Kan. 989, 113 P.3d 248 (2005)—§§ 21.2(f) n.365; 21.5(e) n.149

Bolin, People v., 18 Cal.4th 297, 75 Cal.Rptr.2d 412, 956 P.2d 374 (1998)—§ 22.3(c) n.162

Bolin, People v., 712 P.2d 1002 (Colo.1986)—§ 18.4(d) n.82

Bolin v. State, 736 So.2d 1160 (Fla.1999)—§§ 22.3(a) n.45; 23.2(f) n.90

Boling v. Romer, 101 F.3d 1336 (10th Cir.1996)—§ 3.2(g) n.199

Bolinger, United States v., 940 F.2d 478 (9th Cir.1991)—§§ 26.9(b) n.26, 53

Boll, State v., 2002 SD 114, 651 N.W.2d 710 (S.D.2002)—§ 3.1(c) n.65

Bollenbach v. United States, 326 U.S. 607, 66 S.Ct. 402, 90 L.Ed. 350 (1946)—§ 24.8(a) n.24

Bollig, State v., 232 Wis.2d 561, 605 N.W.2d 199 (2000)—§ 21.4(d) n.138

Bolling, People v., 79 N.Y.2d 317, 582 N.Y.S.2d 950, 591 N.E.2d 1136 (1992)—§ 22.3(d) n.220

Bolling v. Sharpe, 347 U.S. 497, 74 S.Ct. 693, 98 L.Ed. 884 (1954)—§ 13.4(a) n.1

Bollman, Ex parte, 8 U.S. (4 Cranch) 75, 2 L.Ed. 554 (1807)—§ 28.2(a) n.8

Bologna, People v., 67 A.D.2d 1004, 413 N.Y.S.2d 739 (1979)—§ 26.9(c) n.84

Bolt, State v., 142 Ariz. 260, 689 P.2d 519 (1984)—§§ 2.12(c) n.169; 2.12(d) n.198; 2.12(e) n.205; 3.1(c) n.84; 9.4(b) n.57

Bolte, State v., 115 N.J. 579, 560 A.2d 644 (1989)—§ 3.6(a) n.25

Bolton, State v., 274 Kan. 1, 49 P.3d 468 (2002)—§ 22.3(d) n.226

Bolton, State v., 271 Kan. 538, 23 P.3d 824 (2001)—§ 22.3(d) n.255

Bolton, State v., 182 Ariz. 290, 896 P.2d 830 (1995)—§ 22.3(d) n.202

Bolton, United States v., 68 F.3d 396 (10th Cir.1995)—§§ 1.2(c) n.176, 177

Bolton, United States v., 977 F.2d 1196 (7th Cir.1992)—§ 8.11(c) n.47

Bolton, United States v., 893 F.2d 894 (7th Cir.1990)—§§ 8.8(i) n.190; 15.6(f) n.200

Bomar, Commonwealth v., 573 Pa. 426, 826 A.2d 831 (2003)—§§ 6.9(d) n.72; 13.4(e) n.169

Bonahan v. Nebraska, 125 U.S. 692, 8 S.Ct. 1390, 31 L.Ed. 854 (1887)—§ 27.5(c) n.73

Bonanno, In re, 344 F.2d 830 (2d Cir.1965)—§ 8.5(h) n.247

Bonanno, United States v., 452 F.Supp. 743 (N.D.Cal.1978)—§ 26.9(b) n.50

Bonas, United States v., 344 F.3d 945 (9th Cir.2003)—§ 25.2(d) n.25

Boncore, Commonwealth v., 412 Mass. 1013, 593 N.E.2d 227 (1992)—§ 6.9(g) n.149

Bond v. United States, 529 U.S. 334, 120 S.Ct. 1462, 146 L.Ed.2d 365 (2000)—§ 3.2(b) n.94

Bond, United States v., 135 F.3d 1247 (8th Cir.1998)—§ 21.2(g) n.396

Bond v. United States, 77 F.3d 1009 (7th Cir.1996)—§ 9.1(b) n.86

Bondurant, State v., 4 S.W.3d 662 (Tenn.1999)—§§ 15.4(e) n.134, 140

Bone, People v., 82 Ill.2d 282, 45 Ill.Dec. 93, 412 N.E.2d 444 (1980)—§ 17.4(a) n.66

Bone, State v., 354 N.C. 1, 550 S.E.2d 482 (2001)—§§ 3.5(d) n.141; 6.2(c) n.101, 120

Bone v. State, 284 Mont. 293, 944 P.2d 734 (1997)—§§ 21.3(b) n.45, 52

Bonebrake v. Norris, 417 F.3d 938 (8th Cir.2005)—§ 26.4(f) n.105

Bongalis, State v., 180 W.Va. 584, 378 S.E.2d 449 (1989)—§ 22.3(c) n.141

Bongarzone-Suarrcy, People v., 6 N.Y.3d 787, 811 N.Y.S.2d 292, 844 N.E.2d 746 (2006)—§ 6.6(d) n.45

Bonilla Romero, United States v., 836 F.2d 39 (1st Cir.1987)—§ 10.6(d) n.38

Bonin v. Calderon, 77 F.3d 1155 (9th Cir.1996)—§ 11.1(b) n.83

Bonin v. California, 494 U.S. 1039, 110 S.Ct. 1506, 108 L.Ed.2d 641 (1990)—§ 11.9(b) n.69

Bonin, People v., 47 Cal.3d 808, 254 Cal.Rptr. 298, 765 P.2d 460 (1989)—§ 11.9(b) n.86

Bonin, People v., 46 Cal.3d 659, 250 Cal.Rptr. 687, 758 P.2d 1217 (1988)—§ 23.2(a) n.52

Bonneau v. United States, 961 F.2d 17 (1st Cir.1992)—§§ 11.6(d) n.119; 11.10(d) n.192

Bonnenfant v. State, 86 Nev. 393, 469 P.2d 401 (1970)—§ 24.7(e) n.63

Bonner v. Coughlin, 517 F.2d 1311 (7th Cir.1975)—§ 3.9(i) n.176

Bonner, People v., 37 Ill.2d 553, 229 N.E.2d 527 (1967)—§§ 14.4(c) n.55; 14.4(d) n.92

Bonner v. State, 921 So.2d 469 (Ala.Cr.App.2005)—§ 24.7(e) n.44

Bonner, United States v., 440 F.3d 414 (7th Cir.2006)—§ 24.2(a) n.11

Bonner, United States v., 808 F.2d 864 (1st Cir.1986)—§§ 3.1(c) n.74; 3.4(j) n.181

Booker, People v., 208 Mich.App. 163, 527 N.W.2d 42 (1994)—§ 24.9(e) n.58

Booker v. State, 773 So.2d 1079 (Fla.2000)—§ 24.4(d) n.67

Booker v. State, 716 So.2d 1064 (Miss.1998)—§ 22.3(d) n.247

Booker, United States v., 543 U.S. 220, 125 S.Ct. 738, 160 L.Ed.2d 621 (2005)—§§ 13.7(a) n.20; 21.1(h) n.243; 21.2(a) n.7; 26.3(e) n.48; 26.3(g) n.85; 26.4(a) n.3; 26.4(i) n.184; 27.5(d) n.134

Bookhardt, United States v., 277 F.3d 558 (D.C.Cir.2002)—§ 3.1(d) n.98

Boomershine, State v., 85 Ohio App.3d 21, 619 N.E.2d 52 (1993)—§ 25.1(d) n.60

Boone, People v., 22 N.Y.2d 476, 293 N.Y.S.2d 287, 239 N.E.2d 885 (1968)—§ 6.2(c) n.128

Boone v. State, 270 Ark. 83, 603 S.W.2d 410 (1980)—§ 26.10(d) n.91

Boone, State v., 284 Md. 1, 393 A.2d 1361 (1978)—§ 25.4(c) n.40

Boone, State v., 66 N.J. 38, 327 A.2d 661 (1974)—§§ 21.2(h) n.415; 21.5(f) n.157

Boone, United States v., 245 F.3d 352 (4th Cir.2001)—§§ 1.8(e) n.93; 3.10(b) n.74

Boone v. United States, 483 A.2d 1135 (D.C.App.1984)—§ 24.2(a) n.5

Boone, United States v., 543 F.2d 1090 (4th Cir.1976)—§ 21.5(c) n.78

Boon San Chong, United States v., 829 F.2d 1572 (11th Cir.1987)—§ 6.9(g) n.169

Boorigie, State v., 273 Kan. 18, 41 P.3d 764 (2002)—§ 6.4(f) n.122

Booth v. Commonwealth, 675 S.W.2d 856 (Ky.1984)—§ 6.7(b) n.66

Booth, Commonwealth v., 266 Mass. 80, 165 N.E. 29 (1929)—§ 16.4(c) n.52

Booth v. Maryland, 482 U.S. 496, 107 S.Ct. 2529, 96 L.Ed.2d 440 (1987)—§ 26.5(d) n.71

Booth v. State, 903 P.2d 1079 (Alaska App.1995)—§ 25.5(b) n.25

Booton, State v., 114 N.H. 750, 329 A.2d 376 (1974)—§§ 20.2(a) n.7; 20.3(h) n.155

Booze, State v., 684 P.2d 1206 (Okl.Cr.1984)—§ 5.4(b) n.16

Booze, United States v., 293 F.3d 516 (D.C.Cir.2002)—§ 21.3(b) n.62

Boppre, State v., 234 Neb. 922, 453 N.W.2d 406 (1990)—§ 2.6(b) n.37

Borchard, State v., 24 Ohio App.2d 95, 264 N.E.2d 646 (1970)—§ 3.2(d) n.150

Borchardt, United States v., 809 F.2d 1115 (5th Cir.1987)—§ 3.4(a) n.10

Bordeaux, United States v., 400 F.3d 548 (8th Cir.2005)—§ 24.2(e) n.78

Bordeaux, United States v., 121 F.3d 1187 (8th Cir.1997)—§ 25.4(d) n.45

Bordeaux, United States v., 980 F.2d 534 (8th Cir.1992)—§ 24.8(e) n.54

Borden Company, Petition of, 75 F.Supp. 857 (N.D.Ill.1948)—§§ 8.7(b) n.45, 62

Bordenkircher v. Hayes, 434 U.S. 357, 98 S.Ct. 663, 54 L.Ed.2d 604 (1978)—§§ 2.7(a) n.30; 2.10(b) n.12; 13.7(c) n.46; 21.1(b) n.33; 21.2(a) n.14; 21.2(b) n.31; 21.2(c) n.112, 128; 21.3(c) n.165; 21.5(e) n.133

Borders, State v., 255 Kan. 871, 879 P.2d 620 (1994)—§ 26.4(g) n.123

Borders, United States v., 270 F.3d 1180 (8th Cir.2001)—§ 22.3(a) n.16

Bordner, Commonwealth v., 432 Pa. 405, 247 A.2d 612 (1968)—§ 6.10(b) n.27

Borelli, United States v., 336 F.2d 376 (2d Cir.1964)—§ 18.5(a) n.15

Borello, United States v., 624 F.Supp. 150 (E.D.N.Y.1985)—§ 8.11(c) n.47

Borello, United States v., 766 F.2d 46 (2d Cir.1985)—§ 26.4(f) n.91

Boretsky, State v., 186 N.J. 271, 894 A.2d 659 (2006)—§ 6.9(g) n.200

Borghesi, People v., 40 P.3d 15 (Colo.App.2001)—§ 19.3(c) n.198

Boria v. Keane, 83 F.3d 48 (2d Cir.1996)—§ 11.10(b) n.39

Boria v. Keane, 99 F.3d 492 (2d Cir.1996)—§§ 21.3(b) n.74, 78, 94

Borjesson, United States v., 92 F.3d 954 (9th Cir.1996)—§ 17.4(b) n.128

Borre v. United States, 940 F.2d 215 (7th Cir.1991)—§ 26.9(c) n.94

Borrelli, United States v., 621 F.2d 1092 (10th Cir.1980)—§ 7.4(f) n.106

Borrero-Isaza, United States v., 887 F.2d 1349 (9th Cir.1989)—§ 26.4(b) n.11

Borski v. State, 712 So.2d 787 (Fla.App.1998)—§ 3.8(e) n.201

Bortels, United States v., 962 F.2d 558 (6th Cir.1992)—§ 26.9(b) n.47

Bortner, State v., 150 N.H. 504, 841 A.2d 80 (2004)—§ 13.5(b) n.43

Bortnovsky, United States v., 820 F.2d 572 (2d Cir.1987)—§§ 19.4(b) n.14, 21, 31

Borum v. United States, 318 A.2d 590 (D.C.1974)—§ 3.6(b) n.60

Borys, United States v., 169 F.Supp. 366 (D.Alaska 1959)—§ 15.7(h) n.232

Boscarino, State v., 204 Conn. 714, 529 A.2d 1260 (1987)—§§ 17.1(d) n.52, 57

Bosch, United States v., 584 F.2d 1113 (1st Cir.1978)—§ 11.10(b) n.30

Boseman v. State, 263 Ga. 730, 438 S.E.2d 626 (1994)—§§ 18.2(c) n.31; 18.2(e) n.79

Boshell, United States v., 952 F.2d 1101 (9th Cir.1991)—§§ 20.3(b) n.43; 24.3(c) n.100

Boshell, United States v., 728 F.Supp. 632 (E.D.Wash.1990)—§ 13.7(a) n.21

Boss, People v., 182 Misc.2d 700, 701 N.Y.S.2d 891 (Sup.Ct.2000)—§ 23.3(b) n.27

Boss, People v., 261 A.D.2d 1, 701 N.Y.S.2d 342 (1999)—§§ 23.2(a) n.32; 23.2(f) n.108

Boss v. Pierce, 263 F.3d 734 (7th Cir.2001)—§ 24.3(b) n.59

Bosse, United States v., 898 F.2d 113 (9th Cir.1990)—§ 3.10(c) n.96

Bossett v. Walker, 41 F.3d 825 (2d Cir.1994)—§ 2.6(b) n.68

Bost, People v., 770 P.2d 1209 (Colo.1989)—§ 18.4(c) n.40

Boster, State v., 217 Kan. 618, 539 P.2d 294 (1975)—§§ 3.7(d) n.85; 9.1(d) n.115, 128

Bostic, Commonwealth v., 500 Pa. 345, 456 A.2d 1320 (1983)—§ 2.12(d) n.184

Bostic v. State, 805 P.2d 344 (Alaska 1991)—§ 20.6(b) n.29

Bostic, United States v., 713 F.2d 401 (8th Cir.1983)—§ 17.3(e) n.67

Bostick, United States ex rel. v. Peters, 3 F.3d 1023 (7th Cir.1993)—§ 28.3(d) n.85

Boston v. Bowersox, 202 F.3d 1001 (8th Cir.1999)—§ 22.2(d) n.79

Boston, People v., 75 N.Y.2d 585, 555 N.Y.S.2d 27, 554 N.E.2d 64 (1990)—§§ 15.1(f) n.316, 334

Boston, United States v., 508 F.2d 1171 (2d Cir.1974)—§ 6.9(a) n.9

Boston & Maine Railroad, United States v., 380 U.S. 157, 85 S.Ct. 868, 13 L.Ed.2d 728 (1965)—§ 19.4(a) n.8

Boston Herald, Inc. v. Connolly, In re, 321 F.3d 174 (1st Cir.2003)—§ 23.1(d) n.190

Boswell, State v., 111 N.M. 240, 804 P.2d 1059 (1991)—§ 3.5(e) n.193

Bosworth, State v., 451 So.2d 1070 (La.1984)—§ 21.2(g) n.396

Botelho, United States v., 360 F.Supp. 620 (D.Hawai'i 1973)—§§ 3.2(c) n.102; 3.10(e) n.151

Both, People v., 118 Misc. 414, 193 N.Y.S. 591 (Sup.1922)—§ 15.7(b) n.36

Botkin, People v., 132 Cal. 231, 64 P. 286 (1901)—§§ 16.1(a) n.13; 16.4(c) n.84

Boucher, State v., 309 Mont. 514, 48 P.3d 21 (2002)—§ 21.4(e) n.163

Boucher, State v., 718 A.2d 1092 (Me.1998)—§ 17.2(b) n.71

Boucher, State v., 237 Iowa 772, 23 N.W.2d 851 (1946)—§ 15.5(c) n.110

Bouchillon v. Collins, 907 F.2d 589 (5th Cir.1990)—§ 11.10(c) n.126

Bouie v. City of Columbia, 378 U.S. 347, 84 S.Ct. 1697, 12 L.Ed.2d 894 (1964)—§ 17.4(b) n.74

Bouie, State v., 817 So.2d 48 (La.2002)—§ 21.2(c) n.120

Bouie v. State, 559 So.2d 1113 (Fla.1990)—§ 11.9(a) n.29

Boukater, United States v., 409 F.2d 537 (5th Cir.1969)—§ 3.10(b) n.50

Bouknight v. United States, 867 A.2d 245 (D.C.App.2005)—§ 24.11(d) n.39

Boulas v. Superior Court, 188 Cal.App.3d 422, 233 Cal.Rptr. 487 (1986)—§ 11.8(b) n.37

Boulies, People v., 690 P.2d 1253 (Colo.1984)—§ 22.3(e) n.285

Bounds v. Smith, 430 U.S. 817, 97 S.Ct. 1491, 52 L.Ed.2d 72 (1977)—§§ 11.1(b) n.78; 11.2(f) n.230, 235; 28.12(a) n.5

Bounds v. State, 688 So.2d 1362 (Miss.1997)—§§ 22.3(d) n.195, 249

Bourdon v. Loughren, 386 F.3d 88 (2d Cir.2004)—§ 11.2(f) n.240

Bourdon v. State, 28 P.3d 319 (Alaska App.2001)—§ 12.4(d) n.63

Bourexis v. Carroll County Narcotics Task Force, 96 Md.App. 459, 625 A.2d 391 (1993)—§ 21.3(c) n.151

Bourgeois, United States v., 964 F.2d 935 (9th Cir.1992)—§§ 13.4(b) n.57, 60

Bourjaily v. United States, 483 U.S. 171, 107 S.Ct. 2775, 97 L.Ed.2d 144 (1987)—§ 2.8(a) n.6

Bourke, State v., 718 N.W.2d 922 (Minn.2006)—§ 3.4(g) n.128

Bourque, United States v., 541 F.2d 290 (1st Cir.1976)—§ 13.4(e) n.170

Bousley v. United States, 523 U.S. 614, 118 S.Ct. 1604, 140 L.Ed.2d 828 (1998)—§§ 21.4(c) n.83; 21.5(c) n.75; 21.5(e) n.143, 145; 21.6(a) n.78; 28.4(e) n.81; 28.6(d) n.18; 28.9(b) n.36, 39; 28.9(c) n.84

Bousman v. District Court for Clinton County, 630 N.W.2d 789 (Iowa 2001)—§ 3.8(g) n.241

Bouthot, United States v., 878 F.2d 1506 (1st Cir.1989)—§§ 7.4(b) n.31, 32; 21.3(c) n.189; 21.4(d) n.133; 27.3(c) n.48

Boutot, State v., 325 A.2d 34 (Me.1974)—§ 9.1(d) n.135

Boutwell v. State, 256 Ga. 63, 344 S.E.2d 222 (1986)—§§ 6.6(a) n.12; 6.6(b) n.16

Bouye v. State, 699 N.E.2d 620 (Ind.1998)—§ 24.2(a) n.8

Bova, United States v., 350 F.3d 224 (1st Cir.2003)—§ 11.5(f) n.102

Bova, United States v., 493 F.2d 33 (5th Cir.1974)—§§ 17.3(b) n.23; 17.3(d) n.44

Bowden v. Keane, 237 F.3d 125 (2d Cir.2001)—§ 24.1(b) n.29

Bowden v. Kemp, 767 F.2d 761 (11th Cir.1985)—§ 11.2(e) n.151

Bowden v. State, 297 Ark. 160, 761 S.W.2d 148 (1988)—§§ 7.3(b) n.28; 7.3(d) n.77

Bowden, United States v., 380 F.3d 266 (6th Cir.2004)—§ 3.10(f) n.206

Bowe, State v., 77 Hawai'i 51, 881 P.2d 538 (1994)—§ 6.2(c) n.186

Bowe, United States v., 309 F.3d 234 (4th Cir.2002)—§ 21.2(d) n.270

Bowe, United States v., 257 F.3d 336 (4th Cir.2001)—§ 21.2(d) n.274

Bowe, United States v., 698 F.2d 560 (2d Cir.1983)—§ 10.5(f) n.62

Bowen v. Johnston, 306 U.S. 19, 59 S.Ct. 442, 83 L.Ed. 455 (1939)—§§ 16.4(d) n.145; 28.9(c) n.77

Bowen v. State, 606 P.2d 589 (Okla.Crim.1980)—§ 11.5(g) n.115

Bowen v. State, 263 Ind. 558, 334 N.E.2d 691 (1975)—§ 20.6(c) n.89

Bowen v. State, 346 A.2d 172 (Del.1975)—§ 6.10(a) n.3

Bowens v. Superior Court, 1 Cal.4th 36, 2 Cal.Rptr.2d 376, 820 P.2d 600 (1991)—§§ 14.2(d) n.55, 58; 14.4(e) n.114; 15.3(d) n.66

Bowens, United States v., 224 F.3d 302 (4th Cir.2000)—§§ 16.2(d) n.55, 56, 58; 16.2(e) n.68, 74, 89, 90

Bower, In re, 38 Cal.3d 865, 215 Cal.Rptr. 267, 700 P.2d 1269 (1985)—§§ 13.7(c) n.45, 60

Bowerman, State v., 115 Wash.2d 794, 802 P.2d 116 (1990)—§ 21.4(f) n.210

Bowers, Ex parte, 886 S.W.2d 346 (Tex.App.1994)—§ 27.4(f) n.68

Bowers v. Hardwick, 478 U.S. 186, 106 S.Ct. 2841, 92 L.Ed.2d 140 (1986)—§ 2.7(d) n.232

Bowers v. Moore, 266 Ga. 893, 471 S.E.2d 869 (1996)—§ 21.4(e) n.165

Bowers v. State, 320 Md. 416, 578 A.2d 734 (1990)—§ 11.10(c) n.71

Bowers v. State, 565 So.2d 1203 (Ala.Cr.App.1990)—§ 26.1(e) n.99

Bowers v. State, 500 N.E.2d 203 (Ind.1986)—§ 13.5(b) n.38

Bowers, United States v., 432 F.3d 518 (3d Cir.2005)—§ 12.3(a) n.18

Bowers, United States v., 739 F.2d 1050 (6th Cir.1984)—§ 6.10(b) n.23

Bowersmith, State v., 224 Neb. 6, 395 N.W.2d 527 (1986)—§ 6.6(e) n.59

Bowie v. State, 135 S.W.3d 55 (Tex.Crim.App.2004)—§§ 21.5(f) n.163, 171

Bowie v. State, 324 Md. 1, 595 A.2d 448 (1991)—§ 22.3(a) n.23

Bowie v. State, 816 P.2d 1143 (Okl.Cr.1991)—§ 18.4(c) n.45

Bowie v. State, 14 Md.App. 567, 287 A.2d 782 (1972)—§§ 8.11(e) n.95, 97

Bowie, United States v., 892 F.2d 1494 (10th Cir.1990)—§§ 11.9(d) n.202, 233

Bowler v. United States, 480 A.2d 678 (D.C.App.1984)—§ 6.7(b) n.41

Bowler, United States v., 585 F.2d 851 (7th Cir.1978)—§ 21.2(e) n.316

Bowler, United States v., 561 F.2d 1323 (9th Cir.1977)—§ 3.4(e) n.68

Bowles v. Russell, _____ U.S. _____, 127 S.Ct. 2360, 168 L.Ed.2d 96 (2007)—§ 28.10 n.2

Bowles, State v., 530 N.W.2d 521 (Minn.1995)—§ 22.3(b) n.68

Bowles v. United States, 439 F.2d 536 (D.C.Cir.1970)—§ 17.2(d) n.114

Bowling v. Vose, 3 F.3d 559 (1st Cir.1993)—§ 20.6(c) n.75

Bowman, People v., 40 Ill.2d 116, 239 N.E.2d 433 (1968)—§ 21.3(a) n.38

Bowman, State v., 366 S.C. 485, 623 S.E.2d 378 (2005)—§ 10.2(b) n.19

Bowman, State v., 349 N.C. 459, 509 S.E.2d 428 (1998)—§ 22.2(d) n.80

Bowman, State v., 588 A.2d 728 (Me.1991)—§§ 2.6(b) n.69; 17.2(b) n.75; 22.2(e) n.110

Bowman, United States v., 380 F.3d 387 (8th Cir.2004)—§§ 13.5(h) n.180, 211

Bowman, United States v., 348 F.3d 408 (4th Cir.2003)—§ 21.3(b) n.58

Bowman, United States v., 215 F.3d 951 (9th Cir.2000)—§§ 7.4(d) n.72, 73

Bowman, United States v., 907 F.2d 63 (8th Cir.1990)—§ 3.1(d) n.103

Bowman, United States v., 260 U.S. 94, 43 S.Ct. 39, 67 L.Ed. 149 (1922)—§§ 16.4(b) n.24, 26

Bowman, People ex rel. v. Woodward, 63 Ill.2d 382, 349 N.E.2d 57 (1976)—§ 20.4(b) n.37

Bownes, United States v., 405 F.3d 634 (7th Cir.2005)—§§ 21.2(b) n.86; 27.5(c) n.59

Bowring v. Godwin, 551 F.2d 44 (4th Cir.1977)—§ 12.2(d) n.50

Bowser v. State, 816 S.W.2d 518 (Tex.App.1991)—§ 24.5(b) n.23

Bowser v. State, 50 Md.App. 363, 439 A.2d 1 (1981)—§ 5.3(a) n.7

Box, People v., 23 Cal.4th 1153, 99 Cal.Rptr.2d 69, 5 P.3d 130 (2000)—§ 22.3(b) n.94

Box, United States v., 50 F.3d 345 (5th Cir.1995)—§ 23.2(e) n.75

Boyce v. Fernandes, 77 F.3d 946 (7th Cir.1996)—§ 3.3(d) n.154

Boyce, People v., 228 Ill.App.3d 87, 170 Ill.Dec. 65, 592 N.E.2d 501 (1992)—§§ 26.1(d) n.73, 80, 81

Boyce, People v., 113 Ill.App.2d 266, 252 N.E.2d 71 (1969)—§ 7.4(b) n.21

Boyce, United States v., 351 F.3d 1102 (11th Cir.2003)—§ 3.10(a) n.2

Boyce, United States v., 594 F.2d 1246 (9th Cir.1979)—§ 6.9(e) n.88

Boyd, Ex parte, 542 So.2d 1276 (Ala.1989)—§ 3.7(e) n.91

Boyd, Commonwealth v., 451 Pa.Super. 404, 679 A.2d 1284 (1996)—§ 18.4(c) n.68

Boyd, Commonwealth v., 212 Pa.Super. 80, 239 A.2d 853 (1968)—§ 6.7(d) n.144

Boyd v. Dutton, 405 U.S. 1, 92 S.Ct. 759, 30 L.Ed.2d 755 (1972)—§ 11.3(a) n.6

Boyd v. French, 147 F.3d 319 (4th Cir.1998)—§ 24.3(d) n.108

Boyd v. Meachum, 77 F.3d 60 (2d Cir.1996)—§ 25.1(d) n.86

Boyd v. Mintz, 631 F.2d 247 (3d Cir.1980)—§§ 28.3(d) n.82 to 84

Boyd, People v., 88 Ill.App.3d 825, 43 Ill.Dec. 798, 410 N.E.2d 931 (1980)—§ 24.7(e) n.49

Boyd, State v., 202 S.W.3d 393 (Tex.App.2006)—§ 27.3(d) n.59

Boyd, State v., 275 Kan. 271, 64 P.3d 419 (2003)—§ 3.7(c) n.59

Boyd, State v., 221 Conn. 685, 607 A.2d 376 (1992)—§ 1.7(h) n.131

Boyd, State v., 214 Conn. 132, 570 A.2d 1125 (1990)—§§ 14.3(d) n.100; 14.4(e) n.130

Boyd v. State, 321 Md. 69, 581 A.2d 1 (1990)—§ 22.4(c) n.22

Boyd v. State, 51 Md.App. 197, 441 A.2d 1133 (1982)—§ 18.4(c) n.72

Boyd, State v., 29 Wash.App. 584, 629 P.2d 930 (1981)—§ 20.6(b) n.56

Boyd, State v., 128 Ariz. 381, 625 P.2d 970 (1981)—§ 26.10(c) n.78

Boyd, United States v., 480 F.3d 1178 (9th Cir.2007)—§§ 1.2(c) n.176, 177

Boyd, United States v., 86 F.3d 719 (7th Cir.1996)—§ 22.3(d) n.205

Boyd, United States v., 55 F.3d 239 (7th Cir.1995)—§§ 5.4(c) n.38; 27.5(e) n.156

Boyd, United States v., 958 F.2d 247 (8th Cir.1992)—§ 27.5(c) n.83

Boyd, United States v., 446 F.2d 1267 (5th Cir.1971)—§ 22.3(c) n.124

Boyd v. United States, 116 U.S. 616, 6 S.Ct. 524, 29 L.Ed. 746 (1886)—§§ 2.5(f) n.91; 2.8(a) n.10; 2.8(b) n.32; 3.1(a) n.3; 8.7(a) n.1; 8.12(a) n.1

Boyde, People v., 46 Cal.3d 212, 250 Cal.Rptr. 83, 758 P.2d 25 (1988)—§ 17.2(d) n.95

Boyea, State v., 171 Vt. 401, 765 A.2d 862 (Vt.2000)—§ 3.8(d) n.166

Boyer v. Arizona, 455 F.2d 804 (9th Cir.1972)—§ 3.4(c) n.39

Boyer, People v., 48 Cal.3d 247, 256 Cal.Rptr. 96, 768 P.2d 610 (1989)—§§ 6.9(f) n.134; 9.3(e) n.70

Boyer, State v., 103 N.M. 655, 712 P.2d 1 (App.1985)—§§ 11.5(g) n.122; 11.6(a) n.11

Boyette, People v., 29 Cal.4th 381, 127 Cal.Rptr.2d 544, 58 P.3d 391 (2002)—§§ 6.2(c) n.120; 22.3(c) n.154, 157

Boyette v. State, 265 Ark. 707, 580 S.W.2d 473 (1979)—§ 19.6(b) n.20

Boykin v. Alabama, 395 U.S. 238, 89 S.Ct. 1709, 23 L.Ed.2d 274 (1969)—§§ 2.7(a) n.28; 21.4(e) n.153; 21.5(c) n.89

Boykin, State v., 432 N.W.2d 60 (S.D.1988)—§ 6.7(c) n.118

Boykin, United States v., 398 F.2d 483 (3d Cir.1968)—§ 6.9(d) n.78

Boykins, State v., 173 W.Va. 761, 320 S.E.2d 134 (1984)—§§ 7.4(c) n.50; 7.4(d) n.71, 74

Boykins v. United States, 702 A.2d 1242 (D.C.App.1997)—§ 24.10(d) n.49

Boylan, United States v., 898 F.2d 230 (1st Cir.1990)—§ 24.9(f) n.85

Boyle v. Johnson, 93 F.3d 180 (5th Cir.1996)—§ 26.4(b) n.19

Boyle, People v., 161 Ill.App.3d 1054, 113 Ill.Dec. 158, 514 N.E.2d 1169 (1987)—§ 15.6(f) n.203

Boylen, State ex rel. v. Harmon, 107 Ohio St.3d 370, 839 N.E.2d 934 (2006)—§ 13.3(b) n.18

Boyt, People v., 109 Ill.2d 403, 94 Ill.Dec. 438, 488 N.E.2d 264 (1985)—§§ 13.5(b) n.31; 21.2(f) n.368

Boze v. State, 514 N.E.2d 275 (Ind.1987)—§ 25.1(d) n.79

Boze, State v., 482 N.E.2d 276 (Ind. App.1986)—§ 25.1(d) n.60

Bozza v. United States, 330 U.S. 160, 67 S.Ct. 645, 91 L.Ed. 818 (1947)— § 26.7(c) n.27

Brace, United States v., 145 F.3d 247 (5th Cir.1998)—§ 5.2(a) n.19

Bracey, People v., 213 Ill.2d 265, 291 Ill.Dec. 674, 821 N.E.2d 253 (2004)—§ 22.1(h) n.141

Brache v. United States, 165 F.3d 99 (1st Cir.1999)—§ 28.9(b) n.39

Bracht, State v., 573 N.W.2d 176 (S.D.1997)—§§ 21.2(d) n.177; 21.2(e) n.308, 316

Brack v. Wells, 184 Md. 86, 40 A.2d 319 (1944)—§§ 8.4(b) n.52, 84, 88; 13.3(a) n.14

Brackett, State v., 869 S.W.2d 936 (Tenn.Cr.App.1993)—§ 22.1(h) n.149

Bracy v. Gramley, 520 U.S. 899, 117 S.Ct. 1793, 138 L.Ed.2d 97 (1997)—§§ 27.5(e) n.152; 28.7(d) n.27

Bracy, United States v., 67 F.3d 1421 (9th Cir.1995)—§ 18.5(b) n.65

Bracy v. United States, 435 U.S. 1301, 98 S.Ct. 1171, 55 L.Ed.2d 489 (1978)—§§ 15.5(b) n.46, 54, 101; 15.7(e) n.92

Bracy, United States v., 566 F.2d 649 (9th Cir.1977)—§§ 15.5(b) n.49, 59; 15.7(e) n.95

Braddy v. State, 908 S.W.2d 465 (Tex.App.1995)—§§ 16.1(a) n.6; 16.1(g) n.276

Braden, State v., 98 Ohio St.3d 354, 785 N.E.2d 439 (2003)—§ 22.3(e) n.272

Braden v. 30th Judicial Circuit Court of Kentucky, 410 U.S. 484, 93 S.Ct. 1123, 35 L.Ed.2d 443 (1973)— §§ 13.5(f) n.108; 18.4(a) n.22; 27.4(f) n.71; 28.3(a) n.33, 34

Bradfield, State v., 973 S.W.2d 937 (Tenn.Crim.App.1997)—§ 12.2(c) n.43

Bradfield, United States v., 103 F.3d 1207 (5th Cir.1997)—§ 5.3(d) n.42

Bradford, People v., 14 Cal.4th 1005, 60 Cal.Rptr.2d 225, 929 P.2d 544 (1997)—§§ 6.2(c) n.110; 9.5(a) n.25

Bradford, People v., 17 Cal.3d 8, 130 Cal.Rptr. 129, 549 P.2d 1225 (1976)—§§ 16.1(e) n.174, 191, 196, 205; 16.1(f) n.221

Bradford, State v., 700 So.2d 1046 (La.App.1997)—§ 20.3(f) n.110

Bradford v. State, 325 Ark. 278, 927 S.W.2d 329 (1996)—§ 6.4(e) n.62

Bradford, United States v., 237 F.3d 1306 (11th Cir.2001)—§§ 24.2(d) n.46, 50

Bradley, In re, 318 U.S. 50, 63 S.Ct. 470, 87 L.Ed. 608 (1943)—§ 26.7(c) n.28

Bradley, Commonwealth v., 449 Pa. 19, 295 A.2d 842 (1972)—§ 6.8(b) n.57

Bradley v. Cowan, 561 F.2d 1213 (6th Cir.1977)—§ 28.3(d) n.85

Bradley v. Duncan, 315 F.3d 1091 (9th Cir.2002)—§ 5.2(b) n.27

Bradley v. Fairfax, 634 F.2d 1126 (8th Cir.1980)—§§ 8.5(e) n.170; 8.5(h) n.295

Bradley, People v., 12 Ill.App.3d 783, 299 N.E.2d 99 (1973)—§ 7.4(f) n.98

Bradley, People v., 1 Cal.3d 80, 81 Cal.Rptr. 457, 460 P.2d 129 (1969)—§ 3.4(h) n.148

Bradley, People v., 7 Ill.2d 619, 131 N.E.2d 538 (1956)—§ 15.1(f) n.273

Bradley v. School Bd. Of City of Richmond, 416 U.S. 696, 94 S.Ct. 2006, 40 L.Ed.2d 476 (1974)—§ 21.2(d) n.231

Bradley v. State, 109 Nev. 1090, 864 P.2d 1272 (1993)—§ 26.3(f) n.55

Bradley, State v., 236 Neb. 371, 461 N.W.2d 524 (1990)—§§ 6.7(c) n.141; 23.2(a) n.24

Bradley, State v., 246 Kan. 316, 787 P.2d 706 (Kan.1990)—§ 24.11(d) n.12

Bradley v. State, 559 A.2d 1234 (Del.1989)—§§ 6.6(b) n.15; 6.10(c) n.49; 17.2(d) n.94; 17.3(a) n.11

Bradley v. State, 374 So.2d 1154 (Fla.App.1979)—§§ 15.1(d) n.142; 15.1(e) n.260, 261

Bradley, United States v., 455 F.3d 453 (4th Cir.2006)—§§ 21.2(c) n.103, 120; 21.3(d) n.218, 229, 233, 244

Bradley, United States v., 400 F.3d 459 (6th Cir.2005)—§ 21.2(a) n.7

Bradley, United States v., 417 F.3d 1107 (10th Cir.2005)—§ 27.2(c) n.43

Bradley v. United States, 881 A.2d 640 (D.C.App.2005)—§ 21.4(b) n.59

Bradley, United States v., 381 F.3d 641 (7th Cir.2004)—§ 21.4(c) n.86

Bradley, United States v., 173 F.3d 225 (3d Cir.1999)—§ 24.9(f) n.102

Bradley, United States v., 820 F.2d 3 (1st Cir.1987)—§§ 5.1(c) n.34, 37

Bradney, Commonwealth v., 126 Pa. 199, 17 A. 600 (1889)—§ 15.6(d) n.117

Bradshaw, People v., 156 P.3d 452 (Colo.2007)—§§ 6.9(f) n.139; 6.9(g) n.166

Bradshaw, State v., 193 W.Va. 519, 457 S.E.2d 456 (1995)—§ 6.8(b) n.63

Bradshaw v. Stumpf, 545 U.S. 175, 125 S.Ct. 2398, 162 L.Ed.2d 143 (2005)—§§ 17.4(a) n.51; 21.2(a) n.7; 21.3(b) n.86; 21.4(c) n.91; 24.3(d) n.117; 26.4(f) n.111, 112; 28.6(b) n.14

Bradshaw, United States v., 281 F.3d 278 (1st Cir.2002)—§§ 24.9(c) n.20; 24.9(f) n.86

Bradshaw, United States v., 935 F.2d 295 (D.C.Cir.1991)—§ 6.9(b) n.41

Bradshaw, United States v., 787 F.2d 1385 (10th Cir.1986)—§ 22.3(c) n.141

Bradshaw, United States v., 490 F.2d 1097 (4th Cir.1974)—§§ 3.2(c) n.127; 3.2(f) n.184

Brady v. Maryland, 373 U.S. 83, 83 S.Ct. 1194, 10 L.Ed.2d 215 (1963)—§§ 1.5(a) n.12; 2.7(a) n.6, 25; 2.7(c) n.192; 10.5(e) n.50; 19.5(c) n.60; 20.3(m) n.238; 21.2(b) n.64; 21.3(c) n.171, 172, 191; 24.3(b) n.17

Brady v. State, 259 Ga. 573, 385 S.E.2d 653 (1989)—§ 6.9(g) n.200

Brady, United States v., 993 F.2d 177 (9th Cir.1993)—§ 2.12(c) n.173

Brady, United States v., 819 F.2d 884 (9th Cir.1987)—§ 6.6(e) n.86

Brady v. United States, 397 U.S. 742, 90 S.Ct. 1463, 25 L.Ed.2d 747 (1970)—§§ 2.7(a) n.30; 21.2(a) n.6; 21.2(b) n.27; 21.2(c) n.111, 114, 125; 21.2(d) n.270; 21.3(c) n.185; 21.4(b) n.43; 21.4(d) n.152; 21.4(e) n.167; 21.5(a) n.33; 21.6(a) n.7; 22.1(h) n.144; 26.4(c) n.25; 27.5(c) n.66

Brady v. United States, 24 F.2d 405 (8th. Cir.1928)—§ 15.5(a) n.22

Bragan v. Poindexter, 249 F.3d 476 (6th Cir.2001)—§ 13.5(a) n.3

Bragg, State v., 604 A.2d 439 (Me.1992)—§ 6.6(d) n.50

Braggs, People v., 209 Ill.2d 492, 284 Ill.Dec. 682, 810 N.E.2d 472 (2004)—§§ 6.6(c) n.42; 6.9(b) n.41

Braham v. State, 571 P.2d 631 (Alaska 1977)—§ 20.6(b) n.44

Braimah, United States v., 3 F.3d 609 (2d Cir.1993)—§ 21.2(b) n.67

Brainer, United States v., 691 F.2d 691 (4th Cir.1982)—§ 18.3(b) n.2

Brakeall v. Weber, 668 N.W.2d 79 (S.D.2003)—§§ 21.4(d) n.103; 21.5(b) n.67; 21.5(c) n.76

Bram v. United States, 168 U.S. 532, 18 S.Ct. 183, 42 L.Ed. 568 (1897)—§§ 1.7(i) n.157; 2.8(b) n.35; 2.9(d) n.82; 6.2(a) n.17; 6.2(c) n.91; 6.5(a) n.2

Brambles v. Duncan, 330 F.3d 1197 (9th Cir.2003)—§ 28.5(b) n.59

Bramblett v. United States, 231 F.2d 489 (D.C.Cir.1956)—§ 18.5(a) n.13

Brame v. Commonwealth, 252 Va. 122, 476 S.E.2d 177 (1996)—§ 17.4(b) n.124

Brames v. State, 273 Ind. 565, 406 N.E.2d 252 (1980)—§ 3.10(e) n.142

Bramlett, State v., 166 S.C. 323, 164 S.E. 873 (1932)—§ 8.3(h) n.47

Brammeier, State v., 1 Or.App. 612, 464 P.2d 717 (1970)—§ 6.9(d) n.80

Branch, United States v., 91 F.3d 699 (5th Cir.1996)—§ 22.3(b) n.67

Brand, State v., 520 So.2d 114 (La.1988)—§ 5.2(a) n.4

Brand, United States v., 467 F.3d 179 (2d Cir.2006)—§ 5.2(a) n.9

Brandao, United States v., 448 F. Supp.2d 311 (D.Mass.2006)—§ 24.8(b) n.33

Brandborg v. Lucas, 891 F.Supp. 352 (E.D.Tex.1995)—§ 22.3(a) n.7

Brander, People v., 244 Ill. 26, 91 N.E. 59 (1910)—§ 19.1(b) n.24

Brandom v. United States, 431 F.2d 1391 (7th Cir.1970)—§§ 17.3(c) n.36; 17.3(e) n.61

Brandon, People v., 40 Cal.App.4th 1172, 47 Cal.Rptr.2d 383 (1995)—§ 25.2(a) n.9

Brandon, United States v., 17 F.3d 409 (1st Cir.1994)—§ 19.2(b) n.9

Brandwein, Commonwealth v., 435 Mass. 623, 760 N.E.2d 724 (2002)—§ 6.2(c) n.152

Braniff Airways, Inc., In re, 390 F.Supp. 344 (W.D.Tex.1975)—§§ 8.5(d) n.137; 8.5(f) n.211

Braniff Airways, Inc., United States v., 428 F.Supp. 579 (W.D.Tex.1977)—§§ 15.5(b) n.70; 15.7(c) n.55

Branker, United States v., 418 F.2d 378 (2d Cir.1969)—§§ 11.2(g) n.305; 24.5(a) n.10

Branker, United States v., 395 F.2d 881 (2d Cir.1968)—§§ 17.2(f) n.137; 17.3(c) n.37

Brannan, People v., 406 Mich. 104, 276 N.W.2d 14 (1979)—§ 6.8(b) n.40

Brannan v. State, 275 Ga. 70, 561 S.E.2d 414 (2002)—§ 24.3(e) n.127

Branscomb v. State, 299 Ark. 482, 774 S.W.2d 426 (1989)—§ 11.2(e) n.159

Branscome, United States v., 682 F.2d 484 (4th Cir.1982)—§ 22.2(a) n.10

Branstetter, State v., 107 S.W.3d 465 (Mo.App.2003)—§ 18.4(d) n.81

Brantley v. State, 272 Ga. 892, 536 S.E.2d 509 (2000)—§ 26.7(a) n.13

Branzburg v. Hayes, 408 U.S. 665, 92 S.Ct. 2646, 33 L.Ed.2d 626 (1972)—§§ 8.6(a) n.1, 2, 9, 12; 8.8(d) n.47, 50, 60, 64; 8.8(h) n.180; 15.1(c) n.141

Bras, United States v., 483 F.3d 103 (D.C.Cir.2007)—§ 26.4(f) n.93

Brasfield v. United States, 272 U.S. 448, 47 S.Ct. 135, 71 L.Ed. 345 (1926)—§ 24.9(d) n.37

Braskett, State v., 10 Ohio Op.2d 497, 162 N.E.2d 922 (1959)—§ 17.4(a) n.56

Braswell v. United States, 487 U.S. 99, 108 S.Ct. 2284, 101 L.Ed.2d 98 (1988)—§§ 1.3(c) n.22; 1.5(a) n.53; 2.9(i) n.273, 279, 285; 2.10(d) n.161; 8.12(b) n.27; 8.13(d) n.89, 106

Brathwaite, United States v., 458 F.3d 376 (5th Cir.2006)—§§ 6.7(b) n.85; 9.5(b) n.50

Bratis, People v., 73 Cal.App.3d 751, 141 Cal.Rptr. 45 (1977)—§ 24.10(a) n.8

Bratten v. Delaware, 307 F.Supp. 643 (D.Del.1969)—§ 7.4(f) n.103

Braun, State v., 351 N.W.2d 149 (S.D.1984)—§ 26.3(g) n.78

Braun, State v., 82 Wash.2d 157, 509 P.2d 742 (1973)—§§ 6.2(c) n.142; 6.9(c) n.55

Braune, People v., 363 Ill. 551, 2 N.E.2d 839 (1936)—§ 17.2(d) n.93

Brauner, State v., 239 La. 651, 119 So.2d 497 (1960)—§ 9.5(a) n.5

Braunsdorf, State v., 98 Wis.2d 569, 297 N.W.2d 808 (1980)—§ 18.3(c) n.116

Braunstein, United States v., 281 F.3d 982 (9th Cir.2002)—§§ 13.5(h) n.170, 202

Bravo, State v., 158 Ariz. 364, 762 P.2d 1318 (1988)—§ 9.5(d) n.80

Bravo, State v., 131 Ariz. 168, 639 P.2d 358 (App.1981)—§ 22.3(c) n.162

Bravo-Diaz, United States v., 312 F.3d 995 (9th Cir.2002)—§ 28.9(a) n.28

Brawner v. State, 872 So.2d 1 (Miss.2004)—§ 22.3(d) n.230

Braxton, In re, 258 F.3d 250 (4th Cir.2001)—§ 27.4(d) n.59

Braxton, State v., 352 N.C. 158, 531 S.E.2d 428 (2000)—§ 22.3(d) n.216

Braxton v. State, 651 N.E.2d 268 (Ind.1995)—§ 26.10(b) n.21

Braxton v. United States, 852 A.2d 941 (D.C.App.2004)—§ 22.1(g) n.110

Brazel, United States v., 102 F.3d 1120 (11th Cir.1997)—§ 24.1(b) n.18

Brazell, State v., 325 S.C. 65, 480 S.E.2d 64 (1997)—§ 18.1(c) n.28

Brazil, Commonwealth v., 549 Pa. 321, 701 A.2d 216 (1997)—§ 11.5(c) n.47

Brazzel, People v., 18 P.3d 1285 (Colo.2001)—§ 3.10(a) n.1

Breaker, Commonwealth v., 456 Pa. 341, 318 A.2d 354 (1974)—§ 21.3(b) n.134

Breard v. Greene, 523 U.S. 371, 118 S.Ct. 1552, 140 L.Ed.2d 529 (1998)—§ 1.7(c) n.21

Breard v. Netherland, 949 F.Supp. 1255 (E.D.Va.1996)—§ 28.8(b) n.16

Brecheen v. Reynolds, 41 F.3d 1343 (10th Cir.1994)—§ 28.4(b) n.20

Brecht v. Abrahamson, 507 U.S. 619, 113 S.Ct. 1710, 123 L.Ed.2d 353 (1993)—§§ 2.9(h) n.211; 9.6(a) n.46; 27.6(d) n.82, 114; 28.6(g) n.78, 79

Breckenridge, People v., 81 Mich.App. 6, 263 N.W.2d 922 (1978)—§ 19.5(b) n.10

Brede v. Powers, 263 U.S. 4, 44 S.Ct. 8, 68 L.Ed. 132 (1923)—§§ 15.1(b) n.60, 62

Bredy, United States v., 209 F.3d 1193 (10th Cir.2000)—§§ 7.4(c) n.48, 50 to 53

Breed v. Jones, 421 U.S. 519, 95 S.Ct. 1779, 44 L.Ed.2d 346 (1975)—§ 25.1(c) n.23

Breeden, State v., 129 Idaho 813, 932 P.2d 936 (1997)—§ 26.9(b) n.31

Breeden, State v., 333 Md. 212, 634 A.2d 464 (1993)—§ 14.1(d) n.51

Breen, United States v., 243 F.3d 591 (2d Cir.2001)—§ 24.9(f) n.102

Breidenbach, People v., 875 P.2d 879 (Colo.1994)—§§ 6.6(e) n.95; 9.5(b) n.42

Breiner v. Takao, 73 Hawaii 499, 835 P.2d 637 (1992)—§§ 23.1(b) n.69, 80, 88

Breit, State v., 122 N.M. 655, 930 P.2d 792 (1996)—§ 25.4(a) n.7

Breithaupt v. Abram, 352 U.S. 432, 77 S.Ct. 408, 1 L.Ed.2d 448 (1957)—§§ 2.4(f) n.185; 3.1(a) n.14

Breitkreutz, United States v., 977 F.2d 214 (6th Cir.1992)—§ 8.8(f) n.151

Bremmer, People v., 30 Cal.App.3d 1058, 106 Cal.Rptr. 797 (1973)—§ 3.9(j) n.216

Brendlin v. California, _____ U.S. _____, 127 S.Ct. 2400, 168 L.Ed.2d 132 (2007)—§§ 3.8(c) n.69, 96, 105, 110; 3.8(e) n.203; 9.1(d) n.121

Brennan, State v., 627 A.2d 842 (R.I.1993)—§ 11.10(c) n.109

Brennan, United States v., 183 F.3d 139 (2d Cir.1999)—§§ 16.1(b) n.36; 16.1(g) n.283; 16.2(b) n.30; 16.2(c) n.45, 51; 16.2(f) n.105

Brennick, United States v., 405 F.3d 96 (1st Cir.2005)—§ 7.4(e) n.88

Brenson, United States v., 104 F.3d 1267 (11th Cir.1997)—§ 8.5(b) n.19

Brent, State v., 137 N.J. 107, 644 A.2d 583 (1994)—§ 24.8(f) n.98

Breslin, United States v., 916 F.Supp. 438 (E.D.Pa.1996)—§§ 15.5(a) n.4; 15.6(b) n.78; 15.7(b) n.13, 51; 15.7(g) n.199

Bressette, People v., 124 Ill.App.2d 469, 259 N.E.2d 592 (1970)—§ 17.4(c) n.153

Brett, In re, 142 Wash.2d 868, 16 P.3d 601 (2001)—§ 11.10(c) n.127

Brett, State v., 126 Wash.2d 136, 892 P.2d 29 (1995)—§ 19.2(c) n.25

Brett v. United States, 412 F.2d 401 (5th Cir.1969)—§ 3.5(c) n.123

Bretti v. Wainwright, 439 F.2d 1042 (5th Cir.1971)—§ 3.10(f) n.199

Bretz, State v., 166 Mont. 444, 534 P.2d 496 (1975)—§§ 16.1(b) n.36; 16.1(e) n.199

Brewer v. Aiken, 935 F.2d 850 (7th Cir.1991)—§ 11.10(c) n.126

Brewer v. City of Napa, 210 F.3d 1093 (9th Cir.2000)—§ 21.4(a) n.22

Brewer v. Department of Motor Vehicles, 23 Wn.App. 412, 595 P.2d 949 (1979)—§ 6.10(e) n.81

Brewer v. Kimel, 256 F.3d 222 (4th Cir.2001)—§ 17.4(b) n.124

Brewer v. Raines, 670 F.2d 117 (9th Cir.1982)—§ 26.4(g) n.124

Brewer v. Reynolds, 51 F.3d 1519 (10th Cir.1995)—§ 27.6(d) n.146

Brewer v. State, 725 So.2d 106 (Miss.1998)—§ 22.3(d) n.246

Brewer, State v., 328 S.C. 117, 492 S.E.2d 97 (S.C.1997)—§§ 11.5(d) n.68, 84; 11.5(f) n.101

Brewer, State v., 48 Ohio St.3d 50, 549 N.E.2d 491 (1990)—§ 6.2(c) n.176

Brewer, State v., 247 N.W.2d 205 (Iowa 1976)—§§ 22.2(d) n.67, 84

Brewer, United States v., 947 F.2d 404 (9th Cir.1991)—§ 10.5(e) n.55

Brewer v. Williams, 430 U.S. 387, 97 S.Ct. 1232, 51 L.Ed.2d 424 (1977)—§§ 2.9(h) n.215; 6.4(b) n.19; 6.4(d) n.53; 6.4(e) n.60; 6.4(f) n.110; 6.4(g) n.143; 6.7(a) n.7; 6.7(c) n.124; 9.3(e) n.63; 9.5(a) n.28; 11.2(b) n.80; 11.3(a) n.10

Brewer, State ex rel. v. Starcher, 195 W.Va. 185, 465 S.E.2d 185 (W.Va.1995)—§§ 21.2(d) n.219; 21.2(e) n.312; 21.4(g) n.256

Brewington, State v., 352 N.C. 489, 532 S.E.2d 496 (2000)—§§ 6.6(d) n.48; 6.9(f) n.139; 17.2(b) n.38, 71

Brewster, United States v., 408 U.S. 501, 92 S.Ct. 2531, 33 L.Ed.2d 507 (1972)—§ 3.4(a) n.23

Breza, United States v., 308 F.3d 430 (4th Cir.2002)—§ 3.2(d) n.157

Brice, State v., 276 Kan. 758, 80 P.3d 1113 (2003)—§ 22.1(a) n.18

Brickey, State v., 714 P.2d 644 (Utah 1986)—§§ 14.3(c) n.74, 78, 79

Brickey, United States v., 289 F.3d 1144 (9th Cir.2002)—§ 18.3(b) n.51

Bridgeman v. United States, 229 F.3d 589 (7th Cir.2000)—§ 21.2(b) n.82

Bridgeman, United States v., 523 F.2d 1099 (D.C.Cir.1975)—§ 11.6(a) n.62

Bridges v. California, 314 U.S. 252, 62 S.Ct. 190, 86 L.Ed. 192 (1941)—§ 2.3(a) n.48

Bridges v. Chambers, 447 F.3d 994 (7th Cir.2006)—§ 6.2(c) n.163

Bridges, State v., 829 A.2d 247 (Me.2003)—§§ 6.6(f) n.110, 113

Brien, Commonwealth v., 19 Mass.App. 914, 471 N.E.2d 398 (1984)—§§ 15.7(b) n.29, 31

Brien, United States v., 59 F.3d 274 (1st Cir.1995)—§§ 7.4(g) n.117; 7.5(b) n.22

Brien, United States v., 617 F.2d 299 (1st Cir.1980)—§ 15.4(h) n.199

Briggs, Ex parte, 187 S.W.3d 458 (Tex.Crim.App.2005)—§ 21.3(b) n.52

Briggs v. American Air Filter Co., 630 F.2d 414 (5th Cir.1980)—§§ 4.6(b) n.46; 4.6(l) n.178

Briggs v. Goodwin, 569 F.2d 1 (D.C.Cir.1977)—§ 13.5(g) n.120

Briggs, People v., 709 P.2d 911 (Colo.1985)—§§ 9.5(d) n.80, 82

Briggs, State v., 666 N.W.2d 573 (Iowa 2003)—§ 12.2(b) n.31

Briggs, State v., 349 N.J.Super. 496, 793 A.2d 882 (App.Div.2002)—§ 11.8(a) n.20

Briggs, State v., 787 A.2d 479 (R.I.2001)—§ 24.6(e) n.51

Briggs, State v., 756 A.2d 731 (R.I.2000)—§§ 6.2(c) n.168; 6.6(e) n.61

Briggs, State v., 55 Wash.App. 44, 776 P.2d 1347 (1989)—§ 24.9(f) n.93

Briggs, State v., 81 N.M. 581, 469 P.2d 730 (1970)—§ 6.8(a) n.12

Briggs, United States v., 273 F.3d 737 (7th Cir.2001)—§ 6.7(c) n.135

Briggs, United States v., 920 F.2d 287 (5th Cir.1991)—§§ 21.4(f) n.192; 21.5(e) n.125

Briggs, United States v., 514 F.2d 794 (5th Cir.1975)—§§ 19.3(b) n.136; 27.2(d) n.69

Brigham City v. Stuart, 126 S.Ct. 1943, 164 L.Ed.2d 650 (U.S. 2006)—§§ 3.6(b) n.43; 3.6(f) n.142, 145; 4.8(e) n.54

Bright, State v., 776 So.2d 1134 (La.2000)—§ 7.4(e) n.89

Bright v. State, 875 P.2d 100 (Alaska App.1994)—§§ 19.3(a) n.63; 24.1(a) n.11

Bright v. State, 490 A.2d 564 (Del.1985)—§ 16.4(c) n.92

Bright, State v., 229 Kan. 185, 623 P.2d 917 (1981)—§§ 20.6(c) n.82, 87

Brignoni-Ponce, United States v., 422 U.S. 873, 95 S.Ct. 2574, 45 L.Ed.2d 607 (1975)—§§ 3.8(b) n.19; 3.9(f) n.113

Brika, United States v., 416 F.3d 514 (6th Cir.2005)—§ 24.2(a) n.7

Briley, United States v., 726 F.2d 1301 (8th Cir.1984)—§ 3.6(a) n.32

Brill v. Gurich, 965 P.2d 404 (Okl.Cr.1998)—§§ 12.3(b) n.55; 12.3(f) n.142

Brim v. State, 471 N.E.2d 672 (Ind.1984)—§ 22.4(a) n.12

Brimage, People v., 271 N.J.Super. 369, 638 A.2d 904 (App.Div.1994)—§ 21.3(e) n.272

Brimage, State v., 153 N.J. 1, 706 A.2d 1096 (1998)—§ 21.1(g) n.118

Brimah, United States v., 214 F.3d 854 (7th Cir.2000)—§ 3.1(f) n.153

Brinegar v. United States, 338 U.S. 160, 69 S.Ct. 1302, 93 L.Ed. 1879 (1949)—§§ 2.5(f) n.71; 3.3(b) n.30, 45, 58, 62; 3.3(f) n.218; 3.8(f) n.234; 10.5(d) n.40; 13.1(b) n.34; 14.3(a) n.18

Bringham, United States v., 447 F.3d 665 (9th Cir.2006)—§ 26.4(d) n.65

Brings Plenty, State v., 459 N.W.2d 390 (S.D.1990)—§ 9.6(a) n.25

Brinkley, Commonwealth v., 505 Pa. 442, 480 A.2d 980 (1984)—§ 20.5(f) n.83

Brinkley, State v., 193 N.C. 747, 138 S.E. 138 (1927)—§ 18.5(a) n.50

Brinkworth, United States v., 68 F.3d 633 (2d Cir.1995)—§§ 21.6(a) n.78; 26.4(g) n.126

Brinson v. Vaughn, 398 F.3d 225 (3d Cir.2005)—§§ 22.3(d) n.255; 28.5(b) n.59

Briones v. State, 74 Haw. 442, 848 P.2d 966 (1993)—§ 11.10(c) n.117

Briones, United States v., 390 F.3d 610 (8th Cir.2004)—§§ 6.7(c) n.111; 6.8(b) n.49

Brisban, State v., 809 So.2d 923 (La.2002)—§ 3.2(c) n.110

Brisco, State v., 933 So.2d 754 (La.2006)—§ 13.2(a) n.4

Briscoe, People v., 51 Mich.App. 153, 214 N.W.2d 877 (1974)—§ 3.6(c) n.68

Briscoe, United States v., 896 F.2d 1476 (7th Cir.1990)—§ 22.3(d) n.247

Brisendine, People v., 13 Cal.3d 528, 119 Cal.Rptr. 315, 531 P.2d 1099 (1975)—§ 2.12(c) n.133

Briseno, People v., 211 Mich.App. 11, 535 N.W.2d 559 (1995)—§ 27.5(a) n.27

Brisk, United States v., 171 F.3d 514 (7th Cir.1999)—§ 22.3(d) n.216

Brisson v. State, 955 P.2d 888 (Wyo.1998)—§ 26.4(f) n.101

Brisson, State v., 619 A.2d 1099 (R.I.1993)—§§ 20.6(b) n.41, 53

Bristol v. Commonwealth, 272 Va. 568, 636 S.E.2d 460 (2006)—§ 3.5(a) n.4

Bristol, State v., 159 Vt. 334, 618 A.2d 1290 (1992)—§§ 21.3(b) n.59, 80

Brito, United States v., 907 F.2d 392 (2d Cir.1990)—§§ 8.8(f) n.153; 15.5(b) n.58; 15.6(e) n.159; 15.7(c) n.64

Britt v. North Carolina, 404 U.S. 226, 92 S.Ct. 431, 30 L.Ed.2d 400 (1971)—§§ 11.2(d) n.125, 127; 27.1(b) n.16

Britt, State v., 320 N.C. 705, 360 S.E.2d 660 (1987)—§ 24.11(d) n.27

Britt, United States v., 917 F.2d 353 (8th Cir.1990)—§ 21.2(d) n.270

Britt, United States v., 508 F.2d 1052 (5th Cir.1975)—§ 9.1(c) n.101

Britto, Commonwealth v., 433 Mass. 596, 744 N.E.2d 1089 (2001)—§ 24.9(b) n.13

Britton v. Commonwealth, 123 Ky. 411, 96 S.W. 556 (1906)—§ 16.1(d) n.145

Britton, People v., 91 Cal.App.4th 1112, 111 Cal.Rptr.2d 159 (2001)—§ 10.1(b) n.16

Britton, State v., 633 So.2d 1208 (La.1994)—§ 3.2(h) n.203

Britton, State v., 157 W.Va. 711, 203 S.E.2d 462 (1974)—§§ 21.3(a) n.23, 24, 37

Britz v. Thieret, 940 F.2d 226 (7th Cir.1991)—§§ 23.2(f) n.92, 96

Broadwater, United States v., 151 F.3d 1359 (11th Cir.1998)—§ 18.3(b) n.25

Broadway, United States v., 477 F.2d 991 (5th Cir.1973)—§ 7.4(e) n.80

Brocato, People v., 17 Mich.App. 277, 169 N.W.2d 483 (1969)—§ 20.3(i) n.171

Broce, United States v., 488 U.S. 563, 109 S.Ct. 757, 102 L.Ed.2d 927 (1989)—§ 21.6(a) n.61

Brochu, State v., 237 A.2d 418 (Me.1967)—§ 3.10(f) n.200

Brock v. Hudspeth, 111 F.2d 447 (10th Cir.1940)—§ 16.2(g) n.131

Brock, People v., 45 Ill.2d 292, 259 N.E.2d 12 (1970)—§ 21.2(c) n.122

Brock, People v., 149 Mich. 464, 112 N.W. 1116 (1907)—§ 16.1(e) n.196

Brock v. State, 483 So.2d 358 (Miss.1986)—§ 9.6(a) n.51

Brockelman, People v., 933 P.2d 1315 (Colo.1997)—§ 26.9(b) n.76

Brockington v. State, 85 Md.App. 165, 582 A.2d 568 (1990)—§§ 10.3(d) n.66, 67; 10.4(d) n.31

Brockman, State v., 277 Md. 687, 357 A.2d 376 (1976)—§ 21.2(f) n.367

Brocksmith, People v., 162 Ill.2d 224, 205 Ill.Dec. 113, 642 N.E.2d 1230 (1994)—§§ 11.6(a) n.50; 24.8(f) n.121

Brocksmith, United States v., 991 F.2d 1363 (7th Cir.1993)—§ 25.5(a) n.11

Broddus v. State, 693 S.W.2d 459 (Tex.Cr.App.1985)—§ 21.6(b) n.112

Brodes v. State, 279 Ga. 435, 614 S.E.2d 766 (2005)—§ 7.5(a) n.4

Brodeur, State v., 126 N.H. 411, 493 A.2d 1134 (1985)—§ 3.8(b) n.26

Brodie, United States v., 871 F.2d 125 (D.C.Cir.1989)—§§ 20.3(b) n.59; 20.3(c) n.75

Brodson, United States v., 528 F.2d 214 (7th Cir.1975)—§ 15.7(d) n.80

Brody, United States v., 808 F.2d 944 (2d Cir.1986)—§§ 21.2(e) n.316, 317

Brofford v. Marshall, 751 F.2d 845 (6th Cir.1985)—§ 24.9(g) n.126

Brogan, Matter of, 283 Mont. 413, 942 P.2d 100 (1997)—§ 17.4(b) n.125

Brokaw, United States v., 985 F.2d 951 (8th Cir.1993)—§ 3.10(d) n.134

Brokaw, United States v., 60 F.Supp. 100 (S.D.Ill.1945)—§ 13.3(c) n.36

Bromley, Commonwealth v., 862 A.2d 598 (Penn.2004)—§ 26.4(i) n.188

Broncheau, United States v., 597 F.2d 1260 (9th Cir.1979)—§ 19.3(a) n.13

Bronk, United States v., 604 F.Supp. 743 (W.D.Wis.1985)—§§ 20.3(d) n.91, 93

Bronshtein v. Horn, 404 F.3d 700 (3d Cir.2005)—§ 28.4(b) n.19

Bronston v. United States, 409 U.S. 352, 93 S.Ct. 595, 34 L.Ed.2d 568 (1973)—§ 15.7(e) n.130

Brookhart v. Janis, 384 U.S. 1, 86 S.Ct. 1245, 16 L.Ed.2d 314 (1966)—§§ 11.6(a) n.19, 27, 49, 56; 11.6(b) n.73; 21.4(a) n.9, 39

Brookings v. State, 495 So.2d 135 (Fla.1986)—§ 8.5(g) n.229

Brookings, City of v. Thomsen, 84 S.D. 651, 176 N.W.2d 46 (1970)—§§ 1.8(c) n.54; 1.8(d) n.54

Brookins, United States v., 345 F.3d 231 (4th Cir.2003)—§ 3.7(d) n.66

Brooklier, United States v., 685 F.2d 1162 (9th Cir.1982)—§§ 23.1(d) n.144; 23.1(e) n.251

Brooks v. Buscher, 62 F.3d 176 (7th Cir.1995)—§§ 11.2(f) n.249, 250

Brooks, Commonwealth v., 576 Pa. 332, 839 A.2d 245 (2003)—§ 11.10(d) n.204

Brooks, Commonwealth v., 468 Pa. 547, 364 A.2d 652 (1976)—§ 9.4(a) n.7

Brooks v. Dretke, 418 F.3d 430 (5th Cir.2005)—§§ 22.3(c) n.138; 24.9(f) n.85

Brooks v. Florida, 389 U.S. 413, 88 S.Ct. 541, 19 L.Ed.2d 643 (1967)—§§ 6.2(c) n.64, 65, 67, 68

Brooks v. Hopper, 597 F.2d 57 (5th Cir.1979)—§ 11.9(b) n.54

Brooks v. McCaughtry, 380 F.3d 1009 (7th Cir.2004)—§ 11.5(c) n.60

Brooks v. Narick, 161 W.Va. 415, 243 S.E.2d 841 (1978)—§ 21.2(e) n.305

Brooks, People v., 187 Ill.2d 91, 240 Ill.Dec. 607, 718 N.E.2d 88 (1999)—§ 7.4(c) n.49

Brooks, People v., 249 A.D.2d 572, 670 N.Y.S.2d 934 (1998)—§ 15.7(f) n.186

Brooks, People v., 26 Cal.3d 471, 162 Cal.Rptr. 177, 605 P.2d 1306 (1980)—§ 10.6(a) n.8

Brooks, State v., 360 Ark. 499, 202 S.W.3d 508 (2005)—§ 13.2(c) n.56

Brooks v. State, 903 So.2d 691 (Miss.2005)—§§ 7.3(b) n.33; 7.3(d) n.67; 7.3(f) n.111

Brooks, State v., 604 N.W.2d 345 (Minn.2000)—§ 12.2(b) n.31

Brooks v. State, 763 So.2d 859 (Miss.2000)—§ 21.2(h) n.437

Brooks v. State, 325 S.C. 269, 481 S.E.2d 712 (S.C.1997)—§ 21.3(e) n.265

Brooks v. State, 683 N.E.2d 574 (Ind.1997)—§ 6.2(c) n.173

Brooks, State v., 960 S.W.2d 479 (Mo.1997)—§ 22.2(d) n.80

Brooks, State v., 337 N.C. 132, 446 S.E.2d 579 (1994)—§ 10.6(d) n.48

Brooks v. State, 259 Ga. 562, 385 S.E.2d 81 (1989)—§ 11.2(e) n.168

Brooks, State v., 452 So.2d 149 (La.1984)—§ 11.4(d) n.110

Brooks, State v., 224 Tenn. 712, 462 S.W.2d 491 (1970)—§§ 19.6(a) n.2; 19.6(c) n.41

Brooks v. State, 229 A.2d 833 (Del.1967)—§ 6.8(c) n.76

Brooks v. Tennessee, 406 U.S. 605, 92 S.Ct. 1891, 32 L.Ed.2d 358 (1972)—§§ 2.6(d) n.98; 2.10(b) n.40; 11.8(a) n.4, 8; 17.1(f) n.65; 20.4(d) n.61; 24.5(a) n.11; 24.5(d) n.55

Brooks, United States v., 427 F.3d 1246 (10th Cir.2005)—§ 3.4(j) n.202

Brooks, United States v., 285 F.3d 1102 (8th Cir.2002)—§ 3.4(c) n.43

Brooks, United States v., 215 F.3d 842 (8th Cir.2000)—§ 5.2(a) n.8

Brooks, United States v., 175 F.3d 605 (8th Cir.1999)—§ 22.3(c) n.155

Brooks, United States v., 957 F.2d 1138 (4th Cir.1992)—§ 26.4(h) n.159

Brooks, United States v., 677 F.2d 907 (D.C.Cir.1982)—§ 24.9(g) n.122

Brooks v. United States, 267 U.S. 432, 45 S.Ct. 345, 69 L.Ed. 699 (1925)—§ 1.2(c) n.112

Broom v. Mitchell, 441 F.3d 392 (6th Cir.2006)—§§ 7.4(c) n.48, 52

Broom, State v., 40 Ohio St.3d 277, 533 N.E.2d 682 (1988)—§ 11.2(e) n.203

Broom, United States v., 471 F.3d 802 (7th Cir.2006)—§ 7.4(e) n.85

Broome, United States v., 628 F.2d 403 (5th Cir.1980)—§ 21.4(a) n.26

Brosius v. Warden, 278 F.3d 239 (3d Cir.2002)—§ 6.9(g) n.200

Brothers, State v., 12 Or.App. 435, 507 P.2d 398 (1973)—§ 3.4(j) n.186

Brothers v. State, 236 Ala. 448, 183 So. 433 (1938)—§ 19.3(b) n.182

Brotherton, State v., 2 Or.App. 157, 465 P.2d 749 (1970)—§ 3.9(i) n.172

Broughton, State v., 62 Ohio St.3d 253, 581 N.E.2d 541 (1991)—§§ 25.3(a) n.8; 25.4(b) n.17

Brouillard, State v., 745 A.2d 759 (R.I.2000)—§ 6.2(c) n.178

Broussard v. Parish of New Orleans, 318 F.3d 644 (5th Cir.2003)—§§ 2.6(b) n.37; 12.2(b) n.36

Broussard, State v., 816 So.2d 1284 (La.2002)—§§ 3.8(b) n.26; 3.8(d) n.143

Brower v. County of Inyo, 489 U.S. 593, 109 S.Ct. 1378, 103 L.Ed.2d 628 (1989)—§§ 3.2(a) n.30; 3.8(c) n.69, 111

Brown v. Allen, 344 U.S. 443, 73 S.Ct. 397, 97 L.Ed. 469 (1953)—§§ 28.2(c) n.55; 28.2(d) n.76; 28.3(b) n.55; 28.5(a) n.36; 28.6(a) n.1

Brown v. Artuz, 124 F.3d 73 (2d Cir.1997)—§§ 11.6(a) n.51; 11.6(c) n.91, 100; 11.6(d) n.115

Brown v. Board of Levee Commissioners, 50 Miss. 468 (1874)—§ 15.1(c) n.137

Brown v. Butler, 811 F.2d 938 (5th Cir.1987)—§ 6.4(e) n.107

Brown v. Caspari, 186 F.3d 1011 (8th Cir.1999)—§ 6.9(f) n.106

Brown v. Chaney, 469 U.S. 1090, 105 S.Ct. 601, 83 L.Ed.2d 710 (1984)—§ 24.3(b) n.39

Brown, Commonwealth v., 556 Pa. 131, 727 A.2d 541 (1999)—§§ 19.5(b) n.2, 12, 14, 26, 31

Brown, Commonwealth v., 550 Pa. 580, 708 A.2d 81 (1998)—§ 13.2(a) n.3

Brown, Commonwealth v., 544 Pa. 406, 676 A.2d 1178 (1996)—§§ 7.2(d) n.47, 55

Brown v. Commonwealth, 890 S.W.2d 286 (Ky.1994)—§ 3.7(a) n.17

Brown, Commonwealth v., 473 Pa. 458, 375 A.2d 331 (1977)—§ 17.4(a) n.46

Brown, Commonwealth v., 213 Pa.Super. 288, 247 A.2d 802 (1968)—§ 6.4(c) n.41

Brown v. Commonwealth, 76 Pa. 319 (1874)—§ 15.4(a) n.10

Brown, Commonwealth v., 147 Mass. 585, 18 N.E. 587 (1888)—§ 15.4(g) n.171

Brown v. Doe, 2 F.3d 1236 (2d Cir.1993)—§§ 11.6(a) n.7; 11.9(a) n.12; 21.3(b) n.118

Brown v. Frey, 889 F.2d 159 (8th Cir.1989)—§ 26.2(c) n.68

Brown v. Harris, 666 F.2d 782 (2d Cir.1981)—§ 22.2(d) n.83

Brown v. Illinois, 422 U.S. 590, 95 S.Ct. 2254, 45 L.Ed.2d 416 (1975)— §§ 6.7(b) n.96; 9.3(b) n.14; 9.3(c) n.19, 21, 24; 9.4(a) n.3; 9.4(b) n.53; 9.4(d) n.81, 93; 9.5(c) n.65; 10.2(c) n.44

Brown v. Kuhlmann, 142 F.3d 529 (2d Cir.1998)—§ 27.6(d) n.110

Brown v. Louisiana, 447 U.S. 323, 100 S.Ct. 2214, 65 L.Ed.2d 159 (1980)—§§ 2.11(c) n.29, 32

Brown v. Luebbers, 344 F.3d 770 (8th Cir.2003)—§ 6.2(c) n.178

Brown v. Maryland, 25 U.S. (12 Wheat.) 419, 6 L.Ed. 678 (1827)—§ 1.2(c) n.13

Brown v. Mississippi, 297 U.S. 278, 56 S.Ct. 461, 80 L.Ed. 682 (1936)— §§ 2.4(e) n.145; 2.8(c) n.62; 6.2(b) n.23; 6.2(c) n.62

Brown v. New Jersey, 175 U.S. 172, 20 S.Ct. 77, 44 L.Ed. 119 (1899)— § 2.3(b) n.85

Brown v. Ohio, 432 U.S. 161, 97 S.Ct. 2221, 53 L.Ed.2d 187 (1977)— §§ 16.1(f) n.217; 17.4(b) n.69; 17.4(c) n.142; 21.2(d) n.205; 21.3(f) n.447; 25.1(d) n.56

Brown v. Payton, 544 U.S. 133, 125 S.Ct. 1432, 161 L.Ed.2d 334 (2005)—§ 28.6(f) n.69

Brown, People v., 98 N.Y.2d 226, 746 N.Y.S.2d 422, 774 N.E.2d 186 (2002)—§ 20.5(b) n.27

Brown v. People, 1999 WL 717279 (S.D.N.Y.1999)—§ 11.9(d) n.218

Brown, People v., 42 Cal.App.4th 461, 49 Cal.Rptr.2d 652 (1996)— § 9.6(a) n.32

Brown, People v., 172 Ill.2d 1, 216 Ill.Dec. 733, 665 N.E.2d 1290 (1996)—§§ 22.3(c) n.153; 26.4(g) n.141

Brown, People v., 217 App.Div.2d 703, 630 N.Y.S.2d 91 (1995)— §§ 24.10(d) n.46, 48

Brown, People v., 259 Ill.App.3d 579, 197 Ill.Dec. 210, 630 N.E.2d 1334 (1994)—§ 19.3(b) n.180

Brown, People v., 107 Ill.App.3d 742, 63 Ill.Dec. 512, 438 N.E.2d 250 (1982)—§ 16.2(g) n.120

Brown, People v., 53 N.Y.2d 979, 441 N.Y.S.2d 662, 424 N.E.2d 549 (1981)—§ 24.8(e) n.61

Brown, People v., 87 Misc.2d 403, 384 N.Y.S.2d 968 (Sup.Ct.1976)— § 15.2(b) n.24

Brown, People v., 52 Ill.2d 94, 285 N.E.2d 1 (1972)—§ 7.4(e) n.80

Brown v. Perini, 718 F.2d 784 (6th Cir.1983)—§ 21.4(d) n.119

Brown v. Poole, 337 F.3d 1155 (9th Cir.2003)—§ 21.2(e) n.337

Brown v. Sanders, 546 U.S. 212 (2006)—§ 22.2(d) n.75

Brown v. State, 280 Ga. 658, 631 S.E.2d 687 (2006)—§ 21.5(b) n.66

Brown, State v., _____ Wis.2d _____, 716 N.W.2d 906 (2006)—§ 21.4(c) n.90

Brown, State v., 179 Vt. 22, 890 A.2d 79 (2005)—§ 12.1(b) n.33

Brown, State v., 280 Kan. 65, 118 P.3d 1273 (2005)—§ 22.3(b) n.68

Brown, State v., 180 N.J. 572, 853 A.2d 260 (2004)—§ 26.2(b) n.26

Brown, State v., 268 Neb. 943, 689 N.W.2d 347 (2004)—§§ 21.3(e) n.272, 273

Brown v. State, 277 Ga. 573, 592 S.E.2d 666 (2004)—§ 22.1(h) n.133

Brown v. State, 278 Ga. 724, 609 S.E.2d 312 (2004)—§ 6.2(c) n.135

Brown, State v., 356 Ark. 460, 156 S.W.3d 722 (2004)—§ 2.12(d) n.183

Brown v. State, 841 A.2d 1116 (R.I.2004)—§ 18.5(a) n.50

Brown v. State, 67 P.3d 917 (Okla.App.2003)—§ 26.4(i) n.179

Brown, State v., 100 Ohio St.3d 51, 796 N.E.2d 506 (2003)—§ 6.2(c) n.131

Brown, State v., 260 Wis.2d 125, 659 N.W.2d 110 (App.2003)—§ 16.4(d) n.126

Brown v. State, 354 Ark. 30, 117 S.W.3d 598 (2003)—§ 6.2(c) n.113

Brown, State v., 256 Conn. 291, 772 A.2d 1107 (2001)—§§ 22.3(a) n.4; 24.5(b) n.22

Brown v. State, 751 N.E.2d 664 (Ind.2001)—§ 22.3(d) n.250

Brown, State v., 53 S.W.3d 264 (Tenn.Crim.App.2000)—§ 18.4(c) n.35

Brown, State v., 748 A.2d 244 (R.I.2000)—§§ 7.4(c) n.48, 53

Brown v. State, 729 A.2d 259 (Del. 1999)—§ 27.5(d) n.137

Brown v. State, 691 N.E.2d 438 (Ind.1998)—§ 9.1(b) n.35

Brown v. State, 989 P.2d 913 (Okl.Cr.App.1998)—§ 17.2(b) n.75

Brown v. State, 330 Ark. 239, 952 S.W.2d 673 (1997)—§ 27.4(c) n.23

Brown v. State, 684 N.E.2d 529 (Ind.App.1997)—§ 23.2(g) n.125

Brown v. State, 913 S.W.2d 577 (Tex.Cr.App.1996)—§ 27.5(e) n.153

Brown, State v., 235 Conn. 502, 668 A.2d 1288 (1995)—§ 24.9(f) n.86

Brown v. State, 907 S.W.2d 835 (Tex.Cr.App.1995)—§ 25.2(d) n.24

Brown, State v., 339 N.C. 426, 451 S.E.2d 181 (1994)—§ 11.6(a) n.65

Brown v. State, 871 P.2d 56 (Okla.Crim.App.1994)—§ 16.3(b) n.22

Brown v. State, 262 Ga. 728, 425 S.E.2d 856 (1993)—§§ 3.4(j) n.182, 183

Brown, State v., 500 N.W.2d 784 (Minn.1993)—§ 24.5(a) n.9

Brown v. State, 632 So.2d 14 (Ala.1992)—§ 23.2(f) n.90

Brown, State v., 836 S.W.2d 530 (Tenn.1992)—§ 25.4(b) n.22

Brown, State v., 853 P.2d 851 (Utah 1992)—§ 11.9(c) n.149

Brown v. State, 816 P.2d 818 (Wyo.1991)—§ 24.11(d) n.33

Brown, State v., 118 N.J. 595, 573 A.2d 886 (1990)—§ 17.2(d) n.94

Brown v. State, 260 Ga. 153, 391 S.E.2d 108 (1990)—§ 11.2(e) n.175

Brown, State v., 153 Vt. 263, 571 A.2d 643 (1989)—§ 6.9(f) n.135

Brown, State v., 245 Kan. 604, 783 P.2d 1278 (1989)—§ 3.4(i) n.169

Brown, State v., 38 Ohio St.3d 305, 528 N.E.2d 523 (1988)—§ 7.4(b) n.29

Brown, State v., 43 Ohio App.3d 39, 539 N.E.2d 1159 (1988)—§ 18.5(a) n.50

Brown, State v., 177 W.Va. 633, 355 S.E.2d 614 (1987)—§ 22.3(c) n.125

Brown, State v., 496 So.2d 261 (La.1986)—§ 22.3(c) n.133

Brown, State v., 284 S.C. 407, 326 S.E.2d 410 (1985)—§ 26.9(b) n.77

Brown v. State, 657 S.W.2d 797 (Tex.Crim.App.1983)—§§ 2.12(b) n.83; 2.12(c) n.142; 2.12(d) n.192

Brown v. State, 630 S.W.2d 876 (Tex.App.1982)—§§ 11.4(c) n.82, 83

Brown, State v., 2 Ohio App.3d 321, 441 N.E.2d 1126 (1981)—§ 17.4(a) n.47

Brown, State v., 29 Wash.App. 770, 630 P.2d 1378 (1981)—§ 21.4(c) n.80

Brown v. State, 406 So.2d 1262 (Fla.App.1981)—§ 26.9(b) n.16

Brown, State v., 96 Wis.2d 258, 291 N.W.2d 538 (1980)—§ 14.3(c) n.80

Brown v. State, 44 Md.App. 71, 410 A.2d 17 (1979)—§§ 19.1(d) n.51; 19.3(e) n.248

Brown v. State, 285 Md. 105, 400 A.2d 1133 (1979)—§ 19.5(c) n.53

Brown v. State, 367 So.2d 616 (Fla.1979)—§ 21.2(d) n.270

Brown, State v., 371 So.2d 751 (La.1979)—§ 22.3(d) n.186

Brown, State v., 172 Mont. 41, 560 P.2d 533 (1976)—§§ 19.5(c) n.53, 54

Brown, State v., 321 A.2d 478 (Me.1974)—§ 8.11(e) n.102

Brown, State v., 163 Conn. 52, 301 A.2d 547 (1972)—§ 24.8(e) n.69

Brown, State v., 262 Or. 442, 497 P.2d 1191 (1972)—§§ 16.1(f) n.222; 17.4(c) n.144, 153

Brown v. State, 226 Ga. 114, 172 S.E.2d 666 (1970)—§ 6.7(c) n.120

Brown v. State, 457 S.W.2d 917 (Tex.Cr.App.1970)—§ 10.2(c) n.30

Brown v. State, 3 Md.App. 313, 239 A.2d 761 (1968)—§ 6.9(d) n.77

Brown, State v., 103 Vt. 312, 154 A. 579 (1931)—§§ 16.1(b) n.38, 58

Brown v. Sternes, 304 F.3d 677 (7th Cir.2002)—§ 11.10(c) n.126

Brown v. Texas, 443 U.S. 47, 99 S.Ct. 2637, 61 L.Ed.2d 357 (1979)— §§ 3.3(f) n.216; 3.8(c) n.66; 3.8(d) n.176; 3.8(f) n.227

Brown, United States v., 441 F.3d 1330 (11th Cir.2006)—§§ 22.3(c) n.160; 26.4(f) n.108

Brown, United States v., 449 F.3d 154 (D.C.Cir.2006)—§ 6.7(b) n.85

Brown, United States v., 331 F.3d 591 (8th Cir.2003)—§ 21.4(f) n.174

Brown, United States v., 332 F.3d 363 (6th Cir.2003)—§ 19.6(c) n.46

Brown, United States v., 352 F.3d 654 (2d Cir.2003)—§§ 22.3(d) n.199, 220

Brown, United States v., 287 F.3d 965 (10th Cir.2002)—§§ 6.8(d) n.84; 6.9(g) n.185

Brown, United States v., 289 F.3d 989 (7th Cir.2002)—§ 22.3(d) n.250

Brown, United States v., 295 F.3d 152 (1st Cir.2002)—§ 19.2(c) n.38

Brown, United States v., 298 F.3d 392 (5th Cir.2002)—§ 13.7(c) n.63

Brown, United States v., 303 F.3d 582 (5th Cir.2002)—§§ 4.6(m) n.237; 22.3(b) n.68

Brown, United States v., 250 F.3d 811 (3d Cir.2001)—§ 21.3(c) n.172

Brown, United States v., 250 F.3d 907 (5th Cir.2001)—§ 23.1(c) n.107

Brown, United States v., 202 F.3d 691 (4th Cir.2000)—§ 27.6(d) n.127

Brown, United States v., 217 F.3d 247 (5th Cir.2000)—§ 13.5(a) n.5

Brown, United States v., 218 F.3d 415 (5th Cir.2000)—§§ 23.1(b) n.49, 72 to 74, 76 to 78, 80, 89; 27.2(c) n.49

Brown, United States v., 232 F.3d 399 (4th Cir.2000)—§§ 21.2(b) n.82; 27.5(c) n.56

Brown, United States v., 183 F.3d 1306 (11th Cir.1999)—§ 18.3(b) n.53

Brown, United States v., 117 F.3d 471 (11th Cir.1997)—§§ 28.9(a) n.14, 15

Brown, United States v., 700 A.2d 760 (D.C.App.1997)—§ 7.4(c) n.43

Brown v. United States, 675 A.2d 953 (D.C.App.1996)—§ 22.1(b) n.34

Brown, United States v., 43 F.3d 618 (11th Cir.1995)—§ 5.3(b) n.17

Brown, United States v., 64 F.3d 1083 (7th Cir.1995)—§ 9.1(b) n.54

Brown v. United States, 656 A.2d 1133 (D.C.1995)—§ 11.7(e) n.66

Brown, United States v., 16 F.3d 423 (D.C.Cir.1994)—§ 27.5(e) n.151

Brown, United States v., 990 F.2d 397 (8th Cir.1993)—§ 6.6(e) n.67

Brown, United States v., 995 F.2d 1493 (10th Cir.1993)—§§ 19.2(f) n.92, 94

Brown, United States v., 961 F.2d 1039 (2d Cir.1992)—§ 3.10(d) n.136

Brown, United States v., 920 F.2d 1212 (5th Cir.1991)—§ 7.2(d) n.50

Brown, United States v., 823 F.2d 591 (D.C.Cir.1987)—§§ 22.1(g) n.110; 24.9(f) n.104

Brown, United States v., 832 F.2d 991 (7th Cir.1987)—§ 3.1(c) n.78

Brown v. United States, 518 A.2d 415 (D.C.App.1986)—§§ 7.3(b) n.32; 8.8(g) n.179; 8.14(a) n.7

Brown, United States v., 801 F.2d 352 (8th Cir.1986)—§ 8.11(e) n.108

Brown, United States v., 770 F.2d 241 (1st Cir.1985)—§ 18.3(b) n.57

Brown, United States v., 739 F.2d 1136 (7th Cir.1984)—§ 16.2(e) n.78

Brown, United States v., 743 F.2d 1505 (11th Cir.1984)—§ 9.1(b) n.96

Brown, United States v., 699 F.2d 585 (2d Cir.1983)—§§ 7.4(g) n.116; 9.6(a) n.32; 17.2(b) n.55

Brown, United States v., 715 F.2d 387 (8th Cir.1983)—§ 11.7(e) n.70

Brown, United States v., 644 F.2d 101 (2d Cir.1981)—§ 22.3(c) n.130

Brown v. United States, 623 F.2d 54 (9th Cir.1980)—§ 28.9(b) n.70

Brown, United States v., 604 F.2d 557 (8th Cir.1979)—§ 17.4(a) n.47

Brown, United States v., 569 F.2d 236 (5th Cir.1978)—§ 6.8(a) n.33

Brown v. United States, 372 A.2d 557 (D.C.App.1977)—§§ 20.6(b) n.56, 62

Brown v. United States, 551 F.2d 619 (5th Cir.1977)—§ 11.7(a) n.16

Brown v. United States, 565 F.2d 862 (3d Cir.1977)—§ 21.5(d) n.107

Brown, United States v., 540 F.2d 1048 (10th Cir.1976)—§ 7.5(b) n.26

Brown, United States v., 499 F.2d 829 (7th Cir.1974)—§ 21.6(b) n.111

Brown, United States v., 500 F.2d 375 (4th Cir.1974)—§ 21.2(d) n.171

Brown, United States v., 501 F.2d 146 (9th Cir.1974)—§ 7.5(b) n.28

Brown v. United States, 411 U.S. 223, 93 S.Ct. 1565, 36 L.Ed.2d 208 (1973)—§§ 9.1(b) n.83, 85; 9.2(b) n.12

Brown, United States v., 484 F.2d 418 (5th Cir.1973)—§ 4.9(a) n.5

Brown v. United States, 245 F.2d 549 (8th Cir.1957)—§§ 8.8(h) n.185; 15.6(c) n.88

Brown v. United States, 356 U.S. 148, 78 S.Ct. 622, 2 L.Ed.2d 589 (1958)—§ 24.5(a) n.5

Brown v. United States, 359 U.S. 41, 79 S.Ct. 539, 3 L.Ed.2d 609 (1959)—§ 8.4(c) n.113

Brown v. United States, 35 D.C. 548 (1910)—§ 16.4(c) n.55

Brown v. Vance, 637 F.2d 272 (5th Cir.1981)—§ 22.4(a) n.2

Brown v. Walker, 161 U.S. 591, 16 S.Ct. 644, 40 L.Ed. 819 (1896)—§§ 2.8(b) n.35; 2.10(c) n.89; 2.10(d) n.158; 8.10(a) n.7; 8.11(a) n.3

Brown v. Warden, 315 F.3d 1268 (10th Cir.2003)—§ 28.3(a) n.38

Brown v. Wilmot, 572 F.2d 404 (2d Cir.1978)—§ 12.4(d) n.83

Brown & Williamson Tobacco Corp. v. Williams, 62 F.3d 408 (D.C.Cir.1995)—§ 3.4(a) n.23

Browning, People v., 108 Cal.App.3d 117, 166 Cal.Rptr. 293 (1980)—§§ 3.5(d) n.166 to 168, 171

Browning, State v., 333 Mont. 132, 142 P.3d 757 (2006)—§ 21.3(a) n.2

Browning v. State, 32 P.3d 1061 (Wyo.2001)—§ 21.2(d) n.157

Browning, State v., 67 Wash.App. 93, 834 P.2d 84 (1992)—§ 3.10(d) n.136

Browning, State v., 245 Kan. 26, 774 P.2d 935 (1989)—§§ 19.3(a) n.13; 21.4(e) n.163; 21.6(a) n.25

Browning, United States v., 572 F.2d 720 (10th Cir.1978)—§§ 17.3(b) n.18; 19.3(c) n.188

Browning-Ferris Industries v. Kelco Disposal, Inc., 492 U.S. 257, 109 S.Ct. 2909, 106 L.Ed.2d 219 (1989)—§ 2.6(b) n.38

Browning-Ferris Industries of Georgia, United States v., 555 F.Supp. 595 (N.D.Ga.1982)—§ 15.4(e) n.129

Brownlee, United States v., 454 F.3d 131 (3d Cir.2006)—§§ 6.7(a) n.10; 7.4(b) n.23, 25; 7.4(c) n.48, 50 to 53; 7.4(f) n.95, 96

Brown, United States ex rel. v. Warden, 417 F.Supp. 970 (N.D.Ill.1976)—§§ 11.6(c) n.92, 93

Broxton, State v., 49 N.J. 373, 230 A.2d 489 (1967)—§ 10.5(b) n.20

Bruce v. Commonwealth, 418 S.W.2d 645 (Ky.1967)—§ 10.2(c) n.38

Bruce, People v., 102 Mich.App. 573, 302 N.W.2d 238 (1980)—§§ 26.9(b) n.18, 21

Bruce v. State, 781 A.2d 544 (Del.2001)—§§ 18.4(c) n.61, 67

Bruce, State v., 779 P.2d 646 (Utah 1989)—§ 10.2(b) n.20

Bruce v. State, 268 Ind. 180, 375 N.E.2d 1042 (1978)—§§ 7.3(a) n.9; 16.4(b) n.13

Bruce, United States v., 89 F.3d 886 (D.C.Cir.1996)—§ 24.3(d) n.109

Bruce Lindsey (Grand Jury Testimony), In re, 158 F.3d 1263 (D.C.Cir.1998)—§ 8.8(d) n.89

Brule, State v., 127 N.M. 368, 981 P.2d 782 (1999)—§ 13.7(c) n.63

Brum, Commonwealth v., 438 Mass. 103, 777 N.E.2d 1238 (2002)—§§ 6.7(d) n.146; 6.9(f) n.108, 112

Brumfield, State v., 900 A.2d 1151 (R.I.2006)—§ 26.10(b) n.32

Brumley, United States v., 217 F.3d 905 (7th Cir.2000)—§ 21.2(h) n.420

Brummett, United States v., 786 F.2d 720 (6th Cir.1986)—§ 21.2(d) n.178

Brummitt, United States v., 665 F.2d 521 (5th Cir.1981)—§§ 8.3(a) n.10; 8.10(b) n.45

Bruna, State v., 12 Neb.App. 798, 686 N.W.2d 590 (2004)—§ 11.9(c) n.110

Brunet, State v., 174 Vt. 135, 806 A.2d 1007 (2002)—§ 17.4(a) n.31

Brunette, United States v., 256 F.3d 14 (1st Cir.2001)—§ 3.1(c) n.79

Brunetti, State v., 276 Conn. 40, 883 A.2d 1167 (2005)—§ 9.1(b) n.43

Brunetti, United States v., 376 F.3d 93 (2d Cir.2004)—§ 21.2(b) n.93

Bruni v. Lewis, 847 F.2d 561 (9th Cir.1988)—§ 6.9(e) n.97

Brunner v. Collection Div. Of the Utah State Tax Comm'n, 945 P.2d 687 (Utah 1997)—§ 17.4(b) n.138

Bruno v. State, 332 Md. 673, 632 A.2d 1192 (1993)—§ 21.6(c) n.115

Bruno, State v., 157 Vt. 6, 595 A.2d 272 (1991)—§§ 10.6(c) n.22, 23

Bruno v. State, 574 So.2d 76 (Fla.1991)—§ 6.2(c) n.101

Bruno, United States ex rel. v. Herold, 408 F.2d 125 (2d Cir.1969)—§§ 11.6(a) n.42; 11.6(c) n.92; 24.1(b) n.28

Bruns, State v., 429 So.2d 307 (Fla.1983)—§ 24.8(f) n.92

Brunson, People v., 226 A.D.2d 1093, 641 N.Y.S.2d 935 (1996)—§ 15.7(g) n.216

Brunson, People v., 1 Cal.App.3d 226, 81 Cal.Rptr. 726 (1969)—§ 7.4(d) n.76

Brunson, State v., 101 N.J. 132, 501 A.2d 145 (1985)—§ 22.3(d) n.180

Brunson v. State, 182 Ind.App.146, 394 N.E.2d 229 (1979)—§ 11.2(a) n.30

Bruns, State ex rel. v. Clausmeier, 57 N.E. 541 (Ind.1900)—§ 3.5(d) n.158

Bruton, United States v., 647 F.2d 818 (8th Cir.1981)—§ 8.5(g) n.228

Bruton, United States v., 416 F.2d 310 (8th Cir.1969)—§ 9.1(a) n.14

Bruton v. United States, 391 U.S. 123, 88 S.Ct. 1620, 20 L.Ed.2d 476 (1968)—§§ 2.8(b) n.42; 2.9(e) n.106; 2.11(c) n.25; 17.2(b) n.28; 17.2(g) n.141; 17.3(e) n.62

Brutton v. State, 4 Ind. 602 (1853)—§§ 1.6(d) n.286; 19.1(b) n.16

Bruyette, In re, 150 Vt. 557, 556 A.2d 568 (1988)—§ 21.6(a) n.74

Bryan v. Mullin, 335 F.3d 1207 (10th Cir.2003)—§ 11.10(c) n.138

Bryan v. State, 571 A.2d 170 (Del.1990)—§ 6.9(c) n.61

Bryan, State v., 551 A.2d 807 (Del.1988)—§ 6.9(g) n.200

Bryan, United States v., 868 F.2d 1032 (9th Cir.1989)—§ 20.3(a) n.14

Bryan v. United States, 492 F.2d 775 (5th Cir.1974)—§ 21.5(d) n.105

Bryant, Ex parte, 682 So.2d 39 (Ala.1996)—§ 22.4(c) n.28

Bryant, People v., 94 P.3d 624 (Colo.2004)—§ 23.1(c) n.104

Bryant v. State, 841 N.E.2d 1154 (Ind.2006)—§ 26.4(i) n.189

Bryant, State v., 354 S.C. 390, 581 S.E.2d 157 (2003)—§ 22.3(b) n.84

Bryant v. State, 268 Ga. 664, 492 S.E.2d 868 (1997)—§ 22.2(d) n.67

Bryant v. State, 660 N.E.2d 290 (Ind.1995)—§ 17.4(b) n.138

Bryant v. State, 314 Ark. 130, 862 S.W.2d 215 (1993)—§§ 6.8(b) n.51; 6.8(d) n.84; 6.9(c) n.66

Bryant v. State, 565 So.2d 1298 (Fla.1990)—§§ 17.2(b) n.69; 17.2(d) n.95

Bryant, United States v., 991 F.2d 171 (5th Cir.1993)—§ 22.3(c) n.125

Bryant v. United States, 599 A.2d 1107 (D.C.App.1991)—§ 9.4(a) n.36

Bryant, United States v., 439 F.2d 642 (D.C.Cir.1971)—§§ 1.7(i) n.178; 20.6(b) n.64

Bryce, United States v., 287 F.3d 249 (2d Cir.2002)—§ 26.8(b) n.14

Brye, United States v., 146 F.3d 1207 (10th Cir.1998)—§§ 21.2(d) n.180, 181; 21.2(e) n.301

Bryser, United States v., 803 F.Supp. 908 (S.D.N.Y.1992)—§ 11.9(d) n.158

Bryson, State v., 506 S.W.2d 358 (Mo.1974)—§§ 10.2(b) n.20, 21

Bryson v. United States, 396 U.S. 64, 90 S.Ct. 355, 24 L.Ed.2d 264 (1969)—§ 8.10(d) n.90

Bubar, State v., 146 Vt. 398, 505 A.2d 1197 (1985)—§ 26.9(b) n.44

Bubis v. United States, 384 F.2d 643 (9th Cir.1967)—§ 4.6(l) n.179

Buchanan v. Angelone, 103 F.3d 344 (4th Cir.1996)—§ 25.1(d) n.61

Buchanan v. Kentucky, 483 U.S. 402, 107 S.Ct. 2906, 97 L.Ed.2d 336 (1987)—§§ 6.4(f) n.131; 6.7(b) n.104; 6.10(e) n.64; 22.3(c) n.160; 26.4(e) n.82; 26.5(a) n.11

Buchanan, State v., 178 Wis.2d 441, 504 N.W.2d 400 (Wis.Ct.App.1993)—§ 2.12(b) n.82

Buchanan v. State, 561 P.2d 1197 (Alaska 1977)—§§ 14.1(b) n.31; 14.2(c) n.39, 40

Buchanan, State v., 110 Ariz. 285, 518 P.2d 108 (1974)—§ 8.11(d) n.79

Buchanan v. State, 471 S.W.2d 401 (Tex.Cr.App.1971)—§ 3.2(e) n.168

Buchanan, State v., 190 So.2d 594 (Fla.App.1966)—§ 1.8(d) n.48

Buchanan, United States v., 213 F.3d 302 (6th Cir.2000)—§ 22.2(d) n.77

Buchanan, United States v., 59 F.3d 914 (9th Cir.1995)—§§ 21.2(b) n.79; 27.5(c) n.56

Buchanan, United States v., 904 F.2d 349 (6th Cir.1990)—§ 9.3(e) n.68

Buchanan, United States v., 787 F.2d 477 (10th Cir.1986)—§ 15.7(g) n.195

Buchanan, Commonwealth ex rel. v. Verbonitz, 525 Pa. 413, 581 A.2d 172 (Pa.1990)—§ 14.4(c) n.47

Buchanon, United States v., 72 F.3d 1217 (6th Cir.1995)—§§ 3.2(b) n.71; 3.8(c) n.113

Buchner, United States v., 7 F.3d 1149 (5th Cir.1993)—§ 9.1(d) n.124

Buck, State v., 134 P.3d 53 (Mont.2006)—§ 6.9(g) n.167

Buck, United States v., 548 F.2d 871 (9th Cir.1977)—§ 4.9(a) n.5

Buckalew, State v., 561 P.2d 289 (Alaska 1977)—§§ 21.2(c) n.101; 21.3(d) n.221; 27.4(d) n.48

Buckhannon Bd. & Care Home, Inc. v. West Virginia Dep't of Health & Human Resources, 532 U.S. 598, 121 S.Ct. 1835, 149 L.Ed.2d 855 (2001)—§ 13.5(h) n.139

Buckland, State v., 245 Kan. 132, 777 P.2d 745 (1989)—§ 11.3(c) n.63

Buckland, United States v., 289 F.3d 558 (9th Cir.2002)—§ 19.2(e) n.82

Buckles, State v., 636 S.W.2d 914 (Mo.1982)—§ 6.9(f) n.123

Buckles, United States v., 495 F.2d 1377 (8th Cir.1974)—§ 3.10(e) n.168

Bucklew, State v., 973 S.W.2d 83 (Mo.1998)—§§ 6.9(f) n.102, 106; 6.9(g) n.166

Buckley v. Fitzsimmons, 509 U.S. 259, 113 S.Ct. 2606, 125 L.Ed.2d 209 (1993)—§ 13.5(g) n.117

Buckley v. Terhune, 441 F.3d 688 (9th Cir.2006)—§§ 21.2(d) n.158, 194; 21.2(e) n.309, 337

Buckley, United States v., 4 F.3d 552 (7th Cir.1993)—§§ 3.3(c) n.111; 3.4(j) n.212

Buckley, United States v., 847 F.2d 991 (1st Cir.1988)—§§ 11.5(f) n.96; 21.5(a) n.19

Buckley, United States v., 586 F.2d 498 (5th Cir.1978)—§ 20.3(g) n.122

Buckman, State v., 259 Neb. 924, 613 N.W.2d 463 (2000)—§§ 6.7(d) n.145; 21.5(d) n.104; 21.6(a) n.76

Buckman, State v., 236 Mont. 37, 768 P.2d 1361 (1989)—§ 21.4(d) n.119

Buckner, People v., 35 Cal.App.3d 307, 111 Cal.Rptr. 32 (1973)—§ 3.6(b) n.52

Buckner v. Polk, 453 F.3d 195 (4th Cir.2006)—§ 9.6(a) n.47

Buddhu, State v., 264 Conn. 449, 825 A.2d 48 (2003)—§ 3.3(a) n.11

Budzanoski, United States v., 462 F.2d 443 (3d Cir.1972)—§§ 8.5(g) n.227; 15.2(i) n.221

Buege, United States v., 578 F.2d 187 (7th Cir.1978)—§ 24.5(b) n.28

Buehrer, In re, 50 N.J. 501, 236 A.2d 592 (1967)—§§ 1.8(c) n.17; 15.1(d) n.232, 233

Buell v. Mitchell, 274 F.3d 337 (6th Cir.2001)—§§ 22.4(c) n.29; 24.2(a) n.15

Buell, State v., 70 Ohio St.3d 1211, 639 N.E.2d 110 (1994)—§ 11.1(b) n.64

Buell, State v., 22 Ohio St.3d 124, 489 N.E.2d 795 (1986)—§ 7.5(b) n.15

Buenoano v. Singletary, 963 F.2d 1433 (11th Cir.1992)—§ 11.9(d) n.207

Bueno-Hernandez v. State, 724 P.2d 1132 (Wyo.1986)—§ 22.3(d) n.193

Bufalino, United States v., 576 F.2d 446 (2d Cir.1978)—§§ 20.6(b) n.64, 65

Buff v. State, 114 Nev. 1237, 970 P.2d 564 (1998)—§ 17.2(c) n.87

Buffington, Commonwealth v., 574 Pa. 29, 828 A.2d 1024 (2003)—§§ 17.4(a) n.5; 24.8(e) n.50

Buffum, People v., 40 Cal.2d 709, 256 P.2d 317 (1953)—§ 16.4(c) n.88

Buford v. State, 403 So.2d 943 (Fla.1981)—§ 26.1(b) n.32

Buford v. United States, 532 U.S. 59, 121 S.Ct. 1276, 149 L.Ed.2d 197 (2001)—§ 26.6(b) n.28

Bui v. DiPaolo, 170 F.3d 232 (1st Cir.1999)—§§ 6.9(d) n.72; 6.9(g) n.161

Bui v. Haley, 321 F.3d 1304 (11th Cir.2003)—§ 22.3(d) n.232

Buice v. State, 272 Ga. 323, 528 S.E.2d 788 (2000)—§ 13.3(c) n.35

Buie v. McAdory, 322 F.3d 980 (7th Cir.2003)—§ 28.10 n.7

Buie v. State, 633 N.E.2d 250 (Ind.1994)—§ 10.4(b) n.17

Buie v. Sullivan, 923 F.2d 10 (2d Cir.1990)—§ 24.3(h) n.182

Buiel, Commonwealth v., 391 Mass. 744, 463 N.E.2d 1172 (1984)—§ 24.5(c) n.39

Bulger, People v., 462 Mich. 495, 614 N.W.2d 1003 (2000)—§§ 11.1(b) n.66; 11.1(d) n.113

Buljubasic, United States v., 808 F.2d 1260 (7th Cir.1987)—§ 25.2(a) n.6

Bull v. Owens, 595 N.Y.S.2d 535, 191 App.Div.2d 692 (1993)—§ 27.4(b) n.11

Buller, People v., 101 Cal.App.3d 73, 160 Cal.Rptr. 657 (1979)—§ 21.4(c) n.81

Bullington v. Missouri, 451 U.S. 430, 101 S.Ct. 1852, 68 L.Ed.2d 270 (1981)—§§ 17.4(a) n.28; 26.7(a) n.5; 27.3(a) n.5

Bullis, United States v., 77 F.3d 1553 (7th Cir.1996)—§ 13.7(c) n.63

Bullock, People v., 440 Mich. 15, 485 N.W.2d 866 (1992)—§§ 2.12(b) n.83; 2.12(d) n.194; 2.12(e) n.214, 218

Bullock, State v., 272 Mont. 361, 901 P.2d 61 (1995)—§ 9.2(a) n.4

Bullock, United States v., 71 F.3d 171 (5th Cir.1995)—§ 3.4(a) n.13

Bultron v. State, 897 A.2d 758 (Del.2006)—§ 11.4(d) n.115

Bump, United States v., 605 F.2d 548 (10th Cir.1979)—§ 20.4(g) n.109

Bumper v. North Carolina, 391 U.S. 543, 88 S.Ct. 1788, 20 L.Ed.2d 797 (1968)—§§ 3.9(c) n.38; 3.10(b) n.27, 28; 3.10(d) n.103; 9.1(b) n.44; 9.1(c) n.111; 9.2(b) n.12; 10.3(b) n.28, 45; 27.6(d) n.78

Bumpus, State v., 459 N.W.2d 619 (Iowa 1990)—§ 3.3(f) n.204

Bundy, United States v., 392 F.3d 641 (4th Cir.2004)—§ 21.6(b) n.92

Bundy v. Wilson, 815 F.2d 125 (1st Cir.1987)—§ 27.1(a) n.6

Bunnell v. Superior Court, 13 Cal.3d 592, 119 Cal.Rptr. 302, 531 P.2d 1086 (1975)—§ 21.6(c) n.117

Bunner, United States v., 134 F.3d 1000 (10th Cir.1998)—§§ 21.2(b) n.90; 21.2(f) n.365; 21.5(e) n.149

Bunyard, People v., 45 Cal.3d 1189, 249 Cal.Rptr. 71, 756 P.2d 795 (1988)—§§ 23.2(g) n.122, 123

Burch v. Louisiana, 441 U.S. 130, 99 S.Ct. 1623, 60 L.Ed.2d 96 (1979)—§§ 1.5(e) n.222; 2.6(c) n.84; 2.11(c) n.32; 22.1(e) n.89

Burch, United States v., 156 F.3d 1315 (D.C.Cir.1998)—§ 21.2(h) n.439

Burclaff, State v., 138 Vt. 461, 418 A.2d 38 (1980)—§ 19.6(a) n.2

Burdeau v. McDowell, 256 U.S. 465, 41 S.Ct. 574, 65 L.Ed. 1048 (1921)—§ 3.1(h) n.188

Burdell v. Commonwealth, 990 S.W.2d 628 (Ky.1999)—§ 17.2(d) n.95

Burden, People v., 105 Cal.App.3d 917, 166 Cal.Rptr. 542 (1980)—§ 26.9(c) n.90

Burdett, State v., 70 Haw. 85, 762 P.2d 164 (1988)—§ 24.8(e) n.76

Burdin, People v., 171 Mich.App. 520, 430 N.W.2d 772 (1988)—§ 14.3(b) n.49

Burdine v. Johnson, 262 F.3d 336 (5th Cir.2001)—§§ 11.7(d) n.49; 11.10(d) n.199

Burdo, People v., 56 Mich.App. 48, 223 N.W.2d 358 (1974)—§ 3.5(a) n.35

Burford, State v., 163 N.J. 16, 746 A.2d 998 (2000)—§ 21.4(d) n.118

Burgans v. State, 500 N.E.2d 183 (Ind.1986)—§ 6.8(d) n.84

Burge, State v., 195 Conn. 232, 487 A.2d 532 (1985)—§ 6.8(b) n.62

Burge v. State, 443 S.W.2d 720 (Tex.Cr.App.1969)—§ 3.1(e) n.137

Burge, United States v., 407 F.3d 1183 (11th Cir.2005)—§ 26.4(i) n.200

Burgener, People v., 29 Cal.4th 833, 129 Cal.Rptr.2d 747, 62 P.3d 1 (2003)—§ 22.2(d) n.81

Burger v. Kemp, 483 U.S. 776, 107 S.Ct. 3114, 97 L.Ed.2d 638 (1987)—§§ 2.9(g) n.158; 11.9(a) n.6, 28; 11.9(d) n.159, 162, 182, 185, 227, 237; 11.10(c) n.113, 132; 27.6(d) n.112

Burger v. Scott, 317 F.3d 1133 (10th Cir.2003)—§§ 28.5(b) n.58, 59

Burgess v. Griffin, 743 F.2d 1064 (4th Cir.1984)—§ 21.3(f) n.431

Burgess, People v., 946 P.2d 565 (Colo.App.1997)—§ 16.1(a) n.29

Burgess, People v., 107 A.D.2d 703, 484 N.Y.S.2d 58 (1985)—§ 16.1(d) n.138

Burgess, State v., 639 N.W.2d 564 (Iowa 2001)—§ 21.6(a) n.49

Burgess v. State, 723 So.2d 742 (Ala.Crim.App.1997)—§ 15.4(e) n.128

Burgess v. State, 473 So.2d 432 (Miss.1985)—§ 18.2(e) n.71

Burgett v. Texas, 389 U.S. 109, 88 S.Ct. 258, 19 L.Ed.2d 319 (1967)— § 11.1(a) n.27

Burgos v. Murphy, 692 F.Supp. 1571 (S.D.N.Y.1988)—§§ 11.4(a) n.1, 2, 5

Burgos, United States v., 276 F.3d 1284 (11th Cir.2001)—§ 26.4(c) n.35

Burhoe, United States v., 409 F.3d 5 (1st Cir.2005)—§ 3.3(f) n.203

Burk v. State, 848 P.2d 225 (Wyo.1993)—§ 26.1(d) n.87

Burke, Commonwealth v., 566 Pa. 402, 781 A.2d 1136 (Pa.2001)— §§ 20.6(b) n.43; 24.3(b) n.51, 52

Burke v. Commonwealth, 373 Mass. 157, 365 N.E.2d 811 (1977)— §§ 14.3(c) n.68; 14.3(d) n.82

Burke, State v., 153 Wis.2d 445, 451 N.W.2d 739 (1990)—§§ 14.3(d) n.89, 90

Burke v. Town of Walpole, 405 F.3d 66 (1st Cir.2005)—§ 3.5(a) n.64

Burke, United States v., 425 F.3d 400 (7th Cir.2005)—§§ 8.8(h) n.184; 26.5(c) n.60

Burke, United States v., 345 F.3d 416 (6th Cir.2003)—§ 24.2(f) n.87

Burke, United States v., 67 F.3d 1 (1st Cir.1995)—§ 26.3(f) n.64

Burke, United States v., 781 F.2d 1234 (7th Cir.1985)—§ 8.10(d) n.111

Burke, United States v., 700 F.2d 70 (2d Cir.1983)—§ 15.4(h) n.191

Burke, United States v., 517 F.2d 377 (2d Cir.1975)—§ 21.6(b) n.111

Burke, United States v., 506 F.2d 1165 (9th Cir.1974)—§§ 7.5(b) n.13; 9.1(d) n.130

Burkes v. State, 830 S.W.2d 922 (Tex.Cr.App.1991)—§ 3.8(b) n.28

Burket v. Angelone, 208 F.3d 172 (4th Cir.2000)—§§ 6.6(d) n.57; 6.9(a) n.12; 6.9(g) n.161, 166, 200

Burkett v. Cunningham, 826 F.2d 1208 (3d Cir.1987)—§ 18.5(c) n.75

Burkett v. Fulcomer, 951 F.2d 1431 (3d Cir.1991)—§§ 18.5(c) n.75, 84

Burkhalter, United States v., 735 F.2d 1327 (11th Cir.1984)—§ 20.6(b) n.51

Burkhardt, State v., 795 S.W.2d 399 (Mo.1990)—§ 3.3(f) n.212

Burkhart v. State, 301 Ark. 543, 785 S.W.2d 460 (1990)—§ 9.1(a) n.17

Burkhart, State v., 541 S.W.2d 365 (Tenn.1976)—§§ 2.12(e) n.211; 11.5(g) n.110, 111, 120, 121

Burkholder v. State, 491 P.2d 754 (Alaska 1971)—§ 15.5(c) n.134

Burkley, United States v., 591 F.2d 903 (D.C.Cir.1978)—§ 5.3(d) n.42

Burks, State v., 268 Wis.2d 747, 674 N.W.2d 640 (2003)—§ 24.6(a) n.9

Burks v. United States, 437 U.S. 1, 98 S.Ct. 2141, 57 L.Ed.2d 1 (1978)— §§ 2.9(f) n.128; 21.5(e) n.124; 25.4(b) n.10; 27.2(c) n.30

Burnet v. Coronado Oil & Gas Co., 285 U.S. 393, 52 S.Ct. 443, 76 L.Ed. 815 (1932)—§§ 2.9(b) n.7, 21

Burnett, People v., 160 Misc.2d 1005, 612 N.Y.S.2d 774 (N.Y.Sup.1994)—§ 24.3(f) n.146

Burnett, People v., 13 Cal.Rptr.2d 511, 839 P.2d 1020 (1992)—§ 21.4(e) n.161

Burnett v. State, 352 S.C. 589, 576 S.E.2d 144 (2003)—§ 21.5(d) n.102

Burnett v. State, 92 S.W.3d 403 (Tenn.2002)—§ 21.3(b) n.84

Burnett, State v., 351 N.J.Super. 222, 798 A.2d 96 (2002)—§§ 18.4(c) n.40, 47

Burnett v. State, 310 Ark. 202, 832 S.W.2d 848 (Ark.1992)—§§ 11.10(c) n.69, 77, 113

Burnett v. State, 182 Ga.App. 539, 356 S.E.2d 231 (1987)—§§ 11.3(c) n.60, 61

Burnett v. State, 263 Ark. 225, 564 S.W.2d 211 (1978)—§ 10.2(a) n.5

Burnett, State v., 429 S.W.2d 239 (Mo.1968)—§ 6.7(c) n.106

Burnett, State v., 42 N.J. 377, 201 A.2d 39 (1964)—§ 3.3(c) n.140

Burnette, People v., 775 P.2d 583 (Colo.1989)—§ 22.3(e) n.272

Burnett, State ex rel. v. Burke, 22 Wis.2d 486, 126 N.W.2d 91 (1964)—§ 21.4(a) n.2

Burns v. Morton, 134 F.3d 109 (3d Cir.1998)—§ 28.5(b) n.58

Burns v. Ohio, 360 U.S. 257, 79 S.Ct. 1164, 3 L.Ed.2d 1209 (1959)—§ 11.2(d) n.119

Burns, People v., 84 Cal.App.2d 18, 189 P.2d 868 (1948)—§ 22.3(e) n.269

Burns, People v., 242 Mich. 345, 218 N.W. 704 (1928)—§ 16.3(d) n.73

Burns v. Reed, 500 U.S. 478, 111 S.Ct. 1934, 114 L.Ed.2d 547 (1991)—§§ 1.5(f) n.248; 13.5(g) n.116

Burns, State v., 6 S.W.3d 453 (Tenn.1999)—§ 24.8(e) n.70

Burns v. State, 609 So.2d 600 (Fla.1992)—§ 24.4(d) n.50

Burns v. State, 703 S.W.2d 649 (Tex.Cr.App.1985)—§ 24.8(c) n.41

Burns, State v., 322 S.W.2d 736 (Mo.1959)—§ 22.5(a) n.6

Burns, United States v., 15 F.3d 211 (1st Cir.1994)—§ 20.3(c) n.83

Burns, United States v., 37 F.3d 276 (7th Cir.1994)—§ 6.6(e) n.65

Burns v. United States, 501 U.S. 129, 111 S.Ct. 2182, 115 L.Ed.2d 123 (1991)—§§ 26.4(d) n.64; 26.5(c) n.51

Burnsville, City of v. Marsyla, 349 N.W.2d 829 (Minn.1984)—§ 3.10(f) n.199

Burola, People v., 848 P.2d 958 (Colo.1993)—§§ 9.3(e) n.56, 58

Burow, State v., 223 Neb. 867, 394 N.W.2d 665 (1986)—§ 26.10(c) n.60

Burr, United States v., 25 F.Cas. 55 (C.C.Va.1807) (No. 14,693)—§ 15.4(b) n.23

Burr, United States v., 25 Fed.Cas. 49 (D.Va.1807)—§ 22.3(c) n.109

Burrell, State v., 697 N.W.2d 579 (Minn.2005)—§§ 6.9(b) n.17; 6.9(c) n.55

Burrell v. State, 340 Md. 426, 667 A.2d 161 (1995)—§ 13.3(c) n.36

Burrell v. United States, 384 F.3d 22 (2d Cir.2004)—§ 21.4(f) n.213

Burris, State v., 40 S.W.3d 520 (Tenn.Cr.App.2000)—§ 25.1(d) n.77

Burroughs, United States v., 935 F.2d 292 (D.C.Cir.1991)—§ 17.2(b) n.34

Burrows, People v., 220 Cal.App.3d 116, 269 Cal.Rptr. 206 (1990)—§ 11.9(c) n.109

Burrows v. Superior Court, 13 Cal.3d 238, 118 Cal.Rptr. 166, 529 P.2d 590 (1974)—§§ 3.2(j) n.231, 233, 237, 238; 9.1(c) n.112

Burrows, United States v., 48 F.3d 1011 (7th Cir.1995)—§ 3.6(d) n.97

Bursey, United States v., 515 F.2d 1228 (5th Cir.1975)—§ 1.7(g) n.110

Bursey v. United States, 466 F.2d 1059 (9th Cir.1972)—§§ 8.5(d) n.137; 8.8(d) n.51, 58, 63

Burson, United States v., 952 F.2d 1196 (10th Cir.1991)—§ 9.6(a) n.48

Burt, People v., 168 Ill.2d 49, 212 Ill.Dec. 893, 658 N.E.2d 375 (1995)—§ 21.4(d) n.103

Burt v. State, 271 Ark. 245, 608 S.W.2d 15 (1980)—§ 26.9(a) n.5

Burt v. Uchtman, 422 F.3d 557 (7th Cir.2005)—§ 21.4(b) n.59

Burt, United States v., 410 F.3d 1100 (9th Cir.2005)—§ 5.4(c) n.30

Burt, United States v., 619 F.2d 831 (9th Cir.1980)—§ 13.7(c) n.55

Burton v. Johnson, 948 F.2d 1150 (10th Cir.1991)—§ 22.3(c) n.134

Burton, People v., 429 Mich. 133, 413 N.W.2d 413 (1987)—§ 27.4(a) n.2

Burton, State v., 163 W.Va. 40, 254 S.E.2d 129 (1979)—§§ 16.1(g) n.239, 241, 250, 264, 266, 267, 269, 278

Burton v. State, 442 S.W.2d 354 (Tex.Cr.App.1969)—§ 9.1(a) n.24

Burton v. Stewart, ___ U.S. ___, 127 S.Ct. 793, 166 L.Ed.2d 628 (2007)—§§ 28.5(b) n.45; 28.5(c) n.74, 75; 28.5(d) n.82; 28.6(e) n.52

Burton, United States v., 288 F.3d 91 (3d Cir.2002)—§§ 3.8(h) n.251; 9.3(d) n.35

Burton, United States v., 228 F.3d 524 (4th Cir.2000)—§ 3.8(e) n.186

Burton v. United States, 196 U.S. 283, 25 S.Ct. 243, 49 L.Ed. 482 (1905)—§ 24.9(d) n.36

Burton, United States ex rel. v. Cuyler, 439 F.Supp. 1173 (E.D.Pa.1977)—§§ 7.3(d) n.81, 82

Busby v. State, 894 So.2d 88 (Fla.2004)—§§ 22.3(c) n.134, 157

Busby, United States v., 780 F.2d 804 (9th Cir.1986)—§ 5.1(c) n.22

Busch, State v., 76 Ohio St.3d 613, 669 N.E.2d 1125 (1996)—§ 13.2(c) n.61

Busch v. State, 289 Md. 669, 426 A.2d 954 (1981)—§ 19.5(c) n.56

Busch, United States v., 795 F.Supp. 866. (N.D.Ill.1992)—§ 15.7(h) n.246

Buschauer v. State, 106 Nev. 890, 804 P.2d 1046 (1990)—§ 26.5(d) n.69

Buschkopf, State v., 373 N.W.2d 756 (Minn.1985)—§ 3.10(e) n.164

Bush v. Commonwealth, 839 S.W.2d 550 (Ky.1992)—§§ 23.2(d) n.65, 70

Bush v. Commonwealth, 702 S.W.2d 46 (Ky.1986)—§ 21.2(d) n.141

Bush v. Neet, 400 F.3d 849 (10th Cir.2005)—§ 21.3(b) n.71

Bush, State v., 96 Ohio St.3d 235, 773 N.E.2d 522 (2002)—§ 21.5(a) n.23

Bush, United States v., 47 F.3d 511 (2d Cir.1995)—§ 24.9(b) n.12

Bush, United States v., 888 F.2d 1145 (7th Cir.1989)—§ 28.9(a) n.22

Bush, United States v., 466 F.2d 236 (5th Cir.1972)—§ 6.9(b) n.27

Bush v. Williams, 504 So.2d 1060 (1st Cir.1987)—§ 1.8(d) n.46

Bushell's Case, 124 Eng.Rep. 1006 (C.P.1670)—§§ 1.6(b) n.63; 28.1(b) n.13

Bushyhead, United States v., 270 F.3d 905 (9th Cir.2001)—§ 6.5(b) n.25

Busic, United States v., 549 F.2d 252 (2d Cir.1977)—§§ 16.1(b) n.31; 16.2(e) n.64, 65

Bussard v. State, 295 Ark. 72, 747 S.W.2d 71 (1988)—§ 6.4(f) n.136

Busse, State v., 644 N.W.2d 79 (Minn.2002)—§ 21.6(a) n.2

Bustamante, People v., 30 Cal.3d 88, 177 Cal.Rptr. 576, 634 P.2d 927 (1981)—§§ 2.12(a) n.43; 2.12(d) n.195

Bustamante-Gamez, United States v., 488 F.2d 4 (9th Cir.1973)—§ 3.6(b) n.48

Bustamante-Saenz, United States v., 894 F.2d 114 (5th Cir.1990)—§§ 3.6(a) n.5; 6.3(b) n.40

Bustos-Torres v. INS, 898 F.2d 1053 (5th Cir.1990)—§ 6.10(e) n.80

Butala v. State, 664 N.W.2d 333 (Minn.2003)—§ 21.2(b) n.57

Butcher v. Bailey, 753 F.2d 465 (6th Cir.1985)—§§ 8.12(g) n.63; 8.13(a) n.24, 31; 8.13(b) n.58, 62 to 64

Butcher, United States v., 926 F.2d 811 (9th Cir.1991)—§ 3.9(j) n.226

Bute v. Illinois, 333 U.S. 640, 68 S.Ct. 763, 92 L.Ed. 986 (1948)—§§ 2.5(f) n.52; 6.4(a) n.7

Butenko, United States v., 494 F.2d 593 (3d Cir.1974)—§ 4.9(a) n.5

Butera, United States v., 420 F.2d 564 (1st Cir.1970)—§§ 22.2(d) n.72; 22.2(e) n.107

Butler v. Alabama, 608 So.2d 773 (Ala.Cr.App.1992)—§ 26.6(c) n.37

Butler, Commonwealth v., 529 Pa. 7, 601 A.2d 268 (1991)—§ 13.5(a) n.7

Butler v. Cooper, 554 F.2d 645 (4th Cir.1977)—§§ 13.4(b) n.72; 13.4(d) n.159

Butler v. McKellar, 494 U.S. 407, 110 S.Ct. 1212, 108 L.Ed.2d 347 (1990)—§§ 1.5(b) n.76; 2.9(h) n.227; 2.11(e) n.55; 28.6(d) n.25, 28

Butler, People v., 199 Mich.App. 474, 502 N.W.2d 333 (1993)—§ 5.2(b) n.26

Butler, People v., 43 Mich.App. 270, 204 N.W.2d 325 (1972)—§ 27.5(c) n.54

Butler v. State, 392 Md. 169, 896 A.2d 359 (2006)—§ 22.1(g) n.110

Butler, State v., 257 Kan. 1043, 897 P.2d 1007 (1995)—§§ 14.4(e) n.101, 120, 130

Butler v. State, 335 Md. 238, 643 A.2d 389 (1994)—§ 17.4(a) n.19

Butler, State v., 505 N.W.2d 806 (Iowa 1993)—§ 17.4(a) n.23

Butler v. State, 309 Ark. 211, 829 S.W.2d 412 (1992)—§§ 3.6(a) n.25; 10.2(a) n.7

Butler, State v., 496 So.2d 916 (Fla.App.1986)—§ 18.4(c) n.47

Butler v. State, 228 So.2d 421 (Fla.App.1969)—§§ 13.5(b) n.33, 42

Butler, United States v., 295 F.Supp.2d 816 (S.D.Oh.2003)—§ 28.9(a) n.15

Butler, United States v., 297 F.3d 505 (6th Cir.2002)—§ 21.2(d) n.258

Butler, United States v., 249 F.3d 1094 (9th Cir.2001)—§ 6.6(e) n.95

Butler, United States v., 567 F.2d 885 (9th Cir.1978)—§ 24.3(d) n.112

Butler, United States v., 481 F.2d 531 (D.C.Cir.1973)—§ 1.5(k) n.403

Butler v. Wentworth, 24 A. 456, 84 Me. 25 (1891)—§ 15.1(b) n.77

Buttafuoco, People v., 158 Misc.2d 174, 599 N.Y.S.2d 419 (N.Y.Co.Ct.1993)—§ 23.1(b) n.10

Butterfield v. Cook, 817 P.2d 333 (Utah App.1991)—§§ 11.7(e) n.102; 11.10(d) n.192

Butterfield, People v., 258 Cal.App.2d 586, 65 Cal.Rptr. 765 (1968)—§ 6.6(f) n.108

Butterfield, State v., 784 P.2d 153 (Utah 1989)—§ 24.1(a) n.13

Buttersworth v. State, 260 Ga. 795, 400 S.E.2d 908 (1991)—§ 6.10(b) n.33

Butterworth v. Smith, 494 U.S. 624, 110 S.Ct. 1376, 108 L.Ed.2d 572 (1990)—§§ 8.5(a) n.7; 8.5(d) n.120, 152

Buttrum v. State, 249 Ga. 652, 293 S.E.2d 334 (1982)—§ 3.4(b) n.26

Butts v. Heller, 69 Wash.App. 263, 848 P.2d 213 (1993)—§ 27.4(c) n.23

Butts v. State, 273 Ga. 760, 546 S.E.2d 472 (2001)—§ 22.3(c) n.133

Butts, United States v., 630 F.Supp. 1145 (D.Me.1986)—§ 11.10(b) n.43

Butzin v. Wood, 886 F.2d 1016 (8th Cir.1989)—§ 6.7(d) n.154

Buxton, In re, 111 R.I. 480, 304 A.2d 350 (1973)—§§ 8.4(b) n.74; 8.8(a) n.12; 15.1(e) n.266; 15.2(b) n.20

Buzbee v. Donnelly, 96 N.M. 692, 634 P.2d 1244 (1981)—§§ 15.2(c) n.61; 15.2(d) n.97; 15.6(a) n.19, 43; 15.7(f) n.135, 138, 155, 160, 169, 172

Byars v. United States, 273 U.S. 28, 47 S.Ct. 248, 71 L.Ed. 520 (1927)—§ 3.1(a) n.6

Bybee, State v., 1 P.3d 1087 (Utah 2000)—§ 6.9(b) n.18

Bye v. United States, 435 F.2d 177 (2d Cir.1970)—§ 21.4(d) n.118

Byers v. Oklahoma City, 497 P.2d 1302 (Okla.Crim.App.1972)—§ 6.10(a) n.2

Byers, United States v., 740 F.2d 1104 (D.C.Cir.1984)—§§ 6.7(b) n.103; 20.4(e) n.78, 81, 84; 27.5(c) n.95

Byington, State v., 135 Idaho 621, 21 P.3d 943 (App.2001)—§ 19.3(a) n.13

Bymes, State v., 258 Ga. 813, 375 S.E.2d 41 (1989)—§ 6.9(f) n.144

Bynum, Ex parte, 294 Ala. 78, 312 So.2d 52 (1975)—§ 12.4(a) n.12

Bynum v. State, 874 S.W.2d 903 (Tex.App.1994)—§ 19.5(b) n.20

Bynum, United States v., 763 F.2d 474 (1st Cir.1985)—§§ 4.6(d) n.65; 4.6(g) n.129

Bynum v. United States, 262 F.2d 465 (D.C.Cir.1958)—§ 9.4(d) n.98

Byram v. Ozmint, 339 F.3d 203 (4th Cir.2003)—§ 11.10(c) n.138

Byram, United States v., 145 F.3d 405 (1st Cir.1998)—§§ 6.2(c) n.120; 6.6(e) n.76; 9.5(a) n.22

Byrd v. McKaskle, 733 F.2d 1133 (5th Cir.1984)—§ 13.7(c) n.60

Byrd v. State, 58 P.3d 50 (Colo.2002)—§ 26.10(c) n.43

Byrd, State v., 937 P.2d 532 (Utah App.1997)—§ 24.7(i) n.91

Byrd, State v., 63 Ohio St.2d 288, 407 N.E.2d 1384 (1980)—§§ 21.2(c) n.106, 109, 110

Byrd, State v., 378 So.2d 1231 (Fla.1979)—§ 26.9(b) n.27

Byrd, United States v., 413 F.3d 249 (2d Cir.2005)—§§ 21.2(d) n.242, 244; 21.2(e) n.361

Byrd v. United States, 801 A.2d 28 (D.C.App.2002)—§§ 21.2(d) n.167; 21.2(e) n.314

Byrd, United States v., 969 F.2d 106 (5th Cir.1992)—§§ 12.3(a) n.19; 12.4(d) n.71

Byrd v. United States, 579 A.2d 725 (D.C.1990)—§ 3.8(e) n.194

Byrd v. United States, 551 A.2d 96 (D.C.App.1988)—§ 17.3(b) n.27

Byrd, United States v., 765 F.2d 1524 (11th Cir.1985)—§§ 8.11(c) n.35, 37 to 39, 59 to 61, 64, 65

Byrge, State v., 237 Wis.2d 197, 614 N.W.2d 477 (2000)—§ 21.4(d) n.118

Byrne, United States v., 83 F.3d 984 (8th Cir.1996)—§ 24.3(c) n.104

Byrnes, State v., 260 Iowa 765, 150 N.W.2d 280 (1967)—§ 22.2(e) n.110

Byrom v. State, 927 So.2d 709 (Miss.2006)—§ 11.10(c) n.69

Byron, United States v., 994 F.2d 747 (10th Cir.1993)—§§ 15.6(c) n.98, 99

Byrski, United States v., 854 F.2d 955 (7th Cir.1988)—§ 25.2(e) n.38

Bzura, State v., 261 N.J.Super. 602, 619 A.2d 647 (1993)—§ 24.10(c) n.40

C

Caballero, People v., 237 Ill.App.3d 797, 178 Ill.Dec. 505, 604 N.E.2d 1028 (1992)—§ 16.1(e) n.185

Caballes, People v., 221 Ill.2d 282, 851 N.E.2d 26 (2006)—§§ 2.12(b) n.92; 2.12(d) n.186, 193; 2.12(e) n.202

Caballes, People v., 207 Ill.2d 504, 280 Ill.Dec. 277, 802 N.E.2d 202 (2003)—§ 3.8(b) n.59

Caban, United States v., 173 F.3d 89 (2d Cir.1999)—§ 26.4(b) n.23

Cabassa, United States v., 62 F.3d 470 (2d Cir.1995)—§ 9.3(e) n.79

Cabbler v. Superintendent, 528 F.2d 1142 (4th Cir.1975)—§ 3.7(d) n.81

Cabbler v. Superintendent, 374 F.Supp. 690 (E.D.Va.1974)—§ 3.7(f) n.143

Cabell, State v., 176 W.Va. 272, 342 S.E.2d 240 (1986)—§ 21.4(g) n.231

Cabey, In re, 429 F.3d 93 (4th Cir.2005)—§ 28.5(c) n.74

Cable News Network, United States v., 865 F.Supp. 1549 (S.D.Fla.1994)—§ 23.1(c) n.112

Cabral, State v., 275 Conn. 514, 881 A.2d 247 (2005)—§ 9.6(a) n.38

Cabral, United States v., 475 F.2d 715 (1st Cir.1973)—§§ 18.1(c) n.41; 18.4(a) n.21

Cabrales, United States v., 524 U.S. 1, 118 S.Ct. 1772, 141 L.Ed.2d 1 (1998)—§§ 16.2(d) n.53; 16.2(e) n.81

Cabrales, United States v., 109 F.3d 471 (8th Cir.1997)—§ 16.2(e) n.84

Cabrera v. Hinsley, 324 F.3d 527 (7th Cir.2003)—§ 28.3(d) n.82

Cabrera, State v., 891 A.2d 1066 (Del.Super.2005)—§ 21.5(a) n.38

Cabrera-Sarmiento, United States v., 533 F.Supp. 799 (S.D.Fla.1982)—§ 15.4(d) n.100

Cabrera-Teran, United States v., 168 F.3d 141 (5th Cir.1999)—§ 19.3(a) n.13

Cacace, United States v., 529 F.2d 1167 (5th Cir.1976)—§ 4.6(e) n.100

Caceres, Commonwealth v., 413 Mass. 749, 604 N.E.2d 677 (1992)—§ 3.7(e) n.120

Caceres, United States v., 440 U.S. 741, 99 S.Ct. 1465, 59 L.Ed.2d 733 (1979)—§§ 1.7(j) n.229, 230; 3.1(e) n.132

Cade v. One 1987 Dodge Lancer Shelby 4-Door, 125 Idaho 731, 874 P.2d 542 (1994)—§ 5.1(c) n.42

Cadet v. Bulger, 377 F.3d 1173 (11th Cir.2004)—§ 28.3(b) n.66

Cadet, United States v., 727 F.2d 1453 (9th Cir.1984)—§ 20.3(g) n.122

Cadle v. State, 136 Ga.App. 232, 221 S.E.2d 59 (1975)—§ 10.2(c) n.33

Cadman, State v., 476 A.2d 1148 (Me.1984)—§§ 18.2(c) n.37; 18.2(d) n.63; 18.2(e) n.80

Cadorette, State v., 826 A.2d 101 (Vt.2003)—§ 19.2(c) n.27

Cadwallader, People v., 181 Ill.App.3d 488, 130 Ill.Dec. 108, 536 N.E.2d 1319 (1989)—§ 24.8(a) n.20

Cady v. Dombrowski, 413 U.S. 433, 93 S.Ct. 2523, 37 L.Ed.2d 706 (1973)—§§ 2.6(d) n.94; 3.7(e) n.92, 122

Caenen, State v., 270 Kan. 776, 19 P.3d 142 (2001)—§ 6.9(b) n.38

Cafero, United States v., 473 F.2d 489 (3d Cir.1973)—§§ 3.4(g) n.133; 3.4(l) n.247

Caffey v. State, 765 S.W.2d 891 (Tex.App.-San Antonio 1989)—§§ 19.2(c) n.27; 19.5(b) n.21

Caffey, State v., 438 S.W.2d 167 (Mo.1969)—§ 14.2(g) n.101

Caffie, Ex parte, 516 So.2d 831 (Ala.1987)—§§ 26.10(c) n.56, 64

Caffrey v. Solem, 400 N.W.2d 281 (S.D.1987)—§ 11.9(d) n.209

Cage v. Louisiana, 498 U.S. 39, 111 S.Ct. 328, 112 L.Ed.2d 339 (1990)—§§ 1.5(e) n.220; 2.7(a) n.46; 24.8(c) n.40

Cage v. McCaughtry, 305 F.3d 625 (7th Cir.2002)—§ 22.3(c) n.162

Caggiano, United States v., 899 F.2d 99 (1st Cir.1990)—§ 3.3(c) n.94

Caggiano, United States v., 660 F.2d 184 (6th Cir.1981)—§§ 11.9(a) n.30; 22.5(d) n.29, 35

Cagle v. State, 68 Ark.App. 248, 6 S.W.3d 801 (Ark.App.1999)—§ 24.2(e) n.79

Cagle v. State, 507 S.W.2d 121 (Tenn.Crim.App.1973)—§ 16.2(a) n.6

Cahan, People v., 44 Cal.2d 434, 282 P.2d 905 (1955)—§ 3.1(c) n.29

Cahill, People v., 2 N.Y.3d 14, 777 N.Y.S.2d 332, 809 N.E.2d 561 (2003)—§ 22.1(h) n.129

Cahill v. Rushen, 501 F.Supp. 1219 (E.D.Cal.1980)—§ 6.4(e) n.103

Caiazza v. Bally Mfg., Inc., 210 N.J.Super. 7, 509 A.2d 187 (1986)—§§ 8.5(h) n.252, 259, 291

Cain v. Peters, 972 F.2d 748 (7th Cir.1992)—§ 11.5(d) n.66

Cain, State v., 360 Md. 205, 757 A.2d 142 (2000)—§ 16.4(c) n.48

Cain, State v., 400 N.W.2d 582 (Iowa 1987)—§ 6.6(e) n.71

Cain, United States v., 134 F.3d 1345 (8th Cir.1998)—§ 21.2(d) n.198

Cain, United States v., 544 F.2d 1113 (1st Cir.1976)—§ 8.10(e) n.125

Calabrese, United States v., 942 F.2d 218 (3d Cir.1991)—§ 22.3(c) n.133

Calabro, United States v., 467 F.2d 973 (2d Cir.1972)—§ 11.6(a) n.12

Calamia v. City of New York, 879 F.2d 1025 (2d Cir.1989)—§ 3.3(e) n.186

Calandra, United States v., 414 U.S. 338, 94 S.Ct. 613, 38 L.Ed.2d 561 (1974)—§§ 2.9(f) n.134 to 136; 2.9(h) n.209; 2.9(i) n.285; 3.1(b) n.21, 23; 3.1(f) n.142; 8.6(a) n.16 to 18; 8.9(a) n.1; 9.1(a) n.4; 15.2(f) n.151; 15.5(a) n.5, 6, 34; 15.5(b) n.99; 28.3(c) n.70

Calbud, People v., 49 N.Y.2d 389, 426 N.Y.S.2d 238, 402 N.E.2d 1140 (1980)—§§ 15.7(g) n.189, 200 to 202, 206

Calderon v. Coleman, 525 U.S. 141, 119 S.Ct. 500, 142 L.Ed.2d 521 (1998)—§ 28.6(g) n.83

Calderon, People v., 9 Cal.4th 69, 885 P.2d 83, 36 Cal.Rptr.2d 333 (1994)—§ 26.2(b) n.26

Calderon v. Thompson, 523 U.S. 538, 118 S.Ct. 1489, 140 L.Ed.2d 728 (1998)—§§ 28.2(c) n.61, 66; 28.4(e) n.83

Calderon, United States v., 428 F.3d 928 (10th Cir.2005)—§ 27.5(c) n.50

Calderon, United States v., 388 F.3d 197 (6th Cir.2004)—§ 21.2(b) n.86

Calderon, United States v., 243 F.3d 587 (2d Cir.2001)—§ 21.6(a) n.41

Calderon, United States v., 127 F.3d 1314 (11th Cir.1997)—§ 11.4(b) n.40

Calderon-Palomino v. Nichols, 201 Ariz. 419, 36 P.3d 767 (Ariz.App.2001)—§ 24.2(g) n.97

Caldwell v. Cannady, 340 F.Supp. 835 (N.D.Tex.1972)—§ 3.1(g) n.179

Caldwell v. Dretke, 429 F.3d 521 (5th Cir.2006)—§ 28.5(b) n.47

Caldwell v. Mississippi, 472 U.S. 320, 105 S.Ct. 2633, 86 L.Ed.2d 231 (1985)—§§ 1.8(e) n.87; 11.2(e) n.193; 24.7(e) n.47; 26.1(b) n.25; 28.4(c) n.27

Caldwell v. State, 780 A.2d 1037 (Del.2001)—§ 3.4(g) n.128

Caldwell v. State, 971 S.W.2d 663 (Tex.App.1998)—§ 19.1(d) n.69

Caldwell v. State, 443 So.2d 806 (Miss.1983)—§ 10.5(d) n.39

Caldwell, State v., 117 Ariz. 464, 573 P.2d 864 (1977)—§ 7.3(e) n.90

Caldwell, State v., 20 Ariz.App. 331, 512 P.2d 863 (1973)—§ 3.2(d) n.147

Caldwell, United States v., 543 F.2d 1333 (D.C.Cir.1974)—§§ 20.3(b) n.42; 20.3(c) n.71

Caldwell, United States v., 465 F.2d 669 (D.C.Cir.1972)—§ 7.4(g) n.115

Calene v. State, 846 P.2d 679 (Wyo.1993)—§§ 11.7(e) n.63, 69, 72, 73, 76; 11.8 n.1

Calhoon, People v., 897 P.2d 855 (Colo.App.1994)—§ 18.4(d) n.84

Calhoun, State v., 694 So.2d 909 (La.1997)—§ 21.3(b) n.54

Calhoun, State v., 502 So.2d 808 (Ala.1986)—§ 3.2(b) n.33

Calhoun, State v., 18 Ohio St.3d 373, 481 N.E.2d 624 (Ohio 1985)—§ 25.3(a) n.7

Calia, State v., 15 Or.App. 110, 514 P.2d 1354 (1973)—§ 7.5(a) n.7

Caliendo v. Warden of Cal. Men's Colony, 365 F.3d 691 (1st Cir.2004)—§ 24.9(f) n.80

California v. Acevedo, 500 U.S. 565, 111 S.Ct. 1982, 114 L.Ed.2d 619 (1991)—§§ 2.9(b) n.23; 3.5(e) n.207; 3.7(c) n.47

California v. Beheler, 463 U.S. 1121, 103 S.Ct. 3517, 77 L.Ed.2d 1275 (1983)—§ 6.6(e) n.85

California v. Byers, 402 U.S. 424, 91 S.Ct. 1535, 29 L.Ed.2d 9 (1971)—§§ 2.10(d) n.122, 161; 2.12(a) n.21; 6.7(b) n.47; 8.10(a); 8.10(a) n.31; 8.12(c) n.34

California v. Carney, 471 U.S. 386, 105 S.Ct. 2066, 85 L.Ed.2d 406 (1985)—§§ 3.6(a) n.5; 3.7(b) n.34; 3.7(d) n.68

California v. Ciraolo, 476 U.S. 207, 106 S.Ct. 1809, 90 L.Ed.2d 210 (1986)—§ 3.2(c) n.138

California v. Federal Energy Regulatory Commission, 495 U.S. 490, 110 S.Ct. 2024, 109 L.Ed.2d 474 (1990)—§ 1.2(d) n.200

California v. Green, 399 U.S. 149, 90 S.Ct. 1930, 26 L.Ed.2d 489 (1970)—§§ 1.5(c) n.118; 2.6(d) n.99; 2.9(d) n.57; 2.12(a) n.21; 14.1(c) n.38; 14.1(d) n.52; 17.2(b) n.57

California v. Greenwood, 486 U.S. 35, 108 S.Ct. 1625, 100 L.Ed.2d 30 (1988)—§§ 3.1(e) n.126; 3.2(h) n.208

California v. Hodari D., 499 U.S. 621, 111 S.Ct. 1547, 113 L.Ed.2d 690 (1991)—§§ 2.7(d) n.251; 2.9(c) n.48, 51; 3.1(d) n.96; 3.2(h) n.205; 3.3(f) n.205; 3.5(a) n.4; 3.8(c) n.108

California v. Prysock, 453 U.S. 355, 101 S.Ct. 2806, 69 L.Ed.2d 696 (1981)—§§ 6.8(a) n.4, 18

California v. Roy, 519 U.S. 2, 117 S.Ct. 337, 136 L.Ed.2d 266 (1996)—§§ 27.6(d) n.91, 119, 121; 28.6(g) n.86

California v. Superior Court, 482 U.S. 400, 107 S.Ct. 2433, 96 L.Ed.2d 332 (1987)—§§ 3.1(j) n.251; 27.4(f) n.66

California v. Trombetta, 467 U.S. 479, 104 S.Ct. 2528, 81 L.Ed.2d 413 (1984)—§§ 1.5(b) n.67; 2.7(c) n.199; 24.3(e) n.119

California Highway Patrol v. Superior Court, 84 Cal.App.4th 1010, 101 Cal.Rptr.2d 379 (2000)—§ 20.3(g) n.126

Calinda, People v., 83 Misc.2d 520, 372 N.Y.S.2d 479 (1975)—§ 7.4(b) n.29

Calisto, United States v., 838 F.2d 711 (3d Cir.1988)—§ 6.7(c) n.121

Call, State v., 349 N.C. 382, 508 S.E.2d 496 (1998)—§ 14.4(c) n.47

Callabrass, United States v., 458 F.Supp. 964 (S.D.N.Y.1978)—§ 6.4(f) n.126

Callahan, Commonwealth v., 401 Mass. 627, 519 N.E.2d 245 (1988)—§ 6.7(b) n.66

Callahan v. Lash, 381 F.Supp. 827 (N.D.Ind.1974)—§ 23.3(a) n.8

Callahan, People v., 80 N.Y.2d 273, 590 N.Y.S.2d 46, 604 N.E.2d 108 (1992)—§ 21.2(b) n.83

Callahan, State v., 979 S.W.2d 577 (Tenn.1998)—§ 6.8(d) n.84

Callahan, United States v., 534 F.2d 763 (7th Cir.1976)—§§ 8.5(g) n.227; 20.3(b) n.57; 20.3(i) n.168

Callahan, United States v., 18 F.R.D. 486 (D.D.C.1955)—§ 19.4(b) n.39

Callan v. Wilson, 127 U.S. 540, 8 S.Ct. 1301, 32 L.Ed. 223 (1888)—§§ 2.9(d) n.72; 22.1(f) n.91

Callarman, United States v., 273 F.3d 1284 (10th Cir.2001)—§ 3.8(b) n.20

Callens v. State, 471 So.2d 482 (Ala.Crim.App.1984)—§ 14.2(e) n.69

Calliham, State v., 55 P.3d 573 (Utah 2002)—§ 22.3(c) n.104

Callihan v. Commonwealth, 142 S.W.3d 123 (Ky.2004)—§ 6.6(a) n.7

Callins v. Collins, 510 U.S. 1141, 114 S.Ct. 1127, 127 L.Ed.2d 435 (1994)—§§ 2.9(d) n.93; 26.1(b) n.22

Calloway, People v., 29 Cal.3d 666, 175 Cal.Rptr. 596, 631 P.2d 30 (1981)—§ 21.2(e) n.306

Callum, United States v., 404 F.3d 1150 (9th Cir.2005)—§ 4.6(m) n.228

Callum, United States v., 410 F.3d 571 (9th Cir.2005)—§ 4.6(e) n.74

Calvaresi v. United States, 348 U.S. 961, 75 S.Ct. 523, 99 L.Ed. 749 (1955)—§ 1.7(i) n.162

Calvert v. State, 310 N.W.2d 185 (Iowa 1981)—§ 26.10(c) n.63

Calvin's Case, 7 Co. 1, 4b, 77, 1 P. 435 Eng.Rep. 377 (1610)—§ 2.4(b) n.77

Camacho v. Autoridad de Telefonos de Puerto Rico, 868 F.2d 482 (1st Cir.1989)—§ 4.6(l) n.193

Camacho, People v., 23 Cal.4th 824, 98 Cal.Rptr.2d 232, 3 P.3d 878 (2000)—§ 3.2(c) n.111

Camacho, State v., 561 N.W.2d 160 (Minn.1997)—§§ 11.3(b) n.50; 11.5(c) n.61; 11.5(d) n.79

Camacho, United States v., 955 F.2d 950 (4th Cir.1992)—§ 24.2(d) n.48

Camacho v. United States, 407 F.2d 39 (9th Cir.1969)—§ 6.7(c) n.119

Camacho-Bordes, United States v., 94 F.3d 1168 (8th Cir.1996)—§ 28.9(a) n.14

Camara v. Municipal Court, 387 U.S. 523, 87 S.Ct. 1727, 18 L.Ed.2d 930 (1967)—§§ 2.8(b) n.41; 3.1(e) n.129; 3.3(b) n.31; 3.8(a) n.6; 3.8(d) n.179; 3.9(a) n.1; 3.9(b) n.11

Camargo, State v., 126 N.H. 766, 498 A.2d 292 (1985)—§ 2.12(c) n.171

Camarillo-Tello, United States v., 236 F.3d 1024 (9th Cir.2001)—§ 21.2(d) n.170

Cambridge, City of v. Phillips, 415 Mass. 126, 612 N.E.2d 638 (1993)—§§ 13.1(a) n.4; 13.2(b) n.34

Camden County Grand Jury, In re, 10 N.J. 23, 89 A.2d 416 (1952)—§ 8.3(h) n.46

Camera v. Fogg, 658 F.2d 80 (2d Cir.1981)—§ 11.9(d) n.190

Cameron, People v., 73 Misc.2d 790, 342 N.Y.S.2d 773 (1973)—§ 3.2(h) n.206

Cameron, State v., 253 Mont. 95, 830 P.2d 1284 (1992)—§ 21.4(f) n.176

Cameron, United States v., 538 F.2d 254 (9th Cir.1976)—§ 3.9(f) n.102

Caminetti v. United States, 242 U.S. 470, 37 S.Ct. 192, 61 L.Ed. 442 (1917)—§§ 1.2(c) n.109, 115

Caminito, United States ex rel. v. Murphy, 222 F.2d 698 (2d Cir.1955)—§ 6.2(c) n.125

Camirand, State v., 572 A.2d 290 (R.I.1990)—§ 7.4(d) n.71

Cammarano v. State, 602 So.2d 1369 (Fla.App.1992)—§ 24.11(d) n.28

Cammisano, United States v., 546 F.2d 238 (8th Cir.1976)—§ 13.4(c) n.83

Camodeo, United States v., 383 F.2d 770 (2d Cir.1967)—§ 11.2(c) n.99

Campa, United States v., 459 F.3d 1121 (11th Cir.2006)—§§ 23.2(a) n.25, 29, 44

Campa, United States v., 234 F.3d 733 (1st Cir.2000)—§ 3.8(b) n.32

Campagnuolo, United States v., 592 F.2d 852 (5th Cir.1979)—§§ 4.6(b) n.49; 4.6(l) n.205; 8.5(g) n.227; 20.3(m) n.252; 20.6(b) n.42; 24.3(b) n.63

Campana, Commonwealth v., 455 Pa. 622, 314 A.2d 854 (1974)—§ 17.4(c) n.144

Campanale, United States v., 518 F.2d 352 (9th Cir.1975)—§ 16.2(g) n.131

Campaneria v. Reid, 891 F.2d 1014 (2d Cir.1989)—§§ 6.9(b) n.32; 6.9(f) n.100

Campbell v. Commonwealth, 788 S.W.2d 260 (Ky.1990)—§ 16.3(b) n.23

Campbell v. Louisiana, 523 U.S. 392, 118 S.Ct. 1419, 140 L.Ed.2d 551 (1998)—§§ 15.4(c) n.91; 15.4(d) n.121; 15.4(e) n.135

Campbell v. Marshall, 769 F.2d 314 (6th Cir.1985)—§ 21.6(a) n.77

Campbell v. Minnesota, 487 F.2d 1 (8th Cir.1973)—§ 3.4(c) n.38

Campbell, People v., 73 N.Y.2d 481, 541 N.Y.S.2d 756, 539 N.E.2d 584 (1989)—§ 21.6(a) n.2

Campbell, People v., 742 P.2d 302 (Colo.1987)—§§ 18.4(d) n.83, 84

Campbell v. Rice, 408 F.3d 1166 (9th Cir.2005)—§§ 11.9(b) n.90; 11.9(c) n.122; 24.2(a) n.21; 24.2(b) n.26; 27.6(d) n.84

Campbell, State v., 279 Kan. 1, 106 P.3d 1129 (2005)—§ 13.7(a) n.27

Campbell, State v., 965 P.2d 991 (Okl.Cr.App.1998)—§ 17.4(b) n.133

Campbell, State v., 340 N.C. 612, 460 S.E.2d 144 (1995)—§ 24.6(e) n.47

Campbell, State v., 69 Ohio St.3d 38, 630 N.E.2d 339 (1994)—§§ 10.5(c) n.31, 33

Campbell, State v., 127 N.H. 112, 498 A.2d 330 (1985)—§§ 11.2(e) n.189, 214

Campbell, State v., 299 Or. 633, 705 P.2d 694 (1985)—§ 2.12(e) n.199

Campbell, State v., 44 Or.App. 3, 604 P.2d 1266 (1980)—§ 20.6(b) n.34

Campbell, State v., 160 Mont. 111, 500 P.2d 801 (1972)—§ 16.1(g) n.273

Campbell, State v., 210 Mo. 202, 109 S.W. 706 (Mo.1908)—§§ 19.1(b) n.23; 27.6(a) n.9

Campbell, United States v., 410 F.3d 456 (8th Cir.2005)—§ 13.7(c) n.52

Campbell, United States v., 291 F.3d 1169 (9th Cir.2002)—§ 13.5(h) n.138

Campbell, United States v., 106 F.3d 64 (5th Cir.1997)—§ 26.8(b) n.5

Campbell, United States v., 920 F.2d 793 (11th Cir.1991)—§ 3.3(c) n.137

Campbell, United States v., 874 F.2d 838 (1st Cir.1989)—§ 11.3(b) n.38

Campbell, United States v., 843 F.2d 1089 (8th Cir.1988)—§ 3.10(b) n.54

Campbell, United States v., 732 F.2d 1017 (1st Cir.1984)—§§ 3.4(k) n.232; 7.2(b) n.12

Campbell, United States v., 706 F.2d 1138 (11th Cir.1983)—§ 18.3(b) n.36

Campbell, United States v., 431 F.2d 97 (9th Cir.1970)—§ 6.8(d) n.84

Campbell v. United States, 373 U.S. 487, 83 S.Ct. 1356, 10 L.Ed.2d 501 (1963)—§§ 20.3(b) n.43; 24.3(c) n.100

Campbell v. Wood, 18 F.3d 662 (9th Cir.1994)—§ 24.2(b) n.27

Campbell, United States ex rel. v. Rundle, 327 F.2d 153 (3d Cir.1964)—§ 3.3(g) n.239

Camphor v. State, 272 Ga. 408, 529 S.E.2d 121 (2000)—§ 12.3(g) n.159

Campino v. United States, 968 F.2d 187 (2d Cir.1992)—§ 28.9(b) n.38

Campisi, State v., 42 N.J.Super. 138, 126 A.2d 17 (1956)—§ 19.6(b) n.10

Campiti v. Matesanz, 333 F.3d 317 (1st Cir.2003)—§ 28.6(b) n.11

Campiti v. Walonis, 611 F.2d 387 (1st Cir.1979)—§ 4.6(l) n.201

Campodonico v. United States, 222 F.2d 310 (9th Cir.1955)—§ 18.5(c) n.72

Campos v. State, 91 N.M. 745, 580 P.2d 966 (1978)—§ 8.11(e) n.102

Campusano v. United States, 442 F.3d 770 (2d Cir.2006)—§§ 11.6(b) n.80; 27.5(c) n.50

Canaan v. McBride, 395 F.3d 376 (7th Cir.2005)—§§ 11.6(b)   n.84; 11.10(b) n.46

Canada v. State, 104 Nev. 288, 756 P.2d 552 (1988)—§ 3.10(f) n.193

Canada, United States v., 960 F.2d 263 (1st Cir.1992)—§§ 21.2(d) n.166, 174

Canaday, State v., 263 Neb. 566, 641 N.W.2d 13 (2002)—§§ 5.2(a) n.8, 16, 17

Canaday, State v., 117 Ariz. 572, 574 P.2d 60 (App.1977)—§§ 14.4(e) n.135, 136

Canady, United States v., 126 F.3d 352 (2d Cir.1997)—§§ 24.1(a) n.5; 24.2(a) n.10

Canales Gomez, United States v., 358 F.3d 1221 (9th Cir.2004)—§ 4.6(e) n.97

Canal Zone, Government of the v. Castillo, 568 F.2d 405 (5th Cir.1978)—§ 27.5(a) n.14

Canal Zone, Government of the v. Sierra, 594 F.2d 60 (5th Cir.1979)—§ 3.1(i) n.234

Canatella, State v., 96 N.H. 202, 72 A.2d 507 (1950)—§§ 15.7(h) n.224, 229

Canby, State v., 162 W.Va. 666, 252 S.E.2d 164 (1979)—§ 3.5(a) n.13

Cancilla, United States v., 725 F.2d 867 (2d Cir.1984)—§§ 11.9(d) n.175, 220

Cancino v. Craven, 511 F.2d 1371 (9th Cir.1975)—§ 27.5(a) n.15

Candage, State v., 549 A.2d 355 (Me.1988)—§ 3.3(b) n.47

Candelaria-Silva, United States v., 166 F.3d 19 (1st Cir.1999)—§ 22.2(a) n.13

Candelario, United States v., 240 F.3d 1300 (11th Cir.2001)—§§ 19.3(a) n.86, 90, 91

Cane v. State, 560 A.2d 1063 (Del.1989)—§ 18.5(a) n.40

Canedy, State v., 161 Wis.2d 565, 469 N.W.2d 163 (1991)—§ 21.5(a) n.35

Canelo, State v., 139 N.H. 376, 653 A.2d 1097 (1995)—§ 27.3(a) n.7

Canez, State v., 202 Ariz. 133, 42 P.3d 564 (2002)—§§ 3.6(a) n.38; 7.4(c) n.48, 50, 53; 7.4(e) n.86, 89; 22.3(b) n.57; 22.3(d) n.215, 216, 246

Canfield, State v., 154 Wash.2d 698, 116 P.3d 391 (Wash.2005)—§ 26.10(c) n.81

Canfield, United States v., 879 F.2d 446 (8th Cir.1989)—§ 22.2(d) n.74

Canino, United States v., 949 F.2d 928 (7th Cir.1991)—§ 19.4(b) n.30

Canion v. Cole, 210 Ariz. 598, 115 P.3d 1261 (Ariz.2005)—§ 24.3(b) n.80

Cannaday v. State, 455 So.2d 713 (Miss.1984)—§§ 6.4(e) n.61; 6.4(f) n.125

Cannady v. Dugger, 931 F.2d 752 (11th Cir.1991)—§ 6.7(d) n.147

Cannady, United States v., 283 F.3d 641 (4th Cir.2002)—§ 21.3(d) n.218

Cannistraro, United States v., 794 F.Supp. 1313 (D.N.J.1992)—§§ 11.9(a) n.22; 11.9(c) n.141, 143

Cannistraro, United States v., 800 F.Supp. 30 (D.N.J.1992)—§ 15.2(i) n.221

Cannon v. Lockhart, 850 F.2d 437 (8th Cir.1988)—§ 24.9(f) n.97

Cannon, State v., 128 N.J. 546, 608 A.2d 341 (1992)—§§ 1.7(f) n.94, 97

Cannon, State v., 457 So.2d 1177 (La.1984)—§ 26.10(b) n.19

Cannon, United States v., 88 F.3d 1495 (8th Cir.1996)—§ 5.4(c) n.44

Cano v. Municipality of Anchorage, 627 P.2d 660 (Alaska App.1981)—§ 11.5(g) n.111

Cano, State v., 154 Ariz. 447, 743 P.2d 956 (App.1987)—§ 20.3(g) n.126

Cano-Guel, United States v., 167 F.3d 900 (5th Cir.1999)—§ 21.4(f) n.214

Canon, State v., 241 Wis.2d 164, 622 N.W.2d 270 (2001)—§§ 17.4(a) n.39; 25.1(d) n.92

Canon City, City of v. Merris, 137 Colo. 169, 323 P.2d 614 (1958)—§§ 1.8(d) n.60, 71

Cansler v. State, 261 Ga. 693, 409 S.E.2d 504 (1991)—§ 6.2(c) n.152

Cantellano, United States v., 430 F.3d 1142 (11th Cir.2005)—§ 26.4(f) n.108

Canterino v. Wilson, 562 F.Supp. 106 (W.D.Ky.1983)—§ 11.2(f) n.248

Cantero v. State, 612 So.2d 634 (Fla.App.1993)—§ 24.7(e) n.43

Cantizano v. United States, 614 A.2d 870 (D.C.App.1992)—§ 3.2(e) n.160

Canton, Ohio, City of v. Harris, 489 U.S. 378, 109 S.Ct. 1197, 103 L.Ed.2d 412 (1989)—§ 3.1(k) n.270

Cantor, People v., 36 N.Y.2d 106, 365 N.Y.S.2d 509, 324 N.E.2d 872 (1975)—§ 9.4(f) n.118

Cantor, United States v., 328 F.Supp. 561 (E.D.Pa.1971)—§ 4.6(f) n.119

Cantrell v. Commonwealth, 229 Va. 387, 329 S.E.2d 22 (1985)—§§ 13.3(b) n.20; 22.5(a) n.3, 6, 8

Cantrell v. State, 266 Ga. 700, 469 S.E.2d 660 (1996)—§ 24.8(d) n.47

Cantu v. State, 930 S.W.2d 594 (Tex.Crim.App.1996)—§ 11.8(c) n.77

Cantu v. State, 738 S.W.2d 249 (Tex.Cr.App.1987)—§ 7.4(e) n.92

Cantu, United States v., 185 F.3d 298 (5th Cir.1999)—§§ 8.11(c) n.36; 8.11(e) n.108; 13.5(b) n.44, 46

Canty, State v., 278 N.J.Super. 80, 650 A.2d 391 (1994)—§ 10.5(e) n.56

Capaldi, United States v., 134 F.3d 307 (5th Cir.1998)—§ 27.5(c) n.52

Cape v. State, 272 Ind. 609, 400 N.E.2d 161 (1980)—§ 24.2(a) n.7

Capelton, United States v., 350 F.3d 231 (1st Cir.2003)—§§ 5.2(a) n.8; 5.3(d) n.43

Capital Cities/ABC, Inc., In re, 913 F.2d 89 (3d Cir.1990)—§§ 23.1(d) n.166, 212

Caplan, Commonwealth v., 411 Pa. 563, 192 A.2d 894 (1963)—§ 20.1(b) n.31

Caples v. United States, 391 F.2d 1018 (5th Cir.1968)—§ 10.5(a) n.14

Caplin & Drysdale, Chartered v. United States, 491 U.S. 617, 109 S.Ct. 2646, 105 L.Ed.2d 528 (1989)— §§ 11.1(a) n.11, 31; 11.4(c) n.47, 48, 92, 93; 11.9(a) n.14; 26.6(d) n.70, 71

Cappellano, Commonwealth v., 392 Mass. 676, 467 N.E.2d 843 (1984)—§ 17.1(a) n.15

Cappello, United States v., 209 F.Supp. 959 (E.D.N.Y.1962)—§ 17.3(a) n.2

Capps, State v., 276 S.C. 59, 275 S.E.2d 872 (1981)—§ 15.2(d) n.106

Capra, United States v., 501 F.2d 267 (2d Cir.1974)—§ 4.6(j) n.163

Caprio, State v., 819 A.2d 1265 (R.I.2003)—§ 18.4(c) n.78

Capua, United States v., 656 F.2d 1033 (5th Cir.1981)—§ 22.3(a) n.47

Caputo v. Henderson, 541 F.2d 979 (2d Cir.1976)—§ 21.4(d) n.149

Caputo v. Nelson, 455 F.3d 45 (1st Cir.2006)—§ 6.7(c) n.118

Carafas v. LaVallee, 391 U.S. 234, 88 S.Ct. 1556, 20 L.Ed.2d 554 (1968)—§§ 28.2(b) n.31; 28.3(a) n.23

Caraher, State v., 293 Or. 741, 653 P.2d 942 (1982)—§§ 2.12(c) n.178; 2.12(d) n.195

Carbajal, People v., 10 Cal.4th 1114, 899 P.2d 67, 43 Cal.Rptr.2d 681 (1995)—§ 26.9(b) n.31

Carbo v. United States, 82 S.Ct. 662, 7 L.Ed.2d 769 (1962)—§ 12.4(c) n.58

Carbone, United States v., 378 F.2d 420 (2d Cir.1967)—§ 24.10(b) n.31

Carcaise, United States v., 442 F.Supp. 1209 (M.D.Fla.1978)—§§ 15.6(b) n.61; 15.6(c) n.96

Carchman v. Nash, 473 U.S. 716, 105 S.Ct. 3401, 87 L.Ed.2d 516 (1985)—§§ 18.4(c) n.32, 39; 26.10(b) n.13

Card, State v., 137 Idaho 182, 45 P.3d 838 (2002)—§ 3.4(j) n.206

Card, State v., 121 Idaho 425, 825 P.2d 1081 (1991)—§ 22.2(d) n.88

Cardales, United States v., 168 F.3d 548 (1st Cir.1999)—§ 16.4(b) n.31

Cardenas, State v., 146 Wash.2d 400, 47 P.3d 127 (2002)—§§ 3.6(a) n.19; 3.6(b) n.59

Cardenas, United States v., 217 F.3d 491 (7th Cir.2000)—§ 26.6(b) n.28

Cardenas-Alverez, State v., 130 N.M. 386, 25 P.3d 225 (2001)—§ 2.12(b) n.103

Cardinal, State v., 147 Vt. 461, 520 A.2d 984 (1986)—§ 12.3(b) n.65

Cardon, State v., 946 So.2d 171 (La.2007)—§ 13.6(d) n.57

Cardona, United States v., 302 F.3d 494 (5th Cir.2002)—§§ 18.2(b) n.4; 18.2(c) n.31, 36; 18.2(d) n.67; 18.2(e) n.74, 84

Cardona-Rivera, United States v., 904 F.2d 1149 (7th Cir.1990)— §§ 3.1(d) n.98; 3.5(e) n.206

Cardwell, In re, 50 P.3d 897 (Colo.2002)—§ 17.4(b) n.125

Cardwell v. Commonwealth, 209 Va. 68, 161 S.E.2d 787 (1968)— § 6.8(a) n.16

Cardwell v. Lewis, 417 U.S. 583, 94 S.Ct. 2464, 41 L.Ed.2d 325 (1974)—§§ 3.2(f) n.183; 3.7(b) n.30; 3.7(d) n.62

Cardwell, People v., 78 N.Y.2d 996, 575 N.Y.S.2d 267, 580 N.E.2d 753 (1991)—§ 17.2(d) n.97

Cardwell, United States v., 433 F.3d 378 (4th Cir.2005)—§ 17.1(a) n.10

Carella v. California, 491 U.S. 263, 109 S.Ct. 2419, 105 L.Ed.2d 218 (1989)—§§ 27.6(d) n.88, 122

Carey, Commonwealth v., 407 Mass. 528, 554 N.E.2d 1199 (1990)—§ 3.9(k) n.257

Carey v. Musladin, _____ U.S. _____, 127 S.Ct. 649, 166 L.Ed.2d 482 (2006)—§§ 2.7(a) n.13; 24.2(e) n.61, 80; 28.6(f) n.71

Carey v. Saffold, 536 U.S. 214, 122 S.Ct. 2134, 153 L.Ed.2d 260 (2002)—§§ 28.5(b) n.48, 50; 28.11(b) n.34

Carey v. State, 984 P.2d 1098 (Wyo.1999)—§ 6.9(f) n.100

Carey, United States v., 152 F.Supp.2d 415 (S.D.N.Y.2001)—§ 16.2(e) n.69

Carey, United States v., 172 F.3d 1268 (9th Cir.1999)—§ 3.4(j) n.202

Carey, United States v., 943 F.2d 44 (11th Cir.1991)—§ 12.1(a) n.21

Carey, United States v., 746 F.2d 228 (4th Cir.1984)—§§ 18.3(b) n.36, 41

Cargle v. State, 909 P.2d 806 (Okla.Crim.App.1995)—§ 14.1(c) n.45

Carhee, United States v., 27 F.3d 1493 (10th Cir.1994)—§ 10.3(b) n.10

Carignan, State v., 272 N.W.2d 748 (Minn.1978)—§ 16.1(g) n.275

Carignan, United States v., 342 U.S. 36, 72 S.Ct. 97, 96 L.Ed. 48 (1951)—§§ 6.1(c) n.19; 6.2(a) n.19; 6.3(a) n.23; 6.5(a) n.5

Cariola, United States v., 323 F.2d 180 (3d Cir.1963)—§§ 21.4(d) n.122; 28.9(a) n.21

Carkhuff, Commonwealth v., 441 Mass. 122, 804 N.E.2d 317 (2004)—§ 3.9(h) n.169

Carkulis, State ex rel. v. District Court, 229 Mont. 265, 746 P.2d 604 (1987)—§§ 20.4(b) n.20; 20.4(d) n.68; 20.5(f) n.84; 20.5(g) n.97

Carlisle, State v., 280 Ga. 770, 631 S.E.2d 347 (2006)—§ 21.4(a) n.11

Carlisle v. United States, 517 U.S. 416, 116 S.Ct. 1460, 134 L.Ed.2d 613 (1996)—§ 28.9(a) n.17

Carlock, United States v., 606 F.Supp. 491 (E.D.La.1985)—§ 22.3(b) n.55

Carlson v. Ferguson, 9 F.Supp.2d 654 (S.D.W.Va.1998)—§ 28.3(c) n.79

Carlson v. Green, 446 U.S. 14, 100 S.Ct. 1468, 64 L.Ed.2d 15 (1980)—§ 3.1(k) n.278

Carlson v. Landon, 342 U.S. 524, 72 S.Ct. 525, 96 L.Ed. 547 (1952)—§§ 12.3(c) n.81; 12.4(a) n.3

Carlson, People v., 185 Ill.2d 546, 236 Ill.Dec. 786, 708 N.E.2d 372 (1999)—§ 3.1(c) n.79

Carlson, State v., 261 Wis.2d 97, 661 N.W.2d 51 (2003)—§ 22.2(b) n.18

Carlson, State v., 260 Neb. 815, 619 N.W.2d 832 (2000)—§ 21.5(a) n.24

Carlson, State v., 311 Or. 201, 808 P.2d 1002 (1991)—§ 6.6(f) n.108

Carlson, State v., 258 N.W.2d 253 (N.D.1977)—§ 18.4(d) n.90

Carlson, State v., 555 P.2d 269 (Alaska 1976)—§ 21.3(d) n.263

Carlton, State v., 276 Ga. 693, 583 S.E.2d 1 (2003)—§ 18.4(c) n.39

Carlucci, United States v., 288 F.2d 691 (3d Cir.1961)—§ 23.2(g) n.114

Carman v. State, 658 P.2d 131 (Alaska App.1983)—§ 19.3(c) n.189

Carmichael v. State, 228 Ga. 834, 188 S.E.2d 495 (1972)—§ 15.2(b) n.20

Carmichael, United States v., 216 F.3d 224 (2d Cir.2000)—§ 21.3(b) n.74

Carmichael, United States v., 685 F.2d 903 (4th Cir.1982)—§ 15.4(f) n.145

Carmichael, United States v., 489 F.2d 983 (7th Cir.1973)—§§ 3.4(d) n.55, 60

Carmickle, State v., 307 Or. 1, 762 P.2d 290 (1988)—§ 26.1(d) n.89

Carmona, United States v., 873 F.2d 569 (2d Cir.1989)—§§ 6.7(b) n.43; 26.5(a) n.7

Carmona v. United States Bureau of Prisons, 243 F.3d 629 (2d Cir.2001)—§§ 28.9(a) n.10; 28.9(b) n.38

Carmouche, State v., 508 So.2d 792 (La.1987)—§§ 11.9(b) n.82, 87; 11.9(d) n.204

Carnes, United States v., 309 F.3d 950 (6th Cir.2002)—§ 9.1(b) n.46

Carney, Commonwealth v., 31 Mass.App. 250, 576 N.E.2d 691 (1991)—§ 11.10(c) n.89

Carney, State v., 584 N.W.2d 907 (Iowa 1998)—§§ 21.3(b) n.66; 21.4(d) n.128

Carney v. State, 525 So.2d 776 (Miss.1988)—§§ 3.4(j) n.203, 210

Carney, State v., 219 Mont. 412, 714 P.2d 532 (1986)—§ 27.3(c) n.39

Carney, State v., 220 Neb. 906, 374 N.W.2d 59 (1985)—§ 25.3(c) n.25

Carney v. United States, 163 F.2d 784 (9th Cir.1947)—§ 3.2(c) n.119

Carnley v. Cochran, 369 U.S. 506, 82 S.Ct. 884, 8 L.Ed.2d 70 (1962)—§§ 6.9(a) n.8; 11.3(a) n.6, 9, 12, 15; 21.4(e) n.154

Caro, United States v., 248 F.3d 1240 (10th Cir.2001)—§ 3.2(f) n.189

Carolene Products Co., United States v., 304 U.S. 144, 58 S.Ct. 778, 82 L.Ed. 1234 (1938)—§ 2.8(c) n.64

Caron, State v., 155 Vt. 492, 586 A.2d 1127 (1990)—§ 3.3(f) n.212

Caron, United States v., 474 F.2d 506 (5th Cir.1973)—§ 9.6(a) n.15

Carothers, State v., 724 N.W.2d 610 (S.D.2006)—§§ 6.6(d) n.50, 57

Carpenter, In re, 9 Cal.4th 634, 889 P.2d 985, 38 Cal.Rptr.2d 665 (1995)—§ 27.6(d) n.96

Carpenter v. County of Dane, 9 Wis. 274 (1859)—§ 2.12(a) n.10

Carpenter, People v., 21 Cal.4th 1016, 90 Cal.Rptr.2d 607, 988 P.2d 531 (1999)—§§ 22.2(d) n.70; 22.3(c) n.108

Carpenter v. State, 929 P.2d 988 (Okla.Crim.1996)—§ 19.3(a) n.70

Carpenter, State v., 68 Ohio St.3d 59, 623 N.E.2d 66 (1993)—§ 21.2(d) n.229

Carpenter, United States v., 405 F.Supp.2d 85 (2005)—§ 16.2(c) n.52

Carpenter, United States v., 611 F.Supp. 768 (N.D.Ga.1985)—§ 8.11(c) n.55

Carpenter v. Vaughn, 296 F.3d 138 (3d Cir.2002)—§ 11.10(c) n.118

Carpentier, United States v., 526 F.Supp. 292 (E.D.N.Y.1981)—§§ 23.1(d) n.175, 179

Carper v. DeLand, 54 F.3d 613 (10th Cir.1995)—§§ 11.2(f) n.241, 252

Carper, United States v., 24 F.3d 1157 (9th Cir.1994)—§ 26.10(c) n.81

Carper, United States v., 116 F.Supp. 817 (D.D.C.1953)—§ 15.7(h) n.236

Carpticher v. Commonwealth, 641 S.E.2d 486 (Va.2007)—§ 24.11(d) n.21

Carr v. Missouri, 829 S.W.2d 101 (Mo.App.1992)—§ 11.6(a) n.49

Carr, State v., 215 Or. App. 306 (2007)—§ 26.3(g) n.93

Carr v. State, 281 Ga. 43, 635 S.E.2d 767 (2006)—§ 22.3(d) n.176

Carr v. State, 728 N.E.2d 125 (Ind.2000)—§ 3.4(a) n.17

Carr v. State, 655 So.2d 824 (Miss.1995)—§ 23.2(f) n.83

Carr v. State, 284 Md. 455, 397 A.2d 606 (1979)—§§ 20.1(b) n.41; 20.3(i) n.162

Carr, State v., 2 Conn.Cir. 247, 197 A.2d 663 (1963)—§ 3.5(a) n.40

Carr, United States v., 424 F.3d 213 (2d Cir.2005)—§§ 22.1(g) n.98, 125

Carr, United States v., 303 F.3d 539 (4th Cir.2002)—§§ 19.2(c) n.38; 19.3(e) n.237

Carr, United States v., 271 F.3d 172 (4th Cir.2001)—§ 21.4(f) n.174

Carr v. United States, 758 A.2d 944 (D.C.2000)—§ 3.8(c) n.92

Carr, United States v., 80 F.3d 413 (10th Cir.1996)—§§ 21.2(b) n.54; 21.3(b) n.85, 111

Carr, United States v., 939 F.2d 1442 (10th Cir.1991)—§ 9.1(b) n.69

Carr, United States v., 740 F.2d 339 (5th Cir.1984)—§ 21.5(a) n.39

Carradine v. United States, 420 A.2d 1385 (D.C.App.1980)—§ 26.10(a) n.2

Carranza v. State, 266 Ga. 263, 467 S.E.2d 315 (1996)—§ 3.6(a) n.28

Carrasco v. State, 712 S.W.2d 120 (Tex.Cr.App.1986)—§ 3.5(e) n.186

Carrasco, United States v., 257 F.3d 1045 (9th Cir.2001)—§ 18.3(b) n.5

Carrasco, United States v., 786 F.2d 1452 (9th Cir.1986)—§§ 21.3(d) n.263; 21.6(b) n.91, 95

Carrasquillo v. Commonwealth, 422 Mass. 1014, 665 N.E.2d 993 (1996)—§ 17.4(a) n.36

Carrasquillo, People v., 174 Ill.App.3d 1023, 124 Ill.Dec. 622, 529 N.E.2d 603 (1988)—§ 20.6(c) n.80

Carrasquillo, United States v., 667 F.2d 382 (3d Cir.1981)—§§ 18.3(b) n.6, 41

Carraway, United States v., 108 F.3d 745 (7th Cir.1997)—§ 25.2(e) n.38

Carreon, United States v., 872 F.2d 1436 (10th Cir.1989)—§ 3.9(f) n.108

Carrero, United States v., 140 F.3d 327 (1st Cir.1998)—§ 21.2(e) n.319

Carrigan, United States v., 804 F.2d 599 (10th Cir.1986)—§§ 20.2(e) n.86; 20.3(i) n.177

Carrigan, United States v., 778 F.2d 1454 (10th Cir.1985)—§ 21.3(e) n.297

Carriger v. Lewis, 971 F.2d 329 (9th Cir.1992)—§ 13.4(b) n.77

Carriger v. Stewart, 132 F.3d 463 (9th Cir.1997)—§ 28.3(e) n.102

Carriger, United States v., 541 F.2d 545 (6th Cir.1976)—§ 3.2(c) n.107

Carrillo, State v., 156 Ariz. 125, 750 P.2d 883 (1988)—§§ 3.10(a) n.20; 6.2(c) n.182, 183

Carrillo, United States v., 902 F.2d 1405 (9th Cir.1990)—§ 3.3(f) n.211

Carrillo-Bernal, United States v., 58 F.3d 1490 (10th Cir.1995)—§ 27.3(b) n.18

Carrington, State v., 134 Wis.2d 260, 397 N.W.2d 484 (1986)—§ 24.8(e) n.63

Carrington v. United States, 470 F.3d 920 (9th Cir.2006)—§ 28.9(a) n.27

Carrington, United States v., 96 F.3d 1 (1st Cir.1996)—§ 21.4(f) n.171

Carrion, United States v., 488 F.2d 12 (1st Cir.1973)—§ 24.2(g) n.98

Carrizales-Toledo, United States v., 454 F.3d 1142 (10th Cir.2006)—§§ 6.8(b) n.48, 49

Carroll, Commonwealth v., 360 Mass. 580, 276 N.E.2d 705 (1971)—§ 16.4(c) n.55

Carroll, People v., 939 P.2d 452 (Colo.App.1996)—§ 21.6(a) n.57

Carroll, People v., 131 Ill.App.3d 365, 86 Ill.Dec. 603, 475 N.E.2d 982 (1985)—§ 11.10(c) n.70

Carroll, State v., 138 N.H. 687, 645 A.2d 82 (1994)—§ 6.2(c) n.185

Carroll v. State, 517 S.W.2d 13 (1974)—§ 8.4(b) n.46

Carroll, State v., 83 Wash.2d 109, 515 P.2d 1299 (1973)—§ 8.11(d) n.71

Carroll, State v., 81 Wash.2d 95, 500 P.2d 115 (1972)—§ 15.4(b) n.38

Carroll, State v., 55 Wash. 588, 104 P. 814 (1909)—§ 16.1(e) n.199

Carroll v. United States, 354 U.S. 394, 77 S.Ct. 1332, 1 L.Ed.2d 1442 (1957)—§§ 27.2(c) n.26; 27.3(b) n.14

Carroll v. United States, 267 U.S. 132, 45 S.Ct. 280, 69 L.Ed. 543 (1925)—§§ 3.3(b) n.46; 3.5(a) n.38; 3.7(b) n.23

Carrozza, United States v., 4 F.3d 70 (1st Cir.1993)—§ 21.1(h) n.207

Carruthers v. Municipal Court, 110 Cal.App.3d 439, 168 Cal.Rptr. 33 (1980)—§ 20.6(a) n.7

Carruthers, State v., 35 S.W.3d 516 (Tenn.2000)—§§ 11.3(c) n.66, 67; 11.4(b) n.29, 30; 15.5(c) n.109; 23.1(b) n.72, 73, 77, 79, 89

Carruthers v. State, 272 Ga. 306, 528 S.E.2d 217 (2000)—§§ 6.7(c) n.133; 24.7(e) n.61

Carson v. Fischer, 421 F.3d 83 (2d Cir.2005)—§ 24.1(b) n.18

Carson v. Pape, 15 Wis.2d 300, 112 N.W.2d 693 (1961)—§§ 3.5(a) n.39, 40

Carson, People v., 35 Cal.4th 1, 23 Cal.Rptr.3d 482, 104 P.3d 837 (2005)—§ 11.5(d) n.75

Carson v. State, 997 S.W.2d 92 (Mo.App.1999)—§ 18.4(d) n.82

Carson v. State, 271 Ind. 203, 391 N.E.2d 600 (1979)—§ 20.6(b) n.25

Carson, United States v., 455 F.3d 336 (D.C.Cir.2006)—§ 24.9(f) n.103

Carson, United States v., 969 F.2d 1480 (3d Cir.1992)—§§ 4.6(g) n.136; 4.6(i) n.150

Carson, United States v., 793 F.2d 1141 (10th Cir.1986)—§§ 3.10(b) n.41; 9.3(a) n.10; 9.4(b) n.54

Carswell v. State, 279 Ga. 342, 613 S.E.2d 636 (2005)—§ 6.8(b) n.50

Carswell v. State, 268 Ga. 531, 491 S.E.2d 343 (1997)—§ 6.2(c) n.107

Carter, In re, 176 Vt. 322, 848 A.2d 281 (2004)—§§ 6.4(e) n.107, 109; 11.2(b) n.40; 26.4(e) n.83

Carter v. Bell, 218 F.3d 581 (6th Cir.2000)—§§ 7.4(e) n.86; 11.10(c) n.127

Carter v. City of Philadelphia, 181 F.3d 339 (3d Cir.1999)—§ 13.3(e) n.51

Carter, Commonwealth v., 423 Mass. 506, 669 N.E.2d 203 (1996)—§ 22.4(e) n.47

Carter, Commonwealth v., 537 Pa. 233, 643 A.2d 61 (1994)—§§ 10.3(d) n.72; 10.4(d) n.30

Carter v. Commonwealth, 11 Va.App. 569, 400 S.E.2d 540 (1991)—§ 11.9(b) n.84

Carter v. Friel, 415 F.Supp.2d 1314 (D.Utah 2006)—§ 28.5(a) n.25

Carter v. Hopkins, 151 F.3d 872 (8th Cir.1998)—§ 22.3(d) n.220

Carter v. Jury Commission of Greene County, 396 U.S. 320, 90 S.Ct. 518, 24 L.Ed.2d 549 (1970)—§§ 15.4(d) n.103; 22.2(c) n.35

Carter v. Kentucky, 450 U.S. 288, 101 S.Ct. 1112, 67 L.Ed.2d 241 (1981)—§ 24.5(c) n.36

Carter v. Litscher, 275 F.3d 663 (7th Cir.2001)—§ 28.5(b) n.48

Carter v. McCarthy, 806 F.2d 1373 (9th Cir.1986)—§ 21.4(d) n.114

Carter, People v., 36 Cal.4th 1114, 32 Cal.Rptr.3d 759, 117 P.3d 476 (2005)—§§ 7.4(e) n.82; 9.1(d) n.132

Carter, People v., 77 N.Y.2d 95, 564 N.Y.S.2d 992, 566 N.E.2d 119 (1990)—§ 15.3(d) n.65

Carter v. Sowders, 5 F.3d 975 (6th Cir.1993)—§§ 11.6(a) n.21, 24

Carter v. State, 374 Md. 693, 824 A.2d 123 (2003)—§ 26.2(b) n.21

Carter v. State, 367 Md. 447, 788 A.2d 646 (2002)—§ 10.3(b) n.10

Carter v. State, 799 So.2d 40 (Miss.2001)—§ 22.3(d) n.250

Carter, State v., 16 S.W.3d 762 (Tenn.2000)—§§ 6.3(c) n.50; 9.4(a) n.10

Carter, State v., 270 Kan. 426, 14 P.3d 1138 (2000)—§§ 11.6(a) n.27, 48; 21.3(b) n.79

Carter v. State, 730 N.E.2d 155 (Ind.2000)—§ 6.9(b) n.35

Carter v. State, 739 N.E.2d 126 (Ind.2000)—§ 21.5(a) n.8

Carter v. State, 356 Md. 207, 738 A.2d 871 (1999)—§ 24.1(b) n.26

Carter, State v., 208 Wis.2d 142, 560 N.W.2d 256 (1997)—§ 26.8(c) n.29

Carter, State v., 243 Conn. 392, 703 A.2d 763 (1997)—§ 21.4(e) n.155

Carter, State v., 569 N.W.2d 169 (Minn.1997)—§ 3.2(c) n.113

Carter, State v., 955 S.W.2d 548 (Mo.1997)—§ 22.3(c) n.151

Carter, State v., 164 Vt. 545, 674 A.2d 1258 (1996)—§§ 27.6(b) n.47, 49

Carter, State v., 69 Ohio St.3d 57, 630 N.E.2d 355 (1994)—§ 9.1(d) n.120

Carter, State v., 316 Or. 6, 848 P.2d 599 (1993)—§ 3.3(b) n.49

Carter v. State, 261 Ga. 344, 404 S.E.2d 432 (1991)—§§ 17.1(f) n.69, 71

Carter, State v., 810 S.W.2d 197 (Tex.Crim.App.1991)—§ 19.3(a) n.72

Carter v. State, 490 N.E.2d 288 (Ind.1986)—§ 6.2(c) n.122

Carter, State v., 641 S.W.2d 54 (Mo.1982)—§ 20.5(h) n.111

Carter v. State, 389 So.2d 601 (Ala.Cr.App.1980)—§ 26.10(c) n.43

Carter v. State, 418 A.2d 989 (Del.1980)—§ 16.4(c) n.71

Carter, State v., 363 So.2d 893 (La.1978)—§ 14.1(e) n.69

Carter v. State, 18 Md.App. 150, 305 A.2d 856 (1973)—§ 3.3(e) n.190

Carter, State v., 27 N.J.L. 499 (1859)—§ 16.4(c) n.44

Carter v. Texas, 177 U.S. 442, 20 S.Ct. 687, 44 L.Ed. 839 (1900)—§ 15.4(b) n.54

Carter, United States v., 490 F.3d 641 (8th Cir.2007)—§ 26.4(c) n.30

Carter, United States v., 410 F.3d 942 (7th Cir.2005)—§§ 7.4(e) n.84, 89; 7.5(b) n.15, 21

Carter, United States v., 236 F.3d 777 (6th Cir.2001)—§ 24.7(e) n.42

Carter v. United States, 530 U.S. 255, 120 S.Ct. 2159, 147 L.Ed.2d 203 (2000)—§§ 24.8(e) n.67, 86

Carter, United States v., 130 F.3d 1432 (10th Cir.1997)—§§ 11.7(e) n.70; 21.2(f) n.383

Carter v. United States, 684 A.2d 331 (D.C.App.1996)—§ 8.10(a) n.21

Carter, United States v., 14 F.3d 1150 (6th Cir.1994)—§ 9.1(d) n.120

Carter, United States v., 884 F.2d 368 (8th Cir.1989)—§§ 3.10(b) n.64; 3.10(c) n.94; 6.6(e) n.72; 9.5(c) n.67

Carter, United States v., 804 F.2d 508 (9th Cir.1986)—§ 21.5(e) n.127

Carter, United States v., 756 F.2d 310 (3d Cir.1985)—§ 7.4(d) n.72

Carter, United States v., 602 F.2d 799 (7th Cir.1979)—§ 24.9(a) n.11

Carter, United States v., 576 F.2d 1061 (3d Cir.1978)—§ 19.3(c) n.193

Carter, United States v., 454 F.2d 426 (4th Cir.1972)—§§ 8.11(e) n.91; 21.2(e) n.325, 343

Carthrens, People v., 171 App.Div.2d 387, 577 N.Y.S.2d 249 (1991)—§ 24.6(b) n.16

Cartwright v. Maynard, 802 F.2d 1203 (10th Cir.1986)—§§ 11.2(e) n.151, 159, 164

Cartwright, State v., 336 Or. 408, 85 P.3d 305 (2004)—§§ 20.2(d) n.67; 20.3(a) n.18; 24.3(f) n.148

Carty v. Nelson, 426 F.3d 1064 (9th Cir.2005)—§ 28.3(a) n.4

Carufel, State v., 112 R.I. 664, 314 A.2d 144 (1974)—§§ 3.4(h) n.139, 142, 151

Caruso, People v., 116 Ill.Dec. 548, 119 Ill.2d 376, 519 N.E.2d 440 (1987)—§ 2.6(b) n.58

Caruso, United States v., 948 F.Supp. 382 (D.N.J.1996)—§ 24.3(f) n.149

Caruso, United States ex rel. v. Zelinsky, 689 F.2d 435 (3d Cir.1982)—§ 21.3(b) n.106

Caruthers, State v., 22 Kan.App.2d 910, 924 P.2d 1278 (1996)—§ 26.10(c) n.80

Carvell v. United States, 173 F.2d 348 (4th Cir.1949)—§ 28.9(b) n.62

Carver, State v., 32 Kan.App.2d 1070, 95 P.3d 104 (2004)—§ 11.2(c) n.86

Carver, United States v., 160 F.3d 1266 (10th Cir.1998)—§ 21.3(d) n.218

Carwile v. Smith, 874 F.2d 382 (6th Cir.1989)—§§ 21.2(d) n.161; 21.4(g) n.232

Cary, State v., 49 N.J. 343, 230 A.2d 384 (1967)—§ 7.2(c) n.44

Casallas, United States v., 59 F.3d 1173 (11th Cir.1995)—§ 21.4(d) n.104

Casamento, United States v., 887 F.2d 1141 (2d Cir.1989)—§§ 9.6(a) n.38; 24.7(a) n.11

Casanova's, Inc., United States v., 350 F.Supp. 291 (E.D.Wis.1972)—§ 21.4(d) n.127

Casaretto, State v., 818 S.W.2d 313 (Mo.App.1991)—§ 27.3(c) n.23

Casarez v. State, 913 S.W.2d 468 (Tex.Cr.App.1994)—§ 22.3(d) n.199

Casas, United States v., 425 F.3d 23 (1st Cir.2005)—§§ 18.2(b) n.16; 18.3(b) n.36; 18.5(c) n.75

Casas, United States v., 356 F.3d 104 (1st Cir.2004)—§§ 18.1(c) n.24; 18.2(c) n.49

Casazza, People v., 144 Ill.2d 414, 163 Ill.Dec. 497, 581 N.E.2d 651 (1991)—§ 3.6(e) n.126

Case v. Nebraska, 381 U.S. 336, 85 S.Ct. 1486, 14 L.Ed.2d 422 (1965)—§ 28.11(a) n.3

Case, People v., 340 Mich. 526, 65 N.W.2d 803 (1954)—§ 21.5(a) n.36

Case, State v., 412 N.W.2d 1 (Minn.App.1987)—§ 14.2(d) n.64

Casey, State v., 44 P.3d 756 (Utah 2002)—§§ 21.3(f) n.373, 376, 415, 438; 25.1(d) n.63; 27.4(e) n.61

Casey v. State, 732 P.2d 885 (Okla.Crim.App.1987)—§ 6.6(e) n.91

Cash, People v., 28 Cal.4th 703, 122 Cal.Rptr.2d 545, 50 P.3d 332 (2002)—§ 22.3(d) n.199

Cash, United States v., 47 F.3d 1083 (11th Cir.1995)—§§ 11.3(a) n.6, 11; 11.3(b) n.36, 41

Cashaw, In re, 123 Wash.2d 138, 866 P.2d 8 (1994)—§ 26.2(c) n.57

Cashin, United States v., 281 F.2d 669 (2d Cir.1960)—§§ 16.2(b) n.33, 34; 16.3(c) n.28

Casiano, State v., 667 A.2d 1233 (R.I.1995)—§ 26.10(c) n.73

Casiano, United States v., 929 F.2d 1046 (5th Cir.1991)—§ 11.9(c) n.130

Cason, State v., 198 La. 828, 5 So.2d 121 (1941)—§§ 16.1(d) n.139, 142

Caspari v. Bohlen, 510 U.S. 383, 114 S.Ct. 948, 127 L.Ed.2d 236 (1994)—§§ 26.7(a) n.12; 28.5(b) n.65; 28.6(d) n.25; 28.6(e) n.57

Casper v. Ryan, 822 F.2d 1283 (3d Cir.1987)—§ 18.4(c) n.53

Casper, United States v., 541 F.2d 1275 (8th Cir.1976)—§ 17.4(a) n.44

Cassady, Ex parte, 486 So.2d 453 (Ala.1986)—§ 21.2(d) n.148

Cassady, State v., 140 N.H. 46, 662 A.2d 955 (1995)—§ 17.4(a) n.53

Cassamassima v. State, 657 So.2d 906 (Fla.App.1995)—§ 26.9(b) n.72

Cassell, State v., 280 Mont. 397, 932 P.2d 478 (1996)—§ 6.2(c) n.177

Cassett v. Stewart, 406 F.3d 614 (9th Cir.2005)—§ 28.5(a) n.13

Cassidy v. Chertoff, 471 F.3d 67 (2d Cir.2006)—§ 3.9(h) n.171

Cassidy, State v., 567 N.W.2d 707 (Minn.1997)—§ 24.2(d) n.48

Cassidy, United States v., 571 F.2d 534 (10th Cir.1978)—§ 16.4(b) n.13

Cassiere, United States v., 4 F.3d 1006 (1st Cir.1993)—§ 4.6(l) n.208

Cassity, United States v., 807 F.2d 509 (6th Cir.1986)—§ 3.1(c) n.74

Cast, Commonwealth v., 407 Mass. 891, 556 N.E.2d 69 (1990)—§ 2.12(c) n.174

Castaneda v. Partida, 430 U.S. 482, 97 S.Ct. 1272, 51 L.Ed.2d 498 (1977)—§§ 15.4(c) n.83, 87, 88, 90; 15.4(d) n.126; 22.2(c) n.24, 38

Castaneda, People v., 58 Cal.App.3d 165, 129 Cal.Rptr. 755 (1976)— § 3.4(h) n.146

Castaneda, State v., 150 Ariz. 382, 724 P.2d 1 (1986)—§§ 6.9(f) n.102, 107

Castaneda, United States v., 162 F.3d 832 (5th Cir.1998)—§ 13.5(b) n.46

Castellana, United States v., 488 F.2d 65 (5th Cir.1974)—§ 9.3(e) n.48

Castellana, United States v., 500 F.2d 325 (5th Cir.1974)—§ 6.7(b) n.76

Castellano, United States v., 610 F.Supp. 1359 (S.D.N.Y.1985)—§ 16.2(h) n.156

Castellon, People v., 76 Cal.App.4th 1369, 91 Cal.Rptr.2d 204 (1999)— § 3.8(e) n.201

Castille v. Peoples, 489 U.S. 346, 109 S.Ct. 1056, 103 L.Ed.2d 380 (1989)—§ 28.5(a) n.16

Castillo v. McFadden, 399 F.3d 993 (9th Cir.2005)—§ 28.5(a) n.33

Castillo, People v., 80 N.Y.2d 578, 592 N.Y.S.2d 945, 607 N.E.2d 1050 (1992)—§ 10.5(e) n.45

Castillo, People v., 62 A.D.2d 938, 403 N.Y.S.2d 746 (1978)—§ 7.4(c) n.55

Castillo v. State, 614 P.2d 756 (Alaska 1980)—§ 15.7(g) n.213

Castillo, United States v., 496 F.3d 947 (9th Cir.2007)—§ 27.5(c) n.62

Castillo-Basa, United States v., 483 F.3d 890 (9th Cir.2007)—§ 17.4(a) n.38

Castillo-Garcia, United States v., 117 F.3d 1179 (10th Cir.1997)— § 4.6(e) n.89

Castle, United States v., 906 F.2d 134 (5th Cir.1990)—§ 18.3(b) n.23

Castle, United States v., 409 F.2d 1347 (9th Cir.1969)—§ 3.9(f) n.106

Castleberry v. State, 704 S.W.2d 21 (Tex.Cr.App.1984)—§ 21.5(e) n.138

Castle Rock, Town of v. Gonzales, 545 U.S. 748, 125 S.Ct. 2796, 162 L.Ed.2d 658 (2005)—§ 13.2(b) n.37

Castner, United States v., 50 F.3d 1267 (4th Cir.1995)—§ 26.1(f) n.139

Caston v. State, 823 So.2d 473 (Miss.2002)—§§ 18.5(b) n.58, 59, 62, 64, 69

Castonguay, State v., 240 A.2d 747 (Me.1968)—§ 6.2(c) n.105

Castor v. State, 365 So.2d 701 (Fla.1978)—§ 27.5(d) n.120

Castor, United States v., 937 F.2d 293 (7th Cir.1991)—§§ 18.4(c) n.40; 27.4(f) n.71

Castorena-Jaime, United States v., 285 F.3d 916 (10th Cir.2002)—§ 3.7(f) n.131

Castro, Commonwealth v., 438 Mass. 160, 778 N.E.2d 900 (2002)— § 7.4(c) n.49

Castro v. State, 597 So.2d 259 (Fla.1992)—§ 22.5(d) n.36

Castro v. United States, 540 U.S. 375, 124 S.Ct. 786, 157 L.Ed.2d 778 (2004)—§ 28.9(b) n.57

Castro, United States v., 723 F.2d 1527 (11th Cir.1984)—§§ 6.7(d) n.144, 148

Castro, United States v., 413 F.2d 891 (1st Cir.1969)—§ 17.2(b) n.31

Castro-Cervantes, United States v., 927 F.2d 1079 (9th Cir.1990)— §§ 21.1(h) n.233; 21.2(d) n.216

Castro-Gomez, United States v., 233 F.3d 684 (1st Cir.2000)—§ 21.4(d) n.102

Castro-Higuero, United States v., 473 F.3d 880 (8th Cir.2007)—§§ 6.8(a) n.36; 6.9(b) n.32

Caswell, State v., 551 N.W.2d 252 (Minn.App.1996)—§§ 19.5(b) n.26, 40

Caswell, State v., 121 Idaho 801, 828 P.2d 830 (1992)—§ 13.5(b) n.54

Catalfo, United States v., 64 F.3d 1070 (7th Cir.1995)—§ 24.7(e) n.63

Catania, People v., 427 Mich. 447, 398 N.W.2d 343 (1986)—§ 3.10(c) n.87

Catano, United States v., 65 F.3d 219 (1st Cir.1995)—§ 8.11(e) n.92

Cate, State v., 165 Vt. 404, 683 A.2d 1010 (Vt.1996)—§ 26.9(b) n.69

Cater, State v., 1 N.C. (1 Tay.) 310 (1802)—§ 19.1(a) n.4

Cates v. State, 776 S.W.2d 170 (Tex.Cr.App.1989)—§ 6.10(c) n.37

Cates v. Superintendent, 981 F.2d 949 (7th Cir.1992)—§ 11.9(d) n.192

Cates, United States v., 686 F.Supp. 1185 (D.Md.1988)—§ 8.13(b) n.61

Cathey, State v., 241 Kan. 715, 741 P.2d 738 (1987)—§ 6.6(e) n.76

Cathey, United States v., 591 F.2d 268 (5th Cir.1979)—§§ 15.5(b) n.55; 15.7(e) n.106

Catino, United States v., 735 F.2d 718 (2d Cir.1984)—§§ 1.7(j) n.225; 18.5(a) n.25

Catlett, State v., 133 Wash.2d 355, 945 P.2d 700 (1997)—§ 17.4(b) n.120

Catlett, State v., 180 W.Va. 447, 376 S.E.2d 834 (1988)—§ 22.5(b) n.22

Catlett, United States v., 584 F.2d 864 (8th Cir.1978)—§§ 13.4(b) n.43; 13.4(c) n.117, 120

Catlin, People v., 26 Cal.4th 81, 109 Cal.Rptr.2d 31, 26 P.3d 357 (2001)—§§ 17.1(c) n.41; 18.5(b) n.58, 69

Catu, People v., 4 N.Y.3d 242, 792 N.Y.S.2d 887, 825 N.E.2d 1081 (2005)—§ 21.4(d) n.114

Cauble, State v., 563 P.2d 775 (Utah 1977)—§§ 16.1(g) n.235; 16.1(h) n.285, 289, 294, 303

Cauble, United States v., 706 F.2d 1322 (5th Cir.1983)—§ 26.6(d) n.63

Caudill v. Commonwealth, 120 S.W.3d 635 (Ky.2003)—§ 22.2(d) n.67

Caudill v. Jago, 747 F.2d 1046 (6th Cir.1984)—§ 21.2(c) n.117

Caudill v. Scott, 857 F.2d 344 (6th Cir.1988)—§ 2.6(b) n.69

Caudillo, People v., 138 Cal.App.2d 183, 291 P.2d 191 (1955)—§ 5.3(a) n.14

Causey, United States v., 834 F.2d 1277 (6th Cir.1987)—§§ 17.2(c) n.82; 17.2(d) n.113

Cauthern, State v., 778 S.W.2d 39 (Tenn.1989)—§ 6.9(g) n.149

Cavanaugh, People v., 44 Cal.2d 252, 282 P.2d 53 (1955)—§ 16.4(d) n.130

Cavazos, Ex parte, 203 S.W.3d 333 (Tex.Crim.App.2006)—§ 17.4(b) n.73

Cavender, United States v., 228 F.3d 792 (7th Cir.2000)—§ 21.2(d) n.193

Cazares, United States v., 121 F.3d 1241 (9th Cir.1997)—§ 21.4(f) n.171

CBS, In re, 570 F.Supp. 578 (E.D.La.1983)—§ 23.1(c) n.107

CBS, Inc. v. Young, 522 F.2d 234 (6th Cir.1975)—§§ 23.1(b) n.68, 71

Ceballos, United States v., 302 F.3d 679 (7th Cir.2002)—§ 6.2(c) n.128

Ceccolini, United States v., 435 U.S. 268, 98 S.Ct. 1054, 55 L.Ed.2d 268 (1978)—§§ 1.1(a) n.7; 9.4(e) n.104; 9.5(a) n.18; 9.5(d) n.81

Ceccone, People v., 260 Cal.App.2d 886, 67 Cal.Rptr. 499 (1968)—§ 6.6(c) n.17

Cecil, United States v., 836 F.2d 1431 (4th Cir.1988)—§§ 22.2(a) n.5; 22.2(d) n.85

CECOS International, Inc., State v., 38 Ohio St.3d 120, 526 N.E.2d 807 (1988)—§§ 8.5(g) n.221, 229; 8.5(h) n.255

Cedano-Arellano, United States v., 332 F.3d 568 (9th Cir.2003)—§ 20.3(j) n.205

Cederquist, United States v., 641 F.2d 1347 (9th Cir.1981)—§§ 15.6(e) n.152, 158; 15.7(b) n.45

Cefalo, State v., 396 A.2d 233 (Me.1979)—§§ 7.4(c) n.41, 42

Ceja, People v., 204 Ill.2d 332, 273 Ill.Dec. 796, 789 N.E.2d 1228 (2003)—§ 13.2(a) n.4

Ceja v. Stewart, 97 F.3d 1246 (9th Cir.1996)—§ 6.2(c) n.152

Celestine, State v., 452 So.2d 676 (La.1984)—§§ 17.1(b)   n.25; 17.1(d) n.58

Cella, United States v., 568 F.2d 1266 (9th Cir.1977)—§§ 9.2(b) n.13; 10.3(b) n.44

Cellier v. State, 28 Kan.App.2d 508, 18 P.3d 259 (2001)—§ 11.6(d) n.120

Center for National Security Studies v. U.S. Department of Justice, 331 F.3d   918   (D.C.Cir.2003)— §§ 23.1(d) n.197, 206

Centracchio v. Garrity, 198 F.2d 382 (1st Cir.1952)—§ 10.1(c) n.41

Cephas, United States v., 937 F.2d 816 (2d Cir.1991)—§ 18.4(c) n.60

Cerceda, United States v., 139 F.3d 847 (11th Cir.1998)—§§ 22.4(c) n.23, 28, 31

Cere, State v., 125 N.H. 421, 480 A.2d 195 (1984)—§ 22.3(a) n.11

Cerilli, State v., 1998 WL 726486 (R.I.Super.Ct.1998)—§ 15.7(e) n.106

Cernohous, State v., 295 Minn. 491, 205 N.W.2d 680 (1973)—§ 3.4(k) n.225

Cerro v. United States, 872 F.2d 780 (7th Cir.1989)—§§ 11.9(b) n.69, 80; 11.9(d) n.158, 219, 221

Cerrone v. People, 900 P.2d 45 (Colo.1995)—§§ 8.4(a)   n.17; 15.4(a) n.8; 15.4(c) n.94; 15.4(d) n.99

Cerrone, People v., 854 P.2d 178 (Colo.1993)—§§ 8.4(a)   n.17; 15.4(c) n.94; 15.4(d) n.99; 15.4(e) n.128

Certain Chinese Families Benevolent and District Associations, In re, 19 F.R.D.   97   (N.D.Cal.1956)— § 8.7(b) n.35

Certain Interested Individuals v. Pulitzer Publishing Co., 895 F.2d 460 (8th Cir.1990)—§ 4.6(i) n.153

Certain Real Property Located In Romulus, United States v., 977 F.Supp. 833 (E.D.Mich.1997)—§§ 23.1(d) n.196, 201

Cervantes v. Cates, 206 Ariz. 178, 76 P.3d 449 (App.2003)—§ 20.3(g) n.118

Cervantes v. People, 715 P.2d 783 (Colo.1986)—§ 19.2(e) n.54

Cervantes, State v., 118 Or.App. 429, 848 P.2d 118 (1993)—§§ 16.1(g) n.250, 281

Cervantes, United States v., 420 F.3d 792 (8th Cir.2005)—§ 21.2(b) n.82

Cervantes, United States v., 19 F.3d 1151 (7th Cir.1994)—§ 3.1(d) n.103

Cervantes v. Walker, 589 F.2d 424 (9th Cir.1978)—§ 6.6(b) n.16

Cervantes-Pacheco, United States v., 826 F.2d 310 (5th Cir.1987)— § 5.4(a) n.8

Cervantes-Valencia, United States v., 322 F.3d 1060 (9th Cir.2003)— § 21.4(g) n.243

Cervi v. Kemp, 855 F.2d 702 (11th Cir.1988)—§ 6.9(f) n.121

Cervone, United States v., 907 F.2d 332 (2d Cir.1990)—§§ 16.2(h) n.151; 20.6(c) n.76

Cespedes v. Coughlin, 956 F.Supp. 454 (S.D.N.Y.1997)—§ 26.2(c) n.62

Cetlinski, People v., 435 Mich. 742, 460 N.W.2d 534 (1990)—§ 9.6(a) n.38

Chabonian, State v., 50 Wis.2d 574, 185 N.W.2d 289 (1971)—§ 6.4(b) n.26

Chace, State v., 151 N.H. 310, 856 A.2d 1 (2004)—§ 21.4(d) n.128

Chacon, People v., 40 Cal.4th 558, 53 Cal.Rptr.3d 876, 150 P.3d 755 (2007)—§ 5.4(c) n.30

Chacon, State v., 62 N.M. 291, 309 P.2d 230 (1957)—§ 15.1(f) n.276

Chacon, United States v., 663 F.2d 494 (4th Cir.1981)—§ 8.3(a) n.4

Chadd, People v., 28 Cal.3d 739, 170 Cal.Rptr. 798, 621 P.2d 837 (1981)—§ 18.5(a) n.47

Chadwick v. Green, 740 F.2d 897 (11th Cir.1984)—§§ 11.8(c) n.60, 64

Chadwick, United States v., 433 U.S. 1, 97 S.Ct. 2476, 53 L.Ed.2d 538 (1977)—§§ 2.9(d) n.64, 66; 3.2(b) n.45; 3.5(e) n.182, 202; 3.6(e) n.125; 3.7(b) n.31; 3.7(c) n.39

Chadwick, United States v., 393 F.Supp. 763 (D.Mass.1975)—§ 3.3(f) n.196

Chae v. People, 780 P.2d 481 (Colo.1989)—§ 21.2(e) n.294

Chaffin v. Stynchcombe, 412 U.S. 17, 93 S.Ct. 1977, 36 L.Ed.2d 714 (1973)—§ 26.8(c) n.17

Chafin v. State, 246 Ga. 709, 273 S.E.2d 147 (1980)—§ 20.3(h) n.145

Chagnon, State v., 139 N.H. 671, 662 A.2d 944 (1995)—§§ 20.5(f) n.81, 83, 87, 88

Chagra, United States v., 701 F.2d 354 (5th Cir.1983)—§§ 23.1(d) n.137, 139, 140, 145

Chaidez, United States v., 919 F.2d 1193 (7th Cir.1990)—§§ 3.8(b) n.49; 3.10(d) n.134, 135

Chaifetz v. United States, 288 F.2d 133 (D.C.Cir.1960)—§ 18.5(a) n.40

Chaipis v. State Liquor Authority, 44 N.Y.2d 57, 404 N.Y.S.2d 76, 375 N.E.2d 32 (1978)—§§ 21.2(e) n.329, 348

Chaisson, State v., 125 N.H. 810, 486 A.2d 297 (1984)—§ 3.6(a) n.29

Chalikes, State v., 122 Ohio St. 35, 170 N.E. 653 (1930)—§§ 8.8(a) n.9; 16.1(e) n.192

Chalkias, United States v., 971 F.2d 1206 (6th Cir.1992)—§ 18.3(b) n.25

Chalmers, United States v., 410 F.Supp.2d 278 (S.D.N.Y.2006)—§ 20.3(a) n.12

Chamberlain, State v., 263 N.C. 406, 139 S.E.2d 620 (1965)—§ 6.2(a) n.10

Chamberlain, United States v., 163 F.3d 499 (8th Cir.1998)—§ 6.6(b) n.15

Chamberland, State v., 499 A.2d 143 (Me.1985)—§ 26.10(b) n.37

Chamberlin, State v., 162 P.3d 389 (Wash.2007)—§ 22.4(a) n.12

Chamberlin, United States v., 644 F.2d 1262 (9th Cir.1980)—§§ 3.8(d) n.144; 9.4(d) n.82

Chambers, Commonwealth v., 528 Pa. 403, 598 A.2d 539 (1991)—§ 3.4(h) n.142

Chambers v. Florida, 309 U.S. 227, 60 S.Ct. 472, 84 L.Ed. 716 (1940)—§§ 1.5(a) n.59; 1.5(d) n.187; 2.8(c) n.63; 6.2(b) n.34; 6.2(c) n.70, 80, 84

Chambers v. Maroney, 399 U.S. 42, 90 S.Ct. 1975, 26 L.Ed.2d 419 (1970)—§§ 3.1(d) n.102; 3.3(a) n.6; 3.3(d) n.146; 3.5(e) n.200; 3.7(b) n.25; 3.7(f) n.135; 11.8(c) n.51; 27.6(d) n.78

Chambers v. Mississippi, 410 U.S. 284, 93 S.Ct. 1038, 35 L.Ed.2d 297 (1973)—§§ 2.7(a) n.50; 2.7(b) n.87; 2.7(c) n.128, 199; 10.5(f) n.59, 61; 24.4(a) n.4; 24.4(b) n.13; 28.6(g) n.88

Chambers v. NASCO, Inc., 501 U.S. 32, 111 S.Ct. 2123, 115 L.Ed.2d 27 (1991)—§ 1.7(i) n.170

Chambers, People v., 134 Misc.2d 688, 512 N.Y.S.2d 631 (N.Y.Sup.1987)—§ 1.5(k) n.402

Chambers v. People, 682 P.2d 1173 (Colo.1984)—§ 20.3(a) n.14

Chambers v. State, 700 S.W.2d 597 (Tex.Cr.App.1985)—§ 26.10(d) n.96

Chambers v. State, 46 Ala.App. 247, 240 So.2d 370 (1970)—§ 7.3(d) n.66

Chambers, United States v., 441 F.3d 438 (6th Cir.2006)—§ 1.2(c) n.193

Chambers, United States v., 987 F.2d 1331 (8th Cir.1993)—§ 3.1(c) n.71

Chambers, United States ex rel. v. Maroney, 408 F.2d 1186 (3d Cir.1969)—§§ 11.8(c) n.52, 53

Chambless, State v., 682 S.W.2d 227 (Tenn.Cr.App.1984)—§ 15.4(e) n.134

Chamley, State v., 1997 S.D. 107, 568 N.W.2d 607 (1997)—§ 11.5(d) n.74

Champaign, County of v. Anthony, 64 Ill.2d 532, 1 Ill.Dec. 373, 356 N.E.2d 561 (1976)—§ 12.3(g) n.150

Champion v. Ames, 188 U.S. 321, 23 S.Ct. 321, 47 L.Ed. 492 (1903)— §§ 1.2(c) n.101, 103

Chan, United States v., 136 F.3d 1158 (7th Cir.1998)—§ 3.8(c) n.116

Chan, United States v., 97 F.3d 1582 (9th Cir.1996)—§ 21.4(g) n.228

Chance, State v., 236 Conn. 31, 671 A.2d 323 (1996)—§ 24.5(a) n.17

Chancey v. State, 256 Ga. 415, 349 S.E.2d 717 (1986)—§ 16.2(g) n.109

Chandler, Ex parte, 684 S.W.2d 700 (Tex.Cr.App.1985)—§ 21.2(e) n.326

Chandler v. Florida, 449 U.S. 560, 101 S.Ct. 802, 66 L.Ed.2d 740 (1981)— §§ 2.5(f) n.105; 2.6(d) n.99, 100; 2.7(a) n.41; 2.7(c) n.172; 23.3(b) n.14, 23

Chandler v. Fretag, 348 U.S. 3, 75 S.Ct. 1, 99 L.Ed. 4 (1954)—§§ 2.4(e) n.157, 165; 11.1(b) n.84

Chandler v. Miller, 520 U.S. 305, 117 S.Ct. 1295, 137 L.Ed.2d 513 (1997)—§§ 3.9(d) n.68; 3.9(l) n.274

Chandler, People v., 129 Ill.2d 233, 135 Ill.Dec. 543, 543 N.E.2d 1290 (1989)—§§ 11.10(c) n.71, 107

Chandler v. State, 642 S.E.2d 646 (Ga.2007)—§ 22.3(c) n.135

Chandler, State v., 673 N.E.2d 482 (Ind.App.1996)—§ 24.9(c) n.27

Chandler v. United States, 218 F.3d 1305 (11th Cir.2000)—§ 11.10(c) n.127

Chandler, United States v., 72 F.Supp. 230 (D.Mass.1947)—§ 16.4(b) n.27

Chandler v. United States Army, 125 F.3d 1296 (9th Cir.1997)—§ 4.6(m) n.220

Chandler, State ex rel. v. Main, 16 Wis. 398 (1863)—§ 16.4(c) n.115

Chanen, United States v., 549 F.2d 1306 (9th Cir.1977)—§§ 15.5(b) n.36, 62, 68; 15.6(b) n.48; 15.7(c) n.61

Chaney, United States v., 964 F.2d 437 (5th Cir.1992)—§§ 19.2(a) n.5; 19.2(b) n.20

Chaney, United States v., 662 F.2d 1148 (5th Cir.1981)—§ 11.5(c) n.52

Chaney, United States v., 559 F.2d 1094 (7th Cir.1977)—§ 24.9(d) n.47

Chaney v. Wainwright, 561 F.2d 1129 (5th Cir.1977)—§ 6.9(g) n.177

Chang v. United States, 250 F.3d 79 (2d Cir.2001)—§ 24.5(d) n.58

Chang An-Lo, United States v., 851 F.2d 547 (2d Cir.1988)—§ 17.2(e) n.119

Chantal, United States v., 902 F.2d 1018 (1st Cir.1990)—§ 21.6(a) n.78

Chanthadara, United States v., 230 F.3d 1237 (10th Cir.2000)—§ 22.2(d) n.77

Chao v. State, 780 A.2d 1060 (Del.2001)—§ 11.2(e) n.229

Chao v. State, 604 A.2d 1351 (Del.1992)—§ 24.8(f) n.117

Chapa, State v., 127 Idaho 786, 906 P.2d 636 (App.1995)—§ 19.3(a) n.53

Chapa v. State, 729 S.W.2d 723 (Tex.Cr.App.1987)—§ 9.1(d) n.128

Chapa-Garza, United States v., 62 F.3d 118 (5th Cir.1995)—§ 6.9(g) n.166

Chapel, United States v., 55 F.3d 1416 (9th Cir.1995)—§ 3.5(d) n.142

Chapin, State v., 17 Ark. 561 (1856)— §§ 16.2(g) n.110; 16.4(c) n.60

Chapman v. California, 386 U.S. 18, 87 S.Ct. 824, 17 L.Ed.2d 705 (1967)— §§ 1.7(i) n.189; 7.3(f) n.104; 11.5(a) n.9; 11.8(a) n.11; 11.9(b) n.47; 14.4(e) n.132; 15.6(e) n.143; 19.2(e) n.76; 19.3(a) n.96; 24.3(b) n.15; 24.3(d) n.113; 24.5(b) n.25; 27.6(a) n.8, 11; 27.6(c) n.64; 28.6(g) n.80

Chapman, People v., 194 Ill.2d 186, 252 Ill.Dec. 474, 743 N.E.2d 48 (2000)—§ 3.5(a) n.51

Chapman, People v., 261 Cal.App.2d 149, 67 Cal.Rptr. 601 (1968)— § 9.5(d) n.83

Chapman, State v., 210 W.Va. 292, 557 S.E.2d 346 (2001)—§ 21.4(b) n.60

Chapman, State v., 342 N.C. 330, 464 S.E.2d 661 (1995)—§ 24.2(a) n.12

Chapman, State v., 252 Kan. 606, 847 P.2d 1247 (1993)—§ 16.2(g) n.108

Chapman, State v., 111 Idaho 149, 721 P.2d 1248 (1986)—§ 26.10(d) n.86

Chapman, State v., 209 Mont. 57, 679 P.2d 1210 (1984)—§ 24.3(g) n.170

Chapman, State v., 250 A.2d 203 (Me.1969)—§ 3.6(e) n.132

Chapman v. United States, 553 F.2d 886 (5th Cir.1977)—§ 11.5(d) n.71

Chapman v. United States, 365 U.S. 610, 81 S.Ct. 776, 5 L.Ed.2d 828 (1961)—§§ 3.10(e) n.152, 158; 9.1(b) n.36

Chappee v. Vose, 843 F.2d 25 (1st Cir.1988)—§§ 20.6(c) n.74, 77

Chappell v. State, 457 So.2d 995 (Ala.Cr.App.1984)—§ 24.11(d) n.36

Chappell, United States v., 854 F.2d 190 (7th Cir.1988)—§ 16.2(e) n.79

Chapple, State v., 145 Wash.2d 310, 36 P.3d 1025 (2001)—§§ 24.2(c) n.35; 24.5(d) n.58

Chapple, State v., 135 Ariz. 281, 660 P.2d 1208 (1983)—§ 7.5(b) n.23

Charette, State v., 688 A.2d 1286 (R.I.1997)—§ 7.4(e) n.86

Charge to the Grand Jury, 30 Fed.Cas. 992 (C.C.D.Cal.1872) (No. 18,255)—§ 15.1(d) n.154

Charles v. Chandler, 180 F.3d 753 (6th Cir.1999)—§ 28.9(a) n.7

Charles, Commonwealth v., 397 Mass. 1, 489 N.E.2d 679 (1986)—§ 7.3(c) n.61

Charles v. Hickman, 228 F.3d 981 (9th Cir.2000)—§ 17.4(a) n.34

Charles v. Smith, 894 F.2d 718 (5th Cir.1990)—§ 6.9(f) n.111

Charles, United States v., 476 F.3d 492 (7th Cir.2007)—§ 6.2(c) n.114

Charles, United States v., 456 F.3d 249 (1st Cir.2006)—§ 24.4(d) n.30

Charles, United States v., 213 F.3d 10 (1st Cir.2000)—§§ 4.6(c) n.54; 10.6(d) n.48

Charles, United States v., 883 F.2d 355 (5th Cir.1989)—§ 18.3(b) n.5

Charles, United States v., 738 F.2d 686 (5th Cir.1984)—§ 6.6(f) n.114

Charlett, Commonwealth v., 282 Pa.Super. 28, 422 A.2d 659 (1980)—§§ 11.3(b) n.52; 11.5(c) n.51

Charley, United States v., 396 F.3d 1074 (9th Cir.2005)—§§ 6.4(e) n.76; 6.9(g) n.167

Charlotte Observer, In re, 921 F.2d 47 (4th Cir.1990)—§§ 23.1(c) n.102, 104

Charlotte Observer, In re, 882 F.2d 850 (4th Cir.1989)—§§ 23.1(d) n.147, 174; 23.1(e) n.230, 234, 235, 244, 245, 248, 249

Charmer Industries, Inc., United States v., 711 F.2d 1164 (2d Cir.1983)—§ 26.5(c) n.59

Charria, United States v., 919 F.2d 842 (2d Cir.1990)—§ 6.4(f) n.124

Chase v. Robson, 435 F.2d 1059 (7th Cir.1970)—§ 23.1(b) n.71

Chase v. State, 334 Ark. 274, 973 S.W.2d 791 (1998)—§ 6.9(f) n.137

Chase, State v., 588 A.2d 120 (R.I.1991)—§ 17.4(a) n.66

Chase, United States v., 503 F.2d 571 (9th Cir.1974)—§§ 3.9(f) n.90, 97

Chastain, In re, 340 S.C. 356, 532 S.E.2d 264 (2000)—§ 17.4(b) n.125

Chastain v. Civil Service Board of Orlando, 327 So.2d 230 (Fla.App.1976)—§ 1.7(j) n.226

Chastain, People v., 733 P.2d 1206 (Colo.1987)—§ 6.10(b) n.19

Chastang v. State, 83 Ala. 29, 3 So. 304 (1887)—§ 2.12(a) n.9

Chatman v. Mancill, 280 Ga. 253, 626 S.E.2d 102 (2006)—§ 18.5(c) n.84

Chatman, People v., 38 Cal.4th 344, 42 Cal.Rptr.3d 621, 133 P.3d 534 (2006)—§ 22.4(c) n.29

Chatriand, State v., 243 Mont. 375, 792 P.2d 1107 (1990)—§ 10.5(f) n.68

Chauncey v. Second Judicial District Court, 474 F.2d 1238 (9th Cir.1973)—§ 18.4(a) n.17

Chavarria v. State, 876 S.W.2d 388 (Tex.App.1994)—§§ 10.3(b) n.29; 10.4(c) n.20

Chavarria, United States v., 443 F.2d 904 (9th Cir.1971)—§ 6.10(d) n.60

Chaves, United States v., 169 F.3d 687 (11th Cir.1999)—§ 9.1(c) n.102

Chavez v. Illinois State Police, 251 F.3d 612 (7th Cir.2001)—§ 1.11(a) n.8

Chavez v. Martinez, 538 U.S. 760, 123 S.Ct. 1994, 155 L.Ed.2d 984 (2003)—§§ 2.7(d) n.256; 2.9(c) n.51; 2.9(h) n.256; 2.10(b) n.4, 32, 41; 2.10(d) n.144, 156; 6.2(b) n.54; 6.5(a) n.14; 9.5(b) n.47

Chavez, People v., 26 Cal.3d 334, 161 Cal.Rptr. 762, 605 P.2d 401 (1980)—§§ 11.4(a) n.10, 14, 15

Chavez, State v., 668 N.W.2d 89 (S.D.2003)—§§ 10.6(d) n.48; 17.4(a) n.47

Chavez, State v., 77 N.M. 79, 419 P.2d 456 (1966)—§§ 13.7(a) n.24, 28

Chavez, United States v., 204 F.3d 1305 (11th Cir.2000)—§§ 22.1(b) n.43, 44

Chavez, United States v., 902 F.2d 259 (4th Cir.1990)—§ 10.2(a) n.10

Chavez, United States v., 416 U.S. 562, 94 S.Ct. 1849, 40 L.Ed.2d 380 (1974)—§§ 4.6(e) n.73; 4.6(m) n.230, 233

Chavez-Inzunza, State v., 145 Ariz. 362, 701 P.2d 858 (1985)—§ 24.2(d) n.48

Chavez-Marquez, United States v., 66 F.3d 259 (10th Cir.1995)—§§ 10.1(b) n.20; 10.5(f) n.68

Chavez-Martinez v. United States, 407 F.2d 535 (9th Cir.1969)—§ 6.6(a) n.7

Chavez-Palacios, United States v., 30 F.3d 1290 (10th Cir.1994)—§ 27.5(a) n.14

Chavez-Valencia, United States v., 116 F.3d 127 (5th Cir.1997)—§ 10.1(a) n.15

Chavez-Vernaza, United States v., 844 F.2d 1368 (9th Cir.1987)—§ 2.12(c) n.172

Chavira, United States v., 9 F.3d 888 (10th Cir.1993)—§ 3.9(f) n.118

Chavis, Commonwealth v., 415 Mass. 703, 616 N.E.2d 423 (1993)—§ 11.4(c) n.65

Chavis, State v., 31 Wash.App. 784, 644 P.2d 1202 (1982)—§§ 11.5(a) n.7; 11.5(c) n.40, 41, 50; 11.5(d) n.77

Chavis, United States v., 296 F.3d 450 (6th Cir.2002)—§§ 17.1(a) n.14; 17.3(b) n.22; 17.3(d) n.44

Cheatam, State v., 150 Wash.2d 626, 81 P.3d 830 (2003)—§§ 3.5(c) n.122; 7.5(b) n.23

Cheatham, People v., 453 Mich. 1, 551 N.W.2d 355 (1996)—§ 6.9(b) n.42

Cheek v. United States, 498 U.S. 192, 111 S.Ct. 604, 112 L.Ed.2d 617 (1991)—§ 4.6(n) n.260

Cheff v. Schnackenberg, 384 U.S. 373, 86 S.Ct. 1523, 16 L.Ed.2d 629 (1966)—§§ 1.7(i) n.158, 165

Chen, United States v., 439 F.3d 1037 (9th Cir.2006)—§§ 6.10(c) n.56, 57

Chen, United States v., 378 F.3d 151 (2d Cir.2004)—§ 16.1(d) n.143

Chen, United States v., 933 F.2d 793 (9th Cir.1991)—§ 8.8(h) n.184

Cheney, Commonwealth v., 440 Mass. 568, 800 N.E.2d 309 (2003)—§ 13.2(c) n.56

Chenique-Puey, State v., 145 N.J. 334, 678 A.2d 694 (1996)—§ 17.1(d) n.53

Cherrix v. Braxton, 131 F.Supp.2d 756 (E.D.Va.2001)—§§ 28.3(e) n.104; 28.12(b) n.12

Cherrix v. True, 177 F.Supp.2d 485 (E.D.Va.2001)—§ 28.7(d) n.28

Cherry, State v., 341 Ark. 924, 20 S.W.3d 354 (2000)—§ 24.9(f) n.63

Cherry v. State, 302 Ark. 462, 791 S.W.2d 354 (1990)—§ 3.9(j) n.226

Cherry, United States v., 794 F.2d 201 (5th Cir.1986)—§ 9.4(b) n.54

Chesapeake Club v. State, 63 Md. 446 (1885)—§ 2.12(a) n.10

Chesney, United States v., 367 F.3d 1055 (8th Cir.2004)—§ 11.7(e) n.113

Chesney, United States v., 86 F.3d 564 (6th Cir.1996)—§§ 1.2(c) n.142, 145; 22.1(g) n.118; 24.7(e) n.49

Chestaro, United States v., 197 F.3d 600 (2d Cir.1999)—§ 17.4(a) n.6

Chester, State v., 46 R.I. 485, 129 A. 596 (1925)—§ 3.5(a) n.34

Chestnut v. Magnusson, 942 F.2d 820 (1st Cir.1991)—§ 12.2(b) n.27

Chestnut v. State, 669 A.2d 1336 (Me.1996)—§ 18.4(c) n.44

Chestnut, United States ex rel. v. Criminal Court, 442 F.2d 611 (2d Cir.1971)—§§ 8.4(a) n.5; 8.8(i) n.194; 15.4(d) n.112

Chevalier v. State, 730 So.2d 1111 (Miss.1998)—§ 19.5(c) n.62

Chevencek, State v., 127 N.J.L. 476, 23 A.2d 176 (1941)—§ 16.2(g) n.128

Chew, State v., 150 N.J. 30, 695 A.2d 1301 (N.J.1997)—§§ 6.9(g) n.189; 9.5(c) n.68; 27.5(d) n.137

Chiarella, United States v., 184 F.2d 903 (2d Cir.1950)—§ 5.1(c) n.12

Chiavola, United States v., 744 F.2d 1271 (7th Cir.1984)—§ 9.1(a) n.20

Chicago, Burlington, & Quincy R.R. v. Chicago, 166 U.S. 226, 17 S.Ct. 581, 41 L.Ed. 979 (1897)—§§ 2.4(a) n.13; 2.4(d) n.126; 2.5(c) n.26

Chicago, City of v. Morales, 527 U.S. 41, 119 S.Ct. 1849, 144 L.Ed.2d 67 (1999)—§ 1.7(j) n.227

Chicago Council of Lawyers v. Bauer, 522 F.2d 242 (7th Cir.1975)—§§ 23.1(b) n.28, 33

Chicago Magnet Wire Co., People v., 126 Ill.2d 356, 128 Ill.Dec. 517, 534 N.E.2d 962 (1989)—§ 1.2(d) n.200

Chicago, M. St. P. & P. R.R., United States v., 312 U.S. 592, 61 S.Ct. 772, 85 L.Ed. 1064 (1941)—§ 2.9(b) n.28

Chichakly v. United States, 926 F.2d 624 (7th Cir.1991)—§ 21.2(g) n.396

Chicot County Drainage District v. Baxter State Bank, 308 U.S. 371, 60 S.Ct. 317, 84 L.Ed. 329 (1940)—§ 2.11(a) n.3

Chidester, State v., 570 N.W.2d 78 (Iowa 1997)—§§ 22.2(d) n.70, 86

Childers, People v., 20 Mich.App. 639, 174 N.W.2d 565 (1969)—§ 10.1(a) n.4

Childers, State v., 358 S.C. 614, 595 S.E.2d 872 (2004)—§ 11.4(b) n.24

Childers v. State, 656 N.E.2d 514 (Ind.App.1995)—§§ 26.10(d) n.97, 99

Childress v. Humphrey, 329 Ark. 504, 950 S.W.2d 220 (1997)—§ 27.4(a) n.1

Childress v. State, 1 P.3d 1006 (Okla.Crim.App.2000)—§§ 13.7(a) n.5; 13.7(b) n.33

Childress v. State, 266 Ga. 425, 467 S.E.2d 865 (1996)—§ 24.4(d) n.63

Childress, State v., 66 Ohio App.3d 491, 585 N.E.2d 567 (1990)—§ 8.10(d) n.90

Childress, United States v., 58 F.3d 693 (D.C.Cir.1995)—§§ 22.3(b) n.68; 24.9(a) n.4

Childress, United States v., 746 F.Supp. 1122 (D.D.C.1990)—§ 24.10(a) n.18

Childs, Commonwealth v., 23 Mass.App. 33, 499 N.E.2d 299 (1986)—§ 11.10(c) n.99

Childs v. Herbert, 146 F.Supp.2d 317 (S.D.N.Y. 2001)—§ 11.4(c) n.87

Childs, State v., 88 Ohio St.3d 558, 728 N.E.2d 379 (2000)—§ 10.3(b) n.10

Childs, State v., 242 N.J.Super. 121, 576 A.2d 42 (1990)—§§ 15.2(e) n.144; 15.7(b) n.41

Childs, United States v., 447 F.3d 541 (7th Cir.2006)—§ 24.3(b) n.68

Childs, United States v., 944 F.2d 491 (9th Cir.1991)—§ 3.10(d) n.124

Childs v. United States, 267 F.2d 619 (D.C.Cir.1958)—§ 5.4(b) n.17

Chilingirian, United States v., 280 F.3d 704 (6th Cir.2002)—§§ 12.4(d) n.70; 24.10(b) n.26

Chilton, People v., 394 Mich. 34, 228 N.W.2d 210 (1975)—§ 21.4(a) n.23

Chimel v. California, 395 U.S. 752, 89 S.Ct. 2034, 23 L.Ed.2d 685 (1969)—§§ 1.9(b) n.27; 2.5(f) n.77, 82; 2.9(d) n.90; 2.9(g) n.157; 2.11(c) n.26; 3.5(b) n.77; 3.5(e) n.177; 3.6(a) n.20; 3.6(c) n.73; 3.7(a) n.3; 9.4(b) n.49

Chimel v. California, 395 U.S. 752, 89 S.Ct. 1620, 20 L.Ed.2d 476 (1969)—§ 2.8(b) n.42

Chimurenga, United States v., 760 F.2d 400 (2d Cir.1985)—§ 12.3(a) n.18

Chinchic, United States v., 655 F.2d 547 (4th Cir.1981)—§ 25.3(b) n.17

Chinchilla, United States v., 874 F.2d 695 (9th Cir.1989)—§ 22.3(d) n.193

Ching v. United States, 292 F.2d 31 (10th Cir.1961)—§ 15.1(f) n.319

Chinnici, People v., 51 Misc.2d 570, 273 N.Y.S.2d 538 (1966)—§ 3.9(j) n.211

Chintalapalli, State v., 88 Ohio St.3d 43, 723 N.E.2d 111 (2000)—§ 16.4(c) n.103

Chipp, People v., 75 N.Y.2d 327, 553 N.Y.S.2d 72, 552 N.E.2d 608 (1990)—§§ 7.4(c) n.41; 7.4(d) n.69; 10.5(f) n.65

Chippero, State v., 164 N.J. 342, 753 A.2d 701 (2000)—§ 9.4(a) n.18

Chippewa, People v., 751 P.2d 607 (Colo.1988)—§ 21.4(d) n.103

Chipps, United States v., 410 F.3d 438 (8th Cir.2005)—§§ 6.7(c) n.118; 6.7(d) n.153

Chisholm, State v., 565 A.2d 92 (Me.1989)—§ 6.8(d) n.84

Chisholm, United States v., 5 F.R.D. 397 (E.D.Ark.1946)—§ 15.1(f) n.333

Chism, People v., 17 Mich.App. 196, 169 N.W.2d 192 (1969)—§§ 11.2(g) n.261, 281

Chisolm v. State, 529 So.2d 635 (Miss.1988)—§ 22.3(d) n.246

Chitty, United States v., 15 F.3d 159 (11th Cir.1994)—§ 24.4(d) n.42

Chitty, United States v., 760 F.2d 425 (2d Cir.1985)—§§ 26.5(a) n.9, 11

Chmiel, Commonwealth v., 558 Pa. 478, 738 A.2d 406, 558 Pa. 478, 738 A.2d 406 (1999)—§§ 11.7(e) n.87; 11.10(c) n.69

Choat, State v., 178 W.Va. 607, 363 S.E.2d 493 (1987)—§§ 2.12(d) n.181; 3.8(e) n.195

Choate, United States v., 576 F.2d 165 (9th Cir.1978)—§ 4.2(a) n.8

Choate, United States v., 276 F.2d 724 (5th Cir.1960)—§ 15.1(f) n.282

Chojolan, State v., 253 Neb. 591, 571 N.W.2d 621 (1997)—§ 6.2(c) n.163

Chong, State v., 86 Hawai'i 290, 949 P.2d 130 (App.1997)—§§ 15.3(d) n.68; 15.5(c) n.125; 15.6(a) n.10, 39, 43; 15.7(f) n.135

Chouinard, State v., 96 N.M. 658, 634 P.2d 680 (1981)—§ 24.3(e) n.130

Choung v. California, 320 F.Supp. 625 (E.D.Cal.1970)—§§ 19.3(b) n.152, 169

Chrisco v. Shafran, 507 F.Supp. 1312 (D.Del.1981)—§§ 6.4(e) n.92, 93

Chrisicos, State v., 148 N.H. 546, 813 A.2d 513 (2002)—§ 6.7(b) n.42

Chrisman, State v., 100 Wash.2d 814, 676 P.2d 419 (1984)—§ 2.12(a) n.26

Christakis, United States v., 238 F.3d 1164 (9th Cir.2001)—§ 11.9(d) n.194

Christensen, People v., 102 Ill.2d 321, 80 Ill.Dec. 302, 465 N.E.2d 93 (1984)—§ 18.4(c) n.65

Christensen, State v., 582 N.W.2d 675 (S.D.1998)—§ 7.4(e) n.89

Christensen, State v., 244 Mont. 312, 797 P.2d 893 (1990)—§ 3.1(h) n.220

Christensen, United States v., 18 F.3d 822 (9th Cir.1994)—§ 11.5(c) n.61

Christian, People v., 41 Cal.App.4th 986, 48 Cal.Rptr.2d 867 (1996)—§ 11.9(a) n.34

Christian, State v., 657 N.W.2d 186 (Minn.2003)—§ 11.5(d) n.71

Christian v. State, 54 Wis.2d 447, 195 N.W.2d 470 (1972)—§ 21.2(g) n.395

Christian, United States v., 660 F.2d 892 (3d Cir.1981)—§ 27.4(d) n.56

Christian, United States v., 571 F.2d 64 (1st Cir.1978)—§§ 6.9(d) n.73; 6.9(e) n.92

Christiansburg Garment Co. v. EEOC, 434 U.S. 412, 98 S.Ct. 694, 54 L.Ed.2d 648 (1978)—§ 13.5(h) n.169

Christianson v. State, 734 P.2d 1027 (Alaska App.1987)—§ 9.2(c) n.20

Christina L., In re, 149 W.Va. 446, 460 S.E.2d 692 (1995)—§ 24.7(b) n.19

Christmann, People v., 3 Misc.3d 309, 776 N.Y.S.2d 437 (N.Y.J.Ct.2004)—§ 3.7(e) n.126

Christmas v. State, 700 So.2d 262 (Miss.1997)—§ 18.5(a) n.6

Christmas v. State, 632 So.2d 1368 (Fla.1994)—§ 6.10(c) n.35

Christopher v. Florida, 824 F.2d 836 (11th Cir.1987)—§§ 6.9(f) n.132; 6.9(g) n.149, 159, 182

Christopher v. Harbury, 536 U.S. 403, 122 S.Ct. 2179, 153 L.Ed.2d 413 (2002)—§ 11.2(f) n.241

Christopher, State v., 55 Or.App. 544, 639 P.2d 642 (1982)—§ 15.2(j) n.240

Christopher, State v., 134 N.J.Super. 263, 339 A.2d 239 (1977)—§ 20.3(f) n.109

Christopher, United States v., 273 F.3d 294 (3d Cir.2001)—§ 27.5(a) n.7

Christopher K., In re, 217 Ill.2d 348, 299 Ill.Dec. 213, 841 N.E.2d 945 (2005)—§§ 6.9(g) n.166, 174

Christy, State v., 138 N.H. 352, 639 A.2d 261 (1994)—§ 3.3(c) n.111

Chu v. Anne Arundel County, 311 Md. 673, 537 A.2d 250 (1988)—§ 10.1(c) n.45

Chua Han Now v. United States, 730 F.2d 1308 (9th Cir.1984)—§ 16.4(b) n.17

Chubbuck, United States v., 252 F.3d 1300 (11th Cir.2001)—§ 21.4(c) n.77

Chumley, Commonwealth v., 482 Pa. 626, 394 A.2d 497 (1978)—§ 21.4(f) n.172

Chun, United States v., 503 F.2d 533 (9th Cir.1974)—§ 4.6(j) n.171

Chung, State v., 202 Conn. 39, 519 A.2d 1175 (1987)—§§ 6.2(c) n.152, 154

Church v. Powell, 40 N.C.App. 254, 252 S.E.2d 229 (1979)—§ 6.10(e) n.81

Church v. Sullivan, 942 F.2d 1501 (10th Cir.1991)—§ 11.9(d) n.233

Ciak v. State, 278 Ga. 27, 597 S.E.2d 392 (2004)—§ 3.8(d) n.126

Ciak v. United States, 59 F.3d 296 (2d Cir.1995)—§ 11.9(b) n.83

Ciambrone, United States v., 601 F.2d 616 (2d Cir.1979)—§§ 15.2(c) n.66; 15.2(g) n.176; 15.7(f) n.154, 158

Ciancaglini, United States v., 945 F.Supp. 813 (E.D.Pa.1996)—§ 24.7(a) n.1

Cianchetti, United States v., 315 F.2d 584 (2d Cir.1963)—§ 15.2(j) n.238

Cianci, State v., 485 A.2d 565 (R.I.1984)—§ 26.5(c) n.59

Cianfrani, United States v., 573 F.2d 835 (3d Cir.1978)—§ 23.1(e) n.254

Ciapponi, United States v., 77 F.3d 1247 (10th Cir.1996)—§ 21.4(a) n.37

Cicale, United States v., 691 F.2d 95 (2d Cir.1982)—§ 11.4(c) n.64

Ciccone, United States v., 312 F.3d 535 (2d Cir.2002)—§ 12.3(a) n.18

Cicenia v. LaGay, 357 U.S. 504, 78 S.Ct. 1297, 2 L.Ed.2d 1523 (1958)—§§ 6.4(a) n.5; 20.3(m) n.235

Cieslowski, United States v., 410 F.3d 353 (7th Cir.2005)—§§ 11.10(c) n.108; 21.2(d) n.157, 194; 21.3(b) n.71

Cigic, State v., 639 A.2d 251 (N.H.1994)—§ 11.2(c) n.90

Cimino, State v., 126 N.H. 570, 493 A.2d 1197 (1985)—§ 3.7(e) n.121

Cimino, United States v., 381 F.3d 124 (2d Cir.2004)—§§ 21.2(e) n.352 to 354, 356 to 360

Cincotta, Commonwealth v., 6 Mass.App.Ct. 812, 384 N.E.2d 1244 (1979)—§ 7.4(c) n.52

Cintron, Commonwealth v., 435 Mass. 509, 759 N.E.2d 700 (2001)—§ 21.2(f) n.392

Ciochon, People v., 23 Ill.App.3d 363, 319 N.E.2d 332 (1974)—§ 3.2(b) n.51

Cipolla, People v., 163 Misc.2d 144, 619 N.Y.S.2d 939 (County Ct.1994)—§§ 15.4(g) n.149, 150

Cipriano v. City of Houma, 395 U.S. 701, 89 S.Ct. 1897, 23 L.Ed.2d 647 (1969)—§ 2.11(a) n.3

Cipriano, People v., 431 Mich. 315, 429 N.W.2d 781 (1988)—§ 6.3(c) n.50

Cirillo, United States v., 499 F.2d 872 (2d Cir.1974)—§ 4.6(m) n.245

Cisneros, People v., 193 Colo. 380, 566 P.2d 703 (1977)—§ 14.3(d) n.97

Cisneros, State v., 248 Neb. 372, 535 N.W.2d 703 (1995)—§ 22.3(a) n.47

Cisneros, United States v., 385 F.Supp.2d 567 (E.D.Va.2005)—§ 26.4(h) n.156

Cisneros, United States v., 26 F.Supp.2d 24 (1998)—§ 19.5(d) n.75

Cissell, State v., 127 Wis.2d 205, 378 N.W.2d 691 (1985)—§ 13.7(a) n.9

Citizen, State v., 898 So.2d 325 (La.2005)—§ 11.8(c) n.67

Citron, United States v., 853 F.2d 1055 (2d Cir.1988)—§ 17.4(a) n.7

City Court of the City of Tucson, State v., 150 Ariz. 99, 722 P.2d 267 (1986)—§ 22.4(d) n.35

Ciudadanos Unidos De San Juan v. Hidalgo County Grand Jury Commissioners, 622 F.2d 807 (5th Cir.1980)—§ 15.4(d) n.125

Civella, United States v., 666 F.2d 1122 (8th Cir.1981)—§ 15.7(b) n.34

Civella, United States v., 533 F.2d 1395 (8th Cir.1976)—§ 4.6(j) n.162

Civil Rights Cases, 109 U.S. 3, 3 S.Ct. 18, 27 L.Ed. 835 (1883)—§ 1.2(c) n.91

C.J., In re, 166 Ill.2d 264, 209 Ill.Dec. 775, 652 N.E.2d 315 (1995)—§ 24.3(b) n.52

Clabourne v. Lewis, 64 F.3d 1373 (9th Cir.1995)—§§ 9.4(a) n.24; 24.8(f) n.98

Clabourne, State v., 142 Ariz. 335, 690 P.2d 54 (1984)—§ 6.4(f) n.112

Claiborne, United States v., 765 F.2d 784 (9th Cir.1985)—§§ 15.7(b) n.51; 15.7(e) n.124

Claiborne v. United States, 77 F.2d 682 (8th Cir.1935)—§ 8.8(a) n.3

Clair, People v., 2 Cal.4th 629, 7 Cal.Rptr.2d 564, 828 P.2d 705 (1992)—§ 6.4(e) n.63

Clancy, Commonwealth v., 402 Mass. 664, 524 N.E.2d 395 (1988)—§ 24.3(f) n.154

Clanton v. Cooper, 129 F.3d 1147 (10th Cir.1997)—§§ 9.1(a) n.20, 21

Clark v. Commonwealth, 262 Va. 517, 551 S.E.2d 642 (2001)—§§ 20.2(b) n.22; 20.3(m) n.237

Clark, Commonwealth v., 432 Mass. 1, 730 N.E.2d 872 (2000)—§§ 6.2(c) n.166; 6.7(b) n.87

Clark, Commonwealth v., 746 A.2d 1128 (Pa.2000)—§ 27.2(a) n.6

Clark v. Commonwealth, 31 Va.App. 96, 521 S.E.2d 313 (1999)—§§ 3.5(d) n.165, 173

Clark v. Commonwealth, 428 Mass. 1011, 697 N.E.2d 995 (1998)—§ 17.4(b) n.133

Clark, Commonwealth v., 710 A.2d 31, 551 Pa. 258 (1998)—§ 24.5(b) n.23

Clark v. Johnson, 278 F.3d 459 (5th Cir.2002)—§ 28.12(b) n.8

Clark v. Lewis, 1 F.3d 814 (9th Cir.1993)—§ 28.4(e) n.79

Clark v. Mitchell, 425 F.3d 270 (6th Cir.2005)—§ 6.9(b) n.27

Clark v. Murphy, 317 F.3d 1038 (9th Cir.2003)—§ 6.9(g) n.166

Clark, People v., 453 Mich. 572, 556 N.W.2d 820 (1996)—§ 24.8(b) n.27

Clark, People v., 5 Cal.4th 950, 22 Cal.Rptr.2d 689, 857 P.2d 1099 (1993)—§§ 11.9(d) n.174, 208

Clark, People v., 3 Cal.4th 41, 10 Cal.Rptr.2d 554, 833 P.2d 561 (1992)—§§ 7.4(f) n.95; 11.6(a) n.6

Clark, People v., 71 Ill.App.3d 381, 27 Ill.Dec. 680, 389 N.E.2d 911 (1979)—§ 16.1(d) n.139

Clark, People v., 183 Colo. 201, 515 P.2d 1242 (1973)—§ 21.3(d) n.221

Clark v. Prichard, 812 F.2d 991 (5th Cir.1987)—§ 26.9(c) n.82

Clark v. Scott, 70 F.3d 386 (5th Cir.1995)—§ 24.2(d) n.45

Clark, State v., 197 S.W.3d 598 (Mo.2006)—§ 26.4(h) n.154

Clark, State v., 151 N.H. 56, 849 A.2d 143 (2004)—§ 12.4(d) n.63

Clark v. State, 808 N.E.2d 1183 (Ind.2004)—§ 6.2(c) n.152

Clark, State v., 851 So.2d 1055 (La.2003)—§ 3.5(c) n.129

Clark, State v., 20 P.3d 300 (Utah 2001)—§§ 14.3(a) n.6, 8, 9, 11, 30

Clark, State v., 143 Wash.2d 731, 24 P.3d 1006 (2001)—§ 3.4(f) n.107

Clark v. State, 621 N.W.2d 576 (N.D.2001)—§§ 27.6(d) n.127; 28.11(b) n.28

Clark, State v., 162 N.J. 201, 744 A.2d 109 (2000)—§ 11.9(d) n.211

Clark, State v., 128 N.M. 119, 990 P.2d 793 (1999)—§ 22.3(d) n.202

Clark v. State, 271 Ga. 6, 515 S.E.2d 155 (1999)—§ 7.4(d) n.72

Clark, State v., 981 S.W.2d 143 (Mo.1998)—§ 22.3(a) n.23

Clark v. State, 321 S.C. 377, 468 S.E.2d 653 (S.C.1996)—§ 21.2(e) n.334

Clark, State v., 670 So.2d 624 (La.App.1996)—§§ 23.2(a) n.28, 31, 44

Clark v. State, 108 Nev. 324, 831 P.2d 1374 (Nev.1992)—§§ 11.9(a) n.25; 11.9(d) n.174

Clark, State v., 464 N.W.2d 861 (Iowa 1991)—§ 17.2(d) n.94

Clark v. State, 579 So.2d 109 (Fla.1991)—§ 26.9(a) n.7

Clark, State v., 581 So.2d 747 (La.1991)—§ 20.3(b) n.49

Clark v. State, 800 S.W.2d 500 (Tenn.Crim.App.1990)—§ 21.4(e) n.165

Clark, State v., 108 N.M. 288, 772 P.2d 322 (1989)—§ 21.5(a) n.35

Clark v. State, 498 N.E.2d 918 (Ind.1986)—§ 7.4(g) n.116

Clark, State v., 217 Neb. 417, 350 N.W.2d 521 (1984)—§ 21.2(d) n.161

Clark, State v., 475 A.2d 418 (Me.1984)—§ 6.2(c) n.173

Clark, State v., 126 Ariz. 428, 616 P.2d 888 (1980)—§ 14.1(b) n.33

Clark, State v., 312 Minn. 44, 250 N.W.2d 199 (1977)—§ 3.6(b) n.50

Clark, State v., 546 S.W.2d 455 (Mo.App.1976)—§ 14.3(d) n.96

Clark v. State, 256 Ark. 658, 509 S.W.2d 812 (1974)—§ 24.5(b) n.34

Clark, United States v., 43 F.3d 1100 (9th Cir.2006)—§ 16.4(b) n.21

Clark, United States v., 218 F.3d 1092 (9th Cir.2000)—§ 21.2(d) n.158

Clark v. United States, 755 A.2d 1026 (D.C.App.2000)—§ 9.4(f) n.114

Clark, United States v., 84 F.3d 506 (1st Cir.1996)—§ 26.8(c) n.24

Clark, United States v., 982 F.2d 965 (6th Cir.1993)—§ 6.7(b) n.43

Clark, United States v., 988 F.2d 1459 (6th Cir.1993)—§§ 24.4(c) n.24, 27

Clark, United States v., 865 F.2d 1433 (4th Cir.1989)—§ 12.1(a) n.15

Clark, United States v., 847 F.2d 1467 (10th Cir.1988)—§§ 8.13(a) n.16, 23, 26, 27, 29; 8.13(b) n.54

Clark, United States v., 781 F.2d 730 (9th Cir.1986)—§ 21.2(d) n.184

Clark, United States v., 613 F.2d 391 (2d Cir.1979)—§ 24.7(e) n.50

Clark, United States v., 541 F.2d 1016 (4th Cir.1976)—§ 19.3(b) n.181

Clark, United States v., 506 F.2d 416 (5th Cir.1975)—§ 7.4(b) n.33

Clark, United States v., 498 F.2d 535 (2d Cir.1974)—§ 24.1(b) n.30

Clark, United States v., 499 F.2d 802 (4th Cir.1974)—§ 7.3(d) n.76

Clark, United States v., 475 F.2d 240 (2d Cir.1973)—§ 10.5(e) n.46

Clark v. United States, 400 F.2d 83 (9th Cir.1968)—§ 6.6(d) n.58

Clarke v. Neil, 427 F.2d 1322 (6th Cir.1970)—§ 9.1(c) n.108

Clarke, State v., 49 Wis.2d 161, 181 N.W.2d 355 (1970)—§ 16.3(b) n.24

Clarke v. State, 3 Md.App. 447, 240 A.2d 291 (1968)—§ 6.7(b) n.43

Clark, State ex rel. v. Marullo, 352 So.2d 223 (La.1977)—§§ 21.5(a) n.22; 21.5(b) n.67

Clark, United States ex rel. v. Fike, 538 F.2d 750 (7th Cir.1976)—§ 7.4(g) n.118

Class, People v., 67 N.Y.2d 431, 503 N.Y.S.2d 313, 494 N.E.2d 444 (1986)—§ 2.12(a) n.26

Classen, State v., 31 Or.App. 683, 571 P.2d 527 (1977)—§ 7.5(a) n.8

Classic, United States v., 313 U.S. 299, 61 S.Ct. 1031, 85 L.Ed. 1368 (1941)—§ 3.1(l) n.283

Claudio, People v., 59 N.Y.2d 556, 466 N.Y.S.2d 271, 453 N.E.2d 500 (1983)—§ 11.7(a) n.16

Claudio v. Scully, 982 F.2d 798 (2d Cir.1992)—§ 11.10(c) n.90

Clausell, State v., 121 N.J. 298, 580 A.2d 221 (1990)—§ 7.4(f) n.95

Clausell, State v., 474 So.2d 1189 (Fla.1985)—§§ 22.5(c) n.25; 22.5(d) n.29

Clavette, United States v., 135 F.3d 1308 (9th Cir.1998)—§ 22.1(b) n.49

Clavey, United States v., 565 F.2d 111 (7th Cir.1978)—§ 8.5(d) n.135

Clay v. Dormire, 37 S.W.3d 214 (Mo.2000)—§ 28.11(b) n.18

Clay v. State, 757 So.2d 236 (Miss.2000)—§ 12.1(b) n.27

Clay, United States v., 408 F.3d 214 (5th Cir.2005)—§§ 6.8(b) n.51, 57

Clay v. United States, 537 U.S. 522, 123 S.Ct. 1072, 155 L.Ed.2d 88 (2003)—§§ 28.5(b) n.46; 28.9(b) n.46

Clay, United States v., 159 F.Supp.2d 1357 (M.D.Ala.2001)—§ 22.2(a) n.2

Claybrook, State v., 736 S.W.2d 95 (Tenn.1987)—§ 23.2(f) n.82

Clay County Manor, Inc. v. State Department of Health & Environment, 849 S.W.2d 755 (Tenn.1993)—§ 3.9(c) n.49

Claypool, People v., 470 Mich. 715, 684 N.W.2d 278 (2004)—§ 26.4(b) n.22

Clayton, Ex parte, 887 So.2d 856 (Ala.2004)—§ 17.4(a) n.5

Clayton, Matter of, 113 Idaho 817, 748 P.2d 401 (1988)—§ 3.7(e) n.126

Clayton v. Gibson, 199 F.3d 1162 (10th Cir.1999)—§ 6.9(f) n.133

Clayton, State v., 131 S.W.3d 475 (Tenn.Cr.App.2003)—§ 24.9(e) n.57

Clayton v. State, 840 P.2d 18 (Okl.Cr.1992)—§ 7.4(e) n.89

Clear Channel Communications v. Murray, 636 So.2d 818 (Fla.App.1994)—§ 23.1(c) n.107

Cleary v. Bolger, 371 U.S. 392, 83 S.Ct. 385, 9 L.Ed.2d 390 (1963)—§ 6.3(a) n.25

Cleary v. District Court, 704 P.2d 866 (Colo.1985)—§§ 11.4(c) n.57; 11.9(a) n.24; 11.9(c) n.119, 139

Cleary, State v., 175 Vt. 142, 824 A.2d 509 (2003)—§§ 21.4(b) n.65; 21.4(f) n.182; 21.5(c) n.84; 21.6(a) n.78

Cleary, State v., 161 Vt. 403, 641 A.2d 102 (1994)—§ 6.9(b) n.27

Cleburn, People v., 782 P.2d 784 (Colo.1989)—§ 6.6(e) n.65

Clegg, State v., 635 N.W.2d 578 (S.D.2001)—§ 21.4(a) n.24

Cleghorn v. State, 55 Wis.2d 466, 198 N.W.2d 577 (1972)—§ 11.2(c) n.87

Clemente, State v., 166 Conn. 501, 353 A.2d 723 (1974)—§§ 1.7(f) n.90, 94

Clemmer, United States ex rel. v. Mazurkiewicz, 365 F.Supp. 1158 (E.D.Pa.1973)—§ 7.4(f) n.103

Clemmey, Commonwealth v., 447 Mass. 121, 849 N.E.2d 844 (2006)—§ 15.7(f) n.164

Clemons v. Mississippi, 494 U.S. 738, 110 S.Ct. 1441, 108 L.Ed.2d 725 (1990)—§§ 26.1(b) n.16; 27.5(e) n.159; 28.6(d) n.24

Clemons, United States v., 843 F.2d 741 (3d Cir.1988)—§ 22.3(d) n.247

Clemons v. United States, 408 F.2d 1230 (D.C.Cir.1968)—§ 10.5(a) n.15

Clenney, United States v., 434 F.3d 780 (5th Cir.2005)—§ 16.2(d) n.58

Clerk-Magistrate of West Roxbury, Commonwealth v., 439 Mass. 352, 787 N.E.2d 1032 (2003)—§ 13.2(a) n.3

Clermont v. State, 348 Md. 419, 704 A.2d 880 (1998)—§ 26.4(g) n.140

Cleveland, People v., 25 Cal.4th 466, 106 Cal.Rptr. 2d 313, 21 P.3d 1225 (Cal.2001)—§§ 24.9(f) n.75, 104

Cleveland v. State, 417 So.2d 653 (Fla.1982)—§§ 13.6(c) n.35, 39

Cleveland, United States v., 25 Media L.Rep. 2139 (D.La.1997)—§ 24.9(g) n.130

Cleveland v. United States, 329 U.S. 14, 67 S.Ct. 13, 91 L.Ed. 12 (1946)—§ 1.2(c) n.109

Cleveland, City of v. Trzebuckowski, 85 Ohio St.3d 524, 709 N.E.2d 1148 (1999)—§ 13.4(c) n.112

Cleveland, United States ex rel. v. Warden, 544 F.2d 1200 (3d Cir.1976)—§ 11.2(d) n.126

Clewis v. Texas, 386 U.S. 707, 87 S.Ct. 1338, 18 L.Ed.2d 423 (1967)—§§ 6.2(c) n.175; 9.5(c) n.64

Clicque v. United States, 514 F.2d 923 (5th Cir.1975)—§ 21.4(f) n.183

Clifford v. State, 266 Ga. 620, 469 S.E.2d 155 (1996)—§ 24.9(e) n.54

Clifford, United States v., 640 F.2d 150 (8th Cir.1981)—§ 15.4(f) n.145

Clifton, People v., 42 Ill.2d 526, 250 N.E.2d 649 (1969)—§ 3.3(c) n.141

Clifton, State v., 777 A.2d 1272 (R.I.2001)—§ 18.4(c) n.61

Clifton, State v., 134 Ariz. 345, 656 P.2d 634 (App.1982)—§ 15.7(e) n.99

Cline v. Murensky, 174 W.Va. 70, 322 S.E.2d 702 (1984)—§ 17.4(c) n.153

Cline, State v., 617 N.W.2d 277 (Iowa 2000)—§ 3.3(f) n.206

Cline, State v., 122 R.I. 297, 405 A.2d 1192 (1979)—§ 22.5(d) n.35

Cline, United States v., 349 F.3d 1276 (10th Cir.2003)—§ 4.6(m) n.241

Clinger v. State, 533 So.2d 315 (Fla.App.1988)—§ 26.9(b) n.27

Clingman v. State, 23 P.3d 27 (Wyo.2001)—§ 21.2(d) n.178

Clinkscale v. Carter, 375 F.3d 430 (6th Cir.2004)—§ 28.4(c) n.27

Clinton v. Virginia, 377 U.S. 158, 84 S.Ct. 1186, 12 L.Ed.2d 213 (1964)—§ 3.2(a) n.4

Clisby v. Jones, 960 F.2d 925 (11th Cir.1992)—§ 11.2(e) n.171

Cliver v. State, 666 N.E.2d 59 (Ind.1996)—§ 24.10(c) n.40

Closson v. State, 812 P.2d 966 (Alaska 1991)—§§ 13.5(b) n.44, 45

Closure of Preliminary Exam, In re, 200 Mich.App. 566, 505 N.W.2d 24 (1993)—§ 27.5(a) n.23

Cloud, State v., 52 Del. 439, 159 A.2d 588 (1960)—§ 15.1(d) n.219

Clowers v. Sikes, 272 Ga. 463, 532 S.E.2d 98 (2000)—§§ 21.3(a) n.2, 31

Clubb v. State, 350 So.2d 693 (Miss.1977)—§ 7.3(c) n.48

Clutter, United States v., 914 F.2d 775 (6th Cir.1990)—§§ 3.1(h) n.204; 3.10(e) n.148

Clyburn, United States v., 24 F.3d 613 (4th Cir.1994)—§ 3.4(c) n.37

Clymer, United States v., 25 F.3d 824 (9th Cir.1994)—§ 18.3(b) n.26

Clymore, United States v., 245 F.3d 1195 (10th Cir.2001)—§ 10.1(c) n.52

Coady, United States v., 809 F.2d 119 (1st Cir.1987)—§ 24.8(b) n.33

Coates v. City of Cincinnati, 402 U.S. 611, 91 S.Ct. 1686, 29 L.Ed.2d 214 (1971)—§ 2.4(a) n.19

Coates, State v., 241 Mont. 331, 786 P.2d 1182 (Mont.1990)—§ 11.8(c) n.78

Coates v. United States, 413 F.2d 371 (D.C.Cir.1969)—§ 3.5(a) n.7

Coban, State v., 520 So.2d 40 (Fla.1988)—§ 21.4(d) n.103

Cobb, People v., 139 Cal.App.3d 578, 188 Cal.Rptr. 712 (1983)— § 21.3(e) n.272

Cobb, State v., 115 Ariz. 484, 566 P.2d 285 (1977)—§ 6.2(c) n.127

Cobb, State v., 22 Or.App. 510, 539 P.2d 1140 (1975)—§§ 6.7(b) n.65, 67, 70

Cobb, United States v., 185 F.3d 1193 (11th Cir.1999)—§§ 17.2(c) n.84, 87, 92

Cobb, United States v., 144 F.3d 319 (4th Cir.1998)—§ 1.2(c) n.147

Cobbledick v. United States, 309 U.S. 323, 60 S.Ct. 540, 84 L.Ed. 783 (1940)—§§ 27.2(b) n.12; 27.2(e) n.78

Cobbs, People v., 443 Mich. 276, 505 N.W.2d 208 (1993)—§ 21.3(d) n.222

Cobbs v. Robinson, 528 F.2d 1331 (2d Cir.1975)—§§ 15.4(d) n.100, 124

Coble v. Magone, 229 Mont. 45, 744 P.2d 1244 (1987)—§ 27.4(f) n.63

Coccia, United States v., 446 F.3d 233 (1st Cir.2006)—§ 3.7(d) n.88

Cochran, State v., 96 Idaho 862, 538 P.2d 791 (Idaho 1975)—§§ 16.4(c) n.51, 53

Cochran, United States v., 770 F.2d 850 (9th Cir.1985)—§ 22.1(h) n.133

Cockerham v. State, 933 P.2d 537 (Alaska 1997)—§§ 24.3(a) n.11; 26.4(d) n.53; 26.4(f) n.88

Cockerham, United States v., 237 F.3d 1179 (10th Cir.2001)—§§ 21.2(b) n.83; 28.9(b) n.72

Cockrell v. Oberhauser, 413 F.2d 256 (9th Cir.1969)—§ 17.2(b) n.31

Coconino County Superior Court, State v., 139 Ariz. 422, 678 P.2d 1386 (1984)—§§ 15.7(f) n.165, 177

Codd, United States v., 956 F.2d 1109 (11th Cir.1992)—§ 3.8(b) n.28

Coddington v. State, 142 P.3d 437 (Okla.Crim.App.2006)—§§ 6.8(d) n.84; 6.9(b) n.35

Code v. Montgomery, 725 F.2d 1316 (11th Cir.1984)—§ 7.4(g) n.116

Codispoti v. Pennsylvania, 418 U.S. 506, 94 S.Ct. 2687, 41 L.Ed.2d 912 (1974)—§§ 15.1(b) n.85; 22.1(b) n.50

Cody, State v., 236 Neb. 69, 459 N.W.2d 195 (1990)—§ 3.6(a) n.38

Cody v. State, 548 S.W.2d 401 (Tex.Cr.App.1977)—§ 27.5(a) n.28

Coe, State v., 101 Wash.2d 364, 679 P.2d 353 (1984)—§§ 2.12(c) n.139; 2.12(d) n.195

Coe, State v., 101 Wash.2d 772, 684 P.2d 668 (1984)—§§ 20.3(j) n.181; 20.3(k) n.217

Coe, State v., 655 S.W.2d 903 (Tenn.1983)—§ 16.3(g) n.100

Coerper, State v., 199 Wis.2d 216, 544 N.W.2d 423 (1996)—§ 6.9(g) n.147

Coffey v. State, 582 So.2d 608 (Ala.Crim.App.1991)—§ 16.2(e) n.80

Coffey, United States v., 871 F.2d 39 (6th Cir.1989)—§ 26.4(g) n.141

Coffey v. United States, 116 U.S. 436, 6 S.Ct. 437, 29 L.Ed. 684 (1886)—§ 17.4(a) n.25

Coffman, People v., 34 Cal.4th 1, 17 Cal.Rptr.3d 710, 96 P.3d 30 (2004)—§§ 6.2(c) n.166; 6.7(b) n.90; 22.3(c) n.153; 22.4(c) n.29

Cofield, State v., 320 N.C. 297, 357 S.E.2d 622 (1987)—§§ 15.4(e) n.128, 141

Cofield, United States v., 11 F.3d 413 (4th Cir.1993)—§§ 16.2(e) n.68, 74

Cogen v. United States, 278 U.S. 221, 49 S.Ct. 118, 73 L.Ed. 275 (1929)—§ 27.2(d) n.67

Cohane, State v., 193 Conn. 474, 479 A.2d 763 (1984)—§§ 1.7(i) n.202, 205

Cohee v. State, 110 P.3d 267 (Wyo.2005)—§ 21.6(a) n.47

Cohee v. State, 942 P.2d 211 (Okla.Cr.App.1997)—§ 24.9(b) n.13

Cohen v. Beneficial Industrial Loan Corp, 337 U.S. 541, 69 S.Ct. 1221, 93 L.Ed. 1528 (1949)—§ 27.2(c) n.21

Cohen, Commonwealth v., 489 Pa. 167, 413 A.2d 1066 (1980)—§ 23.2(a) n.48

Cohen, Commonwealth v., 221 Pa.Super. 244, 289 A.2d 96 (1972)—§ 6.8(a) n.22

Cohen v. Hurley, 366 U.S. 117, 81 S.Ct. 954, 6 L.Ed.2d 156 (1961)—§§ 2.5(b) n.14; 2.5(c) n.17, 20, 24, 29; 2.5(d) n.32

Cohen, People v., 57 Misc.2d 366, 292 N.Y.S.2d 706 (1968)—§ 3.10(e) n.186

Cohen v. Senkowski, 290 F.3d 485 (2d Cir.2002)—§ 24.2(a) n.5

Cohen, State v., 173 Ariz. 497, 844 P.2d 1147 (1992)—§ 16.2(g) n.138

Cohen, State v., 305 S.C. 432, 409 S.E.2d 383 (1991)—§ 10.3(b) n.38

Cohen v. State, 97 Nev. 166, 625 P.2d 1170 (1981)—§ 11.3(b) n.33

Cohen, United States v., 796 F.2d 20 (2d Cir.1986)—§ 3.9(i) n.184

Cohen, United States v., 444 F.Supp. 1314 (E.D.Pa.1978)—§§ 8.14(a) n.10, 21

Cohen, United States v., 530 F.2d 43 (5th Cir.1976)—§§ 4.6(e) n.82; 6.7(b) n.99, 103

Cohen v. United States, 82 S.Ct. 526, 7 L.Ed.2d 518 (1962)—§ 12.2(a) n.4

Cohens v. Virginia, 19 U.S. (6 Wheat.) 264, 5 L.Ed. 257 (1821)—§§ 1.2(c) n.34, 43

Cohn, State v., 284 So.2d 426 (Fla.App.1973)—§ 3.2(f) n.185

Cohn, State v., 347 S.W.2d 691 (Mo.1961)—§ 3.9(e) n.81

Cohn, United States v., 230 F.Supp. 587 (S.D.N.Y.1964)—§ 17.2(f) n.132

Cohoon, People v., 104 Ill.2d 295, 84 Ill.Dec. 443, 472 N.E.2d 403 (1984)—§ 7.4(e) n.89

Coil, United States v., 442 F.3d 912 (5th Cir.2006)—§§ 10.2(d) n.48; 21.6(a) n.37

Coker, Ex parte, 575 So.2d 43 (Ala.1990)—§ 2.11(a) n.14

Coker v. Georgia, 433 U.S. 584, 97 S.Ct. 2861, 53 L.Ed.2d 982 (1977)—§§ 2.7(c) n.182; 24.1(b) n.22; 26.1(b) n.30

Coker, United States v., 433 F.3d 39 (1st Cir.2005)—§ 6.4(e) n.101

Colacasides, In re, 379 Mich. 69, 150 N.W.2d 1 (1967)—§§ 8.1(c) n.25, 30

Colantoni, Commonwealth v., 396 Mass. 672, 488 N.E.2d 394 (1986)—§ 21.4(c) n.95

Colavito, People v., 639 N.Y.S.2d 996, 87 N.Y.2d 423, 663 N.E.2d 308 (1996)—§§ 20.3(a) n.20; 20.6(b) n.22

Colbert, Ex parte, 805 So.2d 687 (Ala.2001)—§ 12.3(b) n.58

Colbert v. State, 714 P.2d 209 (Okla.Crim.App.1986)—§§ 11.3(c) n.54, 59, 61

Colby, Commonwealth v., 422 Mass. 414, 663 N.E.2d 808 (1996)—§§ 6.2(c) n.133; 6.6(a) n.7; 6.8(b) n.63

Colclasure, People v., 200 Ill.App.3d 1038, 146 Ill.Dec. 742, 558 N.E.2d 705 (1990)—§ 1.7(f) n.93

Cole v. Arkansas, 333 U.S. 196, 68 S.Ct. 514, 92 L.Ed. 644 (1948)—§§ 2.4(e) n.144, 155; 2.6(a) n.21

Cole, Commonwealth v., 585 Pa. 547, 889 A.2d 501 (2005)—§ 7.4(a) n.7

Cole v. Lane, 830 F.2d 104 (7th Cir.1987)—§ 6.2(c) n.92

Cole, People v., 172 Ill.2d 85, 216 Ill.Dec. 718, 665 N.E.2d 1275 (1996)—§ 6.9(g) n.152

Cole, People v., 195 Colo. 483, 584 P.2d 71 (1978)—§ 21.5(f) n.173

Cole v. Slayton, 378 F.Supp. 364 (W.D.Va.1974)—§ 21.3(b) n.115

Cole v. State, 194 S.W.3d 538 (Tex.App.2006)—§ 24.7(e) n.63

Cole, State v., 264 Wis. 2d 540, 665 N.W.2d 328 (2003)—§ 1.2(b) n.4

Cole v. State, 378 Md. 42, 835 A.2d 600 (2003)—§§ 20.2(b) n.20; 20.3(f) n.107

Cole v. State, 842 So.2d 609 (Ala.Crim.App.2002)—§ 21.6(a) n.29

Cole, State v., 180 W.Va. 412, 376 S.E.2d 618 (1988)—§§ 24.9(e) n.52, 58

Cole v. State, 37 Ala.App. 232, 67 So.2d 64 (1953)—§ 16.1(d) n.142

Cole, United States v., 27 F.3d 996 (4th Cir.1994)—§ 27.6(b) n.21

Cole, United States v., 857 F.2d 971 (4th Cir.1988)—§§ 20.3(b) n.56, 57

Cole, United States v., 755 F.2d 748 (11th Cir.1985)—§ 15.1(d) n.171

Cole v. U.S. Department of Agriculture, 133 F.3d 803 (11th Cir.1998)—§ 17.4(b) n.131

Coleman v. Alabama, 399 U.S. 1, 90 S.Ct. 1999, 26 L.Ed.2d 387 (1970)—§§ 2.11(c) n.32; 11.2(b) n.36; 12.1(c) n.48; 14.1(c) n.37; 14.1(d) n.48; 14.2(a) n.13; 14.4(a) n.1; 14.4(c) n.46; 14.4(e) n.124, 131; 27.6(d) n.86

Coleman v. Burnett, 477 F.2d 1187 (D.C.Cir.1973)—§§ 14.2(b) n.30; 14.4(c) n.54; 14.4(e) n.113, 141

Coleman v. Kemp, 778 F.2d 1487 (11th Cir.1985)—§§ 23.2(a) n.16, 19, 25, 26, 29, 32, 39

Coleman v. O'Shea, 184 Misc.2d 238, 707 N.Y.S.2d 308 (2000)—§ 23.3(b) n.27

Coleman v. Painter, 215 W.Va. 592, 600 S.E.2d 304 (2004)—§ 21.4(f) n.213

Coleman, People v., 166 Ill.2d 247, 209 Ill.Dec. 782, 652 N.E.2d 322 (1995)—§ 26.3(f) n.55

Coleman, People v., 48 Cal.3d 112, 255 Cal.Rptr. 813, 768 P.2d 32 (1989)—§§ 23.2(a) n.39, 40

Coleman, People v., 179 Ill.App.3d 410, 128 Ill.Dec. 401, 534 N.E.2d 583 (1989)—§ 24.9(c) n.28

Coleman, People v., 46 Cal.3d 749, 251 Cal.Rptr. 83, 759 P.2d 1260 (1988)—§§ 14.2(g) n.106; 14.4(e) n.123

Coleman, People v., 124 Ill.App.3d 597, 79 Ill.Dec. 923, 464 N.E.2d 827 (1984)—§ 24.3(g) n.167

Coleman, People v., 43 N.Y.2d 222, 401 N.Y.S.2d 57, 371 N.E.2d 819 (1977)—§ 7.3(d) n.67

Coleman, People v., 13 Cal.3d 867, 120 Cal.Rptr. 384, 533 P.2d 1024 (Cal.1975)—§ 26.4(g) n.148

Coleman v. Reilly, 8 Wash.App. 684, 508 P.2d 1035 (1973)—§ 3.6(b) n.60

Coleman v. Saffle, 869 F.2d 1377 (10th Cir.1989)—§ 24.7(e) n.62

Coleman v. Singletary, 30 F.3d 1420 (11th Cir.1994)—§§ 6.9(g) n.155, 161

Coleman, State v., 159 Wash.2d 509, 150 P.3d 1126 (2007)—§ 24.10(c) n.40

Coleman, State v., 85 Ohio St.3d 129, 707 N.E.2d 476 (1999)—§ 22.3(d) n.250

Coleman v. State, 749 So.2d 1003 (Miss.1999)—§§ 20.6(c) n.74, 81

Coleman v. State, 725 So.2d 154 (Miss.1998)—§ 18.1(c) n.36

Coleman v. State, 966 S.W.2d 525 (Tex.Cr.App.1998)—§ 24.3(f) n.146

Coleman, State v., 242 Conn. 523, 700 A.2d 14 (1997)—§§ 24.8(e) n.71; 26.8(c) n.28

Coleman, State v., 128 Idaho 466, 915 P.2d 28 (1996)—§ 14.3(a) n.7

Coleman, State v., 160 Vt. 638, 632 A.2d 21 (1993)—§§ 21.2(d) n.211; 26.9(b) n.20

Coleman, State v., 253 Kan. 335, 856 P.2d 121 (1993)—§ 24.3(c) n.93

Coleman, State v., 227 Neb. 755, 419 N.W.2d 878 (1988)—§ 6.8(d) n.84

Coleman, State v., 202 Conn. 86, 519 A.2d 1201 (1987)—§ 27.2(a) n.5

Coleman v. State, 483 So.2d 680 (Miss.1986)—§§ 21.2(g) n.399; 21.6(a) n.73

Coleman v. State, 553 P.2d 40 (Alaska 1976)—§ 15.2(e) n.145

Coleman v. State, 505 S.W.2d 878 (Tex.Cr.App.1974)—§ 7.4(e) n.86

Coleman v. State, 83 Miss. 290, 35 So. 937 (1904)—§ 16.1(d) n.145

Coleman v. Thompson, 798 F.Supp. 1209 (W.D.Va.1992)—§ 11.10(c) n.154

Coleman v. Thompson, 501 U.S. 722, 111 S.Ct. 2546, 115 L.Ed.2d 640 (1991)—§§ 2.9(g) n.164, 165; 2.9(h) n.234; 11.1(b) n.82; 11.7(a) n.20; 28.4(c) n.27; 28.4(d) n.46; 28.5(a) n.8; 28.12(b) n.15

Coleman, United States v., 208 F.3d 786 (9th Cir.2000)—§§ 6.2(c) n.172; 6.9(f) n.144; 22.1(h) n.146

Coleman, United States v., 149 F.3d 674 (7th Cir.1998)—§ 10.5(f) n.68

Coleman, United States v., 995 F.Supp. 212 (D.Mass.1998)—§§ 15.5(b) n.90; 15.6(b) n.78

Coleman, United States v., 22 F.3d 126 (7th Cir.1994)—§§ 17.1(b) n.37; 26.10(c) n.65

Coleman v. United States, 449 A.2d 327 (D.C.App.1982)—§ 25.2(a) n.10

Coleman, United States ex rel. v. Smith, 395 F.Supp. 1155 (W.D.N.Y.1975)—§ 3.9(j) n.221

Coles, People v., 417 Mich. 523, 339 N.W.2d 440 (1983)—§ 26.3(g) n.80

Coley, State v., 93 Ohio St.3d 253, 754 N.E.2d 1129 (2001)—§§ 17.1(d) n.53, 58

Colgrove v. Battin, 413 U.S. 149, 93 S.Ct. 2448, 37 L.Ed.2d 522 (1973)—§§ 1.7(g) n.111; 22.1(d) n.69

Colkley, United States v., 899 F.2d 297 (4th Cir.1990)—§ 3.4(d) n.51

Collazo v. Estelle, 940 F.2d 411 (9th Cir.1991)—§§ 6.2(b) n.43; 6.2(c) n.154, 161; 6.9(c) n.58

Collazo-Aponte, United States v., 216 F.3d 163 (1st Cir.2000)—§ 22.3(b) n.68

Collemacine, Commonwealth v., 429 Pa. 24, 239 A.2d 296 (1968)— § 15.4(b) n.35

Collette, State v., 199 Conn. 308, 507 A.2d 99 (1986)—§§ 7.4(b) n.23, 24

Collie, People v., 30 Cal.3d 43, 177 Cal.Rptr. 458, 634 P.2d 534 (1981)—§§ 20.2(a) n.2, 9; 20.5(a) n.4

Collier, State v., 277 Mont. 46, 919 P.2d 376 (1996)—§ 21.6(a) n.57

Collier, State v., 553 So.2d 815 (La.1989)—§§ 22.3(d) n.213, 242

Collier v. State, 103 Nev. 563, 747 P.2d 225 (1987)—§ 25.4(a) n.7

Colligan, State v., 679 So.2d 184 (La.App.1996)—§ 24.6(e) n.47

Collin, State v., 687 A.2d 962 (Me.1997)—§§ 16.4(c) n.100, 110; 16.4(d) n.122

Collins v. Brierly, 492 F.2d 735 (3d Cir.1974)—§ 6.9(b) n.44

Collins v. Commodity Futures Trading Commission, 737 F.Supp. 1467 (N.D.Ill.1990)—§ 8.12(e) n.50

Collins, Commonwealth v., 268 Pa. 295, 110 A. 738 (1920)—§§ 16.1(b) n.38; 16.1(e) n.190

Collins v. Fogg, 425 F.Supp. 1339 (E.D.N.Y.1977)—§ 6.9(g) n.163

Collins v. Foster, 299 Or. 90, 698 P.2d 953 (1985)—§ 12.4(a) n.22

Collins v. Harker Heights, 503 U.S. 115, 112 S.Ct. 1061, 117 L.Ed.2d 261 (1992)—§ 2.7(d) n.244

Collins v. Kegans, 802 S.W.2d 702 (Tex.Cr.App.1991)—§ 26.1(e) n.111

Collins, People v., 26 Cal.4th 297, 109 Cal.Rptr.2d 836, 27 P.3d 726 (2001)—§§ 21.1(g) n.138; 22.1(h) n.145

Collins, People v., 32 P.3d 636 (Colo.App.2001)—§§ 14.3(c) n.61, 62

Collins, People v., 438 Mich. 8, 475 N.W.2d 684 (1991)—§§ 2.12(b) n.88; 2.12(c) n.121; 2.12(d) n.192

Collins, People v., 17 Cal.3d 687, 131 Cal.Rptr. 782, 552 P.2d 742 (1976)—§ 22.3(e) n.276

Collins v. State, 897 A.2d 159 (Del.2006)—§ 26.10(c) n.72

Collins v. State, 376 Md. 359, 829 A.2d 992 (2003)—§ 3.8(d) n.152

Collins, State v., 367 Md. 700, 790 A.2d 660 (2002)—§ 3.1(h) n.191

Collins v. State, 639 N.E.2d 653 (Ind.App.1994)—§ 26.10(d) n.94

Collins, State v., 121 Wash.2d 168, 847 P.2d 919 (1993)—§ 3.8(e) n.196

Collins v. State, 854 P.2d 688 (Wyo.1993)—§ 3.8(d) n.152

Collins, State v., 133 N.H. 609, 581 A.2d 69 (1990)—§ 3.10(e) n.183

Collins, State v., 45 Wash.App. 541, 726 P.2d 491 (1986)—§ 19.5(b) n.32

Collins, State v., 470 So.2d 553 (La.App.1985)—§ 22.5(b) n.18

Collins, State v., 479 A.2d 344 (Me.1984)—§ 3.8(d) n.145

Collins, State v., 133 Ariz. 20, 648 P.2d 135 (App.1982)—§ 11.6(a) n.40

Collins, State v., 300 N.C. 142, 265 S.E.2d 172 (1980)—§ 21.2(f) n.384

Collins v. State, 151 Ga.App. 116, 258 S.E.2d 769 (1979)—§ 26.10(b) n.23

Collins, State v., 328 So.2d 674 (La.1976)—§ 7.2(b) n.20

Collins, State v., 297 A.2d 620 (Me.1972)—§ 10.4(b) n.10

Collins, State v., 24 Ohio St.2d 107, 265 N.E.2d 261 (1970)—§ 27.3(c) n.36

Collins, State v., 74 Wash.2d 729, 446 P.2d 325 (1968)—§ 6.8(a) n.23

Collins, State v., 55 Wash.2d 469, 348 P.2d 214 (1960)—§ 13.7(a) n.25

Collins, United States v., 430 F.3d 1260 (10th Cir.2005)—§ 11.10(d) n.201

Collins, United States v., 321 F.3d 691 (8th Cir.2003)—§ 3.7(e) n.126

Collins, United States v., 350 F.3d 773 (8th Cir.2003)—§ 19.6(c) n.46

Collins, United States v., 226 F.3d 457 (6th Cir.2000)—§ 24.9(b) n.13

Collins, United States v., 90 F.3d 1420 (9th Cir.1996)—§§ 18.3(b) n.18; 18.4(c) n.56, 60, 61

Collins, United States v., 972 F.2d 1385 (5th Cir.1992)—§§ 6.6(e) n.90; 13.4(e) n.165; 22.3(b) n.86

Collins, United States v., 949 F.2d 921 (7th Cir.1991)—§ 21.4(b) n.57

Collins, United States v., 920 F.2d 619 (10th Cir.1990)—§ 11.4(c) n.56

Collins, United States v., 462 F.2d 792 (2d Cir.1972)—§ 6.9(f) n.106

Collins v. Youngblood, 497 U.S. 37, 110 S.Ct. 2715, 111 L.Ed.2d 30 (1990)—§§ 2.9(d) n.55, 60

Collins, State ex rel. v. Superior Court, 145 Ariz. 493, 702 P.2d 1338 (1985)—§ 6.2(c) n.99

Collis, State v., 73 Iowa 542, 35 N.W. 625 (1887)—§ 8.4(b) n.78

Collis, United States v., 875 F.Supp. 401 (E.D.Mich.1995)—§ 20.3(b) n.56

Collis, United States v., 766 F.2d 219 (6th Cir.1985)—§ 3.8(c) n.85

Colombo, United States v., 869 F.2d 149 (2d Cir.1989)—§ 24.9(f) n.98

Colombo, United States v., 852 F.2d 19 (1st Cir.1988)—§§ 18.1(c) n.28, 30

Colombo, United States v., 777 F.2d 96 (2d Cir.1985)—§ 12.3(a) n.18

Colon v. Fogg, 603 F.2d 403 (2d Cir.1979)—§ 11.9(d) n.187

Colon, People v., 225 Ill. 2d 125, 310 Ill. Dec. 396, 866 N.E.2d 207 (2007)—§ 17.4(a) n.67

Colon v. Smith, 723 F.Supp. 1003 (S.D.N.Y.1989)—§ 11.2(d) n.131

Colon v. State, 113 Nev. 484, 938 P.2d 714 (1997)—§ 5.2(a) n.4

Colon, United States v., 250 F.3d 130 (2d Cir.2001)—§§ 3.3(e) n.186; 3.8(d) n.174

Colon, United States v., 220 F.3d 48 (2d Cir.2000)—§ 21.2(d) n.191

Colon, United States v., 905 F.2d 580 (2d Cir.1990)—§ 6.4(e) n.109

Colon-Cruz, Commonwealth v., 408 Mass. 533, 562 N.E.2d 797 (1990)—§ 7.4(b) n.35

Colonna, State v., 766 P.2d 1062 (Utah 1988)—§ 5.1(c) n.17

Colonnade Catering Corp. v. United States, 397 U.S. 72, 90 S.Ct. 774, 25 L.Ed.2d 60 (1970)—§ 3.9(c) n.34

Colon Torres, United States v., 382 F.3d 76 (1st Cir.2004)—§§ 11.7(e) n.104, 106

Colorado v. Bannister, 449 U.S. 1, 101 S.Ct. 42, 66 L.Ed.2d 1 (1980)—§ 3.7(b) n.30

Colorado v. Bertine, 479 U.S. 367, 107 S.Ct. 738, 93 L.Ed.2d 739 (1987)—§§ 3.1(d) n.116; 3.1(e) n.129; 3.5(e) n.196; 3.7(d) n.86; 3.7(e) n.96, 102, 103, 112, 115

Colorado v. Connelly, 479 U.S. 157, 107 S.Ct. 515, 93 L.Ed.2d 473 (1986)—§§ 1.5(b) n.69; 1.5(e) n.229; 2.4(e) n.149; 2.9(f) n.116, 118; 3.10(a) n.19; 3.10(b) n.48; 6.2(b) n.50; 6.2(c) n.116; 6.9(b) n.37; 10.4(b) n.13

Colorado v. Spring, 479 U.S. 564, 107 S.Ct. 851, 93 L.Ed.2d 954 (1987)—§§ 6.8(d) n.85; 6.9(b) n.40; 6.9(f) n.126

Colorado Supreme Court, United States v., 189 F.3d 1281 (10th Cir.1999)—§§ 1.7(j) n.257, 258, 260, 264; 8.8(d) n.113

Colorado Supreme Court, United States v., 87 F.3d 1161 (10th Cir.1996)—§§ 8.8(d) n.103; 15.6(b) n.77; 15.7(f) n.134

Colsch, State v., 284 N.W.2d 839 (Minn.1979)—§ 26.9(c) n.88

Colson v. Joyce, 646 F.Supp. 102 (D.Me.1986)—§ 11.1(b) n.60

Colson v. State, 498 A.2d 585 (Me.1985)—§ 11.1(b) n.60

Colson, State v., 262 N.C. 506, 138 S.E.2d 121 (1964)—§ 8.4(b) n.27

Colt, State v., 255 Mont. 399, 843 P.2d 747 (1992)—§ 11.5(c) n.46

Colten v. Kentucky, 407 U.S. 104, 92 S.Ct. 1953, 32 L.Ed.2d 584 (1972)—§§ 1.8(g) n.116; 26.8(c) n.16

Colton, State v., 234 Conn. 683, 663 A.2d 339 (1995)—§ 25.4(a) n.7

Colton, United States v., 231 F.3d 890 (4th Cir.2000)—§ 17.3(b) n.16

Columba-Colella, United States v., 604 F.2d 356 (5th Cir.1979)—§§ 16.4(b) n.19, 34

Columbia Broadcasting Systems, Inc. v. United States District Court, 729 F.2d 1174 (9th Cir.1984)—§ 23.1(c) n.106

Colvin v. Taylor, 324 F.3d 583 (8th Cir.2003)—§ 21.2(d) n.181

Colwell, State v., 994 P.2d 177 (Utah 2000)—§ 22.3(d) n.249

Colyer, United States v., 878 F.2d 469 (D.C.Cir.1989)—§ 3.2(b) n.72

Combs v. Commonwealth, 438 S.W.2d 82 (Ky.1969)—§§ 6.7(a) n.2; 6.7(c) n.106

Combs v. Coyle, 205 F.3d 269 (6th Cir.2000)—§§ 6.5(b) n.25; 9.6(a) n.48

Combs, State v., 945 S.W.2d 770 (Tenn.Cr.App.1996)—§ 26.1(d) n.86

Combs, State v., 398 N.W.2d 563 (Minn.1987)—§ 9.4(f) n.115

Combs, United States v., 369 F.3d 925 (6th Cir.2004)—§ 3.3(d) n.152

Combs, United States v., 672 F.2d 574 (6th Cir.1982)—§ 2.12(c) n.173

Combs, United States v., 634 F.2d 1295 (10th Cir.1980)—§§ 21.3(f) n.426; 25.1(d) n.66

Combs v. United States, 408 U.S. 224, 92 S.Ct. 2284, 33 L.Ed.2d 308 (1972)—§ 9.1(b) n.83

Combs v. Wingo, 465 F.2d 96 (6th Cir.1972)—§§ 6.7(a) n.2; 6.7(c) n.106

Comer v. Schriro, 480 F.3d 960 (9th Cir.2007)—§ 24.2(e) n.67

Comer v. Schriro, 463 F.3d 934 (9th Cir.2006)—§ 27.5(c) n.60

Comer, State v., 165 Ariz. 413, 799 P.2d 333 (1990)—§§ 17.1(a) n.14; 17.1(c) n.45

Comer, State v., 584 A.2d 638 (Me.1990)—§ 21.4(b) n.57

Comi, United States v., 336 F.2d 856 (4th Cir.1964)—§ 3.5(a) n.40

Commissioner of Northern Mariana Islands v. Mendiola, 976 F.2d 475 (9th Cir.1992)—§ 10.3(c) n.52

Commissioner of Revenue v. Mullins, 428 Mass. 406, 702 N.E.2d 1 (1998)—§§ 17.4(b) n.137, 138

Commissioners, Board of v. Backus, 29 How.Pr. 33 (N.Y.Sup.Ct.1864)—§ 5.1(b) n.5

Commonwealth—see opposing party

Comosona, United States v., 848 F.2d 1110 (10th Cir.1988)—§§ 6.9(f) n.135; 18.5(b) n.65

Comosona, United States v., 614 F.2d 695 (10th Cir.1980)—§§ 18.5(b) n.59, 60, 69

Comprehensive Drug Testing, Inc., United States v., 473 F.3d 915 (9th Cir.2006)—§ 3.4(k) n.219

Compton, State v., 333 Or. 274, 39 P.3d 833 (2002)—§ 22.3(c) n.112

Computer Sciences Corp., United States v., 689 F.2d 1181 (4th Cir.1982)—§ 15.7(h) n.240

Comstock, State v., 168 Wis.2d 915, 485 N.W.2d 354 (Wis.1992)—§§ 21.2(f) n.363; 21.3(e) n.265, 276; 21.3(f) n.426, 428, 429; 21.4(a) n.17; 25.1(d) n.55, 64

Conaway v. Polk, 453 F.3d 567 (4th Cir.2006)—§§ 22.3(c) n.102, 120

Concepcion, United States v., 983 F.2d 369 (2d Cir.1992)—§§ 7.4(c) n.54; 7.4(e) n.92

Concepcion, United States v., 942 F.2d 1170 (7th Cir.1991)—§ 3.2(c) n.114

Conde v. State, 860 So.2d 930 (Fla.2003)—§§ 6.2(c) n.90; 6.3(c) n.53

Condit, United States v., 621 F.2d 1096 (10th Cir.1980)—§ 28.9(b) n.30

Condo, United States v., 782 F.2d 1502 (9th Cir.1986)—§ 3.6(f) n.153

Condon, United States v., 170 F.3d 687 (7th Cir.1999)—§ 1.7(j) n.261

Conefrey, Commonwealth v., 410 Mass. 1, 570 N.E.2d 1384 (1991)—§§ 15.6(a) n.9; 15.7(h) n.224, 226, 231

Conerly v. State, 607 So.2d 1153 (Miss.1992)—§ 21.6(a) n.49

Conerly v. State, 544 So.2d 1370 (Miss.1989)—§ 22.3(d) n.213

Coney v. Municipality of Anchorage, 725 P.2d 709 (Alaska 1986)—§ 10.5(c) n.33

Coney, State v., 294 So.2d 82 (Fla.1973)—§§ 20.3(a) n.15, 16, 21

Coney, United States v., 390 F.Supp.2d
844 (D.Neb.2005)—§ 26.4(f) n.104

Coney, United States v., 407 F.3d 871
(7th Cir.2005)—§§ 4.6(k) n.172;
4.6(m) n.238

Confiscation Cases, In re, 74 U.S. (7
Wall.) 454, 19 L.Ed. 196 (1868)—
§§ 1.6(d) n.210; 13.3(c) n.36

Conforte, United States v., 624 F.2d 869
(9th Cir.1980)—§ 22.4(c) n.27

Congdon v. State, 262 Ga. 683, 424
S.E.2d 630 (1993)—§ 22.3(d) n.248

Congo v. State, 409 So.2d 475
(Ala.App.1982)—§ 1.8(d) n.49

Congregation B'Nai Jonah v. Kuriansky,
172 A.D.2d 35, 576 N.Y.S.2d 934
(1991)—§ 8.8(d) n.53

Conkey, Commonwealth v., 443 Mass.
60, 819 N.E.2d 176 (2004)—
§ 10.6(c) n.24

Conkey, Commonwealth v., 430 Mass.
139, 714 N.E.2d 343 (1999)—
§ 7.2(c) n.31

Conklin v. Schofield, 366 F.3d 1191
(11th Cir.2004)—§§ 11.2(e) n.195,
215

Conklin, State v., 115 N.H. 331, 341
A.2d 770 (1975)—§ 3.9(i) n.177

Conley v. Commonwealth, 229 Ky. 358,
17 S.W.2d 201 (1929)—§ 16.3(g)
n.118

Conley, State v., 574 N.W.2d 569
(N.D.1998)—§§ 6.6(b)   n.16;
6.10(e) n.73

Conley v. State, 270 Ark. 886, 607
S.W.2d 328 (1980)—§ 7.5(a) n.8

Conley v. United States, 415 F.3d 183
(1st Cir.2005)—§ 24.3(b) n.49

Conley, United States v., 186 F.3d 7 (1st
Cir.1999)—§ 8.5(e) n.190

Conley, United States v., 156 F.3d 78
(1st Cir.1998)—§ 6.9(f) n.137

Conley, United States v., 779 F.2d 970
(4th Cir.1985)—§ 6.6(b) n.14

Conn v. Gabbert, 526 U.S. 286, 119
S.Ct. 1292, 143 L.Ed.2d 399
(1999)—§§ 3.4(e) n.93; 8.14(a)
n.17

Conn v. State, 831 N.E.2d 828
(Ind.App.2005)—§ 18.4(c) n.67

Conn, State v., 234 Conn. 97, 662 A.2d
68 (1995)—§ 14.4(e) n.107

Conn, State v., 152 Vt. 99, 565 A.2d 246
(1989)—§ 22.1(h) n.134

Conn, State v., 137 Ariz. 148, 669 P.2d
581 (1983)—§ 26.5(a) n.9

Connally v. Georgia, 429 U.S. 245, 97
S.Ct. 546, 50 L.Ed.2d 444 (1977)—
§ 3.4(b) n.28

Connally, State v., 36 N.C.App. 43, 243
S.E.2d 788 (1978)—§ 7.4(c) n.46

Connecticut v. Barrett, 479 U.S. 523,
107 S.Ct. 828, 93 L.Ed.2d 920
(1987)—§§ 2.9(h) n.208; 6.9(e)
n.93; 6.9(g) n.193

Connecticut v. Johnson, 460 U.S. 73,
103 S.Ct. 969, 74 L.Ed.2d 823
(1983)—§ 22.1(a) n.18

Connecticut Board of Pardons v. Dums-
chat, 452 U.S. 458, 101 S.Ct. 2460,
69 L.Ed.2d 158 (1981)—§ 26.2(c)
n.73

Connell, United States v., 869 F.2d 1349
(9th Cir.1989)—§ 6.8(a) n.16

Connelly, State v., 551 N.W.2d 329
(Iowa App.1996)—§ 25.2(e) n.38

Connely, State v., 243 Neb. 319, 499
N.W.2d 65 (1993)—§§ 5.2(a) n.4,
15

Conner v. Auger, 595 F.2d 407 (8th
Cir.1979)—§ 19.2(c) n.32

Conner v. McBride, 375 F.3d 643 (7th
Cir.2004)—§ 11.10(c) n.127

Conner v. State, 67 S.W.3d 192
(Tex.Cr.App.2001)—§ 7.4(e) n.89

Conner v. State, 334 Ark. 457, 982
S.W.2d 655 (1998)—§§ 6.2(c)
n.114; 6.8(b) n.50

Conner, State v., 163 Ariz. 97, 786 P.2d
948 (1990)—§§ 21.2(d) n.242, 270

Conner, State v., 453 N.W.2d 617
(S.D.1990)—§ 14.4(c) n.47

Conner, State v., 295 A.2d 704
(Del.1972)—§§ 8.11(d) n.77, 79

Connery, State v., 441 N.W.2d 651
(N.D.1989)—§§ 6.6(a) n.7; 6.6(e)
n.89

Connery, State v., 100 Nev. 256, 679 P.2d 1266 (1984)—§ 25.2(d) n.34

Connolly, Commonwealth v., 478 Pa. 117, 385 A.2d 1342 (1978)— § 10.4(d) n.29

Connolly, People v., 322 Ill.App.3d 905, 256 Ill.Dec. 382, 751 N.E.2d 1219 (2001)—§ 24.6(b) n.35

Connolly, State v., 700 So.2d 810 (La.1997)—§ 16.3(b) n.22

Connor, Commonwealth v., 392 Mass. 838, 467 N.E.2d 1340 (1984)— §§ 15.7(f) n.139, 170

Connor, People v., 115 Cal.App.4th 669, 9 Cal.Rptr.3d 521 (Cal.App.2004)—§ 26.5(c) n.59

Connor, People v., 270 Cal.App.2d 630, 75 Cal.Rptr. 905 (1969)—§ 6.7(d) n.151

Connor v. State, 803 So.2d 598 (Fla.2001)—§ 27.5(e) n.178

Connor v. State, 29 Fla. 455, 10 So. 891 (1892)—§ 16.4(c) n.48

Connor, United States v., 926 F.2d 81 (1st Cir.1991)—§ 18.3(b) n.51

Conover, State v., 312 Md. 33, 537 A.2d 1167 (1988)—§ 6.7(c) n.133

Conrad, State v., 243 So.2d 174 (Fla.App.1971)—§ 17.4(c) n.149

Conrod v. Davis, 120 F.3d 92 (8th Cir.1997)—§ 3.5(b) n.103

Conroy, State v., 168 Ariz. 373, 814 P.2d 330 (1991)—§ 22.1(h) n.133

Consalvi, In re, 376 Mass. 699, 382 N.E.2d 734 (1978)—§ 3.1(j) n.254

Considine, Commonwealth v., 448 Mass. 295, 860 N.E.2d 673 (2007)—§ 3.9(k) n.253

Consolidated Edison Co. of New York v. Public Service Commission of New York, 447 U.S. 530, 100 S.Ct. 2326, 65 L.Ed.2d 319 (1980)— § 1.2(b) n.4

Constitutional Government v. National Archives, 656 F.2d 856 (D.C.Cir.1981)—§§ 8.5(c) n.73, 103

Consuelo-Gonzalez, United States v., 521 F.2d 259 (9th Cir.1975)— §§ 3.9(j) n.224; 26.9(b) n.26, 64

Consumer Credit Insurance Agency v. United States, 599 F.2d 770 (6th Cir.1979)—§ 8.7(e) n.94

Conte, People v., 421 Mich. 704, 365 N.W.2d 648 (1984)—§§ 6.2(c) n.92, 106

Conte, United States v., 99 F.3d 60 (2d Cir.1996)—§§ 24.5(a) n.7; 26.10(c) n.61

Contee v. United States, 667 A.2d 103 (D.C.App.1995)—§ 6.2(c) n.133

Continental Bank and Trust Co., United States v., 503 F.2d 45 (10th Cir.1974)—§ 8.7(b) n.60

Continental T.V., Inc. v. GTE Sylvania, Inc., 433 U.S. 36, 97 S.Ct. 2549, 53 L.Ed.2d 568 (1977)—§ 2.9(g) n.165

Contos, Commonwealth v., 435 Mass. 19, 754 N.E.2d 647 (2001)— § 6.9(g) n.166

Contreras v. Schiltgen, 122 F.3d 30 (9th Cir.1997)—§ 28.3(a) n.38

Contreras v. State, 838 S.W.2d 594 (Tex.App.1992)—§ 19.3(a) n.63

Contreras, United States v., 108 F.3d 1255 (10th Cir.1997)—§ 13.7(c) n.45

Contreras, United States v., 755 F.2d 733 (9th Cir.1985)—§ 8.11(c) n.39

Contreras, United States v., 776 F.2d 51 (2d Cir.1985)—§ 12.3(a) n.24

Conway, State v., 108 Ohio St.3d 214, 842 N.E.2d 996 (2006)—§ 6.4(e) n.96

Conwell, State v., 141 Wash.2d 901, 10 P.3d 1056 (2000)—§ 21.4(g) n.233

Conyers v. State, 367 Md. 571, 790 A.2d 15 (2002)—§ 24.3(b) n.49

Conyers v. State, 345 Md. 525, 693 A.2d 781 (1997)—§ 17.1(d) n.53

Coogan, State v., 154 Wis.2d 387, 453 N.W.2d 186 (Wis.App.1990)— § 24.11(d) n.21

Cook v. Commonwealth, 826 S.W.2d 329 (Ky.1992)—§§ 3.10(c) n.94; 10.4(c) n.20, 23

Cook v. Morrill, 783 F.2d 593 (5th Cir.1986)—§§ 2.6(b) n.69; 22.2(e) n.110

Cook, State v., 179 N.J. 533, 847 A.2d 530 (2004)—§ 6.8(c) n.65

Cook, State v., 262 Conn. 825, 817 A.2d 670 (2003)—§§ 7.4(c) n.50; 7.4(g) n.118

Cook, State v., 330 N.J.Super. 395, 750 A.2d 91 (2000)—§ 18.4(c) n.60

Cook v. State, 858 S.W.2d 467 (Tex.Cr.App.1993)—§ 22.3(d) n.212

Cook v. State, 37 Ark.App. 27, 823 S.W.2d 916 (1992)—§ 25.4(c) n.40

Cook v. State, 824 S.W.2d 634 (Tex.Cr.App.1991)—§ 26.3(f) n.55

Cook v. State, 710 P.2d 824 (Wyo.1985)—§ 26.1(d) n.75

Cook, State v., 11 Ohio App.3d 237, 464 N.E.2d 577 (1983)—§ 8.10(d) n.106

Cook v. State, 141 Ga.App. 241, 233 S.E.2d 60 (1977)—§ 10.6(d) n.42

Cook, State v., 242 Or. 509, 411 P.2d 78 (1966)—§ 3.10(e) n.175

Cook, United States v., 406 F.3d 485 (7th Cir.2005)—§ 21.2(d) n.157

Cook, United States v., 277 F.3d 82 (1st Cir.2002)—§ 3.8(d) n.175

Cook, United States v., 45 F.3d 388 (10th Cir.1995)—§§ 11.9(b) n.79, 83; 11.10(c) n.101, 117

Cook, United States v., 997 F.2d 1312 (10th Cir.1993)—§ 28.9(b) n.33

Cook, United States v., 880 F.2d 1158 (10th Cir.1989)—§ 12.3(a) n.26

Cook, United States v., 668 F.2d 317 (7th Cir.1982)—§ 21.2(d) n.183

Cook, United States v., 442 F.2d 723 (D.C.Cir.1970)—§ 12.2(b) n.29

Cook, United States v., 17 Wall. 168, 84 U.S. 168, 21 L.Ed. 538 (1872)—§ 19.3(a) n.16

Cooks, People v., 446 Mich. 503, 521 N.W.2d 275 (1994)—§ 24.10(c) n.41

Cooks v. State, 50 Ala.App. 49, 276 So.2d 634 (1973)—§§ 20.3(j) n.181; 20.3(k) n.217

Cooksey v. State, 524 P.2d 1251 (Alaska 1974)—§ 18.1(d) n.49

Cookson, People v., 54 Cal.3d 1091, 2 Cal.Rptr.2d 176, 820 P.2d 278 (1991)—§§ 26.1(f) n.144; 26.9(b) n.33

Cooley v. Commonwealth, 821 S.W.2d 90 (Ky.1991)—§ 25.5(c) n.36

Cooley, State v., 217 Neb. 90, 348 N.W.2d 433 (1984)—§ 26.3(g) n.78

Cooley, United States v., 1 F.3d 985 (10th Cir.1993)—§§ 22.4(c) n.25, 28

Cooley v. United States, 501 F.2d 1249 (9th Cir.1974)—§§ 11.3(b) n.35, 38

Coolidge v. New Hampshire, 403 U.S. 443, 91 S.Ct. 2022, 29 L.Ed.2d 564 (1971)—§§ 3.1(b) n.26; 3.1(h) n.189; 3.2(b) n.31; 3.4(b) n.25; 3.4(k) n.218; 3.6(a) n.1, 20; 3.6(g) n.156; 3.7(b) n.28; 3.7(d) n.61; 3.7(f) n.129, 132; 4.8(e) n.52; 10.3(b) n.15, 47

Coolidge, United States v., 14 U.S. (1 Wheat) 415, 4 L.Ed. 124 (1816)—§ 1.2(c) n.35

Coombs, United States v., 37 U.S. (12 Pet.) 72, 9 L.Ed. 1004 (1838)—§ 1.2(c) n.86

Coombs, United States v., 37 U.S. (12 Pet. 72, 9 L.Ed. 1004 (1838)—§ 1.2(c) n.88

Coon v. Weber, 644 N.W.2d 638 (S.D.2002)—§ 6.2(c) n.172

Coonan, United States v., 839 F.2d 886 (2d Cir.1988)—§ 24.10(a) n.16

Cooney, United States v., 217 F.Supp. 417 (D.Colo.1963)—§ 19.4(b) n.29

Cooper v. California, 386 U.S. 58, 87 S.Ct. 788, 17 L.Ed.2d 730 (1967)—§§ 2.12(a) n.23; 3.7(e) n.92

Cooper, Commonwealth v., 899 S.W.2d 75 (Ky.1995)—§ 6.2(c) n.186

Cooper v. District Court, 133 P.3d 692 (Alaska App.2006)—§§ 1.5(k) n.356; 26.7(b) n.21; 27.4(e) n.62

Cooper v. Fitzharris, 586 F.2d 1325 (9th Cir.1978)—§ 11.10(a) n.12

Cooper v. Griffin, 455 F.2d 1142 (5th Cir.1972)—§§ 6.9(b) n.26, 33

Cooper v. Oklahoma, 517 U.S. 348, 116 S.Ct. 1373, 134 L.Ed.2d 498 (1996)—§§ 2.7(a) n.40; 2.7(c) n.147, 156, 164, 195, 213

Cooper, People v., 156 Misc.2d 483, 593 N.Y.S.2d 733 (Co.Ct.1992)—§ 11.9(d) n.211

Cooper, People v., 398 Mich. 450, 247 N.W.2d 866 (1976)—§ 25.5(b) n.22

Cooper, People v., 53 Cal.2d 755, 3 Cal.Rptr. 148, 349 P.2d 964 (1960)—§ 20.2(a) n.5

Cooper v. State, 281 Ga. 760, 642 S.E.2d 817 (2007)—§ 7.4(e) n.88

Cooper, State v., 281 Ga. 63, 636 S.E.2d 493 (2006)—§ 21.4(f) n.204

Cooper v. State, 277 Ga. 282, 587 S.E.2d 605 (2003)—§ 3.10(b) n.29

Cooper, State v., 124 N.M. 277, 949 P.2d 660 (1997)—§§ 6.2(c) n.178; 6.6(f) n.100

Cooper, State v., 151 N.J. 326, 700 A.2d 306 (1997)—§ 6.2(c) n.100

Cooper v. State, 565 N.W.2d 27 (Minn.App.1997)—§ 11.9(b) n.78

Cooper v. State, 492 So.2d 1059 (Fla.1986)—§ 3.10(e) n.143

Cooper, State v., 167 W.Va. 322, 280 S.E.2d 95 (1981)—§§ 26.10(a) n.4; 26.10(d) n.94

Cooper, State v., 304 N.C. 180, 282 S.E.2d 436 (1981)—§§ 26.9(b) n.24; 26.9(c) n.89

Cooper, State v., 217 N.W.2d 589 (Iowa 1974)—§§ 6.2(c) n.122; 6.9(c) n.54, 56

Cooper, State v., 223 N.W.2d 177 (Iowa 1974)—§ 19.5(b) n.7

Cooper, United States v., 283 F.Supp.2d 1215 (D.Kan.2003)—§ 24.4(d) n.52

Cooper, United States v., 135 F.3d 960 (5th Cir.1998)—§ 13.5(h) n.197

Cooper, United States v., 121 F.3d 130 (3d Cir.1997)—§ 25.4(c) n.28

Cooper, United States v., 70 F.3d 563 (10th Cir.1995)—§ 21.2(e) n.321

Cooper, United States v., 983 F.2d 928 (9th Cir.1993)—§ 24.3(e) n.132

Cooper, United States v., 956 F.2d 960 (10th Cir.1992)—§ 21.6(a) n.33

Cooper, United States v., 942 F.2d 1200 (7th Cir.1991)—§ 17.2(e) n.117

Cooper, United States v., 949 F.2d 737 (5th Cir.1991)—§ 3.7(d) n.69

Cooper, United States v., 800 F.2d 412 (4th Cir.1986)—§§ 6.6(b) n.14; 6.6(e) n.81

Cooper v. United States, 594 F.2d 12 (4th Cir.1979)—§§ 21.2(f) n.371; 21.3(a) n.22; 21.3(c) n.148

Cooper v. United States, 91 F.2d 195 (5th Cir.1937)—§ 26.1(d) n.88

Cooper, United States v., 4 U.S. (4 Dall.) 341, 1 L.Ed. 859 (1800)—§ 2.8(b) n.33

Cooper Industries, Inc. v. Leatherman Tool Group, Inc., 532 U.S. 424, 121 S.Ct. 1678, 149 L.Ed.2d 674 (2001)—§§ 2.6(b) n.41; 27.5(e) n.174

Coopers & Lybrand v. Livesay, 437 U.S. 463, 98 S.Ct. 2454, 57 L.Ed.2d 351 (1978)—§ 27.2(c) n.23

Copas v. Commissioner of Correction, 234 Conn. 139, 662 A.2d 718 (1995)—§ 11.10(d) n.176

Cope, State v., 142 Idaho 492, 129 P.3d 1241 (2006)—§ 21.2(b) n.79

Cope, United States v., 312 F.3d 757 (6th Cir.2002)—§§ 6.4(e) n.91; 6.4(g) n.156

Copeland, State v., 530 So.2d 526 (La.1998)—§ 22.3(c) n.157

Copeland, State v., 928 S.W.2d 828 (Mo.1996)—§ 22.5(b) n.19

Copeland, State v., 765 P.2d 1266 (Utah 1988)—§ 21.2(b) n.48

Copeland, State v., 205 Conn. 201, 530 A.2d 603 (1987)—§ 6.7(c) n.106

Copeland, United States v., 381 F.3d 1101 (11th Cir.2004)—§§ 21.2(b) n.82; 21.2(d) n.150

Copicotto, People v., 50 N.Y.2d 222, 428 N.Y.S.2d 649, 406 N.E.2d 465 (1980)—§§ 20.4(g) n.103, 109

Copley, United States v., 774 F.2d 728 (6th Cir.1985)—§ 18.3(b) n.5

Copley Press Inc. v. San Diego County Superior Court, 228 Cal.App.3d 77, 278 Cal.Rptr. 443 (1991)— § 23.1(d) n.193

Coppa, United States v., 267 F.3d 132 (2d Cir.2001)—§§ 20.3(m) n.254, 255; 24.3(b) n.63, 64

Coppedge v. United States, 311 F.2d 128 (D.C.Cir.1962)—§§ 15.5(b) n.37, 46; 15.7(e) n.92, 124

Coppedge v. United States, 369 U.S. 438, 82 S.Ct. 917, 8 L.Ed.2d 21 (1962)—§§ 1.5(h) n.285; 2.5(f) n.73; 11.2(d) n.135

Coppersmith, United States v., 4 Fed.Cas. 198 (C.C.W.D.Tenn.1880)—§ 1.7(h) n.141

Coppola v. Powell, 878 F.2d 1562 (1st Cir.1989)—§ 9.6(a) n.48

Copson, Commonwealth v., 444 Mass. 609, 830 N.E.2d 193 (2005)— § 18.4(c) n.52

Corallo, United States v., 413 F.2d 1306 (2d Cir.1969)—§ 8.14(a) n.6

Corbett, People v., 190 Colo. 388, 547 P.2d 1264 (1976)—§ 9.4(a) n.15

Corbett, State v., 281 Kan. 294, 130 P.3d 1179 (2006)—§ 24.7(e) n.62

Corbett, United States v., 742 F.2d 173 (5th Cir.1984)—§ 21.4(c) n.66

Corbin v. Broadman, 6 Ariz.App. 436, 433 P.2d 289 (1967)—§ 15.6(a) n.13

Corbin, United States v., 734 F.2d 643 (11th Cir.1984)—§ 18.5(b) n.65

Corbin, State ex rel. v. Superior Court, 155 Ariz. 560, 748 P.2d 1184 (1987)—§ 22.4(c) n.28

Corbitt v. New Jersey, 439 U.S. 212, 99 S.Ct. 492, 58 L.Ed.2d 466 (1978)— §§ 2.6(d) n.99; 21.2(a) n.12; 21.2(b) n.94

Corbitt, United States v., 879 F.2d 224 (7th Cir.1989)—§§ 23.1(d) n.171, 184, 185, 205, 207, 208; 26.5(c) n.59

Cor-Bon Custom Bullet Co., United States v., 287 F.3d 576 (6th Cir.2002)—§§ 19.3(a) n.102, 103; 19.6(c) n.49

Corcoran v. Buss, 483 F.Supp.2d 709 (N.D. Ind. 2007)—§ 22.1(h) n.144

Corcoran v. State, 739 N.E.2d 649 (Ind.2000)—§ 21.2(b) n.42

Cordell, United States v., 924 F.2d 614 (6th Cir.1991)—§ 11.8(c) n.61

Cordell v. Weber, 673 N.W.2d 49 (S.D.2003)—§ 3.5(c) n.122

Cordero, United States v., 668 F.2d 32 (1st Cir.1981)—§§ 16.1(h) n.299, 301

Cordoba v. Hanrahan, 910 F.2d 691 (10th Cir.1990)—§ 6.6(e) n.91

Cordoba-Mosquera, United States v., 212 F.3d 1194 (11th Cir.2000)— § 22.3(d) n.249

Cordoba-Murgas, United States v., 422 F.3d 65 (2d Cir.2005)—§ 19.3(a) n.91

Cordova v. Baca, 346 F.3d 924 (9th Cir.2003)—§ 11.5(a) n.11

Cordova v. People, 880 P.2d 1216 (Colo.1994)—§ 24.8(a) n.10

Cordova v. State, 33 P.3d 142 (Wyo.2001)—§ 3.3(g) n.233

Cordova, State v., 109 N.M. 211, 784 P.2d 30 (1989)—§ 3.3(c) n.96

Cordova, United States v., 157 F.3d 587 (8th Cir.1998)—§ 18.3(b) n.36

Cordova, United States v., 990 F.2d 1035 (8th Cir.1993)—§ 6.7(d) n.153

Cordova, United States v., 89 F.Supp. 298 (E.D.N.Y.1950)—§ 16.4(b) n.7

Cordova-Perez, United States v., 65 F.3d 1552 (9th Cir.1995)—§§ 21.2(e) n.326; 21.4(g) n.250

Cores, United States v., 356 U.S. 405, 78 S.Ct. 875, 2 L.Ed.2d 873 (1958)—§§ 16.2(b) n.24; 16.2(c) n.48

Corey, Commonwealth v., 826 S.W.2d 319 (Ky.1992)—§ 21.3(d) n.262

Corfield v. Coryell, 6 F.Cas. 546 (No 3230) (C.C.E.D.Pa.1823)—§§ 2.3(a) n.17, 19, 21, 41

Cork v. State, 433 So.2d 959 (Ala.App.1983)—§ 22.3(e) n.272

Corley, Commonwealth v., 507 Pa. 540, 491 A.2d 829 (1985)—§ 3.1(h) n.206

Corley, State v., 617 So.2d 1292 (La.App.1993)—§ 15.4(g) n.168

Corley v. State, 585 So.2d 765 (Miss.1991)—§ 21.4(f) n.181

Cornelius, State v., 293 N.W.2d 267 (Iowa 1980)—§ 16.3(b) n.26

Cornell, People v., 466 Mich. 335, 646 N.W.2d 127 (2002)—§ 24.8(e) n.50

Cornell, State v., 179 Ariz. 314, 878 P.2d 1352 (1994)—§§ 11.5(c) n.62, 63; 11.5(g) n.110

Cornett, People v., 685 P.2d 224 (Colo.App.1984)—§§ 24.9(f) n.78; 24.9(g) n.120

Corngold v. United States, 367 F.2d 1 (9th Cir.1966)—§ 3.1(h) n.190

Cornwell, United States v., 625 F.2d 686 (5th Cir.1980)—§ 26.9(a) n.13

Corona, People v., 80 Cal.App.3d 684, 145 Cal.Rptr. 894 (1978)—§ 11.9(d) n.234

Corona, United States v., 108 F.3d 565 (5th Cir.1997)—§ 19.2(b) n.9

Corona, United States v., 34 F.3d 876 (9th Cir.1994)—§§ 16.2(g) n.117, 139, 142

Corona Construction Co. v. Ampress Brick Co., 376 F.Supp. 598 (N.D.Ill.1974)—§ 8.5(h) n.273

Coronado, United States v., 554 F.2d 166 (5th Cir.1977)—§§ 21.4(c) n.78; 21.5(c) n.82, 83; 21.5(d) n.100

Corporacion Insular de Seguros v. Garcia, 876 F.2d 254 (1st Cir.1989)—§ 27.2(e) n.82

Corporan-Cuevas, United States v., 244 F.3d 199 (1st Cir.2001)—§ 19.3(a) n.102

Corporan-Cuevas, United States v., 35 F.3d 953 (4th Cir.1994)—§§ 11.4(c) n.74, 76

Corr, People v., 682 P.2d 20 (Colo.1984)—§§ 2.12(c) n.168; 8.8(g) n.166

Corrado, State v., 81 Wash.App.640, 915 P.2d 1121 (1996)—§ 25.1(d) n.86

Corrado, United States v., 227 F.3d 528 (6th Cir.2000)—§ 24.9(f) n.86

Corral-Corral, United States v., 899 F.2d 927 (10th Cir.1990)—§ 10.3(b) n.13

Corral-Franco, United States v., 848 F.2d 536 (5th Cir.1988)—§ 3.5(a) n.7

Correa, People v., 108 Ill.2d 541, 92 Ill.Dec. 496, 485 N.E.2d 307 (1985)—§ 21.2(g) n.399

Correa, State v., 241 Conn. 322, 696 A.2d 944 (1997)—§ 24.10(c) n.40

Correale v. United States, 479 F.2d 944 (1st Cir.1973)—§ 21.2(e) n.349

Correa-Ventura, United States v., 6 F.3d 1070 (5th Cir.1993)—§ 24.10(c) n.41

Correctional Services Corp. v. Malesko, 534 U.S. 61, 122 S.Ct. 515, 151 L.Ed.2d 456 (2001)—§ 3.1(k) n.278

Correll, State v., 626 S.W.2d 699 (Tenn.1982)—§§ 26.1(d) n.73, 80

Correll v. Thompson, 63 F.3d 1279 (4th Cir.1995)—§ 27.6(d) n.94

Corrugated Container Antitrust, In re, 687 F.2d 52 (5th Cir.1982)—§ 8.5(h) n.271

Corrugated Container Antitrust Litigation, In re, 1981 WL 2136 (S.D.Tex.1981)—§ 8.5(h) n.269

Corsi, State v., 86 N.J. 172, 430 A.2d 210 (1981)—§ 17.2(b) n.75

Cort v. Ash, 422 U.S. 66, 95 S.Ct. 2080, 45 L.Ed.2d 26 (1975)—§ 8.5(i) n.304

Cortes, People v., 181 Ill.2d 249, 229 Ill.Dec. 918, 692 N.E.2d 1129 (1998)—§ 22.3(a) n.43

Cortes, United States v., 922 F.2d 123 (2d Cir.1990)—§§ 6.4(e) n.109; 6.10(c) n.48; 26.5(a) n.11

Cortes, United States v., 588 F.2d 106 (5th Cir.1979)—§ 3.9(g) n.141

Cortez, United States v., 973 F.2d 764 (9th Cir.1992)—§§ 21.6(a) n.59, 64, 78

Cortez, United States v., 935 F.2d 135 (8th Cir.1991)—§ 3.10(b) n.66

Cortez, United States v., 449 U.S. 411, 101 S.Ct. 690, 66 L.Ed.2d 621 (1981)—§§ 3.8(d) n.121, 146

Corthran v. State, 268 Ga. 443, 491 S.E.2d 66 (1997)—§ 21.2(h) n.415

Cortis, State v., 237 Neb. 97, 465 N.W.2d 132 (1991)—§§ 9.1(b) n.69; 9.2(a) n.4

Corum, State v., 663 N.W.2d 151 (N.D.2003)—§ 3.3(c) n.94

Cory, People v., 157 Cal.App.3d 1094, 204 Cal.Rptr. 117 (1984)—§ 24.7(c) n.24

Cory, People v., 26 Cal.App. 735, 148 P. 532 (1915)—§ 16.2(g) n.124

Cory, State v., 204 Or. 235, 282 P.2d 1054 (1955)—§ 13.7(a) n.25

Coryell, State ex rel. v. Gooden, 193 W.Va. 461, 457 S.E.2d 138 (1995)—§ 27.4(f) n.66

Cosby v. Sigler, 435 F.3d 702 (7th Cir.2006)—§ 6.9(f) n.102

Cosentino v. Kelly, 102 F.3d 71 (2d Cir.1996)—§ 24.1(b) n.31

Cosgrove, Commonwealth v., 427 Pa.Super. 553, 629 A.2d 1007 (1993)—§ 17.4(a) n.66

Cosgrove, State v., 186 Conn. 476, 442 A.2d 1320 (1982)—§ 15.2(j) n.240

Coslet, People v., 67 Ill.2d 127, 7 Ill.Dec. 80, 364 N.E.2d 67 (1977)—§ 11.9(d) n.194

Cosner v. See, 129 W.Va. 722, 42 S.E.2d 31 (1947)—§§ 16.3(d) n.56, 59

Coson v. United States, 533 F.2d 1119 (9th Cir.1976)—§ 8.8(a) n.5

Cossel v. Miller, 229 F.3d 649 (7th Cir.2000)—§§ 7.4(c) n.55; 7.4(d) n.74; 7.4(e) n.86

Costa, Commonwealth v., 414 Mass. 618, 609 N.E.2d 465 (1993)—§ 6.9(g) n.149

Costello, State v., 646 N.W.2d 204 (Minn.2002)—§§ 24.9(b) n.12; 27.6(d) n.142

Costello, United States v., 221 F.2d 668 (2d Cir.1955)—§ 15.5(a) n.3

Costello, United States v., 255 F.2d 876 (2d Cir.1958)—§§ 22.3(b) n.74, 82

Costello v. United States, 350 U.S. 359, 76 S.Ct. 406, 100 L.Ed. 397 (1956)—§§ 2.9(d) n.68; 3.1(f) n.143; 15.1(d) n.173; 15.4(g) n.184; 15.5(a) n.1; 15.7(d) n.69; 19.2(f) n.102

Costilla v. State, 146 S.W.3d 213 (Tex.Crim.App.2004)—§ 21.4(a) n.9

Costner v. State, 318 Ark. 806, 887 S.W.2d 533 (1994)—§ 3.4(e) n.67

Cota, United States v., 953 F.2d 753 (2d Cir.1992)—§§ 6.6(d) n.50, 58

Cota-Guerrero, United States v., 907 F.2d 87 (9th Cir.1990)—§ 26.5(a) n.21

Cote, Commonwealth v., 407 Mass. 827, 556 N.E.2d 45 (1990)—§§ 8.8(f) n.145, 147, 150; 8.8(g) n.166

Cote, Commonwealth v., 15 Mass.App.Ct. 229, 444 N.E.2d 1282 (1983)—§§ 3.1(h) n.212; 24.6(b) n.22

Cote, State v., 539 A.2d 628 (Me.1988)—§ 26.9(b) n.19

Cothran, United States v., 302 F.3d 279 (5th Cir.2002)—§§ 19.3(e) n.240; 21.3(b) n.84; 21.5(d) n.102

Cothran, United States v., 855 F.2d 749 (11th Cir.1988)—§ 26.9(b) n.76

Cothren, Ex parte, 705 So.2d 861 (Ala.1997)—§§ 6.9(f) n.133; 6.9(g) n.185

Cotnam, United States v., 88 F.3d 487 (7th Cir.1996)—§ 24.5(b) n.24

Cottle v. State, 733 So.2d 963 (Fla.1999)—§§ 11.10(d) n.177, 178; 21.3(b) n.48, 107

Cotton v. State, 386 Md. 249, 872 A.2d 87 (2005)—§ 3.8(b) n.33

Cotton, United States v., 535 U.S. 625, 122 S.Ct. 1781, 152 L.Ed.2d 860 (2002)—§§ 19.1(e) n.70; 19.2(e) n.78, 83; 19.3(a) n.13, 26, 82, 109, 115; 19.3(e) n.223, 227; 19.5(d) n.86; 19.6(c) n.43; 21.6(a) n.26; 26.4(i) n.176; 27.5(c) n.104; 27.5(d) n.135; 27.6(d) n.113

Cotton, United States v., 261 F.3d 397 (4th Cir.2001)—§§ 19.3(a) n.115; 19.3(e) n.227

Couch v. United States, 409 U.S. 322, 93 S.Ct. 611, 34 L.Ed.2d 548 (1973)—§§ 2.10(c) n.98; 2.10(d) n.116; 3.2(i) n.224; 8.12(e) n.48

Couchman v. State, 3 S.W.3d 155 (Tex.App.1999)—§ 16.1(g) n.283

Coughlan, United States v., 842 F.2d 737 (4th Cir.1988)—§ 8.5(i) n.310

Coughlan v. United States, 391 F.2d 371 (9th Cir.1968)—§ 6.4(f) n.112

Coughlen v. Coots, 5 F.3d 970 (6th Cir.1993)—§ 13.5(a) n.26

Coughlin, United States v., 338 F.Supp. 1328 (E.D.Mich.1972)—§ 3.5(c) n.131

Coulter, State v., 67 S.W.3d 3 (Tenn.Crim.App.2001)—§ 3.6(e) n.139

Coulter v. State, 304 Ark. 527, 804 S.W.2d 348 (Ark.1991)—§§ 11.8(c) n.65, 66

Coulter v. State, 75 Miss. 356, 22 So. 872 (1897)—§ 15.1(d) n.219

Councilman, United States v., 418 F.3d 67 (1st Cir.2005)—§ 4.6(b) n.26

Counsel v. Medley, 104 Ohio St.3d 251, 819 N.E.2d 273 (2004)—§ 21.3(d) n.262

Counselman v. Hitchcock, 142 U.S. 547, 12 S.Ct. 195, 35 L.Ed. 1110 (1892)—§§ 2.8(b) n.35; 2.9(h) n.258; 2.10(b) n.3, 23; 2.12(e) n.207; 8.10(a) n.1, 5; 8.11(a) n.6; 9.5(a) n.11

Countryman, State v., 572 N.W.2d 553 (Iowa 1997)—§§ 6.2(c) n.172, 178; 6.6(d) n.58

County Commissioners, Board of v. Brown, 520 U.S. 397, 117 S.Ct. 1382, 137 L.Ed.2d 626 (1997)—§ 3.1(k) n.269

Coursey v. State, 281 Ga. App. 494, 636 S.E.2d 669 (2006)—§ 22.1(h) n.138

Courtney, People v., 288 Ill.App.3d 1025, 227 Ill.Dec. 271, 687 N.E.2d 521 (1997)—§ 22.5(d) n.37

Courtney, United States v., 463 F.3d 333 (5th Cir.2006)—§§ 6.6(e) n.68, 69; 6.8(b) n.49

Courtney v. United States, 486 F.2d 1108 (9th Cir.1973)—§ 17.2(b) n.55

Courtney, United States v., 236 F.2d 921 (2d Cir.1956)—§ 8.10(e) n.120

Courtois, United States v., 131 F.3d 937 (10th Cir.1997)—§§ 21.2(d) n.257, 258

Cousart v. United States, 618 A.2d 96 (D.C.1992)—§ 3.8(e) n.205

Cousin, Commonwealth v., 449 Mass. 809, 873 N.E.2d 742 (2007)—§§ 22.3(b) n.81, 88

Cousin, Commonwealth v., 585 Pa. 287, 888 A.2d 710 (2005)—§§ 11.6(b) n.77; 11.6(d) n.117

Coutchavlis, United States v., 260 F.3d 1149 (9th Cir.2001)—§ 6.6(d) n.50

Couto, United States v., 311 F.3d 179 (2d Cir.2002)—§§ 11.10(b) n.39; 21.3(b) n.69; 21.4(d) n.135

Couture, State v., 146 Vt. 268, 502 A.2d 846 (1985)—§ 19.3(c) n.195

Couture, State v., 194 Conn. 530, 482 A.2d 300 (1984)—§§ 15.7(f) n.181; 24.7(i) n.91

Covarrubias, State v., 244 Neb. 366, 507 N.W.2d 248 (1993)—§ 22.3(d) n.220

Covelli v. Commissioner of Revenue Services, 239 Conn. 257, 683 A.2d 737 (1996)—§ 17.4(b) n.138

Coveney, United States v., 995 F.2d 578 (5th Cir.1993)—§ 24.4(c) n.24

Coverstone v. Davies, 38 Cal.2d 315, 239 P.2d 876 (1952)—§ 3.5(a) n.37

Covey v. United States, 377 F.3d 903 (8th Cir.2004)—§§ 11.9(d) n.173, 214

Covian-Sandoval, United States v., 462 F.3d 1090 (9th Cir.2006)—§ 21.4(f) n.174

Covington v. Lord, 275 F.Supp.2d 352 (E.D.N.Y.2003)—§ 24.1(b) n.18

Covington v. United States, 698 A.2d 1033 (D.C.App.1997)—§ 12.3(g) n.148

Covington, United States v., 758 F.2d 383 (9th Cir.1985)—§§ 6.9(f) n.141, 142

Covington, United States v., 783 F.2d 1052 (9th Cir.1985)—§§ 6.10(d) n.60, 62

Cowan, State v., 763 So.2d 583 (La.2000)—§ 3.7(c) n.48

Cowan v. Superior Court, 14 Cal.4th 367, 58 Cal.Rptr.2d 458, 926 P.2d 438 (1996)—§§ 18.5(a) n.52; 24.8(f) n.106, 107

Cowan, United States v., 524 F.2d 504 (5th Cir.1975)—§§ 13.3(c) n.43, 44; 21.3(e) n.277

Cowards v. State, 266 Ga. 191, 465 S.E.2d 677 (1996)—§ 12.1(e) n.63

Cowell v. Leapley, 458 N.W.2d 514 (S.D.1990)—§ 28.11(b) n.20

Cowels, Commonwealth v., 425 Mass. 279, 680 N.E.2d 924 (1997)—§ 17.2(c) n.92

Cowles v. State, 23 P.3d 1168 (Alaska 2001)—§ 3.2(e) n.161

Cowles Publishing Co. v. Magistrate Court of First Judicial District, 118 Idaho 753, 800 P.2d 640 (1990)—§§ 1.7(h) n.127; 23.1(d) n.132

Cowley, State v., 408 N.W.2d 758 (S.D.1987)—§ 10.2(d) n.49

Cowley v. Stricklin, 929 F.2d 640 (11th Cir.1991)—§§ 11.2(e) n.158, 161

Cox, Matter of, 553 A.2d 1255 (Me.1989)—§§ 21.3(d) n.219, 233, 236

Cox v. Ballard, 259 Ga. 176, 377 S.E.2d 842 (1989)—§ 28.11(b) n.18

Cox v. Louisiana, 379 U.S. 559, 85 S.Ct. 476, 13 L.Ed.2d 487 (1965)—§ 23.1(a) n.7

Cox v. McBride, 279 F.3d 492 (7th Cir.2002)—§ 28.5(b) n.53

Cox, People v., 53 Cal.3d 618, 280 Cal.Rptr. 692, 809 P.2d 351 (1991)—§ 24.9(g) n.115

Cox v. State, 152 P.3d 244 (Okla.Crim.App.2006)—§§ 18.5(a) n.48; 21.4(f) n.192

Cox v. State, 585 So.2d 182 (Ala.App.1991)—§ 25.2(d) n.26

Cox, State v., 147 Vt. 421, 519 A.2d 1144 (1986)—§ 6.2(c) n.154

Cox v. State, 608 S.W.2d 219 (Tex.Crim.App.1980)—§§ 19.1(d) n.68; 19.3(d) n.204

Cox, United States v., 985 F.2d 427 (8th Cir.1993)—§ 21.2(e) n.303

Cox, United States v., 923 F.2d 519 (7th Cir.1991)—§ 21.4(f) n.214

Cox, United States v., 342 F.2d 167 (5th Cir.1965)—§§ 8.1(a) n.1; 13.3(a) n.9; 13.3(d) n.48; 15.1(a) n.10; 15.1(d) n.169, 174; 15.2(g) n.174

Cox v. Wyrick, 873 F.2d 200 (8th Cir.1989)—§ 20.6(c) n.74

Cox Arizona Publications v. Collins, 175 Ariz. 11, 852 P.2d 1194 (Ariz.1993)—§§ 23.1(b) n.21, 30

Cox Broadcasting Corp. v. Cohn, 420 U.S. 469, 95 S.Ct. 1029, 43 L.Ed.2d 328 (1975)—§§ 1.5(k) n.395; 23.1(c) n.99

Coy v. Iowa, 487 U.S. 1012, 108 S.Ct. 2798, 101 L.Ed.2d 857 (1988)—§§ 2.6(d) n.98; 24.2(e) n.72; 27.6(d) n.83; 27.6(e) n.156

Coyle v. Smith, 221 U.S. 559, 31 S.Ct. 688, 55 L.Ed. 853 (1911)—§ 1.2(b) n.8

Coyle, State v., 119 N.J. 194, 574 A.2d 951 (1990)—§ 3.10(e) n.158

Cozza, State v., 71 Wash.App. 252, 858 P.2d 270 (1993)—§ 19.3(b) n.163

Cozzaglio v. State, 289 Ark. 33, 709 S.W.2d 70 (1986)—§§ 16.1(d) n.132; 17.4(c) n.154

C.P.S. Chemical, State v., 198 N.J.Super. 236, 486 A.2d 944 (1985)—§ 20.3(i) n.160

Crabtree, State v., 198 W.Va. 620, 482 S.E.2d 605 (1996)—§ 24.2(a) n.6

Craft, United States v., 105 F.3d 1123 (6th Cir.1997)—§ 18.5(a) n.50

Crafts, State v., 425 A.2d 194 (Me.1981)—§ 2.12(e) n.211

Craig, In re Petition of, 131 F.3d 99 (2d Cir.1997)—§ 8.5(b) n.38

Craig, In re Petition of, 942 F.Supp. 881 (S.D.N.Y.1996)—§ 8.5(b) n.40

Craig v. Bronson, 202 Conn. 93, 520 A.2d 155 (1987)—§ 21.2(b) n.91

Craig v. Harney, 331 U.S. 367, 67 S.Ct. 1249, 91 L.Ed. 1546 (1947)—§ 23.1(c) n.100

Craig v. People, 986 P.2d 951 (Colo.1999)—§ 21.2(e) n.321

Craig, State v., 262 Mont. 240, 864 P.2d 1240 (1993)—§ 6.2(c) n.141

Craig v. State, 314 Ark. 585, 863 S.W.2d 825 (1993)—§ 25.5(c) n.35

Craig, United States v., 985 F.2d 175 (4th Cir.1993)—§ 27.5(c) n.63

Craig, United States v., 573 F.2d 513 (7th Cir.1978)—§ 16.2(e) n.70

Craig, United States v., 573 F.2d 455 (7th Cir.1977)—§ 6.4(e) n.67

CraigLaMonts v. Superior Court, 95 Cal.App.3d 568, 157 Cal.Rptr. 285 (1979)—§ 11.4(a) n.15

Cramer v. Secretary, Dept. of Corrections, 461 F.3d 1380 (11th Cir.2006)—§ 28.5(b) n.50

Cramer, United States v., 447 F.2d 210 (2d Cir.1971)—§ 15.2(j) n.240

Crandon v. United States, 494 U.S. 152, 110 S.Ct. 997, 108 L.Ed.2d 132 (1990)—§§ 2.9(h) n.206, 207

Crane v. Kentucky, 476 U.S. 683, 106 S.Ct. 2142, 90 L.Ed.2d 636 (1986)—§§ 2.7(a) n.50; 2.7(b) n.94; 2.7(c) n.199; 10.5(a) n.10

Crane, People v., 195 Ill.2d 42, 252 Ill.Dec. 687, 743 N.E.2d 555 (2001)—§§ 18.2(b) n.15; 18.2(c) n.52; 18.2(d) n.67

Crane, People v., 145 Ill.2d 520, 165 Ill.Dec. 703, 585 N.E.2d 99 (1991)—§ 6.9(d) n.79

Crane, United States v., 776 F.2d 600 (6th Cir.1985)—§ 18.3(b) n.7

Crane, United States v., 499 F.2d 1385 (6th Cir.1974)—§ 17.2(b) n.74

Craney, State v., 347 N.W.2d 668 (Iowa 1984)—§ 20.5(h) n.111

Cranford v. Rodriguez, 512 F.2d 860 (10th Cir.1975)—§§ 6.10(d) n.61, 62

Cranford v. Smart, 92 Nev. 89, 545 P.2d 1162 (1976)—§§ 14.2(d) n.62; 14.3(c) n.70

Crank, State v., 13 Ariz.App. 587, 480 P.2d 8 (1971)—§ 14.4(a) n.4

Cranley, United States v., 350 F.3d 617 (7th Cir.2003)—§ 6.6(e) n.78

Crannell, State v., 170 Vt. 387, 750 A.2d 1002 (Vt.2000)—§§ 3.10(b) n.79; 7.4(a) n.7

Craven, State v., 253 Neb. 601, 571 N.W.2d 612 (1997)—§ 3.8(e) n.216

Craven, United States v., 239 F.3d 91 (1st Cir.2001)—§ 19.2(e) n.71

Crawford v. Bannan, 336 F.2d 505 (6th Cir.1964)—§ 3.7(a) n.2

Crawford v. Commonwealth, 22 Va.App. 663, 472 S.E.2d 658 (1996)—§ 19.5(b) n.24

Crawford v. Commonwealth, 824 S.W.2d 847 (Ky.1992)—§ 3.3(d) n.161

Crawford, Commonwealth v., 410 Mass. 75, 571 N.E.2d 7 (1991)—§ 3.3(c) n.93

Crawford, Commonwealth v., 789 S.W.2d 779 (Ky.1990)—§ 21.4(e) n.163

Crawford, People v., 429 Mich. 151, 414 N.W.2d 360 (1987)—§§ 14.2(g) n.95, 96, 100, 101, 107

Crawford v. State, 117 Nev. 718, 30 P.3d 1123 (2001)—§ 21.2(d) n.148

Crawford, State v., 169 Vt. 371, 737 A.2d 366 (1999)—§ 18.4(c) n.68

Crawford, State v., 250 Kan. 174, 824 P.2d 951 (1992)—§ 21.6(a) n.80

Crawford, State v., 246 Kan. 231, 787 P.2d 1180 (1990)—§ 21.2(d) n.172

Crawford v. State, 580 A.2d 571 (Del.1990)—§ 6.9(g) n.183

Crawford, State v., 202 Conn. 443, 521 A.2d 1034 (1987)—§ 18.5(a) n.33

Crawford v. State, 257 Ga. 681, 362 S.E.2d 201 (1987)—§§ 11.2(e) n.190, 197, 203

Crawford v. State, 282 Md. 210, 383 A.2d 1097 (1978)—§ 14.2(e) n.66

Crawford, United States v., 372 F.3d 1048 (9th Cir.2004)—§ 9.4(a) n.48

Crawford, United States v., 323 F.3d 700 (9th Cir.2003)—§§ 9.4(a) n.11, 22

Crawford, United States v., 169 F.3d 590 (9th Cir.1999)—§ 21.4(d) n.110

Crawford, United States v., 462 F.2d 597 (9th Cir.1972)—§ 3.3(c) n.99

Crawford v. Washington, 541 U.S. 36, 124 S.Ct. 1354, 158 L.Ed.2d 177 (2004)—§§ 2.1 n.60; 2.7(b) n.78; 2.8(a) n.25; 2.8(b) n.55; 2.9(a) n.3; 2.9(b) n.15, 22; 2.9(c) n.51, 52; 2.9(d) n.61, 67, 69; 8.3(b) n.15; 14.1(d) n.57, 60; 17.2(b) n.51; 24.2(e) n.77; 24.2(f) n.85; 24.4(a) n.3; 26.4(f) n.92; 28.6(d) n.26

Crawford, State ex rel. v. Superior Court, 549 N.E.2d 374 (Ind.1990)—§§ 20.3(j) n.200; 20.3(k) n.215, 217

Crawley, State v., 187 N.J. 440, 901 A.2d 924 (2006)—§ 3.8(d) n.136

Crawley, State v., 149 N.J. 310, 693 A.2d 859 (1997)—§ 21.2(b) n.67

Crayton, People v., 28 Cal.4th 346, 121 Cal.Rptr.2d 580, 48 P.3d 1136 (2002)—§§ 11.3(a) n.16, 17

Crea, State v., 119 Idaho 352, 806 P.2d 445 (1991)—§ 27.5(e) n.147

Creamer, State v., 161 S.W.3d 420 (Mo.2005)—§§ 21.3(f) n.427; 25.1(d) n.77

Creamer v. State, 447 So.2d 978 (Fla.App.1984)—§ 8.1(c) n.37

Credit, United States v., 95 F.3d 362 (5th Cir.1996)—§ 7.4(e) n.89

Creech, State v., 314 S.C. 76, 441 S.E.2d 635 (S.C.App.1993)—§ 10.5(b) n.18

Creeger, State v., 576 A.2d 757 (Me.1990)—§ 17.2(b) n.40

Creel v. Johnson, 162 F.3d 385 (5th Cir.1998)—§ 6.4(g) n.153

Creel v. State, 493 S.W.2d 814 (Tex.Cr.App.1973)—§ 10.2(c) n.31

Cremer, State v., 234 Kan. 594, 676 P.2d 59 (1984)—§ 14.4(b) n.19

Creque, People v., 72 Ill.2d 515, 22 Ill.Dec. 403, 382 N.E.2d 793 (1978)—§ 15.5(c) n.111

Crespo, State v., 246 Conn. 665, 718 A.2d 925 (1998)—§ 11.9(b) n.78

Crespo de Llano, United States v., 838 F.2d 1006 (9th Cir.1987)—§§ 3.6(e) n.126; 6.2(c) n.96; 11.9(b) n.99

Cresta, United States v., 825 F.2d 538 (1st Cir.1987)—§§ 5.4(a) n.7; 22.3(d) n.200

Crews, Ex parte, 797 So.2d 1119 (Ala.2000)—§ 22.3(d) n.246

Crews, United States v., 445 U.S. 463, 100 S.Ct. 1244, 63 L.Ed.2d 537 (1980)—§ 9.4(d) n.89

Crews v. United States, 369 A.2d 1063 (D.C.App.1977)—§ 9.4(d) n.90

Criden, United States v., 675 F.2d 550 (3d Cir.1982)—§§ 23.1(d) n.136, 138, 139, 141, 146; 23.1(e) n.260, 262

Crider, State v., 341 A.2d 1 (Me.1975)—§ 3.2(c) n.106

Criminal Indictments 76-149 and 77-72, In the Matter of, 469 F.Supp. 666 (M.D.Pa.1978)—§ 8.5(h) n.265

Criminal Investigation, Matter of, 7th District Court No. CS-1, 754 P.2d 633 (Utah 1988)—§ 8.10(d) n.106

Criminal Investigation No. 1, In re, 75 Md.App. 589, 542 A.2d 413 (1988)—§ 8.8(a) n.12

Criminal Investigation No. 1/242Q, In re, 326 Md. 1, 602 A.2d 1220 (1992)—§§ 8.8(d) n.91, 92

Criminal Investigation No. 437 in the Circuit Court for Baltimore City, In re, 316 Md. 66, 557 A.2d 235 (1989)—§§ 8.5(b) n.46, 47; 8.5(e) n.198; 8.5(h) n.238, 247, 252, 276, 286, 291; 15.2(b) n.20

Criminal Investigation No. 465, In re, 80 Md.App. 347, 563 A.2d 1117 (Md.App.1989)—§ 8.13(d) n.109

Criminal Investigation No. 51,843, In re, 119 Md.App. 112, 704 A.2d 464 (1998)—§§ 8.5(h) n.246, 255, 257, 261, 262, 266 to 268, 273

Crimmins, People v., 36 N.Y.2d 230, 367 N.Y.S.2d 213, 326 N.E.2d 787 (1975)—§ 27.6(b) n.45

Criollo, United States v., 962 F.2d 241 (2d Cir.1992)—§ 24.9(c) n.28

Crippen, United States v., 579 F.2d 340 (5th Cir.1978)—§ 19.3(b) n.155

Cripps v. State, 122 Nev. 66, 137 P.3d 1187 (2006)—§ 21.3(d) n.219

Criqui, State v., 105 Kan. 716, 185 P. 1063 (1919)—§ 16.2(a) n.4

Crisafi, State v., 128 N.J. 499, 608 A.2d 317 (1992)—§§ 11.5(c) n.34, 40, 52, 55

Crisci, United States v., 273 F.3d 235 (2d Cir.2001)—§ 19.3(c) n.187

Crisco, United States v., 725 F.2d 1228 (9th Cir.1984)—§§ 6.7(b) n.41; 6.7(c) n.133

Crisconi, United States v., 520 F.Supp. 915 (D.Del.1981)—§ 15.7(b) n.27

Crise, People v., 224 Cal.App.3d Supp. 1, 274 Cal.Rptr. 242 (1990)— § 16.1(a) n.27

Crisona, United States v., 416 F.2d 107 (2d Cir.1969)—§ 20.3(b) n.59

Crisp v. Mayabb, 668 F.2d 1127 (10th Cir.1981)—§ 21.6(a) n.58

Crisp v. State, 271 Ind. 534, 394 N.E.2d 115 (1979)—§ 11.10(c) n.85

Crisp, United States v., 435 F.2d 354 (7th Cir.1970)—§ 6.9(c) n.52

Crist v. Bretz, 437 U.S. 28, 98 S.Ct. 2156, 57 L.Ed.2d 24 (1978)— §§ 2.5(f) n.78; 2.6(c) n.81; 2.6(d) n.95; 25.1(d) n.44

Cristobal, United States v., 293 F.3d 134 (4th Cir.2002)—§§ 6.9(b) n.38, 41

Criswell, United States v., 696 F.2d 636 (8th Cir.1983)—§ 6.4(g) n.154

Crite, People v., 261 Ill.App.3d 1041, 199 Ill.Dec. 648, 634 N.E.2d 487 (1994)—§ 24.8(b) n.28

Crittenden, People v., 149 Ill.App.3d 121, 102 Ill.Dec. 785, 500 N.E.2d 678 (1986)—§ 11.3(b) n.53

Crittendon, United States v., 883 F.2d 326 (4th Cir.1989)—§ 3.8(d) n.153

Crocker, State v., 767 A.2d 88 (R.I.2001)—§ 18.2(c) n.49

Crocker, United States v., 568 F.2d 1049 (3d Cir.1977)—§§ 8.10(c) n.58; 8.10(d) n.112, 113; 19.6(c) n.24

Crocker, United States v., 510 F.2d 1129 (10th Cir.1975)—§ 6.5(e) n.84

Crockett, State v., 110 Nev. 838, 877 P.2d 1077 (1994)—§ 21.2(f) n.383

Crockett v. State, 803 S.W.2d 308 (Tex.Cr.App.1991)—§ 3.2(b) n.71

Crockett, United States v., 514 F.2d 64 (5th Cir.1975)—§ 17.2(a) n.16

Croft, United States v., 124 F.3d 1109 (9th Cir.1997)—§ 24.3(i) n.190

Croken, Commonwealth v., 432 Mass. 266, 733 N.E.2d 1005 (2000)— § 11.9(a) n.20

Cromedy, State v., 158 N.J. 112, 727 A.2d 457 (1999)—§ 7.5(a) n.9

Cromer, Commonwealth v., 365 Mass. 519, 313 N.E.2d 557 (1974)— § 3.1(e) n.131

Cronan ex rel. State v. Cronan, 774 A.2d 866 (R.I.2001)—§§ 13.3(b) n.20, 24, 26; 24.11(c) n.10

Crone v. Cockrell, 324 F.3d 833 (5th Cir.2003)—§ 28.5(d) n.86

Cronic, United States v., 466 U.S. 648, 104 S.Ct. 2039, 80 L.Ed.2d 657 (1984)—§§ 1.5(b) n.69; 1.5(c) n.94, 116, 145; 2.9(f) n.117; 2.9(g) n.161; 11.1(a) n.25; 11.6(a) n.27; 11.7(a)

n.5; 11.7(c) n.30, 33; 11.7(e) n.71; 11.8(c) n.47, 49, 57; 11.10(a) n.17; 11.10(d) n.188; 21.3(a) n.16; 21.3(b) n.42; 24.11(d) n.12

Cronk, Commonwealth v., 396 Mass. 194, 484 N.E.2d 1330 (1985)— § 20.6(b) n.43

Cronk v. Municipal Court, 138 Cal.App.3d 351, 188 Cal.Rptr. 28 (1982)—§ 21.4(a) n.11

Cronk v. State, 443 N.E.2d 882 (Ind.App.1983)—§ 6.7(b) n.74

Crook v. United States, 771 A.2d 355 (D.C.App.2001)—§ 6.7(b) n.87

Crooker v. California, 357 U.S. 433, 78 S.Ct. 1287, 2 L.Ed.2d 1448 (1958)—§§ 6.2(c) n.176; 6.4(a) n.3

Crooker v. United States, 814 F.2d 75 (1st Cir.1987)—§ 18.4(c) n.37

Crooker, United States v., 729 F.2d 889 (1st Cir.1984)—§ 21.3(c) n.174

Crooks, United States v., 826 F.2d 4 (9th Cir.1987)—§ 18.3(b) n.22

Crooks, United States v., 804 F.2d 1441 (9th Cir.1986)—§ 17.4(a) n.36

Crosby v. State, 366 Md. 518, 784 A.2d 1102 (2001)—§ 6.5(b) n.27

Crosby, State v., 34 Conn.App. 261, 641 A.2d 406 (1994)—§ 9.6(a) n.47

Crosby v. State, 232 Ga. 599, 207 S.E.2d 515 (1974)—§ 16.1(d) n.133

Crosby, United States v., 397 F.3d 103 (2d Cir.2005)—§ 27.5(d) n.134

Crosby, United States v., 20 F.3d 480 (D.C.Cir.1994)—§ 27.2(c) n.46

Crosby v. United States, 506 U.S. 255, 113 S.Ct. 748, 122 L.Ed.2d 25 (1993)—§§ 24.2(d) n.42, 49

Crosby, United States v., 713 F.2d 1066 (5th Cir.1983)—§ 18.3(b) n.20

Crosland, United States v., 821 F.Supp. 1123 (E.D.Va.1993)—§ 8.8(f) n.153

Cross v. Cunningham, 87 F.3d 586 (1st Cir.1996)—§ 18.4(c) n.33

Cross, State v., 156 Wash.2d 580, 132 P.3d 80 (2006)—§ 6.9(g) n.154

Cross v. State, 144 S.W.3d 521 (Tex.Crim.App.2004)—§ 6.9(f) n.129

Cross, State v., 270 S.C. 44, 240 S.E.2d 514 (1977)—§ 21.2(c) n.104

Cross v. United States, 893 F.2d 1287 (11th Cir.1990)—§ 11.5(d) n.66

Cross v. United States, 335 F.2d 987 (D.C.Cir.1964)—§§ 17.1(c) n.42; 17.3(e) n.65

Cross v. United States, 325 F.2d 629 (D.C.Cir.1963)—§ 22.1(h) n.133

Crossen, State v., 10 Or.App. 442, 499 P.2d 1357 (1972)—§ 6.6(d) n.56

Crossley, United States v., 224 F.3d 847 (6th Cir.2000)—§§ 6.6(e) n.68; 18.3(b) n.11

Cross, United States ex rel. v. DeRobertis, 811 F.2d 1008 (7th Cir.1987)— § 11.10(d) n.161

Crotty, State v., 17 Conn.App. 395, 553 A.2d 620 (1989)—§ 8.5(g) n.229

Crotwell, United States v., 896 F.2d 437 (10th Cir.1990)—§ 25.2(f) n.51

Crouch, United States v., 51 F.3d 480 (5th Cir.1995)—§ 18.5(b) n.55

Crovedi, People v., 65 Cal.2d 199, 53 Cal.Rptr. 284, 417 P.2d 868 (1966)—§§ 11.1(a) n.12; 11.1(b) n.96; 11.4(c) n.63

Crow, United States v., 37 F.3d 1319 (8th Cir.1994)—§ 15.2(i) n.225

Crowdell, State v., 241 Neb. 216, 487 N.W.2d 273 (1992)—§ 26.1(d) n.87

Crowder, State v., 155 Ariz. 477, 747 P.2d 1176 (1987)—§ 21.4(d) n.110

Crowder, United States v., 543 F.2d 312 (D.C.Cir.1976)—§ 3.4(a) n.14

Crow Dog, United States v., 399 F.Supp. 228 (N.D.Iowa 1975)—§§ 18.1(c) n.32, 34

Crowe, Commonwealth v., 21 Mass.App.Ct. 456, 488 N.E.2d 780 (1986)—§ 14.2(c) n.40

Crowe, State v., 168 S.W.3d 731 (Tenn.2005)—§ 21.4(a) n.23

Crowe, United States v., 516 F.2d 824 (4th Cir.1975)—§ 21.2(d) n.178

Crowell, State v., 149 Wis.2d 859, 440 N.W.2d 352 (1989)—§ 21.5(f) n.163

Crowley, United States v., 236 F.3d 104 (2d Cir.2000)—§ 19.3(b) n.147

Crowson, United States v., 828 F.2d 1427 (9th Cir.1987)—§§ 8.11(c) n.36, 58, 60, 64, 65

Crowthers, United States v., 456 F.2d 1074 (4th Cir.1972)—§§ 13.4(b) n.46, 48

Crozier, United States v., 259 F.3d 503 (6th Cir.2001)—§§ 7.4(c) n.50, 51; 18.4(c) n.67, 73

Cruikshank, United States v., 92 U.S. (2 Otto) 542, 23 L.Ed. 588 (1876)—§§ 19.2(a) n.2; 19.2(c) n.23, 42; 19.2(d) n.45; 19.3(a) n.66; 19.3(b) n.143

Crumley v. City of St. Paul, Minn., 324 F.3d 1003 (8th Cir.2003)—§ 3.1(k) n.264

Crump, State v., 834 S.W.2d 265 (Tenn.1992)—§§ 6.9(f) n.111, 113; 6.9(g) n.158; 9.5(a) n.25

Crutchfield, State v., 306 Ark. 97, 816 S.W.2d 884 (1991)—§ 25.4(c) n.40

Cruthers v. State, 161 Ind. 139, 67 N.E. 930 (1903)—§ 16.4(c) n.81

Cruz v. Commonwealth, 24 Va.App. 454, 482 S.E.2d 880 (1997)—§§ 24.2(d) n.45, 48

Cruz v. Hauck, 627 F.2d 710 (5th Cir.1980)—§ 11.2(f) n.248

Cruz v. Kauai County, 279 F.3d 1064 (9th Cir.2002)—§ 12.1(b) n.38

Cruz v. New York, 481 U.S. 186, 107 S.Ct. 1714, 95 L.Ed.2d 162 (1987)—§§ 2.9(h) n.211; 17.2(b) n.35

Cruz, People v., 44 Cal.3d 1247, 246 Cal.Rptr. 1, 752 P.2d 439 (1988)—§ 21.2(d) n.223

Cruz, State v., 122 P.3d 543 (Utah 2005)—§ 27.5(d) n.137

Cruz, State v., 175 Ariz. 395, 857 P.2d 1249 (1993)—§ 22.3(d) n.245

Cruz, State v., 517 A.2d 237 (R.I.1986)—§§ 22.1(h) n.149; 22.4(b) n.17

Cruz, United States v., 127 F.3d 791 (9th Cir.1997)—§ 5.2(a) n.11

Cruz, United States v., 709 F.2d 111 (1st Cir.1983)—§§ 21.2(d) n.221; 21.2(f) n.363; 21.4(g) n.257

Cruz, United States v., 478 F.2d 408 (5th Cir.1973)—§§ 15.5(b) n.62, 64

Cruzado v. State, 110 Nev. 745, 879 P.2d 1195 (1994)—§ 27.5(c) n.56

Cruz Jimenez, United States v., 894 F.2d 1 (1st Cir.1990)—§§ 3.10(c) n.84; 6.3(b) n.35

Cruz-Martinez, United States v., 436 F.Supp.2d 1157 (S.D.Cal.2006)—§ 24.2(g) n.94

Cruz-Mercado, United States v., 360 F.3d 30 (1st Cir.2004)—§§ 21.2(d) n.250, 258

Cruz-Padilla, United States v., 227 F.3d 1064 (8th Cir.2000)—§ 24.7(e) n.61

Cryar, United States v., 232 F.3d 1318 (10th Cir.2000)—§ 16.2(d) n.58

Cryer, Commonwealth v., 426 Mass. 562, 689 N.E.2d 808 (1998)—§ 6.9(c) n.66

CSC v. State, 2005 WY 106, 118 P.3d 970 (Wyo.2005)—§§ 6.6(c) n.44; 6.6(e) n.70

Cubean, United States v., 611 F.2d 257 (8th Cir.1979)—§ 16.4(d) n.124

Cuciak v. State, 410 So.2d 916 (Fla.1982)—§ 26.10(b) n.26

Cudjo, People v., 6 Cal.4th 585, 25 Cal.Rptr.2d 390, 863 P.2d 635 (1993)—§ 24.3(i) n.188

Cuero Flores, United States v., 276 F.3d 113 (2d Cir.2002)—§ 21.2(d) n.203

Cuervelo, United States v., 949 F.2d 559 (2d Cir.1991)—§§ 5.4(c) n.29, 42

Cuervo, United States v., 354 F.3d 969 (8th Cir.2004)—§ 18.5(a) n.11

Cuevas, State v., 288 N.W.2d 525 (Iowa 1980)—§ 16.3(b) n.23

Cuevas-Sanchez, United States v., 821 F.2d 248 (5th Cir.1987)—§ 3.2(c) n.137

Cuffle, State v., 171 Ariz. 49, 828 P.2d 773 (1992)—§ 21.3(b) n.57

Culberson v. State, 412 So.2d 1184 (Miss.1982)—§§ 11.6(c) n.100; 24.5(d) n.57

Culbert, United States v., 215 F.Supp. 333 (D.C.Mo.1963)—§ 15.1(f) n.332

Culbreath, State v., 30 S.W.3d 309 (Tenn.2000)—§ 27.6(b) n.22

Culkin, State v., 97 Haw. 206, 35 P.3d 233 (2001)—§ 24.9(b) n.12

Culkin, State v., 791 S.W.2d 803 (Mo.Ct.App.1990)—§§ 20.5(f) n.81, 85

Cullen, State v., 39 S.W.3d 899 (Mo.App.2001)—§ 26.7(a) n.13

Cullen, State v., 86 Haw. 1, 946 P.2d 955 (1997)—§§ 12.4(d) n.63; 27.5(d) n.116

Cullen v. United States, 194 F.3d 401 (2d Cir.1999)—§ 21.3(b) n.107

Cullison, State v., 173 N.W.2d 533 (Iowa 1970)—§ 3.9(j) n.199

Culombe v. Connecticut, 367 U.S. 568, 81 S.Ct. 1860, 6 L.Ed.2d 1037 (1961)—§§ 6.1(a) n.1; 6.2(c) n.80, 89, 170

Culotta, State v., 343 So.2d 977 (La.1976)—§ 2.12(e) n.205

Culpepper v. State, 132 Ga.App. 733, 209 S.E.2d 18 (1974)—§ 10.5(c) n.31

Culver v. Director of Corrections, 450 F.Supp.2d 1135 (C.D.Cal.2006)—§ 28.5(b) n.50

Cumbest v. State, 456 So.2d 209 (Miss.1984)—§ 13.7(a) n.29

Cumbie v. State, 345 So.2d 1061 (Fla.1977)—§ 20.6(b) n.18

Cummings, Commonwealth v., 422 Pa.Super. 202, 619 A.2d 316 (1993)—§ 11.10(c) n.87

Cummings, State v., 346 N.C. 291, 488 S.E.2d 550 (1997)—§ 6.8(a) n.16

Cummings v. State, 27 Md.App. 361, 341 A.2d 294 (1975)—§ 6.6(f) n.97

Cummings, State v., 445 S.W.2d 639 (Mo.1969)—§ 7.4(d) n.76

Cummins, State v., 839 P.2d 848 (Utah App.1992)—§ 11.10(c) n.99

Cummiskey v. Superior Court, 3 Cal.4th 1018, 13 Cal.Rptr.2d 551, 839 P.2d 1059 (1992)—§§ 15.7(g) n.202, 213, 214; 27.4(c) n.32

Cunavelis, United States v., 969 F.2d 1419 (2d Cir.1992)—§§ 21.1(h) n.209; 21.3(e) n.286; 21.4(g) n.243

Cunningham v. California, _____ U.S. _____, 127 S.Ct. 856, 166 L.Ed.2d 856 (2007)—§§ 26.3(d) n.28; 26.4(i) n.187

Cunningham, Commonwealth v., 405 Mass. 646, 543 N.E.2d 12 (1989)—§§ 6.8(d) n.84; 6.9(b) n.44

Cunningham v. Diesslin, 92 F.3d 1054 (10th Cir.1996)—§§ 21.2(g) n.396; 21.5(d) n.102

Cunningham v. Hamilton County, 527 U.S. 198, 119 S.Ct. 1915, 144 L.Ed.2d 184 (1999)—§§ 27.2(a) n.6; 27.2(c) n.42

Cunningham, People v., 25 Cal.4th 926, 108 Cal.Rptr.2d 291, 25 P.3d 519 (2001)—§§ 6.9(f) n.133; 7.4(b) n.9; 17.1(d) n.59

Cunningham, People v., 166 Misc.2d 964, 636 N.Y.S.2d 990 (Sup.Ct.1995)—§ 15.7(g) n.221

Cunningham v. State, 341 Ark. 99, 14 S.W.3d 869 (2000)—§ 18.4(c) n.37

Cunningham, State v., 344 N.C. 341, 474 S.E.2d 772 (1996)—§§ 11.4(a) n.1, 2; 11.5(b) n.29; 11.5(d) n.68, 73

Cunningham, State v., 144 Wis.2d 272, 423 N.W.2d 862 (1988)—§ 6.7(c) n.120

Cunningham, State v., 27 Wash.App. 834, 620 P.2d 535 (1980)—§ 23.2(g) n.125

Cunningham, United States v., 292 F.3d 115 (2d Cir.2002)—§ 21.2(b) n.82

Cunningham, United States v., 672 F.2d 1064 (2d Cir.1982)—§§ 11.9(a) n.24; 11.9(c) n.124, 141

Cunningham, United States v., 529 F.2d 884 (6th Cir.1976)—§ 21.5(e) n.138

Cunningham, United States v., 423 F.2d 1269 (4th Cir.1970)—§§ 7.3(c) n.58; 7.4(e) n.89

Cunningham, United States v., 424 F.2d 942 (D.C.Cir.1970)—§ 3.8(b) n.34

Cunningham v. Zant, 928 F.2d 1006 (11th Cir.1991)—§ 11.10(c) n.126

Cunningham, Commonwealth ex rel. v. Maroney, 421 Pa. 157, 218 A.2d 811 (1966)—§ 11.2(c) n.89

Cuomo, United States v., 525 F.2d 1285 (5th Cir.1976)—§ 18.3(b) n.8

Cupit v. Whitley, 28 F.3d 532 (5th Cir.1994)—§ 28.6(g) n.89

Cupp v. Murphy, 412 U.S. 291, 93 S.Ct. 2000, 36 L.Ed.2d 900 (1973)— §§ 3.2(b) n.42, 82, 83; 3.2(g) n.194, 197; 3.5(d) n.139

Cupps, United States v., 503 F.2d 277 (6th Cir.1974)—§ 10.3(b) n.29

Curavoo, State v., 156 Vt. 72, 587 A.2d 963 (1991)—§ 10.1(b) n.21

Curbelo, United States v., 343 F.3d 273 (4th Cir.2003)—§§ 24.9(f) n.103; 27.6(d) n.142

Curby, State v., 553 S.W.2d 566 (Mo.App.1977)—§ 20.5(b) n.29

Curcio, United States v., 712 F.2d 1532 (2d Cir.1983)—§ 21.6(a) n.55

Curcio v. United States, 354 U.S. 118, 77 S.Ct. 1145, 1 L.Ed.2d 1225 (1957)—§ 8.13(d) n.99

Curdgel, People v., 83 N.Y.2d 862, 611 N.Y.S.2d 827, 634 N.E.2d 199 (1994)—§ 21.2(d) n.242

Cure, United States v., 996 F.2d 1136 (11th Cir.1993)—§ 22.3(d) n.250

Curley v. State, 299 Md. 449, 474 A.2d 502 (1984)—§ 18.3(c) n.80

Curley, State v., 253 S.C. 513, 171 S.E.2d 699 (1970)—§ 9.1(a) n.14

Curley v. United States, 160 F.2d 229 (D.C.Cir.1947)—§ 24.6(c) n.37

Curran, United States v., 926 F.2d 59 (1st Cir.1991)—§ 26.4(g) n.114

Currie v. Superior Court, 230 Cal.App.3d 83, 281 Cal.Rptr. 250 (1991)—§ 14.4(c) n.71

Currier, State v., 171 Vt. 181, 758 A.2d 818 (2000)—§ 21.4(g) n.233

Currin v. State, 669 N.E.2d 976 (Ind.1996)—§ 22.3(d) n.250

Curry, People v., 178 Ill.2d 509, 227 Ill.Dec. 395, 687 N.E.2d 877 (1997)—§§ 11.10(c) n.108; 11.10(d) n.173, 174, 177; 21.3(b) n.47, 48, 62

Curry v. State, 930 So.2d 849 (Fla.App.2006)—§§ 24.7(d) n.35; 25.3(c) n.32

Curry, State v., 134 Ohio App.3d 113, 730 N.E.2d 435 (1999)—§ 13.6(d) n.69

Curry, State v., 988 S.W.2d 153 (Tenn.1999)—§§ 13.6(c) n.48, 49

Curry, State v., 118 Wash.2d 911, 829 P.2d 166 (1992)—§ 26.1(f) n.149

Curry, State v., 109 N.J. 1, 532 A.2d 721 (1987)—§§ 9.1(b) n.32; 9.3(d) n.44

Curry v. State, 7 Tex.App. 91 (1879)— § 1.6(d) n.284

Curry v. United States, 658 A.2d 193 (D.C.App.1995)—§ 24.3(b) n.65

Curry, United States v., 751 F.2d 442 (1st Cir.1984)—§ 9.4(b) n.57

Curtis, People v., 113 Ill.2d 136, 100 Ill.Dec. 735, 497 N.E.2d 1004 (1986)—§§ 7.3(a) n.9; 7.3(c) n.41; 7.3(f) n.109

Curtis, People v., 681 P.2d 504 (Colo.1984)—§§ 11.6(c) n.100; 24.5(d) n.57

Curtis, People v., 70 Cal.2d 347, 74 Cal.Rptr. 713, 450 P.2d 33 (1969)— § 3.1(o) n.305

Curtis, State v., 1998 WL 46663 (Conn.Super.1998)—§ 14.2(e) n.72

Curtis, State v., 130 Idaho 522, 944 P.2d 119 (1997)—§ 24.8(e) n.69

Curtis, State v., 552 A.2d 530 (Me.1988)—§ 6.9(g) n.168

Curtis v. State, 175 Ind.App. 76, 370 N.E.2d 385 (Ind.App.1977)— § 26.10(b) n.39

Curtis, State v., 542 P.2d 744 (Utah 1975)—§ 5.2(b) n.24

Curtis, United States v., 344 F.3d 1057 (10th Cir.2003)—§§ 7.4(g) n.112; 13.1(e) n.51; 13.2(a) n.1

Curtis, United States v., 931 F.2d 1011 (4th Cir.1991)—§ 9.4(b) n.73

Curtis, United States v., 562 F.2d 1153 (9th Cir.1977)—§§ 3.2(j) n.244, 247, 260

Curtis, United States v., 506 F.2d 985 (10th Cir.1974)—§ 19.3(b) n.153

Curtiss-Wright Export Corp., United States v., 299 U.S. 304, 57 S.Ct. 216, 81 L.Ed. 255 (1936)—§§ 1.7(c) n.32; 16.4(b) n.23

Curtis, United States ex rel. v. Zelker, 466 F.2d 1092 (2d Cir.1972)—§ 21.2(g) n.406

Curzi, United States v., 867 F.2d 36 (1st Cir.1989)—§ 3.1(c) n.59

Cushing, Commonwealth v., 11 Mass. 67 (1814)—§ 28.1(b) n.17

Cusick v. State, 259 Ark. 720, 536 S.W.2d 119 (1976)—§ 21.4(a) n.23

Custis v. United States, 511 U.S. 485, 114 S.Ct. 1732, 128 L.Ed.2d 517 (1994)—§§ 21.4(e) n.161; 26.4(f) n.98; 26.6(b) n.30; 28.9(b) n.31

Custodio v. State, 373 S.C. 4, 644 S.E.2d 36 (2007)—§ 21.2(f) n.368

Cusumano, United States v., 67 F.3d 1497 (10th Cir.1995)—§ 3.2(b) n.87

Cutchin, United States v., 956 F.2d 1216 (D.C.Cir.1992)—§ 3.8(d) n.171

Cuthrell v. Director, Patuxent Institution, 475 F.2d 1364 (4th Cir.1973)—§§ 21.4(d) n.100, 139

Cutler, United States v., 58 F.3d 825 (2d Cir.1995)—§§ 23.1(b) n.32, 50, 57, 62, 65, 67; 26.9(a) n.3

Cutter v. State, 725 N.E.2d 401 (Ind.2000)—§ 16.1(e) n.191

Cuyler v. Sullivan, 446 U.S. 335, 100 S.Ct. 1708, 64 L.Ed.2d 333 (1980)—§§ 2.9(g) n.158, 171; 2.9(h) n.241; 11.7(b) n.23; 11.9(b) n.44, 57; 11.9(d) n.150; 27.6(d) n.112

Cwikla, People v., 46 N.Y.2d 434, 414 N.Y.S.2d 102, 386 N.E.2d 1070 (1979)—§§ 7.2(b) n.26; 7.2(d) n.49; 24.3(d) n.112

Cymerman, State v., 135 N.J.Super. 591, 343 A.2d 825 (1975)—§ 3.4(c) n.43

Cyphers, United States v., 553 F.2d 1064 (7th Cir.1977)—§ 25.2(a) n.10

Cyprian, United States v., 23 F.3d 1189 (7th Cir.1994)—§§ 13.4(b) n.42; 13.4(c) n.99

Cyr, State v., 588 A.2d 753 (Me.1991)—§§ 18.5(b) n.59, 64, 67

Cyrs, State v., 129 N.H. 497, 529 A.2d 947 (1987)—§§ 11.9(d) n.169, 175, 219

Czachor, State v., 82 N.J. 392, 413 A.2d 593 (1980)—§§ 1.7(i) n.202, 205, 207

Czichray, United States v., 378 F.3d 822 (8th Cir.2004)—§ 6.6(e) n.61

D

D. v. National Society for the Prevention of Cruelty to Children, 1978 App.Cas. 171, [1978] All E.R. 589 (1978)—§ 1.5(c) n.95

Dabney, People v., 172 Misc.2d 458, 659 N.Y.S.2d 717 (1997)—§ 15.2(c) n.80

Daccarett, United States v., 6 F.3d 37 (2d Cir.1993)—§ 3.6(f) n.153

Daccarett-Ghia v. Commissioner, 70 F.3d 621 (D.C.Cir.1995)—§ 27.5(c) n.79

Dace, People v., 114 Ill.App.3d 908, 70 Ill.Dec. 684, 449 N.E.2d 1031 (1983)—§ 20.3(g) n.127

Daddino, United States v., 5 F.3d 262 (7th Cir.1993)—§ 26.7(c) n.35

Daewoo Indus. Co. Ltd., United States v., 591 F.Supp. 157 (D.Or.1984)—§§ 16.3(c) n.34, 35, 38, 39

Daff v. State, 317 Md. 678, 566 A.2d 120 (1989)—§ 25.3(a) n.7

Dagnall, State v., 236 Wis.2d 339, 612 N.W.2d 680 (2000)—§ 6.4(f) n.122

Dagostino v. State, 675 So.2d 194 (Fla.App.1996)—§ 11.5(g) n.124

Dagraca, Commonwealth v., 447 Mass. 546, 854 N.E.2d 1249 (2006)— § 6.8(a) n.7

Dahl, People v., 160 P.3d 301 (Colo.App.2007)—§ 24.9(f) n.101

Dahlin, State v., 289 Mont. 182, 961 P.2d 1247 (1998)—§ 22.1(h) n.135

Dahlstrum, United States v., 655 F.2d 971 (9th Cir.1981)—§ 25.3(a) n.4

Daigger v. State, 268 Ark. 249, 595 S.W.2d 653 (1980)—§ 3.5(e) n.186

Daigre v. Maggio, 705 F.2d 786 (5th Cir.1983)—§ 7.3(b) n.26

Dail, State v., 228 Neb. 653, 424 N.W.2d 99 (1988)—§ 10.6(c) n.31

Dail v. State, 96 Nev. 435, 610 P.2d 1193 (1980)—§ 26.10(c) n.78

Dailey v. State, 828 So.2d 340 (Ala.2001)—§ 22.3(c) n.150

Dailey, United States v., 759 F.2d 192 (1st Cir.1985)—§ 21.2(d) n.243

Dailey, United States v., 524 F.2d 911 (8th Cir.1975)—§ 7.4(c) n.54

Daily, People v., 49 Cal.App.4th 543, 56 Cal.Rptr.2d 787 (1996)—§ 14.3(d) n.94

Daily News, In re Application of, 787 F.Supp. 319 (E.D.N.Y.1992)— §§ 23.1(d) n.164 to 167; 23.1(e) n.219, 242, 246; 23.2(g) n.115

Dakins, United States v., 872 F.2d 1061 (D.C.Cir.1989)—§ 24.9(e) n.58

Daley v. Hett, 113 Ill.2d 75, 99 Ill.Dec. 132, 495 N.E.2d 513 (1986)— § 27.4(d) n.48

Daley v. United States, 231 F.2d 123 (1st Cir.1956)—§ 17.2(a) n.1

Daley, People ex rel. v. Joyce, 126 Ill.2d 209, 127 Ill.Dec. 791, 533 N.E.2d 873 (1988)—§ 22.1(h) n.148

Daley, People ex rel. v. Moran, 94 Ill.2d 41, 67 Ill.Dec. 790, 445 N.E.2d 270 (1983)—§§ 13.2(a) n.3; 21.3(d) n.263

Daley, People ex rel. v. Suria, 112 Ill.2d 26, 96 Ill.Dec. 83, 490 N.E.2d 1288 (1986)—§§ 13.2(c) n.57; 21.3(d) n.263; 21.4(f) n.209; 25.1(d) n.73

Dalia v. United States, 441 U.S. 238, 99 S.Ct. 1682, 60 L.Ed.2d 177 (1979)—§§ 3.3(g) n.244; 3.4(h) n.166; 4.6(b) n.64.50

D'Alimonte v. Kuriansky, 144 A.D.2d 737, 535 N.Y.S.2d 151 (1988)— § 8.7(b) n.33

Dallas v. Arave, 984 F.2d 292 (9th Cir.1993)—§ 26.4(c) n.32

Dallas Morning News Co., In re, 916 F.2d 205 (5th Cir.1990)—§ 22.3(a) n.9

Dalli, United States v., 424 F.2d 45 (2d Cir.1970)—§ 10.5(e) n.58

Dallio v. Spitzer, 343 F.3d 553 (2d Cir.2003)—§ 11.5(c) n.52

Dallmann, State v., 441 N.W.2d 912 (N.D.1989)—§ 3.4(f) n.107

Dally, State ex rel. v. Elliston, 811 S.W.2d 371 (Mo.1991)—§ 27.4(d) n.41

Dalman, State v., 520 N.W.2d 860 (N.D.1994)—§ 27.5(a) n.2

Dalpiaz, United States v., 494 F.2d 374 (6th Cir.1974)—§ 3.9(h) n.159

Daly, State v., 623 N.W.2d 799 (Iowa 2001)—§ 27.5(c) n.112

Daly v. State, 442 So.2d 143 (Ala.App.1983)—§ 15.2(c) n.89

Daly, United States v., 716 F.2d 1499 (9th Cir.1983)—§ 18.3(b) n.11

D'Amato, Commonwealth v., 514 Pa. 471, 526 A.2d 300 (1987)—§ 6.2(c) n.89

Damato, United States v., 554 F.2d 1371 (5th Cir.1977)—§ 15.7(e) n.117

Damiano v. Gaughan, 770 F.2d 1 (1st Cir.1985)—§§ 21.2(c) n.121, 122

Damiano, State v., 124 N.H. 742, 474 A.2d 1045 (1984)—§ 6.2(c) n.169

D'Amico, State v., 299 Mont. 57, 997 P.2d 773 (2000)—§ 21.2(d) n.157

D'Amico For and on Behalf of NLRB v. Industrial Union of Marine & Shipbuilding Workers, 630 F.Supp. 919 (D.Md.1986)—§ 13.5(h) n.146

Dammer, State v., 290 N.W.2d 869 (S.D.1980)—§ 26.10(b) n.34

Damon, State v., 317 A.2d 459 (Me.1974)—§ 16.4(c) n.51

D'Amore, United States v., 56 F.3d 1202 (9th Cir.1995)—§§ 11.4(b) n.18, 21; 11.4(c) n.61, 74, 81, 88

Dampier, State v., 314 N.C. 292, 333 S.E.2d 230 (1985)—§§ 6.4(e) n.63; 6.9(f) n.142

Damron, State v., 151 S.W.3d 510 (Tenn.2004)—§ 6.2(c) n.135

Damron, State v., 213 W.Va. 8, 576 S.E.2d 253 (2002)—§ 21.4(g) n.232

Dancy v. United States, 745 A.2d 259 (D.C.App.2000)—§§ 6.7(a) n.10; 6.7(c) n.118; 17.2(b) n.69

Dancy, United States v., 947 F.2d 1232 (5th Cir.1991)—§ 3.4(e) n.65

Dancy v. United States, 361 F.2d 75 (D.C.Cir.1965)—§ 14.2(b) n.30

D'Andrea, United States v., 497 F.Supp.2d 117 (D. Mass. 2007)—§ 4.4(c) n.9

Daneals, United States v., 370 F.Supp. 1289 (W.D.N.Y.1974)—§ 15.6(c) n.96

Dang v. State, 202 S.W.3d 278 (Tex.App. 2006)—§ 24.7(b) n.20

Dangerfield, State v., 171 N.J. 446, 795 A.2d 250 (2002)—§ 3.3(f) n.204

Daniel v. Cockrell, 283 F.3d 697 (5th Cir.2002)—§ 21.2(g) n.396

Daniel v. State, 78 P.3d 205 (Wyo.2003)—§§ 18.5(c) n.81, 84

Daniel v. State, 189 Ga.App. 835, 377 S.E.2d 914 (1989)—§ 20.3(m) n.252

Daniel, United States v., 3 F.3d 775 (4th Cir.1993)—§ 5.3(d) n.42

Daniel, United States v., 866 F.2d 749 (5th Cir.1989)—§§ 21.6(b) n.86, 88

Daniels v. Burke, 83 F.3d 760 (6th Cir.1996)—§ 22.3(a) n.26

Daniels, Commonwealth v., 531 Pa. 210, 612 A.2d 395 (1992)—§ 6.7(b) n.43

Daniels, People v., 187 Ill.2d 301, 240 Ill.Dec. 668, 718 N.E.2d 149 (1999)—§ 13.3(c) n.35

Daniels, People v., 52 Cal.3d 815, 277 Cal.Rptr. 122, 802 P.2d 906 (1991)—§§ 11.4(a) n.12, 15

Daniels v. State, 110 P.3d 477 (Nev. 2005)—§§ 5.2(a) n.9; 5.2(b) n.26

Daniels, State v., 182 N.J. 80, 861 A.2d 808 (2004)—§ 24.5(d) n.49

Daniels v. State, 17 P.3d 75 (Alaska App.2001)—§ 11.9(c) n.115

Daniels, State v., 172 Ill.2d 154, 216 Ill.Dec. 664, 665 N.E.2d 1221 (1996)—§ 26.1(b) n.27

Daniels v. State, 561 N.E.2d 487 (Ind.1990)—§ 28.11(b) n.15

Daniels, United States v., 281 F.3d 168 (5th Cir.2002)—§ 17.2(d) n.94

Daniels, United States v., 252 F.3d 411 (5th Cir.2001)—§§ 19.6(c) n.46; 27.5(c) n.106

Daniels v. United States, 532 U.S. 374, 121 S.Ct. 1578, 149 L.Ed.2d 590 (2001)—§§ 21.4(e) n.161; 26.4(f) n.100; 26.6(b) n.30; 28.9(b) n.38, 39

Daniels, United States v., 95 F.Supp.2d 1160 (D.Kan.2000) (N.D.N.Y.1997)—§ 19.4(b) n.30

Daniels, United States v., 3 F.3d 25 (1st Cir.1993)—§ 18.4(c) n.73

Daniels, United States v., 5 F.3d 495 (11th Cir.1993)—§ 16.1(h) n.307

Daniels, United States v., 902 F.2d 1238 (7th Cir.1990)—§ 4.6(l) n.200

Daniels, United States v., 821 F.2d 76 (1st Cir.1987)—§ 21.4(b) n.44

Daniels, United States v., 770 F.2d 1111 (D.C.Cir.1985)—§ 17.1(d) n.59

Daniels, United States v., 698 F.2d 221 (4th Cir.1983)—§ 18.1(c) n.35

Daniels, United States v., 11 U.S.C.M.A. 52, 28 C.M.R. 276 (1959)—§ 21.5(f) n.163

Daniels v. Williams, 474 U.S. 327, 106 S.Ct. 662, 88 L.Ed.2d 662 (1986)—§ 2.7 n.1

Daniels v. Woodford, 428 F.3d 1181 (9th Cir.2005)—§§ 11.4(b) n.24, 38

Danielson, United States v., 325 F.3d 1054 (9th Cir.2003)—§§ 11.8(b) n.32, 34, 35

D'Anjou, United States v., 16 F.3d 604 (4th Cir.1994)—§ 6.7(b) n.45

Danks, United States v., 221 F.3d 1037 (8th Cir.1999)—§§ 1.2(c) n.147, 187

Danley, State v., 573 So.2d 691 (Miss.1990)—§ 21.2(d) n.238

Danley v. State, 540 So.2d 619 (Miss.1988)—§ 21.2(d) n.244

Dann, State v., 205 Ariz. 557, 74 P.3d 231 (2003)—§ 24.2(b) n.28

Dann, State v., 167 Vt. 119, 702 A.2d 105 (1997)—§ 22.4(c) n.29

Dannels, State v., 226 Mont. 80, 734 P.2d 188 (1987)—§ 6.6(e) n.91

Dansinger, State v., 521 A.2d 685 (Me.1987)—§ 22.1(h) n.145

D'Antoni, United States v., 874 F.2d 1214 (7th Cir.1989)—§ 5.4(c) n.46

D'Antoni, United States v., 856 F.2d 975 (7th Cir.1988)—§ 6.9(g) n.149

D'Antonio, State v., 274 Conn. 658, 877 A.2d 696 (2005)—§§ 21.3(d) n.234; 22.4(a) n.12; 22.4(c) n.31

D'Antonio, United States v., 801 F.2d 979 (7th Cir.1986)—§ 24.3(i) n.192

Daoud, People v., 462 Mich. 621, 614 N.W.2d 152 (2000)—§§ 6.9(b) n.41, 42, 44

Daoust, United States v., 916 F.2d 757 (1st Cir.1990)—§ 3.2(c) n.127

Daramy v. United States, 733 A.2d 949 (D.C.App.1999)—§ 21.4(d) n.137

Darbey v. State, 79 Ga. 63, 3 S.E. 663 (1887)—§ 11.7(a) n.3

Darby, State v., 556 N.W.2d 311 (S.D.1996)—§ 6.6(d) n.50

Darby, State v., 1996 SD 127, 556 N.W.2d 311 (1996)—§ 6.2(c) n.177

Darby, United States v., 312 U.S. 100, 61 S.Ct. 451, 85 L.Ed. 609 (1941)—§§ 1.2(c) n.113, 124, 154; 2.9(b) n.28

Darden v. Commonwealth, 52 S.W.3d 574 (Ky.2001)—§ 3.8(d) n.153

Darden, Commonwealth v., 441 Pa. 41, 271 A.2d 257 (1970)—§ 6.9(b) n.18

Darden, United States v., 70 F.3d 1507 (8th Cir.1995)—§§ 17.2(c) n.90; 17.3(e) n.57, 58

Darden v. Wainwright, 477 U.S. 168, 106 S.Ct. 2464, 91 L.Ed.2d 144 (1986)—§§ 2.7(a) n.49; 24.7(h) n.85

Dardi, United States v., 330 F.2d 316 (2d Cir.1964)—§ 8.8(f) n.153

Darghty v. State, 530 So.2d 27 (Miss.1988)—§§ 6.2(c) n.116; 20.6(c) n.74, 75

Darling, People v., 95 N.Y.2d 530, 720 N.Y.S.2d 82, 742 N.E.2d 596 (2000)—§ 4.6(e) n.79

Darlington, People v., 105 P.3d 230 (Colo.2005)—§§ 21.4(a) n.24, 31

Darnell, United States v., 716 F.2d 479 (7th Cir.1983)—§ 28.9(a) n.21

Darr v. Burford, 339 U.S. 200, 70 S.Ct. 587, 94 L.Ed. 761 (1950)—§ 28.5(a) n.5

Darren M., In re, 358 Md. 104, 747 A.2d 612 (2000)—§ 13.3(c) n.35

Darroch, State v., 305 N.C. 196, 287 S.E.2d 856 (1982)—§§ 16.4(c) n.39, 105

Darryl H. v. Coler, 801 F.2d 893 (7th Cir.1986)—§ 3.9(d) n.69

Dartmouth College v. Woodward, 17 U.S. (4 Wheat.) 518, 4 L.Ed. 629 (1819)—§ 2.4(b) n.46

Darush, Commonwealth v., 501 Pa. 15, 459 A.2d 727 (1983)—§ 18.5(a) n.50

Darwin v. Connecticut, 391 U.S. 346, 88 S.Ct. 1488, 20 L.Ed.2d 630 (1968)—§§ 6.2(c) n.85; 9.5(c) n.64

Darwin Const. Co., Inc., United States v., 873 F.2d 750 (4th Cir.1989)—§ 8.13(d) n.96

D.A.S., In re, 391 A.2d 255 (D.C.App.1978)—§ 6.9(b) n.18

Dashiell v. State, 374 Md. 85, 821 A.2d 372 (2003)—§ 3.4(i) n.175

Dashner, People v., 77 P.3d 787 (Colo.App.2003)—§ 10.5(e) n.56

Dass, United States v., 849 F.2d 414 (9th Cir.1988)—§ 4.2(b) n.17

Daubert v. Merrell Dow Pharmaceuticals, 509 U.S. 579, 113 S.Ct. 2786, 125 L.Ed.2d 469 (1993)—§ 7.5(b) n.22

Daugherty, People v., 102 Ill.2d 533, 82 Ill.Dec. 315, 468 N.E.2d 969 (1984)—§ 17.2(d) n.93

Daugherty v. State, 44 P.3d 28 (Wyo.2002)—§§ 26.1(e) n.100, 102

Daughtry, People v., 242 App.Div.2d 731, 664 N.Y.S.2d 306 (1997)—§ 24.1(a) n.13

Daulton, State v., 518 N.W.2d 719 (N.D.1994)—§ 24.8(d) n.46

Dauphin Deposit Trust Co., United States v., 385 F.2d 129 (3d Cir.1967)—§ 8.7(b) n.60

Dauzart, State v., 960 So.2d 1079 (La.App.2007)—§ 26.8(c) n.24

D'Avanzo, United States v., 443 F.2d 1224 (2d Cir.1971)—§ 3.2(f) n.174

Davenport, Commonwealth v., 462 Pa. 543, 342 A.2d 67 (1975)—§ 9.4(b) n.69

Davenport, State v., 177 N.J. 288, 827 A.2d 1063 (2003)—§§ 11.5(f) n.98, 99

Davenport v. State, 620 N.W.2d 164 (N.D.2000)—§ 21.4(d) n.138

Davenport, State v., 55 Haw. 90, 516 P.2d 65 (1973)—§ 3.4(j) n.190

Davenport, United States v., 445 F.3d 366 (4th Cir.2006)—§ 26.4(d) n.65

Davenport, United States v., 935 F.2d 1223 (11th Cir.1991)—§§ 18.3(b) n.2, 19

Davenport, United States v., 824 F.2d 1511 (7th Cir.1987)—§ 22.3(b) n.55

David, United States v., 83 F.3d 638 (4th Cir.1996)—§ 27.5(d) n.128

David, United States v., 58 F.3d 113 (4th Cir.1995)—§ 21.2(d) n.223

David D.W., State v., 214 W.Va. 167, 588 S.E.2d 156 (2003)—§ 22.3(c) n.107

David E. Thompson, Inc., United States v., 621 F.2d 1147 (1st Cir.1980)—§ 21.4(a) n.36

Davidoff, United States v., 845 F.2d 1151 (2d Cir.1988)—§ 19.4(b) n.31

Davidovich, People v., 463 Mich. 446, 618 N.W.2d 579 (2000)—§ 21.3(b) n.66

David S., In re, 367 Md. 523, 789 A.2d 607 (2002)—§ 3.8(d) n.134

Davidson, Commonwealth v., 91 Ky. 162, 15 S.W. 53 (1891)—§ 16.3(d) n.58

Davidson v. Dill, 180 Colo. 123, 503 P.2d 157 (1972)—§ 3.1(m) n.289

Davidson v. New Orleans, 96 U.S. (6 Otto) 97, 102, 24 L.Ed. 616 (1877)—§§ 2.4(c) n.101, 116

Davidson, State v., 121 S.W.3d 600 (Tenn.2003)—§ 22.2(b) n.16

Davidson, State v., 351 N.W.2d 8 (Minn.1984)—§ 26.2(b) n.21

Davidson v. State, 48 Ala.App. 446, 265 So.2d 888 (1971)—§ 20.3(i) n.169

Davidson, United States v., 409 F.3d 304 (6th Cir.2005)—§§ 21.2(d) n.197; 21.4(g) n.227

Davidson, United States v., 936 F.2d 856 (6th Cir.1991)—§ 17.2(e) n.118

Davie, State v., 80 Ohio St.3d 311, 686 N.E.2d 245 (1997)—§ 6.9(a) n.12

Davila v. United States, 258 F.3d 448 (6th Cir.2001)—§§ 11.7(e) n.113; 27.5(c) n.63

Davis v. Alaska, 415 U.S. 308, 94 S.Ct. 1105, 39 L.Ed.2d 347 (1974)—§§ 11.7(d) n.47; 23.1(c) n.117; 24.3(a) n.9; 24.4(a) n.5; 24.4(b) n.13

Davis v. Allsbrooks, 778 F.2d 168 (4th Cir.1985)—§ 6.6(f) n.114

Davis v. Brown, 87 N.Y.2d 626, 641 N.Y.S.2d 819, 664 N.E.2d 884 (1996)—§ 27.4(c) n.24

Davis v. Commissioner of Internal Revenue, 81 T.C. 806, 1983 WL 14893 (1983)—§ 8.13(b) n.62

Davis, Commonwealth v., 567 Pa. 135, 786 A.2d 173 (2001)—§ 18.4(c) n.44

Davis, Commonwealth v., 757 A.2d 959 (Pa.Super.2000)—§ 18.4(c) n.44

Davis, Commonwealth v., 462 Pa. 27, 336 A.2d 888 (1975)—§ 9.4(a) n.28

Davis v. Commonwealth, 280 S.W.2d 714 (Ky.1955)—§ 3.5(a) n.32

Davis v. Greiner, 428 F.3d 81 (2d Cir.2006)—§ 21.3(b) n.63

Davis v. Johnson, 158 F.3d 806 (5th Cir.1998)—§ 28.5(b) n.59

Davis v. Kemp, 829 F.2d 1522 (11th Cir.1987)—§ 11.8(c) n.63

Davis v. Mississippi, 394 U.S. 721, 89 S.Ct. 1394, 22 L.Ed.2d 676 (1969)—§§ 3.8(g) n.239; 8.7(c) n.65; 9.4(d) n.97

Davis v. Municipal Court, 46 Cal.3d 64, 249 Cal.Rptr. 300, 757 P.2d 11 (1988)—§ 13.6(b) n.26

Davis v. Murrell, 279 Ga. 584, 619 S.E.2d 662 (2005)—§§ 21.3(b) n.45, 71

Davis v. North Carolina, 384 U.S. 737, 86 S.Ct. 1761, 16 L.Ed.2d 895 (1966)—§§ 6.2(c) n.80, 84, 87, 165; 6.2(d) n.200

Davis, People v., 36 Cal.4th 510, 31 Cal.Rptr.3d 96, 115 P.3d 417 (2005)—§§ 6.7(c) n.118, 141

Davis, People v., 356 Ill.App.3d 940, 292 Ill.Dec. 989, 827 N.E.2d 518 (2005)—§ 18.4(c) n.73

Davis, People v., 472 Mich. 156, 695 N.W.2d 45 (2005)—§ 25.5(c) n.30

Davis v. People, 871 P.2d 769 (Colo.1994)—§§ 11.10(c) n.69, 91, 122, 130

Davis, People v., 442 Mich. 1, 497 N.W.2d 910 (1993)—§ 3.6(f) n.147

Davis, People v., 145 Ill.2d 240, 164 Ill.Dec. 151, 582 N.E.2d 714 (1991)—§ 21.4(d) n.119

Davis, People v., 75 N.Y.2d 517, 554 N.Y.S.2d 460, 553 N.E.2d 1008 (1990)—§ 6.4(f) n.112

Davis, People v., 794 P.2d 159 (Colo.1990)—§§ 22.1(h) n.149; 22.3(d) n.202

Davis, People v., 123 Ill.App.3d 349, 78 Ill.Dec. 705, 462 N.E.2d 824 (1984)—§ 26.10(a) n.3

Davis, People v., 269 Ill. 256, 110 N.E. 9 (1915)—§ 16.4(c) n.51

Davis v. Romney, 55 F.R.D. 337 (E.D.Pa.1972)—§ 8.5(c) n.103

Davis v. Secretary for the Department of Corrections, 341 F.3d 1310 (11th Cir.2003)—§ 28.4(d) n.70

Davis v. Singletary, 853 F.Supp. 1492 (M.D.Fla.1994)—§ 23.2(a) n.27

Davis v. State, 195 S.W.3d 311 (Tex.App.2006)—§ 24.2(e) n.57

Davis, State v., 210 S.W.3d 229 (Mo.App.2006)—§§ 18.4(c) n.31, 34

Davis v. State, 928 So.2d 1089 (Fla.2006)—§ 11.10(c) n.151

Davis, State v., 141 S.W.3d 600 (Tenn.2004)—§ 22.5(d) n.34

Davis, State v., 872 So.2d 250 (Fla.2004)—§ 11.10(c) n.88

Davis, State v., 254 Wis.2d 1, 645 N.W.2d 913 (Wis.2002)—§§ 20.4(e) n.82, 86

Davis v. State, 809 A.2d 565 (Del.2002)—§§ 22.1(h) n.133, 149

Davis, State v., 822 So.2d 161 (La.App.2002)—§ 24.7(b) n.19

Davis, State v., 268 Kan. 661, 998 P.2d 1127 (2000)—§ 6.10(e) n.76

Davis v. State, 272 Ga. 327, 528 S.E.2d 800 (2000)—§ 17.2(b) n.71

Davis v. State, 767 So.2d 986 (Miss.2000)—§ 24.2(a) n.5

Davis v. State, 714 N.E.2d 717 (Ind.App.1999)—§ 19.5(b) n.14

Davis, State v., 751 So.2d 326 (La.App.1999)—§ 14.3(d) n.90

Davis, State v., 979 P.2d 1269 (Kan.1999)—§ 20.6(b) n.45

Davis, State v., 143 N.H. 8, 718 A.2d 1202 (1998)—§ 22.3(a) n.11

Davis v. State, 330 Ark. 76, 953 S.W.2d 559 (1997)—§ 6.4(f) n.137

Davis v. State, 698 So.2d 1182 (Fla.1997)—§§ 6.5(b) n.24; 6.6(c) n.31; 6.8(b) n.51; 6.9(f) n.133

Davis, State v., 76 Ohio St.3d 107, 666 N.E.2d 1099 (1996)—§§ 7.4(c) n.48, 49; 7.4(d) n.69

Davis, State v., 165 Vt. 240, 683 A.2d 1 (1996)—§ 22.4(c) n.29

Davis v. State, 266 Ga. 212, 465 S.E.2d 438 (1996)—§ 10.3(a) n.4

Davis v. State, 325 Ark. 194, 925 S.W.2d 402 (1996)—§ 22.2(d) n.81

Davis, State v., 139 N.H. 185, 650 A.2d 1386 (1994)—§ 16.1(g) n.261

Davis, State v., 229 Conn. 285, 641 A.2d 370 (1994)—§ 26.10(c) n.48

Davis v. State, 872 S.W.2d 743 (Tex.Cr.App.1994)—§ 24.4(d) n.62

Davis, State v., 32 Conn.App. 21, 628 A.2d 11 (1993)—§ 23.2(h) n.129

Davis v. State, 314 Ark. 257, 863 S.W.2d 259 (1993)—§ 11.2(e) n.200

Davis v. State, 333 Md. 27, 633 A.2d 867 (1993)—§ 22.3(a) n.4

Davis, State v., 504 N.W.2d 767 (Minn.1993)—§ 22.3(d) n.199

Davis, State v., 860 S.W.2d 369 (Mo.App.1993)—§ 10.3(d) n.63

Davis v. State, 262 Ga. 578, 422 S.E.2d 546 (1992)—§§ 3.10(e) n.148, 150; 9.3(e) n.67, 72

Davis, State v., 313 Or. 246, 834 P.2d 1008 (1992)—§ 9.1(b) n.79

Davis v. State, 594 So.2d 264 (Fla.1992)—§ 3.10(f) n.196

Davis, State v., 62 Ohio St.3d 326, 581 N.E.2d 1362 (1991)—§ 20.3(f) n.109

Davis v. State, 261 Ga. 221, 403 S.E.2d 800 (1991)—§§ 11.4(a) n.8, 9, 11, 12, 16

Davis, State v., 823 P.2d 367 (1991)—§ 14.3(d) n.92

Davis, State v., 823 S.W.2d 217 (Tenn.Cr.App.1991)—§ 21.3(c) n.174

Davis, State v., 155 Vt. 417, 584 A.2d 1146 (1990)—§§ 21.1(e) n.62, 67; 21.2(c) n.132; 21.3(d) n.222

Davis v. State, 260 Ga. 338, 393 S.E.2d 260 (1990)—§ 24.8(a) n.9

Davis, State v., 446 N.W.2d 785 (Iowa 1989)—§ 6.2(c) n.120

Davis v. State, 520 N.E.2d 1271 (Ind.1988)—§§ 16.1(d) n.154, 155

Davis v. State, 520 So.2d 493 (Miss.1988)—§ 22.1(g) n.115

Davis, State v., 176 W.Va. 454, 345 S.E.2d 549 (1986)—§§ 7.4(c) n.54; 7.4(e) n.89

Davis, State v., 198 Conn. 680, 504 A.2d 1372 (1986)—§§ 7.4(e) n.89; 7.5(a) n.7

Davis v. State, 170 Ga.App. 748, 318 S.E.2d 202 (1984)—§ 25.2(d) n.34

Davis, State v., 192 Conn. 739, 474 A.2d 776 (1984)—§§ 18.2(c) n.37; 18.2(e) n.81

Davis v. State, 275 Ark. 264, 630 S.W.2d 1 (1982)—§ 3.6(a) n.31

Davis, State v., 305 N.C. 400, 290 S.E.2d 574 (1982)—§ 6.9(f) n.108

Davis, State v., 70 Ohio App.2d 48, 434 N.E.2d 285 (1980)—§ 21.2(h) n.437

Davis, State v., 259 N.W.2d 843 (Iowa 1977)—§§ 15.1(b) n.99; 15.4(b) n.35

Davis v. State, 129 Ga.App. 796, 201 S.E.2d 345 (1973)—§ 17.2(e) n.121

Davis, State v., 153 W.Va. 742, 172 S.E.2d 569 (1970)—§ 6.8(a) n.9

Davis, State v., 261 Iowa 1351, 157 N.W.2d 907 (Iowa 1968)—§ 6.6(f) n.108

Davis, State v., 188 So.2d 24 (Fla.App.1966)—§ 13.5(b) n.32

Davis, State v., 203 N.C. 13, 164 S.E. 737 (1932)—§ 16.4(c) n.73

Davis v. Traub, 90 N.M. 498, 565 P.2d 1015 (1977)—§§ 15.7(h) n.233, 235

Davis, United States v., 473 F.3d 680 (6th Cir.2007)—§ 1.2(c) n.176

Davis, United States v., 452 F.3d 991 (8th Cir.2006)—§ 21.5(b) n.66

Davis, United States v., 428 F.3d 802 (9th Cir.2005)—§ 21.5(a) n.43

Davis, United States v., 380 F.3d 821 (5th Cir.2004)—§ 19.3(a) n.91

Davis, United States v., 393 F.3d 540 (5th Cir.2004)—§ 21.2(d) n.242

Davis, United States v., 332 F.3d 1163 (9th Cir.2003)—§ 9.4(a) n.41

Davis, United States v., 285 F.3d 378 (5th Cir.2002)—§ 11.5(d) n.84

Davis, United States v., 306 F.3d 398 (6th Cir.2002)—§ 24.3(b) n.63

Davis, United States v., 239 F.3d 283 (2d Cir.2001)—§ 11.9(d) n.218

Davis, United States v., 247 F.3d 322 (1st Cir.2001)—§ 21.2(d) n.255

Davis, United States v., 270 F.3d 977 (D.C.Cir.2001)—§ 3.9(g) n.146

Davis, United States v., 202 F.3d 1060 (8th Cir.2000)—§ 3.8(c) n.91

Davis, United States v., 174 F.3d 941 (8th Cir.1999)—§ 3.5(a) n.50

Davis, United States v., 184 F.3d 366 (4th Cir.1999)—§ 19.3(e) n.240

Davis, United States v., 154 F.3d 772 (8th Cir.1998)—§ 20.3(i) n.177

Davis, United States v., 112 F.3d 118 (3d Cir.1997)—§ 21.5(e) n.147

Davis, United States v., 902 F.Supp. 98 (E.D.La.1995)—§§ 23.1(b) n.67, 68, 93

Davis, United States v., 30 F.3d 613 (5th Cir.1994)—§ 1.2(c) n.133

Davis v. United States, 512 U.S. 452, 114 S.Ct. 2350, 129 L.Ed.2d 362 (1994)—§§ 6.5(e) n.84; 6.9(g) n.160, 165, 184

Davis v. United States, 641 A.2d 484 (D.C.App.1994)—§§ 8.1(a) n.1; 8.5(d) n.135, 139, 144; 8.5(g) n.229

Davis, United States v., 1 F.3d 606 (7th Cir.1993)—§ 27.2(e) n.89

Davis, United States v., 953 F.2d 1482 (10th Cir.1992)—§ 27.5(a) n.3

Davis, United States v., 958 F.2d 47 (4th Cir.1992)—§§ 11.2(g) n.305, 309

Davis, United States v., 780 F.Supp. 21 (D.D.C.1991)—§ 11.9(a) n.33

Davis, United States v., 932 F.2d 752 (9th Cir.1991)—§ 3.9(j) n.201

Davis, United States v., 900 F.2d 1524 (10th Cir.1990)—§ 21.6(b) n.89

Davis, United States v., 906 F.2d 829 (2d Cir.1990)—§ 25.5(a) n.11

Davis, United States v., 882 F.2d 1334 (8th Cir.1989)—§ 3.7(e) n.108

Davis, United States v., 845 F.2d 412 (2d Cir.1988)—§ 12.1(a) n.17

Davis, United States v., 673 F.Supp. 252 (N.D.Ill.1987)—§§ 8.8(i) n.193; 24.3(b) n.71

Davis, United States v., 809 F.2d 1194 (6th Cir.1987)—§§ 22.3(d) n.229; 24.2(a) n.5

Davis, United States v., 749 F.2d 292 (5th Cir.1985)—§ 3.10(c) n.94

Davis, United States v., 752 F.2d 963 (5th Cir.1985)—§ 17.1(a) n.14

Davis, United States v., 604 F.2d 474 (7th Cir.1979)—§§ 11.4(a) n.2, 5, 6; 11.4(c) n.87

Davis, United States v., 617 F.2d 677 (D.C.Cir.1979)—§ 21.2(h) n.419

Davis v. United States, 367 A.2d 1254 (D.C.App.1976)—§ 24.6(b) n.20

Davis, United States v., 533 F.2d 921 (5th Cir.1976)—§ 18.5(a) n.14

Davis, United States v., 542 F.2d 743 (8th Cir.1976)—§ 3.4(k) n.236

Davis, United States v., 527 F.2d 1110 (9th Cir.1975)—§ 6.7(c) n.106

Davis v. United States, 417 U.S. 333, 94 S.Ct. 2298, 41 L.Ed.2d 109 (1974)—§§ 28.9(a) n.1; 28.9(c) n.81

Davis, United States v., 493 F.2d 502 (5th Cir.1974)—§ 21.4(f) n.199

Davis v. United States, 411 U.S. 233, 93 S.Ct. 1577, 36 L.Ed.2d 216 (1973)—§§ 1.7(f) n.79; 10.2(a) n.8; 15.4(b) n.56, 59; 28.4(d) n.39

Davis, United States v., 482 F.2d 893 (9th Cir.1973)—§ 3.9(h) n.156

Davis, United States v., 346 F.Supp. 435 (S.D.Ill.1972)—§ 3.4(b) n.33

Davis, United States v., 458 F.2d 819 (D.C.Cir.1972)—§ 3.3(b) n.48

Davis, United States v., 459 F.2d 167 (6th Cir.1972)—§ 6.8(d) n.82

Davis, United States v., 423 F.2d 974 (5th Cir.1970)—§ 3.6(e) n.106

Davis v. United States, 327 F.2d 301 (9th Cir.1964)—§ 3.10(e) n.150

Davis v. United States, 328 U.S. 582, 66 S.Ct. 1256, 90 L.Ed. 1453 (1946)— §§ 2.8(c) n.63; 3.9(c) n.38

Davis v. United States, 32 F.2d 860 (9th Cir.1929)—§ 16.1(b) n.81

Davis, United States v., 25 Fed.Cas. 786, No. 14932 (C.C.D.Mass.1837)— § 16.4(b) n.15

Davis v. Warden, 867 F.2d 1003 (7th Cir.1989)—§§ 2.6(b) n.64; 16.1(e) n.208; 22.2(d) n.56

Davis v. Washington, _____ U.S. _____, 126 S.Ct. 2266, 165 L.Ed.2d 224 (U.S.2006)—§§ 2.8(a) n.25; 2.9(c) n.46; 2.9(d) n.67; 2.10(c) n.61

Davis v. Woodford, 446 F.3d 957 (9th Cir.2006)—§ 21.2(d) n.194

Davis v. Zirkelbach, 149 F.3d 614 (7th Cir.1998)—§ 4.6(n) n.258

Davison v. Champlin, 7 Conn. 244 (1828)—§ 1.2(c) n.81

Davison, State v., 280 Ga. 84, 623 S.E.2d 500 (2005)—§ 6.2(c) n.96

Davison, State v., 116 Wash.2d 917, 809 P.2d 1374 (1991)—§ 26.6(c) n.35

Davlin, State v., 263 Neb. 283, 639 N.W.2d 631 (2002)—§ 24.3(e) n.127

Davolt, State v., 207 Ariz. 191, 84 P.3d 456 (2004)—§§ 3.10(b) n.40; 9.3(e) n.62

Dawan v. Lockhart, 31 F.3d 718 (8th Cir.1994)—§§ 11.9(d) n.204, 233

Dawdy, State v., 533 N.W.2d 551 (Iowa 1995)—§ 3.1(o) n.303

Dawdy, United States v., 46 F.3d 1427 (8th Cir.1995)—§ 3.1(o) n.303

Dawes, United States v., 874 F.2d 746 (10th Cir.1989)—§ 11.4(c) n.55

Dawkins, State v., 297 S.C. 386, 377 S.E.2d 298 (1989)—§§ 13.7(c) n.43, 63

Dawkins v. State, 313 Md. 638, 547 A.2d 1041 (1988)—§ 1.11(a) n.5

Dawn, United States v., 900 F.2d 1132 (7th Cir.1990)—§ 18.4(b) n.26

Dawson v. Delaware, 503 U.S. 159, 112 S.Ct. 1093, 117 L.Ed.2d 309 (1992)—§§ 26.1(b) n.24; 26.4(b) n.16; 27.6(d) n.141

Dawson, People v., 154 Mich.App. 260, 397 N.W.2d 277 (1986)—§ 25.4(a) n.7

Dawson v. Scott, 50 F.3d 884 (11th Cir.1995)—§ 28.3(a) n.9

Dawson, State v., 295 Mont. 212, 983 P.2d 916 (1999)—§ 6.6(e) n.91

Dawson v. State, 894 P.2d 672 (Alaska App.1995)—§ 26.9(b) n.47

Dawson, United States v., 193 F.3d 1107 (9th Cir.1999)—§ 21.5(c) n.74

Dawson, United States v., 516 F.2d 796 (9th Cir.1975)—§ 3.9(i) n.185

Dawson v. Wal-Mart Stores, Inc., 781 F.Supp. 1166 (N.D.Miss.1992)— §§ 15.4(b) n.65, 66

Day v. McDonough, 547 U.S. 198, 126 S.Ct. 1675, 164 L.Ed.2d 376 (2006)—§§ 28.5(a) n.24; 28.5(b) n.65; 28.9(b) n.54

Day, State v., 925 A.2d 962 (R.I.2007)— § 24.6(d) n.44

Day, State v., 619 N.W.2d 745 (Minn.2000)—§ 6.9(g) n.149

Day, State v., 233 Conn. 813, 661 A.2d 539 (1995)—§ 11.5(c) n.46

Day, State v., 501 N.W.2d 649 (Minn.App.1993)—§ 24.10(c) n.41

Day v. State, 306 Ark. 520, 816 S.W.2d 852 (1991)—§ 6.9(g) n.183

Day, State v., 147 Vt. 93, 511 A.2d 995 (1986)—§ 26.9(a) n.7

Day, State v., 148 Ariz. 490, 715 P.2d 743 (1986)—§ 7.4(c) n.47

Day v. State, 395 So.2d 119 (Ala.App.1980)—§ 22.1(h) n.138

Day, United States v., 285 F.3d 1167 (9th Cir.2002)—§§ 11.10(d) n.178, 185

Day, United States v., 697 A.2d 31 (D.C.App.1997)—§§ 18.3(c) n.110; 24.3(e) n.126

Daye, Commonwealth v., 435 Mass. 463, 759 N.E.2d 313 (2001)—§ 22.4(c) n.29

Daye, Commonwealth v., 411 Mass. 719, 587 N.E.2d 194 (1992)—§ 20.3(a) n.17

D.B. v. Tewksbury, 545 F.Supp. 896 (D.Or.1982)—§ 12.4(b) n.48

Deal v. State, 626 P.2d 1073 (Alaska 1980)—§ 21.4(a) n.26

Deal v. United States, 508 U.S. 129, 113 S.Ct. 1993, 124 L.Ed.2d 44 (1993)—§ 26.6(b) n.29

De Alba-Conrado, United States v., 481 F.2d 1266 (5th Cir.1973)—§ 15.4(b) n.67

Dean, People v., 103 Misc.2d 480, 426 N.Y.S.2d 418 (City.Ct.1980)—§ 15.1(d) n.212

Dean, People v., 39 Cal.App.3d 875, 114 Cal.Rptr. 555 (1974)—§ 6.7(b) n.89

Dean, State v., 264 Neb. 42, 645 N.W.2d 528 (2002)—§ 22.1(h) n.137

Dean, State v., 273 Kan. 929, 46 P.3d 1130 (2002)—§ 22.3(d) n.246

Dean v. State, 325 Md. 230, 600 A.2d 409 (1992)—§ 13.3(c) n.36

Dean, State v., 163 Wis.2d 503, 471 N.W.2d 310 (App.1991)—§ 11.2(g) n.299

Dean, State v., 148 Vt. 510, 536 A.2d 909 (1987)—§ 18.5(c) n.75

Dean v. State, 478 So.2d 38 (Fla.1985)—§§ 8.7(e) n.89; 9.1(c) n.100

Dean v. State, 291 Md. 198, 434 A.2d 552 (1981)—§ 26.10(c) n.56

Dean v. United States, 278 F.3d 1218 (11th Cir.2002)—§ 28.9(b) n.53

Dean, United States v., 76 F.3d 329 (10th Cir.1996)—§ 26.2(b) n.21

Dean, United States v., 59 F.3d 1479 (5th Cir.1995)—§ 24.6(b) n.32

Dean, United States v., 989 F.2d 1205 (D.C.Cir.1993)—§ 8.13(d) n.94

Dean v. United States, 246 F.2d 335 (8th Cir.1957)—§ 16.1(g) n.241

DeAngelo v. Schiedler, 306 Or. 91, 757 P.2d 1355 (1988)—§§ 26.4(g) n.115, 134

DeAngelo, State v., 113 Or.App. 192, 830 P.2d 630 (1992)—§ 5.4(b) n.19

Dean, State ex rel. v. City Court, 140 Ariz. 75, 680 P.2d 211 (App.1984)—§ 20.3(g) n.126

Dearing v. Commonwealth, 259 Va. 117, 524 S.E.2d 121 (2000)—§ 17.2(c) n.76

Dearmore, United States v., 672 F.2d 738 (9th Cir.1982)—§ 5.2(a) n.9

Deases, State v., 518 N.W.2d 784 (Iowa 1994)—§§ 6.7(b) n.85; 6.10(c) n.50

Death Row Prisoners of Pennsylvania v. Ridge, 106 F.3d 35 (3d Cir.1997)—§ 28.8(b) n.16

Deaton, United States v., 468 F.2d 541 (5th Cir.1972)—§ 6.10(c) n.49

De Beers Consol. Mines, Ltd. v. United States, 325 U.S. 212, 65 S.Ct. 1130, 89 L.Ed. 1566 (1945)—§ 27.4(b) n.6

Deberry v. State, 457 A.2d 744 (Del.1983)—§§ 20.6(b) n.56, 59

Deberry, United States v., 430 F.3d 1294 (10th Cir.2005)—§ 13.4(b) n.69

DeBooy, State v., 996 P.2d 546 (2000)—§§ 3.9(g) n.126, 132, 146

Deborah C., In re, 30 Cal.3d 125, 177 Cal.Rptr. 852, 635 P.2d 446 (1981)—§ 6.10(b) n.19

DeBorde, State v., 121 N.M. 601, 915 P.2d 906 (1996)—§ 26.10(b) n.26

DeBright, United States v., 730 F.2d 1255 (9th Cir.1984)—§§ 27.5(b) n.43, 46

Debro v. State, 821 N.E.2d 367 (Ind.2005)—§§ 21.6(a) n.78; 26.4(f) n.93

Debrow, United States v., 346 U.S. 374, 74 S.Ct. 113, 98 L.Ed. 92 (1953)—§§ 19.1(d) n.63; 19.3(b) n.166

DeCecco v. United States, 485 F.2d 372 (1st Cir.1973)—§ 28.9(a) n.19

December 1988 Term Grand Jury Investigation, In re, 714 F.Supp. 782 (W.D.N.C.1989)—§§ 8.5(h) n.295, 300

Dechaine, State v., 572 A.2d 130 (Me.1990)—§ 24.3(e) n.126

DeCiantis, State v., 813 A.2d 986 (R.I.2003)—§ 26.4(g) n.134

Deck v. Missouri, 544 U.S. 622, 125 S.Ct. 2007, 161 L.Ed.2d 953 (2005)—§§ 24.2(e) n.56; 27.6(d) n.85

Deck v. State, 68 S.W.3d 418 (Mo.2002)—§ 11.10(d) n.159

Deckard, State v., 272 Neb. 410, 722 N.W.2d 55 (2006)—§§ 21.3(b) n.90, 91

Decker, People v., 11 A.D.2d 600, 200 N.Y.S.2d 655 (1960)—§ 15.2(c) n.77

Decker v. State, 734 S.W.2d 393 (Tex.App.1987)—§ 24.7(b) n.20

Decker, United States v., 956 F.2d 773 (8th Cir.1992)—§ 3.1(c) n.71

DeConingh v. State, 433 So.2d 501 (Fla.1983)—§ 6.6(e) n.75

DeCosta, United States v., 435 F.2d 630 (1st Cir.1970)—§ 21.6(a) n.57

DeCoster, United States v., 624 F.2d 196 (D.C.Cir.1976)—§§ 11.7(d) n.38, 39, 42 to 44; 11.8(a) n.23; 11.10(a) n.2, 4 to 6, 15; 11.10(b) n.35, 46

DeCoster, United States v., 487 F.2d 1197 (D.C.Cir.1973)—§ 11.7(d) n.42

De Coteau, United States v., 186 F.3d 1008 (8th Cir.1999)—§ 20.6(b) n.41

Dederich, United States v., 825 F.2d 1317 (9th Cir.1987)—§ 15.6(f) n.189

Dedesma v. State, 806 S.W.2d 928 (Tex.App.1991)—§ 24.11(d) n.16

De Diego, United States v., 511 F.2d 818 (D.C.Cir.1975)—§ 17.3(a) n.9

Dedrick, State v., 132 N.H. 218, 564 A.2d 423 (1989)—§§ 6.3(c) n.49; 6.6(f) n.113; 6.9(f) n.133

Dee v. State, 273 Ga. 739, 545 S.E.2d 912 (2001)—§ 7.4(a) n.7

Deegan v. State, 711 N.W.2d 89 (Minn.2006)—§§ 2.12(d) n.194; 11.1(b) n.71; 27.1(a) n.5; 28.11(b) n.13; 28.12(b) n.13

Deel v. Jago, 967 F.2d 1079 (6th Cir.1992)—§ 23.2(f) n.90

Deere, People v., 41 Cal.3d 353, 222 Cal.Rptr. 13, 710 P.2d 925 (1985)—§ 11.6(a) n.62

Deerfield Speciality Papers, United States v., 501 F.Supp. 796 (E.D.Pa.1980)—§§ 15.2(c) n.61; 15.7(f) n.157, 186

Dees v. State, 676 S.W.2d 403 (Tex.Cr.App.1984)—§ 21.6(a) n.57

Dees, United States v., 467 F.3d 847 (3d Cir.2006)—§ 26.10(d) n.94

Dees, United States v., 125 F.3d 261 (5th Cir.1997)—§ 21.4(a) n.37

DeFabritus, United States v., 605 F.Supp. 1538 (S.D.N.Y.1985)—§ 16.2(f) n.96

Defazio, United States v., 899 F.2d 626 (7th Cir.1990)—§§ 11.9(c) n.117, 118, 143

Deffebaugh, State v., 31 Kan.App.2d 1030, 77 P.3d 1277 (2003)—§ 20.5(b) n.18

Deffenbaugh Industries, Inc., United States v., 957 F.2d 749 (10th Cir.1992)—§ 8.3(b) n.14

Defore, People v., 242 N.Y. 13, 150 N.E. 585 (1926)—§ 1.6(f) n.379

DeFoy v. McCullough, 393 F.3d 439 (3d Cir.2005)—§§ 28.3(a) n.37; 28.5(a) n.39

DeFreece v. State, 848 S.W.2d 150 (Tex.Crim.App.1993)—§§ 11.2(e) n.174, 182

DeFries, United States v., 129 F.3d 1293 (D.C.Cir.1997)—§ 22.2(d) n.80

DeFusco, United States v., 949 F.2d 114 (4th Cir.1991)—§ 21.4(d) n.104

D.E.G., State v., 194 W.Va. 411, 460 S.E.2d 657 (1995)—§ 17.4(c) n.153

DeGarmo, United States v., 450 F.3d 360 (8th Cir.2006)—§ 18.3(b) n.20

DeGay v. State, 741 S.W.2d 445 (Tex.Crim.App.1987)—§§ 26.9(a) n.1, 5

Degen v. United States, 517 U.S. 820, 116 S.Ct. 1777, 135 L.Ed.2d 102 (1996)—§ 27.5(c) n.79

Degnan, State v., 587 A.2d 71 (R.I.1991)—§ 21.4(a) n.24

DeGolyer v. Commonwealth, 314 Mass. 626, 51 N.E.2d 251 (1943)—§§ 15.1(f) n.273, 274, 315

DeGraff, State v., 139 N.M. 211, 131 P.3d 61 (2006)—§ 27.5(d) n.116

De Guair, State v., 108 Haw. 179, 118 P.3d 662 (2005)—§ 21.4(a) n.23

Deilke, State v., 274 Wis.2d 595, 682 N.W.2d 945 (2004)—§§ 18.5(a) n.39; 21.2(d) n.157, 277

Deisch, United States v., 20 F.3d 139 (5th Cir.1994)—§ 19.3(a) n.14

Deitchman, People v., 695 P.2d 1146 (Colo.1985)—§ 3.1(c) n.78

Deitz v. Money, 391 F.3d 804 (6th Cir.2005)—§ 28.4(b) n.19

DeJesus, Commonwealth v., 439 Mass. 616, 790 N.E.2d 231 (2003)— § 9.4(b) n.59

DeJesus, Commonwealth v., 567 Pa. 415, 787 A.2d 394 (2001)— §§ 6.7(c) n.111; 9.5(c) n.68

De Jesus, State v., 216 Neb. 907, 347 N.W.2d 111 (1984)—§ 14.2(g) n.104

DeJesus, United States v., 347 F.3d 500 (3d Cir.2003)—§§ 22.3(d) n.199, 215

DeJesus, United States v., 219 F.3d 117 (2d Cir.2000)—§ 21.2(b) n.76

DeJesus-Abad, United States v., 263 F.3d 5 (2d Cir.2001)—§ 21.4(d) n.102

DeJohn, United States v., 368 F.3d 533 (6th Cir.2004)—§§ 13.7(c) n.43; 18.3(b) n.35; 24.10(c) n.41

DeJongh, United States v., 937 F.2d 1 (1st Cir.1991)—§ 24.4(d) n.32

De La Beckwith v. State, 707 So.2d 547 (Miss.1997)—§ 18.1(c) n.27

De La Beckwith v. State, 615 So.2d 1134 (Miss.1992)—§§ 25.1(d) n.50; 27.2(c) n.62

Delacruz v. State, 280 Ga. 392, 627 S.E.2d 579 (2006)—§ 6.8(a) n.36

De-La-Cruz Castro, United States v., 299 F.3d 5 (1st Cir.2002)— § 21.2(b) n.76

de la Cruz-Paulino, United States v., 61 F.3d 986 (1st Cir.1995)—§ 10.2(a) n.10

De La Fe v. United States, 413 F.2d 543 (5th Cir.1969)—§ 6.8(a) n.36

De la Fuente, United States v., 8 F.3d 1333 (9th Cir.1993)—§ 21.2(d) n.255

Delagarza-Villarreal, United States v., 141 F.3d 133 (5th Cir.1997)— § 27.5(c) n.81

De Lago, People v., 16 N.Y.2d 289, 266 N.Y.S.2d 353, 213 N.E.2d 659 (1965)—§ 3.4(h) n.162

DeLaire, People v., 240 Ill.App.3d 1012, 183 Ill.Dec. 33, 610 N.E.2d 1277 (1993)—§§ 8.7(b) n.35; 8.8(f) n.150

De La Mata, United States v., 266 F.3d 1275 (11th Cir.2001)—§ 18.5(a) n.6

Delaney, Commonwealth v., 442 Mass. 604, 84 N.E.2d 346 (2004)— § 7.2(c) n.31

Delaney v. Commonwealth, 415 Mass. 490, 614 N.E.2d 672 (1993)— § 12.3(g) n.160

Delaney, State v., 187 W.Va. 212, 417 S.E.2d 903 (1992)—§ 3.5(d) n.173

DeLao, State v., 252 Wis.2d 289, 643 N.W.2d 480 (2002)—§§ 20.3(c) n.79; 20.6(b) n.32

Delap v. Dugger, 890 F.2d 285 (11th Cir.1989)—§§ 6.9(g) n.149, 159; 17.4(a) n.28

Dela Pena, People v., 72 F.3d 767 (9th Cir.1995)—§ 6.8(b) n.63

De La Rosa, United States v., 196 F.3d 712 (7th Cir.1999)—§ 20.2(c) n.50

De La Rosa, United States v., 922 F.2d 675 (11th Cir.1991)—§ 3.10(f) n.191

De Larosa, United States v., 450 F.2d 1057 (3d Cir.1971)—§ 17.2(e) n.125

DeLaughter, United States v., 453 F.2d 908 (5th Cir.1972)—§ 24.10(d) n.47

Delaurier, State v., 488 A.2d 688 (R.I.1985)—§ 4.6(m) n.224

De La Vega, United States v., 913 F.2d 861 (11th Cir.1990)—§ 23.2(d) n.69

Delaware v. Prouse, 440 U.S. 648, 99 S.Ct. 1391, 59 L.Ed.2d 660 (1979)—§§ 2.12(a) n.48, 49; 3.8(d) n.177; 3.9(g) n.121; 5.4(b) n.13

Delaware v. Van Arsdall, 475 U.S. 673, 106 S.Ct. 1431, 89 L.Ed.2d 674 (1986)—§§ 1.5(b) n.69; 2.6(c) n.85; 2.9(f) n.116, 117; 2.12(a) n.22; 14.4(e) n.105; 27.6(d) n.76, 83, 146; 27.6(e) n.156

Delay v. United States, 602 F.2d 173 (8th Cir.1979)—§ 13.4(c) n.143

De La Zerda, Commonwealth v., 416 Mass. 247, 619 N.E.2d 617 (1993)—§ 27.5(a) n.2

Delegal, United States v., 678 F.2d 47 (7th Cir.1982)—§ 21.3(e) n.269

DeLeo, People v., 185 App.Div.2d 374, 585 N.Y.S.2d 629 (1992)—§ 27.5(a) n.14

DeLeon v. Aguilar, 127 S.W.3d 1 (Tex.Cr.App.2004)—§ 22.4(c) n.26

DeLeon, United States v., 187 F.3d 60 (1st Cir.1999)—§ 17.2(e) n.116

De Leon-Reyna, United States v., 930 F.2d 396 (5th Cir.1991)—§ 3.1(c) n.59

Delgado v. Souders, 334 Or. 122, 46 P.3d 729 (2002)—§ 22.1(c) n.59

Delgado, State v., 188 N.J. 48, 902 A.2d 888 (2006)—§ 7.5(c) n.50

Delgado, United States v., 350 F.3d 520 (6th Cir.2003)—§§ 22.3(d) n.181; 22.3(e) n.260

Delgado, United States v., 56 F.3d 1357 (11th Cir.1995)—§§ 24.9(c) n.28; 26.4(e) n.82

Delgado-Hernandez, United States v., 420 F.3d 16 (1st Cir.2005)—§ 21.4(f) n.184

Delgado-Miranda, United States v., 951 F.2d 1063 (9th Cir.1991)—§ 18.3(b) n.56

Delgado-Uribe, United States v., 363 F.3d 1077 (10th Cir.2004)—§ 24.6(b) n.27

Delguidice v. New Jersey Racing Comm'n, 100 N.J. 79, 494 A.2d 1007 (1985)—§ 5.1(c) n.41

Delhomme v. Ramirez, 340 F.3d 817 (9th Cir.2003)—§ 28.5(b) n.50

Del Hoyo v. State, 109 Nev. 1216, 866 P.2d 261 (1993)—§§ 18.5(c) n.92; 26.10(b) n.18

Delia, United States v., 944 F.2d 1010 (2d Cir.1991)—§ 16.2(e) n.64

Delisle, State v., 162 Vt. 293, 648 A.2d 632 (1994)—§ 24.8(f) n.111

Delk v. State, 855 S.W.2d 700 (Tex.Crim.App. 1993)—§ 10.4(d) n.32

Delker, United States v., 757 F.2d 1390 (3d Cir.1985)—§§ 12.1(d) n.50; 12.3(a) n.20

Delli Paoli v. United States, 352 U.S. 232, 77 S.Ct. 294, 1 L.Ed.2d 278 (1957)—§ 17.2(b) n.27

Dell'Orfano v. State, 616 So.2d 33 (Fla.1993)—§ 19.3(b) n.163

Dellorfano, State v., 128 N.H. 628, 517 A.2d 1163 (1986)—§ 6.7(b) n.54

Del Muro, United States v., 87 F.3d 1078 (9th Cir.1996)—§ 11.7(e) n.66

DeLoach v. State, 722 So.2d 512 (Miss.1998)—§§ 6.10(b) n.19; 18.2(c) n.31, 53

Delong v. Commonwealth, 234 Va. 357, 362 S.E.2d 669 (1987)—§ 3.2(b) n.35

Delossantos, State v., 211 Conn. 258, 559 A.2d 164 (1989)—§ 3.7(a) n.16

De Los Santos, United States v., 810 F.2d 1326 (5th Cir.1987)—§§ 24.1(b) n.29; 24.3(g) n.171

Delpit, United States v., 94 F.3d 1134 (8th Cir.1996)—§§ 17.1(a) n.9; 17.2(a) n.12

Del Prado-Montero, United States v., 740 F.2d 113 (1st Cir.1984)—§ 21.4(f) n.214

Del Prete, United States v., 567 F.2d 928 (9th Cir.1978)—§ 21.4(e) n.163

Delrio v. State, 866 S.W.2d 304 (Tex.App.1993)—§ 22.3(c) n.162

Del Rosario, United States v., 902 F.2d 55 (D.C.Cir.1990)—§ 21.3(b) n.66

Delta County v. Gladstone, 305 Mich. 50, 8 N.W.2d 908 (1943)—§§ 1.8(d) n.47, 57

DeLuca v. Lord, 77 F.3d 578 (2d Cir.1996)—§§ 11.10(c) n.81, 90

DeLuca v. State, 465 S.W.2d 609 (Mo.1971)—§ 19.3(e) n.245

DeLuca, United States v., 269 F.3d 1128 (10th Cir.2001)—§§ 9.3(b) n.16; 9.3(c) n.17

DeLuca, United States v., 137 F.3d 24 (1st Cir.1998)—§ 24.1(b) n.32

DeLucia, People v., 20 N.Y.2d 275, 282 N.Y.S.2d 526, 229 N.E.2d 211 (1967)—§§ 24.9(g) n.121, 123

DeLuna, State v., 110 Ariz. 497, 520 P.2d 1121 (1974)—§ 11.4(a) n.1

DeLuna, United States v., 584 F.Supp. 139 (W.D.Mo.1984)—§ 11.9(c) n.123

De Luna v. United States, 308 F.2d 140 (5th Cir.1962)—§ 17.2(d) n.107

Del Vecchio v. Illinois Dept. of Corrections, 31 F.3d 1363 (7th Cir.1994)—§§ 6.10(e) n.67; 26.5(a) n.11

DelVerde, Commonwealth v., 398 Mass. 288, 496 N.E.2d 1357 (1986)—§ 21.4(b) n.59

Demarce v. Willrich, 203 Ariz. 502, 56 P.3d 76 (Ariz.App.2002)—§§ 26.1(d) n.91; 27.4(b) n.14

DeMarco, State v., 211 N.J.Super. 421, 511 A.2d 1251 (1986)—§ 25.4(a) n.8

Demarest v. Price, 130 F.3d 922 (10th Cir.1997)—§§ 28.5(a) n.35, 40

DeMarrias v. United States, 444 F.2d 162 (8th Cir.1971)—§ 11.2(c) n.102

DeMarsh, United States v., 360 F.Supp. 132 (E.D.Wis.1973)—§ 3.10(b) n.55

DeMassa v. Nunez, 770 F.2d 1505 (9th Cir.1985)—§ 9.1(c) n.108

DeMassa v. Nunez, 747 F.2d 1283 (9th Cir.1984)—§ 27.2(d) n.73

Demeter, State v., 124 N.J. 374, 590 A.2d 1179 (1991)—§ 3.3(b) n.49

DeMeyers, People v., 183 Mich.App. 286, 454 N.W.2d 202 (1990)—§§ 7.3(c) n.46, 47

DeMichael, United States v., 461 F.3d 414 (3d Cir.2006)—§ 27.5(a) n.3

DeMichael, United States v., 692 F.2d 1059 (7th Cir.1982)—§ 21.2(d) n.148

DeMichel, Commonwealth v., 442 Pa. 553, 277 A.2d 159 (1971)—§ 10.6(c) n.21

Deming v. City of Mobile, 677 So.2d 1233 (Ala.Cr.App.1995)—§ 22.1(b) n.57

Demmith v. Wisconsin Judicial Conference, 166 Wis.2d 649, 480 N.W.2d 502 (1992)—§ 12.2(a) n.6

Democratic County Committee of Bronx County v. Nadjari, 52 A.D.2d 70, 383 N.Y.S.2d 311 (1976)—§ 8.9(a) n.6

DeMonte, In re, 667 F.2d 590 (7th Cir.1981)—§ 8.9(b) n.22

Demoss, People v., 106 A.D.2d 395, 482 N.Y.S.2d 313 (1984)—§ 9.1(b) n.80

Dempsey v. State, 225 Ga. 208, 166 S.E.2d 884 (1969)—§ 6.8(a) n.35

Dempsey, United States v., 724 F.Supp. 573 (N.D.Ill.1989)—§ 11.9(c) n.104

Dempsey, United States v., 830 F.2d 1084 (10th Cir.1987)—§ 22.2(a) n.9

Demus v. United States, 710 A.2d 858 (D.C.App.1998)—§ 21.6(b) n.95

Denham, People v., 41 Ill.2d 1, 241 N.E.2d 415 (1968)—§ 9.1(a) n.15

Denison v. State, 258 Ga. 690, 373 S.E.2d 503 (1988)—§ 22.3(c) n.125

DeNistor, State v., 143 Ariz. 407, 694 P.2d 237 (1985)—§ 21.4(g) n.233

Dennany, People v., 445 Mich. 412, 519 N.W.2d 128 (1994)—§§ 11.5(c) n.46, 47; 11.5(d) n.68; 11.5(f) n.102, 104; 11.5(g) n.110

Dennard, United States v., 722 F.2d 1510 (11th Cir.1984)—§ 18.1(c) n.23

Dennett v. State, 19 Md.App. 376, 311 A.2d 437 (1973)—§ 18.4(c) n.61

Dennis v. Commonwealth, 464 S.W.2d 253 (Ky.1971)—§ 6.7(b) n.71

Dennis, People v., 28 Ill.App.3d 74, 328 N.E.2d 135 (1975)—§ 21.2(c) n.136

Dennis, State v., 893 A.2d 250 (R.I.2006)—§§ 10.4(b) n.17; 10.5(a) n.7

Dennis, State v., 216 W.Va. 331, 607 S.E.2d 437 (2004)—§ 16.4(c) n.56

Dennis v. State, 990 P.2d 277 (Okla.Crim.App.1999)—§ 6.9(c) n.61

Dennis v. State, 696 So.2d 1280 (Fla.App.1997)—§§ 11.7(e) n.76, 84

Dennis, United States v., 843 F.2d 652 (2d Cir.1988)—§ 1.7(j) n.262

Dennis, United States v., 786 F.2d 1029 (11th Cir.1986)—§ 24.10(a) n.17

Dennis, United States v., 804 F.2d 1208 (11th Cir.1986)—§ 22.3(d) n.193

Dennis, United States v., 625 F.2d 782 (8th Cir.1980)—§ 18.5(b) n.64

Dennis v. United States, 384 U.S. 855, 86 S.Ct. 1840, 16 L.Ed.2d 973 (1966)—§§ 8.5(a) n.13; 8.5(g) n.225; 8.5(h) n.235, 267; 20.1(c) n.43

Dennis, United States v., 183 F.2d 201 (2d Cir.1950)—§ 23.2(d) n.64

Dennis v. United States, 339 U.S. 162, 70 S.Ct. 519, 94 L.Ed. 734 (1950)—§ 22.3(c) n.122

Dennison, State v., 115 Wash.2d 609, 801 P.2d 193 (1990)—§ 18.5(a) n.8

Denny v. Commonwealth, 670 S.W.2d 847 (Ky.1984)—§§ 6.4(e) n.69; 6.4(g) n.151; 6.7(c) n.125

Denny, State v., 351 N.W.2d 102 (N.D.1984)—§ 18.5(b) n.58

Denny, United States v., 165 F.2d 668 (7th Cir.1947)—§ 19.3(d) n.203

Denoyer v. Weber, 694 N.W.2d 848 (S.D.2005)—§ 21.3(b) n.74

Densmore, State v., 160 Vt. 131, 624 A.2d 1138 (1993)—§§ 23.1(d) n.171, 182; 26.5(c) n.59

Denson v. State, 112 Nev. 489, 915 P.2d 284 (1996)—§ 26.4(b) n.9

Denson v. United States, 918 A.2d 1193 (D.C.App.2006)—§§ 21.3(b) n.67; 21.4(d) n.116

Dent, State v., 123 Wash.2d 467, 869 P.2d 392 (1994)—§§ 16.1(g) n.246, 256, 262; 16.1(h) n.289, 306, 307; 27.5(e) n.151

Dent, State v., 67 Wash.App. 656, 840 P.2d 202 (1992)—§ 16.1(g) n.269

Dent, United States v., 149 F.3d 180 (3d Cir.1998)—§ 18.4(c) n.53

Denune, State v., 82 Ohio App.3d 497, 612 N.E.2d 768 (1992)—§ 9.1(c) n.100

Denver Justice and Peace v. City of Golden, 405 F.3d 923 (10th Cir.2005)—§ 3.4(i) n.175

DePace, Commonwealth v., 433 Mass. 379, 742 N.E.2d 1054 (2001)—§ 6.5(b) n.25

DePallo v. Burge, 296 F.Supp.2d 282 (E.D.N.Y.2003)—§§ 24.2(a) n.14, 15, 21

DePalma v. State, 225 Ga. 465, 169 S.E.2d 801 (1969)—§ 19.6(b) n.10

DePasquale v. State, 104 Nev. 338, 757 P.2d 367 (1988)—§§ 5.2(b) n.26, 30; 5.2(c) n.43

DePoli, United States v., 628 F.2d 779 (2d Cir.1980)—§ 4.2(a) n.8

Deptula, State v., 34 Conn.App. 1, 639 A.2d 1049 (1994)—§ 27.5(a) n.22

Derby, State v., 131 N.H. 760, 561 A.2d 504 (1989)—§ 6.9(b) n.36

Derksen v. State, 845 P.2d 1383 (Wyo.1993)—§ 19.6(b) n.18

Dermota v. United States, 895 F.2d 1324 (11th Cir.1990)—§ 21.6(a) n.64

DeRoo v. United States, 223 F.3d 919 (8th Cir.2000)—§§ 11.7(e) n.113; 21.2(b) n.83

Derr, State v., 192 W.Va. 165, 451 S.E.2d 731 (1994)—§ 23.2(a) n.47

Derr, United States v., 990 F.2d 1330 (D.C.Cir.1993)—§ 24.3(b) n.41

Derrick v. Peterson, 924 F.2d 813 (9th Cir.1990)—§ 6.2(c) n.183

Derricott v. State, 327 Md. 582, 611 A.2d 592 (1992)—§ 3.8(d) n.146

Derrington v. United States, 488 A.2d 1314 (D.C.1985)—§ 3.10(e) n.143

DeRuggiero, People v., 96 Misc.2d 458, 409 N.Y.S.2d 88 (Sup.Ct.1978)—§ 15.7(h) n.228

DeSantis, People v., 2 Cal.4th 1198, 9 Cal.Rptr.2d 628, 831 P.2d 1210 (1992)—§§ 7.4(d) n.74; 22.2(d) n.68

DeSantis, United States v., 870 F.2d 536 (9th Cir.1989)—§ 6.7(b) n.80

DeSchepper, State v., 304 Minn. 399, 231 N.W.2d 294 (1975)—§§ 17.4(a) n.38, 39

Deschon, State v., 320 Mont. 1, 85 P.3d 756 (2004)—§ 22.3(c) n.125

Desdunes, State v., 576 So.2d 520 (La.App.1990)—§ 19.3(e) n.211

DeShaney v. Winnebago County Dept. of Social Services, 489 U.S. 189, 109 S.Ct. 998, 103 L.Ed.2d 249 (1989)—§ 2.7(d) n.252

Deshawn E. by Charlotte E. v. Safir, 156 F.3d 340 (2d Cir.1998)—§ 6.4(e) n.64

Deshields v. State, 706 A.2d 502 (Del.1998)—§ 22.1(h) n.149

Desir, State v., 766 A.2d 374 (R.I.2001)—§ 21.4(d) n.134

Desir, United States v., 257 F.3d 1233 (11th Cir.2001)—§§ 3.2(b) n.50; 3.7(f) n.130

Desirey, State v., 99 Or.App. 283, 782 P.2d 429 (1989)—§ 10.5(e) n.56

Desist v. United States, 394 U.S. 244, 89 S.Ct. 1030, 22 L.Ed.2d 248 (1969)—§§ 2.11(c) n.19, 20, 23, 26; 2.11(e) n.53; 28.6(d) n.19; 28.6(e) n.42

Deskins v. Commonwealth, 512 S.W.2d 520 (Ky.1974)—§§ 6.4(b) n.25; 20.3(b) n.37

DesLaurier, State v., 230 Conn. 572, 646 A.2d 108 (1994)—§ 6.6(e) n.71

Desmarais, United States v., 967 F.2d 17 (1st Cir.1992)—§ 21.5(a) n.34

Delete Desmarais, United States v., 938 F.2d 347—§ 26.6(d) n.54

Desnoyers, State v., 132 N.M. 756, 55 P.3d 968 (2002)—§ 6.4(g) n.153

DeSousa v. Reno, 190 F.3d 175 (3d Cir.1999)—§ 21.2(d) n.234

DeSouza, Commonwealth v., 428 Mass. 667, 704 N.E.2d 190 (1999)—§ 6.8(a) n.36

Despain v. State, 774 P.2d 77 (Wyo.1989)—§§ 18.1(c) n.36; 18.5(c) n.75

Desper v. State, 173 W.Va. 494, 318 S.E.2d 437 (1984)—§§ 14.4(d) n.83, 84, 88 to 90; 14.4(e) n.113, 142

Desrosiers, State v., 559 A.2d 641 (R.I.1989)—§ 26.10(b) n.22

Dessus, Commonwealth v., 423 Pa. 177, 224 A.2d 188 (1966)—§§ 15.2(d) n.108; 15.4(b) n.47

DeStafano, United States v., 429 F.2d 344 (2d Cir.1970)—§ 17.3(b) n.19

DeStefano v. Woods, 392 U.S. 631, 88 S.Ct. 2093, 20 L.Ed.2d 1308 (1968)—§§ 2.11(c) n.32, 38

DeSumma, Commonwealth v., 522 Pa. 36, 559 A.2d 521 (1989)—§ 19.5(b) n.20

DeSumma, United States v., 272 F.3d 176 (3d Cir.2001)—§§ 9.5(b) n.41, 42

DeTar, United States v., 832 F.2d 1110 (9th Cir.1987)—§ 24.8(f) n.105

DeTemple, United States v., 162 F.3d 279 (4th Cir.1998)—§ 22.4(c) n.23

Deters, United States v., 143 F.3d 577 (10th Cir.1998)—§ 27.2(c) n.44

DeTienne, United States v., 468 F.2d 151 (7th Cir.1972)—§§ 18.1(c) n.37; 18.2(c) n.54

Detlefson, State v., 335 So.2d 371 (Fla.App.1976)—§ 3.2(c) n.132

Detroit Motors, State v., 62 N.J.Super. 386, 163 A.2d 227 (1960)—§ 15.6(d) n.119

Detter, State v., 298 N.C. 604, 260 S.E.2d 567 (1979)—§ 20.3(h) n.155

Dettman, State v., 719 N.W.2d 644 (Minn.2006)—§ 26.4(i) n.203

Deutschendorf v. People, 920 P.2d 53 (Colo.1996)—§ 17.4(b) n.124

De Veau v. United States, 454 A.2d 1308 (D.C.App.1982)—§ 12.4(a) n.7

Devenpeck v. Alford, 543 U.S. 146, 125 S.Ct. 588, 160 L.Ed.2d 537 (2004)—§§ 3.1(d) n.100; 3.5(a) n.46

DeVerney, State v., 592 N.W.2d 837 (Minn.1999)—§ 22.3(d) n.212

Devier v. State, 253 Ga. 604, 323 S.E.2d 150 (1984)—§ 23.2(a) n.46

Devin, People v., 93 Ill.2d 326, 67 Ill.Dec. 63, 444 N.E.2d 102 (1982)—§ 24.2(b) n.25

Devin, State v., 142 P.3d 599 (Wash.2006)—§ 27.5(a) n.7

Devine, State v., 307 Or. 341, 768 P.2d 913 (1989)—§ 3.4(e) n.74

Devine, State v., 114 Ariz. 574, 562 P.2d 1072 (1977)—§ 21.4(c) n.95

Devoe, State v., 430 S.W.2d 164 (Mo.1968)—§ 6.8(a) n.21

Devoney v. State, 717 So.2d 501 (Fla.1998)—§ 24.9(g) n.114

Devore, People v., 402 Ill. 336, 83 N.E.2d 728 (1949)—§§ 16.1(d) n.133; 16.4(c) n.55

Devose v. Norris, 53 F.3d 201 (8th Cir.1995)—§ 22.3(d) n.242

Devot, State v., 66 Utah 319, 242 P. 395 (1925)—§ 16.4(c) n.62

Dew v. United States, 558 A.2d 1112 (D.C.App.1989)—§§ 6.4(f) n.122, 136

Dewalt, United States v., 92 F.3d 1209 (D.C.Cir.1996)—§ 21.4(c) n.78

Dewberry v. State, 4 S.W.3d 735 (Tex.Cr.App.1999)—§ 6.9(b) n.35

Dewberry v. State, 776 S.W.2d 589 (Tex.Cr.App.1989)—§ 22.3(d) n.212

DeWeese, State v., 213 W.Va. 339, 582 S.E.2d 786 (2003)—§§ 6.3(c) n.53, 54; 6.8(a) n.33

DeWitt, People v., 78 Ill.2d 82, 34 Ill.Dec. 319, 397 N.E.2d 1385 (1979)—§ 26.10(b) n.25

Dewitt v. State, 755 N.E.2d 167 (Ind.2001)—§ 21.4(e) n.165

DeWitt, State v., 184 Ariz. 464, 910 P.2d 9 (1996)—§§ 2.12(e) n.205; 3.1(c) n.65

DeWitt, United States v., 366 F.3d 667 (8th Cir.2004)—§§ 21.2(d) n.199; 21.2(e) n.316

Dewitt, United States v., 946 F.2d 1497 (10th Cir.1991)—§ 3.10(f) n.195

Dewitt, United States v., 76 U.S. (9 Wall) 41, 19 L.Ed. 593 (1869)—§§ 1.2(c) n.13, 34

Dexter, State v., 954 S.W.2d 332 (Mo.1997)—§ 27.5(d) n.114

DeZarn, United States v., 157 F.3d 1042 (6th Cir.1998)—§ 15.7(e) n.129

D.F., United States v., 63 F.3d 671 (7th Cir.1995)—§§ 6.2(c) n.187; 6.10(c) n.42, 50

Diacolios, United States v., 837 F.2d 79 (2d Cir.1988)—§ 18.2(c) n.49

Diamond, United States v., 808 F.2d 922 (1st Cir.1987)—§ 3.4(a) n.7

Diamond, United States v., 706 F.2d 105 (2d Cir.1983)—§ 21.2(d) n.178

Diamontopoulas v. State, 140 N.H. 182, 664 A.2d 81 (1995)—§ 21.4(d) n.116

Dias, Commonwealth v., 419 Mass. 698, 646 N.E.2d 1065 (1995)—§ 24.9(e) n.52

Diaz v. Duckworth, 143 F.3d 345 (7th Cir.1998)—§ 27.5(a) n.18

Diaz v. Herbert, 317 F.Supp.2d 462 (S.D.N.Y.2004)—§ 24.2(a) n.5

Diaz, People v., 7 N.Y.3d 831, 857 N.E.2d 47, 823 N.Y.S.2d 752 (2006)—§ 27.5(c) n.72

Diaz, People v., 192 Ill.2d 211, 249 Ill.Dec. 1, 735 N.E.2d 605 (2000)—§ 21.6(a) n.80

Diaz, People v., 10 App.Div.2d 80, 198 N.Y.S.2d 27 (1960)—§ 24.6(a) n.6

Diaz, State v., 274 Conn. 818, 878 A.2d 1078 (2005)—§ 11.3(b) n.45

Diaz, State v., 850 So.2d 435 (Fla.2003)—§ 3.8(b) n.38

Diaz v. State, 118 Nev. 451, 50 P.3d 166 (2002)—§§ 18.4(c) n.60, 73

Diaz, State v., 117 Idaho 392, 788 P.2d 207 (1990)—§ 14.3(c) n.72

Diaz, United States v., 236 F.R.D. 470 (N.D.Cal.2006)—§ 22.3(b) n.55

Diaz, United States v., 248 F.3d 1065 (11th Cir.2001)—§§ 7.4(e) n.92; 17.1(a) n.9; 24.4(d) n.64

Diaz, United States v., 176 F.3d 52 (2d Cir.1999)—§§ 17.2(d) n.95; 17.3(e) n.61, 64; 22.3(d) n.216

Diaz, United States v., 685 F.2d 252 (8th Cir.1982)—§ 16.2(g) n.124

Diaz v. United States, 264 F.Supp. 937 (E.D.La.1967)—§ 6.7(c) n.120

Diaz v. United States, 223 U.S. 442, 32 S.Ct. 250, 56 L.Ed. 500 (1912)—§§ 17.4(b) n.97; 24.2(d) n.40; 25.5(c) n.34

Diaz-Diaz, United States v., 135 F.3d 572 (8th Cir.1998)—§§ 19.2(c) n.37; 27.5(a) n.32

DiBartolomeo v. State, 450 So.2d 925 (Fla.App.1984)—§ 11.2(g) n.277

Di Bella, In re, 518 F.2d 955 (2d Cir.1975)—§ 8.14(c) n.37

DiBella v. United States, 369 U.S. 121, 82 S.Ct. 654, 7 L.Ed.2d 614 (1962)—§§ 27.2(b) n.11; 27.2(c) n.27; 27.2(d) n.71

DiBenedetto, Commonwealth v., 427 Mass. 414, 693 N.E.2d 1007 (1998)—§ 3.6(a) n.12

DiBenedetto, Commonwealth v., 414 Mass. 37, 605 N.E.2d 811 (1992)—§ 14.1(d) n.66

DiBenedetto v. Hall, 272 F.3d 1 (1st Cir.2001)—§ 28.6(f) n.76

DiBernardo, United States v., 880 F.2d 1216 (11th Cir.1989)—§ 17.2(c) n.84

DiBernardo, United States v., 775 F.2d 1470 (11th Cir.1985)—§ 15.5(b) n.59

Dichiarinte, United States v., 445 F.2d 126 (7th Cir.1971)—§ 3.10(f) n.198

Dickens, United States v., 524 F.2d 441 (5th Cir.1975)—§ 5.3(a) n.15

Dickerson v. Louisiana, 816 F.2d 220 (5th Cir.1987)—§ 27.4(f) n.71

Dickerson, State v., 273 Ga. 408, 542 S.E.2d 487 (2001)—§ 20.6(b) n.27

Dickerson, State v., 481 N.W.2d 840 (Minn.1992)—§ 3.2(b) n.91

Dickerson, State v., 313 N.W.2d 526 (Iowa 1981)—§ 3.2(b) n.59

Dickerson v. United States, 530 U.S. 428, 120 S.Ct. 2326, 147 L.Ed.2d 405 (2000)—§§ 2.4(e) n.149; 2.7(d) n.261; 2.9(h) n.212, 243; 2.10(b) n.9; 6.5(d) n.79; 6.5(e) n.87; 6.7(b) n.79; 9.5(b) n.46

Dickerson, United States v., 166 F.3d 667 (4th Cir.1999)—§ 6.5(e) n.86

Dickerson, United States v., 975 F.2d 1245 (7th Cir.1992)—§ 3.10(b) n.49

Dickerson v. Vaughn, 90 F.3d 87 (3d Cir.1996)—§§ 21.3(b) n.45, 72; 21.6(b) n.111

Dickey v. Florida, 398 U.S. 30, 90 S.Ct. 1564, 26 L.Ed.2d 26 (1970)—§§ 2.9(d) n.57; 18.2(c) n.40; 18.4(a) n.7

Dickey, State v., 928 So.2d 1193 (Fla.2006)—§ 21.3(b) n.66

Dickey, State v., 459 N.W.2d 445 (S.D.1990)—§ 6.2(c) n.111

Dickey v. State, 444 P.2d 373 (Wyo.1968)—§ 6.8(a) n.30

Dickey, United States v., 736 F.2d 571 (10th Cir.1984)—§ 17.2(c) n.82

Dickinson v. State, 685 S.W.2d 320 (Tex.Cr.App.1984)—§§ 24.5(b) n.22, 23

Dickson, State v., 4 Haw.App. 614, 673 P.2d 1036 (1983)—§ 11.5(c) n.32

Dickson, United States v., 64 F.3d 409 (8th Cir.1995)—§ 9.1(b) n.81

Dickson, United States v., 712 F.2d 952 (5th Cir.1983)—§ 21.2(d) n.183

Dictado v. Ducharme, 244 F.3d 724 (9th Cir.2001)—§ 28.5(b) n.48

DiDomenico, United States v., 78 F.3d 294 (7th Cir.1996)—§§ 11.8(b) n.44; 22.3(b) n.68

DiDonato, People v., 87 N.Y.2d 992, 642 N.Y.S.2d 616, 665 N.E.2d 186 (1996)—§ 21.6(b) n.112

Diehl, United States v., 276 F.3d 32 (1st Cir.2002)—§ 3.1(c) n.65

Diesen, State v., 297 Mont. 459, 992 P.2d 1287 (2000)—§ 16.1(e) n.174

Di Falco, People v., 44 N.Y.2d 482, 406 N.Y.S.2d 279, 377 N.E.2d 732 (1978)—§§ 15.6(d) n.119; 15.7(c) n.58

DiFrancesco, United States v., 449 U.S. 117, 101 S.Ct. 426, 66 L.Ed.2d 328 (1980)—§§ 2.9(f) n.129, 131; 25.1(b) n.2, 5, 10; 26.3(g) n.90; 26.7(a) n.6; 26.7(b) n.16; 27.3(a) n.5

DiFrisco, State v., 137 N.J. 434, 645 A.2d 734 (1994)—§ 21.2(g) n.396

DiFrisco, State v., 118 N.J. 253, 571 A.2d 914 (1990)—§ 6.2(c) n.148

Diggs, People v., 140 Misc.2d 794, 531 N.Y.S.2d 723 (Dist.Ct.1988)— § 14.4(c) n.64

Diggs v. State, 345 So.2d 815 (Fla.App.1977)—§ 3.1(d) n.110

Diggs v. United States, 906 A.2d 290 (D.C.App.2006)—§§ 7.4(c) n.48, 51, 53

Diggs, United States v., 522 F.2d 1310 (D.C.Cir.1975)—§ 3.3(d) n.180

DiGiacomo, United States v., 579 F.2d 1211 (10th Cir.1978)—§ 6.8(d) n.83

DiGiambattista, Commonwealth v., 442 Mass. 423, 813 N.E.2d 516 (2004)—§§ 6.2(c) n.132; 6.8(c) n.64

DiGiangiemo, United States ex rel. v. Regan, 528 F.2d 1262 (2d Cir.1975)—§§ 10.6(d) n.38, 39, 41; 17.4(a) n.61

DiGilio, United States v., 538 F.2d 972 (3d Cir.1976)—§ 8.8(g) n.169

DiGiovanni v. United States, 810 A.2d 887 (D.C.App.2002)—§§ 6.9(b) n.44, 46; 6.9(c) n.58

DiGirlomo, United States v., 550 F.2d 404 (8th Cir.1977)—§ 4.6(m) n.244

Digirolamo, People v., 179 Ill.2d 24, 227 Ill.Dec. 779, 688 N.E.2d 116 (1997)—§ 16.1(g) n.244

Dignan, State v., 114 W.Va. 275, 171 S.E. 527 (1933)—§ 16.1(e) n.201

Dignoti, State v., 682 A.2d 666 (Me.1996)—§ 3.4(j) n.181

DiGrazia, United States v., 213 F.Supp. 232 (N.D.Ill.1963)—§§ 15.6(b) n.56; 15.7(b) n.15

DiGuiseppe v. Ward, 698 F.2d 602 (2d Cir.1983)—§ 3.9(i) n.177

DiIanni, United States v., 87 F.3d 15 (1st Cir.1996)—§ 26.10(c) n.43

DiJames, United States v., 731 F.2d 758 (11th Cir.1984)—§§ 16.2(b) n.22, 33; 16.2(c) n.39; 16.3(d) n.64

DiLapi, United States v., 651 F.2d 140 (2d Cir.1981)—§ 24.10(d) n.45

DiLeo v. Commissioner of Internal Revenue, 959 F.2d 16 (2d Cir.1992)— §§ 8.5(c) n.90, 96, 97, 113, 117

Dillard v. Commonwealth, 995 S.W.2d 366 (Ky.1999)—§ 17.2(b) n.69

Dillard, People v., 214 A.D.2d 1028, 627 N.Y.S.2d 184 (1995)—§ 15.7(f) n.169

Dillard, United States v., 214 F.3d 88 (2d Cir.2000)—§ 12.3(a) n.18

Dilliner, State v., 212 W.Va. 135, 569 S.E.2d 211 (2002)—§ 24.10(a) n.8

Dillingham v. Commonwealth, 684 S.W.2d 307 (Ky.App.1984)— § 11.10(c) n.116

Dillingham v. United States, 423 U.S. 64, 96 S.Ct. 303, 46 L.Ed.2d 205 (1975)—§ 18.1(c) n.22

Dillon, State v., 74 Ohio St.3d 166, 657 N.E.2d 273 (1995)—§ 11.9(b) n.87

Dillon v. State, 317 Ark. 384, 877 S.W.2d 915 (1994)—§ 25.4(c) n.28

Dillon, State v., 242 Kan. 410, 748 P.2d 856 (1988)—§§ 21.2(f) n.363; 21.4(a) n.17

Dillon, State v., 224 Neb. 503, 398 N.W.2d 718 (1987)—§ 21.2(f) n.388

Dillon v. State, 492 N.E.2d 661 (Ind.1986)—§ 26.5(b) n.29

Dillon, State v., 292 Or. 172, 637 P.2d 602 (1981)—§ 26.9(b) n.31

Dillon, United States v., 938 F.2d 1412 (1st Cir.1991)—§ 12.3(a) n.24

Dillon v. United States, 307 F.2d 445 (9th Cir.1962)—§ 21.2(b) n.48

Dilworth, People v., 169 Ill.2d 195, 214 Ill.Dec. 456, 661 N.E.2d 310 (1996)—§§ 3.9(k) n.254, 258

DiMatteo, People v., 80 Misc.2d 1029, 365 N.Y.S.2d 126 (1975)— § 20.3(c) n.71

Dimatteo, United States v., 759 F.2d 831 (11th Cir.1985)—§ 11.10(d) n.161

Dimeo, State v., 304 Or. 469, 747 P.2d 353 (1987)—§ 4.6(l) n.200

Dimmitt, State v., 665 N.W.2d 692 (N.D.2003)—§§ 21.2(c) n.100; 21.2(d) n.167

DiMuro, United States v., 540 F.2d 503 (1st Cir.1976)—§ 9.4(b) n.59

Dinagen, State v., 639 A.2d 1353 (R.I.1994)—§ 27.6(b) n.43

Dingfelt, Commonwealth v., 227 Pa.Super. 380, 323 A.2d 145 (1974)—§ 3.9(k) n.248

Dingle v. State, 361 Md. 1, 759 A.2d 819 (2000)—§ 22.3(a) n.23

Dingle, United States v., 114 F.3d 307 (D.C.Cir.1997)—§ 24.8(f) n.121

Dingler v. State, 669 So.2d 1024 (Ala.Cr.App.1995)—§ 26.10(c) n.51

Dingler v. State, 233 Ga. 462, 211 S.E.2d 752 (1975)—§ 17.1(f) n.71

Dinitz, United States v., 424 U.S. 600, 96 S.Ct. 1075, 47 L.Ed.2d 267 (1976)—§§ 24.7(a) n.5; 25.2(a) n.3; 25.2(e) n.41; 25.2(f) n.50; 25.4(a) n.4

Dinning v. State, 267 Ga. 879, 485 S.E.2d 464 (1997)—§ 25.4(a) n.8

Di Noi, State v., 59 R.I. 348, 195 A. 497 (1937)—§ 20.1(a) n.9

Dinsmore, State v., 342 Or 1, 147 P.3d 1146 (2006)—§ 21.5(e) n.116

Dionisio, United States v., 410 U.S. 1, 93 S.Ct. 764, 35 L.Ed.2d 67 (1973)—§§ 3.2(b) n.81; 3.2(g) n.190; 7.2(b) n.14; 8.2(c) n.43; 8.4(b) n.50; 8.6(a) n.7, 9, 13, 16, 21, 25; 8.7(a) n.27; 8.7(c) n.63; 8.8(b) n.18; 8.8(h) n.180; 8.10(c) n.70; 15.2(d) n.117; 15.5(a) n.16, 23, 34

Diozzi, United States v., 807 F.2d 10 (1st Cir.1986)—§ 11.9(c) n.117

Di Pasquale, United States v., 864 F.2d 271 (3d Cir.1988)—§ 22.3(d) n.193

Dipentino, United States v., 242 F.3d 1090 (9th Cir.2001)—§ 19.6(c) n.46

DiPietro, United States v., 936 F.2d 6 (1st Cir.1991)—§ 25.2(a) n.7

DiPonio, People v., 20 Mich.App. 658, 174 N.W.2d 572 (1969)—§ 8.1(c) n.26

DiPrete, State v., 682 A.2d 1373 (R.I.1996)—§§ 15.6(a) n.41, 43

DiPrima, United States v., 472 F.2d 550 (1st Cir.1973)—§ 3.10(e) n.143

Di Re, United States v., 332 U.S. 581, 68 S.Ct. 222, 92 L.Ed. 210 (1948)—§§ 3.3(f) n.194, 220; 3.4(i) n.174; 3.7(c) n.53

Dirring v. United States, 370 F.2d 862 (1st Cir.1967)—§ 22.3(e) n.263

Disbrow, People v., 16 Cal.3d 101, 127 Cal.Rptr. 360, 545 P.2d 272 (1976)—§§ 2.12(c) n.119, 125, 166

Disclosure of Evidence, In re Petition for, 63 Ohio St.2d 212, 407 N.E.2d 513 (1980)—§ 8.5(b) n.48

Disclosure of Evidence, Re Petition for, 184 F.Supp. 38 (E.D.Va.1960)—§ 8.5(h) n.297

Disclosure of Grand Jury Testimony, In the Matter of an Application for, 124 N.J. 443, 591 A.2d 614 (1991)—§§ 8.5(h) n.250, 252, 276, 280, 286 to 288

Disclosure of Juror Names and Addresses, In re, 233 Mich.App. 604, 592 N.W.2d 798 (1999)—§§ 23.1(d) n.192; 23.1(e) n.226, 247

Disclosure of Testimony Before Grand Jury, Troia, In re, 580 F.2d 281 (8th Cir.1978)—§ 8.5(h) n.280

Dishman v. Maryland, 352 Md. 279, 721 A.2d 699 (1998)—§ 19.1(c) n.32

Disla, United States v., 805 F.2d 1340 (9th Cir.1986)—§§ 6.7(b) n.42, 54

Dismuke v. United States, 864 F.2d 106 (11th Cir.1989)—§ 21.4(c) n.66

Dispoto, State v., 189 N.J. 108, 913 A.2d 791 (2007)—§ 6.8(b) n.63

Disston, United States v., 612 F.2d 1035 (7th Cir.1980)—§ 20.3(d) n.91

DiStefano, State v., 593 A.2d 1351 (R.I.1991)—§ 22.1(h) n.135

Di Stefano, United States v., 555 F.2d 1094 (2d Cir.1977)—§ 3.6(d) n.85

District Attorney v. Superior Court, 342 Mass. 119, 172 N.E.2d 245 (1961)—§ 26.7(c) n.26

District Attorney v. Watson, 381 Mass. 648, 411 N.E.2d 1274 (1980)—§§ 2.12(b) n.112; 2.12(c) n.121

District Court, People v., 953 P.2d 184 (Colo.1998)—§§ 22.1(h) n.154; 27.4(d) n.51

District Court, People v., 803 P.2d 193 (Colo.1990)—§ 14.3(d) n.87

District Court, People v., 779 P.2d 385 (Colo.1989)—§ 14.3(b) n.51

District Court, People v., 199 Colo. 398, 610 P.2d 490 (1980)—§ 15.2(i) n.214

District Court, People v., 187 Colo. 333, 531 P.2d 626 (1975)—§§ 20.1(a) n.16; 20.4(d) n.67, 71; 20.4(g) n.105

District Court, People v., 187 Colo. 164, 529 P.2d 1335 (1974)—§ 12.4(a) n.5

District Court, State v., 150 Mont. 128, 432 P.2d 93 (1967)—§ 6.6(e) n.71

District Court, 17th Judicial District, People v., 926 P.2d 567 (Colo.1996)—§§ 14.3(a) n.9, 10, 12

District Court for Jackson County, State v., 463 N.W.2d 885 (Iowa 1990)—§ 21.3(d) n.263

District Court of El Paso County, People v., 790 P.2d 332 (Colo.1990)—§§ 20.3(k) n.213; 24.3(c) n.81

District of Columbia v. Clawans, 300 U.S. 617, 57 S.Ct. 660, 81 L.Ed. 843 (1937)—§§ 2.9(d) n.72; 22.1(b) n.37

District of Columbia v. Colts, 282 U.S. 63, 51 S.Ct. 52, 75 L.Ed. 177 (1930)—§ 22.1(b) n.39

District of Columbia v. Houston, 842 A.2d 667 (D.C.App.2004)—§ 13.2(a) n.5

District of Columbia v. John R. Thompson Co., 346 U.S. 100, 73 S.Ct. 1007, 97 L.Ed. 1480 (1953)—§ 13.5(c) n.67

District of Columbia v. Whitley, 640 A.2d 710 (D.C.App.1994)—§ 25.1(d) n.51

Ditmars, State v., 98 Idaho 472, 567 P.2d 17 (1977)—§ 24.2(a) n.11

Ditson, People v., 57 Cal.2d 415, 20 Cal.Rptr. 165, 369 P.2d 714 (1962)—§ 9.5(a) n.6

Ditter, State v., 232 Neb. 600, 441 N.W.2d 622 (1989)—§§ 21.3(b) n.94; 21.3(d) n.220

Ditto v. State, 988 S.W.2d 236 (Tex.Cr.App.1999)—§ 21.2(d) n.227

Divito, State v., 330 Or. 319, 5 P.3d 1103 (2000)—§ 20.3(k) n.213

Dix v. County of Shasta, 963 F.2d 1296 (9th Cir.1992)—§ 1.5(k) n.386

Dixon v. Commonwealth, 270 Va. 34, 613 S.E.2d 398 (2005)—§ 6.6(e) n.95

Dixon v. Commonwealth, 149 S.W.3d 426 (Ky.2004)—§ 6.7(b) n.43

Dixon v. District of Columbia, 394 F.2d 966 (D.C.Cir.1968)—§ 13.5(a) n.9

Dixon, People v., 85 N.Y.2d 218, 623 N.Y.S.2d 813, 647 N.E.2d 1321 (1995)—§ 7.4(b) n.35

Dixon, People v., 392 Mich. 691, 222 N.W.2d 749 (1974)—§ 3.5(c) n.132

Dixon v. Snyder, 266 F.3d 693 (7th Cir.2001)—§ 11.10(c) n.105

Dixon, State v., 112 P.3d 883 (Kan.2005)—§ 24.1(a) n.5

Dixon, State v., 279 Kan. 563, 112 P.3d 883 (2005)—§ 21.2(b) n.63

Dixon v. State, 673 A.2d 1220 (Del.1996)—§§ 22.3(d) n.245, 250

Dixon, State v., 125 N.J. 223, 593 A.2d 266 (1991)—§§ 6.8(d) n.82; 6.9(g) n.150; 15.4(f) n.144

Dixon, State v., 114 Wash.2d 857, 792 P.2d 137 (1990)—§ 18.5(b) n.58

Dixon, State v., 419 N.W.2d 699 (S.D.1988)—§ 17.1(a) n.14

Dixon, State v., 449 So.2d 463 (La.1984)—§ 21.2(g) n.405

Dixon v. State, 605 P.2d 882 (Alaska 1980)—§ 24.2(a) n.6

Dixon v. State, 287 So.2d 698 (Fla.App.1973)—§ 21.3(b) n.56

Dixon, United States v., 187 F.Supp.2d 601 (S.D.W.Va.2002)—§§ 24.3(b) n.80; 26.10(b) n.28

Dixon, United States v., 201 F.3d 1223 (9th Cir.2000)—§ 7.4(g) n.116

Dixon, United States v., 184 F.3d 643 (7th Cir.1999)—§ 17.1(c) n.45

Dixon, United States v., 1 F.3d 1080 (10th Cir.1993)—§ 3.7(d) n.72

Dixon, United States v., 509 U.S. 688, 113 S.Ct. 2849, 125 L.Ed.2d 556 (1993)—§§ 2.9(b) n.23, 29; 2.9(c) n.51, 52; 2.9(d) n.74, 76; 17.4(b) n.82; 24.8(e) n.83; 25.1(b) n.19

Dixon, United States v., 596 F.2d 178 (7th Cir.1979)—§ 19.3(a) n.53

D.J., State ex rel., 817 So.2d 26 (La.2002)—§ 22.1(c) n.64

Djadi v. State, 72 Md.App. 223, 528 A.2d 502 (1987)—§ 11.2(e) n.176

D.M., Matter of, 611 S.W.2d 880 (Tex.App.1980)—§ 25.1(d) n.88

Doan v. Brigano, 237 F.3d 722 (6th Cir.2001)—§ 24.9(f) n.67

Doane v. Commonwealth, 218 Va. 500, 237 S.E.2d 797 (1977)—§ 16.4(c) n.55

Dobbert v. Florida, 432 U.S. 282, 97 S.Ct. 2290, 53 L.Ed.2d 344 (1977)—§§ 23.2(a) n.12, 15; 23.2(f) n.103, 111

Dobbins v. State, 187 S.W.3d 865 (Mo.2006)—§ 21.3(b) n.71

Dobbins, State v., 306 N.C. 342, 293 S.E.2d 162 (1982)—§ 3.4(l) n.242

Dobbs v. Turpin, 142 F.3d 1383 (11th Cir.1998)—§ 11.10(c) n.138

Dobbs, United States v., 449 F.3d 904 (8th Cir.2006)—§ 7.4(f) n.107

Dobbs v. Zant, 963 F.2d 1403 (11th Cir.1991)—§ 24.9(g) n.114

Dobin, United States v., 938 F.2d 867 (8th Cir.1991)—§ 17.3(d) n.56

Dockery, United States v., 965 F.2d 1112 (D.C.Cir.1992)—§§ 21.2(f) n.383; 21.3(c) n.148

Dockery, United States v., 736 F.2d 1232 (8th Cir.1984)—§ 6.6(e) n.72

Doctor v. State, 596 So.2d 442 (Fla.1992)—§ 3.3(b) n.54

Dodd v. State, 993 P.2d 778 (Okla.Crim.App.2000)—§ 20.3(i) n.171

Dodd v. State, 879 P.2d 822 (Okl.Cr.1994)—§ 5.2(a) n.4

Dodd v. United States, 545 U.S. 353, 125 S.Ct. 2478, 162 L.Ed.2d 343 (2005)—§§ 28.5(b) n.56; 28.9(b) n.48, 49

Dodge, Commonwealth v., 428 Mass. 860, 705 N.E.2d 612 (1999)—§ 12.1(b) n.32

Dodge, United States v., 846 F.Supp. 181 (D.Conn.1994)—§ 12.4(d) n.71

Dodge, United States v., 538 F.2d 770 (8th Cir.1976)—§ 7.5(a) n.6

Dodis, State v., 314 N.W.2d 233 (Minn.1982)—§ 20.4(f) n.92

Dodson v. Cooper, 705 P.2d 500 (Colo.1985)—§ 18.4(c) n.70

Dodson, People v., 48 N.Y.2d 36, 421 N.Y.S.2d 47, 396 N.E.2d 194 (1979)—§§ 26.9(a) n.9; 26.9(b) n.34

Dodson, State v., 250 Neb. 584, 550 N.W.2d 347 (1996)—§§ 16.1(h) n.286; 21.3(a) n.35; 21.4(f) n.175

Dodson v. State, 513 A.2d 761 (Del.1986)—§ 6.9(f) n.111

Doe, In re, 107 Hawaii 439, 114 P.3d 945 (2005)—§ 10.3(d) n.63

Doe, In re, 678 F.Supp. 186 (N.D.Ill.1988)—§§ 8.5(c) n.79; 8.5(e) n.186

Doe, In re, 537 F.Supp. 1038 (D.R.I.1982)—§§ 8.5(c) n.92, 93, 95, 104, 105, 113, 115, 116

Doe, In re, 662 F.2d 1073 (4th Cir.1981)—§§ 8.6(b) n.44, 50, 51

Doe v. Borough of Clifton Heights, 719 F.Supp. 382 (E.D.Pa.1989)—§ 1.3(b) n.16

Doe, Commonwealth v., 408 Mass. 764, 563 N.E.2d 1349 (1990)—§ 8.8(g) n.179

Doe, Commonwealth v., 405 Mass. 676, 544 N.E.2d 860 (1989)—§ 8.13(d) n.95

Doe, Commonwealth v., 524 S.W.2d 630 (Ky.1975)—§ 19.3(b) n.182

Doe v. Connell, 179 App.Div.2d 196, 583 N.Y.S.2d 707 (1992)—§ 27.4(c) n.26

Doe v. DiGenova, 779 F.2d 74 (D.C.Cir.1985)—§ 8.8(g) n.163

Doe v. Gonzales, 500 F.Supp.2d 379 (S.D.N.Y. 2007)—§ 4.9(b) n.22

Doe v. Immigration and Naturalization Service, 120 F.3d 200 (9th Cir.1997)—§ 28.9(a) n.29

Doe, People v., 59 N.Y.2d 655, 463 N.Y.S.2d 405, 450 N.E.2d 211 (1983)—§ 8.12(c) n.40

Doe v. Rosenberry, 255 F.2d 118 (2d Cir.1958)—§ 8.5(h) n.300

Doe v. Senechal, 431 Mass. 78, 725 N.E.2d 225 (2000)—§ 3.1(g) n.187

Doe v. Sheriff of DuPage County, 128 F.3d 586 (7th Cir.1997)—§ 3.5(a) n.41

Doe v. Smith, 429 F.3d 706 (7th Cir.2005)—§ 4.6(l) n.207

Doe, State v., 137 Idaho 519, 50 P.3d 1014 (2002)—§ 6.9(c) n.66

Doe v. State, 487 P.2d 47 (Alaska 1971)—§§ 12.4(b) n.50, 52

Doe v. State ex rel Mississippi Department of Corrections, 859 So.2d 350 (2003)—§ 1.11(a) n.7

Doe, United States v., 365 F.3d 150 (2d Cir.2004)—§§ 11.7(e) n.73, 76, 104, 106; 28.9(b) n.41

Doe, United States v., 297 F.3d 76 (2d Cir.2002)—§ 19.3(a) n.117

Doe, United States v., 226 F.3d 672 (6th Cir.2000)—§ 6.2(c) n.163

Doe, United States v., 170 F.3d 1162 (9th Cir.1999)—§ 6.9(g) n.167

Doe, United States v., 149 F.3d 945 (9th Cir.1998)—§ 18.3(b) n.8

Doe, United States v., 155 F.3d 1070 (9th Cir.1998)—§ 6.9(b) n.20

Doe, United States v., 60 F.3d 544 (9th Cir.1995)—§ 6.9(c) n.66

Doe, United States v., 63 F.3d 121 (2d Cir.1995)—§§ 23.1(e) n.224, 226, 244

Doe, United States v., 903 F.2d 16 (D.C.Cir.1990)—§§ 24.7(e) n.61; 24.7(g) n.80

Doe, United States v., 878 F.2d 1546 (1st Cir.1989)—§ 6.7(b) n.54

Doe v. United States, 487 U.S. 201, 108 S.Ct. 2341, 101 L.Ed.2d 184 (1988)—§§ 2.10(b) n.20; 2.10(d) n.105, 107, 137, 147, 160; 8.12(d) n.46; 8.12(f) n.58; 8.13(a) n.6, 42

Doe v. United States, 666 F.2d 43 (4th Cir.1981)—§ 1.5(k) n.397

Doe, United States v., 341 F.Supp. 1350 (S.D.N.Y.1972)—§§ 8.8(e) n.125, 126, 128, 130

Doe, United States v., 455 F.2d 753 (1st Cir.1972)—§ 27.2(e) n.88

Doe, United States v., 405 F.2d 436 (2d Cir.1968)—§ 7.2(c) n.35

Doe (Doe I), United States v., 465 U.S. 605, 104 S.Ct. 1237, 79 L.Ed.2d 552 (1984)—§§ 8.12(f) n.58; 8.13(a) n.12; 8.13(b) n.51; 8.13(c) n.70

Doe (Ellsberg), United States v., 455 F.2d 1270 (1st Cir.1972)—§§ 8.4(c) n.123; 8.8(f) n.145, 149, 152; 27.2(e) n.96

Doe ex rel. Doe v. Little Rock School District, 380 F.3d 349 (8th Cir.2004)—§ 3.9(k) n.256

Doe Grand Jury Investigation, Matter of, 415 Mass. 727, 615 N.E.2d 567 (1993)—§ 8.5(b) n.35

Doe (Popkin), United States v., 460 F.2d 328 (1st Cir.1972)—§§ 8.8(b) n.16, 33; 8.9(b) n.28

Doering v. Fader, 316 Md. 351, 558 A.2d 733 (1989)—§ 27.4(d) n.48

Doering v. State, 313 Md. 384, 545 A.2d 1281 (1988)—§ 3.10(b) n.51

Doe (Schwartz), United States v., 457 F.2d 895 (2d Cir.1972)—§§ 8.7(c) n.67; 8.8(b) n.15

Doe, State ex rel. v. Troisi, 194 W.Va. 28, 459 S.E.2d 139 (1995)—§§ 8.1(a) n.1; 8.4(c) n.129; 8.8(d) n.91, 97

Doggett, People v., 255 Ill.3d 180, 192 Ill.Dec. 768, 625 N.E.2d 923 (1993)—§ 11.9(d) n.208

Doggett, State v., 687 N.W.2d 97 (2004)—§§ 11.10(c) n.116; 21.3(b) n.55

Doggett, United States v., 230 F.3d 160 (5th Cir.2000)—§ 19.2(e) n.71

Doggett v. United States, 505 U.S. 647, 112 S.Ct. 2686, 120 L.Ed.2d 520 (1992)—§§ 18.1(b) n.12, 13; 18.2(b) n.7; 18.2(c) n.36, 42; 18.2(d) n.69; 18.2(e) n.71, 83

Dohm, United States v., 618 F.2d 1169 (5th Cir.1980)—§ 12.1(e) n.63

Dohrmann v. United States, 442 F.3d 1279 (11th Cir.2006)—§ 26.6(c) n.42

Dohrn, State v., 259 N.W.2d 801 (Iowa 1977)—§ 15.4(f) n.144

Doile, State v., 244 Kan. 493, 769 P.2d 666 (1989)—§ 3.1(c) n.78

Dolan, United States v., 120 F.3d 856 (8th Cir.1997)—§ 18.5(a) n.14

Dolbeare, State v., 140 N.H. 84, 663 A.2d 85 (1995)—§ 18.4(c) n.67

Doles v. State, 994 P.2d 315 (Wyo.1999)—§§ 3.2(g) n.198, 199

Doleszny, State v., 2004 Vt. 9, 844 A.2d 773 (Vt.2004)—§ 24.9(b) n.12

Doliner, State v., 96 N.J. 236, 475 A.2d 552 (1984)—§§ 8.5(a) n.5; 8.5(h) n.276, 290

Dombrowski v. Pfister, 380 U.S. 479, 85 S.Ct. 1116, 14 L.Ed.2d 22 (1965)—§ 13.5(e) n.90

Dombrowski, State v., 44 Wis.2d 486, 171 N.W.2d 349 (1969)—§ 16.1(g) n.273

Dome Realty, Inc. v. City of Paterson, 83 N.J. 212, 416 A.2d 334 (1980)—§ 3.9(b) n.28

Domina, United States v., 784 F.2d 1361 (9th Cir.1986)—§ 7.4(g) n.116

Domingo, State v., 82 Hawai'i 265, 921 P.2d 1166 (1996)—§ 21.6(b) n.112

Domingo-Gomez v. People, 125 P.3d 1043 (Colo.2005)—§ 24.7(e) n.55

Dominguez v. Meehan, 140 Ariz. 328, 681 P.2d 911 (1984)—§ 21.4(g) n.245

Dominguez Benitez, United States v., 542 U.S. 74, 124 S.Ct. 2333, 159 L.Ed.2d 157 (2004)—§§ 21.5(c) n.85; 27.5(d) n.129

Don v. Nix, 886 F.2d 203 (8th Cir.1989)—§§ 11.6(a) n.21, 24

Donaghe, United States v., 924 F.2d 940 (9th Cir.1991)—§ 26.10(b) n.27

Donaghy, State v., 171 Vt. 435, 769 A.2d 10 (2000)—§§ 22.3(d) n.212, 217, 255

Donahue v. Armontrout, 820 F.2d 971 (8th Cir.1987)—§ 21.2(d) n.194

Donahue v. City of Sparks, 111 Nev. 1281, 903 P.2d 225 (1995)— § 27.4(c) n.25

Donahue, Commonwealth v., 396 Mass. 590, 487 N.E.2d 1351 (1986)— §§ 24.3(b) n.56; 24.3(d) n.108

Donaldson, State v., 279 Kan. 694, 112 P.3d 99 (2005)—§ 17.3(a) n.8

Donaldson v. State, 305 Md. 522, 505 A.2d 527 (1986)—§ 26.10(d) n.88

Donaldson, United States v., 978 F.2d 381 (7th Cir.1992)—§ 10.3(d) n.66

Donato, United States v., 99 F.3d 426 (D.C.Cir.1996)—§ 24.3(c) n.101

Donato, United States v., 866 F.Supp. 288 (W.D.Va.1994)—§ 16.2(g) n.132

Donato, United States v., 269 F.Supp. 921 (E.D.Pa.1967)—§ 3.10(e) n.183

Dondich, United States v., 460 F.Supp. 849 (N.D.Cal.1978)—§§ 15.7(c) n.54, 56

Donelson, United States v., 450 F.3d 768 (8th Cir.2006)—§ 7.4(c) n.49

Donesay, State v., 270 Kan. 720, 19 P.3d 779 (2001)—§ 22.3(c) n.157

Donlan, United States v., 825 F.2d 653 (2d Cir.1987)—§ 4.6(m) n.238

Donley, State v., 216 W.Va. 368, 607 S.E.2d 474 (W.Va.2004)— § 13.5(c) n.66

Donlin, United States v., 982 F.2d 31 (1st Cir.1992)—§ 3.10(d) n.120

Donnell v. United States, 229 F.2d 560 (5th Cir.1956)—§ 18.5(a) n.26

Donnelly v. DeChristoforo, 416 U.S. 637, 94 S.Ct. 1868, 40 L.Ed.2d 431 (1974)—§§ 2.7(a) n.49; 2.7(b) n.73; 24.7(h) n.84

Donnelly, State v., 242 N.W.2d 295 (Iowa 1976)—§ 16.1(g) n.242

Donnelly v. United States, 185 F.2d 559 (10th Cir.1950)—§ 19.3(a) n.50

Donnes, United States v., 947 F.2d 1430 (10th Cir.1991)—§§ 3.5(e) n.206; 9.1(b) n.76

D'Onofrio, Commonwealth v., 396 Mass. 711, 488 N.E.2d 410 (1986)—§ 3.1(c) n.65

Donohue v. Jenne, 765 So.2d 969 (Fla.App.2000)—§ 12.2(b) n.19

Donovan, Commonwealth v., 392 Mass. 647, 467 N.E.2d 198 (1984)— § 7.3(c) n.56

Donovan, Commonwealth v., 610 S.W.2d 601 (Ky.1980)—§§ 20.4(d) n.73, 74; 27.6(b) n.16

Donovan v. Dewey, 452 U.S. 594, 101 S.Ct. 2534, 69 L.Ed.2d 262 (1981)—§ 3.9(c) n.39

Donovan v. Lone Steer, Inc., 464 U.S. 408, 104 S.Ct. 769, 78 L.Ed.2d 567 (1984)—§§ 3.2(e) n.159, 160; 8.7(a) n.27

Donovan, State v., 305 Or. 332, 751 P.2d 1109 (1988)—§ 17.4(a) n.66

Donovan, United States v., 429 U.S. 413, 97 S.Ct. 658, 50 L.Ed.2d 652 (1977)—§§ 4.6(j) n.169; 4.6(m) n.227, 231

Donovan, United States v., 339 F.2d 404 (7th Cir.1964)—§ 19.3(b) n.178

Donta v. Commonwealth, 858 S.W.2d 719 (Ky.App.1993)—§ 24.2(d) n.46

Doolittle, State v., 155 Ari. 352, 746 P.2d 924 (1987)—§§ 8.10(d) n.90, 106

Dopkowski, State v., 325 Md. 671, 602 A.2d 1185 (1992)—§ 26.3(g) n.76

Dopp, State v., 124 Idaho 481, 861 P.2d 51 (1993)—§§ 21.5(a) n.38, 45

Dorais, United States v., 241 F.3d 1124 (9th Cir.2001)—§ 3.2(c) n.103

Doran, United States v., 882 F.2d 1511 (10th Cir.1989)—§§ 13.7(c) n.45; 18.3(b) n.37

Doran, United States v., 482 F.2d 929 (9th Cir.1973)—§ 3.9(h) n.157

Dorcely, United States v., 454 F.3d 366 (D.C.Cir.2006)—§ 26.4(h) n.154

Dorfman, United States v., 532 F.Supp. 1118 (N.D.Ill.1981)—§§ 15.7(f) n.156, 158

Dorler, Commonwealth v., 403 Pa.Super. 150, 588 A.2d 525 (1991)—§ 27.5(a) n.23

Dorlouis, United States v., 107 F.3d 248 (4th Cir.1997)—§ 18.3(b) n.28

Dorman, United States v., 496 F.2d 438 (4th Cir.1974)—§§ 21.4(a) n.21, 24

Dorman v. United States, 435 F.2d 385 (D.C.Cir.1970)—§§ 3.6(a) n.12, 17

Dorman v. Wainwright, 798 F.2d 1358 (11th Cir.1986)—§ 11.5(b) n.28

Dormire v. Koste, 535 U.S. 967, 122 S.Ct. 1433, 152 L.Ed.2d 378 (2002)—§ 11.9(b) n.73

Dorney, People v., 17 Ill.App.3d 785, 308 N.E.2d 646 (1974)—§ 10.4(c) n.24

Dorough, Ex parte, 773 So.2d 1001 (Ala.2000)—§ 2.6(b) n.42

Dorr, Ex parte, 44 U.S. (3 How.) 103, 11 L.Ed. 514 (1845)—§ 28.2(a) n.8

Dorr, People v., 47 Ill.2d 458, 265 N.E.2d 601 (1970)—§ 8.7(b) n.50

Dorrough, United States v., 927 F.2d 498 (10th Cir.1991)—§ 3.4(e) n.70

Dorrough v. United States, 385 F.2d 887 (5th Cir.1967)—§ 21.4(d) n.108

Dorry v. State, 389 So.2d 1184 (Fla.App.1980)—§ 20.6(c) n.85

Dorsainvil, In re, 119 F.3d 245 (3d Cir.1997)—§ 28.9(a) n.7

Dorsey, In re, 710 A.2d 217 (Del.Super.1998)—§ 27.4(c) n.26

Dorsey v. Kelly, 112 F.3d 50 (2d Cir.1997)—§ 28.5(a) n.34

Dorsey v. State, 115 S.W.3d 842 (Mo.2003)—§§ 21.5(d) n.104; 21.6(a) n.31

Dorsey v. State, 868 So.2d 1192 (Fla.2003)—§ 22.3(d) n.245

Dorsey v. State, 761 A.2d 807 (Del.2000)—§ 3.3(a) n.12

Dorsey v. State, 490 N.E.2d 260 (Ind.1986)—§ 18.4(c) n.36

Dorsey v. State, 276 Md. 638, 350 A.2d 665 (Md.App.1976)—§ 27.6(b) n.48

Dorsey, United States v., 418 F.3d 1038 (9th Cir.2005)—§§ 1.2(c) n.147, 187

Dorsey, United States v., 865 F.2d 1275 (D.C.Cir.1989)—§ 27.5(b) n.42

Dorszynski v. United States, 418 U.S. 424, 94 S.Ct. 3042, 41 L.Ed.2d 855 (1974)—§ 26.3(g) n.69

Doss, People v., 44 Ill.2d 541, 256 N.E.2d 753 (1970)—§ 6.7(c) n.107

Doss, State v., 355 N.W.2d 874 (Iowa 1984)—§ 15.2(f) n.149

Doss, United States v., 563 F.2d 265 (6th Cir.1977)—§§ 8.8(f) n.158; 8.10(c) n.81, 82, 84

Doss, United States v., 545 F.2d 548 (6th Cir.1976)—§ 8.10(c) n.63

Dos Santos, United States v., 979 F.Supp. 949 (E.D.N.Y.1997)—§ 28.9(a) n.20

Doss, United States ex rel. v. Bensinger, 463 F.2d 576 (7th Cir.1972)—§ 6.7(c) n.107

Dotterweich, United States v., 320 U.S. 277, 64 S.Ct. 134, 88 L.Ed. 48 (1943)—§ 24.10(b) n.22

Douangmala, State v., 253 Wis.2d 173, 646 N.W.2d 1 (2002)—§ 21.4(d) n.137

DoubleClick, Inc. Privacy Litig., In re, 154 F.Supp.2d 497 (S.D.N.Y.2001)—§§ 4.8(b) n.17; 4.8(d) n.32

Doucet, State v., 359 So.2d 1239 (La.1977)—§ 10.6(d) n.40

Dougan v. State, 30 Ark. 41 (1875)—§ 16.1(e) n.192

Dougherty, United States v., 473 F.2d 1113 (D.C.Cir.1972)—§§ 22.1(g) n.100, 119

Doughty, State v., 472 N.W.2d 299 (Minn.1991)—§ 9.5(d) n.82

Doughty v. State, 470 N.E.2d 69 (Ind.1984)—§ 22.1(h) n.137

Doughty, State v., 408 A.2d 683 (Me.1979)—§ 10.4(d) n.32

Douglas v. Alabama, 380 U.S. 415, 85 S.Ct. 1074, 13 L.Ed.2d 934 (1965)—§ 24.4(c) n.23

Douglas v. Buder, 412 U.S. 430, 93 S.Ct. 2199, 37 L.Ed.2d 52 (1973)—§ 26.10(a) n.1

Douglas v. California, 372 U.S. 353, 83 S.Ct. 814, 9 L.Ed.2d 811 (1963)—§§ 11.1(b) n.55; 11.1(d) n.102, 106, 107; 11.2(b) n.49, 58; 11.2(f) n.239; 18.5(c) n.77, 80; 27.1(a) n.13; 27.1(b) n.17

Douglas v. State, 481 N.E.2d 107 (Ind.1985)—§ 6.8(d) n.84

Douglas, State v., 260 Or. 60, 488 P.2d 1366 (1971)—§ 3.10(b) n.35

Douglas v. State, 42 Ala.App. 314, 163 So.2d 477 (1963)—§§ 15.2(d) n.97, 105; 15.5(c) n.111

Douglas, State v., 150 Me. 442, 114 A.2d 253 (1955)—§ 15.5(c) n.105

Douglas, United States v., 964 F.2d 738 (8th Cir.1992)—§ 3.8(e) n.193

Douglas, United States v., 874 F.2d 1145 (7th Cir.1989)—§ 25.4(c) n.32

Douglas v. United States, 488 A.2d 121 (D.C.App.1985)—§§ 11.9(a) n.25; 11.9(d) n.217

Douglas v. Warden, 218 Conn. 778, 591 A.2d 399 (1991)—§§ 11.3(c) n.66; 11.4(b) n.28

Douglas Oil Co. of California v. Petrol Stops Northwest, 441 U.S. 211, 99 S.Ct. 1667, 60 L.Ed.2d 156 (1979)—§§ 8.5(h) n.234, 246, 259, 263, 264; 27.2(e) n.98

Dove, United States v., 629 F.2d 325 (4th Cir.1980)—§ 5.1(c) n.26

Dove v. United States, 423 U.S. 325, 96 S.Ct. 579, 46 L.Ed.2d 531 (1976)—§ 27.5(a) n.2

Dow v. Circuit Court of the First Circuit, 995 F.2d 922 (9th Cir.1993)—§ 28.3(a) n.9

Dow, State v., 256 Mont. 126, 844 P.2d 780 (1992)—§ 10.3(b) n.21

Dow Chemical Co. v. United States, 476 U.S. 227, 106 S.Ct. 1819, 90 L.Ed.2d 226 (1986)—§§ 3.2(b) n.60; 3.2(c) n.141; 3.2(e) n.166

Dowd, State v., 478 A.2d 671 (Me.1984)—§ 11.2(a) n.33

Dowd, United States v., 451 F.3d 1244 (11th Cir.2006)—§ 6.9(e) n.88

Dowd, United States ex rel. v. Lane, 574 F.Supp. 972 (N.D.Ill.1983)—§ 24.3(d) n.107

Dowdy, People ex rel. v. Smith, 48 N.Y.2d 477, 423 N.Y.S.2d 862, 399 N.E.2d 894 (1979)—§§ 17.4(a) n.29, 32

Dowell, United States v., 430 F.3d 1100 (10th Cir.2005)—§§ 9.1(a) n.21; 10.3(c) n.52; 10.5(a) n.6

Dowery, People v., 62 Ill.2d 200, 340 N.E.2d 529 (1975)—§ 26.10(c) n.64

Dow Jones & Co., In re, 842 F.2d 603 (2d Cir.1988)—§§ 23.1(b) n.67, 68, 72, 74

Dowling, Commonwealth v., 482 Pa. 608, 394 A.2d 488 (1978)—§ 21.5(b) n.64

Dowling v. United States, 493 U.S. 342, 110 S.Ct. 668, 107 L.Ed.2d 708 (1990)—§§ 2.7(b) n.64; 2.7(c) n.144, 146, 206; 17.4(a) n.5, 33; 17.4(b) n.80

Downer, People v., 192 Colo. 264, 557 P.2d 835 (1976)—§ 8.3(b) n.15

Downer v. State, 543 A.2d 309 (Del.1988)—§ 21.4(f) n.198

Downey, Commonwealth v., 407 Mass. 472, 553 N.E.2d 1303 (1990)—§ 7.4(e) n.84

Downey v. People, 25 P.3d 1200 (Colo.2001)—§ 11.5(f) n.106

Downey, State v., 242 N.J.Super. 367, 576 A.2d 945 (1988)—§ 13.2(c) n.76

Downing, State v., 313 N.C. 164, 326 S.E.2d 256 (1985)—§ 19.6(b) n.20

Downing, United States v., 665 F.2d 404 (1st Cir.1981)—§ 6.7(b) n.42

Downs v. Moore, 801 So.2d 906 (Fla.2001)—§§ 22.4(c) n.29; 22.5(a) n.8

Downs, State v., 361 S.C. 141, 604 S.E.2d 377 (2004)—§ 21.4(a) n.14

Downs, United States v., 230 F.3d 272 (7th Cir.2000)—§§ 7.4(c) n.48, 50, 53; 7.4(d) n.71

Downum v. United States, 372 U.S. 734, 83 S.Ct. 1033, 10 L.Ed.2d 100 (1963)—§§ 25.1(d) n.47; 25.2(d) n.32

Doyen, State v., 676 A.2d 345 (Vt.1996)—§§ 16.4(c) n.51, 53, 57, 80, 86

Doyle v. Johnson, 235 F.3d 956 (5th Cir.2000)—§§ 17.4(b) n.138, 139

Doyle v. Ohio, 426 U.S. 610, 96 S.Ct. 2240, 49 L.Ed.2d 91 (1976)—§§ 1.7(i) n.165; 2.9(h) n.211; 6.5(e) n.94; 7.2(c) n.33; 9.6(a) n.34

Doyle, State v., 272 Kan. 1157, 38 P.3d 650 (2002)—§ 22.3(c) n.157

Doyle v. State, 24 S.W.3d 598 (Tex.App.2000)—§ 24.6(b) n.24

Doyle v. State, 954 P.2d 969 (Wyo.1998)—§§ 6.7(c) n.111; 10.1(a) n.3

Doyle v. State, 112 Nev. 879, 921 P.2d 901 (1996)—§ 22.3(d) n.226

Doyle, United States v., 121 F.3d 1078 (7th Cir.1997)—§§ 25.4(a) n.8, 9

Doyle, United States v., 348 F.2d 715 (2d Cir.1965)—§ 10.2(d) n.46

Dracon, People v., 884 P.2d 712 (Colo.1994)—§ 10.4(b) n.15

Draggo, State v., 65 Ohio St.2d 88, 418 N.E.2d 1343 (1981)—§ 16.1(g) n.245

Drago v. State, 553 S.W.2d 375 (Tex.Cr.App.1977)—§ 3.5(a) n.36

Draheim, Commonwealth v., 447 Mass. 113, 849 N.E.2d 823 (2006)— § 3.2(g) n.195

Drain, People v., 73 N.Y.2d 107, 538 N.Y.S.2d 500, 535 N.E.2d 630 (1989)—§ 9.6(c) n.58

Drake v. Clark, 14 F.3d 351 (7th Cir.1994)—§ 23.2(g) n.121

Drake v. Kemp, 762 F.2d 1449 (11th Cir.1985)—§ 17.4(a) n.50

Drake, People v., 7 N.Y.3d 28, 817 N.Y.S.2d 583, 850 N.E.2d 630 (2006)—§ 7.5(b) n.32

Drake, People v., 785 P.2d 1257 (Colo.1990)—§§ 3.10(b) n.74; 21.4(e) n.165

Drake, People v., 785 P.2d 1253 (Colo.1989)—§ 17.2(b) n.42

Drake, People v., 61 N.Y.2d 359, 474 N.Y.S.2d 276, 462 N.E.2d 376 (1984)—§ 18.5(c) n.75

Drake v. Portuondo, 321 F.3d 338 (2d Cir.2003)—§ 28.7(d) n.28

Drake v. State, 800 So.2d 508 (Miss.2001)—§ 6.6(e) n.59

Drake, State v., 731 A.2d 858 (Me.1999)—§ 6.8(b) n.50

Drake, State v., 343 So.2d 1336 (Fla.App.1977)—§ 3.10(f) n.191

Draper, State v., 162 Ariz. 433, 784 P.2d 259 (1989)—§§ 21.2(b) n.91; 21.4(b) n.49

Draper, State v., 675 S.W.2d 863 (Mo.1984)—§ 22.3(c) n.108

Draper v. United States, 358 U.S. 307, 79 S.Ct. 329, 3 L.Ed.2d 327 (1959)—§§ 3.3(a) n.8; 3.3(b) n.61; 3.3(c) n.122; 3.5(a) n.12

Draper v. Washington, 372 U.S. 487, 83 S.Ct. 774, 9 L.Ed.2d 899 (1963)— §§ 11.2(d) n.124, 125, 133

Drayton, People v., 7 Ill.App.3d 812, 288 N.E.2d 922 (1972)—§ 7.4(f) n.98

Drayton, United States v., 536 U.S. 194, 122 S.Ct. 2105, 153 L.Ed.2d 242 (2002)—§§ 3.8(c) n.104; 3.10(a) n.3; 3.10(b) n.61

Drazen v. New Haven Taxi Cab, 95 Conn. 500, 111 A. 861 (1920)— § 15.1(b) n.73

Dr. Bonham's Case, 8 Co. 113b, 77 Eng.Rep. 646 (1610)—§ 2.4(b) n.76

Dred Scott v. Sandford, 60 U.S. (19 How.) 393, 15 L.Ed.2d 672 (1833)—§ 2.3(a) n.34

Dred Scott v. Sandford, 60 U.S. (19 How.) 393, 15 L.Ed. 691 (1857)— §§ 2.2 n.4; 2.4(c) n.98

Dreier v. United States, 221 U.S. 394, 31 S.Ct. 550, 55 L.Ed. 784 (1911)— § 8.12(b) n.15

Dresner v. County Court, 189 Colo. 374, 540 P.2d 1085 (1975)—§§ 15.1(g) n.360; 15.2(g) n.174

Dressler, State ex rel. v. Circuit Court for Racine County, 163 Wis.2d 622, 472 N.W.2d 532 (Wis.App.1991)— §§ 11.2(e) n.198, 211; 24.3(f) n.139

Dretke v. Haley, 541 U.S. 386, 124 S.Ct. 1847, 158 L.Ed.2d 659 (2004)— §§ 26.2(c) n.70; 26.4(i) n.193; 28.4(e) n.74, 88

Drew, United States v., 894 F.2d 965 (8th Cir.1990)—§ 17.2(b) n.40

Drew v. United States, 331 F.2d 85 (D.C.Cir.1964)—§§ 17.1(c) n.41; 17.1(d) n.49, 50

Drewry v. Commonwealth, 213 Va. 186, 191 S.E.2d 178 (1972)—§ 7.4(e) n.90

Drewry, State v., 139 N.H. 678, 661 A.2d 1181 (1995)—§§ 20.4(b) n.20; 20.4(d) n.73; 20.4(f) n.95

Dreyer, United States v., 533 F.2d 112 (3d Cir.1976)—§ 18.2(e) n.78

Driebel v. City of Milwaukee, 298 F.3d 622 (7th Cir.2002)—§ 3.8(c) n.110

Drinkall, United States v., 749 F.2d 20 (8th Cir.1984)—§ 26.10(a) n.9

Drinkwater v. State, 73 Wis.2d 674, 245 N.W.2d 664 (1976)—§ 21.1(e) n.62

Driskill v. State, 761 P.2d 980 (Wyo.1988)—§ 27.5(b) n.49

Driver, United States v., 776 F.2d 807 (9th Cir.1985)—§ 3.6(a) n.5

Droge, United States v., 961 F.2d 1030 (2d Cir.1992)—§ 22.3(b) n.80

Drollinger v. State, 274 Ind. 5, 408 N.E.2d 1228 (1980)—§ 16.3(b) n.11

Drope v. Missouri, 420 U.S. 162, 95 S.Ct. 896, 43 L.Ed.2d 103 (1975)— §§ 1.5(c) n.169; 2.7(a) n.40; 24.2(e) n.51; 24.2(g) n.90

Drougas, United States v., 748 F.2d 8 (1st Cir.1984)—§ 17.2(f) n.133

Drouhard, State v., 31 Or.App. 1083, 572 P.2d 331 (1977)—§ 3.10(f) n.193

Drown, United States v., 942 F.2d 55 (1st Cir.1991)—§ 21.2(d) n.268

Druce, Commonwealth v., 577 Pa. 581, 848 A.2d 104 (2004)—§ 22.4(c) n.29

Drum, People v., 194 Ill.2d 485, 252 Ill.Dec. 470, 743 N.E.2d 44 (2000)—§ 27.3(c) n.49

Drum, United States v., 569 F.Supp. 605, (M.D.Pa.1984)—§ 15.1(b) n.86

Drumgo v. Superior Court, 8 Cal.3d 930, 106 Cal.Rptr. 631, 506 P.2d 1007 (1973)—§§ 11.4(a) n.4; 27.4(c) n.33

Drumgold, Commonwealth v., 423 Mass. 230, 668 N.E.2d 300 (1996)—§§ 15.6(d) n.121, 126

Drummond, United States v., 69 Fed.Appx. 580 (3d Cir.2003)— § 24.4(d) n.47

Drummond, United States v., 240 F.3d 1333 (11th Cir.2001)—§ 18.3(b) n.5

Drummond, United States v., 481 F.2d 62 (2d Cir.1973)—§ 24.7(i) n.94

Drury v. State, 368 Md. 331, 793 A.2d 567 (2002)—§ 6.7(c) n.106

DSI Associates LLC v. United States, 496 F.3d 175 (2d Cir.2007)— § 26.6(d) n.72

Duarte-Higareda, United States v., 113 F.3d 1000 (9th Cir.1997)— § 24.2(g) n.97

Dubbs v. Head Start, Inc., 336 F.3d 1194 (10th Cir.2003)—§ 3.9(d) n.73

Du Bo, United States v., 186 F.3d 1177 (9th Cir.1999)—§ 19.3(a) n.101

Duboise, Ex parte, 675 So.2d 420 (Ala.1996)—§§ 22.1(h) n.148; 27.4(c) n.28

DuBoise v. State, 520 So.2d 260 (Fla.1988)—§ 6.4(g) n.154

Dubon-Otero, United States v., 76 F.Supp.2d 161 (D.Puerto Rico 1999)—§§ 23.2(a) n.17; 23.2(d) n.69

Dubose, State v., 285 Wis.2d 143, 699 N.W.2d 582 (2005)—§§ 1.5(e) n.234; 7.4(c) n.38

DuBray, State v., 317 Mont. 377, 77 P.3d 247 (2003)—§§ 4.6(l) n.201; 7.4(e) n.90; 7.5(b) n.23

Ducally v. State, 809 A.2d 472 (R.I.2002)—§ 21.4(d) n.137

Ducharme, State v., 601 A.2d 937 (R.I.1991)—§ 17.2(c) n.76

Duck v. State, 61 S.W.3d 135 (Ark.2001)—§ 10.3(b) n.31

Ducker, United States v., 491 F.2d 1190 (5th Cir.1974)—§ 3.7(e) n.91

Duckett v. State, 922 P.2d 631 (Okla.Cr.App.1996)—§ 26.4(g) n.139

Duckworth v. Eagan, 492 U.S. 195, 109 S.Ct. 2875, 106 L.Ed.2d 166 (1989)—§§ 1.5(a) n.35; 6.8(a) n.19

Duckworth v. Serrano, 454 U.S. 1, 102 S.Ct. 18, 70 L.Ed.2d 1 (1981)—§ 28.5(a) n.17

Dudden, United States v., 65 F.3d 1461 (9th Cir.1995)—§ 18.5(b) n.66

Dudley, State v., 264 Kan. 640, 957 P.2d 445 (1998)—§ 6.7(d) n.145

Dudley v. State, 285 Ark. 160, 685 S.W.2d 170 (1985)—§ 11.10(c) n.83

Dudrey v. State, 74 Wis.2d 480, 247 N.W.2d 105 (1976)—§ 21.5(a) n.23

Du Fault, State ex rel. v. Utecht, 220 Minn. 431, 19 N.W.2d 706 (1945)—§ 16.4(d) n.145

Duff, State v., 151 Vt. 433, 563 A.2d 258 (1989)—§ 12.4(a) n.16

Duff, United States v., 76 F.3d 122 (7th Cir.1996)—§ 27.5(b) n.41

Duff, United States v., 529 F.Supp. 148 (N.D.Ill.1981)—§§ 8.10(c) n.68; 15.2(i) n.228; 15.7(d) n.85

Duffel v. Dutton, 785 F.2d 131 (6th Cir.1986)—§ 25.4(c) n.40

Duffield, People v., 387 Mich. 300, 197 N.W.2d 25 (1972)—§ 16.4(c) n.44

Duffy, Ex parte, 607 S.W.2d 507 (Tex.Crim.App.1980)—§ 11.10(c) n.119

Duffy, Commonwealth v., 539 Pa. 141, 650 A.2d 870 (1994)—§ 25.2(e) n.40

Duffy v. State, 271 Ga.App. 668, 610 S.E.2d 620 (2005)—§ 24.7(e) n.69

Duffy, State v., 146 N.H. 648, 778 A.2d 415 (2001)—§ 6.9(a) n.12

Duffy, State v., 300 Mont. 381, 6 P.3d 453 (2000)—§ 18.5(a) n.6

Duffy, State v., 559 N.W.2d 109 (Minn.App.1997)—§ 27.3(c) n.25

Dufresne v. Moran, 729 F.2d 18 (1st Cir.1984)—§ 21.3(b) n.54

Dugan v. Ohio, 277 U.S. 61, 48 S.Ct. 439, 72 L.Ed. 784 (1928)—§ 22.4(a) n.5

Dugas v. Coplan, 428 F.3d 317 (1st Cir.2005)—§ 11.10(c) n.126

Duggan, United States v., 743 F.2d 59 (2d Cir.1984)—§ 4.9(b) n.10

Dugger v. Adams, 489 U.S. 401, 109 S.Ct. 1211, 103 L.Ed.2d 435 (1989)—§§ 28.4(b) n.14; 28.4(e) n.87

Duguay, Commonwealth v., 430 Mass. 397, 720 N.E.2d 458 (1999)—§ 6.7(d) n.145

Duguay, United States v., 93 F.3d 346 (7th Cir.1996)—§§ 3.7(d) n.88, 90

Duhart v. United States, 589 A.2d 895 (D.C.1991)—§§ 3.8(c) n.83, 87

Duke v. Cockrell, 292 F.3d 414 (5th Cir.2002)—§§ 21.4(a) n.23; 21.4(d) n.121

Duke v. State, 260 Ind. 638, 298 N.E.2d 453 (1973)—§ 7.4(g) n.123

Duke, United States v., 255 F.3d 656 (8th Cir.2001)—§ 24.11(d) n.33

Duke, United States v., 229 F.3d 627 (7th Cir.2000)—§ 10.1(c) n.49

Dukes, United States v., 936 F.2d 1281 (D.C.Cir.1991)—§ 21.2(d) n.212

Dukes v. Waitkevitch, 536 F.2d 469 (1st Cir.1976)—§ 22.3(a) n.26

Dukes v. Warden, 406 U.S. 250, 92 S.Ct. 1551, 32 L.Ed.2d 45 (1972)—§ 11.9(d) n.181

Dulworth v. Evans, 442 F.3d 1265 (10th Cir.2006)—§ 28.5(b) n.53

Duma, United States v., 228 F.Supp. 755 (S.D.N.Y.1964)—§ 16.2(f) n.107

Dumaine, State v., 162 Ariz. 392, 783 P.2d 1184 (1989)—§ 1.7(i) n.210

Dumars, State v., 37 Kan.App.2d 600, 154 P.3d 1120 (2007)—§ 27.5(a) n.33

Dumas, Interest of, 357 Pa.Super. 294, 515 A.2d 984 (1986)—§ 3.9(k) n.257

Dumas, State v., 786 So.2d 80 (La.2001)—§ 3.8(e) n.196

Dumas, State v., 145 N.H. 301, 761 A.2d 1063 (2000)—§ 6.9(b) n.24

Dumas, State v., 750 A.2d 420 (R.I.2000)—§ 6.9(g) n.166

Dumas, State v., 363 So.2d 568 (Fla.App.1978)—§ 20.3(k) n.213

Dumbra v. United States, 268 U.S. 435, 45 S.Ct. 546, 69 L.Ed. 1032 (1925)—§ 3.3(b) n.45

Dumbsky v. State, 508 N.E.2d 1274 (Ind.1987)—§ 3.2(f) n.183

Dumes, United States v., 313 F.3d 372 (7th Cir.2002)—§§ 4.6(e) n.97; 4.6(m) n.237

Dumond v. State, 294 Ark. 379, 743 S.W.2d 779 (1988)—§§ 11.9(a) n.15; 11.9(d) n.207

Dumond v. State, 290 Ark. 595, 721 S.W.2d 663 (1986)—§ 20.3(f) n.100

Dumont, State v., 507 A.2d 164 (Me.1986)—§ 26.5(a) n.5

Dunaway v. Commonwealth, 60 S.W.3d 563 (Ky.2001)—§§ 18.2(c) n.37, 49; 18.2(e) n.79; 18.4(c) n.37

Dunaway v. New York, 442 U.S. 200, 99 S.Ct. 2248, 60 L.Ed.2d 824 (1979)—§§ 2.9(g) n.163, 173; 3.3(b) n.36; 3.8(a) n.9; 3.8(b) n.47; 3.8(g) n.243; 6.3(c) n.54; 6.6(d) n.51; 6.6(f) n.107

Dunaway v. United States, 205 F.2d 23 (D.C.Cir.1953)—§ 17.1(b) n.25

Dunbar, In re, 162 Vt. 209, 647 A.2d 316 (Vt.1994)—§ 11.6(a) n.36

Dunbar, United States v., 357 F.3d 582 (6th Cir.2004)—§§ 18.3(b) n.19, 24

Duncan v. Alabama, 881 F.2d 1013 (11th Cir.1989)—§§ 11.9(c) n.129, 133

Duncan v. Henry, 513 U.S. 364, 115 S.Ct. 887, 130 L.Ed.2d 865 (1995)—§ 28.5(a) n.31

Duncan v. Louisiana, 391 U.S. 145, 88 S.Ct. 1444, 20 L.Ed.2d 491 (1968)—§§ 1.5(g) n.266, 268, 269, 271, 275, 277; 1.8(d) n.65; 2.1 n.34; 2.3(a) n.9, 19, 59; 2.3 n.1; 2.4(b) n.22, 57; 2.5(a) n.11, 12; 2.5(b) n.13; 2.5(f) n.53, 77, 78, 83, 89, 99, 101; 2.6(a) n.5, 6, 9, 16, 28; 2.6(b) n.34, 44; 2.6(c) n.75; 2.7(c) n.98, 117, 177; 2.9(d) n.89; 2.11(c) n.32; 15.4(d) n.108; 22.1(a) n.13; 22.1(b) n.30; 22.1(d) n.66; 22.1(g) n.106; 22.2(d) n.51; 22.2(e) n.108; 28.6(e) n.53

Duncan, People v., 78 Cal.App.4th 765, 93 Cal.Rptr.2d 173 (2000)—§ 14.2(g) n.103

Duncan, People v., 462 Mich. 47, 610 N.W.2d 551 (2000)—§ 27.6(d) n.127

Duncan, State v., 802 So.2d 533 (La.2001)—§§ 22.3(d) n.217, 220

Duncan, State v., 435 N.W.2d 384 (Iowa App.1988)—§§ 11.9(d) n.205, 224, 230, 233

Duncan v. State, 291 Ark. 521, 726 S.W.2d 653 (1987)—§ 6.4(e) n.61

Duncan v. State, 281 Md. 247, 378 A.2d 1108 (1977)—§ 3.2(f) n.177

Duncan v. Storie, 869 F.2d 1100 (8th Cir.1989)—§ 3.6(a) n.35

Duncan v. Tennessee, 405 U.S. 127, 92 S.Ct. 785, 31 L.Ed.2d 86 (1972)—§ 19.6(a) n.2

Duncan, United States v., 242 F.3d 940 (10th Cir.2001)—§ 21.2(d) n.252

Duncan, United States v., 704 F.Supp. 820 (N.D.Ill.1989)—§§ 8.13(a) n.25; 8.13(b) n.56, 59, 61

Duncan, United States v., 598 F.2d 839 (4th Cir.1979)—§ 8.8(g) n.165

Duncan, United States v., 456 F.2d 1401 (9th Cir.1972)—§ 8.8(i) n.195

Duncan v. Walker, 533 U.S. 167, 121 S.Ct. 2120, 150 L.Ed.2d 251 (2001)—§§ 28.3(a) n.3; 28.5(a) n.2; 28.5(b) n.49, 60

Duncan, United States ex rel. v. O'Leary, 806 F.2d 1307 (7th Cir.1986)—§§ 11.9(d) n.174, 210

Dunkerley v. Hogan, 579 F.2d 141 (2d Cir.1978)—§ 25.2(d) n.26

Dunkins v. Thigpen, 854 F.2d 394 (11th Cir.1988)—§ 6.9(f) n.144

Dunkle v. State, 139 P.3d 228 (Okla.Crim.App.2006)—§ 6.8(b) n.50

Dunkley, United States v., 911 F.2d 522 (11th Cir.1990)—§ 3.10(e) n.172

Dunlap v. State, 141 Idaho 50, 106 P.3d 376 (2004)—§§ 11.10(b) n.46; 21.3(b) n.89

Dunlap, State v., 395 A.2d 821 (Me.1978)—§ 10.4(c) n.21

Dunlap v. Superior Court, 169 Ariz. 82, 817 P.2d 27 (1991)—§ 14.4(b) n.39

Dunlap v. United States, 250 F.3d 1001 (6th Cir.2001)—§ 28.9(b) n.50

Dunlop v. United States, 165 U.S. 486, 17 S.Ct. 375, 41 L.Ed. 799 (1897)—§§ 24.7(e) n.59; 24.7(i) n.89

Dunn, Ex parte, 514 So.2d 1300 (Ala.1987)—§ 11.10(d) n.192

Dunn, In re, 507 F.2d 195 (1st Cir.1974)—§ 4.6(e) n.102

Dunn v. Colleran, 247 F.3d 450 (3d Cir.2001)—§§ 21.2(d) n.167; 21.2(e) n.280

Dunn, People v., 380 Mich. 693, 158 N.W.2d 404 (1968)—§ 21.3(a) n.34

Dunn v. Roberts, 963 F.2d 308 (10th Cir.1992)—§ 11.2(e) n.189

Dunn v. Roberts, 768 F.Supp. 1442 (D.Kan.1991)—§§ 11.2(e) n.208, 228

Dunn v. State, 262 Ga.App. 643, 586 S.E.2d 352 (2003)—§ 10.1(b) n.16

Dunn, State v., 154 N.C.App. 1, 571 S.E.2d 650 (2002)—§§ 20.3(f) n.107; 20.4(f) n.90, 91

Dunn, State v., 850 P.2d 1201 (Utah 1993)—§§ 25.4(b) n.19, 25

Dunn v. State, 819 S.W.2d 510 (Tex.Crim.App.1991)—§ 11.9(d) n.217

Dunn, State v., 243 Kan. 414, 758 P.2d 718 (1988)—§ 11.2(e) n.228

Dunn v. State, 291 Ark. 131, 722 S.W.2d 595 (1987)—§§ 11.2(e) n.175, 206

Dunn v. State, 721 S.W.2d 325 (Tex.Cr.App.1986)—§ 6.8(a) n.13

Dunn v. State, 292 So.2d 435 (Fla.App.1974)—§ 3.4(j) n.199

Dunn, United States v., 480 U.S. 294, 107 S.Ct. 1134, 94 L.Ed.2d 326 (1987)—§§ 2.9(g) n.160, 163, 180; 3.2(b) n.50; 3.2(c) n.124; 3.2(d) n.156; 3.2(e) n.158

Dunn v. United States, 284 U.S. 390, 52 S.Ct. 189, 76 L.Ed. 356 (1932)—§ 24.10(b) n.20

Dunn v. White, 880 F.2d 1188 (10th Cir.1989)—§ 3.9(i) n.191

Dunne, State v., 124 N.J. 303, 590 A.2d 1144 (1991)—§ 22.1(h) n.154

Dunnigan, United States v., 507 U.S. 87, 113 S.Ct. 1111, 122 L.Ed.2d 445 (1993)—§§ 21.1(e) n.76; 26.4(c) n.28

Dunns, State v., 266 N.J.Super. 349, 629 A.2d 922 (1993)—§ 25.2(d) n.34

Dunn, United States ex rel. v. Casscles, 494 F.2d 397 (2d Cir.1974)— § 21.4(f) n.207

Dunoyair, People v., 660 P.2d 890 (Colo.1983)—§ 24.9(f) n.97

Dunphy v. McKee, 134 F.3d 1297 (7th Cir.1998)—§ 11.7(b) n.29

Dunson, People v., 316 Ill.App.3d 760, 250 Ill.Dec. 77, 737 N.E.2d 699 (2000)—§ 27.6(b) n.22

Dunster, State v., 262 Neb. 329, 631 N.W.2d 879 (2001)—§ 21.2(a) n.8

Dupard, State v., 93 Wash.2d 268, 609 P.2d 961 (1980)—§§ 17.4(a) n.31, 66

Duperry v. Solnit, 261 Conn. 309, 803 A.2d 287 (Conn.2002)—§ 21.4(a) n.15

Dupoint v. United States, 388 F.2d 39 (5th Cir.1967)—§ 22.2(e) n.106

Dupont v. United States, 259 A.2d 355 (D.C.App.1969)—§ 6.8(a) n.28

Dupree v. State, 352 Md. 314, 722 A.2d 52 (1998)—§ 9.6(a) n.35

Dupree, United States v., 323 F.3d 480 (6th Cir.2003)—§ 13.7(c) n.37

Duprey, United States v., 895 F.2d 303 (7th Cir.1989)—§ 7.4(e) n.80

Duquette v. Warden, 154 N.H. 737, 919 A.2d 767 (2007)—§ 26.3(f) n.57

Duran, People v., 179 Colo. 129, 498 P.2d 937 (1972)—§ 21.2(b) n.53

Duran, State v., 156 P.3d 795 (Utah 2007)—§ 3.6(e) n.109

Duran v. Superior Court, 162 Ariz. 206, 782 P.2d 324 (1989)—§ 21.4(f) n.208

Duran, United States v., 957 F.2d 499 (7th Cir.1992)—§§ 3.10(b) n.43, 44, 66; 3.10(e) n.140; 10.5(e) n.55

Durand, In re, 206 Neb. 415, 293 N.W.2d 383 (1980)—§ 6.7(c) n.118

Durant v. United States, 410 F.2d 689 (1st Cir.1969)—§ 21.4(d) n.117

Durante, People v., 97 A.D.2d 851, 469 N.Y.S.2d 18 (1983)—§§ 15.2(c) n.84; 15.7(d) n.90

Durbin v. United States, 221 F.2d 520 (D.C.Cir.1954)—§ 8.8(g) n.169

Duren v. Missouri, 439 U.S. 357, 99 S.Ct. 664, 58 L.Ed.2d 579 (1979)— §§ 22.2(d) n.55, 78

Duren, People v., 9 Cal.3d 218, 107 Cal.Rptr. 157, 507 P.2d 1365 (1973)—§ 3.10(e) n.139

Durham, Commonwealth v., 446 Mass. 212, 843 N.E.2d 1035 (2005)— §§ 20.4(b) n.20; 20.4(f) n.96; 20.5(f) n.85

Durham, Commonwealth v., 57 S.W.3d 829 (Ky.2001)—§ 24.10(a) n.8

Durham, United States v., 287 F.3d 1297 (11th Cir.2002)—§ 24.2(e) n.68

Durham, United States v., 178 F.3d 796 (6th Cir.1999)—§ 21.5(a) n.40

Durham, United States v., 139 F.3d 1325 (10th Cir.1998)—§ 22.2(e) n.102

Durland v. United States, 161 U.S. 306, 16 S.Ct. 508, 40 L.Ed. 709 (1896)— § 1.2(c) n.99

Durling, Commonwealth v., 407 Mass. 108, 551 N.E.2d 1193 (1990)— § 26.10(c) n.72

Durling v. Massachusetts Parole Bd., 789 F.Supp. 457 (D.Mass.1992)— § 26.10(c) n.74

Durnin, United States v., 632 F.2d 1297 (5th Cir.1980)—§§ 18.5(b) n.58, 68

Dusky v. United States, 362 U.S. 402, 80 S.Ct. 788, 4 L.Ed.2d 824 (1960)—§§ 21.4(b) n.63; 24.2(g) n.91

Dustin, Commonwealth v., 373 Mass. 612, 368 N.E.2d 1388 (1977)— § 6.2(c) n.139

Dutchie, State v., 969 P.2d 422 (Utah 1998)—§§ 6.7(b) n.43; 6.9(b) n.20

Duteau, Commonwealth v., 384 Mass. 321, 424 N.E.2d 1119 (1981)— §§ 2.6(b) n.68, 69

Dutkel, United States v., 192 F.3d 893 (9th Cir.1999)—§ 24.9(f) n.85

Dutkiewicz, United States v., 431 F.2d 969 (3d Cir.1970)—§ 6.8(a) n.5

Dutton v. Brown, 812 F.2d 593 (10th Cir.1987)—§ 24.4(d) n.42

Dutton v. Evans, 400 U.S. 74, 91 S.Ct. 210, 27 L.Ed.2d 213 (1970)—§§ 3.3(c) n.107; 17.2(b) n.48

Dutton, State v., 896 S.W.2d 114 (Tenn.1995)—§ 24.8(a) n.8

Dutton, State v., 112 N.J.Super. 402, 271 A.2d 593 (1970)—§ 7.4(f) n.101

Dutton v. State, 91 A. 417, 123 Md. 373 (1914)—§ 15.1(b) n.73

Duuvon, People v., 77 N.Y.2d 541, 569 N.Y.S.2d 346, 571 N.E.2d 654 (1991)—§ 7.4(f) n.96

Duvall, United States v., 537 F.2d 15 (2d Cir.1976)—§§ 6.4(e) n.69; 7.3(b) n.33

Duvernoy, State v., 156 W.Va. 578, 195 S.E.2d 631 (1973)—§ 3.8(b) n.20

Dvoracek, State v., 140 Iowa 266, 118 N.W. 399 (1908)—§ 16.1(d) n.156

Dwire v. State, 381 N.W.2d 871 (Minn.App.1986)—§§ 15.7(h) n.233, 235

Dwyer, Commonwealth v., 448 Mass. 122, 859 N.E.2d 400 (Mass.2006)—§ 24.3(f) n.154

Dwyer, People v., 397 Ill. 599, 74 N.E.2d 882 (1947)—§ 16.4(c) n.50

Dwyer, State v., 229 N.J.Super. 531, 552 A.2d 200 (1989)—§ 11.2(a) n.15

Dyas v. Lockhart, 705 F.2d 993 (8th Cir.1983)—§ 22.4(a) n.4

Dyas v. United States, 376 A.2d 827 (D.C.App.1977)—§§ 7.5(b) n.16, 25, 29

Dydek v. State, 400 So.2d 1255 (Fla.App.1981)—§ 21.4(a) n.23

Dye, People v., 431 Mich. 58, 427 N.W.2d 501 (1988)—§ 24.3(g) n.174

Dye v. State, 717 N.E.2d 5 (Ind.1999)—§ 6.6(d) n.57

Dyer v. Calderon, 151 F.3d 970 (9th Cir.1998)—§ 24.9(f) n.98

Dyer v. Crisp, 613 F.2d 275 (10th Cir.1980)—§ 11.10(b) n.30

Dyer v. State, 34 P.3d 652 (Okla.Crim.App.2001)—§ 21.2(d) n.270

Dyer, State v., 551 N.W.2d 320 (Iowa 1996)—§ 27.5(c) n.73

Dyer, United States v., 325 F.3d 464 (3d Cir.2003)—§ 18.3(b) n.5

Dyer, United States v., 136 F.3d 417 (5th Cir.1998)—§§ 28.9(a) n.20 to 22

Dyess, United States v., 478 F.3d 224 (4th Cir.2007)—§ 21.3(b) n.89

Dyke v. Taylor Implement Manufacturing Co., 391 U.S. 216, 88 S.Ct. 1472, 20 L.Ed.2d 538 (1968)—§§ 3.7(d) n.82; 3.7(e) n.92; 22.1(b) n.35

Dykes, State v., 261 Iowa 1363, 158 N.W.2d 154 (1968)—§ 16.1(e) n.180

Dyle, State v., 899 S.W.2d 607 (Tenn.1995)—§ 7.5(a) n.7

Dymenstein v. State, 720 P.2d 42 (Alaska App.1986)—§ 26.5(a) n.14

Dymo Industries, In re, 300 F.Supp. 532 (N.D.Cal.1969)—§ 15.3(d) n.70

Dymowski, State v., 459 N.W.2d 777 (N.D.1990)—§ 17.3(d) n.55

Dynavac, Inc., United States v., 6 F.3d 1407 (9th Cir.1993)—§§ 8.5(c) n.90, 93, 95, 97, 98, 107, 110

Dyson, State v., 292 Or. 26, 636 P.2d 961 (1981)—§§ 20.6(b) n.42, 45

Dyson v. United States, 815 A.2d 363 (D.C.App.2003)—§§ 6.7(b) n.74, 85

Dzul v. State, 118 Nev. 681, 56 P.3d 875 (2002)—§ 6.10(c) n.46

E

Eaddy v. State, 638 So.2d 22 (Fla.1994)—§ 24.8(f) n.106

Eades v. State, 75 Md.App. 411, 541 A.2d 1001 (1988)—§ 24.9(f) n.65

Eady, State v., 249 Conn. 431, 733 A.2d 112 (1999)—§ 3.3(d) n.159

Eagle, State v., 196 Ariz. 188, 994 P.2d 395 (2000)—§ 26.3(f) n.54

Eagleboy, United States v., 200 F.3d 1137 (8th Cir.1999)—§ 13.4(c) n.82

Eagle Hawk, United States v., 815 F.2d 1213 (8th Cir.1987)—§§ 18.3(b) n.31, 32

Eagleman v. State, 673 N.W.2d 241 (N.D.2004)—§ 21.6(a) n.64

Eaglin v. Welborn, 57 F.3d 496 (7th Cir.1995)—§§ 5.3(c) n.30, 32

Ealey, State v., 959 S.W.2d 605 (Tenn.1997)—§§ 19.4(b) n.14, 21

Ealy v. Littlejohn, 569 F.2d 219 (5th Cir.1978)—§§ 8.8(d) n.54, 58, 77

Earegood, People v., 12 Mich.App. 256, 162 N.W.2d 802 (1968)—§§ 21.1(e) n.82, 86, 90

Earl, Commonwealth v., 393 Mass. 738, 473 N.E.2d 193 (1985)—§ 21.4(e) n.161

Earl, State v., 716 P.2d 803 (Utah 1986)—§ 2.12(a) n.31

Earle, State v., 145 Vt. 650, 497 A.2d 28 (1985)—§ 21.2(d) n.206

Earley, State v., 192 Kan. 167, 386 P.2d 189 (1963)—§ 3.1(f) n.149

Earls v. McCaughtry, 379 F.3d 489 (7th Cir.2004)—§ 11.10(c) n.111

Earls, State v., 116 Wash.2d 364, 805 P.2d 211 (1991)—§§ 6.9(c) n.61, 63

Earls v. State, 496 S.W.2d 464 (Tenn.1973)—§ 3.10(b) n.25

Earls, United States v., 42 F.3d 1321 (10th Cir.1994)—§ 3.4(j) n.182

Early v. Packer, 537 U.S. 3, 123 S.Ct. 362, 154 L.Ed.2d 263 (2002)—§ 28.6(f) n.69

Early, State v., 180 Or.App. 342, 43 P.3d 439 (2002)—§ 19.3(a) n.41

Earnest, In re, 90 F.R.D. 698 (M.D.Ga.1981)—§§ 8.14(a) n.8; 8.14(c) n.36

Earnest v. Dorsey, 87 F.3d 1123 (10th Cir.1996)—§ 25.2(b) n.14

Earnhart, United States v., 683 F.Supp. 717 (W.D.Ark.1987)—§ 19.4(b) n.24

Earp v. Ornoski, 431 F.3d 1158 (9th Cir.2005)—§ 11.10(c) n.149

Eash, State v., 367 So.2d 661 (Fla.App.1979)—§§ 13.6(c) n.31, 35

Easler, State v., 327 S.C. 121, 489 S.E.2d 617 (1997)—§ 6.6(e) n.91

Easley, People v., 192 Ill.2d 307, 249 Ill.Dec. 537, 736 N.E.2d 975 (2000)—§ 22.3(d) n.247

Easley, People v., 148 Ill.2d 281, 170 Ill.Dec. 356, 592 N.E.2d 1036 (1992)—§§ 6.2(c) n.150; 6.6(e) n.83; 6.7(c) n.111

Easley, People v., 46 Cal.3d 712, 250 Cal.Rptr. 855, 759 P.2d 490 (1988)—§§ 11.9(d) n.202, 224, 233

Eason, People v., 435 Mich. 228, 458 N.W.2d 17 (1990)—§ 26.4(d) n.53

East v. Scott, 55 F.3d 996 (5th Cir.1995)—§§ 13.3(b) n.20; 28.7(d) n.28

East, State v., 345 N.C. 535, 481 S.E.2d 652 (1997)—§§ 22.3(a) n.10; 22.3(c) n.112

Eastep v. State, 941 S.W.2d 130 (Tex.Crim.App.1997)—§ 19.5(b) n.27

Easter v. McDonald, 903 S.W.2d 887 (Tex.App.1995)—§ 27.4(b) n.13

Easter v. Norris, 100 F.3d 523 (8th Cir.1996)—§ 21.4(c) n.77

Easter, United States v., 539 F.2d 663 (8th Cir.1976)—§ 11.10(b) n.30

Easterling, State v., 137 P.3d 825, 157 Wash.2d 167 (2006)—§ 24.1(b) n.17

Easterling, United States v., 921 F.2d 1073 (10th Cir.1990)—§ 21.2(d) n.198

Eastern Air Lines, United States v., 923 F.2d 241 (2d Cir.1991)—§ 8.5(c) n.82

Eastern Medical Billing, Inc., United States v., 230 F.3d 600 (3d Cir.2000)—§ 24.9(d) n.45

Easterwood v. State, 273 Kan. 361, 44 P.3d 1209 (2002)—§§ 21.4(c) n.85; 21.5(e) n.143; 28.11(b) n.15

Eastland, United States v., 989 F.2d 760 (5th Cir.1993)—§§ 2.12(c) n.172; 3.2(d) n.146

Eastman, State v., 92 Conn.App. 261, 884 A.2d 442 (2005)—§ 27.5(a) n.15

Eastman Kodak Co., In re, 7 F.R.D. 760 (W.D.N.Y.1947)—§§ 8.7(b) n.30, 57

Eatherton v. State, 810 P.2d 93 (Wyo.1991)—§ 17.4(a) n.34

Eaton v. Commonwealth, 240 Va. 236, 397 S.E.2d 385 (1990)—§ 6.4(e) n.95

Eaton v. Eaton, 119 N.J. 628, 575 A.2d 858 (1990)—§ 21.4(a) n.20

Eaton, State v., 462 A.2d 502 (Me.1983)—§ 14.3(c) n.68

Eaton, State v., 24 Wash.App. 143, 600 P.2d 632 (1979)—§ 19.5(b) n.20

Eaton v. State, 302 A.2d 588 (Me.1973)—§ 1.7(f) n.86

Eaton, United States v., 179 F.3d 1328 (11th Cir.1999)—§ 5.4(c) n.30

Eaton, United States v., 501 F.2d 77 (5th Cir.1974)—§ 19.6(a) n.2

Eaves, United States v., 849 F.2d 363 (8th Cir.1988)—§ 21.4(f) n.171

Ebel, United States v., 299 F.3d 187 (3d Cir.2002)—§§ 21.3(d) n.218; 21.5(c) n.83

Ebens, United States v., 654 F.Supp. 144 (E.D.Mich.1987)—§ 23.2(a) n.43

Eberhart v. United States, 546 U.S. 12, 126 S.Ct. 403, 163 L.Ed.2d 14 (2005)—§ 24.11(b) n.4

Ebersole, United States v., 411 F.3d 517 (4th Cir.2005)—§§ 16.2(e) n.76; 16.2(f) n.104

Eccles, State v., 179 Ariz. 226, 877 P.2d 799 (1994)—§ 26.9(b) n.68

Echavarria v. State, 108 Nev. 734, 839 P.2d 589 (1992)—§ 7.5(b) n.23

Echavarria-Olarte, United States v., 904 F.2d 1391 (9th Cir.1990)—§ 9.6(a) n.15

Echegollen-Barrueta, United States v., 195 F.3d 786 (5th Cir.1999)—§ 21.2(d) n.169

Echeles, United States v., 352 F.2d 892 (7th Cir.1965)—§ 17.2(c) n.78

Echeverria, In re, 141 Wash.2d 323, 6 P.3d 573 (Wash.2000)—§ 26.4(g) n.141

Echeverria v. State, 119 Nev. 41, 62 P.3d 743 (2003)—§§ 21.2(d) n.143; 21.2(e) n.316

Echols v. State, 354 Ark. 530, 127 S.W.3d 486 (2003)—§§ 11.9(a) n.15; 11.9(d) n.173, 230

Echols v. State, 255 Ga. 311, 338 S.E.2d 259 (1986)—§ 15.4(f) n.147

Eckard v. Commonwealth, 20 Va.App. 619, 460 S.E.2d 242 (1995)—§ 18.4(c) n.53

Eckenrod v. State, 67 P.3d 635 (Wyo.2003)—§ 3.8(b) n.43

E. C. Knight Co., United States v., 156 U.S. 1, 15 S.Ct. 249, 39 L.Ed. 325 (1895)—§ 1.2(c) n.124

Eddings v. Oklahoma, 455 U.S. 104, 102 S.Ct. 869, 71 L.Ed.2d 1 (1982)—§§ 26.1(b) n.21; 26.4(g) n.116

Eddy, People v., 349 Mich. 637, 85 N.W.2d 117 (1957)—§ 9.4(e) n.101

Edebohls, People v., 944 P.2d 552 (Colo.App.1996)—§§ 11.9(b) n.92; 11.9(c) n.129

Edelin, United States v., 175 F.Supp.2d 1 (D.D.C.2001)—§ 24.2(e) n.68

Edelman, United States v., 458 F.3d 791 (8th Cir.2006)—§§ 21.2(g) n.399; 21.2(h) n.419

Edelson, United States v., 581 F.2d 1290 (7th Cir.1978)—§ 15.2(i) n.217

Edgar, State v., 281 Kan. 30, 127 P.3d 986 (2006)—§§ 21.4(f) n.181; 21.6(a) n.44

Edgar, United States v., 82 F.3d 499 (1st Cir.1996)—§ 8.8(d) n.93

Edgerton, United States v., 734 F.2d 913 (2d Cir.1984)—§§ 8.10(a) n.21; 8.13(b) n.49

Edlin v. State, 523 So.2d 42 (Miss.1988)—§ 3.7(d) n.70

Edmaiston, State v., 679 S.W.2d 360 (Mo.App.1984)—§ 20.3(a) n.14

Edman, State v., 452 N.W.2d 169 (Iowa 1990)—§ 6.2(c) n.173

Edmo, United States v., 140 F.3d 1289 (9th Cir.1998)—§§ 6.7(a) n.3; 6.7(b) n.41

Edmond v. Goldsmith, 183 F.3d 659 (7th Cir.1999)—§ 3.9(g) n.131

Edmond v. State, 341 S.C. 340, 534 S.E.2d 682 (2000)—§§ 11.10(c) n.116, 118

Edmonds v. Commonwealth, 189 S.W.3d 558 (Ky.2006)—§ 17.1(d) n.53

Edmonds v. State, 372 Md. 314, 812 A.2d 1034 (2002)—§§ 22.3(d) n.221, 226, 250, 255

Edmonds v. State, 138 Md.App. 438, 771 A.2d 1094 (Md.App.2001)— § 24.4(d) n.63

Edmonds, United States v., 240 F.3d 55 (D.C.Cir.2001)—§ 3.8(d) n.141

Edmonds, United States v., 80 F.3d 810 (3d Cir.1996)—§ 27.6(d) n.119

Edmonds, United States v., 870 F.Supp. 1140 (D.D.C.1994)—§§ 24.3(d) n.111, 112

Edmondson v. Pearce, 91 P.3d 605 (Okla.2004)—§§ 1.2(b) n.5, 6

Edmondson, State v., 714 So.2d 1233 (La.1998)—§ 13.5(b) n.36

Edmondson, United States v., 791 F.2d 1512 (11th Cir.1986)—§ 9.4(a) n.33

Edmons, United States v., 432 F.2d 577 (2d Cir.1970)—§ 9.4(d) n.91

Edmonson, People v., 75 N.Y.2d 672, 555 N.Y.S.2d 666, 554 N.E.2d 1254 (1990)—§ 7.4(e) n.87

Edmonson, State v., 257 Neb. 468, 598 N.W.2d 450 (1999)—§ 3.3(a) n.26

Edmonson, State v., 113 Idaho 230, 743 P.2d 459 (1987)—§§ 14.2(d) n.57, 58; 15.2(e) n.142; 15.5(c) n.126; 15.6(a) n.24, 39; 15.6(d) n.107, 123, 128; 15.7(b) n.10, 42; 15.7(h) n.224

Edmonson, United States v., 962 F.2d 1535 (10th Cir.1992)—§§ 15.6(e) n.156, 157

Edmonson, United States v., 659 F.2d 549 (5th Cir.1981)—§ 19.3(c) n.194

Edmunds, Commonwealth v., 526 Pa. 374, 586 A.2d 887 (1991)— §§ 2.12(d) n.195; 2.12(e) n.200

Edmunds v. Won Bae Chang, 509 F.2d 39 (9th Cir.1975)—§ 28.3(a) n.16

Edney, People v., 39 N.Y.2d 620, 385 N.Y.S.2d 23, 350 N.E.2d 400 (1976)—§ 20.5(c) n.55

Edney, United States ex rel. v. Smith, 425 F.Supp. 1038 (E.D.N.Y.1976)—§§ 20.5(c) n.55, 56

Edouard, United States v., 485 F.3d 1324 (11th Cir.2007)—§§ 24.2(g) n.99, 100

Edrozo, State v., 578 N.W.2d 719 (Minn.1998)—§ 6.7(c) n.141

Educational Development Network Corp., United States v., 884 F.2d 737 (3d Cir.1989)—§ 8.5(c) n.87

Education, Board of v. Admiral Heating and Ventilation, Inc., 513 F.Supp. 600 (N.D.Ill.1981)—§ 8.5(h) n.260

Education, Board of v. Nyquist, 590 F.2d 1241 (2d Cir.1979)—§ 22.5(a) n.5

Education, Board of v. Verisario, 143 Ill.App.3d 1000, 97 Ill.Dec. 692, 493 N.E.2d 355 (1986)—§§ 8.5(c) n.71, 97; 8.5(h) n.238, 276, 289, 301; 8.5(i) n.310

Education of Independent School District No. 92, Board of v. Earls, 536 U.S. 822, 122 S.Ct. 2559, 153 L.Ed.2d 735 (2002)—§ 3.9(d) n.68

Education of Independent School District No. 92 of Pottawatomie County, Board of v. Earls, 536 U.S. 822, 122 S.Ct. 2559, 153 L.Ed.2d 735 (2002)—§ 3.9(k) n.261

Edwards v. Arizona, 451 U.S. 477, 101 S.Ct. 1880, 68 L.Ed.2d 378 (1981)—§§ 2.8(b) n.51; 2.9(b) n.43; 2.9(g) n.176; 2.9(h) n.222, 240; 2.11(d) n.47; 3.10(b) n.79; 6.4(e) n.75, 79; 6.9(e) n.91; 6.9(f) n.116; 6.9(g) n.186; 9.6(a) n.30

Edwards v. Balisok, 520 U.S. 641, 117 S.Ct. 1584, 137 L.Ed.2d 906 (1997)—§ 26.2(c) n.65

Edwards v. California, 314 U.S. 160, 62 S.Ct. 164, 86 L.Ed. 119 (1941)—§ 1.7(j) n.236

Edwards v. Carpenter, 529 U.S. 446, 120 S.Ct. 1587, 146 L.Ed.2d 518 (2000)—§§ 11.7(e) n.95; 28.4(d) n.55

Edwards, Commonwealth v., 535 Pa. 575, 637 A.2d 259 (1993)—§ 24.5(c) n.39

Edwards, People v., 96 N.Y.2d 445, 729 N.Y.S.2d 410, 754 N.E.2d 169 (2001)—§§ 21.2(a) n.5, 8

Edwards, People v., 97 Ill.App.3d 407, 52 Ill.Dec. 908, 422 N.E.2d 1117 (1981)—§ 25.3(a) n.7

Edwards, State v., 281 Kan. 1334, 135 P.3d 1251 (2006)—§ 21.6(a) n.64

Edwards, State v., 116 S.W.3d 511 (Mo. 2003)—§§ 6.2(c) n.96; 6.9(g) n.200

Edwards, State v., 810 A.2d 226 (R.I.2002)—§§ 6.6(e) n.71; 6.7(d) n.144

Edwards, State v., 96 Haw. 224, 30 P.3d 238 (2001)—§ 6.4(e) n.84

Edwards v. State, 759 N.E.2d 626 (Ind.2001)—§ 3.5(c) n.130

Edwards, State v., 264 Kan. 177, 955 P.2d 1276 (1998)—§ 22.3(d) n.221

Edwards v. State, 107 Nev. 150, 808 P.2d 528 (1991)—§ 9.4(a) n.36

Edwards v. State, 815 P.2d 670 (Okla.1991)—§ 2.12(d) n.184

Edwards, State v., 214 Conn. 57, 570 A.2d 193 (1990)—§ 3.10(e) n.169

Edwards, State v., 236 Neb. 445, 462 N.W.2d 93 (1990)—§ 21.6(a) n.2

Edwards, State v., 153 Vt. 649, 569 A.2d 1075 (Vt.1989)—§ 20.6(c) n.79

Edwards v. State, 538 So.2d 440 (Fla.1989)—§ 7.3(f) n.115

Edwards, State v., 51 Wash.App. 763, 755 P.2d 821 (1988)—§ 27.5(b) n.49

Edwards, State v., 73 N.C.App. 599, 327 S.E.2d 16 (1985)—§ 11.10(c) n.85

Edwards v. State, 422 So.2d 84 (Fla.App.1982)—§ 1.8(d) n.48

Edwards, State v., 98 Wis.2d 367, 297 N.W.2d 12 (1980)—§ 3.4(g) n.125

Edwards, State v., 279 N.W.2d 9 (Iowa 1979)—§§ 21.2(f) n.383; 27.3(c) n.26

Edwards v. State, 379 So.2d 336 (Ala.App.1979)—§ 19.3(b) n.168

Edwards v. State, 74 Wis.2d 79, 246 N.W.2d 109 (1976)—§ 26.9(b) n.45

Edwards v. State, 51 Wis.2d 231, 186 N.W.2d 193 (1971)—§ 21.4(e) n.165

Edwards v. State, 45 N.J.L. 419 (1883)—§§ 15.1(f) n.273, 274, 289

Edwards, United States v., 342 F.3d 168 (2d Cir.2003)—§ 6.4(g) n.147

Edwards, United States v., 303 F.3d 606 (5th Cir.2002)—§§ 22.3(b) n.67, 70

Edwards, United States v., 72 F.Supp.2d 668 (M.D.La.1999)—§§ 15.4(f) n.145; 22.2(a) n.7

Edwards, United States v., 188 F.3d 230 (4th Cir.1999)—§ 13.4(a) n.11

Edwards v. United States, 523 U.S. 511, 118 S.Ct. 1475, 140 L.Ed.2d 703 (1998)—§ 24.10(a) n.13

Edwards, United States v., 897 F.2d 445 (9th Cir.1990)—§§ 11.6(c) n.100; 24.5(d) n.58

Edwards, United States v., 885 F.2d 377 (7th Cir.1989)—§ 6.7(b) n.50

Edwards, United States v., 823 F.2d 111 (5th Cir.1987)—§§ 23.1(d) n.125, 143, 154

Edwards, United States v., 777 F.2d 364 (7th Cir.1985)—§ 11.2(c) n.99

Edwards, United States v., 716 F.2d 822 (11th Cir.1983)—§ 11.5(c) n.52

Edwards, United States v., 90 F.R.D. 391 (E.D.Va.1981)—§ 20.5(c) n.41

Edwards, United States v., 430 A.2d 1321 (D.C.App.1981)—§§ 12.3(c) n.82; 12.3(d) n.108

Edwards, United States v., 602 F.2d 458 (1st Cir.1979)—§ 3.1(h) n.190

Edwards, United States v., 415 U.S. 800, 94 S.Ct. 1234, 39 L.Ed.2d 771 (1974)—§§ 2.9(h) n.210; 3.5(c) n.107, 118; 3.5(e) n.180; 3.7(f) n.140

Edwards, United States v., 498 F.2d 496 (2d Cir.1974)—§§ 3.9(h) n.155, 158

Edwards, United States v., 441 F.2d 749 (5th Cir.1971)—§ 3.7(d) n.77

Eesley, State v., 225 Wis.2d 248, 591 N.W.2d 846 (1999)—§ 18.4(c) n.40

E.F., In re, 177 Vt. 534, 862 A.2d 239 (2004)—§ 21.6(c) n.118

E.G., Matter of, 482 A.2d 1243 (D.C.1984)—§§ 3.3(d) n.172, 179

Egbuonu, Ex parte, 911 So.2d 748 (Ala.Crim.App.2004)—§ 16.1(d) n.163

Ege v. Yukins, 485 F.3d 364 (6th Cir.2007)—§§ 28.4(d) n.51; 28.5(b) n.54

Egenberger, United States v., 424 F.3d 803 (8th Cir.2005)—§ 21.2(d) n.193

Egerstaffer v. Israel, 726 F.2d 1231 (7th Cir.1984)—§ 26.10(c) n.74

Eggerman, People v., 292 Ill.App.3d 644, 226 Ill.Dec. 493, 685 N.E.2d 948 (1997)—§ 16.1(d) n.155

Eggers, People v., 27 Ill.2d 85, 188 N.E.2d 30 (1963)—§ 11.2(g) n.292

Eggleston v. Pierce County, 148 Wash.2d 760, 64 P.3d 618 (2003)—§ 3.1(k) n.281

Ehly, State v., 317 Or. 66, 854 P.2d 421 (1993)—§ 3.8(e) n.219

Ehrlich, People v., 136 Misc.2d 514, 518 N.Y.S.2d 742 (1987)—§ 15.7(g) n.206

Ehrmann, United States v., 421 F.3d 774 (8th Cir.2005)—§ 22.3(d) n.201

Ehrsam v. Rubenstein, 917 F.2d 764 (3d Cir.1990)—§ 13.7(a) n.23

Eibler, United States v., 991 F.2d 1350 (7th Cir.1993)—§ 21.5(a) n.15

Eichinger, Commonwealth v., 591 Pa. 1, 915 A.2d 1122 (2007)—§ 6.6(e) n.68

Eichstedt, State v., 20 Conn.App. 395, 567 A.2d 1237 (1989)—§§ 24.4(c) n.20, 21

Eight Grand Jury Subpoenae Duces Tecum, In re, 701 F.Supp. 53 (S.D.N.Y.1988)—§ 8.8(e) n.139

Eight Thousand Eight Hundred and Fifty Dollars, United States v., 461 U.S. 555, 103 S.Ct. 2005, 76 L.Ed.2d 143 (1983)—§§ 18.1(a) n.2; 18.5(b) n.54

Einhorn, People v., 75 Misc.2d 183, 346 N.Y.S.2d 986 (1973)—§ 3.4(f) n.112

Eirin, United States v., 778 F.2d 722 (11th Cir.1985)—§ 6.9(e) n.91

Eis, State v., 348 N.W.2d 224 (Iowa 1984)—§ 9.1(d) n.120

Eisemann, Commonwealth v., 276 Pa.Super. 543, 419 A.2d 591 (1980)—§ 13.3(b) n.23

Eisen, United States v., 974 F.2d 246 (2d Cir.1992)—§§ 8.5(i) n.312; 11.9(d) n.217; 15.6(d) n.121; 15.6(f) n.171; 15.7(a) n.3

Eisenberg, In re Application of, 654 F.2d 1107 (5th Cir.1981)—§ 8.5(d) n.126

Eisenberg, United States v., 711 F.2d 959 (11th Cir.1983)—§§ 8.5(f) n.211; 8.5(i) n.307, 308, 314, 316, 321, 322

Eisenman, State v., 153 N.J. 462, 710 A.2d 441 (1998)—§ 26.3(f) n.58

Eisner v. Commonwealth, 375 S.W.2d 825 (Ky.1964)—§ 15.1(d) n.221

Eizember, United States v., 485 F.3d 400 (8th Cir.2007)—§ 24.9(f) n.66

Ekinici, People v., 191 Misc.2d 510, 743 N.Y.S.2d 651 (N.Y.Sup.2002)—§ 27.5(a) n.7

Ekong, People v., 221 Ill.App.3d 559, 164 Ill.Dec. 25, 582 N.W.2d 233 (1991)—§ 8.6(b) n.37

Elaire, State ex rel. v. Blackburn, 424 So.2d 246 (La.1982)—§ 24.8(f) n.100

Elbert, State v., 121 N.H. 43, 424 A.2d 1147 (1981)—§ 15.4(b) n.45

Elder v. Board of Medical Examiners, 241 Cal.App.2d 246, 50 Cal.Rptr. 304 (1966)—§ 3.1(g) n.180

Elder, State v., 815 P.2d 1341 (Utah App.1991)—§§ 3.10(d) n.134; 3.10(e) n.181

Elder, United States v., 90 F.3d 1110 (6th Cir.1996)—§§ 23.2(g) n.123; 24.2(e) n.59

Elders, People v., 63 Ill.App.3d 554, 20 Ill.Dec. 333, 380 N.E.2d 10 (1978)—§ 3.10(e) n.141

Elderts, State v., 62 Haw. 495, 617 P.2d 89 (1980)—§ 9.1(b) n.80

Eldred, State v., 564 N.W.2d 283 (N.D.1997)—§§ 6.6(e) n.91; 14.2(e) n.73

Eldridge v. Atkins, 665 F.2d 228 (8th Cir.1981)—§ 11.10(c) n.119

Eldridge v. United States, 618 A.2d 690 (D.C.App.1992)—§ 21.5(c) n.86

Eldridge, United States v., 302 F.2d 463 (4th Cir.1962)—§ 9.1(d) n.127

Electronic Surveillance, Matter of, 596 F.Supp. 991 (E.D.Mich.1984)—§ 8.5(b) n.40

Eleneki, State v., 92 Hawaii 562, 993 P.2d 1191 (2000)—§ 3.4(h) n.149

Eley, State v., 77 Ohio St.3d 174, 672 N.E.2d 640 (1996)—§ 6.2(c) n.181

El-Gabrowny, United States v., 35 F.3d 63 (2d Cir.1994)—§ 12.3(d) n.97

El-Gawli, United States v., 837 F.2d 142 (3d Cir.1988)—§§ 5.3(d) n.42, 43

El-Hage, United States v., 213 F.3d 74 (2d Cir.2000)—§§ 12.2(c) n.43; 12.3(d) n.97

Elife, United States v., 43 F.R.D. 23 (S.D.N.Y.1967)—§ 20.3(b) n.45

Elkins, State v., 245 Or. 279, 422 P.2d 250 (1966)—§§ 3.5(b) n.104; 3.5(c) n.117

Elkins, United States v., 300 F.3d 638 (6th Cir.2002)—§ 3.4(d) n.51

Elkins v. United States, 364 U.S. 206, 80 S.Ct. 1437, 4 L.Ed.2d 1669 (1960)—§§ 1.7(i) n.164; 3.1(a) n.15; 3.1(c) n.30; 3.1(e) n.122, 133; 25.5(a) n.5

Elko County Grand Jury, In re, 109 F.3d 554 (9th Cir.1997)—§ 8.6(b) n.37

Elksnis, United States v., 259 F.Supp. 236 (S.D.N.Y.1966)—§ 15.4(b) n.36

Elksnis, United States ex rel. v. Gilligan, 256 F.Supp. 244 (S.D.N.Y.1966)—§§ 21.2(c) n.113; 21.3(d) n.229

Eller v. State, 92 N.M. 52, 582 P.2d 824 (1978)—§ 21.4(g) n.233

Ellerbe, State v., 217 La. 639, 47 So.2d 30 (1950)—§§ 16.1(d) n.133; 16.1(e) n.181, 197

Ellerman, United States v., 411 F.3d 941 (8th Cir.2005)—§§ 13.5(b) n.43, 54

Ellett v. State, 883 P.2d 940 (Wyo.1994)—§§ 26.1(e) n.110, 112

Ellingsen, People v., 258 Cal.App.2d 535, 65 Cal.Rptr. 744 (1968)—§§ 6.6(f) n.106, 107

Ellingsworth, State v., 966 P.2d 1220 (Utah App.1998)—§ 3.1(h) n.212

Elliott, State v., 133 N.H. 190, 574 A.2d 1378 (1990)—§ 21.3(b) n.68

Elliott v. State, 687 S.W.2d 359 (Tex.Cr.App.1985)—§ 3.3(c) n.96

Elliott, United States v., 467 F.3d 688 (7th Cir.2006)—§ 18.5(a) n.25

Elliott, United States v., 264 F.3d 1171 (10th Cir.2001)—§§ 21.2(b) n.76; 27.5(c) n.59

Elliott, United States v., 893 F.2d 220 (9th Cir.1990)—§ 3.3(c) n.110

Elliott, United States v., 849 F.2d 554 (11th Cir.1988)—§ 8.8(g) n.167

Elliott, United States v., 266 F.Supp. 318 (S.D.N.Y.1967)—§§ 13.5(c) n.63, 73

Ellis, In re, 356 F.3d 1198 (9th Cir.2004)—§§ 21.3(e) n.282; 21.3(f) n.446; 21.4(g) n.253

Ellis, In re, 294 F.3d 1094 (9th Cir.2002)—§ 21.4(g) n.254

Ellis v. Carlton, 986 S.W.2d 600 (Tenn.Crim.App.1998)—§ 21.6(a) n.64

Ellis, Commonwealth v., 429 Mass. 362, 708 N.E.2d 644 (1999)—§ 22.5(a) n.8

Ellis, Commonwealth v., 534 Pa. 176, 626 A.2d 1137 (Pa.1993)—§§ 11.5(g) n.110, 111, 124

Ellis v. Commonwealth, 227 Va. 419, 317 S.E.2d 479 (1984)—§ 24.2(a) n.20

Ellis, Commonwealth v., 233 Pa.Super. 169, 335 A.2d 512 (1975)—§§ 3.3(f) n.216; 3.8(d) n.132

Ellis v. District of Columbia, 84 F.3d 1413 (D.C.Cir.1996)—§ 26.2(c) n.43

Ellis, People v., 468 Mich. 25, 658 N.W.2d 142 (2003)—§ 22.1(h) n.145

Ellis, People v., 58 N.Y.2d 748, 459 N.Y.S.2d 25, 445 N.E.2d 201 (1982)—§ 6.4(f) n.112

Ellis, People v., 65 Cal.2d 529, 55 Cal.Rptr. 385, 421 P.2d 393 (1966)—§§ 7.2(b) n.29; 7.2(c) n.31, 34

Ellis v. State, 744 N.E.2d 425 (Ind.2001)—§ 21.3(d) n.226

Ellis v. State, 272 Ga. 763, 534 S.E.2d 414 (2000)—§ 11.9(d) n.232

Ellis v. State, 736 N.E.2d 731 (Ind.2000)—§ 26.3(f) n.58

Ellis, State v., 619 A.2d 418 (R.I.1993)—§ 15.5(c) n.109

Ellis v. State, 573 So.2d 724 (Miss.1990)—§ 3.8(e) n.215

Ellis, State v., 748 P.2d 188 (Utah 1987)—§ 17.2(b) n.36

Ellis, State v., 219 Neb. 408, 363 N.W.2d 389 (1985)—§ 7.3(b) n.14

Ellis, United States v., 470 F.3d 275 (6th Cir.2006)—§ 21.5(a) n.43

Ellis, United States v., 121 F.3d 908 (4th Cir.1997)—§ 7.5(b) n.13

Ellis, United States v., 90 F.3d 447 (11th Cir.1996)—§§ 23.1(d) n.170; 27.5(a) n.20

Ellis, United States v., 154 F.R.D. 692 (M.D.Fla.1993)—§ 23.1(d) n.149

Ellis, United States v., 971 F.2d 701 (11th Cir.1992)—§ 3.1(c) n.72

Ellis, United States v., 457 F.2d 1204 (8th Cir.1972)—§ 6.9(e) n.88

Ellis v. United States, 416 F.2d 791 (D.C.Cir.1969)—§ 8.10(e) n.125

Ellison v. Commonwealth, _____ Va. _____, 639 S.E.2d 209 (2007)—§ 17.4(a) n.30

Ellison, State v., 140 P.3d 899 (Ariz.2006)—§ 22.4(c) n.29

Ellison, State v., 213 Ariz. 116, 140 P.3d 899 (2006)—§ 6.9(g) n.166

Ellison v. State, 65 Md.App. 321, 500 A.2d 650 (1985)—§ 8.10(a) n.15

Ellison, United States v., 791 F.2d 821 (10th Cir.1986)—§ 6.6(d) n.50

Ellison, United States v., 798 F.2d 1102 (7th Cir.1986)—§§ 11.9(d) n.210, 213

Ellsworth, State v., 175 W.Va. 64, 331 S.E.2d 503 (1985)—§ 6.9(b) n.20

Elmer v. State, 353 Md. 1, 724 A.2d 625 (1999)—§ 21.2(h) n.426

Elmhurst Milk & Cream Co., People v., 116 Misc.2d 140, 455 N.Y.S.2d 473 (Sup.Ct.1982)—§ 15.4(g) n.171

Elmore, State v., 111 Ohio St.3d 515, 857 N.E.2d 547 (Ohio 2006)—§ 24.9(a) n.8

Elmore, State v., 139 Wash.2d 250, 985 P.2d 289 (1999)—§ 21.4(f) n.176

Elmore, State v., 174 Ariz. 480, 851 P.2d 105 (1992)—§§ 26.9(b) n.16, 20

Elmore v. State, 285 Ark. 42, 684 S.W.2d 263 (1985)—§ 21.3(b) n.107

El-Nobani v. United States, 287 F.3d 417 (6th Cir.2002)—§ 21.4(d) n.135

Elrod, United States v., 441 F.2d 353 (5th Cir.1971)—§§ 3.10(a) n.14; 3.10(b) n.45

El-Sayegh, United States v., 131 F.3d 158 (D.C.Cir.1997)—§ 21.4(b) n.52

Else v. State, 555 P.2d 1210 (Alaska 1976)—§§ 21.4(c) n.93, 94

El-Tabech, State v., 269 Neb. 810, 696 N.W.2d 445 (2005)—§ 24.11(d) n.39

Eltayib, United States v., 88 F.3d 157 (2d Cir.1996)—§ 7.4(e) n.89

Elvik v. State, 114 Nev. 883, 965 P.2d 281 (1998)—§§ 6.2(c) n.147; 6.9(b) n.20

El Vocero de Puerto Rico v. Puerto Rico, 508 U.S. 147, 113 S.Ct. 2004, 124 L.Ed.2d 60 (1993)—§ 23.1(d) n.131

Ely v. Haugh, 172 N.W.2d 144 (Iowa 1969)—§§ 21.5(f) n.157, 174

Ely, State v., 167 Vt. 323, 708 A.2d 1332 (Vt.1997)—§§ 8.11(b) n.22; 8.11(c) n.66 to 68

Ely, State v., 237 Or. 329, 390 P.2d 348 (1964)—§ 6.2(c) n.102

Ely, United States v., 142 F.3d 1113 (9th Cir.1997)—§ 17.4(b) n.119

Ely, United States v., 719 F.2d 902 (7th Cir.1983)—§§ 11.4(a) n.2, 5

Emanuele, United States v., 51 F.3d 1123 (3d Cir.1995)—§ 7.4(c) n.64

Embrey v. Hershberger, 131 F.3d 739 (8th Cir.1997)—§ 28.4(e) n.88

Emerson v. State, 988 P.2d 518 (Wyo.1999)—§ 20.3(a) n.19

Emerson, State v., 149 Vt. 171, 541 A.2d 466 (1987)—§ 7.4(e) n.80

Emerson, State v., 266 Minn. 217, 123 N.W.2d 382 (1963)—§§ 7.2(b) n.16, 17

Emery v. Oregon, 297 Or. 755, 688 P.2d 72 (1984)—§ 3.1(k) n.280

Emery, State v., 636 N.W.2d 116 (Iowa 2001)—§ 21.6(a) n.42

Emery, State v., 156 Vt. 364, 593 A.2d 77 (1991)—§ 26.9(b) n.54

Emery, State v., 131 Ariz. 493, 642 P.2d 838 (1982)—§ 15.4(g) n.178

Emery, United States v., 541 F.2d 887 (1st Cir.1976)—§ 3.2(j) n.248

Emery's Case, 107 Mass. 172 (1871)—§ 2.12(a) n.10

Emmert, United States v., 829 F.2d 805 (9th Cir.1987)—§ 5.1(c) n.36

Emmons v. State, 847 N.E.2d 1035 (Ind.App.2006)—§ 25.1(d) n.88

Emmons, United States v., 24 F.3d 1210 (10th Cir.1994)—§ 3.3(g) n.247

Emond, United States v., 935 F.2d 1511 (7th Cir.1991)—§ 17.2(e) n.119

Emory v. State, 101 Md.App. 585, 647 A.2d 1243 (1994)—§§ 25.4(c) n.34, 38

Emuegbunam, United States v., 268 F.3d 377 (6th Cir.2001)—§§ 1.7(c) n.17, 20

Enas, United States v., 255 F.3d 662 (9th Cir.2001)—§ 25.5(a) n.7

Energy Reserves Group, Inc. v. Kansas Power and Light Co. 459 U.S. 400, 103 S.Ct. 697, 74 L.Ed.2d 589 (1983)—§ 1.2(b) n.4

Eng v. Coughlin, 726 F.Supp. 40 (W.D.N.Y.1989)—§ 8.5(h) n.273

Eng v. Coughlin, 858 F.2d 889 (2d Cir.1988)—§ 26.2(c) n.68

Eng, United States v., 971 F.2d 854 (2d Cir.1992)—§ 9.3(e) n.77

Engberg v. Wyoming, 265 F.3d 1109 (10th Cir.2001)—§ 7.2(b) n.22

Engel, State v., 99 N.J. 453, 493 A.2d 1217 (1985)—§§ 12.1(d) n.53; 12.4(a) n.22, 35, 39; 15.5(c) n.108

Engelhardt, State v., 280 Kan. 113, 119 P.3d 1148 (2005)—§ 24.2(a) n.8

Engelmann, State v., 541 N.W.2d 96 (S.D.1995)—§ 21.5(a) n.19

Engesser, State v., 661 N.W.2d 739 (S.D.2003)—§ 3.5(d) n.142

England v. State, 887 S.W.2d 902 (Tex.Cr.App.1994)—§ 5.2(b) n.24

England, State v., 180 W.Va. 342, 376 S.E.2d 548 (1988)—§ 11.7(e) n.77

England, United States v., 971 F.2d 419 (9th Cir.1992)—§ 4.2(b) n.12

Engle v. Isaac, 456 U.S. 107, 102 S.Ct. 1558, 71 L.Ed.2d 783 (1982)—§§ 2.11(a) n.4; 11.6(a) n.34; 28.2(c) n.40, 47, 49; 28.4(a) n.4, 10; 28.4(d) n.43; 28.4(e) n.71; 28.5(a) n.8

Engleman, United States v., 648 F.2d 473 (8th Cir.1981)—§ 24.8(a) n.19

English v. Artuz, 164 F.3d 105 (2d Cir.1998)—§ 24.1(b) n.17

English v. Cody, 146 F.3d 1257 (10th Cir.1998)—§ 28.4(b) n.20

English, People v., 172 A.D.2d 215, 567 N.Y.S.2d 720 (1991)—§ 16.1(g) n.247

Enmund v. Florida, 458 U.S. 782, 102 S.Ct. 3368, 73 L.Ed.2d 1140 (1982)—§ 2.7(c) n.182

Enoch, People v., 122 Ill.2d 176, 119 Ill.Dec. 265, 522 N.E.2d 1124 (1988)—§§ 6.7(b) n.43; 6.9(f) n.135

Enos v. State, 313 Ark. 683, 858 S.W.2d 72 (1993)—§ 21.3(e) n.266

Enquist v. Oregon Department of Agriculture, 478 F.3d 985 (9th Cir.2007)—§ 2.6(b) n.43

Enright, State v., 303 Mont. 457, 16 P.3d 366 (2000)—§ 17.2(c) n.82

Enslin, United States v., 315 F.3d 1205 (9th Cir.2003)—§ 3.8(e) n.206

Entrekin, State v., 98 Haw. 221, 47 P.3d 336 (2002)—§ 3.5(d) n.142

Environmental Protection, Department of v. Emerson, 616 A.2d 1268 (Me.1992)—§ 3.2(d) n.152

Eperjesi, Commonwealth v., 423 Pa. 455, 224 A.2d 216 (1966)—§ 6.7(d) n.152

Epperly v. Booker, 997 F.2d 1 (4th Cir.1993)—§ 24.3(b) n.61

Epperson v. United States, 471 A.2d 1016 (D.C.App.1984)—§ 24.9(d) n.43

Epperson, United States v., 454 F.2d 769 (4th Cir.1972)—§ 3.2(b) n.52

Epps, People v., 25 Cal.4th 19, 104 Cal.Rptr.2d 572,18 P.3d 2 (2001)—§ 26.6(b) n.17

Epps, State v., 284 N.J.Super. 373, 665 A.2d 412 (1995)—§ 15.7(f) n.170

Epps v. State, 901 F.2d 1481 (8th Cir.1990)—§ 16.3(g) n.108

Epps v. St. Mary's Hospital, 802 F.2d 412 (11th Cir.1986)—§ 4.6(b) n.46

Epton, United States ex rel. v. Nenna, 318 F.Supp. 899 (S.D.N.Y.1970)—§ 15.4(d) n.112

Equihua-Juarez, United States v., 851 F.2d 1222 (9th Cir.1988)—§ 6.10(c) n.56

Ercolano, State v., 79 N.J. 25, 397 A.2d 1062 (1979)—§ 3.1(d) n.101

Erdmann, United States v., 515 F.2d 290 (6th Cir.1975)—§ 4.6(m) n.228

Erdos, United States v., 474 F.2d 157 (4th Cir.1973)—§§ 16.1(e) n.168; 16.4(b) n.12

Erickson v. People, 951 P.2d 919 (Colo.1998)—§§ 19.4(b) n.14, 25

Erickson, State v., 589 N.W.2d 481 (Minn.1999)—§ 22.4(d) n.35

Erickson, State v., 525 N.W.2d 703 (S.D.1994)—§ 10.4(b) n.10

Erickson, State v., 129 N.H. 515, 533 A.2d 23 (1987)—§§ 19.3(a) n.72; 19.5(c) n.54

Erickson, State ex rel. v. West, 42 Minn. 147, 43 N.W. 845 (1889)—§§ 1.8(d) n.56, 64

Ermels, State v., 156 Wash.2d 528, 131 P.3d 299 (2006)—§ 21.5(e) n.149

Ermels, State v., 125 Wash.App. 195, 104 P.3d 67 (2005)—§ 27.5(c) n.64

Ernst, People v., 8 Cal.4th 441, 34 Cal.Rptr.2d 238, 881 P.2d 298 (1994)—§ 22.1(h) n.137

Eroh, People v., 47 Mich.App. 669, 209 N.W.2d 832 (1973)—§ 14.4(b) n.7

Ervin, People v., 22 Cal.4th 48, 91 Cal.Rptr.2d 623, 990 P.2d 506 (2000)—§ 22.3(d) n.225

Ervin, People v., 269 Ill.App.3d 141, 206 Ill.Dec. 350, 645 N.E.2d 355 (1994)—§ 9.1(b) n.70

Ervine's Appeal, 16 Pa. 256 (1851)—§ 2.4(c) n.95

Erving L., United States v., 147 F.3d 1240 (10th Cir.1998)—§§ 6.2(c) n.185; 6.6(c) n.42

Erwin, People v., 20 Cal.App.4th 1542, 25 Cal.Rptr.2d 348 (1993)—§§ 14.4(d) n.85, 87

Esajerre, People v., 35 N.Y.2d 463, 363 N.Y.S.2d 931, 323 N.E.2d 175 (1974)—§§ 21.2(b) n.91; 21.6(b) n.110

Escalanti v. Superior Court, 165 Ariz. 385, 799 P.2d 5 (App.1990)—§ 18.4(c) n.37

Escalera v. Coombe, 852 F.2d 45 (2d Cir.1988)—§§ 20.6(c) n.75, 81

Escalona-Naranjo, State v., 185 Wis.2d 168, 517 N.W.2d 157 (1994)— § 28.11(b) n.29

Escamilla, People v., 65 Cal.App.3d 558, 135 Cal.Rptr. 446 (1976)— § 3.4(b) n.31

Escamilla, United States v., 966 F.2d 465 (9th Cir.1992)—§ 6.2(c) n.114

Escamilla, United States v., 975 F.2d 568 (9th Cir.1992)—§ 21.5(f) n.167

Escandar, United States v., 319 F.Supp. 295 (S.D.Fla.1970)—§ 4.6(e) n.101

Escobar, People v., 168 Ill.App.3d 30, 118 Ill.Dec. 736, 522 N.E.2d 191 (1988)—§ 25.2(a) n.7

Escobar v. State, 699 So.2d 988 (Fla.1997)—§ 6.9(b) n.34

Escobar v. Superior Court, 155 Ariz. 298, 746 P.2d 39 (1987)—§ 15.7(e) n.105

Escobar-de Jesus, United States v., 187 F.3d 148 (1st Cir.1999)—§§ 4.6(e) n.79; 22.3(d) n.216

Escobedo v. Illinois, 378 U.S. 478, 84 S.Ct. 1758, 12 L.Ed.2d 977 (1964)—§§ 2.10(d) n.114; 2.11(c) n.32; 3.10(a) n.10; 6.1(a) n.8; 6.1(c) n.21; 6.4(b) n.21; 6.4(c) n.31; 6.5(a) n.11; 6.5(b) n.21; 6.6(a) n.3; 11.2(b) n.48

Escobedo, State v., 573 N.W.2d 271 (Iowa App.1997)—§ 27.5(d) n.113

Escotto, United States v., 121 F.3d 81 (2d Cir.1997)—§ 24.9(c) n.29

Esieke, United States v., 940 F.2d 29 (2d Cir.1991)—§ 3.9(f) n.110

Eskow, United States v., 279 F.Supp. 556 (S.D.N.Y.1968)—§ 15.5(b) n.52

Eskridge v. Washington State Board, 357 U.S. 214, 78 S.Ct. 1061, 2 L.Ed.2d 1269 (1958)—§ 11.2(d) n.132

Esparaza v. State, 595 So.2d 418 (Miss.1992)—§ 14.2(g) n.106

Esparsen, United States v., 930 F.2d 1461 (10th Cir.1991)—§ 22.3(d) n.214

Esparza-Gonzalez, United States v., 422 F.3d 897 (9th Cir.2005)— §§ 22.3(d) n.180, 210

Espinosa, United States v., 771 F.2d 1382 (10th Cir.1985)—§ 17.2(b) n.39

Espinosa-Guerra, United States v., 805 F.2d 1502 (11th Cir.1986)— § 3.8(b) n.49

Espinoza, Ex parte, 90 S.W.3d 906 (Tex.App.2002)—§§ 12.4(a) n.15, 16, 22

Espinoza v. State, 949 S.W.2d 10 (Tex.App.1997)—§ 18.4(c) n.68

Espinoza, United States v., 256 F.3d 718 (7th Cir.2001)—§ 3.4(h) n.146

Espinoza, United States v., 866 F.2d 1067 (9th Cir.1989)—§ 21.5(d) n.104

Espinoza, United States v., 641 F.2d 153 (4th Cir.1981)—§ 16.3(c) n.31

Espinoza-Cano, United States v., 456 F.3d 1126 (9th Cir.2006)—§ 26.4(i) n.203

Espinoza-Saenz, United States v., 235 F.3d 501 (10th Cir.2000)— § 28.9(b) n.53

Espinoza, United States ex rel. v. Fairman, 813 F.2d 117 (7th Cir.1987)— §§ 6.9(f) n.121, 144

Esposito, State v., 223 Conn. 299, 613 A.2d 242 (1992)—§ 22.3(c) n.104

Esquibel, People v., 49 Cal.Rptr.3d 393, 143 Cal.App.4th 645 (2006)— § 24.1(b) n.27

Esquibel, People v., 143 Cal.App.4th 645, 49 Cal.Rptr.3d 393 (2006)— § 24.1(b) n.29

Esquilin, United States v., 208 F.3d 315 (1st Cir.2000)—§§ 9.5(c) n.67, 68

Essex County Grand Jury Investigation of Seton Hall Fire, In the Matter of, 368 N.J.Super. 269, 845 A.2d 739 (2003)—§ 8.10(c) n.81

Esslinger, State v., 357 N.W.2d 525 (S.D.1984)—§ 7.4(e) n.86

Estelle v. Dorrough, 420 U.S. 534, 95 S.Ct. 1173, 43 L.Ed.2d 377 (1975)—§§ 27.5(c) n.71, 76

Estelle v. Gamble, 429 U.S. 97, 97 S.Ct. 285, 50 L.Ed.2d 251 (1976)— § 2.7(d) n.252

Estelle v. McGuire, 502 U.S. 62, 112 S.Ct. 475, 116 L.Ed.2d 385 (1991)—§§ 2.7(b) n.70; 2.7(c) n.209; 26.2(b) n.20

Estelle v. Smith, 451 U.S. 454, 101 S.Ct. 1866, 68 L.Ed.2d 359 (1981)— §§ 6.4(f) n.131; 6.7(b) n.98; 6.10(c) n.45; 6.10(e) n.64, 66; 20.4(e) n.79; 26.4(e) n.81; 26.5(a) n.9; 28.6(f) n.68

Estelle v. Williams, 425 U.S. 501, 96 S.Ct. 1691, 48 L.Ed.2d 126 (1976)—§§ 2.7(a) n.36; 11.6(a) n.33; 11.6(c) n.102; 24.2(e) n.52, 53

Estep v. State, 901 S.W.2d 491 (Tex.Cr.App.1995)—§ 27.5(c) n.77

Estepa, United States v., 471 F.2d 1132 (2d Cir.1972)—§§ 15.5(b) n.36, 61, 67, 81

Estes, State v., 131 Or.App. 188, 883 P.2d 1335 (1994)—§ 18.4(c) n.50

Estes, State v., 111 Idaho 423, 725 P.2d 128 (1986)—§ 24.7(i) n.87

Estes v. State, 326 So.2d 786 (Miss.1976)—§ 11.8(c) n.59

Estes v. Texas, 381 U.S. 532, 85 S.Ct. 1628, 14 L.Ed.2d 543 (1965)— §§ 2.9(g) n.198; 23.1(a) n.3; 23.3(b) n.21

Estes, United States v., 485 F.2d 1078 (D.C.Cir.1973)—§ 7.3(d) n.83

Estes v. United States, 335 F.2d 609 (5th Cir.1964)—§§ 15.4(a) n.10; 15.4(g) n.176; 15.4(h) n.190

Estese, United States v., 479 F.2d 1273 (6th Cir.1973)—§ 3.6(f) n.150

Estrada, People v., 68 Ill.App.3d 272, 24 Ill.Dec. 924, 386 N.E.2d 128 (1979)—§ 3.9(g) n.127

Estrada, People v., 93 Cal.App.3d 76, 155 Cal.Rptr. 731 (1979)— § 15.4(d) n.98

Estrada, State v., 537 A.2d 983 (R.I.1988)—§ 24.11(d) n.22

Estrada, United States v., 430 F.3d 606 (2d Cir.2005)—§§ 6.7(b) n.74, 85

Estrada, United States v., 256 F.3d 466 (7th Cir.2001)—§ 5.4(a) n.8

Estremera, United States v., 531 F.2d 1103 (2d Cir.1976)—§ 24.3(g) n.162

E.T.C., Juvenile, In re, 141 Vt. 375, 449 A.2d 937 (1982)—§ 6.9(b) n.23

Etheridge v. United States, 241 F.3d 619 (8th Cir.2001)—§ 11.10(c) n.68

Ethington, State v., 121 Ariz. 572, 592 P.2d 768 (1979)—§ 21.2(b) n.78

Eubanks v. Louisiana, 356 U.S. 584, 78 S.Ct. 970, 2 L.Ed.2d 991 (1958)— § 22.2(c) n.30

Eubanks, People v., 14 Cal.4th 580, 59 Cal.Rptr.2d 200, 927 P.2d 310 (1996)—§ 22.5(a) n.8

Euceda-Hernande, United States v., 768 F.2d 1307 (11th Cir.1985)— § 20.6(b) n.34

Euctice, People v., 371 Ill. 159, 20 N.E.2d 83 (1939)—§ 3.8(f) n.230

Eufrasio, United States v., 935 F.2d 553 (3d Cir.1991)—§ 16.2(h) n.157

Euge, United States v., 444 U.S. 707, 100 S.Ct. 874, 63 L.Ed.2d 141 (1980)—§ 7.2(b) n.13

Eugenio, State v., 219 Wis.2d 391, 579 N.W.2d 642 (1998)—§ 20.3(i) n.177

Evans, Ex parte, 690 S.W.2d 274 (Tex.Cr.App.1985)—§ 21.2(g) n.399

Evans, In re, 452 F.2d 1239 (D.C.Cir.1971)—§§ 8.9(b) n.27; 8.14(c) n.38

Evans v. Chavis, _____ U.S. _____, 126 S.Ct. 846, 163 L.Ed.2d 684 (2006)—§ 28.5(b) n.50

Evans, Commonwealth v., 434 Pa. 52, 252 A.2d 689 (1969)—§§ 21.2(c) n.104; 21.3(d) n.220

Evans, Commonwealth v., 190 Pa.Super. 179, 154 A.2d 57 (1959)—§ 15.7(h) n.225

Evans v. Court of Common Pleas, 959 F.2d 1227 (3d Cir.1992)—§ 25.4(c) n.34

Evans v. Cupp, 415 F.2d 844 (9th Cir.1969)—§ 11.10(c) n.115

Evans v. Dowd, 932 F.2d 739 (8th Cir.1991)—§§ 6.2(c) n.120, 125, 160

Evans v. Mitchell, 200 Kan. 290, 436 P.2d 408 (1968)—§ 18.4(a) n.2

Evans, People v., 209 Ill.2d 194, 283 Ill.Dec. 651, 808 N.E.2d 939 (2004)—§ 22.4(d) n.43

Evans, People v., 174 Ill.2d 320, 220 Ill.Dec. 332, 673 N.E.2d 244 (1996)—§ 21.6(a) n.80

Evans, People v., 125 Ill.2d 50, 125 Ill.Dec. 790, 530 N.E.2d 1360 (1988)—§§ 22.3(d) n.216, 220

Evans, People v., 94 Mich.App. 4, 287 N.W.2d 608 (1979)—§ 13.7(b) n.32

Evans, People v., 43 N.Y.2d 160, 400 N.Y.S.2d 810, 371 N.E.2d 528 (1977)—§ 3.5(d) n.140

Evans, People v., 65 Cal.App.3d 924, 134 Cal.Rptr. 436 (1977)—§ 3.2(b) n.65

Evans v. Raines, 534 F.Supp. 791 (D.Ariz.1982)—§ 11.3(b) n.48

Evans, State v., 211 Or.App.162, 154 P.3d 166 (2007)—§ 22.3(a) n.44

Evans v. State, 363 S.C. 495, 611 S.E.2d 510 (2005)—§ 15.4(i) n.215

Evans v. State, 389 Md. 456, 886 A.2d 562 (2005)—§ 19.3(a) n.42

Evans v. State, 277 Ga. 51, 586 S.E.2d 326 (2003)—§ 6.2(c) n.135

Evans v. State, 808 So.2d 92 (Fla.2001)—§ 24.1(a) n.4

Evans, State v., 770 So.2d 1174 (Fla.2000)—§§ 20.2(e) n.107; 20.3(i) n.161

Evans, State v., 352 Md. 496, 723 A.2d 423 (1999)—§ 3.5(b) n.97

Evans, State v., 203 W.Va. 446, 508 S.E.2d 606 (1998)—§ 21.4(a) n.22

Evans v. State, 725 So.2d 613 (Miss.1997)—§ 22.3(c) n.153

Evans, State v., 495 N.W.2d 760 (Iowa 1993)—§ 6.4(e) n.74

Evans, State v., 307 S.C. 477, 415 S.E.2d 816 (1992)—§§ 16.1(a) n.29; 16.1(h) n.285, 289

Evans, State v., 815 S.W.2d 503 (Tenn.1991)—§ 3.4(g) n.125

Evans, State v., 14 Kan.App.2d 591, 796 P.2d 178 (1990)—§ 26.9(b) n.54

Evans, State v., 203 Conn. 212, 523 A.2d 1306 (1987)—§ 6.7(b) n.43

Evans, State v., 223 Neb. 383, 389 N.W.2d 777 (1986)—§ 9.3(e) n.71

Evans v. State, 304 Md. 487, 499 A.2d 1261 (1985)—§§ 7.4(c) n.48, 50; 7.4(e) n.86; 22.3(a) n.43

Evans, State v., 125 Ariz. 401, 610 P.2d 35 (1980)—§ 11.3(a) n.21

Evans, State v., 194 Neb. 559, 234 N.W.2d 199 (1975)—§ 21.3(d) n.260

Evans, State v., 45 Haw. 622, 372 P.2d 365 (1962)—§ 3.10(d) n.127

Evans v. Superior Court, 11 Cal.3d 617, 114 Cal.Rptr. 121, 522 P.2d 681 (1974)—§§ 7.4(g) n.113; 24.3(g) n.162, 163

Evans, United States v., 476 F.3d 1176 (11th Cir.2007)—§ 1.2(c) n.122

Evans, United States v., 352 F.3d 65 (2d Cir.2003)—§ 24.2(a) n.6

Evans, United States v., 282 F.3d 451 (7th Cir.2002)—§ 4.2(b) n.15

Evans, United States v., 62 F.3d 1233 (9th Cir.1995)—§ 16.1(h) n.288

Evans, United States v., 937 F.2d 1534 (10th Cir.1991)—§ 3.8(c) n.86

Evans & Assoc. Const. Co., Inc., United States v., 839 F.2d 656 (10th Cir.1988)—§ 8.5(g) n.228

Evans, State ex rel. v. Columbus Dept. of Law, 83 Ohio St.3d 174, 699 N.E.2d 60 (1998)—§ 13.3(b) n.23

Evenstad v. United States, 494 F.Supp. 146 (D.Minn.1980)—§ 21,4(c) n.76

Everett, In re, 139 Vt. 317, 427 A.2d 349 (1981)—§ 27.4(f) n.66

Everett v. State, 893 So.2d 1278 (Fla.2005)—§§ 6.7(c) n.128, 132

Everett, State v., 472 N.W.2d 864 (Minn.1991)—§§ 22.3(d) n.200, 240

Everett, State v., 372 N.W.2d 235 (Iowa 1985)—§ 21.6(c) n.118

Everett District Justice Ct., State v., 90 Wash.2d 794, 585 P.2d 1177 (1978)—§ 10.1(c) n.45

Everett, State ex rel. v. Hamilton, 175 W.Va. 654, 337 S.E.2d 312 (1985)—§ 24.2(a) n.15

Everhart v. State, 274 Md. 459, 337 A.2d 100 (1975)—§ 9.4(b) n.58

Everroad v. State, 442 N.E.2d 994 (Ind.1982)—§ 3.4(j) n.197

Everson v. Board of Education, 330 U.S. 1, 67 S.Ct. 504, 91 L.Ed. 711 (1947)—§ 2.5(c) n.25

Evitts v. Lucey, 469 U.S. 387, 105 S.Ct. 830, 83 L.Ed.2d 821 (1985)—§§ 1.5(c) n.94; 2.7(a) n.60; 2.7(b) n.86; 2.7(c) n.128; 2.9(c) n.50; 11.1(b) n.36, 37, 45, 53; 11.1(d) n.110, 112, 115; 11.2(b) n.50, 59; 11.7(a) n.7; 11.7(e) n.66; 27.1(b) n.21

Ewain, United States v., 78 F.3d 466 (9th Cir.1996)—§ 3.4(k) n.239

Ewell, United States v., 383 U.S. 116, 86 S.Ct. 773, 15 L.Ed.2d 627 (1966)—§§ 18.1(b) n.9; 18.5(a) n.2

Ewing v. California, 538 U.S. 11, 123 S.Ct. 1179, 155 L.Ed.2d 108 (2003)—§ 26.6(b) n.1

Ewing, United States v., 480 F.2d 1141 (5th Cir.1973)—§ 21.2(d) n.189

Ewing, United States v., 446 F.2d 60 (9th Cir.1971)—§§ 7.3(e) n.86, 99

Ewish v. State, 110 Nev. 221, 871 P.2d 306 (1994)—§ 17.2(b) n.75

Executive Assignment of State Attorney, In re, 298 So.2d 382 (Fla.1974)—§ 8.4(c) n.126

Executive Securities Corp., In re Application of, 702 F.2d 406 (2d Cir.1983)—§ 8.5(h) n.280

Exposito v. State, 891 So.2d 525 (Fla.2004)—§§ 27.3(b) n.17; 27.3(d) n.69

EyeCare Physicians of America, Matter of, 100 F.3d 514 (7th Cir.1996)—§ 3.4(c) n.48

Eyman, State v., 828 S.W.2d 883 (Mo.App.1992)—§§ 8.10(d) n.92; 8.14(a) n.4

Eyster, United States v., 948 F.2d 1196 (11th Cir.1991)—§ 22.2(a) n.2

F

53,082.00 in U.S. Currency, United States v., 985 F.2d 245 (6th Cir.1993)—§ 3.10(f) n.199

Faafiti, State v., 54 Haw. 637, 513 P.2d 697 (1973)—§ 14.4(c) n.58

Fabian, State v., 263 So.2d 773 (Miss.1972)—§ 16.1(g) n.244

Fabiano, People v., 192 Mich.App. 523, 482 N.W.2d 467 (1992)—§ 5.2(b) n.33

Facon v. State, 375 Md. 435, 825 A.2d 1096 (2003)—§ 6.3(c) n.48

Fadayini, United States v., 28 F.3d 1236 (D.C.Cir.1994)—§ 27.5(a) n.14

Fadel, United States v., 844 F.2d 1425 (10th Cir.1988)—§ 5.3(b) n.17

Fafone, Commonwealth v., 416 Mass. 329, 621 N.E.2d 1178 (1993)—§§ 16.4(c) n.64, 100

Fagan, People v., 104 A.D.2d 252, 483 N.Y.S.2d 489 (1984)—§ 17.4(a) n.66

Fagan v. State, 643 S.E.2d 268 (Ga.App.2007)—§ 22.3(c) n.133

Fagan, United States v., 996 F.2d 1009 (9th Cir.1993)—§§ 11.4(c) n.65, 76; 21.2(d) n.219

Fagan v. Washington, 942 F.2d 1155 (7th Cir.1991)—§ 11.10(c) n.117

Faheem-El v. Klincar, 841 F.2d 712 (7th Cir.1988)—§ 12.4(f) n.96

Fahey, State v., 275 N.W.2d 870 (S.D.1979)—§ 14.3(c) n.71

Fahey, United States v., 769 F.2d 829 (1st Cir.1985)—§ 3.2(d) n.147

Fahr, State v., 2001 WL 490738 (Tenn.App.2001)—§ 26.4(b) n.19

Fahy v. Connecticut, 375 U.S. 85, 84 S.Ct. 229, 11 L.Ed.2d 171 (1963)— § 9.4(a) n.39

Fahy v. Horn, 240 F.3d 239 (3d Cir.2001)— § 28.5(b) n.59

Faile, State v., 43 S.C. 52, 20 S.E. 798 (1895)— § 15.1(f) n.273

Failor, Commonwealth v., 564 Pa. 642, 770 A.2d 310 (2001)— § 17.4(c) n.155

Fain, State v., 116 Idaho 82, 774 P.2d 252 (1989)— § 14.3(d) n.94

Fair, State v., 354 N.C. 131, 557 S.E.2d 500 (2001)— §§ 11.7(e) n.100; 22.1(g) n.108; 22.3(c) n.107, 145; 22.3(d) n.202, 221, 250

Fair, State v., 672 A.2d 590 (Me.1996)— § 18.4(c) n.39

Fairbank, People v., 16 Cal.4th 1223, 69 Cal.Rptr.2d 784, 947 P.2d 1321 (1997)— §§ 21.3(b) n.87; 22.3(c) n.162

Fairchild v. State, 349 Ark. 147, 76 S.W.3d 884 (2002)— §§ 6.6(b) n.15; 6.7(d) n.145

Fairchild, United States v., 505 F.2d 1378 (5th Cir.1975)— §§ 9.6(a) n.51; 9.6(b) n.54

Faircloth, Ex parte, 471 So.2d 493 (Ala.1985)— § 24.4(d) n.57

Faircloth, State v., 297 N.C. 100, 253 S.E.2d 890 (1979)— § 16.3(b) n.24

Fairley v. Luman, 281 F.3d 913 (9th Cir.2002)— § 3.5(a) n.65

Fajardo, United States v., 787 F.2d 1523 (11th Cir.1986)— § 24.9(f) n.102

Falange, United States v., 426 F.2d 930 (2d Cir.1970)— §§ 22.3(b) n.76, 81

Falaster, People v., 173 Ill.2d 220, 218 Ill.Dec. 902, 670 N.E.2d 624 (1996)— § 24.1(b) n.24

Falcon, State v., 196 Conn. 557, 494 A.2d 1190 (1985)— §§ 6.4(e) n.69, 77

Falcon, United States v., 347 F.3d 1000 (7th Cir.2003)— §§ 13.7(c) n.43, 63

Falconi v. United States, 280 F. 766 (6th Cir.1922)— § 15.1(b) n.60

Falesbork, United States v., 5 F.3d 715 (4th Cir.1993)— § 26.5(a) n.7

Falk, United States v., 479 F.2d 616 (7th Cir.1973)— §§ 13.4(b) n.37, 46, 49, 55, 61; 13.4(c) n.88, 107; 13.5(a) n.12

Falke, State v., 237 Kan. 668, 703 P.2d 1362 (1985)— § 17.2(c) n.87

Fallis, State v., 205 Neb. 465, 288 N.W.2d 281 (1980)— § 11.4(b) n.27

Fallis, State ex rel. v. Caldwell, 498 P.2d 426 (1972)— § 14.3(c) n.62

Fama v. Commissioner of Correctional Services, 235 F.3d 804 (2d Cir.2000)— § 28.4(b) n.24

Fambo v. Smith, 433 F.Supp. 590 (W.D.N.Y.1977)— §§ 21.3(c) n.173, 174

Famulari, United States v., 447 F.2d 1377 (2d Cir.1971)— § 7.4(g) n.110

Fant, United States v., 974 F.2d 559 (4th Cir.1992)— § 21.2(d) n.246

Far, State v., 51 S.W.3d 222 (Tenn.Cr.App.2001)— § 24.2(d) n.50

Faraday, State v., 268 Conn. 174, 842 A.2d 567 (2004)— §§ 21.4(f) n.218, 220

Farber v. Douglas, 178 W.Va. 491, 361 S.E.2d 456 (W.Va.1985)— §§ 15.7(c) n.54, 58

Farber, State v., 314 N.W.2d 365 (Iowa 1982)— § 3.4(g) n.130

Fare v. Michael C., 442 U.S. 707, 99 S.Ct. 2560, 61 L.Ed.2d 197 (1979)— §§ 6.9(b) n.19; 6.9(c) n.47; 6.9(g) n.170; 6.10(c) n.49

Farese, United States v., 611 F.2d 67 (5th Cir.1980)— § 4.6(m) n.224

Faretta v. California, 422 U.S. 806, 95 S.Ct. 2525, 45 L.Ed.2d 562 (1975)— §§ 1.5(c) n.155, 161; 2.6(a) n.23; 2.9(c) n.51, 52; 11.3(a) n.6; 11.3(b) n.25, 40; 11.5(a) n.1; 11.5(d) n.70, 73, 76; 11.5(e) n.85; 11.5(f) n.94; 11.6(a) n.1, 64; 21.3(a) n.2, 29, 32

Fargo, City of v. Bommersbach, 511 N.W.2d 563 (N.D.1994)—§ 21.4(a) n.41

Fargo, City of v. Wonder, 651 N.W.2d 665 (N.D.2002)—§§ 3.2(g) n.195; 6.7(b) n.42, 54

Farhad, United States v., 190 F.3d 1097 (9th Cir.1999)—§§ 11.5(a) n.17; 11.5(d) n.66

Farina v. United States, 622 A.2d 50 (D.C.App.1993)—§§ 22.1(g) n.115, 126; 27.5(e) n.181

Fariss v. State, 303 Ark. 541, 798 S.W.2d 103 (1990)—§ 17.4(a) n.54

Farley, State v., 192 W.Va. 247, 452 S.E.2d 50 (W.Va. 1994)—§ 10.3(c) n.52

Farley, United States v., 1997 WL 695680 (N.D.Ill.1997)—§§ 19.4(b) n.23, 24

Farmer v. Perrill, 288 F.3d 1254 (10th Cir.2002)—§ 3.9(i) n.189

Farmer v. State, 770 So.2d 953 (Miss.2000)—§ 22.4(a) n.12

Farmer, State v., 259 Kan. 157, 909 P.2d 1154 (1996)—§§ 14.3(a) n.42; 14.3(c) n.63

Farmer, State v., 333 N.C. 172, 424 S.E.2d 120 (1993)—§ 3.8(c) n.83

Farmer, State v., 492 N.W.2d 239 (Iowa App.1992)—§ 16.3(b) n.23

Farmer, State v., 116 Wash.2d 414, 805 P.2d 200 (1991)—§ 22.3(b) n.86

Farmer, United States v., 32 F.3d 369 (8th Cir.1994)—§ 24.1(b) n.19

Farmer, State ex rel. v. Trent, 209 W.Va. 789, 551 S.E.2d 711 (2001)—§§ 21.4(f) n.204; 21.5(b) n.70

Farnam, People v., 28 Cal.4th 107, 121 Cal.Rptr.2d 106, 47 P.3d 988 (2002)—§§ 6.2(c) n.127; 7.4(g) n.114; 24.3(e) n.127

Farnham, State v., 479 A.2d 887 (Me.1984)—§ 21.1(e) n.93

Farnkoff, United States v., 535 F.2d 661 (1st Cir.1976)—§ 24.7(i) n.93

Farnsworth, State v., 240 Mont. 328, 783 P.2d 1365 (Mont.1989)—§ 14.2(d) n.63

Farnsworth, State v., 126 N.H. 656, 497 A.2d 835 (1985)—§ 10.1(a) n.3

Farrar, People v., 52 N.Y.2d 302, 437 N.Y.S.2d 961, 419 N.E.2d 864 (1981)—§ 21.3(e) n.287

Farrar, State v., 309 Or. 132, 786 P.2d 161 (1990)—§ 21.3(c) n.157

Farrar v. State, 187 Ga. 401, 200 S.E. 803 (1939)—§ 15.4(g) n.161

Farrell v. State, 364 Md. 499, 774 A.2d 387 (2001)—§§ 25.2(d) n.33; 25.3(a) n.7

Farrell, State v., 606 N.W.2d 524 (N.D.2000)—§ 21.4(g) n.232

Farrell v. State, 622 N.E.2d 488 (Ind.1993)—§ 7.4(e) n.84

Farris, State v., 109 Ohio St.3d 519, 849 N.E.2d 985 (2006)—§§ 6.6(e) n.95; 6.8(b) n.49; 9.5(b) n.50, 53

Farris v. State, 764 So.2d 411 (Miss.2000)—§ 17.4(a) n.48

Farrow, State v., 61 N.J. 434, 294 A.2d 873 (1972)—§ 7.4(e) n.89

Farruggia v. Hedrick, 174 W.Va. 58, 322 S.E.2d 42 (1984)—§ 6.4(g) n.142

Faruolo, United States v., 506 F.2d 490 (2d Cir.1974)—§ 3.10(b) n.33

Fary, State v., 19 N.J. 431, 117 A.2d 499 (1955)—§§ 8.10(c) n.51; 8.10(d) n.88

Fasano v. Hall, 476 F.Supp. 291 (1979)—§ 18.4(c) n.72

Fasching, State v., 453 N.W.2d 761 (N.D.1990)—§ 6.7(a) n.3

Fassler, People v., 153 Ill.2d 49, 178 Ill.Dec. 782, 605 N.E.2d 576 (1992)—§§ 15.6(d) n.108; 15.7(b) n.23; 15.7(h) n.226, 232

Fatico, United States v., 603 F.2d 1053 (2d Cir.1979)—§ 26.4(g) n.129

Fauber, People v., 2 Cal.4th 792, 9 Cal.Rptr.2d 24, 831 P.2d 249 (1992)—§§ 22.2(d) n.69, 79; 24.9(f) n.85

Faulconbridge v. State, 333 Mont. 186, 142 P.3d 777 (2006)—§ 24.4(d) n.47

Faulder v. Johnson, 81 F.3d 515 (5th Cir.1996)—§ 13.3(b) n.20

Faulisi, United States ex rel. v. Pinkney, 611 F.2d 176 (7th Cir.1979)— § 17.2(b) n.31

Faulk v. State Attorney for Harford County, 52 Md.App. 616, 451 A.2d 936 (1982)—§ 20.2(d) n.79

Faulkner, Ex parte, 221 Ark. 37, 251 S.W.2d 822 (1952)—§§ 8.3(h) n.38, 44

Faulkner, Commonwealth v., 418 Mass. 352, 638 N.E.2d 1 (1994)— §§ 26.4(e) n.80; 26.10(b) n.23, 31

Faulkner, People v., 36 A.D.3d 1071 (N.Y.A.D 3 Dept. 2007)—§ 22.3(c) n.101

Faulkner v. State, 317 Md. 441, 564 A.2d 785 (1989)—§ 9.1(b) n.52

Faulkner, United States v., 439 F.3d 1221 (10th Cir.2006)—§§ 4.6(l) n.201, 202

Faunce, State v., 91 N.J.L. 333, 102 A. 147 (1917)—§ 16.4(c) n.71

Faust, State v., 269 Neb. 749, 696 N.W.2d 420 (2005)—§ 7.4(g) n.110

Faust, State v., 237 Conn. 454, 678 A.2d 910 (1996)—§§ 22.2(d) n.56; 22.3(a) n.43

Favela, State v., 259 Kan. 215, 911 P.2d 792 (1996)—§ 26.3(g) n.88

Favi, State v., 329 Mont. 273, 124 P.3d 164 (2005)—§ 21.5(a) n.40

Favulli, Commonwealth v., 352 Mass. 95, 224 N.E.2d 422 (1967)— § 15.7(c) n.54

Fawley, United States v., 137 F.3d 458 (7th Cir.1998)—§ 27.5(e) n.154

Fay v. New York, 332 U.S. 261, 67 S.Ct. 1613, 91 L.Ed. 2043 (1947)— §§ 15.4(d) n.111, 112; 22.2(d) n.49, 58

Fay v. Noia, 372 U.S. 391, 83 S.Ct. 822, 9 L.Ed.2d 837 (1963)—§§ 28.1(b) n.15; 28.2(a) n.7; 28.2(b) n.25, 27, 31; 28.2(c) n.40, 65; 28.3(b) n.44, 50, 56; 28.4(b) n.12; 28.4(d) n.33; 28.5(a) n.1, 5, 7

Fay, State v., 763 So.2d 473 (Fla.App.2000)—§ 18.4(c) n.37

Fayette, United States v., 388 F.2d 728 (2d Cir.1968)—§ 6.8(a) n.21

Fazio, United States v., 914 F.2d 950 (7th Cir.1990)—§ 9.4(a) n.43

Fazzini, United States v., 871 F.2d 635 (7th Cir.1989)—§§ 11.2(e) n.159; 11.3(a) n.19; 11.4(b) n.30

FDIC v. Ernst & Whinney, 921 F.2d 83 (6th Cir.1990)—§ 8.5(h) n.247

F.D.I.C. v. Meyer, 510 U.S. 471, 114 S.Ct. 996, 127 L.Ed.2d 308 (1994)—§ 3.1(k) n.275

Fearn v. City of Huntsville, 568 So.2d 349 (Ala.Crim.App.1990)— § 19.5(d) n.68

Fears, Commonwealth v., 575 Pa. 281, 836 A.2d 52 (2003)—§ 21.4(a) n.40

Febus, United States v., 218 F.3d 784 (7th Cir.2000)—§ 21.2(d) n.255

Fecteau, State v., 132 N.H. 646, 568 A.2d 1187 (1990)—§ 6.8(d) n.82

Federal Grand Jury, February 1987 Term, Matter of, 677 F.Supp. 26 (D.Me.1988)—§ 8.3(a) n.5

Federal Grand Jury Proceedings, In re, 938 F.2d 1578 (11th Cir.1991)— § 27.5(a) n.20

Federal Grand Jury Proceedings, In re, 760 F.2d 436 (2d Cir.1985)— § 8.5(h) n.300

Federal Savings and Loan Insurance Corp. v. Hardee, 686 F.Supp. 885 (N.D.Fla.1988)—§§ 8.13(b) n.58, 62

Federal Trade Commission v. American Tobacco, 264 U.S. 298, 44 S.Ct. 336, 68 L.Ed. 696 (1924)—§ 8.7(a) n.20

Federick v. State, 902 P.2d 1092 (Okla.Cr.App.1995)—§ 27.6(d) n.145

Fedorov v. United States, 600 A.2d 370 (D.C.App.1991)—§§ 13.4(b) n.41; 13.4(e) n.170; 13.6(c) n.28

Fee v. United States, 207 F.Supp. 674 (W.D.Va.1962)—§ 21.4(d) n.111

Feekes, United States v., 879 F.2d 1562 (7th Cir.1989)—§ 4.6(l) n.201

Feemster, United States v., 98 F.3d 1089 (8th Cir.1996)—§ 22.3(d) n.250

F.E.F., In re, 156 Vt. 503, 594 A.2d 897 (1991)—§ 27.5(a) n.28

Feffer, United States v., 831 F.2d 734 (7th Cir.1987)—§ 10.3(b) n.38

Feguer v. United States, 302 F.2d 214 (8th Cir.1962)—§ 6.3(a) n.19

Feichtinger, United States v., 105 F.3d 1188 (7th Cir.1997)—§ 21.2(d) n.164

Feigenbaum, United States v., 962 F.2d 230 (2d Cir.1992)—§ 21.2(d) n.190

Feinberg, United States v., 502 F.2d 1180 (7th Cir.1974)—§ 20.2(b) n.23

Feist, State v., 708 N.W.2d 870 (N.D.2006)—§§ 21.4(b) n.54; 21.5(c) n.88

Fekete, State v., 120 N.M. 290, 901 P.2d 708 (1995)—§ 6.2(c) n.181

Felder v. Johnson, 204 F.3d 168 (5th Cir.2000)—§ 28.5(b) n.59

Felder v. McCotter, 765 F.2d 1245 (5th Cir.1985)—§ 6.4(e) n.68

Felder, People v., 47 N.Y.2d 287, 418 N.Y.S.2d 295, 391 N.E.2d 1274 (1979)—§ 11.8(c) n.75

Felder, United States v., 548 A.2d 57 (D.C.App.1988)—§ 17.4(a) n.6

Feldman, United States v., 853 F.2d 648 (9th Cir.1988)—§ 26.6(d) n.58

Feldman, United States v., 606 F.2d 673 (6th Cir.1979)—§ 4.6(e) n.79

Feldman, United States v., 366 F.Supp. 356 (D.Hawai'i 1973)—§§ 3.3(g) n.237; 3.4(f) n.104

Felice, United States v., 481 F.Supp. 79 (N.D.Ohio 1978)—§ 15.4(h) n.193

Feliciano, People v., 93 Ill.App.3d 642, 49 Ill.Dec. 134, 417 N.E.2d 824 (1981)—§ 11.3(a) n.12

Feliciano, United States v., 45 F.3d 1070 (7th Cir.1995)—§ 3.8(b) n.11

Felix, United States v., 503 U.S. 378, 112 S.Ct. 1377, 118 L.Ed.2d 25 (1992)—§ 17.4(b) n.86

Felix v. United States, 508 A.2d 101 (D.C.App.1986)—§ 18.4(c) n.37

Felix-Felix, United States v., 275 F.3d 627 (7th Cir.2001)—§ 10.5(f) n.68

Felix-Gutierrez, United States v., 940 F.2d 1200 (9th Cir.1991)—§ 16.4(b) n.34

Felker v. State, 252 Ga. 351, 314 S.E.2d 621 (1984)—§ 15.2(d) n.105

Felker v. Turpin, 518 U.S. 651, 116 S.Ct. 2333, 135 L.Ed.2d 827 (1996)—§§ 28.1(b) n.21; 28.2(a) n.9; 28.5(d) n.90

Fell, United States v., 360 F.3d 135 (2d Cir.2004)—§ 26.5(a) n.12

Fellers, United States v., 397 F.3d 1090 (8th Cir.2005)—§§ 6.8(b) n.49; 9.5(c) n.70

Fellers v. United States, 540 U.S. 519, 124 S.Ct. 1019, 157 L.Ed.2d 1016 (2004)—§§ 6.4(g) n.145; 9.5(c) n.69

Felt, United States v., 502 F.Supp. 71 (D.D.C.1980)—§ 20.4(f) n.88

Feltner v. Columbia Pictures Television, 789 So.2d 453 (Fla.App.2001)—§ 24.7(b) n.19

Felton, People v., 78 N.Y.2d 1063, 576 N.Y.S.2d 89, 581 N.E.2d 1344 (1991)—§ 9.4(f) n.115

Felton, United States v., 811 F.2d 190 (3d Cir.1987)—§§ 18.3(b) n.14, 22

Felton, United States v., 753 F.2d 256 (3d Cir.1985)—§ 3.1(h) n.199

Feltrop, State v., 803 S.W.2d 1 (Mo.1991)—§ 6.6(d) n.50

Felts v. Estelle, 875 F.2d 785 (9th Cir.1989)—§ 24.2(e) n.54

Fender v. State, 74 P.3d 1220 (Wyo.2003)—§ 3.8(e) n.193

Fenin, State v., 154 N.J.Super. 282, 381 A.2d 364 (1977)—§ 9.4(b) n.55

Fennell, United States v., 65 F.3d 812 (10th Cir.1995)—§ 26.4(f) n.91

Fenner v. State, 381 Md. 1, 846 A.2d 1020 (2004)—§§ 6.4(e) n.77; 6.7(b) n.43; 6.10(c) n.39; 12.1(c) n.44, 49; 12.1(e) n.64

Fensterer v. State, 493 A.2d 959 (Del.1985)—§ 18.2(d) n.63

Fenstermaker, Commonwealth v., 515 Pa. 501, 530 A.2d 414 (1987)—§ 23.1(e) n.225

Fenton, State v., 21 Ari.App. 193, 517 P.2d 1086 (1974)—§ 20.6(b) n.17

Fenton, United States v., 367 F.3d 14 (1st Cir.2004)—§§ 17.1(a) n.9; 17.1(d) n.53

Fenton, United States v., 1998 WL 356891 (W.D.Pa.1998)—§§ 15.5(b) n.95, 97; 15.6(b) n.75; 15.7(b) n.13, 32

Fentress, United States v., 792 F.2d 461 (4th Cir.1986)—§ 21.2(d) n.145

Feola, United States v., 651 F.Supp. 1068 (S.D.N.Y.1987)—§§ 15.6(b) n.60; 19.4(b) n.23, 32; 20.3(h) n.157

Ferguson, Ex parte, 822 So.2d 466 (Ala.Crim.App.2000)—§ 12.2(a) n.6

Ferguson, In re, 5 Cal.3d 525, 96 Cal.Rptr. 594, 487 P.2d 1234 (1971)—§ 1.5(b) n.70

Ferguson v. City of Charleston, 308 F.3d 380 (4th Cir.2002)—§§ 3.10(c) n.100; 9.2(c) n.26

Ferguson v. City of Charleston, 532 U.S. 67, 121 S.Ct. 1281, 149 L.Ed.2d 205 (2001)—§§ 3.2(j) n.230; 3.9(a) n.7; 3.9(l) n.275; 3.10(c) n.90

Ferguson v. City of Chicago, 213 Ill.2d 94, 289 Ill.Dec. 679, 820 N.E.2d 455 (2004)—§§ 13.3(c) n.35; 18.5(a) n.35

Ferguson v. Georgia, 365 U.S. 570, 81 S.Ct. 756, 5 L.Ed.2d 783 (1961)—§§ 1.5(c) n.110; 1.6(d) n.257; 11.1(d) n.108; 11.8(a) n.9

Ferguson, People v., 67 N.Y.2d 383, 502 N.Y.S.2d 972, 494 N.E.2d 77 (1986)—§ 11.6(a) n.41

Ferguson, People v., 376 Mich. 90, 135 N.W.2d 357 (1965)—§§ 10.2(a) n.4, 10

Ferguson v. Roper, 400 F.3d 635 (8th Cir.2005)—§ 24.3(e) n.120

Ferguson v. Skrupa, 372 U.S. 726, 83 S.Ct. 1028, 10 L.Ed.2d 93 (1963)—§ 2.4(f) n.182

Ferguson v. State, 143 P.3d 218 (Okla.Crim.App.2006)—§ 21.4(d) n.103

Ferguson v. State, 362 Ark. 547, 210 S.W.3d 53 (2005)—§ 26.2(b) n.26

Ferguson, State v., 2 S.W.3d 912 (Tenn.1999)—§§ 2.12(b) n.84; 2.12(d) n.192; 24.3(e) n.136

Ferguson v. State, 739 So.2d 492 (Miss.1999)—§ 10.3(d) n.71

Ferguson, United States v., 246 F.3d 129 (2d Cir.2001)—§§ 24.6(d) n.45; 24.11(b) n.3; 27.5(e) n.156

Ferguson, United States v., 989 F.2d 202 (6th Cir.1993)—§§ 3.1(d) n.111, 113

Ferguson, United States v., 758 F.2d 843 (2d Cir.1985)—§§ 15.1(f) n.315, 325

Ferguson, United States v., 460 F.Supp. 1 (E.D.Tenn.1977)—§ 19.4(b) n.37

Fern v. Gramley, 99 F.3d 255 (7th Cir.1996)—§ 11.10(d) n.192

Fern, United States v., 155 F.3d 1318 (11th Cir.1998)—§ 19.3(a) n.59

Fernald, State v., 248 A.2d 754 (Me.1968)—§ 21.4(a) n.17

Fernandez v. Cook, 783 P.2d 547 (Utah 1989)—§§ 11.7(e) n.94, 98

Fernandez v. Roe, 286 F.3d 1073 (9th Cir.2002)—§ 22.3(d) n.212

Fernandez, State v., 254 Conn. 637, 758 A.2d 842 (2000)—§ 11.5(f) n.102

Fernandez, State v., 712 So.2d 485 (La.1998)—§ 6.9(b) n.20

Fernandez, United States v., 388 F.3d 1199 (9th Cir.2004)—§§ 4.6(e) n.97; 22.3(d) n.176

Fernandez, United States v., 205 F.3d 1020 (7th Cir.2000)—§§ 21.4(c) n.66, 78; 21.4(d) n.102; 21.5(c) n.83

Fernandez, United States v., 231 F.3d 1240 (9th Cir.2000)—§§ 1.7(j) n.225; 20.3(j) n.205; 27.3(c) n.45

Fernandez, United States v., 960 F.2d 771 (9th Cir.1992)—§ 21.2(d) n.248

Fernandez, United States v., 877 F.2d 1138 (2d Cir.1989)—§ 1.11(a) n.5

Fernandez, United States v., 892 F.2d 976 (11th Cir.1989)—§ 17.3(c) n.34

Fernandez, United States v., 480 F.2d 726 (2d Cir.1973)—§§ 15.4(b) n.68; 16.2(b) n.33

Fernandez, United States v., 456 F.2d 638 (2d Cir.1972)—§ 7.5(a) n.5

Fernandez v. United States, 329 F.2d 899 (9th Cir.1964)—§ 17.3(c) n.29

Fernandez v. United States, 81 S.Ct. 642, 5 L.Ed.2d 683 (1961)—§ 12.4(c) n.59

Fernandez-Alfonso, United States v., 813 F.2d 1571 (9th Cir.1987)—§ 12.3(a) n.27

Fernandez-Ventura, United States v., 132 F.3d 844 (1st Cir.1998)—§ 6.6(c) n.33

Fernando-Granados, State v., 268 Neb. 290, 682 N.W.2d 266 (2004)—§ 6.8(a) n.36

Fernow, State v., 354 N.W.2d 438 (Minn.1984)—§ 18.5(a) n.12

Ferra, United States v., 900 F.2d 1057 (7th Cir.1990)—§ 10.6(c) n.25

Ferrante, State v., 111 N.J.Super. 299, 268 A.2d 301 (1970)—§ 15.2(d) n.93

Ferrara, People v., 99 A.D.2d 257, 472 N.Y.S.2d 407 (1984)—§ 15.2(c) n.80

Ferrara v. United States, 456 F.3d 278 (1st Cir.2006)—§§ 21.3(c) n.174, 183, 190, 192

Ferrara v. United States, 372 F.Supp.2d 108 (D.Mass.2005)—§§ 24.3(b) n.35, 74; 28.9(a) n.3

Ferrara, United States v., 377 F.2d 16 (2d Cir.1967)—§ 6.2(c) n.112

Ferrari, Commonwealth v., 376 Pa.Super. 307, 545 A.2d 1372 (1988)—§ 14.2(d) n.48

Ferrari, State v., 80 N.M. 714, 460 P.2d 244 (1969)—§ 3.4(e) n.76

Ferrario-Pozzi, United States v., 368 F.3d 5 (1st Cir.2004)—§ 26.6(d) n.48

Ferreboeuf, United States v., 632 F.2d 832 (9th Cir.1980)—§ 15.2(i) n.227

Ferreira v. Secretary, Dept. of Corrections, 494 F.3d 1286 (11th Cir.2007)—§ 28.5(b) n.45

Ferrell, People v., 277 Ill.App.3d 74, 213 Ill.Dec. 646, 659 N.E.2d 992 (1995)—§ 26.9(b) n.55

Ferrell v. State, 318 Md. 235, 567 A.2d 937 (1990)—§ 17.4(a) n.6

Ferrette, State v., 18 Ohio St.3d 106, 480 N.E.2d 399 (1985)—§ 6.10(c) n.35

Ferretti, United States v., 508 F.Supp. 913 (E.D.Pa.1981)—§ 15.5(b) n.62

Ferretti, United States v., 635 F.2d 1089 (3d Cir.1980)—§ 1.7(g) n.110

Ferri, United States v., 652 F.2d 325 (3d Cir.1981)—§ 28.9(b) n.70

Ferri, United States v., 357 F.Supp. 487 (W.D.Wis.1973)—§ 3.7(e) n.124

Ferris, Matter of, 512 F.Supp. 91 (D.C.Nev.1981)—§§ 8.5(d) n.137, 139; 8.5(f) n.211

Ferro, People v., 63 N.Y.2d 316, 482 N.Y.S.2d 237, 472 N.E.2d 13 (1984)—§ 6.7(c) n.106

Ferro, United States v., 321 F.3d 756 (8th Cir.2003)—§ 27.2(c) n.44

Ferron, State v., 219 Wis.2d 481, 579 N.W.2d 654 (1998)—§ 22.3(c) n.112

Ferrone, United States v., 438 F.2d 381 (3d Cir.1971)—§§ 3.1(o) n.308; 3.4(e) n.96

Ferry, People v., 237 Cal.App.2d 880, 47 Cal.Rptr. 324 (1965)—§ 11.2(g) n.273

Feurtado, United States v., 191 F.3d 420 (4th Cir.1999)—§§ 18.3(b) n.54; 21.2(b) n.74

Fex v. Michigan, 507 U.S. 43, 113 S.Ct. 1085, 122 L.Ed.2d 406 (1993)—§ 18.4(c) n.55

Fialk, United States v., 5 F.3d 250 (7th Cir.1993)—§ 9.3(e) n.64

Fidler, Commonwealth v., 377 Mass. 192, 385 N.E.2d 513 (1979)—§§ 24.9(g) n.127, 130

Fidler, United States v., 419 F.3d 1026 (9th Cir.2005)—§ 12.1(a) n.8

Fiedeke, United States v., 384 F.3d 407 (7th Cir.2004)—§ 5.2(a) n.8

Field, State v., 132 N.H. 760, 571 A.2d 1276 (1990)—§§ 3.1(f) n.156; 21.2(d) n.227

Fields v. Attorney General, 956 F.2d 1290 (4th Cir.1992)—§§ 11.9(a) n.12; 11.9(d) n.217

Fields v. Brown, 431 F.3d 1186 (9th Cir.2005)—§ 22.3(c) n.135

Fields v. Gibson, 277 F.3d 1203 (10th Cir.2002)—§§ 21.2(g) n.395; 21.3(b) n.89

Fields v. Leapley, 30 F.3d 986 (8th Cir.1994)—§ 9.6(a) n.38

Fields, People v., 13 Cal.4th 289, 52 Cal.Rptr.2d 282, 914 P.2d 832 (1996)—§ 25.4(d) n.45

Fields, People v., 88 Ill.App.3d 821, 44 Ill.Dec. 86, 410 N.E.2d 1178 (1980)—§ 11.9(d) n.218

Fields, People v., 8 Ill.App.3d 1045, 291 N.E.2d 258 (1972)—§ 21.2(d) n.209

Fields v. Soloff, 920 F.2d 1114 (2d Cir.1990)—§§ 13.3(d) n.46; 15.1(d) n.171; 15.2(b) n.20; 15.6(c) n.93

Fields, State v., 265 Conn. 184, 827 A.2d 690 (2003)—§§ 6.2(c) n.71; 6.9(f) n.106, 113

Fields, State v., 662 N.W.2d 242 (N.D.2003)—§ 3.8(d) n.144

Fields v. State, 349 Ark. 122, 76 S.W.3d 868 (2002)—§ 7.4(c) n.46

Fields, State v., 249 Wis.2d 292, 638 N.W.2d 897 (2001)—§ 19.2(c) n.31

Fields, State v., 196 Ariz. 580, 2 P.3d 670 (Ariz.App.1999)—§ 20.3(g) n.125

Fields v. State, 923 P.2d 624 (Okl.Cr.1996)—§ 21.4(e) n.161

Fields, State v., 49 Or.App. 1033, 621 P.2d 651 (1980)—§ 26.10(c) n.83

Fields, State v., 390 So.2d 128 (Fla.1980)—§ 19.3(a) n.67

Fields, United States v., 483 F.3d 313 (5th Cir.2007)—§§ 26.4(f) n.109; 26.4(i) n.179

Fields, United States v., 371 F.3d 910 (7th Cir.2004)—§ 10.6(a) n.6

Fields, United States v., 324 F.3d 1025 (8th Cir.2003)—§ 26.9(b) n.48

Fields, United States v., 113 F.3d 313 (2d Cir.1997)—§§ 3.3(c) n.143; 3.6(a) n.19; 9.1(b) n.75

Fields v. United States, 698 A.2d 485 (D.C.App.1997)—§ 18.4(c) n.58

Fields v. United States, 963 F.2d 105 (6th Cir.1992)—§ 21.1(h) n.207

Fields, United States v., 766 F.2d 1161 (7th Cir.1985)—§ 21.2(d) n.151

Fields, United States v., 466 F.2d 119 (2d Cir.1972)—§ 12.4(d) n.87

Fields v. Wyrick, 706 F.2d 879 (8th Cir.1983)—§ 6.4(f) n.130

Fields v. Wyrick, 682 F.2d 154 (8th Cir.1982)—§ 6.9(e) n.96

Fierro, Ex parte, 934 S.W.2d 370 (Tex.Cr.App.1996)—§ 28.11(b) n.16

Fierro, State v., 166 Ariz. 539, 804 P.2d 72 (1990)—§§ 7.4(d) n.74; 7.4(g) n.111

Fifth Avenue Peace Parade Committee v. Hoover, 327 F.Supp. 238 (S.D.N.Y.1971)—§ 10.1(c) n.33

Figueroa, State v., 257 Conn. 192, 777 A.2d 587 (2001)—§ 22.3(e) n.272

Figueroa, State v., 639 A.2d 495 (R.I.1994)—§ 21.3(b) n.69

Figueroa, United States v., 757 F.2d 466 (2d Cir.1985)—§ 4.6(e) n.85

Figueroa, United States v., 666 F.2d 1375 (11th Cir.1982)—§ 19.6(c) n.40

Figueroa, United States v., 618 F.2d 934 (2d Cir.1980)—§ 17.2(e) n.127

Fikes v. Alabama, 352 U.S. 191, 77 S.Ct. 281, 1 L.Ed.2d 246 (1957)—§§ 6.2(c) n.80, 81, 84, 169

Filippatos, United States v., 307 F.Supp. 564 (S.D.N.Y.1969)—§ 15.5(a) n.22

Filippi, United States v., 918 F.2d 244 (1st Cir.1990)—§ 24.3(h) n.182

Filkin, State v., 242 Neb. 276, 494 N.W.2d 544 (1993)—§ 3.5(e) n.196

Fillinger v. State, 349 So.2d 714 (Fla.App.1977)—§ 6.2(c) n.112

Filmore v. State, 813 A.2d 1112 (Del.2003)—§§ 22.3(a) n.5, 13

Final Grand Jury Report Concerning the Torrington Police Department, In re, 197 Conn. 698, 501 A.2d 377 (1985)—§§ 8.5(b) n.47, 48; 8.5(h) n.239, 245, 246, 258, 261

Finch, State v., 137 Wash.2d 792, 975 P.2d 967 (1999)—§ 24.2(e) n.57

Finch v. United States, 433 U.S. 676, 97 S.Ct. 2909, 53 L.Ed.2d 1048 (1977)—§§ 25.1(d) n.52; 25.3(e) n.41

Finch v. Vaughn, 67 F.3d 909 (11th Cir.1995)—§§ 21.2(e) n.334; 21.3(b) n.71

Fine, United States v., 975 F.2d 596 (9th Cir.1992)—§ 21.2(d) n.210

Finetti v. Harris, 609 F.2d 594 (2d Cir.1979)—§ 12.4(d) n.84

Fink v. Ryan, 174 Ill.2d 302, 220 Ill.Dec. 369, 673 N.E.2d 281 (1996)—§ 3.5(d) n.146

Fink, United States v., 502 F.2d 1 (5th Cir.1974)—§ 20.3(i) n.177

Finley, State v., 219 W.Va. 747, 639 S.E.2d 839 (2006)—§ 24.2(e) n.65

Finley, State v., 273 Kan. 237, 42 P.3d 723 (2002)—§ 24.3(e) n.127

Finley, State v., 268 Kan. 557, 998 P.2d 95 (2000)—§ 24.3(h) n.179

Finley v. State, 295 Ark. 357, 748 S.W.2d 643 (1988)—§ 18.4(c) n.73

Finley, State v., 177 W.Va. 554, 355 S.E.2d 47 (1987)—§§ 22.3(a) n.43; 23.2(f) n.82

Finley, United States v., 705 F.Supp. 1297 (N.D.Ill.1988)—§ 15.4(h) n.188

Finn v. Schiller, 72 F.3d 1182 (4th Cir.1996)—§§ 8.5(i) n.304, 305

Finnell, State v., 115 Ohio App.3d 583, 685 N.E.2d 1267 (1996)—§ 3.2(c) n.98

Fioravanti, United States v., 412 F.2d 407 (3d Cir.1969)—§ 24.9(d) n.45

Fiorillo, United States v., 376 F.2d 180 (2d Cir.1967)—§ 6.6(f) n.100

Fire, State v., 145 Wash.2d 152, 34 P.3d 1218 (2001)—§ 22.3(c) n.157

First Charleston Corp., Ex parte v. Evans, 329 S.C. 31, 495 S.E.2d 423 (1998)—§§ 23.1(e) n.230, 247

First Defense Legal Aid v. City of Chicago, 319 F.3d 967 (7th Cir.2003)—§ 6.9(c) n.66

First National Bank of Tulsa v. U.S. Department of Justice, 865 F.2d 217 (10th Cir.1989)—§§ 8.8(d) n.54, 68, 71

Fisch, United States v., 474 F.2d 1071 (9th Cir.1973)—§ 3.2(b) n.47

Fischbach and Moore, United States v., 576 F.Supp. 1384 (W.D.Pa.1983)—§ 20.3(f) n.110

Fischbach and Moore, Inc., United States v., 776 F.2d 839 (9th Cir.1985)—§§ 8.5(h) n.260; 27.2(e) n.98

Fischer, People v., 53 N.Y.2d 178, 440 N.Y.S.2d 872, 423 N.E.2d 349 (1981)—§ 8.3(b) n.13

Fischer, State v., 285 A.2d 417 (Del.1971)—§ 18.3(c) n.111

Fischer v. United States, 529 U.S. 667, 120 S.Ct. 1780, 146 L.Ed.2d 707 (2000)—§ 1.2(c) n.196

Fischetti v. Johnson, 384 F.3d 140 (3d Cir.2004)—§§ 11.3(c) n.66, 69; 11.4(d) n.115

Fischetti, United States v., 450 F.2d 34 (5th Cir.1971)—§ 19.5(d) n.69

Fish, United States v., 388 F.3d 284 (7th Cir.2004)—§ 5.4(c) n.30

Fish, United States v., 34 F.3d 488 (7th Cir.1994)—§§ 11.9(b) n.90, 91

Fish, United States v., 432 F.2d 107 (4th Cir.1970)—§ 6.6(c) n.38

Fisher v. City of Eupora, 587 So.2d 878 (Miss.1991)—§§ 11.2(e) n.197, 212, 213

Fisher v. City of San Jose, 475 F.3d 1049 (9th Cir.2007)—§ 3.8(c) n.101

Fisher, Commonwealth v., 564 Pa. 505, 769 A.2d 1116 (2001)—§ 7.4(e) n.87

Fisher, Commonwealth v., 354 Mass. 549, 238 N.E.2d 525 (1968)— § 6.9(d) n.70

Fisher v. Gibson, 282 F.3d 1283 (10th Cir.2002)—§§ 11.10(c) n.71, 75, 113

Fisher, People v., 220 Mich.App. 133, 559 N.W.2d 318 (1996)—§§ 16.1(f) n.224; 16.2(e) n.75, 80

Fisher, People v., 281 Ill.App.3d 395, 217 Ill.Dec. 349, 667 N.E.2d 142 (1996)—§ 24.9(c) n.24

Fisher v. Roe, 263 F.3d 906 (9th Cir.2001)—§ 24.2(a) n.8

Fisher, State v., 99 Ohio St.3d 127, 789 N.E.2d 222 (2003)—§ 24.9(b) n.12

Fisher, State v., 145 Wash.2d 209, 35 P.3d 366 (2001)—§ 12.1(b) n.38

Fisher v. State, 690 A.2d 917 (Del.1996)—§ 24.9(g) n.118

Fisher, State v., 259 Ill.App.3d 445, 198 Ill.Dec. 359, 632 N.E.2d 689 (1994)—§ 25.4(d) n.45

Fisher, State v., 176 Ariz. 69, 859 P.2d 179 (1993)—§ 21.2(b) n.63

Fisher, State v., 210 Conn. 619, 556 A.2d 596 (1989)—§§ 6.8(c) n.70, 71

Fisher, State v., 318 N.C. 512, 350 S.E.2d 334 (1986)—§ 6.8(b) n.55

Fisher, State v., 141 Ariz. 227, 686 P.2d 750 (1984)—§ 24.11(d) n.16

Fisher, State v., 279 N.W.2d 265 (Iowa 1979)—§ 10.4(b) n.11

Fisher, State v., 2 Kan.App.2d 353, 579 P.2d 167 (1978)—§ 27.2(c) n.63

Fisher v. State, 259 Ind. 633, 291 N.E.2d 76 (1973)—§ 3.2(f) n.181

Fisher, State v., 112 N.J.Super. 319, 271 A.2d 24 (1970)—§ 15.6(d) n.127

Fisher v. United States, 779 A.2d 348 (D.C.App.2001)—§§ 6.10(d) n.60, 63

Fisher, United States v., 232 F.3d 301 (2d Cir.2000)—§§ 21.2(b) n.79; 27.5(c) n.56

Fisher, United States v., 137 F.3d 1158 (9th Cir.1998)—§ 12.1(a) n.19

Fisher, United States v., 106 F.3d 622 (5th Cir.1997)—§ 19.3(c) n.189

Fisher, United States v., 871 F.2d 444 (3d Cir.1989)—§§ 15.6(f) n.184, 185, 187

Fisher, United States v., 692 F.Supp. 495 (E.D.Pa.1988)—§§ 15.7(b) n.25, 32

Fisher, United States v., 772 F.2d 371 (7th Cir.1985)—§ 21.6(b) n.86

Fisher v. United States, 425 U.S. 391, 96 S.Ct. 1569, 48 L.Ed.2d 39 (1976)—§§ 2.10(d) n.105, 146, 160; 8.12(a) n.8; 8.12(b) n.23, 26; 8.12(e) n.49; 8.12(f) n.55; 8.13(a) n.1; 8.13(c) n.74; 8.13(d) n.88; 20.4(b) n.17

Fisher, United States v., 6 U.S. (2 Cranch) 358, 2 L.Ed. 304 (1805)— § 1.2(c) n.13

Fisher v. Volz, 496 F.2d 333 (3d Cir.1974)—§ 3.6(a) n.13

Fisk, State v., 966 P.2d 860 (Utah App.1998)—§ 14.1(a) n.2

Fisk, State v., 165 Vt. 260, 682 A.2d 937 (1996)—§ 21.4(a) n.27

Fitch, United States v., 964 F.2d 571 (6th Cir.1992)—§§ 8.11(e) n.108; 13.5(b) n.43, 46

Fitterer, State v., 652 N.W.2d 908 (N.D.2002)—§ 10.1(b) n.19

Fitz v. State, 275 Ga. 349, 566 S.E.2d 668 (2002)—§ 6.9(g) n.166

Fitzgerald v. Estelle, 505 F.2d 1334 (5th Cir.1974)—§ 11.10(a) n.5

Fitzgerald v. Greene, 150 F.3d 357 (4th Cir.1998)—§ 22.3(c) n.135

Fitzgerald, State v., 165 Vt. 343, 683 A.2d 10 (1996)—§ 6.7(b) n.70

Fitzgerald, State v., 137 N.H. 23, 622 A.2d 1245 (1993)—§ 17.4(b) n.136

Fitzgerald v. State, 166 Ga.App. 307, 304 S.E.2d 114 (1983)—§ 15.5(c) n.103

Fitzgerald v. United States, 530 A.2d 1129 (D.C.App.1987)—§ 11.9(c) n.130

Fitzgerald v. Withrow, 292 F.3d 500 (6th Cir.2002)—§§ 22.1(h) n.133, 140

Fitzhugh, United States v., 78 F.3d 1326 (8th Cir.1996)—§§ 21.6(a) n.51, 64

Fitzpatrick v. State, 900 So.2d 495 (Fla.2005)—§§ 6.6(d) n.48; 7.4(c) n.48

Fitzpatrick, State v., 102 Ohio St.3d 321, 810 N.E.2d 927 (2004)—§§ 21.4(c) n.90; 22.1(h) n.133

Fitzpatrick, State v., 172 Vt. 111, 772 A.2d 1093 (2001)—§§ 13.2(c) n.63, 65

Fitzpatrick, State v., 464 So.2d 1185 (Fla.1985)—§ 22.5(d) n.29

Fitzpatrick v. United States, 178 U.S. 304, 20 S.Ct. 944, 44 L.Ed. 1078 (1900)—§ 15.1(b) n.53

Fitzpatrick v. Wainwright, 800 F.2d 1057 (11th Cir.1986)—§ 11.3(b) n.37

Fitzsimmons v. State, 48 Md.App. 193, 426 A.2d 4 (1981)—§ 19.3(a) n.51

Flack, State v., 260 Mont. 181, 860 P.2d 89 (1993)—§ 6.7(c) n.118

Flaherty, United States v., 76 F.3d 967 (8th Cir.1996)—§ 17.2(b) n.64

Flamer v. Delaware, 68 F.3d 710 (3d Cir.1995)—§ 6.9(g) n.197

Flamer v. Delaware, 585 A.2d 736 (Del.1990)—§ 2.11(a) n.14

Flanagan, Commonwealth v., 578 Pa. 587, 854 A.2d 489 (2004)—§ 21.4(c) n.86

Flanagan v. State, 109 Nev. 50, 846 P.2d 1053 (1993)—§ 26.4(b) n.18

Flanagan v. United States, 465 U.S. 259, 104 S.Ct. 1051, 79 L.Ed.2d 288 (1984)—§ 27.2(c) n.38

Flanakin, United States v., 25 Fed.Cas. 1105 (Super.Ct.Ark.Terr.1825)—§§ 8.4(b) n.52, 102; 15.1(d) n.156

Flannery, United States v., 451 F.2d 880 (1st Cir.1971)—§ 24.9(d) n.48

Flansburg, State v., 345 Md. 694, 694 A.2d 462 (1997)—§ 26.10(b) n.31

Flatt, People v., 82 Ill.2d 250, 45 Ill.Dec. 158, 412 N.E.2d 509 (1980)—§ 27.3(d) n.67

Flaxman, United States v., 304 F.Supp. 1301 (S.D.N.Y.1969)—§§ 16.2(b) n.16, 33

Fleck, State v., 281 Minn. 247, 161 N.W.2d 309 (1968)—§ 16.1(f) n.221

Fleck, United States v., 413 F.3d 883 (8th Cir.2005)—§§ 6.7(b) n.73; 6.7(d) n.145

Fleeger, Commonwealth v., 292 Pa.Super. 310, 437 A.2d 60 (1981)—§ 26.10(b) n.37

Flegel, State v., 485 N.W.2d 210 (S.D.1992)—§ 10.6(a) n.6

Fleming, Ex parte, 814 So.2d 302 (Ala.Crim.App.2001)—§§ 12.3(b) n.65, 70

Fleming v. Collins, 954 F.2d 1109 (5th Cir.1992)—§ 6.7(b) n.87

Fleming v. Collins, 917 F.2d 850 (5th Cir.1990)—§ 6.6(e) n.86

Fleming v. Kemp, 837 F.2d 940 (11th Cir.1988)—§ 6.4(f) n.136

Fleming, People v., 900 P.2d 19 (Colo.1995)—§ 18.4(d) n.91

Fleming, People v., 36 Ill.App.3d 612, 345 N.E.2d 10 (1975)—§ 9.1(b) n.62

Fleming v. State, 814 So.2d 310 (Ala.Crim.App.2001)—§§ 19.5(b) n.29, 38; 19.5(d) n.68

Fleming v. State, 269 Ga. 245, 497 S.E.2d 211 (1998)—§§ 15.2(j) n.236; 22.3(b) n.86; 22.3(c) n.133

Fleming, State v., 726 So.2d 113 (Miss.1998)—§ 17.4(b) n.120

Fleming v. State, 284 Ark. 307, 681 S.W.2d 390 (1984)—§ 6.9(d) n.72

Flemmi, United States v., 245 F.3d 24 (1st Cir.2001)—§ 8.8(f) n.153

Flemmi, United States v., 225 F.3d 78 (1st Cir.2000)—§§ 6.2(c) n.106; 8.11(e) n.98, 100; 13.5(b) n.58

Flemming, State v., 184 Ariz. 110, 907 P.2d 496 (1995)—§ 26.10(b) n.16

Fletcher v. District Court of Jefferson County, 213 Iowa 822, 238 N.W. 290 (1931)—§ 16.3(d) n.75

Fletcher, People v., 260 Mich.App. 531, 679 N.W.2d 127 (2004)—§ 24.9(f) n.67

Fletcher, People v., 156 Ill.App.3d 405, 108 Ill.Dec. 929, 509 N.E.2d 625 (1987)—§ 24.7(e) n.71

Fletcher v. State, 277 Ga. 795, 596 S.E.2d 132 (2004)—§ 7.4(e) n.82

Fletcher, State v., 348 N.C. 292, 500 S.E.2d 668 (1998)—§ 6.9(g) n.155

Fletcher, United States v., 121 F.3d 187 (5th Cir.1997)—§ 7.4(e) n.89

Fletcher, United States v., 74 F.3d 49 (4th Cir.1996)—§ 20.2(b) n.23

Fletcher, United States v., 965 F.2d 781 (9th Cir.1992)—§ 22.2(d) n.70

Fletcher v. Weir, 455 U.S. 603, 102 S.Ct. 1309, 71 L.Ed.2d 490 (1982)—§ 9.6(a) n.45

Flewitt, United States v., 874 F.2d 669 (9th Cir.1989)—§ 11.5(d) n.73

Flieger v. Delo, 16 F.3d 878 (8th Cir.1994)—§§ 11.6(a) n.31; 11.6(c) n.100; 11.10(c) n.84

Flippo, State v., 212 W.Va. 560, 575 S.E.2d 170 (2002)—§ 3.6(e) n.134

Flippo v. West Virginia, 528 U.S. 11, 120 S.Ct. 7, 145 L.Ed.2d 16 (1999)—§ 3.6(e) n.134

Flittie v. Solem, 775 F.2d 933 (8th Cir.1985)—§ 17.4(a) n.42

Flonnory v. State, 893 A.2d 507 (Del.2006)—§ 24.4(c) n.21

Flonnory v. State, 778 A.2d 1044 (Del.2001)—§ 24.9(f) n.105

Flood v. Kuhn, 407 U.S. 258, 92 S.Ct. 2099, 32 L.Ed.2d 728 (1972)—§ 2.9(b) n.27

Florance, State v., 270 Or. 169, 527 P.2d 1202 (1974)—§§ 3.5(b) n.103; 3.5(c) n.116

Florea, United States v., 541 F.2d 568 (6th Cir.1976)—§ 1.7(i) n.177

Florence, State v., 306 Minn. 442, 239 N.W.2d 892 (1976)—§ 14.2(d) n.47

Florence, United States v., 456 F.2d 46 (4th Cir.1972)—§ 22.2(e) n.105

Flores v. Estelle, 578 F.2d 80 (5th Cir.1978)—§ 21.2(c) n.106

Flores, People v., 168 Ill.App.3d 284, 119 Ill.Dec. 46, 522 N.E.2d 708 (1988)—§ 20.6(c) n.77

Flores, People v., 12 Cal.3d 85, 115 Cal.Rptr. 225, 524 P.2d 353 (1974)—§§ 3.8(d) n.148, 149

Flores, State v., 245 Neb. 179, 512 N.W.2d 128 (1994)—§ 10.1(b) n.21

Flores v. State, 485 N.E.2d 890 (Ind.1985)—§§ 19.5(c) n.54, 61

Flores, State v., 280 Or. 273, 570 P.2d 965 (1977)—§ 2.12(d) n.198

Flores, State v., 9 Ariz.App. 502, 454 P.2d 172 (1969)—§ 6.9(d) n.79

Flores, United States v., 149 F.3d 1272 (10th Cir.1998)—§ 7.4(e) n.82

Flores, United States v., 289 U.S. 137, 53 S.Ct. 580, 77 L.Ed. 1086 (1933)—§§ 16.4(b) n.6, 8

Flores-Chapa, United States v., 48 F.3d 156 (5th Cir.1995)—§ 24.7(e) n.41

Flores-Montano, United States v., 541 U.S. 149, 124 S.Ct. 1582, 158 L.Ed.2d 311 (2004)—§ 3.9(f) n.107

Florez, State v., 134 N.J. 570, 636 A.2d 1040 (1994)—§ 5.3(b) n.28

Florez, United States v., 447 F.3d 145 (2d Cir.2006)—§§ 18.5(a) n.25, 26, 31

Florida v. Bostick, 501 U.S. 429, 111 S.Ct. 2382, 115 L.Ed.2d 389 (1991)—§§ 2.9(g) n.163; 3.8(c) n.74, 100

Florida v. Casal, 462 U.S. 637, 103 S.Ct. 3100, 77 L.Ed.2d 277 (1983)—§ 2.12(a) n.22

Florida v. Jimeno, 500 U.S. 248, 111 S.Ct. 1801, 114 L.Ed.2d 297 (1991)—§§ 3.10(f) n.187, 192, 197

Florida v. J.L., 529 U.S. 266, 120 S.Ct. 1375, 146 L.Ed.2d 254 (2000)— §§ 3.6(d) n.95; 3.8(d) n.165; 3.8(e) n.192

Florida v. Meyers, 466 U.S. 380, 104 S.Ct. 1852, 80 L.Ed.2d 381 (1984)—§ 3.7(b) n.30

Florida v. Nixon, 543 U.S. 175, 125 S.Ct. 551, 160 L.Ed.2d 565 (2004)—§§ 11.6(a) n.54; 11.6(b) n.71; 11.6(d) n.116

Florida v. Riley, 488 U.S. 445, 109 S.Ct. 693, 102 L.Ed.2d 835 (1989)— §§ 3.2(a) n.22; 3.2(c) n.139; 10.3(b) n.37

Florida v. Rodriguez, 469 U.S. 1, 105 S.Ct. 308, 83 L.Ed.2d 165 (1984)— § 3.8(d) n.147

Florida v. Royer, 460 U.S. 491, 103 S.Ct. 1319, 75 L.Ed.2d 229 (1983)—§§ 3.3(b) n.47; 3.5(a) n.8; 3.8(b) n.19, 48, 54; 3.8(c) n.72

Florida v. Thomas, 532 U.S. 774, 121 S.Ct. 1905, 150 L.Ed.2d 1 (2001)— § 27.2(a) n.5

Florida v. Wells, 495 U.S. 1, 110 S.Ct. 1632, 109 L.Ed.2d 1 (1990)— §§ 3.1(d) n.116; 3.7(e) n.104, 109, 117

Florida v. White, 526 U.S. 559, 119 S.Ct. 1555, 143 L.Ed.2d 748 (1999)—§ 3.7(d) n.73

Florida Department of Health and Rehabilitative Services v. Florida Nursing Home Association, 450 U.S. 147, 101 S.Ct. 1032, 67 L.Ed.2d 132 (1981)—§ 2.9(b) n.26

Florida Rule of Criminal Procedure 3.220, In re Amendment of, 550 So.2d 1097 (Fla.1990)—§ 20.2(e) n.107

Flournoy v. State, 131 Ga.App. 171, 205 S.E.2d 473 (1974)—§ 3.10(b) n.32

Flournoy, State ex rel. v. Wren, 108 Ariz. 356, 498 P.2d 444 (1972)— § 3.5(b) n.101

Flower, State v., 161 Ariz. 283, 778 P.2d 1179 (1989)—§§ 6.9(g) n.150, 159

Flowers, Commonwealth v., 5 Mass.App.Ct. 557, 365 N.E.2d 839 (1977)—§ 11.3(b) n.35

Flowers v. Fiore, 359 F.3d 24 (1st Cir.2004)—§ 3.8(b) n.27

Flowers, People v., 138 Ill.2d 218, 149 Ill.Dec. 304, 561 N.E.2d 674 (1990)—§ 2.11(a) n.14

Flowers v. State, 738 N.E.2d 1051 (Ind.2000)—§ 7.4(g) n.111

Flowers, United States v., 441 F.3d 900 (10th Cir.2006)—§ 27.6(b) n.20

Floyd, People v., 1 Cal.3d 694, 83 Cal.Rptr. 608, 464 P.2d 64 (1970)— §§ 7.4(f) n.99; 17.2(b) n.49

Floyd, People v., 26 N.Y.2d 558, 312 N.Y.S.2d 193, 260 N.E.2d 815 (1970)—§ 3.6(c) n.75

Floyd v. State, 902 So.2d 775 (Fla.2005)—§ 24.3(b) n.35

Floyd v. State, 272 Ga. 65, 525 S.E.2d 683 (2000)—§ 22.3(d) n.202

Floyd v. State, 983 S.W.2d 273 (Tex.Cr.App.1998)—§ 18.5(a) n.50

Floyd v. State, 412 So.2d 826 (Ala.Crim.App.1981)—§ 11.1(b) n.87

Floyd v. State, 1 Tenn.Cr.App. 106, 430 S.W.2d 888 (1968)—§ 6.8(a) n.32

Floyd, United States v., 428 F.3d 513 (3d Cir.2005)—§ 21.2(d) n.255

Floyd, United States v., 108 F.3d 202 (9th Cir.1997)—§§ 21.4(e) n.161; 21.6(b) n.87

Floyd, United States v., 1 F.3d 867 (9th Cir.1993)—§§ 21.2(d) n.250; 21.4(g) n.239

Floyd v. United States, 860 F.2d 999 (10th Cir.1988)—§ 10.1(c) n.40

Floyd, United States v., 228 F.2d 913 (7th Cir.1956)—§ 16.2(f) n.106

Flummerfelt, State v., 235 Kan. 609, 684 P.2d 363 (1984)—§ 3.5(a) n.22

Flynn, People v., 79 N.Y.2d 879, 581 N.Y.S.2d 160, 589 N.E.2d 383 (1992)—§ 20.3(a) n.18

Flynt v. Commonwealth, 105 S.W.3d 415 (Ky.2003)—§§ 13.6(c) n.27, 28

Foehrer, People v., 197 Ill.App.3d 754, 144 Ill.Dec. 161, 555 N.E.2d 58 (1990)—§ 26.10(c) n.58

Fogarty, State v., 128 N.J. 59, 607 A.2d 624 (1992)—§ 5.1(c) n.40

Fogg, United States v., 409 F.3d 1022 (8th Cir.2005)—§ 21.2(b) n.76

Fogg, United States v., 652 F.2d 551 (5th Cir.1981)—§ 15.5(b) n.65

Folding Carton Antitrust Litigation, In re, 609 F.2d 867 (7th Cir.1979)— § 8.10(a) n.21

Foley, Commonwealth v., 445 Mass. 1001, 833 N.E.2d 130 (2005)— § 6.7(b) n.66

Foley v. Connelie, 435 U.S. 291, 98 S.Ct. 1067, 55 L.Ed.2d 287 (1978)—§ 1.9(e) n.127

Follansbee v. Plymouth Dist. Court, 151 N.H. 365, 856 A.2d 740 (2004)— § 12.2(b) n.38

Fong Foo v. United States, 369 U.S. 141, 82 S.Ct. 671, 7 L.Ed.2d 629 (1962)—§§ 13.2(c) n.53; 25.1(d) n.84; 25.3(d) n.36; 27.3(a) n.2

Fonseca-Martinez, United States v., 36 F.3d 62 (9th Cir.1994)—§ 27.5(e) n.175

Fontaine v. United States, 411 U.S. 213, 93 S.Ct. 1461, 36 L.Ed.2d 169 (1973)—§§ 11.3(a) n.8; 21.5(d) n.95; 28.9(b) n.63

Fontana v. United States, 262 F. 283 (8th Cir.1919)—§ 19.3(b) n.150

Fontanez, United States v., 878 F.2d 33 (2d Cir.1989)—§ 24.2(a) n.7

Font-Ramirez, United States v., 944 F.2d 42 (1st Cir.1991)—§ 17.2(c) n.88

Foo v. State, 106 Haw. 102, 102 P.3d 346 (2004)—§§ 21.4(d) n.100, 138

Foont v. United States, 93 F.3d 76 (2d Cir.1996)—§§ 28.9(a) n.20, 21

Foote, State v., 149 N.H. 323, 821 A.2d 1072 (2003)—§ 22.1(h) n.137

Foote v. United States, 670 A.2d 366 (D.C.App.1996)—§ 22.1(b) n.42

Footman, United States v., 215 F.3d 145 (1st Cir.2000)—§§ 4.6(l) n.200, 201

Forbert v. State, 437 So.2d 1079 (Fla.1983)—§ 21.2(e) n.294

Forbes, Commonwealth v., 450 Pa. 185, 299 A.2d 268 (1973)—§ 21.3(b) n.82

Forbes, State v., 203 Neb. 349, 278 N.W.2d 615 (1979)—§ 14.3(d) n.84

Forbes, United States v., 816 F.2d 1006 (5th Cir.1987)—§ 22.3(d) n.250

Forbes, State ex rel. v. Canady, 197 W.Va. 37, 475 S.E.2d 37 (1996)— §§ 27.3(c) n.28; 27.4(d) n.40

Forbes, State ex rel. v. Kaufman, 185 W.Va. 72, 404 S.E.2d 763 (W.Va. 1991)—§ 21.2(d) n.158

Ford v. Ford, 749 F.2d 681 (11th Cir.1985)—§ 11.9(d) n.193

Ford v. Georgia, 498 U.S. 411, 111 S.Ct. 850, 112 L.Ed.2d 935 (1991)— §§ 22.3(d) n.220; 28.4(b) n.18

Ford v. Norris, 67 F.3d 162 (8th Cir.1995)—§ 27.6(d) n.141

Ford v. Parratt, 638 F.2d 1115 (8th Cir.1981)—§ 21.3(b) n.54

Ford, People v., 86 N.Y.2d 397, 633 N.Y.S.2d 270, 657 N.E.2d 265 (1995)—§ 21.3(b) n.66

Ford v. Seabold, 841 F.2d 677 (6th Cir.1988)—§§ 22.2(d) n.67, 82, 83

Ford v. State, 122 Nev. 796, 138 P.3d 500 (2006)—§ 6.9(g) n.178

Ford v. State, 158 S.W.3d 488 (Tex.Crim.App.2005)—§ 10.3(b) n.10

Ford v. State, 69 P.3d 407 (Wyo.2003)— §§ 21.2(d) n.167, 225

Ford, State v., 306 Mont. 517, 39 P.3d 108 (2001)—§§ 22.3(d) n.220; 27.5(c) n.89

Ford, State v., 144 N.H. 57, 738 A.2d 937 (1999)—§§ 6.2(c) n.107; 6.6(b) n.16

Ford, State v., 539 N.W.2d 214 (Minn.1995)—§ 22.3(b) n.68

Ford v. State, 262 Ga. 558, 423 S.E.2d 245 (1992)—§ 22.3(d) n.242

Ford v. State, 256 Ga. 375, 349 S.E.2d 361 (1986)—§ 7.3(b) n.33

Ford, State v., 108 Ariz. 404, 499 P.2d 699 (1972)—§ 6.10(d) n.60

Ford, United States v., 176 F.3d 376 (6th Cir.1999)—§ 6.4(g) n.156

Ford, United States v., 56 F.3d 265 (D.C.Cir.1995)—§ 3.6(d) n.96

Ford, United States v., 986 F.2d 57 (4th Cir.1993)—§ 3.7(e) n.105

Ford, United States v., 993 F.2d 249 (D.C.Cir.1993)—§ 21.5(a) n.2

Ford, United States v., 870 F.2d 729 (D.C.Cir.1989)—§§ 17.2(c) n.82, 84, 90

Ford, United States v., 830 F.2d 596 (6th Cir.1987)—§§ 23.1(b) n.83; 27.2(b) n.13

Ford v. Wainwright, 477 U.S. 399, 106 S.Ct. 2595, 91 L.Ed.2d 335 (1986)—§§ 1.8(e) n.98; 26.1(b) n.33; 28.6(d) n.21

Ford v. Warden, 111 Nev. 872, 901 P.2d 123 (1995)—§ 26.4(b) n.15

Forde, Commonwealth v., 392 Mass. 453, 466 N.E.2d 510 (1984)— § 6.9(c) n.55

Fore, United States v., 169 F.3d 104 (2d Cir.1999)—§ 11.3(b) n.45

Foree, United States v., 43 F.3d 1572 (11th Cir.1995)—§ 3.3(c) n.100

Forella, United States ex rel. v. Follette, 405 F.2d 680 (2d Cir.1969)— §§ 6.4(b) n.23; 6.4(e) n.59

Foreman, State v., 662 N.E.2d 929 (Ind.1996)—§ 3.2(e) n.160

Foreman v. State, 200 Ga.App. 400, 408 S.E.2d 178 (1991)—§ 24.11(d) n.12

Forest, United States v., 355 F.3d 942 (6th Cir.2004)—§§ 4.6(a) n.15; 22.2(d) n.75

Forgy v. Norris, 64 F.3d 399 (8th Cir.1995)—§§ 19.3(a) n.70; 19.3(b) n.169

Forker, United States v., 928 F.2d 365 (11th Cir.1991)—§ 3.6(a) n.5

Fornia-Castillo, United States v., 408 F.3d 52 (1st Cir.2005)—§ 6.6(e) n.91

Forrest, United States v., 402 F.3d 678 (6th Cir.2005)—§§ 13.7(c) n.47; 18.4(c) n.35

Forrest, United States v., 429 F.3d 73 (4th Cir.2005)—§ 1.2(c) n.193

Forrester, United States v., 495 F.3d 1041 (9th Cir.2007)—§§ 4.4(b) n.3; 4.4(d) n.15; 4.7(c) n.22

Forsyth, State v., 587 P.2d 1387 (Utah 1978)—§ 27.2(c) n.63

Forsythe, People v., 84 Ill.App.3d 643, 40 Ill.Dec. 357, 406 N.E.2d 58 (1980)—§ 20.6(b) n.45

Fort, People v., 248 Ill.App.3d 301, 187 Ill.Dec. 854, 618 N.E.2d 445 (1993)—§ 23.2(e) n.75

Fort, State v., 101 N.J. 123, 501 A.2d 140 (1985)—§ 21.2(b) n.62

Fort, United States v., 472 F.3d 1106 (9th Cir.2007)—§ 24.3(c) n.86

Forte, State v., 360 N.C. 427, 629 S.E.2d 137 (2006)—§ 6.9(g) n.157

Forte, State v., 154 Vt. 46, 572 A.2d 941 (1990)—§ 27.4(d) n.49

Fortenberry, United States v., 914 F.2d 671 (5th Cir.1990)—§ 17.1(a) n.14

Fortier, State v., 146 N.H. 784, 780 A.2d 1243 (2001)—§ 24.10(c) n.41

Fortier, State v., 113 Ariz. 332, 553 P.2d 1206 (1976)—§ 9.4(b) n.51

Fortin, State v., 178 N.J. 540, 843 A.2d 974 (2004)—§§ 19.3(a) n.38; 22.3(a) n.23

Fortini v. Murphy, 257 F.3d 39 (1st Cir.2001)—§ 28.6(f) n.76

Fort Lauderdale v. Byrd, 242 So.2d 494 (Fla.App.1970)—§ 1.8(d) n.45

Fort Lauderdale, City of v. Mattlin, 566 So.2d 1330 (Fla.App.1990)— § 1.8(d) n.69

Fortner v. State, 825 So.2d 876 (Ala.App.2001)—§ 28.11(b) n.19

Fortner, State v., 182 W.Va. 345, 387 S.E.2d 812 (1989)—§ 27.5(b) n.48

Fort Wayne Books, Inc. v. Indiana, 489 U.S. 46, 109 S.Ct. 916, 103 L.Ed.2d 34 (1989)—§ 27.2(a) n.5

Foss, State v., 556 N.W.2d 540 (Minn.1996)—§ 13.2(c) n.60

Fosselman, People v., 33 Cal.3d 572, 189 Cal.Rptr. 855, 659 P.2d 1144 (1983)—§ 11.7(e) n.81

Foster v. Booher, 296 F.3d 947 (10th Cir.2002)—§ 28.3(a) n.37

Foster v. California, 394 U.S. 440, 89 S.Ct. 1127, 22 L.Ed.2d 402 (1969)—§§ 7.4(b) n.14; 7.4(d) n.66

Foster v. Illinois, 332 U.S. 134, 67 S.Ct. 1716, 91 L.Ed. 1955 (1947)— § 2.11(a) n.5

Foster, People v., 271 Ill.App.3d 562, 207 Ill.Dec. 881, 648 N.E.2d 337 (1995)—§ 20.6(c) n.79

Foster, People v., 200 A.D.2d 196, 613 N.Y.S.2d 616 (1994)—§ 10.3(d) n.72

Foster, People v., 176 Ill.App.3d 406, 531 N.E.2d 93, 125 Ill.Dec. 914 (1988)—§ 25.1(d) n.66

Foster, People v., 119 Ill.2d 69, 115 Ill.Dec. 557, 518 N.E.2d 82 (1987)—§ 6.9(f) n.106

Foster, People v., 19 N.Y.2d 150, 278 N.Y.S.2d 603, 225 N.E.2d 200 (1967)—§§ 21.4(f) n.197, 198

Foster, State v., 845 N.E.2d 470 (Ohio 2006)—§ 26.4(i) n.190

Foster, State v., 845 So.2d 393 (La.App.2003)—§§ 15.7(d) n.78, 79

Foster v. State, 116 Nev. 1088, 13 P.3d 61 (Nev.2000)—§ 5.4(b) n.17

Foster, State v., 135 Wash.2d 441, 957 P.2d 712 (1998)—§ 2.12(e) n.210

Foster, State v., 560 N.W.2d 194 (N.D.1997)—§ 18.4(d) n.91

Foster, State v., 484 N.W.2d 113 (N.D.1992)—§ 26.7(c) n.37

Foster v. State, 614 So.2d 455 (Fla.1992)—§ 22.3(c) n.121

Foster v. State, 464 So.2d 1214 (Fla.App.1984)—§ 24.7(d) n.29

Foster v. State, 70 Wis.2d 12, 233 N.W.2d 411 (1975)—§§ 18.1(d) n.48, 50

Foster, United States v., 904 F.2d 20 (9th Cir.1990)—§ 11.2(a) n.27

Foster, United States v., 783 F.2d 1082 (D.C.Cir.1986)—§ 24.6(b) n.28

Fotopoulos v. State, 608 So.2d 784 (Fla.1992)—§ 22.3(d) n.250

Fouche, United States v., 833 F.2d 1284 (9th Cir.1987)—§ 6.9(g) n.183

Fouche, United States v., 776 F.2d 1398 (9th Cir.1985)—§ 6.3(b) n.36

Fountain, United States v., 840 F.2d 509 (7th Cir.1988)—§§ 15.6(f) n.189 to 191; 18.3(b) n.56

Fountain, United States v., 777 F.2d 351 (7th Cir.1985)—§ 21.4(f) n.174

Fountaine v. Mullen, 117 R.I. 262, 366 A.2d 1138 (1976)—§§ 12.4(a) n.5, 22

Fournier, People v., 793 P.2d 1176 (Colo.1990)—§ 3.4(c) n.43

Fourth Street Pharmacy v. United States Department of Justice, 836 F.2d 1137 (8th Cir.1988)—§ 21.2(e) n.329

Foust, State v., 105 Ohio St.3d 137, 823 N.E.2d 836 (2004)—§ 6.8(d) n.82

Foutz, United States v., 540 F.2d 733 (4th Cir.1976)—§§ 17.1(b) n.25; 17.1(e) n.60

Fowler, Ex parte, 574 So.2d 745 (Ala.1990)—§ 23.2(a) n.19

Fowler v. Bauman, 663 So.2d 438 (La.App.1995)—§ 24.9(c) n.27

Fowler, People v., 1 Cal.3d 335, 82 Cal.Rptr. 363, 461 P.2d 643 (1969)—§§ 7.3(a) n.7, 8

Fowler, State v., 353 N.C. 599, 548 S.E.2d 684 (2001)—§§ 7.4(g) n.112, 120

Fowler v. State, 566 So.2d 1194 (Miss.1990)—§ 6.9(e) n.87

Fowler v. United States, 411 A.2d 618 (D.C.App.1980)—§§ 11.3(b) n.35; 11.5(c) n.41

Fowler, United States v., 605 F.2d 181 (5th Cir.1979)—§§ 11.3(c) n.54, 59

Fowler, United States v., 476 F.2d 1091 (7th Cir.1973)—§ 6.8(c) n.80

Fowlie, United States v., 24 F.3d 1059 (9th Cir.1994)—§§ 15.7(h) n.224, 246

Fox, Commonwealth v., 422 Pa.Super. 224, 619 A.2d 327 (1993)—§ 14.4(c) n.57

Fox, Commonwealth v., 476 Pa. 475, 383 A.2d 199 (1978)—§ 11.9(d) n.218

Fox v. Ohio, 46 U.S. (5 How.) 410, 12 L.Ed. 213 (1847)—§§ 1.2(c) n.39, 43

Fox, People v., 319 Ill. 606, 150 N.E. 347 (1925)—§ 6.2(a) n.7

Fox v. State, 176 W.Va. 677, 347 S.E.2d 197 (1986)—§§ 26.9(b) n.30; 26.10(a) n.2

Fox, United States v., 393 F.3d 52 (1st Cir.2004)—§ 6.7(b) n.85

Fox, United States v., 889 F.2d 357 (1st Cir.1989)—§ 21.2(d) n.211

Fox, United States v., 721 F.2d 32 (2d Cir.1983)—§§ 8.13(a) n.22, 24

Fox, United States v., 403 F.2d 97 (2d Cir.1968)—§ 6.8(a) n.6

Fox v. Ward, 200 F.3d 1286 (10th Cir.2000)—§§ 6.9(f) n.133; 17.2(b) n.69

Fox Film Corp. v. Muller, 296 U.S. 207, 56 S.Ct. 183, 80 L.Ed. 158 (1935)—§ 2.12(a) n.46

Fox, State ex rel. v. La Porte Circuit Court, 236 Ind. 69, 138 N.E.2d 875 (1956)—§ 16.3(f) n.91

Foxworth, United States v., 599 F.2d 1 (1st Cir.1979)—§§ 15.4(b) n.67; 22.2(d) n.89

Foy, State v., 574 N.W.2d 337 (Iowa 1998)—§ 21.2(d) n.223

Foy, United States v., 28 F.3d 464 (5th Cir.1994)—§ 25.1(d) n.65

F.P. v. State, 528 So.2d 1253 (Fla.App.1988)—§ 3.9(k) n.258

Fraction, United States v., 795 F.2d 12 (3d Cir.1986)—§ 6.2(c) n.107

Frady, United States v., 456 U.S. 152, 102 S.Ct. 1584, 71 L.Ed.2d 816 (1982)—§§ 27.5(d) n.132; 28.4(d) n.44; 28.9(b) n.38

Fragoso v. Fell, 210 Ariz. 427, 111 P.3d 1027 (App.2005)—§ 12.2(b) n.31

Frampton, State v., 737 P.2d 183 (Utah 1987)—§§ 11.3(b) n.42; 11.5(c) n.43, 54

Frampton, State v., 95 Wash.2d 469, 627 P.2d 922 (1981)—§ 21.2(a) n.19

France, People v., 159 Misc.2d 869, 608 N.Y.S.2d 1006 (Sup.Ct. 1994)—§ 20.3(f) n.103

Francis, Commonwealth v., 374 Mass. 750, 374 N.E.2d 1207 (1978)—§ 18.4(c) n.72

Francis v. Franklin, 471 U.S. 307, 105 S.Ct. 1965, 85 L.Ed.2d 344 (1985)—§ 2.7(a) n.43

Francis v. Henderson, 425 U.S. 536, 96 S.Ct. 1708, 48 L.Ed.2d 149 (1976)—§§ 11.6(a) n.32; 15.4(i) n.204; 28.4(d) n.40

Francis, People v., 166 Misc.2d 476, 634 N.Y.S.2d 639 (Sup.Ct.1995)—§ 15.7(g) n.214

Francis, State v., 282 Kan. 120, 145 P.3d 48 (2006)—§ 3.4(f) n.118

Francis, State v., 104 Ohio St.3d 490, 820 N.E.2d 355 (2004)—§ 21.4(d) n.137

Francis v. State, 808 So.2d 110 (Fla.2001)—§ 22.3(d) n.250

Francis, United States v., 646 F.2d 251 (6th Cir.1981)—§ 10.1(c) n.50

Francisco v. Gathright, 419 U.S. 59, 95 S.Ct. 257, 42 L.Ed.2d 226 (1974)—§ 28.5(a) n.12

Francisco, United States v., 35 F.3d 116 (4th Cir.1994)—§ 24.7(i) n.86

Franciscus, Commonwealth v., 551 Pa. 376, 710 A.2d 1112 (1998)—§ 6.4(g) n.153

Franco, People v., 86 N.Y.2d 493, 634 N.Y.S.2d 38, 657 N.E.2d 1321 (1995)—§ 15.2(h) n.192

Franco v. State, 918 A.2d 1158 (Del.2007)—§ 26.4(f) n.93

Franco, State v., 750 A.2d 415 (R.I.2000)—§§ 15.2(b) n.26; 15.5(c) n.112, 114; 15.6(d) n.127; 15.6(f) n.189

Franco, State v., 96 Wash.2d 816, 639 P.2d 1320 (1982)—§ 24.10(c) n.41

Franco, United States v., 136 F.3d 622 (9th Cir.1998)—§ 24.10(b) n.26

Franco, United States v., 163 F.3d 1359 (11th Cir.1998)—§ 27.5(e) n.148

Franco, United States v., 909 F.2d 1042 (7th Cir.1990)—§ 5.3(d) n.43

Francois v. Dolan, 95 N.Y.2d 33, 709 N.Y.S.2d 898, 731 N.E.2d 614 (2000)—§ 21.4(a) n.11

Francois v. Henderson, 850 F.2d 231 (5th Cir.1988)—§ 28.3(a) n.3

Francois v. State, 695 So.2d 695 (1997)—§ 26.10(d) n.92

Franco-Lopez, United States v., 312 F.3d 984 (9th Cir.2002)— §§ 21.2(b) n.48; 21.2(d) n.157, 165

Franco-Martinez, United States v., 271 F.3d 764 (8th Cir.2001)—§ 21.2(d) n.161

Frank v. Blackburn, 646 F.2d 873 (5th Cir.1980)—§ 21.2(c) n.131

Frank v. Magnum, 237 U.S. 309, 35 S.Ct. 582, 59 L.Ed. 969 (1915)— § 28.3(b) n.50

Frank v. Maryland, 359 U.S. 360, 79 S.Ct. 804, 3 L.Ed.2d 877 (1959)— §§ 3.9(b) n.9, 13

Frank, State v., 803 So.2d 1 (La.2001)— §§ 11.2(g) n.261, 270

Frank v. Superior Court, 48 Cal.3d 632, 257 Cal.Rptr. 550, 770 P.2d 1119 (1989)—§ 17.1(d) n.58

Frank, United States v., 36 F.3d 898 (9th Cir.1994)—§ 21.3(d) n.218

Frank, United States v., 901 F.2d 846 (10th Cir.1990)—§ 22.3(c) n.127

Frank, United States v., 864 F.2d 992 (3d Cir.1988)—§ 3.1(d) n.95

Frank v. United States, 395 U.S. 147, 89 S.Ct. 1503, 23 L.Ed.2d 162 (1969)—§ 22.1(b) n.36

Franklin v. Anderson, 434 F.3d 412 (6th Cir.2006)—§§ 11.10(c) n.96; 11.10(d) n.171; 28.4(b) n.18, 19

Franklin, Commonwealth v., 376 Mass. 885, 385 N.E.2d 227 (1978)— §§ 13.4(b) n.33, 36, 40

Franklin v. Duncan, 70 F.3d 75 (9th Cir.1995)—§ 24.7(e) n.57

Franklin v. Johnson, 290 F.3d 1223 (9th Cir.2002)—§§ 11.10(c) n.113; 11.10(d) n.162

Franklin v. Kearney, 814 So.2d 462 (Fla.App.2001)—§ 27.2(c) n.64

Franklin, People v., 167 Ill.2d 1, 212 Ill.Dec. 153, 656 N.E.2d 750 (1995)—§ 17.4(a) n.46

Franklin, People v., 135 Ill.2d 78, 142 Ill.Dec. 152, 552 N.E.2d 743 (1990)—§§ 22.3(b) n.73, 86

Franklin, State v., 184 N.J. 516, 878 A.2d 757 (2005)—§ 27.6(d) n.126

Franklin v. State, 138 S.W.3d 351 (Tex.Cr.App.2004)—§ 22.3(c) n.142

Franklin, State v., 618 So.2d 171 (Fla.1993)—§ 24.8(a) n.25

Franklin, State v., 299 S.C. 133, 382 S.E.2d 911 (1989)—§ 6.7(c) n.118

Franklin, State v., 174 W.Va. 469, 327 S.E.2d 449 (1985)—§ 24.2(e) n.79

Franklin, State v., 194 Neb. 630, 234 N.W.2d 610 (1975)—§§ 14.3(d) n.102, 105; 14.4(e) n.119

Franklin v. State, 6 Md.App. 572, 252 A.2d 487 (1969)—§ 6.8(b) n.52

Franklin, United States v., 148 F.3d 451 (5th Cir.1998)—§ 18.3(b) n.36

Franklin et al. v. District of Columbia, 163 F.3d 625 (D.C.Cir.1998)— § 26.2(c) n.63

Franklyn, United States v., 157 F.3d 90 (2d Cir.1998)—§ 22.3(d) n.220

Franks v. Delaware, 438 U.S. 154, 98 S.Ct. 2674, 57 L.Ed.2d 667 (1978)—§§ 1.9(b) n.19; 3.4(d) n.49; 13.5(h) n.171; 23.1(d) n.195

Franks v. State, 140 P.3d 557 (Okla.Crim.App.2006)—§ 13.7(a) n.29

Franks v. State, 268 Ga. 238, 486 S.E.2d 594 (1997)—§ 6.7(b) n.45

Franky-Ortiz, United States v., 230 F.3d 405 (1st Cir.2000)—§ 21.2(b) n.74

Fransaw v. Lynaugh, 810 F.2d 518 (5th Cir.1987)—§§ 21.5(e) n.119; 25.1(d) n.76

Franzen, State v., 495 N.W.2d 714 (Iowa 1993)—§§ 25.1(d) n.66; 25.4(d) n.48

Franzi v. Superior Court, 139 Ariz. 556, 679 P.2d 1043 (1984)—§§ 8.8(a) n.12, 13; 15.6(c) n.88

Fraser, Commonwealth v., 410 Mass. 541, 573 N.E.2d 979 (1991)— § 3.8(c) n.82

Fraser v. Nationwide Mut. Ins., 135 F.Supp.2d 623 (E.D. Pa. 2001)— § 4.8(d) n.32

Fraser v. Nationwide Mutual Insurance Co., 352 F.3d 107 (3d Cir.2003)— § 4.6(b) n.25

Fraser v. United States, 834 F.2d 911 (11th Cir.1987)—§ 27.2(e) n.93

Fratello, United States v., 44 F.R.D. 444 (S.D.N.Y.1968)—§ 20.4(g) n.110

Fraternal Order of Eagles Aerie 0337 Buckeye, State v., 58 Ohio St.3d 166, 569 N.E.2d 478 (Ohio.1991)— § 27.3(d) n.67

Fraternal Order of Eagles Sheridan v. State ex rel. Forwood, 126 P.3d 847 (Wyo.2006)—§ 13.5(c) n.63

Fraternal Order of Police v. Newark, 216 N.J.Super. 461, 524 A.2d 430 (1987)—§ 3.9(l) n.271

Frazier v. Cupp, 394 U.S. 731, 89 S.Ct. 1420, 22 L.Ed.2d 684 (1969)— §§ 3.10(d) n.104, 128; 3.10(e) n.171; 6.2(c) n.121, 128; 6.4(c) n.45; 17.2(b) n.39; 24.7(a) n.11, 12

Frazier v. Huffman, 343 F.3d 780 (6th Cir.2003)—§ 11.10(c) n.127

Frazier v. Montana State Dep't of Corrections, 277 Mont. 82, 920 P.2d 93 (1996)—§ 26.1(f) n.150

Frazier, State v., 336 Mont. 81, 153 P.3d 18 (2007)—§ 21.4(f) n.173

Frazier, State v., 622 N.W.2d 246 (S.D.2001)—§ 6.8(b) n.50

Frazier v. State, 257 Ga. 690, 362 S.E.2d 351 (1987)—§ 22.5(d) n.29

Frazier, State v., 99 Wash.2d 180, 661 P.2d 126 (1983)—§ 24.9(c) n.20

Frazier, State v., 162 W.Va. 602, 252 S.E.2d 39 (1979)—§ 15.7(h) n.233

Frazier v. Superior Court of Santa Cruz County, 5 Cal.3d 287, 95 Cal.Rptr. 798, 486 P.2d 694 (1971)— §§ 16.3(b) n.16; 27.4(c) n.31

Frazier, United States v., 408 F.3d 1102 (8th Cir.2005)—§ 9.6(a) n.48

Frazier, United States v., 340 F.3d 5 (1st Cir.2003)—§ 21.2(d) n.177

Frazier, United States v., 280 F.3d 835 (8th Cir.2002)—§§ 22.1(d) n.79; 22.3(e) n.289; 24.9(f) n.103

Frazier, United States v., 880 F.2d 878 (6th Cir.1989)—§§ 17.4(a) n.6, 36

Frazier, United States v., 476 F.2d 891 (D.C.Cir.1973)—§ 6.9(e) n.83

Frazier v. Wilkinson, 842 F.2d 42 (2d Cir.1988)—§ 28.3(a) n.35

Frazier-El, United States v., 204 F.3d 553 (4th Cir.2000)—§ 11.5(d) n.69

Frechette, United States v., 456 F.3d 1 (1st Cir.2006)—§ 22.1(h) n.133

Frederick, People v., 45 N.Y.2d 520, 410 N.Y.S.2d 555, 382 N.E.2d 1332 (1978)—§ 21.5(d) n.104

Frederick, United States v., 583 F.2d 273 (6th Cir.1978)—§ 25.5(a) n.16

Frederick v. Warden, 308 F.3d 192 (2d Cir.2002)—§ 21.2(b) n.83

Fredericks, United States v., 586 F.2d 470 (5th Cir.1978)—§ 9.1(a) n.20

Fredette v. State, 428 A.2d 395 (Me.1981)—§ 12.4(a) n.5

Fredrick v. State, 755 N.E.2d 1078 (Ind.2001)—§ 6.4(g) n.161

Fredriksson, United States v., 893 F.2d 1404 (D.C.Cir.1990)—§ 24.5(d) n.50

Freedle, State v., 1 Hawai'i App. 396, 620 P.2d 740 (1980)—§§ 15.5(c) n.121; 15.7(g) n.205

Freedman v. American Online, 412 F.Supp.2d 174 (D. Conn. 2005)— § 4.4(b) n.6

Freeland, State v., 295 Or. 367, 667 P.2d 509 (1983)—§ 14.2(d) n.57

Freeman v. City of Dallas, 242 F.3d 642 (5th Cir.2001)—§ 3.9(b) n.28

Freeman, Commonwealth v., 573 Pa. 532, 827 A.2d 385 (2003)—§§ 27.5(c) n.91; 27.5(d) n.113

Freeman, Commonwealth v., 563 Pa. 82, 757 A.2d 903 (2000)—§ 3.8(c) n.118

Freeman, Commonwealth v., 407 Mass. 279, 552 N.E.2d 553 (1990)—§ 15.7(b) n.17

Freeman, State v., 113 Or.App. 246, 831 P.2d 84 (1992)—§ 27.5(a) n.28

Freeman v. State, 194 Ga.App. 905, 392 S.E.2d 330 (1990)—§§ 19.4(b) n.9; 24.8(c) n.41

Freeman, State v., 319 N.C. 609, 356 S.E.2d 765 (1987)—§ 1.7(i) n.208

Freeman v. State, 723 S.W.2d 727 (Tex.Cr.App.1986)—§ 6.9(f) n.135

Freeman, State v., 236 Kan. 274, 689 P.2d 885 (1984)—§ 18.5(c) n.75

Freeman, United States v., 479 F.3d 743 (10th Cir.2007)—§ 26.9(b) n.63

Freeman, United States v., 816 F.2d 558 (10th Cir.1987)—§ 5.3(a) n.7

Freeman, United States v., 524 F.2d 337 (7th Cir.1975)—§ 4.7(d) n.29

Freeman v. United States, 227 F. 732 (2d Cir.1915)—§ 22.4(e) n.50

Freese, State v., 116 Nev. 337, 997 P.2d 122 (2000)—§§ 21.4(c) n.70; 21.4(e) n.163

Frega, United States v., 179 F.3d 793 (9th Cir.1999)—§§ 13.7(c) n.43; 22.5(d) n.34

Fregoso, United States v., 60 F.3d 1314 (8th Cir.1995)—§§ 4.7(b) n.10; 4.7(c) n.26

Freidus, United States v., 135 F.R.D. 52 (S.D.N.Y.1991)—§§ 8.12(g) n.64; 8.13(a) n.27, 29

Freie, United States v., 545 F.2d 1217 (9th Cir.1976)—§ 3.2(a) n.13

Freije v. State, 709 N.E.2d 323 (Ind.1999)—§ 21.2(d) n.194

Freitas, United States v., 856 F.2d 1425 (9th Cir.1988)—§ 3.1(c) n.74

Freitas, United States v., 800 F.2d 1451 (9th Cir.1986)—§§ 3.1(c) n.74; 3.4(g) n.135; 3.4(l) n.248

French v. Jones, 332 F.3d 430 (6th Cir.2003)—§§ 11.10(d) n.198, 201, 203

French, United States v., 974 F.2d 687 (6th Cir.1992)—§ 3.8(b) n.40

French, United States v., 787 F.2d 1381 (9th Cir.1986)—§ 27.2(c) n.51

French, United States v., 683 F.2d 1189 (8th Cir.1982)—§ 19.2(a) n.5

Frensley v. State, 291 Ark. 268, 724 S.W.2d 165 (1987)—§ 7.4(g) n.122

Freshment, State v., 309 Mont. 154, 43 P.3d 968 (2002)—§§ 17.1(d) n.58; 17.1(e) n.60; 22.3(c) n.112

Frey v. Fulcomer, 974 F.2d 348 (3d Cir.1992)—§ 11.10(c) n.107

Frey, People v., 103 Ill.2d 327, 82 Ill.Dec. 661, 469 N.E.2d 195 (1984)—§ 22.1(h) n.137

Frias, People v., 219 App.Div.2d 479, 631 N.Y.S.2d 160 (1995)—§ 24.8(a) n.9

Frias v. State, 547 N.E.2d 809 (Ind.1989)—§ 24.3(g) n.161

Frick, United States v., 490 F.2d 666 (5th Cir.1973)—§ 9.2(c) n.27

Fried, In re, 161 F.2d 453 (2d Cir.1947)—§§ 1.5(f) n.247; 15.5(a) n.22

Friedland, United States v., 441 F.2d 855 (2d Cir.1971)—§ 9.3(d) n.38

Friedman v. Commissioner of Public Safety, 473 N.W.2d 828 (Minn.1991)—§ 2.12(d) n.194

Friedman, State v., 93 Haw. 63, 996 P.2d 268 (2000)—§ 22.1(h) n.133

Friedman, State v., 225 Mont. 373, 732 P.2d 1322 (1987)—§ 26.10(b) n.37

Friedman, United States v., 366 F.3d 975 (9th Cir.2004)—§ 27.2(c) n.44

Friedman, United States v., 300 F.3d 111 (2d Cir.2002)—§ 4.6(b) n.50

Friedman, United States v., 909 F.2d 705 (2d Cir.1990)—§ 24.7(i) n.92

Friedman, United States v., 837 F.2d 48 (2d Cir.1988)—§ 12.3(a) n.23

Friedman, United States v., 532 F.2d 928 (3d Cir.1976)—§ 8.7(b) n.60

Friedman, State ex rel. v. Provaznik, 668 S.W.2d 76 (Mo.1984)—§§ 8.6(b) n.46; 8.8(d) n.88

Friel, State v., 500 A.2d 631 (Me.1985)—§ 25.2(e) n.40

Friel, United States v., 588 F.Supp. 1173 (E.D.Pa.1984)—§ 11.10(c) n.129

Friend, United States v., 50 F.3d 548 (8th Cir.1995)—§ 10.6(d) n.48

Frierson v. City of Terrell, 2003 WL 21355969 (N.D.Tex.2003)— § 8.10(e) n.124

Frierson, People v., 39 Cal.3d 803, 218 Cal.Rptr. 73, 705 P.2d 396 (1985)— § 11.6(a) n.27

Frierson, United States v., 945 F.2d 650 (3d Cir.1991)—§§ 21.1(h) n.233; 21.2(d) n.210

Frink v. State, 597 P.2d 154 (Alaska 1979)—§§ 15.5(c) n.126; 15.7(f) n.134, 152

Frisbie v. Collins, 342 U.S. 519, 72 S.Ct. 509, 96 L.Ed. 541 (1952)—§§ 3.1(j) n.243, 244; 9.4(d) n.92

Frisbie v. United States, 157 U.S. 160, 15 S.Ct. 586, 39 L.Ed. 657 (1895)— §§ 8.4(b) n.50, 71

Frisby, United States v., 258 F.3d 46 (1st Cir.2001)—§ 21.2(d) n.177

Frisby v. United States, 79 F.3d 29 (6th Cir.1996)—§ 27.2(d) n.74

Frisco, People v., 119 P.3d 1093 (Colo.2005)—§ 11.9(c) n.115

Fritschen, State v., 247 Kan. 592, 802 P.2d 558 (1990)—§ 6.6(c) n.32

Fritschler, People v., 81 Misc.2d 106, 364 N.Y.S.2d 801 (1975)—§ 3.9(h) n.154

Fritz v. Spalding, 682 F.2d 782 (9th Cir.1982)—§ 11.5(d) n.71

Fritz v. State, 811 P.2d 1353 (Okla.Crim.App.1991)—§ 18.5(b) n.71

Fritz, State v., 204 Conn. 156, 527 A.2d 1157 (1987)—§§ 17.4(a) n.48, 62

Fritz v. State, 730 P.2d 530 (Okla.Cr.App.1986)—§ 22.3(d) n.176

Fritz, State v., 72 Or.App. 409, 695 P.2d 972 (1985)—§ 20.3(c) n.77

Fritz, State v., 21 Wash.App. 354, 585 P.2d 173 (1978)—§ 11.5(d) n.71

Fritz, United States v., 852 F.2d 1175 (9th Cir.1988)—§§ 15.2(c) n.62, 66

Frohnmayer, State ex rel. v. Sams, 293 Or. 385, 648 P.2d 364 (1982)— § 8.4(b) n.29

Froistad v. State, 641 N.W.2d 86 (N.D.2002)—§§ 21.4(f) n.174, 178, 179; 21.5(a) n.8

Frometa, Commonwealth v., 520 Pa. 552, 555 A.2d 92 (1989)—§ 21.3(b) n.66

Frosch, State v., 816 So.2d 269 (La.2002)—§§ 3.1(d) n.98; 3.3(f) n.206

Frost, Ex parte, 848 So.2d 1021 (Ala.Crim.2002)—§ 12.3(b) n.61

Frost, United States v., 125 F.3d 346 (6th Cir.1997)—§ 24.9(f) n.86

Fruchter, United States v., 411 F.3d 377 (2d Cir.2005)—§§ 26.6(d) n.51, 54

Frumento, United States v., 552 F.2d 534 (3d Cir.1977)—§ 27.5(a) n.31

Fry, People v., 92 P.3d 970 (Colo.2004)—§ 14.1(d) n.65

Fry, People v., 271 Cal.App.2d 350, 76 Cal.Rptr. 718 (1969)—§ 3.10(d) n.112

Fry v. Pliler, _____ U.S. _____, 127 S.Ct. 2321, 168 L.Ed.2d 16 (2007)—§§ 2.7(b) n.75; 27.6(d) n.76; 28.6(g) n.86, 88, 91

Fry, State v., 131 Wis.2d 153, 388 N.W.2d 565 (1986)—§§ 2.12(c) n.167; 3.7(a) n.13, 19

Fry, United States v., 831 F.2d 664 (6th Cir.1987)—§ 26.5(c) n.56

Frye v. Settle, 168 F.Supp. 7 (D.C.Mo.1958)—§ 15.1(f) n.333

Frye, United States v., 738 F.2d 196 (7th Cir.1984)—§ 21.4(c) n.82

Fryer v. State, 68 S.W.3d 628 (Tex.Cr.App.2002)—§ 26.5(d) n.63

Fryer v. United States, 243 F.3d 1004 (7th Cir.2001)—§ 28.6(e) n.63

F.S.J., United States v., 265 F.3d 764 (9th Cir.2001)—§ 13.2(a) n.2

FTC v. American National Cellular, 868 F.2d 315 (9th Cir.1989)—§ 22.5(a) n.10

FTC v. Carter, 464 F.Supp. 633 (D.D.C.1979)—§ 8.7(a) n.25

F.T.C. v. Netscape Communications Corp, 196 F.R.D. 559 (N.D.Cal. 2000)—§ 4.8(c) n.22

Fuccillo, United States v., 808 F.2d 173 (1st Cir.1987)—§ 3.1(c) n.72

Fudge, United States v., 325 F.3d 910 (7th Cir.2003)—§§ 4.6(e) n.74, 97

Fuente v. State, 549 So.2d 652 (Fla.1989)—§ 18.4(c) n.60

Fuessenich, State v., 50 Conn.App. 187, 717 A.2d 801 (1998)—§ 26.10(c) n.65

Fuesting, United States v., 845 F.2d 664 (7th Cir.1988)—§§ 18.5(b) n.58, 59

Fugate v. Commonwealth, 62 S.W.3d 15 (Ky.2001)—§ 24.2(b) n.27

Fugate v. Head, 261 F.3d 1206 (11th Cir.2001)—§ 11.10(c) n.113

Fuget, United States v., 984 F.2d 943 (8th Cir.1993)—§ 3.10(e) n.172

Fuhrmann, State v., 257 N.W.2d 619 (Iowa 1977)—§ 19.5(b) n.33

Fukagawa, State v., 100 Haw. 498, 60 P.3d 899 (2002)—§ 13.2(c) n.77

Fukusaku, State v., 85 Hawai'i 462, 946 P.2d 32 (1997)—§ 20.3(a) n.20

Fulkman, People v., 235 Cal.App.3d 555, 28 Cal.Rptr. 728 (1991)—§ 3.5(b) n.101

Fulks, State v., 566 N.W.2d 418 (N.D.1997)—§ 18.4(d) n.91

Fuller, In re, 345 N.C. 157, 478 S.E.2d 641 (1996)—§ 21.3(d) n.263

Fuller v. Diesslin, 868 F.2d 604 (3d Cir.1989)—§ 11.4(c) n.56

Fuller v. Israel, 421 F.Supp. 582 (E.D.Ill.1976)—§ 11.9(a) n.42

Fuller v. M.G. Jewelry, 950 F.2d 1437 (9th Cir.1991)—§ 3.5(c) n.130

Fuller v. Oregon, 417 U.S. 40, 94 S.Ct. 2116, 40 L.Ed.2d 642 (1974)—§§ 11.2(h) n.318; 26.1(f) n.149; 26.9(b) n.28

Fuller, People v., 96 N.Y.2d 881, 756 N.E.2d 61, 730 N.Y.S.2d 773 (2001)—§ 25.4(d) n.45

Fuller, State v., 182 N.J. 174, 862 A.2d 1130 (2004)—§ 22.3(d) n.199

Fuller, State v., 308 Md. 547, 520 A.2d 1315 (1987)—§ 26.10(c) n.73

Fuller, United States v., 374 F.3d 617 (8th Cir.2004)—§ 9.1(d) n.125

Fuller, United States v., 312 F.3d 287 (7th Cir.2002)—§ 21.2(g) n.395

Fuller, United States v., 86 F.3d 105 (7th Cir.1996)—§ 18.3(b) n.20

Fuller, United States v., 942 F.2d 454 (8th Cir.1991)—§ 18.3(b) n.25

Fuller, United States v., 769 F.2d 1095 (5th Cir.1985)—§ 21.5(c) n.74

Full Gospel Tabernacle, In the Matter of v. Attorney General, 142 A.D.2d 489, 536 N.Y.S.2d 201 (1988)—§ 8.8(d) n.53

Fullwood v. Lee, 290 F.3d 663 (4th Cir.2002)—§ 28.6(f) n.77

Fullwood, State v., 323 N.C. 371, 373 S.E.2d 518 (1988)—§ 22.3(d) n.202

Fulton, State v., 57 Ohio St.3d 120, 566 N.E.2d 1195 (1991)—§ 22.2(d) n.66

Fulton, United States v., 5 F.3d 605 (2d Cir.1993)—§§ 11.9(a) n.13; 11.9(c) n.144, 145; 11.9(d) n.175, 219 to 221

Fults, State v., 719 S.W.2d 46 (Mo.App.1986)—§ 19.3(b) n.148

Fultz, United States v., 146 F.3d 1102 (9th Cir.1998)—§ 9.1(b) n.95

Funches, United States v., 135 F.3d 1405 (11th Cir.1998)—§ 22.1(g) n.117

Funches, United States v., 84 F.3d 249 (7th Cir.1996)—§§ 7.4(d) n.69; 7.4(f) n.99

Funderbird-Day, People v., 225 A.D.2d 498, 640 N.Y.S.2d 42 (N.Y.App.Div.1996)—§ 24.4(c) n.24

Funk v. Commonwealth, 8 Va.App. 91, 379 S.E.2d 371 (1989)—§ 11.2(e) n.175

Funk v. United States, 290 U.S. 371, 54 S.Ct. 212, 78 L.Ed. 369 (1933)— §§ 1.7(h) n.133, 143; 1.7(i) n.156

Funston, In re, 133 Misc. 620, 233 N.Y.S. 81 (Sup.Ct.1929)— §§ 15.1(d) n.152, 249

Furen, State v., 118 So.2d 6 (Fla.1960)—§ 1.7(f) n.106

Furey v. Hyland, 395 F.Supp. 1356 (D.N.J.1975)—§ 28.3(a) n.22

Furlett, United States v., 974 F.2d 839 (7th Cir.1992)—§ 17.4(b) n.125

Furlong, State ex rel. v. County Court for Waukesha County, 47 Wis.2d 515, 177 N.W.2d 333 (1970)— § 14.3(a) n.20

Furman v. Georgia, 408 U.S. 238, 92 S.Ct. 2726, 33 L.Ed.2d 346 (1972)—§§ 2.6(b) n.41; 2.9(d) n.93; 12.4(a) n.8; 26.1(b) n.10

Furman, United States v., 507 F.Supp. 848 (1981)—§ 15.7(f) n.186

Furr v. State, 297 Ark. 233, 761 S.W.2d 160 (1988)—§§ 21.4(f) n.173, 184

Furrow, United States v., 229 F.3d 805 (9th Cir.2000)—§ 3.4(j) n.182

Furtado v. State, 623 P.2d 770 (Wyo.1981)—§ 21.1(e) n.67

Furutani, State v., 76 Haw. 172, 873 P.2d 51 (1994)—§§ 24.9(f) n.93, 94; 24.9(g) n.114

Fuselier v. State, 468 So.2d 45 (Miss.1985)—§§ 20.3(a) n.15, 16; 22.3(c) n.147

Fusko, United States v., 869 F.2d 1048 (7th Cir.1989)—§§ 5.2(a) n.11; 5.2(c) n.43

Fuson v. State, 105 N.M. 632, 735 P.2d 1138 (1987)—§ 22.3(c) n.104

Futernick v. Sumpter Township, 78 F.3d 1051 (6th Cir.1996)—§§ 13.4(c) n.80, 130; 13.4(e) n.174

Fuzer, United States v., 18 F.3d 517 (7th Cir.1994)—§ 21.2(e) n.326

G

Gabaldon, United States v., 91 F.3d 91 (10th Cir.1996)—§ 27.5(e) n.156

Gabay, United States v., 923 F.2d 1536 (11th Cir.1991)—§ 17.1(a) n.10

Gabbidon, People v., 116 Misc.2d 127, 455 N.Y.S.2d 244 (Sup.Ct.1982)— § 18.4(c) n.37

Gable, People v., 647 P.2d 246 (Colo.App.1982)—§ 15.5(c) n.125

Gaboriault, Commonwealth v., 439 Mass. 84, 785 N.E.2d 691 (2003)— § 6.8(c) n.73

Gabow v. Commonwealth, 34 S.W.3d 63 (Ky.2000)—§ 17.2(b) n.50

Gabriel v. State, 925 P.2d 234 (Wyo.1996)—§§ 24.4(d) n.30, 55

Gacy, People v., 125 Ill.2d 117, 125 Ill.Dec. 770, 530 N.E.2d 1340 (1988)—§ 11.9(d) n.207

Gaddis, United States v., 877 F.2d 605 (7th Cir.1989)—§ 20.3(g) n.120

Gaddy, State v., 313 Ark. 677, 858 S.W.2d 81 (1993)—§§ 21.2(d) n.206; 21.2(e) n.308

Gaertner, United States v., 583 F.2d 308 (7th Cir.1978)—§ 21.6(a) n.57

Gafford, State v., 172 Mont. 380, 563 P.2d 1129 (1977)—§ 20.3(h) n.144

Gaggi, United States v., 811 F.2d 47 (2d Cir.1987)—§ 23.2(h) n.129

Gagnon, Commonwealth v., 408 Mass. 185, 557 N.E.2d 728 (1990)— §§ 24.4(c) n.20, 21

Gagnon v. Scarpelli, 411 U.S. 778, 93 S.Ct. 1756, 36 L.Ed.2d 656 (1973)—§§ 1.10(a) n.17; 1.11(a) n.2, 4; 2.7(a) n.60, 62; 2.7(b) n.86; 2.7(c) n.213; 2.9(g) n.199; 2.9(i) n.284; 11.1(a) n.29; 11.1(b) n.35, 38, 44, 47, 88 to 90; 11.2(b) n.56, 61, 78; 13.6(d) n.65; 18.5(c) n.89; 26.4(e) n.78; 26.10(b) n.11; 26.10(c) n.67

Gagnon, United States v., 470 U.S. 522, 105 S.Ct. 1482, 84 L.Ed.2d 486 (1985)—§§ 2.7(a) n.35; 2.7(b) n.96; 24.2(a) n.3, 18

Gainer, People v., 19 Cal.3d 835, 139 Cal.Rptr. 861, 566 P.2d 997 (1977)—§ 24.9(d) n.43

Gaines, Commonwealth v., 4 Va. 172, 2 Va.Cas. (4 Va.) 172 (1819)—§ 16.4(c) n.115

Gaines, People v., 105 Ill.2d 79, 85 Ill.Dec. 269, 473 N.E.2d 868 (1984)—§§ 11.7(e) n.65, 94

Gaines, State v., 770 So.2d 1221 (Fla.2000)—§§ 1.7(f) n.93; 27.3(d) n.67

Gaines, State v., 688 So.2d 679 (La.App.1997)—§ 25.4(c) n.28

Gaines v. State, 215 Ala. 361, 110 So. 601 (1926)—§ 15.1(d) n.219

Gaines, United States v., 295 F.3d 293 (2d Cir.2002)—§§ 6.2(c) n.107, 175

Gaines, United States v., 888 F.2d 1122 (6th Cir.1989)—§§ 21.2(d) n.161, 198

Gaines, United States v., 555 F.2d 618 (7th Cir.1977)—§ 6.3(b) n.43

Gaines v. Washington, 277 U.S. 81, 48 S.Ct. 468, 72 L.Ed. 793 (1928)—§§ 2.4(e) n.160; 15.1(c) n.141

Gaitan, State v., 536 N.W.2d 11 (Minn.1995)—§ 22.3(d) n.226

Gaither v. Commonwealth, 963 S.W.2d 621 (Ky.1997)—§ 21.6(a) n.36

Gaither, United States v., 245 F.3d 1064 (9th Cir.2001)—§ 21.4(f) n.175

Gaither v. United States, 413 F.2d 1061 (D.C.Cir.1969)—§§ 15.1(d) n.162; 15.6(c) n.97; 15.6(d) n.116; 15.6(f) n.200

Gaito v. Brierley, 485 F.2d 86 (3d Cir.1973)—§ 24.2(e) n.54

Gaitor v. State, 106 Nev. 785, 801 P.2d 1372 (1990)—§§ 7.3(a) n.9; 7.4(f) n.96

Galanis, United States v., 43 Crim.L.Rptr. 2030 (S.D.N.Y.1988)—§ 8.5(i) n.325

Galante, United States v., 547 F.2d 733 (2d Cir.1976)—§ 9.1(b) n.65

Galati, United States v., 230 F.3d 254 (7th Cir.2000)—§§ 7.4(e) n.82; 10.2(b) n.26

Galberth, United States v., 846 F.2d 983 (5th Cir.1988)—§ 3.10(b) n.54

Galbreath, State v., 525 N.W.2d 424 (Iowa 1994)—§ 21.4(f) n.174

Galceran, United States v., 301 F.3d 927 (8th Cir.2002)—§§ 6.6(c) n.37; 6.6(d) n.46

Gale, People v., 9 Cal.3d 788, 108 Cal.Rptr. 852, 511 P.2d 1204 (1973)—§ 3.7(e) n.125

Gale, People v., 24 A.D.2d 697, 261 N.Y.S.2d 839 (1965)—§ 15.5(c) n.127

Galen v. County of Los Angeles, 477 F.3d 652 (9th Cir.2007)—§ 12.2(a) n.4

Gales, State v., 265 Neb. 598, 658 N.W.2d 604 (2003)—§ 26.4(i) n.179

Galford, Commonwealth v., 413 Mass. 364, 597 N.E.2d 410 (1992)—§ 6.9(f) n.144

Gallagher, People v., 55 Mich.App. 613, 223 N.W.2d 92 (1974)—§ 3.10(f) n.203

Gallarelli, Commonwealth v., 399 Mass. 17, 502 N.E.2d 516 (1987)—§ 24.3(b) n.40

Gallarelli v. United States, 441 F.2d 1402 (3d Cir.1971)—§§ 21.3(a) n.4, 12, 20; 21.3(b) n.50

Gallego, People v., 430 Mich. 443, 424 N.W.2d 470 (1988)—§ 13.5(b) n.53

Gallegos v. City of Colorado Springs, 114 F.3d 1024 (10th Cir.1997)—§ 3.8(b) n.31

Gallegos v. City of Los Angeles, 308 F.3d 987 (9th Cir.2002)—§ 3.8(b) n.45

Gallegos v. Louisiana Code of Criminal Procedures, 858 F.2d 1091 (5th Cir.1988)—§ 26.9(c) n.83

Gallegos v. Nebraska, 342 U.S. 55, 72 S.Ct. 141, 96 L.Ed. 86 (1951)—§§ 6.2(c) n.163; 6.3(c) n.46

Gallegos, People v., 293 Ill.App.3d 873, 228 Ill.Dec. 351, 689 N.E.2d 223 (1997)—§§ 16.1(g) n.235, 241

Gallegos, State v., 141 N.M. 185, 152 P.3d 828 (2007)—§§ 17.1(d) n.54, 56

Gallegos, State v., 109 N.M. 55, 781 P.2d 783 (N.M.App.1989)—§ 19.5(b) n.27

Gallegos, State v., 92 N.M. 370, 588 P.2d 1045 (App.1978)—§§ 20.4(b) n.36, 40, 42

Gallegos, United States v., 387 F.3d 794 (9th Cir.2004)—§ 21.2(b) n.79

Gallicchio, State v., 51 N.J. 313, 240 A.2d 166 (1968)—§ 6.7(c) n.119

Gallie v. Wainwright, 362 So.2d 936 (Fla.1978)—§ 12.4(d) n.79

Gallimore v. State, 944 P.2d 939 (Okla.Cr.App.1997)—§ 27.4(c) n.23

Gallington, United States v., 488 F.2d 637 (8th Cir.1973)—§ 21.3(d) n.234

Gallion v. State, 517 So.2d 1364 (Miss.1987)—§§ 20.6(b) n.22, 31

Gallo, People v., 54 Ill.2d 343, 297 N.E.2d 569 (1973)—§ 18.5(a) n.37

Gallo, State v., 279 So.2d 71 (Fla.App.1973)—§ 3.4(e) n.72

Gallo, United States v., 654 F.Supp. 463 (E.D.N.Y.1987)—§ 20.3(b) n.38

Gallo, United States v., 394 F.Supp. 310 (D.Conn.1975)—§§ 15.3(d) n.68, 72; 15.5(b) n.69

Gallo-Vasquez v. United States, 402 F.3d 793 (7th Cir.2005)—§ 21.3(b) n.47

Galloway v. Josey, 507 So.2d 590 (Fla.1987)—§ 27.4(f) n.66

Galloway v. State, 371 Md. 379, 809 A.2d 653 (2002)—§ 24.10(b) n.35

Galloway, State v., 133 N.J. 631, 628 A.2d 735 (1993)—§ 24.8(a) n.10

Galloway, State v., 16 Kan.App.2d 54, 817 P.2d 1124 (1991)—§ 24.2(d) n.48

Galloway, State v., 275 N.W.2d 736 (Iowa 1979)—§ 7.5(b) n.23

Galloway, United States v., 316 F.3d 624 (6th Cir.2003)—§§ 6.6(a) n.7; 6.6(e) n.93

Galloway, United States v., 963 F.2d 1388 (10th Cir.1992)—§ 24.1(b) n.26

Gallup, State v., 500 N.W.2d 437 (Iowa 1993)—§§ 5.4(b) n.18; 24.8(e) n.50

Gallup, State v., 520 S.W.2d 619 (Mo.App.1975)—§§ 16.1(d) n.138, 154

Galo, United States v., 239 F.3d 572 (3d Cir.2001)—§ 26.4(i) n.196

Galvan, State v., 374 N.W.2d 269 (Minn.1985)—§ 20.3(j) n.202

Galvez, State v., 214 Ariz. 154, 150 P.3d 241 (App.2006)—§ 18.4(c) n.53

Galvin, People v., 127 Ill.2d 153, 129 Ill.Dec. 72, 535 N.E.2d 837 (1989)—§§ 3.8(e) n.191, 197

Gama-Bastidas, United States v., 222 F.3d 779 (10th Cir.2000)—§§ 19.3(e) n.210, 235, 236, 244, 246

Gambino, United States v., 59 F.3d 353 (2d Cir.1995)—§§ 18.3(b) n.26, 43

Gambino, United States v., 864 F.2d 1064 (3d Cir.1988)—§ 11.9(d) n.159

Gambino v. United States, 275 U.S. 310, 48 S.Ct. 137, 72 L.Ed. 293 (1927)—§ 3.1(a) n.7

Gamble v. Commonwealth, 68 S.W.3d 367 (Ky.2002)—§ 22.3(c) n.157

Gamble v. Oklahoma, 583 F.2d 1161 (10th Cir.1978)—§ 28.3(d) n.89

Gamble, State v., 211 W.Va. 125, 563 S.E.2d 790 (2001)—§ 18.4(c) n.53

Gamble v. State, 318 Md. 120, 567 A.2d 95 (1989)—§ 2.12(d) n.186

Gamble v. State, 257 Ga. 325, 357 S.E.2d 792 (1987)—§§ 22.3(d) n.212, 242, 245

Gamble, United States v., 327 F.3d 662 (8th Cir.2003)—§ 21.2(b) n.53

Gamble, United States v., 473 F.2d 1274 (7th Cir.1973)—§ 3.6(d) n.89

Gamboa, United States v., 439 F.3d 796 (8th Cir.2006)—§§ 18.2(b) n.14; 18.3(b) n.38, 50

Gamboa, United States v., 166 F.3d 1327 (11th Cir.1999)—§§ 21.1(h) n.226; 21.3(e) n.272, 279

Gambrel, State v., 20 Kan.App.2d 944, 894 P.2d 235 (1995)—§ 26.1(d) n.86

Gambrell, State v., 318 N.C. 249, 347 S.E.2d 390 (1986)—§ 11.2(e) n.174

Gambrill, United States v., 449 F.2d 1148 (D.C.Cir.1971)—§ 7.4(c) n.56

Games v. State, 743 N.E.2d 1132 (Ind.2001)—§ 21.6(a) n.65

Gamez, United States v., 301 F.3d 1138 (9th Cir.2002)—§§ 6.2(c) n.154, 174

Gamez-Orduno, United States v., 235 F.3d 453 (9th Cir.2000)—§§ 9.1(b) n.74; 10.5(e) n.50; 13.7(c) n.43

Gandia-Maysonet, United States v., 227 F.3d 1 (1st Cir.2000)—§ 21.4(c) n.88

Ganger v. Peyton, 379 F.2d 709 (4th Cir.1967)—§§ 22.5(a) n.6, 9

Gann v. Smith, 318 F.Supp. 409 (N.D.Miss.1970)—§ 10.2(c) n.37

Gann, United States v., 732 F.2d 714 (9th Cir.1984)—§ 13.7(c) n.52

Gannett Co. v. State, 565 A.2d 895 (Del.1989)—§ 27.2(d) n.68

Gannett Co. v. State, 571 A.2d 735 (Del.1989)—§§ 22.3(b) n.68; 23.1(d) n.132, 135, 191

Gannett Co., Inc. v. DePasquale, 443 U.S. 368, 99 S.Ct. 2898, 61 L.Ed.2d 608 (1979)—§§ 2.6(a) n.16; 23.1(d) n.120, 136; 23.1(e) n.220, 252; 24.1(a) n.2; 24.1(b) n.15

Gannon v. State, 704 A.2d 272 (Del.1998)—§§ 2.12(b) n.104; 2.12(c) n.151; 2.12(e) n.200

Gansz v. People, 888 P.2d 256 (Colo.1995)—§§ 13.1(a) n.25, 27

Gant, State v., 231 Conn. 43, 646 A.2d 835 (1994)—§§ 14.4(c) n.74; 14.4(e) n.107

Gant, United States v., 17 F.3d 935 (7th Cir.1994)—§ 9.6(a) n.36

Gant, United States v., 759 F.2d 484 (5th Cir.1985)—§ 3.1(c) n.56

Gantley, United States v., 172 F.3d 422 (6th Cir.1999)—§ 25.2(a) n.7

Gantt v. Roe, 389 F.3d 908 (9th Cir.2004)—§ 24.3(b) n.35

Ganus, People v., 185 Ill.2d 355, 236 Ill.Dec. 1, 706 N.E.2d 875 (1998)—§ 11.10(c) n.129

Gapen, State v., 104 Ohio St.3d 358, 819 N.E.2d 1047 (2004)—§ 6.9(g) n.200

Garber, State v., 674 N.W.2d 320 (S.D.2004)—§ 21.4(e) n.158

Garber, United States v., 413 F.2d 284 (2d Cir.1969)—§ 27.2(c) n.51

Garbutt, State v., 173 Vt. 277, 790 A.2d 444 (2001)—§ 6.6(e) n.93

Garcia, Ex parte, 100 S.W.3d 243 (Tex.App.2001)—§ 12.2(a) n.6

Garcia, Ex parte, 682 S.W.2d 581 (Tex.Cr.App.1985)—§ 21.2(d) n.211

Garcia v. Bertsch, 470 F.3d 748 (8th Cir.2006)—§ 24.1(b) n.19

Garcia v. Bunnell, 33 F.3d 1193 (9th Cir.1994)—§§ 11.9(b) n.69, 85; 11.9(d) n.208

Garcia, Commonwealth v., 585 Pa. 160, 888 A.2d 633 (2005)—§ 24.5(c) n.39

Garcia, People v., 36 Cal.4th 777, 31 Cal.Rptr.3d 541, 115 P.3d 1191 (2005)—§ 24.2(a) n.8

Garcia, People v., 17 P.3d 820 (Colo.App.2000)—§ 18.4(c) n.64

Garcia, People v., 77 Cal.App.4th 1269, 92 Cal.Rptr.2d 339 (2000)—§ 22.3(d) n.201

Garcia v. People, 997 P.2d 1 (Colo.2000)—§ 24.9(f) n.104

Garcia, People v., 940 P.2d 357 (Colo.1997)—§ 24.8(f) n.119

Garcia, People v., 84 N.Y.2d 336, 618 N.Y.S.2d 621, 642 N.E.2d 1077 (1994)—§ 26.3(f) n.64

Garcia, People v., 826 P.2d 1259 (Colo.1992)—§ 24.8(e) n.55

Garcia, People v., 698 P.2d 801 (Colo.1985)—§§ 22.5(a) n.4; 22.5(d) n.31

Garcia, People v., 36 Cal.3d 539, 205 Cal.Rptr. 265, 684 P.2d 826 (1984)—§ 6.2(c) n.147

Garcia v. San Antonio Metro. Transit Authority, 469 U.S. 528, 105 S.Ct. 1005, 83 L.Ed.2d 1016 (1985)—§§ 2.9(b) n.22, 24

Garcia v. Singletary, 13 F.3d 1487 (11th Cir.1994)—§ 6.6(e) n.81

Garcia, State v., 358 N.C. 382, 597 S.E.2d 724 (2004)—§§ 6.6(c) n.31; 6.6(d) n.45

Garcia, State v., 582 N.W.2d 879 (Minn.1998)—§ 21.2(e) n.321

Garcia v. State, 981 S.W.2d 683 (Tex.Crim.App.1998)—§§ 19.2(c) n.35; 19.3(b) n.161

Garcia, State v., 121 N.M. 544, 915 P.2d 300 (1996)—§ 21.4(c) n.88

Garcia, State v., 233 Conn. 44, 658 A.2d 947 (1995)—§ 27.2(c) n.61

Garcia v. State, 827 S.W.2d 937 (Tex.Cr.App.1992)—§ 3.1(d) n.112

Garcia, State v., 235 Neb. 53, 453 N.W.2d 469 (1990)—§ 7.4(e) n.90

Garcia v. State, 492 So.2d 360 (Fla.1986)—§§ 11.6(a) n.24; 11.6(d) n.124, 125

Garcia, State v., 500 N.E.2d 158 (Ind.1986)—§ 3.9(g) n.135

Garcia v. State, 667 P.2d 1148 (Wyo.1983)—§§ 14.4(d) n.86; 14.4(e) n.127

Garcia v. State, 454 S.W.2d 400 (Tex.Crim.App.1970)—§ 8.5(g) n.222

Garcia v. Superior Court, 14 Cal.4th 953, 59 Cal.Rptr.2d 858, 928 P.2d 572 (1997)—§ 26.4(f) n.101

Garcia, United States v., 401 F.3d 1008 (9th Cir.2005)—§ 21.5(a) n.43

Garcia, United States v., 340 F.3d 1013 (9th Cir.2003)—§ 12.4(d) n.75

Garcia, United States v., 232 F.3d 1309 (10th Cir.2000)—§ 4.6(e) n.97

Garcia, United States v., 182 F.3d 1165 (10th Cir.1999)—§ 5.2(a) n.9

Garcia, United States v., 78 F.3d 1457 (10th Cir.1996)—§ 27.6(b) n.20

Garcia, United States v., 65 F.3d 17 (4th Cir.1995)—§§ 10.1(c) n.47; 13.5(h) n.204

Garcia, United States v., 42 F.2d 604 (10th Cir.1994)—§ 21.4(a) n.22

Garcia, United States v., 991 F.2d 489 (8th Cir.1993)—§ 22.2(d) n.85

Garcia, United States v., 995 F.2d 556 (5th Cir.1993)—§ 18.3(b) n.9

Garcia, United States v., 897 F.2d 1413 (7th Cir.1990)—§§ 3.10(f) n.193; 10.3(b) n.32

Garcia, United States v., 909 F.2d 1346 (9th Cir.1990)—§ 21.2(g) n.396

Garcia, United States v., 890 F.2d 355 (11th Cir.1989)—§ 3.10(b) n.34

Garcia, United States v., 778 F.2d 1558 (11th Cir.1986)—§ 18.3(b) n.25

Garcia, United States v., 676 F.2d 1086 (5th Cir.1982)—§ 1.8(f) n.100

Garcia, United States v., 694 F.2d 294 (1st Cir.1982)—§ 21.2(e) n.299

Garcia, United States v., 625 F.2d 162 (7th Cir.1980)—§ 24.2(e) n.60

Garcia, United States v., 544 F.2d 681 (3d Cir.1976)—§ 21.2(d) n.182

Garcia, United States v., 519 F.2d 1343 (9th Cir.1975)—§ 13.6(d) n.55

Garcia, United States v., 431 F.2d 134 (9th Cir.1970)—§ 6.8(c) n.79

Garcia, United States v., 272 F.Supp. 286 (S.D.N.Y.1967)—§ 10.3(b) n.25

Garcia, United States v., 377 F.2d 321 (2d Cir.1967)—§ 6.4(b) n.27

Garcia-Contreras, State v., 191 Ariz. 144, 953 P.2d 536 (1998)—§§ 24.2(d) n.47; 27.6(d) n.84

Garcia-Martinez, United States v., 254 F.3d 16 (1st Cir.2001)—§ 18.3(b) n.5

Garcia-Rosa, United States v., 876 F.2d 209 (1st Cir.1989)—§ 9.1(b) n.51

Garcia-Trigo v. United States, 671 F.2d 147 (5th Cir.1982)—§ 21.5(b) n.71

Garcia-Valenzuela, United States v., 232 F.3d 1003 (9th Cir.2000)— § 21.6(a) n.60

Garden v. State, 815 A.2d 327 (Del.2003)—§§ 7.4(g) n.111; 7.5(a) n.9; 7.5(b) n.23

Gardiner, In re, 31 Misc. 364, 64 N.Y.S. 760 (Cty.Ct.1900)—§ 15.1(d) n.249

Gardiner, State v., 636 A.2d 710 (R.I.1994)—§ 7.5(b) n.21

Gardiner v. United States, 114 F.3d 734 (8th Cir.1997)—§ 21.5(e) n.147

Gardiner, United States v., 955 F.2d 1492 (11th Cir.1992)—§§ 12.1(a) n.18; 17.1(c) n.45

Gardner v. Barnett, 175 F.3d 580 (7th Cir.1999)—§ 22.3(a) n.23

Gardner v. Bradenton Herald, 413 So.2d 10 (Fla.1982)—§ 23.1(c) n.119

Gardner v. Broderick, 392 U.S. 273, 88 S.Ct. 1913, 20 L.Ed.2d 1082 (1968)—§§ 2.10(b) n.41; 8.10(f) n.130

Gardner v. California, 393 U.S. 367, 89 S.Ct. 580, 21 L.Ed.2d 601 (1969)— §§ 11.2(d) n.122, 125, 126

Gardner v. City of Columbus, 841 F.2d 1272 (6th Cir.1988)—§ 1.8(d) n.74

Gardner v. City of Newburgh, 2 Johns. Ch. 162 (N.Y.1816)—§ 2.4(b) n.81

Gardner v. Florida, 430 U.S. 349, 97 S.Ct. 1197, 51 L.Ed.2d 393 (1977)—§§ 1.8(e) n.96, 97; 2.7(a) n.54; 2.7(b) n.90; 2.7(c) n.198; 26.1(b) n.26; 26.4(d) n.40; 26.4(g) n.117; 26.5(c) n.41

Gardner, State v., 8 S.W.3d 66 (Mo.1999)—§ 13.7(c) n.63

Gardner v. State, 332 Ark. 33, 963 S.W.2d 590 (1998)—§ 13.7(c) n.60

Gardner, State v., 126 Idaho 428, 885 P.2d 1144 (Idaho Ct.App.1994)— § 24.3(b) n.77

Gardner, State v., 844 P.2d 293 (Utah 1992)—§ 21.2(b) n.48

Gardner, State v., 741 S.W.2d 1 (Mo.1987)—§ 10.2(b) n.19

Gardner, State v., 311 N.C. 489, 319 S.E.2d 591 (1984)—§ 6.2(c) n.107

Gardner, State v., 626 S.W.2d 721 (Tenn.Crim.App.1981)—§ 11.2(g) n.281

Gardner, State v., 600 S.W.2d 614 (Mo.App.1980)—§ 14.3(c) n.64

Gardner, United States v., 480 F.2d 929 (10th Cir.1973)—§ 3.5(c) n.111

Garfield, State v., 552 P.2d 129 (Utah 1976)—§ 21.4(g) n.232

Garguilo, United States v., 554 F.2d 59 (2d Cir.1977)—§ 19.6(b) n.12

Garibay, United States v., 143 F.3d 534 (9th Cir.1998)—§ 6.8(a) n.36

Garib-Bazain, United States v., 222 F.3d 17 (1st Cir.2000)—§ 27.2(c) n.57

Garland, Ex parte, 71 U.S. (4 Wallace) 333, 18 L.Ed. 366 (1866)— § 26.2(c) n.72

Garland v. Cox, 472 F.2d 875 (4th Cir.1973)—§§ 11.8(c) n.54, 55

Garland v. State, 788 N.E.2d 425 (Ind.2003)—§ 22.4(c) n.29

Garland, State v., 617 S.W.2d 176 (Tenn.Crim.App.1981)—§ 20.6(b) n.45

Garlotte v. Fordice, 515 U.S. 39, 115 S.Ct. 1948, 132 L.Ed.2d 36 (1995)—§ 28.3(a) n.36

Garmon v. Johnson, 243 Ga. 855, 257 S.E.2d 276 (1979)—§ 15.1(f) n.273

Garmon v. Lockhart, 938 F.2d 120 (8th Cir.1991)—§ 21.3(b) n.71

Garmon, State v., 972 S.W.2d 706 (Tenn.Crim.1998)—§ 18.4(c) n.59

Garner v. Jones, 529 U.S. 244, 120 S.Ct. 1362, 146 L.Ed.2d 236 (2000)— § 1.7(j) n.227

Garner, People v., 72 Cal.App.3d 214, 139 Cal.Rptr. 838 (1977)— § 13.4(c) n.101

Garner, State v., 270 Conn. 458, 853 A.2d 478 (2004)—§§ 7.4(c) n.48, 51

Garner, State v., 260 Neb. 41, 614 N.W.2d 319 (2000)—§ 6.2(c) n.105

Garner v. State, 314 A.2d 908 (Del.Supr.1973)—§§ 9.4(d) n.80, 88

Garner, United States v., 338 F.3d 78 (1st Cir.2003)—§ 9.1(b) n.55

Garner, United States v., 837 F.2d 1404 (7th Cir.1987)—§ 16.2(h) n.157

Garner v. United States, 424 U.S. 648, 96 S.Ct. 1178, 47 L.Ed.2d 370 (1976)—§§ 1.5(c) n.95; 2.10(b) n.7

Garner, State ex rel. v. Gray, 59 Wis.2d 323, 208 N.W.2d 161 (1973)— § 18.4(c) n.48

Garnick v. Miller, 81 Nev. 372, 403 P.2d 850 (1965)—§ 11.3(b) n.38

Garofalo, People v., 71 App.Div.2d 782, 419 N.Y.S.2d 784 (1979)— § 27.3(d) n.64

Garofalo, United States v., 496 F.2d 510 (8th Cir.1974)—§ 3.3(e) n.191

Garrard, State v., 170 Ohio App.3d 487, 867 N.E.2d 887 (Ohio App.2007)— § 27.5(d) n.128

Garrett, People v., 179 Ill.2d 239, 227 Ill.Dec. 921, 688 N.E.2d 614 (1997)—§ 7.3(b) n.36

Garrett, People v., 139 Ill.2d 189, 151 Ill.Dec. 329, 564 N.E.2d 784 (1990)—§ 22.3(d) n.215

Garrett v. State, 737 N.E.2d 388 (Ind.2000)—§ 21.6(c) n.118

Garrett, State v., 14 Kan.App.2d 8, 780 P.2d 168 (1989)—§ 26.9(b) n.29

Garrett, State v., 182 W.Va. 166, 386 S.E.2d 823 (1989)—§ 22.3(a) n.29

Garrett v. State, 466 N.E.2d 8 (Ind.1984)—§ 9.1(b) n.47

Garrett v. State, 682 S.W.2d 301 (Tex.Crim.App.1984)—§ 6.8(a) n.8

Garrett, State v., 16 Ariz.App. 427, 493 P.2d 1232 (1972)—§ 12.4(a) n.5

Garrett v. State, 270 P.2d 1101 (Okla.Crim.App.1954)—§§ 3.4(e) n.91, 95

Garrett, United States v., 238 F.3d 293 (5th Cir.2000)—§ 20.6(b) n.36

Garrett, United States v., 179 F.3d 1143 (9th Cir.1999)—§ 11.4(c) n.74

Garrett, United States v., 149 F.3d 1018 (9th Cir.1998)—§ 11.4(d) n.110

Garrett, United States v., 961 F.2d 743 (8th Cir.1992)—§ 17.2(d) n.100

Garrett, United States v., 797 F.2d 656 (8th Cir.1986)—§§ 15.7(d) n.66, 71

Garrett v. United States, 471 U.S. 773, 105 S.Ct. 2407, 85 L.Ed.2d 764 (1985)—§§ 6.4(e) n.100; 17.4(b) n.91, 99

Garrett, State ex rel. v. Dally, 188 S.W.3d 111 (Mo.App.2006)— § 18.4(d) n.90

Garrey, Commonwealth v., 436 Mass. 422, 765 N.E.2d 725 (2002)— §§ 22.3(d) n.221, 250; 22.3(e) n.274

Garrison, State v., 118 Wash.2d 870, 827 P.2d 1388 (1992)—§ 3.4(d) n.51

Garrison v. State, 88 Md.App. 475, 594 A.2d 1264 (1991)—§ 24.7(a) n.10

Garrison, United States v., 849 F.2d 103 (4th Cir.1988)—§§ 22.3(d) n.229, 247

Garrity v. New Jersey, 385 U.S. 493, 87 S.Ct. 616, 17 L.Ed.2d 562 (1967)— §§ 2.10(b) n.7, 39; 8.10(e) n.123

Garrity v. New Jersey, 385 U.S. 511, 87 S.Ct. 636, 17 L.Ed.2d 586 (1967)— § 8.10(f) n.130

Garrow, State v., 480 N.W.2d 256 (Iowa 1992)—§ 3.10(c) n.84

Garsson, United States v., 291 F. 646 (S.D.N.Y.1923)—§§ 1.5(e) n.207; 1.6(e) n.322; 20.1(b) n.23

Gartin, State v., 271 N.W.2d 902 (Iowa 1978)—§ 15.4(b) n.36

Gartland, State v., 149 N.J. 456, 694 A.2d 564 (1997)—§§ 27.5(a) n.1, 22

Garvin, Commonwealth v., 448 Pa. 258, 293 A.2d 33 (1972)—§ 9.4(d) n.77

Garvin, State v., 242 Conn. 296, 699 A.2d 921 (Conn.1997)—§ 21.2(d) n.223

Gary, Ex parte, 895 S.W.2d 465 (Tex.App.1995)—§ 27.4(c) n.24

Gary v. State, 760 So.2d 743 (Miss.2000)—§§ 18.5(c) n.84; 24.6(d) n.43

Gary, State v., 348 N.C. 510, 501 S.E.2d 57 (1998)—§ 11.4(b) n.24

Gary, State v., 78 N.C.App. 29, 337 S.E.2d 70 (1985)—§ 15.4(e) n.139

Gary v. State, 471 N.E.2d 695 (Ind.1984)—§ 6.2(c) n.107

Gary, United States v., 291 F.3d 30 (D.C.Cir.2002)—§§ 13.7(c) n.45; 21.2(d) n.206

Gary, United States v., 74 F.3d 304 (1st Cir.1996)—§ 13.4(a) n.11

Gary v. United States, 499 A.2d 815 (D.C.App.1985)—§ 24.2(b) n.24

Garza v. Lappin, 253 F.3d 918 (7th Cir.2001)—§ 28.9(a) n.7

Garza, People v., 92 Ill.App.3d 723, 48 Ill.Dec. 44, 415 N.E.2d 1328 (1981)—§§ 14.2(d) n.58; 20.4(b) n.36

Garza, State v., 150 Wash.2d 360, 77 P.3d 347 (2003)—§ 24.2(d) n.48

Garza, State v., 256 Neb. 752, 592 N.W.2d 485 (1999)—§ 17.1(d) n.53

Garza v. State, 974 S.W.2d 251 (Tex.App.1998)—§ 2.6(b) n.69

Garza, State v., 563 N.W.2d 406 (S.D.1997)—§ 7.4(e) n.89

Garza, United States v., 608 F.2d 659 (5th Cir.1979)—§ 24.7(e) n.38

Garza-Juarez, United States v., 992 F.2d 896 (9th Cir.1993)—§ 5.4(b) n.18

Gaskin v. State, 618 So.2d 103 (Miss.1993)—§ 21.4(c) n.73

Gaskins, State v., 210 W.Va. 580, 558 S.E.2d 579 (2001)—§ 21.6(a) n.25

Gaskins, United States v., 485 F.2d 1046 (D.C.Cir.1973)—§ 21.4(f) n.214

Gasparro, State v., 194 Conn. 96, 480 A.2d 509 (1984)—§ 18.2(d) n.63

Gasper v. District Court, 74 Idaho 388, 264 P.2d 679 (1953)—§ 15.2(e) n.141

Gastelum-Almeida, United States v., 298 F.3d 1167 (9th Cir.2002)— §§ 13.7(c) n.43; 18.3(b) n.5

Gaston v. Palmer, 447 F.3d 1165 (9th Cir.2006)—§ 28.5(b) n.50

Gaston, State v., 198 Conn. 435, 503 A.2d 594 (1986)—§ 18.2(b) n.25

Gaston, United States v., 357 F.3d 77 (D.C.Cir.2004)—§ 6.7(b) n.43

Gatch, State v., 669 So.2d 676 (La.App.1996)—§ 16.1(g) n.235

Gates, People v., 434 Mich. 146, 452 N.W.2d 627 (1990)—§ 17.4(a) n.62

Gates, State v., 299 S.C. 92, 382 S.E.2d 886 (1989)—§ 21.2(f) n.368

Gates, State v., 466 S.W.2d 681 (Mo.1971)—§ 11.2(c) n.90

Gates, United States v., 967 F.2d 497 (11th Cir.1992)—§ 5.3(d) n.42

Gates, United States v., 557 F.2d 1086 (5th Cir.1977)—§§ 11.3(c) n.55; 20.3(b) n.43

Gateway 2000, Inc. v. Limoges, 552 N.W.2d 591 (S.D.1996)—§§ 3.2(e) n.163; 3.6(f) n.154

Gatewood, United States v., 230 F.3d 186 (6th Cir.2000)—§ 26.4(h) n.159

Gatlin v. United States, 833 A.2d 995 (D.C.App.2003)—§ 9.1(c) n.103

Gatti, In re Conduct of, 330 Or. 517, 8 P.3d 966 (2000)—§ 6.4(e) n.91

Gattis v. State, 697 A.2d 1174 (Del.1997)—§ 22.3(d) n.228

Gatto, United States v., 763 F.2d 1040 (9th Cir.1985)—§§ 20.3(a) n.7, 12; 20.6(a) n.6

Gaudin, United States v., 515 U.S. 506, 115 S.Ct. 2310, 132 L.Ed.2d 444 (1995)—§§ 2.9(d) n.55, 66; 16.1(g) n.246; 22.1(a) n.16, 17; 24.10(a) n.6; 27.5(d) n.126; 28.6(e) n.62

Gaughran, State v., 260 N.J.Super. 283, 615 A.2d 1293 (1992)—§§ 1.7(i) n.204; 15.5(b) n.45; 15.7(f) n.142, 175

Gaul, Commonwealth v., 590 Pa. 175, 912 A.2d 252 (2006)—§ 6.7(c) n.111

Gault, In re, 387 U.S. 1, 87 S.Ct. 1428, 18 L.Ed.2d 527 (1967)—§§ 2.4(b) n.57; 2.8(b) n.41; 2.8(c) n.75; 6.9(g) n.172; 6.10(e) n.75; 11.1(b) n.58; 25.1(c) n.24

Gault, State v., 551 N.W.2d 719 (Minn.App.1996)—§§ 8.11(c) n.66, 69

Gault, United States v., 141 F.3d 1399 (10th Cir.1998)—§ 22.2(d) n.77

Gauthier, People v., 28 Mich.App. 318, 184 N.W.2d 488 (1970)—§ 17.2(b) n.46

Gautier, State v., 871 A.2d 347 (R.I. 2005)—§ 26.10(d) n.98

Gauze, People v., 15 Cal.3d 709, 125 Cal.Rptr. 773, 542 P.2d 1365 (1975)—§ 11.6(a) n.26

Gaviria, United States v., 805 F.2d 1108 (2d Cir.1986)—§§ 3.9(f) n.91, 94

Gawron v. Roberts, 113 Idaho 330, 743 P.2d 983 (1987)—§ 26.10(b) n.16

Gay v. State, 562 So.2d 283 (Ala.Crim.App.1990)—§§ 11.2(e) n.157, 159

Gay, United States v., 240 F.3d 1222 (10th Cir.2001)—§ 3.6(b) n.59

Gay, United States v., 774 F.2d 368 (10th Cir.1985)—§ 6.7(b) n.73

Gay, United States v., 567 F.2d 916 (9th Cir.1978)—§§ 17.2(c) n.84, 86

Gay, United States v., 577 F.2d 465 (8th Cir.1978)—§ 19.3(b) n.149

Gayle, United States v., 967 F.2d 483 (11th Cir.1992)—§§ 19.2(c) n.24; 19.2(f) n.92; 19.3(a) n.53, 64

Gayler v. State, 957 P.2d 855 (Wyo.1998)—§ 27.5(d) n.116

Gaytan, United States v., 74 F.3d 545 (5th Cir.1996)—§§ 3.4(e) n.84; 4.6(e) n.80; 19.2(c) n.25

Gayther, People v., 110 Cal.App.3d 79, 167 Cal.Rptr. 700 (1980)—§ 26.1(d) n.81

Gbemisola, United States v., 225 F.3d 753 (D.C.Cir.2000)—§§ 3.2(j) n.262; 4.6(a) n.15

G.C., In re State in Interest of, 121 N.J.Super. 108, 296 A.2d 102 (1972)—§ 3.9(k) n.246

G.E., In re, 879 A.2d 672 (D.C.App.2005)—§ 6.9(f) n.134

Geaneas v. Willets, 911 F.2d 579 (11th Cir.1990)—§ 13.4(a) n.29

Gearns, People v., 14 Misc.2d 1010, 180 N.Y.S.2d 875 (Mag.Ct.1958)—§ 15.1(b) n.99

Geary, Commonwealth v., 352 Mass. 427, 226 N.E.2d 253 (1967)—§ 6.8(a) n.33

Gebbie, United States v., 294 F.3d 540 (3d Cir.2002)—§§ 21.2(d) n.150, 158; 21.2(e) n.325

Gebro, United States v., 948 F.2d 1118 (9th Cir.1991)—§§ 12.1(a) n.14; 12.3(a) n.27

Gecas, United States v., 120 F.3d 1419 (11th Cir.1997)—§§ 2.1 n.55; 2.10(c) n.51, 52, 55, 61, 85

Geders v. United States, 425 U.S. 80, 96 S.Ct. 1330, 47 L.Ed.2d 592 (1976)—§§ 11.8(a) n.5; 11.10(d) n.205; 24.4(d) n.28; 27.6(d) n.109

Gedutis, State v., 163 Vt. 591, 653 A.2d 761 (1994)—§ 26.10(b) n.25

Gee, People v., 99 N.Y.2d 158, 753 N.Y.S.2d 19, 782 N.E.2d 1155 (2002)—§ 7.4(f) n.106

Gee v. State, 110 Ga.App. 439, 138 S.E.2d 700 (1964)—§ 16.2(g) n.113

Geelan, United States v., 520 F.2d 585 (9th Cir.1975)—§§ 18.2(c) n.48; 18.2(d) n.69

Geelan, United States v., 509 F.2d 737 (8th Cir.1974)—§ 15.4(b) n.68

Geeslin, Ex parte, 505 So.2d 1246 (Ala.1986)—§ 24.3(b) n.58

Gefroh, State v., 458 N.W.2d 479 (N.D.1990)—§§ 18.5(c) n.87, 90

Geibel, United States v., 369 F.3d 682 (2d Cir.2004)—§§ 16.1(f) n.213; 16.1(g) n.282

Geiger v. State, 532 So.2d 1298 (Fla.App.1988)—§§ 18.5(a) n.39; 21.2(d) n.278

Geisendorfer, People v., 991 P.2d 308 (Colo.App.1999)—§ 27.6(d) n.127

Geisler, State v., 222 Conn. 672, 610 A.2d 1225 (1992)—§ 9.4(a) n.38

Geisser, Petition of, 627 F.2d 745 (5th Cir.1980)—§§ 21.2(e) n.327, 346

Geisser v. United States, 513 F.2d 862 (5th Cir.1975)—§ 21.2(e) n.338

Geittmann, United States v., 733 F.2d 1419 (10th Cir.1984)—§ 6.4(g) n.142

Gelb, United States v., 881 F.2d 1155 (2d Cir.1989)—§§ 22.2(d) n.66, 76

Gelbard v. United States, 408 U.S. 41, 92 S.Ct. 2357, 33 L.Ed.2d 179 (1972)—§§ 8.9(b) n.14; 14.4(b) n.39; 15.5(b) n.98; 15.7(d) n.80

Gelfand v. People, 196 Colo. 487, 586 P.2d 1331 (1978)—§ 21.2(h) n.415

Gelhaar v. State, 58 Wis.2d 547, 207 N.W.2d 88 (1973)—§ 6.6(e) n.63

Gelinas, State v., 147 N.H. 437, 790 A.2d 138 (2002)—§ 5.2(a) n.20

Gell-Iren, United States v., 146 F.3d 827 (10th Cir.1998)—§ 6.8(b) n.57

Gementera, United States v., 379 F.3d 596 (9th Cir.2004)—§ 26.9(b) n.78

Genao, United States v., 281 F.3d 305 (1st Cir.2002)—§ 6.7(b) n.72

Gendreau, State v., 106 R.I. 332, 259 A.2d 855 (1969)—§ 6.8(a) n.31

Genesee Chief, The, 53 U.S. (10 How.) 443, 13 L.Ed. 1058 (1851)—§ 2.9(b) n.16

Genre, State v., 712 N.W.2d 624 (N.D.2006)—§§ 6.6(e) n.91; 21.2(h) n.419

Gentile, Commonwealth v., 437 Mass. 569, 773 N.E.2d 428 (2002)—§ 3.3(f) n.211

Gentile v. State Bar of Nevada, 501 U.S. 1030, 111 S.Ct. 2720, 115 L.Ed.2d 888 (1991)—§§ 23.1(a) n.4; 23.1(b) n.24, 27, 37

Gentile, United States v., 816 F.2d 1157 (7th Cir.1987)—§ 17.4(a) n.45

Gentile, United States v., 610 F.2d 541 (8th Cir.1979)—§ 26.10(c) n.51

Gentry v. Deuth, 456 F.3d 687 (6th Cir.2006)—§§ 28.2(b) n.31; 28.3(a) n.28

Gentry v. Roe, 320 F.3d 891 (9th Cir.2002)—§ 11.10(c) n.91

Gentry, State v., 363 S.C. 93, 610 S.E.2d 494 (2005)—§§ 19.2(c) n.22; 19.2(e) n.55; 19.3(e) n.222

Georgacarakos, United States v., 988 F.2d 1289 (1st Cir.1993)—§§ 16.2(c) n.45, 49

George v. Commonwealth, 242 Va. 264, 411 S.E.2d 12 (1991)—§ 22.3(c) n.133

George, People v., 69 Mich.App. 403, 245 N.W.2d 65 (1976)—§ 21.5(f) n.161

George, State v., 264 Neb. 26, 645 N.W.2d 777 (2002)—§ 13.7(c) n.64

George, State v., 557 N.W.2d 575 (Minn.1997)—§ 3.10(a) n.8

George v. State, 397 N.E.2d 1027 (Ind.App.1979)—§ 20.5(f) n.78

George, United States v., 403 F.3d 470 (7th Cir.2005)—§ 26.6(c) n.42

George, United States v., 987 F.2d 1428 (9th Cir.1993)—§ 6.9(b) n.34

George, United States v., 971 F.2d 1113 (4th Cir.1992)—§§ 9.3(e) n.65, 81; 10.6(b) n.12

George, United States v., 975 F.2d 72 (2d Cir.1992)—§ 3.1(c) n.72

George, United States v., 975 F.2d 1431 (9th Cir.1992)—§ 7.5(b) n.21

George, United States v., 869 F.2d 333 (7th Cir.1989)—§ 21.3(b) n.66

George, United States v., 883 F.2d 1407 (9th Cir.1989)—§§ 3.6(a) n.19; 3.10(b) n.44

George, United States v., 444 F.2d 310 (6th Cir.1971)—§ 8.14(c) n.35

George Anthony W., State v., 200 W.Va. 86, 488 S.E.2d 361 (1996)—§ 6.3(c) n.53

George J., State v., 910 A.2d 931, 280 Conn. 551 (2006)—§ 22.3(d) n.204

Georgeoff, State v., 163 Ariz. 434, 788 P.2d 1185 (1990)—§ 21.2(d) n.177

Georgia v. McCollum, 505 U.S. 42, 112 S.Ct. 2348, 120 L.Ed.2d 33 (1992)—§ 22.3(d) n.203

Georgia v. Rachel, 384 U.S. 780, 86 S.Ct. 1783, 16 L.Ed.2d 925 (1966)—§ 13.5(d) n.86

Georgia v. Randolph, _____ U.S. _____, 126 S.Ct. 1515, 164 L.Ed.2d 208 (2006)—§§ 3.10(d) n.117, 119

Gerace, United States v., 997 F.2d 1293 (9th Cir.1993)—§ 21.2(d) n.192

Gerald, State v., 113 N.J. 40, 549 A.2d 792 (1988)—§ 6.9(g) n.183

Gerchberg, People v., 131 Cal.App.3d 618, 181 Cal.Rptr. 505 (1982)— § 16.4(c) n.53

Gerdes, State v., 233 Neb. 528, 446 N.W.2d 224 (1989)—§ 17.4(a) n.42

Gerena, United States v., 677 F.Supp. 1266 (D.Conn.1987)—§ 15.4(d) n.123

Gerhardt, State v., 97 Idaho 603, 549 P.2d 262 (1976)—§ 10.2(a) n.11

Gerisch v. Meadows, 278 Ga. 641, 604 S.E.2d 462 (2004)—§ 21.6(a) n.62

Gerlaugh v. Commonwealth, 156 S.W.3d 747 (Ky.2005)—§ 7.4(c) n.50

Gerlaugh v. Lewis, 898 F.Supp. 1388 (D.Ariz.1995)—§ 24.8(f) n.98

Germain v. State, 363 Md. 511, 769 A.2d 931 (2001)—§ 26.5(c) n.59

Germano, State v., 559 A.2d 1031 (R.I.1989)—§ 3.3(c) n.109

Germany v. United States, 2001 ICJ 466 (June 27, 2001)—§ 1.7(c) n.28

Germonto, State v., 868 P.2d 50 (Utah 1993)—§§ 17.3(b) n.12, 14

Germosen, People v., 86 N.Y.2d 822, 633 N.Y.S.2d 472, 657 N.E.2d 493 (1995)—§ 15.2(c) n.83

Gernie, United States v., 252 F.2d 664 (2d Cir.1958)—§ 21.5(f) n.164

Gerns, State v., 145 N.J. 216, 678 A.2d 634 (1996)—§§ 21.2(d) n.158, 264

Gerry, United States v., 845 F.2d 34 (1st Cir.1988)—§ 3.6(d) n.99

Gershon v. Broomfield, 131 Ariz. 507, 642 P.2d 852 (1982)—§§ 8.2(b) n.23; 8.2(c) n.42

Gerstein v. Pugh, 420 U.S. 103, 95 S.Ct. 854, 43 L.Ed.2d 54 (1975)— §§ 2.6(b) n.33; 2.7(b) n.82; 2.7(c) n.226; 2.7(d) n.244; 3.1(j) n.241, 252; 3.3(a) n.23, 24; 3.5(a) n.47; 9.4(a) n.9; 12.3(d) n.106; 12.4(a) n.31; 13.5(e) n.96; 14.2(a) n.4; 15.1(b) n.25, 39, 115; 15.1(c) n.141; 26.10(b) n.41

Gersten v. Rundle, 833 F.Supp. 906 (S.D.Fla.1993)—§ 8.8(h) n.185

Gersten v. Senkowski, 426 F.3d 588 (2d Cir.2005)—§§ 11.10(c) n.126, 152

Gervato, United States v., 474 F.2d 40 (3d Cir.1973)—§ 3.4(g) n.131

Gessert, State v., 21 Minn. 369 (1875)— § 16.4(c) n.44

Gessler, State ex rel. v. Mazzone, 212 W.Va. 368, 572 S.E.2d 891 (2002)—§§ 21.3(f) n.426, 432; 25.1(d) n.73

Gethers, People v., 86 N.Y.2d 159, 630 N.Y.S.2d 281, 654 N.E.2d 102 (1995)—§ 9.4(d) n.82

Gethers, State v., 197 Conn. 369, 497 A.2d 408 (1985)—§§ 2.12(e) n.211; 11.4(d) n.112; 11.5(g) n.110

Gethers, State v., 193 Conn. 526, 480 A.2d 435 (1984)—§ 11.5(c) n.32

Getsy, State v., 84 Ohio St.3d 180, 702 N.E.2d 866 (1998)—§ 13.2(a) n.5

Geyer, Commonwealth v., 546 Pa. 586, 687 A.2d 815 (1996)—§ 17.4(c) n.153

Ghent, People v., 43 Cal.3d 739, 43 Cal.3d 739, 239 Cal.Rptr. 82, 739 P.2d 1250 (1987)—§ 1.7(c) n.16

Gher v. District Court, 183 Colo. 316, 516 P.2d 643 (1973)—§§ 8.8(e) n.131, 138

Gholston, People v., 332 Ill.App.3d 179, 265 Ill.Dec. 509, 772 N.E.2d 880 (2002)—§ 28.11(b) n.15

Giacalone v. Lucas, 445 F.2d 1238 (6th Cir.1971)—§ 3.6(d) n.86

Giannattasio, United States v., 979 F.2d 98 (7th Cir.1992)—§§ 13.2(a) n.4; 13.2(c) n.56

Giannetta, United States v., 909 F.2d 571 (1st Cir.1990)—§ 3.9(j) n.220

Giardino v. Bourbeau, 193 Conn. 116, 475 A.2d 298 (1984)—§ 18.4(c) n.50

Gibbons, State v., 105 N.J. 67, 519 A.2d 350 (1987)—§ 5.3(a) n.5

Gibbons, United States v., 1995 WL 121297 (S.D.N.Y.1995)—§§ 15.5(b) n.95, 96

Gibbs, Commonwealth v., 520 Pa. 151, 553 A.2d 409 (1989)—§ 6.9(f) n.134

Gibbs, State v., 254 Conn. 578, 758 A.2d 327 (2000)—§§ 22.2(a) n.8; 22.2(d) n.76, 77

Gibbs, State v., 253 Neb. 241, 570 N.W.2d 326 (1997)—§ 27.2(c) n.62

Gibbs v. State, 238 Neb. 268, 470 N.W.2d 558 (1991)—§§ 14.2(g) n.93, 96

Gibbs, United States v., ____ F.3d ____, 2007 WL 3131667 (6th Cir.2007)—§ 26.3(f) n.59

Gibbs, United States v., 182 F.3d 408 (6th Cir.1999)—§§ 22.3(d) n.176, 245

Gibson, Commonwealth v., 547 Pa. 71, 688 A.2d 1152 (1997)—§ 6.3(c) n.49

Gibson, Commonwealth v., 389 Pa.Super. 518, 567 A.2d 724 (1989)—§ 1.11(a) n.5

Gibson, Commonwealth v., 368 Mass. 518, 333 N.E.2d 400 (1975)—§ 15.2(d) n.106

Gibson v. County of Washoe, 290 F.3d 1175 (9th Cir.2002)—§ 12.2(d) n.50

Gibson v. Florida Legislative Investigation Committee, 372 U.S. 539, 83 S.Ct. 889, 9 L.Ed.2d 929 (1963)—§ 8.8(d) n.64

Gibson v. Halleck, 254 F.Supp. 159 (D.D.C.1966)—§ 14.4(c) n.65

Gibson v. State, 758 So.2d 782 (La.2000)—§ 3.3(b) n.59

Gibson v. State, 334 S.C. 515, 514 S.E.2d 320 (1999)—§§ 21.3(c) n.174; 24.3(b) n.77

Gibson v. State, 731 So.2d 1087 (Miss.1998)—§ 13.7(a) n.5

Gibson v. State, 261 Ga. 313, 404 S.E.2d 781 (1991)—§ 3.10(b) n.66

Gibson v. State, 803 S.W.2d 316 (Tex.Cr.App.1991)—§ 21.2(e) n.306

Gibson v. State, 555 So.2d 784 (Ala.Cr.App.1989)—§ 24.3(c) n.82

Gibson, State v., 228 Neb. 455, 422 N.W.2d 570 (1988)—§§ 6.6(e) n.65; 6.7(c) n.121

Gibson, State v., 68 N.J. 499, 348 A.2d 769 (1975)—§ 21.2(b) n.81

Gibson, State v., 132 Iowa 53, 106 N.W. 270 (1906)—§ 16.1(d) n.141

Gibson v. Turpin, 270 Ga. 855, 513 S.E.2d 186 (1999)—§ 28.12(b) n.13

Gibson, United States v., 434 F.3d 1234 (11th Cir.2006)—§ 26.4(i) n.201

Gibson, United States v., 356 F.3d 761 (7th Cir.2004)—§§ 21.2(b) n.83, 86; 21.6(a) n.67

Gibson v. United States, 271 F.3d 247 (6th Cir.2001)—§ 24.4(d) n.65

Gibson, United States v., 135 F.3d 257 (2d Cir.1998)—§ 7.4(e) n.88

Gibson, United States v., 135 F.3d 1124 (6th Cir.1998)—§ 21.2(g) n.394

Gibson, United States v., 55 F.3d 173 (5th Cir.1995)—§ 24.8(a) n.9

Gibson, United States v., 480 F.Supp. 339 (S.D.Ohio 1979)—§ 15.4(g) n.149

Gibson, United States v., 392 F.2d 373 (4th Cir.1968)—§§ 6.6(c) n.20; 6.6(f) n.105

Giddins v. State, 393 Md. 1, 899 A.2d 139 (2006)—§ 25.2(a) n.5

Gideon v. Wainwright, 372 U.S. 335, 83
S.Ct. 792, 9 L.Ed.2d 799 (1963)—
§§ 2.3 n.2; 2.5(b) n.14; 2.6(a) n.5;
2.6(b) n.34; 2.7(c) n.110; 2.9(d)
n.94; 2.9(g) n.189, 192; 6.4(a) n.11;
11.1(a) n.19; 11.2(a) n.6; 11.2(e)
n.143; 11.2(f) n.238; 11.2(g) n.257;
11.5(a) n.5; 11.8(a) n.13; 27.6(d)
n.69

Giebler, State v., 22 Wash.App. 640, 591
P.2d 465 (1979)—§ 21.2(d) n.222

Gieger, United States v., 190 F.3d 661
(5th Cir.1999)—§ 24.10(b) n.26

Giessinger, State v., 235 Neb. 140, 454
N.W.2d 289 (1990)—§ 10.2(a) n.1

Gifford, State v., 595 A.2d 1049
(Me.1991)—§ 19.2(b) n.17

Gigante, United States v., 85 F.3d 83 (2d
Cir.1996)—§ 12.1(a) n.7

Gigley, United States v., 213 F.3d 509
(10th Cir.2000)—§§ 21.5(a) n.40,
45

Giglio v. United States, 405 U.S. 150,
92 S.Ct. 763, 31 L.Ed.2d 104
(1972)—§§ 15.7(e) n.109, 113;
24.3(d) n.108

Gigot, United States v., 147 F.3d 1193
(10th Cir.1998)—§§ 21.4(c) n.77;
21.5(c) n.83

Gil, State v., 543 A.2d 1296
(R.I.1988)—§ 6.9(f) n.135

Gil, United States v., 142 F.3d 1398
(11th Cir.1998)—§§ 17.4(a) n.5, 34

Gilbert v. California, 388 U.S. 263, 87
S.Ct. 1951, 18 L.Ed.2d 1178
(1967)—§§ 7.2(b) n.11; 7.3(b) n.10;
7.3(c) n.51; 7.3(f) n.103; 7.4(a) n.2;
10.3(d) n.59

Gilbert v. Lockhart, 930 F.2d 1356 (8th
Cir.1991)—§§ 11.5(c) n.55, 57

Gilbert, People v., 199 N.Y. 10, 92 N.E.
85 (1910)—§§ 19.1(a) n.12; 19.3(a)
n.50

Gilbert, State v., 103 S.W.3d 743
(Mo.2003)—§§ 6.2(c) n.102; 6.9(a)
n.12

Gilbert v. State, 951 P.2d 98
(Okl.Cr.1997)—§§ 6.2(c) n.152;
6.7(b) n.43; 6.9(a) n.12

Gilbert, State v., 68 Wash.App. 379, 842
P.2d 1029 (1993)—§ 25.4(b) n.22

Gilbert, United States v., 266 F.3d 1180
(9th Cir.2001)—§ 13.5(a) n.6

Gilbert, United States v., 181 F.3d 152
(1st Cir.1999)—§ 1.2(c) n.122

Gilbert, United States v., 198 F.3d 1293
(11th Cir.1999)—§§ 13.5(h) n.130,
156, 159, 160, 163, 166, 168, 178,
183; 15.3(d) n.63; 15.7(f) n.138,
143

Gilbert, United States v., 425 F.2d 490
(D.C.Cir.1969)—§§ 12.3(g) n.149;
12.4(c) n.60

Gilbert v. United States, 359 F.2d 285
(9th Cir.1966)—§ 16.1(h) n.311

Gilberts, State v., 497 N.W.2d 93
(N.D.1993)—§ 3.7(a) n.17

Gilbreath v. Wallace, 292 Ala. 267, 292
So.2d 651 (1974)—§§ 2.12(b) n.91;
2.12(e) n.212

Gilchrist v. Commonwealth, 227 Va.
540, 317 S.E.2d 784 (1984)—
§ 20.3(m) n.237

Gilchrist v. O'Keefe, 260 F.3d 87 (2d
Cir.2001)—§§ 11.4(b) n.29; 11.4(d)
n.115

Gilchrist v. State, 340 Md. 606, 667
A.2d 876 (1995)—§§ 22.3(d) n.192,
237

Gilchrist, United States v., 130 F.3d
1131 (3d Cir.1997)—§ 21.2(e)
n.322

Gilday v. Callahan, 866 F.Supp. 611
(D.Mass.1994)—§§ 23.2(d) n.64,
69, 70

Gildea, State v., 240 Neb. 780, 484
N.W.2d 467 (1992)—§ 21.2(d)
n.191

Giles, United States v., 967 F.2d 382
(10th Cir.1992)—§ 6.9(g) n.162

Giles v. United States, 400 A.2d 1051
(D.C.1979)—§ 3.5(a) n.8

Gill v. Commonwealth, 7 S.W.3d 365
(Ky.1999)—§ 23.2(a) n.39

Gill, State v., 681 N.W.2d 832
(N.D.2004)—§ 26.6(c) n.40

Gill v. State ex rel. Mobley, 242 Ark. 797, 416 S.W.2d 269 (1967)—§ 8.1(c) n.37

Gill, United States v., 55 F.2d 399 (D.N.M.1931)—§§ 15.1(f) n.272, 273, 282

Gillard, State v., 78 Ohio St.3d 548, 679 N.E.2d 276 (1997)—§ 11.1(b) n.64

Gillard, State v., 64 Ohio St.3d 304, 595 N.E.2d 878 (1992)—§ 11.9(b) n.83

Gillaum, United States v., 355 F.3d 982 (7th Cir.2004)—§ 6.2(c) n.177

Gillen, United States v., 449 F.3d 898 (8th Cir.2006)—§ 21.4(g) n.227

Gillespie, People v., 136 Ill.2d 496, 145 Ill.Dec. 915, 557 N.E.2d 894 (Ill. 1990)—§ 5.3(c) n.35

Gillespie, People v., 42 Mich.App. 679, 202 N.W.2d 552 (1972)—§§ 11.2(g) n.292, 293

Gillespie, State v., 445 N.W.2d 661 (S.D.1989)—§ 6.6(d) n.58

Gillespie v. State, 440 So.2d 8 (Fla.App.1983)—§ 24.8(f) n.96

Gillespie, State v., 227 So.2d 550 (Fla.App.1969)—§ 24.3(b) n.71

Gillespie, United States v., 974 F.2d 796 (7th Cir.1992)—§§ 8.4(c) n.138; 8.10(d) n.98, 105, 110 to 113

Gillette, United States v., 189 F.2d 449 (2d Cir.1951)—§§ 16.2(g) n.108, 110, 113, 114

Gilliam, People v., 172 Ill.2d 484, 218 Ill.Dec. 884, 670 N.E.2d 606 (1996)—§ 16.1(g) n.256

Gilliam, State v., 274 S.C. 324, 262 S.E.2d 923 (1980)—§ 26.9(b) n.75

Gilliam, United States v., 975 F.2d 1050 (4th Cir.1992)—§§ 11.9(b) n.54, 99

Gilliard, Commonwealth v., 36 Mass.App. 183, 629 N.E.2d 349 (1994)—§ 8.14(a) n.7

Gillis, People v., 474 Mich. 105, 712 N.W.2d 419 (2006)—§ 13.7(a) n.5

Gillis v. State, 333 Md. 69, 633 A.2d 888 (1993)—§ 17.4(a) n.47

Gill, State ex rel. v. Irons, 207 W.Va. 199, 530 S.E.2d 460 (2000)—§ 21.4(d) n.103

Gillum v. State, 681 P.2d 87 (Okl.Cr.1984)—§ 21.2(h) n.431

Gilman, State v., 489 A.2d 1100 (Me.1985)—§ 24.7(b) n.19

Gilman, State v., 105 Idaho 891, 673 P.2d 1085 (Idaho App.1983)—§ 24.8(f) n.119

Gilmore v. Marks, 799 F.2d 51 (3d Cir.1986)—§ 28.3(d) n.87

Gilmore, People v., 222 Mich.App. 442, 564 N.W.2d 158 (1997)—§§ 20.3(j) n.188, 195

Gilmore, People v., 101 Ill.App.2d 447, 243 N.E.2d 473 (1968)—§ 19.6(b) n.12

Gilmore, State v., 193 Wis.2d 403, 535 N.W.2d 21 (App.1995)—§ 4.6(i) n.153

Gilmore v. Taylor, 508 U.S. 333, 113 S.Ct. 2112, 124 L.Ed.2d 306 (1993)—§§ 24.8(f) n.95; 28.6(d) n.25; 28.6(e) n.55

Gilmore v. Zimmerman, 793 F.2d 564 (3d Cir.1986)—§ 25.1(d) n.71

Gilnite, State v., 202 Conn. 369, 521 A.2d 547 (1987)—§§ 21.4(a) n.26; 21.6(b) n.84

Gilreath v. Head, 234 F.3d 547 (11th Cir.2000)—§ 11.6(a) n.62

Gilreath v. Mitchell, 705 F.2d 109 (4th Cir.1983)—§ 6.2(b) n.39

Giltner, State v., 56 Haw. 374, 537 P.2d 14 (1975)—§ 3.8(e) n.192

Gimelstob, United States v., 475 F.2d 157 (3d Cir.1973)—§ 17.3(e) n.57

Ginanni, State v., 174 W.Va. 580, 328 S.E.2d 187 (1985)—§ 23.2(a) n.48

Ginsberg v. Abrams, 702 F.2d 48 (2d Cir.1984)—§ 28.3(a) n.18

Ginsberg, State ex rel. v. Naum, 173 W.Va. 510, 318 S.E.2d 454 (1984)—§ 13.3(a) n.8

Giordano, United States v., 416 U.S. 505, 94 S.Ct. 1820, 40 L.Ed.2d 341 (1974)—§§ 4.6(e) n.90; 4.6(m) n.229, 232; 9.4(b) n.61

Giordenello v. United States, 357 U.S. 480, 78 S.Ct. 1245, 2 L.Ed.2d 1503 (1958)—§§ 3.1(f) n.148; 3.5(a) n.56

Giorgi, United States v., 840 F.2d 1022 (1st Cir.1988)—§§ 15.6(f) n.192; 21.2(d) n.206

Giovanelli, United States v., 998 F.2d 116 (2d Cir.1993)—§ 10.1(c) n.47

Gipe, United States v., 672 F.2d 777 (9th Cir.1982)—§ 16.4(d) n.122

Gipson, People v., 203 Ill.2d 298, 272 Ill.Dec. 1, 786 N.E.2d 540 (2003)—§§ 3.7(e) n.118; 10.3(b) n.19

Gipson v. State, 609 P.2d 1038 (Alaska 1980)—§§ 20.4(b) n.36, 40

Gipson v. State, 375 So.2d 514 (Ala.1979)—§ 8.11(e) n.98

Gipson v. State, 575 P.2d 782 (Alaska 1978)—§ 14.4(e) n.135

Gipson, United States v., 835 F.2d 1323 (10th Cir.1988)—§ 21.6(a) n.35

Gipson, United States v., 693 F.2d 109 (10th Cir.1982)—§§ 11.4(c) n.62; 11.5(c) n.57

Giraldi, United States v., 86 F.3d 1368 (5th Cir.1996)—§ 27.5(e) n.154

Girard, United States v., 744 F.2d 1170 (5th Cir.1984)—§ 18.5(a) n.14

Giraud, State v., 258 Conn. 631, 783 A.2d 1019 (2001)—§ 24.3(i) n.189

Girgenti, United States v., 197 F.2d 218 (3d Cir.1952)—§ 8.8(a) n.6

Girouard, Commonwealth v., 436 Mass. 657, 766 N.E.2d 873 (2002)—§§ 6.6(b) n.16; 6.9(g) n.167

Gissendaner v. State, 272 Ga. 704, 532 S.E.2d 677 (2000)—§ 22.2(d) n.94

Gissendanner v. Wainwright, 482 F.2d 1293 (5th Cir.1973)—§ 9.3(d) n.39

Gitlow v. New York, 268 U.S. 652, 45 S.Ct. 625, 69 L.Ed. 1138 (1925)—§§ 2.4(d) n.127; 2.5(c) n.25

Gittens, People v., 110 A.D.2d 908, 488 N.Y.S.2d 457 (1985)—§ 9.1(d) n.136

Givens, State v., 776 So.2d 443 (La.2001)—§§ 21.2(f) n.383; 22.3(d) n.212

Givens, State v., 252 Or. 477, 449 P.2d 151 (1969)—§ 6.8(c) n.67

Givner v. State, 210 Md. 484, 124 A.2d 764 (1956)—§ 3.9(b) n.12

Giwa, United States v., 831 F.2d 538 (5th Cir.1987)—§ 18.3(b) n.5

Gladden, People v., 118 Misc.2d 831, 462 N.Y.S.2d 115 (Sup.Ct.1983)—§ 15.7(g) n.207

Gladney, United States v., 48 F.3d 309 (8th Cir.1995)—§ 3.3(c) n.93

Glaesman, State v., 545 N.W.2d 178 (N.D.1996)—§ 27.5(e) n.168

Glanzer v. Glanzer, 347 F.3d 1212 (11th Cir.2003)—§ 4.6(b) n.48

Glasper v. State, 914 So.2d 708 (Miss.2005)—§ 6.2(c) n.100

Glaspie v. Little, 564 N.W.2d 651 (N.D.1997)—§ 26.1(f) n.150

Glaspy, Commonwealth v., 532 Pa. 572, 616 A.2d 1359 (1992)—§ 22.3(a) n.26

Glass, People v., 464 Mich. 266, 627 N.W.2d 261 (2001)—§ 14.2(d) n.49

Glass, People v., 239 Ill.App.3d 916, 179 Ill.Dec. 823, 606 N.E.2d 655 (1992)—§ 16.1(g) n.261

Glass, People v., 94 Ill.App.3d 69, 49 Ill.Dec. 600, 418 N.E.2d 454 (1981)—§ 8.10(c) n.76

Glass, State v., 279 Ga. 696, 620 S.E.2d 371 (2005)—§§ 7.4(c) n.49; 21.5(c) n.88

Glass, State v., 136 S.W.3d 496 (Mo.2004)—§§ 6.8(b) n.41, 47; 19.3(a) n.42, 44

Glass v. State, 853 P.2d 972 (Wyo.1993)—§ 6.6(e) n.81

Glass, State v., 583 P.2d 872 (Alaska 1978)—§ 2.12(b) n.88

Glasser, United States v., 773 F.2d 1553 (11th Cir.1985)—§ 18.3(b) n.23

Glasser v. United States, 315 U.S. 60, 62 S.Ct. 457, 86 L.Ed. 680 (1942)—§§ 11.7(a) n.4; 11.9(a) n.1; 11.9(b) n.45; 11.9(d) n.155, 160, 180; 22.2(d) n.45

Glatzmayer, State v., 789 So.2d 297 (Fla.2001)—§ 6.9(g) n.166

Glaubman, People v., 175 Colo. 41, 485 P.2d 711 (1971)—§ 3.5(c) n.112

Glaum, United States v., 356 F.3d 169 (1st Cir.2004)—§§ 5.2(a) n.6, 9

Gleason, Commonwealth v., 567 Pa. 111, 785 A.2d 983 (2001)—§ 3.8(b) n.20

Gleason, State v., 277 Kan. 624, 88 P.3d 218 (2004)—§ 11.9(d) n.209

Gleason, United States v., 616 F.2d 2 (2d Cir.1979)—§ 20.3(c) n.74

Glen, People v., 30 N.Y.2d 252, 331 N.Y.S.2d 656, 282 N.E.2d 614 (1972)—§ 3.3(g) n.241

Glen, United States v., 418 F.3d 181 (2d Cir.2005)—§ 21.2(b) n.48

Glenn v. Commonwealth, 633 S.E.2d 205, 48 Va.App. 556 (2006)—§ 27.5(c) n.50

Glenn, People v., 56 Cal.App.4th 886, 65 Cal.Rptr.2d 797 (1997)—§ 14.4(b) n.42

Glenn, State v., 267 Ark. 501, 592 S.W.2d 116 (1980)—§ 27.3(d) n.64

Glenn v. United States, 391 A.2d 772 (D.C.App.1978)—§ 21.4(a) n.39

Glenna, United States v., 878 F.2d 967 (7th Cir.1989)—§ 3.10(b) n.72

Glickstein v. United States, 222 U.S. 139, 32 S.Ct. 71, 56 L.Ed. 128 (1911)—§§ 8.10(d) n.90; 8.11(a) n.8

Glinsey, United States v., 209 F.3d 386 (5th Cir.2000)—§ 21.5(c) n.86

Globe v. State, 877 So.2d 663 (Fla.2004)—§ 6.9(f) n.106

Globe Communications Corp., State v., 648 So.2d 110 (Fla.1994)—§ 23.1(c) n.119

Globe Newspaper Co., In re, 920 F.2d 88 (1st Cir.1990)—§§ 22.3(b) n.68; 23.1(d) n.192; 27.4(d) n.57

Globe Newspaper Co., In re, 729 F.2d 47 (1st Cir.1984)—§§ 23.1(d) n.145, 175, 188; 23.1(e) n.222, 228, 246, 250, 255

Globe Newspaper Co. v. Commonwealth, 264 Va. 622, 570 S.E.2d 809 (2002)—§ 23.1(d) n.173

Globe Newspaper Co. v. Superior Court, 457 U.S. 596, 102 S.Ct. 2613, 73 L.Ed.2d 248 (1982)—§§ 1.5(k) n.396; 2.6(d) n.98; 23.1(d) n.123; 23.1(e) n.214; 23.3(a) n.2; 24.1(b) n.24

Glosson, State v., 462 So.2d 1082 (Fla.1985)—§§ 5.4(a) n.5; 5.4(c) n.46

Glover v. Cain, 128 F.3d 900 (5th Cir.1997)—§ 28.4(d) n.67

Glover v. Miro, 262 F.3d 268 (4th Cir.2001)—§§ 11.8(c) n.64; 11.10(c) n.105

Glover, State v., 35 Ohio St.3d 18, 517 N.E.2d 900 (Ohio 1988)—§ 25.2(e) n.42

Glover, United States v., 431 F.3d 744 (11th Cir.2005)—§ 6.9(b) n.27

Glover v. United States, 531 U.S. 198, 121 S.Ct. 696, 148 L.Ed.2d 604 (2001)—§§ 11.10(d) n.181, 183; 26.4(e) n.75

Glover, United States v., 957 F.2d 1004 (2d Cir.1992)—§ 3.8(b) n.49

Glover, United States v., 506 F.2d 291 (2d Cir.1974)—§ 17.2(b) n.66

Gloves, Inc. v. Berger, 198 F.R.D. 6 (D.Mass.2000)—§ 8.13(d) n.115

Gluzman, United States v., 154 F.3d 49 (2d Cir.1998)—§ 22.2(a) n.2

G.M. Leasing Corp. v. United States, 429 U.S. 338, 97 S.Ct. 619, 50 L.Ed.2d 530 (1977)—§§ 3.6(f) n.152; 3.7(d) n.75

Go-Bart Importing Co. v. United States, 282 U.S. 344, 51 S.Ct. 153, 75 L.Ed. 374 (1931)—§§ 2.1 n.53; 2.9(g) n.163; 3.4(f) n.102; 3.10(b) n.26

Gobert, United States v., 139 F.3d 436 (5th Cir.1998)—§ 21.4(f) n.171

Gockley, United States ex rel. v. Myers, 450 F.2d 232 (3d Cir.1971)—§ 9.4(a) n.16

Godbold v. State, 336 Ark. 251, 983 S.W.2d 939 (1999)—§ 6.7(d) n.145

Goddard, State ex rel. v. Gravano, 210 Ariz. 101, 108 P.3d 251 (Ariz.App.2005)—§ 25.1(c) n.40

Godfrey, State v., 204 Ga.App. 58, 418 S.E.2d 383 (1992)—§ 27.4(f) n.67

Godfrey, State v., 170 W.Va. 25, 289 S.E.2d 660 (1981)—§ 26.5(c) n.50

Godinez v. Moran, 509 U.S. 389, 113 S.Ct. 2680, 125 L.Ed.2d 321 (1993)—§§ 11.3(b) n.49; 11.5(c) n.59; 11.5(d) n.78, 83; 11.6(a) n.26; 21.4(b) n.64; 24.2(g) n.91

Godoy, United States v., 821 F.2d 1498 (11th Cir.1987)—§ 18.3(b) n.18

Godwin, United States v., 272 F.3d 659 (4th Cir.2001)—§ 24.6(e) n.52

Godwin v. United States, 687 F.2d 585 (2d Cir.1982)—§§ 21.4(c) n.82; 21.4(f) n.207

Goehring, State v., 374 N.W.2d 882 (N.D.1985)—§ 10.2(a) n.2

Goeke v. Branch, 514 U.S. 115, 115 S.Ct. 1275, 131 L.Ed.2d 152 (1995)—§§ 27.1(a) n.13; 27.5(c) n.84; 28.6(b) n.14; 28.6(d) n.25

Goene v. State, 577 So.2d 1306 (Fla.1991)—§ 26.7(c) n.37

Goetz, People v., 131 Misc.2d 1, 502 N.Y.S.2d 577 (1986)—§ 15.2(c) n.81

Gogarty, United States v., 533 F.2d 93 (2d Cir.1976)—§ 13.6(d) n.56

Goings, United States v., 200 F.3d 539 (8th Cir.2000)—§§ 21.2(d) n.167; 21.2(e) n.304

Goins v. Angelone, 226 F.3d 312 (4th Cir.2000)—§ 22.3(a) n.26

Goins v. State, 672 So.2d 30 (Fla.1996)—§ 21.4(g) n.232

Goins, United States v., 437 F.3d 644 (7th Cir.2006)—§ 9.3(e) n.62

Gold, United States v., 470 F.Supp. 1336 (N.D.Ill.1979)—§§ 15.6(b) n.49, 61; 15.7(b) n.10; 15.7(c) n.54, 55, 58; 15.7(f) n.152

Goldberg v. Kelly, 397 U.S. 254, 90 S.Ct. 1011, 25 L.Ed.2d 287 (1970)—§ 12.2(a) n.9

Goldberg, State v., 872 A.2d 378 (Vt. 2005)—§ 3.3(d) n.152

Goldberg, United States v., 67 F.3d 1092 (3d Cir.1995)—§§ 11.3(c) n.56, 58, 62, 66, 67; 11.4(b) n.29, 30; 11.4(d) n.118; 11.5(c) n.31, 51

Goldberg, United States v., 862 F.2d 101 (6th Cir.1988)—§ 21.5(c) n.74

Goldberg, United States v., 830 F.2d 459 (3d Cir.1987)—§§ 16.2(b) n.16; 16.2(e) n.78; 16.4(b) n.28

Goldberg v. United States, 425 U.S. 94, 96 S.Ct. 1338, 47 L.Ed.2d 603 (1976)—§§ 24.3(c) n.99, 100

Goldberg, United States ex rel. v. Warden, 622 F.2d 60 (3d Cir.1980)—§ 21.2(d) n.214

Golden, State v., 226 Neb. 863, 415 N.W.2d 469 (1987)—§ 21.4(d) n.106

Goldhammer, Commonwealth v., 507 Pa. 236, 489 A.2d 1307 (1985)—§ 18.5(a) n.21

Goldman, United States v., 451 F.Supp. 518 (S.D.N.Y.1978)—§§ 15.5(b) n.54; 15.7(e) n.104

Goldman, United States v., 563 F.2d 501 (1st Cir.1977)—§ 9.6(a) n.38

Goldman v. United States, 316 U.S. 129, 62 S.Ct. 993, 86 L.Ed. 1322 (1942)—§ 4.6(a) n.18

Goldsby v. United States, 160 U.S. 70, 16 S.Ct. 216, 40 L.Ed. 343 (1895)—§ 14.4(c) n.47

Goldsmith, Commonwealth v., 438 Pa. 83, 263 A.2d 322 (1970)—§ 6.8(a) n.34

Goldsmith v. State, 337 Md. 112, 651 A.2d 866 (1995)—§ 24.3(a) n.11

Goldsmith v. Superior Court, 152 Cal.App.3d 76, 199 Cal.Rptr. 366 (1984)—§§ 8.13(e) n.116; 20.4(b) n.33

Goldsmith v. United States, 277 F.2d 335 (D.C.Cir.1960)—§ 6.3(b) n.33

Goldstein, United States v., 442 F.3d 777 (2d Cir.2006)—§ 24.10(c) n.40

Goldstein, United States v., 502 F.2d 526 (3d Cir.1974)—§§ 19.3(b) n.162; 19.5(d) n.69; 19.6(b) n.15

Goldstein, United States v., 120 F.2d 485 (2d Cir.1941)—§ 10.3(b) n.42

Goldston, People v., 470 mich. 523, 470 Mich. 523, 682 N.W.2d 479 (2004)—§ 2.12(b) n.107

Goldswer, People v., 39 N.Y.2d 656, 385 N.Y.S.2d 274, 350 N.E.2d 604 (1976)—§§ 16.3(d) n.65; 16.3(g) n.115

Goliday, People v., 8 Cal.3d 771, 106 Cal.Rptr. 113, 505 P.2d 537 (1973)—§ 24.3(g) n.173

Golino, State v., 201 Conn. 435, 518 A.2d 57 (1986)—§ 18.5(a) n.9

Gollihar v. State, 46 S.W.3d 243 (Tex.Cr.App.2001)—§§ 19.6(b) n.22; 19.6(c) n.41

Gollott v. State, 646 So.2d 1297 (Miss.1994)—§ 27.5(a) n.8

Golphin, State v., 352 N.C. 364, 533 S.E.2d 168 (2000)—§§ 6.7(b) n.43; 9.1(a) n.14; 10.2(b) n.19; 17.2(b) n.64; 22.3(d) n.247

Golston, State v., 71 Ohio St.3d 224, 643 N.E.2d 109 (Ohio 1994)—§ 27.5(a) n.14

Gomes, Commonwealth v., 355 Mass. 479, 245 N.E.2d 429 (1969)—§ 6.10(e) n.78

Gomes, State v., 764 A.2d 125 (R.I.2001)—§ 3.3(d) n.175

Gomes, State v., 79 Hawai'i 32, 897 P.2d 959 (1995)—§ 21.5(a) n.43

Gomes, State v., 604 A.2d 1249 (R.I.1992)—§ 7.4(b) n.35

Gomes, United States v., 177 F.3d 76 (1st Cir.1999)—§ 11.10(c) n.91

Gometz, United States v., 730 F.2d 475 (7th Cir.1984)—§ 22.2(a) n.7

Gomez v. Ahitow, 29 F.3d 1128 (7th Cir.1994)—§§ 11.9(c) n.132, 133

Gomez v. Berge, 434 F.3d 940 (7th Cir.2006)—§§ 21.4(a) n.26; 21.6(a) n.14

Gomez v. Collins, 993 F.2d 96 (5th Cir.1993)—§ 11.5(g) n.126

Gomez v. Layton, 394 F.2d 764 (D.C.Cir.1968)—§ 3.1(n) n.297

Gomez, State v., 778 So.2d 549 (La.2001)—§ 26.5(d) n.74

Gomez, State v., 122 N.M. 777, 932 P.2d 1 (1997)—§§ 2.12(b) n.104; 2.12(c) n.118; 2.12(d) n.192, 195

Gomez, State v., 887 P.2d 853 (Utah 1994)—§ 26.4(d) n.54

Gomez, United States v., 326 F.3d 971 (8th Cir.2003)—§ 21.2(d) n.219

Gomez, United States v., 271 F.3d 779 (8th Cir.2001)—§§ 21.2(d) n.167, 236, 237

Gomez, United States v., 276 F.3d 694 (5th Cir.2001)—§ 9.1(d) n.128

Gomez, United States v., 237 F.3d 238 (3d Cir.2000)—§ 8.10(d) n.98

Gomez, United States v., 191 F.3d 1214 (10th Cir.1999)—§ 24.3(e) n.135

Gomez, United States v., 67 F.3d 1515 (10th Cir.1995)—§ 4.6(k) n.173

Gomez, United States v., 927 F.2d 1530 (11th Cir.1991)—§§ 6.9(f) n.131, 133

Gomez, United States v., 947 F.2d 737 (5th Cir.1991)—§ 10.5(a) n.6

Gomez v. United States, 490 U.S. 858, 109 S.Ct. 2237, 104 L.Ed.2d 923 (1989)—§ 27.6(b) n.32

Gomez, United States v., 770 F.2d 251 (1st Cir.1985)—§ 9.1(b) n.53

Gomez, United States v., 584 F.Supp. 1185 (D.R.I.1984)—§ 11.9(a) n.22

Gomez-Olmeda, United States v., 296 F.Supp.2d 71 (D, Puerto Rico 2003)—§ 19.3(a) n.27

Gomm v. Cook, 754 P.2d 1226 (Utah App.1988)—§ 27.4(f) n.63

Gompf v. State, 120 P.3d 980 (Wyo.2005)—§ 6.6(e) n.61

Gonczy, United States v., 357 F.3d 50 (1st Cir.2004)—§ 21.2(d) n.169

Gondolfi v. Clinger, 352 Ark. 156, 98 S.W.3d 812 (2003)—§ 18.4(c) n.40

Gonsalves, United States v., 121 F.3d 1416 (11th Cir.1997)—§ 21.2(d) n.255

Gonsalves, United States v., 675 F.2d 1050 (9th Cir.1982)—§ 18.5(a) n.31

Gonzales v. Landon, 350 U.S. 920, 76 S.Ct. 210, 100 L.Ed. 806 (1955)—§ 26.10(c) n.46

Gonzales, People v., 987 P.2d 239 (Colo.1999)—§ 6.7(a) n.23

Gonzales, People v., 679 P.2d 1085 (Colo.1984)—§ 18.4(d) n.84

Gonzales v. Raich, 545 U.S. 1, 125 S.Ct. 2195, 162 L.Ed.2d 1 (2005)—§§ 1.2(c) n.117, 145, 188; 1.2(d) n.201

Gonzales, State v., 138 N.M. 271, 119 P.3d 151 (2005)—§ 22.5(d) n.36

Gonzales v. State, 67 S.W.3d 910 (Tex.Cr.App.2002)—§ 6.9(g) n.178

Gonzales, State v., 638 S.W.2d 841 (Tenn.Crim.App.1982)—§§ 15.2(d) n.106; 15.5(c) n.103

Gonzales, State v., 96 N.M. 513, 632 P.2d 748 (1981)—§ 8.4(b) n.74

Gonzales v. State, 605 S.W.2d 278 (Tex.Cr.App.1980)—§ 11.9(d) n.186

Gonzales v. State, 582 P.2d 630 (Alaska 1978)—§ 18.5(c) n.75

Gonzales v. State, 507 P.2d 1277 (Okla.Cr.App.1973)—§ 3.7(f) n.147

Gonzales v. Thomas, 99 F.3d 978 (10th Cir.1996)—§ 22.3(c) n.135

Gonzales, United States v., 339 F.3d 725 (8th Cir.2003)—§ 21.6(a) n.40

Gonzales, United States v., 227 F.3d 520 (6th Cir.2000)—§ 24.9(g) n.114

Gonzales, United States v., 164 F.3d 1285 (10th Cir.1999)—§§ 9.1(a) n.21, 22; 20.3(i) n.176; 20.6(b) n.19, 34, 41

Gonzales, United States v., 137 F.3d 1431 (10th Cir.1998)—§ 18.3(b) n.37

Gonzales, United States v., 121 F.3d 928 (5th Cir.1997)—§§ 19.3(a) n.58, 59

Gonzales, United States v., 65 F.3d 814 (10th Cir.1995)—§ 21.3(c) n.148

Gonzales, United States v., 979 F.2d 711 (9th Cir.1992)—§ 9.1(d) n.127

Gonzales, United States v., 897 F.2d 1312 (5th Cir.1990)—§ 18.3(b) n.26

Gonzales, United States v., 842 F.2d 748 (5th Cir.1988)—§ 3.10(b) n.54

Gonzales, United States v., 852 F.2d 1214 (9th Cir.1988)—§ 12.3(a) n.27

Gonzales Claudio, United States v., 806 F.2d 334 (2d Cir.1986)—§ 12.1(a) n.15

Gonzales-Morales, 138 Wash.2d 374, 979 P.2d 826 (1999)—§ 11.8(c) n.78

Gonzalez, Commonwealth v., 519 Pa. 116, 546 A.2d 26 (1988)—§ 6.6(e) n.91

Gonzalez v. Crosby, 545 U.S. 524, 125 S.Ct. 2641, 162 L.Ed.2d 480 (2005)—§§ 28.5(d) n.91; 28.9(b) n.59

Gonzalez v. Kokot, 314 F.3d 311 (7th Cir.2002)—§ 13.5(a) n.26

Gonzalez, People v., 38 Cal.4th 932, 44 Cal.Rptr.3d 237, 135 P.3d 649 (2006)—§§ 7.4(b) n.28; 7.4(d) n.70; 7.4(e) n.82

Gonzalez, People v., 34 Cal.4th 1111, 23 Cal.Rptr.3d 295, 104 P.3d 98 (2005)—§ 6.9(g) n.167

Gonzalez, People v., 201 A.D.2d 414, 607 N.Y.S.2d 670 (1994)—§ 15.6(d) n.120

Gonzalez, People v., 178 Mich.App. 526, 444 N.W.2d 228 (1989)—§ 14.3(d) n.94

Gonzalez, People v., 68 N.Y.2d 950, 510 N.Y.S.2d 86, 502 N.E.2d 1001 (1986)—§§ 10.3(a) n.5; 10.5(d) n.42

Gonzalez, People v., 47 N.Y.2d 606, 419 N.Y.S.2d 913, 393 N.E.2d 987 (1979)—§ 11.2(c) n.102

Gonzalez v. Phillips, 147 F.Supp.2d 791 (E.D.Mich.2001)—§ 28.7(c) n.17

Gonzalez v. Pliler, 341 F.3d 897 (9th Cir.2003)—§ 24.2(e) n.68

Gonzalez v. Quinones, 211 F.3d 735 (2d Cir.2000)—§ 24.1(b) n.18

Gonzalez v. Secretary for Dept. of Corrections, 366 F.3d 1253 (11th Cir.2004)—§ 28.10 n.1

Gonzalez v. State, 340 Or. 452, 134 P.3d 955 (2006)—§ 21.3(b) n.68

Gonzalez v. State, 117 S.W.3d 831 (Tex.Crim.App.2003)—§ 11.9(c) n.117

Gonzalez v. State, 627 So.2d 63 (Fla.App.1993)—§ 24.9(e) n.58

Gonzalez, State v., 853 P.2d 526 (Alaska 1993)—§§ 8.11(b) n.21, 32

Gonzalez, State v., 825 P.2d 920 (Alaska 1992)—§ 2.10(d) n.109

Gonzalez v. State, 578 So.2d 729 (Fla.App.1991)—§ 10.4(c) n.23

Gonzalez, State v., 206 Conn. 213, 537 A.2d 460 (1988)—§ 6.9(b) n.14

Gonzalez, State v., 206 Conn. 391, 538 A.2d 210 (1988)—§§ 22.3(d) n.193, 249

Gonzalez v. State, 392 So.2d 334 (Fla.App.1981)—§ 26.9(c) n.81

Gonzalez, State v., 75 N.J. 181, 380 A.2d 1128 (1977)—§ 10.6(d) n.49

Gonzalez, United States v., 311 F.3d 440 (1st Cir.2002)—§ 21.6(a) n.25

Gonzalez, United States v., 259 F.3d 355 (5th Cir.2001)—§ 21.2(b) n.76

Gonzalez, United States v., 202 F.3d 20 (1st Cir.2000)—§§ 21.3(b) n.66; 21.4(d) n.135

Gonzalez, United States v., 183 F.3d 1315 (11th Cir.1999)—§ 17.2(b) n.71

Gonzalez, United States v., 113 F.3d 1026 (9th Cir.1997)—§§ 11.4(b) n.20, 21, 36

Gonzalez, United States v., 927 F.Supp. 768 (D.Del.1996)—§§ 23.1(d) n.174, 176, 181, 209, 210, 212

Gonzalez, United States v., 58 F.3d 459 (9th Cir.1995)—§ 13.3(c) n.44

Gonzalez, United States v., 969 F.2d 999 (11th Cir.1992)—§ 3.3(b) n.45

Gonzalez, United States v., 970 F.2d 1095 (2d Cir.1992)—§ 21.5(a) n.40

Gonzalez, United States v., 804 F.2d 691 (11th Cir.1986)—§ 17.2(d) n.97

Gonzalez, United States v., 748 F.2d 74 (2d Cir.1984)—§ 18.3(b) n.5

Gonzalez, United States v., 671 F.2d 441 (11th Cir.1982)—§ 18.3(b) n.7

Gonzalez-Acosta, United States v., 989 F.2d 384 (10th Cir.1993)—§ 10.5(e) n.55

Gonzalez-Aguilar, United States v., 446 F. Supp.2d 1099 (D.Ariz.2006)—§ 24.2(g) n.93

Gonzalez-Arimont, United States v., 268 F.3d 8 (1st Cir.2001)—§ 21.6(a) n.57

Gonzalez-Basulto, United States v., 898 F.2d 1011 (5th Cir.1990)—§§ 3.2(b) n.72; 3.10(f) n.195

Gonzalez Edeza, United States v., 359 F.3d 1246 (10th Cir.2004)—§ 19.6(c) n.46

Gonzalez-Faguaga, State v., 266 Neb. 72, 662 N.W.2d 581 (2003)—§ 21.6(a) n.78

Gonzalez-Flores, United States v., 418 F.3d 1093 (9th Cir.2005)—§ 27.6(b) n.31

Gonzalez, Inc., United States v., 412 F.3d 1102 (9th Cir.2005)—§§ 4.6(e) n.97, 99, 101; 9.1(c) n.100

Gonzalez-Lauzan, United States v., 437 F.3d 1128 (11th Cir.2006)—§ 6.8(b) n.49

Gonzalez-Lerma, United States v., 71 F.3d 1537 (10th Cir.1995)—§ 27.6(b) n.20

Gonzalez-Lopez, United States v., _____ U.S. _____, 126 S.Ct. 2557, 165 L.Ed.2d 409 (2006)—§§ 2.6(e) n.110; 2.7(b) n.76, 79; 11.1(a) n.11, 25; 11.4(b) n.42; 11.4(c) n.49; 11.7(d) n.38, 54; 11.9(c) n.122; 27.6(d) n.104, 116, 132

Gonzalez-Lopez, United States v., 399 F.3d 924 (8th Cir.2005)—§§ 11.4(c) n.56; 27.6(d) n.143

Gonzalez-Maldonado, United States v., 115 F.3d 9 (1st Cir.1997)—§ 24.7(a) n.14

Gonzalez-Mares, United States v., 752 F.2d 1485 (9th Cir.1985)—§§ 6.4(e) n.107; 6.7(b) n.66; 6.10(c) n.48

Gonzalez-Mercado, United States v., 402 F.3d 294 (1st Cir.2005)—§ 21.2(a) n.7

Gonzalez-Rodriguez, United States v., 513 F.2d 928 (9th Cir.1975)—§ 3.2(j) n.268

Gonzalez-Sanchez, United States v., 825 F.2d 572 (1st Cir.1987)—§ 21.2(d) n.242

Gonzalez-Sandoval, United States v., 894 F.2d 1043 (9th Cir.1990)—§§ 6.7(b) n.54; 6.10(c) n.56; 9.5(a) n.20; 9.5(b) n.42, 44

Gonzalez-Vazquez, United States v., 219 F.3d 37 (1st Cir.2000)—§§ 21.2(b) n.58; 21.3(b) n.110

Gooch, United States v., 6 F.3d 673 (9th Cir.1993)—§ 3.6(a) n.5

Gooch v. United States, 609 A.2d 259 (D.C.App.1992)—§§ 17.1(a) n.15; 17.1(b) n.27

Good, State v., 309 Mont. 113, 43 P.3d 948 (2002)—§§ 18.2(e) n.79; 22.3(c) n.108, 157

Good v. State, 723 S.W.2d 734 (Tex.Cr.App.1986)—§ 24.5(b) n.33

Good, State v., 10 Ariz.App. 556, 460 P.2d 662 (1969)—§§ 15.6(a) n.17; 15.6(d) n.124; 15.7(b) n.14, 21, 35

Goodacre, United States v., 793 F.2d 1124 (9th Cir.1986)—§ 5.1(c) n.26

Goodall, United States v., 236 F.3d 700 (D.C.Cir.2001)—§ 21.1(h) n.210

Goodall v. United States, 759 A.2d 1077 (D.C.App.2000)—§ 21.3(b) n.71

Goodall v. United States, 584 A.2d 560 (D.C.App.1990)—§ 21.2(d) n.162

Good Bird v. United States, 752 F.2d 349 (8th Cir.1985)—§ 21.5(c) n.74

Goodchild, State ex rel. v. Burke, 27 Wis.2d 244, 133 N.W.2d 753 (1965)—§ 10.5(c) n.27

Goodine v. Griffin, 309 F.Supp. 590 (S.D.Ga.1970)—§ 12.2(a) n.1

Gooding v. Stotts, 856 F.Supp. 1504 (D.Kan.1994)—§ 25.3(c) n.25

Gooding v. United States, 529 A.2d 301 (D.C.App.1987)—§ 21.5(a) n.39

Gooding v. United States, 416 U.S. 430, 94 S.Ct. 1780, 40 L.Ed.2d 250 (1974)—§§ 3.3(b) n.39; 3.4(g) n.129

Goodlett, United States v., 3 F.3d 976 (6th Cir.1993)—§ 11.7(e) n.84

Goodley, State v., 381 So.2d 1180 (Fla.App.1980)—§ 3.8(h) n.247

Goodman, Ex parte, 152 S.W.3d 67 (Tex.Cr.App.2004)—§ 25.2(f) n.49

Goodman, State v., 2002 WL 274639 (Oh.App.2002)—§ 25.1(d) n.69

Goodman, State v., 696 So.2d 940 (Fla.App.1997)—§ 25.1(d) n.50

Goodman, United States v., 165 F.3d 169 (2d Cir.1999)—§ 21.2(b) n.86

Goodman, United States v., 285 F.2d 378 (5th Cir.1960)—§ 17.3(b) n.20

Goodman v. United States, 108 F.2d 516 (9th Cir.1939)—§ 8.5(d) n.128

Goodmuth v. State, 302 Md. 613, 490 A.2d 682 (1985)—§ 24.9(d) n.43

Goodrich, State v., 256 N.W.2d 506 (Minn.1977)—§ 3.7(d) n.85

Goodrich, State v., 116 N.H. 477, 363 A.2d 425 (1976)—§ 21.2(d) n.162

Goodroad, State v., 563 N.W.2d 126 (S.D.1997)—§§ 6.5(b) n.30; 9.6(a) n.35

Goodroad, State v., 442 N.W.2d 246 (S.D.1989)—§§ 5.2(a) n.4, 10

Goodroe v. State, 224 Ga.App. 378, 480 S.E.2d 378 (1997)—§ 24.2(b) n.27

Goodson, State v., 412 So.2d 1077 (La.1982)—§ 23.2(f) n.82

Goodson, United States v., 204 F.3d 508 (4th Cir.2000)—§ 13.3(c) n.44

Goodwin, In re, 146 Wash.2d 861, 50 P.3d 618 (2002)—§ 21.2(d) n.221

Goodwin, Commonwealth v., 414 Mass. 88, 605 N.E.2d 827 (1993)—§ 26.4(f) n.88

Goodwin v. Johnson, 224 F.3d 450 (5th Cir.2000)—§ 6.9(g) n.166

Goodwin, State v., 681 N.W.2d 847 (S.D.2004)—§ 21.5(c) n.88

Goodwin v. State, 263 Ark. 856, 568 S.W.2d 3 (1978)—§ 20.2(c) n.50

Goodwin, United States v., 317 F.3d 293 (D.C.Cir.2003)—§ 26.4(b) n.22

Goodwin, United States v., 457 U.S. 368, 102 S.Ct. 2485, 73 L.Ed.2d 74 (1982)—§§ 2.7(a) n.20; 2.9(h) n.232; 13.5(a) n.3, 4; 13.6(c) n.34; 13.7(c) n.41, 51; 26.8(b) n.12

Gooljar, People v., 80 A.D.2d 860, 436 N.Y.S.2d 754 (1981)—§ 27.6(b) n.44

Goolsby v. Hutto, 691 F.2d 199 (4th Cir.1982)—§ 25.1(d) n.52

Goossens, United States v., 84 F.3d 697 (4th Cir.1996)—§§ 12.1(a) n.7; 12.4(d) n.66

Gopman, In re, 531 F.2d 262 (5th Cir.1976)—§§ 8.14(d) n.55, 56

Gordils, United States v., 982 F.2d 64 (2d Cir.1992)—§ 3.6(a) n.19

Gordon, In re, 534 F.2d 197 (9th Cir.1976)—§ 8.9(b) n.21

Gordon, Commonwealth v., 543 Pa. 513, 673 A.2d 866 (1996)—§ 27.3(c) n.33

Gordon, Commonwealth v., 410 Mass. 498, 574 N.E.2d 974 (1991)—§§ 21.3(d) n.263; 25.1(d) n.60

Gordon, Commonwealth v., 254 P.Super. 267, 254 Pa.Super. 267, 385 A.2d 1013 (1978)—§ 14.4(e) n.112

Gordon v. Justice Court, 12 Cal.3d 323, 115 Cal.Rptr. 632, 525 P.2d 72 (1974)—§ 1.5(g) n.281

Gordon, People v., 50 Cal.3d 1223, 270 Cal.Rptr. 451, 792 P.2d 251 (1990)—§ 7.4(c) n.47

Gordon, People v., 76 N.Y.2d 595, 561 N.Y.S.2d 903, 563 N.E.2d 274 (1990)—§ 7.4(f) n.99

Gordon v. State, 97 P.3d 64 (Wyo.2004)—§ 6.2(c) n.173

Gordon, State v., 262 Wis.2d 380, 663 N.W.2d 765 (2003)—§ 21.6(c) n.118

Gordon v. State, 704 So.2d 107 (Fla.1997)—§ 22.2(d) n.81

Gordon, State v., 913 P.2d 350 (Utah 1996)—§ 11.9(a) n.18

Gordon v. State, 469 So.2d 795 (Fla.App.1985)—§ 11.7(e) n.80

Gordon v. State, 684 S.W.2d 888 (Mo.App.1985)—§ 11.9(d) n.202

Gordon, State v., 221 Kan. 253, 559 P.2d 312 (1977)—§ 9.1(c) n.102

Gordon v. State, 102 Ga. 673, 29 S.E. 444 (1897)—§ 15.1(d) n.225

Gordon, United States v., 480 F.3d 1205 (10th Cir.2007)—§ 21.2(b) n.85

Gordon, United States v., 291 F.3d 181 (2d Cir.2002)—§ 27.5(d) n.117

Gordon, United States v., 173 F.3d 761 (10th Cir.1999)—§ 3.10(f) n.188

Gordon, United States v., 974 F.2d 1110 (9th Cir.1992)—§§ 9.5(e) n.85, 87

Gordon, United States v., 895 F.2d 932 (4th Cir.1990)—§ 3.8(c) n.75

Gordon, United States v., 901 F.2d 48 (5th Cir.1990)—§ 3.4(e) n.71

Gordon, United States v., 844 F.2d 1397 (9th Cir.1988)—§§ 19.3(c) n.184, 189

Gordon, United States v., 817 F.2d 1538 (11th Cir.1987)—§§ 13.4(b) n.42, 72; 22.3(d) n.251

Gordon, United States v., 829 F.2d 119 (D.C.Cir.1987)—§ 24.2(b) n.27

Gordon, United States v., 540 F.2d 452 (9th Cir.1976)—§ 3.9(j) n.205

Gordon-Nikkar, United States v., 518 F.2d 972 (5th Cir.1975)—§ 22.2(d) n.87

Gore v. State, 599 So.2d 978 (Fla.1992)—§ 24.4(d) n.55

Gore v. State, 573 So.2d 87 (Fla.App.1991)—§ 23.3(b) n.27

Gore v. United States, 357 U.S. 386, 78 S.Ct. 1280, 2 L.Ed.2d 1405 (1958)—§§ 2.7(c) n.115; 2.9(d) n.76; 25.1(b) n.14

Gorecki, United States v., 813 F.2d 40 (3d Cir.1987)—§ 17.1(a) n.10

Gorg, People v., 157 Cal.App.2d 515, 321 P.2d 143 (1958)—§ 3.4(e) n.76

Gorham v. Franzen, 760 F.2d 786 (7th Cir.1985)—§§ 6.9(d) n.72; 27.6(d) n.93

Gori v. United States, 367 U.S. 364, 81 S.Ct. 1523, 6 L.Ed.2d 901 (1961)—§ 25.2(e) n.43

Gorman, United States v., 355 F.2d 151 (2d Cir.1965)—§ 3.10(b) n.58

Gornto, United States v., 792 F.2d 1028 (11th Cir.1986)—§ 17.4(a) n.6

Gorski, United States v., 852 F.2d 692 (2d Cir.1988)—§ 9.3(e) n.81

Gortmaker, State v., 295 Or. 505, 668 P.2d 354 (1983)—§§ 15.4(b) n.55; 15.6(a) n.6

Gorwell, State v., 339 Md. 203, 661 A.2d 718 (1995)—§§ 22.1(h) n.157; 25.2(d) n.25

Goseland, State v., 256 Kan. 729, 887 P.2d 1109 (1994)—§ 24.9(f) n.68

Gosnell, State v., 62 S.W.3d 740 (Tenn.Cr.App.2001)—§§ 6.6(d) n.48; 6.7(c) n.141

Goss, People v., 446 Mich. 587, 521 N.W.2d 312 (1994)—§ 17.4(a) n.58

Goss v. State, 730 So.2d 568 (Miss.1998)—§§ 21.2(f) n.383; 21.3(d) n.219

Goss, State v., 245 Kan. 189, 777 P.2d 781 (1989)—§ 18.2(b) n.18

Goss, United States v., 329 F.2d 180 (4th Cir.1964)—§ 17.3(c) n.31

Gossett, State v., 120 Ariz. 44, 583 P.2d 1364 (1978)—§ 21.6(c) n.115

Goswick, State v., 142 Ariz. 582, 691 P.2d 673 (1984)—§ 11.10(c) n.62

Gottfried, United States v., 165 F.2d 360 (2d Cir.1948)—§ 22.2(e) n.107

Gotti, United States v., 753 F.Supp. 443 (E.D.N.Y.1990)—§§ 23.1(e) n.232, 236, 246, 248

Gotti, United States v., 794 F.2d 773 (2d Cir.1986)—§ 12.1(a) n.17

Gottlieb v. State, 697 A.2d 400 (Del.1997)—§ 27.2(c) n.62

Goudreau, United States v., 854 F.2d 1097 (8th Cir.1988)—§ 6.6(b) n.15

Gougis, United States v., 374 F.2d 758 (7th Cir.1967)—§ 17.3(d) n.45

Gould, State v., 562 N.W.2d 518 (Minn.1997)—§ 26.3(f) n.54

Goulding, United States v., 26 F.3d 656 (7th Cir.1994)—§ 13.4(d) n.162

Gouled v. United States, 255 U.S. 298, 41 S.Ct. 261, 65 L.Ed. 647 (1921)—§§ 2.8(b) n.36; 3.2(i) n.214; 3.4(a) n.1; 3.10(c) n.89; 10.6(c) n.26

Goupil, State v., _____ N.H. _____, 908 A.2d 1256 (2006)—§ 6.6(e) n.67

Gouveia, United States v., 467 U.S. 180, 104 S.Ct. 2292, 81 L.Ed.2d 146 (1984)—§§ 7.3(b) n.15; 11.2(b) n.47; 18.1(c) n.35; 18.5(b) n.57; 21.3(a) n.11

Gove, Commonwealth v., 366 Mass. 351, 320 N.E.2d 900 (1974)—§ 18.1(c) n.33

Governing Board of Mountain View School District v. Metcalf, 36 Cal.App.3d 546, 111 Cal.Rptr. 724 (1974)—§§ 3.1(g) n.181, 182

Governor, State ex rel. v. Engler, 85 F.3d 1205 (6th Cir.1996)—§ 27.4(d) n.46

Govin, People v., 213 Ill.App.3d 928, 157 Ill.Dec. 381, 572 N.E.2d 450 (1991)—§ 16.4(c) n.104

Govro, United States v., 833 F.2d 135 (9th Cir.1987)—§ 25.3(a) n.4

Gowan v. Smith, 157 Mich. 443, 122 N.W. 286 (1909)—§ 13.2(b) n.34

Gowdy, State v., 88 Ohio St.3d 387, 727 N.E.2d 579 (2000)—§§ 22.3(d) n.250, 251

Gower, United States v., 447 F.2d 187 (5th Cir.1971)—§ 15.6(c) n.96

Grades v. Boles, 398 F.2d 409 (4th Cir.1968)—§ 21.3(a) n.5

Grady v. Corbin, 495 U.S. 508, 110
S.Ct. 2084, 109 L.Ed.2d 548
(1990)—§§ 2.9(d) n.74; 17.4(b)
n.78, 113; 17.4(c) n.142; 25.1(b)
n.19

Grady, State v., 619 S.W.2d 139
(Tenn.1979)—§ 15.3(d) n.72

Grady, United States v., 544 F.2d 598
(2d Cir.1976)—§ 18.5(a) n.37

Graewe, United States v., 689 F.2d 54
(6th Cir.1982)—§ 12.3(g) n.150

Grage, State v., 2001 WL 1580495
(Iowa App.2001)—§ 24.7(g) n.83

Graham v. Collins, 506 U.S. 461, 113
S.Ct. 892, 122 L.Ed.2d 260
(1993)—§§ 2.9(f) n.126; 26.1(b)
n.21; 28.6(e) n.40, 54

Graham, Commonwealth v., 661 A.2d
1367, 541 Pa. 173 (1995)—
§ 26.3(f) n.66

Graham v. Connor, 490 U.S. 386, 109
S.Ct. 1865, 104 L.Ed.2d 443
(1989)—§§ 2.7(d) n.237, 244, 258;
3.1(k) n.274; 3.5(a) n.73

Graham v. Johnson, 94 F.3d 958 (5th
Cir.1996)—§ 28.5(a) n.35

Graham v. O'Dwyer, 198 App.D.2d 505,
604 N.Y.S.2d 199 (1993)—
§ 27.4(b) n.11

Graham, People v., 67 A.D.2d 172, 415
N.Y.S.2d 714 (1979)—§ 7.4(b) n.30

Graham v. People, 134 Colo. 290, 302
P.2d 737 (1956)—§§ 16.2(a) n.6;
16.4(c) n.39

Graham v. Smith, 602 F.2d 1078 (2d
Cir.1979)—§ 17.4(b) n.71

Graham, State v., 153 Wash.2d 400, 103
P.3d 1238 (2005)—§ 17.4(b) n.73

Graham, State v., 273 Kan. 844, 46 P.3d
1177 (2002)—§ 3.2(f) n.178

Graham, State v., 311 Mont. 500, 57
P.3d 54 (2002)—§ 21.5(a) n.40

Graham, State v., 259 Neb. 966, 614
N.W.2d 266 (2000)—§ 5.3(d) n.40

Graham v. State, 325 Md. 398, 601 A.2d
131 (1992)—§ 3.8(d) n.143

Graham v. State, 34 Ark.App. 126, 806
S.W.2d 32 (1991)—§§ 16.4(d)
n.128, 137

Graham v. State, 535 N.E.2d 1152
(Ind.1989)—§ 6.6(d) n.45

Graham, State v., 135 Ariz. 209, 660
P.2d 460 (1983)—§ 6.9(e) n.86

Graham, State v., 240 So.2d 486
(Fla.App.1970)—§ 6.8(c) n.66

Graham v. State, 252 Ind. 367, 249
N.E.2d 25 (1969)—§ 24.11(b) n.8

Graham, United States v., 323 F.3d 603
(8th Cir.2003)—§ 13.5(a) n.5

Graham, United States v., 257 F.3d 143
(2d Cir.2001)—§§ 23.1(d) n.204,
207, 210, 211

Graham, United States v., 275 F.3d 490
(6th Cir.2001)—§ 17.1(a) n.16

Graham, United States v., 91 F.3d 213
(D.C.Cir.1996)—§§ 11.4(b) n.20,
21, 35, 40; 21.2(h) n.419

Graham, United States v., 982 F.2d 273
(8th Cir.1992)—§ 3.8(h) n.247

Graham, United States v., 538 F.2d 261
(9th Cir.1976)—§§ 18.4(a) n.18, 19

Grammas, United States v., 371 F.3d
281 (5th Cir.2004)—§ 21.3(b) n.54

Grammatikos, United States v., 633 F.2d
1013 (2d Cir.1980)—§§ 16.1(g)
n.261; 20.6(b) n.56, 59, 64, 65;
24.3(e) n.131; 26.6(d) n.53

Gramolini, United States v., 301 F.Supp.
39 (D.R.I.1969)—§§ 8.4(c) n.130;
15.3(d) n.68; 15.5(b) n.70

Grana, People v., 185 Colo. 126, 527
P.2d 543 (1974)—§ 3.7(e) n.100

Granados v. State, 85 S.W.3d 217
(Tex.Crim.App.2002)—§ 9.1(b)
n.47

Granberry v. Greer, 481 U.S. 129, 107
S.Ct. 1671, 95 L.Ed.2d 119
(1987)—§§ 28.5(a) n.40; 28.5(b)
n.65

Granbery v. District Court, 187 Colo.
316, 531 P.2d 390 (1975)—§ 8.5(a)
n.13

Granby, State v., 283 Mont. 193, 939
P.2d 1006 (1997)—§ 24.6(b) n.32

Grandia, United States v., 18 F.3d 184
(2d Cir.1994)—§ 21.4(a) n.8

Grandinetti, United States v., 564 F.2d 723 (5th Cir.1977)—§ 21.2(d) n.171

Grandison, Commonwealth v., 433 Mass. 135, 741 N.E.2d 25 (2001)— § 3.8(d) n.141

Grandison v. State, 305 Md. 685, 506 A.2d 580 (1986)—§§ 16.2(g) n.109, 120, 138

Grand Jury, In re, 286 F.3d 153 (3d.Cir.2002)—§§ 8.6(b) n.61, 62

Grand Jury, In re, 215 F.3d 430 (4th Cir.2000)—§§ 13.5(h) n.129, 168, 173

Grand Jury, In re, 737 So.2d 1 (La.1999)—§§ 8.5(b) n.45, 48; 8.5(e) n.198

Grand Jury, In re, 111 F.3d 1066 (3d Cir.1997)—§§ 4.6(m) n.220; 8.4(c) n.123; 8.5(d) n.158; 27.2(e) n.87

Grand Jury, In re, 79-01, 489 F.Supp. 844 (N.D.Ga.1980)—§ 15.2(e) n.138

Grand Jury, In re, 446 F.Supp. 1132 (N.D.Tex.1978)—§ 8.14(a) n.11

Grand Jury 11-84, In re, 799 F.2d 1321 (9th Cir.1986)—§ 8.9(b) n.31

Grand Jury 87-3 Subpoena Duces Tecum, In re, 955 F.2d 229 (4th Cir.1992)—§§ 8.8(d) n.52, 67, 75

Grand Jury 87-3 Subpoena Duces Tecum, In re, 884 F.2d 772 (4th Cir.1989)—§ 8.8(a) n.8

Grand Jury 89-4-72, In re, 932 F.2d 481 (6th Cir.1991)—§ 8.5(h) n.300

Grand Jury 89-4 Subpoena Duces Tecum, In re, 727 F.Supp. 265 (E.D.Va.1989)—§§ 8.13(d) n.87, 93, 97

Grand Jury 91-1, In re, 790 F.Supp. 109 (E.D.Va.1992)—§ 11.9(a) n.32

Grand Jury 95-1, In re, 118 F.3d 1433 (10th Cir.1997)—§ 8.5(h) n.262

Grand Jury Appearance by Larry Loigman, In the Matter of, 183 N.J. 133, 870 A.2d 249 (2005)—§ 8.4(b) n.91

Grand Jury, C. Schmidt & Sons, Inc., In re, 619 F.2d 1022 (3d Cir.1980)— §§ 8.8(b) n.29; 8.8(e) n.132; 8.8(h) n.182, 187; 27.2(e) n.88

Grand Jury Disclosure, In re, 550 F.Supp. 1171 (E.D.Va.1982)— § 8.5(c) n.95

Grand Jury Empaneled January 21, 1975, In re, 536 F.2d 1009 (3d Cir.1976)—§§ 8.14(d) n.52, 58

Grand Jury Empaneled on April 6, 1993, In re, 869 F.Supp. 298 (D.N.J.1994)—§§ 8.13(d) n.103, 105

Grand Jury Empaneling of the Special Grand Jury, In re, 171 F.3d 826 (3d Cir.1999)—§§ 8.8(b) n.24; 8.8(d) n.53

Grand Jury Empanelled February 14, 1978, In the Matter of, 597 F.2d 851 (3d Cir.1979)—§§ 8.12(e) n.53; 27.3(c) n.41

Grand Jury Empanelled March 8, 1983, In re, 579 F.Supp. 189 (E.D.Tenn.1984)—§ 23.1(d) n.156

Grand Jury Empanelled May 1988, Freligh, In re, 894 F.2d 881 (7th Cir.1989)—§§ 8.11(d) n.85, 86

Grand Jury Fall Term, A.D. 1991, 624 So.2d 291 (1993)—§ 8.5(h) n.281

Grand Jury (Garcia-Rosell), In re, 889 F.2d 220 (9th Cir.1989)—§ 8.11(b) n.32

Grand Jury Impaneled January 21, 1975 (Freedman), In re, 529 F.2d 543 (3d Cir.1976)—§§ 8.8(a) n.8, 9

Grand Jury Impanelled January 21, 1981, In re, 535 F.Supp. 537 (D.N.J.1982)—§ 8.6(b) n.33

Grand Jury Impanelled October 2, 1978, In re, 510 F.Supp. 112 (D.D.C.1981)—§§ 8.5(c) n.93, 105

Grand Jury Investigation, In re, 182 F.3d 668 (9th Cir.1999)—§§ 8.14(d) n.44; 27.2(c) n.56

Grand Jury Investigation, In re, 55 F.3d 350 (8th Cir.1995)—§§ 8.5(c) n.95; 8.5(h) n.246, 250; 27.2(e) n.98

Grand Jury Investigation, In re, 974 F.2d 1068 (9th Cir.1992)—§ 27.5(e) n.146

Grand Jury Investigation, In re, 61 Ohio Misc.2d 583, 580 N.E.2d 868 (Com.Pl.1991)—§ 8.5(b) n.37

Grand Jury Investigation, In re, 407 Mass. 916, 556 N.E.2d 363 (1990)—§ 8.8(d) n.101

Grand Jury Investigation, In re, 746 F.Supp. 866 (E.D.Wis.1990)— § 8.7(b) n.38

Grand Jury Investigation, In re, 774 F.2d 34 (2d Cir.1985)—§§ 8.5(b) n.67; 8.5(i) n.310

Grand Jury Investigation, In re, 610 F.2d 202 (5th Cir.1980)—§§ 8.4(c) n.123; 8.5(c) n.72, 78; 8.5(d) n.127; 8.5(i) n.307, 316, 318 to 320, 324, 325; 27.2(e) n.77

Grand Jury Investigation, In re, 459 F.Supp. 1335 (E.D.Pa.1978)— § 8.7(b) n.59

Grand Jury Investigation, In re, 425 F.Supp. 717 (S.D.Fla.1977)— § 8.8(b) n.30

Grand Jury Investigation, In re, 436 F.Supp. 818 (W.D.Pa.1977)— §§ 8.14(a) n.11; 8.14(d) n.49, 54, 59

Grand Jury Investigation, In re, 486 F.2d 1013 (3d Cir.1973)—§ 8.11(d) n.76

Grand Jury Investigation, In the Matter of a, 427 Mass. 221, 692 N.E.2d 56 (1998)—§§ 8.7(d) n.71, 77, 79, 81

Grand Jury Investigation v. John Doe, In re, 399 F.3d 527 (2d Cir.2005)— § 8.8(d) n.89

Grand Jury Investigation, United States v., 417 F.Supp. 389 (E.D.Pa.1976)—§ 8.8(b) n.26

Grand Jury Investigation (90-3-2), Matter of, 748 F.Supp. 1188 (E.D.Mich.1990)—§§ 8.5(c) n.73; 8.5(i) n.304, 306, 319, 320, 325

Grand Jury Investigation (Balistrieri), In re, 503 F.Supp. 1112 (E.D.Wis.1980)—§§ 8.5(f) n.211; 15.4(a) n.10

Grand Jury Investigation (Braun), In re, 600 F.2d 420 (3d Cir.1979)— § 8.3(a) n.5

Grand Jury Investigation (Bruno), In re, 545 F.2d 385 (3d Cir.1976)— § 8.8(b) n.25

Grand Jury Investigation, Detroit Police Department Special Fund, In re, 922 F.2d 1266 (6th Cir.1991)— § 8.11(d) n.84

Grand Jury Investigation (DiLoreto), In re, 903 F.2d 180 (3d Cir.1990)— § 8.5(c) n.76

Grand Jury Investigation, General Motors Corp., In re, 32 F.R.D. 175 (S.D.N.Y.1963)—§§ 8.7(b) n.45; 8.8(f) n.149

Grand Jury Investigation (Heller), In re, 921 F.2d 1184 (11th Cir.1991)— § 8.12(e) n.54

Grand Jury Investigation (Jackson), In re, 696 F.2d 449 (6th Cir.1982)— § 8.9(a) n.4

Grand Jury Investigation (New Jersey State Commission of Investigation), In re, 630 F.2d 996 (3d Cir.1980)— § 8.5(c) n.93

Grand Jury Investigation No. 2184-86, In re, 219 N.J.Super. 90, 529 A.2d 1041 (1987)—§§ 8.7(b) n.61; 8.7(c) n.70

Grand Jury Investigation (Pflaumer), In re, 53 F.R.D. 464 (E.D.Pa.1971)— § 8.8(e) n.132

Grand Jury Investigation (Sturgis), In re, 412 F.Supp. 943 (E.D.Pa.1976)— §§ 8.6(b) n.39, 41

Grand Jury Investigation (United States), In re, 599 F.2d 1224 (3d Cir.1979)—§§ 8.6(b) n.44, 50, 51

Grand Jury, January 1969, In re, 315 F.Supp. 662 (D.Md.1970)— §§ 8.3(h) n.47; 15.1(d) n.172

Grand Jury, Leahy, In re, 735 F.2d 1230 (10th Cir.1984)—§ 8.9(b) n.23

Grand Jury Matter, In re, 789 F.Supp. 693 (D.Md.1992)—§§ 8.8(d) n.94; 11.9(a) n.21; 11.9(d) n.197

Grand Jury Matter, In re, 762 F.Supp. 333 (S.D.Fla.1991)—§ 8.6(b) n.37

Grand Jury Matter, In re, 926 F.2d 348 (4th Cir.1991)—§ 8.8(d) n.91

Grand Jury Matter, In re, 495 F.Supp. 127 (E.D.Pa.1980)—§ 8.5(h) n.296

Grand Jury Matter, Re, 516 F.Supp. 27 (E.D.Pa.1981)—§ 8.5(e) n.198

Grand Jury Matter (Backiel), In re, 906 F.2d 78 (3d Cir.1990)—§§ 8.5(b) n.58; 8.8(d) n.91; 8.9(b) n.33; 23.1(d) n.160

Grand Jury Matter (Catania), In re, 682 F.2d 61 (3d Cir.1982)—§§ 8.5(c) n.73, 85, 100

Grand Jury Matter (District Council 33), In re, 770 F.2d 36 (3d Cir.1985)—§ 8.8(b) n.28

Grand Jury Matter (Doe), In re, 798 F.2d 91 (3d Cir.1986)—§ 8.9(b) n.30

Grand Jury Matter (Garden Court Nursing Home), In re, 697 F.2d 511 (3d Cir.1982)—§§ 8.5(c) n.80, 81

Grand Jury Matter (Gronowicz), In re, 764 F.2d 983 (3d Cir.1985)—§§ 8.8(a) n.11; 8.8(d) n.57, 59

Grand Jury Matters, In re, 751 F.2d 13 (1st Cir.1984)—§§ 8.8(d) n.97, 98

Grand Jury No. 91-1, In re, 795 F.Supp. 1057 (D.Colo.1992)—§ 8.6(b) n.37

Grand Jury of Hennepin County, In re, 271 N.W.2d 817 (Minn.1978)—§ 8.3(h) n.38

Grand Jury of Wabasha County, In re, 309 Minn. 148, 244 N.W.2d 253 (1976)—§ 15.1(e) n.265

Grand Jury Proceeding, In re, 842 F.2d 1229 (11th Cir.1988)—§§ 8.8(d) n.54, 66, 68, 69, 71; 8.9(a) n.11

Grand Jury Proceeding, In re, 721 F.2d 1221 (9th Cir.1983)—§ 8.8(b) n.31

Grand Jury Proceeding, In re, 479 F.Supp. 93 (E.D.N.Y.1979)—§ 8.5(e) n.182

Grand Jury Proceeding, In re, 309 F.2d 440 (3d Cir.1962)—§ 8.5(h) n.303

Grand Jury Proceeding, Grand Jury 1988-2 (Cherney), In re, 898 F.2d 565 (7th Cir.1990)—§ 8.8(d) n.90

Grand Jury Proceeding (John Doe), In re, 13 F.3d 459 (1st Cir.1994)—§ 8.11(d) n.87

Grand Jury Proceeding (Nigro), In re, 705 F.2d 1224 (10th Cir.1982)—§ 8.10(b) n.45

Grand Jury Proceedings, In re, 219 F.3d 175 (2d Cir.2000)—§ 8.8(d) n.90

Grand Jury Proceedings, In re, 87 F.3d 377 (9th Cir.1996)—§ 8.6(b) n.52

Grand Jury Proceedings, In re, 55 F.3d 1012 (5th Cir.1995)—§ 8.13(d) n.112

Grand Jury Proceedings, In re, 43 F.3d 966 (5th Cir.1994)—§ 27.2(e) n.91

Grand Jury Proceedings, In re, 861 F.Supp. 386 (D.Md.1994)—§ 8.6(b) n.33

Grand Jury Proceedings, In re, 988 F.2d 211 (1st Cir.1992)—§ 8.9(b) n.22

Grand Jury Proceedings, In re, 707 F.Supp. 1207 (D.Hawai'i 1989)—§§ 8.7(b) n.33, 38, 42, 46, 61; 8.9(a) n.10

Grand Jury Proceedings, In re, 873 F.2d 238 (9th Cir.1989)—§ 8.3(a) n.1

Grand Jury Proceedings, In re, 851 F.2d 860 (6th Cir.1988)—§§ 8.5(c) n.90, 91, 95, 97, 107, 108

Grand Jury Proceedings, In re, 859 F.2d 1021 (1st Cir.1988)—§ 8.14(d) n.50

Grand Jury Proceedings, In re, 814 F.2d 61 (1st Cir.1987)—§§ 8.5(d) n.145, 147, 148; 8.8(e) n.132; 8.8(f) n.146, 149, 153, 161, 162; 27.2(e) n.96; 27.5(a) n.20

Grand Jury Proceedings, In re, 791 F.2d 663 (8th Cir.1986)—§ 8.8(d) n.91

Grand Jury Proceedings, In re, 776 F.2d 1099 (2d Cir.1985)—§§ 8.8(d) n.55, 66, 68, 69

Grand Jury Proceedings, In re, 558 F.Supp. 532 (W.D.Va.1983)—§§ 1.7(g) n.111; 8.5(d) n.145, 148

Grand Jury Proceedings, In re, 658 F.2d 782 (10th Cir.1981)—§ 15.2(h) n.187

Grand Jury Proceedings, In re, 664 F.2d 423 (5th Cir.1981)—§ 8.9(b) n.32

Grand Jury Proceedings, In re, 497 F.Supp. 979 (E.D.Pa.1980)— § 8.11(c) n.45

Grand Jury Proceedings, In re, 632 F.2d 1033 (3d Cir.1980)— § 27.2(e) n.95

Grand Jury Proceedings, In re, 601 F.2d 162 (5th Cir.1979)—§§ 8.7(a) n.24; 8.7(b) n.38; 8.12(c) n.38

Grand Jury Proceedings, In re, 445 F.Supp. 349 (D.R.I.1978)— §§ 8.5(e) n.182, 188

Grand Jury Proceedings, In re, 428 F.Supp. 273 (E.D.Mich.1976)— §§ 8.14(d) n.41, 54

Grand Jury Proceedings (86-2), In re, 640 F.Supp. 988 (E.D.Mich.1986)—§ 8.10(c) n.65

Grand Jury Proceedings 89-8, Matter of, 742 F.Supp. 1154 (S.D.Fla.1990)— § 8.13(d) n.87

Grand Jury Proceedings at Chattanoogo, Tennessee, In re, 649 F.2d 387 (6th Cir.1981)—§ 27.2(e) n.98

Grand Jury Proceedings, August 1984, Matter of, 757 F.2d 108 (7th Cir.1984)—§ 8.11(c) n.48

Grand Jury Proceedings (Bank of Nova Scotia), In re, 691 F.2d 1384 (11th Cir.1982)—§ 8.8(b) n.31

Grand Jury Proceedings (Bowe), In re, 694 F.2d 1256 (11th Cir.1982)— § 8.8(d) n.88

Grand Jury Proceedings (Caucus Distributors), In re, 871 F.2d 156 (1st Cir.1989)—§§ 8.3(a) n.2, 4

Grand Jury Proceedings (Doe), In re, 790 F.Supp. 422 (E.D.N.Y.1992)— §§ 8.4(b) n.29; 8.4(c) n.127; 8.11(d) n.87

Grand Jury Proceedings (Doe), In re, 708 F.Supp. 492 (E.D.N.Y.1988)— §§ 8.13(d) n.96, 100

Grand Jury Proceedings (Doe), In re, 575 F.Supp. 197 (N.D.Ohio 1983)—§ 8.14(a) n.10

Grand Jury Proceedings (Duffy), In re Matter of, 473 F.2d 840 (8th Cir.1973)—§§ 8.6(b) n.41, 47

Grand Jury Proceedings (Garrett), In re, 773 F.2d 1071 (9th Cir.1985)— § 8.9(b) n.29

Grand Jury Proceedings GJ-76-4 and GJ-75-3, In re, 800 F.2d 1293 (4th Cir.1986)—§§ 8.5(h) n.247, 259, 260

Grand Jury Proceedings (G.J. 80-264-2), In re, 514 F.Supp. 90 (E.D.Pa.1981)—§§ 8.8(b) n.26, 27

Grand Jury Proceedings (Goodman), In re, 33 F.3d 1060 (9th Cir.1994)— §§ 8.8(d) n.90, 91, 93

Grand Jury Proceedings, Grand Jury No. 87-4, In re, 856 F.2d 685 (4th Cir.1988)—§ 8.9(b) n.23

Grand Jury Proceedings (Gravel), In re, 605 F.2d 750 (5th Cir.1979)— § 8.11(d) n.87

Grand Jury Proceedings (Greentree), In re, 644 F.2d 348 (5th Cir.1981)— § 8.11(a) n.8

Grand Jury Proceedings Involving Eve Rosahn, In re, 671 F.2d 690 (2d Cir.1982)—§ 8.7(d) n.83

Grand Jury Proceedings Involving Vickers, In re, 38 F.Supp.2d 159 (D.N.H.1998)—§§ 8.7(c) n.70; 8.7(d) n.77, 82, 83

Grand Jury Proceedings, John Doe, In re, 943 F.2d 132 (1st Cir.1991)— §§ 8.11(d) n.84, 86, 87

Grand Jury Proceedings, John Doe, In re, 862 F.2d 430 (2d Cir.1988)— §§ 8.8(d) n.95; 8.11(d) n.85, 87

Grand Jury Proceedings (John Doe), In re, 754 F.2d 154 (6th Cir.1985)— §§ 8.8(b) n.31; 8.8(d) n.91

Grand Jury Proceedings (John Doe Co., Inc.), In re, 838 F.2d 624 (1st Cir.1988)—§§ 8.13(d) n.103, 108

Grand Jury Proceedings (Katsouros), In re, 613 F.2d 1171 (D.C.Cir.1979)— § 8.9(b) n.22

Grand Jury Proceedings, Lahey, In re, 914 F.2d 1372 (9th Cir.1990)— § 8.11(d) n.84

Grand Jury Proceedings (Macklen), In re, 525 F.Supp. 831 (D.S.C.1981)—§§ 8.9(b) n.26, 30

Grand Jury Proceedings (Manges), In re, 745 F.2d 1250 (9th Cir.1984)—§ 8.12(e) n.54

Grand Jury Proceedings (Marsoner), In re, 40 F.3d 959 (9th Cir.1994)—§ 8.13(a) n.7

Grand Jury Proceedings (McNabb), In re, 658 F.2d 211 (3d Cir.1981)—§ 8.8(b) n.30

Grand Jury Proceedings, Miller Brewing Co., In re, 687 F.2d 1079 (7th Cir.1982)—§§ 8.5(c) n.101; 8.5(h) n.250, 294; 8.8(e) n.125; 27.2(e) n.98

Grand Jury Proceedings (Mills), In re, 686 F.2d 135 (3d Cir.1982)—§§ 8.7(d) n.79, 83

Grand Jury Proceedings (No. 93-2), In re, 142 F.3d 1416 (11th Cir.1998)—§ 8.9(a) n.4

Grand Jury Proceedings of Guarino, Matter of, 104 N.J. 218, 516 A.2d 1063 (1986)—§ 8.12(g) n.66

Grand Jury Proceedings (PHE, Inc.), In re, 640 F.Supp. 149 (E.D.N.C.1986)—§§ 8.8(e) n.132; 8.8(g) n.167

Grand Jury Proceedings (Pressman), In re, 586 F.2d 724 (9th Cir.1978)—§ 8.8(f) n.155

Grand Jury Proceedings Relative to Perl, In re, 838 F.2d 304 (8th Cir.1988)—§§ 8.5(c) n.100; 8.5(h) n.270

Grand Jury Proceedings (Samuelson), In re, 763 F.2d 321 (8th Cir.1985)—§ 8.10(a) n.17

Grand Jury Proceedings (Scarce), In re, 5 F.3d 397 (9th Cir.1993)—§§ 8.8(d) n.48, 57, 65, 82

Grand Jury Proceedings (Schofield), In re, 507 F.2d 963 (3d Cir.1975)—§§ 8.5(f) n.211; 8.8(b) n.29

Grand Jury Proceedings (Schofield I), In re, 486 F.2d 85 (3d Cir.1973)—§§ 8.2(c) n.42, 43; 8.4(c) n.128; 8.5(c) n.76; 8.8(b) n.21

Grand Jury Proceedings (Sealed Case), In re, 867 F.2d 562 (9th Cir.1989)—§§ 8.12(e) n.50; 27.2(e) n.84

Grand Jury Proceedings (Shiffman), In re, 576 F.2d 703 (6th Cir.1978)—§ 8.12(b) n.21

Grand Jury Proceedings (Soto-Davila), In re, 96 F.R.D. 409 (D.Puerto Rico 1983)—§ 8.8(b) n.31

Grand Jury Proceedings, Special Grand Jury, In re, 89-2, 1993 WL 245557 (D.Colo.1993)—§ 8.3(h) n.47

Grand Jury Proceedings, Special Grand Jury 89-2, In re, 813 F.Supp. 1451 (D.Colo.1992)—§§ 8.3(h) n.47; 15.1(d) n.172

Grand Jury Proceedings, Storer Communications, Inc., In re, 810 F.2d 580 (6th Cir.1987)—§§ 8.8(d) n.50, 82

Grand Jury Proceedings: Subpoena Duces Tecum (Danbom), In re, 827 F.2d 301 (8th Cir.1987)—§§ 8.7(b) n.58; 8.8(c) n.46

Grand Jury Proceedings Subpoena to Vargas, In re, 723 F.2d 1461 (10th Cir.1983)—§ 27.2(e) n.90

Grand Jury Proceedings (Trimiew), In re, 9 F.3d 1389 (9th Cir.1993)—§ 8.11(c) n.48

Grand Jury Proceedings (T.S.), In re, 816 F.Supp. 1196 (W.D.Ky.1993)—§§ 8.7(d) n.71, 75, 76

Grand Jury Proceedings (Under Seal), In re, 102 F.3d 748 (4th Cir.1996)—§ 8.6(b) n.52

Grand Jury Proceedings (United States Steel-Clairton Works), In re, 525 F.2d 151 (3d Cir.1975)—§ 8.8(a) n.7

Grand Jury Proceedings (U.S. v. Law Firm Z), In re, 857 F.2d 707 (10th Cir.1988)—§ 8.7(b) n.45

Grand Jury Proceedings (Williams), In re, 995 F.2d 1013 (11th Cir.1993)—§§ 8.6(b) n.55, 56, 58, 60

Grand Jury Proceedings (Wilson), In re, 760 F.2d 26 (1st Cir.1985)—§§ 8.8(d) n.91, 93

Grand Jury Proceedings (Worobyzt), In re, 522 F.2d 196 (5th Cir.1975)—§ 8.9(b) n.21

Grand Jury Report, In re, 204 Wis. 409, 235 N.W. 789 (1931)—§ 8.3(h) n.42

Grand Jury Sitting in Cedar Rapids, Iowa, In re, 734 F.Supp. 875 (N.D.Iowa 1990)—§ 8.3(h) n.38

Grand Jury Subpoena, In re, 198 F.Supp.2d 1113 (D.Alaska 2002)—§§ 8.6(b) n.33, 56

Grand Jury Subpoena, In re, 223 F.3d 213 (3d Cir.2000)—§§ 8.8(b) n.24; 8.8(d) n.93

Grand Jury Subpoena, In re, 190 F.3d 375 (5th Cir.1999)—§ 27.2(e) n.90

Grand Jury Subpoena, In re, 119 F.3d 750 (9th Cir.1997)—§ 27.2(e) n.95

Grand Jury Subpoena, In re, 21 F.3d 226 (8th Cir.1994)—§ 8.12(c) n.41

Grand Jury Subpoena, In re, 973 F.2d 45 (1st Cir.1992)—§§ 8.12(b) n.21; 8.12(g) n.63; 8.13(a) n.17

Grand Jury Subpoena, In re, 920 F.2d 235 (4th Cir.1990)—§§ 8.5(c) n.85 to 87, 89, 100; 8.7(b) n.49; 8.8(c) n.45

Grand Jury Subpoena, In re, 836 F.2d 1468 (4th Cir.1988)—§§ 8.6(b) n.56 to 59

Grand Jury Subpoena, In re, 831 F.2d 225 (11th Cir.1987)—§ 8.8(d) n.88

Grand Jury Subpoena, In re, 626 F.Supp. 1057 (D.P.R.1986)—§ 8.7(b) n.35

Grand Jury Subpoena, In re, 739 F.2d 1354 (8th Cir.1984)—§ 8.10(c) n.65

Grand Jury Subpoena, In re, 167 N.J.Super. 471, 401 A.2d 258 (1979)—§ 8.7(b) n.46

Grand Jury Subpoena, In the Matter of a, 411 Mass. 489, 583 N.E.2d 241 (1992)—§ 27.2(e) n.90

Grand Jury Subpoena v. McDougal, In re, 97 F.3d 1090 (8th Cir.1996)—§§ 8.5(b) n.58, 59; 8.14(a) n.10; 23.1(d) n.160

Grand Jury Subpoena 92-1(SJ), In re, 31 F.3d 826 (9th Cir.1994)—§ 27.5(e) n.176

Grand Jury Subpoena American Broadcasting Companies, Inc., In re, 947 F.Supp. 1314 (E.D.Ark.1996)—§§ 8.8(d) n.47, 82

Grand Jury Subpoena, April 18, 2003, 383 F.3d 905 (9th Cir.2004)—§§ 8.13(a) n.44, 45

Grand Jury Subpoena c/d 91R0052-11, In re, 142 F.R.D. 122 (M.D.N.C.1992)—§§ 8.8(d) n.94; 8.13(b) n.60; 11.9(a) n.21

Grand Jury Subpoena Dated August 9, 2000, In re, 218 F.Supp.2d 544 (S.D.N.Y.2002)—§§ 8.6(b) n.34, 56

Grand Jury Subpoena Dated December 19, 1978, In re, 599 F.2d 504 (2d Cir.1979)—§§ 8.6(b) n.44, 47, 50

Grand Jury Subpoena Dated Jan. 4, 1984 In re, 750 F.2d 223 (2d Cir.1984)—§ 8.8(d) n.57

Grand Jury Subpoena Dated January 30, 1986 to Bronx Democratic Party, In re, 784 F.2d 116 (2d Cir.1986)—§ 27.2(e) n.90

Grand Jury Subpoena Dated June 5, In re, 825 F.2d 231 (9th Cir.1987)—§ 27.2(e) n.83

Grand Jury Subpoena Dated November 12, 1991, In re, 957 F.2d 807 (11th Cir.1992)—§§ 8.13(d) n.114, 115

Grand Jury Subpoena Dated November 14, 1989, In re, 728 F.Supp. 368 (W.D.Pa.1990)—§ 8.6(b) n.33

Grand Jury Subpoena Dated Oct. 22, 1991, Matter of, 959 F.2d 1158 (2d Cir.1992)—§§ 8.13(a) n.28; 8.13(d) n.94, 109

Grand Jury Subpoena Dated October 22, 2001, In re, 282 F.3d 156 (2d Cir.2002)—§§ 8.6(b) n.50; 8.8(d) n.92

Grand Jury Subpoena, Deguerin, In re, 926 F.2d 1423 (5th Cir.1991)— § 8.8(d) n.90

Grand Jury Subpoena (Doe), In re, 72 F.3d 271 (2d Cir.1995)—§§ 8.5(d) n.135, 137

Grand Jury Subpoena Duces Tecum, In re, 31 F.Supp.2d 542 (N.D.W.Va.1998)—§ 13.5(h) n.142

Grand Jury Subpoena Duces Tecum, In re, 112 F.3d 910 (8th Cir.1997)— §§ 8.8(d) n.89; 27.3(c) n.41

Grand Jury Subpoena Duces Tecum, In re, 955 F.2d 670 (11th Cir.1992)— § 8.3(a) n.2

Grand Jury Subpoena Duces Tecum, In re, 797 F.2d 676 (8th Cir.1986)— § 8.5(d) n.147

Grand Jury Subpoena Duces Tecum, In re, 143 N.J.Super. 526, 363 A.2d 936 (1976)—§§ 8.7(b) n.30, 36, 54; 8.8(b) n.30

Grand Jury Subpoena Duces Tecum, In re, 342 F.Supp. 709 (D.Md.1972)— §§ 8.7(b) n.31, 35, 40, 43, 57

Grand Jury Subpoena Duces Tecum Addressed to Provision Salesmen and Distributors Union, Local 627, In re, 203 F.Supp. 575 (S.D.N.Y.1961)—§§ 8.7(b) n.36, 42, 50, 55

Grand Jury Subpoena Duces Tecum (Armada Petroleum), In re, 520 F.Supp. 253 (S.D.Tex.1981)—§ 8.8(e) n.137

Grand Jury Subpoena Duces Tecum (Arrington), In re, 782 F.Supp. 1518 (N.D.Ala.1992)—§§ 8.8(d) n.56, 68; 8.10(a) n.11; 8.13(a) n.25; 8.13(b) n.59

Grand Jury Subpoena Duces Tecum (Corrado Bros.), In re, 367 F.Supp. 1126 (D.Del.1973)—§§ 8.7(b) n.37, 40, 41, 48, 53

Grand Jury Subpoena Duces Tecum Dated April 19, 1991, In re, 945 F.2d 1221 (2d Cir.1991)—§ 8.6(b) n.54

Grand Jury Subpoena Duces Tecum Dated April 23, 1981 v. United States, In re, 657 F.2d 5 (2d Cir.1981)—§ 8.13(d) n.112

Grand Jury Subpoena Duces Tecum Dated April 23, 1981, In re, 522 F.Supp. 977 (S.D.N.Y.1981)— § 8.13(d) n.109

Grand Jury Subpoena Duces Tecum Dated December 9, 1983, In re, 575 F.Supp. 1219 (E.D.Pa.1983)— §§ 8.5(b) n.40; 8.5(d) n.148

Grand Jury Subpoena Duces Tecum Dated January 2, 1985 (Simels), In re, 767 F.2d 26 (2d Cir.1985)— §§ 8.8(f) n.149, 155, 157, 161

Grand Jury Subpoena Duces Tecum Dated May 9, 1990, In re, 741 F.Supp. 1059 (S.D.N.Y.1990)— §§ 8.8(f) n.153, 159; 8.12(g) n.64

Grand Jury Subpoena Duces Tecum Dated May 29, 1987, In re, 834 F.2d 1128 (2d Cir.1987)—§ 8.12(e) n.54

Grand Jury Subpoena Duces Tecum Dated November 13, 1984, In re, 605 F.Supp. 174 (E.D.N.Y.1985)— §§ 8.12(b) n.20; 8.12(g) n.64

Grand Jury Subpoena Duces Tecum Dated November 13, 1984, In re, 616 F.Supp. 1159 (E.D.N.Y.1985)—§§ 8.13(a) n.16, 27

Grand Jury Subpoena Duces Tecum Dated November 15, 1993, In re, 846 F.Supp. 11 (S.D.N.Y.1994)— §§ 8.7(b) n.34; 8.8(b) n.42

Grand Jury Subpoena Duces Tecum Dated October 29, 1992, In re, 1 F.3d 87 (2d Cir.1993)—§§ 8.12(g) n.67 to 69; 8.13(a) n.16, 24, 25, 31

Grand Jury Subpoena Duces Tecum Issued on June 9, 1982, In re, 697 F.2d 277 (10th Cir.1983)—§ 8.8(b) n.30

Grand Jury Subpoena Duces Tecum Issued to Southern Motor Carriers Rate Conference, Inc., In re, 405 F.Supp. 1192 (N.D.Ga.1975)—

§§ 8.7(b) n.41, 45, 50, 59, 61; 8.8(a) n.7

Grand Jury Subpoena Duces Tecum (M.G. Allen), In re, 391 F.Supp. 991 (D.R.I.1975)—§§ 8.7(b) n.36, 40, 41, 46, 47, 53

Grand Jury Subpoena Duces Tecum served on the Museum of Modern Art, In the Matter of, 93 N.Y.2d 729, 697 N.Y.S.2d 538, 719 N.E.2d 897 (1999)—§ 8.6(b) n.37

Grand Jury Subpoena Duces Tecum (Underhill), In re, 781 F.2d 64 (6th Cir.1986)—§ 8.12(c) n.41

Grand Jury Subpoena For Attorney Representing Criminal Defendant Reyes-Requena, In re, 913 F.2d 1118 (5th Cir.1990)—§§ 8.8(d) n.94, 97, 98

Grand Jury Subpoena (Huntington Beach Police Department), In re, 75 F.3d 446 (9th Cir.1996)—§ 8.11(c) n.52

Grand Jury Subpoena Issued to Bailin, In re, 51 F.3d 203 (9th Cir.1995)— § 27.2(e) n.90

Grand Jury Subpoena Issued to First National Bank of Maryland, In re, 436 F.Supp. 46 (D.Md.1977)— § 8.8(c) n.44

Grand Jury Subpoena, John Doe No. 4, In re v. John Doe No. 1, 103 F.3d 234 (2d Cir.1996)—§ 23.1(d) n.158

Grand Jury Subpoena, Judith Miller, In re, 438 F.3d 1138 (D.C.Cir.2006)— § 8.5(c) n.75

Grand Jury Subpoena (Kent), In re, 646 F.2d 963 (5th Cir.1981)—§ 8.12(e) n.52

Grand Jury Subpoena (Miller), In re, 397 F.3d 964 (D.C.Cir.2005)— §§ 8.8(d) n.81, 83, 85

Grand Jury Subpoena (Model Magazine), In re, 829 F.2d 1291 (4th Cir.1987)—§§ 8.7(b) n.33, 61

Grand Jury Subpoena (Newparent, Inc.), In re, 274 F.3d 563 (1st Cir.2001)— § 8.5(d) n.159

Grand Jury Subpoena of Glenn Lincoln, In re, 767 F.2d 1130 (5th Cir.1985)—§ 8.13(a) n.21

Grand Jury Subpoena of Rochon, In re, 686 F.Supp. 195 (N.D.Ill.1988)— § 8.8(e) n.131

Grand Jury Subpoena of Stewart, In re, 156 A.D.2d 294, 548 N.Y.S.2d 679 (1989)—§§ 8.4(c) n.129; 8.8(d) n.98

Grand Jury Subpoena (Psychological Treatment Records), In re, 710 F.Supp. 999 (D.N.J.1989)— § 8.6(b) n.33

Grand Jury Subpoena (Roach), In re, 138 F.3d 442 (1st Cir.1998)—§ 8.6(b) n.61

Grand Jury Subpoenas, In re, 144 F.3d 653 (10th Cir.1998)—§ 8.10(a) n.6

Grand Jury Subpoenas, In re, 123 F.3d 695 (1st Cir.1997)—§§ 27.2(e) n.89, 92

Grand Jury Subpoenas, In re, 818 F.2d 330 (5th Cir.1987)—§ 27.2(e) n.95

Grand Jury Subpoenas, In re, 387 So.2d 1140 (La.1980)—§ 8.14(a) n.7

Grand Jury Subpoenas (Anderson), In re, 906 F.2d 1485 (10th Cir.1990)— §§ 8.7(b) n.36; 8.8(d) n.90, 91

Grand Jury Subpoenas, April, 1978, In re, 581 F.2d 1103 (4th Cir.1978)— §§ 8.5(i) n.310; 8.8(e) n.132, 137, 139, 143; 27.2(e) n.94, 95; 27.4(c) n.29

Grand Jury Subpoenas Dated December 7 and 8, Issued to Bob Stover, Chief of Albuquerque Police Dept. v. United States, In re, 40 F.3d 1096 (10th Cir.1994)—§§ 8.11(c) n.52; 27.2(e) n.85

Grand Jury Subpoenas Dated December 10, 1987, In re, 926 F.2d 847 (9th Cir.1991)—§§ 3.4(a) n.22; 8.7(e) n.91, 94

Grand Jury Subpoenas Dated June 27, 1991, In re, 772 F.Supp. 326 (N.D.Tex.1991)—§ 8.12(c) n.38

Grand Jury Subpoenas Dated March 19, 2002 and August 2, 2002 (Mercator Corp.), In re, 318 F.3d 379 (2d Cir.2003)—§ 8.6(b) n.50

Grand Jury Subpoenas Duces Tecum Dated Aug. 1986, In re, 658 F.Supp. 474 (D.Md.1987)—§ 8.13(a) n.25

Grand Jury Subpoenas Duces Tecum Dated June 13, 1983, In re, 722 F.2d 981 (2d Cir.1983)—§ 8.13(b) n.49

Grand Jury Subpoenas Duces Tecum (Farber), In the Matter of, 241 N.J.Super. 18, 574 A.2d 449 (1989)—§ 8.8(d) n.88

Grand Jury Subpoenas Duces Tecum (Rice), In re, 483 F.Supp. 1085 (D.Minn.1979)—§ 8.9(a) n.4

Grand Jury Subpoena Served on Crown Video Unlimited, Inc., In re, 630 F.Supp. 614 (E.D.N.C.1986)—§ 8.8(d) n.52

Grand Jury Subpoena Served on Doe, In re, 889 F.2d 384 (2d Cir.1989)—§ 4.6(i) n.156

Grand Jury Subpoena Served on Meserve, Mumper & Hughes, In re, 62 F.3d 1222 (9th Cir.1995)—§§ 8.6(b) n.56, 58 to 60

Grand Jury Subpoena Served Upon Doe, In re, 781 F.2d 238 (2d Cir.1986)—§§ 8.8(d) n.91, 95, 96; 8.14(a) n.8

Grand Jury Subpoena Served Upon Niren, In re, 784 F.2d 939 (9th Cir.1986)—§ 27.2(e) n.90

Grand Jury Subpoenas for Locals 17, 135, 257, & 608, In re, 72 N.Y.2d 307, 532 N.Y.S.2d 722, 528 N.E.2d 1195 (1988)—§§ 8.8(d) n.54, 66, 68, 73

Grand Jury Subpoenas Issued May 3, 1994 for Nash, In re Matter of, 858 F.Supp. 132 (1994)—§§ 8.8(d) n.98; 8.8(f) n.148, 157

Grand Jury Subpoenas Served February 27, 1984, In re, 599 F.Supp. 1006 (E.D.Wash.1984)—§§ 8.13(a) n.21, 22, 31, 32

Grand Jury Subpoenas Served Upon Doe, In re Matter of, 142 Misc.2d 229, 536 N.Y.S.2d 926 (Sup.Ct.1988)—§ 8.6(b) n.52

Grand Jury Subpoenas Served Upon Doe, In re Matter of, 536 N.Y.S.2d 926, 142 Misc.2d 229 (Sup.Ct.1988)—§ 8.6(b) n.44

Grand Jury Subpoena to John Doe, In re, 41 F.Supp.2d 616 (W.D.Va.1999)—§ 8.10(a) n.11

Grand Jury Subpoena (Under Seal), In re, 175 F.3d 332 (4th Cir.1999)—§§ 8.8(e) n.123, 132, 135, 138, 139; 8.8(f) n.160

Grand Jury Summoned Oct. 12, 1970, In re, 321 F.Supp. 238 (N.D.Ohio 1970)—§ 8.5(d) n.145

Grand Jury Testimony, Doe, In re, 832 F.2d 60 (5th Cir.1987)—§ 8.5(h) n.265

Grand Jury Transcripts, In re, 309 F.Supp. 1050 (S.D.Ohio 1970)—§ 8.5(h) n.298

Grand Jury (Vigil), In re, 524 F.2d 209 (10th Cir.1975)—§§ 8.8(g) n.170; 8.9(b) n.29

Grand Jury Which Presented Criminal Indictments 76-149 to 77-72, In re, 469 F.Supp. 666 (M.D.Pa.1978)—§ 8.5(c) n.94

Grand Rapids, City of v. Impens, 414 Mich. 667, 327 N.W.2d 278 (1982)—§ 6.10(b) n.24

Grand Trunk Railway, United States v., 225 Fed. 283 (W.D.N.Y.1915)—§ 16.2(g) n.129

Granello, United States v., 365 F.2d 990 (2d Cir.1966)—§ 17.2(a) n.22

Grant v. City of Long Beach, 315 F.3d 1081 (9th Cir.2002)—§ 3.3(d) n.162

Grant, Commonwealth v., 572 Pa. 48, 813 A.2d 726 (2002)—§ 28.4(d) n.57

Grant, People v., 445 Mich. 535, 520 N.W.2d 123 (1994)—§ 27.5(d) n.137

Grant v. Sheriff, 95 Nev. 211, 591 P.2d 1145 (1979)—§ 15.5(c) n.122

Grant, State v., 361 N.J.Super. 349, 825 A.2d 577 (2003)—§ 15.6(a) n.17

Grant, State v., 274 Ga. 826, 561 S.E.2d 94 (2002)—§ 19.2(c) n.25

Grant, State v., 67 Ohio St.3d 465, 620 N.E.2d 50 (1993)—§ 20.6(b) n.27

Grant v. State, 73 Wis.2d 441, 243 N.W.2d 186 (1976)—§ 21.2(d) n.186

Grant, State v., 102 N.J.Super. 164, 245 A.2d 528 (1968)—§ 7.4(b) n.18

Grant v. United States, 856 A.2d 1131 (D.C.App.2004)—§ 18.4(c) n.40

Grant, United States v., 349 F.3d 192 (5th Cir.2003)—§ 9.1(d) n.120

Grant, United States v., 117 F.3d 788 (5th Cir.1997)—§ 21.5(a) n.11

Grant, United States v., 816 F.2d 440 (9th Cir.1987)—§ 26.1(e) n.120

Grant-Chase v. Commissioner, 145 F.3d 431 (1st Cir.1998)—§ 6.9(g) n.189

Grantham, Ex parte, 613 So.2d 1260 (Ala.1993)—§ 25.4(c) n.37

Grantham v. State, 214 Miss. 756, 59 So.2d 344 (1952)—§ 15.6(d) n.117

Granviel v. Lynaugh, 881 F.2d 185 (5th Cir.1989)—§§ 6.7(b) n.105; 11.2(e) n.176, 178, 179; 20.4(e) n.82

Grap, United States v., 368 F.3d 824 (8th Cir.2004)—§ 21.2(d) n.217

Grass, United States v., 239 F.Supp.2d 535 (M.D.Pa.2003)—§§ 1.7(j) n.262; 11.8(b) n.40

Grau v. United States, 287 U.S. 124, 53 S.Ct. 38, 77 L.Ed. 212 (1932)—§ 3.3(b) n.57

Gravatt, United States v., 868 F.2d 585 (3d Cir.1989)—§ 11.2(g) n.305

Gravel, State v., 135 N.H. 172, 601 A.2d 678 (1991)—§ 9.5(b) n.42

Graves v. Cockrell, 351 F.3d 156 (5th Cir.2003)—§ 28.4(d) n.62

Graves v. Dretke, 442 F.3d 334 (5th Cir.2006)—§ 24.3(b) n.35

Graves, State v., 126 S.W.3d 873 (Tenn.2003)—§§ 14.1(b) n.31, 36

Graves, State v., 668 N.W.2d 860 (Iowa 2003)—§ 24.7(e) n.46

Graves v. State, 112 Nev. 118, 912 P.2d 234 (1996)—§ 11.3(b) n.44

Graves, State v., 60 N.J. 441, 291 A.2d 2 (1972)—§ 6.10(c) n.37

Graves, United States v., 374 F.3d 80 (2d Cir.2004)—§ 21.2(d) n.148

Graves, United States v., 106 F.3d 342 (10th Cir.1997)—§ 21.4(f) n.179

Graves, United States v., 98 F.3d 258 (7th Cir.1996)—§§ 21.4(d) n.151; 21.5(f) n.170

Graves v. United States, 472 A.2d 395 (D.C.App.1984)—§ 17.2(c) n.86

Graves v. United States, 490 A.2d 1086 (D.C.App.1984)—§§ 18.2(b) n.17; 18.2(c) n.35; 18.2(d) n.63; 18.2(e) n.79

Gravitt v. United States, 523 F.2d 1211 (5th Cir.1975)—§ 18.1(c) n.38

Grawien, State v., 123 Wis.2d 428, 367 N.W.2d 816 (App.1985)—§ 2.12(e) n.218

Gray v. Commissioner of Internal Revenue, 708 F.2d 243 (6th Cir.1983)—§ 21.4(a) n.20

Gray v. Commonwealth, 226 Va. 591, 311 S.E.2d 409 (1984)—§ 22.3(c) n.102

Gray v. District Court, 884 P.2d 286 (Colo.1994)—§§ 20.4(f) n.92; 20.5(c) n.55

Gray v. Maryland, 523 U.S. 185, 118 S.Ct. 1151, 140 L.Ed.2d 294 (1998)—§§ 17.2(b) n.60, 70

Gray v. Mississippi, 481 U.S. 648, 107 S.Ct. 2045, 95 L.Ed.2d 622 (1987)—§§ 22.3(c) n.148; 27.6(d) n.106, 134

Gray v. Netherland, 518 U.S. 152, 116 S.Ct. 2074, 135 L.Ed.2d 457 (1996)—§§ 26.4(d) n.48; 28.5(a) n.32; 28.6(d) n.25; 28.6(e) n.46, 58

Gray v. North Dakota Game and Fish Dept., 706 N.W.2d 614 (N.D.2005)—§ 17.4(b) n.123

Gray, People v., 214 Ill.2d 1, 291 Ill.Dec. 263, 823 N.E.2d 555 (2005)— § 21.2(e) n.325

Gray, People v., 158 Misc.2d 597, 601 N.Y.S.2d 526 (1993)—§ 15.2(c) n.80

Gray, People v., 69 Mich.App. 685, 245 N.W.2d 165 (1976)—§ 7.3(c) n.47

Gray v. Raines, 662 F.2d 569 (9th Cir.1981)—§§ 2.6(a) n.22; 19.2(c) n.29

Gray, State v., 217 W.Va. 591, 619 S.E.2d 104 (2005)—§ 21.2(f) n.392

Gray v. State, 368 Md. 529, 796 A.2d 697 (2002)—§ 24.4(c) n.20

Gray v. State, 728 So.2d 36 (Miss.1998)—§§ 19.3(b) n.147; 19.3(e) n.211

Gray, State v., 129 Idaho 784, 932 P.2d 907 (Idaho App.1997)—§ 24.9(a) n.10

Gray, State v., 958 S.W.2d 302 (Ark.1997)—§ 27.3(c) n.32

Gray, State v., 239 Neb. 1024, 479 N.W.2d 796 (1992)—§ 24.6(b) n.28

Gray v. State, 317 Md. 250, 562 A.2d 1278 (1989)—§ 22.3(d) n.230

Gray v. State, 549 So.2d 1316 (Miss.1989)—§ 17.1(b) n.35

Gray v. State, 249 Ind. 629, 231 N.E.2d 793 (1967)—§ 5.4(b) n.16

Gray, United States v., 410 F.3d 338 (7th Cir.2005)—§ 4.6(e) n.97

Gray, United States v., 78 F.Supp.2d 524 (E.D.Va.1999)—§ 3.4(j) n.202

Gray, United States v., 105 F.3d 956 (5th Cir.1997)—§ 24.7(b) n.20

Gray, United States v., 659 F.2d 1296 (5th Cir.1981)—§ 6.6(e) n.94

Gray, United States v., 448 F.2d 164 (9th Cir.1971)—§ 13.2(c) n.57

Graybeal v. State, 13 Md.App. 557, 284 A.2d 37 (1971)—§ 6.7(d) n.146

Gray-Bey v. United States, 201 F.3d 866 (7th Cir.2000)—§ 28.9(b) n.55

Graybill, State v., 695 P.2d 725 (Alaska 1985)—§ 26.3(g) n.79

Grayer v. State, 234 Ark. 548, 353 S.W.2d 148 (1962)—§ 18.5(a) n.47

Grayhurst, State v., 852 A.2d 491 (R.I.2004)—§§ 6.7(d) n.145, 153

Grayned v. City of Rockford, 408 U.S. 104, 92 S.Ct. 2294, 33 L.Ed.2d 222 (1972)—§ 26.9(b) n.15

Grayson, Ex parte, 479 So.2d 76 (Ala.1985)—§§ 11.2(e) n.184, 207, 210

Grayson v. King, 460 F.3d 1328 (11th Cir.2006)—§ 24.3(b) n.80

Grayson, People v., 58 Ill.2d 260, 319 N.E.2d 43 (1974)—§ 17.4(a) n.67

Grayson, United States v., 438 U.S. 41, 98 S.Ct. 2610, 57 L.Ed.2d 582 (1978)—§§ 21.1(e) n.74; 26.4(c) n.27; 26.8(c) n.27

Gray, State ex rel. v. McClure, 161 W.Va. 488, 242 S.E.2d 704 (1978)—§ 21.2(f) n.362

Grazier, Commonwealth v., 481 Pa. 622, 393 A.2d 335 (1978)—§§ 17.4(a) n.64; 25.5(b) n.23

Greatwalker, United States v., 285 F.3d 727 (8th Cir.2002)—§ 21.2(e) n.321

Greco v. State, 307 Md. 470, 515 A.2d 220 (1986)—§ 16.2(e) n.80

Greeley, State v., 178 N.J. 38, 834 A.2d 1016 (2003)—§ 21.6(b) n.84

Green v. Arn, 809 F.2d 1257 (6th Cir.1987)—§ 11.10(d) n.200

Green v. Artuz, 990 F.Supp. 267 (S.D.N.Y.1998)—§ 28.7(d) n.28

Green v. Baldwin, 204 Or.App. 351, 129 P.3d 734 (2006)—§ 28.11(b) n.21

Green v. Butler, 420 F.3d 689 (7th Cir.2003)—§ 3.6(b) n.43

Green v. Commonwealth, 262 Va. 105, 546 S.E.2d 446 (2001)—§§ 22.3(c) n.105, 154

Green, Commonwealth v., 551 Pa. 88, 709 A.2d 382 (1998)—§§ 11.7(e) n.73, 78, 83

Green, Commonwealth v., 420 Mass. 771, 652 N.E.2d 572 (1995)— § 22.3(d) n.223

Green, Commonwealth v., 126 Pa. 531, 17 A. 878 (1889)—§ 15.1(d) n.161

Green v. Georgia, 442 U.S. 95, 99 S.Ct. 2150, 60 L.Ed.2d 738 (1979)— §§ 1.8(e) n.87; 24.4(a) n.5; 26.4(g) n.116

Green, People v., 187 A.D.2d 528, 589 N.Y.S.2d 916 (1993)—§ 15.2(c) n.79

Green, People v., 56 N.Y.2d 427, 452 N.Y.S.2d 389, 437 N.E.2d 1146 (1982)—§ 24.8(e) n.50

Green, People v., 112 Mich.App. 655, 317 N.W.2d 212 (1981)— § 26.10(c) n.71

Green, People v., 83 Ill.App.3d 982, 39 Ill.Dec. 339, 404 N.E.2d 930 (1980)—§ 19.6(b) n.22

Green v. Petit, 222 Ind. 467, 54 N.E.2d 281 (1944)—§ 12.1(b) n.25

Green, State v., 283 Kan. 531, 153 P.3d 1216 (2007)—§ 21.4(f) n.184

Green, State v., 108 P.3d 710 (Utah 2005)—§ 18.5(a) n.45

Green v. State, 279 Ga. 455, 614 S.E.2d 751 (2005)—§ 7.4(b) n.29

Green v. State, 362 Ark. 459, 209 S.W.3d 339 (2005)—§§ 21.5(d) n.101; 27.5(d) n.119

Green v. State, 119 Nev. 542, 80 P.3d 93 (Nev.2003)—§ 24.8(d) n.47

Green, State v., 253 Wis.2d 356, 646 N.W.2d 298 (2002)—§ 24.3(f) n.158

Green v. State, 274 Ga. 686, 558 S.E.2d 707 (2002)—§ 17.2(d) n.95

Green v. State, 275 Ga. 569, 570 S.E.2d 207 (2002)—§ 3.4(b) n.33

Green, State v., 367 Md. 61, 785 A.2d 1275 (2001)—§ 27.3(b) n.17

Green v. State, 330 Ark. 458, 956 S.W.2d 849 (1997)—§§ 22.3(d) n.247, 249

Green v. State, 688 So.2d 301 (Fla.1996)—§§ 3.1(c) n.72; 27.6(b) n.45

Green, State v., 540 N.W.2d 649 (Iowa 1995)—§ 3.3(b) n.47

Green v. State, 620 So.2d 188 (Fla.1993)—§§ 11.1(d) n.128; 11.2(b) n.66

Green v. State, 835 S.W.2d 142 (Tex.App.1992)—§ 7.4(e) n.89

Green, State v., 133 N.H. 249, 575 A.2d 1308 (1990)—§ 3.10(b) n.49

Green, State v., 236 Neb. 33, 458 N.W.2d 472 (1990)—§ 22.1(g) n.115

Green, State v., 324 N.C. 238, 376 S.E.2d 727 (1989)—§ 22.3(d) n.230

Green, State v., 493 So.2d 1178 (La.1986)—§§ 20.4(b) n.30, 32

Green v. State, 463 So.2d 1139 (Fla.1985)—§ 17.4(a) n.31

Green v. State, 682 S.W.2d 271 (Tex.Cr.App.1984)—§ 6.8(d) n.84

Green, State v., 395 So.2d 532 (Fla.1981)—§§ 23.3(b) n.18, 27

Green, State v., 44 Or.App. 253, 605 P.2d 746 (1980)—§ 19.5(b) n.44

Green, State v., 49 Or.App. 949, 621 P.2d 67 (1980)—§ 27.5(c) n.88

Green, State v., 275 So.2d 184 (La.1973)—§ 12.4(a) n.21

Green v. State, 161 Tex.Crim. 131, 275 S.W.2d 110 (1955)—§ 3.4(e) n.90

Green, State v., 128 Or. 49, 273 P. 381 (1929)—§ 6.2(a) n.12

Green v. Travis, 414 F.3d 288 (2d Cir.2005)—§ 22.3(d) n.218

Green, United States v., 435 F.3d 1265 (10th Cir.2006)—§ 22.2(d) n.70

Green, United States v., 405 F.3d 1180 (10th Cir.2005)—§ 21.2(a) n.7

Green, United States v., 407 F.3d 434 (1st Cir.2005)—§ 22.3(c) n.160

Green, United States v., 388 F.3d 918 (6th Cir.2004)—§ 11.4(d) n.117

Green, United States v., 293 F.3d 855 (5th Cir.2002)—§ 3.9(h) n.168

Green, United States v., 272 F.3d 748 (5th Cir.2001)—§ 6.7(b) n.40

Green, United States v., 507 U.S. 545, 113 S.Ct. 1835, 123 L.Ed.2d 260 (1993)—§ 27.5(a) n.2

Green, United States v., 592 A.2d 985 (D.C.App.1991)—§ 6.9(f) n.146

Green v. United States, 580 A.2d 1325 (D.C.App.1990)—§ 7.4(e) n.86

Green, United States v., 670 F.2d 1148 (D.C.Cir.1981)—§§ 3.3(f) n.202; 10.5(e) n.57

Green, United States v., 24 U.S.C.M.A. 299, 1 M.J. 453 (1976)—§ 21.3(d) n.261

Green, United States v., 523 F.2d 968 (9th Cir.1975)—§ 9.4(a) n.47

Green, United States v., 525 F.2d 386 (8th Cir.1975)—§ 7.5(b) n.10

Green, United States v., 474 F.2d 1385 (5th Cir.1973)—§ 3.9(e) n.76

Green v. United States, 365 U.S. 301, 81 S.Ct. 653, 5 L.Ed.2d 670 (1961)—§ 26.4(g) n.136

Green, United States v., 350 U.S. 415, 76 S.Ct. 522, 100 L.Ed. 494 (1956)—§ 1.2(c) n.132

Green v. United States, 355 U.S. 184, 78 S.Ct. 221, 21 L.Ed.2d 199 (1957)—§§ 2.1 n.43, 54; 15.1(b) n.23; 21.5(e) n.117; 25.1(b) n.4; 25.4(d) n.41

Green v. United States, 356 U.S. 165, 78 S.Ct. 632, 2 L.Ed.2d 672 (1958)—§ 15.1(b) n.83

Greenawalt v. Stewart, 105 F.3d 1287 (9th Cir.1997)—§ 28.7(c) n.21

Greene v. Georgia, 519 U.S. 145, 117 S.Ct. 578, 136 L.Ed.2d 507 (1996)—§ 27.5(e) n.143

Greene v. Grievance Committee, 54 N.Y.2d 118, 444 N.Y.S.2d 883, 429 N.E.2d 390 (1981)—§ 1.7(j) n.245

Greene, State v., 274 Conn. 134, 874 A.2d 750 (2005)—§ 21.4(d) n.120

Greene v. State, 343 Ark. 526, 37 S.W.3d 579 (2001)—§ 26.5(d) n.74

Greene, State v., 137 N.H. 126, 623 A.2d 1342 (1993)—§ 24.10(c) n.40

Greene, State v., 209 Conn. 458, 551 A.2d 1231 (1988)—§ 17.1(d) n.53

Greene, State v., 92 N.M. 347, 588 P.2d 548 (1978)—§ 6.9(f) n.110

Greene, United States v., 250 F.3d 471 (6th Cir.2001)—§§ 3.3(c) n.94; 3.4(f) n.120

Greene, United States v., 995 F.2d 793 (8th Cir.1993)—§§ 15.4(d) n.124; 22.2(d) n.89

Greene, United States v., 591 F.2d 471 (8th Cir.1979)—§ 10.5(a) n.15

Greene v. United States, 454 F.2d 783 (9th Cir.1971)—§ 5.4(c) n.46

Greener, United States v., 979 F.2d 517 (7th Cir.1992)—§ 21.1(h) n.226

Greenholtz v. Inmates of Nebraska Penal and Correctional Complex, 442 U.S. 1, 99 S.Ct. 2100, 60 L.Ed.2d 668 (1979)—§§ 2.7(a) n.63; 11.1(a) n.33; 26.2(c) n.38

Greenleaf, State v., 591 N.W.2d 488 (Minn.1999)—§§ 6.7(b) n.43; 15.5(c) n.126; 15.6(d) n.127; 17.2(d) n.94; 21.2(b) n.75; 22.3(d) n.205

Greenlee v. State, 725 So.2d 816 (Miss.1998)—§ 6.7(b) n.61

Greenlee, State v., 228 Kan. 712, 620 P.2d 1132 (1980)—§§ 13.6(b) n.18, 19

Greenman, United States v., 700 F.2d 1377 (11th Cir.1983)—§ 21.2(f) n.366

Greenpeace, Inc., United States v., 314 F.Supp.2d 1252 (S.D.Fla.2004)—§ 22.1(b) n.47

Greenslit, State v., 151 Vt. 225, 559 A.2d 672 (1989)—§§ 3.5(b) n.96; 12.5(b) n.33

Greenwald, State v., 109 Nev. 808, 858 P.2d 36 (1993)—§ 2.12(d) n.181

Greenwald v. Wisconsin, 390 U.S. 519, 88 S.Ct. 1152, 20 L.Ed.2d 77 (1968)—§ 6.2(c) n.167

Greenway v. State, 207 Ga.App. 511, 428 S.E.2d 415 (1993)—§ 24.11(d) n.19

Greenwood, People v., 174 Colo. 500, 484 P.2d 1217 (1971)—§ 3.7(d) n.84

Greenwood, State v., 665 N.E.2d 579 (Ind.1996)—§ 18.4(c) n.53

Greenwood v. Wolchik, 149 Vt. 441, 544 A.2d 1156 (1988)—§ 23.1(d) n.196

Greenwood, City of v. Peacock, 384 U.S. 808, 86 S.Ct. 1800, 16 L.Ed.2d 944 (1966)—§ 13.5(d) n.84

Greer v. Miller, 483 U.S. 756, 107 S.Ct. 3102, 97 L.Ed.2d 618 (1987)— § 9.6(a) n.35

Greer, People v., 212 Ill.2d 192, 288 Ill.Dec. 153, 817 N.E.2d 511 (2004)—§ 21.5(d) n.104

Greer, People v., 91 Mich.App. 18, 282 N.W.2d 819 (1979)—§ 10.2(a) n.4

Greer, State v., 635 N.W.2d 82 (Minn.2001)—§ 22.3(a) n.4

Greer, State v., 39 Ohio St.3d 236, 530 N.E.2d 382 (1988)—§§ 1.7(f) n.102; 10.1(b) n.20

Greer, State v., 66 Ohio St.2d 139, 420 N.E.2d 982 (1981)—§ 8.5(h) n.236

Greer, State v., 238 N.C. 325, 77 S.E.2d 917 (1953)—§ 19.1(a) n.11

Greer v. Texas, 999 S.W.2d 484 (Tex.App.1999)—§ 26.3(g) n.78

Greer, United States v., 285 F.3d 158 (2d Cir.2002)—§ 24.2(a) n.5

Greer, United States v., 137 F.3d 247 (5th Cir.1998)—§ 15.6(b) n.75

Greer, United States v., 968 F.2d 433 (5th Cir.1992)—§§ 22.3(a) n.7; 22.3(c) n.136

Greeson, State v., 336 Mont. 1, 152 P.3d 695 (2007)—§ 26.9(b) n.25

Greever, United States v., 134 F.3d 777 (6th Cir.1998)—§ 18.5(a) n.31

Gregg v. Georgia, 428 U.S. 153, 96 S.Ct. 2909, 49 L.Ed.2d 859 (1976)— §§ 2.8(a) n.21; 2.9(d) n.93; 12.4(a) n.19; 21.2(a) n.18; 26.1(b) n.11, 14

Gregg, United States v., 463 F.3d 160 (2d Cir.2006)—§ 21.6(a) n.18

Gregg v. United States, 394 U.S. 489, 89 S.Ct. 1134, 22 L.Ed.2d 442 (1969)—§ 26.5(b) n.33

Gregory v. Ashcroft, 501 U.S. 452, 111 S.Ct. 2395, 115 L.Ed.2d 410 (1991)—§§ 2.5(f) n.55, 60, 61

Gregory, Commonwealth v., 263 Va. 134, 557 S.E.2d 715 (2002)— § 6.9(f) n.144

Gregory, People v., 59 Ill.2d 111, 319 N.E.2d 483 (1974)—§ 19.3(b) n.159

Gregory, People v., 30 Mich. 371 (1874)—§ 15.4(b) n.75

Gregory v. State, 540 N.E.2d 585 (Ind.1989)—§ 6.10(b) n.14

Gregory v. State, 353 N.W.2d 777 (S.D.1984)—§ 21.4(c) n.92

Gregory, State v., 66 N.J. 510, 333 A.2d 257 (1975)—§ 1.7(i) n.205

Gregory, State v., 223 N.C. 415, 27 S.E.2d 140 (1943)—§ 19.1(a) n.10

Gregory, United States v., 245 F.3d 160 (2d Cir.2001)—§§ 21.2(d) n.224; 21.2(e) n.361

Gregory, United States v., 74 F.3d 819 (7th Cir.1996)—§ 11.6(a) n.31

Gregory, United States v., 891 F.2d 732 (9th Cir.1989)—§ 6.6(e) n.62

Gregory, United States v., 656 F.2d 1132 (5th Cir.1981)—§ 27.2(c) n.52

Gregory v. United States, 369 F.2d 185 (D.C.Cir.1966)—§ 20.3(i) n.176

Gregory-Bey v. Hanks, 332 F.3d 1036 (7th Cir.2003)—§§ 7.4(e) n.90, 92

Greiff, State v., 141 Wash.2d 910, 10 P.3d 390 (2000)—§ 20.3(i) n.161

Greig, United States v., 967 F.2d 1018 (5th Cir.1992)—§§ 11.9(b) n.82, 84; 11.9(d) n.217, 224

Grekis, Commonwealth v., 411 Pa.Super. 513, 601 A.2d 1284 (1992)—§§ 19.5(b) n.30, 38

Grell, State v., 212 Ariz. 516, 135 P.3d 696 (Ariz.2006)—§ 26.4(h) n.156

Grell v. United States, 112 F.2d 861 (8th Cir.1940)—§ 13.4(a) n.4

Grendon v. Burnham, 146 Me. 387, 82 A.2d 773 (1951)—§ 15.1(d) n.251

Grenier, State v., 158 Vt. 153, 605 A.2d 853 (1992)—§ 26.4(g) n.125

Grennan, People v., 284 A.D. 657, 134 N.Y.S.2d 676 (1954)—§§ 16.3(d) n.70, 71

Greschner, United States v., 802 F.2d 373 (10th Cir.1986)—§ 24.4(d) n.39

Gressler, People v., 235 A.D.2d 599, 652 N.Y.S.2d 792 (1997)—§ 19.5(b) n.22

Gretzler v. Stewart, 112 F.3d 992 (9th Cir.1997)—§ 28.6(e) n.61

Grewell, State v., 45 Ohio St.3d 4, 543 N.E.2d 93 (1989)—§§ 15.2(j) n.235, 240

Grey, State v., 147 N.J. 4, 685 A.2d 923 (1996)—§ 24.10(b) n.27

Grey, State v., 274 Mont. 206, 907 P.2d 951 (1995)—§ 6.8(c) n.64

Grey Bear, United States v., 828 F.2d 1286 (8th Cir.1987)—§ 17.2(a) n.23

Greybull, State v., 579 N.W.2d 161 (N.D.1998)—§§ 6.9(g) n.157, 166

Greyson v. Kellam, 937 F.2d 1409 (9th Cir.1991)—§ 25.4(a) n.9

Grice v. United States, 146 F.2d 849 (4th Cir.1945)—§ 3.10(b) n.56

Grieco v. Meachum, 533 F.2d 713 (1st Cir.1976)—§ 6.4(b) n.25

Grieco, People v., 44 Ill.2d 407, 255 N.E.2d 897 (1970)—§ 19.3(b) n.151

Grier v. State, 351 Md. 241, 718 A.2d 211 (1998)—§§ 9.6(a) n.36, 48

Grier, United States v., 449 F.3d 558 (3d Cir.2006)—§ 26.4(h) n.155

Grievance Committee of Hartford County Bar v. Broder, 112 Conn. 269, 152 A. 292 (1930)—§§ 15.1(b) n.73, 78

Grievance Comm. of Toledo Bar Ass'n, Petition of, 47 Ohio St.3d 611, 548 N.E.2d 916 (1989)—§ 8.5(h) n.300

Griffey v. Lindsey, 345 F.3d 1058 (9th Cir.2003)—§ 7.4(e) n.87

Griffin, Ex parte, 679 S.W.2d 15 (Tex.Cr.App.1984)—§§ 21.2(g) n.402, 403

Griffin v. California, 380 U.S. 609, 85 S.Ct. 1229, 14 L.Ed.2d 106 (1965)—§§ 1.5(c) n.104; 2.10(b) n.42; 8.10(f) n.127; 17.2(d) n.111; 24.5(a) n.4; 24.5(b) n.18; 26.4(c) n.34

Griffin v. Delo, 33 F.3d 895 (8th Cir.1994)—§ 2.7(a) n.10

Griffin v. Illinois, 351 U.S. 12, 76 S.Ct. 585, 100 L.Ed. 891 (1956)—§§ 2.4(a) n.8; 2.7(c) n.119, 122; 2.9(d) n.84; 11.1(d) n.104; 11.2(d) n.118; 11.2(e) n.139; 11.2(f) n.237; 11.2(g) n.257; 12.2(b) n.21; 12.4(d) n.78; 27.1(b) n.14

Griffin v. Johnson, 350 F.3d 956 (9th Cir.2003)—§ 28.4(e) n.76

Griffin, People v., 135 Misc.2d 775, 517 N.Y.S.2d 366 (Sup.Ct.Kings County 1987)—§ 15.2(c) n.81

Griffin, People v., 727 P.2d 55 (Colo.1986)—§ 9.4(b) n.57

Griffin v. Santagata, 168 App.Div.2d 557, 562 N.Y.S.2d 778 (1990)—§ 27.4(c) n.19

Griffin v. State, 280 Ga. 683, 631 S.E.2d 671 (2006)—§ 6.9(f) n.106

Griffin v. State, 361 S.C. 173, 604 S.E.2d 394 (2004)—§ 21.2(g) n.399

Griffin, State v., 814 A.2d 1003 (Me.2003)—§ 6.7(b) n.42

Griffin, State v., 211 W.Va. 508, 566 S.E.2d 645 (2002)—§ 22.3(c) n.112

Griffin, State v., 136 N.C.App. 531, 525 S.E.2d 793 (N.C.App.2000)—§§ 16.3(a) n.5; 16.3(e) n.79

Griffin, State v., 83 Haw. 105, 924 P.2d 1211 (1996)—§ 27.5(e) n.157

Griffin, State v., 117 N.M. 745, 877 P.2d 551 (1994)—§ 24.11(b) n.3

Griffin, State v., 116 N.M. 689, 866 P.2d 1156 (1993)—§ 24.9(a) n.10

Griffin, State v., 848 S.W.2d 464 (Mo.1993)—§§ 6.7(b) n.100; 14.1(d) n.55, 67

Griffin, State v., 122 Idaho 733, 838 P.2d 862 (1992)—§ 26.4(c) n.32

Griffin v. State, 607 So.2d 1197 (Miss.1992)—§ 22.3(d) n.249

Griffin v. State, 557 So.2d 542 (Miss.1990)—§ 11.2(e) n.211

Griffin v. State, 565 So.2d 918 (Fla.App.1990)—§ 11.4(a) n.2

Griffin v. State, 540 N.E.2d 1187 (Ind.1989)—§ 21.6(a) n.65

Griffin v. State, 545 So.2d 729 (Miss.1989)—§ 17.4(a) n.36

Griffin, State v., 756 S.W.2d 475 (Mo.1988)—§§ 3.3(f) n.206; 3.10(e) n.149

Griffin v. State, 493 N.E.2d 439 (Ind.1986)—§ 7.4(g) n.118

Griffin v. United States, 878 A.2d 1195 (D.C.App.2005)—§ 6.6(e) n.91

Griffin, United States v., 84 F.3d 912 (7th Cir.1996)—§§ 24.11(d) n.27, 31

Griffin, United States v., 922 F.2d 1343 (8th Cir.1990)—§§ 6.6(e) n.65; 6.6(f) n.109

Griffin, United States v., 814 F.2d 806 (1st Cir.1987)—§ 16.2(g) n.108

Griffin, United States v., 827 F.2d 1108 (7th Cir.1987)—§ 3.4(j) n.183

Griffin, United States v., 699 F.2d 1102 (11th Cir.1983)—§§ 11.7(e) n.89, 90, 92

Griffin, United States v., 502 F.2d 959 (6th Cir.1974)—§ 9.3(e) n.61

Griffin v. Wisconsin, 483 U.S. 868, 107 S.Ct. 3164, 97 L.Ed.2d 709 (1987)—§§ 3.9(a) n.5; 3.9(j) n.218, 223; 3.9(l) n.277; 26.9(b) n.59

Griffis v. State, 759 So.2d 668 (Fla.2000)—§ 27.5(c) n.83

Griffith v. Kentucky, 479 U.S. 314, 107 S.Ct. 708, 93 L.Ed.2d 649 (1987)—§§ 2.11(a) n.11; 2.11(d) n.45, 50

Griffith v. Slinkard, 146 Ind. 117, 44 N.E. 1001 (1896)—§ 13.5(g) n.110

Griffith v. State, 55 S.W.3d 598 (Tex.Crim.App.2001)—§§ 6.4(e) n.63; 6.5(b) n.25; 6.7(b) n.41

Griffith, State v., 97 Idaho 52, 539 P.2d 604 (1975)—§§ 1.7(f) n.86, 93, 101

Griffith, United States v., 756 F.2d 1244 (6th Cir.1985)—§§ 15.6(b) n.62, 78; 15.7(b) n.16, 20

Griggs v. Allegheny County, 369 U.S. 84, 82 S.Ct. 531, 7 L.Ed.2d 585 (1962)—§ 2.5(c) n.26

Griggs, People v., 152 Ill.2d 1, 178 Ill.Dec. 1, 604 N.E.2d 257 (1992)—§§ 6.9(c) n.63; 19.5(c) n.60

Griggs, State v., 103 Ohio St.3d 85, 814 N.E.2d 51 (2004)—§ 21.4(e) n.161

Griggs, United States v., 713 F.2d 672 (11th Cir.1983)—§ 24.3(b) n.58

Griggs-Ryan v. Smith, 904 F.2d 112 (1st Cir.1990)—§ 4.6(l) n.201

Grijalva, State v., 111 Ariz. 476, 533 P.2d 533 (1975)—§ 3.8(g) n.241

Grilli, State v., 304 Minn. 80, 230 N.W.2d 445 (1975)—§ 5.3(b) n.23

Grillot v. State, 353 Ark. 294, 107 S.W.3d 136 (2003)—§ 6.8(b) n.63

Grimes v. McAnulty, 957 S.W.2d 223 (Ky.1997)—§ 27.4(c) n.24

Grimes, United States v., 142 F.3d 1342 (11th Cir.1998)—§§ 6.9(g) n.200; 18.5(a) n.6

Grimes, United States v., 438 F.2d 391 (6th Cir.1971)—§ 5.4(a) n.8

Griminger, People v., 71 N.Y.2d 635, 529 N.Y.S.2d 55, 524 N.E.2d 409 (1988)—§ 2.12(c) n.174

Grimm, State v., 165 W.Va. 547, 270 S.E.2d 173 (W.Va.1980)—§ 20.6(b) n.31

Grimmond, United States v., 137 F.3d 823 (4th Cir.1998)—§ 18.2(c) n.51

Grimsley, State v., 3 Ohio App.3d 265, 444 N.E.2d 1071 (1982)—§ 22.1(h) n.138

Grisanti, United States v., 4 F.3d 173 (2d Cir.1993)—§ 17.4(b) n.132

Grisby, State v., 97 Wash.2d 493, 647 P.2d 6 (1982)—§§ 6.7(c) n.118; 17.2(b) n.49

Grisham v. Hagan, 361 U.S. 278, 80 S.Ct. 310, 4 L.Ed.2d 279 (1960)—§ 15.1(b) n.92

Grisham, United States v., 63 F.3d 1074 (11th Cir.1995)—§§ 22.2(d) n.56, 80

Grissom v. State, 121 P.3d 127 (Wyo.2005)—§ 6.7(d) n.145

Grissom, State v., 251 Kan. 851, 840 P.2d 1142 (1992)—§§ 3.2(c) n.98; 3.2(f) n.175; 9.1(d) n.126

Griswold v. Connecticut, 381 U.S. 479, 85 S.Ct. 1678, 14 L.Ed.2d 510 (1965)—§§ 2.3(b) n.91; 2.3 n.1; 2.4(f) n.188

Griswold, People v., 54 Ill.App.3d 246, 11 Ill.Dec. 938, 369 N.E.2d 392 (1977)—§ 7.4(c) n.48

Groban, In re, 352 U.S. 330, 77 S.Ct. 510, 1 L.Ed.2d 376 (1957)—§§ 8.6(a) n.24; 8.14(a) n.1; 15.5(a) n.29

Groff, State v., 323 N.W.2d 204 (Iowa 1982)—§ 3.4(b) n.30

Grogan, State v., 373 So.2d 1300 (La.1979)—§ 9.4(a) n.19

Groh v. Ramirez, 540 U.S. 551, 124 S.Ct. 1284, 157 L.Ed.2d 1068 (2004)—§§ 3.1(c) n.75; 3.4(e) n.73; 3.4(f) n.119; 3.4(l) n.241, 243

Groome, Commonwealth v., 435 Mass. 201, 755 N.E.2d 1224 (2001)—§§ 6.6(d) n.57, 58; 6.6(e) n.68; 6.9(e) n.88; 6.9(g) n.200

Grooms, State v., 353 N.C. 50, 540 S.E.2d 713 (2000)—§ 18.2(c) n.53

Groover v. State, 458 So.2d 226 (Fla.1984)—§ 21.2(h) n.425

Groppi v. Wisconsin, 400 U.S. 505, 91 S.Ct. 490, 27 L.Ed.2d 571 (1971)—§§ 2.7(a) n.34; 2.7(b) n.91; 16.3(b) n.7; 23.2(a) n.2

Grosbois, In re, 109 Cal. 445, 42 P. 444 (1895)—§ 15.1(g) n.359

Groscost, State v., 355 N.W.2d 32 (Iowa 1984)—§ 24.3(c) n.91

Grose, State v., 387 N.W.2d 182 (Minn.App.1986)—§§ 15.7(d) n.85; 15.7(g) n.215

Grosh, State v., 387 N.W.2d 503 (S.D.1986)—§ 21.5(a) n.30

Groshart v. United States, 392 F.2d 172 (9th Cir.1968)—§ 6.8(a) n.16

Gross, State v., 97 Ohio St.3d 121, 776 N.E.2d 1061 (2002)—§ 7.4(b) n.29

Gross, State v., 134 Md.App. 528, 760 A.2d 725 (2000)—§§ 11.6(d) n.120; 11.10(c) n.96

Gross, United States v., 41 F.Supp.2d 1096 (C.D.Cal.1999)—§ 15.2(c) n.69

Gross, United States v., 276 F.2d 816 (2d Cir.1960)—§ 16.1(h) n.298

Grossberg, State v., 705 A.2d 608 (Super.Ct.Del.1997)—§§ 23.1(b) n.62, 66, 67, 87

Grossfeld v. Commodity Futures Trading Comm'n, 137 F.3d 1300 (11th Cir.1998)—§ 17.4(b) n.131

Grossman, Ex parte, 267 U.S. 87, 45 S.Ct. 332, 69 L.Ed. 527 (1925)—§ 26.2(c) n.72

Grossman v. State, 457 P.2d 226 (Alaska 1969)—§§ 5.1(a) n.2; 5.2(b) n.23, 29; 5.2(d) n.55; 5.3(a) n.9

Grosso v. United States, 390 U.S. 62, 88 S.Ct. 709, 19 L.Ed.2d 906 (1968)—§ 8.12(c) n.32

Grossoehme v. Cordell, 904 S.W.2d 392 (Mo.App.1995)—§ 26.9(b) n.34

Grosvenor v. State, 874 So.2d 1176 (Fla.2004)—§ 11.10(d) n.175

Grosvenor, State v., 402 N.W.2d 402 (Iowa 1987)—§ 10.6(c) n.23

Groth, United States v., 682 F.2d 578 (6th Cir.1982)—§ 22.1(h) n.141

Groton v. United Steelworkers of America, 254 Conn. 35, 757 A.2d 501 (2000)—§ 21.4(a) n.21

Grove, People v., 455 Mich. 439, 566 N.W.2d 547 (1997)—§§ 21.3(e) n.272, 288

Groves, United States v., 369 F.3d 1178 (10th Cir.2004)—§ 21.2(b) n.82

Grubb v. State, 734 N.E.2d 589 (Ind.App.2000)—§ 26.10(c) n.66

Grubbs, United States v., 547 U.S. 90, 126 S.Ct. 1494, 164 L.Ed.2d 195 (2006)—§§ 3.1(b) n.25; 3.3(g) n.242

Gruberg, United States v., 493 F.Supp. 234 (S.D.N.Y.1979)—§ 16.3(c) n.46

Grubor Enterprises, Inc. v. Kortidis, 201 Mich.App. 625, 506 N.W.2d 614 (1993)—§ 24.4(d) n.46

Grumman Aerospace Corp. v. Titanium Metals Corp. of America, 554 F.Supp. 771 (S.D.N.Y.1982)—§ 8.5(h) n.269

Grunewald, United States v., 233 F.2d 556 (2d Cir.1956)—§ 2.10(c) n.100

Grunewald v. United States, 353 U.S. 391, 77 S.Ct. 963, 1 L.Ed.2d 931 (1957)—§§ 1.7(i) n.161; 2.10(d) n.130; 8.10(a) n.19; 8.10(c) n.76; 8.10(f) n.129; 18.5(a) n.14

Grusse, In re, 402 F.Supp. 1232 (D.Conn.1975)—§§ 8.8(g) n.170, 172; 8.9(b) n.33; 8.11(c) n.48

Gryger v. Burke, 334 U.S. 728, 68 S.Ct. 1256, 92 L.Ed. 1683 (1948)—§§ 26.6(b) n.7; 26.7(d) n.39

Grzelak, State v., 215 Wis.2d 577, 573 N.W.2d 538 (App.1997)—§ 18.4(c) n.39

Guadalupe-Garza, United States v., 421 F.2d 876 (9th Cir.1970)—§ 3.9(f) n.98

Guadarrama, United States v., 128 F.Supp.2d 1202 (E.D.Wis.2001)—§ 3.4(e) n.98

Guadarrama, United States v., 742 F.2d 487 (9th Cir.1984)—§ 21.4(a) n.21

Guajardo, State v., 135 N.H. 401, 605 A.2d 217 (1992)—§ 6.7(c) n.133

Gualandi, People v., 21 Ill.App.3d 992, 316 N.E.2d 195 (1974)—§ 3.4(j) n.184

Guam v. Snaer, 758 F.2d 1341 (9th Cir.1985)—§ 6.8(a) n.17

Guam, People of Territory of v. Muna, 999 F.2d 397 (9th Cir.1993)—§§ 7.4(a) n.5; 15.6(f) n.181

Guapi, United States v., 144 F.3d 1393 (11th Cir.1998)—§ 3.8(c) n.102

Guarin, United States v., 898 F.2d 1120 (6th Cir.1990)—§ 21.1(e) n.86

Guay, State v., 130 N.H. 413, 543 A.2d 910 (1988)—§§ 7.4(c) n.41, 48, 50, 51

Guay, United States v., 108 F.3d 545 (4th Cir.1997)—§§ 6.9(b) n.32, 34

Guerin, People v., 769 P.2d 1068 (Colo.1989)—§ 3.6(a) n.5

Guernsey, People v., 80 Cal.App.2d 463, 180 P.2d 27 (1947)—§ 16.1(d) n.154

Guerra, People v., 37 Cal.4th 1067, 40 Cal.Rptr.3d 118, 129 P.3d 321 (2006)—§§ 6.2(c) n.120, 178

Guerra, State v., 562 N.W.2d 10 (Minn.App.1997)—§§ 19.5(b) n.9, 12, 13

Guerrero, United States v., 938 F.2d 725 (7th Cir.1991)—§ 17.2(d) n.94

Guerro, United States v., 694 F.2d 898 (2d Cir.1982)—§ 21.6(b) n.111

Guess, State v., 613 So.2d 406 (Fla.1992)—§ 10.5(b) n.18

Guess, United States v., 745 F.2d 1286 (9th Cir.1984)—§ 17.3(d) n.55

Guest v. United States, 867 A.2d 208 (D.C.App.2005)—§ 24.3(b) n.51

Guest, United States v., 383 U.S. 745, 86 S.Ct. 1170, 16 L.Ed.2d 239 (1966)—§ 1.2(c) n.92

Guevara v. Superior Court, 7 Cal.App.3d 531, 86 Cal.Rptr. 657 (1970)—§ 3.6(d) n.88

Guevara, United States v., 277 F.3d 111 (2d Cir.2001)—§ 19.2(e) n.71

Guevara, United States v., 941 F.2d 1299 (4th Cir.1991)—§ 21.2(b) n.88

Guevara, United States v., 823 F.2d 446 (11th Cir.1987)—§ 22.3(e) n.279

Guichard, United States v., 779 F.2d 1139 (5th Cir.1986)—§ 21.4(f) n.178

Guido, State v., 698 A.2d 729 (R.I.1997)—§§ 8.6(b) n.37; 8.7(a) n.28; 8.7(d) n.74

Guido, United States v., 251 F.2d 1 (7th Cir.1958)—§ 3.2(i) n.218

Guidry v. Dretke, 397 F.3d 306 (5th Cir.2005)—§ 6.9(c) n.58

Guilder v. State, 794 S.W.2d 765 (Tex.App.1990)—§ 20.3(j) n.195

Guillette, United States v., 547 F.2d 743 (2d Cir.1976)—§§ 15.5(b) n.50, 54; 15.7(e) n.104

Guilmette, People v., 1 Cal.App.4th 1534, 2 Cal.Rptr.2d 750 (1991)—§ 6.7(c) n.142

Guilty Plea Cases, 395 Mich. 96, 235 N.W.2d 132 (1975)—§§ 21.4(b) n.54; 21.4(c) n.67; 21.4(d) n.103; 21.4(e) n.161; 21.4(f) n.172

Guinan v. Armontrout, 909 F.2d 1224 (8th Cir.1990)—§ 11.2(e) n.155

Guinn, United States v., 454 F.2d 29 (5th Cir.1972)—§ 3.3(c) n.95

Guiteau, United States v., 1 Mackey 498 (1882)—§ 16.1(d) n.145

Gulledge, State v., 326 S.C. 220, 487 S.E.2d 590 (1997)—§ 20.3(a) n.19

Gulledge, State v., 257 Kan. 915, 896 P.2d 378 (1995)—§ 17.4(b) n.138

Gulledge, United States v., 469 F.2d 713 (5th Cir.1972)—§ 3.2(f) n.176

Gullett v. State, 233 Ind. 6, 116 N.E.2d 234 (1953)—§ 19.5(c) n.59

Gulley, State v., 155 Vt. 65, 580 A.2d 980 (1990)—§ 24.4(d) n.61

Gullick, State v., 118 N.H. 912, 396 A.2d 554 (1978)—§ 6.9(e) n.92

Gumm, State v., 99 Idaho 549, 585 P.2d 959 (1978)—§§ 19.3(b) n.137, 159

Gunning, State v., 183 Conn. 299, 439 A.2d 339 (1981)—§ 15.7(g) n.205

Gunsby v. Wainwright, 596 F.2d 654 (5th Cir.1979)—§ 21.2(h) n.425

Gunter, Commonwealth v., 565 Pa. 79, 771 A.2d 767 (2001)—§§ 21.4(a) n.23; 21.4(e) n.163; 21.5(a) n.24

Gunwall, State v., 106 Wash.2d 54, 720 P.2d 808 (1986)—§§ 2.12(a) n.43; 2.12(b) n.104, 109; 2.12(e) n.200, 205

Gupta, United States v., 183 F.3d 615 (7th Cir.1999)—§ 6.7(b) n.57

Gurleski v. United States, 405 F.2d 253 (5th Cir.1968)—§ 17.2(d) n.110

Gurley, People v., 23 Cal.App.3d 536, 100 Cal.Rptr. 407 (1972)—§ 6.9(b) n.36

Gurley v. State, 906 So.2d 1264 (Fla.App.2005)—§ 26.4(i) n.196

Gurney, United States v., 558 F.2d 1202 (5th Cir.1977)—§ 23.1(d) n.167

Gurolla, United States v., 333 F.3d 944 (9th Cir.2003)—§ 5.2(a) n.10

Gurtenstein, People v., 69 Cal.App.3d 441, 138 Cal.Rptr. 161 (1977)—§ 3.10(b) n.34

Gurule, People v., 28 Cal.4th 557, 123 Cal.Rptr.2d 345, 51 P.3d 224 (2002)—§§ 6.2(c) n.140; 21.2(b) n.63

Gurule, United States v., 437 F.2d 239 (10th Cir.1970)—§ 8.7(b) n.36

Gusman, State v., 125 Idaho 805, 874 P.2d 1112 (1993)—§ 17.4(a) n.53

Gustafson, In re, 619 F.2d 1354 (9th Cir.1980)—§ 24.7(i) n.97

Gustafson v. Florida, 414 U.S. 260, 94 S.Ct. 488, 38 L.Ed.2d 456 (1973)—§ 3.5(b) n.79

Gustafson, State v., 76 Ohio St.3d 425, 668 N.E.2d 435 (1996)—§ 17.4(b) n.124

Gustafson v. State, 854 P.2d 751 (Alaska App.1993)—§§ 15.2(e) n.142; 15.7(f) n.169, 176

Guste, State ex rel. v. K-Mart Corporation, 462 So.2d 616 (La.1985)—§ 13.4(c) n.114

Guthrie, State v., 205 W.Va. 326, 518 S.E.2d 83 (1999)—§ 6.7(d) n.145

Guthrie, State v., 194 W.Va. 657, 461 S.E.2d 163 (W.Va.1995)—§ 24.6(c) n.40

Gutierrez v. McGinnis, 389 F.3d 300 (2d Cir.2004)—§ 28.6(g) n.90

Gutierrez, People v., 28 Cal.4th 1083, 124 Cal.Rptr.2d 373, 52 P.3d 572 (2002)—§§ 9.6(a) n.19; 17.1(d) n.53; 22.3(d) n.218

Gutierrez, People v., 622 P.2d 547 (Colo.1981)—§ 21.5(a) n.35

Gutierrez, State v., 136 N.M. 779, 105 P.3d 332 (App.2004)—§ 10.1(a) n.2

Gutierrez, United States v., 343 F.3d 415 (5th Cir.2003)—§ 5.2(a) n.8

Gutierrez, United States v., 351 F.3d 897 (8th Cir.2003)—§ 11.5(f) n.98

Gutierrez, United States v., 990 F.2d 472 (9th Cir.1993)—§ 13.4(b) n.72

Gutierrez-Gonzalez, United States v., 184 F.3d 1160 (10th Cir.1999)—§ 5.4(c) n.30

Gutierrez-Mederos, United States v., 965 F.2d 800 (9th Cir.1992)— §§ 3.10(f) n.191, 197

Gutierrez-Zamarano, United States v., 23 F.3d 235 (9th Cir.1994)— § 25.4(c) n.32

Gutknecht v. United States, 396 U.S. 295, 90 S.Ct. 506, 24 L.Ed.2d 532 (1970)—§§ 13.4(b) n.49; 28.9(c) n.82

Guy v. City of Oklahoma City, 760 P.2d 1312 (Okla.App.1988)—§ 26.1(f) n.144

Guy, Commonwealth v., 441 Mass. 96, 803 N.E.2d 707 (2004)—§ 6.7(b) n.43

Guy, State v., 172 Wis.2d 86, 492 N.W.2d 311 (1992)—§ 2.12(d) n.186

Guy v. State, 282 Ark. 424, 668 S.W.2d 952 (1984)—§ 17.1(f) n.69

Guy, United States v., 924 F.2d 702 (7th Cir.1991)—§ 22.2(d) n.81

Guyton v. State, 272 Ga. 529, 531 S.E.2d 94 (2000)—§ 7.4(c) n.48

Guzek, State v., 322 Or. 245, 906 P.2d 272 (1995)—§ 26.5(d) n.74

Guzek, State v., 310 Or. 299, 797 P.2d 1031 (1990)—§ 21.3(c) n.157

Guzman, Commonwealth v., 446 Mass. 344, 845 N.E.2d 270 (2006)— § 13.2(c) n.69

Guzman v. Morris, 644 F.2d 1295 (9th Cir.1981)—§ 21.2(d) n.208

Guzman, People v., 76 N.Y.2d 1, 556 N.Y.S.2d 7, 555 N.E.2d 259 (1990)—§ 22.3(c) n.100

Guzman v. State, 868 So.2d 498 (Fla.2003)—§ 24.3(d) n.111

Guzman v. State, 85 S.W.3d 242 (Tex.Cr.App.2002)—§ 22.3(d) n.228

Guzman, State v., 752 A.2d 1 (R.I.2000)—§§ 3.3(d) n.167, 169

Guzman v. State, 644 So.2d 996 (Fla.1994)—§§ 11.9(c) n.124; 11.9(d) n.213

Guzman, State v., 122 Idaho 981, 842 P.2d 660 (1992)—§ 3.1(c) n.57

Guzman, State v., 166 Wis.2d 577, 480 N.W.2d 446 (1992)—§ 3.9(j) n.205

Guzman v. State, 283 Ark. 112, 672 S.W.2d 656 (1984)—§ 3.10(b) n.38

Guzman, United States v., 318 F.3d 1191 (10th Cir.2003)—§ 21.2(d) n.244

Guzman, United States v., 75 F.3d 1090 (6th Cir.1996)—§ 3.2(b) n.93

Guzman, United States v., 85 F.3d 823 (1st Cir.1996)—§§ 18.4(b) n.26; 25.5(a) n.11

Gwinn, United States v., 219 F.3d 326 (4th Cir.2000)—§ 3.6(d) n.84

Gwynn, Commonwealth v., 555 Pa. 86, 723 A.2d 143 (1998)—§ 6.9(f) n.144

Gyant v. State, 21 Md.App. 674, 321 A.2d 815 (1974)—§ 19.5(c) n.51

Gyles v. State, 901 P.2d 1143 (Alaska 1995)—§ 26.10(c) n.62

H

Haag v. State, 591 So.2d 614 (Fla.1992)—§ 1.7(h) n.132

Haanio, State v., 94 Haw. 405, 16 P.3d 246 (2001)—§ 24.8(f) n.120

Haas, Commonwealth v., 373 Mass. 545, 369 N.E.2d 692 (1977)— § 9.5(b) n.33

Haas, State v., 188 Md. 63, 51 A.2d 647 (1947)—§ 20.1(a) n.9

Haas, United States v., 583 F.2d 216 (5th Cir.1978)—§ 19.3(a) n.47

Haase, State v., 446 N.W.2d 62 (S.D.1989)—§§ 16.1(h) n.305, 307

Haase v. United States, 800 F.2d 123 (7th Cir.1986)—§ 21.5(c) n.74

Haas, State ex rel. v. Schwabe, 276 Or. 853, 556 P.2d 1366 (1976)— § 27.4(d) n.40

Habbena, State v., 372 N.W.2d 450 (S.D.1985)—§ 26.5(a) n.8

Habeas Corpus of Rowe, In re Complaint in, 67 Ohio St.2d 115, 423 N.E.2d 167 (1981)—§ 27.4(f) n.66

Haberski, State v., 449 A.2d 373 (Me.1982)—§§ 8.4(b) n.74; 15.4(h) n.200; 15.4(i) n.214

Habig, United States v., 390 U.S. 222, 88 S.Ct. 926, 19 L.Ed.2d 1055 (1968)—§ 18.5(a) n.6

Hack v. State, 141 Wis. 346, 124 N.W. 492 (1910)—§ 15.1(f) n.293

Haddad, State v., 767 So.2d 682 (La.2000)—§ 24.4(c) n.21

Haddad, United States v., 462 F.3d 783 (7th Cir.2006)—§ 5.2(a) n.9

Haddock, State v., 257 Kan. 964, 897 P.2d 152 (1995)—§ 6.6(f) n.114

Haddock, United States v., 961 F.2d 933 (10th Cir.1992)—§ 25.4(c) n.28

Haddon, United States v., 927 F.2d 942 (7th Cir.1991)—§ 6.2(c) n.183

Haden, United States v., 397 F.2d 460 (7th Cir.1968)—§ 3.10(c) n.88

Hadix v. Johnson, 694 F.Supp. 259 (E.D.Mich.1988)—§§ 11.2(f) n.248, 249

Hadley v. State, 322 Ark. 472, 910 S.W.2d 675 (1995)—§ 26.3(f) n.55

Hafford, State v., 252 Conn. 274, 746 A.2d 150 (2000)—§ 6.9(f) n.138

Hagans v. State, 316 Md. 429, 559 A.2d 792 (1989)—§ 24.8(f) n.117

Hage, State v., 258 Mont. 498, 853 P.2d 1251 (1993)—§ 24.9(g) n.114

Hagege, United States v., 437 F.3d 943 (9th Cir.2006)—§ 25.2(b) n.14

Hageman, State v., 307 N.C. 1, 296 S.E.2d 433 (1982)—§ 5.2(a) n.4

Hagen v. Commonwealth, 437 Mass. 374, 772 N.E.2d 32 (2002)—§§ 13.1(a) n.27; 13.3(a) n.1

Hagen, United States v., 782 F.Supp. 1351 (D.Neb.1991)—§ 19.3(a) n.71

Hagenkord v. State, 100 Wis.2d 452, 302 N.W.2d 421 (1981)—§ 24.8(e) n.52

Hager, People v., 69 N.Y.2d 141, 512 N.Y.S.2d 794, 505 N.E.2d 237 (1987)—§ 6.7(a) n.3

Hager, People v., 124 Misc.2d 123, 476 N.Y.S.2d 442 (Co.Ct.1984)—§ 15.7(g) n.208

Hager, State v., 630 N.W.2d 828 (Iowa 2001)—§ 21.3(e) n.272

Hager v. United States, 856 A.2d 1143 (D.C.App.2004)—§§ 6.4(g) n.153; 7.5(b) n.21, 29

Hager, United States v., 985 F.2d 945 (8th Cir.1993)—§ 21.2(d) n.193

Hagez v. State, 110 Md.App. 194, 676 A.2d 992 (1996)—§ 24.4(c) n.27

Haggard v. United States, 369 F.2d 968 (8th Cir.1966)—§ 17.3(b) n.17

Haggerty, Commonwealth v., 400 Mass. 437, 509 N.E.2d 1163 (1987)—§ 11.10(c) n.126

Hagmann, United States v., 950 F.2d 175 (5th Cir.1991)—§§ 19.2(b) n.13; 19.2(c) n.22; 19.3(a) n.49

Hagner v. United States, 54 F.2d 446 (D.C.Cir.1931)—§ 16.1(a) n.23

Hahn, People v., 183 Mich.App. 465, 455 N.W.2d 310 (1989)—§ 14.4(e) n.104

Hahn, United States v., 359 F.3d 1315 (10th Cir.2004)—§§ 21.2(b) n.86; 27.5(c) n.63

Haight v. Commonwealth, 938 S.W.2d 243 (Ky.1996)—§ 21.2(e) n.314

Haight v. Commonwealth, 760 S.W.2d 84 (Ky.1988)—§ 21.2(d) n.161

Haigler, State v., 334 S.C. 623, 515 S.E.2d 88 (1999)—§ 22.3(d) n.246

Haigler v. United States, 531 A.2d 1236 (D.C.App.1987)—§ 18.4(c) n.61

Hain v. Mullin, 436 F.3d 1168 (10th Cir.2006)—§§ 11.2(b) n.75; 28.12(b) n.8

Hairston, United States v., 46 F.3d 361 (4th Cir.1995)—§ 26.1(f) n.145

Hairston v. United States, 500 A.2d 994 (D.C.App.1985)—§§ 6.7(b) n.64, 69

Haislip, State v., 237 Kan. 461, 701 P.2d 909 (1985)—§§ 22.3(e) n.276, 279

Hajtic, State v., 724 N.W.2d 449 (Iowa 2006)—§ 17.1(a) n.14

Halacy v. Steen, 670 A.2d 1371 (Me.1996)—§§ 23.1(d) n.185; 26.5(c) n.59

Halbert v. Michigan, 545 U.S. 605, 125 S.Ct. 2582, 162 L.Ed.2d 552 (2005)—§§ 1.11(a) n.4; 11.1(b) n.65; 11.1(d) n.117; 11.2(b) n.60; 27.1(a) n.6, 13; 27.1(b) n.18; 27.5(c) n.68; 28.12(a) n.1, 2

Halbert, United States v., 436 F.2d 1226 (9th Cir.1970)—§ 6.3(b) n.35

Haldeman, United States v., 559 F.2d 31 (D.C.Cir.1976)—§ 23.2(e) n.75

Hale v. Gibson, 227 F.3d 1298 (10th Cir.2000)—§ 11.9(d) n.170

Hale v. Henkel, 201 U.S. 43, 26 S.Ct. 370, 50 L.Ed. 652 (1906)— §§ 2.8(b) n.35; 8.2(c) n.32; 8.4(b) n.54, 69, 76; 8.4(c) n.121; 8.6(a) n.25; 8.7(a) n.7; 8.7(b) n.29, 32; 8.8(a) n.1; 8.12(a) n.7; 8.12(b) n.10; 15.1(d) n.173

Hale, State v., 277 Wis.2d 593, 691 N.W.2d 637 (2005)—§ 27.6(e) n.159

Hale v. State, 343 Ark. 62, 31 S.W.3d 850 (2000)—§§ 27.5(d) n.119; 27.5(e) n.170

Hale, State v., 136 N.H. 42, 611 A.2d 630 (1992)—§ 10.1(b) n.24

Hale, State v., 453 N.W.2d 704 (Minn.1990)—§ 6.7(b) n.43

Hale, United States v., 422 U.S. 171, 95 S.Ct. 2133, 45 L.Ed.2d 99 (1975)— §§ 1.7(i) n.161, 165

Haley v. Ohio, 332 U.S. 596, 68 S.Ct. 302, 92 L.Ed. 224 (1948)— §§ 6.2(b) n.41; 6.2(c) n.84, 90, 163, 165; 6.4(a) n.2

Haley, People v., 34 Cal.4th 283, 17 Cal.Rptr.3d 877, 96 P.3d 170 (2004)—§ 6.7(c) n.111

Haley, State v., 538 So.2d 679 (La.App.1989)—§ 11.3(b) n.44

Haley, United States v., 758 F.2d 1294 (8th Cir.1985)—§ 3.4(f) n.120

Haley, United States v., 504 F.Supp. 1124 (E.D.Pa.1981)—§ 16.3(c) n.37

Haliburton v. State, 514 So.2d 1088 (Fla.1987)—§ 6.9(c) n.61

Hall, Ex parte, 844 So.2d 571 (Ala.2002)—§ 12.4(a) n.24

Hall, Commonwealth v., 549 Pa. 269, 701 A.2d 190 (1997)—§ 6.9(c) n.66

Hall v. Commonwealth, 817 S.W.2d 228 (Ky.1991)—§ 17.2(b) n.62

Hall, Commonwealth v., 366 Mass. 790, 323 N.E.2d 319 (1975)—§ 9.4(b) n.62

Hall v. Earthlink Network, Inc., 396 F.3d 500 (2d Cir.2005)—§ 4.6(b) n.40

Hall v. Henderson, 672 A.2d 1047 (D.C.App.1996)—§ 26.2(c) n.43

Hall v. Luebbers, 341 F.3d 706 (8th Cir.2003)—§ 21.2(f) n.383

Hall v. Luebbers, 296 F.3d 685 (8th Cir.2002)—§ 28.4(e) n.83

Hall v. Moore, 253 F.3d 624 (11th Cir.2001)—§ 11.2(b) n.55

Hall, People v., 152 N.H. 374, 877 A.2d 222 (2005)—§ 22.4(c) n.29

Hall, People v., 194 Ill.2d 305, 252 Ill.Dec. 653, 743 N.E.2d 521 (2000)—§ 18.3(c) n.65

Hall, People v., 218 Cal.App.3d 1102, 267 Cal.Rptr. 494 (1990)— §§ 11.3(a) n.16; 11.5(c) n.49

Hall, People v., 435 Mich. 599, 460 N.W.2d 520 (1990)—§§ 14.3(d) n.101, 103, 105; 14.4(e) n.120, 125, 129

Hall, People v., 114 Ill.2d 376, 102 Ill.Dec. 322, 499 N.E.2d 1335 (1986)—§ 22.4(c) n.24

Hall v. State, 225 S.W.3d 524 (Tex.Cr.App.2007)—§§ 24.8(e) n.69, 75

Hall, State v., 154 N.H. 180, 908 A.2d 766 (2006)—§ 28.12(b) n.13

Hall v. State, 849 N.E.2d 466 (Ind.2006)—§ 21.5(c) n.93

Hall, State v., 268 Neb. 91, 679 N.W.2d 760 (2004)—§ 21.4(d) n.111

Hall v. State, 67 S.W.3d 870 (Tex.Cr.App.2002)—§ 6.4(g) n.153

Hall, State v., 148 N.H. 671, 813 A.2d 501 (2002)—§ 6.2(c) n.132

Hall v. State, 13 S.W.3d 115 (Tex.App.2000)—§ 24.5(b) n.23

Hall v. State, 226 Ga.App. 298, 485 S.E.2d 800 (1997)—§ 16.1(g) n.270

Hall, State v., 955 S.W.2d 198 (Mo.1997)—§ 22.3(a) n.5

Hall, State v., 616 So.2d 664 (La.1993)—§ 22.3(a) n.11

Hall v. State, 851 P.2d 1262 (Wyo.1993)—§ 13.5(b) n.36

Hall, State v., 246 Kan. 728, 793 P.2d 737 (Kan.1990)—§§ 19.2(b) n.17, 19; 19.2(c) n.24; 19.3(e) n.219; 19.6(b) n.18

Hall v. State, 539 So.2d 1338 (Miss.1989)—§ 1.7(f) n.90

Hall, State v., 179 W.Va. 398, 369 S.E.2d 701 (1988)—§ 6.2(c) n.78

Hall v. State, 497 So.2d 1145 (Ala.Crim.App.1986)—§ 18.5(a) n.51

Hall v. State, 255 Ga. 267, 336 S.E.2d 812 (1985)—§ 6.9(g) n.183

Hall, State v., 145 Vt. 299, 487 A.2d 166 (1984)—§ 18.5(c) n.82

Hall, State v., 93 N.J. 552, 461 A.2d 1155 (1983)—§ 3.8(g) n.242

Hall v. State, 47 Md.App. 590, 425 A.2d 227 (1981)—§ 6.4(g) n.154

Hall v. State, 273 Ind. 507, 405 N.E.2d 530 (1980)—§ 16.3(b) n.14

Hall v. State, 176 Ind.App. 59, 374 N.E.2d 62 (1978)—§ 24.3(b) n.42

Hall, State v., 249 N.W.2d 843 (Iowa 1977)—§§ 15.3(d) n.68; 24.3(b) n.61

Hall v. State, 138 Ga.App. 20, 225 S.E.2d 705 (1976)—§ 24.7(a) n.15

Hall v. State, 264 Ind. 448, 346 N.E.2d 584 (1976)—§ 6.9(b) n.23

Hall, State v., 235 N.W.2d 702 (Iowa 1975)—§§ 15.6(a) n.6, 8; 15.6(d) n.107; 15.7(f) n.133, 136

Hall, State v., 114 N.C. 909, 19 S.E. 602 (1894)—§ 16.4(c) n.44

Hall, United States v., 419 F.3d 980 (9th Cir.2005)—§ 26.10(c) n.71

Hall v. United States, 371 F.3d 969 (7th Cir.2004)—§§ 11.9(d) n.173, 229

Hall, United States v., 324 F.3d 720 (D.C.Cir.2003)—§§ 11.7(e) n.70; 24.11(d) n.20

Hall, United States v., 212 F.3d 1016 (7th Cir.2000)—§ 21.3(b) n.112

Hall, United States v., 181 F.3d 1057 (9th Cir.1999)—§ 18.3(b) n.26

Hall, United States v., 152 F.3d 381 (5th Cir.1998)—§§ 6.3(b) n.36; 6.4(f) n.137; 26.4(g) n.139, 141, 146

Hall, United States v., 77 F.3d 398 (11th Cir.1996)—§ 24.7(e) n.45

Hall, United States v., 93 F.3d 1337 (7th Cir.1996)—§ 6.2(c) n.183

Hall, United States v., 989 F.2d 711 (4th Cir.1993)—§ 22.3(c) n.100

Hall, United States v., 969 F.2d 1102 (D.C.Cir.1992)—§§ 3.10(a) n.21; 3.10(b) n.45

Hall, United States v., 854 F.2d 1269 (11th Cir.1988)—§ 24.11(d) n.35

Hall, United States v., 739 F.2d 96 (2d Cir.1984)—§ 3.5(d) n.141

Hall, United States v., 632 F.2d 500 (5th Cir.1980)—§ 19.3(b) n.160

Hall, United States v., 536 F.2d 313 (10th Cir.1976)—§ 24.9(a) n.4

Hall, United States v., 488 F.2d 193 (9th Cir.1973)—§ 4.6(a) n.4

Hall, United States v., 421 F.2d 540 (2d Cir.1969)—§§ 3.5(a) n.6; 6.6(c) n.26; 6.6(e) n.62

Haller, United States v., 837 F.2d 84 (2d Cir.1988)—§§ 21.4(b) n.52; 23.1(e) n.225, 261

Hallford v. State, 548 So.2d 526 (Ala.Crim.App.1988)—§ 1.8(e) n.91

Halliman, United States v., 923 F.2d 873 (D.C.Cir.1991)—§ 17.3(b) n.21

Hallinan v. Mitchell, 418 F.Supp. 1056 (N.D. Cal. 1976)—§ 4.6(n) n.257

Halling, People v., 203 Misc. 428, 122 N.Y.S.2d 543 (1953)—§ 16.4(a) n.1

Hallman, United States v., 365 F.2d 289 (3d Cir.1966)—§ 3.9(j) n.225

Hallmark v. Cartwright, 742 F.2d 584 (10th Cir.1984)—§ 7.3(c) n.61

Hall, United States ex rel. v. Lane, 804 F.2d 79 (7th Cir.1986)—§ 7.3(b) n.14

Halner v. Commonwealth, 378 Mass. 388, 392 N.E.2d 529 (1979)— § 20.3(h) n.156

Halper, United States v., 490 U.S. 435, 109 S.Ct. 1892, 104 L.Ed.2d 487 (1989)—§§ 2.1 n.54; 17.4(b) n.115; 25.1(b) n.19; 25.1(c) n.28

Halsey, State v., 218 N.J.Super. 149, 526 A.2d 1165 (1987)—§ 23.1(e) n.243

Halter, United States v., 411 F.3d 949 (8th Cir.2005)—§ 21.5(b) n.66

Halton, State v., 535 N.W.2d 734 (N.D.1995)—§ 21.2(d) n.191

Halvorsen, State v., 79 S.D. 209, 110 N.W.2d 132 (1961)—§ 8.1(c) n.25

Halvorson, State v., 346 N.W.2d 704 (N.D.1984)—§ 6.6(f) n.100

Ham v. South Carolina, 409 U.S. 524, 93 S.Ct. 848, 35 L.Ed.2d 46 (1973)—§ 22.3(a) n.17

Ham, United States v., 58 F.3d 78 (4th Cir.1995)—§ 25.4(d) n.45

Hamann, State v., 90 Ohio App.3d 654, 630 N.E.2d 384 (1993)—§ 26.9(c) n.89

Hamann v. State, 324 N.W.2d 906 (Iowa 1982)—§ 24.3(d) n.111

Hamblen v. State, 527 So.2d 800 (Fla.1988)—§ 11.5(d) n.84

Hambrick, United States v., 225 F.3d 656, 2000 WL 1062039 (4th Cir.2000)—§§ 4.4(b) n.6; 4.4(c) n.9; 4.8(f) n.69

Hamdan v. Rumsfeld, 548 U.S. _____, 126 S.Ct. 2749, 165 L.Ed.2d 723 (2006)—§§ 1.7(c) n.52; 24.2(a) n.2; 28.2(a) n.16

Hamdi v. Rumsfeld, 542 U.S. 507, 124 S.Ct. 2633, 159 L.Ed.2d 578 (2004)—§§ 28.2(a) n.14, 17

Hameed, People v., 88 N.Y.2d 232, 644 N.Y.S.2d 466, 666 N.E.2d 1339 (1996)—§§ 22.3(d) n.229, 230

Hamel, Petition of, 137 N.H. 488, 629 A.2d 802 (1993)—§ 12.4(d) n.81

Hamer v. United States, 259 F.2d 274 (9th Cir.1958)—§§ 22.3(b) n.52, 72, 86

Hamili, State v., 87 Haw. 102, 952 P.2d 390 (1998)—§ 27.4(d) n.48

Hamilton v. Alabama, 368 U.S. 52, 82 S.Ct. 157, 7 L.Ed.2d 114 (1961)— §§ 1.4(g) n.144; 11.2(b) n.41

Hamilton, Commonwealth v., 411 Mass. 313, 582 N.E.2d 929 (1991)— § 22.3(d) n.249

Hamilton, Commonwealth v., 445 Pa. 292, 285 A.2d 172 (1971)—§ 6.7(c) n.107

Hamilton v. Ford, 969 F.2d 1006 (11th Cir.1992)—§§ 11.9(b) n.54, 90

Hamilton v. Groose, 28 F.3d 859 (8th Cir.1994)—§§ 11.5(d) n.66, 69

Hamilton, People v., 465 Mich. 526, 638 N.W.2d 92 (2002)—§ 3.5(a) n.22

Hamilton, People v., 666 P.2d 152 (Colo.1983)—§ 1.8(f) n.103

Hamilton, People v., 188 Colo. 250, 533 P.2d 919 (1975)—§ 3.3(e) n.184

Hamilton, State v., 681 So.2d 1217 (La.1996)—§ 24.5(b) n.23

Hamilton v. State, 320 Ark. 346, 896 S.W.2d 877 (1995)—§ 27.2(c) n.64

Hamilton v. State, 677 So.2d 1254 (Ala.Cr.App.1995)—§ 24.3(d) n.107

Hamilton, State v., 228 Conn. 234, 636 A.2d 760 (1994)—§§ 11.4(c) n.73, 77, 86

Hamilton v. State, 556 So.2d 685 (Miss.1990)—§ 3.4(e) n.72

Hamilton, State v., 107 N.M. 186, 754 P.2d 857 (1988)—§ 25.1(d) n.88

Hamilton, State v., 104 N.M. 614, 725 P.2d 590 (1986)—§ 14.4(a) n.4

Hamilton, United States v., 391 F.3d 1066 (9th Cir.2004)—§§ 11.10(d) n.201, 203

Hamilton, United States v., 334 F.3d 170 (2d Cir.2003)—§ 17.3(c) n.34

Hamilton, United States v., 128 F.3d 996 (6th Cir.1997)—§ 20.6(c) n.79

Hamilton, United States v., 46 F.3d 271 (3d Cir.1995)—§§ 18.3(b) n.31, 32

Hamilton, United States v., 708 F.2d 1412 (9th Cir.1983)—§ 18.5(c) n.90

Hamilton, United States v., 553 F.2d 63 (10th Cir.1977)—§ 21.5(a) n.52

Hamlin v. Barrett, 335 So.2d 898 (Miss.1976)—§ 21.2(d) n.219

Hamlin, United States v., 319 F.3d 666 (4th Cir.2003)—§ 3.8(b) n.25

Hamling v. United States, 418 U.S. 87, 94 S.Ct. 2887, 41 L.Ed.2d 590 (1974)—§§ 19.2(a) n.3; 19.3(a) n.45; 22.3(a) n.21

Hamm, State v., 807 S.W.2d 692 (Mo.App.1991)—§ 27.5(a) n.28

Hamm, State v., 121 N.J. 109, 577 A.2d 1259 (1990)—§§ 15.1(d) n.234; 22.1(b) n.43

Hamm v. State, 301 Ark. 154, 782 S.W.2d 577 (1990)—§ 24.8(a) n.16

Hamm, State v., 423 N.W.2d 379 (Minn.1988)—§ 2.12(e) n.216

Hamm, State v., 348 A.2d 268 (Me.1975)—§ 9.1(d) n.136

Hammad, United States v., 858 F.2d 834 (2d Cir.1988)—§ 6.4(e) n.91

Hammell, State v., 147 N.H. 313, 787 A.2d 850 (2001)—§ 13.7(a) n.6

Hammell v. Warden, 146 N.H. 557, 776 A.2d 740 (2001)—§ 13.3(c) n.36

Hammer v. Dagenhart, 247 U.S. 251, 38 S.Ct. 529, 62 L.Ed. 101 (1918)—§ 1.2(c) n.124

Hammerman, United States v., 528 F.2d 326 (4th Cir.1975)—§§ 15.1(f) n.321, 322; 21.2(e) n.322, 332

Hammers v. State, 337 P.2d 1097 (Okl.Crim.1959)—§§ 15.6(d) n.105; 15.7(b) n.41

Hammett, United States v., 236 F.3d 1054 (9th Cir.2001)—§ 3.2(c) n.127

Hammitt v. State, 225 Ga.App. 21, 482 S.E.2d 437 (1997)—§ 20.6(a) n.8

Hammon, People v., 15 Cal.4th 1117, 65 Cal.Rptr.2d 1, 938 P.2d 986 (1997)—§§ 24.3(a) n.11; 24.3(f) n.156

Hammond v. Brown, 323 F.Supp. 326 (N.D.Ohio 1971)—§ 8.3(h) n.53

Hammond v. D.C. Board of Parole, 756 A.2d 896 (D.C.App.2000)—§ 26.8(c) n.31

Hammond, People v., 357 Ill. 182, 191 N.E. 327 (1934)—§ 15.4(b) n.23

Hammond, State v., 144 N.H. 401, 742 A.2d 532 (1999)—§§ 6.6(d) n.48; 6.6(e) n.59

Hammond v. State, 569 A.2d 81 (Del.1989)—§ 6.6(e) n.71

Hammond, United States v., 351 F.3d 765 (6th Cir.2003)—§ 3.4(d) n.51

Hammond, United States v., 286 F.3d 189 (4th Cir.2002)—§§ 4.6(b) n.44, 50; 4.6(l) n.201

Hammond, United States v., 419 F.2d 166 (4th Cir.1969)—§§ 7.2(c) n.36; 7.2(d) n.52

Hammons v. Scott, 423 F.Supp. 618 (N.D.Cal.1976)—§ 3.1(m) n.290

Hammontree, State v., 363 So.2d 1364 (La.1978)—§ 19.5(b) n.10

Hampe, Commonwealth v., 419 Mass. 514, 646 N.E.2d 387 (1995)—§ 12.2(c) n.41

Hampton, People v., 696 P.2d 765 (Colo.1985)—§§ 20.6(c) n.82, 89

Hampton v. State, 141 P.3d 101 (Wyo.2006)—§ 26.6(c) n.39

Hampton, State v., 163 S.W.3d 903 (Mo.2005)—§ 22.3(d) n.255

Hampton, State v., 274 Wis.2d 379, 683 N.W.2d 14 (2004)—§§ 21.4(g) n.232; 21.5(c) n.88

Hampton v. State, 357 Ark. 473, 183 S.W.3d 148 (2004)—§ 18.5(a) n.11

Hampton v. State, 86 S.W.3d 603 (Tex.Cr.App.2002)—§ 24.3(b) n.64

Hampton, State v., 207 Wis.2d 367, 558 N.W.2d 884 (1996)—§ 25.4(a) n.8

Hampton v. State, 623 P.2d 318 (Alaska 1981)—§ 20.6(b) n.31

Hampton, State v., 61 N.J. 250, 294 A.2d 23 (1972)—§ 10.5(a) n.8

Hampton, United States v., 260 F.3d 832 (8th Cir.2001)—§ 3.6(a) n.31

Hampton, United States v., 775 F.2d 1479 (11th Cir.1985)—§§ 8.11(b) n.29; 8.11(c) n.35

Hampton v. United States, 425 U.S. 484, 96 S.Ct. 1646, 48 L.Ed.2d 113 (1976)—§§ 5.1(a) n.4; 5.1(c) n.20; 5.4(c) n.34

Hampton v. United States, 269 A.2d 441 (D.C.App.1970)—§ 24.7(a) n.1

Hamrick, State v., 110 N.C.App. 60, 428 S.E.2d 830 (1993)—§ 25.1(d) n.66

Hamsley, State v., 672 S.W.2d 437 (Tenn.Crim.App.1984)—§ 16.1(g) n.246

Hamstead, State ex rel. v. Dostert, 173 W.Va. 133, 313 S.E.2d 409 (1984)—§ 13.2(a) n.3

Hana, People v., 443 Mich. 202, 504 N.W.2d 166 (1993)—§ 6.10(e) n.76

Hance, State v., _____ Vt. _____, 910 A.2d 874 (2006)—§ 12.2(b) n.31

Hance, State v., 157 Vt. 222, 596 A.2d 365 (1991)—§ 21.2(b) n.76

Hancock v. State, 26 Ark.App. 107, 760 S.W.2d 391 (1988)—§§ 11.2(g) n.261, 292

Hancock v. White, 378 F.2d 479 (1st Cir.1967)—§ 6.4(b) n.30

Hand, United States v., 913 F.2d 854 (10th Cir.1990)—§ 21.2(d) n.172

Hand, United States v., 863 F.2d 1100 (3d Cir.1988)—§ 26.6(c) n.35

Handa, United States v., 122 F.3d 690 (9th Cir.1997)—§ 21.5(e) n.147

Handtmann, State v., 437 N.W.2d 830 (N.D.1989)—§ 9.3(e) n.58

Handwerker, People v., 816 N.Y.S.2d 824, 12 Misc.3d 19 (N.Y.Sup.2006)—§ 24.7(e) n.46

Handy, State v., 326 N.C. 532, 391 S.E.2d 159 (1990)—§§ 21.5(a) n.24, 30, 38, 40

Handy, United States v., 753 F.2d 1487 (9th Cir.1985)—§ 12.4(d) n.69

Haner, State v., 95 Wash.2d 858, 631 P.2d 381 (1981)—§ 21.3(e) n.296

Haney v. Sharp, 1 Dana 442, 31 Ky. 442 (1833)—§ 1.2(c) n.81

Hang, United States v., 75 F.3d 1275 (8th Cir.1996)—§§ 24.3(f) n.142, 150

Hang Le-Thy Tran, United States v., 433 F.3d 472 (6th Cir.2006)—§ 3.4(e) n.68

Hankerson v. State, 723 N.W.2d 232 (Minn.2006)—§ 26.7(b) n.20

Hankey, United States v., 203 F.3d 1160 (9th Cir.2000)—§ 6.9(c) n.61

Hankins, State v., 232 Neb. 608, 441 N.W.2d 854 (1989)—§§ 6.9(b) n.27; 24.3(f) n.154

Hankins, United States v., 565 F.2d 1344 (5th Cir.1978)—§ 8.12(b) n.20

Hankish, United States v., 502 F.2d 71 (4th Cir.1974)—§ 16.2(f) n.104

Hanks v. State, 13 Tex.App. 289 (1882)—§§ 16.4(c) n.106, 109

Hanna v. Plumer, 380 U.S. 460, 85 S.Ct. 1136, 14 L.Ed.2d 8 (1965)—§ 1.7(f) n.97

Hanna, State v., 180 W.Va. 598, 378 S.E.2d 640 (1989)—§ 23.3(b) n.29

Hannah v. Larche, 363 U.S. 420, 80 S.Ct. 1502, 4 L.Ed.2d 1307 (1960)—§ 15.5(a) n.23

Hannah, State v., 312 N.C. 286, 322 S.E.2d 148 (1984)—§ 7.4(g) n.110

Hannah v. State, 336 So.2d 1317 (Miss.1976)—§§ 15.7(b) n.50; 15.7(h) n.225

Hannah, State ex rel. v. Seier, 654 S.W.2d 894 (Mo.1983)—§ 27.4(d) n.39

Hannon v. State, 84 P.3d 320 (Wyo.2004)—§§ 6.6(c) n.37; 6.6(d) n.48

Hannon, State v., 636 N.W.2d 796 (Minn.2001)—§§ 6.9(f) n.134; 6.9(g) n.166

Hansel, People v., 1 Cal.4th 1211, 4 Cal.Rptr.2d 888, 824 P.2d 694 (1992)—§ 14.4(b) n.43

Hansen, People v., 95 N.Y.2d 227, 715 N.Y.S.2d 369, 738 N.E.2d 773 (2000)—§§ 15.5(c) n.130; 15.6(f) n.204; 19.2(e) n.54; 19.3(a) n.13; 21.6(a) n.43

Hansen, State v., 138 Idaho 791, 69 P.3d 1052 (2003)—§§ 3.10(b) n.72; 6.7(c) n.128

Hansen, State v., 243 Wis.2d 328, 627 N.W.2d 195 (2001)—§ 25.5(b) n.25

Hansen v. State, 845 P.2d 449 (Alaska App.1993)—§ 24.8(e) n.69

Hansen v. State, 592 So.2d 114 (Miss.1991)—§ 14.1(b) n.32

Hansen, State v., 105 Idaho 816, 673 P.2d 416 (1983)—§ 5.2(a) n.4

Hansen, United States v., 422 F.Supp. 430 (D.Wis.1976)—§ 19.3(b) n.136

Hansford, State v., 219 Wis.2d 226, 580 N.W.2d 171 (1998)—§ 22.1(d) n.79

Hanson v. Circuit Court, 591 F.2d 404 (7th Cir.1979)—§ 28.3(a) n.26

Hanson v. Commonwealth, 29 Va.App. 69, 509 S.E.2d 543 (Va.App.1999)—§ 20.3(c) n.75

Hanson v. Passer, 13 F.3d 275 (8th Cir.1994)—§ 11.2(h) n.312

Hanson, People v., 283 Mont. 316, 940 P.2d 1166 (1997)—§ 27.5(d) n.120

Hanson v. Phillips, 442 F.3d 789 (2d Cir.2006)—§§ 21.5(c) n.92; 27.5(c) n.87

Hanson, State v., 23 Cal.4th 355, 97 Cal.Rptr.2d 58, 1 P.3d 650 (2000)—§ 26.7(b) n.20

Hanson, State v., 181 W.Va. 353, 382 S.E.2d 547 (1989)—§§ 6.2(c) n.102; 8.11(e) n.95, 97

Hanson, State v., 136 Wis.2d 195, 401 N.W.2d 771 (1987)—§ 6.9(c) n.61

Hanson, United States v., 339 F.3d 983 (D.C.Cir.2003)—§§ 5.2(a) n.9; 21.3(b) n.45

Hanson, United States v., 237 F.3d 961 (8th Cir.2001)—§ 6.6(d) n.49

Hanson, United States v., 472 F.Supp. 1049 (D.Minn.1979)—§ 15.4(d) n.98

Hanson, United States v., 28 F. 74 (C.C.Me.1886)—§ 15.4(b) n.35

Hansz, State v., 167 Or.App. 147, 5 P.3d 1109 (2000)—§§ 19.3(b) n.145, 152; 19.5(c) n.52

Harbaugh, State v., 123 Idaho 835, 853 P.2d 580 (1993)—§ 21.5(a) n.24

Harber, United States v., 53 F.3d 236 (9th Cir.1995)—§ 24.9(f) n.80

Harbin, United States v., 250 F.3d 532 (7th Cir.2001)—§ 22.3(d) n.172

Harbin, United States v., 601 F.2d 773 (5th Cir.1979)—§ 20.6(b) n.16

Harbison, State v., 315 N.C. 175, 337 S.E.2d 504 (1985)—§ 11.6(a) n.48

Harbolt, United States v., 426 F.2d 1346 (5th Cir.1970)—§ 16.2(e) n.78

Harbour, United States v., 809 F.2d 384 (7th Cir.1987)—§ 24.5(a) n.8

Hardcastle v. Horn, 368 F.3d 246 (3d Cir.2004)—§ 28.2(b) n.31

Harden v. Johnson, 280 Ga. 464, 629 S.E.2d 259 (2006)—§ 21.5(d) n.101

Harden, People v., 54 Mich.App. 353, 220 N.W.2d 785 (1974)—§ 3.6(f) n.149

Harden, State v., 750 S.W.2d 666 (Mo.App.1988)—§ 15.4(b) n.55

Hardesty v. Hamburg Township, 461 F.3d 646 (6th Cir.2006)—§ 3.2(c) n.127

Hardesty, State v., 129 Wash.2d 303, 915 P.2d 1080 (1996)—§§ 21.4(g) n.256; 26.7(c) n.37

Hardiman v. State, 726 N.E.2d 1201 (Ind.2000)—§ 7.4(c) n.53

Hardin, People v., 217 Ill.2d 289, 298 Ill.Dec. 770, 840 N.E.2d 1205 (2005)—§§ 11.7(a) n.10; 11.7(e) n.67

Hardin v. State, 269 Ga. 1, 494 S.E.2d 647 (1998)—§ 6.6(e) n.69

Hardin v. State, 265 Ind. 635, 358 N.E.2d 134 (1976)—§ 5.4(b) n.16

Harding v. Davis, 878 F.2d 1341 (11th Cir.1989)—§§ 11.5(c) n.52; 11.10(d) n.193

Harding v. Lewis, 834 F.2d 853 (9th Cir.1987)—§§ 11.5(c) n.61, 62; 11.10(b) n.43

Harding, People v., 443 Mich. 693, 506 N.W.2d 482 (1993)—§ 17.4(b) n.98

Harding, State v., 137 Ariz. 278, 670 P.2d 383 (1983)—§ 11.5(c) n.61

Hardman, State v., 121 Idaho 873, 828 P.2d 902 (Idaho App.1992)—§§ 14.4(e) n.115; 24.11(d) n.21, 23

Hardnett v. Marshall, 25 F.3d 875 (9th Cir.1994)—§ 28.6(g) n.89

Hardwick v. Crosby, 320 F.3d 1127 (11th Cir.2003)—§ 11.10(c) n.127

Hardwick v. Doolittle, 558 F.2d 292 (5th Cir.1977)—§§ 13.7(c) n.54, 66

Hardy, Ex parte, 804 So.2d 298 (Ala.2000)—§ 17.2(d) n.94

Hardy v. Commonwealth, 17 Va.App. 677, 440 S.E.2d 434 (1994)—§ 9.1(d) n.126

Hardy, People v., 2 Cal.4th 86, 5 Cal.Rptr.2d 796, 825 P.2d 781 (1992)—§§ 11.9(a) n.25; 22.3(d) n.176

Hardy, State v., 353 N.C. 122, 540 S.E.2d 334 (2000)—§ 22.3(d) n.249

Hardy v. State, 655 So.2d 1245 (1995)—§ 11.3(a) n.18

Hardy, State v., 293 N.C. 105, 235 S.E.2d 828 (1977)—§§ 20.3(i) n.168; 24.3(b) n.71, 73

Hardy, United States v., 37 F.3d 753 (1st Cir.1994)—§ 24.5(b) n.27

Hardy, United States v., 762 F.Supp. 1403 (D.Hawai'i 1991)—§§ 19.2(b) n.9; 19.3(c) n.188

Hardy v. United States, 375 U.S. 277, 84 S.Ct. 424, 11 L.Ed.2d 331 (1964)—§ 11.2(d) n.130

Hardy, People ex rel. v. Sielaff, 79 N.Y.2d 618, 584 N.Y.S.2d 742, 595 N.E.2d 817 (1992)—§ 27.4(f) n.65

Hare v. State, 467 N.E.2d 7 (Ind.1984)—§ 16.3(b) n.21

Hare, United States v., 269 F.3d 859 (7th Cir.2001)—§§ 21.2(b) n.76, 88; 21.2(d) n.272; 21.2(e) n.357; 21.3(c) n.148

Hare, United States v., 49 F.3d 447 (8th Cir.1995)—§ 21.2(h) n.419

Hare, United States v., 873 F.2d 796 (5th Cir.1989)—§§ 12.1(a) n.15; 12.3(d) n.97

Harford County Education Ass'n v. Board of Education, 281 Md. 574, 380 A.2d 1041 (1977)—§ 5.2(a) n.4

Harfst, United States v., 168 F.3d 398 (10th Cir.1999)—§ 11.10(d) n.168

Hargis, State v., 328 So.2d 479 (Fla.App.1976)—§ 8.11(e) n.95

Hargrave v. Wainwright, 804 F.2d 1182 (11th Cir.1986)—§ 6.10(e) n.67

Hargrove, State v., 273 Kan. 314, 45 P.3d 376 (2002)—§ 18.4(c) n.35

Hargrove, State v., 330 So.2d 895 (La.1976)—§ 7.4(b) n.33

Haring v. Prosise, 462 U.S. 306, 103 S.Ct. 2368, 76 L.Ed.2d 595 (1983)—§ 21.6(a) n.18

Harisiades v. Shaughnessy, 342 U.S. 580, 72 S.Ct. 512, 96 L.Ed. 586 (1952)—§ 15.1(b) n.14

Harjo v. State, 882 P.2d 1067 (Okla.Crim.App.1994)—§ 3.5(d) n.141

Harkins, In re, 624 F.2d 1160 (3d Cir.1980)—§§ 8.9(b) n.22, 23

Harlan, People v., 109 P.3d 616 (Colo.2005)—§ 24.9(f) n.69

Harlan, J., dissenting in Miranda v. Arizona, 384 U.S. 436, 86 S.Ct. 1602, 16 L.Ed.2d 694 (1966)—§ 2.9(g) n.195

Harlee v. District of Columbia, 558 A.2d 351 (D.C.App.1989)—§ 22.2(d) n.82

Harley, United States v., 990 F.2d 1340 (D.C.Cir.1993)—§ 24.8(e) n.86

Harling v. United States, 387 A.2d 1101 (D.C.App.1978)—§§ 11.4(a) n.1; 11.4(b) n.46

Harlow v. Fitzgerald, 457 U.S. 800, 102 S.Ct. 2727, 73 L.Ed.2d 396 (1982)—§§ 3.1(k) n.260; 4.6(n) n.259

Harlow, United States v., 444 F.3d 1255 (10th Cir.2006)—§ 24.7(i) n.90

Harman v. Frye, 188 W.Va. 611, 425 S.E.2d 566 (1992)—§§ 13.3(b) n.18; 13.3(f) n.57

Harman v. Mohn, 683 F.2d 834 (4th Cir.1982)—§ 21.2(b) n.54

Harmelin v. Michigan, 501 U.S. 957, 111 S.Ct. 2680, 115 L.Ed.2d 836 (1991)—§§ 1.5(h) n.290; 2.4(a) n.20; 2.6(c) n.85; 2.9(b) n.6, 9; 2.9(d) n.55, 93

Harmison, People v., 124 Ill.App.3d 236, 79 Ill.Dec. 598, 463 N.E.2d 1373 (1984)—§ 19.3(b) n.136

Harmon, Commonwealth v., 469 Pa. 490, 366 A.2d 895 (1976)— § 10.6(b) n.12

Harmon v. McVicar, 95 F.3d 620 (7th Cir.1996)—§ 24.4(c) n.24

Harmon v. State, 224 Ga.App. 890, 482 S.E.2d 730 (1997)—§ 20.3(f) n.104

Harmon, State v., 575 N.W.2d 635 (N.D.1997)—§§ 11.4(b) n.20, 25, 27; 11.4(d) n.117; 11.5(c) n.54

Harms, State v., 233 Neb. 882, 449 N.W.2d 1 (1989)—§§ 3.1(e) n.135; 9.1(c) n.100; 9.1(d) n.120

Harned v. Henderson, 588 F.2d 12 (2d Cir.1978)—§ 21.4(c) n.76

Harned, State v., 281 Kan. 1023, 135 P.3d 1169 (2006)—§§ 21.4(c) n.74, 89, 92; 21.5(a) n.26

Harnish v. State, 531 A.2d 1264 (Me.1987)—§§ 12.3(b) n.34; 12.4(a) n.5, 16, 27

Harold v. State, 450 So.2d 910 (Fla.App.1984)—§ 11.2(c) n.89

Harper, Ex parte, 594 So.2d 1181 (Ala.1991)—§§ 1.7(h) n.132; 19.3(a) n.57

Harper v. District Court, 484 P.2d 891 (Okla.Crim.App.1971)—§ 14.3(c) n.77

Harper, People v., 32 Mich.App. 73, 188 N.W.2d 254 (1971)—§ 21.5(e) n.120

Harper, State v., 855 S.W.2d 474 (Mo.Ct.App.1993)—§ 16.1(g) n.274

Harper, State v., 778 S.W.2d 836 (Mo.App. S.D.1989)—§ 16.1(h) n.306

Harper, State v., 33 Wash.App. 507, 655 P.2d 1199 (1982)—§ 11.6(a) n.49

Harper, State v., 57 Wis.2d 543, 205 N.W.2d 1 (1973)—§ 10.2(a) n.17

Harper, United States v., 928 F.2d 894 (9th Cir.1991)—§ 3.9(j) n.219

Harper, United States v., 901 F.2d 471 (5th Cir.1990)—§ 28.9(c) n.77

Harper, United States v., 729 F.2d 1216 (9th Cir.1984)—§ 26.1(b) n.32

Harr, State v., 156 W.Va. 492, 194 S.E.2d 652 (1973)—§§ 10.5(b) n.17; 10.5(f) n.62

Harrell, State v., 182 Wis.2d 408, 513 N.W.2d 676 (App.1994)—§ 21.4(f) n.201

Harrell v. State, 647 So.2d 1016 (Fla.App.1994)—§ 24.5(b) n.34

Harrell, United States v., 894 F.2d 120 (5th Cir.1990)—§ 6.6(c) n.33

Harrelson, United States v., 754 F.2d 1153 (5th Cir.1985)—§ 22.4(c) n.22

Harries v. Bell, 417 F.3d 631 (6th Cir.2005)—§§ 11.10(b) n.46; 11.10(c) n.127

Harrigan, United States v., 557 F.2d 879 (1st Cir.1977)—§ 4.6(m) n.243

Harrill, State v., 289 N.C. 186, 221 S.E.2d 325 (1976)—§ 21.2(h) n.437

Harrington, Ex parte, 883 S.W.2d 396 (Tex.App.1994)—§ 26.9(a) n.14

Harrington v. California, 395 U.S. 250, 89 S.Ct. 1726, 23 L.Ed.2d 284 (1969)—§§ 27.6(d) n.80; 27.6(e) n.153

Harrington, People v., 29 N.Y.2d 498, 323 N.Y.S.2d 971, 272 N.E.2d 482 (1971)—§ 7.3(f) n.109

Harrington v. State, 659 N.W.2d 509 (Iowa 2003)—§ 24.3(b) n.58

Harrington, State v., 705 A.2d 998 (R.I.1997)—§ 27.2(c) n.62

Harrington, State v., 5 N.C.App. 622, 169 S.E.2d 32 (1969)—§§ 15.1(f) n.279, 316, 327

Harrington, State v., 128 Vt. 242, 260 A.2d 692 (Vt.1969)—§§ 2.6(b) n.58; 16.4(c) n.86, 89, 105

Harrington, United States v., 354 F.3d 178 (2004)—§ 21.5(c) n.83

Harrington, United States v., 923 F.2d 1371 (9th Cir.1991)—§ 6.2(c) n.140

Harrington, United States v., 947 F.2d 956 (D.C.Cir.1991)—§ 26.3(b) n.11

Harris, In re, 5 Cal.4th 813, 21 Cal.Rptr.2d 373, 855 P.2d 391 (1993)—§ 28.11(b) n.18

Harris, In re, 221 U.S. 274, 31 S.Ct. 557, 55 L.Ed. 732 (1911)—§ 8.13(a) n.3

Harris v. Alabama, 513 U.S. 504, 115 S.Ct. 1031, 130 L.Ed.2d 1004 (1995)—§§ 26.1(b) n.15; 26.2(b) n.10

Harris v. Arkansas, 322 Ark. 167, 907 S.W.2d 729 (1995)—§ 26.6(b) n.19

Harris v. Champion, 15 F.3d 1538 (10th Cir.1994)—§§ 18.5(c) n.81, 84

Harris, Commonwealth v., 572 Pa. 489, 817 A.2d 1033 (2002)—§ 22.3(d) n.202

Harris v. Commonwealth, 262 Va. 407, 551 S.E.2d 606 (2001)—§ 3.8(e) n.192

Harris, Commonwealth v., 409 Mass. 461, 567 N.E.2d 899 (1991)—§§ 22.3(d) n.242, 248

Harris, Commonwealth v., 395 Mass. 296, 479 N.E.2d 690 (1985)—§ 7.4(b) n.19

Harris, Commonwealth v., 387 Mass. 758, 443 N.E.2d 1287 (1982)—§ 3.10(b) n.79

Harris v. District Court, 843 P.2d 1316 (Colo.1993)—§§ 14.1(c) n.45, 46

Harris v. Hutchinson, 209 F.3d 325 (4th Cir.2000)—§ 28.5(b) n.59

Harris v. McRae, 448 U.S. 297, 100 S.Ct. 2671, 65 L.Ed.2d 784 (1980)—§ 13.5(h) n.122

Harris v. New York, 401 U.S. 222, 91 S.Ct. 643, 28 L.Ed.2d 1 (1971)—§§ 2.9(h) n.208; 2.10(b) n.24; 6.5(e) n.93; 9.1(a) n.19; 9.5(a) n.21; 9.6(a) n.5; 10.1(b) n.28; 10.5(c) n.32; 21.2(h) n.429

Harris v. Oklahoma, 433 U.S. 682, 97 S.Ct. 2912, 53 L.Ed.2d 1054 (1977)—§§ 16.1(f) n.217; 17.4(b) n.75

Harris, People v., 363 Ill.App.3d 586, 300 Ill.Dec. 244, 843 N.E.2d 502 (2006)—§ 22.1(h) n.134

Harris, People v., 99 N.Y.2d 202, 753 N.Y.S.2d 437, 783 N.E.2d 502 (2002)—§§ 11.9(d) n.230, 233

Harris, People v., 206 Ill.2d 1, 276 Ill.Dec. 419, 794 N.E.2d 314 (2002)—§ 22.3(d) n.191

Harris, People v., 222 App.Div.2d 522, 635 N.Y.S.2d 258 (1995)—§ 24.2(a) n.12

Harris, People v., 164 Ill.2d 322, 207 Ill.Dec. 400, 647 N.E.2d 893 (1994)—§ 22.3(d) n.245

Harris, People v., 14 Cal.App.4th 984, 18 Cal.Rptr.2d 92 (1993)—§ 11.6(a) n.21

Harris, People v., 10 Cal.App.4th 672, 12 Cal.Rptr.2d 758 (1992)—§ 24.1(a) n.4

Harris, People v., 77 N.Y.2d 434, 568 N.Y.S.2d 702, 570 N.E.2d 1051 (1991)—§ 9.4(a) n.38

Harris, People v., 47 Cal.3d 1047, 255 Cal.Rptr. 352, 767 P.2d 619 (1989)—§ 17.2(b) n.75

Harris, People v., 36 Cal.3d 36, 201 Cal.Rptr. 782, 679 P.2d 433 (1984)—§ 22.2(d) n.63

Harris, People v., 15 Cal.3d 384, 124 Cal.Rptr. 536, 540 P.2d 632 (1975)—§§ 3.8(b) n.44; 3.8(d) n.150; 11.6(a) n.45; 11.6(d) n.124, 125

Harris v. Pulley, 885 F.2d 1354 (9th Cir.1989)—§ 13.4(b) n.77

Harris v. Reed, 894 F.2d 871 (7th Cir.1990)—§ 11.10(c) n.80

Harris v. Reed, 489 U.S. 255, 109 S.Ct. 1038, 103 L.Ed.2d 308 (1989)—§§ 28.4(b) n.24; 28.4(c) n.27

Harris v. Rivera, 454 U.S. 339, 102 S.Ct. 460, 70 L.Ed.2d 530 (1981)—§ 24.10(b) n.32

Harris v. South Carolina, 338 U.S. 68, 69 S.Ct. 1354, 93 L.Ed. 1815 (1949)—§§ 6.2(c) n.79; 6.4(a) n.2

Harris, State v., 279 Kan. 163, 105 P.3d 1258 (2005)—§ 6.2(c) n.134

Harris, State v., 104 P.3d 1250 (Utah 2004)—§§ 25.2(d) n.24; 27.2(c) n.62

Harris v. State, 160 Md.App. 78, 862 A.2d 516 (2004)—§ 24.10(d) n.48

Harris, State v., 272 Wis.2d 80, 680 N.W.2d 737 (2004)—§§ 21.3(c) n.178, 181

Harris, State v., 264 Neb. 856, 652 N.W.2d 585 (2002)—§ 22.3(c) n.162

Harris v. State, 806 So.2d 1127 (Miss.2002)—§ 21.3(b) n.61

Harris, State v., 294 Mont. 397, 983 P.2d 881 (1999)—§ 13.4(c) n.105

Harris, State v., 156 N.J. 122, 716 A.2d 458 (1998)—§§ 16.3(g) n.111, 116; 23.2(c) n.59; 23.2(g) n.123

Harris v. State, 687 So.2d 29 (Fla.App.1997)—§ 11.3(a) n.18

Harris, State v., 109 Ohio App.3d 873, 673 N.E.2d 237 (1996)—§ 27.5(a) n.29

Harris v. State, 107 Md.App. 399, 668 A.2d 938 (1995)—§ 27.2(c) n.56

Harris, State v., 282 N.J.Super. 409, 660 A.2d 539 (1995)—§ 22.2(d) n.74

Harris, State v., 521 N.W.2d 348 (Minn.1994)—§ 24.7(i) n.88

Harris, State v., 227 Conn. 751, 631 A.2d 309 (1993)—§ 24.3(a) n.11

Harris v. State, 841 P.2d 597 (Okla.Crim.App.1992)—§§ 14.1(b) n.31; 14.2(f) n.92

Harris v. State, 260 Ga. 860, 401 S.E.2d 263 (1991)—§ 9.4(b) n.70

Harris, State v., 436 N.W.2d 364 (Iowa 1989)—§ 3.6(g) n.162

Harris, State v., 157 Ariz. 35, 754 P.2d 1139 (1988)—§ 22.3(d) n.220

Harris v. State, 312 Md. 225, 539 A.2d 637 (1988)—§ 24.7(c) n.23

Harris v. State, 519 N.E.2d 1253 (Ind.App.1988)—§ 24.8(a) n.3

Harris, State v., 333 N.W.2d 873 (Minn.1983)—§ 3.3(f) n.202

Harris v. State, 608 S.W.2d 229 (Tex.Cr.App.1980)—§ 26.9(b) n.19

Harris, State v., 91 Wash.2d 145, 588 P.2d 720 (1978)—§ 24.3(g) n.171

Harris v. State, 142 Ga.App. 37, 234 S.E.2d 798 (1977)—§ 14.2(g) n.98

Harris, State v., 256 Wis. 93, 39 N.W.2d 912 (1949)—§ 3.3(b) n.51

Harris, State v., 3 Del. 559 (1841)—§ 19.1(a) n.7

Harris v. Superior Court, 19 Cal.3d 786, 140 Cal.Rptr. 318, 567 P.2d 750 (1977)—§§ 11.4(a) n.11, 13; 27.4(c) n.33

Harris, United States v., 491 F.3d 440 (D.C.Cir.2007)—§ 27.5(e) n.169

Harris, United States v., 376 F.3d 1282 (11th Cir.2004)—§§ 13.6(d) n.56; 18.3(b) n.9

Harris, United States v., 293 F.3d 970 (6th Cir.2002)—§ 19.3(a) n.29

Harris v. United States, 536 U.S. 545, 122 S.Ct. 2406, 153 L.Ed.2d 524 (2002)—§§ 19.3(a) n.28, 30, 119; 26.3(c) n.21; 26.4(i) n.180

Harris, United States v., 221 F.3d 1048 (8th Cir.2000)—§ 6.9(f) n.144

Harris v. United States, 738 A.2d 269 (D.C.App.1999)—§ 24.9(g) n.130

Harris v. United States, 1998 WL 26187 (S.D.N.Y.1998)—§ 20.3(j) n.195

Harris, United States v., 70 F.3d 1001 (8th Cir.1995)—§§ 21.1(h) n.233; 21.2(d) n.216

Harris, United States v., 25 F.3d 1275 (5th Cir.1994)—§ 1.2(c) n.148

Harris, United States v., 995 F.2d 532 (4th Cir.1993)—§ 7.5(b) n.18

Harris v. United States, 602 A.2d 1140 (D.C.App.1992)—§ 24.11(d) n.34

Harris v. United States, 612 A.2d 198 (D.C.App.1992)—§§ 26.4(f) n.89; 26.10(c) n.48, 63

Harris, United States v., 956 F.2d 177 (8th Cir.1992)—§ 3.3(d) n.162

Harris, United States v., 973 F.2d 333 (4th Cir.1992)—§§ 8.11(c) n.45, 58; 21.2(d) n.150

Harris, United States v., 928 F.2d 1113 (11th Cir.1991)—§ 3.10(f) n.197

Harris, United States v., 914 F.2d 927 (7th Cir.1990)—§ 6.2(c) n.113

Harris, United States v., 882 F.2d 902 (4th Cir.1989)—§ 21.1(e) n.86

Harris, United States v., 683 F.2d 322 (9th Cir.1982)—§§ 11.3(b) n.36, 38

Harris, United States v., 534 F.2d 95 (7th Cir.1976)—§ 3.10(e) n.170

Harris, United States v., 543 F.2d 1247 (9th Cir.1976)—§§ 20.3(b) n.23, 50

Harris, United States v., 528 F.2d 914 (4th Cir.1975)—§§ 6.7(b) n.75; 7.5(b) n.11

Harris, United States v., 403 U.S. 573, 91 S.Ct. 2075, 29 L.Ed.2d 723 (1971)—§§ 3.3(a) n.2; 3.3(b) n.64; 3.3(c) n.104

Harris v. United States, 404 U.S. 1232, 92 S.Ct. 10, 30 L.Ed.2d 25 (1971)—§ 12.4(d) n.80

Harris v. United States, 413 F.2d 316 (9th Cir.1969)—§ 27.2(e) n.86

Harris v. United States, 390 U.S. 234, 88 S.Ct. 992, 19 L.Ed.2d 1067 (1968)—§§ 3.5(c) n.108; 3.7(e) n.92

Harris v. United States, 400 F.2d 264 (5th Cir.1968)—§ 5.4(a) n.7

Harris v. United States, 382 U.S. 162, 86 S.Ct. 352, 15 L.Ed.2d 240 (1965)—§§ 8.3(a) n.8; 8.4(c) n.113

Harris v. United States, 331 U.S. 145, 67 S.Ct. 1098, 91 L.Ed. 1399 (1947)—§§ 2.8(c) n.65; 3.4(j) n.200; 3.6(c) n.70; 3.9(b) n.20

Harris v. Vasquez, 949 F.2d 1497 (9th Cir.1990)—§ 24.3(d) n.112

Harris v. Washington, 404 U.S. 55, 92 S.Ct. 183, 30 L.Ed.2d 212 (1971)—§ 17.4(a) n.21

Harris v. Wright, 93 F.3d 581 (9th Cir.1996)—§ 6.9(b) n.23

Harris Methodist Ft. Worth, United States v., 970 F.2d 94 (5th Cir.1992)—§§ 3.9(c) n.49, 58, 59

Harrison v. Commonwealth, 244 Va. 576, 423 S.E.2d 160 (1992)—§ 6.9(b) n.28

Harrison v. Commonwealth, 559 S.W.2d 744 (Ky.App.1977)—§ 19.6(b) n.12

Harrison, People v., 81 Misc.2d 144, 364 N.Y.S.2d 760 (Sup.Ct.1975)—§ 20.3(h) n.157

Harrison v. Ryan, 909 F.2d 84 (3d Cir.1990)—§ 22.3(d) n.212

Harrison, State v., 148 Wash.2d 550, 61 P.3d 1104 (2003)—§ 21.2(e) n.318

Harrison, State v., 118 N.J. Super. 299, 287 A.2d 229 (1962)—§ 20.3(k) n.220

Harrison, United States v., 241 F.3d 289 (2d Cir.2001)—§§ 21.4(d) n.102; 21.5(c) n.83

Harrison, United States v., 213 F.3d 1206 (9th Cir.2000)—§ 6.4(f) n.122

Harrison, United States v., 113 F.3d 135 (8th Cir.1997)—§ 21.5(e) n.147

Harrison, United States v., 34 F.3d 886 (9th Cir.1994)—§ 6.2(c) n.113

Harrison, United States v., 432 F.2d 1328 (D.C.Cir.1970)—§ 3.5(b) n.100

Harrison v. United States, 392 U.S. 219, 88 S.Ct. 2008, 20 L.Ed.2d 1047 (1968)—§§ 9.5(a) n.29; 9.5(d) n.74; 10.2(c) n.41; 24.5(a) n.7

Harrolle v. State, 763 P.2d 126 (Okl.Crim. 1988)—§§ 7.4(b) n.23; 7.4(f) n.96

Harry Alexander, Inc., Application of, 8 F.R.D. 559 (S.D.N.Y.1949)—§ 8.7(b) n.61

Harryman v. Estelle, 616 F.2d 870 (5th Cir.1980)—§§ 6.7(b) n.69; 27.6(d) n.93

Harry Shapiro Jr. Realty & Investment Co., State ex rel. v. Cloyd, 615 S.W.2d 41 (Mo.1981)—§ 8.10(a) n.14

Hart v. Attorney General, 323 F.3d 884 (11th Cir.2003)—§ 6.9(c) n.58

Hart v. Gomez, 174 F.3d 1067 (9th Cir.1999)—§ 11.10(c) n.84

Hart v. Marion Correctional Institution, 927 F.2d 256 (6th Cir.1991)—§ 21.4(d) n.150

Hart, People v., 93 N.Y.2d 825, 687 N.Y.S.2d 617, 710 N.E.2d 263 (1999)—§ 17.4(b) n.133

Hart, State v., 723 N.W.2d 254 (Minn.2006)—§ 13.2(c) n.60

Hart v. State, 62 P.3d 566 (Wyo.2003)—§§ 11.9(a) n.32; 22.5(d) n.34

Hart v. State, 116 Nev. 558, 1 P.3d 969 (2000)—§§ 21.5(a) n.24, 28

Hart, State v., 139 N.J.Super. 565, 354 A.2d 679 (1976)—§§ 15.2(e) n.145; 15.6(a) n.36; 15.7(b) n.36, 41, 49

Hart, United States v., 963 F.2d 1278 (9th Cir.1992)—§ 5.4(c) n.42

Hart, United States v., 779 F.Supp. 883 (E.D.Mich.1991)—§§ 15.7(c) n.58; 15.7(h) n.246

Hart, United States v., 729 F.2d 662 (10th Cir.1984)—§ 24.4(c) n.20

Hart, United States v., 513 F.Supp. 657 (E.D.Pa.1981)—§ 15.7(g) n.205

Harte-Hanks Newspapers, United States v., 254 F.2d 366 (5th Cir.1958)—§ 10.1(c) n.37

Hartfield, State v., 290 Or. 583, 624 P.2d 588 (1981)—§ 15.2(i) n.223

Hartford, State v., 132 N.H. 580, 567 A.2d 577 (1989)—§ 25.2(d) n.24

Hartgraves, People v., 31 Ill.2d 375, 202 N.E.2d 33 (1964)—§ 6.2(c) n.113

Hartinger, State ex rel. v. Court of Common Pleas, 84 Ohio App. 241, 86 N.E.2d 810 (1948)—§ 16.3(d) n.55

Hartless v. State, 327 Md. 558, 611 A.2d 581 (App.1992)—§ 20.4(e) n.78

Hartley, State v., 103 N.J. 252, 511 A.2d 80 (1986)—§§ 6.9(f) n.102; 9.5(a) n.25

Hartley v. United States, 4 Tenn. 45 (1816)—§ 1.2(c) n.82

Hartman v. Bagley, 492 F.3d 347 (6th Cir.2007)—§ 27.5(e) n.169

Hartman v. Lee, 283 F.3d 190 (4th Cir.2002)—§ 19.2(c) n.26

Hartman v. State, 176 Ind.App. 375, 376 N.E.2d 100 (1978)—§ 11.5(e) n.91

Hartmann, United States v., 958 F.2d 774 (7th Cir.1992)—§ 8.11(e) n.108

Hartog, State v., 440 N.W.2d 852 (Iowa 1989)—§ 1.2(b) n.5

Hartridge v. United States, 896 A.2d 198 (D.C.Cir.2006)—§§ 18.2(b) n.16; 18.2(c) n.50; 18.2(e) n.76, 80

Harts v. Indiana, 732 F.2d 95 (7th Cir.1984)—§ 28.3(a) n.19

Hartsfield v. State, 722 P.2d 717 (Okl.Crim.1986)—§ 7.4(g) n.118

Hartwell, United States v., 436 F.3d 174 (3d Cir.2006)—§ 3.9(h) n.156

Hartwig, State v., 123 Wis.2d 278, 366 N.W.2d 866 (1985)—§ 6.9(f) n.103

Harvey v. Horan, 278 F.3d 370 (4th Cir.2002)—§§ 1.5(e) n.207; 28.3(e) n.104

Harvey v. Horan, 285 F.3d 298 (4th Cir.2002)—§ 2.7(d) n.231

Harvey v. McCaughtry, 11 F.3d 691 (7th Cir.1993)—§ 11.9(c) n.126

Harvey, People v., 174 Mich.App. 58, 435 N.W.2d 456 (1989)—§ 16.4(c) n.53

Harvey, People v., 41 Ill.App.3d 869, 354 N.E.2d 393 (1976)—§ 10.2(b) n.29

Harvey v. Shillinger, 76 F.3d 1528 (10th Cir.1996)—§ 26.4(g) n.147

Harvey v. South Dakota, 526 F.2d 840 (8th Cir.1975)—§ 28.3(a) n.20

Harvey v. State, 751 N.E.2d 254 (Ind.App.2001)—§§ 3.9(j) n.207; 12.1(b) n.32

Harvey v. State, 887 S.W.2d 174 (Tex.App.1994)—§§ 23.2(a) n.21, 31, 32

Harvey v. State, 835 P.2d 1074 (Wyo.1992)—§§ 1.7(h) n.127; 26.4(g) n.134

Harvey, State v., 121 N.J. 407, 581 A.2d 483 (1990)—§§ 6.9(f) n.102; 6.9(g) n.174

Harvey v. State, 213 Tenn. 608, 376 S.W.2d 497 (1964)—§ 16.1(g) n.264

Harvey, United States v., 2 F.3d 1318 (3d Cir.1993)—§ 16.4(b) n.25

Harvey, United States v., 3 F.3d 1294 (9th Cir.1993)—§§ 3.3(d) n.167, 169

Harvey, United States v., 961 F.2d 1361 (8th Cir.1992)—§ 3.2(b) n.71

Harvey, United States v., 897 F.2d 1300 (5th Cir.1990)—§ 3.4(i) n.175

Harvey, United States v., 869 F.2d 1439 (11th Cir.1989)—§§ 8.11(e) n.100, 107

Harvey, United States v., 791 F.2d 294 (4th Cir.1986)—§§ 21.2(d) n.156, 217

Harvey, United States v., 540 F.2d 1345 (8th Cir.1976)—§ 4.6(l) n.182

Harvin, State v., 345 S.C. 190, 547 S.E.2d 497 (2001)—§ 6.4(e) n.84

Harwell v. State, 22 Tex.App. 251, 2 S.W. 606 (1886)—§ 1.6(d) n.284

Harwood, State v., 45 Or.App. 931, 609 P.2d 1312 (1980)—§ 15.7(f) n.161

Harwood, State v., 94 Idaho 615, 495 P.2d 160 (1972)—§ 10.3(b) n.29

Haselden, State v., 357 N.C. 1, 577 S.E.2d 594 (2003)—§ 24.7(e) n.61

Haselden v. State, 386 So.2d 624 (Fla.App.1980)—§ 19.3(e) n.247

Hashagen v. United States, 283 F.2d 345 (9th Cir.1960)—§ 8.10(e) n.120

Haska v. State, 240 Ga.App. 527, 523 S.E.2d 589 (1999)—§ 19.3(b) n.147

Haskell, Commonwealth v., 438 Mass. 790, 784 N.E.2d 625 (2003)—§§ 3.8(b) n.27; 6.7(a) n.3; 10.6(c) n.29

Haskell, State v., 645 A.2d 619 (Me.1994)—§ 3.1(d) n.114

Haskins v. Commonwealth, 44 Va.App. 1, 602 S.E.2d 402 (2004)—§ 24.6(c) n.40

Haskins, People v., 48 A.D.2d 480, 369 N.Y.S.2d 869 (1975)—§ 3.9(k) n.262

Haskins, State v., 262 Kan. 728, 942 P.2d 16 (1997)—§ 21.2(g) n.396

Haskins v. State, 264 Ark. 454, 572 S.W.2d 411 (1978)—§ 27.5(c) n.98

Has No Horses, United States v., 261 F.3d 744 (8th Cir.2001)—§§ 21.2(d) n.167, 169, 174

Hassan v. Lubbock Independent School District, 55 F.3d 1075 (5th Cir.1995)—§ 3.9(k) n.255

Hassan, State v., 108 P.3d 695 (Utah 2004)—§ 22.1(h) n.133

Hastamorir, United States v., 881 F.2d 1551 (11th Cir.1989)—§ 3.2(f) n.173

Hasting, United States v., 739 F.2d 1269 (7th Cir.1984)—§ 22.3(a) n.14

Hasting, United States v., 461 U.S. 499, 103 S.Ct. 1974, 76 L.Ed.2d 96 (1983)—§§ 1.7(i) n.169, 182, 187; 15.6(e) n.136; 15.6(f) n.196; 27.6(e) n.155

Hastings, State v., 119 Wash.2d 229, 830 P.2d 658 (1992)—§ 3.10(c) n.84

Hastings, United States v., 126 F.3d 310 (4th Cir.1997)—§§ 13.4(b) n.68; 13.4(c) n.86, 117; 13.4(d) n.162

Hastings, United States v., 695 F.2d 1278 (11th Cir.1983)—§ 23.3(b) n.19

Hastings, United States v., 681 F.2d 706 (11th Cir.1982)—§ 27.2(c) n.48

Hatch v. State, 958 S.W.2d 813 (Tex.Cr.App.1997)—§ 22.1(h) n.157

Hatch, United States v., 931 F.2d 1478 (11th Cir.1991)—§ 3.2(d) n.157

Hatchett v. State, 503 N.E.2d 398 (Ind.1987)—§ 22.3(d) n.176

Hatchie, State v., 166 P.3d 698 (Wash.2007)—§ 26.3(g) n.93

Hatfield, United States v., 108 F.3d 67 (4th Cir.1997)—§ 17.4(b) n.128

Hathaway, United States v., 318 F.3d 1001 (10th Cir.2003)—§§ 19.3(a) n.102, 104, 115

Hathman, State v., 65 Ohio St.3d 403, 604 N.E.2d 743 (1992)—§ 3.7(e) n.118

Hatley v. State, 289 Ark. 130, 709 S.W.2d 812 (1986)—§ 6.9(f) n.106

Hatten, United States v., 68 F.3d 257 (8th Cir.1995)—§ 3.2(b) n.50

Hattery, People v., 109 Ill.2d 449, 94 Ill.Dec. 514, 488 N.E.2d 513 (1985)—§§ 11.6(a) n.27; 11.10(d) n.194

Hattney, State v., 279 Ga. 88, 610 S.E.2d 44 (2005)—§ 7.4(c) n.46

Hatton, State v., 95 Idaho 856, 522 P.2d 64 (1974)—§ 21.2(h) n.415

Hauck v. State, 36 P.3d 597 (Wyo.2001)—§ 24.2(a) n.15

Hauge v. District Court, 307 Mont. 195, 36 P.3d 947 (2001)—§ 3.4(f) n.120

Haught, State v., 122 Idaho 104, 831 P.2d 946 (App.1992)—§ 3.7(a) n.14

Hauk, United States v., 412 F.3d 1179 (10th Cir.2005)—§ 3.6(d) n.95

Hauring, United States v., 790 F.2d 1570 (11th Cir.1986)—§ 21.2(b) n.58

Hauser, State v., 150 P.3d 296 (Idaho App. 2006)—§ 22.3(c) n.108

Hauser, State v., 342 N.C. 382, 464 S.E.2d 443 (1995)—§ 3.2(h) n.213

Hausman, United States v., 894 F.2d 686 (5th Cir.1990)—§ 18.3(b) n.5

Havener, United States v., 905 F.2d 3 (1st Cir.1990)—§ 21.2(d) n.161

Havens v. Indiana, 793 F.2d 143 (7th Cir.1986)—§ 22.5(a) n.6

Havens, United States v., 446 U.S. 620, 100 S.Ct. 1912, 64 L.Ed.2d 559 (1980)—§§ 1.5(b) n.68; 2.9(f) n.116, 141; 9.6(a) n.7

Havier, United States v., 155 F.3d 1090 (9th Cir.1998)—§ 27.5(e) n.179

Hawk, Ex parte, 321 U.S. 114, 64 S.Ct. 448, 88 L.Ed. 572 (1944)—§§ 28.5(a) n.4, 6

Hawk v. Berkemer, 610 F.2d 445 (6th Cir.1979)—§ 21.5(e) n.118

Hawk, State v., 616 N.W.2d 527 (Iowa 2000)—§ 21.5(b) n.64

Hawkes, Commonwealth v., 362 Mass. 786, 291 N.E.2d 411 (1973)—§ 3.8(e) n.214

Hawkins, Commonwealth v., 586 Pa. 366, 894 A.2d 716 (2006)—§ 11.10(c) n.86

Hawkins, Commonwealth v., 553 Pa. 76, 718 A.2d 265 (1998)—§ 9.2(d) n.39

Hawkins v. Comparet-Cassani, 251 F.3d 1230 (9th Cir.2001)—§ 24.2(e) n.68

Hawkins v. Mullin, 291 F.3d 658 (10th Cir.2002)—§ 28.7(c) n.18

Hawkins, People v., 643 N.Y.S.2d 634, 228 A.D.2d 450 (1996)—§ 25.2(a) n.6

Hawkins, People v., 10 Cal.4th 920, 42 Cal.Rptr.2d 636, 897 P.2d 574 (1995)—§ 17.1(e) n.61

Hawkins, People v., 212 Ill.App.3d 973, 157 Ill.Dec. 30, 571 N.E.2d 1049 (1991)—§ 11.10(c) n.111

Hawkins, State v., 117 Idaho 285, 787 P.2d 271 (1990)—§§ 21.5(a) n.23, 30

Hawkins v. Superior Court, 22 Cal.3d 584, 150 Cal.Rptr. 435, 586 P.2d 916 (1978)—§§ 14.2(d) n.56; 15.3(d) n.64, 65

Hawkins v. United States, 902 A.2d 99 (D.C.2006)—§ 3.8(e) n.201

Hawkins, United States v., 59 F.3d 723 (8th Cir.1995)—§ 3.5(a) n.9

Hawkins, United States v., 905 F.2d 1489 (11th Cir.1990)—§ 27.6(b) n.40

Hawkins, United States v., 566 F.2d 1006 (5th Cir.1978)—§§ 15.4(b) n.65, 66

Hawkman v. Parratt, 661 F.2d 1161 (8th Cir.1981)—§§ 21.3(b) n.53, 116

Hawley v. State, 614 P.2d 1349 (Alaska 1980)—§§ 20.6(b) n.33, 34

Hawthorne, People v., 474 Mich. 174, 713 N.W.2d 724 (2006)—§ 27.6(b) n.42

Hawthorne, United States v., 982 F.2d 1186 (8th Cir.1992)—§ 3.10(b) n.33

Hawthorne, United States v., 502 F.2d 1183 (3d Cir.1974)—§§ 21.5(d) n.106, 107

Hay v. Commonwealth, 432 S.W.2d 641 (Ky.1968)—§ 10.2(c) n.39

Hay, United States v., 527 F.2d 990 (10th Cir.1975)—§§ 18.1(c) n.23; 18.2(c) n.43

Hayden, United States v., 260 F.3d 1062 (9th Cir.2001)—§ 6.6(d) n.48

Hayes v. Commonwealth, 25 S.W.3d 463 (Ky.2000)—§ 6.4(f) n.124

Hayes v. Commonwealth, 698 S.W.2d 827 (Ky.1985)—§§ 2.6(b) n.58, 61; 16.4(c) n.105

Hayes, Commonwealth v., 245 Pa.Super. 521, 369 A.2d 750 (1976)—§ 21.4(c) n.79

Hayes v. Cowan, 547 F.2d 42 (6th Cir.1976)—§ 21.2(b) n.34

Hayes v. Florida, 470 U.S. 811, 105 S.Ct. 1643, 84 L.Ed.2d 705 (1985)—§§ 3.8(b) n.47, 57; 3.8(g) n.244, 245

Hayes v. Missouri, 120 U.S. 68, 7 S.Ct. 350, 30 L.Ed. 578 (1887)—§ 2.5(f) n.50

Hayes, People v., 139 Ill.2d 89, 151 Ill.Dec. 348, 564 N.E.2d 803 (1990)—§§ 7.3(b) n.33, 36

Hayes, State v., 170 Vt. 618, 752 A.2d 16 (2000)—§ 5.2(b) n.25

Hayes v. State, 355 Md. 615, 735 A.2d 1109 (1999)—§§ 22.3(e) n.272, 275, 277

Hayes v. State, 269 Ark. 47, 598 S.W.2d 91 (1980)—§ 11.9(d) n.186

Hayes v. State, 470 S.W.2d 950 (Tn.Cr.App.1971)—§ 24.7(c) n.25

Hayes v. State, 46 Wis.2d 93, 175 N.W.2d 625 (1970)—§ 7.3(d) n.65

Hayes, United States v., 236 F.3d 891 (7th Cir.2001)—§ 13.4(b) n.58

Hayes, United States v., 190 F.3d 939 (9th Cir.1999)—§ 6.4(e) n.64

Hayes, United States v., 40 F.3d 362 (11th Cir.1994)—§ 18.1(c) n.23

Hayes, United States v., 385 F.2d 375 (4th Cir.1967)—§ 6.9(d) n.72

Hayles v. State, 180 Ga.App. 860, 350 S.E.2d 793 (1986)—§ 24.8(f) n.96

Hayman, United States v., 342 U.S. 205, 72 S.Ct. 263, 96 L.Ed. 232 (1952)—§§ 28.9(a) n.2, 4

Haynes v. Anderson, 597 So.2d 615 (Miss.1992)—§ 10.1(c) n.51

Haynes v. Cain, 298 F.3d 375 (5th Cir.2002)—§ 11.10(c) n.91

Haynes, People v., 192 Ill.2d 437, 249 Ill.Dec. 779, 737 N.E.2d 169 (2000)—§ 28.11(b) n.14

Haynes v. State, 934 So.2d 983 (Miss.2006)—§ 6.9(f) n.139

Haynes, State v., 288 Or. 59, 602 P.2d 272 (1979)—§ 6.4(f) n.115

Haynes, United States v., 301 F.3d 669 (6th Cir.2002)—§§ 3.3(a) n.12; 6.2(c) n.96

Haynes v. United States, 390 U.S. 85, 88 S.Ct. 722, 19 L.Ed.2d 923 (1968)—§ 21.6(a) n.58

Haynes v. Washington, 373 U.S. 503, 83 S.Ct. 1336, 10 L.Ed.2d 513 (1963)—§§ 6.2(c) n.59, 63, 177; 6.2(d) n.197; 6.4(a) n.12

Haynie, State v., 116 N.M. 746, 867 P.2d 416 (1994)—§ 25.4(b) n.22

Haynie, State v., 240 Ga. 866, 242 S.E.2d 713 (1978)—§§ 3.5(d) n.166, 172

Haynie, United States v., 637 F.2d 227 (4th Cir.1980)—§ 3.2(b) n.53

Hays v. Marano, 114 A.D.2d 387, 493 N.Y.S.2d 904 (1985)—§§ 23.1(c) n.102, 104

Hays, State v., 253 Neb. 467, 570 N.W.2d 823 (1997)—§ 21.4(a) n.38

Hays, State v., 256 Kan. 48, 883 P.2d 1093 (Kan.1994)—§ 24.9(b) n.12

Hays, State v., 173 Wis.2d 439, 496 N.W.2d 645 (1992)—§ 26.9(a) n.7

Hayward, People v., 98 Mich.App. 332, 296 N.W.2d 250 (1980)—§ 20.6(b) n.39

Hayward, State v., 327 Or. 397, 963 P.2d 667 (1998)—§ 21.3(c) n.162

Haywood, People v., 60 Ill.App.3d 236, 17 Ill.Dec. 329, 376 N.E.2d 328 (1978)—§ 14.1(d) n.54

Haywood, State v., 232 Neb. 97, 439 N.W.2d 511 (1989)—§§ 6.2(c) n.127; 6.8(b) n.57

Haywood, United States v., 324 F.3d 514 (7th Cir.2003)—§ 9.1(d) n.133

Haywood v. United States, 584 A.2d 552 (D.C.1990)—§ 3.3(e) n.189

Haywood, United States ex rel. v. O'Leary, 827 F.2d 52 (7th Cir.1987)—§ 7.4(g) n.110

Hazard, State v., 785 A.2d 1111 (R.I.2001)—§§ 22.3(c) n.99; 24.2(a) n.5

Hazel v. Commonwealth, 833 S.W.2d 831 (Ky.1992)—§ 3.4(k) n.228

Hazel, People v., 252 Cal.App.2d 412, 60 Cal.Rptr. 437 (1967)—§ 6.6(c) n.21

Hazel v. United States, 303 F.Supp.2d 753 (E.D.Va.2004)—§ 24.3(b) n.54

Hazel, United States v., 696 F.2d 473 (6th Cir.1983)—§ 13.4(c) n.116

Hazelwood, State v., 866 P.2d 827 (Alaska 1993)—§ 10.3(c) n.57

Hazen, State v., 131 N.H. 196, 552 A.2d 77 (1988)—§ 3.3(c) n.109

Head v. Hill, 277 Ga. 255, 587 S.E.2d 613 (2004)—§ 26.4(h) n.156

Head, State v., 971 S.W.2d 49 (Tenn.Crim.App.1997)—§§ 21.3(c) n.148, 157

Head, United States v., 586 F.2d 508 (5th Cir.1978)—§ 15.2(j) n.237

Headley, State v., 6 Ohio St.3d 475, 453 N.E.2d 716 (1983)—§ 19.5(b) n.46

Heald v. Mullaney, 505 F.2d 1241 (1st Cir.1974)—§§ 17.4(a) n.11; 24.10(a) n.7, 18

Health of Weehawken, Board of v. New York Central Railroad Co., 10 N.J. 294, 90 A.2d 729 (1952)—§§ 15.1(d) n.231, 242

Healy, United States v., 376 U.S. 75, 84 S.Ct. 553, 11 L.Ed.2d 527 (1964)—§ 1.2(c) n.112

Heaps v. State, 30 P.3d 109 (Alaska App.2001)—§ 24.8(f) n.116

Heaps, United States v., 39 F.3d 479 (4th Cir.1994)—§§ 16.2(e) n.84; 16.3(c) n.37

Heard, In re, _____ So.2d _____, 2007 WL 80876 (Ala.2007)—§ 24.10(b) n.27

Heard, People v., 187 Ill.2d 36, 240 Ill.Dec. 577, 718 N.E.2d 58 (1999)—§ 22.3(d) n.220

Hearst, United States v., 638 F.2d 1190 (9th Cir.1980)—§§ 11.9(a) n.38; 11.9(d) n.168, 207, 234

Hearst, United States v., 563 F.2d 1331 (9th Cir.1977)—§§ 3.9(i) n.195; 6.4(g) n.154, 163

Hearst, United States v., 412 F.Supp. 863 (N.D.Cal.1975)—§ 20.5(c) n.42

Heart of Atlanta Motel, Inc. v. United States, 379 U.S. 241, 85 S.Ct. 348, 13 L.Ed.2d 258 (1964)—§ 1.2(c) n.154

Hearty, People v., 644 P.2d 302 (Colo.1982)—§ 3.4(a) n.22

Heath v. Alabama, 474 U.S. 82, 106 S.Ct. 433, 88 L.Ed.2d 387 (1985)—§§ 1.2(b) n.10; 25.5(a) n.3; 25.5(c) n.29

Heath v. Jones, 941 F.2d 1126 (11th Cir.1991)—§§ 16.4(c) n.85, 104

Heath, State v., 320 Mont. 211, 89 P.3d 947 (2004)—§ 22.3(c) n.112

Heath, State v., 264 Kan. 557, 957 P.2d 449 (Kan.1998)—§ 27.5(d) n.113

Heath, State v., 122 Ariz. 36, 592 P.2d 1302 (1979)—§§ 6.7(b) n.62, 64

Heath, United States v., 259 F.3d 522 (6th Cir.2001)—§§ 3.2(c) n.107; 9.1(b) n.81

Heaton, State v., 958 P.2d 911 (Utah 1998)—§§ 11.3(b) n.34; 11.5(c) n.55

Heaton, State v., 225 Neb. 702, 407 N.W.2d 780 (1987)—§ 26.10(a) n.3

Heavrin v. State, 675 N.E.2d 1075 (Ind.1996)—§§ 6.2(c) n.132; 24.8(a) n.8; 27.5(c) n.89

Heavrin, United States v., 330 F.3d 723 (6th Cir.2003)—§§ 13.5(h) n.146, 153, 178

Hebebrand v. State, 129 Ohio St. 574, 196 N.E. 412 (1935)—§§ 8.4(b) n.46, 74

Heberly, State v., 120 Ariz. 541, 587 P.2d 260 (App.1978)—§ 3.7(c) n.42

Hebert, State v., 277 Kan. 61, 82 P.3d 470 (2004)—§§ 6.7(a) n.5; 6.7(b) n.32

Hebert, United States v., 131 F.3d 514 (5th Cir.1997)—§ 1.2(d) n.235

Heck v. Humphrey, 512 U.S. 477, 114 S.Ct. 2364, 129 L.Ed.2d 383 (1994)—§§ 3.1(k) n.261, 262

Heckenkamp, United States v., 482 F.3d 1142 (9th Cir.2007)—§ 3.9(k) n.265

Hector, United States v., 474 F.3d 1150 (9th Cir.2007)—§ 3.4(l) n.244

Hedaithy, United States v., 392 F.3d 580 (3d Cir.2004)—§§ 13.4(b) n.69; 19.3(e) n.241

Hedge, United States v., 462 F.2d 220 (5th Cir.1972)—§ 8.8(g) n.168

Hedgepeth, United States v., 434 F.3d 609 (3d Cir.2006)—§ 19.5(d) n.75

Hedrick v. State, 430 N.E.2d 1150 (Ind.1982)—§ 15.5(c) n.109

Hedrick v. True, 443 F.3d 342 (4th Cir.2006)—§ 28.4(b) n.19

Hedrick, United States v., 922 F.2d 396 (7th Cir.1991)—§ 3.2(h) n.212

Heffernan v. State, 278 Ark. 325, 645 S.W.2d 666 (1983)—§ 24.9(a) n.4

Heffner v. State, 530 N.E.2d 297 (Ind.1988)—§§ 3.3(e) n.185; 6.4(e) n.68

Heffran, State v., 129 Wis.2d 156, 384 N.W.2d 351 (1986)—§ 6.10(c) n.48

Heflin v. United States, 358 U.S. 415, 79 S.Ct. 451, 3 L.Ed.2d 407 (1959)—§§ 28.9(a) n.3; 28.9(b) n.30

Hefner, People v., 70 Ill.App.3d 693, 27 Ill.Dec. 96, 388 N.E.2d 1059 (1979)—§ 7.5(a) n.8

Heggy v. Heggy, 944 F.2d 1537 (10th Cir.1991)—§ 4.6(n) n.256

Hegler v. Borg, 50 F.3d 1472 (9th Cir.1995)—§ 27.6(d) n.84

Heidecke, United States v., 900 F.2d 1155 (7th Cir.1990)—§§ 1.7(j) n.225; 13.5(a) n.7

Heiler, People v., 79 Mich.App. 714, 262 N.W.2d 890 (1977)—§§ 21.2(f) n.383, 385

Heiman v. State, 511 N.E.2d 458 (Ind.1987)—§§ 7.3(c) n.48; 7.4(e) n.89

Heimel, People v., 812 P.2d 1177 (Colo.1991)—§ 3.9(h) n.156

Heimerle, In re, 788 F.Supp. 700 (E.D.N.Y.1992)—§ 8.5(d) n.139

Heine, United States v., 920 F.2d 552 (8th Cir.1990)—§ 11.5(f) n.96

Heiner, State v., 683 P.2d 629 (Wyo.1984)—§ 6.10(b) n.22

Heinsen, State v., 138 N.M. 441, 121 P.3d 1040 (2005)—§ 13.3(c) n.40

Heinz, People v., 197 Colo. 102, 589 P.2d 931 (1979)—§ 21.4(d) n.111

Heinz, United States v., 983 F.2d 609 (5th Cir.1993)—§§ 1.7(j) n.262; 6.4(e) n.91

Heirens, People v., 4 Ill.2d 131, 122 N.E.2d 231 (1954)—§ 21.3(b) n.96

Heirtzler, State v., 147 N.H. 344, 789 A.2d 634 (2001)—§ 6.10(c) n.36

Heisler v. Hynes, 42 N.Y.2d 250, 397 N.Y.S.2d 727, 366 N.E.2d 817 (1977)—§§ 8.4(b) n.26; 8.8(g) n.165

Heisman, United States v., 503 F.2d 1284 (8th Cir.1974)—§ 3.10(e) n.166

Heitman, State v., 262 Neb. 185, 629 N.W.2d 542 (2001)—§ 5.2(a) n.17

Heitman v. State, 815 S.W.2d 681 (Tex.Crim.App.1991)—§§ 2.12(c) n.133, 139, 143, 149, 151, 153, 155; 2.12(d) n.192, 195

Heitzman, State v., 107 N.J. 603, 527 A.2d 439 (1987)—§ 21.4(d) n.126

Heldt, United States v., 745 F.2d 1275 (9th Cir.1984)—§ 6.9(e) n.91

Helena Parents Commission v. Lewis & Clark County Commissioners, 277 Mont. 367, 922 P.2d 1140 (1996)—§ 13.2(a) n.3

Helfend, People v., 1 Cal.App.3d 873, 82 Cal.Rptr. 295 (1969)—§ 6.10(d) n.58

Heller v. New York, 413 U.S. 483, 93 S.Ct. 2789, 37 L.Ed.2d 745 (1973)—§ 3.4(a) n.7

Heller, United States v., 785 F.2d 1524 (11th Cir.1986)—§ 24.9(g) n.118

Helliger, People v., 96 N.Y.2d 462, 754 N.E.2d 756, 729 N.Y.S.2d 654 (2001)—§ 25.4(d) n.45

Helmenstein, State v., 620 N.W.2d 581 (N.D.2000)—§ 6.6(e) n.61

Helmsley, United States v., 985 F.2d 1202 (2d Cir.1993)—§ 24.3(d) n.107

Helmsley, United States v., 941 F.2d 71 (2d Cir.1991)—§ 8.11(c) n.44

Helm, State ex rel. v. Superior Court, 90 Ariz. 133, 367 P.2d 6 (1961)—§ 20.1(a) n.8

Helmstetter, People v., 914 P.2d 474 (Colo.App.1995)—§§ 18.4(c) n.37, 39

Helstoski v. Meanor, 442 U.S. 500, 99 S.Ct. 2445, 61 L.Ed.2d 30 (1979)—§ 27.2(c) n.32

Helstoski, United States v., 635 F.2d 200 (3d Cir.1980)—§ 15.7(d) n.79

Helstoski, United States v., 442 U.S. 477, 99 S.Ct. 2432, 61 L.Ed.2d 12 (1979)—§ 27.3(c) n.45

Helstrom, People v., 50 A.D.2d 685, 375 N.Y.S.2d 189 (1975)—§ 6.9(c) n.50

Helton, United States v., 314 F.3d 812 (6th Cir.2003)—§ 3.1(c) n.78

Heltzel, State v., 552 N.E.2d 31 (Ind.1990)—§§ 8.5(b) n.19; 8.5(d) n.123

Helvering v. Mitchell, 303 U.S. 391, 58 S.Ct. 630, 82 L.Ed. 917 (1938)—§ 25.1(c) n.21

Hemingway v. Henderson, 754 F.Supp. 296 (E.D.N.Y.1991)—§ 11.6(a) n.51

Hemingway, People ex rel. v. Elrod, 60 Ill.2d 74, 322 N.E.2d 837 (1975)—§§ 1.5(a) n.20; 12.2(a) n.12; 12.3(b) n.57, 58, 67

Hemler v. Superior Court, 44 Cal.App.3d 430, 118 Cal.Rptr. 564 (1975)—§ 3.3(g) n.230

Hemlin, State v., 151 Or.App. 481, 950 P.2d 336 (1997)—§ 26.3(f) n.55

Hemmings, United States v., 258 F.3d 587 (7th Cir.2001)—§§ 18.3(b) n.5, 28

Hempele, State v., 120 N.J. 182, 576 A.2d 793 (1990)—§§ 2.12(b) n.103, 105; 2.12(c) n.119, 124, 127, 144, 158

Henderson v. Kibbe, 431 U.S. 145, 97 S.Ct. 1730, 52 L.Ed.2d 203 (1977)—§§ 11.6(a) n.34; 24.8(b) n.30

Henderson v. Lane, 613 F.2d 175 (7th Cir.1980)—§ 24.2(b) n.25

Henderson v. Morgan, 426 U.S. 637, 96 S.Ct. 2253, 49 L.Ed.2d 108 (1976)—§§ 2.7(a) n.28; 21.4(c) n.68

Henderson, People v., 211 Ill.2d 90, 284 Ill.Dec. 278, 809 N.E.2d 1224 (2004)—§ 21.4(g) n.221

Henderson, People v., 33 Ill.2d 225, 210 N.E.2d 483 (1965)—§ 3.10(a) n.15

Henderson v. Quarterman, 460 F.3d 654 (5th Cir.2006)—§ 6.4(e) n.100

Henderson v. Singletary, 968 F.2d 1070 (11th Cir.1992)—§ 6.9(g) n.155

Henderson, State v., 139 N.M. 595, 136 P.3d 1005 (2006)—§ 14.1(d) n.66

Henderson, State v., 245 Wis.2d 345, 629 N.W.2d 613 (2001)—§ 3.4(h) n.165

Henderson v. State, 272 Ga. 621, 532 S.E.2d 398 (2000)—§ 22.3(c) n.112

Henderson, State v., 527 N.W.2d 827 (Minn.1995)—§ 26.1(e) n.131

Henderson, State v., 215 Iowa 276, 243 N.W. 289 (1932)—§ 19.1(c) n.29

Henderson, United States v., 409 F.3d 1293 (11th Cir.2005)—§ 22.2(d) n.86

Henderson v. United States, 527 A.2d 1262 (D.C.App.1987)—§ 7.4(e) n.89

Henderson v. United States, 476 U.S. 321, 106 S.Ct. 1871, 90 L.Ed.2d 299 (1986)—§ 18.3(b) n.26

Henderson, United States v., 721 F.2d 662 (9th Cir.1983)—§ 2.12(c) n.172

Henderson v. United States, 349 F.2d 712 (D.C.Cir.1965)—§ 13.7(a) n.15

Henderson v. United States, 237 F.2d 169 (5th Cir.1956)—§ 5.1(c) n.26

Hendley v. Commonwealth, 573 S.W.2d 662 (Ky.1978)—§ 20.3(b) n.42

Hendricks, Commonwealth v., 376 Pa.Super. 381, 546 A.2d 79 (1988)—§ 24.8(b) n.29

Hendricks, People v., 43 Cal.3d 584, 238 Cal.Rptr. 66, 737 P.2d 1350 (1987)—§ 6.2(c) n.173

Hendricks v. State, 331 Mont. 47, 128 P.3d 1017 (2006)—§ 11.9(d) n.173

Hendricks v. State, 871 A.2d 1118 (Del.2005)—§ 24.3(e) n.136

Hendricks, State v., 173 Vt. 132, 787 A.2d 1270 (2001)—§ 21.4(g) n.251

Hendricks, United States v., 319 F.3d 993 (7th Cir.2003)—§ 3.8(d) n.134

Hendricks, United States v., 661 F.2d 38 (5th Cir.1981)—§ 18.4(b) n.26

Hendrickson, State v., 584 N.W.2d 774 (Minn.App.1998)—§ 6.7(b) n.85

Hendrickson, State v., 444 N.W.2d 468 (Iowa 1989)—§ 22.1(g) n.127

Hendrickson v. State, 290 Ark. 319, 719 S.W.2d 420 (1986)—§ 9.6(a) n.9

Hendrickson, State v., 217 Mont. 1, 701 P.2d 1368 (1985)—§ 3.4(c) n.36

Hendrickson v. State, 285 Ark. 462, 688 S.W.2d 295 (1985)—§ 6.9(g) n.162

Hendrix, State v., 782 S.W.2d 833 (Tenn.1989)—§ 3.6(e) n.116

Henke, United States v., 222 F.3d 633 (9th Cir.2000)—§§ 11.9(c) n.116; 11.9(d) n.205

Henley v. Jenne, 796 So.2d 1273 (Fla.App.2001)—§ 12.2(a) n.5

Henley v. State, 576 S.W.2d 66 (Tex.Crim.App.1978)—§ 23.2(g) n.124

Henley v. Taylor, 324 Ark. 114, 918 S.W.2d 713 (1996)—§ 12.3(b) n.58

Henley, United States v., 238 F.3d 1111 (9th Cir.2001)—§§ 24.9(g) n.118, 122

Henley, United States v., 984 F.2d 1040 (9th Cir.1993)—§§ 6.6(e) n.59; 6.7(b) n.54

Henne, People v., 165 Ill.App.3d 315, 116 Ill.Dec. 296, 518 N.E.2d 1276 (1988)—§ 11.6(c) n.100

Hennessey, People v., 37 Cal.App.4th 1830, 44 Cal.Rptr.2d 792 (1995)—§ 26.3(f) n.65

Hennessey, State v., 142 N.H. 149, 697 A.2d 930 (1997)—§§ 17.3(a) n.7; 17.3(e) n.64

Hennessey, State v., 405 N.W.2d 846 (Iowa 1987)—§ 24.9(f) n.97

Hennessey, United States v., 575 F.Supp. 119 (N.D.N.Y.1984)—§ 11.2(g) n.264

Hennigan v. State, 746 P.2d 360 (Wyo.1987)—§§ 15.2(j) n.233; 15.3(d) n.65; 15.5(a) n.2; 15.6(g) n.217

Henning, State v., 273 Wis.2d 352, 681 N.W.2d 871 (2004)—§ 25.4(b) n.18

Hennington v. State, 702 So.2d 403 (Miss.1997)—§§ 6.6(e) n.78; 6.10(c) n.37

Henry v. Dees, 658 F.2d 406 (5th Cir.1981)—§§ 6.7(c) n.118; 6.9(b) n.24

Henry v. Kernan, 177 F.3d 1152 (9th Cir.1999)—§ 9.6(a) n.27

Henry v. Kernan, 197 F.3d 1021 (9th Cir.1999)—§§ 6.2(c) n.139; 9.6(a) n.22

Henry v. Mississippi, 379 U.S. 443, 85 S.Ct. 564, 13 L.Ed.2d 408 (1965)—§§ 10.2(a) n.12; 11.6(a) n.30, 31; 28.4(b) n.16; 28.4(d) n.36

Henry v. Page, 223 F.3d 477 (7th Cir.2000)—§ 24.3(e) n.127

Henry v. Poole, 409 F.3d 48 (2d Cir.2005)—§§ 11.10(b) n.38; 11.10(c) n.89

Henry v. Ryan, 775 F.Supp. 247 (N.D.Ill.1991)—§§ 8.7(d) n.71, 77, 78, 80, 82

Henry, State v., 189 Ariz. 542, 944 P.2d 57 (1997)—§§ 11.4(b) n.27; 11.4(c) n.79; 11.5(d) n.66, 67

Henry v. State, 265 Ga. 732, 462 S.E.2d 737 (1995)—§ 22.2(d) n.70

Henry, State v., 733 S.W.2d 127 (Tenn.Crim.App.1987)—§ 11.2(g) n.279

Henry v. State, 276 S.C. 515, 280 S.E.2d 536 (1981)—§ 26.9(b) n.76

Henry, United States v., 113 F.3d 37 (5th Cir.1997)—§ 21.4(b) n.42

Henry, United States v., 893 F.2d 46 (3d Cir.1990)—§ 21.4(d) n.104

Henry, United States v., 749 F.2d 203 (5th Cir.1984)—§ 5.3(c) n.37

Henry, United States v., 447 U.S. 264, 100 S.Ct. 2183, 65 L.Ed.2d 115 (1980)—§§ 2.9(h) n.217; 6.4(e) n.79; 6.4(f) n.132; 6.4(g) n.149, 150; 6.7(c) n.139

Henry, United States v., 615 F.2d 1223 (9th Cir.1980)—§§ 18.5(b) n.61, 68

Henry, United States v., 604 F.2d 908 (5th Cir.1979)—§§ 15.1(b) n.13, 14

Henry v. United States, 361 U.S. 98, 80 S.Ct. 168, 4 L.Ed.2d 134 (1959)—§§ 3.3(a) n.1, 5; 3.3(b) n.43; 3.5(a) n.2; 3.8(d) n.129

Hensley, In re, 184 Ga.App. 625, 362 S.E.2d 432 (1987)—§ 15.4(g) n.170

Hensley v. Municipal Court, 411 U.S. 345, 93 S.Ct. 1571, 36 L.Ed.2d 294 (1973)—§ 28.3(a) n.8

Hensley, State v., 608 So.2d 664 (La.App.1992)—§ 7.2(d) n.47

Hensley, United States v., 469 U.S. 221, 105 S.Ct. 675, 83 L.Ed.2d 604 (1985)—§§ 3.8(b) n.14, 27, 33, 55; 3.8(c) n.96; 3.8(d) n.172; 3.8(e) n.202

Henson v. Commonwealth, 20 S.W.3d 466 (Ky.1999)—§ 6.2(c) n.96

Henson v. State, 94 Ark.App. 163, 227 S.W.3d 450 (2006)—§ 24.5(d) n.47

Henson, United States v., 945 F.2d 430 (1st Cir.1991)—§ 18.4(c) n.40

Henson, United States v., 848 F.2d 1374 (6th Cir.1988)—§ 3.3(g) n.225

Hentz v. State, 503 So.2d 262 (Miss.1987)—§ 21.2(d) n.242

Hepperle, United States v., 810 F.2d 836 (8th Cir.1987)—§ 3.7(b) n.36

Herald, In re, 734 F.2d 93 (2d Cir.1984)—§§ 23.1(d) n.144; 23.1(e) n.226

Herb v. Pitcairn, 324 U.S. 117, 65 S.Ct. 459, 89 L.Ed. 789 (1945)—§ 2.12(a) n.47

Herberman, United States v., 583 F.2d 222 (5th Cir.1978)—§§ 16.2(c) n.42; 16.2(e) n.76

Herbert v. Billy, 160 F.3d 1131 (6th Cir.1998)—§ 17.4(b) n.124

Herbert, United States v., 698 F.2d 981 (9th Cir.1983)—§§ 15.4(f) n.145; 16.3(c) n.47

Herbert v. United States, 340 A.2d 802 (D.C.App.1975)—§ 11.6(a) n.37

Herbest, State v., 551 A.2d 442 (Me.1988)—§ 3.2(e) n.161

Herdan, People v., 42 Cal.App.3d 300, 116 Cal.Rptr. 641 (1974)—§ 3.3(d) n.149

Heredia, State v., 144 Idaho 95, 156 P.3d 1193 (2007)—§ 21.4(d) n.110

Heredia, State v., 493 A.2d 831 (R.I.1985)—§§ 15.6(a) n.33; 15.6(d) n.120

Hereford, State v., 224 Wis.2d 605, 592 N.W.2d 247 (1999)—§ 11.6(a) n.43

Herem, State v., 384 N.W.2d 880 (Minn.1986)—§ 6.6(f) n.104

Hergott, Ex parte, 588 So.2d 911 (Ala.1991)—§ 10.6(a) n.6

Heritage, State v., 152 Wash.2d 210, 95 P.3d 345 (2004)—§ 6.10(c) n.51

Herman v. State, 396 So.2d 222 (Fla.App.1981)—§ 15.4(g) n.163

Herman, United States v., 576 F.2d 1139 (5th Cir.1978)—§ 18.2(e) n.76

Herman, United States v., 544 F.2d 791 (5th Cir.1977)—§ 21.2(h) n.417

Hermanek, United States v., 289 F.3d 1076 (9th Cir.2002)—§§ 4.6(i) n.149; 4.6(k) n.174; 4.6(m) n.241

Hern v. State, 862 S.W.2d 179 (Tex.App.1993)—§ 25.1(d) n.73

Hernandez v. Municipal Court, 49 Cal.3d 713, 263 Cal.Rptr. 513, 781 P.2d 547 (1989)—§§ 2.6(b) n.51, 65; 16.1(b) n.84; 16.1(c) n.125; 16.1(e) n.205, 210; 22.2(e) n.109

Hernandez v. New York, 500 U.S. 352, 111 S.Ct. 1859, 114 L.Ed.2d 395 (1991)—§§ 22.3(d) n.193, 221, 227, 236

Hernandez, People v., 30 Cal.4th 1, 131 Cal.Rptr.2d 514, 64 P.3d 800 (2003)—§ 24.9(f) n.102

Hernandez, People v., 207 App.Div.2d 719, 616 N.Y.S.2d 587 (1994)—§ 24.8(a) n.10

Hernandez, People v., 70 N.Y.2d 833, 523 N.Y.S.2d 442, 517 N.E.2d 1328 (1987)—§ 7.4(e) n.90

Hernandez, People v., 229 Cal.App.2d 143, 40 Cal.Rptr. 100 (1964)—§§ 3.9(j) n.202, 212

Hernandez v. State, 127 S.W.3d 768 (Tex.Crim.App.2004)—§ 18.5(a) n.37

Hernandez v. State, 118 Nev. 513, 50 P.3d 1100 (2002)—§ 13.7(a) n.5

Hernandez v. State, 357 Md. 204, 742 A.2d 952 (1999)—§ 22.3(a) n.13

Hernandez v. State, 750 So.2d 50 (Fla.App.1999)—§ 11.9(d) n.224

Hernandez v. State, 988 S.W.2d 770 (Tex.Cr.App.1999)—§§ 2.12(e) n.214; 11.1(a) n.12

Hernandez, State v., 115 N.M. 6, 846 P.2d 312 (1993)—§ 22.4(b) n.20

Hernandez, State v., 218 Conn. 458, 590 A.2d 112 (1991)—§ 24.6(e) n.51

Hernandez, State v., 167 Ariz. 236, 805 P.2d 1057 (1990)—§ 24.8(d) n.46

Hernandez v. Texas, 347 U.S. 475, 74 S.Ct. 667, 98 L.Ed. 866 (1954)—§§ 15.4(c) n.87, 90

Hernandez, United States v., 476 F.3d 791 (9th Cir.2007)—§ 9.6(a) n.35

Hernandez, United States v., 183 F.Supp.2d 468 (D.P.R.2002)—§ 3.4(g) n.124

Hernandez, United States v., 2002 WL 1205058 (S.D.Fla.2002)—§ 11.9(d) n.224

Hernandez, United States v., 242 F.3d 110 (2d Cir.2001)—§ 27.5(c) n.63

Hernandez, United States v., 203 F.3d 614 (9th Cir.2000)—§§ 11.5(a) n.11; 11.5(d) n.83; 21.3(a) n.2; 21.6(a) n.78

Hernandez, United States v., 234 F.3d 252 (5th Cir.2000)—§ 21.4(d) n.106

Hernandez, United States v., 189 F.3d 785 (9th Cir.1999)—§§ 16.1(e) n.178; 16.1(g) n.283; 16.2(c) n.51

Hernandez, United States v., 109 F.3d 1450 (9th Cir.1997)—§ 24.3(e) n.125

Hernandez, United States v., 79 F.3d 1193 (D.C.Cir.1996)—§§ 21.2(b) n.57; 21.4(b) n.49

Hernandez, United States v., 7 F.3d 944 (10th Cir.1993)—§ 3.2(h) n.207

Hernandez, United States v., 972 F.2d 885 (8th Cir.1992)—§ 21.2(d) n.217

Hernandez, United States v., 976 F.2d 929 (5th Cir.1992)—§ 3.2(b) n.72

Hernandez, United States v., 948 F.2d 316 (7th Cir.1991)—§ 9.5(a) n.20

Hernandez, United States v., 901 F.2d 1217 (5th Cir.1990)—§ 3.7(a) n.16

Hernandez, United States v., 779 F.2d 456 (8th Cir.1985)—§ 24.7(a) n.15

Hernandez, United States v., 608 F.2d 741 (9th Cir.1979)—§ 24.1(b) n.27

Hernandez, United States v., 574 F.2d 1362 (5th Cir.1978)—§§ 6.9(c) n.51; 6.9(g) n.150

Hernandez, United States v., 486 F.2d 614 (7th Cir.1973)—§ 3.8(d) n.169

Hernandez-Cano, United States v., 808 F.2d 779 (11th Cir.1987)—§§ 9.3(e) n.57, 70

Hernandez-Escarsega, United States v., 886 F.2d 1560 (9th Cir.1989)—§ 20.2(e) n.86

Hernandez-Fundora, United States v., 49 F.3d 848 (2d Cir.1995)—§ 16.4(d) n.121

Hernandez-Fundora, United States v., 58 F.3d 802 (2d Cir.1995)—§ 16.4(b) n.13

Hernandez-Gonzalez, United States v., 608 F.2d 1240 (9th Cir.1979)—§ 24.3(h) n.180

Hernandez-Hernandez, United States v., 431 F.3d 1212 (9th Cir.2005)—§ 26.4(i) n.203

Hernandez-Lebron, United States v., 23 F.3d 600 (1st Cir.1994)—§ 11.9(c) n.129

Hernandez-Merado, State v., 124 Wash.2d 368, 879 P.2d 283 (1994)—§ 1.2(d) n.200

Hernandez-Rodriguez, United States v., 443 F.3d 138 (1st Cir.2006)—§ 17.2(c) n.76

Hernandez-Uribe v. United States, 515 F.2d 20 (8th Cir.1975)—§ 17.4(a) n.56

Hernandez-Urista, United States v., 9 F.3d 82 (10th Cir.1993)—§§ 24.3(f) n.140, 141

Hernandez-Wilson, United States v., 186 F.3d 1 (1st Cir.1999)—§ 21.4(d) n.104

Herndon, United States v., 156 F.3d 629 (6th Cir.1998)—§§ 24.9(f) n.86; 24.9(g) n.126

Hernly v. United States, 832 F.2d 980 (7th Cir.1987)—§ 8.5(h) n.266

Herr, People v., 86 N.Y.2d 638, 635 N.Y.S.2d 159, 658 N.E.2d 1032 (1995)—§§ 11.9(a) n.18; 11.9(d) n.209

Herren, State v., 212 Neb. 706, 325 N.W.2d 151 (1982)—§ 21.3(b) n.91

Herrera v. Collins, 506 U.S. 390, 113 S.Ct. 853, 122 L.Ed.2d 203 (1993)—§§ 1.5(e) n.206, 207; 2.7(b) n.69; 2.7(c) n.147, 148, 161; 2.7(d) n.233; 2.9(f) n.119; 24.11(d) n.15; 26.2(c) n.75; 28.3(e) n.98; 28.4(e) n.76; 28.8(a) n.11

Herrera v. Lemaster, 225 F.3d 1176 (10th Cir.2000)—§ 28.3(c) n.80

Herrera, State v., 187 N.J. 493, 902 A.2d 177 (2006)—§§ 7.4(c) n.38, 50; 7.4(f) n.95; 7.5(c) n.46

Herrera v. State, 64 P.3d 724 (Wyo.2003)—§ 21.2(d) n.172

Herrera, State v., 183 Ariz. 642, 905 P.2d 1377 (App.1995)—§ 11.7(e) n.102

Herrera v. State, 594 So.2d 275 (Fla.1992)—§§ 5.3(d) n.44, 45

Herrera, State v., 93 N.M. 442, 601 P.2d 75 (App.1979)—§ 15.7(f) n.135

Herrera, United States v., 412 F.3d 577 (5th Cir.2005)—§ 21.3(b) n.62

Herrera, United States v., 265 F.3d 349 (6th Cir.2001)—§ 21.6(b) n.95

Herrera, United States v., 948 F.2d 1046 (7th Cir.1991)—§ 26.4(g) n.129

Herrera, United States v., 640 F.2d 958 (9th Cir.1981)—§ 21.2(b) n.41

Herrera-Figueroa, United States v., 918 F.2d 1430 (9th Cir.1990)—§§ 6.4(e) n.107; 26.4(e) n.83

Herrera-Ordones, United States v., 190 F.3d 504 (7th Cir.1999)—§ 16.2(c) n.51

Herrera-Soto, United States v., 961 F.2d 645 (7th Cir.1992)—§ 12.4(d) n.68

Herrick, State v., 588 N.W.2d 847 (N.D.1999)—§ 3.1(c) n.63

Herring v. Meachum, 11 F.3d 374 (2d Cir.1993)—§ 24.1(a) n.5

Herring v. New York, 422 U.S. 853, 95 S.Ct. 2550, 45 L.Ed.2d 593 (1975)—§§ 1.5(c) n.119; 11.7(c) n.37; 11.8(a) n.2, 3, 7; 24.7(b) n.18

Herring v. Secretary, Dep't. Of Corrections, 397 F.3d 1338 (11th Cir.2005)—§ 11.10(c) n.127

Herring v. State, 691 So.2d 948 (Miss.1997)—§ 18.1(c) n.21

Herring, State v., 210 Conn. 78, 554 A.2d 686 (1989)—§ 18.4(c) n.50

Herring, State v., 209 Conn. 52, 547 A.2d 6 (1988)—§ 13.3(c) n.40

Herring, State v., 21 Ohio App.3d 18, 486 N.E.2d 119 (1984)—§ 23.2(a) n.42

Herrington v. State, 690 So.2d 1132 (Miss.1997)—§ 24.9(d) n.43

Herrman, State v., 316 Mont. 198, 70 P.3d 738 (2003)—§§ 11.7(e) n.82; 28.4(d) n.57

Herrman, State v., 2003 MT 149, 316 Mont. 198, 70 P.3d 738 (2003)— § 22.3(a) n.35

Herrold, United States v., 962 F.2d 1131 (3d Cir.1992)—§§ 9.3(e) n.76; 9.4(b) n.66

Herron, People v., 215 Ill.2d 167, 294 Ill.Dec. 55, 830 N.E.2d 467 (2005)—§ 27.5(d) n.137

Herron, United States v., 215 F.3d 812 (8th Cir.2000)—§ 3.1(c) n.77

Hersch, State v., 445 N.W.2d 626 (N.D.1989)—§ 18.5(a) n.49

Hescock, State v., 98 Wash.App. 600, 989 P.2d 1251 (1999)—§ 25.4(d) n.44

Heslop v. State, 202 Md. 123, 95 A.2d 880 (1953)—§ 16.3(b) n.14

Hess v. Medlock, 820 F.2d 1368 (4th Cir.1987)—§ 17.4(a) n.5

Hess, State v., 680 N.W.2d 314 (S.D.2004)—§ 3.6(a) n.11

Hess v. State, 794 So.2d 1249 (Fla.2001)—§ 6.9(g) n.200

Hess, United States v., 982 F.2d 181 (6th Cir.1992)—§ 27.2(d) n.70

Hessen, State v., 145 N.J. 441, 678 A.2d 1082 (1996)—§§ 21.1(g) n.118; 21.3(c) n.150

Hessling, United States v., 845 F.2d 617 (6th Cir.1988)—§ 3.2(b) n.47

Hester, People v., 271 Ill.App.3d 954, 208 Ill.Dec. 690, 649 N.E.2d 1351 (1995)—§ 19.5(b) n.23

Hester v. United States, 265 U.S. 57, 44 S.Ct. 445, 68 L.Ed. 898 (1924)— §§ 3.2(d) n.143; 3.2(h) n.201

Hetzko, State v., 283 So.2d 49 (Fla.App.1973)—§ 3.6(f) n.148

Hewes, State v., 558 A.2d 696 (Me.1989)—§§ 6.6(c) n.40; 6.6(f) n.112

Hewes, United States v., 729 F.2d 1302 (11th Cir.1984)—§§ 17.2(c) n.87, 90; 17.3(e) n.57, 64

Hewett v. State, 613 So.2d 1305 (Fla.1993)—§ 26.9(b) n.33

Hewitt, State v., 689 P.2d 22 (Utah 1984)—§ 22.3(c) n.108

Hewitt v. State, 43 Fla. 194, 30 So. 795 (1901)—§§ 16.3(d) n.55, 57

Hewlett, United States v., 395 F.3d 458 (D.C.Cir.2005)—§ 10.2(a) n.2

Hezzie R., Interest of, 219 Wis.2d 848, 580 N.W.2d 660 (1998)—§ 22.1(c) n.64

Hibbard, State v., 273 N.W.2d 172 (S.D.1978)—§§ 20.6(c) n.89, 90

Hibl, State v., 290 Wis.2d 595, 714 N.W.2d 194 (2006)—§ 7.4(b) n.33

Hickey v. State, 109 Nev. 22, 846 P.2d 289 (1993)—§ 11.5(c) n.52

Hickey, State v., 317 N.C. 457, 346 S.E.2d 646 (1986)—§ 11.2(e) n.192

Hickey v. State, 484 So.2d 1271 (Fla.App.1986)—§ 24.7(b) n.20

Hickey, United States v., 367 F.3d 888 (9th Cir.2004)—§ 27.2(c) n.40

Hickey, United States v., 997 F.Supp. 1206 (N.D.Cal.1998)—§ 23.1(d) n.170

Hickman, People v., 470 Mich. 602, 684 N.W.2d 267 (2004)—§ 7.3(b) n.29

Hickman, State v., 205 Ariz. 192, 68 P.3d 418 (Ariz.2003)—§§ 22.3(c) n.157; 27.6(b) n.21

Hickman v. Taylor, 329 U.S. 495, 67 S.Ct. 385, 91 L.Ed. 451 (1947)—§§ 8.6(b) n.40, 48, 51; 20.3(j) n.182

Hickman, United States v., 179 F.3d 230 (5th Cir.1999)—§§ 1.2(d) n.202, 210

Hickman, United States v., 151 F.3d 446 (5th Cir.1998)—§ 7.4(e) n.89

Hicks v. Miranda, 422 U.S. 332, 95 S.Ct. 2281, 45 L.Ed.2d 223 (1975)—§ 13.5(e) n.101

Hicks v. Oklahoma 447 U.S. 343, 100 S.Ct. 2227, 65 L.Ed.2d 175 (1980)—§ 2.4(b) n.60

Hicks, People v., 98 N.Y.2d 185, 746 N.Y.S.2d 441, 774 N.E.2d 205 (2002)—§ 21.2(d) n.241

Hicks, People v., 49 Ill.App.3d 421, 7 Ill.Dec. 279, 364 N.E.2d 440 (1977)—§ 3.4(e) n.97

Hicks v. State, 812 So.2d 179 (Miss.2002)—§§ 18.2(e) n.76; 22.3(d) n.246

Hicks, State v., 55 S.W.3d 515 (Tenn.2001)—§ 3.9(g) n.124

Hicks, State v., 1999 WL 997297, 1999 Ohio 916 (1999)—§ 26.9(b) n.25

Hicks, State v., 330 S.C. 207, 499 S.E.2d 209 (1998)—§ 22.3(d) n.245

Hicks, State v., 333 N.C. 467, 428 S.E.2d 167 (1993)—§ 10.4(b) n.16

Hicks v. State, 860 S.W.2d 419 (Tex.Crim.App.1993)—§§ 8.10(c) n.68; 8.14(b) n.31; 19.3(b) n.140

Hicks, State v., 241 Neb. 357, 488 N.W.2d 359 (1992)—§ 10.2(a) n.1

Hicks v. State, 421 So.2d 510 (Fla.1982)—§ 19.3(a) n.18

Hicks v. State, 96 Nev. 82, 605 P.2d 219 (1980)—§ 9.1(b) n.80

Hicks, State v., 233 N.C. 511, 64 S.E.2d 871 (1951)—§ 16.4(c) n.71

Hicks v. Straub, 377 F.3d 538 (6th Cir.2004)—§ 28.4(b) n.19

Hicks, United States v., 283 F.3d 380 (D.C.Cir.2002)—§ 28.9(b) n.53

Hicks, United States v., 978 F.2d 722 (D.C.Cir.1992)—§ 10.2(b) n.28

Hicks, United States v., 947 F.2d 1356 (9th Cir.1991)—§ 22.3(b) n.80

Hicks, United States v., 693 F.2d 32 (5th Cir.1982)—§§ 13.6(d) n.55, 56

Hicks v. United States, 382 F.2d 158 (D.C.Cir.1967)—§§ 6.6(d) n.46; 6.6(f) n.107

Hidalgo, People v., 91 N.Y.2d 733, 698 N.E.2d 46, 675 N.Y.S.2d 327 (1998)—§ 27.5(c) n.52

Hidalgo, State v., 668 So.2d 1188 (La.App.1996)—§ 24.3(b) n.38

Hider, State v., 715 A.2d 942 (Me.1998)—§§ 17.4(a) n.68; 17.4(b) n.120

Hien Van Tieu, United States v., 279 F.3d 917 (10th Cir.2002)—§§ 19.6(c) n.50, 51

Higby, State v., 26 Wash.App. 457, 613 P.2d 1192 (1980)—§ 21.6(c) n.116

Higdon v. United States, 627 F.2d 893 (9th Cir.1980)—§§ 26.9(b) n.26, 38; 26.9(c) n.81

Higgenbotham, State v., 271 Kan. 582, 23 P.3d 874 (2001)—§ 23.2(a) n.25

Higginbotham, State v., 174 Vt. 640, 816 A.2d 547 (2002)—§ 18.4(c) n.58

Higginbotham v. State, 807 S.W.2d 732 (Tex.Cr.App.1991)—§ 27.6(b) n.55

Higgins v. People, 868 P.2d 371 (Colo.1994)—§ 19.5(b) n.20

Higgins, State v., 265 Conn. 35, 826 A.2d 1126 (2003)—§ 24.2(e) n.64

Higgins, State v., 796 A.2d 50 (Me.2002)—§ 6.6(d) n.48

Higgins, United States v., 2 F.3d 1094 (10th Cir.1993)—§ 6.6(e) n.68

Higgins, United States v., 987 F.2d 543 (8th Cir.1993)—§ 12.2(a) n.4

Higgins, United States v., 428 F.2d 232 (7th Cir.1970)—§ 3.4(e) n.74

Higgins v. United States, 209 F.2d 819 (D.C.Cir.1954)—§ 3.10(b) n.53

Higgins v. Wainwright, 424 F.2d 177 (5th Cir.1970)—§ 7.2(c) n.30

Higgs, United States v., 353 F.3d 281 (4th Cir.2003)—§§ 19.3(a) n.27, 103, 128; 26.4(f) n.109

Higgs, United States v., 713 F.2d 39 (3d Cir.1983)—§ 20.3(m) n.239

High, State v., 225 Neb. 690, 407 N.W.2d 776 (1987)—§ 22.1(h) n.133

High v. State, 573 S.W.2d 807 (Tex.Crim.App.1978)—§ 11.2(c) n.99

Highfill, United States v., 334 F.Supp. 700 (E.D.Ark.1971)—§ 3.4(j) n.211

Highland Park v. Curtis, 83 Ill.App.2d 218, 226 N.E.2d 870 (1967)—§ 1.8(d) n.58

Highland Sales Corp. v. Vance, 244 Ind. 20, 186 N.E.2d 682 (1962)—§ 13.4(c) n.116

Highsaw v. State, 758 P.2d 336 (Okl.Crim. 1988)—§ 7.4(c) n.48

Hightower, State v., 146 N.J. 239, 680 A.2d 649 (1996)—§§ 24.9(d) n.32; 24.9(f) n.102

Hightower, State v., 661 A.2d 948 (R.I.1995)—§ 27.5(c) n.103

Hightower, State v., 214 N.J.Super. 43, 518 A.2d 482 (1986)—§ 11.6(a) n.46

Hiibel v. Sixth Judicial District Court, 542 U.S. 177, 124 S.Ct. 2451, 159 L.Ed.2d 292 (2004)—§§ 1.7(j) n.255; 3.3(f) n.216; 3.8(b) n.56; 3.8(e) n.222; 6.7(b) n.51; 8.10(a) n.26

Hildwin v. Florida, 490 U.S. 638, 109 S.Ct. 2055, 104 L.Ed.2d 728 (1989)—§§ 26.1(b) n.15; 26.2(b) n.2; 26.6(b) n.11

Hill v. Braxton, 277 F.3d 701 (4th Cir.2002)—§ 28.5(b) n.57

Hill v. Brigano, 199 F.3d 833 (6th Cir.1999)—§ 6.9(f) n.131

Hill v. California, 401 U.S. 797, 91 S.Ct. 1106, 28 L.Ed.2d 484 (1971)—§§ 3.10(a) n.18; 3.10(d) n.133

Hill v. Commonwealth, 125 S.W.3d 221 (Ky.2004)—§§ 11.5(g) n.110, 112

Hill, Commonwealth v., 264 Va. 315, 568 S.E.2d 673 (Va.2002)—§ 22.3(a) n.33

Hill v. Levy, 117 Cal.App.2d 667, 256 P.2d 622 (1953)—§ 3.5(a) n.39

Hill v. Lockhart, 28 F.3d 832 (8th Cir.1994)—§ 11.10(c) n.90

Hill v. Lockhart, 894 F.2d 1009 (8th Cir.1990)—§ 21.3(b) n.69

Hill v. Lockhart, 474 U.S. 52, 106 S.Ct. 366, 88 L.Ed.2d 203 (1985)—§§ 11.10(a) n.24; 21.3(b) n.43; 21.6(a) n.71

Hill v. McDonough, _____ U.S. _____, 126 S.Ct. 2096, 165 L.Ed.2d 44 (2006)—§ 28.3(b) n.67

Hill, People v., 353 Ill.App.3d 961, 289 Ill.Dec. 485, 819 N.E.2d 1285 (Ill.App.2004)—§ 25.2(a) n.7

Hill, People v., 17 Cal.4th 800, 952 P.2d 673, 72 Cal.Rptr.2d 656 (1998)—§ 24.7(e) n.61

Hill, People v., 3 Cal.4th 959, 13 Cal.Rptr.2d 475, 839 P.2d 984 (1992)—§ 6.8(d) n.84

Hill, People v., 433 Mich. 464, 446 N.W.2d 140 (1989)—§ 14.3(a) n.30

Hill, People v., 429 Mich. 382, 415 N.W.2d 193 (1987)—§§ 6.6(a) n.7; 6.6(e) n.68

Hill, People v., 12 Cal.3d 731, 117 Cal.Rptr. 393, 528 P.2d 1 (1974)—§§ 3.4(k) n.221; 21.6(b) n.84

Hill, People v., 70 Cal.2d 678, 76 Cal.Rptr. 225, 452 P.2d 329 (1969)—§ 6.6(d) n.45

Hill, State v., 368 S.C. 649, 630 S.E.2d 274 (2006)—§ 24.3(b) n.80

Hill, State v., 204 Ariz. 442, 65 P.3d 90 (2003)—§ 6.7(c) n.142

Hill v. State, 90 S.W.3d 308 (Tex.Cr.App.2002)—§ 22.1(d) n.79

Hill, State v., 174 Vt. 566, 816 A.2d 440 (2002)—§ 6.10(c) n.48

Hill, State v., 264 Va. 541, 570 S.E.2d 805 (2002)—§ 3.1(o) n.303

Hill, State v., 146 N.H. 568, 781 A.2d 979 (2001)—§§ 9.6(a) n.47; 13.7(a) n.5

Hill, State v., 255 Neb. 173, 583 N.W.2d 20 (1998)—§ 14.3(d) n.92

Hill, State v., 201 W.Va. 95, 491 S.E.2d 765 (1997)—§ 17.4(c) n.156

Hill v. State, 339 Md. 275, 661 A.2d 1164 (1995)—§ 22.3(a) n.13

Hill v. State, 898 P.2d 155 (Okl.Cr.1995)—§ 21.5(f) n.157

Hill, State v., 314 S.C. 330, 444 S.E.2d 255 (1994)—§ 27.3(c) n.51

Hill v. State, 827 S.W.2d 860 (Tex.Cr.App.1992)—§ 22.3(d) n.252

Hill v. State, 305 Ark. 193, 805 S.W.2d 651 (1991)—§ 11.2(g) n.261

Hill, State v., 247 Kan. 377, 799 P.2d 997 (1990)—§ 21.2(d) n.188

Hill v. State, 517 N.E.2d 784 (Ind.1988)—§ 24.7(d) n.35

Hill v. State, 499 N.E.2d 1103 (Ind.1986)—§ 21.1(e) n.67

Hill v. State, 719 S.W.2d 199 (Tex.Cr.App.1986)—§ 26.10(c) n.50

Hill, State v., 196 Conn. 667, 495 A.2d 699 (1985)—§ 22.3(a) n.23

Hill v. State, 470 N.E.2d 1332 (Ind.1984)—§ 6.9(e) n.86

Hill, State v., 688 P.2d 450 (Utah 1984)—§ 13.7(a) n.29

Hill, State v., 614 S.W.2d 744 (Mo.App.1981)—§ 15.5(c) n.110

Hill, State v., 204 Neb. 743, 285 N.W.2d 229 (1979)—§§ 21.5(a) n.23, 55

Hill v. State, 366 So.2d 318 (Ala.1979)—§§ 2.12(b) n.82; 2.12(d) n.187; 2.12(e) n.208

Hill, State v., 268 S.C. 390, 234 S.E.2d 219 (1977)—§ 14.2(e) n.66

Hill, State v., 211 Kan. 287, 507 P.2d 342 (1973)—§ 20.1(a) n.15

Hill v. State, 253 Ark. 512, 487 S.W.2d 624 (1972)—§ 16.2(e) n.80

Hill v. Texas, 316 U.S. 400, 62 S.Ct. 1159, 86 L.Ed. 1559 (1942)— § 22.2(c) n.30

Hill, United States v., 322 F.Supp.2d 1081 (C.D.Cal.2004)—§ 3.4(j) n.202

Hill v. United States, 858 A.2d 435 (D.C.App.2004)—§ 6.7(c) n.111

Hill, United States v., 279 F.3d 731 (9th Cir.2002)—§ 19.3(a) n.101

Hill, United States v., 252 F.3d 919 (7th Cir.2001)—§§ 11.4(d) n.117; 11.5(c) n.58

Hill, United States v., 197 F.3d 436 (10th Cir.1999)—§ 22.2(d) n.80

Hill, United States v., 146 F.3d 337 (6th Cir.1998)—§ 22.3(d) n.245

Hill, United States v., 60 F.3d 672 (10th Cir.1995)—§§ 3.1(f) n.140; 9.6(c) n.66

Hill v. United States, 664 A.2d 347 (D.C.App.1995)—§ 9.1(b) n.77

Hill, United States v., 19 F.3d 984 (5th Cir.1994)—§§ 3.4(f) n.105; 3.4(k) n.219

Hill, United States v., 893 F.Supp. 1039 (N.D.Fla.1994)—§ 23.1(b) n.89

Hill, United States v., 967 F.2d 226 (6th Cir.1992)—§§ 7.4(g) n.116; 10.3(d) n.66

Hill, United States v., 976 F.2d 132 (3d Cir.1992)—§ 24.3(c) n.88

Hill, United States v., 855 F.2d 664 (10th Cir.1988)—§ 3.6(a) n.5

Hill, United States v., 738 F.2d 152 (6th Cir.1984)—§ 22.3(a) n.11

Hill, United States v., 626 F.2d 1301 (5th Cir.1980)—§ 5.3(d) n.42

Hill v. United States, 367 A.2d 110 (D.C.App.1976)—§ 7.4(b) n.29

Hill, United States v., 545 F.2d 1191 (9th Cir.1976)—§ 3.8(e) n.209

Hill v. United States, 418 F.2d 449 (D.C.Cir.1968)—§ 10.5(e) n.49

Hill v. United States, 368 U.S. 424, 82 S.Ct. 468, 7 L.Ed.2d 417 (1962)— §§ 21.5(b) n.71; 26.4(g) n.142; 28.3(b) n.63; 28.9(c) n.76, 78

Hill, United States v., 26 Fed.Cas. 315 (C.C.D.Va.1809)—§§ 15.1(d) n.152, 166

Hill v. Wainwright, 617 F.2d 375 (5th Cir.1980)—§ 18.4(a) n.14

Hillary, People v., 28 Cal.Rptr.2d 415 (App.1994)—§ 5.2(b) n.28

Hillary, United States v., 106 F.3d 1170 (4th Cir.1997)—§ 21.5(e) n.147

Hillegas v. Sams, 349 F.2d 859 (5th Cir.1965)—§ 13.5(f) n.107

Hilleshiem, State v., 291 N.W.2d 314 (Iowa 1980)—§ 3.8(d) n.184

Hilley, Ex parte, 484 So.2d 485 (Ala.1985)—§ 3.1(h) n.204

Hillhouse, People v., 27 Cal.4th 469, 117 Cal.Rptr.2d 45, 40 P.3d 754 (2002)—§ 21.2(b) n.63

Hilliard v. Beto, 465 F.2d 829 (5th Cir.1972)—§ 21.5(d) n.99

Hilliard, Commonwealth v., 270 Va. 42, 613 S.E.2d 579 (2005)—§ 6.9(g) n.166

Hilliard, Commonwealth v., 471 Pa. 318, 370 A.2d 322 (1977)—§ 6.4(f) n.115

Hilliard v. State, 259 Ark. 81, 531 S.W.2d 463 (1976)—§ 11.7(e) n.92

Hillman, People v., 834 P.2d 1271 (Colo.1992)—§ 3.2(h) n.211

Hillman, State v., 749 A.2d 758 (Me.2000)—§ 21.5(a) n.35

Hills, People v., 78 Ill.2d 500, 36 Ill.Dec. 682, 401 N.E.2d 523 (1980)—§ 26.10(d) n.93

Hills v. Washington, 441 F.3d 1374 (11th Cir.2006)—§§ 28.4(c) n.31; 28.5(a) n.39

Hillsborough County v. Martinez, 483 So.2d 540 (Fla.App.1986)—§ 1.5(f) n.248

Hillstrom, United States v., 533 F.2d 209 (5th Cir.1976)—§ 3.9(g) n.140

Hill, United States ex rel. v. Ternullo, 510 F.2d 844 (2d Cir.1975)—§ 21.4(d) n.146

Hillyard, People v., 197 Colo. 83, 589 P.2d 939 (1979)—§ 9.4(a) n.20

Hilton, Commonwealth v., 443 Mass. 597, 823 N.E.2d 383 (2005)—§§ 6.4(g) n.151, 152; 6.9(b) n.24, 44

Hilton, United States v., 534 F.2d 556 (3d Cir.1976)—§ 8.8(g) n.164

Himes v. Thompson, 336 F.3d 848 (9th Cir.2003)—§ 28.6(f) n.77

Himler, United States v., 797 F.2d 156 (3d Cir.1986)—§ 12.3(a) n.19

Himmelfarb v. United States, 175 F.2d 924 (9th Cir.1949)—§ 19.4(b) n.33

Himmerick, State v., 499 N.W.2d 568 (N.D.1993)—§ 24.6(b) n.32

Hinchey, State v., 181 Ariz. 307, 890 P.2d 602 (1995)—§§ 21.5(e) n.119; 26.7(a) n.8

Hin Chow, State v., 77 Hawaii 241, 883 P.2d 663 (1994)—§ 27.5(e) n.162

Hinckley, United States v., 672 F.2d 115 (D.C.Cir.1982)—§§ 6.7(b) n.42, 70; 9.6(b) n.55

Hinderman, State v., 665 S.W.2d 699 (Mo.App.1984)—§ 24.5(b) n.34

Hinds, In re, 90 N.J. 604, 449 A.2d 483 (1982)—§§ 23.1(b) n.10, 32

Hinds, Commonwealth v., 437 Mass. 54, 768 N.E.2d 1067 (2002)—§ 3.10(f) n.199

Hinds, United States v., 856 F.2d 438 (1st Cir.1988)—§ 3.4(e) n.78

Hines, People v., 165 Ill.App.3d 289, 116 Ill.Dec. 382, 518 N.E.2d 1362 (1988)—§ 23.2(f) n.108

Hines v. State, 425 So.2d 589 (Fla.App.1982)—§ 24.7(e) n.73

Hines, United States v., 955 F.2d 1449 (11th Cir.1992)—§ 19.3(b) n.181

Hines, United States v., 455 F.2d 1317 (D.C.Cir.1971)—§§ 7.4(d) n.71; 17.2(d) n.109

Hinkel, State v., 365 N.W.2d 774 (Minn.1985)—§ 3.4(e) n.98

Hinkle, United States v., 307 F.Supp. 117 (D.D.C.1969)—§ 14.4(c) n.52

Hinners, State v., 471 N.W.2d 841 (Iowa 1991)—§ 21.2(b) n.76

Hinojosa v. State, 781 N.E.2d 677 (Ind.2003)—§ 8.5(h) n.269

Hinton v. District Court, 693 P.2d 1277 (Okl.Cr.1984)—§ 17.4(b) n.98

Hinton v. State, 36 Md.App. 52, 373 A.2d 39 (1977)—§ 17.4(a) n.42

Hinton, United States v., 222 F.3d 664 (9th Cir.2000)—§ 4.2(c) n.20

Hinton, United States v., 543 F.2d 1002 (2d Cir.1976)—§§ 15.7(d) n.66, 67

Hinton, United States v., 268 F.Supp. 728 (E.D.La.1967)—§ 16.3(c) n.42

Hinton, United States v., 219 F.2d 324 (7th Cir.1955)—§ 3.4(e) n.75

Hintzman, United States v., 806 F.2d 840 (8th Cir.1986)—§ 15.6(f) n.189

Hipolite Egg Co. v. United States, 220 U.S. 45, 31 S.Ct. 364, 55 L.Ed. 364 (1911)—§ 1.2(c) n.107

Hipps, State v., 348 N.C. 377, 501 S.E.2d 625 (1998)—§ 6.7(b) n.69

Hires v. State, 882 So.2d 225 (Miss.2004)—§ 27.5(c) n.85

Hironaka, State v., 99 Haw. 198, 53 P.3d 806 (2002)—§ 13.2(c) n.77

Hirsch, State v., 245 Neb. 31, 511 N.W.2d 69 (1994)—§ 18.5(a) n.6

Hirschkop v. Snead, 594 F.2d 356 (4th Cir.1979)—§§ 23.1(b) n.27, 31 to 33, 50

Hiss v. Department of Justice, 441 F.Supp. 69 (S.D.N.Y.1977)— § 8.5(b) n.40

Hitch, People v., 12 Cal.3d 641, 117 Cal.Rptr. 9, 527 P.2d 361 (1974)— §§ 20.6(b) n.60, 64

Hitch v. Pima County Superior Court, 146 Ariz. 588, 708 P.2d 72 (1985)— §§ 11.9(a) n.21; 11.9(d) n.197

Hitchcock, United States v., 286 F.3d 1064 (9th Cir.2002)—§ 3.4(g) n.125

Hitchcock v. Wainwright, 745 F.2d 1332 (11th Cir.1984)—§ 21.1(e) n.62

Hitchings, In re, 6 Cal.4th 97, 24 Cal.Rptr.2d 74, 860 P.2d 466 (1993)—§ 24.9(f) n.64

Hitt, State v., 273 Kan. 224, 42 P.3d 732 (2002)—§ 26.4(i) n.200

Hix, State v., 38 Ohio St.3d 129, 527 N.E.2d 784 (1988)—§ 11.2(e) n.176

H.J. Inc. v. Northwestern Bell Telephone Co., 492 U.S. 229, 109 S.Ct. 2893, 106 L.Ed.2d 195 (1989)—§ 16.2(h) n.150

Hlady, State v., 43 Or.App. 921, 607 P.2d 733 (1979)—§ 3.5(e) n.185

Hlavacek, State v., 185 W.Va. 371, 407 S.E.2d 375 (1991)—§ 3.1(c) n.77

Hoag v. New Jersey, 356 U.S. 464, 78 S.Ct. 829, 2 L.Ed.2d 913 (1958)— § 17.4(a) n.61

Hoag v. State, 728 S.W.2d 375 (Tex.Cr.App.1987)—§ 3.8(d) n.175

Hoang, State v., 86 Hawai'i 48, 947 P.2d 360 (1997)—§ 13.7(a) n.27

Hoang v. State, 872 S.W.2d 694 (Tex.Cr.App.1993)—§ 25.1(d) n.88

Hoa Quoc Ta, United States v., 221 Fed.Appx. 938 (11th Cir.2007)— § 25.2(e) n.46

Hobble, State v., 126 Wash.2d 283, 892 P.2d 85 (1995)—§ 2.12(e) n.213

Hobbs v. Commonwealth, 306 Ky. 66, 206 S.W.2d 48 (1947)—§ 16.3(d) n.75

Hobbs, People v., 7 Cal.4th 948, 30 Cal.Rptr.2d 651, 873 P.2d 1246 (1994)—§ 3.4(c) n.48

Hobby v. United States, 468 U.S. 339, 104 S.Ct. 3093, 82 L.Ed.2d 260 (1984)—§§ 15.4(d) n.117; 15.4(e) n.131

Hobley, State v., 752 So.2d 771 (La.1999)—§§ 6.9(f) n.139; 22.3(d) n.246

Hobson, People v., 39 N.Y.2d 479, 384 N.Y.S.2d 419, 348 N.E.2d 894 (1976)—§§ 6.4(e) n.84, 85

Hobson, United States v., 672 F.2d 825 (11th Cir.1982)—§§ 11.9(c) n.105, 142

Hocker, State v., 113 Ariz. 450, 556 P.2d 784 (1976)—§§ 10.5(a) n.12; 15.2(e) n.141; 15.7(b) n.33

Hockridge, United States v., 573 F.2d 752 (2d Cir.1978)—§§ 24.9(g) n.112; 24.10(d) n.45

Hoctel, United States v., 154 F.3d 506 (5th Cir.1998)—§ 21.6(a) n.35

Hodgdon v. United States, 365 F.2d 679 (8th Cir.1966)—§§ 12.2(b) n.19; 12.2(c) n.41

Hodge v. Hurley, 426 F.3d 368 (6th Cir.2005)—§§ 11.10(c) n.118; 24.7(e) n.52

Hodge, People v., 53 N.Y.2d 313, 441 N.Y.S.2d 231, 423 N.E.2d 1060 (1981)—§ 14.4(e) n.137

Hodge, State v., 248 Conn. 207, 726 A.2d 531 (1999)—§§ 22.3(d) n.199, 249, 250

Hodge v. State, 332 Ark. 377, 965 S.W.2d 766 (1998)—§ 9.1(c) n.100

Hodge, State v., 118 N.M. 410, 882 P.2d 1 (1994)—§§ 21.6(b) n.83, 96; 27.5(c) n.50

Hodge, United States v., 412 F.3d 479 (3d Cir.2005)—§§ 21.2(b) n.57; 21.2(d) n.178

Hodge, United States v., 259 F.3d 549 (6th Cir.2001)—§§ 21.5(a) n.38; 21.5(c) n.83; 21.5(d) n.104

Hodges, People v., 27 Cal. 340 (1865)— § 16.2(g) n.110

Hodges v. State, 678 So.2d 1049 (Ala.1996)—§ 3.8(e) n.210

Hodges v. State, 265 Ga. 870, 463 S.E.2d 16 (1995)—§ 6.6(a) n.7

Hodges v. State, 904 P.2d 334 (Wyo.1995)—§ 24.6(b) n.28

Hodges, State v., 252 Kan. 989, 851 P.2d 352 (1993)—§ 9.1(d) n.120

Hodges, State v., 815 S.W.2d 151 (Tenn.1991)—§ 21.3(e) n.286

Hodges, State v., 43 Or.App. 547, 603 P.2d 1205 (1979)—§ 3.6(e) n.140

Hodges, United States v., 460 F.3d 646 (5th Cir.2006)—§ 26.10(b) n.32

Hodges, United States v., 936 F.2d 371 (8th Cir.1991)—§ 5.1(c) n.37

Hodges, United States v., 556 F.2d 366 (5th Cir.1977)—§ 16.2(g) n.127

Hodgin v. State, 702 So.2d 113 (Miss.1997)—§ 21.4(a) n.38

Hodgson, State v., 108 Wash.2d 662, 740 P.2d 848 (1987)—§ 18.5(a) n.6

Hodson, State v., 907 P.2d 1155 (Utah 1995)—§ 3.5(b) n.102

Hoeft, State v., 594 N.W.2d 323 (S.D.1999)—§ 21.4(a) n.26

Hoekstra, State v., 286 N.W.2d 127 (S.D.1979)—§§ 15.5(c) n.108, 113; 15.6(a) n.6, 7, 44; 15.7(e) n.99, 106

Hoeplinger, State v., 206 Conn. 278, 537 A.2d 1010 (1988)—§ 9.5(d) n.75

Hoey v. State, 965 So.2d 360 (Fla.App.2007)—§ 26.9(b) n.33

Hoey, State v., 77 Hawai'i 51, 881 P.2d 504 (1994)—§ 6.9(g) n.189

Hoffa v. United States, 385 U.S. 293, 87 S.Ct. 408, 17 L.Ed.2d 374 (1966)— §§ 3.2(j) n.235; 3.4(k) n.235; 3.10(c) n.81; 6.2(c) n.149; 6.4(e) n.66; 6.6(a) n.5; 6.7(c) n.136; 11.8(b) n.28; 21.2(b) n.72

Hoffa, United States v., 349 F.2d 20 (6th Cir.1965)—§ 15.4(g) n.149

Hoffard, People v., 10 Cal.4th 1170, 43 Cal.Rptr. 827, 899 P.2d 896 (1995)—§ 21.4(f) n.204

Hoffer, People v., 106 Ill.2d 186, 88 Ill.Dec. 20, 478 N.E.2d 335 (1985)—§ 17.4(a) n.42

Hoffman v. Arave, 455 F.3d 926 (9th Cir.2006)—§ 21.3(b) n.100

Hoffman v. Arave, 236 F.3d 523 (9th Cir.2001)—§§ 6.4(e) n.109; 6.10(e) n.67; 11.7(e) n.64, 65, 71, 96; 28.4(b) n.20

Hoffman v. Leeke, 903 F.2d 280 (4th Cir.1990)—§ 11.9(d) n.192

Hoffman, People v., 205 Mich.App. 1, 518 N.W.2d 817 (1994)—§ 8.10(d) n.107

Hoffman, State v., 314 Mont. 155, 64 P.3d 1013 (2003)—§ 6.9(b) n.36

Hoffman, State v., 348 N.C. 548, 500 S.E.2d 718 (1998)—§ 22.3(d) n.212

Hoffman v. State, 474 So.2d 1178 (Fla.1985)—§ 21.2(d) n.242

Hoffman, State v., 273 Ark. 111, 617 S.W.2d 16 (1981)—§ 3.3(a) n.12

Hoffman, United States v., 832 F.2d 1299 (1st Cir.1987)—§ 24.7(i) n.93

Hoffman v. United States, 341 U.S. 479, 71 S.Ct. 814, 95 L.Ed. 1118 (1951)—§§ 8.10(a) n.8, 9; 15.1(b) n.22; 24.5(a) n.2

Hoffner, State v., 102 Ohio St.3d 358, 811 N.E.2d 48 (2004)—§ 6.6(e) n.61

Hogan v. Mayor of Chattanooga, 2 Shannon Cas 339 (1877)—§ 15.1(d) n.227

Hogan, People v., 31 Cal.3d 815, 183 Cal.Rptr. 817, 647 P.2d 93 (1982)—§ 6.2(c) n.104

Hogan v. State, 139 P.3d 907 (Okl.Cr.App.2006)—§ 25.4(d) n.45

Hogan, State v., 336 N.J.Super. 319, 764 A.2d 1012 (2001)—§§ 15.7(g) n.200, 215, 216

Hogan, State v., 144 N.J. 216, 676 A.2d 533 (1996)—§§ 15.3(d) n.68; 15.6(a) n.25, 27; 15.7(f) n.133, 136, 139, 149, 152, 162, 169, 172, 176, 180, 182

Hogan v. State, 158 Ga.App. 495, 280 S.E.2d 891 (1981)—§ 26.10(d) n.92

Hogan, United States v., 712 F.2d 757 (2d Cir.1983)—§§ 8.1(a) n.2; 15.5(b) n.57; 15.6(b) n.58; 15.6(d) n.104; 15.6(e) n.152, 155; 15.7(b) n.14, 16, 19, 35

Hogg, State v., 118 N.H. 262, 385 A.2d 844 (1978)—§ 25.5(b) n.23

Hoggard, United States v., 254 F.3d 744 (6th Cir.2001)—§ 3.10(c) n.98

Hohensee, State v., 650 S.W.2d 268 (Mo.App.1982)—§ 5.4(c) n.46

Hohle, State v., 510 N.W.2d 847 (Iowa 1994)—§ 7.5(a) n.7

Hohn v. United States, 524 U.S. 236, 118 S.Ct. 1969, 141 L.Ed.2d 242 (1998)—§ 28.10 n.6

Hoines v. Barney's Club, Inc., 28 Cal.3d 603, 170 Cal.Rptr. 42, 620 P.2d 628 (1980)—§ 13.5(a) n.22

Hoitt v. Vitek, 361 F.Supp. 1238 (D.N.H.1973)—§ 3.9(i) n.186

Hoke v. Henderson, 4 Dev. (N.C.) 1 (1833)—§ 2.4(c) n.95

Hoke v. United States, 227 U.S. 308, 33 S.Ct. 281, 57 L.Ed. 523 (1913)—§§ 1.2(c) n.105, 108

Holbrook v. Flynn, 475 U.S. 560, 106 S.Ct. 1340, 89 L.Ed.2d 525 (1986)—§§ 2.7(a) n.36; 24.2(e) n.62

Holbrook v. State, 877 So.2d 525 (Miss.App.2004)—§§ 16.2(a) n.10; 16.2(e) n.74

Holbrook, United States v., 368 F.3d 415 (4th Cir.2004)—§ 21.2(e) n.361

Holcomb, State v., 128 Idaho 296, 912 P.2d 664 (1995)—§ 19.4(b) n.10

Holcomb, State v., 156 Vt. 251, 590 A.2d 894 (Vt.1991)—§ 19.3(c) n.190

Holcomb v. State, 254 Ga. 124, 326 S.E.2d 760 (1985)—§ 6.2(c) n.172

Holdaway, United States v., 1999 WL 1076114 (D.Mass.1999)—§ 20.4(e) n.84

Holden, State v., 346 N.C. 404, 488 S.E.2d 514 (1997)—§ 27.5(d) n.114

Holden, State v., 321 N.C. 125, 362 S.E.2d 513 (1987)—§ 24.7(d) n.35

Holden, United States v., 963 F.2d 1114 (8th Cir.1992)—§ 22.3(b) n.80

Holder v. State, 354 Ark. 364, 124 S.W.3d 439 (2003)—§ 22.3(d) n.235

Holder v. United States, 150 U.S. 91, 14 S.Ct. 10, 37 L.Ed. 1010 (1893)—§§ 24.4(d) n.57, 59, 63

Holdren v. Legursky, 16 F.3d 57 (4th Cir.1994)—§ 19.3(a) n.45

Hole v. State, 851 N.E.2d 302 (Ind.2006)—§§ 21.2(b) n.76; 21.2(d) n.194

Holeman, State v., 103 Wash.2d 426, 693 P.2d 89 (1985)—§ 3.6(a) n.35

Holland, Commonwealth v., 410 Mass. 248, 571 N.E.2d 625 (1991)—§§ 10.3(d) n.63, 72

Holland v. Commonwealth, 679 S.W.2d 832 (Ky.App.1984)—§ 11.10(c) n.111

Holland, Commonwealth v., 480 Pa. 202, 389 A.2d 1026 (1978)—§ 7.2(d) n.48

Holland v. Horn, 150 F.Supp.2d 706 (E.D.Pa.2001)—§ 11.2(e) n.173

Holland v. Illinois, 493 U.S. 474, 110 S.Ct. 803, 107 L.Ed.2d 905 (1990)—§§ 2.9(d) n.55, 57; 22.2(c) n.26; 22.2(d) n.59, 60, 65; 22.3(d) n.188

Holland v. Jackson, 542 U.S. 649, 124 S.Ct. 2736, 159 L.Ed.2d 683 (2004)—§ 11.10(d) n.159

Holland v. McGinnis, 963 F.2d 1044 (7th Cir.1992)—§§ 6.2(c) n.125, 128; 9.5(c) n.65

Holland, People v., 179 Mich.App. 184, 445 N.W.2d 206 (1989)—§§ 20.4(c) n.48; 20.5(b) n.25

Holland, People v., 121 Ill.2d 136, 117 Ill.Dec. 109, 520 N.E.2d 270 (1987)—§ 6.9(c) n.55

Holland v. State, 773 So.2d 1065 (Fla.2000)—§ 6.9(f) n.135

Holland v. State, 322 S.C. 111, 470 S.E.2d 378 (S.C.1996)—§ 21.2(d) n.161

Holland, State v., 921 P.2d 430 (Utah 1996)—§§ 21.3(b) n.42; 21.4(b) n.65

Holland v. State, 587 So.2d 848 (Miss.1991)—§ 6.9(g) n.183

Holland, United States v., 214 F.3d 523 (4th Cir.2000)—§§ 13.5(h) n.201, 207

Holland v. United States, 584 A.2d 13 (D.C.App.1990)—§ 21.4(d) n.110

Holland, United States v., 510 F.2d 453 (9th Cir.1975)—§ 3.8(d) n.128

Holland, United States v., 378 F.Supp. 144 (E.D.Pa.1974)—§§ 3.2(g) n.192, 193

Holland ex rel. Overdorff v. Harrington, 268 F.3d 1179 (10th Cir.2001)—§ 3.4(h) n.166

Holler v. Commonwealth, 220 Va. 961, 265 S.E.2d 715 (1980)—§ 21.4(g) n.232

Holley, State v., 604 A.2d 772 (R.I.1992)—§ 7.4(e) n.92

Holley, United States v., 986 F.2d 100 (5th Cir.1993)—§ 18.3(b) n.41

Holley, United States v., 502 F.2d 273 (4th Cir.1974)—§ 7.5(a) n.5

Holliday, United States v., 457 F.3d 121 (1st Cir.2006)—§ 7.4(b) n.26

Holliday, United States v., 474 F.2d 320 (10th Cir.1973)—§ 3.3(g) n.232

Holliman, State v., 214 Conn. 38, 570 A.2d 680 (1990)—§ 7.4(b) n.34

Holliness v. State, 467 N.E.2d 4 (Ind.1984)—§ 22.1(h) n.134

Hollingsworth, United States v., 27 F.3d 1196 (7th Cir.1994)—§§ 5.1(c) n.29, 33; 5.2(a) n.19

Hollis, State v., 161 Vt. 87, 633 A.2d 1362 (1993)—§§ 3.1(d) n.99; 3.5(a) n.45

Holloman v. Commonwealth, 37 S.W.3d 764 (Ky. 2001)—§ 26.3(f) n.66

Holloman, State v., 835 S.W.2d 42 (Tenn.Cr.App.1992)—§ 19.3(b) n.182

Holloman, State v., 240 Kan. 589, 731 P.2d 294 (1987)—§ 6.2(c) n.96

Holloman, State v., 197 Neb. 139, 248 N.W.2d 15 (1976)—§ 3.6(g) n.160

Holloway v. Arkansas, 435 U.S. 475, 98 S.Ct. 1173, 55 L.Ed.2d 426 (1978)—§§ 11.9(a) n.41; 11.9(b) n.43; 21.3(b) n.130, 131, 138; 27.6(d) n.113, 131

Holloway, Commonwealth v., 559 Pa. 258, 739 A.2d 1039 (1999)—§ 22.3(d) n.253

Holloway v. Horn, 355 F.3d 707 (3d Cir.2004)—§§ 22.3(d) n.217, 255

Holloway, People v., 33 Cal.4th 96, 14 Cal.Rptr.3d 212, 91 P.3d 164 (2004)—§§ 6.2(c) n.113; 6.6(d) n.49, 50

Holloway, People v., 50 Cal.3d.1098, 269 Cal.Rptr. 530, 790 P.2d 1327 (1990)—§ 24.9(f) n.78

Holloway, State v., 209 Conn. 636, 553 A.2d 166 (1989)—§ 22.3(d) n.216

Holloway v. State, 293 Ark. 438, 738 S.W.2d 796 (1987)—§ 10.6(a) n.1

Holloway, State v., 19 N.M. 528, 146 P. 1066 (1914)—§§ 16.3(d) n.55, 56

Holloway v. United States, 526 U.S. 1, 119 S.Ct. 966, 143 L.Ed.2d 1 (1999)—§ 1.2(c) n.149

Holloway, United States v., 991 F.2d 370 (7th Cir.1993)—§ 8.3(a) n.9

Holloway v. Wolff, 482 F.2d 110 (8th Cir.1973)—§ 3.10(b) n.69

Holloway v. Woodard, 655 F.Supp. 1245 (W.D.N.C.1987)—§ 28.3(d) n.84

Hollywood Motor Car Co., United States v., 458 U.S. 263, 102 S.Ct. 3081, 73 L.Ed.2d 754 (1982)—§ 27.2(c) n.35

Holman v. Kemna, 212 F.3d 413 (8th Cir.2000)—§ 6.9(f) n.131

Holman v. Page, 102 F.3d 872 (7th Cir.1996)—§ 11.10(d) n.181

Holman, State v., 721 N.W.2d 452 (S.D.2006)—§ 6.2(c) n.103

Holman v. State, 772 S.W.2d 722 (Mo.App.1989)—§ 26.10(d) n.93

Holman, State v., 221 Neb. 730, 380 N.W.2d 304 (1986)—§ 3.3(f) n.219

Holman, State v., 486 So.2d 500 (Ala.1986)—§ 21.2(d) n.223

Holman v. Superior Court, 29 Cal.3d 480, 174 Cal.Rptr. 506, 629 P.2d 14 (1981)—§ 14.4(c) n.62

Holman, United States v., 314 F.3d 837 (7th Cir.2002)—§ 11.6(a) n.48

Holman, United States v., 728 F.2d 809 (6th Cir.1984)—§ 21.2(f) n.363

Holmes v. Burr, 486 F.2d 55 (9th Cir.1973)—§ 4.3(b) n.6

Holmes v. Gray, 526 F.2d 622 (7th Cir.1975)—§ 17.1(c) n.44

Holmes v. Kucynda, 321 F.3d 1069 (11th Cir.2003)—§ 3.10(b) n.24

Holmes, People v., 32 Cal.4th 432, 9 Cal.Rptr.3d 678, 84 P.3d 366 (2004)—§ 21.4(f) n.174

Holmes, People v., 292 Ill.App.3d 855, 227 Ill.Dec. 53, 686 N.E.2d 1209 (1997)—§§ 16.1(g) n.236; 16.1(h) n.303

Holmes v. South Carolina, _____ U.S. _____, 126 S.Ct. 1727, 164 L.Ed.2d 503 (2006)—§§ 2.7(a) n.50; 2.7(b) n.94; 24.4(a) n.5

Holmes, State v., 278 Kan. 603, 102 P.3d 406 (2004)—§ 10.6(c) n.24

Holmes, State v., 818 A.2d 1054 (Me.2003)—§ 22.1(h) n.132

Holmes v. State, 671 N.E.2d 841 (Ind.1996)—§ 24.9(a) n.5

Holmes, State v., 374 N.W.2d 457 (Minn.App.1985)—§ 24.2(a) n.15

Holmes, State v., 276 N.W.2d 823 (Iowa 1979)—§ 26.1(d) n.82

Holmes, State v., 270 N.W.2d 51 (S.D.1978)—§ 21.4(c) n.80

Holmes v. State, 59 Wis.2d 488, 208 N.W.2d 815 (1973)—§ 7.4(e) n.80

Holmes, United States v., 521 F.2d 859 (5th Cir.1975)—§§ 3.2(j) n.249, 257, 259

Holmes, United States v., 18 U.S. (5 Wheat.) 412, 5 L.Ed. 122 (1820)—§ 16.4(b) n.7

Holmgren, Commonwealth v., 421 Mass. 224, 656 N.E.2d 577 (Mass.1995)—§§ 17.4(a) n.30; 26.10(c) n.48

Holsey v. State, 253 Ind. 437, 254 N.E.2d 859 (1970)—§ 16.3(g) n.105

Holt, United States v., 417 F.3d 1172 (11th Cir.2005)—§ 28.9(a) n.27

Holt v. United States, 218 U.S. 245, 31 S.Ct. 2, 54 L.Ed. 1021 (1910)—§ 7.2(a) n.5

Holtkamp, State v., 588 S.W.2d 183 (Mo.App.1979)—§ 19.4(a) n.5

Holton, State v., 126 S.W.3d 845 (Tenn.2004)—§ 19.3(a) n.42

Holton, United States v., 116 F.3d 1536 (D.C.Cir.1997)—§ 23.2(h) n.126

Holtzman, People v., 234 Mich.App. 166, 593 Mich.App. 166, 593 N.W.2d 617 (1999)—§§ 20.3(b) n.22, 49; 20.3(j) n.186, 188, 194; 20.5(f) n.72, 84

Holyfield, United States v., 802 F.2d 846 (6th Cir.1986)—§ 18.3(b) n.36

Holy Land Foundation, United States v., 493 F.3d 469 (5th Cir.2007)—§ 26.6(d) n.69

Holzer, United States v., 848 F.2d 822 (7th Cir.1988)—§ 12.4(d) n.67

Holzman, United States v., 871 F.2d 1496 (9th Cir.1989)—§§ 3.5(c) n.105; 3.8(d) n.143

Home Depot, Inc. v. Guste, 773 F.2d 616 (5th Cir.1985)—§ 13.4(c) n.114

Homick, United States v., 964 F.2d 899 (9th Cir.1992)—§ 4.6(h) n.147

Honer, United States v., 225 F.3d 549 (5th Cir.2000)—§§ 7.4(c) n.48, 50 to 52; 7.4(e) n.93

Honeycutt, People v., 20 Cal.3d 150, 141 Cal.Rptr. 698, 570 P.2d 1050 (1977)—§ 6.8(b) n.43

Honeycutt, State v., 96 S.W.3d 85 (Mo.2003)—§ 13.2(c) n.59

Honken, United States v., 378 F.Supp.2d 880 (N.D.Iowa.2004)—§ 22.3(b) n.68

Honken, United States v., 378 F.Supp.2d 1010 (N.D.Iowa 2004)—§ 24.2(e) n.68

Honneus, United States v., 508 F.2d 566 (1st Cir.1974)—§ 16.1(g) n.262

Honomichl, State v., 410 N.W.2d 544 (S.D.1987)—§ 17.2(d) n.95

Hood v. Carsten, 267 Ga. 579, 481 S.E.2d 525 (1997)—§ 12.3(g) n.159

Hood v. State, 185 S.W.3d 445 (Tex.Cr.App.2006)—§ 26.8(b) n.14

Hood v. State, 111 Nev. 335, 890 P.2d 797 (1995)—§ 21.2(b) n.78

Hood, State v., 245 Kan. 367, 780 P.2d 160 (1989)—§§ 22.3(d) n.246, 247, 249

Hood v. State, 523 So.2d 302 (Miss.1988)—§§ 15.5(c) n.114; 15.6(a) n.32

Hood, State v., 242 Kan. 115, 744 P.2d 816 (1987)—§ 22.1(h) n.157

Hood, United States v., 469 F.3d 7 (1st Cir.2006)—§ 18.3(b) n.25

Hook v. McDade, 89 F.3d 350 (7th Cir.1996)—§ 22.4(c) n.29

Hook, State v., 623 N.W.2d 865 (Iowa 2001)—§ 21.4(b) n.42

Hook v. State, 315 Md. 25, 553 A.2d 233 (1989)—§§ 13.3(c) n.36; 24.8(f) n.92

Hook, State v., 433 S.W.2d 41 (1968)—§ 16.2(e) n.80

Hook, State v., 174 Minn. 590, 219 N.W. 926 (1928)—§ 21.5(f) n.162

Hooker, People v., 113 Misc.2d 159, 448 N.Y.S.2d 363 (Sup.Ct.1982)—§ 15.2(c) n.85

Hooker, United States v., 841 F.2d 1225 (4th Cir.1988)—§§ 19.2(c) n.36; 19.2(f) n.92, 94, 99; 19.3(a) n.49, 57, 58, 75; 19.3(b) n.140; 19.3(e) n.238

Hooker, United States v., 607 F.2d 286 (9th Cir.1979)—§ 18.4(a) n.15

Hooker, United States v., 418 F.Supp. 476 (M.D.Pa.1976)—§ 12.1(c) n.49

Hooks, United States v., 848 F.2d 785 (7th Cir.1988)—§ 24.3(i) n.191

Hooks, United States v., 780 F.2d 1526 (10th Cir.1986)—§ 24.6(c) n.40

Hooks v. Ward, 184 F.3d 1206 (10th Cir.1999)—§ 24.8(f) n.93

Hooper v. State, 680 N.W.2d 89 (Minn.2004)—§ 22.4(c) n.23

Hooper, State v., 101 Wis.2d 517, 305 N.W.2d 110 (1981)—§ 14.3(b) n.52

Hooper, United States v., 432 F.2d 604 (D.C.Cir.1970)—§ 27.5(b) n.42

Hoopii, State v., 68 Haw. 246, 710 P.2d 1193 (1985)—§ 11.2(e) n.159

Hooshmand, United States v., 931 F.2d 725 (11th Cir.1991)—§ 3.3(g) n.225

Hoover, People v., 119 P.3d 564 (Colo.App.2005)—§ 12.4(d) n.79

Hoover v. Slayton, 341 F.Supp. 317 (W.D.Va.1972)—§ 7.4(f) n.99

Hoover, State v., 594 S.W.2d 743 (Tenn.Crim.App.1979)—§§ 23.2(a) n.38, 41

Hope, People v., 184 Ill.2d 39, 234 Ill.Dec. 379, 702 N.E.2d 1282 (1998)—§ 22.3(a) n.30

Hope, People v., 147 Ill.2d 315, 168 Ill.Dec. 103, 589 N.E.2d 503 (1992)—§ 22.3(d) n.242

Hope, State v., 215 Conn. 570, 577 A.2d 1000 (1990)—§ 17.4(a) n.5

Hope v. United States, 108 F.3d 119 (7th Cir.1997)—§ 28.9(b) n.56

Hope, United States v., 102 F.3d 114 (5th Cir.1996)—§ 10.2(b) n.25

Hopkins v. Cockrell, 325 F.3d 579 (5th Cir.2003)—§ 6.2(c) n.140

Hopkins, People v., 52 Ill.2d 1, 284 N.E.2d 283 (1972)—§ 10.6(d) n.46

Hopkins v. Reeves, 524 U.S. 88, 118 S.Ct. 1895, 141 L.Ed.2d 76 (1998)—§§ 17.4(b) n.76; 24.8(f) n.115

Hopkins v. State, 759 N.E.2d 633 (Ind.2001)—§ 27.6(d) n.127

Hopkins v. State, 799 So.2d 874 (Miss.2001)—§ 6.6(e) n.89

Hopkins v. State, 352 Md. 146, 721 A.2d 231 (1998)—§ 7.2(b) n.10

Hopkins v. State, 263 Ga. 354, 434 S.E.2d 459 (1993)—§ 6.9(f) n.141

Hopkins v. State, 582 N.E.2d 345 (Ind.1991)—§ 7.5(a) n.8

Hopkins v. State, 24 Md.App. 53, 329 A.2d 738 (1974)—§§ 15.3(d) n.70; 15.4(g) n.168, 171, 172, 185

Hopkins, United States v., 433 F.2d 1041 (5th Cir.1970)—§ 6.8(b) n.59

Hopkins v. United States, 344 F.2d 229 (8th Cir.1965)—§ 15.4(b) n.36

Hopkins v. United States, 171 U.S. 578, 19 S.Ct. 40, 43 L.Ed. 290 (1898)—§ 1.2(c) n.123

Hopkinson v. Shillinger, 866 F.2d 1185 (10th Cir.1989)—§ 11.8(c) n.60

Hopkinson v. State, 679 P.2d 1008 (Wyo.1984)—§ 22.4(b) n.20

Hopkinson v. State, 632 P.2d 79 (Wyo.1981)—§§ 16.2(a) n.10; 16.4(c) n.63

Hoppe, State v., 261 Wis.2d 294, 661 N.W.2d 407 (2003)—§ 6.2(c) n.184

Hopper v. Evans, 456 U.S. 605, 102 S.Ct. 2049, 72 L.Ed.2d 367 (1982)—§ 24.8(f) n.98

Hopper v. Hampton, 244 Ga. 361, 260 S.E.2d 73 (1979)—§ 19.2(e) n.54

Hopper, State v., 118 Wash.2d 151, 822 P.2d 775 (1992)—§§ 19.2(c) n.22; 19.3(a) n.52

Hopper v. State, 205 Tenn. 246, 326 S.W.2d 448 (1959)—§ 16.1(d) n.142

Hoppett, The, 11 U.S. (7 Cranch) 389, 3 L.Ed. 380 (1813)—§ 19.2(a) n.2

Hopson v. State, 625 So.2d 395 (Miss.1993)—§ 9.1(b) n.80

Hopson, State v., 112 Ariz. 497, 543 P.2d 1126 (1975)—§ 26.4(g) n.141

Hopson v. State, 201 Tenn. 337, 299 S.W.2d 11 (1957)—§ 16.1(g) n.278

Hopson, United States v., 39 F.3d 795 (7th Cir.1994)—§§ 26.10(c) n.43, 49

Hopt v. Utah, 110 U.S. 574, 4 S.Ct. 202, 28 L.Ed. 262 (1884)—§§ 6.2(a) n.16; 24.2(a) n.5

Horan, In re, 271 Va. 258, 634 S.E.2d 675 (2006)—§ 13.2(a) n.5

Horelick, United States ex rel. v. Criminal Court, 366 F.Supp. 1140 (S.D.N.Y.1973)—§ 3.1(o) n.306

Horn v. Banks, 536 U.S. 266, 122 S.Ct. 2147, 153 L.Ed.2d 301 (2002)—§§ 28.6(a) n.3; 28.6(b) n.11, 12

Horn, People v., 790 P.2d 816 (Colo.1990)—§ 6.6(d) n.57

Horn, United States v., 187 F.3d 781 (8th Cir.1999)—§ 3.4(f) n.116

Horn, United States v., 29 F.3d 754 (1st Cir.1994)—§§ 27.3(b) n.16; 27.4(b) n.14; 27.4(d) n.52

Horn, United States v., 970 F.2d 728 (10th Cir.1992)—§ 9.3(e) n.58

Horn, United States v., 583 F.2d 1124 (10th Cir.1978)—§ 25.2(e) n.38

Hornaday, United States v., 392 F.3d 1306 (11th Cir.2004)—§ 1.2(c) n.173

Hornbeck, State v., 492 S.W.2d 802 (Mo.1973)—§ 10.3(b) n.31

Hornbeck, State ex rel. v. Durflinger, 73 Ohio St. 154, 76 N.E. 291 (1905)— § 16.3(d) n.53

Hornbuckle, State v., 769 S.W.2d 89 (Mo.1989)—§ 7.4(d) n.74

Horne v. State, 825 So.2d 627 (Miss.2002)—§§ 22.3(d) n.212, 249, 250

Horne, State v., 140 N.H. 90, 663 A.2d 92 (1995)—§ 21.5(a) n.24

Horne, United States v., 987 F.2d 833 (D.C.Cir.1993)—§§ 21.2(g) n.395; 21.4(d) n.104; 21.5(a) n.43

Horner, State v., 112 Ariz. 432, 543 P.2d 118 (1975)—§ 15.7(g) n.203

Horness, State v., 600 N.W.2d 294 (Iowa 1999)—§§ 21.2(d) n.167, 169

Hornsby, State v., 8 Rob. (La.) 554 (1844)—§ 19.1(b) n.13

Horowitz, In re, 482 F.2d 72 (2d Cir.1973)—§§ 8.7(a) n.2, 10, 24; 8.7(b) n.34, 39, 44

Horowitz, United States v., 756 F.2d 1400 (9th Cir.1985)—§ 18.5(b) n.65

Horr, United States v., 963 F.2d 1124 (8th Cir.1992)—§ 4.6(l) n.201

Horrocks, State v., 17 P.3d 1145 (Utah App.2001)—§ 25.1(d) n.77

Horse, State v., 644 N.W.2d 211 (S.D.2002)—§§ 6.9(b) n.22, 23

Horsley, United States v., 864 F.2d 1543 (11th Cir.1989)—§ 22.3(d) n.245

Horton v. California, 496 U.S. 128, 110 S.Ct. 2301, 110 L.Ed.2d 112 (1990)—§§ 3.1(d) n.93; 3.2(b) n.32, 38; 3.4(k) n.223, 231, 237; 3.6(g) n.159, 166, 168; 3.7(d) n.64; 3.7(f) n.133, 145; 4.8(e) n.52, 55

Horton, Commonwealth v., 434 Mass. 823, 753 N.E.2d 119 (2001)— § 24.1(a) n.4

Horton v. Dugger, 895 F.2d 714 (11th Cir.1990)—§ 11.5(d) n.72

Horton v. Goose Creek School District, 690 F.2d 470 (5th Cir.1982)— § 3.2(b) n.71

Horton v. Mayle, 408 F.3d 570 (9th Cir.2005)—§ 24.3(b) n.35

Horton, People v., 11 Cal.4th 1068, 47 Cal.Rptr.2d 516, 906 P.2d 478 (1995)—§§ 11.4(a) n.8 to 10, 12, 15; 26.4(f) n.107

Horton, People v., 65 Ill.2d 413, 3 Ill.Dec. 436, 358 N.E.2d 1121 (1976)—§§ 14.1(a) n.3; 14.4(c) n.49

Horton, State v., 305 Mont. 242, 25 P.3d 886 (2001)—§ 21.2(b) n.60

Horton, State v., 203 W.Va. 9, 506 S.E.2d 46 (1998)—§ 6.2(c) n.122

Horton v. State, 584 So.2d 764 (Miss.1991)—§ 21.5(c) n.88

Horton, United States v., 845 F.2d 1414 (7th Cir.1988)—§§ 11.9(d) n.208, 210

Horton v. Zant, 941 F.2d 1449 (11th Cir.1991)—§ 11.10(c) n.80

Horwat, Commonwealth v., 511 Pa. 398, 515 A.2d 514 (1986)—§ 7.2(d) n.48

Horwitz, United States v., 622 F.2d 1101 (2d Cir.1980)—§ 27.3(c) n.44

Horzempa v. State, 292 Ala. 140, 290 So.2d 220 (1974)—§ 3.3(c) n.126

Hosea, State v., 199 W.Va. 62, 483 S.E.2d 62 (1996)—§ 21.6(b) n.102

Hosey, State v., 134 Idaho 883, 11 P.3d 1101 (2000)—§ 21.6(b) n.84

Hosford, United States v., 782 F.2d 936 (11th Cir.1986)—§§ 22.5(c) n.26, 27

Hoskins v. Maricle, 150 S.W.3d 1 (Ky.2004)—§§ 21.3(e) n.268, 270, 281

Hoskins, State v., 199 Ariz. 127, 14 P.3d 997 (2000)—§ 7.4(f) n.100

Hoskins v. State, 702 So.2d 202 (Fla.1997)—§ 22.2(d) n.68

Hoskins, State v., 292 Minn. 111, 193 N.W.2d 802 (1972)—§ 6.9(b) n.36

Hoskins, United States v., 243 F.3d 407 (7th Cir.2001)—§ 11.3(c) n.62

Hoslett, United States v., 998 F.2d 648 (9th Cir.1993)—§ 18.3(b) n.25

Hosteen, State v., 122 N.M. 228, 923 P.2d 595 (App.1996)—§ 11.7(e) n.72

Hoster, United States v., 988 F.2d 1374 (5th Cir.1993)—§ 21.4(d) n.104

Hott v. Yarbrough, 112 Tex. 179, 245 S.W. 676 (Tex.1922)—§ 8.4(b) n.88

Houchin v. State, 581 N.E.2d 1228 (Ind.1991)—§ 3.6(a) n.31

Houck, Commonwealth v., 233 Pa.Super. 512, 335 A.2d 389 (1975)—§ 13.2(c) n.77

Hough, State v., 571 N.W.2d 578 (Minn.App.1997)—§ 6.2(c) n.154

Houghton v. State, 6 P.3d 643 (Wyo.2000)—§ 6.4(f) n.137

Houle v. State, 482 N.W.2d 24 (N.D.1992)—§ 21.4(d) n.119

Hourigan v. Commonwealth, 962 S.W.2d 860 (Ky.1998)—§ 6.6(e) n.89

Housden v. Leverette, 161 W.Va. 324, 241 S.E.2d 810 (1978)—§ 11.8(c) n.54

House v. Bell, _____ U.S. _____, 126 S.Ct. 2064, 165 L.Ed.2d 1 (2006)—§§ 28.3(e) n.99, 101; 28.4(e) n.77

House, People v., 141 Ill.2d 323, 152 Ill.Dec. 572, 566 N.E.2d 259 (1990)—§ 6.2(c) n.89

House, People v., 98 Ill.App.3d 304, 53 Ill.Dec. 777, 424 N.E.2d 412 (1981)—§ 26.10(c) n.50

House v. State, 44 S.W.3d 508 (Tenn.2001)—§ 21.3(b) n.45

House, State v., 127 N.M. 151, 978 P.2d 967 (N.M.1999)—§§ 16.1(h) n.287; 16.3(d) n.71; 16.3(g) n.119, 129; 23.2(a) n.43

House, State v., 124 N.M. 564, 953 P.2d 737 (1997)—§ 23.2(a) n.43

House v. State, 380 So.2d 940 (Ala.1979)—§ 19.6(b) n.19

House, State v., 260 Or. 138, 489 P.2d 381 (1971)—§ 19.4(b) n.10

House, United States v., 939 F.2d 659 (8th Cir.1991)—§ 6.9(e) n.88

House, United States v., 524 F.2d 1035 (3d Cir.1975)—§ 3.10(e) n.181

Housel v. Head, 238 F.3d 1289 (11th Cir.2001)—§ 11.10(c) n.127

Houser, State v., 241 Neb. 525, 490 N.W.2d 168 (1992)—§§ 3.10(b) n.76; 6.7(b) n.73

Houston v. Moore, 18 U.S. (5 Wheat) 1, 5 L.Ed. 19 (1820)—§§ 1.2(c) n.43, 79

Houston, People v., 174 Ill.App.3d 584, 124 Ill.Dec. 472, 529 N.E.2d 292 (1988)—§§ 14.2(e) n.72, 76

Houston, State v., 122 N.C.App. 648, 471 S.E.2d 127 (1996)—§ 27.5(c) n.102

Houston, State v., 197 W.Va. 215, 475 S.E.2d 307 (1996)—§§ 5.2(a) n.4; 5.3(d) n.43

Houston v. State, 299 Ark. 7, 771 S.W.2d 16 (1989)—§ 3.4(a) n.15

Hovanec, People v., 76 Ill.App.3d 401, 394 N.E.2d 1340 (1979)—§ 14.3(d) n.91

Hove, United States v., 848 F.2d 137 (9th Cir.1988)—§ 3.1(c) n.79

Hovey v. Ayers, 458 F.3d 892 (9th Cir.2006)—§ 13.1(b) n.33

Hovey, People v., 44 Cal.3d 543, 244 Cal.Rptr. 121, 749 P.2d 776 (1988)—§ 6.4(e) n.95

Hovey, State v., 106 N.M. 300, 742 P.2d 512 (1987)—§§ 23.3(b) n.27, 28

Hovey v. Superior Court, 28 Cal.3d 1, 168 Cal.Rptr. 128, 616 P.2d 1301 (1980)—§§ 1.7(i) n.202, 207; 1.8(e) n.91

Hovind, State v., 431 N.W.2d 366 (Iowa 1988)—§§ 21.2(d) n.242; 21.2(h) n.423

Howard, Ex parte, 710 So.2d 460 (Ala.1997)—§ 17.4(a) n.42

Howard v. Beto, 466 F.2d 1356 (5th Cir.1972)—§ 21.3(b) n.56

Howard v. Bouchard, 405 F.3d 459 (6th Cir.2005)—§§ 7.4(b) n.33; 7.4(d) n.70; 28.4(c) n.31; 28.6(f) n.77

Howard, People v., 92 P.3d 445 (Colo.2004)—§§ 6.6(c) n.31; 6.6(e) n.61

Howard, People v., 16 Cal.4th 1081, 946 P.2d 828, 68 Cal.Rptr.2d 870 (1997)—§ 26.10(d) n.90

Howard v. Senkowski, 986 F.2d 24 (2d Cir.1993)—§ 22.3(d) n.228

Howard, State v., 127 Wash.App. 862, 113 P.3d 511 (2005)—§ 24.10(c) n.40

Howard v. State, 710 So.2d 456 (Ala.Crim.App.1996)—§ 25.4(d) n.46

Howard, State v., 176 Wis.2d 921, 501 N.W.2d 9 (1993)—§ 9.1(d) n.120

Howard v. State, 106 Nev. 713, 800 P.2d 175 (1990)—§ 24.7(e) n.50

Howard, State v., 110 N.J. 113, 539 A.2d 1203 (1988)—§ 21.4(d) n.118

Howard, State v., 295 S.C. 462, 369 S.E.2d 132 (1988)—§ 17.2(b) n.38

Howard v. State, 181 Ga.App. 187, 351 S.E.2d 550 (1986)—§§ 16.1(g) n.275, 280

Howard, State v., 373 N.W.2d 596 (Minn.1985)—§ 3.6(a) n.35

Howard, State v., 56 Ohio St.2d 328, 383 N.E.2d 912 (1978)—§ 20.5(e) n.69

Howard, United States v., 480 F.3d 1005, 2007 WL 900125 (9th Cir.2007)—§ 24.2(e) n.66

Howard v. United States, 374 F.3d 1068 (11th Cir.2004)—§§ 28.6(d) n.36; 28.6(e) n.49; 28.9(b) n.49

Howard, United States v., 381 F.3d 873 (9th Cir.2004)—§ 21.3(b) n.54

Howard, United States v., 218 F.3d 556 (6th Cir.2000)—§§ 18.2(e) n.84; 22.4(c) n.29

Howard v. United States, 135 F.3d 506 (7th Cir.1998)—§ 21.4(f) n.179

Howard, United States v., 80 F.3d 1194 (7th Cir.1996)—§ 24.9(c) n.28

Howard, United States v., 894 F.2d 1085 (9th Cir.1990)—§§ 21.2(d) n.198, 200, 201

Howard, United States v., 867 F.2d 548 (9th Cir.1989)—§§ 8.8(h) n.184; 15.6(f) n.192

Howard, United States v., 577 F.2d 269 (5th Cir.1978)—§ 18.5(c) n.75

Howe, State v., 129 N.H. 120, 523 A.2d 94 (1987)—§ 7.4(c) n.52

Howe v. State, 589 P.2d 421 (Alaska 1979)—§ 20.3(h) n.143

Howell, Ex parte, 34 Okl.Cr. 126, 245 P. 66 (1926)—§ 12.4(a) n.5

Howell, Commonwealth v., 394 Mass. 654, 477 N.E.2d 126 (1985)— § 7.4(b) n.9

Howell v. Mississippi, 543 U.S. 440, 125 S.Ct. 856, 160 L.Ed.2d 873 (2005)—§§ 24.8(f) n.91, 95

Howell, People v., 60 Ill.2d 117, 324 N.E.2d 403 (1975)—§ 14.2(g) n.97

Howell v. State, 185 S.W.3d 319 (Tenn.2006)—§§ 21.2(b) n.57; 21.4(a) n.38

Howell v. State, 860 So.2d 704 (Miss.2003)—§§ 7.4(c) n.51; 7.4(d) n.69

Howell v. State, 350 Ark. 552, 89 S.W.3d 343 (2002)—§ 3.3(d) n.161

Howell, State v., 254 Neb. 247, 575 N.W.2d 861 (1998)—§ 17.4(b) n.124

Howell v. State, 882 P.2d 1086 (Okla.Crim.App.1994)—§ 14.1(d) n.55

Howell, State v., 868 S.W.2d 238 (Tenn.1993)—§ 22.3(a) n.4

Howell, State v., 838 S.W.2d 158 (Mo.App.1992)—§ 9.6(a) n.35

Howell, State v., 222 Mont. 136, 720 P.2d 1174 (1986)—§ 26.10(b) n.18

Howell, State v., 707 P.2d 115 (Utah 1985)—§ 21.2(d) n.212

Howell, State v., 56 Or.App. 6, 641 P.2d 37 (1982)—§ 20.5(b) n.25

Howell v. State, 48 Md.App. 89, 425 A.2d 1361 (1981)—§ 11.5(e) n.87

Howell v. State, 632 P.2d 1223 (Okla.Cr.App.1981)—§ 26.2(b) n.15

Howell v. State, 421 A.2d 892 (Del.1980)—§ 26.5(c) n.49

Howell, State v., 226 Kan. 511, 601 P.2d 1141 (1979)—§ 19.3(a) n.57

Howell v. State, 271 Md. 378, 318 A.2d 189 (1974)—§ 3.7(a) n.6

Howell v. State, 5 Md.App. 337, 247 A.2d 291 (1968)—§ 6.7(c) n.108

Howell, United States v., 425 F.3d 971 (11th Cir.2005)—§ 10.1(c) n.48

Howell, United States v., 936 F.Supp. 767 (D.Kan.1996)—§ 11.4(c) n.56

Howell v. United States, 455 A.2d 1371 (D.C.App.1983)—§ 27.5(a) n.3

Howell, United States v., 719 F.2d 1258 (5th Cir.1983)—§ 18.3(b) n.7

Howerton v. State, 640 P.2d 566 (Okla.Crim.1982)—§ 11.9(d) n.211

Howie v. Commonwealth, 222 Va. 625, 283 S.E.2d 197 (1981)— §§ 26.10(b) n.38; 26.10(d) n.86

Howington, State v., 907 S.W.2d 403 (Tenn.1995)—§§ 8.11(e) n.97, 101, 104, 109, 110; 13.5(b) n.36, 39

Howle, United States v., 166 F.3d 1166 (11th Cir.1999)—§§ 21.2(b) n.76; 21.2(d) n.152

Howlett v. State, 51 Md.App. 162, 441 A.2d 1112 (1982)—§ 26.10(c) n.57

Hoyer v. State, 180 Wis. 407, 193 N.W. 89 (1923)—§ 2.12(a) n.9

Hoyne, People ex rel. v. Newcomer, 284 Ill. 315, 120 N.E. 244 (1918)— § 13.3(c) n.36

Hoyt v. United States, 273 F. 792 (2d Cir.1921)—§ 27.6(b) n.12

Hristler, United States v., 396 F.3d 1044 (9th Cir.2005)—§ 13.5(h) n.147

Hsia, United States v., 131 F.Supp.2d 195 (D.D.C.2001)—§ 8.11(c) n.55

Hsu, United States v., 852 F.2d 407 (9th Cir.1988)—§ 6.9(f) n.106

Hsu v. United States, 392 A.2d 972 (D.C.App.1978)—§§ 11.3(b) n.32 to 34, 38; 11.5(c) n.36, 54, 55; 19.3(b) n.155

Huang, United States v., 178 F.3d 184 (3d Cir.1999)—§§ 21.2(d) n.249, 255, 257

Huante, People v., 143 Ill.2d 61, 156 Ill.Dec. 756, 571 N.E.2d 736 (1991)—§ 21.3(b) n.66

Hubanks v. Frank, 392 F.3d 926 (7th Cir.2004)—§§ 24.3(e) n.120; 28.7(d) n.26

Hubbard, Commonwealth v., 777 S.W.2d 882 (Ky.1989)—§ 13.3(b) n.20

Hubbard, State v., 267 Neb. 316, 673 N.W.2d 567 (2004)—§ 22.4(c) n.29

Hubbard, State v., 48 P.3d 953 (Utah 2002)—§§ 7.4(e) n.82; 7.5(b) n.21

Hubbard v. State, 112 Nev. 946, 920 P.2d 991 (1996)—§ 18.5(a) n.50

Hubbard v. United States, 514 U.S. 695, 115 S.Ct. 1754, 131 L.Ed.2d 779 (1995)—§§ 2.9(b) n.17; 8.3(b) n.14

Hubbard, United States v., 650 F.2d 293 (D.C.Cir.1980)—§ 23.1(d) n.188

Hubbard, United States v., 603 F.2d 137 (10th Cir.1979)—§ 27.5(c) n.100

Hubbell v. State, 754 N.E.2d 884 (Ind.2001)—§ 7.4(f) n.95

Hubbell, United States v., 530 U.S. 27, 120 S.Ct. 2037, 147 L.Ed.2d 24 (2000)—§§ 2.10(c) n.94; 8.12(d) n.47; 8.12(g) n.71, 77; 8.13(a) n.33; 8.13(b) n.65; 8.13(c) n.79; 9.5(b) n.52; 15.7(d) n.78

Hubbell, United States v., 167 F.3d 552 (D.C.Cir.1999)—§§ 8.13(a) n.10, 14, 44; 8.13(b) n.58, 61; 8.13(c) n.77, 81

Huberts, United States v., 637 F.2d 630 (9th Cir.1980)—§§ 3.1(f) n.145; 15.5(a) n.9

Huckaby, State v., 15 Wash. App. 280, 549 P.2d 35 (1976)—§ 3.6(b) n.53

Huckaby, United States v., 43 F.3d 135 (5th Cir.1995)—§ 26.5(c) n.59

Huckelbury v. State, 337 So.2d 400 (Fla.App.1976)—§ 11.8(c) n.75

Hudacek, United States v., 24 F.3d 143 (11th Cir.1994)—§ 27.5(b) n.40

Huddleston v. Commonwealth, 171 Ky. 310, 188 S.W. 398 (1916)— § 16.4(c) n.54

Huddleston, United States v., 194 F.3d 214 (1st Cir.1999)—§ 24.11(d) n.28

Huddleston, State ex rel. v. Sawyer, 324 Or. 597, 932 P.2d 1145 (1997)— § 26.4(g) n.137

Hudgens v. State, 324 Ark. 169, 919 S.W.2d 939 (1996)—§ 26.8(b) n.14

Hudgens, United States v., 798 F.2d 1234 (9th Cir.1986)—§§ 6.6(a) n.7; 6.6(d) n.45

Hudgins v. State, 292 Md. 342, 438 A.2d 928 (1982)—§§ 26.9(b) n.20; 26.9(c) n.93

Hudson v. Hunt, 235 F.3d 892 (4th Cir.2000)—§ 11.10(c) n.92

Hudson v. Louisiana, 450 U.S. 40, 101 S.Ct. 970, 67 L.Ed.2d 30 (1981)— § 25.4(b) n.14

Hudson v. McMillian, 503 U.S. 1, 112 S.Ct. 995, 117 L.Ed.2d 156 (1992)—§§ 2.9(d) n.87, 93

Hudson v. Michigan, _____ U.S. _____, 126 S.Ct. 2159, 165 L.Ed.2d 56 (2006)—§§ 3.1(c) n.89; 3.1(f) n.163; 3.4(h) n.138; 3.4(l) n.244; 3.6(b) n.64; 9.3(b) n.15; 9.3(c) n.30; 9.3(e) n.58

Hudson v. Palmer, 468 U.S. 517, 104 S.Ct. 3194, 82 L.Ed.2d 393 (1984)—§ 3.9(i) n.179

Hudson, People v., 195 Ill.2d 117, 253 Ill.Dec. 712, 745 N.E.2d 1246 (2001)—§ 22.3(d) n.228

Hudson v. Rushen, 686 F.2d 826 (9th Cir.1982)—§ 11.4(b) n.28

Hudson, State v., 346 S.C. 139, 551 S.E.2d 253 (2001)—§ 6.2(c) n.90

Hudson, State v., 129 Idaho 478, 927 P.2d 451 (App.1996)—§ 24.8(d) n.46

Hudson, State v., 331 N.C. 122, 415 S.E.2d 732 (1992)—§ 21.2(f) n.383

Hudson v. State, 675 S.W.2d 507 (Tex.Cr.App.1984)—§§ 7.4(b) n.23; 7.4(f) n.96

Hudson v. State, 268 Ind. 310, 375 N.E.2d 195 (1978)—§ 11.9(d) n.188

Hudson, State v., 295 N.C. 427, 245 S.E.2d 686 (1978)—§§ 14.2(c) n.40; 14.2(g) n.99

Hudson, State v., 508 S.W.2d 707 (Mo.1974)—§ 7.4(f) n.96

Hudson, United States v., 207 F.3d 852 (6th Cir.2000)—§ 26.10(d) n.90

Hudson, United States v., 210 F.3d 1184 (10th Cir.2000)—§§ 6.6(c) n.31, 33

Hudson v. United States, 522 U.S. 93, 118 S.Ct. 488, 139 L.Ed.2d 450 (1997)—§§ 2.1 n.54; 17.4(b) n.116; 25.1(b) n.19; 25.1(c) n.31, 39

Hudson, United States v., 100 F.3d 1409 (9th Cir.1996)—§ 3.1(d) n.119

Hudson, United States v., 11 U.S. (7 Cranch) 32, 3 L.Ed. 259 (1812)— § 1.2(c) n.35

Hudson v. Warden, 117 Nev. 387, 22 P.3d 1154 (2001)—§ 21.4(d) n.101

Hudson, United States ex rel. v. Cannon, 529 F.2d 890 (7th Cir.1976)— § 9.5(d) n.80

Huebner v. State, 103 Nev. 29, 731 P.2d 1330 (1987)—§ 6.3(c) n.49

Huerstel, State v., 206 Ariz. 93, 75 P.3d 698 (2003)—§§ 6.2(c) n.113, 163

Huey, United States v., 76 F.3d 638 (5th Cir.1996)—§ 22.3(d) n.205

Huff, Commonwealth v., 540 Pa. 535, 658 A.2d 1340 (1995)—§ 27.5(c) n.82

Huff v. Commonwealth, 213 Va. 710, 194 S.E.2d 690 (1973)—§ 3.3(g) n.234

Huff v. State, 325 Md. 55, 599 A.2d 428 (1991)—§ 17.4(b) n.113

Huff, State v., 180 W.Va. 75, 375 S.E.2d 438 (1988)—§§ 21.5(a) n.38, 39

Huff, United States v., 959 F.2d 731 (8th Cir.1992)—§§ 5.4(c) n.44; 13.4(e) n.165

Huffaker, State v., 493 N.W.2d 832 (Iowa 1992)—§ 22.2(d) n.76

Huffhines, United States v., 967 F.2d 314 (9th Cir.1992)—§ 3.2(c) n.103

Huffman v. Pursue, Limited, 420 U.S. 592, 95 S.Ct. 1200, 43 L.Ed.2d 482 (1975)—§ 13.5(e) n.94

Hufford, United States v., 539 F.2d 32 (9th Cir.1976)—§ 3.2(j) n.243

Hufnagel, People v., 745 P.2d 242 (Colo.1987)—§ 3.6(c) n.82

Huggins, People v., 38 Cal.4th 175, 41 Cal.Rptr.3d 593, 131 P.3d 995 (2006)—§§ 6.4(g) n.154; 7.4(c) n.51; 9.6(a) n.35

Hughes v. Booker, 220 F.3d 346 (5th Cir.2000)—§§ 11.2(c) n.106, 107

Hughes, Commonwealth v., 380 Mass. 583, 404 N.E.2d 1239 (1980)—§§ 8.13(e) n.116; 20.4(b) n.28, 33

Hughes v. Idaho State Board of Corrections, 800 F.2d 905 (9th Cir.1986)—§ 28.4(d) n.65

Hughes, People v., 27 Cal.4th 287, 116 Cal.Rptr.2d 401, 39 P.3d 432 (2002)—§ 24.8(f) n.98

Hughes, People v., 767 P.2d 1201 (Colo.1989)—§ 3.1(d) n.103

Hughes v. Rizzo, 282 F.Supp. 881 (E.D.Pa.1968)—§ 3.1(n) n.301

Hughes v. State, 347 Ark. 696, 66 S.W.3d 645 (2002)—§ 25.3(c) n.30

Hughes v. State, 807 So.2d 426 (Miss.2001)—§ 24.2(b) n.27

Hughes, State v., 233 Wis.2d 280, 607 N.W.2d 621 (2000)—§ 3.6(e) n.112

Hughes, State v., 136 N.C.App. 92, 524 S.E.2d 63 (1999)—§ 19.3(a) n.13

Hughes v. State, 735 So.2d 238 (Miss.1999)—§ 7.4(a) n.7

Hughes v. State, 346 Md. 80, 695 A.2d 132 (1997)—§ 6.7(b) n.45

Hughes v. State, 112 Nev. 84, 910 P.2d 254 (1996)—§ 27.5(b) n.47

Hughes v. State, 217 Ga.App. 766, 458 S.E.2d 911 (1995)—§ 24.9(c) n.21

Hughes, State v., 653 So.2d 748 (La.App.1995)—§ 11.8(c) n.70

Hughes v. State, 897 S.W.2d 285 (Tex.Cr.App.1994)—§ 9.1(d) n.132

Hughes v. State, 843 S.W.2d 591 (Tex.Cr.App.1992)—§ 3.4(e) n.91

Hughes v. State, 259 Ga. 227, 378 S.E.2d 853 (1989)—§ 6.7(a) n.3

Hughes, State v., 713 S.W.2d 11 (Mo.App.1986)—§ 26.6(b) n.21

Hughes v. State, 437 A.2d 559 (Del.1981)—§§ 23.1(b) n.32; 24.5(b) n.33

Hughes, State v., 41 Ohio St.2d 208, 324 N.E.2d 731 (1975)—§ 1.7(f) n.105

Hughes v. United States, 689 A.2d 1206 (D.C.App.1997)—§ 27.6(d) n.142

Hughes, United States v., 15 F.3d 798 (8th Cir.1994)—§ 3.8(e) n.196

Hughes, United States v., 964 F.2d 536 (6th Cir.1992)—§ 27.5(b) n.45

Hughes, United States v., 970 F.2d 227 (7th Cir.1992)—§ 27.5(e) n.145

Hughes, United States v., 911 F.2d 113 (8th Cir.1990)—§ 22.3(d) n.247

Hughes, United States v., 429 F.2d 1293 (10th Cir.1970)—§ 8.5(c) n.81

Hughey, United States v., 147 F.3d 423 (5th Cir.1998)—§§ 11.4(c) n.63, 73

Huginski, State v., 139 Vt. 95, 422 A.2d 935 (1980)—§ 16.4(c) n.60

Hugueley, State v., 185 S.W.3d 356 (Tenn.2006)—§§ 22.3(a) n.46; 22.3(c) n.102

Huguenin, United States v., 950 F.2d 23 (1st Cir.1991)—§ 22.3(b) n.80

Huguet, State v., 369 So.2d 1331 (La.1979)—§ 19.4(a) n.8

Huguez v. United States, 406 F.2d 366 (9th Cir.1968)—§§ 3.9(f) n.105; 7.2(c) n.43

Huguley v. People, 195 Colo. 259, 577 P.2d 746 (1978)—§ 10.3(d) n.71

Huie, United States v., 593 F.2d 14 (5th Cir.1979)—§ 4.2(a) n.8

Huihui v. Shimoda, 64 Haw. 527, 644 P.2d 968 (1982)—§§ 12.3(b) n.46; 12.3(g) n.153

Hulbert, State v., 265 Mont. 317, 877 P.2d 25 (1994)—§ 3.3(c) n.97

Hull, Ex parte, 312 U.S. 546, 61 S.Ct. 640, 85 L.Ed. 1034 (1941)—§ 11.2(f) n.231

Hull, State v., 210 Conn. 481, 556 A.2d 154 (1989)—§ 9.6(a) n.51

Hull v. State, 699 S.W.2d 220 (Tex.Cr.App.1985)—§ 18.2(d) n.62

Hull, United States v., 419 F.3d 762 (8th Cir.2005)—§§ 6.7(c) n.118; 6.9(f) n.139

Hullum, State v., 273 Kan. 282, 43 P.3d 806 (2002)—§ 6.9(g) n.189

Hulstine v. Morris, 819 F.2d 861 (8th Cir.1987)—§ 19.2(c) n.27

Hummel, State v., 483 N.W.2d 68 (Minn.1992)—§ 24.3(b) n.72

Humphrey v. Commonwealth, 962 S.W.2d 870 (Ky.1998)—§§ 11.7(e) n.66, 70, 79

Humphrey, People v., 132 P.3d 352 (Colo.2006)—§§ 6.2(c) n.183; 6.8(d) n.84

Humphrey v. State, 290 Md. 164, 428 A.2d 440 (1981)—§ 26.10(c) n.50

Humphrey, State v., 217 Kan. 352, 537 P.2d 155 (1975)—§§ 20.3(a) n.15, 21; 20.3(g) n.127

Humphrey v. United States, 888 F.2d 1546 (11th Cir.1989)—§ 13.7(c) n.52

Humphreys, State v., 251 Or. 63, 444 P.2d 476 (1968)—§ 6.8(a) n.10

Hundley v. Ashworth, 181 W.Va. 379, 382 S.E.2d 573 (1989)—§ 18.5(b) n.69

Hunnel, State v., 125 Idaho 623, 873 P.2d 877 (1994)—§ 11.5(c) n.52

Hunnicutt v. State, 531 S.W.2d 618 (Tex.Cr.App.1976)—§ 10.2(c) n.30

Hunsberger, Commonwealth v., 523 Pa. 92, 565 A.2d 152 (1989)—§ 9.6(a) n.51

Hunsucker v. Phinney, 497 F.2d 29 (5th Cir.1974)—§§ 10.1(c) n.37, 39

Hunt v. Mitchell, 261 F.3d 575 (6th Cir.2001)—§§ 11.8(c) n.64; 11.10(d) n.204

Hunt v. National Broadcasting Co., 872 F.2d 289 (9th Cir.1989)—§ 23.1(c) n.107

Hunt, People v., 442 Mich. 359, 501 N.W.2d 151 (1993)—§ 14.3(d) n.85

Hunt v. Roth, 648 F.2d 1148 (8th Cir.1981)—§§ 2.6(b) n.37; 12.3(c) n.87; 12.3(e) n.114

Hunt, State v., 275 Kan. 811, 69 P.3d 571 (2003)—§ 7.4(c) n.47

Hunt, State v., 357 N.C. 257, 582 S.E.2d 593 (2003)—§§ 19.3(a) n.42, 44

Hunt, State v., 615 N.W.2d 294 (Minn.2000)—§ 24.3(b) n.49

Hunt v. State, 613 So.2d 893 (Fla.1992)—§§ 21.2(d) n.242; 21.2(e) n.308

Hunt, State v., 115 N.J. 330, 558 A.2d 1259 (1989)—§ 22.3(a) n.35

Hunt, State v., 150 Vt. 483, 555 A.2d 369 (1988)—§ 6.9(g) n.176

Hunt, State v., 91 N.J. 338, 450 A.2d 952 (1982)—§§ 2.12(b) n.104; 2.12(c) n.119, 121

Hunt, State v., 57 Idaho 122, 62 P.2d 1372 (1936)—§ 15.6(a) n.6

Hunt v. Texas, 994 S.W.2d 206 (Tex.App.1999)—§ 19.3(e) n.221

Hunt, United States v., 372 F.3d 1010 (8th Cir.2004)—§ 6.7(d) n.148

Hunt, United States v., 205 F.3d 931 (6th Cir.2000)—§ 21.5(d) n.104

Hunt, United States v., 171 F.3d 1192 (8th Cir.1999)—§ 5.4(c) n.44

Hunt v. United States, 2 F.3d 96 (5th Cir.1993)—§ 10.1(c) n.40

Hunt, United States v., 749 F.2d 1078 (4th Cir.1984)—§ 5.3(a) n.7

Hunt, United States v., 496 F.2d 888 (5th Cir.1974)—§ 3.4(d) n.59

Hunt, United States v., 505 F.2d 931 (5th Cir.1974)—§ 9.2(c) n.28

Hunt, United States v., 366 F.Supp. 172 (N.D.Tex.1973)—§ 3.7(f) n.144

Hunte, United States v., 193 F.3d 173 (3d Cir.1999)—§ 21.2(b) n.74

Hunter, In re, 520 F.Supp. 1020 (W.D.Mo.1981)—§§ 8.5(i) n.318, 324

Hunter v. Aispuro, 982 F.2d 344 (9th Cir.1992)—§ 28.4(c) n.27

Hunter, Commonwealth v., 426 Mass. 715, 690 N.E.2d 815 (1998)— § 6.3(c) n.53

Hunter v. District Court, 190 Colo. 48, 543 P.2d 1265 (1975)—§§ 14.3(a) n.25, 41; 14.3(b) n.52, 53

Hunter v. Fogg, 616 F.2d 55 (2d Cir.1980)—§ 21.4(d) n.146

Hunter, State v., 140 N.M. 406, 143 P.3d 168 (2006)—§ 21.3(b) n.58

Hunter, State v., 141 Or.App. 73, 918 P.2d 104 (1996)—§§ 19.2(a) n.1; 19.2(b) n.20; 19.2(d) n.46

Hunter v. State, 676 N.E.2d 14 (Ind.1996)—§ 21.5(a) n.24

Hunter v. State, 684 So.2d 625 (Miss.1996)—§ 24.7(e) n.70

Hunter, State v., 313 S.C. 53, 437 S.E.2d 41 (1993)—§ 22.5(a) n.1

Hunter, State v., 840 S.W.2d 850 (Mo.1992)—§ 11.5(g) n.112

Hunter, State v., 586 So.2d 319 (Fla.1991)—§ 5.1(c) n.34

Hunter v. State, 82 Md.App. 679, 573 A.2d 85 (1990)—§§ 11.1(b) n.91; 24.7(e) n.57

Hunter v. State, 590 P.2d 888 (Alaska 1979)—§ 6.6(c) n.34

Hunter, United States v., 13 F.Supp.2d 586 (D.Vt.1998)—§ 19.4(b) n.28

Hunter, United States v., 692 A.2d 1370 (D.C.App.1997)—§§ 7.4(b) n.23; 27.5(a) n.32

Hunter, United States v., 672 F.2d 815 (10th Cir.1982)—§§ 16.3(c) n.36, 40

Hunter v. United States, 272 F. 235 (4th Cir.1921)—§ 15.1(b) n.71

Huntley, United States v., 535 F.2d 1400 (5th Cir.1976)—§ 27.6(d) n.110

Huntsville, City of v. Shanes, 645 So.2d 339 (Ala.App.1994)—§ 27.3(c) n.30

Hurley, United States v., 63 F.3d 1 (1st Cir.1995)—§ 19.3(a) n.68

Hurlich, United States v., 293 F.3d 1223 (10th Cir.2002)—§ 21.4(d) n.106

Hursey, State v., 176 Ariz. 330, 861 P.2d 615 (1993)—§ 22.5(b) n.19

Hurst, State v., 688 N.E.2d 402 (Ind.1997)—§ 17.4(b) n.136

Hurst, United States v., 228 F.3d 751 (6th Cir.2000)—§§ 3.7(d) n.77; 6.9(g) n.154

Hurtado v. California, 110 U.S. 516, 4 S.Ct. 111, 28 L.Ed.2d 232 (1884)— §§ 2.3(b) n.83; 2.4(a) n.12; 2.4(c) n.88, 101, 109, 115; 2.4(d) n.119, 124, 125; 2.4(e) n.171; 2.4 n.3; 2.5(f) n.94; 2.6(b) n.33; 2.7(c) n.104, 175; 2.7(d) n.241; 8.2(b) n.15; 14.2(a) n.1; 15.1(b) n.64; 15.1(c) n.123, 124; 15.4(d) n.110

Hurtado, United States v., 905 F.2d 74 (5th Cir.1990)—§ 10.4(c) n.23

Hurwitz, United States v., 968 F.2d 1212 (4th Cir.1992)—§ 5.4(b) n.19

Huser, State ex rel. v. Rasmussen, 84 Wis.2d 600, 267 N.W.2d 285 (1978)—§ 14.4(c) n.57

Huskey, State v., 82 S.W.3d 297 (Tenn.App. 2002)—§ 11.4(b) n.46

Husky, United States v., 924 F.2d 223 (11th Cir.1991)—§ 26.6(c) n.36

Huss v. Graves, 252 F.3d 952 (8th Cir.2001)—§ 25.2(e) n.45

Hussein, People v., 150 Misc.2d 119, 568 N.Y.S.2d 296 (Sup.Ct.1991)— §§ 15.4(h) n.190, 193

Husske v. Commonwealth, 252 Va. 203, 476 S.E.2d 920 (1996)—§ 6.6(e) n.78

Huston, People v., 88 N.Y.2d 400, 646 N.Y.S.2d 69, 668 N.E.2d 1362 (1996)—§§ 15.6(a) n.29; 15.6(d) n.128; 15.7(b) n.27, 35; 15.7(c) n.59, 63, 64

Husty v. United States, 282 U.S. 694, 51 S.Ct. 240, 75 L.Ed. 629 (1931)— § 3.7(c) n.44

Hutcherson v. United States, 345 F.2d 964 (D.C.Cir.1965)—§ 13.7(a) n.15

Hutcheson, State v., 177 W.Va. 391, 352 S.E.2d 143 (1986)—§ 6.3(c) n.49

Hutchings, United States v., 757 F.2d 11 (2d Cir.1985)—§§ 21.1(e) n.78; 21.2(c) n.132

Hutchins, People v., 147 Cal.App.4th 992, 55 Cal.Rptr.3d 105 (2007)— § 22.3(d) n.236

Hutchins v. State, 493 N.E.2d 444 (Ind.1986)—§ 22.1(h) n.138

Hutchinson v. People, 742 P.2d 875 (Colo.1987)—§ 20.4(f) n.91

Hutchinson v. State, 292 Md. 367, 438 A.2d 1335 (1982)—§§ 20.3(f) n.108; 26.10(c) n.53, 55

Hutchison, State v., 957 S.W.2d 757 (Mo.1997)—§§ 6.5(b) n.26; 9.6(a) n.38

Hutto v. Ross, 429 U.S. 28, 97 S.Ct. 202, 50 L.Ed.2d 194 (1976)—§ 21.2(h) n.424

Hutul, United States v., 416 F.2d 607 (7th Cir.1969)—§§ 17.2(d) n.95; 17.3(e) n.64

Huu Thanh Nguyen v. Garcia, 477 F.3d 716 (9th Cir.2007)—§ 6.7(b) n.102

Huynh v. King, 95 F.3d 1052 (11th Cir.1996)—§ 11.10(c) n.81

Huynh Thi Anh v. Levi, 586 F.2d 625 (6th Cir.1978)—§ 1.7(c) n.16

Hyatt, Commonwealth v., 419 Mass. 815, 647 N.E.2d 1168 (1995)— §§ 7.5(a) n.9; 26.8(c) n.25

Hyatt, State v., 355 N.C. 642, 566 S.E.2d 61 (2002)—§§ 6.9(c) n.61; 6.9(g) n.166

Hyde v. State, 275 Ga. 693, 572 S.E.2d 562 (2002)—§ 3.2(f) n.176

Hyde, State v., 352 N.C. 37, 530 S.E.2d 281 (2000)—§ 6.2(c) n.152

Hyde, State v., 186 Ariz. 252, 921 P.2d 655 (1996)—§ 14.1(a) n.2

Hyde, United States v., 520 U.S. 670, 117 S.Ct. 1630, 137 L.Ed.2d 935 (1997)—§§ 21.2(f) n.363; 21.4(g) n.230, 252; 21.5(a) n.4

Hyde v. United States, 225 U.S. 347, 32 S.Ct. 793, 56 L.Ed. 1114 (1912)— §§ 16.2(g) n.109, 121

Hyder, State ex rel. v. Superior Court of Maricopa County, 128 Ariz. 253, 625 P.2d 316 (1981)—§ 8.13(a) n.18

Hyder, State ex rel. v. Superior Ct., 128 Ariz. 216, 624 P.2d 1264 (1981)— § 27.4(d) n.40

Hyde, United States ex rel. v. McMann, 263 F.2d 940 (2d Cir.1959)— § 12.2(c) n.41

Hygh, State v., 711 P.2d 264 (Utah 1985)—§ 1.7(j) n.234

Hyler v. State, 98 Nev. 47, 639 P.2d 560 (1982)—§ 26.10(c) n.69

Hylton v. Eighth Judicial District Court, 103 Nev. 418, 743 P.2d 622 (1987)—§ 25.2(d) n.34

Hylton, United States v., 294 F.3d 130 (D.C.Cir.2002)—§ 11.10(c) n.105

Hymon v. State, 121 Nev. 200, 111 P.3d 1092 (Nev.2005)—§ 24.2(e) n.68

Hynes v. Lerner, 44 N.Y.2d 329, 405 N.Y.S.2d 649, 376 N.E.2d 1294 (1978)—§ 8.8(f) n.145

Hynes v. Tomei, 92 N.Y.2d 613, 684 N.Y.S.2d 177, 706 N.E.2d 1201 (1998)—§ 21.2(a) n.5

Hyten, United States v., 5 F.3d 1154 (8th Cir.1993)—§ 3.3(e) n.182

I

Iaea v. Sunn, 800 F.2d 861 (9th Cir.1986)—§§ 21.2(g) n.399; 21.3(b) n.82; 21.4(b) n.44

Iafornaro, State v., 336 Mont. 489, 155 P.3d 1238 (2007)—§ 21.4(c) n.67

I & O Publishing Co., Inc. v. C.I.R., 131 F.3d 1314 (9th Cir.1997)— § 17.4(b) n.130

Ianniello, People v., 21 N.Y.2d 418, 288 N.Y.S.2d 462, 235 N.E.2d 439 (1968)—§§ 8.14(a) n.12; 8.14(c) n.36

Ianniello, United States v., 740 F.Supp. 171 (S.D.N.Y.1990)—§ 24.3(f) n.147

Iannone, People v., 45 N.Y.2d 589, 412 N.Y.S.2d 110, 384 N.E.2d 656 (1978)—§§ 19.1(a) n.8; 19.2(f) n.99, 104; 19.3(b) n.147

Ibanez, United States v., 924 F.2d 427 (2d Cir.1991)—§ 26.4(g) n.129

Ibar v. State, 938 So.2d 451 (Fla.2006)—§ 7.3(b) n.14

Ibarra, In re, 34 Cal.3d 277, 193 Cal.Rptr. 538, 666 P.2d 980 (1983)—§ 21.2(b) n.59

Ibarra, United States v., 955 F.2d 1405 (10th Cir.1992)—§ 9.3(e) n.66

Ibarra, United States v., 948 F.2d 903 (5th Cir.1991)—§ 3.10(f) n.192

Ibn-Tamas v. United States, 368 A.2d 520 (D.C.App.1977)—§ 21.3(b) n.137

Ibuos, State v., 75 Haw. 118, 857 P.2d 576 (1993)—§ 22.1(h) n.137

ICS Cybernetics, Inc., In re, 107 B.R. 821 (Bkrtcy.N.Y.1989)—§ 8.13(a) n.20

Idaho v. Wright, 497 U.S. 805, 110 S.Ct. 3139, 111 L.Ed.2d 638 (1990)—§ 2.8(a) n.6

Idowu, United States v., 74 F.3d 387 (2d Cir.1996)—§ 17.4(b) n.140

Ienco, United States v., 182 F.3d 517 (7th Cir.1999)—§§ 9.4(e) n.107, 110

Igbonwa, United States v., 120 F.3d 437 (3d Cir.1997)—§ 21.2(e) n.329

Iglesias, Commonwealth v., 426 Mass. 574, 689 N.E.2d 1315 (1998)—§ 6.9(b) n.32

Iglesias, State v., 185 Wis.2d 117, 517 N.W.2d 175 (1994)—§ 12.2(a) n.4

Iglesias, United States v., 881 F.2d 1519 (9th Cir.1989)—§§ 20.3(f) n.103, 105

Ignot, State v., 701 So.2d 1001 (La.App.1997)—§ 19.5(b) n.8

I.J., In re, 906 A.2d 249 (D.C.App.2006)—§ 6.6(e) n.73

Ikaika, State v., 67 Haw. 563, 698 P.2d 281 (1985)—§§ 6.7(b) n.63; 6.9(f) n.133

Iles, United States v., 906 F.2d 1122 (6th Cir.1990)—§ 11.4(b) n.21

Illingworth v. Municipal Court, 102 Cal.App.3d 19, 164 Cal.Rptr. 53 (1980)—§ 27.4(c) n.36

Illinois v. Abbott & Associates, 460 U.S. 557, 103 S.Ct. 1356, 75 L.Ed.2d 281 (1983)—§ 8.5(h) n.278

Illinois v. Allen, 397 U.S. 337, 90 S.Ct. 1057, 25 L.Ed.2d 353 (1970)—§§ 2.7(a) n.37; 11.4(b) n.29; 24.2(a) n.2; 24.2(c) n.31

Illinois v. Andreas, 463 U.S. 765, 103 S.Ct. 3319, 77 L.Ed.2d 1003 (1983)—§§ 3.2(b) n.38, 44; 3.5(e) n.211

Illinois v. Caballes, 543 U.S. 405, 125 S.Ct. 834, 160 L.Ed.2d 842 (2005)—§§ 3.2(b) n.67, 70, 71; 3.8(b) n.58

Illinois v. Fisher, 540 U.S. 544, 124 S.Ct. 1200, 157 L.Ed.2d 1060 (2004)—§ 24.3(e) n.124

Illinois v. Gates, 462 U.S. 213, 103 S.Ct. 2317, 76 L.Ed.2d 527 (1983)—§§ 1.5(a) n.35; 2.9(g) n.152, 153, 163, 166, 179; 3.1(c) n.76; 3.3(a) n.8, 22; 3.3(b) n.68; 3.3(c) n.80; 3.3(d) n.155; 3.8(d) n.164

Illinois v. Krull, 480 U.S. 340, 107 S.Ct. 1160, 94 L.Ed.2d 364 (1987)—§§ 2.9(f) n.135, 138; 3.1(b) n.24; 3.1(c) n.60; 3.3(b) n.76

Illinois v. Lafayette, 462 U.S. 640, 103 S.Ct. 2605, 77 L.Ed.2d 65 (1983)—§§ 3.5(c) n.114, 132; 3.5(e) n.195; 3.7(d) n.87; 3.7(e) n.97, 114

Illinois v. Lidster, 540 U.S. 419, 124 S.Ct. 885, 157 L.Ed.2d 843 (2004)—§§ 3.8(f) n.238; 3.9(g) n.148

Illinois v. McArthur, 531 U.S. 326, 121 S.Ct. 946, 148 L.Ed.2d 838 (2001)—§§ 3.6(a) n.24; 3.6(e) n.128

Illinois v. Perkins, 496 U.S. 292, 110 S.Ct. 2394, 110 L.Ed.2d 243 (1990)—§§ 2.9(g) n.180; 6.7(c) n.140; 6.10(b) n.31

Illinois v. Rodriguez, 497 U.S. 177, 110 S.Ct. 2793, 111 L.Ed.2d 148 (1990)—§§ 3.10(d) n.132; 3.10(e) n.162

Illinois v. Sarbaugh, 552 F.2d 768 (7th Cir.1977)—§ 8.5(h) n.259

Illinois v. Somerville, 410 U.S. 458, 93 S.Ct. 1066, 35 L.Ed.2d 425 (1973)—§§ 25.2(c) n.20; 25.2(d) n.28

Illinois, United States v., 619 F.2d 668 (7th Cir.1980)—§ 22.1(h) n.156

Illinois v. Vitale, 447 U.S. 410, 100 S.Ct. 2260, 65 L.Ed.2d 228 (1980)—§§ 17.4(b) n.77, 85

Illinois v. Wardlow, 528 U.S. 119, 120 S.Ct. 673, 145 L.Ed.2d 570 (2000)—§§ 3.3(f) n.206; 3.8(c) n.103; 3.8(d) n.137

Illinois v. Washington, 469 U.S. 1022, 105 S.Ct. 442, 83 L.Ed.2d 367 (1984)—§§ 11.9(d) n.168, 174

Illinois Migrant Council v. Pilliod, 398 F.Supp. 882 (N.D.Ill.1975)—§ 3.8(c) n.97

Imbler v. Pachtman, 424 U.S. 409, 96 S.Ct. 984, 47 L.Ed.2d 128 (1976)—§§ 1.5(f) n.248; 13.5(g) n.113, 114

Imbruglia, State v., 913 A.2d 1022 (R.I.2007)—§ 7.4(e) n.82

Imlay, State v., 249 Mont. 82, 813 P.2d 979 (1991)—§ 26.9(b) n.69

Immerman, Commonwealth v., 391 Pa.Super. 569, 571 A.2d 1062 (1990)—§ 20.6(c) n.74

Immigration and Naturalization Service v. Delgado, 466 U.S. 210, 104 S.Ct. 1758, 80 L.Ed.2d 247 (1984)—§§ 3.8(c) n.98; 6.6(e) n.72

Imngren, United States v., 98 F.3d 811 (4th Cir.1996)—§ 17.4(b) n.124

Impounded, In re, 178 F.3d 150 (3d Cir.1999)—§ 8.10(b) n.45

Impounded, 277 F.3d 407 (3d Cir.2002)—§ 8.5(e) n.199

Impounded, 241 F.3d 308 (3d Cir.2001)—§ 8.8(d) n.97

Ince, United States v., 21 F.3d 576 (4th Cir.1994)—§ 27.6(b) n.14

Index Funds, Inc. v. Hagopian, 512 F.Supp. 1122 (S.D.N.Y.1981)— § 8.5(c) n.95

Indianapolis, City of v. Edmond, 531 U.S. 32, 121 S.Ct. 447, 148 L.Ed.2d 333 (2000)—§§ 3.2(b) n.70; 3.9(a) n.6; 3.9(c) n.41; 3.9(f) n.118; 3.9(g) n.131, 145

Indianapolis, City of v. Edmond, 531 U.S. 47, 99 S.Ct. 2637, 61 L.Ed.2d 357 (1979)—§ 3.5(d) n.163

Individual Subpoena to Appear at Waukesha County, State ex rel. v. Davis, 281 Wis.2d 431, 697 N.W.2d 803 (2005)—§ 8.1(c) n.28

Industrias Cardoen, Ltda. v. United States, 983 F.2d 49 (5th Cir.1993)— § 10.1(c) n.40

Indvik, State v., 382 N.W.2d 623 (N.D.1986)—§ 11.2(e) n.176

Iness v. State, 606 S.W.2d 306 (Tex.Cr.App.1980)—§ 24.3(b) n.41

Infante-Ruiz, United States v., 13 F.3d 498 (1st Cir.1994)—§§ 9.1(d) n.127; 9.3(e) n.66

Infelise, United States v., 934 F.2d 103 (7th Cir.1991)—§§ 12.1(a) n.8; 12.3(d) n.97

Inge v. Commonwealth, 217 Va. 360, 228 S.E.2d 563 (1976)—§ 7.4(a) n.7

Ingenito, State v., 87 N.J. 204, 432 A.2d 912 (1981)—§ 17.4(a) n.58

Ingersoll v. State, 96 P.3d 1046 (Wyo.2004)—§§ 10.2(d) n.48; 21.5(a) n.55

Ingle v. State, 294 Ark. 353, 742 S.W.2d 939 (1988)—§§ 21.3(b) n.132, 135

Ingle, United States v., 454 F.3d 1082 (10th Cir.2006)—§ 12.3(a) n.18

Ingle, United States v., 157 F.3d 1147 (8th Cir.1998)—§ 6.4(e) n.64

Ingleton, State v., 663 So.2d 443 (La.App.1995)—§ 19.3(b) n.180

Ingraham, United States v., 832 F.2d 229 (1st Cir.1987)—§ 12.1(e) n.66

Ingram, Ex parte, 675 So.2d 863 (Ala.1996)—§ 24.11(b) n.7

Ingram, Commonwealth v., 455 Pa. 198, 316 A.2d 77 (1974)—§ 21.4(c) n.70

Ingram, People v., 984 P.2d 597 (Colo.1999)—§ 6.7(b) n.85

Ingram, People v., 439 Mich. 288, 484 N.W.2d 241 (1992)—§ 21.5(c) n.76

Ingram, State v., 279 Kan. 745, 113 P.3d 228 (2005)—§ 9.3(e) n.56

Ingram v. State, 253 Ga. 622, 323 S.E.2d 801 (1984)—§§ 7.2(b) n.28; 22.2(d) n.85

Ingram, United States v., 446 F.3d 1332 (11th Cir.2006)—§§ 18.1(c) n.43; 18.2(b) n.17; 18.2(c) n.36, 53

Ingram, United States v., 979 F.2d 1179 (7th Cir.1992)—§ 21.2(d) n.217

Ingram v. United States, 592 A.2d 992 (D.C.App.1991)—§ 17.3(e) n.57

Ingram v. United States, 272 F.2d 567 (4th Cir.1959)—§ 17.3(c) n.32

Inman, People v., 765 P.2d 577 (Colo.1988)—§ 3.5(e) n.198

Inmates of Attica Correctional Facility v. Rockefeller, 477 F.2d 375 (2d Cir.1973)—§ 13.3(a) n.2

Inmates of the Allegheny County Jail v. Pierce, 612 F.2d 754 (3d Cir.1979)—§ 12.2(d) n.50

Inmon, United States v., 568 F.2d 326 (3d Cir.1977)—§ 24.5(a) n.10

Innamorati, United States v., 996 F.2d 456 (1st Cir.1993)—§ 24.3(b) n.69

Innes v. Dalsheim, 864 F.2d 974 (2d Cir.1988)—§ 8.11(e) n.110

INS v. Jean, 496 U.S. 154, 110 S.Ct. 2316, 110 L.Ed.2d 134 (1990)—§ 13.5(h) n.194

I.N.S. v. Lopez-Mendoza, 468 U.S. 1032, 104 S.Ct. 3479, 82 L.Ed.2d 778 (1984)—§§ 1.3(c) n.22; 3.1(b) n.24; 3.1(g) n.184; 3.1(i) n.238; 3.1(j) n.241

INS v. St. Cyr, 533 U.S. 289, 121 S.Ct. 2271, 150 L.Ed.2d 347 (2001)—§§ 28.2(a) n.12; 28.3(b) n.39

Inscore, State v., 219 W.Va. 443, 634 S.E.2d 389 (2006)—§ 18.5(c) n.92

Inspect and Copy Grand Jury Materials, In re Petition to, 735 F.2d 1261 (11th Cir.1984)—§§ 8.4(c) n.130; 8.5(b) n.39; 8.5(h) n.300

Inspection of Titan Tire, In re, 637 N.W.2d 115 (Iowa 2001)—§ 3.9(c) n.57

Interfaith Hospital v. People, 71 Misc.2d 910, 337 N.Y.S.2d 358 (Sup.Ct.1972)—§§ 8.7(e) n.91, 92

International Harvester Co. v. Commonwealth, 124 Ky. 543, 99 S.W. 637 (1907)—§ 16.4(c) n.71

International Paper Co., United States v., 457 F.Supp. 571 (S.D.Tex.1978)—§ 8.2(c) n.42

International Union, UMW v. Bagwell, 512 U.S. 821, 114 S.Ct. 2552, 129 L.Ed.2d 642 (1994)—§§ 22.1(b) n.48; 22.1(c) n.58

Interstate Circuit, Inc. v. Dallas, 390 U.S. 676, 88 S.Ct. 1298, 20 L.Ed.2d 225 (1968)—§ 2.5(c) n.25

Interstate Dress Carriers, Inc., United States v., 280 F.2d 52 (2d Cir.1960)—§§ 8.5(c) n.96, 97

Inthavong v. Lamarque, 420 F.3d 1055 (9th Cir.2005)—§ 28.6(g) n.90

Inthavong, State v., 402 N.W.2d 799 (Minn.1987)—§§ 15.7(g) n.201, 204

Intogna, State v., 101 Ariz. 275, 419 P.2d 59 (1966)—§§ 6.6(c) n.20; 6.6(f) n.102; 6.7(d) n.152

Investigating Grand Jury of Chester County, In re, 518 Pa. 485, 544 A.2d 924 (1988)—§ 8.3(b) n.13

Investigating Grand Jury of Philadelphia County, In re, 527 Pa. 432, 593 A.2d 402 (1991)—§§ 8.14(d) n.41, 47, 54, 56, 57

Investigation Before April 1975 Grand Jury, In re, 531 F.2d 600 (D.C.Cir.1976)—§ 8.14(d) n.58

Investigation of World Arrangements, In re, 107 F.Supp. 628 (D.D.C.1952)—§ 8.4(c) n.118

Investigative Grand Jury Proceedings on April 10, 1979, In re, 480 F.Supp. 162 (N.D.Ohio 1979)—§§ 8.14(d) n.52, 54

Inzirillo, In re, 542 F.2d 90 (1st Cir.1976)—§ 8.8(f) n.148

Iorizzo, United States v., 786 F.2d 52 (2d Cir.1986)—§ 11.9(d) n.204

Iovieno v. Commissioner of Correction, 242 Conn. 689, 699 A.2d 1003 (1997)—§ 28.11(a) n.9

Iovinelli, United States v., 276 F.Supp. 629 (N.D.Ill.1967)—§ 20.3(b) n.48

Iovino, State v., 524 A.2d 556 (R.I.1987)—§ 25.3(c) n.25

Iowa v. Tovar, 541 U.S. 77, 124 S.Ct. 1379, 158 L.Ed.2d 209 (2004)—§§ 11.3(a) n.3, 4, 14; 11.3(b) n.39; 11.5(a) n.12; 21.3(a) n.33

Iowa Department of Transportation v. Iowa District Court, 670 N.W.2d 114 (2003)—§ 21.2(e) n.329

Iowa District Court, State v., 568 N.W.2d 505 (Iowa 1997)—§§ 8.4(b) n.93, 109; 8.4(c) n.133; 13.2(a) n.3; 13.3(d) n.47; 13.3(f) n.58

Iowa District Court, State v., 308 N.W.2d 27 (Iowa 1981)—§ 26.1(d) n.71

Iowa Supreme Court Attorney Disciplinary Board v. Howe, 706 N.W.2d 360 (Iowa 2005)—§ 21.3(c) n.197

Iowa Supreme Court Attorney Disciplinary Board v. Zenor, 707 N.W.2d 176 (2005)—§ 21.3(c) n.197

Iozia, United States v., 13 F.R.D. 335 (S.D.N.Y.1952)—§ 20.2(d) n.67

Ippolito, United States v., 774 F.2d 1482 (9th Cir.1985)—§ 4.6(e) n.97

Ira I., Commonwealth v., 439 Mass. 805, 791 N.E.2d 894 (2003)—§§ 6.6(e) n.70; 6.10(c) n.36

Ireland, State v., 126 N.J.L. 444, 20 A.2d 69 (1941)—§ 18.5(a) n.17

Iribe-Perez, United States v., 129 F.3d 1167 (10th Cir.1997)—§§ 22.3(c) n.101; 27.6(d) n.142

Irish, State v., 223 Neb. 814, 394 N.W.2d 879 (1986)—§ 21.4(d) n.106

Irizarry, State v., 111 Wash.2d 591, 763 P.2d 432 (1988)—§ 19.5(b) n.27

Iron Moccasin, United States v., 878 F.2d 226 (8th Cir.1989)—§ 22.3(d) n.193

Irons, People v., 20 Ill.App.3d 125, 312 N.E.2d 664 (1974)—§ 7.4(d) n.68

Iron Thunder, State v., 272 N.W.2d 299 (S.D.1978)—§ 10.3(d) n.63

Irvin v. Dowd, 366 U.S. 717, 81 S.Ct. 1639, 6 L.Ed.2d 751 (1961)—§§ 2.7(b) n.91; 22.3(c) n.109, 116; 23.1(a) n.5; 23.2(f) n.99

Irvin v. Dowd, 359 U.S. 394, 79 S.Ct. 825, 3 L.Ed.2d 900 (1959)—§§ 28.4(c) n.25; 28.5(a) n.7

Irvin v. State, 345 Ark. 541, 49 S.W.3d 635 (2001)—§ 22.4(c) n.29

Irvine v. California, 347 U.S. 128, 74 S.Ct. 381, 98 L.Ed. 561 (1954)—§§ 2.4(f) n.184; 3.1(a) n.13

Irvine, State v., 1996 S.D. 43, 547 N.W.2d 177 (1996)—§ 11.5(d) n.69

Irvine, United States v., 756 F.2d 708 (9th Cir.1985)—§ 8.11(e) n.93

Irving, State v., 114 N.J. 427, 555 A.2d 575 (1989)—§ 20.4(c) n.48

Irwin, United States v., 654 F.2d 671 (10th Cir.1981)—§ 19.3(a) n.14

Irwin, United States v., 612 F.2d 1182 (9th Cir.1980)—§ 11.8(b) n.34

Isa, United States v., 923 F.2d 1300 (8th Cir.1991)—§ 4.9(b) n.8

Isaac, State v., 131 N.M. 235, 34 P.3d 624 (N.M.App.2001)—§§ 15.2(h) n.187; 25.1(d) n.45

Isaac, State v., 696 So.2d 813 (Fla.App.1997)—§§ 27.3(c) n.39; 27.4(d) n.51

Isaac v. State, 605 N.E.2d 144 (Ind.1992)—§ 26.10(b) n.34

Isaacs v. State, 259 Ga. 717, 386 S.E.2d 316 (1989)—§ 15.6(f) n.203

Isaacs, State v., 24 Ohio App.2d 115, 265 N.E.2d 327 (1970)—§ 9.1(a) n.25

Isaacs, United States v., 493 F.2d 1124 (7th Cir.1974)—§ 17.2(a) n.20

Isaacs v. United States, 283 F.2d 587 (10th Cir.1960)—§ 10.2(a) n.9

Isaacson, People v., 44 N.Y.2d 511, 406 N.Y.S.2d 714, 378 N.E.2d 78 (1978)—§§ 5.4(c) n.44, 46

Isaacson, United States v., 853 F.Supp. 83 (E.D.N.Y.1994)—§§ 11.9(c) n.123, 124

Isadore, In re, 151 Wash.2d 294, 88 P.3d 390 (2004)—§ 21.2(e) n.337

Isaiah, United States v., 434 F.3d 513 (6th Cir.2006)—§§ 13.5(h) n.158, 178

Isgro, United States v., 974 F.2d 1091 (9th Cir.1992)—§§ 15.5(b) n.94; 15.6(b) n.80; 15.7(a) n.8

Ishmael, United States v., 343 F.3d 741 (5th Cir.2003)—§ 28.9(b) n.33

Isla, People v., 96 A.D.2d 789, 466 N.Y.S.2d 16 (1983)—§ 15.7(f) n.187

Ismaili, United States v., 828 F.2d 153 (3d Cir.1987)—§§ 18.5(b) n.59, 68; 20.2(e) n.83

Isom, State v., 306 Or. 587, 761 P.2d 524 (1988)—§§ 2.12(a) n.26; 6.9(c) n.61

Israel, State v., 78 Hawaii 66, 890 P.2d 303 (1995)—§§ 19.2(a) n.1, 6; 19.2(c) n.27; 19.2(f) n.98; 19.3(a) n.70; 19.3(b) n.145

Italiano, State v., 18 Ohio St.3d 38, 479 N.E.2d 857 (1985)—§ 5.2(a) n.4

Italiano, United States v., 837 F.2d 1480 (11th Cir.1988)—§§ 19.2(d) n.46; 19.2(f) n.93, 98

Iverson, State v., 664 N.W.2d 346 (Minn.2003)—§ 21.6(a) n.78

Ives, State v., 568 N.W.2d 710 (Minn.1997)—§ 11.8(c) n.60

Ivester, United States v., 316 F.3d 955 (9th Cir.2003)—§ 24.1(b) n.18

Ivey v. State, 82 Nev. 448, 420 P.2d 853 (1966)—§ 15.5(c) n.135

Ivy v. Caspari, 173 F.3d 1136 (8th Cir.1999)—§ 21.4(c) n.76

Ivy v. Pontesso, 328 F.3d 1057 (9th Cir.2003)—§ 28.9(a) n.5

Ivy, State v., 188 S.W.3d 132 (Tenn.2006)—§§ 22.3(b) n.68, 70

Ivy, United States v., 83 F.3d 1266 (10th Cir.1996)—§§ 20.6(b) n.17, 27

I.W.I., Inc., People v., 176 Ill.App.3d 951, 126 Ill.Dec. 374, 531 N.E.2d 1001 (1988)—§ 8.12(g) n.63

Izazaga v. Superior Court, 54 Cal.3d 356, 285 Cal.Rptr. 231, 815 P.2d 304 (1991)—§§ 20.4(a) n.11 to 13; 20.4(b) n.14, 20; 20.4(d) n.64, 66, 69, 73; 20.5(e) n.68, 69; 24.3(c) n.92

Izquierdo, United States v., 448 F.3d 1269 (11th Cir.2006)—§ 21.5(a) n.54

J

Jaben v. United States, 381 U.S. 214, 85 S.Ct. 1365, 14 L.Ed.2d 345 (1965)—§ 3.3(d) n.145

Jablonski, People v., 37 Cal.4th 774, 38 Cal.Rptr.3d 98, 126 P.3d 938 (2006)—§ 6.2(c) n.159

Jack, State v., 125 P.3d 311 (Alaska 2005)—§ 16.4(c) n.114

Jackman, United States v., 46 F.3d 1240 (2d Cir.1995)—§ 22.2(d) n.76

Jackson, Ex parte, 674 So.2d 1365 (Ala.1994)—§ 24.2(a) n.11

Jackson, Ex parte, 614 So.2d 405 (Ala. 1993)—§ 27.4(c) n.21

Jackson, Ex parte, 96 U.S. 727, 24 L.Ed. 877, 1877 WL 18454 (1877)—§§ 3.2(a) n.10; 4.2(a) n.1

Jackson, In re, 170 Cal.App.3d 773, 216 Cal.Rptr. 539 (1985)—§ 27.4(f) n.68

Jackson v. Albany Appeal Bureau Unit, 442 F.3d 51 (2d Cir.2006)—§ 28.10 n.1

Jackson v. Bailey, 221 Conn. 498, 605 A.2d 1350 (1992)—§ 22.1(b) n.51

Jackson v. Coalter, 337 F.3d 74 (1st Cir.2003)—§ 28.3(a) n.9

Jackson v. Commonwealth, 187 S.W.3d 300 (Ky.2006)—§ 6.9(g) n.167

Jackson, Commonwealth v., 447 Mass. 603, 855 N.E.2d 1097 (2006)—§ 6.9(f) n.139

Jackson, Commonwealth v., 432 Mass. 82, 731 N.E.2d 1066 (2000)—§§ 6.2(c) n.169; 6.9(b) n.27

Jackson, Commonwealth v., 255 Va. 552, 499 S.E.2d 276 (1998)—§ 21.4(a) n.22

Jackson v. Commonwealth, 255 Va. 625, 499 S.E.2d 538 (1998)—§ 6.9(c) n.63

Jackson v. Commonwealth, 499 S.E.2d 538 (Va.1998)—§ 24.6(b) n.23

Jackson, Commonwealth v., 336 Pa.Super. 609, 486 A.2d 431 (1984)—§ 11.10(c) n.116

Jackson, Commonwealth v., 388 Mass. 98, 445 N.E.2d 1033 (1983)—§ 24.3(b) n.39

Jackson, Commonwealth v., 459 Pa. 669, 331 A.2d 189 (1975)—§§ 3.3(b) n.70; 3.3(d) n.164; 9.4(a) n.8

Jackson v. Denno, 378 U.S. 368, 84 S.Ct. 1774, 12 L.Ed.2d 908 (1964)—§§ 2.7(a) n.9, 21; 2.7(c) n.114, 195; 2.9(h) n.208; 6.2(c) n.166; 10.5(a) n.1; 10.5(b) n.23; 10.6(a) n.5; 17.2(b) n.30; 21.6(a) n.5

Jackson v. Duckworth, 112 F.3d 878 (7th Cir.1997)—§ 28.5(a) n.19

Jackson v. Edwards, 404 F.3d 612 (2d Cir.2005)—§ 28.5(a) n.33

Jackson v. Fogg, 589 F.2d 108 (2d Cir.1978)—§ 7.3(f) n.115

Jackson v. Indiana, 406 U.S. 715, 92 S.Ct. 1845, 32 L.Ed.2d 435 (1972)—§ 12.3(d) n.102

Jackson v. Jamrog, 411 F.3d 615 (6th Cir.2005)—§ 26.2(c) n.50

Jackson v. Meadows, 157 Ga.App. 569, 278 S.E.2d 8 (1981)—§ 24.8(b) n.29

Jackson, People v., 150 Wash.2d 251, 76 P.3d 217 (2003)—§ 3.2(j) n.256

Jackson, People v., 39 P.3d 1174 (Colo.2002)—§ 3.8(c) n.89

Jackson, People v., 96 Cal.App.4th 1265, 117 Cal.Rptr.2d 886 (2002)—§ 14.4(b) n.42

Jackson, People v., 98 N.Y.2d 555, 750 N.Y.S.2d 561, 780 N.E.2d 162 (2002)—§ 7.4(d) n.69

Jackson, People v., 13 Cal.4th 1164, 56 Cal.Rptr.2d 49, 920 P.2d 1254 (1996)—§ 24.10(a) n.19

Jackson, People v., 78 N.Y.2d 638, 578 N.Y.S.2d 483, 585 N.E.2d 795 (1991)—§ 1.7(h) n.127

Jackson, People v., 161 Ill.App.3d 573, 113 Ill.Dec. 410, 515 N.E.2d 219 (1987)—§ 11.10(d) n.192

Jackson, People v., 37 Cal.3d 826, 210 Cal.Rptr. 623, 694 P.2d 736 (1985)—§ 21.4(f) n.198

Jackson, People v., 167 Cal.App.3d 829, 213 Cal.Rptr. 521 (1985)—§ 11.9(a) n.20

Jackson, People v., 150 Cal.App.3d Supp. 1, 198 Cal.Rptr. 135 (1983)—§ 16.1(a) n.27

Jackson, People v., 69 Ill.2d 252, 13 Ill.Dec. 667, 371 N.E.2d 602 (1977)—§ 1.7(f) n.102

Jackson, People v., 391 Mich. 323, 217 N.W.2d 22 (1974)—§§ 7.3(b) n.31; 7.4(e) n.80

Jackson v. Ray, 390 F.3d 1254 (10th Cir.2004)—§§ 18.2(c) n.31, 42; 18.2(e) n.76, 81

Jackson v. Rose, 4 Va. 34 (1815)—§ 1.2(c) n.81

Jackson, State v., 107 Ohio St.3d 300, 839 N.E.2d 362 (2006)—§§ 6.9(g) n.149, 157, 166

Jackson v. State, 146 P.3d 1149 (Okla.Crim.App.2006)—§ 6.7(b) n.90

Jackson, State v., 107 Ohio St.3d 53, 836 N.E.2d 1173 (2005)—§ 22.3(a) n.23

Jackson, State v., 280 Kan. 16, 118 P.3d 1238 (2005)—§ 6.2(c) n.135

Jackson v. State, 852 So.2d 941 (Fla.App. 2003)—§ 19.3(a) n.38

Jackson, State v., 178 Or.App. 233, 36 P.3d 500 (2001)—§ 24.1(a) n.11

Jackson v. State, 364 Md. 192, 772 A.2d 273 (2001)—§ 26.4(b) n.11

Jackson v. State, 770 A.2d 506 (Del.2001)—§ 24.3(b) n.49

Jackson v. State, 272 Ga. 191, 528 S.E.2d 232 (2000)—§§ 6.6(d) n.49; 6.10(b) n.14

Jackson v. State, 272 Ga. 782, 534 S.E.2d 796 (2000)—§ 18.2(e) n.77

Jackson v. State, 358 Md. 259, 747 A.2d 1199 (2000)—§§ 13.5(b) n.37; 27.2(c) n.47

Jackson v. State, 732 So.2d 187 (Miss.1999)—§§ 11.1(b) n.79, 83

Jackson v. State, 330 Ark. 126, 954 S.W.2d 894 (1997)—§ 22.3(d) n.216

Jackson v. State, 902 P.2d 1292 (Wyo.1995)—§ 21.2(d) n.180

Jackson, State v., 75 Wash.App. 537, 879 P.2d 307 (1994)—§ 24.9(f) n.73

Jackson, State v., 188 Wis.2d 537, 525 N.W.2d 165 (1994)—§ 24.9(e) n.54

Jackson v. State, 643 A.2d 1360 (Del.1994)—§ 3.5(c) n.122

Jackson v. State, 614 So.2d 965 (Miss.1993)—§ 18.1(c) n.22

Jackson, State v., 857 P.2d 267 (Utah App.1993)—§ 25.3(c) n.25

Jackson, State v., 78 Ohio App.3d 479, 605 N.E.2d 426 (1992)—§§ 19.5(b) n.14, 43

Jackson v. State, 597 N.E.2d 950 (Ind.1992)—§ 3.7(a) n.13

Jackson v. State, 556 So.2d 335 (Miss.1990)—§ 16.1(g) n.259

Jackson v. State, 760 S.W.2d 505 (Mo.App.1988)—§ 19.5(b) n.11

Jackson, State v., 128 Wis.2d 356, 382 N.W.2d 429 (1986)—§ 26.9(b) n.33

Jackson v. State, 284 Ark. 478, 683 S.W.2d 606 (1985)—§ 6.2(c) n.176

Jackson v. State, 465 So.2d 1375 (Fla.App.1985)—§ 11.4(b) n.30

Jackson v. State, 483 N.E.2d 1374 (Ind.1985)—§ 11.4(a) n.1

Jackson, State v., 102 Wash.2d 432, 688 P.2d 136 (1984)—§ 3.3(c) n.82

Jackson, State v., 351 N.W.2d 352 (Minn.1984)—§ 6.7(c) n.106

Jackson, State v., 450 So.2d 621 (La.1984)—§ 22.3(b) n.88

Jackson, State v., 206 Mont. 338, 672 P.2d 255 (Mont.1983)—§ 2.12(d) n.192

Jackson, State v., 234 Kan. 84, 670 P.2d 1327 (1983)—§ 26.10(c) n.76

Jackson v. State, 421 So.2d 15 (Fla.App.1982)—§ 24.7(e) n.63

Jackson v. State, 441 N.E.2d 29 (Ind.App.1982)—§ 11.5(f) n.104

Jackson v. State, 628 S.W.2d 120 (Tex.App.1981)—§§ 26.10(a) n.5; 26.10(c) n.50

Jackson, State v., 50 Ohio St.2d 253, 364 N.E.2d 236 (1977)—§ 21.3(c) n.148

Jackson, State v., 223 N.W.2d 229 (Iowa 1974)—§ 24.11(d) n.32

Jackson, State v., 213 Kan. 219, 515 P.2d 1108 (1973)—§§ 10.6(c) n.22, 23

Jackson, State v., 280 N.C. 122, 185 S.E.2d 202 (1971)—§ 3.5(c) n.105

Jackson v. State, 90 Ala. 590, 8 So. 862 (1891)—§ 16.1(e) n.190

Jackson v. Superior Court of San Francisco, 13 Cal.App.3d 440, 91 Cal.Rptr. 565 (1970)—§ 16.3(d) n.51

Jackson, United States v., 473 F.3d 660 (6th Cir.2007)—§ 18.2(e) n.71

Jackson, United States v., 462 F.3d 899 (8th Cir.2006)—§ 21.4(d) n.104

Jackson, United States v., 368 F.3d 59 (2d Cir.2004)—§ 26.4(i) n.193

Jackson, United States v., 327 F.3d 273 (4th Cir.2003)—§§ 13.4(c) n.143; 13.5(a) n.5; 19.3(a) n.29

Jackson, United States v., 345 F.3d 59 (2d Cir.2003)—§ 5.2(a) n.9

Jackson, United States v., 345 F.3d 638 (8th Cir.2003)—§ 4.6(e) n.97

Jackson, United States v., 280 F.3d 403 (4th Cir.2002)—§ 6.6(e) n.91

Jackson, United States v., 300 F.3d 740 (7th Cir.2002)—§ 3.8(e) n.196

Jackson, United States v., 207 F.3d 910 (7th Cir.2000)—§§ 4.6(d) n.68; 4.6(e) n.80; 4.6(m) n.241

Jackson, United States v., 213 F.3d 1269 (10th Cir.2000)—§ 10.5(d) n.42

Jackson, United States v., 181 F.3d 740 (6th Cir.1999)—§ 26.8(b) n.14

Jackson, United States v., 189 F.3d 655 (7th Cir.1999)—§ 13.2(a) n.2

Jackson, United States v., 60 F.3d 128 (2d Cir.1995)—§§ 24.4(d) n.49, 64

Jackson, United States v., 32 F.3d 1101 (7th Cir.1994)—§ 26.4(d) n.65

Jackson, United States v., 155 F.R.D. 664 (D.Kan.1994)—§ 24.3(f) n.150

Jackson, United States v., 863 F.Supp. 1449 (D.Kan.1994)—§§ 8.8(f) n.156; 15.2(i) n.219, 221, 222, 224

Jackson, United States v., 886 F.2d 838 (7th Cir.1989)—§§ 6.4(e) n.106; 26.4(e) n.82

Jackson, United States v., 845 F.2d 1262 (5th Cir.1988)—§ 12.3(a) n.23

Jackson, United States v., 818 F.2d 345 (5th Cir.1987)—§ 3.1(c) n.77

Jackson, United States v., 823 F.2d 4 (2d Cir.1987)—§ 12.3(d) n.97

Jackson, United States v., 825 F.2d 853 (5th Cir.1987)—§§ 3.1(c) n.59; 3.9(f) n.93

Jackson, United States v., 835 F.2d 1195 (7th Cir.1987)—§ 1.11(a) n.5

Jackson, United States v., 836 F.2d 324 (7th Cir.1987)—§ 6.6(e) n.76

Jackson, United States v., 805 F.2d 457 (2d Cir.1986)—§ 13.7(a) n.29

Jackson, United States v., 757 F.2d 1486 (4th Cir.1985)—§ 20.3(d) n.91

Jackson, United States v., 778 F.2d 933 (2d Cir.1985)—§ 17.4(a) n.45

Jackson v. United States, 404 A.2d 911 (D.C.App.1979)—§ 6.4(f) n.127

Jackson, United States v., 588 F.2d 1046 (5th Cir.1979)—§ 4.6(b) n.43

Jackson, United States v., 549 F.2d 517 (8th Cir.1977)—§§ 17.2(c) n.88, 92; 17.2(e) n.125

Jackson, United States v., 563 F.2d 1145 (4th Cir.1977)—§§ 21.3(e) n.266; 21.4(g) n.240

Jackson, United States v., 533 F.2d 314 (6th Cir.1976)—§ 3.5(a) n.4

Jackson, United States v., 508 F.2d 1001 (7th Cir.1975)—§§ 18.2(c) n.52; 20.3(h) n.150

Jackson, United States v., 476 F.2d 249 (7th Cir.1973)—§§ 3.8(b) n.46; 7.2(d) n.45, 46

Jackson, United States v., 482 F.2d 1167 (10th Cir.1973)—§ 16.2(b) n.16

Jackson v. United States, 412 F.2d 149 (D.C.Cir.1969)—§ 7.4(f) n.102

Jackson, United States v., 390 U.S. 570, 88 S.Ct. 1209, 20 L.Ed.2d 138 (1968)—§§ 21.2(a) n.2; 21.2(b) n.25; 21.2(c) n.125; 22.1(h) n.144; 26.8(c) n.19

Jackson v. United States, 395 F.2d 615 (D.C.Cir.1968)—§ 22.3(c) n.132

Jackson v. United States, 359 F.2d 260 (D.C.Cir.1966)—§§ 19.6(c) n.34, 38, 39; 24.7(e) n.55

Jackson v. Virginia, 443 U.S. 307, 99 S.Ct. 2781, 61 L.Ed.2d 560 (1979)—§§ 24.6(b) n.14; 24.6(c) n.38; 27.5(e) n.169; 28.3(c) n.73; 28.3(e) n.93

Jackson v. Walker, 585 F.2d 139 (5th Cir.1978)—§ 13.7(c) n.52

Jackson v. Washington, 270 Va. 269, 619 S.E.2d 92 (2005)—§§ 11.10(c) n.118; 24.2(e) n.54

Jackson v. Weber, 637 N.W.2d 19 (S.D.2001)—§ 11.7(a) n.10

Jackson v. Ylst, 921 F.2d 882 (9th Cir.1990)—§ 11.2(e) n.183

Jackson-Bey, United States v., 302 F.Supp.2d 621 (E.D.Va.2004)—§ 28.9(b) n.50

Jackson, United States ex rel. v. Follette, 462 F.2d 1041 (2d Cir.1972)— § 25.4(d) n.44

Jaco, State v., 156 S.W.3d 775 (Mo.2005)—§ 26.4(d) n.52

Jaco v. State, 120 S.W.3d 828 (Tenn.2003)—§ 21.4(d) n.119

Jacob, State v., 253 Neb. 950, 574 N.W.2d 117 (1998)—§ 16.3(b) n.22

Jacobowitz, United States v., 877 F.2d 162 (2d Cir.1989)—§ 7.2(c) n.30

Jacobo-Zavala, United States v., 241 F.3d 1009 (8th Cir.2001)— § 13.3(c) n.44

Jacobs, Commonwealth v., 52 Mass.App. 38, 750 N.E.2d 1028 (2001)—§ 17.3(b) n.27

Jacobs v. Commonwealth, 870 S.W.2d 412 (Ky.1994)—§§ 11.6(a) n.26; 23.2(a) n.40, 43, 48

Jacobs v. Hopper, 238 Ga. 461, 233 S.E.2d 169 (1977)—§ 28.11(b) n.14

Jacobs, People v., 43 Cal.3d 472, 233 Cal.Rptr. 323, 729 P.2d 757 (1987)—§ 3.10(e) n.150

Jacobs v. Singletary, 952 F.2d 1282 (11th Cir.1992)—§§ 6.6(f) n.102; 6.9(f) n.113; 6.9(g) n.150

Jacobs v. State, 128 P.3d 1085 (Okla.Crim.App.2006)—§ 9.4(b) n.50

Jacobs v. State, 20 P.3d 382 (Utah 2001)—§ 21.4(b) n.59

Jacobs, State v., 803 So.2d 933 (La.2001)—§§ 22.3(d) n.212, 220

Jacobs, State v., 129 N.M. 448, 10 P.3d 127 (2000)—§ 7.4(b) n.33

Jacobs v. State, 787 S.W.2d 397 (Tex.Cr.App. App. 1990)—§ 6.2(c) n.115

Jacobs, United States v., 431 F.3d 99 (3d Cir.2005)—§§ 6.6(c) n.37; 6.6(d) n.49

Jacobs, United States v., 4 F.3d 603 (8th Cir.1993)—§ 13.7(b) n.34

Jacobs, United States v., 986 F.2d 1231 (8th Cir.1993)—§ 3.4(d) n.58

Jacobs, United States v., 531 F.2d 87 (2d Cir.1978)—§§ 1.7(i) n.194; 1.7(j) n.231; 8.10(d) n.113

Jacobs, United States v., 531 F.2d 87 (2d Cir.1976)—§ 8.4(c) n.131

Jacobs, United States v., 547 F.2d 772 (2d Cir.1976)—§ 8.10(d) n.112

Jacobsen, United States v., 466 U.S. 109, 104 S.Ct. 1652, 80 L.Ed.2d 85 (1984)—§§ 3.1(h) n.195, 198; 3.2(a) n.28; 3.2(b) n.46; 3.5(e) n.212; 4.2(a) n.4

Jacobson v. State, 476 So.2d 1282 (Fla.1985)—§ 3.8(b) n.31

Jacobson v. United States, 503 U.S. 540, 112 S.Ct. 1535, 118 L.Ed.2d 174 (1992)—§§ 5.1(c) n.20; 5.2(a) n.1, 15; 5.2(c) n.43; 5.3(b) n.17; 5.3(d) n.43; 5.4(b) n.19

Jacobson, United States v., 916 F.2d 467 (8th Cir.1990)—§ 5.4(b) n.18

Jacobson, United States v., 691 F.2d 110 (2d Cir.1982)—§ 15.7(c) n.61

Jacquez-Beltran, United States v., 326 F.3d 661 (5th Cir.2003)— §§ 19.3(e) n.240, 241

Jaeger, State v., 886 P.2d 53 (Utah 1994)—§§ 14.3(c) n.61, 73

Jafek, State v., 141 Idaho 71, 106 P.3d 397 (2005)—§ 21.2(d) n.242

Jaffee v. Redmond, 518 U.S. 1, 116 S.Ct. 1923, 135 L.Ed.2d 337 (1996)— § 27.2(e) n.84

Jager, People v., 145 Cal.App.2d 792, 303 P.2d 115 (1956)—§ 9.2(d) n.44

Jaggers v. United States, 482 A.2d 786 (D.C.App.1984)—§ 17.1(d) n.58

Jahnke v. State, 682 P.2d 991 (Wyo.1984)—§ 22.3(a) n.5

Jahnke v. State, 692 P.2d 911 (Wyo.1984)—§ 6.9(b) n.20

Jaimez, State v., 817 P.2d 822 (Utah App.1991)—§ 14.1(c) n.45

Jake, United States v., 281 F.3d 123 (3d Cir.2002)—§ 18.5(a) n.50

Jalbert v. United States, 375 F.2d 125 (5th Cir.1967)—§ 24.10(a) n.18

Jamail v. State, 787 S.W.2d 372 (Tex.Cr.App.1990)—§ 6.9(e) n.97

James v. Harrison, 389 F.3d 450 (2004)—§ 11.10(d) n.201

James v. Illinois, 493 U.S. 307, 110 S.Ct. 648, 107 L.Ed.2d 676 (1990)—§§ 1.5(a) n.35; 1.5(b) n.88; 9.6(a) n.49

James v. Kentucky, 466 U.S. 341, 104 S.Ct. 1830, 80 L.Ed.2d 346 (1984)—§ 24.5(c) n.37

James v. Louisiana, 382 U.S. 36, 86 S.Ct. 151, 15 L.Ed.2d 30 (1965)—§ 3.6(c) n.72

James v. Newspaper Agency Corp., 591 F.2d 579 (10th Cir.1979)—§ 4.6(b) n.46

James v. People, 727 P.2d 850 (Colo.1986)—§ 22.4(a) n.12

James, People v., 19 Cal.3d 99, 137 Cal.Rptr. 447, 561 P.2d 1135 (1977)—§ 3.10(b) n.64

James v. Rodriguez, 553 F.2d 59 (10th Cir.1977)—§ 13.7(c) n.67

James v. State, 699 N.W.2d 723 (Minn.2005)—§§ 21.2(d) n.227; 21.4(d) n.114

James, State v., 276 Kan. 737, 79 P.3d 169 (2003)—§§ 6.6(e) n.71; 16.4(c) n.85

James, State v., 797 A.2d 732 (Me.2002)—§ 26.10(c) n.74

James v. State, 613 N.E.2d 15 (Ind.1993)—§ 24.2(a) n.8

James, State v., 626 So.2d 259 (Fla.App.1993)—§ 25.3(a) n.7

James v. State, 289 Ark. 560, 712 S.W.2d 919 (1986)—§ 21.5(e) n.119

James v. State, 711 P.2d 111 (Okl.Cr.1985)—§ 6.2(c) n.107

James, State v., 329 So.2d 713 (La.1976)—§ 27.3(c) n.29

James, State v., 203 Md. 113, 100 A.2d 12 (1953)—§ 16.4(c) n.52

James v. Strange, 407 U.S. 128, 92 S.Ct. 2027, 32 L.Ed.2d 600 (1972)—§ 11.2(h) n.320

James, United States v., 353 F.3d 606 (8th Cir.2003)—§ 3.10(e) n.172

James, United States v., 257 F.3d 1173 (10th Cir.2001)—§§ 13.4(b) n.69; 27.5(e) n.182

James, United States v., 210 F.3d 1342 (11th Cir.2000)—§ 21.4(c) n.78

James, United States v., 113 F.3d 721 (7th Cir.1997)—§§ 6.6(e) n.68; 27.5(e) n.164

James, United States v., 40 F.3d 850 (7th Cir.1994)—§ 3.2(c) n.128

James, United States v., 555 F.2d 992 (D.C.Cir.1977)—§ 3.5(e) n.205

James, United States v., 532 F.2d 1161 (7th Cir.1976)—§ 21.2(g) n.413

James, United States v., 493 F.2d 323 (2d Cir.1974)—§ 15.7(d) n.81

James v. United States, 418 F.2d 1150 (D.C.Cir.1969)—§ 9.4(b) n.60

James v. Whitley, 39 F.3d 607 (5th Cir.1994)—§§ 15.4(e) n.128, 141

James B. Beam Distilling Co. v. Georgia, 501 U.S. 529, 111 S.Ct. 2439, 115 L.Ed.2d 481 (1991)—§§ 2.11(a) n.3, 8; 2.11(e) n.63

James C. Gould, Ex parte, 99 Cal. 360, 33 P. 1112 (1893)—§ 2.12(a) n.9

James Daniel Good Real Property, United States v., 510 U.S. 43, 114 S.Ct. 492, 126 L.Ed.2d 490 (1993)—§§ 2.7(c) n.226; 2.7(d) n.243, 244; 26.4(d) n.69; 26.6(d) n.68

Jamieson, People v., 436 Mich. 61, 461 N.W.2d 884 (1990)—§§ 1.7(h) n.129; 5.3(b) n.26

Jamison, People v., 197 Ill.2d 135, 258 Ill.Dec. 514, 756 N.E.2d 788 (2001)—§ 13.7(a) n.5

Jamison, People v., 181 Ill.2d 24, 228 Ill.Dec. 920, 690 N.E.2d 995 (1998)—§ 21.4(b) n.59

Jamison v. State, 918 S.W.2d 889 (Mo.App.1996)—§ 18.4(c) n.57

Jamison, State v., 482 N.W.2d 409 (Iowa 1992)—§ 3.4(e) n.91

Jamison v. United States, 600 A.2d 65 (D.C.App.1991)—§ 26.1(d) n.89

Jamison, United States v., 505 F.2d 407 (D.C.Cir.1974)—§§ 13.7(c) n.55, 65; 21.5(e) n.131

Jancsek, State v., 302 Or. 270, 730 P.2d 14 (1986)—§§ 8.12(e) n.50; 8.12(g) n.67, 69; 8.13(a) n.25

Jandak v. Village of Brookfield, 520 F.Supp. 815 (N.D. Ill.1981)—§§ 4.6(b) n.51; 4.6(l) n.203

Janes v. State, 350 Md. 284, 711 A.2d 1319 (1998)—§ 17.4(a) n.53

Janiec, United States v., 464 F.2d 126 (3d Cir.1972)—§ 26.5(a) n.18

Janik, United States v., 723 F.2d 537 (7th Cir.1983)—§ 18.3(b) n.5

Janis v. Commonwealth, 22 Va.App. 646, 472 S.E.2d 649 (1996)—§ 3.1(c) n.79

Janis, United States v., 428 U.S. 433, 96 S.Ct. 3021, 49 L.Ed.2d 1046 (1976)—§§ 3.1(b) n.24; 3.1(g) n.175; 9.6(c) n.63

Janney v. United States, 206 F.2d 601 (4th Cir.1953)—§ 3.2(d) n.144

Jannotti, United States v., 673 F.2d 578 (3d Cir.1982)—§ 5.4(b) n.21

Jansen, In re, 444 Mass. 112, 826 N.E.2d 186 (2005)—§§ 3.1(h) n.225; 3.5(d) n.165; 24.3(f) n.154

Janto, State v., 92 Haw. 19, 986 P.2d 306 (1999)—§ 6.2(c) n.172

Janus Industries, United States v., 48 F.3d 1548 (10th Cir.1995)—§ 3.3(b) n.55

Januszewski, State v., 182 Conn. 142, 438 A.2d 679 (1980)—§ 3.8(d) n.144

Januszewski, United States v., 777 F.2d 108 (2d Cir.1985)—§ 21.2(d) n.166

Jaques, In re, 761 F.2d 302 (6th Cir.1985)—§ 8.3(a) n.2

Jaramillo v. Stewart, 340 F.3d 877 (9th Cir.2003)—§ 28.7(c) n.17

Jaramillo, United States v., 42 F.3d 920 (5th Cir.1995)—§ 24.11(d) n.34

Jaramillo, United States v., 891 F.2d 620 (7th Cir.1989)—§ 10.6(b) n.12

Jaroma, State v., 139 N.H. 611, 660 A.2d 1131 (1995)—§ 21.6(c) n.118

Jarrad, United States v., 754 F.2d 1451 (9th Cir.1985)—§§ 3.9(j) n.226; 7.4(c) n.48

Jarrell v. Balkcom, 735 F.2d 1242 (11th Cir.1984)—§§ 6.2(c) n.110; 6.8(b) n.63

Jarrell, United States v., 147 F.3d 315 (4th Cir.1998)—§ 18.3(b) n.25

Jarrett, United States v., 705 F.2d 198 (7th Cir.1983)—§ 13.4(a) n.27

Jasin, United States v., 280 F.3d 355 (3d Cir.2002)—§§ 24.11(d) n.20, 35

Jaskolski v. Daniels, 427 F.3d 456 (7th Cir.2005)—§ 8.5(e) n.175

Jasper, People v., 17 P.3d 807 (Colo.2001)—§§ 21.3(e) n.272, 273

Jasper v. State, 871 So.2d 729 (Miss.2004)—§§ 21.2(h) n.415, 420

Jasper v. State, 61 S.W.3d 413 (Tex.Cr.App.2001)—§ 22.3(d) n.202

Jaster, State v., 690 N.W.2d 213 (N.D.2004)—§ 22.3(c) n.129

Jaswal, United States v., 47 F.3d 539 (2d Cir.1995)—§ 19.2(c) n.25

Javier M., State v., 131 N.M. 1, 33 P.3d 1 (2001)—§§ 6.6(e) n.67, 91

Javor v. United States, 724 F.2d 831 (9th Cir.1984)—§ 11.10(d) n.199

Jawara, United States v., 474 F.3d 565 (9th Cir.2007)—§ 17.1(b) n.27

Jawara, United States v., 462 F.3d 1173 (9th Cir.2006)—§§ 17.1(a) n.7, 14; 17.1(b) n.37

Jaworski, People v., 387 Mich. 21, 194 N.W.2d 868 (1972)—§ 21.4(e) n.164

J. Clyde K., In re, 192 Cal.App.3d 710, 237 Cal.Rptr. 550 (1987)—§ 9.1(a) n.20

J.D., People v., 989 P.2d 762 (Colo.1999)—§ 6.6(b) n.16

J.D., State v., 86 Wash.App. 501, 937 P.2d 630 (1997)—§ 27.5(a) n.24

J.D. and D.R.D. v. State, 558 P.2d 402 (Okl.Cr.1976)—§ 9.4(a) n.25

J.D.F., Interest of, 553 N.W.2d 585 (Iowa 1996)—§§ 6.7(b) n.80; 9.3(e) n.70; 9.5(b) n.31, 35

J.D.H., Ex parte, 797 So.2d 1130 (Ala.2001)—§ 6.8(b) n.53

Jeannotte, State v., 133 Wash.2d 847, 947 P.2d 1192 (1997)—§ 26.3(g) n.88

J.E.B. v. Alabama ex rel. T.B., 511 U.S. 127, 114 S.Ct. 1419, 128 L.Ed.2d 89 (1994)—§ 22.3(d) n.194

Jeff, State v., 761 So.2d 574 (La.App.1999)—§ 11.8(c) n.70

Jefferies, State v., 333 N.C. 501, 428 S.E.2d 150 (1993)—§ 15.4(e) n.129

Jefferies, United States v., 908 F.2d 1520 (11th Cir.1990)—§ 21.1(h) n.220

Jeffers, People v., 188 Cal.App.3d 840, 233 Cal.Rptr. 692 (1987)— § 26.1(d) n.81

Jeffers v. United States, 432 U.S. 137, 97 S.Ct. 2207, 53 L.Ed.2d 168 (1977)—§ 17.4(b) n.110

Jeffers, United States v., 520 F.2d 1256 (7th Cir.1975)—§§ 11.9(d) n.202, 205, 206

Jeffers, United States v., 342 U.S. 48, 72 S.Ct. 93, 96 L.Ed. 59 (1951)— §§ 3.1(g) n.166; 3.3(a) n.15, 16; 3.6(e) n.114; 9.1(b) n.82; 9.2(b) n.12; 10.3(b) n.47

Jefferson v. Morgan, 962 F.2d 1185 (6th Cir.1992)—§ 15.4(c) n.90

Jefferson, People v., 934 P.2d 870 (Colo.App.1996)—§§ 19.5(b) n.9, 12, 31

Jefferson, People v., 43 A.D.2d 112, 350 N.Y.S.2d 3 (1973)—§ 3.10(c) n.97

Jefferson v. State, 189 S.W.3d 305 (Tex.Cr.App.2006)—§ 24.10(c) n.40

Jefferson, State v., 315 Mont. 146, 69 P.3d 641 (2003)—§§ 18.2(b) n.13; 18.2(e) n.76

Jefferson v. State, 807 So.2d 1222 (Miss.2002)—§ 24.2(d) n.45

Jefferson, State v., 574 N.W.2d 268 (Iowa 1997)—§ 11.4(b) n.24

Jefferson, State v., 938 S.W.2d 1 (Tenn.Crim.App.1996)—§ 18.3(c) n.68

Jefferson v. State, 108 Nev. 953, 840 P.2d 1234 (1992)—§ 21.4(a) n.11

Jefferson v. State, 595 So.2d 38 (Fla.1992)—§ 22.3(d) n.252

Jefferson, State v., 319 Md. 674, 574 A.2d 918 (1990)—§ 18.4(c) n.73

Jefferson v. State, 556 So.2d 1016 (Miss.1989)—§§ 15.1(f) n.324; 19.2(d) n.46; 19.3(a) n.13

Jefferson v. State, 141 Ga.App. 712, 234 S.E.2d 333 (1977)—§ 24.3(b) n.57

Jefferson, United States v., 569 F.2d 260 (5th Cir.1978)—§ 22.3(a) n.49

Jeffries, State v., 430 N.W.2d 728 (Iowa 1988)—§§ 24.8(d) n.43; 24.8(f) n.99

Jeffries, United States v., 265 F.3d 556 (7th Cir.2001)—§ 21.4(e) n.161

J.E.G., In re, 144 Vt. 309, 476 A.2d 130 (1984)—§ 6.2(c) n.163

Jeleniewski, State v., 147 N.H. 462, 791 A.2d 188 (2002)—§§ 6.4(e) n.68, 77; 6.9(g) n.157; 11.2(b) n.46; 21.3(e) n.265; 22.4(c) n.29

Jelle v. State, 119 P.3d 403 (Wyo.2005)—§ 6.6(e) n.91

Jelliff, State v., 251 N.W.2d 1 (N.D.1977)—§ 27.3(c) n.22

Jemmerson v. State, 80 Ga. 111, 5 S.E. 131 (1888)—§ 16.4(c) n.52

Jencks v. United States, 353 U.S. 657, 77 S.Ct. 1007, 1 L.Ed.2d 1103 (1957)—§§ 1.7(i) n.160; 24.3(c) n.83

Jendrzejewski, People v., 455 Mich. 495, 566 N.W.2d 530 (1997)— § 23.2(f) n.106

Jenich, State v., 94 Wis.2d 74, 292 N.W.2d 348 (1980)—§ 27.2(c) n.64

Jenison, State v., 122 R.I. 142, 405 A.2d 3 (R.I.1979)—§§ 15.4(d) n.100, 103, 124; 15.4(i) n.214

Jenison, United States v., 485 F.Supp. 655 (S.D.Fla.1979)—§ 15.4(d) n.123

Jenkins v. Anderson, 447 U.S. 231, 100 S.Ct. 2124, 65 L.Ed.2d 86 (1980)—§§ 9.6(a) n.39; 24.5(a) n.7

Jenkins v. Artuz, 294 F.3d 284 (2d Cir.2002)—§ 24.3(d) n.107

Jenkins v. Delaware, 395 U.S. 213, 89 S.Ct. 1677, 23 L.Ed.2d 253 (1969)—§§ 2.11(a) n.8; 2.11(c) n.37, 39, 41

Jenkins v. Fourth Judicial District Court, 109 Nev. 337, 849 P.2d 1055 (Nev.1993)—§ 25.1(d) n.62

Jenkins v. Garrison, 265 Ga. 42, 453 S.E.2d 698 (1995)—§ 27.4(f) n.66

Jenkins v. Georgia, 65 Ga.App. 16, 14 S.E.2d 594 (1941)—§ 8.10(c) n.51

Jenkins, People v., 22 Cal.4th 900, 95 Cal.Rptr.2d 377, 997 P.2d 1044 (2000)—§§ 3.10(e) n.172; 9.1(a) n.14, 17, 20

Jenkins, State v., 182 N.J. 112, 801 A.2d 827 (2004)—§ 22.3(e) n.280

Jenkins v. State, 375 Md. 284, 825 A.2d 1008 (2003)—§ 24.9(f) n.78

Jenkins v. State, 348 Ark. 686, 75 S.W.3d 180 (2002)—§ 6.9(b) n.23

Jenkins, State v., 204 W.Va. 347, 512 S.E.2d 860 (1998)—§ 17.4(c) n.153

Jenkins, State v., 845 S.W.2d 787 (Tenn.Cr.App.1992)—§ 24.9(c) n.29

Jenkins v. State, 301 Ark. 586, 786 S.W.2d 566 (1990)—§ 21.6(b) n.90

Jenkins, State v., 148 Ariz. 463, 715 P.2d 716 (1986)—§ 11.9(d) n.224

Jenkins v. State, 214 So.2d 470 (Miss.1968)—§ 6.8(a) n.38

Jenkins, United States v., 92 F.3d 430 (6th Cir.1996)—§§ 3.10(d) n.134; 18.3(b) n.25

Jenkins, United States v., 986 F.2d 76 (4th Cir.1993)—§ 3.9(h) n.168

Jenkins, United States v., 938 F.2d 934 (9th Cir.1991)—§§ 6.2(c) n.76 to 78

Jenkins, United States v., 904 F.2d 549 (10th Cir.1990)—§§ 8.8(f) n.150; 26.6(d) n.58

Jenkins v. United States, 541 A.2d 1269 (D.C.App.1988)—§ 1.7(i) n.202

Jenkins, United States v., 420 U.S. 358, 95 S.Ct. 1006, 43 L.Ed.2d 250 (1975)—§ 25.3(e) n.38

Jenkins v. United States, 392 F.2d 303 (10th Cir.1968)—§ 16.1(h) n.306

Jenne, State v., 156 Vt. 283, 591 A.2d 85 (1991)—§ 22.2(d) n.67

Jennette, State v., 706 S.W.2d 614 (1986)—§ 2.12(d) n.185

Jennings, Ex parte, 91 Tex.Crim. 612, 240 S.W. 942 (App.1922)—§ 8.8(b) n.30

Jennings, State v., 252 Wis.2d 228, 647 N.W.2d 142 (2002)—§§ 2.12(b) n.82; 6.9(g) n.166

Jennings v. State, 116 Nev. 488, 998 P.2d 557 (Nev.2000)—§ 19.5(b) n.33

Jennings, State v., 216 Conn. 647, 583 A.2d 915 (1990)—§ 24.8(a) n.18

Jennings v. State, 276 Ark. 217, 633 S.W.2d 373 (1982)—§ 1.7(f) n.100

Jennings v. Superior Court, 66 Cal.2d 867, 59 Cal.Rptr. 440, 428 P.2d 304 (1967)—§§ 14.4(d) n.95; 14.4(e) n.108

Jennings, United States v., 855 F.Supp. 1427 (M.D.Pa.1994)—§§ 11.4(b) n.28, 29

Jennings, United States v., 991 F.2d 725 (11th Cir.1993)—§§ 15.4(g) n.167; 15.4(i) n.213

Jennings, United States v., 960 F.2d 1488 (9th Cir.1992)—§ 20.3(a) n.12

Jennings, State ex rel. v. Nurre, 72 Ohio St.3d 596, 651 N.E.2d 1006 (1995)—§ 27.4(b) n.11

Jensen v. DeLand, 795 P.2d 619 (Utah 1989)—§ 11.7(e) n.65

Jensen, State v., 378 N.W.2d 710 (Iowa 1985)—§ 26.10(b) n.19

Jerez, United States v., 108 F.3d 684 (7th Cir.1997)—§§ 3.8(c) n.101, 106

Jermyn v. Horn, 266 F.3d 257 (3d Cir.2001)—§ 11.10(c) n.127

Jeronimo, United States v., 398 F.3d 1149 (9th Cir.2005)—§ 21.2(b) n.82

Jeronimo-Bautista, United States v., 425 F.3d 1266 (10th Cir.2005)—§ 1.2(c) n.193

Jerrell C.J., In re, 283 Wis.2d 145, 699 N.W.2d 110 (2005)—§§ 6.2(c) n.163; 6.8(c) n.64; 10.3(c) n.52

Jerry, United States v., 487 F.2d 600 (3d Cir.1973)—§ 21.5(a) n.45

Jersey City Ed. Ass'n, In re, 115 N.J.Super. 42, 278 A.2d 206 (A.D. 1971)—§ 15.1(d) n.242

Jerskey v. State, 546 P.2d 173 (1976)—§ 2.10(d) n.116

Jessen, In re, 738 F.Supp. 960 (W.D.N.C.1990)—§ 15.1(b) n.86

Jessen, State v., 130 Ariz. 1, 633 P.2d 410 (1981)—§ 15.2(c) n.62

Jessup, Petition of, 50 Del. 530, 136 A.2d 207 (1957)—§§ 8.5(b) n.37; 15.2(b) n.20

Jessup, United States v., 966 F.2d 1354 (10th Cir.1992)—§ 26.5(a) n.8

Jessup, United States v., 757 F.2d 378 (1st Cir.1985)—§ 12.3(a) n.24

Jetblue Airways Corp. Privacy Litigation, In re, 379 F.Supp.2d 299 (E.D.N.Y. 2005)—§ 4.8(b) n.14

Jeter, United States v., 315 F.3d 445 (5th Cir.2002)—§§ 21.3(d) n.218; 21.3(e) n.265, 279

Jett, State v., 474 N.W.2d 741 (S.D.1991)—§§ 11.7(e) n.63, 79

Jewell v. Commonwealth, 725 S.W.2d 593 (Ky.1987)—§ 21.4(d) n.151

Jewell v. Hempleman, 210 Wis. 265, 246 N.W. 441 (1933)—§ 3.3(b) n.56

Jewett, State v., 146 Vt. 221, 500 A.2d 233 (1985)—§§ 2.12(a) n.31, 38; 2.12(d) n.195

J.G., State in Interest of, 151 N.J. 565, 701 A.2d 1260 (1997)—§ 3.5(d) n.144

J.H., In re, 928 A.2d 643 (D.C.Dist.2007)—§ 24.6(c) n.41

J.H., People v., 136 Ill.2d 1, 143 Ill.Dec. 889, 554 N.E.2d 961 (1990)—§ 15.6(d) n.120

Jhirad v. Ferrandina, 536 F.2d 478 (2d Cir.1976)—§ 18.5(a) n.25

Ji, State v., 251 Kan. 3, 832 P.2d 1176 (Kan.1992)—§§ 23.3(b) n.27, 28

Jibben v. State, 901 P.2d 1099 (Wyo.1995)—§ 26.10(b) n.19

Jideonwo v. INS, 224 F.3d 692 (7th Cir.2000)—§§ 21.2(d) n.232, 233; 21.2(e) n.321; 21.3(b) n.68

Jimenez, People v., 21 Cal.3d 595, 147 Cal.Rptr. 172, 580 P.2d 672 (1978)—§ 10.4(b) n.9

Jimenez, State v., 188 N.J. 390, 908 A.2d 181 (2006)—§ 26.4(h) n.156

Jimenez, State v., 987 S.W.2d 886 (Tex.Cr.App.1999)—§ 21.4(d) n.134

Jimenez, State v., 935 P.2d 920 (Ariz.App.1996)—§ 27.5(c) n.50

Jimenez, United States v., 256 F.3d 330 (5th Cir.2001)—§ 13.5(b) n.36

Jimenez, United States v., 780 F.2d 975 (11th Cir.1986)—§§ 24.4(d) n.57, 61

Jiminez, People v., 863 P.2d 981 (Colo.1993)—§§ 6.9(b) n.24, 41

Jiminez v. State, 144 P.3d 903 (Okla.Crim.App.2006)—§ 21.3(b) n.107

Jiminez, United States v., 478 F.3d 929 (8th Cir.2007)—§ 6.9(b) n.28

Jiminez, United States v., 983 F.2d 1020 (11th Cir.1993)—§ 22.3(d) n.216

Jiminez v. Walker, 458 F.3d 130 (2d Cir.2006)—§ 28.6(f) n.77

Jiminez-Nova, United States v., 243 F.3d 192 (5th Cir.2001)—§§ 1.7(c) n.17, 20

Jiosa v. State, 755 N.E.2d 605 (Ind.2001)—§ 24.4(d) n.62

J.J., In the Interest of, 540 Pa. 274, 656 A.2d 1355 (1995)—§ 27.5(c) n.82

J.J.K., United States v., 76 F.3d 870 (7th Cir.1996)—§ 27.2(c) n.45

J.M., In re, 619 A.2d 497 (D.C.1992)—§§ 3.8(c) n.79; 3.10(b) n.42

J.M., State v., 718 So.2d 316 (Fla.App.1998)—§ 13.2(c) n.56

J.M.L., People ex rel., 726 N.W.2d 621 (S.D.2007)—§ 6.8(d) n.84

Joao, State v., 53 Haw. 226, 491 P.2d 1089 (1971)—§§ 15.6(a) n.13, 16, 17; 15.6(d) n.107, 124; 15.7(b) n.27

Jobe, State v., 486 N.W.2d 407 (Minn.1992)—§ 6.5(b) n.26

Joe, United States v., 928 F.2d 99 (4th Cir.1991)—§ 22.3(d) n.213

Jogi v. Voges, 425 F.3d 367 (7th Cir.2005)—§§ 1.7(c) n.20, 38

John, State v., 210 Conn. 652, 557 A.2d 93 (1989)—§ 14.4(b) n.7

John, United States v., 508 F.2d 1134 (8th Cir.1975)—§ 15.2(j) n.237

John Bad Elk v. United States, 177 U.S. 529, 20 S.Ct. 729, 44 L.Ed. 874 (1900)—§ 3.1(o) n.302

John Doe, United States v., 471 U.S. 1001, 105 S.Ct. 1861, 85 L.Ed.2d 155 (1985)—§ 8.12(g) n.64

John Doe Agency v. John Doe Corp., 493 U.S. 146, 110 S.Ct. 471, 107 L.Ed.2d 462 (1989)—§ 20.2(d) n.78

John Doe Grand Jury Investigation, In the Matter of, 418 Mass. 549, 637 N.E.2d 858 (1994)—§ 8.13(d) n.95

John Doe Grand Jury Investigation, Matter of, 410 Mass. 596, 574 N.E.2d 373 (1991)—§ 8.8(d) n.50

John Doe, Inc. I, United States v., 481 U.S. 102, 107 S.Ct. 1656, 95 L.Ed.2d 94 (1987)—§§ 1.5(c) n.95, 166; 2.9(h) n.206; 8.5(e) n.180; 8.5(h) n.279, 283; 8.5(i) n.310

John Doe Number 1, United States v., 272 F.3d 116 (2d Cir.2001)—§ 11.4(b) n.28

John Doe Trader Number One, In re, 894 F.2d 240 (7th Cir.1990)—§ 4.6(b) n.42

Johns v. Shulsen, 717 P.2d 1336 (Utah 1986)—§ 17.4(a) n.30

Johns v. State, 274 Ga. 23, 549 S.E.2d 68 (2001)—§ 6.7(d) n.145

Johns, State v., 679 S.W.2d 253 (Mo.1984)—§§ 3.10(b) n.52; 3.10(f) n.205

Johns v. State, 19 Ind. 421 (1862)—§§ 16.4(c) n.60, 62

Johns, United States v., 948 F.2d 599 (9th Cir.1991)—§ 3.3(c) n.143

Johns, United States v., 891 F.2d 243 (9th Cir.1989)—§ 9.3(d) n.39

Johns, United States v., 469 U.S. 478, 105 S.Ct. 881, 83 L.Ed.2d 890 (1985)—§§ 3.5(e) n.206; 3.7(b) n.26; 3.7(c) n.45, 48; 3.7(f) n.138

Johns, United States v., 707 F.2d 1093 (9th Cir.1983)—§ 9.2(c) n.33

Johns-Manville Corp., United States v., 213 F.Supp. 65 (E.D.Pa.1962)—§§ 8.4(c) n.134; 8.8(g) n.169

Johnson, Ex parte, 669 So.2d 205 (Ala.1995)—§ 21.2(f) n.363

Johnson, Ex parte, 620 So.2d 709 (Ala.1993)—§§ 6.8(c) n.66; 7.4(d) n.76

Johnson, Ex parte, 522 So.2d 234 (Ala.1988)—§ 6.9(c) n.59

Johnson, In re, 47 Va.App. 503, 624 S.E.2d 696 (2006)—§ 24.11(d) n.47

Johnson, In re, 1 Cal.4th 689, 4 Cal.Rptr.2d 170, 822 P.2d 1317 (1992)—§ 11.8(c) n.75

Johnson, In re, 62 Cal.2d 325, 42 Cal.Rptr. 228, 398 P.2d 420 (1965)—§ 21.3(a) n.32

Johnson v. Avery, 393 U.S. 483, 89 S.Ct. 747, 21 L.Ed.2d 718 (1969)—§§ 11.2(f) n.232, 242

Johnson v. Beto, 466 F.2d 478 (5th Cir.1972)—§ 21.2(f) n.393

Johnson v. Cadillac Plastic Group, Inc., 930 F.Supp. 1437 (D.Colo.1996)—§ 1.7(j) n.262

Johnson v. California, 545 U.S. 162, 125 S.Ct. 2410, 162 L.Ed.2d 129 (2005)—§ 22.3(d) n.211

Johnson v. Commissioner of Correction, 60 Conn.App. 1, 758 A.2d 442 (2000)—§ 18.4(c) n.70

Johnson v. Commissioner of Correction, 218 Conn. 403, 589 A.2d 1214 (1991)—§ 28.11(b) n.18

Johnson, Commonwealth v., 447 Mass. 1018, 856 N.E.2d 822 (2006)— § 21.2(f) n.383

Johnson v. Commonwealth, 103 S.W.3d 687 (Ky.2003)—§§ 21.4(b) n.65; 21.4(e) n.165

Johnson v. Commonwealth, 120 S.W.3d 704 (Ky.2003)—§ 21.2(b) n.76

Johnson, Commonwealth v., 574 Pa. 5, 828 A.2d 1009 (2003)—§ 11.8(a) n.12

Johnson, Commonwealth v., 576 Pa. 23, 838 A.2d 663 (2003)—§ 22.2(d) n.81

Johnson, Commonwealth v., 565 Pa. 51, 771 A.2d 751 (2001)—§ 22.1(h) n.133

Johnson v. Commonwealth, 259 Va. 654, 529 S.E.2d 769 (2000)— § 3.3(g) n.222

Johnson, Commonwealth v., 727 A.2d 1089 (Pa.1999)—§ 24.3(b) n.38

Johnson, Commonwealth v., 550 Pa. 298, 705 A.2d 830 (1998)— §§ 27.2(c) n.60, 62

Johnson, Commonwealth v., 420 Mass. 458, 650 N.E.2d 1257 (1995)— § 7.4(c) n.38

Johnson, Commonwealth v., 542 Pa. 384, 668 A.2d 97 (1995)—§§ 7.2(c) n.30, 31

Johnson v. Commonwealth, 221 Va. 736, 273 S.E.2d 784 (1981)— § 25.4(d) n.44

Johnson v. Commonwealth, 208 Va. 481, 158 S.E.2d 725 (1968)— § 7.2(b) n.15

Johnson v. Commonwealth, 86 Ky. 122, 5 S.W. 365 (1887)—§ 16.4(c) n.47

Johnson v. Dretke, 442 F.3d 901 (5th Cir.2006)—§ 28.5(d) n.87

Johnson v. Dretke, 394 F.3d 332 (5th Cir.2004)—§ 24.3(b) n.35

Johnson v. Duckworth, 793 F.2d 898 (7th Cir.1986)—§ 21.3(b) n.79

Johnson v. Duckworth, 650 F.2d 122 (7th Cir.1981)—§ 22.3(e) n.284

Johnson v. Dugger, 911 F.2d 440 (11th Cir.1990)—§ 11.10(c) n.80

Johnson v. Dugger, 817 F.2d 726 (11th Cir.1987)—§§ 7.4(b) n.23; 7.4(f) n.96

Johnson v. Eisentrager, 339 U.S. 763, 70 S.Ct. 936, 94 L.Ed. 1255 (1950)— § 1.7(c) n.54

Johnson v. Hendricks, 314 F.3d 159 (3d Cir.2002)—§ 28.5(b) n.59

Johnson v. Karnes, 198 F.3d 589 (6th Cir.1999)—§ 25.2(d) n.24

Johnson v. Larabida Children's Hospital, 372 F.3d 894 (7th Cir.2004)— § 3.1(h) n.190

Johnson v. Louisiana, 406 U.S. 356, 92 S.Ct. 1620, 32 L.Ed.2d 152 (1972)—§§ 1.5(e) n.222; 2.5(f) n.99, 101; 9.4(a) n.23; 9.4(d) n.84; 22.1(e) n.83

Johnson v. Mabry, 752 F.2d 313 (8th Cir.1985)—§ 21.3(b) n.53

Johnson v. Manson, 196 Conn. 309, 493 A.2d 846 (1985)—§ 27.4(f) n.66

Johnson v. McCaughtry, 92 F.3d 585 (7th Cir.1996)—§ 22.2(d) n.67

Johnson v. Mississippi, 486 U.S. 578, 108 S.Ct. 1981, 100 L.Ed.2d 575 (1988)—§§ 26.1(b) n.24; 26.4(f) n.106

Johnson v. Mississippi, 403 U.S. 212, 91 S.Ct. 1778, 29 L.Ed.2d 423 (1971)—§§ 2.7(c) n.200; 22.4(a) n.10

Johnson v. Nevada, 118 Nev. 787, 59 P.3d 450 (Nev.2002)—§ 26.4(i) n.179

Johnson v. New Jersey, 384 U.S. 719, 86 S.Ct. 1772, 16 L.Ed.2d 882 (1966)—§§ 2.11(c) n.32, 37; 6.2(c) n.155; 6.4(c) n.37; 6.5(b) n.34; 9.5(a) n.16

Johnson v. Pataki, 91 N.Y.2d 214, 668 N.Y.S.2d 978, 691 N.E.2d 1002 (1997)—§ 13.3(e) n.49

Johnson, People v., 38 Cal.4th 1096, 45 Cal.Rptr.3d 1 (2006), 136 P.3d 804—§ 22.3(d) n.255

Johnson, People v., 142 Cal.App.4th 776, 48 Cal.Rptr.3d 439 (2006)—§ 24.3(b) n.35

Johnson, People v., 208 Ill.2d 53, 281 Ill.Dec. 1, 803 N.E.2d 405 (2004)—§§ 24.7(i) n.91; 27.5(d) n.137

Johnson, People v., 1 N.Y.3d 252, 771 N.Y.S.2d 64, 803 N.E.2d 385 (2003)—§ 3.7(e) n.107

Johnson, People v., 466 Mich. 491, 647 N.W.2d 480 (2002)—§§ 5.2(b) n.24, 28

Johnson, People v., 116 Nev. 78, 993 P.2d 44 (2000)—§ 3.10(f) n.192

Johnson, People v., 999 P.2d 825 (Colo.2000)—§ 21.2(d) n.239

Johnson v. People, 939 P.2d 817 (Colo.1997)—§§ 18.4(c) n.51, 53

Johnson, People v., 89 N.Y.2d 905, 653 N.Y.S.2d 265, 675 N.E.2d 1217 (1996)—§ 21.4(f) n.197

Johnson, People v., 232 A.D.2d 220, 648 N.Y.S.2d 30 (1996)—§ 25.2(a) n.9

Johnson, People v., 6 Cal.4th 1, 23 Cal.Rptr.2d 593, 859 P.2d 673 (1993)—§§ 6.9(g) n.182, 183

Johnson, People v., 81 N.Y.2d 828, 595 N.Y.S.2d 385, 611 N.E.2d 286 (1993)—§ 7.4(f) n.97

Johnson, People v., 3 Cal.4th 1183, 14 Cal.Rptr.2d 702, 842 P.2d 1 (1992)—§§ 2.12(a) n.69; 7.2(c) n.30; 24.8(d) n.46

Johnson, People v., 149 Ill.2d 118, 171 Ill.Dec. 401, 594 N.E.2d 253 (1992)—§ 7.4(e) n.82

Johnson, People v., 227 Ill.App.3d 800, 169 Ill.Dec. 858, 592 N.E.2d 345 (1992)—§ 11.7(b) n.29

Johnson, People v., 237 Ill.App.3d 860, 178 Ill.Dec. 659, 605 N.E.2d 98 (1992)—§ 9.1(b) n.81

Johnson, People v., 191 Mich.App. 222, 477 N.W.2d 426 (1991)—§§ 26.10(d) n.97, 99

Johnson, People v., 47 Cal.3d 576, 253 Cal.Rptr. 710, 764 P.2d 1087 (1988)—§§ 17.1(b) n.27; 17.1(d) n.53

Johnson, People v., 427 Mich. 98, 398 N.W.2d 219 (1986)—§§ 14.3(d) n.84; 19.3(a) n.67

Johnson, People v., 96 Ill.App.3d 763, 52 Ill.Dec. 369, 422 N.E.2d 50 (1981)—§ 6.4(e) n.68

Johnson, People v., 97 Ill.App.3d 1055, 53 Ill.Dec. 402, 423 N.E.2d 1206 (1981)—§ 15.7(c) n.61

Johnson, People v., 26 Cal.3d 557, 162 Cal.Rptr. 431, 606 P.2d 738 (1980)—§ 11.6(a) n.44

Johnson, People v., 69 Ill.App.3d 248, 25 Ill.Dec. 732, 387 N.E.2d 388 (1979)—§§ 19.1(d) n.51; 19.3(a) n.57; 19.5(b) n.44

Johnson, People v., 77 Mich.App. 426, 258 N.W.2d 504 (1977)—§ 8.14(c) n.37

Johnson, People v., 34 Ill.App.3d 38, 339 N.E.2d 325 (1975)—§ 19.6(b) n.16

Johnson v. People, 172 Colo. 72, 470 P.2d 37 (1970)—§ 7.4(b) n.20

Johnson, People v., 70 Cal.2d 469, 74 Cal.Rptr. 889, 450 P.2d 265 (1969)—§ 6.2(c) n.103

Johnson, People v., 70 Cal.2d 541, 75 Cal.Rptr. 401, 450 P.2d 865 (1969)—§§ 6.9(d) n.72; 9.4(a) n.44; 10.3(c) n.56

Johnson, People v., 38 Ill.2d 399, 231 N.E.2d 447 (1967)—§ 10.2(a) n.16

Johnson, People v., 356 Mich. 619, 97 N.W.2d 739 (1959)—§ 20.1(a) n.9

Johnson v. Pinchack, 392 F.3d 551 (3d Cir.2004)—§§ 28.4(b) n.19; 28.4(c) n.27

Johnson v. Puckett, 929 F.2d 1067 (5th Cir.1991)—§ 15.4(e) n.141

Johnson v. Quander, 440 F.3d 489 (D.C.Cir.2006)—§§ 3.9(i) n.190; 3.9(j) n.236, 238, 241

Johnson v. Raftevold, 505 N.W.2d 110 (N.D.1993)—§ 27.4(f) n.63

Johnson v. Ross, 955 F.2d 178 (2d Cir.1992)—§§ 7.4(a) n.7; 7.4(d) n.74

Johnson v. Sayre, 158 U.S. 109, 15 S.Ct. 773, 39 L.Ed. 914 (1895)— § 15.1(b) n.93

Johnson v. Stagner, 781 F.2d 758 (9th Cir.1986)—§ 18.4(c) n.33

Johnson, State v., 155 P.3d 183 (Wash.App.2007)—§ 24.9(f) n.97

Johnson, State v., 207 S.W.3d 24 (Mo.2006)—§ 6.2(c) n.151

Johnson, State v., 182 N.J. 232, 864 A.2d 400 (2005)—§ 21.4(d) n.114

Johnson v. State, 827 N.E.2d 547 (Ind.2005)—§ 24.11(d) n.39

Johnson v. State, 903 So.2d 888 (Fla.2005)—§ 6.2(c) n.128

Johnson v. State, 904 So.2d 162 (Miss.2005)—§ 7.4(c) n.48

Johnson, State v., 276 Ga. 78, 576 S.E.2d 831 (2003)—§§ 20.4(e) n.78, 84

Johnson v. State, 68 S.W.3d 644 (Tex.Cr.App.2002)—§ 6.2(c) n.107

Johnson, State v., 171 N.J. 192, 793 A.2d 619 (2002)—§§ 3.2(b) n.34; 3.2(c) n.130

Johnson, State v., 367 Md. 418, 788 A.2d 628 (2002)—§ 24.10(b) n.26

Johnson v. State, 641 N.W.2d 912 (Minn.2002)—§ 21.2(d) n.256

Johnson, State v., 814 So.2d 390 (Fla.2002)—§§ 3.1(c) n.63; 8.5(i) n.310

Johnson, State v., 823 So.2d 917 (La.2002)—§ 24.8(f) n.100

Johnson v. State, 117 Nev. 153, 17 P.3d 1008 (Nev.2001)—§ 11.6(a) n.26

Johnson, State v., 274 Ga. 511, 555 S.E.2d 710 (2001)—§§ 18.2(d) n.63, 67; 18.2(e) n.82

Johnson, State v., 232 Wis.2d 679, 605 N.W.2d 846 (2000)—§ 13.7(c) n.45

Johnson, State v., 253 Conn. 1, 751 A.2d 298 (2000)—§ 21.4(b) n.59

Johnson v. State, 734 N.E.2d 242 (Ind.2000)—§ 21.5(d) n.101

Johnson v. State, 765 A.2d 926 (Del.2000)—§ 11.7(e) n.73

Johnson, State v., 231 Wis.2d 58, 604 N.W.2d 902 (1999)—§ 14.3(c) n.80

Johnson v. State, 337 Ark. 196, 987 S.W.2d 694 (1999)—§ 22.1(h) n.137

Johnson v. State, 750 So.2d 22 (Fla.1999)—§ 22.3(d) n.253

Johnson v. State, 711 A.2d 18 (Del.1998)—§§ 19.3(a) n.5, 65; 19.5(b) n.4; 19.5(d) n.85

Johnson, State v., 207 Wis.2d 239, 558 N.W.2d 375 (1997)—§ 21.4(f) n.192

Johnson, State v., 346 N.C. 119, 484 S.E.2d 372 (1997)—§ 24.9(c) n.29

Johnson, State v., 197 W.Va. 575, 476 S.E.2d 522 (1996)—§ 17.4(c) n.153

Johnson v. State, 267 Ga. 77, 475 S.E.2d 595 (1996)—§ 26.1(e) n.98

Johnson, State v., 267 Ga. 305, 477 S.E.2d 579 (1996)—§§ 25.2(a) n.7, 10

Johnson v. State, 675 N.E.2d 678 (Ind.1996)—§ 22.5(b) n.20

Johnson v. State, 683 So.2d 607 (Fla.App.1996)—§ 26.9(c) n.87

Johnson v. State, 922 P.2d 1384 (Wyo.1996)—§ 21.4(d) n.138

Johnson, State v., 258 Kan. 61, 899 P.2d 1050 (1995)—§ 21.2(d) n.178

Johnson, State v., 258 Kan. 607, 907 P.2d 140 (1995)—§§ 21.3(f) n.402, 406

Johnson v. State, 660 So.2d 648 (Fla.1995)—§ 24.7(e) n.49

Johnson, State v., 664 So.2d 94 (La.1995)—§§ 13.3(c) n.38; 27.6(b) n.44

Johnson v. State, 666 So.2d 784 (Miss.1995)—§ 18.3(c) n.111

Johnson, State v., 667 A.2d 110 (Me.1995)—§ 26.9(c) n.80

Johnson v. State, 905 P.2d 818 (Okla.Crim.App.1995)—§§ 3.10(d) n.126; 24.4(c) n.26

Johnson, State v., 75 Wash.App. 692, 879 P.2d 984 (1994)—§ 2.12(c) n.176

Johnson, State v., 314 S.C. 161, 442 S.E.2d 191 (1994)—§ 19.5(c) n.60

Johnson, State v., 242 Neb. 924, 497 N.W.2d 28 (1993)—§ 21.2(f) n.383

Johnson, State v., 257 Mont. 157, 848 P.2d 496 (1993)—§§ 16.1(g) n.235, 270; 16.1(h) n.304, 305, 308, 312

Johnson, State v., 269 N.J.Super. 276, 635 A.2d 527 (1993)—§§ 11.6(a) n.24; 11.6(d) n.115

Johnson, State v., 856 P.2d 1064 (Utah 1993)—§ 26.4(f) n.91

Johnson, State v., 1993 WL 205242 (Minn.App.1993)—§ 21.3(f) n.360

Johnson, State v., 127 N.J. 458, 606 A.2d 315 (1992)—§ 5.4(c) n.39

Johnson, State v., 158 Vt. 344, 612 A.2d 1114 (1992)—§§ 17.1(d) n.53; 17.1(f) n.69

Johnson v. State, 834 S.W.2d 922 (Tenn.1992)—§ 21.5(c) n.91

Johnson, State v., 219 Conn. 557, 594 A.2d 933 (1991)—§ 3.3(c) n.108

Johnson v. State, 806 P.2d 1282 (Wyo.1991)—§ 22.1(h) n.154

Johnson, State v., 823 P.2d 484 (Utah App.1991)—§§ 11.9(c) n.126, 145

Johnson, State v., 120 N.J. 263, 576 A.2d 834 (1990)—§ 9.3(e) n.71

Johnson, State v., 302 S.C. 243, 395 S.E.2d 167 (1990)—§ 3.1(c) n.77

Johnson, State v., 558 So.2d 325 (La.App.1990)—§ 24.3(i) n.188

Johnson v. State, 299 Ark. 223, 772 S.W.2d 322 (1989)—§ 6.8(a) n.26

Johnson, State v., 441 N.W.2d 460 (Minn.1989)—§§ 15.3(d) n.64, 68; 15.6(a) n.26; 15.6(d) n.111, 122; 15.7(b) n.51; 15.7(g) n.221

Johnson, State v., 40 Ohio St.3d 130, 532 N.E.2d 1295 (1988)—§§ 21.4(d) n.106, 146

Johnson, State v., 295 S.C. 215, 367 S.E.2d 700 (1988)—§ 5.2(a) n.4

Johnson v. State, 529 So.2d 577 (Miss.1988)—§§ 11.2(e) n.198, 207, 211

Johnson v. State, 761 P.2d 484 (Okla.Crim.App.1988)—§ 22.3(d) n.193

Johnson v. State, 291 Ark. 260, 724 S.W.2d 160 (1987)—§ 3.2(c) n.134

Johnson v. State, 513 N.E.2d 650 (Ind.1987)—§ 6.2(c) n.96

Johnson, State v., 748 P.2d 1069 (Utah 1987)—§ 3.9(j) n.201

Johnson, State v., 221 Mont. 503, 719 P.2d 1248 (Mont.1986)—§§ 2.12(d) n.192, 195

Johnson, State v., 317 N.C. 193, 344 S.E.2d 775 (1986)—§ 16.3(g) n.105

Johnson, State v., 714 S.W.2d 752 (Mo.App.1986)—§ 11.6(a) n.31

Johnson v. State, 174 Ga.App. 579, 330 S.E.2d 791 (1985)—§ 20.3(c) n.64

Johnson v. State, 472 N.E.2d 892 (Ind.1985)—§ 7.3(b) n.14

Johnson v. State, 475 So.2d 1136 (Miss.1985)—§ 6.8(b) n.57

Johnson v. State, 476 So.2d 1195 (Miss.1985)—§ 23.2(a) n.51

Johnson, State v., 702 S.W.2d 65 (Mo.1985)—§§ 22.5(c) n.25; 22.5(d) n.29, 30

Johnson v. State, 171 Ga.App. 851, 321 S.E.2d 402 (1984)—§ 11.10(c) n.85

Johnson v. State, 460 So.2d 954 (Fla.App.1984)—§§ 21.3(f) n.427; 25.1(d) n.63, 72

Johnson, State v., 673 S.W.2d 877 (Tenn.Crim.App.1984)—§ 16.1(g) n.276

Johnson v. State, 676 S.W.2d 416 (Tex.Crim.App.1984)—§ 11.5(d) n.71

Johnson v. State, 378 So.2d 335 (Fla.App.1980)—§ 21.2(d) n.227

Johnson v. State, 611 P.2d 1137 (Okla.Crim.App.1980)—§ 16.1(d) n.132

Johnson, State v., 37 Or.App. 209, 586 P.2d 811 (1978)—§ 6.4(f) n.128

Johnson v. State, 269 Ind. 370, 380 N.E.2d 1236 (1978)—§ 6.7(b) n.72

Johnson v. State, 282 Md. 314, 384 A.2d 709 (1978)—§ 6.3(c) n.50

Johnson v. State, 267 Ind. 256, 369 N.E.2d 623 (1977)—§ 22.3(e) n.283

Johnson v. State, 30 Md.App. 280, 352 A.2d 349 (1976)—§ 3.10(b) n.39

Johnson, State v., 74 Wis.2d 169, 246 N.W.2d 503 (1976)—§§ 13.4(c) n.85, 91, 123

Johnson, State v., 219 Kan. 847, 549 P.2d 1370 (1976)—§ 20.6(b) n.17

Johnson v. State, 265 Ind. 470, 355 N.E.2d 240 (1976)—§ 24.8(f) n.109

Johnson, State v., 306 So.2d 724 (La.1975)—§ 3.6(d) n.87

Johnson, State v., 16 Or.App. 560, 519 P.2d 1053 (1974)—§§ 10.1(b) n.19, 21, 22; 10.6(a) n.7

Johnson, State v., 216 N.W.2d 337 (Iowa 1974)—§ 24.9(a) n.4

Johnson v. State, 262 Ind. 164, 313 N.E.2d 535 (1974)—§ 18.3(c) n.109

Johnson v. State, 496 S.W.2d 72 (Tex.Cr.App.1973)—§ 9.4(d) n.94

Johnson, State v., 31 Ohio St.2d 106, 285 N.E.2d 751 (1972)—§ 22.2(d) n.85

Johnson, State v., 61 N.J. 351, 294 A.2d 245 (1972)—§ 12.4(a) n.10

Johnson, State v., 87 S.D. 43, 202 N.W.2d 132 (1972)—§ 6.10(c) n.41

Johnson, State v., 6 Or.App. 195, 487 P.2d 115 (1971)—§ 16.1(d) n.158

Johnson, State v., 28 N.J. 133, 145 A.2d 313 (1958)—§ 20.1(a) n.14

Johnson, State v., 26 Idaho 609, 144 P. 784 (1914)—§ 24.1(b) n.20

Johnson v. Sublett, 63 F.3d 926 (9th Cir.1995)—§§ 7.3(e) n.102; 7.4(a) n.7; 7.4(g) n.117

Johnson v. Superior Court, 15 Cal.3d 248, 124 Cal.Rptr. 32, 539 P.2d 792 (1975)—§§ 15.2(b) n.36; 15.2(c) n.61; 15.7(d) n.85; 15.7(f) n.131; 27.4(c) n.32

Johnson, United States v., 437 F.3d 69 (D.C.Cir.2006)—§ 3.3(g) n.225

Johnson, United States v., 463 F.3d 803 (8th Cir.2006)—§ 21.4(g) n.256

Johnson, United States v., 362 F.Supp.2d 1043 (N.D.Iowa 2005)—§ 24.4(d) n.53

Johnson, United States v., 378 F.Supp.2d 1051 (N.D.Iowa 2005)—§ 26.4(f) n.110

Johnson, United States v., 399 F.3d 1297 (11th Cir.2005)—§ 12.3(a) n.18

Johnson v. United States, 544 U.S. 295, 125 S.Ct. 1571, 161 L.Ed.2d 542 (2005)—§§ 26.4(f) n.101; 28.5(d) n.87; 28.9(b) n.49

Johnson v. United States, 362 F.3d 636 (9th Cir.2004)—§ 28.9(b) n.58

Johnson, United States v., 380 F.3d 1013 (7th Cir.2004)—§ 9.3(e) n.84

Johnson, United States v., 325 F.3d 205 (4th Cir.2003)—§ 13.7(c) n.45

Johnson, United States v., 326 F.3d 1018 (8th Cir.2003)—§ 3.8(c) n.89

Johnson, United States v., 338 F.3d 918 (8th Cir.2003)—§ 6.4(g) n.153

Johnson, United States v., 351 F.3d 254 (6th Cir.2003)—§ 6.2(c) n.96

Johnson, United States v., 352 F.3d 339 (8th Cir.2003)—§ 6.4(e) n.100

Johnson, United States v., 241 F.3d 1049 (8th Cir.2001)—§ 21.2(d) n.255

Johnson, United States v., 246 F.3d 749 (5th Cir.2001)—§ 21.4(f) n.192

Johnson, United States v., 248 F.3d 655 (7th Cir.2001)—§ 24.2(g) n.97

Johnson, United States v., 260 F.3d 919 (8th Cir.2001)—§ 28.4(e) n.85

Johnson, United States v., 212 F.3d 1313 (D.C.Cir.2000)—§ 10.6(a) n.2

Johnson v. United States, 746 A.2d 349 (D.C.App.2000)—§ 11.4(c) n.89

Johnson, United States v., 169 F.3d 1092 (8th Cir.1999)—§§ 6.9(e) n.97; 21.2(b) n.74

Johnson, United States v., 171 F.3d 139 (2d Cir.1999)—§ 13.5(a) n.5

Johnson, United States v., 171 F.3d 601 (8th Cir.1999)—§ 4.2(b) n.15

Johnson, United States v., 187 F.3d 1129 (9th Cir.1999)—§§ 21.2(d) n.172, 174

Johnson, United States v., 196 F.3d 1000 (9th Cir.1999)—§§ 18.4(c) n.56, 57

Johnson, United States v., 21 F.Supp.2d 329 (S.D.N.Y.1998)—§ 19.4(b) n.28

Johnson, United States v., 132 F.3d 628 (11th Cir.1998)—§§ 21.2(d) n.177; 21.2(e) n.308, 316

Johnson, United States v., 130 F.3d 1420 (10th Cir.1997)—§§ 19.3(c) n.193, 196

Johnson v. United States, 520 U.S. 461, 117 S.Ct. 1544, 137 L.Ed.2d 718 (1997)—§§ 19.2(e) n.81; 19.3(a) n.99, 118, 125; 24.8(c) n.38; 27.5(d) n.123; 27.6(b) n.33; 27.6(d) n.115

Johnson v. United States, 701 A.2d 1085 (D.C.App.1997)—§ 22.3(c) n.104

Johnson, United States v., 47 F.3d 272 (8th Cir.1995)—§ 6.8(d) n.84

Johnson, United States v., 16 F.3d 69 (5th Cir.1994)—§§ 3.6(c) n.79, 83

Johnson, United States v., 22 F.3d 106 (6th Cir.1994)—§ 1.2(c) n.147

Johnson v. United States, 636 A.2d 978 (D.C.App.1994)—§ 22.1(g) n.118

Johnson, United States v., 991 F.2d 1287 (7th Cir.1993)—§ 3.9(f) n.92

Johnson, United States v., 994 F.2d 980 (2d Cir.1993)—§ 9.4(b) n.73

Johnson, United States v., 953 F.2d 1167 (9th Cir.1992)—§§ 18.4(c) n.45, 59, 73

Johnson, United States v., 954 F.2d 1015 (5th Cir.1992)—§ 6.4(f) n.133

Johnson, United States v., 970 F.2d 907 (D.C.Cir.1992)—§ 20.6(c) n.76

Johnson, United States v., 944 F.2d 396 (8th Cir.1991)—§§ 3.4(e) n.65, 68

Johnson, United States v., 893 F.2d 451 (1st Cir.1990)—§ 24.7(g) n.83

Johnson, United States v., 903 F.2d 1219 (9th Cir.1990)—§ 24.5(d) n.56

Johnson, United States v., 873 F.2d 1137 (8th Cir.1989)—§ 22.3(d) n.213

Johnson, United States v., 888 F.2d 1255 (8th Cir.1989)—§ 21.4(f) n.171

Johnson, United States v., 862 F.2d 1135 (5th Cir.1988)—§ 3.5(e) n.205

Johnson, United States v., 820 F.2d 1065 (9th Cir.1987)—§§ 7.4(d) n.74; 17.1(d) n.58

Johnson, United States v., 826 F.2d 913 (9th Cir.1987)—§ 21.4(g) n.228

Johnson, United States v., 624 F.Supp. 1191 (E.D.Pa.1986)—§§ 11.6(a) n.62; 11.10(c) n.82

Johnson, United States v., 802 F.2d 833 (5th Cir.1986)—§§ 18.5(b) n.64, 69

Johnson v. United States, 805 F.2d 1284 (7th Cir.1986)—§ 28.9(c) n.77

Johnson, United States v., 805 F.2d 1518 (11th Cir.1986)—§ 6.9(f) n.134

Johnson, United States v., 752 F.2d 206 (6th Cir.1985)—§ 20.2(e) n.86

Johnson, United States v., 732 F.2d 379 (4th Cir.1984)—§§ 18.5(c) n.81, 84

Johnson, United States v., 713 F.2d 633 (11th Cir.1983)—§ 17.2(c) n.90

Johnson, United States v., 457 U.S. 537, 102 S.Ct. 2579, 73 L.Ed.2d 202 (1982)—§§ 2.11(a) n.9, 13; 2.11(c) n.42, 43

Johnson, United States v., 577 F.2d 1304 (5th Cir.1978)—§ 13.4(b) n.45

Johnson, United States v., 582 F.2d 335 (5th Cir.1978)—§ 21.2(d) n.181

Johnson, United States v., 584 F.2d 148 (6th Cir.1978)—§ 24.9(a) n.4

Johnson, United States v., 527 F.2d 1328 (5th Cir.1976)—§ 11.2(c) n.102

Johnson, United States v., 537 F.2d 1170 (4th Cir.1976)—§§ 21.5(e) n.129, 138

Johnson v. United States, 539 F.2d 1241 (9th Cir.1976)—§ 21.2(b) n.53

Johnson, United States v., 475 F.2d 977 (D.C.Cir.1973)—§ 3.4(j) n.194

Johnson, United States v., 478 F.2d 1129 (5th Cir.1973)—§ 17.2(b) n.54

Johnson, United States v., 455 F.2d 932 (5th Cir.1972)—§ 6.10(e) n.71

Johnson, United States v., 461 F.2d 285 (10th Cir.1972)—§ 3.3(g) n.225

Johnson, United States v., 461 F.2d 1165 (5th Cir.1972)—§ 7.4(h) n.128

Johnson, United States v., 452 F.2d 1363 (D.C.Cir.1971)—§ 7.4(e) n.90

Johnson, United States v., 426 F.2d 1112 (7th Cir.1970)—§ 6.8(a) n.11

Johnson v. United States, 356 F.2d 680 (8th Cir.1966)—§ 17.1(e) n.62

Johnson, United States v., 383 U.S. 169, 86 S.Ct. 749, 15 L.Ed.2d 681 (1966)—§ 3.4(a) n.23

Johnson v. United States, 207 F.2d 314 (5th Cir.1953)—§ 3.1(i) n.227

Johnson, United States v., 165 F.2d 42 (3d Cir.1947)—§ 16.2(g) n.130

Johnson, United States v., 323 U.S. 273, 65 S.Ct. 249, 89 L.Ed. 236 (1944)—§§ 16.2(b) n.15; 16.2(f) n.97

Johnson v. United States, 333 U.S. 10, 68 S.Ct. 367, 92 L.Ed. 436 (1948)—§§ 3.3(a) n.17, 20; 3.3(b) n.50, 53, 68; 3.6(e) n.104, 114; 3.10(a) n.6; 3.10(b) n.31

Johnson v. Wainwright, 806 F.2d 1479 (11th Cir.1986)—§ 7.5(b) n.25

Johnson v. Zerbst, 304 U.S. 458, 58 S.Ct. 1019, 82 L.Ed. 1461 (1938)—§§ 2.4(e) n.139; 2.8(b) n.37; 2.9(d) n.94; 3.10(a) n.4; 6.4(f) n.119; 6.9(c) n.62; 11.1(a) n.13; 11.2(a) n.5; 11.3(a) n.7, 9, 14; 11.3(c) n.58; 16.1(h) n.293; 18.2(a) n.2; 21.3(a) n.31; 21.6(a) n.16; 28.3(b) n.52; 28.4(d) n.34; 28.11(a) n.4

Johnson, State ex rel. v. Roth, 276 Or. 883, 557 P.2d 230 (1976)—§ 15.2(j) n.241

Johnston v. Love, 940 F.Supp. 738 (E.D.Pa.1996)—§ 24.3(d) n.111

Johnston, State v., 150 N.H. 448, 839 A.2d 830 (2004)—§ 3.2(c) n.129

Johnston, State v., 17 Conn.App. 226, 551 A.2d 1264 (1988)—§ 26.10(c) n.57

Johnston, United States v., 199 F.3d 1015 (9th Cir.1999)—§ 21.2(e) n.325

Johnston, United States v., 690 F.2d 638 (7th Cir.1982)—§ 22.5(c) n.24

Johnston, United States v., 497 F.2d 397 (9th Cir.1974)—§ 3.2(b) n.48

Johnston v. United States, 351 U.S. 215, 76 S.Ct. 739, 100 L.Ed. 1097 (1956)—§ 16.2(b) n.19

Joiner v. State, 245 Ga.App. 415, 537 S.E.2d 792 (2000)—§ 11.10(c) n.86

Joiner v. State, 231 Ga.App. 61, 497 S.E.2d 642 (1998)—§ 16.1(g) n.278

Joint Anti-Fascist Refugee Committee v. McGrath, 341 U.S. 123, 71 S.Ct. 624, 95 L.Ed. 817 (1951)—§§ 2.4(a) n.9; 2.7(c) n.116, 123, 205; 2.8(c) n.59

Jojola, State v., 140 N.M. 660, 146 P.3d 305 (2006)—§ 24.2(a) n.7

Jolley v. State, 282 Md. 353, 384 A.2d 91 (1978)—§ 27.2(c) n.60

Jolly v. State, 358 Ark. 180, 189 S.W.3d 40 (2004)—§ 26.4(f) n.105

Jonathan B., State v., 124 N.M. 620, 954 P.2d 52 (1997)—§ 21.5(c) n.88

Jones, Ex parte, 456 So.2d 380 (Ala.1984)—§ 26.2(b) n.9

Jones, In re, 264 S.C. 286, 214 S.E.2d 816 (1975)—§ 3.3(b) n.52

Jones v. Barnes, 463 U.S. 745, 103 S.Ct. 3308, 77 L.Ed.2d 987 (1983)—§§ 1.5(c) n.116, 154; 11.4(c) n.58; 11.6(a) n.5, 8, 10, 15, 18 to 20, 22, 23, 29, 35; 11.6(c) n.88, 95, 102, 109, 110, 112; 11.7(a) n.6; 21.4(a) n.9; 27.1(a) n.11, 13

Jones v. Berry, 722 F.2d 443 (9th Cir.1983)—§ 3.10(f) n.205

Jones v. Cardwell, 686 F.2d 754 (9th Cir.1982)—§ 6.10(c) n.49

Jones, Commonwealth v., 886 A.2d 689 (Pa.Super.2005)—§ 18.4(c) n.67

Jones, Commonwealth v., 439 Mass. 249, 786 N.E.2d 1197 (2003)—§ 6.9(g) n.167

Jones v. Commonwealth, 995 S.W.2d 363 (Ky.1999)—§ 21.2(d) n.223

Jones, Commonwealth v., 546 Pa. 161, 683 A.2d 1181 (1996)—§ 6.7(b) n.90

Jones, Commonwealth v., 542 Pa. 464, 668 A.2d 491 (1995)—§§ 17.2(d) n.94; 17.3(e) n.58

Jones, Commonwealth v., 530 Pa. 591, 610 A.2d 931 (1992)—§ 24.9(a) n.11

Jones v. Commonwealth, 230 Va. 14, 334 S.E.2d 536 (1985)—§ 1.7(k) n.273

Jones, Commonwealth v., 457 Pa. 423, 322 A.2d 119 (1974)—§ 3.3(d) n.174

Jones v. Commonwealth, 185 Va. 335, 38 S.E.2d 444 (1946)—§ 26.9(b) n.54

Jones v. Cunningham, 371 U.S. 236, 83 S.Ct. 373, 9 L.Ed.2d 285 (1963)— §§ 28.2(a) n.7; 28.3(a) n.6

Jones v. Dretke, 375 F.3d 352 (5th Cir.2004)—§ 22.3(c) n.150

Jones v. French, 535 U.S. 1109, 122 S.Ct. 2324, 153 L.Ed.2d 153 (2002)—§ 11.10(d) n.198

Jones v. Gasch, 404 F.2d 1231 (D.C.Cir.1967)—§§ 16.3(c) n.31, 35, 36, 45

Jones v. Ivory, 255 Ga. 20, 334 S.E.2d 666 (1985)—§ 11.9(d) n.209

Jones v. Jago, 575 F.2d 1164 (6th Cir.1978)—§ 24.3(b) n.46

Jones v. Jamrog, 414 F.3d 585 (6th Cir.2005)—§ 11.5(d) n.68

Jones v. Jones, 163 F.3d 285 (5th Cir.1998)—§ 11.10(d) n.189

Jones v. Kemp, 794 F.2d 1536 (11th Cir.1986)—§§ 7.3(b) n.28; 7.3(c) n.39

Jones v. Murray, 962 F.2d 302 (4th Cir.1992)—§ 26.9(c) n.82

Jones, People v., 219 Ill.2d 1, 300 Ill.Dec. 709, 845 N.E.2d 598 (2006)—§ 21.2(h) n.423

Jones, People v., 369 Ill.App.3d 452, 861 N.E.2d 276 (2006)—§ 24.9(f) n.71

Jones, People v., 364 Ill.App.3d 1, 846 N.E.2d 947 (2005)—§ 11.2(c) n.86

Jones, People v., 30 Cal.4th 1084, 135 Cal.Rptr.2d 370, 70 P.3d 359 (2003)—§ 7.5(b) n.15

Jones, People v., 207 Ill.2d 122, 278 Ill.Dec. 45, 797 N.E.2d 640 (2003)—§ 24.10(b) n.26

Jones, People v., 467 Mich. 301, 651 N.W.2d 906 (2002)—§ 12.4(d) n.63

Jones, People v., 95 N.Y.2d 721, 723 N.Y.S.2d 761, 746 N.E.2d 1053 (2001)—§§ 3.3(e) n.188; 10.1(b) n.31

Jones, People v., 284 A.D.2d 277, 726 N.Y.S.2d 853 (N.Y.2001)— § 24.1(b) n.18

Jones, People v., 236 Mich.App. 396, 600 N.W.2d 652 (1999)—§ 8.11(e) n.93

Jones, People v., 17 Cal.4th 279, 70 Cal.Rptr.2d 793, 949 P.2d 890 (1998)—§§ 6.2(c) n.102, 114; 22.3(d) n.247

Jones, People v., 15 Cal.4th 119, 61 Cal.Rptr.2d 386, 931 P.2d 960 (1997)—§ 24.9(f) n.86

Jones, People v., 53 Cal.3d 1115, 282 Cal.Rptr. 465, 811 P.2d 757 (1991)—§§ 11.5(g) n.112; 11.6(a) n.48

Jones, People v., 121 Ill.2d 21, 117 Ill.Dec. 164, 520 N.E.2d 325 (1988)—§§ 11.9(d) n.158, 186

Jones, People v., 47 N.Y.2d 409, 418 N.Y.S.2d 359, 391 N.E.2d 1335 (1979)—§ 24.1(b) n.29

Jones, People v., 44 N.Y.2d 76, 404 N.Y.S.2d 85, 375 N.E.2d 41 (1978)—§ 21.3(c) n.175

Jones, People v., 61 A.D.2d 264, 402 N.Y.S.2d 28 (1978)—§ 6.10(b) n.26

Jones, People v., 33 Ill.App.3d 1025, 339 N.E.2d 519 (1975)—§ 15.2(j) n.240

Jones, People v., 9 Cal.3d 546, 108 Cal.Rptr. 345, 510 P.2d 705 (1973)—§§ 2.6(b) n.51, 65; 22.2(e) n.109

Jones v. Richards, 776 F.2d 1244 (4th Cir.1985)—§§ 13.3(b) n.20; 22.5(a) n.9

Jones v. Robbins, 74 Mass. (8 Gray) 329 (1857)—§§ 2.4(c) n.93; 2.4(d) n.123

Jones v. Robbins, 74 Mass. 329, 8 Gray 329 (1857)—§§ 15.1(b) n.56, 64; 15.1(c) n.123; 15.1(d) n.185, 215

Jones v. Smith, 772 F.2d 668 (11th Cir.1985)—§ 7.5(a) n.5

Jones, State v., 283 Kan. 186, 151 P.3d 22 (2007)—§ 6.6(d) n.58

Jones v. State, 134 P.3d 150 (Okl.2006)—§ 22.3(c) n.157

Jones, State v., 159 Wash.2d 231, 149 P.3d 636 (2006)—§ 26.4(i) n.196

Jones, State v., 922 So.2d 508 (La.2006)—§ 22.1(d) n.79

Jones, State v., 216 W.Va. 392, 607 S.E.2d 498 (W.Va.2004)—§ 6.9(e) n.97

Jones v. State, 119 S.W.3d 766 (Tex.Crim.App.2003)—§ 9.5(c) n.68

Jones, State v., 818 A.2d 649 (R.I.2003)—§ 7.4(e) n.82

Jones v. State, 841 So.2d 115 (Miss.2003)—§§ 3.3(e) n.182; 6.7(b) n.41; 22.4(c) n.29

Jones, State v., 203 Ariz. 1, 49 P.3d 273 (2002)—§§ 3.5(c) n.129; 3.8(g) n.241; 6.8(c) n.64

Jones, State v., 355 N.C. 117, 558 S.E.2d 97 (2002)—§§ 22.3(c) n.145; 24.7(i) n.92

Jones, State v., 274 Ga. 287, 553 S.E.2d 612 (2001)—§§ 18.5(a) n.8, 40

Jones v. State, 344 Ark. 682, 42 S.W.3d 536 (2001)—§§ 6.8(b) n.50; 6.9(g) n.155

Jones v. State, 272 Ga. 900, 537 S.E.2d 80 (2000)—§§ 16.1(g) n.276; 16.1(h) n.312, 313

Jones v. State, 747 So.2d 249 (Miss.1999)—§ 21.6(a) n.57

Jones v. State, 982 S.W.2d 386 (Tex.Crim.App.1998)—§ 22.3(c) n.155

Jones, State v., 347 N.C. 193, 491 S.E.2d 641 (1997)—§ 22.3(a) n.5

Jones, State v., 566 N.W.2d 317 (Minn.1997)—§§ 6.2(c) n.132; 6.9(b) n.20

Jones v. State, 937 P.2d 55, 113 Nev. 454 (1997)—§ 24.7(i) n.90

Jones v. State, 343 Md. 584, 683 A.2d 520 (1996)—§ 22.3(d) n.252

Jones, State v., 556 N.W.2d 903 (Minn.1996)—§§ 7.4(e) n.86; 24.9(d) n.43

Jones v. State, 944 S.W.2d 642 (Tex.Cr.App.1996)—§ 6.2(c) n.173

Jones, State v., 143 N.J. 4, 667 A.2d 1043 (1995)—§ 3.6(a) n.22

Jones, State v., 193 W.Va. 378, 456 S.E.2d 459 (1995)—§ 9.4(a) n.7

Jones, State v., 234 Conn. 324, 662 A.2d 1199 (1995)—§ 26.2(b) n.26

Jones, State v., 340 Md. 235, 666 A.2d 128 (1995)—§ 17.4(b) n.124

Jones, State v., 516 N.W.2d 545 (Minn.1994)—§ 27.5(a) n.14

Jones v. State, 314 Ark. 289, 862 S.W.2d 242 (1993)—§ 7.5(b) n.21

Jones, State v., 490 N.W.2d 787 (Iowa 1992)—§ 22.2(c) n.39

Jones v. State, 584 So.2d 917 (Ala.Crim.App.1991)—§ 10.5(b) n.18

Jones, State v., 49 Ohio St.3d 51, 550 N.E.2d 469 (1990)—§ 26.9(b) n.46

Jones v. State, 319 Md. 279, 572 A.2d 169 (1990)—§ 3.8(c) n.96

Jones, State v., 327 N.C. 439, 396 S.E.2d 309 (1990)—§ 26.4(h) n.159

Jones v. State, 795 S.W.2d 171 (Tex.Crim.App.1990)—§ 6.7(a) n.3

Jones v. State, 105 Nev. 124, 771 P.2d 154 (1989)—§ 21.4(a) n.22

Jones, State v., 151 Wis.2d 488, 444 N.W.2d 760 (1989)—§ 1.11(a) n.5

Jones, State v., 231 Neb. 47, 435 N.W.2d 167 (1989)—§ 5.1(c) n.26

Jones, State v., 418 N.W.2d 782 (N.D.1988)—§ 26.10(d) n.90

Jones v. State, 728 S.W.2d 469 (Tex.App.1987)—§ 11.9(c) n.133

Jones v. State, 288 Ark. 375, 705 S.W.2d 874 (1986)—§ 21.4(f) n.174

Jones, State v., 125 N.H. 490, 484 A.2d 1070 (1984)—§ 6.9(e) n.87

Jones v. State, 298 Md. 634, 471 A.2d 1055 (1984)—§ 16.4(c) n.57

Jones v. State, 353 N.W.2d 781 (S.D.1984)—§ 11.10(c) n.88

Jones v. State, 449 So.2d 253 (Fla.1984)—§ 11.4(d) n.112

Jones v. State, 450 So.2d 186 (Ala.App.1984)—§ 27.2(c) n.66

Jones, State v., 461 So.2d 97 (Fla.1984)—§ 6.10(b) n.19

Jones, State v., 233 Kan. 170, 660 P.2d 965 (1983)—§§ 14.3(c) n.60; 14.4(d) n.77, 98

Jones v. State, 445 N.E.2d 98 (1983)—§ 20.2(e) n.94

Jones v. State, 660 P.2d 634 (Okla.Crim.App.1983)—§§ 14.3(a) n.32, 37

Jones, State v., 51 Md.App. 321, 443 A.2d 967 (1982)—§ 16.4(c) n.57

Jones, State v., 128 Ariz. 378, 625 P.2d 967 (1981)—§ 26.10(c) n.58

Jones v. State, 398 So.2d 1312 (Miss.1981)—§ 25.2(a) n.9

Jones, State v., 26 Wash.App. 1, 612 P.2d 404 (1980)—§ 19.5(b) n.7

Jones, State v., 96 Nev. 71, 605 P.2d 202 (1980)—§ 19.6(b) n.13

Jones, State v., 180 Conn. 443, 429 A.2d 936 (1980)—§§ 22.5(a) n.4; 22.5(b) n.19; 22.5(d) n.34, 38

Jones v. State, 269 Ark. 119, 598 S.W.2d 748 (1980)—§ 27.5(e) n.170

Jones, State v., 416 A.2d 676 (R.I.1980)—§§ 5.2(a) n.4; 5.3(a) n.6; 5.3(d) n.42

Jones v. State, 270 Ind. 285, 385 N.E.2d 426 (1979)—§§ 15.4(g) n.161; 15.4(h) n.186

Jones, State v., 281 N.W.2d 13 (Iowa 1979)—§ 24.1(a) n.10

Jones, State v., 558 S.W.2d 233 (Mo.App.1977)—§ 9.4(a) n.26

Jones, State v., 325 So.2d 235 (La.1975)—§ 9.4(d) n.85

Jones, State v., 37 Ohio St.2d 21, 306 N.E.2d 409 (1974)—§ 6.9(e) n.91

Jones, State v., 110 Ariz. 546, 521 P.2d 978 (1974)—§ 7.4(e) n.90

Jones, State v., 122 N.J.Super. 585, 301 A.2d 185 (1973)—§ 3.7(d) n.80

Jones, State v., 209 Kan. 526, 498 P.2d 65 (1972)—§§ 20.6(b) n.26, 28, 34

Jones v. State, 484 S.W.2d 745 (Tex.Cr.App.1972)—§ 10.2(c) n.30

Jones v. State, 481 P.2d 169 (Okla.Crim.App.1971)—§ 14.3(c) n.75

Jones v. State, 47 Wis.2d 642, 178 N.W.2d 42 (1970)—§ 6.8(a) n.35

Jones, State v., 240 Or. 129, 400 P.2d 524 (1965)—§§ 16.1(g) n.241, 246, 248, 250, 270, 272

Jones v. State, 185 Md. 481, 45 A.2d 350 (1946)—§ 16.3(g) n.100

Jones v. State, 89 Ind. 82 (1883)—§ 24.9(g) n.109

Jones v. Sterling, 210 Ariz. 308, 110 P.3d 1271 (2005)—§§ 13.4(a) n.10; 13.4(b) n.67

Jones v. Superior Court, 4 Cal.3d 660, 94 Cal.Rptr. 289, 483 P.2d 1241 (1971)—§§ 14.3(b) n.45, 49; 14.3(d) n.91

Jones v. Superior Court, 58 Cal.2d 56, 22 Cal.Rptr. 879, 372 P.2d 919 (1962)—§§ 20.4(b) n.37; 20.4(d) n.54, 65; 20.4(e) n.75; 20.4(f) n.91

Jones v. Thomas, 491 U.S. 376, 109 S.Ct. 2522, 105 L.Ed.2d 322 (1989)—§§ 2.9(h) n.211; 26.7(c) n.30

Jones, United States v., 472 F.3d 905 (D.C.Cir.2007)—§ 21.5(a) n.5

Jones, United States v., 454 F.3d 642 (7th Cir.2006)—§§ 7.4(c) n.52; 7.4(e) n.92; 18.4(c) n.56

Jones, United States v., 455 F.3d 134 (2d Cir.2006)—§ 17.3(b) n.13

Jones, United States v., 469 F.3d 563 (6th Cir.2006)—§ 21.5(f) n.166

Jones, United States v., 471 F.3d 868 (8th Cir.2006)—§ 3.7(e) n.128

Jones, United States v., 482 F.3d 60 (2d Cir.2006)—§ 17.3(c) n.34

Jones, United States v., 149 Fed. Appx. 954 (11th Cir.2005)—§§ 4.3(c) n.18, 20

Jones, United States v., 149 Fed.Appx. 954 (11th Cir.2005)—§ 4.4(c) n.9

Jones, United States v., 399 F.3d 640 (6th Cir.2005)—§ 13.4(e) n.169

Jones v. United States, 879 A.2d 970 (D.C.App.2005)—§ 7.4(e) n.92

Jones, United States v., 381 F.3d 615 (7th Cir.2004)—§ 21.5(d) n.104

Jones, United States v., 332 F.3d 688 (3d Cir.2003)—§ 26.4(i) n.200

Jones, United States v., 335 F.3d 527 (6th Cir.2003)—§ 3.10(d) n.117

Jones, United States v., 286 F.3d 1146 (9th Cir.2002)—§ 3.10(b) n.66

Jones, United States v., 266 F.3d 804 (8th Cir.2001)—§ 6.7(b) n.43

Jones, United States v., 269 F.3d 919 (8th Cir.2001)—§ 3.8(d) n.147

Jones v. United States, 779 A.2d 277 (D.C.App.2001)—§ 6.7(b) n.50

Jones, United States v., 209 F.3d 991 (7th Cir.2000)—§ 21.2(d) n.258

Jones, United States v., 213 F.3d 1253 (10th Cir.2000)—§ 17.1(d) n.59

Jones v. United States, 224 F.3d 1251 (11th Cir.2000)—§ 11.10(c) n.105

Jones, United States v., 231 F.3d 508 (9th Cir.2000)—§ 5.1(c) n.22

Jones, United States v., 235 F.3d 1231 (10th Cir.2000)—§§ 19.3(a) n.89, 91, 92

Jones v. United States, 529 U.S. 848, 120 S.Ct. 1904, 146 L.Ed.2d 902 (2000)—§ 1.2(c) n.179

Jones, United States v., 36 F.Supp.2d 304 (E.D.Va.1999)—§§ 1.2(d) n.202, 241, 247

Jones, United States v., 187 F.3d 210 (1st Cir.1999)—§ 3.2(b) n.33

Jones v. United States, 526 U.S. 227, 119 S.Ct. 1215, 143 L.Ed.2d 311 (1999)—§§ 1.2(c) n.149; 1.6(b) n.29; 19.2(e) n.70; 19.3(a) n.24; 26.4(i) n.167, 199

Jones v. United States, 527 U.S. 373, 119 S.Ct. 2090, 144 L.Ed.2d 370 (1999)—§ 24.9(d) n.31

Jones v. United States, 747 A.2d 558 (D.C.App.1999)—§ 6.7(b) n.54

Jones, United States v., 84 F.3d 1206 (9th Cir.1996)—§ 27.5(e) n.169

Jones, United States v., 56 F.3d 581 (5th Cir.1995)—§ 18.3(b) n.43

Jones, United States v., 58 F.3d 688 (D.C.Cir.1995)—§ 21.2(d) n.262

Jones, United States v., 72 F.3d 1324 (7th Cir.1995)—§ 9.3(e) n.56

Jones v. United States, 669 A.2d 724 (D.C.App.1995)—§ 27.2(c) n.59

Jones, United States v., 16 F.3d 487 (2d Cir.1994)—§ 17.3(c) n.28

Jones, United States v., 27 F.3d 50 (2d Cir.1994)—§ 26.4(f) n.101

Jones, United States v., 31 F.3d 1304 (4th Cir.1994)—§ 3.2(j) n.261

Jones, United States v., 997 F.2d 1475 (D.C.Cir.1993)—§ 26.4(c) n.26

Jones, United States v., 979 F.2d 317 (3d Cir.1992)—§ 21.5(a) n.43

Jones, United States v., 938 F.2d 737 (7th Cir.1991)—§§ 11.5(b) n.27, 30

Jones, United States v., 900 F.2d 512 (2d Cir.1990)—§ 11.9(d) n.222

Jones, United States v., 907 F.2d 456 (4th Cir.1990)—§§ 7.3(c) n.62; 7.4(d) n.71

Jones v. United States, 566 A.2d 44 (D.C.1989)—§ 3.8(d) n.154

Jones, United States v., 839 F.2d 1041 (5th Cir.1988)—§§ 17.2(c) n.82; 17.2(d) n.109; 24.5(b) n.35

Jones, United States v., 846 F.2d 358 (6th Cir.1988)—§ 3.10(b) n.74

Jones, United States v., 759 F.2d 633 (8th Cir.1985)—§ 3.8(e) n.202

Jones, United States v., 722 F.2d 632 (11th Cir.1983)—§ 26.7(c) n.37

Jones, United States v., 641 F.2d 425 (6th Cir.1981)—§ 3.10(b) n.36

Jones, United States v., 630 F.2d 1073 (5th Cir.1980)—§ 8.12(e) n.51

Jones, United States v., 612 F.2d 453 (9th Cir.1979)—§ 20.3(m) n.252

Jones, United States v., 524 F.2d 834 (D.C.Cir.1975)—§ 18.2(c) n.55

Jones, United States v., 475 F.2d 723 (5th Cir.1973)—§ 3.10(b) n.38

Jones, United States v., 43 F.R.D. 511 (D.D.C.1967)—§§ 16.3(c) n.32, 41

Jones v. United States, 342 F.2d 863 (D.C.Cir.1964)—§§ 8.10(c) n.56, 73; 15.7(d) n.81

Jones v. United States, 362 U.S. 257, 80 S.Ct. 725, 4 L.Ed.2d 697 (1960)— §§ 3.3(b) n.66; 3.3(c) n.84, 101; 9.1(a) n.3; 9.1(b) n.63; 9.1(c) n.104, 111; 9.1(d) n.114; 9.2(a) n.1; 9.2(b) n.12; 10.1(a) n.7; 10.3(b) n.30

Jones v. United States, 357 U.S. 493, 78 S.Ct. 1253, 2 L.Ed.2d 1514 (1958)—§§ 3.1(d) n.104; 3.6(a) n.1

Jordan, In re, 913 So.2d 775 (La.2005)— §§ 24.3(b) n.35; 24.7(i) n.98

Jordan, Commonwealth v., 439 Mass. 47, 785 N.E.2d 368 (2003)— § 22.3(d) n.197

Jordan v. Commonwealth, 217 Va. 57, 225 S.E.2d 661 (1976)—§ 21.2(e) n.306

Jordan v. Lefevre, 206 F.3d 196 (2d Cir.2000)—§§ 22.3(d) n.236, 255

Jordan, People v., 108 Cal.App.4th 349, 133 Cal.Rptr.2d 434 (2003)— § 24.3(b) n.49

Jordan, People v., 241 Ill.App.3d 464, 181 Ill.Dec. 553, 608 N.E.2d 626 (1993)—§ 27.5(a) n.14

Jordan v. State, 242 Ga.App. 408, 530 S.E.2d 42 (2000)—§ 16.1(g) n.283

Jordan, State v., 116 N.M. 76, 860 P.2d 206 (App.1993)—§ 27.4(f) n.63

Jordan v. State, 207 Ga.App. 710, 429 S.E.2d 97 (1993)—§ 24.9(f) n.68

Jordan v. State, 297 S.C. 52, 374 S.E.2d 683 (1988)—§ 21.2(d) n.177

Jordan, State v., 40 N.C.App. 412, 252 S.E.2d 857 (1979)—§ 9.1(d) n.131

Jordan v. State, 221 Md. 134, 156 A.2d 453 (1959)—§ 15.1(f) n.323

Jordan, United States v., 357 F.Supp.2d 889 (E.D.Va.2005)—§ 26.4(f) n.110

Jordan, United States v., 291 F.3d 1091 (9th Cir.2002)—§§ 19.3(a) n.88, 89, 114, 117

Jordan, United States v., 846 F.Supp. 895 (D.Nev.1994)—§§ 16.2(g) n.117, 139

Jordan, United States v., 958 F.2d 1085 (D.C.Cir.1992)—§ 3.8(c) n.89

Jordan, United States v., 915 F.2d 563 (9th Cir.1990)—§ 18.3(b) n.43

Jordan, United States v., 870 F.2d 1310 (7th Cir.1989)—§§ 21.2(d) n.217; 21.4(d) n.120, 133; 21.6(a) n.74

Jordan, United States v., 810 F.2d 262 (D.C.Cir.1987)—§ 24.7(a) n.13

Jordan v. United States, 421 F.2d 493 (9th Cir.1970)—§ 6.8(a) n.23

Jorn, United States v., 400 U.S. 470, 91 S.Ct. 547, 27 L.Ed.2d 543 (1971)— §§ 22.3(e) n.267; 25.2(a) n.4; 25.2(b) n.12; 25.2(d) n.22; 25.2(e) n.44

Jose C., People v., 127 Misc.2d 689, 487 N.Y.S.2d 499 (Co.Ct.1985)— § 15.2(h) n.192

Joseph, State v., 109 Haw. 482, 128 P.3d 795 (2006)—§ 6.8(a) n.33

Joseph v. State, 636 So.2d 777 (Fla.App.1994)—§ 22.3(d) n.199

Joseph, State v., 114 R.I. 596, 337 A.2d 523 (1975)—§ 3.3(c) n.91

Joseph, United States v., 333 F.3d 587 (5th Cir.2003)—§ 24.2(e) n.68

Joshlin, State v., 752 So.2d 834 (La.2000)—§ 16.2(a) n.10

Joshua v. DeWitt, 341 F.3d 430 (6th Cir.2003)—§ 3.8(d) n.171

Josleyn, United States v., 99 F.3d 1182 (1st Cir.1996)—§ 16.1(a) n.6

Jost, State v., 219 Neb. 162, 361 N.W.2d 526 (1985)—§ 21.4(f) n.193

Joubert v. Nebraska Board of Pardons, 87 F.3d 966 (8th Cir.1996)— § 26.2(c) n.76

Joubert, State v., 603 A.2d 861 (Me.1992)—§ 6.10(b) n.15

Joubert, State v., 235 Neb. 230, 455 N.W.2d 117 (1990)—§ 21.3(b) n.74

Journet, United States v., 544 F.2d 633 (2d Cir.1976)—§ 21.5(c) n.80

Journey v. State, 257 Ark. 1007, 521 S.W.2d 210 (1975)—§ 25.5(b) n.28

Journigan v. Duffy, 552 F.2d 283 (9th Cir.1977)—§ 21.6(a) n.58

Joyce, State v., 243 Conn. 282, 705 A.2d 181 (1997)—§ 9.4(b) n.68

Joyce, State v., 229 Conn. 10, 639 A.2d 1007 (1994)—§ 3.2(b) n.54

Joyce, United States v., 330 F.Supp.2d 527 (E.D.Pa.2004)—§ 11.9(c) n.126

Joyce, United States v., 357 F.3d 921 (9th Cir.2004)—§ 21.2(b) n.82

Joyce, United States v., 499 F.2d 9 (7th Cir.1974)—§§ 17.2(d) n.99; 20.6(b) n.28

Joyner v. State, 736 N.E.2d 232 (Ind.2000)—§§ 6.7(b) n.73; 22.3(c) n.135

Joyner v. State, 303 So.2d 60 (Fla.App.1974)—§ 3.4(j) n.185

Joyner, United States v., 201 F.3d 61 (2d Cir.2000)—§ 22.2(d) n.81

Joyner, United States v., 539 F.2d 1162 (8th Cir.1976)—§ 6.5(b) n.26

J.R.M., In re, 487 S.W.2d 502 (Mo.1972)—§ 9.1(d) n.129

J.S., State v., 222 N.J.Super. 247, 536 A.2d 769 (1988)—§ 19.5(b) n.22

Juarez, State v., 572 N.W.2d 286 (Minn.1997)—§ 6.5(b) n.25

Juarez, State v., 570 A.2d 1118 (R.I.1990)—§ 20.3(a) n.19

Juarez, State v., 161 Ariz. 76, 775 P.2d 1140 (1989)—§ 11.1(b) n.91

Juda, United States v., 46 F.3d 961 (9th Cir.1995)—§ 3.1(i) n.236

Judd, Ex parte, 694 So.2d 1294 (Ala.1997)—§ 24.1(b) n.18

Judd v. Vose, 813 F.2d 494 (1st Cir.1987)—§ 6.4(e) n.77

Judge v. State, 321 S.C. 554, 471 S.E.2d 146 (S.C.1996)—§§ 21.3(b) n.47, 101

Judge, United States v., 864 F.2d 1144 (5th Cir.1989)—§ 3.7(e) n.120

Judge, United States v., 625 F.Supp. 901 (D.Hawai'i 1986)—§ 11.9(a) n.33

Judge Hunter's Special Grand Jury, In re, 667 F.2d 724 (8th Cir.1981)— § 8.5(h) n.302

Judicial Inquiry and Review Comm'n v. Elliott, 272 Va. 97, 630 S.E.2d 485 (2006)—§ 13.5(b) n.44

Judicial Watch v. United States Department of Commerce, 196 F.R.D. 1 (D.D.C.2000)—§ 8.13(a) n.42

Judon, United States v., 472 F.3d 575 (8th Cir.2007)—§ 6.2(c) n.107

Juillet, People v., 439 Mich. 34, 475 N.W.2d 786 (1991)—§§ 5.2(b) n.24, 29

Julian, State v., 244 Kan. 101, 765 P.2d 1104 (1988)—§ 18.4(d) n.89

Julien, People v., 47 P.3d 1194 (Colo.2002)—§ 22.4(c) n.29

July 1973 Grand Jury, In re, 374 F.Supp. 1334 (N.D.Ill.1973)—§§ 8.8(e) n.130, 140

Jungbauer, State v., 348 N.W.2d 344 (Minn.1984)—§ 6.2(c) n.112

Jungers, People v., 127 Cal.App.4th 698, 25 Cal.Rptr.3d 873 (2005)— § 26.9(b) n.44

Juniors, State v., 915 So.2d 291 (La. 2005)—§ 22.3(c) n.127

Junkin, State v., 123 Ariz. 288, 599 P.2d 244 (1979)—§ 27.5(c) n.110

Jurado, People v., 38 Cal.4th 72, 41 Cal.Rptr.3d 319 (Cal.2006)— § 22.3(a) n.46

Jurado, People v., 4 Cal.App.4th 1217, 6 Cal.Rptr.2d 242 (1992)—§ 25.1(d) n.60

Jurado-Gutierrez v. Greene, 190 F.3d 1135 (10th Cir.1999)—§ 21.2(d) n.234

Jureidini, United States v., 846 F.2d 964 (4th Cir.1988)—§§ 21.2(d) n.213; 21.2(e) n.324

Jurek v. Estelle, 593 F.2d 672 (5th Cir.1979)—§ 6.9(b) n.24

Jurek, State v., 52 Ohio App.3d 30, 556 N.E.2d 1191 (1989)—§ 5.4(c) n.46

Jurek v. Texas, 428 U.S. 262, 96 S.Ct. 2950, 49 L.Ed.2d 929 (1976)—§ 26.1(b) n.16

Jurn, United States v., 766 F.2d 465 (11th Cir.1985)—§ 18.3(b) n.8

Jury Service Resource Center v. De Muniz, 340 Or. 423, 134 P.3d 948 (2006)—§§ 22.2(d) n.76; 22.3(b) n.55

Justice v. State, 550 N.E.2d 809 (Ind.App.1990)—§ 26.10(c) n.48

Justice Court of Las Vegas Township, State v., 112 Nev. 803, 919 P.2d 401 (1996)—§§ 14.3(a) n.7; 14.4(c) n.63

Justice, Department of v. Reporter's Committee for Freedom of the Press, 489 U.S. 749, 109 S.Ct. 1468, 103 L.Ed.2d 774 (1989)—§ 3.2(j) n.241

Justices of Boston Municipal Court v. Lydon, 466 U.S. 294, 104 S.Ct. 1805, 80 L.Ed.2d 311 (1984)—§§ 2.6(c) n.84; 24.6(b) n.31; 25.1(e) n.95; 25.4(c) n.26; 27.4(f) n.72; 28.3(a) n.11

Justice, United States Dep't of v. Julian, 486 U.S. 1, 108 S.Ct. 1606, 100 L.Ed.2d 1 (1988)—§§ 26.5(c) n.47, 54, 57

Juvenile #1, United States v., 38 F.3d 470 (9th Cir.1994)—§§ 26.9(b) n.22, 24

J.W. Goldsmith, Jr., Grant Co. v. United States, 254 U.S. 505, 41 S.Ct. 189, 65 L.Ed. 376 (1921)—§ 2.9(d) n.75

K

Kabbaby, United States v., 672 F.2d 857 (11th Cir.1982)—§ 15.6(b) n.57

Kachar, People v., 400 Mich. 78, 252 N.W.2d 807 (1977)—§ 7.4(c) n.57

Kacy, In re, 68 Cal.App.4th 704, 80 Cal.Rptr.2d 432 (1998)—§ 26.9(b) n.65

Kaczmarek v. State, 120 Nev. 314, 91 P.3d 16 (2004)—§ 6.4(c) n.48

Kaczynski, State v., 258 Wis.2d 653, 654 N.W.2d 300 (Wis.App.2002)—§ 26.4(c) n.35

Kaczynski, United States v., 239 F.3d 1108 (9th Cir.2001)—§§ 11.5(d) n.71; 11.6(a) n.26

Kaczynski, United States v., 923 F.Supp. 161 (D.Mont.1996)—§§ 15.4(h) n.188, 197

Kadish, In re, 377 F.Supp. 951 (N.D.Ill.1974)—§ 8.8(e) n.139

Kadivar, State v., 460 So.2d 391 (Fla.App.1984)—§ 22.5(a) n.12

Kahan, United States v., 415 U.S. 239, 94 S.Ct. 1179, 39 L.Ed.2d 297 (1974)—§§ 9.2(a) n.7; 10.5(c) n.37

Kahlbaun, State v., 64 Haw. 197, 638 P.2d 309 (1981)—§ 15.2(e) n.126

Kahlenbeck v. State, 719 N.E.2d 1213 (Ind.1999)—§ 6.2(c) n.173

Kahn v. United States, 414 F.Supp.2d 210 (E.D.N.Y.2006)—§ 28.9(b) n.50

Kahn, United States v., 415 U.S. 143, 94 S.Ct. 977, 39 L.Ed.2d 225 (1974)—§§ 4.6(e) n.84, 91

Kaiser, People v., 32 P.3d 480 (Colo.2001)—§§ 6.8(c) n.74; 6.9(b) n.24

Kaiser, State v., 504 N.W.2d 96 (S.D.1993)—§ 10.2(b) n.19

Kaiser, State v., 469 N.W.2d 316 (Minn.1991)—§§ 21.5(a) n.35, 55

Kaiser, United States v., 893 F.2d 1300 (11th Cir.1990)—§ 21.6(a) n.63

Kalal, State ex rel. v. Dane County, 271 Wis.2d 633, 681 N.W.2d 110 (2004)—§§ 13.2(a) n.3; 13.3(b) n.25, 26

Kalina v. Fletcher, 522 U.S. 118, 118 S.Ct. 502, 139 L.Ed.2d 471 (1997)—§§ 3.1(k) n.257; 3.5(a) n.60, 61; 13.5(g) n.118

Kaluna, State v., 55 Haw. 361, 520 P.2d 51 (1974)—§§ 2.12(d) n.195; 2.12(e) n.219; 3.1(e) n.126; 3.5(c) n.115

Kaluza, State v., 272 Mont. 404, 901 P.2d 107 (1995)—§ 3.3(c) n.98

Kalwa, People v., 306 Ill.App.3d 601, 239 Ill.Dec. 726, 714 N.E.2d 1023 (1999)—§ 16.1(d) n.138

Kamer, United States v., 781 F.2d 1380 (9th Cir.1986)—§ 21.2(d) n.150

Kaminski, People v., 58 N.Y.2d 886, 460 N.Y.S.2d 495, 447 N.E.2d 43 (1983)—§ 19.5(b) n.25

Kammer v. State, 748 S.W.2d 844 (Mo.App.1988)—§ 27.4(f) n.67

Kamoga, United States v., 177 F.3d 617 (7th Cir.1999)—§ 21.1(h) n.199

Kampiles, United States v., 609 F.2d 1233 (7th Cir.1979)—§§ 6.6(f) n.114; 16.1(g) n.274; 16.1(h) n.309

Kandirakis, United States v., 441 F.Supp.2d 282 (D.Mass.2006)—§ 26.4(f) n.104

Kane v. Garcia Espitia, _____ U.S. _____, 126 S.Ct. 407, 163 L.Ed.2d 10 (2005)—§ 11.5(e) n.92

Kane, State v., 87 Hawai'i 71, 951 P.2d 934 (1998)—§ 6.7(b) n.85

Kane, State v., 218 Conn. 151, 588 A.2d 179 (1991)—§ 10.4(b) n.11

Kane, United States v., 646 F.2d 4 (1st Cir.1981)—§ 27.3(c) n.44

Kaneshiro, State ex rel. v. Huddy, 82 Haw. 188, 921 P.2d 108 (1996)—§§ 27.4(b) n.13; 27.4(d) n.51

Kang, People v., 107 Cal.App.4th 43, 131 Cal.Rptr.2d 447 (Cal.App.2003)—§ 27.5(c) n.83

Kang, State v., 859 So.2d 649 (La.2003)—§ 22.3(c) n.108

Kang, United States v., 934 F.2d 621 (5th Cir.1991)—§ 5.3(a) n.7

Kansas v. Hendricks, 521 U.S. 346, 117 S.Ct. 2072, 138 L.Ed.2d 501 (1997)—§§ 25.1(c) n.36; 26.6(e) n.80

Kansas v. Marsh, _____ U.S. _____, 126 S.Ct. 2516, 165 L.Ed.2d 429 (2006)—§§ 1.5(e) n.237; 1.11(a) n.4; 22.1(a) n.27; 26.4(h) n.158; 26.4(i) n.179

Kanuck v. Meehan, 165 Ariz. 282, 798 P.2d 420 (1990)—§ 26.10(b) n.26

Kapadia v. Tally, 229 F.3d 641 (7th Cir.2000)—§ 26.4(b) n.20

Kaplan v. Ritter, 71 N.Y.2d 222, 525 N.Y.S.2d 1, 519 N.E.2d 802 (1987)—§ 25.5(b) n.28

Kaplan, United States v., 832 F.2d 676 (1st Cir.1987)—§ 24.8(b) n.34

Kaplan, United States v., 554 F.2d 577 (3d Cir.1977)—§ 20.3(m) n.252

Kappos v. State, 465 N.E.2d 1092 (Ind.1984)—§ 23.2(a) n.46

Karaffa, Commonwealth v., 551 Pa. 173, 709 A.2d 887 (1998)—§ 27.6(b) n.17

Karassik, People v., 90 Misc.2d 839, 396 N.Y.S.2d 765 (Sup.Ct.1977)—§ 15.7(g) n.216

Karathanos, United States v., 531 F.2d 26 (2d Cir.1976)—§§ 9.4(e) n.107, 111

Karathanos, United States v., 399 F.Supp. 185 (E.D.N.Y.1975)—§ 3.3(c) n.112

Karcher v. Daggett, 462 U.S. 725, 103 S.Ct. 2653, 77 L.Ed.2d 133 (1983)—§ 2.8(a) n.16

Kargar, State v., 679 A.2d 81 (Me.1996)—§§ 13.2(c) n.75, 78

Karlen, State v., 589 N.W.2d 594 (S.D.1999)—§ 18.2(b) n.17

Karnes v. Commonwealth, 125 Va. 758, 99 S.E. 562 (1919)—§ 16.1(e) n.200

Karo, United States v., 468 U.S. 705, 104 S.Ct. 3296, 82 L.Ed.2d 530 (1984)—§§ 3.2(j) n.251; 3.3(g) n.243; 3.4(e) n.85; 4.3(a) n.5; 9.1(b) n.51

Karp, State v., 527 N.W.2d 912 (S.D.1995)—§ 26.3(f) n.64

Karp, United States v., 484 F.Supp. 157 (S.D.N.Y.1980)—§ 8.13(b) n.49

Karr, State ex rel. v. McCarty, 187 W.Va. 201, 417 S.E.2d 120 (W.Va. 1992)—§ 22.5(c) n.24

Karsseboom, United States v., 881 F.2d 604 (9th Cir.1989)—§ 18.3(b) n.12

Kaschik, Commonwealth v., 235 Pa.Super. 388, 344 A.2d 519 (1975)—§ 3.3(c) n.113

Kasel, State v., 488 N.W.2d 706 (Iowa 1992)—§ 6.9(g) n.151

Kasold, State v., 110 Ariz. 563, 521 P.2d 995 (1974)—§ 3.3(g) n.229

Kassner v. Fremont Mutual Insurance Co., 47 Mich.App. 264, 209 N.W.2d 490 (1973)—§§ 3.1(g) n.186, 187

Kastanis, State v., 848 P.2d 673 (Utah 1993)—§§ 12.4(a) n.22, 32, 36

Kastigar v. United States, 406 U.S. 441, 92 S.Ct. 1653, 32 L.Ed.2d 212 (1972)—§§ 2.10(b) n.4, 23, 37; 8.6(a) n.3; 8.10(a) n.22; 8.10(c) n.62; 8.11(a) n.1, 13; 11.8(b) n.35

Kastigar, Zicarelli v. New Jersey, 406 U.S. 472, 92 S.Ct. 1670, 32 L.Ed.2d 234 (1972)—§ 8.11(b) n.16

Kat, United States v., 178 F.3d 368 (5th Cir.1999)—§§ 20.6(b) n.41, 42

Kater v. Maloney, 459 F.3d 56 (1st Cir.2006)—§ 22.3(a) n.22

Katin, United States v., 109 F.R.D. 406 (D.Mass.1986)—§§ 8.12(g) n.64; 8.13(a) n.24

Katz, In re, 476 F.Supp.2d 572 (W.D.Va.2007)—§ 24.7(d) n.33

Katz, In re, 623 F.2d 122 (2d Cir.1980)—§ 8.13(a) n.21

Katz v. United States, 389 U.S. 347, 88 S.Ct. 507, 19 L.Ed.2d 576 (1967)— §§ 2.8(b) n.41; 2.10(d) n.148; 2.11(c) n.26; 3.2(a) n.12; 3.2(b) n.55, 86; 3.10(c) n.83; 4.3(a) n.3; 4.5 n.4; 4.6(a); 9.1(b) n.89

Katzman v. Victoria's Secret Catalogue (Courtroom TV), 923 F.Supp. 580 (S.D.N.Y.1996)—§ 23.3(b) n.27

Katzopoulos, United States v., 437 F.3d 569 (6th Cir.2006)—§ 26.4(f) n.93

Kaufman, United States v., 858 F.2d 994 (5th Cir.1988)—§§ 17.2(d) n.98; 17.3(b) n.21

Kaufman v. United States, 394 U.S. 217, 89 S.Ct. 1068, 22 L.Ed.2d 227 (1969)—§§ 2.9(h) n.215; 28.2(c) n.40, 41, 43; 28.2(d) n.83; 28.9(a) n.3; 28.9(b) n.32, 38, 66, 68

Kaufmann, United States v., 783 F.2d 708 (7th Cir.1986)—§ 24.3(d) n.111

Kaupp v. Texas, 538 U.S. 626, 123 S.Ct. 1843, 155 L.Ed.2d 814 (2003)— §§ 3.8(g) n.244; 9.4(a) n.4

Kavanagh, United States v., 572 F.2d 9 (1st Cir.1978)—§ 7.5(a) n.6

Kave, In re, 760 F.2d 343 (1st Cir.1985)—§ 8.13(a) n.20

Kavoukian, United States v., 315 F.3d 139 (2d Cir.2002)—§ 19.3(e) n.218

Kawa, State v., 270 Neb. 992, 708 N.W.2d 662 (2006)—§ 11.9(c) n.112

Kawakita v. United States, 343 U.S. 717, 72 S.Ct. 950, 96 L.Ed. 1249 (1952)—§ 16.4(b) n.27

Kawamura v. State, 299 Md. 276, 473 A.2d 438 (1984)—§ 2.12(b) n.91

Kay, State v., 717 P.2d 1294 (Utah 1986)—§§ 21.2(d) n.221; 21.3(d) n.222

Kay, United States v., 359 F.3d 738 (5th Cir.2004)—§ 19.3(b) n.152

Kay v. United States, 421 F.2d 1007 (9th Cir.1970)—§ 17.2(b) n.40

Kaylor, United States v., 877 F.2d 658 (8th Cir.1989)—§ 9.1(b) n.79

Kealaiki, State v., 95 Hawai'i 309, 22 P.3d 588 (2001)—§ 21.6(b) n.84

Kear v. United States, 369 F.2d 78 (9th Cir.1966)—§ 6.8(a) n.26

Kearney, United States v., 451 F.Supp. 33 (S.D.N.Y.1978)—§ 19.3(c) n.187

Keating v. Hood, 191 F.3d 1053 (9th Cir.1999)—§ 27.6(d) n.127

Keaton v. State, 253 Ga. 70, 316 S.E.2d 452 (1984)—§ 5.2(a) n.14

Keaton, State ex rel. v. Circuit Court, 475 N.E.2d 1146 (Ind.1985)—§§ 20.3(j) n.181; 20.3(k) n.217

Keats v. State, 115 P.3d 1110 (Wyo.2005)—§§ 11.7(e) n.66, 72; 28.4(d) n.57

Kee v. City of Rowlett, 247 F.3d 206 (5th Cir.2001)—§ 4.6(a) n.9

Keeble v. United States, 412 U.S. 205, 93 S.Ct. 1993, 36 L.Ed.2d 844 (1973)—§ 24.8(f) n.88

Keefe, State ex rel. v. Schmiege, 251 Wis. 79, 28 N.W.2d 345 (1947)—§ 1.8(d) n.43

Keeling v. Commonwealth, 178 Ky. 624, 199 S.W. 789 (1918)—§ 16.3(d) n.77

Keen, United States v., 104 F.3d 1111 (9th Cir.1996)—§§ 11.3(b) n.41; 11.5(c) n.55

Keenan, State v., 81 Ohio St.3d 133, 689 N.E.2d 929 (1998)—§ 11.9(c) n.112

Keenan, State v., 66 Ohio St.3d 402, 613 N.E.2d 203 (1993)—§ 24.7(i) n.86

Keenan, State ex rel. v. Calabrese, 69 Ohio St.3d 176, 631 N.E.2d 119 (1994)—§ 27.2(c) n.62

Keene, Matter of, 95 Wash.2d 203, 622 P.2d 360 (1980)—§ 21.4(c) n.88

Keene, State v., 630 N.W.2d 579 (Iowa 2001)—§ 21.4(f) n.183

Keene, State v., 81 Ohio St.3d 646, 693 N.E.2d 246 (1998)—§ 13.4(b) n.72

Keene, State ex rel. v. Jordan, 192 W.Va. 131, 451 S.E.2d 432 (1994)—§ 27.4(c) n.19

Keeney v. Tamayo-Reyes, 504 U.S. 1, 112 S.Ct. 1715, 118 L.Ed.2d 318 (1992)—§§ 28.5(a) n.28; 28.7(c) n.14

Keeran, State v., 5 R.I. 497 (1858)—§ 2.4(c) n.95

Keeton v. State, 749 S.W.2d 861 (Tex.Cr.App.1988)—§ 22.3(d) n.250

Keffer, State v., 860 P.2d 1118 (Wyo.1993)—§§ 24.8(d) n.43; 24.8(e) n.58

Keindl, People v., 68 N.Y.2d 410, 509 N.Y.S.2d 790, 502 N.E.2d 577 (1986)—§ 19.3(b) n.163

Keith, State v., 160 Vt. 257, 628 A.2d 1247 (1993)—§ 6.9(b) n.35

Keith, State v., 507 N.E.2d 245 (Ind.App.1987)—§ 25.1(d) n.69

Keith v. State, 612 P.2d 977 (Alaska 1980)—§ 15.5(b) n.56

Keith, United States v., 605 F.2d 462 (9th Cir.1979)—§§ 19.3(a) n.47, 48

Keith, People ex rel. v. Keith, 38 Ill.2d 405, 231 N.E.2d 387 (1967)—§ 6.10(e) n.77

Kelch v. Director Nevada Dep't of Prisons, 107 Nev. 827, 822 P.2d 1094 (1991)—§ 26.2(c) n.79

Kelekolio, State v., 74 Haw. 479, 849 P.2d 58 (1993)—§§ 6.2(c) n.132; 10.5(a) n.10

Kell, State v., 276 Ga. 423, 577 S.E.2d 551 (2003)—§§ 16.2(a) n.1; 16.2(c) n.45

Kelleher v. Henderson, 531 F.2d 78 (2d Cir.1976)—§§ 21.4(b) n.46; 21.4(d) n.151

Kellen v. State, 49 Ala.App. 475, 273 So.2d 235 (1972)—§ 3.3(g) n.245

Keller, In re, 213 Mont. 196, 693 P.2d 1211 (1984)—§ 23.1(b) n.33

Keller v. Larkins, 251 F.3d 408 (3d Cir.2001)—§ 28.5(a) n.33

Keller v. People, 29 P.3d 290 (Colo.2000)—§ 21.2(d) n.158

Keller, People v., 214 A.D.2d 825, 625 N.Y.S.2d 325 (1995)—§ 15.7(b) n.17

Keller, People v., 79 Cal.App. 612, 250 P. 585 (1926)—§ 16.1(d) n.142

Keller, State v., 695 N.W.2d 703 (N.D.2005)—§§ 24.8(e) n.50; 24.8(f) n.98, 116

Keller, United States v., 413 F.3d 706 (8th Cir.2005)—§ 1.11(a) n.7

Keller, United States v., 902 F.2d 1391 (9th Cir.1990)—§ 21.2(d) n.211

Keller v. United States, 213 U.S. 138, 29 S.Ct. 470, 53 L.Ed. 737 (1909)—§§ 1.2(c) n.95, 115

Keller, State ex rel. v. Criminal Court, 262 Ind. 420, 317 N.E.2d 433 (Ind.1974)—§§ 20.2(a) n.5, 8, 10; 20.4(d) n.73, 74; 20.4(g) n.108; 20.5(a) n.2, 5

Kelley, In re, 433 A.2d 704 (D.C.App.1981)—§§ 8.7(d) n.86; 8.8(b) n.30; 8.8(g) n.178, 179

Kelley, State v., 517 N.W.2d 905 (Minn.1994)—§§ 24.9(f) n.72; 24.9(g) n.118

Kelley v. State, 539 N.E.2d 8 (Ind.1989)—§ 19.5(b) n.10

Kelley, State v., 206 Conn. 323, 537 A.2d 483 (1988)—§§ 21.6(a) n.41, 42; 21.6(b) n.84

Kelley v. State, 482 N.E.2d 701 (Ind.1985)—§§ 6.7(d) n.146; 6.9(f) n.100

Kelley v. State, 169 Ga.App. 917, 315 S.E.2d 916 (1984)—§ 20.3(b) n.37

Kelley v. State, 184 Tenn. 143, 197 S.W.2d 545 (1946)—§ 3.10(d) n.107

Kelley, United States v., 446 F.3d 688 (7th Cir.2006)—§ 26.10(c) n.71

Kelley, United States v., 402 F.3d 39 (1st Cir.2005)—§ 18.4(c) n.69

Kelley, United States v., 140 F.3d 596 (5th Cir.1998)—§ 4.6(e) n.97

Kelley, United States v., 712 F.2d 884 (1st Cir.1983)—§ 22.4(c) n.22

Kellogg v. Scurr, 741 F.2d 1099 (8th Cir.1984)—§ 11.10(c) n.88

Kellogg, State v., 534 N.W.2d 431 (Iowa 1995)—§ 12.4(d) n.83

Kellogg, State v., 263 N.W.2d 539 (Iowa 1978)—§§ 11.7(e) n.70, 77

Kelly v. Lynaugh, 862 F.2d 1126 (5th Cir.1988)—§§ 6.9(f) n.102, 106, 111, 114

Kelly v. Meachum, 950 F.Supp. 461 (D.Conn.1996)—§ 24.3(f) n.154

Kelly, People v., 209 A.D.2d 436, 618 N.Y.S.2d 822 (1994)—§ 20.3(a) n.18

Kelly, People v., 51 Cal.3d 931, 275 Cal.Rptr. 160, 800 P.2d 516 (1990)—§ 6.8(a) n.14

Kelly, People v., 62 N.Y.2d 516, 478 N.Y.S.2d 834, 467 N.E.2d 498 (1984)—§ 20.6(b) n.57

Kelly v. Robinson, 479 U.S. 36, 107 S.Ct. 353, 93 L.Ed.2d 216 (1986)—§§ 1.5(k) n.381; 26.9(c) n.82

Kelly v. South Carolina, 534 U.S. 246, 122 S.Ct. 726, 151 L.Ed.2d 670 (2002)—§ 2.7(b) n.90

Kelly, State v., 631 N.W.2d 167 (N.D.2001)—§ 17.4(b) n.133

Kelly, State v., 752 A.2d 188 (Me.2000)—§ 7.5(b) n.17

Kelly, State v., 45 Conn.App. 142, 695 A.2d 1 (1997)—§§ 23.1(e) n.230, 231

Kelly, State v., 186 Wis.2d 580, 522 N.W.2d 222 (Wis.App.1994)—§ 22.3(d) n.200

Kelly, State v., 435 N.W.2d 807 (Minn.1989)—§ 6.6(e) n.65

Kelly, State v., 68 Haw. 213, 708 P.2d 820 (1985)—§ 3.2(j) n.252

Kelly, State v., 362 So.2d 1071 (La.1978)—§ 7.4(c) n.49

Kelly, State v., 439 S.W.2d 487 (Mo.1969)—§ 6.10(b) n.25

Kelly v. State, 415 P.2d 187 (Okl.Cr.1966)—§ 10.3(b) n.23

Kelly, United States v., 329 F.3d 624 (8th Cir.2003)—§ 6.9(g) n.166

Kelly, United States v., 337 F.3d 897 (7th Cir.2003)—§§ 21.2(d) n.242; 21.2(e) n.352

Kelly, United States v., 312 F.3d 328 (7th Cir.2002)—§ 21.4(a) n.12

Kelly, United States v., 91 F.Supp.2d 580 (S.D.N.Y.2000)—§ 24.3(b) n.63

Kelly, United States v., 991 F.2d 1308 (7th Cir.1993)—§ 6.6(e) n.89

Kelly, United States v., 913 F.2d 261 (6th Cir.1990)—§ 3.10(f) n.191

Kelly, United States v., 790 F.2d 130 (D.C.Cir.1986)—§ 12.4(d) n.64

Kelly, United States v., 708 F.2d 121 (3d Cir.1983)—§ 4.6(l) n.200

Kelly, United States v., 556 F.2d 257 (5th Cir.1977)—§ 13.4(b) n.56

Kelly, United States v., 414 F.Supp. 1131 (W.D.Mo.1976)—§ 3.10(e) n.174

Kelly, United States v., 529 F.2d 1365 (8th Cir.1976)—§ 9.2(b) n.13

Kelly, United States v., 55 F.2d 67 (2d Cir.1932)—§ 3.5(d) n.157

Kelsey, United States v., 951 F.2d 1196 (10th Cir.1991)—§§ 6.9(c) n.58; 6.9(g) n.200

Kelter, State v., 71 Wash.2d 52, 426 P.2d 500 (1967)—§ 6.4(c) n.40

Kelty, State v., _____ Wis.2d _____, 716 N.W.2d 886 (2006)—§ 21.6(a) n.65

Kember, United States v., 648 F.2d 1354 (D.C.Cir.1980)—§ 8.9(b) n.32

Kemmerlin, State v., 356 N.C. 446, 573 S.E.2d 870 (2002)—§ 6.6(d) n.57

Kemmler, In re, 136 U.S. 436, 10 S.Ct. 930, 34 L.Ed. 519 (1890)— §§ 2.3(b) n.83, 84

Kemp v. Simpson, 278 Ga. 439, 603 S.E.2d 267 (2004)—§§ 19.3(a) n.13; 21.6(a) n.64

Kemp, State v., 199 Conn. 473, 507 A.2d 1387 (1986)—§ 7.5(b) n.21

Kemper, United States v., 908 F.2d 33 (6th Cir.1990)—§ 21.4(g) n.226

Kemp, State ex rel. v. Hodge, 629 S.W.2d 353 (Mo.1982)—§ 18.4(d) n.85

Kendall, United States v., 665 F.2d 126 (7th Cir.1981)—§ 19.4(b) n.22

Kenna v. U.S. District Court for the Central District of California, 435 F.3d 1011 (9th Cir.2006)— §§ 26.5(d) n.61; 26.7(b) n.21; 27.4(e) n.61

Kennard, People v., 175 Colo. 479, 488 P.2d 563 (1971)—§ 3.10(f) n.202

Kennard v. State, 177 Md. 549, 10 A.2d 710 (1940)—§ 24.9(a) n.2

Kennedy v. Cardwell, 487 F.2d 101 (6th Cir.1973)—§ 24.2(e) n.70

Kennedy, Commonwealth v., 413 Pa.Super. 95, 604 A.2d 1036 (1992)—§ 24.3(f) n.156

Kennedy v. Fairman, 618 F.2d 1242 (7th Cir.1980)—§ 6.4(f) n.129

Kennedy v. Frazier, 178 W.Va. 10, 357 S.E.2d 43 (1987)—§ 21.4(f) n.216

Kennedy v. Lockyer, 379 F.3d 1041 (9th Cir.2004)—§ 11.2(d) n.130

Kennedy v. Mendoza-Martinez, 372 U.S. 144, 83 S.Ct. 554, 9 L.Ed.2d 644 (1963)—§§ 17.4(b) n.117; 22.1(c) n.58; 25.1(c) n.25

Kennedy, State v., 788 A.2d 174 (Me.2002)—§ 10.2(a) n.2

Kennedy, State v., 152 N.J. 413, 705 A.2d 757 (1998)—§ 21.4(d) n.110

Kennedy, State v., 333 S.C. 426, 510 S.E.2d 714 (1998)—§ 6.9(g) n.166

Kennedy, State v., 251 Neb. 337, 557 N.W.2d 33 (1996)—§ 21.4(f) n.176

Kennedy v. State, 325 Ark. 3, 923 S.W.2d 274 (1996)—§ 6.2(c) n.163

Kennedy v. State, 839 P.2d 667 (Okla.Crim.App.1992)—§§ 14.3(a) n.25, 27

Kennedy, State v., 247 N.J.Super. 21, 588 A.2d 834 (1991)—§ 13.4(b) n.72

Kennedy, State v., 97 N.J. 278, 478 A.2d 723 (1984)—§ 6.4(f) n.112

Kennedy v. State, 253 Ga. 132, 317 S.E.2d 822 (1984)—§§ 17.2(f) n.133; 17.3(e) n.57

Kennedy, State v., 295 Or. 260, 666 P.2d 1316 (1983)—§§ 2.12(a) n.26; 2.12(c) n.139

Kennedy, United States v., 372 F.3d 686 (4th Cir.2004)—§§ 8.10(c) n.84, 86; 8.10(d) n.90

Kennedy, United States v., 81 F.Supp.2d 1103 (D. Kan. 2000)—§§ 4.4(b) n.6; 4.8(f) n.69

Kennedy, United States v., 122 F.Supp.2d 1195 (N.D.Okla.2000)— § 8.13(d) n.87

Kennedy, United States v., 61 F.3d 494 (6th Cir.1995)—§§ 9.3(e) n.57, 64, 72

Kennedy, United States v., 618 F.2d 557 (9th Cir.1980)—§ 12.3(c) n.84

Kennedy, United States v., 573 F.2d 657 (9th Cir.1978)—§ 6.6(f) n.112

Kennedy, United States v., 548 F.2d 608 (5th Cir.1977)—§ 22.2(a) n.10

Kennerly, State v., 337 S.C. 617, 524 S.E.2d 837 (1999)—§ 24.9(f) n.106

Kenney, State v., 973 S.W.2d 536 (Mo.App.1998)—§ 14.2(g) n.105

Kenney v. State, 837 P.2d 664 (Wyo.1993)—§ 11.9(b) n.100

Kenney, State v., 327 Md. 354, 609 A.2d 337 (1992)—§ 22.1(h) n.156

Kenney, United States v., 992 F.2d 32 (3d Cir.1993)—§ 24.5(a) n.10

Kenney, United States v., 911 F.2d 315 (9th Cir.1990)—§§ 11.9(c) n.108, 111, 112

Kennon v. State, 248 Kan. 515, 809 P.2d 546 (1991)—§ 27.4(f) n.66

Kenny, In re, 715 F.2d 51 (2d Cir.1983)—§ 8.12(c) n.40

Kenny, State v., 523 A.2d 853 (R.I. 1987)—§ 25.1(d) n.90

Kenny, United States v., 645 F.2d 1323 (9th Cir.1981)—§ 6.4(e) n.91

Kenny, United States v., 462 F.2d 1205 (3d Cir.1972)—§ 3.1(f) n.145

Kenosha, County of v. C & S Management, Inc., 223 Wis.2d 373, 588 N.W.2d 236 (1999)—§ 13.4(c) n.102

Kent v. Cupp, 8 Or.App. 137, 492 P.2d 507 (1972)—§ 21.5(a) n.57

Kent v. United States, 383 U.S. 541, 86 S.Ct. 1045, 16 L.Ed.2d 84 (1966)—§ 13.7(b) n.34

Kent v. United States, 272 F.2d 795 (1st Cir.1959)—§ 21.2(b) n.49

Kentucky v. Dennison, 65 U.S. (24 How.) 66, 16 L.Ed. 717 (1860)—§ 3.1(j) n.250

Kentucky v. Stincer, 482 U.S. 730, 107 S.Ct. 2658, 96 L.Ed.2d 631 (1987)—§§ 1.5(c) n.118; 24.2(a) n.17; 24.3(a) n.5

Kentucky Whip & Collar Co. v. Illinois Cen.R.R. Co., 299 U.S. 334, 57 S.Ct. 277, 81 L.Ed. 270 (1937)—§ 1.2(c) n.113

Kentz, United States v., 251 F.3d 835 (9th Cir.2001)—§ 12.1(a) n.12

Kepner v. United States, 195 U.S. 100, 24 S.Ct. 797, 49 L.Ed. 114 (1904)—§§ 25.1(d) n.81; 25.1(e) n.93; 27.3(a) n.2

Kepple, State v., 151 N.H. 661, 866 A.2d 959 (2005)—§ 4.6(c) n.54

Ker v. California, 374 U.S. 23, 83 S.Ct. 1623, 10 L.Ed.2d 726 (1963)—§§ 2.5(e) n.43; 2.5(f) n.53, 77, 86, 90; 2.6(a) n.2, 4; 3.1(e) n.124; 3.3(f) n.195; 3.4(h) n.140; 3.6(b) n.45

Ker v. Illinois, 119 U.S. 436, 7 S.Ct. 225, 30 L.Ed. 421 (1886)—§§ 3.1(j) n.240, 242

Kerby, State v., 141 N.M. 413, 156 P.3d 704 (2007)—§ 18.5(a) n.51

Kercheval v. United States, 274 U.S. 220, 47 S.Ct. 582, 71 L.Ed. 1009 (1927)—§§ 21.5(a) n.19; 21.5(f) n.156

Kerdachi, United States v., 756 F.2d 349 (5th Cir.1985)—§ 21.4(b) n.52

Keresztury, United States v., 293 F.3d 750 (5th Cir.2002)—§§ 21.2(d) n.177, 236

Kerley, United States v., 753 F.2d 617 (7th Cir.1985)—§ 23.3(b) n.19

Kernats v. O'Sullivan, 35 F.3d 1171 (7th Cir.1994)—§ 3.8(c) n.107

Kerns, State v., 187 W.Va. 620, 420 S.E.2d 891 (1992)—§ 1.7(h) n.134

Kerr v. Farrey, 95 F.3d 472 (7th Cir.1996)—§ 26.9(b) n.54

Kerr, State v., 181 Wis.2d 372, 511 N.W.2d 586 (1994)—§ 14.3(a) n.8

Kerr v. United States Dist. Court, 426 U.S. 394, 96 S.Ct. 2119, 48 L.Ed.2d 725 (1976)—§ 27.4(b) n.17

Kerrigan, United States v., 514 F.2d 35 (9th Cir.1975)—§ 4.6(e) n.99

Kershner, United States v., 432 F.2d 1066 (5th Cir.1970)—§ 6.8(a) n.10

Kessel, People v., 61 Cal.App.3d 322, 132 Cal.Rptr. 126 (1976)—§ 13.2(c) n.64

Kesser v. Cambra, 465 F 3d 351 (9th Cir.2006)—§ 22.3(d) n.193

Kesser v. Cambra, 465 F.3d 351 (9th Cir.2006)—§ 22.3(d) n.242

Kessler v. State, 752 So.2d 545 (Fla.1999)—§ 23.2(f) n.90

Kessler, United States v., 692 F.2d 584 (9th Cir.1982)—§ 7.4(f) n.96

Keszthelyi, United States v., 308 F.3d 557 (6th Cir.2002)—§ 3.4(j) n.215

Ketchum, State v., 97 Haw. 107, 34 P.3d 1006 (2001)—§§ 6.6(e) n.95; 6.7(b) n.54

Ketterer, State v., 111 Ohio St.3d 70, 855 N.E.2d 48 (2006)—§§ 21.3(b) n.89; 21.4(b) n.59

Ketterer, State v., 248 Minn. 173, 79 N.W.2d 136 (1956)—§§ 1.8(c) n.54; 1.8(d) n.52

Kettering, United States v., 861 F.2d 675 (11th Cir.1988)—§§ 21.2(d) n.142; 21.2(f) n.386

Keup, State v., 265 Neb. 96, 655 N.W.2d 25 (2003)—§ 3.4(k) n.227

Kevil, State v., 111 Ariz. 240, 527 P.2d 285 (1974)—§ 20.1(a) n.15

Key v. State, 325 Ark. 73, 923 S.W.2d 865 (1996)—§ 6.2(c) n.169

Key, State v., 388 N.W.2d 866 (N.D.1986)—§ 27.5(a) n.14

Keyes v. State, 708 So.2d 540 (Miss.1998)—§ 17.4(b) n.124

Keys v. Hey, 164 W.Va. 132, 260 S.E.2d 837 (1979)—§ 16.3(g) n.108

Keys, State v., 293 Mont. 81, 973 P.2d 812 (1999)—§ 21.2(b) n.53

Keys v. State, 283 So.2d 919 (Miss.1973)—§ 10.2(c) n.40

Kezerle, United States v., 99 F.3d 867 (7th Cir.1996)—§ 26.3(f) n.60

Khaalis v. United States, 408 A.2d 313 (D.C.App.1979)—§§ 15.4(h) n.186; 24.2(a) n.7

Kham, State v., 689 S.W.2d 324 (Tex.App.1985)—§ 25.1(d) n.66

Khan, United States v., 461 F.3d 477 (4th Cir.2006)—§ 13.4(e) n.169

Khan, United States v., 869 F.2d 661 (2d Cir.1989)—§ 21.5(c) n.86

Khan, United States v., 822 F.2d 451 (4th Cir.1987)—§ 25.1(d) n.89

Khattak, United States v., 273 F.3d 557 (3d Cir.2001)—§ 21.2(b) n.76

Khorey, Commonwealth v., 521 Pa. 1, 555 A.2d 100 (1989)—§ 15.6(f) n.204

Khounsavanh, United States v., 113 F.3d 279 (1st Cir.1997)—§ 27.5(e) n.178

Kiam, United States v., 432 F.3d 524 (3d Cir.2005)—§ 6.7(b) n.57

Kibbe v. DuBois, 269 F.3d 26 (1st Cir.2001)—§ 9.6(a) n.38

Kidd, People v., 178 Ill.2d 92, 227 Ill.Dec. 463, 687 N.E.2d 945 (1997)—§§ 11.3(b) n.36, 37, 41, 42

Kidd, People v., 147 Ill.2d 510, 169 Ill.Dec. 258, 591 N.E.2d 431 (1992)—§ 6.9(g) n.198

Kidd, People v., 129 Ill.2d 432, 136 Ill.Dec. 18, 544 N.E.2d 704 (1989)—§§ 6.4(e) n.96; 6.4(f) n.122

Kido, State v., 102 Haw. 369, 76 P.3d 612 (Haw.App.2003)—§ 24.5(a) n.13

Kiefaber, In re, 774 F.2d 969 (9th Cir.1985)—§ 8.5(i) n.308

Kiefer, State v., 90 Md. 165, 44 A. 1043 (1899)—§ 15.1(g) n.358

Kiendra v. Hadden, 763 F.2d 69 (2d Cir.1985)—§ 18.4(c) n.32

Kiett, State v., 121 N.J. 483, 582 A.2d 630 (1990)—§ 21.5(c) n.88

Kikumura, United States v., 947 F.2d 72 (3d Cir.1991)—§ 11.4(c) n.76

Kikumura, United States v., 918 F.2d 1084 (3d Cir.1990)—§ 26.4(h) n.155

Kikuyama, United States v., 109 F.3d 536 (9th Cir.1997)—§ 21.4(d) n.106

Kile, State v., 96 Okla.Crim. 148, 250 P.2d 233 (1952)—§ 14.3(c) n.57

Kilgo, In re, 484 F.2d 1215 (4th Cir.1973)—§ 8.11(d) n.75

Kilgore, United States v., 518 F.2d 496 (5th Cir.1975)—§ 4.6(e) n.112

Kilgroe, United States v., 959 F.2d 802 (9th Cir.1992)—§ 6.6(e) n.76

Killean, State v., 185 Ari. 270, 915 P.2d 1225 (1996)—§ 20.6(c) n.75

Killebrew, People v., 416 Mich. 189, 330 N.W.2d 834 (1982)—§§ 21.3(d) n.221; 21.4(g) n.233

Kills Enemy, United States v., 3 F.3d 1201 (8th Cir.1993)—§§ 3.9(j) n.206; 12.1(b) n.32

Kilpatrick, United States v., 821 F.2d 1456 (10th Cir.1987)—§§ 15.6(e) n.151, 153

Kilpatrick, United States v., 594 F.Supp. 1324 (D.Colo.1984)—§ 1.7(i) n.191

Kilpatrick, United States v., 575 F.Supp. 325 (D.Colo.1983)—§§ 15.2(i) n.219, 220, 223; 15.6(e) n.137

Kilpatrick, United States v., 16 F. 765 (W.D.N.C.1883)—§§ 8.4(b) n.95, 102

Kilroy, United States v., 27 F.3d 679 (D.C.Cir.1994)—§§ 8.11(c) n.44; 8.11(e) n.94, 105; 10.3(c) n.57

Kilvington, People v., 104 Cal. 86, 37 P. 799 (1894)—§ 3.5(a) n.11

Kim, State v., 239 Mont. 189, 779 P.2d 512 (1989)—§ 10.4(c) n.23

Kim v. State, 434 N.W.2d 263 (Minn.1989)—§ 21.5(a) n.8

Kim, United States v., 292 F.3d 969 (9th Cir.2002)—§ 6.6(e) n.68

Kim, United States v., 246 F.3d 186 (2d Cir.2001)—§ 16.2(e) n.91

Kim, United States v., 25 F.3d 1426 (9th Cir.1994)—§ 26.5(a) n.8

Kim, United States v., 896 F.2d 678 (2d Cir.1990)—§§ 21.1(h) n.233; 21.2(d) n.216

Kim, United States v., 415 F.Supp. 1252 (D.Hawai'i 1976)—§ 3.2(b) n.56

Kimball, Commonwealth v., 555 Pa. 299, 724 A.2d 326 (1999)—§ 11.10(c) n.86

Kimball, United States v., 884 F.2d 1274 (9th Cir.1989)—§§ 9.5(a) n.28; 9.5(d) n.80

Kimberlin, United States v., 805 F.2d 210 (7th Cir.1986)—§ 17.4(a) n.45

Kimble v. State, 539 P.2d 73 (Alaska 1975)—§ 7.4(b) n.29

Kimbrell v. Cockrell, 311 F.3d 361 (5th Cir.2002)—§ 28.5(b) n.53

Kimbro, State v., 197 Conn. 219, 496 A.2d 498 (1985)—§ 2.12(d) n.195

Kimbrough, United States v., 477 F.3d 144 (4th Cir.2007)—§§ 6.10(b) n.14, 34

Kimler, United States v., 335 F.3d 1132 (10th Cir.2003)—§ 3.9(j) n.239

Kimmel, United States v., 672 F.2d 720 (9th Cir.1982)—§§ 11.5(c) n.52 to 54; 11.5(f) n.105; 11.5(g) n.111

Kimmelman v. Morrison, 477 U.S. 365, 106 S.Ct. 2574, 91 L.Ed.2d 305 (1986)—§§ 11.10(c) n.102; 11.10(d) n.179; 28.3(c) n.77; 28.3(d) n.90; 28.4(d) n.54

Kimmons, United States v., 965 F.2d 1001 (11th Cir.1992)—§§ 3.6(a) n.19; 3.6(d) n.98

Kimpel, State v., 665 So.2d 990 (Ala.App.1995)—§ 27.3(c) n.27

Kincade, United States v., 379 F.3d 813 (9th Cir.2004)—§§ 3.2(g) n.198; 3.9(i) n.190

Kincaid, United States v., 898 F.2d 110 (9th Cir.1990)—§ 27.5(b) n.46

Kincaide, United States v., 145 F.3d 771 (6th Cir.1998)—§ 4.6(k) n.173

Kinchen, State v., 243 Conn. 690, 707 A.2d 1255 (1998)—§§ 13.2(a) n.3; 13.2(c) n.56

Kinderman, State v., 271 Minn. 405, 136 N.W.2d 577 (1965)—§ 3.10(e) n.145

Kindle, United States v., 88 F.3d 535 (8th Cir.1996)—§ 28.9(a) n.15

Kindle, United States v., 925 F.2d 272 (8th Cir.1991)—§§ 11.9(d) n.226, 232

Kindred v. Spears, 894 F.2d 1477 (5th Cir.1990)—§ 26.2(c) n.40

Kindred v. State, 521 N.E.2d 320 (Ind.1988)—§ 22.5(a) n.12

Kindred v. State, 524 N.E.2d 279 (Ind.1988)—§§ 11.3(b) n.38; 17.1(a) n.14

King v. Commonwealth, 142 S.W.3d 645 (Ky.2004)—§§ 7.4(c) n.48, 51, 53; 7.4(e) n.91

King, Commonwealth v., 554 Pa. 331, 721 A.2d 763 (1998)—§§ 17.1(d) n.53; 17.2(d) n.95

King, Commonwealth v., 374 Mass. 5, 372 N.E.2d 196 (1977)—§§ 13.4(c) n.92, 95, 123

King v. Hawkins, 266 Ga. 655, 469 S.E.2d 30 (1996)—§ 21.4(f) n.184

King v. Kemna, 266 F.3d 816 (8th Cir.2001)—§ 11.10(c) n.113

King v. Moore, 312 F.3d 1365 (11th Cir.2002)—§ 11.2(b) n.75

King v. Moore, 196 F.3d 1327 (11th Cir.1999)—§ 22.3(d) n.228

King, People v., 16 P.3d 807 (Colo.2001)—§ 3.8(b) n.28

King v. People, 728 P.2d 1264 (Colo.1986)—§ 11.3(c) n.67

King, People v., 79 App.Div.2d 992, 434 N.Y.S.2d 462 (1981)—§ 24.3(b) n.48

King, People v., 412 Mich. 145, 312 N.W.2d 629 (1981)—§§ 14.3(b) n.48 to 50

King, People v., 27 Cal. 507 (1863)— § 19.1(a) n.7

King v. Second National Bank and Trust Co., 234 Ala. 106, 173 So. 498 (1937)—§§ 8.4(b) n.83, 85, 88

King, State v., 48 P.3d 396 (Wyo.2002)—§ 25.1(d) n.60

King v. State, 808 So.2d 1237 (Fla.2002)—§ 24.3(e) n.127

King, State v., 353 N.C. 457, 546 S.E.2d 575 (2001)—§ 22.3(d) n.246

King v. State, 273 Ga. 258, 539 S.E.2d 783 (2000)—§ 22.3(b) n.86

King v. State, 270 Ga. 367, 509 S.E.2d 32 (1998)—§ 21.5(d) n.98

King, State v., 576 N.W.2d 369 (Iowa 1998)—§§ 21.2(e) n.308, 316

King, State v., 708 A.2d 1014 (Me.1998)—§§ 6.9(g) n.157, 161

King, State v., 130 Wash.2d 517, 925 P.2d 606 (1996)—§ 26.10(c) n.61

King, State v., 205 Wis.2d 81, 555 N.W.2d 189 (1996)—§ 27.5(d) n.138

King v. State, 323 Ark. 558, 916 S.W.2d 725 (1996)—§ 7.4(e) n.92

King, State v., 316 Ore. 437, 852 P.2d 190 (1993)—§ 24.10(c) n.41

King v. State, 580 So.2d 1182 (Miss.1991)—§ 24.9(a) n.11

King, State v., 30 Or.App. 223, 566 P.2d 1204 (1977)—§ 20.6(b) n.45

King v. State, 262 Ark. 342, 557 S.W.2d 386 (1977)—§ 2.12(d) n.183

King v. State, 553 P.2d 529 (Okla.Crim.App.1976)—§§ 21.4(b) n.54; 21.4(e) n.161; 21.4(g) n.231, 237

King v. State, 473 S.W.2d 43 (Tex.Cr.App.1971)—§§ 15.1(f) n.272 to 275, 282, 309, 334

King, State v., 140 W.Va. 362, 84 S.E.2d 313 (1954)—§ 18.5(a) n.40

King v. State, 236 Ind. 268, 139 N.E.2d 547 (1957)—§ 15.4(b) n.36

King, State v., 342 Mo. 975, 119 S.W.2d 277 (Mo.1938)—§ 15.4(b) n.38

King v. Superior Court, 107 Cal.App.4th 929, 132 Cal.Rptr.2d 585 (2003)— §§ 11.3(c) n.66; 11.4(b) n.29, 30

King, United States v., 338 F.3d 794 (7th Cir.2003)—§ 18.1(c) n.36

King, United States v., 246 F.3d 1166 (9th Cir.2001)—§ 21.4(f) n.207

King, United States v., 257 F.3d 1013 (9th Cir.2001)—§§ 21.4(f) n.207; 21.5(a) n.18

King, United States v., 227 F.3d 732 (6th Cir.2000)—§§ 3.2(c) n.106; 3.4(j) n.184; 9.1(b) n.58

King, United States v., 234 F.3d 126 (2d Cir.2000)—§ 21.5(c) n.83

King, United States v., 140 F.3d 76 (2d Cir.1998)—§§ 23.1(e) n.219, 246, 251

King, United States v., 148 F.3d 968 (8th Cir.1998)—§ 7.4(f) n.96

King, United States v., 126 F.3d 394 (2d Cir.1997)—§§ 13.7(c) n.45, 52

King, United States v., 55 F.3d 1193 (6th Cir.1995)—§ 4.2(a) n.7

King, United States v., 911 F.Supp. 113 (S.D.N.Y.1995)—§ 23.1(d) n.165

King, United States v., 478 F.2d 494 (9th Cir.1973)—§ 4.6(m) n.218

King, United States v., 321 F.Supp. 614 (W.D.Tex.1970)—§ 7.3(g) n.124

King v. Warickshall, 168 Eng.Rep. 234, L. Leach Cr. Cases 263 (K.B.1783)—§ 6.2(a) n.4

Kingsbury v. United States, 520 A.2d 686 (D.C.App.1987)—§ 22.2(d) n.79

Kingsley v. United States, 968 F.2d 109 (1st Cir.1992)—§ 21.2(e) n.300

Kingston, United States v., 971 F.2d 481 (10th Cir.1992)—§ 15.7(d) n.82

King, The v. Coombis, 168 Eng.Rep. 296 (Ex.1785)—§ 16.4(c) n.44

Kington, United States v., 875 F.2d 1091 (5th Cir.1989)—§ 18.3(b) n.22

Kington, United States v., 835 F.2d 106 (5th Cir.1988)—§ 27.3(d) n.67

Kington, United States v., 801 F.2d 733 (5th Cir.1986)—§§ 3.2(j) n.240; 8.5(b) n.33; 8.8(g) n.166; 27.3(d) n.67

Kinkade, State v., 140 Ariz. 91, 680 P.2d 801 (1984)—§ 17.2(d) n.93

Kinnebrew v. State, 132 Ala. 8, 31 So. 567 (1902)—§ 15.6(d) n.119

Kinnersley v. State, 494 N.W.2d 698 (Iowa 1993)—§ 21.4(d) n.119

Kinney v. Lenon, 425 F.2d 209 (9th Cir.1970)—§ 12.2(c) n.42

Kinney, United States v., 953 F.2d 863 (4th Cir.1992)—§ 3.10(d) n.134

Kinsella v. United States, 361 U.S. 234, 80 S.Ct. 297, 4 L.Ed.2d 268 (1960)—§ 15.1(b) n.91

Kinser v. Commonwealth, 741 S.W.2d 648 (Ky.1987)—§ 17.2(b) n.74

Kinsey, State v., 173 Conn. 344, 377 A.2d 1095 (1977)—§ 10.3(d) n.63

Kirby, In re, 101 Ohio St.3d 312, 804 N.E.2d 476 (2004)—§ 21.4(f) n.209

Kirby v. Illinois, 406 U.S. 682, 92 S.Ct. 1877, 32 L.Ed.2d 411 (1972)—§§ 2.9(b) n.44; 2.9(h) n.211; 3.10(b) n.76; 6.4(c) n.47; 6.4(d) n.58; 6.4(e) n.65, 71, 83; 7.3(b) n.13; 8.14(a) n.3; 11.1(c) n.99; 11.2(b) n.44, 48; 12.1(c) n.47; 21.3(a) n.3, 11

Kirby, People v., 440 Mich. 485, 487 N.W.2d 404 (1992)—§ 22.1(h) n.149

Kirby, State v., 280 Conn. 361, 908 A.2d 506 (2006)—§§ 6.5(b) n.25; 6.6(e) n.61

Kirby, United States v., 418 F.3d 621 (6th Cir.2005)—§ 26.10(c) n.71

Kirchoff, State v., 452 N.W.2d 801 (Iowa 1990)—§ 21.4(e) n.163

Kirk v. Louisiana, 536 U.S. 635, 122 S.Ct. 2458, 153 L.Ed.2d 599 (2002)—§ 3.6(a) n.4

Kirk v. State, 41 Tenn. 344 (1860)—§ 16.3(f) n.95

Kirk, United States v., 105 F.3d 997 (5th Cir.1997)—§ 1.2(c) n.144

Kirkland v. State, 274 Ga. 778, 560 S.E.2d 6 (2002)—§ 22.3(c) n.102

Kirkley, People v., 60 Ill.App.3d 746, 18 Ill.Dec. 251, 377 N.E.2d 540 (1978)—§ 14.2(g) n.98

Kirkpatrick, State v., 94 Nev. 628, 584 P.2d 670 (1978)—§ 19.3(b) n.178

Kirksey v. State, 112 Nev. 980, 923 P.2d 1102 (1996)—§ 21.6(a) n.78

Kirtdoll, State v., 281 Kan. 1138, 136 P.3d 417 (2006)—§ 6.9(a) n.12

Kirtley, United States v., 5 F.3d 1110 (7th Cir.1993)—§ 26.10(b) n.23

Kiser, Application of, 83 S.D. 272, 158 N.W.2d 596 (1968)—§ 3.8(f) n.233

Kiser, State v., 158 Vt. 403, 610 A.2d 135 (1997)—§ 20.3(a) n.20

Kiser, United States v., 948 F.2d 418 (8th Cir.1991)—§ 9.1(d) n.127

Kishel v. State, 287 So.2d 414 (Fla.App.1974)—§ 9.1(b) n.43

Kisling, United States v., 334 F.3d 734 (8th Cir.2003)—§§ 12.1(a) n.6; 12.1(d) n.58

Kisner v. State, 209 Md. 524, 122 A.2d 102 (1956)—§ 16.1(h) n.285

Kissick, United States v., 69 F.3d 1048 (10th Cir.1995)—§ 11.10(c) n.105

Kitchen, People v., 159 Ill.2d 1, 201 Ill.Dec. 1, 636 N.E.2d 433 (1994)— § 22.3(d) n.249

Kitchen v. State, 87 Md.App. 299, 589 A.2d 575 (1991)—§ 26.10(c) n.49

Kitchen v. United States, 227 F.3d 1014 (7th Cir.2000)—§§ 11.2(b) n.52; 11.6(d) n.120

Kitchens, United States v., 114 F.3d 29 (4th Cir.1997)—§ 3.2(c) n.103

Kitt v. United States, 904 A.2d 348 (D.C.App.2006)—§ 6.7(c) n.133

Kittel, State v., 203 Or.App. 736, 127 P.3d 1204 (2006)—§ 24.2(a) n.16

Kitto, State v., 373 N.W.2d 307 (Minn.1985)—§ 22.3(b) n.91

Kivela v. Department of Treasury, 449 Mich. 220, 536 N.W.2d 498 (1995)—§§ 2.12(d) n.192, 194; 2.12(e) n.202

Kivioja, State v., 225 Wis.2d 271, 592 N.W.2d 220—§ 21.5(a) n.43

Kizer, People v., 318 Ill.App.3d 238, 251 Ill.Dec. 925, 741 N.E.2d 1103 (2000)—§ 2.11(a) n.14

Kjorsvik, State v., 117 Wash.2d 93, 812 P.2d 86 (1991)—§§ 19.3(a) n.46; 19.3(e) n.243, 244

K.L., State v., 663 A.2d 21 (Me.1995)— § 21.6(b) n.95

Kladouris, United States v., 964 F.2d 658 (7th Cir.1992)—§ 11.9(a) n.7

Klamath Falls, City of v. Winters, 289 Or. 757, 619 P.2d 217 (1980)— § 13.7(a) n.26

Klarfeld v. United States, 944 F.2d 583 (9th Cir.1991)—§ 3.9(h) n.169

Klattenhoff, State v., 71 Haw. 598, 801 P.2d 548 (Haw.1990)—§ 8.5(d) n.156

Kleba, People v., 110 Ill.App.3d 345, 66 Ill.Dec. 179, 442 N.E.2d 605 (1982)—§§ 11.4(c) n.62, 79, 84

Klee, United States v., 494 F.2d 394 (9th Cir.1974)—§§ 11.5(g) n.116, 118

Kleeman v. United States Parole Comm'n., 125 F.3d 725 (9th Cir.1997)—§ 24.8(e) n.54

Kleen, State v., 491 S.W.2d 244 (Mo.1973)—§ 16.4(c) n.49

Kleen Laundry & Cleaners, Inc., United States v., 381 F.Supp. 519 (E.D.N.Y.1974)—§§ 8.4(b) n.25, 26; 8.8(g) n.164; 15.3(d) n.64

Klein, In re, 776 F.2d 628 (7th Cir.1985)—§§ 8.8(d) n.88, 91, 95; 27.2(e) n.89

Klein v. Harris, 667 F.2d 274 (2d Cir.1981)—§ 8.10(e) n.121

Klein, State v., 560 N.W.2d 198 (N.D.1997)—§ 21.5(a) n.3

Klein v. United States, 880 F.2d 250 (10th Cir.1989)—§ 28.9(a) n.21

Klem, State v., 438 N.W.2d 798 (N.D.1989)—§ 24.1(b) n.26

Klessig, State v., 211 Wis.2d 194, 564 N.W.2d 716 (1997)—§ 11.5(c) n.32

Kleypas, State v., 272 Kan. 894, 40 P.3d 139 (2001)—§ 22.3(d) n.202

Klimavicius-Viloria, United States v., 144 F.3d 1249 (9th Cir.1998)— § 16.4(d) n.121

Klimczak, State v., 159 Conn. 608, 268 A.2d 372 (1970)—§ 6.9(g) n.149

Kline, Commonwealth v., 234 Pa.Super. 12, 335 A.2d 361 (1975)—§ 3.3(g) n.246

Kline, State v., 155 Or.App. 96, 963 P.2d 697 (Or.App.1998)—§ 26.9(b) n.55

Kline, United States ex rel. v. Lane, 707 F.Supp. 368 (N.D.Ill.1989)— § 14.2(d) n.58

Klingbeil, United States v., 410 F.Supp. 1235 (W.D.Wis.1976)—§ 16.2(f) n.104

Klinge, State v., 92 Haw. 577, 994 P.2d 509 (2000)—§ 24.10(c) n.41

Klingenberg, People v., 172 Ill.2d 270, 216 Ill.Dec. 813, 665 N.E.2d 1370 (1996)—§§ 17.4(a) n.7, 8

Klingler v. United States, 409 F.2d 299 (8th Cir.1969)—§ 3.1(d) n.98

Klitzman, Klitzman, and Gallagher v. Krut, 591 F.Supp. 258 (D.N.J. 1984)—§ 3.4(a) n.22

Klobuchir, Commonwealth v., 486 Pa. 241, 405 A.2d 881 (1979)—§§ 21.5(e) n.112, 122, 123

Klobuchir v. Commonwealth of Pennsylvania, 639 F.2d 966 (3d Cir.1981)—§ 21.5(e) n.119

Klopfer v. North Carolina, 386 U.S. 213, 87 S.Ct. 988, 18 L.Ed.2d 1 (1967)—§§ 2.5(f) n.53; 2.6(a) n.8; 18.1(a) n.1, 2, 7; 18.1(b) n.11; 18.2(b) n.22

Klos v. Haskell, 48 F.3d 81 (2d Cir.1995)—§ 26.1(e) n.113

Klosterman, State v., 114 Ohio App.3d 327, 683 N.E.2d 100 (1996)—§ 3.1(c) n.79

Klosterman, United States v., 248 F.2d 191 (3d Cir.1957)—§ 5.1(c) n.31

Klubock, United States v., 832 F.2d 664 (1st Cir.1987)—§ 8.8(d) n.101

Klubock, United States v., 639 F.Supp. 117 (D.Mass.1986)—§ 24.3(f) n.147

Kluger, In re, 827 F.2d 868 (2d Cir.1987)—§ 8.5(c) n.94

Knaak, People v., 112 Misc.2d 83, 446 N.Y.S.2d 154 (Sup.Ct.1981)—§ 15.2(c) n.86

Knaff, People v., 196 Ill.2d 460, 752 N.E.2d 1123, 256 Ill.Dec. 881 (2001)—§§ 25.3(a) n.8; 25.3(c) n.30

Knaff, State v., 128 Oh.App.3d 90, 713 N.E.2d 1112 (1998)—§ 25.1(d) n.67

Knapp, In re, 536 So.2d 1330 (Miss.1988)—§ 8.10(c) n.65

Knapp, People v., 113 App.Div.2d 154, 495 N.Y.S.2d 985 (1985)—§ 24.1(a) n.11

Knapp, State v., 285 Wis.2d 86, 700 N.W.2d 899 (2005)—§§ 2.12(b) n.82, 83; 9.5(b) n.53

Knapp, State v., 40 Kan. 148, 19 P. 728 (1888)—§§ 16.3(d) n.55, 62

Knapp, United States v., 25 F.3d 451 (7th Cir.1994)—§ 22.3(b) n.74

Knappenberger v. State, 278 Ark. 382, 647 S.W.2d 417 (1983)—§§ 11.7(e) n.88, 89

Knapstad, State v., 107 Wash.2d 346, 729 P.2d 48 (1986)—§ 14.2(d) n.64

Kneefe v. Sullivan, 2 Or.App. 152, 465 P.2d 741 (1970)—§ 16.1(e) n.200

Kneeland, United States v., 148 F.3d 6 (1st Cir.1998)—§ 11.4(d) n.110

Knese v. State, 85 S.W.3d 628 (Mo.2002)—§§ 11.10(c) n.75; 11.10(d) n.171; 22.3(c) n.154

Knese, State v., 985 S.W.2d 759 (Mo.1999)—§ 6.9(b) n.36

Kniep, State v., 87 Ohio App.3d 681, 622 N.E.2d 1138 (1993)—§ 8.8(f) n.145

Knight v. Jacobson, 300 F.3d 1272 (11th Cir.2002)—§ 3.5(a) n.22

Knight, People v., _____ P.3d _____, 2006 WL 3437553 (Colo.App.2006)—§ 24.2(e) n.58

Knight v. Schofield, 292 F.3d 709 (11th Cir.2002)—§ 28.5(b) n.59

Knight, State v., 183 N.J. 449, 874 A.2d 546 (2005)—§§ 6.2(c) n.79; 21.6(a) n.39

Knight, State v., 701 N.W.2d 83 (Iowa 2005)—§ 21.4(f) n.207

Knight v. State, 381 Md. 517, 850 A.2d 1179 (2004)—§ 6.2(c) n.107

Knight, State v., 266 Conn. 658, 835 A.2d 47 (2003)—§ 24.10(b) n.35

Knight, State v., 145 N.J. 233, 678 A.2d 642 (1996)—§ 24.3(b) n.49

Knight, State v., 283 N.J.Super. 98, 661 A.2d 298 (App.Div.1995)—§ 2.12(c) n.176

Knight, State v., 168 Wis.2d 509, 484 N.W.2d 540 (1992)—§ 11.7(e) n.102

Knight, State v., 168 W.Va. 615, 285 S.E.2d 401 (1981)—§ 22.5(a) n.8

Knight, State v., 616 S.W.2d 593 (Tenn.1981)—§ 16.1(d) n.139

Knight, State v., 1 N.C. 143 (1799)— §§ 16.4(c) n.107, 110

Knight, United States v., 96 F.3d 307 (8th Cir.1996)—§ 21.6(a) n.59

Knight, United States v., 867 F.2d 1285 (11th Cir.1989)—§ 21.2(h) n.419

Knight v. United States, 611 F.2d 918 (1st Cir.1979)—§ 21.2(g) n.400

Knight, United States v., 443 F.2d 174 (6th Cir.1971)—§ 11.8(c) n.54

Knight Publishing, In re, 743 F.2d 231 (4th Cir.1984)—§ 23.1(e) n.261

Knights, State v., 482 A.2d 436 (Me.1984)—§ 6.9(b) n.27

Knights, United States v., 534 U.S. 112, 122 S.Ct. 587, 151 L.Ed.2d 497 (2001)—§§ 3.5(d) n.145; 3.9(a) n.8; 3.9(c) n.41; 3.9(j) n.216, 230; 26.9(b) n.61

Knights, United States v., 968 F.2d 1483 (2d Cir.1992)—§ 21.2(d) n.245

Knobel, People v., 94 N.Y.2d 226, 701 N.Y.S.2d 695, 723 N.E.2d 550 (1999)—§ 18.5(a) n.24

Knoll, United States v., 16 F.3d 1313 (2d Cir.1994)—§ 3.1(h) n.191

Knoll Associates, Inc. v. Federal Trade Commission, 397 F.2d 530 (7th Cir.1968)—§§ 3.1(g) n.178; 3.1(h) n.218

Knop v. Johnson, 977 F.2d 996 (6th Cir.1992)—§§ 11.2(f) n.241, 248, 249, 251, 252

Knott, United States v., 256 F.3d 20 (1st Cir.2001)—§§ 13.5(h) n.145, 169

Knotts, State v., 187 W.Va. 795, 421 S.E.2d 917 (W.Va. 1992)—§ 9.6(a) n.23

Knotts, United States v., 460 U.S. 276, 103 S.Ct. 1081, 75 L.Ed.2d 55 (1983)—§§ 3.2(b) n.84; 3.2(j) n.253

Knotts, State ex rel. v. Watt, 186 W.Va. 518, 413 S.E.2d 173 (1991)— §§ 15.6(d) n.119; 15.7(c) n.52, 53

Knowles v. Iowa, 525 U.S. 113, 119 S.Ct. 484, 142 L.Ed.2d 492 (1998)—§§ 3.5(a) n.9; 3.5(b) n.92; 3.7(a) n.11; 12.5(b) n.29

Knowles, State v., 946 S.W.2d 791 (Mo.App.1997)—§ 24.8(a) n.8

Knowles, United States v., 147 F.Supp. 19 (D.D.C.1957)—§§ 15.4(g) n.171, 175

Knowlton, State v., 123 Idaho 916, 854 P.2d 259 (1993)—§§ 22.4(b) n.16; 22.4(c) n.22

Knox, State v., 307 Mont. 1, 36 P.3d 383 (2001)—§ 21.2(d) n.141

Knox v. State, 340 S.C. 81, 530 S.E.2d 887 (2000)—§ 21.3(b) n.71

Knox, State v., 609 So.2d 803 (La.1992)—§ 22.3(d) n.192

Knox v. State, 234 Md. 203, 198 A.2d 285 (1964)—§ 21.5(f) n.164

Knox, United States v., 950 F.2d 516 (8th Cir.1991)—§ 11.5(f) n.102

Knox, United States v., 839 F.2d 285 (6th Cir.1988)—§ 6.6(e) n.92

Knuckles, People v., 165 Ill.2d 125, 209 Ill.Dec. 1, 650 N.E.2d 974 (1995)— §§ 20.4(f) n.91; 20.5(c) n.54, 56; 20.5(h) n.112

Knuckles, United States v., 581 F.2d 305 (2d Cir.1978)—§ 19.6(c) n.39

Knudson, State v., 499 N.W.2d 872 (N.D.1993)—§ 3.4(g) n.128

Knudson, State v., 51 Wis.2d 270, 187 N.W.2d 321 (1971)—§ 14.4(d) n.86

Knutson, State v., 168 Wash. 633, 12 P.2d 923 (1932)—§ 16.2(a) n.1

Koblan, United States v., 478 F.3d 1324 (11th Cir.2007)—§ 27.5(a) n.7

Kobli, United States v., 172 F.2d 919 (3d Cir.1949)—§§ 1.5(i) n.305; 24.1(b) n.20

Kobrosky, United States v., 711 F.2d 449 (1st Cir.1983)—§ 21.5(a) n.19

Koczuk, United States v., 166 F.Supp.2d 757 (E.D.N.Y.2001)—§ 26.4(h) n.154

Kodiak, City of v. Samaniego, 83 P.3d 1077 (Alaska 2004)—§ 3.8(b) n.18

Koedatich, State v., 112 N.J. 225, 548 A.2d 939 (1988)—§§ 11.5(a) n.20; 24.9(g) n.118

Koelzer, People v., 222 Cal.App.2d 20, 34 Cal.Rptr. 718 (1963)—§ 9.5(a) n.9

Koenig v. State, 597 So.2d 256 (Fla.1992)—§ 21.4(f) n.177

Koenig, United States v., 912 F.2d 1190 (9th Cir.1990)—§ 12.3(a) n.27

Koennecke, State v., 274 Or. 169, 545 P.2d 127 (1976)—§ 24.3(g) n.160

Koepplin, State v., 213 Mont. 55, 689 P.2d 921 (1984)—§ 21.3(b) n.58

Koerth, United States v., 312 F.3d 862 (7th Cir.2002)—§ 3.3(c) n.100

Koger v. State, 117 Nev. 138, 17 P.3d 428 (2001)—§ 6.8(b) n.51

Koh, United States v., 199 F.3d 632 (2d Cir.1999)—§ 13.5(a) n.6

Kohler v. Englade, 470 F.3d 1104 (5th Cir.2006)—§ 3.2(g) n.195

Kohn v. State, 336 N.W.2d 292 (Minn.1983)—§ 8.12(b) n.22

Kokal v. State, 901 So.2d 766 (Fla.2005)—§ 24.11(d) n.23

Kolberg v. State, 829 So.2d 29 (Miss.2002)—§ 22.3(c) n.157

Kolbet, State v., 638 N.W.2d 653 (Iowa 2001)—§ 22.4(c) n.29

Kolender v. Lawson, 461 U.S. 352, 103 S.Ct. 1855, 75 L.Ed.2d 903 (1983)—§§ 3.3(f) n.216, 219

Kolodziej, United States v., 706 F.2d 590 (5th Cir.1983)—§ 4.6(l) n.200

Kolton, People v., 219 Ill.2d 353, 302 Ill.Dec. 386 (2006)—§ 24.8(e) n.71

Konefal, United States v., 566 F.Supp. 698 (N.D.N.Y.1983)—§ 20.3(b) n.50

Konigsberg, State v., 33 N.J. 367, 164 A.2d 740 (1960)—§§ 12.3(b) n.32; 12.4(a) n.1, 16, 17, 22, 23, 33, 42

Konigsberg v. Vincent, 526 F.2d 131 (2d Cir.1975)—§ 11.5(c) n.52

Konkol, State v., 256 Wis.2d 725, 649 N.W.2d 300 (App.2002)—§ 20.3(h) n.142

Konop v. Hawaiian Airlines, Inc., 302 F.3d 868 (9th Cir.2002)—§§ 4.6(b) n.25, 30

Kon Yu-Leung, United States v., 910 F.2d 33 (2d Cir.1990)—§ 3.10(b) n.78

Koon, State v., 704 So.2d 756 (La.1997)—§ 6.9(f) n.133

Koon v. United States, 518 U.S. 81, 116 S.Ct. 2035, 135 L.Ed.2d 392 (1996)—§ 26.3(g) n.70

Koontz v. Glossa, 731 F.2d 365 (6th Cir.1984)—§ 19.2(c) n.29

Koontz, State v., 145 Wash.2d 650, 41 P.3d 475 (2002)—§ 24.9(c) n.25

Koopmans, State v., 210 Wis.2d 670, 563 N.W.2d 528 (1997)—§ 24.2(a) n.11

Koota v. Colombo, 17 N.Y.2d 147, 269 N.Y.S.2d 393, 216 N.E.2d 568 (1966)—§§ 8.8(a) n.12; 8.8(b) n.30

Kopituk, United States v., 690 F.2d 1289 (11th Cir.1982)—§ 24.7(e) n.73

Koput, State v., 142 Wis.2d 370, 418 N.W.2d 804 (1988)—§ 6.6(d) n.58

Kordenbrock v. Scroggy, 919 F.2d 1091 (6th Cir.1990)—§§ 11.2(e) n.204, 208

Kordosky, United States v., 921 F.2d 722 (7th Cir.1991)—§ 3.7(e) n.105

Korematsu v. United States, 584 F.Supp. 1406 (N.D.Cal.1984)—§ 28.9(a) n.16

Koren, State ex rel. v. Grogan, 68 Ohio St.3d 590, 629 N.E.2d 446 (1994)—§ 27.4(c) n.21

Korman, United States v., 614 F.2d 541 (6th Cir.1980)—§ 3.6(e) n.119

Korn, United States v., 138 F.3d 1239 (8th Cir.1998)—§ 26.4(d) n.65

Kornahrens v. Evatt, 66 F.3d 1350 (4th Cir.1995)—§ 11.10(c) n.110

Kornegay, United States v., 410 F.3d 89 (1st Cir.2005)—§ 10.3(b) n.44

Korolkov, United States v., 870 F.Supp. 60 (S.D.N.Y.1994)—§§ 16.2(e) n.68, 71, 78; 16.2(f) n.107

Korsen, State v., 141 Idaho 445, 111 P.3d 130 (2005)—§ 27.5(a) n.7

Korth, State v., 650 N.W.2d 528 (S.D.2002)—§§ 11.2(c) n.90, 96

Kortkamp, State v., 560 N.W.2d 93 (Minn.App.1997)—§ 26.4(d) n.52

Korum, State v., 157 Wash.2d 614, 141 P.3d 13 (2006)—§ 21.2(b) n.45

Korwan, Commonwealth v., 448 Mass 304, 860 N.E.2d 931 (2007)— § 6.6(e) n.61

Korzep v. Superior Court, 155 Ariz. 303, 746 P.2d 44 (App.1987)— §§ 15.5(b) n.45; 15.5(c) n.112, 114; 15.6(a) n.29, 32; 15.7(e) n.127

Korzuch, State v., 186 Ariz. 190, 920 P.2d 312 (1996)—§ 26.9(a) n.14

Kosal v. State, 204 Ga.App. 708, 420 S.E.2d 621 (1992)—§ 20.3(f) n.110

Koshnevis, United States v., 979 F.2d 691 (9th Cir.1992)—§ 3.10(b) n.46

Kosik, United States ex rel. v. Napoli, 814 F.2d 1151 (7th Cir.1987)— § 7.4(c) n.62

Koskela, United States v., 86 F.3d 122 (8th Cir.1996)—§ 26.2(b) n.21

Kosovsky, United States v., 506 F.Supp. 43 (1980)—§ 8.5(g) n.215

Kossakowski v. People, 177 Ill. 563, 53 N.E. 115 (1899)—§ 16.4(c) n.51

Kossin v. United States, 235 F.2d 188 (6th Cir.1956)—§ 15.1(f) n.319

Kothe v. State, 152 S.W.3d 54 (Tex.Cr.App.2004)—§ 9.1(d) n.131

Kotila v. Commonwealth, 114 S.W.3d 226 (Ky.2003)—§ 6.9(g) n.167

Kotleakos v. United States, 328 U.S. 750, 66 S.Ct. 1239, 90 L.Ed. 1557 (1946)—§ 28.6(g) n.81

Kotredes, State v., 838 A.2d 331 (Me.2003)—§ 18.5(a) n.41

Kott v. United States, 163 F.2d 984 (5th Cir.1947)—§§ 5.1(c) n.13; 16.2(g) n.124

Kotteakos v. United States, 328 U.S. 750, 66 S.Ct. 1239, 90 L.Ed. 1557 (1946)—§§ 15.6(e) n.138; 19.6(c) n.26; 27.6(b) n.38, 53

Kouba, United States v., 632 F.Supp. 937 (D.N.D.1986)—§ 15.5(b) n.65

Koubriti, United States v., 307 F.Supp.2d 891 (E.D.Mich.2004)— §§ 23.1(b) n.70, 88

Koubriti, United States v., 336 F.Supp.2d 676 (E.D.Mich.2004)— § 24.3(b) n.35

Kovac, United States v., 795 F.2d 1509 (9th Cir.1986)—§ 9.1(d) n.129

Kovack, State v., 91 N.J. 476, 453 A.2d 521 (1982)—§ 21.2(e) n.332

Kovacs v. Cooper, 336 U.S. 77, 69 S.Ct. 448, 93 L.Ed. 513 (1949)—§ 1.2(b) n.5

Kovaleski, United States v., 406 F.Supp. 267 (E.D.Mich.1976)—§§ 8.8(f) n.157, 158

Kow, United States v., 58 F.3d 423 (9th Cir.1995)—§ 3.1(c) n.72

Kowalski, People v., 196 Cal.App.3d 174, 242 Cal.Rptr. 32 (1987)— §§ 14.2(e) n.77; 14.2(f) n.91

Kowalski v. Tesmer, 543 U.S. 125, 125 S.Ct. 564, 160 L.Ed.2d 519 (2004)—§§ 11.1(b) n.65; 28.12(a) n.1

Koza v. State, 102 Nev. 181, 718 P.2d 671 (1986)—§§ 6.7(c) n.118; 6.9(f) n.127

KPNX Broadcasting v. Superior Court, 139 Ariz. 246, 678 P.2d 431 (1984)—§§ 23.1(b) n.68, 71

Kradenych, People v., 83 Ill.App.3d 547, 39 Ill.Dec. 104, 404 N.E.2d 488 (1980)—§ 20.6(b) n.33

Kraft, State v., 539 N.W.2d 56 (N.D.1995)—§ 13.4(e) n.170

Kraft v. State, 100 Idaho 671, 603 P.2d 1005 (1979)—§ 11.7(e) n.86

Kragness, United States v., 830 F.2d 842 (8th Cir.1987)—§ 24.5(b) n.28

Kramar, State v., 149 Wis.2d 767, 440 N.W.2d 317 (1989)—§§ 6.9(f) n.133; 6.9(g) n.155, 162

Kramer, State v., 248 Wis.2d 1009, 637 N.W.2d 35 (2001)—§ 13.4(c) n.84

Kramer v. State, 619 So.2d 274 (Fla.1993)—§§ 22.3(d) n.245, 247

Kramer, United States v., 827 F.2d 1174 (8th Cir.1987)—§ 18.3(b) n.56

Kramer v. Village of North Fond du Lac, 384 F.3d 856 (7th Cir.2004)—§§ 5.4(c) n.30; 13.4(c) n.84

Krankel, United States v., 164 F.3d 1046 (7th Cir.1998)—§ 6.4(f) n.137

Krasny, United States v., 607 F.2d 840 (9th Cir.1979)—§ 24.11(d) n.28

Kraus, State v., 397 N.W.2d 671 (Iowa 1986)—§ 21.3(b) n.98

Kraus, United States v., 137 F.3d 447 (7th Cir.1998)—§§ 21.3(d) n.225; 21.3(e) n.270; 21.4(a) n.12

Krause v. Commonwealth, 206 S.W.3d 922 (Ky.2006)—§ 3.10(c) n.98

Kraushaar, State v., 264 Kan. 667, 957 P.2d 1106 (1998)—§ 14.3(d) n.98

Kraushaar, State v., 470 N.W.2d 509 (Minn.1991)—§ 24.9(c) n.29

Krebs v. Schwarz, 212 Wis.2d 127, 568 N.W.2d 26 (Wis.App.1997)—§ 26.9(b) n.55

Krebs, State v., 504 N.W.2d 580 (S.D.1993)—§ 9.1(d) n.120

Krejcarek, United States v., 453 F.3d 1290 (10th Cir.2006)—§ 21.4(d) n.131

Krejci, State v., 458 N.W.2d 407 (Minn.1990)—§ 11.5(c) n.41

Kress, State v., 636 N.W.2d 12 (Iowa 2001)—§ 21.4(d) n.118

Kretz Equipment Co., United States v., 56 A.F.T.R.2d ¶ 85-5135, 1985 WL 1489 (N.D.Ind.1985)—§ 8.13(a) n.25

Kretzer, State v., 898 S.W.2d 639 (Mo.App.1995)—§§ 11.9(b) n.88; 11.9(d) n.202

Krieger v. Commonwealth, 38 Va.App. 569, 567 S.E.2d 557 (2002)—§ 11.1(b) n.39

Kriho, People v., 996 P.2d 158 (Colo.App.1999)—§ 24.9(f) n.106

Krimstock v. Kelly, 306 F.3d 40 (2d Cir.2002)—§ 10.1(c) n.52

Krison, State v., 63 Ill.App.3d 531, 380 N.E.2d 449 (1978)—§ 14.2(e) n.67

Kristel, United States v., 762 F.Supp. 1100 (S.D.N.Y.1991)—§§ 8.11(c) n.45; 8.11(e) n.106

Krochta v. Commonwealth, 429 Mass. 711, 711 N.E.2d 142 (1999)—§ 17.4(a) n.31

Kroehler v. Scott, 391 F.Supp. 1114 (E.D.Pa.1975)—§ 3.2(e) n.167

Krogness, State v., 238 Or. 135, 388 P.2d 120 (1963)—§ 3.1(e) n.136

Krosch, State v., 642 N.W.2d 713 (Minn.2002)—§ 24.3(e) n.122

Krout, United States v., 66 F.3d 1420 (5th Cir.1995)—§ 4.6(e) n.98

Krueger, People v., 466 Mich. 50, 643 N.W.2d 223 (2002)—§§ 24.2(e) n.76; 27.6(b) n.59

Krueger, State v., 224 Wis.2d 59, 588 N.W.2d 921 (1999)—§§ 13.2(a) n.3; 13.2(c) n.56

Krueger, United States v., 415 F.3d 766 (7th Cir.2005)—§ 6.4(e) n.96

Kruelski, State v., 250 Conn. 1, 737 A.2d 377 (1999)—§ 25.3(a) n.7

Krug, State v., 187 Neb. 551, 192 N.W.2d 163 (1971)—§ 21.5(a) n.56

Krulewitch v. United States, 336 U.S. 440, 69 S.Ct. 716, 93 L.Ed. 790 (1949)—§§ 16.2(g) n.133; 17.2(e) n.115

Krull v. State, 211 Ga.App. 37, 438 S.E.2d 152 (1993)—§ 24.6(c) n.39

Kubick, United States v., 205 F.3d 1117 (9th Cir.1999)—§ 21.5(c) n.83

Kuchinski, United States v., 469 F.3d 853 (9th Cir.2006)—§ 21.6(b) n.85

Kuehn, United States v., 562 F.2d 427 (7th Cir.1977)—§ 8.11(d) n.80

Kuespert, United States v., 773 F.2d 1066 (9th Cir.1985)—§ 9.1(b) n.96

Kuhl v. United States, 370 F.2d 20 (9th Cir.1966)—§ 11.10(c) n.68

Kuhlmann v. Wilson, 477 U.S. 436, 106 S.Ct. 2616, 91 L.Ed.2d 364 (1986)—§§ 2.9(f) n.119; 6.4(g) n.160; 28.5(c) n.71; 28.5(d) n.80

Kuhn v. Proctor, 141 Idaho 459, 111 P.3d 144 (2005)—§ 21.4(a) n.21

Kuhn, State v., 74 Wash. App. 787, 875 P.2d 1225 (1994)—§ 27.5(a) n.24

Kula, State v., 260 Neb. 183, 616 N.W.2d 313 (2000)—§ 6.2(c) n.186

Kula, State v., 252 Neb. 471, 562 N.W.2d 717 (1997)—§ 27.5(d) n.116

Kulp, United States v., 365 F.Supp. 747 (E.D.Pa.1973)—§ 7.4(e) n.86

Kummer, State v., 481 N.W.2d 437 (N.D.1992)—§ 5.2(b) n.33

Kummer, United States v., 89 F.3d 1536 (11th Cir.1996)—§ 21.4(g) n.230

Kunish, Commonwealth v., 529 Pa. 206, 602 A.2d 849 (1992)—§ 26.7(c) n.36

Kunkle, Ex parte, 852 S.W.2d 499 (Tex.Crim.App.1993)—§§ 11.10(c) n.69, 80, 110

Kuntu, People v., 196 Ill.2d 105, 256 Ill.Dec. 500, 752 N.E.2d 380 (2001)—§ 22.3(c) n.127

Kuntz, State v., 160 Wis.2d 722, 467 N.W.2d 531 (1991)—§ 26.3(f) n.54

Kuntz, United States v., 908 F.2d 655 (10th Cir.1990)—§ 21.2(d) n.252

Kupec v. State, 835 P.2d 359 (Wyo.1992)—§§ 26.1(f) n.144; 26.10(d) n.91

Kurnava v. United States, 222 F.Supp. 822 (W.D.Mo.1963)—§ 15.1(b) n.115

Kurt, United States v., 986 F.2d 309 (9th Cir.1993)—§ 3.1(c) n.74

Kurtzman, People v., 46 Cal.3d 322, 250 Cal.Rptr. 244, 758 P.2d 572 (1988)—§ 24.8(d) n.46

Kurzer, United States v., 534 F.2d 511 (2d Cir.1976)—§§ 8.11(a) n.15; 8.11(b) n.29

Kussmaul, United States v., 987 F.2d 345 (6th Cir.1993)—§ 5.2(a) n.17

KUTV v. Wilkinson, 686 P.2d 456 (Utah.1984)—§§ 23.1(c) n.108, 109

Kuzmichev, State v., 132 Idaho 536, 976 P.2d 462 (1999)—§ 6.6(d) n.48

Kwak, State v., 80 Hawai'i 297, 909 P.2d 1112 (1995)—§§ 16.1(g) n.250, 276, 277; 16.1(h) n.309

Kwan, United States v., 407 F.3d 1005 (9th Cir.2005)—§ 28.9(a) n.21

Kye Soo Lee, United States v., 962 F.2d 430 (5th Cir.1992)—§ 3.3(e) n.189

Kye Soo Lee, United States v., 898 F.2d 1034 (5th Cir.1990)—§ 9.1(d) n.127

Kyger v. Carlton, 146 F.3d 374 (6th Cir.1998)—§§ 6.9(f) n.144; 6.9(g) n.166

Kyle v. State, 312 Ark. 274, 849 S.W.2d 935 (1993)—§§ 26.9(b) n.33, 35

Kyle v. United States, 759 A.2d 192 (D.C.App.2000)—§ 21.4(f) n.183

Kyle, United States v., 469 F.2d 547 (D.C.Cir.1972)—§ 22.3(b) n.90

Kyles, State v., 269 Wis.2d 1, 675 N.W.2d 449 (2004)—§ 3.8(e) n.195

Kyles, State v., 513 So.2d 265 (La.1987)—§ 24.3(h) n.179

Kyles, United States v., 40 F.3d 519 (2d Cir.1994)—§§ 22.3(a) n.15, 26

Kyles v. Whitley, 514 U.S. 419, 115 S.Ct. 1555, 131 L.Ed.2d 490 (1995)—§§ 24.3(b) n.20, 30, 50; 27.6(d) n.75; 28.4(d) n.68; 28.6(g) n.87

Kyllo v. United States, 533 U.S. 27, 121 S.Ct. 2038, 150 L.Ed.2d 94 (2001)—§§ 2.8(b) n.51; 2.9(d) n.99; 3.2(b) n.62, 70, 85

Kysar, State v., 116 Idaho 992, 783 P.2d 859 (1989)—§ 3.3(d) n.164

L

L.A., In the Matter of, 270 Kan. 879, 21 P.3d 952 (2001)—§ 6.10(c) n.36

Laaman v. United States, 973 F.2d 107 (2d Cir.1992)—§ 9.4(b) n.59

Laatsch, Commonwealth v., 541 Pa. 169, 661 A.2d 1365 (1995)—§ 6.2(c) n.107

LaBare, United States v., 191 F.3d 60 (1st Cir.1999)—§ 6.4(g) n.153

Labarre, State v., 115 Ariz. 444, 565 P.2d 1305 (App.1977)—§ 20.4(g) n.105

La Belle, People v., 18 N.Y.2d 405, 276 N.Y.S.2d 105, 222 N.E.2d 727 (1966)—§ 17.2(b) n.69

Labelle v. State, 720 S.W.2d 101 (Tex.Cr.App.1986)—§ 26.10(b) n.23

LaBlanc v. People, 177 Colo. 250, 493 P.2d 1089 (1972)—§ 7.4(d) n.71

LaBonte, United States v., 520 U.S. 751, 117 S.Ct. 1673, 137 L.Ed.2d 1001 (1997)—§ 13.2(a) n.2

Labonville, State v., 126 N.H. 451, 492 A.2d 1376 (1985)—§§ 11.9(a) n.14; 11.9(d) n.234

LaBranche, State v., 118 N.H. 176, 385 A.2d 108 (1978)—§ 27.6(b) n.55

Labrum, State v., 881 P.2d 900 (Utah App.1994)—§ 11.7(e) n.65

Lace v. United States, 736 F.2d 48 (2d Cir.1984)—§ 11.9(a) n.20

Lacey, United States v., 86 F.3d 956 (10th Cir.1996)—§§ 8.11(c) n.36, 47; 26.4(b) n.23

Lacey, United States v., 648 F.2d 441 (5th Cir.1981)—§ 26.10(d) n.85

LaChance v. Reno, 13 F.3d 586 (2d Cir.1994)—§ 26.10(d) n.93

LaChance, United States v., 817 F.2d 1491 (11th Cir.1987)—§§ 11.5(e) n.88; 11.5(g) n.110

LaChappell, State v., 222 Neb. 112, 382 N.W.2d 343 (1986)—§ 6.9(g) n.154

Lackawanna County District Attorney v. Coss, 532 U.S. 394, 121 S.Ct. 1567, 149 L.Ed.2d 608 (2001)— §§ 11.1(a) n.27; 21.4(e) n.161; 26.4(f) n.100; 26.6(b) n.30; 28.3(a) n.38; 28.3(b) n.60

Lackey v. State, 574 S.W.2d 97 (Tex.Crim.App.1978)—§§ 15.1(f) n.315, 323

Lackey, United States v., 334 F.3d 1224 (10th Cir.2003)—§ 6.7(b) n.85

LaCrosse v. Commodity Futures Trading Comm'n, 137 F.3d 925 (7th Cir.1998)—§ 17.4(b) n.125

Lacy v. People, 775 P.2d 1 (Colo.1989)—§§ 21.4(c) n.88; 21.4(e) n.165; 21.4(f) n.204

Lacy v. State, 345 Ark. 63, 44 S.W.3d 296 (2001)—§§ 6.7(a) n.28; 6.9(f) n.135

Lacy, State v., 187 Ariz. 340, 929 P.2d 1288 (1996)—§§ 6.2(c) n.108; 18.5(a) n.8

Lacy, State v., 196 W.Va. 104, 468 S.E.2d 719 (1996)—§ 3.4(j) n.189

Lacy v. State, 629 So.2d 688 (Ala.App.1993)—§ 22.3(c) n.161

Lacy v. State, 608 P.2d 19 (Alaska 1980)—§§ 3.8(f) n.232, 236

Ladd, State v., 210 W.Va. 413, 557 S.E.2d 820 (2001)—§ 22.5(a) n.8

Ladd, United States v., 218 F.3d 701 (7th Cir.2000)—§§ 23.1(d) n.177; 23.1(e) n.222, 224

Ladner, State v., 613 S.W.2d 951 (Mo.App.1981)—§ 19.3(a) n.67

Ladsen, People v., 111 Misc.2d 374, 444 N.Y.S.2d 362 (1981)—§ 15.2(h) n.192

La Duca, People v., 172 App.Div.2d 1054, 569 N.Y.S.2d 308 (1991)— § 15.4(g) n.149

LaFay, United States ex rel. v. Fritz, 455 F.2d 297 (2d Cir.1972)—§ 21.2(g) n.405

Laferriere v. State, 697 A.2d 1301 (Me.1997)—§ 21.3(b) n.42

LaFevers v. Gibson, 238 F.3d 1263 (10th Cir.2001)—§§ 28.3(e) n.100; 28.5(d) n.88

Lafferty, State v., 749 P.2d 1239 (Utah 1988)—§ 11.6(a) n.50

LaFlamme, State v., 170 Mont. 202, 551 P.2d 1011 (1976)—§ 3.10(f) n.195

LaFollette v. Commonwealth, 915 S.W.2d 747 (Ky.1996)—§ 3.2(b) n.61

LaFontaine, United States v., 210 F.3d 125 (2d Cir.2000)—§ 12.1(a) n.17

Laforest, State v., 140 N.H. 286, 665 A.2d 1083 (1995)—§ 21.2(b) n.91

LaFortune v. District Court, 972 P.2d 868 (Okla.Crim.App.1998)— §§ 14.4(c) n.63; 14.4(d) n.84

LaFountain, State v., 138 N.H. 225, 636 A.2d 1028 (1994)—§ 6.8(d) n.84

LaFrance v. Bohlinger, 499 F.2d 29 (1st Cir.1974)—§§ 9.1(a) n.22; 10.5(a) n.6

LaFrance, United States v., 879 F.2d 1 (1st Cir.1989)—§ 3.8(h) n.252

LaFrankie, People v., 858 P.2d 702 (Colo.1993)—§ 6.6(e) n.72

LaFreniere, United States v., 236 F.3d 41 (1st Cir.2001)—§ 5.2(a) n.8

LaFromboise, State v., 542 N.W.2d 110 (N.D.1996)—§ 27.5(c) n.71

LaFuente, United States v., 991 F.2d 1406 (8th Cir.1993)—§ 24.11(d) n.30

Lagana, Commonwealth v., 510 Pa. 477, 509 A.2d 863 (1986)—§ 10.6(d) n.38

Lagares, State v., 127 N.J. 20, 601 A.2d 690 (1992)—§ 1.7(j) n.218

Lagat, State v., 97 Haw. 492, 40 P.3d 894 (2002)—§ 13.2(a) n.4

Lage, United States v., 183 F.3d 374 (5th Cir.1999)—§ 3.7(e) n.118

Lagow, United States v., 66 F.Supp. 738 (S.D.N.Y.1946)—§ 3.10(e) n.178

LaGrone, United States v., 43 F.3d 332 (7th Cir.1994)—§§ 3.10(b) n.76; 6.4(f) n.136; 6.7(c) n.120; 6.9(g) n.200

Laguer, Commonwealth v., 36 Mass.App.Ct. 310, 630 N.E.2d 618 (1994)—§ 24.9(f) n.73

Lahr, People v., 147 Ill.2d 379, 168 Ill.Dec. 139, 589 N.E.2d 539 (1992)—§ 3.5(a) n.23

Lainez-Leiva, United States v., 129 F.3d 89 (2d Cir.1997)—§ 18.4(b) n.26

Lake, State v., 180 W.Va. 628, 378 S.E.2d 670 (1989)—§ 21.2(g) n.395

Lake, United States v., 985 F.2d 265 (6th Cir.1993)—§ 19.5(d) n.72

Lakes v. Goodloe, 195 Ky. 240, 242 S.W. 632 (1922)—§ 15.1(d) n.222

Lakeside v. Oregon, 435 U.S. 333, 98 S.Ct. 1091, 55 L.Ed.2d 319 (1978)—§§ 2.10(c) n.96; 24.5(c) n.38

Lakhani, United States v., 480 F.3d 171 (3d Cir.2007)—§§ 5.2(a) n.9; 5.4(c) n.46

Laliberte, People v., 246 Ill.App.3d 159, 186 Ill.Dec. 9, 615 N.E.2d 813 (1993)—§§ 9.5(b) n.42, 44

LaLonde v. County of Riverside, 204 F.3d 947 (9th Cir.2000)—§ 3.8(b) n.32

Lam v. Kelchner, 304 F.3d 256 (3d Cir.2002)—§§ 6.2(c) n.73; 6.3(a) n.1; 9.5(a) n.8

Lam, State v., 75 Haw. 195, 857 P.2d 585 (1993)—§ 25.2(a) n.9

Lamantia, United States v., 59 F.3d 705 (7th Cir.1995)—§§ 15.6(c) n.89, 94; 15.6(e) n.156, 158, 165

LaMar, State v., 95 Ohio St.3d 181, 767 N.E.2d 166 (2002)—§ 13.4(e) n.169

Lamar v. United States, 240 U.S. 60, 36 S.Ct. 255, 60 L.Ed. 526 (1916)—§§ 19.3(a) n.110; 27.5(c) n.105

Lamas, State v., 143 Ariz. 564, 694 P.2d 1178 (1985)—§ 21.4(d) n.118

Lamas, United States v., 930 F.2d 1099 (5th Cir.1991)—§ 9.3(e) n.71

Lamb v. Anderson, 147 P.3d 736 (Alaska 2006)—§ 21.4(a) n.21

Lamb v. Kontgias, 169 Md.App. 466, 901 A.2d 860 (2006)—§§ 21.3(f) n.422; 26.7(b) n.22; 27.4(e) n.62

Lamb, People v., 136 Cal.App.4th 575, 40 Cal.Rptr.3d 609 (2006)—§ 20.5(h) n.100

Lamb v. State, 89 Nev. 570, 516 P.2d 1405 (1973)—§ 3.10(f) n.189

Lamb, United States v., 945 F.Supp. 441 (N.D.N.Y. 1996)—§ 4.4(c) n.12

Lamb, United States v., 575 F.2d 1310 (10th Cir.1978)—§ 7.2(d) n.54

Lambert, Ex parte, 519 So.2d 899 (Ala.1987)—§ 20.3(c) n.82

Lambert v. Blackwell, 387 F.3d 210 (3d Cir.2004)—§ 28.7(a) n.4

Lambert v. Blackwell, 962 F.Supp. 1521 (E.D.Pa.1997)—§ 28.7(c) n.20

Lambert v. California, 355 U.S. 225, 78 S.Ct. 240, 2 L.Ed.2d 228 (1957)—§§ 2.4(a) n.19; 2.7(d) n.232

Lambert, State v., 775 A.2d 1140 (Me.2001)—§§ 21.5(a) n.38, 40, 45

Lambert, State v., 705 A.2d 957 (R.I.1997)—§§ 6.8(d) n.84; 6.9(b) n.20

Lambert v. State, 286 Ark. 408, 692 S.W.2d 238 (1985)—§ 26.7(c) n.36

Lambert v. State, 196 Md. 57, 75 A.2d 327 (1950)—§ 9.1(b) n.66

Lambert, United States v., 887 F.2d 1568 (11th Cir.1989)—§ 10.3(b) n.10

Lambert, United States v., 771 F.2d 83 (6th Cir.1985)—§§ 4.6(d) n.65; 4.6(e) n.78

Lambert v. United States, 600 F.2d 476 (5th Cir.1979)—§ 21.4(c) n.87

Lambeth v. State, 562 So.2d 575 (Ala.1990)—§§ 5.3(a) n.11; 5.3(d) n.43

Lambey, United States v., 974 F.2d 1389 (4th Cir.1992)—§§ 21.4(g) n.226; 21.5(a) n.43

Lambrechts, People v., 69 Ill.2d 544, 14 Ill.Dec. 445, 372 N.E.2d 641 (1977)—§§ 21.4(g) n.236, 240

Lambrechts, State v., 585 A.2d 645 (R.I.1991)—§ 24.8(f) n.105

Lambrix v. Singletary, 520 U.S. 518, 117 S.Ct. 1517, 137 L.Ed.2d 771 (1997)—§§ 28.6(b) n.10, 13; 28.6(d) n.30

LaMere, State v., 298 Mont. 358, 2 P.3d 204 (2000)—§§ 22.2(d) n.79; 27.6(d) n.142

LaMere, State v., 272 Mont. 355, 900 P.2d 926 (1995)—§ 21.2(d) n.169

Lamia, United States v., 429 F.2d 373 (2d Cir.1970)—§ 6.8(a) n.6

Lamkin v. State, 165 Tex.Crim. 11, 301 S.W.2d 922 (1957)—§ 15.4(g) n.166

Lam Kwong-Wah, United States v., 924 F.2d 298 (D.C.Cir.1991)—§ 24.3(c) n.89

Lamon, State v., 262 Wis.2d 747, 664 N.W.2d 607 (2003)—§ 22.3(d) n.250

Lamp v. Farrier, 763 F.2d 994 (8th Cir.1985)—§ 6.9(f) n.135

Lamp, State v., 322 N.W.2d 48 (Iowa 1982)—§ 6.9(g) n.162

Lampazianie, United States v., 251 F.3d 519 (5th Cir.2001)—§ 21.5(d) n.103

Lamphere v. State, 348 N.W.2d 212 (Iowa 1984)—§ 27.5(d) n.113

Lampitok, People v., 207 Ill.2d 231, 278 Ill.Dec. 244, 798 N.E.2d 91 (2003)—§ 26.9(b) n.66

Lanari v. People, 827 P.2d 495 (Colo.1992)—§ 1.5(b) n.70

Lancaster, Ex parte, 206 Ala. 60, 89 So. 721 (1921)—§ 16.3(d) n.51

Lancaster v. Adams, 324 F.3d 423 (6th Cir.2003)—§ 22.3(d) n.213

Lancaster, People v., 69 N.Y.2d 20, 511 N.Y.S.2d 559, 503 N.E.2d 990 (1986)—§§ 15.7(f) n.179; 15.7(g) n.217

Lancaster, State v., 25 Ohio St.2d 83, 267 N.E.2d 291 (1971)—§ 10.2(a) n.14

Lancaster v. Stubblefield, 985 S.W.2d 854 (Mo.App.1998)—§ 18.4(c) n.39

Lance W., In re, 37 Cal.3d 873, 210 Cal.Rptr. 631, 694 P.2d 744 (1985)—§§ 3.1(e) n.126; 9.2(d) n.38

Lanchester v. Pennsylvania State Horse Racing Commission, 16 Pa.Cmwlth. 85, 325 A.2d 648 (1974)—§ 3.9(c) n.43

Lanci, United States v., 669 F.2d 391 (6th Cir.1982)—§ 27.2(c) n.31

Lancto, State v., 155 Vt. 168, 582 A.2d 448 (1990)—§ 6.6(e) n.59

Land v. State, 262 Ga. 898, 426 S.E.2d 370 (1993)—§ 26.9(b) n.53

Landa, People v., 30 Cal.App.3d 487, 106 Cal.Rptr. 329 (1973)—§ 3.7(d) n.83

Landaw, United States v., 727 F.Supp. 481 (N.D.Ind.1989)—§ 24.8(e) n.86

Landenberger v. State, 519 So.2d 712 (Fla.App.1988)—§ 8.10(a) n.15

Landers v. State, 229 S.W.3d 532 (Tex.App.2007)—§ 22.5(b) n.18

Landers v. State, 550 S.W.2d 272 (Tex.Crim.1977)—§ 2.12(e) n.211

Landis, State v., 308 Mont. 354, 43 P.3d 298 (2002)—§ 22.4(c) n.29

Landmark Communications, Inc. v. Virginia, 435 U.S. 829, 98 S.Ct. 1535, 56 L.Ed.2d 1 (1978)—§ 23.1(c) n.118

Landrum, State v., 53 Ohio St.3d 107, 559 N.E.2d 710 (1990)—§ 19.3(a) n.70

Landry v. Attorney General, 429 Mass. 336, 709 N.E.2d 1085 (1999)— § 3.2(g) n.198

Landry, State v., 339 So.2d 8 (La.1976)—§ 10.6(c) n.30

Lane v. Brown, 372 U.S. 477, 83 S.Ct. 768, 9 L.Ed.2d 892 (1963)— §§ 11.2(d) n.121, 134

Lane, People v., 56 N.Y.2d 1, 451 N.Y.S.2d 6, 436 N.E.2d 456 (1982)—§ 17.1(c) n.45

Lane v. State, 274 Ga. 751, 559 S.E.2d 455 (2002)—§ 24.7(c) n.26

Lane, State v., 262 Kan. 373, 940 P.2d 422 (1997)—§ 6.2(c) n.178

Lane, State v., 328 N.C. 598, 403 S.E.2d 267 (1991)—§ 3.10(f) n.204

Lane v. State, 388 So.2d 1022 (Fla.1980)—§§ 16.1(a) n.6; 16.4(c) n.45, 85, 92, 93, 98; 16.4(d) n.120, 133

Lane, State v., 60 Ohio St.2d 112, 397 N.E.2d 1338 (1979)—§ 24.1(a) n.11

Lane, State v., 77 Wash.2d 860, 467 P.2d 304 (1970)—§ 6.7(b) n.74

Lane, United States v., 252 F.3d 905 (7th Cir.2005)—§ 12.3(a) n.18

Lane, United States v., 866 F.2d 103 (4th Cir.1989)—§ 22.3(d) n.249

Lane, United States v., 474 U.S. 438, 106 S.Ct. 725, 88 L.Ed.2d 814 (1986)—§§ 17.3(b) n.25; 27.6(b) n.15, 24

Lane v. Williams, 455 U.S. 624, 102 S.Ct. 1322, 71 L.Ed.2d 508 (1982)—§ 27.5(a) n.17

Laney, People v., 115 Cal.App.3d 508, 171 Cal.Rptr. 493 (1981)—§ 15.4(i) n.217

Laney v. State, 379 Md. 522, 842 A.2d 773 (2004)—§ 3.2(c) n.102

Laney v. State, 271 Ga. 194, 515 S.E.2d 610 (1999)—§ 22.3(d) n.220

Lang, Commonwealth v., 517 Pa. 390, 537 A.2d 1361 (1988)—§ 8.8(f) n.145

Lang v. United States, 474 F.3d 348 (6th Cir.2007)—§ 28.9(b) n.60

Lang, United States v., 364 F.3d 1210 (10th Cir.2004)—§ 19.3(a) n.29

Lang, United States v., 8 F.3d 268 (5th Cir.1993)—§ 10.5(a) n.12

Lang, United States v., 792 F.2d 1235 (4th Cir.1986)—§§ 8.13(a) n.26, 29

Lang, United States v., 644 F.2d 1232 (7th Cir.1981)—§§ 15.4(a) n.22; 15.6(c) n.98, 100

Lang, United States v., 527 F.2d 1264 (4th Cir.1975)—§ 9.1(b) n.66

Langdon v. Board of Liquor Control, 98 Ohio App. 535, 130 N.E.2d 430 (1954)—§ 5.1(c) n.42

Lange, Ex parte, 85 U.S. (18 Wall.) 163, 21 L.Ed. 872 (1873)—§§ 25.1(b) n.6; 25.1(c) n.20; 26.7(c) n.23; 28.3(b) n.43

Lange, Ex parte, 85 U.S. 163, 21 L.Ed. 872 (1873)—§ 2.1 n.54

Lange, State v., 495 N.W.2d 105 (Iowa.1992)—§ 25.3(a) n.5

Lange, State v., 158 Wis.2d 609, 463 N.W.2d 390 (App. 1990)—§ 3.2(d) n.157

Langford v. State, 332 Ark. 54, 962 S.W.2d 358 (1998)—§ 3.4(e) n.76

Langford, State v., 248 Mont. 420, 813 P.2d 936 (1991)—§ 21.3(b) n.53

Langford v. Superior Court, 43 Cal.3d 21, 233 Cal.Rptr. 387, 729 P.2d 822 (1987)—§ 3.4(h) n.166

Langford, United States v., 369 F.Supp. 1107 (N.D.Ill.1973)—§ 26.10(b) n.36

Langill, State v., 567 A.2d 440 (Me.1989)—§ 19.3(a) n.73

Langlands, State v., 276 Ga. 721, 583 S.E.2d 18 (2003)—§ 6.9(f) n.134

Langley, State v., 314 Or. 247, 839 P.2d 692 (1992)—§ 27.5(e) n.149

Langley, United States v., 848 F.2d 152 (11th Cir.1988)—§ 7.3(b) n.33

Langley, United States v., 466 F.2d 27 (6th Cir.1972)—§ 9.4(b) n.64

Langone, State v., 127 N.H. 49, 498 A.2d 731 (1985)—§ 18.2(b) n.20

Lanier v. South Carolina, 474 U.S. 25, 106 S.Ct. 297, 88 L.Ed.2d 23 (1985)—§ 9.4(a) n.33

Lanier, State v., 2007 WL 1806070 (Ohio App.2007)—§ 25.2(d) n.34

Lanier v. State, 486 P.2d 981 (Alaska 1971)—§§ 11.6(a) n.31; 11.6(c) n.95

Lankford v. Idaho, 500 U.S. 110, 111 S.Ct. 1723, 114 L.Ed.2d 173 (1991)—§§ 2.7(a) n.54; 2.7(b) n.90; 2.7(c) n.193, 198, 204, 205, 208, 213; 26.4(d) n.55

Lankford, State v., 127 Idaho 608, 903 P.2d 1305 (1995)—§§ 21.2(e) n.314, 316

Lankford, State v., 116 Idaho 860, 781 P.2d 197 (Idaho 1989)—§ 24.11(d) n.25

Lankford, United States v., 196 F.3d 563 (5th Cir.1999)—§§ 1.2(c) n.170, 172; 17.3(b) n.13

Lanoue, Commonwealth v., 326 Mass. 559, 95 N.E.2d 925 (1950)—§ 16.4(c) n.53

Lanoue, United States v., 137 F.3d 656 (1st Cir.1998)—§§ 17.4(a) n.3, 5

Lanoue, United States v., 71 F.3d 966 (1st Cir.1995)—§§ 4.6(b) n.51; 4.6(l) n.201, 203

Lansden, State v., 144 Wash.2d 654, 30 P.3d 483 (2001)—§ 3.4(f) n.103

Lanza v. New York, 370 U.S. 139, 82 S.Ct. 1218, 8 L.Ed.2d 384 (1962)—§ 3.9(i) n.174

Lanza, United States v., 260 U.S. 377, 43 S.Ct. 141, 67 L.Ed. 314 (1922)—§ 25.5(a) n.1

Lanzotti, United States v., 90 F.3d 1217 (7th Cir.1996)—§ 25.4(b) n.18

LaPage, United States v., 441 F.Supp. 824 (N.D.N.Y.1977)—§ 8.12(c) n.39

L.A.P.D. v. United Reporting Publ'g. Corp., 528 U.S. 32, 120 S.Ct. 483, 145 L.Ed.2d 451 (1999)—§ 23.1(d) n.197

LaPena-Juarez, United States v., 214 F.3d 594 (5th Cir.2000)—§ 18.3(b) n.5

LaPierre, United States v., 998 F.2d 1460 (9th Cir.1993)—§§ 6.6(e) n.69; 6.7(c) n.121; 7.3(a) n.9; 7.3(c) n.58

Laplume, State v., 118 R.I. 670, 375 A.2d 938 (1977)—§ 16.4(c) n.72

LaPoint v. State, 650 S.W.2d 821 (Tex.Cr.App.1983)—§ 6.6(f) n.102

Lapointe, State v., 237 Conn. 694, 678 A.2d 942 (1996)—§§ 6.2(c) n.120, 127; 6.6(f) n.113

Lapp v. Department of Transp., 2001 ND 140, 632 N.W.2d 419 (N.D.2001)—§ 3.7(e) n.126

Lara v. Johnson, 141 F.3d 239 (5th Cir.1998)—§§ 18.4(c) n.50; 28.3(b) n.64

Lara v. State, 25 P.3d 507 (Wyo.2001)—§ 6.2(d) n.202

Lara, State v., 258 Neb. 996, 607 N.W.2d 487 (2000)—§ 9.1(b) n.76

Lara, United States v., 541 U.S. 193, 124 S.Ct. 1628, 158 L.Ed.2d 420 (2004)—§ 25.5(a) n.9

Lara, United States v., 181 F.3d 183 (1st Cir.1999)—§ 21.2(b) n.74

Lara, United States v., 520 F.2d 460 (D.C.Cir.1975)—§§ 18.2(c) n.30, 34; 18.2(e) n.73

Larabee, State v., 69 Oh.St.3d 357, 632 N.E.2d 511 (1994)—§ 27.3(c) n.22

Lares-Valdez, United States v., 939 F.2d 688 (9th Cir.1991)—§ 6.8(d) n.82

Larimore v. State, 339 Ark. 167, 3 S.W.3d 680 (1999)—§ 12.4(d) n.81

Lark, Commonwealth v., 505 Pa. 126, 477 A.2d 857 (1984)—§§ 6.7(b) n.41; 6.7(c) n.131; 6.9(a) n.7

Lark, Commonwealth v., 482 Pa. 292, 393 A.2d 1112 (1978)—§ 6.4(f) n.126

Lark, State v., 117 N.J. 331, 567 A.2d 197 (1989)—§ 2.11(a) n.14

Larkin, People v., 52 Cal.App.3d 346, 125 Cal.Rptr. 137 (1975)—§ 3.8(c) n.93

Larkin, United States v., 978 F.2d 964 (7th Cir.1992)—§§ 7.3(b) n.31; 7.4(c) n.56; 7.4(d) n.71; 7.5(b) n.14, 25; 8.8(g) n.175

Larocco, State v., 794 P.2d 460 (Utah 1990)—§ 3.1(e) n.126

LaRosa, State v., 112 R.I. 571, 313 A.2d 375 (1974)—§ 9.3(c) n.20

LaRose, State v., 286 Minn. 517, 174 N.W.2d 247 (1970)—§ 6.10(b) n.12

Larrazolo, United States v., 869 F.2d 1354 (9th Cir.1989)—§§ 15.6(e) n.156, 157, 160, 164; 15.7(b) n.44; 15.7(g) n.197

Larrison v. United States, 24 F.2d 82 (7th Cir.1928)—§ 24.11(d) n.29

Larry v. Hicks, 268 Ga. 487, 491 S.E.2d 373 (1997)—§§ 11.3(a) n.20; 21.3(a) n.34

Larry, State v., 345 N.C. 497, 481 S.E.2d 907 (1997)—§§ 22.3(a) n.5, 6

Larry v. State, 477 N.E.2d 94 (Ind.1985)—§ 21.4(f) n.192

Larry Harmon Pictures Corp. v. Williams Restaurant Corp., 929 F.2d 662 (Fed.Cir.1991)—§ 1.2(c) n.94

Larsen, In re, 571 Pa. 457, 812 A.2d 640 (Pa.Spec.Trib.2002)—§ 17.4(b) n.125

Larsen, State v., 442 N.W.2d 840 (Minn.App.1989)—§§ 16.1(g) n.244, 277

Larson v. State, 572 So.2d 1368 (Fla.1991)—§§ 21.6(a) n.80; 26.9(a) n.1; 26.9(b) n.26, 76

Larson, State v., 240 Mont. 203, 783 P.2d 416 (1989)—§ 24.8(f) n.107

Larson v. State, 104 Nev. 691, 766 P.2d 261 (1988)—§ 21.3(b) n.101

Larson v. State, 614 P.2d 776 (Alaska 1980)—§ 21.4(c) n.81

Larson, United States v., 302 F.3d 1016 (9th Cir.2002)—§ 21.6(c) n.120

Larson, United States v., 978 F.2d 1021 (8th Cir.1992)—§ 3.10(b) n.34

Lartey, United States v., 716 F.2d 955 (2d Cir.1983)—§ 8.7(e) n.93

LaRue, State v., 619 N.W.2d 395 (Iowa 2000)—§§ 11.9(c) n.112; 21.6(a) n.76; 27.5(c) n.63

Larue, State v., 68 Haw. 575, 722 P.2d 1039 (1986)—§ 24.9(g) n.126

Lasaga, State v., 269 Conn. 454, 848 A.2d 1149 (2004)—§ 21.6(a) n.45

Lash, United States v., 937 F.2d 1077 (6th Cir.1991)—§ 24.9(d) n.40

Lashwood, State v., 384 N.W.2d 319 (S.D.1986)—§ 21.4(f) n.173

Laskay, State v., 103 N.M. 799, 715 P.2d 72 (N.M.App.1986)—§ 15.4(g) n.168

Lasky, United States v., 600 F.2d 765 (9th Cir.1979)—§ 15.2(c) n.61

LaSpina, United States v., 299 F.3d 165 (2d Cir.2002)—§ 18.5(a) n.14

Lass, State v., 228 N.W.2d 758 (Iowa 1975)—§ 19.4(b) n.22

Lassek, People v., 122 P.3d 1029 (Colo.App.2005)—§§ 26.3(g) n.88; 26.4(f) n.93; 26.5(d) n.70

Lassiter v. Department of Social Services, 452 U.S. 18, 101 S.Ct. 2153, 68 L.Ed.2d 640 (1981)—§ 11.1(b) n.39

Lassor, State v., 555 A.2d 339 (R.I.1989)—§ 24.4(d) n.31

Laster v. State, 313 Md. 548, 546 A.2d 472 (1988)—§ 18.4(c) n.44

Laswell v. Frey, 45 F.3d 1011 (6th Cir.1995)—§ 27.4(f) n.72

Latham, People v., 90 N.Y.2d 795, 666 N.Y.S.2d 557, 689 N.E.2d 527 (1997)—§ 21.4(e) n.155

Latham, United States v., 874 F.2d 852 (1st Cir.1989)—§ 24.2(d) n.48

Lather, State v., 110 Ohio St.3d 270, 853 N.E.2d 279 (2006)—§ 6.9(d) n.72

Lathers v. United States, 396 F.2d 524 (5th Cir.1968)—§ 6.8(a) n.17

Lathrop v. Hauptly, 86 Wash. 199, 149 P. 705 (1915)—§ 16.3(d) n.51

Lathrop, United States v., 17 Johns Rep. 4 (1819)—§§ 1.2(c) n.40, 81

Latimore, Commonwealth v., 423 Mass. 129, 667 N.E.2d 818 (1996)—§§ 21.3(c) n.152, 157; 21.3(f) n.362

Latimore, United States ex rel. v. Sielaff, 561 F.2d 691 (7th Cir.1977)—§ 24.1(b) n.21

LaTray, State v., 220 Mont. 358, 715 P.2d 52 (1986)—§ 21.3(b) n.54

Latshaw, Commonwealth v., 481 Pa. 298, 392 A.2d 1301 (1978)—§ 3.10(d) n.137

Latta v. Fitzharris, 521 F.2d 246 (9th Cir.1975)—§§ 3.9(j) n.200, 209

Lattany, United States v., 982 F.2d 866 (3d Cir.1992)—§ 18.3(b) n.43

Lattanzio, People v., 134 Misc.2d 469, 511 N.Y.S.2d 521 (Sup.Ct.1987)—§ 15.2(c) n.86

Lauersen, United States v., 348 F.3d 329 (2d Cir.2003)—§ 22.4(c) n.29

Laureano, People v., 87 N.Y.2d 640, 642 N.Y.S.2d 150, 664 N.E.2d 1212 (1996)—§ 26.3(f) n.54

Laureano, State v., 101 Wash.2d 745, 682 P.2d 889 (1984)—§ 7.5(a) n.8

Lauria, Commonwealth v., 29 Mass.App. 542, 562 N.E.2d 1367 (1990)—§ 18.3(c) n.109

Laurie, State v., 139 N.H. 325, 653 A.2d 549 (1995)—§ 24.3(b) n.40

Laurie, State v., 135 N.H. 438, 606 A.2d 1077 (1992)—§ 6.9(f) n.106

Laury, United States v., 985 F.2d 1293 (5th Cir.1993)—§ 9.6(a) n.38

LaValle, People v., 3 N.Y.3d 88, 783 N.Y.S.2d 485, 817 N.E.2d 341 (2004)—§§ 2.12(b) n.111; 24.9(d) n.31

LaVallee v. Delle Rose, 410 U.S. 690, 93 S.Ct. 1203, 35 L.Ed.2d 637 (1973)—§ 28.7(a) n.2

LaVallee v. Justices in the Hampton Superior Court, 442 Mass. 228, 812 N.E.2d 895 (2004)—§§ 11.8(c) n.69, 70; 12.1(c) n.49

LaValley, United States v., 957 F.2d 1309 (6th Cir.1992)—§ 22.1(b) n.42

Lavariega, People v., 175 Ill.2d 153, 221 Ill.Dec. 840, 676 N.E.2d 643 (1997)—§ 17.4(b) n.124

Lave v. Dretke, 416 F.3d 372 (5th Cir.2005)—§ 28.7(d) n.28

La Velle, Commonwealth v., 414 Mass. 146, 605 N.E.2d 852 (1993)—§ 15.5(c) n.115

LaVigne v. State, 812 P.2d 217 (Alaska 1991)—§§ 11.6(c) n.100; 11.6(d) n.124, 126; 24.5(d) n.57

Lavoie, State v., 562 A.2d 146 (Me.1989)—§ 6.9(f) n.108

Lawal, United States v., 231 F.3d 1045 (7th Cir.2000)—§ 6.2(c) n.178

Lawes, United States v., 292 F.3d 123 (2d Cir.2002)—§§ 22.3(a) n.10, 34

Law Firm of Zimmerman and Schwartz, United States v., 738 F.Supp. 407 (D.Colo.1990)—§ 15.6(e) n.157

Lawhorn, State v., 762 S.W.2d 820 (Mo.1988)—§ 7.5(b) n.21

Lawler, State v., 221 Wis. 423, 267 N.W. 65 (1936)—§ 15.2(e) n.141

Lawley, People v., 27 Cal.4th 102, 115 Cal.Rptr.2d 614, 38 P.3d 461 (2002)—§ 22.1(c) n.62

Lawlor, United States v., 406 F.3d 37 (1st Cir.2005)—§ 10.6(b) n.10

Lawlor, United States v., 168 F.3d 633 (2d Cir.1999)—§ 21.2(d) n.199

Lawn v. United States, 355 U.S. 339, 78 S.Ct. 311, 2 L.Ed.2d 321 (1958)—§§ 3.1(f) n.144; 15.5(a) n.5, 8, 9; 15.7(d) n.84

Lawn Builders of New England, Inc., United States v., 856 F.2d 388 (1st Cir.1988)—§§ 8.13(d) n.98, 100, 103

Lawrence v. Florida, _____ U.S. _____, 127 S.Ct. 1079, 166 L.Ed.2d 924 (2007)—§§ 28.5(b) n.51, 60

Lawrence, People v., 4 Cal.3d 273, 93 Cal.Rptr. 204, 481 P.2d 212 (1971)—§ 7.4(e) n.81

Lawrence, State v., 112 Idaho 149, 730 P.2d 1069 (1986)—§ 24.11(d) n.27

Lawrence, State v., 260 La. 169, 255 So.2d 729 (1971)—§§ 10.1(a) n.9, 13

Lawrence v. Texas, 539 U.S. 558, 123 S.Ct. 2472, 156 L.Ed.2d 508 (2003)—§§ 2.7(c) n.180, 181

Lawrence, United States v., 349 F.3d 109 (3d Cir.2003)—§§ 7.4(c) n.49; 7.4(e) n.89

Lawrence, United States v., 308 F.3d 623 (6th Cir.2002)—§ 18.3(b) n.6

Lawrence, United States v., 248 F.3d 300 (4th Cir.2001)—§ 24.2(f) n.83

Lawrence, United States v., 179 F.3d 343 (5th Cir.1999)—§ 13.2(a) n.2

Lawrence, United States v., 952 F.2d 1034 (8th Cir.1992)—§§ 6.7(b) n.46; 21.2(h) n.420

Laws, People v., 218 Mich.App. 447, 554 N.W.2d 586 (1996)—§§ 14.3(b) n.50; 14.4(c) n.62, 71

Laws, State v., 801 S.W.2d 68 (Mo.1990)—§ 3.3(c) n.97

Lawson, People v., 67 Ill.2d 449, 10 Ill.Dec. 478, 367 N.E.2d 1244 (1977)—§ 18.5(b) n.67

Lawson, People v., 84 Misc.2d 24, 374 N.Y.S.2d 270 (Sup.Ct.1975)— § 15.7(g) n.207

Lawson, State v., 159 N.C.App. 534, 583 S.E.2d 354 (N.C.App.2003)— § 11.7(e) n.107

Lawson, State v., 64 Ohio St.3d 336, 595 N.E.2d 902 (1992)—§ 13.4(e) n.170

Lawson v. State, 604 S.W.2d 91 (Tex.Crim.App.1979)—§ 11.5(c) n.41

Lawson, United States v., 670 F.2d 923 (10th Cir.1982)—§ 26.9(b) n.42

Lawson, United States v., 653 F.2d 299 (7th Cir.1981)—§ 16.1(h) n.305

Lawson, United States v., 502 F.Supp. 158 (D.Md.1980)—§§ 15.5(b) n.37; 15.6(b) n.61

Lawson, United States v., 545 F.2d 557 (7th Cir.1975)—§ 4.6(m) n.228

Lawton, United States v., 193 F.3d 1087 (9th Cir.1999)—§§ 21.1(h) n.233; 21.2(d) n.216

Lay v. State, 110 Nev. 1189, 886 P.2d 448 (1994)—§§ 15.7(f) n.134, 169

Lay, United States v., 456 F.Supp.2d 869 (S.D.Tx.2006)—§ 27.5(a) n.7

Layeni, United States v., 90 F.3d 514 (D.C.Cir.1996)—§ 5.1(c) n.34

Layman, State v., 214 S.W.3d 442 (Tenn.2007)—§§ 13.1(a) n.26, 27; 13.3(c) n.40; 13.6(a) n.9; 13.6(b) n.17; 21.3(f) n.371

Laymon v. State, 280 Kan. 430, 122 P.3d 326 (2005)—§ 11.10(c) n.95

Layne, United States v., 973 F.2d 1417 (8th Cir.1992)—§ 6.6(e) n.91

Layton, People v., 29 Cal.App.3d 349, 105 Cal.Rptr. 509 (1972)—§ 6.6(e) n.74

Layton v. State, 150 P.3d 173 (Wyo.2007)—§ 18.4(c) n.68

Layton, State v., 189 W.Va. 470, 432 S.E.2d 740 (1993)—§§ 11.5(e) n.86; 24.3(d) n.109

Layton, United States v., 564 F.Supp. 1391 (D.Or.1983)—§ 20.3(b) n.50

Layton, United States v., 720 F.2d 548 (9th Cir.1983)—§ 27.3(c) n.45

Layton, United States v., 509 F.Supp. 212 (N.D.Cal.1981)—§§ 16.4(b) n.27, 34

Lazarchick, State v., 314 N.J.Super. 500, 715 A.2d 365 (1998)—§ 13.3(b) n.15

Lazaroff, State v., 77 Ohio St.3d 237, 673 N.E.2d 1273 (1997)—§ 21.6(a) n.28

Lea, United States v., 400 F.3d 1115 (8th Cir.2005)—§ 21.2(a) n.7

Lea, United States v., 360 F.3d 401 (2d Cir.2004)—§ 12.4(d) n.74

Leach v. State, 311 Ark. 485, 845 S.W.2d 11 (1993)—§ 6.2(c) n.114

Leach, State v., 53 Wash.App. 322, 766 P.2d 1116 (1989)—§ 19.2(c) n.36

Leach, State v., 113 Wash.2d 679, 782 P.2d 552 (1989)—§ 19.3(a) n.58

Leach, State v., 113 Wash.2d 735, 782 P.2d 1035 (1989)—§ 3.10(d) n.125

Leahey, United States v., 434 F.2d 7 (1st Cir.1970)—§ 1.7(j) n.231

Leahy, Commonwealth v., 445 Mass. 481, 838 N.E.2d 1220 (2005)—§ 6.9(g) n.153

Leahy, United States v., 438 F.3d 328 (3d Cir.2006)—§ 26.6(d) n.51

Leahy v. United States, 272 F.2d 487 (9th Cir.1959)—§ 3.6(g) n.170

Leake, United States v., 998 F.2d 1359 (6th Cir.1993)—§ 3.3(d) n.152

Leaming, Commonwealth v., 432 Pa. 326, 247 A.2d 590 (1968)—§ 9.5(b) n.56

Leap, Commonwealth v., 179 S.W.3d 809 (Ky.2005)—§ 13.7(c) n.45

Lear v. Cowan, 220 F.3d 825 (7th Cir.2000)—§ 11.10(c) n.76

Leary, United States v., 378 F.Supp.2d 482 (D.Del.2005)—§ 24.11(d) n.19

Leary, United States v., 846 F.2d 592 (10th Cir.1988)—§§ 3.1(c) n.72; 3.10(f) n.198, 199

Leasure, United States v., 319 F.3d 1092 (9th Cir.2003)—§ 3.3(g) n.225

Leasure, United States v., 122 F.3d 837 (9th Cir.1997)—§ 6.6(c) n.33

Leathers, United States v., 354 F.3d 955 (8th Cir.2004)—§ 13.5(a) n.5

Leavell v. Commonwealth, 737 S.W.2d 695 (Ky.1987)—§ 3.3(f) n.198

Leavitt v. Howard, 462 F.2d 992 (1st Cir.1972)—§§ 3.10(b) n.57, 59

Leavitt, State v., 103 R.I. 273, 237 A.2d 309 (1968)—§ 10.2(a) n.13

Lebanon & Big Spring Turnpike Co. v. State, 141 Tenn. 675, 214 S.W. 819 (1918)—§§ 15.1(d) n.227, 228

Lebbing, State v., 158 N.J.Super. 209, 385 A.2d 938 (1978)—§§ 13.6(d) n.68, 69, 71

Lebedun v. Commonwealth, 27 Va.App. 697, 501 S.E.2d 427 (1998)—§ 24.6(b) n.23

Lebel v. Swincicki, 354 Mich. 427, 93 N.W.2d 281 (1958)—§ 2.12(a) n.13

Lebell, People v., 89 Cal.App.3d 772, 152 Cal.Rptr. 840 (1979)—§ 6.4(e) n.68

LeBlanc, Commonwealth v., 433 Mass. 549, 744 N.E.2d 33 (2001)—§ 6.2(c) n.178

LeBlanc, State v., 186 Ariz. 437, 924 P.2d 441 (1996)—§ 24.8(d) n.47

LeBlanc, United States v., 762 F.2d 502 (6th Cir.1985)—§ 21.2(d) n.186

LeBlanc v. United States, 391 F.2d 916 (1st Cir.1968)—§ 9.4(d) n.88

Lebroke, State v., 589 A.2d 941 (Me.1991)—§ 27.2(c) n.62

Lebron v. State, 894 So.2d 849 (Fla. 2005)—§ 26.4(f) n.93

LeBrun, United States v., 363 F.3d 715 (8th Cir.2004)—§ 6.2(c) n.102

Lech, United States v., 895 F.Supp. 586 (S.D.N.Y.1995)—§ 11.9(a) n.33

LeClair, Commonwealth v., 445 Mass. 734, 840 N.E.2d 510 (2006)—§ 6.9(f) n.139

LeClaire, State v., _____ Vt. _____, 819 A.2d 719 (2003)—§ 6.6(e) n.78

LeCroy v. Hanlon, 713 S.W.2d 335 (Tex.1986)—§ 2.12(c) n.150

Ledbetter v. Edwards, 35 F.3d 1062 (6th Cir.1994)—§§ 6.2(c) n.125, 127

Ledbetter, State v., 275 Conn. 534, 881 A.2d 290 (2005)—§§ 7.4(c) n.60; 7.4(f) n.96

Ledbetter, State v., 240 Conn. 317, 692 A.2d 713 (1997)—§ 27.5(c) n.89

Ledda v. State, 564 A.2d 1125 (Del.1989)—§ 3.10(e) n.172

Ledezma v. State, 626 N.W.2d 134 (Iowa 2001)—§ 1.7(c) n.20

Ledrow, People v., 53 Mich.App. 511, 220 N.W.2d 336 (1974)—§ 21.2(b) n.78

Leduc, State v., 40 Conn.App. 233, 670 A.2d 1309 (1996)—§ 24.3(f) n.154

Lee, Commonwealth v., 541 Pa. 260, 662 A.2d 645 (1995)—§ 24.5(a) n.17

Lee v. Commonwealth, 547 S.W.2d 792 (Ky.App.1977)—§ 10.6(a) n.2

Lee v. County Court, 27 N.Y.2d 432, 318 N.Y.S.2d 705, 267 N.E.2d 452 (1971)—§§ 20.4(e) n.78, 80, 85; 20.5(c) n.39

Lee v. Dep't of Justice, 413 F.3d 53 (D.C.Cir.2005)—§ 8.8(d) n.82

Lee v. Ferraro, 284 F.3d 1188 (11th Cir.2002)—§ 3.1(d) n.98

Lee v. Illinois, 476 U.S. 530, 106 S.Ct. 2056, 90 L.Ed.2d 514 (1986)—§§ 17.2(b) n.59; 27.6(d) n.83

Lee v. Kemna, 534 U.S. 362, 122 S.Ct. 877, 151 L.Ed.2d 820 (2002)—§ 28.4(b) n.21

Lee, People v., 196 Ill.2d 368, 256 Ill.Dec. 775, 752 N.E.2d 1017 (2001)—§ 20.2(d) n.74

Lee, People v., 87 Ill.2d 182, 57 Ill.Dec. 563, 429 N.E.2d 461 (1981)—§ 17.2(d) n.97

Lee, People v., 88 Ill.App.3d 396, 43 Ill.Dec. 646, 410 N.E.2d 646 (1980)—§ 26.10(c) n.78

Lee, People v., 48 Ill.2d 272, 269 N.E.2d 488 (1971)—§ 3.8(e) n.225

Lee, State v., 265 Neb. 663, 658 N.W.2d 669 (2003)—§ 3.8(d) n.145

Lee v. State, 97 S.W.3d 9 (Mo.App.2002)—§ 18.4(d) n.94

Lee, State v., 787 So.2d 1020 (La.App.2001)—§§ 23.1(b) n.71, 77

Lee, State v., 15 S.W.3d 921 (Tex.Cr.App.2000)—§ 25.2(b) n.15

Lee v. State, 115 Nev. 207, 985 P.2d 164 (1999)—§ 27.5(c) n.56

Lee, State v., 131 Idaho 600, 961 P.2d 1203 (1998)—§ 24.9(e) n.58

Lee, State v., 191 Ariz. 542, 959 P.2d 799 (1998)—§ 17.3(a) n.8

Lee, State v., 132 Wash.2d 498, 939 P.2d 1223 (1997)—§§ 21.2(b) n.76; 27.3(c) n.24

Lee v. State, 903 S.W.2d 845 (Tex.App.1995)—§§ 16.1(h) n.312, 313

Lee, State v., 10 Haw.App. 192, 862 P.2d 295 (1993)—§ 26.9(a) n.5

Lee v. State, 262 Ga. 593, 423 S.E.2d 249 (1992)—§ 9.6(a) n.38

Lee, State v., 461 N.W.2d 245 (1990)—§ 20.3(a) n.19

Lee v. State, 501 So.2d 591 (Fla.1987)—§ 21.2(d) n.165

Lee v. State, 683 S.W.2d 8 (Tex.Cr.App.1985)—§ 12.3(g) n.159

Lee, State v., 142 Ariz. 210, 689 P.2d 153 (1984)—§ 11.6(a) n.61

Lee v. Stickman, 357 F.3d 338 (3d Cir.2004)—§§ 28.3(a) n.9, 28; 28.5(a) n.19

Lee, United States v., 413 F.3d 622 (7th Cir.2005)—§ 6.9(g) n.166

Lee, United States v., 359 F.3d 194 (3d Cir.2004)—§ 4.6(l) n.199

Lee, United States v., 317 F.3d 26 (1st Cir.2003)—§§ 3.8(b) n.26, 37; 24.10(c) n.40

Lee, United States v., 356 F.3d 831 (8th Cir.2003)—§§ 3.10(a) n.1; 3.10(b) n.72

Lee, United States v., 90 F.Supp.2d 1324 (D.N.M.2000)—§ 20.4(d) n.63

Lee, United States v., 972 F.Supp. 1330 (D.Kan.1997)—§ 19.4(b) n.28

Lee v. United States, 668 A.2d 822 (D.C.App.1995)—§ 24.8(e) n.86

Lee, United States v., 818 F.2d 302 (4th Cir.1987)—§ 18.3(b) n.5

Lee, United States v., 743 F.2d 1240 (8th Cir.1984)—§ 17.2(e) n.116

Lee, United States v., 699 F.2d 466 (9th Cir.1982)—§ 6.6(e) n.59

Lee v. United States, 432 U.S. 23, 97 S.Ct. 2141, 53 L.Ed.2d 80 (1977)—§§ 25.2(f) n.47; 25.3(a) n.1

Lee, United States v., 539 F.2d 606 (6th Cir.1976)—§ 22.1(h) n.132

Lee, United States v., 513 F.2d 423 (D.C.Cir.1975)—§ 11.2(b) n.53

Lee, United States v., 274 U.S. 559, 47 S.Ct. 746, 71 L.Ed. 1202 (1927)—§ 3.2(b) n.49

Leecan v. Lopes, 893 F.2d 1434 (2d Cir.1990)—§ 9.6(a) n.36

Leecan, State v., 198 Conn. 517, 504 A.2d 480 (1986)—§§ 9.6(a) n.44; 11.7(e) n.71, 74, 88, 93

Leep, State v., 212 W.Va. 57, 569 S.E.2d 133 (2002)—§ 24.6(e) n.51

Leeper v. United States, 579 A.2d 695 (D.C.App.1990)—§ 22.3(e) n.272

Leese, United States v., 176 F.3d 740 (3d Cir.1999)—§ 6.6(e) n.68

Leeson, United States ex rel. v. Damon, 496 F.2d 718 (2d Cir.1974)—§ 21.4(d) n.150

Lefcourt v. Legal Aid Society, 445 F.2d 1150 (2d Cir.1971)—§ 21.3(b) n.107

Lefebre, People v., 5 P.3d 295 (Colo.2000)—§§ 22.3(c) n.115, 155

LeFebvre, State v., 875 P.2d 431 (Okla.Crim.App.1994)—§§ 20.6(a) n.10; 20.6(b) n.43

Lefever, State v., 67 N.C.App. 419, 313 S.E.2d 599 (1984)—§ 24.5(b) n.24

Lefkowitz v. Cunningham, 431 U.S. 801, 97 S.Ct. 2132, 53 L.Ed.2d 1 (1977)—§§ 2.10(b) n.41; 8.10(f) n.130

Lefkowitz v. Fair, 816 F.2d 17 (1st Cir.1987)—§ 28.3(a) n.18

Lefkowitz v. Newsome, 420 U.S. 283, 95 S.Ct. 886, 43 L.Ed.2d 196 (1975)—§§ 21.6(b) n.84, 99

Lefkowitz v. Turley, 414 U.S. 70, 94 S.Ct. 316, 38 L.Ed.2d 274 (1973)—§§ 2.9(h) n.258; 2.10(b) n.41; 8.10(f) n.130; 26.10(c) n.59

Lefkowitz, United States v., 285 U.S. 452, 52 S.Ct. 420, 76 L.Ed. 877 (1932)—§§ 3.2(a) n.7; 3.2(i) n.215; 3.5(b) n.87

Lefthand, State v., 488 N.W.2d 799 (Minn.1992)—§§ 6.4(f) n.122; 6.9(c) n.61

Legato, United States v., 480 F.2d 408 (5th Cir.1973)—§ 3.9(h) n.159

Leger, State v., 936 So.2d 108 (La.2006)—§§ 6.7(a) n.28; 6.8(b) n.50; 6.9(g) n.166, 167; 7.4(c) n.48, 50, 51, 53

Legg, State v., 633 N.W.2d 763 (Iowa 2001)—§ 3.2(c) n.118

Legg, State v., 207 W.Va. 686, 536 S.E.2d 110 (2000)—§ 21.6(b) n.84

Legg, United States v., 18 F.3d 240 (4th Cir.1994)—§ 3.4(k) n.228

Leggett, United States v., 162 F.3d 237 (3d Cir.1998)—§ 24.5(d) n.58

Leggio, People v., 133 Misc.2d 320, 507 N.Y.S.2d 131 (Sup.Ct.1986)—§ 15.2(c) n.79

Lego, People v., 116 Ill.2d 323, 107 Ill.Dec. 647, 507 N.E.2d 800 (1987)—§ 20.4(b) n.20

Lego v. Twomey, 404 U.S. 477, 92 S.Ct. 619, 30 L.Ed.2d 618 (1972)—§§ 2.7(a) n.21; 2.12(a) n.23; 3.4(d) n.63; 10.3(b) n.49; 10.3(c) n.54; 10.4(b) n.4; 10.5(a) n.3

LeGrande v. Commonwealth, 494 S.W.2d 726 (Ky.1973)—§ 15.7(b) n.36

LeGrande, State v., 346 N.C. 718, 487 S.E.2d 727 (1997)—§§ 11.3(a) n.20; 11.3(b) n.48

Legree, United States v., 205 F.3d 724 (4th Cir.2000)—§ 26.4(e) n.76

Lehder-Rivas, United States v., 955 F.2d 1510 (11th Cir.1992)—§ 23.2(a) n.27

Lehman, State v., 130 Or. 132, 279 P. 283 (1929)—§ 16.1(e) n.194

Lehman, United States v., 887 F.2d 1328 (7th Cir.1989)—§§ 8.12(c) n.39, 41

Lehr, State v., 201 Ariz. 509, 38 P.3d 1172 (2002)—§ 7.4(d) n.74

Lehr, State v., 258 N.W.2d 158 (Iowa 1977)—§ 3.4(e) n.76

Lei, State v., 95 Haw. 278, 21 P.3d 880 (2001)—§ 13.2(c) n.59

Lei, State v., 95 Hawai'i 278, 21 P.3d 880 (2001)—§ 21.6(b) n.96

Leichtfuss, United States v., 331 F.Supp. 723 (N.D.Ill.1971)—§ 20.3(i) n.168

Leichtnam, United States v., 948 F.2d 370 (7th Cir.1991)—§ 19.6(c) n.40

Leigh v. McGuire, 613 F.2d 380 (2d Cir.1979)—§ 4.6(m) n.226

Leigh, State v., 178 Kan. 549, 289 P.2d 774 (1955)—§ 22.5(a) n.6

Leis v. Flynt, 439 U.S. 438, 99 S.Ct. 698, 58 L.Ed.2d 717 (1979)—§ 11.4(c) n.56

Leisure, United States v., 377 F.3d 910 (8th Cir.2004)—§ 22.4(c) n.29

Leisure, United States v., 844 F.2d 1347 (8th Cir.1988)—§ 24.3(c) n.95

Leitheiser, State v., 331 Mont. 464, 133 P.3d 185 (2006)—§ 21.2(d) n.177

Leja, United States v., 448 F.3d 86 (1st Cir.2006)—§ 22.1(h) n.134

Lejarde-Rada, United States v., 319 F.3d 1288 (11th Cir.2003)—§ 21.4(e) n.163

Leka v. Portuondo, 257 F.3d 89 (2d Cir.2001)—§ 24.3(b) n.65

Lekas, State v., 201 Kan. 579, 442 P.2d 11 (1968)—§ 6.10(c) n.49

Leland v. Oregon, 343 U.S. 790, 72 S.Ct. 1002, 96 L.Ed. 1302 (1952)— § 2.4(e) n.168

Lemcool, People v., 445 Mich. 491, 518 N.W.2d 437 (1994)—§§ 20.4(d) n.72 to 74

Lemieux v. Kerby, 931 F.2d 1391 (10th Cir.1991)—§ 12.2(b) n.27

Lemke, Ex parte, 13 S.W.3d 791 (Tex.Cr.App.2000)—§§ 21.3(b) n.48, 107

Lemon v. Supreme Court, 245 N.Y. 24, 156 N.E. 84 (1927)—§ 20.1(a) n.2

Lemons, United States v., 941 F.2d 309 (5th Cir.1991)—§ 19.3(c) n.198

Lem Woon v. Oregon, 229 U.S. 586, 33 S.Ct. 783, 57 L.Ed. 1340 (1913)— §§ 2.4(e) n.160; 14.2(a) n.2; 15.1(c) n.141

Lennick, United States v., 917 F.2d 974 (7th Cir.1990)—§ 6.6(e) n.69

Lenoci, United States v., 377 F.3d 246 (2d Cir.2004)—§§ 21.2(d) n.148, 177

Lent v. Wells, 861 F.2d 972 (6th Cir.1988)—§ 24.5(b) n.26

Lentsch, United States v., 369 F.3d 948 (6th Cir.2004)—§ 19.3(a) n.102

Lentz, State v., 70 Ohio St.3d 527, 639 N.E.2d 784 (1994)—§ 11.7(e) n.67

Lenwell v. State, 156 Ind.App. 41, 294 N.E.2d 643 (1973)—§ 21.3(b) n.49

Lenz v. True, 370 F.Supp.2d 446 (W.D.Va.2005)—§ 24.9(f) n.69

Lenz v. Winburn, 51 F.3d 1540 (11th Cir.1995)—§ 9.1(b) n.51

Leocal v. Ashcroft, 543 U.S. 1, 125 S.Ct. 377, 160 L.Ed.2d 371 (2004)— § 12.3(a) n.18

Leon, State v., 142 Idaho 705, 132 P.3d 462 (Idaho App.2006)—§ 26.5(d) n.70

Leon, United States v., 468 U.S. 897, 104 S.Ct. 3405, 82 L.Ed.2d 677 (1984)—§§ 1.5(a) n.51; 1.11(a) n.3; 2.9(f) n.137; 2.9(h) n.211, 215; 2.9(i) n.274, 280; 2.12(b) n.115; 3.1(b) n.24; 3.1(c) n.55; 3.3(a) n.27; 3.4(d) n.50

Leon v. Wainwright, 734 F.2d 770 (11th Cir.1984)—§ 9.5(c) n.65

Leonard v. Hammond, 804 F.2d 838 (4th Cir.1986)—§ 28.3(a) n.3

Leonard, People v., 66 A.D.2d 805, 410 N.Y.S.2d 885 (1978)—§ 7.4(c) n.54

Leonard, State v., 104 Ohio St.3d 54, 818 N.E.2d 229 (2004)—§ 6.2(c) n.178

Leonard, State v., 209 W.Va. 98, 543 S.E.2d 655 (2000)—§ 18.5(a) n.40

Leonard v. State, 114 Nev. 1196, 969 P.2d 288 (1998)—§ 22.3(d) n.202

Leonard v. State, 146 Ga.App. 439, 246 S.E.2d 450 (1978)—§ 20.3(h) n.144

Leonard, United States v., 817 F.Supp. 286 (E.D.N.Y.1992)—§ 24.3(f) n.150

Leonard v. United States, 378 U.S. 544, 84 S.Ct. 1696, 12 L.Ed.2d 1028 (1964)—§ 22.3(c) n.101

Leonard v. United States, 277 F.2d 834 (9th Cir.1960)—§ 24.7(a) n.15

Leonardis, State v., 73 N.J. 360, 375 A.2d 607 (1977)—§§ 1.7(j) n.218; 13.6(b) n.22; 13.6(c) n.42

Leonard, People ex rel. v. Papp, 386 Mich. 672, 194 N.W.2d 693 (1972)—§ 13.2(c) n.57

Leon-Delfis, United States v., 203 F.3d 103 (1st Cir.2000)—§ 6.4(f) n.130

Leone, People v., 44 N.Y.2d 315, 405 N.Y.S.2d 642, 376 N.E.2d 1287 (1978)—§ 8.3(a) n.3

Leone, United States v., 215 F.3d 253 (2d Cir.2000)—§ 11.7(e) n.73

Leon Guerrero, United States v., 847 F.2d 1363 (9th Cir.1988)—§§ 6.2(c) n.92, 94

Leong Yau v. Carden, 23 Haw. 362 (1916)—§ 13.5(g) n.111

Leonti, United States v., 326 F.3d 1111 (9th Cir.2003)—§ 11.2(b) n.40

Leos-Maldonado, United States v., 302 F.3d 1061 (9th Cir.2002)—§ 19.3(e) n.239

Lepczynski, People v., 240 App.Div.2d 593, 659 N.Y.S.2d 53 (1997)—§ 24.2(b) n.27

Lepe, People v., 57 Cal.App.4th 977, 67 Cal.Rptr.2d 525 (1997)—§ 14.1(d) n.66

Lepe, People v., 164 Cal.App.3d 685, 211 Cal.Rptr. 432 (1985)—§§ 22.5(a) n.4; 22.5(b) n.20; 22.5(d) n.37

Le Pera, United States v., 443 F.2d 810 (9th Cir.1971)—§ 22.3(c) n.125

Leppert, State v., 656 N.W.2d 718 (N.D.2003)—§ 3.9(i) n.190

Leppo, United States v., 634 F.2d 101 (3d Cir.1980)—§ 27.2(c) n.31

Le Rose, United States v., 219 F.3d 335 (4th Cir.2000)—§ 21.2(d) n.253

Lescard, State v., 128 N.H. 495, 517 A.2d 1158 (1986)—§§ 6.6(e) n.71; 6.6(f) n.101; 6.7(b) n.41; 6.7(c) n.131

Lesko v. Lehman, 925 F.2d 1527 (3d Cir.1991)—§§ 21.2(g) n.401; 24.5(b) n.23

Leslie v. State, 36 S.W.3d 34 (Tenn.2000)—§ 11.4(b) n.29

Leslie, State v., 147 Ariz. 38, 708 P.2d 719 (1985)—§ 18.2(c) n.59

Lesnick, State v., 84 Wash.2d 940, 530 P.2d 243 (1975)—§ 3.1(g) n.169

Lessary, State v., 75 Haw. 446, 865 P.2d 150 (1994)—§ 17.4(b) n.88

Lester v. Mayor, 77 Ga. 143 (1886)—§ 8.4(b) n.88

Lester v. State, 145 Ga.App. 847, 244 S.E.2d 880 (1978)—§ 3.1(h) n.207

Lester, State v., 294 N.C. 220, 240 S.Ed.2d 391 (1978)—§ 14.2(c) n.39

Lett v. State, 51 Md.App. 668, 445 A.2d 1050 (1982)—§§ 16.1(a) n.28, 29

Letters v. Commonwealth, 346 Mass. 403, 193 N.E.2d 578 (1963)—§ 21.1(e) n.94

Lettley v. State, 358 Md. 26, 746 A.2d 392 (2000)—§ 11.9(d) n.205

Leung, United States v., 40 F.3d 577 (2d Cir.1994)—§§ 8.8(f) n.150, 151, 154, 162

Leuthavone, State v., 640 A.2d 515 (R.I.1994)—§§ 6.8(d) n.84; 6.9(b) n.32

Levasseur, State v., 538 A.2d 764 (Me.1988)—§§ 19.3(a) n.72, 73

Levasseur, United States v., 816 F.2d 37 (2d Cir.1987)—§§ 3.2(c) n.98, 101

Levato, State v., 186 Ariz. 441, 924 P.2d 445 (1996)—§§ 11.6(a) n.21; 24.2(a) n.10

Levendoski, People v., 100 Ill.App.3d 755, 55 Ill.Dec. 867, 426 N.E.2d 1241 (1981)—§ 6.7(d) n.156

Leventhal, United States v., 961 F.2d 936 (11th Cir.1992)—§ 8.8(d) n.90

Leverage Funding Systems, United States v., 637 F.2d 645 (9th Cir.1980)—§§ 15.6(c) n.98, 100

Levesque, State v., 281 A.2d 570 (Me.1971)—§ 8.5(a) n.5

Levine, United States v., 80 F.3d 129 (5th Cir.1996)—§ 3.3(d) n.171

Levine, United States v., 546 F.2d 658 (5th Cir.1977)—§ 17.2(a) n.15

Levine, United States v., 457 F.2d 1186 (10th Cir.1972)—§ 15.7(b) n.45

Levine v. United States, 362 U.S. 610, 80 S.Ct. 1038, 4 L.Ed.2d 989 (1960)—§§ 8.4(c) n.113; 8.5(b) n.60; 15.6(b) n.71; 24.1(a) n.3, 7

Levine v. United States District Court, 764 F.2d 590 (9th Cir.1985)—§§ 23.1(b) n.28, 71, 72, 76, 78, 80 to 82, 85

Levingston v. Washoe County, 114 Nev. 306, 956 P.2d 84 (1998)—§ 17.4(b) n.120

Levinson v. Attorney General, 321 F.Supp. 984 (E.D.Pa.1970)—§ 8.8(a) n.11

Levinson, Commonwealth v., 480 Pa. 273, 389 A.2d 1062 (1978)—§ 15.6(c) n.102

Levinson, Commonwealth v., 239 Pa.Super. 387, 362 A.2d 1080 (1976)—§ 15.7(h) n.225

Levinson, United States v., 405 F.2d 971 (6th Cir.1968)—§ 8.14(a) n.6

Leviston v. Black, 843 F.2d 302 (8th Cir.1988)—§§ 6.6(b) n.16; 6.6(e) n.81

Leviton, United States v., 193 F.2d 848 (2d Cir.1951)—§ 6.3(a) n.20

Levitt, State v., 36 N.J. 266, 176 A.2d 465 (1961)—§ 24.9(g) n.118

Levitt, United States v., 799 F.2d 505 (9th Cir.1986)—§ 26.10(a) n.6

Levy, State v., 156 Wash.2d 709, 132 P.3d 1076 (2006)—§ 27.6(d) n.97

Levy, United States v., 374 F.3d 1023 (11th Cir.2004)—§ 21.2(d) n.174

Levy, United States v., 25 F.3d 146 (2d Cir.1994)—§§ 11.9(b) n.91, 92; 11.9(c) n.129, 146; 11.9(d) n.168, 170, 175, 189, 201, 213, 222, 223, 225

Levy, United States v., 577 F.2d 200 (3d Cir.1978)—§ 11.8(b) n.33

Lewallen, In re, 23 Cal.3d 274, 152 Cal.Rptr. 528, 590 P.2d 383 (1979)—§§ 21.2(c) n.126, 131

Lewandowski v. Makel, 949 F.2d 884 (6th Cir.1991)—§ 11.10(d) n.175

Lewellen v. State, 265 Ind. 483, 358 N.E.2d 115 (1976)—§ 19.6(b) n.10

Lewin, Commonwealth v., 405 Mass. 566, 542 N.E.2d 275 (1989)—§ 1.9(b) n.19

Lewinski, Commonwealth v., 367 Mass. 889, 329 N.E.2d 738 (1975)—§ 20.3(i) n.169

Lewis, Ex parte, 2007 WL 2285475 (Tex.Cr.App.2007)—§ 25.2(b) n.15

Lewis, Ex parte, 587 S.W.2d 697 (Tex.Cr.App.1979)—§§ 21.3(c) n.174, 183

Lewis, In re, 389 Mich. 668, 209 N.W.2d 203 (1973)—§ 21.4(a) n.22

Lewis v. Alexander, 11 F.3d 1349 (6th Cir.1993)—§§ 11.6(a) n.46; 11.6(b) n.66; 11.10(c) n.83, 119, 130, 131

Lewis v. Casey, 518 U.S. 343, 116 S.Ct. 2174, 135 L.Ed.2d 606 (1996)—§§ 11.2(f) n.241, 244, 253; 27.1(a) n.13; 28.12(a) n.4, 6

Lewis, Commonwealth v., 399 Mass. 761, 506 N.E.2d 891 (1987)—§ 21.6(c) n.118

Lewis, Commonwealth v., 443 Pa. 305, 279 A.2d 26 (1971)—§ 13.4(a) n.10

Lewis v. Continental Bank Corp., 494 U.S. 472, 110 S.Ct. 1249, 108 L.Ed.2d 400 (1990)—§ 27.5(a) n.19

Lewis v. Iowa District Court, 555 N.W.2d 216 (1996)—§ 11.8(c) n.66

Lewis v. Lane, 832 F.2d 1446 (7th Cir.1987)—§§ 11.10(c) n.80; 11.10(d) n.161

Lewis v. Lewis, 321 F.3d 824 (9th Cir.2003)—§ 22.3(d) n.236

Lewis, People v., 39 Cal.4th 970, 47 Cal.Rptr.3d 467, 140 P.3d 775 (2006)—§ 24.2(a) n.10

Lewis, People v., 26 Cal.4th 334, 110 Cal.Rptr.2d 272, 28 P.3d 34 (2001)—§§ 6.8(b) n.50, 57; 6.9(b) n.20

Lewis, People v., 157 Misc.2d 937, 599 N.Y.S.2d 777 (1993)—§ 15.6(c) n.95

Lewis, People v., 88 Ill.2d 129, 58 Ill.Dec. 895, 430 N.E.2d 1346 (1981)—§ 15.3(a) n.20

Lewis, People v., 73 Ill.App.3d 361, 25 Ill.Dec. 436, 386 N.E.2d 910 (1979)—§ 13.4(b) n.72

Lewis, People v., 183 Colo. 236, 516 P.2d 416 (1973)—§ 15.6(d) n.119

Lewis v. Peterson, 329 F.3d 934 (7th Cir.2003)—§ 28.4(e) n.85

Lewis v. State, 279 Ga. 756, 620 S.E.2d 778 (2005)—§ 21.4(b) n.59

Lewis, State v., 363 S.C. 37, 609 S.E.2d 515 (2005)—§§ 7.4(g) n.112, 116

Lewis v. State, 150 P.3d 1060 (Okla.Crim.App.2004)—§ 17.4(b) n.73

Lewis v. State, 747 A.2d 1191 (Me.2000)—§ 27.5(a) n.9

Lewis, State v., 123 Idaho 336, 848 P.2d 394 (1993)—§ 3.2(i) n.225

Lewis, State v., 188 W.Va. 85, 422 S.E.2d 807 (1992)—§§ 27.3(b) n.17; 27.4(b) n.12; 27.4(c) n.28

Lewis, State v., 611 A.2d 69 (Me.1992)—§ 3.10(f) n.204

Lewis v. State, 554 N.E.2d 1133 (Ind.1990)—§ 7.4(f) n.96

Lewis, State v., 539 So.2d 1199 (La.1989)—§ 21.2(h) n.425

Lewis, State v., 129 N.H. 787, 533 A.2d 358 (1987)—§ 6.9(g) n.200

Lewis, State v., 293 S.C. 107, 359 S.E.2d 66 (1987)—§ 22.3(d) n.247

Lewis, State v., 321 N.C. 42, 361 S.E.2d 728 (1987)—§ 24.9(c) n.28

Lewis v. State, 664 S.W.2d 345 (Tex.Cr.App.1984)—§ 9.1(d) n.120

Lewis, State v., 632 P.2d 547 (Alaska App.1981)—§§ 20.6(b) n.28, 34, 36

Lewis, State v., 115 Ariz. 530, 566 P.2d 678 (1977)—§ 3.5(b) n.102

Lewis v. State, 166 Ind.App. 553, 337 N.E.2d 516 (1975)—§ 26.6(b) n.15

Lewis v. State, 259 Ind. 431, 288 N.E.2d 138 (1972)—§ 6.9(g) n.178

Lewis v. State, 132 Miss. 200, 96 So. 169 (1923)—§ 15.2(i) n.223

Lewis, United States v., 476 F.3d 369 (5th Cir.2007)—§ 21.2(d) n.206

Lewis, United States v., 406 F.3d 11 (1st Cir.2005)—§ 4.6(b) n.50

Lewis, United States v., 411 F.3d 838 (7th Cir.2005)—§ 20.3(i) n.177

Lewis, United States v., 368 F.3d 1102 (9th Cir.2004)—§ 25.4(a) n.9

Lewis, United States v., 391 F.3d 989 (9th 2004)—§ 11.9(c) n.134

Lewis v. United States, 518 U.S. 322, 116 S.Ct. 2163, 135 L.Ed.2d 590 (1996)—§ 22.1(b) n.53

Lewis, United States v., 53 F.3d 29 (4th Cir.1995)—§ 20.5(c) n.46

Lewis, United States v., 979 F.2d 1372 (9th Cir.1992)—§ 21.2(d) n.165

Lewis, United States v., 980 F.2d 555 (9th Cir.1992)—§ 18.3(b) n.50

Lewis, United States v., 875 F.2d 444 (5th Cir.1989)—§ 21.5(c) n.74

Lewis, United States v., 837 F.2d 415 (9th Cir.1988)—§ 22.3(d) n.247

Lewis, United States v., 738 F.2d 916 (8th Cir.1984)—§ 3.3(d) n.149

Lewis v. United States, 446 A.2d 837 (D.C.App.1982)—§ 11.9(d) n.218

Lewis v. United States, 430 A.2d 528 (D.C.App.1981)—§ 11.4(c) n.66

Lewis v. United States, 393 A.2d 109 (D.C.App.1978)—§ 24.3(b) n.62

Lewis, United States v., 556 F.2d 446 (6th Cir.1977)—§ 6.6(f) n.114

Lewis, United States v., 511 F.2d 798 (D.C.Cir.1975)—§ 20.2(b) n.23

Lewis v. United States, 517 F.2d 236 (9th Cir.1975)—§§ 8.8(d) n.50, 65

Lewis v. United States, 501 F.2d 418 (9th Cir.1974)—§ 8.8(d) n.65

Lewis v. United States, 385 U.S. 206, 87 S.Ct. 424, 17 L.Ed.2d 312 (1966)—§§ 3.2(c) n.104; 3.10(c) n.82

Lewis v. United States, 74 F.2d 173 (9th Cir.1934)—§ 6.2(a) n.14

Lewis v. United States, 279 U.S. 63, 49 S.Ct. 257, 73 L.Ed. 615 (1929)—§ 22.2(e) n.104

Lewis v. United States, 146 U.S. 370, 13 S.Ct. 136, 36 L.Ed. 1011 (1892)—§§ 22.3(a) n.2; 24.2(a) n.2, 5

Leyda, State v., 157 Wash.2d 335, 138 P.3d 610 (2006)—§§ 13.7(a) n.6; 17.4(b) n.73

Leyland, United States v., 277 F.3d 628 (2d Cir.2002)—§ 21.6(a) n.64

Leyra v. Denno, 347 U.S. 556, 74 S.Ct. 716, 98 L.Ed. 948 (1954)—§§ 2.4(e) n.146; 6.2(c) n.79, 143, 167; 9.5(c) n.61

Leyva, State v., 951 P.2d 738 (Utah 1997)—§§ 6.9(a) n.12; 6.9(g) n.159, 185

Li, United States v., 206 F.3d 78 (1st Cir.2000)—§ 6.6(e) n.94

Li, United States v., 115 F.3d 125 (2d Cir.1997)—§ 26.4(g) n.138

Liakos, State v., 142 N.H. 726, 709 A.2d 187 (1998)—§ 17.4(b) n.124

Liang, Commonwealth v., 434 Mass. 131, 747 N.E.2d 112 (2001)—§§ 20.3(j) n.195, 198, 202; 20.5(f) n.83; 24.3(b) n.52

Libby, Commonwealth v., 358 Mass. 617, 266 N.E.2d 641 (1971)—§ 16.1(d) n.132

Libby, United States v., 429 F.Supp.2d 1 (D.D.C.2006)—§§ 20.3(a) n.12; 24.3(b) n.52

Liberal, Kansas, City of v. Witherspoon, 28 Kan.App.2d 649, 20 P.3d 727 (2001)—§ 8.10(e) n.126

Liberatore, In re, 574 F.2d 78 (2d Cir.1978)—§ 8.8(b) n.32

Liberman, In re, 293 Or. 457, 650 P.2d 83 (1982)—§ 12.1(b) n.25

Library of Congress v. Shaw, 478 U.S. 310, 106 S.Ct. 2957, 92 L.Ed.2d 250 (1986)—§ 13.5(h) n.123

Libretti v. United States, 516 U.S. 29, 116 S.Ct. 356, 133 L.Ed.2d 271 (1995)—§§ 21.4(e) n.156; 21.4(f) n.171; 26.2(b) n.2; 26.6(d) n.50

Licari, State v., 659 N.W.2d 243 (Minn.2003)—§§ 3.10(d) n.136; 3.10(e) n.158

Licavoli, United States v., 604 F.2d 613 (9th Cir.1979)—§ 8.10(e) n.125

Licavoli, United States v., 456 F.Supp. 960 (N.D.Ohio 1978)—§ 4.6(i) n.158

Licciardi, Commonwealth v., 387 Mass. 670, 443 N.E.2d 386 (1982)—§ 24.10(a) n.18

Lichti v. State, 827 N.E.2d 82 (Ind.App.2005)—§ 10.4(b) n.16

Liciaga v. Court of Common Pleas, 523 Pa. 258, 566 A.2d 246 (1989)—§§ 14.3(b) n.45; 14.3(c) n.57, 65, 67

Liddell, State v., 672 N.W.2d 805 (Iowa 2003)—§ 22.1(h) n.133

Liddy, In re, 506 F.2d 1293 (D.C.Cir.1974)—§ 8.10(c) n.63

Liddy, United States v., 542 F.2d 76 (D.C.Cir.1976)—§ 25.5(a) n.11

Lieberman, United States ex rel. v. Washington, 1995 WL 513516 (N.D.Ill.1995)—§ 23.2(d) n.70

Liefert, State v., 309 Mont. 19, 43 P.3d 329 (2002)—§§ 21.4(b) n.44; 21.4(d) n.131

Liegakos v. Cooke, 106 F.3d 1381 (7th Cir.1997)—§ 28.6(f) n.76

Lien v. Class, 574 N.W.2d 601 (S.D.1998)—§§ 15.7(f) n.141; 21.3(b) n.53

Lifshitz, United States v., 369 F.3d 173 (2d Cir.2004)—§ 26.9(b) n.48

Liggins, State v., 524 N.W.2d 181 (Iowa 1994)—§§ 16.4(c) n.98; 16.4(d) n.123, 131, 132, 139, 140

Lightbourne v. Dugger, 829 F.2d 1012 (11th Cir.1987)—§ 6.9(g) n.159

Lightfoot, United States v., 483 F.3d 876 (8th Cir.2007)—§ 18.3(b) n.36

Ligori, United States v., 658 F.2d 130 (3d Cir.1981)—§ 21.2(d) n.190

Liistro v. Robinson, 170 Conn. 116, 365 A.2d 109 (1976)—§ 12.3(b) n.63

Lileikis, United States v., 899 F.Supp. 802 (D.Mass.1995)—§ 2.10(d) n.109

Liles v. Saffle, 945 F.2d 333 (10th Cir.1991)—§§ 11.2(e) n.153, 158, 159

Liljeberg v. Health Services Acquisition Corp., 486 U.S. 847, 108 S.Ct. 2194, 100 L.Ed.2d 855 (1988)—§ 22.4(c) n.31

Lill, United States v., 511 F.Supp. 50 (S.D.W.Va.1980)—§§ 15.6(b) n.55; 15.7(h) n.241

Lillard, United States v., 929 F.2d 500 (9th Cir.1991)—§ 3.1(d) n.109

Liller, United States v., 999 F.2d 61 (2d Cir.1993)—§ 17.4(b) n.95

Lillie, United States v., 989 F.2d 1054 (9th Cir.1993)—§ 11.4(c) n.56

Lillios v. New Hampshire, 788 F.2d 60 (1st Cir.1986)—§§ 28.3(a) n.16, 19

Lilly v. State, 649 A.2d 1055 (Del.1994)—§ 24.8(e) n.50

Lilly, United States v., 901 F.Supp. 25 (D.Mass.1995)—§ 26.9(c) n.79

Linares v. State, 266 Ga. 812, 471 S.E.2d 208 (1996)—§ 6.2(c) n.139

Lincoln, State v., 165 Vt. 570, 680 A.2d 110 (1996)—§ 22.4(c) n.28

Lincoln, United States v., 494 F.2d 833 (9th Cir.1974)—§ 3.9(f) n.86

Lind, People v., 370 Ill. 131, 18 N.E.2d 189 (1938)—§ 3.10(b) n.44

Lindberg, United States v., 220 F.3d 1120 (9th Cir.2000)—§§ 13.5(h) n.149, 150, 161, 162, 168, 172, 183, 187

Lindberg v. United States, 363 F.2d 438 (9th Cir.1966)—§ 16.3(c) n.36

Lindell, State v., 245 Wis.2d 689, 629 N.W.2d 223 (2001)—§§ 22.3(c) n.112, 133, 157; 27.6(b) n.21

Linderman, United States v., 20 F.R.D. 459 (D.Mont.1957)—§ 19.1(d) n.44

Lindh v. Murphy, 521 U.S. 320, 117 S.Ct. 2059, 138 L.Ed.2d 481 (1997)—§ 28.2(c) n.39

Lindh, State v., 161 Wis.2d 324, 468 N.W.2d 168 (1991)—§ 6.9(g) n.155

Lindh, United States v., 198 F.Supp.2d 739 (E.D.Va.2002)—§ 23.1(b) n.80

Lindsay, People v., 10 Cal.App.4th 1642, 13 Cal.Rptr.2d 676 (1992)—§ 26.9(b) n.24

Lindsay v. State, 606 So.2d 652 (Fla.App.1992)—§§ 26.9(b) n.22, 78

Lindsay, United States v., 506 F.2d 166 (D.C.Cir.1974)—§ 3.6(a) n.19

Lindsey, People v., 201 Ill.2d 45, 265 Ill.Dec. 616, 772 N.E.2d 1268 (2002)—§ 24.2(f) n.87

Lindsey v. State, 939 So.2d 743 (2005)—§ 11.2(c) n.107

Lindsey v. State, 86 Ark.App. 297, 184 S.W.3d 458 (2004)—§ 18.4(c) n.32

Lindsey, State v., 632 N.W.2d 652 (Minn.2001)—§§ 7.4(e) n.83; 24.1(b) n.20

Lindsey v. State, 254 Ga. 444, 330 S.E.2d 563 (1985)—§ 11.2(e) n.174

Lindsey, State v., 284 N.W.2d 368 (Minn.1979)—§§ 20.6(b) n.19; 20.6(c) n.82, 85

Lindsey v. State, 38 Ohio St. 507 (1882)—§§ 16.4(c) n.49, 62

Lindsey v. United States, 911 A.2d 824 (D.C.App.2006)—§ 6.6(b) n.16

Lindsey, United States v., 782 F.2d 116 (8th Cir.1986)—§§ 17.1(b) n.25; 17.1(d) n.53

Lineberger, State v., 342 N.C. 599, 467 S.E.2d 24 (1996)—§ 21.2(f) n.389

Linehan, Matter of, 557 N.W.2d 171 (Minn.1996)—§ 17.4(b) n.134

Linen Supply Companies, Application of, 15 F.R.D. 115 (S.D.N.Y.1953)—§§ 8.7(b) n.43, 44, 55

Linetsky, United States v., 533 F.2d 192 (5th Cir.1976)—§§ 15.7(g) n.205; 17.4(a) n.41

Lingar, State v., 726 S.W.2d 728 (Mo.1987)—§§ 3.2(f) n.174; 16.1(g) n.264, 276; 22.3(c) n.112

Link v. Luebbers, 469 F.3d 1197 (8th Cir.2006)—§ 11.10(c) n.96

Link, United States v., 238 F.3d 106 (1st Cir.2001)—§ 3.3(c) n.132

Linkey v. State, 46 Md.App. 312, 416 A.2d 286 (1980)—§ 21.6(c) n.120

Linkletter v. Walker, 381 U.S. 618, 85 S.Ct. 1731, 14 L.Ed.2d 601 (1965)—§§ 2.11(a) n.1; 2.11(b) n.15; 3.1(b) n.19

Linn v. State, 505 P.2d 1270 (Wyo.1973)—§§ 16.2(g) n.114; 16.4(c) n.60

Linnear, United States v., 40 F.3d 215 (7th Cir.1994)—§ 26.5(a) n.7

Linscott, State v., 521 A.2d 701 (Me.1987)—§§ 8.10(a) n.14, 15

Linton v. Perini, 656 F.2d 207 (6th Cir.1981)—§§ 11.4(c) n.64, 71

Linton, State v., 156 Wash.2d 777, 132 P.3d 127 (2006)—§ 25.4(d) n.45

Linton, United States v., 502 F.Supp. 861 (D.Nev.1980)—§§ 15.5(b) n.55, 57; 15.7(b) n.31; 15.7(f) n.154

Linzy, People v., 78 Ill.2d 106, 34 Ill.Dec. 326, 398 N.E.2d 1 (1979)—§§ 1.7(i) n.204; 15.2(e) n.142, 144; 15.7(b) n.11

Lionberg, State v., 533 A.2d 1172 (R.I.1987)—§ 6.9(f) n.138

Lipke, State v., 186 Wis.2d 358, 521 N.W.2d 444 (1994)—§ 27.5(a) n.25

Lippert, People v., 79 Mich.App. 730, 263 N.W.2d 268 (1977)—§ 21.5(a) n.25

Lippert, United States v., 740 F.2d 457 (6th Cir.1984)—§ 21.1(e) n.62

Lippold, United States v., 175 F.Supp.2d 537 (S.D.N.Y.2001)—§ 12.4(d) n.74

Lipps v. State, 254 Ind. 141, 258 N.E.2d 622 (1970)—§ 6.10(b) n.15

Lipscomb v. State, 700 P.2d 1298 (Alaska App.1985)—§ 15.7(f) n.172

Lipscomb, United States v., 435 F.2d 795 (5th Cir.1970)—§ 3.5(e) n.194

Lipsky, State v., 608 P.2d 1241 (Utah 1980)—§ 26.5(c) n.45

Liquid Sugars, Inc., United States v., 158 F.R.D. 466 (E.D.Cal.1994)—§§ 20.3(a) n.20; 20.3(f) n.105, 106; 20.3(g) n.125

Lira, United States v., 515 F.2d 68 (2d Cir.1975)—§ 3.1(j) n.246

Lisak v. Florida, 433 So.2d 487 (Fla.1983)—§ 25.1(d) n.88

Lisenba v. California, 314 U.S. 219, 62 S.Ct. 280, 86 L.Ed. 166 (1941)—§§ 2.4 n.5; 6.2(b) n.45, 52; 21.2(b) n.72

Lisk, United States v., 522 F.2d 228 (7th Cir.1975)—§§ 9.1(b) n.84; 9.1(d) n.124

Lisle v. State, 113 Nev. 679, 941 P.2d 459 (1997)—§ 17.2(e) n.116

Litaker v. State, 784 S.W.2d 739 (Tex.App.1990)—§ 24.5(b) n.33

Litchfield, United States v., 959 F.2d 1514 (10th Cir.1992)—§ 11.9(a) n.21

Liteky v. United States, 510 U.S. 540, 114 S.Ct. 1147, 127 L.Ed.2d 474 (1994)—§§ 22.4(a) n.14; 22.4(b) n.18

Litherland, State v., 12 P.3d 92 (2000)—§ 11.10(c) n.76

Litteral, State v., 110 N.M. 138, 793 P.2d 268 (1990)—§ 16.4(d) n.137

Litteral, United States v., 910 F.2d 547 (9th Cir.1990)—§ 3.6(a) n.10

Little v. Armontrout, 835 F.2d 1240 (8th Cir.1987)—§§ 11.2(e) n.183, 188, 191, 203, 210, 212

Little, People v., 59 Cal.App.4th 426, 68 Cal.Rptr.2d 907 (1997)—§ 20.3(a) n.16

Little v. State, 475 N.E.2d 677 (Ind.1985)—§ 7.3(b) n.29

Little, United States v., 851 A.2d 1280 (D.C.App.2004)—§ 6.6(d) n.53

Little, United States v., 18 F.3d 1499 (10th Cir.1994)—§ 3.8(c) n.78

Little v. United States, 613 A.2d 880 (D.C.App.1992)—§ 22.3(d) n.214

Little, United States v., 735 F.2d 1049 (8th Cir.1984)—§ 9.1(b) n.83

Little, United States v., 753 F.2d 1420 (9th Cir.1984)—§ 17.2(c) n.82

Little v. United States, 524 F.2d 335 (8th Cir.1975)—§ 15.1(d) n.171

Little v. Warden, 117 Nev. 845, 34 P.3d 540 (2001)—§§ 21.4(d) n.118; 27.6(b) n.19

Littlefield, Ex parte, 343 S.C. 212, 540 S.E.2d 81 (2000)—§§ 13.1(a) n.10, 26

Littlefield, In re, 5 Cal.4th 122, 19 Cal.Rptr.2d 248, 851 P.2d 42 (1993)—§ 20.3(a) n.15

Littlefield, United States v., 105 F.3d 527 (9th Cir.1997)—§§ 21.6(a) n.49, 80

Littlefield, United States v., 752 F.2d 1429 (9th Cir.1985)—§ 24.9(f) n.78

Littlejohn v. State, 593 So.2d 20 (Miss.1992)—§§ 11.9(b) n.80; 11.9(d) n.179, 202

Littlejohn, State v., 199 Conn. 631, 508 A.2d 1376 (1986)—§ 18.5(a) n.51

Littlejohn, United States v., 224 F.3d 960 (9th Cir.2000)—§§ 21.4(d) n.129, 130

Littlejohn v. United States, 705 A.2d 1077 (D.C.1997)—§ 8.10(a) n.23

Littlesun, United States v., 444 F.3d 1196 (9th Cir.2006)—§ 26.4(f) n.93

Little, United States ex rel. v. Twomey, 477 F.2d 767 (7th Cir.1973)—§ 18.2(c) n.48

Lively, State v., 130 Wash.2d 1, 921 P.2d 1035 (1996)—§§ 5.3(d) n.40, 41

Lively v. State, 326 Ark. 398, 930 S.W.2d 339 (1996)—§ 27.4(c) n.23

Liveoak, United States v., 377 F.3d 859 (8th Cir.2004)—§ 21.5(d) n.104

Livermore, People v., 30 Cal.App.3d 1073, 106 Cal.Rptr. 822 (1973)—§ 3.4(h) n.146

Livings v. Davis, 465 So.2d 507 (Fla.1985)—§ 16.4(c) n.114

Livingston v. Johnson, 107 F.3d 297 (5th Cir.1997)—§ 24.8(f) n.91

Livingston v. Murdaugh, 183 F.3d 300 (4th Cir.1999)—§ 25.4(d) n.44

Livingston v. State, 519 So.2d 1218 (Miss.1988)—§ 7.3(b) n.34

Livorsi, United States v., 180 F.3d 76 (2d Cir.1999)—§§ 21.4(f) n.174; 21.4(g) n.228

Llanes v. State, 603 So.2d 1294 (Fla.App.1992)—§ 24.3(c) n.92

Llewelyn, People v., 136 Misc.2d 525, 518 N.Y.S.2d 881 (Sup.Ct.1987)—§§ 15.5(b) n.45; 15.7(e) n.105, 124

Lloyd v. State, 258 Ga. 645, 373 S.E.2d 1 (1988)—§ 21.3(b) n.107

Lloyd, State v., 22 Or.App. 254, 538 P.2d 1278 (1975)—§§ 6.6(b) n.15; 9.4(a) n.17

Lloyd, United States v., 398 F.3d 978 (7th Cir.2005)—§ 28.9(b) n.58

Lloyd, United States v., 10 F.3d 1197 (6th Cir.1993)—§ 10.6(d) n.48

Lo, United States v., 231 F.3d 471 (9th Cir.2000)—§ 18.5(a) n.50

Loayza, United States v., 107 F.3d 257 (4th Cir.1997)—§§ 19.2(f) n.98; 19.3(b) n.140; 19.4(a) n.2

Lobatos v. State, 875 P.2d 716 (Wyo.1994)—§ 3.3(b) n.55

Locascio, United States v., 6 F.3d 924 (2d Cir.1993)—§§ 11.9(c) n.108, 111, 118, 121, 138, 142; 24.7(e) n.73

Lochiatto, In re, 497 F.2d 803 (1st Cir.1974)—§ 8.9(b) n.23

LoCicero, People v., 453 Mich. 496, 556 N.W.2d 498 (1996)—§ 9.3(c) n.26

Locke, United States v., 482 F.3d 764 (5th Cir.2007)—§ 26.9(b) n.72

Lockert v. State, 271 Ind. 226, 391 N.E.2d 613 (1979)—§ 21.2(b) n.41

Lockett v. Ohio, 438 U.S. 586, 98 S.Ct. 2954, 57 L.Ed.2d 973 (1978)—§§ 24.5(b) n.29; 26.1(b) n.19; 26.4(g) n.116

Lockett v. State, 517 So.2d 1346 (Miss.1987)—§§ 22.3(d) n.246, 250

Lockett v. State, 459 So.2d 246 (Miss.1984)—§ 6.9(d) n.72

Lockett, United States v., 406 F.3d 207 (3d Cir.2005)—§§ 10.2(a) n.2; 21.2(b) n.86

Lockett, United States v., 526 F.2d 1110 (7th Cir.1975)—§ 18.2(e) n.74

Lockhart v. Fretwell, 506 U.S. 364, 113 S.Ct. 838, 122 L.Ed.2d 180 (1993)—§§ 2.11(e) n.59; 11.10(d) n.169, 182; 26.4(e) n.75; 28.6(b) n.7

Lockhart v. McCree, 476 U.S. 162, 106 S.Ct. 1758, 90 L.Ed.2d 137 (1986)—§§ 22.2(d) n.65; 22.3(a) n.31; 22.3(c) n.159; 22.3(d) n.188

Lockhart v. Nelson, 488 U.S. 33, 109 S.Ct. 285, 102 L.Ed.2d 265 (1988)—§ 25.4(c) n.35

Lockhart, State v., 830 A.2d 433 (Me.2003)—§§ 6.7(b) n.90; 6.9(g) n.157, 166

Lockhart v. Terhune, 250 F.3d 1223 (9th Cir.2001)—§ 11.9(d) n.194

Locklear, State v., 349 N.C. 118, 505 S.E.2d 277 (1998)—§§ 22.3(d) n.193, 217

Locklear, State v., 331 N.C. 720, 417 S.E.2d 445 (1992)—§ 24.8(a) n.21

Locklear, United States v., 97 F.3d 196 (7th Cir.1996)—§§ 19.2(c) n.37; 19.3(a) n.15

Locks v. Sumner, 703 F.2d 403 (9th Cir.1983)—§ 24.9(d) n.38

Lockwood, State v., 160 Vt. 547, 632 A.2d 655 (1993)—§ 26.10(a) n.5

Lockwood, United States v., 416 F.3d 604 (7th Cir.2005)—§ 21.2(b) n.76

Lockyer v. Andrade, 538 U.S. 63, 123 S.Ct. 1166, 155 L.Ed.2d 144 (2003)—§§ 28.6(f) n.69, 72, 73

LoConte v. Dugger, 847 F.2d 745 (11th Cir.1988)—§§ 21.2(b) n.53; 21.4(b) n.44

Lodermeier v. Class, 1996 S.D. 134, 555 N.W.2d 618 (1996)—§ 22.4(a) n.12

Lodermeier, State v., 481 N.W.2d 614 (S.D.1992)—§ 3.2(c) n.127

Lodowski v. State, 302 Md. 691, 490 A.2d 1228 (1985)—§ 21.3(f) n.422

Loe, United States v., 248 F.3d 449 (5th Cir.2001)—§ 24.10(c) n.41

Loftin, State v., 276 S.C. 48, 275 S.E.2d 575 (1981)—§ 3.10(e) n.153

Lofton, United States v., 233 F.3d 313 (4th Cir.2000)—§ 24.11(d) n.30

Logan v. State, 729 N.E.2d 125 (Ind.2000)—§ 7.4(b) n.30

Logan v. State, 690 S.W.2d 311 (Tex.App.1985)—§§ 11.5(c) n.34, 36, 38, 52

Logan, United States v., 210 F.3d 820 (8th Cir.2000)—§ 17.2(b) n.71

Logan v. United States, 144 U.S. 263, 12 S.Ct. 617, 36 L.Ed. 429 (1892)—§ 1.7(h) n.141

Loggins v. Frey, 786 F.2d 364 (8th Cir.1986)—§ 11.6(a) n.49

Logner v. North Carolina, 260 F.Supp. 970 (M.D.N.C.1966)—§ 6.2(c) n.173

Lo-Ji Sales, Inc. v. New York, 442 U.S. 319, 99 S.Ct. 2319, 60 L.Ed.2d 920 (1979)—§§ 3.1(c) n.69; 3.4(b) n.32

Lomas, State v., 114 Nev. 313, 955 P.2d 678 (1998)—§ 17.4(b) n.124

Lombardi, State v., 8 Wis.2d 421, 99 N.W.2d 829 (1959)—§ 13.2(b) n.36

Lombardo, United States v., 241 U.S. 73, 36 S.Ct. 508, 60 L.Ed. 897 (1916)—§§ 16.1(d) n.144; 16.2(c) n.38

Lombardozzi, United States v., 436 F.2d 878 (2d Cir.1971)—§ 21.5(a) n.45

Lombrano v. Superior Court, 124 Ariz. 525, 606 P.2d 15 (1980)—§ 25.1(d) n.76

Lonchar v. Thomas, 517 U.S. 314, 116 S.Ct. 1293, 134 L.Ed.2d 440 (1996)—§§ 28.5(b) n.42; 28.7(d) n.28

London, United States v., 66 F.3d 1227 (1st Cir.1995)—§ 4.6(i) n.156

Lonedog, United States v., 929 F.2d 568 (10th Cir.1991)—§ 24.7(e) n.43

Lonergan, State v., 213 Conn. 74, 566 A.2d 677 (1989)—§ 2.12(a) n.3

Long v. District Court, 385 U.S. 192, 87 S.Ct. 362, 17 L.Ed.2d 290 (1966)—§§ 11.2(d) n.121, 126

Long v. District of Columbia, 469 F.2d 927 (D.C.Cir.1972)—§ 3.1(n) n.298

Long, State v., 276 Kan. 297, 75 P.3d 1217 (2003)—§ 18.5(a) n.33

Long, State v., 190 Wis.2d 386, 526 N.W.2d 826 (App.1994)—§ 6.9(g) n.161

Long, State v., 227 Mont. 199, 738 P.2d 487 (1987)—§ 21.4(c) n.95

Long, State v., 721 P.2d 483 (Utah 1986)—§§ 7.4(c) n.47; 7.5(a) n.7; 17.1(d) n.59

Long, State v., 408 So.2d 1221 (La.1982)—§ 14.4(e) n.115

Long v. State, 109 Ohio St. 77, 141 N.E. 691 (1923)—§ 27.6(b) n.12

Long, United States v., 900 F.2d 1270 (8th Cir.1990)—§§ 18.3(b) n.22, 27

Long, United States v., 866 F.2d 402 (11th Cir.1989)—§ 3.10(b) n.52

Long, United States v., 852 F.2d 975 (7th Cir.1988)—§§ 6.2(c) n.92, 94; 21.4(d) n.120, 133

Long, United States v., 857 F.2d 436 (8th Cir.1988)—§ 11.10(b) n.45

Long, United States v., 524 F.2d 660 (9th Cir.1975)—§ 3.10(d) n.109

Long v. United States, 424 F.2d 799 (D.C.Cir.1969)—§ 7.3(d) n.78

Long, United States v., 323 F.2d 468 (6th Cir.1963)—§ 21.5(f) n.162

Longbehn, United States v., 850 F.2d 450 (8th Cir.1988)—§§ 6.6(e) n.65; 6.6(f) n.110; 6.8(a) n.22

Longhibler v. State, 832 S.W.2d 908 (Mo.1992)—§§ 24.8(f) n.104, 105, 113

Longhorn, State v., 310 Mont. 172, 49 P.3d 48 (2002)—§§ 18.2(e) n.79, 84

Longley, State v., 119 Me. 535, 112 A. 260 (1921)—§§ 16.1(b) n.38; 16.1(e) n.190

Longoria, United States v., 177 F.3d 1179 (10th Cir.1999)—§ 4.6(a) n.10

Longoria, United States v., 113 F.3d 975 (9th Cir.1997)—§ 21.4(c) n.66

Long, State ex rel. v. Justice Court, Lake County, 335 Mont. 219, 156 P.3d 5 (Mont.2007)—§§ 22.1(h) n.149; 27.4(d) n.58

Longworth, State v., 313 S.C. 360, 438 S.E.2d 219 (1993)—§ 23.2(c) n.62

Lonis v. State, 998 P.2d 441 (Alaska App.2000)—§ 16.3(g) n.101

Loo, State v., 94 Haw. 207, 10 P.3d 728 (2000)—§ 6.6(e) n.91

Looney v. State, 797 So.2d 429 (Ala.Crim.App.2001)—§ 21.6(a) n.30

Loosli, State v., 130 Idaho 398, 941 P.2d 1299 (Idaho 1997)—§ 6.6(d) n.50

Loper v. Beto, 405 U.S. 473, 92 S.Ct. 1014, 31 L.Ed.2d 374 (1972)—§ 11.1(a) n.27

Loper, State ex rel. v. Stack, 291 So.2d 207 (1974)—§ 12.4(a) n.29

Lopes, State v., 805 So.2d 124 (La.2001)—§ 24.2(g) n.97

Lopes, State v., 289 N.J.Super. 460, 673 A.2d 1379 (1995)—§ 13.6(c) n.42

Lopez, In re, 62 Cal.2d 368, 42 Cal.Rptr. 188, 398 P.2d 380 (1965)—§ 1.5(a) n.20

Lopez, Commonwealth v., 447 Mass. 625, 856 N.E.2d 163 (2006)—§ 21.6(c) n.118

Lopez, Commonwealth v., 426 Mass. 657, 690 N.E.2d 809 (1998)—§ 21.4(e) n.161

Lopez v. Davis, 531 U.S. 230, 121 S.Ct. 714, 148 L.Ed.2d 635 (2001)—§ 26.2(c) n.54

Lopez v. Department of Justice, 393 F.3d 1345 (D.C. Cir.2005)—§ 8.5(c) n.86

Lopez, People v., 6 N.Y.3d 248, 811 N.Y.S.2d 623, 844 N.E.2d 1145 (2006)—§§ 21.2(b) n.76, 79

Lopez, People v., 16 App.Div.3d 258, 791 N.Y.S.2d 111 (2005)—§ 27.5(c) n.63

Lopez v. People, 113 P.3d 713 (Colo.2005)—§ 26.4(i) n.201

Lopez, People v., 155 Cal.App.3d 813, 202 Cal.Rptr. 333 (1984)—§§ 22.5(d) n.34, 36

Lopez, People v., 41 Colo.App. 206, 587 P.2d 792 (1978)—§ 18.4(d) n.85

Lopez, People v., 71 Cal.App.3d 568, 138 Cal.Rptr. 36 (1977)—§§ 11.5(c) n.35, 36, 39, 42

Lopez, People v., 60 Cal.2d 223, 32 Cal.Rptr. 424, 384 P.2d 16 (1963)—§§ 6.2(a) n.13; 20.3(l) n.225

Lopez, State v., 138 N.M. 521, 123 P.3d 754 (N.M.2005)—§ 26.4(i) n.188

Lopez, State v., 269 Conn. 799, 850 A.2d 143 (2004)—§ 21.4(c) n.92

Lopez v. State, 888 So.2d 693 (Fla.App.2004)—§ 20.2(e) n.95

Lopez, State v., 78 Hawai'i 433, 896 P.2d 889 (1995)—§ 9.3(e) n.80

Lopez, State v., 886 P.2d 1105 (Utah 1994)—§ 7.4(e) n.93

Lopez v. State, 105 Nev. 68, 769 P.2d 1276 (1989)—§ 24.9(f) n.97

Lopez v. State, 536 So.2d 226 (Fla.1988)—§ 21.2(d) n.242

Lopez v. Thompson, 202 F.3d 1110 (9th Cir.2000)—§ 11.5(c) n.50

Lopez, United States v., 474 F.3d 1208 (9th Cir.2007)—§ 13.5(a) n.6

Lopez, United States v., 437 F.3d 1059 (10th Cir.2006)—§§ 6.2(c) n.113; 9.5(c) n.65

Lopez, United States v., 443 F.3d 1280 (10th Cir.2006)—§ 3.8(c) n.73

Lopez, United States v., 385 F.3d 245 (2d Cir.2004)—§ 21.5(a) n.13

Lopez, United States v., 300 F.3d 46 (1st Cir.2002)—§§ 4.6(e) n.97, 117

Lopez, United States v., 106 F.3d 309 (9th Cir.1997)—§ 11.8(b) n.42

Lopez, United States v., 514 U.S. 549, 115 S.Ct. 1624, 131 L.Ed.2d 626 (1995)—§§ 1.2(b) n.4; 1.2(c) n.117, 126, 128, 138, 157; 1.2(d) n.202; 2.5(f) n.55

Lopez, United States v., 4 F.3d 1455 (9th Cir.1993)—§§ 11.6(a) n.7; 11.8(b) n.37, 38

Lopez, United States v., 6 F.3d 1281 (7th Cir.1993)—§§ 17.2(c) n.82, 88

Lopez, United States v., 779 F.Supp. 13 (S.D.N.Y.1991)—§§ 8.5(d) n.135; 8.5(h) n.247

Lopez, United States v., 761 F.2d 632 (11th Cir.1985)—§ 9.1(c) n.101

Lopez, United States v., 581 F.2d 1338 (9th Cir.1978)—§§ 22.1(e) n.88; 22.1(h) n.160

Lopez, United States v., 328 F.Supp. 1077 (E.D.N.Y.1971)—§ 3.9(h) n.152

Lopez v. United States, 373 U.S. 427, 83 S.Ct. 1381, 10 L.Ed.2d 462 (1963)—§§ 3.2(j) n.236; 3.10(c) n.91; 4.6(l) n.196

Lopez v. Wilson, 426 F.3d 339 (6th Cir.2005)—§§ 11.1(b) n.71, 83

Lopez-Arias, United States v., 344 F.3d 623 (6th Cir.2003)—§ 3.8(b) n.28

Lopez-Armenta, United States v., 400 F.3d 1173 (9th Cir.2005)—§ 21.2(b) n.79

Lopez-Gonzales, United States v., 688 F.2d 1275 (9th Cir.1982)—§ 26.3(g) n.74

Lopez-Gutierrez, United States v., 83 F.3d 1235 (10th Cir.1996)—§§ 15.6(b) n.78; 15.6(f) n.186, 187; 15.7(b) n.30

Lopez-Lopez, United States v., 282 F.3d 1 (1st Cir.2002)—§ 7.4(f) n.101

Lopez-Martinez, United States v., 725 F.2d 471 (9th Cir.1984)—§ 9.6(c) n.66

Lopez-Soto, United States v., 205 F.3d 1101 (9th Cir.2000)—§ 3.1(d) n.117

Lord, In re, 152 Wash.2d 182, 94 P.3d 952 (2004)—§§ 21.2(d) n.167; 21.2(e) n.297

Lord v. Kelley, 223 F.Supp. 684 (D.Mass.1963)—§ 10.1(c) n.34

Lord, State v., 128 Wash.App. 216, 114 P.3d 1241 (2005)—§ 24.2(e) n.79

Lord v. State, 107 Nev. 28, 806 P.2d 548 (1991)—§ 17.2(b) n.49

Lord, State v., 117 Wash.2d 829, 822 P.2d 177 (1991)—§§ 26.4(g) n.140, 146

Lord, United States v., 711 F.2d 887 (9th Cir.1983)—§ 24.3(i) n.190

Lordan, State v., 116 N.H. 479, 363 A.2d 201 (1976)—§ 21.2(d) n.229

Lorenz, State v., 152 Wash.2d 22, 93 P.3d 133 (2004)—§§ 6.6(a) n.7; 6.6(c) n.31; 6.6(e) n.61

Lorenz, State v., 622 N.W.2d 243 (S.D.2001)—§§ 3.2(c) n.108, 135

Lorenzana v. Superior Court, 9 Cal.3d 626, 108 Cal.Rptr. 585, 511 P.2d 33 (1973)—§ 3.2(c) n.110

Lorenzini, United States v., 71 F.3d 1489 (9th Cir.1995)—§ 26.9(b) n.28

Lorenzo, United States v., 995 F.2d 1448 (9th Cir.1993)—§ 22.5(d) n.30

Los Alamos, County of v. Tapia, 109 N.M. 736, 790 P.2d 1017 (1990)—§§ 25.3(a) n.7; 25.3(c) n.28

Los Angeles, City of v. Heller, 475 U.S. 796, 106 S.Ct. 1571, 89 L.Ed.2d 806 (1986)—§ 3.1(k) n.272

Los Angeles, City of v. Superior Court, 82 Cal.App.4th 819, 98 Cal.Rptr.2d 564 (2000)—§ 20.2(d) n.77

Los Angeles County, California v. Rettele, 127 S.Ct. 1989, 167 L.Ed.2d 974 (U.S. 2007)—§ 3.4(i) n.175

Los Angeles Police Protective League v. Gates, 907 F.2d 879 (9th Cir.1990)—§ 3.2(c) n.118

Los Angeles Times v. Superior Court, 114 Cal.App.4th 247, 7 Cal.Rptr.3d 524 (2003)—§§ 8.5(b) n.46, 54

Losavio v. Kikel, 187 Colo. 148, 529 P.2d 306 (1974)—§§ 8.3(g) n.33; 8.4(c) n.116

Losavio v. Mayber, 178 Colo. 184, 496 P.2d 1032 (1972)—§§ 22.3(b) n.73, 88

Losavio, People ex rel. v. J.L., 195 Colo. 494, 580 P.2d 23 (1978)—§§ 8.5(a) n.5; 8.14(d) n.60

Losey v. Frank, 268 F.Supp.2d 1066 (E.D.Wis.2003)—§ 25.4(b) n.19

Losing, United States v., 601 F.2d 351 (8th Cir.1979)—§ 11.2(d) n.138

Losson, State v., 262 Mont. 342, 865 P.2d 255 (1993)—§ 21.5(e) n.119

Lotsch, United States v., 102 F.2d 35 (2d Cir.1939)—§ 24.7(i) n.96

Lott, In re, 424 F.3d 446 (6th Cir.2005)—§§ 28.5(d) n.88; 28.10 n.1

Lott v. State, 150 P.3d 337, 334 Mont. 270 (2006)—§ 28.11(b) n.22

Lott v. State, 334 Mont. 270, 150 P.3d 337 (2006)—§ 28.11(b) n.20

Lott, State v., 152 N.H. 436, 879 A.2d 1167 (2005)—§ 4.6(l) n.205

Lott, United States v., 298 F.3d 969 (10th Cir.2002)—§ 19.3(a) n.104

Lott, United States v., 310 F.3d 1231 (10th Cir.2002)—§§ 11.4(b) n.35, 38, 41

Lott v. United States, 367 U.S. 421, 81 S.Ct. 1563, 6 L.Ed.2d 940 (1961)—§ 21.6(b) n.82

Lotter, State v., 266 Neb. 758, 669 N.W.2d 438 (2003)—§ 24.11(d) n.39

Lotter, State v., 255 Neb. 889, 587 N.W.2d 673 (1999)—§ 22.4(a) n.4

Loucious v. Sheriff, 94 Nev. 98, 575 P.2d 598 (1978)—§ 15.5(c) n.122

Louden, Commonwealth v., 569 Pa. 245, 803 A.2d 1181 (2002)—§§ 18.5(b) n.58, 65

Loud Hawk, United States v., 474 U.S. 302, 106 S.Ct. 648, 88 L.Ed.2d 640 (1986)—§§ 18.2(b) n.26; 18.2(c) n.57, 58; 18.5(c) n.78

Loud Hawk, United States v., 628 F.2d 1139 (9th Cir.1979)—§§ 20.6(b) n.59, 63, 66

Loudner, State v., 77 N.C.App. 453, 335 S.E.2d 78 (1985)—§ 19.6(b) n.19

Loughead, State v., 726 N.W.2d 859 (N.D.2007)—§ 6.6(e) n.91

Loughery, United States v., 908 F.2d 1014 (D.C.Cir.1990)—§§ 21.3(b) n.45, 60

Loui v. Board of Medical Examiners, 78 Hawai'i 21, 889 P.2d 705 (1995)— § 17.4(b) n.125

Louis v. C.I.R., 170 F.3d 1232 (9th Cir.1999)—§ 17.4(b) n.130

Louis, United States v., 814 F.2d 852 (2d Cir.1987)—§ 18.3(b) n.25

Louis Carreau, Inc., United States v., 42 F.R.D. 408 (S.D.N.Y.1967)— § 20.1(b) n.32

Louisell v. Director, 178 F.3d 1019 (8th Cir.1999)—§ 6.7(a) n.28

Louisiana ex rel. Francis v. Resweber, 329 U.S. 459, 67 S.Ct. 374, 91 L.Ed. 422 (1947)—§§ 1.5(h) n.290; 2.4(b) n.67; 2.4(e) n.158

Louisiana State Bar Ass'n v. Paige, 456 So.2d 990 (La.1984)—§ 21.4(a) n.22

Louissant, People v., 240 A.D.2d 433, 658 N.Y.S.2d 390 (1997)— § 15.7(b) n.19

Louis Trauth Dairy, Inc., United States v., 1994 WL 876373 (S.D.Ohio 1994)—§ 8.5(g) n.215

Louisville & Nashville Railroad v. Commonwealth, 175 Ky. 372, 194 S.W. 315 (Ky.1917)—§ 15.1(d) n.242

Louk, State v., 171 W.Va. 639, 301 S.E.2d 596 (W.Va.1983)—§ 8.5(h) n.245

Lourido, People v., 70 N.Y.2d 428, 522 N.Y.S.2d 98, 516 N.E.2d 1212 (1987)—§ 24.9(c) n.27

Louviere, State v., 833 So.2d 885 (La.2002)—§ 21.4(a) n.11

Loux v. United States, 389 F.2d 911 (9th Cir.1968)—§ 15.2(j) n.238

Lovaglia, United States v., 954 F.2d 811 (2d Cir.1992)—§ 21.2(d) n.186

Lovasco, United States v., 431 U.S. 783, 97 S.Ct. 2044, 52 L.Ed.2d 752 (1977)—§§ 2.7(a) n.19; 2.7(b) n.85; 2.7(c) n.128, 158, 203; 18.1(c) n.20; 18.5(b) n.54

Lovato v. New Mexico, 242 U.S. 199, 37 S.Ct. 107, 61 L.Ed. 244 (1916)— § 25.2(d) n.31

Love, People v., 24 Ill.App.3d 477, 321 N.E.2d 419 (1974)—§ 9.4(d) n.88

Love, People v., 56 Cal.2d 720, 16 Cal.Rptr. 777, 366 P.2d 33 (1961)— § 16.3(b) n.24

Love v. Reilly, 924 F.2d 1492 (9th Cir.1991)—§ 13.5(h) n.190

Love, State v., 88 S.W.3d 511 (Mo.App.2002)—§ 14.2(d) n.50

Love, State v., 227 Wis.2d 60, 594 N.W.2d 806 (1999)—§§ 11.9(d) n.178, 183

Love, State v., 267 Kan. 600, 986 P.2d 358 (1999)—§ 7.4(e) n.84

Love v. State, 468 N.E.2d 519 (Ind.1984)—§§ 13.4(a) n.24, 27; 13.4(b) n.33

Love v. State, 630 P.2d 21 (Alaska App.1981)—§ 21.5(a) n.23

Love v. State, 211 Miss. 606, 52 So.2d 470 (1951)—§ 19.3(a) n.54

Love, United States v., 767 F.2d 1052 (4th Cir.1985)—§ 9.6(a) n.48

Love, United States v., 746 F.2d 477 (9th Cir.1984)—§ 7.4(e) n.87

Love, United States v., 597 F.2d 81 (6th Cir.1979)—§ 25.3(b) n.18

Lovegren, State v., 310 Mont. 358, 51 P.3d 471 (2002)—§ 3.8(b) n.18

Lovelace v. Commonwealth, 258 Va. 588, 522 S.E.2d 856 (1999)— § 3.5(b) n.98

Lovelace v. Commonwealth, 272 Ky. 52, 113 S.W.2d 853 (1938)— § 15.2(h) n.190

Lovelace, State v., 140 Idaho 73, 90 P.3d 298 (2004)—§ 27.6(d) n.150

Lovelace, State v., 140 Idaho 53, 90 P.3d 278 (Idaho 2003)—§§ 19.3(a) n.42, 44

Lovelace, State v., 227 Kan. 348, 607 P.2d 49 (1980)—§ 16.1(g) n.247

Loveland v. Hatcher, 231 F.3d 640 (9th Cir.2000)—§ 28.4(c) n.27

Lovell v. City of Griffin, 303 U.S. 444, 58 S.Ct. 666, 82 L.Ed. 949 (1938)— § 2.5(c) n.25

Lovell v. State, 347 Md. 623, 702 A.2d 261 (1997)—§§ 21.2(b) n.53; 21.3(b) n.79; 21.4(c) n.70, 71; 22.2(d) n.77, 85; 24.2(e) n.57

Lovett v. State, 330 Ark. 33, 952 S.W.2d 644 (1997)—§ 19.5(b) n.10

Lovett, United States v., 328 U.S. 303, 66 S.Ct. 1073, 90 L.Ed. 1252 (1946)—§ 2.9(d) n.83

Loving, People v., 67 Cal.App.3d Supp. 12, 136 Cal.Rptr. 851 (1977)—§ 25.2(d) n.26

Lovins, State v., 177 Or.App. 534, 33 P.3d 1060 (2001)—§ 24.7(b) n.19

Lovitt v. True, 403 F.3d 171 (4th Cir.2005)—§§ 24.3(b) n.53; 24.3(e) n.120

Lovitz, People v., 127 Ill.App.3d 390, 82 Ill.Dec. 356, 468 N.E.2d 1010 (1984)—§ 11.10(c) n.77

L.O.W. v. District Court, 623 P.2d 1253 (Colo.1981)—§§ 12.4(b) n.48, 53

Low, United States v., 887 F.2d 232 (9th Cir.1989)—§ 3.8(c) n.89

Lowe v. Duckworth, 663 F.2d 42 (7th Cir.1981)—§ 28.5(a) n.19

Lowe, People v., 969 P.2d 746 (Colo.App.1998)—§§ 20.4(c) n.48, 50; 20.5(b) n.25

Lowe v. State, 650 So.2d 969 (Fla.1994)—§ 6.10(b) n.13

Lowe v. State, 805 S.W.2d 368 (Tenn.1991)—§ 26.4(i) n.166

Lowe v. State, 14 Kan.App.2d 119, 783 P.2d 1313 (1989)—§ 18.5(a) n.51

Lowe, State v., 21 W.Va. 782, 45 Am.Rep. 570 (1883)—§§ 16.1(c) n.118; 16.1(e) n.192

Lowe, United States v., 654 F.2d 562 (9th Cir.1981)—§ 26.9(b) n.57

Lowe-Bey v. Groose, 28 F.3d 816 (8th Cir.1994)—§§ 11.7(e) n.71, 95

Lowenburg v. United States, 156 F.2d 22 (10th Cir.1946)—§ 19.3(a) n.71

Lowenfield v. Phelps, 484 U.S. 231, 108 S.Ct. 546, 98 L.Ed.2d 568 (1988)—§ 24.9(d) n.46

Lowery v. Anderson, 138 F.Supp.2d 1123 (S.D.Ind.2001)—§ 11.2(b) n.75

Lowery v. Cardwell, 575 F.2d 727 (9th Cir.1978)—§ 11.6(a) n.22

Lowery v. City of Boaz, 393 So.2d 534 (Ala.Cr.App.1981)—§§ 1.8(d) n.58, 78

Lowery, Commonwealth v., 305 Pa.Super. 66, 451 A.2d 245 (1982)—§ 3.10(d) n.124

Lowery v. State, 547 N.E.2d 1046 (Ind.1989)—§ 22.3(a) n.43

Lowery v. State, 499 S.W.2d 160 (Tex.Cr.App.1973)—§ 3.10(b) n.37

Lowery, United States v., 166 F.3d 1119 (11th Cir.1999)—§§ 1.7(j) n.261 to 263; 6.4(e) n.91; 21.2(b) n.74

Lowe, State ex rel. v. Nelson, 202 So.2d 232 (Fla.App.1967)—§ 8.10(d) n.88

Lowrey v. State, 705 So.2d 1367 (Fla.1998)—§ 22.3(c) n.162

Lowry, State v., 295 Or. 337, 667 P.2d 996 (Or.1983)—§§ 2.12(a) n.31, 43; 2.12(c) n.168

Lowry, United States v., 971 F.2d 55 (7th Cir.1992)—§ 11.9(c) n.126

Lowther, State v., 434 N.W.2d 747 (S.D.1989)—§ 3.9(e) n.75

Loyal, State v., 386 N.J.Super. 162, 899 A.2d 1009 (N.J.Sup.2006)—§ 24.7(d) n.35

Loyal, State v., 164 N.J. 418, 753 A.2d 1073 (2000)—§ 11.9(c) n.105

Loyd, State v., 269 Neb. 762, 696 N.W.2d 860 (2005)—§ 27.2(c) n.57

Loyd, State v., 425 So.2d 710 (La.1982)—§ 6.10(b) n.30

Loyd, United States v., 743 F.2d 1555 (11th Cir.1984)—§§ 17.3(e) n.64; 24.3(c) n.102

Loye, State v., 670 N.W.2d 141 (Iowa 2003)—§§ 21.2(b) n.79; 21.4(d) n.103

Loyer, People v., 169 Mich.App. 105, 425 N.W.2d 714 (1988)—§ 24.3(f) n.143

Lozada v. Deeds, 964 F.2d 956 (9th Cir.1992)—§§ 11.6(d)   n.119; 11.10(d) n.192

Lozada v. Warden, 223 Conn. 834, 613 A.2d 818 (1992)—§ 11.7(a) n.10

Lozano, State v., 76 Wash.App. 116, 882 P.2d 1191 (1994)—§ 9.5(b) n.44

Lozano, State v., 616 So.2d 73 (Fla.App.1993)—§§ 16.3(g) n.108, 109

Luanglath, State v., 863 A.2d 631 (R.I.2005)—§§ 22.1(h)   n.156; 24.9(d) n.40

Lucas, Commonwealth v., 195 S.W.3d 403 (Ky.2006)—§ 6.6(d) n.56

Lucas, People v., 12 Cal.4th 415, 48 Cal.Rptr.2d 525, 907 P.2d 373 (1995)—§ 13.2(a) n.5

Lucas, People v., 132 Ill.2d 399, 139 Ill.Dec. 447, 548 N.E.2d 1003 (1989)—§§ 6.9(f) n.135; 9.6(a) n.38

Lucas v. State, 274 Ga. 640, 555 S.E.2d 440 (2001)—§ 22.3(c) n.153

Lucas, State v., 353 N.C. 568, 548 S.E.2d 712 (2001)—§ 19.3(a) n.38

Lucas v. State, 273 Ga. 88, 538 S.E.2d 44 (2000)—§ 6.9(g) n.166

Lucas, State v., 23 Kan.App.2d 5, 926 P.2d 242 (1996)—§ 24.2(a) n.11

Lucas v. Turner, 725 F.2d 1095 (7th Cir.1984)—§§ 8.5(h) n.247, 269

Lucas, United States v., 429 F.3d 1154 (7th Cir.2005)—§ 21.4(f) n.192

Lucas v. United States, 963 F.2d 8 (2d Cir.1992)—§ 21.5(c) n.74

Lucas, United States v., 932 F.2d 1210 (8th Cir.1991)—§ 19.3(e) n.244

Lucas v. United States, 408 F.2d 835 (9th Cir.1969)—§§ 6.6(e)   n.69; 6.6(f) n.106

Luce v. United States, 469 U.S. 38, 105 S.Ct. 460, 83 L.Ed.2d 443 (1984)—§ 24.5(d) n.53

Lucente, People v., 116 Ill.2d 133, 107 Ill.Dec. 214, 506 N.E.2d 1269 (1987)—§ 3.4(d) n.63

Lucero v. Gunter, 17 F.3d 1347 (10th Cir.1994)—§ 3.9(i) n.185

Lucero v. Kerby, 133 F.3d 1299 (10th Cir.1998)—§ 6.2(c) n.127

Lucero v. Kerby, 7 F.3d 1520 (10th Cir.1993)—§ 21.2(d) n.227

Luciano, State v., 739 A.2d 222 (R.I.1999)—§ 7.4(e) n.86

Luciano v. State, 906 S.W.2d 523 (Tex.Cr.App.1995)—§ 27.5(c) n.74

Luciano, United States v., 414 F.3d 174 (1st Cir.2005)—§ 26.4(f) n.93

Lucido v. Superior Court, 51 Cal.3d 335, 272 Cal.Rptr. 767, 795 P.2d 1223 (1990)—§§ 17.4(a)   n.31,   66; 26.10(d) n.98

Lucious, State v., 271 Ga. 361, 518 S.E.2d 677 (1999)—§ 20.4(g) n.109

Luck, State v., 15 Ohio St.3d 150, 472 N.E.2d 1097 (1984)—§ 6.4(f) n.115

Luckett v. State, 259 Ind. 174, 284 N.E.2d 738 (1972)—§ 3.8(d) n.131

Luckhart v. State, 736 N.E.2d 227 (Ind.2000)—§ 6.2(c) n.125

Ludlow v. State, 761 P.2d 1293 (Okla.Crim.1988)—§ 11.6(a) n.49

Ludwick, State v., 197 W.Va. 70, 475 S.E.2d 70 (1996)—§ 24.5(a) n.17

Ludwig v. Massachusetts, 427 U.S. 618, 96 S.Ct. 2781, 49 L.Ed.2d 732 (1976)—§§ 2.6(c) n.83; 22.1(f) n.92

Ludwig, State v., 124 Wis.2d 600, 369 N.W.2d 722 (1985)—§ 21.3(b) n.107

Lue, United States v., 134 F.3d 79 (2d Cir.1998)—§ 1.7(c) n.13

Lueck, United States v., 678 F.2d 895 (11th Cir.1982)—§ 6.6(e) n.93

Luepke, United States v., 495 F.3d 443 (7th Cir.2007)—§§ 26.3(g) n.94; 26.4(g) n.141; 27.6(b) n.21

Lueth, United States v., 807 F.2d 719 (8th Cir.1986)—§ 3.4(d) n.58

Lufkins v. Solem, 716 F.2d 532 (8th Cir.1983)—§ 10.5(b) n.18

Lugo, Commonwealth v., 406 Mass. 565, 548 N.E.2d 1263 (1990)—§ 24.3(g) n.170

Lugo v. Munoz, 682 F.2d 7 (1st Cir.1982)—§ 24.3(b) n.62

Lugo, United States v., 361 F.Supp.2d 91 (E.D.N.Y.2005)—§ 24.2(a) n.11

Lugo, United States v., 978 F.2d 631 (10th Cir.1992)—§§ 3.7(a) n.13; 3.7(e) n.111, 122

Luisi, United States v., 482 F.3d 43 (1st Cir.2007)—§ 5.1(c) n.37

Lujan, United States v., 324 F.3d 27 (1st Cir.2003)—§ 21.2(d) n.165

Lujano-Perez, United States v., 274 F.3d 219 (5th Cir.2001)—§§ 21.4(c) n.66; 21.5(c) n.83

Lujan, United States ex rel. v. Gengler, 510 F.2d 62 (2d Cir.1975)—§ 3.1(j) n.245

Luke, State v., 134 Idaho 294, 1 P.3d 795 (2000)—§§ 6.2(c) n.107; 6.8(d) n.84

Lukehart v. State, 776 So.2d 906 (Fla.2000)—§§ 6.2(c) n.151; 6.7(c) n.131; 6.9(f) n.139

Luken v. Scott, 71 F.3d 192 (5th Cir.1995)—§ 26.2(c) n.63

Luker, United States v., 395 F.3d 830 (8th Cir.2003)—§ 6.7(b) n.86

Lukity, People v., 460 Mich. 484, 596 N.W.2d 607 (1999)—§ 27.6(b) n.42

Lukse, United States v., 286 F.3d 906 (6th Cir.2002)—§ 21.2(d) n.266

Luloff, United States v., 15 F.3d 763 (8th Cir.1994)—§ 27.2(c) n.59

Lumitap, United States v., 111 F.3d 81 (9th Cir.1997)—§ 24.2(b) n.29

Luna, Commonwealth v., 410 Mass. 131, 571 N.E.2d 603 (1991)— § 10.5(f) n.68

Luna v. Massachusetts, 354 F.3d 108 (1st Cir.2004)—§ 6.2(c) n.185

Luna v. Pico, 356 F.3d 481 (2d Cir.2004)—§ 6.8(b) n.57

Luna v. Russell, 70 Ohio St.3d 561, 639 N.E.2d 1168 (1994)—§ 27.4(f) n.67

Luna v. State, 788 N.E.2d 832 (Ind.2003)—§ 6.6(d) n.48

Luna, United States v., 165 F.3d 316 (5th Cir.1999)—§§ 1.2(c) n.145, 147

Lundberg, Commonwealth v., 422 Pa.Super. 495, 619 A.2d 1066 (1993)—§ 26.3(f) n.57

Lundgren, State v., 653 N.E.2d 304, 73 Ohio St.3d 474 (1995)—§ 24.7(i) n.90

Lung v. State, 420 P.2d 158 (Okla.Crim.App.1966)—§ 6.7(d) n.143

Lupi v. Commonwealth, 434 Mass. 1018, 750 N.E.2d 1013 (2001)— § 25.1(d) n.49

Lupino v. United States, 268 F.2d 799 (8th Cir.1959)—§ 1.2(c) n.116

Luros, United States v., 243 F.Supp. 160 (N.D.Iowa 1965)—§ 16.3(c) n.28

Lurry, People v., 77 Ill.App.3d 108, 32 Ill.Dec. 853, 395 N.E.2d 1234 (1979)—§ 24.7(g) n.80

Lusk, State v., 37 P.3d 1103 (Utah 2001)—§ 18.5(a) n.45

Lussier, United States v., 71 F.3d 456 (2d Cir.1995)—§§ 11.9(c) n.126, 131, 132, 140; 11.9(d) n.206

Luster v. State, 515 So.2d 1177 (Miss.1987)—§ 22.3(e) n.284

Lustig v. United States, 338 U.S. 74, 69 S.Ct. 1372, 93 L.Ed. 1819 (1949)— § 3.1(i) n.231

Lutes v. State, 517 So.2d 541 (Miss.1987)—§ 23.2(a) n.46

Luton, State v., 83 Hawai'i 443, 927 P.2d 844 (1996)—§§ 6.2(c) n.152; 6.4(e) n.63, 77

Lutry, State v., 938 S.W.2d 431 (Tenn.Crim.App.1996)—§ 13.6(c) n.41

Lutz, Commonwealth v., 508 Pa. 297, 495 A.2d 928 (1985)—§§ 13.6(c) n.27, 28

Luv Pharmacy, State v., 118 N.H. 398, 388 A.2d 190 (1978)—§ 16.4(c) n.83

Luxenberg, United States v., 374 F.2d 241 (6th Cir.1967)—§ 8.10(d) n.87

Lybarger, State v., 165 S.W.3d 180 (Mo.App.2005)—§§ 18.4(c) n.41, 43

Lydia v. State, 109 S.W.3d 495 (Tex.Cr.App.2003)—§ 22.3(a) n.5

Lyell v. Renico, 470 F.3d 1177 (6th Cir.2006)—§ 22.4(a) n.15

Lykins v. State, 288 Md. 71, 415 A.2d 1113 (1980)—§ 15.7(c) n.53

Lyles v. Estelle, 658 F.2d 1015 (5th Cir.1981)—§ 11.5(d) n.77

Lyman, State v., 230 Neb. 457, 432 N.W.2d 43 (1988)—§ 21.4(d) n.106

Lynce v. Mathis, 519 U.S. 433, 117 S.Ct. 891, 137 L.Ed.2d 63 (1997)—§ 26.1(e) n.96

Lynch, People v., 95 N.Y.2d 243, 715 N.Y.S.2d 691, 738 N.E.2d 1172 (2000)—§§ 22.1(g) n.108; 22.3(c) n.107, 128, 157

Lynch, People v., 410 Mich. 343, 301 N.W.2d 796 (1981)—§ 13.5(c) n.72

Lynch, State v., 330 Mont. 74, 125 P.3d 1148 (2005)—§ 13.7(a) n.5

Lynch v. State, 877 So.2d 1254 (Miss.2004)—§ 22.3(d) n.249

Lynch, State v., 98 Ohio St.3d 514, 787 N.E.2d 1185 (2003)—§§ 6.6(d) n.48; 6.6(e) n.61

Lynch, State v., 770 A.2d 840 (R.I.2001)—§ 7.4(e) n.82

Lynch, State v., 248 Neb. 234, 533 N.W.2d 905 (1995)—§ 27.2(c) n.62

Lynch, State v., 655 So.2d 470 (La.App.1995)—§ 14.3(d) n.102

Lynch, State v., 796 P.2d 1150 (Okla.1990)—§ 11.8(c) n.65

Lynch, State v., 79 N.J. 327, 399 A.2d 629 (1979)—§ 2.12(d) n.189

Lynch, State v., 528 S.W.2d 454 (Mo.App.1975)—§ 9.4(d) n.79

Lynch, United States v., 181 F.3d 330 (2d Cir.1999)—§ 25.3(c) n.20

Lynch, United States v., 162 F.3d 732 (2d Cir.1998)—§§ 25.3(c) n.25, 30

Lynch, United States v., 934 F.2d 1226 (11th Cir.1991)—§ 3.1(f) n.153

Lynch v. United States, 557 A.2d 580 (D.C.App.1989)—§ 12.3(a) n.6

Lynch v. United States, 534 A.2d 658 (D.C.App.1987)—§ 12.3(d) n.113

Lynde, In re, 922 F.2d 1448 (10th Cir.1991)—§ 8.5(h) n.266

Lynn, People v., 89 Ill.App.3d 712, 44 Ill.Dec. 939, 412 N.E.2d 15 (1980)—§ 22.5(a) n.12

Lynn v. Reinstein, 205 Ariz. 186, 68 P.3d 412 (Ariz.2003)—§ 26.5(d) n.74

Lynn v. United States, 365 F.3d 1225 (11th Cir.2004)—§ 28.9(b) n.39

Lynn v. West, 134 F.3d 582 (4th Cir.1998)—§ 17.4(b) n.138

Lynumn v. Illinois, 372 U.S. 528, 83 S.Ct. 917, 9 L.Ed.2d 922 (1963)—§§ 6.2(c) n.97, 164

Lyons, Commonwealth v., 409 Mass. 16, 564 N.E.2d 390 (1990)—§ 2.12(c) n.178

Lyons v. Oklahoma, 322 U.S. 596, 64 S.Ct. 1208, 88 L.Ed. 1481 (1944)—§§ 6.2(b) n.36; 9.5(c) n.59

Lyons v. Pearce, 298 Or. 569, 694 P.2d 978 (1985)—§ 21.4(a) n.39

Lyons v. State, 105 Nev. 317, 775 P.2d 219 (1989)—§ 21.4(f) n.198

Lyons v. State, 787 P.2d 460 (Okl.Crim.App. 1989)—§ 3.1(d) n.109

Lyons, United States v., 352 F.Supp.2d 1231 (M.D.Fla.2004)—§ 24.3(b) n.74

Lyons v. United States, 833 A.2d 481 (D.C.App.2003)—§§ 7.4(b) n.23, 24

Lyons, United States v., 898 F.2d 210 (1st Cir.1990)—§§ 3.2(c) n.114; 21.6(c) n.118

Lyons, State ex rel. v. Dep't of Health & Social Services, 105 Wis.2d 146, 312 N.W.2d 868 (1981)—§ 26.10(a) n.5

Lytle, State v., 715 S.W.2d 910 (Mo.1986)—§ 6.2(c) n.146

M

M., In re, 3 Cal.3d 16, 89 Cal.Rptr. 33, 473 P.2d 737 (1970)—§§ 12.4(b) n.45, 52

Maag v. Wessler, 960 F.2d 773 (9th Cir.1991)—§ 3.5(a) n.22

Maass, State v., 178 Wis.2d 63, 502 N.W.2d 913 (Wis.App.1993)—§ 27.3(c) n.44

Mabra, State v., 61 Wis.2d 613, 213 N.W.2d 545 (1974)—§ 9.2(b) n.10

Mabry v. Johnson, 467 U.S. 504, 104 S.Ct. 2543, 81 L.Ed.2d 437 (1984)—§§ 2.7(a) n.31; 21.2(f) n.387; 28.3(a) n.7

M.A.C., In re, 761 A.2d 32 (D.C.App.2000)—§§ 6.9(b) n.24; 7.4(f) n.96

M.A.C. v. Harrison County Family Court, 566 So.2d 472 (Miss.1990)—§ 6.9(b) n.22

MacCallum, People v., 925 P.2d 758 (Colo.1996)—§ 27.3(c) n.48

Maccini, United States v., 721 F.2d 840 (1st Cir.1983)—§ 24.7(a) n.10

MacCollom, United States v., 426 U.S. 317, 96 S.Ct. 2086, 48 L.Ed.2d 666 (1976)—§§ 11.2(d) n.120, 136; 28.11(a) n.7

MacDonald v. Musick, 425 F.2d 373 (9th Cir.1970)—§ 13.5(a) n.18

MacDonald v. State, 778 A.2d 1064 (Del.2001)—§§ 21.2(b) n.54, 83; 21.3(b) n.54

MacDonald, State v., 129 N.H. 13, 523 A.2d 35 (1986)—§ 3.10(f) n.193

MacDonald, United States v., 456 U.S. 1, 102 S.Ct. 1497, 71 L.Ed.2d 696 (1982)—§§ 2.9(c) n.51; 18.1(c) n.31; 18.2(b) n.23

MacDonald, United States v., 435 U.S. 850, 98 S.Ct. 1547, 56 L.Ed.2d 18 (1978)—§§ 21.6(b) n.104; 27.2(c) n.34

Mace, State v., 921 P.2d 1372 (Utah 1996)—§ 21.6(b) n.84

Maceo, United States v., 873 F.2d 1 (1st Cir.1989)—§§ 15.5(b) n.54, 92; 15.7(e) n.110

Mace, State ex rel. v. Circuit Court, 193 Wis.2d 208, 532 N.W.2d 720 (1995)—§ 27.4(c) n.25

MacFarlane v. Walter, 179 F.3d 1131 (9th Cir.1999)—§ 12.2(b) n.27

Mach v. Stewart, 137 F.3d 630 (9th Cir.1997)—§ 27.6(d) n.142

Machado, United States v., 195 F.3d 454 (9th Cir.1999)—§ 22.3(d) n.173

Machetti v. Linahan, 679 F.2d 236 (11th Cir.1982)—§§ 15.4(d) n.123, 124

Machia, State v., 155 Vt. 192, 583 A.2d 556 (1990)—§ 22.1(h) n.156

Machibroda v. United States, 368 U.S. 487, 82 S.Ct. 510, 7 L.Ed.2d 473 (1962)—§§ 28.9(b) n.63, 64

Machor, United States v., 879 F.2d 945 (1st Cir.1989)—§§ 24.4(d) n.44; 24.7(f) n.78

Machuca-Barrera, United States v., 261 F.3d 425 (5th Cir.2001)—§ 3.9(f) n.118

Macino, United States v., 486 F.2d 750 (7th Cir.1973)—§ 18.2(c) n.31

Mack, People v., 190 Mich.App. 7, 475 N.W.2d 830 (1991)—§ 11.2(f) n.250

Mack, People v., 105 Ill.2d 103, 85 Ill.Dec. 281, 473 N.E.2d 880 (1984)—§§ 21.3(c) n.152; 21.3(f) n.362

Mack v. Peters, 80 F.3d 230 (7th Cir.1996)—§ 17.2(c) n.84

Mack, State v., 903 S.W.2d 623 (Mo.Ct.App.1995)—§ 16.1(h) n.285

Mack v. State, 375 So.2d 476 (Ala.App.1981)—§ 20.2(a) n.6

Mack, United States v., 258 F.3d 548 (6th Cir.2001)—§ 21.5(a) n.59

Mack, United States v., 669 F.2d 28 (1st Cir.1982)—§ 18.3(b) n.14

Mack, United States v., 249 F.2d 321 (7th Cir.1957)—§ 17.3(a) n.8

Mackall v. Angelone, 131 F.3d 442 (4th Cir.1997)—§ 11.1(b) n.83

Mackell v. Palermo, 59 Misc.2d 760, 300 N.Y.S.2d 459 (1969)—§ 7.2(d) n.57

MacKenzie, United States v., 601 F.2d 221 (5th Cir.1979)—§ 6.10(e) n.71

Mackey v. Montrym, 443 U.S. 1, 99 S.Ct. 2612, 61 L.Ed.2d 321 (1979)—§ 1.5(c) n.125

Mackey v. State, 357 S.C. 666, 595 S.E.2d 241 (2004)—§ 13.3(c) n.35

Mackey, State v., 553 S.W.2d 337 (Tenn.1977)—§§ 1.7(i) n.202, 206

Mackey, United States v., 114 F.3d 470 (4th Cir.1997)—§ 27.6(d) n.96

Mackey, United States v., 117 F.3d 24 (1st Cir.1997)—§ 24.3(i) n.190

Mackey, United States v., 405 F.Supp. 854 (E.D.N.Y.1975)—§ 15.7(d) n.82

Mackey, United States v., 474 F.2d 55 (4th Cir.1973)—§ 7.4(f) n.106

Mackey v. United States, 401 U.S. 667, 91 S.Ct. 1160, 28 L.Ed.2d 404 (1971)—§§ 2.11(c) n.42; 2.11(e) n.53; 28.1(a) n.3; 28.6(e) n.38

Mackin v. United States, 117 U.S. 348, 6 S.Ct. 777, 29 L.Ed. 909 (1886)—§§ 15.1(b) n.30, 63; 15.1(d) n.142, 214

Mackins, United States v., 218 F.3d 263 (3d Cir.2000)—§ 21.4(f) n.208

Macklin, United States v., 900 F.2d 948 (6th Cir.1990)—§ 6.2(c) n.178

Macklin, United States v., 902 F.2d 1320 (8th Cir.1990)—§ 10.5(f) n.62

Macklin, United States v., 523 F.2d 193 (2d Cir.1975)—§§ 8.8(i) n.190; 15.4(i) n.215; 15.6(f) n.200

Mackrill v. State, 100 P.3d 361 (Wyo.2004)—§§ 6.7(b) n.75, 87

MacLean v. State Board of Retirement, 432 Mass. 339, 733 N.E.2d 1053 (2000)—§§ 17.4(b) n.118, 127

MacNeill, Commonwealth v., 399 Mass. 71, 502 N.E.2d 938 (1987)—§ 6.9(b) n.23

Macomber v. Hannigan, 15 F.3d 155 (10th Cir.1994)—§ 26.8(c) n.24

Macon Telegraph Publishing Company, In re, 900 F.Supp. 489 (M.D.Ga.1995)—§§ 23.1(d) n.197, 199, 201, 213

MacPheat v. Mahoney, 299 Mont. 46, 997 P.2d 753 (2000)—§ 12.2(b) n.27

MacWade v. Kelly, 460 F.3d 260 (2d Cir.2006)—§ 3.9(h) n.170

Macy, State ex rel. v. Owens, 934 P.2d 343 (Okla.Cr.App.1997)—§ 27.4(d) n.51

Maday, State v., 179 Wis.2d 346, 507 N.W.2d 365 (App.1993)—§ 20.4(b) n.42

Maddocks, State v., 80 N.J. 98, 402 A.2d 224 (1979)—§ 13.6(c) n.43

Maddox v. Elzie, 238 F.3d 437 (D.C.Cir.2001)—§ 13.5(a) n.5

Maddox v. State, 278 Ga. 823, 607 S.E.2d 587 (2005)—§ 21.5(a) n.24

Maddox, United States v., 388 F.3d 1356 (10th Cir.2004)—§ 3.6(d) n.101

Maddox, United States v., 48 F.3d 555 (D.C.Cir.1995)—§§ 21.4(a) n.12; 21.4(f) n.215

Maddox, United States v., 492 F.2d 104 (5th Cir.1974)—§ 5.1(c) n.25

Madeley v. State, 488 S.W.2d 416 (Tex.Cr.App.1972)—§ 3.7(a) n.7

Madeoy, United States v., 652 F.Supp. 371 (D.D.C.1987)—§ 19.4(b) n.24

Mader, United States v., 251 F.3d 1099 (6th Cir.2001)—§ 21.5(a) n.11

Madera, State v., 198 Conn. 92, 503 A.2d 136 (1985)—§ 21.6(b) n.112

Madison v. Parker, 104 F.3d 765 (5th Cir.1997)—§ 26.2(c) n.62

Madison, People v., 121 Ill.2d 195, 117 Ill.Dec. 213, 520 N.E.2d 374 (1988)—§ 3.1(c) n.61

Madison, State v., 163 Vt. 360, 658 A.2d 536 (1995)—§ 27.5(e) n.180

Madison, State v., 109 N.J. 223, 536 A.2d 254 (1988)—§§ 7.4(c) n.61; 7.4(e) n.90

Madison, State v., 64 Ohio St.2d 322, 415 N.E.2d 272 (1980)—§ 14.1(d) n.67

Madoch, United States v., 149 F.3d 596 (7th Cir.1998)—§ 6.6(e) n.65

Madrid v. State, 910 P.2d 1340 (Wyo.1996)—§§ 14.1(b) n.32; 14.4(d) n.83

Madrid, State v., 108 Idaho 736, 702 P.2d 308 (1985)—§ 24.8(e) n.69

Madrid, State v., 91 N.M. 375, 574 P.2d 594 (1978)—§ 3.10(d) n.108

Madrigal v. Bagley, 413 F.3d 548 (6th Cir.2005)—§ 28.6(g) n.90

Madril v. Superior Court, 15 Cal.3d 73, 123 Cal.Rptr. 465, 539 P.2d 33 (1975)—§ 10.6(c) n.30

Madruga-Jiminez, State v., 485 So.2d 462 (Fla.App.1986)—§ 9.5(b) n.39

Madson, People v., 638 P.2d 18 (Colo.1981)—§ 3.8(g) n.241

Maestas v. State, 987 S.W.2d 59 (Tex.Cr.App.1999)—§ 6.9(f) n.101

Maestas, United States v., 2 F.3d 1485 (10th Cir.1993)—§§ 10.3(b) n.17, 18

Maestras, State v., 332 Mont. 140, 136 P.3d 514 (2006)—§ 6.9(g) n.166

Maez, United States v., 872 F.2d 1444 (10th Cir.1989)—§ 3.6(a) n.38

Magallanez, United States v., 408 F.3d 672 (10th Cir.2005)—§ 26.4(h) n.154

Magana v. Hofbauer, 263 F.3d 542 (6th Cir.2001)—§ 11.10(d) n.178

Magana, United States v., 127 F.3d 1 (1st Cir.1997)—§ 24.4(d) n.37

Magana-Pizano v. INS, 200 F.3d 603 (9th Cir.1999)—§ 21.2(d) n.234

Magda, United States v., 409 F.Supp. 734 (S.D.N.Y.1976)—§ 10.6(d) n.48

Magda, United States v., 547 F.2d 756 (2d Cir.1976)—§§ 3.8(d) n.135, 141

Magdaniel-Mora, United States v., 746 F.2d 715 (11th Cir.1984)—§ 6.6(e) n.94

Magee, Commonwealth v., 423 Mass. 381, 668 N.E.2d 339 (1996)—§§ 6.2(c) n.104; 6.6(f) n.110, 112; 6.9(b) n.29

Magee v. State, 542 So.2d 228 (Miss.1989)—§ 7.3(b) n.30

Magee, State v., 304 Or. 261, 744 P.2d 250 (1987)—§ 2.12(c) n.146

Maggard v. State, 27 Kan.App.2d 1060, 11 P.3d 89 (2000)—§ 28.11(b) n.21

Maggard, United States v., 573 F.2d 926 (6th Cir.1978)—§ 17.4(a) n.58

Maggio v. Fulford, 462 U.S. 111, 103 S.Ct. 2261, 76 L.Ed.2d 794 (1983)—§§ 27.5(e) n.165; 28.7(a) n.2

Maggio, United States v., 514 F.2d 80 (5th Cir.1975)—§ 21.5(d) n.106

Maggitt, United States v., 778 F.2d 1029 (5th Cir.1985)—§ 10.3(b) n.13

Magini, United States v., 973 F.2d 261 (4th Cir.1992)—§ 11.9(a) n.16

Magluta, United States v., 418 F.3d 1166 (11th Cir.2005)—§ 17.4(a) n.36

Maguire, In re, 571 F.2d 675 (1st Cir.1978)—§ 7.2(b) n.15

Maguire, United States v., 918 F.2d 254 (1st Cir.1990)—§ 3.3(d) n.173

Maguire v. United States, 396 F.2d 327 (9th Cir.1968)—§ 6.8(b) n.51

Magwood, In re, 113 F.3d 1544 (11th Cir.1997)—§ 28.5(d) n.86

Magwood v. Smith, 791 F.2d 1438 (11th Cir.1986)—§§ 11.2(e) n.176, 181

Magwood, State v., 290 Md. 615, 432 A.2d 446 (1981)—§ 24.9(a) n.6

Mahady, United States v., 512 F.2d 521 (3d Cir.1975)—§ 8.12(b) n.20

Mahaffey, People v., 128 Ill.2d 388, 132 Ill.Dec. 366, 539 N.E.2d 1172 (1989)—§ 17.2(b) n.38

Mahan v. State, 541 N.W.2d 918 (Iowa App.1995)—§ 26.2(c) n.59

Mahar, Commonwealth v., 442 Mass. 11, 809 N.E.2d 989 (2004)—§§ 21.3(b) n.75, 99, 102

Mahavier v. State, 644 S.W.2d 129 (Tex.App.1982)—§ 15.2(i) n.223

Mahboubian, People v., 74 N.Y.2d 174, 544 N.Y.S.2d 769, 543 N.E.2d 34 (1989)—§§ 17.2(b) n.69; 17.2(d) n.94

Mahdi, United States v., 777 A.2d 814 (D.C.App.2001)—§§ 13.5(a) n.3, 17; 13.7(c) n.52

Mahler, People v., 329 Mich. 155, 45 N.W.2d 14 (1950)—§ 21.4(a) n.1

Mahoney, United States v., 508 F.Supp. 263 (E.D.Pa.1981)—§ 15.5(b) n.60

Mai, State v., 294 Or. 269, 656 P.2d 315 (1982)—§§ 20.6(c) n.84, 85, 87

Maidwell, State v., 137 Idaho 424, 50 P.3d 439 (2002)—§ 18.5(a) n.12

Maier, State v., 423 A.2d 235 (Me.1980)—§ 26.10(c) n.44

Maier, State v., 13 N.J. 235, 99 A.2d 21 (1953)—§ 15.1(d) n.232

Maine v. Baldwin, 305 A.2d 555 (Me.1973)—§ 16.4(d) n.134

Maine v. Moulton, 474 U.S. 159, 106 S.Ct. 477, 88 L.Ed.2d 481 (1985)—§§ 2.8(b) n.51; 2.9(h) n.216, 217, 240, 247; 6.4(e) n.94; 6.4(g) n.146

Maine v. Superior Court, 68 Cal.2d 375, 66 Cal.Rptr. 724, 438 P.2d 372 (1968)—§§ 23.2(a) n.41, 49, 53; 27.4(c) n.37

Mainelli, State v., 543 A.2d 1311 (R.I.1988)—§§ 15.7(b) n.45, 46

Maine Lobster Co., United States v., 160 F.Supp. 122 (D.Me.1957)—§ 15.4(g) n.149

Mainiero v. Jordan, 105 F.3d 361 (7th Cir.1997)—§ 24.3(f) n.154

Mainiero v. Liburdi, 214 Conn. 717, 573 A.2d 1207 (1990)—§ 21.4(d) n.119

Mainor v. State, 259 Ga. 803, 387 S.E.2d 882 (1990)—§ 6.8(b) n.56

Maise, State v., 805 So.2d 1141 (La.2002)—§§ 6.6(f) n.100; 6.10(c) n.41

Maisley, State v., 215 W.Va. 582, 600 S.E.2d 294 (2004)—§ 13.6(d) n.67

Maisonet, State v., 166 N.J. 9, 763 A.2d 1254 (2001)—§ 24.2(e) n.54

Major v. State, 83 P.3d 468 (Wyo.2004)—§§ 21.3(b) n.84; 21.4(a) n.27; 21.5(a) n.38

Major v. State, 814 So.2d 424 (Fla.2002)—§§ 21.3(b) n.71; 21.4(d) n.131

Makaila, State v., 79 Haw. 40, 897 P.2d 967 (1995)—§ 27.5(a) n.8

Maki, State v., 291 Minn. 427, 192 N.W.2d 811 (1971)—§§ 14.3(c) n.60, 71

Makres, United States v., 937 F.2d 1282 (7th Cir.1991)—§ 21.6(a) n.64

Malani, State v., 59 Haw. 167, 578 P.2d 236 (1978)—§ 7.3(c) n.48

Malatesta, United States v., 583 F.2d 748 (5th Cir.1978)—§ 15.6(b) n.57

Malave, People v., 124 Misc.2d 210, 476 N.Y.S.2d 422 (Sup.Ct.1984)—§§ 15.7(b) n.48; 15.7(g) n.221

Malave, State v., 250 Conn. 722, 737 A.2d 442 (1999)—§ 24.4(c) n.21

Malave, United States v., 22 F.3d 145 (7th Cir.1994)—§ 21.4(f) n.176

Malcolm, State v., 257 Conn. 653, 778 A.2d 134 (2001)—§ 21.4(d) n.137

Malcolm v. United States, 332 A.2d 917 (D.C.App.1975)—§§ 10.3(b) n.11, 12, 14

Malcom v. Payne, 281 F.3d 951 (9th Cir.2002)—§ 28.5(b) n.48

Maldonado v. State, 93 N.M. 670, 604 P.2d 363 (1979)—§ 15.6(a) n.8

Maldonado-Rivera, United States v., 922 F.2d 934 (2d Cir.1990)—§§ 11.3(b) n.37, 38; 15.4(d) n.123; 16.3(c) n.40

Malede v. United States, 767 A.2d 267 (D.C.App.2001)—§ 11.9(d) n.170

Maleng v. Cook, 490 U.S. 488, 109 S.Ct. 1923, 104 L.Ed.2d 540 (1989)—§§ 28.3(a) n.5, 14, 29

Mali v. Keeper of the Common Jail, 120 U.S. 1, 7 S.Ct. 385, 30 L.Ed. 565 (1887)—§ 16.4(b) n.8

Malicoat v. Mullen, 426 F.3d 1241 (10th Cir.2005)—§ 11.10(c) n.96

Malinovsky v. Court of Common Pleas of Lorain County, 7 F.3d 1263 (6th Cir.1993)—§ 25.3(a) n.8

Malinowski, Commonwealth v., 543 Pa. 350, 671 A.2d 674 (1996)—§ 27.3(c) n.33

Malinski v. New York, 324 U.S. 401, 65 S.Ct. 781, 89 L.Ed. 1029 (1945)—§§ 2.4(a) n.10; 2.4(e) n.180; 2.4 n.4; 2.5(f) n.53; 2.7(c) n.99, 120, 174; 2.8(c) n.59; 2.9(d) n.89; 6.2(c) n.67; 6.4(a) n.2

Malinski v. State, 794 N.E.2d 1071 (Ind.2003)—§ 6.9(c) n.61

Mallak v. State, 308 Mont. 314, 42 P.3d 794 (2002)—§ 21.4(d) n.136

Mallett v. Bowersox, 160 F.3d 456 (8th Cir.1998)—§ 22.2(d) n.56

Mallett v. Missouri, 494 U.S. 1009, 110 S.Ct. 1308, 108 L.Ed.2d 484 (1990)—§§ 16.3(g) n.128; 22.2(d) n.74

Mallett v. State, 769 S.W.2d 77 (Mo.1989)—§§ 16.3(g) n.100, 108, 119, 124; 22.2(d) n.74

Mallette, State v., 159 Conn. 143, 267 A.2d 438 (1970)—§ 7.4(d) n.77

Malley v. Briggs, 475 U.S. 335, 106 S.Ct. 1092, 89 L.Ed.2d 271 (1986)—§§ 3.1(c) n.79; 3.1(k) n.259

Mallon, Commonwealth v., 356 Pa.Super. 493, 515 A.2d 1 (1986)—§ 15.3(d) n.65

Mallory v. United States, 354 U.S. 449, 77 S.Ct. 1356, 1 L.Ed.2d 1479 (1957)—§§ 1.7(c) n.47; 1.7(i) n.164, 167; 3.3(b) n.68; 6.3(a) n.10

Malloy, Commonwealth v., 579 Pa. 425, 856 A.2d 767 (2004)—§ 6.9(e) n.87

Malloy v. Hogan, 378 U.S. 1, 84 S.Ct. 1489, 12 L.Ed.2d 653 (1964)—§§ 1.2(c) n.11; 1.5(c) n.104; 1.5(d) n.179, 183, 195; 2.4(e) n.145, 149; 2.5(a) n.8; 2.5(c) n.22; 2.5(f) n.53, 57, 62, 77, 90; 2.6(a) n.6, 7; 2.6(b) n.34; 2.10(d) n.135; 6.2(b) n.24; 6.5(a) n.9; 8.10(a) n.12; 8.10(b) n.47

Malo, State v., 577 A.2d 332 (Me.1990)—§ 21.4(f) n.207

Malone v. Malone, 591 P.2d 296 (Okla.1979)—§ 26.4(d) n.54

Malone, State v., 568 A.2d 1378 (R.I.1990)—§ 21.2(d) n.242

Malone v. United States, 482 A.2d 768 (D.C.App.1984)—§ 18.4(c) n.73

Malone v. United States, 502 F.2d 554 (9th Cir.1974)—§§ 26.9(b) n.43, 54

Maloney v. State, 684 N.E.2d 488 (Ind.1997)—§ 21.4(e) n.163

Malpiedi, United States v., 62 F.3d 465 (2d Cir.1995)—§ 11.9(d) n.231

Maltais, United States v., 403 F.3d 550 (8th Cir.2005)—§ 3.8(d) n.158

Malufau, State v., 80 Haw. 126, 906 P.2d 612 (1995)—§ 25.4(b) n.22

Malveaux, People v., 50 Cal.App.4th 1425, 59 Cal.Rptr.2d 371 (1996)—§ 25.1(d) n.87

Malvo, State v., 357 So.2d 1084 (La.1978)—§ 15.6(c) n.96

Mamacos, Commonwealth v., 409 Mass. 635, 568 N.E.2d 1139 (1991)—§ 3.7(e) n.126

Manarite, United States v., 314 F.Supp. 607 (S.D.N.Y.1970)—§ 3.6(c) n.79

Manbeck, United States v., 744 F.2d 360 (4th Cir.1984)—§§ 3.8(b) n.30; 6.6(f) n.104; 9.1(d) n.124

Mance, Commonwealth v., 539 Pa. 282, 652 A.2d 299 (1995)—§ 5.4(b) n.19

Mancero-Londono, United States v., 912 F.2d 373 (9th Cir.1990)—§ 9.3(e) n.65

Manchester, State v., 545 So.2d 528 (La.1989)—§ 21.2(g) n.401

Manchester v. U.S. Department of Justice, 823 F.Supp. 1259 (E.D.Pa.1993)—§ 8.5(b) n.35

Manchester Farming Partnership, United States v., 315 F.3d 1176 (9th Cir.2003)—§§ 13.5(h) n.169 to 171

Mancias, United States v., 350 F.3d 800 (8th Cir.2003)—§ 18.3(b) n.11

Mancilla, People v., 250 Ill.App.3d 353, 189 Ill.Dec. 846, 620 N.E.2d 1163 (1993)—§ 24.3(h) n.176

Mancini, United States v., 8 F.3d 104 (1st. Cir.1993)—§ 9.1(c) n.103

Manck, State v., 385 Md.App. 581, 870 A.2d 196 (2005)—§§ 27.3(b) n.17; 27.4(d) n.45

Mancusi v. DeForte, 392 U.S. 364, 88 S.Ct. 2120, 20 L.Ed.2d 1154 (1968)—§§ 3.2(e) n.158; 9.1(a) n.5; 9.1(b) n.92; 9.1(c) n.97, 111

Mandacina v. United States, 328 F.3d 995 (8th Cir.2003)—§ 28.9(b) n.53

Mandan, City of v. Baer, 578 N.W.2d 559 (N.D.1998)—§ 24.2(a) n.5

Mandanici, United States v., 205 F.3d 519 (2d Cir.2000)—§§ 28.6(e) n.63; 28.9(a) n.24

Mandel, United States v., 914 F.2d 1215 (9th Cir.1990)—§ 20.3(g) n.125

Mandel, United States v., 862 F.2d 1067 (4th Cir.1988)—§ 28.9(a) n.19

Mandel, United States v., 431 F.Supp. 90 (D.Md.1977)—§ 16.3(b) n.23

Mandel, United States v., 415 F.Supp. 1033 (D.Md.1976)—§§ 15.4(h) n.195, 197; 15.7(f) n.152, 155, 180; 23.2(e) n.73

Mandicino, State v., 509 N.W.2d 481 (Iowa 1993)—§ 16.1(a) n.29

Mandile, Commonwealth v., 397 Mass. 410, 492 N.E.2d 74 (1986)—§ 6.2(c) n.108

Mandujano, United States v., 425 U.S. 564, 96 S.Ct. 1768, 48 L.Ed.2d 212 (1976)—§§ 6.6(a) n.10; 8.10(a) n.6; 8.10(c) n.51, 58, 62, 63, 74, 82; 8.10(d) n.89; 8.14(a) n.2; 9.6(c) n.65; 11.1(c) n.100

Manduley v. Superior Court, 27 Cal.4th 537, 117 Cal.Rptr.2d 168, 41 P.3d 3 (2002)—§ 13.2(a) n.6

Maness v. Meyers, 419 U.S. 449, 95 S.Ct. 584, 42 L.Ed.2d 574 (1975)—§§ 2.10(b) n.4; 8.10(a) n.2; 8.14(a) n.13; 11.1(b) n.85

Manfredi, United States v., 789 F.Supp. 961 (N.D.Ind.1992)—§§ 16.2(e) n.74, 75

Manfredi, United States v., 275 F.2d 588 (2d Cir.1960)—§ 17.3(c) n.30

Manfro, People v., 150 Misc.2d 1080, 571 N.Y.S.2d 986 (Sup.Ct.1991)—§§ 15.7(f) n.178, 187

Mangialino, People v., 75 Misc.2d 698, 348 N.Y.S.2d 327 (1973)—§ 3.4(f) n.108

Manglitz, United States v., 773 F.2d 1463 (4th Cir.1985)—§§ 8.5(e) n.190; 21.4(f) n.176

Manglitz, United States v., 590 F.Supp. 177 (D.Md.1984)—§ 8.5(b) n.40

Mangual-Corchado, United States v., 139 F.3d 34 (1st Cir.1998)—§ 15.7(e) n.106

Mangum, People v., 48 P.3d 568 (Colo.2002)—§§ 6.5(b) n.24; 6.6(e) n.95

Mangum, United States v., 100 F.3d 164 (D.C.Cir.1996)—§§ 26.2(b) n.21, 26

Mangum, United States v., 871 F.Supp. 1486 (D.D.C.1995)—§ 24.3(g) n.169

Manley v. Georgia, 279 U.S. 1, 49 S.Ct. 215, 73 L.Ed. 575 (1929)—§ 2.4(e) n.137

Manley, State v., 142 Idaho 338, 127 P.3d 954 (2005)—§ 25.2(e) n.46

Mann, State v., 271 Conn. 300, 857 A.2d 329 (2004)—§§ 3.6(f) n.155; 3.8(e) n.186

Mann, State v., 131 N.M. 459, 39 P.3d 124 (2002)—§ 24.9(f) n.70

Mann, State v., 129 N.M. 600, 11 P.3d 564 (2000)—§ 24.9(g) n.121

Mann, State v., 602 N.W.2d 785 (Iowa 1999)—§ 21.6(a) n.79

Mann, State v., 959 S.W.2d 503 (Tenn.1997)—§ 21.2(b) n.42

Mann, State v., 512 N.W.2d 528 (Iowa 1994)—§ 22.4(c) n.22

Mann v. Thalacker, 246 F.3d 1092 (8th Cir.2001)—§§ 6.9(g) n.154; 22.4(a) n.4, 13

Mann, United States v., 161 F.3d 840 (5th Cir.1998)—§§ 17.2(b) n.44; 17.3(d) n.47; 18.5(a) n.14

Mann, United States v., 61 F.3d 326 (5th Cir.1995)—§ 20.3(j) n.206

Manna, State v., 534 N.W.2d 642 (Iowa 1995)—§ 10.1(a) n.3

Manna, State v., 130 N.H. 306, 539 A.2d 284 (1988)—§ 17.1(c) n.45

Manna v. U.S. Department of Justice, 815 F.Supp. 798 (D.N.J.1993)—§ 8.5(b) n.35

Mannes v. Gillespie, 967 F.2d 1310 (9th Cir.1992)—§ 27.4(f) n.72

Manney, State v., 24 N.J. 571, 133 A.2d 313 (1957)—§§ 8.5(a) n.3; 15.6(c) n.90; 15.6(g) n.217; 15.7(h) n.224, 225

Mannhalt v. Reed, 847 F.2d 576 (9th Cir.1988)—§§ 11.9(a) n.13; 11.9(d) n.219

Manning v. Bowersox, 310 F.3d 571 (8th Cir.2002)—§§ 6.4(e) n.68; 6.4(g) n.161

Manning v. Municipal Court, 372 Mass. 315, 361 N.E.2d 1274 (1977)—§ 13.2(a) n.3

Manning, People v., 182 Ill.2d 193, 230 Ill.Dec. 933, 695 N.E.2d 423 (1998)—§ 6.7(c) n.141

Manning v. State, 122 P.3d 628 (Utah 2005)—§ 21.2(b) n.76

Manning, State v., 885 So.2d 1044 (La.2004)—§ 6.9(b) n.27

Manning v. State, 735 So.2d 323 (Miss.1999)—§ 23.2(f) n.90

Manning v. State, 726 So.2d 1152 (Miss.1998)—§ 22.3(d) n.246

Mannon v. State, 98 Nev. 224, 645 P.2d 433 (Nev.1982)—§ 11.9(d) n.203

Manns v. State, 122 S.W.3d 171 (Tex.Crim.App.2003)—§ 6.4(g) n.153

Manor, United States v., 936 F.2d 1238 (11th Cir.1991)—§§ 6.6(c) n.41; 6.6(e) n.66

Mans, United States v., 999 F.2d 966 (6th Cir.1993)—§ 3.7(a) n.14

Mansel v. State, 805 P.2d 677 (Okl.Crim.App. 1991)—§ 10.5(a) n.7

Mansfield v. State, 758 So.2d 636 (Fla.2000)—§ 6.6(d) n.49

Manson v. Brathwaite, 432 U.S. 98, 97 S.Ct. 2243, 53 L.Ed.2d 140 (1977)—§§ 2.7(c) n.194; 2.9(g) n.178, 181; 7.4(b) n.36; 10.3(d) n.70, 72

Manson v. State, 101 Wis.2d 413, 304 N.W.2d 729 (1981)—§ 19.3(c) n.187

Manson v. State, 349 So.2d 67 (1977)—§ 19.3(a) n.67

Mansoori, United States v., 304 F.3d 635 (7th Cir.2002)—§§ 4.6(m) n.237; 6.3(b) n.36, 43; 22.3(b) n.68

Mantel, People v., 88 Misc.2d 439, 388 N.Y.S.2d 565 (1976)—§ 13.4(c) n.136

Manuszak, United States v., 438 F.Supp. 613 (D.Pa.1977)—§ 4.6(m) n.225

Manzanares, State v., 100 N.M. 621, 674 P.2d 511 (1983)—§ 17.4(b) n.109

Manzella, United States v., 791 F.2d 1263 (7th Cir.1986)—§ 5.1(c) n.27

Mapes, United States v., 59 M.J. 60 (C.M.A.2003)—§ 8.11(c) n.48

Maple, United States v., 348 F.3d 260 (D.C.Cir.2003)—§ 3.7(e) n.121

Maples, United States v., 501 F.2d 985 (4th Cir.1974)—§§ 26.3(g) n.73; 26.4(b) n.12

Mapp v. Ohio, 367 U.S. 643, 81 S.Ct. 1684, 6 L.Ed.2d 1081 (1961)—§§ 2.4(f) n.185; 2.5(e) n.44; 2.5(f) n.53; 2.6(a) n.2; 2.6(b) n.34; 2.9(b) n.20; 2.11(a) n.6; 2.12(c) n.170; 3.1(a) n.17; 3.1(e) n.123; 9.2(d) n.35

Mapp, United States v., 170 F.3d 328 (2d Cir.1999)—§ 6.4(e) n.101

Mar, People v., 28 Cal.4th 1201, 124 Cal.Rptr.2d 161, 52 P.3d 95 (2002)—§ 24.2(e) n.68

Mara, United States v., 410 U.S. 19, 93 S.Ct. 774, 35 L.Ed.2d 99 (1973)—§§ 3.2(b) n.82; 3.2(g) n.191; 7.2(b) n.13; 8.6(a) n.22; 8.7(c) n.64; 8.8(b) n.17

Maragh, People v., 94 N.Y.2d 569, 708 N.Y.S.2d 44, 729 N.E.2d 701 (2000)—§§ 24.9(f) n.70; 24.9(g) n.121

Maragh, United States v., 894 F.2d 415 (D.C.Cir.1990)—§§ 3.8(c) n.83, 88

Maraj, United States v., 947 F.2d 520 (1st Cir.1991)—§ 24.8(a) n.25

Marallo, State v., 175 Vt. 469, 817 A.2d 1271 (2002)—§ 6.7(a) n.3

Marano v. Holland, 179 W.Va. 156, 366 S.E.2d 117 (1988)—§ 9.4(e) n.108

Maraziti, In re, 233 N.J.Super. 488, 559 A.2d 447 (1989)—§ 24.3(f) n.156

Marberry v. State, 686 S.W.2d 31 (Mo.App.1984)—§ 11.10(d) n.161

Marbley, State v., 20 Kan.App.2d 34, 882 P.2d 1004 (1994)—§ 22.3(d) n.222

Marbly, People v., 85 Ill.App.3d 935, 41 Ill.Dec. 223, 407 N.E.2d 721 (1980)—§ 27.3(c) n.26

Marbury v. Madison, 5 U.S. (1 Cranch) 137, 2 L.Ed. 60 (1802)—§ 1.7(b) n.1

Marcello, United States v., 370 F.Supp.2d 745 (N.D.Ill.2005)—§ 12.1(f) n.86

Marcello, United States v., 212 F.3d 1005 (7th Cir.2000)—§ 28.9(b) n.51

March, State v., 265 Neb. 447, 658 N.W.2d 20 (2003)—§ 10.6(c) n.21

March, United States v., 999 F.2d 456 (10th Cir.1993)—§ 10.4(b) n.15

Marchand, United States v., 564 F.2d 983 (2d Cir.1977)—§§ 9.4(b) n.63; 9.4(c) n.74

Marchant, United States v., 55 F.3d 509 (10th Cir.1995)—§ 9.1(c) n.113

Marchant, United States v., 774 F.2d 888 (8th Cir.1985)—§ 16.2(b) n.16

Marchese, United States v., 438 F.2d 452 (2d Cir.1971)—§ 22.1(g) n.115

Marchetti v. United States, 390 U.S. 39, 88 S.Ct. 697, 19 L.Ed.2d 889 (1968)—§§ 2.10(c) n.100; 8.10(a) n.58; 8.12(c) n.31

Marchildon, United States v., 519 F.2d 337 (8th Cir.1975)—§ 6.9(b) n.30

Marchwinski v. Howard, 60 Fed.Appx. 601 (6th Cir.2003)—§ 3.9(d) n.68

Marchwinski v. Howard, 309 F.3d 330 (6th Cir.2002)—§ 3.9(d) n.68

Marchwinski v. Howard, 113 F.Supp.2d 1134 (E.D.Mich.2000)—§ 3.9(d) n.68

Marc Rich & Co., A.G., In re, 707 F.2d 663 (2d Cir.1983)—§ 8.8(i) n.192

Marcus, United States ex rel. v. Hess, 317 U.S. 537, 63 S.Ct. 379, 87 L.Ed. 443 (1943)—§ 25.1(c) n.22

Marcy, People v., 628 P.2d 69 (Colo.1981)—§ 13.7(a) n.27

Marden, State v., 673 A.2d 1304 (Me.1996)—§ 6.9(g) n.154

Mardian, United States v., 546 F.2d 973 (D.C.Cir.1976)—§ 17.2(e) n.118

Maree, United States v., 934 F.2d 196 (9th Cir.1991)—§ 24.9(f) n.70

Marek, Ex parte, 556 So.2d 375 (Ala.1989)—§ 9.6(a) n.44

Mareska v. State, 534 N.E.2d 246 (Ind.App.1989)—§ 2.6(b) n.64

Marez, People v., 39 P.3d 1190 (Colo.2002)—§§ 21.4(d) n.114, 131

Margalli-Olvera v. INS, 43 F.3d 345 (8th Cir.1994)—§ 21.2(e) n.329

Margiotta, United States v., 646 F.2d 729 (2d Cir.1981)—§§ 19.3(c) n.185, 186

Mariani, United States v., 851 F.2d 595 (2d Cir.1988)—§§ 8.11(c) n.59, 64

Marinari, United States v., 32 F.3d 1209 (7th Cir.1994)—§ 24.9(e) n.53

Marin-Buitrago, United States v., 734 F.2d 889 (2d Cir.1984)—§ 3.3(a) n.25

Marine v. State, 607 A.2d 1185 (Del.1992)—§§ 6.6(c) n.31; 6.9(b) n.20

Marines, United States v., 535 F.2d 552 (10th Cir.1976)—§ 21.2(d) n.211

Marini, State v., 638 A.2d 507 (1994)—§ 10.4(b) n.10

Marino v. Ragen, 332 U.S. 561, 68 S.Ct. 240, 92 L.Ed. 170 (1947)— § 28.5(a) n.18

Marino, State v., 100 Wash.2d 719, 674 P.2d 171 (1984)—§§ 16.1(g) n.243, 248, 274

Marino, United States v., 277 F.3d 11 (1st Cir.2002)—§ 22.3(d) n.193

Marino, United States v., 868 F.2d 549 (3d Cir.1989)—§ 5.3(b) n.16

Marino v. Vasquez, 812 F.2d 499 (9th Cir.1987)—§ 24.9(g) n.121

Marion, People v., 275 Ill.App.3d 494, 212 Ill.Dec. 117, 656 N.E.2d 440 (1995)—§ 26.10(c) n.76

Marion, People v., 182 Colo. 435, 514 P.2d 327 (1973)—§ 19.5(b) n.10

Marion, United States v., 535 F.2d 697 (2d Cir.1976)—§§ 1.7(c) n.10; 4.6(c) n.54

Marion, United States v., 404 U.S. 307, 92 S.Ct. 455, 30 L.Ed.2d 468 (1971)—§§ 2.7(a) n.19; 2.7(b) n.73, 85; 2.7(c) n.128; 2.9(c) n.50; 18.1(c) n.19; 18.2(b) n.24; 18.5(a) n.1; 18.5(b) n.53

Marionneaux, United States v., 514 F.2d 1244 (5th Cir.1975)—§ 17.2(a) n.9

Markham, People v., 49 Cal.3d 63, 260 Cal.Rptr. 273, 775 P.2d 1042 (1989)—§ 10.4(b) n.8

Markham, United States v., 191 F.2d 936 (7th Cir.1951)—§ 24.7(e) n.68

Markle, State v., 118 Wash.2d 424, 823 P.2d 1101 (1992)—§§ 19.5(b) n.2, 14, 26

Markling, United States v., 7 F.3d 1309 (7th Cir.1993)—§§ 9.3(d) n.43; 9.4(b) n.66

Markman, Commonwealth v., _____ Pa. _____, 916 A.2d 586 (2007)— § 17.2(b) n.71

Marks v. United States, 430 U.S. 188, 97 S.Ct. 990, 51 L.Ed.2d 260 (1977)—§§ 6.8(b) n.48; 26.4(d) n.57; 28.6(d) n.33

Marku, State v., 176 Vt. 607, 850 A.2d 993 (2004)—§ 21.4(c) n.81

Markum, United States v., 4 F.3d 891 (10th Cir.1993)—§ 26.4(c) n.30

Marler, United States v., 756 F.2d 206 (1st Cir.1985)—§§ 18.1(c) n.31; 18.5(b) n.64, 69

Marlow, State v., 334 N.C. 273, 432 S.E.2d 275 (1993)—§ 21.2(f) n.386

Marlow v. State, 538 So.2d 804 (Ala.Crim.App.1988)—§ 11.2(e) n.148

Marlowe, State v., 89 S.W.3d 464 (Mo.2002)—§ 22.3(d) n.232

Marone v. United States, 10 F.3d 65 (2d Cir.1993)—§ 22.1(h) n.133

Marque, United States v., 521 F.Supp. 359 (S.D.N.Y.1981)—§ 20.6(b) n.52

Marquette, State ex rel. v. Police Court of City of Deer Lodge, 86 Mont. 297, 283 P. 430 (1929)—§ 1.8(d) n.64

Marquez, People v., 1 Cal.4th 553, 3 Cal.Rptr.2d 710, 822 P.2d 418 (1992)—§ 7.4(d) n.71

Marquez, State v., 124 N.M. 409, 951 P.2d 1070 (N.M.App.1997)— §§ 19.5(b) n.8, 11, 24

Marquez v. State, 921 S.W.2d 217 (Tex.Cr.App.1996)—§ 22.1(h) n.138

Marquez, United States v., 410 F.3d 612 (9th Cir.2005)—§ 3.9(h) n.166

Marquez, United States v., 909 F.2d 738 (2d Cir.1990)—§ 21.2(b) n.53

Marquez, United States v., 319 F.Supp. 1016 (S.D.N.Y.1970)—§ 17.2(d) n.113

Marquis, State v., 525 A.2d 1041 (Me.1987)—§ 2.12(e) n.199

Marren, United States v., 919 F.2d 61 (7th Cir.1990)—§ 11.9(c) n.120

Marrera, United States v., 768 F.2d 201 (7th Cir.1985)—§§ 11.9(d) n.168, 207, 226, 234

Marrero, United States v., 705 F.2d 652 (2d Cir.1983)—§ 18.3(b) n.32

Marrero-Ortiz, United States v., 160 F.3d 768 (1st Cir.1998)—§§ 22.3(b) n.68; 26.3(f) n.64

Marrero-Rivera, United States v., 124 F.3d 342 (1st Cir.1997)—§§ 21.3(b) n.79; 21.5(a) n.43

Marron v. United States, 275 U.S. 192, 48 S.Ct. 74, 72 L.Ed. 231 (1927)—§§ 2.8(b) n.36; 3.4(f) n.99; 3.4(k) n.216

Marroquin, United States v., 885 F.2d 1240 (5th Cir.1989)—§ 18.3(b) n.11

Marrow v. United States, 772 F.2d 525 (9th Cir.1985)—§ 21.5(d) n.103

Marrowbone, United States v., 211 F.3d 452 (8th Cir.2000)—§§ 22.3(d) n.247, 249

Marsch v. Commonwealth, 743 S.W.2d 830 (Ky.1987)—§ 22.3(c) n.133

Marsh v. Alabama, 326 U.S. 501, 66 S.Ct. 276, 90 L.Ed. 265 (1946)—§ 3.1(h) n.209

Marsh v. Chambers, 463 U.S. 783, 103 S.Ct. 3330, 77 L.Ed.2d 1019 (1983)—§ 2.9(d) n.102

Marsh, People v., 36 Cal.3d 134, 202 Cal.Rptr. 92, 679 P.2d 1033 (1984)—§ 21.2(b) n.48

Marsh, State v., 132 Or.App. 416, 888 P.2d 580 (1995)—§§ 14.2(d) n.54, 57

Marsh v. State, 95 N.M. 224, 620 P.2d 878 (1980)—§§ 16.2(a) n.11; 16.2(g) n.125; 16.4(c) n.39

Marshall v. Barlow's, Inc., 436 U.S. 307, 98 S.Ct. 1816, 56 L.Ed.2d 305 (1978)—§§ 2.9(i) n.272; 3.2(e) n.163; 3.9(c) n.36

Marshall v. Casey, 174 W.Va. 204, 324 S.E.2d 346 (1984)—§ 12.3(d) n.105

Marshall v. Cathel, 428 F.3d 452 (3d Cir.2005)—§§ 11.10(c) n.127, 151

Marshall v. Commonwealth, 60 S.W.3d 513 (Ky.2001)—§ 22.1(h) n.134

Marshall v. Hendricks, 307 F.3d 36 (3d Cir.2002)—§ 28.3(d) n.86

Marshall v. Jerrico, Inc., 446 U.S. 238, 100 S.Ct. 1610, 64 L.Ed.2d 182 (1980)—§ 22.5(a) n.1

Marshall v. Lonberger, 459 U.S. 422, 103 S.Ct. 843, 74 L.Ed.2d 646 (1983)—§§ 21.4(c) n.92; 26.2(b) n.24, 25; 26.6(b) n.19; 28.7(a) n.2

Marshall, People v., 50 Cal.3d 907, 269 Cal.Rptr. 269, 790 P.2d 676 (1990)—§ 6.8(c) n.65

Marshall, People v., 82 Mich.App. 92, 266 N.W.2d 678 (1978)—§ 22.1(c) n.61

Marshall, State v., 144 Wash.2d 266, 27 P.3d 192 (2001)—§ 21.5(a) n.47

Marshall v. State, 963 P.2d 1 (Okla.Cr.App.1998)—§§ 21.3(b) n.89, 115

Marshall, State v., 123 N.J. 1, 586 A.2d 85 (1991)—§ 3.2(e) n.162

Marshall, State v., 414 So.2d 684 (La.1982)—§ 11.9(a) n.6

Marshall v. State, 381 So.2d 276 (Fla.App.1980)—§ 19.6(b) n.11

Marshall, United States v., 348 F.3d 281 (1st Cir.2003)—§ 3.10(f) n.198

Marshall, United States v., 132 F.3d 63 (D.C.Cir.1998)—§§ 20.3(a) n.20; 20.3(g) n.134; 20.6(b) n.22, 26, 42

Marshall, United States v., 856 F.2d 896 (7th Cir.1988)—§ 18.5(a) n.31

Marshall, United States v., 519 F.Supp. 751 (E.D.Wis.1981)—§ 26.5(a) n.12

Marshall, United States v., 609 F.2d 152 (5th Cir.1980)—§§ 10.6(b) n.14, 16

Marshall, United States v., 532 F.2d 1279 (9th Cir.1976)—§ 20.3(g) n.132

Marshall v. United States, 414 U.S. 417, 94 S.Ct. 700, 38 L.Ed.2d 618 (1974)—§ 13.6(b) n.23

Marshall v. United States, 355 F.2d 999 (9th Cir.1966)—§ 1.2(c) n.114

Marshall v. United States, 360 U.S. 310, 79 S.Ct. 1171, 3 L.Ed.2d 1250 (1959)—§§ 1.7(i) n.159; 22.3(c) n.119; 23.2(f) n.95; 24.9(f) n.89

Marshank, United States v., 777 F.Supp. 1507 (N.D.Cal.1991)—§ 11.8(b) n.37

Marston's, Inc. v. Strand, 114 Ariz. 260, 560 P.2d 778 (1977)—§ 8.8(g) n.165

Martel v. State, 221 Md. 294, 157 A.2d 437 (1960)—§ 16.1(e) n.180

Martel-Martines, United States v., 988 F.2d 855 (8th Cir.1993)—§ 3.10(f) n.192

Martens, Commonwealth v., 398 Mass. 674, 500 N.E.2d 282 (1986)— § 18.4(c) n.53

Martenson, United States v., 178 F.3d 457 (7th Cir.1999)—§ 26.7(b) n.19

Marti, State v., 147 N.H. 168, 784 A.2d 1193 (2001)—§ 25.4(a) n.7

Marti, State v., 143 N.H. 608, 732 A.2d 414 (1999)—§ 13.7(c) n.60

Marti, State v., 290 N.W.2d 570 (Iowa 1980)—§§ 19.4(a) n.8; 19.4(b) n.20, 30

Martin, In re, 44 Cal.3d 1, 241 Cal.Rptr. 263, 744 P.2d 374 (1987)— §§ 24.3(h) n.176 to 178

Martin v. Beto, 397 F.2d 741 (5th Cir.1968)—§ 2.6(b) n.71

Martin v. Bissonette, 118 F.3d 871 (1st Cir.1997)—§ 24.1(b) n.27

Martin, Commonwealth v., 447 Mass. 274, 850 N.E.2d 555 (2006)— §§ 7.4(b) n.25; 7.4(c) n.41; 7.4(f) n.94

Martin, Commonwealth v., 444 Mass. 213, 827 N.E.2d 198 (2005)— §§ 2.12(e) n.200, 208; 9.5(b) n.53

Martin, Commonwealth v., 425 Mass. 718, 683 N.E.2d 280 (1997)— §§ 11.5(d) n.84; 11.5(e) n.89

Martin, Commonwealth v., 423 Mass. 496, 668 N.E.2d 825 (1996)— §§ 8.10(a) n.23; 8.10(e) n.125

Martin, Commonwealth v., 417 Mass. 187, 629 N.E.2d 297 (1994)— § 24.1(b) n.26

Martin v. Commonwealth, 11 Va.App. 397, 399 S.E.2d 623 (1990)— § 24.2(e) n.70

Martin, Commonwealth v., 358 Mass. 282, 264 N.E.2d 366 (1970)— § 3.10(d) n.110

Martin, Commonwealth v., 379 Pa. 587, 109 A.2d 325 (1954)—§ 24.9(e) n.51

Martin v. Consultants and Administrators, 966 F.2d 1078 (7th Cir.1992)—§ 8.5(c) n.83

Martin v. Darnell, 960 S.W.2d 838 (Tex.App.1997)—§ 20.2(b) n.20

Martin v. Flanagan, 259 Conn. 487, 789 A.2d 979 (2002)—§ 8.10(e) n.126

Martin v. Hunter's Lessee, 14 U.S. (1 Wheat) 304, 4 L.Ed. 97 (1816)— §§ 1.2(c) n.79; 1.7(b) n.1

Martin v. Kemp, 760 F.2d 1244 (11th Cir.1985)—§ 21.2(b) n.54

Martin v. Leverette, 161 W.Va. 547, 244 S.E.2d 39 (1978)—§ 22.5(a) n.12

Martin v. Musteen, 303 Ark. 656, 799 S.W.2d 540 (1990)—§ 20.2(d) n.79

Martin v. Ohio, 480 U.S. 228, 107 S.Ct. 1098, 94 L.Ed.2d 267 (1987)— §§ 1.5(d) n.198; 2.7(a) n.44; 2.7(c) n.142, 148, 167, 170; 2.9(d) n.66

Martin v. Parker, 11 F.3d 613 (6th Cir.1993)—§ 24.7(e) n.63

Martin, People v., 102 Ill.2d 412, 80 Ill.Dec. 776, 466 N.E.2d 228 (1984)—§§ 6.2(c) n.128; 6.9(c) n.55

Martin, People v., 94 Mich.App. 649, 290 N.W.2d 48 (1980)—§ 3.5(a) n.42

Martin, People v., 9 Cal.3d 687, 108 Cal.Rptr. 809, 511 P.2d 1161 (1973)—§§ 3.3(b) n.73; 21.6(c) n.118

Martin, People v., 2 Cal.3d 822, 87 Cal.Rptr. 709, 471 P.2d 29 (1970)— § 7.3(f) n.116

Martin, People v., 45 Cal.2d 755, 290 P.2d 855 (1955)—§§ 2.12(a) n.13; 9.2(d) n.36

Martin v. Reinstein, 195 Ariz. 293, 987 P.2d 779 (App.1999)—§ 12.3(b) n.32

Martin v. Rose, 744 F.2d 1245 (6th Cir.1984)—§§ 11.10(c) n.72, 81; 11.10(d) n.194

Martin v. Sheriff, Clark County, 88 Nev. 303, 496 P.2d 754 (1972)—§ 14.3(d) n.84

Martin, State v., 723 N.W.2d 613 (Minn.2006)—§ 24.2(b) n.28

Martin, State v., 103 Ohio St.3d 385, 816 N.E.2d 227 (2004)—§§ 11.5(g) n.112, 119

Martin v. State, 277 Ga. 227, 587 S.E.2d 650 (2003)—§ 6.7(b) n.85

Martin, State v., 367 Md. 53, 785 A.2d 1270 (2001)—§§ 13.3(c) n.36; 25.3(a) n.8

Martin v. State, 839 So.2d 665 (Ala.App.2001)—§ 24.3(b) n.49

Martin, State v., 145 N.H. 362, 761 A.2d 516 (2000)—§ 10.3(b) n.19

Martin v. State, 736 N.E.2d 1213 (Ind.2000)—§ 6.2(c) n.178

Martin v. State, 271 Ga. 301, 518 S.E.2d 898 (1999)—§ 6.2(c) n.107

Martin, State v., 595 N.W.2d 214 (Minn.App.1999)—§ 26.10(c) n.66

Martin, State v., 959 P.2d 982 (Okla.Crim.App.1998)—§ 14.2(e) n.85

Martin, State v., 567 N.W.2d 62 (Minn.App.1997)—§ 15.4(h) n.200

Martin, State v., 950 S.W.2d 20 (Tenn.1997)—§ 6.4(f) n.131

Martin v. State, 316 Ark. 715, 875 S.W.2d 81 (1994)—§ 27.5(c) n.89

Martin v. State, 635 So.2d 1352 (Miss.1994)—§ 21.2(d) n.161

Martin, State v., 243 Neb. 368, 500 N.W.2d 512 (1993)—§ 6.2(c) n.107

Martin, State v., 607 So.2d 775 (La.Ct.App.1992)—§ 10.3(c) n.55

Martin v. State, 537 N.E.2d 491 (Ind.1989)—§ 21.2(h) n.420

Martin, State v., 553 A.2d 1264 (Me.1989)—§ 3.2(c) n.125

Martin, State v., 755 S.W.2d 337 (Mo.App.1988)—§ 24.9(f) n.94

Martin, State v., 201 Conn. 74, 513 A.2d 116 (1986)—§§ 11.9(b) n.54, 79; 11.9(d) n.169

Martin, State v., 315 N.C. 667, 340 S.E.2d 326 (1986)—§§ 3.3(d) n.161; 6.3(c) n.53

Martin, State v., 197 Conn. 17, 495 A.2d 1028 (1985)—§ 21.5(a) n.20

Martin v. State, 630 S.W.2d 952 (Tex.Crim.App.1982)—§ 11.5(e) n.90

Martin, State v., 94 Wash.2d 1, 614 P.2d 164 (1980)—§ 21.4(f) n.210

Martin, State v., 288 Or. 643, 607 P.2d 171 (1980)—§ 26.7(b) n.20

Martin, State v., 282 Or. 583, 580 P.2d 536 (1978)—§§ 26.9(b) n.52; 26.9(c) n.87

Martin v. State, 517 P.2d 1389 (Alaska 1974)—§§ 12.3(b) n.58, 62

Martin v. Struthers, 319 U.S. 141, 63 S.Ct. 862, 87 L.Ed. 1313 (1943)—§ 2.5(f) n.72

Martin v. Texas, 200 U.S. 316, 26 S.Ct. 338, 50 L.Ed. 497 (1906)—§ 15.4(d) n.107

Martin, United States v., 408 F.3d 1089 (8th Cir.2005)—§ 28.9(b) n.50

Martin, United States v., 369 F.3d 1046 (8th Cir.2004)—§ 6.6(e) n.69

Martin, United States v., 382 F.3d 840 (8th Cir.2004)—§ 26.10(c) n.71

Martin, United States v., 332 F.3d 827 (5th Cir.2003)—§ 8.11(d) n.71

Martin, United States v., 287 F.3d 609 (7th Cir.2002)—§§ 13.3(c) n.45; 21.3(e) n.279

Martin, United States v., 297 F.3d 1308 (11th Cir.2002)—§ 3.1(c) n.71

Martin, United States v., 147 F.3d 529 (7th Cir.1998)—§ 21.6(a) n.25

Martin, United States v., 128 F.3d 1188 (7th Cir.1997)—§ 26.6(c) n.35

Martin, United States v., 25 F.3d 211 (4th Cir.1994)—§§ 21.2(d) n.255, 258

Martin, United States v., 25 F.3d 293 (6th Cir.1994)—§§ 11.5(b) n.23, 25, 30

Martin, United States v., 982 F.2d 1236 (8th Cir.1993)—§§ 10.2(b) n.27, 28

Martin, United States v., 965 F.2d 839 (10th Cir.1992)—§§ 11.9(d) n.187, 189

Martin v. United States, 567 A.2d 896 (D.C.App.1989)—§ 9.1(b) n.45

Martin, United States v., 781 F.2d 671 (9th Cir.1985)—§ 6.6(e) n.71

Martin, United States v., 704 F.2d 267 (6th Cir.1983)—§ 22.1(h) n.136

Martin, United States v., 480 F.Supp. 880 (S.D.Tex.1979)—§§ 15.6(b) n.58, 61

Martin v. United States, 462 F.2d 60 (5th Cir.1972)—§ 7.4(d) n.71

Martin v. Wainwright, 770 F.2d 918 (11th Cir.1985)—§§ 6.2(c) n.146; 6.4(f) n.112; 6.9(g) n.159

Martin v. Warden, 993 F.2d 824 (11th Cir.1993)—§ 18.1(a) n.2

Martindell v. International Telephone & Telegraph Corp., 594 F.2d 291 (2d Cir.1979)—§§ 8.6(b) n.53 to 55

Martineau, People v., 185 Colo. 194, 523 P.2d 126 (1974)—§ 3.8(d) n.136

Martineau v. Perrin, 601 F.2d 1196 (1st Cir.1979)—§ 24.1(a) n.13

Martinelli, United States v., 62 M.J. 52 (2005)—§ 16.4(b) n.25

Martinez, Commonwealth v., 431 Mass. 168, 726 N.E.2d 913 (2000)—§ 6.5(b) n.29

Martinez, Commonwealth v., 420 Mass. 622, 651 N.E.2d 380 (1995)—§ 15.7(c) n.64

Martinez v. Court of Appeal of California, 528 U.S. 152, 120 S.Ct. 684, 145 L.Ed.2d 597 (2000)—§§ 11.2(b) n.65; 11.5(a) n.16; 27.1(a) n.3

Martinez v. Johnson, 104 F.3d 769 (5th Cir.1997)—§ 28.7(d) n.26

Martinez v. Nygaard, 831 F.2d 822 (9th Cir.1987)—§ 3.8(c) n.85

Martinez, People v., 22 Cal.4th 750, 94 Cal.Rptr.2d 381, 996 P.2d 32 (2000)—§ 18.1(c) n.25

Martinez, People v., 970 P.2d 469 (Colo.1998)—§§ 20.4(b) n.20; 20.4(d) n.73; 20.4(f) n.95; 20.5(f) n.83, 84

Martinez, People v., 164 Misc.2d 314, 624 N.Y.S.2d 783 (Sup.Ct.1995)—§ 15.7(b) n.49

Martinez, People v., 81 N.Y.2d 810, 595 N.Y.S.2d 376, 611 N.E.2d 277 (1993)—§ 21.4(f) n.197

Martinez, People v., 82 N.Y.2d 436, 604 N.Y.S.2d 932, 624 N.E.2d 1027 (1993)—§ 24.1(b) n.29

Martinez, People v., 172 App.Div.2d 428, 568 N.Y.S.2d 940 (1991)—§ 24.1(a) n.5

Martinez, People v., 71 N.Y.2d 937, 528 N.Y.S.2d 813, 524 N.E.2d 134 (1988)—§ 24.3(c) n.95

Martinez, State v., 276 Kan. 527, 78 P.3d 769 (2003)—§ 3.2(g) n.195

Martinez, State v., 26 P.3d 203 (Utah 2001)—§ 21.3(b) n.45

Martinez v. State, 17 S.W.3d 677 (Tex.Crim.App.2000)—§ 10.1(b) n.23

Martinez, State v., 196 Ariz. 451, 999 P.2d 795 (2000)—§ 22.3(c) n.112

Martinez, State v., 127 N.M. 207, 979 P.2d 718 (1999)—§ 6.2(c) n.105

Martinez, State v., 255 Kan. 464, 874 P.2d 617 (1994)—§ 14.4(c) n.47

Martinez, State v., 624 A.2d 291 (R.I.1993)—§ 7.4(e) n.90

Martinez, State v., 294 S.C. 72, 362 S.E.2d 641 (1987)—§ 22.3(d) n.250

Martinez, State v., 97 N.M. 585, 642 P.2d 188 (App.1982)—§ 15.7(b) n.11

Martinez, State v., 59 Haw. 366, 580 P.2d 1282 (1978)—§ 26.9(c) n.83

Martinez v. Superior Court, 29 Cal.3d 574, 174 Cal.Rptr. 701, 629 P.2d 502 (1981)—§§ 23.2(a) n.54, 55

Martinez v. Superior Court, 26 Ariz.App. 386, 548 P.2d 1198 (1976)—§ 12.4(a) n.20

Martinez, United States v., 462 F.3d 903 (8th Cir.2006)—§§ 6.6(e) n.95; 7.4(c) n.48, 50, 53

Martinez, United States v., 376 F.Supp.2d 1168 (D.N.M.2004)— § 18.4(c) n.46

Martinez, United States v., 277 F.3d 517 (4th Cir.2002)—§§ 21.4(f) n.170; 21.4(g) n.228

Martinez, United States v., 143 F.3d 1266 (9th Cir.1998)—§ 21.2(b) n.86

Martinez, United States v., 87 F.3d 731 (5th Cir.1996)—§ 24.3(c) n.101

Martinez, United States v., 949 F.2d 1117 (11th Cir.1992)—§ 3.10(f) n.192

Martinez, United States v., 967 F.2d 1343 (9th Cir.1992)—§ 9.6(a) n.10

Martinez, United States v., 979 F.2d 1424 (10th Cir.1992)—§§ 5.1(c) n.26, 28, 36

Martinez, United States v., 981 F.2d 867 (6th Cir.1992)—§ 19.3(a) n.59

Martinez, United States v., 901 F.2d 374 (4th Cir.1990)—§ 16.2(b) n.16

Martinez, United States v., 837 F.2d 861 (9th Cir.1988)—§ 18.5(c) n.76

Martinez, United States v., 749 F.2d 623 (11th Cir.1984)—§ 18.3(b) n.26

Martinez, United States v., 630 F.2d 361 (5th Cir.1980)—§ 11.9(d) n.233

Martinez, United States v., 486 F.2d 15 (5th Cir.1973)—§ 21.4(b) n.55

Martinez-Fuerte, United States v., 428 U.S. 543, 96 S.Ct. 3074, 49 L.Ed.2d 1116 (1976)—§§ 3.8(c) n.99; 3.8(d) n.178, 183; 3.9(f) n.119; 3.9(g) n.124

Martinez-Martinez, United States v., 369 F.3d 1076 (9th Cir.2004)— §§ 18.3(b) n.18, 32; 22.3(c) n.112

Martinez-Martinez, United States v., 69 F.3d 1215 (1st Cir.1995)—§ 21.4(a) n.38

Martinez-Medina, United States v., 279 F.3d 105 (1st Cir.2002)—§§ 24.7(e) n.54, 67

Martinez-Miramontes, United States v., 494 F.2d 808 (9th Cir.1974)— § 3.2(f) n.179

Martinez-Moncivais, United States v., 14 F.3d 1030 (5th Cir.1994)— § 24.9(g) n.114

Martinez-Salazar, United States v., 528 U.S. 304, 120 S.Ct. 774, 145 L.Ed.2d 792 (2000)—§§ 22.3(c) n.157; 27.6(b) n.21

Martinez-Zayas, United States v., 857 F.2d 122 (3d Cir.1988)—§ 3.4(b) n.30

Martini, State v., 144 N.J. 603, 677 A.2d 1106 (2006)—§ 28.11(a) n.10

Martini, State v., 131 N.J. 176, 619 A.2d 1208 (1993)—§ 6.9(g) n.174

Martin Linen Supply Co., United States v., 430 U.S. 564, 97 S.Ct. 1349, 51 L.Ed.2d 642 (1977)—§§ 13.2(c) n.54; 15.1(b) n.21; 22.1(a) n.18; 25.1(d) n.84; 25.3(c) n.24

Martino, Commonwealth v., 412 Mass. 267, 588 N.E.2d 651 (1992)— § 3.6(e) n.126

Martino, United States v., 825 F.2d 754 (3d Cir.1987)—§ 8.10(d) n.113

Martino, United States v., 648 F.2d 367 (5th Cir.1981)—§§ 15.7(b) n.19; 20.6(b) n.50; 24.3(c) n.94

Martinson, United States v., 809 F.2d 1364 (9th Cir.1987)—§ 10.1(c) n.43

Martin, State ex rel. v. Michell, 188 So.2d 684 (Fla.App.1966)— § 8.4(b) n.19

Martin-Trigona, United States v., 767 F.2d 35 (2d Cir.1985)—§ 12.1(a) n.7

Martir, United States v., 782 F.2d 1141 (2d Cir.1986)—§§ 12.1(a) n.11; 12.3(a) n.24

Martley v. State, 519 P.2d 544 (Okla.Cr.App.1974)—§ 12.4(a) n.12

Martorano, Commonwealth v., 559 Pa. 533, 741 A.2d 1221 (1999)— § 25.4(a) n.7

Marts, United States v., 986 F.2d 1216 (8th Cir.1993)—§ 3.4(h) n.142

Martucci, People v., 153 A.D.2d 866, 545 N.Y.S.2d 385 (1989)— § 15.2(c) n.83

Marvin, United States v., 211 F.3d 778 (3d Cir.2000)—§§ 11.2(c) n.96, 99, 102

Marx v. Gumbinner, 905 F.2d 1503 (11th Cir.1990)—§ 3.3(d) n.153

Marx, People v., 54 Cal.App.3d 100, 126 Cal.Rptr. 350 (1975)—§ 7.2(b) n.19

Marx v. United States, 930 F.2d 1246 (7th Cir.1991)—§ 21.5(b) n.69

Marxen, United States v., 410 F.3d 326 (6th Cir.2005)—§ 3.8(d) n.152

Mary D. v. Watt, 190 W.Va. 341, 438 S.E.2d 521 (1992)—§ 15.2(f) n.148

Maryland v. Brown, 295 F.Supp. 63 (D.Md.1969)—§§ 2.6(b) n.59; 16.1(b) n.65, 77, 79, 80; 16.3(d) n.65; 16.3(g) n.108

Maryland v. Buie, 494 U.S. 325, 110 S.Ct. 1093, 108 L.Ed.2d 276 (1990)—§§ 2.9(g) n.163, 169, 181; 3.4(j) n.187; 3.6(d) n.92; 3.7(e) n.127

Maryland v. Craig, 497 U.S. 836, 110 S.Ct. 3157, 111 L.Ed.2d 666 (1990)—§§ 1.5(c) n.118; 1.5(e) n.218; 1.5(k) n.412; 2.6(d) n.99; 2.12(e) n.210; 24.2(e) n.74

Maryland v. Dyson, 527 U.S. 465, 119 S.Ct. 2013, 144 L.Ed.2d 442 (1999)—§ 3.7(b) n.33

Maryland v. Garrison, 480 U.S. 79, 107 S.Ct. 1013, 94 L.Ed.2d 72 (1987)— §§ 3.3(b) n.45; 3.4(e) n.79; 3.4(j) n.186; 3.10(d) n.133

Maryland v. Macon, 472 U.S. 463, 105 S.Ct. 2778, 86 L.Ed.2d 370 (1985)—§ 3.2(e) n.162

Maryland v. Pringle, 540 U.S. 366, 124 S.Ct. 795, 157 L.Ed.2d 769 (2003)—§§ 3.3(b) n.69; 3.3(f) n.197; 14.3(a) n.22

Maryland v. Soper, 270 U.S. 9, 46 S.Ct. 185, 70 L.Ed. 449 (1926)— §§ 13.5(d) n.79, 81

Maryland v. Wilson, 519 U.S. 408, 117 S.Ct. 882, 137 L.Ed.2d 41 (1997)— §§ 3.5(b) n.93; 3.8(e) n.204; 12.5(b) n.30

Maryland v. Wirtz, 392 U.S. 183, 88 S.Ct. 2017, 20 L.Ed.2d 1020 (1968)—§ 1.2(c) n.155

Marzolf, State v., 79 N.J. 167, 398 A.2d 849 (1979)—§ 21.2(d) n.212

Marzullo, United States v., 780 F.Supp. 658 (W.D.Mo.1991)—§ 12.4(d) n.71

Masat, United States v., 896 F.2d 88 (5th Cir.1990)—§ 22.3(b) n.80

Mascarenas, State v., 129 N.M. 230, 4 P.3d 1221 (2000)—§ 27.5(d) n.114

Mascarenas v. State, 80 N.M. 537, 458 P.2d 789 (1969)—§§ 14.4(c) n.64; 14.4(e) n.127, 128

Masciale v. United States, 356 U.S. 386, 78 S.Ct. 827, 2 L.Ed.2d 859 (1958)—§§ 5.2(a) n.1; 5.2(b) n.36

Masciola v. United States, 469 F.2d 1057 (3d Cir.1972)—§ 21.2(g) n.395

Mascual-Cruz, United States v., 387 F.3d 1 (1st Cir.2004)—§§ 21.2(b) n.52, 53, 57

Maseratti, United States v., 1 F.3d 330 (5th Cir.1993)—§ 22.3(d) n.220

Mash v. Commonwealth, 769 S.W.2d 42 (Ky.1989)—§ 3.5(a) n.36

Mash, State v., 328 N.C. 61, 399 S.E.2d 307 (1991)—§ 22.3(a) n.7

Mashburn, United States v., 406 F.3d 303 (4th Cir.2005)—§ 6.8(b) n.49

Masilko, State v., 226 Neb. 45, 409 N.W.2d 322 (1987)—§ 11.2(g) n.264

Mask, United States v., 330 F.3d 330 (5th Cir.2003)—§ 3.8(c) n.76

Maske v. United States, 785 A.2d 687 (D.C.App.2001)—§ 21.4(f) n.176

Masloski, People v., 25 Cal.4th 1212, 108 Cal.Rptr.2d 484, 25 P.3d 681 (2001)—§ 21.2(d) n.223

Mason, Ex parte, 711 So.2d 468 (Ala.1998)—§ 27.5(e) n.169

Mason, In re, 116 Ohio App.3d 451, 688 N.E.2d 552 (1996)—§ 12.3(b) n.66

Mason v. Mitchell, 320 F.3d 604 (6th Cir.2003)—§ 11.10(c) n.138

Mason v. Mitchell, 536 U.S. 901, 122 S.Ct. 2354, 153 L.Ed.2d 177 (2002)—§ 11.10(d) n.198

Mason, People v., 308 App.Div.2d 317, 764 N.Y.S.2d 80 (2003)—§ 24.2(a) n.7

Mason, People v., 5 Cal.3d 759, 97 Cal.Rptr. 302, 488 P.2d 630 (1971)—§ 3.9(j) n.214

Mason v. Pulliam, 557 F.2d 426 (5th Cir.1977)—§ 3.10(f) n.204

Mason, State v., 150 N.H. 53, 834 A.2d 339 (2003)—§§ 17.3(b) n.27; 27.6(b) n.26

Mason, State v., 283 Mont. 149, 941 P.2d 437 (1997)—§ 18.5(a) n.47

Mason v. State, 302 Md. 434, 488 A.2d 955 (1985)—§ 21.1(a) n.7

Mason, State v., 34 Wash.App. 514, 663 P.2d 137 (1983)—§ 1.8(d) n.44

Mason, State v., 56 Or.App. 164, 641 P.2d 1139 (1982)—§ 26.10(c) n.82

Mason, State v., 641 P.2d 1139 (1982)— § 26.10(c) n.84

Mason, State v., 305 So.2d 523 (La.1974)—§ 19.1(c) n.29

Mason, United States v., 869 F.2d 414 (8th Cir.1989)—§ 8.12(g) n.63

Mason, United States v., 372 F.Supp. 651 (N.D.Ohio 1973)—§ 18.4(c) n.60

Masonheimer, Ex parte, 220 S.W.3d 494 (Tex.Cr.App.2007)—§ 27.4(f) n.70

Masqua, State v., 210 Kan. 419, 502 P.2d 728 (1972)—§ 9.1(b) n.66

Massa, People v., 271 Ill.App.3d 75, 207 Ill.Dec. 667, 648 N.E.2d 123 (1995)—§§ 11.9(a) n.25; 11.9(d) n.217

Massa, United States v., 686 F.2d 526 (7th Cir.1982)—§ 16.1(g) n.256

Massachusetts v. Painten, 389 U.S. 560, 88 S.Ct. 660, 19 L.Ed.2d 770 (1968)—§ 3.1(d) n.96

Massachusetts v. Painten, 368 F.2d 142 (1st Cir.1966)—§ 3.1(d) n.94

Massachusetts v. Sheppard, 468 U.S. 981, 104 S.Ct. 3424, 82 L.Ed.2d 737 (1984)—§ 3.1(c) n.64

Massachusetts v. Upton, 466 U.S. 727, 104 S.Ct. 2085, 80 L.Ed.2d 721 (1984)—§§ 2.12(a) n.26, 51; 3.3(a) n.22; 3.3(c) n.86

Massameno v. Statewide Grievance Committee, 234 Conn. 539, 663 A.2d 317 (1995)—§§ 13.2(a) n.3; 13.2(f) n.108

Massara v. United States, 538 U.S. 500, 123 S.Ct. 1690, 155 L.Ed.2d 714 (2003)—§ 28.9(b) n.40

Massard, People v., 139 A.D.2d 927, 528 N.Y.S.2d 954 (1988)— §§ 15.2(c) n.84; 15.7(d) n.90

Massaro v. United States, 538 U.S. 500, 123 S.Ct. 1690, 155 L.Ed.2d 714 (2003)—§§ 11.7(e) n.78, 91, 101, 103; 28.4(d) n.58

Massen v. State, 41 Wis.2d 245, 163 N.W.2d 616 (1969)—§ 7.3(f) n.112

Massey v. Mullen, 117 R.I. 272, 366 A.2d 1144 (1976)—§ 12.4(a) n.40

Massey, State v., 316 N.C. 558, 342 S.E.2d 811 (1986)—§ 6.10(b) n.14

Massey, United States v., 89 F.3d 1433 (11th Cir.1996)—§ 24.8(a) n.19

Massiah v. United States, 377 U.S. 201, 84 S.Ct. 1199, 12 L.Ed.2d 246 (1964)—§§ 6.4(b) n.15; 6.4(g) n.141; 6.7(a) n.8; 7.3(a) n.4

Massie, People v., 19 Cal.4th 550, 79 Cal.Rptr.2d 816, 967 P.2d 29 (1998)—§§ 22.2(d) n.80, 81

Massingill v. State, 8 S.W.3d 733 (Tex.Cr.App.1999)—§§ 11.2(b) n.52; 27.6(d) n.84

Massino, United States v., 657 F.Supp. 101 (S.D.N.Y.1987)—§ 4.6(e) n.110

Mast v. Superior Court of Yavapai County, 102 Ariz. 225, 427 P.2d 917 (1967)—§ 16.3(d) n.57

Mastberg, United States v., 503 F.2d 465 (9th Cir.1974)—§ 3.9(f) n.101

Master v. State, 702 P.2d 375 (Okl.Crim.App.1985)—§ 17.2(d) n.96

Master Key Litigation, In re, 507 F.2d 292 (9th Cir.1974)—§ 8.10(e) n.120

Masterson, United States v., 529 F.2d 30 (9th Cir.1976)—§ 7.5(a) n.6

Master, State ex rel. v. Cleveland, 75 Ohio St.3d 23, 661 N.E.2d 180 (1996)—§ 13.3(a) n.7

Mastin v. Senkowski, 297 F.Supp.2d 558 (W.D.N.Y.2003)—§ 24.4(c) n.21

Mastracchio v. Moran, 698 A.2d 706 (R.I.1997)—§ 24.3(b) n.32

Mastrangelo, United States v., 733 F.2d 793 (11th Cir.1984)—§ 18.3(b) n.11

Mastrangelo, United States v., 662 F.2d 946 (2d Cir.1981)—§ 25.2(d) n.34

Mastrian v. Hedman, 326 F.2d 708 (8th Cir.1964)—§ 12.2(a) n.1

Mastrodonato, People v., 75 N.Y.2d 18, 550 N.Y.S.2d 580, 549 N.E.2d 1151 (1989)—§ 4.6(i) n.153

Mastroianni, United States v., 749 F.2d 900 (1st Cir.1984)—§§ 11.8(b) n.32, 35

Mata v. Sumner, 696 F.2d 1244 (9th Cir.1983)—§ 7.4(e) n.78

Mata-Abundiz, United States v., 717 F.2d 1277 (9th Cir.1983)—§§ 6.7(b) n.42; 6.10(c) n.54

Matafeo, State v., 71 Haw. 183, 787 P.2d 671 (1990)—§§ 24.3(e) n.134, 136

Matautia, State v., 81 Hawai'i 76, 912 P.2d 573 (App.1996)—§§ 19.5(b) n.26, 40

Matchopatow, United States v., 259 F.3d 847 (7th Cir.2001)—§ 21.2(d) n.167

Mateo, People v., 453 Mich. 203, 551 N.W.2d 891 (1996)—§ 27.6(a) n.7

Matey, State v., 153 N.H. 263, 891 A.2d 592 (2006)—§ 6.4(e) n.100

Mathe, State v., 102 Wash.2d 537, 688 P.2d 859 (1984)—§ 3.10(e) n.154

Matheny v. Commonwealth, 37 S.W.3d 756 (Ky.2001)—§ 21.2(f) n.363

Matheny, People v., 46 P.3d 453 (Colo.2002)—§§ 6.6(d) n.46, 48

Mathews v. Diaz, 426 U.S. 67, 96 S.Ct. 1883, 48 L.Ed.2d 478 (1976)—§ 15.1(b) n.16

Mathews v. Eldridge, 424 U.S. 319, 96 S.Ct. 893, 47 L.Ed.2d 18 (1976)—§§ 2.4(b) n.73; 2.7(b) n.67; 2.7(c) n.215; 11.1(b) n.40; 11.2(e) n.144; 26.4(d) n.60

Mathews v. United States, 485 U.S. 58, 108 S.Ct. 883, 99 L.Ed.2d 54 (1988)—§§ 5.1(c) n.20; 5.3(c) n.34

Mathis v. Hood, 937 F.2d 790 (2d Cir.1991)—§ 11.9(d) n.217

Mathis v. State, 112 N.M. 744, 819 P.2d 1302 (1991)—§§ 20.3(a) n.16; 20.6(b) n.43

Mathis v. State, 734 P.2d 312 (Okla.Crim.App.1987)—§ 16.1(g) n.250

Mathis v. State, 419 So.2d 774 (Fla.App.1982)—§ 16.1(h) n.286

Mathis, United States v., 264 F.3d 321 (3d Cir.2001)—§§ 7.4(e) n.92; 7.5(b) n.23

Mathis, United States v., 96 F.3d 1577 (11th Cir.1996)—§ 22.3(d) n.250

Mathis v. United States, 391 U.S. 1, 88 S.Ct. 1503, 20 L.Ed.2d 381 (1968)—§§ 6.6(b) n.13; 6.6(e) n.80; 6.10(c) n.43

Mathison, United States v., 157 F.3d 541 (8th Cir.1998)—§ 22.4(c) n.30

Matias, State v., 57 Haw. 96, 550 P.2d 900 (1976)—§ 17.3(d) n.55

Matko, State ex rel. v. Ziegler, 154 W.Va. 872, 179 S.E.2d 735 (1971)—§§ 8.4(b) n.109; 8.5(a) n.3

Matlock v. State, 732 So.2d 168 (Miss.1999)—§ 21.6(a) n.64

Matlock, United States v., 675 F.2d 981 (8th Cir.1982)—§ 19.1(d) n.43

Matlock, United States v., 415 U.S. 164, 94 S.Ct. 988, 39 L.Ed.2d 242 (1974)—§§ 3.10(d) n.105; 4.4(e) n.19; 10.4(c) n.19; 10.5(d) n.38

Matney v. Armontrout, 956 F.2d 824 (8th Cir.1992)—§ 6.9(c) n.63

Matson, State v., 260 Kan. 366, 921 P.2d 790 (1996)—§§ 6.9(g) n.154; 19.5(b) n.33

Matta-Ballesteros v. Henman, 896 F.2d 255 (7th Cir.1990)—§ 3.1(j) n.247

Mattarolo, United States v., 209 F.3d 1153 (9th Cir.2000)—§ 3.8(e) n.193

Mattatall, State v., 603 A.2d 1098 (R.I.1992)—§ 9.6(a) n.32

Mattatall, State v., 525 A.2d 49 (R.I.1987)—§ 6.4(g) n.148

Mattes, State v., 175 Wis.2d 572, 499 N.W.2d 711 (1993)—§ 16.1(g) n.247

Matthew v. Johnson, 201 F.3d 353 (5th Cir.2000)—§ 24.3(b) n.76

Matthews, Ex parte, 933 S.W.2d 134 (Tex.Cr.App.1996)—§ 18.5(a) n.6

Matthews, Ex parte, 601 So.2d 52 (Ala.1992)—§ 6.2(c) n.113

Matthews, In re, 345 S.C. 638, 550 S.E.2d 311 (2001)—§ 17.4(b) n.134

Matthews v. Commonwealth, 168 S.W.3d 14 (Ky.2005)—§§ 6.9(f) n.101; 10.4(b) n.15

Matthews, Commonwealth v., 406 Mass. 380, 548 N.E.2d 843 (1990)— § 22.2(d) n.70

Matthews, Commonwealth v., 167 Mass. 173, 45 N.E. 92 (1896)—§ 16.1(e) n.194

Matthews, People v., 22 Mich.App. 619, 178 N.W.2d 94 (1970)—§ 6.9(d) n.76

Matthews v. State, 350 S.C. 272, 565 S.E.2d 766 (2002)—§ 11.10(c) n.118

Matthews, State v., 81 Oh.St.3d. 375, 691 N.E.2d 1041 (1998)—§ 27.3(d) n.59

Matthews v. State, 313 Ark. 327, 854 S.W.2d 339 (1993)—§§ 7.4(d) n.76; 22.4(c) n.23

Matthews, State v., 295 N.C. 265, 245 S.E.2d 727 (1978)—§ 7.3(b) n.29

Matthews, State v., 217 Kan. 654, 538 P.2d 637 (1975)—§ 3.9(i) n.194

Matthews, State v., 218 So.2d 743 (Miss.1969)—§ 15.5(c) n.103

Matthews, United States v., 411 F.3d 1210 (11th Cir.2005)—§ 4.6(k) n.172

Mattis v. Reno, 212 F.3d 31 (1st Cir.2000)—§ 21.2(d) n.234

Mattox, State v., 280 Kan. 473, 124 P.3d 6 (2005)—§ 6.9(f) n.139

Mattson, People v., 50 Cal.3d 826, 268 Cal.Rptr. 802, 789 P.2d 983 (1990)—§ 10.6(c) n.23

Mattson, People v., 37 Cal.3d 85, 207 Cal.Rptr. 278, 688 P.2d 887 (1984)—§ 6.9(f) n.99

Mattson, People v., 51 Cal.2d 777, 336 P.2d 937 (1959)—§§ 11.5(g) n.118, 119

Mattson, United States v., 671 F.2d 1020 (7th Cir.1982)—§ 1.2(c) n.134

Maturo, United States v., 982 F.2d 57 (2d Cir.1992)—§ 3.1(i) n.229

Maugaotega, State v., 107 Haw. 399, 114 P.3d 905 (2005)—§ 26.4(i) n.188

Maulden v. State, 617 So.2d 298 (Fla.1993)—§ 9.3(e) n.82

Maulding v. State, 296 Ark. 328, 757 S.W.2d 916 (1988)—§ 7.4(c) n.51

Maull, United States v., 773 F.2d 1479 (8th Cir.1985)—§ 12.1(a) n.14

Maunsell, State v., 170 Vt. 543, 743 A.2d 580 (1999)—§ 21.5(e) n.119

Maupin, State v., 859 S.W.2d 313 (Tenn.1993)—§ 25.4(b) n.22

Maupin, State v., 63 Wash.App. 887, 822 P.2d 355 (Wash.App. 1992)— § 7.4(e) n.86

Maurello, People v., 932 P.2d 851 (Colo.App.1997)—§ 17.4(b) n.138

Mauricio v. Duckworth, 840 F.2d 454 (7th Cir.1988)—§ 20.4(g) n.105

Mauro, State v., 159 Ariz. 186, 766 P.2d 59 (1988)—§ 2.12(e) n.205

Mauro, United States v., 436 U.S. 340, 98 S.Ct. 1834, 56 L.Ed.2d 329 (1978)—§§ 18.4(c) n.39, 40, 44, 72

Mauro, United States v., 507 F.2d 802 (2d Cir.1974)—§§ 10.1(a) n.8, 11, 15

Maves, State v., 358 N.W.2d 805 (S.D.1984)—§§ 17.2(f) n.133; 17.3(a) n.7

Mavredakis, Commonwealth v., 430 Mass. 848, 725 N.E.2d 169 (2000)—§§ 2.12(e) n.208, 214

Max, State v., 263 N.W.2d 685 (S.D.1978)—§ 3.6(d) n.90

Maxey, State v., 125 Idaho 505, 873 P.2d 150 (1994)—§ 21.3(a) n.32

Maxfield, State v., 125 Wash.2d 378, 886 P.2d 123 (1994)—§ 3.2(c) n.129

Maxwell v. City of New York, 102 F.3d 664 (2d Cir.1996)—§ 3.9(g) n.124

Maxwell v. Dow, 176 U.S. 581, 20 S.Ct. 448, 44 L.Ed. 597 (1900)— §§ 2.3(b) n.86; 2.4(d) n.128; 2.5(f) n.51; 2.6(b) n.34; 22.1(a) n.10; 22.1(e) n.80

Maxwell, State v., 165 Or.App. 467, 998 P.2d 680 (2000)—§ 19.3(b) n.147

Maxwell v. Superior Court, 30 Cal.3d 606, 180 Cal.Rptr. 177, 639 P.2d 248 (1982)—§ 11.9(a) n.15

Maxwell, United States v., 446 F.3d 1210 (11th Cir.2006)—§ 1.2(c) n.193

Maxwell, United States v., 386 F.3d 1042 (11th Cir.2004)—§ 1.2(c) n.145

Maxwell, United States v., 351 F.3d 35 (1st Cir.2003)—§ 18.3(b) n.26

Maxwell, United States v., 160 F.3d 1071 (6th Cir.1998)—§ 22.3(d) n.200

Maxwell, United States v., 45 M.J. 406 (C.A.A.F. 1996)—§§ 4.4(c) n.9, 12

May, Commonwealth v., 587 Pn.184, 898 A.2d 559 (2006)—§ 11.10(c) n.96

May, People v., 859 P.2d 879 (Colo.1993)—§§ 6.9(b) n.33, 41

May, State v., 334 N.C. 609, 434 S.E.2d 180 (1993)—§§ 9.5(b) n.42, 43

May v. State, 718 S.W.2d 495 (Mo.1986)—§ 11.3(b) n.42

May, United States v., 413 F.3d 841 (8th Cir.2005)—§ 26.6(c) n.42

May 18, 1981 Grand Jury, In the Matter of the, 602 F.Supp. 772 (E.D.N.Y.1985)—§ 8.5(e) n.198

Mayans, United States v., 17 F.3d 1174 (9th Cir.1994)—§ 24.2(g) n.98

Mayberry v. Pennsylvania, 400 U.S. 455, 91 S.Ct. 499, 27 L.Ed.2d 532 (1971)—§§ 2.7(a) n.33; 2.7(c) n.200; 22.4(a) n.6

Mayberry, State v., 787 A.2d 135 (Me.2001)—§ 3.5(a) n.54

Mayberry, United States v., 896 F.2d 1117 (8th Cir.1990)—§ 20.3(d) n.93

Maybury, United States v., 274 F.2d 899 (2d Cir.1960)—§§ 13.2(c) n.51; 24.10(b) n.31

Mayer, In re, 2006 WL 20526 (D.N.J. 2006)—§ 15.2(b) n.53

Mayer v. City of Chicago, 404 U.S. 189, 92 S.Ct. 410, 30 L.Ed.2d 372 (1971)—§§ 1.8(d) n.61, 62, 77; 11.1(d) n.122; 11.2(a) n.13; 11.2(d) n.124, 125

Mayer, State v., 139 Idaho 643, 84 P.3d 579 (App.2001)—§ 19.3(b) n.147

Mayer, United States v., 235 U.S. 55, 35 S.Ct. 16, 59 L.Ed. 129 (1914)— § 28.9(a) n.18

Mayes v. City of Columbus, 105 Ohio App.3d 728, 664 N.E.2d 1340 (1995)—§ 15.7(f) n.136

Mayes v. State, 887 P.2d 1288 (Okla.Cr.App.1994)—§ 24.9(a) n.6

Mayes v. State, 604 A.2d 839 (Del.1992)—§§ 26.3(g) n.76; 26.4(f) n.89

Mayes v. State, 264 Ark. 283, 571 S.W.2d 420 (1978)—§ 7.4(b) n.24

Mayes, United States v., 917 F.2d 457 (10th Cir.1990)—§§ 17.2(d) n.109; 18.3(b) n.36

Mayes, United States v., 670 F.2d 126 (9th Cir.1982)—§§ 8.5(e) n.182, 193

Mayes, United States v., 552 F.2d 729 (6th Cir.1977)—§§ 3.10(b) n.36, 42; 6.3(b) n.40; 9.4(a) n.7

Mayette, State v., 204 Conn. 571, 529 A.2d 673 (1987)—§ 7.4(e) n.92

Mayfield, Commonwealth v., 398 Mass. 615, 500 N.E.2d 774 (1986)—§ 15.7(e) n.100

Mayfield, People v., 14 Cal.4th 668, 60 Cal.Rptr.2d 1, 928 P.2d 485 (1997)—§ 6.6(f) n.100

Mayfield v. State, 612 So.2d 1120 (Miss.1992)—§§ 14.1(c) n.42, 44; 14.2(c) n.39

Mayfield v. State, 293 Ark. 216, 736 S.W.2d 12 (1987)—§ 6.8(a) n.16

Mayfield v. United States, 504 F.Supp.2d 1023 (D. Or. 2007)—§ 4.9(b) n.16

Mayfield, United States v., 189 F.3d 895 (9th Cir.1999)—§§ 17.2(b) n.71; 17.2(c) n.76; 17.2(d) n.93, 106

Mayle v. Felix, 545 U.S. 644, 125 S.Ct. 2562, 162 L.Ed.2d 582 (2005)—§§ 28.5(b) n.64; 28.9(b) n.52

Mayle v. Ferguson, 174 W.Va. 430, 327 S.E.2d 409 (1985)—§ 18.5(c) n.81

Maynard v. Meachum, 545 F.2d 273 (1st Cir.1976)—§§ 11.4(d) n.112; 11.5(c) n.34; 11.5(f) n.104

Maynard v. State, 47 Ga.App. 221, 170 S.E. 265 (1933)—§ 16.1(e) n.180

Mayo v. Cockrell, 287 F.3d 336 (5th Cir.2002)—§ 11.2(b) n.53

Mayo v. Head, 280 Ga. 793, 631 S.E.2d 108 (2006)—§ 13.3(a) n.1

Mayo v. Henderson, 13 F.3d 528 (2d Cir.1994)—§§ 11.10(c) n.95, 117

Mayo, State v., 125 N.H. 200, 480 A.2d 85 (1984)—§ 22.1(g) n.116

Mayo v. State, 258 A.2d 269 (Me.1969)—§ 16.1(d) n.155

Mayo v. State, 36 Ala.App. 557, 60 So.2d 860 (1952)—§ 15.1(d) n.250

Mayo, United States v., 394 F.3d 1271 (9th Cir.2005)—§ 3.7(a) n.16

Mayo, United States v., 705 F.2d 62 (2d Cir.1983)—§ 19.3(d) n.202

Mayo v. United States, 425 F.Supp. 119 (E.D.Ill.1977)—§ 10.6(d) n.43

Mayomi, United States v., 873 F.2d 1049 (7th Cir.1989)—§ 4.2(b) n.16

Mays, State v., 277 Kan. 359, 85 P.3d 1208 (2004)—§ 6.9(b) n.38

Mays v. State, 308 Ark. 39, 822 S.W.2d 846 (1992)—§ 10.3(b) n.10

Mays, United States v., 69 F.3d 116 (6th Cir.1995)—§§ 11.9(c) n.115, 140

Mayze, State v., 280 Ga. 5, 622 S.E.2d 836 (2005)—§§ 16.1(d) n.163; 16.1(e) n.199; 16.2(a) n.10

Mazurek v. State, 10 P.3d 531 (Wyo.2000)—§ 21.2(b) n.75

Mazzaferro, United States v., 865 F.2d 450 (1st Cir.1989)—§ 21.2(c) n.131

Mazzan v. Warden, 116 Nev. 48, 993 P.2d 25 (2000)—§§ 24.3(b) n.58, 80

Mazzone, State v., 212 W.Va. 368, 572 S.E.2d 891 (2002)—§ 21.2(e) n.321

McAdoo v. Elo, 365 F.3d 487 (6th Cir.2004)—§§ 21.2(b) n.48; 21.3(b) n.45; 21.4(d) n.119

McAlear, State v., 519 N.W.2d 596 (S.D.1994)—§§ 21.3(f) n.426; 25.1(d) n.63

McAleney v. United States, 539 F.2d 282 (1st Cir.1976)—§§ 21.2(g) n.403, 414

McAllister, State v., 184 N.J. 17, 875 A.2d 866 (2005)—§ 8.5(d) n.156

McAllister v. State, 807 A.2d 1119 (Del.2002)—§ 6.6(e) n.61

McAlonan, People v., 22 Cal.App.3d 982, 99 Cal.Rptr. 733 (1972)—§ 13.2(c) n.56

McAlpine, United States v., 919 F.2d 1461 (10th Cir.1990)—§§ 3.10(d) n.109; 3.10(e) n.162

McAnderson, United States v., 914 F.2d 934 (7th Cir.1990)—§§ 22.2(d) n.76; 22.3(e) n.266

McAnulty, State v., 184 Ariz. 399, 909 P.2d 466 (1995)—§ 24.4(c) n.26

McArthur v. Robinson, 98 F.R.D. 672 (E.D.Ark.1983)—§ 8.5(c) n.81

McArthur v. State, 671 So.2d 867 (Fla.App.1996)—§ 20.6(b) n.32

McArthur, State v., 296 So.2d 97 (Fla.App.1974)—§ 15.2(j) n.237

McAvoy v. Shufrin, 401 Mass. 593, 518 N.E.2d 513 (1988)—§ 13.3(b) n.24

McAvoy v. State, 314 Md. 509, 551 A.2d 875 (1989)—§ 6.7(a) n.3

McBain, State v., 30 Or.App. 1055, 569 P.2d 630 (1977)—§ 7.2(d) n.53

McBride, Commonwealth v., 528 Pa. 153, 595 A.2d 589 (1991)— § 14.1(a) n.4

McBride, State v., 252 Neb. 866, 567 N.W.2d 136 (1997)—§ 21.4(a) n.41

McBride v. State, 838 S.W.2d 248 (Tex.Crim.App.1992)—§§ 11.2(e) n.190, 209, 228

McBride v. State, 477 A.2d 174 (Del.1984)—§§ 22.3(a) n.5; 22.3(b) n.86

McBride, State v., 287 Or. 315, 599 P.2d 449 (1979)—§§ 5.1(c) n.10; 5.3(c) n.31, 38

McBride, United States v., 362 F.2d 360 (6th Cir.2004)—§ 11.3(a) n.19

McBride, United States v., 801 F.2d 1045 (8th Cir.1986)—§ 3.8(d) n.160

McCahill, State v., 261 Conn. 492, 811 A.2d 667 (2002)—§§ 12.4(d) n.63, 81

McCain v. Gramley, 96 F.3d 288 (7th Cir.1996)—§ 22.3(d) n.226

McCain, United States v., 556 F.2d 253 (5th Cir.1977)—§ 6.4(g) n.144

McCall v. People, 623 P.2d 397 (Colo.1981)—§ 3.6(a) n.33

McCall, State v., 101 N.M. 616, 686 P.2d 958 (App.1983)—§ 15.4(h) n.188

McCalvin, People v., 55 Ill.2d 161, 302 N.E.2d 342 (1973)—§ 21.3(b) n.143

McCambridge v. City of Little Rock, 298 Ark. 219, 766 S.W.2d 909 (1989)—§ 3.1(k) n.280

McCandless v. State, 425 S.W.2d 636 (Tex.Cr.App.1968)—§ 6.8(a) n.32

McCandless v. Vaughn, 172 F.3d 255 (3d Cir.1999)—§ 18.4(c) n.33

McCann, People v., 122 P.3d 1085 (Colo.App.2005)—§ 26.8(c) n.28

McCann, State v., 200 Ariz. 27, 21 P.3d 845 (2001)—§§ 21.4(e) n.161; 26.6(b) n.30

McCann, United States ex rel. v. Thompson, 144 F.2d 604 (2d Cir.1944)— § 15.6(c) n.98

McCants, Commonwealth v., 450 Pa. 245, 299 A.2d 283 (1973)—§ 3.4(g) n.126

McCard v. State, 78 P.3d 1040 (Wyo.2003)—§§ 21.5(a) n.40, 42; 27.5(e) n.155

McCardle, Ex parte, 74 U.S. (7 Wall.) 506, 19 L.Ed. 264 (1869)— § 28.2(b) n.22

McCarrick v. State, 553 So.2d 1373 (Fla.App.1989)—§ 26.10(d) n.97

McCart v. State, 387 So.2d 232 (Ala.App.1980)—§ 16.4(c) n.86

McCarter v. State, 363 Md. 705, 770 A.2d 195 (2001)—§ 11.2(b) n.42

McCarthy v. Arndstein, 262 U.S. 355, 43 S.Ct. 562, 67 L.Ed. 1023 (1923)—§ 2.12(a) n.10

McCarthy v. Arndstein, 266 U.S. 34, 45 S.Ct. 16, 69 L.Ed. 158 (1924)— §§ 2.10(b) n.4; 2.10(d) n.122

McCarthy, State v., 819 A.2d 335 (Me.2003)—§ 6.2(c) n.100

McCarthy v. State, 65 S.W.3d 47 (Tex.Cr.App.2001)—§ 6.9(f) n.141

McCarthy, State v., 258 Mont. 51, 852 P.2d 111 (1993)—§ 9.1(d) n.122

McCarthy, State v., 197 Conn. 247, 496 A.2d 513 (1985)—§ 22.2(d) n.77

McCarthy v. United States, 320 F.3d 1230 (11th Cir.2003)—§ 21.4(d) n.131

McCarthy v. United States, 394 U.S. 459, 89 S.Ct. 1166, 22 L.Ed.2d 418 (1969)—§§ 1.7(i) n.163, 167; 21.4(c) n.97; 21.5(b) n.62; 21.5(c) n.77

McCartney, State v., 55 Ohio App.3d 170, 563 N.E.2d 350 (1988)— § 16.1(h) n.286

McCarty v. State, 114 P.3d 1089 (Okla.Cr.App.2005)—§ 24.3(e) n.132

McCarty, State v., 140 Wash.2d 420, 998 P.2d 296 (2000)—§§ 19.2(c) n.25; 19.3(e) n.244

McCarty v. State, 904 P.2d 110 (Okl.Crim.App.1995)—§ 9.4(a) n.26

McCarty v. State, 107 N.M. 651, 763 P.2d 360 (1988)—§§ 20.6(c) n.76, 79, 80

McCarty, United States v., 475 F.3d 39 (1st Cir.2007)—§ 6.6(e) n.61

McCarty, United States v., 862 F.2d 143 (7th Cir.1988)—§ 19.3(b) n.156

McCarver v. Lee, 221 F.3d 583 (4th Cir.2000)—§ 28.7(c) n.23

McCary, Ex parte, 528 So.2d 1133 (Ala.1988)—§ 6.2(c) n.128

McCauley, People v., 163 Ill.2d 414, 206 Ill.Dec. 671, 645 N.E.2d 923 (1994)—§ 6.9(c) n.61

McChristian, People v., 245 Cal.App.2d 891, 54 Cal.Rptr. 324 (1966)—§ 14.3(a) n.24

McClain, State v., 258 Kan. 176, 899 P.2d 993 (1995)—§§ 14.2(g) n.95, 105; 14.3(d) n.93

McClamrock v. State, 374 So.2d 1076 (Fla.App.1979)—§ 19.3(b) n.166

McClamrock, State v., 295 So.2d 715 (Fla.App.1974)—§ 3.10(b) n.79

McClanahan, State v., 212 Kan. 208, 510 P.2d 153 (1973)—§ 22.1(g) n.115

McClary, People v., 20 Cal.3d 218, 142 Cal.Rptr. 163, 571 P.2d 620 (1977)—§ 6.9(f) n.109

McClary, State v., 679 N.W.2d 455 (N.D.2004)—§ 24.10(b) n.26

McClatchy Newspapers, In re, 288 F.3d 369 (9th Cir.2002)—§§ 23.1(d) n.174; 23.1(e) n.224

McClatchy Newspapers v. Superior Court, 44 Cal.3d 1162, 245 Cal.Rptr. 774, 751 P.2d 1329 (1988)—§§ 8.3(h) n.36, 41; 8.5(a) n.5

McCleary, State v., 116 Ariz. 244, 568 P.2d 1142 (1977)—§ 3.6(e) n.131

McClellan, People v., 6 Cal.4th 367, 24 Cal.Rptr.2d 739, 862 P.2d 739 (1993)—§ 21.5(a) n.15

McClellan v. State, 359 So.2d 869 (Fla.App.1978)—§ 3.1(e) n.139

McClellan v. State, 53 Wis.2d 724, 193 N.W.2d 711 (1972)—§ 6.8(a) n.13

McClelland v. McGrath, 31 F. Supp.2d 616 (N.D. Ill. 1998)—§§ 4.6(l) n.186, 214

McClendon v. Story County Sheriff's Office, 403 F.3d 510 (8th Cir.2005)—§ 3.4(k) n.219

McCleskey v. Kemp, 481 U.S. 279, 107 S.Ct. 1756, 95 L.Ed.2d 262 (1987)—§§ 1.5(j) n.312; 13.4(b) n.68, 77; 24.7(e) n.61; 26.4(b) n.10

McCleskey v. Zant, 499 U.S. 467, 111 S.Ct. 1454, 113 L.Ed.2d 517 (1991)—§§ 2.9(f) n.119, 122; 24.11(d) n.17; 28.4(d) n.64; 28.5(d) n.78

McCline, People v., 442 Mich. 127, 499 N.W.2d 341 (1993)—§ 22.4(e) n.51

McCloskey, Commonwealth v., 443 Pa. 117, 277 A.2d 764 (1971)—§ 8.14(c) n.37

McCloud, State v., 357 So.2d 1132 (La.1978)—§§ 14.2(g) n.99; 15.5(c) n.107

McCloud, United States v., 127 F.3d 1284 (10th Cir.1997)—§ 3.4(h) n.151

McClure, State v., 184 W.Va. 418, 400 S.E.2d 853 (1990)—§ 22.3(a) n.50

McClure, State v., 277 S.C. 432, 289 S.E.2d 158 (1982)—§ 14.2(e) n.69

McClure v. Thompson, 323 F.3d 1233 (9th Cir.2003)—§ 11.10(b) n.42

McClure, United States v., 734 F.2d 484 (10th Cir.1984)—§§ 17.2(d) n.95, 113; 20.3(b) n.55

McCluskie, State v., 611 A.2d 975 (Me.1992)—§ 6.9(d) n.72

McClusky, Ex parte, 40 F. 71 (C.C.D.Ark.1889)—§ 15.1(f) n.276

McCollins, People v., 126 Ill.App.3d 1083, 82 Ill.Dec. 134, 468 N.E.2d 196 (1984)—§ 27.3(c) n.39

McCollom, United States v., 651 F.Supp. 1217 (N.D.Ill.1987)—§ 8.12(g) n.63

McCollum v. Board of Education, 333 U.S. 203, 68 S.Ct. 461, 92 L.Ed. 649 (1948)—§ 2.5(f) n.72

McCollum, State v., 334 N.C. 208, 433 S.E.2d 144 (1993)—§ 22.3(d) n.252

McConahy, United States v., 505 F.2d 770 (7th Cir.1974)—§ 18.4(a) n.15

McConaughy v. Lockhart, 310 Ark. 686, 840 S.W.2d 166 (1992)—§ 11.7(e) n.76

McConico v. Alabama, 919 F.2d 1543 (11th Cir.1990)—§§ 11.9(a) n.7; 11.9(d) n.194

McConkie, State v., 755 A.2d 1075 (Me.2000)—§ 6.2(c) n.139

McConnell, United States v., 903 F.2d 566 (8th Cir.1990)—§ 3.6(c) n.76

McConnell, United States v., 842 F.2d 105 (5th Cir.1988)—§§ 12.1(a) n.8; 12.2(b) n.19

McConnell, United States v., 749 F.2d 1441 (10th Cir.1984)—§ 17.2(c) n.90

McCoo v. State, 921 So.2d 450 (Ala.2005)—§ 26.10(d) n.85

McCorkendale, State v., 267 Kan. 263, 979 P.2d 1239 (1999)—§ 6.9(g) n.155

McCorkle v. State, 95 Md.App. 31, 619 A.2d 186 (1993)—§ 25.2(d) n.34

McCormick, People v., 859 P.2d 846 (Colo.1993)—§§ 17.4(c) n.153; 21.2(d) n.242

McCormick v. State, 803 N.E.2d 1108 (Ind.2004)—§§ 22.3(d) n.214, 221, 228, 248

McCormick, State v., 246 Neb. 890, 523 N.W.2d 697 (1994)—§ 27.5(a) n.32

McCormick, State v., 778 S.W.2d 48 (Tenn.1989)—§ 6.4(e) n.64

McCormick, State v., 385 N.W.2d 121 (S.D.1986)—§ 26.10(b) n.22

McCormick, State v., 273 N.W.2d 624 (Minn.1978)—§ 16.4(c) n.53

McCormick, United States v., 502 F.2d 281 (9th Cir.1974)—§ 3.7(a) n.5

McCottrell, People v., 117 Ill.App.2d 1, 254 N.E.2d 284 (1969)—§ 6.8(c) n.72

McCown, State v., 113 Or.App. 627, 833 P.2d 1321 (1992)—§§ 16.1(e) n.194; 16.1(h) n.308

McCown, United States v., 711 F.2d 1441 (9th Cir.1983)—§ 18.3(b) n.5

McCoy v. Commission of Internal Revenue, 696 F.2d 1234 (9th Cir.1983)—§ 8.13(b) n.62

McCoy v. Court of Appeals of Wisconsin, 486 U.S. 429, 108 S.Ct. 1895, 100 L.Ed.2d 440 (1988)—§§ 11.2(c) n.83, 87, 89, 100, 101

McCoy, People v., 207 Ill.2d 352, 278 Ill.Dec. 551, 799 N.E.2d 269 (2003)—§ 24.10(b) n.34

McCoy, People v., 40 Cal.App.4th 778, 47 Cal.Rptr.2d 599 (1995)—§ 22.2(d) n.67

McCoy, People v., 9 Cal.App.4th 1578, 12 Cal.Rptr.2d 476 (1992)—§ 27.5(a) n.22

McCoy, State v., 320 N.C. 581, 359 S.E.2d 764 (1987)—§ 22.2(d) n.74

McCoy, State v., 100 Idaho 753, 605 P.2d 517 (1980)—§ 24.3(b) n.65

McCoy, State v., 91 W.Va. 262, 111 S.E. 125 (1922)—§ 16.1(b) n.83

McCoy, United States v., 323 F.3d 1114 (9th Cir.2003)—§§ 1.2(c) n.130, 145

McCoy v. United States, 266 F.3d 1245 (11th Cir.2001)—§§ 19.2(e) n.82; 19.3(a) n.90, 98

McCoy v. United States, 781 A.2d 765 (D.C.App.2001)—§§ 7.4(c) n.50; 7.4(e) n.93

McCoy, United States v., 215 F.3d 102 (D.C.Cir.2000)—§§ 21.5(a) n.38, 43

McCoy, United States v., 848 F.2d 743 (6th Cir.1988)—§ 22.3(d) n.247

McCoy v. Wisconsin Court of Appeals, 137 Wis.2d 90, 403 N.W.2d 449 (1987)—§ 11.2(c) n.101

McCra, Commonwealth v., 427 Mass. 564, 694 N.E.2d 849 (1998)—§ 6.9(b) n.23

McCraney v. State, 180 Ind.App. 190, 388 N.E.2d 283 (1979)—§ 11.4(c) n.81

McCranie, United States v., 703 F.2d 1213 (10th Cir.1983)—§ 3.2(b) n.66

McCrary, State v., 253 Ga. 747, 325 S.E.2d 151 (1985)—§ 17.4(c) n.155

McCrary, State v., 97 N.M. 306, 639 P.2d 593 (1982)—§ 14.3(d) n.84

McCraw v. State, 476 P.2d 370 (Okla.Crim.App.1970)—§§ 11.2(g) n.265, 298

McCray v. Illinois, 386 U.S. 300, 87 S.Ct. 1056, 18 L.Ed.2d 62 (1967)—§§ 2.7(a) n.21; 2.9(g) n.198; 3.3(c) n.79, 88, 139; 10.5(e) n.43; 24.3(g) n.166

McCray, People v., 245 Mich.App. 631, 630 N.W.2d 633 (Mich.App.2001)—§ 20.5(b) n.25

McCray, State v., 332 S.C. 536, 506 S.E.2d 301 (1998)—§§ 6.9(g) n.167; 22.3(d) n.206

McCray v. State, 738 So.2d 911 (Ala.Crim.App.1998)—§§ 15.5(c) n.112; 15.7(b) n.28

McCreary v. State, 582 So.2d 425 (Miss.1991)—§ 26.9(b) n.75

McCreary-Redd, United States v., 475 F.3d 718 (6th Cir.2007)—§§ 21.4(c) n.78; 21.4(f) n.192

McCrimmon v. United States, 853 A.2d 154 (D.C.App.2004)—§ 11.9(d) n.230

McCrory v. State, 342 So.2d 897 (Miss.1977)—§ 2.12(d) n.187

McCrory, United States v., 930 F.2d 63 (D.C.Cir.1991)—§§ 3.1(f) n.153, 154

McCroy, State v., 259 Neb. 709, 613 N.W.2d 1 (2000)—§ 11.8(c) n.77

McCullar v. State, 696 S.W.2d 579 (1985)—§ 19.1(b) n.19

McCullar v. State, 676 S.W.2d 587 (Tex.Crim.App.1984)—§ 26.10(d) n.90

McCullough, Commonwealth v., 501 Pa. 423, 461 A.2d 1229 (1983)—§ 14.3(d) n.101

McCullough v. Maryland, 17 U.S. (4 Wheat.) 316, 4 L.Ed. 579 (1819)—§§ 1.2(c) n.33, 34

McCullough, State v., 49 Wash.App. 546, 744 P.2d 641 (1987)—§ 8.11(b) n.32

McCully, United States v., 407 F.3d 931 (8th Cir.2005)—§ 26.4(i) n.201

McCurdy, United States v., 40 F.3d 1111 (10th Cir.1994)—§ 6.7(c) n.120

McCurry, State v., 228 Neb. 841, 424 N.W.2d 364 (1988)—§ 6.2(c) n.96

McCurry v. State, 538 P.2d 100 (Alaska 1975)—§ 20.3(h) n.141

McCutcheon, State v., 162 Ariz. 54, 781 P.2d 31 (1989)—§ 7.5(b) n.23

McDade, United States v., 28 F.3d 283 (3d Cir.1994)—§ 27.2(c) n.33

McDaniel v. State, 271 Ga. 552, 522 S.E.2d 648 (1999)—§ 21.3(d) n.221

McDaniel v. State, 356 So.2d 1151 (Miss.1978)—§ 24.3(b) n.57

McDaniel, State v., 44 Ohio App.2d 163, 337 N.E.2d 173 (1975)—§ 3.2(e) n.172

McDaniel, United States v., 482 F.2d 305 (8th Cir.1973)—§§ 8.11(b) n.28; 8.11(c) n.37, 55 to 57, 61; 15.7(d) n.78; 24.3(i) n.193

McDermott, People v., 28 Cal.4th 946, 123 Cal.Rptr.2d 654, 51 P.3d 874 (2002)—§§ 22.3(d) n.202, 220

McDermott, State v., 962 P.2d 136 (Wyo.1998)—§ 21.4(b) n.45

McDermott, State v., 131 N.H. 495, 554 A.2d 1302 (1989)—§ 6.2(c) n.140

McDermott, United States v., 277 F.3d 240 (2d Cir.2002)—§ 19.6(c) n.32

McDile, United States v., 914 F.2d 1059 (8th Cir.1990)—§ 3.1(c) n.78

McDole v. State, 339 Ark. 391, 6 S.W.3d 74 (1999)—§§ 20.2(e) n.82; 20.3(m) n.236

McDole v. State, 283 So.2d 553 (Fla.1973)—§ 10.4(b) n.8

McDonald v. Arkansas, 501 F.2d 385 (8th Cir.1974)—§ 3.3(d) n.172

McDonald v. District Court, 195 Colo. 159, 576 P.2d 169 (Colo.1978)—§§ 14.4(d) n.84, 87, 88; 14.4(e) n.109

McDonald v. Johnson, 139 F.3d 1056 (5th Cir.1998)—§ 28.7(c) n.23

McDonald v. Moore, 353 F.2d 106 (5th Cir.1965)—§ 6.10(a) n.5

McDonald, People v., 227 Ill.App.3d 92, 169 Ill.Dec. 84, 590 N.E.2d 1003 (1992)—§ 24.2(d) n.45

McDonald, People v., 125 Ill.2d 182, 125 Ill.Dec. 781, 530 N.E.2d 1351 (1988)—§ 22.3(d) n.242

McDonald, People v., 37 Cal.3d 351, 208 Cal.Rptr. 236, 690 P.2d 709 (1984)—§ 7.5(b) n.23

McDonald v. Pless, 238 U.S. 264, 35 S.Ct. 783, 59 L.Ed. 1300 (1915)—§ 24.9(g) n.111

McDonald, State v., 143 Wash.2d 506, 22 P.3d 791 (2001)—§ 11.5(f) n.106

McDonald v. State, 61 Md.App. 461, 487 A.2d 306 (1985)—§§ 16.1(a) n.1; 16.4(d) n.144

McDonald, State v., 231 Or. 24, 361 P.2d 1001 (1961)—§ 3.1(f) n.146

McDonald, State v., 109 Wis. 506, 85 N.W. 502 (1901)—§ 16.1(e) n.191

McDonald, United States v., 740 F.Supp. 757 (D.Alaska 1990)—§§ 16.3(c) n.40, 42

McDonald v. United States, 335 U.S. 451, 69 S.Ct. 191, 93 L.Ed. 153 (1948)—§§ 3.2(c) n.114; 3.6(e) n.114; 9.1(b) n.39, 56; 9.2(c) n.17

McDonnell, State v., 313 Or. 478, 837 P.2d 941 (1992)—§ 21.3(c) n.157

McDonnell, State v., 310 Or. 98, 794 P.2d 780 (1990)—§§ 21.3(c) n.152; 21.3(f) n.361

McDonnell v. United States, 4 F.3d 1227 (3d Cir.1993)—§ 8.5(b) n.35

McDonough, State v., 631 N.W.2d 373 (Minn.2001)—§§ 6.9(f) n.134; 22.3(d) n.247

McDonough, United States v., 56 F.3d 381 (2d Cir.1995)—§ 23.2(h) n.127

McDonough, United States v., 603 F.2d 19 (7th Cir.1979)—§ 16.1(h) n.311

McDonough Power Equipment, Inc. v. Greenwood, 464 U.S. 548, 104 S.Ct. 845, 78 L.Ed.2d 663 (1984)—§ 24.9(f) n.95

McDougal v. State, 277 Ga. 493, 591 S.E.2d 788 (2004)—§§ 6.6(d) n.53; 6.9(f) n.137, 139; 6.9(g) n.162

McDougall v. Dixon, 921 F.2d 518 (4th Cir.1990)—§ 11.8(c) n.78

McDougle v. State, 355 So.2d 1386 (Miss.1978)—§ 6.9(f) n.111

McDoulett v. State, 685 P.2d 978 (Okl.Cr.1984)—§ 7.5(a) n.7

McDowell v. Chesney, 2004 WL 1376591 (D.Del.2004)—§ 28.3(a) n.34

McDowell, State v., 272 Wis.2d 488, 681 N.W.2d 500 (2004)—§ 11.10(b) n.45

McDowell, State v., 824 A.2d 948 (Del.2003)—§ 18.4(c) n.53

McDowell v. State, 807 So.2d 413 (Miss.2001)—§ 7.4(e) n.90

McDowell, State v., 242 Conn. 648, 699 A.2d 987 (1997)—§§ 17.4(a) n.31, 66

McDowell, State v., 685 A.2d 252 (R.I.1996)—§ 24.4(d) n.54

McDowell, State v., 329 N.C. 363, 407 S.E.2d 200 (1991)—§ 3.10(a) n.22

McDowell, State v., 102 Wash.2d 341, 685 P.2d 595 (1984)—§ 13.7(c) n.43

McDowell, United States v., 250 F.3d 1354 (11th Cir.2001)—§ 6.6(e) n.93

McDowell, United States v., 888 F.2d 285 (3d Cir.1989)—§§ 8.5(e) n.182, 191

McDowell v. United States, 484 U.S. 980, 108 S.Ct. 478, 98 L.Ed.2d 492 (1987)—§ 11.5(c) n.52

McDowell, United States v., 814 F.2d 245 (6th Cir.1987)—§§ 11.3(b) n.42; 11.5(c) n.32, 34, 38, 39, 42, 46, 47, 52; 11.5(d) n.81, 84

McDowell v. United States, 383 F.2d 599 (8th Cir.1967)—§ 3.2(d) n.145

McDowney, State v., 49 N.J. 471, 231 A.2d 359 (1967)—§ 16.4(d) n.138

McDuff v. State, 939 S.W.2d 607 (Tex.Cr.App.1997)—§ 3.2(f) n.174

McDuffee, People v., 187 Ill.2d 481, 241 Ill.Dec. 603, 719 N.E.2d 732 (1999)—§ 22.4(d) n.33

M.C.E., United States v., 232 F.3d 1252 (9th Cir.2000)—§ 27.2(c) n.45

McElderry, State v., 422 N.W.2d 23 (Minn.Ct.App.1988)—§ 26.1(d) n.89

McElhaney, United States v., 469 F.3d 382 (5th Cir.2006)—§ 21.2(b) n.59

McElhiney, United States v., 275 F.3d 928 (10th Cir.2001)—§ 24.9(d) n.48

McElmurry v. State, 60 P.3d 4 (Okla.Cr.App.2002)—§§ 22.3(d) n.200, 220

McElrath, State v., 322 N.C. 1, 366 S.E.2d 442 (1988)—§ 24.6(b) n.29

McElreavy, State v., 157 Vt. 18, 595 A.2d 1332 (1991)—§ 6.6(e) n.59

McElroy v. State, 247 Ga. 355, 276 S.E.2d 38 (1981)—§ 26.10(b) n.40

McElroy, State v., 71 R.I. 379, 46 A.2d 397 (1946)—§§ 16.1(d) n.137; 16.2(g) n.120, 124

McElroy v. United States, 361 U.S. 281, 80 S.Ct. 305, 4 L.Ed.2d 282 (1960)—§ 15.1(b) n.92

McElvaine v. Brush, 142 U.S. 155, 12 S.Ct. 156, 35 L.Ed. 971 (1891)—§ 2.3(b) n.83

McFadden v. Garraghty, 820 F.2d 654 (4th Cir.1987)—§ 6.9(f) n.144

McFadden, State v., 216 S.W.3d 673 (Mo.2007)—§ 22.3(d) n.245

McFadden, United States v., 630 F.2d 963 (3d Cir.1980)—§ 11.4(c) n.78

McFarlan v. District Court, 718 P.2d 247 (Colo.1986)—§ 22.5(b) n.22

McFarlan, People v., 42 N.Y.2d 896, 397 N.Y.S.2d 1003, 366 N.E.2d 1357 (1977)—§ 8.10(c) n.61

McFarland v. Scott, 512 U.S. 849, 114 S.Ct. 2568, 129 L.Ed.2d 666 (1994)—§ 28.12(b) n.8

McFarland v. Smith, 611 F.2d 414 (2d Cir.1979)—§ 24.7(e) n.61

McFarland v. State, 707 So.2d 166 (Miss.1997)—§§ 22.3(d) n.242, 246; 23.2(f) n.90

McFarland v. State, 928 S.W.2d 482 (1996)—§ 11.10(d) n.199

McFarland, State v., 127 Wash.2d 322, 899 P.2d 1251 (1995)—§ 11.7(e) n.85

McFarland, State v., 175 W.Va. 205, 332 S.E.2d 217 (1985)—§ 6.7(b) n.72

McFarland v. Yukins, 356 F.3d 688 (6th Cir.2004)—§§ 11.9(b) n.53; 11.9(d) n.153, 231

McFarlane, United States v., 309 F.3d 510 (8th Cir.2002)—§§ 8.11(e) n.104, 106

McFayden, United States v., 865 F.2d 1306 (D.C.Cir.1989)—§ 3.9(g) n.125

McFerguson v. United States, 770 A.2d 66 (D.C.2001)—§§ 3.8(d) n.175; 9.3(e) n.59

McFerron, Commonwealth v., 680 S.W.2d 924 (Ky.1984)—§ 22.2(d) n.63

McFerron, United States v., 163 F.3d 952 (6th Cir.1998)—§ 27.6(d) n.141

McGahan v. State, 606 P.2d 396 (Alaska 1980)—§ 19.5(b) n.14

McGath, State v., 370 N.W.2d 882 (Minn.1985)—§ 24.2(a) n.20

McGautha v. California, 402 U.S. 183, 91 S.Ct. 1454, 28 L.Ed.2d 711 (1971)—§§ 2.7(a) n.14, 56; 2.7(c) n.118, 126, 163; 2.9(d) n.89, 97; 2.10(c) n.99; 24.5(a) n.14; 26.2(b)

n.19; 26.4(g) n.122, 143, 144; 26.6(d) n.60

McGavic, United States v., 337 F.2d 317 (6th Cir.1964)—§ 9.4(a) n.2

McGee, Commonwealth v., 560 Pa. 324, 744 A.2d 754 (2000)—§ 17.4(b) n.133

McGee, People v., 38 Cal.4th 682, 42 Cal.Rptr.3d 899, 133 P.3d 1054 (2006)—§ 26.4(i) n.198

McGee v. State, 105 Nev. 718, 782 P.2d 1329 (1989)—§ 9.6(c) n.59

McGee, State v., 757 S.W.2d 321 (Mo.App.1988)—§ 14.2(d) n.50

McGee, United States v., 408 F.3d 966 (7th Cir.2005)—§ 24.3(c) n.103

McGee, United States v., 7 F.3d 1496 (10th Cir.1993)—§ 21.1(h) n.233

McGee, United States v., 108 F.Supp. 909 (D.C.Wyo.1952)—§ 16.2(g) n.127

McGhee, State v., 280 N.W.2d 436 (Iowa 1979)—§ 24.11(d) n.28

McGhee, State v., 350 So.2d 370 (La.1977)—§ 7.3(c) n.59

McGill, State v., 234 Wis.2d 560, 609 N.W.2d 795 (2000)—§§ 3.8(e) n.185, 198

McGinnis v. Johnson, 181 F.3d 686 (5th Cir.1999)—§ 22.2(d) n.80

McGinnis v. M.I. Harris, Inc., 486 F.Supp. 750 (N.D.Tex.1980)—§ 15.4(b) n.69

McGinnis v. Royster, 410 U.S. 263, 93 S.Ct. 1055, 35 L.Ed.2d 282 (1973)—§ 12.2(b) n.27

McGinnis, State v., 335 Or. 243, 64 P.3d 1123 (2003)—§§ 9.5(a) n.30; 9.5(d) n.75

McGinnis v. State, 28 Tenn. (9 Humph) 43, 49 Am.Doc 697 (1848)—§§ 15.1(d) n.227 to 229; 15.1(f) n.273

McGinnis v. Wine, 959 S.W.2d 437 (Ky.1998)—§ 25.4(d) n.44

McGlade v. State, 941 So.2d 1185 (Fla.App.2006)—§ 12.4(d) n.63

McGlocklin, United States v., 8 F.3d 1037 (6th Cir.1993)—§§ 21.4(f) n.204; 21.5(c) n.74

McGlory, United States v., 968 F.2d 309 (3d Cir.1992)—§ 26.4(f) n.85

McGoldrick, United States v., 796 F.Supp. 178 (E.D.Pa.1992)—§ 24.3(f) n.147

McGovern, People v., 307 Ill. 373, 138 N.E. 632 (1923)—§ 16.4(c) n.50

McGovern, United States v., 822 F.2d 739 (8th Cir.1987)—§ 21.3(e) n.265

McGowan, People v., 127 Cal.App. 39, 14 P.2d 1036 (1932)—§ 16.4(c) n.55

McGowan v. State, 742 So.2d 1183 (App.1999)—§ 16.1(e) n.175

McGowan v. State, 706 So.2d 231 (Miss.1997)—§§ 6.2(c) n.170; 6.9(b) n.24; 21.5(f) n.168; 22.3(c) n.157

McGowan v. State, 599 N.E.2d 589 (Ind.1992)—§ 3.5(a) n.62

McGowen v. State, 25 S.W.3d 741 (Tex.App.2000)—§ 24.7(a) n.1

McGrath, Commonwealth v., 508 Pa. 250, 495 A.2d 517 (1985)—§ 6.6(d) n.48

McGrath, United States v., 613 F.2d 361 (2d Cir.1979)—§ 9.1(d) n.122

McGraw v. Holland, 257 F.3d 513 (6th Cir.2001)—§ 6.9(g) n.149

McGraw, State v., 129 N.J. 68, 608 A.2d 1335 (N.J.1992)—§ 24.4(c) n.21

McGraw v. State, 260 So.2d 457 (Miss.1972)—§ 20.2(a) n.7

McGregor v. Gibson, 248 F.3d 946 (10th Cir.2001)—§ 28.6(f) n.76

McGregor v. Gibson, 219 F.3d 1245 (10th Cir.2000)—§ 6.9(b) n.38

McGregor v. State, 754 P.2d 1216 (Okla.Crim.App.1988)—§ 11.2(e) n.168

McGrew, State v., 38 Or.App. 493, 590 P.2d 755 (1979)—§ 6.9(c) n.49

McGriff, Ex parte, 908 So.2d 1024 (Ala.2004)—§ 26.2(b) n.8

McGrone, State v., 798 So.2d 519 (Miss.2001)—§ 24.3(e) n.127

McGruder, State v., 123 N.M. 302, 940 P.2d 150 (1997)—§ 7.4(c) n.48

McGuinness v. Commonwealth, 423 Mass. 1003, 667 N.E.2d 818 (1996)—§ 27.2(c) n.65

McGuire, Commonwealth v., 19 Mass.App. 1013, 476 N.E.2d 632 (1985)—§§ 15.7(f) n.169, 184

McGuire, United States v., 307 F.3d 1192 (9th Cir.2002)—§§ 4.6(e) n.96; 4.6(m) n.237, 241

McGuire, United States v., 200 F.3d 668 (10th Cir.1999)—§ 7.5(a) n.6

McGuire, United States v., 45 F.3d 1177 (8th Cir.1995)—§ 15.7(d) n.68

McGuirk, Commonwealth v., 376 Mass. 338, 380 N.E.2d 662 (1978)—§ 21.4(c) n.76

McHenry v. State, 820 N.E.2d 124 (Ind.2005)—§ 22.3(c) n.133

McIlwain v. United States, 568 A.2d 470 (D.C.App.1989)—§ 6.6(e) n.61

McInnis, People v., 6 Cal.3d 821, 100 Cal.Rptr. 618, 494 P.2d 690 (1972)—§ 9.4(d) n.95

McIntire, People v., 23 Cal.3d 742, 153 Cal.Rptr. 237, 591 P.2d 527 (1979)—§ 5.1(c) n.37

McIntire v. State, 717 N.E.2d 96 (Ind.1999)—§ 17.4(b) n.94

McIntosh, State v., 213 Ariz. 579, 146 P.3d 80 (Ariz.App.2006)—§ 24.9(e) n.60

McIntosh v. State, 296 Ark. 167, 753 S.W.2d 273 (1988)—§ 3.10(a) n.2

McIntosh, State v., 199 Conn. 155, 506 A.2d 104 (1986)—§ 24.8(f) n.92

McIntosh, United States v., 857 F.2d 466 (8th Cir.1988)—§ 3.10(b) n.37

McIntosh, United States v., 612 F.2d 835 (4th Cir.1979)—§§ 21.2(e) n.326, 333, 344

McIntyre, People v., 36 N.Y.2d 10, 364 N.Y.S.2d 837, 324 N.E.2d 322 (1974)—§ 11.5(b) n.25

McIntyre v. State, 266 Ga. 7, 463 S.E.2d 476 (1995)—§ 27.6(d) n.147

McIntyre v. State, 309 Md. 607, 526 A.2d 30 (1987)—§ 6.2(c) n.163

McIntyre, United States v., 997 F.2d 687 (10th Cir.1993)—§ 22.3(c) n.125

McJunkin, Commonwealth v., 11 Mass.App.Ct. 609, 418 N.E.2d 1259 (1981)—§§ 15.7(f) n.136, 152, 175

McKamey v. Roach, 55 F.3d 1236 (6th Cir.1995)—§ 4.3(b) n.9

McKane v. Durston, 153 U.S. 684, 14 S.Ct. 913, 38 L.Ed. 867 (1894)— §§ 12.4(d) n.76; 27.1(a) n.1

McKaskle v. Vela, 464 U.S. 1053, 104 S.Ct. 736, 79 L.Ed.2d 195 (1984)— § 28.5(a) n.34

McKaskle v. Wiggins, 465 U.S. 168, 104 S.Ct. 944, 79 L.Ed.2d 122 (1984)—§§ 11.5(a) n.10; 11.5(d) n.81; 11.5(f) n.95; 11.5(g) n.109; 27.6(d) n.103

McKay v. Collins, 12 F.3d 66 (5th Cir.1994)—§§ 19.2(c) n.26, 31; 19.3(a) n.57

McKay, People v., 27 Cal.4th 601, 117 Cal.Rptr.2d 236, 41 P.3d 59 (2002)—§ 3.1(e) n.129

McKee v. Harris, 649 F.2d 927 (2d Cir.1981)—§§ 11.4(b) n.19, 24, 26, 36, 38; 11.4(d) n.111

McKee, State v., 330 Mont. 249, 127 P.3d 445 (2006)—§§ 6.6(e) n.95; 6.9(b) n.22

McKeehan, State v., 894 S.W.2d 216 (Mo.App.1995)—§§ 19.5(b) n.27, 37

McKeeth v. State, 140 Idaho 847, 103 P.3d 460 (2004)—§ 21.3(b) n.72

McKeiver v. Pennsylvania, 403 U.S. 528, 91 S.Ct. 1976, 29 L.Ed.2d 647 (1971)—§§ 12.4(b) n.47; 22.1(c) n.63

McKendry v. State, 641 So.2d 45 (Fla.1994)—§ 26.1(d) n.76

McKenna, Ex parte, 655 So.2d 989 (Ala.1995)—§ 25.1(d) n.49

McKenna, Commonwealth v., 355 Mass. 313, 244 N.E.2d 560 (1969)— § 6.4(f) n.115

McKenna v. State, 780 S.W.2d 797 (Tex.Cr.App.1989)—§ 21.6(b) n.84

McKenna v. State, 101 Nev. 338, 705 P.2d 614 (1985)—§ 21.2(h) n.423

McKenney, State v., 98 Idaho 551, 568 P.2d 1213 (1977)—§ 11.2(c) n.90

McKenzie, People v., 263 Ill.App.3d 716, 200 Ill.Dec. 564, 635 N.E.2d 903 (1994)—§ 11.10(c) n.76

McKenzie v. Risley, 801 F.2d 1519 (9th Cir.1986)—§ 21.2(f) n.369

McKenzie, State v., 197 W.Va. 429, 475 S.E.2d 521 (1996)—§§ 6.9(f) n.144; 6.9(g) n.200; 24.4(d) n.51

McKenzie, State v., 532 N.W.2d 210 (Minn.1995)—§§ 22.1(h) n.149; 24.8(a) n.7

McKenzie, State v., 186 Mont. 481, 608 P.2d 428 (1980)—§ 10.3(b) n.21

McKenzie v. State, 145 Ga.App. 224, 243 S.E.2d 646 (1978)—§ 16.2(a) n.1

McKenzie, United States v., 735 F.2d 907 (5th Cir.1984)—§ 23.1(c) n.107

McKenzie, United States v., 678 F.2d 629 (5th Cir.1982)—§§ 15.2(e) n.142; 15.2(h) n.187; 15.6(b) n.53, 62; 15.6(d) n.129; 15.7(b) n.11, 33, 36, 42 to 44

McKeon, United States v., 738 F.2d 26 (2d Cir.1984)—§ 11.9(c) n.142

McKeown, State v., 249 Kan. 506, 819 P.2d 644 (1991)—§ 3.8(c) n.96

McKessor, State v., 246 Kan. 1, 785 P.2d 1332 (1990)—§ 7.3(b) n.14

McKevitt v. Pallasch, 339 F.3d 530 (7th Cir.2003)—§ 8.8(d) n.82

McKibben, State v., 239 Kan. 574, 722 P.2d 518 (1986)—§§ 22.5(d) n.32, 34, 36

McKie, United States v., 112 F.3d 626 (3d Cir.1997)—§§ 21.2(f) n.370; 27.5(b) n.40

McKim, State v., 215 S.W.3d 781 (Tenn.2007)—§ 27.2(b) n.19

McKines, United States v., 933 F.2d 1412 (8th Cir.1991)—§§ 3.10(b) n.67; 3.10(f) n.197

McKinley v. City of Mansfield, 404 F.3d 418 (6th Cir.2005)—§§ 8.10(e) n.124; 8.11(a) n.8

McKinley, United States v., 485 F.2d 1059 (D.C.Cir.1973)—§ 7.2(d) n.47

McKinnell, United States v., 888 F.2d 669 (10th Cir.1989)—§ 18.3(b) n.51

McKinney, State v., 273 Neb. 346, 730 N.W.2d 74 (2007)—§§ 3.5(d) n.165, 175; 6.6(d) n.57; 6.9(g) n.200; 24.3(f) n.154

McKinney, State v., 272 Kan. 331, 33 P.3d 234 (2001)—§ 24.2(a) n.8

McKinney v. State, 553 N.E.2d 860 (Ind.App.1990)—§§ 16.4(c) n.98; 16.4(d) n.121, 123, 126, 134, 135, 139

McKinney, United States v., 395 F.3d 837 (8th Cir.2004)—§ 18.4(c) n.69

McKinney, United States v., 822 F.2d 946 (10th Cir.1987)—§§ 24.10(d) n.45, 48

McKinnon, United States v., 985 F.2d 525 (11th Cir.1993)—§ 4.6(a) n.9

McKinnon, United States v., 721 F.2d 19 (1st Cir.1983)—§§ 1.7(c) n.10; 4.6(h) n.147; 4.6(i) n.156

McKintrush v. State, 334 Ark. 390, 978 S.W.2d 293 (1998)—§ 22.3(d) n.235

McKissack, State v., 625 N.E.2d 1246 (Ind.App.1993)—§ 25.3(c) n.25

McKissick, United States v., 204 F.3d 1282 (10th Cir.2000)—§ 24.2(e) n.68

McKneely, United States v., 69 F.3d 1067 (10th Cir.1995)—§ 27.5(c) n.100

McKneely, United States v., 6 F.3d 1447 (10th Cir.1993)—§ 9.1(d) n.120

McKnight v. State, 320 S.C. 356, 465 S.E.2d 352 (1995)—§ 11.10(d) n.200

McKnight, State v., 52 N.J. 35, 243 A.2d 240 (1968)—§ 1.5(a) n.39

McKnight v. United States, 183 F.2d 977 (D.C.Cir.1950)—§ 3.6(g) n.169

McKorkle v. State, 305 So.2d 361 (Miss.1974)—§ 16.1(d) n.138

McKoy v. North Carolina, 494 U.S. 433, 110 S.Ct. 1227, 108 L.Ed.2d 369 (1990)—§ 26.1(b) n.21

McKoy, State v., 323 N.C. 1, 372 S.E.2d 12 (1988)—§§ 6.2(c) n.169, 173

McKoy, United States v., 78 F.3d 446 (9th Cir.1996)—§ 24.3(c) n.88

McKune v. Lile, 536 U.S. 24, 122 S.Ct. 2017, 153 L.Ed.2d 47 (2002)—§§ 2.10(b) n.48; 26.4(c) n.35; 26.9(b) n.70

McLain, United States v., 823 F.2d 1457 (11th Cir.1987)—§§ 11.9(a) n.13; 11.9(d) n.223

McLaughlin v. Bronson, 206 Conn. 267, 537 A.2d 1004 (1988)—§ 26.2(c) n.79

McLaughlin, Commonwealth v., 364 Mass. 211, 303 N.E.2d 338 (1973)—§ 17.2(b) n.43

McLaughlin v. District Court, 915 P.2d 919 (Okla.Crim.App.1996)—§ 14.4(d) n.75

McLaughlin v. North Carolina, 494 U.S. 1021, 110 S.Ct. 1463, 108 L.Ed.2d 601 (1990)—§ 22.2(c) n.41

McLaughlin, People v., 80 N.Y.2d 466, 591 N.Y.S.2d 966, 606 N.E.2d 1357 (1992)—§§ 16.1(a) n.1, 2; 16.4(d) n.117, 126, 131, 133

McLaughlin v. Royster, 346 F.Supp. 297 (E.D.Va.1972)—§§ 21.3(b) n.51, 74

McLaughlin, State v., 307 S.C. 19, 413 S.E.2d 819 (1992)—§ 3.3(f) n.209

McLaughlin, State v., 323 N.C. 68, 372 S.E.2d 49 (1988)—§ 22.2(c) n.41

McLaughlin, United States v., 126 F.3d 130 (3d Cir.1997)—§ 19.6(c) n.39

McLaughlin, United States v., 957 F.2d 12 (1st Cir.1992)—§ 8.11(e) n.109

McLaurin, United States v., 57 F.3d 823 (9th Cir.1995)—§ 17.4(a) n.19

McLean, State v., 815 A.2d 799 (Me.2002)—§ 22.3(c) n.157

McLean, State v., 294 N.C. 623, 242 S.E.2d 814 (1978)—§ 6.7(c) n.108

McLean, United States v., 409 F.3d 492 (1st Cir.2005)—§ 6.7(d) n.145

McLee, United States v., 436 F.3d 751 (7th Cir.2006)—§§ 4.6(e) n.95; 4.6(k) n.174

McLellan v. State, 696 So.2d 928 (Fla.App.1997)—§ 24.7(e) n.54

McLemore, People v., 27 Cal.App.4th 601, 32 Cal.Rptr.2d 687 (1994)—§ 24.10(c) n.40

McLemore, People v., 411 Mich. 691, 311 N.W.2d 720 (1981)—§ 18.4(c) n.40

McLemore, United States v., 28 F.3d 1160 (11th Cir.1994)—§ 1.2(d) n.270

McLennan, United States v., 672 F.2d 239 (1st Cir.1982)—§ 19.3(a) n.59

McLeod, Ex parte, 272 S.C. 373, 252 S.E.2d 126 (1979)—§ 8.4(b) n.27

McLeod, Commonwealth v., 394 Mass. 727, 477 N.E.2d 972 (1985)—§ 15.4(g) n.173

McLeod v. Ohio, 381 U.S. 356, 85 S.Ct. 1556, 14 L.Ed.2d 682 (1965)—§§ 6.4(b) n.18; 6.4(e) n.78

McLeod v. State, 718 So.2d 727 (Ala.1998)—§ 6.2(c) n.107

McLeod v. State, 581 So.2d 1144 (Ala.Crim.App.1990)—§ 11.2(e) n.211

McLeod, State v., 1 Ohio St.2d 60, 203 N.E.2d 349 (1964)—§ 6.4(b) n.29

McLeod, United States v., 53 F.3d 322 (11th Cir.1995)—§§ 11.3(c) n.58; 11.4(b) n.28, 29

McLeod, United States v., 493 F.2d 1186 (7th Cir.1974)—§ 4.6(b) n.41

McLernon, United States v., 746 F.2d 1098 (6th Cir.1984)—§ 24.3(h) n.182

McLindon v. United States, 329 F.2d 238 (D.C.Cir.1964)—§ 9.4(e) n.103

McMahan, State v., 821 S.W.2d 110 (Mo.App.1991)—§ 22.3(b) n.73

McMahan, United States v., 495 F.3d 410 (7th Cir.2007)—§ 26.4(c) n.30

McMahon v. Fulcomer, 821 F.2d 934 (3d Cir.1987)—§§ 11.4(b) n.19, 36; 11.5(c) n.49, 50, 52

McMahon v. State, 569 S.W.2d 753 (Mo.1978)—§§ 21.2(g) n.405, 407

McMahon v. State, 582 S.W.2d 786 (Tex.Cr.App.1978)—§ 9.1(a) n.14

McMahon, State v., 116 Ariz. 129, 568 P.2d 1027 (1977)—§ 9.4(d) n.83

McMahon, United States v., 104 F.3d 638 (4th Cir.1997)—§§ 24.4(d) n.59, 63

McMahon, United States v., 938 F.2d 1501 (1st Cir.1991)—§§ 8.5(g) n.224; 8.5(h) n.265

McManaman, United States v., 606 F.2d 919 (10th Cir.1979)—§ 18.5(b) n.65

McManis, People v., 26 Cal.App.3d 608, 102 Cal.Rptr. 889 (1972)—§ 20.3(i) n.162

McMann v. Richardson, 397 U.S. 759, 90 S.Ct. 1441, 25 L.Ed.2d 763 (1970)—§§ 9.5(d) n.76; 10.2(d) n.50, 51; 11.10(b) n.31, 36; 21.3(a) n.17; 21.3(b) n.39; 21.6(a) n.4

McMaster v. Retirement System, 362 S.C. 362, 608 S.E.2d 843 (2005)—§ 17.4(b) n.121

McMaster, State v., 206 Wis.2d 30, 556 N.W.2d 673 (1996)—§ 17.4(b) n.124

McMillan v. Pennsylvania, 477 U.S. 79, 106 S.Ct. 2411, 91 L.Ed.2d 67 (1986)—§§ 2.7(a) n.57; 2.7(c) n.165; 26.4(h) n.150; 26.4(i) n.162

McMillan, State v., 43 Conn.App. 698, 685 A.2d 1138 (1996)—§ 27.3(c) n.56

McMiller, People v., 389 Mich. 425, 208 N.W.2d 451 (1973)—§ 21.5(e) n.113

McMillian v. Monroe County, 520 U.S. 781, 117 S.Ct. 1734, 138 L.Ed.2d 1 (1997)—§ 3.1(k) n.267

McMorran v. State, 118 Nev. 379, 46 P.3d 81 (2002)—§ 10.4(c) n.23

McMorris, State v., 213 Wis.2d 156, 570 N.W.2d 384 (1997)—§ 7.3(f) n.113

McMullin v. South Carolina Dep't of Revenue & Taxation, 321 S.C. 475, 469 S.E.2d 600 (1996)—§ 17.4(b) n.138

McMullin v. State, 442 So.2d 155 (Ala.App.1983)—§ 20.3(m) n.236

McMurty, People v., 64 Misc.2d 63, 314 N.Y.S.2d 194 (N.Y.City Crim.Ct.1970)—§§ 1.9(b) n.19, 27

McNabb v. United States, 142 F.2d 904 (6th Cir.1944)—§§ 1.7(i) n.155; 6.3(a) n.3, 5

McNabb v. United States, 318 U.S. 332, 63 S.Ct. 608, 87 L.Ed. 819 (1943)—§§ 1.7(h) n.152; 1.7(i) n.153, 166; 2.8(c) n.59; 6.3(a) n.4

McNair v. Campbell, 416 F.3d 1291 (11th Cir.2005)—§§ 24.9(f) n.69; 28.4(c) n.31; 28.5(a) n.33

McNair v. Commonwealth, 37 Va.App. 687, 561 S.E.2d 26 (2002)—§§ 11.3(c) n.66; 11.4(d) n.115

McNair, People v., 87 N.Y.2d 772, 642 N.Y.S.2d 597, 665 N.E.2d 167 (1996)—§ 26.1(e) n.98

McNally v. Hill, 293 U.S. 131, 55 S.Ct. 24, 79 L.Ed. 238 (1934)—§ 28.3(a) n.32

McNally, United States v., 473 F.2d 934 (3d Cir.1973)—§ 3.3(a) n.11

McNamara, United States v., 74 F.3d 514 (4th Cir.1996)—§ 11.10(c) n.109

McNaught, State v., 238 Kan. 567, 713 P.2d 457 (1986)—§ 24.2(e) n.79

McNeal, In re, 99 Wash.App. 617, 994 P.2d 890 (2000)—§ 11.1(b) n.50

McNeal, State v., 337 So.2d 178 (La.1976)—§ 6.8(c) n.70

McNeal, United States v., 955 F.2d 1067 (6th Cir.1992)—§ 9.1(b) n.70

McNeely v. Blanas, 336 F.3d 822 (9th Cir.2003)—§§ 18.2(c) n.28; 18.2(d) n.64

McNeil v. State, 112 Md.App. 434, 685 A.2d 839 (1996)—§§ 27.3(c) n.34, 36

McNeil, State v., 155 Wis.2d 24, 454 N.W.2d 742 (1990)—§ 6.4(e) n.67

McNeil v. Wisconsin, 501 U.S. 171, 111 S.Ct. 2204, 115 L.Ed.2d 158 (1991)—§§ 1.5(c) n.94, 104; 1.5(e) n.229; 6.4(e) n.67, 97; 6.4(f) n.139, 140; 6.9(f) n.125; 6.9(g) n.196

McNeill, People v., 81 Mich.App. 368, 265 N.W.2d 334 (1978)—§ 7.3(c) n.47

McNerny, State v., 239 Neb. 887, 479 N.W.2d 454 (1992)—§ 26.3(f) n.57

McNulty, United States v., 47 F.3d 100 (4th Cir.1995)—§ 4.3(b) n.10

McParlin, State v., 422 A.2d 742 (R.I.1980)—§ 19.6(b) n.14

McPhail, Commonwealth v., 547 Pa. 519, 692 A.2d 139 (1997)— § 25.5(c) n.36

McPhail, State v., 213 Conn. 161, 567 A.2d 812 (1989)—§ 14.4(e) n.127

McPherson v. Barksdale, 640 F.2d 780 (6th Cir.1981)—§ 21.2(e) n.289

McPherson v. McPherson, 112 Idaho 402, 732 P.2d 371 (App.1987)— § 8.10(a) n.14

McQuaid, State v., 147 N.J. 464, 688 A.2d 584 (1997)—§ 21.3(b) n.60

McQuay, State v., 154 Wis.2d 116, 452 N.W.2d 377 (1990)—§§ 21.2(d) n.165, 186, 211

McQueen v. Blackburn, 755 F.2d 1174 (5th Cir.1985)—§§ 11.4(d) n.112; 11.5(f) n.102

McQueen v. Commonwealth, 669 S.W.2d 519 (Ky.1984)—§ 22.2(d) n.83

McQueen, People v., 52 N.Y.2d 1025, 438 N.Y.S.2d 299, 420 N.E.2d 97 (1981)—§ 22.1(h) n.138

McQueen, People v., 18 N.Y.2d 337, 274 N.Y.S.2d 886, 221 N.E.2d 550 (1966)—§ 6.2(c) n.122

McQueen v. Swenson, 498 F.2d 207 (8th Cir.1974)—§§ 11.10(a)   n.15; 11.10(c) n.60

McQueen, United States v., 108 F.3d 64 (4th Cir.1997)—§ 21.2(d) n.159

McRae, People v., 469 Mich. 704, 678 N.W.2d 425 (2004)—§ 6.10(b) n.13

McRae, People v., 195 A.D.2d 180, 607 N.Y.S.2d 624 (1994)—§§ 10.3(a) n.2; 10.3(d) n.63

McRae, United States v., 156 F.3d 708 (6th Cir.1998)—§ 10.2(b) n.28

McRae v. United States, 420 F.2d 1283 (D.C.Cir.1969)—§§ 10.6(c) n.31, 32, 35

McReavy, People v., 436 Mich. 197, 462 N.W.2d 1 (1990)—§ 9.6(a) n.38

McSurely, United States v., 473 F.2d 1178 (D.C.Cir.1972)—§ 3.1(g) n.183

McVeigh, United States v., 153 F.3d 1166 (10th Cir.1998)—§§ 23.2(a) n.18, 21, 47

McVeigh, United States v., 106 F.3d 325 (10th Cir.1997)—§§ 27.3(b) n.16; 27.4(d) n.59

McVeigh, United States v., 119 F.3d 806 (10th Cir.1997)—§§ 23.1(d) n.167, 171, 172, 188, 209

McVeigh, United States v., 958 F.Supp. 512 (D.Colo.1997)—§ 24.4(d) n.53

McVeigh, United States v., 918 F.Supp. 1467 (W.D.Okla.1996)—§§ 23.2(a) n.14, 28, 34, 43

McVeigh, United States v., 896 F.Supp. 1549 (W.D.Okla.1995)—§§ 8.7(c) n.70; 8.8(i) n.195; 15.4(b) n.43

McVeigh v. United States, 78 U.S. (11 Wall.) 259, 20 L.Ed. 80 (1870)— § 24.5(d) n.42

McWaine, United States v., 243 F.3d 871 (5th Cir.2001)—§ 3.3(c) n.111

McWeeney, United States v., 454 F.3d 1030 (9th Cir.2006)—§ 3.10(f) n.204

Meachum v. Fano, 427 U.S. 215, 96 S.Ct. 2532, 49 L.Ed.2d 451 (1976)—§ 13.6(d) n.72

Mead, State v., 105 S.W.3d 552 (Mo.App.2003)—§ 27.5(d) n.137

Meadors, State v., 121 N.M. 38, 908 P.2d 731 (1995)—§§ 24.8(d) n.43; 24.8(e) n.69

Meadows v. Commonwealth, 35 Va.App. 298, 544 S.E.2d 876 (2001)—§ 20.3(c) n.77

Meadows v. State, 849 S.W.2d 748 (Tenn.1993)—§ 2.11(a) n.14

Means, State v., 367 S.C. 374, 626 S.E.2d 348 (2006)—§ 19.5(b) n.44

Means, United States v., 133 F.3d 444 (6th Cir.1998)—§ 28.9(b) n.45

Means, United States v., 409 F.Supp. 115 (D.N.D.1976)—§ 16.1(b) n.39

Mears v. State, 533 N.E.2d 140 (Ind.1989)—§ 3.10(e) n.149

Meaton v. United States, 328 F.2d 379 (5th Cir.1964)—§§ 21.4(d) n.123, 124

M.E.B., In re, 638 A.2d 1123 (D.C.1993)—§§ 3.8(b) n.45; 3.8(d) n.173

Mechanik, United States v., 475 U.S. 66, 106 S.Ct. 938, 89 L.Ed.2d 50 (1986)—§§ 2.9(h) n.215; 15.2(f) n.151; 15.2(i) n.226; 15.4(i) n.207; 15.5(a) n.15; 15.5(b) n.71, 74; 15.6(b) n.72; 15.6(e) n.130; 15.6(f) n.172; 15.7(h) n.228, 242; 19.3(a) n.107; 27.2(c) n.41; 27.6(b) n.27; 27.6(d) n.113, 139

Mechler v. Procunier, 754 F.2d 1294 (5th Cir.1985)—§ 14.1(d) n.68

Mechtel, State v., 176 Wis.2d 87, 499 N.W.2d 662 (1993)—§ 10.6(d) n.48

Medberry v. Crosby, 351 F.3d 1049 (11th Cir.2003)—§ 28.2(b) n.34

Medeiros, Commonwealth v., 395 Mass. 336, 479 N.E.2d 1371 (1985)—§ 6.8(d) n.84

Medeiros, People v., 25 Cal.App.4th 1260, 31 Cal.Rptr.2d 83 (1994)—§ 26.9(b) n.35

Medellin v. Dretke, 544 U.S. 660, 125 S.Ct. 2088, 161 L.Ed.2d 982 (2005)—§§ 1.7(c) n.26; 28.3(b) n.65

Medellin v. Texas, _____ U.S. _____, 127 S.Ct. 2129, 167 L.Ed.2d 862 (2007)—§ 1.7(c) n.36

Meders v. State, 260 Ga. 49, 389 S.E.2d 320 (1990)—§§ 15.4(c) n.96; 22.2(d) n.94

Medillin, Ex parte, 223 S.W.3d 315 (2006)—§ 1.7(c) n.36

Medina, In re, 109 F.3d 1556 (11th Cir.1997)—§ 28.7(c) n.21

Medina v. California, 505 U.S. 437, 112 S.Ct. 2572, 120 L.Ed.2d 353 (1992)—§§ 1.5(c) n.169; 1.5(d) n.199; 2.6(d) n.105; 2.7(a) n.40; 2.7(b) n.65, 69, 71; 2.7(c) n.140, 143, 145, 147, 156, 166, 190, 210, 211, 214; 11.1(b) n.41; 11.2(e) n.144, 193; 24.2(g) n.91; 26.4(d) n.66

Medina v. People, 114 P.3d 845 (Colo.2005)—§ 24.9(b) n.14

Medina, People v., 25 P.3d 1216 (Colo.2001)—§§ 6.2(c) n.98, 154; 9.5(c) n.65

Medina, People v., 71 Ill.2d 254, 16 Ill.Dec. 447, 375 N.E.2d 78 (1978)—§ 6.9(b) n.15

Medina, State v., 349 N.J.Super. 108, 793 A.2d 68 (2002)—§ 22.1(b) n.43

Medina, State v., 228 Conn. 281, 636 A.2d 351 (1994)—§ 6.7(b) n.72

Medina v. State, 747 S.W.2d 509 (Tex.App.1988)—§ 11.3(a) n.8

Medina, United States v., 175 Fed.Appx. 541 (3d Cir.2006)—§ 25.2(d) n.33

Medina, United States v., 118 F.3d 371 (5th Cir.1997)—§ 11.7(e) n.70

Medina, United States v., 944 F.2d 60 (2d Cir.1991)—§ 3.6(a) n.19

Medina, United States v., 775 F.2d 1398 (11th Cir.1985)—§ 12.3(a) n.23

Medina-Cervantes, United States v., 690 F.2d 715 (5th Cir.1982)—§ 21.2(c) n.132

Medina-Flores, United States v., 477 F.2d 225 (10th Cir.1973)—§ 9.1(d) n.116

Medina-Juarez, State v., 34 P.3d 187 (Utah 2001)—§ 11.10(c) n.113

Medina-Ramos, United States v., 834 F.2d 874 (10th Cir.1987)—§ 16.2(b) n.33

Medjuck, United States v., 156 F.3d 916 (9th Cir.1998)—§ 16.4(b) n.31

Medley, Commonwealth v., 531 Pa. 279, 612 A.2d 430 (1992)—§ 6.6(f) n.101

Medley, United States v., 476 F.3d 835 (10th Cir.2007)—§ 26.7(b) n.19

Medrano, State v., 67 S.W.3d 892 (Tex.Cr.App.2002)—§ 27.3(c) n.39

Medrano v. State, 914 P.2d 804 (Wyo.1996)—§ 3.8(b) n.53

Meechaicum v. Fountain, 696 F.2d 790 (10th Cir.1983)—§ 2.6(b) n.37

Meegan, People v., 60 A.D.2d 961, 401 N.Y.S.2d 602 (1978)—§ 15.5(c) n.126

Meehan, Commonwealth v., 377 Mass. 552, 387 N.E.2d 527 (1979)— §§ 9.5(b) n.31, 57; 9.5(c) n.65

Meek v. State, 636 So.2d 543 (Fla.App.1994)—§ 8.11(d) n.71

Meeker, State v., 143 Ariz. 256, 693 P.2d 911 (1984)—§ 7.3(c) n.48

Meeker, United States v., 411 F.3d 736 (6th Cir.2005)—§§ 26.4(d) n.65; 26.5(d) n.76

Meeks v. Bergen, 749 F.2d 322 (6th Cir.1984)—§§ 11.6(a)   n.46; 11.10(d) n.161

Meeks v. State, 341 Ark. 620, 19 S.W.3d 25 (2000)—§ 12.4(d) n.63

Meeks, State v., 205 Kan. 261, 469 P.2d 302 (1970)—§ 7.4(f) n.99

Meers, State v., 257 Neb. 398, 598 N.W.2d 435 (1999)—§ 16.1(h) n.294

Meester, United States v., 762 F.2d 867 (11th Cir.1985)—§ 17.2(f) n.136

Megargel, State v., 143 N.J. 484, 673 A.2d 259 (1996)—§ 27.5(e) n.158

Megel v. Commonwealth, 262 Va. 531, 551 S.E.2d 638 (2001)—§ 3.9(i) n.180

Mehciz, United States v., 437 F.2d 145 (9th Cir.1971)—§ 3.5(e) n.201

Mehmedi, People v., 69 N.Y.2d 759, 513 N.Y.S.2d 100, 505 N.E.2d 610 (1987)—§ 24.2(b) n.26

Mehner, State v., 480 N.W.2d 872 (Iowa 1992)—§ 3.4(e) n.71

Mehring v. State, 860 P.2d 1101 (Wyo.1993)—§§ 21.2(g) n.396; 21.4(c) n.73; 21.4(g) n.232

Meinhold v. United States Dep't of Defense, 123 F.3d 1275 (9th Cir.1997)—§ 13.5(h) n.182

Meinster, United States v., 484 F.Supp. 442 (S.D.Fla.1980)—§ 22.3(e) n.274

Meister v. People, 31 Mich. 99 (1875)— § 1.6(d) n.209

Meister, State v., 866 S.W.2d 485 (1993)—§ 2.6(b) n.43

Mejia, State v., 233 Conn. 215, 658 A.2d 571 (1995)—§ 24.9(b) n.12

Mejia v. State, 328 Md. 522, 616 A.2d 356 (1992)—§ 22.3(d) n.193

Mejia, United States v., 356 F.3d 470 (2d Cir.2004)—§ 24.2(a) n.7

Mejia, United States v., 69 F.3d 309 (9th Cir.1995)—§ 9.3(e) n.68

Mejia, United States v., 953 F.2d 461 (9th Cir.1991)—§§ 3.10(b) n.24; 3.10(f) n.193; 10.3(b) n.29; 10.4(c) n.23; 10.5(f) n.68

Mejia-Mendoza, People v., 965 P.2d 777 (Colo.1998)—§ 6.8(a) n.36

Melancon, United States v., 972 F.2d 566 (5th Cir.1992)—§ 27.5(c) n.56

Melanson, United States v., 691 F.2d 579 (1st Cir.1981)—§ 6.4(g) n.151

Melbourne v. State, 679 So.2d 759 (Fla.1996)—§ 22.3(d) n.253

Melendez v. City of New York, 109 A.D.2d 13, 489 N.Y.S.2d 741 (1985)—§ 8.5(h) n.278

Melendez, Commonwealth v., 544 Pa. 323, 676 A.2d 226 (1996)—§ 3.8(b) n.15

Melendez, People v., 102 P.3d 315 (Colo.2004)—§ 24.4(d) n.62

Melendez, United States v., 301 F.3d 27 (1st Cir.2002)—§ 10.3(b) n.10

Melendez, United States v., 228 F.3d 19 (1st Cir.2000)—§ 6.6(e) n.76

Melendez, United States v., 57 F.3d 238 (2d Cir.1995)—§ 24.7(i) n.96

Melendez-Carrion, United States v., 820 F.2d 56 (2d Cir.1987)—§ 12.3(d) n.97

Melgar, United States v., 139 F.3d 1005 (4th Cir.1998)—§ 6.9(g) n.200

Mello v. State, 93 Nev. 662, 572 P.2d 533 (1977)—§ 18.3(c) n.89

Mello v. Superior Court, 117 R.I. 578, 370 A.2d 1262 (1977)—§§ 12.3(b) n.73; 12.3(g) n.155

Melock, People v., 149 Ill.2d 423, 174 Ill.Dec. 857, 599 N.E.2d 941 (1992)—§ 6.2(c) n.133

Melone, State v., 299 Mont. 442, 2 P.3d 233 (2000)—§ 21.4(d) n.111

Melson, State v., 638 S.W.2d 342 (Tenn.1982)—§ 11.5(g) n.111

Melton, State v., 239 Neb. 790, 478 N.W.2d 341 (1992)—§ 3.10(b) n.46

Melton, State v., 239 Neb. 506, 476 N.W.2d 842 (1991)—§ 6.6(e) n.71

Melton v. State, 713 S.W.2d 107 (Tex.Cr.App.1986)—§ 5.1(c) n.34

Melvin, In re, 550 F.2d 674 (1st Cir.1977)—§§ 8.5(c) n.79; 8.7(d) n.85

Melvin, In re, 546 F.2d 1 (1st Cir.1976)—§§ 8.4(b) n.25; 8.4(c) n.127; 8.8(g) n.175, 177

Melvin, State v., 65 N.J. 1, 319 A.2d 450 (1974)—§ 6.8(a) n.14

Melvin, United States v., 27 F.3d 710 (1st Cir.1994)—§ 24.10(a) n.11

Melvins, State v., 155 N.J.Super. 316, 382 A.2d 925 (1978)—§ 20.4(f) n.89

Mempa v. Rhay, 389 U.S. 128, 88 S.Ct. 254, 19 L.Ed.2d 336 (1967)—§§ 6.10(e) n.72; 11.2(a) n.12; 11.2(b) n.36, 54; 18.5(c) n.87; 26.4(d) n.45; 26.4(e) n.73; 26.4(g) n.118

Memro, People v., 11 Cal.4th 786, 47 Cal.Rptr.2d 219, 905 P.2d 1305 (1995)—§ 24.3(e) n.125

Mena v. City of Simi Valley, 226 F.3d 1031 (9th Cir.2000)—§§ 9.1(b) n.33, 61

Mena v. State, 504 S.W.2d 410 (Tex.Cr.App.1974)—§ 3.3(d) n.158

Mena, United States v., 863 F.2d 1522 (11th Cir.1989)—§ 24.5(b) n.35

Menard v. Saxbe, 498 F.2d 1017 (D.C.Cir.1974)—§ 3.1(m) n.296

Mencer, State v., 798 S.W.2d 543 (Tenn.Crim.App.1990)—§§ 19.2(d) n.49; 19.3(a) n.8, 75; 19.4(a) n.2

Mendell, United States v., 447 F.2d 639 (7th Cir.1971)—§ 16.1(g) n.250

Mendenhall, United States v., 446 U.S. 544, 100 S.Ct. 1870, 64 L.Ed.2d 497 (1980)—§§ 3.5(a) n.8; 3.8(c) n.68; 3.10(b) n.43, 54

Mendez v. People, 986 P.2d 275 (Colo.1999)—§ 3.3(b) n.53

Mendez, United States v., 102 F.3d 126 (5th Cir.1996)—§ 22.1(h) n.137

Mendez-Rodriguez, United States v., 450 F.2d 1 (9th Cir.1971)—§ 24.3(h) n.180

Mendia, United States v., 731 F.2d 1412 (9th Cir.1984)—§§ 9.1(b) n.89; 9.1(d) n.124

Mendiola, Commonwealth v., 976 F.2d 475 (9th Cir.1992)—§§ 6.2(c) n.167; 10.5(a) n.6

Mendiola v. Schomig, 224 F.3d 589 (7th Cir.2000)—§ 28.7(a) n.4

Mendocino Environmental Center v. Mendocino County, 192 F.3d 1283 (9th Cir.1999)—§ 3.3(f) n.196

Mendonza v. Commonwealth, 423 Mass. 771, 673 N.E.2d 22 (1996)—§§ 12.3(d) n.96; 12.3(f) n.137

Mendoza v. Carey, 449 F.3d 1065 (9th Cir.2006)—§ 28.5(b) n.59

Mendoza, People v., 468 Mich. 527, 664 N.W.2d 685 (Mich.2003)—§ 24.8(e) n.54

Mendoza, People v., 24 Cal.4th 130, 99 Cal.Rptr.2d 485, 6 P.3d 150 (2000)—§§ 17.1(a) n.15; 17.1(e) n.63

Mendoza, People v., 82 N.Y.2d 415, 604 N.Y.S.2d 922, 624 N.E.2d 1017 (1993)—§ 10.1(b) n.30

Mendoza, State v., 157 Wash.2d 582, 141 P.3d 49 (2006)—§ 21.5(a) n.49

Mendoza v. State, _____ Nev. _____, 130 P.3d 176 (2006)—§ 6.8(a) n.36

Mendoza, State v., 227 Wis.2d 838, 596 N.W.2d 736 (1999)—§ 22.3(c) n.155

Mendoza, State v., 80 Wis.2d 122, 258 N.W.2d 260 (1977)—§ 16.3(f) n.95

Mendoza, United States v., 78 F.3d 460 (9th Cir.1996)—§§ 8.11(e) n.104, 109

Mendoza-Burciaga, United States v., 981 F.2d 192 (5th Cir.1992)—§§ 3.6(d) n.99; 22.3(c) n.125

Mendoza-Cecelia, United States v., 963 F.2d 1467 (11th Cir.1992)—§§ 6.2(c) n.113; 6.4(e) n.77

Mendoza-Cepeda, United States v., 250 F.3d 626 (8th Cir.2001)—§ 3.10(a) n.15

Mendoza-Gonzalez, United States v., 318 F.3d 663 (5th Cir.2003)—§ 3.10(f) n.192

Mendoza-Prado, United States v., 314 F.3d 1099 (9th Cir.2002)—§ 5.2(a) n.10

Mendoza-Salgado, United States v., 964 F.2d 993 (10th Cir.1992)—§ 11.7(b) n.29

Mendoza-Solorio, State v., 108 Wash.App. 823, 33 P.3d 411 (2001)—§ 19.2(c) n.40

Menefield v. Borg, 881 F.2d 696 (9th Cir.1989)—§ 11.5(c) n.64

Menendez, United States v., 612 F.2d 51 (2d Cir.1979)—§§ 16.1(h) n.295, 306, 311

Meneses, State v., 731 So.2d 375 (La.App.1999)—§ 19.6(b) n.15

Menillo, State v., 159 Conn. 264, 268 A.2d 667 (1970)—§§ 12.4(a) n.15, 16, 25, 26, 34, 35, 43

Menke v. State, 740 S.W.2d 861 (Tex.App.1987)—§ 24.3(c) n.91

Menna v. New York, 423 U.S. 61, 96 S.Ct. 241, 46 L.Ed.2d 195 (1975)—§ 21.6(a) n.13

Mennenga, People v., 195 Ill.App.3d 204, 141 Ill.Dec. 858, 551 N.E.2d 1386 (1990)—§ 15.2(h) n.187

Menon, United States v., 24 F.3d 550 (3d Cir.1994)—§§ 3.4(j) n.212; 3.4(k) n.228

Mensah, State v., 424 N.W.2d 453 (Iowa 1988)—§ 21.4(f) n.174

Mentz, United States v., 840 F.2d 315 (6th Cir.1988)—§§ 18.3(b) n.10, 19, 25

Menuey, State v., 239 Neb. 513, 476 N.W.2d 846 (1991)—§ 22.3(e) n.285

Menzies, State v., 845 P.2d 220 (Utah 1992)—§ 27.5(e) n.156

Mercado, United States v., 349 F.3d 708 (2d Cir.2003)—§ 21.4(e) n.162

Mercado, United States v., 307 F.3d 1226 (10th Cir.2002)—§ 3.2(f) n.178

Mercedes, United States v., 254 F.3d 433 (2d Cir.2001)—§ 12.3(a) n.24

Mercedes-Amparo, United States v., 980 F.2d 17 (1st Cir.1992)—§ 21.2(e) n.308

Mercer, People v., 257 Cal.App.2d 244, 64 Cal.Rptr. 861 (1967)—§ 6.7(d) n.154

Mercer v. State, 450 S.W.2d 715 (Tex.Civ.App.1970)—§ 3.9(k) n.242

Mercer, State v., 249 N.C. 371, 106 S.E.2d 866 (1959)—§ 15.2(h) n.185

Mercer, United States v., 691 F.2d 343 (7th Cir.1982)—§ 21.2(d) n.162

Merchant, People v., 260 Cal.App.2d 875, 67 Cal.Rptr. 459 (1968)—§ 6.6(f) n.100

Merchant v. State, 4 P.3d 184 (Wyo.2000)—§ 18.4(c) n.71

Mercier, Commonwealth v., 451 Pa. 211, 302 A.2d 337 (1973)—§ 6.7(c) n.108

Meredith, People v., 209 Mich.App. 403, 531 N.W.2d 749 (1995)—§§ 16.2(a) n.11; 16.2(g) n.124, 128, 132

Meredith, People v., 29 Cal.3d 682, 175 Cal.Rptr. 612, 631 P.2d 46 (1981)—§§ 20.4(b) n.32, 34

Merino, State v., 81 Hawai'i 198, 915 P.2d 672 (1996)—§ 21.4(a) n.23

Meriwether, United States v., 917 F.2d 955 (6th Cir.1990)—§§ 4.6(b) n.25; 4.6(m) n.216

Merkt, United States v., 794 F.2d 950 (5th Cir.1986)—§ 7.4(e) n.89

Merle v. United States, 683 A.2d 755 (D.C.App.1996)—§ 26.10(a) n.5

Meron, State v., 675 N.W.2d 537 (Iowa 2004)—§§ 21.4(e) n.161; 21.5(c) n.88

Merriam, United States v., 108 F.3d 1162 (9th Cir.1997)—§ 17.4(b) n.128

Merrill, Commonwealth v., 80 Mass. (14 Gray) 415 (1860)—§ 1.6(d) n.246

Merrill, People v., 2 Park Crim 590 (N.Y.Sup.Ct.1855)—§ 16.4(c) n.110

Merrill, State v., 252 Neb. 736, 566 N.W.2d 742 (1997)—§ 27.6(b) n.44

Merrill, State v., 155 Vt. 422, 584 A.2d 1129 (Vt.1990)—§§ 11.3(a) n.12; 11.3(b) n.38

Merrill v. State, 130 Ga.App. 745, 204 S.E.2d 632 (1974)—§§ 17.2(d) n.103; 17.2(e) n.124

Merritt, People v., 396 Mich. 67, 238 N.W.2d 31 (1976)—§§ 20.6(c) n.84, 85, 89

Merritt, United States v., 988 F.2d 1298 (2d Cir.1993)—§ 21.2(d) n.178

Mers v. State, 482 N.E.2d 778 (1985)—§ 2.12(d) n.198

Mers, United States v., 701 F.2d 1321 (11th Cir.1983)—§§ 5.1(c) n.26; 11.8 n.1

Mersino, People v., 237 Cal.App.2d 265, 46 Cal.Rptr. 821 (1965)—§ 8.5(d) n.127

Mersman, People v., 148 P.3d 199 (Colo.App.2006)—§ 22.3(a) n.44

Mesa v. California, 489 U.S. 121, 109 S.Ct. 959, 103 L.Ed.2d 99 (1989)—§ 13.5(d) n.82

Mesa v. United States, 875 A.2d 79 (D.C.App.2005)—§ 6.8(a) n.36

Mesarosh v. United States, 352 U.S. 1, 77 S.Ct. 1, 1 L.Ed.2d 1 (1956)—§ 1.7(i) n.162

Meshell v. State, 739 S.W.2d 246 (Tex.Cr.App.1987)—§ 18.3(c) n.64

Mespoulede, United States v., 597 F.2d 329 (2d Cir.1979)—§ 17.4(a) n.6

Messano, Appeal of, 16 N.J. 142, 106 A.2d 537 (1954)—§ 8.3(h) n.47

Messelt, State v., 178 Wis.2d 320, 504 N.W.2d 362 (App.1993)—§ 16.3(b) n.26

Messer v. Kemp, 831 F.2d 946 (11th Cir.1987)—§ 11.2(e) n.154

Messick v. State, 209 Ga.App. 459, 433 S.E.2d 595 (1993)—§ 24.8(e) n.76

Messier, State v., 101 N.M. 582, 686 P.2d 272 (N.M.App.1984)—§ 25.2(d) n.34

Messina, United States v., 388 F.2d 393 (2d Cir.1968)—§§ 6.6(e) n.69; 6.8(a) n.30

Messino, United States v., 181 F.3d 826 (7th Cir.1999)—§ 11.9(c) n.123

Messino, United States v., 55 F.3d 1241 (7th Cir.1995)—§ 21.3(c) n.194

Messino, United States v., 852 F.Supp. 652 (N.D.Ill.1994)—§§ 11.9(c) n.137, 140

Mestas, State v., 93 N.M. 765, 605 P.2d 1164 (N.M.App.1980)—§ 27.2(c) n.63

Metcalf v. State, 635 So.2d 11 (Fla.1994)—§ 5.4(c) n.36

Metcalf v. State, 284 Ark. 223, 681 S.W.2d 344 (1984)—§§ 6.9(f) n.130, 134

Metcalfe, People v., 202 Ill.2d 544, 270 Ill.Dec. 69, 782 N.E.2d 263 (2002)—§ 22.3(c) n.162

Metellus v. State, 900 So.2d 491 (Fla.2005)—§ 21.2(d) n.270

Metheny v. State, 359 Md. 576, 755 A.2d 1088 (2000)—§§ 21.4(f) n.172, 184, 193

Metoyer v. United States, 250 F.2d 30 (D.C.Cir.1957)—§ 6.3(a) n.13

Mettetal v. State, 615 So.2d 600 (Miss.1993)—§§ 3.10(e) n.140, 141

Metts v. State, 270 Ga. 481, 511 S.E.2d 508 (1999)—§ 6.7(b) n.43

Metz, Commonwealth v., 534 Pa. 341, 633 A.2d 125 (1993)—§ 10.2(b) n.29

Meuli, United States v., 8 F.3d 1481 (10th Cir.1993)—§ 24.9(d) n.43

Meunier, In re, 145 Vt. 414, 491 A.2d 1019 (1985)—§§ 21.2(d) n.177, 178; 21.2(e) n.308, 316

Mexico v. United States, 2004 ICJ 12 (March 31)—§ 1.7(c) n.28

Meyer v. Sargent, 854 F.2d 1110 (8th Cir.1988)—§§ 11.4(d) n.117; 11.5(c) n.43, 54

Meyer v. State, 119 Nev. 554, 80 P.3d 447 (Nev.2003)—§§ 24.9(f) n.70, 85

Meyer, State v., 167 Vt. 608, 708 A.2d 1343 (1998)—§ 3.4(g) n.130

Meyer, State v., 330 N.C. 738, 412 S.E.2d 339 (1992)—§ 21.5(a) n.35

Meyer, United States v., 359 F.3d 820 (6th Cir.2004)—§ 7.4(c) n.46

Meyer, United States v., 157 F.3d 1067 (7th Cir.1998)—§ 13.5(b) n.47

Meyer, United States v., 810 F.2d 1242 (D.C.Cir.1987)—§ 13.7(c) n.44

Meyers v. Gillis, 93 F.3d 1147 (3d Cir.1996)—§§ 21.3(b) n.71; 21.4(d) n.119; 21.4(f) n.204

Meyers, People v., 158 Ill.2d 46, 196 Ill.Dec. 646, 630 N.E.2d 811 (1994)—§ 19.4(a) n.6

Meyers, People v., 617 P.2d 808 (Colo.1980)—§§ 15.2(e) n.142; 15.7(b) n.10, 42

Meyers, People v., 46 Ill.2d 149, 263 N.E.2d 81 (1970)—§ 11.9(d) n.194

Meyers v. State, 124 P.3d 710 (Wyo.2005)—§§ 21.4(a) n.26; 21.6(a) n.52

Meyers v. State, 265 Ga. 149, 454 S.E.2d 490 (1995)—§ 11.9(d) n.186

Meyers, State v., 223 Neb. 773, 393 N.W.2d 533 (1986)—§ 6.6(e) n.78

Meyers, United States v., 95 F.3d 1475 (10th Cir.1996)—§ 15.5(b) n.90

Meyrick, State v., 313 Or. 125, 831 P.2d 666 (1992)—§ 11.3(b) n.37

Meza-Gonzalez, United States v., 394 F.3d 587 (8th Cir.2005)—§§ 22.3(d) n.246, 250

Mezquita v. State, 354 Ark. 433, 125 S.W.3d 161 (2003)—§§ 7.4(g) n.111, 114

Mezy, People v., 453 Mich. 269, 551 N.W.2d 389 (1996)—§§ 25.5(b) n.22, 27

Mezzanatto, United States v., 513 U.S. 196, 115 S.Ct. 797, 130 L.Ed.2d 697 (1995)—§§ 21.2(h) n.438; 27.5(c) n.57

Miami Herald Publishing Co. v. Marko, 352 So.2d 518 (Fla.1977)—§§ 8.3(h) n.39, 51

Miami Herald Publishing Co. v. Morphonios, 467 So.2d 1026 (Fla.App.1985)—§§ 23.1(c) n.102, 104

Miami Herald Publishing Co., State ex rel. v. McIntosh, 340 So.2d 904 (Fla.1976)—§ 23.1(c) n.109

Miami Valley Broadcasting Corp., State ex rel. v. Kessler, 64 Ohio St.2d 165, 413 N.E.2d 1203 (1980)—§ 23.3(b) n.27

Michael, In re, 326 U.S. 224, 66 S.Ct. 78, 90 L.Ed. 30 (1945)—§ 8.3(b) n.13

Michael v. Louisiana, 350 U.S. 91, 76 S.Ct. 158, 100 L.Ed. 83 (1955)—§§ 15.4(b) n.78 to 80

Michael v. State, 115 P.3d 517 (Alaska 2005)—§ 26.3(g) n.88

Michael v. State, 918 So.2d 798 (Miss.App.2005)—§ 22.1(g) n.118

Michael v. State, 805 P.2d 371 (Alaska 1991)—§ 19.6(c) n.23

Michael, State v., 2 Md.App. 750, 237 A.2d 782 (Md.1968)—§ 1.7(f) n.107

Michael B. v. Superior Court, 103 Cal.App.4th 1384, 127 Cal.Rptr.2d 454 (2002)—§§ 8.4(b) n.20; 8.4(c) n.123; 8.8(b) n.31

Michael H. v. Gerald D., 491 U.S. 110, 109 S.Ct. 2333, 105 L.Ed.2d 91 (1991)—§ 2.8(a) n.16

Michael J., State v., 274 Conn. 321, 875 A.2d 510 (2005)—§ 25.2(b) n.15

Michaels, Commonwealth v., 39 Mass.App. 646, 659 N.E.2d 1209 (1996)—§ 26.10(b) n.23

Michaels, People v., 28 Cal.4th 486, 122 Cal.Rptr.2d 285, 49 P.3d 1032 (2002)—§§ 6.9(g) n.154; 13.7(c) n.43; 21.4(a) n.11

Michaelson, United States v., 552 F.2d 472 (2d Cir.1977)—§§ 21.2(d) n.183; 21.5(a) n.54

Michaud, State v., 724 A.2d 1222 (Me.1998)—§ 6.6(e) n.71

Michaud, United States v., 268 F.3d 728 (9th Cir.2001)—§§ 3.6(a) n.40; 6.9(f) n.130

Micheaux v. Collins, 911 F.2d 1083 (5th Cir.1990)—§ 21.4(d) n.103

Michel v. United States, 507 F.2d 461 (2d Cir.1974)—§ 21.4(d) n.135

Micheli, United States v., 487 F.2d 429 (1st Cir.1973)—§ 3.4(j) n.191

Michelle's Lounge, United States v., 39 F.3d 684 (7th Cir.1994)—§ 26.6(d) n.69

Michelsen, United States v., 141 F.3d 867 (8th Cir.1998)—§§ 21.2(b) n.76; 27.5(c) n.62

Michigan v. Chesternut, 486 U.S. 567, 108 S.Ct. 1975, 100 L.Ed.2d 565 (1988)—§§ 2.9(g) n.163; 3.8(c) n.77

Michigan v. Clifford, 464 U.S. 287, 104 S.Ct. 641, 78 L.Ed.2d 477 (1984)—§§ 3.9(e) n.75, 77, 79, 80

Michigan v. DeFillippo, 443 U.S. 31, 99 S.Ct. 2627, 61 L.Ed.2d 343 (1979)—§§ 1.7(k) n.273; 2.12(a) n.21; 3.3(b) n.75

Michigan v. Doran, 439 U.S. 282, 99 S.Ct. 530, 58 L.Ed.2d 521 (1978)—§§ 2.12(a) n.21; 3.1(j) n.248

Michigan v. Dyer, 425 Mich. 572, 390 N.W.2d 645 (1986)—§ 24.4(c) n.21

Michigan v. Harvey, 494 U.S. 344, 110 S.Ct. 1176, 108 L.Ed.2d 293 (1990)—§§ 2.9(h) n.217, 225, 227 to 229; 9.6(a) n.28

Michigan v. Jackson, 475 U.S. 625, 106 S.Ct. 1404, 89 L.Ed.2d 631 (1986)—§§ 2.9(g) n.176; 2.9(h) n.224; 6.4(e) n.62, 77; 6.4(f) n.135; 6.9(f) n.121; 6.9(g) n.194; 9.6(a) n.29; 11.2(b) n.80; 11.3(a) n.10

Michigan v. Long, 463 U.S. 1032, 103 S.Ct. 3469, 77 L.Ed.2d 1201 (1983)—§§ 2.12(a) n.22, 50; 3.5(b) n.95; 3.6(d) n.94; 3.8(e) n.217, 224; 12.5(b) n.32; 28.4(c) n.27

Michigan v. Lucas, 500 U.S. 145, 111 S.Ct. 1743, 114 L.Ed.2d 205 (1991)—§§ 1.5(e) n.209; 20.6(c) n.73; 24.4(a) n.8

Michigan v. Mosley, 423 U.S. 96, 96 S.Ct. 321, 46 L.Ed.2d 313 (1975)—§§ 2.9(g) n.178; 2.9(h) n.224; 2.12(a) n.21, 22; 6.7(c) n.116; 6.9(f) n.98

Michigan v. Payne, 412 U.S. 47, 93 S.Ct. 1966, 36 L.Ed.2d 736 (1973)—§§ 2.11(c) n.27; 2.12(a) n.21

Michigan v. Sanders, 38 Mich. 218 (1878)—§ 5.1(b) n.7

Michigan v. Summers, 452 U.S. 692, 101 S.Ct. 2587, 69 L.Ed.2d 340 (1981)—§§ 2.12(a) n.21; 3.4(i) n.176

Michigan v. Thomas, 458 U.S. 259, 102 S.Ct. 3079, 73 L.Ed.2d 750 (1982)—§ 3.7(b) n.30

Michigan v. Tucker, 417 U.S. 433, 94 S.Ct. 2357, 41 L.Ed.2d 182 (1974)—§§ 2.10(c) n.97; 2.10(d) n.108, 114; 6.5(b) n.31; 9.5(a) n.14; 9.5(d) n.78

Michigan v. Tyler, 436 U.S. 499, 98 S.Ct. 1942, 56 L.Ed.2d 486 (1978)—§§ 2.12(a) n.21; 3.6(e) n.136; 3.9(e) n.74

Michigan Dept. of State Police v. Sitz, 496 U.S. 444, 110 S.Ct. 2481, 110 L.Ed.2d 412 (1990)—§§ 2.6(d) n.99; 3.9(g) n.133

Miciotto v. United States, 198 F.2d 951 (D.C.Cir.1952)—§ 17.2(a) n.25

Mickelson, State v., 18 Or.App. 647, 526 P.2d 583 (1974)—§ 3.3(e) n.188

Mickelson, United States v., 378 F.3d 810 (8th Cir.2004)—§ 17.2(c) n.82

Mickens v. Taylor, 535 U.S. 162, 122 S.Ct. 1237, 152 L.Ed.2d 291 (2002)—§§ 11.4(b) n.32; 11.4(c) n.48, 68; 11.9(b) n.70; 11.9(d) n.151, 171, 228; 21.3(b) n.138

Mickens, United States v., 926 F.2d 1323 (2d Cir.1991)—§ 3.6(d) n.99

Mickle, People v., 54 Cal.3d 140, 284 Cal.Rptr. 511, 814 P.2d 290 (1991)—§ 6.2(c) n.76

Mickle, State v., 56 Haw. 23, 525 P.2d 1108 (Hawaii 1974)—§ 11.2(g) n.271

Micklos, Commonwealth v., 448 Pa.Super. 560, 672 A.2d 796 (1996)—§ 25.3(a) n.7

Middendorf v. Henry, 425 U.S. 25, 96 S.Ct. 1281, 47 L.Ed.2d 556 (1976)—§ 11.1(b) n.80

Middlebrooks, State v., 840 S.W.2d 317 (Tenn.1992)—§ 6.3(c) n.50

Middlebrooks, State v., 236 Ga. 52, 222 S.E.2d 343 (1976)—§ 14.2(c) n.39

Middleton v. McNeil, 541 U.S. 433, 124 S.Ct. 1830, 158 L.Ed.2d 701 (2004)—§ 24.8(b) n.36

Middleton, State v., 995 S.W.2d 443 (Mo.1999)—§§ 7.4(c) n.48, 53

Middleton, State v., 299 N.J.Super. 22, 690 A.2d 623 (1997)—§ 25.2(a) n.6

Middleton v. State, 49 Md.App. 286, 431 A.2d 734 (1981)—§§ 20.6(c) n.82, 86, 87

Middleton, State v., 69 S.C. 72, 48 S.E. 35 (1904)—§ 6.2(a) n.9

Midgett, United States v., 342 F.3d 321 (4th Cir.2003)—§ 11.6(d) n.123

Midgley, United States v., 142 F.3d 174 (3d Cir.1998)—§ 18.5(a) n.36

Midland Asphalt Corp., Matter of, 616 F.Supp. 223 (W.D.N.Y.1985)—§ 8.7(b) n.59

Midland Asphalt Corp. v. United States, 489 U.S. 794, 109 S.Ct. 1494, 103 L.Ed.2d 879 (1989)—§§ 15.5(b) n.75; 15.6(f) n.173, 197; 27.2(c) n.40

Midland Asphalt Corp., United States v., 840 F.2d 1040 (2d Cir.1988)— § 15.6(f) n.173

Midulla v. State, 410 So.2d 637 (Fla.App.1982)—§ 26.10(c) n.76

Miele, United States v., 989 F.2d 659 (3d Cir.1993)—§ 26.5(a) n.15

Mierz, State v., 127 Wash.2d 460, 901 P.2d 286 (1995)—§ 9.4(f) n.115

Miggins, United States v., 302 F.3d 384 (6th Cir.2002)—§ 3.3(g) n.247

Miguel, United States v., 952 F.2d 285 (9th Cir.1991)—§ 6.8(a) n.20

Mikalajunas, United States v., 186 F.3d 490 (4th Cir.1999)—§ 28.4(e) n.88

Mikell, United States v., 163 F.Supp.2d 720 (E.D.Mich.2001)—§ 16.2(e) n.90

Mikenas v. State, 460 So.2d 359 (Fla.App.1985)—§ 21.3(b) n.58

Mikhel, In re, 453 F.3d 1137 (9th Cir.2006)—§§ 24.4(d) n.53, 66

Mikolajczyk, United States v., 137 F.3d 237 (5th Cir.1998)—§ 11.5(f) n.106

Mikulewicz, State v., 462 A.2d 497 (Me.1983)—§ 6.2(c) n.173

Milam v. State, 240 Ala. 314, 198 So. 863 (1940)—§§ 16.1(d) n.133; 16.1(e) n.179

Milam, United States v., 443 F.3d 382 (4th Cir.2006)—§ 26.4(i) n.201

Milani, United States ex rel. v. Pate, 425 F.2d 6 (7th Cir.1970)—§ 6.4(b) n.24

Milano v. State, 790 So.2d 179 (Miss.2001)—§ 22.2(d) n.88

Milano, United States v., 443 F.2d 1022 (10th Cir.1971)—§§ 14.2(g) n.97, 99

Milanovich v. United States, 275 F.2d 716 (4th Cir.1960)—§ 24.4(d) n.43

Milashoski, State v., 163 Wis.2d 72, 471 N.W.2d 42 (1991)—§ 3.2(h) n.207

Milbourn, People v., 435 Mich. 630, 461 N.W.2d 1 (1990)—§ 26.3(g) n.80

Miles v. Dorsey, 61 F.3d 1459 (10th Cir.1995)—§§ 21.3(b) n.84; 21.3(d) n.228

Miles v. Sheriff, 266 Va. 110, 581 S.E.2d 191 (2003)—§ 11.6(d) n.119

Miles v. State, 348 Ark. 544, 75 S.W.3d 677 (2002)—§ 6.9(a) n.12

Miles v. State, 350 Ark. 243, 85 S.W.3d 907 (2002)—§ 21.2(d) n.242

Miles, United States v., 480 F.2d 1217 (9th Cir.1973)—§ 3.9(h) n.168

Milestone, United States v., 626 F.2d 264 (3d Cir.1980)—§ 19.5(d) n.74

Milette, State v., 702 A.2d 1165 (R.I.1997)—§ 9.1(d) n.128

Miley v. United States, 477 A.2d 720 (D.C.App.1984)—§§ 6.6(f) n.102; 6.7(b) n.66

Milhollin, People v., 751 P.2d 43 (Colo.1988)—§ 6.6(e) n.71

Milian-Rodriguez, United States v., 828 F.2d 679 (11th Cir.1987)—§ 10.2(a) n.9

Milken, United States v., 780 F.Supp. 123 (S.D.N.Y.1991)—§ 23.1(d) n.152

Millan, People v., 69 N.Y.2d 514, 516 N.Y.S.2d 168, 508 N.E.2d 903 (1987)—§ 9.2(a) n.6

Millan, People v., 47 Ill.App.3d 296, 5 Ill.Dec. 500, 361 N.E.2d 823 (1977)—§ 20.6(b) n.42

Millan, United States v., 4 F.3d 1038 (2d Cir.1993)—§ 12.3(d) n.97

Millay, State v., 787 A.2d 129 (Me.2001)—§§ 6.7(a) n.3; 6.9(g) n.155

Miller, State ex rel., 168 W.Va. 745, 285 S.E.2d 500 (W.Va.1981)—§§ 1.7(i) n.204; 8.2(c) n.26; 8.4(b) n.89; 8.4(c) n.112; 15.2(c) n.70, 71; 15.2(e) n.136; 15.3(d) n.68; 15.6(a) n.27; 15.7(c) n.59, 63

Miller v. Champion, 262 F.3d 1066 (10th Cir.2001)—§ 11.10(d) n.176

Miller, Commonwealth v., 399 Pa.Super. 180, 582 A.2d 4 (1990)—§ 24.3(a) n.5

Miller v. Comm'r of Correction, 242 Conn. 745, 700 A.2d 1108 (1997)—§ 28.3(e) n.103

Miller v. Dugger, 838 F.2d 1530 (11th Cir.1988)—§ 6.2(c) n.181

Miller v. Fenton, 474 U.S. 104, 106 S.Ct. 445, 88 L.Ed.2d 405 (1985)—§§ 1.5(d) n.179; 6.2(b) n.43; 28.7(b) n.11

Miller v. New Jersey State Dept. of Corrections, 145 F.3d 616 (3d Cir.1998)—§ 28.5(b) n.59

Miller v. Pate, 386 U.S. 1, 87 S.Ct. 785, 17 L.Ed.2d 690 (1967)—§ 24.3(b) n.23

Miller, People v., 113 P.3d 743 (Colo.2005)—§ 27.5(d) n.113

Miller, People v., 75 P.3d 1108 (Colo.2003)—§ 3.1(c) n.77

Miller, People v., 91 N.Y.2d 372, 670 N.Y.S.2d 978, 694 N.E.2d 61 (1998)—§ 21.4(f) n.213

Miller, People v., 65 N.Y.2d 502, 493 N.Y.S.2d 96, 482 N.E.2d 892 (1985)—§ 21.5(e) n.140

Miller, People v., 33 Cal.3d 545, 189 Cal.Rptr. 519, 658 P.2d 1320 (1983)—§ 21.6(b) n.84

Miller, People v., 121 Mich.App. 691, 329 N.W.2d 460 (1982)—§ 22.1(h) n.160

Miller, People v., 19 Ill.App.3d 161, 310 N.E.2d 808 (1974)—§ 3.10(e) n.157

Miller, State v., 717 N.W.2d 614 (S.D.2006)—§ 21.4(a) n.41

Miller v. State, 380 Md. 1, 843 A.2d 803 (2004)—§ 10.1(a) n.3

Miller v. State, 770 N.E.2d 763 (Ind.2002)—§§ 6.2(c) n.123, 127

Miller v. State, 29 P.3d 1077 (Okla.Crim.App.2001)—§ 6.4(e) n.61

Miller, State v., 798 So.2d 947 (La.2001)—§ 3.8(b) n.37

Miller, State v., 55 Conn.App.185, 738 A.2d 1142 (1999)—§ 11.5(c) n.32

Miller v. State, 720 N.E.2d 696 (Ind.1999)—§§ 21.4(a) n.14, 16

Miller, State v., 186 Ariz. 314, 921 P.2d 1151 (1996)—§ 9.4(a) n.25

Miller, State v., 194 W.Va. 3, 459 S.E.2d 114 (1995)—§ 27.5(d) n.137

Miller, State v., 339 N.C. 663, 455 S.E.2d 137 (1995)—§§ 15.4(b) n.59, 74

Miller v. State, 664 So.2d 1066 (Fla.App.1995)—§ 26.9(c) n.80

Miller, State v., 277 N.J.Super. 122, 649 A.2d 94 (1994)—§ 18.4(c) n.73

Miller, State v., 175 Wis.2d 204, 499 N.W.2d 215 (1993)—§§ 26.9(b) n.24, 26

Miller, State v., 253 Mont. 395, 833 P.2d 1040 (1992)—§ 21.5(a) n.57

Miller, State v., 488 N.W.2d 235 (Minn.1992)—§ 26.3(f) n.66

Miller v. State, 827 P.2d 875 (Okla.Crim.App.1992)—§§ 19.3(a) n.2; 19.3(b) n.151

Miller, State v., 160 Wis.2d 646, 467 N.W.2d 118 (1991)—§§ 11.9(c) n.114, 124

Miller, State v., 571 So.2d 603 (La.1990)—§ 17.4(a) n.34

Miller, State v., 110 Wash.2d 528, 756 P.2d 122 (1988)—§ 21.2(e) n.299

Miller, State v., 157 Ariz. 129, 755 P.2d 434 (1988)—§§ 16.4(c) n.100, 110

Miller, State v., 231 Mont. 497, 757 P.2d 1275 (Mont.1988)—§ 1.5(b) n.70

Miller, State v., 429 N.W.2d 26 (S.D.1988)—§ 3.4(e) n.87

Miller, State v., 202 Conn. 463, 522 A.2d 249 (1987)—§ 7.4(e) n.92

Miller v. State, 496 N.E.2d 1297 (Ind.1986)—§ 6.9(b) n.44

Miller v. State, 174 Ga.App. 42, 329 S.E.2d 252 (1985)—§ 16.1(d) n.132

Miller, State v., 175 W.Va. 616, 336 S.E.2d 910 (1985)—§ 11.2(b) n.36

Miller v. State, 444 So.2d 523 (Fla.App.1984)—§ 26.10(c) n.72

Miller, State v., 674 S.W.2d 279 (Tenn.1984)—§ 26.5(a) n.21

Miller v. State, 273 Ind. 493, 405 N.E.2d 909 (1980)—§ 20.6(b) n.46

Miller v. State, 617 P.2d 516 (Alaska 1980)—§ 21.4(a) n.17

Miller v. State, 584 S.W.2d 758 (Tenn.1979)—§ 2.12(c) n.150

Miller v. State, 262 Ark. 223, 555 S.W.2d 563 (Ark.1977)—§ 1.7(f) n.98

Miller, State v., 17 Or.App. 352, 521 P.2d 1330 (1974)—§§ 10.1(b) n.20, 25, 26

Miller v. State, 54 Ala.App. 230, 307 So.2d 40 (1974)—§ 3.3(g) n.235

Miller v. State, 272 Md. 249, 322 A.2d 527 (1974)—§ 21.2(e) n.308

Miller, State v., 282 N.C. 633, 194 S.E.2d 353 (1973)—§ 9.4(f) n.117

Miller v. State, 249 Ark. 3, 457 S.W.2d 848 (1970)—§ 24.2(e) n.54

Miller, State v., 254 Or. 244, 458 P.2d 1017 (1969)—§§ 15.3(d) n.65, 67

Miller v. State, 94 Okl.Cr. 411, 237 P.2d 166 (1951)—§ 3.4(e) n.86

Miller v. State, 42 Fla. 266, 28 So. 208 (Fla.1900)—§ 15.7(h) n.228

Miller, State v., 14 Del. 564, 32 A. 137 (1892)—§ 16.1(g) n.246

Miller, State v., 15 Minn. 344 (1870)— § 16.3(d) n.57

Miller v. Stewart, 231 F.3d 1248 (9th Cir.2000)—§ 11.3(b) n.50

Miller, United States v., 450 F.3d 270 (7th Cir.2006)—§ 6.2(c) n.96

Miller v. United States, 150 F.Supp.2d 871 (E.D.N.C.2001)—§ 11.6(b) n.82

Miller, United States v., 111 F.3d 747 (10th Cir.1997)—§§ 16.1(g) n.246, 255, 258, 260, 262; 16.1(h) n.292, 293

Miller, United States v., 116 F.3d 641 (2d Cir.1997)—§§ 4.6(c) n.54; 6.9(f) n.138; 19.5(d) n.72

Miller, United States v., 14 F.3d 761 (2d Cir.1994)—§ 27.2(c) n.55

Miller, United States v., 952 F.2d 866 (5th Cir.1992)—§§ 25.4(b) n.17; 25.4(c) n.32, 34

Miller, United States v., 910 F.2d 1321 (6th Cir.1990)—§§ 6.10(c) n.41; 21.2(d) n.246

Miller, United States v., 891 F.2d 1265 (7th Cir.1989)—§ 5.4(c) n.42

Miller, United States v., 812 F.2d 543 (9th Cir.1987)—§ 10.6(c) n.23

Miller, United States v., 797 F.2d 336 (6th Cir.1986)—§§ 17.4(a) n.31, 66

Miller, United States v., 800 F.2d 129 (7th Cir.1986)—§ 3.10(e) n.181

Miller, United States v., 471 U.S. 130, 105 S.Ct. 1811, 85 L.Ed.2d 99 (1985)—§§ 19.5(d) n.77; 19.6(c) n.31

Miller, United States v., 753 F.2d 19 (3d Cir.1985)—§ 12.4(d) n.69

Miller, United States v., 579 F.Supp. 862 (S.D.Fla.1984)—§ 23.1(d) n.180

Miller, United States v., 624 F.2d 1198 (3d Cir.1980)—§§ 11.4(c) n.57; 11.9(a) n.24; 11.9(c) n.119

Miller, United States v., 650 F.2d 169 (9th Cir.1980)—§ 19.3(c) n.194

Miller, United States v., 565 F.2d 1273 (3d Cir.1977)—§ 21.2(d) n.178

Miller, United States v., 425 U.S. 435, 96 S.Ct. 1619, 48 L.Ed.2d 71 (1976)—§§ 3.2(j) n.229; 8.5(d) n.156; 8.7(a) n.28; 9.1(c) n.109

Miller v. United States, 357 U.S. 301, 78 S.Ct. 1190, 2 L.Ed.2d 1332 (1958)—§§ 1.7(c) n.47; 3.1(e) n.125; 3.4(h) n.144; 3.6(b) n.49, 63

Miller v. Warden, 16 Md.App. 614, 299 A.2d 862 (1973)—§ 11.3(c) n.57

Miller-El v. Cockrell, 537 U.S. 322, 123 S.Ct. 1029, 154 L.Ed.2d 931 (2003)—§§ 22.3(d) n.239; 28.2(b) n.33; 28.10 n.4

Miller-El v. Dretke, 545 U.S. 231, 125 S.Ct. 2317, 162 L.Ed.2d 196 (2005)—§§ 22.3(d) n.209, 233, 241, 257; 28.7(a) n.3

Millhouse, Commonwealth v., 255 Pa.Super. 206, 386 A.2d 581 (1978)—§ 15.4(b) n.49

Millican, United States v., 600 F.2d 273 (5th.Cir.1979)—§ 14.2(g) n.106

Milligan, Ex parte, 71 U.S. (4 Wall.) 2, 18 L.Ed. 281 (1866)—§ 15.1(b) n.88

Milligan v. State, 135 N.C.App. 781, 522 S.E.2d 330 (1999)—§ 25.1(c) n.31

Milliken, Commonwealth v., 450 Pa. 310, 300 A.2d 78 (1973)—§ 1.7(i) n.206

Milliorn, State v., 794 S.W.2d 181 (Mo.1990)—§ 9.3(e) n.81

Millner, State v., 409 N.W.2d 642 (N.D.1987)—§§ 21.5(a) n.24, 35, 45

Mills v. Commonwealth, 996 S.W.2d 473 (Ky.1999)—§ 6.9(f) n.111

Mills v. Commonwealth, 14 Va.App. 459, 418 S.E.2d 718 (1992)—§ 10.4(b) n.15

Mills v. Maryland, 486 U.S. 367, 108 S.Ct. 1860, 100 L.Ed.2d 384 (1988)—§ 28.6(d) n.35

Mills v. Municipal Court, 10 Cal.3d 288, 110 Cal.Rptr. 329, 515 P.2d 273 (1973)—§ 2.12(c) n.159

Mills, People v., 178 N.Y. 274, 70 N.E. 786 (1904)—§ 5.1(b) n.5

Mills, State v., 211 W.Va. 532, 566 S.E.2d 891 (2002)—§ 22.3(c) n.108

Mills, State v., 57 Conn.App. 202, 748 A.2d 318 (2000)—§ 24.7(e) n.73

Mills, State v., 62 Ohio St.3d 357, 582 N.E.2d 972 (1992)—§ 9.1(d) n.126

Mills, State v., 238 Kan. 189, 707 P.2d 1079 (1985)—§§ 18.5(a) n.6, 22

Mills, State v., 6 N.C.App. 347, 170 S.E.2d 189 (1969)—§ 6.7(c) n.106

Mills v. Superior Court, 42 Cal.3d 951, 232 Cal.Rptr. 141, 728 P.2d 211 (1986)—§ 14.4(b) n.32

Mills, United States v., 446 F.Supp.2d 1115 (C.D.Cal.2006)—§ 26.4(f) n.108

Mills, United States v., 412 F.3d 325 (2d Cir.2005)—§ 6.4(e) n.102

Mills, United States v., 280 F.3d 915 (9th Cir.2002)—§ 24.9(f) n.103

Mills, United States v., 315 F.3d 1 (1st Cir.2002)—§ 21.2(d) n.175

Mills, United States v., 199 F.3d 184 (5th Cir.1999)—§ 21.4(f) n.178

Mills, United States v., 138 F.3d 928 (11th Cir.1998)—§ 27.6(d) n.100

Mills, United States v., 995 F.2d 480 (4th Cir.1993)—§ 15.5(a) n.4

Mills, United States v., 925 F.2d 455 (D.C.Cir.1991)—§ 13.7(a) n.23

Mills, United States v., 895 F.2d 897 (2d Cir.1990)—§ 11.5(f) n.103

Mills, United States v., 704 F.2d 1553 (11th Cir.1983)—§ 18.1(c) n.35

Mills, United States v., 641 F.2d 785 (9th Cir.1981)—§ 8.5(g) n.228

Mills, United States v., 32 U.S. (7 Peters) 138, 8 L.Ed. 636 (1833)—§ 19.2(a) n.2

Milner v. State, 658 So.2d 500 (Ala.Civ.App.1994)—§ 17.4(b) n.138

Milner, United States v., 155 F.3d 697 (3d Cir.1998)—§§ 21.2(d) n.219; 21.2(e) n.323

Milone v. Camp, 22 F.3d 693 (7th Cir.1994)—§§ 11.6(d) n.123; 11.10(b) n.43

Milstein, United States v., 401 F.3d 53 (2d Cir.2005)—§§ 19.6(c) n.39, 51

Milton, People v., 826 P.2d 1282 (Colo.1992)—§ 3.10(f) n.193

Milton, State v., 178 N.J. 421, 840 A.2d 835 (2004)—§ 24.9(e) n.56

Milton, United States v., 153 F.3d 891 (8th Cir.1998)—§ 4.6(e) n.98

Milton v. Wainwright, 407 U.S. 371, 92 S.Ct. 2174, 33 L.Ed.2d 1 (1972)—§ 27.6(d) n.79

Milwaukee, City of v. Arrieh, 211 Wis.2d 764, 565 N.W.2d 291 (Wis.App.1997)—§ 2.6(b) n.43

Mincey v. Arizona, 437 U.S. 385, 98 S.Ct. 2408, 57 L.Ed.2d 290 (1978)—§§ 2.7(d) n.264; 2.9(f) n.147; 2.10(b) n.22; 3.6(e) n.133; 6.2(c) n.166; 9.1(a) n.18; 9.6(a) n.26

Mincey v. Head, 206 F.3d 1106 (11th Cir.2000)—§§ 6.9(g) n.169; 21.4(a) n.14; 24.3(b) n.49

Mincey, People v., 2 Cal.4th 408, 6 Cal.Rptr.2d 822, 827 P.2d 388 (1992)—§ 24.9(f) n.68

Miner v. Atlass, 363 U.S. 641, 80 S.Ct. 1300, 4 L.Ed.2d 1462 (1960)—§ 1.7(g) n.111

Miner, United States v., 484 F.2d 1075 (9th Cir.1973)—§ 3.9(h) n.157

Minet, People v., 296 N.Y. 315, 73 N.E.2d 529 (1947)—§ 15.7(h) n.237

Ming He, United States v., 94 F.3d 782 (2d Cir.1996)—§§ 1.7(i) n.194, 198, 200; 21.2(d) n.258

Mingo, State v., 77 N.J. 576, 392 A.2d 590 (1978)—§ 20.4(f) n.91

Minifield, Commonwealth v., 225 Pa.Super. 149, 310 A.2d 366 (1973)—§ 11.4(c) n.81

Minjares-Alvarez, United States v., 264 F.3d 980 (10th Cir.2001)—§§ 1.7(c) n.17; 6.9(b) n.30

Minjarez, People v., 81 P.3d 348 (Colo.2003)—§§ 6.6(c) n.31; 6.6(f) n.113

Minkoff, In re, 349 F.Supp. 154 (D.C.R.I.1972)—§ 8.5(f) n.211

Minneapolis, City of v. Buschette, 307 Minn. 60, 240 N.W.2d 500 (1976)—§ 13.4(c) n.94

Minnesota v. Carter, 525 U.S. 83, 119 S.Ct. 469, 142 L.Ed.2d 373 (1998)—§§ 2.9(c) n.53; 4.4(e) n.22; 9.1(b) n.71; 9.1(c) n.98

Minnesota v. Dickerson, 508 U.S. 366, 113 S.Ct. 2130, 124 L.Ed.2d 334 (1993)—§§ 2.9(d) n.98, 99; 3.2(b) n.89, 90; 3.5(e) n.206; 3.8(e) n.212; 27.5(a) n.10

Minnesota v. Murphy, 465 U.S. 420, 104 S.Ct. 1136, 79 L.Ed.2d 409 (1984)—§§ 6.6(a) n.8; 6.6(e) n.77; 6.10(c) n.49; 8.10(d) n.97; 26.9(b) n.67; 26.10(c) n.61

Minnesota v. Olson, 495 U.S. 91, 110 S.Ct. 1684, 109 L.Ed.2d 85 (1990)—§§ 3.6(a) n.18; 4.4(e) n.23; 9.1(b) n.59, 68, 93

Minnesota Mining & Manufacturing Co., United States v., 249 F.Supp. 594 (E.D.Ill.1966)—§ 21.4(a) n.33

Minnesota State Bar v. Divorce Assistance Association, 311 Minn. 276, 248 N.W.2d 733 (1976)—§ 8.12(b) n.21

Minnick v. Mississippi, 498 U.S. 146, 111 S.Ct. 486, 112 L.Ed.2d 489 (1990)—§§ 2.9(b) n.43; 2.9(h) n.207, 223; 2.9(i) n.277; 6.5(e) n.90; 6.9(f) n.118

Minniefield v. State, 539 N.E.2d 464 (Ind.1989)—§ 22.3(d) n.248

Minor, Commonwealth v., 89 Ky. 555, 13 S.W. 5 (1890)—§ 15.2(d) n.106

Minor, United States v., 228 F.3d 352 (4th Cir.2000)—§ 10.1(c) n.49

Minore, United States v., 292 F.3d 1109 (9th Cir.2002)—§§ 19.3(e) n.240; 21.4(c) n.76, 96

Minter, State v., 111 N.C.App. 40, 432 S.E.2d 146 (1993)—§§ 15.5(c) n.111; 15.7(e) n.105

Minton v. State, 269 Ind. 39, 378 N.E.2d 639 (1978)—§ 22.3(e) n.283

Mira v. Marshall, 806 F.2d 636 (6th Cir.1986)—§ 19.2(c) n.31

Miramontez, United States v., 995 F.2d 56 (5th Cir.1993)—§§ 8.5(h) n.238, 262

Miranda v. Arizona, 384 U.S. 436, 86 S.Ct. 1602, 16 L.Ed.2d 694 (1966)—§§ 1.10(c) n.55; 2.5(f) n.73; 2.7(c) n.179; 2.8(b) n.42; 2.8(c) n.59; 2.9(d) n.82; 2.9(f) n.133; 2.9(g) n.192, 194, 197; 2.9(h) n.214, 218, 236; 2.9(i) n.273, 274, 277, 281; 2.10(b) n.10; 2.10(c) n.96, 100; 2.10(d) n.135, 157; 2.11(a) n.6; 3.5(a) n.6; 3.10(b) n.65; 6.1(a) n.6; 6.1(b) n.11; 6.1(c) n.22; 6.2(b) n.48; 6.2(c) n.118; 6.2(d) n.188; 6.4(b) n.22; 6.4(c) n.36; 6.4(d) n.49; 6.4(e) n.80; 6.5(a) n.12; 6.6(a) n.1; 6.7(a) n.1; 6.8(a) n.1; 6.9(a) n.2; 6.10(a) n.1; 7.2(a) n.2; 7.3(a) n.3; 7.3(d) n.64; 10.3(c) n.55; 10.4(b) n.12; 11.1(c) n.97; 11.2(b) n.48; 11.3(a) n.13

Miranda v. Bennett, 322 F.3d 171 (2d Cir.2003)—§ 28.6(f) n.76

Miranda v. Clark County, 319 F.3d 465 (9th Cir.2003)—§ 11.8(c) n.79

Miranda, People v., 23 Cal.4th 340, 1 P.3d 73, 96 Cal.Rptr.2d 758 (2000)—§ 14.4(b) n.30

Miranda, People v., 44 Cal.3d 57, 241 Cal.Rptr. 594, 744 P.2d 1127 (1987)—§ 6.4(g) n.163

Miranda, State v., 672 N.W.2d 753 (Iowa 2003)—§§ 6.6(e) n.65; 6.6(f) n.101

Miranda, State v., 777 So.2d 1173 (Fla.App.2001)—§ 20.3(a) n.20

Miranda, United States v., 248 F.3d 434 (5th Cir.2001)—§§ 17.2(c) n.87; 17.2(f) n.136

Miranda, United States v., 986 F.2d 1283 (9th Cir.1993)—§ 18.3(b) n.20

Miranda, United States v., 526 F.2d 1319 (2d Cir.1975)—§§ 20.6(b) n.51, 52, 58, 63, 64

Miranda-Olivas, People v., 41 P.3d 658 (Colo.2001)—§§ 6.2(c) n.96, 152

Miravalles, United States v., 280 F.3d 1328 (11th Cir.2002)—§ 3.2(c) n.107

Mireles, United States v., 570 F.2d 1287 (5th Cir.1978)—§ 10.2(b) n.25

Mireles v. Waco, 502 U.S. 9, 112 S.Ct. 286, 116 L.Ed.2d 9 (1991)—§ 2.9(h) n.265

Mirenda, People v., 57 N.Y.2d 261, 455 N.Y.S.2d 752, 442 N.E.2d 49 (1982)—§§ 11.5(g) n.110, 111

Mirquet, State v., 914 P.2d 1144 (Utah 1996)—§§ 6.6(c) n.33; 6.6(e) n.59

Misener, In re, 38 Cal.3d 543, 213 Cal.Rptr. 569, 698 P.2d 637 (1985)—§ 20.4(b) n.20

Misenheimer v. State, 27 P.3d 273 (Wyo.2001)—§ 13.4(e) n.169

Miskimins, State v., 435 N.W.2d 217 (S.D. 1989)—§ 9.4(f) n.117

Miskinis, United States v., 966 F.2d 1263 (9th Cir.1992)—§§ 11.9(d) n.214, 229

Mispagel, State v., 207 Mo. 557, 106 S.W. 513 (1907)—§§ 16.1(d) n.139, 142

Misquadace, State v., 644 N.W.2d 65 (Minn.2002)—§ 21.3(e) n.288

Mississippi Publishers Corp. v. Coleman, 515 So.2d 1163 (Miss.1987)—§§ 2.6(b) n.62, 64; 23.1(e) n.239, 254, 256

Missoulian, State ex rel. v. Montana Twenty-First Judicial District Court, 281 Mont. 285, 933 P.2d 829 (1997)—§§ 23.1(b) n.89; 23.1(e) n.227

Missouri v. Durham, 822 S.W.2d 453 (Mo.App.1991)—§ 25.5(b) n.22

Missouri v. Holland, 252 U.S. 416, 40 S.Ct. 382, 64 L.Ed. 641 (1920)—§ 1.7(c) n.13

Missouri v. Hunter, 459 U.S. 359, 103 S.Ct. 673, 74 L.Ed.2d 535 (1983)—§§ 17.4(b) n.91; 26.7(c) n.29

Missouri v. Jenkins, 515 U.S. 70, 115 S.Ct. 2038, 132 L.Ed.2d 63 (1995)—§ 2.9(d) n.61

Missouri v. Lewis, 101 U.S. (11 Otto) 22, 25 L.Ed. 989 (1879)—§§ 2.3(b) n.83; 2.5(f) n.50

Missouri v. Seibert, 542 U.S. 600, 124 S.Ct. 2601, 159 L.Ed.2d 643 (2004)—§§ 2.9(h) n.267; 2.10(b) n.24; 6.8(b) n.44; 9.5(a) n.27; 9.5(c) n.72

Mitchell, Commonwealth v., 943 S.W.2d 625 (Ky.1997)—§ 24.9(d) n.48

Mitchell, Commonwealth v., 355 S.W.2d 686 (Ky.1962)—§ 3.9(g) n.122

Mitchell v. Esparza, 540 U.S. 12, 124 S.Ct. 7, 157 L.Ed.2d 263 (2003)—§§ 19.6(c) n.49; 27.6(d) n.124

Mitchell v. Gibson, 262 F.3d 1036 (10th Cir.2001)—§ 6.9(g) n.167

Mitchell v. Mason, 325 F.3d 732 (6th Cir.2003)—§§ 11.10(d) n.198, 204, 205

Mitchell, People v., 2 N.Y.3d 272, 778 N.Y.S.2d 427, 810 N.E.2d 879 (2004)—§ 7.3(b) n.31

Mitchell, People v., 152 Ill.2d 274, 178 Ill.Dec. 354, 604 N.E.2d 877 (1992)—§§ 22.3(d) n.249, 250

Mitchell, People v., 431 Mich. 744, 432 N.W.2d 715 (1988)—§ 21.4(f) n.192

Mitchell v. Scully, 746 F.2d 951 (2d Cir.1984)—§ 21.4(c) n.81

Mitchell, State v., 353 N.C. 309, 543 S.E.2d 830 (2001)—§§ 6.8(b) n.50, 57, 58

Mitchell v. State, 792 So.2d 192 (Miss.2001)—§§ 3.3(f) n.206; 3.5(c) n.124

Mitchell v. State, 982 P.2d 717 (Wyo.1999)—§ 6.8(b) n.50

Mitchell, State v., 573 N.W.2d 239 (Iowa 1997)—§ 22.3(c) n.100

Mitchell v. State, 963 S.W.2d 532 (Tex.App.1996)—§ 25.4(a) n.8

Mitchell v. State, 109 Nev. 137, 848 P.2d 1060 (1993)—§ 21.5(a) n.38

Mitchell v. State, 609 So.2d 416 (Miss.1992)—§ 3.10(b) n.46

Mitchell v. State, 105 Nev. 735, 782 P.2d 1340 (1989)—§ 17.3(b) n.27

Mitchell v. State, 541 N.E.2d 265 (Ind.1989)—§ 6.6(e) n.59

Mitchell v. State, 295 Ark. 341, 750 S.W.2d 936 (1988)—§ 22.3(d) n.245

Mitchell, State v., 204 Conn. 187, 527 A.2d 1168 (1987)—§§ 3.8(b) n.45; 7.4(b) n.22

Mitchell, State v., 147 Vt. 218, 514 A.2d 1047 (1986)—§ 13.3(c) n.38

Mitchell, State v., 200 Conn. 323, 512 A.2d 140 (1986)—§§ 14.4(c) n.66, 72

Mitchell, State v., 682 S.W.2d 918 (Tenn.1984)—§ 17.4(b) n.98

Mitchell, State v., 104 Idaho 493, 660 P.2d 1336 (1983)—§§ 14.3(c) n.63; 14.3(d) n.101

Mitchell, State v., 278 So.2d 48 (La.1973)—§ 9.1(a) n.16

Mitchell v. State, 3 Tenn.Cr.App. 153, 458 S.W.2d 630 (1970)—§ 6.8(b) n.58

Mitchell, United States v., 429 F.3d 952 (10th Cir.2005)—§ 9.1(b) n.53

Mitchell, United States v., 216 F.3d 1126 (D.C.Cir.2000)—§ 11.8(c) n.77

Mitchell v. United States, 746 A.2d 877 (D.C.App.2000)—§ 6.7(d) n.150

Mitchell, United States v., 178 F.3d 904 (7th Cir.1999)—§ 21.2(b) n.74

Mitchell v. United States, 526 U.S. 314, 119 S.Ct. 1307, 143 L.Ed.2d 424 (1999)—§§ 2.10(b) n.43; 2.10(c) n.76, 94; 21.4(e) n.157; 21.4(f) n.189; 21.4(g) n.260; 24.5(b) n.32; 26.4(c) n.33

Mitchell, United States v., 136 F.3d 1192 (8th Cir.1998)—§ 21.2(d) n.172

Mitchell v. United States, 609 A.2d 1099 (D.C.App.1992)—§ 9.1(d) n.120

Mitchell, United States v., 951 F.2d 1291 (D.C.Cir.1991)—§§ 3.8(e) n.195; 9.1(d) n.122; 10.1(b) n.20

Mitchell v. United States, 569 A.2d 177 (D.C.App.1990)—§§ 16.4(d) n.117, 119, 131, 133, 134

Mitchell, United States v., 812 F.2d 1250 (9th Cir.1987)—§ 9.5(e) n.87

Mitchell, United States v., 777 F.2d 248 (5th Cir.1985)—§§ 11.3(c) n.66; 11.4(c) n.82

Mitchell, United States v., 778 F.2d 1271 (7th Cir.1985)—§§ 13.4(b) n.60; 13.4(c) n.143

Mitchell, United States v., 397 F.Supp. 166 (D.C.1974)—§ 1.7(f) n.80

Mitchell, United States v., 179 F.Supp. 636 (D.D.C.1959)—§ 3.8(b) n.42

Mitchell, United States v., 322 U.S. 65, 64 S.Ct. 896, 88 L.Ed. 1140 (1944)—§ 6.3(a) n.22

Mitchell v. W.T. Grant Co., 416 U.S. 600, 94 S.Ct. 1895, 40 L.Ed.2d 406 (1974)—§ 14.2(a) n.6

Mitchell, United States ex rel. v. Fairman, 750 F.2d 806 (7th Cir.1984)—§§ 18.2(b) n.25; 18.2(c) n.52; 18.2(d) n.63

Mitchell, United States ex rel. v. Thompson, 56 F.Supp. 683 (S.D.N.Y.1944)—§ 11.4(a) n.6

Mitrione, United States v., 357 F.3d 712 (7th Cir.2004)—§ 24.11(d) n.29

Mittelman, United States v., 999 F.2d 440 (9th Cir.1993)—§ 3.4(a) n.22

Mittender v. Adams, 376 F.3d 520 (6th Cir.2004)—§ 7.4(d) n.76

Mitzel v. Tate, 267 F.3d 524 (6th Cir.2001)—§ 6.4(e) n.76

Mixon, United States v., 977 F.2d 921 (5th Cir.1992)—§ 22.3(d) n.250

Miyasaki, State v., 62 Haw. 269, 614 P.2d 915 (1980)—§§ 2.12(e) n.215; 8.11(b) n.21, 26

Miyashiro, State v., 90 Haw. 489, 979 P.2d 85 (1999)—§ 24.9(d) n.35

Miyashiro, State v., 3 Haw.App. 229, 647 P.2d 302 (1982)—§§ 16.1(h) n.285, 289, 308

Mizell, United States v., 488 F.2d 97 (5th Cir.1973)—§ 21.6(b) n.112

MLB v. SLJ, 519 U.S. 102, 117 S.Ct. 555, 136 L.Ed.2d 473 (1996)—§ 11.1(d) n.113

M.L.C., State v., 933 P.2d 380 (Utah 1997)—§ 12.4(b) n.48

M.M.R.Corp., United States v., 954 F.2d 1040 (5th Cir.1992)—§ 24.11(d) n.30

Moats, State v., 906 S.W.2d 431 (Tenn.1995)—§§ 24.6(d) n.42, 45

Moats, State v., 156 Wis.2d 74, 457 N.W.2d 299 (1990)—§§ 14.4(b) n.25, 36

Moavenzadeh, State v., 135 Wash.2d 359, 956 P.2d 1097 (1998)—§§ 19.2(d) n.49; 19.3(a) n.8, 49, 75; 19.3(e) n.219

Moberg v. State, 810 S.W.2d 190 (Tex.Cr.App.1991)—§ 3.10(e) n.156

Mobile Materials, United States v., 871 F.2d 902 (10th Cir.1989)—§§ 19.2(f) n.97; 19.4(a) n.4

Mobley, Commonwealth v., 160 S.W.3d 783 (Ky.2005)—§ 3.3(f) n.200

Mobley v. State, 270 Md. 76, 310 A.2d 803 (1973)—§ 3.3(d) n.165

Mobley, United States v., 40 F.3d 688 (4th Cir.1994)—§§ 6.7(b) n.80, 85

Moczygemba v. State, 532 S.W.2d 636 (Tex.Crim.1976)—§ 15.2(c) n.62

Moderacki, United States v., 280 F.Supp. 633 (D.Del.1968)—§ 3.10(b) n.75

Modesto, People v., 62 Cal.2d 436, 42 Cal.Rptr. 417, 398 P.2d 753 (1965)—§ 6.4(c) n.43

Modica, State v., 58 Haw. 249, 567 P.2d 420 (1977)—§ 13.7(a) n.27

Modica, United States v., 663 F.2d 1173 (2d Cir.1981)—§ 24.7(i) n.92

Modrowski v. Mote, 322 F.3d 965 (7th Cir.2003)—§ 28.5(b) n.59

Moe, In re, 62 Haw. 613, 617 P.2d 1222 (1980)—§ 8.4(c) n.112

Moe, People v., 227 A.D.2d 253, 642 N.Y.S.2d 656 (1996)—§ 15.7(f) n.172

Moe, State v., 581 N.W.2d 468 (N.D.1998)—§§ 18.4(c) n.53; 18.4(d) n.84

Moeck, State v., 280 Wis.2d 277, 695 N.W.2d 783 (2005)—§ 25.2(d) n.24

Moeckly, United States v., 769 F.2d 453 (8th Cir.1985)—§ 16.1(g) n.260

Moehlenkamp, United States v., 557 F.2d 126 (7th Cir.1977)—§ 27.5(a) n.5

Moeller, State v., 616 N.W.2d 424 (S.D.2000)—§ 22.3(a) n.5

Moeller, State v., 396 N.W.2d 320 (S.D.1986)—§ 5.3(b) n.18

Moeller, United States v., 80 F.3d 1053 (5th Cir.1996)—§ 22.3(d) n.249

Moeller, United States v., 402 F.Supp. 49 (D.Conn.1975)—§ 8.9(b) n.25

Moeller v. Weber, 689 N.W.2d 1 (S.D.2004)—§ 13.2(a) n.5

Moen, State v., 150 Wash.2d 221, 76 P.3d 721 (2003)—§ 21.3(c) n.148

Moetamedi, United States v., 46 F.3d 225 (2d Cir.1995)—§ 3.4(f) n.120

Moffett, Commonwealth v., 383 Mass. 201, 418 N.E.2d 585 (1981)—§§ 11.2(c) n.90, 92

Moffett v. Wainwright, 512 F.2d 496 (5th Cir.1975)—§ 3.10(e) n.167

Mohabir, United States v., 624 F.2d 1140 (2d Cir.1980)—§§ 1.7(i) n.194; 6.4(f) n.123

Mohawk, United States v., 20 F.3d 1480 (9th Cir.1994)—§ 18.5(c) n.82

Moher, United States v., 445 F.2d 584 (2d Cir.1971)—§ 7.3(d) n.68

Mohney, United States v., 949 F.2d 1397 (6th Cir.1991)—§§ 9.1(c) n.101; 24.3(i) n.193; 24.4(d) n.48, 52

Mohney, United States v., 476 F.Supp. 421 (D.Hawai'i 1979)—§ 16.3(c) n.49

Mohr v. State, 584 So.2d 426 (Miss.1991)—§ 6.9(g) n.171

Mohr, State v., 150 Ariz. 564, 724 P.2d 1233 (1986)—§§ 16.1(g) n.266, 267

Mojica-Baez, United States v., 229 F.3d 292 (1st Cir.2000)—§§ 19.2(e) n.82; 19.3(a) n.88, 92, 98, 99

Moleno-Trevino, United States v., 432 F.3d 1181 (10th Cir.2005)—§ 21.1(h) n.213

Moleterno v. Nelson, 114 F.3d 629 (7th Cir.1997)—§§ 28.5(a) n.15, 34

Molinaro v. New Jersey, 396 U.S. 365, 90 S.Ct. 498, 24 L.Ed.2d 586 (1970)—§ 27.5(c) n.73

Molinas v. Comm'r of Corrections, 231 Conn. 514, 652 A.2d 481 (1994)—§ 26.1(f) n.144

Moll, People v., 26 N.Y.S.2d 1, 307 N.Y.S.2d 876, 256 N.E.2d 185 (1970)—§ 17.2(b) n.56

Moll v. United States, 413 F.2d 1233 (5th Cir.1969)—§ 6.8(c) n.75

Mollica, State v., 114 N.J. 329, 554 A.2d 1315 (1989)—§§ 2.12(c) n.175, 176

Mollicone, State v., 654 A.2d 311 (R.I.1995)—§ 15.6(a) n.32

Moloney, United States v., 287 F.3d 236 (2d Cir.2002)—§ 21.6(a) n.25

Momon v. State, 18 S.W.3d 152 (Tenn.1999)—§§ 11.6(d) n.115, 124, 126

Momon v. State, 18 S.W.3d 152 (Tenn.Sup.Ct.1990)—§ 11.6(c) n.100

Monaco, People v., 474 Mich. 48, 710 N.W.2d 46 (2006)—§ 18.5(a) n.11

Monaco, United States v., 702 F.2d 860 (11th Cir.1983)—§ 26.8(b) n.5

Monclavo-Cruz, United States v., 662 F.2d 1285 (9th Cir.1981)—§ 3.7(a) n.12

Mondesir, State v., 891 A.2d 856 (R.I.2006)—§ 10.1(a) n.3

Mondragon, United States v., 228 F.3d 978 (9th Cir.2000)—§§ 21.2(d) n.178; 21.2(e) n.316

Monell v. New York City Department of Social Services, 436 U.S. 658, 98 S.Ct. 2018, 56 L.Ed.2d 611 (1978)—§ 3.1(k) n.265

Monge v. California, 524 U.S. 721, 118 S.Ct. 2246, 141 L.Ed.2d 615 (1998)—§§ 26.6(b) n.14, 27; 26.7(a) n.13; 26.7(d) n.41

Mongelli, United States v., 2 F.3d 29 (2d Cir.1993)—§ 8.3(a) n.2

Monia, United States v., 317 U.S. 424, 63 S.Ct. 409, 87 L.Ed. 376 (1943)—§§ 2.10(b) n.33; 8.10(d) n.93

Monica, Commonwealth v., 528 Pa. 266, 597 A.2d 600 (1991)—§ 11.3(a) n.11

Monk, Ex parte, 557 So.2d 832 (Ala.1989)—§ 1.8(e) n.94

Monk, State v., 291 N.C. 37, 229 S.E.2d 163 (1976)—§ 9.1(d) n.126

Monreal v. State, 947 S.W.2d 559 (Tex.Crim.App.1997)—§ 11.9(a) n.21

Monroe v. Kuhlman, 436 F.Supp.2d 474 (E.D.N.Y.2006)—§ 24.9(c) n.23

Monroe v. Pape, 365 U.S. 167, 81 S.Ct. 473, 5 L.Ed.2d 492 (1961)—§ 3.1(k) n.258

Monroe, People v., 925 P.2d 767 (Colo.1996)—§§ 7.4(g) n.112, 116

Monroe, People v., 125 Misc.2d 550, 480 N.Y.S.2d 259 (Sup.Ct.1984)—§§ 15.6(a) n.25, 27, 29; 15.7(e) n.127; 15.7(f) n.170

Monroe, State v., 142 N.H. 857, 711 A.2d 878 (1998)—§ 6.8(b) n.63

Monroe, United States v., 353 F.3d 1346 (11th Cir.2003)—§ 21.5(c) n.84

Monsalve, State v., 133 N.H. 268, 574 A.2d 1384 (1990)—§ 24.3(i) n.190

Monsanto, United States v., 491 U.S. 600, 109 S.Ct. 2657, 105 L.Ed.2d 512 (1989)—§§ 11.4(c) n.93; 26.6(d) n.70

Monson v. Carver, 928 P.2d 1017 (Utah 1996)—§ 26.4(e) n.80

Monson, State v., 518 N.W.2d 171 (N.D.1994)—§§ 26.9(b) n.16, 44

Monsoor, United States v., 77 F.3d 1031 (7th Cir.1996)—§ 13.4(d) n.162

Montague, State v., 55 N.J. 387, 262 A.2d 398 (1970)—§§ 20.1(a) n.16; 20.3(j) n.200

Montague, United States v., 40 F.3d 1251 (D.C.Cir.1994)—§ 26.4(c) n.30

Montalban, State v., 810 So.2d 1106 (La.2002)—§ 21.3(b) n.66

Montalvo, United States v., 331 F.3d 1052 (9th Cir.2003)—§ 28.9(b) n.37

Montalvo-Murillo, United States v., 495 U.S. 711, 110 S.Ct. 2072, 109 L.Ed.2d 720 (1990)—§§ 12.3(a) n.20, 27

Montana v. Egelhoff, 518 U.S. 37, 116 S.Ct. 2013, 135 L.Ed.2d 361 (1996)—§§ 2.7(d) n.232; 24.4(a) n.5

Montana v. Hall, 481 U.S. 400, 107 S.Ct. 1825, 95 L.Ed.2d 354 (1987)—§§ 17.4(b) n.102; 25.4(b) n.16

Montana, United States v., 199 F.3d 947 (7th Cir.1999)—§ 11.9(d) n.183

Montana, United States v., 958 F.2d 516 (2d Cir.1992)—§ 6.9(g) n.150

Montana Department of Revenue v. Kurth Ranch, 511 U.S. 767, 114 S.Ct. 1937, 128 L.Ed.2d 767 (1994)—§§ 17.4(b) n.137; 25.1(c) n.30; 25.5(a) n.8

Montano, United States v., 472 F.3d 1202 (10th Cir.2007)—§ 21.2(b) n.86

Montano, United States v., 398 F.3d 1276 (11th Cir.2005)—§ 28.4(e) n.84

Monteagudo, Commonwealth v., 427 Mass. 484, 693 N.E.2d 1381 (1998)—§ 5.4(c) n.29

Monteiro, United States v., 270 F.3d 465 (7th Cir.2001)—§ 26.9(b) n.66

Monteleone, United States v., 804 F.2d 1004 (7th Cir.1986)—§ 8.3(a) n.7

Montelongo v. State, 681 S.W.2d 47 (Tex.Crim.App.1984)—§ 6.9(g) n.162

Monteririo, Commonwealth v., 4 Mass.App.Ct. 349, 348 N.E.2d 449 (1976)—§ 3.2(e) n.161

Montes-Cardenas, United States v., 746 F.2d 771 (11th Cir.1984)—§ 17.1(a) n.15

Montez, United States v., 952 F.2d 854 (9th Cir.1992)—§ 3.1(f) n.157

Montgomery v. Bagley, 482 F.Supp.2d 919 (N.D.Oh.2007)—§§ 24.3(b) n.35, 41; 24.5(b) n.25

Montgomery v. Greer, 956 F.2d 677 (7th Cir.1992)—§ 7.4(e) n.93

Montgomery, People v., 112 Ill.2d 517, 98 Ill.Dec. 353, 494 N.E.2d 475 (1986)—§ 10.5(c) n.35

Montgomery, People v., 96 Ill.App.3d 994, 52 Ill.Dec. 545, 422 N.E.2d 226 (1981)—§ 19.6(b) n.17

Montgomery v. Petersen, 846 F.2d 407 (7th Cir.1988)—§§ 11.10(c) n.111, 126

Montgomery, State v., 254 Conn. 694, 759 A.2d 995 (2000)—§ 9.6(a) n.41

Montgomery v. State, 176 So.2d 331 (Fla.1965)—§ 6.4(c) n.38

Montgomery, State v., 115 La. 155, 38 So. 949 (1905)—§ 16.1(e) n.192

Montgomery, United States v., 441 F.Supp.2d 58 (D.D.C. 2006)—§ 16.2(c) n.52

Montgomery, United States v., 390 F.3d 1013 (7th Cir.2004)—§ 6.8(c) n.65

Montgomery, United States v., 262 F.3d 233 (4th Cir.2001)—§§ 6.4(e) n.101, 104

Montgomery, United States v., 150 F.3d 983 (9th Cir.1998)—§§ 7.3(c) n.57; 7.4(g) n.110

Montgomery, United States v., 990 F.2d 266 (7th Cir.1993)—§ 15.7(b) n.43

Montgomery, United States v., 714 F.2d 201 (1st Cir.1983)—§ 6.7(b) n.30

Montgomery, United States v., 628 F.2d 414 (5th Cir.1980)—§§ 15.1(f) n.322, 334

Montiel, State v., 122 P.3d 571 (Utah 2005)—§§ 21.3(e) n.266, 270, 281

Montilla, United States v., 870 F.2d 549 (9th Cir.1989)—§ 21.6(a) n.64

Montilla-Rivera, United States v., 115 F.3d 1060 (1st Cir.1997)—§ 24.11(d) n.35

Montione, Commonwealth v., 554 Pa. 121, 720 A.2d 738 (1998)—§ 18.4(c) n.61

Montos, United States v., 421 F.2d 215 (5th Cir.1970)—§§ 10.6(a) n.6; 10.6(c) n.19

Montoya v. Collins, 955 F.2d 279 (5th Cir.1992)—§§ 6.4(f) n.136; 24.8(f) n.91

Montoya, People v., 255 Cal.App.2d 137, 63 Cal.Rptr. 73 (1967)—§ 3.5(a) n.62

Montoya v. Scott, 65 F.3d 405 (5th Cir.1995)—§§ 24.9(d) n.40, 48

Montoya, State v., 887 P.2d 857 (Utah 1994)—§ 21.6(b) n.102

Montoya, United States v., 45 F.3d 1286 (9th Cir.1995)—§§ 8.11(c) n.59, 64

Montoya, United States v., 827 F.2d 143 (7th Cir.1987)—§§ 18.3(b) n.21, 25

Montoya de Hernandez, United States v., 473 U.S. 531, 105 S.Ct. 3304, 87 L.Ed.2d 381 (1985)—§ 3.9(f) n.109

Montoya-Ortiz, United States v., 7 F.3d 1171 (5th Cir.1993)—§ 26.5(a) n.8

Monzon, United States v., 359 F.3d 110 (2d Cir.2004)—§ 27.5(c) n.63

Monzon, United States v., 869 F.2d 338 (7th Cir.1989)—§ 6.7(b) n.70

Moody, Ex parte, 991 S.W.2d 856 (Tex.Cr.App.1999)—§ 21.3(b) n.71

Moody v. Daggett, 429 U.S. 78, 97 S.Ct. 274, 50 L.Ed.2d 236 (1976)—§§ 18.5(c) n.91; 26.10(b) n.17

Moody, People v., 716 So.2d 592 (Miss.1998)—§ 21.3(e) n.289

Moody, State v., 282 Kan. 181, 144 P.3d 612 (2006)—§ 21.4(d) n.114

Moody v. State, 716 So.2d 562 (Miss.1998)—§ 13.6(c) n.28

Moody, State v., 345 N.C. 563, 481 S.E.2d 629 (1997)—§ 6.9(b) n.27

Moody, United States v., 206 F.3d 609 (6th Cir.2000)—§§ 11.7(a) n.16; 21.3(a) n.10

Moody, United States v., 977 F.2d 1425 (11th Cir.1992)—§§ 3.4(f) n.107; 4.6(h) n.147

Moody, United States v., 762 F.Supp. 1485 (N.D.Ga.1991)—§ 23.2(a) n.26

Moody, United States v., 762 F.Supp. 1491 (N.D.Ga.1991)—§ 16.3(g) n.101

Moody, United States v., 746 F.Supp. 1090 (M.D.Ga.1990)—§§ 23.1(d) n.167, 188

Moody v. United States, 497 F.2d 359 (7th Cir.1974)—§ 1.7(i) n.177

Moog Industries, Inc. v. FTC, 355 U.S. 411, 78 S.Ct. 377, 2 L.Ed.2d 370 (1958)—§ 13.2(b) n.41

Moomau, State ex rel. v. Hamilton, 184 W.Va. 251, 400 S.E.2d 259 (1990)—§ 27.4(d) n.48

Moon, State v., 841 S.W.2d 336 (Tenn.Crim.App.1992)—§ 3.3(c) n.95

Moon v. State, 258 Ga. 748, 375 S.E.2d 442 (1988)—§§ 18.4(c) n.45, 59

Moon, State v., 178 N.C. 715, 100 S.E. 614 (1919)—§ 16.4(c) n.47

Mooney v. Holohan, 294 U.S. 103, 55 S.Ct. 340, 79 L.Ed. 791 (1935)—§§ 2.4(e) n.135; 2.7(a) n.47; 2.7(c) n.158; 24.3(b) n.13; 24.3(d) n.105

Mooney, State v., 218 Conn. 85, 588 A.2d 145 (1991)—§ 3.2(h) n.203

Mooney v. State, 817 S.W.2d 693 (Tex.Cr.App.1991)—§ 22.3(c) n.112

Mooney v. State, 615 S.W.2d 776 (Tex.Cr.App.1981)—§ 21.4(a) n.26

Mooney, United States v., 654 F.2d 482 (7th Cir.1981)—§§ 21.2(d) n.188, 191

Moore, In re Petition of, 336 So.2d 736 (Miss.1976)—§ 8.3(h) n.50

Moore, Matter of, 116 Wash.2d 30, 803 P.2d 300 (1991)—§ 21.6(a) n.80

Moore v. Arizona, 414 U.S. 25, 94 S.Ct. 188, 38 L.Ed.2d 183 (1973)—§ 18.2(e) n.71

Moore v. Bryant, 348 F.3d 238 (7th Cir.2003)—§§ 21.3(b) n.47, 60

Moore v. City of East Cleveland, 431 U.S. 494, 97 S.Ct. 1932, 52 L.Ed.2d 531 (1977)—§ 2.4(a) n.19

Moore v. Commonwealth, 27 Va.App. 192, 497 S.E.2d 908 (1998)—§ 19.3(a) n.38

Moore, Commonwealth v., 534 Pa. 527, 633 A.2d 1119 (1993)—§ 10.3(d) n.65

Moore v. Commonwealth, 523 S.W.2d 635 (Ky.1975)—§ 16.1(d) n.138

Moore v. Dempsey, 261 U.S. 86, 43 S.Ct. 265, 67 L.Ed. 543 (1923)—§§ 2.4(b) n.60; 2.4(d) n.130; 2.5(d) n.36; 2.8(c) n.62; 28.3(b) n.49

Moore v. Dugger, 856 F.2d 129 (11th Cir.1988)—§ 6.2(c) n.178

Moore v. Hinton, 513 F.2d 781 (5th Cir.1975)—§ 21.4(d) n.128

Moore v. Hopper, 389 F.Supp. 931 (M.D.Ga.1974)—§ 6.2(c) n.126

Moore v. Illinois, 434 U.S. 220, 98 S.Ct. 458, 54 L.Ed.2d 424 (1977)— §§ 7.3(b) n.25; 7.3(c) n.55; 7.3(e) n.101; 7.4(g) n.109; 11.2(b) n.80; 27.6(d) n.79

Moore v. Illinois, 408 U.S. 786, 92 S.Ct. 2562, 33 L.Ed.2d 706 (1972)— § 20.3(m) n.235

Moore v. Jamieson, 451 Pa. 299, 306 A.2d 283 (1973)—§ 11.8(c) n.74

Moore v. Johnson, 225 F.3d 495 (5th Cir.2000)—§ 11.2(e) n.212

Moore v. Kemp, 809 F.2d 702 (11th Cir.1987)—§§ 11.2(e) n.163, 185, 195, 197, 203, 208, 209

Moore v. McCormick, 260 Mont. 305, 858 P.2d 1254 (1993)—§ 12.4(d) n.63

Moore v. New York, 333 U.S. 565, 68 S.Ct. 705, 92 L.Ed. 881 (1948)— § 22.2(d) n.50

Moore, People v., 207 Ill.2d 68, 278 Ill.Dec. 36, 797 N.E.2d 631 (2003)—§ 11.7(e) n.68

Moore, People v., 266 Ill.App.3d 791, 203 Ill.Dec. 883, 640 N.E.2d 1256 (1994)—§ 10.3(d) n.66

Moore, People v., 138 Ill.2d 162, 149 Ill.Dec. 278, 561 N.E.2d 648 (1990)—§ 17.4(a) n.53

Moore, People v., 180 Mich.App. 301, 446 N.W.2d 834 (1989)—§ 14.4(d) n.97

Moore, People v., 46 N.Y.2d 1, 412 N.Y.S.2d 795, 385 N.E.2d 535 (1978)—§ 16.1(e) n.196

Moore, People v., 57 Cal.App.3d 437, 129 Cal.Rptr. 279 (1976)— §§ 21.3(a) n.4, 14

Moore, People v., 20 Cal.App.3d 444, 97 Cal.Rptr. 601 (1971)—§ 6.9(b) n.35

Moore, People v., 69 Cal.2d 674, 72 Cal.Rptr. 800, 446 P.2d 800 (1968)—§ 3.1(g) n.173

Moore, People v., 64 Cal.App. 328, 221 P. 665 (1923)—§ 27.6(b) n.12

Moore v. Purkett, 275 F.3d 685 (8th Cir.2001)—§ 11.8(a) n.3

Moore v. Quarterman, 454 F.3d 484 (5th Cir.2006)—§ 28.5(a) n.35

Moore v. State, 390 Md. 343, 889 A.2d 325 (2006)—§§ 11.2(e) n.149, 168, 173, 183, 187, 203, 229

Moore v. State, 933 So.2d 910 (Miss.2006)—§ 10.3(c) n.52

Moore v. State, 123 P.3d 1081 (Alaska App.2005)—§ 11.4(b) n.27

Moore, State v., 638 N.W.2d 735 (Iowa 2002)—§ 21.4(b) n.42

Moore v. State, 272 Ga. 359, 528 S.E.2d 793 (2000)—§ 6.9(g) n.167

Moore, State v., 343 S.C. 282, 540 S.E.2d 445 (2000)—§§ 7.4(c) n.54; 7.4(f) n.95

Moore, State v., 81 Ohio St.3d 22, 689 N.E.2d 1 (1998)—§ 22.3(c) n.151

Moore, State v., 678 N.E.2d 1258 (Ind.1997)—§§ 11.10(d) n.171; 21.4(a) n.40

Moore v. State, 321 Ark. 249, 903 S.W.2d 154 (1995)—§ 6.9(g) n.185

Moore v. State, 900 P.2d 996 (Okla.Cr.App.1995)—§§ 7.4(d) n.71; 22.3(d) n.258

Moore v. State, 215 Ga.App. 626, 451 S.E.2d 534 (1994)—§ 24.9(d) n.43

Moore, State v., 882 S.W.2d 253 (Mo.App.1994)—§ 19.3(a) n.63

Moore v. State, 263 Ga. 11, 427 S.E.2d 766 (1993)—§ 22.3(d) n.240

Moore, State v., 74 Ohio App.3d 334, 598 N.E.2d 1224 (1991)— §§ 20.2(d) n.77; 20.3(b) n.49

Moore, State v., 329 N.C. 245, 404 S.E.2d 845 (1991)—§§ 15.4(c) n.96; 15.4(e) n.128

Moore, State v., 438 N.W.2d 101 (Minn.1989)—§ 22.3(d) n.250

Moore, State v., 776 S.W.2d 933 (Tenn.1989)—§ 3.8(c) n.86

Moore v. State, 297 Ark. 296, 761 S.W.2d 894 (1988)—§ 3.4(e) n.78

Moore, State v., 321 N.C. 327, 364 S.E.2d 648 (1988)—§§ 11.2(e) n.189, 190, 208, 220, 228

Moore v. State, 534 So.2d 557 (Miss.1988)—§ 5.2(a) n.4

Moore, State v., 319 N.C. 645, 356 S.E.2d 336 (1987)—§ 16.3(b) n.23

Moore v. State, 740 P.2d 731 (Okla.Crim.App.1987)—§ 20.3(m) n.237

Moore v. State, 493 So.2d 1301 (Miss.1986)—§ 6.9(d) n.67

Moore v. State, 498 N.E.2d 1 (Ind.1986)—§ 6.9(f) n.104

Moore v. State, 172 Ga.App. 844, 324 S.E.2d 760 (1984)—§§ 24.9(f) n.68, 78

Moore, State v., 38 N.C.App. 239, 247 S.E.2d 670 (1978)—§§ 19.2(d) n.49; 19.3(e) n.219

Moore v. State, 83 Wis.2d 285, 265 N.W.2d 540 (1978)—§§ 11.5(g) n.110, 113

Moore, State v., 575 S.W.2d 253 (Mo.App.1978)—§ 27.5(d) n.121

Moore v. State, 142 Ga.App. 145, 235 S.E.2d 577 (1977)—§ 11.5(e) n.89

Moore, State v., 300 So.2d 492 (La.1974)—§ 7.3(c) n.46

Moore v. State, 105 Ariz. 510, 467 P.2d 904 (1970)—§§ 20.2(b) n.25; 20.4(b) n.27; 20.5(a) n.7

Moore v. Student Affairs Committee of Troy State University, 284 F.Supp. 725 (M.D.Ala.1968)—§§ 3.9(k) n.243, 263

Moore, United States v., 452 F.3d 382 (5th Cir.2006)—§ 24.3(c) n.89

Moore, United States v., 208 F.3d 577 (7th Cir.2000)—§ 20.5(g) n.89

Moore, United States v., 184 F.3d 790 (8th Cir.1999)—§§ 15.5(b) n.52; 17.3(b) n.12

Moore v. United States, 724 A.2d 1198 (D.C.App.1999)—§§ 18.4(c) n.35; 21.6(a) n.57

Moore, United States v., 149 F.3d 773 (8th Cir.1998)—§§ 19.3(c) n.196, 197

Moore, United States v., 41 F.3d 370 (8th Cir.1994)—§ 4.6(m) n.228

Moore, United States v., 936 F.2d 287 (6th Cir.1991)—§ 10.6(a) n.2

Moore, United States v., 936 F.2d 1508 (7th Cir.1991)—§ 24.2(a) n.15

Moore, United States v., 949 F.2d 68 (2d Cir.1991)—§ 26.5(c) n.60

Moore, United States v., 916 F.2d 1131 (6th Cir.1990)—§ 21.3(e) n.269

Moore, United States v., 917 F.2d 215 (6th Cir.1990)—§§ 3.10(d) n.111; 17.2(e) n.119; 24.3(f) n.140

Moore, United States v., 817 F.2d 1105 (4th Cir.1987)—§ 3.8(e) n.191

Moore, United States v., 786 F.2d 1308 (5th Cir.1986)—§ 7.5(b) n.15

Moore, United States v., 706 F.2d 538 (5th Cir.1983)—§§ 11.4(b) n.26; 11.4(c) n.83

Moore, United States v., 671 F.2d 139 (5th Cir.1982)—§ 11.2(g) n.304

Moore, United States v., 637 F.2d 1194 (8th Cir.1981)—§ 21.3(e) n.269

Moore v. United States, 592 F.2d 753 (4th Cir.1979)—§ 21.4(d) n.115

Moore, United States v., 613 F.2d 1029 (D.C.Cir.1979)—§ 25.1(d) n.52

Moore, United States v., 562 F.2d 106 (1st Cir.1977)—§§ 3.2(j) n.245, 246, 255, 258, 264

Moore v. United States, 353 A.2d 16 (D.C.App.1976)—§§ 20.6(b) n.62, 64

Moore, United States v., 554 F.2d 1086 (D.C.Cir.1976)—§ 10.2(a) n.17

Moore, United States v., 522 F.2d 1068 (9th Cir.1975)—§ 3.3(c) n.144

Moore v. United States, 432 F.2d 730 (3d Cir.1970)—§§ 11.8(c) n.53, 62; 11.10(b) n.30

Moore v. Wainwright, 633 F.2d 406 (5th Cir.1980)—§ 11.2(d) n.130

Moorehead, State v., 699 N.W.2d 667 (Iowa 2005)—§ 6.4(e) n.63

Moorman, State v., 320 N.C. 387, 358 S.E.2d 502 (1987)—§ 11.10(c) n.71

Moorman v. Thalacker, 83 F.3d 970 (8th Cir.1996)—§ 26.2(c) n.62

Mootispaw v. Eckstein, 76 Ohio St.3d 383, 667 N.E.2d 1197 (1996)— § 13.3(a) n.7

Morais, State v., 359 N.J.Super. 123, 819 A.2d 424 (N.J.Super.2003)— § 24.7(e) n.62

Morales, Commonwealth v., 508 Pa. 51, 494 A.2d 367 (1985)—§ 22.1(h) n.151

Morales v. Greiner, 273 F.Supp.2d 236 (E.D.N.Y.2003)—§ 28.4(d) n.70

Morales, People v., 48 Cal.3d 527, 257 Cal.Rptr. 64, 770 P.2d 244 (1989)— § 22.2(d) n.80

Morales, People v., 121 App.Div.2d 240, 503 N.Y.S.2d 374 (1986)— § 24.9(g) n.126

Morales, People v., 65 N.Y.2d 997, 494 N.Y.S.2d 95, 484 N.E.2d 124 (1985)—§ 6.6(e) n.91

Morales, People v., 43 A.D.2d 917, 352 N.Y.S.2d 938 (1974)—§ 7.4(f) n.95

Morales, State v., 232 Conn. 707, 657 A.2d 585 (1995)—§§ 24.3(e) n.130, 136

Morales, United States v., 994 F.2d 386 (7th Cir.1993)—§ 26.5(a) n.7

Morales, United States v., 923 F.2d 621 (8th Cir.1991)—§ 3.5(e) n.190

Morales, United States v., 868 F.2d 1562 (11th Cir.1989)—§§ 3.6(e) n.127; 17.2(a) n.2; 17.2(f) n.132; 17.3(b) n.21

Morales, United States v., 861 F.2d 396 (3d Cir.1988)—§ 3.10(e) n.172

Morales, United States v., 834 F.2d 35 (2d Cir.1987)—§ 6.10(c) n.38

Morales-Diaz, United States v., 925 F.2d 535 (1st Cir.1991)—§ 22.3(c) n.101

Morales-Rosales, United States v., 838 F.2d 1359 (5th Cir.1988)— § 21.6(a) n.25

Morales-Zamora, United States v., 914 F.2d 200 (10th Cir.1990)—§ 3.2(b) n.71

Moran v. Burbine, 475 U.S. 412, 106 S.Ct. 1135, 89 L.Ed.2d 410 (1986)—§§ 1.5(c) n.135; 2.7(a) n.16; 6.4(e) n.86; 6.4(f) n.116; 6.9(c) n.61; 6.9(g) n.147; 21.3(a) n.11

Moran v. Godinez, 40 F.3d 1567 (9th Cir.1994)—§ 11.5(c) n.61

Moran v. State, 213 S.W.3d 917 (Tex.Crim.App.2007)—§ 6.9(f) n.133

Moran, State v., 711 N.W.2d 915 (N.D.2006)—§§ 18.2(b) n.16; 18.2(e) n.77, 84

Moran, State v., 820 A.2d 381 (Del.2002)—§ 13.7(c) n.60

Moran v. State, 268 Ga. 816, 493 S.E.2d 126 (1997)—§ 12.4(d) n.81

Moran v. Territory, 14 Okla. 544, 78 P. 111 (1904)—§§ 16.1(d) n.145; 16.2(a) n.3

Moran, United States v., 452 F.3d 1167 (10th Cir.2006)—§ 21.4(f) n.170

Moran, United States v., 214 F.3d 950 (8th Cir.2000)—§ 3.10(e) n.166

Moran, United States v., 998 F.2d 1368 (6th Cir.1993)—§ 18.3(b) n.25

Moran, United States v., 759 F.2d 777 (9th Cir.1985)—§ 18.5(b) n.69

Morant, State v., 758 S.W.2d 110 (Mo.App.1988)—§ 24.9(d) n.38

Morasse, Commonwealth v., 446 Mass. 113, 842 N.E.2d 909 (2006)— § 26.1(e) n.123

Morato, State v., 619 N.W.2d 655 (S.D.2000)—§ 6.6(e) n.59

Mordenti v. State, 894 So.2d 161 (Fla.2004)—§ 24.3(b) n.35

Mordican, People v., 64 Ill.2d 257, 1 Ill.Dec. 71, 356 N.E.2d 71 (1976)— § 10.6(d) n.47

Morehead, United States v., 959 F.2d 1489 (10th Cir.1992)—§ 27.5(b) n.40

Moreland, United States v., 258 U.S. 433, 42 S.Ct. 368, 66 L.Ed. 700 (1922)—§§ 15.1(b) n.59; 15.1(d) n.142, 211

Morell, United States v., 524 F.2d 550 (2d Cir.1975)—§§ 20.6(b) n.52, 53

Moreno v. Baca, 431 F.3d 633 (9th Cir.2005)—§ 26.9(b) n.66

Moreno v. Baskerville, 249 Va. 16, 452 S.E.2d 653 (1995)—§§ 16.4(c) n.57, 64, 100; 16.4(d) n.145

Moreno v. State, 858 S.W.2d 453 (Tex.Cr.App.1993)—§ 10.3(b) n.10

Moreno, United States v., 233 F.3d 937 (7th Cir.2000)—§ 3.10(a) n.2

Moreno, United States v., 897 F.2d 26 (2d Cir.1990)—§§ 3.8(c) n.84; 3.10(b) n.72

Moreno, United States v., 475 F.2d 44 (5th Cir.1973)—§ 3.9(h) n.150

Moreno-Flores, United States v., 33 F.3d 1164 (9th Cir.1994)—§ 6.7(b) n.41

Moreno-Morales, United States v., 815 F.2d 725 (1st Cir.1987)—§§ 8.3(b) n.13; 23.2(b) n.56; 23.2(d) n.64, 65, 70; 23.2(f) n.106

Moreton, United States v., 25 F.R.D. 262 (W.D.N.Y.1960)—§ 17.2(f) n.131

Moretti, State v., 521 A.2d 1003 (R.I.1987)—§ 3.1(h) n.205

Morey v. Doud, 354 U.S. 457, 77 S.Ct. 1344, 1 L.Ed.2d 1485 (1957)—§ 2.9(b) n.25

Morgan, In re, 377 F.Supp. 281 (S.D.N.Y.1974)—§§ 8.7(b) n.31, 47, 49, 53; 8.8(e) n.131, 139

Morgan v. Foster, 208 Ga. 630, 68 S.E.2d 583 (1952)—§ 26.9(b) n.17

Morgan v. Illinois, 504 U.S. 719, 112 S.Ct. 2222, 119 L.Ed.2d 492 (1992)—§§ 2.7(b) n.90; 2.7(c) n.200, 213; 22.3(a) n.32; 22.3(c) n.152; 26.1(b) n.28

Morgan, People v., 212 Ill.2d 148, 288 Ill.Dec. 166, 817 N.E.2d 524 (2004)—§ 24.11(d) n.28

Morgan, People v., 197 Ill.2d 404, 259 Ill.Dec. 405, 758 N.E.2d 813 (2001)—§ 6.2(c) n.163

Morgan v. Rhay, 78 Wash.2d 116, 470 P.2d 180 (1970)—§ 11.2(g) n.264

Morgan v. State, 139 P.3d 1272 (Alaska App.2006)—§ 22.4(e) n.49

Morgan, State v., 316 Mont. 509, 74 P.3d 1047 (2003)—§ 21.5(a) n.26

Morgan v. State, 275 Ga. 222, 564 S.E.2d 192 (2002)—§ 6.9(f) n.101

Morgan, State v., 559 N.W.2d 603 (Iowa 1997)—§§ 2.6(b) n.64; 22.2(e) n.109

Morgan v. State, 703 So.2d 832 (Miss.1997)—§ 5.2(a) n.4

Morgan v. State, 587 N.E.2d 680 (Ind.1992)—§§ 6.2(c) n.114, 115

Morgan, State v., 389 So.2d 364 (La.1980)—§§ 26.9(b) n.74, 76

Morgan, United States v., 435 F.3d 660 (6th Cir.2006)—§ 3.10(e) n.166

Morgan, United States v., 384 F.3d 439 (7th Cir.2004)—§ 18.3(b) n.51

Morgan, United States v., 254 F.3d 424 (2d Cir.2001)—§ 21.5(a) n.19

Morgan, United States v., 230 F.3d 1067 (8th Cir.2000)—§§ 21.6(a) n.64, 78

Morgan, United States v., 958 F.2d 847 (8th Cir.1992)—§ 21.2(b) n.48

Morgan, United States v., 936 F.2d 1561 (10th Cir.1991)—§ 3.8(c) n.96

Morgan, United States v., 346 U.S. 502, 74 S.Ct. 247, 98 L.Ed. 248 (1954)—§ 28.9(a) n.12

Morgano, United States v., 39 F.3d 1358 (7th Cir.1994)—§§ 16.2(h) n.151; 26.1(f) n.139; 26.3(f) n.59

Morganroth, In re, 718 F.2d 161 (6th Cir.1983)—§ 8.10(a) n.14

Morgenstern, United States v., 933 F.2d 1108 (2d Cir.1991)—§ 24.3(e) n.128

Morgenthau v. Marks, 177 App.Div.2d 131, 581 N.Y.S.2d 296 (1992)—§ 27.4(d) n.41

Morgese, People v., 94 Ill.App.3d 638, 50 Ill.Dec. 130, 418 N.E.2d 1124 (1981)—§§ 11.2(a) n.27; 11.3(a) n.2

Moriarty, United States v., 962 F.Supp. 217 (D. Mass. 1997)—§ 4.6(b) n.25

Morin, State v., 71 Haw. 159, 785 P.2d 1316 (1990)—§§ 21.4(a) n.26; 21.6(b) n.111

Morlan v. State, 499 N.E.2d 1084 (Ind.1986)—§ 21.4(d) n.116

Morley, Commonwealth v., 545 Pa. 420, 681 A.2d 1254 (1996)—§ 20.4(e) n.82

Morman, Commonwealth v., 373 Pa.Super. 360, 541 A.2d 356 (1988)—§ 27.4(f) n.67

Morningstar, State v., 207 N.W.2d 772 (Iowa 1973)—§§ 15.4(b) n.35, 36

Morrell, People v., 134 Misc.2d 1011, 513 N.Y.S.2d 925 (Sup.Ct.1987)— §§ 15.2(e) n.143; 15.7(g) n.214

Morrell v. State, 575 P.2d 1200 (Alaska 1978)—§ 20.4(b) n.30

Morrill, State v., 197 Conn. 507, 498 A.2d 76 (1985)—§ 8.10(c) n.63

Morris, In re Contempt of, 110 Ohio App.3d 475, 674 N.E.2d 761 (1996)—§ 27.5(a) n.28

Morris v. Dretke, 413 F.3d 484 (5th Cir.2005)—§ 28.5(a) n.35

Morris v. Mathews, 475 U.S. 237, 106 S.Ct. 1032, 89 L.Ed.2d 187 (1986)—§§ 17.4(b) n.71; 25.4(b) n.20, 21; 25.4(d) n.43

Morris, People v., 107 Cal.App.4th 402, 131 Cal.Rptr.2d 872 (2003)— § 27.6(d) n.105

Morris, People v., 450 Mich. 316, 537 N.W.2d 842 (1995)—§ 26.3(f) n.64

Morris, People v., 162 Misc.2d 742, 621 N.Y.S.2d 434 (1994)—§ 24.8(a) n.7

Morris, People v., 53 Cal.3d 152, 279 Cal.Rptr. 720, 807 P.2d 949 (1991)—§ 6.6(e) n.63

Morris, People v., 135 Ill.2d 540, 143 Ill.Dec. 215, 554 N.E.2d 150 (1990)—§ 19.3(a) n.16

Morris v. Reynolds, 264 F.3d 38 (2d Cir.2001)—§§ 21.2(d) n.205; 21.3(f) n.430; 25.1(d) n.70

Morris v. Slappy, 461 U.S. 1, 103 S.Ct. 1610, 75 L.Ed.2d 610 (1983)— §§ 1.5(c) n.145; 1.5(k) n.418; 11.4(b) n.43; 11.4(c) n.80; 11.8(c) n.52

Morris, State v., 157 Ohio App.3d 395, 811 N.E.2d 577 (2004)—§ 24.1(a) n.5

Morris v. State, 795 A.2d 653 (Del.2002)—§ 24.7(e) n.46

Morris, State v., 744 A.2d 850 (R.I.2000)—§ 7.5(b) n.25

Morris, State v., 49 Conn.App. 409, 716 A.2d 897 (1998)—§ 19.5(b) n.24

Morris, State v., 165 Vt. 111, 680 A.2d 90 (1996)—§ 3.3(c) n.114

Morris v. State, 667 So.2d 982 (Fla.App.1996)—§ 11.5(d) n.80

Morris, State v., 126 Wash.2d 306, 892 P.2d 734 (1995)—§ 18.4(c) n.58

Morris, State v., 255 Kan. 964, 880 P.2d 1244 (1994)—§§ 6.9(g) n.161; 10.3(c) n.52

Morris v. State, 595 So.2d 840 (Miss.1991)—§§ 19.3(b) n.160, 161, 164

Morris v. State, 59 Md.App. 659, 477 A.2d 1206 (1984)—§§ 20.5(h) n.112, 114

Morris v. State, 246 Ga. 510, 272 S.E.2d 254 (1980)—§ 8.7(b) n.46

Morris v. State, 228 Ga. 39, 184 S.E.2d 82 (1971)—§ 6.8(a) n.9

Morris v. State, 184 So.2d 199 (Fla.App.1966)—§ 7.2(b) n.24

Morris, United States v., 470 F.3d 596 (6th Cir.2006)—§§ 21.2(e) n.326; 21.3(a) n.25

Morris, United States v., 287 F.3d 985 (10th Cir.2002)—§§ 6.9(b) n.38, 41

Morris, United States v., 116 F.3d 501 (D.C.Cir.1997)—§ 21.5(e) n.147

Morris v. United States, 73 F.3d 216 (8th Cir.1996)—§ 21.2(d) n.178

Morris v. United States, 399 F.Supp. 720 (D.Va.1975)—§ 26.4(b) n.12

Morris v. Woodford, 273 F.3d 826 (9th Cir.2001)—§ 21.2(b) n.63

Morris v. Ylst, 447 F.3d 735 (9th Cir.2006)—§ 24.3(b) n.49

Morrisette v. Commonwealth, 264 Va. 386, 569 S.E.2d 47 (2002)—§§ 18.5(b) n.58, 69

Morrison v. Olson, 487 U.S. 654, 108 S.Ct. 2597, 101 L.Ed.2d 569 (1988)—§§ 1.2(c) n.47, 49; 8.8(a) n.7; 13.3(f) n.62

Morrison, People v., 148 Misc.2d 61, 559 N.Y.S.2d 1013 (N.Y.Sup.1990)—§ 24.3(f) n.146

Morrison v. State, 280 Ga. 222, 626 S.E.2d 500 (2006)—§ 18.4(c) n.64

Morrison, State v., 351 N.W.2d 359 (Minn.1984)—§ 6.9(e) n.91

Morrison, State v., 33 Or.App. 9, 575 P.2d 988 (1978)—§ 20.6(b) n.62

Morrison, State v., 298 Minn. 179, 213 N.W.2d 629 (1974)—§ 11.10(c) n.85

Morrison, United States v., 529 U.S. 598, 120 S.Ct. 1740, 146 L.Ed.2d 658 (2000)—§§ 1.2(c) n.92, 167; 1.2(d) n.202

Morrison, United States v., 967 F.2d 264 (8th Cir.1992)—§ 21.5(a) n.57

Morrison, United States v., 946 F.2d 484 (7th Cir.1991)—§ 24.3(f) n.141

Morrison, United States v., 449 U.S. 361, 101 S.Ct. 665, 66 L.Ed.2d 564 (1981)—§ 11.8(b) n.30

Morrison, United States v., 535 F.2d 223 (3d Cir.1976)—§§ 24.3(h) n.176, 177

Morrison, United States v., 536 F.2d 286 (9th Cir.1976)—§§ 19.3(a) n.47, 56; 19.3(e) n.235, 250

Morrison v. United States, 491 F.2d 344 (8th Cir.1974)—§ 3.3(d) n.159

Morrison, United States v., 43 F.R.D. 516 (S.D.Ill.1967)—§ 20.3(b) n.48

Morrissette v. Commonwealth, 380 Mass. 197, 402 N.E.2d 492 (1980)—§§ 15.7(b) n.28, 33

Morrissette, United States v., 429 F.3d 318 (1st Cir.2005)—§ 21.4(b) n.59

Morrissey, In re, 168 F.3d 134 (4th Cir.1999)—§ 23.1(b) n.49

Morrissey v. Brewer, 408 U.S. 471, 92 S.Ct. 2593, 33 L.Ed.2d 484 (1972)—§§ 2.7(a) n.62; 2.7(c) n.173, 198, 213; 2.9(g) n.199; 2.9(i) n.284, 286; 3.1(f) n.161; 3.9(j) n.210, 213; 12.3(d) n.107; 13.6(d) n.64; 18.5(c) n.88; 26.2(c) n.51; 26.4(e) n.78; 26.10(b) n.12; 26.10(c) n.68

Morris Thrift Pharmacy, In re, 397 So.2d 1301 (La.1981)—§ 8.12(c) n.40

Morrow, Ex parte, 952 S.W.2d 530 (Tex.Cr.App.1997)—§§ 21.2(b) n.42; 21.3(b) n.66

Morrow, State v., 75 S.W.3d 919 (Tenn.2002)—§ 22.1(h) n.145

Morrow, State v., 968 S.W.2d 100 (Mo.1998)—§ 22.3(d) n.246

Morrow, State v., 237 Neb. 653, 467 N.W.2d 63 (1991)—§ 22.3(d) n.247

Morrow, United States v., 177 F.3d 272 (5th Cir.1999)—§ 18.5(a) n.6

Morrow, United States v., 925 F.2d 779 (4th Cir.1991)—§ 19.5(d) n.72

Morrow, United States v., 914 F.2d 608 (4th Cir.1990)—§ 21.2(b) n.57

Morse v. C.I.R., 419 F.3d 829 (8th Cir.2005)—§ 17.4(a) n.15

Morse, Commonwealth v., 427 Mass. 117, 691 N.E.2d 566 (1998)—§ 6.6(c) n.31

Morse v. Municipal Court, 13 Cal.3d 149, 118 Cal.Rptr. 14, 529 P.2d 46 (1974)—§ 13.6(c) n.37

Morse, People v., 70 Cal.2d 711, 76 Cal.Rptr. 391, 452 P.2d 607 (1969)—§§ 6.4(c) n.39; 6.7(b) n.63, 64

Morse, State v., 125 N.H. 403, 480 A.2d 183 (1984)—§ 3.6(a) n.16

Morse, State v., 127 Ariz. 25, 617 P.2d 1141 (1980)—§ 21.2(f) n.392

Morse, United States v., 36 F.3d 1070 (11th Cir.1994)—§ 21.4(d) n.130

Mortimer, People v., 46 A.D.2d 275, 361 N.Y.S.2d 955 (1974)—§ 3.10(d) n.115

Morton v. State, 684 P.2d 144 (Alaska App.1984)—§ 24.3(f) n.145

Morton, United States v., 412 F.3d 901 (8th Cir.2005)—§ 21.2(d) n.244

Morton, United States v., 391 F.3d 274 (D.C.Cir.2004)—§ 6.7(c) n.135

Morton v. United States, 734 A.2d 178 (D.C.App.1999)—§ 9.1(b) n.72

Morton Bldgs., Inc. v. Rezultz, Inc., 127 N.J. 227, 603 A.2d 946 (1992)— § 24.4(d) n.46

Morton Provision Co., United States v., 294 F.Supp. 385 (D.Del.1968)— § 9.1(c) n.100

Morton Salt Co., United States v., 338 U.S. 632, 70 S.Ct. 357, 94 L.Ed. 401 (1950)—§§ 8.6(a) n.11; 8.7(a) n.26; 15.1(b) n.20

Mosburg, State v., 13 Kan.App.2d 257, 768 P.2d 313 (1989)—§ 26.9(b) n.55

Mosby v. State, 249 Ark. 17, 457 S.W.2d 836 (1970)—§§ 11.5(g) n.113, 120

Moscony, United States v., 927 F.2d 742 (3d Cir.1991)—§§ 11.9(c) n.105, 108, 111, 115, 124, 140

Moseley v. Commonwealth, 27 Ky.L.Rptr. 214, 84 S.W. 748 (1905)—§ 16.1(b) n.83

Moseley, State v., 587 So.2d 46 (La.App.1991)—§§ 23.2(a) n.38, 39, 41

Mosely, United States v., 810 F.2d 93 (6th Cir.1987)—§ 22.3(d) n.181

Moser, In re, 6 Cal.4th 342, 24 Cal.Rptr.2d 723, 862 P.2d 723 (1993)—§§ 21.4(d) n.118; 21.5(c) n.88

Moser v. Richmond County Board of Comm'rs, 263 Ga. 63, 428 S.E.2d 71 (1993)—§ 17.4(b) n.125

Moses v. Helgemoe, 562 F.2d 62 (1st Cir.1976)—§ 14.4(e) n.136

Moses v. Kennedy, 219 F.Supp. 762 (D.D.C.1963)—§ 13.3(a) n.3

Moses, State v., 280 Kan. 939, 127 P.3d 330 (2006)—§ 21.5(c) n.88

Moses, State v., 159 Vt. 294, 618 A.2d 478 (1992)—§§ 26.9(a) n.1; 26.9(c) n.89

Moses v. State, 814 S.W.2d 437 (Tex.App.1991)—§ 24.3(f) n.146

Moskovits, United States v., 86 F.3d 1303 (3d Cir.1996)—§ 26.4(c) n.30

Moskowitz, United States v., 581 F.2d 14 (2d Cir.1978)—§ 7.4(e) n.90

Mosley, In re, 1 Cal.3d 913, 83 Cal.Rptr. 809, 464 P.2d 473 (1970)— § 21.4(a) n.39

Mosley, People v., 198 Cal.App.3d 1167, 244 Cal.Rptr. 264 (1988)— § 26.10(b) n.23

Mosley, State v., 200 S.W.3d 624 (Tenn.Cr.App.2006)—§ 24.2(c) n.35

Mosley, United States v., 965 F.2d 906 (10th Cir.1992)—§ 5.4(c) n.43

Mosquera, United States v., 95 F.3d 1012 (11th Cir.1996)—§ 18.3(b) n.5

Mosquera, United States v., 816 F.Supp. 168 (E.D.N.Y.1993)—§ 24.2(g) n.97

Moss v. District Court of Tulsa, 756 P.2d 1250 (Okla.Crim.App.1988)— § 14.4(b) n.10

Moss v. Hofbauer, 286 F.3d 851 (6th Cir.2002)—§§ 11.10(c) n.90, 113

Moss, State v., 921 P.2d 1021 (Utah App.1996)—§ 25.1(d) n.73

Moss v. United States, 323 F.3d 445 (6th Cir.2003)—§§ 11.9(d) n.173, 192

Moss, United States v., 252 F.3d 993 (8th Cir.2001)—§ 19.2(e) n.68

Moss, United States v., 217 F.3d 426 (6th Cir.2000)—§ 18.3(b) n.59

Moss, United States v., 963 F.2d 673 (4th Cir.1992)—§ 3.6(f) n.144

Moss, United States v., 887 F.2d 333 (1st Cir.1989)—§ 12.3(a) n.24

Most, State v., 578 N.W.2d 250 (Iowa App.1998)—§ 27.5(e) n.147

Most, United States v., 876 F.2d 191 (D.C.Cir.1989)—§§ 3.2(b) n.92; 3.10(b) n.31; 3.10(e) n.172, 177; 9.1(b) n.91

Mota v. Buchanan, 26 Ariz.App. 246, 547 P.2d 517 (1976)—§ 20.3(i) n.176

Mota, United States v., 982 F.2d 1384 (9th Cir.1993)—§§ 3.1(e) n.129; 3.5(b) n.97

Moten, United States v., 582 F.2d 654 (2d Cir.1978)—§ 8.5(h) n.268

Motes v. United States, 178 U.S. 458, 20 S.Ct. 993, 44 L.Ed. 1150 (1900)—§ 27.6(c) n.61

Motions of Dow Jones and Co., In re, 142 F.3d 496 (D.C.Cir.1998)—§§ 8.5(c) n.72, 73; 23.1(d) n.156, 159 to 162

Motion to Quash a Grand Jury Subpoena (Bekins Storage Co.), In the Matter of a, 118 Misc.2d 173, 460 N.Y.S.2d 684 (Sup.Ct.1983)—§ 8.6(b) n.49

Motion to Testify Before Grand Jury, In re, 864 F.2d 1559 (11th Cir.1989)—§ 23.1(d) n.156

Motley v. State, 273 Ga. 732, 546 S.E.2d 468 (2001)—§ 21.4(e) n.163

Motley, United States v., 655 F.2d 186 (9th Cir.1981)—§ 13.7(c) n.68

Motor Vehicles, Department of v. McLeod, 106 Nev. 852, 801 P.2d 1390 (1990)—§ 6.10(e) n.81

Mott v. State, 407 N.W.2d 581 (Iowa 1987)—§§ 11.10(b) n.40; 21.3(b) n.64

Motz, United States v., 936 F.2d 1021 (9th Cir.1991)—§ 3.4(j) n.197

Moulder, United States v., 141 F.3d 568 (5th Cir.1998)—§ 21.5(e) n.149

Moulton v. State, 486 S.W.2d 334 (Tex.Cr.App.1971)—§ 10.2(c) n.35

Moultrie, United States v., 340 A.2d 828 (D.C.App.1975)—§ 8.4(c) n.134

Mountjoy, State v., 257 Kan. 163, 891 P.2d 376 (1995)—§ 27.3(a) n.7

Mounts, People v., 784 P.2d 792 (Colo.1990)—§ 6.2(c) n.115

Mourad, United States v., 729 F.2d 195 (2d Cir.1984)—§ 6.4(g) n.151

Moure-Ortiz, United States v., 184 F.3d 1 (1st Cir.1999)—§§ 21.3(e) n.271, 286; 21.4(g) n.243

Moussaoui, United States v., 365 F.3d 292 (4th Cir.2004)—§ 24.3(h) n.182

Moussazadeh, Ex parte, 64 S.W.3d 404 (Tex.Cr.App.2001)—§ 21.2(g) n.396

Mouzon, State v., 326 S.C. 199, 485 S.E.2d 918 (1997)—§ 24.7(c) n.26

Movants to Quash Grand Jury Subpoenas Issued in Multicounty Grand Jury Case No. CJ-92-4110 v. Powers, 839 P.2d 655 (Okla.1992)—§ 8.8(d) n.56

Moya-Gomez, United States v., 860 F.2d 706 (7th Cir.1988)—§§ 11.3(b) n.42; 11.4(d) n.112; 11.5(c) n.32, 53, 54, 56; 11.5(f) n.103

Moyd, State v., 1 Haw.App. 439, 619 P.2d 1107 (1980)—§§ 16.3(b) n.24, 26

Moylan, United States v., 417 F.2d 1002 (4th Cir.1969)—§ 22.1(g) n.115

Mroczko, People v., 35 Cal.3d 86, 197 Cal.Rptr. 52, 672 P.2d 835 (1983)—§ 11.9(c) n.131

M.S. Ali v. United States, 581 A.2d 368 (D.C.App.1990)—§ 11.5(e) n.86

Muca, United States v., 945 F.2d 88 (4th Cir.1991)—§ 6.4(f) n.124

Muegge, United States v., 225 F.3d 1267 (11th Cir.2000)—§ 6.6(e) n.72

Muehler v. Mena, 544 U.S. 93, 125 S.Ct. 1465, 161 L.Ed.2d 299 (2005)—§§ 2.9(g) n.163; 3.4(i) n.179, 180; 3.8(b) n.61

Mueller v. Angelone, 181 F.3d 557 (4th Cir.1999)—§ 6.9(g) n.166

Mueller, People v., 851 P.2d 211 (Colo.App.1992)—§ 21.6(a) n.57

Mueller, People v., 109 Ill.2d 378, 94 Ill.Dec. 524, 488 N.E.2d 523 (1985)—§ 17.4(c) n.150

Mueller v. State, 837 N.E.2d 198 (Ind.App.2005)—§ 11.2(d) n.119

Mueller, United States v., 902 F.2d 336 (5th Cir.1990)—§§ 3.3(b) n.53; 10.3(a) n.2

Muench, United States v., 153 F.3d 1298 (11th Cir.1998)—§ 16.2(e) n.68

Muentner, State v., 138 Wis.2d 374, 406 N.W.2d 415 (1987)—§§ 18.5(a) n.51; 24.8(f) n.110

Mugnano v. Painter, 212 W.Va. 831, 575 S.E.2d 590 (2002)—§ 21.2(d) n.178

Muhammad v. Close, 540 U.S. 749, 124 S.Ct. 1303, 158 L.Ed.2d 32 (2004)—§ 28.3(b) n.67

Muhammad, State v., 182 N.J. 551, 868 A.2d 302 (2005)—§ 9.6(a) n.44

Muhammad, State v., 145 N.J. 23, 678 A.2d 164 (1996)—§§ 2.12(b) n.104, 105; 2.12(e) n.206; 26.5(d) n.67

Muhammad, State v., 678 A.2d 164 (1996)—§ 26.5(d) n.70

Muhammad, United States v., 120 F.3d 688 (7th Cir.1997)—§ 6.9(g) n.185

Muhammad F., In re, 94 N.Y.2d 136, 700 N.Y.S.2d 77, 722 N.E.2d 45 (1999)—§ 3.8(d) n.182

Muick, United States v., 167 F.3d 1162 (7th Cir.1999)—§§ 6.9(g) n.147, 200

Muise, State v., 103 N.M. 382, 707 P.2d 1192 (App.1985)—§ 14.2(d) n.50

Mukai, United States v., 26 F.3d 953 (9th Cir.1994)—§§ 21.1(h) n.209; 21.4(g) n.226, 243

Mulcahey, People v., 155 Ill.2d 549, 187 Ill.Dec. 455, 617 N.E.2d 1176 (1993)—§ 21.2(d) n.270

Mulder, United States v., 808 F.2d 1346 (9th Cir.1987)—§ 3.2(c) n.103

Mulderig, United States v., 120 F.3d 534 (5th Cir.1997)—§ 18.5(a) n.50

Muldowney, State v., 60 N.J. 594, 292 A.2d 26 (1972)—§ 3.4(f) n.101

Mullane v. Central Hanover Bank & Trust Co., 339 U.S. 306, 70 S.Ct. 652, 94 L.Ed. 865 (1950)—§ 2.7(c) n.123

Mullaney v. Wilbur, 421 U.S. 684, 95 S.Ct. 1881, 44 L.Ed.2d 508 (1975)—§§ 2.7(a) n.44; 2.7(b) n.74

Mullen, State v., 216 N.W.2d 375 (Iowa 1974)—§ 5.2(b) n.24

Mulligan v. Kemp, 771 F.2d 1436 (11th Cir.1985)—§ 11.10(c) n.124

Mulligan, United States v., 520 F.2d 1327 (6th Cir.1975)—§§ 14.1(b) n.33; 14.2(b) n.29

Mulligan, United States v., 488 F.2d 732 (9th Cir.1973)—§§ 3.6(d) n.87; 9.1(d) n.125

Mullings v. State, 917 S.W.2d 334 (Tex.App.1996)—§ 15.4(g) n.153

Mullins, United States v., 315 F.3d 449 (5th Cir.2002)—§ 11.6(d) n.115

Mullreed v. Kroop, 425 F.2d 1095 (6th Cir.1970)—§ 21.5(e) n.118

Mulroy, People v., 108 Misc.2d 907, 439 N.Y.S.2d 61 (Sup.1979)—§ 15.4(g) n.149

Multaler, State v., 252 Wis.2d 54, 643 N.W.2d 437 (2002)—§ 17.3(b) n.13

Mu'Min v. Commonwealth, 239 Va. 433, 389 S.E.2d 886 (1990)—§ 6.2(c) n.176

Mu'Min v. Virginia, 500 U.S. 415, 111 S.Ct. 1899, 114 L.Ed.2d 493 (1991)—§§ 2.6(c) n.84; 2.7(b) n.92; 2.7(c) n.157, 172; 6.5(e) n.91; 22.3(a) n.22; 22.3(c) n.118; 23.2(f) n.85, 98

Mundelein, Village of v. Aaron, 67 Ill.Dec. 765, 112 Ill.App.3d 134, 445 N.E.2d 57 (1983)—§ 1.8(d) n.70

Mundt, United States v., 508 F.2d 904 (10th Cir.1974)—§§ 6.10(d) n.59, 63

Mungia, State v., 119 S.W.3d 814 (Tex.Crim.App.2003)—§ 13.2(c) n.56

Municipal Court, People v., 27 Cal.App.3d 193, 103 Cal.Rptr. 645 (1972)—§ 13.3(b) n.20

Municipal Court (Runyan), People v., 20 Cal.3d 523, 142 Cal.Rptr. 609, 574 P.2d 425 (1978)—§§ 20.2(a) n.5; 20.2(e) n.106

Muniz v. Hoffman, 422 U.S. 454, 95 S.Ct. 2178, 45 L.Ed.2d 319 (1975)—§ 22.1(b) n.46

Muniz, People v., 91 N.Y.2d 570, 673 N.Y.S.2d 358, 696 N.E.2d 182 (1998)—§ 21.2(b) n.76

Muniz v. State, 672 S.W.2d 804 (Tex.Cr.App.1984)—§ 3.3(d) n.177

Muniz-Caudillo, State v., 185 Ariz. 261, 914 P.2d 1353 (1996)—§ 24.2(d) n.45

Muniz-Melchor, United States v., 894 F.2d 1430 (5th Cir.1990)— § 3.10(b) n.64

Munkus v. Furlong, 170 F.3d 980 (10th Cir.1999)—§ 11.5(b) n.25

Munn v. Pate, 489 P.2d 534 (Okl.Cr.1971)—§ 17.4(a) n.12

Munn, State v., 56 S.W.3d 486 (Tenn.2001)—§§ 3.9(i) n.195; 6.6(d) n.57

Munn, State ex rel. v. McKelvey, 733 S.W.2d 765 (Mo.1987)—§ 8.11(e) n.95

Munoz, State v., 136 N.M. 235, 96 P.3d 796 (N.M.App.2004)—§§ 24.8(d) n.45; 24.8(e) n.69

Munoz, State v., 305 Mont. 139, 23 P.3d 922 (2001)—§ 21.2(e) n.297

Munoz, State v., 126 N.M. 535, 972 P.2d 847 (1998)—§ 6.2(c) n.182

Munoz, State v., 233 Conn. 106, 659 A.2d 683 (1995)—§ 14.3(a) n.8

Munoz, State v., 182 Ariz. 528, 898 P.2d 477 (App.1994)—§ 13.4(e) n.168

Munoz v. State, 629 So.2d 90 (Fla.1993)—§§ 5.2(b) n.24; 5.3(b) n.18; 5.3(d) n.41

Munoz, United States v., 408 F.3d 222 (5th Cir.2005)—§ 21.2(d) n.174

Munoz, United States v., 233 F.3d 410 (6th Cir.2000)—§ 21.4(f) n.185

Munoz, United States v., 150 F.3d 401 (5th Cir.1998)—§ 19.6(c) n.39

Munoz, United States v., 894 F.2d 292 (8th Cir.1990)—§ 17.3(d) n.47

Munoz v. United States, 325 F.2d 23 (9th Cir.1963)—§ 3.4(h) n.145

Munsch, State v., 287 S.C. 313, 338 S.E.2d 329 (1985)—§ 21.4(a) n.26

Munson, People v., 171 Ill.2d 158, 215 Ill.Dec. 125, 662 N.E.2d 1265 (1996)—§§ 22.3(d) n.245, 246; 26.4(d) n.52

Munson v. State, 123 P.3d 1042 (Alaska 2005)—§ 6.9(g) n.149

Munson, State v., 594 N.W.2d 128 (Minn.1999)—§§ 6.9(f) n.134, 136; 6.9(g) n.166

Munson, State v., 972 P.2d 418 (Utah 1998)—§ 21.6(a) n.46

Muratella, State v., 240 Neb. 567, 483 N.W.2d 128 (1992)—§ 26.1(e) n.123

Murch v. Mottram, 409 U.S. 41, 93 S.Ct. 71, 34 L.Ed.2d 194 (1972)— §§ 11.6(a) n.35; 28.4(d) n.37

Murchison, In re, 349 U.S. 133, 75 S.Ct. 623, 99 L.Ed. 942 (1955)— §§ 2.7(c) n.122, 201; 8.1(c) n.29

Murchison, State v., 687 N.W.2d 725 (N.D.2004)—§ 22.4(c) n.29

Murchison, State v., 541 N.W.2d 435 (N.D.1995)—§ 18.2(e) n.76

Murchu v. United States, 926 F.2d 50 (1st Cir.1991)—§ 22.3(d) n.193

Murdoch, United States v., 290 U.S. 389, 54 S.Ct. 223, 78 L.Ed. 381 (1933)—§ 8.10(b) n.40

Murdock v. Memphis, 87 U.S. (20 Wall) 590, 22 L.Ed. 429 (1875)— § 2.12(a) n.46

Murdock v. Pennsylvania, 319 U.S. 105, 63 S.Ct. 870, 87 L.Ed. 1292 (1943)—§ 2.5(c) n.28

Murdock v. State, 311 S.C. 16, 426 S.E.2d 740 (1992)—§ 11.10(c) n.108

Murdock, United States v., 63 F.3d 1391 (6th Cir.1995)—§§ 4.6(b) n.47; 4.6(m) n.221

Murdock, United States v., 928 F.2d 293 (8th Cir.1991)—§§ 3.10(e) n.168; 7.4(e) n.90; 7.4(g) n.117

Murdock, United States v., 548 F.2d 599 (5th Cir.1977)—§§ 13.4(b) n.58, 60

Murgas, United States v., 967 F.Supp. 695 (S.D.N.Y.1997)—§ 20.3(d) n.91

Murgia v. Municipal Court, 15 Cal.3d 286, 124 Cal.Rptr. 204, 540 P.2d 44 (1975)—§§ 13.4(a) n.7, 26; 13.4(c) n.87

Muriel, United States v., 111 F.3d 975 (1st Cir.1997)—§ 21.5(a) n.43

Muriel-Cruz, United States v., 412 F.3d 9 (1st Cir.2005)—§ 21.4(b) n.61

Muriithi, State v., 273 Kan. 952, 46 P.3d 1145 (2002)—§§ 21.3(b) n.66; 21.4(d) n.134

Murillo, United States v., 288 F.3d 1126 (9th Cir.2002)—§ 18.3(b) n.38

Murillo, United States v., 709 F.2d 1298 (9th Cir.1983)—§ 26.6(d) n.73

Murphy, Commonwealth v., 448 Mass. 452, 862 N.E.2d 30 (2007)— § 6.4(g) n.153

Murphy v. Commonwealth, 50 S.W.3d 173 (Ky.2001)—§ 17.2(b) n.32

Murphy v. District Court, 14 N.D. 542, 105 N.W. 728 (1905)—§§ 16.3(g) n.99, 100, 103

Murphy v. Florida, 421 U.S. 794, 95 S.Ct. 2031, 44 L.Ed.2d 589 (1975)—§§ 2.7(a) n.34; 2.7(b) n.91; 22.3(c) n.118; 23.2(f) n.96, 97, 104; 23.3(b) n.22

Murphy v. Holland, 845 F.2d 83 (4th Cir.1988)—§ 6.4(f) n.137

Murphy v. Hunt, 455 U.S. 478, 102 S.Ct. 1181, 71 L.Ed.2d 353 (1982)— § 12.1(a) n.15

Murphy v. People, 863 P.2d 301 (Colo.1993)—§ 11.9(d) n.218

Murphy, People v., 51 Cal. 376 (1876)— § 16.1(e) n.180

Murphy, State v., 91 Ohio St.3d 516, 747 N.E.2d 765 (2001)—§§ 6.9(d) n.75; 6.9(g) n.157, 161; 7.4(e) n.82; 22.3(d) n.250

Murphy v. State, 807 So.2d 603 (Ala.Crim.2001)—§ 12.2(a) n.6

Murphy v. State, 267 Ga. 120, 475 S.E.2d 907 (1996)—§ 17.4(b) n.120

Murphy, State v., 342 N.C. 813, 467 S.E.2d 428 (1996)—§§ 6.8(b) n.50; 6.9(g) n.149

Murphy, State v., 537 N.W.2d 492 (Minn.App.1995)—§ 27.2(c) n.66

Murphy v. State, 110 Nev. 194, 871 P.2d 916 (1994)—§ 18.5(a) n.6

Murphy, State v., 125 Idaho 456, 872 P.2d 719 (1994)—§§ 21.2(b) n.76; 27.5(c) n.58

Murphy, State v., 315 Ark. 68, 864 S.W.2d 842 (1993)—§ 13.2(c) n.56

Murphy v. State, 766 S.W.2d 246 (Tex.Crim.App.1989)—§ 6.9(g) n.167

Murphy, State v., 110 N.J. 20, 538 A.2d 1235 (1988)—§§ 15.4(g) n.150, 178 to 180, 182; 15.4(i) n.216, 218; 15.6(d) n.112; 15.6(f) n.204

Murphy v. State, 453 N.E.2d 219 (Ind.1983)—§ 13.7(c) n.45

Murphy v. Superior Court, 142 Ariz. 273, 689 P.2d 532 (1984)— § 20.2(e) n.95

Murphy, United States v., 483 F.3d 639 (9th Cir.2007)—§§ 22.1(e) n.88; 22.1(h) n.160

Murphy v. United States, 282 F.3d 940 (7th Cir.2002)—§ 28.9(b) n.39

Murphy, United States v., 241 F.3d 447 (6th Cir.2001)—§ 18.3(b) n.20

Murphy, United States v., 768 F.2d 1518 (7th Cir.1985)—§§ 15.5(b) n.41; 24.3(c) n.94

Murphy, United States v., 506 F.2d 529 (9th Cir.1974)—§ 3.10(e) n.179

Murphy, United States v., 41 U.S. (16 Pet.) 203, 10 L.Ed. 937 (1842)— § 24.5(d) n.41

Murphy v. Waterfront Commission of New York Harbor, 378 U.S. 52, 84 S.Ct. 1594, 12 L.Ed.2d 678 (1964)—§§ 1.5(d) n.182, 186; 1.5(h) n.289; 1.5 n.2; 2.10(b) n.4; 2.10(c) n.52, 68; 2.10(d) n.103, 159;

8.10(b) n.40, 41; 8.11(a) n.4, 10; 8.11(c) n.35; 8.12(b) n.11; 25.5(a) n.5

Murr, State v., 35 Ohio App.3d 159, 520 N.E.2d 264 (1987)—§ 26.10(b) n.34

Murr v. United States, 200 F.3d 895 (6th Cir.2000)—§ 17.2(e) n.122

Murray v. Carrier, 477 U.S. 478, 106 S.Ct. 2639, 91 L.Ed.2d 397 (1986)—§§ 11.6(a) n.16; 11.10(c) n.100; 28.4(d) n.52, 59; 28.4(e) n.72; 28.5(d) n.81

Murray, Commonwealth v., 348 Pa.Super. 439, 502 A.2d 624 (1985)—§ 14.4(e) n.119

Murray v. Earle, 405 F.3d 278 (5th Cir.2005)—§§ 6.2(c) n.163; 6.6(c) n.42, 44; 6.6(e) n.81

Murray v. Giarratano, 492 U.S. 1, 109 S.Ct. 2765, 106 L.Ed.2d 1 (1989)—§§ 2.6(d) n.105; 11.1(b) n.77; 11.1(c) n.101; 11.1(d) n.120; 11.2(b) n.64; 11.2(f) n.242, 243, 245; 27.1(b) n.22; 28.11(a) n.9; 28.12(a) n.2

Murray v. Giarratano, 492 U.S. 1, 109 S.Ct. 2765, 106 L.Ed.2d 397 (1986)—§ 28.8(a) n.3

Murray v. Hildreth, 61 F.2d 483 (5th Cir.1932)—§ 16.4(b) n.10

Murray, People v., 5 Misc.3d 636, 785 N.Y.S.2d 675 (N.Y.Sup.2004)—§ 26.4(i) n.191

Murray v. Regier, 872 So.2d 217 (Fla.2002)—§ 21.2(d) n.196

Murray, State v., 254 Conn. 472, 757 A.2d 578 (Conn.2000)—§ 24.9(f) n.104

Murray, State v., 184 Ariz. 9, 906 P.2d 542 (1995)—§§ 17.3(e) n.57, 58

Murray, State v., 510 N.W.2d 107 (N.D.1994)—§ 6.6(c) n.31

Murray v. State, 528 P.2d 739 (Okl.Cr.1974)—§ 17.2(b) n.54

Murray v. United States, 145 F.3d 1249 (11th Cir.1998)—§ 28.10 n.7

Murray v. United States, 487 U.S. 533, 108 S.Ct. 2529, 101 L.Ed.2d 472 (1988)—§§ 2.9(g) n.163; 9.3(c) n.22; 9.3(d) n.42; 9.3(e) n.56, 74; 9.4(b) n.57, 66, 72; 10.6(a) n.2

Murray's Lessee v. Hoboken Land and Improvement Co., 59 U.S. (18 How.) 272, 25 L.Ed. 372 (1855)—§§ 2.4(b) n.32, 53, 55, 60; 2.4(c) n.99, 114; 2.7(c) n.101; 15.1(c) n.122, 129

Murtishaw, People v., 29 Cal.3d 733, 175 Cal.Rptr. 738, 631 P.2d 446 (1981)—§ 22.3(b) n.87

Muse, United States v., 633 F.2d 1041 (2d Cir.1980)—§ 18.1(c) n.24

Musgrove v. State, 638 So.2d 1347 (Ala.Crim.App.1992)—§ 26.5(b) n.27

Musser, United States v., 873 F.2d 1513 (D.C.Cir.1989)—§ 22.1(b) n.42

Mussey, State v., 893 A.2d 701 (N.H.2006)—§ 24.7(i) n.90

Mustafa, United States v., 238 F.3d 485 (3d Cir.2001)—§ 21.5(c) n.83

Mustread v. Gilmore, 966 F.2d 1148 (7th Cir.1992)—§ 21.3(c) n.174

Musumeci, State v., 717 A.2d 56 (R.I.1998)—§ 20.6(b) n.43

Mutchler, United States v., 559 F.2d 955 (5th Cir.1977)—§ 22.3(a) n.48

Muzevsky, United States v., 760 F.2d 83 (4th Cir.1985)—§ 24.2(d) n.45

Muzika, United States v., 986 F.2d 1050 (7th Cir.1993)—§ 21.3(d) n.263

Myer, State v., 441 N.W.2d 762 (Iowa 1989)—§ 3.10(f) n.204

Myers v. Collins, 8 F.3d 249 (5th Cir.1993)—§ 11.5(g) n.126

Myers, Commonwealth v., 51 Mass.App.Ct. 627, 748 N.E.2d 471 N.E.3d 471 (2001)—§ 11.5(b) n.30

Myers v. Commonwealth, 363 Mass. 843, 298 N.E.2d 819 (1973)—§§ 14.3(a) n.30, 31, 33, 35 to 37; 14.3(b) n.46; 14.4(d) n.93

Myers v. Frazier, 173 W.Va. 658, 319 S.E.2d 782 (1984)—§§ 21.2(f) n.363; 21.4(g) n.248

Myers v. Johnson, 76 F.3d 1330 (5th Cir.1996)—§ 27.6(d) n.140

Myers, State v., 258 Neb. 300, 603 N.W.2d 378 (1999)—§ 22.3(d) n.220

Myers, State v., 204 W.Va. 449, 513 S.E.2d 676 (1998)—§§ 21.2(d) n.177; 21.2(e) n.297

Myers, State v., 117 Wash.2d 332, 815 P.2d 761 (1991)—§ 3.4(c) n.39

Myers, State v., 158 Wis.2d 356, 461 N.W.2d 777 (1990)—§ 25.4(b) n.24

Myers v. State, 510 N.E.2d 1360 (Ind.1987)—§§ 6.3(c) n.50; 6.8(a) n.10

Myers, State v., 82 N.C.App. 299, 346 S.E.2d 273 (N.C.1986)—§ 25.5(b) n.24

Myers, State v., 407 A.2d 307 (Me.1979)—§ 19.3(c) n.195

Myers v. State, 3 Md.App. 534, 240 A.2d 288 (1968)—§ 6.6(e) n.59

Myers, United States v., 308 F.3d 251 (3d Cir.2002)—§§ 3.6(c) n.76, 82

Myers, United States v., 123 F.3d 350 (6th Cir.1997)—§§ 6.4(e) n.64; 6.6(a) n.11; 8.4(c) n.143; 8.10(d) n.105, 110, 111, 113

Myers, United States v., 692 F.2d 823 (2d Cir.1982)—§ 5.4(b) n.21

Myers, United States v., 510 F.Supp. 323 (E.D.N.Y.1980)—§§ 15.4(h) n.186, 188, 196

Myers, United States v., 550 F.2d 1036 (5th Cir.1977)—§§ 20.6(b) n.39; 20.6(c) n.82

Myhre, State v., 633 N.W.2d 186 (S.D.2001)—§ 6.6(c) n.40

Myrick, Commonwealth v., 468 Pa. 155, 360 A.2d 598 (1976)—§ 11.6(a) n.28

Myrick, State v., 102 Wash.2d 506, 688 P.2d 151 (1984)—§ 2.12(e) n.205

N

949 Erie Street, Racine, Wisconsin, Matter of, 824 F.2d 538 (7th Cir.1987)—§§ 10.1(c) n.39; 10.6(c) n.19, 21

NAACP v. Alabama ex rel. Patterson, 357 U.S. 449, 78 S.Ct. 1163, 2 L.Ed.2d 1488 (1958)—§§ 8.8(d) n.64; 9.1(a) n.2

Nabbefeld v. State, 83 Wis.2d 515, 266 N.W.2d 292 (1978)—§§ 14.1(d) n.55, 56

Nabors, United States v., 707 F.2d 1294 (11th Cir.1983)—§ 8.9(b) n.28

Nachtigal, United States v., 507 U.S. 1, 113 S.Ct. 1072, 122 L.Ed.2d 374 (1993)—§§ 22.1(b) n.41, 44

Nadler, State v., 151 N.H. 244, 855 A.2d 490 (2004)—§§ 18.5(a) n.24; 18.5(b) n.56

Naeole, State v., 80 Hawai'i 419, 910 P.2d 732 (1996)—§ 3.2(b) n.50

Nafzger, United States v., 965 F.2d 213 (7th Cir.1992)—§ 9.4(a) n.41

Nafzger, United States v., 974 F.2d 906 (7th Cir.1992)—§ 3.8(d) n.175

Nagel, State v., 87 N.M. 434, 535 P.2d 641 (1975)—§ 17.4(a) n.37

Nagelberg, United States v., 434 F.2d 585 (2d Cir.1970)—§ 17.1(a) n.9

Nagra, United States v., 147 F.3d 875 (9th Cir.1998)—§ 21.3(c) n.172

Nai Cheng Chen v. Immigration and Naturalization Service, 537 F.2d 566 (1st Cir.1976)—§ 6.10(e) n.80

Najjar, United States v., 283 F.3d 1306 (11th Cir.2002)—§ 18.5(a) n.50

Najjar, United States v., 300 F.3d 466 (4th Cir.2002)—§§ 9.3(d) n.38; 13.5(a) n.8; 17.2(d) n.94

Nall v. State, 85 Nev. 1, 448 P.2d 826 (1969)—§ 19.5(b) n.10

Namet v. United States, 373 U.S. 179, 83 S.Ct. 1151, 10 L.Ed.2d 278 (1963)—§ 24.4(c) n.22

Nance, United States v., 236 F.3d 820 (7th Cir.2000)—§§ 19.2(e) n.71, 82; 19.3(a) n.99

Nanfito v. United States, 20 F.2d 376 (8th Cir.1927)—§ 15.5(a) n.22

Nanfro, United States v., 64 F.3d 98 (2d Cir.1995)—§ 4.6(d) n.65

Nanni, United States v., 59 F.3d 1425 (2d Cir.1995)—§ 8.11(c) n.43

Nantelle, People v., 215 Mich.App. 77, 544 N.W.2d 667 (1996)—§ 26.3(f) n.55

Napier v. State, 276 Ga. 769, 583 S.E.2d 825 (2003)—§ 22.3(a) n.23

Napier, United States v., 233 F.3d 394 (6th Cir.2000)—§ 21.6(b) n.94

Napolitano, United States v., 761 F.2d 135 (2d Cir.1985)—§ 18.3(b) n.5

Nappi, United States v., 243 F.3d 758 (3d Cir.2001)—§ 26.4(d) n.65

Napue v. Illinois, 360 U.S. 264, 79 S.Ct. 1173, 3 L.Ed.2d 1217 (1959)—§§ 2.7(c) n.203; 24.3(d) n.107

Napue, United States v., 834 F.2d 1311 (7th Cir.1987)—§ 20.3(l) n.232

Naranjo, People v., 840 P.2d 319 (Colo.1992)—§§ 11.6(d) n.115, 123

Naranjo, United States v., 52 F.3d 245 (9th Cir.1995)—§ 26.4(b) n.22

Naranjo, United States v., 14 F.3d 145 (2d Cir.1994)—§ 16.2(f) n.104

Narciso, United States v., 446 F.Supp. 252 (E.D.Mich.1977)—§ 15.2(d) n.117

Nardolillo, State v., 698 A.2d 195 (R.I.1997)—§ 6.3(c) n.53

Nardone v. United States, 302 U.S. 379, 58 S.Ct. 275, 82 L.Ed. 314 (1937)—§ 4.5 n.1

Nardone v. United States, 308 U.S. 338, 60 S.Ct. 266, 84 L.Ed. 307 (1939)—§§ 9.3(a) n.2, 8; 10.3(b) n.33

Narvaez, United States v., 38 F.3d 162 (5th Cir.1994)—§ 26.4(g) n.129

Narvaiz v. State, 840 S.W.2d 415 (Tex.Crim.App.1992)—§ 23.2(a) n.47

Nash v. Israel, 707 F.2d 298 (7th Cir.1983)—§ 21.4(c) n.76

Nash, People v., 418 Mich. 196, 341 N.W.2d 439 (1983)—§§ 2.12(c) n.121; 2.12(e) n.212

Nash, State v., 279 Ga. 646, 619 S.E.2d 684 (2005)—§ 6.7(b) n.42

Nash, State v., 143 Ariz. 392, 694 P.2d 222 (1985)—§§ 11.10(c) n.62, 72; 11.10(d) n.195

Nash, United States v., 563 F.2d 1166 (5th Cir.1977)—§ 6.6(e) n.72

Nash, United States v., 447 F.2d 1382 (4th Cir.1971)—§ 17.4(a) n.39

Nason, State v., 498 A.2d 252 (Me.1985)—§ 3.2(c) n.134

Nason, United States v., 9 F.3d 155 (1st Cir.1993)—§ 17.2(c) n.82

Natal, People v., 75 N.Y.2d 379, 553 N.Y.S.2d 650, 553 N.E.2d 239 (1990)—§ 8.7(e) n.89

Nathan, United States v., 816 F.2d 230 (6th Cir.1987)—§ 8.8(g) n.165

Nathan L., In re, 146 N.H. 614, 776 A.2d 1277 (2001)—§ 24.8(f) n.120

Nathanson v. State, 554 P.2d 456 (Alaska 1976)—§ 3.2(d) n.151

Nathanson v. United States, 290 U.S. 41, 54 S.Ct. 11, 78 L.Ed. 159 (1933)—§ 3.3(c) n.84

Nation v. State, 445 N.E.2d 565 (Ind.1983)—§ 11.3(a) n.12

Nation v. State, 426 N.E.2d 436 (Ind.App.1981)—§ 11.5(b) n.25

National Broadcasting Co., In re Application of, 828 F.2d 340 (6th Cir.1987)—§§ 23.1(d) n.149, 150, 174

National Broadcasting Co. v. Cooperman, 116 A.D.2d 287, 501 N.Y.S.2d 405 (1986)—§ 23.1(b) n.71

National Broadcasting Company, State ex rel. v. Court of Common Pleas, 52 Ohio St.3d 104, 556 N.E.2d 1120 (1990)—§§ 23.1(b) n.88, 89, 93; 23.1(c) n.100, 103

National Commodity and Barter Association v. United States, 951 F.2d 1172 (10th Cir.1991)—§§ 8.8(d) n.54, 68 to 71; 27.2(e) n.86

National Treasury Employees Union v. Von Raab, 489 U.S. 656, 109 S.Ct. 1384, 103 L.Ed.2d 685 (1989)—§ 3.9(l) n.273

National Window Glass Workers, In re, 287 F. 219 (N.D.Ohio 1922)—§ 8.8(f) n.157

Nat'l Broadcasting Co. v. U.S. Dept. of Justice, 735 F.2d 51 (2d Cir.1984)—§ 4.3(a) n.5

Nattier, United States v., 127 F.3d 655 (8th Cir.1997)—§ 19.3(c) n.189

Natwig v. Webster, 562 F.Supp. 225 (D.R.I.1983)—§ 15.2(g) n.176

Naucke, State v., 829 S.W.2d 445 (Mo.1992)—§ 2.12(d) n.188

Naugle, United States v., 879 F.Supp. 262 (E.D.N.Y.1995)—§ 24.2(a) n.11

Naujoks, State v., 637 N.W.2d 101 (Iowa 2001)—§ 9.4(b) n.59

Naulls, People v., 937 P.2d 778 (Colo.App.1996)—§ 18.4(d) n.92

Nava v. State, 450 So.2d 606 (Fla.1984)—§ 20.6(c) n.82

Nava-Ramirez, United States v., 210 F.3d 1128 (10th Cir.2000)—§ 9.1(d) n.120

Navarro-Botello, United States v., 912 F.2d 318 (9th Cir.1990)—§ 21.2(b) n.85

Navarroli, People v., 121 Ill.2d 516, 118 Ill.Dec. 414, 521 N.E.2d 891 (1988)—§ 13.5(b) n.31

Navarro-Vargas, United States v., 408 F.3d 1184 (9th Cir.2005)—§§ 15.2(g) n.179, 180; 15.6(b) n.86

Navarro-Vargas, United States v., 367 F.3d 896 (9th Cir.2004)—§ 15.2(g) n.176

Nave v. State, 808 P.2d 991 (Okla.Cr.App.1991)—§ 7.4(e) n.84

Nawrocki, People v., 6 Mich.App. 46, 150 N.W.2d 516 (1967)—§ 3.10(f) n.201

Naydihor, State v., 270 Wis.2d 585, 678 N.W.2d 220 (2004)—§ 21.2(d) n.174

Nazarenus, United States v., 983 F.2d 1480 (8th Cir.1993)—§ 22.3(c) n.125

Neal v. Cain, 141 F.3d 207 (5th Cir.1998)—§ 17.4(a) n.19

Neal, Commonwealth v., 387 Pa.Super. 165, 563 A.2d 1236 (1989)—§ 11.3(b) n.53

Neal v. Delaware, 103 U.S. 370, 26 L.Ed. 567 (1880)—§ 22.2(c) n.23

Neal, People v., 31 Cal.4th 63, 1 Cal.Rptr.3d 650, 72 P.3d 280 (2003)—§ 6.9(f) n.130

Neal v. Puckett, 286 F.3d 230 (5th Cir.2002)—§§ 11.10(a) n.29; 11.10(c) n.127

Neal v. State, 150 S.W.3d 169 (Tex.Cr.App.2004)—§ 13.5(a) n.7

Neal v. State, 703 S.W.2d 570 (Mo.App.1986)—§ 11.10(c) n.84

Neal, State v., 353 N.W.2d 83 (Iowa 1984)—§ 7.4(e) n.90

Neal, State v., 476 S.W.2d 547 (Mo.1972)—§ 6.10(a) n.3

Neal v. Texas, 870 F.2d 312 (5th Cir.1989)—§§ 11.3(b) n.38; 11.3(c) n.56; 11.4(c) n.87

Neal, United States v., 93 F.3d 219 (6th Cir.1996)—§ 25.3(a) n.8

Neal, United States v., 990 F.2d 355 (8th Cir.1993)—§ 5.1(c) n.26

Neaves v. State, 767 S.W.2d 784 (Tex.Cr.App.1989)—§ 17.4(a) n.36

Nebraska Free Press Association v. Stuart, 427 U.S. 539, 96 S.Ct. 2791, 49 L.Ed.2d 683 (1976)—§§ 23.1(a) n.1; 23.1(b) n.90; 23.1(c) n.94; 23.3(b) n.22

Neckopulos, People v., 284 Ill.App.3d 660, 219 Ill.Dec. 904, 672 N.E.2d 757 (1996)—§ 26.10(c) n.61

Neder v. United States, 527 U.S. 1, 119 S.Ct. 1827, 144 L.Ed.2d 35 (1999)—§§ 19.2(e) n.61; 19.3(a) n.80; 24.8(c) n.38; 27.6(d) n.91, 113, 120; 27.6(e) n.159

Needles, United States v., 472 F.2d 652 (2d Cir.1973)—§§ 21.2(d) n.207, 211; 21.5(a) n.39

Needs, State v., 333 S.C. 134, 508 S.E.2d 857 (1998)—§ 13.2(a) n.3

Neel v. Holden, 886 P.2d 1097 (Utah 1994)—§ 26.4(g) n.125

Neeley, State v., 748 P.2d 1091 (Utah 1988)—§ 22.4(c) n.26

Neeley v. State, 261 Ind. 434, 305 N.E.2d 434 (1974)—§§ 1.7(f) n.90, 93

Neely, People v., 6 Cal.4th 877, 864 P.2d 460, 26 Cal.Rptr.2d 189 (1993)—§ 24.10(a) n.10

Neely, State v., 1 S.W.3d 679 (Tenn.Crim.App.1999)—§§ 18.5(a) n.39; 21.2(d) n.278

Neely, United States v., 38 F.3d 458 (9th Cir.1994)—§ 21.4(d) n.106

Neff, United States v., 212 F.2d 297 (3d Cir.1954)—§ 8.8(a) n.6

Neher, State v., 213 S.W.3d 44 (Mo.2007)—§ 21.6(a) n.63

Neil v. Biggers, 409 U.S. 188, 93 S.Ct. 375, 34 L.Ed.2d 401 (1972)— §§ 7.4(a) n.7; 7.4(b) n.35; 7.4(c) n.39, 45; 7.4(d) n.71; 10.3(d) n.69

Neill v. Gibson, 278 F.3d 1044 (10th Cir.2001)—§ 24.3(d) n.108

Neill v. State, 896 P.2d 537 (Okla.Cr.App.1994)—§ 24.9(a) n.4

Neill v. State, 827 P.2d 884 (Okla.Crim.App.1992)—§§ 17.2(d) n.97; 17.3(d) n.54

Neiss, State v., 260 Neb. 691, 619 N.W.2d 222 (2000)—§ 26.7(a) n.13

Neitz v. People, 170 Colo. 428, 462 P.2d 498 (1969)—§ 6.8(c) n.67

Nelsen, State v., 390 N.W.2d 589 (Iowa 1986)—§§ 6.4(e) n.68; 6.4(g) n.144

Nelson, In re, 19 S.D. 214, 102 N.W. 885 (1902)—§§ 16.3(d) n.55, 57, 60 to 62

Nelson v. Alabama, 292 F.3d 1291 (11th Cir.2002)—§§ 11.5(c) n.54, 55

Nelson v. California, 346 F.2d 73 (9th Cir.1965)—§§ 11.6(a) n.29, 31; 11.6(b) n.66; 11.6(c) n.110, 112

Nelson, Commonwealth v., 841 S.W.2d 628 (Ky.1992)—§ 15.4(f) n.144

Nelson v. Follette, 430 F.2d 1055 (2d Cir.1970)—§ 17.2(b) n.60

Nelson v. Fulcomer, 911 F.2d 928 (3d Cir.1990)—§§ 6.7(c) n.111, 141

Nelson v. Lane County, 304 Or. 97, 743 P.2d 692 (1987)—§ 3.9(g) n.135

Nelson v. Mollen, 175 A.D.2d 518, 573 N.Y.S.2d 99 (1991)—§ 8.5(h) n.266

Nelson v. O'Neil, 402 U.S. 622, 91 S.Ct. 1723, 29 L.Ed.2d 222 (1971)— § 17.2(b) n.52

Nelson, People v., 127 Misc.2d 583, 486 N.Y.S.2d 979 (Sup.1985)— § 15.7(g) n.212

Nelson v. Roylston, 137 Ariz. 272, 669 P.2d 1349 (App.1983)—§ 15.7(e) n.93

Nelson v. State, 850 So.2d 514 (Fla.2003)—§§ 6.2(c) n.130, 151; 6.9(g) n.149

Nelson, State v., 822 So.2d 796 (La.App.2002)—§ 10.4(b) n.16

Nelson, State v., 263 Kan. 115, 946 P.2d 1355 (1997)—§ 27.3(c) n.21

Nelson, State v., 221 Conn. 635, 605 A.2d 1381 (1992)—§ 21.4(e) n.161

Nelson v. State, 578 So.2d 694 (Fla.1991)—§ 9.1(d) n.136

Nelson, State v., 23 Conn.App. 215, 579 A.2d 1104 (1990)—§ 21.2(d) n.229

Nelson, State v., 435 N.W.2d 344 (Iowa 1989)—§ 6.9(b) n.22

Nelson v. State, 398 So.2d 421 (Ala.Crim.App.1981)—§ 6.4(f) n.126

Nelson v. State, 628 P.2d 884 (Alaska 1981)—§ 15.5(c) n.116

Nelson v. State, 274 Ind. 218, 409 N.E.2d 637 (1980)—§ 27.5(d) n.120

Nelson, State v., 92 Wis.2d 855, 285 N.W.2d 924 (1979)—§ 16.4(c) n.39

Nelson, State v., 14 Wash.App. 658, 545 P.2d 36 (1975)—§§ 20.4(d) n.71; 20.4(g) n.105

Nelson, United States v., 277 F.3d 164 (2d Cir.2002)—§§ 22.1(h) n.146, 161; 22.3(c) n.104, 161; 22.3(d) n.210; 27.5(c) n.63

Nelson, United States v., 222 F.3d 545 (9th Cir.2000)—§ 21.2(d) n.177

Nelson, United States v., 137 F.3d 1094 (9th Cir.1998)—§§ 22.2(d) n.66, 76

Nelson, United States v., 837 F.2d 1519 (11th Cir.1988)—§ 21.2(d) n.183

Nelson, United States v., 718 F.2d 315 (9th Cir.1983)—§ 22.2(a) n.10

Nelson-Rodriguez, United States v., 319 F.3d 12 (1st Cir.2003)—§§ 18.5(c) n.75; 21.2(d) n.263, 264; 24.7(e) n.61; 24.7(i) n.86

Nembhard, United States v., 676 F.2d 193 (6th Cir.1982)—§§ 15.5(b) n.60, 61

Nemes, United States v., 555 F.2d 51 (2d Cir.1977)—§ 8.11(c) n.41

Nemeti, State v., 472 N.W.2d 477 (S.D.1991)—§§ 3.10(b) n.43, 74

Nenno v. State, 970 S.W.2d 549 (Tex.Cr.App.1998)—§§ 6.6(d) n.46, 48

Nepstead, United States v., 424 F.2d 269 (9th Cir.1970)—§ 3.4(g) n.124

Nerber, United States v., 222 F.3d 597 (9th Cir.2000)—§§ 4.6(a) n.10; 4.6(l) n.199; 9.1(c) n.98

Nersesian, United States v., 824 F.2d 1294 (2d Cir.1987)—§ 24.7(i) n.92

Nesbit, State v., 978 S.W.2d 872 (Tenn.1998)—§ 26.5(d) n.74

Nesbitt v. Hopkins, 86 F.3d 118 (8th Cir.1996)—§ 17.4(a) n.8

Nesbitt, State v., 264 Neb. 612, 650 N.W.2d 766 (2002)—§§ 17.4(a) n.2, 34; 21.4(a) n.41

Nesbitt, United States v., 852 F.2d 1502 (7th Cir.1988)—§ 18.3(b) n.28

Neset, State v., 462 N.W.2d 175 (N.D.1990)—§§ 10.2(a) n.7, 10

Nesler, People v., 16 Cal.4th 561, 66 Cal.Rptr.2d 454, 941 P.2d 87 (1997)—§§ 24.8(f) n.120; 24.9(g) n.114

Nesser, State ex rel. v. Pennoyer, 887 S.W.2d 394 (Mo.1994)—§ 27.4(f) n.68

Nethery v. State, 692 S.W.2d 686 (Tex.Crim.App. 1985)—§ 16.3(b) n.21

Netling, State v., 46 Wn.App. 461, 731 P.2d 11 (1987)—§ 25.1(d) n.62

Netto, Commonwealth v., 438 Mass. 686, 783 N.E.2d 439 (2003)—§ 6.2(c) n.58

Netz, United States v., 758 F.2d 1308 (8th Cir.1985)—§ 16.1(g) n.259

Neubauer, Commonwealth v., 142 Pa.Super. 528, 16 A.2d 450 (1940)—§ 16.4(c) n.70

Neudorff, State v., 170 Wis.2d 608, 489 N.W.2d 689 (App.1992)—§§ 19.2(c) n.30; 19.5(b) n.10, 12, 36

Neuendorf, State v., 509 N.W.2d 743 (Iowa 1993)—§ 22.3(c) n.157

Neulander, State v., 173 N.J. 193, 801 A.2d 255 (2002)—§§ 23.1(c) n.104, 107

Neuman, State v., 179 W.Va. 580, 371 S.E.2d 77 (1988)—§§ 11.6(c) n.100; 24.5(d) n.57

Neumann, United States v., 887 F.2d 880 (8th Cir.1989)—§§ 10.1(b) n.20, 23

Neuroth, United States v., 809 F.2d 339 (6th Cir.1987)—§ 27.6(b) n.40

Nevada, Marcum v. Sheriff, Clark County, 85 Nev. 175, 451 P.2d 845 (1969)—§ 14.4(d) n.99

Nevarez-Diaz, United States v., 648 F.Supp. 1226 (N.D.Ind.1986)—§§ 11.1(b) n.39; 11.7(a) n.10

Nevels v. Parratt, 596 F.2d 344 (8th Cir.1979)—§ 24.2(a) n.7

Nevers v. Killinger, 169 F.3d 352 (6th Cir.1999)—§§ 23.2(a) n.15, 17; 23.2(f) n.108

Neverson, United States v., 463 F.2d 1224 (D.C.Cir.1972)—§ 7.4(f) n.101

Neville, State v., 346 N.W.2d 425 (S.D.1984)—§ 2.12(a) n.26

Neville, State v., 312 N.W.2d 723 (S.D.1981)—§ 2.12(a) n.27

Nevitt, In re, 117 F. 448 (8th Cir.1902)—§ 8.3(a) n.3

Nevitt, People v., 76 Mich.App. 402, 256 N.W.2d 612 (1977)—§ 14.3(c) n.73

Nevius v. State, 101 Nev. 238, 699 P.2d 1053 (1985)—§ 7.5(a) n.8

Nevius v. Sumner, 105 F.3d 453 (9th Cir.1996)—§ 11.7(e) n.95

New, People v., 427 Mich. 482, 398 N.W.2d 358 (1986)—§§ 10.2(d) n.48, 49; 21.6(a) n.53

New, State v., 276 Mont. 529, 917 P.2d 919 (1996)—§ 9.3(d) n.35

New, United States v., 491 F.3d 369 (8th Cir.2007)—§§ 24.3(c) n.89, 97

Newark, City of v. Pulverman, 12 N.J. 105, 95 A.2d 889 (1953)—§ 1.8(d) n.64

Newberry v. Commonwealth, 192 Va. 819, 66 S.E.2d 841 (1951)— § 16.3(d) n.56

Newberry, People v., 166 Ill.2d 310, 209 Ill.Dec. 748, 652 N.E.2d 288 (1995)—§ 24.3(e) n.136

Newberry v. United States, 256 U.S. 232, 41 S.Ct. 469, 65 L.Ed. 913 (1921)—§ 1.2(b) n.4

Newcomb v. Ingle, 944 F.2d 1534 (10th Cir.1991)—§ 4.6(b) n.47

Newcomer v. Commonwealth, 220 Va. 64, 255 S.E.2d 485 (1979)— § 16.3(b) n.6

Newell, State v., 212 Ariz. 389, 132 P.3d 833 (2006)—§§ 6.2(c) n.102, 152; 6.9(g) n.179

Newell, United States v., 315 F.3d 510 (5th Cir.2002)—§ 11.9(c) n.134

New England Telephone & Telegraph Co. v. District Attorney, 374 Mass. 569, 373 N.E.2d 960 (1978)— § 4.6(g) n.141

Newhart v. State, 669 N.E.2d 953 (Ind.1996)—§ 9.6(a) n.38

New Haven Grand Jury, In re, 604 F.Supp. 453 (D.Conn.1985)— §§ 8.4(b) n.91, 94, 95, 100, 102, 103, 105; 15.2(b) n.53

New Jersey v. Crews, 208 N.J.Super. 224, 505 A.2d 198 (1986)— § 24.4(c) n.27

New Jersey v. Portash, 440 U.S. 450, 99 S.Ct. 1292, 59 L.Ed.2d 501 (1979)—§§ 2.9(f) n.146; 2.10(b) n.22; 8.11(a) n.14; 9.2(a) n.9; 9.6(a) n.24; 10.5(c) n.34; 21.2(h) n.432; 24.5(d) n.54

New Jersey v. T.L.O., 469 U.S. 325, 105 S.Ct. 733, 83 L.Ed.2d 720 (1985)— §§ 3.1(h) n.211; 3.9(k) n.244, 251

New Jersey in the Interest of S.G., State of, 175 N.J. 132, 814 A.2d 612 (2003)—§§ 11.9(c) n.140, 149; 11.9(d) n.179

Newman v. Lance, 129 Idaho 98, 922 P.2d 395 (1996)—§ 27.4(d) n.51

Newman, State v., 235 Kan. 29, 680 P.2d 257 (1984)—§§ 27.3(c) n.40, 49

Newman, United States v., 912 F.2d 1119 (9th Cir.1990)—§§ 21.4(c) n.77, 92; 21.4(f) n.204

Newman, United States v., 849 F.2d 156 (5th Cir.1988)—§ 5.3(a) n.9

Newman, United States v., 733 F.2d 1395 (10th Cir.1984)—§ 4.6(e) n.97

Newman, United States v., 549 F.2d 240 (2d Cir.1977)—§ 27.4(b) n.9

Newman v. United States, 382 F.2d 479 (D.C.Cir.1967)—§§ 13.7(b) n.33; 21.3(c) n.150

New Mexico ex rel. Ortiz v. Reed, 524 U.S.357, 118 S.Ct. 1860, 141 L.Ed.2d 131 (1998)—§ 3.1(j) n.255

New Mexico Press Assoc., State ex rel. v. Kaufman, 98 N.M. 261, 648 P.2d 300 (1982)—§ 23.1(c) n.101

Newnam, State v., 409 N.W.2d 79 (N.D.1987)—§ 6.3(c) n.50

Newsday, Inc., In re Application of, 895 F.2d 74 (2d Cir.1990)—§ 23.1(d) n.201

News-Journal Corp. v. Foxman, 939 F.2d 1499 (11th Cir.1991)— § 23.1(b) n.89

Newsom, State v., 414 N.W.2d 354 (Iowa 1987)—§ 6.4(f) n.137

Newsom, United States v., 9 F.3d 337 (4th Cir.1993)—§ 16.2(e) n.69

Newsome, State v., 238 Conn. 588, 682 A.2d 972 (1996)—§§ 24.9(f) n.63, 78

Newsome, State v., 778 S.W.2d 34 (Tenn.1989)—§ 1.7(i) n.210

Newsome, United States v., 475 F.3d 1221 (11th Cir.2007)—§ 6.7(b) n.87

Newsome, United States v., 894 F.2d 852 (6th Cir.1990)—§ 21.2(d) n.202

New State Ice Co. v. Liebmann, 285 U.S. 262, 52 S.Ct. 371, 76 L.Ed. 747 (1932)—§§ 2.5(f) n.92; 2.6(d) n.101; 2.12(c) n.153

Newton v. Commonwealth, 760 S.W.2d 100 (Ky.App.1988)—§ 26.2(b) n.26

Newton v. Kemna, 354 F.3d 776 (8th Cir.2004)—§ 28.7(d) n.26

Newton, People v., 764 P.2d 1182 (Colo.1988)—§ 18.4(c) n.68

Newton v. State, 205 Ga.App. 762, 423 S.E.2d 707 (1992)—§ 27.5(a) n.15

Newton, United States v., 369 F.3d 659 (2d Cir.2004)—§§ 6.6(e) n.65; 6.7(b) n.76, 87

Newton, United States v., 756 F.2d 53 (8th Cir.1985)—§ 24.9(f) n.81

Newton, United States v., 68 F.Supp. 952 (W.D.Va.1946)—§ 16.1(d) n.137

Newton, Town of v. Rumery, 480 U.S. 386, 107 S.Ct. 1187, 94 L.Ed.2d 405 (1987)—§ 13.5(a) n.25

New York v. Belton, 453 U.S. 454, 101 S.Ct. 2860, 69 L.Ed.2d 768 (1981)—§§ 2.9(g) n.157, 163, 168, 172, 174, 175, 177; 3.5(e) n.188; 3.6(c) n.80; 3.7(a) n.8; 12.5(b) n.27

New York v. Burger, 482 U.S. 691, 107 S.Ct. 2636, 96 L.Ed.2d 601 (1987)—§§ 3.1(d) n.116; 3.9(c) n.40; 3.9(g) n.129

New York v. Class, 475 U.S. 106, 106 S.Ct. 960, 89 L.Ed.2d 81 (1986)—§§ 2.12(a) n.26; 3.2(f) n.183, 185, 187; 3.9(g) n.123

New York v. Harris, 495 U.S. 14, 110 S.Ct. 1640, 109 L.Ed.2d 13 (1990)—§ 9.4(a) n.34

New York v. Hill, 528 U.S. 110, 120 S.Ct. 659, 145 L.Ed.2d 560 (2000)—§§ 11.6(a) n.25, 38, 44; 11.6(c) n.99; 18.4(c) n.33, 66, 67

New York v. P.J. Video, Inc., 475 U.S. 868, 106 S.Ct. 1610, 89 L.Ed.2d 871 (1986)—§ 3.3(b) n.41

New York v. Quarles, 467 U.S. 649, 104 S.Ct. 2626, 81 L.Ed.2d 550 (1984)—§§ 2.7(c) n.179; 2.9(h) n.211, 231; 6.5(e) n.93; 6.6(e) n.84; 6.7(b) n.79; 9.5(b) n.40

New York v. United States, 505 U.S. 144, 112 S.Ct. 2408, 120 L.Ed.2d 120 (1992)—§ 2.5(f) n.55

New York Central & Hudson River Railroad Co. v. United States, 212 U.S. 481, 29 S.Ct. 304, 53 L.Ed. 613 (1909)—§ 15.1(b) n.18

New York, City of v. Gentile, 248 A.D.2d 382, 669 N.Y.S.2d 854 (1998)—§ 20.3(m) n.236

New York News, Inc. v. Office of Special State Prosecutor, 153 A.D.2d 512, 544 N.Y.S.2d 151 (1989)—§ 8.5(b) n.35

New York State Comm'n on Government Integrity v. Congel, 156 A.D.2d 274, 548 N.Y.S.2d 663 (1989)—§ 8.7(b) n.45

New York State National Organization for Women v. Terry, 886 F.2d 1339 (2d Cir.1989)—§ 8.12(b) n.21

New York Telephone, United States v., 434 U.S. 159, 98 S.Ct. 364, 54 L.Ed.2d 376 (1977)—§§ 4.6(l) n.181; 4.7(c) n.19

New York Times Co., Matter of, 828 F.2d 110 (2d Cir.1987)—§§ 23.1(d) n.172, 174, 176; 23.1(e) n.222, 223; 27.2(d) n.68

New York Times Co. v. Gonzales, 459 F.3d 160 (2d Cir.2006)—§§ 8.5(d) n.159; 8.8(d) n.85, 86

New York Times Company v. Gonzales, 382 F.Supp.2d 475 (S.D.N.Y.2005)—§ 8.8(d) n.47

Nguyen, State v., _____ Kan. _____, 133 P.3d 1259 (2006)—§ 6.8(b) n.50

Nguyen, State v., 173 Vt. 598, 795 A.2d 538 (2002)—§ 24.2(g) n.97

Nguyen, United States v., 465 F.3d 1128 (9th Cir.2006)—§ 21.4(a) n.21

Nguyen, United States v., 413 F.3d 1170 (10th Cir.2005)—§ 5.2(a) n.17

Nguyen v. United States, 539 U.S. 69, 123 S.Ct. 2130, 156 L.Ed.2d 64 (2003)—§ 27.5(d) n.136

Nguyen, United States v., 250 F.3d 643 (8th Cir.2001)—§ 6.9(b) n.34

Nguyen, United States v., 155 F.3d 1219 (10th Cir.1998)—§§ 6.2(c) n.107, 120

Nguyen v. United States, 114 F.3d 699 (8th Cir.1997)—§ 21.2(b) n.56

Niblack, State v., 220 Conn. 270, 596 A.2d 407 (1991)—§§ 14.2(g) n.107; 21.2(c) n.135; 21.3(d) n.220, 234

Nicaragua v. Reagan, 859 F.2d 929 (D.C.Cir.1988)—§ 1.7(c) n.32

Nicholas v. Goord, 430 F.3d 652 (2d Cir.2005)—§§ 3.2(g) n.198; 3.5(d) n.145; 3.9(i) n.190; 3.9(j) n.240

Nicholas, People v., 98 N.Y.2d 749, 751 N.Y.S.2d 820, 781 N.E.2d 884 (2002)—§ 22.3(c) n.108

Nicholas v. People, 973 P.2d 1213 (Colo.1999)—§ 6.9(b) n.22

Nicholas v. Sammons, 178 W.Va. 631, 363 S.E.2d 516 (1987)—§ 22.5(a) n.8

Nichols v. Butler, 953 F.2d 1550 (11th Cir.1992)—§§ 11.6(d)   n.115; 11.10(b) n.43

Nichols v. Commonwealth, 142 S.W.3d 683 (Ky.2004)—§ 6.2(c) n.173

Nichols v. Scott, 69 F.3d 1255 (5th Cir.1995)—§ 17.4(a) n.50

Nichols, State v., 111 Haw. 327, 141 P.3d 974 (2006)—§ 27.5(d) n.139

Nichols, State v., 201 Ariz. 234, 33 P.3d 1172 (App.2001)—§§ 19.3(a) n.39, 40, 42

Nichols, State v., 325 S.C. 111, 481 S.E.2d 118 (1997)—§ 13.3(b) n.20

Nichols, State v., 698 A.2d 521 (Me.1997)—§ 11.7(e) n.63

Nichols, State v., 1997 Me. 178, 698 A.2d 521 (1997)—§ 11.7(e) n.78

Nichols, State v., 877 S.W.2d 722 (Tenn.1994)—§ 16.1(h) n.287

Nichols v. State, 528 So.2d 1282 (Fla.App.1988)—§ 26.9(b) n.73

Nichols, United States v., 438 F.3d 437 (4th Cir.2006)—§ 26.5(a) n.11

Nichols, United States v., 248 F.Supp.2d 1027 (D.Kan.2003)—§ 22.3(b) n.55

Nichols, United States v., 344 F.3d 793 (8th Cir.2003)—§§ 3.4(e) n.78; 3.4(k) n.221

Nichols, United States v., 169 F.3d 1255 (10th Cir.1999)—§ 20.6(b) n.40

Nichols, United States v., 56 F.3d 403 (2d Cir.1995)—§ 24.2(d) n.46

Nichols v. United States, 511 U.S. 738, 114 S.Ct. 1921, 128 L.Ed.2d 745 (1994)—§§ 11.2(a) n.21; 26.4(f) n.97

Nichols, United States v., 979 F.2d 402 (6th Cir.1992)—§§ 3.1(f) n.153, 154

Nichols, United States v., 937 F.2d 1257 (7th Cir.1991)—§ 18.5(b) n.65

Nichols, United States v., 841 F.2d 1485 (10th Cir.1988)—§ 26.6(d) n.45

Nicholson v. State, 157 Md.App. 304, 850 A.2d 1204 (2004)—§ 25.1(d) n.77

Nicholson, State v., 355 N.C. 1, 558 S.E.2d 109 (2002)—§ 22.3(d) n.215

Nicholson, State v., 148 Wis.2d 353, 435 N.W.2d 298 (Wis.App.1988)—§ 24.8(f) n.92

Nicholson v. State, 523 So.2d 68 (Miss.1988)—§§ 7.3(c) n.54; 7.4(e) n.89

Nicholson, State v., 174 W.Va. 573, 328 S.E.2d 180 (1985)—§ 6.9(b) n.24

Nicholson, United States v., 231 F.3d 445 (8th Cir.2000)—§ 21.2(d) n.167

Nickel v. Hannigan, 97 F.3d 403 (10th Cir.1996)—§ 6.2(c) n.178

Nickels, United States v., 502 F.2d 1173 (7th Cir.1974)—§ 8.8(a) n.5

Nickens, People v., 470 Mich. 622, 685 N.W.2d 657 (2004)—§ 24.8(e) n.61

Nickerson, Commonwealth v., 386 Mass. 54, 434 N.E.2d 992 (1982)—§ 9.6(a) n.44

Nicklasson, State v., 967 S.W.2d 596 (Mo.1998)—§ 22.3(d) n.245

Nickolai v. State, 708 P.2d 1292 (Alaska App.1985)—§ 23.2(a) n.29

Nickols v. Gagnon, 454 F.2d 467 (7th Cir.1971)—§ 11.2(c) n.87

Nickopoulous, People v., 26 Mich.App. 297, 182 N.W.2d 83 (1970)—§ 20.5(b) n.25

Nicks v. State, 598 N.E.2d 520 (Ind.1992)—§ 9.6(a) n.35

Nicks v. United States, 835 F.Supp. 151 (S.D.N.Y.1993)—§§ 28.9(a) n.20, 21

Nicolella, Commonwealth v., 307 Pa.Super. 96, 452 A.2d 1055 (1982)—§ 11.4(c) n.78

Nicolosi, United States v., 885 F.Supp. 50 (E.D.N.Y.1995)—§ 8.7(d) n.82

Nieblas, United States v., 115 F.3d 703 (9th Cir.1997)—§§ 6.6(e) n.78; 6.10(e) n.71; 26.10(c) n.61

Niedelman, United States v., 356 F.Supp. 979 (S.D.N.Y.1973)—§ 15.6(c) n.97

Niedziejko, State ex rel. v. Coffey, 22 Wis.2d 392, 126 N.W.2d 96 (1964)—§§ 8.1(c) n.25, 28

Nields, State v., 93 Ohio St.3d 6, 752 N.E.2d 859 (2001)—§ 6.9(f) n.135

Nielsen, Petitioner, 131 U.S. 176, 9 S.Ct. 672, 33 L.Ed. 118 (1889)—§ 28.3(b) n.48

Nielsen v. Oregon, 212 U.S. 315, 29 S.Ct. 383, 53 L.Ed. 528 (1909)—§§ 16.4(c) n.39, 83

Nielson, People v., 187 Ill.2d 271, 240 Ill.Dec. 650, 718 N.E.2d 131 (1999)—§§ 6.9(f) n.101; 6.9(g) n.151

Niemotko v. Maryland, 340 U.S. 268, 71 S.Ct. 328, 95 L.Ed. 280 (1951)—§ 2.5(f) n.72

Nienhardt, State v., 196 Wis.2d 161, 537 N.W.2d 123 (1995)—§ 26.9(b) n.76

Nienhouse v. Superior Court, 42 Cal.App.4th 83, 49 Cal.Rptr.2d 573 (1996)—§ 14.4(c) n.49

Nieto, State v., 129 N.M. 688, 12 P.3d 442 (2000)—§ 6.6(d) n.50

Nieves, People v., 36 N.Y.2d 396, 369 N.Y.S.2d 50, 330 N.E.2d 26 (1975)—§ 3.4(e) n.98

Nieves-Rivera, United States v., 961 F.2d 15 (1st Cir.1992)—§ 26.1(d) n.77

Nika v. State, 951 P.2d 1047 (Nev.1997)—§ 6.7(b) n.45

Nikas, Commonwealth v., 431 Mass. 453, 727 N.E.2d 1166 (2000)—§§ 21.4(c) n.88, 98

Nikolaev v. Weber, 705 N.W.2d 72 (S.D.2005)—§§ 21.3(b) n.66; 21.4(d) n.134

Niles, City of v. Howard, 12 Ohio St.3d 162, 466 N.E.2d 539 (1984)—§§ 1.8(c) n.49; 1.8(d) n.48

Nims, United States v., 524 F.2d 123 (5th Cir.1975)—§ 17.3(c) n.41

Nippon Paper Industries, United States v., 109 F.3d 1 (1st Cir.1997)—§§ 16.4(b) n.17, 19

Nitschmann, People v., 35 Cal.App.4th 677, 41 Cal.Rptr.2d 325 (1995)—§ 6.8(a) n.26

Nivens v. Gilchrist, 319 F.3d 151 (4th Cir.2003)—§ 17.4(b) n.140

Nivens, People v., 239 Ill.App.3d 1, 177 Ill.Dec. 901, 603 N.E.2d 1275 (1992)—§ 24.2(d) n.47

Niver, United States v., 689 F.2d 520 (5th Cir.1982)—§ 27.5(b) n.44

Nivica, United States v., 887 F.2d 1110 (1st Cir.1989)—§ 24.3(f) n.142

Nix, People v., 453 Mich. 619, 556 N.W.2d 866 (1996)—§ 25.3(c) n.28

Nix v. State, 653 P.2d 1093 (Alaska App.1982)—§ 15.4(g) n.178

Nix, United States v., 21 F.3d 347 (9th Cir.1994)—§§ 8.5(b) n.66, 67

Nix v. Whiteside, 475 U.S. 157, 106 S.Ct. 988, 89 L.Ed.2d 123 (1986)—§§ 1.5(c) n.136; 11.6(a) n.22; 11.10(b) n.41; 11.10(d) n.160, 184; 24.3(d) n.109; 24.5(d) n.46

Nix v. Williams, 467 U.S. 431, 104 S.Ct. 2501, 81 L.Ed.2d 377 (1984)—§§ 2.9(f) n.140; 9.3(c) n.22; 9.3(e) n.45, 54; 9.5(a) n.28; 9.5(b) n.54; 10.3(b) n.43; 10.3(c) n.56; 10.4(b) n.5; 10.4(d) n.28

Nixon v. Singletary, 758 So.2d 618 (Fla.2000)—§ 21.4(a) n.9

Nixon v. State, 994 P.2d 324 (Wyo.1999)—§ 23.2(a) n.42

Nixon, State v., 599 A.2d 66 (Me.1991)—§ 6.7(c) n.111

Nixon v. State, 572 So.2d 1336 (Fla.1990)—§ 24.7(e) n.62

Nixon, United States v., 779 F.2d 126 (2d Cir.1985)—§ 18.3(b) n.9

Nixon, United States v., 634 F.2d 306 (5th Cir.1981)—§ 18.1(c) n.37

Nixon, United States v., 418 U.S. 683, 94 S.Ct. 3090, 41 L.Ed.2d 1039 (1974)—§§ 1.5(a) n.26; 1.5(c) n.117; 1.5(e) n.209; 8.8(b) n.37; 20.2(d) n.67; 24.3(f) n.146; 27.2(e) n.82

Nixon v. Warner Communications, Inc., 435 U.S. 589, 98 S.Ct. 1306, 55 L.Ed.2d 570 (1978)—§§ 23.1(d) n.203; 23.3(b) n.24

Noah, United States v., 130 F.3d 490 (1st Cir.1997)—§ 11.5(d) n.71

Nobel, United States v., 696 F.2d 231 (3d Cir.1982)—§ 22.4(c) n.30

Noble v. Kelly, 246 F.3d 93 (2d Cir.2001)—§ 20.6(c) n.80

Noble, State v., 253 Wis.2d 206, 646 N.W.2d 38 (2002)—§ 8.1(c) n.26

Noble v. State, 240 Kan. 162, 727 P.2d 473 (1986)—§ 21.4(g) n.232

Noble v. State, 478 S.W.2d 83 (Tex.Cr.App.1972)—§ 6.8(a) n.12

Noble, United States v., 367 F.3d 681 (7th Cir.2004)—§ 26.7(a) n.13

Nobles, State v., 357 N.C. 433, 584 S.E.2d 765 (2003)—§ 26.4(f) n.108

Nobles, United States v., 422 U.S. 225, 95 S.Ct. 2160, 45 L.Ed.2d 141 (1975)—§§ 1.5(a) n.26; 1.5(e) n.209; 1.7(i) n.160; 20.3(i) n.174; 20.3(j) n.187, 210; 20.4(b) n.15; 20.5(f) n.74; 20.6(c) n.71; 24.3(c) n.90

Noe, United States v., 821 F.2d 604 (11th Cir.1987)—§§ 20.3(b) n.60; 20.6(b) n.23

Noel v. Norris, 322 F.3d 500 (8th Cir.2003)—§ 28.3(e) n.104

Noel v. State, 113 Idaho 92, 741 P.2d 728 (1987)—§§ 14.2(e) n.72, 76; 14.2(g) n.107

Noffsinger v. State, 850 P.2d 647 (Alaska App.1993)—§ 26.9(c) n.89

Noggle v. Marshall, 706 F.2d 1408 (6th Cir.1983)—§ 20.5(c) n.55

Noia, United States ex rel. v. Fay, 300 F.2d 345 (2d Cir.1962)—§ 22.1(h) n.161

Nolan, Commonwealth v., 579 Pa. 300, 855 A.2d 834 (2004)—§ 17.4(c) n.143

Nolan v. Henshaw, 681 P.2d 1118 (Okl.Crim. 1984)—§§ 13.5(b) n.31; 13.6(d) n.53

Nolan-Cooper, United States v., 155 F.3d 221 (3d Cir.1998)—§§ 5.4(c) n.29; 21.2(d) n.180, 182; 21.2(e) n.323

Noland v. French, 134 F.3d 208 (4th Cir.1998)—§§ 6.5(b) n.30; 9.6(a) n.51

Noline, People v., 917 P.2d 1256 (Colo.1996)—§§ 14.2(d) n.51; 14.3(c) n.68, 70; 14.3(d) n.82

Noling, State v., 98 Ohio St.3d 44, 781 N.E.2d 88 (2002)—§ 22.3(d) n.202

Noll, Commonwealth v., 443 Pa.Super. 602, 662 A.2d 1123 (1995)—§ 27.3(c) n.42

Nollette v. State, 118 Nev. 341, 46 P.3d 87 (2002)—§ 21.4(d) n.138

Noltie, State v., 116 Wash.2d 831, 809 P.2d 190 (1991)—§§ 19.2(b) n.12; 19.3(a) n.72

Nom, Commonwealth v., 426 Mass. 152, 686 N.E.2d 1017 (1997)—§ 6.9(g) n.183

Nontestimonial Identification Order Directed to R.H., In re, 171 Vt. 227, 762 A.2d 1239 (2000)—§ 3.8(g) n.241

Norby, State v., 122 Wash.2d 258, 858 P.2d 210 (1993)—§ 18.5(b) n.58

Norcross v. State, 816 A.2d 757 (Del.2003)—§§ 6.2(c) n.128; 6.9(g) n.155

Norcutt, State v., 139 P.3d 1066 (Utah App.2006)—§ 14.2(g) n.106

Nordahl, State v., 2004 N.D. 106, 680 N.W.2d 247 (2004)—§ 26.1(f) n.144

Nordquist, State v., 309 N.W.2d 109 (N.D.1981)—§ 15.7(f) n.185

Nordstrom v. Cruikshank, 142 P.3d 1247, 213 Ariz. 434 (2006)—§ 26.2(b) n.6

Noreikis, United States v., 481 F.2d 1177 (7th Cir.1973)—§ 3.4(h) n.151

Noren, State v., 704 P.2d 568 (Utah 1985)—§ 24.6(b) n.25

Norfolk, State v., 221 Neb. 810, 381 N.W.2d 120 (1986)—§§ 6.8(a) n.9; 6.9(b) n.44

Norgaard, State v., 201 Mont. 165, 653 P.2d 483 (1982)—§ 6.4(f) n.112

Norgaard, United States v., 959 F.2d 136 (9th Cir.1992)—§ 21.2(d) n.227

Noriega, State v., 261 Kan. 440, 932 P.2d 940 (1997)—§ 7.5(a) n.7

Noriega, United States v., 117 F.3d 1206 (11th Cir.1997)—§ 24.3(d) n.112

Noriega, United States v., 764 F.Supp. 1480 (S.D.Fla.1991)—§ 4.6(b) n.50

Noriega, United States v., 746 F.Supp. 1548 (S.D.Fla.1990)—§ 23.2(e) n.73

Noriega (In re Cable News Network), United States v., 917 F.2d 1543 (11th Cir.1990)—§ 23.1(c) n.108

Normal, Town of v. Bowsky, 142 Ill.App.3d 760, 97 Ill.Dec. 1, 492 N.E.2d 204 (1986)—§§ 1.8(d) n.65, 79

Norman v. Ducharme, 871 F.2d 1483 (9th Cir.1989)—§ 6.4(f) n.124

Norman, People v., 14 Cal.3d 929, 123 Cal.Rptr. 109, 538 P.2d 237 (1975)—§§ 2.12(c) n.126, 128

Norman, State v., 118 Ariz. 23, 574 P.2d 491 (1978)—§ 21.4(c) n.77

Norrell, Commonwealth v., 423 Mass. 725, 673 N.E.2d 19 (1996)—§ 13.2(c) n.51

Norrid, State v., 611 N.W.2d 866 (N.D.2000)—§ 7.4(f) n.96

Norris v. Alabama, 294 U.S. 587, 55 S.Ct. 579, 79 L.Ed. 1074 (1935)—§ 22.2(c) n.28

Norris, People v., 214 Ill.2d 92, 291 Ill.Dec. 629, 824 N.E.2d 205 (2005)—§ 13.3(c) n.40

Norris v. Risley, 878 F.2d 1178 (9th Cir.1989)—§ 24.2(e) n.79

Norris, State v., 48 P.3d 872 (Utah 2001)—§ 3.3(d) n.147

Norris, State v., 768 So.2d 1070 (Fla.2000)—§ 12.1(b) n.26

Norris, State v., 244 Kan. 326, 768 P.2d 296 (1989)—§§ 6.9(b) n.35; 6.9(f) n.144

Norris v. State, 498 N.E.2d 1203 (Ind.1986)—§ 6.9(e) n.88

Norris, State v., 577 S.W.2d 941 (Mo.App.1979)—§ 7.2(b) n.23

Norris, United States v., 428 F.3d 907 (9th Cir.2005)—§ 6.6(d) n.57

North, In re, 16 F.3d 1234 (1994)—§ 8.3(h) n.47

North v. Russell, 427 U.S. 328, 96 S.Ct. 2709, 49 L.Ed.2d 534 (1976)—§§ 1.3(c) n.22; 1.5(g) n.278; 2.6(d) n.91; 11.2(a) n.4

North, United States v., 910 F.2d 843 (1990)—§§ 8.11(c) n.35, 37, 46, 49, 60

North Carolina v. Alford, 400 U.S. 25, 91 S.Ct. 160, 27 L.Ed.2d 162 (1970)—§§ 2.7(a) n.29; 2.7(c) n.157; 21.3(b) n.95; 21.3(c) n.186; 21.4(e) n.168; 21.4(f) n.205; 21.5(c) n.90

North Carolina v. Butler, 441 U.S. 369, 99 S.Ct. 1755, 60 L.Ed.2d 286 (1979)—§§ 2.9(g) n.178, 179; 6.9(a) n.10; 6.9(d) n.68, 69; 6.9(e) n.82; 6.9(g) n.169

North Carolina v. Pearce, 395 U.S. 711, 89 S.Ct. 2072, 23 L.Ed.2d 656 (1969)—§§ 2.4(b) n.57; 2.7(a) n.53, 61; 2.9(d) n.76; 2.9(g) n.190; 2.9(h) n.212, 219, 246; 2.11(a) n.6; 2.11(c) n.27; 13.7(c) n.36; 21.2(c) n.127; 21.5(e) n.136; 25.1(b) n.7; 26.4(c) n.24; 26.7(a) n.1; 26.8(a) n.1; 27.1(b) n.23

Northfield Insurance Co. v. Derma Clinic, Inc., 440 F.3d 86 (2d Cir.2006)—§ 21.4(a) n.21

North Georgia Finishing, Inc. v. Di-Chem, Inc., 419 U.S. 601, 95 S.Ct. 719, 42 L.Ed.2d 751 (1975)—§ 14.2(a) n.6

Northrop, State v., 213 Conn. 405, 568 A.2d 439 (1990)—§ 6.9(b) n.27

Northrop v. Trippett, 265 F.3d 372 (6th Cir.2001)—§ 28.3(d) n.91

Northwest Airlines, Inc. v. Transport Workers Union, 451 U.S. 77, 101 S.Ct. 1571, 67 L.Ed.2d 750 (1981)—§ 1.7(h) n.135

Norton v. State, 43 P.3d 404 (Okla.Crim.App.2002)—§§ 14.4(a) n.4; 14.4(e) n.135

Norton v. State, 307 Ark. 336, 820 S.W.2d 272 (1991)—§ 10.3(b) n.38

Norton v. United States, 581 F.2d 390 (4th Cir.1978)—§ 3.1(k) n.277

Norvell v. Illinois, 373 U.S. 420, 83 S.Ct. 1366, 10 L.Ed.2d 456 (1963)—§ 11.2(d) n.126

Norwood, State v., 344 N.C. 511, 476 S.E.2d 349 (1996)—§ 22.3(d) n.202

Norwood, State ex rel. v. Drumm, 691 S.W.2d 238 (Mo.1985)—§ 13.3(c) n.38

Nova, People v., 206 A.D.2d 132, 618 N.Y.S.2d 645 (1994)—§ 20.3(a) n.18

Novak, Commonwealth v., 233 Pa.Super. 236, 335 A.2d 773 (1975)—§ 3.3(g) n.233

Novak v. State, 130 Ga.App. 780, 204 S.E.2d 491 (1974)—§ 9.1(b) n.85

Novak, United States v., 903 F.2d 883 (2d Cir.1990)—§ 11.8(c) n.76

Novak, United States v., 918 F.2d 107 (10th Cir.1990)—§§ 24.7(a) n.7, 16

Novak, United States v., 715 F.2d 810 (3d Cir.1983)—§§ 18.3(b) n.28, 35

Novaton, United States v., 271 F.3d 968 (11th Cir.2001)—§ 24.2(d) n.48

November 1979 Grand Jury, In re, 616 F.2d 1021 (7th Cir.1980)—§ 27.2(e) n.97

November 1992 Special Grand Jury, In re, 836 F.Supp. 615 (N.D.Ind.1993)—§§ 8.5(e) n.174, 188

Novembrino, State v., 105 N.J. 95, 519 A.2d 820 (1987)—§§ 2.12(b) n.114; 2.12(c) n.159, 166; 2.12(e) n.219

Novo, Commonwealth v., 442 Mass. 262, 812 N.E.2d 1169 (2004)—§§ 6.2(c) n.138; 6.8(d) n.82

Nowells, Commonwealth v., 390 Mass. 621, 458 N.E.2d 1186 (1983)—§ 3.3(c) n.114

Noy v. State, 83 P.3d 545 (Alaska 2003)—§ 25.3(b) n.15

N.S., State v., 98 Wash.App. 910, 991 P.2d 133 (2000)—§ 24.8(f) n.108

Nuccio, State v., 454 So.2d 93 (La.1984)—§ 21.4(d) n.111

Nuckols, United States v., 606 F.2d 566 (5th Cir.1979)—§§ 21.2(b) n.53, 55; 21.5(d) n.103

Nudd v. Burrows, 91 U.S. 426, 23 L.Ed. 286 (1875)—§§ 1.7(h) n.145, 146

Nunes v. Mueller, 350 F.3d 1045 (9th Cir.2003)—§§ 21.3(a) n.4; 21.3(b) n.47, 108

Nunez, Commonwealth v., 446 Mass. 54, 841 N.E.2d 1250 (2006)—§ 26.4(f) n.93

Nunez, State v., 138 Idaho 636, 67 P.3d 831 (2003)—§ 3.3(g) n.247

Nunez, State v., 129 N.M. 63, 2 P.3d 264 (1999)—§§ 17.4(b) n.120; 25.1(c) n.40

Nunez, United States v., 19 F.3d 719 (1st Cir.1994)—§§ 10.1(a) n.15; 10.2(a) n.11

Nunez, United States v., 889 F.2d 1564 (6th Cir.1989)—§ 24.9(c) n.28

Nunez-Rios, United States v., 622 F.2d 1093 (2d Cir.1980)—§ 5.4(c) n.46

Nunley, State v., 923 S.W.2d 911 (Mo.1996)—§ 21.2(d) n.161

Nunn v. Georgia, 1 Ga. 243 (1846)—§§ 15.1(d) n.152, 162

Nunn, United States v., 940 F.2d 1148 (8th Cir.1991)—§ 5.3(a) n.9

Nunn, United States v., 622 F.2d 802 (5th Cir.1980)—§ 15.1(b) n.86

Nururdin, United States v., 8 F.3d 1187 (7th Cir.1993)—§ 24.5(a) n.9

Nutall, United States v., 180 F.3d 182 (5th Cir.1999)—§§ 17.2(b) n.71; 17.2(c) n.90

Nutley, State v., 24 Wis.2d 527, 129 N.W.2d 155 (1964)—§ 17.2(e) n.130

Nutt v. State, 312 Ark. 247, 848 S.W.2d 427 (1993)—§ 22.3(a) n.5

Nwamu, In re, 421 F.Supp. 1361 (S.D.N.Y.1976)—§§ 8.7(e) n.91, 95

Nye v. State, 639 So.2d 1383 (Ala.App. 1993)—§ 19.3(b) n.181

NYNEX Corp., United States v., 781 F.Supp. 19 (D.D.C.1991)—§ 22.1(b) n.49

O

1-95-CV-553-P1 v. 1-95-CV-553-D1, 75 F.3d 135 (2d Cir.1996)—§ 21.2(e) n.281

192 Coin-Operated Video Machines, State v., 338 S.C. 176, 525 S.E.2d 872 (2000)—§ 3.1(g) n.169

1969 Plymouth Roadrunner, In re, 455 S.W.2d 466 (Mo.1970)—§ 3.4(f) n.111

1979 Grand Jury Subpoena, In re, 478 F.Supp. 59 (M.D.La.1979)—§ 8.8(a) n.7

1997 Grand Jury, In re, 215 F.3d 430 (4th Cir.2000)—§§ 13.5(h) n.183, 202

$124,570 United States Currency, United States v., 873 F.2d 1240 (9th Cir.1989)—§ 3.9(h) n.155

Oakes v. United States, 400 F.3d 92 (1st Cir.2005)—§§ 28.4(c) n.31; 28.9(b) n.43

Oakley, State v., 245 Wis.2d 447, 629 N.W.2d 200 (2001)—§§ 21.4(a) n.26; 26.9(b) n.55

Oakley, State v., 245 Wis.2d 449, 629 N.W.2d 200 (2001)—§ 21.6(a) n.48

Oaks, People v., 169 Ill.2d 409, 215 Ill.Dec. 188, 662 N.E.2d 1328 (1996)—§§ 6.2(c) n.107, 113

Oaks, United States v., 508 F.2d 1403 (9th Cir.1974)—§§ 13.4(a) n.10; 13.4(b) n.60

Oates, People v., 698 P.2d 811 (Colo.1985)—§ 2.12(c) n.174

Oatman, State v., 275 Mont. 139, 911 P.2d 213 (1996)—§ 27.5(e) n.150

Obado v. State of New Jersey, 328 F.3d 716 (3d Cir.2003)—§§ 28.3(a) n.17; 28.9(a) n.11

O'Banner, People v., 215 Ill.App.3d 778, 159 Ill.Dec. 201, 575 N.E.2d 1261 (1991)—§ 11.10(c) n.73

Oberlin, United States v., 718 F.2d 894 (9th Cir.1983)—§ 27.5(a) n.5

Obershaw, Commonwealth v., 435 Mass. 794, 762 N.E.2d 276 (2002)—§ 6.9(g) n.162

Obregon v. United States, 423 A.2d 200 (D.C.App.1980)—§§ 15.4(d) n.98, 100, 126

O'Bremski, State v., 70 Wash.2d 425, 423 P.2d 530 (1967)—§ 9.3(d) n.34

O'Brian, Commonwealth v., 445 Mass. 720, 840 N.E.2d 500 (2006)—§ 6.2(c) n.100

O'Brien, Commonwealth v., 432 Mass. 578, 736 N.E.2d 841 (2000)— § 6.6(e) n.71

O'Brien v. O'Brien, 899 So.2d 1133 (Fla. App. 5 Dist. 2005)— § 4.6(a) n.19

O'Brien v. State, 88 Nev. 488, 500 P.2d 693 (1972)— § 17.3(d) n.46

O'Brien v. State, 6 Tex.App. 665 (1879)— § 5.1(b) n.7

O'Brien, United States v., 895 F.2d 810 (1st Cir.1990)— § 12.3(a) n.28

O'Brien, United States v., 618 F.2d 1234 (7th Cir.1980)— § 21.2(h) n.419

O'Brien v. United States, 386 U.S. 345, 87 S.Ct. 1158, 18 L.Ed.2d 94 (1967)— § 11.8(b) n.26

O'Brien v. Wainwright, 738 F.2d 1139 (11th Cir.1984)— §§ 7.2(c) n.31; 7.4(c) n.50, 52; 7.4(e) n.89

Obstein, State v., 52 N.J. 516, 247 A.2d 5 (1968)— §§ 12.4(a) n.35, 44

O'Callahan v. Parker, 395 U.S. 258, 89 S.Ct. 1683, 23 L.Ed.2d 291 (1969)— §§ 15.1(b) n.95, 98

Ocampo, United States v., 890 F.2d 1363 (7th Cir.1989)— § 3.8(b) n.27

Ocasio, Commonwealth v., 434 Mass. 1, 746 N.E.2d 469 (2001)— §§ 3.4(l) n.242; 10.3(b) n.10

Ocasio, People v., 134 A.D.2d 293, 520 N.Y.S.2d 620 (1987)— § 10.5(f) n.65

Occhicone v. State, 570 So.2d 902 (Fla.1990)— § 24.7(a) n.8

Ochana v. Flores, 347 F.3d 266 (7th Cir.2003)— § 3.5(a) n.9

Ochoa, People v., 26 Cal.4th 398, 110 Cal.Rptr.2d 324, 28 P.3d 78 (2001)— §§ 6.7(b) n.69; 22.2(d) n.85; 22.2(e) n.111

Ochoa, People v., 19 Cal.4th 353, 79 Cal.Rptr.2d 408, 966 P.2d 442 (1998)— § 7.4(e) n.85

Ochoa v. Sirmons, 485 F.3d 538 (10th Cir.2007)— § 28.5(d) n.85

Ochoa v. State, 848 P.2d 1359 (Wyo.1993)— § 21.6(a) n.31

Ochoa-Gaytan, United States v., 265 F.3d 837 (9th Cir.2001)— § 21.1(h) n.213

Ochoa-Vasquez, United States v., 428 F.3d 1015 (11th Cir.2005)— § 22.3(b) n.69

O'Connell v. State, 742 N.E.2d 943 (Ind.2001)— § 7.4(f) n.101

O'Connell, State v., 36 Conn.App. 135, 648 A.2d 168 (1994)— § 27.2(c) n.44

O'Connell v. State, 480 So.2d 1284 (Fla.1985)— § 22.3(c) n.147

O'Connell, United States v., 841 F.2d 1408 (8th Cir.1988)— §§ 3.8(d) n.175; 4.6(e) n.97

O'Connell v. United States, 40 F.2d 201 (2d Cir.1930)— § 8.10(c) n.63

O'Connor, Commonwealth v., 406 Mass. 112, 546 N.E.2d 336 (1989)— §§ 3.5(a) n.22; 9.3(e) n.65, 78; 10.4(c) n.25

O'Connor v. Johnson, 287 N.W.2d 400 (Minn.1979)— § 3.4(a) n.22

O'Connor v. Ortega, 480 U.S. 709, 107 S.Ct. 1492, 94 L.Ed.2d 714 (1987)— §§ 3.9(l) n.268; 4.4(e) n.17

O'Connor v. State, 855 F.Supp. 303 (C.D.Cal.1994)— § 26.9(b) n.54

O'Daniel, State v., 62 Haw. 518, 616 P.2d 1383 (1980)— § 15.7(g) n.213

Odedo, United States v., 154 F.3d 937 (9th Cir.1998)— § 21.4(c) n.66

O'Dell v. Commonwealth, 234 Va. 672, 364 S.E.2d 491 (1988)— § 11.2(e) n.184

O'Dell, Commonwealth v., 392 Mass. 445, 466 N.E.2d 828 (1984)— § 15.5(c) n.115

O'Dell v. Netherland, 521 U.S. 151, 117 S.Ct. 1969, 138 L.Ed.2d 351 (1997)— §§ 26.4(d) n.56; 28.6(b) n.9; 28.6(d) n.31; 28.6(e) n.59

O'Dell, State v., 71 Idaho 64, 225 P.2d 1020 (1950)— § 1.8(c) n.10

Odhinn v. State, 82 P.3d 715 (Wyo.2003)— §§ 18.4(c) n.60, 61

Odiaga, State v., 125 Idaho 384, 871 P.2d 801 (1994)— § 14.2(d) n.50

Odle v. Superior Court, 32 Cal.3d 932, 187 Cal.Rptr. 455, 654 P.2d 225 (1982)—§ 27.4(c) n.31

Odoardi, Commonwealth v., 397 Mass. 28, 489 N.E.2d 674 (1986)—§§ 26.10(b) n.18, 38

Odofin, United States v., 929 F.2d 56 (2d Cir.1991)—§ 3.9(f) n.110

O'Doherty, People v., 70 N.Y.2d 479, 522 N.Y.S.2d 498, 517 N.E.2d 213 (1987)—§ 20.6(b) n.39

Odom v. State, 403 So.2d 936 (Fla.1981)—§ 24.4(d) n.63

Odom, United States v., 888 F.2d 1014 (4th Cir.1989)—§ 17.2(d) n.97

Odom, United States v., 674 F.2d 228 (4th Cir.1982)—§ 18.4(c) n.60

Odom, United States v., 526 F.2d 339 (5th Cir.1976)—§§ 3.9(g) n.138, 139

Odoms, State v., 117 Or.App. 1, 844 P.2d 217 (1992)—§ 26.6(e) n.82

Odoms v. State, 102 Nev. 27, 714 P.2d 568 (1986)—§ 9.1(b) n.47

O'Donnell, United States v., 539 F.2d 1233 (9th Cir.1976)—§ 21.6(a) n.57

Odufowora, United States v., 814 F.2d 73 (1st Cir.1987)—§ 12.1(a) n.18

Offutt v. United States, 348 U.S. 11, 75 S.Ct. 11, 99 L.Ed. 11 (1954)—§§ 1.5(i) n.297; 1.7(i) n.158, 166

Ogbudimkpa v. Ashcroft, 342 F.3d 207 (3d Cir.2003)—§ 1.7(c) n.16

Ogbuehi, United States v., 18 F.3d 807 (9th Cir.1994)—§ 27.6(b) n.16

Ogbuh, United States v., 982 F.2d 1000 (6th Cir.1993)—§ 3.6(e) n.111

Ogden, United States v., 572 F.2d 501 (5th Cir.1978)—§ 6.9(d) n.72

Ogden, United States v., 485 F.2d 536 (9th Cir.1973)—§ 3.1(h) n.191

Ogle v. State, 698 N.E.2d 1146 (Ind.1998)—§ 6.8(b) n.50

Ogles, United States v., 440 F.3d 1095 (9th Cir.2006)—§ 25.3(a) n.7

Oglesby, State v., 298 S.C. 279, 379 S.E.2d 891 (1989)—§ 22.3(d) n.242

Oglesby, United States v., 764 F.2d 1273 (7th Cir.1985)—§ 17.2(d) n.101

Oglialoro, Commonwealth v., 525 Pa. 250, 579 A.2d 1288 (1990)—§ 3.2(c) n.140

O'Hagen, State v., 189 N.J. 140, 914 A.2d 267 (2007)—§ 3.5(d) n.156

Ohanian, Commonwealth v., 373 Mass. 839, 370 N.E.2d 695 (1977)—§ 19.6(b) n.10

O'Hara, State v., 627 A.2d 1001 (Me.1993)—§ 22.3(a) n.23

O'Hara, United States v., 301 F.3d 563 (7th Cir.2002)—§§ 13.7(c) n.63; 24.3(b) n.67

O'Hara, United States v., 960 F.2d 11 (2d Cir.1992)—§ 21.5(a) n.43

Ohayon, United States v., 483 F.3d 1281 (11th Cir.2007)—§ 17.4(a) n.6

Ohio v. Johnson, 467 U.S. 493, 104 S.Ct. 2536, 81 L.Ed.2d 425 (1984)—§§ 17.4(a) n.22, 43; 17.4(b) n.113; 21.2(d) n.205; 21.3(f) n.426, 432, 447; 25.1(d) n.57; 25.4(d) n.46

Ohio v. Reiner, 532 U.S. 17, 121 S.Ct. 1252, 149 L.Ed.2d 158 (2001)—§ 8.10(a) n.18

Ohio v. Roberts, 448 U.S. 56, 100 S.Ct. 2531, 65 L.Ed.2d 597 (1980)—§§ 2.8(a) n.6; 14.1(d) n.57; 17.2(b) n.58; 28.6(d) n.26

Ohio v. Robinette, 519 U.S. 33, 117 S.Ct. 417, 136 L.Ed.2d 347 (1996)—§§ 2.9(g) n.163; 2.9(h) n.241; 3.8(c) n.115, 119; 3.10(b) n.62

Ohio Adult Parole Authority, et al. v. Woodard, 523 U.S. 272, 118 S.Ct. 1244, 140 L.Ed.2d 387 (1998)—§§ 2.10(b) n.13; 26.2(c) n.69, 77; 27.1(b) n.21

Ohio ex rel. Eaton v. Price, 364 U.S. 263, 80 S.Ct. 1463, 4 L.Ed.2d 1708 (1960)—§ 2.5(b) n.14

Ohio State ex rel Hartinger v. Court of Common Pleas, 84 Ohio App. 241, 86 N.E.2d 810 (1948)—§ 16.3(d) n.59

Ohler v. United States, 529 U.S. 753, 120 S.Ct. 1851, 146 L.Ed.2d 826 (2000)—§§ 27.5(c) n.111, 112

Oimen v. McCaughtry, 130 F.3d 809 (7th Cir.1997)—§§ 11.4(b) n.27; 11.4(d) n.112

Ojala, United States v., 544 F.2d 940 (8th Cir.1976)—§§ 13.4(b) n.70; 13.4(c) n.117, 121

Ojaniemi, People v., 93 Mich.App. 200, 285 N.W.2d 816 (1979)— § 26.10(b) n.22

Ojeda Rios, United States v., 495 U.S. 257, 110 S.Ct. 1845, 109 L.Ed.2d 224 (1990)—§§ 4.6(k) n.174; 4.6(m) n.239

Ojeda Rios, United States v., 875 F.2d 17 (2d Cir.1989)—§ 4.6(i) n.149

Ojeda Rios, United States v., 846 F.2d 167 (2d Cir.1988)—§ 12.3(d) n.97

Okafor, United States v., 285 F.3d 842 (9th Cir.2002)—§ 6.2(c) n.107

O'Kane, United States v., 439 F.Supp. 211 (S.D.Fla.1977)—§ 8.8(g) n.175

Okeani v. Superior Court, 178 Ariz. 180, 871 P.2d 727 (Ariz.App.1993)— § 27.2(c) n.64

O'Kelley v. State, 278 Ga. 564, 604 S.E.2d 509 (2004)—§ 6.4(e) n.77

Oken v. State, 378 Md. 179, 835 A.2d 1105 (2003)—§ 26.4(i) n.179

Oken v. State, 327 Md. 628, 612 A.2d 258 (1992)—§§ 3.6(f) n.144; 9.1(b) n.52; 9.3(e) n.57

Oklahoma Press Publishing Co. v. Walling, 327 U.S. 186, 66 S.Ct. 494, 90 L.Ed. 614 (1946)—§§ 8.7(a) n.23; 8.7(b) n.32; 8.7(c) n.66; 8.8(b) n.19

Oklahoma Publishing Co. v. City of Moore, 682 P.2d 754 (Okla.1984)— § 1.7(k) n.270

Oklahoma Publishing Co. v. District Court, 430 U.S. 308, 97 S.Ct. 1045, 51 L.Ed.2d 355 (1977)—§§ 23.1(c) n.98, 105

Oklahoma Tax Commission v. Texas Co., 336 U.S. 342, 69 S.Ct. 561, 93 L.Ed. 721 (1949)—§ 2.9(b) n.25

Okonkwo v. Lacy, 104 F.3d 21 (2d Cir.1997)—§ 24.1(b) n.15

Okoronkwo, United States v., 46 F.3d 426 (5th Cir.1995)—§ 22.3(a) n.15

Oksoktaruk v. State, 619 P.2d 480 (Alaska 1980)—§ 26.10(c) n.56

Olafisoye v. United States, 857 A.2d 1078 (D.C.App.2004)—§ 22.1(b) n.42

Olander, State v., 575 N.W.2d 658 (N.D.1998)—§ 27.5(d) n.137

Olano, United States v., 62 F.3d 1180 (9th Cir.1995)—§ 24.9(f) n.85

Olano, United States v., 507 U.S. 725, 113 S.Ct. 1770, 123 L.Ed.2d 508 (1993)—§§ 11.3(c) n.57, 65; 22.3(e) n.285; 24.9(f) n.84; 27.5(d) n.122

Olatunji, United States v., 872 F.2d 1161 (3d Cir.1989)—§ 19.2(a) n.5

Old Chief v. United States, 519 U.S. 172, 117 S.Ct. 644, 136 L.Ed.2d 574 (1997)—§§ 27.5(e) n.147; 28.6(e) n.63

Olden v. Kentucky, 488 U.S. 227, 109 S.Ct. 480, 102 L.Ed.2d 513 (1988)—§ 24.4(b) n.13

Oldroyd, State v., 685 P.2d 551 (Utah 1984)—§ 24.8(f) n.92

O'Leary, State v., 128 N.H. 661, 517 A.2d 1174 (1986)—§ 21.2(f) n.388

O'Leary v. Superior Court, 816 P.2d 163 (Alaska 1991)—§ 8.4(c) n.112

Olesen, United States v., 920 F.2d 538 (8th Cir.1990)—§ 21.4(g) n.257

Olibrices v. State, 929 So.2d 1176 (Fla.2006)—§ 22.3(d) n.199

Olin Corp., United States v., 465 F.Supp. 1120 (S.D.N.Y.1979)—§ 15.7(f) n.157

Olinger, People v., 176 Ill.2d 326, 223 Ill.Dec. 588, 680 N.E.2d 321 (1997)—§ 24.3(d) n.116

Oliphant, State v., 47 Conn.App. 271, 702 A.2d 1206 (1997)—§§ 11.3(b) n.37; 11.4(b) n.23; 11.5(f) n.96, 106

Olis, United States v., 450 F.3d 583 (5th Cir.2006)—§ 12.4(d) n.67

Olish, State v., 164 W.Va. 712, 266 S.E.2d 134 (1980)—§§ 21.5(a) n.24, 28

Olivares, United States v., 292 F.3d 196 (4th Cir.2002)—§ 26.7(a) n.4

Olivares-Rangel, United States v., 458 F.3d 1104 (10th Cir.2006)— § 9.1(a) n.30

Olivas, State v., 122 Wash.2d 73, 856 P.2d 1076 (1993)—§§ 3.5(d) n.145; 21.4(d) n.138

Oliver, In re, 333 U.S. 257, 68 S.Ct. 499, 92 L.Ed. 682 (1948)—§§ 2.4(e) n.154; 2.6(a) n.15, 17; 24.1(a) n.1, 3, 7

Oliver, People v., 111 Mich.App. 734, 314 N.W.2d 740 (1981)—§ 21.2(h) n.423

Oliver, People v., 63 Mich.App. 509, 234 N.W.2d 679 (1975)—§ 3.9(i) n.187

Oliver v. State, 147 P.3d 410 (Utah 2006)—§ 21.4(b) n.59

Oliver, United States v., 363 F.3d 1061 (10th Cir.2004)—§ 3.7(c) n.48

Oliver, United States v., 60 F.3d 547 (9th Cir.1994)—§ 1.2(c) n.148

Oliver, United States v., 931 F.2d 463 (8th Cir.1991)—§ 26.9(b) n.65

Oliver v. United States, 466 U.S. 170, 104 S.Ct. 1735, 80 L.Ed.2d 214 (1984)—§§ 2.9(c) n.51, 52; 2.9(g) n.156, 172, 174; 3.2(c) n.122; 3.2(d) n.153

Oliver, United States v., 683 F.2d 224 (7th Cir.1982)—§ 12.4(g) n.100

Oliver v. United States, 384 A.2d 642 (D.C.App.1978)—§ 1.7(i) n.206

Oliver v. United States, 239 F.2d 818 (8th Cir.1957)—§ 3.9(f) n.89

Oliver v. Wainwright, 782 F.2d 1521 (11th Cir.1986)—§ 27.5(e) n.180

Olivera, People v., 164 Ill.2d 382, 207 Ill.Dec. 433, 647 N.E.2d 926 (1995)—§ 6.9(f) n.137

Oliver, United States ex rel. v. Vincent, 498 F.2d 340 (2d Cir.1974)— § 21.2(g) n.413

Olkon, State v., 299 N.W.2d 89 (Minn.1980)—§§ 15.7(f) n.135, 163

Ollie, United States v., 442 F.3d 1135 (8th Cir.2006)—§§ 6.6(d) n.49; 6.8(b) n.49

Olmstead, United States v., 698 F.2d 224 (4th Cir.1983)—§ 6.2(c) n.176

Olmstead v. United States, 277 U.S. 438, 48 S.Ct. 564, 72 L.Ed. 944, 66 A.L.R. 376 (1928)—§§ 1.5(a) n.61; 1.6(f) n.391; 1.7(h) n.142; 2.8(b) n.36; 4.3(a) n.1

Olney v. United States, 433 F.2d 161 (9th Cir.1970)—§ 10.5(e) n.57

Oloyede, United States v., 982 F.2d 133 (4th Cir.1992)—§ 3.4(a) n.22

Olsen v. Correiro, 189 F.3d 52 (1st Cir.1999)—§ 21.4(a) n.22

Olsen v. Delmore, 48 Wash.2d 545, 295 P.2d 324 (1956)—§ 13.7(a) n.24

Olsen v. Koppy, 593 N.W.2d 762 (N.D.1999)—§§ 13.2(a) n.3; 13.3(b) n.19

Olsen v. State, 67 P.3d 536 (Wyo.2003)—§ 26.5(d) n.74

Olsen, State v., 159 Vt. 448, 620 A.2d 1272 (1992)—§ 3.3(e) n.182

Olsen, State v., 462 N.W.2d 474 (S.D.1990)—§§ 14.3(c) n.63; 14.3(d) n.96

Olson, State v., 311 Mont. 270, 55 P.3d 935 (2002)—§§ 3.6(d) n.96, 97; 9.4(a) n.41

Olson, State v., 449 N.W.2d 251 (S.D.1989)—§ 6.10(c) n.40

Olson, United States v., 450 F.3d 655 (7th Cir.2006)—§ 21.2(h) n.420

Olson, United States v., 408 F.3d 366 (7th Cir.2005)—§ 3.3(c) n.117

Olson, United States v., 262 F.3d 795 (8th Cir.2001)—§§ 19.3(a) n.101, 114

Olson, United States v., 846 F.2d 1103 (7th Cir.1988)—§ 19.3(a) n.62

Olunloyo, United States v., 10 F.3d 578 (8th Cir.1993)—§ 27.5(b) n.45

Olvis, United States v., 97 F.3d 739 (4th Cir.1996)—§ 13.4(b) n.69

O'Malley, United States v., 786 F.2d 786 (7th Cir.1986)—§ 11.9(c) n.140

Omalza v. State, 911 P.2d 286 (Okla.Crim.App.1995)—§§ 16.1(a) n.6, 17; 16.1(g) n.246; 16.1(h) n.292; 16.4(d) n.142

Oman v. State, 737 N.E.2d 1131 (Ind.2000)—§§ 3.9(l) n.276; 8.1(c) n.33; 8.7(a) n.26

O'Meara v. Gottsfield, 174 Ariz. 576, 851 P.2d 1375 (1993)—§ 15.7(g) n.205

Omechinski, State v., 196 W.Va. 41, 468 S.E.2d 173 (1996)—§ 24.4(d) n.39

Omer, United States v., 395 F.3d 1087 (9th Cir.2005)—§ 19.3(a) n.130

One (1) 43 Foot Sailing Vessel, United States v., 405 F.Supp. 879 (S.D.Fla.1975)—§ 3.9(g) n.137

One (1) 1994 Dodge Truck Automobile, United States v., 197 W.Va. 665, 478 S.E.2d 118 (1996)—§ 17.4(b) n.120

One, 1980 Cadillac, State v., 21 P.3d 212 (Utah 2001)—§ 17.4(b) n.120

One 1958 Plymouth Sedan v. Pennsylvania, 380 U.S. 693, 85 S.Ct. 1246, 14 L.Ed.2d 170 (1965)—§ 3.1(g) n.165

One 1965 Econoline, In re, 109 Ariz. 433, 511 P.2d 168 (1973)—§ 3.7(f) n.148

One 1987 Toyota Pickup, State v., 233 Neb. 670, 447 N.W.2d 243 (1989)—§ 3.9(g) n.124

O'Neal v. Delo, 44 F.3d 655 (8th Cir.1995)—§§ 15.4(d) n.100, 124

O'Neal v. Lampert, 199 F.Supp.2d 1064 (D.Or.2002)—§ 28.5(b) n.62

O'Neal v. McAninch, 513 U.S. 432, 115 S.Ct. 992, 130 L.Ed.2d 947 (1995)—§§ 27.6(b) n.51, 54; 28.6(g) n.84

O'Neal, State v., 87 Ohio St.3d 402, 721 N.E.2d 73 (2000)—§ 22.3(d) n.250

O'Neal v. United States, 222 F.2d 411 (D.C.Cir.1955)—§ 10.1(b) n.17

One Assortment of 89 Firearms, United States v., 465 U.S. 354, 104 S.Ct. 1099, 79 L.Ed.2d 361 (1984)—§§ 1.5(f) n.251; 17.4(a) n.25, 26; 25.1(c) n.33

O'Neil, State v., 261 Conn. 49, 801 A.2d 730 (2002)—§ 24.9(d) n.48

O'Neil, United States v., 118 F.3d 65 (2d Cir.1997)—§ 11.9(d) n.170

O'Neil v. Vermont, 144 U.S. 323, 12 S.Ct. 693, 36 L.Ed. 450 (1892)—§§ 2.3(a) n.9; 2.3(b) n.83, 85

O'Neill, People v., 803 P.2d 164 (Colo.1990)—§ 22.3(a) n.35

O'Neill, United States v., 437 F.3d 654 (7th Cir.2006)—§§ 21.2(c) n.118; 21.3(d) n.225; 21.3(e) n.283

O'Neill, United States v., 497 F.2d 1020 (6th Cir.1974)—§ 4.6(e) n.111

One Lot Emerald Cut Stones v. United States, 409 U.S. 232, 93 S.Ct. 489, 34 L.Ed.2d 438 (1972)—§§ 17.4(a) n.25, 35; 25.1(c) n.22

One Parcel of Real Property, United States v., 960 F.2d 200 (1st Cir.1992)—§ 13.5(h) n.185

One Star, United States v., 465 F.3d 828 (8th Cir.2006)—§ 9.6(a) n.35

Ong, United States v., 541 F.2d 331 (2d Cir.1976)—§ 17.3(c) n.38

On Lee v. United States, 343 U.S. 747, 72 S.Ct. 967, 96 L.Ed. 1270 (1952)—§§ 3.10(c) n.80; 4.6(l) n.197

Ontiveros, State v., 82 Haw. 446, 923 P.2d 388 (1996)—§§ 17.4(b) n.124; 27.2(c) n.60

Opinion of the Justices, 137 N.H. 100, 623 A.2d 1334 (1993)—§§ 22.3(e) n.265, 276, 279

Opinion of the Justices, 121 N.H. 531, 431 A.2d 144 (1981)—§ 26.9(b) n.41

Opinion of the Justices to the Governor, 373 Mass. 915, 371 N.E.2d 422 (1977)—§ 8.14(a) n.20

Oplinger, United States v., 150 F.3d 1061 (9th Cir.1998)—§ 9.6(a) n.48

Oppel v. Lopes, 200 Conn. 553, 512 A.2d 888 (1986)—§ 21.4(c) n.90

Oppel v. Meachum, 851 F.2d 34 (2d Cir.1988)—§ 21.4(c) n.88

Opper v. United States, 348 U.S. 84, 75 S.Ct. 158, 99 L.Ed. 101 (1954)—§ 17.2(f) n.135

Opperman, State v., 247 N.W.2d 673 (S.D.1976)—§§ 2.12(a) n.26, 28; 3.7(e) n.95

Opperman, State v., 89 S.D. 25, 228 N.W.2d 152 (1975)—§ 2.12(a) n.24

Opsta, United States v., 659 F.2d 848 (8th Cir.1981)—§ 19.3(a) n.46

Oquendo, State v., 223 Conn. 635, 613 A.2d 1300 (1992)—§§ 2.12(e) n.213; 3.8(c) n.109; 27.6(c) n.67

Orange, In re, 152 Wash.2d 795, 100 P.3d 291 (2005)—§ 24.1(a) n.11

Orange, United States v., 447 F.3d 792 (9th Cir.2006)—§ 22.2(d) n.76

Orazio v. Dugger, 876 F.2d 1508 (11th Cir.1989)—§ 11.10(c) n.125

Orbino, United States v., 981 F.2d 1035 (9th Cir.1992)—§ 18.3(b) n.5

Order Authorizing Roving Interception, In re, 349 F.3d 1132 (9th Cir.2003)—§ 4.6(g) n.139

Order on Prosecution of Criminal Appeals by Tenth Judicial Circuit Public Defender, In re, 561 So.2d 1130 (Fla.1990)—§ 11.8(c) n.69

Ordunez v. Bean, 579 S.W.2d 911 (Tex.Cr.App.1979)—§ 27.4(c) n.23

O'Rear, People v., 220 Cal.App.2d Supp. 927, 34 Cal.Rptr. 61 (1963)—§ 13.2(c) n.71

Oreck, People v., 74 Cal.App.2d 215, 168 P.2d 186 (1946)—§ 13.4(c) n.100

O'Regan v. Schermerhorn, 25 N.J.Misc. 1, 50 A.2d 10 (1946)—§§ 15.1(d) n.162, 166

Oregon v. Bradshaw, 462 U.S. 1039, 103 S.Ct. 2830, 77 L.Ed.2d 405 (1983)—§ 6.9(f) n.128

Oregon v. Elstad, 470 U.S. 298, 105 S.Ct. 1285, 84 L.Ed.2d 222 (1985)—§§ 2.9(f) n.143; 2.10(b) n.24; 2.10(c) n.101; 6.8(b) n.46; 9.4(a) n.42; 9.5(a) n.19; 9.5(b) n.38

Oregon v. Guzek, 546 U.S. 517, 126 S.Ct. 1226, 163 L.Ed.2d 1112 (2006)—§§ 26.1(b) n.21, 24

Oregon v. Hass, 420 U.S. 714, 95 S.Ct. 1215, 43 L.Ed.2d 570 (1975)—§§ 2.9(f) n.142; 2.12(a) n.21 to 23, 26; 9.6(a) n.20

Oregon v. Kennedy, 456 U.S. 667, 102 S.Ct. 2083, 72 L.Ed.2d 416 (1982)—§§ 2.12(a) n.26; 25.2(b) n.13; 25.2(c) n.19; 25.4(a) n.5

Oregon v. Mathiason, 429 U.S. 492, 97 S.Ct. 711, 50 L.Ed.2d 714 (1977)—§§ 6.6(c) n.23, 36; 6.6(d) n.47

Oregon v. Wilson, 323 Ore. 498, 918 P.2d 826 (1996)—§ 27.6(d) n.84

Oregon City Elks Lodge No. 1189, State v., 17 Or.App. 124, 520 P.2d 900 (1974)—§ 3.2(e) n.164

Oregonian Publishing Co. v. United States District Court, 920 F.2d 1462 (9th Cir.1990)—§§ 21.4(b) n.52; 23.1(d) n.183

O'Reilly v. United States, 486 F.2d 208 (8th Cir.1973)—§ 3.7(d) n.71

Oren, State v., 160 Vt. 245, 627 A.2d 337 (1993)—§ 27.3(d) n.59

Orena, United States v., 986 F.2d 628 (2d Cir.1993)—§§ 12.2(b) n.30; 12.3(a) n.21

Oreye, United States v., 263 F.3d 669 (7th Cir.2001)—§§ 11.3(c) n.62; 11.5(f) n.104, 105

Organek, United States v., 65 F.3d 60 (6th Cir.1995)—§ 26.3(g) n.93

Organizacion JD Ltda. v. United States Dep't of Justice, 18 F.3d 91 (2d Cir.1994)—§ 4.6(n) n.247

Organizacion Jd Ltda. v. U.S. Dept. of Justice, 124 F.3d 354 (2d Cir.1997)—§ 4.8(c) n.23

Oriakhi, United States v., 57 F.3d 1290 (4th Cir.1995)—§ 4.6(e) n.97

Orians, State v., 335 Or. 257, 66 P.3d 468 (2003)—§ 13.2(c) n.68

Original Grand Jury Investigation, In re, 89 Ohio St.3d 544, 733 N.E.2d 1135 (2000)—§ 8.8(d) n.88

Orin, People v., 13 Cal.3d 937, 120 Cal.Rptr. 65, 533 P.2d 193 (1975)—§ 13.2(c) n.63

Orisnord, United States v., 483 F.3d 1169 (11th Cir.2007)—§ 5.2(a) n.8

Orjuela, United States v., 809 F.Supp. 193 (E.D.N.Y.1992)—§§ 15.5(b) n.90, 94; 15.6(b) n.74; 15.7(a) n.8; 15.7(e) n.101

Orlandez-Gamboa, United States v., 320 F.3d 328 (2d Cir.2003)—§ 21.2(h) n.420

Orlando, United States ex rel. v. Fay, 350 F.2d 967 (2d Cir.1965)—§ 24.1(b) n.20

Orlosky, People v., 40 Cal.App.3d 935, 115 Cal.Rptr. 598 (1974)—§ 2.12(c) n.171

Orman v. Cain, 228 F.3d 616 (5th Cir.2000)—§ 21.4(f) n.207

Orme v. State, 677 So.2d 258 (Fla.1996)—§ 6.9(b) n.35

Ormsby, United States v., 252 F.3d 844 (6th Cir.2001)—§ 21.6(b) n.94

Ornelas v. United States, 517 U.S. 690, 116 S.Ct. 1657, 134 L.Ed.2d 911 (1996)—§§ 27.5(e) n.173, 174, 178

Ornelas v. United States, 840 F.2d 890 (11th Cir.1988)—§ 15.1(f) n.324

Ornelas-Ledesma, United States v., 16 F.3d 714 (7th Cir.1994)—§§ 1.5(j) n.324; 10.6(b) n.15

Orona v. District Court, 184 Colo. 55, 518 P.2d 839 (1974)—§ 12.4(a) n.22

Orosco, State v., 113 N.M. 780, 833 P.2d 1146 (1992)—§ 27.5(c) n.100

Orozco v. Day, 281 Mont. 341, 934 P.2d 1009 (1997)—§§ 26.2(c) n.63; 27.4(f) n.63

Orozco v. Texas, 394 U.S. 324, 89 S.Ct. 1095, 22 L.Ed.2d 311 (1969)—§§ 6.6(c) n.22; 6.6(e) n.64; 6.7(b) n.84; 9.5(a) n.12

Orozco, United States v., 630 F.Supp. 1418 (S.D.Cal.1986)—§ 15.7(d) n.80

Orr v. People, 803 P.2d 509 (Colo.1990)—§§ 3.9(g) n.134, 135

Orr, State v., 262 Kan. 312, 940 P.2d 42 (1997)—§§ 6.9(b) n.20; 27.5(e) n.180

Orr, State v., 123 Idaho 55, 844 P.2d 684 (1992)—§ 21.5(e) n.127

ORS, Inc., United States v., 997 F.2d 628 (9th Cir.1993)—§ 19.3(b) n.156

Orso, United States v., 266 F.3d 1030 (9th Cir.2001)—§§ 6.5(b) n.24; 6.7(c) n.111; 9.5(c) n.67

Orso, United States v., 234 F.3d 436 (9th Cir.2000)—§ 9.5(c) n.68

Orta, United States v., 760 F.2d 887 (8th Cir.1985)—§ 12.3(a) n.22

Ortega v. O'Leary, 843 F.2d 258 (7th Cir.1988)—§§ 11.6(c) n.100; 11.6(d) n.126; 27.6(d) n.95

Ortega, People v., 209 Ill.2d 354, 283 Ill.Dec. 530, 808 N.E.2d 496 (2004)—§ 11.9(c) n.115

Ortega, State v., 198 N.J.Super. 161, 486 A.2d 904 (1985)—§ 20.4(f) n.98

Ortega-Ascanio, United States v., 376 F.3d 879 (8th Cir.2004)—§ 21.5(a) n.46

Ortega-Rodriguez v. United States, 507 U.S. 234, 113 S.Ct. 1199, 122 L.Ed.2d 581 (1993)—§§ 27.5(c) n.69, 72, 74

Orth, State v., 178 W.Va. 303, 359 S.E.2d 136 (1987)—§ 13.2(a) n.3

Ortiz, Commonwealth v., 435 Mass. 569, 760 N.E.2d 282 (2002)—§ 6.2(c) n.147

Ortiz, People v., 51 Cal.3d 975, 275 Cal.Rptr. 191, 800 P.2d 547 (1990)—§§ 11.4(b) n.23; 11.4(c) n.61, 70

Ortiz, People v., 76 N.Y.2d 652, 563 N.Y.S.2d 20, 564 N.E.2d 630 (1990)—§ 11.9(d) n.203

Ortiz v. State, 869 A.2d 285 (Del.2005)—§ 26.2(b) n.8

Ortiz, State v., 252 Conn. 533, 747 A.2d 487 (2000)—§ 7.4(b) n.11

Ortiz v. State, 933 S.W.2d 102 (Tex.Cr.App.1996)—§§ 21.3(f) n.428; 21.4(g) n.248; 21.5(a) n.7; 25.1(d) n.65

Ortiz, United States v., 315 F.3d 873 (8th Cir.2002)—§§ 17.2(b) n.69, 71; 17.2(d) n.95; 17.2(f) n.133; 22.3(a) n.22, 35

Ortiz, United States v., 82 F.3d 1066 (D.C.Cir.1996)—§ 11.6(c) n.100

Ortiz, United States v., 993 F.2d 204 (10th Cir.1993)—§§ 26.4(f) n.91; 26.5(a) n.14

Ortiz, United States v., 422 U.S. 891, 95 S.Ct. 2585, 45 L.Ed.2d 623 (1975)—§§ 3.3(b) n.49; 3.9(f) n.116

Ortiz, United States v., 496 F.2d 705 (2d Cir.1974)—§ 5.3(a) n.12

Ortiz-Santiago, United States v., 211 F.3d 146 (1st Cir.2000)—§ 21.2(d) n.157

Ortiz-Torres, United States v., 449 F.3d 61 (1st Cir.2006)—§ 21.2(b) n.57

Oruche, United States v., 484 F.3d 590 (D.C.Cir.2007)—§ 24.3(c) n.98

Oryang v. State, 642 So.2d 979 (Ala.Crim.App.1993)—§ 16.3(b) n.22

Orzechowski, United States v., 547 F.2d 978 (7th Cir.1976)—§ 17.3(b) n.12

Osakalumi, State v., 194 W.Va. 758, 461 S.E.2d 504 (1995)—§ 24.3(e) n.136

Osband, People v., 13 Cal.4th 622, 55 Cal.Rptr.2d 26, 919 P.2d 640 (1996)—§§ 24.8(a) n.20; 27.6(b) n.43

Osborn v. Shillinger, 861 F.2d 612 (10th Cir.1988)—§ 11.10(c) n.71

Osborn, State v., 345 Ark. 196, 45 S.W.3d 373 (2001)—§§ 16.1(a) n.26; 16.2(e) n.80

Osborn v. State, 806 P.2d 259 (Wyo.1991)—§ 27.5(b) n.49

Osborne v. Ohio, 495 U.S. 103, 110 S.Ct. 1691, 109 L.Ed.2d 98 (1990)—§ 28.4(b) n.21

Osborne v. State, 754 N.E.2d 916 (Ind.2001)—§§ 6.9(f) n.137; 24.4(d) n.64

Osborne, State v., 301 S.C. 363, 392 S.E.2d 178 (1990)—§ 6.2(c) n.96

Osborne v. State, 304 Md. 323, 499 A.2d 170 (1985)—§ 21.2(g) n.394

Osborne, State v., 102 Wash.2d 87, 684 P.2d 683 (1984)—§ 21.4(c) n.79

Osborne, United States v., 68 F.3d 94 (5th Cir.1995)—§ 24.1(b) n.18

Osborne, United States v., 931 F.2d 1139 (7th Cir.1991)—§ 21.2(d) n.219

Osborne, United States v., 591 F.2d 413 (8th Cir.1978)—§ 21.5(e) n.112

Osburn, State v., 211 Kan. 248, 505 P.2d 742 (1973)—§ 24.10(a) n.17

Oseni, United States v., 996 F.2d 186 (7th Cir.1993)—§ 25.4(a) n.9

Oses v. Massachusetts, 961 F.2d 985 (1st Cir.1992)—§ 11.5(f) n.98

O'Shea, Commonwealth v., 456 Pa. 288, 318 A.2d 713 (1974)—§ 6.6(c) n.27

O'Shea, United States v., 447 F.Supp. 330 (S.D.Fla.1978)—§§ 15.2(f) n.151; 15.5(a) n.4

Osorio, United States v., 801 F.Supp. 966 (D.Conn.1992)—§ 15.4(d) n.123

Osorio, United States v., 929 F.2d 753 (1st Cir.1991)—§§ 21.3(b) n.110; 24.3(b) n.51, 68

Osorio, United States v., 949 F.2d 38 (2d Cir.1991)—§ 9.1(b) n.78

Osorio-Pena, United States v., 247 F.3d 14 (1st Cir.2001)—§ 11.7(e) n.70

Osslo, In re, 51 Cal.2d 371, 334 P.2d 1 (1958)—§ 26.1(d) n.89

Ostafin v. State, 564 N.W.2d 616 (N.D.1997)—§ 21.2(e) n.324

Ostafin v. State, 1997 N.D. 102, 564 N.W.2d 616 (1997)—§ 21.2(b) n.67

Osteen, United States v., 254 F.3d 521 (4th Cir.2001)—§ 25.1(d) n.49

Osterburg, United States v., 423 F.2d 704 (9th Cir.1970)—§ 6.8(b) n.56

Osterloth, State v., 299 Mont. 517, 1 P.3d 946 (2000)—§ 21.2(g) n.394

Ostler, State v., 31 P.3d 528 (Utah 2001)—§ 21.3(f) n.419

Ostman v. Eight Judicial District Court, 107 Nev. 563, 816 P.2d 458 (Nev.1991)—§ 15.7(f) n.174

Ostrander, State ex rel. v. Wilt, 164 W.Va. 184, 262 S.E.2d 420 (1980)—§ 26.10(b) n.16

O'Sullivan v. Boerckel, 526 U.S. 838, 119 S.Ct. 1728, 144 L.Ed.2d 1 (1999)—§§ 28.5(a) n.2, 38

Otello, People v., 48 A.D.2d 169, 368 N.Y.S.2d 592 (1975)—§ 15.2(c) n.77

Otinger, Ex parte, 493 So.2d 1362 (Ala.1986)—§ 21.2(d) n.219

O'Tinger v. State, 342 So.2d 1343 (Ala.Crim.App.1977)—§ 6.2(c) n.104

Otis, Commonwealth v., 364 Pa.Super. 464, 528 A.2d 249 (1987)—§ 14.3(a) n.31

O'Toole, Commonwealth v., 351 Mass. 627, 223 N.E.2d 87 (1967)—§ 6.6(c) n.37

Otte, State v., 887 So.2d 1186 (Fla.2004)—§ 4.6(c) n.54

Otte, State v., 74 Ohio St.3d 555, 660 N.E.2d 711 (1996)—§§ 9.1(d) n.132, 136

Ouber v. Guarino, 293 F.3d 19 (1st Cir.2002)—§§ 11.10(a) n.29; 11.10(c) n.90

Ouellette, State v., 145 N.H. 489, 764 A.2d 914 (2000)—§§ 19.3(a) n.38, 41

Oughterson, State v., 99 Haw. 244, 54 P.3d 415 (2002)—§ 13.2(c) n.75

Ouimette v. Moran, 942 F.2d 1 (1st Cir.1991)—§§ 24.3(d) n.107, 111

Ouimette, United States v., 137 F.3d 24 (1st Cir.1998)—§ 22.3(b) n.70

Ouk, State v., 516 N.W.2d 180 (Minn.1994)—§ 6.8(d) n.84

Outen, United States v., 286 F.3d 622 (2d Cir.2002)—§ 26.4(h) n.159

Outerbridge v. State, 947 So.2d 279 (Miss.2006)—§§ 7.4(c) n.49, 50, 53

Outland, United States v., 476 F.2d 581 (6th Cir.1973)—§ 3.3(g) n.238

Outlaw, State v., 216 Conn. 492, 582 A.2d 751 (1990)—§ 14.1(d) n.64

Outlaw, State v., 326 N.C. 467, 390 S.E.2d 336 (1990)—§§ 21.4(a) n.22, 23

Outten, State v., 206 So.2d 392 (Fla.1968)—§ 6.4(c) n.44

Ovalle, United States v., 136 F.3d 1092 (6th Cir.1998)—§§ 22.2(a) n.13; 22.2(c) n.44; 22.2(d) n.95

Overman, People v., 126 Cal.App.4th 1344, 24 Cal.Rptr.3d 798 (2005)—§ 24.8(f) n.106

Overmyer, United States v., 899 F.2d 457 (6th Cir.1990)—§ 8.11(c) n.46

Overstock Book Co. v. Barry, 436 F.2d 1289 (2d Cir.1970)—§ 3.4(a) n.6

Overton v. State, 801 So.2d 877 (Fla.2001)—§ 22.3(c) n.106

Owen v. City of Independence, 445 U.S. 622, 100 S.Ct. 1398, 63 L.Ed.2d 673 (1980)—§ 3.1(k) n.271

Owen, State v., 129 Idaho 920, 935 P.2d 183 (1997)—§ 19.2(c) n.37

Owen, State v., 696 So.2d 715 (Fla.1997)—§ 6.9(g) n.161

Owen v. State, 596 So.2d 985 (Fla.1992)—§ 6.4(e) n.76

Owen v. State, 560 So.2d 207 (Fla.1990)—§ 6.9(g) n.159

Owen v. State, 656 S.W.2d 458 (Tex.Cr.App.1983)—§ 24.5(b) n.34

Owen, State v., 5 N.C. 452, 1 Mur. 452 (1810)—§§ 1.6(d) n.282; 19.1(a) n.5

Owen F., In re, 70 Md.App. 678, 523 A.2d 627 (1987)—§ 9.5(b) n.42

Owens v. Kelley, 681 F.2d 1362 (11th Cir.1982)—§§ 26.9(b) n.66; 26.9(c) n.83

Owens, People v., 969 P.2d 704 (Colo.1999)—§ 6.8(a) n.5

Owens, People v., 69 N.Y.2d 585, 516 N.Y.S.2d 619, 509 N.E.2d 314 (1987)—§ 24.8(a) n.21

Owens, People v., 74 Mich.App. 191, 253 N.W.2d 706 (1977)—§ 20.6(b) n.44

Owens, People v., 126 Ill.App.2d 379, 261 N.E.2d 785 (1970)—§ 7.4(b) n.21

Owens v. State, 399 Md. 388, 924 A.2d 1072 (2007)—§ 22.3(a) n.4

Owens v. State, 906 A.2d 989 (Md.App.2006)—§ 22.3(c) n.162

Owens v. State, 354 Ark. 644, 128 S.W.3d 445 (2003)—§ 13.4(b) n.42

Owens, State v., 643 N.W.2d 735 (S.D.2002)—§§ 6.2(c) n.125, 127

Owens v. State, 322 Md. 616, 589 A.2d 59 (1991)—§§ 9.1(b) n.86, 91

Owens, State v., 148 Wis.2d 922, 436 N.W.2d 869 (1989)—§§ 6.2(c) n.111, 182

Owens v. State, 463 So.2d 408 (Fla.App.1985)—§ 11.10(c) n.70

Owens, State v., 54 N.J. 153, 254 A.2d 97 (1969)—§ 15.1(d) n.234

Owens v. United States, 387 F.3d 607 (7th Cir.2004)—§ 11.10(d) n.181

Owens, United States v., 933 F.Supp. 76 (D.Mass.1996)—§ 20.3(m) n.254

Owens, United States v., 996 F.2d 59 (5th Cir.1993)—§ 21.6(a) n.25

Owens, United States v., 782 F.2d 146 (10th Cir.1986)—§ 3.10(e) n.156

Owens, United States v., 332 A.2d 752 (D.C.App.1975)—§ 19.3(a) n.55

Owens Against Coker, In re Complaint of, 810 A.2d 172 (Pa.Super.2002)—§ 13.3(b) n.19

Owens-El v. Robinson, 442 F.Supp. 1368 (W.D.Pa.1978)—§ 11.5(e) n.92

Ownbey v. Morgan, 256 U.S. 94, 41 S.Ct. 433, 65 L.Ed. 837 (1921)—§§ 2.4(e) n.174; 2.7(c) n.110

Ownes v. State, 825 So.2d 861 (Ala.Crim.App.2001)—§ 19.3(e) n.245

Oxendine, State v., 303 N.C. 235, 278 S.E.2d 200 (1981)—§§ 15.4(g) n.167, 169

Oxley, State v., 127 N.H. 407, 503 A.2d 756 (1985)—§ 3.3(f) n.213

Oyegbola, United States v., 961 F.2d 11 (1st Cir.1992)—§ 21.2(d) n.193

Oyler v. Boles, 368 U.S. 448, 82 S.Ct. 501, 7 L.Ed.2d 446 (1962)—§§ 2.7(a) n.58; 13.4(a) n.8, 9; 13.4(b) n.51; 13.4(c) n.79; 13.4(d) n.146; 26.6(b) n.7, 9, 12; 26.7(d) n.39

Oyoghok v. Anchorage, 641 P.2d 1267 (Alaska App.1982)—§ 26.9(b) n.76

Ozar, United States v., 50 F.3d 1440 (8th Cir.1995)—§ 4.6(h) n.147

Ozuna, United States v., 170 F.3d 654 (6th Cir.1999)—§ 6.6(e) n.93

P

Paaaina, State v., 67 Haw. 408, 689 P.2d 754 (1984)—§ 26.5(c) n.49

Pabian, United States v., 704 F.2d 1533 (11th Cir.1983)—§§ 15.2(c) n.66; 15.2(h) n.187

Paccione, United States v., 949 F.2d 1183 (2d Cir.1991)—§ 22.3(b) n.68

Pace, Ex parte, 775 So.2d 814 (Ala.2000)—§§ 11.4(a) n.2; 11.4(c) n.56

Pace v. DiGugliemo, 544 U.S. 408, 125 S.Ct. 1807, 161 L.Ed.2d 669 (2005)—§§ 28.5(b) n.48, 60

Pace, People v., 102 Mich.App. 522, 302 N.W.2d 216 (1980)—§§ 20.6(b) n.31, 42

Pace, State v., 67 N.J. 222, 337 A.2d 33 (1975)—§ 6.10(c) n.48

Pace, United States v., 201 F.3d 1116 (9th Cir.2000)—§§ 27.2(b) n.13; 27.2(c) n.59

Pace v. United States, 705 A.2d 673 (D.C.App.1998)—§§ 19.5(b) n.15, 17, 24, 30; 19.6(b) n.15

Pace, United States v., 955 F.2d 270 (5th Cir.1992)—§§ 3.2(c) n.126; 3.2(e) n.165

Pace, United States v., 898 F.2d 1218 (7th Cir.1990)—§ 3.8(b) n.32

Pace, United States v., 833 F.2d 1307 (9th Cir.1987)—§§ 6.4(e) n.69; 6.10(b) n.16

Pacee v. State, 306 Ark. 563, 816 S.W.2d 856 (1991)—§ 22.3(d) n.220

Pacella, United States v., 622 F.2d 640 (2d Cir.1980)—§ 8.9(b) n.28

Pacente, United States v., 490 F.2d 661 (7th Cir.1973)—§ 17.1(e) n.64

Pachay, United States v., 711 F.2d 488 (2d Cir.1983)—§ 22.1(h) n.160

Pacheco, State v., 141 N.M. 340, 155 P.3d 745 (2007)—§ 24.9(f) n.76

Pacheco, United States v., 434 F.3d 106 (1st Cir.2006)—§ 24.7(d) n.35

Pacheco-Ortiz, United States v., 889 F.2d 301 (1st Cir.1989)—§§ 1.7(j) n.236; 8.10(d) n.110, 113

Pacific and Southern Co., Inc., Matter of, 257 Ga. 484, 361 S.E.2d 159 (1987)—§ 23.1(e) n.239

Pacific Mutual Life Insurance Co. v. Haslip, 499 U.S. 1, 111 S.Ct. 1032, 113 L.Ed.2d 1 (1991)—§§ 2.4(b) n.21 to 23, 28, 31; 2.4(c) n.112; 2.4(e) n.178; 2.7(c) n.129, 141, 148, 149, 163; 2.9(d) n.66, 92

Pack, People v., 224 Ill.2d 144, 862 N.E.2d 938 (Ill.2007)—§ 28.11(b) n.21

Pack, People v., 179 Misc. 316, 39 N.Y.S.2d 302 (Sup.Ct.1942)—§ 15.2(h) n.192

Packel v. Mirarchi, 458 Pa. 602, 327 A.2d 53 (1974)—§ 8.4(b) n.109

Packer v. Hill, 277 F.3d 1092 (9th Cir.2002)—§ 24.9(d) n.48

Packer, United States v., 730 F.2d 1151 (8th Cir.1984)—§ 27.6(d) n.93

Packwood, United States v., 848 F.2d 1009 (9th Cir.1988)—§§ 8.11(e) n.108; 21.2(d) n.242

Paddy v. United States, 143 F.2d 847 (9th Cir.1944)—§ 6.3(a) n.7

Padgett v. Donald, 401 F.3d 1273 (11th Cir.2005)—§§ 3.2(g) n.195, 199

Padgett, State v., 410 N.W.2d 143 (N.D.1987)—§ 18.5(b) n.69

Padgett v. State, 717 S.W.2d 55 (Tex.Cr.App.1986)—§ 24.10(a) n.15

Padie v. State, 594 P.2d 50 (Alaska 1979)—§ 18.5(a) n.51

Padilla, People v., 907 P.2d 601 (Colo.1995)—§§ 26.4(f) n.101; 26.4(g) n.127

Padilla, State v., 139 N.M. 700, 137 P.3d 640 (App.2006)—§ 18.4(c) n.32

Padilla, State v., 132 N.M. 247, 46 P.3d 1247 (2002)—§§ 24.2(b) n.27; 27.5(c) n.63

Padilla, State v., 84 Wash.App. 523, 928 P.2d 1141 (1997)—§ 25.4(d) n.46

Padilla, State v., 122 N.M. 92, 920 P.2d 1046 (1996)—§ 24.5(b) n.31

Padilla, State v., 176 Ariz. 81, 859 P.2d 191 (App.1993)—§ 11.9(d) n.186

Padilla v. Superior Court, 133 Ariz. 488, 652 P.2d 561 (App.1982)—§ 26.10(b) n.16

Padilla, United States v., 415 F.3d 211 (1st Cir.2005)—§§ 26.9(a) n.1; 27.5(d) n.128

Padilla, United States v., 387 F.3d 1087 (9th Cir.2004)—§ 6.7(c) n.123

Padilla, United States v., 203 F.3d 156 (2d Cir.2000)—§§ 11.8(a) n.3; 11.8(b) n.29

Padilla, United States v., 23 F.3d 1220 (7th Cir.1994)—§ 21.5(c) n.86

Padilla, United States v., 508 U.S. 77, 113 S.Ct. 1936, 123 L.Ed.2d 635 (1993)—§ 9.2(c) n.34

Padilla, United States v., 819 F.2d 952 (10th Cir.1987)—§§ 6.7(b) n.90; 11.3(b) n.24, 33; 11.5(c) n.52; 18.2(c) n.49

Padilla, United States v., 520 F.2d 526 (1st Cir.1975)—§ 4.6(l) n.199

Padilla ex rel Newman v. Bush, 233 F.Supp.2d 564 (S.D.N.Y.2002)—§ 11.8(b) n.44

Padilla-Galarza, United States v., 351 F.3d 594 (1st Cir.2003)—§§ 21.4(c) n.73; 21.4(f) n.207; 21.5(b) n.66

Padilla-Martinez, United States v., 762 F.2d 942 (11th Cir.1985)—§ 11.9(c) n.113

Padin, United States v., 787 F.2d 1071 (6th Cir.1986)—§ 24.3(c) n.99

Padron v. State, 328 So.2d 216 (Fla.App.1976)—§ 3.10(d) n.121

Paez v. State, 681 S.W.2d 34 (Tex.Cr.App.1984)—§ 6.10(c) n.37

Pagan v. United States, 353 F.3d 1343 (11th Cir.2003)—§ 27.2(c) n.25

Page v. Palmateer, 336 Or. 379, 84 P.3d 133 (2004)—§ 28.11(b) n.15

Page, People v., 296 A.D.2d 427, 745 N.Y.S.2d 193 (2002)—§ 24.3(b) n.68

Page, People v., 88 N.Y.2d 1, 643 N.Y.S.2d 1, 665 N.E.2d 1041 (1996)—§§ 22.1(h) n.135; 22.3(e) n.272

Page, People v., 155 Ill.2d 232, 185 Ill.Dec. 475, 614 N.E.2d 1160 (1993)—§ 10.6(d) n.45

Page, State v., 709 N.W.2d 739 (S.D.2006)—§ 22.4(c) n.29

Page, State v., 709 A.2d 1042 (R.I.1998)—§ 6.9(b) n.38

Page v. State, 615 N.E.2d 894 (Ind.1993)—§ 21.3(b) n.80

Page, State v., 386 N.W.2d 330 (Minn.App.1986)—§ 4.6(b) n.49

Page, United States v., 167 F.3d 325 (6th Cir.1999)—§ 1.2(c) n.172

Page, United States v., 69 F.3d 482 (11th Cir.1995)—§ 27.5(a) n.14

Page v. United States, 884 F.2d 300 (7th Cir.1989)—§ 11.10(c) n.117

Page, United States v., 808 F.2d 723 (10th Cir.1987)—§ 15.6(e) n.158

Page, United States v., 661 F.2d 1080 (5th Cir.1981)—§ 22.1(h) n.137

Paget, State v., 134 Or.App. 476, 896 P.2d 1 (1995)—§ 16.1(d) n.139

Pagliari, People v., 47 Ill.App.3d 708, 7 Ill.Dec. 787, 365 N.E.2d 72 (1977)—§ 9.4(f) n.113

Paige, State v., 316 N.C. 630, 343 S.E.2d 848 (1986)—§ 7.5(a) n.8

Paige v. United States, 493 F.2d 22 (9th Cir.1974)—§ 15.4(b) n.66

Pailin, State v., 576 A.2d 1384 (R.I.1990)—§ 7.4(f) n.101

Paille, People v., 383 Mich. 621, 178 N.W.2d 465 (1970)—§§ 14.3(a) n.35; 14.3(b) n.48; 14.3(c) n.63

Paine v. McCarthy, 527 F.2d 173 (9th Cir.1975)—§ 18.4(a) n.14

Painter v. State, 157 Md.App. 1, 848 A.2d 692 (2004)—§§ 18.4(c) n.35, 37, 72

Painter v. State, 762 P.2d 990 (Okla.1988)—§§ 11.3(c) n.59, 66

Paiz, State v., 777 S.W.2d 575 (Tex.App.1989)—§ 16.4(c) n.104

Pakacki, Commonwealth v., 587 Pa. 511, 901 A.2d 983 (2006)—§ 6.6(e) n.91

Palacio, People v., 240 Ill.App.3d 1078, 180 Ill.Dec. 862, 607 N.E.2d 1375 (1993)—§ 27.5(a) n.23

Paladino, United States v., 401 F.3d 471 (7th Cir.2005)—§ 27.5(d) n.134

Palazo, People v., 556 N.Y.S.2d 432, 147 Misc.2d 829 (N.Y.Sup.1990)—§ 26.5(b) n.27

Palazzolo v. Gorcyca, 244 F.3d 512 (6th Cir.2001)—§§ 25.3(a) n.9; 25.4(d) n.48

Palenkas, State v., 188 Ariz. 201, 933 P.2d 1269 (1996)—§ 24.7(e) n.57

Paleo, State v., 200 Ariz. 42, 22 P.3d 35 (2001)—§ 22.3(d) n.210

Palermo, State v., 224 Kan. 275, 579 P.2d 718 (1978)—§§ 16.4(c) n.64, 100

Palermo v. United States, 360 U.S. 343, 79 S.Ct. 1217, 3 L.Ed.2d 1287 (1959)—§§ 6.5(e) n.88; 20.3(b) n.52, 53; 24.3(c) n.101

Palermo v. Warden, 545 F.2d 286 (2d Cir.1976)—§§ 21.2(e) n.324, 340

Palfy v. Cardwell, 448 F.2d 328 (6th Cir.1971)—§ 11.6(a) n.62

Palko v. Connecticut, 302 U.S. 319, 58 S.Ct. 149, 82 L.Ed. 288 (1937)—§§ 2.4(e) n.143, 152; 2.4 n.1; 2.5(a) n.6, 10; 2.5(c) n.18, 27; 2.6(b) n.34;

2.7(c) n.106, 175; 22.1(a) n.10, 11

Pall v. State, 632 So.2d 1084 (Fla.App.1994)—§ 11.3(a) n.16

Palladino, United States v., 347 F.3d 29 (2d Cir.2003)—§§ 21.2(d) n.158, 204

Pallais, United States v., 921 F.2d 684 (7th Cir.1990)—§ 3.6(a) n.5

Pallotta, United States v., 433 F.2d 594 (1st Cir.1970)—§ 21.2(g) n.401

Palma, United States v., 760 F.2d 475 (3d Cir.1985)—§ 26.6(c) n.40

Palma-Ruedas, United States v., 121 F.3d 841 (3d Cir.1997)—§§ 16.2(c) n.45, 49

Palm Beach Newspapers Inc. v. Burk, 504 So.2d 378 (Fla.1987)— § 23.1(d) n.187

Palmentere v. Campbell, 205 F.Supp. 261 (W.D.Mo.1962)—§ 8.5(a) n.10

Palmer v. Grammer, 863 F.2d 588 (8th Cir.1988)—§ 25.4(c) n.28

Palmer, People v., 162 Ill.2d 465, 205 Ill.Dec. 506, 643 N.E.2d 797 (1994)—§§ 11.10(b) n.39; 21.3(b) n.115

Palmer, People v., 194 Colo. 186, 570 P.2d 251 (1977)—§ 7.4(c) n.56

Palmer, People v., 41 Ill.2d 571, 244 N.E.2d 173 (1969)—§ 7.3(b) n.12

Palmer v. State, 118 Nev. 823, 59 P.3d 1192 (2002)—§ 21.4(d) n.114

Palmer, State v., 638 N.W.2d 18 (N.D.2002)—§ 22.2(d) n.79

Palmer, State v., 206 W.Va. 306, 524 S.E.2d 661 (1999)—§§ 21.2(d) n.206; 21.2(f) n.363

Palmer, State v., 334 N.C. 104, 431 S.E.2d 172 (1993)—§ 6.4(f) n.124

Palmer v. State, 626 A.2d 1358 (Del.1993)—§ 6.9(g) n.178

Palmer, State v., 860 P.2d 339 (Utah App.1993)—§ 2.10(d) n.109

Palmer v. State, 486 N.E.2d 477 (Ind.1985)—§ 11.2(e) n.180

Palmer, State v., 270 Ind. 493, 386 N.E.2d 946 (1979)—§ 27.4(d) n.48

Palmer, State v., 35 Or.App. 125, 580 P.2d 592 (1978)—§ 11.5(e) n.88

Palmer, State v., 293 N.C. 633, 239 S.E.2d 406 (1977)—§§ 19.1(d) n.66; 19.3(b) n.151

Palmer v. Thompson, 403 U.S. 217, 91 S.Ct. 1940, 29 L.Ed.2d 438 (1971)—§ 2.3 n.1

Palmer, United States v., 456 F.3d 484 (5th Cir.2006)—§ 21.4(f) n.192

Palmer, United States v., 122 F.3d 215 (5th Cir.1997)—§ 25.2(a) n.7

Palmer, United States v., 603 F.2d 1286 (8th Cir.1979)—§ 3.8(d) n.184

Palmieri v. New York, 779 F.2d 861 (2d Cir.1985)—§ 8.6(b) n.54

Palmigiano v. Travisono, 317 F.Supp. 776 (D.R.I.1970)—§ 3.9(i) n.196

Palmore v. United States, 411 U.S. 389, 93 S.Ct. 1670, 36 L.Ed.2d 342 (1973)—§ 1.2(c) n.15

Palomba, United States v., 31 F.3d 1456 (9th Cir.1994)—§§ 18.3(b) n.5; 27.5(b) n.46

Palomo, United States v., 80 F.3d 138 (5th Cir.1996)—§ 26.4(e) n.76

Palow, United States v., 777 F.2d 52 (1st Cir.1985)—§ 5.3(a) n.14

Palumbo, United States v., 897 F.2d 245 (7th Cir.1990)—§ 8.11(c) n.58

Pambianchi, State v., 139 Conn. 543, 95 A.2d 695 (1953)—§ 16.4(c) n.55

Panah, People v., 35 Cal.4th 395, 25 Cal.Rptr.3d 672, 107 P.3d 790 (2005)—§ 6.7(b) n.90

Panarella, United States v., 277 F.3d 678 (3d Cir.2002)—§§ 19.3(e) n.210, 241, 243; 21.6(a) n.25

Panesenko v. State, 706 P.2d 273 (Wyo.1985)—§ 26.10(c) n.43

Panetta, United States v., 436 F.Supp. 114 (E.D.Pa.1977)—§ 17.4(a) n.58

Panetti, Commonwealth v., 406 Mass. 230, 547 N.E.2d 46 (1989)— § 3.2(c) n.112

Panetti v. Quarterman, _____ U.S. _____, 127 S.Ct. 2842, _____ L.Ed.2d _____ (2007)—§§ 28.5(c) n.73; 28.7(a) n.5

Panetti, State v., 891 S.W.2d 281 (Tex.App.1994)—§ 6.9(g) n.161

Panico, People v., 111 A.D.2d 358, 489 N.Y.S.2d 122 (1985)—§ 8.8(h) n.189

Panizzon, People v., 13 Cal.4th 68, 51 Cal.Rptr.2d 851, 913 P.2d 1061 (1996)—§§ 21.2(b) n.86; 27.5(c) n.56

Pannell v. United States, 320 F.2d 698 (D.C.Cir.1963)—§§ 12.1(b) n.29; 12.2(b) n.18

P. (Anonymous), People v., 21 N.Y.2d 1, 286 N.Y.S.2d 225, 233 N.E.2d 255 (1967)—§§ 6.6(c) n.19, 21, 33; 6.6(e) n.63; 6.6(f) n.98

Pantoja, People v., 28 Mich.App. 681, 184 N.W.2d 762 (1970)—§ 6.6(f) n.105

Pantojas, In re, 628 F.2d 701 (1st Cir.1980)—§§ 8.8(b) n.31; 8.8(h) n.186

Pantojas, In re, 639 F.2d 822 (1st Cir.1980)—§§ 8.3(a) n.5; 8.8(g) n.175

Pantone, United States v., 634 F.2d 716 (3d Cir.1980)—§ 8.11(c) n.47

Pantos v. City and County of San Francisco, 151 Cal.App.3d 258, 198 Cal.Rptr. 489 (1984)—§ 22.3(b) n.62

Panzardi-Alvarez v. United States, 879 F.2d 975 (1st Cir.1989)—§§ 11.4(c) n.56; 22.4(c) n.29

Paolello, Commonwealth v., 542 Pa. 47, 665 A.2d 439 (1995)—§ 23.2(g) n.123

Papachristou v. City of Jacksonville, 405 U.S. 156, 92 S.Ct. 839, 31 L.Ed.2d 110 (1972)—§ 1.8(d) n.61

Papaleo, United States v., 853 F.2d 16 (1st Cir.1988)—§ 21.2(f) n.388

Pappaconstantinou v. State, 352 Md. 167, 721 A.2d 241 (1998)—§ 6.2(c) n.186

Pappas, United States v., 409 F.3d 828 (7th Cir.2005)—§ 21.2(b) n.89

Paquette v. Commonwealth, 440 Mass. 121, 795 N.E.2d 521 (2003)—§§ 12.3(g) n.158, 160

Paradies, United States v., 98 F.3d 1266 (11th Cir.1996)—§ 22.2(a) n.13

Paradis, United States v., 351 F.3d 21 (1st Cir.2003)—§ 3.6(d) n.99

Paradise, Ex parte, 477 So.2d 948 (Ala.1985)—§ 21.3(b) n.134

Paradise, State v., 213 Conn. 388, 567 A.2d 1221 (1990)—§ 24.5(d) n.58

Paradiso v. United States, 689 F.2d 28 (2d Cir.1982)—§ 21.5(e) n.110

Paradiso v. United States, 482 F.2d 409 (3d Cir.1973)—§ 21.2(g) n.398

Paradyne Corp., In re, 803 F.2d 604 (11th Cir.1986)—§ 11.9(b) n.89

Paraiso v. United States, 207 U.S. 368, 28 S.Ct. 127, 52 L.Ed. 249 (1907)—§ 19.1(a) n.3

Para-Professional Law Clinic, United States ex rel. v. Kane, 656 F.Supp. 1099 (E.D.Pa.1987)—§§ 11.2(f) n.248, 251

Parda, State v., 142 Vt. 261, 455 A.2d 323 (1982)—§ 12.4(e) n.89

Pardo, United States v., 25 F.3d 1187 (3d Cir.1994)—§ 27.5(b) n.45

Pardons, Board of v. Allen, 482 U.S. 369, 107 S.Ct. 2415, 96 L.Ed.2d 303 (1987)—§ 26.2(c) n.39

Pardue v. State, 363 Ark. 567, 215 S.W.3d 650 (2005)—§§ 21.4(b) n.59; 21.4(f) n.175, 176

Pardue, United States v., 363 F.3d 695 (8th Cir.2004)—§ 18.4(c) n.35

Pare, State v., 253 Conn. 611, 755 A.2d 180 (2000)—§§ 24.9(e) n.52; 27.6(d) n.142

Paredes-Batista, United States v., 140 F.3d 367 (2d Cir.1998)—§ 18.4(c) n.56

Paredez, State v., 136 N.M. 533, 101 P.3d 799 (2004)—§§ 21.3(b) n.68, 70; 21.4(d) n.137

Parfait, State v., 693 So.2d 1232 (La.App.1997)—§ 24.6(b) n.17

Parham v. J.R., 442 U.S. 584, 99 S.Ct. 2493, 61 L.Ed.2d 101 (1979)— § 2.7(c) n.216

Parham, People v., 60 Cal.2d 378, 33 Cal.Rptr. 497, 384 P.2d 1001 (1963)—§ 3.5(b) n.102

Parham v. State, 262 Ark. 241, 555 S.W.2d 943 (1977)—§§ 10.2(a) n.2, 15

Parhms, United States v., 424 F.2d 152 (9th Cir.1970)—§ 7.2(c) n.32

Paris, People v., 48 Cal.App.3d 766, 122 Cal.Rptr. 272 (1975)—§ 3.3(d) n.159

Park v. California, 202 F.3d 1146 (9th Cir.2000)—§ 28.4(b) n.22

Park v. State, 230 Ga.App. 274, 495 S.E.2d 886 (1998)—§§ 3.5(d) n.165, 166

Park, United States v., 531 F.2d 754 (5th Cir.1976)—§ 17.1(a) n.12

Parke v. Raley, 506 U.S. 20, 113 S.Ct. 517, 121 L.Ed.2d 391 (1992)— §§ 21.4(e) n.161; 21.5(c) n.75; 26.6(b) n.12, 30

Parker, In re, 49 F.3d 204 (6th Cir.1995)—§ 28.10 n.1

Parker, In re, 357 So.2d 508 (La.1978)— § 2.12(e) n.208

Parker v. Arkansas, 498 U.S. 883, 111 S.Ct. 218, 112 L.Ed.2d 186 (1990)—§ 25.4(b) n.17

Parker, Commonwealth v., 919 A.2d 943 (Pa.2007)—§ 24.7(a) n.9

Parker, Commonwealth v., 165 Mass. 526, 43 N.E. 499 (1896)—§ 16.4(c) n.55

Parker v. Gladden, 385 U.S. 363, 87 S.Ct. 468, 17 L.Ed.2d 420 (1966)— § 24.9(f) n.91

Parker v. Head, 244 F.3d 831 (11th Cir.2001)—§ 24.9(f) n.85

Parker v. Moody, 446 S.W.2d 596 (Mo.1969)—§ 16.3(g) n.99

Parker v. Norris, 64 F.3d 1178 (8th Cir.1995)—§ 25.4(b) n.17

Parker v. North Carolina, 397 U.S. 790, 90 S.Ct. 1458, 25 L.Ed.2d 785 (1970)—§§ 21.2(a) n.9; 21.6(a) n.9; 27.5(c) n.66

Parker v. Parratt, 662 F.2d 479 (8th Cir.1981)—§ 11.9(d) n.191

Parker, People v., 57 N.Y.2d 815, 455 N.Y.S.2d 600, 441 N.E.2d 1118 (1982)—§ 24.2(d) n.45

Parker, People v., 374 Ill. 524, 30 N.E.2d 11 (1940)—§§ 8.4(b) n.91, 101; 15.2(b) n.53

Parker, People v., 397 Ill. 305, 74 N.E.2d 523 (1947)—§§ 8.4(b) n.101, 103; 15.2(b) n.53

Parker v. Randolph, 442 U.S. 62, 99 S.Ct. 2132, 60 L.Ed.2d 713 (1979)—§ 17.2(b) n.33

Parker v. Ross, 470 F.2d 1092 (4th Cir.1972)—§ 15.3(d) n.67

Parker v. Roth, 202 Neb. 850, 278 N.W.2d 106 (1979)—§§ 12.3(d) n.100, 104

Parker v. Singletary, 974 F.2d 1562 (11th Cir.1992)—§ 6.9(f) n.119

Parker v. State, 182 S.W.3d 923 (Tex.Crim.App.2006)—§ 9.1(d) n.133

Parker v. State, 277 Ga.App. 155, 626 S.E.2d 152 (2006)—§ 12.4(c) n.60

Parker v. State, 843 So.2d 871 (Fla.2003)—§ 12.3(g) n.160

Parker v. State, 365 Md. 299, 778 A.2d 1096 (2001)—§ 22.3(d) n.249

Parker v. State, 780 So.2d 210 (Fla.App.2001)—§ 12.3(b) n.44

Parker v. State, 790 So.2d 1033 (Fla.2001)—§ 21.3(c) n.150

Parker, State v., 139 Wash.2d 486, 987 P.2d 73 (1999)—§ 3.7(a) n.17

Parker v. State, 698 N.E.2d 737 (1998)—§ 7.4(e) n.82

Parker v. State, 917 P.2d 980 (Okla.Crim.App.1996)—§§ 19.2(c) n.22, 31; 19.2(e) n.55; 19.3(a) n.2, 8, 10

Parker, State v., 334 Md. 576, 640 A.2d 1104 (1994)—§ 21.2(e) n.335

Parker v. State, 587 So.2d 1072 (Ala.Crim.App.1991)—§ 23.2(a) n.42

Parker v. State, 302 Ark. 509, 790 S.W.2d 894 (1990)—§ 26.2(b) n.15

Parker, State v., 181 W.Va. 619, 383 S.E.2d 801 (1989)—§ 6.3(c) n.53

Parker v. State, 437 N.W.2d 65 (Minn.1989)—§ 24.11(d) n.31

Parker v. State, 745 S.W.2d 934 (Tex.App.1988)—§ 24.9(c) n.27

Parker, State v., 221 Neb. 570, 379 N.W.2d 259 (1986)—§ 24.10(c) n.41

Parker v. State, 693 S.W.2d 640 (Tex.App.1985)—§ 11.10(c) n.115

Parker v. State, 100 Nev. 264, 679 P.2d 1271 (1984)—§§ 21.3(b) n.79; 21.5(a) n.16

Parker v. State, 454 So.2d 910 (Miss.1984)—§ 11.8(a) n.10

Parker, State v., 55 Wis.2d 131, 197 N.W.2d 742 (1972)—§ 6.9(b) n.34

Parker, United States v., 439 F.3d 81 (2d Cir.2006)—§§ 11.2(g) n.261, 299

Parker, United States v., 262 F.3d 415 (4th Cir.2001)—§ 6.6(e) n.61

Parker, United States v., 877 F.2d 327 (5th Cir.1989)—§ 23.2(a) n.47

Parker, United States v., 848 F.2d 61 (5th Cir.1988)—§ 12.1(e) n.63

Parker v. United States, 400 F.2d 248 (9th Cir.1968)—§ 7.4(d) n.77

Parkerson v. State, 156 Ga.App. 440, 274 S.E.2d 799 (1980)—§ 26.9(b) n.23

Parker, State ex rel. v. Roberds, 155 Kan. 165, 123 P.2d 806 (1942)—§ 16.3(f) n.95

Parkinson, State v., 389 A.2d 1 (Me.1978)—§ 10.2(a) n.7

Parklane Hosiery Co., Inc. v. Shore, 439 U.S. 322, 99 S.Ct. 645, 58 L.Ed.2d 552 (1979)—§ 1.5(g) n.276

Parks v. Commonwealth, 89 S.W.3d 395 (Ky.2002)—§ 18.4(c) n.67

Parks v. State, 275 Ga. 320, 565 S.E.2d 447 (2002)—§ 24.2(a) n.14

Parks, State v., 331 N.C. 649, 417 S.E.2d 467 (1992)—§§ 11.2(e) n.158, 160, 201, 204

Parks, State v., 324 N.C. 420, 378 S.E.2d 785 (1989)—§ 22.3(a) n.5

Parks, State v., 437 P.2d 642 (Alaska 1968)—§§ 15.5(c) n.118, 119, 121

Parks, United States v., 285 F.3d 1133 (9th Cir.2002)—§§ 9.1(d) n.126; 17.2(b) n.71

Parmar, State v., 231 Neb. 687, 437 N.W.2d 503 (1989)—§ 3.1(c) n.72

Paroutian, United States v., 299 F.2d 486 (2d Cir.1962)—§ 9.1(b) n.53

Parr, State v., 208 W.Va. 555, 542 S.E.2d 69 (2000)—§ 21.4(f) n.216

Parr v. United States, 351 U.S. 513, 76 S.Ct. 912, 100 L.Ed. 1377 (1956)—§§ 16.3(d) n.51; 27.2(a) n.5; 27.2(c) n.28, 51

Parra v. Municipal Court, 83 Cal.App.3d 690, 148 Cal.Rptr. 203 (1978)—§ 27.4(c) n.34

Parra, People v., 30 Cal.App.3d 729, 106 Cal.Rptr. 531 (1973)—§ 3.6(f) n.151

Parra, United States v., 2 F.3d 1058 (10th Cir.1993)—§ 3.6(c) n.78

Parren v. State, 309 Md. 260, 523 A.2d 597 (1987)—§ 11.5(g) n.112

Parretti v. United States, 122 F.3d 758 (9th Cir.1997)—§ 3.1(j) n.256

Parris, People v., 83 N.Y.2d 342, 610 N.Y.S.2d 464, 632 N.E.2d 870 (1994)—§ 3.3(d) n.157

Parrish v. Fulcomer, 150 F.3d 326 (3d Cir.1998)—§ 22.1(h) n.144

Parry v. Rosemeyer, 64 F.3d 110 (3d Cir.1995)—§ 21.4(d) n.116

Parsley v. State, 557 N.E.2d 1331 (Ind.1990)—§ 7.4(d) n.74

Parsley v. Superior Court, 9 Cal.3d 934, 109 Cal.Rptr. 563, 513 P.2d 611 (1973)—§ 3.4(h) n.163

Parsons, State v., 181 W.Va. 131, 381 S.E.2d 246 (1989)—§ 6.9(b) n.24

Parsons, United States v., 396 F.3d 1015 (8th Cir.2005)—§ 21.2(a) n.7

Parsons, United States v., 367 F.3d 409 (5th Cir.2004)—§ 27.5(a) n.5

Parsons, United States ex rel. v. Adams, 336 F.Supp. 340 (D.C.Conn.1971)—§ 24.7(c) n.24

Parson, United States ex rel. v. Anderson, 354 F.Supp. 1060 (D.Del.1972)—§ 3.5(c) n.129

Partida Parra, United States v., 859 F.2d 629 (9th Cir.1988)—§ 25.1(d) n.72

Partin v. Commonwealth, 168 S.W.3d 23 (Ky.2005)—§§ 15.4(g) n.170, 176

Partin, United States v., 320 F.Supp. 275 (E.D.La.1970)—§ 15.4(g) n.181

Partridge v. Two Unknown Police Officers, 791 F.2d 1182 (5th Cir.1986)—§ 12.2(d) n.50

Partyka, United States v., 561 F.2d 118 (8th Cir.1977)—§ 13.7(c) n.59

Pascall, State v., 49 Ohio App.2d 18, 358 N.E.2d 1368 (1972)—§ 21.2(d) n.224

Pascarella, United States v., 84 F.3d 61 (2d Cir.1996)—§§ 11.4(d) n.117; 11.5(c) n.55

Pasch, People v., 152 Ill.2d 133, 178 Ill.Dec. 38, 604 N.E.2d 294 (1992)—§ 24.11(b) n.7

Pasciuti, United States v., 803 F.Supp. 563 (D.N.H.1992)—§ 23.1(b) n.30

Pasdon v. City of Peabody, 417 F.3d 225 (1st Cir.2005)—§ 6.6(f) n.100

Paskett, United States v., 950 F.2d 705 (11th Cir.1992)—§§ 9.5(e) n.84, 87, 88

Passarella, United States v., 788 F.2d 377 (6th Cir.1986)—§ 4.6(l) n.205

Passman, State v., 345 So.2d 874 (1977)—§ 20.3(h) n.146

Passodelis, United States v., 615 F.2d 975 (3d Cir.1980)—§ 16.1(g) n.238

Pastorini, State v., 226 Ga.App. 260, 486 S.E.2d 399 (Ga.1997)—§ 27.3(c) n.39

Paszko, Commonwealth v., 391 Mass. 164, 461 N.E.2d 222 (1984)—§ 20.5(f) n.82

Patane, United States v., 542 U.S. 630, 124 S.Ct. 2620, 159 L.Ed.2d 667 (2004)—§§ 2.9(f) n.143; 2.9(h) n.267; 2.10(b) n.24; 9.5(a) n.27; 9.5(b) n.48

Patane, United States v., 304 F.3d 1013 (10th Cir.2002)—§§ 3.3(d) n.147, 150

Pate v. Municipal Court, 11 Cal.App.3d 721, 89 Cal.Rptr. 893 (1970)—§ 3.2(c) n.112

Pate v. Robinson, 383 U.S. 375, 86 S.Ct. 836, 15 L.Ed.2d 815 (1966)—§§ 1.5(c) n.169; 21.4(b) n.58

Patel, Ex parte, 879 So.2d 532 (Ala.2003)—§ 12.4(a) n.22

Patel, State v., 280 Ga. 181, 626 S.E.2d 121 (2006)—§ 21.3(b) n.71

Paternostro, United States v., 966 F.2d 907 (5th Cir.1992)—§ 11.5(c) n.64

Patino, United States v., 830 F.2d 1413 (7th Cir.1987)—§ 9.4(a) n.42

Patler v. Slayton, 503 F.2d 472 (4th Cir.1974)—§§ 24.3(b) n.46, 47

Patriarca, United States v., 948 F.2d 789 (1st Cir.1991)—§ 12.2(b) n.30

Patricelli, State v., 324 N.W.2d 351 (Minn.1982)—§ 3.6(a) n.36

Patrick v. Camden County Prosecutor, 630 F.2d 206 (3d Cir.1980)—§§ 21.2(d) n.177; 21.2(e) n.290

Patrick, Commonwealth v., 477 Pa. 284, 383 A.2d 935 (1978)—§ 11.7(e) n.67

Patrick v. State, 108 P.3d 838 (Wyo.2005)—§ 26.4(e) n.76

Patrick v. State, 349 S.C. 203, 562 S.E.2d 609 (2002)—§§ 13.7(c) n.39, 60

Patrick, United States v., 959 F.2d 991 (D.C.Cir.1992)—§§ 3.10(d) n.111; 3.10(f) n.193

Patrick v. United States, 524 F.2d 1109 (7th Cir.1975)—§§ 8.11(d) n.83, 85

Patry, Commonwealth v., 48 Mass.App.Ct. 470, 722 N.E.2d 979 (2000)—§ 24.1(a) n.5

Patten, State v., 137 N.H. 627, 631 A.2d 921 (1993)—§ 12.1(e) n.61

Patterson v. Dahm, 769 F.Supp. 1103 (D.Neb.1991)—§§ 11.10(c) n.86, 89

Patterson v. Faircloth, 256 Ga. 489, 350 S.E.2d 243 (1986)—§§ 16.3(f) n.84, 91

Patterson v. Gomez, 223 F.3d 959 (9th Cir.2000)—§ 21.2(b) n.83

Patterson v. Haskins, 470 F.3d 645 (6th Cir.2006)—§ 25.4(c) n.34

Patterson v. Illinois, 487 U.S. 285, 108 S.Ct. 2389, 101 L.Ed.2d 261 (1988)—§§ 6.4(f) n.117, 120, 138; 11.3(a) n.3, 4; 11.3(b) n.47

Patterson v. LeMaster, 130 N.M. 179, 21 P.3d 1032 (2001)—§§ 7.4(c) n.54; 7.4(f) n.95

Patterson v. McLean Credit Union, 491 U.S. 164, 109 S.Ct. 2363, 105 L.Ed.2d 132 (1989)—§ 2.9(b) n.25

Patterson v. New York, 432 U.S. 197, 97 S.Ct. 2319, 53 L.Ed.2d 281 (1977)—§§ 1.5(d) n.198; 2.7(a) n.44; 2.7(b) n.69, 71; 2.7(c) n.148, 156, 157, 168, 169, 190, 211, 221; 2.9(d) n.66; 26.4(d) n.68; 26.4(h) n.151

Patterson, People v., 217 Ill.2d 407, 299 Ill.Dec. 157, 841 N.E.2d 889 (2005)—§ 9.6(a) n.38

Patterson, People v., 146 Ill.2d 445, 167 Ill.Dec. 1045, 588 N.E.2d 1175 (1992)—§§ 6.6(b) n.14; 6.6(e) n.82

Patterson, State v., 236 Conn. 561, 674 A.2d 416 (1996)—§§ 26.4(d) n.61; 26.5(b) n.36

Patterson, State v., 237 Neb. 198, 465 N.W.2d 743 (1991)—§ 27.5(a) n.14

Patterson, State v., 582 A.2d 1204 (Me.1990)—§ 3.9(g) n.126

Patterson v. State, 747 P.2d 535 (Alaska App.1987)—§ 15.4(g) n.178

Patterson v. State, 500 N.E.2d 1191 (Ind.1986)—§ 21.4(b) n.57

Patterson, State v., 192 Neb. 308, 220 N.W.2d 235 (1974)—§ 3.6(e) n.109

Patterson v. State, 4 Tenn.Cr.App. 657, 475 S.W.2d 201 (1971)—§ 10.2(c) n.36

Patterson, State v., 28 Ohio St.2d 181, 277 N.E.2d 201 (1971)—§ 8.5(h) n.232

Patterson, United States v., 381 F.3d 859 (9th Cir.2004)—§§ 21.3(f) n.426; 21.4(g) n.255; 25.1(d) n.68

Patterson, United States v., 277 F.3d 709 (4th Cir.2002)—§ 18.3(b) n.32

Patterson, United States v., 278 F.3d 315 (4th Cir.2002)—§ 3.4(j) n.186

Patterson, United States v., 292 F.3d 615 (9th Cir.2002)—§ 3.3(d) n.159

Patterson, United States v., 211 F.3d 927 (5th Cir.2000)—§ 28.9(b) n.50

Patterson, United States v., 65 F.3d 68 (7th Cir.1995)—§ 3.7(a) n.18

Patterson, United States v., 26 F.3d 1127 (D.C.Cir.1994)—§ 22.1(d) n.79

Patterson, United States v., 819 F.2d 1495 (9th Cir.1987)—§ 24.5(b) n.35

Patterson v. United States, 324 F.2d 310 (5th Cir.1963)—§ 17.3(e) n.66

Patti, United States v., 337 F.3d 1317 (11th Cir.2003)—§ 21.6(a) n.46

Patton v. People, 35 P.3d 124 (Colo.2001)—§ 21.6(a) n.63

Patton, State v., 37 Kan.App. 166, 150 P.3d 328 (2007)—§§ 27.5(c) n.53, 57

Patton v. State, 810 N.E.2d 690 (Ind.2004)—§ 21.4(c) n.95

Patton v. State, 517 N.E.2d 374 (Ind.1987)—§ 21.4(f) n.209

Patton, United States v., 451 F.3d 615 (10th Cir.2006)—§§ 1.2(c) n.130, 142, 144, 147, 183, 184, 194; 1.2(d) n.239

Patton v. United States, 281 U.S. 276, 50 S.Ct. 253, 74 L.Ed. 854 (1930)—§§ 22.1(h) n.130; 24.6(a) n.3, 5

Patton v. Yount, 467 U.S. 1025, 104 S.Ct. 2885, 81 L.Ed.2d 847 (1984)—§§ 2.7(b) n.92; 22.3(c) n.113, 118; 23.2(f) n.87, 101, 105; 28.7(a) n.2; 28.7(b) n.7, 8

Patty v. Board of Medical Examiners, 9 Cal.3d 356, 107 Cal.Rptr. 473, 508 P.2d 1121 (1973)—§ 5.1(c) n.41

Paty v. State, 276 So.2d 195 (Fla.App.1973)—§ 3.2(c) n.100

Patzer, United States v., 277 F.3d 1080 (9th Cir.2002)—§ 9.4(a) n.33

Paul, In re, 270 Ga. 680, 513 S.E.2d 219 (1999)—§§ 6.2(c) n.185; 6.10(b) n.15

Paul v. Davis, 424 U.S. 693, 96 S.Ct. 1155, 47 L.Ed.2d 405 (1976)— § 3.1(m) n.291

Paul, State v., 716 N.W.2d 329 (Minn.2006)—§ 6.9(f) n.139

Paul, State v., 792 A.2d 42 (R.I.2002)— § 6.7(b) n.72

Paul, State v., 783 So.2d 1042 (Fla.2001)—§ 12.3(b) n.55

Paul v. State, 272 Ga. 845, 537 S.E.2d 58 (2000)—§ 27.5(d) n.119

Paul, State v., 548 N.W.2d 260 (Minn.1996)—§ 3.6(a) n.27

Paul, United States v., 274 F.3d 155 (5th Cir.2001)—§ 26.9(b) n.57

Pauley, State v., 12 Wis. 537 (1860)— § 16.1(e) n.198

Paulin, People v., 61 Misc.2d 289, 305 N.Y.S.2d 607 (1968)—§ 6.6(f) n.110

Paulino, United States v., 299 F.Supp.2d 332 (S.D.N.Y.2004)—§ 24.3(b) n.57

Paulino v. United States, 352 F.3d 1056 (6th Cir.2003)—§ 28.9(a) n.6

Paulino, United States v., 996 F.2d 1541 (3d Cir.1993)—§ 26.4(f) n.89

Paulman, People v., 5 N.Y.3d 122, 800 N.Y.S.2d 96, 833 N.E.2d 239 (2005)—§ 6.8(b) n.49

Paul, People ex rel. v. Harvey, 9 Ill.App.3d 209, 292 N.E.2d 124 (1972)—§ 24.9(e) n.56

Paulsen v. Manson, 203 Conn. 484, 525 A.2d 1315 (1987)—§§ 21.4(c) n.92; 21.4(f) n.203, 204

Paulsen, State v., 286 N.W.2d 157 (Iowa 1979)—§§ 15.6(g) n.215; 15.7(b) n.44

Paulson v. State, 28 S.W.3d 570 (Tex.Cr.App.2000)—§ 24.8(c) n.40

Paulson, State v., 313 Or. 346, 833 P.2d 1278 (1992)—§ 3.6(f) n.141

Paulson, State v., 106 Wis.2d 96, 315 N.W.2d 350 (1982)—§ 24.8(b) n.28

Paulson v. State, 257 So.2d 303 (Fla.App.1972)—§ 9.4(d) n.100

Pau'u, State v., 72 Haw. 505, 824 P.2d 833 (1992)—§ 9.4(a) n.41

Pavao, Commonwealth v., 423 Mass. 798, 672 N.E.2d 531 (1996)— § 22.1(h) n.134

Pavey v. State, 764 N.E.2d 692 (Ind.App.2002)—§ 24.7(a) n.17

Pawlyk, State v., 115 Wash.2d 457, 800 P.2d 338 (1990)—§§ 20.5(c) n.55, 56; 20.5(h) n.102

Paxton v. State, 255 Ind. 264, 263 N.E.2d 636 (1970)—§ 3.7(a) n.4

Payette, State v., 557 A.2d 72 (R.I.1989)—§ 7.5(a) n.8

Payne v. Arkansas, 356 U.S. 560, 78 S.Ct. 844, 2 L.Ed.2d 975 (1958)— §§ 6.2(b) n.26; 6.2(c) n.64, 70, 74, 175; 27.6(d) n.68

Payne, People v., 88 N.Y.2d 172, 643 N.Y.S.2d 949, 666 N.E.2d 542 (1996)—§ 22.3(d) n.237

Payne, People v., 282 Ill.App.3d 307, 217 Ill.Dec. 554, 667 N.E.2d 643 (1996)—§ 8.7(d) n.84

Payne, People v., 424 Mich. 475, 381 N.W.2d 391 (1985)—§ 3.4(b) n.26

Payne v. Rees, 738 F.2d 118 (6th Cir.1984)—§ 18.5(b) n.58

Payne v. Robinson, 207 Conn. 565, 541 A.2d 504 (1988)—§ 3.1(f) n.156

Payne, State v., 149 S.W.3d 20 (Tenn.2004)—§ 6.6(d) n.57

Payne v. State, 355 S.C. 642, 586 S.E.2d 857 (2003)—§ 24.5(b) n.35

Payne, State v., 260 Conn. 446, 797 A.2d 1088 (2002)—§ 24.7(e) n.41

Payne, State v., 273 Kan. 466, 44 P.3d 419 (2002)—§ 3.5(c) n.105

Payne, State v., 219 Conn. 93, 591 A.2d 1246 (1991)—§ 7.4(g) n.108

Payne, State v., 404 So.2d 1055 (Fla.1981)—§ 21.2(d) n.226

Payne v. Tennessee, 501 U.S. 808, 111 S.Ct. 2597, 115 L.Ed.2d 720 (1991)—§§ 2.9(b) n.6 to 8, 19, 22, 24, 27 to 29, 34; 2.9(c) n.48; 2.9(h) n.241; 26.5(d) n.71, 72

Payne, United States v., 63 F.3d 1200 (2d Cir.1995)—§ 24.3(b) n.62

Payne, United States v., 2 F.3d 706 (6th Cir.1993)—§§ 17.4(a) n.53; 24.7(f) n.78

Payne, United States v., 954 F.2d 199 (4th Cir.1992)—§ 6.7(c) n.118

Payne, United States v., 962 F.2d 1228 (6th Cir.1992)—§§ 5.4(c) n.37; 22.3(d) n.247

Payne v. United States, 516 A.2d 484 (D.C.App.1986)—§ 17.2(e) n.119

Payne v. United States, 508 F.2d 1391 (5th Cir.1975)—§ 3.4(g) n.130

Payner, United States v., 447 U.S. 727, 100 S.Ct. 2439, 65 L.Ed.2d 468 (1980)—§§ 1.7(i) n.181, 199; 9.1(c) n.110; 9.2(b) n.16

Payner, United States v., 434 F.Supp. 113 (N.D.Ohio 1977)—§ 1.7(i) n.186

Payton v. County of Carroll, 473 F.3d 845 (7th Cir.2007)—§ 12.2(b) n.38

Payton v. New York, 445 U.S. 573, 100 S.Ct. 1371, 63 L.Ed.2d 639 (1980)—§§ 1.9(b) n.27; 2.9(d) n.57, 86; 2.9(i) n.275; 2.11(d) n.44; 3.6(a) n.3; 6.4(e) n.73; 9.4(a) n.35

Payton, United States v., 168 F.3d 1103 (8th Cir.1999)—§ 21.5(a) n.11

Payton, United States v., 615 F.2d 922 (1st Cir.1980)—§ 6.4(f) n.123

Payton, United States v., 363 F.2d 996 (2d Cir.1966)—§ 15.5(b) n.61

Paz, State v., 118 Idaho 542, 798 P.2d 1 (1990)—§ 22.2(d) n.88

Pazden v. Maurer, 424 F.3d 303 (3d Cir.2005)—§ 11.4(d) n.110

Peacock, United States v., 654 F.2d 339 (5th Cir.1981)—§ 16.2(h) n.151

Pearce v. Pearce, 63 Eng.Rep. 950 (1846)—§ 1.5(b) n.88

Pearl v. State, 996 P.2d 688 (Wyo.2000)—§ 11.1(b) n.52

Pearson, People v., 356 Ill.App.3d 390, 292 Ill.Dec. 663, 826 N.E.2d 1099 (2005)—§ 22.3(a) n.11

Pearson v. State, 740 So.2d 346 (Miss.App.1999)—§ 19.5(c) n.60

Pearson, State v., 858 S.W.2d 879 (Tenn.1993)—§§ 18.5(a) n.51, 52; 24.8(f) n.106; 26.4(d) n.63

Pearson, State v., 818 P.2d 581 (Utah App.1991)—§ 21.2(h) n.437

Pearson v. State, 537 N.E.2d 25 (Ind.1989)—§ 6.9(f) n.144

Pearson v. State, 308 Minn. 287, 241 N.W.2d 490 (1976)—§ 26.10(b) n.39

Peart, State v., 621 So.2d 780 (La.1993)—§ 11.8(c) n.67

Pease v. District Court, 708 P.2d 800 (Colo.1985)—§§ 22.5(a) n.5; 22.5(d) n.31

Pease, State v., 233 Mont. 65, 758 P.2d 764 (Mont.1988)—§ 26.9(b) n.51

Pease, State v., 531 N.E.2d 1207 (Ind.App.1988)—§ 27.3(c) n.36

Pease, State v., 520 A.2d 698 (Me.1987)—§ 3.6(a) n.5

Pease, United States v., 240 F.3d 938 (11th Cir.2001)—§ 11.10(c) n.123

Peat, Marwick Mitchell & Co. v. Superior Court, 200 Cal.App.3d 272, 245 Cal.Rptr. 873 (1988)—§ 8.11(c) n.51

Peats v. State, 213 Ind. 560, 12 N.E.2d 270 (1938)—§ 16.1(d) n.145

Peavler, State v., 88 N.M. 125, 537 P.2d 1387 (1975)—§ 14.2(g) n.99

Peavy v. United States, 31 F.3d 1341 (6th Cir.1994)—§ 21.5(d) n.104

Pebworth v. Conte, 489 F.2d 266 (9th Cir.1974)—§ 21.4(d) n.143

Peck, State v., 140 N.H. 333, 666 A.2d 962 (1995)—§ 24.8(e) n.50

Pecoraro, State v., 196 Conn. 305, 493 A.2d 180 (1985)—§ 26.10(c) n.53

Pederson v. State, 692 N.W.2d 452 (Minn.2005)—§ 27.5(e) n.177

Pedraza, United States v., 27 F.3d 1515 (10th Cir.1994)—§ 23.2(a) n.42

Pedro Archuleta, In re, 432 F.Supp. 583 (S.D.N.Y.1977)—§ 8.8(g) n.171

Pedroza, United States v., 269 F.3d 821 (7th Cir.2001)—§ 18.3(b) n.28

Peek v. Kemp, 784 F.2d 1479 (11th Cir.1986)—§ 22.3(e) n.279

Peek v. Mitchell, 419 F.2d 575 (6th Cir.1970)—§ 13.3(a) n.9

Peele, State v., 58 S.W.3d 701 (Tenn.2001)—§ 21.5(a) n.21

Peeler, State v., 267 Conn. 611, 841 A.2d 181 (2004)—§ 22.3(d) n.250

Peeler, State v., 265 Conn. 460, 828 A.2d 1216 (2003)—§§ 11.9(c) n.117, 122

Peeples, People v., 155 Ill.2d 422, 186 Ill.Dec. 341, 616 N.E.2d 294 (1993)—§ 22.2(d) n.56

Peeples v. State, 234 Ga.App. 454, 507 S.E.2d 197 (1998)—§ 24.6(b) n.24

Peete, United States v., 919 F.2d 1168 (6th Cir.1990)—§ 26.9(b) n.57

Peevy, People v., 17 Cal.4th 1184, 73 Cal.Rptr.2d 865, 953 P.2d 1212 (1998)—§ 9.6(a) n.19

Peglera, United States v., 33 F.3d 412 (4th Cir.1994)—§ 21.2(d) n.219

Peguero v. United States, 526 U.S. 23, 119 S.Ct. 961, 143 L.Ed.2d 18 (1999)—§§ 11.6(d) n.119; 27.6(b) n.30; 28.9(c) n.80

Peiffer v. State, 88 S.W.3d 439 (Mo.2002)—§ 21.3(f) n.426

Peitsmeyer v. State, 21 P.3d 733 (Wyo.2001)—§ 21.4(a) n.23

Pejsa, State v., 75 Wash.App. 139, 876 P.2d 963 (1994)—§ 16.1(b) n.95

Pelayo-Landero, United States v., 285 F.3d 491 (6th Cir.2002)—§ 3.4(e) n.70

Pelican, State v., 154 Vt. 496, 580 A.2d 942 (1990)—§ 22.2(d) n.62

Pelkey, State v., 109 Wash.2d 484, 745 P.2d 854 (1987)—§ 19.5(b) n.35

Pelland v. Rhode Island, 317 F.Supp.2d 86 (D.R.I.2004)—§ 26.9(b) n.76

Pellegrine v. Commonwealth, 844 N.E. 2d 608 (Mass.2006)—§ 25.2(a) n.7

Pellerito, United States v., 878 F.2d 1535 (1st Cir.1989)—§§ 21.2(g) n.405; 21.4(b) n.44

Pelletier, State v., 541 A.2d 1296 (Me.1988)—§ 3.2(j) n.264

Pelletier, United States v., 469 F.3d 194 (1st Cir.2006)—§ 3.6(b) n.65

Pelletier, United States v., 898 F.2d 297 (2d Cir.1990)—§§ 8.11(e) n.99, 107, 109

Pellon, United States v., 475 F.Supp. 467 (S.D.N.Y.1979)—§ 8.11(e) n.103

Peloquin, United States v., 810 F.2d 911 (9th Cir.1987)—§ 18.5(a) n.36

Peltier v. State, 657 N.W.2d 238 (N.D.2003)—§ 21.2(d) n.227

Peltier, United States v., 422 U.S. 531, 95 S.Ct. 2313, 45 L.Ed.2d 374 (1975)—§§ 2.11(c) n.21, 26; 3.1(c) n.49

Pelton, United States v., 835 F.2d 1067 (4th Cir.1987)—§§ 6.2(c) n.96, 107

Pelton, United States v., 578 F.2d 701 (8th Cir.1978)—§§ 8.5(g) n.227; 20.3(l) n.233

Peltz v. People, 728 P.2d 1271 (Colo.1986)—§ 17.2(d) n.97

Pelullo, United States v., 399 F.3d 197 (3d Cir.2005)—§§ 24.3(b) n.54, 61

Pelullo, United States v., 173 F.3d 131 (3d Cir.1999)—§ 10.2(c) n.42

Pelullo, United States v., 14 F.3d 881 (3d Cir.1994)—§ 17.4(a) n.58

Pembaur v. Cincinnati, 475 U.S. 469, 106 S.Ct. 1292, 89 L.Ed.2d 452 (1986)—§ 3.1(k) n.268

Pemberton, Commonwealth v., 256 Pa.Super. 297, 389 A.2d 1132 (1978)—§ 7.4(c) n.46

Pemberton, United States v., 121 F.3d 1157 (8th Cir.1997)—§ 21.5(e) n.134

Pena v. State, 98 P.3d 857 (Wyo.2004)—§§ 6.9(g) n.149, 185; 10.4(b) n.15

Pena, State v., 93 Ohio App.3d 367, 638 N.E.2d 626 (1994)—§ 26.4(g) n.125

Pena, State v., 16 Conn.App. 518, 548 A.2d 445 (1988)—§ 11.7(b) n.29

Pena, United States v., 314 F.3d 1152 (9th Cir.2003)—§ 21.4(c) n.66

Pena, United States v., 227 F.3d 23 (2d Cir.2000)—§§ 20.3(g) n.122; 26.5(c) n.60

Pena, United States v., 961 F.2d 333 (2d Cir.1992)—§ 10.5(f) n.69

Pena, United States v., 949 F.2d 751 (5th Cir.1991)—§§ 24.11(d) n.16, 23, 35

Pena, United States v., 897 F.2d 1075 (11th Cir.1990)—§ 6.9(g) n.159

Pena, United States v., 920 F.2d 1509 (10th Cir.1990)—§ 3.10(f) n.195

Pena, United States v., 527 F.2d 1356 (5th Cir.1976)—§ 18.2(e) n.81

Pena-Corea, United States v., 165 F.3d 819 (11th Cir.1999)—§§ 18.4(c) n.42, 50

Penagaricano-Soler, United States v., 911 F.2d 833 (1st Cir.1990)— § 13.4(b) n.58

Pena-Lora, State v., 710 A.2d 1262 (R.I.1998)—§ 10.5(d) n.42

Pena-Lora, United States v., 225 F.3d 17 (1st Cir.2000)—§§ 17.2(d) n.94, 95

Pendergraft, People v., 45 Ill.App.3d 954, 4 Ill.Dec. 553, 360 N.E.2d 489 (1977)—§ 21.3(b) n.103

Pendleton, State v., 706 N.W.2d 500 (Minn.2005)—§ 17.4(a) n.50

Pendleton, City of v. Standerfer, 297 Or. 725, 688 P.2d 68 (1984)— §§ 11.1(d) n.128; 11.2(a) n.34

Peng, United States v., 766 F.2d 82 (2d Cir.1985)—§ 11.9(a) n.23

Penix, United States v., 516 F.Supp. 248 (W.D.Okla.1981)—§ 19.4(b) n.22

Penkaty, State v., 708 N.W.2d 185 (Minn.2006)—§§ 15.4(g) n.162; 15.7(b) n.30, 40

Penn v. Commonwealth, 13 Va.App. 399, 412 S.E.2d 189 (1991)— § 3.5(a) n.36

Penn, State v., 61 Ohio St.3d 720, 576 N.E.2d 790 (1991)—§ 9.1(c) n.100

Penn, United States v., 721 F.2d 762 (11th Cir.1983)—§ 26.10(c) n.74

Penn, United States v., 2 Crim L Rptr 3139 (D.C.Ct.Gen.Sess.1968)— § 12.1(d) n.55

Pennekamp v. Florida, 328 U.S. 331, 66 S.Ct. 1029, 90 L.Ed. 1295 (1946)— § 1.5(h) n.287

Pennell v. State, 602 A.2d 48 (Del.1991)—§ 3.7(f) n.131

Pennell, United States v., 737 F.2d 521 (6th Cir.1984)—§ 24.9(f) n.85

Penner, State v., 100 N.M. 377, 671 P.2d 38 (App.1983)—§§ 15.2(c) n.84; 15.7(d) n.90

Pennick v. State, 453 So.2d 542 (Fla.App.1984)—§§ 16.1(g) n.274, 277

Pennington v. Commonwealth, 577 S.W.2d 19 (Ky.App.1978)— § 20.6(b) n.25

Pennington, State v., 154 N.J. 344, 712 A.2d 1133 (1998)—§ 21.2(f) n.391

Pennington, State v., 115 N.M. 372, 851 P.2d 494 (N.M.App.1993)— § 22.5(d) n.32

Pennington, State v., 179 W.Va. 139, 365 S.E.2d 803 (1987)—§ 22.5(a) n.8

Pennington v. State, 308 Md. 727, 521 A.2d 1216 (1987)—§ 16.4(c) n.57

Pennington v. State, 286 Ark. 503, 697 S.W.2d 85 (1985)—§ 21.5(a) n.20

Pennington, United States v., 287 F.3d 739 (8th Cir.2002)—§ 3.4(j) n.182

Pennsalt Chemicals Corp., United States v., 260 F.Supp. 171 (E.D.Pa.1966)—§ 8.8(e) n.144

Penn, State ex rel. v. Norblad, 323 Or. 464, 918 P.2d 426 (1996)— § 27.4(d) n.47

Pennsylvania v. Bruder, 488 U.S. 9, 109 S.Ct. 205, 102 L.Ed.2d 172 (1988)—§ 6.6(e) n.89

Pennsylvania v. Collins, 420 Pa.Super. 358, 616 A.2d 1012 (1992)— § 24.4(c) n.21

Pennsylvania v. Finley, 481 U.S. 551, 107 S.Ct. 1990, 95 L.Ed.2d 539 (1987)—§§ 2.6(d) n.105; 11.1(b) n.64, 75; 11.1(d) n.119; 11.2(b) n.63; 11.2(c) n.85, 109; 11.2(f) n.243, 246; 11.7(a) n.17; 27.1(a) n.13; 28.11(a) n.9; 28.12(a) n.2; 28.12(b) n.15

Pennsylvania v. Homoki, 413 Pa.Super. 490, 605 A.2d 829 (1992)— § 26.10(b) n.40

Pennsylvania v. Labron, 518 U.S. 938, 116 S.Ct. 2485, 135 L.Ed.2d 1031 (1996)—§ 3.7(b) n.38

Pennsylvania v. Mimms, 434 U.S. 106, 98 S.Ct. 330, 54 L.Ed.2d 331 (1977)—§§ 2.9(g) n.163; 3.5(b) n.93; 3.8(e) n.200, 218; 12.5(b) n.30

Pennsylvania v. Muniz, 496 U.S. 582, 110 S.Ct. 2638, 110 L.Ed.2d 528 (1990)—§§ 1.5(c) n.104; 2.10(b) n.5; 6.7(a) n.3, 29; 6.7(b) n.33; 6.7(c) n.126; 8.10(a); 8.10(a) n.28, 32, 38; 8.13(a) n.8; 9.5(b) n.44

Pennsylvania v. Nelson, 350 U.S. 497, 76 S.Ct. 477, 100 L.Ed. 640 (1956)—§§ 1.2(c) n.42; 1.2(d) n.200

Pennsylvania v. Ritchie, 480 U.S. 39, 107 S.Ct. 989, 94 L.Ed.2d 40 (1987)—§§ 2.6(e) n.114; 2.7(a) n.24; 2.7(b) n.88; 20.3(m) n.237; 24.2(a) n.15; 24.3(a) n.3, 8; 24.3(b) n.75; 24.3(f) n.153

Pennsylvania Board of Probation and Parole v. Scott, 524 U.S. 357, 118 S.Ct. 2014, 141 L.Ed.2d 344 (1998)—§§ 3.1(b) n.24; 3.1(f) n.160; 26.10(c) n.64

Pennsylvania Coal v. Mahon, 260 U.S. 393, 43 S.Ct. 158, 67 L.Ed. 322 (1922)—§ 2.5(c) n.26

Pennycooke, United States v., 65 F.3d 9 (3d Cir.1995)—§ 11.6(c) n.100

Pen Register and Trap/Trace Device with Cell Site Location Authority, In re Application for, 396 F.Supp.2d 747 (S.D. Tex. 2005)—§§ 4.7(c) n.16, 18, 21

Penrod, People v., 316 Ill.App.3d 713, 249 Ill.Dec. 951, 737 N.E.2d 341 (2000)—§ 18.4(d) n.80

Penry v. Johnson (Penry II), 532 U.S. 782, 121 S.Ct. 1910, 150 L.Ed.2d 9 (2001)—§§ 6.10(e) n.67; 26.1(b) n.25; 28.6(f) n.67; 28.6(g) n.86, 91

Penry v. Lynaugh, 492 U.S. 302, 109 S.Ct. 2934, 106 L.Ed.2d 256 (1989)—§§ 2.11(e) n.55; 26.1(b) n.21; 28.6(d) n.22; 28.6(e) n.41; 28.6(f) n.67

Pens v. Bail, 902 F.2d 1464 (9th Cir.1990)—§ 6.2(c) n.140

Penson v. Ohio, 488 U.S. 75, 109 S.Ct. 2934, 106 L.Ed.2d 256 (1989)— §§ 2.7(b) n.74; 11.6(d) n.120

Penson v. Ohio, 488 U.S. 75, 109 S.Ct. 346, 102 L.Ed.2d 300 (1988)— §§ 1.5(c) n.94, 119; 11.2(c) n.114; 27.6(d) n.108, 130

Penta, United States v., 898 F.2d 815 (1st Cir.1990)—§§ 18.3(b) n.23; 21.2(h) n.420

People—see opposing party

Peoples v. Campbell, 377 F.3d 1208 (11th Cir.2004)—§ 6.6(d) n.48

Peoples, People v., 8 P.3d 577 (Colo.App.2000)—§ 27.6(d) n.127

Peoples, People v., 51 Cal.App.4th 1592, 60 Cal.Rptr.2d 173 (1997)— § 11.9(c) n.109

Peoples v. United States, 403 F.3d 844 (7th Cir.2005)—§ 11.7(e) n.86

Pepe, United States v., 367 F.Supp. 1365 (D.Conn.1973)—§ 15.7(d) n.81

Peplow, State v., 307 Mont. 172, 36 P.3d 922 (2001)—§ 21.4(a) n.12

Peppers, People v., 172 Colo. 556, 475 P.2d 337 (1970)—§ 3.4(e) n.77

Peppers v. State, 261 Ga. 338, 404 S.E.2d 788 (1991)—§ 24.9(d) n.40

Peppers, United States v., 302 F.3d 120 (3d Cir.2002)—§§ 11.5(c) n.32, 52; 11.5(d) n.83

Perala, State v., 130 P.3d 852 (Wash.App.2006)—§ 22.4(c) n.30

Peralta, United States v., 849 F.2d 625 (D.C.Cir.1988)—§ 12.3(a) n.23

Perank, State v., 858 P.2d 927 (Utah 1992)—§ 21.6(a) n.32

Percell, United States v., 526 F.2d 189 (9th Cir.1975)—§ 15.7(e) n.117

Percevault, United States v., 490 F.2d 126 (2d Cir.1974)—§§ 20.3(d) n.92; 20.3(i) n.168

Percy, State v., 548 A.2d 408 (Vt.1998)—§ 24.3(f) n.154

Percy, State v., 146 Vt. 475, 507 A.2d 955 (Vt.1986)—§ 24.7(e) n.48

Percy, United States v., 250 F.3d 720 (9th Cir.2001)—§§ 6.3(b) n.36; 6.4(e) n.76; 6.4(f) n.122

Perdomo, United States v., 929 F.2d 967 (3d Cir.1991)—§§ 24.3(b) n.55; 24.3(d) n.111

Perdue, United States v., 8 F.3d 1455 (10th Cir.1993)—§ 6.6(e) n.95

Pere, United States v., 960 F.2d 1569 (11th Cir.1992)—§ 20.6(b) n.42

Perea, United States v., 986 F.2d 633 (2d Cir.1993)—§§ 3.5(e) n.192; 3.7(a) n.16; 9.3(e) n.65, 66

Pereira, People v., 26 N.Y.2d 265, 309 N.Y.S.2d 901, 258 N.E.2d 194 (1970)—§ 3.10(c) n.95

Perelman v. State, 115 Nev. 190, 981 P.2d 1199 (1999)—§ 18.5(a) n.11

Peretz v. United States, 501 U.S. 923, 111 S.Ct. 2661, 115 L.Ed.2d 808 (1991)—§ 27.5(c) n.96

Perez, Commonwealth v., 411 Mass. 249, 581 N.E.2d 1010 (1991)— § 6.9(f) n.146

Perez v. Marshall, 119 F.3d 1422 (9th Cir.1997)—§ 24.9(f) n.102

Perez, People v., 83 N.Y.2d 269, 631 N.E.2d 570, 609 N.Y.S.2d 564 (1994)—§ 19.5(b) n.46

Perez, People v., 21 Cal.App.4th 214, 26 Cal.Rptr.2d 691 (1993)—§ 24.10(c) n.40

Perez, People v., 62 Cal.2d 769, 44 Cal.Rptr. 326, 401 P.2d 934 (1965)—§ 5.3(c) n.31

Perez, State v., 912 A.2d 944 (Vt.2006)—§ 24.8(f) n.98

Perez v. State, 919 So.2d 347 (Fla.2005)—§ 6.6(d) n.46

Perez v. State, 748 N.E.2d 853 (Ind.2001)—§ 11.10(c) n.105

Perez, State v., 85 S.W.3d 817 (Tex.Crim.App.1992)—§ 10.5(f) n.68

Perez, State v., 235 Neb. 796, 457 N.W.2d 448 (1990)—§ 21.4(b) n.56

Perez, State v., 464 So.2d 737 (La.1985)—§ 8.4(b) n.78

Perez, State v., 95 N.M. 262, 620 P.2d 1287 (1980)—§ 24.9(e) n.53

Perez, State v., 182 Neb. 680, 157 N.W.2d 162 (1968)—§ 6.8(a) n.27

Perez v. Sullivan, 793 F.2d 249 (10th Cir.1986)—§ 18.5(c) n.75

Perez, United States v., 280 F.3d 318 (3d Cir.2002)—§§ 16.1(g) n.255, 257, 259; 24.8(c) n.38

Perez, United States v., 217 F.3d 323 (5th Cir.2000)—§ 18.3(b) n.5

Perez, United States v., 940 F.Supp. 540 (S.D.N.Y.1996)—§ 16.2(h) n.152

Perez, United States v., 67 F.3d 1371 (9th Cir.1995)—§§ 15.2(i) n.220, 225

Perez, United States v., 845 F.2d 100 (5th Cir.1988)—§§ 18.3(b) n.5, 6

Perez, United States v., 776 F.2d 797 (9th Cir.1985)—§ 6.7(b) n.43

Perez, United States v., 733 F.2d 1026 (2d Cir.1984)—§ 6.3(b) n.42

Perez, United States v., 440 F.Supp. 272 (N.D.Ohio 1977)—§ 3.6(e) n.131

Perez v. United States, 402 U.S. 146, 91 S.Ct. 1357, 28 L.Ed.2d 686 (1971)—§§ 1.2(c) n.117, 151, 152, 155

Perez, United States v., 22 U.S. (9 Wheat) 579, 6 L.Ed. 165 (1824)— §§ 2.8(b) n.33; 25.2(c) n.16

Perez-Arellano v. Smith, 279 F.3d 791 (9th Cir.2002)—§ 13.5(h) n.140

Perez-Bustamante, United States v., 963 F.2d 48 (5th Cir.1992)—§ 6.2(c) n.81

Perez-Carrera, United States v., 243 F.3d 42 (1st Cir.2001)—§ 21.2(e) n.321

Perez-Casillas, United States v., 593 F.Supp. 794 (D.Puerto Rico 1984)—§ 23.2(d) n.65

Perez-Garcia, United States v., 56 F.3d 1 (1st Cir.1995)—§ 19.6(c) n.39

Perez-Hernandez, United States v., 672 F.2d 1380 (11th Cir.1982)—§§ 15.4(c) n.85; 15.4(e) n.128, 129

Perez-Leon, United States v., 757 F.2d 866 (7th Cir.1985)—§ 5.3(a) n.13

Perez-Lopez, United States v., 348 F.3d 839 (9th Cir.2003)—§ 6.8(a) n.36

Perez-Macias, United States v., 335 F.3d 421 (5th Cir.2003)—§ 11.2(a) n.25

Perez-Reveles, United States v., 715 F.2d 1348 (9th Cir.1983)—§ 18.3(b) n.53

Perez-Tavares, People v., 238 A.D.2d 446, 656 N.Y.S.2d 352 (1997)—§ 15.2(c) n.78

Perez, United States ex rel. v. Warden, 286 F.3d 1059 (8th Cir.2002)—§ 28.9(a) n.5

Perholtz, United States v., 836 F.2d 554 (D.C.Cir.1987)—§ 12.4(d) n.69

Perillo v. Johnson, 79 F.3d 441 (5th Cir.1996)—§§ 8.14(d) n.53; 11.9(d) n.192, 225

Perillo v. State, 758 S.W.2d 567 (Tex.Crim.1988)—§ 11.9(d) n.204

Perkins v. Court of Appeals, 738 S.W.2d 276 (Tex.Cr.App.1987)—§§ 21.2(d) n.219; 21.2(f) n.363

Perkins v. State, 279 Ga. 506, 614 S.E.2d 92 (2005)—§ 25.1(d) n.90

Perkins, State v., 271 Conn. 218, 856 A.2d 917 (2004)—§ 24.6(b) n.28

Perkins v. State, 226 Ga.App. 613, 487 S.E.2d 365 (1997)—§§ 11.7(e) n.66, 67

Perkins, State v., 248 Kan. 760, 811 P.2d 1142 (1991)—§ 6.2(c) n.148

Perkins, State v., 444 N.W.2d 34 (S.D.1989)—§ 6.6(d) n.45

Perkins, State v., 108 Wash.2d 212, 737 P.2d 250 (1987)—§ 21.4(d) n.122

Perkins, State v., 219 Neb. 491, 364 N.W.2d 20 (1985)—§§ 6.9(g) n.155; 22.2(d) n.83

Perkins, State v., 141 Ariz. 278, 686 P.2d 1248 (1984)—§§ 7.4(f) n.96; 22.4(a) n.12

Perkins, State v., 353 N.W.2d 557 (Minn.1984)—§ 22.1(g) n.115

Perkins, State v., 337 So.2d 1145 (La.1976)—§ 20.3(b) n.42

Perkins, United States v., 108 F.3d 512 (4th Cir.1997)—§ 27.5(d) n.117

Perkins, United States v., 748 F.2d 1519 (11th Cir.1984)—§ 24.9(f) n.96

Perkinson v. State, 273 Ga. 491, 542 S.E.2d 92 (2001)—§ 25.5(c) n.36

Perlaza, United States v., 439 F.3d 1149 (9th Cir.2006)—§ 22.1(a) n.18

Perlin, In re, 589 F.2d 260 (7th Cir.1978)—§§ 8.5(e) n.170, 172; 15.7(c) n.56

Perlman v. United States, 247 U.S. 7, 38 S.Ct. 417, 62 L.Ed. 950 (1918)—§ 27.2(e) n.80

Perlos, People v., 436 Mich. 305, 462 N.W.2d 310 (1990)—§ 3.2(j) n.230

Pernillo-Fuentes, United States v., 252 F.3d 1030 (9th Cir.2001)—§§ 19.3(a) n.114, 123

Pero, State v., 590 N.W.2d 319 (Minn.1999)—§§ 13.3(c) n.40; 21.3(e) n.265

Perreault, Commonwealth v., 930 A.2d 553 (Pa.Sup.2007)—§ 26.9(b) n.20

Perrigo, State v., 640 A.2d 1074 (Me.1994)—§ 3.3(d) n.147

Perrin, State v., 897 So.2d 749 (La.App.2005)—§ 24.6(e) n.51

Perry, In re, 19 Wis. 676 (1865)—§ 12.4(a) n.6

Perry, Commonwealth v., 418 Mass. 808, 641 N.E.2d 1313 (1994)—§ 15.1(f) n.327

Perry v. Commonwealth, 839 S.W.2d 268 (Ky.1992)—§ 24.8(f) n.98

Perry v. Leeke, 488 U.S. 272, 109 S.Ct. 594, 102 L.Ed.2d 624 (1989)— §§ 1.5(c) n.104; 2.9(g) n.170; 11.8(a) n.3, 6; 24.4(d) n.28; 24.5(d) n.45

Perry v. Norris, 879 F.Supp. 1503 (E.D.Ark.1995)—§§ 24.3(f) n.145; 24.11(d) n.12; 28.3(e) n.103

Perry, People v., 199 A.D.2d 889, 605 N.Y.S.2d 790 (1993)—§ 15.6(c) n.102

Perry, People v., 47 Ill.2d 402, 266 N.E.2d 330 (1971)—§ 3.6(c) n.74

Perry v. Rent-A-Ride, Inc., 505 A.2d 424 (R.I.1986)—§ 21.4(a) n.21

Perry v. State, 357 Md. 37, 741 A.2d 1162 (Ct.App.1999)—§ 11.10(d) n.181

Perry, State v., 879 S.W.2d 609 (Mo.App.1994)—§ 24.3(b) n.36

Perry, State v., 605 So.2d 94 (Fla.App.1992)—§ 12.4(a) n.16

Perry, State v., 610 So.2d 746 (La.1992)—§ 2.12(c) n.139

Perry v. State, 303 Ark. 100, 794 S.W.2d 141 (1990)—§ 1.8(f) n.103

Perry, State v., 502 So.2d 543 (La.1986)—§ 9.1(b) n.43

Perry, State v., 168 W.Va. 324, 284 S.E.2d 861 (1981)—§§ 19.6(b) n.19, 21

Perry, United States v., 479 F.3d 885 (D.C.Cir.2007)—§ 24.1(b) n.18

Perry, United States v., 731 F.2d 985 (D.C.Cir.1984)—§ 17.2(a) n.12

Persak, State v., 256 Mont. 404, 847 P.2d 280 (1993)—§§ 21.2(e) n.308, 316

Persico, In re, 491 F.2d 1156 (2d Cir.1974)—§ 8.9(b) n.21

Persico, United States v., 164 F.3d 796 (2d Cir.1999)—§ 21.5(a) n.10

Persinger, Commonwealth v., 532 Pa. 317, 615 A.2d 1305 (1992)— § 21.4(d) n.106

Persinger, State v., 62 Wash.2d 362, 382 P.2d 497 (1963)—§ 17.2(d) n.102

Person, State v., 34 Ohio Misc. 97, 298 N.E.2d 922 (1973)—§§ 3.2(c) n.113; 10.3(b) n.32

Personal Restraint of Clements, In re, 154 Wash.2d 1020, 120 P.3d 548 (2005)—§ 21.4(f) n.208

Personal Restraint of VanDelft, In re, 147 P.3d 573, 158 Wash.2d 731 (2006)—§ 26.4(i) n.190

Pervaz, United States v., 118 F.3d 1 (1st Cir.1997)—§ 4.6(l) n.185

Pesina v. Johnson, 913 F.2d 53 (2d Cir.1990)—§ 28.5(a) n.37

Peskin, United States v., 527 F.2d 71 (7th Cir.1975)—§ 13.4(c) n.117

Peter, United States v., 310 F.3d 709 (11th Cir.2002)—§§ 19.3(e) n.240, 241; 28.9(a) n.19

Peters v. Gunn, 33 F.3d 1190 (9th Cir.1994)—§§ 11.5(c) n.38; 11.5(d) n.84

Peters v. Kiff, 407 U.S. 493, 92 S.Ct. 2163, 33 L.Ed.2d 83 (1972)— §§ 1.7(c) n.12; 15.4(d) n.102, 113; 15.4(e) n.133; 22.2(c) n.26; 22.2(d) n.61; 22.2(f) n.116

Peters v. New York, 392 U.S. 40, 88 S.Ct. 1889, 20 L.Ed.2d 917 (1968)—§§ 3.1(d) n.104; 3.3(f) n.201; 3.5(a) n.9; 3.8(b) n.35

Peters, People v., 449 Mich. 515, 537 N.W.2d 160 (1995)—§§ 27.5(a) n.3, 7

Peters v. Secretary of Health and Human Serv., 934 F.2d 693 (6th Cir.1991)—§ 13.5(h) n.147

Peters, State v., 244 Wis.2d 470, 628 N.W.2d 797 (Wis.2001)—§ 24.2(f) n.87

Peters, State v., 237 Wis.2d 741, 615 N.W.2d 655 (2000)—§ 21.4(a) n.6

Peters, State v., 855 S.W.2d 345 (Mo.1993)—§ 24.10(b) n.29

Peters, State v., 315 So.2d 678 (La.1975)—§ 10.4(b) n.9

Peters, United States v., 435 F.3d 746 (7th Cir.2006)—§ 6.9(g) n.167

Peters, United States v., 937 F.2d 1422 (9th Cir.1991)—§ 20.6(c) n.75

Peters, United States v., 617 F.2d 503 (7th Cir.1980)—§ 22.3(e) n.268

Petersen v. Farnsworth, 371 F.3d 1219 (10th Cir.2004)—§ 12.5(a) n.2

Petersen, United States v., 777 F.2d 482 (9th Cir.1985)—§ 11.10(d) n.199

Peterson, Ex parte, 890 So.2d 990 (Ala.2004)—§ 21.5(e) n.151

Peterson v. City of Long Beach, 24 Cal.3d 238, 155 Cal.Rptr. 360, 594 P.2d 477 (1979)—§ 1.7(j) n.226

Peterson, People v., 74 Ill.2d 478, 23 Ill.Dec. 554, 384 N.E.2d 348 (1978)—§ 26.10(c) n.82

Peterson, People v., 98 Misc.2d 637, 414 N.Y.S.2d 436 (1978)—§ 24.3(b) n.66

Peterson, People v., 93 Mich. 27, 52 N.W. 1039 (1892)—§ 16.3(d) n.53

Peterson, State v., 110 P.3d 699 (Utah 2005)—§ 3.8(e) n.221

Peterson, State v., 663 N.W.2d 417 (Iowa 2003)—§ 6.6(b) n.16

Peterson, State v., 137 Idaho 255, 47 P.3d 378 (App.2002)—§§ 18.4(c) n.44, 60

Peterson, State v., 30 S.W.3d 209 (Mo.App.2000)—§ 18.4(c) n.47

Peterson, State v., 739 So.2d 561 (Fla.1999)—§ 3.3(c) n.89

Peterson, State v., 344 N.C. 172, 472 S.E.2d 730 (1996)—§ 6.9(c) n.66

Peterson v. State, 671 So.2d 647 (Miss.1996)—§§ 19.3(a) n.15, 54

Peterson v. State, 674 N.E.2d 528 (Ind.1996)—§ 2.12(c) n.146

Peterson, State v., 97 Wash.2d 864, 651 P.2d 211 (1982)—§ 21.3(e) n.266

Peterson, State v., 90 Wash.2d 423, 585 P.2d 66 (1978)—§ 18.4(c) n.44

Peterson, United States v., 414 F.3d 825 (7th Cir.2005)—§§ 6.8(b) n.47; 21.5(d) n.104

Peterson, United States v., 225 F.3d 1167 (10th Cir.2000)—§§ 21.2(d) n.158, 180

Peterson, United States v., 233 F.3d 101 (1st Cir.2000)—§ 13.4(e) n.169

Peterson, United States v., 867 F.2d 1110 (8th Cir.1989)—§ 3.4(j) n.203

Peterson, United States v., 812 F.2d 486 (9th Cir.1987)—§§ 3.1(i) n.236; 4.6(c) n.62

Peterson v. Utah Board of Pardons, 931 P.2d 147 (Utah Ct.App.1997)—§ 26.2(c) n.46

Peterson v. Williams, 85 F.3d 39 (2d Cir.1996)—§ 24.1(b) n.18

Pethel v. McBride, 219 W.Va. 578, 638 S.E.2d 727 (2006)—§§ 18.4(c) n.33, 46; 21.6(a) n.57

Petite v. United States, 361 U.S. 529, 80 S.Ct. 450, 4 L.Ed.2d 490 (1960)—§ 25.5(a) n.13

Petitioner, Brief of, 2002 WL 264766 (2002)—§ 19.3(e) n.230

Petito, United States v., 671 F.2d 68 (2d Cir.1982)—§ 8.3(a) n.7

Petraborg v. United States, 432 F.2d 1194 (7th Cir.1970)—§ 21.2(g) n.401

Petralia, People v., 62 N.Y.2d 47, 476 N.Y.S.2d 56, 464 N.E.2d 424 (1984)—§ 10.5(f) n.64

Petrillo, United States v., 237 F.3d 119 (2d Cir.2000)—§ 24.11(d) n.28

Petrol Stops Northwest v. Continental Oil Co., 647 F.2d 1005 (9th Cir.1981)—§ 8.5(c) n.94

Pettaway v. Plummer, 943 F.2d 1041 (9th Cir.1991)—§ 17.4(a) n.15

Petti, United States v., 973 F.2d 1441 (9th Cir.1992)—§§ 3.4(e) n.84; 4.6(e) n.80

Pettiford v. State, 619 N.E.2d 925 (Ind.1993)—§ 6.2(c) n.178

Pettiford v. United States, 700 A.2d 207 (D.C.App.1997)—§§ 21.3(b) n.41, 52

Pettigrew, United States v., 455 F.3d 1164 (10th Cir.2006)—§ 9.5(c) n.68

Pettigrew, United States v., 468 F.3d 626 (10th Cir.2006)—§ 9.5(c) n.67

Pettis, People v., 12 Ill.App.3d 123, 298 N.E.2d 372 (1973)—§ 9.4(d) n.96

Pettit v. State, 612 So.2d 1381 (Fla.App.1992)—§ 20.3(f) n.108

Pettit, State v., 227 Neb. 218, 417 N.W.2d 3 (1987)—§ 2.12(d) n.181

Pettitt, State v., 93 Wash.2d 288, 609 P.2d 1364 (1980)—§ 13.2(h) n.143

Petty v. City of El Dorado, 270 Kan. 847, 19 P.3d 167 (2001)—§ 13.6(a) n.6

Petty v. Smith, 279 Ga. 273, 612 S.E.2d 276 (2005)—§§ 21.3(b) n.60; 21.6(a) n.28

Petty, United States v., 1 F.3d 695 (8th Cir.1993)—§ 11.7(e) n.77

Petty, United States v., 982 F.2d 1365 (9th Cir.1993)—§§ 26.4(f) n.85, 90, 103

Petz, United States v., 764 F.2d 1390 (11th Cir.1985)—§ 11.9(c) n.130

Peveler v. United States, 269 F.3d 693 (6th Cir.2001)—§ 28.4(e) n.84

Peyatt v. Kopp, 189 W.Va. 114, 428 S.E.2d 535 (1993)—§§ 14.4(d) n.88; 14.4(e) n.112

Peyton v. Rowe, 391 U.S. 54, 88 S.Ct. 1549, 20 L.Ed.2d 426 (1968)— § 28.3(a) n.31

Pfeifer, United States v., 371 F.3d 430 (8th Cir.2004)—§ 21.4(d) n.125

Pforzheimer, United States v., 826 F.2d 200 (2d Cir.1987)—§§ 2.12(c) n.172; 24.10(a) n.11

Phabsomphou, State v., 530 N.W.2d 876 (Minn.App.1995)—§ 26.10(c) n.79

Phan v. Commonwealth, 18 Va.App. 360, 444 S.E.2d 9 (1994)— § 19.5(c) n.60

Pharmatrak Privacy Litigation, In re, 329 F.3d 9 (1st Cir.2003)— §§ 4.4(d) n.16; 4.6(b) n.37; 4.6(o) n.263; 4.7(c) n.14

Phea v. Benson, 95 F.3d 660 (8th Cir.1996)—§ 22.2(d) n.80

Pheaster, United States v., 544 F.2d 353 (9th Cir.1976)—§§ 6.7(c) n.106, 109; 6.9(f) n.114; 19.1(d) n.65

Pheil, State v., 152 Wis.2d 523, 449 N.W.2d 858 (1989)—§ 23.2(c) n.63

PHE, Inc., In re, 790 F.Supp. 1310 (W.D.Ky.1992)—§§ 8.8(c) n.43, 44; 8.8(d) n.52, 67, 75; 24.3(f) n.149

Phelps v. Duckworth, 757 F.2d 811 (7th Cir.1985)—§ 9.6(a) n.38

Phelps, State v., 131 Idaho 249, 953 P.2d 999 (1998)—§ 14.3(d) n.96

Phelps, State v., 241 Neb. 707, 490 N.W.2d 676 (1992)—§ 16.1(g) n.270

Phelps, State v., 215 Mont. 217, 696 P.2d 447 (1985)—§ 6.2(c) n.110

Phelps, State v., 297 N.W.2d 769 (N.D.1980)—§ 26.5(c) n.52

Phelps, United States v., 443 F.2d 246 (5th Cir.1971)—§ 6.6(f) n.113

Philadelphia County Investigating Grand Jury XII, In re, 529 Pa. 471, 605 A.2d 318 (1992)—§ 8.14(d) n.50

Philadelphia Electric Co. v. Anaconda American Brass Co., 41 F.R.D. 518 (E.D.Pa.1967)—§ 8.5(d) n.126

Philip S., Commonwealth v., 414 Mass. 804, 611 N.E.2d 226 (1993)— § 6.9(g) n.178

Phillip, United States v., 948 F.2d 241 (6th Cir.1991)—§ 24.3(b) n.42

Phillips v. Hust, 477 F.3d 1070 (9th Cir.2007)—§ 28.12(a) n.6

Phillips, People v., 371 Ill.App. 3d 948, 309 Ill.Dec. 582 (Ill.App.2007)— § 24.5(d) n.52

Phillips, People v., 217 Ill.2d 270, 298 Ill.Dec. 759, 840 N.E.2d 1194 (2005)—§ 21.6(c) n.118

Phillips, People v., 88 A.D.2d 672, 450 N.Y.S.2d 925 (1982)—§ 15.2(c) n.78

Phillips v. Smith, 485 F.Supp. 1365 (S.D.N.Y.1980)—§ 22.3(c) n.139

Phillips, State v., 204 S.W.3d 729 (Mo.App.2006)—§§ 19.3(a) n.13; 19.3(e) n.244, 248

Phillips, State v., 138 N.M. 730, 126 P.3d 546 (N.M.App.2005)— § 26.10(c) n.72

Phillips v. State, 275 Ga. 595, 571 S.E.2d 361 (2002)—§ 22.4(c) n.29

Phillips, State v., 940 S.W.2d 512 (Mo.1997)—§ 24.3(b) n.41

Phillips, State v., 74 Ohio St.3d 72, 656 N.E.2d 643 (1995)—§ 17.4(a) n.46

Phillips v. State, 612 So.2d 557 (Fla.1992)—§ 6.4(e) n.76

Phillips, State v., 152 Ariz. 533, 733 P.2d 1116 (Ariz. 1987)—§ 21.3(e) n.284

Phillips v. State, 492 N.E.2d 10 (Ind.1986)—§ 6.9(f) n.102

Phillips v. State, 493 So.2d 350 (Miss.1986)—§ 5.1(c) n.18

Phillips, State v., 465 So.2d 794 (La.App.1985)—§ 24.3(f) n.149

Phillips, State v., 672 S.W.2d 427 (Tenn.Cr.App.1984)—§§ 22.5(a) n.6; 22.5(b) n.15

Phillips v. State, 29 Wis.2d 521, 139 N.W.2d 41 (1966)—§ 6.3(c) n.53

Phillips, State v., 42 Wash.2d 137, 253 P.2d 919 (1953)—§ 16.2(a) n.1

Phillips, United States v., 195 F.Supp.2d 893 (E.D.Mich.2001)—§ 24.2(g) n.97

Phillips, United States v., 239 F.3d 829 (7th Cir.2001)—§§ 17.2(e) n.121; 17.3(d) n.55; 22.2(a) n.12

Phillips, United States v., 732 F.Supp. 255 (D.Mass.1990)—§ 12.1(a) n.16

Phillips, United States v., 664 F.2d 971 (5th Cir.1981)—§ 22.3(e) n.279

Phillips, United States v., 599 F.2d 134 (6th Cir.1979)—§ 17.1(d) n.48

Phillips, United States v., 497 F.2d 1131 (9th Cir.1974)—§ 3.10(c) n.96

Phillips v. United States, 502 F.2d 227 (4th Cir.1974)—§ 17.4(a) n.19

Phillips, United States v., 478 F.2d 743 (5th Cir.1973)—§ 4.2(a) n.10

Phillips, United States v., 375 F.2d 75 (7th Cir.1967)—§ 10.2(b) n.26

Phillips Petroleum Co., United States v., 435 F.Supp. 610 (N.D.Okla.1977)—§§ 15.6(b) n.61; 15.7(f) n.152, 187

Philpott, State v., 882 S.W.2d 394 (Tenn.Crim.App.1994)—§ 10.5(f) n.62

Phinney, State v., 348 N.W.2d 466 (S.D.1984)—§ 7.4(c) n.48

Phinney, State v., 117 N.H. 145, 370 A.2d 1153 (1977)—§ 10.4(b) n.10

Phipps, People v., 83 Ill.2d 87, 46 Ill.Dec. 164, 413 N.E.2d 1277 (1980)—§ 27.3(c) n.44

Phipps, State v., 959 S.W.2d 538 (Tenn.1997)—§§ 13.7(c) n.64; 26.8(b) n.14

Phipps, United States v., 319 F.3d 177 (5th Cir.2003)—§ 18.3(b) n.5

Phipps, United States ex rel. v. Follette, 428 F.2d 912 (2d Cir.1970)—§ 7.4(b) n.8

Phoenix, State v., 428 So.2d 262 (1982)—§ 1.8(f) n.103

Photogrammetric Data Services, Inc., United States v., 259 F.3d 229 (4th Cir.2001)—§§ 6.6(e) n.62; 17.2(b) n.45

Piancone, United States v., 506 F.2d 748 (3d Cir.1974)—§ 24.9(a) n.7

Piankhy v. Cuyler, 703 F.2d 728 (3d Cir.1983)—§ 11.3(a) n.12

Piazzola v. Watkins, 442 F.2d 284 (5th Cir.1971)—§§ 3.9(k) n.245; 3.10(e) n.185

Picard v. Connor, 404 U.S. 270, 92 S.Ct. 509, 30 L.Ed.2d 438 (1971)—§§ 28.5(a) n.10, 27

Piccirillo v. New York, 400 U.S. 548, 91 S.Ct. 520, 27 L.Ed.2d 596 (1971)—§ 2.9(d) n.77

Pichardo, People v., 1 N.Y.3d 126, 769 N.Y.S.2d 791, 802 N.E.2d 141 (2003)—§ 21.2(d) n.194

Pickar, State v., 453 N.W.2d 783 (N.D.1990)—§§ 6.2(c) n.102, 166, 171

Pickens v. Gibson, 206 F.3d 988 (10th Cir.2000)—§ 6.9(f) n.139

Pickens, People v., 61 Cal.App. 405, 214 P. 1027 (1923)—§ 27.6(b) n.13

Pickens, State v., 109 Ohio App.3d 147, 671 N.E.2d 1116 (1996)—§§ 13.6(d) n.56, 69

Pickens, State v., 335 N.C. 717, 440 S.E.2d 552 (1994)—§ 17.2(d) n.93

Pickens, State v., 183 W.Va. 261, 395 S.E.2d 505 (1990)—§§ 15.7(b) n.40; 15.7(g) n.219

Pickens v. State, 96 Wis.2d 549, 292 N.W.2d 601 (1980)—§ 11.5(d) n.82

Pickens v. Tucker, 851 F.Supp. 363 (8th Cir.1994)—§ 26.2(c) n.76

Pickett, United States v., 353 F.3d 62 (D.C.Cir.2004)—§§ 19.3(a) n.117, 129

Picketts, United States v., 655 F.2d 837 (7th Cir.1981)—§§ 8.10(c) n.62, 74

Pidcock, State v., 306 Or. 335, 759 P.2d 1092 (1988)—§ 3.2(h) n.203

Pielago, United States v., 135 F.3d 703 (11th Cir.1998)—§ 8.11(e) n.92

Pierce, Commonwealth v., 515 Pa. 153, 527 A.2d 973 (1987)—§ 11.10(a) n.12

Pierce v. State, 761 N.E.2d 821 (Ind.2002)—§§ 6.2(c) n.100, 130, 146

Pierce, State v., 173 Vt. 151, 787 A.2d 1284 (2001)—§§ 3.8(b) n.17; 3.8(c) n.96

Pierce v. State, 209 Ga.App. 366, 433 S.E.2d 641 (1993)—§ 20.3(f) n.110

Pierce, State v., 439 N.W.2d 435, 231 Neb. 966 (1989)—§ 24.7(e) n.74

Pierce, State v., 126 N.H. 84, 489 A.2d 109 (1985)—§ 3.3(d) n.173

Pierce, State v., 474 A.2d 182 (Me.1984)—§§ 17.1(a) n.15; 17.1(d) n.53

Pierce v. State, 125 Ga.App. 490, 188 S.E.2d 181 (1972)—§ 16.3(b) n.20

Pierce v. Underwood, 487 U.S. 552, 108 S.Ct. 2541, 101 L.Ed.2d 490 (1988)—§§ 13.5(h) n.164, 214; 27.5(e) n.140

Pierce v. United States, 705 A.2d 1086 (D.C.App.1997)—§§ 21.4(b) n.57, 65

Pierce, United States v., 60 F.3d 886 (1st Cir.1995)—§ 17.4(b) n.140

Pierce, People ex rel. v. Thomas, 70 Misc.2d 629, 334 N.Y.S.2d 666 (Sup.Ct.1972)—§ 14.4(c) n.52

Pierpoint, Matter of, 271 Kan. 620, 24 P.3d 128 (2001)—§ 11.1(b) n.93

Pierre, In the Matter of, 118 Wash.2d 321, 823 P.2d 492 (1992)—§ 2.11(a) n.14

Pierre, State v., 842 So.2d 321 (La.2003)—§§ 22.1(h) n.134, 137

Pierre, United States v., 958 F.2d 1304 (5th Cir.1992)—§ 3.9(f) n.120

Pierre, United States v., 974 F.2d 1355 (D.C.Cir.1992)—§§ 22.1(g) n.98, 125

Pierre, United States v., 932 F.2d 377 (5th Cir.1991)—§§ 3.10(b) n.41; 9.4(b) n.54

Pierro v. Turner, 95 Okla.Crim. 425, 247 P.2d 291 (1952)—§ 15.2(h) n.185

Pierson v. Ray, 386 U.S. 547, 87 S.Ct. 1213, 18 L.Ed.2d 288 (1967)—§ 3.1(k) n.259

Pierson v. State, 338 A.2d 571 (Del.1975)—§ 3.3(g) n.231

Pierson v. State, 210 Kan. 367, 502 P.2d 721 (1972)—§ 18.4(d) n.85

Pietras, United States v., 501 F.2d 182 (8th Cir.1974)—§ 17.1(a) n.10

Pietri v. State, 644 So.2d 1347 (Fla.1994)—§ 23.2(f) n.83

Pigman v. Evansville Press, 537 N.E.2d 547 (Ind.App.1989)—§§ 8.5(b) n.35; 8.5(c) n.71, 78

Pigott, State v., 331 N.C. 199, 415 S.E.2d 555 (1992)—§ 15.4(b) n.66

Pike v. State, 164 S.W.3d 257 (Tenn.2005)—§ 28.11(a) n.10

Pike, State v., 712 P.2d 277 (Utah 1985)—§ 24.9(f) n.81

Pike, State v., 49 Or.App. 67, 618 P.2d 1315 (1980)—§§ 26.9(a) n.1, 6

Pike, State v., 65 Me. 111 (1876)—§ 24.9(g) n.109

Pilarinos, United States v., 864 F.2d 253 (2d Cir.1988)—§§ 5.1(c) n.34, 37

Pilcher v. State, 355 Ark. 369, 136 S.W.3d 766 (2003)—§ 6.2(c) n.107

Pilkington v. United States, 315 F.2d 204 (4th Cir.1963)—§ 21.4(d) n.141

Pilliteri, In re, 420 F.Supp. 913 (W.D.Pa.1976)—§§ 8.8(b) n.26, 28

Pillor, United States v., 387 F.Supp.2d 1053 (N.D.Cal.2005)—§ 1.2(c) n.174

Pillsbury Co. v. Conboy, 459 U.S. 248, 103 S.Ct. 608, 74 L.Ed.2d 430 (1983)—§ 8.11(d) n.81

Pilotti, People v., 170 Misc.2d 118, 647 N.Y.S.2d 453 (Sup.Ct.1796)—§ 15.7(b) n.17

Pimental, United States v., 367 F.Supp.2d 143 (D.Mass.2005)—§ 26.4(h) n.154

Pimental, United States v., 380 F.3d 575 (2004)—§ 8.5(e) n.174

Pimentel, United States v., 810 F.2d 366 (2d Cir.1987)—§ 9.3(e) n.56

Pina, Commonwealth v., 406 Mass. 540, 549 N.E.2d 106 (1990)—§ 10.1(b) n.20

Pina, State v., 90 N.M. 181, 561 P.2d 43 (1977)—§ 19.4(a) n.5

Pinckney, State v., 306 N.W.2d 726 (Iowa 1981)—§ 27.5(c) n.98

Pinder, State v., 114 P.3d 551 (Utah 2005)—§ 24.11(d) n.23

Pinder, State v., 250 Conn. 385, 736 A.2d 857 (1999)—§§ 6.2(c) n.113; 6.6(c) n.35

Pinder, State v., 128 N.H. 66, 514 A.2d 1241 (1986)—§ 3.2(d) n.153

Pineiro, United States v., 470 F.3d 200 (5th Cir.2006)—§ 26.7(b) n.19

Pinela, State v., 458 N.W.2d 795 (S.D.1990)—§ 6.9(b) n.34

Pinizzotto v. Superior Court, 257 Cal.App.2d 582, 65 Cal.Rptr. 74 (1968)—§ 14.4(b) n.7

Pink, State v., 270 Kan. 728, 20 P.3d 31 (2001)—§§ 6.9(g) n.166; 22.3(d) n.246

Pinkerton v. State, 784 P.2d 671 (Alaska App.1989)—§§ 8.10(a) n.29; 8.10(d) n.114 to 116

Pinkerton v. United States, 328 U.S. 640, 66 S.Ct. 1180, 90 L.Ed. 1489 (1946)—§ 16.2(g) n.138

Pinkham, State v., 955 S.W.2d 956 (Tenn.1997)—§ 13.6(c) n.45

Pinkney v. Keane, 920 F.2d 1090 (2d Cir.1990)—§ 10.6(d) n.41

Pinkney v. State, 350 Md. 201, 711 A.2d 205 (1998)—§§ 24.2(d) n.44, 47

Pinkney, State v., 33 Ohio Misc. 183, 290 N.E.2d 923 (1972)—§ 3.1(m) n.296

Pinkus v. United States, 436 U.S. 293, 98 S.Ct. 1808, 56 L.Ed.2d 293 (1978)—§ 27.5(b) n.37

Pinnell, People v., 43 Cal.App.3d 627, 117 Cal.Rptr. 913 (1974)—§ 15.4(b) n.55

Pino v. State, 849 P.2d 716 (Wyo.1993)—§ 24.11(d) n.22

Pino, United States v., 855 F.2d 357 (6th Cir.1988)—§ 3.7(a) n.16

Pino, United States v., 729 F.2d 1357 (11th Cir.1984)—§ 3.9(f) n.100

Pino, United States v., 708 F.2d 523 (10th Cir.1983)—§§ 15.5(b) n.36; 15.6(b) n.58; 15.6(e) n.152

Pinson, United States v., 321 F.3d 558 (6th Cir.2003)—§§ 3.3(a) n.11; 3.3(c) n.93

Pinter, United States v., 971 F.2d 554 (10th Cir.1992)—§ 21.2(d) n.241

Pinto v. Pierce, 389 U.S. 31, 88 S.Ct. 192, 19 L.Ed.2d 31 (1967)—§§ 10.5(b) n.18, 22

Pioletti, State v., 246 Kan. 49, 785 P.2d 963 (1990)—§ 14.3(d) n.85

Piper, State v., 663 N.W.2d 894 (Iowa 2003)—§§ 13.2(c) n.61, 66

Pipkins v. State, 592 So.2d 947 (Miss.1991)—§ 3.3(c) n.94

Pirillo v. Takiff, 462 Pa. 511, 341 A.2d 896 (1975)—§ 8.14(d) n.56

Pirkey, State v., 203 Or. 697, 281 P.2d 698 (1955)—§ 13.7(a) n.26

Pirman, State ex rel. v. Money, 69 Ohio St.3d 591, 635 N.E.2d 26 (1994)—§ 27.4(f) n.65

Pirolli, United States v., 742 F.2d 1382 (11th Cir.1984)—§ 17.2(d) n.98

Pirtle, Matter of, 136 Wash.2d 467, 965 P.2d 593 (1998)—§ 6.7(b) n.41

Pirtle v. Morgan, 313 F.3d 1160 (9th Cir.2002)—§§ 11.10(c) n.75, 151; 28.6(f) n.76

Pisano v. Shillinger, 814 P.2d 274 (Wyo.1991)—§§ 12.3(b) n.63; 12.4(f) n.96

Pitner, United States v., 307 F.3d 1178 (9th Cir.2002)—§ 18.3(b) n.22

Pitsonbarger v. Gramley, 103 F.3d 1293 (7th Cir.1996)—§§ 18.4(c) n.76, 77

Pitsonbarger, People v., 205 Ill.2d 444, 275 Ill.Dec. 838, 793 N.E.2d 609 (2002)—§ 22.3(d) n.202

Pitt, State v., 390 Md. 697, 891 A.2d 697 (2006)—§ 21.2(h) n.439

Pitt, United States v., 193 F.3d 751 (3d Cir.1999)—§ 5.4(c) n.46

Pittman, State v., 360 Ark. 273, 200 S.W.3d 893 (2005)—§ 6.7(c) n.129

Pittman v. State, 277 Ga. 475, 592 S.E.2d 72 (2004)—§ 6.8(d) n.84

Pittman v. State, 337 S.C. 597, 524 S.E.2d 623 (1999)—§ 21.4(d) n.103

Pittman, United States v., 411 F.3d 813 (7th Cir.2005)—§ 9.4(b) n.58

Pittman, United States v., 82 F.3d 152 (7th Cir.1996)—§ 24.3(c) n.104

Pitts v. State, 259 Ga. 745, 386 S.E.2d 351 (1989)—§ 6.9(e) n.97

Pitts, United States v., 6 F.3d 1366 (9th Cir.1993)—§ 3.3(g) n.247

Pitts v. United States, 763 F.2d 197 (6th Cir.1985)—§ 21.5(c) n.74

Pittsburgh Action Against Rape, In re, 494 Pa. 15, 428 A.2d 126 (1981)—§ 20.3(l) n.226

Pittsburgh Plate Glass Co. v. United States, 360 U.S. 395, 79 S.Ct. 1237, 3 L.Ed.2d 1323 (1959)—§§ 8.5(g) n.225; 8.5(h) n.267

Pixley, Commonwealth v., 42 Mass.App. 927, 677 N.E.2d 273 (1997)—§ 24.9(c) n.20

Pizarro v. Bartlett, 776 F.Supp. 815 (S.D.N.Y.1991)—§ 11.4(b) n.23

Pizzarello v. United States, 408 F.2d 579 (2d Cir.1969)—§ 3.1(g) n.177

Pizzuto v. Arave, 280 F.3d 949 (9th Cir.2002)—§ 6.10(e) n.67

P.J. Video, People v., 68 N.Y.2d 296, 501 N.E.2d 556, 508 N.Y.S.2d 907 (1986)—§§ 2.12(b) n.104; 2.12(e) n.200, 213

Place, United States v., 462 U.S. 696, 103 S.Ct. 2637, 77 L.Ed.2d 110 (1983)—§§ 3.1(h) n.196; 3.2(a) n.29; 3.2(b) n.67; 3.5(b) n.103; 3.8(b) n.36; 3.8(h) n.249; 4.2(b) n.14

Placek, People v., 184 Ill.2d 370, 235 Ill.Dec. 44, 704 N.E.2d 393 (1998)—§ 5.2(a) n.9

Plambeck, State v., 182 S.W.3d 365 (Tex.Crim.App.2005)—§ 13.2(c) n.58

Planned Parenthood of Southeastern Pennsylvania v. Casey, 505 U.S. 833, 112 S.Ct. 2791, 120 L.Ed.2d 674 (1992)—§§ 2.7(d) n.255; 2.9(b) n.5, 9, 19 to 21, 25, 39, 40

Plant, State v., 165 Vt. 617, 686 A.2d 941 (1996)—§ 12.3(g) n.148

Plant, State v., 236 Neb. 317, 461 N.W.2d 253 (1990)—§ 3.6(f) n.149

Plante, In re, 171 Vt. 310, 762 A.2d 873 (2000)—§ 21.3(b) n.102

Plante, State v., 623 A.2d 166 (Me.1993)—§ 20.3(a) n.19

Plante v. State, 203 Ga.App. 33, 416 S.E.2d 316 (1992)—§ 24.3(f) n.154

Plante, State v., 134 N.H. 585, 594 A.2d 165 (1991)—§ 3.9(h) n.169

Plaster v. United States, 789 F.2d 289 (4th Cir.1986)—§§ 8.11(e) n.99, 101

Platou, Commonwealth v., 455 Pa. 258, 312 A.2d 29 (1973)—§§ 2.12(a) n.18; 3.4(j) n.193

Platt v. Minnesota Mining and Manufacturing Co., 376 U.S. 240, 84 S.Ct. 769, 11 L.Ed.2d 674 (1964)—§§ 16.2(b) n.36; 16.3(c) n.31, 33, 48

Platt, People v., 81 P.3d 1060 (Colo.2004)—§ 6.6(f) n.100

Platt, State v., 158 Vt. 423, 610 A.2d 139 (1992)—§ 21.2(e) n.300

Platt, State v., 154 Vt. 179, 574 A.2d 789 (1990)—§ 3.4(d) n.58

Platt, State v., 193 La. 928, 192 So. 659 (La.1939)—§ 8.4(b) n.109

Platteville Area Apartment Ass'n v. City of Platteville, 179 F.3d 574 (7th Cir.1999)—§ 3.9(b) n.21

Plattner, United States v., 330 F.2d 271 (2d Cir.1964)—§ 11.5(b) n.24

Plautz, People v., 28 Mich.App. 621, 184 N.W.2d 761 (1970)—§§ 16.1(g) n.245, 275

Plch, State v., 149 N.H. 608, 826 A.2d 534 (2003)—§ 6.9(f) n.131

Pleasant, United States v., 125 F.Supp.2d 173 (E.D.Va.2000)—§§ 19.3(c) n.187; 19.5(d) n.75

Pleasant, United States v., 730 F.2d 657 (11th Cir.1984)—§ 21.2(f) n.383

Pledger, State v., 896 P.2d 1226 (Utah 1995)—§§ 14.3(a) n.10, 27

Plewniak, United States v., 947 F.2d 1284 (5th Cir.1991)—§ 11.9(c) n.132

Pliler v. Ford, 542 U.S. 225, 124 S.Ct. 2441, 159 L.Ed.2d 338 (2004)—§ 28.5(a) n.23

Plitman, United States v., 194 F.3d 59 (2d Cir.1999)—§ 11.6(a) n.49

Ploof, State v., 162 Vt. 560, 649 A.2d 774 (Vt.1994)—§§ 11.5(c) n.62; 11.5(d) n.73

Ploof, United States v., 851 F.2d 7 (1st Cir.1988)—§ 12.3(a) n.19

Plumlee v. Sue del Papa, 465 F.3d 910 (9th Cir.2006)—§ 11.4(b) n.24

Plumlee v. Sue del Papa, 426 F.3d 1095 (9th Cir.2005)—§ 11.4(d) n.110

Plumman, United States v., 409 F.3d 919 (8th Cir.2005)—§§ 6.6(e) n.59; 6.7(c) n.118

Plummer, United States v., 221 F.3d 1298 (11th Cir.2000)—§ 16.4(b) n.25

Plummer, United States v., 941 F.2d 799 (9th Cir.1991)—§ 8.11(e) n.105

Podde, United States v., 105 F.3d 813 (2d Cir.1997)—§ 18.5(a) n.52

Podgurski, Commonwealth v., 386 Mass. 385, 436 N.E.2d 150 (1982)—§ 3.2(f) n.184

Poe v. State, 389 So.2d 154 (Ala.Cr.App.1980)—§ 27.5(c) n.102

Poe v. Ullman, 367 U.S. 497, 81 S.Ct. 1752, 6 L.Ed.2d 989 (1961)—§§ 1.2(b) n.4; 2.3(b) n.91; 2.4(f) n.182; 13.5(c) n.68

Poe, United States v., 713 F.2d 579 (10th Cir.1983)—§ 24.4(d) n.58

Poehlman, United States v., 217 F.3d 692 (9th Cir.2000)—§§ 5.2(a) n.8, 16

Poellnitz, United States v., 372 F.3d 562 (3d Cir.2004)—§ 21.4(a) n.21

Poggemiller, United States v., 375 F.3d 686 (8th Cir.2004)—§ 3.7(a) n.16

Pogue, United States v., 19 F.3d 663 (D.C.Cir.1994)—§ 27.5(a) n.3

Pohlhammer, State v., 78 Wis.2d 516, 254 N.W.2d 478 (1977)—§§ 18.5(a) n.39; 21.2(d) n.278

Poindexter, United States v., 727 F.Supp. 1470 (D.D.C.1989)—§§ 20.3(a) n.12; 20.3(b) n.50; 20.3(g) n.122, 125

Pointer, People v., 151 Cal.App.3d 1128, 199 Cal.Rptr. 357 (1984)—§ 26.9(b) n.55

Pointer v. Texas, 380 U.S. 400, 85 S.Ct. 1065, 13 L.Ed.2d 923 (1965)—§§ 2.5(b) n.14, 15; 2.5(c) n.17, 19; 2.5(d) n.31; 2.5(e) n.39; 2.5(f) n.53, 58, 100; 2.6(a) n.6, 10; 2.6(b) n.34; 17.2(b) n.29; 24.2(a) n.1

Pointer v. United States, 151 U.S. 396, 14 S.Ct. 410, 38 L.Ed. 208 (1894)—§§ 17.2(a) n.24; 22.3(a) n.2; 22.3(d) n.181

Polan, United States v., 970 F.2d 1280 (3d Cir.1992)—§§ 19.3(a) n.16, 17

Polanco v. United States Drug Enforcement Admin., 158 F.3d 647 (2d Cir.1998)—§ 10.1(c) n.49

Poland v. Arizona, 476 U.S. 147, 106 S.Ct. 1749, 90 L.Ed.2d 123 (1986)—§ 26.7(a) n.9

Poland, State v., 782 So.2d 556 (La.2001)—§ 8.5(b) n.45

Polander, People v., 41 P.3d 698 (Colo.2001)—§ 6.6(c) n.33

Police Com'r of City of New York, Application of, 131 Misc.2d 695, 501 N.Y.S.2d 568 (1986)—§ 8.5(h) n.286

Polichemi, United States v., 201 F.3d 858 (7th Cir.2000)—§ 22.3(c) n.128

Polikov v. Neth, 270 Neb. 29, 699 N.W.2d 802 (2005)—§§ 13.2(a) n.3; 13.6(b) n.20

Poling, State v., 207 W.Va. 299, 531 S.E.2d 678 (2000)—§§ 3.2(c) n.110; 10.6(a) n.6

Politte v. United States, 852 F.2d 924 (7th Cir.1988)—§ 21.2(b) n.53

Polizzi, United States v., 500 F.2d 856 (9th Cir.1974)—§ 16.3(c) n.43

Polk, People v., 21 Ill.2d 594, 174 N.E.2d 393 (1961)—§§ 8.8(a) n.12, 13

Polk v. State, 612 So.2d 381 (Miss.1992)—§ 11.2(e) n.190

Polk, United States v., 433 F.2d 644 (5th Cir.1970)—§ 3.2(f) n.186

Pollack, United States v., 91 F.3d 331 (2d Cir.1996)—§ 21.2(d) n.264

Pollack, United States v., 534 F.2d 964 (D.C.Cir.1976)—§ 20.3(m) n.252

Pollack, United States v., 427 F.2d 1168 (5th Cir.1970)—§ 7.4(f) n.101

Pollard, United States v., 389 F.3d 101 (4th Cir.2004)—§§ 11.2(a) n.25, 26

Pollard, United States v., 215 F.3d 643 (6th Cir.2000)—§ 9.1(b) n.74

Pollard, United States v., 959 F.2d 1011 (D.C.Cir.1992)—§ 21.2(b) n.59

Pollard v. United States, 352 U.S. 354, 77 S.Ct. 481, 1 L.Ed.2d 393 (1957)—§ 18.5(c) n.74

Pollard, State ex rel. v. Criminal Court, 263 Ind. 236, 329 N.E.2d 573 (1975)—§§ 8.7(a) n.19; 8.10(c) n.51; 8.10(d) n.107

Pollen, United States v., 978 F.2d 78 (3d Cir.1992)—§ 21.6(a) n.63

Pollitt, State v., 205 Conn. 132, 531 A.2d 125 (1987)—§§ 7.4(d) n.74; 24.5(a) n.9

Pollock, United States v., 726 F.2d 1456 (9th Cir.1984)—§§ 9.2(c) n.33; 18.3(b) n.5, 53

Pomerantz, People v., 46 N.Y.2d 240, 413 N.Y.S.2d 288, 385 N.E.2d 1218 (1978)—§ 8.8(h) n.189

Pomeroy, United States v., 822 F.2d 718 (8th Cir.1987)—§ 18.2(c) n.49

Pompa-Ortiz, People v., 27 Cal.3d 519, 165 Cal.Rptr. 851, 612 P.2d 941 (1980)—§§ 14.4(e) n.108, 120, 122, 125, 129

Pomranz, United States v., 43 F.3d 156 (5th Cir.1995)—§§ 16.2(b) n.16; 16.2(g) n.109, 139

Pona, State v., 926 A.2d 592 (R.I. 2007)—§ 22.3(d) n.246

Ponce v. Craven, 409 F.2d 621 (9th Cir.1969)—§ 3.2(b) n.34

Pond, Commonwealth v., 24 Mass.App. 546, 510 N.E.2d 783 (1987)—§§ 15.7(e) n.100, 120, 127

Ponder, People v., 54 N.Y.2d 160, 445 N.Y.S.2d 57, 429 N.E.2d 735 (1981)—§ 2.12(d) n.198

Ponds, United States v., 290 F.Supp.2d 71 (D.D.C.2003)—§ 8.13(c) n.83

Pontbriand, State v., 178 Vt. 120, 878 A.2d 227 (Vt.2005)—§§ 6.2(c) n.154; 6.6(e) n.71

Ponte-Alfonzo, State v., 348 N.W.2d 734 (Minn.1984)—§ 6.8(d) n.84

Ponticelli v. State, 593 So.2d 483 (Fla.1991)—§ 6.2(c) n.140

Pool, Ex parte, 738 S.W.2d 285 (Tex.Cr.App.1987)—§ 21.3(b) n.60

Pool v. McKune, 267 Kan. 797, 987 P.2d 1073 (1999)—§ 3.9(i) n.192

Pool v. United States, 344 F.2d 943 (9th Cir.1965)—§ 22.1(h) n.136

Poole, Ex parte, 497 So.2d 537 (1986)—§ 24.9(f) n.93

Poole v. Goodno, 335 F.3d 705 (8th Cir.2003)—§ 22.1(c) n.60

Poole v. State, 846 So.2d 370 (Ala.Crim.App.2001)—§§ 19.3(a) n.39, 42, 43

Poole, State v., 499 N.W.2d 31 (Minn.1993)—§ 3.4(f) n.106

Poole, State v., 321 Md. 482, 583 A.2d 265 (1991)—§ 21.2(e) n.338

Poole v. State, 60 Wis.2d 152, 208 N.W.2d 328 (1973)—§ 16.4(c) n.103

Poole, United States v., 407 F.3d 767 (6th Cir.2005)—§§ 13.7(c) n.45, 52

Poole v. United States, 630 A.2d 1109 (D.C.App.1993)—§ 10.4(d) n.30

Poole, United States v., 794 F.2d 462 (9th Cir.1986)—§ 6.7(b) n.54

Poole, United States v., 495 F.2d 115 (D.C.Cir.1974)—§ 6.9(b) n.36

Poole, People ex rel. v. Hesterberg, 43 Misc. 510, 89 N.Y.S. 498 (1904)— § 13.5(c) n.60

Pooler, State v., 141 Me. 274, 43 A.2d 353 (1945)—§ 16.4(c) n.72

Poore v. State, 531 So.2d 161 (Fla.1988)—§§ 26.1(e) n.100, 101

Poor Thunder v. United States, 810 F.2d 817 (8th Cir.1987)—§ 28.9(c) n.77

Pope, Commonwealth v., 392 Mass. 493, 467 N.E.2d 117 (1984)— §§ 15.4(b) n.45; 17.3(e) n.64

Pope v. Illinois, 481 U.S. 497, 107 S.Ct. 1918, 95 L.Ed.2d 439 (1987)— §§ 27.6(d) n.89, 121

Pope, State v., 318 Mont. 383, 80 P.3d 1232 (Mont.2003)—§ 28.11(b) n.33

Pope, State v., 192 Neb. 755, 224 N.W.2d 521 (1974)—§§ 10.6(c) n.18, 20

Pope, United States v., 452 F.3d 338 (5th Cir.2006)—§ 3.1(c) n.68

Pope v. United States, 739 A.2d 819 (D.C.App.1999)—§ 12.3(a) n.6

Pope v. United States, 372 F.2d 710 (8th Cir.1967)—§ 20.4(e) n.82

Porcher, Commonwealth v., 26 Mass.App.Ct. 517, 529 N.E.2d 1348 (1988)—§ 20.6(c) n.83

Porreca, Commonwealth v., 528 Pa. 46, 595 A.2d 23 (1991)—§ 21.4(g) n.232

Porro, State v., 175 N.J.Super 49, 417 A.2d 573 (1980)—§ 8.10(c) n.83

Portalatin v. Graham, 478 F.Supp.2d 385 (E.D.N.Y.2007)—§ 26.4(i) n.197

Porter, Commonwealth v., 51 Mass. 263 (1845)—§ 1.6(d) n.235

Porter v. Coughlin, 421 F.3d 141 (2d Cir.2005)—§§ 17.4(b) n.133; 25.1(c) n.40

Porter v. Gramley, 112 F.3d 1308 (7th Cir.1997)—§ 28.5(a) n.34

Porter, People v., 156 Ill.2d 218, 189 Ill.Dec. 413, 620 N.E.2d 381 (Ill.1993)—§ 25.5(b) n.22

Porter v. Singletary, 14 F.3d 554 (11th Cir.1994)—§§ 11.9(d) n.202, 226; 11.10(c) n.66

Porter, State v., 150 Wash.2d 732, 82 P.3d 234 (2004)—§ 24.8(d) n.44

Porter, State v., 241 Conn. 57, 698 A.2d 739 (1997)—§ 26.5(a) n.4

Porter, State v., 326 N.C. 489, 391 S.E.2d 144 (1990)—§§ 22.3(d) n.247, 250

Porter v. State, 564 So.2d 1060 (Fla.1990)—§ 21.5(a) n.2

Porter, State v., 209 Neb. 722, 310 N.W.2d 926 (1981)—§ 26.5(a) n.1

Porter v. State, 400 So.2d 5 (Fla.1981)— § 15.4(a) n.10

Porter v. State, 271 Ind. 180, 391 N.E.2d 801 (1979)—§§ 15.4(b) n.45, 47

Porter v. State, 94 Nev. 142, 576 P.2d 275 (1978)—§§ 7.5(b) n.21, 27

Porter v. United States, 769 A.2d 143 (D.C.App.2001)—§ 18.5(a) n.36

Porter, United States v., 924 F.2d 395 (1st Cir.1991)—§ 7.4(e) n.90

Porter, United States v., 807 F.2d 21 (1st Cir.1986)—§ 25.4(c) n.32

Porter, United States v., 764 F.2d 1 (1st Cir.1985)—§ 6.9(g) n.162

Porter, United States v., 711 F.2d 1397 (7th Cir.1983)—§ 8.12(c) n.37

Porter, United States v., 544 F.2d 936 (8th Cir.1976)—§ 27.6(b) n.58

Porter v. Wainwright, 805 F.2d 930 (11th Cir.1986)—§§ 15.4(g) n.167; 15.4(i) n.213; 15.6(f) n.189, 192

Porterfield, State v., 746 S.W.2d 441 (Tenn.1988)—§ 17.2(b) n.38

Porterfield, United States v., 624 F.2d 122 (10th Cir.1980)—§ 11.10(a) n.14

Porter, State ex rel. v. Recht, 211 W.Va. 396, 566 S.E.2d 283 (2002)— § 17.3(b) n.13

Portes, United States v., 786 F.2d 758 (7th Cir.1985)—§§ 12.1(a) n.15; 12.3(a) n.23, 24; 12.3(e) n.115

Porth v. Templar, 453 F.2d 330 (10th Cir.1971)—§ 26.9(b) n.56

Portillo-Cano, United States v., 192 F.3d 1246 (9th Cir.1999)—§ 21.2(b) n.83

Portland, City of v. Lodi, 308 Or. 468, 782 P.2d 415 (1989)—§ 1.8(d) n.48

Portuondo v. Agard, 529 U.S. 61, 120 S.Ct. 1119, 146 L.Ed.2d 47 (2000)—§§ 24.5(d) n.48; 24.7(e) n.58

Posada-Rios, United States v., 158 F.3d 832 (5th Cir.1998)—§§ 6.2(c) n.148; 6.9(g) n.166

Posado, United States v., 57 F.3d 428 (5th Cir.1995)—§ 10.5(d) n.39

Posey, People v., 32 Cal.4th 193, 8 Cal.Rptr.3d 551, 82 P.3d 755 (2004)—§§ 16.1(g) n.235, 252; 22.2(e) n.109

Posey, State v., 40 Ohio St.3d 420, 534 N.E.2d 61 (1988)—§§ 3.2(e) n.164; 3.10(c) n.87

Posey v. United States, 416 F.2d 545 (5th Cir.1969)—§ 15.2(i) n.195

Posner, United States v., 865 F.2d 654 (5th Cir.1989)—§ 5.3(a) n.14

Pospisil, United States v., 186 F.3d 1023 (8th Cir.1999)—§ 22.3(d) n.248

Post, State v., 118 Wash.2d 596, 826 P.2d 172 (1992)—§§ 6.6(e) n.79; 6.7(b) n.100; 6.10(c) n.38; 6.10(e) n.69

Post, State v., 32 Ohio St.3d 380, 513 N.E.2d 754 (1987)—§ 21.4(f) n.207

Postal, United States v., 589 F.2d 862 (5th Cir.1979)—§ 16.4(b) n.17

Post-Newsweek Stations, Florida, Inc., In re, 370 So.2d 764 (Fla.1979)— § 23.3(b) n.19

Poston, United States v., 902 F.2d 90 (D.C.Cir.1990)—§§ 11.4(c) n.62; 11.8(c) n.61

Potash Litigation, In re, 896 F.Supp. 916 (D.Minn.1995)—§§ 8.5(c) n.83; 8.5(d) n.126

Potter v. State, 547 A.2d 595 (Del.Supr.1988)—§ 11.3(c) n.66

Potts v. State, 261 Ga. 716, 410 S.E.2d 89 (1991)—§ 17.4(b) n.109

Potts v. State, 259 Ga. 812, 388 S.E.2d 678 (1990)—§ 15.4(b) n.56

Potts, United States v., 297 F.2d 68 (6th Cir.1961)—§ 3.2(c) n.115

Pou, United States v., 484 F.Supp. 972 (S.D.Fla.1979)—§ 19.3(a) n.53

Pough v. United States, 442 F.3d 959 (6th Cir.2006)—§ 21.3(b) n.102

Poulas v. United States, 95 F.2d 412 (9th Cir.1938)—§ 3.3(f) n.217

Poulicakos, State v., 131 N.H. 709, 559 A.2d 1341 (1989)—§ 12.1(d) n.51

Pouncey, State v., 29 Wash.App. 629, 630 P.2d 932 (1981)—§ 21.2(c) n.107

Powell, In re, 117 Wash.2d 175, 814 P.2d 635 (1991)—§ 26.4(d) n.61

Powell v. Alabama, 287 U.S. 45, 53 S.Ct. 55, 77 L.Ed. 158 (1932)— §§ 2.4(a) n.13; 2.4(d) n.126; 2.4(e) n.138, 157, 175; 2.5(c) n.23; 2.5(f) n.45, 96; 2.7(c) n.106, 111; 2.9(d) n.94; 8.14(a) n.14; 11.1(a) n.3; 11.1(b) n.85; 11.4(c) n.52; 11.5(a) n.4; 11.7(a) n.2; 11.7(d) n.48; 11.8(c) n.48; 11.10(d) n.187

Powell v. Allstate Ins. Co., 652 So.2d 354 (Fla.1995)—§ 24.9(g) n.118

Powell v. Collins, 332 F.3d 376 (6th Cir.2003)—§ 11.2(e) n.215

Powell v. Commonwealth, 267 Va. 107, 590 S.E.2d 537 (2004)—§§ 22.5(a) n.11 to 13

Powell v. Graham, 185 S.W.3d 624 (Ky.2006)—§ 27.4(b) n.16

Powell v. Katzenbach, 359 F.2d 234 (D.C.Cir.1965)—§ 13.3(a) n.3

Powell v. Lambert, 357 F.3d 871 (9th Cir.2004)—§ 28.4(b) n.19

Powell v. Nevada, 511 U.S. 79, 114 S.Ct. 1280, 128 L.Ed.2d 1 (1994)—§§ 2.11(e) n.63; 3.5(a) n.52; 9.4(a) n.10

Powell v. Pappagianis, 108 N.H. 523, 238 A.2d 733 (1968)—§§ 15.1(d) n.251; 15.2(b) n.20

Powell, People v., 67 Cal.2d 32, 59 Cal.Rptr. 817, 429 P.2d 137 (1967)—§ 16.2(a) n.5

Powell, People v., 87 Cal. 348, 25 P. 481 (1891)—§§ 16.3(d) n.55, 60, 62; 16.3(g) n.119

Powell, State v., 907 A.2d 242 (Md.2006)—§ 22.1(h) n.134

Powell, State v., 266 Kan. 282, 971 P.2d 340 (1998)—§ 14.3(b) n.52

Powell v. State, 206 Ga.App. 36, 424 S.E.2d 333 (1992)—§ 9.6(a) n.47

Powell, State v., 598 So.2d 454 (La.App.1992)—§§ 16.1(g) n.235; 16.1(h) n.304

Powell v. State, 85 Md.App. 330, 583 A.2d 1114 (1991)—§§ 14.2(g) n.105, 107

Powell, State v., 34 Wash.App. 791, 664 P.2d 1 (1983)—§ 19.5(b) n.33

Powell v. State, 86 Wis.2d 51, 271 N.W.2d 610 (1978)—§ 7.4(c) n.41

Powell v. State, 23 Md.App. 666, 329 A.2d 413 (1974)—§ 20.6(b) n.28

Powell v. Superior Court, 232 Cal.App.3d 785, 283 Cal.Rptr. 777 (1991)—§§ 23.2(a) n.29, 30, 52, 53; 27.4(c) n.31, 37

Powell, United States v., 354 F.3d 362 (5th Cir.2003)—§ 21.5(c) n.83

Powell, United States v., 226 F.3d 1181 (10th Cir.2000)—§§ 22.3(c) n.134, 135

Powell v. United States, 684 A.2d 373 (D.C.App.1996)—§ 24.8(d) n.47

Powell, United States v., 929 F.2d 1190 (7th Cir.1991)—§§ 9.1(a) n.29; 9.1(d) n.125, 127

Powell, United States v., 823 F.2d 996 (6th Cir.1987)—§§ 15.5(b) n.64, 66

Powell, United States v., 469 U.S. 57, 105 S.Ct. 471, 83 L.Ed.2d 461 (1984)—§ 24.10(b) n.24

Powell, United States v., 498 F.2d 890 (9th Cir.1974)—§ 16.1(g) n.263

Powell v. Zuckert, 366 F.2d 634 (D.C.Cir.1966)—§ 3.1(i) n.235

Power, Commonwealth v., 420 Mass. 410, 650 N.E.2d 87 (1995)—§§ 26.9(b) n.16, 22, 23, 26, 58

Power, State v., 886 So.2d 952 (Fla.2004)—§ 24.9(g) n.129

Powers v. Commonwealth, 426 Mass. 534, 694 N.E.2d 324 (1998)—§ 17.4(b) n.124

Powers v. Lord, 462 F.Supp.2d 371 (W.D.N.Y.2006)—§ 28.4(d) n.57

Powers v. Ohio, 499 U.S. 400, 111 S.Ct. 1364, 113 L.Ed.2d 411 (1991)—§§ 15.4(c) n.92; 15.4(i) n.205; 22.2(c) n.25; 22.3(d) n.190

Powers, State v., 654 N.W.2d 667 (Minn.2003)—§ 22.3(d) n.177

Powers, State v., 952 P.2d 997 (Okla.Crim.App.1997)—§ 27.4(d) n.51

Powers v. State, 147 Ga.App. 459, 249 S.E.2d 292 (1978)—§ 7.4(c) n.55

Powers, United States v., 439 F.2d 373 (4th Cir.1971)—§ 3.2(f) n.188

Powers v. United States, 223 U.S. 303, 32 S.Ct. 281, 56 L.Ed. 448 (1912)—§ 6.5(a) n.4

Poyner v. Murray, 964 F.2d 1404 (4th Cir.1992)—§ 11.2(e) n.171

Poynter v. State, 749 N.E.2d 1122 (Ind.2001)—§§ 11.3(c) n.67; 11.4(d) n.117

Poyson, State v., 198 Ariz. 70, 7 P.3d 79 (2000)—§ 6.2(c) n.178

Poywing, People v., 90 Misc.2d 197, 393 N.Y.S.2d 888 (1977)— §§ 7.3(d) n.75, 79

Pozo, People v., 746 P.2d 523 (Colo.1987)—§§ 21.3(b) n.64, 68

Prado, Commonwealth v., 481 Pa. 485, 393 A.2d 8 (1978)—§§ 14.3(a) n.30; 14.3(c) n.72

Prandy-Binett, United States v., 995 F.2d 1069 (D.C.Cir.1993)— § 3.3(b) n.55

Prasertphong, State v., 206 Ariz. 70, 75 P.3d 675 (2003)—§ 3.3(g) n.248

Prater, Commonwealth v., 431 Mass. 86, 725 N.E.2d 233 (2000)—§ 22.2(d) n.76

Prater, People v., 170 Misc.2d 327, 648 N.Y.S.2d 228 (1996)—§ 15.4(a) n.10

Pratt, Commonwealth v., 240 S.W.2d 635 (Ky.1951)—§ 16.3(d) n.73

Pratt, State v., 641 A.2d 732 (R.I.1994)—§ 3.4(f) n.120

Pratt, State v., 309 Or. 205, 785 P.2d 350 (1990)—§ 3.3(e) n.185

Pratt v. State, 9 Md.App. 220, 263 A.2d 247 (1970)—§ 6.10(b) n.24

Pratt, United States v., 438 F.3d 1264 (11th Cir.2006)—§ 10.3(b) n.10

Pratt, United States v., 913 F.2d 982 (1st Cir.1990)—§ 5.3(d) n.42

Pratt, United States v., 657 F.2d 218 (8th Cir.1981)—§ 21.6(a) n.68

Pray, State v., 30 Nev. 206, 94 P. 218 (1908)—§ 16.1(e) n.181

Praylow v. Martin, 761 F.2d 179 (4th Cir.1985)—§§ 11.8(c) n.57; 21.3(b) n.42

Preate, United States v., 91 F.3d 10 (3d Cir.1996)—§ 27.5(a) n.20

Preate, United States v., 927 F.Supp. 163 (M.D.Pa.1996)—§§ 23.1(d) n.165, 168, 185

Preciado-Robles, United States v., 964 F.2d 882 (9th Cir.1992)—§§ 3.9(f) n.118, 120

Precise, State v., 129 N.J. 451, 609 A.2d 1280 (1992)—§ 28.11(b) n.20

Preece, State v., 181 W.Va. 633, 383 S.E.2d 815 (1989)—§§ 6.6(e) n.89; 6.6(f) n.108

Prejean v. Smith, 889 F.2d 1391 (5th Cir.1989)—§ 16.3(g) n.108

Premises Known as 608 Taylor Ave., Apartment 302, Pittsburgh, Pa., United States v., 584 F.2d 1297 (3d Cir.1978)—§ 27.2(d) n.76

Prentice, State v., 170 N.C.App. 593, 613 S.E.2d 498 (N.C.App.2005)— § 18.4(c) n.39

Prentiss, United States v., 256 F.3d 971 (10th Cir.2001)—§§ 19.3(a) n.102, 103; 19.6(c) n.51

Prentiss, United States v., 273 F.3d 1277 (10th Cir.2001)—§ 19.3(a) n.105

Prescott, People v., 66 N.Y.2d 216, 495 N.Y.S.2d 955, 486 N.E.2d 813 (1985)—§ 21.6(a) n.56

Prescott, United States v., 42 F.3d 1165 (8th Cir.1994)—§ 19.3(c) n.190

Prescott, United States v., 581 F.2d 1343 (9th Cir.1978)—§ 3.1(o) n.309

Presentment by Camden Court, In re, 10 N.J. 23, 89 A.2d 416 (1952)— § 8.4(b) n.72

Presentment of Camden County Grand Jury, In re, 34 N.J. 378, 169 A.2d 465 (1961)—§ 8.3(h) n.40

Presentment to Superior Court, Hudson County, In re, 14 N.J.Super. 542, 82 A.2d 496 (1951)—§ 15.1(d) n.155

Presha, State v., 163 N.J. 304, 748 A.2d 1108 (2000)—§ 6.9(g) n.178

President v. State, 925 S.W.2d 866 (Mo.App.1996)—§ 27.5(c) n.85

Presley v. State, 792 So.2d 950 (Miss.2001)—§ 21.2(d) n.245

Presley v. State, 750 S.W.2d 602 (Mo.Ct.App.1988)—§ 11.10(c) n.99

Presley v. State, 498 So.2d 832 (Miss.1986)—§ 21.4(d) n.111

Presnell v. Georgia, 439 U.S. 14, 99 S.Ct. 235, 58 L.Ed.2d 207 (1978)— § 19.6(c) n.49

Presnell v. Zant, 959 F.2d 1524 (11th Cir.1992)—§ 6.7(b) n.103

Press v. United States District Court, 705 F.2d 1143 (9th Cir.1983)— § 23.1(e) n.233

Pressel, State v., 2 Or.App. 477, 468 P.2d 915 (1970)—§§ 6.8(a) n.28; 6.9(b) n.34

Press-Enterprise Co. v. Superior Court of California, 478 U.S. 1, 106 S.Ct. 2735, 92 L.Ed.2d 1 (1986)— §§ 2.9(d) n.59; 23.1(d) n.125, 127; 23.1(e) n.221; 24.1(a) n.6

Press-Enterprise Co. v. Superior Court (Press Enterprise I), 464 U.S. 501, 104 S.Ct. 819, 78 L.Ed.2d 629 (1984)—§§ 22.3(a) n.6, 8; 23.1(d) n.126; 23.1(e) n.217; 24.1(a) n.2

Presser, United States v., 844 F.2d 1275 (6th Cir.1988)—§ 20.3(m) n.256

Pressley, Ex parte, 770 So.2d 143 (Ala.2000)—§ 22.3(d) n.215

Pressley, People v., 804 P.2d 226 (Colo.App.1990)—§ 24.3(f) n.156

Prest, People v., 105 A.D.2d 1078, 482 N.Y.S.2d 172 (1984)—§ 15.2(c) n.85

Preston v. State, 700 S.W.2d 227 (Tex.Cr.App.1985)—§ 1.8(f) n.100

Preston, State v., 411 A.2d 402 (Me.1980)—§ 9.5(b) n.36

Preston v. State, 260 So.2d 501 (Fla.1972)—§ 24.7(c) n.24

Preston v. United States, 376 U.S. 364, 84 S.Ct. 881, 11 L.Ed.2d 777 (1964)—§§ 3.2(a) n.11; 3.5(c) n.106

Preuss, People v., 920 P.2d 859 (Colo.App.1995)—§ 26.10(d) n.96

Prevost, State v., 141 N.H. 559, 689 A.2d 121 (1997)—§ 19.5(c) n.56

Prewitt v. State, 755 So.2d 537 (Miss.App.1999)—§ 20.6(b) n.27

Price v. Commonwealth, 31 S.W.3d 885 (Ky.2000)—§ 24.7(e) n.38

Price v. Georgia, 398 U.S. 323, 90 S.Ct. 1757, 26 L.Ed.2d 300 (1970)— §§ 25.4(d) n.42; 27.6(d) n.72

Price v. Johnston, 334 U.S. 266, 68 S.Ct. 1049, 92 L.Ed. 1356 (1948)— § 28.5(d) n.76

Price, People v., 54 N.Y.2d 557, 446 N.Y.S.2d 906, 431 N.E.2d 267 (1981)—§ 3.1(e) n.138

Price, State v., 385 Md. 261, 868 A.2d 252 (2005)—§ 18.3(c) n.80

Price, State v., 61 Conn.App. 417, 767 A.2d 107 (2001)—§ 27.6(d) n.127

Price, State v., 306 Mont. 381, 34 P.3d 112 (2001)—§ 18.2(c) n.56

Price v. State, 725 N.E.2d 82 (Ind.2000)—§ 22.3(d) n.200

Price, State v., 333 S.C. 267, 510 S.E.2d 215 (1998)—§ 17.4(b) n.124

Price, State v., 940 S.W.2d 534 (Mo.App.1997)—§§ 19.5(b) n.12, 30

Price, State v., 94 Wash.2d 810, 620 P.2d 994 (1980)—§ 20.6(b) n.37

Price, State v., 108 N.J.Super. 272, 260 A.2d 877 (1970)—§ 15.5(c) n.108

Price v. Superior Court, 25 Cal.4th 1046, 108 Cal.Rptr.2d 409, 25 P.3d 618 (2001)—§§ 2.6(b) n.51, 63, 65, 67, 69; 16.1(c) n.125; 16.1(e) n.199, 210; 22.2(e) n.111

Price v. Time, Inc., 416 F.3d 1327 (11th Cir.2005)—§ 8.8(d) n.82

Price v. Turner, 260 F.3d 1144 (9th Cir.2001)—§§ 4.3(b) n.8, 11

Price, United States v., 265 F.3d 1097 (10th Cir.2001)—§§ 17.1(a) n.10; 19.2(e) n.82; 26.3(f) n.63

Price, United States v., 95 F.3d 364 (5th Cir.1996)—§§ 21.2(d) n.257, 258

Price, United States v., 51 F.3d 175 (9th Cir.1995)—§ 26.4(f) n.101

Price, United States v., 888 F.2d 1206 (7th Cir.1989)—§ 3.4(i) n.178

Price, United States v., 750 F.2d 363 (5th Cir.1985)—§§ 17.4(a) n.7, 18, 42

Price, United States v., 448 F.Supp. 503 (D.Colo.1978)—§ 20.3(h) n.151

Price, United States v., 573 F.2d 356 (5th Cir.1978)—§§ 15.4(b) n.65; 22.3(a) n.50

Price, United States v., 383 U.S. 787, 86 S.Ct. 1152, 16 L.Ed.2d 267 (1966)—§ 4.6(l) n.206

Price v. Vincent, 538 U.S. 634, 123 S.Ct. 1848, 155 L.Ed.2d 877 (2003)—§§ 21.3(f) n.432; 25.3(c) n.25, 32; 28.6(f) n.69

Priddy, Commonwealth v., 184 S.W.3d 501 (Ky.2006)—§ 10.5(d) n.39

Pride, People v., 3 Cal.4th 195, 10 Cal.Rptr.2d 636, 833 P.2d 643 (1992)—§ 16.3(b) n.25

Priest, State v., 128 Idaho 6, 909 P.2d 624 (1995)—§ 24.7(a) n.7

Priest, State v., 615 A.2d 244 (Me.1992)—§ 26.3(f) n.64

Priestley v. State, 446 P.2d 405 (Wyo.1968)—§ 6.6(f) n.104

Priet v. State, 45 Md.App. 1, 410 A.2d 1107 (1980)—§ 21.4(c) n.92

Prieto v. Quarterman, 456 F.3d 511 (5th Cir.2006)—§§ 28.4(c) n.31; 28.5(b) n.59

Prieto-Villa, United States v., 910 F.2d 601 (9th Cir.1990)—§ 10.6(a) n.2

Primeaux v. State, 88 P.3d 893 (Okl.Crim.App.2004)—§ 19.3(a) n.42

Primus, State v., 312 S.C. 256, 440 S.E.2d 128 (S.C.1994)—§ 6.5(b) n.24

Prince v. Alabama, 507 F.2d 693 (5th Cir.1975)—§§ 18.4(a) n.11, 17

Prince, State v., 160 Ariz. 268, 772 P.2d 1121 (1989)—§ 6.9(g) n.163

Prince v. United States, 825 A.2d 928 (D.C.2003)—§ 3.3(e) n.185

Prince, United States v., 204 F.3d 1021 (10th Cir.2000)—§ 21.2(d) n.180

Prince, United States v., 533 F.2d 205 (5th Cir.1976)—§ 21.4(a) n.23

Prince, United States v., 491 F.2d 655 (5th Cir.1974)—§ 3.9(f) n.91

Princeton, State ex rel. City of v. Buckner, 180 W.Va. 457, 377 S.E.2d 139 (1988)—§ 1.2(b) n.6

Principie, United States v., 531 F.2d 1132 (2d Cir.1976)—§ 4.6(e) n.86

Prior, United States v., 107 F.3d 654 (8th Cir.1997)—§ 21.4(b) n.65

Privett v. State, 635 S.W.2d 746 (Tex.App.1982)—§§ 11.5(c) n.36, 49, 50; 11.5(f) n.105

Probasco, People v., 795 P.2d 1330 (Colo.1990)—§ 6.6(e) n.59

Probst, State v., 247 Kan. 196, 795 P.2d 393 (1990)—§ 3.1(c) n.70

Proceedings Before Federal Grand Jury for District of Nevada, In re, 487 F.Supp. 1098 (D.Nev.1980)—§§ 8.5(e) n.198; 8.5(h) n.296, 297, 299

Proceedings of Multicounty Grand Jury, In re, 847 P.2d 812 (Okla.1993)—§§ 8.5(b) n.55; 23.1(d) n.156, 159

Prochilo, United States v., 187 F.3d 221 (1st Cir.1999)—§§ 11.4(b) n.20, 36

Procter & Gamble, United States v., 356 U.S. 677, 78 S.Ct. 983, 2 L.Ed.2d 1077 (1958)—§§ 8.5(a) n.6; 8.5(h) n.236, 256, 260, 262, 267; 8.8(e) n.118, 127; 15.2(i) n.197; 20.1(b) n.17

Procter & Gamble Co., United States v., 187 F.Supp. 55 (D.N.J.1960)—§§ 8.8(e) n.124, 126, 127, 130

Procter & Gamble Co., United States v., 19 F.R.D. 122 (D.N.J.1956)—§ 8.8(e) n.127

Procter & Gamble Co., United States v., 180 F.Supp. 195 (D.N.J.1959)—§ 8.5(i) n.311

Proctor, People v., 4 Cal.4th 499, 15 Cal.Rptr.2d 340, 842 P.2d 1100 (1992)—§ 16.3(b) n.21

Proctor v. State, 291 Ark. 459, 725 S.W.2d 827 (1987)—§ 21.5(d) n.104

Proctor, State v., 535 S.W.2d 141 (Mo.App.1976)—§ 7.2(b) n.27

Proctor, United States v., 166 F.3d 396 (1st Cir.1999)—§ 11.5(b) n.30

Proctor v. United States, 338 F.2d 533 (D.C.Cir.1964)—§ 6.3(a) n.17

Procunier v. Atchley, 400 U.S. 446, 91 S.Ct. 485, 27 L.Ed.2d 524 (1971)—§ 6.2(c) n.158

Procunier v. Martinez, 416 U.S. 396, 94 S.Ct. 1800, 40 L.Ed.2d 224 (1974)—§§ 3.9(i) n.193; 11.2(f) n.242

Production of Records to Grand Jury, In re, 618 F.Supp. 440 (D.Mass.1985)—§ 8.6(b) n.33

Proetto, Commonwealth v., 771 A.2d 823 (Pa. Super. Ct. 2001)—§ 4.6(l) n.205

Professional Check Service, Inc. v. Dutton, 560 So.2d 755 (Ala.1990)—§ 13.3(a) n.7

Proffitt v. Florida, 428 U.S. 242, 96 S.Ct. 2960, 49 L.Ed.2d 913 (1976)—§ 26.1(b) n.15

Proffitt v. Wainwright, 685 F.2d 1227 (11th Cir.1982)—§§ 24.2(b) n.30; 26.4(f) n.108

Profit, State v., 591 N.W.2d 451 (Minn.1999)—§ 17.1(a) n.6

Profitt v. Waldron, 831 F.2d 1245 (5th Cir.1987)—§ 11.10(c) n.126

Progress Club v. State, 12 Ga.App. 174, 76 S.E. 1029 (1913)—§ 15.1(d) n.242

Prohibition, In re Petition for Writ of, 312 Md. 280, 539 A.2d 664 (1988)—§ 27.4(d) n.49

Projansky, United States v., 465 F.2d 123 (2d Cir.1972)—§ 16.3(c) n.34

Projansky, United States v., 44 F.R.D. 550 (S.D.N.Y.1968)—§ 20.3(c) n.64

Prokos v. State, 266 Ark. 50, 582 S.W.2d 36 (1979)—§§ 19.5(b) n.32; 19.6(a) n.4

Promise, United States v., 255 F.3d 150 (4th Cir.2001)—§ 19.2(e) n.71

Pronovost, People v., 773 P.2d 555 (Colo.1989)—§§ 20.6(c) n.76 to 78, 80

Property Clerk, New York City Police Department v. Madden, 138 Misc.2d 1023, 526 N.Y.S.2d 710 (N.Y.Sup. 1988)—§ 1.7(k) n.272

Property Seized From Terrel, In the Matter of, 639 N.W.2d 18 (Iowa 2002)—§ 2.6(b) n.42

Prophet v. United States, 602 A.2d 1087 (D.C.1992)—§ 3.3(d) n.169

Propps, State v., 190 N.W.2d 408 (Iowa 1971)—§ 24.10(a) n.14

Propst v. State, 335 Ark. 448, 983 S.W.2d 405 (1998)—§ 21.3(b) n.45

Prouse, United States v., 945 F.2d 1017 (8th Cir.1991)—§ 3.1(d) n.98

Provenzano v. Singletary, 148 F.3d 1327 (11th Cir.1998)—§§ 11.10(c) n.68, 87

Provenzano v. State, 616 So.2d 428 (Fla.1993)—§ 22.4(b) n.20

Provenzano, United States v., 688 F.2d 194 (3d Cir.1982)—§§ 15.2(j) n.229; 17.2(d) n.95

Provenzano, United States v., 620 F.2d 985 (3d Cir.1980)—§ 8.11(c) n.47

Provenzano, United States v., 440 F.Supp. 561 (S.D.N.Y.1977)—§§ 15.5(b) n.57, 69

Providence Journal Co., In re, 820 F.2d 1342 (1st Cir.1986)—§ 23.1(c) n.113

Providence Journal Co. v. Superior Court, 593 A.2d 446 (R.I.1991)—§ 22.3(a) n.9

Provost, United States v., 969 F.2d 617 (8th Cir.1992)—§ 24.11(d) n.28

Prowell v. State, 741 N.E.2d 704 (Ind.2001)—§ 21.3(b) n.45

Prude, People v., 66 Ill.2d 470, 6 Ill.Dec. 689, 363 N.E.2d 371 (1977)—§ 6.8(d) n.84

Pruden, United States v., 398 F.3d 241 (3d Cir.2005)—§ 6.8(b) n.50

Prudhomme v. Superior Court, 2 Cal.3d 320, 85 Cal.Rptr. 129, 466 P.2d 673 (1970)—§§ 20.2(a) n.9; 20.4(d) n.66

Pruett, In re, 133 F.3d 275 (4th Cir.1997)—§ 28.7(d) n.28

Pruett v. Norris, 153 F.3d 579 (8th Cir.1998)—§§ 23.2(a) n.15, 18

Pruitt v. State, 834 N.E.2d 90 (Ind.2005)—§ 26.4(h) n.156

Pruitt, State v., 805 A.2d 177 (Del.2002)—§ 13.1(e) n.53

Pruneda-Gonzalez, United States v., 953 F.2d 190 (5th Cir.1992)—§ 5.4(a) n.9

Pryor v. State, 314 Ark. 212, 861 S.W.2d 544 (1993)—§ 21.4(a) n.22

Pryor v. State, 349 So.2d 1063 (Miss.1977)—§ 20.3(h) n.147

P.S., In re, 175 Ill.2d 79, 221 Ill.Dec. 853, 676 N.E.2d 656 (1997)— §§ 2.12(b) n.103; 17.4(b) n.120

Public Defender Commission, State ex rel. v. Bonacker, 706 S.W.2d 449 (Mo.1986)—§ 11.9(a) n.30

Puckett, State v., 240 Kan. 393, 729 P.2d 458 (1986)—§ 14.3(a) n.42

Puckett, United States v., 61 F.3d 1092 (4th Cir.1995)—§ 21.4(d) n.104

Pueblo School Dist. No. 70 v. Toth, 924 P.2d 1094 (Colo.App.1996)— § 2.6(b) n.43

Puerto Rico v. Branstad, 483 U.S. 219, 107 S.Ct. 2802, 97 L.Ed.2d 187 (1987)—§ 3.1(j) n.250

Pugach v. Klein, 193 F.Supp. 630 (S.D.N.Y.1961)—§§ 13.2(a) n.1; 13.3(a) n.3

Pugh, People v., 157 Ill.2d 1, 191 Ill.Dec. 10, 623 N.E.2d 255 (1993)—§§ 11.10(c) n.105; 21.4(f) n.207

Pugh v. Rainwater, 572 F.2d 1053 (5th Cir.1978)—§ 12.2(b) n.34

Pugh v. Rainwater, 557 F.2d 1189 (5th Cir.1977)—§ 12.2(b) n.32

Pugh v. State, 103 Md.App. 624, 654 A.2d 888 (1995)—§§ 11.9(b) n.61, 88

Pugh, State v., 53 Ohio St.2d 153, 372 N.E.2d 1351 (1978)—§ 14.2(g) n.98

Pugh v. State, 271 Md. 701, 319 A.2d 542 (1974)—§ 25.3(c) n.21

Pugh, United States ex rel. v. Pate, 401 F.2d 6 (7th Cir.1968)—§ 3.4(c) n.46

Puglia, United States v., 8 F.3d 478 (7th Cir.1993)—§§ 8.9(a) n.12; 15.2(i) n.227; 15.5(a) n.9

Pugliese v. Perrin, 731 F.2d 85 (1st Cir.1984)—§ 17.4(a) n.19

Pugliese, United States v., 805 F.2d 1117 (2d Cir.1986)—§§ 26.4(d) n.61; 26.4(f) n.102

Pugliese, United States v., 346 F.2d 861 (2d Cir.1965)—§ 5.3(d) n.41

Puglisi, People v., 51 A.D.2d 695, 380 N.Y.S.2d 221 (1976)—§ 9.4(f) n.112

Puiatti v. State, 521 So.2d 1106 (Fla.1988)—§ 17.2(b) n.38

Pulaski County Circuit-Chancery Court, State v., 316 Ark. 473, 872 S.W.2d 854 (1994)—§ 27.4(d) n.41

Pulaski County Circuit Court, State v., 327 Ark. 287, 938 S.W.2d 815 (1997)—§ 27.4(d) n.50

Pulido, United States v., 879 F.2d 1255 (5th Cir.1989)—§ 11.2(d) n.130

Pullen, United States v., 721 F.2d 788 (11th Cir.1983)—§ 6.10(b) n.16

Pulley v. Harris, 465 U.S. 37, 104 S.Ct. 871, 79 L.Ed.2d 29 (1984)— § 26.1(b) n.17

Pulley v. State, 287 Md. 406, 412 A.2d 1244 (1980)—§ 27.2(c) n.62

Punch, United States v., 709 F.2d 889 (5th Cir.1983)—§ 21.4(c) n.66

Pungitore, United States v., 910 F.2d 1084 (3d Cir.1990)—§ 11.9(c) n.126

Pupo, United States v., 841 F.2d 1235 (4th Cir.1988)—§§ 19.3(e) n.235, 245

Purcell, People v., 201 Ill.2d 542, 268 Ill.Dec. 429, 778 N.E.2d 695 (2002)—§ 12.4(a) n.22

Purcell, People v., 325 Ill.App.3d 551, 259 Ill.Dec. 487, 758 N.E.2d 895 (2001)—§ 12.4(a) n.27

Purcell, State v., 110 Nev. 1389, 887 P.2d 276 (1994)—§ 24.6(d) n.45

Purcell v. United States, 594 A.2d 527 (D.C.App.1991)—§ 17.4(b) n.96

Purdy, State v., 491 N.W.2d 402 (N.D.1992)—§§ 22.3(a) n.6; 22.3(d) n.176

Purdy v. United States, 208 F.3d 41 (2d Cir.2000)—§§ 21.3(b) n.76 to 78, 109

Purkett v. Elem, 514 U.S. 765, 115 S.Ct. 1769, 131 L.Ed.2d 834 (1995)— §§ 22.3(d) n.224, 235

Purnell v. Missouri Department of Corrections, 753 F.2d 703 (8th Cir.1985)—§ 28.5(a) n.34

Purnell, State v., 161 N.J. 44, 735 A.2d 513 (1999)—§ 28.11(b) n.15

Purnett, United States v., 910 F.2d 51 (2d Cir.1990)—§ 11.5(c) n.61

Purrington, State v., 122 N.H. 458, 446 A.2d 451 (1982)—§ 15.2(j) n.235

Purry, United States v., 545 F.2d 217 (D.C.Cir.1976)—§ 3.8(b) n.29

Pursley, State v., 238 Kan. 253, 710 P.2d 1231 (1985)—§ 6.10(b) n.13

Pursley, United States v., 474 F.3d 757 (10th Cir.2007)—§ 18.4(c) n.75

Purvis v. Dugger, 932 F.2d 1413 (11th Cir.1991)—§ 6.6(d) n.50

Puryear, State v., 121 Ariz. 359, 590 P.2d 475 (App.1979)—§§ 19.3(a) n.70; 19.3(b) n.147; 19.3(e) n.211, 254

Putnam v. State, 995 P.2d 632 (Wyo.2000)—§§ 3.8(d) n.133; 9.1(d) n.128

Pye v. State, 269 Ga. 779, 505 S.E.2d 4 (1998)—§ 22.3(d) n.246

Pyle v. Sommerville, 186 W.Va. 177, 411 S.E.2d 696 (1991)—§ 7.4(e) n.86

Pyle v. State, 340 Ark. 53, 8 S.W.3d 491 (2000)—§ 21.2(f) n.383

Pyle, State v., 19 Ohio St.2d 64, 249 N.E.2d 826 (1969)—§ 6.10(a) n.2

Pyles, Commonwealth v., 423 Mass. 717, 672 N.E.2d 96 (1996)— § 21.3(d) n.263

Pyles v. Johnson, 136 F.3d 986 (5th Cir.1998)—§ 27.6(d) n.96

Pyles v. State, 755 S.W.2d 98 (Tex.Cr.App.1988)—§ 3.3(e) n.189

Pyron v. State, 330 Ark. 88, 953 S.W.2d 874 (1997)—§ 17.4(b) n.124

Q

Q.N., State ex rel., 179 N.J. 165, 843 A.2d 1140 (2004)—§ 6.9(g) n.178

Quach, United States v., 302 F.3d 1096 (9th Cir.2002)—§§ 21.2(d) n.167, 267

Quackenbush, People v., 88 N.Y.2d 534, 647 N.Y.S.2d 150, 670 N.E.2d 434 (1996)—§ 3.7(d) n.80

Quackenbush, People v., 687 P.2d 448 (Colo.1984)—§§ 18.4(c) n.31, 34

Quadra v. Superior Court, 403 F.Supp. 486 (S.D.Cal.1975)—§ 8.4(a) n.8

Quadrini v. Clusen, 864 F.2d 577 (7th Cir.1989)—§ 6.4(f) n.124

Qualls v. State, 961 P.2d 765 (Nev.1998)—§ 27.5(e) n.147

Quam, United States v., 367 F.3d 1006 (8th Cir.2004)—§ 8.10(d) n.98

Quarles, People v., 88 Ill.App.3d 340, 43 Ill.Dec. 497, 410 N.E.2d 497 (1980)—§ 3.5(c) n.131

Quarrier, Ex parte, 2 W. Va. 569 (1866)—§ 1.2(c) n.40

Quartararo, People v., 200 A.D.2d 160, 612 N.Y.S.2d 635 (1994)— § 23.2(a) n.40

Quartermaine, United States v., 913 F.2d 910 (11th Cir.1990)—§§ 12.3(a) n.19, 23, 24; 12.3(d) n.97

Quash a Grand Jury Subpoena Duces Tecum, Dated Dec. 28, 1992, In re Application to, 157 Misc.2d 432, 597 N.Y.S.2d 557 (Sup.Ct.1993)— §§ 8.13(a) n.30, 31; 8.13(b) n.59

Quash a Subpoena Duces Tecum in Grand Jury Proceedings, In re Application to, 56 N.Y.2d 348, 452 N.Y.S.2d 361, 437 N.E.2d 1118 (1982)—§ 8.6(b) n.49

Quatermain, United States v., 613 F.2d 38 (3d Cir.1980)—§§ 8.11(e) n.102, 103

Quatsling, State v., 24 Ariz.App. 105, 536 P.2d 226 (1975)—§ 3.2(b) n.63

Quattlebaum, State v., 338 S.C. 441, 527 S.E.2d 105 (S.C.2000)—§§ 11.8(b) n.33, 36

Quedens v. State, 280 Ga. 355, 629 S.E.2d 197 (2006)—§ 6.6(e) n.61

Queen v. Boyles, 1 B & S 311, 121 Eng.Rept. 730 (K.B.1861)—§ 8.10(a) n.7

Queen, Commonwealth v., 536 Pa. 315, 639 A.2d 443 (1994)—§ 3.8(d) n.171

Queen, State v., 91 N.C. 659 (1884)—§ 15.1(f) n.276

Quercia v. United States, 289 U.S. 466, 53 S.Ct. 698, 77 L.Ed. 1321 (1933)—§§ 24.6(e) n.46, 50

Querubin v. Commonwealth, 440 Mass. 108, 795 N.E.2d 534 (2003)—§§ 12.1(d) n.51, 58; 12.2(a) n.14

Quezada, People v., 731 P.2d 730 (Colo.1987)—§ 6.9(f) n.106

Quezada, United States v., 944 F.2d 903 (4th Cir.1991)—§ 3.10(a) n.21

Quick, State v., 659 N.W.2d 701 (Minn.2003)—§ 3.4(g) n.128

Quigley, United States v., 53 F.3d 909 (8th Cir.1995)—§ 1.2(c) n.134

Quinlan, United States v., 473 F.3d 273 (6th Cir.2007)—§§ 21.5(a) n.38, 40

Quinn, In re, 174 Vt. 562, 816 A.2d 425 (2002)—§ 21.3(b) n.83

Quinn, In re, 525 F.2d 222 (1st Cir.1975)—§ 8.9(b) n.29

Quinn, People v., 183 Colo. 245, 516 P.2d 420 (1973)—§ 14.4(c) n.63

Quinn, State v., 930 P.2d 267 (Utah 1996)—§ 27.3(c) n.35

Quinn, State v., 169 Wis.2d 620, 486 N.W.2d 542 (Wis.App.1992)—§ 27.5(e) n.164

Quinn, United States v., 359 F.3d 666 (4th Cir.2004)—§ 19.3(e) n.237

Quinn, United States v., 357 F.Supp. 1348 (N.D.Ga.1973)—§§ 14.2(b) n.30; 14.4(e) n.112

Quinn v. United States, 349 U.S. 155, 75 S.Ct. 668, 99 L.Ed. 964 (1955)—§ 2.10(c) n.95

Quinones, Commonwealth v., 414 Mass. 423, 608 N.E.2d 724 (1993)—§ 21.4(e) n.161

Quinones, United States v., 196 F.Supp.2d 416 (S.D.N.Y.2002)—§ 2.7(c) n.195

Quinones, United States v., 313 F.3d 49 (2d Cir.2002)—§§ 1.5(e) n.207; 2.7(c) n.143, 183, 184; 28.3(e) n.104

Quinones, United States v., 906 F.2d 924 (2d Cir.1990)—§§ 25.1(d) n.61; 25.4(d) n.46

Quinones, United States v., 516 F.2d 1309 (1st Cir.1975)—§§ 17.1(a) n.15; 17.3(d) n.43

Quinonez, State v., 735 P.2d 159 (Colo.1987)—§ 21.3(e) n.284

Quintal, State v., 479 A.2d 117 (R.I.1984)—§ 20.6(b) n.43

Quintana, United States v., 508 F.2d 867 (7th Cir.1975)—§ 4.6(m) n.237

Quintanilla, United States v., 2 F.3d 1469 (7th Cir.1993)—§§ 17.3(d) n.52; 24.3(i) n.185

Quintano v. People, 105 P.3d 585 (Colo.2005)—§ 17.4(b) n.73

Quintero v. Bell, 368 F.3d 892 (6th Cir.2004)—§ 11.10(d) n.171

Quintero v. Bell, 256 F.3d 409 (6th Cir.2001)—§ 11.10(d) n.171

Quintero, People v., 657 P.2d 948 (Colo.1983)—§ 3.1(c) n.53

Quintero, State v., 480 N.W.2d 50 (Iowa 1992)—§ 6.2(c) n.95

Quintero, United States v., 38 F.3d 1317 (3d Cir.1994)—§ 4.6(m) n.238

Quintero, United States v., 937 F.2d 95 (2d Cir.1991)—§§ 21.2(d) n.210, 211

Quintero, United States v., 157 F.3d 1038 (6th Cir.1988)—§ 26.3(f) n.51

Quiovers, United States v., 539 F.2d 744 (D.C.Cir.1976)—§ 24.3(e) n.126

Quirin, Ex parte, 317 U.S. 1, 63 S.Ct. 2, 87 L.Ed. 3 (1942)—§ 15.1(b) n.90

Quiroz, United States v., 13 F.3d 505 (2d Cir.1993)—§ 6.9(e) n.94

Quispe, Commonwealth v., 433 Mass. 508, 744 N.E.2d 21 (2001)—§ 13.2(c) n.56

Quitog, State v., 85 Haw. 128, 938 P.2d 559 (1997)—§ 25.2(a) n.6

Quoting Kirby v. Illinois, 406 U.S. 682, 92 S.Ct. 1877, 32 L.Ed.2d 411 (1972)—§ 6.4(e) n.61

QWest Corp. v. Minnesota Public Utilities Commission, 427 F.3d 1061 (8th Cir.2005)—§ 2.6(b) n.42

R

R., People v., 160 Misc.2d 142, 607 N.Y.S.2d 887 (1994)—§ 16.2(a) n.14

R.A.B., In re, 197 Ill.2d 358, 259 Ill.Dec. 24, 757 N.E.2d 887 (2001)—§ 22.1(h) n.137

Rabago, State v., 103 Haw. 236, 81 P.3d 1151 (2003)—§ 24.10(c) n.41

Rabb, Commonwealth v., 431 Mass. 123, 725 N.E.2d 1036 (2000)—§ 17.4(b) n.73

Rabb, United States v., 680 F.2d 294 (3d Cir.1982)—§§ 18.3(b) n.5, 6

Rabin, State v., 495 So.2d 257 (Fla.App.1986)—§§ 8.6(b) n.44, 48

Rabinowitz, United States v., 339 U.S. 56, 70 S.Ct. 430, 94 L.Ed. 653 (1950)—§§ 2.8(c) n.65; 2.9(d) n.60, 90; 3.6(c) n.71

Rabon, State v., 45 Wash.App. 832, 727 P.2d 995 (1986)—§ 1.8(d) n.49

Rachmiel, In the Matter of, 90 N.J. 646, 449 A.2d 505 (1982)—§ 23.1(b) n.10

Racine v. State, 51 Ala.App. 484, 286 So.2d 890 (1973)—§ 3.8(d) n.140

Rackley, United States v., 742 F.2d 1266 (11th Cir.1984)—§ 24.6(c) n.40

Rackstraw, United States v., 7 F.3d 1476 (10th Cir.1993)—§ 24.5(a) n.8

Radcliff, United States v., 331 F.3d 1153 (10th Cir.2003)—§ 4.6(m) n.228

Raddatz, United States v., 447 U.S. 667, 100 S.Ct. 2406, 65 L.Ed.2d 424 (1980)—§§ 1.4(g) n.163; 2.7(c) n.218; 10.6(b) n.9

Raddatz, United States v., 592 F.2d 976 (7th Cir.1979)—§ 10.6(b) n.11

Radetsky, United States v., 535 F.2d 556 (10th Cir.1976)—§§ 8.5(d) n.127; 19.2(f) n.91

Radford v. Lovelace, 212 S.W.3d 72 (Ky.2006)—§ 25.2(e) n.39

Radford v. State, 360 So.2d 1303 (Fla.App.1978)—§ 27.5(c) n.98

Radford v. Stewart, 320 F.Supp. 826 (D.Mont.1970)—§ 20.4(d) n.68

Radford, United States v., 452 F.2d 332 (7th Cir.1971)—§ 22.1(h) n.150

Radi, State v., 185 Mont. 38, 604 P.2d 318 (1979)—§ 26.5(b) n.26

Radio & Television News Assn. v. United States, 781 F.2d 1443 (9th Cir.1986)—§ 23.1(b) n.68

Radio Corp. of America, Application of, 13 F.R.D. 167 (S.D.N.Y.1952)—§§ 8.7(b) n.30; 8.8(a) n.7

Rado, State v., 14 Conn.App. 322, 541 A.2d 124 (1988)—§ 8.1(c) n.30

Radtke, People v., 153 Misc.2d 554, 581 N.Y.S.2d 712 (1992)—§ 24.3(f) n.150

Rae v. State, 884 P.2d 163 (Alaska App.1994)—§ 24.2(e) n.70

Raffel v. United States, 271 U.S. 494, 46 S.Ct. 566, 70 L.Ed. 1054 (1926)—§ 9.6(a) n.40

Raffield, United States v., 82 F.3d 611 (4th Cir.1996)—§ 16.4(b) n.13

Raffoul, United States v., 826 F.2d 218 (3d Cir.1987)—§ 23.1(e) n.261

Raftery, United States v., 534 F.2d 854 (9th Cir.1976)—§ 9.6(c) n.57

Ragghianti, United States v., 527 F.2d 586 (9th Cir.1975)—§ 17.1(e) n.63

Ragland, State v., 105 N.J. 189, 519 A.2d 1361 (1986)—§§ 22.1(g) n.98, 125, 127

Raglin, State v., 83 Ohio St.3d 253, 699 N.E.2d 482 (1998)—§ 6.8(d) n.84

Ragsdale, State v., 381 So.2d 492 (La.1980)—§ 3.2(c) n.111

Ragsdale, United States v., 470 F.2d 24 (5th Cir.1972)—§ 3.3(e) n.189

Raheem v. Kelly, 257 F.3d 122 (2d Cir.2001)—§§ 7.4(c) n.64; 7.4(d) n.71

Raheem v. State, 275 Ga. 87, 560 S.E.2d 680 (2002)—§§ 3.6(a) n.32; 22.3(d) n.221

Rahman, United States v., 861 F.Supp. 266 (S.D.N.Y.1994)—§§ 11.9(c) n.112, 118

Rahme, United States v., 813 F.2d 31 (2d Cir.1987)—§ 3.2(c) n.103

Rahn, United States v., 511 F.2d 290 (10th Cir.1975)—§ 3.3(g) n.224

Railway Express Agency v. New York, 336 U.S. 106, 69 S.Ct. 463, 93 L.Ed. 533 (1949)—§ 13.4(c) n.125

Raimondo, United States v., 721 F.2d 476 (4th Cir.1983)—§ 26.6(d) n.53

Raineri, United States v., 670 F.2d 702 (7th Cir.1982)—§ 15.4(b) n.63

Raines, United States v., 243 F.3d 419 (8th Cir.2001)—§ 3.2(c) n.128

Rainey v. Michigan Department of Corrections, 41 Mich.App. 313, 199 N.W.2d 829 (1972)—§ 18.4(c) n.54

Rains v. State, 173 Neb. 586, 114 N.W.2d 399 (1962)—§ 20.2(e) n.83

Rairdon v. State, 557 N.W.2d 318 (Minn.1996)—§ 24.7(i) n.90

Rajappa v. State, 200 Ga.App. 372, 408 S.E.2d 163 (1991)—§ 3.10(e) n.148

Rakas v. Illinois, 439 U.S. 128, 99 S.Ct. 421, 58 L.Ed.2d 387 (1978)—§§ 2.9(f) n.139; 2.9(g) n.165, 193; 4.4(e) n.21; 9.1(a) n.5, 7; 9.1(b) n.32, 45, 46, 67; 9.1(c) n.105; 9.1(d) n.117; 9.2(a) n.5; 9.2(b) n.14

Raleigh v. State, 932 So.2d 1054 (Fla.2006)—§ 24.3(d) n.118

Rambo, United States v., 365 F.3d 906 (10th Cir.2004)—§§ 6.7(c) n.115; 6.9(f) n.100; 6.9(g) n.152

Ramey, People v., 152 Ill.2d 41, 178 Ill.Dec. 19, 604 N.E.2d 275 (1992)—§ 10.6(c) n.21

Ramirez v. People, 682 P.2d 1181 (Colo.1984)—§ 21.4(c) n.78

Ramirez, State v., 636 N.W.2d 740 (Iowa 2001)—§§ 21.3(b) n.66; 21.4(d) n.134

Ramirez v. State, 739 So.2d 568 (Fla.1999)—§§ 6.6(d) n.49; 6.8(b) n.43; 6.9(a) n.6

Ramirez, State v., 62 Wash.App. 301, 814 P.2d 227 (1991)—§ 24.8(a) n.9

Ramirez, State v., 817 P.2d 774 (Utah 1991)—§§ 7.4(c) n.60; 10.6(a) n.2, 6

Ramirez, United States v., 420 F.3d 134 (2d Cir.2005)—§§ 16.2(d) n.58; 16.2(e) n.64, 76

Ramirez, United States v., 324 F.3d 1225 (11th Cir.2003)—§ 19.3(e) n.243

Ramirez, United States v., 523 U.S. 65, 118 S.Ct. 992, 140 L.Ed.2d 191 (1998)—§§ 3.4(h) n.138, 143, 157, 160; 3.6(b) n.46, 61

Ramirez, United States v., 112 F.3d 849 (7th Cir.1997)—§ 4.6(d) n.68

Ramirez, United States v., 91 F.3d 1297 (9th Cir.1996)—§ 9.6(c) n.66

Ramirez, United States v., 884 F.2d 1524 (1st Cir.1989)—§ 22.2(a) n.10

Ramirez, United States v., 524 F.2d 283 (10th Cir.1975)—§§ 18.2(d) n.67; 18.4(a) n.16, 18

Ramirez-Benitez, United States v., 292 F.3d 22 (1st Cir.2002)—§ 21.4(c) n.66

Ramirez-Burgos, United States v., 44 F.3d 17 (1st Cir.1995)—§ 27.2(c) n.54

Ramirez-Cortez, United States v., 213 F.3d 1149 (9th Cir.2000)—§ 18.3(b) n.37

Ramirez-Hernandez, United States v., 449 F.3d 824 (8th Cir.2006)—§ 21.2(g) n.396

Ramirez-Martinez, United States v., 273 F.3d 903 (9th Cir.2001)—§§ 19.3(c) n.188, 191; 22.3(d) n.252

Ramirez-Rangel, United States v., 103 F.3d 1501 (9th Cir.1997)—§ 26.4(b) n.21

Ramirez-Sandoval, United States v., 872 F.2d 1392 (9th Cir.1989)— §§ 9.4(e) n.106 to 110

Ramirez-Valencia, United States v., 202 F.3d 1106 (9th Cir.2000)—§ 5.4(c) n.30

Ramon v. Cupp, 423 F.2d 248 (9th Cir.1970)—§ 3.7(b) n.24

Ramos, People v., 34 Cal.4th 494, 21 Cal.Rptr.3d 575, 101 P.3d 478 (2004)—§ 21.4(b) n.59

Ramos, People v., 13 P.3d 295 (Colo.2000)—§ 3.8(d) n.122

Ramos, People v., 223 A.D.2d 495, 637 N.Y.S.2d 93 (1996)—§ 15.7(g) n.208

Ramos, People v., 63 N.Y.2d 640, 479 N.Y.S.2d 510, 468 N.E.2d 692 (1984)—§ 21.2(g) n.399

Ramos, People v., 30 A.D.2d 848, 292 N.Y.S.2d 938 (1968)—§ 21.2(b) n.78

Ramos v. Rogers, 170 F.3d 560 (6th Cir.1999)—§ 21.5(d) n.104

Ramos, State v., 149 N.H. 118, 818 A.2d 1228 (2003)—§ 17.1(f) n.71

Ramos v. State, 806 P.2d 822 (Wyo.1991)—§§ 6.7(c) n.133; 10.5(b) n.18

Ramos, State v., 553 A.2d 1059 (R.I.1989)—§§ 3.5(d) n.173; 20.6(c) n.78

Ramos, United States v., 443 F.3d 304 (3d Cir.2006)—§ 3.8(d) n.131

Ramos, United States v., 462 F.3d 329 (4th Cir.2006)—§ 5.2(a) n.8

Ramsay v. Harrison, 119 Va. 682, 89 S.E. 977 (1916)—§ 16.3(b) n.6

Ramsay, State v., 146 Vt. 70, 499 A.2d 15 (1985)—§ 26.5(c) n.52

Ramsden v. United States, 2 F.3d 322 (9th Cir.1993)—§ 10.1(c) n.39

Ramseur v. Beyer, 983 F.2d 1215 (3d Cir.1992)—§§ 15.4(c) n.96; 15.4(e) n.139, 141; 15.4(i) n.206; 22.2(c) n.39, 42, 43

Ramseur, State v., 106 N.J. 123, 524 A.2d 188 (1987)—§§ 1.7(i) n.210; 15.4(c) n.96; 15.4(e) n.139, 140

Ramsey, Commonwealth v., 744 S.W.2d 418 (Ky.1987)—§ 3.7(a) n.17

Ramsey, State v., 844 A.2d 715 (R.I.2004)—§ 6.2(c) n.146

Ramsey, United States v., 165 F.3d 980 (D.C.Cir.1999)—§ 21.2(b) n.74

Ramsey, United States v., 999 F.2d 348 (8th Cir.1993)—§ 10.3(d) n.66

Ramsey v. United States, 569 A.2d 142 (D.C.App.1990)—§ 11.7(e) n.94

Ramsey, United States v., 785 F.2d 184 (7th Cir.1986)—§§ 8.14(a) n.8, 11

Ramsey, United States v., 431 U.S. 606, 97 S.Ct. 1972, 52 L.Ed.2d 617 (1977)—§ 3.9(f) n.85

Ramsey, United States v., 538 F.2d 415 (D.C.Cir.1976)—§ 3.9(f) n.88

Ramstad, United States v., 219 F.3d 1263 (10th Cir.2000)—§ 10.6(a) n.6

Randall v. State, 356 S.C. 639, 591 S.E.2d 608 (2004)—§ 21.3(b) n.66

Randall v. State, 806 So.2d 185 (Miss.2001)—§ 24.7(i) n.91

Randall v. State, 474 N.E.2d 76 (Ind.1985)—§ 7.4(d) n.72

Randazzo, People v., 15 N.Y.2d 526, 254 N.Y.S.2d 99, 202 N.E.2d 549 (1964)—§ 3.9(j) n.201

Randel, United States v., 8 F.3d 1526 (10th Cir.1993)—§§ 21.2(d) n.141; 21.2(f) n.383

Randell, United States v., 924 F.Supp. 557 (S.D.N.Y.1996)—§ 8.5(c) n.81

Randle, State v., 252 Wis.2d 743, 647 N.W.2d 324 (2002)—§ 16.4(d) n.142

Randle v. State, 847 S.W.2d 576 (Tex.Cr.App.1993)—§ 21.3(b) n.110

Randle, State v., 179 W.Va. 242, 366 S.E.2d 750 (1988)—§ 6.2(c) n.132

Randle, United States v., 324 F.3d 550 (7th Cir.2003)—§ 21.2(d) n.157

Randle, United States v., 966 F.2d 1209 (7th Cir.1992)—§ 10.5(f) n.67

Randolph v. People of the State of California, 380 F.3d 1133 (9th Cir.2004)—§§ 6.4(g) n.153; 22.2(d) n.76, 82

Randolph v. State, 463 So.2d 186 (Fla.1984)—§§ 24.4(d) n.31, 48

Randolph, State v., 316 N.W.2d 508 (Minn.1982)—§§ 26.1(d) n.90, 91

Randolph, State v., 139 Mo.App. 314, 123 S.W. 61 (1909)—§ 15.5(c) n.105

Randolph, United States v., 230 F.3d 243 (6th Cir.2000)—§ 21.2(b) n.48

Randy G., In re, 26 Cal.4th 556, 110 Cal.Rptr.2d 516, 28 P.3d 239 (2001)—§ 3.9(k) n.252

Ranes, People v., 58 Mich.App. 268, 227 N.W.2d 312 (1975)—§ 20.3(i) n.171

Raney, United States v., 342 F.3d 551 (7th Cir.2003)—§ 3.10(f) n.199

Rangel v. Florida, 692 So.2d 277 (Fla.App.1997)—§ 26.3(g) n.95

Rangel-Reyes v. United States, _____ U.S. _____, 126 S.Ct. 2873, 165 L.Ed.2d 910 (2006)—§ 26.4(i) n.193

Ranger Electronic Communications, Inc., United States v., 210 F.3d 627 (6th Cir.2000)—§ 13.5(h) n.147

Ranghelle, People v., 69 N.Y.2d 56, 511 N.Y.S.2d 580, 503 N.E.2d 1011 (1986)—§ 20.6(b) n.53

Raniere, United States v., 895 F.Supp. 699 (D.N.J.1995)—§ 8.13(d) n.103

Ranke v. United States, 873 F.2d 1033 (7th Cir.1989)—§ 21.4(a) n.23

Rankin v. State, 338 Ark. 723, 1 S.W.3d 14 (1999)—§ 6.2(c) n.170

Rankin v. State, 329 Ark. 379, 948 S.W.2d 397 (1997)—§ 10.2(b) n.18

Rankin v. State, 636 So.2d 652 (Miss.1994)—§ 3.5(e) n.192

Rankin, United States v., 779 F.2d 956 (3d Cir.1986)—§ 11.4(c) n.64

Ransome v. State, 373 Md. 99, 816 A.2d 901 (2003)—§ 3.8(e) n.186

Ranta v. State, 288 Mont. 391, 958 P.2d 670 (1998)—§ 26.4(e) n.77

Rantz, United States v., 862 F.2d 808 (10th Cir.1988)—§§ 11.6(a) n.22; 11.6(d) n.115

Rapanos, United States v., 115 F.3d 367 (6th Cir.1997)—§ 27.5(e) n.156

Rapert, United States v., 813 F.2d 182 (8th Cir.1987)—§ 26.10(c) n.58

Raphael, United States v., 786 F.Supp. 355 (S.D.N.Y.1992)—§§ 8.8(f) n.154, 156

Rapier, Ex parte, 143 U.S. 110, 12 S.Ct. 374, 36 L.Ed. 93 (1892)—§§ 1.2(c) n.97, 100

Rardon, State v., 327 Mont. 228, 115 P.3d 182 (2005)—§ 21.2(d) n.174

Rardon, State v., 313 Mont. 321, 61 P.3d 132 (2002)—§ 21.2(d) n.174

Rardon, State v., 296 Mont. 19, 986 P.2d 424 (1999)—§ 21.2(d) n.167

Rascon v. State, 47 Ariz. 501, 57 P.2d 304 (1936)—§ 21.5(f) n.154

Rascon, United States v., 922 F.2d 584 (10th Cir.1990)—§§ 9.1(d) n.136; 10.1(a) n.3

Rascon-Ortiz, United States v., 994 F.2d 749 (10th Cir.1993)—§ 3.2(f) n.182

Rashad v. Burt, 108 F.3d 677 (6th Cir.1997)—§ 17.4(b) n.73

Rashad, United States v., 331 F.3d 908 (D.C.Cir.2003)—§§ 11.7(e) n.73, 104, 106; 28.9(b) n.41

Rashad v. Walsh, 300 F.3d 27 (1st Cir.2002)—§§ 18.1(c) n.36; 18.2(c) n.36; 18.2(d) n.63; 18.2(e) n.84

Rashard, United States v., 396 F.3d 398 (D.C.Cir.2005)—§ 21.4(f) n.215

Rashed, United States v., 234 F.3d 1280 (D.C.Cir.2000)—§ 25.5(a) n.11

Rasinski, State v., 472 N.W.2d 645 (Minn.1991)—§ 26.1(d) n.90

Rasinsky, State v., 527 N.W.2d 593 (Minn.App. 1995)—§ 26.3(f) n.55

Rassmussen, State v., 92 Idaho 731, 449 P.2d 837 (1969)—§ 6.7(b) n.43

Rastelli, United States v., 870 F.2d 822 (2d Cir.1989)—§§ 24.9(e) n.55; 25.3(b) n.18

Rastrom v. Robbins, 440 F.2d 1251 (1st Cir.1971)—§ 11.8(c) n.59

Rasul v. Bush, 542 U.S. 466, 124 S.Ct. 2686, 159 L.Ed.2d 548 (2004)—§ 28.2(a) n.16

Raszkiewicz, United States v., 169 F.3d 459 (7th Cir.1999)—§ 22.2(d) n.70

Ratcliff, People v., 778 P.2d 1371 (Colo.1989)—§ 3.1(d) n.98

Ratcliff, United States v., 245 F.3d 1246 (11th Cir.2001)—§ 18.5(a) n.37

Rath, United States v., 406 F.2d 757 (6th Cir.1969)—§ 15.7(h) n.227

Rathbun v. United States, 355 U.S. 107, 78 S.Ct. 161, 2 L.Ed.2d 134 (1957)—§ 4.6(b) n.45

Ratley, State v., 253 Kan. 394, 855 P.2d 943 (1993)—§ 13.5(b) n.55

Ratliff v. State, 690 S.W.2d 597 (Tex.Cr.App.1985)—§ 22.3(a) n.6

Ratner, State v., 948 So.2d 700 (Fla.2007)—§ 27.3(c) n.45

Rattley v. Irelan, 197 F.2d 585 (D.C.Cir.1952)—§ 15.1(f) n.309

Rattray v. Brown, 261 F.Supp.2d 149 (E.D.N.Y.2003)—§ 11.7(e) n.108

Rau, State v., 129 N.H. 126, 523 A.2d 98 (1987)—§§ 26.10(a) n.6; 26.10(b) n.20

Raudebaugh v. State, 135 Idaho 602, 21 P.3d 924 (Idaho 2001)—§ 11.10(d) n.162

Raulerson v. United States, 901 F.2d 1009 (11th Cir.1990)—§ 21.2(d) n.176

Raulerson v. Wainwright, 732 F.2d 803 (11th Cir.1984)—§ 11.5(b) n.27

Raulston, State v., 707 N.W.2d 464 (N.D.2005)—§ 21.4(d) n.103

Rave, State v., 326 Mont. 398, 109 P.3d 753 (2005)—§ 21.4(c) n.67

Raven v. Deukmejian, 52 Cal.3d 336, 276 Cal.Rptr. 326, 801 P.2d 1077 (1990)—§ 2.12(a) n.69

Ravin v. State, 537 P.2d 494 (Alaska 1975)—§ 2.12(b) n.112

Rawlings v. Kentucky, 448 U.S. 98, 100 S.Ct. 2556, 65 L.Ed.2d 633 (1980)—§§ 3.2(b) n.96; 3.5(d) n.135; 3.6(e) n.118, 120; 9.1(a) n.5, 8; 9.1(b) n.60, 87; 9.1(c) n.107; 9.1(d) n.123; 9.4(a) n.7, 21, 30; 12.5(b) n.35

Rawlings, State v., 893 P.2d 1063 (Utah App.1995)—§ 26.9(a) n.14

Rawlings, State v., 121 Idaho 930, 829 P.2d 520 (1992)—§ 3.1(d) n.96

Rawlins v. Georgia, 201 U.S. 638, 26 S.Ct. 560, 50 L.Ed. 899 (1906)—§ 22.2(d) n.48

Ray v. Duckworth, 881 F.2d 512 (7th Cir.1989)—§ 6.2(c) n.135

Ray, People v., 13 Cal.4th 313, 52 Cal.Rptr.2d 296, 914 P.2d 846 (1996)—§ 6.7(d) n.153

Ray, People v., 65 N.Y.2d 282, 491 N.Y.S.2d 283, 480 N.E.2d 1065 (1985)—§ 6.10(b) n.20

Ray v. Rose, 535 F.2d 966 (6th Cir.1976)—§ 11.9(a) n.42

Ray, State v., 659 N.W.2d 736 (Minn.2003)—§ 6.9(g) n.181

Ray, State v., 272 Ga. 450, 531 S.E.2d 705 (2000)—§ 6.2(c) n.105

Ray v. State, 133 Idaho 96, 982 P.2d 931 (1999)—§§ 21.3(b) n.66; 21.4(d) n.138

Ray v. State, 679 N.E.2d 1364 (Ind.App.1997)—§§ 12.3(b) n.58, 59

Ray, State v., 241 Neb. 551, 489 N.W.2d 558 (1992)—§ 6.2(c) n.147

Ray, State v., 151 N.C. 710, 66 S.E. 204 (1909)—§ 16.4(c) n.47

Ray v. United States, 481 U.S. 736, 107 S.Ct. 2093, 95 L.Ed.2d 693 (1987)—§ 27.5(b) n.38

Ray, United States v., 828 F.2d 399 (7th Cir.1987)—§ 21.4(c) n.78

Ray, United States v., 234 F.Supp. 371 (D.D.C.1964)—§ 16.3(c) n.44

Rayborn v. Coughlin, In re, 202 App.Div.2d 591, 609 N.Y.S.2d 271 (1994)—§ 26.3(f) n.57

Rayborn v. Scully, 858 F.2d 84 (2d Cir.1988)—§ 18.2(c) n.49

Rayburn House Office Building, Room 2113, United States v., 2007 WL 2275237 (D.C.Cir.2007)—§ 3.4(a) n.24

Raye, State v., 281 Wis.2d 339, 697 N.W.2d 407 (Wis.2005)—§ 24.9(e) n.56

Rayes, State v., 142 N.H. 496, 703 A.2d 1381 (1997)—§ 13.2(a) n.4

Rayford v. State, 125 S.W.3d 521 (Tex.Crim.App.2003)—§ 10.4(c) n.23

Ray J. McDermott & Co., Inc., In re, 622 F.2d 166 (5th Cir.1980)—§ 8.5(h) n.303

Raymond, Commonwealth v., 424 Mass. 382, 676 N.E.2d 824 (1997)—§§ 6.2(c) n.96; 6.8(d) n.84; 6.9(g) n.158

Raynor, United States v., 989 F.Supp. 43 (D.D.C.1997)—§§ 21.2(b) n.86; 27.5(c) n.56

R.C., People v., 108 Ill.2d 349, 91 Ill.Dec. 606, 483 N.E.2d 1241 (1985)—§ 6.9(f) n.109

R.C. v. State, 760 P.2d 501 (Alaska 1988)—§ 27.5(c) n.101

R.D., State v., 169 N.J. 551, 781 A.2d 37 (2001)—§ 24.9(f) n.86

Re, United States v., 313 F.Supp. 442 (S.D.N.Y.1970)—§ 8.7(e) n.94

Rea v. Commonwealth, 14 Va.App. 940, 421 S.E.2d 464 (1992)—§ 25.1(d) n.66

Rea v. United States, 350 U.S. 214, 76 S.Ct. 292, 100 L.Ed. 233 (1956)—§§ 1.7(i) n.163; 3.1(a) n.16

Rea-Beltran, United States v., 457 F.3d 695 (7th Cir.2006)—§ 21.4(f) n.184

Read, United States v., 778 F.2d 1437 (9th Cir.1985)—§ 21.2(d) n.222

Ready, State v., 252 Neb. 816, 565 N.W.2d 728 (1997)—§ 3.8(c) n.116

Reagan v. Norris, 279 F.3d 651 (8th Cir.2002)—§ 28.4(d) n.56

Reagan, People v., 395 Mich. 306, 235 N.W.2d 581 (1975)—§§ 13.5(b) n.34, 40, 41

Reagan, State v., 35 N.C.App. 140, 240 S.E.2d 805 (1978)—§ 3.10(e) n.160

Real Property at 633 East 640 North, Orem, Utah, State v., 994 P.2d 1254 (Utah 2000)—§ 26.6(d) n.75

Real Property at 15324 County Highway E, United States v., 332 F.3d 1070 (7th Cir.2003)—§ 3.1(c) n.79

Rease v. Commonwealth, 227 Va. 289, 316 S.E.2d 148 (1984)—§ 26.10(b) n.20

Reasor v. State, 12 S.W.3d 813 (Tex.Crim.App.2000)—§ 3.10(b) n.74

Reasor, United States v., 418 F.3d 466 (5th Cir.2005)—§ 21.4(f) n.192

Reass v. United States, 99 F.2d 752 (4th Cir.1938)—§ 16.1(d) n.137

Reaves v. State, 242 Ga. 542, 250 S.E.2d 376 (1978)—§ 15.5(c) n.103

Reaves, State v., 254 N.W.2d 488 (Iowa 1977)—§ 21.4(c) n.92

Reavley, State v., 318 Mont. 150, 79 P.3d 270 (2003)—§ 6.4(e) n.64

Rebmann, United States v., 226 F.3d 521 (6th Cir.2000)—§ 21.4(e) n.156

Recio, United States v., 371 F.3d 1093 (9th Cir.2004)—§ 27.5(d) n.128

Reck v. Pate, 367 U.S. 433, 81 S.Ct. 1541, 6 L.Ed.2d 948 (1961)—§§ 6.2(c) n.64, 66, 80, 81, 84

Reckmeyer, United States v., 786 F.2d 1216 (4th Cir.1986)—§ 21.2(d) n.186

Records of Various Distributing, Inc., In re Custodian of, 927 F.2d 244 (6th Cir.1991)—§§ 8.13(d) n.103, 104, 108

Rector v. Johnson, 120 F.3d 551 (5th Cir.1997)—§§ 24.3(b) n.57; 28.7(d) n.26

Recupero, People v., 73 N.Y.2d 877, 538 N.Y.S.2d 234, 535 N.E.2d 287 (1988)—§§ 21.3(b) n.132, 141

Red Bird, United States v., 287 F.3d 709 (8th Cir.2002)—§ 6.4(e) n.101

Redd, People v., 173 Ill.2d 1, 218 Ill.Dec. 861, 670 N.E.2d 583 (1996)—§ 11.3(a) n.19

Redd v. Sowders, 809 F.2d 1266 (6th Cir.1987)—§ 18.2(c) n.30

Redd v. State, 264 Ga. 399, 444 S.E.2d 776 (1994)—§§ 11.9(c) n.112, 130

Reddick, State v., 224 Conn. 445, 619 A.2d 453 (1993)—§ 7.4(g) n.121

Reddick, State v., 207 Conn. 323, 541 A.2d 1209 (1988)—§ 9.1(b) n.45

Redding, Commonwealth v., 382 Mass. 154, 414 N.E.2d 347 (1980)— § 24.3(b) n.63

Redding, State v., 274 Ga. 831, 561 S.E.2d 79 (2002)—§§ 18.2(d) n.68; 18.2(e) n.82

Redding, State v., 213 Neb. 887, 331 N.W.2d 811 (1983)—§ 24.8(f) n.96

Redding v. State, 10 Md.App. 601, 272 A.2d 70 (1971)—§ 7.3(d) n.66

Reddish, State v., 181 N.J. 553, 859 A.2d 1173 (2004)—§ 11.5(a) n.18

Reddish, State v., 189 N.J. 553, 859 A.2d 1173 (2004)—§ 11.5(c) n.39

Redditt v. State, 337 Md. 621, 655 A.2d 390 (1995)—§§ 24.4(d) n.33, 64

Red Elk, United States v., 955 F.Supp. 1170 (S.D.1997)—§§ 15.6(a) n.43; 15.6(e) n.160; 15.7(b) n.24, 26

Redfearn, United States v., 906 F.2d 352 (8th Cir.1990)—§§ 16.2(a) n.1; 16.2(e) n.77

Redford, State v., 242 Kan. 658, 750 P.2d 1013 (1988)—§§ 16.1(d) n.138, 154

Redinger, State v., 64 N.J. 41, 312 A.2d 129 (1973)—§ 17.4(a) n.39

Redlich, State v., 322 Mont. 476, 97 P.3d 1090 (2004)—§ 9.1(b) n.75

Redmon, United States v., 138 F.3d 1109 (7th Cir.1998)—§ 3.2(h) n.212

Redmond v. Kingston, 240 F.3d 590 (7th Cir.2001)—§ 24.4(b) n.13

Redmond, People v., 67 Ill.2d 242, 10 Ill.Dec. 250, 367 N.E.2d 703 (1977)—§ 14.3(d) n.90

Redmond v. People, 180 Colo. 24, 501 P.2d 1051 (1972)—§ 6.9(c) n.59

Redmond v. United States, 829 A.2d 229 (D.C.App.2003)—§ 7.4(g) n.110

Redondo-Lemos, United States v., 955 F.2d 1296 (9th Cir.1992)— § 13.2(g) n.136

Reece v. Georgia, 350 U.S. 85, 76 S.Ct. 167, 100 L.Ed. 77 (1955)— §§ 2.7(a) n.26; 15.4(b) n.78, 81; 27.5(c) n.94

Reece, United States v., 797 F.Supp. 843 (D.Colo.1992)—§ 9.6(a) n.25

Reece, United States v., 614 F.2d 1259 (10th Cir.1980)—§ 8.5(e) n.172

Reed v. Becka, 333 S.C. 676, 511 S.E.2d 396 (App.1999)—§ 21.3(f) n.360

Reed v. City and County of Honolulu, 76 Hawai'i 219, 873 P.2d 98 (1994)—§ 14.3(b) n.45

Reed v. Farley, 512 U.S. 339, 114 S.Ct. 2291, 129 L.Ed.2d 277 (1994)— §§ 18.2(e) n.72; 18.4(c) n.33; 28.3(b) n.62

Reed, People v., 132 P.3d 347 (Colo.2006)—§§ 16.1(f) n.226; 16.1(g) n.235

Reed v. People, 745 P.2d 235 (Colo.1987)—§ 18.4(c) n.32

Reed v. Ross, 468 U.S. 1, 104 S.Ct. 2901, 82 L.Ed.2d 1 (1984)— §§ 15.1(c) n.141; 28.4(d) n.47

Reed v. Roylston, 22 Ariz.App. 118, 524 P.2d 513 (1974)—§ 3.8(d) n.145

Reed, State v., _____ N.W.2d _____, 2007 WL 2389774 (Minn.2007)— § 27.5(d) n.137

Reed, State v., 215 W.Va. 220, 599 S.E.2d 643 (2004)—§ 17.4(c) n.145

Reed, State v., 266 Neb. 641, 668 N.W.2d 245 (2003)—§§ 18.4(c) n.60, 75

Reed, State v., 355 N.C. 150, 558 S.E.2d 167 (2002)—§ 22.3(c) n.112

Reed v. State, 748 N.E.2d 381 (Ind.2001)—§§ 21.2(h) n.426; 24.3(i) n.190

Reed, State v., 686 A.2d 1067 (Me.1996)—§ 17.4(a) n.31

Reed, State v., 77 Hawai'i 72, 881 P.2d 1218 (1994)—§ 5.2(b) n.25

Reed, State v., 133 N.J. 237, 627 A.2d 630 (1993)—§§ 6.9(c) n.60, 61

Reed v. State, 560 So.2d 203 (Fla.1990)—§ 11.6(a) n.50

Reed v. State, 506 So.2d 277 (1987)—§ 19.5(c) n.58

Reed, State v., 237 Kan. 685, 703 P.2d 756 (1985)—§ 26.3(f) n.64

Reed v. State, 35 Md.App. 472, 372 A.2d 243 (1978)—§ 2.12(d) n.187

Reed, State v., 284 So.2d 574 (La.1973)—§ 3.2(h) n.204

Reed v. State, 126 Ga.App. 323, 190 S.E.2d 587 (1972)—§ 3.4(e) n.88

Reed, United States v., 349 F.3d 457 (7th Cir.2003)—§ 9.4(a) n.17

Reed, United States v., 15 F.3d 928 (9th Cir.1994)—§ 9.4(b) n.59

Reed, United States v., 924 F.2d 1014 (11th Cir.1991)—§ 26.6(d) n.48

Reed, United States v., 910 F.2d 621 (9th Cir.1990)—§ 18.4(c) n.50

Reed, United States v., 773 F.2d 477 (2d Cir.1985)—§ 16.2(e) n.61

Reed, United States v., 639 F.2d 896 (2d Cir.1981)—§ 19.3(c) n.195

Reed v. United States, 383 A.2d 316 (D.C.App.1978)—§ 15.4(g) n.174

Reed Enterprises v. Corcoran, 354 F.2d 519 (D.C.Cir.1965)—§ 16.2(f) n.100

Rees, State v., 748 A.2d 976 (Me.2000)—§§ 6.2(b) n.51; 6.2(c) n.179

Reese, Commonwealth v., 520 Pa. 29, 549 A.2d 909 (1988)—§ 3.4(j) n.192

Reese, State v., 91 N.M. 76, 570 P.2d 614 (N.M.App.1977)—§§ 15.6(a) n.12, 18; 15.7(e) n.93, 105, 115, 121

Reese, State v., 112 Wash. 507, 192 P. 934 (1920)—§ 16.1(e) n.196

Reese, United States v., 561 F.2d 894 (D.C.Cir.1977)—§ 8.10(e) n.118

Reese, United States v., 463 F.2d 830 (D.C.Cir.1972)—§ 12.2(c) n.44

Reeves, State v., 714 So.2d 696 (La.1998)—§ 6.7(c) n.118

Reeves v. State, 564 N.E.2d 550 (Ind.App.1991)—§ 11.10(c) n.108

Reeves v. State, 241 Ga. 44, 243 S.E.2d 24 (1978)—§ 6.9(g) n.157

Reeves, United States v., 255 F.3d 208 (5th Cir.2001)—§§ 21.2(d) n.167, 174

Reeves, United States v., 83 F.3d 203 (8th Cir.1996)—§ 24.4(c) n.24

Reeves, United States v., 892 F.2d 1223 (5th Cir.1990)—§ 11.9(d) n.222

Reeves, United States v., 674 F.2d 739 (8th Cir.1982)—§ 11.4(c) n.84

Reffett v. State, 571 N.E.2d 1227 (Ind.1991)—§ 21.2(f) n.363

Regan, United States v., 103 F.3d 1072 (2d Cir.1997)—§ 8.8(h) n.189

Regan, United States v., 706 F.Supp. 1102 (S.D.N.Y.1989)—§ 8.5(e) n.189

Reggio, State v., 84 S.D. 687, 176 N.W.2d 62 (1970)—§ 14.4(b) n.7

Regina v. Garner, 169 Eng.Rep. 267, 1 Den.C.C. 329 (Ct.Crim.App.1848)—§ 6.2(a) n.8

Regina v. Moore, 169 Eng.Rep. 608, 2 Den.C.C. 522 (Ct.Crim.App.1852)—§ 6.2(a) n.6

Regional Consulting Services for Economic and Community Development, Inc., United States v., 766 F.2d 870 (4th Cir.1985)—§ 27.2(d) n.73

Register, State v., 323 S.C. 471, 476 S.E.2d 153 (1996)—§§ 6.2(c) n.132; 6.9(g) n.177

Register, State v., 308 S.C. 534, 419 S.E.2d 771 (1992)—§ 27.4(e) n.60

Register, United States v., 182 F.3d 820 (11th Cir.1999)—§§ 11.9(c) n.120; 22.3(e) n.277

Register, United States v., 931 F.2d 308 (5th Cir.1991)—§ 9.4(b) n.73

Reichert v. State, 134 P.3d 268 (Wyo.2006)—§§ 21.2(g) n.399; 21.5(a) n.24

Reichle, Commonwealth v., 404 Pa.Super. 1, 589 A.2d 1140 (1991)—§ 26.3(g) n.95

Reid v. Colorado, 187 U.S. 137, 23 S.Ct. 92, 47 L.Ed.2d 108 (1902)—§ 1.2(c) n.107

Reid, Commonwealth v., 571 Pa. 1, 811 A.2d 530 (2002)—§ 3.10(b) n.66

Reid v. Oklahoma, 101 F.3d 628 (10th Cir.1996)—§ 28.4(e) n.88

Reid, State v., 213 S.W.3d 792 (Tenn.2006)—§ 22.4(c) n.29

Reid, State v., 277 Conn. 764, 894 A.2d 963 (2006)—§ 21.4(c) n.88

Reid, State v., 254 Conn. 540, 757 A.2d 482 (2000)—§ 7.4(e) n.90

Reid, State v., 155 Ariz. 399, 747 P.2d 560 (1987)—§ 22.1(h) n.156

Reid, United States v., 53 U.S. (12 How.) 361, 13 L.Ed. 1023 (1851)—§ 1.7(h) n.141

Reiff v. State, 41 Wis.2d 369, 164 N.W.2d 249 (1969)—§ 21.5(a) n.56

Reifler, United States v., 446 F.3d 65 (2d Cir.2006)—§§ 26.6(c) n.35, 42

Reilley, United States v., 948 F.2d 648 (10th Cir.1991)—§ 11.2(a) n.27

Reilly, Commonwealth v., 324 Pa. 558, 188 A. 574 (1936)—§§ 16.1(b) n.38; 16.3(a) n.5; 16.3(d) n.53, 56 to 58, 76

Reilly v. State, 557 So.2d 1365 (Fla.1990)—§ 22.3(c) n.117

Reilly, United States v., 224 F.3d 986 (9th Cir.2000)—§§ 6.7(b) n.74, 85; 9.3(e) n.62

Reilly, United States v., 76 F.3d 1271 (2d Cir.1996)—§ 3.1(c) n.65

Reimnitz v. State's Attorney, 761 F.2d 405 (7th Cir.1985)—§ 1.6(h) n.456

Reina v. United States, 364 U.S. 507, 81 S.Ct. 260, 5 L.Ed.2d 249 (1960)—§ 8.10(a) n.13

Reinert v. Larkins, 379 F.3d 76 (3d Cir.2004)—§ 6.6(e) n.75

Reinhardt, People v., 42 Misc.2d 45, 247 N.Y.S.2d 708 (1964)—§ 10.3(b) n.24

Reinhardt v. State, 263 Ga. 113, 428 S.E.2d 333 (1993)—§ 6.6(e) n.75

Reinholz, United States v., 245 F.3d 765 (8th Cir.2001)—§ 3.3(b) n.72

Reinier, State v., 628 N.W.2d 460 (Iowa 2001)—§§ 3.10(c) n.98, 99

Reis, United States v., 788 F.2d 54 (1st Cir.1986)—§ 20.3(h) n.156

Reitmeyer, United States v., 356 F.3d 1313 (10th Cir.2004)—§ 18.5(a) n.11

Reittinger v. Commonwealth, 260 Va. 232, 532 S.E.2d 25 (2000)—§ 3.8(c) n.117

Reldan, State v., 185 N.J.Super. 494, 449 A.2d 1317 (1982)—§ 16.4(d) n.119

Rem, United States v., 984 F.2d 806 (7th Cir.1993)—§ 3.2(h) n.203

Reme, United States v., 738 F.2d 1156 (11th Cir.1984)—§ 18.1(c) n.35

Remick, State v., 149 N.H. 745, 829 A.2d 1079 (2003)—§ 6.5(b) n.25

Remigio, United States v., 767 F.2d 730 (10th Cir.1985)—§ 3.4(h) n.147

Remington v. Montana Dept. Of Corrections and Human Servs., 255 Mont. 480, 844 P.2d 50 (1992)—§ 27.4(f) n.63

Remington, People v., 217 Cal.App.3d 423, 266 Cal.Rptr. 183 (1990)—§ 16.1(a) n.27

Remiro, People v., 89 Cal.App.3d 809, 153 Cal.Rpt. 89 (1979)—§ 16.3(g) n.108

Remmer v. United States, 347 U.S. 227, 74 S.Ct. 450, 98 L.Ed. 654 (1954)—§§ 24.9(f) n.70, 77

Renda v. King, 347 F.3d 550 (3d Cir.2003)—§ 6.5(a) n.17

Rendel v. Mummert, 106 Ariz. 233, 474 P.2d 824 (1970)—§§ 12.3(b) n.73; 12.3(g) n.151, 152

Rendell-Baker v. Kohn, 457 U.S. 830, 102 S.Ct. 2764, 73 L.Ed.2d 418 (1982)—§ 3.9(k) n.253

Renfro v. State, 785 P.2d 491 (Wyo.1990)—§ 26.6(c) n.40

Renick, United States v., 273 F.3d 1009 (11th Cir.2001)—§ 24.11(b) n.4

Reno, State v., 150 N.H. 466, 840 A.2d 786 (2004)—§ 3.2(f) n.182

R. Enterprises, Inc., United States v., 498 U.S. 292, 111 S.Ct. 722, 112 L.Ed.2d 795 (1991)—§§ 8.4 n.1; 8.7(d) n.78; 8.8(b) n.34; 15.2(f) n.151; 24.3(f) n.146

Renton v. State, 265 Ark. 223, 577 S.W.2d 594 (1979)—§ 12.4(a) n.30

Report and Recommendation of June 5, 1972 Grand Jury Concerning Transmission of Evidence to the House of Representatives, In re, 370 F.Supp. 1219 (D.D.C.1974)—§§ 8.3(h) n.38, 39; 8.5(h) n.301; 15.1(d) n.172

Reporters Comm. For Freedom of the Press, In re, 773 F.2d 1325 (D.C.Cir.1985)—§ 23.1(d) n.134

Report of Grand Jury, In re, 152 Fla. 154, 11 So.2d 316 (1943)—§ 8.3(h) n.40

Report of Grand Jury, Jefferson County, In re, 533 So.2d 873 (Fla.App.1988)—§§ 15.6(d) n.121, 123

Report of Grand Jury of Baltimore City, In re, 152 Md. 616, 137 A. 370 (1927)—§§ 8.3(h) n.38, 44

Report of Grand Jury of Carroll County, In re, 39 Md.App. 472, 386 A.2d 1246 (1978)—§ 8.3(h) n.38

Report of Grand Jury of Marshall County, In re, 108 Ill.App.3d 232, 63 Ill.Dec. 953, 438 N.E.2d 1316 (1982)—§ 8.3(h) n.50

Report of Grand Jury (Shoemaker), In re, 123 Utah 458, 260 P.2d 521 (1953)—§ 8.3(h) n.44

Report of the Grand Jury, Jefferson County, In re, 533 So.2d 873 (Fla.App.1988)—§ 8.5(i) n.312

Repository Division of Thompson Newspapers, Inc., State ex rel. The v. Unger, 28 Ohio St.3d 418, 504 N.E.2d 37 (1986)—§§ 23.1(d) n.144; 23.1(e) n.247

Request for Access to Grand Jury Materials (Hastings), In re, 833 F.2d 1438 (11th Cir.1987)—§§ 8.5(h) n.275, 301

Resek v. State, 706 P.2d 288 (Alaska 1985)—§ 11.2(b) n.57

Resendez-Mendez, United States v., 251 F.3d 514 (5th Cir.2001)—§ 26.8(b) n.14

Resendiz, In re, 25 Cal.4th 230, 105 Cal.Rptr.2d 431, 19 P.3d 1171 (2001)—§§ 21.3(b) n.68, 69

Resendiz-Ponce, United States v., _____ U.S. _____, 127 S.Ct. 782, 166 L.Ed.2d 591 (2007)— §§ 19.2(a) n.5; 19.2(f) n.108; 19.3(a) n.60, 131; 19.3(b) n.157; 27.6(d) n.113

Resendiz-Ponce, United States v., 425 F.3d 729 (9th Cir.2005)—§ 19.3(a) n.130

Residence Located at 218 Third Street, United States v., 805 F.2d 256 (7th Cir.1986)—§ 8.5(b) n.33

Resio, State v., 148 Wis.2d 687, 436 N.W.2d 603 (1989)—§ 22.1(h) n.133

Resnover v. Pearson, 754 F.Supp. 1374 (N.D.Ind.1991)—§ 22.5(a) n.12

Resolution Trust Corp. v. Lopez, 794 F.Supp. 1 (D.D.C.1992)—§ 8.12(c) n.37

Respass, State v., 256 Conn. 165, 770 A.2d 471 (2001)—§ 3.3(c) n.93

Resper v. United States, 793 A.2d 450 (D.C.App.2002)—§ 6.6(c) n.37

Resper v. United States, 527 A.2d 1257 (D.C.App.1987)—§§ 26.10(a) n.3, 7

Respondent's Brief before the Supreme Court, 2002 WL 463382 (2002)— § 19.3(e) n.225

Respondent's Reply Brief, 2002 WL 535148 (2002)—§ 19.3(e) n.233

Ressin, People v., 620 P.2d 717 (Colo.1980)—§ 26.10(c) n.65

Reston v. F.C.C., 492 F.Supp. 697 (D.D.C.1980)—§ 4.6(l) n.194

Restrepo, United States v., 994 F.2d 173 (5th Cir.1993)—§ 10.4(b) n.15

Restrepo, United States v., 966 F.2d 964 (5th Cir.1992)—§§ 9.4(b) n.66, 73

Restrepo, United States v., 946 F.2d 654 (9th Cir.1991)—§ 26.4(d) n.61

Retirement Bd. Of Employees' Retirement System v. Azar, 721 A.2d 872 (R.I.1998)—§ 17.4(b) n.127

Rettenberger, State v., 984 P.2d 1009 (Utah 1999)—§§ 6.2(c) n.132, 148, 169, 183

Reuscher v. State, 887 S.W.2d 588 (Mo.1994)—§§ 28.11(a)   n.9; 28.11(b) n.19

Revelo, State v., 256 Conn. 494, 775 A.2d 260 (2001)—§ 21.2(c) n.134

Revels, State v., 221 Wis.2d 315, 585 N.W.2d 602 (1998)—§§ 20.4(b) n.20, 36; 20.4(d) n.72; 20.4(f) n.95

Revere, State v., 232 La. 184, 94 So.2d 25 (1957)—§§ 15.7(h) n.234, 235

Revere, Pa., Commonwealth v., 585 Pa. 262, 888 A.2d 694 (2005)—§ 3.8(b) n.45

Review of Habeas Corpus Proceedings, In re, 313 Ark. 168, 852 S.W.2d 791 (1993)—§ 27.4(f) n.63

Rewak v. United States, 512 F.2d 1184 (9th Cir.1975)—§ 28.9(a) n.19

Rewald, United States v., 889 F.2d 836 (9th Cir.1989)—§ 24.7(e) n.69

Rewis, United States v., 969 F.2d 985 (11th Cir.1992)—§ 21.2(d) n.186

Rex v. Sullivan, 194 Colo. 568, 575 P.2d 408 (1978)—§ 14.4(d) n.88

Rex v. Warickshall, Leach's Crown Cases 263 (1783)—§ 1.6(d) n.207

Rexach, United States v., 896 F.2d 710 (2d Cir.1990)—§§ 21.2(d) n.245, 261, 264

Rex Trailer Co. v. United States, 350 U.S. 148, 76 S.Ct. 219, 100 L.Ed. 149 (1956)—§ 25.1(c) n.22

Rey v. State, 897 S.W.2d 333 (Tex.Crim.App.1995)—§§ 11.2(e) n.187; 27.6(d) n.145

Rey, United States v., 811 F.2d 1453 (11th Cir.1987)—§ 5.4(a) n.8

Reyes, Commonwealth v., 764 S.W.2d 62 (Ky.1989)—§ 21.2(f) n.368

Reyes v. State, 978 P.2d 635 (Alaska App.1999)—§ 26.7(b) n.20

Reyes v. State, 741 S.W.2d 414 (Tex.Cr.App.1987)—§ 9.4(b) n.54

Reyes, United States v., 353 F.3d 148 (2d Cir.2003)—§ 6.7(b) n.85

Reyes, United States v., 283 F.3d 446 (2d Cir.2002)—§§ 3.2(c) n.129; 3.9(j) n.206

Reyes, United States v., 313 F.3d 1152 (9th Cir.2002)—§ 21.2(d) n.249

Reyes, United States v., 239 F.3d 722 (5th Cir.2001)—§ 5.2(a) n.11

Reyes, United States v., 225 F.3d 71 (1st Cir.2000)—§ 6.7(b) n.45

Reyes, United States v., 922 F.Supp. 818 (S.D.N.Y. 1996)—§ 4.6(b) n.25

Reyes-Alvarado, United States v., 963 F.2d 1184 (9th Cir.1992)— § 17.2(b) n.34

Reyes-Platero, United States v., 224 F.3d 1112 (9th Cir.2000)— §§ 11.7(e) n.73, 76; 21.6(a) n.40

Reyes-Requena v. United States, 243 F.3d 893 (5th Cir.2001)— §§ 28.9(a) n.6; 28.9(b) n.55

Reyna v. State, 33 P.3d 1129 (Wyo.2001)—§§ 21.3(b) n.53; 21.4(f) n.174

Reyna, United States v., 130 F.3d 104 (5th Cir.1997)—§ 21.4(c) n.66

Reyna-Segovia, United States v., 125 F.3d 645 (8th Cir.1997)—§ 21.5(a) n.59

Reyna-Tapia, United States v., 328 F.3d 1114 (9th Cir.2003)—§ 21.4(a) n.37

Reynolds v. Commonwealth, 133 Va. 760, 112 S.E. 707 (1922)— § 27.6(b) n.12

Reynolds v. Sims, 377 U.S. 533, 84 S.Ct. 1362, 12 L.Ed.2d 506 (1964)—§ 25.5(c) n.32

Reynolds, State v., 264 Conn. 1, 824 A.2d 611 (2003)—§ 6.9(e) n.81

Reynolds, State v., 264 Conn. 1, 836 A.2d 224 (2003)—§ 3.8(c) n.76

Reynolds v. State, 994 S.W.2d 944 (Mo.1999)—§ 21.4(d) n.119

Reynolds v. State, 327 Md. 494, 610 A.2d 782 (1992)—§ 1.7(h) n.132

Reynolds v. State, 592 So.2d 1082 (Fla.1992)—§§ 3.10(b) n.39, 68

Reynolds, State v., 124 N.J. 559, 592 A.2d 194 (1991)—§ 15.4(g) n.172

Reynolds, State v., 819 S.W.2d 322 (Mo.1991)—§§ 1.7(h) n.132; 27.5(b) n.48

Reynolds, State v., 218 Neb. 753, 359 N.W.2d 93 (1984)—§ 18.4(c) n.40

Reynolds, State v., 101 Conn. 224, 125 A. 636 (1924)—§ 2.12(a) n.9

Reynolds, United States v., 956 F.2d 192 (9th Cir.1992)—§ 12.4(d) n.65

Reynolds, United States v., 762 F.2d 489 (6th Cir.1985)—§§ 6.4(e) n.69; 6.6(a) n.7; 6.6(c) n.31

Reynolds v. United States, 98 U.S. 145, 8 Otto 145, 25 L.Ed. 244 (1878)—§ 23.2(f) n.93

Reynoso, People v., 31 Cal.4th 903, 3 Cal.Rptr.3d 769, 74 P.3d 852 (2003)—§ 22.3(d) n.238

Reynoso, United States v., 239 F.3d 143 (2d Cir.2000)—§ 26.3(c) n.19

Reynoso-Hernandez, State v., 816 A.2d 826 (Me.2003)—§ 10.3(b) n.10

Rezin, United States v., 322 F.3d 443 (7th Cir.2003)—§ 28.9(b) n.42

Rezk, State v., 150 N.H. 483, 840 A.2d 758 (2004)—§§ 6.2(c) n.94, 102

Rezk, State v., 135 N.H. 599, 609 A.2d 391 (1992)—§ 7.4(e) n.92

Reznick, People v., 491 N.E.2d 444 (Ill.App.1986)—§ 26.7(c) n.34

R.H., In re, 568 Pa. 1, 791 A.2d 331 (2002)—§ 6.10(c) n.36

R.H. v. State, 777 P.2d 204 (Alaska App.1989)—§ 6.10(e) n.76

Rheuark v. Shaw, 628 F.2d 297 (5th Cir.1980)—§ 18.5(c) n.81

Rhiger, United States v., 315 F.3d 1283 (10th Cir.2003)—§ 3.6(e) n.131

Rhind, United States v., 289 F.3d 690 (11th Cir.2002)—§ 3.8(e) n.219

Rhinehart, State v., 312 S.C. 36, 430 S.E.2d 536 (1993)—§ 26.9(a) n.7

Rhiner, State v., 352 N.W.2d 258 (Iowa 1984)—§ 6.2(c) n.103

Rhines, State v., 548 N.W.2d 415 (S.D.1996)—§§ 6.8(a) n.16, 17; 6.9(d) n.70

Rhines, State v., 1996 SD 55, 548 N.W.2d 415 (1996)—§ 6.8(a) n.6

Rhines v. Weber, 544 U.S. 269, 125 S.Ct. 1528, 161 L.Ed.2d 440 (2005)—§ 28.5(a) n.24

Rhoades v. State, 675 N.E.2d 698 (Ind.1996)—§ 21.4(f) n.184

Rhoades, State v., 121 Idaho 63, 822 P.2d 960 (1991)—§ 20.5(h) n.100

Rhoads, United States v., 617 F.2d 1313 (8th Cir.1980)—§ 20.3(g) n.132

Rhoda, State v., 23 Ark. 156 (1861)—§ 16.1(e) n.191

Rhode Island v. Innis, 446 U.S. 291, 100 S.Ct. 1682, 64 L.Ed.2d 297 (1980)—§§ 3.10(b) n.79; 6.7(a) n.4

Rhode Island Grand Jury Subpoena, In the Matter of a, 414 Mass. 104, 605 N.E.2d 840 (1993)—§ 27.2(e) n.90

Rhodes, United States v., 253 F.3d 800 (5th Cir.2001)—§ 21.2(d) n.193

Rhodes, United States v., 62 F.3d 1449 (D.C.Cir.1995)—§ 17.2(b) n.62

Rhodes, United States v., 913 F.2d 839 (10th Cir.1990)—§§ 21.2(g) n.396; 21.4(d) n.104

Rhodes, United States v., 779 F.2d 1019 (4th Cir.1985)—§ 6.7(d) n.152

Rhodes, United States v., 631 F.2d 43 (5th Cir.1980)—§ 24.9(b) n.18

Rhodes, United States v., 569 F.2d 384 (5th Cir.1978)—§ 24.3(b) n.48

Rhodus, People v., 870 P.2d 470 (Colo.1994)—§ 22.3(c) n.142

Ribowsky, People v., 77 N.Y.2d 284, 567 N.Y.S.2d 392, 568 N.E.2d 1197 (1991)—§ 24.10(a) n.18

Ricard, United States v., 563 F.2d 45 (2d Cir.1977)—§ 13.7(c) n.59

Ricardo, United States v., 619 F.2d 1124 (5th Cir.1980)—§ 16.4(b) n.19

Ricci v. Arlington Heights, 116 F.3d 288 (7th Cir.1997)—§ 3.5(a) n.20

Ricci, State v., 704 A.2d 210 (R.I.1997)—§ 13.4(c) n.98

Ricco, People v., 56 N.Y.2d 320, 452 N.Y.S.2d 340, 437 N.E.2d 1097 (1982)—§ 9.6(b) n.55

Rice v. Collins, 546 U.S. 333, 126 S.Ct. 969, 163 L.Ed.2d 824 (2006)—§§ 22.3(d) n.247, 257; 28.6(f) n.69

Rice v. Cooper, 148 F.3d 747 (7th Cir.1998)—§ 6.9(b) n.38

Rice v. Marshall, 816 F.2d 1126 (6th Cir.1987)—§ 11.10(c) n.111

Rice, People v., 69 N.Y.2d 781, 513 N.Y.S.2d 108, 505 N.E.2d 618 (1987)—§ 20.3(h) n.145

Rice, People v., 40 Colo.App. 357, 579 P.2d 647 (1978)—§ 11.5(e) n.92

Rice, State v., 329 Ark. 219, 947 S.W.2d 3 (1997)—§ 27.3(c) n.23

Rice v. State, 429 So.2d 686 (Ala.Cr.App.1983)—§ 26.10(b) n.40

Rice v. State, 192 So.2d 698 (Miss.1966)—§ 16.1(e) n.201

Rice v. State, 204 Ark. 236, 161 S.W.2d 401 (1942)—§ 15.4(g) n.170

Rice, United States v., 489 F.Supp.2d 1312 (S.D.Ala.2007)—§ 22.3(b) n.55

Rice, United States v., 659 F.2d 524 (5th Cir.1981)—§ 13.4(c) n.121

Rice v. Wood, 77 F.3d 1138 (9th Cir.1996)—§§ 24.2(a) n.11; 24.2(b) n.24; 27.6(d) n.84

Rich, Ex parte, 194 S.W.3d 508 (Tex.Crim.App.2006)—§ 21.2(e) n.321

Richard, State v., 228 Neb. 872, 424 N.W.2d 859 (1988)—§§ 7.4(c) n.48, 50; 7.4(g) n.111

Richard A. Vaughn, DDS, P.C. v. Baldwin, 950 F.2d 331 (6th Cir.1991)—§§ 3.10(f) n.199, 204

Richard L., In re, 479 A.2d 103 (R.I.1984)—§ 7.4(f) n.98

Richards, In re, 213 F.3d 773 (3d Cir.2000)—§§ 13.3(c) n.36, 38, 41

Richards, Commonwealth v., 458 Pa. 455, 327 A.2d 63 (1974)—§ 3.3(b) n.71

Richards v. Commonwealth, 107 Va. 881, 59 S.E. 1104 (1908)—§ 16.1(b) n.83

Richards, State v., 640 N.W.2d 480 (S.D.2002)—§ 21.4(d) n.103

Richards, State v., 274 Mont. 180, 906 P.2d 222 (1995)—§§ 17.1(a) n.14; 17.1(e) n.61; 17.3(e) n.58, 64

Richards, State v., 464 N.W.2d 540 (Minn.1990)—§ 15.6(a) n.28

Richards, State v., 740 P.2d 1314 (Utah 1987)—§ 12.2(b) n.27

Richards, United States v., 707 F.2d 995 (8th Cir.1983)—§§ 18.2(d) n.67; 18.2(e) n.81

Richards, United States v., 500 F.2d 1025 (9th Cir.1974)—§§ 3.8(b) n.41, 43; 3.10(b) n.49

Richards v. Wisconsin, 520 U.S. 385, 117 S.Ct. 1416, 137 L.Ed.2d 615 (1997)—§§ 2.6(c) n.85; 2.9(g) n.163, 181; 3.4(h) n.156, 167; 3.6(b) n.58

Richardson, Ex parte, 678 So.2d 1046 (Ala.1995)—§ 21.2(d) n.217

Richardson, In re, 100 Wash.2d 669, 675 P.2d 209 (1983)—§§ 11.9(b) n.78, 79, 83; 11.9(d) n.169

Richardson v. District Court, 632 P.2d 595 (Colo.1981)—§§ 20.2(b) n.25; 20.4(b) n.27; 20.4(d) n.67; 20.5(a) n.7; 24.3(c) n.93

Richardson v. Marsh, 481 U.S. 200, 107 S.Ct. 1702, 95 L.Ed.2d 176 (1987)—§§ 1.5(b) n.93; 1.11(a) n.2; 2.9(i) n.277, 278; 17.2(b) n.36, 61; 24.4(a) n.2

Richardson, People v., 189 Ill.2d 401, 245 Ill.Dec. 109, 727 N.E.2d 362 (2000)—§ 22.3(d) n.220

Richardson v. State, 381 Md. 348, 849 A.2d 487 (2004)—§ 11.3(b) n.35

Richardson v. State, 717 N.E.2d 32 (Ind.1999)—§ 17.4(b) n.88

Richardson v. State, 706 So.2d 1349 (Fla.1998)—§§ 21.2(h) n.415, 423

Richardson v. State, 673 A.2d 144 (Del.1996)—§ 7.4(c) n.48

Richardson, State v., 514 N.W.2d 573 (Minn.App.1994)—§ 9.6(a) n.44

Richardson v. State, 841 P.2d 603 (Okla.Crim.App.1992)—§ 3.1(f) n.159

Richardson, State v., 156 Wis.2d 128, 456 N.W.2d 830 (1990)—§ 3.8(e) n.193

Richardson, State v., 204 Conn. 654, 529 A.2d 1236 (1987)—§ 3.3(c) n.144

Richardson v. State, 508 So.2d 289 (Ala.Crim.App.1987)—§ 24.9(d) n.40

Richardson, State v., 316 N.C. 594, 342 S.E.2d 823 (1986)—§ 6.2(c) n.115

Richardson v. State, 622 S.W.2d 852 (Tex.Cr.App.1981)—§ 26.10(a) n.4

Richardson v. State Board of Control, 98 N.J.L. 690, 121 A. 457 (1923)— §§ 15.1(f) n.316, 323

Richardson, United States v., 427 F.3d 1128 (8th Cir.2005)—§ 6.7(c) n.121

Richardson, United States v., 233 F.3d 1285 (11th Cir.2000)—§ 24.9(b) n.12

Richardson v. United States, 526 U.S. 813, 119 S.Ct. 1707, 143 L.Ed.2d 985 (1999)—§§ 19.3(a) n.68; 24.10(c) n.42

Richardson, United States v., 87 F.3d 706 (5th Cir.1996)—§ 26.3(f) n.51

Richardson, United States v., 849 F.2d 439 (9th Cir.1988)—§ 3.9(j) n.226

Richardson, United States v., 856 F.2d 644 (4th Cir.1988)—§ 13.6(c) n.40

Richardson, United States v., 764 F.2d 1514 (11th Cir.1985)—§ 10.5(f) n.67

Richardson v. United States, 468 U.S. 317, 104 S.Ct. 3081, 82 L.Ed.2d 242 (1984)—§§ 2.9(d) n.77; 24.6(b) n.31; 25.1(b) n.14; 25.1(e) n.97; 25.4(c) n.27; 27.2(c) n.30

Richardson, United States v., 388 F.2d 842 (6th Cir.1968)—§ 7.2(b) n.18

Richardson, United States ex rel. v. Rundle, 461 F.2d 860 (3d Cir.1972)—§ 3.8(e) n.189

Richburg v. Morgenthau, 184 A.D.2d 316, 584 N.Y.S.2d 830 (App.Div.1992)—§ 8.5(h) n.265

Richey v. Smith, 515 F.2d 1239 (5th Cir.1975)—§§ 10.1(c) n.32, 35, 38, 40

Richey, State v., 195 La. 319, 196 So. 545 (1940)—§ 15.1(e) n.266

Richman, Commonwealth v., 458 Pa. 167, 320 A.2d 351 (1974)—§ 7.3(b) n.33

Richman, United States v., 600 F.2d 286 (1st Cir.1979)—§ 18.2(e) n.80

Richmond v. Polk, 375 F.3d 309 (4th Cir.2004)—§ 22.3(c) n.153

Richmond v. State, 554 P.2d 1217 (Wyo.1976)—§ 14.3(c) n.74

Richmond, United States v., 735 F.2d 208 (6th Cir.1984)—§ 18.3(b) n.11

Richmond Newspapers v. Commonwealth, 222 Va. 574, 281 S.E.2d 915 (1981)—§§ 23.1(d) n.136, 140

Richmond Newspapers v. Virginia, 448 U.S. 555, 100 S.Ct. 2814, 65 L.Ed.2d 973 (1980)—§§ 1.5(i) n.299, 301; 16.1(b) n.54; 23.1(c) n.109; 23.1(d) n.122, 141, 163; 23.1(e) n.240; 24.1(a) n.2

Richter v. Fairbanks, 903 F.2d 1202 (8th Cir.1990)—§ 22.1(b) n.43

Richter, State v., 220 Neb. 551, 371 N.W.2d 125 (1985)—§§ 21.4(a) n.23, 24; 21.4(f) n.179

Richter v. Thomas County Commission, 152 Ga.App. 332, 262 S.E.2d 604 (1979)—§ 8.4(b) n.106

Rickard, People v., 761 P.2d 188 (Colo.1988)—§§ 8.5(b) n.45; 8.5(e) n.167, 183, 186, 187; 8.5(i) n.312, 313; 15.6(d) n.123, 126; 15.6(e) n.134

Rickard, People v., 99 Ill.App.3d 914, 55 Ill.Dec. 144, 425 N.E.2d 1317 (1981)—§ 6.5(b) n.26

Rickard, State v., 420 So.2d 303 (Fla.1982)—§ 3.2(c) n.134

Ricketts v. Adamson, 483 U.S. 1, 107 S.Ct. 2680, 97 L.Ed.2d 1 (1987)—§§ 8.11(e) n.93; 21.2(d) n.269; 21.2(e) n.357; 21.2(f) n.364; 21.3(f) n.423, 432; 25.1(d) n.54, 75

Ricks, State v., 122 Idaho 856, 840 P.2d 400 (App.1992)—§§ 14.1(d) n.55, 59, 63, 67

Ricks, State v., 816 P.2d 125 (Alaska 1991)—§ 3.6(c) n.77

Ricks, United States v., 882 F.2d 885 (4th Cir.1989)—§ 17.4(a) n.47

Ricks, United States v., 802 F.2d 731 (4th Cir.1986)—§ 22.3(d) n.179

Rico, Commonwealth v., 551 Pa. 526, 711 A.2d 990 (1998)—§ 22.3(d) n.193

Rico-Villalobos v. Giusto, 339 Or. 197, 118 P.3d 246 (2005)—§ 12.4(a) n.38

Riddick v. Edmiston, 894 F.2d 586 (3d Cir.1990)—§ 6.4(f) n.124

Riddle v. Cockrell, 288 F.3d 713 (5th Cir.2002)—§ 22.5(c) n.24

Riddle v. Mondragon, 83 F.3d 1197 (10th Cir.1996)—§ 12.2(d) n.50

Riddle, People v., 141 Ill.App.3d 97, 95 Ill.Dec. 448, 489 N.E.2d 1176 (1986)—§§ 14.2(g) n.96, 101

Riddle, State v., 330 Or. 471, 8 P.3d 980 (2000)—§§ 20.5(h) n.109, 113

Riddle, United States v., 249 F.3d 529 (6th Cir.2001)—§ 1.2(c) n.175

Riddley v. State, 777 So.2d 31 (Miss.2000)—§ 11.1(b) n.91

Rideau v. Louisiana, 373 U.S. 723, 83 S.Ct. 1417, 10 L.Ed.2d 663 (1963)—§§ 2.7(b) n.91; 23.2(a) n.6

Rideau, State v., 376 So.2d 1251 (La.1979)—§§ 26.10(b) n.29; 26.10(c) n.75

Rideau v. Whitley, 237 F.3d 472 (5th Cir.2000)—§§ 15.4(i) n.203; 27.6(d) n.107; 28.5(b) n.41

Rideout v. State, 122 P.3d 201 (Wyo.2005)—§ 3.6(a) n.24

Rideout v. Superior Court, 67 Cal.2d 471, 62 Cal.Rptr. 581, 432 P.2d 197 (1967)—§§ 14.3(a) n.13, 24

Ridlington v. State, 93 P.3d 471 (Alaska App.2004)—§ 25.1(d) n.61

Riebesehl v. Commonwealth, 434 S.W.2d 41 (Ky.1968)—§ 20.6(b) n.34

Riederer, State ex rel. v. Mason, 810 S.W.2d 541 (Mo.App.1991)—§ 27.4(c) n.23

Rieger, State v., 290 Neb. 904, 708 N.W.2d 630 (2006)—§ 18.4(c) n.44

Rieger, State v., 12 Neb.App. 444, 695 N.W.2d 678 (2005)—§ 18.4(c) n.63

Riel, People v., 22 Cal.4th 1153, 96 Cal.Rptr.2d 1, 998 P.2d 969 (2000)—§§ 3.9(i) n.195; 21.2(b) n.75

Riera, United States v., 298 F.3d 128 (2d Cir.2002)—§ 21.2(d) n.177

Ries, People v., 28 Ill.App.3d 698, 329 N.E.2d 243 (1975)—§ 21.4(a) n.39

Ries, United States v., 100 F.3d 1469 (9th Cir.1996)—§ 11.4(c) n.56

Rietveld, State v., 151 Or.App. 318, 948 P.2d 758 (1997)—§ 27.3(d) n.59

Rife v. D.T. Corner, Inc., 641 N.W.2d 761 (Iowa 2002)—§ 3.5(a) n.28

Rigabar v. Broome, 658 So.2d 1038 (Fla.App.1995)—§ 21.4(f) n.210

Riggins v. McMackin, 935 F.2d 790 (6th Cir.1991)—§ 21.5(c) n.92

Riggins v. Nevada, 504 U.S. 127, 112 S.Ct. 1810, 118 L.Ed.2d 479 (1992)—§ 2.7(d) n.234

Riggs v. Humphrey, 334 Ark. 231, 972 S.W.2d 946 (1998)—§ 27.5(e) n.167

Riggs v. State, 339 Ark. 111, 3 S.W.3d 305 (1999)—§ 6.6(e) n.75

Riggs, United States v., 287 F.3d 221 (1st Cir.2002)—§ 21.2(d) n.167

Righter v. State, 704 A.2d 262 (Del.1997)—§ 9.1(b) n.61

Riley v. Deeds, 56 F.3d 1117 (9th Cir.1995)—§ 27.6(d) n.147

Riley v. Dretke, 362 F.3d 302 (5th Cir.2004)—§ 11.2(e) n.226

Riley v. Gray, 674 F.2d 522 (6th Cir.1982)—§§ 28.3(d) n.82, 85

Riley, People v., 70 N.Y.2d 523, 522 N.Y.S.2d 842, 517 N.E.2d 520 (1987)—§ 7.4(f) n.98

Riley v. State, 278 Ga. 677, 604 S.E.2d 488 (2004)—§ 6.2(c) n.120

Riley v. State, 711 N.E.2d 489 (Ind.1999)—§ 5.2(a) n.9

Riley, State v., 242 N.J.Super. 113, 576 A.2d 39 (1990)—§ 8.11(e) n.99

Riley v. State, 496 A.2d 997 (Del.1985)—§ 22.3(a) n.7

Riley, State v., 97 N.J.Super. 542, 235 A.2d 503 (1967)—§ 15.6(c) n.97

Riley v. Taylor, 1998 WL 172856 (D.Del.1998)—§ 23.2(g) n.121

Riley, United States v., 991 F.2d 120 (4th Cir.1993)—§ 18.3(b) n.26

Riley, United States v., 968 F.2d 422 (5th Cir.1992)—§ 3.6(e) n.127

Riley, United States v., 554 F.2d 1282 (4th Cir.1977)—§ 4.2(a) n.9

Riley, State ex rel. v. Rudloff, 212 W.Va. 767, 575 S.E.2d 377 (2002)— § 12.2(d) n.50

Riley, United States ex rel. v. Franzen, 653 F.2d 1153 (7th Cir.1981)— § 6.9(g) n.176

Rimmer v. State, 825 So.2d 304 (Fla.2002)—§§ 3.4(k) n.221; 7.4(c) n.50; 7.4(d) n.74; 7.4(e) n.89, 90

Rinaldi v. United States, 434 U.S. 22, 98 S.Ct. 81, 54 L.Ed.2d 207 (1977)— §§ 13.3(c) n.42; 25.5(a) n.15

Rinaldi v. Yeager, 384 U.S. 305, 86 S.Ct. 1497, 16 L.Ed.2d 577 (1966)—§ 11.2(h) n.320

Rinaldo, State v., 36 Wash.App. 86, 673 P.2d 614 (1983)—§ 2.10(d) n.116

Rinard, United States v., 956 F.2d 85 (5th Cir.1992)—§ 11.7(e) n.63

Riner v. Commonwealth, 268 Va. 296, 601 S.E.2d 555 (2004)—§§ 13.3(b) n.20; 24.7(d) n.36

Riner v. Crawford, 415 F.Supp.2d 1207 (D.Nev.2006)—§ 28.5(a) n.25

Ring v. Arizona, 536 U.S. 584, 122 S.Ct. 2428, 153 L.Ed.2d 556 (2002)— §§ 2.9(b) n.25; 19.3(a) n.22; 22.1(a) n.23, 27; 22.3(c) n.158; 26.1(b)

n.15; 26.2(b) n.2, 4; 26.4(h) n.157; 26.4(i) n.177; 27.6(d) n.149

Ring, State v., 204 Ariz. 534, 65 P.3d 915 (Ariz.2003)—§§ 26.4(i) n.179; 27.6(d) n.150

Ring v. State, 320 Ark. 128, 894 S.W.2d 944 (1995)—§ 6.9(g) n.178

Ringer, State v., 100 Wash.2d 686, 674 P.2d 1240 (1983)—§ 2.12(c) n.168

Ringling, United States v., 988 F.2d 504 (4th Cir.1993)—§§ 21.2(d) n.242; 21.2(e) n.325

Ringo, State v., 30 S.W.3d 811 (Mo.2000)—§ 6.9(c) n.63

Ringold, United States v., 335 F.3d 1168 (10th Cir.2003)—§ 3.8(c) n.82

Rinn, United States v., 586 F.2d 113 (9th Cir.1978)—§ 20.6(b) n.29

Rinto v. State, 628 S.W.2d 159 (Tex.App.1982)—§ 26.10(c) n.50

Riojas v. State, 530 S.W.2d 298 (Tex.Cr.App.1975)—§§ 10.2(b) n.23, 24

Rios, Commonwealth v., 412 Mass. 208, 588 N.E.2d 6 (1992)—§ 27.6(c) n.67

Rios, People v., 16 Cal.3d 351, 128 Cal.Rptr. 5, 546 P.2d 293 (1976)— § 21.6(b) n.84

Rios v. State, 733 P.2d 242 (Wyo.1987)—§§ 16.4(c) n.39, 53, 57 to 59

Rios-Cruz, United States v., 376 F.3d 303 (5th Cir.2004)—§ 11.2(a) n.26

Rios-Ortiz, United States v., 830 F.2d 1067 (9th Cir.1987)—§ 21.5(a) n.34

Rioux, United States v., 97 F.3d 648 (2d Cir.1996)—§§ 22.2(d) n.77, 80

Ripinsky, United States v., 20 F.3d 359 (9th Cir.1994)—§ 26.6(d) n.48

Ripkowski v. State, 61 S.W.3d 378 (Tex.Crim.App.2001)—§§ 6.4(f) n.131; 6.7(b) n.105; 6.9(b) n.41

Ripley, State v., 548 N.W.2d 24 (N.D.1996)—§ 18.4(d) n.85

Rippo v. State, 113 Nev. 1239, 946 P.2d 1017 (1997)—§ 22.4(c) n.29

Riser, People v., 47 Cal.2d 566, 305 P.2d 1 (1956)—§ 20.1(b) n.26

Risinger, State v., 297 Ark. 405, 762 S.W.2d 787 (1989)—§ 3.6(d) n.84

Risk, State v., 598 N.W.2d 642 (Minn.1999)—§§ 2.12(d) n.194; 6.9(g) n.189

Ristaino v. Ross, 424 U.S. 589, 96 S.Ct. 1017, 47 L.Ed.2d 258 (1976)— §§ 2.9(g) n.162, 169; 2.9(h) n.241; 22.3(a) n.24

Rister, People v., 803 P.2d 483 (Colo.1990)—§ 3.9(g) n.135

Rita v. State, 674 N.E.2d 968 (Ind.1996)—§ 20.2(e) n.94

Rita v. United States, _____ U.S. _____, 127 S.Ct. 2456, 168 L.Ed.2d 203 (2007)—§§ 26.3(g) n.86, 87, 93; 26.4(i) n.185; 27.5(e) n.157

Ritchie v. State, 809 N.E.2d 258 (Ind.2004)—§ 26.4(i) n.179

Rith, United States v., 164 F.3d 1323 (10th Cir.1999)—§ 6.6(e) n.61

Ritsema, United States v., 89 F.3d 392 (7th Cir.1996)—§§ 21.2(e) n.312; 21.4(g) n.258; 25.1(d) n.64

Ritter, United States v., 456 F.2d 178 (10th Cir.1972)—§ 6.9(b) n.28

Rivas, People v., 13 P.3d 315 (Colo.2000)—§ 6.9(f) n.139

Rivas, United States v., 377 F.3d 195 (2d Cir.2004)—§ 24.3(b) n.35

Rivas, United States v., 157 F.3d 364 (5th Cir.1998)—§ 3.9(f) n.108

Rivas v. United States, 368 F.2d 703 (9th Cir.1966)—§ 3.9(f) n.103

Riveiro, Commonwealth v., 393 Mass. 224, 471 N.E.2d 43 (1984)— § 10.5(b) n.21

Rivera v. Collins, 934 F.2d 658 (5th Cir.1991)—§ 6.7(b) n.103

Rivera, Commonwealth v., 429 Mass. 620, 710 N.E.2d 950 (1999)— § 3.6(d) n.84

Rivera, Commonwealth v., 425 Mass. 633, 682 N.E.2d 636 (1997)— § 10.5(c) n.33

Rivera, People v., 94 N.Y.2d 908, 707 N.Y.S.2d 620, 729 N.E.2d 339 (2000)—§ 24.2(a) n.15

Rivera, People v., 233 Ill.App.3d 69, 174 Ill.Dec. 226, 598 N.E.2d 423 (1992)—§ 3.8(b) n.32

Rivera, People v., 792 P.2d 786 (Colo.1990)—§ 4.6(l) n.200

Rivera, People v., 60 N.Y.2d 110, 468 N.Y.S.2d 601, 456 N.E.2d 492 (1983)—§ 25.5(c) n.33

Rivera, People v., 72 Ill.App.3d 1027, 28 Ill.Dec. 669, 390 N.E.2d 1259 (1979)—§§ 15.5(c) n.113; 15.6(a) n.8, 18

Rivera, People v., 56 A.D.2d 701, 392 N.Y.S.2d 516 (1977)—§ 19.5(b) n.25

Rivera, People v., 22 N.Y.2d 453, 293 N.Y.S.2d 271, 239 N.E.2d 873 (1968)—§ 7.4(b) n.19

Rivera v. Pugh, 194 F.3d 1064 (9th Cir.1999)—§ 17.4(b) n.124

Rivera v. State, 851 N.E.2d 299 (Ind.2006)—§ 21.2(b) n.76

Rivera, State v., 210 Ariz. 188, 109 P.3d 83 (2005)—§ 21.2(b) n.63

Rivera, State v., 106 Haw. 146, 102 P.3d 1044 (2004)—§ 26.4(i) n.197

Rivera, State v., 277 Kan. 109, 83 P.3d 169 (2004)—§§ 18.2(c) n.53; 18.2(d) n.66

Rivera, State v., 108 Wash.App. 645, 32 P.3d 292 (2001)—§ 27.6(b) n.21

Rivera v. State, 846 P.2d 1 (Wyo.1993)—§§ 5.2(a) n.15; 5.2(c) n.43; 5.4(c) n.37, 43

Rivera, State v., 250 Conn. 188, 736 A.2d 790 (1990)—§§ 8.3(b) n.15; 8.5(b) n.46; 8.5(d) n.126

Rivera, United States v., 412 F.3d 562 (4th Cir.2005)—§ 17.2(e) n.123

Rivera, United States v., 357 F.3d 290 (3d Cir.2004)—§§ 21.2(d) n.194; 21.2(e) n.316

Rivera, United States v., 347 F.3d 850 (10th Cir.2003)—§§ 19.3(a) n.102, 104

Rivera, United States v., 248 F.3d 677 (7th Cir.2001)—§ 3.6(e) n.115

Rivera, United States v., 164 F.3d 130 (2d Cir.1999)—§ 21.2(d) n.194

Rivera, United States v., 201 F.3d 99 (2d Cir.1999)—§ 26.4(c) n.35

Rivera, United States v., 153 F.3d 809 (7th Cir.1998)—§ 4.6(k) n.174

Rivera, United States v., 944 F.2d 1563 (11th Cir.1991)—§ 9.6(a) n.48

Rivera, United States v., 900 F.2d 1462 (10th Cir.1990)—§ 27.6(b) n.60

Rivera, United States v., 879 F.2d 1247 (5th Cir.1989)—§ 21.2(d) n.211

Rivera, United States v., 844 F.2d 916 (2d Cir.1988)—§§ 18.3(b) n.14, 22

Rivera-Guerrero, United States v., 377 F.3d 1064 (9th Cir.2004)— § 27.2(c) n.43

Rivera-Puig v. Garcia-Rosario, 983 F.2d 311 (1st Cir.1992)—§ 23.1(d) n.132

Rivera-Rosario, United States v., 300 F.3d 1 (1st Cir.2002)—§ 4.6(e) n.97

Rivera-Santiago, United States v., 107 F.3d 960 (1st Cir.1997)—§ 27.6(d) n.97

Rivera-Santiago, United States v., 872 F.2d 1073 (1st Cir.1989)— §§ 15.6(e) n.152, 155; 15.6(f) n.185

Rivera-Ventura, United States v., 72 F.3d 277 (2d Cir.1995)—§§ 18.5(a) n.11, 25

Rivers, People v., 166 Misc.2d 98, 631 N.Y.S.2d 509 (Sup.Ct. 1995)— § 15.2(c) n.79

Rivers, State v., 634 A.2d 1261 (Me.1993)—§ 5.2(a) n.4

Rivers v. United States, 416 F.3d 1319 (11th Cir.2005)—§ 28.9(b) n.49

Riverside, County of v. McLaughlin, 500 U.S. 44, 111 S.Ct. 1661, 114 L.Ed.2d 49 (1991)—§§ 2.9(g) n.163; 3.5(a) n.49; 14.2(a) n.5

Rivery, Commonwealth v., 441 Mass. 358, 805 N.E.2d 942 (2004)— § 24.5(c) n.39

Rivest, State v., 106 Wis.2d 406, 316 N.W.2d 395 (1982)—§ 21.2(e) n.358

Rivieccio, United States v., 919 F.2d 812 (2d Cir.1990)—§§ 8.11(c) n.59, 64; 15.7(d) n.77

Rizzo v. Goode, 423 U.S. 362, 96 S.Ct. 598, 46 L.Ed.2d 561 (1976)— §§ 3.1(l) n.286; 3.1(n) n.299

Rizzo, People v., 40 N.Y.2d 425, 386 N.Y.S.2d 878, 353 N.E.2d 841 (1976)—§ 3.9(c) n.51

Rizzo, United States v., 492 F.2d 443 (2d Cir.1974)—§ 4.6(j) n.167

Rizzo, United States v., 373 F.Supp. 204 (S.D.N.Y.1973)—§§ 19.2(f) n.98; 19.3(b) n.133

R.L., State ex rel. v. Bedell, 192 W.Va. 435, 452 S.E.2d 893 (W.Va.1994)—§§ 15.1(d) n.252, 253

RMI Industries, United States v., 599 F.2d 1183 (3d Cir.1979)—§ 8.5(g) n.215

Roach, State v., 172 N.J. 19, 796 A.2d 214 (2002)—§ 3.8(e) n.214

Roach, State v., 293 Mont. 311, 975 P.2d 817 (1999)—§ 21.4(d) n.106

Roach, State v., 146 N.J. 208, 680 A.2d 634 (1996)—§§ 6.2(c) n.124; 6.9(c) n.56

Roache, State v., 148 N.H. 45, 803 A.2d 572 (2002)—§ 6.9(c) n.61

Roaden v. Kentucky, 413 U.S. 496, 93 S.Ct. 2796, 37 L.Ed.2d 757 (1973)—§ 3.6(g) n.173

Roadifer, State v., 346 N.W.2d 438 (S.D.1984)—§ 7.3(c) n.50

Roane, Commonwealth v., 459 Pa. 389, 329 A.2d 286 (1974)—§ 6.9(b) n.23

Roan Eagle, United States v., 867 F.2d 436 (8th Cir.1989)—§§ 22.3(d) n.214, 230, 246, 250

Roark, State ex rel. v. Casey, 169 W.Va. 280, 286 S.E.2d 702 (1982)— § 21.3(d) n.219

Robaina, United States v., 39 F.3d 858 (8th Cir.1994)—§ 24.3(i) n.185

Robbins v. California, 453 U.S. 420, 101 S.Ct. 2841, 69 L.Ed.2d 744 (1981)—§ 2.9(g) n.167

Robbins, Commonwealth v., 431 Mass. 442, 727 N.E.2d 1157 (2000)—§§ 21.4(b) n.59; 21.4(c) n.88

Robbins, People v., 54 Ill.App.3d 298, 12 Ill.Dec. 80, 369 N.E.2d 577 (1977)—§ 9.4(a) n.43

Robbins, State v., 272 Kan. 158, 32 P.3d 171 (2001)—§ 18.4(c) n.44

Robbins, State v., 319 N.C. 465, 356 S.E.2d 279 (1987)—§ 6.9(g) n.149

Robbins, State v., 218 Mont. 107, 708 P.2d 227 (1985)—§ 18.2(c) n.49

Robbins, United States v., 179 F.3d 1268 (10th Cir.1999)—§ 13.5(h) n.200

Robbins v. United States, 476 F.2d 26 (10th Cir.1973)—§ 14.4(c) n.65

Roberson v. Commonwealth, 913 S.W.2d 310 (Ky.1994)—§ 18.4(c) n.67

Roberson v. Connecticut, 501 F.2d 305 (2d Cir.1974)—§§ 12.4(d) n.83; 26.10(c) n.52

Roberson v. State, 54 Ark.App. 230, 925 S.W.2d 820 (1996)—§ 25.4(c) n.37

Roberson, State v., 78 Wash.App. 600, 897 P.2d 443 (1995)—§ 18.4(c) n.31

Roberson v. United States, 901 F.2d 1475 (8th Cir.1990)—§ 21.5(c) n.74

Robert v. State, 613 S.W.2d 291 (Tex.Cr.App.1981)—§ 26.10(a) n.4

Robert Hawthorne, Inc. v. County Investigating Grand Jury, 488 Pa. 373, 412 A.2d 556 (1980)—§§ 1.7(i) n.204; 8.4(c) n.128; 8.8(b) n.30

Robert Hawthorne, Inc. v. Director of Internal Revenue, 406 F.Supp. 1098 (E.D.Pa.1975)—§§ 8.2(c) n.42; 8.4(b) n.26; 8.4(c) n.134; 8.5(e) n.171, 173; 8.8(e) n.123, 132

Robert Howard, Jr., In re v. State, 710 So.2d 460 (Ala.1997)—§ 25.5(c) n.36

Roberts, Ex parte, 662 So.2d 229 (Ala.1995)—§ 25.4(b) n.24

Roberts v. Collins, 544 F.2d 168 (4th Cir.1976)—§ 21.2(d) n.215

Roberts v. Illinois Liquor Control Commission, 58 Ill.App.2d 171, 206 N.E.2d 799 (1965)—§ 5.1(c) n.42

Roberts v. LaVallee, 389 U.S. 40, 88 S.Ct. 194, 19 L.Ed.2d 41 (1967)—§§ 11.2(d) n.123, 129; 28.5(a) n.11

Roberts v. Louisiana, 428 U.S. 325, 96 S.Ct. 3001, 49 L.Ed.2d 974 (1976)—§ 26.1(b) n.20

Roberts v. Love, 231 Ark. 886, 333 S.W.2d 897 (1960)—§ 1.7(f) n.98

Roberts, People v., 214 Ill.2d 106, 291 Ill.Dec. 674, 824 N.E.2d 250 (2005)—§§ 22.3(e) n.272, 280

Roberts v. Russell, 392 U.S. 293, 88 S.Ct. 1921, 20 L.Ed.2d 1100 (1968)—§ 2.11(c) n.25

Roberts v. Secretary of State, 334 Ark. 244, 973 S.W.2d 797 (1998)—§ 27.5(e) n.165

Roberts, State v., 369 S.C. 580, 632 S.E.2d 871 (2006)—§ 24.2(b) n.29

Roberts v. State, 278 Ga. 541, 604 S.E.2d 500 (2004)—§ 22.3(d) n.247

Roberts v. State, 352 Ark. 489, 102 S.W.3d 482 (2003)—§ 6.2(c) n.101

Roberts, State v., 686 So.2d 722 (Fla.App.1997)—§ 27.4(d) n.51

Roberts v. State, 263 Ga. 764, 438 S.E.2d 905 (1994)—§ 11.4(a) n.8

Roberts v. State, 263 Ga. 807, 439 S.E.2d 911 (Ga.1994)—§§ 11.6(a) n.37, 50; 11.10(c) n.84

Roberts, State v., 160 Vt. 385, 631 A.2d 835 (1993)—§§ 6.2(c) n.100, 112

Roberts v. State, 196 Ga.App. 450, 396 S.E.2d 81 (1990)—§ 20.3(f) n.103

Roberts, State v., 32 Ohio St.3d 225, 513 N.E.2d 720 (1987)—§§ 6.8(b) n.60; 6.10(c) n.49

Roberts v. State, 149 Ga.App. 667, 255 S.E.2d 126 (1979)—§ 19.6(b) n.13

Roberts, United States v., 1 F.Supp.2d 601 (E.D.La.1998)—§ 16.4(b) n.7

Roberts, United States v., 5 F.3d 365 (9th Cir.1993)—§ 21.4(d) n.119

Roberts, United States v., 14 F.3d 502 (10th Cir.1993)—§ 10.3(c) n.52

Roberts, United States v., 986 F.2d 1026 (6th Cir.1993)—§§ 3.1(d) n.95; 3.8(b) n.16

Roberts, United States v., 726 F.Supp. 1359 (D.D.C.1989)—§ 13.7(a) n.22

Roberts, United States v., 852 F.2d 671 (2d Cir.1988)—§ 9.3(e) n.77

Roberts, United States v., 811 F.2d 257 (4th Cir.1987)—§ 20.3(d) n.93

Roberts, United States v., 747 F.2d 537 (9th Cir.1984)—§ 3.2(c) n.129

Roberts v. United States, 445 U.S. 552, 100 S.Ct. 1358, 63 L.Ed.2d 622 (1980)—§§ 21.1(e) n.97; 26.4(c) n.31

Roberts, United States v., 481 F.Supp. 1385 (C.D.Cal.1980)—§§ 15.2(b) n.44, 50, 56; 15.6(b) n.50, 61; 15.7(f) n.187

Roberts, United States v., 600 F.2d 815 (D.C.Cir.1978)—§ 21.1(e) n.96

Roberts v. United States, 491 F.2d 1236 (3d Cir.1974)—§ 21.4(d) n.114

Roberts, United States v., 264 F.Supp. 622 (S.D.N.Y.1966)—§ 19.3(b) n.166

Roberts v. United States, 320 U.S. 264, 64 S.Ct. 113, 88 L.Ed. 41 (1943)—§ 26.10(d) n.90

Robertson v. Goldman, 179 W.Va. 453, 369 S.E.2d 888 (1988)—§ 12.2(b) n.26

Robertson v. Hanks, 140 F.3d 707 (7th Cir.1998)—§ 24.8(f) n.92

Robertson, People v., 255 Cal.Rptr. 631, 48 Cal.3d 18, 767 P.2d 1109 (1989)—§ 24.2(b) n.27

Robertson, People v., 40 Colo.App. 386, 577 P.2d 314 (1978)—§ 10.2(a) n.6

Robertson, State v., 182 S.W.3d 747 (Mo.App.2006)—§ 18.4(c) n.73

Robertson, State v., 279 Kan. 291, 109 P.3d 1174 (2005)—§ 6.9(f) n.137

Robertson, State v., 30 Kan.App.2d 639, 44 P.3d 1283 (2002)—§§ 11.4(b) n.31; 11.9(b) n.55, 78; 11.9(d) n.217

Robertson, State v., 254 Conn. 739, 760 A.2d 82 (2000)—§ 17.2(b) n.40

Robertson v. State, 699 N.E.2d 697 (Ind.App.1998)—§ 2.11(a) n.14

Robertson, State v., 712 So.2d 8 (La.1998)—§§ 6.2(c) n.147; 6.9(g) n.154

Robertson v. State, 596 A.2d 1345 (Del.1991)—§ 24.5(b) n.26

Robertson v. State, 541 S.W.2d 608 (Tex.Cr.App.1976)—§ 3.7(e) n.110

Robertson v. State, 84 Nev. 559, 445 P.2d 352 (1968)—§ 15.2(d) n.95

Robertson v. State, 64 Fla. 437, 60 So. 118 (1912)—§ 24.1(b) n.20

Robertson v. Superintendent of Wise Correctional Unit, 248 Va. 232, 445 S.E.2d 116 (1994)—§ 26.3(f) n.56

Robertson, United States v., 45 F.3d 1423 (10th Cir.1995)—§§ 21.3(e) n.269, 270, 272; 22.1(h) n.135

Robertson, United States v., 514 U.S. 669, 115 S.Ct. 1732, 131 L.Ed.2d 714 (1995)—§ 1.2(c) n.172

Robertson, United States v., 21 F.3d 1030 (10th Cir.1994)—§§ 3.4(f) n.106; 3.4(j) n.208

Robertson, United States v., 810 F.2d 254 (D.C.Cir.1987)—§ 18.3(b) n.5

Robertson, United States v., 698 F.2d 703 (5th Cir.1983)—§ 21.4(a) n.41

Robertson, United States v., 582 F.2d 1356 (5th Cir.1978)—§ 21.2(h) n.419

Robertson, United States v., 504 F.2d 289 (5th Cir.1974)—§ 4.6(m) n.228

Robin, State v., 115 Ariz. 9, 562 P.2d 1376 (1977)—§ 21.4(c) n.92

Robinette v. State, 741 N.E.2d 1162 (Ind.2001)—§ 9.6(a) n.51

Robinette, State v., 80 Ohio St.3d 234, 685 N.E.2d 762 (1997)—§§ 3.8(c) n.118; 3.10(b) n.62

Robins v. State, 106 Nev. 611, 798 P.2d 558 (1990)—§ 17.3(b) n.27

Robinson, Ex parte, 641 S.W.2d 552 (Tex.Cr.App.1982)—§ 27.2(c) n.65

Robinson v. California, 370 U.S. 660, 82 S.Ct. 1417, 8 L.Ed.2d 758 (1962)—§§ 2.4(a) n.19; 2.4(f) n.182; 2.6(a) n.3; 26.1(b) n.9

Robinson v. Commonwealth, 445 Mass. 280, 837 N.E.2d 241 (2005)—§§ 10.5(e) n.56, 58

Robinson v. Commonwealth, 17 Va.App. 551, 439 S.E.2d 622 (1994)—§ 25.4(a) n.8

Robinson v. Crist, 278 F.3d 862 (8th Cir.2002)—§ 28.6(f) n.76

Robinson v. Neil, 409 U.S. 505, 93 S.Ct. 876, 35 L.Ed.2d 29 (1973)—§ 2.11(c) n.35

Robinson v. Norris, 60 F.3d 457 (8th Cir.1995)—§ 11.2(b) n.52

Robinson v. Oklahoma Employment Sec. Comm'n, 932 P.2d 1120 (Okla.1997)—§ 16.1(a) n.24

Robinson, People v., 187 Ill.2d 461, 719 N.E.2d 662 (Ill.1999)—§§ 27.5(a) n.3, 7

Robinson, People v., 53 Cal.App.4th 270, 61 Cal.Rptr.2d 587 (1997)—§ 11.4(a) n.15

Robinson, People v., 286 Ill.App.3d 903, 222 Ill.Dec. 164, 676 N.E.2d 1368 (1997)—§ 26.4(f) n.88

Robinson, People v., 167 Ill.2d 53, 212 Ill.Dec. 256, 656 N.E.2d 1090 (1995)—§ 26.6(b) n.12

Robinson, People v., 79 Ill.2d 147, 37 Ill.Dec. 267, 402 N.E.2d 157 (1979)—§ 11.9(a) n.31

Robinson, People v., 66 Misc.2d 639, 323 N.Y.S.2d 573 (Sup.1971)—§ 8.14(a) n.6

Robinson, People v., 22 Mich.App. 124, 177 N.W.2d 234 (1970)—§ 6.6(f) n.110

Robinson v. Percy, 738 F.2d 214 (7th Cir.1984)—§ 6.7(b) n.43

Robinson v. Polk, 438 F.3d 350 (4th Cir.2006)—§ 24.9(f) n.69

Robinson v. State, 278 Ga. 134, 598 S.E.2d 466 (2004)—§ 22.3(d) n.175

Robinson, State v., 249 Wis.2d 553, 638 N.W.2d 564 (2002)—§ 19.3(c) n.198

Robinson, State v., 618 N.W.2d 306 (Iowa 2000)—§ 21.6(a) n.64

Robinson v. State, 761 So.2d 209 (Miss.2000)—§ 22.3(d) n.245

Robinson, State v., 138 Wash.2d 753, 982 P.2d 590 (1999)—§§ 11.6(c) n.100; 11.6(d) n.115, 123

Robinson v. State, 693 N.E.2d 548 (Ind.1998)—§ 20.3(k) n.213

Robinson, State v., 237 Conn. 238, 676 A.2d 384 (1996)—§ 22.3(d) n.220

Robinson, State v., 230 Conn. 591, 646 A.2d 118 (1994)—§ 24.4(d) n.64

Robinson v. State, 317 Ark. 17, 875 S.W.2d 837 (1994)—§ 10.3(d) n.63

Robinson, State v., 158 Vt. 286, 611 A.2d 852 (1992)—§ 6.2(c) n.181

Robinson, State v., 233 Neb. 729, 448 N.W.2d 386 (1989)—§ 6.4(g) n.161

Robinson v. State, 520 So.2d 1 (Fla.1988)—§ 24.7(e) n.61

Robinson v. State, 307 Md. 738, 517 A.2d 94 (1986)—§ 17.4(a) n.36

Robinson, State v., 389 N.W.2d 401 (Iowa 1986)—§ 23.2(a) n.48

Robinson v. State, 477 N.E.2d 883 (Ind.1985)—§ 15.6(d) n.121

Robinson v. State, 453 N.E.2d 280 (Ind.1983)—§ 8.10(d) n.116

Robinson, State v., 618 S.W.2d 754 (Tenn.Crim.App.1981)—§§ 20.3(i) n.169; 20.3(j) n.201; 20.3(k) n.220

Robinson, State v., 190 Mont. 145, 619 P.2d 813 (1980)—§ 26.10(c) n.49

Robinson v. State, 373 So.2d 898 (Fla.1979)—§§ 21.5(b) n.64, 66

Robinson, State v., 290 N.C. 56, 224 S.E.2d 174 (1976)—§ 24.3(d) n.109

Robinson, State v., 544 P.2d 545 (Okla.Crim.App.1975)—§§ 10.6(c) n.31, 33

Robinson v. State, 69 Fla. 521, 68 So. 649 (1915)—§ 19.3(b) n.137

Robinson, State v., 14 Minn. 447 (1869)—§ 16.1(e) n.190

Robinson v. Trast, 128 F.Supp.2d 710 (D.Kan.2001)—§ 6.9(f) n.112

Robinson, United States v., 473 F.3d 487 (2d Cir.2007)—§ 27.2(c) n.58

Robinson, United States v., 482 F.3d 244 (3d Cir.2007)—§ 26.4(f) n.93

Robinson, United States v., 455 F.3d 602 (6th Cir.2006)—§§ 18.2(e) n.76; 18.4(b) n.26; 18.4(c) n.50; 21.2(b) n.79

Robinson v. United States, 416 F.3d 645 (7th Cir.2005)—§ 28.5(b) n.45

Robinson v. United States, 878 A.2d 1273 (D.C.App.2005)—§ 22.3(d) n.255

Robinson, United States v., 367 F.3d 278 (5th Cir.2004)—§§ 19.3(a) n.27, 127, 128; 27.6(d) n.150

Robinson v. United States, 825 A.2d 318 (D.C.App.2003)—§ 20.3(a) n.11

Robinson v. United States, 769 A.2d 747 (D.C.App.2001)—§ 13.4(b) n.76

Robinson, United States v., 62 F.3d 1325 (11th Cir.1995)—§ 3.2(b) n.61

Robinson, United States v., 20 F.3d 1030 (9th Cir.1994)—§ 26.1(f) n.139

Robinson, United States v., 893 F.2d 1244 (11th Cir.1990)—§ 26.10(c) n.82

Robinson, United States v., 913 F.2d 712 (9th Cir.1990)—§§ 11.3(a) n.8, 16; 11.3(b) n.44; 11.4(d) n.112; 11.5(b) n.29; 11.5(c) n.52

Robinson, United States v., 485 U.S. 25, 108 S.Ct. 864, 99 L.Ed.2d 23 (1988)—§§ 2.9(f) n.118; 2.9(g) n.154; 9.6(a) n.36; 24.5(b) n.30; 24.7(f) n.77

Robinson v. United States, 478 A.2d 1065 (D.C.App.1984)—§ 18.5(b) n.64

Robinson, United States v., 651 F.2d 1188 (6th Cir.1981)—§ 19.3(c) n.188

Robinson, United States v., 414 U.S. 218, 94 S.Ct. 467, 38 L.Ed.2d 427 (1973)—§§ 1.11(a) n.3; 2.9(g) n.163, 177; 2.12(a) n.20; 3.1(e) n.129; 3.5(b) n.78; 3.5(e) n.179, 184; 12.5(b) n.26

Robinson, United States v., 479 F.2d 300 (7th Cir.1973)—§ 3.10(d) n.130

Robinson, United States v., 471 F.2d 1082 (D.C.Cir.1972)—§§ 3.5(b) n.82, 83

Robinson, United States v., 439 F.2d 553 (D.C.Cir.1970)—§§ 6.2(c) n.140; 6.3(b) n.42

Robinson, United States v., 311 F.Supp. 1063 (W.D.Mo.1969)—§§ 13.4(c) n.111, 126; 13.4(e) n.171

Robinson v. United States, 172 Fed. 105 (8th Cir.1909)—§ 16.2(g) n.123

Robinson, United States ex rel. v. Housewright, 525 F.2d 988 (7th Cir.1975)—§§ 21.2(c) n.106; 21.4(b) n.46

Robinson, United States ex rel. v. Israel, 603 F.2d 635 (7th Cir.1979)—§ 21.2(d) n.195

Robinson, United States ex rel. v. McGinnis, 593 F.Supp. 175 (C.D.Ill.1984)—§ 20.6(c) n.89

Robledo, People v., 832 P.2d 249 (Colo.1992)—§ 6.10(c) n.51

Robledo-Kinney, State v., 615 N.W.2d 25 (Minn.2000)—§ 21.2(h) n.437

Robles, United States v., 45 F.3d 1 (1st Cir.1995)—§ 3.9(f) n.108

Robran, State v., 119 Idaho 285, 805 P.2d 491 (App.1991)—§§ 19.2(a) n.1, 6; 19.2(b) n.20; 19.3(e) n.244, 245

Robtoy v. Kincheloe, 871 F.2d 1478 (9th Cir.1989)—§ 21.2(a) n.19

Roccasecca, State v., 130 N.J.Super. 585, 328 A.2d 35 (1974)—§§ 10.6(c) n.21, 24, 28

Rocco v. State, 267 Ga.App. 900, 601 S.E.2d 189 (2004)—§ 12.1(b) n.32

Rocha, United States v., 916 F.2d 219 (5th Cir.1990)—§ 17.2(c) n.88

Rocha v. United States, 288 F.2d 545 (9th Cir.1961)—§ 16.4(b) n.33

Roche v. Davis, 291 F.3d 473 (7th Cir.2002)—§ 11.10(c) n.118

Roche v. State, 913 So.2d 306 (Miss. 2005)—§§ 7.4(b) n.10; 7.4(c) n.51, 52

Roche, United States v., 415 F.3d 614 (7th Cir.2005)—§ 26.4(f) n.93

Rochester, State v., 301 S.C. 196, 391 S.E.2d 244 (1990)—§ 6.2(c) n.113

Rochester, State v., 105 N.J.Super. 529, 253 A.2d 558 (1969)—§ 15.1(d) n.231

Rochin v. California, 342 U.S. 165, 72 S.Ct. 205, 96 L.Ed. 183 (1952)— §§ 2.4(e) n.164; 2.4(f) n.183, 187, 190; 2.4 n.6; 2.7(a) n.16; 2.7(c) n.109, 158, 174, 202, 206; 2.7(d) n.236, 252; 3.1(a) n.12; 3.4(a) n.8; 7.2(c) n.42

Rock v. Arkansas, 483 U.S. 44, 107 S.Ct. 2704, 97 L.Ed.2d 37 (1987)— §§ 1.5(b) n.72; 1.5(e) n.219; 2.7(a) n.39; 2.7(b) n.95; 2.7(c) n.128, 171, 179; 8.10(c) n.72; 11.6(a) n.51; 20.4(d) n.62; 24.4(a) n.5; 24.5(d) n.43, 44; 28.6(d) n.20

Rocker, State v., 130 Iowa 239, 106 N.W. 645 (1906)—§ 15.6(d) n.119

Rockholt, State v., 96 N.J. 570, 476 A.2d 1236 (1984)—§§ 5.2(b) n.24; 5.3(d) n.40

Rockl, State v., 130 Wash.App. 293, 122 P.3d 759 (2005)—§ 16.3(c) n.30

Rockman, United States ex rel. v. DeRobertis, 717 F.Supp. 553 (N.D.Ill.1989)—§ 24.7(e) n.62

Rockwell International Corp., United States v., 924 F.2d 928 (9th Cir.1991)—§ 1.7(j) n.235

Roddy v. State, 339 S.C. 29, 528 S.E.2d 418 (2000)—§ 21.2(g) n.394

Roddy v. Superior Court, 151 Cal.App.4th 1115, 60 Cal.Rptr.3d 307 (Cal.App.2007)—§ 22.3(b) n.55

Rodgers, Commonwealth v., 21 Va.App. 745, 467 S.E.2d 813 (1996)— § 27.3(c) n.39

Rodgers v. Commonwealth, 227 Va. 605, 318 S.E.2d 298 (1984)— § 6.2(c) n.147

Rodgers, People v., 92 Ill.2d 283, 65 Ill.Dec. 929, 442 N.E.2d 240 (1982)—§§ 15.2(d) n.105; 15.5(c) n.110

Rodgers v. State, 948 So.2d 655 (Fla.2006)—§ 26.4(f) n.93

Rodgers, State v., 237 Neb. 506, 466 N.W.2d 537 (1991)—§ 10.2(b) n.19

Rodgers, State v., 119 Wis.2d 102, 349 N.W.2d 453 (1984)—§ 3.6(a) n.33

Rodgers, State v., 347 So.2d 610 (Fla.1977)—§ 22.3(c) n.162

Rodgers, United States v., 18 F.3d 1425 (8th Cir.1994)—§ 17.4(a) n.36

Rodgers, United States v., 466 U.S. 475, 104 S.Ct. 1942, 80 L.Ed.2d 492 (1984)—§ 8.3(b) n.14

Rodgers, United States v., 732 F.2d 625 (8th Cir.1984)—§ 17.1(b) n.28

Rodgers, United States v., 150 U.S. 249, 14 S.Ct. 109, 37 L.Ed. 1071 (1893)—§§ 16.4(b) n.7, 8

Rodia, United States v., 194 F.3d 465 (3d Cir.1999)—§ 1.2(c) n.145

Rodman, United States v., 446 F.Supp.2d 487 (D.S.C.2006)— § 24.2(g) n.95

Rodney, People v., 85 N.Y.2d 289, 624 N.Y.S.2d 95, 648 N.E.2d 471 (1995)—§ 6.7(b) n.43

Rodney, United States v., 956 F.2d 295 (D.C.Cir.1992)—§ 3.10(f) n.196

Rodrequez-Felix, United States v., 450 F.3d 1117 (10th Cir.2006)— § 11.2(e) n.212

Rodrigues v. Haw., 469 U.S. 1078, 105 S.Ct. 580, 83 L.Ed.2d 691 (1984)— § 25.3(d) n.34

Rodrigues, State v., 67 Haw. 70, 679 P.2d 615 (1984)—§ 25.3(d) n.34

Rodrigues, United States v., 347 F.3d 818 (9th Cir.2003)—§ 11.9(a) n.27

Rodriguez v. Burk, 637 So.2d 317 (Fla.Ct.App.1994)—§ 27.4(c) n.24

Rodriguez v. Chandler, 382 F.3d 670 (7th Cir.2004)—§ 27.6(d) n.143

Rodriguez v. Commonwealth, 107 S.W.3d 215 (Ky.2003)—§ 7.4(f) n.96

Rodriguez, Commonwealth v., 431 Mass. 804, 731 N.E.2d 71 (2000)— § 22.3(d) n.245

Rodriguez v. Commonwealth, 20 Va.App. 122, 455 S.E.2d 724 (1995)—§ 7.5(b) n.26

Rodriguez, People v., 112 P.3d 693 (Colo.2005)—§ 22.1(d) n.79

Rodriguez, People v., 95 N.Y.2d 497, 719 N.Y.S.2d 208, 741 N.E.2d 882 (2000)—§ 11.5(g) n.124

Rodriguez, People v., 192 Mich.App. 1, 480 N.W.2d 287 (1991)—§§ 27.5(c) n.54, 63

Rodriguez, People v., 69 N.Y.2d 159, 513 N.Y.S.2d 75, 505 N.E.2d 586 (1987)—§ 9.1(b) n.89

Rodriguez, State v., 139 N.M. 450, 134 P.3d 737 (N.M.2006)—§ 24.9(e) n.59

Rodriguez, State v., 138 N.M. 21, 116 P.3d 92 (2005)—§ 25.1(d) n.88

Rodriguez, State v., 146 Wash.2d 260, 45 P.3d 541 (2002)—§ 24.2(e) n.58

Rodriguez, State v., 47 Conn.App. 91, 702 A.2d 906 (1997)—§ 18.3(c) n.109

Rodriguez, State v., 261 Kan. 1, 927 P.2d 463 (1996)—§ 18.4(c) n.60

Rodriguez v. State, 906 S.W.2d 70 (Tex.App.1995)—§§ 11.2(e) n.220, 228

Rodriguez, State v., 254 Kan. 768, 869 P.2d 631 (1994)—§§ 18.4(c) n.67; 18.4(d) n.93

Rodriguez, State v., 877 S.W.2d 106 (Mo.1994)—§ 3.9(g) n.128

Rodriguez, State v., 317 Or. 27, 854 P.2d 399 (1993)—§ 2.12(c) n.174

Rodriguez v. State, 129 Ariz. 67, 628 P.2d 950 (1981)—§ 27.2(c) n.64

Rodriguez v. State, 597 S.W.2d 917 (Tex.Crim.1980)—§ 15.4(b) n.47

Rodriguez, State v., 37 Or.App. 355, 587 P.2d 487 (1978)—§ 6.4(g) n.144

Rodriguez, United States v., 406 F.3d 1261 (11th Cir.2005)—§§ 27.5(d) n.128, 134

Rodriguez, United States v., 356 F.3d 254 (2d Cir.2004)—§ 6.7(b) n.43

Rodriguez, United States v., 260 F.3d 416 (5th Cir.2001)—§ 24.7(e) n.57

Rodriguez, United States v., 197 F.3d 156 (5th Cir.1999)—§§ 21.3(d) n.218, 227

Rodriguez, United States v., 162 F.3d 135 (1st Cir.1998)—§§ 21.1(e) n.64; 21.2(b) n.42; 26.5(a) n.5

Rodriguez, United States v., 112 F.3d 26 (1st Cir.1997)—§ 21.5(e) n.147

Rodriguez, United States v., 114 F.3d 46 (5th Cir.1997)—§ 21.5(e) n.147

Rodriguez, United States v., 931 F.Supp. 907 (D.Mass.1996)—§ 15.5(a) n.4

Rodriguez, United States v., 1996 WL 479441 (S.D.N.Y.1996)—§§ 15.5(b) n.90, 94

Rodriguez, United States v., 67 F.3d 1312 (7th Cir.1995)—§ 16.2(g) n.124

Rodriguez, United States v., 69 F.3d 136 (7th Cir.1995)—§ 10.5(f) n.68

Rodriguez, United States v., 993 F.2d 1170 (5th Cir.1993)—§ 6.9(f) n.130

Rodriguez, United States v., 968 F.2d 130 (2d Cir.1992)—§§ 11.9(c) n.130, 131; 11.9(d) n.207

Rodriguez, United States v., 976 F.2d 592 (9th Cir.1992)—§ 3.9(f) n.115

Rodriguez, United States v., 950 F.2d 85 (2d Cir.1991)—§ 12.3(a) n.19

Rodriguez, United States v., 888 F.2d 519 (7th Cir.1989)—§ 3.10(e) n.140

Rodriguez, United States v., 858 F.2d 809 (1st Cir.1988)—§ 5.3(d) n.42

Rodriguez, United States v., 776 F.2d 1509 (11th Cir.1985)—§ 22.2(d) n.76

Rodriguez, United States v., 429 F.Supp. 520 (S.D.N.Y.1977)—§ 21.5(e) n.132

Rodriguez, United States v., 182 F.Supp. 479 (S.D.Cal.1960)—§ 16.4(b) n.33

Rodriguez-Aguirre, United States v., 414 F.3d 1177 (10th Cir.2005)—§ 10.1(c) n.52

Rodriguez-Aguirre, United States v., 264 F.3d 1195 (10th Cir.2001)—§ 10.1(c) n.49

Rodriguez-Arreola, United States v., 270 F.3d 611 (8th Cir.2001)— § 9.1(d) n.119

Rodriguez-Berrios, United States v., 376 F.Supp.2d 118 (D.P.R.2005)— § 20.3(i) n.177

Rodriguez-Fernandez v. Wilkinson, 654 F.2d 1382 (10th Cir.1981)— § 15.1(b) n.16

Rodriguez-Franco, United States v., 749 F.2d 1555 (11th Cir.1985)— § 18.3(b) n.19

Rodriguez-Garcia, United States v., 983 F.2d 1563 (10th Cir.1993)— § 3.10(b) n.72

Rodriguez-Gonzales, United States v., 358 F.3d 1156 (9th Cir.2004)— § 26.4(i) n.195

Rodriguez-Gonzalez v. United States, 378 F.2d 256 (9th Cir.1967)— § 3.9(f) n.87

Rodriguez-Luna, United States v., 937 F.2d 1208 (7th Cir.1991)— § 21.3(b) n.71

Rodriguez-Morales, United States v., 929 F.2d 780 (1st Cir.1991)— §§ 3.7(d) n.88; 3.7(e) n.99

Rodriguez-Moreno, United States v., 526 U.S. 275, 119 S.Ct. 1239, 143 L.Ed.2d 388 (1999)— §§ 16.2(c) n.50; 16.2(d) n.54; 16.2(e) n.88

Rodriguez-Nuez, United States v., 919 F.2d 461 (7th Cir.1990)— § 21.1(h) n.233

Rodriguez-Preciado, United States v., 399 F.3d 1118 (9th Cir.2005)— § 6.8(b) n.50

Rodriquez, State v., 272 Neb. 930, 726 N.W.2d 157 (2007)— § 6.7(d) n.144

Rodriquez, State v., 731 A.2d 726 (R.I.1999)— § 7.4(c) n.51

Rodriquez v. United States, 395 U.S. 327, 89 S.Ct. 1715, 23 L.Ed.2d 340 (1969)— §§ 11.6(b) n.80; 11.6(d) n.119

Rodwell, Commonwealth v., 394 Mass. 694, 477 N.E.2d 385 (1985)— § 6.10(b) n.16

Roe v. Commonwealth, 271 Va. 453, 628 S.E.2d 526 (2006)— § 13.3(c) n.40

Roe v. Flores-Ortega, 528 U.S. 470, 120 S.Ct. 1029, 145 L.Ed.2d 985 (2000)— §§ 11.6(b) n.78; 11.6(d) n.119; 21.3(b) n.145

Roe v. Marcotte, 193 F.3d 72 (2d Cir.1999)— § 3.9(i) n.190

Roe v. Texas Dept. of Protective & Reg. Services, 299 F.3d 395 (5th Cir.2002)— § 3.9(d) n.73

Roe v. United States Attorney, 618 F.2d 980 (2d Cir.1980)— § 21.2(e) n.341

Roe v. Wade, 410 U.S. 113, 93 S.Ct. 705, 35 L.Ed.2d 147 (1973)— § 2.7(c) n.181

Roebke, United States v., 333 F.3d 911 (8th Cir.2003)— § 22.3(d) n.221

Roebuck v. State, 277 Ga. 200, 586 S.E.2d 651 (2003)— § 18.5(b) n.69

Roeder, State v., 209 Or.App. 199, 147 P.3d 363 (2006)— § 17.4(b) n.136

Roeder v. State, 768 S.W.2d 745 (Tex.App.1988)— § 2.12(b) n.83

Roethe, United States v., 418 F.Supp. 1118 (E.D.Wis.1976)— § 15.4(g) n.164

Rogan, State v., 91 Haw. 405, 984 P.2d 1231 (1999)— § 25.4(a) n.7

Rogel, State v., 116 Ariz. 114, 568 P.2d 421 (1977)— § 21.2(d) n.165

Rogers v. Commonwealth, 86 S.W.3d 29 (Ky.2002)— § 6.2(c) n.183

Rogers v. McMackin, 884 F.2d 252 (6th Cir.1989)— § 17.2(b) n.31

Rogers, People v., 48 N.Y.2d 167, 422 N.Y.S.2d 18, 397 N.E.2d 709 (1979)— § 6.4(e) n.84

Rogers, People v., 18 Ill.App.3d 940, 310 N.E.2d 854 (1974)— § 10.3(b) n.35

Rogers, People v., 34 A.D.2d 598, 308 N.Y.S.2d 274 (1970)— § 16.3(d) n.71

Rogers, People v., 14 Mich.App. 207, 165 N.W.2d 337 (1968)— § 6.6(e) n.67

Rogers v. Richmond, 365 U.S. 534, 81 S.Ct. 735, 5 L.Ed.2d 760 (1961)—§§ 1.5(c) n.104; 1.5(d) n.179, 183, 195; 2.4(e) n.147; 2.10(d) n.135; 6.2(b) n.38; 6.2(c) n.95

Rogers, State v., 188 S.W.3d 593 (Tenn.2006)—§ 6.8(b) n.50

Rogers, State v., 355 N.C. 420, 562 S.E.2d 859 (2002)—§§ 7.4(e) n.89; 22.3(d) n.207

Rogers v. State, 247 Ga.App. 219, 543 S.E.2d 81 (2000)—§ 27.5(d) n.137

Rogers, State v., 352 N.C. 119, 529 S.E.2d 671 (2000)—§ 11.8(c) n.60

Rogers, State v., 161 Vt. 236, 638 A.2d 569 (1993)—§ 3.2(c) n.136

Rogers, State v., 313 Or. 356, 836 P.2d 1308 (1992)—§§ 11.2(e) n.195, 205, 212, 228

Rogers v. State, 537 N.E.2d 481 (Ind.1989)—§ 7.4(b) n.24

Rogers, State v., 573 S.W.2d 710 (Mo.App.1978)—§ 10.4(c) n.20

Rogers, State v., 27 Ohio.Op.2d 105, 198 N.E.2d 796 (1963)—§ 9.4(e) n.108

Rogers, United States v., 387 F.3d 925 (7th Cir.2004)—§§ 21.5(a) n.44; 21.6(a) n.37

Rogers, United States v., 150 F.3d 851 (8th Cir.1998)—§ 3.4(e) n.67

Rogers, United States v., 118 F.3d 466 (6th Cir.1997)—§§ 18.5(b) n.65, 68, 69

Rogers, United States v., 121 F.3d 12 (1st Cir.1997)—§ 5.2(a) n.17

Rogers, United States v., 126 F.3d 655 (5th Cir.1997)—§ 7.4(c) n.64

Rogers, United States v., 9 F.3d 1025 (2d Cir.1993)—§ 11.9(c) n.121

Rogers, United States v., 960 F.2d 1501 (10th Cir.1992)—§ 24.3(b) n.67

Rogers, United States v., 899 F.2d 917 (10th Cir.1990)—§§ 6.6(e) n.81; 6.10(c) n.48

Rogers, United States v., 906 F.2d 189 (5th Cir.1990)—§ 6.2(c) n.102

Rogers, United States v., 921 F.2d 975 (10th Cir.1990)—§§ 6.4(e) n.107; 26.5(a) n.11

Rogers, United States v., 636 F.Supp. 237 (D.Colo.1986)—§§ 19.3(a) n.65; 19.3(b) n.154

Rogers v. United States, 483 A.2d 277 (D.C.App.1984)—§ 6.9(f) n.137

Rogers v. United States, 609 F.2d 1315 (9th Cir.1979)—§ 25.2(e) n.38

Rogers v. United States, 422 U.S. 35, 95 S.Ct. 2091, 45 L.Ed.2d 1 (1975)—§ 24.8(a) n.25

Rogers, United States v., 475 F.2d 821 (7th Cir.1973)—§ 17.3(d) n.56

Rogers, United States v., 455 F.2d 407 (5th Cir.1972)—§ 14.2(g) n.98

Rogers, United States v., 289 F.Supp. 726 (D.Conn.1968)—§§ 21.3(b) n.92, 93

Rogers v. United States, 330 F.2d 535 (5th Cir.1964)—§ 6.3(a) n.18

Rogers v. United States, 340 U.S. 367, 71 S.Ct. 438, 95 L.Ed. 344 (1951)—§§ 2.10(c) n.52; 8.10(a) n.6; 8.10(e) n.117, 118; 24.4(c) n.15

Rogers v. Zant, 13 F.3d 384 (11th Cir.1994)—§ 11.7(c) n.35

Rogers, United States ex rel. v. Warden, 381 F.2d 209 (2d Cir.1967)—§ 21.6(b) n.98

Rogowicz v. O'Connell, 147 N.H. 270, 786 A.2d 841 (2001)—§ 13.3(b) n.20

Rohrig, United States v., 98 F.3d 1506 (6th Cir.1996)—§ 3.6(f) n.146

Rojas-Contreras, United States v., 474 U.S. 231, 106 S.Ct. 555, 88 L.Ed.2d 537 (1985)—§ 18.3(b) n.11

Rojas-Martinez, United States v., 968 F.2d 415 (5th Cir.1992)—§ 6.2(c) n.148

Rojas-Tapia, United States v., 446 F.3d 1 (1st Cir.2006)—§ 6.9(b) n.27

Rojo-Alvarez, United States v., 944 F.2d 959 (1st Cir.1991)—§ 3.7(a) n.16

Roldan, People v., 35 Cal.4th 646, 27 Cal.Rptr.3d 360, 110 P.3d 289 (2005)—§§ 6.4(g) n.154; 6.7(b) n.66; 6.7(c) n.135

Rollie, State v., 585 S.W.2d 78 (Mo.App.1979)—§§ 16.2(g) n.108, 113, 114

Rolling v. State, 695 So.2d 278 (Fla.1997)—§§ 23.2(a) n.25, 27, 38, 39, 41

Rolling v. State, 673 So.2d 812 (Ala.App.1995)—§ 27.5(c) n.103

Rollins, People v., 759 P.2d 816 (Colo.App.1988)—§ 21.2(h) n.423

Rollins, State v., 188 S.W.3d 553 (Tenn.2006)—§§ 6.8(c) n.65; 24.4(c) n.20

Rollins v. State, 277 Ga. 488, 591 S.E.2d 796 (2004)—§ 21.3(b) n.69

Rollins, State v., 245 Conn. 700, 714 A.2d 1217 (1998)—§ 6.9(f) n.120

Rollins, United States v., 862 F.2d 1282 (7th Cir.1988)—§§ 10.5(f) n.67; 17.2(d) n.98

Rollins, United States v., 522 F.2d 160 (2d Cir.1975)—§§ 3.3(d) n.150; 10.2(a) n.10

Rollinson, State v., 203 Conn. 641, 526 A.2d 1283 (1987)—§ 15.3(a) n.17

Rollison v. State, 346 S.C. 506, 552 S.E.2d 290 (2001)—§ 21.4(f) n.198

Rollman v. State, 887 So.2d 1233 (Fla.2004)—§ 21.2(e) n.312

Roman, State v., 70 Haw. 351, 772 P.2d 113 (1989)—§ 6.9(e) n.97

Roman v. State, 475 So.2d 1228 (Fla.1985)—§ 6.2(c) n.169

Roman, United States v., 121 F.3d 136 (3d Cir.1997)—§ 21.2(d) n.242

Roman, United States v., 822 F.2d 261 (2d Cir.1987)—§ 18.3(b) n.35

Roman Catholic Archbishop of Los Angeles v. Superior Court, 131 Cal.App.4th 417, 32 Cal.Rptr.3d 209 (2005)—§ 8.8(d) n.53

Romanello, United States v., 425 F.Supp. 304 (D.Conn.1975)—§ 15.7(d) n.80

Romano v. Gibson, 278 F.3d 1145 (10th Cir.2002)—§ 11.10(c) n.91

Romano v. Oklahoma, 512 U.S. 1, 114 S.Ct. 2004, 129 L.Ed.2d 1 (1994)—§ 26.4(f) n.106

Romano v. State, 272 Ga. 238, 527 S.E.2d 184 (2000)—§ 21.4(f) n.182

Romano, United States v., 825 F.2d 725 (2d Cir.1987)—§ 26.4(d) n.61

Romero v. Furlong, 215 F.3d 1107 (10th Cir.2000)—§ 21.4(c) n.71

Romero v. Lynaugh, 884 F.2d 871 (5th Cir.1989)—§§ 11.10(c) n.80, 91

Romero, State v., 95 Wash.App. 323, 975 P.2d 564 (1999)—§ 11.5(g) n.124

Romero, State v., 279 Mont. 58, 926 P.2d 717 (1996)—§ 19.5(c) n.51

Romero, State v., 578 N.E.2d 673 (Ind.1991)—§§ 11.9(c) n.119, 137, 139

Romero, State v., 224 Mont. 431, 730 P.2d 1157 (1986)—§ 3.7(b) n.36

Romero, United States v., 360 F.3d 1248 (10th Cir.2004)—§§ 13.3(c) n.44; 21.3(e) n.297

Romero, United States v., 967 F.2d 63 (2d Cir.1992)—§ 27.2(c) n.47

Romero, United States v., 836 F.2d 39 (1st Cir.1987)—§ 25.3(d) n.34

Romero, United States v., 780 F.2d 981 (11th Cir.1986)—§ 11.9(b) n.99

Romero, United States v., 676 F.2d 406 (9th Cir.1982)—§ 26.9(c) n.89

Romero, United States v., 585 F.2d 391 (9th Cir.1978)—§ 15.5(a) n.4

Romero-Galue, United States v., 757 F.2d 1147 (11th Cir.1985)—§ 16.4(b) n.9

Romero-Tamayo, United States v., 212 F.3d 729 (2d Cir.2000)—§ 21.3(e) n.265

Romine v. Head, 253 F.3d 1349 (11th Cir.2001)—§ 28.6(f) n.76

Romley, State ex rel. v. Rayes, 206 Ariz. 58, 75 P.3d 148 (App. 2003)—§ 12.3(e) n.120

Romley, State ex rel. v. Superior Court, 183 Ariz. 139, 901 P.2d 1169 (1995)—§§ 24.2(d) n.45; 27.4(d) n.51

Rompilla v. Beard, 545 U.S. 374, 125 S.Ct. 2456, 162 L.Ed.2d 360 (2005)—§§ 11.10(b) n.46; 11.10(c) n.126, 140; 11.10(d) n.165; 28.6(f) n.69

Ronald E., In re, 19 Cal.3d 315, 137 Cal.Rptr. 781, 562 P.2d 684 (1977)—§ 21.4(c) n.88

Ronald W., People v., 24 N.Y.2d 732, 302 N.Y.S.2d 260, 249 N.E.2d 882 (1969)—§ 6.10(c) n.41

Ronda, United States v., 455 F.3d 1273 (11th Cir.2006)—§ 24.9(f) n.102

Rondeau, United States v., 430 F.3d 44 (1st Cir.2005)—§ 26.10(c) n.71

Rondon, United States v., 204 F.3d 376 (2d Cir.2000)—§ 11.8(c) n.77

Roney v. State, 819 P.2d 286 (Okla.Crim.App.1991)—§ 3.2(f) n.178

Roofener, People v., 95 Ill.App.3d 342, 50 Ill.Dec. 872, 420 N.E.2d 189 (1981)—§§ 11.3(b) n.48; 11.6(a) n.6, 12

Rook, Complaint of, 276 Or. 695, 556 P.2d 1351 (1976)—§ 21.3(c) n.151

Rooks, State v., 401 A.2d 943 (Del.1979)—§ 10.4(b) n.11

Root v. Gauper, 438 F.2d 361 (8th Cir.1971)—§§ 3.6(f) n.141, 144

Root, People v., 87 Misc.2d 482, 384 N.Y.S.2d 951 (Sup.Ct.1976)—§ 15.2(c) n.77

Roper v. Simmons, 543 U.S. 551, 125 S.Ct. 1183, 161 L.Ed.2d 1 (2005)—§§ 2.7(c) n.182, 185; 26.1(b) n.35

Roper v. State, 258 Ga. 847, 375 S.E.2d 600 (1989)—§§ 6.4(f) n.136, 137

Roper, United States v., 716 F.2d 611 (4th Cir.1983)—§ 18.4(b) n.24

Roper, United States v., 681 F.2d 1354 (11th Cir.1982)—§ 3.6(a) n.39

Ropp, United States v., 347 F.Supp.2d 831 (C.D. Cal. 2004)—§ 4.6(a) n.21

Roque, United States v., 421 F.3d 118 (2d Cir.2005)—§ 21.2(b) n.86

Rosa v. McCray, 396 F.3d 210 (2d Cir.2005)—§ 6.7(b) n.43

Rosa, State v., 575 A.2d 727 (Me.1990)—§§ 26.4(g) n.114, 127

Rosa, United States v., 123 F.3d 94 (2d Cir.1997)—§§ 21.2(b) n.85; 27.5(c) n.52

Rosa, United States v., 17 F.3d 1531 (2d Cir.1994)—§§ 16.1(g) n.249, 263

Rosa, United States v., 11 F.3d 315 (2d Cir.1993)—§ 7.4(e) n.84

Rosa, United States v., 891 F.2d 1074 (3d Cir.1989)—§ 24.3(c) n.88

Rosado, In re, 441 F.Supp. 1081 (S.D.N.Y.1977)—§§ 8.9(b) n.29; 8.14(c) n.37

Rosahn, In re, 671 F.2d 690 (2d Cir.1982)—§ 8.5(b) n.58

Rosales v. Dretke, 444 F.3d 703 (5th Cir.2006)—§ 28.4(b) n.19

Rosales, People v., 68 Cal.2d 299, 66 Cal.Rptr. 1, 437 P.2d 489 (1968)—§ 3.6(b) n.57

Rosales-Lopez v. United States, 451 U.S. 182, 101 S.Ct. 1629, 68 L.Ed.2d 22 (1981)—§§ 1.7(i) n.159; 22.3(a) n.12

Rosa-Ortiz, United States v., 348 F.3d 33 (1st Cir.2003)—§ 19.3(e) n.241

Rosario, Commonwealth v., 422 Mass. 48, 661 N.E.2d 71 (1996)—§ 6.3(c) n.52

Rosario, Commonwealth v., 545 Pa. 4, 679 A.2d 756 (1996)—§ 21.4(g) n.249

Rosario, United States v., 962 F.2d 733 (7th Cir.1992)—§ 3.10(d) n.134

Rosario, United States v., 864 F.2d 1064 (3d Cir.1988)—§ 11.9(d) n.226

Rosario-Diaz, United States v., 202 F.3d 54 (1st Cir.2000)—§ 6.3(b) n.40

Rosario-Peralta, United States v., 175 F.3d 48 (1st Cir.1999)—§ 20.6(b) n.47

Rosas v. State, 147 P.3d 1101 (Nev.2007)—§ 24.8(f) n.98

Roscoe v. State, 345 S.C. 16, 546 S.E.2d 417 (2001)—§ 21.5(c) n.76

Roscoe, State v., 184 Ariz. 484, 910 P.2d 635 (1996)—§ 7.5(b) n.15

Rose v. Clark, 478 U.S. 570, 106 S.Ct. 3101, 92 L.Ed.2d 460 (1986)— §§ 1.5(b) n.76; 27.6(d) n.87, 101

Rose v. Lundy, 455 U.S. 509, 102 S.Ct. 1198, 71 L.Ed.2d 379 (1982)— §§ 28.2(d) n.81; 28.5(a) n.9, 21; 28.5(c) n.72

Rose v. Mitchell, 443 U.S. 545, 99 S.Ct. 2993, 61 L.Ed.2d 739 (1979)— §§ 2.7(c) n.201; 2.9(g) n.190; 15.1(c) n.141; 15.4(c) n.83, 84; 15.4(d) n.104; 15.4(e) n.130; 15.4(i) n.201; 27.6(d) n.107; 28.2(c) n.43, 49; 28.3(c) n.75

Rose v. Nickeson, 29 Conn.Sup. 102, 273 A.2d 290 (1970)—§ 12.4(f) n.96

Rose v. Palmateer, 395 F.3d 1108 (9th Cir.2005)—§ 28.5(a) n.33

Rose, State v., 748 A.2d 1283 (R.I.2000)—§§ 3.4(f) n.117; 24.9(b) n.17, 18

Rose, State v., 75 Wash.App. 28, 876 P.2d 925 (1994)—§ 3.2(b) n.57

Rose, State v., 604 A.2d 24 (Me.1992)— § 6.4(f) n.136

Rose, United States v., 357 F.3d 615 (6th Cir.2004)—§§ 21.4(c) n.78; 21.4(f) n.178

Rose, United States v., 362 F.3d 1059 (8th Cir.2004)—§ 7.4(e) n.82

Rose v. United States, 629 A.2d 526 (D.C.App.1993)—§ 9.1(b) n.70

Rose, United States v., 791 F.2d 1477 (11th Cir.1986)—§§ 12.1(a) n.7; 12.2(a) n.4

Rose, United States v., 669 F.2d 23 (1st Cir.1982)—§ 4.6(a) n.4

Rose, United States v., 215 F.2d 617 (3d Cir.1954)—§§ 8.5(a) n.8; 8.5(d) n.137

Roseberry, People v., 465 Mich. 713, 641 N.W.2d 558 (2002)—§ 11.1(a) n.27

Roseboro, State v., 221 Conn. 430, 604 A.2d 1286 (1992)—§ 6.2(c) n.166

Roseboro, United States v., 87 F.3d 642 (4th Cir.1996)—§ 24.3(c) n.101

Roselle, People v., 84 N.Y.2d 350, 618 N.Y.S.2d 753, 643 N.E.2d 72 (1994)—§ 17.4(a) n.54

Roselli, United States v., 432 F.2d 879 (9th Cir.1970)—§ 17.2(a) n.21

Rosemond v. State, 104 Nev. 286, 756 P.2d 1180 (1988)—§ 21.4(d) n.106

Rosen, United States v., 365 F.Supp.2d 1126 (C.D. Cal.2005)—§ 16.2(c) n.51

Rosenbaum v. State, 4 Ind. 599 (1853)— §§ 1.6(d) n.287; 19.1(b) n.17

Rosenberg v. United States, 346 U.S. 273, 73 S.Ct. 1173, 97 L.Ed. 1607 (1953)—§§ 1.9(b) n.10, 11

Rosencranz v. United States, 356 F.2d 310 (1st Cir.1966)—§§ 3.2(c) n.117; 9.1(b) n.40

Rosencranz v. United States, 334 F.2d 738 (1st Cir.1964)—§ 9.2(c) n.21

Rosengard, United States v., 949 F.2d 905 (7th Cir.1991)—§ 6.10(c) n.41

Rosenthal, United States v., 454 F.3d 943 (9th Cir.2006)—§§ 24.9(f) n.79, 85; 24.9(g) n.119

Rosenthal, United States v., 793 F.2d 1214 (11th Cir.1986)—§ 3.1(i) n.232

Rosenthal, State ex rel. v. Poe, 98 S.W.3d 194 (Tex.Crim.App.2003)—§§ 23.3(b) n.16; 24.9(f) n.76

Rosenwald v. United States, 898 F.2d 585 (7th Cir.1990)—§ 11.9(d) n.202

Rosin, United States v., 892 F.2d 649 (7th Cir.1990)—§ 19.6(c) n.23

Rosine, State v., 233 Kan. 663, 664 P.2d 852 (1983)—§ 2.12(d) n.184

Ross, Commonwealth v., 465 Pa. 421, 350 A.2d 836 (1976)—§ 11.4(c) n.85

Ross v. Heyne, 638 F.2d 979 (7th Cir.1980)—§ 11.9(a) n.27

Ross v. Moffitt, 417 U.S. 600, 94 S.Ct. 2437, 41 L.Ed.2d 341 (1974)—§§ 11.1(b) n.61, 62, 95; 11.1(d) n.103, 109; 11.2(b) n.51, 62; 11.7(a) n.12; 12.2(b) n.24; 18.5(c) n.79; 27.1(a) n.13

Ross v. Neff, 905 F.2d 1349 (10th Cir.1990)—§ 3.5(a) n.23

Ross v. Oklahoma, 487 U.S. 81, 108 S.Ct. 2273, 101 L.Ed.2d 80 (1988)—§ 22.3(c) n.156

Ross v. Sirica, 380 F.2d 557 (D.C.Cir.1967)—§§ 14.2(b) n.26, 30

Ross, State v., 269 Conn. 213, 849 A.2d 648 (2004)—§ 22.3(c) n.157

Ross, State v., 166 Vt. 630, 699 A.2d 47 (1997)—§ 27.2(c) n.64

Ross, State v., 230 Conn. 183, 646 A.2d 1318 (1994)—§§ 16.4(c) n.57, 59, 78, 84

Ross, State v., 829 S.W.2d 948 (Mo.1992)—§§ 22.5(d) n.33, 36

Ross, State v., 472 N.W.2d 651 (Minn.1991)—§ 22.1(h) n.133

Ross v. State, 300 Ark. 369, 779 S.W.2d 161 (Ark.1989)—§ 16.3(g) n.108

Ross v. State, 308 Md. 337, 519 A.2d 735 (1987)—§§ 19.1(c) n.29; 19.3(b) n.134

Ross v. State, 254 Ga. 22, 326 S.E.2d 194 (1985)—§ 6.4(e) n.77

Ross, State v., 6 Ohio App.3d 25, 452 N.E.2d 339 (1982)—§§ 15.6(d) n.119; 15.7(c) n.54, 56

Ross, State v., 108 Ariz. 245, 495 P.2d 841 (1972)—§ 21.4(d) n.119

Ross v. United States, 339 F.3d 483 (6th Cir.2003)—§§ 17.2(c) n.84, 87, 88

Ross, United States v., 123 F.3d 1181 (9th Cir.1997)—§ 9.6(a) n.35

Ross, United States v., 77 F.3d 1525 (7th Cir.1996)—§ 18.5(a) n.50

Ross, United States v., 33 F.3d 1507 (11th Cir.1994)—§§ 11.9(a) n.27; 11.9(c) n.115

Ross, United States v., 9 F.3d 1182 (7th Cir.1993)—§ 26.10(c) n.60

Ross, United States v., 713 F.2d 389 (8th Cir.1983)—§ 4.6(l) n.188

Ross, United States v., 456 U.S. 798, 102 S.Ct. 2157, 72 L.Ed.2d 572 (1982)—§ 3.7(c) n.43

Ross, United States v., 511 F.2d 757 (5th Cir.1975)—§§ 20.3(g) n.123, 132

Ross, United States v., 503 F.2d 940 (5th Cir.1974)—§ 26.10(a) n.8

Ross, United States v., 205 F.2d 619 (10th Cir.1953)—§ 16.2(f) n.99

Ross v. U.S., 511 U.S. 1124, 114 S.Ct. 2129, 128 L.Ed.2d 860 (1994)—§ 26.10(c) n.60

Ross v. U.S. Marshal for Eastern Dist. of Oklahoma, 168 F.3d 1190 (10th Cir.1999)—§ 18.5(a) n.25

Ross v. Wainwright, 738 F.2d 1217 (11th Cir.1984)—§§ 11.10(c) n.72; 11.10(d) n.195

Rossbach, State v., 288 N.W.2d 714 (Minn.1980)—§ 16.4(c) n.44

Rosse, State v., 478 N.W.2d 482 (Minn.1991)—§ 6.6(e) n.86

Rossi, People v., 80 N.Y.2d 952, 590 N.Y.S.2d 872, 605 N.E.2d 359 (1992)—§§ 9.3(a) n.1; 9.3(d) n.36

Rossi, State v., 146 Ariz. 359, 706 P.2d 371 (1985)—§ 7.4(e) n.80

Rossignol, State v., 627 A.2d 524 (Me.1993)—§§ 6.7(b) n.54; 6.9(f) n.111

Rostad, Commonwealth v., 410 Mass. 618, 574 N.E.2d 381 (1991)—§ 3.5(e) n.196

Rostenkowski, United States v., 59 F.3d 1291 (D.C.Cir.1995)—§ 15.2(i) n.222

Roston, United States v., 986 F.2d 1287 (9th Cir.1993)—§ 11.4(c) n.77

Roth v. State, 788 A.2d 101 (Del.2001)—§ 6.7(c) n.118

Roth, State v., 305 N.W.2d 501 (Iowa 1981)—§ 2.12(d) n.186

Rothman, Commonwealth v., 222 Pa.Super. 385, 294 A.2d 783 (1972)—§ 21.2(c) n.123

Rothman, State v., 70 Haw. 546, 779 P.2d 1 (Hawaii 1989)—§ 2.12(b) n.88

Rothman, United States v., 492 F.2d 1260 (9th Cir.1973)—§§ 3.5(e) n.178; 3.10(b) n.40, 68

Rothrock, United States v., 806 F.2d 318 (1st Cir.1986)—§ 24.7(e) n.61

Roucchio v. Coughlin, 923 F.Supp. 360 (E.D.N.Y.1996)—§ 26.1(e) n.113

Roundtree, Commonwealth v., 469 Pa. 241, 364 A.2d 1359 (1976)—§ 18.1(d) n.45

Roundtree v. Felton, 656 So.2d 584 (Fla.App.1995)—§ 27.4(f) n.68

Roundtree v. State, 546 So.2d 1042 (Fla.1989)—§ 22.3(d) n.242

Rourke, United States v., 74 F.3d 802 (7th Cir.1996)—§ 21.2(d) n.150

Rousan, State v., 961 S.W.2d 831 (Mo.1998)—§§ 6.2(c) n.90; 22.3(c) n.146

Rouse v. Foster, 672 F.2d 649 (8th Cir.1982)—§ 21.4(d) n.151

Rouse v. Lee, 339 F.3d 238 (4th Cir.2003)—§ 28.5(b) n.59

Rouse, State v., 206 Neb. 371, 293 N.W.2d 83 (1980)—§§ 21.4(d) n.151; 21.5(b) n.68

Rouse, State v., 290 N.W.2d 911 (Iowa 1980)—§§ 14.2(g) n.93, 94, 97

Rouse, United States v., 148 F.3d 1040 (8th Cir.1998)—§ 3.1(h) n.197

Rouse v. United States, 359 F.2d 1014 (D.C.Cir.1966)—§§ 10.2(b) n.28; 10.6(c) n.25

Rousseau v. State, 855 S.W.2d 666 (Tex.Crim.App.1993)—§ 15.4(e) n.140

Roviaro v. United States, 353 U.S. 53, 77 S.Ct. 623, 1 L.Ed.2d 639 (1957)—§§ 1.7(i) n.160; 24.3(g) n.164

Rowan v. Owens, 752 F.2d 1186 (7th Cir.1984)—§ 9.6(a) n.38

Rowan, State v., 694 So.2d 1052 (La.App.1997)—§ 24.3(b) n.62

Rowe v. Griffin, 676 F.2d 524 (11th Cir.1982)—§ 13.5(e) n.95

Rowe, State v., 479 A.2d 1296 (Me.1984)—§ 6.2(c) n.172

Rowe, State v., 480 A.2d 778 (Me.1984)—§ 17.2(b) n.67

Rowe, State v., 93 Wash.2d 277, 609 P.2d 1348 (1980)—§ 13.2(h) n.146

Rowe, United States v., 414 F.3d 271 (2d Cir.2005)—§ 16.2(f) n.104

Rowe, United States v., 92 F.3d 928 (9th Cir.1996)—§ 6.3(b) n.36

Rowell, United States v., 903 F.2d 899 (2d Cir.1990)—§ 2.12(c) n.173

Rowell, United States v., 612 F.2d 1176 (7th Cir.1980)—§ 3.1(d) n.97

Rower v. State, 264 Ga. 323, 443 S.E.2d 839 (1994)—§ 20.5(h) n.116

Rowerdink, People v., 756 P.2d 986 (Colo.1988)—§ 3.3(c) n.141

Rowland, People v., 8 N.Y.2d 342, 834 N.Y.S.2d 58, 865 N.E.2d 1224 (2007)—§ 21.2(d) n.194

Rowland v. State, 118 Nev. 31, 39 P.3d 114 (2002)—§ 24.7(e) n.54

Rowland, State v., 110 Ohio App.3d 562, 674 N.E.2d 1219 (1996)—§ 26.9(b) n.40

Rowland, United States v., 341 F.3d 774 (8th Cir.2003)—§§ 3.7(d) n.79; 3.8(e) n.197

Rowsey v. Lee, 327 F.3d 335 (4th Cir.2003)—§ 13.4(c) n.96

Roy v. Lampert, 465 F.3d 964 (9th Cir.2006)—§ 28.5(b) n.61

Roy, State v., 681 So.2d 1230 (La.1996)—§ 22.3(a) n.30

Roy, State v., 151 Vt. 17, 557 A.2d 884 (1989)—§ 19.3(a) n.45

Roy, United States v., 869 F.2d 1427 (11th Cir.1989)—§§ 3.1(d) n.103; 3.3(b) n.47

Roy, United States v., 830 F.2d 628 (7th Cir.1987)—§§ 18.4(c) n.60, 73

Roy, United States v., 771 F.2d 54 (2d Cir.1985)—§§ 18.4(c) n.38, 40

Roy, United States v., 734 F.2d 108 (2d Cir.1984)—§ 9.1(d) n.133

Royal, United States v., 174 F.3d 1 (1st Cir.1999)—§§ 22.2(a) n.7; 22.2(d) n.76

Royal, United States v., 100 F.3d 1019 (1st Cir.1996)—§ 22.3(b) n.54

Royal Health Care Services v. Jefferson-Pilot Ins. Co., 924 F.2d 215 (11th Cir.1991)—§ 4.6(b) n.46

Royall, Ex parte, 117 U.S. 241, 6 S.Ct. 734, 29 L.Ed. 868 (1886)—§ 28.5(a) n.3

Roye v. United States, 772 A.2d 837 (D.C.App.2001)—§ 21.2(e) n.297

Royer, State v., 632 N.W.2d 905 (Iowa 2001)—§ 21.4(f) n.192

Royster, State v., 57 N.J. 472, 273 A.2d 574 (1971)—§ 7.3(f) n.110

Royster v. State, 108 Ga.App. 269, 132 S.E.2d 830 (1963)—§ 16.1(g) n.272

Rubanowitz, People v., 688 P.2d 231 (Colo.1984)—§ 22.2(d) n.72

Rubbo, United States v., 396 F.3d 1330 (11th Cir.2005)—§ 21.2(b) n.86

Rubenstein, State v., 40 Ohio App.3d 57, 531 N.E.2d 732 (1987)—§ 11.6(a) n.62

Rubenstein, United States v., 151 F.2d 915 (2d Cir.1945)—§ 27.6(b) n.37

Rubics, People v., 136 Cal.App.4th 452, 38 Cal.Rptr.3d 886 (2006)—§ 26.6(c) n.36

Rubin v. Gee, 292 F.3d 396 (4th Cir.2002)—§§ 11.9(d) n.214, 235

Rubin v. State, 325 Md. 552, 602 A.2d 677 (1992)—§ 9.3(e) n.57

Rubin, United States v., 37 F.3d 49 (2d Cir.1994)—§ 24.2(a) n.12

Rubin, United States v., 559 F.2d 975 (5th Cir.1977)—§ 8.10(c) n.76

Rubin, United States v., 474 F.2d 262 (3d Cir.1973)—§§ 3.6(e) n.111, 113

Rubio v. State, 939 P.2d 238 (Wyo.1997)—§§ 6.2(c) n.163; 6.9(b) n.18

Rubio v. Superior Court, 24 Cal.3d 93, 154 Cal.Rptr. 734, 593 P.2d 595 (1979)—§ 22.2(d) n.70

Rucker, People v., 26 Cal.3d 368, 162 Cal.Rptr. 13, 605 P.2d 843 (1980)—§ 6.7(b) n.42

Rucker v. State, 320 Ark. 643, 899 S.W.2d 447 (1995)—§ 19.5(b) n.33

Rucker, United States v., 435 F.2d 950 (8th Cir.1971)—§ 6.10(c) n.35

Rudas, United States v., 905 F.2d 38 (2d Cir.1990)—§§ 22.3(d) n.193, 234

Rudberg, United States v., 122 F.3d 1199 (9th Cir.1997)—§ 24.7(e) n.51

Rude v. State, 851 P.2d 15 (Wyo.1993)—§ 21.4(f) n.192

Rude v. State, 851 P.2d 20 (Wyo.1993)—§ 21.2(b) n.57

Rudisill, State v., 20 N.C.App. 313, 201 S.E.2d 368 (1973)—§ 3.4(h) n.146

Rudnick, People v., 878 P.2d 16 (Colo.App.1993)—§ 24.9(f) n.72

Rudolph v. State, 829 P.2d 269 (Wyo.1992)—§ 24.3(f) n.140

Rue, State v., 175 N.J. 1, 811 A.2d 425 (2002)—§§ 11.2(b) n.76; 11.2(c) n.93

Rue, United States v., 819 F.2d 1488 (8th Cir.1987)—§§ 8.13(a) n.16, 25

Rueben, United States v., 974 F.2d 580 (5th Cir.1992)—§ 12.3(a) n.24

Ruebke, State v., 240 Kan. 493, 731 P.2d 842 (1987)—§§ 23.2(a) n.24, 38, 39

Ruehrup, United States v., 333 F.2d 641 (7th Cir.1964)—§§ 16.1(d) n.141; 16.2(e) n.77

Ruelas, United States v., 106 F.3d 1416 (9th Cir.1997)—§ 21.2(b) n.84

Ruelas-Arreguin, United States v., 219 F.3d 1056 (9th Cir.2000)—§§ 16.1(h) n.307; 16.2(c) n.51

Ruesga-Martinez, United States v., 534 F.2d 1367 (9th Cir.1976)—§ 13.7(c) n.40

Ruff v. State, 65 Wis.2d 713, 223 N.W.2d 446 (1974)—§ 16.3(b) n.23

Ruff, United States v., 984 F.2d 635 (5th Cir.1993)—§ 3.3(g) n.225

Ruffin v. Commonwealth, 62 Va. (21 Grat.) 790 (1871)—§ 16.1(e) n.200

Ruffin v. Commonwealth, 62 Va. 791 (1871)—§ 16.1(e) n.182

Ruffin v. Kemp, 767 F.2d 748 (11th Cir.1985)—§§ 11.9(d) n.184, 192; 21.3(b) n.134

Ruffin v. United States, 524 A.2d 685 (D.C.App.1987)—§ 18.2(c) n.50

Ruffner, United States v., 51 F.2d 579 (D.Md.1931)—§ 3.10(e) n.176

Rufus, State v., 338 Ark. 305, 993 S.W.2d 490 (1999)—§ 3.4(d) n.50

Rugerio v. United States, 330 F.Supp.2d 900 (E.D.Mich.2004)—§ 11.9(d) n.173

Ruggeri, State v., 19 Utah 2d 216, 429 P.2d 969 (1967)—§§ 8.10(d) n.87, 88

Ruggiero, United States v., 100 F.3d 284 (2d Cir.1996)—§ 26.4(f) n.91

Ruggiero, United States v., 754 F.2d 927 (11th Cir.1985)—§ 17.4(a) n.36

Ruggiero, United States v., 726 F.2d 913 (2d Cir.1984)—§§ 24.10(a) n.1, 18, 19

Ruhbayan, United States v., 325 F.3d 197 (4th Cir.2003)—§ 17.4(a) n.38

Ruhe, United States v., 191 F.3d 376 (4th Cir.1999)—§§ 3.4(k) n.220; 9.3(d) n.35

Ruhm v. State, 496 P.2d 809 (Okl.Cr.1972)—§ 10.3(b) n.22

Ruigomez, United States v., 702 F.2d 61 (5th Cir.1983)—§ 3.5(c) n.109

Ruimveld v. Birkett, 404 F.3d 1006 (6th Cir.2005)—§ 27.6(d) n.85

Ruiz v. Craven, 425 F.2d 235 (9th Cir.1970)—§ 9.4(a) n.41

Ruiz v. Norris, 868 F.Supp. 1471 (E.D.Ark.1994)—§ 23.2(g) n.121

Ruiz, State v., 106 Idaho 336, 678 P.2d 1109 (1984)—§§ 14.3(c) n.60, 67, 71

Ruiz v. State, 265 Ark. 875, 582 S.W.2d 915 (1979)—§ 23.2(a) n.28

Ruiz v. Superior Court, 26 Cal.App.4th 935, 31 Cal.Rptr.2d 741 (1994)—§ 14.3(a) n.17

Ruiz, United States v., 536 U.S. 622, 122 S.Ct. 2450, 153 L.Ed.2d 586 (2002)—§§ 11.3(b) n.46; 20.3(m) n.258; 21.2(b) n.66; 21.3(c) n.176; 24.3(b) n.79; 27.5(c) n.57, 67

Ruiz, United States v., 241 F.3d 1157 (9th Cir.2001)—§ 21.2(b) n.65

Ruiz-Castro, United States v., 125 F.Supp.2d 411 (D.Hawaii 2000)—§ 19.2(e) n.71

Ruiz-Estrada, United States v., 312 F.3d 398 (8th Cir.2002)—§ 3.6(e) n.127

Ruiz-Estrella, United States v., 481 F.2d 723 (2d Cir.1973)—§ 3.9(h) n.157

Rumery, United States v., 698 F.2d 764 (5th Cir.1983)—§ 21.2(g) n.399

Ruminer, United States v., 786 F.2d 381 (10th Cir.1986)—§§ 21.2(h) n.427; 21.5(f) n.175

Rummel v. Estelle, 445 U.S. 263, 100 S.Ct. 1133, 63 L.Ed.2d 382 (1980)—§§ 2.8(a) n.16; 13.2(h) n.145; 21.2(b) n.38

Rummer, State v., 189 W.Va. 369, 432 S.E.2d 39 (1993)—§§ 9.6(a) n.16, 31

Rumsfeld v. Padilla, 542 U.S. 426, 124 S.Ct. 2711, 159 L.Ed.2d 513 (2004)—§§ 28.2(a) n.15, 17

Runck v. State, 497 N.W.2d 74 (N.D.1993)—§§ 18.4(c) n.37, 40

Runions, State v., 100 Wash.2d 52, 665 P.2d 1358 (1983)—§ 8.11(b) n.32

Runyan, United States v., 275 F.3d 449 (5th Cir.2001)—§ 3.1(h) n.197

Rupe, State v., 108 Wash.2d 734, 743 P.2d 210 (1987)—§ 22.2(d) n.67

Rupe, State v., 101 Wash.2d 664, 683 P.2d 571 (1984)—§§ 6.8(a) n.10; 6.8(b) n.63; 6.8(d) n.84

Rupert, State v., 649 A.2d 1013 (R.I.1994)—§ 27.5(d) n.113

Ruple, State v., 437 So.2d 873 (La.App.1983)—§§ 15.1(d) n.142; 15.1(e) n.261; 15.1(f) n.288

Rupley, United States v., 706 F.Supp. 751 (D.Nev.1989)—§ 26.6(d) n.53

Rupnick, State v., 280 Kan. 720, 125 P.3d 541 (2005)—§ 6.6(e) n.68

Ruppel, United States v., 666 F.2d 261 (5th Cir.1982)—§§ 8.8(f) n.146; 24.8(a) n.7

Ruppuhn, People v., 25 Mich.App. 62, 180 N.W.2d 900 (1970)—§ 6.8(a) n.12

Ruscoe, State v., 212 Conn. 223, 563 A.2d 267 (1989)—§§ 3.4(h) n.151; 3.4(j) n.201; 3.4(k) n.228

Rusen, State ex rel. v. Hill, 193 W.Va. 133, 454 S.E.2d 427 (1994)— §§ 20.6(a) n.10; 20.6(b) n.37, 40, 43; 27.4(d) n.41, 50

Rush v. State, 749 So.2d 1024 (Miss.1999)—§ 21.2(e) n.325

Rush, United States v., 738 F.2d 497 (1st Cir.1984)—§§ 18.3(b) n.14, 43

Rush v. United States, 559 F.2d 455 (7th Cir.1977)—§ 11.2(d) n.138

Rushen v. Spain, 464 U.S. 114, 104 S.Ct. 453, 78 L.Ed.2d 267 (1983)— §§ 24.2(a) n.9; 24.2(b) n.25, 26; 27.6(d) n.84; 28.7(b) n.9

Rusher, United States v., 966 F.2d 868 (4th Cir.1992)—§ 9.1(d) n.120

Rushworth v. Registrar of Motor Vehicles, 413 Mass. 265, 596 N.E.2d 340 (1992)—§ 17.4(b) n.118

Rusk, United States v., 96 F.3d 777 (5th Cir.1996)—§ 17.4(b) n.128

Russell, In re, 726 F.2d 1007 (4th Cir.1984)—§§ 23.1(b) n.75, 82, 89

Russell v. Douthitt, 261 Ind. 428, 304 N.E.2d 793 (1973)—§ 11.1(b) n.48

Russell v. Parratt, 543 F.2d 1214 (8th Cir.1976)—§ 13.7(b) n.34

Russell, People v., 34 N.Y.2d 261, 357 N.Y.S.2d 415, 313 N.E.2d 732 (1974)—§ 3.3(b) n.74

Russell, State v., 384 N.J.Super. 586, 895 A.2d 1163 (2006)—§ 24.2(e) n.58

Russell, State v., 248 Neb. 723, 539 N.W.2d 8 (1995)—§ 26.3(f) n.64

Russell, State v., 125 Wash.2d 24, 882 P.2d 747 (1994)—§§ 9.5(b) n.42, 44

Russell, State v., 477 N.W.2d 886 (Minn.1991)—§§ 1.5(j) n.330; 2.12(c) n.140

Russell v. State, 727 S.W.2d 573 (Tex.Cr.App.1987)—§ 6.9(g) n.183

Russell v. State, 717 S.W.2d 7 (Tex.Cr.App.1986)—§§ 3.8(c) n.76; 10.3(b) n.39

Russell, State v., 229 Kan. 124, 622 P.2d 658 (1981)—§ 25.5(b) n.28

Russell, State v., 261 N.W.2d 490 (Iowa 1978)—§ 6.9(b) n.28

Russell v. State, 270 Ind. 55, 383 N.E.2d 309 (1978)—§ 11.5(d) n.71

Russell, United States v., 205 F.3d 768 (5th Cir.2000)—§§ 11.3(a) n.13; 11.10(d) n.200

Russell, United States v., 221 F.3d 615 (4th Cir.2000)—§ 11.10(c) n.123

Russell, United States v., 109 F.3d 1503 (10th Cir.1997)—§§ 20.6(b) n.41, 42; 20.6(c) n.67

Russell, United States v., 411 U.S. 423, 93 S.Ct. 1637, 36 L.Ed.2d 366 (1973)—§§ 1.7(i) n.171; 2.7(a) n.16; 2.7(c) n.202; 3.1(j) n.247; 3.1(o) n.307; 5.1(c) n.20; 5.2(a) n.1; 5.2(b) n.37; 5.3(a) n.8; 5.4(a) n.11; 5.4(c) n.31

Russell v. United States, 408 F.2d 1280 (D.C.Cir.1969)—§ 7.3(b) n.22

Russell v. United States, 369 U.S. 749, 82 S.Ct. 1038, 8 L.Ed.2d 240 (1962)—§§ 19.2(b) n.16; 19.2(c) n.24, 42; 19.2(d) n.45, 46, 48; 19.2(f) n.90, 95, 108; 19.3(a) n.111; 19.3(b) n.138; 19.4(a) n.3

Russell, State ex rel. v. Jones, 293 Or. 312, 647 P.2d 904 (1982)— §§ 6.4(e) n.109; 11.1(b) n.91

Russo, In re, 53 F.R.D. 564 (C.D.Cal.1971)—§§ 8.2(a) n.4; 8.2(c) n.26; 8.5(a) n.9; 8.5(d) n.139

Russo, In re, 448 F.2d 369 (9th Cir.1971)—§ 8.8(f) n.152

Russo, People v., 439 Mich. 584, 487 N.W.2d 698 (1992)—§ 3.3(g) n.228

Russo, United States v., 110 F.3d 948 (2d Cir.1997)—§ 24.8(a) n.18

Russo, United States v., 741 F.2d 1264 (11th Cir.1984)—§ 18.3(b) n.54

Russo, United States v., 527 F.2d 1051 (10th Cir.1975)—§ 4.6(e) n.87

Russotti, United States v., 717 F.2d 27 (2d Cir.1983)—§ 25.5(c) n.35

Russo, United States ex rel. v. Attorney General, 780 F.2d 712 (7th Cir.1986)—§ 11.2(c) n.86

Rutan, United States v., 956 F.2d 827 (8th Cir.1992)—§ 21.2(b) n.85

Ruth, United States v., 65 F.3d 599 (7th Cir.1995)—§ 9.1(b) n.48

Ruthenberg v. United States, 245 U.S. 480, 38 S.Ct. 168, 62 L.Ed. 414 (1918)—§ 22.2(e) n.104

Rutherford v. Blankenship, 468 F.Supp. 1357 (W.D.Va.1979)—§ 21.2(b) n.61

Rutherford, United States v., 824 F.2d 831 (10th Cir.1987)—§ 3.3(f) n.206

Rutledge v. State, 525 N.E.2d 326 (Ind.1988)—§ 6.10(b) n.16

Rutledge v. United States, 517 U.S. 292, 116 S.Ct. 1241, 134 L.Ed.2d 419 (1996)—§§ 17.4(b) n.111; 24.8(e) n.57; 25.4(b) n.21; 27.5(b) n.39

Rutledge, United States v., 900 F.2d 1127 (7th Cir.1990)—§§ 6.2(c) n.92, 94

Rutti v. State, 100 P.3d 394 (Wyo.2004)—§§ 21.2(d) n.206; 21.6(a) n.75, 76

Rutzinski, State v., 241 Wis.2d 729, 623 N.W.2d 516 (2001)—§ 3.8(d) n.166

Rutz, United States ex rel. v. Levy, 268 U.S. 390, 45 S.Ct. 516, 69 L.Ed. 1010 (1925)—§ 14.3(c) n.67

Ruzzano, United States v., 247 F.3d 688 (7th Cir.2001)—§§ 22.4(c) n.29, 30

R.W., State v., 115 N.J.Super. 286, 279 A.2d 709 (1971)—§ 6.10(e) n.74

R.W.S., In re, 728 N.W.2d 326 (N.D.2007)—§ 7.4(g) n.112

Ryals v. State, 794 So.2d 161 (Miss.2001)—§ 6.7(b) n.64

Ryan v. Commodity Futures Trading Comm'n, 145 F.3d 910 (7th Cir.1998)—§ 17.4(b) n.125

Ryan, Commonwealth v., 5 S.W.3d 113 (Ky.1999)—§ 21.4(a) n.14

Ryan v. Palmateer, 108 P.3d 1127, 338 Or. 278 (2005)—§ 27.6(d) n.151

Ryan, People v., 451 Mich. 30, 545 N.W.2d 612 (1996)—§ 13.5(a) n.5

Ryan, People v., 19 N.Y.2d 100, 278 N.Y.S.2d 199, 224 N.E.2d 710 (1966)—§ 22.3(e) n.280

Ryan v. Roman Catholic Bishop of Providence, 787 A.2d 1191 (R.I.2002)—§ 26.5(c) n.59

Ryan, State v., 257 Neb. 635, 601 N.W.2d 473 (1999)—§ 22.4(a) n.4

Ryan v. State, 479 N.E.2d 517 (Ind.1985)—§ 21.2(d) n.177

Ryan, United States v., 236 F.3d 1268 (10th Cir.2001)—§ 3.1(f) n.153

Ryan, United States v., 894 F.2d 355 (10th Cir.1990)—§ 16.2(c) n.45

Ryan, United States v., 448 F.Supp. 810 (S.D.N.Y.1978)—§ 20.4(g) n.108

Ryan, United States v., 402 U.S. 530, 91 S.Ct. 1580, 29 L.Ed.2d 85 (1971)—§ 27.2(e) n.81

Ryan, People ex rel. v. Roe, 201 Ill.2d 552, 268 Ill.Dec. 435, 778 N.E.2d 701 (2002)—§ 21.2(e) n.349

Ryans, United States v., 903 F.2d 731 (10th Cir.1990)—§ 6.4(e) n.91

Ryan-Webster, United States v., 353 F.3d 353 (4th Cir.2003)—§ 13.7(a) n.5

Rybar, United States v., 103 F.3d 273 (3d Cir.1995)—§§ 1.2(c) n.119, 194

Ryder v. State, 83 P.3d 856 (Okla.Crim.App.2004)—§ 21.3(d) n.234

Rylander, United States v., 460 U.S. 752, 103 S.Ct. 1548, 75 L.Ed.2d 521 (1983)—§ 8.13(d) n.100

Ryon v. State, 29 Md.App. 62, 349 A.2d 393 (1975)—§ 9.4(a) n.18

Rytman, United States v., 475 F.2d 192 (5th Cir.1973)—§ 3.4(f) n.110

Rzepphiewski, Commonwealth v., 431 Mass. 48, 725 N.E.2d 210 (2000)—§ 21.5(c) n.94

S

6918 North Tyron Street, Charlotte, N.C., United States v., 672 F.Supp. 890 (W.D.N.C.1987)—§ 8.5(c) n.115

$639,558 in U.S. Currency, United States v., 955 F.2d 712 (D.C.Cir.1992)—§ 9.3(e) n.66

Saade, United States v., 652 F.2d 1126 (1st Cir.1981)—§§ 13.4(b) n.42; 13.4(c) n.117

Saadeh, United States v., 61 F.3d 510 (7th Cir.1995)—§ 6.7(b) n.73

Saadiq v. State, 387 N.W.2d 315 (Iowa 1986)—§ 21.4(d) n.125

Saadya, United States v., 750 F.2d 1419 (9th Cir.1985)—§ 22.1(h) n.135

Saari, United States v., 272 F.3d 804 (6th Cir.2001)—§ 3.6(a) n.38

Saathoff, State v., 29 P.3d 236 (Alaska 2001)—§ 18.5(a) n.11

Saathoff v. State, 891 S.W.2d 264 (Tex.Crim.App.1994)—§ 19.3(a) n.67

Saavedra v. State, 622 So.2d 952 (Fla.1993)—§ 10.4(c) n.23

Saavedra, State v., 406 N.W.2d 667 (N.D.1987)—§ 26.9(a) n.1

Saavedra, State v., 396 N.W.2d 304 (N.D.1986)—§ 9.4(f) n.116

Saavedra, United States v., 223 F.3d 85 (2d Cir.2000)—§§ 16.1(d) n.131; 16.2(b) n.30; 16.2(d) n.58; 16.2(e) n.91, 92; 16.2(h) n.158

Sababu, United States v., 891 F.2d 1308 (7th Cir.1989)—§ 4.6(b) n.50

Sabalos, State v., 178 Ariz. 420, 874 P.2d 977 (1994)—§ 27.4(d) n.42

Sabater, United States v., 830 F.2d 7 (2d Cir.1987)—§ 7.4(g) n.124

Sabbath v. United States, 391 U.S. 585, 88 S.Ct. 1755, 20 L.Ed.2d 828 (1968)—§ 3.4(h) n.146

Sabino, United States v., 274 F.3d 1053 (6th Cir.2001)—§§ 18.3(b) n.38, 43

Sablan, United States v., 461 F. Supp.2d 1239 (D.Colo.2006)—§ 26.4(h) n.156

Sablowski v. United States, 403 F.2d 347 (10th Cir.1968)—§ 3.1(e) n.134

Sabri v. United States, 541 U.S. 600, 124 S.Ct. 1941, 158 L.Ed.2d 891 (2004)—§§ 1.2(c) n.130, 195

Sacarakis, Commonwealth v., 196 Pa.Super. 455, 175 A.2d 127 (1961)—§ 16.3(f) n.90

Sacco, United States v., 428 F.2d 264 (9th Cir.1970)—§ 13.4(c) n.135

Sackler v. Sackler, 15 N.Y.2d 40, 255 N.Y.S.2d 83, 203 N.E.2d 481 (1964)—§ 3.1(h) n.221

Sacramento Bee v. U.S. District Court, 656 F.2d 477 (9th Cir.1981)—§ 23.1(e) n.242

Sacramento, County of v. Lewis, 523 U.S. 833, 118 S.Ct. 1708, 140 L.Ed.2d 1043 (1998)—§§ 2.7(d) n.236, 239, 249, 265; 3.5(a) n.72; 3.8(c) n.111

Sadeghi v. United States, 46 Fed.Cl. 660 (2000)—§ 21.2(e) n.281

Sadler v. State, 846 P.2d 377 (Okl.Cr.1993)—§ 6.4(f) n.124

Saechao, United States v., 418 F.3d 1073 (9th Cir.2005)—§ 26.9(b) n.68

Saenz v. Roe, 526 U.S. 489, 119 S.Ct. 1518, 143 L.Ed.2d 689 (1999)—§§ 2.3(a) n.26; 2.3(b) n.80

Saferian, Commonwealth v., 366 Mass. 89, 315 N.E.2d 878 (1974)—§§ 11.10(a) n.4; 11.10(c) n.119

Saffeels, United States v., 982 F.2d 1199 (8th Cir.1992)—§ 3.8(d) n.152

Saffle v. Parks, 494 U.S. 484, 110 S.Ct. 1257, 108 L.Ed.2d 415 (1990)—§§ 2.11(e) n.55; 28.6(c) n.15; 28.6(d) n.25; 28.6(e) n.40, 46

Saffold, People v., 465 Mich. 268, 631 N.W.2d 320 (2001)—§ 21.4(e) n.161

Safford v. Warden, 223 Conn. 180, 612 A.2d 1161 (1992)—§ 21.2(c) n.135

Saft, United States v., 558 F.2d 1073 (2d Cir.1977)—§ 21.5(a) n.30

Sage, United States v., 92 F.3d 101 (2d Cir.1996)—§ 1.2(c) n.174

S.A. Healy Co. v. Occupational Safety & Health Review Comm'n, 138 F.3d 686 (7th Cir.1998)—§ 17.4(b) n.131

Saiken, People v., 49 Ill.2d 504, 275 N.E.2d 381 (1971)—§ 3.1(e) n.138

Saiken, United States ex rel. v. Bensinger, 489 F.2d 865 (7th Cir.1973)—§ 3.3(c) n.116

Sailer, United States v., 552 F.2d 213 (8th Cir.1977)—§ 11.2(e) n.226

Sailor v. State, 733 So.2d 1057 (Fla.App.1999)—§§ 2.6(b) n.69; 16.3(d) n.54, 70, 71

Saintignon v. State, 616 N.E.2d 369 (Ind.1993)—§ 6.8(b) n.58

Saintil, United States v., 705 F.2d 415 (11th Cir.1983)—§ 18.3(b) n.22

Sairafi, United States v., 801 F.2d 691 (4th Cir.1986)—§ 18.3(b) n.5

Saiz v. Ortiz, 392 F.3d 1166 (10th Cir.2004)—§ 28.7(a) n.4

Saiz, People v., 620 P.2d 15 (Colo.1980)—§ 6.9(g) n.178

Sakarias, In re, 35 Cal.4th 140, 25 Cal.Rptr.3d 265, 106 P.3d 931 (2005)—§ 26.4(f) n.111

Sakellson, State v., 379 N.W.2d 779 (N.D.1985)—§ 3.4(h) n.147

Saks, United States v., 426 F.Supp. 812 (S.D.N.Y.1976)—§§ 8.5(c) n.96, 99, 107

Salaam, People v., 83 N.Y.2d 51, 607 N.Y.S.2d 899, 629 N.E.2d 371 (1993)—§ 6.9(g) n.178

Salahuddin v. State, 277 Ga. 561, 592 S.E.2d 410 (2004)—§§ 18.2(c) n.38; 18.2(e) n.76, 81

Salaiscooper v. District Court, 117 Nev. 892, 34 P.3d 509 (2001)—§§ 13.4(c) n.93; 13.6(c) n.28

Salameh, United States v., 152 F.3d 88 (2d Cir.1998)—§ 21.2(e) n.325

Salameh, United States v., 856 F.Supp. 781 (S.D.N.Y.1994)—§§ 11.9(c) n.112, 131

Salameh, United States v., 992 F.2d 445 (2d Cir.1993)—§§ 23.1(b) n.69, 71, 72, 77, 80

Salamone, United States v., 800 F.2d 1216 (3d Cir.1986)—§§ 22.3(c) n.136, 155

Salanitro, United States v., 437 F.Supp. 240 (D.Neb.1977)—§§ 8.5(e) n.198; 8.5(h) n.297

Salazar, People v., 136 Misc.2d 992, 519 N.Y.S.2d 589 (Sup.Ct.1987)—§ 15.2(c) n.77

Salazar, United States v., 453 F.3d 911 (7th Cir.2006)—§ 21.2(d) n.174

Salazar, United States v., 323 F.3d 852 (10th Cir.2003)—§ 21.6(a) n.38

Salazar, United States v., 805 F.2d 1394 (9th Cir.1986)—§ 9.1(d) n.122

Salazar Robles, United States v., 207 F.3d 648 (9th Cir.2000)—§ 16.2(c) n.51

Salcido, State v., 22 Ariz.App. 167, 525 P.2d 298 (1974)—§ 3.8(b) n.20

Saldana v. New York, 850 F.2d 117 (2d Cir.1988)—§ 15.6(f) n.181

Saldana v. State, 846 P.2d 604 (Wyo.1993)—§§ 2.12(b) n.82, 91; 2.12(c) n.119, 120

Saldana v. United States, 365 U.S. 646, 81 S.Ct. 783, 5 L.Ed.2d 855 (1961)—§ 1.7(i) n.162

Salem, City of v. Jungblut, 83 Or.App. 540, 732 P.2d 919 (1987)—§ 1.8(d) n.45

Salemme, United States v., 985 F.Supp. 197 (D.Mass.1997)—§ 11.2(g) n.305

Salemo, United States v., 61 F.3d 214 (3d Cir.1995)—§§ 11.3(b) n.27; 11.5(c) n.49; 26.4(e) n.74

Salerno, United States v., 505 U.S. 317, 112 S.Ct. 2503, 120 L.Ed.2d 255 (1992)—§ 24.3(i) n.196

Salerno, United States v., 481 U.S. 739, 107 S.Ct. 2095, 95 L.Ed.2d 697 (1987)—§§ 1.5(c) n.169; 2.7(d) n.236, 243; 12.2(a) n.4; 12.3(c) n.80, 88; 12.3(d) n.94, 110

Salerno, United States v., 829 F.2d 345 (2d Cir.1987)—§§ 12.3(c) n.89; 12.3(d) n.113

Sales v. Harris, 675 F.2d 532 (2d Cir.1982)—§ 7.4(e) n.93

Salgado, State v., 257 Conn. 394, 778 A.2d 24 (Conn.2001)—§ 24.10(d) n.47

Salgado, State v., 126 N.M. 691, 974 P.2d 661 (1999)—§§ 7.4(e) n.82, 84

Salgado, United States v., 292 F.3d 1169 (9th Cir.2002)—§§ 6.7(b) n.43; 6.10(c) n.55

Salina, City of v. Amador, 279 Kan. 266, 106 P.3d 1139 (2005)—§ 25.1(e) n.96

Salinas, United States v., 373 F.3d 161 (1st Cir.2004)—§§ 16.2(c) n.52; 16.2(d) n.59, 60; 16.2(e) n.89, 90

Salinas-Cano, United States v., 959 F.2d 861 (10th Cir.1992)—§§ 3.10(d) n.136; 3.10(e) n.169

Saling, United States v., 205 F.3d 764 (5th Cir.2000)—§§ 21.2(d) n.177, 178

Salinger v. Loisel, 265 U.S. 224, 44 S.Ct. 519, 68 L.Ed. 989 (1924)—§§ 16.2(f) n.94; 28.5(c) n.68

Salisbury, United States ex rel. v. Blackburn, 792 F.2d 498 (5th Cir.1986)—§ 21.4(c) n.82

Sallis, State v., 574 N.W.2d 15 (Iowa 1998)—§ 6.7(b) n.43

Salman, Commonwealth v., 387 Mass. 160, 439 N.E.2d 245 (1982)—§ 15.7(e) n.107

Salmon v. Commonwealth, 32 Va.App. 586, 529 S.E.2d 815 (2000)—§ 22.3(b) n.86

Salmon, State v., 216 Mo. 466, 115 S.W. 1106 (1909)—§ 15.7(h) n.239

Salmonese, United States v., 352 F.3d 608 (2d Cir.2003)—§§ 18.5(a) n.14, 30

Salmons, State v., 203 W.Va. 561, 509 S.E.2d 842 (1998)—§§ 20.3(k) n.220; 24.11(b) n.7; 27.5(c) n.93

Salovitz, United States v., 701 F.2d 17 (2d Cir.1983)—§ 24.7(a) n.1

Saltzman, State v., 871 So.2d 1087 (La.2004)—§ 6.6(c) n.31

Salvador, United States v., 740 F.2d 752 (9th Cir.1984)—§ 9.1(b) n.80

Salvador v. United States, 505 F.2d 1348 (8th Cir.1974)—§ 24.7(e) n.61

Salvati, Commonwealth v., 420 Mass. 499, 650 N.E.2d 782 (1995)—§ 24.3(g) n.168

Salvucci, United States v., 448 U.S. 83, 100 S.Ct. 2547, 65 L.Ed.2d 619 (1980)—§§ 9.2(a) n.4; 10.5(c) n.29, 36

Salyer, Interest of, 44 Ill.App.3d 854, 3 Ill.Dec. 648, 358 N.E.2d 1333 (1977)—§ 3.10(e) n.147

Salyer, People v., 80 P.3d 831 (Colo.App.2003)—§ 27.6(d) n.147

Salyers, State v., 239 Neb. 1002, 480 N.W.2d 173 (1992)—§§ 26.9(a) n.1; 26.9(b) n.16

Salyers, United States v., 160 F.3d 1152 (7th Cir.1998)—§ 6.6(c) n.32

Salzmann, State v., 119 Or.App. 217, 850 P.2d 1122 (1993)—§ 27.2(c) n.66

Salzmann, United States v., 548 F.2d 395 (2d Cir.1976)—§ 18.4(a) n.15

Samango, United States v., 607 F.2d 877 (9th Cir.1979)—§§ 15.5(b) n.37, 38, 50, 55, 69; 15.6(b) n.59; 15.7(d) n.88; 15.7(e) n.94

Samango, United States v., 450 F.Supp. 1097 (D.Hawai'i 1978)—§§ 15.6(a) n.1; 15.6(b) n.61

Sambursky v. State, 723 N.W.2d 524 (N.D.2006)—§ 21.4(d) n.119

Samkas, In re, 80 Ohio App.3d 240, 608 N.E.2d 1172 (1992)—§ 26.3(f) n.55

Sammons v. Rodgers, 785 F.2d 1343 (5th Cir.1986)—§ 28.3(a) n.10

Sammons, United States v., 918 F.2d 592 (6th Cir.1990)—§ 22.4(c) n.23

Samora, State v., 99 P.3d 858 (Utah 2004)—§ 26.8(c) n.29

Sample v. Eyman, 469 F.2d 819 (9th Cir.1972)—§ 6.9(b) n.29

Samples, United States v., 713 F.2d 298 (7th Cir.1983)—§ 18.3(b) n.12

Sampson, United States v., 448 F.Supp.2d 692 (E.D.Va.2006)— § 16.2(e) n.74

Sampson, United States v., 385 F.3d 183 (2d Cir.2004)—§ 17.1(c) n.43

Sampson, United States v., 661 F.Supp. 514 (W.D.Pa.1987)—§ 24.3(i) n.188

Sams, State v., 293 Or. 385, 648 P.2d 364 (1982)—§§ 8.4(c) n.127; 8.11(d) n.87

Samson v. California, _____ U.S. _____, 126 S.Ct. 2193, 165 L.Ed.2d 250 (2006)—§§ 1.11(a) n.3; 3.5(d) n.145; 3.9(a) n.3; 3.9(j) n.232, 237; 26.9(b) n.62

Samuel, Commonwealth v., 398 Mass. 93, 495 N.E.2d 279 (1986)— § 22.3(d) n.200

Samuel, State v., 252 Wis.2d 26, 643 N.W.2d 423 (2002)—§§ 9.1(a) n.22; 10.5(a) n.6

Samuel, State v., 74 Haw. 141, 838 P.2d 1374 (1992)—§§ 11.6(a) n.48; 24.8(a) n.8

Samuels v. Mackell, 401 U.S. 66, 91 S.Ct. 764, 27 L.Ed.2d 688 (1971)— §§ 13.5(e) n.93, 97

Samuels, People v., 49 N.Y.2d 218, 424 N.Y.S.2d 892, 400 N.E.2d 1344 (1980)—§ 6.4(f) n.112

Sanabria, State v., 192 Conn. 671, 474 A.2d 760 (1984)—§ 14.2(d) n.48

Sanabria v. United States, 437 U.S. 54, 98 S.Ct. 2170, 57 L.Ed.2d 43 (1978)—§§ 2.9(f) n.128; 25.3(c) n.24; 27.3(a) n.2

San Antonio Independent School District v. Rodriguez, 411 U.S. 1, 93 S.Ct. 1278, 36 L.Ed.2d 16 (1973)— § 12.3(d) n.98

Sanborn, People v., 133 Cal.App.4th 1462, 35 Cal.Rptr.3d 592 (2005)— § 24.10(d) n.46

Sanborn v. State, 474 So.2d 309 (Fla.App.1985)—§ 24.3(d) n.109

Sanchell v. Parratt, 530 F.2d 286 (8th Cir.1976)—§ 10.3(d) n.66

Sanchez, Commonwealth v., 552 Pa. 570, 716 A.2d 1221 (1998)— § 3.1(e) n.139

Sanchez v. Duncan, 282 F.3d 78 (2d Cir.2002)—§ 24.2(a) n.5

Sanchez v. Mondragon, 858 F.2d 1462 (10th Cir.1988)—§§ 11.5(c) n.40; 11.5(f) n.101

Sanchez, People v., 161 Ill.App.3d 586, 113 Ill.Dec. 404, 515 N.E.2d 213 (1987)—§ 11.9(d) n.174

Sanchez, People v., 65 N.Y.2d 436, 492 N.Y.S.2d 577, 482 N.E.2d 56 (1985)—§ 24.2(d) n.39

Sanchez, People v., 125 Misc.2d 394, 479 N.Y.S.2d 602 (Sup.Ct.1984)— § 15.7(g) n.210

Sanchez, People v., 83 Cal. App. 3d Supp. l, 147 Cal.Rptr. 850 (1978)— § 24.8(b) n.29

Sanchez, People v., 65 Cal.2d 814, 56 Cal.Rptr. 648, 423 P.2d 800 (1967)—§ 10.5(a) n.9

Sanchez v. State, 142 P.3d 1134 (Wyo.2006)—§ 24.7(b) n.20

Sanchez, State v., _____ Kan. _____, 144 P.3d 718 (2006)—§ 9.6(a) n.36

Sanchez v. State, 165 S.W.3d 707 (Tex.Cr.App.2005)—§ 22.3(a) n.3

Sanchez, State v., 146 Wash.2d 339, 46 P.3d 774 (2002)—§ 21.2(d) n.165

Sanchez, State v., 130 N.M. 602, 28 P.3d 1143 (N.M.App.2001)—§ 26.10(b) n.26

Sanchez, State v., 129 N.M. 284, 6 P.3d 486 (2000)—§§ 22.3(e) n.272; 24.9(f) n.102

Sanchez, State v., 201 Wis.2d 219, 548 N.W.2d 69 (1996)—§ 11.10(d) n.168

Sanchez, State v., 120 N.M. 247, 901 P.2d 178 (1995)—§ 22.3(c) n.142

Sanchez, State v., 129 N.J. 261, 609 A.2d 400 (1992)—§ 6.4(f) n.121

Sanchez v. State, 707 S.W.2d 575 (Tex.Cr.App.1986)—§ 9.6(a) n.44

Sanchez v. State, 702 S.W.2d 258 (Tex.App.1985)—§ 24.2(a) n.22

Sanchez, United States v., 269 F.3d 1250 (11th Cir.2001)—§§ 19.3(a) n.88, 90, 98, 99, 103

Sanchez, United States v., 138 F.3d 1410 (11th Cir.1998)—§§ 5.2(a) n.6; 5.4(c) n.44

Sanchez, United States v., 156 F.3d 875 (8th Cir.1998)—§ 22.2(d) n.85

Sanchez, United States v., 74 F.3d 562 (5th Cir.1996)—§ 22.3(b) n.68

Sanchez v. United States, 50 F.3d 1448 (9th Cir.1995)—§§ 21.6(a) n.77; 24.3(b) n.77

Sanchez, United States v., 24 F.3d 1259 (10th Cir.1994)—§ 7.4(e) n.84

Sanchez v. United States, 782 F.2d 928 (11th Cir.1986)—§ 22.1(h) n.160

Sanchez, United States v., 509 F.2d 886 (6th Cir.1975)—§ 3.4(k) n.239

Sanchez-Berrios, United States v., 424 F.3d 65 (1st Cir.2005)—§ 5.3(d) n.42

Sanchez-Cervantes, United States v., 282 F.3d 664 (9th Cir.2002)— § 28.9(b) n.35

Sanchez-Llamas v. Oregon, _____ U.S. _____, 126 S.Ct. 2669, 165 L.Ed.2d 557 (2006)—§§ 1.7(c) n.40; 3.1(b) n.25; 6.2(c) n.86; 6.8(d) n.87; 28.3(b) n.65; 28.4(a) n.6

Sanchez-Lopez, United States v., 879 F.2d 541 (9th Cir.1989)— §§ 19.3(c) n.198; 22.2(d) n.77

Sanchez-Sotelo, United States v., 8 F.3d 202 (5th Cir.1993)—§ 24.7(e) n.72

Sanders v. City of Birmingham, 669 So.2d 236 (Ala.App.1995)— § 19.5(c) n.51

Sanders v. Commonwealth, 801 S.W.2d 665 (Ky.1990)—§ 22.3(c) n.133

Sanders v. Craven, 488 F.2d 478 (9th Cir.1973)—§ 10.2(d) n.48

Sanders v. Lamarque, 357 F.3d 943 (9th Cir.2004)—§ 24.9(f) n.104

Sanders, People v., 342 Ill.App.3d 374, 276 Ill.Dec. 976, 795 N.E.2d 329 (2003)—§ 25.2(d) n.25

Sanders, People v., 11 Cal.4th 475, 46 Cal.Rptr.2d 751, 905 P.2d 420 (1995)—§§ 16.3(b) n.26; 23.2(a) n.54

Sanders, People v., 58 A.D.2d 525, 395 N.Y.S.2d 190 (1977)—§ 7.2(b) n.21

Sanders v. Robert Bosch Corp., 38 F.3d 736 (4th Cir.1994)—§ 4.6(b) n.46

Sanders v. State, 280 Ga. 780, 631 S.E.2d 344 (2006)—§ 13.3(c) n.40

Sanders, State v., 269 Neb. 895, 697 N.W.2d 657 (Neb.2005)—§ 22.3(b) n.55

Sanders, State v., 92 Ohio St.3d 245, 750 N.E.2d 90 (2001)—§§ 22.3(c) n.100, 155

Sanders, State v., 341 S.C. 386, 534 S.E.2d 696 (2000)—§ 11.9(c) n.117

Sanders, State v., 294 Mont. 539, 982 P.2d 1015 (1999)—§ 21.2(d) n.167

Sanders, State v., 258 Kan. 409, 904 P.2d 951 (1997)—§ 22.3(d) n.240

Sanders, State v., 263 Kan. 317, 949 P.2d 1084 (1997)—§ 22.3(d) n.250

Sanders v. State, 669 So.2d 356 (1996)—§ 19.5(c) n.51

Sanders, State v., 331 Md. 378, 628 A.2d 209 (1993)—§§ 21.3(e) n.271; 21.4(g) n.234

Sanders, State v., 260 N.J.Super. 491, 616 A.2d 1345 (1992)—§§ 11.9(c) n.137; 11.9(d) n.186, 233

Sanders, State v., 235 Neb. 183, 455 N.W.2d 108 (1990)—§§ 7.4(d) n.68, 72

Sanders v. State, 585 A.2d 117 (Del.1990)—§§ 2.12(c) n.139, 155, 157

Sanders, State v., 95 N.C.App. 56, 381 S.E.2d 827 (1989)—§ 5.3(c) n.30

Sanders v. State, 179 Ga.App. 168, 345 S.E.2d 677 (1986)—§ 21.5(a) n.1

Sanders v. State, 57 Md.App. 156, 469 A.2d 476 (1984)—§ 2.12(c) n.175

Sanders v. State, 429 So.2d 245 (1983)—§§ 2.12(c) n.144; 2.12(d) n.189

Sanders v. State, 612 P.2d 1363 (Okla.Crim.App.1980)—§ 11.4(c) n.87

Sanders, State v., 35 Or.App. 503, 582 P.2d 22 (1978)—§ 26.6(e) n.82

Sanders v. State, 259 Ark. 329, 532 S.W.2d 752 (1976)—§ 9.4(a) n.27

Sanders v. State, 69 Wis.2d 242, 230 N.W.2d 845 (1975)—§ 16.3(g) n.108

Sanders, State v., 8 Wash.App. 306, 506 P.2d 892 (1973)—§ 3.6(f) n.146

Sanders v. State, 85 Ind. 318 (1882)— § 28.1(c) n.26

Sanders v. United States, 252 F.3d 1329 (Fed.Cir.2001)—§§ 12.4(d) n.61; 21.2(e) n.281

Sanders, United States v., 211 F.3d 711 (2d Cir.2000)—§§ 13.5(a) n.5, 7

Sanders v. United States, 567 A.2d 55 (D.C.App.1989)—§ 6.9(g) n.159

Sanders, United States v., 669 F.2d 609 (9th Cir.1982)—§ 18.4(c) n.68

Sanders v. United States, 339 A.2d 373 (D.C.1975)—§ 3.5(a) n.65

Sanders v. United States, 373 U.S. 1, 83 S.Ct. 1068, 10 L.Ed.2d 148 (1963)—§§ 28.2(c) n.40, 42; 28.5(c) n.69; 28.5(d) n.77

Sanders v. Woodford, 373 F.3d 1054 (9th Cir.2004)—§ 22.2(d) n.75

Sanderson, United States v., 595 F.2d 1021 (5th Cir.1979)—§ 21.5(d) n.101

Sanders, United States ex rel. v. Rowe, 460 F.Supp. 1128 (N.D.Ill.1978)— § 6.4(e) n.68

Sandin v. Conner, 515 U.S. 472, 115 S.Ct. 2293, 132 L.Ed.2d 418 (1995)—§§ 26.1(e) n.113; 26.2(c) n.41, 61, 80

Sandini, United States v., 888 F.2d 300 (3d Cir.1989)—§§ 17.2(b) n.39; 17.2(e) n.121

Sandini, United States v., 816 F.2d 869 (3d Cir.1987)—§ 26.6(d) n.58

Sandler, Commonwealth v., 368 Mass. 729, 335 N.E.2d 903 (1975)— § 9.1(b) n.54

Sandles, United States v., 23 F.3d 1121 (7th Cir.1994)—§§ 11.5(c) n.41, 55; 11.5(d) n.67

Sandor, State v., 218 W.Va. 469, 624 S.E.2d 906 (2005)—§ 11.5(c) n.53

Sandoval v. Calderon, 241 F.3d 765 (9th Cir.2000)—§§ 17.1(d) n.53; 24.7(e) n.61; 26.4(b) n.17

Sandoval, People v., 974 P.2d 1012 (Colo. Ct. App. 1998)—§ 26.7(c) n.34

Sandoval, People v., 4 Cal.4th 155, 14 Cal.Rptr.2d 342, 841 P.2d 862 (1992)—§§ 17.1(c) n.45; 17.1(d) n.52

Sandoval, People v., 733 P.2d 319 (Colo.1987)—§ 22.3(c) n.113

Sandoval, United States v., 390 F.3d 1294 (10th Cir.2004)—§§ 21.5(a) n.41, 42

Sandoval-Lopez, United States v., 409 F.3d 1193 (9th Cir.2005)— § 11.6(b) n.80

Sandoval-Lopez, United States v., 122 F.3d 797 (9th Cir.1997)— §§ 21.2(b) n.90; 21.2(e) n.352; 21.5(e) n.150

Sandoval-Mendoza, United States v., 472 F.3d 645 (9th Cir.2006)— § 5.2(a) n.9

Sandstrom v. Montana, 442 U.S. 510, 99 S.Ct. 2450, 61 L.Ed.2d 39 (1979)— § 2.7(a) n.43

Sandstrom, State v., 225 Kan. 717, 595 P.2d 324 (1979)—§ 20.5(f) n.77

Sandstrom, People ex rel. v. District Court, 904 P.2d 874 (Colo.1995)— §§ 3.3(c) n.138; 27.4(d) n.51

Sandvik v. United States, 177 F.3d 1269 (11th Cir.1999)—§ 28.9(b) n.50

Sandy, Commonwealth v., 257 Va. 87, 509 S.E.2d 492 (1999)—§ 21.2(f) n.383

Sandy v. Fifth Judicial Dist. Ct., 113 Nev. 435, 935 P.2d 1148 (1997)— § 27.4(c) n.28

Sanford v. State, 331 Ark. 334, 962 S.W.2d 335 (1998)—§§ 6.9(b) n.20, 27; 22.3(d) n.250

Sanford, United States v., 429 U.S. 14, 97 S.Ct. 20, 50 L.Ed.2d 17 (1976)—§§ 25.1(d) n.83; 25.3(d) n.35

Sanges, United States v., 144 U.S. 310, 12 S.Ct. 609, 36 L.Ed. 445 (1892)—§ 27.3(b) n.11

Sangineto-Miranda, United States v., 859 F.2d 1501 (6th Cir.1988)—§§ 4.6(b) n.49; 4.6(l) n.205; 9.5(b) n.42; 22.3(d) n.216

Saniti, United States v., 604 F.2d 603 (9th Cir.1979)—§ 7.4(f) n.106

San Jose Charter of Hells Angels v. San Jose, 402 F.3d 962 (9th Cir.2005)—§ 3.4(k) n.219

San Juan-Cruz, United States v., 314 F.3d 384 (9th Cir.2002)—§ 6.8(a) n.16

San Juan Star Co., In re, 662 F.2d 108 (1st Cir.1981)—§ 23.1(b) n.82

Sanna v. Dipaolo, 265 F.3d 1 (1st Cir.2001)—§ 6.9(f) n.127

San Pedro v. United States, 79 F.3d 1065 (11th Cir.1996)—§ 21.2(e) n.329

Sansome, State v., 133 Miss. 428, 97 So. 753 (1923)—§ 15.1(d) n.219

Sansone v. United States, 380 U.S. 343, 85 S.Ct. 1004, 13 L.Ed.2d 882 (1965)—§ 24.8(f) n.97

Sansui v. Gonzales, 474 F.3d 341 (6th Cir.2007)—§ 21.4(d) n.134

Santa, United States v., 180 F.3d 20 (2d Cir.1999)—§ 3.1(h) n.215

Santa Clara County v. Southern Pacific Railroad Co., 118 U.S. 394, 6 S.Ct. 1132, 30 L.Ed. 118 (1886)—§ 15.1(b) n.20

Santa Cruz, City of v. Municipal Court, 49 Cal.3d 74, 260 Cal.Rptr. 520, 776 P.2d 222 (1989)—§ 27.4(c) n.30

Santamaria v. Horsley, 133 F.3d 1242 (9th Cir.1998)—§ 17.4(a) n.34

Santana, Commonwealth v., 420 Mass. 205, 649 N.E.2d 717 (1995)—§ 3.2(f) n.180

Santana, State v., 133 N.H. 798, 586 A.2d 77 (1991)—§ 3.6(e) n.111

Santana, United States v., 6 F.3d 1 (1st Cir.1993)—§ 5.4(c) n.36

Santana, United States v., 427 U.S. 38, 96 S.Ct. 2406, 49 L.Ed.2d 300 (1976)—§§ 3.6(a) n.16, 34

Santaniello, Commonwealth v., 369 Mass. 606, 341 N.E.2d 259 (1976)—§ 8.9(a) n.6

Santelli, State v., 159 Vt. 442, 621 A.2d 222 (1992)—§ 22.3(c) n.104

Santeramo, United States v., 45 F.3d 622 (2d Cir.1995)—§ 19.3(a) n.47

Santiago, In re, 533 F.2d 727 (1st Cir.1976)—§§ 8.8(h) n.181; 8.11(d) n.75

Santiago, Commonwealth v., 394 Mass. 25, 474 N.E.2d 154 (1985)—§ 21.2(g) n.405

Santiago, State v., 275 Conn. 192, 881 A.2d 222 (2005)—§ 17.4(a) n.46

Santiago v. State, 644 N.W.2d 425 (Minn.2002)—§ 17.3(b) n.27

Santiago, State v., 245 Conn. 301, 715 A.2d 1 (1998)—§§ 6.9(e) n.85; 14.4(c) n.74; 14.4(e) n.101; 24.9(f) n.86

Santiago, State v., 240 Conn. 97, 689 A.2d 1108 (1997)—§ 17.4(b) n.133

Santiago, State v., 206 Wis.2d 3, 556 N.W.2d 687 (1996)—§ 6.8(a) n.36

Santiago, United States v., 410 F.3d 193 (5th Cir.2005)—§§ 10.6(a) n.2; 21.6(b) n.96

Santiago, United States v., 229 F.3d 313 (1st Cir.2000)—§ 21.5(a) n.40

Santiago, United States v., 46 F.3d 885 (9th Cir.1995)—§§ 20.3(a) n.12; 24.7(e) n.61

Santiago, United States v., 826 F.2d 499 (7th Cir.1987)—§ 12.1(a) n.20

Santiago-Martinez, United States v., 58 F.3d 422 (9th Cir.1995)—§ 22.3(d) n.202

Santiago Soto, United States v., 825 F.2d 616 (1st Cir.1997)—§§ 21.3(f) n.432; 25.1(d) n.71

Santiago (WOKR-TV), People v., 185 Misc.2d 138, 712 N.Y.S.2d 244 (2000)—§ 23.3(b) n.27

Santillanes, State v., 130 N.M. 464, 27 P.3d 456 (2001)—§ 13.7(a) n.29

Santillanes v. State, 115 N.W. 215, 849 P.2d 358 (1993)—§ 1.2(b) n.5

Santillanes, United States v., 848 F.2d 1103 (10th Cir.1988)—§§ 3.8(b) n.20; 3.8(e) n.215

Santo, United States v., 225 F.3d 92 (1st Cir.2000)—§ 21.4(d) n.102

Santobello v. New York, 404 U.S. 257, 92 S.Ct. 495, 30 L.Ed.2d 427 (1971)—§§ 1.10(a) n.17; 1.10(c) n.84; 2.7(a) n.32; 6.2(c) n.94; 13.5(b) n.29; 13.6(d) n.52; 21.1(b) n.33; 21.2(b) n.29; 21.2(d) n.140; 21.2(e) n.279, 315; 21.2(g) n.397; 21.3(c) n.186; 21.3(f) n.429; 21.5(d) n.99; 21.5(e) n.110

Santobello, People v., 39 A.D.2d 654, 331 N.Y.S.2d 776 (1972)— § 21.2(e) n.300

Santoli, Commonwealth v., 424 Mass. 837, 680 N.E.2d 1116 (1997)— §§ 7.5(a) n.4; 7.5(b) n.23

Santora, United States v., 583 F.2d 453 n.10 (9thCir. 1978)—§ 4.6(l) n.192

Santoro, United States v., 647 F.Supp. 153 (E.D.N.Y.1986)—§§ 15.2(i) n.222, 224

Santos v. Kolb, 880 F.2d 941 (7th Cir.1989)—§ 21.3(b) n.66

Santos, People v., 147 Cal.App.4th 965, 55 Cal.Rptr.3d 1 (2007)—§ 24.2(a) n.6

Santos, United States v., 201 F.3d 953 (7th Cir.2000)—§ 11.4(c) n.88

Santos-Garcia, United States v., 313 F.3d 1073 (8th Cir.2002)—§ 6.2(c) n.100

Santosky v. Kramer, 455 U.S. 745, 102 S.Ct. 1388, 71 L.Ed.2d 599 (1982)—§ 1.5(e) n.221

Santtini, United States v., 963 F.2d 585 (3d Cir.1992)—§ 27.4(d) n.55

Santucci, State v., 210 W.Va. 483, 557 S.E.2d 890 (2001)—§ 22.1(h) n.134

Santucci, United States v., 674 F.2d 624 (7th Cir.1982)—§ 8.8(g) n.174

Sanwick, State v., 713 P.2d 707 (Utah 1986)—§ 26.5(a) n.6

Saperstein, In re, 30 N.J.Super. 373, 104 A.2d 842 (1954)—§§ 8.1(a) n.3; 8.2(b) n.20

Sapia, People v., 41 N.Y.2d 160, 391 N.Y.S.2d 93, 359 N.E.2d 688 (1976)—§ 24.3(i) n.188

Sapienza v. Vincent, 534 F.2d 1007 (2d Cir.1976)—§ 28.5(a) n.19

Sapio v. State, 223 So.2d 759 (Fla.App.1969)—§ 11.2(g) n.298

Sapp, People v., 31 Cal.4th 240, 2 Cal.Rptr.3d 554, 73 P.3d 433 (2003)—§ 6.9(f) n.139

Sapp, State v., 105 Ohio St.3d 104, 822 N.E.2d 1239 (2004)—§ 6.2(c) n.152

Sa'ra, People v., 117 P.3d 51 (Colo.App.2004)—§§ 17.4(b) n.132; 18.4(d) n.95

Sarette, State v., 134 N.H. 133, 589 A.2d 125 (1991)—§ 21.5(a) n.35

Sargent, State v., 111 Wash.2d 641, 762 P.2d 1127 (1988)—§§ 6.4(e) n.103; 6.7(b) n.66; 6.10(c) n.49

Sarkissian, United States v., 841 F.2d 959 (9th Cir.1988)—§ 4.9(b) n.8

Sarmiento, United States v., 786 F.2d 665 (5th Cir.1986)—§§ 5.1(c) n.34; 21.6(b) n.84

Sarmiento, United States v., 744 F.2d 755 (11th Cir.1984)—§ 24.7(e) n.39

Sarno, United States v., 1998 WL 547302 (N.D.Ill.1998)—§ 11.7(e) n.65

Sarracino, United States v., 340 F.3d 1148 (10th Cir.2003)—§ 17.2(b) n.60

Sarsoun, United States v., 834 F.2d 1358 (7th Cir.1987)—§ 11.2(g) n.305

Sartain v. United States, 303 F.2d 859 (9th Cir.1962)—§ 3.10(e) n.172

Sartin, Commonwealth v., 708 A.2d 121 (Pa.Sup.1998)—§ 27.2(d) n.68

Sarvis, United States v., 523 F.2d 1177 (D.C.Cir.1975)—§ 18.2(d) n.64

Sassen, State v., 240 Neb. 773, 484 N.W.2d 469 (1992)—§ 3.1(d) n.98

Sasso, United States v., 59 F.3d 341 (2d Cir.1995)—§§ 24.3(c) n.101; 26.3(g) n.93

Deleted Sasso, United States v., 59 F.3d 341 (2d Cir.1995)—§ 26.3(g) n.93

Sassower v. Sheriff of Westchester County, 824 F.2d 184 (2d Cir.1987)—§ 13.3(b) n.20

Satcher v. Commonwealth, 244 Va. 220, 421 S.E.2d 821 (1992)—§§ 17.1(a) n.15; 17.1(d) n.53

Saterlee v. Wolfenburger, 453 F.3d 362 (6th Cir.2006)—§ 28.2(b) n.31

Saternus, State v., 127 Wis.2d 460, 381 N.W.2d 290 (1986)—§§ 5.2(a) n.4; 5.3(d) n.41

Sattazahn v. Pennsylvania, 537 U.S. 101, 123 S.Ct. 732, 154 L.Ed.2d 588 (2003)—§§ 19.3(a) n.20; 25.2(e) n.35; 25.4(d) n.45; 26.7(a) n.10

Satter v. Leapley, 977 F.2d 1259 (8th Cir.1992)—§ 25.4(c) n.34

Satter v. Solem, 422 N.W.2d 425 (S.D.1988)—§ 6.8(b) n.60

Satterfield v. Johnson, 434 F.3d 185 (3d Cir.2006)—§ 28.5(b) n.48

Satterfield, State v., 182 W.Va. 365, 387 S.E.2d 832 (1989)—§§ 13.2(a) n.4; 13.7(c) n.45

Satterfield, United States v., 743 F.2d 827 (11th Cir.1984)—§§ 9.3(e) n.71, 72, 75; 26.6(c) n.40

Satterfield, United States v., 572 F.2d 687 (9th Cir.1978)—§ 7.2(b) n.25

Satterfield v. Zahradnick, 572 F.2d 443 (4th Cir.1978)—§ 11.2(e) n.141

Satterwhite v. Texas, 486 U.S. 249, 108 S.Ct. 1792, 100 L.Ed.2d 284 (1988)—§§ 27.6(d) n.81, 146; 27.6(e) n.156

Saucier v. Katz, 533 U.S. 194, 121 S.Ct. 2151, 150 L.Ed.2d 272 (2001)— § 3.1(k) n.274

Sauerheber v. State, 698 N.E.2d 796 (Ind.1998)—§§ 6.9(g) n.167, 200; 18.2(b) n.16

Saul, Commonwealth v., 260 Mass. 97, 156 N.E. 679 (1927)—§ 16.1(d) n.137

Sauls, State v., 356 N.W.2d 516 (Iowa 1984)—§ 17.2(d) n.93

Saulsbury, United States ex rel. v. Greer, 702 F.2d 651 (7th Cir.1983)— § 9.6(a) n.36

Saunders, Commonwealth v., 50 Mass.App.Ct. 865, 744 N.E.2d 74 (2001)—§ 11.1(a) n.27

Saunders v. Lowry, 58 F.2d 158 (5th Cir.1932)—§ 13.4(a) n.4

Saunders, State v., 992 P.2d 951 (Utah 1999)—§ 22.3(a) n.23

Saunders, State v., 75 N.J. 200, 381 A.2d 333 (1977)—§ 2.12(c) n.157

Saunders, State v., 102 Ariz. 565, 435 P.2d 39 (1967)—§§ 6.6(e) n.59; 6.6(f) n.103

Saunders, United States v., 957 F.2d 1488 (8th Cir.1992)—§ 3.4(f) n.115

Saunders v. United States, 508 A.2d 92 (D.C.App.1986)—§ 26.10(d) n.86

Sauve, State v., 164 Vt. 134, 666 A.2d 1164 (1995)—§§ 13.2(c) n.59, 61, 62, 66

Sauve, State v., 159 Vt. 566, 621 A.2d 1296 (1993)—§§ 12.3(b) n.67, 71; 12.3(g) n.160

Savage v. Estelle, 924 F.2d 1459 (9th Cir.1990)—§§ 11.5(d) n.80, 81

Savage, United States v., 978 F.2d 1136 (9th Cir.1992)—§ 21.2(f) n.383

Savage, United States v., 561 F.2d 554 (4th Cir.1977)—§ 21.5(a) n.29

Savage, United States v., 564 F.2d 728 (5th Cir.1977)—§ 4.6(l) n.187

Savard, State v., 659 A.2d 1265 (Me.1995)—§ 17.4(b) n.124

Savell, United States v., 546 F.2d 43 (5th Cir.1977)—§ 6.8(a) n.29

Savides, United States v., 787 F.2d 751 (1st Cir.1986)—§ 15.4(f) n.145

Savinon-Acosta, United States v., 232 F.3d 265 (1st Cir.2000)—§ 21.4(b) n.59

Savoca, United States v., 739 F.2d 220 (6th Cir.1984)—§ 3.3(a) n.12

Savoie, State v., 128 N.J.Super. 329, 320 A.2d 164 (1974)—§ 13.4(c) n.109

Savory, United States ex rel. v. Lane, 832 F.2d 1011 (7th Cir.1987)—§ 9.6(a) n.48

Savva, State v., 159 Vt. 75, 616 A.2d 774 (1991)—§ 3.7(a) n.16

Sawyer, People v., 57 N.Y.2d 12, 453 N.Y.S.2d 418, 438 N.E.2d 1133 (1982)—§§ 11.4(b) n.27; 11.4(d) n.118; 11.5(c) n.40, 42, 49, 56

Sawyer v. Smith, 497 U.S. 227, 110 S.Ct. 2822, 111 L.Ed.2d 193 (1990)—§§ 2.9(f) n.127; 2.11(e) n.55; 28.6(c) n.15; 28.6(d) n.25; 28.6(e) n.50, 59

Sawyer, State v., 156 S.W.3d 531 (Tenn.2005)—§ 6.7(c) n.133

Sawyer, State v., 227 Conn. 566, 630 A.2d 1064 (1993)—§ 24.8(d) n.46

Sawyer, United States v., 239 F.3d 31 (1st Cir.2001)—§§ 28.9(a) n.18, 23

Sawyer, United States v., 210 F.2d 169 (3d Cir.1954)—§ 5.1(a) n.3

Sawyer v. Whitley, 505 U.S. 333, 112 S.Ct. 2514, 120 L.Ed.2d 269 (1992)—§§ 2.9(f) n.119, 122; 28.4(e) n.86; 28.7(c) n.19

Saxena, United States v., 229 F.3d 1 (1st Cir.2000)—§§ 21.2(d) n.174; 21.5(c) n.83

Saxton, 30 Utah, State v., 2d 456, 519 P.2d 1340 (1974)—§ 16.4(c) n.49

Sayakhom, United States v., 186 F.3d 928 (9th Cir.1999)—§ 21.2(h) n.419

Sayan, United States v., 968 F.2d 55 (D.C.Cir.1992)—§ 11.9(d) n.222

Sayavong, People v., 83 N.Y.2d 702, 613 N.Y.S.2d 343, 635 N.E.2d 1213 (1994)—§§ 15.7(h) n.226, 230

Sayerwinnie, State v., 157 P.3d 137 (Okla.Cr.App.2007)—§ 27.3(c) n.50

Saykally, United States v., 777 F.2d 1286 (7th Cir.1985)—§ 26.10(b) n.35

Saylor, State v., 223 Neb. 694, 392 N.W.2d 789 (1986)—§ 6.6(c) n.31

Sayre, State v., 566 N.W.2d 193 (Iowa 1997)—§ 21.6(c) n.118

Sazenski, United States v., 833 F.2d 741 (8th Cir.1987)—§ 17.2(a) n.14

Sbordone, Commonwealth v., 424 Mass. 802, 678 N.E.2d 1184 (1997)—§§ 3.4(j) n.206, 209

Scaife, United States v., 749 F.2d 338 (6th Cir.1984)—§§ 1.2(c) n.133; 17.3(d) n.42; 18.3(b) n.7

Scales, State v., 261 Kan. 734, 933 P.2d 737 (1997)—§ 26.4(d) n.54

Scales, State v., 518 N.W.2d 587 (Minn.1994)—§ 6.8(c) n.64

Scales v. State, 13 Md.App. 474, 284 A.2d 45 (1971)—§ 3.2(b) n.35

Scales, United States v., 903 F.2d 765 (10th Cir.1990)—§§ 3.1(c) n.59, 65

Scalf, United States v., 708 F.2d 1540 (10th Cir.1983)—§§ 6.9(f) n.141, 143

Scalissi v. State, 759 N.E.2d 618 (Ind.2001)—§ 6.2(c) n.181

Scalzitti, United States v., 578 F.2d 507 (3d Cir.1978)—§ 22.1(h) n.160

Scanlon, State v., 174 Mont. 139, 569 P.2d 368 (Mont.1976)—§ 15.5(c) n.118

Scarborough v. Principi, 541 U.S. 401, 124 S.Ct. 1856, 158 L.Ed.2d 674 (2004)—§ 13.5(h) n.147

Scarborough v. United States, 431 U.S. 563, 97 S.Ct. 1963, 52 L.Ed.2d 582 (1977)—§§ 1.2(c) n.138, 140

Scardamaglia, Commonwealth v., 410 Mass. 375, 573 N.E.2d 5 (1991)—§ 9.2(b) n.15

Scarfo, United States v., 180 F.Supp.2d 572 (D.N.J. 2001)—§ 4.6(a) n.20

Scarfo, United States v., 850 F.2d 1015 (3d Cir.1988)—§ 22.3(b) n.68

Scarlet, State v., 800 So.2d 220 (Fla.2001)—§ 26.10(c) n.66

Scarpa v. DuBois, 38 F.3d 1 (1st Cir.1994)—§§ 11.10(d) n.171, 189

Scarpa, United States v., 897 F.2d 63 (2d Cir.1990)—§§ 6.4(f) n.118; 6.9(c) n.66; 6.9(d) n.70

Scasino, United States v., 513 F.2d 47 (5th Cir.1975)—§ 4.6(e) n.88

Scelza, State v., 134 Vt. 385, 359 A.2d 660 (1976)—§§ 21.5(a) n.27, 55

Schaaf, State v., 169 Ariz. 323, 819 P.2d 909 (1991)—§ 18.4(c) n.63

Schabert, State v., 218 Minn. 1, 15 N.W.2d 585 (1944)—§ 6.2(b) n.37

Schad v. Arizona, 501 U.S. 624, 111 S.Ct. 2491, 115 L.Ed.2d 555 (1991)—§§ 2.7(a) n.45; 2.7(c) n.133, 139, 156, 159, 161, 165, 190, 195, 228; 24.8(f) n.90; 24.10(c) n.36; 26.1(b) n.25

Schade v. State, 53 P.3d 551 (Wyo.2002)—§§ 18.5(c) n.75; 21.2(d) n.141

Schaefer, State v., 157 Vt. 339, 599 A.2d 337 (1991)—§ 23.1(d) n.196

Schaeffer, State v., 782 S.W.2d 68 (Mo.App.1989)—§ 14.2(g) n.107

Schafer, People v., 946 P.2d 938 (Colo.1997)—§ 9.1(b) n.40

Schafer, State ex rel. v. Fenton, 104 Ariz. 160, 449 P.2d 939 (1969)—§ 13.2(c) n.72

Schaffer v. United States, 362 U.S. 511, 80 S.Ct. 945, 4 L.Ed.2d 921 (1960)—§§ 17.3(c) n.33; 17.3(d) n.53

Schall v. Martin, 467 U.S. 253, 104 S.Ct. 2403, 81 L.Ed.2d 207 (1984)—§§ 12.3(f) n.132; 12.4(b) n.49

Schamberg, State v., 146 N.J.Super. 559, 370 A.2d 482 (1977)—§§ 15.6(a) n.28; 15.6(d) n.123; 15.7(b) n.27, 33

Schandl, United States v., 947 F.2d 462 (11th Cir.1991)—§ 22.3(b) n.80

Schappel, United States v., 445 F.2d 716 (D.C.Cir.1971)—§ 11.2(e) n.227

Scharf, United States v., 267 F.Supp. 19 (S.D.N.Y.1967)—§ 20.3(b) n.47

Scharfman, United States v., 448 F.2d 1352 (2d Cir.1971)—§ 3.4(f) n.109

Scheckel v. State, 655 N.E.2d 506 (Ind.1995)—§§ 21.1(e) n.85, 93, 98

Scheffer, United States v., 523 U.S. 303, 118 S.Ct. 1261, 140 L.Ed.2d 413 (1998)—§ 24.4(a) n.5

Schell, United States v., 775 F.2d 559 (4th Cir.1985)—§§ 22.5(a) n.3; 22.5(b) n.14

Schell v. Witek, 218 F.3d 1017 (9th Cir.2000)—§§ 11.4(b) n.36, 40; 11.4(c) n.70, 87, 88

Schellert v. State, 569 S.W.2d 735 (Mo.1978)—§ 21.2(d) n.162

Schenkman, People v., 46 N.Y.2d 232, 413 N.Y.S.2d 284, 385 N.E.2d 1214 (1978)—§ 8.8(h) n.189

Scher v. United States, 305 U.S. 251, 59 S.Ct. 174, 83 L.Ed. 151 (1938)—§ 3.7(c) n.44

Schermerhorn, State v., 211 W.Va. 376, 566 S.E.2d 263 (2002)—§ 22.3(c) n.104

Schertz, State v., 330 N.W.2d 1 (Iowa 1983)—§ 19.5(b) n.32

Scherzer, State v., 301 N.J.Super. 363, 694 A.2d 196 (1997)—§§ 15.2(d) n.93; 15.5(c) n.108; 15.7(f) n.177

Scheve v. United States, 184 F.2d 695 (D.C.Cir.1950)—§ 17.2(a) n.24

Schick v. United States, 195 U.S. 65, 24 S.Ct. 826, 49 L.Ed. 99 (1904)—§ 22.1(b) n.38

Schier, United States v., 438 F.3d 1104 (11th Cir.2006)—§ 24.3(c) n.85

Schiff, United States v., 876 F.2d 272 (2d Cir.1989)—§ 26.9(b) n.53

Schilb v. Kuebel, 404 U.S. 357, 92 S.Ct. 479, 30 L.Ed.2d 502 (1971)—§§ 2.6(b) n.35, 36; 2.6(d) n.99; 12.2(a) n.1; 12.2(b) n.36; 12.3(c) n.79

Schillberg, State ex rel. v. Cascade District Court, 94 Wash.2d 772, 621 P.2d 115 (1980)—§ 13.6(c) n.44

Schilleci, United States v., 545 F.2d 519 (5th Cir.1977)—§ 24.8(a) n.21

Schillerstrom v. State, 180 Ariz. 468, 885 P.2d 156 (1994)—§ 17.4(b) n.125

Schimmel, United States v., 950 F.2d 432 (7th Cir.1991)—§ 26.10(b) n.19

Schindelar v. Michaud, 411 F.2d 80 (10th Cir.1969)—§ 3.5(a) n.40

Schindele, State v., 540 N.W.2d 139 (N.D.1995)—§ 27.3(c) n.48

Schinzing, State v., 342 N.W.2d 105 (Minn.1983)—§ 1.8(f) n.103

Schipani, United States v., 315 F.Supp. 253 (E.D.N.Y.1970)—§ 3.1(f) n.153

Schipani, United States v., 289 F.Supp. 43 (E.D.N.Y.1968)—§ 9.3(d) n.41

Schirber v. State, 142 P.3d 1169 (Wyo.2006)—§ 3.4(k) n.227

Schiro v. Farley, 510 U.S. 222, 114 S.Ct. 783, 127 L.Ed.2d 47 (1994)—§§ 17.4(a) n.20; 26.7(a) n.11

Schlagenhauf v. Holder, 379 U.S. 104, 85 S.Ct. 234, 13 L.Ed.2d 152 (1964)—§ 27.4(b) n.18

Schlansky, United States v., 709 F.2d 1079 (6th Cir.1983)—§ 8.13(a) n.17

Schledwitz v. United States, 169 F.3d 1003 (6th Cir.1999)—§ 24.3(b) n.36

Schleis, United States v., 582 F.2d 1166 (8th Cir.1978)—§ 3.5(e) n.197

Schleiss v. State, 71 Wis.2d 733, 239 N.W.2d 68 (1976)—§ 17.4(a) n.45

Schlette, United States v., 842 F.2d 1574 (9th Cir.1988)—§§ 23.1(d) n.202; 26.5(c) n.59

Schlicher v. (NFN) Peters, I & I, 103 F.3d 940 (10th Cir.1996)—§§ 3.2(g) n.198, 199

Schlick v. Superior Court, 4 Cal.4th 310, 14 Cal.Rptr.2d 406, 841 P.2d 926 (1992)—§ 10.6(c) n.31

Schlund, State v., 249 Neb. 173, 542 N.W.2d 421 (1996)—§ 27.2(c) n.62

Schlup v. Delo, 513 U.S. 298, 115 S.Ct. 851, 130 L.Ed.2d 808 (1995)—§§ 1.5(e) n.206; 2.9(f) n.119, 122; 28.3(e) n.99; 28.4(e) n.75; 28.7(c) n.20

Schmerber v. California, 384 U.S. 757, 86 S.Ct. 1826, 16 L.Ed.2d 908 (1966)—§§ 2.4(f) n.189, 190; 2.10(b) n.16; 2.10(d) n.105, 106, 118, 137, 140, 158; 3.2(a) n.2; 3.2(b) n.78; 3.3(b) n.40; 3.4(a) n.10, 11; 3.5(c) n.127; 3.5(d) n.169; 3.6(a) n.23; 3.9(b) n.10, 18; 3.9(f) n.103; 6.7(b) n.34; 7.2(a) n.1; 7.2(c) n.30; 7.3(a) n.2; 8.7(d) n.73, 74; 8.12(d) n.42

Schmick, State v., 62 Or.App. 227, 660 P.2d 693 (1983)—§§ 11.3(c) n.59, 60, 66; 11.4(c) n.80

Schmid, State v., 487 N.W.2d 539 (Minn.App.1992)—§§ 24.3(e) n.128, 130

Schmid, State v., 84 N.J. 535, 423 A.2d 615 (1980)—§ 2.12(b) n.107

Schmidgall, United States v., 25 F.3d 1523 (11th Cir.1994)—§ 8.11(c) n.42

Schmidt, United States v., 935 F.2d 1440 (4th Cir.1991)—§ 13.4(a) n.27

Schmidt, United States v., 816 F.2d 1477 (10th Cir.1987)—§ 8.13(b) n.59

Schmidt, United States v., 760 F.2d 828 (7th Cir.1985)—§ 21.6(c) n.118

Schminkey, State v., 597 N.W.2d 785 (Iowa 1999)—§ 21.4(f) n.206

Schmitt, United States v., 784 F.2d 880 (8th Cir.1986)—§ 11.4(c) n.55

Schmoll, People v., 383 Ill. 280, 48 N.E.2d 933 (1943)—§ 3.10(f) n.194

Schmuck v. United States, 489 U.S. 705, 109 S.Ct. 1443, 103 L.Ed.2d 734 (1989)—§§ 24.8(e) n.51, 62; 24.8(f) n.119

Schmuck, United States v., 840 F.2d 384 (7th Cir.1988)—§ 24.8(e) n.82

Schneble v. Florida, 405 U.S. 427, 92 S.Ct. 1056, 31 L.Ed.2d 340 (1972)—§ 27.6(d) n.80

Schneckloth v. Bustamonte, 412 U.S. 218, 93 S.Ct. 2041, 36 L.Ed.2d 854 (1973)—§§ 2.6(d) n.94; 2.9(f) n.118, 119, 123; 2.9(h) n.215; 2.9(i) n.272; 3.9(c) n.38; 3.9(j) n.215; 3.10(a) n.7; 3.10(b) n.23; 9.4(b)

n.52; 10.4(c) n.26; 11.5(b) n.25; 28.2(b) n.28; 28.2(c) n.49, 50, 52, 60, 67; 28.2(d) n.86; 28.3(c) n.69

Schneider v. Lynaugh, 835 F.2d 570 (5th Cir.1988)—§ 6.7(b) n.105

Schneider, People v., 25 P.3d 755 (Colo.2001)—§§ 21.5(a) n.19, 50

Schneider, People v., 133 Colo. 173, 292 P.2d 982 (1956)—§ 8.10(d) n.88

Schneider v. State, 725 N.W.2d 516 (Minn.2007)—§ 22.4(c) n.29

Schneider, State v., 263 Neb. 318, 640 N.W.2d 8 (2002)—§ 21.4(d) n.138

Schneider, State v., 126 Idaho 624, 888 P.2d 798 (1995)—§§ 27.5(c) n.71, 83

Schneider, State v., 402 N.W.2d 779 (Minn.1987)—§§ 20.4(f) n.90, 92

Schneider, United States v., 395 F.3d 78 (2d Cir.2005)—§§ 13.5(h) n.148, 153, 159, 168, 175 to 177, 211

Schneiderhan, United States v., 404 F.3d 73 (1st Cir.2005)—§ 24.3(c) n.89

Schneiderman v. United States, 320 U.S. 118, 63 S.Ct. 1333, 87 L.Ed. 1796 (1943)—§ 26.10(c) n.46

Schnelle v. State, 103 S.W.3d 165 (Mo.App.2003)—§ 11.10(c) n.109

Schnorenberg v. United States, 23 F.2d 38 (7th Cir.1927)—§ 3.2(c) n.120

Schoelerman, State v., 315 N.W.2d 67 (Iowa 1982)—§§ 11.7(e) n.78, 80

Schoels v. State, 114 Nev. 981, 966 P.2d 735 (1998)—§ 21.4(a) n.12

Schoenwetter v. State, 931 So.2d 857 (Fla.2006)—§ 6.6(d) n.49

Schoffner, State v., 248 Mont. 260, 811 P.2d 548 (1991)—§ 3.3(d) n.168

Scholl, State v., 227 Neb. 572, 419 N.W.2d 137 (1988)—§§ 21.3(b) n.45, 60

Scholl, United States v., 166 F.3d 964 (9th Cir.1999)—§ 20.6(c) n.74

Schonbrun, United States ex rel. v. Commanding Officer, 403 F.2d 371 (2d Cir.1968)—§ 13.3(a) n.5

Schoolcraft, United States v., 879 F.2d 64 (3d Cir.1989)—§ 13.5(a) n.5

Schoondermark, People v., 759 P.2d 715 (Colo.1988)—§ 9.4(b) n.73

Schoonover, State v., 293 Mont. 54, 973 P.2d 230 (1999)—§ 21.2(d) n.177

Schopp, State v., 653 So.2d 1016 (Fla.1995)—§ 20.6(b) n.18

Schorr v. State, 499 P.2d 450 (Okla.Crim.App.1972)—§ 3.10(b) n.70

Schram, People v., 283 Ill.App.3d 1056, 220 Ill.Dec. 225, 672 N.E.2d 1237 (1996)—§ 27.2(c) n.31

Schrantz, People v., 50 Mich.App. 227, 213 N.W.2d 257 (1973)—§ 20.4(e) n.80

Schreane, United States v., 331 F.3d 548 (6th Cir.2003)—§§ 18.2(c) n.51; 18.2(d) n.67

Schrier v. Halford, 60 F.3d 1309 (8th Cir.1995)—§§ 11.2(f) n.241, 244

Schriro v. Landrigan, _____ U.S. _____, 127 S.Ct. 1933, 167 L.Ed.2d 836 (2007)—§§ 11.6(a) n.62; 11.10(c) n.123; 28.7(c) n.22

Schriro v. Smith, 546 U.S. 6, 126 S.Ct. 7, 163 L.Ed.2d 6 (2005)—§ 26.4(h) n.156

Schriro v. Summerlin, 542 U.S. 348, 124 S.Ct. 2519, 159 L.Ed.2d 442 (2004)—§ 28.6(e) n.52

Schroeder, State v., 279 Kan. 104, 105 P.3d 1237 (2005)—§ 17.4(a) n.5

Schroeder, State v., 450 N.W.2d 423 (N.D.1990)—§ 3.3(a) n.8

Schroeder, State v., 112 So.2d 257 (Fla.1959)—§ 15.2(d) n.108

Schroff, State v., 206 Conn. 182, 536 A.2d 952 (1988)—§ 9.5(c) n.65

Schroff, State v., 198 Conn. 405, 503 A.2d 167 (1986)—§ 17.1(c) n.45

Schrushy, United States v., 366 F.Supp.2d 1134 (N.D.Ala.2005)—§ 8.8(h) n.184

Schuck v. State, 865 So.2d 1111 (Miss.2003)—§ 6.9(b) n.35

Schueler, State v., 488 A.2d 481 (Me.1985)—§ 6.2(c) n.109

Schuh, United States v., 289 F.3d 968 (7th Cir.2002)—§ 21.5(d) n.106

Schuler, United States v., 813 F.2d 978 (9th Cir.1987)—§ 24.5(b) n.33

Schultz v. Lainson, 234 Iowa 606, 13 N.W.2d 326 (1944)—§ 16.4(c) n.55

Schultz v. Page, 313 F.3d 1010 (7th Cir.2002)—§ 11.2(e) n.154

Schultz v. State, 497 N.E.2d 531 (Ind.1986)—§ 11.2(e) n.211

Schulz, State v., 409 N.W.2d 655 (S.D.1987)—§§ 21.4(f) n.174, 177

Schumacher v. Hopkins, 83 F.3d 1034 (8th Cir.1996)—§ 26.4(e) n.82

Schuman, United States v., 127 F.3d 815 (9th Cir.1997)—§§ 21.2(b) n.86; 27.5(c) n.63

Schumann, United States v., 861 F.2d 1234 (11th Cir.1988)—§ 27.5(a) n.3

Schuster, United States v., 769 F.2d 337 (6th Cir.1985)—§§ 21.3(f) n.426; 25.1(d) n.66

Schutter v. Soong, 76 Haw. 187, 873 P.2d 66 (1994)—§ 26.4(g) n.141

Schwab v. State, 814 So.2d 402 (Fla.2002)—§ 22.4(c) n.30

Schwander v. Blackburn, 750 F.2d 494 (5th Cir.1985)—§ 11.10(c) n.84

Schwartz, State v., 14 Ariz.App. 531, 484 P.2d 1060 (1971)—§ 19.4(b) n.10

Schwartz v. Texas, 344 U.S. 199, 73 S.Ct. 232, 97 L.Ed. 231 (1952)— § 4.5 n.2

Schwartz, United States v., 274 F.3d 1220 (9th Cir.2001)—§ 28.9(b) n.50

Schwartz v. United States Department of Justice, 494 F.Supp. 1268 (E.D.Pa.1980)—§§ 15.4(a) n.10; 15.4(g) n.164; 15.4(h) n.196

Schwartzmiller v. Winters, 99 Idaho 18, 576 P.2d 1052 (1978)—§ 24.3(b) n.65

Schwartz, State ex rel. v. Kennedy, 120 N.M. 619, 904 P.2d 1044 (1995)— § 17.4(b) n.124

Schwarz, United States v., 283 F.3d 76 (2d Cir.2002)—§§ 11.9(c) n.147; 11.9(d) n.175, 194, 199

Schwebke, State v., 253 Wis.2d 1, 644 N.W.2d 666 (2002)—§ 13.7(a) n.5

Schweitzer, State v., 171 N.J.Super. 82, 407 A.2d 1276 (1979)—§ 8.7(d) n.85

Schwimmer, United States v., 882 F.2d 22 (2d Cir.1989)—§§ 8.11(b) n.32; 8.11(c) n.47

Schwimmer v. United States, 232 F.2d 855 (8th Cir.1956)—§ 8.7(b) n.51

Sciortino v. Zampano, 385 F.2d 132 (2d Cir.1967)—§ 14.2(b) n.18

Scipio v. State, 928 So.2d 1138 (Fla.2006)—§§ 20.2(e) n.107, 108; 20.3(i) n.161; 20.6(b) n.18, 20

Scoggins, Commonwealth v., 439 Mass. 571, 789 N.E.2d 1080 (2003)— § 6.9(g) n.166

Scoggins v. State, 691 So.2d 1185 (Fla.App.1997)—§§ 24.9(d) n.38, 39

Scoggins v. State, 111 N.M. 122, 802 P.2d 631 (1990)—§ 24.3(e) n.133

Scoleri, Commonwealth v., 415 Pa. 218, 202 A.2d 521 (1964)—§ 21.3(b) n.120

Scopo, United States v., 19 F.3d 777 (2d Cir.1994)—§ 3.1(d) n.112

Scotland, State v., 58 Haw. 474, 572 P.2d 497 (1977)—§ 15.5(c) n.118

Scott v. Anderson, 958 F.Supp. 330 (N.D.Ohio 1997)—§ 28.8(b) n.16

Scott, Commonwealth v., 561 Pa. 617, 752 A.2d 871 (2000)—§ 6.8(b) n.50

Scott, Commonwealth v., 430 Mass. 351, 718 N.E.2d 1248 (1999)— § 6.8(c) n.78

Scott v. Harris, 127 S.Ct. 1769, 167 L.Ed.2d 686 (U.S. 2007)—§ 3.5(a) n.74

Scott v. Illinois, 440 U.S. 367, 99 S.Ct. 1158, 59 L.Ed.2d 383 (1979)— §§ 1.10(a) n.17; 2.6(d) n.95; 2.9(i) n.277, 279, 285; 11.1(a) n.14, 30; 11.1(d) n.125; 11.2(a) n.11, 29

Scott v. Louisiana, 934 F.2d 631 (5th Cir.1991)—§§ 11.2(e) n.190, 211

Scott, People v., 186 Ill.2d 283, 238 Ill.Dec. 36, 710 N.E.2d 833 (1999)—§ 22.1(h) n.134

Scott, People v., 15 Cal.4th 1188, 65 Cal.Rptr.2d 240, 939 P.2d 354 (1997)—§ 17.4(b) n.98

Scott, People v., 79 N.Y.2d 474, 583 N.Y.S.2d 920, 593 N.E.2d 1328 (1992)—§§ 2.12(c) n.177; 2.12(d) n.195; 3.2(d) n.155; 3.9(c) n.40

Scott, People v., 150 Misc.2d 297, 568 N.Y.S.2d 857 (Sup.Ct.1991)— § 15.7(f) n.170

Scott, People v., 70 N.Y.2d 420, 522 N.Y.S.2d 94, 516 N.E.2d 1208 (1987)—§ 22.3(d) n.212

Scott, People v., 124 Misc.2d 357, 476 N.Y.S.2d 999 (1984)—§ 15.2(c) n.81

Scott, People v., 70 A.D.2d 601, 416 N.Y.S.2d 83 (1979)—§ 15.7(d) n.85

Scott, People v., 21 Cal.3d 284, 145 Cal.Rptr. 876, 578 P.2d 123 (1978)—§ 3.5(d) n.168

Scott, People v., 93 Misc.2d 1074, 405 N.Y.S.2d 169 (1978)—§ 17.4(a) n.68

Scott, People v., 43 Cal.App.3d 723, 117 Cal.Rptr. 925 (1974)—§ 3.1(h) n.216

Scott v. Ryan, 548 P.2d 235 (Utah 1976)—§ 12.3(b) n.60

Scott v. State, 175 Md.App. 130, 926 A.2d 792 (2007)—§ 22.4(c) n.29

Scott v. State, 366 Md. 121, 782 A.2d 862 (2001)—§§ 3.10(b) n.60, 67

Scott, State v., 33 S.W.3d 746 (Tenn.2000)—§ 11.2(e) n.190

Scott, State v., 584 N.W.2d 412 (Minn.1998)—§ 6.7(b) n.69

Scott v. State, 593 N.E.2d 198 (Ind.1992)—§§ 11.2(e) n.220, 228

Scott v. State, 602 So.2d 830 (Miss.1992)—§ 7.4(g) n.118

Scott v. State, 298 Ark. 214, 766 S.W.2d 428 (1989)—§ 11.3(a) n.12

Scott v. State, 359 So.2d 1355 (Miss.1978)—§ 20.3(i) n.176

Scott, State v., 24 Ari.App. 203, 537 P.2d 40 (1975)—§ 20.6(c) n.82

Scott v. State, 519 P.2d 774 (Alaska 1974)—§§ 2.12(d) n.195; 20.4(d) n.56

Scott v. State, 251 Ark. 918, 475 S.W.2d 699 (1972)—§ 6.8(b) n.54

Scott, United States v., 450 F.3d 863 (9th Cir.2006)—§ 12.1(b) n.32

Scott, United States v., 469 F.3d 1335 (10th Cir.2006)—§ 21.2(d) n.167

Scott, United States v., 270 F.3d 30 (1st Cir.2001)—§§ 3.8(d) n.143; 9.3(e) n.83; 16.2(c) n.52; 18.3(b) n.26

Scott, United States v., 19 F.3d 1238 (7th Cir.1994)—§ 10.5(e) n.55

Scott, United States v., 975 F.2d 927 (1st Cir.1992)—§ 3.2(h) n.209

Scott, United States v., 909 F.2d 488 (11th Cir.1990)—§§ 11.4(d) n.110; 11.6(a) n.22; 11.10(b) n.45

Scott v. United States, 559 A.2d 745 (D.C.App.1989)—§§ 22.4(c) n.28, 31

Scott, United States v., 854 F.2d 697 (5th Cir.1988)—§ 24.9(f) n.98

Scott, United States v., 665 F.2d 874 (9th Cir.1981)—§ 3.7(e) n.121

Scott v. United States, 436 U.S. 128, 98 S.Ct. 1717, 56 L.Ed.2d 168 (1978)—§§ 3.1(d) n.91; 3.6(g) n.171; 4.6(m) n.219, 234

Scott, United States v., 437 U.S. 82, 98 S.Ct. 2187, 57 L.Ed.2d 65 (1978)— §§ 1.5(e) n.224; 1.5(f) n.251; 2.9(b) n.7; 2.9(d) n.76; 2.9(f) n.128; 13.2(c) n.58; 21.2(d) n.270; 25.1(b) n.19; 25.3(a) n.2, 3; 27.3(a) n.6

Scott, United States v., 578 F.2d 1186 (6th Cir.1978)—§ 7.5(a) n.5

Scott, United States v., 520 F.2d 697 (9th Cir.1975)—§ 9.2(b) n.11

Scott, United States v., 524 F.2d 465 (5th Cir.1975)—§ 20.3(m) n.252

Scott, United States v., 413 F.2d 932 (7th Cir.1969)—§ 17.2(a) n.19

Scott v. United States, 419 F.2d 264 (D.C.Cir.1969)—§§ 21.1(e) n.69, 73, 87, 100

Scott v. Wainwright, 698 F.2d 427 (11th Cir.1983)—§ 11.7(b) n.29

Scotti, United States v., 47 F.3d 1237 (2d Cir.1995)—§ 24.3(c) n.102

Screws v. United States, 325 U.S. 91, 65 S.Ct. 1031, 89 L.Ed. 1495 (1945)— §§ 2.10(d) n.144; 3.1(l) n.282, 284; 25.5(b) n.20

Screws Antitrust Litigation, In re, 91 F.R.D. 47 (D.Mass.1981)— §§ 8.5(h) n.248, 255, 257, 271

Scroggins, State v., 297 Minn. 144, 210 N.W.2d 55 (1973)—§ 3.5(c) n.113

Scroggins, United States v., 361 F.3d 1075 (8th Cir.2004)—§ 3.4(h) n.162

Scroggins, United States v., 965 F.2d 480 (7th Cir.1992)—§ 21.2(d) n.211

Scroggins, United States v., 880 F.2d 1204 (11th Cir.1989)—§§ 21.2(d) n.210; 26.1(c) n.42

Scruggs, United States v., 356 F.3d 539 (4th Cir.2004)—§§ 21.2(e) n.355; 21.2(h) n.439; 21.5(f) n.169

Scudder, Ex parte, 789 So.2d 837 (Ala.2001)—§ 11.5(a) n.17

Scully, United States v., 225 F.2d 113 (2d Cir.1955)—§§ 8.10(c) n.71 to 73

Scurr v. Moore, 647 F.2d 854 (8th Cir.1981)—§ 24.2(c) n.35

Sczubelek, United States v., 402 F.3d 175 (3d Cir.2005)—§ 3.2(g) n.198

Seacott, United States v., 15 F.3d 1380 (7th Cir.1994)—§ 26.3(g) n.94

Sealed Case, In re, 310 F.3d 717 (Foreign Int. Surv. Ct. Rev.2003)— § 4.9(b) n.16

Sealed Case, In re, 283 F.3d 349 (D.C.Cir.2002)—§ 21.4(c) n.95

Sealed Case, In re, 244 F.3d 961 (D.C.Cir.2001)—§§ 21.2(d) n.262, 265

Sealed Case, In re, 250 F.3d 764 (D.C.Cir.2001)—§§ 8.5(h) n.242; 8.5(i) n.310

Sealed Case, In re, 199 F.3d 522 (D.C.Cir.2000)—§ 23.1(d) n.156

Sealed Case, In re, 877 F.2d 83 (D.C.Cir.1989)—§§ 8.12(b) n.21; 8.13(d) n.87, 96

Sealed Case, In re, 827 F.2d 776 (D.C.Cir.1987)—§ 8.8(a) n.7

Sealed Case, In re, 832 F.2d 1268 (D.C.Cir.1987)—§§ 8.8(i) n.192; 8.12(g) n.67; 8.13(a) n.32

Sealed Case, In re, 676 F.2d 793 (D.C.Cir.1982)—§§ 8.6(b) n.44, 48, 51, 52

Sealed Case, In re, 655 F.2d 1298 (D.C.Cir.1981)—§ 27.2(e) n.91

Sealed Case (Government Records), In re, 950 F.2d 736 (D.C.Cir.1991)— §§ 8.12(b) n.16; 8.13(d) n.87, 109, 111, 113, 114

Sealed Case No. 98-3077, In re, 151 F.3d 1059 (D.C.Cir.1998)— §§ 8.5(c) n.74; 8.5(f) n.213; 8.5(i) n.307, 314, 316, 317, 321, 322, 324

Sealed Case No. 99-3091, In re, 192 F.3d 995 (D.C.Cir.1999)—§ 8.5(c) n.75

Sealed Juvenile 1, United States v., 255 F.3d 213 (5th Cir.2001)—§ 3.5(a) n.9

Sealed Motion, In re, 880 F.2d 1367 (D.C.Cir.1989)—§§ 8.5(d) n.139, 140

Seals, United States v., 987 F.2d 1102 (5th Cir.1993)—§§ 3.2(b) n.72; 9.3(e) n.65

Sealy v. State, 277 Ga. 617, 593 S.E.2d 335 (2004)—§ 22.2(f) n.115

Search of 4801 Fyler Avenue, Matter of, 879 F.2d 385 (8th Cir.1989)— § 10.1(c) n.39

Search of Kitty's East, In re the Matter of the, 905 F.2d 1367 (10th Cir.1990)—§§ 10.1(c) n.32, 36; 27.2(d) n.72

Search of Law Office, Residence, United States v., 341 F.3d 404 (5th Cir.2003)—§ 10.1(c) n.42

Search of Music City Marketing, United States v., 212 F.3d 920 (6th Cir.2000)—§ 10.1(c) n.34

Search of the Office Suites for World and Islam Studies, In the Matter of the, 925 F.Supp. 738 (M.D.Fla.1996)—§ 23.1(d) n.199

Search Warrant for Second Floor Bedroom, In re, 489 F.Supp. 207 (D.R.I.1980)—§ 8.5(c) n.87

Search Warrant For Secretarial Area Outside Office of Gunn, In re, 855 F.2d 569 (8th Cir.1988)—§§ 3.4(c) n.47, 48; 23.1(d) n.196

Search Warrants Issued on June 11, 1988 (Unisys), In the Matter of, 710 F.Supp. 701 (D.Minn.1989)—§§ 23.1(e) n.222, 225

Search Warrant (the Washington Post Co.), In the Matter of Application and Affidavit for a v. Hughes, 923 F.2d 324 (4th Cir.1991)—§ 23.1(d) n.211

Searcy, United States v., 233 F.3d 1096 (8th Cir.2000)—§§ 5.2(a) n.6; 21.1(h) n.199

Searle v. Juvenile Court for Williamson County, 188 S.W.3d 547 (Tenn.2006)—§ 27.5(c) n.87

Sears v. Cottrell, 5 Mich. 251 (1858)—§ 2.4(c) n.95

Sears, People v., 49 Ill.2d 14, 273 N.E.2d 380 (1971)—§§ 8.4(b) n.107; 8.4(c) n.125; 15.2(b) n.39, 54

Sears, State v., 208 W.Va. 700, 542 S.E.2d 863 (2000)—§ 21.3(e) n.272

Sears v. State, 262 Ga. 805, 426 S.E.2d 553 (1993)—§ 22.2(d) n.94

Sears v. United States, 343 F.2d 139 (5th Cir.1965)—§§ 5.3(c) n.37; 5.4(a) n.6

Sears, People ex rel. v. Romiti, 50 Ill.2d 51, 277 N.E.2d 705 (1971)—§§ 15.2(i) n.223; 15.4(h) n.198; 15.6(g) n.215

Sears, Roebuck and Co., United States v., 719 F.2d 1386 (9th Cir.1983)—§§ 15.2(e) n.142; 15.5(b) n.49; 15.6(b) n.79, 80; 15.6(d) n.129; 15.7(b) n.43

Sears, Roebuck and Co., United States v., 518 F.Supp. 179 (C.D.Cal.1981)—§ 15.6(b) n.61

Seaton, Ex parte, 580 S.W.2d 593 (Tex.Cr.App.1979)—§ 19.1(d) n.68

Seattle v. Mesiani, 110 Wash.2d 454, 755 P.2d 775 (1988)—§ 2.12(e) n.218

Seattle, City of v. Gerry, 76 Wash.2d 689, 458 P.2d 548 (1969)—§ 6.8(a) n.36

Seattle, City of v. Hogan, 53 Wash.App. 387, 766 P.2d 1134 (1989)—§ 1.8(d) n.48

Seattle, City of v. Lewis, 70 Wash.App. 715, 855 P.2d 327 (1993)—§ 22.1(a) n.26

Seattle, City of v. Wandler, 60 Wash.App. 309, 803 P.2d 833 (1991)—§ 1.8(d) n.48

Seattle, City of v. Williams, 101 Wash.2d 445, 680 P.2d 1051 (1984)—§ 22.1(h) n.132

Seattle Times Co. v. Rhinehart, 467 U.S. 20, 104 S.Ct. 2199, 81 L.Ed.2d 17 (1984)—§ 23.1(d) n.187

Seawell, United States v., 550 F.2d 1159 (9th Cir.1977)—§ 24.9(d) n.32

Seay v. State, 286 So.2d 532 (Fla.1973)—§ 15.4(b) n.47

Seay v. State, 21 Ala.App. 339, 108 So. 620 (1925)—§ 16.1(d) n.158

Sebastian, United States v., 497 F.2d 1267 (2d Cir.1974)—§ 10.5(e) n.53

Sebetich, United States v., 776 F.2d 412 (3d Cir.1985)—§ 7.4(g) n.118

S.E.C. v. Dresser, 628 F.2d 1368 (D.C.Cir.1980)—§§ 8.5(c) n.90, 91

SEC v. ESM Government Securities, Inc., 645 F.2d 310 (5th Cir.1981)—§ 3.10(c) n.96

S.E.C. v. Everest, 87 F.R.D. 100 (S.D.N.Y.1980)—§ 8.5(c) n.98

S.E.C. v. Palmisano, 135 F.3d 860 (2d Cir.1998)—§§ 17.4(b) n.131; 25.1(c) n.40

Sechrest v. State, 101 Nev. 360, 705 P.2d 626 (1985)—§§ 6.9(g) n.168, 183

Sechrist, United States v., 640 F.2d 81 (7th Cir.1981)—§§ 7.3(b) n.14; 18.3(b) n.8

SEC, United States ex rel. v. Carter, 907 F.2d 484 (5th Cir.1990)—§ 22.5(a) n.10

Seda, United States v., 978 F.2d 779 (2d Cir.1992)—§§ 19.3(c) n.193, 197

Sederburg, State v., 25 S.W.3d 172 (Mo.App.2000)—§§ 18.4(d) n.89, 93

Sedgwick v. Superior Court, 584 F.2d 1044 (D.C.Cir.1978)—§ 27.3(c) n.26

Sedillo, United States v., 496 F.2d 151 (9th Cir.1974)—§ 3.2(b) n.33

Sedlak v. Dick, 256 Kan. 779, 887 P.2d 1119 (1995)—§ 27.4(d) n.43

See v. City of Seattle, 387 U.S. 541, 87 S.Ct. 1737, 18 L.Ed.2d 943 (1967)—§§ 3.2(a) n.9; 3.9(c) n.33; 8.7(a) n.14, 27; 8.7(b) n.32

Seefeldt, State v., 51 N.J. 472, 242 A.2d 322 (1968)—§ 6.6(c) n.37

Seek v. State, 330 Ark. 833, 957 S.W.2d 709 (1997)—§ 21.2(g) n.396

Seeley, United States v., 331 F.3d 471 (5th Cir.2003)—§ 9.1(d) n.133

Seeright, United States v., 978 F.2d 842 (4th Cir.1992)—§ 8.11(e) n.93

Segarra, State v., 388 So.2d 1017 (Fla.1980)—§ 21.2(d) n.226

Segars, State v., 172 N.J. 481, 799 A.2d 541 (2002)—§ 3.8(c) n.62

Segerstrom v. State, 301 Ark. 314, 783 S.W.2d 847 (1990)—§§ 6.2(c) n.61; 6.9(b) n.24

Segien, United States v., 114 F.3d 1014 (10th Cir.1997)—§ 26.4(i) n.164

Segura v. United States, 468 U.S. 796, 104 S.Ct. 3380, 82 L.Ed.2d 599 (1984)—§§ 3.6(e) n.122; 9.3(c) n.23; 9.4(b) n.56

Seibel, State v., 163 Wis.2d 164, 471 N.W.2d 226 (1991)—§§ 2.12(b) n.80; 2.12(c) n.141

Seiber, State v., 56 Ohio St.3d 4, 564 N.E.2d 408 (1990)—§ 22.3(d) n.202

Seibert v. Commonwealth, 22 Va.App. 40, 467 S.E.2d 838 (1996)—§ 14.2(c) n.37

Seidlitz, United States v., 589 F.2d 152 (4th Cir.1978)—§ 4.6(a) n.13

Seifert, State v., 151 Vt. 66, 557 A.2d 494 (1989)—§ 24.3(e) n.126

Seifert, United States v., 648 F.2d 557 (9th Cir.1980)—§ 15.5(b) n.55

Seiffert, In re, 446 F.Supp. 1153 (N.D.N.Y.1978)—§ 8.7(b) n.47

Selby, Commonwealth v., 420 Mass. 656, 651 N.E.2d 843 (1995)—§§ 6.2(c) n.127; 6.9(g) n.155

Selby, People v., 148 Misc.2d 447, 561 N.Y.S.2d 123 (Sup.1990)—§ 16.1(a) n.20

Self, Commonwealth v., 802 S.W.2d 940 (Ky.App.1990)—§§ 16.1(h) n.300; 25.3(a) n.8

Self, United States v., 410 F.2d 984 (10th Cir.1969)—§ 3.1(e) n.134

Selikoff, People v., 35 N.Y.2d 227, 360 N.Y.S.2d 623, 318 N.E.2d 784 (1974)—§§ 21.1(b) n.34; 21.1(c) n.41

Seling v. Young, 531 U.S. 250, 121 S.Ct. 727, 148 L.Ed.2d 734 (2001)—§§ 17.4(b) n.117; 25.1(c) n.42

Sell, Commonwealth v., 504 Pa. 46, 470 A.2d 457 (1983)—§§ 2.12(c) n.150; 9.2(a) n.4

Sell v. United States, 539 U.S. 166, 123 S.Ct. 2174, 156 L.Ed.2d 197 (2003)—§§ 2.7(d) n.235, 266; 24.2(g) n.92; 27.2(c) n.42

Sellers v. Broadwater, 176 W.Va. 232, 342 S.E.2d 198 (1986)—§ 21.2(f) n.363

Sellers, State v., 273 N.C. 641, 161 S.E.2d 15 (1968)—§ 21.4(a) n.24

Sellers, United States v., 566 F.2d 884 (4th Cir.1977)—§ 7.5(b) n.14

Sellers, United States v., 483 F.2d 37 (5th Cir.1973)—§ 3.3(c) n.128

Sellers v. United States, 89 S.Ct. 36, 21 L.Ed.2d 64 (1968)—§ 12.4(d) n.80

Selley v. State, 403 So.2d 427 (Fla.App.1980)—§ 19.3(e) n.245

Sells, United States v., 477 F.3d 1226 (10th Cir.2007)—§ 21.2(e) n.326

Sells, United States v., 463 F.3d 1148 (10th Cir.2006)—§§ 3.4(f) n.121, 122

Sells Engineering, Inc., United States v., 463 U.S. 418, 103 S.Ct. 3133, 77 L.Ed.2d 743 (1983)—§§ 8.5(e) n.178; 8.5(h) n.274; 15.6(b) n.72

Selsor v. Kaiser, 81 F.3d 1492 (10th Cir.1996)—§ 11.9(b) n.53

Selsor v. Kaiser, 22 F.3d 1029 (10th Cir.1994)—§ 28.4(e) n.78

Semkiw, United States v., 712 F.2d 891 (3d Cir.1983)—§ 8.11(c) n.55

Semler, United States v., 883 F.2d 832 (9th Cir.1989)—§§ 21.3(e) n.286; 21.4(g) n.244

Semon v. Turner, 289 F.Supp. 803 (C.D.Utah 1968)—§ 21.2(g) n.408

Sena, Commonwealth v., 441 Mass. 822, 809 N.E.2d 505 (2004)—§ 22.2(d) n.80

Sena, Commonwealth v., 429 Mass. 590, 709 N.E.2d 1111 (1999)—§ 20.6(c) n.75

Sena, State v., 105 N.M. 686, 736 P.2d 491 (1987)—§§ 24.11(d) n.22, 37

Senate of Puerto Rico v. United States Department of Justice, 823 F.2d 574 (D.C.Cir.1987)—§§ 8.5(c) n.100, 102, 103, 106

Senate Select Committee on Ethics v. Packwood, 845 F.Supp. 17 (D.D.C.1994)—§§ 8.12(g) n.67 to 69

Senecal, State v., 145 Vt. 554, 497 A.2d 349 (1985)—§ 10.5(f) n.68

Seng, Commonwealth v., 436 Mass. 537, 766 N.E.2d 492 (2002)—§§ 3.5(c) n.109; 6.8(c) n.79

Senior, Commonwealth v., 433 Mass. 453, 744 N.E.2d 614 (2001)—§ 6.5(b) n.26

Sensback v. State, 720 N.E.2d 1160 (Ind.1999)—§ 21.1(e) n.98

Senske, State v., 692 N.W.2d 743 (Minn.App.2005)—§ 26.4(i) n.189

Seper, Matter of, 705 F.2d 1499 (9th Cir.1983)—§ 8.10(e) n.119

September 1971 Grand Jury (Mara), In re, 454 F.2d 580 (7th Cir.1971)—§ 8.8(b) n.20

September, 1975 Special Grand Jury, Matter of, 435 F.Supp. 538 (N.D.Ind.1977)—§ 8.12(b) n.20

September 1978 Grand Jury (II), In re, 640 F.2d 49 (7th Cir.1980)—§ 8.6(b) n.52

Sepulveda, Commonwealth v., 579 Pa. 217, 855 A.2d 783 (2004)—§§ 6.6(e) n.59; 6.7(b) n.90

Sepulveda v. State, 90 S.W.3d 633 (Tenn.2002)—§ 11.10(c) n.118

Sepulveda v. United States, 330 F.3d 55 (1st Cir.2003)—§ 28.6(e) n.45

Sepulveda, United States v., 15 F.3d 1161 (1st Cir.1993)—§§ 24.4(d) n.44, 58

Sepulveda-Contreras, United States v., 466 F.3d 166 (1st Cir.2006)—§ 24.2(a) n.11

Sequoia Books, Inc., People v., 160 Ill.App.3d 315, 112 Ill.Dec. 54, 513 N.E.2d 468 (1987)—§ 24.10(a) n.18

Serfass v. United States, 420 U.S. 377, 95 S.Ct. 1055, 43 L.Ed.2d 265 (1975)—§§ 25.1(d) n.48, 82; 25.3(d) n.33; 27.3(a) n.3

Sergeant, People v., 193 A.D.2d 417, 597 N.Y.S.2d 350 (1993)—§ 15.7(g) n.215

Serl, State v., 269 N.W.2d 785 (S.D.1978)—§ 15.4(b) n.36

Serlin, United States v., 707 F.2d 953 (7th Cir.1983)—§ 6.9(f) n.108

Serna, People v., 71 Cal.App.3d 229, 139 Cal.Rptr. 426 (1977)—§§ 13.4(c) n.86, 88

Serna, State v., 167 Ariz. 373, 807 P.2d 1109 (1991)—§ 24.11(d) n.28

Serna v. Superior Court, 40 Cal.3d 239, 219 Cal.Rptr. 420, 707 P.2d 793 (1985)—§§ 18.1(c) n.25, 26

Serna-Villarreal, United States v., 352
F.3d 225 (5th Cir.2003)—§ 18.2(e)
n.85

Serra v. Michigan Department of Corrections, 4 F.3d 1348 (6th
Cir.1993)—§§ 11.9(a) n.23; 11.9(c)
n.112, 115, 126; 11.9(d) n.203

Serrano, In re, 10 Cal.4th 447, 41
Cal.Rptr.2d 695, 895 P.2d 936
(1995)—§ 27.4(f) n.63

Serrano, People v., 93 N.Y.2d 73, 688
N.Y.S.2d 90, 710 N.E.2d 655
(1999)—§ 3.3(c) n.143

Serrano, United States v., 406 F.3d 1208
(10th Cir.2005)—§ 24.3(h) n.176

Serrano, United States v., 938 F.2d 1058
(9th Cir.1991)—§ 21.2(b) n.85

Serrano, United States v., 870 F.2d 1 (1st
Cir.1989)—§§ 8.11(c) n.46, 59, 63,
65

Serrano-Beauvaix, United States v., 400
F.3d 50 (1st Cir.2005)—§ 27.5(d)
n.134

Serubo, United States v., 604 F.2d 807
(3d Cir.1979)—§§ 15.2(i) n.223;
15.5(b) n.37; 15.6(b) n.52, 62;
15.6(d) n.104; 15.7(b) n.14, 19, 35

Service v. Dulles, 354 U.S. 363, 77 S.Ct.
1152, 1 L.Ed.2d 1403 (1957)—
§ 1.7(j) n.229

Seschillie, United States v., 310 F.3d
1208 (9th Cir.2002)—§ 24.4(d)
n.50

Sessions, State v., 621 N.W.2d 751
(Minn.2001)—§ 24.2(a) n.9

Sesslin, People v., 68 Cal.2d 418, 67
Cal.Rptr. 409, 439 P.2d 321
(1968)—§ 9.4(d) n.99

Sesson v. State, 563 S.W.2d 799
(Tenn.Cr.App.1978)—§ 24.1(a)
n.10

Setaro, People v., 44 A.D.2d 847, 355
N.Y.S.2d 796 (1974)—§ 23.3(a) n.8

Setien, State v., 173 Vt. 576, 795 A.2d
1135 (2002)—§ 21.4(d) n.111

Setters, State v., 305 Mont. 253, 25 P.3d
893 (2001)—§ 21.2(b) n.60

Settles, People v., 46 N.Y.2d 154, 412
N.Y.S.2d 874, 385 N.E.2d 612
(1978)—§ 7.3(d) n.72

Settles v. State, 584 So.2d 1260
(Miss.1991)—§ 24.5(d) n.52

Sevencan v. Herbert, 342 F.3d 69 (2d
Cir.2003)—§ 24.1(b) n.29

Severino, United States v., 800 F.2d 42
(2d Cir.1986)—§§ 21.4(a) n.12;
22.3(d) n.182

Sevier v. State, 596 So.2d 771
(Fla.App.1992)—§ 24.11(d) n.23

Sevigny, People v., 679 P.2d 1070
(Colo.1984)—§ 18.4(c) n.67

Sexton v. California, 189 U.S. 319, 23
S.Ct. 543, 189 U.S. 319 (1903)—
§ 1.2(c) n.44

Sexton, Commonwealth v., 485 Pa. 17,
400 A.2d 1289 (1979)—§ 7.4(g)
n.115

Sexton, State v., 256 Kan. 344, 886 P.2d
811 (1994)—§ 27.5(d) n.113

Seymour, State v., 183 Wis.2d 683, 515
N.W.2d 874 (1994)—§ 24.10(c)
n.40

S.F., In re, 414 Pa.Super. 529, 607 A.2d
793 (1992)—§ 3.9(k) n.258

Sgro v. United States, 287 U.S. 206, 53
S.Ct. 138, 77 L.Ed. 260 (1932)—
§§ 3.3(g) n.223; 3.4(g) n.123

S.H., State v., 159 Wis.2d 730, 465
N.W.2d 238 (1990)—§ 24.3(f)
n.154

Shabazz, In re, 200 F.Supp.2d 578
(D.S.C.2002)—§§ 3.2(g) n.199;
8.7(d) n.80, 82

Shabazz v. State, 440 So.2d 1200
(Ala.Crim.App.1983)—§ 12.3(b)
n.65

Shabazz, United States v., 883 F.Supp.
422 (D.Minn.1995)—§ 4.6(l) n.199

Shabazz, 246 Conn. 746, 719 A.2d 440
(1998)—§ 22.4(c) n.22

Shackelford, People v., 37 Colo.App.
317, 546 P.2d 964 (1976)—§ 3.8(e)
n.210

Shackelford, State v., 634 A.2d 1292
(Me.1993)—§ 7.3(b) n.14

Shackleford v. Commonwealth, 262 Va. 196, 547 S.E.2d 899 (2001)—§ 6.8(a) n.16

Shacklett, United States v., 921 F.2d 580 (5th Cir.1991)—§ 21.5(c) n.83

Shackley, State v., 750 S.W.2d 99 (Mo.App.1988)—§ 24.9(f) n.97

Shade v. City of Farmington, 309 F.3d 1054 (8th Cir.2002)—§§ 3.9(k) n.255, 256

Shade v. Pennsylvania Department of Transportation, 394 F.Supp. 1237 (M.D.Pa.1975)—§ 13.6(b) n.25

Shadwick v. City of Tampa, 407 U.S. 345, 92 S.Ct. 2119, 32 L.Ed.2d 783 (1972)—§§ 1.3(c) n.22; 1.8(c) n.8; 1.8(d) n.61; 2.6(d) n.93; 3.4(b) n.29; 3.5(a) n.57

Shaeffer, State v., 89 Mo. 271, 1 S.W. 293 (1886)—§ 16.4(c) n.48

Shafer v. Bowersox, 329 F.3d 637 (8th Cir.2003)—§ 6.4(f) n.137

Shagloak v. State, 597 P.2d 142 (Alaska 1979)—§ 26.7(b) n.20

Shaheed v. State, 276 Ga. 291, 578 S.E.2d 119 (2003)—§ 21.5(a) n.1

Shaheed v. State, 274 Ga. 716, 559 S.E.2d 466 (2002)—§ 24.2(a) n.11

Shahid v. State, 276 Ga. 543, 579 S.E.2d 724 (2003)—§ 22.5(a) n.4

Shahryar, United States v., 719 F.2d 1522 (11th Cir.1983)—§ 18.3(b) n.5

Shaibu, United States v., 920 F.2d 1423 (9th Cir.1990)—§ 3.10(b) n.24

Shaker, United States v., 279 F.3d 494 (7th Cir.2002)—§ 21.5(a) n.10

Shakir, United States v., 113 F.Supp.2d 1182 (M.D.Tenn.2000)—§ 1.7(j) n.225

Shaktman v. State, 553 So.2d 148 (1989)—§ 2.12(b) n.88

Shamaeizadeh v. Cunigan, 338 F.3d 535 (6th Cir.2003)—§ 9.1(b) n.41

Shanbarger v. Macy, 77 F.3d 1424 (2d Cir.1996)—§ 22.2(d) n.85

Shanea J., In re the Matter of, 150 Cal.App.3d 831, 198 Cal.Rptr. 228 (1984)—§ 25.1(d) n.88

Shanks v. State, 672 So.2d 1207 (Miss.1996)—§ 21.4(d) n.119

Shannon v. Newland, 410 F.3d 1083 (9th Cir.2005)—§ 28.5(b) n.53

Shannon, People v., 683 P.2d 792 (Colo.1984)—§ 20.6(b) n.43

Shannon v. United States, 512 U.S. 573, 114 S.Ct. 2419, 129 L.Ed.2d 459 (1994)—§ 22.1(g) n.118

Shapiro, United States v., 669 F.2d 593 (9th Cir.1982)—§ 5.1(c) n.29

Shapiro v. United States, 335 U.S. 1, 68 S.Ct. 1375, 92 L.Ed. 1787 (1948)—§ 8.12(c) n.30

Shareef, United States v., 100 F.3d 1491 (10th Cir.1996)—§ 3.1(h) n.217

Shargel, In re, 742 F.2d 61 (2d Cir.1984)—§ 8.8(d) n.92

Sharkey v. State, 672 N.E.2d 937 (Ind.App.1996)—§ 27.5(c) n.107

Sharp, State v., 708 A.2d 1328 (R.I.1998)—§ 14.1(d) n.68

Sharp v. State, 908 S.W.2d 752 (Mo.App.1995)—§§ 21.3(f) n.389, 403, 404

Sharpe, State v., 304 N.W.2d 220 (1981)—§ 19.5(b) n.28

Sharpe, State v., 284 N.C. 157, 200 S.E.2d 44 (1973)—§ 3.2(g) n.196

Sharpe, United States v., 438 F.3d 1257 (11th Cir.2006)—§§ 24.6(b) n.36; 24.11(a) n.1

Sharpe, United States v., 470 U.S. 675, 105 S.Ct. 1568, 84 L.Ed.2d 605 (1985)—§§ 2.9(g) n.179; 3.8(b) n.40, 51

Sharpless, State v., 189 W.Va. 169, 429 S.E.2d 56 (W.Va.1993)—§ 13.5(b) n.56

Shashaty, State v., 205 Conn. 39, 529 A.2d 1308 (1987)—§ 6.6(d) n.46

Shatney, State v., 572 A.2d 872 (R.I.1990)—§ 18.4(c) n.61

Shattell, People v., 179 A.D.2d 896, 578 N.Y.S.2d 694 (1992)—§ 23.3(b) n.29

Shaughnessy v. United States ex rel. Mezei, 345 U.S. 206, 73 S.Ct. 625, 97 L.Ed. 956 (1953)—§§ 1.5(a) n.59; 1.5(h) n.287; 2.8(c) n.59, 75

Shaw v. Murphy, 532 U.S. 223, 121 S.Ct. 1475, 149 L.Ed.2d 420 (2001)—§ 11.2(f) n.233

Shaw, People v., 180 Ill.App.3d 1091, 129 Ill.Dec. 799, 536 N.E.2d 849 (1989)—§ 6.2(c) n.113

Shaw, People v., 89 Ill.App.3d 69, 44 Ill.Dec. 237, 411 N.E.2d 143 (1980)—§ 11.3(b) n.52

Shaw, State v., 259 Kan. 3, 910 P.2d 809 (1996)—§ 21.4(f) n.177

Shaw v. State, 476 So.2d 22 (Miss.1985)—§ 3.10(e) n.172

Shaw, State v., 96 Idaho 897, 539 P.2d 250 (1975)—§ 16.4(c) n.103

Shaw v. State, 2 Tex.App. 487 (1877)—§ 1.6(d) n.283

Shaw, United States v., 94 F.3d 438 (8th Cir.1996)—§ 4.6(e) n.97

Shaw, United States v., 701 F.2d 367 (5th Cir.1983)—§ 9.6(a) n.38

Shea, Commonwealth v., 401 Mass. 731, 519 N.E.2d 1283 (1988)—§ 15.6(a) n.44

Shea v. Louisiana, 470 U.S. 51, 105 S.Ct. 1065, 84 L.Ed.2d 38 (1985)—§§ 2.11(a) n.10; 2.11(d) n.46

Shea, United States v., 150 F.3d 44 (1st Cir.1998)—§§ 6.7(b) n.74, 85

Shead, United States v., 568 F.2d 678 (10th Cir.1978)—§ 26.10(d) n.94

Shedelbower v. Estelle, 885 F.2d 570 (9th Cir.1989)—§ 6.7(c) n.111

Shedrick v. State, 10 Md.App. 579, 271 A.2d 773 (1970)—§ 6.6(e) n.75

Sheehan, United States v., 874 F.Supp. 31 (D.Mass.1994)—§ 27.5(a) n.3

Sheets, State v., 291 N.W.2d 35 (Iowa 1980)—§ 27.5(c) n.100

Sheff v. State, 329 So.2d 270 (Fla.1976)—§ 9.4(c) n.75

Shell, United States v., 961 F.2d 138 (9th Cir.1992)—§ 18.1(c) n.23

Shelley v. Kraemer, 334 U.S. 1, 68 S.Ct. 836, 92 L.Ed. 1161 (1948)—§ 3.1(h) n.223

Shelley, People v., 156 Cal.App.3d 521, 202 Cal.Rptr. 874 (1984)—§ 11.4(d) n.110

Shelton, State v., 692 N.E.2d 947 (Ind.App.1998)—§ 27.3(a) n.7

Shelton, State v., 621 So.2d 769 (La.1993)—§ 21.4(e) n.161

Shelton v. State, 287 Ark. 322, 699 S.W.2d 728 (1985)—§ 6.6(f) n.104

Shelton, State v., 368 P.2d 817 (Alaska 1962)—§ 15.5(c) n.120

Shelton, United States v., 337 F.3d 529 (5th Cir.2003)—§§ 3.10(d) n.109; 3.10(e) n.139

Shelton, United States v., 588 F.2d 1242 (9th Cir.1978)—§ 24.3(b) n.68

Shelton v. United States, 246 F.2d 571 (5th Cir.1957)—§§ 21.2(b) n.30; 21.3(c) n.185; 21.4(b) n.43

Shenberg, United States v., 89 F.3d 1461 (11th Cir.1996)—§§ 17.4(a) n.34; 24.10(a) n.17

Shenberg, United States v., 817 F.Supp. 118 (S.D.Fla.1993)—§ 23.1(d) n.202

Shepard v. Attorney General, 409 Mass. 398, 567 N.E.2d 187 (1991)—§§ 13.2(a) n.3; 13.3(a) n.1, 7

Shepard, United States v., 462 F.3d 847 (8th Cir.2006)—§ 18.3(b) n.25

Shepard v. United States, 544 U.S. 13, 125 S.Ct. 1254, 161 L.Ed.2d 205 (2005)—§§ 2.8(a) n.24; 26.4(i) n.192, 194, 202, 203

Shephard v. Scheeler, 701 So.2d 1308 (La.1997)—§ 21.4(a) n.21

Shephard, State v., 255 Iowa 1218, 124 N.W.2d 712 (1963)—§ 3.10(e) n.138

Shephard v. Superior Court, 180 Cal.App.3d 23, 225 Cal.Rptr. 328 (1986)—§ 11.6(a) n.45

Shephard, United States v., 4 F.3d 647 (8th Cir.1993)—§ 26.4(b) n.23

Shepherd, State v., 989 P.2d 503 (Utah App.1999)—§ 22.3(d) n.197

Shepherd, State v., 235 Neb. 426, 455 N.W.2d 566 (1990)—§ 21.5(b) n.64

Shepherd, United States v., 102 F.3d 558 (D.C.Cir.1996)—§ 11.4(c) n.77

Sheppard v. Maxwell, 384 U.S. 333, 86 S.Ct. 1507, 16 L.Ed.2d 600 (1966)—§§ 2.7(a) n.7, 52; 23.1(b) n.8, 29, 31, 86; 23.1(c) n.95; 23.2(a) n.22; 23.2(d) n.66; 23.2(g) n.119; 23.3(a) n.3

Sheppard v. Rees, 909 F.2d 1234 (9th Cir.1989)—§ 19.2(c) n.30

Sheppard, State v., 679 So.2d 899 (La.1996)—§ 21.3(b) n.42

Sheppard, State v., 253 Mont. 118, 832 P.2d 370 (1992)—§§ 24.8(f) n.92, 117

Sheppard, United States v., 901 F.2d 1230 (5th Cir.1990)—§ 9.4(b) n.54

Sheppard & White v. City of Jacksonville, 827 So.2d 925 (2002)—§ 11.8(c) n.66

Sherbert v. Verner, 374 U.S. 398, 83 S.Ct. 1790, 10 L.Ed.2d 965 (1963)—§ 3.9(c) n.44

Sherburne, United States v., 249 F.3d 1121 (9th Cir.2001)—§§ 13.5(h) n.123, 165, 168, 169

Sheridan, State v., 121 Iowa 164, 96 N.W. 730 (1903)—§ 2.12(a) n.10

Sheriff v. Fernandez, 97 Nev. 61, 624 P.2d 13 (1981)—§ 15.5(c) n.121

Sheriff v. Marcum, 105 Nev. 824, 783 P.2d 1389 (1989)—§ 15.2(c) n.74

Sheriff v. Marcus, 116 Nev. 188, 995 P.2d 1016 (2000)—§ 13.3(c) n.37

Sheriff, Clark County v. Keeney, 106 Nev. 213, 791 P.2d 55 (1990)—§§ 15.2(e) n.144; 15.7(b) n.42

Sheriff, Clark County v. Killman, 100 Nev. 619, 691 P.2d 434 (1984)—§ 13.7(a) n.26

Sheriff, Clark County v. Roylance, 110 Nev. 334, 871 P.2d 359 (1994)—§ 14.2(g) n.99

Sheriff, Clark County v. Terpstra, 111 Nev. 860, 899 P.2d 548 (1995)—§ 14.2(f) n.89

Sheriff, Clark County v. Warner, 112 Nev. 1234, 926 P.2d 775 (1996)—§ 8.14(a) n.7

Sheriff, Humboldt County v. Lang, 104 Nev. 539, 763 P.2d 56 (1988)—§ 14.3(d) n.92

Sheriff of Clark County v. Richardson, 103 Nev. 180, 734 P.2d 735 (1987)—§ 14.3(d) n.99

Sheriff, Washoe County v. Hawkins, 104 Nev. 70, 752 P.2d 769 (1988)—§§ 5.2(b) n.26; 5.3(a) n.6

Sheriff, Washoe County v. Middleton, 112 Nev. 956, 112 Nev. 956, 921 P.2d 282 (1996)—§§ 14.3(a) n.9, 10, 13

Sherlin, United States v., 67 F.3d 1208 (6th Cir.1995)—§ 24.3(b) n.54

Sherman, People v., _____ P.3d _____, 2006 WL 3314976 (Colo.App.2006)—§ 24.8(f) n.92

Sherman, State v., 931 So.2d 286 (La.2006)—§§ 3.5(d)   n.137; 12.5(b) n.36

Sherman v. State, 326 Ark. 153, 931 S.W.2d 417 (1996)—§ 27.2(c) n.31

Sherman, United States v., 150 F.3d 306 (3d Cir.1998)—§§ 13.7(a) n.5, 28, 29

Sherman, United States v., 200 F.2d 880 (2d Cir.1952)—§ 5.3(d) n.40

Sherman v. United States, 356 U.S. 369, 78 S.Ct. 819, 2 L.Ed.2d 848 (1958)—§§ 5.1(c) n.20, 23; 5.2(a) n.1, 2, 13; 5.2(b) n.26, 31; 5.2(c) n.40 to 42; 5.3(a) n.3; 5.3(b) n.17, 18; 5.4(c) n.28

Sherrell, United States v., 979 F.2d 1315 (8th Cir.1992)—§ 3.4(e) n.67

Sherrick v. State, 167 Ind. 345, 79 N.E. 193 (1906)—§ 19.4(b) n.9

Sherriff, United States v., 546 F.2d 604 (5th Cir.1977)—§ 19.4(b) n.25

Sherrill v. Wyrick, 524 F.2d 186 (8th Cir.1975)—§ 11.10(c) n.84

Sherroan v. Commonwealth, 142 S.W.3d 7 (Ky.2004)—§§ 22.3(a) n.33; 22.3(c) n.153

Sherrod v. State, 280 Ga. 275, 627
S.E.2d 36 (2006)—§ 22.1(a) n.18

Sherrod, United States v., 445 F.3d 980
(7th Cir.2006)—§ 6.9(g) n.157

Sherwood v. State, 717 N.E.2d 131
(Ind.1999)—§§ 11.5(d)   n.83;
11.5(g) n.119

Sherwood, United States v., 527 F.Supp.
1001 (W.D.N.Y.1981)—§§ 20.3(b)
n.37, 59

Shick, People v., 318 Ill.App.3d 899,
253 Ill.Dec. 125, 744 N.E.2d 858
(2001)—§ 22.5(d) n.36

Shiel v. United States, 515 A.2d 405
(D.C.App.1986)—§ 13.7(c) n.43

Shields v. State, 269 Ga. 177, 496 S.E.2d
719 (1998)—§ 6.7(b) n.41

Shields v. State, 722 So.2d 584
(Miss.1998)—§§ 25.4(b) n.22, 24

Shields v. State, 374 A.2d 816
(Del.1977)—§§ 21.2(f) n.366, 383

Shifflett, United States v., 798 F.Supp.
354 (W.D.Va.1992)—§§ 20.3(m)
n.239, 251, 255

Shillcutt v. Gagnon, 602 F.Supp. 1280
(E.D.Wis.1985)—§ 24.9(g) n.114

Shillinger v. Haworth, 70 F.3d 1132
(10th Cir.1995)—§ 11.8(b) n.33

Shillitani v. United States, 384 U.S. 364,
86 S.Ct. 1531, 16 L.Ed.2d 622
(1966)—§§ 8.3(a) n.3, 4, 6; 15.1(b)
n.82

Shinault, United States v., 147 F.3d 1266
(10th Cir.1998)—§ 22.2(d) n.75

Shine, People v., 187 A.D.2d 950, 590
N.Y.S.2d   965
(N.Y.App.Div.1992)—§ 5.4(c) n.46

Shinkle, People v., 51 N.Y.2d 417, 434
N.Y.S.2d 918, 415 N.E.2d 909
(1980)—§ 11.9(d) n.211

Shipley v. State, 570 A.2d 1159
(Del.1990)—§§ 6.2(c) n.182; 6.6(d)
n.46

Shipp, People v., 96 Ill.App.2d 364, 239
N.E.2d 296 (1968)—§ 6.10(c) n.36

Shirley, State v., 117 Ariz. 105, 570 P.2d
1278 (1977)—§ 3.1(f) n.159

Shirley, United States v., 884 F.2d 1130
(9th Cir.1989)—§ 24.3(f) n.141

Shivaee v. Commonwealth, 270 Va.
112, 613 S.E.2d 570 (2005)—
§ 17.4(b) n.134

Shives, State v., 601 S.W.2d 22
(Mo.App.1980)—§§ 15.2(j) n.238;
27.5(c) n.101

Shoatz, Commonwealth v., 469 Pa. 545,
366 A.2d 1216 (1976)—§§ 7.3(d)
n.80; 7.3(e) n.92

Shober, United States v., 489 F.Supp.
393 (E.D.Pa.1979)—§§ 15.1(b)
n.115; 15.2(e) n.128, 143; 15.5(b)
n.53

Shoemaker, Commonwealth v., 226
Pa.Super. 203, 313 A.2d 342
(1973)—§ 26.5(a) n.21

Shoemaker, State v., 276 S.C. 86, 275
S.E.2d 878 (1981)—§ 19.3(b) n.149

Shoemaker, United States v., 542 F.2d
561 (10th Cir.1976)—§ 6.3(b) n.40

Shoff, State v., 118 N.C.App. 724, 456
S.E.2d 875 (1995)—§ 27.2(c) n.66

Shofler, State v., 9 Kan.App.2d 696, 687
P.2d 29 (1984)—§ 19.3(e) n.218

Shoher, United States v., 555 F.Supp.
346 (S.D.N.Y.1983)—§ 20.3(h)
n.150

Shomo, State v., 129 N.J. 248, 609 A.2d
394 (1992)—§§ 24.10(d) n.46, 48

Shondel, State v., 22 Utah 2d 343, 453
P.2d 146 (1969)—§ 13.7(a) n.24

Shongutsie v. State, 827 P.2d 361
(Wyo.1992)—§ 11.9(b) n.100

Shonubi, United States v., 103 F.3d 1085
(2d Cir.1997)—§§ 26.4(b) n.7;
26.4(h) n.154

Shore, State v., 522 A.2d 1215
(R.I.1987)—§ 10.1(c) n.45

Shore, State v., 206 N.C. 743, 175 S.E.
116 (1934)—§ 16.1(d) n.142

Shorette v. State, 402 A.2d 450
(Me.1979)—§ 21.5(c) n.88

Shorney, State v., 524 P.2d 69
(Okla.App.1974)—§ 1.7(k) n.271

Short, State v., 333 S.C. 473, 511 S.E.2d
358 (1999)—§ 22.3(d) n.205

Short, State v., 131 N.J. 47, 618 A.2d
316 (1993)—§ 24.8(f) n.110

Short v. State, 211 So.2d 545 (Miss.1968)—§ 7.4(b) n.18

Short v. United States, 471 F.3d 686 (6th Cir.2006)—§ 21.3(b) n.42

Short, United States v., 671 F.2d 178 (6th Cir.1982)—§§ 8.5(g) n.227; 15.5(a) n.4

Shorter, United States v., 328 F.3d 167 (4th Cir.2003)—§§ 3.4(d) n.51, 58

Shorter v. Waters, 275 Ga. 581, 571 S.E.2d 373 (2002)—§ 11.10(c) n.117

Short Horn, State v., 427 N.W.2d 361 (S.D.1988)—§ 26.9(b) n.21

Shortsleeves, State v., 580 A.2d 145 (Me.1990)—§ 27.6(b) n.44

Shorty, People v., 731 P.2d 679 (Colo.1987)—§ 3.2(c) n.128

Shotikare v. United States, 779 A.2d 335 (D.C.App.2001)—§§ 17.1(c) n.45; 17.1(d) n.53

Showalter, State v., 427 N.W.2d 166 (Iowa 1988)—§§ 3.2(c) n.121, 125

Showers v. State, 407 So.2d 169 (Ala.1981)—§ 24.9(d) n.38

Showery v. Samaniego, 814 F.2d 200 (5th Cir.1987)—§§ 17.4(a) n.31, 61

Showker v. State, 146 Ga.App. 862, 247 S.E.2d 515 (1978)—§ 27.6(b) n.44

Shrader v. State, 101 Nev. 499, 706 P.2d 834 (1985)—§ 5.4(b) n.17

Shreck, People v., 107 P.3d 1048 (Colo.2004)—§ 18.4(d) n.90

Shreveport Rate Cases, 234 U.S. 342, 34 S.Ct. 833, 58 L.Ed. 1341 (1914)—§ 1.2(c) n.122

Shreves, State v., 313 Mont. 252, 60 P.3d 991 (Mont.2002)—§ 26.4(c) n.35

Shryock, United States v., 342 F.3d 948 (9th Cir.2003)—§§ 4.6(e) n.98; 22.3(b) n.68; 23.1(e) n.221; 24.1(a) n.10

Shuck, United States v., 895 F.2d 962 (4th Cir.1990)—§§ 8.10(c) n.68; 8.10(d) n.90

Shuey, People v., 13 Cal.3d 835, 120 Cal.Rptr. 83, 533 P.2d 211 (1975)—§ 9.4(b) n.55

Shuford, United States v., 454 F.2d 772 (4th Cir.1971)—§ 17.2(c) n.79

Shuler, State v., 344 S.C. 604, 545 S.E.2d 805 (2001)—§ 22.3(d) n.202

Shulman, United States v., 466 F.Supp. 293 (S.D.N.Y.1979)—§ 15.2(c) n.69

Shuman, Commonwealth v., 391 Mass. 345, 462 N.E.2d 80 (1984)—§ 5.2(a) n.4

Shunk, United States v., 113 F.3d 31 (5th Cir.1997)—§ 28.6(e) n.63

Shupe v. Sigler, 230 F.Supp. 601 (D.Neb.1964)—§§ 21.3(a) n.4, 6

Shushan v. United States, 117 F.2d 110 (5th Cir.1941)—§ 15.2(j) n.238

Shute v. State of Texas, 117 F.3d 233 (5th Cir.1997)—§ 21.6(a) n.62

Shvarts, United States v., 90 F.Supp.2d 219 (E.D.N.Y.2000)—§ 20.3(m) n.253

Si, United States v., 343 F.3d 1116 (9th Cir.2003)—§ 5.2(a) n.8

Sibbach v. Wilson, 312 U.S. 1, 61 S.Ct. 422, 85 L.Ed. 479 (1941)—§ 1.7(f) n.98

Sibilia, State v., 88 N.J.Super. 546, 212 A.2d 869 (1965)—§ 8.10(c) n.57

Sibley v. Culliver, 377 F.3d 1196 (11th Cir.2004)—§ 28.5(b) n.48

Sibron v. New York, 392 U.S. 40, 88 S.Ct. 1889, 20 L.Ed.2d 917 (1968)—§§ 3.5(d) n.133; 3.8(e) n.207; 27.5(a) n.11; 28.3(a) n.24

Siciliano v. Vose, 834 F.2d 29 (1st Cir.1987)—§ 11.6(c) n.100

Sidebotham, State v., 124 N.H. 682, 474 A.2d 1377 (1984)—§§ 2.12(e) n.199; 9.2(a) n.4

Sidebottom v. Delo, 46 F.3d 744 (8th Cir.1995)—§ 24.5(b) n.24

Sides, Ex parte, 501 So.2d 1262 (Ala.1986)—§ 21.2(d) n.244

Sidman, United States v., 470 F.2d 1158 (9th Cir.1972)—§ 17.2(b) n.75

Siebert, Ex parte, 555 So.2d 780 (Ala.1989)—§§ 6.2(c) n.115; 6.8(a) n.10

Siebert, People v., 450 Mich. 500, 537 N.W.2d 891 (1995)—§ 21.4(g) n.247

Siebold, Ex parte, 100 U.S. 371, 25 L.Ed. 717 (1879)—§ 28.3(b) n.47

Siegal, United States ex rel. v. Follette, 290 F.Supp. 632 (S.D.N.Y.1968)—§ 12.2(a) n.1

Siegel v. New York, 691 F.2d 620 (2d Cir.1982)—§ 21.5(d) n.104

Siegel, United States v., 477 F.3d 87 (3d Cir.2007)—§ 26.4(i) n.201

Siegfried, State v., 274 N.W.2d 113 (Minn.1978)—§ 1.7(j) n.217

Siegmund, In re Extradition of, 887 F.Supp. 1383 (D.Nev.1995)—§ 27.4(f) n.66

Sierb, People v., 456 Mich. 519, 581 N.W.2d 219 (1998)—§§ 13.2(c) n.56; 25.2(e) n.38

Sierp, State v., 260 Ind. 57, 292 N.E.2d 245 (1973)—§ 1.7(h) n.134

Sierra v. State, 100 Nev. 614, 691 P.2d 431 (1984)—§ 21.4(d) n.103

Sifrit v. State, 383 Md. 77, 857 A.2d 65 (2004)—§§ 13.5(b) n.45; 17.4(a) n.50

Sigerson, State v., 282 So.2d 649 (Fla.App.1973)—§ 10.5(e) n.47

Sigh, State v., 38 Del. 362, 192 A. 682 (1937)—§ 16.2(g) n.114

Sigma International, United States v., 300 F.3d 1278 (11th Cir.2002)—§ 15.6(e) n.137

Sigman v. Whyte, 165 W.Va. 356, 268 S.E.2d 603 (1980)—§ 26.10(c) n.45

Sikora, United States v., 635 F.2d 1175 (6th Cir.1980)—§ 6.4(e) n.93

Sikora, State ex rel. v. District Court, 154 Mont. 241, 462 P.2d 897 (1969)—§ 20.5(b) n.29

Silagy, People v., 101 Ill.2d 147, 77 Ill.Dec. 792, 461 N.E.2d 415 (1984)—§ 11.5(d) n.84

Silagy v. Peters, 905 F.2d 986 (7th Cir.1990)—§§ 11.2(e) n.171; 22.2(d) n.67

Silanskas, Commonwealth v., 433 Mass. 678, 746 N.E.2d 445 (2001)—§ 6.9(b) n.35

Silber v. United States, 370 U.S. 717, 82 S.Ct. 1287, 8 L.Ed.2d 798 (1962)—§§ 19.2(e) n.77; 19.3(e) n.227

Silbert v. United States, 275 F.Supp. 765 (D.Md.1967)—§ 10.1(c) n.36

Sileven, United States v., 985 F.2d 962 (8th Cir.1993)—§ 3.10(c) n.84

Silhan, State v., 302 N.C. 223, 275 S.E.2d 450 (1981)—§ 19.4(b) n.29

Silien, United States v., 825 F.2d 320 (11th Cir.1987)—§ 13.4(c) n.98

Silmon v. Travis, 95 N.Y.2d 470, 718 N.Y.S.2d 704, 741 N.E.2d 501 (2000)—§ 21.4(f) n.220

Silva, Commonwealth v., 21 Mass.App. 536, 488 N.E.2d 34 (1986)—§ 5.1(c) n.37

Silva, United States v., 430 F.3d 1096 (10th Cir.2005)—§ 21.3(b) n.71

Silva, United States v., 247 F.3d 1051 (9th Cir.2001)—§ 9.1(b) n.34

Silva, United States v., 122 F.3d 412 (7th Cir.1997)—§ 21.5(a) n.43

Silva v. Woodford, 279 F.3d 825 (9th Cir.2002)—§ 11.10(c) n.127

Silveira v. Santos, 490 A.2d 969 (R.I.1985)—§ 21.4(a) n.20

Silver, In re, 273 Ga. 727, 545 S.E.2d 886 (2001)—§ 21.4(a) n.22

Silver, People v., 466 Mich. 386, 646 N.W.2d 150 (2002)—§ 24.8(f) n.98

Silver, State v., 314 S.C. 483, 431 S.E.2d 250 (1993)—§ 6.6(e) n.89

Silver, United States v., 83 F.3d 289 (9th Cir.1996)—§ 26.9(a) n.12

Silverman, United States v., 976 F.2d 1502 (6th Cir.1992)—§ 26.4(f) n.86

Silverman, United States v., 430 F.2d 106 (2d Cir.1970)—§ 19.2(f) n.98

Silverman v. United States, 365 U.S. 505, 81 S.Ct. 679, 5 L.Ed.2d 734 (1961)—§ 3.2(a) n.1

Silvern, United States v., 484 F.2d 879 (7th Cir.1973)—§ 24.9(d) n.43

Silvernail, State v., 25 Wash.App. 185, 605 P.2d 1279 (1980)—§ 3.8(f) n.237

Silvers, United States v., 90 F.3d 95 (4th Cir.1996)—§ 25.4(b) n.21

Silverthorne v. United States, 400 F.2d 627 (9th Cir.1968)—§ 15.4(h) n.186

Silverthorne Lumber Co. v. United States, 251 U.S. 385, 40 S.Ct. 182, 64 L.Ed. 319 (1920)—§§ 2.8(b) n.36; 8.9(a) n.8; 9.1(c) n.99; 9.3(a) n.7; 9.4(b) n.67; 9.6(a) n.2; 15.1(b) n.21; 15.5(a) n.9

Silvestain, United States v., 668 F.2d 1161 (10th Cir.1982)—§ 8.12(e) n.51

Silvestri, United States v., 787 F.2d 736 (1st Cir.1986)—§ 9.3(e) n.71

Simac, People v., 161 Ill.2d 297, 204 Ill.Dec. 192, 641 N.E.2d 416 (1994)—§ 7.4(g) n.125

Simants v. State, 202 Neb. 828, 277 N.W.2d 217 (1979)—§ 24.9(a) n.11

Simelton v. Frank, 446 F.3d 666 (7th Cir.2006)—§ 21.2(g) n.394

Simington v. Shimp, 60 Ohio App.2d 402, 398 N.E.2d 812 (1978)—§§ 8.3(h) n.45, 50

Simmers v. State, 943 P.2d 1189 (Wyo.1997)—§ 6.2(c) n.182

Simmon v. Commonwealth, 191 S.W.3d 557 (Ky.2006)—§ 11.6(b) n.77

Simmonds, United States v., 262 F.3d 468 (5th Cir.2001)—§ 3.6(g) n.163

Simmons v. Bowersox, 235 F.3d 1124 (8th Cir.2001)—§§ 6.2(c) n.147; 6.5(b) n.28

Simmons v. Commonwealth, 746 S.W.2d 393 (Ky.1988)—§ 11.2(e) n.198

Simmons, Commonwealth v., 383 Mass. 46, 417 N.E.2d 1193 (1981)—§ 7.4(a) n.7

Simmons v. Lockhart, 814 F.2d 504 (8th Cir.1987)—§ 23.2(f) n.106

Simmons v. Mississippi, 568 So.2d 1192 (Miss.1990)—§ 16.1(b) n.36

Simmons, People v., 75 N.Y.2d 738, 551 N.Y.S.2d 196, 550 N.E.2d 449 (1989)—§ 9.3(a) n.1

Simmons, People v., 105 Ill.App.3d 402, 61 Ill.Dec. 282, 434 N.E.2d 435 (1982)—§ 15.7(b) n.28

Simmons v. South Carolina, 512 U.S. 154, 114 S.Ct. 2187, 129 L.Ed.2d 133 (1994)—§§ 2.7(b) n.90; 26.1(b) n.25; 26.4(g) n.116; 28.6(d) n.32

Simmons, State v., 140 N.M. 311, 142 P.3d 899 (2006)—§ 21.2(d) n.150

Simmons, State v., 714 N.W.2d 264 (Iowa 2006)—§ 6.7(b) n.90

Simmons v. State, 934 So.2d 1100 (Fla.2006)—§§ 7.4(a) n.7; 7.5(b) n.21

Simmons v. State, 869 So.2d 995 (Miss.2004)—§ 19.3(a) n.42

Simmons, State v., 944 S.W.2d 165 (Mo.1997)—§§ 6.2(c) n.152; 24.7(i) n.91

Simmons v. State, 333 Md. 547, 636 A.2d 463 (1994)—§ 2.12(d) n.188

Simmons, State v., 308 S.C. 80, 417 S.E.2d 92 (1992)—§ 7.5(a) n.8

Simmons, State v., 260 Ga. 92, 390 S.E.2d 43 (1990)—§ 6.4(e) n.77

Simmons, United States v., 374 F.3d 313 (5th Cir.2004)—§ 17.2(f) n.133

Simmons, United States v., 964 F.2d 763 (8th Cir.1992)—§ 26.5(a) n.15

Simmons, United States v., 912 F.2d 1215 (10th Cir.1990)—§ 12.1(a) n.18

Simmons v. United States, 554 A.2d 1167 (D.C.App.1989)—§ 22.1(b) n.55

Simmons, United States v., 536 F.2d 827 (9th Cir.1976)—§§ 18.2(e) n.77, 79

Simmons, United States v., 537 F.2d 1260 (4th Cir.1976)—§ 21.2(d) n.240

Simmons v. United States, 390 U.S. 377, 88 S.Ct. 967, 19 L.Ed.2d 1247 (1968)—§§ 7.4(a) n.6; 7.4(b) n.15; 7.4(c) n.44; 9.1(a) n.27; 9.2(a) n.2; 10.1(b) n.27; 10.5(c) n.30; 12.1(e)

n.65; 17.4(b) n.114; 24.4(a) n.9; 24.5(a) n.10

Simms v. Oedekoven, 839 P.2d 381 (Wyo.1992)—§§ 12.2(a) n.12; 12.3(b) n.57

Simms v. Simms, 175 U.S. 162, 20 S.Ct. 58, 44 L.Ed. 115 (1899)—§§ 1.2(c) n.15; 16.4(b) n.5

Simms v. State, 905 S.W.2d 720 (Tex.App.1995)—§ 19.1(d) n.69

Simms, State v., 201 Conn. 395, 518 A.2d 35 (1986)—§ 15.4(h) n.190

Simms v. United States, 634 A.2d 442 (D.C.App.1993)—§ 24.10(c) n.40

Simon, Commonwealth v., 526 Pa. 69, 584 A.2d 895 (1990)—§ 8.3(a) n.4

Simon, People v., 25 Cal.4th 1082, 108 Cal.Rptr.2d 385, 25 P.3d 598 (2001)—§§ 16.1(g) n.254; 16.1(h) n.291, 306

Simon, People v., 45 Cal.2d 645, 290 P.2d 531 (1955)—§ 3.5(d) n.136

Simon v. State, 679 So.2d 617 (Miss.1996)—§ 22.3(d) n.216

Simon v. State, 633 So.2d 407 (Miss.1993)—§§ 16.3(g) n.108, 113; 22.2(d) n.74

Simon, State v., 297 N.W.2d 206 (1980)—§ 11.5(e) n.92

Simon, State v., 79 N.J. 191, 398 A.2d 861 (1979)—§ 24.10(a) n.8

Simon v. State, 515 P.2d 1161 (Okla.Crim.App.1973)—§§ 3.4(c) n.44, 45

Simon, United States v., 995 F.2d 1236 (3d Cir.1993)—§§ 27.6(b) n.17, 40

Simon, United States v., 453 F.2d 111 (8th Cir.1971)—§ 17.1(b) n.28

Simon & Schuster v. New York Crime Victims Board, 502 U.S. 105, 112 S.Ct. 501, 116 L.Ed.2d 476 (1991)—§ 1.5(k) n.382

Simone, United States v., 14 F.3d 833 (3d Cir.1994)—§§ 23.1(d) n.133, 140, 153

Simone, United States v., 627 F.Supp. 1264 (D.N.J.1986)—§ 8.10(d) n.113

Simoneau, State v., 176 Vt. 15, 833 A.2d 1280 (2003)—§ 3.8(b) n.29

Simons, State v., 214 Or. App. 675 (2007)—§ 24.6(c) n.41

Simons, United States v., 206 F.3d 392 (4th Cir.2000)—§ 4.4(e) n.18

Simonson v. Cahn, 27 N.Y.2d 1, 313 N.Y.S.2d 97, 261 N.E.2d 246 (1970)—§§ 15.1(f) n.276; 15.3(d) n.64

Simon, United States ex rel. v. Murphy, 349 F.Supp. 818 (E.D.Pa.1972)—§§ 11.9(a) n.14; 21.3(b) n.107, 137

Simpson v. Bouker, 249 F.3d 1204 (10th Cir.2001)—§ 17.4(b) n.138

Simpson, Commonwealth v., 562 Pa. 255, 754 A.2d 1264 (Pa.2000)—§ 24.6(d) n.43

Simpson v. Commonwealth, 759 S.W.2d 224 (Ky.1988)—§ 21.5(e) n.119

Simpson v. Commonwealth, 227 Va. 557, 318 S.E.2d 386 (1984)—§ 6.9(b) n.27

Simpson v. Florida, 403 U.S. 384, 91 S.Ct. 1801, 29 L.Ed.2d 549 (1971)—§§ 10.6(d) n.44; 17.4(a) n.59

Simpson v. Langston, 281 Ark. 458, 664 S.W.2d 872 (1984)—§§ 8.3(h) n.46; 15.1(g) n.358

Simpson v. Matesanz, 175 F.3d 200 (1st Cir.1999)—§§ 28.4(e) n.82; 28.9(b) n.39

Simpson v. Owens, 207 Ariz. 261, 85 P.3d 478 (App.2004)—§§ 12.3(d) n.105; 12.3(e) n.124; 12.4(a) n.22, 27

Simpson v. State, 874 So.2d 575 (Ala.Crim.App.2003)—§ 24.2(d) n.45

Simpson v. State, 678 So.2d 712 (Miss.1996)—§ 21.5(d) n.102

Simpson v. State, 876 P.2d 690 (Okla.Cr.App.1994)—§§ 27.6(a) n.7; 27.6(b) n.41

Simpson, State v., 846 S.W.2d 724 (Mo.1993)—§§ 14.2(g) n.107; 19.5(b) n.37

Simpson v. State, 92 Ga. 41, 17 S.E. 984 (1893)—§§ 16.4(c) n.45, 69

Simpson, United States v., 439 F.3d 490 (8th Cir.2006)—§ 9.4(b) n.50

Simpson v. United States, 632 A.2d 374 (D.C.App.1993)—§ 9.6(a) n.32

Simpson, United States v., 995 F.2d 109 (7th Cir.1993)—§ 16.1(h) n.288

Simpson, United States v., 974 F.2d 845 (7th Cir.1992)—§ 6.7(b) n.77

Simpson, United States v., 910 F.2d 154 (4th Cir.1990)—§ 25.4(c) n.32

Simpson, United States v., 813 F.2d 1462 (9th Cir.1987)—§§ 4.6(e) n.98; 5.4(c) n.29

Simpson, United States v., 475 F.2d 934 (D.C.Cir.1973)—§§ 21.3(b) n.144; 21.5(d) n.102

Simpson, United States v., 460 F.2d 515 (9th Cir.1972)—§ 22.1(g) n.115

Sims v. Georgia, 385 U.S. 538, 87 S.Ct. 639, 17 L.Ed.2d 593 (1967)—§ 10.6(a) n.4

Sims v. Livesay, 970 F.2d 1575 (6th Cir.1992)—§§ 11.10(c) n.125, 128

Sims, People v., 192 Ill.2d 592, 249 Ill.Dec. 610, 736 N.E.2d 1048 (2000)—§§ 3.3(d) n.177; 3.3(f) n.209

Sims, People v., 5 Cal.4th 405, 20 Cal.Rptr.2d 537, 853 P.2d 992 (1993)—§§ 6.9(f) n.137, 139

Sims, People v., 244 Ill.App.3d 966, 184 Ill.Dec. 135, 612 N.E.2d 1011 (1993)—§ 16.4(d) n.137

Sims v. Roland, 414 F.3d 1148 (9th Cir.2005)—§§ 22.3(b) n.70; 24.9(f) n.86

Sims, State v., 851 So.2d 1039 (La.2003)—§ 3.1(o) n.303

Sims v. State, 688 So.2d 337 (Fla.App.1996)—§ 26.9(c) n.79

Sims, State v., 426 So.2d 148 (La.1983)—§ 3.7(e) n.126

Sims v. State, 502 S.W.2d 730 (Tex.Cr.App.1973)—§ 10.2(c) n.32

Sims, United States v., 296 F.3d 284 (4th Cir.2002)—§ 3.8(d) n.135

Sims v. United States, 607 F.2d 757 (6th Cir.1979)—§ 26.10(d) n.90

Sims v. United States, 405 F.2d 1381 (D.C.Cir.1968)—§ 22.3(c) n.132

Sims, United States v., 161 F. 1008 (5th Cir.1907)—§ 15.1(b) n.77

Simuel, State v., 357 S.C. 378, 593 S.E.2d 178 (2004)—§ 19.3(a) n.41

Sinadinos, Matter of, 760 F.2d 167 (7th Cir.1985)—§ 8.8(b) n.33

Sinclair, State v., 46 Wash.App. 433, 730 P.2d 742 (1986)—§§ 11.4(b) n.31; 11.9(b) n.55

Sinclair, United States v., 109 F.3d 1527 (10th Cir.1997)—§ 24.11(d) n.30

Sinclair v. United States, 279 U.S. 749, 49 S.Ct. 471, 73 L.Ed. 938 (1929)—§ 13.4(e) n.171

Sincock v. State, 76 P.3d 323 (Wyo.2003)—§ 6.4(g) n.153

Sindelar v. State, 932 P.2d 730 (Wyo.1997)—§ 24.8(e) n.50

Sine, United States v., 461 F.Supp. 565 (D.S.C.1978)—§ 12.4(d) n.77

Singer, People v., 226 Cal.App.3d 23, 275 Cal.Rptr. 911 (1990)—§ 11.9(d) n.224

Singer, United States v., 970 F.2d 1414 (5th Cir.1992)—§ 3.4(j) n.198

Singer, United States v., 660 F.2d 1295 (8th Cir.1981)—§§ 15.6(b) n.54; 15.7(b) n.45

Singer v. United States, 380 U.S. 24, 85 S.Ct. 783, 13 L.Ed.2d 630 (1965)—§§ 22.1(a) n.14; 22.1(h) n.153; 24.1(a) n.14; 24.6(a) n.8

Singletary, United States v., 268 F.3d 196 (3d Cir.2001)—§ 1.2(c) n.142

Singleterry, United States v., 683 F.2d 122 (5th Cir.1982)—§ 22.2(a) n.10

Singleton, Commonwealth v., 439 Pa. 185, 266 A.2d 753 (1970)—§§ 6.8(a) n.13, 15

Singleton v. Commonwealth, 306 Ky. 454, 208 S.W.2d 325 (1948)—§ 15.1(f) n.276

Singleton v. Lefkowitz, 583 F.2d 618 (2d Cir.1978)—§ 24.3(h) n.182

Singleton v. Lockhart, 871 F.2d 1395 (8th Cir.1989)—§ 22.2(d) n.80

Singleton, State v., 218 W.Va. 180, 624 S.E.2d 527 (2005)—§ 6.6(e) n.59

Singleton, State v., 340 Ark. 710, 13 S.W.3d 584 (2000)—§§ 21.4(a) n.11; 22.1(h) n.149

Singleton, State v., 284 S.C. 388, 326 S.E.2d 153 (1985)—§ 6.8(a) n.14

Singleton, State v., 352 So.2d 191 (La.1977)—§ 17.2(d) n.97

Singleton, United States v., 165 F.3d 1297 (10th Cir.1999)—§§ 13.2(a) n.27; 21.2(b) n.71

Singleton, United States v., 182 F.3d 7 (D.C.Cir.1999)—§ 12.3(a) n.18

Singleton, United States v., 144 F.3d 1343 (10th Cir.1998)—§ 21.2(b) n.69

Singleton, United States v., 987 F.2d 1444 (9th Cir.1993)—§ 9.2(a) n.6

Singleton, United States v., 460 F.2d 1148 (2d Cir.1972)—§ 20.2(e) n.83

Siniard v. State, 491 So.2d 1062 (Ala.Crim.App.1986)—§§ 11.3(c) n.54, 66

Sinistaj v. Burt, 66 F.3d 804 (6th Cir.1995)—§§ 22.1(h) n.138, 140

Sioux Falls Argus Leader v. Miller, 610 N.W.2d 76 (2000)—§ 23.1(b) n.68

Sioux Falls, City of v. Bohner, 86 S.D. 527, 199 N.W.2d 499 (1972)—§ 1.8(d) n.56

Sipe, United States v., 388 F.3d 471 (5th Cir.2004)—§ 24.3(b) n.35

Siripongs, People v., 45 Cal.3d 548, 247 Cal.Rptr. 729, 754 P.2d 1306 (1988)—§ 4.6(b) n.42

Sirois, Commonwealth v., 437 Mass. 845, 777 N.E.2d 125 (2002)—§ 6.8(b) n.50

Sisca, United States v., 503 F.2d 1337 (2d Cir.1974)—§ 10.1(a) n.12

Sisk v. State, 290 So.2d 608 (Miss.1974)—§§ 10.5(a) n.11, 13

Sisk v. State, 232 Ind. 214, 110 N.E.2d 627 (1953)—§ 15.4(b) n.49

Sisneros v. State, 121 P.3d 790 (Wyo.2005)—§ 18.2(d) n.64

Sisneros, State v., 137 Ariz. 323, 670 P.2d 721 (1983)—§ 14.2(d) n.58

Sisson, State v., 567 N.W.2d 839 (N.D.1997)—§ 21.6(a) n.80

Sistrunk v. Lyons, 646 F.2d 64 (3d Cir.1981)—§ 2.6(b) n.37

Sites, Commonwealth v., 427 Pa. 486, 235 A.2d 387 (1967)—§ 6.6(f) n.109

Sites v. State, 300 Md. 702, 481 A.2d 192 (1984)—§ 7.3(c) n.50

Sithithongtham, United States v., 192 F.3d 1119 (8th Cir.1999)—§ 22.3(c) n.108

Sitton, United States v., 968 F.2d 947 (9th Cir.1992)—§§ 15.5(b) n.90; 15.7(e) n.107, 115

Sitz v. Department of State Police, 443 Mich. 744, 506 N.W.2d 209 (1993)—§§ 2.12(c) n.133; 2.12(d) n.192

Siu Kuen Ma, United States v., 290 F.3d 1002 (9th Cir.2002)—§ 21.4(e) n.163

Sivels, People v., 60 Ill.2d 102, 324 N.E.2d 422 (1975)—§ 21.1(e) n.67

Sivels v. State, 741 N.E.2d 1197 (Ind.2001)—§§ 13.2(c) n.59; 25.2(e) n.38

Siverson v. O'Leary, 764 F.2d 1208 (7th Cir.1985)—§ 11.10(d) n.200

Sixth Judicial District Court, State v., 114 Nev. 739, 964 P.2d 48 (1998)—§§ 14.2(d) n.62; 14.3(c) n.70

Sizemore v. State, 483 N.E.2d 56 (Ind.1985)—§ 3.1(h) n.206

Sizemore v. State, 272 Ind. 26, 395 N.E.2d 783 (Ind.1979)—§ 16.1(g) n.248

Skaff, State v., 152 Wis.2d 48, 447 N.W.2d 84 (1989)—§ 26.5(c) n.44

Skaggs v. Commonwealth, 694 S.W.2d 672 (Ky.1985)—§ 6.2(c) n.107

Skaggs v. State, 676 So.2d 897 (Miss.1996)—§ 18.2(b) n.12

Skaggs, State v., 551 So.2d 831 (La.App.1989)—§ 5.3(a) n.5

Skakel, State v., 276 Conn. 633, 888 A.2d 985 (2006)—§ 6.10(b) n.16

Skalsky, United States v., 857 F.2d 172 (3d Cir.1988)—§§ 8.11(e) n.93; 13.5(b) n.36

Skarie, United States v., 971 F.2d 317 (9th Cir.1992)—§§ 5.2(a) n.16; 5.3(b) n.17

Skaro, State v., 474 N.W.2d 711 (N.D.1991)—§ 24.11(d) n.21

Skeddle, United States v., 989 F.Supp. 912 (N.D.Ohio 1997)—§ 20.3(j) n.194

Skeens, United States v., 449 F.2d 1066 (D.C.Cir.1971)—§ 24.3(g) n.169

Skelley, United States v., 501 F.2d 447 (7th Cir.1974)—§ 19.5(d) n.81

Skelton, State v., 247 Kan. 34, 795 P.2d 349 (1990)—§§ 3.2(f) n.183; 7.4(d) n.74; 10.2(b) n.19

Skidmore, State v., 15 S.W.3d 502 (Tenn.Crim.App.1999)—§§ 13.6(c) n.46, 50

Skidmore, United States v., 998 F.2d 372 (6th Cir.1993)—§§ 21.2(e) n.300; 21.3(e) n.271

Skillern v. State, 890 S.W.2d 849 (Tex.App.1994)—§§ 16.1(a) n.1, 2

Skillicorn, State v., 944 S.W.2d 877 (Mo.1997)—§ 24.9(c) n.20

Skinner v. Oklahoma ex rel. Williamson, 316 U.S. 535, 62 S.Ct. 1110, 86 L.Ed. 1655 (1942)—§ 13.4(a) n.2

Skinner, People v., 52 N.Y.2d 24, 436 N.Y.S.2d 207, 417 N.E.2d 501 (1980)—§ 6.4(f) n.112

Skinner v. Railway Labor Executives Ass'n, 489 U.S. 602, 109 S.Ct. 1402, 103 L.Ed.2d 639 (1989)—§§ 3.1(h) n.190; 3.2(b) n.69, 79; 3.2(g) n.195; 3.9(l) n.272; 8.7(d) n.73

Skinner v. State, 113 Nev. 49, 930 P.2d 748 (1997)—§ 21.4(d) n.119

Skinner v. State, 575 A.2d 1108 (Del.1990)—§ 18.2(e) n.81

Skinner, United States v., 972 F.2d 171 (7th Cir.1992)—§§ 3.1(c) n.57, 79

Skipper v. South Carolina, 476 U.S. 1, 106 S.Ct. 1669, 90 L.Ed.2d 1 (1986)—§§ 26.1(b) n.21; 26.4(d) n.57; 26.4(g) n.116

Skipwith, United States v., 482 F.2d 1272 (5th Cir.1973)—§ 3.9(h) n.151

Skiriotes v. Florida, 313 U.S. 69, 61 S.Ct. 924, 85 L.Ed. 1193 (1941)—§§ 16.4(c) n.39, 113

Skjonsby, State v., 319 N.W.2d 764 (N.D.1982)—§§ 15.7(f) n.134, 166; 24.8(f) n.92

Sklar, State v., 317 A.2d 160 (Me.1974)—§§ 2.12(b) n.106; 2.12(e) n.212

Skramstad, United States v., 649 F.2d 1259 (8th Cir.1981)—§ 3.3(c) n.114

Skrine, People v., 125 A.D.2d 507, 509 N.Y.S.2d 589 (1986)—§ 15.2(c) n.79

Skrivanek v. State, 356 Md. 270, 739 A.2d 12 (1999)—§ 5.4(c) n.44

Skurtal, United States v., 341 F.3d 921 (9th Cir.2003)—§ 11.2(c) n.96

Slack v. McDaniel, 529 U.S. 473, 120 S.Ct. 1595, 146 L.Ed.2d 542 (2000)—§§ 28.5(c) n.72; 28.10 n.3, 5

Slade v. State, 270 Ga. 305, 509 S.E.2d 618 (1998)—§ 22.3(d) n.250

Slamon, State v., 73 Vt. 212, 50 A. 1097 (1901)—§ 2.12(a) n.10

Slapnicka, State v., 376 N.W.2d 33 (N.D.1985)—§ 21.6(a) n.80

Slappy, State v., 522 So.2d 18 (Fla.1988)—§ 22.3(d) n.245

Slater, Commonwealth v., 242 Pa.Super. 255, 363 A.2d 1257 (1976)—§ 3.3(c) n.115

Slater, State v., 169 Conn. 38, 362 A.2d 499 (1975)—§ 21.5(a) n.35

Slater, United States v., 971 F.2d 626 (10th Cir.1992)—§ 6.2(c) n.78

Slaton, Commonwealth v., 530 Pa. 207, 608 A.2d 5 (1992)—§ 3.10(c) n.96

Slaton v. State, 510 N.E.2d 1343 (Ind.1987)—§§ 7.4(b) n.23; 7.4(f) n.96

Slaughter v. Parker, 450 F.3d 224 (6th Cir.2006)—§ 24.9(b) n.14

Slaughter v. State, 969 P.2d 990 (Okla.Crim.App.1998)—§ 11.7(e) n.94

Slaughter-House Cases, 83 U.S. (16 Wall) 36, 21 L.Ed. 394 (1872)—§§ 2.2 n.5; 2.3(a) n.15 to 17, 26, 36; 2.3(b) n.76; 2.5(f) n.49

Slavin, People v., 1 N.Y.3d 392, 775 N.Y.S.2d 210, 807 N.E.2d 259 (2004)—§§ 7.2(b) n.28; 8.12(d) n.44

Slawson v. State, 619 So.2d 255 (Fla.1993)—§ 6.9(g) n.183

Sledge, United States v., 546 F.2d 1120 (4th Cir.1977)—§§ 6.8(c) n.69, 71

Sleeper v. Spencer, 453 F.Supp.2d 204 (D.Mass.2006)—§ 24.3(b) n.54

Slemmer, State v., 170 Ariz. 174, 823 P.2d 41 (1991)—§ 2.11(a) n.14

Slepicoff, United States v., 524 F.2d 1244 (5th Cir.1975)—§ 15.7(g) n.195

Slifco, People v., 162 Mich.App. 758, 413 N.W.2d 102 (1987)—§ 16.1(d) n.138

Sliker, United States v., 751 F.2d 477 (2d Cir.1984)—§ 11.2(d) n.131

Slimskey, State v., 257 Conn. 842, 779 A.2d 723 (2001)—§§ 20.3(g) n.124; 20.3(m) n.237

Sliney v. State, 699 So.2d 662 (Fla.1997)—§ 6.9(a) n.6

Sloan, Commonwealth v., _____ Pa. _____, 907 A.2d 460 (2006)—§ 18.3(c) n.118

Sloan v. Pugh, 351 F.3d 1319 (10th Cir.2003)—§ 13.5(h) n.128

Sloan, United States v., 293 F.3d 1066 (8th Cir.2002)—§ 3.5(e) n.186

Sloan, United States v., 776 F.2d 926 (10th Cir.1985)—§ 11.2(e) n.173

Slobodian, State v., 57 N.J. 18, 268 A.2d 849 (1970)—§ 6.9(g) n.162

Slochower v. Board of Higher Education, 350 U.S. 551, 76 S.Ct. 637, 100 L.Ed. 692 (1956)—§ 3.9(c) n.46

Slocum, United States v., 708 F.2d 587 (11th Cir.1983)—§ 3.4(j) n.202

Slocum, United States v., 464 F.2d 1180 (3d Cir.1972)—§ 24.1(b) n.30

Sloley, United States v., 464 F.3d 355 (2d Cir.2006)—§ 21.1(h) n.213

Slye v. United States, 602 A.2d 135 (D.C.App.1992)—§ 24.3(c) n.95

Smaage, State v., 547 N.W.2d 916 (N.D.1996)—§ 16.3(b) n.23

Smack, United States v., 347 F.3d 533 (3d Cir.2003)—§ 21.3(b) n.89

Smagula, State v., 133 N.H. 600, 578 A.2d 1215 (1990)—§ 24.3(e) n.129

Smalis v. Pennsylvania, 476 U.S. 140, 106 S.Ct. 1745, 90 L.Ed.2d 116 (1986)—§ 25.3(c) n.29

Small, People v., 157 Misc.2d 673, 598 N.Y.S.2d 431 (Sup.Ct.1993)—§ 15.7(g) n.207

Small, State v., 762 So.2d 1071 (La.2000)—§ 3.3(b) n.55

Small, State v., 988 S.W.2d 671 (Tenn.1999)—§ 11.5(f) n.103

Small, United States v., 209 F.Supp.2d 1114 (D.Colo.2002)—§ 18.4(c) n.46

Small, United States v., 74 F.3d 1276 (D.C.Cir.1996)—§ 24.7(a) n.11

Smalley, United States v., 294 F.3d 1030 (8th Cir.2002)—§ 26.4(i) n.200

Smalley, United States v., 754 F.2d 944 (11th Cir.1985)—§ 17.1(a) n.14

Smalls v. Batista, 191 F.3d 272 (2d Cir.1999)—§ 24.9(d) n.48

Smalls, State v., 201 Or.App. 652, 120 P.3d 506 (2005)—§ 11.1(d) n.121

Smallwood, Commonwealth v., 379 Mass. 878, 401 N.E.2d 802 (1980)—§ 6.4(e) n.70

Smallwood, People v., 42 Cal.3d 415, 228 Cal.Rptr. 913, 722 P.2d 197 (1986)—§ 17.1(e) n.63

Smallwood, State v., 264 Kan. 69, 955 P.2d 1209 (1998)—§ 21.2(b) n.45

Smallwood v. State, 584 So.2d 733 (Miss.1991)—§ 15.4(g) n.169

Smallwood, United States v., 920 F.2d 1231 (5th Cir.1991)—§§ 21.1(h) n.233; 21.2(d) n.211

Smart v. Alaska, 146 P.3d 15 (Alaska.2006)—§ 28.11(b) n.20

Smart v. State, 352 Ark. 522, 104 S.W.3d 386 (2003)—§ 6.6(d) n.45

Smart, State v., 136 N.H. 639, 622 A.2d 1197 (N.H.1993)—§§ 23.3(a) n.9; 23.3(b) n.29

Smart, United States v., 278 F.3d 1168 (10th Cir.2002)—§ 4.6(c) n.52

Smays, People v., 156 Misc.2d 621, 594 N.Y.S.2d 101 (1993)—§ 8.14(b) n.33

Smiley, In re, 66 Cal.2d 606, 58 Cal.Rptr. 579, 427 P.2d 179 (1967)—§ 11.2(g) n.264

Smiley, Commonwealth v., 431 Mass. 477, 727 N.E.2d 1182 (2000)—§ 21.2(h) n.419

Smith, In re, 285 F.3d 6 (D.C.Cir.2002)—§ 28.9(a) n.6

Smith, In re, 888 F.2d 167 (D.C.Cir.1989)—§§ 10.1(c) n.38, 42

Smith v. Alabama, 124 U.S. 465, 8 S.Ct. 564, 31 L.Ed. 508 (1888)—§ 2.9(d) n.60

Smith v. Allwright, 321 U.S. 649, 64 S.Ct. 757, 88 L.Ed. 987 (1944)—§§ 2.9(b) n.6, 7, 13, 25

Smith v. Anderson, 689 F.2d 59 (6th Cir.1982)—§ 11.9(b) n.56

Smith v. Baldwin, 466 F.3d 805 (9th Cir.2006)—§ 24.3(h) n.176

Smith v. Bennett, 365 U.S. 708, 81 S.Ct. 895, 6 L.Ed.2d 39 (1961)—§ 11.2(d) n.119

Smith v. Black, 904 F.2d 950 (5th Cir.1990)—§ 24.3(d) n.111

Smith v. City of Hemst, 394 F.3d 689 (9th Cir.2005)—§ 3.5(a) n.70

Smith v. Coiner, 473 F.2d 877 (4th Cir.1973)—§ 7.4(b) n.22

Smith v. Commonwealth, 633 S.E.2d 188, 48 Va.App. 521 (2006)—§ 24.2(g) n.91

Smith v. Commonwealth, 40 Va.App. 595, 580 S.E.2d 481 (2003)—§ 24.7(e) n.40

Smith, Commonwealth v., 575 Pa. 203, 836 A.2d 5 (2003)—§ 3.2(h) n.207

Smith v. Commonwealth, 420 Mass. 291, 649 N.E.2d 744 (1995)—§ 22.2(d) n.74

Smith, Commonwealth v., 414 Mass. 437, 608 N.E.2d 1018 (1993)—§ 15.7(h) n.222

Smith, Commonwealth v., 412 Mass. 823, 593 N.E.2d 1288 (Mass.1992)—§§ 9.5(a) n.23; 9.5(c) n.66; 10.4(b) n.10, 17

Smith, Commonwealth v., 532 Pa. 177, 615 A.2d 321 (Pa.1992)—§ 25.4(a) n.7

Smith v. Commonwealth, 734 S.W.2d 437 (Ky.1987)—§§ 11.2(e) n.212, 213; 15.4(e) n.139

Smith v. Commonwealth, 222 Va. 700, 284 S.E.2d 590 (1981)—§ 26.10(d) n.90

Smith, Commonwealth v., 350 Mass. 600, 215 N.E.2d 897 (1966)—§ 22.3(b) n.75

Smith v. Daily Mail Pub. Co., 443 U.S. 97, 99 S.Ct. 2667, 61 L.Ed.2d 399 (1979)—§§ 23.1(c) n.115, 116

Smith v. DeRobertis, 758 F.2d 1151 (7th Cir.1985)—§ 17.2(f) n.133

Smith v. Doe, 538 U.S. 84, 123 S.Ct. 1140, 155 L.Ed.2d 164 (2003)—§§ 25.1(c) n.40, 43

Smith v. Dugger, 840 F.2d 787 (11th Cir.1988)—§ 11.10(c) n.83

Smith v. Endell, 860 F.2d 1528 (9th Cir.1988)—§ 6.9(f) n.134

Smith v. Gohmert, 962 S.W.2d 590 (Tex.Cr.App.1998)—§ 27.4(c) n.23

Smith v. Groose, 205 F.3d 1045 (8th Cir.2000)—§ 17.4(a) n.50

Smith v. Hall, 874 F.Supp. 441 (D.Mass.1995)—§§ 15.6(d) n.117; 15.7(b) n.50

Smith v. Hightower, 693 F.2d 359 (5th Cir.1982)—§ 15.1(d) n.251

Smith v. Hooey, 393 U.S. 374, 89 S.Ct. 575, 21 L.Ed.2d 607 (1969)—§§ 2.6(d) n.95; 2.9(i) n.276, 286; 18.1(b) n.8; 18.4(a) n.3

Smith v. Illinois, 469 U.S. 91, 105 S.Ct. 490, 83 L.Ed.2d 488 (1984)—§§ 2.9(h) n.210, 225; 6.9(f) n.140; 6.9(g) n.180

Smith v. Illinois, 390 U.S. 129, 88 S.Ct. 748, 19 L.Ed.2d 956 (1968)—§ 24.4(b) n.13

Smith v. Katzenbach, 351 F.2d 810 (D.C.Cir.1965)—§ 10.1(c) n.37

Smith v. Leis, 165 Ohio App.3d 581, 847 N.E.2d 485 (2006)—§ 12.4(e) n.91

Smith v. Leis, 106 Ohio St.3d 309, 835 N.E.2d 5 (2005)—§ 12.2(b) n.31

Smith v. Lockhart, 923 F.2d 1314 (8th Cir.1991)—§ 11.4(b) n.24

Smith v. Mabry, 564 F.2d 249 (8th Cir.1977)—§§ 18.4(a) n.11, 12

Smith v. Maryland, 442 U.S. 735, 99 S.Ct. 2577, 61 L.Ed.2d 220 (1979)—§§ 4.3(c) n.15; 4.5 n.6; 4.7(a) n.1

Smith v. Maryland, 59 U.S. (18 How.) 71, 15 L.Ed. 269 (1855)—§ 3.1(a) n.8

Smith v. Massachusetts, 543 U.S. 462, 125 S.Ct. 1129, 160 L.Ed.2d 914 (2005)—§§ 25.3(c) n.19, 25, 31

Smith v. Massey, 235 F.3d 1259 (10th Cir.2000)—§ 24.3(d) n.108

Smith v. McCormick, 914 F.2d 1153 (9th Cir.1990)—§ 11.2(e) n.172

Smith v. McCotter, 786 F.2d 697 (5th Cir.1986)—§ 21.4(f) n.204

Smith v. McRay, 907 So.2d 575 (Fla.App.2005)—§ 12.1(b) n.32

Smith v. Mullin, 379 F.3d 919 (10th Cir.2004)—§§ 6.9(b) n.27; 11.10(b) n.46; 11.10(c) n.127, 153

Smith v. Murray, 477 U.S. 527, 106 S.Ct. 2661, 91 L.Ed.2d 434 (1986)—§§ 2.9(f) n.119, 122; 11.10(a) n.23; 11.10(c) n.94; 28.4(e) n.73

Smith v. Newsome, 876 F.2d 1461 (11th Cir.1989)—§ 28.4(d) n.65

Smith v. O'Grady, 312 U.S. 329, 61 S.Ct. 572, 85 L.Ed. 859 (1941)—§ 21.4(c) n.69

Smith v. Ohio, 494 U.S. 541, 110 S.Ct. 1288, 108 L.Ed.2d 464 (1990)—§§ 3.2(h) n.203; 3.5(e) n.176

Smith v. Parman, 101 Kan. 115, 165 P. 663 (1917)—§ 13.5(g) n.111

Smith, People v., 40 Cal.4th 483, 54 Cal.Rptr.3d 245, 150 P.3d 1224 (2007)—§§ 6.2(c) n.132, 178; 6.8(b) n.50

Smith, People v., 478 Mich. 64, 731 N.W.2d 411 (2007)—§ 24.8(e) n.54

Smith, People v., 121 P.3d 243 (Colo.App.2005)—§ 26.8(c) n.28

Smith, People v., 132 Cal.App.4th 924, 33 Cal.Rptr.3d 918 (2005)—§ 22.1(h) n.141

Smith, People v., 185 Ill.2d 532, 236 Ill.Dec. 779, 708 N.E.2d 365 (1999)—§ 1.5(e) n.243

Smith, People v., 188 Ill.2d 335, 242 Ill.Dec. 274, 721 N.E.2d 553 (1999)—§ 24.2(d) n.45

Smith, People v., 921 P.2d 80 (Colo.App.1996)—§ 27.3(d) n.59

Smith, People v., 84 N.Y.2d 998, 622 N.Y.S.2d 507, 646 N.E.2d 809 (1994)—§ 15.2(c) n.83

Smith, People v., 206 App.Div.2d 102, 618 N.Y.S.2d 649 (1994)—§ 24.3(c) n.91

Smith, People v., 870 P.2d 617 (Colo.App.1994)—§ 9.4(f) n.115

Smith, People v., 6 Cal.4th 684, 25 Cal.Rptr.2d 122, 863 P.2d 192 (1993)—§ 11.4(b) n.19

Smith, People v., 237 Ill.App.3d 901, 178 Ill.Dec. 666, 605 N.E.2d 105 (1992)—§ 24.3(f) n.150

Smith, People v., 165 Ill.App.3d 603, 116 Ill.Dec. 402, 518 N.E.2d 1382 (1988)—§ 24.10(a) n.8

Smith, People v., 423 Mich. 427, 378 N.W.2d 384 (1985)—§§ 1.8(c) n.14, 15

Smith, People v., 111 Ill.App.3d 494, 67 Ill.Dec. 329, 444 N.E.2d 565 (1982)—§ 11.4(b) n.26

Smith, People v., 91 Ill.App.3d 242, 46 Ill.Dec. 698, 414 N.E.2d 751 (1980)—§§ 16.1(g) n.279, 280

Smith, People v., 67 Cal.App.3d 638, 136 Cal.Rptr. 764 (1977)—§ 3.10(e) n.173

Smith, People v., 18 Ill.App.3d 851, 310 N.E.2d 796 (1974)—§ 19.6(b) n.20

Smith, People v., 185 Colo. 369, 524 P.2d 607 (1974)—§ 20.1(a) n.15

Smith, People v., 5 Ill.App.3d 642, 283 N.E.2d 736 (1972)—§ 6.4(b) n.24

Smith, People v., 7 Cal.3d 282, 101 Cal.Rptr. 893, 496 P.2d 1261 (1972)—§ 3.9(b) n.30

Smith, People v., 7 Ill.App.3d 143, 287 N.E.2d 174 (1972)—§ 21.4(d) n.128

Smith, People v., 43 Mich.App. 400, 204 N.W.2d 308 (1972)—§ 3.10(e) n.180

Smith, People v., 5 Ill.App.3d 341, 275 N.E.2d 480 (1971)—§ 3.1(e) n.135

Smith, People v., 173 Colo. 10, 475 P.2d 627 (1970)—§ 6.7(d) n.147

Smith v. Phillips, 455 U.S. 209, 102 S.Ct. 940, 71 L.Ed.2d 78 (1982)—§§ 2.6(b) n.46; 2.9(g) n.171; 22.3(b) n.91; 22.3(c) n.120, 126, 138; 24.9(f) n.83

Smith v. Richert, 35 F.3d 300 (7th Cir.1994)—§§ 8.13(a) n.28; 8.13(b) n.61

Smith v. Robbins, 528 U.S. 259, 120 S.Ct. 746, 145 L.Ed.2d 756 (2000)—§§ 2.6(d) n.103; 2.7(b) n.80; 11.2(c) n.103, 116; 11.7(d) n.49; 11.10(d) n.169; 27.1(b) n.20

Smith v. Robbins, 528 U.S. 259, 120 S.Ct. 940, 71 L.Ed. 756 (2000)—§ 11.6(d) n.120

Smith v. Singletary, 170 F.3d 1051 (11th Cir.1999)—§ 11.10(c) n.109

Smith v. State, 918 A.2d 1144 (Del.2007)—§§ 6.9(b) n.20, 24

Smith, State v., 332 Mont. 386, 138 P.3d 799 (2006)—§ 5.2(a) n.8

Smith, State v., 269 Neb. 773, 696 N.W.2d 871 (2005)—§§ 7.4(c) n.52, 53

Smith v. State, 279 Ga. 396, 614 S.E.2d 79 (2005)—§ 13.3(c) n.38

Smith, State v., 339 Or. 515, 124 P.3d 261 (2005)—§ 11.4(c) n.91

Smith v. State, 149 S.W.3d 667 (Tex.Cr.App.2004)—§§ 22.2(d) n.70; 22.2(f) n.117

Smith, State v., 322 Mont. 206, 95 P.3d 137 (2004)—§§ 13.2(a) n.4; 13.7(a) n.29

Smith, State v., 322 Mont. 466, 97 P.3d 567 (2004)—§ 9.1(b) n.75

Smith v. State, 375 Md. 365, 825 A.2d 1055 (2003)—§ 22.1(h) n.145

Smith, State v., 38 P.3d 1149 (Alaska 2002)—§ 6.6(e) n.59

Smith v. State, 275 Ga. 261, 564 S.E.2d 441 (2002)—§§ 18.2(c) n.50; 18.2(d) n.65; 18.2(e) n.76

Smith, State v., 346 N.J.Super. 233, 787 A.2d 276 (2002)—§§ 24.2(d) n.45; 24.2(e) n.58

Smith v. State, 770 N.E.2d 290 (Ind.2002)—§ 21.2(b) n.48

Smith, State v., 816 A.2d 57 (Me.2002)—§ 17.4(b) n.122

Smith, State v., 167 N.J. 158, 770 A.2d 255 (2001)—§ 24.7(e) n.42

Smith v. State, 367 Md. 348, 787 A.2d 152 (2001)—§ 24.5(b) n.27

Smith v. State, 744 N.E.2d 437 (Ind.2001)—§ 3.5(c) n.129

Smith, State v., 24 S.W.3d 274 (Tenn. 2000)—§ 27.5(d) n.137

Smith, State v., 87 Ohio St.3d 424, 721 N.E.2d 93 (2000)—§ 16.1(e) n.175

Smith, State v., 352 N.C. 531, 532 S.E.2d 773 (2000)—§§ 21.4(a) n.40; 21.4(d) n.103; 22.3(c) n.147

Smith, State v., 193 Ariz. 452, 974 P.2d 431 (1999)—§ 6.9(f) n.139

Smith v. State, 745 So.2d 922 (Ala.App.1999)—§ 14.4(e) n.112

Smith, State v., 996 S.W.2d 845 (Tenn.Crim.App.1999)—§ 19.3(a) n.13

Smith, State v., 134 Wash.2d 849, 953 P.2d 810 (1998)—§ 21.6(b) n.112

Smith, State v., 155 N.J. 83, 713 A.2d 1033 (1998)—§ 3.3(c) n.90

Smith v. State, 116 Md.App. 43, 695 A.2d 575 (Md.App.1997)— §§ 16.1(a) n.17; 16.1(g) n.235, 236, 259, 264, 266, 267, 269; 16.1(h) n.294, 303, 305

Smith, State v., 268 Ga. 75, 485 S.E.2d 491 (1997)—§ 27.3(b) n.16

Smith v. State, 329 S.C. 280, 494 S.E.2d 626 (1997)—§ 21.4(d) n.119

Smith v. State, 686 N.E.2d 1264 (Ind.1997)—§ 21.2(a) n.8

Smith, State v., 700 So.2d 493 (La.1997)—§ 28.11(b) n.21

Smith, State v., 546 N.W.2d 916 (Iowa 1996)—§ 6.6(c) n.42

Smith, State v., 662 A.2d 1171 (R.I.1995)—§§ 15.6(a) n.42; 15.7(g) n.203

Smith v. State, 666 So.2d 810 (Miss.1995)—§ 11.9(b) n.83

Smith, State v., 74 Wash.App. 844, 875 P.2d 1249 (1994)—§ 26.3(f) n.55

Smith, State v., 136 N.J. 245, 642 A.2d 978 (1994)—§§ 13.2(a) n.3; 13.3(c) n.36

Smith v. State, 641 So.2d 1319 (Fla.1994)—§§ 11.5(b) n.23, 27, 30

Smith v. State, 646 So.2d 538 (Miss.1994)—§ 16.1(h) n.309

Smith, State v., 269 N.J.Super. 86, 634 A.2d 576 (1993)—§ 15.7(f) n.168

Smith, State v., 222 Conn. 1, 608 A.2d 63 (1992)—§§ 22.3(d) n.249, 250

Smith, State v., 312 Ore. 561, 822 P.2d 1193 (1992)—§ 27.5(c) n.73

Smith, State v., 834 S.W.2d 915 (Tenn.1992)—§ 9.5(a) n.23

Smith, State v., 120 Idaho 77, 813 P.2d 888 (1991)—§§ 3.7(a) n.12; 3.7(e) n.99, 108

Smith v. State, 565 N.E.2d 1059 (Ind.1991)—§§ 3.6(d) n.96; 10.2(b) n.19

Smith v. State, 588 A.2d 305 (Me.1991)—§ 11.5(f) n.96

Smith v. State, 588 So.2d 561 (Ala.Crim.App.1991)—§ 11.9(d) n.209

Smith, State v., 810 S.W.2d 155 (Tenn.Cr.App.1991)—§ 24.4(d) n.58

Smith, State v., 115 Wash.2d 775, 801 P.2d 975 (1990)—§ 3.10(b) n.34

Smith v. State, 790 S.W.2d 794 (Tex.App.1990)—§ 22.3(d) n.246

Smith, State v., 45 Ohio St.3d 255, 544 N.E.2d 239 (1989)—§ 3.8(c) n.84

Smith, State v., 105 Nev. 293, 774 P.2d 1037 (1989)—§§ 6.7(a) n.3; 17.4(a) n.42

Smith, State v., 244 Kan. 283, 767 P.2d 1302 (1989)—§ 21.2(d) n.217

Smith, State v., 316 Md. 223, 557 A.2d 1343 (1989)—§ 18.4(c) n.32

Smith v. State, 550 So.2d 406 (Miss.1989)—§ 18.2(d) n.65

Smith, State v., 777 P.2d 464 (Utah 1989)—§ 21.4(d) n.118

Smith, State v., 110 Wash.2d 658, 756 P.2d 722 (1988)—§ 3.1(h) n.193

Smith, State v., 207 Conn. 152, 540 A.2d 679 (1988)—§ 1.7(i) n.208

Smith, State v., 243 Kan. 715, 763 P.2d 632 (1988)—§ 3.1(h) n.212

Smith v. State, 296 Ark. 451, 757 S.W.2d 554 (1988)—§ 6.3(c) n.49

Smith, State v., 421 N.W.2d 315 (Minn.1988)—§§ 2.6(b) n.58, 61; 16.4(c) n.39, 45, 83, 105; 16.4(d) n.121, 138, 139

Smith v. State, 757 S.W.2d 14 (Tenn.Crim.App.1988)—§ 14.2(c) n.40

Smith, State v., 200 Conn. 465, 512 A.2d 189 (1986)—§§ 6.2(c) n.116; 7.4(g) n.112

Smith, State v., 301 Or. 681, 725 P.2d 894 (1986)—§ 2.12(c) n.146

Smith v. State, 306 Md. 1, 506 A.2d 1165 (1986)—§ 26.10(d) n.85

Smith v. State, 308 Md. 162, 517 A.2d 1081 (1986)—§ 26.4(b) n.8

Smith, State v., 317 N.C. 100, 343 S.E.2d 518 (1986)—§§ 6.6(c) n.40; 6.9(b) n.22

Smith v. State, 492 So.2d 1063 (Fla.1986)—§ 6.9(f) n.100

Smith v. State, 64 Md.App. 625, 498 A.2d 284 (1985)—§ 26.4(d) n.54

Smith v. State, 101 Nev. 167, 697 P.2d 113 (1985)—§ 16.4(c) n.89

Smith, State v., 315 N.C. 76, 337 S.E.2d 833 (1985)—§§ 1.7(i) n.202, 206

Smith v. State, 475 N.E.2d 1139 (Ind.1985)—§ 23.2(g) n.122

Smith, State v., 699 P.2d 711 (Utah 1985)—§ 18.1(c) n.36

Smith v. State, 703 S.W.2d 641 (Tex.Cr.App.1985)—§ 22.3(a) n.23

Smith, State v., 140 Ariz. 355, 681 P.2d 1374 (1984)—§§ 11.4(a) n.7; 11.8(c) n.68

Smith, State v., 195 N.J.Super. 468, 480 A.2d 236 (1984)—§ 13.2(c) n.77

Smith, State v., 353 N.W.2d 338 (S.D.1984)—§§ 18.4(c) n.47, 70

Smith, State v., 92 N.J. 143, 455 A.2d 1117 (1983)—§ 13.6(c) n.42

Smith v. State, 51 Md.App. 408, 443 A.2d 985 (1982)—§ 27.5(b) n.49

Smith, State v., 418 So.2d 515 (La.1982)—§ 20.3(h) n.155

Smith, State v., 102 Idaho 108, 626 P.2d 206 (1981)—§§ 19.2(b) n.19, 21

Smith, State v., 617 P.2d 232 (Okla.Crim.App.1980)—§ 14.3(d) n.99

Smith, State v., 122 Ariz. 50, 592 P.2d 1316 (1979)—§ 24.5(b) n.33

Smith, State v., 123 Ari. 243, 599 P.2d 199 (1979)—§§ 20.6(b) n.18; 20.6(c) n.84, 87

Smith, State v., 123 Ariz. 231, 599 P.2d 187 (1979)—§ 20.3(a) n.21

Smith, State v., 357 So.2d 798 (La.1978)—§ 7.3(d) n.77

Smith, State v., 88 Wash.2d 127, 559 P.2d 970 (1977)—§ 3.5(e) n.204

Smith v. State, 344 A.2d 251 (Del.1975)—§ 14.2(c) n.40

Smith, State v., 84 Wash.2d 498, 527 P.2d 674 (1974)—§§ 1.7(f) n.93, 103

Smith v. State, 258 Ind. 415, 281 N.E.2d 803 (1972)—§ 5.4(b) n.16

Smith, State v., 260 So.2d 489 (Fla.1972)—§ 3.5(d) n.175

Smith v. State, 228 Miss. 476, 87 So.2d 917 (1956)—§ 3.5(a) n.39

Smith v. State, 18 Okla.Crim.Rep. 603, 18 Okla.Crim. 603, 197 Pac. 712 (1921)—§ 16.1(e) n.192

Smith v. State, 42 Fla. 605, 28 So. 758 (1900)—§§ 16.1(e) n.198; 16.2(a) n.5

Smith, State v., 138 Ala. 111, 35 So. 42 (1903)—§ 14.3(a) n.23

Smith v. Stegall, 385 F.3d 993 (6th Cir.2004)—§§ 21.2(b) n.48; 21.2(d) n.177

Smith, United States v., 445 F.3d 713 (3d Cir.2006)—§ 26.9(b) n.43

Smith, United States v., 452 F.3d 323 (4th Cir.2006)—§ 21.2(d) n.150

Smith, United States v., 415 F.3d 682 (7th Cir.2005)—§ 18.3(b) n.27

Smith, United States v., 417 F.3d 483 (5th Cir.2005)—§§ 21.3(d) n.218; 21.3(e) n.297

Smith, United States v., 419 F.3d 521 (6th Cir.2005)—§ 27.5(c) n.80

Smith, United States v., 422 F.3d 715 (8th Cir.2005)—§ 21.1(h) n.199

Smith, United States v., 429 F.3d 620 (6th Cir.2005)—§ 21.5(d) n.104

Smith, United States v., 373 F.3d 561 (4th Cir.2004)—§ 18.5(a) n.11

Smith, United States v., 389 F.3d 944 (9th Cir.2004)—§ 3.7(a) n.10

Smith, United States v., 344 F.3d 479 (6th Cir.2003)—§ 21.2(b) n.82

Smith v. United States, 801 A.2d 958 (D.C. App.2002)—§ 19.6(c) n.46

Smith, United States v., 245 F.3d 538 (6th Cir.2001)—§ 8.10(a) n.17

Smith v. United States, 768 A.2d 577 (D.C.App.2001)—§ 22.1(b) n.42

Smith, United States v., 218 F.3d 777 (7th Cir.2000)—§ 6.9(e) n.88

Smith, United States v., 223 F.3d 554 (7th Cir.2000)—§ 4.6(g) n.136

Smith, United States v., 231 F.3d 800 (11th Cir.2000)—§§ 13.4(b) n.38; 13.4(e) n.167, 169

Smith, United States v., 184 F.3d 415 (5th Cir.1999)—§ 21.5(c) n.83

Smith, United States v., 135 F.3d 963 (5th Cir.1998)—§§ 8.8(d) n.47, 82

Smith, United States v., 140 F.3d 1325 (10th Cir.1998)—§ 21.2(d) n.173

Smith, United States v., 155 F.3d 1051 (9th Cir.1998)—§ 4.6(b) n.31

Smith, United States v., 156 F.3d 1046 (10th Cir.1998)—§§ 7.4(e) n.84, 89; 7.5(b) n.21

Smith, United States v., 160 F.3d 117 (2d Cir.1998)—§§ 21.4(f) n.170, 171; 21.4(g) n.259

Smith, United States v., 123 F.3d 140 (3d Cir.1997)—§§ 23.1(d) n.125, 156, 159, 162, 204

Smith, United States v., 131 F.3d 1392 (10th Cir.1997)—§ 3.5(a) n.56

Smith, United States v., 73 F.3d 1414 (6th Cir.1996)—§ 3.5(a) n.40

Smith, United States v., 77 F.3d 511 (D.C.Cir.1996)—§ 24.3(b) n.49

Smith, United States v., 79 F.3d 1208 (D.C.Cir.1996)—§ 12.3(a) n.20

Smith, United States v., 103 F.3d 531 (7th Cir.1996)—§ 21.5(e) n.147

Smith v. United States, 687 A.2d 581 (D.C.App.1996)—§ 26.7(c) n.36

Smith, United States v., 13 F.3d 1421 (10th Cir.1994)—§ 19.3(b) n.145

Smith, United States v., 31 F.3d 1294 (4th Cir.1994)—§§ 4.6(e) n.102; 24.3(c) n.100

Smith, United States v., 3 F.3d 1088 (7th Cir.1993)—§ 6.6(e) n.95

Smith, United States v., 7 F.3d 1164 (5th Cir.1993)—§ 9.6(c) n.66

Smith, United States v., 995 F.2d 662 (7th Cir.1993)—§§ 11.4(c) n.57; 11.9(a) n.24; 11.9(c) n.111, 119, 139

Smith, United States v., 973 F.2d 1374 (8th Cir.1992)—§ 3.10(b) n.37

Smith, United States v., 982 F.2d 757 (2d Cir.1992)—§ 11.8(c) n.60

Smith v. United States, 586 A.2d 684 (D.C.App.1991)—§ 6.7(b) n.71

Smith, United States v., 924 F.2d 889 (9th Cir.1991)—§ 24.3(f) n.142

Smith, United States v., 930 F.2d 1081 (5th Cir.1991)—§ 3.10(d) n.110

Smith, United States v., 907 F.2d 42 (6th Cir.1990)—§ 11.5(e) n.86

Smith, United States v., 912 F.2d 322 (9th Cir.1990)—§ 25.1(c) n.40

Smith, United States v., 918 F.2d 1551 (11th Cir.1990)—§§ 17.2(c) n.82; 17.2(e) n.116; 17.2(f) n.133

Smith v. United States, 876 F.2d 655 (8th Cir.1989)—§ 21.6(a) n.77

Smith v. United States, 542 A.2d 823 (D.C.App.1988)—§ 24.9(d) n.40

Smith, United States v., 787 F.2d 111 (3d Cir.1986)—§§ 23.1(d) n.141, 157, 164, 166, 202

Smith, United States v., 793 F.2d 85 (3d Cir.1986)—§ 12.4(d) n.69

Smith v. United States, 491 A.2d 1144 (D.C.App.1985)—§ 20.3(c) n.77

Smith, United States v., 757 F.2d 1161 (11th Cir.1985)—§ 5.3(c) n.36

Smith, United States v., 776 F.2d 1104 (3d Cir.1985)—§§ 19.4(b) n.25; 23.1(d) n.177, 186; 23.1(e) n.224

Smith, United States v., 580 F.Supp. 1418 (D.N.J.1984)—§§ 8.11(c) n.37, 41, 55

Smith, United States v., 687 F.2d 147 (6th Cir.1982)—§ 8.8(g) n.174

Smith, United States v., 643 F.2d 942 (2d Cir.1981)—§ 3.1(d) n.109

Smith, United States v., 578 F.2d 1227 (8th Cir.1978)—§ 24.4(d) n.44

Smith, United States v., 550 F.2d 277 (5th Cir.1977)—§§ 11.9(d) n.188; 22.3(e) n.266

Smith, United States v., 552 F.2d 257 (8th Cir.1977)—§ 15.5(b) n.60

Smith, United States v., 354 A.2d 510 (D.C.App.1976)—§ 13.6(c) n.36

Smith, United States v., 473 F.2d 1148 (D.C.Cir.1972)—§ 7.4(g) n.115

Smith, United States v., 440 F.2d 521 (7th Cir.1971)—§ 21.5(c) n.75

Smith v. United States, 375 F.2d 243 (5th Cir.1967)—§ 13.3(a) n.3

Smith v. United States, 384 F.2d 649 (8th Cir.1967)—§ 11.2(c) n.101

Smith v. United States, 360 U.S. 1, 79 S.Ct. 991, 3 L.Ed.2d 1041 (1959)—§§ 15.1(f) n.273, 303

Smith v. United States, 94 U.S. 97, 24 L.Ed. 32 (1876)—§§ 27.5(c) n.72, 73

Smith v. Wainwright, 664 F.2d 1194 (11th Cir.1981)—§ 21.1(e) n.62

Smith v. Walls, 276 F.3d 340 (7th Cir.2002)—§ 28.5(b) n.48

Smith v. White, 815 F.2d 1401 (11th Cir.1987)—§§ 11.9(d) n.204, 205

Smith v. Zant, 855 F.2d 712 (11th Cir.1988)—§ 6.9(b) n.26

Smithers v. State, 826 So.2d 916 (Fla.2002)—§ 17.1(a) n.4

Smith, Estate of v. Marasco, 318 F.3d 497 (3d Cir.2003)—§ 3.2(c) n,127

Smith Grading and Paving, Inc., United States v., 760 F.2d 527 (4th Cir.1985)—§ 20.3(m) n.239

Smith, United States ex rel. v. Baldi, 344 U.S. 561, 73 S.Ct. 391, 97 L.Ed. 549 (1953)—§ 11.2(e) n.140

Smith, United States ex rel. v. Lane, 794 F.2d 287 (7th Cir.1986)—§ 11.8(c) n.61

Smith, United States ex rel. v. Twomey, 486 F.2d 736 (7th Cir.1973)—§ 12.4(d) n.86

Smocum, People v., 99 N.Y.2d 418, 757 N.Y.S.2d 239, 786 N.E.2d 1275 (2003)—§§ 22.3(d) n.221, 234

Smothers, State v., 605 S.W.2d 128 (Mo.1980)—§ 20.6(b) n.45

Smuda, State v., 419 N.W.2d 166 (N.D.1988)—§ 24.2(b) n.24

Smullen, State v., 118 N.J. 408, 571 A.2d 1305 (1990)—§§ 21.4(f) n.174; 21.5(a) n.35

Smylie v. State, 823 N.E.2d 679 (Ind.2005)—§ 26.4(i) n.189

Smyth v. Lubbers, 398 F.Supp. 777 (W.D.Mich.1975)—§§ 3.9(k) n.264, 265

Smyth, State v., 286 Or. 293, 593 P.2d 1166 (1979)—§ 2.12(e) n.210

Smyth, United States v., 104 F.Supp. 283 (N.D.Cal.1952)—§§ 8.4(b) n.50; 8.4(c) n.112, 117; 8.5(a) n.2; 15.2(b) n.20; 15.4(b) n.32; 15.6(c) n.91

Smythe, State v., 72 Haw. 217, 811 P.2d 1100 (1991)—§ 21.4(a) n.22

Snead v. Stringer, 454 U.S. 988, 102 S.Ct. 535, 70 L.Ed.2d 402 (1981)—§ 28.2(c) n.49

Snead, United States v., 527 F.2d 590 (4th Cir.1975)—§ 16.2(g) n.131

Sneed, United States v., 34 F.3d 1570 (10th Cir.1994)—§§ 5.4(c) n.43, 48

Sneed, State ex rel. v. Long, 871 S.W.2d 148 (Tenn.1994)—§ 27.4(f) n.66

Snelgrove v. State, 292 Ark. 116, 728 S.W.2d 497 (1987)—§ 21.4(f) n.173

Snell v. Lockhart, 14 F.3d 1289 (8th Cir.1994)—§§ 23.2(a) n.16, 25

Snell, State v., _____ R.I. _____, 892 A.2d 108 (2006)—§ 24.2(e) n.55

Snell, United States v., 899 F.Supp. 17 (D.Mass.1995)—§§ 20.3(m) n.251, 253, 254

Snethen v. Nix, 885 F.2d 456 (8th Cir.1989)—§ 6.10(b) n.14

Snider, United States v., 957 F.2d 703 (9th Cir.1992)—§§ 21.3(e) n.284; 21.4(g) n.240

Snipes v. State, 733 So.2d 1000 (Fla.1999)—§§ 6.2(c) n.185; 19.5(c) n.50

Snipes v. United States, 507 A.2d 159 (D.C.App.1986)—§ 21.2(d) n.141

Snodgrass, Commonwealth v., 831 S.W.2d 176 (Ky.1992)—§ 22.3(d) n.246

Snow, In re, 120 U.S. 274, 7 S.Ct. 556, 30 L.Ed. 658 (1887)—§ 28.3(b) n.48

Snow v. Commonwealth, 404 Mass. 1007, 537 N.E.2d 578 (1989)— § 12.1(d) n.51

Snow, People v., 39 Ill.App.3d 887, 350 N.E.2d 875 (1976)—§ 6.6(e) n.68

Snow, People v., 386 Mich. 586, 194 N.W.2d 314 (1972)—§ 21.1(e) n.61

Snow v. State, 800 So.2d 472 (Miss.2001)—§§ 6.7(c) n.121, 123; 6.7(d) n.147, 152; 6.9(b) n.31

Snow, United States v., 234 F.3d 187 (4th Cir.2000)—§ 21.2(d) n.257

Snow, United States v., 919 F.2d 1458 (10th Cir.1990)—§ 3.3(g) n.225

Snow, United States v., 748 F.2d 928 (4th Cir.1984)—§ 27.5(c) n.83

Snow, United States v., 552 F.2d 165 (6th Cir.1977)—§ 7.5(b) n.12

Snowden v. Hughes, 321 U.S. 1, 64 S.Ct. 397, 88 L.Ed. 497 (1944)— § 13.4(d) n.148

Snowden v. State, 672 A.2d 1017 (Del.1996)—§ 24.3(b) n.73

Snowman, State v., 698 A.2d 1057 (Me.1997)—§ 27.5(a) n.9

Snyder, Commonwealth v., 413 Mass. 521, 597 N.E.2d 1363 (1992)— § 3.9(k) n.257

Snyder v. Massachusetts, 291 U.S. 97, 54 S.Ct. 330, 78 L.Ed. 674 (1934)— §§ 1.5(k) n.417; 2.4(e) n.156, 165; 2.6(b) n.34; 2.7(c) n.148, 161, 163, 210, 222; 22.1(a) n.10; 24.2(a) n.4

Snyder v. State, 500 N.E.2d 154 (Ind.1986)—§ 21.4(a) n.12

Snyder v. Sumner, 960 F.2d 1448 (9th Cir.1992)—§ 18.4(c) n.37

Snyder, United States v., 235 F.3d 42 (1st Cir.2000)—§ 22.4(c) n.28

Snyder, United States v., 852 F.2d 471 (9th Cir.1988)—§ 3.5(c) n.129

Snyder, United States v., 707 F.2d 139 (5th Cir.1983)—§ 11.9(c) n.105

Snype, United States v., 441 F.3d 119 (2d Cir.2006)—§ 13.4(a) n.28

Sobamowo, United States v., 892 F.2d 90 (D.C.Cir.1989)—§ 24.2(a) n.8

Sober v. Crist, 644 F.2d 807 (9th Cir.1981)—§ 21.4(c) n.82

Soberon, United States v., 929 F.2d 935 (3d Cir.1991)—§§ 15.6(e) n.164; 15.7(e) n.110

Sobin, United States v., 56 F.3d 1423 (D.C.Cir.1995)—§ 26.1(f) n.145

Sobin v. United States, 606 A.2d 1029 (D.C.App.1992)—§§ 24.1(a) n.5; 24.1(b) n.18

Sochor v. State, 619 So.2d 285 (Fla.1993)—§ 18.5(a) n.8

Society of Good Neighbors v. Van Antwerp, 324 Mich. 22, 36 N.W.2d 308 (1949)—§ 13.4(a) n.5

Sockwell, Ex parte, 675 So.2d 38 (Ala.1995)—§ 22.3(d) n.228

Sockwell v. Blackburn, 748 F.2d 979 (5th Cir.1984)—§ 6.10(b) n.11

Sockwell v. State, 675 So.2d 4 (Ala.Crim.App.1993)—§ 11.9(a) n.27

Socony-Vacuum Oil Co., United States v., 310 U.S. 150, 60 S.Ct. 811, 84 L.Ed. 1129 (1940)—§ 24.7(e) n.61

Soderling, United States v., 970 F.2d 529 (9th Cir.1992)—§ 21.3(e) n.284

Soffar v. Johnson, 237 F.3d 411 (5th Cir.2000)—§§ 6.9(g) n.166, 189

Sohnleitner, Commonwealth v., 884 A.2d 307 (Pa.Super.2005)— §§ 13.6(c) n.28, 31, 43

Sohrab, People v., 59 Cal.App.4th 89, 68 Cal.Rptr.2d 89 (1997)— § 11.3(a) n.17

Sokolow, United States v., 490 U.S. 1, 109 S.Ct. 1581, 104 L.Ed.2d 1 (1989)—§§ 2.9(i) n.272; 3.8(d) n.124, 127, 146

Sokolow, United States v., 808 F.2d 1366 (9th Cir.1987)—§ 3.8(c) n.92

Solan, United States v., 792 F.Supp. 99 (M.D.Fla.1992)—§ 16.2(f) n.106

Solano, State v., 150 Ariz. 398, 724 P.2d 17 (1986)—§ 21.2(b) n.57

Solano, United States v., 605 F.2d 1141 (9th Cir.1979)—§ 17.4(b) n.106

Solano-Godines, United States v., 120 F.3d 957 (9th Cir.1997)—§ 6.10(e) n.80

Solberg v. Superior Court, 19 Cal.3d 182, 137 Cal.Rptr. 460, 561 P.2d 1148 (1977)—§ 22.4(d) n.36

Soldal v. Cook County, 506 U.S. 56, 113 S.Ct. 538, 121 L.Ed.2d 450 (1992)—§§ 3.2(a) n.27; 3.7(f) n.131; 3.10(f) n.199

Solem v. Helm, 463 U.S. 277, 103 S.Ct. 3001, 77 L.Ed.2d 637 (1983)—§§ 2.4(a) n.20; 2.9(d) n.55; 13.2(h) n.145; 26.3(g) n.72

Solem v. Stumes, 465 U.S. 638, 104 S.Ct. 1338, 79 L.Ed.2d 579 (1984)—§§ 2.9(h) n.227, 228; 2.11(d) n.48; 6.9(f) n.116

Solina, United States v., 733 F.2d 1208 (7th Cir.1984)—§ 11.5(c) n.64

Solina v. United States, 709 F.2d 160 (2d Cir.1983)—§§ 11.8(c) n.75; 11.9(d) n.175

Solis, United States v., 299 F.3d 420 (5th Cir.2002)—§ 3.10(f) n.194

Solis, United States v., 536 F.2d 880 (9th Cir.1976)—§ 3.2(b) n.64

Soller, State v., 181 S.W.3d 645 (Tenn. 2005)—§ 21.3(e) n.271

Solomon, State v., 107 Haw. 117, 111 P.3d 12 (2005)—§ 21.5(c) n.88

Solomon v. State, 323 Ark. 178, 913 S.W.2d 288 (1996)—§§ 6.6(e) n.71; 24.4(d) n.54

Solomon, United States v., 29 F.3d 961 (5th Cir.1994)—§ 16.1(h) n.288

Solomon, United States v., 679 F.2d 1246 (8th Cir.1982)—§ 11.8(b) n.36

Solomon, United States v., 688 F.2d 1171 (7th Cir.1982)—§ 18.5(b) n.63

Solorio v. United States, 483 U.S. 435, 107 S.Ct. 2924, 97 L.Ed.2d 364 (1987)—§§ 15.1(b) n.96 to 98

Solorzano, People v., 63 Cal.Rptr.3d 659, 153 Cal.App.4th 1026 (2007)—§ 24.3(g) n.163

Solorzano v. State, 397 Md. 661, 919 A.2d 652 (2007)—§§ 21.2(e) n.282; 21.4(g) n.246

Somer v. United States, 138 F.2d 790 (2d Cir.1943)—§§ 9.3(e) n.47; 9.4(c) n.76

Somerlot, State v., 209 W.Va. 125, 544 S.E.2d 52 (2000)—§ 18.4(c) n.56

Somers, United States v., 496 F.2d 723 (3d Cir.1974)—§§ 19.6(c) n.30, 38

Somerville v. State, 703 A.2d 629 (Del.1997)—§ 21.5(d) n.102

Sommers v. Commonwealth, 843 S.W.2d 879 (Ky.1992)—§ 11.2(e) n.210

Sonka, State v., 893 S.W.2d 388 (Mo.App.1995)—§ 22.5(a) n.12

Sons v. Superior Court, 125 Cal.App.4th 110, 22 Cal.Rptr.3d 647 (2005)—§ 25.4(a) n.7

Sophanthavong v. Palmateer, 378 F.3d 859 (9th Cir.2004)—§ 21.2(g) n.399

Sorenson, State v., 441 N.W.2d 455 (Minn.1989)—§ 3.2(d) n.153

Sorenson, State v., 758 P.2d 466 (Utah App.1988)—§§ 16.4(d) n.123, 140

Soria v. State, 933 S.W.2d 46 (Tex.Crim.App.1996)—§§ 20.4(e) n.85; 20.5(c) n.39

Soria-Garcia, United States v., 947 F.2d 900 (10th Cir.1991)—§ 6.8(a) n.16

Soriano, State v., 68 Or.App. 642 (1984)—§§ 2.12(e) n.215; 8.11(b) n.21, 25

Soriano, United States v., 346 F.3d 963 (9th Cir.2003)—§ 3.10(b) n.67

Soriano-Hernandez, United States v., 310 F.3d 1099 (8th Cir.2002)—§ 21.6(a) n.49

Sorino, State v., 108 Haw. 162, 118 P.3d 645 (2005)—§ 21.4(d) n.137

Sorrells v. United States, 287 U.S. 435, 53 S.Ct. 210, 77 L.Ed. 413 (1932)—§§ 5.1(b) n.8; 5.1(c) n.11, 20; 5.2(a) n.1, 3; 5.2(b) n.32; 5.2(c) n.44;

5.3(b) n.25; 5.4(c) n.27

Sosa, State v., 122 N.M. 446, 926 P.2d 299 (1996)—§ 26.4(c) n.32

Sosa, United States v., 469 F.2d 271 (9th Cir.1972)—§ 3.9(f) n.104

Sosbe, People v., 789 P.2d 1113 (Colo.1990)—§ 3.1(d) n.95

Sossamon v. State, 816 S.W.2d 340 (Tex. Cr. 1991)—§ 6.2(c) n.102

Soto, Commonwealth v., 431 Mass. 340, 727 N.E.2d 811 (2000)—§ 21.4(d) n.137

Soto, People v., 62 Mich.App. 370, 233 N.W.2d 545 (1975)—§ 27.5(c) n.54

Soto, United States v., 988 F.2d 1548 (10th Cir.1993)—§ 9.1(d) n.128

Soto, United States v., 953 F.2d 263 (6th Cir.1992)—§ 6.7(b) n.42

Soto, United States v., 574 F.Supp. 986 (D.Conn.1983)—§ 8.14(a) n.12

Sotomayor, United States v., 592 F.2d 1219 (2d Cir.1979)—§ 4.6(c) n.54

Soto-Olivas, United States v., 44 F.3d 788 (9th Cir.1995)—§ 17.4(b) n.132

Soucy v. New Hampshire, 127 N.H. 451, 506 A.2d 288 (1985)—§ 3.1(k) n.280

Soule, State v., 168 Ariz. 134, 811 P.2d 1071 (1991)—§ 5.3(c) n.35

Soura, State v., 118 Idaho 232, 796 P.2d 109 (1990)—§ 6.9(g) n.162

Sousa, United States v., 468 F.3d 42 (1st Cir.2006)—§ 5.4(c) n.30

Souter v. Jones, 395 F.3d 577 (6th Cir.2005)—§ 28.5(b) n.62

South Carolina v. Gathers, 490 U.S. 805, 109 S.Ct. 2207, 104 L.Ed.2d 876 (1989)—§§ 2.9(b) n.17; 26.5(d) n.71

South Carolina Press Assoc., In re, 946 F.2d 1037 (4th Cir.1991)—§§ 23.1(e) n.219, 230; 27.5(a) n.20

South Dakota v. Dole, 483 U.S. 203, 107 S.Ct. 2793, 97 L.Ed.2d 193 (1987)—§ 1.3(b) n.16

South Dakota v. Neville, 459 U.S. 553, 103 S.Ct. 916, 74 L.Ed.2d 748 (1983)—§§ 2.10(d) n.137; 2.12(a) n.26, 27; 6.7(b) n.41; 6.7(c) n.127; 7.2(a) n.8; 7.2(c) n.30; 9.6(a) n.36

South Dakota v. Opperman, 428 U.S. 364, 96 S.Ct. 3092, 49 L.Ed.2d 1000 (1976)—§§ 2.6(d) n.94; 2.12(a) n.24, 25; 3.5(c) n.132; 3.7(d) n.79; 3.7(e) n.93

Southerland, United States v., 466 F.3d 1083 (D.C.Cir.2006)—§§ 3.4(h) n.138; 3.6(b) n.66

Southern Ry. Co. v. United States, 222 U.S. 20, 32 S.Ct. 2, 56 L.Ed. 72 (1911)—§ 1.2(c) n.122

Southward v. State, 293 So.2d 343 (Miss.1974)—§ 15.4(g) n.167

Southway Discount Center v. Moore, 315 F.Supp. 617 (N.D.Ala.1970)—§ 1.8(d) n.45

Southwell, United States v., 432 F.3d 1050 (9th Cir.2005)—§ 22.1(a) n.25

Souza, Commonwealth v., 42 Mass.App. 186, 675 N.E.2d 432 (1997)—§§ 19.5(b) n.14, 35; 19.5(c) n.52

Soviero v. United States, 967 F.2d 791 (2d Cir.1992)—§ 10.1(c) n.48

Sowell v. Bradshaw, 372 F.3d 821 (6th Cir.2004)—§ 22.1(h) n.133

Sowels v. State, 45 S.W.3d 690 (Tex.Ct.App.2001)—§ 11.2(c) n.86

Sowers, State ex rel. v. Olwell, 64 Wash.2d 828, 394 P.2d 681 (1964)—§§ 20.4(b) n.30, 32, 34

Soychak, Commonwealth v., 221 Pa.Super. 458, 289 A.2d 119 (1972)—§ 3.2(e) n.165

Spaeth, State v., 552 N.W.2d 187 (Minn.1996)—§ 21.2(d) n.211

Spagnuolo, United States v., 469 F.3d 39 (1st Cir.2006)—§ 18.3(b) n.50

Spagnuolo, United States v., 515 F.2d 818 (9th Cir.1975)—§ 10.5(e) n.52

Spagnuolo, United States v., 168 F.2d 768 (2d Cir.1948)—§ 16.1(g) n.250

Spain v. State, 386 Md. 145, 872 A.2d 25 (2005)—§ 24.7(e) n.54

Spalding, People v., 17 Mich.App. 73, 169 N.W.2d 163 (1969)—§ 14.2(f) n.89

Spanbauer v. Burke, 374 F.2d 67 (7th Cir.1966)—§ 11.3(b) n.33

Spang, State v., 310 Mont. 52, 48 P.3d 727 (2002)—§ 6.9(g) n.166

Spann, People v., 56 N.Y.2d 469, 452 N.Y.S.2d 869, 438 N.E.2d 402 (1982)—§ 19.5(b) n.21

Spann v. State, 704 N.W.2d 486 (Minn.2005)—§§ 27.5(c) n.51, 54

Spann v. United States, 551 A.2d 1347 (D.C.App.1988)—§ 6.7(c) n.119

Spano v. New York, 360 U.S. 315, 79 S.Ct. 1202, 3 L.Ed.2d 1265 (1959)—§§ 1.5(d) n.187; 2.4(e) n.146; 2.8(c) n.58; 6.2(c) n.144; 6.4(a) n.6

Sparf and Hansen v. United States, 156 U.S. 51, 15 S.Ct. 273, 39 L.Ed. 343 (1895)—§§ 1.6(c) n.145; 1.6(d) n.242; 22.1(a) n.16; 22.1(g) n.113; 24.8(f) n.97

Sparklin, State v., 296 Or. 85, 672 P.2d 1182 (1983)—§ 2.12(c) n.167

Sparks, People v., 221 Ill.App.3d 546, 164 Ill.Dec. 106, 582 N.E.2d 314 (1991)—§ 19.3(a) n.65

Sparks, State v., 641 S.E.2d 339 (N.C.App.2007)—§ 26.10(d) n.99

Sparks v. State, 110 P.3d 486 (Nev. 2005)—§ 21.2(d) n.242

Sparks v. State, 121 Nev. 107, 110 P.3d 486 (2005)—§ 21.2(e) n.361

Sparks v. State, 140 Idaho 292, 92 P.3d 542 (2004)—§ 11.9(d) n.173

Sparks v. State, 338 So.2d 550 (Fla.App.1976)—§ 21.4(c) n.92

Sparks, United States v., 67 F.3d 1145 (4th Cir.1995)—§ 21.5(a) n.34

Sparks, United States v., 20 F.3d 476 (D.C.Cir.1994)—§ 21.2(d) n.258

Spaziano v. Florida, 468 U.S. 447, 104 S.Ct. 3154, 82 L.Ed.2d 340 (1984)—§§ 1.8(e) n.87; 15.1(f) n.301; 18.5(a) n.42; 22.1(a) n.19; 24.8(f) n.88, 102; 26.1(b) n.15

Spearman v. State, 744 N.E.2d 545 (Ind.2001)—§ 26.2(b) n.21

Spears v. Commonwealth, 134 S.W.3d 12 (Ky.2003)—§§ 21.6(a) n.64, 79

Spears v. Greiner, 459 F.3d 200 (2d Cir.2006)—§ 24.9(d) n.49

Spears v. State, 272 Ind. 647, 403 N.E.2d 828 (1980)—§ 20.5(f) n.77

Spears v. Stewart, 283 F.3d 992 (9th Cir.2002)—§ 28.8(b) n.16

Spears, United States v., 159 F.3d 1081 (7th Cir.1998)—§§ 13.5(a) n.5, 6

Specht v. Patterson, 386 U.S. 605, 87 S.Ct. 1209, 18 L.Ed.2d 326 (1967)—§§ 2.7(a) n.57, 58; 26.4(d) n.46; 26.4(g) n.121; 26.4(i) n.161

Special Counsel Investigation, In re, 332 F.Supp.2d 26 (D.D.C.2004)—§§ 8.8(d) n.61, 81, 82

Special Feb. 1977 Grand Jury, In re, 581 F.2d 1262 (7th Cir.1978)—§ 8.14(d) n.53

Special February 1971 Grand Jury (Conlisk), 490 F.2d 894 (7th Cir.1973)—§ 8.5(h) n.298

Special February 1975 Grand Jury (Baggot), In re, 662 F.2d 1232 (7th Cir.1981)—§§ 8.5(c) n.80, 82, 84, 113, 114

Special Federal Grand Jury, Matter of, 809 F.2d 1023 (3d Cir.1987)—§ 7.2(b) n.12

Special Grand Jury 89-2, In re, 143 F.3d 565 (10th Cir.1998)—§ 8.5(h) n.265

Special Grand Jury (Gimbel), In re, 480 F.Supp. 174 (E.D.Wis.1979)—§§ 8.14(d) n.54, 59

Special Grand Jury No. 1, Matter of, 465 F.Supp. 800 (D.Md.1978)—§ 8.12(b) n.20

Special Grand Jury No. 81-1 (Harvey, In re, 676 F.2d 1005 (4th Cir.1982)—§ 8.14(a) n.12

Special Grand Jury Proceedings (Goodman & Chesnoff), In re, 871 F.Supp. 391 (D.Nev.1994)—§§ 8.8(f) n.148, 154

Special Investigation No. 231, In re, 295 Md. 366, 455 A.2d 442 (1983)— § 8.14(d) n.59

Special Investigation No. 249, In re, 296 Md. 201, 461 A.2d 1082 (Md.App.1983)—§ 8.8(b) n.31

Special March 1981 Grand Jury (Almond Pharmacy), In re, 753 F.2d 575 (7th Cir.1985)—§§ 8.5(b) n.68; 8.5(c) n.95 to 97, 100, 103, 107, 109, 114, 115, 117; 8.5(i) n.310

Special Proceedings, In re, 373 F.3d 37 (1st Cir.2004)—§§ 8.8(d) n.81, 83

Speck, People v., 41 Ill.2d 177, 242 N.E.2d 208 (1968)—§ 23.2(f) n.84

Spector v. State, 289 Md. 407, 425 A.2d 197 (1981)—§ 19.4(b) n.30

Spector, United States v., 326 F.2d 345 (7th Cir.1963)—§ 17.2(a) n.14

Speed, State v., 265 Kan. 26, 961 P.2d 13 (Kan.1998)—§§ 11.4(b) n.24; 24.2(e) n.79

Speelman, United States v., 431 F.3d 1226 (9th Cir.2005)—§§ 21.2(b) n.82; 21.2(d) n.158

Speiser v. Randall, 357 U.S. 513, 78 S.Ct. 1332, 2 L.Ed.2d 1460 (1958)—§§ 1.5(d) n.190; 2.5(c) n.24

Speller, People v., 46 Ill.App.3d 208, 4 Ill.Dec. 780, 360 N.E.2d 1155 (1977)—§ 18.5(a) n.50

Speller, State v., 345 N.C. 600, 481 S.E.2d 284 (1997)—§ 24.2(a) n.14

Spence, Commonwealth v., 534 Pa. 233, 627 A.2d 1176 (1993)—§ 22.3(d) n.218

Spence v. Superintendent, Great Meadow Correctional Facility, 219 F.3d 162 (2d Cir.2000)—§§ 21.2(d) n.244; 28.4(e) n.88

Spencer v. Kemna, 523 U.S. 1, 118 S.Ct. 978, 140 L.Ed.2d 43 (1998)— §§ 27.5(a) n.1, 12, 16, 19; 28.3(a) n.30

Spencer, People v., 272 A.D.2d 682, 708 N.Y.S.2d 488 (2000)—§ 3.4(j) n.204

Spencer v. State, 118 P.3d 978 (Wyo.2005)—§ 21.2(d) n.194

Spencer, State v., 149 N.H. 622, 826 A.2d 546 (2003)—§§ 6.7(c) n.118; 6.9(c) n.49

Spencer v. State, 615 So.2d 688 (Fla.1993)—§ 22.3(c) n.100

Spencer v. State, 805 S.W.2d 677 (Mo.App.1990)—§ 27.5(c) n.103

Spencer v. State, 501 S.W.2d 799 (Tenn.1973)—§ 24.8(e) n.70

Spencer v. State of Texas, 385 U.S. 554, 87 S.Ct. 648, 17 L.Ed.2d 606 (1967)—§§ 2.7(c) n.157, 210; 26.2(b) n.18, 20; 26.6(b) n.19

Spencer, United States v., 955 F.2d 814 (2d Cir.1992)—§ 9.6(a) n.32

Spencer, United States v., 618 F.2d 605 (9th Cir.1980)—§ 24.3(c) n.102

Sperling, United States ex rel. v. Fitzpatrick, 426 F.2d 1161 (2d Cir.1970)—§ 3.1(f) n.157

Spero, United States v., 331 F.3d 57 (2d Cir.2003)—§ 19.3(b) n.147

Spevack v. Klein, 385 U.S. 511, 87 S.Ct. 625, 17 L.Ed.2d 574 (1967)— §§ 2.10(b) n.4, 45; 2.10(c) n.96; 2.10(d) n.161; 3.9(c) n.45

Sphere Casual Wear, Inc. v. International Leisure Apparel, Inc., 1994 WL 67851 (S.D.N.Y.1994)— § 8.13(b) n.62

Spicer v. State, 921 So.2d 292 (Miss.2006)—§ 10.1(a) n.2

Spicuzza, Ex parte, 903 S.W.2d 381 (Tex.App.1995)—§ 11.7(b) n.29

Spiegel v. City of Chicago, 106 F.3d 209 (7th Cir.1997)—§ 3.8(c) n.107

Spiegel, State v., 710 So.2d 13 (Fla.App.1998)—§ 8.11(d) n.80

Spiezer, People v., 316 Ill.App.3d 75, 249 Ill.Dec. 192, 735 N.E.2d 1017 (2000)—§§ 20.4(f) n.91; 20.5(h) n.109

Spiller, State v., 778 S.W.2d 825 (Mo.App.1989)—§ 11.6(a) n.36

Spillers v. State, 84 Nev. 23, 436 P.2d 18 (1968)—§ 13.7(a) n.24

Spillman, United States v., 924 F.2d 721 (7th Cir.1991)—§ 21.3(e) n.283

Spillman v. United States, 413 F.2d 527 (9th Cir.1969)—§ 13.4(c) n.143

Spillone, United States v., 879 F.2d 514 (9th Cir.1989)—§§ 15.5(b) n.53, 56, 79; 15.6(f) n.183, 197; 15.7(e) n.101, 122

Spina, State v., 99 S.W.3d 596 (Tenn.Crim.App.2002)—§ 16.2(d) n.60

Spine, United States v., 945 F.2d 143 (6th Cir.1991)—§ 22.3(b) n.80

Spinelli v. Collins, 992 F.2d 559 (5th Cir.1993)—§ 21.2(g) n.394

Spinelli v. United States, 393 U.S. 410, 89 S.Ct. 584, 21 L.Ed.2d 637 (1969)—§§ 2.9(g) n.153; 3.3(a) n.8; 3.3(b) n.63; 3.3(c) n.78, 81, 103, 121

Spinkellink v. Wainwright, 578 F.2d 582 (5th Cir.1978)—§ 2.6(a) n.20

Spinner, United States v., 180 F.3d 514 (3d Cir.1999)—§§ 19.3(a) n.13, 101; 19.3(e) n.218

Spinosa, United States v., 982 F.2d 620 (1st Cir.1992)—§ 3.4(d) n.58

Spirko v. Commonwealth, 480 S.W.2d 169 (Ky.1972)—§ 9.1(b) n.55

Spirko, State ex rel. v. Judges of Court of Appeals, 27 Ohio St.3d 13, 501 N.E.2d 625 (1986)—§ 27.1(b) n.16

Spitaleri, People v., 9 N.Y.2d 168, 212 N.Y.S.2d 53, 173 N.E.2d 35 (1961)—§§ 21.5(f) n.157, 174

Spitznas v. Boone, 464 F.3d 1213 (10th Cir.2006)—§ 28.5(d) n.91

Spivey, State v., 81 Ohio St.3d 405, 692 N.E.2d 151 (1998)—§ 21.4(b) n.57

Spivey, State v., 700 S.W.2d 812 (Mo.1985)—§ 22.2(d) n.69

Splunge v. Clark, 960 F.2d 705 (7th Cir.1992)—§ 22.3(d) n.249

Spock, United States v., 416 F.2d 165 (1st Cir.1969)—§§ 24.10(a) n.3, 18

Sponsler, People v.,1 Dak. 289, 46 N.W. 459 (Dakota 1876)—§§ 15.1(b) n.73, 77

Spoonmore v. State, 411 N.E.2d 146 (Ind.App.1980)—§ 16.1(d) n.138

Spotted Blanket, State v., 288 Mont. 126, 955 P.2d 1347 (1998)—§ 21.6(a) n.32

Spotts, State v., 257 Neb. 44, 595 N.W.2d 259 (1999)—§ 17.4(b) n.120

Spotz, Commonwealth v., 562 Pa. 498, 756 A.2d 1139 (2000)—§§ 11.9(a) n.21; 11.9(d) n.170; 17.3(a) n.3; 17.4(c) n.143

Spradlin, State v., 12 S.W.3d 432 (Tenn.2000)—§§ 8.11(e) n.98, 100; 13.5(b) n.54

Sprague, State v., 146 N.H. 334, 771 A.2d 583 (2001)—§§ 18.4(c) n.59, 61

Spreitz, State v., 202 Ariz. 1, 39 P.3d 525 (2002)—§ 11.7(e) n.88

Spreitzer, People v., 123 Ill.2d 1, 121 Ill.Dec. 224, 525 N.E.2d 30 (1988)—§§ 11.9(d) n.178, 179

Spreitzer v. Peters, 114 F.3d 1435 (7th Cir.1997)—§ 11.9(d) n.170

Spriggs, Commonwealth v., 463 Pa. 375, 344 A.2d 880 (1975)—§ 6.8(a) n.6

Spring, United States v., 80 F.3d 1450 (10th Cir.1996)—§§ 18.3(b) n.38, 43

Springer v. Commonwealth, 998 S.W.2d 439 (Ky.1999)—§§ 6.2(c) n.132; 6.9(f) n.108

Springer, United States v., 51 F.3d 861 (9th Cir.1995)—§ 12.1(a) n.18

Springer, United States v., 946 F.2d 1012 (2d Cir.1991)—§ 3.8(c) n.82

Springs, United States v., 936 F.2d 1330 (D.C.Cir.1991)—§ 3.10(f) n.197

Sprosty v. Buchler, 79 F.3d 635 (7th Cir.1996)—§ 6.6(e) n.65

Sproul, State v., 544 A.2d 743 (Me.1988)—§ 16.3(f) n.89

Sprouse, People v., 983 P.2d 771 (Colo.1999)—§ 5.2(a) n.17

Sprouts, United States v., 282 F.3d 1037 (8th Cir.2002)—§ 18.2(e) n.76

Sprovieri, People v., 95 Ill.App.2d 10, 238 N.E.2d 115 (1968)—§ 3.6(a) n.11

Spruill, United States v., 292 F.3d 207 (5th Cir.2002)—§ 21.2(b) n.83

Spruill, United States v., 296 F.3d 580 (7th Cir.2002)—§ 6.4(f) n.136

Spruill, United States v., 118 F.3d 221 (4th Cir.1997)—§ 19.3(a) n.8

Spry, State v., 21 P.3d 675 (Utah App.2001)—§§ 20.2(b) n.21; 20.3(a) n.11, 17; 20.5(a) n.7

Spry v. State, 796 So.2d 229 (Miss.2001)—§ 21.4(b) n.59

Spunaugle v. State, 946 P.2d 246 (Okl.Cr.1997)—§§ 17.2(b) n.69; 17.2(d) n.94

Spy Factory, United States v., 951 F.Supp. 450 (S.D.N.Y.1997)— § 16.3(c) n.40

Square v. State, 283 Ala. 548, 219 So.2d 377 (1968)—§ 6.8(a) n.17

Squartino, United States v., 778 F.2d 734 (11th Cir.1985)—§ 15.4(h) n.196

Squillacote, United States v., 221 F.3d 542 (4th Cir.2000)—§§ 4.9(b) n.10; 5.2(a) n.17

Sriram, United States v., 482 F.3d 956 (7th Cir.2007)—§ 13.5(h) n.141

Staats, State v., 658 N.W.2d 207 (Minn.2003)—§§ 6.9(f) n.137, 139

Stacey, State v., 482 So.2d 1350 (1985)—§ 11.10(c) n.116

Stach v. State, 97 Tex.Crim. 280, 260 S.W. 569 (1924)—§ 2.12(a) n.7

Stack v. Boyle, 342 U.S. 1, 72 S.Ct. 1, 96 L.Ed. 3 (1951)—§§ 2.6(b) n.36; 12.2(a) n.3; 12.2(b) n.17; 12.3(a) n.2; 12.3(c) n.86; 27.2(c) n.24

Stackhouse v. State, 298 Md. 203, 468 A.2d 333 (1983)—§ 3.6(c) n.82

Stacy, State v., 104 Vt. 379, 160 A. 257 (1932)—§ 2.12(a) n.10

Stafford v. Harrison, 766 F.Supp. 1014 (D.Kan.1991)—§ 26.9(b) n.54

Stafford v. Love, 726 P.2d 894 (Okla.1986)—§ 11.2(e) n.206

Stafford, People v., 325 Ill.App.3d 1069, 259 Ill.Dec. 635, 759 N.E.2d 115 (2001)—§ 19.3(a) n.10

Stafford, People v., 434 Mich. 125, 450 N.W.2d 559 (1990)—§ 14.3(b) n.49

Stafford v. State, 455 So.2d 385 (Fla.1984)—§ 26.10(a) n.7

Stafford, State v., 213 Kan. 152, 515 P.2d 769 (1973)—§§ 14.4(c) n.65; 20.3(k) n.220

Stafford, United States v., 136 F.3d 1109 (7th Cir.1998)—§ 22.3(d) n.199

Stafford, United States v., 697 F.2d 1368 (11th Cir.1983)—§ 18.3(b) n.28

Staggs, United States v., 881 F.2d 1527 (10th Cir.1989)—§§ 19.2(b) n.17, 20; 19.2(c) n.22; 19.2(f) n.106; 19.3(a) n.68

Staggs, United States v., 553 F.2d 1073 (7th Cir.1977)—§ 20.5(c) n.43

Stagner, Commonwealth v., 3 S.W.3d 738 (Ky.1999)—§ 21.4(b) n.44

Stahl v. State, 109 Nev. 442, 851 P.2d 436 (1993)—§§ 21.2(d) n.162; 21.4(g) n.233

Stahl, State v., 240 Neb. 501, 482 N.W.2d 829 (Neb. 1992)— §§ 5.3(a) n.15; 5.3(d) n.43

Stallings, State v., 658 N.W.2d 106 (Iowa 2003)—§ 22.1(h) n.133

Stallworth, Commonwealth v., 566 Pa. 349, 781 A.2d 110 (2001)— §§ 6.6(f) n.100; 6.7(b) n.90

Stallworth v. State, 797 So.2d 905 (Miss.2001)—§§ 6.2(c) n.145; 6.7(d) n.145

Stamm, State v., 16 Wash.App. 603, 559 P.2d 1 (1976)—§ 20.6(a) n.2

Stamper v. Commonwealth, 228 Va. 707, 324 S.E.2d 682 (1985)— §§ 5.2(a) n.4; 22.4(c) n.30

Stampley, State v., 127 N.M. 426, 982 P.2d 477 (1999)—§§ 7.4(c) n.48; 7.4(g) n.110

Stamps v. State, 515 N.E.2d 507 (Ind.1987)—§ 22.3(d) n.249

Stanaway, People v., 446 Mich. 643, 521 N.W.2d 557 (1994)—§§ 24.3(a) n.11; 24.3(f) n.157

Standard Drywall Inc. v. United States, 668 F.2d 156 (2d Cir.1982)—§§ 27.2(d) n.72, 73

Standard Jury Instructions—Criminal Report No. 90-2, In re, 575 So.2d 1276 (Fla.1991)—§§ 8.4(b) n.98; 15.1(e) n.266; 15.2(b) n.20, 24; 15.2(e) n.128 to 132, 135, 137; 15.2(f) n.148

Standard Oil Co., United States v., 316 F.2d 884 (7th Cir.1963)—§ 8.8(g) n.168

Standefer v. State, 59 S.W.3d 177 (Tex.Cr.App.2001)—§ 22.3(a) n.5

Standefer, United States v., 2007 WL 2301760 (S.D.Cal. 2007)—§ 4.8(b) n.13

Standefer v. United States, 447 U.S. 10, 100 S.Ct. 1999, 64 L.Ed.2d 689 (1980)—§ 24.10(b) n.23

Standen v. State, 101 Nev. 725, 710 P.2d 718 (1985)—§ 21.5(f) n.157

Standerford v. State, 928 S.W.2d 688 (Tex.App.1996)—§ 16.3(b) n.22

Standish, People v., 38 Cal.4th 858, 43 Cal.Rptr.3d 785, 135 P.3d 32 (2006)—§§ 14.2(g) n.94, 101

Standlee v. Rhay, 557 F.2d 1303 (9th Cir.1977)—§ 17.4(a) n.30

Standley v. Department of Justice, 835 F.2d 216 (9th Cir.1987)—§ 8.5(c) n.76

Standley v. Warden, 115 Nev. 333, 990 P.2d 783 (1999)—§§ 21.3(d) n.219, 233

Standridge v. State, 357 Ark. 105, 161 S.W.3d 815 (2004)—§ 6.8(d) n.84

Stands, United States v., 105 F.3d 1565 (8th Cir.1997)—§ 19.6(b) n.15

Stanfield, United States v., 109 F.3d 976 (4th Cir.1997)—§ 3.8(e) n.202

Stanford v. Commonwealth, 734 S.W.2d 781 (Ky.1987)—§ 6.9(f) n.138

Stanford v. Parker, 266 F.3d 442 (6th Cir.2001)—§ 17.2(b) n.71

Stanford v. Texas, 379 U.S. 476, 85 S.Ct. 506, 13 L.Ed.2d 431 (1965)—§ 3.4(f) n.113

Stanford, United States v., 589 F.2d 285 (7th Cir.1978)—§§ 8.5(e) n.182, 186

Stanford Daily v. Zurcher, 353 F.Supp. 124 (N.D.Cal.1972)—§ 3.4(a) n.19

Stanga, State v., 617 N.W.2d 486 (S.D.2000)—§ 6.9(c) n.58

Staniford, United States v., 148 F.3d 864 (7th Cir.1998)—§ 21.5(a) n.12

Stanislaw, State v., 153 Vt. 517, 573 A.2d 286 (1990)—§§ 6.9(c) n.64; 6.9(g) n.162

Stanley, Commonwealth v., 265 Pa.Super. 194, 401 A.2d 1166 (1979)—§§ 19.5(b) n.6, 18

Stanley v. Georgia, 394 U.S. 557, 89 S.Ct. 1243, 22 L.Ed.2d 542 (1969)—§ 3.4(k) n.224

Stanley, People v., 56 P.3d 1241 (Colo.App.2002)—§ 11.5(c) n.32

Stanley, State v., 120 Wash.App. 312, 85 P.3d 395 (2004)—§ 24.9(f) n.102

Stanley, State v., 223 Conn. 674, 613 A.2d 788 (1992)—§ 10.4(b) n.15

Stanley v. State, 313 Md. 50, 542 A.2d 1267 (1988)—§ 22.3(d) n.220

Stanley, State v., 288 N.C. 19, 215 S.E.2d 589 (1975)—§ 1.7(i) n.208

Stanley v. State, 19 Md.App. 507, 313 A.2d 847 (1974)—§§ 3.3(c) n.109, 124, 131

Stanley, United States v., 483 U.S. 669, 107 S.Ct. 3054, 97 L.Ed.2d 550 (1987)—§ 2.9(h) n.206

Stanley, United States v., 765 F.2d 1224 (5th Cir.1985)—§ 5.4(c) n.37

Stanley Williams, In re, 7 Cal.4th 572, 29 Cal.Rptr.2d 64, 870 P.2d 1072 (1994)—§ 24.3(i) n.188

Stano v. Dugger, 921 F.2d 1125 (11th Cir.1991)—§§ 11.3(b) n.31; 11.5(b) n.25; 11.5(c) n.41, 52, 53

Stano v. Dugger, 889 F.2d 962 (11th Cir.1989)—§ 21.3(b) n.42

Stano, State v., 159 P.3d 931 (Kan.2007)—§§ 14.1(d) n.66, 68

Stansbury v. California, 511 U.S. 318, 114 S.Ct. 1526, 128 L.Ed.2d 293 (1994)—§§ 6.5(e) n.90; 6.6(a) n.8, 12; 6.6(c) n.32

Stansbury, People v., 9 Cal.4th 824, 38 Cal.Rptr.2d 394, 889 P.2d 588 (1995)—§§ 6.6(d) n.50, 58

Stansfield, United States v., 101 F.3d 909 (3d Cir.1996)—§ 24.9(g) n.118

Stanton, In re, 682 A.2d 655 (D.C.App.1996)—§ 21.3(b) n.107

Stanton, People v., 241 A.D.2d 687, 660 N.Y.S.2d 169 (1997)—§ 15.7(g) n.218

Stanton, Commonwealth ex rel. v. Francies, 250 Pa. 496, 95 A. 527 (1915)—§ 15.1(f) n.273

Staples v. United States, 320 F.2d 817 (5th Cir.1963)—§ 3.5(a) n.42

Stapleton v. State, 565 S.W.2d 532 (Tex.Cr.App.1978)—§ 27.6(b) n.23

Star, United States v., 470 F.2d 1214 (9th Cir.1972)—§ 8.8(f) n.150

Starcher, State v., 195 W.Va. 185, 465 S.E.2d 185 (1995)—§ 27.5(e) n.166

Stargel v. State, 210 Ga.App. 619, 436 S.E.2d 786 (1993)—§§ 20.4(b) n.23, 39; 20.5(h) n.116

Starkey v. Swenson, 370 F.Supp. 594 (E.D.Mo.1974)—§ 12.4(d) n.86

Starks, People v., 106 Ill.2d 441, 88 Ill.Dec. 35, 478 N.E.2d 350 (1985)—§ 13.5(b) n.34

Starks v. State, 658 So.2d 183 (Fla.App.1995)—§ 26.9(a) n.9

Starks, United States v., 6 F.R.D. 43 (S.D.N.Y.1946)—§ 19.1(a) n.11

Starling v. State, 242 Ga.App. 685, 530 S.E.2d 757 (Ga.App.2000)—§§ 16.1(g) n.277, 281

Starr, Commonwealth v., 541 Pa. 564, 664 A.2d 1326 (1995)—§§ 11.3(b) n.42; 11.5(c) n.37, 45; 11.5(d) n.77, 84

Starr, People v., 37 Ill.App.3d 495, 346 N.E.2d 410 (1976)—§ 10.6(d) n.49

Starr, State v., 259 Kan. 713, 915 P.2d 72 (1996)—§§ 19.5(b) n.7, 8

Starr, State ex rel. v. Halbritter, 183 W.Va. 350, 395 S.E.2d 773 (1990)—§§ 15.6(d) n.116; 27.4(c) n.21

Stassi, United States v., 583 F.2d 122 (3d Cir.1978)—§ 21.5(d) n.106

Stastny, State v., 223 Neb. 903, 395 N.W.2d 492 (1986)—§ 21.4(d) n.119

State, In re, 139 N.H. 705, 661 A.2d 766 (1995)—§§ 27.4(b) n.17; 27.4(d) n.48

State—see opposing party

State Grand Jury Investigation, Matter of, 197 Colo. 460, 593 P.2d 967 (1979)—§ 8.5(h) n.231

State, Indiana Dep't of Revenue v. Adams, 762 N.E.2d 728 (Ind.2002)—§ 3.1(g) n.176

State, In re v. Wilson, 632 N.W.2d 225 (Minn.2001)—§ 18.4(d) n.90

Staten v. Neal, 880 F.2d 962 (7th Cir.1989)—§§ 8.11(e) n.91, 107; 21.2(e) n.343

Staten, State v., 238 Neb. 13, 469 N.W.2d 112 (1991)—§ 3.5(c) n.109

Staten, United States v., 450 F.3d 384 (9th Cir.2006)—§ 26.4(h) n.155

Staten v. United States, 562 A.2d 90 (D.C.1989)—§§ 3.7(a) n.17, 19

State Police Litigation, In re, 888 F. Supp 1235 (D. Conn. 1995)—§ 4.6(b) n.25

State-Record Company, Inc., In re The, 917 F.2d 124 (4th Cir.1990)—§§ 23.1(d) n.209, 212; 23.1(e) n.230

States v. Flanakin, 25 Fed.Cas 1105 (Super.Ct.Ark.Terr.1825)—§ 15.1(d) n.166

States v. Hubbard, 650 F.2d 293 (D.C.Cir.1980)—§ 27.2(d) n.69

State's Attorney, Office of v. Office of Attorney General, 138 Vt. 10, 409 A.2d 599 (1979)—§ 13.3(e) n.50

State, State ex rel. v. Gustke, 205 W.Va. 72, 516 S.E.2d 283 (1999)—§ 3.5(a) n.24

State, State ex rel. v. Hill, 201 W.Va. 95, 491 S.E.2d 765 (1997)—§§ 18.5(b) n.62; 27.4(d) n.42

Staton, People v., 154 Ill.App.3d 230, 107 Ill.Dec. 398, 507 N.E.2d 62 (1987)—§ 11.10(c) n.116

Staton, People v., 94 Misc.2d 1002, 406 N.Y.S.2d 242 (1978)—§ 14.4(c) n.57

Staufer, United States v., 38 F.3d 1103 (9th Cir.1994)—§§ 5.2(a) n.6; 26.4(b) n.22

Staula, United States v., 80 F.3d 596 (1st Cir.1996)—§ 18.3(b) n.26

Staves, United States v., 383 F.3d 977 (9th Cir.2004)—§ 4.6(l) n.201

Stavricos, State v., 506 S.W.2d 51 (Mo.App.1974)—§ 3.2(d) n.148

Stawicki v. Israel, 778 F.2d 380 (7th Cir.1985)—§ 6.2(c) n.151

Stayton, United States v., 791 F.2d 17 (2d Cir.1986)—§ 18.3(b) n.7

St. Clair v. Commonwealth, 140 S.W.3d 510 (Ky.2004)—§ 18.4(c) n.44

St. Clair, United States v., 855 F.2d 518 (8th Cir.1988)—§ 24.9(f) n.96

St. Cloud v. Class, 1996 S.D. 64, 550 N.W.2d 70 (1996)—§§ 22.2(d) n.66, 85

Stead, United States v., 745 F.2d 1170 (8th Cir.1984)—§§ 18.1(c) n.36; 18.3(b) n.5

Steadman, People v., 82 N.Y.2d 1, 603 N.Y.S.2d 382, 623 N.E.2d 509 (1993)—§§ 24.3(d) n.107, 111

Steagald v. United States, 451 U.S. 204, 101 S.Ct. 1642, 68 L.Ed.2d 38 (1981)—§§ 2.9(i) n.272; 3.6(a) n.14

Steckel v. State, 711 A.2d 5 (Del.1998)—§ 6.9(g) n.166

Steckler v. United States, 7 F.2d 59 (2d Cir.1925)—§ 24.10(b) n.21

Steele, State v., 261 Neb. 541, 624 N.W.2d 1 (2001)—§ 18.4(c) n.44

Steele, State v., 620 P.2d 1026 (Wyo.1980)—§ 21.4(a) n.21

Steele, United States v., 933 F.2d 1313 (6th Cir.1991)—§ 8.3(b) n.14

Steele, United States v., 727 F.2d 580 (6th Cir.1984)—§ 11.8(b) n.34

Steele, United States v., 461 F.2d 1148 (9th Cir.1972)—§§ 13.4(c) n.88, 118; 13.5(a) n.12

Steele v. United States, 267 U.S. 498, 45 S.Ct. 414, 69 L.Ed. 757 (1925)—§§ 3.2(b) n.40; 3.4(e) n.64

Steeves, United States v., 525 F.2d 33 (8th Cir.1975)—§ 3.3(g) n.226

Steffel v. Thompson, 415 U.S. 452, 94 S.Ct. 1209, 39 L.Ed.2d 505 (1974)—§ 13.5(e) n.98

Stegall, State v., 124 Wash.2d 719, 881 P.2d 979 (1994)—§ 22.1(h) n.156

Steiger, United States v., 318 F.3d 1039 (11th Cir.2003)—§§ 4.6(b) n.25; 4.6(m) n.216

Steigler, In re, 250 A.2d 379 (Del.1969)—§ 12.4(a) n.22

Steigler v. Anderson, 496 F.2d 793 (3d Cir.1974)—§ 3.9(e) n.82

Steigler v. Superior Court, 252 A.2d 300 (Del.1969)—§§ 3.1(f) n.152; 6.6(e) n.67; 12.4(a) n.21; 15.5(c) n.103, 105

Stein v. KPMG, 486 F.3d 753 (2d Cir.2007)—§ 11.4(c) n.106

Stein v. New York, 346 U.S. 156, 73 S.Ct. 1077, 97 L.Ed. 1522 (1953)—§§ 2.7(c) n.114; 6.2(c) n.71, 177; 10.5(a) n.2

Stein, State v., 70 N.J. 369, 360 A.2d 347 (1976)—§ 6.8(a) n.22

Stein v. State, 514 S.W.2d 927 (Tex.Cr.App.1974)—§ 10.2(c) n.34

Stein, State v., 203 Kan. 638, 456 P.2d 1 (1969)—§ 3.10(e) n.184

Stein, United States v., 495 F.Supp.2d 390 (S.D.N.Y. 2007)—§ 11.4(c) n.106

Stein, United States v., 435 F.Supp.2d 330 (S.D.N.Y.2006)—§ 11.4(c) n.101

Stein, United States v., 452 F.Supp.2d 281 (S.D.N.Y.2006)—§ 11.4(c) n.106

Steinberg, In re, 837 F.2d 527 (1st Cir.1988)—§ 8.12(g) n.63

Steinberg, People v., 148 Cal.App.2d 855, 307 P.2d 634 (1957)—§ 3.5(a) n.29

Steinberger v. District Court, 198 Colo. 59, 596 P.2d 755 (1979)—§ 8.11(b) n.32

Steiner v. State, 763 N.E.2d 1024 (Ind.App.2002)—§ 12.1(b) n.32

Steinert, United States v., 470 F.Supp.2d 627 (E.D. Va.2007)—§ 26.10(c) n.81

Steingut, In the Matter of v. Gold, 42 N.Y.2d 311, 397 N.Y.S.2d 765, 366 N.E.2d 854 (1977)—§§ 8.8(a) n.9; 16.1(e) n.187; 16.1(g) n.245, 247

Steinhorn, United States v., 927 F.2d 195 (4th Cir.1991)—§ 12.4(d) n.69

Steinhorst v. State, 412 So.2d 332 (Fla.1982)—§§ 24.4(d) n.40, 61

Steinkoetter, United States v., 633 F.2d 719 (6th Cir.1980)—§ 24.7(e) n.66

Steinmetz, People v., 287 Ill.App.3d 1, 222 Ill.Dec. 682, 678 N.E.2d 89 (1997)—§ 24.2(e) n.54

Steinolfson, State v., 483 N.W.2d 182 (N.D.1992)—§ 21.3(e) n.284

Stelly, State v., 149 La. 1022, 90 So. 390 (1922)—§§ 16.1(d) n.145; 16.2(a) n.3

Stenger, State v., 111 Wash.2d 516, 760 P.2d 357 (1988)—§§ 11.9(a) n.32; 22.5(b) n.19

Stenson, State v., 169 Vt. 590, 738 A.2d 567 (1999)—§ 6.9(g) n.167

Stenson, State v., 132 Wash.2d 668, 940 P.2d 1239 (1997)—§§ 11.4(b) n.25; 11.5(d) n.66, 68, 69

Stephan v. State, 711 P.2d 1156 (Alaska 1985)—§ 6.8(c) n.64

Stephan, State ex rel. v. Finney, 251 Kan. 559, 836 P.2d 1169 (1992)—§ 27.4(d) n.43

Stephan, State ex rel. v. Smith, 242 Kan. 336, 747 P.2d 816 (Kan.1987)—§ 11.8(c) n.65

Stephens, Ex parte, 171 Ohio St. 323, 170 N.E.2d 735 (1960)—§ 15.1(f) n.273

Stephens v. Attorney General of California, 23 F.3d 248 (9th Cir.1994)—§ 10.6(d) n.48

Stephens v. Borg, 59 F.3d 932 (9th Cir.1995)—§ 19.2(c) n.27

Stephens v. Hall, 407 F.3d 1195 (11th Cir.2005)—§ 24.3(d) n.116

Stephens v. State, 911 So.2d 424 (Miss.2005)—§§ 24.6(c) n.41; 24.9(a) n.10; 27.5(d) n.116

Stephens v. State, 806 S.W.2d 812 (Tex.Cr.App.1990)—§ 25.4(b) n.23

Stephens, State v., 118 Me. 237, 107 A. 296 (1919)—§ 16.4(c) n.47

Stephens, United States v., 421 F.3d 503 (7th Cir.2005)—§§ 22.3(d) n.218, 219

Stephens, United States v., 206 F.3d 914 (9th Cir.2000)—§§ 3.8(c) n.102, 103

Stephens, United States v., 906 F.2d 251 (6th Cir.1990)—§§ 21.2(g) n.396; 21.5(a) n.43

Stephens, United States v., 609 F.2d 230 (5th Cir.1980)—§ 11.6(a) n.49

Stephenson v. State, 864 N.E.2d 1022 (Ind.2007)—§ 24.2(e) n.69

Stephenson v. State, 801 So.2d 34 (Ala.Crim.2000)—§ 18.4(c) n.39

Stephenson v. State, 645 So.2d 161 (Fla.App.1994)—§ 10.5(a) n.7

Stephenson, State v., 878 S.W.2d 530 (Tenn.1994)—§§ 6.9(c) n.61; 26.4(g) n.135, 141

Stephenson, United States v., 183 F.3d 110 (2d Cir.1999)—§ 21.2(b) n.74

Stephenson, United States v., 924 F.2d 753 (8th Cir.1991)—§ 6.6(e) n.92

Stephenson, United States v., 895 F.2d 867 (2d Cir.1990)—§§ 16.3(c) n.31, 45

Stepney, United States v., 246 F.Supp.2d 1069 (2003)—§ 11.9(c) n.116

Stepteau, People v., 81 N.Y.2d 799, 595 N.Y.S.2d 371, 611 N.E.2d 272 (1993)—§ 15.2(c) n.82

Sterling, State v., 759 So.2d 60 (La.2000)—§ 3.4(e) n.78

Sterling, State v., 685 A.2d 432 (Me.1996)—§ 17.4(b) n.126

Sterling, United States v., 283 F.3d 216 (4th Cir.2002)—§§ 9.5(b) n.41, 42

Stern v. United States District Court, 214 F.3d 4 (1st Cir.2000)—§§ 1.7(j) n.257, 260, 261, 263; 8.8(d) n.110

Stern, State ex rel. v. Mascio, 75 Ohio St.3d 422, 662 N.E.2d 370 (1996)— § 21.4(a) n.26

Steuding, People v., 6 N.Y.2d 214, 189 N.Y.S.2d 166, 160 N.E.2d 468 (1959)—§§ 8.10(c) n.51, 53

Steurer, State v., 37 Ohio App.2d 51, 66 O.O.2d 89, 306 N.E.2d 425 (1973)—§ 13.4(c) n.108

Steve Jackson Games, Inc. v. United States Secret Service, 36 F.3d 457 (5th Cir.1994)—§§ 4.6(b) n.25; 4.6(m) n.216

Stevens, In re, 119 Cal.App.4th 1228, 15 Cal.Rptr.3d (2004)—§ 26.9(b) n.57

Stevens v. Kansas City, 146 Mo. 460, 48 S.W. 658 (1898)—§ 1.8(d) n.53

Stevens, People v., 461 Mich. 655, 610 N.W.2d 881 (2000)—§ 21.2(h) n.439

Stevens, People v., 460 Mich. 626, 597 N.W.2d 53 (1999)—§ 9.3(e) n.58

Stevens, People v., 151 A.D.2d 704, 542 N.Y.S.2d 754 (1989)—§ 15.2(c) n.85

Stevens, People v., 642 P.2d 39 (Colo.App.1981)—§ 22.5(d) n.33

Stevens, People v., 183 Colo. 399, 517 P.2d 1336 (1973)—§ 3.8(b) n.33

Stevens, People v., 5 Cal.2d 92, 53 P.2d 133 (1935)—§ 11.7(b) n.25

Stevens, State v., 278 Conn. 1, 845 A.2d 771 (2006)—§ 21.2(d) n.222

Stevens v. State, 365 S.C. 309, 617 S.E.2d 366 (2005)—§ 21.3(b) n.54

Stevens v. State, 770 N.E.2d 739 (Ind.2002)—§ 22.3(b) n.57

Stevens v. State, 806 So.2d 1031 (Miss.2001)—§ 22.3(d) n.221

Stevens, State v., 126 Idaho 822, 892 P.2d 889 (1995)—§ 25.2(d) n.24

Stevens, State v., 311 Or. 119, 806 P.2d 92 (1991)—§§ 10.4(b) n.11; 10.4(c) n.20

Stevens v. State, 409 So.2d 1051 (Fla.1982)—§ 26.10(c) n.54

Stevens v. State, 242 Ga. 34, 247 S.E.2d 838 (1978)—§ 20.3(i) n.170

Stevens v. State, 582 P.2d 621 (Alaska 1978)—§ 20.6(b) n.31

Stevens, State v., 98 Idaho 131, 559 P.2d 310 (1977)—§ 21.4(c) n.95

Stevens v. State, 34 Md.App. 164, 366 A.2d 414 (1976)—§ 17.4(a) n.40

Stevens, United States v., 177 F.3d 579 (6th Cir.1999)—§ 25.2(d) n.33

Stevens, United States v., 935 F.2d 1380 (3d Cir.1991)—§§ 7.4(c) n.47; 7.4(e) n.89

Stevens, United States v., 918 F.2d 1383 (8th Cir.1990)—§ 21.1(h) n.220

Stevens, United States v., 510 F.2d 1101 (5th Cir.1975)—§ 8.9(b) n.30

Stevenson v. Lewis, 384 F.3d 1069 (9th Cir.2004)—§ 2.6(b) n.68

Stevenson v. Newsome, 774 F.2d 1558 (11th Cir.1985)—§ 11.9(c) n.123

Stevenson, People v., 60 Mich.App. 614, 231 N.W.2d 476 (1975)—§ 21.2(b) n.78

Stevenson, State v., 652 N.W.2d 735 (S.D.2002)—§ 21.2(d) n.242

Stevenson v. State, 782 A.2d 249 (Del.2001)—§§ 22.4(c) n.22, 23

Stevenson v. State, 709 A.2d 619 (Del.1998)—§ 22.4(c) n.29

Steven William T., Matter of, 201 W.Va. 654, 499 S.E.2d 876 (1997)— § 6.9(b) n.23

Stever, State v., 107 N.J. 543, 527 A.2d 408 (1987)—§ 6.7(b) n.41

Stevison, State v., 721 So.2d 843 (La.1999)—§ 11.2(a) n.30

Stewart, Ex parte, 853 So.2d 901 (Ala.2002)—§ 6.4(e) n.76

Stewart v. LaGrand, 526 U.S. 115, 119 S.Ct. 1018, 143 L.Ed.2d 196 (1999)—§ 28.4(d) n.56

Stewart v. Martinez-Villareal, 523 U.S. 637, 118 S.Ct. 1618, 140 L.Ed.2d 849 (1998)—§ 28.5(c) n.72

Stewart v. Maryland, 275 Md. 258, 340 A.2d 290 (1975)—§ 16.1(e) n.200

Stewart, People v., 33 Cal.4th 425, 15 Cal.Rptr.3d 656, 93 P.3d 271 (2004)—§ 22.3(c) n.146

Stewart, People v., 242 Ill.App.3d 599, 182 Ill.Dec. 773, 610 N.E.2d 197 (1993)—§ 26.10(c) n.65

Stewart, People v., 52 Mich.App. 477, 217 N.W.2d 894 (1974)—§ 13.2(c) n.57

Stewart, People v., 10 Ill.App.3d 187, 293 N.E.2d 169 (1973)—§ 3.7(f) n.139

Stewart v. Peters, 958 F.2d 1379 (7th Cir.1992)—§§ 21.4(f)   n.204; 21.5(c) n.92

Stewart v. Smith, 536 U.S. 856, 122 S.Ct. 2578, 153 L.Ed.2d 762 (2002)—§ 28.4(b) n.23

Stewart v. State, 44 S.W.3d 582 (Tex.Crim.App.2001)—§ 16.1(d) n.142

Stewart v. State, 754 N.E.2d 492 (Ind.2001)—§ 6.9(b) n.23

Stewart, State v., 598 N.W.2d 773 (N.D.1999)—§ 17.4(b) n.129

Stewart, State v., 321 Or. 1, 892 P.2d 1013 (1995)—§ 26.4(f) n.101

Stewart v. State, 662 So.2d 552 (Miss.1995)—§ 22.3(d) n.219

Stewart, State v., 486 N.W.2d 444 (Ct.App.1992)—§§ 15.1(f) n.288; 15.7(b) n.17

Stewart v. State, 562 So.2d 1365 (Ala.Crim.App.1989)—§ 11.2(e) n.162

Stewart, State v., 530 So.2d 1263 (La.App.1988)—§ 24.9(g) n.116

Stewart v. State, 757 P.2d 388 (Okla.Crim.App.1988)—§ 22.3(c) n.162

Stewart v. State, 289 Ark. 272, 711 S.W.2d 787 (1986)—§ 3.1(c) n.70

Stewart, State v., 692 S.W.2d 295 (Mo.1985)—§ 22.3(c) n.106

Stewart v. State, 420 So.2d 862 (Fla.1982)—§ 11.7(e) n.83

Stewart v. State, 282 Md. 557, 386 A.2d 1206 (1978)—§ 27.2(c) n.62

Stewart, State v., 175 Mont. 286, 573 P.2d 1138 (1977)—§ 16.4(b) n.13

Stewart v. State, 170 Ind.App. 696, 354 N.E.2d 749 (1976)—§ 18.1(c) n.24

Stewart v. State, 21 Md.App. 346, 319 A.2d 621 (1974)—§ 16.2(a) n.11

Stewart v. State, 51 So.2d 494 (Fla.1951)—§ 24.7(e) n.65

Stewart, State v., 60 Wis. 587, 19 N.W. 429 (1884)—§ 16.1(e) n.190

Stewart, United States v., 468 F.Supp.2d 261 (D.Mass.2007)—§ 26.9(b) n.63

Stewart, United States v., 451 F.3d 1071 (9th Cir.2006)—§ 1.2(c) n.194

Stewart, United States v., 388 F.3d 1079 (7th Cir.2004)—§§ 3.8(b) n.37; 6.8(b) n.49

Stewart, United States v., 306 F.3d 295 (6th Cir.2002)—§§ 19.3(a) n.86, 88 to 90, 99; 27.6(d) n.113

Stewart, United States v., 256 F.3d 231 (4th Cir.2001)—§ 16.1(h) n.293

Stewart, United States v., 185 F.3d 112 (3d Cir.1999)—§ 5.4(c) n.30

Stewart, United States v., 198 F.3d 984 (7th Cir.1999)—§ 21.5(d) n.102

Stewart, United States v., 104 F.3d 1377 (D.C.Cir.1997)—§ 12.1(a) n.19

Stewart v. United States, 668 A.2d 857 (D.C.App.1995)—§§ 6.9(f) n.102, 111

Stewart, United States v., 20 F.3d 911 (8th Cir.1994)—§ 11.5(c) n.52

Stewart, United States v., 972 F.2d 216 (8th Cir.1992)—§ 10.2(d) n.48

Stewart, United States v., 867 F.2d 581 (10th Cir.1989)—§ 3.4(h) n.166

Stewart, United States v., 700 F.2d 702 (11th Cir.1983)—§ 22.1(h) n.157

Stewart Clinical Labs, United States v., 652 F.2d 804 (9th Cir.1981)—§ 19.5(d) n.84

Stewart on Behalf of Tineo, United States ex rel. v. Kelly, 870 F.2d 854 (2d Cir.1989)—§§ 11.9(c) n.104, 115

Stewart, United States ex rel. v. Hewitt, 517 F.2d 993 (3d Cir.1975)—§ 25.2(e) n.42

Stice v. State, 799 P.2d 1204 (Wyo.1990)—§§ 21.4(c) n.77; 21.4(f) n.182; 21.5(c) n.88

Stiefel, State v., 256 So.2d 581 (Fla.App.1972)—§ 17.4(a) n.60

Stillings, State v., 238 Mont. 478, 778 P.2d 406 (1989)—§§ 18.5(a) n.10, 24

Stillwell, State v., 175 N.J.Super. 244, 418 A.2d 267 (1980)—§ 18.5(a) n.47

Stilson v. State, 278 Mont. 20, 924 P.2d 238 (1996)—§ 21.6(a) n.63

Stilson v. United States, 250 U.S. 583, 40 S.Ct. 28, 63 L.Ed. 1154 (1919)—§ 22.3(d) n.166

Stiltner, State v., 80 Wash.2d 47, 491 P.2d 1043 (1971)—§ 23.2(a) n.26

Stine, United States v., 646 F.2d 839 (3d Cir.1981)—§ 26.9(c) n.90

Stinson, People v., 186 App.Div.2d 23, 587 N.Y.S.2d 631 (1992)—§ 24.5(c) n.39

Stinson, State v., 278 Ga. 377, 602 S.E.2d 654 (2004)—§ 21.5(a) n.1

Stipetich, Commonwealth v., 539 Pa. 428, 652 A.2d 1294 (1995)—§ 21.2(d) n.142

Stirling, United States v., 571 F.2d 708 (2d Cir.1978)—§ 21.2(h) n.419

Stirone v. United States, 361 U.S. 212, 80 S.Ct. 270, 4 L.Ed.2d 252 (1960)—§§ 1.2(c) n.133; 1.5(g) n.270; 19.2(e) n.77; 19.2(f) n.89, 108; 19.3(a) n.95; 19.3(e) n.227; 19.5(d) n.73, 79; 19.6(a) n.3; 19.6(c) n.28, 33

Stitely, People v., 35 Cal.4th 514, 26 Cal.Rptr.3d 1, 108 P.3d 182 (2005)—§§ 6.9(g) n.157, 161

Stites v. State, 829 N.E.2d 527 (Ind.2005)—§ 21.2(e) n.321

Stith, People v., 69 N.Y.2d 313, 514 N.Y.S.2d 201, 506 N.E.2d 911 (1987)—§ 9.3(e) n.56

Stith, United States v., 479 F.2d 315 (8th Cir.1973)—§ 14.2(b) n.29

Stiver, United States v., 9 F.3d 298 (3d Cir.1993)—§ 3.4(k) n.219

St. James v. People, 948 P.2d 1028 (Colo.1997)—§§ 21.2(e) n.308, 316; 27.5(e) n.166

St. John, State v., 282 Conn. 260, 919 A.2d 452 (2007)—§§ 7.4(c) n.53; 7.4(f) n.96

St. Joseph Stock Yards Co. v. United States, 298 U.S. 38, 56 S.Ct. 720, 80 L.Ed. 1033 (1936)—§ 2.9(b) n.6

St. Marks, State v., 312 Mont. 468, 59 P.3d 1113 (2002)—§§ 3.3(a) n.22; 10.3(b) n.11

Stobaugh v. State, 298 Ark. 577, 769 S.W.2d 26 (1989)—§ 21.2(g) n.395

Stobaugh, United States v., 420 F.3d 796 (8th Cir.2005)—§ 21.2(b) n.86

Stock, People v., 15 Ill.App.3d 722, 304 N.E.2d 646 (1973)—§ 7.4(b) n.22

Stock, State v., 361 N.W.2d 280 (S.D.1985)—§§ 18.5(b) n.58, 67

Stocker, Commonwealth v., 424 Pa.Super. 189, 622 A.2d 333 (1993)—§§ 24.11(d) n.22, 37

Stocks, United States v., 104 F.3d 308 (9th Cir.1997)—§ 26.4(e) n.78

Stockwell v. State, 98 Idaho 797, 573 P.2d 116 (1977)—§§ 14.3(d) n.88; 27.4(b) n.14

Stockwell, United States v., 743 F.2d 123 (2d Cir.1984)—§§ 18.3(b) n.20; 20.4(e) n.80

Stoddard, State v., 206 Conn. 157, 537 A.2d 446 (1988)—§ 6.9(c) n.61

Stoeckle, State v., 41 Wis.2d 378, 164 N.W.2d 303 (1969)—§ 14.2(g) n.100

Stoia v. United States, 22 F.3d 766 (7th Cir.1994)—§ 27.5(c) n.107

Stokes, People v., 951 Y.Y.2d 633, 722 N.Y.S.2d 217, 744 N.E.2d 1153 (2001)—§ 11.2(c) n.96

Stokes, People v., 88 N.Y.2d 618, 648 N.Y.S.2d 863, 671 N.E.2d 1260 (1996)—§§ 16.4(c) n.76, 92, 98

Stokes v. State, 379 Md. 618, 843 A.2d 64 (Md.App.2004)—§§ 22.3(e) n.285; 27.6(d) n.96

Stokes v. Wabash R.R. Co., 355 Mo. 602, 197 S.W.2d 304 (1946)— § 1.8(d) n.57

Stolar, In re, 397 F.Supp. 520 (S.D.N.Y.1975)—§ 8.8(g) n.172

Stolt-Nielsen, S.A. v. United States, 442 F.3d 177 (3d Cir.2006)—§§ 13.5(b) n.50 to 52

Stone v. Commonwealth, 217 S.W.3d 233 (Ky.2007)—§§ 21.3(a) n.4, 6, 13, 16

Stone v. Cupp, 39 Or.App. 473, 592 P.2d 1044 (1979)—§ 21.2(e) n.316

Stone v. Estelle, 556 F.2d 1242 (5th Cir.1977)—§ 9.6(b) n.54

Stone v. Godbehere, 894 F.2d 1131 (9th Cir.1990)—§ 26.7(c) n.34

Stone v. Hope, 488 P.2d 616 (1971)— § 14.2(d) n.49

Stone, People v., 269 Mich.App. 240, 712 N.W.2d 165 (2005)— §§ 18.4(c) n.62, 63

Stone, People v., 293 Mich. 658, 292 N.W. 520 (1940)—§ 21.5(a) n.36

Stone v. Powell, 428 U.S. 465, 96 S.Ct. 3037, 49 L.Ed.2d 1067 (1976)— §§ 1.3(c) n.22; 2.9(f) n.119, 120, 135; 2.9(g) n.190; 2.9(h) n.209; 2.12(a) n.20; 3.1(b) n.24, 26; 3.1(c) n.40, 47; 6.4(d) n.55; 28.2(b) n.22, 28; 28.2(c) n.40, 46, 48, 49; 28.2(d) n.72, 74, 89; 28.3(c) n.68

Stone v. Shea, 113 N.H. 174, 304 A.2d 647 (1973)—§ 3.1(f) n.155

Stone v. State, 348 Ark. 661, 74 S.W.3d 591 (2002)—§ 10.4(c) n.23

Stone v. State, 344 Md. 97, 685 A.2d 441 (1996)—§§ 18.4(c) n.72; 24.2(d) n.47

Stone v. State, 321 Ark. 46, 900 S.W.2d 515 (1995)—§ 6.7(d) n.153

Stone v. Superior Court, 31 Cal.3d 503, 183 Cal.Rptr. 647, 646 P.2d 809 (1982)—§ 24.10(d) n.46

Stone, United States v., 976 F.2d 909 (4th Cir.1992)—§§ 8.12(b) n.22; 8.13(a) n.28; 8.13(b) n.54; 8.13(d) n.98, 110

Stone, United States v., 866 F.2d 359 (10th Cir.1989)—§ 3.2(b) n.72

Stone, United States v., 813 F.2d 1536 (9th Cir.1987)—§ 18.3(b) n.20

Stoneman, United States v., 870 F.2d 102 (3d Cir.1989)—§ 28.9(a) n.18

Stoner v. California, 376 U.S. 483, 84 S.Ct. 889, 11 L.Ed.2d 856 (1964)— §§ 3.2(a) n.5; 3.10(d) n.102, 131; 3.10(e) n.155; 9.1(b) n.37

Stoner v. Graddick, 751 F.2d 1535 (11th Cir.1985)—§§ 18.5(b) n.62, 68, 69

St. Onge, State v., 392 A.2d 47 (Me.1978)—§ 7.4(c) n.50

Stoots v. State, 205 Tenn. 59, 325 S.W.2d 532 (1959)—§ 15.1(d) n.255

Stopher v. Commonwealth, 57 S.W.3d 787 (Ky.2001)—§ 22.3(c) n.154

Storch, State v., 66 Ohio St.3d 280, 612 N.E.2d 305 (1993)—§ 2.12(e) n.210

Storer, State v., 583 A.2d 1016 (Me.1990)—§ 9.4(b) n.59

Storer Broadcasting Co., State ex rel. v. Gorenstein, 131 Wis.2d 342, 388 N.W.2d 633 (1986)—§ 27.4(c) n.27

Storer Communications, Application of, 828 F.2d 330 (6th Cir.1987)— § 24.3(b) n.73

Storey, United States v., 2 F.3d 1037 (10th Cir.1993)—§§ 15.6(b) n.84; 15.6(f) n.202

Storm, People v., 28 Cal.4th 1007, 124 Cal.Rptr.2d 110, 52 P.3d 52 (2002)—§§ 6.9(f) n.144, 145

Storm, State v., 141 N.J. 245, 661 A.2d 790 (1995)—§ 13.3(b) n.19

Storm v. State, 736 P.2d 1000 (Okla.Crim.App.1987)—§ 6.9(f) n.106

Storms, People v., 155 Ill.2d 498, 187 Ill.Dec. 467, 617 N.E.2d 1188 (1993)—§ 22.4(c) n.29

Story, Commonwealth v., 476 Pa. 391, 383 A.2d 155 (1978)—§§ 27.6(b) n.46, 50, 52, 55, 59

Story, United States v., 439 F.3d 226 (5th Cir.2006)—§ 21.2(b) n.77

Story, United States v., 891 F.2d 988 (2d Cir.1989)—§ 21.2(e) n.321

Stott, State v., 171 N.J. 343, 794 A.2d 120 (2002)—§ 6.6(e) n.71

Stott, State v., 6 Neb.App. 677, 576 N.W.2d 843 (1998)—§ 11.2(a) n.27

Stott, State v., 243 Neb. 967, 503 N.W.2d 822 (1993)—§§ 9.1(b) n.45; 9.1(d) n.120

Stotts, State v., 144 Ariz. 72, 695 P.2d 1110 (1985)—§ 26.9(a) n.4

Stoudmire, In re, 145 Wash.2d 258, 36 P.3d 1005 (2001)—§ 21.5(c) n.91

Stoudmire, In re, 141 Wash.2d 342, 5 P.3d 1240 (2000)—§ 21.6(a) n.33

Stouffer v. State, 147 P.3d 245 (Okla.Cr.App.2006)—§ 22.3(a) n.46

Stough, State v., 273 Kan. 113, 41 P.3d 281 (2002)—§ 21.5(a) n.23

Stout v. People, 171 Colo. 142, 464 P.2d 872 (1970)—§ 24.7(e) n.54

Stout, State v., 305 Or. 34, 749 P.2d 1174 (1988)—§ 15.5(c) n.107

Stout, State v., 172 W.Va. 763, 310 S.E.2d 695 (1983)—§ 14.4(e) n.137

Stout, State ex rel. v. Craytor, 753 P.2d 1365 (Okla.Crim.App.1988)—§ 21.2(f) n.388

Stoval, People v., 40 Ill.2d 109, 239 N.E.2d 441 (1968)—§ 11.9(a) n.1

Stovall v. Denno, 388 U.S. 293, 87 S.Ct. 1967, 18 L.Ed.2d 1199 (1967)—§§ 1.5(b) n.77; 2.7(a) n.15; 2.11(c) n.22, 28, 30, 36, 40; 7.1(c) n.30; 7.2(c) n.38; 7.4(a) n.3; 7.5(a) n.2; 9.1(a) n.26; 10.3(d) n.62, 68

Stovall, United States ex rel. v. Denno, 355 F.2d 731 (2d Cir.1966)—§ 7.4(b) n.17

Stover, Ex parte, 946 S.W.2d 343 (Tex.Crim.App.1997)—§ 26.10(d) n.94

Stover, State v., 140 Idaho 927, 104 P.3d 969 (2005)—§ 26.4(i) n.188

Stow v. Murashige, 389 F.3d 880 (9th Cir.2004)—§ 25.3(b) n.15

Stow, State v., 136 N.H. 598, 620 A.2d 1023 (1993)—§ 11.2(e) n.189

Stow, State v., 83 N.J.L. 14, 84 A. 1063 (1912)—§ 16.4(c) n.68

Stowers, State v., 3 Wash.App. 766, 479 P.2d 145 (1970)—§ 24.10(a) n.18

Stoyko, Commonwealth v., 504 Pa. 455, 475 A.2d 714 (1984)—§ 11.10(b) n.43

St. Paul, City of v. Whidby, 295 Minn. 129, 203 N.W.2d 823 (1972)—§§ 1.8(d) n.65, 70, 79

St. Petersburg, City of v. Reed, 330 So.2d 256 (Fla.App.1976)—§ 1.7(j) n.226

St. Pierre, Commonwealth v., 377 Mass. 650, 387 N.E.2d 1135 (1979)—§§ 15.5(c) n.115; 15.6(a) n.26; 15.7(e) n.94; 20.3(i) n.177

St. Pierre, State v., 1997 ME 107, 693 A.2d 1137 (1997)—§ 24.10(c) n.41

Straach, United States v., 987 F.2d 232 (5th Cir.1993)—§§ 24.9(d) n.42, 47

Strada, United States v., 393 F.Supp. 19 (W.D.Mo.1974)—§ 26.9(b) n.52

Strada, United States v., 503 F.2d 1081 (8th Cir.1974)—§ 26.10(b) n.35

Strader v. Garrison, 611 F.2d 61 (4th Cir.1979)—§ 21.2(g) n.399

Stradley, State v., 127 Idaho 203, 899 P.2d 416 (1995)—§ 20.6(c) n.87

Strain, People v., 194 Ill.2d 467, 252 Ill.Dec. 65, 742 N.E.2d 315 (2000)—§ 22.3(a) n.23

Strain, State v., 779 P.2d 221 (Utah 1989)—§§ 6.2(c) n.105; 6.8(a) n.20

Strain, United States v., 396 F.3d 689 (5th Cir.2005)—§§ 16.2(d) n.55; 16.2(e) n.64

Straka, State v., 116 Wash.2d 859, 810 P.2d 888 (1991)—§ 20.6(b) n.19

Stralla, People v., 14 Cal.2d 617, 96 P.2d 941 (1939)—§ 16.4(c) n.39

Strand Amusement Co. v. Commonwealth, 241 Ky. 48, 43 S.W.2d 321 (1931)—§ 13.4(a) n.5

Strange, State v., 772 S.W.2d 440 (Tenn.Crim.App.1989)—§ 7.3(b) n.29

Strassheim v. Daily, 221 U.S. 280, 31 S.Ct. 558, 55 L.Ed. 735 (1911)—§ 16.4(c) n.75

Stratton, Commonwealth v., 231 Pa.Super. 91, 331 A.2d 741 (1974)—§ 3.8(d) n.134

Stratton, State v., 5 Ohio App.3d 228, 451 N.E.2d 520 (1982)—§ 19.3(c) n.184

Stratton, United States v., 779 F.2d 820 (2d Cir.1985)—§§ 22.1(h) n.156; 24.9(f) n.103

Stratton, United States v., 649 F.2d 1066 (5th Cir.1981)—§ 16.3(d) n.64

Strauder v. West Virginia, 100 U.S. (10 Otto) 303, 25 L.Ed. 664 (1879)—§§ 1.6(d) n.227; 15.4(d) n.107; 22.2(c) n.22

Straughter, State v., 261 Kan. 481, 932 P.2d 387 (1997)—§§ 6.7(c) n.118; 9.6(a) n.35

Strauss, State v., 119 Wash.2d 401, 832 P.2d 78 (1992)—§ 26.4(f) n.90

Strauss, United States v., 563 F.2d 127 (4th Cir.1977)—§§ 21.5(a) n.19, 31

Strayer, State v., 242 Kan. 618, 750 P.2d 390 (1988)—§ 6.7(b) n.72

Streater, State v., 233 N.J.Super. 537, 559 A.2d 473 (1989)—§ 16.4(d) n.144

Streck, United States v., 958 F.2d 141 (6th Cir.1992)—§ 8.11(c) n.43

Streebing, United States v., 987 F.2d 368 (6th Cir.1993)—§ 21.2(d) n.142

Streep v. United States, 160 U.S. 128, 16 S.Ct. 244, 40 L.Ed. 365 (1895)—§ 18.5(a) n.25

Street, People v., 316 Ill.App.3d 205, 249 Ill.Dec. 227, 735 N.E.2d 1052 (2000)—§ 25.2(c) n.21

Street v. Surdyka, 492 F.2d 368 (4th Cir.1974)—§ 3.5(a) n.22

Street, United States v., 472 F.3d 1298 (11th Cir.2006)—§§ 6.8(a) n.7, 22; 6.8(b) n.49

Strehl v. District Court, 558 P.2d 597 (Utah 1976)—§ 15.7(f) n.134

Streifel, United States v., 781 F.2d 953 (1st Cir.1986)—§ 6.6(e) n.90

Streiff, State v., 673 N.W.2d 831 (Minn.2004)—§ 21.3(d) n.263

Streitenberger v. Sheriff, Clark County, 93 Nev. 689, 572 P.2d 931 (1977)—§§ 14.2(g) n.93, 96

Strickland, Commonwealth v., 457 Pa. 631, 326 A.2d 379 (1974)—§ 9.1(b) n.49

Strickland, People v., 363 Ill.App.3d 598, 300 Ill.Dec. 297, 843 N.E.2d 897 (2006)—§ 24.2(e) n.57

Strickland, People v., 211 Ill.App.3d 183, 155 Ill.Dec. 591, 569 N.E.2d 1202 (1991)—§ 26.9(a) n.7

Strickland, State v., 243 Conn. 339, 703 A.2d 109 (1997)—§ 26.10(c) n.81

Strickland, State v., 683 So.2d 218 (La.1996)—§ 24.8(a) n.17

Strickland, State v., 36 Or.App. 119, 584 P.2d 310 (1978)—§ 7.4(b) n.24

Strickland v. State, 280 Ala. 31, 189 So.2d 771 (1965)—§ 11.3(a) n.19

Strickland, United States v., 902 F.2d 937 (11th Cir.1990)—§§ 3.10(f) n.190, 192

Strickland v. Washington, 466 U.S. 668, 104 S.Ct. 2052, 80 L.Ed.2d 674 (1984)—§§ 2.6(e) n.110; 2.9(e) n.104; 2.9(g) n.152; 11.1(a) n.25; 11.4(b) n.39; 11.4(c) n.89; 11.6(b) n.68; 11.7(c) n.31, 34; 11.8(a) n.6, 17; 11.8(c) n.56; 11.9(d) n.166; 11.10(a) n.1, 12, 15, 16; 11.10(c) n.62, 78, 121, 122; 11.10(d) n.157; 21.3(b) n.41, 88; 21.6(a) n.72; 24.3(b) n.28; 26.4(e) n.75; 28.6(f) n.66

Strickler, Commonwealth v., 563 Pa. 47, 757 A.2d 884 (2000)—§ 3.8(c) n.119

Strickler v. Greene, 527 U.S. 263, 119 S.Ct. 1936, 144 L.Ed.2d 286 (1999)—§§ 20.2(c) n.50; 24.3(b) n.21, 33, 51; 28.4(d) n.61, 69

Strickler, United States v., 490 F.2d 378 (9th Cir.1974)—§ 3.8(b) n.24

Stricklin, United States v., 591 F.2d 1112 (5th Cir.1979)—§ 18.3(b) n.53

Strifler, United States v., 851 F.2d 1197 (9th Cir.1988)—§ 3.4(d) n.58

Stringer v. Black, 503 U.S. 222, 112 S.Ct. 1130, 117 L.Ed.2d 367 (1992)—§§ 2.11(e) n.55, 60; 27.6(d) n.90; 28.6(b) n.8; 28.6(d) n.23

Stringer v. State, 491 So.2d 837 (Miss.1986)—§ 2.12(c) n.159

Stringer v. State, 372 So.2d 378 (Ala.Crim.App.1979)—§ 15.4(b) n.74

Stringer v. Williams, 161 F.3d 259 (5th Cir.1998)—§ 17.4(a) n.31

Strmel, United States v., 744 F.2d 1086 (5th Cir.1984)—§ 9.1(d) n.131

Stromberg, United States v., 268 F.2d 256 (2d Cir.1959)—§ 20.3(b) n.51

Strong, State v., 158 Vt. 56, 605 A.2d 510 (1992)—§ 17.4(b) n.124

Strong, State v., 493 N.W.2d 834 (Iowa 1992)—§ 3.4(a) n.10

Strong, State v., 110 N.J. 583, 542 A.2d 866 (1988)—§§ 8.11(c) n.67 to 69

Strongsville v. Waiwood, 62 Ohio App.3d 521, 577 N.E.2d 63 (1989)—§ 22.5(a) n.12

Stroop, United States v., 121 F.R.D. 269 (E.D.N.C.1988)—§§ 20.3(h) n.150, 152

Stroud, Commonwealth v., 375 Mass. 265, 376 N.E.2d 849 (1978)— § 6.9(f) n.107

Stroud, People v., 208 Ill.2d 398, 281 Ill.Dec. 545, 804 N.E.2d 510 (2004)—§ 21.4(a) n.4

Stroud, State v., 106 Wash.2d 144, 720 P.2d 436 (1986)—§§ 2.12(b) n.90; 2.12(e) n.205, 212; 3.7(a) n.19

Stroud v. Superior Court, 23 Cal.4th 952, 98 Cal.Rptr.2d 677, 4 P.3d 933 (2000)—§ 14.2(f) n.88

Stroud v. United States, 251 U.S. 15, 40 S.Ct. 50, 64 L.Ed. 103 (1919)— § 3.9(i) n.173

Stroup, State v., 101 Idaho 54, 607 P.2d 1328 (1980)—§ 26.3(g) n.78

Strouse v. Leonardo, 928 F.2d 548 (2d Cir.1991)—§§ 11.9(b) n.87; 24.7(i) n.86

Strouse, United States v., 286 F.3d 767 (5th Cir.2002)—§§ 15.6(b) n.72, 74; 15.7(e) n.108

Strouther v. Commonwealth, 92 Va. 789, 22 S.E. 852 (1895)—§ 16.4(c) n.115

Strozier v. Newsome, 926 F.2d 1100 (11th Cir.1991)—§§ 11.3(b) n.30, 34; 11.5(c) n.42

Strozier v. Newsome, 871 F.2d 995 (11th Cir.1989)—§§ 11.5(c) n.32, 40, 52, 55

Strunk v. United States, 412 U.S. 434, 93 S.Ct. 2260, 37 L.Ed.2d 56 (1973)—§§ 18.1(e) n.55; 18.2(c) n.38, 41; 27.6(d) n.72

Strunk, United States v., 467 F.2d 969 (7th Cir.1972)—§ 18.1(e) n.54

Stuard, State v., 176 Ariz. 589, 863 P.2d 881 (1993)—§ 17.1(f) n.69

Stuart, State v., 279 Wis.2d 659, 695 N.W.2d 259 (2005)—§ 14.1(d) n.65

Stuart, State v., 544 N.W.2d 158 (N.D.1996)—§ 13.2(c) n.56

Stuart v. State, 127 Idaho 806, 907 P.2d 783 (1995)—§ 24.3(e) n.132

Stuart, State v., 194 Mo. 345, 92 S.W. 878 (1906)—§ 16.4(c) n.47

Stuart v. State, 35 Tex.Crim. 440, 34 S.W. 118 (Tex.Crim.App.1896)— § 15.6(d) n.117

Stubblefield, State v., 249 Neb. 436, 543 N.W.2d 743 (1996)—§ 17.4(b) n.138

Stubbs, People v., 25 Ill.App.3d 181, 323 N.E.2d 26 (1974)—§ 10.5(e) n.58

Stubbs v. State, 114 Nev. 1412, 972 P.2d 843 (1998)—§ 21.2(d) n.172

Stubbs, United States v., 279 F.3d 402 (6th Cir.2002)—§ 21.2(b) n.83

Stubbs, United States v., 281 F.3d 109 (3d Cir.2002)—§§ 11.5(c) n.56; 11.5(f) n.104

Stubbs, United States v., 944 F.2d 828 (11th Cir.1991)—§§ 6.7(c) n.141, 142; 9.6(a) n.35

Studer v. State, 799 S.W.2d 263 (Tex.Crim.App.1990)—§§ 19.1(d) n.69; 19.2(e) n.55; 19.3(e) n.221

Studnicka, United States v., 777 F.2d 652 (11th Cir.1985)—§ 18.3(b) n.38

Stumes v. Solem, 752 F.2d 317 (8th Cir.1985)—§§ 6.9(e) n.97; 6.9(f) n.102

Stumpf v. Mitchell, 367 F.3d 594 (6th Cir.2004)—§§ 17.4(a) n.49, 50; 21.4(f) n.187

Stumpf, State v., 481 N.W.2d 887 (Minn.App.1992)—§ 9.6(a) n.25

Stumpf v. State, 749 P.2d 880 (Alaska 1988)—§ 15.7(e) n.106

Stumpf, United States v., 900 F.2d 842 (5th Cir.1990)—§ 21.5(c) n.74

Stump, State ex rel. v. Johnson, 217 W.Va. 733, 619 S.E.2d 246 (2005)—§ 21.2(e) n.329

Sturdivant, People v., 412 Mich. 92, 312 N.W.2d 622 (1981)—§ 26.10(d) n.91

Sturgeon v. State, 719 N.E.2d 1173 (Ind.1999)—§ 22.4(c) n.29

Sturgess v. United States, 633 A.2d 56 (D.C.App.1993)—§§ 24.3(g) n.168, 172

Sturgis, People v., 58 Ill.2d 211, 317 N.E.2d 545 (1974)—§§ 10.1(b) n.28; 10.5(c) n.33

Sturm, People v., 37 Cal.4th 1218, 39 Cal.Rptr.3d 799, 129 P.3d 10 (2006)—§ 24.6(e) n.52

Sturman, United States v., 49 F.3d 1275 (7th Cir.1995)—§ 12.1(a) n.12

Sturman, United States v., 951 F.2d 1466 (6th Cir.1991)—§ 19.2(f) n.91

Stuttley, United States v., 103 F.3d 684 (8th Cir.1996)—§ 21.2(f) n.383

Styles, People v., 90 Misc.2d 861, 395 N.Y.S.2d 1007 (1977)—§ 7.3(d) n.77

Styles v. State, 474 So.2d 185 (Ala.Crim.App.1985)—§ 19.5(b) n.7

Styskal, State v., 242 Neb. 26, 493 N.W.2d 313 (1992)—§ 26.9(c) n.94

Suarez, United States v., 263 F.3d 468 (6th Cir.2001)—§§ 6.9(g) n.167; 13.7(c) n.43

Suarez, United States v., 906 F.2d 977 (4th Cir.1990)—§ 4.6(k) n.174

Suarez-Rosario, United States v., 237 F.3d 1164 (9th Cir.2001)—§ 24.6(b) n.23

Subin v. Ulmer, 131 N.M. 350, 36 P.3d 441 (App.2001)—§ 11.2(e) n.229

Subpoena & Order Directing Probation Officer to Produce Records, In re, 737 F.Supp. 30 (W.D.N.C.1990)—§ 26.5(c) n.59

Subpoena Duces Tecum Dated April 23, 1981, 522 F.Supp. 977 (S.D.N.Y.1981)—§ 8.13(d) n.113

Subpoena Issued to Erato, In re, 2 F.3d 11 (2d Cir.1993)—§ 8.11(d) n.75

Subpoena to Testify Before Grand Jury Directed to Custodian of Records, In re, 864 F.2d 1559 (11th Cir.1989)—§§ 8.5(c) n.86; 8.5(d) n.147

Suco, State v., 521 So.2d 1100 (Fla.1988)—§ 9.1(b) n.41

Sudds v. Texas, 140 S.W.3d 813 (2004)—§ 16.1(g) n.282

Sugar, State v., 108 N.J. 151, 527 A.2d 1377 (1987)—§ 9.3(e) n.80

Sugar, State v., 100 N.J. 214, 495 A.2d 90 (1985)—§ 10.4(c) n.25

Sugar, State v., 84 N.J. 1, 417 A.2d 474 (1980)—§ 8.9(a) n.7

Suggs v. State, 923 So.2d 419 (Fla.2005)—§ 6.4(g) n.153

Suggs, United States v., 374 F.3d 508 (7th Cir.2004)—§ 21.5(d) n.104

Suggs v. United States, 391 F.2d 971 (D.C.Cir.1968)—§ 11.2(c) n.98

Sugimoto, State v., 62 Haw. 259, 614 P.2d 386 (1980)—§ 20.6(b) n.24

Suleiman, United States v., 208 F.3d 32 (2d Cir.2000)—§ 27.5(a) n.32

Sullivan, Ex parte, 779 So.2d 1157 (Ala.2000)—§§ 25.2(d) n.33; 27.4(d) n.39

Sullivan, In the Matter of, 185 A.D.2d 440, 586 N.Y.S.2d 322 (1992)—§§ 23.1(b) n.58, 63, 81

Sullivan v. Alabama, 666 F.2d 478 (11th Cir.1982)—§ 6.7(d) n.143

Sullivan v. Askew, 348 So.2d 312 (Fla.1977)—§ 26.2(c) n.74

Sullivan v. City of Norwalk, 28 Conn.App. 449, 612 A.2d 114 (App. 1992)—§ 3.4(h) n.151

Sullivan, Commonwealth v., 425 Mass. 449, 681 N.E.2d 1184 (1997)—§ 2.11(a) n.14

Sullivan v. Louisiana, 508 U.S. 275, 113 S.Ct. 2078, 124 L.Ed.2d 182 (1993)—§§ 2.7(a) n.46; 24.8(c) n.40; 27.6(d) n.111, 117

Sullivan v. Murphy, 478 F.2d 938 (D.C.Cir.1973)—§§ 3.1(m) n.292, 295

Sullivan, People v., 59 Cal.Rptr.3d 876, 151 Cal.App.4th 524 (2007)—§ 24.3(g) n.163

Sullivan, State v., 97 Haw. 259, 36 P.3d 803 (2001)—§ 22.1(b) n.44

Sullivan v. State, 115 Nev. 383, 990 P.2d 1258 (1999)—§ 21.2(d) n.174

Sullivan v. State, 585 N.W.2d 782 (Minn.1998)—§ 6.6(d) n.45

Sullivan, State v., 541 A.2d 450 (R.I.1988)—§ 18.5(a) n.44

Sullivan v. State, 246 Ga. 426, 271 S.E.2d 823 (1980)—§§ 15.4(b) n.47, 49

Sullivan, State v., 159 La. 589, 105 So. 631 (La.1925)—§ 8.4(b) n.88

Sullivan, United States v., 451 F.3d 884 (D.C. Cir.2006)—§ 1.2(c) n.193

Sullivan, United States v., 85 F.3d 743 (1st Cir.1996)—§ 24.5(b) n.22

Sullivan, United States v., 919 F.2d 1403 (10th Cir.1990)—§ 20.5(c) n.46

Sullivan, State ex rel. v. Patterson, 64 Ariz. 40, 165 P.2d 309 (1946)—§§ 16.3(d) n.55, 70, 71

Sumdum v. State, 612 P.2d 1018 (Alaska 1980)—§ 3.10(e) n.159

Sumlin, United States v., 271 F.3d 274 (D.C.Cir.2001)—§ 5.2(a) n.9

Summerlin v. Schriro, 427 F.3d 623 (9th Cir.2005)—§§ 11.6(a) n.26, 62; 11.10(c) n.127, 151

Summers, People v., 291 Ill.App. 656, 226 Ill.Dec. 8, 684 N.E.2d 1004 (1997)—§ 26.3(f) n.67

Summers v. Schriro, 481 F.3d 710 (9th Cir.2007)—§ 28.5(b) n.44

Summers v. State, 148 P.3d 778 (Nev.2006)—§§ 26.4(f) n.93, 109

Summers, State v., 642 So.2d 742 (Fla.1994)—§ 26.10(d) n.92

Sumner v. Mata, 455 U.S. 591, 102 S.Ct. 1303, 71 L.Ed.2d 480 (1982)—§ 28.7(b) n.6

Sumner v. Mata, 449 U.S. 539, 101 S.Ct. 764, 66 L.Ed.2d 722 (1981)—§ 28.7(a) n.2

Sumner v. Shuman, 483 U.S. 66, 107 S.Ct. 2716, 97 L.Ed.2d 56 (1987)—§ 26.1(b) n.20

Sumner, State v., 178 Conn. 163, 422 A.2d 299 (1979)—§ 19.3(b) n.149

Sumner v. State, 132 Tex.Cr.R. 281, 104 S.W.2d 45 (1937)—§ 15.4(i) n.214

Sumpter v. State, 312 S.C. 221, 439 S.E.2d 842 (1994)—§ 22.3(d) n.250

Sunal v. Large, 332 U.S. 174, 67 S.Ct. 1588, 91 L.Ed. 1982 (1947)—§ 28.9(c) n.74

Sundance v. Municipal Court, 42 Cal.3d 1101, 232 Cal.Rptr. 814, 729 P.2d 80 (1986)—§ 13.2(h) n.147

Sunday, People v., 275 Cal.App.2d 473, 79 Cal.Rptr. 752 (1969)—§ 6.7(c) n.116

Sundberg, State v., 235 Mont. 115, 765 P.2d 736 (1988)—§ 3.3(a) n.11

Sundby, United States v., 186 F.3d 873 (8th Cir.1999)—§ 10.6(a) n.8

Sundel, State v., 121 R.I. 638, 402 A.2d 585 (1979)—§ 3.6(b) n.56

Sunderman v. Warnken, 251 Wis. 471, 29 N.W.2d 496 (1947)—§ 3.9(b) n.21

Sun Myung Moon, United States v., 718 F.2d 1210 (2d Cir.1983)—§ 24.5(d) n.50

Sun Myung Moon, United States v., 532 F.Supp. 1360 (S.D.N.Y.1982)— §§ 15.2(b) n.50; 15.7(f) n.145, 185

Sun Oil v. Wortman, 486 U.S. 717, 108 S.Ct. 2117, 100 L.Ed.2d 743 (1988)—§ 2.7(c) n.163

Sunrhodes, United States v., 831 F.2d 1537 (10th Cir.1987)—§ 26.6(c) n.40

Superintendent, Mass. Correctional Inst. v. Hill, 472 U.S. 445, 105 S.Ct. 2768, 86 L.Ed.2d 356 (1985)— § 26.2(c) n.64

Superior Court, People v., 28 Cal.4th 798, 123 Cal.Rptr.2d 31, 50 P.3d 743 (2002)—§ 22.4(d) n.43

Superior Court, People v., 25 Cal.4th 703, 107 Cal.Rptr.2d 323, 23 P.3d 563 (2001)—§ 3.4(a) n.22

Superior Court, People v., 23 Cal.4th 183, 96 Cal.Rptr.2d 463, 999 P.2d 686 (2000)—§ 21.4(d) n.137

Superior Court, People v., 13 Cal.4th 497, 53 Cal.Rptr.2d 789, 917 P.2d 628 (1996)—§§ 13.2(c) n.62; 26.3(c) n.19

Superior Court, People v., 235 Cal.App.3d 1261, 1 Cal.Rptr.2d 333 (1991)—§ 27.4(d) n.41

Superior Court, People v., 19 Cal.3d 338, 138 Cal.Rptr. 66, 562 P.2d 1315 (1977)—§ 13.4(c) n.93

Superior Court, People v., 15 Cal.3d 729, 125 Cal.Rptr. 798, 542 P.2d 1390 (1975)—§ 6.9(g) n.163

Superior Court, People v., 11 Cal.3d 59, 113 Cal.Rptr. 21, 520 P.2d 405 (1974)—§§ 13.6(b) n.21; 13.6(c) n.45

Superior Court, People v., 11 Cal.3d 793, 114 Cal.Rptr. 596, 523 P.2d 636 (1974)—§ 21.4(d) n.136

Superior Court, People v., 3 Cal.3d 807, 91 Cal.Rptr. 729, 478 P.2d 449 (1970)—§ 3.3(f) n.203

Superior Court, People v., 3 Cal.App.3d 648, 83 Cal.Rptr. 732 (1970)— § 3.10(e) n.151

Superior Court, People v., 2 Cal.App.3d 131, 82 Cal.Rptr. 507 (1969)— § 3.2(e) n.162

Superior Court, State v., 125 Ariz. 575, 611 P.2d 928 (1980)—§ 21.4(g) n.245

Superior Court, State v., 119 Ariz. 286, 580 P.2d 747 (App.1978)— § 15.7(g) n.201

Superior Court, State v., 2 Ariz.App. 458, 409 P.2d 742 (1966)— § 11.6(a) n.6

Superior Court (Fairbank), People v., 192 Cal.App.3d 32, 237 Cal.Rptr. 158 (1987)—§§ 20.4(b) n.30, 31, 34

Superior Court (Mouchaourab), People v., 78 Cal.App.4th 403, 92 Cal.Rptr.2d 829 (2000)—§§ 15.2(i) n.213; 15.5(c) n.127; 15.7(a) n.2

Suppa, United States v., 799 F.2d 115 (3d Cir.1986)—§ 12.1(a) n.15

Surette, State v., 130 N.H. 531, 544 A.2d 823 (1988)—§ 24.10(a) n.8

Surge, State v., 122 Wash.App. 448, 94 P.3d 345 (2004)—§ 3.2(g) n.200

Surina v. Buckalew, 629 P.2d 969 (Alaska 1981)—§§ 8.11(e) n.95, 100

Surland v. State, 392 Md. 17, 895 A.2d 1034 (2006)—§§ 27.5(a) n.6, 8

Susi, Commonwealth v., 394 Mass. 784, 477 N.E.2d 995 (1985)—§ 22.3(c) n.97

Susskind, United States v., 4 F.3d 1400 (6th Cir.1993)—§ 8.7(e) n.91

Susskind, United States v., 965 F.2d 80 (6th Cir.1992)—§ 8.7(e) n.93

Sustaita, United States v., 1 F.3d 950 (9th Cir.1993)—§ 26.5(c) n.44

Sutherland, People v., 194 Ill.2d 289, 252 Ill.Dec. 56, 742 N.E.2d 306 (2000)—§ 11.10(c) n.126

Sutherland, People v., 17 Cal.App.4th 602, 21 Cal.Rptr.2d 752 (1993)—§ 24.10(c) n.40

Sutherland, State v., 329 Or. 359, 987 P.2d 501 (1999)—§ 12.3(b) n.58

Sutherland, United States v., 929 F.2d 765 (1st Cir.1991)—§ 2.12(c) n.172

Sutherlin v. Sutherlin, 27 Ind.App. 301, 61 N.E. 206 (1901)—§ 15.1(b) n.77

Sutphin, State v., 107 N.M. 126, 753 P.2d 1314 (1988)—§ 22.3(d) n.176

Sutter, United States v., 340 F.3d 1022 (9th Cir.2003)—§ 18.3(b) n.26

Sutton, Commonwealth v., 485 Pa. 47, 400 A.2d 1305 (1979)—§ 23.2(g) n.124

Sutton, People v., 36 Mich.App. 604, 194 N.W.2d 3 (1971)—§ 16.1(h) n.306

Sutton v. State, 784 So.2d 1239 (Fla.App.2001)—§ 18.5(a) n.33

Sutton, State v., 231 Neb. 30, 434 N.W.2d 689 (1989)—§ 10.3(b) n.29

Sutton, State v., 197 Conn. 485, 498 A.2d 65 (1985)—§ 21.5(e) n.138

Sutton, United States v., 961 F.2d 476 (4th Cir.1992)—§§ 19.3(e) n.245, 249

Sutton, United States v., 794 F.2d 1415 (9th Cir.1986)—§ 21.2(d) n.217

Sutton, United States v., 607 F.2d 220 (8th Cir.1979)—§ 26.10(b) n.38

Sutton, United States v., 421 F.2d 1394 (5th Cir.1970)—§ 26.10(a) n.4

Sutton v. United States, 267 F.2d 271 (4th Cir.1959)—§ 9.3(d) n.33

Svacina, United States v., 137 F.3d 1179 (10th Cir.1998)—§§ 21.1(h) n.228; 21.2(d) n.210

Svoboda, State v., 205 Neb. 175, 287 N.W.2d 41 (1980)—§§ 21.2(c) n.120; 21.3(d) n.220

Swacker, United States v., 628 F.2d 1250 (9th Cir.1980)—§§ 18.5(b) n.58, 59

Swackhammer v. State, 808 P.2d 219 (Wyo.1991)—§ 26.10(c) n.73

Swaim, State v., 412 N.W.2d 568 (Iowa 1987)—§§ 6.4(f) n.137; 6.9(f) n.139

Swain v. Alabama, 380 U.S. 202, 85 S.Ct. 824, 13 L.Ed.2d 759 (1965)—§§ 22.2(c) n.32; 22.3(c) n.97; 22.3(d) n.163, 171, 184

Swain v. Pressley, 430 U.S. 372, 97 S.Ct. 1224, 51 L.Ed.2d 411 (1977)—§ 28.2(a) n.4

Swain v. State, 275 Ga. 150, 563 S.E.2d 122 (2002)—§§ 6.9(g) n.166; 22.3(d) n.176

Swain v. State, 527 S.W.2d 119 (Tenn.1975)—§ 12.4(d) n.81

Swain, State v., 267 Or. 527, 517 P.2d 684 (1974)—§§ 10.6(c) n.31, 33

Swan, In re, 92 Ill.App.3d 856, 48 Ill.Dec. 70, 415 N.E.2d 1354 (1981)—§ 8.3(a) n.8

Swan, United States v., 275 F.3d 272 (3d Cir.2002)—§ 26.3(f) n.60

Swanberg, United States v., 370 F.3d 622 (6th Cir.2004)—§ 21.2(b) n.79

Swanigan, State v., 279 Kan. 18, 106 P.3d 39 (2005)—§§ 6.2(c) n.107, 127, 169; 9.5(c) n.68

Swanigan v. United States, 853 A.2d 742 (D.C.App.2004)—§ 18.4(c) n.65

Swann v. Huntsville, 471 So.2d 1268 (Ala.Crim.App.1985)—§ 11.1(b) n.87

Swann, United States v., 526 F.2d 147 (9th Cir.1975)—§ 4.6(m) n.228

Swanquist, United States v., 125 F.3d 573 (7th Cir.1997)—§ 12.4(d) n.87

Swanson, People v., 308 Ill.App.3d 708, 242 Ill.Dec. 351, 721 N.E.2d 630 (1999)—§ 19.3(b) n.152

Swanson, United States v., 341 F.3d 524 (6th Cir.2003)—§§ 3.7(d) n.67; 6.6(e) n.91

Swanson, United States v., 509 F.2d 1205 (8th Cir.1975)—§ 13.4(c) n.106

Swartz, State v., 88 Ohio St.3d 131, 723 N.E.2d 1084 (2000)—§ 18.5(a) n.11

Swartz, State v., 541 N.W.2d 533 (Iowa App.1995)—§§ 25.4(a) n.9; 25.4(c) n.37

Swartz v. State, 506 N.W.2d 792 (Iowa App.1993)—§ 24.3(d) n.112

Swartz, United States v., 975 F.2d 1042 (4th Cir.1992)—§ 11.9(d) n.190

Swearingen Aviation Corp., In re, 486 F.Supp. 9 (D.Md.1979)—§ 8.5(d) n.147

Swearingen Aviation Corp., In re, 605 F.2d 125 (4th Cir.1979)—§ 8.5(d) n.126

Sweatt, State v., 333 N.C. 407, 427 S.E.2d 112 (1993)—§ 6.6(e) n.71

Sweeney v. Carter, 361 F.3d 327 (7th Cir.2004)—§ 6.8(a) n.33

Sweeney, State v., 151 N.H. 666, 867 A.2d 441 (2005)—§§ 11.5(b) n.30; 19.4(b) n.10

Sweeney, State v., 178 Vt. 1, 869 A.2d 137 (2005)—§ 22.1(h) n.138

Sweeney v. State, 704 N.E.2d 86 (Ind.1998)—§ 18.4(c) n.40

Sweeney, State v., 203 Iowa 1305, 214 N.W. 735 (1927)—§§ 16.1(d) n.145; 16.2(a) n.4

Sweeney, United States v., 878 F.2d 68 (2d Cir.1989)—§ 21.2(g) n.395

Sweeny, People v., 57 Ill.App.3d 879, 15 Ill.Dec. 317, 373 N.E.2d 663 (1978)—§ 7.3(c) n.59

Sweet v. Delo, 125 F.3d 1144 (8th Cir.1997)—§§ 11.1(b) n.83; 11.10(d) n.181; 28.3(c) n.80

Sweet v. State, 191 Ga.App. 516, 382 S.E.2d 376 (1989)—§ 14.2(e) n.66

Sweet v. United States, 449 A.2d 315 (D.C.App.1982)—§ 15.4(d) n.98

Sweeting, United States v., 933 F.2d 962 (11th Cir.1991)—§ 6.7(b) n.46

Sweezy v. State, 167 P.3d 79 (Alaska App.2007)—§ 26.1(d) n.89

Sweig, United States v., 316 F.Supp. 1148 (S.D.N.Y.1970)—§§ 8.5(i) n.319, 324; 15.4(h) n.188, 191, 194

Swenson v. Bosler, 386 U.S. 258, 87 S.Ct. 996, 18 L.Ed.2d 33 (1967)—§ 11.1(b) n.70

Swenson, State v., 217 Neb. 820, 352 N.W.2d 149 (1984)—§ 5.2(a) n.10

Swepston, United States v., 987 F.2d 1510 (10th Cir.1993)—§ 3.2(d) n.157

Swift, People v., 32 A.D.2d 183, 300 N.Y.S.2d 639 (1969)—§ 6.8(c) n.77

Swift, State v., 251 Neb. 204, 556 N.W.2d 243 (1996)—§ 3.4(g) n.125

Swift, State v., 290 N.C. 383, 226 S.E.2d 652 (1976)—§ 19.4(b) n.20

Swift v. United States, 196 U.S. 375, 25 S.Ct. 276, 49 L.Ed. 518 (1905)—§ 1.2(c) n.126

Swift & Co. v. Wickham, 382 U.S. 111, 86 S.Ct. 258, 15 L.Ed.2d 194 (1965)—§ 2.9(b) n.22

Swims, State v., 212 W.Va. 263, 569 S.E.2d 784 (2002)—§ 22.3(c) n.99

Swindall, United States v., 107 F.3d 831 (11th Cir.1997)—§§ 28.6(e) n.47; 28.9(a) n.18

Swindall, United States v., 971 F.2d 1531 (11th Cir.1992)—§ 15.7(d) n.79

Swinehart, Commonwealth v., 541 Pa. 500, 664 A.2d 957 (1995)—§ 8.11(c) n.67

Swinehart, United States v., 614 F.2d 853 (3d Cir.1980)—§ 21.2(d) n.245

Swingler, United States v., 758 F.2d 477 (10th Cir.1985)—§ 17.2(d) n.97

Swinney, United States v., 970 F.2d 494 (8th Cir.1992)—§ 22.3(d) n.250

Swint, United States v., 223 F.3d 249 (3d Cir.2000)—§ 21.2(d) n.222

Swinton, State v., 268 Conn. 781, 847 A.2d 921 (2004)—§ 6.4(g) n.153

Swoopes, State v., 223 Neb. 914, 395 N.W.2d 500 (1986)—§ 7.4(e) n.84

Swoopes v. Sublett, 196 F.3d 1008 (9th Cir.1999)—§ 28.5(a) n.39

Swope, State v., 939 S.W.2d 491 (Mo.App.1997)—§ 27.3(c) n.39

Sword v. State, 746 P.2d 423 (Wyo.1987)—§ 21.6(a) n.53

S.W.T., In re, 277 N.W.2d 507 (Minn.1979)—§ 6.9(b) n.16

Syal, United States v., 963 F.2d 900 (6th Cir.1992)—§§ 21.4(c) n.95; 21.5(c) n.83

Sykes, State v., 412 N.W.2d 578 (Iowa 1987)—§ 3.4(j) n.198

Sykes, United States v., 292 F.3d 495 (6th Cir.2002)—§ 21.4(e) n.156

Sykes, United States v., 7 F.3d 1331 (7th Cir.1993)—§ 22.4(b) n.20

Sylvester, United States v., 143 F.3d 923 (5th Cir.1998)—§ 24.9(f) n.85

Sylvester, United States v., 848 F.2d 520 (5th Cir.1988)—§ 6.6(e) n.91

Syme, United States v., 276 F.3d 131 (3d Cir.2002)—§§ 19.3(a) n.98; 19.6(c) n.46; 27.5(c) n.106

Symington, United States v., 195 F.3d 1080 (9th Cir.1999)—§ 24.9(f) n.75

Synder v. Massachusetts, 291 U.S. 97, 54 S.Ct. 330, 78 L.Ed. 674 (1934)—§ 2.4 n.2

Synodinos, United States v., 218 F.Supp. 479 (D.Utah 1963)—§ 16.3(c) n.47

Syphers, United States v., 426 F.3d 461 (1st Cir.2005)—§ 3.4(g) n.124

Syverston, State v., 597 N.W.2d 644 (N.D.1999)—§ 7.4(e) n.86

Szabo v. Walls, 313 F.3d 392 (7th Cir.2002)—§ 26.4(f) n.109

Szuchon v. Lehman, 273 F.3d 299 (3d Cir.2001)—§ 22.3(c) n.146

Szymaniak, United States v., 934 F.2d 434 (2d Cir.1991)—§ 6.9(f) n.134

T

2000-2001 District Grand Jury, In re, 22 P.3d 922 (Colo.2001)—§ 8.3(h) n.49

2000-2001 District Grand Jury, In the Matter of the, 97 P.3d 921 (Colo.2004)—§ 8.3(h) n.52

$273,969.04 U.S. Currency, United States v., 164 F.3d 462 (9th Cir.1999)—§ 17.4(b) n.120

Taberer v. Armstrong World Industries, Inc., 954 F.2d 888 (3d Cir.1992)—§§ 8.3(a) n.6, 7

Tabor, State v., _____ So.2d _____, 2007 WL 1653113 (La.App.2007)—§ 27.5(d) n.118

Tabor v. State, 161 S.W.3d 862 (Mo.App.2005)—§§ 18.4(d) n.86, 88

Tachibana v. State, 79 Haw. 226, 900 P.2d 1293 (Haw.1995)—§ 24.5(d) n.57

Tachibana, State v., 67 Haw. 573, 698 P.2d 287 (1985)—§§ 21.4(f) n.173, 176; 21.4(g) n.232; 21.5(a) n.24

Tackno v. Blackburn, 571 F.2d 1383 (5th Cir.1978)—§ 28.3(d) n.85

Taffe, United States v., 36 F.3d 1047 (11th Cir.1994)—§ 21.4(f) n.171

Tagala v. State, 812 P.2d 604 (Alaska App.1991)—§ 22.3(b) n.73

Tagbering, United States v., 985 F.2d 946 (8th Cir.1993)—§ 3.1(c) n.71

Tager, United States v., 638 F.2d 167 (10th Cir.1980)—§§ 8.5(e) n.182, 188

Taggart v. State, 595 N.E.2d 256 (Ind.1992)—§ 17.2(b) n.62

Taggart, United States v., 334 F.Supp. 206 (D.Del.1971)—§ 3.5(c) n.110

Taggert, State v., 443 S.W.2d 168 (Mo.1969)—§ 6.8(c) n.76

Taglia, United States v., 922 F.2d 413 (7th Cir.1991)—§§ 11.7(e) n.69, 70, 85, 86

Taglia, United States v., 925 F.2d 1031 (7th Cir.1991)—§ 21.2(d) n.238

Tague v. Louisiana, 444 U.S. 469, 100 S.Ct. 652, 62 L.Ed.2d 622 (1980)—§§ 6.9(a) n.11; 6.9(b) n.13; 6.9(d) n.71

Tague v. Puckett, 874 F.2d 1013 (5th Cir.1989)—§ 11.2(d) n.128

Taillon, State v., 470 N.W.2d 226 (N.D.1991)—§ 6.2(c) n.160

Tajeddini, United States v., 945 F.2d 458 (1st Cir.1991)—§ 11.2(b) n.53

Taketa, United States v., 923 F.2d 665 (9th Cir.1991)—§§ 3.9(l) n.270; 9.2(c) n.32

Talamante v. Romero, 620 F.2d 784 (10th Cir.1980)—§§ 15.5(b) n.50, 52

Talao, United States v., 222 F.3d 1133 (9th Cir.2000)—§ 11.8(b) n.41

Talavera, State v., 127 Idaho 700, 905 P.2d 633 (1995)—§ 17.4(b) n.124

Talavera, State v., 243 So.2d 595 (Fla.1971)—§ 17.2(c) n.80

Talbot, Commonwealth v., 444 Mass. 586, 830 N.E.2d 177 (2005)—§§ 11.2(b) n.40; 26.4(e) n.83

Talbott, United States v., 902 F.2d 1129 (4th Cir.1990)—§ 3.4(k) n.228

Taliaferro v. Locke, 182 Cal.App.2d 752, 6 Cal.Rptr. 813 (1960)—§ 13.3(a) n.7

Taliaferro v. State, 295 Md. 376, 456 A.2d 29 (1983)—§§ 20.5(b) n.14; 20.6(c) n.82, 86

Talley v. State, 200 Ga.App. 442, 408 S.E.2d 463 (1991)—§ 10.6(d) n.45

Talley, State v., 112 Ari. 268, 540 P.2d 1249 (1975)—§ 20.6(c) n.86

Talley, United States v., 275 F.3d 560 (6th Cir.2001)—§ 6.7(b) n.79

Talley, United States v., 164 F.3d 989 (6th Cir.1999)—§ 22.3(b) n.68

Tamari, United States v., 454 F.3d 1259 (11th Cir.2006)—§ 3.4(e) n.91

Tamble, People v., 5 Cal.App.4th 815, 7 Cal.Rptr.2d 446 (1992)—§§ 16.1(b) n.31, 36; 16.1(e) n.205, 210

Tamerius, State v., 234 Neb. 121, 449 N.W.2d 535 (1989)—§ 6.2(c) n.112

Tamme v. Commonwealth, 973 S.W.2d 13 (Ky.1998)—§ 18.1(c) n.27

Tamura, United States v., 694 F.2d 591 (9th Cir.1982)—§ 3.4(k) n.219

Tankleff v. Senkowski, 135 F.3d 235 (2d Cir.1998)—§§ 9.5(c) n.68; 22.3(d) n.212, 254; 27.6(d) n.141

Tannehill, State v., 341 Or. 205, 141 P.3d 584 (2006)—§ 21.6(b) n.84

Tanner, People v., 45 Cal.App.3d 345, 119 Cal.Rptr. 407 (1975)—§ 21.2(h) n.415

Tanner, State v., 210 Or.App. 70, 150 P.3d 31 (Or.App.2006)—§ 26.4(i) n.191

Tanner v. State, 242 Ga. 437, 249 S.E.2d 238 (1978)—§ 22.3(e) n.265

Tanner, United States v., 941 F.2d 574 (7th Cir.1991)—§ 18.4(b) n.23

Tanner v. United States, 483 U.S. 107, 107 S.Ct. 2739, 97 L.Ed.2d 90 (1987)—§§ 24.9(f) n.71; 24.9(g) n.124

Tanner, United States v., 279 F.Supp. 457 (N.D.Ill.1967)—§§ 19.4(b) n.24, 26

Tanso, Commonwealth v., 411 Mass. 640, 583 N.E.2d 1247 (1992)—§§ 7.3(c) n.59; 14.1(d) n.59

Tantalo, United States v., 680 F.2d 903 (2d Cir.1982)—§ 15.7(d) n.67

Tanu, United States v., 589 F.2d 82 (2d Cir.1978)—§ 18.1(c) n.40

Tanzella, State v., 226 Conn. 601, 628 A.2d 973 (1993)—§§ 19.5(b) n.30, 32

Tapia, State v., 159 Ariz. 284, 767 P.2d 5 (1988)—§§ 6.2(c) n.107, 120

Tapio, State v., 459 N.W.2d 406 (S.D.1990)—§§ 6.8(a) n.20; 9.1(b) n.76

Taplette, State v., 545 So.2d 985 (La.1989)—§ 3.6(a) n.19

Tapley v. Collins, 211 F.3d 1210 (11th Cir.2000)—§ 4.6(n) n.258

Tapp v. Lucas, 658 F.2d 383 (5th Cir.1981)—§ 17.4(b) n.71

Tapscott v. State, 106 Md.App. 109, 664 A.2d 42 (1995)—§ 19.2(c) n.35

Tapson, State v., 307 Mont. 428, 41 P.3d 305 (2001)—§ 24.2(a) n.6

Tarallo, United States ex rel. v. La-Vallee, 433 F.2d 4 (2d Cir.1970)—§ 17.3(d) n.46

Tarango-Hinojos, United States v., 791 F.2d 1174 (5th Cir.1986)—§ 3.3(f) n.214

Tarantino, State v., 587 A.2d 1095 (Me.1991)—§ 2.12(c) n.146

Tarantino, State v., 322 N.C. 386, 368 S.E.2d 588 (1988)—§§ 3.2(b) n.57; 3.2(e) n.165

Tarantino, United States v., 846 F.2d 1384 (D.C.Cir.1988)—§ 20.3(d) n.93

Tarpkin v. State, 236 Ga. 67, 222 S.E.2d 364 (1976)—§ 14.4(e) n.135

Tarr v. State, 486 A.2d 672 (Del.1984)—§ 25.1(d) n.63

Tart, Commonwealth v., 408 Mass. 249, 557 N.E.2d 1123 (1990)—§ 6.6(e) n.63

Tarumoto, State v., 62 Haw. 298, 614 P.2d 397 (1980)—§§ 11.3(c) n.54 to 56, 60

Tarver, Ex parte, 725 S.W.2d 195 (Tex.Cr.App.1986)—§ 17.4(a) n.66

Tasco, Commonwealth v., 227 Pa.Super. 144, 323 A.2d 831 (1974)—§ 9.1(b) n.64

Tasios v. Reno, 204 F.3d 544 (4th Cir.2000)—§ 21.2(d) n.234

Tassin v. Cain, 482 F.Supp.2d 764 (E.D.La.2007)—§ 24.3(d) n.110

Tata v. State, 486 N.E.2d 1025 (Ind.1986)—§ 9.3(a) n.1

Tate, People v., 45 Ill.2d 540, 259 N.E.2d 791 (1970)—§ 6.6(c) n.38

Tate v. Short, 401 U.S. 395, 91 S.Ct. 668, 28 L.Ed.2d 130 (1971)—§§ 12.2(b) n.23; 26.1(f) n.141

Tate v. State, 912 So.2d 919 (Miss.2005)—§ 5.3(a) n.4

Tate v. Wood, 963 F.2d 20 (2d Cir.1992)—§ 21.6(a) n.77

Tateo, United States v., 377 U.S. 463, 84 S.Ct. 1587, 12 L.Ed.2d 448 (1964)—§ 25.4(a) n.3

Tattered Cover, Inc. v. City of Thornton, 44 P.3d 1044 (Colo.2002)—§ 3.4(a) n.20

Tatum, State v., 642 So.2d 523 (Ala.App.1994)—§ 27.3(c) n.36

Tatum, State v., 219 Conn. 721, 595 A.2d 322 (1991)—§ 7.4(g) n.116

Tatum, State v., 291 N.C. 73, 229 S.E.2d 562 (1976)—§§ 11.2(e) n.141, 220

Tatum, United States v., 943 F.2d 370 (4th Cir.1991)—§§ 11.9(a) n.16; 11.9(b) n.80; 11.9(d) n.194, 213

Taubman, State ex rel. v. Huston, 19 S.D. 644, 104 N.W. 451 (1905)—§ 16.1(d) n.157

Tauil-Hernandez, United States v., 88 F.3d 576 (8th Cir.1996)—§ 26.5(a) n.8

Taus v. Senkowski, 293 F.Supp.2d 238 (E.D.N.Y.2003)—§ 24.3(b) n.54

Tavarez, State v., 572 A.2d 276 (R.I.1990)—§ 10.4(c) n.20

Taveras v. Smith, 463 F.3d 141 (2d Cir.2006)—§ 27.5(c) n.86

Taveras v. Smith, 388 F.Supp.2d 256 (S.D.N.Y.2005)—§§ 11.6(b) n.80; 27.1(b) n.22

Tavolacci, United States v., 895 F.2d 1423 (D.C.Cir.1990)—§§ 3.5(e) n.190; 3.8(b) n.36, 41; 3.8(c) n.89

Taylor, In re, 171 F.3d 185 (4th Cir.1999)—§ 28.5(c) n.74

Taylor, In re, 567 F.2d 1183 (2d Cir.1977)—§§ 8.14(d) n.52, 59

Taylor, In re Commitment of, 272 Wis.2d 642, 679 N.W.2d 893 (Wis.App.2004)—§ 28.4(d) n.70

Taylor v. Alabama, 457 U.S. 687, 102 S.Ct. 2664, 73 L.Ed.2d 314 (1982)—§§ 9.4(a) n.6, 13, 24, 26

Taylor v. Bowersox, 329 F.3d 963 (8th Cir.2003)—§ 21.2(d) n.161

Taylor v. Cisneros, 913 F.Supp. 314 (1995)—§ 2.6(b) n.43

Taylor v. City of Pine Bluff, 226 Ark. 309, 289 S.W.2d 679 (1956)—§ 13.4(c) n.122

Taylor v. Commonwealth, 182 S.W.3d 521 (Ky.2006)—§§ 6.6(e) n.91; 6.7(c) n.134; 6.7(d) n.144

Taylor v. Commonwealth, 175 S.W.3d 68 (Ky.2005)—§ 24.9(f) n.96

Taylor, Commonwealth v., 565 Pa. 140, 771 A.2d 1261 (2001)—§§ 3.4(j) n.184, 189; 3.8(e) n.195

Taylor, Commonwealth v., 428 Mass. 623, 704 N.E.2d 170 (1999)— § 13.2(c) n.56

Taylor, Commonwealth v., 426 Mass. 189, 687 N.E.2d 631 (1997)— § 3.3(f) n.210

Taylor, Commonwealth v., 32 Mass.App. 570, 591 N.E.2d 1108 (1992)—§§ 14.1(d) n.63, 66

Taylor, Commonwealth v., 259 Pa.Super. 484, 393 A.2d 929 (1978)—§ 27.6(b) n.23

Taylor v. Commonwealth, 274 Ky. 51, 118 S.W.2d 140 (1938)—§§ 8.10(c) n.51, 53, 56

Taylor v. Cruikshank, 214 Ariz. 40, 148 P.3d 84 (App.2006)—§ 18.5(a) n.23

Taylor v. Hayes, 418 U.S. 488, 94 S.Ct. 2697, 41 L.Ed.2d 897 (1974)— §§ 15.1(b) n.85; 22.4(a) n.8

Taylor v. Hopper, 596 F.2d 1284 (5th Cir.1979)—§ 11.5(d) n.72

Taylor v. Illinois, 484 U.S. 400, 108 S.Ct. 646, 98 L.Ed.2d 798 (1988)— §§ 1.5(b) n.86; 2.6(c) n.84; 2.9(f) n.117; 10.5(f) n.63; 11.6(a) n.17 to 21, 29, 36, 37, 39; 11.6(c) n.96, 101; 11.10(b) n.43; 20.4(a) n.2; 20.6(c) n.69; 24.2(b) n.27; 24.3(f) n.152; 24.4(a) n.7; 24.4(d) n.60

Taylor v. Kentucky, 436 U.S. 478, 98 S.Ct. 1930, 56 L.Ed.2d 468 (1978)—§§ 1.5(d) n.186, 191; 24.8(c) n.40

Taylor v. Kincheloe, 920 F.2d 599 (9th Cir.1990)—§§ 13.7(c) n.59; 21.5(e) n.119, 122

Taylor v. Louisiana, 419 U.S. 522, 95 S.Ct. 692, 42 L.Ed.2d 690 (1975)— §§ 1.7(i) n.165; 2.6(b) n.46; 2.8(b) n.53; 15.4(d) n.109; 22.1(g) n.107; 22.2(d) n.54

Taylor, People v., 41 P.3d 681 (Colo.2002)—§§ 3.8(b) n.18; 6.6(e) n.95

Taylor, People v., 191 Misc.2d 672, 743 N.Y.S.2d 253 (N.Y.Sup.2002)— § 22.2(b) n.16

Taylor, People v., 244 Ill.App.3d 460, 183 Ill.Dec. 891, 612 N.E.2d 543 (1993)—§ 24.1(a) n.4

Taylor, People v., 159 Mich.App. 468, 406 N.W.2d 859 (1987)— §§ 20.2(c) n.48; 20.3(m) n.237; 20.6(b) n.17, 21

Taylor, People v., 39 N.Y.2d 649, 385 N.Y.S.2d 270, 350 N.E.2d 600 (1976)—§ 22.2(d) n.73

Taylor, People v., 12 Cal.3d 686, 117 Cal.Rptr. 70, 527 P.2d 622 (1974)— § 17.4(a) n.65

Taylor, People v., 8 Cal.3d 174, 104 Cal.Rptr. 350, 501 P.2d 918 (1972)—§ 9.6(a) n.12

Taylor, People v., 52 Ill.2d 293, 287 N.E.2d 673 (1972)—§ 7.4(f) n.102

Taylor, People v., 50 Ill.2d 136, 277 N.E.2d 878 (1971)—§ 10.6(c) n.34

Taylor, People v., 247 Cal.App.2d 11, 55 Cal.Rptr. 521 (1966)—§ 6.4(c) n.42

Taylor v. Rhode Island, 101 F.3d 780 (1st Cir.1996)—§§ 26.1(f) n.150; 26.9(c) n.83

Taylor v. Riddle, 563 F.2d 133 (4th Cir.1977)—§ 6.9(g) n.154

Taylor v. Sherrill, 169 Ariz. 335, 819 P.2d 921 (1991)—§ 17.4(b) n.96

Taylor v. State, 156 P.3d 739 (Utah 2007)—§ 26.4(f) n.93

Taylor, State v., 863 N.E.2d 917 (Ind.App.2007)—§ 24.6(d) n.44

Taylor v. State, 840 N.E.2d 324 (Indiana 2006)—§ 24.10(c) n.40

Taylor v. State, 388 Md. 385, 879 A.2d 1074 (2005)—§§ 6.2(c) n.112; 21.6(c) n.114

Taylor v. State, 849 A.2d 405 (Del.2004)—§ 24.4(d) n.47

Taylor, State v., 875 So.2d 58 (La.2004)—§ 22.3(a) n.5

Taylor v. State, 74 P.3d 1236 (Wyo.2003)—§§ 19.3(a) n.13; 21.6(a) n.37

Taylor v. State, 822 A.2d 1052 (Del.2003)—§ 3.5(c) n.109

Taylor v. State, 855 So.2d 1 (Fla.2003)—§ 3.8(b) n.47

Taylor, State v., 63 Conn.App. 386, 776 A.2d 1154 (2001)—§ 18.4(c) n.68

Taylor v. State, 274 Ga. 269, 553 S.E.2d 598 (2001)—§§ 6.2(c) n.107; 6.9(g) n.166; 9.5(b) n.41, 42

Taylor, State v., 354 N.C. 28, 550 S.E.2d 141 (2001)—§§ 6.4(e) n.69, 77; 11.2(b) n.46

Taylor v. State, 789 So.2d 787 (Miss.2001)—§§ 6.2(c) n.152; 6.8(b) n.50; 6.8(c) n.68

Taylor v. State, 7 P.3d 15 (Wyo.2000)— § 3.4(j) n.211

Taylor v. State, 10 S.W.3d 673 (Tex.Cr.App.2000)—§ 2.11(a) n.14

Taylor v. State, 998 P.2d 1225 (Okla.Crim.App.2000)—§ 11.10(c) n.69

Taylor, State v., 594 N.W.2d 158 (Minn.1999)—§ 7.4(f) n.104

Taylor v. State, 733 So.2d 251 (Miss.1999)—§ 22.3(d) n.207

Taylor, State v., 944 S.W.2d 925 (Mo.1997)—§ 24.7(e) n.60

Taylor, State v., 239 Conn. 481, 687 A.2d 489 (1996)—§ 7.4(e) n.89

Taylor v. State, 672 So.2d 1246 (Miss. 1996)—§ 18.1(c) n.29

Taylor, State v., 929 S.W.2d 209 (Mo.1996)—§§ 21.2(d) n.161; 21.4(b) n.42; 21.4(f) n.174

Taylor v. State, 656 So.2d 104 (Miss.1995)—§ 22.3(c) n.127

Taylor, State v., 621 A.2d 1252 (R.I.1993)—§ 10.3(b) n.10

Taylor, State v., 490 N.W.2d 536 (Iowa 1992)—§§ 16.1(a) n.27, 29

Taylor, State v., 51 Ohio App.3d 173, 555 N.E.2d 649 (1988)—§ 18.4(c) n.70

Taylor v. State, 172 Ga.App. 827, 324 S.E.2d 788 (1984)—§ 20.3(g) n.126

Taylor, State v., 80 N.J. 353, 403 A.2d 889 (1979)—§ 21.4(d) n.107

Taylor v. State, 92 Nev. 158, 547 P.2d 674 (1976)—§ 9.6(c) n.66

Taylor, State v., 112 Ariz. 68, 537 P.2d 938 (1975)—§ 20.3(h) n.145

Taylor, State v., 538 P.2d 310 (Utah 1975)—§ 18.4(d) n.87

Taylor, State v., 60 Wis.2d 506, 210 N.W.2d 873 (1973)—§ 10.3(b) n.36

Taylor v. State, 229 Ga. 536, 192 S.E.2d 249 (Ga.1972)—§ 11.2(e) n.141

Taylor, State v., 456 S.W.2d 9 (Mo.1970)—§ 7.3(d) n.65

Taylor, United States v., 413 F.3d 1146 (10th Cir.2005)—§ 21.2(a) n.7

Taylor, United States v., 414 F.3d 528 (4th Cir.2005)—§ 26.4(e) n.76

Taylor, United States v., 353 F.3d 868 (10th Cir.2003)—§ 18.3(b) n.20

Taylor, United States v., 240 F.3d 425 (4th Cir.2001)—§ 18.3(b) n.5

Taylor, United States v., 248 F.3d 506 (6th Cir.2001)—§ 3.6(a) n.32

Taylor, United States v., 253 F.3d 1115 (8th Cir.2001)—§ 17.2(d) n.105

Taylor, United States v., 258 F.3d 815 (8th Cir.2001)—§ 21.2(d) n.150

Taylor, United States v., 173 F.3d 538 (6th Cir.1999)—§§ 18.4(c) n.37, 73

Taylor, United States v., 186 F.3d 1332 (11th Cir.1999)—§ 17.2(b) n.71

Taylor, United States v., 139 F.3d 924 (D.C.Cir.1998)—§§ 11.9(d) n.170, 218, 223

Taylor, United States v., 77 F.3d 368 (11th Cir.1996)—§§ 21.2(d) n.172; 21.2(e) n.297

Taylor, United States v., 13 F.3d 986 (6th Cir.1994)—§ 24.3(c) n.88

Taylor v. United States, 985 F.2d 844 (6th Cir.1993)—§ 11.9(d) n.223

Taylor v. United States, 603 A.2d 451 (D.C.App.1992)—§ 17.2(a) n.23

Taylor, United States v., 956 F.2d 572 (6th Cir.1992)—§ 3.8(c) n.76

Taylor, United States v., 975 F.2d 402 (7th Cir.1992)—§ 10.5(c) n.31

Taylor, United States v., 933 F.2d 307 (5th Cir.1991)—§§ 11.3(a) n.16; 11.5(c) n.65; 11.5(f) n.104, 105

Taylor, United States v., 934 F.2d 218 (9th Cir.1991)—§ 3.9(f) n.120

Taylor, United States v., 917 F.2d 1402 (6th Cir.1990)—§ 3.8(c) n.92

Taylor, United States v., 707 F.Supp. 696 (S.D.N.Y.1989)—§§ 20.3(b) n.58; 20.3(h) n.151

Taylor, United States v., 487 U.S. 326, 108 S.Ct. 2413, 101 L.Ed.2d 297 (1988)—§§ 18.3(b) n.58, 59

Taylor, United States v., 821 F.2d 1377 (9th Cir.1987)—§ 18.3(b) n.32

Taylor, United States v., 828 F.2d 630 (10th Cir.1987)—§§ 16.1(g) n.238, 263

Taylor, United States v., 798 F.2d 1337 (10th Cir.1986)—§§ 15.6(f) n.184 to 187, 193

Taylor, United States v., 799 F.2d 126 (4th Cir.1986)—§ 6.7(b) n.50

Taylor, United States v., 749 F.2d 1511 (11th Cir.1985)—§§ 13.7(c) n.52, 53

Taylor, United States v., 657 F.2d 92 (6th Cir.1981)—§ 11.9(a) n.13

Taylor, United States v., 507 F.2d 166 (5th Cir.1975)—§ 25.3(b) n.18

Taylor v. United States, 414 U.S. 17, 94 S.Ct. 194, 38 L.Ed.2d 174 (1973)—§§ 2.7(a) n.38; 11.4(b) n.29; 24.2(d) n.37

Taylor v. United States, 259 A.2d 835 (D.C.1969)—§ 3.5(a) n.31

Taylor v. United States, 286 U.S. 1, 52 S.Ct. 466, 76 L.Ed. 951 (1932)—§§ 3.2(a) n.6; 3.2(b) n.40; 3.2(c) n.116

Taylor v. Warden, 905 P.2d 277 (Utah 1995)—§ 22.1(h) n.137

Taylor v. Whitley, 933 F.2d 325 (5th Cir.1991)—§ 21.6(a) n.64

Taylor B., Matter of, 201 W.Va. 60, 491 S.E.2d 607 (1997)—§ 21.2(e) n.328

Tchibassa, United States v., 452 F.3d 918 (D.C.Cir.2006)—§ 18.2(c) n.49

Teague v. Lane, 489 U.S. 288, 109 S.Ct. 1060, 103 L.Ed.2d 334 (1989)—§§ 2.9(b) n.11; 2.9(f) n.125, 127; 2.9(h) n.215; 2.11(a) n.6, 12;

2.11(d) n.51; 2.11(e) n.54; 26.4(d) n.49; 28.2(d) n.74, 77, 82; 28.4(d) n.48; 28.6(a) n.2; 28.8(a) n.9; 28.9(b) n.34

Teague, State v., 680 S.W.2d 785 (Tenn.1984)—§ 21.4(a) n.22

Teague, United States v., 953 F.2d 1525 (11th Cir.1992)—§§ 11.6(a) n.51; 11.6(c) n.91, 92, 105; 11.6(d) n.123; 24.5(d) n.58

Teale, People v., 70 Cal.2d 497, 75 Cal.Rptr. 172, 450 P.2d 564 (1969)—§ 3.7(f) n.134

Tedeschi, United States v., 774 F.2d 511 (1st Cir.1985)—§ 18.3(b) n.52

Tedesco, United States v., 726 F.2d 1216 (7th Cir.1984)—§§ 18.3(b) n.26, 32

Tedford, United States v., 875 F.2d 446 (5th Cir.1989)—§ 3.10(b) n.67

Teemer, United States v., 394 F.3d 59 (1st Cir.2005)—§ 6.6(c) n.33

Teeter, United States v., 257 F.3d 14 (1st Cir.2001)—§§ 21.2(b) n.76, 86; 27.5(c) n.56, 63

Tehan v. United States ex rel. Shott, 382 U.S. 406, 86 S.Ct. 459, 15 L.Ed.2d 453 (1966)—§§ 1.5(d) n.182; 1.5(e) n.211; 2.10(d) n.124, 131

Teitloff, United States v., 55 F.3d 391 (8th Cir.1995)—§§ 3.1(c) n.63, 65

Tejada, United States v., 956 F.2d 1256 (2d Cir.1992)—§§ 3.1(f) n.153; 26.5(a) n.8

Tejeda, Commonwealth v., 2003 Pa.Super. 378, 834 A.2d 619 (2003)—§ 25.2(e) n.39

Tejeda, State v., 677 N.W.2d 744 (Iowa 2004)—§§ 11.4(b) n.20, 35

Telemaque, United States v., 244 F.3d 1247 (11th Cir.2001)—§§ 21.3(d) n.227; 21.4(c) n.66

Telfaire, United States v., 469 F.2d 552 (D.C.Cir.1972)—§ 7.5(a) n.3

Telink v. United States, 24 F.3d 42 (9th Cir.1994)—§ 28.9(a) n.21

Tellez, United States v., 882 F.2d 141 (5th Cir.1989)—§ 21.1(e) n.86

Tello, United States v., 707 F.2d 85 (4th Cir.1983)—§ 24.6(e) n.51

Templeman, United States v., 965 F.2d 617 (8th Cir.1992)—§§ 9.3(a) n.1; 9.3(d) n.36

Templeman, United States v., 938 F.2d 122 (8th Cir.1991)—§ 3.6(e) n.111

Templin, Commonwealth v., 568 Pa. 306, 795 A.2d 959 (2002)—§§ 6.2(c) n.112, 160

Tempo Trucking and Transfer Corp. v. Dickson, 405 F.Supp. 506 (E.D.N.Y.1975)—§ 21.4(a) n.22

Tennard v. Dretke, _____ U.S. _____, 124 S.Ct. 2562, 159 L.Ed.2d 384 (2004)—§ 28.10 n.4

Tennessee v. Garner, 471 U.S. 1, 105 S.Ct. 1694, 85 L.Ed.2d 1 (1985)—§§ 1.5(a) n.51; 1.7(j) n.214; 1.11(a) n.3; 2.9(d) n.79; 3.1(d) n.119; 3.5(a) n.69

Tennessee v. Street, 471 U.S. 409, 105 S.Ct. 2078, 85 L.Ed.2d 425 (1985)—§ 17.2(b) n.65

Tennessee Department of Human Services v. Vaughn, 595 S.W.2d 62 (Tenn.1980)—§ 1.7(f) n.87

Tennin, State v., 674 N.W.2d 403 (2004)—§ 11.2(h) n.319

Tennors, State v., 923 So.2d 823 (La.App.2006)—§ 22.3(e) n.268

Tenriero, State v., 183 N.J.Super. 519, 444 A.2d 623 (1981)—§ 15.1(d) n.234

Teresinski, People v., 26 Cal.3d 457, 162 Cal.Rptr. 44, 605 P.2d 874 (1980)—§ 3.8(d) n.125

Terkeltoub, In re, 256 F.Supp. 683 (S.D.N.Y.1966)—§ 8.6(b) n.47

Terraciano, United States ex rel. v. Montanye, 493 F.2d 682 (2d Cir.1974)—§ 3.9(c) n.52

Terranova, In re, 495 F.Supp. 837 (E.D.Wis.1980)—§§ 15.2(b) n.50; 15.7(f) n.145

Terrell, People v., 185 Ill.2d 467, 236 Ill.Dec. 723, 708 N.E.2d 309 (1998)—§ 22.3(a) n.22

Terrell v. State, 276 Ga. 34, 572 S.E.2d 595 (2002)—§§ 19.3(a) n.40, 42, 44

Terrell v. State, 271 Ga. 783, 523 S.E.2d 294 (1999)—§ 22.3(c) n.125

Terrell, State v., 283 N.W.2d 529 (Minn.1979)—§ 10.5(e) n.48

Terrell, United States v., 983 F.2d 653 (5th Cir.1993)—§ 12.1(a) n.20

Terrigno, United States v., 838 F.2d 371 (9th Cir.1988)—§ 26.9(b) n.58

Terrill, State v., 242 Wis.2d 415, 625 N.W.2d 353 (Wis.App.2001)—§ 25.1(d) n.55

Territory v. Hale, 13 N.M. 181, 81 P. 583 (1905)—§ 16.1(d) n.142

Terry, Commonwealth v., 513 Pa. 381, 521 A.2d 398 (1987)—§§ 1.7(i) n.202, 207

Terry v. Duckworth, 715 F.2d 1217 (7th Cir.1983)—§§ 18.2(c) n.36; 18.2(d) n.67

Terry v. Le Fevre, 862 F.2d 409 (2d Cir.1988)—§ 6.9(g) n.162

Terry v. Ohio, 392 U.S. 1, 88 S.Ct. 1868, 20 L.Ed.2d 889 (1968)—§§ 1.6(h) n.453; 1.9(b) n.21; 1.10(c) n.56; 2.9(g) n.198; 3.1(b) n.20; 3.2(a) n.21; 3.3(b) n.33; 3.3(f) n.208, 215; 3.4(i) n.173; 3.5(a) n.3; 3.5(b) n.84 to 86, 89, 94; 3.6(d) n.93; 3.8(a) n.2; 3.9(a) n.2; 3.9(f) n.114; 3.9(h) n.149; 4.8(c) n.26; 10.3(b) n.15; 12.5(b) n.31

Terry, People v., 312 Ill.App.3d 984, 245 Ill.Dec. 587, 728 N.E.2d 669 (2000)—§ 24.7(e) n.43

Terry v. Potter, 111 F.3d 454 (6th Cir.1997)—§ 25.4(d) n.44

Terry v. Rees, 985 F.2d 283 (6th Cir.1993)—§§ 11.2(e) n.183, 190

Terry v. State, 602 N.E.2d 535 (Ind.App.1992)—§ 25.4(c) n.32

Terry, State v., 5 Ohio App.2d 122, 214 N.E.2d 114 (1966)—§ 3.8(a) n.10

Terry, United States v., 131 F.3d 138 (4th Cir.1997)—§ 27.3(c) n.23

Terry, United States v., 60 F.3d 1541 (11th Cir.1995)—§ 22.2(d) n.86

Terry, United States v., 17 F.3d 575 (2d Cir.1994)—§ 22.5(a) n.10

Terry, United States v., 911 F.2d 272 (9th Cir.1990)—§§ 17.3(d) n.44, 52

Terry, United States v., 916 F.2d 157 (4th Cir.1990)—§ 26.5(b) n.26

Terzado-Madruga, United States v., 897 F.2d 1099 (11th Cir.1990)—§ 6.4(e) n.95

Tesfaye v. State, 275 Ga. 439, 569 S.E.2d 849 (2002)—§ 17.3(b) n.13

Teslim, United States v., 869 F.2d 316 (7th Cir.1989)—§§ 3.8(c) n.96; 24.7(e) n.62

Test, United States v., 550 F.2d 577 (10th Cir.1976)—§ 15.4(d) n.98

Test v. United States, 420 U.S. 28, 95 S.Ct. 749, 42 L.Ed.2d 786 (1975)—§ 22.3(b) n.54

Testa, United States v., 33 F.3d 747 (7th Cir.1994)—§ 21.2(h) n.426

Tevlin, Commonwealth v., 433 Mass. 305, 741 N.E.2d 827 (2001)—§ 6.4(g) n.153

Texas v. Brown, 460 U.S. 730, 103 S.Ct. 1535, 75 L.Ed.2d 502 (1983)—§§ 3.2(b) n.46; 3.4(k) n.221; 3.5(e) n.206; 3.6(g) n.158

Texas v. Cobb, 532 U.S. 162, 121 S.Ct. 1335, 149 L.Ed.2d 321 (2001)—§§ 6.4(e) n.98; 6.4(f) n.135

Texas v. McCullough, 475 U.S. 134, 106 S.Ct. 976, 89 L.Ed.2d 104 (1986)—§§ 2.9(h) n.220, 241; 13.7(c) n.49, 51; 26.8(b) n.9

Texas, United States v., 339 U.S. 707, 70 S.Ct. 918, 94 L.Ed. 1221 (1950)—§ 1.2(b) n.8

Texas v. United States Steel Corp., 546 F.2d 626 (5th Cir.1977)—§§ 8.5(c) n.94; 8.5(h) n.260

Texas v. White, 423 U.S. 67, 96 S.Ct. 304, 46 L.Ed.2d 209 (1975)—§§ 2.12(a) n.22; 3.7(b) n.30; 3.7(f) n.136

Texas Co., Application of, 27 F.Supp. 847 (E.D.Ill.1939)—§ 8.8(b) n.15

Texas Industries v. Radcliff Materials, Inc., 451 U.S. 630, 101 S.Ct. 2061, 68 L.Ed.2d 500 (1981)—§ 1.7(h) n.136

Thacker v. Commonwealth, 310 Ky. 702, 221 S.W.2d 682 (1949)—§ 3.1(h) n.190

Thaggard, State v., 527 N.W.2d 804 (Minn.1995)—§ 6.2(c) n.113

Thai, United States v., 29 F.3d 785 (2d Cir.1994)—§ 22.3(b) n.68

Thanos v. State, 282 Md. 709, 387 A.2d 286 (1978)—§§ 19.5(c) n.55; 19.6(b) n.22

Tharp, Commonwealth v., 562 Pa. 231, 754 A.2d 1251 (2000)—§ 22.1(h) n.149

Tharp v. State, 362 Md. 77, 763 A.2d 151 (2000)—§ 20.2(e) n.82

Thatcher, People v., 638 P.2d 760 (Colo.1981)—§ 20.2(c) n.50

Thatsaphone v. Weber, 137 F.3d 1041 (8th Cir.1998)—§§ 6.2(c) n.182; 6.6(c) n.42

Thayer v. People, 2 Doug. 417 (Mich.1847)—§ 15.4(b) n.35

Thayer, State v., 528 So.2d 67 (Fla. 4th DCA 1988)—§ 22.3(b) n.60

Theis v. State, 117 Nev. 744, 30 P.3d 1140 (2001)—§ 18.4(c) n.39

Theodor v. Superior Court, 8 Cal.3d 77, 104 Cal.Rptr. 226, 501 P.2d 234 (1972)—§§ 3.4(d) n.53, 54, 61

Theodosopoulos, United States v., 48 F.3d 1438 (7th Cir.1995)—§ 24.11(d) n.35

Theofel v. Farey-Jones, 359 F.3d 1066 (9th Cir.2004)—§ 4.8(d) n.33

Theron, United States v., 782 F.2d 1510 (10th Cir.1986)—§ 18.3(b) n.18

Therriault, State v., 485 A.2d 986 (Me.1984)—§ 21.2(f) n.383

Therrien, Commonwealth v., 359 Mass. 500, 269 N.E.2d 687 (1971)—§ 21.5(e) n.121

Thetford, State v., 109 Wash.2d 392, 745 P.2d 496 (1987)—§ 3.4(d) n.56

Thevis, United States v., 665 F.2d 616 (5th Cir.1982)—§§ 7.3(c) n.39; 24.3(i) n.192

Thevis, United States v., 84 F.R.D. 47 (N.D.Ga.1979)—§ 20.3(b) n.37

Thevis, United States v., 474 F.Supp. 117 (N.D.Ga.1979)—§§ 19.4(b) n.20, 26, 35

Thibodeau, State v., 496 A.2d 635 (Me.1985)—§ 6.6(f) n.104

Thibodeau, State v., 317 A.2d 172 (Me.1974)—§ 3.10(e) n.163

Thickstun, United States v., 110 F.3d 1394 (9th Cir.1997)—§ 5.2(a) n.19

Thiel v. Southern Pacific Co., 328 U.S. 217, 66 S.Ct. 984, 90 L.Ed. 1181 (1946)—§ 22.2(d) n.47

Thiele, United States v., 314 F.3d 399 (9th Cir.2002)—§ 28.9(b) n.31

Thielsen, State v., 675 N.W.2d 429 (S.D.2004)—§ 21.5(a) n.43

Thiem v. Commonwealth, 269 S.W.2d 195 (Ky.1954)—§ 16.4(a) n.1

Thierfelder, State v., 174 Wis.2d 213, 495 N.W.2d 669 (1993)—§ 17.4(b) n.96

Thierman, United States v., 678 F.2d 1331 (9th Cir.1982)—§ 6.9(g) n.149

Thies v. State, 178 Wis. 98, 189 N.W. 539 (1922)—§ 14.1(a) n.4

Thigpen v. Cory, 804 F.2d 893 (6th Cir.1986)—§§ 7.4(b) n.31; 7.4(c) n.54, 57

Thigpen v. Roberts, 468 U.S. 27, 104 S.Ct. 2916, 82 L.Ed.2d 23 (1984)— §§ 13.7(c) n.38, 50

Thigpen v. State, 49 Ala.App. 233, 270 So.2d 666 (1972)—§§ 20.2(a) n.2, 6

Thigpen v. State, 462 P.2d 270 (Okl.Cr.1969)—§ 10.2(a) n.10

Thill, State v., 691 N.W.2d 230 (N.D.2005)—§ 24.3(e) n.126

Thin Elk, State v., 2005 SD 106, 705 N.W.2d 613 (S.D.2005)—§ 21.4(f) n.176

Third Statewide Grand Jury, In re, 360 So.2d 4 (Fla.App.1978)—§ 8.11(a) n.8

Thiret, People v., 685 P.2d 193 (Colo.1984)—§§ 3.10(f) n.199, 207

Thoma, United States v., 713 F.2d 604 (10th Cir.1983)—§ 7.5(a) n.6

Thomas, Ex parte, 601 So.2d 56 (Ala.1992)—§ 22.3(d) n.246

Thomas, In re, 434 A.2d 503 (Me.1981)—§ 8.4(b) n.90

Thomas v. Arn, 474 U.S. 140, 106 S.Ct. 466, 88 L.Ed.2d 435 (1985)— §§ 1.7(i) n.175, 193

Thomas v. Borg, 159 F.3d 1147 (9th Cir.1998)—§ 22.2(d) n.76

Thomas v. Commonwealth, 244 Va. 1, 419 S.E.2d 606 (1992)—§ 23.2(a) n.42

Thomas, Commonwealth v., 353 Mass. 429, 233 N.E.2d 25 (1967)— § 14.2(c) n.40

Thomas v. Foltz, 818 F.2d 476 (6th Cir.1987)—§§ 11.9(d) n.193, 224; 21.3(b) n.139

Thomas v. Lockhart, 738 F.2d 304 (8th Cir.1984)—§ 21.3(b) n.53

Thomas, People v., 438 Mich. 448, 475 N.W.2d 288 (1991)—§§ 14.3(d) n.96, 98

Thomas, People v., 131 Ill.2d 104, 137 Ill.Dec. 1, 545 N.E.2d 654 (1989)— § 11.9(d) n.202

Thomas, People v., 51 N.Y.2d 466, 434 N.Y.S.2d 941, 415 N.E.2d 931 (1980)—§§ 24.4(c) n.20, 27

Thomas, People v., 12 Cal.App.3d 1102, 91 Cal.Rptr. 867 (1970)—§ 3.10(b) n.73

Thomas, People v., 41 Ill.2d 122, 242 N.E.2d 177 (1968)—§ 21.4(d) n.123

Thomas, State v., 213 Ariz. 499, 144 P.3d 513 (2006)—§ 22.4(d) n.34

Thomas, State v., 280 Kan. 526, 124 P.3d 48 (2005)—§ 3.6(a) n.16

Thomas, State v., 267 Neb. 339, 673 N.W.2d 897 (2004)—§ 6.9(g) n.157

Thomas, State v., 274 Wis. 2d 513, 683 N.W.2d 497 (2004)—§ 1.2(b) n.5

Thomas v. State, 894 So.2d 126 (Fla.2004)—§ 6.9(b) n.24

Thomas, State v., 369 Md. 202, 798 A.2d 566 (2002)—§§ 22.3(a) n.4, 23

Thomas, State v., 794 A.2d 990 (R.I.2002)—§ 21.4(b) n.59

Thomas, State v., 262 Neb. 138, 629 N.W.2d 503 (2001)—§ 17.4(b) n.140

Thomas v. State, 274 Ga. 492, 555 S.E.2d 693 (2001)—§ 18.2(d) n.60

Thomas v. State, 346 S.C. 140, 551 S.E.2d 254 (2001)—§§ 11.9(c) n.134; 11.9(d) n.192; 21.3(b) n.133, 140

Thomas, State v., 232 Wis.2d 714, 605 N.W.2d 836 (2000)—§§ 21.4(f) n.177; 21.5(a) n.24

Thomas v. State, 784 S.2d 247 (Miss.App.2000)—§ 16.1(g) n.277

Thomas v. State, 114 Nev. 1127, 967 P.2d 1111 (1998)—§ 22.3(d) n.249

Thomas v. State, 268 Ga. 135, 485 S.E.2d 783 (1997)—§ 6.9(a) n.6

Thomas, State v., 285 Mont. 112, 946 P.2d 140 (1997)—§ 21.4(d) n.114

Thomas v. State, 113 Md.App. 1, 686 A.2d 676 (1996)—§ 25.2(e) n.38

Thomas, State v., 128 Wash.2d 553, 910 P.2d 475 (1996)—§ 24.5(d) n.58

Thomas, State v., 257 Kan. 228, 891 P.2d 417 (1995)—§ 24.11(d) n.16

Thomas, State v., 540 N.W.2d 658 (Iowa 1995)—§ 3.1(c) n.72

Thomas, State v., 637 So.2d 1272 (La.App.1994)—§ 20.3(k) n.213

Thomas v. State, 263 Ga. 85, 428 S.E.2d 564 (1993)—§ 3.9(i) n.184

Thomas v. State, 614 So.2d 468 (Fla. 1993)—§ 3.5(b) n.97

Thomas, State v., 187 W.Va. 686, 421 S.E.2d 227 (1992)—§ 3.3(b) n.68

Thomas v. State, 593 So.2d 219 (Fla.1992)—§ 21.2(d) n.165

Thomas v. State, 811 S.W.2d 201 (Tex.App.1991)—§ 7.4(e) n.90

Thomas, State v., 818 S.W.2d 350 (Tenn.Crim.App. 1991)—§ 3.4(j) n.193

Thomas v. State, 788 S.W.2d 887 (Tex.App.1990)—§ 7.4(e) n.90

Thomas, State v., 780 S.W.2d 379 (Tenn.Crim.App.1989)—§ 7.4(f) n.95

Thomas v. State, 784 P.2d 237 (Wyo.1989)—§ 7.5(a) n.8

Thomas v. State, 517 So.2d 1285 (Miss.1987)—§ 22.3(d) n.220

Thomas, State v., 148 Ariz. 225, 714 P.2d 395 (1986)—§ 6.2(c) n.105

Thomas v. State, 456 So.2d 454 (Fla.1984)—§ 6.2(c) n.173

Thomas, State v., 61 Ohio St.2d 254, 400 N.E.2d 897, 15 O.O.3d 262 (1980)—§ 17.4(b) n.98

Thomas, State v., 34 Or.App. 187, 578 P.2d 452 (1978)—§ 27.3(c) n.22

Thomas, State v., 529 S.W.2d 379 (Mo.1975)—§ 14.3(c) n.72

Thomas, State v., 114 N.J.Super. 360, 276 A.2d 391 (1971)—§ 21.2(d) n.229

Thomas, State v., 236 N.C. 454, 73 S.E.2d 283 (1952)—§§ 15.1(d) n.156, 249

Thomas v. State, 107 Ala. 61, 17 So. 941 (1895)—§ 15.1(d) n.219

Thomas v. Texas, 212 U.S. 278, 29 S.Ct. 393, 53 L.Ed. 512 (1909)—§ 22.2(c) n.27

Thomas, United States v., 410 F.3d 1235 (10th Cir.2005)—§§ 13.7(c) n.45, 52

Thomas, United States v., 417 F.3d 1053 (9th Cir.2005)—§§ 11.6(b) n.77; 11.6(d) n.117

Thomas, United States v., 367 F.3d 194 (4th Cir.2004)—§ 21.4(f) n.192

Thomas, United States v., 389 F.3d 424 (3d Cir.2004)—§ 21.4(c) n.81

Thomas, United States v., 303 F.3d 138 (2d Cir.2002)—§ 22.3(d) n.255

Thomas, United States v., 249 F.3d 725 (8th Cir.2001)—§ 3.7(e) n.128

Thomas, United States v., 263 F.3d 805 (8th Cir.2001)—§ 3.1(c) n.74

Thomas, United States v., 274 F.3d 655 (2d Cir.2001)—§§ 19.2(e) n.82; 19.3(a) n.91

Thomas v. United States, 766 A.2d 50 (D.C.App.2001)—§§ 21.3(b) n.71; 21.4(d) n.131

Thomas, United States v., 221 F.3d 430 (3d Cir.2000)—§ 28.9(b) n.53

Thomas, United States v., 116 F.3d 606 (2d Cir.1997)—§§ 22.1(g) n.109, 118; 24.9(f) n.75, 104; 24.10(a) n.4

Thomas, United States v., 77 F.3d 989 (7th Cir.1996)—§ 26.3(f) n.64

Thomas, United States v., 97 F.3d 1499 (D.C.Cir.1996)—§ 24.3(c) n.88

Thomas, United States v., 55 F.3d 144 (4th Cir.1995)—§§ 18.2(c) n.51; 18.4(a) n.9

Thomas, United States v., 11 F.3d 620 (6th Cir.1993)—§ 3.7(a) n.19

Thomas, United States v., 11 F.3d 1392 (7th Cir.1993)—§ 6.7(c) n.118

Thomas, United States v., 987 F.2d 697 (11th Cir.1993)—§ 24.6(b) n.27

Thomas, United States v., 992 F.2d 201 (8th Cir.1993)—§ 11.7(e) n.70

Thomas, United States v., 955 F.2d 207 (4th Cir.1992)—§ 9.3(e) n.59

Thomas, United States v., 961 F.2d 1110 (3d Cir.1992)—§§ 21.1(h) n.233; 21.2(d) n.216

Thomas, United States v., 934 F.2d 840 (7th Cir.1991)—§ 26.1(d) n.88

Thomas, United States v., 946 F.2d 73 (8th Cir.1991)—§ 24.9(d) n.48

Thomas, United States v., 893 F.2d 482 (2d Cir.1990)—§ 3.6(e) n.111

Thomas, United States v., 900 F.2d 37 (4th Cir.1990)—§ 24.10(b) n.26

Thomas, United States v., 884 F.2d 540 (10th Cir.1989)—§ 13.7(a) n.23

Thomas v. United States, 544 A.2d 1260 (D.C.1988)—§ 25.3(b) n.18

Thomas, United States v., 788 F.2d 1250 (7th Cir.1986)—§ 18.3(b) n.27

Thomas, United States v., 757 F.2d 1359 (2d Cir.1985)—§ 3.2(b) n.72

Thomas, United States v., 593 F.2d 615 (5th Cir.1979)—§ 8.5(e) n.173

Thomas, United States v., 536 F.2d 1253 (8th Cir.1976)—§ 7.3(d) n.69

Thomas v. United States, 391 F.Supp. 202 (W.D.Pa.1975)—§ 26.10(b) n.37

Thomas, United States v., 444 F.2d 919 (D.C.Cir.1971)—§§ 19.2(f) n.108; 19.3(a) n.70; 19.3(e) n.253; 19.5(d) n.69

Thomas, United States v., 449 F.2d 1177 (D.C.Cir.1971)—§ 24.9(d) n.43

Thomas, United States v., 453 F.2d 141 (9th Cir.1971)—§ 17.2(c) n.87

Thomas v. United States, 418 F.2d 567 (5th Cir.1969)—§ 17.3(b) n.14

Thomas, United States v., 396 F.2d 310 (2d Cir.1968)—§ 6.10(b) n.21

Thomas v. Varner, 428 F.3d 491 (3d Cir.2005)—§ 28.7(c) n.17

Thomas v. Wainwright, 767 F.2d 738 (11th Cir.1985)—§ 11.4(b) n.21

Thomas v. Whitworth, 136 F.3d 756 (11th Cir.1998)—§ 27.6(b) n.34

Thomas v. Wyrick, 535 F.2d 407 (8th Cir.1976)—§ 11.10(a) n.13

Thomas J., In re, 372 Md. 50, 811 A.2d 310 (2002)—§ 18.1(a) n.2

Thomas, State ex rel. v. Crouch, 603 S.W.2d 532 (1980)—§ 14.3(d) n.84

Thomas, State ex rel. v. Schneider, 212 Ariz. 292, 130 P.3d 991 (App.2005)—§ 8.8(d) n.89

Thompkins v. Cohen, 965 F.2d 330 (7th Cir.1992)—§ 11.9(d) n.223

Thompkins, People v., 121 Ill.2d 401, 117 Ill.Dec. 927, 521 N.E.2d 38 (1988)—§§ 6.4(e) n.70; 6.9(g) n.162

Thompkins, State v., 75 Ohio St. 3d 558, 664 N.E.2d 926 (1996)—§ 1.2(b) n.5

Thompkins, State v., 318 N.W.2d 194 (Iowa 1982)—§§ 20.6(b) n.19, 27

Thompson, In re, 141 Wash.2d 712, 10 P.3d 380 (2000)—§§ 21.4(f) n.198; 21.6(a) n.63

Thompson v. Battaglia, 458 F.3d 614 (7th Cir.2006)—§ 6.2(c) n.178

Thompson v. Blackburn, 776 F.2d 118 (5th Cir.1985)—§§ 21.6(a) n.79, 80

Thompson v. Calderon, 120 F.3d 1045 (9th Cir.1997)—§ 17.4(a) n.50

Thompson v. City of Lawrence, 58 F.3d 1511 (10th Cir.1995)—§ 3.6(a) n.30

Thompson v. City of Louisville, 362 U.S. 199, 80 S.Ct. 624, 4 L.Ed.2d 654 (1960)—§§ 1.8(d) n.61; 2.4(e) n.136

Thompson v. Commonwealth, 147 S.W.3d 22 (Ky.2004)—§§ 19.3(a) n.13; 21.4(b) n.62

Thompson v. Commonwealth, 50 S.W.3d 204 (Ky.2001)—§§ 21.4(b) n.59, 65

Thompson, Commonwealth v., 431 Mass. 108, 725 N.E.2d 556 (2000)—§§ 9.6(a) n.38, 48

Thompson, Commonwealth v., 427 Mass. 729, 696 N.E.2d 105 (1998)—§ 7.4(f) n.96

Thompson, Commonwealth v., 538 Pa. 297, 648 A.2d 315 (1994)—§ 14.1(d) n.59

Thompson, Commonwealth v., 335 Pa.Super. 332, 484 A.2d 159 (Pa.Super. 1984)—§ 5.2(b) n.28

Thompson v. Cox, 352 F.2d 488 (10th Cir.1965)—§ 6.4(c) n.38

Thompson v. Keohane, 516 U.S. 99, 116 S.Ct. 457, 133 L.Ed.2d 383 (1995)—§§ 27.5(e) n.177; 28.7(b) n.12

Thompson v. Louisiana, 469 U.S. 17, 105 S.Ct. 409, 83 L.Ed.2d 246 (1984)—§§ 2.1 n.53; 3.6(e) n.138

Thompson v. Macon-Bibb County Hosp. Auth., 246 Ga. 777, 273 S.E.2d 19 (1980)—§ 8.3(h) n.53

Thompson v. McManus, 512 F.2d 769 (8th Cir.1975)—§ 3.10(b) n.51

Thompson v. Mississippi, 914 F.2d 736 (5th Cir.1990)—§ 7.4(b) n.35

Thompson v. Missouri Bd. of Parole, 929 F.2d 396 (8th Cir.1991)—§ 28.3(a) n.34

Thompson v. Oklahoma, 487 U.S. 815, 108 S.Ct. 2687, 101 L.Ed.2d 702 (1988)—§§ 2.7(c) n.182, 189

Thompson, People v., 820 P.2d 1160 (Colo.App.1991)—§ 3.4(a) n.10

Thompson, People v., 50 Cal.3d 134, 266 Cal.Rptr. 309, 785 P.2d 857 (1990)—§ 6.2(c) n.132

Thompson, State v., 143 Idaho 155, 139 P.3d 757 (Idaho App.2006)—§ 27.6(d) n.127

Thompson v. State, 277 Ga. 102, 586 S.E.2d 231 (2003)—§§ 16.1(g) n.282, 283

Thompson, State v., 842 So.2d 330 (La.2003)—§ 3.3(f) n.202

Thompson v. State, 761 N.E.2d 467 (Ind.App.2002)—§ 24.8(e) n.61

Thompson, State v., 781 So.2d 1221 (La.2001)—§ 20.3(l) n.226

Thompson, State v., 343 Ark. 135, 34 S.W.3d 33 (2000)—§ 24.8(e) n.50

Thompson, State v., 349 N.C. 483, 508 S.E.2d 277 (1998)—§ 12.3(b) n.77

Thompson, State v., 708 A.2d 192 (Vt.1998)—§ 21.4(b) n.60

Thompson, State v., 190 Ariz. 555, 950 P.2d 1176 (App.1997)—§ 20.6(c) n.81

Thompson v. State, 322 Ark. 586, 910 S.W.2d 694 (Ark.1995)—§ 24.3(c) n.82

Thompson, State v., 504 N.W.2d 315 (N.D.1993)—§ 21.2(d) n.161

Thompson, State v., 158 Vt. 452, 613 A.2d 192 (1992)—§ 26.8(c) n.30

Thompson v. State, 595 So.2d 16 (Fla.1992)—§ 6.8(a) n.16

Thompson v. State, 565 So.2d 1311 (Fla.1990)—§§ 15.2(j) n.238, 241; 15.4(a) n.10

Thompson, State v., 231 Neb. 771, 438 N.W.2d 131 (1989)—§§ 9.4(d) n.86; 17.3(a) n.7

Thompson, State v., 237 Mont. 384, 773 P.2d 722 (1989)—§ 6.7(a) n.3

Thompson v. State, 548 So.2d 198 (Fla.1989)—§§ 6.2(c) n.169; 22.3(d) n.213, 250

Thompson, State v., 768 S.W.2d 239 (Tenn.1989)—§ 22.2(d) n.76

Thompson, State v., 114 Idaho 746, 760 P.2d 1162 (1988)—§ 2.12(d) n.196

Thompson, State v., 146 Wis.2d 554, 431 N.W.2d 716 (1988)—§ 24.8(e) n.65

Thompson v. State, 748 P.2d 526 (Okla.Cr.App.1988)—§ 24.8(f) n.92

Thompson v. State, 257 Ga. 386, 359 S.E.2d 664 (1987)—§ 11.7(e) n.78

Thompson, State v., 516 So.2d 349 (La.1987)—§§ 22.3(d) n.247, 250

Thompson v. State, 483 So.2d 690 (Miss.1986)—§ 7.3(c) n.39

Thompson v. State, 62 Md.App. 190, 488 A.2d 995 (1985)—§ 9.1(b) n.95

Thompson, State v., 197 Conn. 67, 495 A.2d 1054 (1985)—§ 26.4(g) n.127

Thompson, State v., 19 Ohio App.3d 261, 483 N.E.2d 1207 (1984)— § 18.4(c) n.47

Thompson, State v., 3 Kan.App.2d 426, 596 P.2d 174 (1979)—§ 19.6(b) n.14

Thompson v. State, 453 P.2d 314 (Okla.Crim.App.1969)—§ 3.5(a) n.30

Thompson v. Superior Court, 53 Cal.App.4th 480, 61 Cal.Rptr.2d 785 (1997)—§§ 20.3(b) n.32; 20.3(i) n.161; 20.5(f) n.72, 73

Thompson, United States v., 403 F.3d 1037 (8th Cir.2005)—§ 21.2(d) n.167

Thompson, United States v., 237 F.3d 1258 (10th Cir.2001)—§ 21.2(f) n.365

Thompson, United States v., 210 F.3d 855 (8th Cir.2000)—§ 4.6(e) n.97

Thompson, United States v., 130 F.3d 676 (5th Cir.1997)—§ 5.3(d) n.43

Thompson, United States v., 76 F.3d 442 (2d Cir.1996)—§§ 24.9(b) n.15; 27.6(b) n.18

Thompson, United States v., 35 F.3d 100 (2d Cir.1994)—§ 6.9(g) n.200

Thompson, United States v., 944 F.2d 1331 (7th Cir.1991)—§§ 8.8(f) n.150; 24.5(d) n.58

Thompson, United States v., 837 F.2d 673 (5th Cir.1988)—§ 3.5(c) n.124

Thompson, United States v., 827 F.2d 1254 (9th Cir.1987)—§§ 22.3(d) n.229, 231; 24.2(a) n.5

Thompson, United States v., 680 F.2d 1145 (7th Cir.1982)—§ 21.5(a) n.30

Thompson, United States v., 612 F.2d 233 (6th Cir.1979)—§ 13.7(c) n.59

Thompson, United States v., 576 F.2d 784 (9th Cir.1978)—§ 15.5(b) n.56

Thompson, United States v., 483 F.2d 527 (3d Cir.1973)—§ 22.4(b) n.20

Thompson, United States v., 452 F.2d 1333 (D.C.Cir.1971)—§§ 12.3(a) n.6; 12.4(d) n.87

Thompson v. United States, 382 F.2d 390 (9th Cir.1967)—§ 6.6(d) n.46

Thompson, United States v., 251 U.S. 407, 40 S.Ct. 289, 64 L.Ed. 333 (1920)—§§ 15.2(h) n.187, 188

Thompson v. United States, 155 U.S. 271, 15 S.Ct. 73, 39 L.Ed. 146 (1894)—§ 25.2(d) n.30

Thompson v. Utah, 170 U.S. 343, 18 S.Ct. 620, 42 L.Ed. 1061 (1898)— §§ 22.1(a) n.5; 22.1(d) n.65

Thomson, State v., 123 Wash.2d 877, 872 P.2d 1097 (1994)—§ 27.5(e) n.150

Thomson, United States v., 936 F.2d 1249 (11th Cir.1991)—§ 4.7(e) n.34

Thoreen, United States v., 653 F.2d 1332 (9th Cir.1981)—§ 7.4(g) n.125

Thoresen, United States v., 428 F.2d 654 (9th Cir.1970)—§ 15.2(j) n.241

Thorn, People v., 138 Cal.App. 714, 33 P.2d 5 (1934)—§ 19.4(b) n.9

Thornburg, People v., 173 Colo. 230, 477 P.2d 372 (1970)—§ 10.1(a) n.4

Thornburgh v. Abbott, 490 U.S. 401, 109 S.Ct. 1874, 104 L.Ed.2d 459 (1989)—§ 3.9(i) n.197

Thorne v. Dep't of Public Safety, 774 P.2d 1326 (Alaska 1989)— §§ 24.3(e) n.134, 136

Thorne v. State, 269 Ark. 556, 601 S.W.2d 886 (1980)—§§ 11.4(c) n.76, 77, 82, 86

Thorne, United States v., 153 F.3d 130 (4th Cir.1998)—§§ 21.4(d) n.114; 21.5(c) n.86

Thornes v. State, 310 S.C. 306, 426 S.E.2d 764 (1993)—§ 21.3(b) n.53

Thornton v. State, 145 S.W.3d 228 (Tex.Cr.App.2004)—§ 9.6(c) n.66

Thornton, State v., 10 S.W.3d 229 (Tenn.App.1999)—§ 22.4(c) n.29

Thornton, State v., 140 N.H. 532, 669 A.2d 791 (1995)—§§ 21.4(c) n.74, 88; 21.4(f) n.207

Thornton v. State, 264 Ga. 563, 449 S.E.2d 98 (1994)—§ 15.4(b) n.49

Thornton v. State, 317 Ark. 257, 878 S.W.2d 378 (1994)—§ 18.1(c) n.28

Thornton v. United States, 541 U.S. 615, 124 S.Ct. 2127, 158 L.Ed.2d 905 (2004)—§§ 3.7(a) n.14, 20

Thornton, United States v., 327 F.3d 268 (3d Cir.2003)—§§ 11.7(e) n.104, 106

Thornton, United States v., 1 F.3d 149 (3d Cir.1993)—§§ 17.2(a) n.12; 24.3(b) n.51

Thornton, United States v., 746 F.2d 39 (D.C.Cir.1984)—§ 3.1(c) n.65

Thornton v. United States, 357 A.2d 429 (D.C.App.1976)—§ 11.6(a) n.22

Thoro Products Co., Inc., People v., 70 P.3d 1188 (Colo.2003)—§ 18.5(a) n.11

Thorpe, State v., 274 N.C. 457, 164 S.E.2d 171 (1968)—§ 6.9(b) n.25

Thorpe, United States v., 471 F.3d 652 (6th Cir.2006)—§§ 13.4(b) n.65, 72

Thorson v. State, 721 So.2d 590 (Miss.1998)—§ 22.3(d) n.199

Thorson v. State, 653 So.2d 876 (Miss.1994)—§ 16.2(a) n.4

Thorup, State v., 659 So.2d 1116 (Fla.App.1995)—§ 27.4(d) n.42

Though in State v. Flynn, 92 Wis.2d 427, 285 N.W.2d 710 (1979)—§ 3.8(e) n.222

Three Grand Jury Subpoenas, Ducus Tecum Dated January 29, 1999, In re, 191 F.3d 173 (2d Cir.1999)—§§ 8.13(d) n.87, 114

Thrift, State v., 312 S.C. 282, 440 S.E.2d 341 (1994)—§§ 8.11(b) n.21; 15.6(d) n.126; 15.6(e) n.134; 15.7(b) n.18; 21.2(e) n.325; 21.5(d) n.104

Thriftimart, Inc., United States v., 429 F.2d 1006 (9th Cir.1970)—§ 3.9(b) n.32

Thrunk, State v., 157 N.J.Super. 265, 384 A.2d 906 (App.Div.1978)—§ 15.2(d) n.93

Thunder, United States v., 438 F.3d 866 (8th Cir.2006)—§ 24.1(b) n.24

Thurlow, State v., 485 A.2d 960 (Me.1984)—§ 24.6(b) n.22

Thurlow, United States v., 44 F.3d 46 (1st Cir.1995)—§ 26.9(b) n.24

Thurman, State v., 846 P.2d 1256 (Utah 1993)—§§ 27.5(e) n.142, 178

Thurman v. State, 861 S.W.2d 96 (Tex.App. - Hous.1993)—§ 8.7(d) n.74

Thurman, United States v., 687 F.2d 11 (3d Cir.1982)—§ 16.2(g) n.108

Thurmond, State v., 195 Ga.App. 369, 393 S.E.2d 518 (1990)—§ 27.3(d) n.59

Thurmond, United States ex rel. v. Mancusi, 275 F.Supp. 508 (E.D.N.Y.1967)—§§ 21.2(g) n.404, 409; 21.5(d) n.109

Thurow, People v., 203 Ill.2d 352, 272 Ill.Dec. 185, 786 N.E.2d 1019 (2003)—§§ 19.3(a) n.42, 43

Thurston, State v., 781 P.2d 1296 (Utah App.1989)—§ 21.2(d) n.165

Tibbetts, State v., 92 Ohio St.3d 146, 749 N.E.2d 226 (2001)—§ 6.9(f) n.137

Tibboel, United States v., 753 F.2d 608 (7th Cir.1985)—§§ 18.3(b) n.28, 41

Tibbs v. Florida, 457 U.S. 31, 102 S.Ct. 2211, 72 L.Ed.2d 652 (1982)—§§ 24.6(d) n.43; 25.4(b) n.15; 25.4(c) n.30

Tibbs v. State, 819 P.2d 1372 (Okla.Crim.App.1991)—§ 11.2(e) n.211

Tibiatowski, State v., 590 N.W.2d 305 (Minn.1999)—§§ 6.6(b) n.16; 6.10(c) n.40

Tidwell, People v., 95 Ill.App.3d 489, 51 Ill.Dec. 413, 420 N.E.2d 827 (1981)—§ 26.10(c) n.84

Tidwell v. Superior Court, 17 Cal.App.3d 780, 95 Cal.Rptr. 213 (1971)—§ 3.10(b) n.78

Tierney, In re, 465 F.2d 806 (5th Cir.1972)—§§ 8.11(d) n.76; 8.14(c) n.35

Tighe, United States v., 266 F.3d 1187 (9th Cir.2001)—§ 26.4(i) n.200

Tijerina, United States v., 412 F.2d 661 (10th Cir.1969)—§§ 23.1(b) n.71, 76, 78

Tileston v. Ullman, 318 U.S. 44, 63 S.Ct. 493, 87 L.Ed. 603 (1943)—§ 9.1(a) n.2

Tilghman, State v., 385 N.J.Super. 45, 895 A.2d 1207 (2006)—§ 24.7(a) n.6

Tilghman, United States v., 134 F.3d 414 (D.C.Cir.1998)—§ 24.6(e) n.52

Tili, State v., 148 Wash.2d 350, 60 P.3d 1192 (2003)—§ 17.4(a) n.36

Tillema v. Long, 253 F.3d 494 (9th Cir.2001)—§ 28.5(b) n.48

Tilley, United States v., 964 F.2d 66 (1st Cir.1992)—§ 21.2(d) n.249

Tillis, People v., 18 Cal.4th 284, 75 Cal.Rptr.2d 447, 956 P.2d 409 (1998)—§ 20.4(a) n.12

Tillman, State v., 220 Conn. 487, 600 A.2d 738 (1991)—§ 22.2(d) n.68

Tillman, State v., 750 P.2d 546 (Utah 1987)—§ 22.2(d) n.63

Tillman, State v., 122 N.J.Super. 137, 299 A.2d 419 (1973)—§ 24.4(d) n.38

Tillman, United States ex rel. v. Alldredge, 350 F.Supp. 189 (E.D.Pa.1972)—§ 21.3(b) n.117

Tilmon, United States v., 19 F.3d 1221 (7th Cir.1994)—§ 3.8(b) n.26

Tilson, State v., 794 A.2d 465 (R.I.2002)—§§ 13.7(c) n.43, 63

Timas, State v., 82 Haw. 499, 923 P.2d 916 (Haw.App.1996)—§ 27.5(a) n.8

Timberlake v. Davis, 418 F.3d 702 (7th Cir.2005)—§§ 11.10(c) n.127, 151

Timberlake, United States v., 559 F.2d 1375 (5th Cir.1977)—§ 5.3(d) n.42

Times Mirror Co. v. United States, 873 F.2d 1210 (9th Cir.1989)—§§ 23.1(d) n.197, 198, 200, 201, 208

Times Publishing Co. v. State, 632 So.2d 1072 (Fla.App.1994)—§§ 23.1(c) n.101, 103

Times-World Corporation, In re, 25 Va.App. 405, 488 S.E.2d 677 (1997)—§§ 23.1(d) n.148; 23.1(e) n.230, 231, 234, 245

Timko, Commonwealth v., 491 Pa. 32, 417 A.2d 620 (1980)—§ 3.5(e) n.187

Timmendequas, State v., 161 N.J. 515, 737 A.2d 55 (1999)—§§ 6.6(e) n.61; 16.3(g) n.116, 132; 23.2(c) n.59

Timmins, United States v., 301 F.3d 974 (9th Cir.2002)—§ 21.4(b) n.58

Timmreck, United States v., 441 U.S. 780, 99 S.Ct. 2085, 60 L.Ed.2d 634 (1979)—§§ 21.4(d) n.145; 21.5(c) n.73; 28.9(a) n.3; 28.9(c) n.79

Timoteo, State v., 87 Haw. 108, 952 P.2d 865 (1997)—§§ 18.5(a) n.46, 52; 24.8(f) n.104

Tinch, State v., 84 Ohio App.3d 111, 616 N.E.2d 529 (1992)—§ 16.1(e) n.191

Tincher, State v., 181 W.Va. 183, 381 S.E.2d 382 (1989)—§ 7.4(e) n.89

Tindle v. United States, 778 A.2d 1077 (D.C.App.2001)—§ 6.9(f) n.134

Tindle, United States v., 860 F.2d 125 (4th Cir.1988)—§ 22.3(d) n.229

Tinetti v. Wittke, 479 F.Supp. 486 (E.D.Wis.1979)—§ 3.5(c) n.130

Tinghitella v. California, 718 F.2d 308 (9th Cir.1983)—§ 18.4(c) n.39

Tingle, United States v., 658 F.2d 1332 (9th Cir.1981)—§§ 6.2(c) n.105, 107

Tinker v. Hanks, 255 F.3d 444 (7th Cir.2001)—§ 28.5(b) n.48

Tinkham, State v., 143 N.H. 73, 719 A.2d 580 (1998)—§ 6.10(c) n.36

Tinoco, People v., 185 Ill.App.3d 816, 133 Ill.Dec. 760, 541 N.E.2d 1198 (1989)—§ 20.6(c) n.83

Tinsley v. Borg, 895 F.2d 520 (9th Cir.1990)—§ 22.3(c) n.136

Tinsley v. United States, 868 A.2d 867 (D.C.App.2005)—§ 24.1(b) n.27

Tinson, United States v., 23 F.3d 1010 (6th Cir.1994)—§ 21.2(b) n.58

Tin Trung Ngo, People v., 14 Cal.4th 30, 57 Cal.Rptr.2d 456, 924 P.2d 97 (1996)—§ 11.8(c) n.77

Tippins v. Walker, 77 F.3d 682 (2d Cir.1996)—§ 11.10(d) n.199

Tipton, People v., 78 Ill.2d 477, 36 Ill.Dec. 687, 401 N.E.2d 528 (1980)—§ 5.1(a) n.3

Tipton, United States v., 11 F.3d 602 (6th Cir.1993)—§ 7.5(a) n.6

Tisdale, United States v., 952 F.2d 934 (6th Cir.1992)—§§ 6.4(e) n.107; 26.4(e) n.83

Tisler, People v., 103 Ill.2d 226, 82 Ill.Dec. 613, 469 N.E.2d 147 (1984)—§§ 2.12(b) n.82, 90 to 92; 2.12(c) n.121; 3.3(c) n.132

Tisnado v. United States, 547 F.2d 452 (9th Cir.1976)—§ 28.9(b) n.33

Tison v. Arizona, 481 U.S. 137, 107 S.Ct. 1676, 95 L.Ed.2d 127 (1987)—§ 26.1(b) n.31

Tison, State v., 142 Ariz. 446, 690 P.2d 747 (1984)—§ 10.2(b) n.18

Titemore, United States v., 437 F.3d 251 (2d Cir.2006)—§ 6.6(e) n.61

Titlbach, United States v., 339 F.3d 692 (8th Cir.2003)—§§ 18.2(b) n.15; 18.3(b) n.25

Titterington, United States v., 374 F.3d 453 (6th Cir.2004)—§ 19.3(a) n.16

Titus, State v., 707 So.2d 706 (Fla.1998)—§ 3.2(c) n.106

Titus v. State, 963 P.2d 258 (Alaska 1998)—§ 24.9(g) n.126

Titus, United States v., 445 F.2d 577 (2d Cir.1971)—§ 3.6(d) n.87

T.J.K., In re, 598 N.W.2d 781 (N.D.1999)—§ 10.6(a) n.6

Tkacz, State v., 258 Wis.2d 611, 654 N.W.2d 37 (2002)—§ 11.9(c) n.128

T.M., State ex rel., 166 N.J. 319, 765 A.2d 735 (2001)—§ 21.4(f) n.192

Tobias v. State, 884 S.W.2d 571 (Tex.App.1994)—§§ 19.5(b) n.43, 45

Tobin, United States v., 840 F.2d 867 (11th Cir.1988)—§ 18.3(b) n.36

Tobon-Hernandez, United States v., 845 F.2d 277 (11th Cir.1988)—§§ 21.2(d) n.213; 21.2(e) n.299

Tocco, United States v., 135 F.3d 116 (2d Cir.1998)—§ 1.2(c) n.175

Today's Bookstore, State v., 86 Ohio App.3d 810, 621 N.E.2d 1283 (1993)—§ 20.3(j) n.195

Todd, Commonwealth v., 408 Mass. 724, 563 N.E.2d 211 (1990)—§ 10.5(a) n.8

Todd v. State, 566 N.E.2d 67 (Ind.App.1991)—§§ 19.2(c) n.28; 19.2(d) n.46

Todd, State v., 56 N.C.App. 116, 286 S.E.2d 849 (1982)—§ 3.7(a) n.15

Todd, United States v., 446 F.3d 1062 (10th Cir.2006)—§ 24.6(b) n.36

Todd, United States v., 424 F.3d 525 (7th Cir.2005)—§ 11.5(c) n.54

Todd, United States v., 964 F.2d 925 (9th Cir.1992)—§ 25.4(b) n.17

Todisco, Commonwealth v., 363 Mass. 445, 294 N.E.2d 860 (1973)—§§ 3.4(e) n.69; 4.6(b) n.49

Todisco, United States v., 667 F.2d 255 (2d Cir.1981)—§§ 11.4(c) n.76, 78, 83; 11.6(a) n.13

Tokars, United States v., 95 F.3d 1520 (11th Cir.1996)—§ 22.3(d) n.228

Tokars, United States v., 839 F.Supp. 1578 (N.D.Ga.1993)—§ 16.3(g) n.114

Tolbert v. Page, 182 F.3d 677 (9th Cir.1999)—§ 22.3(d) n.197

Tolbert, State v., 381 Md. 539, 850 A.2d 1192 (2004)—§§ 6.8(b) n.63; 10.4(b) n.15

Tolbert, State v., 60 Ohio St.3d 89, 573 N.E.2d 617 (1991)—§ 17.4(b) n.98

Tolbert v. State, 315 Md. 13, 553 A.2d 228 (1989)—§ 22.3(d) n.212

Tolentino, Commonwealth v., 422 Mass. 515, 663 N.E.2d 846 (1996)— §§ 22.2(d) n.66, 75

Toler v. Wyrick, 563 F.2d 372 (8th Cir.1977)—§ 21.2(c) n.106

Toles v. Gibson, 269 F.3d 1167 (10th Cir.2001)—§ 6.9(f) n.139

Toles v. State, 947 P.2d 180 (Okl.Cr.1997)—§ 22.3(c) n.100

Toles, United States v., 297 F.3d 959 (10th Cir.2002)—§§ 6.2(c) n.120; 6.4(e) n.95

Toliver, United States v., 330 F.3d 607 (3d Cir.2003)—§ 27.6(d) n.84

Tollefson, State v., 660 N.W.2d 575 (N.D.2003)—§ 3.8(e) n.214

Tollett v. Henderson, 411 U.S. 258, 93 S.Ct. 1602, 36 L.Ed.2d 235 (1973)—§§ 10.2(d) n.47; 11.6(a) n.32; 11.10(c) n.63; 15.3(d) n.71; 21.6(a) n.10; 28.4(a) n.7

Tollette v. State, 280 Ga. 100, 621 S.E.2d 742 (2005)—§ 11.10(c) n.88

Tolliver, State v., 268 Neb. 920, 689 N.W.2d 567 (2004)—§ 7.4(e) n.90

Tolliver v. State, 273 Ga. 785, 546 S.E.2d 525 (2001)—§§ 6.6(a) n.7; 6.7(b) n.64

Tolliver, United States v., 116 F.3d 120 (5th Cir.1997)—§ 27.5(b) n.42

Tolliver, United States v., 569 F.2d 724 (2d Cir.1978)—§ 7.3(c) n.61

Tolman, State v., 775 P.2d 422 (Utah App.1989)—§ 14.2(d) n.50

Tolson v. State, 900 A.2d 639 (Del.2006)—§ 6.7(c) n.133

Tolson, State v., 274 Kan. 558, 56 P.3d 279 (2002)—§ 3.6(a) n.19

Tolson, United States v., 988 F.2d 1494 (7th Cir.1993)—§ 21.4(f) n.171

Tolson, United States v., 28 Fed.Cas. 200 (No. 16530) (C.C.D.C.1803)— § 16.1(d) n.130

Tom, United States v., 330 F.3d 83 (1st Cir.2003)—§ 5.2(a) n.9

Tomaszewski, United States v., 833 F.2d 1532 (11th Cir.1987)—§ 3.3(b) n.45

Tomblin v. State, 128 Ga.App. 823, 198 S.E.2d 366 (1973)—§ 3.4(e) n.66

Tomeny, United States v., 144 F.3d 749 (11th Cir.1998)—§ 21.6(a) n.63

Tomlin, State v., 266 Conn. 608, 835 A.2d 12 (2003)—§§ 24.8(e) n.69, 75; 24.8(f) n.98; 27.6(d) n.99

Tomlin v. State, 695 So.2d 157 (Ala.1996)—§ 25.4(a) n.8

Tomlin, State v., 299 S.C. 294, 384 S.E.2d 707 (1989)—§ 22.3(d) n.242

Tompkins v. State, 705 P.2d 836 (Wyo.1985)—§ 21.6(b) n.112

Tompkins v. Superior Court, 59 Cal.2d 65, 27 Cal.Rptr. 889, 378 P.2d 113 (1963)—§ 3.6(b) n.43

Toner, United States v., 728 F.2d 115 (2d Cir.1984)—§ 22.2(d) n.87

Toney, Ex parte, 11 Mo. 661 (1848)— § 28.1(c) n.26

Tongue, State v., 170 Vt. 409, 753 A.2d 356 (2000)—§§ 10.5(f) n.68; 10.6(a) n.2

Tonkin v. Michael, 349 F.Supp. 78 (D.V.I.1972)—§ 13.3(b) n.19

Tonn, State v., 195 Iowa 94, 191 N.W. 530 (1923)—§ 2.12(a) n.10

Tonry, United States v., 605 F.2d 144 (5th Cir.1979)—§ 26.9(b) n.57

Tonzola, State v., 159 Vt. 491, 621 A.2d 243 (1993)—§ 6.6(e) n.76

Toohey, People v., 438 Mich. 265, 475 N.W.2d 16 (1991)—§ 3.7(e) n.108

Toohey v. United States, 404 F.2d 907 (9th Cir.1968)—§ 6.7(b) n.43

Tookes, State v., 67 Haw. 608, 699 P.2d 983 (1985)—§ 5.4(c) n.29

Toomer, State v., 395 So.2d 1320 (La.1981)—§ 24.4(d) n.42

Toomey, State v., 126 Vt. 123, 223 A.2d 473 (1966)—§ 12.4(a) n.5

Toone, State v., 823 S.W.2d 744 (Tex.App.1992)—§ 2.12(c) n.175

Toothman, United States v., 137 F.3d 1393 (9th Cir.1998)—§ 21.4(d) n.104

Tootick, United States v., 952 F.2d 1078 (9th Cir.1991)—§ 17.2(d) n.94

Torbet v. United Airlines, 298 F.3d 1087 (9th Cir.2002)—§ 3.9(h) n.156

Torgerson, State v., 611 N.W.2d 182 (N.D.2000)—§ 22.2(d) n.79

Toribio Lugo, United States v., 376 F.3d 33 (1st Cir.2004)—§ 25.2(d) n.25

Toro v. Fairman, 940 F.2d 1065 (7th Cir.1991)—§ 21.3(b) n.74

Torquato, United States v., 602 F.2d 564 (3d Cir.1979)—§§ 13.4(b) n.44; 13.4(c) n.86

Torres, In re, 177 Vt. 507, 861 A.2d 1055 (Vt.2004)—§ 21.6(a) n.50

Torres, Commonwealth v., 441 Mass. 499, 806 N.E.2d 895 (2004)—§ 12.1(d) n.59

Torres, People v., 452 Mich. 43, 549 N.W.2d 540 (1996)—§ 25.4(b) n.12

Torres, People v., 245 Ill.App.3d 297, 184 Ill.Dec. 311, 613 N.E.2d 338 (1993)—§§ 15.6(a) n.10, 20, 39; 15.6(d) n.107, 123; 15.7(f) n.141

Torres, People v., 209 Ill.App.3d 314, 154 Ill.Dec. 157, 568 N.E.2d 157 (1991)—§ 11.10(c) n.107

Torres, State v., 280 Kan. 309, 121 P.3d 429 (2005)—§ 6.6(d) n.48

Torres, State v., 208 Ariz. 340, 93 P.3d 1056 (2004)—§§ 11.4(b) n.35, 40

Torres, State v., 66 Ohio St.2d 340, 421 N.E.2d 1288 (1981)—§ 24.5(a) n.17

Torres, United States v., 282 F.3d 1241 (10th Cir.2002)—§§ 28.9(a) n.15, 28

Torres, United States v., 128 F.3d 38 (2d Cir.1997)—§ 22.3(c) n.161

Torres, United States v., 129 F.3d 710 (2d Cir.1997)—§ 21.5(d) n.102

Torres, United States v., 1994 WL 48820 (S.D.N.Y.1994)—§§ 15.5(b) n.94, 95; 15.6(e) n.160

Torres, United States v., 999 F.2d 376 (9th Cir.1993)—§ 21.2(b) n.85

Torres, United States v., 977 F.2d 321 (7th Cir.1992)—§ 26.5(a) n.21

Torres, United States v., 926 F.2d 321 (3d Cir.1991)—§ 3.1(f) n.153

Torres, United States v., 901 F.2d 205 (2d Cir.1990)—§ 24.8(e) n.65

Torres, United States v., 908 F.2d 1417 (9th Cir.1990)—§§ 4.6(d) n.65; 4.6(e) n.98

Torres, United States v., 751 F.2d 875 (7th Cir.1984)—§ 4.6(a) n.5

Torres-Arboledo v. State, 524 So.2d 403 (Fla.1988)—§ 24.5(d) n.58

Torres-Echavarria, United States v., 129 F.3d 692 (2d Cir.1997)—§ 21.3(e) n.279

Torres-Palma, United States v., 290 F.3d 1244 (10th Cir.2002)—§ 24.2(f) n.83

Torres-Rodriguez, United States v., 930 F.2d 1375 (9th Cir.1991)—§§ 11.4(b) n.23, 36; 11.4(c) n.71

Torres-Rosa, United States v., 209 F.3d 4 (1st Cir.2000)—§§ 21.2(d) n.161; 21.5(a) n.38, 40

Torrie, State v., 794 A.2d 82 (Me.2002)—§ 25.2(e) n.38

Tortora, United States v., 922 F.2d 880 (1st Cir.1990)—§§ 12.1(a) n.16, 20; 12.3(a) n.21

Tortora, United States v., 464 F.2d 1202 (2d Cir.1972)—§ 24.2(d) n.43

Tortorello, United States v., 480 F.2d 764 (2d Cir.1973)—§ 4.6(e) n.83

Tortorello, United States v., 342 F.Supp. 1029 (S.D.N.Y.1972)—§ 4.6(f) n.125

Tot v. United States, 319 U.S. 463, 63 S.Ct. 1241, 87 L.Ed. 1519 (1943)—§§ 2.4(e) n.137, 177

Toth v. State, 297 So.2d 53 (Fla.App.1974)—§ 21.5(f) n.157

Toth, United States ex rel. v. Quarles, 350 U.S. 11, 76 S.Ct. 1, 100 L.Ed. 8 (1955)—§§ 15.1(b) n.88, 89, 94

Toups, In re, 773 So.2d 709 (La.2000)—§ 22.5(a) n.8

Toure v. United States, 24 F.3d 444 (2d Cir.1994)—§ 10.1(c) n.47

Tourtellotte, State v., 88 Wash.2d 579, 564 P.2d 799 (1977)—§§ 21.2(e) n.293, 310; 21.2(f) n.363

Tousant, United States v., 619 F.2d 810 (9th Cir.1980)—§ 18.5(b) n.64

Toushin, United States v., 714 F.Supp. 1452 (M.D.Tenn.1989)—§§ 16.3(c) n.44, 49

Toussaint v. State, 755 So.2d 170 (Fla.App.2000)—§ 19.5(b) n.28

Toussie v. United States, 397 U.S. 112, 90 S.Ct. 858, 25 L.Ed.2d 156 (1970)—§§ 18.5(a) n.3, 11

Tower, People v., 215 Mich.App. 318, 544 N.W.2d 752 (1996)—§§ 14.3(a) n.9, 14; 14.3(d) n.99

Tower v. Phillips, 979 F.2d 807 (11th Cir.1992)—§ 21.3(b) n.105

Towery, State v., 186 Ariz. 168, 920 P.2d 290 (1996)—§ 14.1(c) n.45

Towler, People v., 31 Cal.3d 105, 181 Cal.Rptr. 391, 641 P.2d 1253 (1982)—§ 15.6(f) n.171

Townes, People v., 41 N.Y.2d 97, 390 N.Y.S.2d 893, 359 N.E.2d 402 (1976)—§§ 9.4(f) n.116, 118

Townley, United States v., 665 F.2d 579 (5th Cir.1982)—§ 18.5(b) n.63

Towns v. Smith, 395 F.3d 251 (Sixth Cir.2005)—§ 11.10(c) n.84

Towns, United States v., 19 F.Supp.2d 64 (W.D.N.Y.1998)—§ 20.5(c) n.43

Townsend v. Burke, 334 U.S. 736, 68 S.Ct. 1252, 92 L.Ed. 1690 (1948)—§§ 2.7(a) n.55; 26.4(d) n.45; 26.4(e) n.71; 26.4(f) n.95

Townsend v. Sain, 372 U.S. 293, 83 S.Ct. 745, 9 L.Ed.2d 770 (1963)—§§ 2.4(e) n.146; 6.2(b) n.44; 6.2(c) n.172; 28.3(e) n.92; 28.7(a) n.1; 28.7(c) n.22

Townsend v. State, 355 Ark. 248, 134 S.W.3d 545 (2003)—§ 13.7(c) n.48

Townsend, State v., 147 Wash.2d 606, 57 P.3d 255 (2002)—§ 4.6(l) n.205

Townsend v. State, 350 Ark. 129, 85 S.W.3d 526 (2002)—§ 11.9(b) n.78

Townsend, State v., 186 W.Va. 283, 412 S.E.2d 477 (1991)—§ 3.2(c) n.125

Townsend, State v., 211 Conn. 215, 558 A.2d 669 (1989)—§ 23.2(a) n.15

Townsend v. Superior Court, 15 Cal.3d 774, 126 Cal.Rptr. 251, 543 P.2d 619 (1975)—§§ 11.6(a) n.25, 44; 18.1(d) n.46

Townsend, United States v., 897 F.2d 989 (9th Cir.1990)—§§ 12.1(a) n.9; 12.3(a) n.23

T.R., In re, 52 Ohio St.3d 6, 556 N.E.2d 439 (1990)—§§ 27.2(d) n.68; 27.4(e) n.60

Tracey, Commonwealth v., 416 Mass. 528, 624 N.E.2d 84 (1993)—§§ 5.3(c) n.31; 5.3(d) n.42

Tracey, People v., 221 Mich.App. 321, 561 N.W.2d 133 (1997)—§ 25.2(a) n.6

Trade-Mark Cases, 100 U.S. 82, 25 L.Ed. 550 (1879)—§ 1.2(c) n.93

Trader Roe, Matter of, 720 F.Supp. 645 (N.D.Ill.1989)—§ 8.12(g) n.67

Traeger, United States v., 289 F.3d 461 (7th Cir.2002)—§§ 7.4(b) n.28; 7.4(d) n.69

Traficant, United States v., 368 F.3d 646 (6th Cir.2004)—§ 25.1(c) n.40

Traficante, State v., 636 A.2d 692 (R.I.1994)—§ 21.2(h) n.419

Trahan v. Estelle, 544 F.2d 1305 (5th Cir.1977)—§§ 21.3(a) n.18, 19

Trahan, State v., 797 So.2d 38 (La.2001)—§ 21.4(g) n.233

Trahan, State v., 229 Neb. 683, 428 N.W.2d 619 (1988)—§ 3.2(h) n.212

Trainer, United States v., 265 F.Supp.2d 589 (D.Md.2003)—§ 26.9(b) n.43

Traitz, United States v., 871 F.2d 368 (3d Cir.1989)—§ 4.6(m) n.228

Trammel, United States v., 813 F.2d 946 (7th Cir.1987)—§ 18.4(c) n.40

Trammell, State v., 278 Kan. 265, 92 P.3d 1101 (2004)—§§ 7.4(e) n.83, 93

Trammell v. State, 751 N.E.2d 283 (Ind.App.2001)—§ 26.9(b) n.55

Trammell v. State, 162 Tex.Crim. 543, 287 S.W.2d 487 (1956)—§ 2.12(a) n.13

Trammell, United States v., 133 F.3d 1343 (10th Cir.1998)—§ 25.5(a) n.11

Tramunti, United States v., 513 F.2d 1087 (2d Cir.1975)—§ 3.7(c) n.42

Tran v. Superior Court, 92 Cal.App.4th 1149, 112 Cal.Rptr.2d 506 (2001)—§ 11.2(g) n.290

Tranakos, United States v., 911 F.2d 1422 (10th Cir.1990)—§§ 18.2(c) n.50; 18.3(b) n.36

Tranakos, United States v., 690 F.Supp. 971 (D.Wyo.1988)—§ 15.4(d) n.123

Trancoso, People v., 776 P.2d 374 (Colo.1989)—§ 18.4(d) n.87

Transfiguracion, United States v., 442 F.3d 1222 (9th Cir.2006)—§ 21.2(e) n.309

Trapp, People v., 46 Misc.2d 642, 260 N.Y.S.2d 305 (1965)—§ 13.2(c) n.70

Trapp, United States v., 257 F.3d 1053 (9th Cir.2001)—§ 21.2(d) n.167

Trap Rock Industries v. Kohl, 59 N.J. 471, 284 A.2d 161 (1971)—§ 15.2(f) n.149

Trask v. Robbins, 421 F.2d 773 (1st Cir.1970)—§ 7.4(b) n.19

Travaglia, Commonwealth v., 541 Pa. 108, 661 A.2d 352 (1995)—§ 17.2(b) n.69

Travis v. State, 328 Ark. 442, 944 S.W.2d 96 (1997)—§ 24.6(b) n.20

Travis, State v., 125 Idaho 1, 867 P.2d 234 (1994)—§ 26.10(c) n.63

Travis, State v., 568 A.2d 316 (R.I.1990)—§ 3.3(d) n.170

Travis, United States v., 735 F.2d 1129 (9th Cir.1984)—§§ 15.1(f) n.324; 21.2(e) n.316

Travis v. United States, 364 U.S. 631, 81 S.Ct. 358, 5 L.Ed.2d 340 (1961)—§§ 16.2(b) n.27, 28; 16.2(c) n.40, 48; 16.2(f) n.101

Trawitzki, State v., 244 Wis.2d 523, 628 N.W.2d 801 (2001)—§ 17.3(b) n.13

Traylor, Commonwealth v., 43 Mass.App.Ct. 239, 681 N.E.2d 1249 (1997)—§ 24.7(e) n.55

Traylor, State v., 360 S.C. 74, 600 S.E.2d 523 (2004)—§§ 7.4(c) n.48, 50, 53; 7.4(e) n.91

Traylor v. State, 596 So.2d 957 (Fla.1992)—§§ 2.12(c) n.151, 153, 155, 158, 159; 2.12(d) n.195

Traylor v. State, 165 Ga.App. 226, 299 S.E.2d 911 (1983)—§ 15.2(d) n.105

Treadway, People v., 182 Colo. 239, 512 P.2d 275 (1973)—§ 3.3(c) n.90

Treadway, United States v., 445 F.Supp. 959 (N.D.Tex.1978)—§§ 15.6(b) n.61; 15.7(c) n.59, 60

Treece v. State, 313 Md. 665, 547 A.2d 1054 (1988)—§§ 11.6(a) n.26, 46; 11.6(c) n.106

Treesh, State v., 90 Ohio St.3d 460, 739 N.E.2d 749 (2001)—§§ 6.8(a) n.25; 6.9(b) n.38

Treff, United States v., 924 F.2d 975 (10th Cir.1991)—§ 11.5(g) n.110

Trejo, United States v., 136 F.3d 826 (D.C.Cir.1998)—§ 5.2(a) n.8

Trenkler v. United States, 268 F.3d 16 (1st Cir.2001)—§ 28.9(b) n.50

Trennell, United States v., 290 F.3d 881 (7th Cir.2002)—§ 19.3(a) n.92

Trent, State v., 79 N.J. 251, 398 A.2d 1271 (1979)—§ 22.3(e) n.279

Trepal v. State, 621 So.2d 1361 (Fla.1993)—§ 9.1(b) n.41

Trepanier, State v., 600 A.2d 1311 (R.I. 1991)—§ 21.2(f) n.383

Tressler, State v., 503 S.W.2d 13 (1973)—§ 15.2(d) n.95

Trest v. Cain, 522 U.S. 87, 118 S.Ct. 478, 139 L.Ed.2d 444 (1997)— § 28.4(c) n.29

Trevino, People v., 72 Cal.App.3d 686, 140 Cal.Rptr. 243 (1977)—§ 3.5(b) n.99

Trevino, United States v., 89 F.3d 187 (4th Cir.1996)—§ 26.5(c) n.59

Trevino, United States v., 556 F.2d 1265 (5th Cir.1977)—§ 20.3(a) n.13

Trevino-Martinez, United States v., 86 F.3d 65 (5th Cir.1996)—§ 5.4(c) n.30

Triana v. United States, 205 F.3d 36 (2d Cir.2000)—§§ 11.9(d) n.175, 207

Tribble, State v., 892 A.2d 232 (Vt.2005)—§§ 11.4(d) n.110; 11.5(c) n.55; 11.6(a) n.12

Trice v. United States, 662 A.2d 891 (D.C.App.1995)—§§ 6.7(b) n.80, 81

Triestman, United States v., 178 F.3d 624 (2d Cir.1999)—§ 26.7(b) n.19

Triestman v. United States, 124 F.3d 361 (2d Cir.1997)—§ 28.9(a) n.7

Triggs, People v., 8 Cal.3d 884, 106 Cal.Rptr. 408, 506 P.2d 232 (1973)—§ 3.2(e) n.170

Trigones, Commonwealth v., 397 Mass. 633, 492 N.E.2d 1146 (1986)— § 14.1(d) n.59

Trigon, Inc., State v., 657 N.W.2d 441 (Iowa 2003)—§§ 6.6(e) n.68; 6.10(c) n.50

Trimble v. Gordon, 430 U.S. 762, 97 S.Ct. 1459, 52 L.Ed.2d 31 (1977)— § 2.9(d) n.88

Trimble, State v., 371 N.W.2d 921 (Minn.App.1985)—§ 24.7(e) n.46

Trimble, United States v., 986 F.2d 394 (10th Cir.1993)—§ 4.8(d) n.28

Trindle v. State, 326 Md. 25, 602 A.2d 1232 (1992)—§§ 16.4(c) n.57, 59, 83

Triplett, People v., 68 Mich.App. 531, 243 N.W.2d 665 (1976)—§ 21.5(e) n.138

Triplett, State v., 187 W.Va. 760, 421 S.E.2d 511 (1992)—§ 11.7(e) n.76

Triplett, United States v., 828 F.2d 1195 (6th Cir.1987)—§§ 21.5(a) n.34, 39

Tripp, People v., 208 Ill.App.3d 1006, 153 Ill.Dec. 811, 567 N.E.2d 769 (1991)—§ 25.3(a) n.7

Trochinski, State v., 253 Wis.2d 38, 644 N.W.2d 891 (2002)—§ 21.4(c) n.71

Trombley, State v., 147 Vt. 371, 518 A.2d 20 (1986)—§ 6.9(f) n.134

Trombly, In re, 160 Vt. 215, 627 A.2d 855 (1993)—§ 11.6(a) n.50

Trompeter, State v., 555 N.W.2d 468 (Iowa 1996)—§§ 18.5(b) n.56, 58

Tropiano, United States v., 50 F.3d 157 (2d Cir.1995)—§ 9.1(d) n.132

Tropp, United States v., 725 F.Supp. 482 (D.Wyo.1989)—§§ 8.8(g) n.164, 165

Trostle, State v., 191 Ariz. 4, 951 P.2d 869 (1997)—§ 22.3(d) n.250

Trotter, People v., 84 Ill.App.2d 388, 228 N.E.2d 467 (1967)—§ 24.7(e) n.63

Troup v. State, 51 Okla.Crim. 438, 2 P.2d 591 (1931)—§ 16.2(a) n.1

Troupe, State v., 237 Conn. 284, 677 A.2d 917 (1996)—§§ 20.6(b) n.19; 24.4(d) n.42

Troupe, State v., 891 S.W.2d 808 (Mo.1995)—§ 27.5(c) n.71

Trowbridge, Commonwealth v., 419 Mass. 750, 647 N.E.2d 413 (1995)—§ 15.7(f) n.164

Trowbridge v. State, 502 P.2d 495 (Okla.Crim.1972)—§ 11.2(e) n.141

Troxell, State v., 78 S.W.3d 866 (Tenn.2002)—§ 3.10(f) n.188

Troxler Hosiery Co., Inc., United States v., 681 F.2d 934 (4th Cir.1982)— § 22.1(b) n.49

Troy, State v., 124 Idaho 211, 858 P.2d 750 (1993)—§§ 6.2(c) n.100, 153

Trudeau, People v., 385 Mich. 276, 187 N.W.2d 890 (1971)—§ 3.5(c) n.125

True, State v., 236 Neb. 274, 460 N.W.2d 668 (1990)—§ 26.5(c) n.43

True, State v., 330 A.2d 787 (Me.1975)—§§ 16.1(g) n.246, 273; 16.1(h) n.285

True, United States v., 250 F.3d 410 (6th Cir.2001)—§§ 13.5(h) n.147, 211

Trueber, United States v., 238 F.3d 79 (1st Cir.2001)—§§ 18.2(c) n.52; 18.2(d) n.61; 18.2(e) n.81

Trueblood v. Davis, 301 F.3d 784 (7th Cir.2002)—§ 21.4(d) n.131

Truesdale, Commonwealth v., 449 Pa. 325, 296 A.2d 829 (1972)—§§ 12.3(e) n.121; 12.4(a) n.9

Truesdale v. Moore, 142 F.3d 749 (4th Cir.1998)—§ 22.2(d) n.85

Truesdale, United States v., 211 F.3d 898 (5th Cir.2000)—§§ 13.5(h) n.135, 148, 162, 163, 174, 183, 186, 202, 208, 211, 213, 215

Truglio, United States v., 493 F.2d 574 (4th Cir.1974)—§ 21.3(b) n.133

Truitt, State v., 500 So.2d 355 (La.1987)—§§ 11.7(e) n.77, 84

Trujillo, People v., 49 P.3d 316 (Colo.2002)—§ 9.6(a) n.49

Trujillo, People v., 773 P.2d 1086 (Colo.1989)—§ 6.9(f) n.145

Trujillo, People v., 154 Cal.App.3d 1077, 202 Cal.Rptr. 832 (1984)—§ 26.6(b) n.22

Trujillo v. State, 880 P.2d 575 (Wyo.1994)—§§ 14.1(b) n.33; 14.4(e) n.101; 24.6(b) n.32

Trujillo, State v., 95 N.M. 535, 624 P.2d 44 (1981)—§ 3.4(j) n.213

Trujillo, United States v., 714 F.2d 102 (11th Cir.1983)—§§ 22.1(g) n.116; 24.7(e) n.49

Trujillo v. United States, 377 F.2d 266 (5th Cir.1967)—§ 21.4(d) n.119

Trujillo v. Wyoming, 2 P.3d 567 (Wyo.2000)—§ 11.4(b) n.30

Trull, State v., 509 S.E.2d 178 (1998)—§ 23.2(f) n.83

Trulock v. Freeh, 275 F.3d 391 (4th Cir.2001)—§§ 3.10(b) n.26; 3.10(e) n.166

Trump, State ex rel. v. Hott, 187 W.Va. 749, 421 S.E.2d 500 (1992)—§ 27.4(d) n.49

Trunell v. State, 487 So.2d 820 (Miss.1986)—§ 2.12(e) n.211

Truong Dinh Hung, United States v., 629 F.2d 908 (4th Cir.1980)—§ 4.9(a) n.5

Trupiano v. United States, 334 U.S. 699, 68 S.Ct. 1229, 92 L.Ed. 1663 (1948)—§ 3.1(g) n.167

Trusky v. State, 7 P.3d 5 (Wyo.2000)—§ 20.4(f) n.92

Trussell v. Bowersox, 447 F.3d 588 (8th Cir.2006)—§§ 24.2(a) n.11; 26.1(d) n.79

Tryon, State ex rel. v. Mason, 679 S.W.2d 268 (Mo.1984)—§ 18.4(c) n.60

Tsanas, United States v., 572 F.2d 340 (2d Cir.1978)—§ 24.8(d) n.46

Tsavaris, State v., 382 So.2d 56 (Fla.App.1980)—§ 8.12(e) n.54

Tsosie, United States v., 966 F.2d 1357 (10th Cir.1992)—§ 27.2(c) n.53

T.T.C., Matter of, 583 A.2d 986 (D.C.1990)—§ 3.8(c) n.90

T.T.T., Matter of, 365 A.2d 366 (D.C.App.1976)—§ 6.9(f) n.103

Tuchman, State v., 242 Conn. 345, 699 A.2d 952 (1997)—§ 17.4(b) n.129

Tucker, Ex parte, 454 So.2d 552 (Ala.1984)—§ 22.3(c) n.102

Tucker v. Holland, 174 W.Va. 409, 327 S.E.2d 388 (1985)—§§ 21.3(b) n.79, 107

Tucker, State v., 259 Wis.2d 484, 657 N.W.2d 374 (2003)—§ 22.3(b) n.70

Tucker, State v., 145 N.H. 723, 765 A.2d 1058 (2001)—§§ 6.7(d) n.148; 9.5(e) n.84, 87, 88

Tucker, State v., 330 Or. 85, 997 P.2d 182 (2000)—§§ 3.1(h) n.190; 10.3(b) n.10

Tucker, State v., 81 Ohio St.3d 431, 692 N.E.2d 171 (1998)—§ 6.7(c) n.121

Tucker, State v., 136 N.J. 158, 642 A.2d 401 (1994)—§ 3.2(h) n.205

Tucker, State v., 315 Or. 321, 845 P.2d 904 (1993)—§ 21.3(c) n.157

Tucker, State v., 626 So.2d 707 (La.1993)—§§ 2.12(a) n.78; 2.12(b) n.80

Tucker, State v., 331 N.C. 12, 414 S.E.2d 548 (1992)—§§ 6.9(g) n.162; 17.2(b) n.68

Tucker, State v., 131 N.H. 526, 557 A.2d 270 (1989)—§ 6.6(e) n.71

Tucker, State v., 101 N.J.Super. 380, 244 A.2d 353 (1968)—§ 12.4(a) n.41

Tucker, United States v., 419 F.3d 719 (8th Cir.2005)—§ 21.2(g) n.394

Tucker, United States v., 305 F.3d 1193 (10th Cir.2002)—§ 3.9(j) n.229

Tucker, United States v., 243 F.3d 499 (8th Cir.2001)—§§ 22.3(c) n.142; 24.9(f) n.97

Tucker, United States v., 28 F.3d 1420 (6th Cir.1994)—§§ 5.4(c) n.38, 39, 46

Tucker, United States v., 8 F.3d 673 (9th Cir.1993)—§§ 18.5(c) n.81, 84

Tucker v. United States, 569 A.2d 162 (D.C.App.1990)—§ 18.4(c) n.39

Tucker, United States v., 836 F.2d 334 (7th Cir.1988)—§§ 22.3(d) n.230; 24.2(a) n.5

Tucker, United States v., 773 F.2d 136 (7th Cir.1985)—§ 11.5(g) n.120

Tucker, United States v., 404 U.S. 443, 92 S.Ct. 589, 30 L.Ed.2d 592 (1972)—§§ 11.1(a) n.27; 26.4(f) n.96; 26.5(a) n.19

Tucor International, Inc., United States v., 238 F.3d 1171 (9th Cir.2001)—§ 13.5(h) n.154

Tueller, United States v., 349 F.3d 1239 (10th Cir.2003)—§ 3.7(e) n.113

Tueros v. Greiner, 343 F.3d 587 (2d Cir.2003)—§ 11.9(d) n.173

Tufts, People v., 717 P.2d 485 (Colo.1986)—§ 10.3(b) n.31

Tufts, State v., 136 N.H. 517, 618 A.2d 818 (1992)—§ 26.5(c) n.52

Tufts, State v., 56 N.H. 137 (1875)—§ 13.3(c) n.36

Tuggle v. Netherland, 79 F.3d 1386 (4th Cir.1996)—§ 27.6(d) n.146

Tuilaepa v. California, 512 U.S. 967, 114 S.Ct. 2630, 129 L.Ed.2d 750 (1994)—§ 26.1(b) n.18

Tuipuapua, State v., 83 Haw. 141, 925 P.2d 311 (1996)—§ 17.4(b) n.120

Tuitt v. Fair, 822 F.2d 166 (1st Cir.1987)—§§ 11.3(a) n.20; 11.5(c) n.43; 11.5(d) n.69

Tukes v. Dugger, 911 F.2d 508 (11th Cir.1990)—§§ 3.10(a) n.21; 6.6(f) n.114

Tuller v. Neal, 886 P.2d 279 (Colo.1994)—§ 11.7(e) n.76

Tullo, State v., 366 A.2d 843 (Me.1976)—§ 2.12(e) n.208

Tulsa, City of v. Haley, 554 P.2d 102 (Okla.Crim.1976)—§ 19.3(b) n.151

Tumey v. Ohio, 273 U.S. 510, 47 S.Ct. 437, 71 L.Ed. 749 (1927)—§§ 2.4(d) n.131; 2.4(e) n.165; 2.5(d) n.36; 2.7(a) n.33; 2.7(b) n.74; 22.4(a) n.1; 27.6(d) n.70

Tune, State v., 13 N.J. 203, 98 A.2d 881 (1953)—§§ 20.1(a) n.14; 20.1(b) n.24, 26, 31, 38

Tunender, State v., 182 Neb. 701, 157 N.W.2d 165 (1968)—§ 21.2(g) n.399

Tung, People v., 30 Cal.App.4th 1607, 36 Cal.Rptr.2d 727 (1994)—§ 21.1(g) n.118

Tungland, State v., 281 N.W.2d 646 (Minn.1979)—§ 5.2(a) n.4

Tunnessen, United States v., 763 F.2d 74 (2d Cir.1985)—§ 18.3(b) n.37

Tunney, State v., 129 Wash.2d 336, 917 P.2d 95 (1996)—§ 19.3(e) n.245

Tunning, United States v., 69 F.3d 107 (6th Cir.1995)—§§ 21.4(f) n.175, 184, 185, 207

Tupko, State v., 161 Conn. 20, 282 A.2d 911 (1971)—§ 21.4(a) n.27

Turcotte, United States v., 515 F.3d 145 (2d Cir.1975)—§ 17.3(e) n.58

Ture, State v., 632 N.W.2d 621 (Minn.2001)—§ 3.7(e) n.118

Turentine v. Miller, 80 F.3d 222 (7th Cir.1996)—§§ 28.3(d) n.83, 89

Turgeon, State v., 161 Vt. 561, 641 A.2d 88 (1993)—§ 21.2(e) n.334

Turk, United States v., 526 F.2d 654 (5th Cir.1976)—§§ 3.7(f) n.133; 9.6(c) n.60

Turkette, United States v., 452 U.S. 576, 101 S.Ct. 2524, 69 L.Ed.2d 246 (1981)—§ 16.2(h) n.148

Turkish, United States v., 623 F.2d 769 (2d Cir.1980)—§§ 24.3(i) n.186, 187, 190

Turley, State v., 149 Wash.2d 395, 69 P.3d 338 (2003)—§ 21.5(e) n.152

Turley v. State, 74 Neb. 471, 104 N.W. 934 (1995)—§ 22.3(c) n.162

Turley, State v., 128 Wis.2d 39, 381 N.W.2d 309 (1986)—§ 25.3(c) n.25

Turmelle, State v., 132 N.H. 148, 562 A.2d 196 (1989)—§ 2.12(c) n.174

Turnage, People v., 162 Ill.2d 299, 205 Ill.Dec. 118, 642 N.E.2d 1235 (1994)—§ 10.3(b) n.13

Turnbaugh, State v., 174 Vt. 532, 811 A.2d 662 (2002)—§§ 12.4(a) n.1, 16, 22, 43

Turnbeaugh, People v., 116 Ill.App.3d 199, 71 Ill.Dec. 862, 451 N.E.2d 1016 (1983)—§ 3.9(h) n.167

Turnbull, United States v., 888 F.2d 636 (9th Cir.1989)—§ 11.5(g) n.112

Turner v. Arkansas, 407 U.S. 366, 92 S.Ct. 2096, 32 L.Ed.2d 798 (1972)—§ 17.4(a) n.16

Turner v. Calderon, 281 F.3d 851 (9th Cir.2002)—§ 21.3(b) n.80

Turner v. Commonwealth, 259 Va. 816, 528 S.E.2d 112 (2000)—§ 11.9(d) n.208

Turner v. Commonwealth, 914 S.W.2d 343 (Ky.1996)—§ 26.1(d) n.86

Turner v. Commonwealth, 767 S.W.2d 557 (Ky.1988)—§ 3.5(d) n.173

Turner v. Fouche, 396 U.S. 346, 90 S.Ct. 532, 24 L.Ed.2d 567 (1970)—§§ 13.4(b) n.73; 22.2(c) n.36

Turner v. Louisiana, 379 U.S. 466, 85 S.Ct. 546, 13 L.Ed.2d 424 (1965)—§ 24.9(f) n.90

Turner v. Marshall, 63 F.3d 807 (9th Cir.1995)—§ 22.3(d) n.197

Turner v. Murray, 476 U.S. 28, 106 S.Ct. 1683, 90 L.Ed.2d 27 (1986)—§§ 1.8(e) n.90; 2.9(g) n.159, 168, 171; 22.3(a) n.28

Turner v. Pennsylvania, 338 U.S. 62, 69 S.Ct. 1352, 93 L.Ed. 1810 (1949)—§§ 6.2(c) n.79, 84

Turner, People v., 5 N.Y.3d 476, 806 N.Y.S.2d 154, 840 N.E.2d 124 (2005)—§ 11.10(c) n.116

Turner, People v., 34 Cal.4th 406, 20 Cal.Rptr.3d 182, 99 P.3d 505 (2004)—§ 21.3(e) n.291

Turner, People v., 8 Cal.4th 137, 32 Cal.Rptr.2d 762, 878 P.2d 521 (1994)—§§ 3.2(f) n.175; 3.7(e) n.123

Turner, State v., 936 So.2d 89 (La.2006)—§ 26.4(h) n.156

Turner, State v., 267 Conn. 414, 838 A.2d 947 (2004)—§ 6.6(d) n.48

Turner, State v., 630 N.W.2d 601 (Iowa 2001)—§ 6.6(e) n.95

Turner v. State, 818 So.2d 1186 (Miss. 2001)—§ 11.2(c) n.86

Turner, State v., 252 Conn. 714, 751 A.2d 372 (2000)—§ 24.7(e) n.57

Turner v. State, 114 Nev. 682, 962 P.2d 1223 (1998)—§ 22.4(c) n.28

Turner, State v., 980 P.2d 1188 (Utah App.1998)—§ 25.1(d) n.73

Turner v. State, 682 N.E.2d 491 (Ind.1997)—§ 24.8(a) n.7

Turner v. State, 267 Ga. 149, 476 S.E.2d 252 (1996)—§ 6.4(e) n.77

Turner, State v., 550 N.W.2d 622 (Minn.1996)—§ 27.4(c) n.27

Turner, State v., 257 Kan. 19, 891 P.2d 317 (1995)—§§ 26.10(c) n.64, 65

Turner v. State, 655 A.2d 309 (Del.1995)—§ 24.9(d) n.42

Turner, State v., 561 A.2d 869 (R.I.1989)—§§ 7.4(c) n.50, 52

Turner, State v., 136 Wis.2d 333, 401 N.W.2d 827 (1987)—§ 6.9(f) n.104

Turner, State v., 433 A.2d 397 (Me.1981)—§ 24.5(b) n.34

Turner, State v., 223 Kan. 707, 576 P.2d 644 (1978)—§ 14.3(d) n.88

Turner, State v., 32 Or.App. 61, 573 P.2d 326 (1977)—§ 6.4(g) n.144

Turner v. State, 76 Wis.2d 1, 250 N.W.2d 706 (1977)—§§ 6.2(c) n.135; 16.3(b) n.25

Turner, State v., 190 Neb. 261, 207 N.W.2d 382 (1973)—§ 3.3(d) n.165

Turner v. State, 499 S.W.2d 182 (Tex.Cr.App.1973)—§ 3.2(c) n.109

Turner, State v., 186 Neb. 424, 183 N.W.2d 763 (1971)—§§ 21.2(c) n.101; 21.4(e) n.165

Turner, State v., 247 Or. 301, 429 P.2d 565 (1967)—§ 26.7(b) n.20

Turner v. State, 87 Fla. 155, 99 So. 334 (1924)—§ 16.3(d) n.73

Turner v. Tennessee, 940 F.2d 1000 (6th Cir.1991)—§ 13.7(c) n.44

Turner, United States v., 367 F.Supp.2d 319 (E.D.N.Y.2005)—§§ 12.1(f) n.80, 93, 97

Turner, United States v., 389 F.3d 111 (4th Cir.2004)—§ 22.3(c) n.133

Turner, United States v., 209 F.3d 1198 (10th Cir.2000)—§§ 4.6(a) n.9, 11

Turner, United States v., 761 A.2d 845 (D.C.App.2000)—§ 6.6(d) n.53

Turner, United States v., 157 F.3d 552 (8th Cir.1998)—§§ 6.9(b) n.27, 36, 41

Turner, United States v., 104 F.3d 1180 (9th Cir.1997)—§ 13.4(b) n.58

Turner, United States v., 93 F.3d 276 (7th Cir.1996)—§ 17.1(b) n.25

Turner, United States v., 44 F.3d 900 (10th Cir.1995)—§ 26.9(b) n.57

Turner, United States v., 28 F.3d 981 (9th Cir.1994)—§ 3.5(c) n.122

Turner, United States v., 926 F.2d 883 (9th Cir.1991)—§ 3.4(c) n.41

Turner, United States v., 881 F.2d 684 (9th Cir.1989)—§ 21.4(d) n.104

Turner, United States v., 528 F.2d 143 (9th Cir.1975)—§§ 4.6(e) n.98; 4.6(h) n.147

Turner v. United States, 396 U.S. 398, 90 S.Ct. 642, 24 L.Ed.2d 610 (1970)—§§ 2.4(b) n.58; 21.4(f) n.185

Turner v. United States, 325 F.2d 988 (8th Cir.1964)—§ 15.1(f) n.321

Turner v. Weber, 635 N.W.2d 587 (S.D.2001)—§ 21.5(d) n.104

Turner-Bey, State v., 812 S.W.2d 799 (Mo.App.1991)—§§ 15.2(j) n.237, 238

Turner, State ex rel. v. Frankel, 322 Ore. 363, 908 P.2d 293 (1995)—§ 27.4(c) n.24

Turner, State ex rel. v. Maggio, 463 So.2d 1304 (La.1985)—§ 21.2(g) n.396

Turner, State ex rel. v. McDonald, 676 S.W.2d 371 (Tex.Cr.App.1984)—§ 22.1(h) n.149

Turning Bear, United States v., 357 F.3d 730 (8th Cir.2004)—§ 24.2(e) n.75

Turnquest v. Wainwright, 651 F.2d 331 (5th Cir.1981)—§§ 11.9(d) n.184 to 186

Turns, United States v., 198 F.3d 584 (6th Cir.2000)—§ 24.11(d) n.34

Turoff, United States v., 853 F.2d 1037 (2d Cir.1988)—§ 17.2(a) n.9

Turpin v. State, 206 Ind. 345, 189 N.E. 403 (1934)—§ 15.2(e) n.142

Turrentine v. State, 965 P.2d 955 (Okl.Cr.App.1998)—§ 22.3(d) n.249

Tutein, United States v., 122 F.Supp.2d 575 (D.Virgin Islands 2000)—§ 19.3(c) n.187

Tutino, United States v., 883 F.2d 1125 (2d Cir.1989)—§ 17.2(e) n.125

Tutt v. State, 267 Ga. 49, 472 S.E.2d 306 (1996)—§ 21.6(a) n.57

Tuttle, State v., 650 N.W.2d 20 (S.D.2002)—§§ 6.2(c) n.113, 129; 6.9(g) n.185

Tuttle, State v., 460 N.W.2d 157 (S.D.1990)—§ 26.6(c) n.41

Tuttle, State v., 713 P.2d 703 (Utah 1985)—§ 27.5(c) n.77

Tuttle v. State, 158 Me. 150, 180 A.2d 608 (1962)—§§ 15.1(f) n.272 to 274

Tweed, United States v., 503 F.2d 1127 (7th Cir.1974)—§ 9.6(a) n.11

Tweedell v. State, 218 Ga.App. 518, 462 S.E.2d 181 (1995)—§ 11.7(e) n.72

Tweedy v. State, 380 Md.App. 475, 845 A.2d 1215 (2004)—§§ 24.2(a) n.11; 24.2(d) n.50

Tweeten, State v., 679 N.W.2d 287 (N.D.2004)—§ 18.3(c) n.111

Twentieth Century Fox Film Corp., United States v., 882 F.2d 656 (2d Cir.1989)—§ 22.1(b) n.49

Twentieth Century-Fox Film Corp., United States v., 700 F.Supp. 1242 (S.D.N.Y.1988)—§ 8.5(g) n.221

Twigg, United States v., 588 F.2d 373 (3d Cir.1978)—§§ 5.1(a) n.4; 5.4(c) n.45

Twillie v. State, 892 So.2d 187 (Miss.2004)—§ 21.6(a) n.67

Twining v. New Jersey, 211 U.S. 78, 29 S.Ct. 14, 53 L.Ed.2d 97 (1908)—§§ 2.3(b) n.86, 87; 2.4(a) n.16; 2.4(b) n.23; 2.4(d) n.129; 2.4 n.6; 2.5(f) n.51; 2.6(b) n.34; 2.7(c) n.110, 151, 175; 6.2(b) n.24; 6.5(a) n.6

Twitchell v. Commonwealth, 74 U.S. (7 Wall.) 321, 19 L.Ed. 223 (1868)—§ 2.4(c) n.107

Twitchell, State v., 8 Utah 2d 314, 333 P.2d 1075 (1959)—§ 13.7(a) n.25

Twitty, United States v., 44 F.3d 410 (6th Cir.1995)—§§ 26.10(a) n.7, 9

Two Grand Jury Subpoenae Duces Tecum, In re, 793 F.2d 69 (2d Cir.1986)—§ 8.12(b) n.21

Two Grand Jury Subpoenae Duces Tecum, In re, 769 F.2d 52 (2d Cir.1985)—§ 27.2(e) n.87

Two Guys from Harrison-Allentown, Inc. v. McGinley, 366 U.S. 582, 81 S.Ct. 1135, 6 L.Ed.2d 551 (1961)—§§ 13.4(a) n.8, 32

Twohig v. Blackmer, 121 N.M. 746, 918 P.2d 332 (1996)—§§ 23.1(b) n.69, 71, 72

Twohig, State v., 238 Neb. 92, 469 N.W.2d 344 (1991)—§ 3.8(c) n.88

Twyford, State v., 94 Ohio St.3d 340, 763 N.E.2d 122 (2002)—§ 22.3(c) n.153

TXO Production Corp. v. Alliance Resources, 509 U.S. 443, 113 S.Ct. 2711, 125 L.Ed.2d 366 (1993)—§ 2.7(d) n.233

Tyburski, People v., 445 Mich. 606, 518 N.W.2d 441 (1994)—§§ 23.2(f) n.91, 92

Tye, State v., 276 Ga. 559, 580 S.E.2d 528 (2003)—§§ 3.2(c) n.130; 3.10(b) n.36

Tye, State v., 248 Wis.2d 530, 636 N.W.2d 473 (2001)—§ 3.4(c) n.42

Tykarsky, United States v., 446 F.3d 458 (3d Cir.2006)—§ 6.8(c) n.65

Tyler v. Berodt, 877 F.2d 705 (8th Cir.1989)—§ 4.3(b) n.8

Tyler v. Cain, 533 U.S. 656, 121 S.Ct. 2478, 150 L.Ed.2d 632 (2001)—§§ 28.5(b) n.52; 28.5(d) n.83; 28.5(e) n.93; 28.6(e) n.51

Tyler v. Commonwealth, 21 Va.App. 702, 467 S.E.2d 294 (1996)—§ 24.10(b) n.30

Tyler, Commonwealth v., 402 Pa.Super. 429, 587 A.2d 326 (1991)—§§ 14.4(d) n.85, 86; 14.4(e) n.115

Tyler, People v., 802 P.2d 1153 (Colo.App.1990)—§ 15.6(f) n.203

Tyler, People v., 46 N.Y.2d 251, 413 N.Y.S.2d 295, 385 N.E.2d 1224 (1978)—§ 8.8(h) n.189

Tyler, People v., 399 Mich. 564, 250 N.W.2d 467 (1977)—§ 3.9(e) n.80

Tyler v. Purkett, 413 F.3d 696 (8th Cir.2005)—§ 24.3(e) n.120

Tyler v. State, 265 Ark. 822, 581 S.W.2d 328 (1979)—§ 11.4(c) n.84

Tyler, State v., 587 S.W.2d 918 (Mo.App.1979)—§ 22.5(a) n.12

Tyler v. State, 476 S.W.2d 611 (Mo.1972)—§ 21.5(a) n.57

Tyler v. United States, 705 A.2d 270 (D.C.App.1997)—§ 27.5(a) n.25

Tyler, United States v., 878 F.2d 753 (3d Cir.1989)—§ 7.5(c) n.48

Tyler v. United States, 397 F.2d 565 (5th Cir.1968)—§ 24.9(a) n.8

Tynan, People v., 701 P.2d 80 (Colo.App.1984)—§ 8.5(c) n.80

Tynes, Commonwealth v., 400 Mass. 369, 510 N.E.2d 244 (1987)— § 6.10(b) n.17

Tyree v. State, 262 Ga. 395, 418 S.E.2d 16 (1992)—§§ 22.3(b) n.91; 22.5(b) n.19

Tyrell, In re, 8 Cal.4th 68, 32 Cal.Rptr.2d 33, 876 P.2d 519 (1994)—§ 3.1(g) n.172

Tyrrell, State v., 234 Neb. 901, 453 N.W.2d 104 (1990)—§ 9.4(d) n.95

Tyson, Ex parte, 784 So.2d 357 (Ala.2000)—§§ 3.1(c) n.74; 3.4(e) n.72

Tyson v. State, 619 N.E.2d 276 (Ind.App.1993)—§ 1.10(d) n.155

Tyson v. State, 593 N.E.2d 175 (Ind.1992)—§ 12.4(d) n.63

Tyson v. Trigg, 50 F.3d 436 (7th Cir.1995)—§§ 15.4(i)   n.209; 20.6(c) n.73, 76

Tyson, United States v., 470 F.2d 381 (D.C.Cir.1972)—§ 5.4(b) n.24

U

Ubiles, United States v., 224 F.3d 213 (3d Cir.2000)—§ 3.8(d) n.167

Udziela, United States v., 671 F.2d 995 (7th Cir.1982)—§§ 1.7(i) n.177; 15.5(b) n.36, 46, 49, 50, 52, 54; 15.7(e) n.94 to 96, 104, 124

Uganiza, State v., 68 Haw. 28, 702 P.2d 1352 (1985)—§ 6.7(c) n.111

Ulestad, State v., 127 Wash.App. 209, 111 P.3d 276 (2005)—§ 24.2(f) n.89

Ulibarri, People v., 671 P.2d 1325 (Colo.App.1983)—§ 14.2(e) n.69

Ulibarri, State v., 128 N.M. 686, 997 P.2d 818 (2000)—§§ 15.6(f) n.203; 15.7(g) n.189, 201

Ulibarri, State v., 128 N.M. 546, 994 P.2d 1164 (1999)—§ 2.11(a) n.14

Ullah, United States v., 976 F.2d 509 (9th Cir.1992)—§ 22.1(h) n.160

Ullery, People v., 984 P.2d 586 (Colo.1999)—§§ 20.5(c) n.55; 20.5(f) n.80

Ullery v. State, 988 P.2d 332 (Okl.Cr.App.1999)—§ 18.4(c) n.44

Ullmann v. United States, 350 U.S. 422, 76 S.Ct. 497, 100 L.Ed. 511 (1956)—§§ 2.9(d) n.77; 2.10(b) n.25; 2.10(c) n.52, 68, 89, 90, 96; 2.10(d) n.130; 8.11(a) n.5

Ulloa, United States v., 882 F.2d 41 (2d Cir.1989)—§ 5.2(a) n.19

Ullring, State v., 741 A.2d 1065 (Me.1999)—§ 3.9(j) n.207

Ulster County Court v. Allen, 442 U.S. 140, 99 S.Ct. 2213, 60 L.Ed.2d 777 (1979)—§§ 28.4(c) n.25, 26

Under Griffin v. California, 380 U.S. 609, 85 S.Ct. 1229, 14 L.Ed.2d 106 (1965)—§ 15.7(d) n.89

Under Seal, United States v., 757 F.2d 600 (4th Cir.1985)—§ 27.5(a) n.32

(Under Seal), United States v., 745 F.2d 834 (4th Cir.1984)—§ 8.12(g) n.64

Underwood, In re, 9 Cal.3d 345, 107 Cal.Rptr. 401, 508 P.2d 721 (1973)—§ 12.3(b) n.75

Underwood v. Johnson, 651 So.2d 760 (Fla.App.1995)—§ 27.4(c) n.23

Underwood v. State, 708 So.2d 18 (Miss.1998)—§ 22.3(d) n.202

Underwood, State v., 228 Kan. 294, 615 P.2d 153 (1980)—§ 21.4(a) n.27

Underwood, United States v., 717 F.2d 482 (9th Cir.1983)—§ 9.1(b) n.79

Ungar v. Sarafite, 376 U.S. 575, 84 S.Ct. 841, 11 L.Ed.2d 921 (1964)— § 11.4(c) n.72

Unger, United States v., 665 F.2d 251 (8th Cir.1981)—§ 21.2(g) n.411

Unger, United States v., 469 F.2d 1283 (7th Cir.1972)—§ 3.3(d) n.151

Uniformed Sanitation Men Association v. Commissioner of Sanitation, 392 U.S. 280, 88 S.Ct. 1917, 20 L.Ed.2d 1089 (1968)—§§ 2.10(b) n.41; 8.10(f) n.130

United v. Jackson, 327 F.3d 273 (4th Cir.2003)—§ 19.3(a) n.32

United Bhd. of Carpenters v. United States, 330 U.S. 395, 67 S.Ct. 775, 91 L.Ed. 973 (1947)—§ 22.1(a) n.18

United Electrical Radio & Machine Workers of America, Application of, 111 F.Supp. 858 (S.D.N.Y.1953)—§ 8.3(h) n.38

United Mine Workers of America v. Bagwell, 512 U.S. 821, 114 S.Ct. 2552, 129 L.Ed.2d 642 (1994)—§ 8.5(b) n.59

United Shoe Machinery Corp., In re, 73 F.Supp. 207 (D.Mass.1947)—§ 8.7(b) n.55

United States, Application of, 427 F.2d 639 (9th Cir.1970)—§ 4.6(g) n.140

United States, Ex parte, 287 U.S. 241, 53 S.Ct. 129, 77 L.Ed. 283 (1932)—§ 3.5(a) n.61

United States, In re, 441 F.3d 44 (1st Cir.2006)—§ 15.6(g) n.216

United States, In re, 441 F.Supp.2d 816 (S.D. Tex 2006)—§ 4.3(c) n.18

United States, In re, 397 F.3d 274 (5th Cir.2005)—§ 13.4(b) n.69

United States, In re, 426 F.3d 1 (1st Cir.2005)—§§ 1.7(i) n.193; 22.2(a) n.2; 22.2(d) n.91, 97

United States, In re, 345 F.3d 450 (7th Cir.2003)—§§ 13.3(c) n.41, 43; 21.3(e) n.280; 27.4(d) n.54

United States, In re, 878 F.2d 153 (5th Cir.1989)—§ 20.3(i) n.177

United States, In re, 834 F.2d 283 (2d Cir.1987)—§§ 20.3(b) n.38, 54 to 56

United States, In re, 610 F.2d 1148 (3d Cir.1979)—§ 4.7(a) n.2

United States, In re Application of the, 416 F.Supp.2d 13 (D.D.C. 2006)—§ 4.7(c) n.13

United States, In re Application of the, 396 F.Supp.2d 294 (E.D.N.Y. 2005)—§ 4.7(c) n.21

United States, In re Application of the, 402 F.Supp.2d 597 (D. Md. 2005)—§ 4.7(c) n.21

United States Coin and Currency, United States v., 401 U.S. 715, 91 S.Ct. 1041, 28 L.Ed.2d 434 (1971)—§§ 2.11(c) n.33; 28.6(e) n.39

United States Currency in the Amount of $228,536.00, United States v., 895 F.2d 908 (2d Cir.1990)—§ 21.4(d) n.132

United States District Court, United States v., 407 U.S. 297, 92 S.Ct. 2125, 32 L.Ed.2d 752 (1972)—§ 4.9(a) n.3

United States District Court, United States v., 444 F.2d 651 (6th Cir.1971)—§ 4.9(a) n.2

United States District Court, United States v., 238 F.2d 713 (4th Cir.1956)—§ 8.8(b) n.15

United States District Court (DeLorean), United States v., 717 F.2d 478 (9th Cir.1983)—§ 20.2(d) n.80

United States District Court For The Eastern District Of California, United States v., 464 F.3d 1065 (9th Cir.2006)—§§ 22.1(h) n.154; 27.4(d) n.58

United States—see opposing party

United States for a Material Witness Warrant, In re Application of the, 213 F.Supp.2d 287 (S.D.N.Y.2002)—§ 12.4(g) n.102

United States for an Order Authorizing Disclosure of Certain Matters Before the Regular Friday 7/1/96 Grand Jury, In re Application of, 1998 WL 817759 (E.D.N.Y.1998)—§ 8.5(c) n.116

United States for an Order Authorizing the Release of Prospective Cell Site Information, In re Application of the, 407 F.Supp.2d 134 (D.D.C. Jan. 11, 2006)—§ 4.7(c) n.21

United States for an Order Authorizing Use of A Pen Register, In re Application of, 396 F.Supp.2d 45 (D. Mass. 2005)—§§ 4.4(d) n.14; 4.6(b) n.33; 4.7(c) n.13

United States For a Nunc Pro Tunc Order For Disclosure of Telecommunications Records, In re Application of, 352 F. Supp.2d 45 (D.Mass. 2005)—§ 4.8(e) n.55

United States for Disclosure, Petition of, 518 F.Supp. 163 (E.D.Wis.1981)— § 8.8(e) n.142

United States for Disclosure of Grand Jury Matters, Petition of, 510 F.Supp. 585 (E.D.Wis.1981)— § 8.5(h) n.255

United States Gypsum Co., United States v., 333 U.S. 364, 68 S.Ct. 525, 92 L.Ed. 746 (1948)— § 27.5(e) n.162

United States Industries v. United States District Court, 345 F.2d 18 (9th Cir.1965)—§ 8.5(h) n.260

United States of America, In re, 846 F.Supp. 1555 (M.D. Fla. 1994)— § 4.7(b) n.11

United States Securities and Exchange Commission v. First Jersey Securities, Inc., 843 F.2d 74 (2d Cir.1988)—§§ 8.13(a) n.16, 27

United States, United States ex rel. v. Ellis, 121 F.3d 908 (4th Cir.1997)— § 24.3(b) n.36

Universal C.I.T. Credit Co., United States v., 344 U.S. 218, 73 S.Ct. 227, 97 L.Ed. 260 (1952)— § 17.3(b) n.15

Universal Manufacturing Co. v. United States, 508 F.2d 684 (8th Cir.1975)—§ 8.8(e) n.123

Universal Manufacturing Co., United States v., 525 F.2d 808 (8th Cir.1975)—§§ 8.4(b) n.26; 8.5(e) n.173

Universal Milk Bottle Service, United States v., 85 F.Supp. 622 (N.D.Ohio 1949)—§ 19.4(b) n.33

Universita, United States v., 192 F.Supp. 154 (S.D.N.Y.1961)—§ 14.2(b) n.26

University of Colorado v. Derdeyn, 863 P.2d 929 (Colo.1993)—§ 3.9(k) n.267

University of North Carolina v. Foy, 3 N.C. 310, 2 Hayw. (N.C.) 310 (1804)—§§ 2.4(b) n.38; 2.4(c) n.95

University of Pennsylvania v. Equal Employment Opportunity Commission, 493 U.S. 182, 110 S.Ct. 577, 107 L.Ed.2d 571 (1990)—§§ 8.8(d) n.47, 80

Unnamed Defendant, State v., 150 Wis.2d 352, 441 N.W.2d 696 (1989)—§§ 8.1(c) n.32; 13.2(a) n.3

Unnamed Petitioners, State ex rel. v. Connors, 136 Wis.2d 118, 401 N.W.2d 782 (1987)—§ 13.2(a) n.3

Unruh, United States v., 855 F.2d 1363 (9th Cir.1987)—§ 11.9(d) n.208

Updike v. People, 92 Colo. 125, 18 P.2d 472 (1933)—§ 16.4(c) n.48

Upham, United States v., 168 F.3d 532 (1st Cir.1999)—§ 3.2(h) n.212

Upham, State ex rel. v. Bonebrake, 303 Or. 361, 736 P.2d 1020 (1987)— § 20.3(i) n.177

Upjohn Company v. United States, 449 U.S. 383, 101 S.Ct. 677, 66 L.Ed.2d 584 (1981)—§§ 8.6(b) n.51; 8.12(b) n.28

Upshaw v. United States, 335 U.S. 410, 69 S.Ct. 170, 93 L.Ed. 100 (1948)— § 6.3(a) n.8

Upshur, Commonwealth v., 882 A.2d 499 (Pa.Super.Ct.2005)—§ 23.1(d) n.180

Upshur v. United States, 742 A.2d 887 (D.C.App.1999)—§ 21.4(c) n.95

Upton, Commonwealth v., 394 Mass. 363, 476 N.E.2d 548 (1985)— §§ 2.12(a) n.26; 3.3(c) n.82

Upton v. State, 343 Ark. 543, 36 S.W.3d 740 (2001)—§ 6.8(b) n.63

Upton, United States v., 91 F.3d 677 (5th Cir.1996)—§ 27.5(b) n.40

Upton, United States v., 856 F.Supp. 727 (E.D.N.Y.1994)—§ 19.4(a) n.2

Upton, United States v., 763 F.Supp. 232 (S.D.Ohio 1991)—§ 4.6(b) n.41

Urbigkit v. State, 67 P.3d 1207 (Wyo.2003)—§ 3.3(c) n.111

Uresti v. Lynaugh, 821 F.2d 1099 (5th Cir.1987)—§§ 21.3(b) n.82, 84

Uriarte, State v., 194 Ariz. 275, 981 P.2d 575 (1998)—§ 24.4(d) n.54

Urias, State v., 609 P.2d 1326 (Utah 1980)—§ 27.6(b) n.43

Uribe, United States v., 890 F.2d 554 (1st Cir.1989)—§ 4.6(m) n.237

Uribe-Londo, United States v., 409 F.3d 1 (1st Cir.2005)—§ 21.3(d) n.218

Ursery, United States v., 109 F.3d 1129 (6th Cir.1997)—§ 24.5(b) n.22

Ursery, United States v., 518 U.S. 267, 116 S.Ct. 2135, 135 L.Ed.2d 549 (1996)—§§ 25.1(b) n.17; 25.1(c) n.32

Usenia, State v., 599 A.2d 1026 (R.I.1991)—§ 20.3(j) n.202

Usher, United States v., 703 F.2d 956 (6th Cir.1983)—§ 21.2(b) n.53

Usry, State v., 205 Conn. 298, 533 A.2d 212 (1987)—§ 6.9(e) n.88

Ussery, People v., 24 Ill.App.3d 864, 321 N.E.2d 718 (1974)—§ 3.5(a) n.5

U.S. Telecom Ass'n v. F.C.C., 227 F.3d 450 (D.C. Cir.2000)—§§ 4.3(c) n.17, 18

Utica Daw's Drug Co., People v., 16 A.D.2d 12, 225 N.Y.S.2d 128 (1962)—§§ 13.4(a) n.24; 13.4(b) n.35; 13.4(c) n.115

Utley, State v., 956 S.W.2d 489 (Tenn.1997)—§ 18.1(c) n.22

Uttecht v. Brown, _____ U.S. _____, 127 S.Ct. 2218, 167 L.Ed.2d 1014 (2007)—§§ 22.3(c) n.146; 28.6(f) n.69

Utterback, State v., 240 Neb. 981, 485 N.W.2d 760 (1992)—§ 3.4(d) n.58

Utz v. Cullinane, 520 F.2d 467 (D.C.Cir.1975)—§ 1.7(k) n.270

Uwaezhoke, United States v., 995 F.2d 388 (3d Cir.1993)—§ 22.3(d) n.226

V

Vaden v. State, 768 P.2d 1102 (Alaska 1989)—§ 5.4(c) n.47

Vader, State v., 114 N.J.Super. 260, 276 A.2d 151 (1971)—§ 3.9(e) n.75

Vaise v. Delaval, 99 Eng.Rep. 944 (KB 1785)—§ 24.9(g) n.108

Valadez, United States v., 267 F.3d 395 (5th Cir.2001)—§ 3.8(b) n.38

Valdes, United States v., 876 F.2d 1554 (11th Cir.1989)—§ 3.7(d) n.71

Valdez v. Cockrell, 274 F.3d 941 (5th Cir.2001)—§ 28.7(a) n.4

Valdez v. Gunter, 988 F.2d 91 (10th Cir.1993)—§ 24.2(a) n.8

Valdez v. People, 966 P.2d 587 (Colo.1998)—§ 22.3(d) n.216

Valdez, People v., 911 P.2d 703 (Colo.App.1996)—§§ 27.5(a) n.2, 3

Valdez, People v., 789 P.2d 406 (Colo.1990)—§ 11.1(d) n.128

Valdez v. Scully, 627 F.Supp. 714 (S.D.N.Y.1986)—§ 11.10(c) n.111

Valdez v. State, 900 P.2d 363 (Okla.Crim.App.1995)—§ 6.4(e) n.95

Valdez, State v., 83 N.M. 632, 495 P.2d 1079 (1972)—§ 16.3(d) n.53

Valdez v. State, 83 N.M. 720, 497 P.2d 231 (1972)—§ 16.3(f) n.90

Valdez v. United States, 906 A.2d 284 (D.C.App.2006)—§ 21.5(c) n.94

Valdez, United States v., 146 F.3d 547 (8th Cir.1998)—§ 6.9(f) n.139

Valdez, United States v., 931 F.2d 1448 (11th Cir.1991)—§ 3.1(d) n.109

Valdez v. Ward, 219 F.3d 1222 (10th Cir.2000)—§§ 6.4(f) n.140; 6.8(a) n.36

Valdez-Sanchez, United States v., 414 F.3d 539 (5th Cir.2005)—§ 21.2(d) n.206

Vale v. Louisiana, 399 U.S. 30, 90 S.Ct. 1969, 26 L.Ed.2d 409 (1970)—§ 3.6(e) n.105

Valen, United States v., 479 F.2d 467 (3d Cir.1973)—§ 3.1(h) n.190

Valencia, State v., 118 Ariz. 136, 575 P.2d 335 (1977)—§ 7.5(a) n.8

Valencia, United States v., 826 F.2d 169 (2d Cir.1987)—§ 27.3(c) n.45

Valencia, United States v., 669 F.2d 37 (2d Cir.1981)—§ 5.1(c) n.30

Valensia, United States v., 299 F.3d 1068 (9th Cir.2002)—§ 21.4(e) n.156

Valenti, State v., 772 A.2d 127 (R.I.2001)—§ 9.6(b) n.54

Valentin v. State, 685 N.E.2d 1100 (Ind.App.1997)—§ 2.12(b) n.83

Valentine v. Konteh, 395 F.3d 626 (6th Cir.2005)—§ 19.3(b) n.171

Valentine, State v., 208 W.Va. 513, 541 S.E.2d 603 (2000)—§ 21.5(c) n.83

Valentine, State v., 506 S.W.2d 406 (1974)—§ 16.1(g) n.241

Valentine, State v., 264 Or. 54, 504 P.2d 84 (1972)—§ 3.4(h) n.141

Valenzuela, State v., 590 So.2d 89 (La.App.1991)—§ 4.6(b) n.49

Valenzuela-Bernal, United States v., 458 U.S. 858, 102 S.Ct. 3440, 73 L.Ed.2d 1193 (1982)—§§ 2.7(a) n.18; 2.7(b) n.73, 94; 24.3(b) n.26; 24.3(h) n.181

Valenzuela-Puentes, United States v., 479 F.3d 1220 (10th Cir.2007)—§ 24.2(g) n.96

Valera, State v., 74 Haw. 424, 848 P.2d 376 (1993)—§§ 6.10(e) n.69; 26.5(a) n.8

Valle v. State, 132 P.3d 181 (Wyo.2006)—§ 21.4(d) n.134

Vallejo, United States v., 237 F.3d 1008 (9th Cir.2001)—§ 6.8(a) n.36

Vallejos, State v., 123 N.M. 739, 945 P.2d 957 (1997)—§§ 5.2(b) n.24, 33

Vallejos, State v., 118 N.M. 572, 883 P.2d 1269 (N.M. 1994)—§ 10.3(c) n.57

Valles, People v., 62 N.Y.2d 36, 476 N.Y.S.2d 50, 464 N.E.2d 418 (1984)—§§ 15.7(f) n.179; 15.7(g) n.215, 217

Valley v. State, 765 So.2d 721 (Fla.App. 5 Dist. Jul 05, 2000)—§ 11.9(b) n.53

Valley, State v., 252 Mont. 489, 830 P.2d 1255 (1992)—§ 3.3(d) n.158

Vallo v. State, 726 P.2d 1045 (Wyo.1986)—§ 21.6(c) n.120

Valona, United States v., 834 F.2d 1334 (7th Cir.1987)—§ 18.5(b) n.65

Valpredo, State v., 75 Wash.2d 368, 450 P.2d 979 (1969)—§ 6.10(b) n.11

Van Ackeren, State v., 242 Neb. 479, 495 N.W.2d 630 (1993)—§ 24.8(c) n.39

Van Alstine, State v., 305 Minn. 276, 232 N.W.2d 899 (1975)—§ 15.4(b) n.35

Van Atta v. Scott, 27 Cal.3d 424, 166 Cal.Rptr. 149, 613 P.2d 210 (1980)—§ 12.1(d) n.56

Van Buren, United States v., 804 F.2d 888 (6th Cir.1986)—§ 21.4(c) n.78

Vance v. Holland, 177 W.Va. 607, 355 S.E.2d 396 (1987)—§ 26.2(c) n.46

Vance v. State, 620 N.E.2d 687 (Ind.1993)—§ 9.1(b) n.80

Van Cleave, State v., 674 N.E.2d 1293 (Ind.1996)—§ 11.10(d) n.176

Van Cleave, State v., 239 Kan. 117, 716 P.2d 580 (1986)—§§ 11.7(e) n.72, 88, 92

Vandebogart, State v., 139 N.H. 145, 652 A.2d 671 (1994)—§§ 3.3(f) n.211; 27.6(b) n.47

VandeHoek v. Weber, 724 N.W.2d 858 (S.D.2006)—§ 21.2(d) n.167

Vandenberg, State v., 134 N.M. 566, 81 P.3d 19 (2003)—§§ 3.8(e) n.199; 3.10(a) n.2

Vandenberg v. Superior Court, 8 Cal.App.3d 1048, 87 Cal.Rptr. 876 (1970)—§§ 3.10(d) n.121; 3.10(e) n.144, 146

Vanderbilt v. Collins, 994 F.2d 189 (5th Cir.1993)—§ 25.4(c) n.33

Vandervort, State v., 276 Kan. 164, 72 P.3d 925 (2003)—§ 6.6(d) n.45

Van Doren, United States v., 182 F.3d 1077 (9th Cir.1999)—§ 21.5(c) n.83

Van Dyken, State v., 242 Mont. 415, 791 P.2d 1350 (1990)—§ 25.2(e) n.37

Van Engel, United States v., 15 F.3d 623 (7th Cir.1993)—§ 11.8(b) n.29

Van Engel, United States v., 809 F.Supp. 1360 (E.D.Wis.1992)—§§ 8.5(i) n.313; 8.8(g) n.167; 15.6(c) n.96

Vang, State v., 700 N.W.2d 491 (Minn.App.2005)—§ 25.3(a) n.7

Van Hook v. Anderson, 444 F.3d 830 (6th Cir.2006)—§ 6.9(f) n.134

Van Hooser, State v., 266 Or. 19, 511 P.2d 359 (1973)—§ 27.6(b) n.45

Van Horn v. City of Trenton, 80 N.J. 528, 404 A.2d 615 (1979)— § 8.10(d) n.106

Van Horn, United States v., 277 F.3d 48 (1st Cir.2002)—§ 5.3(a) n.4

Van Horn, United States v., 976 F.2d 1180 (8th Cir.1992)—§ 21.2(d) n.177

Van Horn, United States v., 789 F.2d 1492 (11th Cir.1986)—§§ 4.6(e) n.110; 4.6(i) n.156

Vanisi v. State, 117 Nev. 330, 22 P.3d 1164 (Nev.2001)—§§ 11.5(d) n.71, 83

Van Kirk, State v., 306 Mont. 215, 32 P.3d 735 (2001)—§§ 6.7(b) n.41; 27.6(b) n.57

Van Krieken, United States v., 39 F.3d 227 (9th Cir.1994)—§ 11.5(c) n.53

Van Leeuwen, United States v., 397 U.S. 249, 90 S.Ct. 1029, 25 L.Ed.2d 282 (1970)—§§ 3.7(b) n.27; 3.8(h) n.246; 3.9(f) n.89; 4.2(a) n.3; 4.2(b) n.13

Van Lufkins, United States v., 676 F.2d 1189 (8th Cir.1982)—§ 6.3(b) n.40

VanMeter, United States v., 278 F.3d 1156 (10th Cir.2002)—§§ 4.6(e) n.89, 97, 99; 4.6(i) n.153

Van Metre, State v., 176 W.Va. 365, 342 S.E.2d 450 (1986)—§ 22.3(c) n.101

Van Nguyen, State v., 253 Conn. 639, 756 A.2d 833 (2000)—§§ 24.4(d) n.38, 57

Van Oster v. Kansas, 272 U.S. 465, 47 S.Ct. 133, 71 L.Ed. 354 (1926)— § 2.9(d) n.75

Vanover, Commonwealth v., 689 S.W.2d 11 (Ky.1985)—§ 6.9(f) n.106

Vanover, State v., 721 A.2d 430 (R.I.1998)—§ 7.4(g) n.110

Van Patten v. Deppisch, 434 F.3d 1038 (7th Cir.2006)—§§ 11.10(d) n.201; 24.2(f) n.89

Van Pelt, State v., 247 Mont. 99, 805 P.2d 549 (1991)—§§ 24.3(f) n.141, 145

Van Poyck, United States v., 77 F.3d 285 (9th Cir.1996)—§§ 4.6(b) n.51; 4.6(l) n.201

Van Roekel, State v., 472 N.W.2d 919 (S.D.1991)—§ 22.1(h) n.154

Van Someren, United States v., 118 F.3d 1214 (8th Cir.1997)—§ 18.3(b) n.24

Vanterpool, United States v., 394 F.2d 697 (2d Cir.1968)—§ 6.8(c) n.73

VanThournout, United States v., 100 F.3d 590 (8th Cir.1996)— §§ 21.2(e) n.308, 325

Van Tran v. Lindsey, 212 F.3d 1143 (9th Cir.2000)—§ 7.4(d) n.69

Van Tuyl, Commonwealth v., 58 Ky. 1, 71 Am.Dec. 455 (1858)—§ 16.4(c) n.48

VanWagner, State v., 504 N.W.2d 746 (Minn.1993)—§ 6.6(e) n.59

Van Zant v. Waddell, 2 Yerg (Tenn.) 260 (1829)—§ 2.4(b) n.39

Vao Sok, Commonwealth v., 435 Mass. 743, 761 N.E.2d 923 (2002)— § 6.9(c) n.61

Varble v. Commonwealth, 125 S.W.3d 246 (Ky.2004)—§ 22.3(a) n.33

Varela, United States v., 968 F.2d 259 (2d Cir.1992)—§§ 9.6(c) n.58, 61, 63

Vargas, State v., 127 Ariz. 59, 618 P.2d 229 (1980)—§ 21.2(h) n.433

Vargus, State v., 118 R.I. 113, 373 A.2d 150 (1977)—§ 6.9(d) n.70

Varie, State v., 135 Idaho 848, 26 P.3d 31 (2001)—§ 6.9(g) n.166

Vario, United States v., 943 F.2d 236 (2d Cir.1991)—§ 22.3(b) n.68

Varkoni, United States v., 645 F.2d 453 (5th Cir.1981)—§ 19.3(e) n.252

Varner v. Alabama, 497 So.2d 1135 (Ala.Cr.App.1986)—§ 26.6(c) n.37

Varnum, People v., 66 Cal.2d 808, 59 Cal.Rptr. 108, 427 P.2d 772 (1967)—§ 9.1(a) n.11

Vasey, United States v., 834 F.2d 782 (9th Cir.1987)—§§ 3.1(c) n.65; 3.7(a) n.12

Vasky, State v., 218 N.J.Super. 487, 528 A.2d 61 (1987)—§ 15.5(c) n.110

Vasquez v. Hillery, 474 U.S. 254, 106 S.Ct. 617, 88 L.Ed.2d 598 (1986)—§§ 2.11(a) n.4; 15.2(g) n.176; 15.3(d) n.71; 15.4(i) n.202; 15.6(d) n.114; 27.6(d) n.107; 28.5(a) n.35; 28.5(b) n.41

Vasquez, People v., 45 Cal.Rptr.3d 372, 39 Cal.4th 47, 137 P.3d 199 (2006)—§ 22.5(a) n.6

Vasquez, People v., 133 Misc.2d 963, 509 N.Y.S.2d 458 (N.Y.Sup.1986)—§ 18.3(c) n.109

Vasquez, State v., 148 Wash.2d 303, 59 P.3d 648 (2002)—§ 17.4(a) n.53

Vasquez v. State, 990 P.2d 476 (Wyo.1999)—§§ 3.7(a) n.14; 6.7(d) n.145

Vasquez, State v., 129 N.J. 189, 609 A.2d 29 (1992)—§§ 1.7(j) n.218; 21.1(g) n.118

Vasquez, United States v., 7 F.3d 81 (5th Cir.1993)—§ 28.9(b) n.69

Vasquez, United States v., 995 F.2d 40 (5th Cir.1993)—§ 11.9(c) n.114

Vasquez, United States v., 953 F.2d 176 (5th Cir.1992)—§ 3.6(e) n.111

Vasquez, United States v., 966 F.2d 254 (7th Cir.1992)—§ 11.9(c) n.112

Vasquez, United States v., 918 F.2d 329 (2d Cir.1990)—§§ 17.3(d) n.46; 18.3(b) n.36

Vasquez, United States v., 858 F.2d 1387 (9th Cir.1988)—§ 10.2(a) n.7

Vasquez-Aerreola, State v., 327 Ark. 617, 940 S.W.2d 451 (1997)—§ 21.3(d) n.263

Vasquez-Castillo, United States v., 258 F.3d 1207 (10th Cir.2001)—§ 3.9(g) n.130

Vasquez-Ramirez, In re, 443 F.3d 692 (9th Cir.2006)—§§ 21.4(a) n.12; 21.4(g) n.255

Vasquez-Velasco, United States v., 471 F.2d 294 (9th Cir.1973)—§ 21.5(a) n.45

Vassar v. State, 99 P.3d 987 (Wyo.2004)—§ 3.7(c) n.49

Vastine, United States v., 363 F.2d 853 (3d Cir.1966)—§ 24.10(b) n.28

Vastola, United States v., 989 F.2d 1318 (3d Cir.1993)—§ 4.6(m) n.241

Vastola, United States v., 915 F.2d 865 (3d Cir.1990)—§§ 4.6(i) n.149; 4.6(m) n.238

Vaughan, United States v., 13 F.3d 1186 (8th Cir.1994)—§ 21.6(a) n.64

Vaughn v. Commonwealth, 485 S.W.2d 497 (Ky.1972)—§ 15.6(d) n.117

Vaughn v. Rutledge, 265 Ga. 773, 462 S.E.2d 132 (1995)—§ 26.10(b) n.29

Vaughn, State v., 199 Conn. 557, 508 A.2d 430 (1986)—§§ 7.4(e) n.80; 7.4(g) n.116

Vaughn, State v., 101 Wash.2d 604, 682 P.2d 878 (1984)—§ 7.4(c) n.43

Vaughn, United States v., 370 F.3d 1049 (10th Cir.2004)—§ 18.3(b) n.8

Vaughn, United States v., 80 F.3d 549 (D.C.Cir.1996)—§ 5.2(a) n.17

Vauzanges, People v., 158 Ill.2d 509, 199 Ill.Dec. 731, 634 N.E.2d 1085 (1994)—§ 3.3(c) n.143

Vavages, United States v., 151 F.3d 1185 (9th Cir.1998)—§ 24.3(h) n.179

Vaval, United States v., 404 F.3d 144 (2d Cir.2005)—§§ 21.2(d) n.177; 21.2(e) n.317

Vazquez, People v., 194 Ill.App.3d 516, 141 Ill.Dec. 469, 551 N.E.2d 656 (1990)—§ 11.10(c) n.99

Vazquez, United States v., 271 F.3d 93 (3d Cir.2001)—§ 27.5(d) n.128

Vazquez, United States v., 113 F.3d 383 (2d Cir.1997)—§ 12.1(a) n.12

Vazquez, United States v., 857 F.2d 857 (1st Cir.1988)—§ 6.7(c) n.114

Vazquez-Garcia, United States v., 340 F.3d 632 (8th Cir.2003)—§ 21.5(a) n.59

Veatch, United States v., 674 F.2d 1217 (9th Cir.1981)—§ 3.1(h) n.220

Vega v. People, 893 P.2d 107 (Colo.1995)—§ 26.4(i) n.164

Vega, People v., 51 A.D.2d 33, 379 N.Y.S.2d 419 (1976)—§ 7.2(d) n.56

Vega v. Rubin, 73 A.D.2d 658, 423 N.Y.S.2d 193 (1979)—§ 16.1(f) n.221

Vega v. Suthers, 195 F.3d 573 (10th Cir.1999)—§ 5.1(c) n.16

Vega, United States v., 438 F.3d 801 (7th Cir.2006)—§ 12.1(a) n.14

Vega, United States v., 241 F.3d 910 (7th Cir.2001)—§ 21.2(b) n.84

Vega, United States v., 221 F.3d 789 (5th Cir.2000)—§§ 9.1(b) n.46, 54

Vega, United States v., 860 F.2d 779 (7th Cir.1988)—§ 18.3(b) n.38

Vega, United States v., 589 F.2d 1147 (2d Cir.1978)—§ 9.6(b) n.54

Vega-Figueroa, United States v., 234 F.3d 744 (1st Cir.2000)—§§ 6.7(c) n.114; 6.10(b) n.16

Vega-Martinez, United States v., 425 F.3d 15 (1st Cir.2005)—§ 21.2(b) n.57

Vega-Penarete, United States v., 137 F.R.D. 233 (E.D.N.C.1991)—§ 20.5(c) n.47

Veiman, State v., 249 Neb. 875, 546 N.W.2d 785 (1996)—§ 6.6(c) n.33

Veitch, People v., 128 Cal.App.3d 460, 180 Cal.Rptr. 412 (1982)—§ 24.6(d) n.42

Vejar-Urias, United States v., 165 F.3d 337 (5th Cir.1999)—§ 17.2(b) n.71

Vejvoda, State v., 231 Neb. 668, 438 N.W.2d 461 (1989)—§§ 16.1(g) n.250; 16.1(h) n.312

Vela v. Superior Court of Los Angeles, 208 Cal.App.3d 141, 255 Cal.Rptr. 921 (1989)—§ 20.3(j) n.194

Velarde-Gomez, United States v., 269 F.3d 1023 (9th Cir.2001)—§§ 6.5(b) n.25; 9.5(a) n.20

Velasco, United States v., 953 F.2d 1467 (7th Cir.1992)—§§ 8.11(c) n.60, 64; 8.11(e) n.106

Velasco-Medina, United States v., 305 F.3d 839 (9th Cir.2002)—§§ 19.3(a) n.123; 19.3(e) n.210, 239

Velasquez, United States v., 304 F.3d 237 (3d Cir.2002)—§ 26.3(f) n.59

Velasquez, United States v., 885 F.2d 1076 (3d Cir.1989)—§§ 6.2(c) n.127; 6.9(c) n.55; 6.9(f) n.138

Velasquez, United States v., 890 F.2d 717 (5th Cir.1989)—§§ 18.3(b) n.5, 20

Velasquez, United States v., 772 F.2d 1348 (7th Cir.1985)—§§ 17.2(a) n.9; 17.3(c) n.38

Velez v. Schmer, 724 F.2d 249 (1st Cir.1984)—§ 7.4(f) n.95

Velez, United States v., 46 F.3d 688 (7th Cir.1995)—§ 24.7(e) n.64

Velez Carrero, United States v., 77 F.3d 11 (1st Cir.1996)—§ 21.2(e) n.316

Velsicol Chemical Corp., United States v., 498 F.Supp. 1255 (D.D.C.1980)—§ 21.2(b) n.45

Venegas, United States v., 800 F.2d 868 (9th Cir.1986)—§§ 15.7(b) n.31, 32

Venhaus v. Brown, 286 Ark. 229, 691 S.W.2d 141 (1985)—§ 13.3(f) n.58

Vento, United States v., 533 F.2d 838 (3d Cir.1976)—§§ 4.6(i) n.157, 160

Ventresca, United States v., 380 U.S. 102, 85 S.Ct. 741, 13 L.Ed.2d 684 (1965)—§§ 3.3(a) n.14, 21; 3.3(e) n.181; 9.4(b) n.65; 10.3(b) n.11

Ventura v. State, 794 So.2d 553 (Fla.2001)—§ 24.3(d) n.116

Ventura v. State, 801 S.W.2d 225 (Tex.App.1990)—§ 11.2(e) n.220

Ventura-Cruel, United States v., 356 F.3d 55 (1st Cir.2003)—§§ 21.4(f) n.170; 21.4(g) n.261; 25.1(d) n.71

Vera Cruz v. City of Escondido, 139 F.3d 659 (9th Cir.1997)—§ 3.5(a) n.70

Vercillo v. Commodity Futures Trading Comm'n, 147 F.3d 548 (7th Cir.1998)—§ 17.4(b) n.125

Verdoorn, United States v., 528 F.2d 103 (8th Cir.1976)—§ 21.2(h) n.436

Verdugo-Urquidez, United States v., 494 U.S. 259, 110 S.Ct. 1056, 108 L.Ed.2d 222 (1990)—§§ 3.1(g) n.185; 3.1(i) n.237

Verduzco, United States v., 330 F.3d 1182 (9th Cir.2003)—§ 21.4(a) n.22

Verduzco-Martinez, United States v., 186 F.3d 1208 (10th Cir.1999)—§ 17.2(b) n.71

Vergara, United States v., 791 F.Supp. 1095 (N.D.W.Va.1992)—§ 8.11(e) n.110

Verhoef, State v., 627 N.W.2d 437 (S.D.2001)—§ 22.3(c) n.157

Veri, United States v., 108 F.3d 1311 (10th Cir.1997)—§§ 21.4(g) n.226, 243

Vericker, In re, 446 F.2d 244 (2d Cir.1971)—§ 8.11(d) n.76

Vermont Agency of Natural Resources v. United States ex rel. Stevens, 529 U.S. 765, 120 S.Ct. 1858, 146 L.Ed.2d 836 (2000)—§ 13.3(b) n.29

Vernatter, State ex rel. v. Warden, 207 W.Va. 11, 528 S.E.2d 207 (1999)—§ 21.5(c) n.76

Vernier v. State, 909 P.2d 1344 (Wyo.1996)—§§ 19.3(b) n.161, 163

Vernon v. Alabama, 313 U.S. 547, 61 S.Ct. 1092, 85 L.Ed. 1513 (1941)—§ 6.2(c) n.83

Vernon, State v., 218 Neb. 539, 356 N.W.2d 887 (1984)—§ 22.1(h) n.134

Vernon, State v., 45 N.C.App. 486, 263 S.E.2d 340 (1980)—§ 1.7(j) n.234

Vernonia School District 47J v. Acton—§ 3.9(k)

Vernonia School District 47J v. Acton, 515 U.S. 646, 115 S.Ct. 2386, 132 L.Ed.2d 564 (1995)—§§ 3.9(a) n.5; 3.9(k) n.259

Verrecchia, State v., 766 A.2d 377 (R.I.2001)—§§ 18.2(c) n.53; 18.2(e) n.76, 80

Verrusio, United States v., 803 F.2d 885 (7th Cir.1986)—§§ 8.11(e) n.108; 21.2(d) n.244

Verstoppen, State v., 185 Wis.2d 728, 519 N.W.2d 653 (Wis.App.1994)—§ 26.10(c) n.48

Vertner v. State, 272 Ind. 550, 400 N.E.2d 134 (1980)—§ 21.4(c) n.96

Verweire, State ex rel. v. Moore, 211 S.W.3d 89 (Mo.2007)—§ 21.4(f) n.192

Vescovo Special Grand Jury, In re, 473 F.Supp. 1335 (C.D.Cal.1979)—§ 8.5(d) n.148

Vest, United States v., 116 F.3d 1179 (7th Cir.1997)—§ 24.4(b) n.13

Vest, United States v., 125 F.3d 676 (8th Cir.1997)—§ 21.2(b) n.59

Vest, United States v., 813 F.2d 477 (1st Cir.1987)—§ 4.6(m) n.220

Vetere, United States v., 663 F.Supp. 381 (S.D.N.Y.1987)—§§ 15.5(b) n.57; 15.6(f) n.184

Via, State v., 146 Ariz. 108, 704 P.2d 238 (1985)—§ 22.3(a) n.7

Via v. Superintendent, 643 F.2d 167 (4th Cir.1981)—§ 21.5(d) n.101

Vick v. Williams, 233 F.3d 213 (4th Cir.2000)—§ 25.1(c) n.31

Vickers, State v., 148 Wash.2d 91, 59 P.3d 58 (2002)—§ 7.4(e) n.82

Vickers, State v., 985 S.W.2d 1 (Tenn.Crim.App.1997)—§ 17.4(a) n.55

Vickers v. State, 878 S.W.2d 329 (Tex. 1994)—§ 10.1(b) n.19

Vickers, State v., 159 Ariz. 532, 768 P.2d 1177 (1989)—§§ 6.6(b) n.16; 6.7(b) n.68

Vicory v. State, 802 N.E.2d 426 (Ind.2004)—§ 26.10(c) n.81

Victor v. Nebraska, 511 U.S. 1, 114 S.Ct. 1239, 127 L.Ed.2d 583 (1994)—§§ 1.5(e) n.220; 2.7(a) n.46; 24.8(c) n.40

Victor, State v., 242 Neb. 306, 494 N.W.2d 565 (1993)—§ 28.11(a) n.9

Victor, State v., 235 Neb. 770, 457 N.W.2d 431 (1990)—§ 6.6(d) n.50

Victor, United States v., 973 F.2d 975 (1st Cir.1992)—§ 24.4(c) n.25

Victory Distributors v. Ayer Dist. Court, 435 Mass. 136, 755 N.E.2d 273 (2001)—§ 13.3(b) n.25

Vida, United States v., 370 F.2d 759 (6th Cir.1966)—§ 17.3(e) n.67

Vidakovich, United States v., 911 F.2d 435 (10th Cir.1990)—§ 21.5(a) n.2

Viduya, People v., 703 P.2d 1281 (Colo.1985)—§ 6.6(a) n.12

Vielguth, United States v., 502 F.2d 1257 (9th Cir.1974)—§ 8.9(b) n.27

Viera, United States v., 819 F.2d 498 (5th Cir.1987)—§ 24.3(h) n.179

Viernes, State v., 92 Haw. 130, 988 P.2d 195 (1999)—§ 13.2(c) n.77

Viers, State v., 86 Nev. 385, 469 P.2d 53 (1970)—§ 27.3(a) n.7

Vigil, State v., 97 N.M. 749, 643 P.2d 618 (1982)—§ 26.10(c) n.70

Vigil, United States v., 561 F.2d 1316 (9th Cir.1977)—§ 17.2(c) n.81

Vigne, State v., 820 So.2d 533 (La.2002)—§§ 6.9(d) n.70; 9.3(e) n.77

Vigorito, In re, 499 F.2d 1351 (2d Cir.1974)—§ 10.1(c) n.42

Vihko v. Commonwealth, 10 Va.App. 498, 393 S.E.2d 413 (1990)—§§ 8.3(h) n.39; 15.2(j) n.237; 15.6(d) n.120

Vilardi, People v., 76 N.Y.2d 67, 556 N.Y.S.2d 518, 555 N.E.2d 915 (1990)—§§ 24.3(b) n.37, 40

Vilhotti, United States v., 323 F.Supp. 425 (S.D.N.Y.1971)—§ 3.2(c) n.123

Villafuerte v. Stewart, 111 F.3d 616 (9th Cir.1997)—§§ 24.8(f) n.91; 28.3(c) n.80

Villalba-Alvarado, United States v., 345 F.3d 1007 (8th Cir.2003)—§ 9.5(b) n.41

Villalobos, People v., 193 Ill.2d 229, 250 Ill.Dec. 17, 737 N.E.2d 639 (2000)—§ 6.9(g) n.200

Villalobos, United States v., 333 F.3d 1070 (9th Cir.2003)—§ 21.5(c) n.83

Villalpando v. Reagan, 211 Ariz. 305, 121 P.3d 172 (Ariz.App.2005)—§ 22.5(a) n.3

Villamonte-Marquez, United States v., 462 U.S. 579, 103 S.Ct. 2573, 77 L.Ed.2d 22 (1983)—§ 3.9(g) n.142

Villano v. United States, 310 F.2d 680 (10th Cir.1962)—§ 9.1(c) n.103

Villanueva v. United States, 346 F.3d 55 (2d Cir.2003)—§ 28.9(b) n.58

Villanueva, United States v., 32 F.Supp.2d 635 (S.D.N.Y. 1998)—§ 4.6(l) n.183

Villa-Perez, State v., 835 S.W.2d 897 (Mo.1992)—§ 3.2(f) n.179

Villareal, People v., 262 Cal.App.2d 438, 68 Cal.Rptr. 610 (1968)—§ 3.9(j) n.203

Villarman-Oviedo, United States v., 325 F.3d 1 (1st Cir.2003)—§§ 4.6(e) n.97; 12.1(a) n.15

Villarreal, People v., 152 Ill.2d 368, 178 Ill.Dec. 400, 604 N.E.2d 923 (1992)—§ 9.4(f) n.115

Villarreal, People v., 100 Mich.App. 379, 298 N.W.2d 738 (1980)—§ 11.9(d) n.190

Villarreal, United States v., 963 F.2d 770 (5th Cir.1992)—§§ 3.5(e) n.206; 4.2(a) n.5

Villarreal-Tamayo, United States v., 467 F.3d 630 (7th Cir.2006)—§ 21.4(d) n.111

Villasenor-Cesar, United States v., 114 F.3d 970 (9th Cir.1997)—§ 21.1(h) n.213

Villegas, State v., 101 Ariz. 465, 420 P.2d 940 (1966)—§ 24.6(b) n.27

Villegas, United States v., 911 F.2d 623 (11th Cir.1990)—§ 26.5(a) n.7

Vinal, State v., 198 Conn. 644, 504 A.2d 1364 (1986)—§ 17.2(d) n.93

Vincennes, City of v. Emmons, 841 N.E.2d 155 (Ind.2006)—§ 9.1(b) n.41

Vincent, State v., 36 La.Ann. 770 (1884)—§ 15.2(h) n.185

Vincent, United States v., 416 F.3d 593 (7th Cir.2005)—§ 15.7(e) n.119

Vincent, United States v., 520 F.2d 1272 (2d Cir.1975)—§ 24.1(b) n.29

Vincik, State v., 436 N.W.2d 350 (Iowa 1989)—§§ 9.3(e) n.56, 64, 82

Vincik, State v., 398 N.W.2d 788 (Iowa 1987)—§§ 6.2(c) n.172, 180

Vincze v. Sheriff, 86 Nev. 474, 470 P.2d 427 (1970)—§ 16.4(c) n.89

Vinegra, State v., 73 N.J. 484, 376 A.2d 150 (1977)—§§ 8.2(c) n.26; 8.10(d) n.87

Vinge, State v., 81 Haw. 309, 916 P.2d 1210 (1996)—§ 24.8(f) n.100

Vingelli v. United States, 992 F.2d 449 (2d Cir.1993)—§ 8.8(d) n.90

Vinieris, United States v., 606 F.Supp. 1390 (S.D.N.Y.1985)—§ 16.1(g) n.251

Vinson, State v., 182 S.W.3d 709 (Mo.App.2006)—§ 18.4(c) n.73

Vinson, United States v., 414 F.3d 924 (8th Cir.2005)—§§ 13.5(b) n.54; 18.4(c) n.46; 21.2(b) n.76

Virag v. Hynes, 54 N.Y.2d 437, 446 N.Y.S.2d 196, 430 N.E.2d 1249 (1981)—§§ 8.8(a) n.13; 8.8(b) n.30

Virdin v. State, 780 A.2d 1024 (Del.2001)—§ 6.9(b) n.36

Virgen-Chavarin, United States v., 350 F.3d 1122 (10th Cir.2003)—§ 21.1(a) n.4

Virgen-Moreno, United States v., 265 F.3d 276 (5th Cir.2001)—§ 6.7(b) n.42

Virgil, United States v., 444 F.3d 447 (5th Cir.2006)—§ 11.5(c) n.49

Virgin, State v., 137 P.3d 787 (Utah 2006)—§§ 14.3(a) n.9; 14.3(b) n.54; 14.3(c) n.63

Virginia, Ex parte, 100 U.S. (10 Otto) 339, 25 L.Ed. 676 (1880)—§ 15.4(c) n.82

Virginia, Commonwealth of v. State of West Virginia, 246 U.S. 565, 38 S.Ct. 400, 59 L.Ed. 1272 (1918)—§ 1.2(b) n.8

Virginia Department of Corrections v. Clark, 227 Va. 525, 318 S.E.2d 399 (1984)—§ 11.10(c) n.122

Virginia Erection Corp., United States v., 335 F.2d 868 (4th Cir.1964)—§ 22.3(e) n.285

Virgin Islands, Government of v. Duberry, 923 F.2d 317 (3d Cir.1991)—§ 18.3(b) n.7

Virgin Islands, Government of v. Edinborough, 625 F.2d 472 (3d Cir.1980)—§ 24.4(d) n.54

Virgin Islands, Government of v. Fahie, 419 F.3d 249 (3d Cir.2005)—§§ 20.3(j) n.211; 20.6(b) n.43; 24.3(b) n.74

Virgin Islands, Government of v. Forte, 865 F.2d 59 (3d Cir.1989)—§§ 11.10(c) n.82; 22.3(d) n.192

Virgin Islands, Government of v. George, 741 F.2d 643 (3d Cir.1984)—§ 26.4(i) n.166

Virgin Islands, Government of v. James, 934 F.2d 468 (3d Cir.1991)—§§ 11.4(b) n.21; 11.4(d) n.116; 11.5(c) n.34

Virgin Islands, Government of v. Martinez, 780 F.2d 302 (3d Cir.1985)—§ 24.3(b) n.60

Virgin Islands, Government of v. Sanes, 57 F.3d 338 (3d Cir.1995)—§§ 7.4(b) n.37; 7.4(c) n.48, 52

Virgin Islands, Government of v. Scotland, 614 F.2d 360 (3d Cir.1980)—§§ 21.2(f) n.377, 380, 383, 384

Virgin Islands, Government of v. Smith, 615 F.2d 964 (3d Cir.1980)—§ 24.3(i) n.188

Virgin Islands, Government of v. Testamark, 570 F.2d 1162 (3d Cir.1978)—§ 20.6(b) n.57

Virgin Islands, Government of v. Weatherwax, 77 F.3d 1425 (3d Cir.1996)—§§ 11.6(a) n.37, 40, 41; 11.6(b) n.67, 74; 11.6(c) n.91, 103, 104; 11.10(c) n.69

Virgin Islands, Government of v. Zepp, 748 F.2d 125 (3d Cir.1984)—§§ 11.9(c) n.145; 11.9(d) n.213, 214, 222

Virgin Islands, Government of the v. Josiah, 641 F.2d 1103 (3d Cir.1981)—§ 25.4(b) n.22

Virgin Islands, Government of the v. Mills, 956 F.2d 443 (3d Cir.1992)—§ 24.3(h) n.182

Virgin Islands, Government of the v. Walker, 261 F.3d 370 (3d Cir.2001)—§§ 21.2(c) n.132; 21.3(d) n.218

Visage v. State, 664 So.2d 1101 (Fla.App.1995)—§ 11.5(d) n.79

Vispi, United States v., 545 F.2d 328 (2d Cir.1976)—§ 18.1(c) n.42

Visser, In re, 968 F.2d 1319 (D.C.Cir.1992)—§ 13.3(f) n.61

Vita, United States v., 294 F.2d 524 (2d Cir.1961)—§ 6.3(a) n.14

Vitale, State v., 197 Conn. 396, 497 A.2d 956 (1985)—§ 6.4(g) n.154

Vitarelli v. Seaton, 359 U.S. 535, 79 S.Ct. 968, 3 L.Ed.2d 1012 (1959)—§ 1.7(j) n.229

Vite-Espinoza, United States v., 342 F.3d 462 (6th Cir.2003)—§ 9.3(e) n.56

Vitek v. State, 750 N.E.2d 346 (Ind.2001)—§ 9.6(b) n.54

Vitoratos v. Maxwell, 351 F.2d 217 (6th Cir.1965)—§ 11.2(b) n.43

Viverito, Commonwealth v., 422 Mass. 228, 661 N.E.2d 1304 (1996)—§ 14.2(g) n.96

Vlahos, United States v., 33 F.3d 758 (7th Cir.1994)—§§ 22.5(d) n.30; 27.3(b) n.16, 18

Vlcek, People v., 114 Ill.App.2d 74, 252 N.E.2d 377 (1969)—§ 6.10(b) n.17

Vogel v. Commonwealth of Pennsylvania, 790 F.2d 368 (3d Cir.1986)—§ 25.4(c) n.28

Vogel, State v., 428 N.W.2d 272 (S.D.1988)—§ 3.2(c) n.109

Vogelsberg, State v., 724 N.W.2d 649 (Wis.App.2006)—§§ 24.2(e) n.75, 78

Vogl, United States v., 374 F.3d 976 (10th Cir.2004)—§ 18.3(b) n.25

Void v. State, 325 Md. 386, 601 A.2d 124 (1992)—§ 24.3(f) n.140

Voigt, State v., 734 N.W. 2d 787 (N.D. 2007)—§ 25.2(a) n.9

Voigt, United States v., 89 F.3d 1050 (3d Cir.1996)—§§ 11.8(b) n.37; 11.9(c) n.111, 112, 124

Voisine, Commonwealth v., 414 Mass. 772, 610 N.E.2d 926 (1993)—§ 3.6(a) n.32

Volanty v. Lynaugh, 874 F.2d 243 (5th Cir.1989)—§§ 11.2(e) n.154, 165

Volk, State v., 291 So.2d 643 (Fla.App.1974)—§ 3.7(d) n.85

Volpe, United States v., 224 F.3d 72 (2d Cir.2000)—§ 21.1(h) n.213

Volson v. Blackburn, 794 F.2d 173 (5th Cir.1986)—§ 11.2(e) n.152

VonBergen, State v., 317 Mont. 445, 77 P.3d 537 (2003)—§ 10.1(a) n.3

von Bulow, State v., 475 A.2d 995 (R.I.1984)—§ 20.3(j) n.206

VonderAhe v. Howland, 508 F.2d 364 (9th Cir.1974)—§ 3.4(f) n.105

Von Eichelberger v. United States, 252 F.2d 184 (9th Cir.1958)—§ 18.5(a) n.12

Von Moltke v. Gillies, 332 U.S. 708, 68 S.Ct. 316, 92 L.Ed. 309 (1948)—§§ 11.3(a) n.9; 11.3(b) n.23

Vonn, United States v., 535 U.S. 55, 122 S.Ct. 1043, 152 L.Ed.2d 90 (2002)—§§ 19.3(e) n.233; 21.5(c) n.84, 87; 27.5(d) n.115

Vonn, United States v., 224 F.3d 1152 (9th Cir.2000)—§ 21.5(c) n.83

Von Neumann, United States v., 474 U.S. 242, 106 S.Ct. 610, 88 L.Ed.2d 587 (1986)—§ 18.1(a) n.2

Vontress, State v., 266 Kan. 248, 970 P.2d 42 (1998)—§§ 17.3(b) n.13; 19.2(b) n.9

Voorhees, State v., 596 N.W.2d 241 (Minn.1999)—§§ 15.4(g) n.162, 165

Vortis, United States v., 785 F.2d 327 (D.C.Cir.1986)—§ 12.3(a) n.23

Voshart, State v., 39 Wis.2d 419, 159 N.W.2d 1 (1968)—§ 3.1(g) n.170

Voss v. State, 856 N.E.2d 1211 (Ind.2006)—§ 22.4(c) n.28

Vroman v. Brigano, 346 F.3d 598 (6th Cir.2003)—§ 28.5(b) n.59

Vujosevic v. Rafferty, 844 F.2d 1023 (3d Cir.1988)—§ 6.9(f) n.113

W

W.A., State v., 184 N.J. 45, 875 A.2d 882 (2005)—§ 24.2(a) n.5

Wabash, St. Louis, and Pacific Railway, People v., 12 Ill.App. 263 (1883)—§ 1.6(d) n.210

Wabaunsee v. State, 554 P.2d 36 (Okla.Cr.App.1976)—§ 22.1(h) n.138

Wacker, State v., 268 Neb. 787, 688 N.W.2d 357 (2004)—§§ 13.5(b) n.57; 13.7(d) n.69

Wacker, United States v., 72 F.3d 1453 (10th Cir.1995)—§ 25.4(b) n.18

Waddell, State v., 655 N.W.2d 803 (Minn.2003)—§ 6.3(c) n.53

Waddell, United States v., 112 U.S. 76, 5 S.Ct. 35, 28 L.Ed. 673 (1884)—§ 15.1(b) n.64

Wade v. Hunter, 336 U.S. 684, 69 S.Ct. 834, 93 L.Ed. 974 (1949)—§§ 25.1(b) n.9; 25.2(d) n.29

Wade v. Lockhart, 763 F.2d 999 (8th Cir.1985)—§ 11.2(g) n.273

Wade v. State, 802 So.2d 1023 (Miss.2001)—§ 21.1(e) n.62

Wade, State v., 105 Nev. 206, 772 P.2d 1291 (1989)—§ 18.4(c) n.36

Wade v. State, 490 N.E.2d 1097 (Ind.1986)—§ 7.2(b) n.19

Wade v. United States, 504 U.S. 181, 112 S.Ct. 1840, 118 L.Ed.2d 524 (1992)—§§ 21.1(h) n.182; 21.2(d) n.251

Wade, United States v., 388 U.S. 218, 87 S.Ct. 1926, 18 L.Ed.2d 1149 (1967)—§§ 1.10(c) n.57; 2.9(g) n.192, 195, 196; 2.9(h) n.211, 236; 2.11(a) n.6; 2.11(c) n.31; 6.7(b) n.35; 7.1(a) n.6; 7.1(b) n.20; 7.1(c) n.28; 7.2(b) n.9; 7.2(c) n.40; 7.3(a) n.1; 7.3(c) n.49; 7.3(d) n.63; 7.4(a) n.1; 7.5(a) n.1; 9.1(a) n.23; 9.4(d) n.87; 9.5(c) n.71; 10.3(d) n.58, 60, 61; 10.4(d) n.27; 27.6(d) n.79

Wadle, People v., 97 P.3d 932 (Colo.2004)—§ 24.9(f) n.85

Wadley v. Commonwealth, 98 Va. 803, 35 S.E. 452 (1900)—§ 15.2(d) n.106

Wadlington, United States v., 233 F.3d 1067 (8th Cir.2000)—§ 8.8(g) n.168

Wadsworth, United States v., 830 F.2d 1500 (9th Cir.1987)—§§ 11.4(b) n.20; 11.4(c) n.84

Wafai v. People, 750 P.2d 37 (Colo.1988)—§§ 16.3(f) n.90, 94

Wagner, State v., 315 Mont. 498, 68 P.3d 840 (2003)—§ 3.8(c) n.82

Wagner, United States v., 103 F.3d 551 (7th Cir.1996)—§ 11.2(c) n.106

Wagner, United States v., 996 F.2d 906 (7th Cir.1993)—§ 21.4(d) n.104

Wagner, United States v., 884 F.2d 1090 (8th Cir.1989)—§ 3.10(c) n.87

Wahl, United States v., 290 F.3d 370 (D.C.Cir.2002)—§ 24.6(b) n.26

Wahlert, State v., 379 N.W.2d 10 (Iowa 1985)—§ 26.10(c) n.79

Waidla, People v., 22 Cal.4th 690, 94 Cal.Rptr.2d 396, 996 P.2d 46 (2000)—§§ 6.9(f) n.129, 139

Wainwright v. Cottle, 414 U.S. 895, 94 S.Ct. 221, 38 L.Ed.2d 138 (1973)—§§ 11.1(d) n.114, 121

Wainwright v. Greenfield, 474 U.S. 284, 106 S.Ct. 634, 88 L.Ed.2d 623 (1986)—§§ 6.5(b) n.25; 9.6(a) n.51

Wainwright v. New Orleans, 392 U.S. 598, 88 S.Ct. 2243, 20 L.Ed.2d 1322 (1968)—§§ 3.1(o) n.304; 3.5(a) n.44

Wainwright, State v., 18 Kan.App.2d 449, 856 P.2d 163 (1993)—§ 11.2(e) n.190

Wainwright v. Sykes, 433 U.S. 72, 97 S.Ct. 2497, 53 L.Ed.2d 594 (1977)—§§ 11.6(a) n.31, 52; 28.2(c) n.40; 28.4(a) n.3, 5, 6, 9; 28.4(d) n.38, 42

Wainwright v. Torna, 455 U.S. 586, 102 S.Ct. 1300, 71 L.Ed.2d 475 (1982)—§§ 11.1(b) n.94; 11.7(a) n.11

Wainwright v. Witt, 469 U.S. 412, 105 S.Ct. 844, 83 L.Ed.2d 841 (1985)—§§ 22.3(c) n.144; 26.1(b) n.28; 27.5(e) n.153; 28.7(b) n.10

Waits v. People, 724 P.2d 1329 (Colo.1986)—§ 21.4(c) n.77

Wajda, State v., 296 Minn. 29, 206 N.W.2d 1 (1973)—§ 10.4(b) n.8

Wake v. Barker, 514 S.W.2d 692 (Ky.1974)—§ 2.12(e) n.211

Wakefield, State v., 130 Wash.2d 464, 925 P.2d 183 (1996)—§ 21.3(d) n.222

Walberg v. Israel, 766 F.2d 1071 (7th Cir.1985)—§ 11.9(d) n.176

Walborn, United States v., 730 F.2d 192 (5th Cir.1984)—§ 18.4(b) n.25

WALB-TV, Inc. v. Gibson, 269 Ga. 564, 501 S.E.2d 821 (1998)—§ 23.3(b) n.18

Walck v. Edmondson, 472 F.3d 1227 (10th Cir.2007)—§ 25.2(d) n.33

Wald, United States v., 208 F.3d 902 (10th Cir.2000)—§ 3.10(f) n.188

Waldbaum, Inc., United States v., 593 F.Supp. 967 (E.D.N.Y.1984)—§§ 15.4(g) n.176, 177, 181; 15.4(h) n.188

Waldemer v. United States, 911 F.Supp. 1105 (S.D.Ill.1996)—§ 19.5(d) n.82

Walden, United States v., 490 F.2d 372 (4th Cir.1974)—§ 1.2(d) n.251

Walden, United States v., 464 F.2d 1015 (4th Cir.1972)—§§ 16.1(f) n.213; 16.2(g) n.116, 139

Walder v. United States, 347 U.S. 62, 74 S.Ct. 354, 98 L.Ed. 503 (1954)—§§ 9.6(a) n.3; 9.6(b) n.52; 9.6(c) n.56; 28.3(c) n.71

Waldner, State v., 692 N.W.2d 187 (S.D.2005)—§ 21.2(d) n.167

Waldrip v. Head, 279 Ga. 826, 620 S.E.2d 829 (2005)—§ 24.3(b) n.49

Waldron, State v., 218 W.Va. 450, 624 S.E.2d 887 (2005)—§ 21.3(e) n.265

Waldron v. United States, 219 F.2d 37 (D.C.Cir.1955)—§ 10.2(b) n.27

Waldrop v. State, 506 So.2d 273 (Miss.1987)—§ 11.10(c) n.98

Waley v. Johnston, 316 U.S. 101, 62 S.Ct. 964, 86 L.Ed. 1302 (1942)—§ 28.3(b) n.53

Walk, United States v., 533 F.2d 417 (9th Cir.1975)—§§ 20.3(b) n.38, 57

Walker, Commonwealth v., 421 Mass. 90, 653 N.E.2d 1080 (1995)—§§ 7.4(b) n.23; 7.5(b) n.21

Walker, Commonwealth v., 470 Pa. 534, 368 A.2d 1284 (1977)—§ 6.9(f) n.103

Walker v. Crosby, 341 F.3d 1240 (11th Cir.2003)—§ 28.5(b) n.50

Walker v. Davis, 840 F.2d 834 (11th Cir.1988)—§ 22.5(c) n.24

Walker v. Girdich, 410 F.3d 120 (2d Cir.2005)—§ 22.3(d) n.214

Walker v. Lockhart, 807 F.2d 136 (8th Cir.1986)—§ 11.10(c) n.84

Walker, People v., 308 Ill.App.3d 435, 241 Ill.Dec. 842, 720 N.E.2d 297 (1999)—§ 25.4(a) n.7

Walker, People v., 461 Mich. 908, 603 N.W.2d 784 (1999)—§ 13.2(c) n.51

Walker, People v., 54 Cal.3d 1013, 1 Cal.Rptr.2d 902, 819 P.2d 861 (1991)—§ 21.2(e) n.349

Walker, People v., 119 Ill.2d 465, 116 Ill.Dec. 675, 519 N.E.2d 890 (Ill.1988)—§ 1.7(f) n.94

Walker, People v., 666 P.2d 113 (Colo.1983)—§ 20.3(g) n.126

Walker, People v., 84 Ill.2d 512, 50 Ill.Dec. 718, 419 N.E.2d 1167 (1981)—§ 21.5(e) n.141

Walker, People v., 189 Colo. 545, 542 P.2d 1283 (1975)—§ 17.1(c) n.45

Walker, People v., 385 Mich. 565, 189 N.W.2d 234 (1971)—§§ 14.3(a) n.35; 14.4(b) n.36

Walker, People v., 50 Misc.2d 751, 271 N.Y.S.2d 447 (1966)—§ 13.4(e) n.171

Walker, People v., 14 N.Y.2d 901, 252 N.Y.S.2d 96, 200 N.E.2d 779 (1964)—§§ 13.4(e) n.172; 13.5(a) n.14, 16

Walker v. Sauvinet, 92 U.S. (2 Otto) 90, 23 L.Ed. 678 (1875)—§§ 2.3(b) n.83; 2.4(c) n.108; 2.4(d) n.120

Walker v. Schneider, 477 N.W.2d 167 (N.D.1991)—§§ 14.1(a)   n.4; 14.3(c) n.78, 80

Walker v. State, 195 S.W.3d 250 (Tex.Cr.App.2006)—§§ 11.10(c) n.75, 98; 22.3(a) n.35

Walker v. State, 201 S.W.3d 841 (Tex.App.2006)—§ 18.4(c) n.40

Walker v. State, 161 Md.App. 253, 868 A.2d 898 (2005)—§ 11.10(d) n.195

Walker v. State, 913 So.2d 198 (Miss.2005)—§ 9.1(d) n.132

Walker v. State, 881 So.2d 820 (Miss.2004)—§ 5.4(c) n.32

Walker, State v., 276 Kan. 939, 80 P.3d 1132 (2003)—§ 6.9(g) n.166

Walker v. State, 740 So.2d 873 (Miss.1999)—§ 22.3(d) n.216

Walker v. State, 933 P.2d 327 (Okla.Crim.App.1997)—§ 11.7(e) n.94

Walker, State v., 887 P.2d 971 (Alaska App.1994)—§ 27.3(d) n.59

Walker v. State, 621 N.E.2d 627 (Ind.1993)—§§ 15.4(g) n.168, 171

Walker, State v., 188 W.Va. 661, 425 S.E.2d 616 (1992)—§ 23.2(f) n.92

Walker, State v., 242 Neb. 99, 493 N.W.2d 329 (1992)—§ 6.2(c) n.137

Walker, State v., 154 Wis.2d 158, 453 N.W.2d 127 (1990)—§§ 3.6(a) n.5; 22.3(d) n.245, 252

Walker, State v., 236 Neb. 155, 459 N.W.2d 527 (1990)—§ 3.10(e) n.170

Walker v. State, 303 Ark. 401, 797 S.W.2d 447 (1990)—§ 6.7(c) n.121

Walker, State v., 567 So.2d 581 (La.1990)—§§ 15.5(b) n.45; 15.5(c) n.112; 15.6(a) n.26 to 28

Walker v. State, 781 P.2d 838 (Okla.Crim.App.1989)—§§ 21.6(c) n.118; 22.1(h) n.158

Walker v. State, 102 Nev. 290, 720 P.2d 700 (1986)—§§ 6.6(b) n.15; 6.10(c) n.51

Walker, State v., 236 N.W.2d 292 (Iowa 1975)—§ 13.4(c) n.110

Walker v. State, 255 Ind. 65, 262 N.E.2d 641 (1970)—§ 5.4(b) n.16

Walker v. State, 249 Ind. 551, 233 N.E.2d 483 (1968)—§ 6.2(c) n.102

Walker, State v., 265 N.C. 482, 144 S.E.2d 419 (1965)—§ 1.8(d) n.70

Walker, United States v., 490 F.3d 1282 (11th Cir.2007)—§§ 22.3(d) n.197, 252

Walker, United States v., 447 F.3d 999 (7th Cir.2006)—§ 26.4(d) n.65

Walker, United States v., 255 F.3d 540 (8th Cir.2001)—§§ 18.4(b) n.26; 18.4(c) n.50

Walker, United States v., 272 F.3d 407 (7th Cir.2001)—§§ 6.2(c) n.107; 6.9(g) n.166

Walker, United States v., 112 F.3d 163 (4th Cir.1997)—§ 21.2(d) n.223

Walker v. United States, 115 F.3d 603 (8th Cir.1997)—§ 21.4(f) n.171

Walker, United States v., 98 F.3d 944 (7th Cir.1996)—§ 21.2(e) n.321

Walker, United States v., 910 F.Supp. 861 (N.D.N.Y.1995)—§§ 20.5(h) n.102, 109, 110

Walker, United States v., 931 F.2d 1066 (5th Cir.1991)—§ 3.7(e) n.105

Walker, United States v., 915 F.2d 480 (9th Cir.1990)—§§ 11.4(b) n.18, 28; 11.4(c) n.75, 88

Walker, United States v., 839 F.2d 1483 (11th Cir.1988)—§ 11.8(b) n.37

Walker v. United States, 481 A.2d 1308 (D.C.App.1984)—§ 21.4(a) n.26

Walker, United States v., 653 F.2d 1343 (9th Cir.1981)—§ 19.3(c) n.194

Walker, United States v., 535 F.2d 896 (5th Cir.1976)—§ 9.4(b) n.50

Walker, United States v., 538 F.2d 266 (9th Cir.1976)—§§ 20.3(b) n.59, 60

Walker, United States v., 491 F.2d 236 (9th Cir.1974)—§ 14.4(e) n.110

Walker, United States v., 473 F.2d 136 (D.C.Cir.1972)—§ 21.3(d) n.234

Walker v. United States, 418 F.2d 1116 (D.C.Cir.1969)—§ 24.8(f) n.121

Wall, State v., 348 N.C. 671, 502 S.E.2d 585 (1998)—§§ 21.2(e) n.321; 26.3(f) n.55

Wall, United States v., 92 F.3d 1444 (6th Cir.1996)—§§ 1.2(d) n.202, 235

Wall, United States v., 371 F.2d 398 (6th Cir.1967)—§ 15.7(e) n.130

Wallace v. City of Chicago, 440 F.3d 421 (7th Cir.2006)—§ 2.7(a) n.10

Wallace, Commonwealth v., 582 Pa. 234, 870 A.2d 838 (2005)—§ 21.2(d) n.227

Wallace, Commonwealth v., 417 Mass. 126, 627 N.E.2d 935 (Mass. 1994)—§§ 7.4(e) n.92; 10.4(d) n.32

Wallace, Commonwealth v., 356 Mass. 92, 248 N.E.2d 246 (1969)—§§ 3.1(i) n.226; 6.10(d) n.60

Wallace v. Morrison, 87 F.3d 1271 (11th Cir.1996)—§ 22.3(d) n.228

Wallace, People v., 33 Cal.4th 738, 16 Cal.Rptr.3d 96, 93 P.3d 1037 (2004)—§ 21.4(a) n.22

Wallace, People v., 724 P.2d 670 (Colo.1986)—§ 6.6(e) n.91

Wallace, State v., 105 Hawai'i 131, 94 P.3d 1275 (2004)—§§ 6.6(f) n.114; 6.9(e) n.88

Wallace v. State, 373 Md. 69, 816 A.2d 883 (2003)—§ 3.5(c) n.124

Wallace, State v., 351 N.C. 481, 528 S.E.2d 326 (2000)—§§ 23.2(a) n.27, 29

Wallace v. State, 768 So.2d 1247 (Fla.App.2000)—§ 24.7(e) n.61

Wallace, State v., 345 N.C. 462, 480 S.E.2d 673 (1997)—§§ 21.2(f) n.363; 21.3(e) n.265

Wallace, State v., 80 Haw. 382, 910 P.2d 695 (1996)—§ 25.4(c) n.39

Wallace, State v., 146 N.J. 576, 684 A.2d 1355 (1996)—§§ 13.6(b) n.25; 13.6(c) n.41

Wallace, State v., 258 Kan. 639, 908 P.2d 1267 (1995)—§ 11.9(d) n.211

Wallace v. State, 893 P.2d 504 (Okla.Cr.App.1995)—§ 27.5(c) n.60

Wallace, State v., 475 N.W.2d 197 (Iowa 1991)—§ 24.8(f) n.92

Wallace, State v., 43 Ohio St.2d 1, 330 N.E.2d 697 (1975)—§ 1.7(f) n.104

Wallace, State v., 321 So.2d 349 (La.1975)—§ 8.10(d) n.88

Wallace, State v., 285 So.2d 796 (La.1973)—§§ 7.3(c) n.46; 7.4(e) n.90

Wallace, United States v., 408 F.3d 1046 (8th Cir.2005)—§ 26.4(f) n.93

Wallace, United States v., 323 F.3d 1109 (8th Cir.2003)—§§ 6.6(e) n.68, 72

Wallace, United States v., 276 F.3d 360 (7th Cir.2002)—§ 11.9(d) n.175

Wallace, United States v., 22 F.3d 84 (4th Cir.1994)—§§ 21.2(d) n.258, 259

Wallace, United States v., 848 F.2d 1464 (9th Cir.1988)—§ 24.3(c) n.96

Wallace v. United States, 475 A.2d 401 (D.C.App.1984)—§ 26.10(b) n.19

Wallach, United States v., 935 F.2d 445 (2d Cir.1991)—§ 25.4(a) n.8

Wallach, United States v., 870 F.2d 902 (2d Cir.1989)—§ 15.6(f) n.185

Wallen v. State, 863 S.W.2d 34 (Tenn.1993)—§ 21.4(e) n.161

Waller v. Florida, 397 U.S. 387, 90 S.Ct. 1184, 25 L.Ed.2d 435 (1970)—§§ 1.8(d) n.61, 63; 2.11(c) n.34; 25.5(c) n.31

Waller v. Georgia, 467 U.S. 39, 104 S.Ct. 2210, 81 L.Ed.2d 31 (1984)—§§ 2.6(a) n.16; 12.3(f) n.145; 24.1(a) n.6, 12; 27.6(d) n.110

Waller, United States v., 426 F.3d 838 (6th Cir.2005)—§ 9.1(b) n.81

Walley, Commonwealth v., 262 Pa.Super. 496, 396 A.2d 1280 (1978)—§ 11.6(a) n.44

Walley v. State, 353 Ark. 586, 112 S.W.3d 349 (2003)—§ 3.2(c) n.131

Walling, United States v., 974 F.2d 140 (10th Cir.1992)—§ 18.4(c) n.33

Wallis v. Spencer, 202 F.3d 1126 (9th Cir.2000)—§ 3.9(d) n.72

Walls v. Bowersox, 151 F.3d 827 (8th Cir.1998)—§ 11.10(c) n.130

Walls, People v., 117 Mich.App. 691, 324 N.W.2d 136 (1982)—§ 14.3(c) n.71

Walls v. State, 24 Ga.App. 697, 102 S.E. 43 (1920)—§ 27.6(b) n.13

Walls, United States v., 225 F.3d 858 (7th Cir.2000)—§ 17.2(b) n.69

Walsh, Commonwealth v., 255 Mass. 317, 151 N.E. 300 (1926)—§ 15.4(b) n.73

Walsh v. State, 166 S.W.3d 641 (Tenn.2005)—§§ 24.9(g) n.120, 122

Walsh, State v., 143 Wash.2d 1, 17 P.3d 591 (2001)—§ 21.2(e) n.321

Walsh, State v., 495 N.W.2d 602 (Minn.1993)—§ 6.6(e) n.91

Walsh, United States v., 194 F.3d 37 (2d Cir.1999)—§ 19.4(b) n.30

Walsh, United States v., 7 F.3d 1064 (1st Cir.1993)—§ 21.5(e) n.119

Walston, State v., 140 N.C.App. 327, 536 S.E.2d 630 (2000)—§§ 19.6(b) n.18; 19.6(c) n.39

Walter v. United States, 447 U.S. 649, 100 S.Ct. 2395, 65 L.Ed.2d 410 (1980)—§§ 3.1(h) n.194; 3.5(c) n.126

Walters, In re, 15 Cal.3d 738, 126 Cal.Rptr. 239, 543 P.2d 607 (1975)—§§ 3.5(a) n.48, 53

Walters v. Edgar, 900 F.Supp. 197 (N.D.Ill.1995)—§§ 11.2(f) n.249, 251

Walters v. National Association of Radiation Survivors, 473 U.S. 305, 105 S.Ct. 3180, 87 L.Ed.2d 220 (1985)—§§ 1.5(c) n.135; 11.1(b) n.93

Walters, People v., 148 P.3d 331 (Colo.App.2006)—§ 24.7(e) n.40

Walters, People v., 196 Misc.2d 78, 763 N.Y.S.2d 715 (Sup.Ct.2003)—§ 19.3(a) n.42

Walters v. State, 720 So.2d 856 (Miss.1998)—§ 22.3(d) n.249

Walters, State v., 426 N.W.2d 136 (Iowa 1988)—§§ 16.3(g) n.100 to 102

Walters, State v., 436 So.2d 66 (Fla.1983)—§ 19.3(a) n.69

Walters, United States v., 309 F.3d 589 (9th Cir.2002)—§§ 11.4(c) n.56; 27.6(d) n.143

Walters, United States v., 269 F.3d 1207 (10th Cir.2001)—§ 21.6(a) n.77

Walther, State v., 240 Wis.2d 619, 623 N.W.2d 205 (2000)—§ 20.3(g) n.122

Walton v. Arizona, 497 U.S. 639, 110 S.Ct. 3047, 111 L.Ed.2d 511 (1990)—§§ 22.1(a) n.27; 26.1(b) n.22; 26.4(h) n.156

Walton v. Briley, 361 F.3d 431 (7th Cir.2004)—§ 24.1(a) n.11

Walton v. Roanoke, 204 Va. 678, 133 S.E.2d 315 (1963)—§ 2.12(e) n.208

Walton, State v., 41 S.W.3d 75 (Tenn.2001)—§§ 6.6(e) n.59; 6.7(d) n.155; 9.5(b) n.41, 42

Walton, State v., 227 Conn. 32, 630 A.2d 990 (1993)—§ 16.2(g) n.138

Walton, State v., 227 Neb. 559, 418 N.W.2d 589 (1988)—§§ 22.3(d) n.240, 250

Walton, State v., 424 N.W.2d 444 (Iowa 1988)—§ 7.4(b) n.23

Walton v. State, 481 So.2d 1197 (Fla.1985)—§ 17.2(b) n.49

Walton, United States v., 56 F.3d 551 (4th Cir.1995)—§ 9.4(b) n.73

Walton, United States v., 10 F.3d 1024 (3d Cir.1993)—§§ 6.2(c) n.140; 10.3(c) n.52

Walton, United States v., 411 F.2d 283 (9th Cir.1969)—§ 5.4(b) n.25

Walton v. United States, 334 F.2d 343 (10th Cir.1964)—§§ 6.3(a) n.12, 21

Wamget v. State, 67 S.W.3d 851 (Tex.Cr.App.2001)—§ 22.3(d) n.193

Wandick, United States ex rel. v. Chrans, 869 F.2d 1084 (7th Cir.1989)—§ 22.1(h) n.133

Wang, United States v., 222 F.3d 234 (6th Cir.2000)—§§ 1.2(c) n.177, 178

Wangrow v. United States, 399 F.2d 106 (8th Cir.1968)—§§ 3.4(e) n.89, 92

Wannamaker, State v., 346 S.C. 495, 552 S.E.2d 284 (2001)—§ 6.9(g) n.166

Wansley v. Miller, 353 F.Supp. 42 (E.D.Va.1973)—§ 23.2(a) n.39

Wansley v. State, 256 Ga. 624, 352 S.E.2d 368 (1987)—§ 22.3(b) n.86

War Bonnett, State v., 229 Neb. 681, 428 N.W.2d 508 (1988)—§ 21.4(d) n.110

Ward v. Commonwealth, 62 S.W.3d 399 (Ky.App.2001)—§§ 18.4(c) n.40, 67

Ward, Commonwealth v., 426 Mass. 290, 688 N.E.2d 227 (1997)—§ 6.2(c) n.173

Ward, Commonwealth v., 412 Mass. 395, 590 N.E.2d 173 (1992)—§ 6.9(b) n.23

Ward v. Commonwealth, 695 S.W.2d 404 (Ky.1985)—§§ 22.3(a) n.5; 22.3(c) n.127

Ward, Commonwealth v., 17 Mass.App. 985, 459 N.E.2d 122 (1984)—§ 15.7(e) n.110

Ward v. Commonwealth, 205 Va. 564, 138 S.E.2d 293 (1964)—§ 6.4(c) n.46

Ward, Commonwealth v., 308 Ky. 666, 215 S.W.2d 565 (1948)—§ 16.2(a) n.5

Ward v. Monroeville, 409 U.S. 57, 93 S.Ct. 80, 34 L.Ed.2d 267 (1972)—§§ 1.5(i) n.298; 2.7(c) n.201; 22.4(a) n.3

Ward, People v., 302 Ill.App.3d 550, 236 Ill.Dec. 285, 707 N.E.2d 130 (1998)—§ 19.4(b) n.25

Ward, People v., 234 A.D.2d 723, 651 N.Y.S.2d 649 (1996)—§ 15.2(c) n.78

Ward, People v., 63 Ill.App.3d 864, 20 Ill.Dec. 674, 380 N.E.2d 883 (1978)—§ 7.4(f) n.104

Ward, People v., 72 Ill.2d 379, 21 Ill.Dec. 178, 381 N.E.2d 256 (1978)—§ 17.4(a) n.38

Ward, People v., 32 Ill.App.3d 781, 336 N.E.2d 205 (1975)—§ 22.5(a) n.6

Ward, People v., 37 A.D.2d 174, 323 N.Y.S.2d 316 (1971)—§§ 15.4(g) n.169; 15.4(h) n.196

Ward v. State, 810 N.E.2d 1042 (Ind.2004)—§ 23.2(a) n.48

Ward, State v., 354 N.C. 231, 555 S.E.2d 251 (2001)—§§ 22.3(b) n.86; 22.3(c) n.147

Ward, State v., 231 Wis.2d 723, 604 N.W.2d 517 (2000)—§§ 3.1(c) n.62; 3.3(a) n.25

Ward, State v., 257 Neb. 377, 597 N.W.2d 614 (1999)—§ 18.2(b) n.27

Ward, State v., 123 Wash.2d 488, 869 P.2d 1062 (1994)—§ 21.4(d) n.138

Ward, State v., 624 A.2d 485 (Me.1993)—§ 3.3(c) n.108

Ward v. State, 248 Ga. 60, 281 S.E.2d 503 (1981)—§ 26.9(b) n.23

Ward v. State, 290 Md. 76, 427 A.2d 1008 (1981)—§ 6.4(e) n.105

Ward, State v., 569 S.W.2d 249 (Mo.App.1978)—§ 19.3(a) n.53

Ward v. State, 2 Mo. 120 (1829)— §§ 8.2(c) n.31; 8.4(b) n.55; 8.4(c) n.121

Ward v. Texas, 316 U.S. 547, 62 S.Ct. 1139, 86 L.Ed. 1663 (1942)— §§ 6.2(b) n.35; 6.2(c) n.70, 81, 165

Ward, United States v., 23 F.3d 1303 (8th Cir.1994)—§ 3.8(e) n.193

Ward, United States v., 682 F.2d 876 (10th Cir.1982)—§ 3.4(i) n.169

Ward, United States v., 448 U.S. 242, 100 S.Ct. 2636, 65 L.Ed.2d 742 (1980)—§§ 1.8(d) n.72; 2.10(b) n.27; 25.1(c) n.26

Ward, United States v., 488 F.2d 162 (9th Cir.1973)—§ 3.8(b) n.18

Warden v. Hayden, 387 U.S. 294, 87 S.Ct. 1642, 18 L.Ed.2d 782 (1967)—§§ 2.1 n.53; 3.2(i) n.219; 3.4(a) n.2; 3.5(c) n.121; 3.6(a) n.16; 3.6(c) n.67; 3.6(g) n.157; 8.7(a) n.4; 28.4(c) n.25

Warden v. Palermo, 431 U.S. 911, 97 S.Ct. 2166, 53 L.Ed.2d 221 (1977)—§ 27.5(a) n.2

Wardenburg, State v., 261 Iowa 1395, 158 N.W.2d 147 (Iowa 1968)— §§ 16.1(g) n.243, 273, 279, 280

Wardius v. Oregon, 412 U.S. 470, 93 S.Ct. 2208, 37 L.Ed.2d 82 (1973)— §§ 2.7(a) n.22; 20.4(a) n.3

Wardlaw, People v., 6 N.Y.3d 556, 816 N.Y.S.2d 399, 849 N.E.2d 258 (2006)—§ 11.5(c) n.49

Ware v. Commonwealth, 537 S.W.2d 174 (Ky.1976)—§ 17.2(d) n.96

Ware v. Gagnon, 659 F.2d 809 (7th Cir.1981)—§ 26.10(b) n.33

Ware, State v., 498 N.W.2d 454 (Minn.1993)—§§ 11.6(a) n.21; 11.6(d) n.124 to 126; 24.9(e) n.58

Ware, United States v., 161 F.3d 414 (6th Cir.1998)—§ 21.2(b) n.74

Ware, United States v., 897 F.2d 1538 (10th Cir.1990)—§ 4.6(g) n.129

Ware, United States v., 914 F.2d 997 (7th Cir.1990)—§ 3.2(f) n.178

Ware, United States v., 890 F.2d 1008 (8th Cir.1989)—§ 3.10(f) n.191

Warfield, United States v., 97 F.3d 1014 (8th Cir.1996)—§§ 17.2(e) n.121; 24.4(c) n.20

Wargo, State v., 168 Vt. 231, 719 A.2d 407 (1998)—§ 21.5(a) n.20

Waring v. State, 670 P.2d 357 (Alaska 1983)—§ 9.2(c) n.20

Warlick v. Commonwealth, 215 Va. 263, 208 S.E.2d 746 (1974)— § 9.4(a) n.46

Warlick, United States v., 742 F.2d 113 (4th Cir.1984)—§ 22.3(b) n.83

Warneke, United States v., 199 F.3d 906 (7th Cir.1999)—§ 12.3(d) n.97

Warnell, Ex parte, 606 S.W.2d 923 (Tex.Cr.App.1980)—§ 19.1(b) n.23

Warner v. Ford, 752 F.2d 622 (11th Cir.1985)—§§ 11.10(c) n.72; 11.10(d) n.195

Warner v. Orange Co. Dept. of Probation, 173 F.3d 120 (2d Cir.1999)— § 26.9(b) n.54

Warner v. Orange County Dep't of Probation, 870 F.Supp. 69 (S.D.N.Y.1994)—§ 26.9(c) n.83

Warner v. State, 773 N.E.2d 239 (Ind.2002)—§ 3.2(c) n.128

Warner v. State, 28 P.3d 21 (Wyo.2001)—§§ 18.2(d) n.67; 18.2(e) n.80

Warner, State v., 762 So.2d 507 (Fla.2000)—§§ 21.3(d) n.222; 22.4(c) n.29

Warner, State v., 86 N.M. 219, 521 P.2d 1168 (1974)—§ 14.2(g) n.101

Warner v. United States, 975 F.2d 1207 (6th Cir.1992)—§ 21.3(b) n.71

Warner, United States v., 894 F.2d 957 (8th Cir.1990)—§ 3.3(c) n.87

Warner, United States v., 843 F.2d 401 (9th Cir.1988)—§ 3.10(e) n.158

Warner v. Zent, 997 F.2d 116 (6th Cir.1993)—§ 19.2(c) n.27

Warner-Lambert Co., People v., 51 N.Y.2d 295, 434 N.Y.S.2d 159, 414 N.E.2d 660 (1980)—§§ 15.5(c) n.116, 122

Warrant Dated December 14, 1990 and Records Seized from 3273 Hubbard, Detroit, Michigan on December 17, 1990, In re, 961 F.2d 1241 (6th Cir.1992)—§ 27.2(d) n.74

Warren v. City of Enterprise, 641 So.2d 1312 (Ala.Crim.App.1994)—§§ 11.2(g) n.265, 281

Warren v. Lewis, 365 F.3d 529 (6th Cir.2004)—§ 21.4(b) n.59

Warren v. Richland County Circuit Court, 223 F.3d 454 (7th Cir.2000)—§§ 21.4(f) n.218 to 220

Warren, State v., 78 P.3d 590 (Utah 2003)—§ 3.8(e) n.197

Warren, State v., 9 Neb.App. 60, 608 N.W.2d 617 (2000)—§ 27.6(d) n.127

Warren, State v., 348 N.C. 80, 499 S.E.2d 431 (1998)—§ 6.9(f) n.144

Warren, State v., 115 N.J. 433, 558 A.2d 1312 (1989)—§ 21.4(g) n.246

Warren, State v., 304 Or. 428, 746 P.2d 711 (1987)—§ 20.3(a) n.18

Warren, State v., 103 N.M. 472, 709 P.2d 194 (1985)—§ 3.5(a) n.39

Warren, State v., 313 N.C. 254, 328 S.E.2d 256 (1985)—§ 17.4(c) n.156

Warren, State v., 230 Kan. 385, 635 P.2d 1236 (1981)—§ 7.5(b) n.21

Warren, State v., 31 Or.App. 1121, 572 P.2d 341 (1977)—§ 20.6(b) n.26

Warren, State v., 312 A.2d 535 (Me.1973)—§§ 15.4(g) n.163, 164

Warren, United States v., 16 F.3d 247 (8th Cir.1994)—§§ 9.4(b) n.57; 15.2(i) n.217

Warren, United States v., 25 F.3d 890 (9th Cir.1994)—§ 22.3(d) n.181

Warren, United States v., 42 F.3d 647 (D.C.Cir.1994)—§ 3.4(e) n.70

Warren, United States v., 984 F.2d 325 (9th Cir.1993)—§§ 16.4(d) n.121, 124

Warren, United States v., 982 F.2d 287 (8th Cir.1992)—§ 22.3(d) n.182

Warren, State ex rel. v. Schwarz, 219 Wis.2d 615, 579 N.W.2d 698 (1998)—§§ 21.4(f) n.218, 219

Warrick v. State, 302 Md. 162, 486 A.2d 189 (1985)—§ 20.3(i) n.162

Warrick v. Superior Court, 35 Cal.4th 1011, 29 Cal.Rptr.3d 2, 112 P.3d 2 (2005)—§ 27.4(c) n.30

Warrick v. United States, 551 A.2d 1332 (D.C.1988)—§ 26.4(g) n.141

Warshak v. United States, 490 F.3d 455 (6th Cir.2007)—§§ 4.4(c) n.7; 4.8(d) n.38

Warwick, United States v., 167 F.3d 965 (6th Cir.1999)—§ 5.4(c) n.38

Warwick, City of v. Robalewski, 120 R.I. 119, 385 A.2d 669 (1978)—§ 12.4(b) n.56

Wascom, Commonwealth v., 236 Pa.Super. 157, 344 A.2d 630 (1975)—§ 3.8(d) n.142

Washburn, United States v., 383 F.3d 638 (7th Cir.2004)—§ 3.3(c) n.106

Washington v. Chrisman, 455 U.S. 1, 102 S.Ct. 812, 70 L.Ed.2d 778 (1982)—§§ 2.9(g) n.163, 168, 177; 2.12(a) n.26; 3.6(d) n.102

Washington v. Clemmer, 339 F.2d 715 (D.C.Cir.1964)—§ 14.4(b) n.31

Washington v. Commonwealth, 34 S.W.3d 376 (Ky.2000)—§ 22.3(d) n.245

Washington v. Commonwealth, 228 Va. 535, 323 S.E.2d 577 (1984)—§ 6.8(b) n.56

Washington v. Davis, 426 U.S. 229, 96 S.Ct. 2040, 48 L.Ed.2d 597 (1976)—§ 13.4(d) n.155

Washington v. Meachum, 238 Conn. 692, 680 A.2d 262 (1996)—§ 3.9(i) n.198

Washington, People v., 101 Ill.2d 104, 77 Ill.Dec. 770, 461 N.E.2d 393 (1984)—§§ 11.9(a) n.18; 11.9(d) n.174, 211

Washington, People v., 134 Mich.App. 504, 351 N.W.2d 577 (1984)— § 16.1(a) n.20

Washington v. Recuenco, _____ U.S. _____, 126 S.Ct. 2546, 165 L.Ed.2d 466 (2006)—§§ 19.3(a) n.37; 27.6(d) n.125, 149; 27.6(e) n.160

Washington v. Smith, 219 F.3d 620 (7th Cir.2000)—§ 11.10(c) n.126

Washington v. Sobina, 475 F.3d 162 (3d Cir.2007)—§§ 18.1(d) n.48; 21.6(a) n.57

Washington v. State, 808 N.E.2d 617 (Ind.2004)—§§ 6.2(c) n.117; 6.8(d) n.84; 6.9(g) n.155

Washington v. State, 844 A.2d 293 (Del.2004)—§ 21.2(f) n.392

Washington, State v., 614 So.2d 711 (La.1993)—§ 24.7(b) n.20

Washington, State v., 866 S.W.2d 950 (Tenn.1993)—§ 13.6(b) n.18

Washington, State v., 315 S.C. 108, 432 S.E.2d 448 (1992)—§ 7.4(e) n.80

Washington v. State, 836 P.2d 673 (Okla.Crim.App.1992)—§§ 11.2(e) n.151, 158, 205, 207, 209

Washington v. State, 419 So.2d 1100 (Fla.App.1982)—§ 11.9(d) n.191

Washington, State v., 375 So.2d 1162 (La.1979)—§ 22.3(d) n.186

Washington, State v., 83 Wis.2d 808, 266 N.W.2d 597 (1978)—§§ 8.1(c) n.27, 30; 8.8(b) n.30; 27.4(d) n.42

Washington v. Strickland, 693 F.2d 1243 (5th Cir.1982)—§§ 11.10(a) n.3, 12, 15, 20; 11.10(c) n.121, 122

Washington v. Superior Court, 180 Ariz. 91, 881 P.2d 1196 (App.1994)— § 21.5(a) n.19

Washington v. Texas, 388 U.S. 14, 87 S.Ct. 1920, 18 L.Ed.2d 1019 (1967)—§§ 2.6(a) n.11, 14, 18; 10.5(f) n.60; 24.3(f) n.151; 24.3(i) n.185

Washington, United States v., 480 F.3d 309 (5th Cir.2007)—§ 21.4(b) n.42

Washington, United States v., 404 F.3d 834 (4th Cir.2005)—§ 26.4(i) n.195

Washington, United States v., 198 F.3d 721 (8th Cir.1999)—§§ 11.6(a) n.41; 11.6(b) n.86

Washington, United States v., 151 F.3d 1354 (11th Cir.1998)—§ 3.8(c) n.102

Washington, United States v., 106 F.3d 983 (D.C.Cir.1997)—§ 5.1(c) n.38

Washington, United States v., 12 F.3d 1128 (D.C.Cir.1994)—§ 3.3(f) n.204

Washington, United States v., 957 F.2d 559 (8th Cir.1992)—§§ 6.6(e) n.90, 92

Washington, United States v., 969 F.2d 1073 (D.C.Cir.1992)—§§ 21.4(f) n.171, 174

Washington v. United States, 585 A.2d 167 (D.C.App.1991)—§§ 3.6(a) n.19; 3.6(f) n.144

Washington, United States v., 819 F.2d 221 (9th Cir.1987)—§ 22.3(a) n.23

Washington, United States v., 797 F.2d 1461 (9th Cir.1986)—§§ 11.4(c) n.57; 11.9(a) n.24; 11.9(c) n.119, 139

Washington, United States v., 705 F.2d 489 (D.C.Cir.1983)—§§ 13.4(a) n.23; 22.1(g) n.115; 24.2(b) n.24

Washington, United States v., 573 F.2d 1121 (9th Cir.1978)—§ 27.2(c) n.52

Washington v. United States, 377 A.2d 1348 (D.C.App.1977)—§ 7.3(d) n.81

Washington, United States v., 431 U.S. 181, 97 S.Ct. 1814, 52 L.Ed.2d 238 (1977)—§§ 2.9(h) n.231; 8.10(c) n.70; 8.10(d) n.95, 108

Washington, Commonwealth ex rel. v. Maroney, 427 Pa. 599, 235 A.2d 349 (1967)—§ 11.10(c) n.88

Washington Massage Foundation v. Nelson, 87 Wash.2d 948, 558 P.2d 231 (1976)—§ 3.9(c) n.50

Washington Post, Application of, 1992 WL 233354 (D.D.C.1992)— § 23.1(d) n.193

Washington Post, In re, 807 F.2d 383 (4th Cir.1986)—§§ 21.4(b) n.52; 23.1(d) n.151, 175, 183

Washington Post v. Robinson, 935 F.2d 282 (D.C.Cir.1991)—§§ 21.4(b) n.52; 23.1(d) n.183; 23.1(e) n.226, 261

Washington Post Co., Application of, 576 F.Supp. 76 (D.D.C.1983)—§§ 23.1(d) n.164, 169; 23.1(e) n.242

Washman, United States v., 66 F.3d 210 (9th Cir.1995)—§ 21.5(a) n.3

Wasman v. United States, 468 U.S. 559, 104 S.Ct. 3217, 82 L.Ed.2d 424 (1984)—§§ 13.7(c) n.49, 51; 26.8(b) n.6

Wassillie, State v., 606 P.2d 1279 (Alaska 1980)—§ 12.4(d) n.62

Wasson, State v., 125 N.M. 656, 964 P.2d 820 (App.1998)—§ 13.7(a) n.29

Watchmaker, United States v., 761 F.2d 1459 (11th Cir.1985)—§ 15.7(d) n.80

Waters, People v., 328 Ill.App.3d 117, 262 Ill.Dec. 77, 764 N.E.2d 1194 (Ill.App.2002)—§ 24.11(d) n.39

Waters v. State, 281 Ga. 119, 636 S.E.2d 538 (2006)—§ 6.7(c) n.121

Waters, State v., 296 Mont. 101, 987 P.2d 1142 (1999)—§ 2.11(a) n.14

Waters v. State, 320 Md. 52, 575 A.2d 1244 (1990)—§ 10.3(b) n.38

Waters v. Thomas, 46 F.3d 1506 (11th Cir.1995)—§§ 11.10(c) n.84, 91, 131

Watford, United States v., 468 F.3d 891 (6th Cir.2006)—§§ 18.2(b) n.16; 18.2(c) n.51; 22.3(d) n.235

Watkins, Ex parte, 28 U.S. (3 Pet.) 193, 7 L.Ed. 650 (1830)—§ 28.3(b) n.41

Watkins v. Commonwealth, 238 Va. 341, 385 S.E.2d 50 (1989)—§ 4.6(l) n.200

Watkins v. Kassulke, 90 F.3d 138 (6th Cir.1996)—§§ 11.6(a) n.41; 11.6(c) n.95, 108

Watkins, People v., 468 Mich. 233, 661 N.W.2d 553 (2003)—§ 21.4(e) n.159

Watkins v. Solem, 571 F.2d 435 (8th Cir.1978)—§ 21.2(b) n.47

Watkins v. Sowders, 449 U.S. 341, 101 S.Ct. 654, 66 L.Ed.2d 549 (1981)—§§ 2.6(c) n.84; 10.5(a) n.16; 10.5(b) n.19, 25

Watkins, State v., 99 Ohio St.3d 12, 788 N.E.2d 635 (2003)—§ 21.4(e) n.165

Watkins, State v., 114 N.J. 259, 553 A.2d 1344 (1989)—§ 22.3(d) n.212

Watkins v. State, 296 Ark. 345, 756 S.W.2d 907 (1988)—§ 3.2(f) n.183

Watkins, United States v., 179 F.3d 489 (6th Cir.1999)—§ 3.1(c) n.74

Watkins, United States v., 85 F.3d 498 (10th Cir.1996)—§ 21.2(h) n.419

Watkins, United States v., 983 F.2d 1413 (7th Cir.1993)—§ 24.2(c) n.35

Watley, State v., 109 N.M. 619, 788 P.2d 375 (App.1989)—§§ 20.6(c) n.78, 83

Watley, United States v., 987 F.2d 841 (D.C.Cir.1993)—§§ 21.4(d) n.104; 21.5(a) n.43

Watley v. Williams, 218 F.3d 1156 (10th Cir.2000)—§ 20.6(c) n.76

Watson v. DiSabato, 933 F.Supp. 390 (D.N.J.1996)—§ 26.2(c) n.44

Watson, People v., 22 Cal.4th 220, 91 Cal.Rptr.2d 822, 990 P.2d 1031 (2000)—§ 5.2(b) n.24

Watson, People v., 85 Ill.App.3d 649, 40 Ill.Dec. 781, 406 N.E.2d 1148 (1980)—§ 8.3(b) n.13

Watson, State v., 159 Wash.2d 215, 149 P.3d 361 (2006)—§ 21.3(d) n.220

Watson v. State, 892 A.2d 366 (Del.2005)—§ 9.1(d) n.131

Watson, State v., 151 N.H. 537, 864 A.2d 1095 (2004)—§ 3.10(b) n.51

Watson v. State, 274 Ga. 689, 558 S.E.2d 704 (2002)—§ 22.1(h) n.144

Watson, State v., 620 N.W.2d 233 (Iowa 2000)—§§ 11.9(b) n.83; 11.9(d) n.204

Watson, State v., 47 Conn.App. 794, 707 A.2d 1278 (1998)—§ 11.9(b) n.86

Watson v. State, 900 S.W.2d 60 (Tex.Cr.App.1995)—§ 17.4(b) n.95

Watson v. State, 762 S.W.2d 591 (Tex.Crim.App.1988)—§§ 6.9(f) n.113; 6.9(g) n.150, 158

Watson, State v., 173 W.Va. 553, 318 S.E.2d 603 (1984)—§ 7.4(e) n.89

Watson v. State, 235 Ga. 461, 219 S.E.2d 763 (1975)—§ 24.8(f) n.96

Watson, State v., 165 Conn. 577, 345 A.2d 532 (1973)—§ 3.8(b) n.39

Watson, United States v., 483 F.3d 828 (D.C.Cir.2007)—§ 22.3(d) n.202

Watson, United States v., 988 F.2d 544 (5th Cir.1993)—§ 21.2(d) n.254

Watson, United States v., 950 F.2d 505 (8th Cir.1991)—§§ 9.3(d) n.38, 39

Watson, United States v., 591 F.2d 1058 (5th Cir.1979)—§ 6.3(b) n.35

Watson, United States v., 599 F.2d 1149 (2d Cir.1979)—§§ 18.1(c) n.23, 24, 42

Watson, United States v., 587 F.2d 365 (7th Cir.1978)—§§ 7.5(b) n.17, 24

Watson, United States v., 423 U.S. 411, 96 S.Ct. 820, 46 L.Ed.2d 598 (1976)—§§ 1.3(f) n.82; 2.9(d) n.57, 73, 78, 90; 3.5(a) n.14; 3.6(a) n.6; 3.10(b) n.63

Watson v. Walker, 447 Mass. 1014, 854 N.E.2d 1247 (2006)—§ 13.2(a) n.3

Watt v. People, 126 Ill. 9, 18 N.E. 340 (1888)—§§ 16.1(e) n.196; 16.1(g) n.247

Watt, State v., 186 W.Va. 518, 413 S.E.2d 173 (1991)—§ 15.6(e) n.134

Wattenburg v. United States, 388 F.2d 853 (9th Cir.1968)—§ 3.2(c) n.133

Watton, State v., 164 Ariz. 323, 793 P.2d 80 (1990)—§ 21.2(b) n.86

Watts v. Brewer, 340 F.Supp. 378 (S.D.Iowa 1972)—§ 21.4(d) n.142

Watts v. Gerking, 111 Or. 641, 222 P. 318 (1924)—§ 13.5(g) n.111

Watts v. Indiana, 338 U.S. 49, 69 S.Ct. 1347, 93 L.Ed. 1801 (1949)—§§ 1.5(c) n.104; 1.5(d) n.189, 195; 2.4(e) n.147; 2.9(i) n.273, 277; 6.2(b) n.28, 46; 6.2(c) n.79, 82; 6.5(a) n.7; 9.5(a) n.7

Watts v. State, 99 S.W.3d 604 (Tex.Cr.App.2003)—§ 24.6(e) n.51

Watts, State v., 750 P.2d 1219 (Utah 1988)—§§ 2.12(c) n.179; 10.3(b) n.38

Watts, United States v., 519 U.S. 148, 117 S.Ct. 633, 136 L.Ed.2d 554 (1997)—§§ 26.4(a) n.3; 26.4(b) n.8, 9; 26.4(h) n.153; 26.5(a) n.20

Watts v. United States, 362 A.2d 706 (D.C.App.1976)—§ 22.1(g) n.126

Watts v. United States, 297 A.2d 790 (D.C.1972)—§ 3.7(a) n.11

Waucaush v. United States, 380 F.3d 251 (6th Cir.2004)—§§ 21.4(c) n.86; 21.4(f) n.174; 21.5(c) n.75; 21.6(a) n.78

Waugh v. Commonwealth, 605 S.W.2d 43 (Ky.App.1980)—§ 10.6(c) n.31

Waugh, State v., 238 Kan. 537, 712 P.2d 1243 (1986)—§§ 6.2(c) n.147; 6.4(e) n.77

Waugh v. State, 564 S.W.2d 654 (Tenn.1978)—§§ 14.2(c) n.37; 14.4(b) n.7

Waupekenay, United States v., 973 F.2d 1533 (10th Cir.1992)—§ 9.4(f) n.115

Way v. United States, 285 F.2d 253 (10th Cir.1960)—§ 15.5(b) n.52

Waye v. Murray, 884 F.2d 765 (4th Cir.1989)—§ 11.2(e) n.171

Wayne v. United States, 318 F.2d 205 (D.C.Cir.1963)—§ 3.6(f) n.147

Wayne Prosecuting Attorney v. Wayne County Circuit Judge, 387 Mich. 784 (1972)—§ 8.4(b) n.109

Wayne W., Commonwealth v., 414 Mass. 218, 606 N.E.2d 1323 (1993)—§ 6.10(e) n.76

Wayrynen v. Class, 586 N.W.2d 499 (S.D.1998)—§ 21.3(b) n.115

Wayte v. United States, 470 U.S. 598, 105 S.Ct. 1524, 84 L.Ed.2d 547 (1985)—§§ 8.8(d) n.68; 13.2(g) n.134; 13.4(b) n.47; 13.4(d) n.156; 13.5(a) n.15

WBZ-TV4 v. District Attorney for Suffolk District, 408 Mass. 595, 562 N.E.2d 817 (1990)—§§ 8.5(b) n.35; 8.5(c) n.79

W.C., In re, 167 Ill.2d 307, 212 Ill.Dec. 563, 657 N.E.2d 908 (1995)—§§ 6.9(b) n.18, 20, 27, 42

Wead v. State, 129 S.W.3d 126 (Tex.Cr.App.2004)—§ 24.5(b) n.22

Weatherford v. Bursey, 429 U.S. 545, 97 S.Ct. 837, 51 L.Ed.2d 30 (1977)—§§ 11.8(b) n.24; 20.3(m) n.236; 21.2(f) n.378; 21.3(c) n.149; 24.3(b) n.44; 26.4(d) n.50

Weathers v. State, 105 Nev. 199, 772 P.2d 1294 (1989)—§ 6.7(c) n.111

Weathers, United States v., 21 F.Supp. 763 (N.D.Ga.1937)—§ 15.2(j) n.238

Weatherspoon, United States v., 410 F.3d 1142 (9th Cir.2005)—§ 24.7(e) n.73

Weaver v. Bowersox, 438 F.3d 832 (8th Cir.2006)—§ 24.7(e) n.72

Weaver v. Bowersox, 241 F.3d 1024 (8th Cir.2001)—§ 22.3(d) n.228

Weaver, People v., 26 Cal.4th 876, 111 Cal.Rptr.2d 2, 29 P.3d 103 (2001)—§ 6.2(c) n.178

Weaver, People v., 44 Cal.App.4th 154, 51 Cal.Rptr.2d 602 (1996)—§ 14.4(b) n.42

Weaver v. Schaaf, 520 S.W.2d 58 (Mo.1975)—§ 25.5(c) n.35

Weaver v. State, 894 So.2d 178 (Fla.2004)—§§ 11.4(b) n.46; 24.2(e) n.68

Weaver v. State, 339 Ark. 97, 3 S.W.3d 323 (1999)—§ 5.3(c) n.35

Weaver, United States v., 267 F.3d 231 (3d Cir.2001)—§§ 22.2(d) n.77, 85

Weaver, United States v., 216 F.3d 693 (8th Cir.2000)—§ 21.2(d) n.264

Weaver, United States v., 8 F.3d 1240 (7th Cir.1993)—§ 3.8(b) n.31

Weaver, United States v., 882 F.2d 1128 (7th Cir.1989)—§ 18.4(c) n.40

Weaver v. United States, 454 F.2d 315 (7th Cir.1971)—§ 21.4(d) n.116

Webb v. Commonwealth, 32 Va.App. 337, 528 S.E.2d 138 (2000)—§ 11.8(c) n.66

Webb v. Commonwealth, 204 Va. 24, 129 S.E.2d 22 (1963)—§ 14.2(c) n.37

Webb v. Henlery, 209 Ga. 447, 74 S.E.2d 7 (1953)—§§ 15.1(d) n.182; 15.1(f) n.282

Webb v. McCullough, 828 F.2d 1151 (6th Cir.1987)—§ 3.9(k) n.244

Webb, People v., 6 Cal.4th 494, 24 Cal.Rptr.2d 779, 862 P.2d 779 (1993)—§§ 20.3(j) n.195; 24.3(f) n.156

Webb, People v., 186 Cal.App.3d 401, 230 Cal.Rptr. 755 (1986)—§ 21.2(b) n.96

Webb, People v., 36 Cal.App.3d 460, 111 Cal.Rptr. 524 (1973)—§ 3.4(h) n.146

Webb, State v., 358 N.C. 92, 591 S.E.2d 505 (2004)—§ 11.2(h) n.320

Webb, State v., 570 N.W.2d 913 (Iowa 1997)—§§ 18.4(c) n.40, 44

Webb, State v., 186 Ariz. 560, 925 P.2d 701 (Ariz.App.1996)—§ 24.10(b) n.30

Webb, State v., 323 Ark. 80, 913 S.W.2d 259 (1996)—§ 27.4(c) n.20

Webb v. State, 663 A.2d 452 (Del.1995)—§ 24.8(f) n.96

Webb, State v., 160 Wis.2d 622, 467 N.W.2d 108 (1991)—§§ 14.3(d) n.92, 101, 105; 14.4(e) n.115, 117 to 119, 129; 27.2(b) n.19

Webb v. State, 586 So.2d 954 (Ala.1991)—§ 22.3(a) n.23

Webb, State v., 790 P.2d 65 (Utah App.1990)—§§ 11.9(b) n.86; 11.9(d) n.191, 232

Webb v. State, 756 P.2d 293 (Alaska 1988)—§ 6.9(c) n.50

Webb v. State, 760 S.W.2d 263 (Tex.Cr.App.1988)—§§ 3.3(d) n.157; 7.4(d) n.72

Webb v. Texas, 409 U.S. 95, 93 S.Ct. 351, 34 L.Ed.2d 330 (1972)—§§ 2.7(a) n.51; 2.7(b) n.93; 10.5(f) n.59; 24.3(h) n.175

Webb, United States v., 403 F.3d 373 (6th Cir.2005)—§ 21.4(c) n.66

Webb, United States v., 755 F.2d 382 (5th Cir.1985)—§§ 6.7(b) n.42, 66, 90; 6.9(f) n.141; 6.10(b) n.16

Webber v. District Court, 895 P.2d 728 (Okla.Crim.App.1995)—§ 27.4(c) n.28

Webber, State v., 292 N.W.2d 5 (Minn.1980)—§ 16.3(g) n.100

Weber, State v., 159 Wash.2d 252, 149 P.3d 646 (2006)—§ 26.4(i) n.200

Weber, State v., 140 Idaho 89, 90 P.3d 314 (2004)—§ 21.4(e) n.161

Weber v. State, 547 A.2d 948 (Del.1988)—§ 22.4(c) n.22

Weber, United States v., 437 F.2d 327 (3d Cir.1970)—§ 17.1(b) n.26

Webster v. District Court of Oklahoma County, 473 P.2d 277 (Okla.Crim.App.1970)—§ 14.3(d) n.85

Webster, People v., 54 Cal.3d 411, 285 Cal.Rptr. 31, 814 P.2d 1273 (1991)—§ 3.7(e) n.121

Webster, State v., 32 P.3d 976 (Utah App.2001)—§ 20.2(d) n.70

Webster v. State, 604 A.2d 1364 (Del. 1992)—§ 21.5(a) n.53

Webster v. State, 300 Ark. 169, 777 S.W.2d 849 (1989)—§ 3.10(e) n.169

Webster v. State, 299 Md. 581, 474 A.2d 1305 (1984)—§§ 2.12(a) n.77; 2.12(b) n.82; 2.12(d) n.190; 7.3(b) n.36; 7.4(d) n.69

Webster v. State, 59 Del. (9 Storey) 54, 213 A.2d 298 (1965)—§ 6.3(c) n.52

Webster, United States v., 392 F.3d 787 (5th Cir.2004)—§ 28.9(b) n.71

Webster, United States v., 162 F.3d 308 (5th Cir.1998)—§§ 13.2(a) n.5; 13.4(b) n.72

Webster, United States v., 125 F.3d 1024 (7th Cir.1997)—§ 19.3(a) n.45

Webster, United States v., 750 F.2d 307 (5th Cir.1984)—§ 3.3(e) n.188

Webster, United States v., 639 F.2d 174 (4th Cir.1981)—§ 15.4(b) n.67

Webster, United States v., 649 F.2d 346 (5th Cir.1981)—§ 5.3(a) n.7

Wedalowski, United States v., 572 F.2d 69 (2d Cir.1978)—§ 25.1(d) n.49

Weddell, United States v., 800 F.2d 1404 (5th Cir.1986)—§ 24.3(h) n.178

Wedmore v. State, 235 Ind. 341, 133 N.E.2d 842 (1956)—§ 18.4(a) n.1

Weedon v. State, 501 S.W.2d 336 (Tex.Cr.App.1973)—§ 6.6(c) n.37

Weeks, Ex parte, 531 So.2d 643 (Ala.1988)—§ 6.2(c) n.107

Weeks v. Angelone, 528 U.S. 225, 120 S.Ct. 727, 145 L.Ed.2d 727 (2000)—§ 24.8(a) n.23

Weeks v. Angelone, 176 F.3d 249 (4th Cir.1999)—§§ 6.9(f) n.102, 106

Weeks v. Snyder, 219 F.3d 245 (3d Cir.2000)—§ 28.7(a) n.4

Weeks, State v., 141 N.H. 248, 681 A.2d 86 (1996)—§ 26.4(f) n.101

Weeks v. State, 190 Ga.App. 373, 378 S.E.2d 895 (1989)—§ 11.9(d) n.233

Weeks v. United States, 232 U.S. 383, 34 S.Ct. 341, 58 L.Ed. 652 (1914)—§§ 1.7(i) n.196; 2.8(b) n.35; 2.12(a) n.9; 3.1(a) n.5; 3.10(e) n.161

Weems v. State, 268 Ga. 142, 485 S.E.2d 767 (1997)—§ 3.5(d) n.166

Weems, United States v., 322 F.3d 18 (1st Cir.2003)—§ 3.6(a) n.19

Weems, United States v., 49 F.3d 528 (9th Cir.1995)—§ 25.4(b) n.18

Weems v. United States, 217 U.S. 349, 30 S.Ct. 544, 54 L.Ed. 793 (1910)—§§ 2.9(d) n.64, 87

Weeren, People v., 26 Cal.3d 654, 163 Cal.Rptr. 255, 607 P.2d 1279 (1980)—§ 16.4(c) n.114

Weese, State v., 424 A.2d 705 (Me.1981)—§ 11.9(b) n.61

Weichert v. United States, 458 F.Supp.2d 57 (N.D.N.Y.2006)—§ 28.9(a) n.21

Weide, State v., 155 Wis.2d 537, 455 N.W.2d 899 (1990)—§ 3.5(e) n.193

Weidul, State v., 628 A.2d 135 (Me.1993)—§ 24.9(d) n.43

Weigand v. United States, 380 F.3d 890 (6th Cir.2004)—§ 28.9(b) n.49

Wein, State v., 80 N.J. 491, 404 A.2d 302 (1979)—§ 19.3(a) n.57

Weinberg, United States v., 439 F.2d 743 (9th Cir.1971)—§§ 8.8(b) n.16; 8.14(c) n.35

Weiner, United States v., 418 F.Supp. 941 (M.D.Pa.1976)—§§ 8.8(b) n.25, 29

Weingartner, United States v., 485 F.Supp. 1167 (D.N.J.1979)—§§ 15.5(a) n.31; 15.5(b) n.35

Weinstein v. Bradford, 423 U.S. 147, 96 S.Ct. 347, 46 L.Ed.2d 350 (1975)—§ 27.5(a) n.19

Weinstein, People v., 254 A.D.2d 83, 680 N.Y.S.2d 204 (App.Div.1998)—§ 19.3(a) n.63

Weinstein, United States v., 511 F.2d 622 (2d Cir.1975)—§§ 8.5(c) n.90; 27.4(d) n.46

Weinstein, United States v., 452 F.2d 704 (2d Cir.1971)—§ 13.2(c) n.56

Weir, In re, 520 F.2d 662 (9th Cir.1975)—§ 8.11(c) n.48

Weir, In re, 495 F.2d 879 (9th Cir.1974)—§ 8.9(a) n.4

Weisenberger, People v., 183 Colo. 353, 516 P.2d 1128 (1973)—§ 3.2(c) n.121

Weiskerger, Commonwealth v., 520 Pa. 305, 554 A.2d 10 (1989)—§§ 5.3(c) n.31; 5.3(d) n.44

Weiss, In re, 703 F.2d 653 (2d Cir.1983)—§ 8.3(b) n.13

Weiss, Commonwealth v., 565 Pa. 504, 776 A.2d 958 (2001)—§ 22.3(c) n.112

Weiss, State v., 155 Vt. 558, 587 A.2d 73 (1990)—§ 3.4(g) n.128

Weiss v. United States, 510 U.S. 163, 114 S.Ct. 752, 127 L.Ed.2d 1 (1994)—§§ 2.7(c) n.133, 148

Weiss, United States v., 7 F.3d 1088 (2d Cir.1993)—§ 27.2(c) n.57

Welborn, United States v., 849 F.2d 980 (5th Cir.1988)—§ 20.6(b) n.45

Welch v. Commonwealth, 149 S.W.3d 407 (Ky.2004)—§§ 6.6(e) n.81; 6.10(c) n.51

Welch, Commonwealth v., 345 Mass. 366, 187 N.E.2d 813 (1963)—§ 16.4(c) n.54

Welch, People v., 5 Cal.4th 228, 19 Cal.Rptr.2d 520, 851 P.2d 802 (1993)—§§ 26.3(g) n.93; 26.9(c) n.81

Welch v. Sirmons, 2006 WL 1681358 (10th Cir.2006)—§ 26.5(d) n.73

Welch v. State, 93 S.W.3d 50 (Tex.Crim.App.2002)—§ 3.10(e) n.172

Welch v. State, 330 Ark. 158, 955 S.W.2d 181 (1997)—§ 3.7(e) n.118

Welch, State v., 28 Ohio St.2d 31, 274 N.E.2d 756 (1971)—§ 15.1(f) n.315

Welch, State v., 4 Or.App. 225, 476 P.2d 822 (1970)—§ 6.7(c) n.107

Welch v. State, 66 Tex.Crim. 525, 147 S.W. 572 (1912)—§§ 15.4(g) n.166, 169

Welch, United States v., 97 F.3d 142 (6th Cir.1996)—§§ 17.2(e) n.116; 17.2(f) n.131

Welch v. United States, 466 A.2d 829 (D.C.App.1983)—§ 24.2(b) n.28

Welch, United States v., 656 F.2d 1039 (5th Cir.1981)—§ 16.2(h) n.157

Welch, United States v., 455 F.2d 211 (2d Cir.1972)—§ 6.10(d) n.60

Welker, State v., 157 Wash.2d 557, 141 P.3d 8 (2006)—§ 18.4(c) n.40

Welker, State v., 127 Wash.App. 222, 110 P.3d 1167 (2005)—§ 18.4(c) n.39

Wellington v. Comm'r, Dept. of Corrections. 140 N.H. 399, 666 A.2d 969 (1995)—§ 21.3(b) n.71

Wellington, United States v., 417 F.3d 284 (2d Cir.2005)—§ 21.6(c) n.118

Wellman, State v., 128 N.H. 340, 513 A.2d 944 (1986)—§ 3.3(d) n.170

Wellman, State v., 102 Kan. 503, 170 P.2d 1052 (1918)—§ 16.4(c) n.52

Wellnitz v. Page, 420 F.2d 935 (10th Cir.1970)—§ 21.2(g) n.395

Wells v. Indiana, 848 N.E.2d 1133 (Ind.App.2006)—§ 22.2(d) n.67

Wells v. Sacks, 115 Ohio App. 219, 184 N.E.2d 449 (1962)—§ 15.1(f) n.334

Wells, State v., 638 N.W.2d 456 (Minn.App.2002)—§§ 18.4(c) n.58, 66

Wells, State v., 78 Haw. 373, 894 P.2d 70 (1995)—§§ 25.3(a) n.8; 27.3(d) n.61

Wells, State v., 94 Ohio App.3d 48, 640 N.E.2d 217 (1994)—§ 18.4(c) n.68

Wells, State v., 539 So.2d 464 (Fla.1989)—§ 3.10(f) n.192

Wells, State v., 466 So.2d 291 (Fla.App.1985)—§ 15.1(e) n.260

Wells v. State, 474 A.2d 846 (Me.1984)—§ 27.4(f) n.68

Wells, State v., 20 S.C.L. 687, 2 Hill (S.C.) 687 (Ct.App. 1835)—§ 1.2(c) n.82

Wells, United States v., 211 F.3d 988 (6th Cir.2000)—§ 21.2(d) n.157

Wells, United States v., 163 F. 313 (D.Idaho 1908)—§§ 15.7(b) n.48, 50

Welsand, United States v., 993 F.2d 1366 (8th Cir.1993)—§ 12.1(a) n.7

Welsh, United States v., 15 F.R.D. 189 (D.D.C.1953)—§ 17.2(a) n.13

Welsh v. Wisconsin, 466 U.S. 740, 104 S.Ct. 2091, 80 L.Ed.2d 732 (1984)—§§ 1.8(c) n.8; 3.1(d) n.119; 3.6(a) n.16, 21; 3.6(e) n.112, 129; 3.6(f) n.143

Welty, United States v., 674 F.2d 185 (3d Cir.1982)—§§ 11.3(b) n.33; 11.4(b) n.19; 11.4(c) n.65, 67; 11.5(c) n.39, 52, 56; 11.5(f) n.101

Weltzin, State v., 630 N.W.2d 406 (Minn.2001)—§ 22.1(b) n.57

Welwood, State v., 258 Conn. 425, 780 A.2d 924 (2001)—§§ 21.2(b) n.84; 26.9(a) n.9

Wenatchee v. Durham, 43 Wash.App. 547, 718 P.2d 819 (1986)—§ 1.8(f) n.103

Wende, People v., 25 Cal.3d 436, 158 Cal.Rptr. 839, 600 P.2d 1071 (1979)—§ 11.2(c) n.91

Wendling v. Commonwealth, 143 Ky. 587, 137 S.W. 205 (1911)—§ 20.1(a) n.9

Wendte v. State, Board of Real Estate Appraisers, 70 P.3d 1089 (Alaska 2003)—§ 17.4(b) n.125

Wengert v. State, 364 Md. 76, 771 A.2d 389 (2001)—§§ 3.6(f) n.149; 3.6(g) n.158

Weninger, United States v., 624 F.2d 163 (10th Cir.1980)—§§ 11.3(c) n.54, 59; 11.5(e) n.88

Wentz, Commonwealth v., 280 Pa.Super. 427, 421 A.2d 796 (1980)—§ 11.3(c) n.55

Wenzel v. Enright, 68 Ohio St.3d 63, 623 N.E.2d 69 (1993)—§ 27.2(c) n.66

Werber, United States v., 51 F.3d 342 (2d Cir.1995)—§ 26.7(c) n.35

Werblow, People v., 241 N.Y. 55, 148 N.E. 786 (1925)—§ 16.4(c) n.88

Werbrouck, United States v., 589 F.2d 273 (7th Cir.1978)—§ 14.1(a) n.2

Werdell v. Turzynski, 128 Ill.App.2d 139, 262 N.E.2d 833 (1970)—§ 15.1(b) n.73

Werker, United States v., 535 F.2d 198 (2d Cir.1976)—§§ 21.3(d) n.218, 262

Werking, United States v., 915 F.2d 1404 (10th Cir.1990)—§ 3.8(c) n.114

Werner, State v., 831 A.2d 183 (R.I.2003)—§ 3.6(a) n.19

Werner, State v., 9 S.W.3d 590 (Mo.2000)—§§ 6.6(c) n.37; 6.6(d) n.53

Werner, State v., 615 A.2d 1010 (R.I.1992)—§ 2.12(d) n.198

Werner, United States v., 317 F.3d 1168 (10th Cir.2003)—§ 21.2(d) n.173

Werner, United States v., 620 F.2d 922 (2d Cir.1980)—§§ 17.1(b) n.27, 29, 30

Wernert v. Arn, 819 F.2d 613 (6th Cir.1987)—§ 6.9(g) n.162

Wesbrook v. State, 29 S.W.3d 103 (Tex.Crim.App.2000)—§ 6.4(g) n.161

Wesco, Inc., State v., _____ Vt. _____, 911 A.2d 281 (2006)—§§ 13.2(a) n.5; 13.4(b) n.67

Wesela, United States v., 223 F.3d 656 (7th Cir.2000)—§ 3.10(b) n.51

Wesley v. State, 521 So.2d 1283 (Miss.1988)—§ 6.7(b) n.43

Wesley, United States v., 293 F.3d 541 (D.C.Cir.2002)—§ 3.7(a) n.14

Wesley College v. Pitts, 974 F.Supp. 375 (D. Del. 1997)—§ 4.6(b) n.25

West, In re, 154 Wash.2d 204, 110 P.3d 1122 (2005)—§ 21.6(a) n.67

West, In re, 10 N.D. 464, 88 N.W. 88 (1901)—§ 12.4(a) n.5

West v. Commonwealth, 887 S.W.2d 338 (Ky.1994)—§§ 6.9(c) n.61; 27.5(a) n.21

West v. Director of Department of Corrections, 639 S.E.2d 190 (Va.2007)—§ 27.5(b) n.48

West v. Johnson, 92 F.3d 1385 (5th Cir.1996)—§ 6.9(g) n.154

West, People v., 81 N.Y.2d 370, 599 N.Y.S.2d 484, 615 N.E.2d 968 (1993)—§ 6.4(e) n.84

West v. State, 160 Ga.App. 855, 287 S.E.2d 694 (1982)—§ 26.9(b) n.44

West v. Thomson Newspapers, 872 P.2d 999 (Utah 1994)—§ 2.12(d) n.195

West v. United States, 866 A.2d 74 (D.C.App.2005)—§§ 6.4(g) n.153; 7.4(e) n.85

West, United States v., 219 F.3d 1171 (10th Cir.2000)—§ 3.10(f) n.189

West v. United States, 659 A.2d 1260 (D.C.App.1995)—§ 27.5(a) n.2

West, United States v., 2 F.3d 66 (4th Cir.1993)—§ 21.2(e) n.352

West, United States v., 898 F.2d 1493 (11th Cir.1990)—§ 24.9(d) n.43

West, United States v., 877 F.2d 281 (4th Cir.1989)—§§ 11.5(d) n.73; 24.2(c) n.35

West v. Virginia Dep't of Corrections, 847 F.Supp. 402 (W.D.Va.1994)—§ 26.1(e) n.111

West v. Waters, 272 Ga. 591, 533 S.E.2d 88 (2000)—§§ 11.10(c) n.116, 118

Westbrook v. Arizona, 384 U.S. 150, 86 S.Ct. 1320, 16 L.Ed.2d 429 (1966)—§ 11.5(c) n.60

Westbrook, Commonwealth v., 484 Pa. 534, 400 A.2d 160 (1979)—§ 11.9(a) n.29

Westbrook, United States v., 780 F.2d 1185 (5th Cir.1986)—§ 12.1(a) n.8

West Coast News Co., United States v., 30 F.R.D. 13 (W.D.Mich.1962)—§§ 16.2(f) n.100; 16.3(c) n.49

West Covina, City of v. Perkins, 525 U.S. 234, 119 S.Ct. 678, 142 L.Ed.2d 636 (1999)—§§ 3.4(l) n.250; 10.1(c) n.46

Westenberg, Ex parte, 167 Cal. 309, 139 P. 674 (1914)—§ 15.1(b) n.73

Westerdahl, United States v., 945 F.2d 1083 (9th Cir.1991)—§ 24.3(i) n.190

Westerfield, State v., 567 N.W.2d 863 (S.D.1997)—§ 20.5(f) n.80

Westerheide v. State, 831 So.2d 93 (Fla.2002)—§ 17.4(b) n.134

Westerman v. Cary, 125 Wash.2d 277, 892 P.2d 1067 (1994)—§§ 12.1(b) n.25; 12.2(a) n.10, 11; 12.3(b) n.76

Westerman, State v., 945 P.2d 695 (Utah App.1997)—§ 26.6(c) n.35

West Indies Transport, Inc., United States v., 127 F.3d 299 (3d Cir.1997)—§ 5.4(c) n.30

Westling, State v., 145 Wash.2d 607, 40 P.3d 669 (2002)—§ 17.4(b) n.73

Westly v. Johnson, 83 F.3d 714 (5th Cir.1996)—§ 24.3(b) n.62

Westly v. State, 754 S.W.2d 224 (Tex.Crim.App.1988)—§ 6.9(b) n.27

Westmoreland v. Columbia Broadcasting System, Inc., 752 F.2d 16 (2d Cir.1984)—§ 23.3(b) n.19

Westmoreland, United States v., 122 F.3d 431 (7th Cir.1997)—§ 13.4(a) n.27

Westmoreland, United States v., 41 F.R.D. 419 (S.D.Ind.1967)—§ 20.3(d) n.94

Weston v. Kernan, 50 F.3d 633 (9th Cir.1995)—§§ 25.2(a) n.7; 25.2(f) n.51

Weston v. State, 2 S.W.3d 111 (Mo.App.1999)—§ 21.3(b) n.66

Weston, United States v., 448 F.2d 626 (9th Cir.1971)—§ 26.5(a) n.14

West Virginia v. Douglass, 20 W.Va. 770 (1882)—§ 1.5(b) n.88

Wetherbee, State v., 177 Vt. 274, 866 A.2d 527 (2004)—§ 27.2(d) n.76

Wethered, State v., 110 Wash.2d 466, 755 P.2d 797 (1988)—§§ 3.10(b) n.71, 76; 9.5(b) n.44

Wetherington v. Carlisle, 273 Ga. 854, 547 S.E.2d 559 (2001)—§ 21.5(b) n.67

Wetterlin, United States v., 583 F.2d 346 (7th Cir.1978)—§ 21.4(c) n.77

Wetzel, State v., 456 N.W.2d 115 (N.D.1990)—§ 3.9(g) n.126

Wexler v. New York State Tax Commission, 527 N.Y.S.2d 876, 139 A.D.2d 890 (1988)—§ 8.5(e) n.161

Wexler, United States v., 31 F.3d 117 (3d Cir.1994)—§ 27.4(d) n.59

Whalen, United States v., 976 F.2d 1346 (10th Cir.1992)—§ 21.2(b) n.54

Whaley, State v., 305 S.C. 138, 406 S.E.2d 369 (1991)—§ 7.5(b) n.23

Whaley v. State, 686 S.W.2d 950 (Tex.Cr.App.1985)—§ 3.3(c) n.132

Wharton, People v., 74 N.Y.2d 921, 550 N.Y.S.2d 260, 549 N.E.2d 462 (1989)—§ 7.4(b) n.10

Wharton v. State, 734 So.2d 985 (Miss.1998)—§ 24.9(b) n.12

Whatley v. State, 270 Ga. 296, 509 S.E.2d 45 (1998)—§ 22.3(c) n.162

Wheat, State v., 907 So.2d 461 (Ala.2005)—§ 27.5(a) n.7

Wheat v. United States, 486 U.S. 153, 108 S.Ct. 1692, 100 L.Ed.2d 140 (1988)—§§ 2.6(e) n.111; 8.14(d) n.48; 11.1(a) n.31; 11.4(c) n.55, 59; 11.9(c) n.103

Wheat, United States v., 813 F.2d 1399 (9th Cir.1987)—§§ 21.2(b) n.58; 21.3(c) n.148

Wheel v. Robinson, 34 F.3d 60 (2d Cir.1994)—§§ 8.8(h) n.185; 24.9(f) n.86, 87

Wheeler, Application of, 81 Nev. 495, 406 P.2d 713 (1965)—§ 12.4(a) n.22

Wheeler, People v., 43 Cal.App.3d 898, 118 Cal.Rptr. 205 (1974)—§ 3.8(d) n.130

Wheeler v. State, 160 Md.App. 566, 864 A.2d 1058 (2005)—§ 12.3(f) n.140

Wheeler, State v., 285 Mont. 400, 948 P.2d 698 (1997)—§ 21.6(a) n.50

Wheeler, State v., 108 Wash.2d 230, 737 P.2d 1005 (1987)—§ 6.7(b) n.42

Wheeler, State v., 468 So.2d 978 (Fla.1985)—§ 5.3(d) n.43

Wheeler v. State, 24 Wis. 52 (1869)—§ 16.3(d) n.61

Wheeler, United States v., 435 U.S. 313, 98 S.Ct. 1079, 55 L.Ed.2d 303 (1978)—§ 25.5(a) n.6

Wheeler, United States ex rel. v. Flood, 269 F.Supp. 194 (E.D.N.Y.1967)—§§ 14.1(b) n.30; 14.2(b) n.26

Whipple v. Duckworth, 957 F.2d 418 (7th Cir.1992)—§ 5.3(c) n.32

Whipple, People v., 97 N.Y.2d 1, 734 N.Y.S.2d 549, 760 N.E.2d 337 (N.Y.2001)—§ 24.6(b) n.22

Whipple, People v., 9 Cow. 707 (N.Y.1827)—§ 15.1(b) n.77

Whipple, State v., 324 S.C. 43, 476 S.E.2d 683 (S.C.1996)—§ 21.3(c) n.148

Whipple, State v., 57 Vt. 637 (1885)— § 15.2(h) n.185

Whiskey Cases, 99 U.S. 594, 25 L.Ed. 399 (1878)—§ 21.2(b) n.72

Whisler, People v., 724 P.2d 648 (Colo.1986)—§ 9.1(b) n.95

Whisnant, People v., 103 Mich.App. 772, 303 N.W.2d 887 (1981)— § 3.9(h) n.167

Whitaker, People v., 64 N.Y.2d 347, 486 N.Y.S.2d 895, 476 N.E.2d 294 (1985)—§ 3.2(g) n.192

Whitaker, State v., 215 Conn. 739, 578 A.2d 1031 (1990)—§§ 6.9(b) n.22; 6.9(g) n.177

Whitaker, State v., 202 Conn. 259, 520 A.2d 1018 (1987)—§ 24.3(c) n.93

Whitaker, United States v., 127 F.3d 595 (7th Cir.1997)—§§ 21.2(d) n.146; 21.2(f) n.362

Whitaker, United States v., 447 F.2d 314 (D.C.Cir.1971)—§§ 24.8(e) n.81, 84

Whitchurch, State v., 155 Vt. 134, 577 A.2d 690 (1990)—§§ 26.9(b) n.46; 26.9(c) n.84

White v. Bowersox, 206 F.3d 776 (8th Cir.2000)—§ 28.4(b) n.18

White v. City of Markham, 310 F.3d 989 (7th Cir.2002)—§ 3.8(c) n.107

White, Commonwealth v., 589 Pa. 642, 910 A.2d 648 (2006)—§ 22.4(c) n.28

White, Commonwealth v., 374 Mass. 132, 371 N.E.2d 777 (1977)— §§ 9.5(b) n.32, 34

White, Commonwealth v., 228 Pa.Super. 23, 324 A.2d 469 (1974)—§ 10.6(b) n.12

White, Commonwealth v., 459 Pa. 84, 327 A.2d 40 (1974)—§ 9.1(b) n.81

White, Commonwealth v., 353 Mass. 409, 232 N.E.2d 335 (1967)— § 6.10(b) n.13

White v. Coplan, 399 F.3d 18 (1st Cir.2005)—§ 24.4(b) n.13

White v. Godinez, 301 F.3d 796 (7th Cir.2002)—§ 11.10(c) n.49

White v. Johnson, 153 F.3d 197 (5th Cir.1998)—§ 27.6(d) n.146

White v. Kelso, 261 Ga. 32, 401 S.E.2d 733 (1991)—§ 11.7(e) n.98

White v. Kendrick, 1 Brev (S.C.) 469 (1805)—§ 2.4(c) n.93

White v. Maryland, 373 U.S. 59, 83 S.Ct. 1050, 10 L.Ed.2d 193 (1963)—§§ 6.4(a) n.8; 6.4(c) n.32; 6.4(h) n.168; 11.2(b) n.42; 21.3(a) n.2

White, People v., 196 App.Div.2d 641, 601 N.Y.S.2d 355 (1993)— § 24.7(i) n.96

White, People v., 73 N.Y.2d 468, 541 N.Y.S.2d 749, 539 N.E.2d 577 (1989)—§ 11.5(g) n.124

White, People v., 180 Ill.App.3d 781, 129 Ill.Dec. 641, 536 N.E.2d 481 (1989)—§§ 15.7(e) n.115, 124

White, People v., 117 Ill.2d 194, 111 Ill.Dec. 288, 512 N.E.2d 677 (1987)—§ 3.6(a) n.15

White, People v., 32 N.Y.2d 393, 345 N.Y.S.2d 513, 298 N.E.2d 659 (1973)—§§ 18.1(d) n.51; 21.2(b) n.91; 21.6(b) n.109, 110

White, People v., 390 Mich. 245, 212 N.W.2d 222 (1973)—§ 16.1(f) n.223

White v. Schotten, 201 F.3d 743 (6th Cir.2000)—§ 11.2(b) n.60

White, State v., 110 Haw. 79, 129 P.3d 1107 (2006)—§ 26.4(i) n.188

White v. State, 208 S.W.3d 467 (Tex.Cr.App.2006)—§ 24.10(c) n.40

White, State v., 340 Or.624, 147 P.3d 313 (2006)—§ 17.4(b) n.73

White, State v., 321 Mont. 45, 88 P.3d 1258 (2004)—§ 21.5(a) n.48

White, State v., 114 S.W.3d 469 (Tenn.2003)—§ 11.9(c) n.149

White, State v., 275 Kan. 580, 67 P.3d 138 (2003)—§§ 17.2(b) n.71; 17.2(d) n.94

White v. State, 374 Md. 232, 821 A.2d 459 (2003)—§ 6.7(b) n.41

White v. State, 772 N.E.2d 408 (Ind.2002)—§ 6.7(d) n.145

White, State v., 44 S.W.3d 838 (Mo.App.2001)—§§ 11.5(d) n.66; 11.5(f) n.103

White, State v., 326 N.J.Super. 304, 741 A.2d 143 (1999)—§§ 15.2(b) n.24, 27

White, State v., 587 N.W.2d 240 (Iowa 1998)—§ 21.4(d) n.106

White v. State, 330 Ark. 720, 957 S.W.2d 683 (1997)—§ 18.5(c) n.87

White, State v., 129 Wash.2d 105, 915 P.2d 1099 (1996)—§ 3.6(a) n.30

White, State v., 674 So.2d 1018 (La.App.1996)—§ 24.10(a) n.17

White, State v., 660 So.2d 664 (Fla.1995)—§ 3.1(h) n.215

White, State v., 229 Conn. 125, 640 A.2d 572 (1994)—§ 7.3(b) n.14

White, State v., 246 Neb. 346, 518 N.W.2d 923 (1994)—§ 11.6(c) n.100

White v. State, 263 Ga. 94, 428 S.E.2d 789 (1993)—§ 9.1(b) n.69

White, State v., 857 S.W.2d 344 (Mo.App.1993)—§ 26.3(f) n.65

White, State v., 188 W.Va. 534, 425 S.E.2d 210 (1992)—§ 26.1(e) n.99

White, State v., 331 N.C. 604, 419 S.E.2d 557 (N.C.1992)—§ 20.4(b) n.40

White, State v., 838 S.W.2d 140 (Mo.App.1992)—§§ 18.5(a) n.39; 21.2(d) n.278

White, State v., 239 Neb. 554, 477 N.W.2d 24 (1991)—§ 18.5(a) n.8

White, State v., 160 Ariz. 24, 770 P.2d 328 (1989)—§ 7.4(g) n.116

White v. State, 773 P.2d 211 (Alaska App.1989)—§§ 11.9(d) n.169, 209

White, State v., 85 N.C.App. 81, 354 S.E.2d 324 (1987)—§ 25.4(a) n.7

White v. State, 497 N.E.2d 893 (Ind.1986)—§ 21.4(d) n.103

White, State v., 234 Kan. 340, 673 P.2d 1106 (1983)—§ 18.4(c) n.59

White, State v., 337 N.W.2d 517 (Iowa 1983)—§ 11.7(e) n.73

White, State v., 325 N.W.2d 76, 109 Wis.2d 64 (App.1982)—§ 19.3(a) n.13

White, State v., 53 Or.App. 856, 632 P.2d 1363 (1981)—§ 11.4(c) n.64

White v. State, 577 P.2d 1056 (Alaska 1978)—§ 20.6(b) n.56

White, State v., 26 Ariz.App. 505, 549 P.2d 600 (1976)—§ 3.9(h) n.158

White, State v., 195 La. 1028, 197 So. 745 (1940)—§ 19.3(a) n.17

White, State v., 316 Mo. 576, 292 S.W. 411 (1927)—§ 6.2(a) n.11

White v. Texas, 310 U.S. 530, 60 S.Ct. 1032, 84 L.Ed. 1342 (1940)—§§ 6.2(c) n.83, 165

White, United States v., 408 F.3d 399 (8th Cir.2005)—§ 21.4(f) n.171

White, United States v., 431 F.3d 431 (5th Cir.2005)—§ 24.2(g) n.93

White, United States v., 366 F.3d 291 (4th Cir.2004)—§ 21.5(d) n.100

White, United States v., 367 F.3d 968 (8th Cir.2004)—§ 21.2(d) n.161

White v. United States, 863 A.2d 839 (D.C.App.2004)—§§ 21.5(a) n.38, 40, 41

White, United States v., 326 F.3d 1135 (10th Cir.2003)—§ 9.3(e) n.56

White, United States v., 307 F.3d 336 (5th Cir.2002)—§ 11.7(e) n.113

White, United States v., 244 F.3d 1199 (10th Cir.2001)—§ 26.9(b) n.57

White, United States v., 258 F.3d 374 (5th Cir.2001)—§ 21.2(b) n.84

White, United States v., 270 F.3d 356 (6th Cir.2001)—§§ 6.6(e) n.61; 13.6(c) n.27

White, United States v., 174 F.3d 290 (2d Cir.1999)—§§ 11.4(b) n.22; 11.9(d) n.217

White, United States v., 116 F.3d 948 (1st Cir.1997)—§ 26.6(d) n.47

White, United States v., 689 A.2d 535 (D.C.App.1997)—§ 13.2(c) n.56

White, United States v., 855 F.Supp. 13 (D.Mass.1994)—§§ 23.1(d) n.179; 23.1(e) n.232, 233, 245, 251

White, United States v., 985 F.2d 271 (6th Cir.1993)—§ 18.2(e) n.76

White, United States v., 997 F.2d 1213 (7th Cir.1993)—§ 21.4(e) n.153

White, United States v., 972 F.2d 590 (5th Cir.1992)—§ 24.10(b) n.30

White, United States v., 936 F.2d 1326 (D.C.Cir.1991)—§ 17.4(a) n.6

White, United States v., 914 F.2d 747 (6th Cir.1990)—§ 25.2(a) n.10

White, United States v., 887 F.2d 267 (D.C.Cir.1989)—§ 16.2(e) n.75

White, United States v., 890 F.2d 1012 (8th Cir.1989)—§ 3.2(e) n.171

White, United States v., 890 F.2d 1413 (8th Cir.1989)—§ 3.1(c) n.65

White v. United States, 858 F.2d 416 (8th Cir.1988)—§ 21.6(a) n.77

White v. United States, 484 A.2d 553 (D.C.App.1984)—§ 18.2(c) n.49

White, United States v., 724 F.2d 714 (8th Cir.1984)—§ 21.2(d) n.190

White, United States v., 750 F.2d 726 (8th Cir.1984)—§ 20.3(h) n.156

White, United States v., 611 F.2d 531 (5th Cir.1980)—§§ 16.1(g) n.238; 16.4(d) n.117, 124, 127, 130; 24.6(b) n.27

White, United States v., 401 U.S. 745, 91 S.Ct. 1122, 28 L.Ed.2d 453 (1971)—§§ 3.2(a) n.20, 25; 3.2(j) n.234; 3.10(c) n.83; 4.3(b) n.6; 4.6(l) n.198; 6.2(c) n.149

White, United States v., 454 F.2d 435 (7th Cir.1971)—§ 20.3(i) n.177

White, United States v., 322 U.S. 694, 64 S.Ct. 1248, 88 L.Ed. 1542 (1944)—§§ 2.9(i) n.273; 2.10(d) n.161; 8.12(a) n.6; 8.12(b) n.17

Whiteaker v. State, 808 P.2d 270 (Alaska App.1991)—§ 24.10(d) n.46

Whitehead v. Cowan, 263 F.3d 708 (7th Cir.2001)—§ 6.7(a) n.28

Whitehead, People v., 143 A.D.2d 1066, 533 N.Y.S.2d 753 (N.Y.1988)—§ 10.5(e) n.56

Whitehead, People v., 116 Ill.2d 425, 108 Ill.Dec. 376, 508 N.E.2d 687 (1987)—§ 6.10(b) n.14

Whitehead v. State, 220 S.W.3d 171 (Tex.App. 2007)—§ 22.4(c) n.30

Whitehead v. State, 777 So.2d 781 (Ala.Crim.App.1999)—§ 17.2(c) n.83

Whitehead, United States v., 238 F.3d 949 (8th Cir.2001)—§ 22.3(d) n.176

Whitehead, United States v., 200 F.3d 634 (9th Cir.2000)—§ 6.5(b) n.25

Whitehead, United States v., 849 F.2d 849 (4th Cir.1988)—§ 3.2(b) n.72

Whitehead, United States v., 539 F.2d 1023 (4th Cir.1976)—§§ 17.2(a) n.26; 17.3(a) n.7

Whitehead, State ex rel. v. Vescovi-Dial, 124 N.M. 375, 950 P.2d 818 (N.M.App.1997)—§§ 14.1(a) n.2; 14.1(d) n.49; 14.2(e) n.85

Whitehorn, United States v., 829 F.2d 1225 (2d Cir.1987)—§ 9.3(e) n.76

Whitehouse v. United States District Court, 53 F.3d 1349 (1st Cir.1995)—§§ 1.7(i) n.197; 8.8(d) n.105

Whitehurst, People v., 25 N.Y.2d 389, 306 N.Y.S.2d 673, 254 N.E.2d 905 (1969)—§ 10.3(a) n.2

Whiteley, State v., 124 Idaho 261, 858 P.2d 800 (1993)—§ 10.4(c) n.20

Whiteley v. Warden, 401 U.S. 560, 91 S.Ct. 1031, 28 L.Ed.2d 306 (1971)—§§ 3.3(c) n.84; 3.3(e) n.183; 3.4(c) n.35; 3.5(a) n.59, 63; 3.8(d) n.170

White Ready-Mix Concrete Co., United States v., 509 F.Supp. 747 (N.D.Ohio 1981)—§ 8.5(h) n.268

Whiteside v. Superior Court, 25 Cal.App.3d 1021, 102 Cal.Rptr. 381 (1972)—§ 16.3(g) n.106

White, State ex rel. v. Gray, 57 Wis.2d 17, 203 N.W.2d 638 (1973)— § 21.2(b) n.54

Whitfield, People v., 217 Ill.2d 177, 298 Ill.Dec. 545, 840 N.E.2d 658 (2005)—§§ 21.2(d) n.194; 21.2(e) n.349; 21.4(d) n.114, 150

Whitfield, People v., 81 N.Y.2d 904, 597 N.Y.S.2d 641, 613 N.E.2d 547 (1993)—§ 10.3(b) n.31

Whitfield, People v., 40 Ill.2d 308, 239 N.E.2d 850 (1968)—§ 21.3(b) n.106

Whitfield v. State, 867 A.2d 168 (Del.2005)—§ 17.3(b) n.13

Whitfield v. State, 287 Md. 124, 411 A.2d 415 (App.1980)—§ 6.7(b) n.78

Whitfield, United States v., 939 F.2d 1071 (D.C.Cir.1991)—§§ 3.10(d) n.134, 136; 3.10(e) n.143

Whiting v. United States, 296 F.2d 512 (1st Cir.1961)—§ 5.3(a) n.13

Whitley v. Senkowski, 317 F.3d 223 (2d Cir.2003)—§ 28.5(b) n.62

Whitley, United States v., 759 F.2d 327 (4th Cir.1985)—§§ 21.5(e) n.127, 137

Whitlock, People v., 174 Ill.App.3d 749, 124 Ill.Dec. 263, 528 N.E.2d 1371 (1988)—§ 14.2(d) n.50

Whitlow, United States v., 287 F.3d 638 (7th Cir.2002)—§ 21.2(d) n.274

Whitman v. Superior Court, 54 Cal.3d 1063, 2 Cal.Rptr.2d 160, 820 P.2d 262 (1991)—§§ 14.3(a) n.35; 14.4(b) n.30, 32

Whitmore v. Arkansas, 495 U.S. 149, 110 S.Ct. 1717, 109 L.Ed.2d 135 (1990)—§ 27.1(a) n.13

Whitmore, State v., 221 Neb. 450, 378 N.W.2d 150 (1985)—§ 6.7(b) n.70

Whitner, United States v., 219 F.3d 289 (3d Cir.2000)—§ 3.3(b) n.60

Whitney, In re, 421 F.2d 337 (1st Cir.1970)—§ 12.4(f) n.95

Whitney v. California, 274 U.S. 357, 47 S.Ct. 641, 71 L.Ed. 1095 (1927)— § 2.4(d) n.127

Whitrock, State v., 161 Wis.2d 960, 468 N.W.2d 696 (1991)—§§ 3.10(d) n.134; 9.1(b) n.69

Whitsell, State v., 262 La. 165, 262 So.2d 509 (1972)—§ 8.1(c) n.37

Whitsey v. State, 796 S.W.2d 707 (Tex.Cr.App.1989)—§ 27.5(e) n.164

Whitt, People v., 36 Cal.3d 724, 205 Cal.Rptr. 810, 685 P.2d 1161 (1984)—§ 6.10(b) n.16

Whitt, State v., 649 S.E.2d 258, [2007 WL 1039066] (W.Va.2007)— § 24.4(c) n.20

Whittaker, State v., 568 N.W.2d 440 (Minn.1997)—§ 15.4(g) n.178

Whitten, United States v., 706 F.2d 1000 (9th Cir.1983)—§ 3.6(d) n.100

Whittey, State v., 149 N.H. 463, 821 A.2d 1086 (2003)—§ 22.4(c) n.29

Whittington, State v., 260 Kan. 873, 926 P.2d 237 (1996)—§§ 13.2(c) n.56; 14.1(a) n.2

Whittington v. State, 680 S.W.2d 505 (Tex.App.1984)—§ 14.2(d) n.58

Whittington, State v., 142 N.J.Super. 45, 359 A.2d 881 (1976)—§ 10.4(c) n.21

Whittle, State v., 989 P.2d 52 (Utah 1999)—§ 15.6(f) n.203

Whittle, State v., 156 Ariz. 405, 752 P.2d 494 (1988)—§§ 24.8(f) n.92, 121

Whittlesey v. State, 326 Md. 502, 606 A.2d 225 (1992)—§ 17.4(b) n.98

Whitus v. Balkcom, 333 F.2d 496 (5th Cir.1964)—§ 11.6(a) n.30

Whorton v. Bockting, _____ U.S. _____, 127 S.Ct. 1173, 167 L.Ed.2d 1 (2007)—§ 28.6(d) n.27

Wren v. United States, 517 U.S. 806, 116 S.Ct. 1769, 135 L.Ed.2d 89 (1996)—§§ 1.5(j) n.324; 3.1(d) n.115; 3.4(k) n.239; 3.5(b) n.88, 97; 3.5(e) n.196; 3.6(g) n.172; 3.7(a) n.9; 3.7(f) n.149; 3.8(c) n.115; 3.9(h) n.155; 3.9(j) n.226; 10.3(b) n.16; 12.5(b) n.34

Wichita, City of v. Lucero, 255 Kan. 437, 874 P.2d 1144 (1994)— § 26.1(f) n.144

Wick v. Baldwin, 36 N.E. 671, 51 Ohio St. 51 (1894)—§ 15.1(b) n.77

Wickard v. Filburn, 317 U.S. 111, 63 S.Ct. 82, 87 L.Ed. 122 (1942)— §§ 1.2(c) n.127, 154, 161

Wicker, United States v., 848 F.2d 1059 (10th Cir.1988)—§ 20.6(b) n.38

Wickham, People v., 53 P.3d 691 (Colo.App.2001)—§ 6.2(c) n.154

Wickham, United States v., 30 F.3d 1252 (9th Cir.1994)—§ 18.4(b) n.26

Wicks, People v., 76 N.Y.2d 128, 556 N.Y.S.2d 970, 556 N.E.2d 409 (1990)—§ 14.4(e) n.136

Wicks, State v., 576 NW2d 518 (1998)—§ 11.9(b) n.55

Wicks, State v., 576 N.W.2d 518 (1998)—§ 11.9(d) n.217

Wicks, State v., 1998 ND 76, 576 N.W.2d 518 (1998)—§ 11.4(b) n.30

Wicks v. State, 270 Ark. 781, 606 S.W.2d 366 (1980)—§ 27.5(d) n.119

Wicktor, United States v., 403 F.Supp.2d 964 (D.Ariz.2005)—§ 14.4(c) n.64

Wideman, Commonwealth v., 478 Pa. 102, 385 A.2d 1334 (1978)— § 9.5(b) n.35

Widmer-Baum, State v., 653 N.W.2d 351 (Iowa 2002)—§ 18.4(c) n.44

Wiegers, State v., 373 N.W.2d 1 (S.D.1985)—§ 24.3(h) n.176

Wiegmann, State v., 350 Md. 585, 714 A.2d 841 (1998)—§ 3.1(o) n.303

Wiernasz, State v., 584 N.W.2d 1 (Minn.1998)—§§ 6.6(c) n.37; 6.6(d) n.49

Wiggins v. Corcoran, 288 F.3d 629 (4th Cir.2002)—§ 11.10(c) n.127

Wiggins v. Procunier, 753 F.2d 1318 (5th Cir.1985)—§ 11.5(c) n.52

Wiggins v. Smith, 539 U.S. 510, 123 S.Ct. 2527, 156 L.Ed.2d 471 (2003)—§§ 11.10(b) n.39, 46; 11.10(c) n.133; 11.10(d) n.163; 28.6(f) n.69

Wiggins, State v., 334 N.C. 18, 431 S.E.2d 755 (1993)—§§ 14.2(g) n.97; 22.3(d) n.247

Wiggins v. State, 386 So.2d 46 (Fla.App.1980)—§ 26.9(b) n.26

Wiggins, United States v., 131 F.3d 1440 (11th Cir.1997)—§ 21.4(c) n.71

Wiggins, United States v., 905 F.2d 51 (4th Cir.1990)—§ 21.2(b) n.85

Wigginton v. State, 668 So.2d 763 (Miss.1996)—§ 26.1(e) n.113

Wika, State v., 464 N.W.2d 630 (S.D.1991)—§ 21.4(a) n.27

Wilcher v. State, 863 So.2d 719 (2003)—§ 28.4(d) n.70

Wilcher v. State, 697 So.2d 1087 (Miss.1997)—§ 6.4(f) n.136

Wilcher v. State, 876 S.W.2d 466 (Tex.App.1994)—§ 3.9(k) n.258

Wilcox, Commonwealth v., 437 Mass. 33, 767 N.E.2d 1061 (2002)— §§ 15.6(c) n.100, 102

Wilcox v. Hopkins, 249 F.3d 720 (8th Cir.2001)—§ 21.3(b) n.45

Wilcox, People v., 303 Mich. 287, 6 N.W.2d 518 (1942)—§ 8.1(c) n.26

Wilcox, State v., 808 P.2d 1028 (Utah 1991)—§§ 19.3(b) n.135, 163

Wilcox, State v., 104 N.C. 847, 10 S.E. 453 (1889)—§ 15.4(g) n.169

Wilcox, United States v., 357 F.Supp. 514 (E.D.Pa.1973)—§ 9.1(b) n.42

Wilcox, United States ex rel. v. Johnson, 555 F.2d 115 (3d Cir.1977)— § 11.6(a) n.22

Wild, United States v., 551 F.2d 418 (D.C.Cir.1977)—§§ 18.5(a) n.51; 21.6(a) n.23

Wildberger v. State, 74 Md.App. 107, 536 A.2d 718 (1988)—§ 3.9(d) n.69

Wildenstein, State v., 91 N.M. 550, 577 P.2d 448 (1978)—§ 11.2(d) n.126

Wilderness, United States v., 160 F.3d 1173 (7th Cir.1998)—§ 6.9(g) n.178

Wilding v. State, 674 So.2d 114 (Fla.1996)—§ 24.9(f) n.80

Wild, State ex rel. v. Otis, 257 N.W.2d 361 (Minn.1977)—§ 8.4(b) n.88

Wilen, State v., 4 Neb.App. 132, 539 N.W.2d 650 (1995)—§ 27.3(c) n.56

Wiles, State v., 59 Ohio St.3d 71, 571 N.E.2d 97 (1991)—§ 6.2(c) n.128

Wiles, United States v., 106 F.3d 1516 (10th Cir.1997)—§ 25.4(c) n.28

Wiley v. Couzens, 38 N.Y.2d 731, 381 N.Y.S.2d 39, 343 N.E.2d 757 (1975)—§ 24.10(d) n.47

Wiley, People v., 156 Ill.2d 464, 190 Ill.Dec. 736, 622 N.E.2d 766 (1993)—§ 22.3(d) n.220

Wiley, State v., 232 Neb. 642, 441 N.W.2d 629 (1989)—§ 21.3(b) n.137

Wiley, United States v., 997 F.2d 378 (8th Cir.1993)—§§ 8.11(b) n.29; 9.5(b) n.45

Wiley, United States v., 267 F.2d 453 (7th Cir.1959)—§ 21.2(a) n.22

Wilhelm v. Boggs, 290 F.3d 822 (6th Cir.2002)—§ 3.10(e) n.152

Wilhelmi v. Director of Department of Transportation, 498 N.W.2d 150 (N.D.1993)—§ 3.5(d) n.142

Wilk, People v., 124 Ill.2d 93, 529 N.E.2d 218 (1988)—§ 27.5(c) n.107

Wilkerson, Commonwealth v., 436 Mass. 137, 763 N.E.2d 508 (2002)—§ 3.1(h) n.215

Wilkerson, People v., 123 Ill.App.3d 527, 79 Ill.Dec. 1, 463 N.E.2d 139 (1984)—§ 22.5(b) n.23

Wilkerson v. State, 173 S.W.3d 521 (Tex.Crim.App.2005)—§ 6.10(c) n.52

Wilkerson, State v., 948 S.W.2d 440 (Mo.App.1997)—§ 11.3(a) n.21

Wilkerson, United States v., 208 F.3d 794 (9th Cir.2000)—§ 22.4(c) n.29

Wilkerson, United States v., 170 F.3d 1040 (11th Cir.1999)—§ 18.3(b) n.9

Wilkerson, United States v., 84 F.3d 692 (4th Cir.1996)—§§ 7.4(b) n.9; 7.4(c) n.48, 62

Wilkerson v. Wyrick, 806 F.2d 161 (8th Cir.1986)—§ 19.2(c) n.31

Wilkes, State v., 233 N.C. 645, 65 S.E.2d 129 (1951)—§ 1.8(d) n.59

Wilkes, United States v., 130 F.Supp.2d 222 (D.Mass.2001)—§ 19.2(f) n.92

Wilkes v. United States, 631 A.2d 880 (D.C.App.1993)—§ 9.6(a) n.50

Wilkett v. State, 753 P.2d 383 (Okla.Crim.App.1988)—§ 18.4(c) n.73

Wilkett v. United States, 655 F.2d 1007 (10th Cir.1981)—§§ 16.1(h) n.300; 25.3(a) n.8

Wilkey v. State, 203 Ga.App. 1, 416 S.E.2d 350 (Ga.App. 1992)—§ 5.3(d) n.42

Wilkey v. Superior Court, 115 Ariz. 526, 566 P.2d 327 (App.1977)—§ 15.6(c) n.91

Wilkins v. Bowersox, 933 F.Supp. 1496 (W.D.Mo.1996)—§ 11.3(b) n.48

Wilkins v. Erickson, 505 F.2d 761 (9th Cir.1974)—§ 21.4(e) n.166

Wilkins v. May, 872 F.2d 190 (7th Cir.1989)—§ 6.5(e) n.97

Wilkins, People v., 68 N.Y.2d 269, 508 N.Y.S.2d 893, 501 N.E.2d 542 (1986)—§§ 15.6(f) n.177, 204

Wilkins v. State, 104 P.3d 85 (Wyo.2005)—§ 10.3(c) n.52

Wilkins v. State, 879 So.2d 61 (Fla.App.2004)—§ 12.1(b) n.32

Wilkins, State v., 267 Kan. 355, 985 P.2d 690 (1999)—§ 18.5(a) n.22

Wilkins, State v., 240 Conn. 489, 692 A.2d 1233 (1997)—§ 3.8(b) n.30

Wilkins, State v., 534 So.2d 705 (Fla.1988)—§ 13.7(c) n.45

Wilkins, State v., 144 Vt. 22, 473 A.2d 295 (1983)—§ 5.2(b) n.24

Wilkins, State v., 64 Ohio St.2d 382, 415 N.E.2d 303 (1980)—§ 24.8(f) n.98

Wilkins v. United States, 441 U.S. 468, 99 S.Ct. 1829, 60 L.Ed.2d 365 (1979)—§ 11.2(b) n.67

Wilkinson v. Austin, 545 U.S. 209, 125 S.Ct. 2384, 162 L.Ed.2d 174 (2005)—§§ 26.2(c) n.42, 63

Wilkinson v. Dotson, 544 U.S. 74, 125 S.Ct. 1242, 161 L.Ed.2d 253 (2005)—§§ 28.1(a) n.3; 28.3(b) n.67

Wilkinson, State v., 136 N.H. 170, 612 A.2d 926 (1992)—§ 3.3(d) n.158

Wilkinson, United States v., 53 F.3d 757 (6th Cir.1995)—§ 4.6(m) n.240

Wilkinson, United States v., 926 F.2d 22 (1st Cir.1991)—§ 3.2(h) n.212

Wilkinson, United States v., 460 F.2d 725 (5th Cir.1972)—§ 6.10(b) n.23

Wilks v. Israel, 627 F.2d 32 (7th Cir.1980)—§§ 11.4(d) n.110, 113; 22.4(c) n.24

Will v. Michigan Dep't of State Police, 491 U.S. 58, 109 S.Ct. 2304, 105 L.Ed.2d 45 (1989)—§ 3.1(k) n.266

Will v. United States, 389 U.S. 90, 88 S.Ct. 269, 19 L.Ed.2d 305 (1967)—§§ 27.4(b) n.8; 27.4(d) n.44

Willaman, United States v., 437 F.3d 354 (3d Cir.2006)—§§ 6.6(e) n.61; 18.3(b) n.9

Willard, State v., 144 Ohio App.3d 767, 761 N.E.2d 688 (2001)—§ 24.7(i) n.91

Willbright v. Smith, 745 F.2d 779 (2d Cir.1984)—§ 21.4(f) n.204

Will County Grand Jury, In re, 152 Ill.2d 381, 178 Ill.Dec. 406, 604 N.E.2d 929 (1992)—§§ 2.12(e) n.205; 8.7(d) n.84, 86

Willcoxon, People v., 80 P.3d 817 (Colo.App.2002)—§ 24.9(c) n.22

Willett v. Lockhart, 37 F.3d 1265 (8th Cir.1994)—§ 28.3(d) n.82

William, State v., 248 Kan. 389, 807 P.2d 1292 (1991)—§ 6.6(d) n.58

Williams, Ex parte, 780 So.2d 673 (Ala.2000)—§ 6.2(c) n.112

Williams, Ex parte, 704 S.W.2d 773 (Tex.Cr.App.1986)—§ 21.4(d) n.119

Williams, In re, 444 F.3d 233 (4th Cir.2006)—§ 28.5(c) n.74

Williams, In re, 766 F.Supp. 358 (W.D.Pa.1991)—§ 8.8(d) n.82

Williams v. Bagley, 380 F.3d 932 (6th Cir.2004)—§ 28.7(d) n.26

Williams v. Beto, 354 F.2d 698 (5th Cir.1965)—§ 11.10(a) n.8

Williams v. Chrans, 957 F.2d 487 (7th Cir.1992)—§ 22.3(d) n.246

Williams v. Chrans, 945 F.2d 926 (7th Cir.1991)—§ 21.3(b) n.84

Williams, Commonwealth v., 439 Mass. 678, 790 N.E.2d 662 (2003)—§ 8.7(d) n.81

Williams v. Commonwealth, 24 Va.App. 577, 484 S.E.2d 153 (1997)—§ 24.9(b) n.13

Williams v. Commonwealth, 16 Va.App. 928, 434 S.E.2d 343 (1993)—§ 20.3(m) n.236

Williams, Commonwealth v., 388 Pa.Super. 153, 565 A.2d 160 (Pa.Super.1989)—§§ 8.8(h) n.184, 189

Williams v. Commonwealth, 234 Va. 168, 360 S.E.2d 361 (1987)—§ 6.2(c) n.111

Williams, Commonwealth v., 504 Pa. 511, 475 A.2d 1283 (1984)—§ 6.9(b) n.20

Williams v. Commonwealth, 261 S.W.2d 416 (Ky.1953)—§ 3.4(e) n.94

Williams, Commonwealth v., 56 Mass. (2 Cush.) 582 (1849)—§ 1.6(d) n.209

Williams v. District Court, El Paso County, 700 P.2d 549 (Colo.1985)—§ 8.8(d) n.91

Williams v. Duffy, 270 Ga. 580, 513 S.E.2d 212 (1999)—§§ 21.3(b) n.66, 71

Williams v. Florida, 399 U.S. 78, 90 S.Ct. 1893, 26 L.Ed.2d 446 (1970)—§§ 1.5(c) n.141, 145; 1.8(e) n.88; 2.1 n.59; 2.5(f) n.90, 99, 102; 2.6(a) n.6; 2.6(b) n.32, 49; 2.6(c) n.77; 2.6(d) n.97; 2.9(d) n.55, 57, 59; 2.9(e) n.105; 2.9(i) n.271; 2.10(b) n.14; 16.1(b) n.55, 59, 70; 20.1(d) n.56; 20.4(a) n.1; 20.4(b) n.22; 20.4(c) n.43; 20.4(d) n.52; 20.5(b) n.26, 28; 22.1(d) n.67; 22.3(e) n.288; 24.4(a) n.8

Williams v. Henderson, 289 So.2d 74 (La.1974)—§ 21.6(a) n.57

Williams v. Illinois, 399 U.S. 235, 90 S.Ct. 2018, 26 L.Ed.2d 586 (1970)—§§ 2.7(c) n.135; 2.9(d) n.88; 12.2(b) n.22; 26.1(f) n.140

Williams v. Lawrence, 273 Ga. 295, 540 S.E.2d 599 (2001)—§ 26.10(c) n.73

Williams v. Meachum, 948 F.2d 863 (2d Cir.1991)—§§ 11.9(c) n.124, 132

Williams v. Missouri, 640 F.2d 140 (8th Cir.1981)—§ 21.2(b) n.41

Williams v. New York, 337 U.S. 241, 69 S.Ct. 1079, 93 L.Ed. 1337 (1949)—§§ 2.7(a) n.53 to 55; 2.7(c) n.191; 26.4(a) n.1; 26.5(a) n.2; 26.8(b) n.7

Williams v. Ohio, 547 F.2d 40 (6th Cir.1976)—§ 6.2(c) n.135

Williams v. Oklahoma, 358 U.S. 576, 79 S.Ct. 421, 3 L.Ed.2d 516 (1959)—§ 26.7(d) n.38

Williams, People v., 40 Cal.4th 287, 148 P.3d 47, 52 Cal.Rptr.3d 268 (2006)—§ 24.9(f) n.69

Williams, People v., 475 Mich. 245, 716 N.W.2d 208 (2006)—§§ 18.2(b) n.18; 18.2(c) n.53

Williams, People v., 25 Cal.4th 441, 106 Cal.Rptr.2d 295, 21 P.3d 1209 (2001)—§§ 22.1(g) n.109; 24.9(f) n.104

Williams, People v., 241 Mich.App. 519, 616 N.W.2d 710 (2000)—§ 22.3(b) n.67

Williams, People v., 188 Ill.2d 365, 242 Ill.Dec. 260, 721 N.E.2d 539 (1999)—§ 21.4(d) n.120

Williams, People v., 987 P.2d 232 (Colo.1999)—§ 14.3(c) n.70

Williams, People v., 16 Cal.4th 153, 66 Cal.Rptr.2d 123, 940 P.2d 710 (1997)—§ 7.4(g) n.114

Williams, People v., 16 Cal.4th 635, 66 Cal.Rptr.2d 573, 941 P.2d 752 (1997)—§ 6.2(c) n.99

Williams, People v., 226 Mich.App. 568, 576 N.W.2d 390 (1997)—§ 27.3(c) n.25

Williams, People v., 46 Cal.App.4th 1767, 54 Cal.Rptr.2d 521 (1996)—§ 24.9(a) n.8

Williams, People v., 173 Ill.2d 48, 218 Ill.Dec. 916, 670 N.E.2d 638 (1996)—§ 22.3(c) n.112

Williams, People v., 196 Mich.App. 656, 493 N.W.2d 507 (1992)—§ 5.2(b) n.29

Williams, People v., 143 Ill.2d 477, 160 Ill.Dec. 437, 577 N.E.2d 762 (1991)—§ 12.4(d) n.81

Williams, People v., 138 Ill.2d 377, 150 Ill.Dec. 498, 563 N.E.2d 385 (1990)—§ 10.6(c) n.34

Williams, People v., 213 Cal.App.3d 1186, 262 Cal.Rptr. 303 (1989)—§ 14.4(c) n.53

Williams, People v., 44 Cal.3d 883, 245 Cal.Rptr. 336, 751 P.2d 395 (1988)—§ 11.10(d) n.162

Williams, People v., 136 A.D.2d 132, 526 N.Y.S.2d 581 (1988)—§ 15.7(g) n.212

Williams, People v., 62 N.Y.2d 285, 476 N.Y.S.2d 788, 465 N.E.2d 327 (1984)—§ 6.9(b) n.24

Williams, People v., 97 Ill.2d 252, 73 Ill.Dec. 360, 454 N.E.2d 220 (1983)—§ 2.12(e) n.211

Williams, People v., 92 Ill.2d 109, 64 Ill.Dec. 939, 440 N.E.2d 843 (1982)—§§ 11.3(c) n.54, 56

Williams, People v., 87 Ill.2d 161, 57 Ill.Dec. 589, 429 N.E.2d 487 (1981)—§§ 20.2(b) n.25; 20.4(b) n.27; 20.5(a) n.7

Williams, People v., 55 Ill.App.3d 752, 13 Ill.Dec. 234, 370 N.E.2d 1261 (1977)—§ 20.6(c) n.82

Williams, People v., 77 Mich.App. 119, 258 N.W.2d 68 (1977)—§ 24.11(d) n.22

Williams, People v., 16 Ill.App.3d 440, 306 N.E.2d 678 (1973)—§ 10.3(b) n.27

Williams, People v., 3 Cal.3d 853, 92 Cal.Rptr. 6, 478 P.2d 942 (1971)— §§ 7.3(c) n.59, 60

Williams, People v., 2 Cal.3d 894, 88 Cal.Rptr. 208, 471 P.2d 1008 (1970)—§§ 11.6(a) n.12, 37

Williams, People v., 269 Cal.App.2d 879, 75 Cal.Rptr. 348 (1969)— § 21.2(c) n.117

Williams, People v., 25 Ill.2d 562, 185 N.E.2d 686 (1962)—§ 10.5(c) n.27

Williams, People v., 368 Mich. 494, 118 N.W.2d 391 (1962)—§ 10.2(b) n.28

Williams v. Poulos, 11 F.3d 271 (1st Cir.1993)—§§ 4.6(l) n.201; 4.6(n) n.261

Williams v. Smith, 591 F.2d 169 (2d Cir.1979)—§§ 21.4(d) n.144, 147, 148

Williams v. Spears, 814 So.2d 1167 (Fla.App.2002)—§ 12.3(b) n.38

Williams, State v., 953 So.2d 91 (La.App.2007)—§ 26.1(f) n.144

Williams, State v., 392 Md. 194, 896 A.2d 973 (2006)—§ 24.3(b) n.52

Williams v. State, 125 P.3d 627 (Nev.2005)—§ 22.2(c) n.44

Williams v. State, 363 Ark. 395, 214 S.W.3d 829 (2005)—§ 6.8(b) n.50

Williams v. State, 811 N.E.2d 462 (Ind.App.2004)—§ 26.4(b) n.11

Williams, State v., 97 S.W.3d 462 (Mo.2003)—§ 22.3(d) n.247

Williams, State v., 99 Ohio St.3d 439, 793 N.E.2d 446 (2003)—§§ 6.9(c) n.61, 66

Williams v. State, 375 Md. 404, 825 A.2d 1078 (2003)—§ 6.3(c) n.50

Williams, State v., 171 N.J. 151, 793 A.2d 594 (2002)—§§ 22.3(e) n.274, 276, 278

Williams, State v., 172 N.J. 361, 799 A.2d 470 (2002)—§ 17.4(c) n.153

Williams, State v., 249 Wis.2d 492, 637 N.W.2d 733 (2002)—§ 21.2(d) n.174

Williams v. State, 275 Ga. 622, 571 S.E.2d 385 (2002)—§ 7.4(e) n.82

Williams v. State, 372 Md. 386, 813 A.2d 231 (2002)—§ 9.3(e) n.56

Williams, State v., 592 N.W.2d 844 (Iowa App.2002)—§ 11.9(a) n.20

Williams, State v., 652 N.W.2d 844 (Iowa App.2002)—§ 11.9(d) n.224

Williams v. State, 762 N.E.2d 1216 (Ind.2002)—§ 17.4(c) n.144

Williams v. State, 774 N.E.2d 889 (Ind.2002)—§ 7.4(c) n.48

Williams v. State, 364 Md. 160, 771 A.2d 1082 (2001)—§§ 20.2(d) n.63; 20.3(k) n.220

Williams v. State, 792 So.2d 1207 (Fla.2001)—§ 24.9(f) n.102

Williams v. State, 794 So.2d 181 (Miss.2001)—§ 22.3(d) n.215

Williams v. State, 794 So.2d 1019 (Miss.2001)—§§ 6.6(d) n.58; 17.1(a) n.14

Williams, State v., 237 Wis.2d 591, 614 N.W.2d 11 (App.2000)—§ 22.3(c) n.162

Williams v. State, 272 Ga. 335, 528 S.E.2d 518 (2000)—§ 22.3(d) n.250

Williams v. State, 761 So.2d 149 (Miss.2000)—§ 5.3(a) n.5

Williams v. State, 271 Ga. 323, 519 S.E.2d 232 (1999)—§ 22.3(d) n.235

Williams v. State, 338 Ark. 178, 992 S.W.2d 89 (1999)—§§ 17.2(e) n.119; 17.2(f) n.132

Williams v. State, 736 So.2d 699 (Fla.App.1999)—§ 24.1(a) n.4

Williams, State v., 132 Wash.2d 248, 937 P.2d 1052 (1997)—§ 17.4(a) n.53

Williams v. State, 268 Ga. 488, 491 S.E.2d 377 (Ga.1997)—§ 25.4(a) n.9

Williams, State v., 299 N.J.Super. 264, 690 A.2d 1082 (1997)—§ 26.10(c) n.56

Williams v. State, 690 N.E.2d 162 (Ind.1997)—§ 26.3(f) n.51

Williams, State v., 198 Wis.2d 516, 544 N.W.2d 406 (1996)—§§ 14.1(a) n.4; 14.3(d) n.91

Williams, State v., 249 Neb. 582, 544 N.W.2d 350 (1996)—§ 3.8(e) n.210

Williams, State v., 321 S.C. 327, 468 S.E.2d 626 (1996)—§ 16.4(d) n.137

Williams v. State, 667 So.2d 15 (Miss.1996)—§ 14.1(c) n.43

Williams v. State, 669 N.E.2d 956 (Ind.1996)—§ 6.7(c) n.141

Williams v. State, 669 N.E.2d 1372 (Ind.1996)—§§ 22.3(d) n.219, 245

Williams v. State, 927 S.W.2d 903 (Mo.App.1996)—§ 26.10(b) n.18

Williams, State v., 535 N.W.2d 277 (Minn.1995)—§ 6.9(g) n.161

Williams, State v., 525 N.W.2d 538 (Minn.1994)—§ 22.2(d) n.77

Williams v. State, 634 N.E.2d 849 (Ind.App.1994)—§§ 16.1(g) n.245, 264; 16.1(h) n.300

Williams, State v., 227 Conn. 101, 629 A.2d 402 (1993)—§§ 6.6(e) n.91; 6.9(a) n.6; 6.9(d) n.67

Williams, State v., 243 Neb. 959, 503 N.W.2d 561 (1993)—§ 24.8(e) n.50

Williams, State v., 334 N.C. 440, 434 S.E.2d 588 (1993)—§§ 6.9(a) n.12; 6.9(d) n.72

Williams, State v., 623 So.2d 462 (Fla.1993)—§ 5.4(c) n.36

Williams, State v., 250 Kan. 730, 829 P.2d 892 (1992)—§ 13.7(a) n.29

Williams v. State, 326 Md. 367, 605 A.2d 103 (1992)—§§ 11.10(d) n.175; 21.3(b) n.62

Williams v. State, 601 So.2d 1062 (Ala.Crim.App.1991)—§ 9.1(b) n.76

Williams v. State, 574 So.2d 876 (Ala.Crim.App.1990)—§§ 11.9(d) n.202, 204, 205

Williams, State v., 181 W.Va. 150, 381 S.E.2d 265 (1989)—§§ 7.3(f) n.115, 116

Williams v. State, 533 N.E.2d 1193 (Ind.1989)—§ 18.4(c) n.67

Williams v. State, 258 Ga. 281, 368 S.E.2d 742 (1988)—§ 6.9(g) n.162

Williams v. State, 525 N.E.2d 337 (Ind.1988)—§ 6.2(c) n.135

Williams, State v., 166 Ariz. 132, 800 P.2d 1240 (1987)—§§ 7.4(b) n.35; 11.2(e) n.151, 154

Williams, State v., 203 Conn. 159, 523 A.2d 1284 (1987)—§§ 7.4(e) n.82, 90, 92; 11.9(c) n.130

Williams, State v., 205 Conn. 456, 534 A.2d 230 (1987)—§ 22.1(h) n.139

Williams, State v., 200 Conn. 310, 511 A.2d 1000 (1986)—§ 17.2(c) n.87

Williams, State v., 314 N.C. 337, 333 S.E.2d 708 (1985)—§ 6.9(f) n.135

Williams, State v., 465 So.2d 1229 (Fla.1985)—§ 22.3(c) n.132

Williams v. State, 491 A.2d 1129 (Del.1985)—§ 21.2(h) n.428

Williams v. State, 349 N.W.2d 58 (S.D.1984)—§ 21.3(b) n.94

Williams v. State, 675 S.W.2d 754 (Tex.Cr.App.1984)—§ 7.4(d) n.69

Williams, State v., 681 S.W.2d 948 (Mo.App.1984)—§ 11.5(g) n.121

Williams v. State, 692 S.W.2d 671 (Tex.Cr.App.1984)—§ 6.3(c) n.53

Williams, State v., 93 N.J. 39, 459 A.2d 641 (1983)—§§ 23.1(d) n.138, 145

Williams v. State, 427 So.2d 768 (Fla.App.1983)—§§ 11.4(b) n.19; 11.5(d) n.77, 82

Williams v. State, 658 P.2d 499 (Okla.Cr.App.1983)—§ 24.7(e) n.38

Williams, State v., 305 N.W.2d 428 (Iowa 1981)—§ 19.5(b) n.23

Williams v. State, 406 So.2d 86 (Fla.App.1981)—§ 26.10(a) n.6

Williams v. State, 616 P.2d 881 (Alaska 1980)—§ 11.3(b) n.24

Williams, State v., 23 Wash.App. 694, 598 P.2d 731 (1979)—§§ 16.4(d) n.144; 27.5(c) n.99

Williams, State v., 80 N.J. 472, 404 A.2d 34 (1979)—§§ 20.4(f) n.97; 20.4(g) n.108, 109; 20.5(f) n.85

Williams, State v., 121 Ari. 218, 589 P.2d 461 (App.1979)—§ 20.6(c) n.85

Williams v. State, 600 P.2d 741 (Alaska 1979)—§§ 20.6(b) n.26, 28

Williams, State v., 16 Wash.App. 868, 560 P.2d 1160 (1977)—§ 3.5(b) n.102

Williams v. State, 342 So.2d 1328 (Ala.1977)—§§ 15.4(b) n.45, 59

Williams v. State, 549 S.W.2d 183 (Tex.Crim.App.1977)—§ 11.5(e) n.91

Williams v. State, 264 Ind. 664, 348 N.E.2d 623 (1976)—§ 9.4(a) n.10

Williams, State v., 307 Minn. 191, 239 N.W.2d 222 (1976)—§ 7.2(b) n.22

Williams v. State, 341 So.2d 214 (Fla.App.1976)—§ 21.2(e) n.339

Williams, State v., 115 N.H. 437, 343 A.2d 29 (1975)—§ 12.1(e) n.60

Williams v. State, 316 So.2d 267 (Fla.1975)—§ 21.4(f) n.172

Williams, State v., 260 La. 1153, 258 So.2d 534 (1972)—§ 24.2(b) n.30

Williams, State v., 262 La. 160, 262 So.2d 507 (1972)—§ 6.8(b) n.61

Williams, State v., 486 S.W.2d 468 (Mo.1972)—§§ 3.9(j) n.208; 6.10(c) n.49

Williams, State v., 182 N.W.2d 396 (Iowa 1970)—§ 6.4(d) n.54

Williams v. State, 44 Ala.App. 618, 217 So.2d 830 (1969)—§ 11.2(c) n.88

Williams, State v., 248 Or. 85, 432 P.2d 679 (1967)—§ 3.10(b) n.71

Williams v. State, 226 Md. 614, 174 A.2d 719 (1961)—§ 3.8(f) n.231

Williams, State v., 210 N.C. 159, 185 S.E. 661 (1936)—§ 19.3(b) n.178

Williams v. State, 188 Ind. 283, 123 N.E. 209 (1919)—§§ 15.6(d) n.117; 15.7(b) n.50; 15.7(h) n.228

Williams v. Superior Court, 46 Cal.App.4th 320, 53 Cal.Rptr.2d 832 (1996)—§§ 11.4(a) n.11, 15; 27.5(a) n.22

Williams v. Superior Court, 49 Cal.3d 736, 263 Cal.Rptr. 503, 781 P.2d 537 (1989)—§ 22.2(d) n.56

Williams v. Superior Court, 36 Cal.3d 441, 204 Cal.Rptr. 700, 683 P.2d 699 (1984)—§§ 17.1(b) n.25; 17.1(e) n.63

Williams v. Superior Court, 130 Ariz. 209, 635 P.2d 497 (1981)—§§ 21.3(f) n.429; 25.1(d) n.63

Williams v. Superior Court, 226 Cal.App.2d 666, 38 Cal.Rptr. 291 (1964)—§ 11.2(g) n.293

Williams v. Taylor, 529 U.S. 420, 120 S.Ct. 1479, 146 L.Ed.2d 435 (2000)—§ 28.7(c) n.15

Williams, United States v., 435 F.3d 1148 (9th Cir.2006)—§ 6.8(b) n.49

Williams, United States v., 445 F.3d 1302 (11th Cir.2006)—§ 26.6(c) n.42

Williams, United States v., 449 F.3d 635 (5th Cir.2006)—§§ 24.10(c) n.40; 25.4(d) n.45

Williams v. United States, 396 F.3d 1340 (11th Cir.2005)—§ 11.7(e) n.113

Williams, United States v., 429 F.3d 767 (8th Cir.2005)—§ 6.8(c) n.65

Williams, United States v., 365 F.3d 399 (5th Cir.2004)—§ 3.8(c) n.84

Williams, United States v., 372 F.3d 96 (2d Cir.2004)—§ 11.9(d) n.231

Williams, United States v., 340 F.3d 563 (8th Cir.2003)—§ 7.4(c) n.52

Williams, United States v., 354 F.3d 497 (6th Cir.2003)—§ 3.1(h) n.201

Williams, United States v., 264 F.3d 561 (5th Cir.2001)—§§ 22.2(c) n.43; 22.2(d) n.56; 22.3(d) n.247

Williams, United States v., 272 F.3d 845 (7th Cir.2001)—§§ 21.2(d) n.146; 21.2(f) n.362; 22.3(d) n.245

Williams, United States v., 274 F.3d 1079 (6th Cir.2001)—§ 16.2(e) n.90

Williams, United States v., 233 F.3d 592 (D.C.Cir.2000)—§ 24.11(d) n.30

Williams, United States v., 181 F.3d 945 (8th Cir.1999)—§§ 6.7(b) n.74, 87

Williams, United States v., 198 F.3d 988 (7th Cir.1999)—§ 21.2(e) n.320

Williams, United States v., 132 F.3d 1055 (5th Cir.1998)—§ 13.5(h) n.206

Williams, United States v., 103 F.3d 1093 (2d Cir.1997)—§ 24.6(b) n.22

Williams, United States v., 104 F.3d 213 (8th Cir.1997)—§ 21.4(d) n.120

Williams, United States v., 97 F.3d 240 (8th Cir.1996)—§§ 17.2(f) n.136; 17.3(e) n.64

Williams, United States v., 47 F.3d 658 (4th Cir.1995)—§ 21.2(b) n.44

Williams, United States v., 23 F.3d 629 (2d Cir.1994)—§ 21.4(a) n.37

Williams, United States v., 3 F.3d 69 (3d Cir.1993)—§ 3.3(d) n.147

Williams, United States v., 504 U.S. 36, 112 S.Ct. 1735, 118 L.Ed.2d 352 (1992)—§§ 1.5(g) n.270; 1.7(i) n.171, 195; 8.2(c) n.41; 8.4(c) n.111, 114, 135; 8.5(b) n.41; 8.6(b) n.60; 8.8(b) n.36; 8.8(d) n.104, 114; 8.10(d) n.112; 15.2(b) n.38; 15.5(a) n.4, 9, 12, 30; 15.5(b) n.43, 73, 80; 15.6(a) n.19; 15.6(b) n.46, 63; 15.7(d) n.83; 15.7(e) n.102; 15.7(f) n.138, 140; 19.3(a) n.61; 27.6(d) n.113

Williams, United States v., 792 F.Supp. 1120 (S.D.Ind.1992)—§ 20.3(m) n.250

Williams, United States v., 951 F.2d 853 (7th Cir.1992)—§ 3.10(b) n.79

Williams, United States v., 962 F.2d 1218 (6th Cir.1992)—§§ 3.8(e) n.219; 20.3(b) n.43

Williams, United States v., 935 F.2d 1531 (8th Cir.1991)—§ 12.1(a) n.21

Williams, United States v., 945 F.2d 192 (7th Cir.1991)—§ 3.8(c) n.86

Williams, United States v., 951 F.2d 1287 (D.C.Cir.1991)—§ 10.6(a) n.7

Williams, United States v., 899 F.2d 898 (10th Cir.1990)—§ 15.6(f) n.197

Williams, United States v., 874 F.2d 968 (5th Cir.1989)—§§ 8.10(d) n.90, 113

Williams, United States v., 880 F.2d 804 (4th Cir.1989)—§ 21.2(d) n.210

Williams, United States v., 822 F.2d 1174 (D.C.Cir.1987)—§ 3.2(b) n.92

Williams, United States v., 788 F.2d 1213 (6th Cir.1986)—§§ 16.2(e) n.69, 72, 74, 79

Williams, United States v., 737 F.2d 594 (7th Cir.1984)—§ 3.4(d) n.51

Williams, United States v., 738 F.2d 172 (7th Cir.1984)—§ 18.5(b) n.65

Williams, United States v., 684 F.2d 296 (4th Cir.1982)—§ 18.5(a) n.50

Williams, United States v., 687 F.2d 290 (9th Cir.1982)—§ 3.4(j) n.190

Williams, United States v., 642 F.2d 136 (5th Cir.1981)—§ 21.4(a) n.25

Williams, United States v., 656 F.2d 357 (8th Cir.1981)—§ 21.2(e) n.317

Williams, United States v., 622 F.2d 830 (5th Cir.1980)—§ 3.1(c) n.51

Williams, United States v., 631 F.2d 198 (3d Cir.1980)—§ 11.6(c) n.92

Williams v. United States, 404 A.2d 189 (D.C.App.1979)—§ 19.3(b) n.147

Williams, United States v., 580 F.2d 578 (D.C.Cir.1978)—§ 8.9(b) n.27

Williams, United States v., 534 F.2d 119 (8th Cir.1976)—§ 21.5(e) n.127

Williams, United States v., 372 F.Supp. 65 (D.S.D.1974)—§ 3.9(g) n.124

Williams, United States v., 455 F.2d 361 (9th Cir.1972)—§ 24.2(a) n.14

Williams v. United States, 401 U.S. 646, 91 S.Ct. 1148, 28 L.Ed.2d 388 (1971)—§§ 1.5(e) n.212; 2.9(f) n.124; 2.11(c) n.24, 26

Williams, United States v., 436 F.2d 1166 (9th Cir.1970)—§ 7.4(g) n.119

Williams v. United States, 328 F.2d 669 (5th Cir.1964)—§ 6.2(c) n.103

Williams v. United States, 273 F.2d 781 (9th Cir.1959)—§ 6.3(a) n.16

Williams v. United States, 265 F. 625 (8th Cir.1920)—§ 27.6(b) n.13

Williams v. Warden, 217 Conn. 419, 586 A.2d 582 (1991)—§§ 11.9(a) n.29; 11.9(d) n.194

Williams v. Weldon, 826 F.2d 1018 (11th Cir.1987)—§ 7.4(d) n.69

Williams v. Woodford, 306 F.3d 665 (9th Cir.2002)—§ 11.10(c) n.138

Williams-Davis, United States v., 90 F.3d 490 (D.C.Cir.1996)— §§ 20.3(i) n.163; 24.9(f) n.68, 85; 24.9(g) n.116

Williamsen v. People, 735 P.2d 176 (Colo.1987)—§§ 17.4(a) n.27, 53

Williamson v. Gregoire, 151 F.3d 1180 (9th Cir.1998)—§ 28.3(a) n.21

Williamson v. Lee Optical, 348 U.S. 483, 75 S.Ct. 461, 99 L.Ed. 563 (1955)—§ 13.4(c) n.125

Williamson v. Moore, 221 F.3d 1177 (11th Cir.2000)—§ 24.3(b) n.49

Williamson v. State, 669 A.2d 95 (Del.1995)—§ 27.5(b) n.47

Williamson, State v., 253 Kan. 163, 853 P.2d 56 (1993)—§ 13.2(c) n.56

Williamson v. State, 812 P.2d 384 (Okla.Crim.App.1991)—§§ 11.2(e) n.184, 212

Williamson, State v., 307 Or. 621, 772 P.2d 404 (1989)—§ 3.10(b) n.34

Williamson, State v., 14 Conn.App. 108, 552 A.2d 815 (1988)—§ 24.3(e) n.128

Williamson v. State, 201 N.W.2d 490 (Iowa 1972)—§ 7.4(f) n.98

Williamson v. United States, 512 U.S. 594, 114 S.Ct. 2431, 129 L.Ed.2d 476 (1994)—§ 24.4(a) n.2

Williamson v. United States, 311 F.2d 441 (5th Cir.1962)—§ 5.4(a) n.3

Williams (Terry) v. Taylor, 529 U.S. 362, 120 S.Ct. 1495, 146 L.Ed.2d 389 (2000)—§§ 11.10(c) n.98, 125; 11.10(d) n.181, 183, 186; 28.6(f) n.64, 75; 28.7(b) n.13

Williams, United States ex rel. v. Franzen, 687 F.2d 944 (7th Cir.1982)— § 11.9(d) n.186

Williams, United States ex rel. v. McMann, 436 F.2d 103 (2d Cir.1970)—§§ 21.5(e) n.115, 137

Willie v. Maggio, 737 F.2d 1372 (5th Cir.1984)—§ 6.9(f) n.141

Willie v. State, 738 So.2d 217 (Miss.1999)—§ 21.6(a) n.62

Willie, United States v., 941 F.2d 1384 (10th Cir.1991)—§ 11.5(c) n.54

Willingham, Ex parte, 695 So.2d 148 (Ala.1996)—§ 24.3(b) n.52

Willingham v. Morgan, 395 U.S. 402, 89 S.Ct. 1813, 23 L.Ed.2d 396 (1969)—§ 13.5(d) n.80

Willis, Commonwealth v., 716 S.W.2d 224 (Ky.1986)—§§ 2.12(d) n.188; 2.12(e) n.210

Willis v. Commonwealth, 339 S.W.2d 174 (Ky.1960)—§§ 16.1(g) n.275, 277

Willis v. Kemp, 838 F.2d 1510 (11th Cir.1988)—§ 22.2(d) n.67

Willis v. O'Brien, 151 W.Va. 628, 153 S.E.2d 178 (1967)—§§ 16.1(e) n.198; 16.2(a) n.5

Willis, People v., 215 Ill.2d 517, 294 Ill.Dec. 581, 831 N.E.2d 531 (2005)—§§ 3.5(a) n.52; 9.4(a) n.10

Willis, People v., 27 Cal.4th 811, 118 Cal.Rptr.2d 301, 43 P.3d 130 (2002)—§ 22.3(d) n.252

Willis, People v., 28 Cal.4th 22, 120 Cal.Rptr.2d 105, 46 P.3d 898 (2002)—§ 10.3(b) n.13

Willis, State v., 915 A.2d 208 (2006)— §§ 17.1(a) n.14; 17.1(c) n.45; 17.3(d) n.51

Willis, State v., 820 A.2d 1216 (Me.2003)—§ 21.5(a) n.3

Willis, State v., 123 N.M. 55, 933 P.2d 854 (1997)—§ 21.5(e) n.119

Willis, State v., 559 N.W.2d 693 (Minn.1997)—§ 26.3(f) n.51

Willis v. State, 263 Ga. 597, 436 S.E.2d 204 (1993)—§ 24.6(d) n.42

Willis, State v., 332 N.C. 151, 420 S.E.2d 158 (1992)—§§ 17.2(b) n.40, 41

Willis, State v., 145 Vt. 459, 494 A.2d 108 (1985)—§ 6.6(e) n.62

Willis, State v., 250 N.W.2d 428 (Iowa 1977)—§ 19.4(b) n.24

Willis, State v., 260 La. 439, 256 So.2d 436 (1972)—§ 9.1(a) n.14

Willis, State v., 71 Conn. 293, 41 A. 820 (1898)—§ 9.5(a) n.1

Willis, United States v., 257 F.3d 636 (6th Cir.2001)—§ 24.11(d) n.30

Willis, United States v., 958 F.2d 60 (5th Cir.1992)—§ 18.3(b) n.51

Willis, United States v., 33 F.R.D. 510 (S.D.N.Y.1963)—§ 19.4(b) n.24

Willis v. Zant, 720 F.2d 1212 (11th Cir.1982)—§ 22.3(d) n.186

Willman, Commonwealth v., 434 Pa. 489, 255 A.2d 534 (1969)—§ 6.6(f) n.111

Willoughby, State v., 181 Ariz. 530, 892 P.2d 1319 (Ariz.1995)—§§ 16.1(a) n.1, 2; 16.4(c) n.93; 16.4(d) n.117, 120, 123, 126, 135, 142

Willoughby, State v., 507 A.2d 1060 (Me.1986)—§ 24.3(f) n.147

Willoughby, United States v., 860 F.2d 15 (2d Cir.1988)—§§ 4.6(b) n.50; 4.6(l) n.201

Wills, State v., 244 Kan. 62, 765 P.2d 1114 (1988)—§§ 21.2(d) n.158, 188, 191; 21.2(e) n.299

Wills, United States v., 88 F.3d 704 (9th Cir.1996)—§§ 22.3(d) n.216; 24.9(d) n.42

Willsey v. State, 698 N.E.2d 784 (Ind.1998)—§ 6.5(b) n.30

Wilmart, State v., 234 Neb. 320, 450 N.W.2d 703 (1990)—§§ 3.10(b) n.79; 9.3(e) n.67, 81

Wilmette, Village of v. Michels, 137 Ill.App.3d 1001, 92 Ill.Dec. 615, 485 N.E.2d 426 (1985)—§ 1.8(d) n.48

Wilmoth, State v., 104 Ohio App.3d 539, 662 N.E.2d 863 (1995)—§ 20.6(c) n.87

Wilmoth, State v., 22 Wash.App. 419, 589 P.2d 1270 (1979)—§ 22.1(c) n.60

Wilshire, State v., 509 A.2d 444 (R.I.1986)—§ 15.6(f) n.203

Wilson, Ex parte, 114 U.S. 417, 5 S.Ct. 935, 29 L.Ed. 89 (1885)—§§ 2.1 n.43; 2.9(d) n.55; 15.1(b) n.41; 15.1(d) n.151; 28.3(b) n.45

Wilson, In re, 442 F.3d 872 (5th Cir.2006)—§ 28.5(b) n.59

Wilson v. Arkansas, 514 U.S. 927, 115 S.Ct. 1914, 131 L.Ed.2d 976 (1995)—§§ 2.8(b) n.51; 2.9(d) n.61; 3.1(d) n.119; 3.4(h) n.138; 3.6(b) n.47

Wilson v. Beard, 426 F.3d 653 (3d Cir.2005)—§§ 22.3(d) n.255; 28.5(b) n.54

Wilson v. City of Boston, 421 F.3d 45 (1st Cir.2005)—§ 3.3(e) n.187

Wilson v. Commonwealth, 199 S.W.3d 175 (Ky.2006)—§§ 6.6(c) n.31; 6.9(g) n.200

Wilson, Commonwealth v., 443 Mass. 122, 819 N.E.2d 919 (2004)—§ 18.4(c) n.72

Wilson, Commonwealth v., 430 Mass. 440, 720 N.E.2d 464 (1999)—§§ 21.2(h) n.419, 423

Wilson, Commonwealth v., 529 Pa. 268, 602 A.2d 1290 (1992)—§ 24.3(f) n.156

Wilson v. Commonwealth, 839 S.W.2d 17 (Ky.App.1992)—§§ 21.3(f) n.400, 401, 405, 407

Wilson, Commonwealth v., 399 Mass. 455, 504 N.E.2d 1060 (1987)—§ 18.4(c) n.31

Wilson v. Commonwealth, 695 S.W.2d 854 (Ky.1985)—§ 7.4(b) n.30

Wilson, Commonwealth v., 450 Pa. 296, 301 A.2d 823 (1973)—§ 7.4(d) n.68

Wilson v. Coon, 808 F.2d 688 (8th Cir.1987)—§§ 6.6(b) n.15; 6.6(f) n.108

Wilson v. Czerniak, 355 F.3d 1151 (9th Cir.2004)—§ 25.4(d) n.45

Wilson v. Department of Revenue, 169 Ill.2d 306, 214 Ill.Dec. 849, 662 N.E.2d 415 (1996)—§ 17.4(b) n.138

Wilson v. Gaffney, 454 F.2d 142 (10th Cir.1972)—§ 7.3(b) n.11

Wilson v. Gray, 345 F.2d 282 (9th Cir.1965)—§ 11.6(a) n.49

Wilson v. Henderson, 742 F.2d 741 (2d Cir.1984)—§ 6.4(g) n.159

Wilson v. Layne, 526 U.S. 603, 119 S.Ct. 1692, 143 L.Ed.2d 818 (1999)—§§ 3.4(j) n.207; 3.6(a) n.41

Wilson v. McGinnis, 413 F.3d 196 (2d Cir.2005)—§ 21.4(d) n.106

Wilson v. Mintzes, 761 F.2d 275 (6th Cir.1985)—§ 11.4(c) n.70

Wilson v. Mitchell, 250 F.3d 388 (6th Cir.2001)—§§ 7.4(c) n.53; 18.2(c) n.36, 49

Wilson v. O'Leary, 895 F.2d 378 (7th Cir.1990)—§ 6.10(b) n.34

Wilson, People v., 181 Ill.2d 409, 299 Ill.Dec. 896, 692 N.E.2d 1107 (1998)—§ 26.3(f) n.67

Wilson, People v., 164 Ill.2d 436, 207 Ill.Dec. 417, 647 N.E.2d 910 (1994)—§ 8.8(g) n.165

Wilson v. People, 708 P.2d 792 (Colo.1985)—§§ 21.4(c) n.77; 21.4(f) n.179

Wilson, People v., 268 Cal.App.2d 581, 74 Cal.Rptr. 131 (1968)—§ 3.3(g) n.228

Wilson v. State, 936 So.2d 357 (Miss.2006)—§ 6.7(d) n.145

Wilson v. State, 121 Nev. 345, 114 P.3d 285 (Nev.2005)—§ 18.4(c) n.44

Wilson, State v., 138 N.M. 551, 123 P.3d 784 (N.M.App.2005)—§ 27.5(a) n.26

Wilson v. State, 904 So.2d 987 (Miss.2004)—§ 13.2(a) n.4

Wilson, State v., 149 Wash.2d 1, 65 P.3d 657 (2003)—§§ 20.6(b) n.43, 46

Wilson v. State, 277 Ga. 195, 586 S.E.2d 669 (2003)—§ 11.7(e) n.69

Wilson v. State, 845 So.2d 142 (Fla.2003)—§ 21.2(c) n.132

Wilson v. State, 363 Md. 333, 768 A.2d 675 (2001)—§ 24.3(b) n.49

Wilson, State v., 31 S.W.3d 189 (Tenn.2000)—§§ 21.5(b) n.64, 68

Wilson, State v., 235 Wis.2d 177, 612 N.W.2d 368 (2000)—§ 14.3(c) n.61

Wilson, State v., 267 Kan. 530, 986 P.2d 365 (1999)—§§ 14.3(b) n.52; 14.4(b) n.18

Wilson v. State, 271 Ga. 811, 525 S.E.2d 339 (1999)—§ 22.3(c) n.133

Wilson v. State, 234 Ga.App. 375, 506 S.E.2d 882 (1998)—§ 19.3(b) n.179

Wilson, State v., 573 N.W.2d 248 (Iowa 1998)—§ 18.5(a) n.21

Wilson, State v., 252 Neb. 637, 564 N.W.2d 241 (1997)—§§ 11.5(c) n.52; 11.5(g) n.111

Wilson v. State, 693 So.2d 616 (Fla.App.1997)—§ 25.2(a) n.9

Wilson, State v., 680 So.2d 411 (Fla.1996)—§ 25.4(b) n.22

Wilson, State v., 685 So.2d 1063 (La.1996)—§ 26.1(b) n.32

Wilson, State v., 535 N.W.2d 597 (Minn.1995)—§ 24.9(f) n.86

Wilson, State v., 658 So.2d 521 (Fla.1995)—§§ 21.2(e) n.288; 21.5(c) n.86

Wilson, State v., 179 Wis.2d 660, 508 N.W.2d 44 (App.1993)—§ 10.3(d) n.66

Wilson v. State, 825 S.W.2d 155 (Tex.App.1992)—§ 19.3(b) n.164

Wilson v. State, 592 So.2d 993 (Miss. 1991)—§ 6.9(f) n.144

Wilson, State v., 459 N.W.2d 457 (S.D.1990)—§§ 21.4(d) n.110, 150

Wilson v. State, 574 So.2d 1324 (Miss.1990)—§§ 7.3(c) n.61; 7.4(d) n.76

Wilson v. State, 574 So.2d 1338 (Miss.1990)—§ 11.8(c) n.66

Wilson, State v., 149 Wis.2d 878, 440 N.W.2d 534 (1989)—§ 18.5(b) n.68

Wilson, State v., 240 Kan. 606, 731 P.2d 306 (1987)—§§ 19.2(d) n.49; 19.2(e) n.54; 19.3(a) n.15, 62, 75

Wilson, State v., 311 N.C. 117, 316 S.E.2d 46 (1984)—§§ 13.2(f) n.99; 13.4(c) n.114

Wilson v. State, 451 So.2d 724 (Miss.1984)—§ 10.5(b) n.24

Wilson v. State, 246 Ga. 62, 268 S.E.2d 895 (1980)—§ 24.3(b) n.73

Wilson v. State, 621 P.2d 1173 (Okl.Cr.App.1980)—§ 26.10(c) n.60

Wilson, State v., 58 Ohio St.2d 52, 388 N.E.2d 745 (1979)—§ 21.6(a) n.58

Wilson v. State, 378 So.2d 1258 (Fla.App.1979)—§ 21.5(c) n.88

Wilson v. State, 372 A.2d 198 (Del.1977)—§ 24.3(d) n.111

Wilson v. State, 59 Wis.2d 269, 208 N.W.2d 134 (1973)—§ 14.4(c) n.56

Wilson v. State, 155 Ind.App. 100, 291 N.E.2d 570 (1973)—§ 21.3(b) n.49

Wilson, State v., 22 Utah 2d 361, 453 P.2d 158 (1969)—§ 18.4(d) n.92

Wilson v. State, 16 Okla.Cr. 471, 184 P. 603 (1919)—§ 16.4(c) n.47

Wilson, United States v., 429 F.3d 455 (3d Cir.2005)—§ 21.5(a) n.38

Wilson, United States v., 392 F.3d 1055 (9th Cir.2004)—§ 13.5(b) n.36

Wilson, United States v., 281 F.Supp.2d 827 (E.D.Va.2003)—§ 11.2(a) n.26

Wilson, United States v., 237 F.3d 827 (7th Cir.2001)—§ 4.6(d) n.68

Wilson, United States v., 262 F.3d 305 (4th Cir.2001)—§ 13.5(a) n.6

Wilson, United States v., 2001 WL 798018 (S.D.N.Y.2001)—§§ 16.2(d) n.55; 16.2(e) n.76; 16.3(c) n.35, 44

Wilson, United States v., 184 F.3d 798 (8th Cir.1999)—§ 21.6(a) n.80

Wilson, United States v., 159 F.3d 280 (7th Cir.1998)—§ 1.11(a) n.7

Wilson, United States v., 116 F.3d 1066 (5th Cir.1997)—§ 19.6(b) n.15

Wilson, United States v., 81 F.3d 1300 (4th Cir.1996)—§§ 21.4(c) n.74; 21.5(a) n.43

Wilson, United States v., 26 F.3d 142 (D.C.Cir.1994)—§ 16.1(h) n.287

Wilson, United States v., 2 F.3d 226 (7th Cir.1993)—§ 3.5(c) n.105

Wilson v. United States, 606 A.2d 1017 (D.C.App.1992)—§ 21.2(d) n.139

Wilson v. United States, 592 A.2d 1009 (D.C.App.1991)—§ 21.3(d) n.222

Wilson, United States v., 938 F.2d 785 (7th Cir.1991)—§ 3.7(e) n.118

Wilson, United States v., 953 F.2d 116 (4th Cir.1991)—§§ 3.8(c) n.101, 113

Wilson, United States v., 894 F.2d 1245 (11th Cir.1990)—§ 24.11(d) n.23

Wilson, United States v., 884 F.2d 1121 (8th Cir.1989)—§ 22.3(d) n.248

Wilson, United States v., 838 F.2d 1081 (9th Cir.1988)—§ 6.3(b) n.36

Wilson, United States v., 571 F.Supp. 1422 (S.D.N.Y.1983)—§ 20.3(h) n.157

Wilson, United States v., 719 F.2d 1491 (10th Cir.1983)—§ 18.4(c) n.37

Wilson, United States v., 720 F.2d 608 (9th Cir.1983)—§ 18.3(b) n.9

Wilson, United States v., 657 F.2d 755 (5th Cir.1981)—§ 17.2(d) n.95

Wilson, United States v., 614 F.2d 1224 (9th Cir.1980)—§§ 1.7(j) n.225; 8.7(e) n.94

Wilson, United States v., 629 F.2d 439 (6th Cir.1980)—§ 24.10(a) n.8

Wilson, United States v., 536 F.2d 883 (9th Cir.1976)—§ 9.1(b) n.84

Wilson, United States v., 540 F.2d 1100 (D.C.Cir.1976)—§§ 9.2(c) n.22; 10.1(c) n.47, 50, 52

Wilson, United States v., 342 A.2d 27 (D.C.App.1975)—§ 13.4(c) n.94

Wilson, United States v., 420 U.S. 332, 95 S.Ct. 1013, 43 L.Ed.2d 232 (1975)—§§ 2.1 n.43, 54; 25.3(e) n.37; 27.3(a) n.4; 27.3(b) n.19

Wilson, United States v., 479 F.2d 936 (7th Cir.1973)—§ 3.3(d) n.160

Wilson v. United States, 215 F.Supp. 661 (W.D.Va.1963)—§ 11.4(a) n.6

Wilson v. United States, 221 U.S. 361, 31 S.Ct. 538, 55 L.Ed. 771 (1911)— § 8.12(b) n.14

Wilson v. United States, 149 U.S. 60, 13 S.Ct. 765, 37 L.Ed. 650 (1893)— §§ 2.10(d) n.127, 130; 17.2(d) n.112; 24.5(a) n.4

Wilson v. United States, 162 U.S. 613, 16 S.Ct. 895, 40 L.Ed. 1090 (1896)—§ 1.7(i) n.157

Wilson v. Webster, 467 F.2d 1282 (9th Cir.1972)—§ 3.1(m) n.294

Wilson v. Webster, 315 F.Supp. 1104 (C.D.Cal.1970)—§ 3.1(n) n.300

Wims, People v., 10 Cal.4th 293, 41 Cal.Rptr.2d 241, 895 P.2d 77 (1995)—§ 26.4(i) n.164

Winberry v. Salisbury, 5 N.J. 240, 74 A.2d 406 (1950)—§ 1.7(f) n.94

Winchester v. Stein, 135 Wash.2d 835, 959 P.2d 1077 (1998)—§ 17.4(b) n.119

Winchester, United States v., 407 F.Supp. 261 (D.Del.1975)— §§ 15.6(c) n.97; 19.3(b) n.153

Winckler, State v., 260 N.W.2d 356 (S.D.1977)—§§ 9.1(c) n.99; 16.4(c) n.69

Wind, United States v., 527 F.2d 672 (6th Cir.1975)—§ 12.3(f) n.144

Windham, Ex parte, 634 S.W.2d 718 (Tex.Crim.App.1982)—§§ 11.4(c) n.79, 80, 85

Windham v. State, 118 Nev. 226, 43 P.3d 993 (2002)—§§ 18.4(c) n.53, 54

Windsor, People v., 207 Mich.App. 221, 523 N.W.2d 881 (1994)—§ 17.4(a) n.48

Windsor v. State, 338 Ark. 649, 1 S.W.3d 20 (1999)—§ 21.2(b) n.75

Winebrenner v. United States, 147 F.2d 322 (8th Cir.1945)—§§ 16.2(g) n.130; 24.9(f) n.63

Winfield v. Div. of Pari-Mutual Wagering, 477 So.2d 544 (Fla.1985)— § 8.5(d) n.156

Winfrey v. State, 293 Ark. 342, 738 S.W.2d 391 (1987)—§ 20.3(b) n.51

Winfrey, United States v., 915 F.2d 212 (6th Cir.1990)—§ 3.8(c) n.89

Winfrey v. Wyrick, 836 F.2d 406 (8th Cir.1987)—§ 6.2(c) n.120

Wing v. State, 579 P.2d 196 (Okl.Cr.1978)—§ 10.2(b) n.19

Wingfield v. State, 197 S.W.3d 922 (Tex.App.2006)—§ 24.2(a) n.7

Winkler v. Keane, 7 F.3d 304 (2d Cir.1993)—§§ 11.9(d) n.207, 225

Winkler, People v., 71 N.Y.2d 592, 528 N.Y.S.2d 360, 523 N.E.2d 485 (1988)—§§ 11.9(a) n.14; 11.9(d) n.234

Winn, United States v., 969 F.2d 642 (8th Cir.1992)—§ 3.10(b) n.43

Winograd, People v., 68 N.Y.2d 383, 509 N.Y.S.2d 512, 502 N.E.2d 189 (1986)—§ 4.6(c) n.54

Winsett, People v., 153 Ill.2d 335, 180 Ill.Dec. 109, 606 N.E.2d 1186 (1992)—§ 9.5(a) n.25

Winship, In re, 397 U.S. 358, 90 S.Ct. 1068, 25 L.Ed.2d 368 (1970)— §§ 1.5(e) n.213; 2.3(a) n.58, 59; 2.3(b) n.91; 2.4(b) n.57, 58; 2.7(a) n.8, 42; 2.7(c) n.164; 10.4(a) n.1; 16.1(g) n.265; 26.10(c) n.42; 28.3(c) n.74

Winship, United States v., 724 F.2d 1116 (5th Cir.1984)—§§ 16.1(g) n.256, 263; 16.1(h) n.292, 293, 295

Winslow, People v., 26 Ill.App.3d 1035, 325 N.E.2d 426 (1975)—§ 3.8(d) n.133

Winsor, United States v., 846 F.2d 1569 (9th Cir.1988)—§ 3.1(c) n.59

Winston v. Commonwealth, 268 Va. 564, 604 S.E.2d 21 (2004)— § 7.4(b) n.9

Winston v. Lee, 470 U.S. 753, 105 S.Ct. 1611, 84 L.Ed.2d 662 (1985)— §§ 3.1(d) n.119; 3.3(b) n.40; 3.4(a) n.10, 16; 3.5(d) n.170

Winston, State v., 300 Minn. 314, 219 N.W.2d 617 (1974)—§ 12.1(e) n.62

Winston, United States v., 373 F.Supp. 1005 (E.D.Mich.1974)—§ 3.4(k) n.232

Winter, United States v., 663 F.2d 1120 (1st Cir.1981)—§ 8.11(e) n.102

Winter, United States v., 348 F.2d 204 (2d Cir.1965)—§ 8.10(c) n.74

Winters v. Cook, 489 F.2d 174 (5th Cir.1973)—§§ 11.6(a) n.30; 11.6(c) n.90, 93, 101, 106

Winters, People v., 171 Cal.App.2d Supp. 876, 342 P.2d 538 (1959)— § 13.4(b) n.72

Wireman v. State, 432 N.E.2d 1343 (Ind.1982)—§ 15.4(f) n.144

Wisconsin v. Mitchell, 508 U.S. 476, 113 S.Ct. 2194, 124 L.Ed.2d 436 (1993)—§ 26.4(b) n.13

Wisconsin Professional Police Ass'n v. Public Service Commission, 555 N.W.2d 179 (Wisc. App. 1996)— § 4.7(d) n.27

Wisconsin Public Intervenor v. Mortier, 501 U.S. 597, 111 S.Ct. 2476, 115 L.Ed.2d 532 (1991)—§ 1.2(d) n.200

Wise v. Commonwealth, 230 Va. 322, 337 S.E.2d 715 (1985)—§ 22.3(c) n.127

Wise v. Murphy, 275 A.2d 205 (D.C.App.1971)—§ 8.8(g) n.178

Wise, People v., 194 Misc.2d 481, 752 N.Y.S.2d 837 (N.Y.Sup.2002)— § 24.11(d) n.39

Wise, People v., 236 A.D.2d 739, 654 N.Y.S.2d 210 (1997)—§ 15.2(c) n.78

Wise, People v., 18 Mich.App. 21, 170 N.W.2d 487 (1969)—§ 22.3(c) n.162

Wise v. State, 708 N.W.2d 66 (Iowa 2006)—§§ 21.5(d) n.104; 21.6(a) n.78

Wise, State v., 879 S.W.2d 494 (Mo.1994)—§§ 11.5(c) n.61, 63

Wise, State v., 305 Or. 78, 749 P.2d 1179 (1988)—§ 10.6(a) n.2

Wise, United States v., 221 F.3d 140 (5th Cir.2000)—§ 5.2(a) n.9

Wise, United States v., 179 F.3d 184 (5th Cir.1999)—§ 21.6(b) n.92

Wise, United States v., 976 F.2d 393 (8th Cir.1992)—§§ 26.4(f) n.86, 103

Wisehart v. Davis, 408 F.3d 321 (7th Cir.2005)—§§ 24.3(b) n.49; 24.9(f) n.81

Wiseman v. State, 223 S.W.3d 45 (Tex.App.2006)—§ 24.2(e) n.66

Wiseman v. State, _____ S.W.3d _____, 2006 WL 2773088 (Tex.App.2006)—§ 27.6(d) n.85

Wiseman, United States v., 297 F.3d 975 (10th Cir.2002)—§ 28.9(b) n.43

Wiseman, United States v., 172 F.3d 1196 (10th Cir.1999)—§§ 7.4(e) n.84; 15.2(e) n.144

Wiser v. People, 732 P.2d 1139 (Colo.1987)—§§ 24.9(f) n.80; 24.9(g) n.121

Withers, United States v., 972 F.2d 837 (7th Cir.1992)—§ 3.8(c) n.89

Witherspoon v. Illinois, 391 U.S. 510, 88 S.Ct. 1770, 20 L.Ed.2d 776 (1968)—§ 22.3(c) n.143

Witherspoon, State v., 402 So.2d 1184 (Fla.1981)—§ 19.6(a) n.2

Witherspoon v. United States, 557 A.2d 587 (D.C.App.1989)—§ 11.4(b) n.19

Witherspoon v. United States, 633 F.2d 1247 (6th Cir.1980)—§ 21.4(a) n.39

Withrow v. Larkin, 421 U.S. 35, 95 S.Ct. 1456, 43 L.Ed.2d 712 (1975)— § 22.4(a) n.11

Withrow v. Williams, 507 U.S. 680, 113 S.Ct. 1745, 123 L.Ed.2d 407 (1993)—§§ 1.5(b) n.90; 2.4(e) n.149; 2.9(f) n.119; 2.10(d) n.108,

124, 131; 28.3(c) n.78

Witkowski, State v., 163 Wis.2d 985, 473 N.W.2d 512 (1991)—§ 27.5(a) n.2

Witmer v. State, 394 So.2d 1096 (Fla.App.1981)—§ 20.3(h) n.143

Witness Before the Special Grand Jury 2000-2, In re, 288 F.3d 289 (7th Cir.2002)—§ 8.8(d) n.89

Witt v. Moran, 572 A.2d 261 (R.I.1990)—§§ 12.3(b) n.55; 12.3(f) n.142

Witt v. State, 892 P.2d 132 (Wyo.1995)—§ 10.5(a) n.7

Witte, State v., 308 Minn. 214, 245 N.W.2d 438 (1976)—§ 21.5(b) n.66

Witte v. United States, 515 U.S. 389, 115 S.Ct. 2199, 132 L.Ed.2d 351 (1995)—§§ 26.4(a) n.3; 26.7(d) n.39, 40

Wittebort, People v., 81 Mich.App. 529, 265 N.W.2d 404 (1978)—§ 14.1(d) n.56

Witten v. Pitman, 613 F.Supp. 63 (S.D.Fla.1985)—§ 16.4(b) n.12

Wittig, United States v., 425 F.Supp.2d 1196 (D.Kan.2006)—§ 24.9(c) n.22

Wittrock, In re Petition of, 649 A.2d 1053 (Del.1994)—§ 27.4(b) n.11

Wittsell, State v., 275 Kan. 442, 66 P.3d 831 (Kan.2003)—§ 25.2(b) n.15

W.M., In re, 851 A.2d 431 (D.C.App.2004)—§ 17.4(b) n.135

WMUR Channel 9, Petition of, 148 N.H. 644, 813 A.2d 455 (N.H.2002)— § 23.3(b) n.20

Woerner v. Justice Court of Reno Township, 116 Nev. 518, 1 P.3d 377 (Nev.2000)—§ 14.2(g) n.103

Wofford v. Scott, 177 F.3d 1236 (11th Cir.1999)—§ 28.9(a) n.7

Woirhaye v. Montana Fourth Judicial District Court, 292 Mont. 185, 972 P.2d 800 (1998)—§ 22.1(f) n.96

Wojdak, Commonwealth v., 502 Pa. 359, 466 A.2d 991 (1983)— § 14.3(d) n.98

Wolak, United States v., 923 F.2d 1193 (6th Cir.1991)—§ 6.6(e) n.69

Wolbrecht v. Commonwealth, 955 S.W.2d 533 (Ky.1997)—§ 19.5(b) n.12

Wold v. State, 430 N.W.2d 171 (Minn.1988)—§ 6.9(b) n.27

Wold, United States v., 979 F.2d 632 (8th Cir.1992)—§ 3.4(d) n.58

Woldt v. People, 64 P.3d 256 (Colo.2003)—§ 27.6(d) n.150

Wolf v. Colorado, 338 U.S. 25, 69 S.Ct. 1359, 93 L.Ed. 1782 (1949)— §§ 1.3(c) n.22; 1.9(b) n.45; 2.4(e) n.142, 151, 179; 2.5(f) n.53, 70, 71; 2.6(a) n.2; 2.6(b) n.34; 2.7(c) n.174; 3.1(a) n.9; 3.1(e) n.121

Wolf, State v., 605 N.W.2d 381 (Minn.2000)—§ 16.1(e) n.190

Wolf, United States v., 879 F.2d 1320 (6th Cir.1989)—§ 6.9(f) n.121

Wolf, United States v., 813 F.2d 970 (9th Cir.1987)—§ 6.2(c) n.153

Wolfe v. Brigano, 232 F.3d 499 (6th Cir.2000)—§ 22.3(c) n.104

Wolfe, People v., 114 Cal.App.4th 177, 7 Cal.Rptr.3d 483 (Cal.App.2003)—§ 27.6(d) n.98

Wolfe v. State, 743 So.2d 380 (Miss.1999)—§ 19.5(c) n.56

Wolfe v. State, 326 S.C. 158, 485 S.E.2d 367 (1997)—§ 21.3(b) n.45

Wolfe, State v., 46 Wis.2d 478, 175 N.W.2d 216 (1970)—§§ 21.2(c) n.101; 21.3(d) n.220

Wolfenbarger v. Commonwealth, 936 S.W.2d 770 (Ky.App.1996)— § 16.1(a) n.29

Wolfer, State v., 39 Wash.App. 287, 693 P.2d 154 (1984)—§ 6.10(c) n.36

Wolff v. McDonnell, 418 U.S. 539, 94 S.Ct. 2963, 41 L.Ed.2d 935 (1974)—§§ 3.9(i) n.175; 11.1(b) n.92; 11.2(f) n.234, 242; 13.6(d) n.70; 26.2(c) n.60, 66

Wolff, State v., 237 Conn. 633, 678 A.2d 1369 (1996)—§§ 11.3(b) n.41, 42, 44; 11.5(c) n.61

Wolff, State v., 438 N.W.2d 199 (S.D.1989)—§ 21.6(a) n.80

Wolff, United States v., 241 F.3d 1055 (8th Cir.2001)—§ 19.2(e) n.74

Wolff, United States v., 127 F.3d 84 (D.C.Cir.1997)—§§ 21.2(e) n.308, 316

Wolfle v. United States, 291 U.S. 7, 54 S.Ct. 279, 78 L.Ed. 617 (1934)—§ 1.7(h) n.149

Wolfs v. Britton, 509 F.2d 304 (8th Cir.1975)—§§ 11.8(c) n.55, 59, 62

Wolfs, State v., 312 Or. 646, 826 P.2d 623 (Or.1992)—§ 25.2(f) n.48

Wolfson, United States v., 55 F.3d 58 (2d Cir.1995)—§§ 23.1(d) n.170, 189, 208

Wolk, United States v., 337 F.3d 997 (8th Cir.2003)—§§ 6.3(b) n.36; 6.6(e) n.61

Wolkow, State v., 110 Kan. 722, 205 P. 639 (1922)—§ 16.4(c) n.64

Wollan, State v., 303 N.W.2d 253 (Minn.1981)—§ 8.4(b) n.37

Wolverton, State v., 193 Wis.2d 234, 533 N.W.2d 167 (1995)—§§ 14.4(a) n.4; 14.4(c) n.49; 14.4(e) n.102

Womack, State v., 145 N.J. 576, 679 A.2d 606 (1996)—§ 15.7(f) n.149

Womack v. State, 281 Ala. 499, 205 So.2d 579 (1967)—§ 6.2(c) n.113

Womack, United States v., 542 F.2d 1047 (9th Cir.1976)—§ 6.9(c) n.58

Wong, United States v., 2 F.3d 927 (9th Cir.1993)—§ 26.4(b) n.8

Wong, United States v., 431 U.S. 174, 97 S.Ct. 1823, 52 L.Ed.2d 231 (1977)—§§ 2.10(b) n.33; 8.10(d) n.90

Wong Ching Hing, United States v., 867 F.2d 754 (2d Cir.1989)—§ 21.6(b) n.92

Wong Doo v. United States, 265 U.S. 239, 44 S.Ct. 524, 68 L.Ed. 999 (1924)—§ 28.5(d) n.76

Wong Sun v. United States, 371 U.S. 471, 83 S.Ct. 407, 9 L.Ed.2d 441 (1963)—§§ 3.3(a) n.7; 3.3(b) n.68; 3.3(f) n.207; 7.3(f) n.107; 9.1(a) n.29; 9.2(c) n.18; 9.3(a) n.9; 9.4(a) n.1, 40; 9.4(e) n.105

Wong Took, State v., 147 Wash. 190, 265 Pac. 459 (1928)—§ 16.4(c) n.54

Wong Wing v. United States, 163 U.S. 228, 16 S.Ct. 977, 41 L.Ed. 140 (1896)—§§ 15.1(b) n.14, 15, 58

Wong Yang Sung v. McGrath, 339 U.S. 33, 70 S.Ct. 445, 94 L.Ed. 616 (1950)—§ 2.7(c) n.123

Wood, In re, 833 F.2d 113 (8th Cir.1987)—§§ 8.4(b) n.93, 110; 8.4(c) n.125; 15.2(b) n.39

Wood, In re, 430 F.Supp. 41 (S.D.N.Y.1977)—§§ 8.8(g) n.170 to 172

Wood v. Bartholomew, 516 U.S. 1, 116 S.Ct. 7, 133 L.Ed.2d 1 (1995)—§§ 24.3(b) n.45, 49

Wood, Commonwealth v., 389 Mass. 552, 451 N.E.2d 714 (1983)—§ 3.4(j) n.210

Wood v. Georgia, 450 U.S. 261, 101 S.Ct. 1097, 67 L.Ed.2d 220 (1981)—§§ 11.9(a) n.10, 11; 11.9(b) n.62

Wood v. Georgia, 370 U.S. 375, 82 S.Ct. 1364, 8 L.Ed.2d 569 (1962)—§§ 1.5(g) n.270; 8.4(b) n.52, 104, 105; 15.1(a) n.8; 15.5(a) n.23; 23.1(b) n.91

Wood v. Hancock Co. Sheriff's Dept., 354 F.3d 57 (1st Cir.2003)—§ 3.5(c) n.130

Wood v. Morris, 87 Wash.2d 501, 554 P.2d 1032 (1976)—§§ 21.4(d) n.103; 21.4(e) n.165

Wood, People v., 135 P.3d 744 (Colo.2006)—§ 6.7(d) n.145

Wood v. State, 11 P.3d 1249 (Okla.Crim.App.2000)—§ 6.4(f) n.130

Wood, State v., 132 Idaho 88, 967 P.2d 702 (1998)—§ 22.4(c) n.29

Wood, State v., 924 S.W.2d 342 (Tenn.1996)—§ 18.1(c) n.24

Wood, State v., 148 Vt. 479, 536 A.2d 902 (1987)—§§ 9.1(b) n.32; 9.2(a) n.4

Wood v. State, 287 Ark. 203, 697 S.W.2d 884 (1985)—§ 19.6(b) n.19

Wood, State v., 457 So.2d 206 (La.App.1984)—§§ 2.12(d) n.183, 196

Wood, State v., 48 Ohio App.2d 339, 357 N.E.2d 1106 (1976)—§ 14.2(g) n.97

Wood, State v., 190 Kan. 778, 378 P.2d 536 (1963)—§ 2.12(a) n.18

Wood, State v., 53 N.H. 484 (1873)— § 15.2(i) n.223

Wood, United States v., 364 F.3d 704 (6th Cir.2004)—§§ 16.2(f) n.105, 107

Wood, United States v., 378 F.3d 342 (4th Cir.2004)—§§ 21.2(d) n.153 to 155

Wood v. United States, 622 A.2d 67 (D.C.App.1993)—§ 13.6(d) n.73

Wood, United States v., 981 F.2d 536 (D.C.Cir.1992)—§ 3.2(h) n.205

Wood, United States v., 950 F.2d 638 (10th Cir.1991)—§ 27.2(c) n.31

Wood, United States v., 879 F.2d 927 (D.C.Cir.1989)—§ 3.4(h) n.151

Wood v. Zahradnick, 578 F.2d 980 (4th Cir.1978)—§ 11.10(a) n.14

Woodahl, State ex rel. v. District Court, 166 Mont. 31, 530 P.2d 780 (1975)—§ 8.4(c) n.116

Woodall v. Commonwealth, 63 S.W.3d 104 (Ky.2001)—§ 22.3(d) n.250

Woodall, State v., 100 Wash.2d 74, 666 P.2d 364 (1983)—§ 3.3(c) n.100

Woodard v. Collins, 898 F.2d 1027 (5th Cir.1990)—§ 21.3(b) n.42

Woodard v. Hutchins, 464 U.S. 377, 104 S.Ct. 752, 78 L.Ed.2d 541 (1984)— § 28.5(d) n.79

Woodard, United States v., 291 F.3d 95 (1st Cir.2002)—§§ 11.5(c) n.54; 11.5(f) n.103

Woodby v. Immigration and Naturalization Service, 385 U.S. 276, 87 S.Ct. 483, 17 L.Ed.2d 362 (1966)— § 26.10(c) n.46

Woodcock, State v., 719 A.2d 32 (Vt.1998)—§ 12.3(b) n.38

Woodel, State ex rel. v. Wallace, 89 Or.App. 478, 750 P.2d 178 (1988)—§ 15.2(j) n.233

Woodford v. Garceau, 538 U.S. 202, 123 S.Ct. 1398, 155 L.Ed.2d 363 (2003)—§ 28.5(b) n.63

Woodford v. Ngo, _____ U.S. _____, 126 S.Ct. 2378, 165 L.Ed.2d 368 (2006)—§ 28.5(a) n.14

Woodford v. State, 752 N.E.2d 1278 (Ind.2001)—§ 3.7(d) n.78

Woodford v. State, 544 N.E.2d 1355 (Ind.1989)—§ 21.4(e) n.161

Woodford v. Visciotti, 537 U.S. 19, 123 S.Ct. 357, 154 L.Ed.2d 279 (2002)—§§ 11.10(a) n.29; 28.6(f) n.69

Woodland, State v., 945 P.2d 665 (Utah 1997)—§§ 18.1(c) n.28, 29

Woodland Oil Co., People v., 153 Mich.App. 799, 396 N.W.2d 541 (1986)—§ 14.4(b) n.6

Woodley, United States v., 9 F.3d 774 (9th Cir.1993)—§ 24.3(b) n.63

Wood, Matter of v. Hughes, 9 N.Y.2d 144, 212 N.Y.S.2d 33, 173 N.E.2d 21 (1961)—§ 8.3(h) n.45

Woodruff, State v., 676 So.2d 975 (Fla.1996)—§ 27.3(c) n.23

Woodruff v. State, 846 P.2d 1124 (Okla.Crim.App.1993)—§ 14.3(a) n.10

Woodruff v. State, 360 So.2d 49 (Fla.App.1978)—§ 24.4(d) n.41

Woodrum, United States v., 202 F.3d 1 (1st Cir.2000)—§§ 3.10(d) n.101, 106

Woods, Ex parte, 789 So.2d 941 (Ala.2001)—§§ 6.9(f) n.101, 106; 6.9(g) n.157

Woods, In re, 154 Wash.2d 400, 114 P.3d 607 (2005)—§ 24.2(e) n.79

Woods, In re, 20 Ill.App.3d 641, 314 N.E.2d 606 (1974)—§ 9.4(d) n.88

Woods, Commonwealth v., 427 Mass. 169, 693 N.E.2d 123 (1998)— § 6.4(f) n.131

Woods, Commonwealth v., 419 Mass. 366, 645 N.E.2d 1153 (1995)— § 6.7(b) n.45

Woods, Commonwealth v., 444 Pa.Super. 321, 663 A.2d 803 (1995)—§ 18.4(c) n.60

Woods v. Commonwealth, 287 Ky. 312, 152 S.W.2d 997 (1941)—§ 22.3(e) n.280

Woods v. Kuhlmann, 977 F.2d 74 (2d Cir.1992)—§§ 24.1(b) n.19, 27

Woods, People v., 21 Cal.4th 668, 88 Cal.Rptr.2d 88, 981 P.2d 1019 (1999)—§ 3.9(j) n.226

Woods, State v., 280 Ga. 758, 632 S.E.2d 654 (2006)—§ 6.2(c) n.151

Woods v. State, 114 Nev. 468, 958 P.2d 91 (1998)—§ 21.2(b) n.97

Woods, State v., 283 Mont. 359, 942 P.2d 88 (1997)—§ 6.6(b) n.16

Woods, State v., 723 S.W.2d 488 (Mo.App.1986)—§§ 14.1(c) n.42, 44

Woods, State v., 374 N.W.2d 92 (S.D.1985)—§ 6.9(g) n.158

Woods v. Thieret, 5 F.3d 244 (7th Cir.1993)—§§ 24.2(e) n.58, 60

Woods, United States v., 213 F.3d 1021 (8th Cir.2000)—§ 3.8(c) n.62

Woods, United States v., 907 F.2d 1540 (5th Cir.1990)—§ 6.4(e) n.107

Woodson v. North Carolina, 428 U.S. 280, 96 S.Ct. 2978, 49 L.Ed.2d 944 (1976)—§§ 12.4(a) n.18; 26.1(b) n.12

Woodson, State v., 338 Md. 322, 658 A.2d 272 (1995)—§ 25.2(e) n.37

Woodsum, State v., 137 N.H. 198, 624 A.2d 1342 (1993)—§ 21.2(h) n.437

Woodward v. Commonwealth, 147 S.W.3d 63 (Ky.2004)—§ 22.3(c) n.100

Woodward, Commonwealth v., 157 Mass. 516, 32 N.E. 939 (1893)— § 15.2(b) n.20

Woodward v. Morrissey, 991 P.2d 1042 (Okl.Cr.App.1999)—§§ 13.6(c) n.39; 21.3(c) n.148

Woodward, People v., 4 Cal.4th 376, 14 Cal.Rptr.2d 434, 841 P.2d 954 (1992)—§ 24.1(b) n.18

Woodward, United States v., 387 F.3d 1329 (11th Cir.2004)—§ 21.4(a) n.37

Woody, State v., 613 N.W.2d 215 (Iowa 2000)—§ 21.6(a) n.80

Woody, State v., 29 Ohio App.3d 364, 505 N.E.2d 646 (1986)—§ 19.5(b) n.31

Woody v. State, 445 S.W.2d 288 (Mo.1969)—§ 21.3(a) n.18

Woody, United States v., 55 F.3d 1257 (7th Cir.1995)—§ 3.7(a) n.19

Woolard, State v., 12 Ohio N.P.(n.s.) 395, 22 Ohio Dec. 652 (1910)— § 15.2(b) n.20

Wooldridge, Commonwealth v., 19 Mass.App.Ct. 162, 472 N.E.2d 970 (1985)—§ 11.9(c) n.133

Woolery, United States v., 735 F.2d 818 (5th Cir.1984)—§ 7.4(d) n.72

Wooley v. United States, 697 A.2d 777 (D.C.App.1997)—§ 19.6(c) n.23

Woolfolk, United States v., 399 F.3d 590 (4th Cir.2005)—§§ 18.2(b) n.12; 18.3(b) n.5

Woolley, United States v., 123 F.3d 627 (7th Cir.1997)—§§ 21.2(b) n.76; 27.5(c) n.56, 61

Woolridge, State v., 357 N.C. 544, 592 S.E.2d 191 (2003)—§ 10.6(c) n.22

Woolsey, People v., 139 Ill.2d 157, 151 Ill.Dec. 309, 564 N.E.2d 764 (1990)—§ 13.3(c) n.40

Woolverton v. Multi-County Grand Jury, Oklahoma County, 859 P.2d 1112 (Okla.Crim.App.1993)— §§ 8.7(d) n.71, 75, 84, 86

Woosley, United States v., 361 F.3d 924 (6th Cir.2004)—§ 21.6(b) n.94

Woosley v. United States, 478 F.2d 139 (8th Cir.1973)—§ 26.3(g) n.75

Wooten, State v., 227 Conn. 677, 631 A.2d 271 (1993)—§ 7.4(b) n.23

Wooten, United States v., 688 F.2d 941 (4th Cir.1982)—§ 18.3(b) n.11

Woratzeck v. Stewart, 118 F.3d 648 (9th Cir.1997)—§ 28.5(d) n.86

Workman v. Bell, 245 F.3d 849 (6th Cir.2001)—§ 26.2(c) n.78

Workman v. Bell, 178 F.3d 759 (6th Cir.1998)—§ 20.3(i) n.177

Workman v. Commonwealth, 580 S.W.2d 206 (Ky.1979)—§§ 13.5(b) n.34, 39, 42

Workman v. Mullin, 342 F.3d 1100 (10th Cir.2003)—§ 22.3(c) n.112

Workman, State v., 344 N.C. 482, 476 S.E.2d 301 (1996)—§ 17.2(d) n.95

Workman v. Tate, 957 F.2d 1339 (6th Cir.1992)—§§ 11.10(c) n.125, 128

Workman, United States v., 80 F.3d 688 (2d Cir.1996)—§§ 4.3(b) n.7; 4.6(l) n.201

Worley, State v., 179 W.Va. 403, 369 S.E.2d 706 (1988)—§§ 6.2(c) n.128; 9.1(b) n.45

Worley, United States v., 193 F.3d 380 (6th Cir.1999)—§ 3.10(b) n.38

Worrell Enterprises, Inc., In re, 14 Va.App. 671, 419 S.E.2d 271 (1992)—§ 23.1(d) n.187

Worthen v. Meachum, 842 F.2d 1179 (10th Cir.1988)—§§ 21.4(d) n.146, 147; 21.5(c) n.92

Worthen v. State, 964 P.2d 904 (Okl.Cr.App.1998)—§ 17.4(b) n.133

Worthington v. State, 58 Md. 403 (1882)—§ 16.4(c) n.55

Wortman, Commonwealth v., 929 S.W.2d 199 (Ky.App.1996)—§§ 14.1(a) n.3; 14.1(b) n.33; 14.4(d) n.84 to 86

Wozniak, United States v., 126 F.3d 105 (2d Cir.1997)—§§ 19.5(d) n.83; 19.6(c) n.40

Wray v. State, 472 So.2d 1119 (Ala.1985)—§ 26.10(a) n.8

Wren, State v., 234 Neb. 291, 450 N.W.2d 684 (1990)—§ 26.7(b) n.18

Wrenn v. Sheriff, 87 Nev. 85, 482 P.2d 289 (1971)—§ 14.3(b) n.45

Wrest, People v., 3 Cal.4th 1088, 13 Cal.Rptr.2d 511, 839 P.2d 1020 (1992)—§ 21.3(b) n.89

Wright v. Angelone, 151 F.3d 151 (4th Cir.1998)—§ 28.7(c) n.21

Wright v. Commonwealth, 953 S.W.2d 611 (Ky.App.1997)—§ 18.4(c) n.58

Wright, Commonwealth v., 362 Pa.Super. 464, 524 A.2d 970 (1987)—§ 22.1(h) n.138

Wright, Commonwealth v., 234 Pa.Super. 83, 339 A.2d 103 (1975)—§ 9.6(b) n.53

Wright, Commonwealth v., 460 Pa. 247, 332 A.2d 809 (1975)—§ 9.4(a) n.29

Wright, Commonwealth v., 158 Mass. 149, 33 N.E. 82 (1893)—§ 3.5(a) n.18

Wright v. Cowan, 149 F.Supp.2d 523 (C.D.Ill.2001)—§ 22.5(b) n.18

Wright v. Estelle, 572 F.2d 1071 (5th Cir.1978)—§ 27.6(d) n.95

Wright v. Hall, 281 Ga. 318, 638 S.E.2d 270 (2006)—§ 21.6(a) n.41

Wright v. Illinois & Miss. Tel. Co., 20 Iowa 195 (1866)—§ 24.9(g) n.110

Wright v. Lockhart, 914 F.2d 1093 (8th Cir.1990)—§ 23.2(h) n.129

Wright v. McAdory, 536 So.2d 897 (Miss.1988)—§§ 8.11(b) n.21, 25

Wright, People v., 86 N.Y.2d 591, 635 N.Y.S.2d 136, 658 N.E.2d 1009 (1995)—§ 24.3(b) n.49

Wright, People v., 441 Mich. 140, 490 N.W.2d 351 (1992)—§ 6.9(c) n.61

Wright, People v., 45 Cal.3d 1126, 248 Cal.Rptr. 600, 755 P.2d 1049 (1988)—§ 7.5(a) n.7

Wright, People v., 431 Mich. 282, 430 N.W.2d 133 (1988)—§ 6.7(b) n.101

Wright, People v., 43 Cal.3d 487, 233 Cal.Rptr. 69, 729 P.2d 260 (1987)—§ 21.6(c) n.118

Wright, People v., 194 Colo. 448, 573 P.2d 551 (1978)—§§ 21.2(d) n.163; 21.4(g) n.233

Wright, People v., 41 Ill.App.3d 364, 353 N.E.2d 711 (1976)—§ 11.2(g) n.279

Wright, People v., 41 Ill.2d 170, 242 N.E.2d 180 (1968)—§ 3.2(c) n.108

Wright, People v., 249 Cal.App.2d 692, 57 Cal.Rptr. 781 (1967)—§§ 6.10(c) n.36, 42

Wright v. Secretary, Dep't of Corr., 278 F.3d 1245 (11th Cir.2002)—§ 28.6(f) n.77

Wright, State v., 699 N.W.2d 782 (Minn.App.2005)—§ 27.2(a) n.6

Wright, State v., 261 Neb. 277, 622 N.W.2d 676 (2001)—§ 13.7(a) n.5

Wright, State v., 30 S.W.3d 906 (Mo.App.2000)—§ 22.3(c) n.162

Wright v. State, 267 Ga. 496, 480 S.E.2d 13 (1997)—§ 11.9(d) n.213

Wright v. State, 658 N.E.2d 563 (Ind.App.1995)—§ 24.8(e) n.74

Wright v. State, 851 P.2d 12 (Wyo.1993)—§ 5.2(a) n.4

Wright, State v., 598 So.2d 561 (La.App.1992)—§§ 24.11(d) n.28, 32

Wright v. State, 586 So.2d 1024 (Fla.1991)—§ 22.3(d) n.246

Wright v. State, 106 Nev. 647, 799 P.2d 548 (1990)—§ 7.3(e) n.85

Wright, State v., 207 Conn. 276, 542 A.2d 299 (1988)—§ 21.4(d) n.103

Wright v. State, 307 Md. 552, 515 A.2d 1157 (1986)—§ 21.2(h) n.439

Wright v. State, 473 So.2d 1277 (Fla.1985)—§ 24.4(d) n.62

Wright v. State, 707 P.2d 153 (Wyo.1985)—§ 26.3(g) n.78

Wright, State v., 354 N.W.2d 615 (Minn.App.1984)—§ 26.10(d) n.92

Wright v. State, 421 So.2d 1324 (Ala.Crim.App.1982)—§ 15.5(c) n.111

Wright v. State, 266 Ind. 327, 363 N.E.2d 1221 (1977)—§ 21.2(h) n.437

Wright, State v., 87 Wash.2d 783, 557 P.2d 1 (1976)—§§ 20.6(b) n.19, 57

Wright v. State, 552 P.2d 1157 (Okl.Crim.App.1976)—§ 3.1(e) n.130

Wright v. State, 46 Wis.2d 75, 175 N.W.2d 646 (1970)—§§ 7.3(e) n.86, 99

Wright, State v., 274 N.C. 84, 161 S.E.2d 581 (1968)—§ 7.3(f) n.117

Wright, United States v., 343 F.3d 849 (6th Cir.2003)—§ 3.3(g) n.225

Wright, United States v., 248 F.3d 765 (8th Cir.2001)—§§ 19.2(e) n.71; 19.3(a) n.88, 89, 114, 117

Wright, United States v., 128 F.3d 1274 (8th Cir.1997)—§ 1.2(c) n.172

Wright, United States v., 43 F.3d 491 (10th Cir.1994)—§§ 21.2(b) n.59; 21.6(a) n.77

Wright, United States v., 962 F.2d 953 (9th Cir.1992)—§ 6.9(g) n.200

Wright, United States v., 932 F.2d 868 (10th Cir.1991)—§ 3.7(a) n.16

Wright, United States v., 873 F.2d 437 (1st Cir.1989)—§ 21.2(d) n.210

Wright v. United States, 732 F.2d 1048 (2d Cir.1984)—§ 22.5(a) n.6

Wright, United States v., 744 F.2d 1127 (5th Cir.1984)—§ 26.10(a) n.7

Wright, United States v., 667 F.2d 793 (9th Cir.1982)—§ 15.7(g) n.197

Wright, United States v., 449 F.2d 1355 (D.C.Cir.1971)—§ 3.2(b) n.50

Wright, United States v., 365 F.2d 135 (7th Cir.1966)—§ 15.1(d) n.171

Wright v. West, 505 U.S. 277, 112 S.Ct. 2482, 120 L.Ed.2d 225 (1992)—§§ 28.6(a) n.2; 28.6(f) n.65

Wrightsil, State v., 13 Ariz.App. 111, 474 P.2d 470 (1970)—§ 14.2(g) n.101

Wright, State ex rel. v. Ohio Adult Parole Authority, 75 Oh.St.3d 82, 661 N.E.2d 728 (1996)—§ 26.10(c) n.64

Wrinkles v. State, 749 N.E.2d 1179 (Ind.2001)—§ 24.2(e) n.69

Wrzesinski, State v., 334 Mont. 157, 145 P.3d 985 (2006)—§ 6.6(e) n.91

Wujkowski, United States v., 929 F.2d 981 (4th Cir.1991)—§§ 8.12(g) n.67; 8.13(d) n.109, 112

Wukawitz, State v., 662 N.W.2d 517 (Minn.2003)—§ 21.2(e) n.300

Wuliger, United States v., 981 F.2d 1497 (6th Cir.1992)—§ 9.6(a) n.15

Wunder v. State, 705 P.2d 333 (Wyo.1985)—§ 6.6(e) n.62

Wuornos v. State, 676 So.2d 966 (Fla.1995)—§ 21.4(e) n.165

Wurth v. Emro Marketing Co., 125 Ohio App.3d 494, 708 N.E.2d 1057 (1998)—§§ 8.5(a) n.5, 10; 8.5(b) n.47; 8.5(h) n.266

Wyatt v. State, 23 S.W.3d 18 (Tex.Cr.App.2000)—§ 24.3(b) n.68

Wyatt v. State, 24 S.W.3d 319 (Tenn.2000)—§§ 19.2(a) n.6; 19.2(e) n.54; 19.2(f) n.92; 19.3(b) n.152

Wyatt v. State, 272 Ga. 490, 532 S.E.2d 390 (2000)—§ 6.9(f) n.139

Wyatt v. State, 498 A.2d 1088 (Del.1985)—§ 26.6(c) n.36

Wyatt, United States v., 179 F.3d 532 (7th Cir.1999)—§ 6.9(f) n.106

Wyatt, United States v., 102 F.3d 241 (7th Cir.1996)—§ 3.5(c) n.132

Wybierala, State v., 305 Minn. 455, 235 N.W.2d 197 (1975)—§ 3.9(c) n.48

Wyckoff, State v., 31 N.J.L. 65 (1864)—§§ 16.4(c) n.60, 62

Wydermyer, United States v., 51 F.3d 319 (2d Cir.1995)—§§ 19.1(a) n.9, 10; 19.2(f) n.94; 19.3(e) n.244

Wyman v. James, 400 U.S. 309, 91 S.Ct. 381, 27 L.Ed.2d 408 (1971)—§ 3.9(d) n.61

Wynehamer v. People, 13 N.Y. 378 (1856)—§ 2.4(c) n.94

Wynn, United States v., 292 F.3d 226 (5th Cir.2002)—§ 28.9(b) n.50

Wynne v. State, 676 S.W.2d 650 (Tex.App.1984)—§ 20.3(m) n.237

Wynne, United States v., 993 F.2d 760 (10th Cir.1993)—§ 6.6(e) n.91

Wyoming v. Houghton, 526 U.S. 295, 119 S.Ct. 1297, 143 L.Ed.2d 408 (1999)—§§ 2.9(d) n.61, 90; 3.4(j) n.196; 3.7(a) n.17; 3.7(c) n.57

Wyrick v. District Court, 839 P.2d 1376 (Okla.Crim.App.1992)—§§ 14.4(d) n.93; 14.4(e) n.109

Wyrick v. Fields, 459 U.S. 42, 103 S.Ct. 394, 74 L.Ed.2d 214 (1982)—§ 6.9(e) n.95

Wyrick, State v., 62 S.W.3d 751 (Tenn.Cr.App.2001)—§ 26.6(b) n.17

X

Xenia, City of v. Wallace, 37 Ohio St.3d 216, 524 N.E.2d 889 (1988)—§ 10.1(b) n.21

Y

Yager, People v., 640 N.Y.S.2d 642, 226 A.D.2d 830 (N.Y.App.Div. 1996)—§ 24.4(c) n.21

Yagow, United States v., 953 F.2d 427 (8th Cir.1992)—§§ 11.5(c) n.32, 34, 42, 52

Yakus v. United States, 321 U.S. 414, 64 S.Ct. 660, 88 L.Ed. 834 (1944)—§ 27.5(c) n.89

Yanagita, United States v., 552 F.2d 940 (2d Cir.1977)—§ 8.9(b) n.30

Yancey v. State, 98 Ga.App. 797, 107 S.E.2d 265 (1959)—§ 16.3(b) n.11

Yancey, United States v., 827 F.2d 83 (7th Cir.1987)—§ 11.10(c) n.77

Yanetta v. State, 320 So.2d 23 (Fla.App.1975)—§ 20.3(g) n.127

Yang, State v., 201 Wis.2d 725, 549 N.W.2d 769 (1996)—§ 24.9(e) n.54

Yarborough v. Alvarado, 541 U.S. 652, 124 S.Ct. 2140, 158 L.Ed.2d 938 (2004)—§§ 3.8(c) n.80; 6.6(c) n.43; 28.6(f) n.70

Yarborough v. Gentry, 540 U.S. 1, 124 S.Ct. 1, 157 L.Ed.2d 1 (2003)—§§ 11.10(c) n.78, 93, 97

Yarborough v. Keane, 101 F.3d 894 (2d Cir.1996)—§ 27.6(d) n.84

Yarborough, United States v., 400 F.3d 17 (D.C.Cir.2005)—§ 24.9(d) n.50

Yarbough, State v., 100 N.J. 627, 498 A.2d 1239 (1985)—§ 26.3(f) n.58

Yarbrough v. Commonwealth, 262 Va. 388, 551 S.E.2d 306 (2001)—§ 22.3(d) n.247

Yarbrough, State v., 95 Ohio St.3d 227, 767 N.E.2d 216 (2002)—§ 22.2(d) n.85

Yarnell, State v., 324 Mont. 164, 102 P.3d 34 (2004)—§ 21.6(a) n.34

Yasak, United States v., 884 F.2d 996 (7th Cir.1989)—§§ 21.6(b) n.92, 96

Yaselli v. Goff, 275 U.S. 503, 48 S.Ct. 155, 72 L.Ed. 395 (1927)—§ 13.5(g) n.112

Yashar, United States v., 166 F.3d 873 (7th Cir.1999)—§ 18.5(a) n.11

Yater, United States v., 756 F.2d 1058 (5th Cir.1985)—§ 21.6(b) n.90

Yates v. Aiken, 484 U.S. 211, 108 S.Ct. 534, 98 L.Ed.2d 546 (1988)—§ 1.5(e) n.213

Yates v. Evatt, 500 U.S. 391, 111 S.Ct. 1884, 114 L.Ed.2d 432 (1991)—§§ 27.6(d) n.88, 122

Yates, State v., 169 Vt. 20, 726 A.2d 483 (1999)—§§ 21.4(f) n.172, 185

Yates v. State, 792 P.2d 187 (Wyo.1990)—§ 26.1(d) n.88

Yates, State v., 111 Wash.2d 793, 765 P.2d 291 (1988)—§§ 20.4(b) n.20; 20.4(f) n.88, 96; 20.5(f) n.81, 85

Yates, United States v., 438 F.3d 1307 (11th Cir.2006)—§§ 24.2(e) n.78; 24.2(f) n.84, 86

Yates v. United States, 227 F.2d 848 (9th Cir.1955)—§ 8.3(a) n.7

Yaw v. State, 632 S.W.2d 768 (Tex.Crim.App.1982)—§ 20.2(e) n.82

Ybarra v. Illinois, 444 U.S. 85, 100 S.Ct. 338, 62 L.Ed.2d 238 (1979)—§§ 3.2(b) n.69; 3.4(i) n.172

Yeager, State ex rel. v. Trent, 203 W. Va. 716, 510 S.E.2d 790 (1998)—§ 20.3(g) n.127

Yeagin, United States v., 927 F.2d 798 (5th Cir.1991)—§§ 3.10(b) n.67, 74

Yee v. Duncan, 463 F.3d 893 (9th Cir.2006)—§ 22.3(d) n.245

Yefsky, United States v., 994 F.2d 885 (1st Cir.1993)—§§ 17.1(a) n.9; 19.3(a) n.46, 49; 19.3(b) n.153

Yehling, United States v., 456 F.3d 1236 (10th Cir.2006)—§ 18.5(c) n.85

Yeje-Cabrera, United States v., 430 F.3d 1 (1st Cir.2005)—§§ 24.9(f) n.103; 26.4(f) n.104

Yelder v. State, 575 So.2d 137 (Ala.1991)—§ 11.10(d) n.171

Yellen, People v., 739 P.2d 1384 (Colo.1987)—§ 18.4(c) n.44

Yellow Freight System, Inc., United States v., 637 F.2d 1248 (9th Cir.1980)—§§ 15.1(b) n.26, 34, 36, 39, 70, 74, 76, 81

Yellowwolf v. Morris, 536 F.2d 813 (9th Cir.1976)—§ 21.4(d) n.143

Yeloushan v. United States, 339 F.2d 533 (5th Cir.1964)—§ 16.1(h) n.285

Yemitan, United States v., 70 F.3d 746 (2d Cir.1995)—§§ 21.2(b) n.87; 21.4(g) n.226

Yeoman, People v., 31 Cal.4th 93, 2 Cal.Rptr.3d 186, 72 P.3d 1166 (2003)—§§ 7.4(e) n.92; 7.4(f) n.101

Yesil, United States v., 991 F.2d 1527 (11th Cir.1992)—§§ 21.2(d) n.246; 21.2(e) n.306, 308; 21.4(g) n.225

Yick Wo v. Hopkins, 118 U.S. 356, 6 S.Ct. 1064, 30 L.Ed. 220 (1886)—§§ 13.4(a) n.3; 15.1(b) n.14

Yielding, In re, 599 F.2d 251 (8th Cir.1979)—§ 21.3(e) n.266

Yim, In re, 139 Wash.2d 581, 989 P.2d 512 (1999)—§§ 3.3(a) n.25; 21.4(d) n.134

Yizar, United States v., 956 F.2d 230 (11th Cir.1992)—§ 17.3(d) n.47

Ykema, United States v., 887 F.2d 697 (6th Cir.1989)—§ 21.2(d) n.213

Ylst v. Nunnemaker, 501 U.S. 797, 111 S.Ct. 2590, 115 L.Ed.2d 706 (1991)—§§ 28.4(c) n.27, 28

Yoh, State v., 180 Vt. 317, 910 A.2d 853 (2006)—§§ 6.9(f) n.100; 27.5(d) n.137

Yohey v. Collins, 985 F.2d 222 (5th Cir.1993)—§§ 11.2(e) n.183, 207

Yonn, United States v., 702 F.2d 1341 (11th Cir.1983)—§ 4.6(l) n.199

York, In re, 9 Cal.4th 1133, 40 Cal.Rptr.2d 308, 892 P.2d 804 (1995)—§ 12.1(b) n.32

York v. Director of Revenue, 186 S.W.3d 267 (Mo.2006)—§ 3.3(e) n.182

York, State v., 705 A.2d 692 (Me.1997)—§ 9.6(a) n.32

York, United States v., 428 F.3d 1325 (11th Cir.2005)—§§ 15.4(h) n.195, 198

York, United States v., 357 F.3d 14 (1st Cir.2004)—§ 26.9(b) n.73

York v. United States, 785 A.2d 651 (D.C.App.2001)—§ 22.4(c) n.29

York, United States v., 933 F.2d 1343 (7th Cir.1991)—§ 6.4(g) n.161

Yorn v. Superior Court, 90 Cal.App.3d 669, 153 Cal.Rptr. 295 (1979)—§ 27.4(c) n.33

Yost v. State, 149 Neb. 584, 31 N.W.2d 538 (1948)—§ 16.1(d) n.139

Yoswick v. State, 347 Md. 228, 700 A.2d 251 (1997)—§§ 21.3(b) n.45, 71; 21.4(d) n.119

Yother, State v., 253 Mont. 128, 831 P.2d 1347 (1992)—§ 21.2(d) n.165

You, United States v., 382 F.3d 958 (9th Cir.2004)—§ 25.2(a) n.10

Young, Ex parte, 684 S.W.2d 704 (Tex.Cr.App.1985)—§ 21.2(e) n.326

Young, Commonwealth v., 561 Pa. 34, 748 A.2d 166 (1999)—§§ 7.4(e) n.89, 92

Young v. Dretke, 356 F.3d 616 (5th Cir.2004)—§ 11.10(d) n.186

Young v. Harper, 520 U.S. 143, 117 S.Ct. 1148, 137 L.Ed.2d 270 (1997)—§§ 26.1(e) n.96; 26.2(c) n.52

Young v. Hayes, 218 F.3d 850 (8th Cir.2000)—§ 26.2(c) n.78

Young v. Herring, 917 F.2d 858 (5th Cir.1990)—§§ 7.4(c) n.54, 55, 57; 7.4(e) n.89

Young v. Hubbard, 673 F.2d 132 (5th Cir.1982)—§§ 12.4(d) n.81, 84

Young v. Lockhart, 892 F.2d 1348 (8th Cir.1989)—§ 11.5(c) n.56

Young v. Mabry, 596 F.2d 339 (8th Cir.1979)—§ 18.4(c) n.60

Young v. People, 30 P.3d 202 (Colo.2001)—§ 21.5(c) n.88

Young, People v., 94 N.Y.2d 171, 701 N.Y.S.2d 309, 723 N.E.2d 58 (1999)—§§ 26.8(c) n.25, 29

Young, People v., 153 Ill.2d 383, 180 Ill.Dec. 229, 607 N.E.2d 123 (1992)—§§ 6.4(e) n.77; 6.9(f) n.142

Young, People v., 137 Misc.2d 400, 520 N.Y.S.2d 924 (1987)—§ 15.2(c) n.80

Young, People v., 6 Ill.App.3d 119, 285 N.E.2d 159 (1972)—§ 7.4(b) n.20

Young, People v., 21 Mich.App. 684, 176 N.W.2d 420 (1970)—§ 10.3(d) n.64

Young v. Prince George's County, 355 F.3d 751 (4th Cir.2004)—§ 3.8(b) n.29

Young v. Ragen, 337 U.S. 235, 69 S.Ct. 1073, 93 L.Ed. 1333 (1949)—§ 28.11(a) n.1

Young v. Runnels, 435 F.3d 1038 (9th Cir.2006)—§ 11.8(c) n.77

Young v. Russell, 332 S.W.2d 629 (Ky.1960)—§ 12.4(a) n.22

Young, State v., 196 S.W.3d 85 (Tenn.2006)—§ 22.4(e) n.47

Young, State v., 294 Wis.2d 1, 717 N.W.2d 729 (2006)—§ 3.8(d) n.136

Young, State v., 710 N.W.2d 272 (Minn.2006)—§ 7.4(e) n.90

Young v. State, 731 So.2d 1120 (Miss.1999)—§ 21.5(d) n.104

Young v. State, 645 So.2d 965 (Fla.1994)—§ 24.9(c) n.21

Young v. State, 109 Nev. 205, 849 P.2d 336 (1993)—§ 3.2(e) n.168

Young, State v., 626 So.2d 655 (Fla.1993)—§§ 11.4(d) n.116, 118; 11.5(c) n.49, 51

Young, State v., 853 P.2d 327 (Utah 1993)—§§ 26.4(g) n.133, 146

Young, State v., 122 Idaho 278, 833 P.2d 911 (1992)—§ 26.10(b) n.31

Young v. State, 308 Ark. 647, 826 S.W.2d 814 (1992)—§ 5.3(d) n.44

Young, State v., 249 Mont. 257, 815 P.2d 590 (1991)—§ 24.3(i) n.197

Young, State v., 37 Ohio St.3d 249, 525 N.E.2d 1363 (1988)—§ 3.3(g) n.227

Young v. State, 103 Nev. 233, 737 P.2d 512 (1987)—§ 22.3(d) n.176

Young, State v., 149 Ariz. 580, 720 P.2d 965 (Ariz.App.1986)—§§ 15.6(a) n.36; 15.7(g) n.220

Young, State v., 317 N.C. 396, 346 S.E.2d 626 (1986)—§ 6.9(f) n.135

Young, State v., 173 W.Va. 1, 311 S.E.2d 118 (1983)—§ 23.2(g) n.121

Young v. State, 297 Md. 286, 465 A.2d 1149 (1983)—§§ 22.5(d) n.32, 34, 36

Young, State v., 89 Wash.2d 613, 574 P.2d 1171 (1978)—§ 6.9(a) n.9

Young, State v., 112 Ariz. 361, 542 P.2d 20 (1975)—§ 21.4(d) n.138

Young, State v., 234 Ga. 488, 216 S.E.2d 586 (1975)—§ 3.9(k) n.247

Young, State v., 273 Minn. 240, 141 N.W.2d 15 (Minn.1966)—§ 26.10(d) n.94

Young, United States v., 315 F.3d 911 (8th Cir.2003)—§ 11.9(d) n.173

Young, United States v., 350 F.3d 1302 (11th Cir.2003)—§ 3.2(b) n.53

Young, United States v., 287 F.3d 1352 (11th Cir.2002)—§ 11.5(d) n.71

Young, United States v., 223 F.3d 905 (8th Cir.2000)—§§ 21.2(h) n.419, 439

Young, United States v., 20 F.3d 758 (7th Cir.1994)—§ 24.3(b) n.55

Young, United States v., 814 F.2d 392 (7th Cir.1987)—§ 18.3(b) n.9

Young, United States v., 822 F.2d 1234 (2d Cir.1987)—§ 22.2(d) n.81

Young, United States v., 470 U.S. 1, 105 S.Ct. 1038, 84 L.Ed.2d 1 (1985)—§§ 24.7(b) n.21; 24.7(e) n.52; 24.7(f) n.75; 27.5(d) n.132

Young, United States v., 494 F.Supp. 57 (E.D.Tex.1980)—§ 8.5(h) n.296

Young, United States v., 512 F.2d 321 (4th Cir.1975)—§§ 3.3(d) n.176; 9.4(d) n.78

Young, United States v., 482 F.2d 993 (5th Cir.1973)—§§ 11.4(b) n.18, 20, 25, 36

Young v. United States ex rel. Vuitton et Fils, S.A., 481 U.S. 787, 107 S.Ct. 2124, 95 L.Ed.2d 740 (1987)—§§ 1.7(i) n.158; 13.3(b) n.20; 22.5(a) n.10; 27.6(b) n.34

Young v. Weston, 344 F.3d 973 (9th Cir.2003)—§ 17.4(b) n.134

Youngblood, State v., 117 Idaho 160, 786 P.2d 551 (1990)—§ 3.2(b) n.36

Youngblood, United States v., 379 F.2d 365 (2d Cir.1967)—§ 8.5(g) n.224

Youngblood v. West Virginia, _____ U.S. _____, 126 S.Ct. 2188, 165 L.Ed.2d 269 (2006)—§ 24.3(b) n.51

Youngblood, State ex rel. v. Sanders, 212 W.Va. 885, 575 S.E.2d 864 (2002)—§ 11.9(c) n.116

Younger v. Gilmore, 404 U.S. 15, 92 S.Ct. 250, 30 L.Ed.2d 142 (1971)—§ 11.2(f) n.233

Younger v. Harris, 401 U.S. 37, 91 S.Ct. 746, 27 L.Ed.2d 669 (1971)—§ 13.5(e) n.92

Younger, United States v., 398 F.3d 1179 (9th Cir.2005)—§ 6.9(g) n.166

Younghaus v. State, 90 So.2d 308 (Fla.1956)—§ 12.4(d) n.63

Young, United States ex rel. v. Lane, 768 F.2d 834 (7th Cir.1985)—§ 25.3(c) n.22

Yount v. Patton, 710 F.2d 956 (3d Cir.1983)—§§ 6.7(d) n.143, 154

Yount, State v., 853 S.W.2d 6 (Tex.Cr.App.1993)—§ 24.8(f) n.107

Yousef, United States v., 327 F.3d 56 (2d Cir.2003)—§§ 6.4(f) n.136; 16.4(b) n.25

Yowell, State v., 513 S.W.2d 397 (Mo.1974)—§ 10.2(b) n.22

Yuch, In re, 437 F.Supp. 775 (E.D.Pa.1977)—§ 8.9(b) n.33

Yuknavich, United States v., 419 F.3d 1302 (11th Cir.2005)—§ 26.9(b) n.66

Yu-Leung, United States v., 51 F.3d 1116 (2d Cir.1995)—§ 22.4(c) n.24

Yung v. Walker, 468 F.3d 169 (2d Cir.2006)—§ 24.1(b) n.29

Yunis, United States v., 859 F.2d 953 (D.C.Cir.1988)—§ 6.9(b) n.44

Yurick v. State, 184 N.J. 70, 875 A.2d 898 (2005)—§ 13.3(e) n.49

Z

Zabawa, United States v., 39 F.3d 279 (10th Cir.1994)—§ 13.2(a) n.4

Zabriskie, United States v., 415 F.3d 1139 (10th Cir.2005)—§§ 24.9(d) n.48; 27.6(d) n.98

Zacarias v. United States, 884 A.2d 83 (D.C.2005)—§ 19.6(c) n.39

Zacek v. Brewer, 241 N.W.2d 41 (Iowa 1976)—§ 24.3(b) n.77

Zachodni, State v., 466 N.W.2d 624 (S.D.1991)—§§ 3.10(e) n.172; 3.10(f) n.204

Zack v. State, 911 So.2d 1190 (Fla.2005)—§ 26.2(b) n.8

Zackson, United States v., 6 F.3d 911 (2d Cir.1993)—§ 11.9(a) n.12

Zadvydas v. Davis, 533 U.S. 678, 121 S.Ct. 2491, 150 L.Ed.2d 653 (2001)—§ 28.9(a) n.8

Zafiro v. United States, 506 U.S. 534, 113 S.Ct. 933, 122 L.Ed.2d 317 (1993)—§§ 17.2(d) n.104; 17.3(e) n.61

Zagorski v. State, 983 S.W.2d 654 (Tenn.1998)—§§ 11.6(a) n.62, 64

Zagorski, State v., 701 S.W.2d 808 (Tenn.1985)—§§ 22.5(c) n.25, 27

Zagranski, Commonwealth v., 408 Mass. 278, 558 N.E.2d 933 (1990)—§ 3.3(d) n.162

Zagrodny, Commonwealth v., 443 Mass. 93, 819 N.E.2d 565 (2004)—§ 6.9(b) n.24

Zaha, State v., 44 Or.App. 103, 605 P.2d 306 (1980)—§§ 11.4(c) n.82, 85

Zajac, United States v., 62 F.3d 145 (6th Cir.1995)—§ 26.4(c) n.30

Zakharov, United States v., 468 F.3d 1171 (9th Cir.2006)—§ 6.3(b) n.36

Zakrzewski, Commonwealth v., 460 Pa. 528, 333 A.2d 898 (1975)—§ 21.2(e) n.308

Zamarripa, United States v., 905 F.2d 337 (10th Cir.1990)—§§ 21.1(h) n.233; 21.2(d) n.216

Zambrano v. City of Tustin, 885 F.2d 1473 (9th Cir.1989)—§ 1.7(j) n.262

Zamora, People v., 18 Cal.3d 538, 134 Cal.Rptr. 784, 557 P.2d 75 (1976)—§ 18.5(a) n.49

Zamora, State v., 129 Idaho 817, 933 P.2d 106 (1997)—§ 22.4(c) n.29

Zanabria, United States v., 74 F.3d 590 (5th Cir.1996)—§ 9.6(a) n.48

Zancauske, State v., 804 S.W.2d 851 (Mo.App.1991)—§ 6.6(d) n.57

Zane, People v., 152 A.D.2d 976, 543 N.Y.S.2d 777 (1989)—§ 19.3(a) n.62

Zangger, United States v., 848 F.2d 923 (8th Cir.1988)—§§ 15.7(g) n.195; 19.2(f) n.93; 19.3(a) n.15, 58

Zannino, United States v., 895 F.2d 1 (1st Cir.1990)—§ 4.6(e) n.110

Zanter, State v., 535 N.W.2d 624 (Minn.1995)—§§ 3.3(g) n.248; 27.3(c) n.57

Zap v. United States, 328 U.S. 624, 66 S.Ct. 1277, 90 L.Ed. 1477 (1946)—§§ 3.9(c) n.42; 3.10(a) n.5

Zapata, United States v., 18 F.3d 971 (1st Cir.1994)—§§ 9.3(e) n.56, 65, 82

Zapata, United States v., 997 F.2d 751 (10th Cir.1993)—§ 3.10(b) n.42

Zapien, People v., 4 Cal.4th 929, 17 Cal.Rptr.2d 122, 846 P.2d 704 (1993)—§§ 14.1(d) n.63, 64

Zappulla v. New York, 391 F.3d 462 (2d Cir.2004)—§ 6.8(b) n.50

Zarate, State v., 264 Neb. 690, 651 N.W.2d 215 (2002)—§§ 21.3(b) n.64, 66; 21.4(d) n.137

Zavala, United States v., 839 F.2d 523 (9th Cir.1988)—§ 24.3(b) n.54

Zayas, People v., 217 N.Y. 78, 111 N.E. 465 (1916)—§§ 16.4(c) n.81, 86

Zazzara, United States v., 626 F.2d 135 (9th Cir.1980)—§ 11.7(a) n.16

Z.C.B., In re, 669 N.W.2d 478 (N.D.2003)—§ 6.9(b) n.23

Zdiarstek, State v., 53 Wis.2d 776, 193 N.W.2d 833 (1972)—§ 24.8(e) n.60

Zebe v. State, 112 Nev. 1482, 929 P.2d 927 (1996)—§ 21.2(e) n.325

Zedner v. United States, _____ U.S. _____, 126 S.Ct. 1976, 164 L.Ed.2d 749 (2006)—§§ 18.3(b) n.37, 46, 51; 27.6(b) n.35

Zehr, People v., 103 Ill.2d 472, 83 Ill.Dec. 128, 469 N.E.2d 1062 (1984)—§ 22.3(a) n.11

Zehrbach, United States v., 47 F.3d 1252 (3d Cir.1995)—§ 27.6(b) n.18

Zehrung v. State, 569 P.2d 189 (Alaska 1977)—§ 10.4(c) n.20

Zeigler, United States v., 19 F.3d 486 (10th Cir.1994)—§ 1.2(c) n.133

Zell v. State, 15 Ohio App. 446 (1922)— § 15.4(g) n.167

Zeller, State ex rel. v. Montgomery Circuit Court, 223 Ind. 476, 62 N.E.2d 149 (1945)—§ 27.4(b) n.6

Zemtsov, Commonwealth v., 443 Mass. 36, 818 N.E.2d 1057 (2004)— §§ 17.1(d) n.53; 17.2(e) n.119; 17.2(f) n.132

Zemunski, State v., 230 Neb. 613, 433 N.W.2d 170 (1988)—§ 22.1(h) n.138

Zenone, United States v., 153 F.3d 725 (4th Cir.1998)—§ 7.4(a) n.7

Zentgraf, United States v., 20 F.3d 906 (8th Cir.1994)—§ 26.10(c) n.73

Zerduche, United States v., 133 Fed. Appx. 599, 2005 WL 1052357 (11th Cir.2005)—§ 24.9(f) n.102

Zerilli v. United States, 706 F.2d 877 (8th Cir.1983)—§ 16.2(e) n.79

Zermeno, United States v., 66 F.3d 1058 (9th Cir.1995)—§ 9.1(b) n.48

Zeuli, United States v., 137 F.2d 845 (2d Cir.1943)—§ 16.2(g) n.127

Zhao, State v., 157 Wash.2d 188, 137 P.3d 835 (2006)—§ 21.4(f) n.202

Ziang Sung Wan v. United States, 266 U.S. 1, 45 S.Ct. 1, 69 L.Ed. 131 (1924)—§§ 6.2(a) n.20; 6.2(c) n.84, 167

Zicarelli v. Dietz, 633 F.2d 312 (3d Cir.1980)—§§ 2.6(b) n.54, 63, 69, 71, 72; 16.1(b) n.31; 16.1(e) n.208; 22.2(d) n.74; 22.2(e) n.110

Zicarelli v. Gray, 543 F.2d 466 (3d Cir.1976)—§§ 2.6(b) n.68, 72; 22.2(e) n.109

Zicarelli v. New Jersey State Commission of Investigation, 406 U.S. 472, 92 S.Ct. 1670, 32 L.Ed.2d 234 (1972)—§§ 2.6(d) n.99; 8.10(b) n.43

Zickert, United States v., 955 F.2d 665 (11th Cir.1992)—§ 21.4(g) n.228

Zidell, United States v., 323 F.3d 412 (6th Cir.2003)—§§ 16.2(e) n.90, 91

Ziegler, Commonwealth v., 286 Pa.Super. 26, 428 A.2d 220 (1981)—§ 26.10(b) n.21

Zielezinski, United States v., 740 F.2d 727 (9th Cir.1984)—§§ 15.6(b) n.56; 15.7(d) n.66, 68, 72, 74, 76

Zillges, United States v., 978 F.2d 369 (7th Cir.1992)—§§ 11.4(b) n.20, 40; 11.4(c) n.67, 74; 27.6(d) n.148

Zimmer, State v., 19 Kan.App.2d 617, 873 P.2d 1381 (1994)—§ 27.5(a) n.27

Zimmerman, People v., 44 Ill.App.3d 601, 3 Ill.Dec. 317, 358 N.E.2d 715 (1976)—§ 3.1(g) n.171

Zimmerman, State v., 539 N.W.2d 49 (N.D.1995)—§ 17.4(b) n.124

Zimmermann v. Board of Professional Responsibility, 764 S.W.2d 757 (Tenn.1989)—§ 23.1(b) n.32

Zinn v. District Court of Morton County, 17 N.D. 135, 114 N.W. 472 (1908)—§§ 16.3(d) n.78; 16.3(g) n.102

Zito, State v., 333 Mont. 312, 143 P.3d 108 (2006)—§ 6.7(c) n.130

Zmayefski, State v., 836 A.2d 191 (R.I.2003)—§§ 18.2(b) n.17; 18.2(c) n.53

Zoller v. State, 282 Ark. 380, 669 S.W.2d 434 (1984)—§ 21.4(b) n.52

Zook, Commonwealth v., 532 Pa. 79, 615 A.2d 1 (1992)—§§ 14.2(g) n.93, 94

Zook, People v., 177 Ill.App.3d 62, 126 Ill.Dec. 439, 531 N.E.2d 1066 (1988)—§ 14.3(c) n.57

Zuber, Commonwealth v., 466 Pa. 453, 353 A.2d 441 (1976)—§ 21.2(e) n.349

Zuber, United States v., 118 F.3d 101 (2d Cir.1997)—§ 24.2(e) n.66

Zubke, People v., 469 Mich. 80, 664 N.W.2d 751 (2003)—§ 25.5(b) n.27

Zucconi, State v., 50 N.J. 361, 235 A.2d 193 (1967)—§ 6.6(e) n.71

Zucconi, State v., 93 N.J.Super. 380, 226 A.2d 16 (1967)—§ 6.10(a) n.6

Zukowski, United States v., 851 F.2d 174 (7th Cir.1988)—§§ 18.1(c) n.36; 18.3(b) n.5

Zuniga, In re, 714 F.2d 632 (6th Cir.1983)—§ 8.12(b) n.22

Zuniga, People v., 31 Ill.2d 429, 202 N.E.2d 31 (1964)—§ 6.4(f) n.111

Zuniga, State v., 257 Wis.2d 625, 652 N.W.2d 423 (App.2002)—§ 21.2(e) n.358

Zupan, State v., 184 A.D.2d 888, 585 N.Y.S.2d 545 (1992)—§ 15.7(f) n.176

Zupancic, State v., 192 Colo. 231, 557 P.2d 1195 (1976)—§ 19.3(b) n.134

Zuppo v. State, 807 A.2d 545 (Del.2002)—§ 11.5(d) n.72

Zurcher v. Stanford Daily, 35 Record 415 (1980)—§ 3.4(a) n.21

Zurcher v. Stanford Daily, 436 U.S. 547, 98 S.Ct. 1970, 56 L.Ed.2d 525 (1978)—§§ 3.4(a) n.18; 3.4(f) n.114; 8.3(c) n.19

Zurita, State v., 133 N.H. 719, 584 A.2d 758 (1990)—§ 6.8(a) n.36

Zurla v. State, 109 N.M. 640, 789 P.2d 588 (1990)—§ 18.2(c) n.35

Zweibon v. Mitchell, 516 F.2d 594 (D.C. Cir.1975)—§ 4.9(a) n.5

Zylstra v. Corporation of Charleston, 1 Bay (S.C.) 382 (1794)—§ 2.4(c) n.93

Zylstra, United States v., 713 F.2d 1332 (7th Cir.1983)—§§ 16.3(c) n.40, 44, 45

Table of Laws and Rules

UNITED STATES CONSTITUTION

Art.	This Work Sec.	Note
I	2.1	
I	13.3(c)	43
I	28.1(b)	
I	28.2(a)	
I, § 3	1.2(c)	24
I, § 6, cl. 1	3.4(a)	23
I, § 7, cl. 3	2.1	10
I, § 8	1.2(c)	
I, § 8	1.2(c)	14
I, § 8	2.12(b)	84
I, § 8	16.4(b)	7
I, § 8, cl. 4	1.2(c)	12
I, § 8, cl. 6	1.2(c)	21
I, § 8, cl. 6	1.2(c)	36
I, § 8, cl. 6	1.2(c)	37
I, § 8, cl. 10	1.2(c)	22
I, § 8, cl. 17	1.2(c)	15
I, § 8, cl. 17	1.2(c)	23
I, § 8, cl. 17	1.2(c)	34
I, § 8, cl. 18	1.2(c)	16
I, § 9	2.1	
I, § 9	2.1	21
I, § 9	2.12(c)	178
I, § 9	28.2(a)	
I, § 9. cl. 2	28.2(a)	2
I, § 9, cl. 2	2.1	9
I, § 10	2.1	
I, § 10	2.1	34
I, § 10	2.2	
I, § 10	2.3(a)	15
I, § 10, cl. 1	2.1	11
I, § 38, cl. 4	1.2(c)	87
II	1.2(c)	
II	13.3(b)	29
II	23.1(b)	85
II, § 1, cl. 1	1.2(c)	45
II, § 2, cl. 1	1.2(c)	48
II, § 2, cl. 2	1.2(c)	47
II, § 3	1.2(c)	46
II, § 3	13.3(c)	43
II, § 4	1.2(c)	26
III	1.2(c)	14
III	1.2(c)	64
III	1.2(c)	65
III	2.1	26
III	2.4(c)	

UNITED STATES CONSTITUTION

Art.	This Work Sec.	Note
III	2.6(b)	
III	7.3(g)	
III	7.4(h)	
III	10.6(b)	
III	12.1(a)	14
III	13.3(b)	29
III	16.1(b)	44
III	16.1(b)	55
III	16.1(c)	101
III	16.1(c)	118
III	16.1(c)	127
III	16.1(d)	
III	16.2(e)	89
III	18.4(c)	66
III	18.4(c)	75
III	21.4(a)	37
III	24.6(a)	
III	27.5(a)	1
III	27.5(d)	
III(a)	18.4(c)	
III, § 1	1.2(c)	
III, § 1	1.2(c)	62
III, § 2	1.2(c)	
III, § 2	15.1(b)	
III, § 2	15.1(b)	47
III, § 2	16.1(b)	
III, § 2	16.1(b)	85
III, § 2	16.1(c)	100
III, § 2	16.1(d)	
III, § 2	16.1(e)	166
III, § 2	16.2(b)	
III, § 2	16.2(f)	
III, § 2	22.1(a)	6
III, § 2	25.1(d)	89
III, § 2, cl. 1	1.2(c)	63
III, § 2, cl. 3	1.2(c)	61
III, § 2, cl. 3	2.1	12
III, § 2, cl. 3	2.1	13
III, § 2, cl. 3	16.1(b)	43
III, § 2, cl. 3	22.1(f)	
III, § 3	2.1	14
III, § 3	26.6(d)	44
IV	1.2(c)	
IV	2.3(a)	
IV	2.3(a)	13
IV	2.3(a)	67
IV	2.3(b)	

UNITED STATES CONSTITUTION

Art.	This Work Sec.	Note
IV	11.2(f)	241
IV	18.4(c)	75
IV, § 1	1.2(c)	14
IV, § 2	2.3(a)	22
IV, § 2	2.3(a)	23
IV, § 2	3.1(j)	249
IV, cl. 2	2.3(a)	13
IV, § 3	1.2(c)	14
IV, § 3	16.4(b)	5
IV, § 3, cl. 2	1.2(c)	15
V	8.10(a)	
V	15.1(b)	64
VI	1.7(b)	
VI	2.1	
VI, cl. 2	1.2(c)	17
VI, cl. 3	2.1	15

Amend.	This Work Sec.	Note
I	1.6(f)	384
I	2.1	26
I	2.2	
I	2.3(a)	8
I	2.3(a)	15
I	2.3(b)	82
I	2.4(d)	127
I	2.4(e)	
I	2.5(c)	24
I	2.5(c)	25
I	2.5(c)	29
I	2.5(f)	
I	2.6(c)	76
I	2.8(a)	11
I	2.8(a)	25
I	2.8(c)	
I	2.10(c)	52
I	3.1(i)	
I	3.3(b)	41
I	3.4(a)	
I	3.4(a)	20
I	3.4(c)	
I	3.6(g)	
I	3.10(c)	84
I	4.9(b)	
I	5.4(c)	
I	8.4(b)	103
I	8.4(b)	104
I	8.5(b)	
I	8.5(b)	57
I	8.5(d)	121
I	8.5(d)	123
I	8.5(d)	152
I	8.5(d)	159

UNITED STATES CONSTITUTION

Amend.	This Work Sec.	Note
I	8.5(i)	325
I	8.6(b)	
I	8.8	
I	8.13(a)	25
I	11.2(f)	233
I	11.2(f)	241
I	12.2(d)	
I	13.4(c)	121
I	13.5(a)	13
I	13.5(a)	15
I	13.5(b)	
I	13.5(e)	
I	18.1(b)	
I	21.4(b)	52
I	22.1(b)	42
I	22.2(d)	76
I	22.3(b)	55
I	22.3(b)	68
I	22.3(d)	202
I	23.1	
I	23.3(a)	
I	23.3(b)	27
I	24.1(b)	24
I	26.4(b)	17
I	26.9(b)	26
I	26.9(b)	54
I	27.5(e)	
II	2.1	26
II	2.3(a)	50
II	2.3(a)	68
II	3.1(i)	
III	2.1	26
III	2.3(a)	68
IV	1.2(c)	
IV	1.3(b)	11
IV	1.3(c)	22
IV	1.4(g)	139
IV	1.5(b)	
IV	1.5(h)	
IV	1.5(h)	294
IV	1.5(h)	296
IV	1.5(j)	334
IV	1.5(k)	370
IV	1.7(b)	
IV	1.7(c)	
IV	1.7(i)	180
IV	1.7(i)	196
IV	1.7(j)	234
IV	1.8(c)	8
IV	1.8(d)	61
IV	1.9(b)	12
IV	1.9(b)	24

| UNITED STATES CONSTITUTION | | | UNITED STATES CONSTITUTION | | |
| | This Work | | | This Work | |
Amend.	Sec.	Note	Amend.	Sec.	Note
IV	2.1		IV	3.6(g)	
IV	2.4(b)	50	IV	3.7	
IV	2.4(b)	54	IV	3.8	
IV	2.4(c)		IV	3.9	
IV	2.4(c)	104	IV	3.10	
IV	2.4(e)		IV	4.1	
IV	2.4(f)	187	IV	4.2(a)	
IV	2.5(e)	44	IV	4.2(b)	
IV	2.5(f)		IV	4.3(a)	
IV	2.5(f)	91	IV	4.3(b)	
IV	2.6(a)	2	IV	4.3(c)	
IV	2.6(c)	76	IV	4.4(a)	
IV	2.6(c)	85	IV	4.4(b)	
IV	2.6(d)		IV	4.4(c)	12
IV	2.6(e)		IV	4.4(d)	
IV	2.7		IV	4.4(e)	
IV	2.8(a)	25	IV	4.5	
IV	2.8(b)		IV	4.6(b)	
IV	2.8(b)	34	IV	4.6(b)	29
IV	2.8(c)		IV	4.6(e)	80
IV	2.9		IV	4.6(g)	
IV	2.10(d)		IV	4.6(l)	
IV	2.11(b)		IV	4.6(l)	199
IV	2.11(b)	18	IV	4.6(m)	
IV	2.11(c)		IV	4.7(a)	
IV	2.11(c)	37	IV	4.7(b)	
IV	2.11(d)		IV	4.7(c)	22
IV	2.12		IV	4.8(a)	
IV	3.1		IV	4.8(c)	
IV	3.2		IV	4.8(d)	
IV	3.3(a)		IV	4.8(e)	
IV	3.3(b)		IV	4.8(e)	52
IV	3.3(b)	76	IV	4.9(a)	
IV	3.3(c)		IV	5.2(b)	
IV	3.3(d)		IV	5.4(b)	15
IV	3.3(e)		IV	6.2(b)	
IV	3.3(e)	186	IV	6.3(c)	54
IV	3.3(f)	205	IV	6.4(b)	17
IV	3.3(f)	216	IV	6.4(d)	
IV	3.3(f)	219	IV	6.5(a)	20
IV	3.3(g)		IV	6.6(c)	33
IV	3.4		IV	6.6(d)	54
IV	3.5		IV	6.6(e)	
IV	3.6(a)	9	IV	6.7(b)	51
IV	3.6(a)	42	IV	6.7(b)	52
IV	3.6(b)	43	IV	6.10(e)	67
IV	3.6(b)	46	IV	7.3(b)	14
IV	3.6(b)	47	IV	7.4(b)	
IV	3.6(c)		IV	8.1(c)	
IV	3.6(d)		IV	8.3(c)	22
IV	3.6(e)	127	IV	8.5(d)	
IV	3.6(f)	154	IV	8.7	

UNITED STATES CONSTITUTION

Amend.	Sec.	This Work Note
IV	8.8(b)	
IV	8.8(c)	45
IV	8.8(e)	132
IV	8.8(f)	147
IV	8.8(g)	173
IV	8.9(a)	
IV	8.10(a)	37
IV	8.11(a)	15
IV	8.12	
IV	9.1(a)	5
IV	9.1(a)	9
IV	9.1(b)	61
IV	9.1(b)	72
IV	9.1(b)	73
IV	9.1(b)	75
IV	9.1(b)	83
IV	9.1(c)	98
IV	9.1(c)	100
IV	9.1(d)	
IV	9.1(d)	128
IV	9.2(a)	
IV	9.2(b)	
IV	9.2(c)	20
IV	9.2(d)	
IV	9.3(b)	
IV	9.3(c)	
IV	9.3(e)	58
IV	9.3(e)	62
IV	9.4(a)	9
IV	9.4(a)	33
IV	9.4(a)	42
IV	9.4(d)	
IV	9.4(e)	
IV	9.4(f)	
IV	9.5(a)	
IV	9.5(c)	
IV	9.5(e)	
IV	9.6(a)	16
IV	9.6(a)	32
IV	9.6(a)	49
IV	9.6(b)	
IV	9.6(c)	61
IV	10.1(b)	20
IV	10.1(b)	21
IV	10.2(a)	2
IV	10.3(b)	49
IV	10.4(b)	
IV	10.4(c)	18
IV	10.5(c)	
IV	10.6(c)	24
IV	10.6(d)	45
IV	11.2(f)	241

UNITED STATES CONSTITUTION

Amend.	Sec.	This Work Note
IV	11.8(b)	27
IV	11.10(c)	
IV	11.10(d)	181
IV	12.1(b)	32
IV	12.1(b)	38
IV	12.2(a)	10
IV	12.2(d)	
IV	12.3(b)	78
IV	12.4(g)	
IV	12.5(b)	
IV	14.2(a)	5
IV	14.2(a)	8
IV	14.2(a)	9
IV	14.2(a)	12
IV	14.3(a)	36
IV	15.1(b)	21
IV	15.1(b)	115
IV	15.1(f)	271
IV	15.2(d)	
IV	15.5(a)	9
IV	15.5(b)	99
IV	17.4(b)	114
IV	20.2(d)	63
IV	20.6(b)	
IV	21.2(b)	68
IV	21.6(a)	18
IV	21.6(b)	107
IV	21.6(c)	120
IV	24.4(a)	
IV	26.5(a)	8
IV	26.9(b)	61
IV	26.9(b)	66
IV	26.9(c)	88
IV	26.10(c)	
IV	27.5(e)	178
IV	27.6(d)	
IV	28.2(c)	
IV	28.2(d)	86
IV	28.3(c)	79
IV	28.3(d)	83
IV	28.3(d)	85
IV	28.3(d)	86
IV	28.4(d)	
IV	28.9(b)	
V	1.3	
V	1.5	
V	1.7	
V	1.8	
V	2.1	
V	2.2	
V	2.3	
V	2.4	

UNITED STATES CONSTITUTION

Amend.	This Work Sec.	Note
V	2.5	
V	2.6	
V	2.7	
V	2.8	
V	2.9	
V	2.10	
V	2.11	
V	2.12	
V	3.1	
V	3.2	
V	3.3	
V	3.4	
V	3.5	
V	3.10	
V	6.1	
V	6.2	
V	6.3	
V	6.4	
V	6.5	
V	6.7	
V	6.8	
V	6.9	
V	6.10	
V	7.1	
V	7.2	
V	7.3	
V	8.2	
V	8.4	
V	8.5	
V	8.7	
V	8.8	
V	8.10	
V	8.11	
V	8.12	
V	8.13	
V	8.14	
V	9.1	
V	9.2	
V	9.4	
V	9.5	
V	9.6	
V	10.3	
V	10.4	
V	10.5	
V	10.6	
V	11.1	
V	11.2	
V	11.6	
V	11.8	
V	11.10	
V	12.1	
V	12.3	

UNITED STATES CONSTITUTION

Amend.	This Work Sec.	Note
V	13.1	
V	13.4	
V	13.5	
V	14.2	
V	14.3	
V	15.1	
V	15.2	
V	15.4	
V	15.5	
V	15.6	
V	15.7	
V	17.1	
V	17.2	
V	17.4	
V	18.3	
V	18.5	
V	19.2	
V	19.3	
V	19.5	
V	19.6	
V	20.2	
V	20.4	
V	21.1	
V	21.2	
V	21.3	
V	21.4	
V	22.1	
V	22.2	
V	24.2	
V	24.3	
V	24.4	
V	24.5	
V	24.10	
V	24.11	
V	25.1	
V	25.2	
V	25.5	
V	26.4	
V	26.5	
V	26.7	
V	26.9	
V	27.2	
V	27.3	
V	28.3	
V	28.5	
V	28.6	
V	28.9	
VI	1.3	
VI	1.5	
VI	1.7	
VI	1.8	
VI	2.1	

UNITED STATES CONSTITUTION		
	This Work	
Amend.	Sec.	Note
VI	2.4	
VI	2.5	
VI	2.6	
VI	2.7	
VI	2.8	
VI	2.9	
VI	2.10	
VI	2.12	
VI	3.4	
VI	3.10	
VI	6.4	
VI	6.5	
VI	6.6	
VI	6.7	
VI	6.9	
VI	6.10	
VI	7.3	
VI	8.3	
VI	8.5	
VI	8.6	
VI	8.8	
VI	8.10	
VI	8.12	
VI	8.14	
VI	9.1	
VI	9.5	
VI	9.6	
VI	10.5	
VI	11.1	
VI	11.2	
VI	11.3	
VI	11.4	
VI	11.5	
VI	11.6	
VI	11.7	
VI	11.8	
VI	11.9	
VI	11.10	
VI	12.1	
VI	13.6	
VI	14.1	
VI	14.2	
VI	14.4	
VI	15.1	
VI	15.3	
VI	15.4	
VI	15.6	
VI	16.1	
VI	16.2	
VI	16.3	
VI	16.4	
VI	17.2	

UNITED STATES CONSTITUTION		
	This Work	
Amend.	Sec.	Note
VI	17.4	
VI	18.1	
VI	18.2	
VI	18.3	
VI	18.4	
VI	18.5	
VI	19.1	
VI	19.2	
VI	19.3	
VI	20.3	
VI	20.4	
VI	20.5	
VI	20.6	
VI	21.1	
VI	21.2	
VI	21.3	
VI	21.6	
VI	22.1	
VI	22.2	
VI	22.3	
VI	23.1	
VI	23.2	
VI	24.1	
VI	24.2	
VI	24.3	
VI	24.4	
VI	24.5	
VI	24.6	
VI	24.7	
VI	24.9	
VI	25.1	
VI	26.1	
VI	26.2	
VI	26.4	
VI	26.6	
VI	26.10	
VI	27.2	
VI	27.5	
VI	27.6	
VI	28.3	
VI	28.4	
VI	28.5	
VI	28.6	
VI	28.8	
VI	28.9	
VI	28.12	
VII	2.1	47
VII	2.3(a)	
VII	2.3(a)	68
VII	2.3(a)	69
VII	2.4(c)	
VII	2.4(d)	120

UNITED STATES CONSTITUTION

Amend.	This Work Sec.	Note
VII	22.1(a)	8
VIII	1.3(b)	
VIII	1.5(e)	
VIII	1.8(e)	98
VIII	2.1	
VIII	2.4(a)	20
VIII	2.4(e)	
VIII	2.6(a)	3
VIII	2.6(b)	41
VIII	2.6(c)	85
VIII	2.7(a)	2
VIII	2.7(b)	90
VIII	2.7(c)	
VIII	2.7(d)	233
VIII	2.7(d)	243
VIII	2.9(d)	93
VIII	2.12(a)	
VIII	3.9(i)	181
VIII	11.1(b)	
VIII	11.2(f)	236
VIII	12.1(e)	63
VIII	12.2(a)	
VIII	12.2(b)	
VIII	12.2(b)	35
VIII	12.2(b)	38
VIII	12.3(a)	
VIII	12.3(b)	
VIII	12.3(c)	79
VIII	12.3(e)	
VIII	12.3(f)	
VIII	12.3(g)	
VIII	12.4(a)	
VIII	12.4(d)	
VIII	12.4(f)	96
VIII	13.2(h)	145
VIII	13.4(e)	166
VIII	24.11(d)	
VIII	25.1(c)	34
VIII	26.1(b)	20
VIII	26.3(g)	72
VIII	26.4(d)	
VIII	26.4(f)	
VIII	26.4(g)	
VIII	26.5(d)	73
VIII	26.6(d)	
VIII	26.9(b)	77
VIII	28.3(b)	66
VIII	28.3(e)	
VIII	28.4(d)	56
VIII	28.6(d)	
VIII	28.6(e)	56
VIII	28.6(f)	69

UNITED STATES CONSTITUTION

Amend.	This Work Sec.	Note
VIII	28.6(f)	72
VIII	28.9(a)	7
VIII	28.12(a)	3
IX	2.1	
IX	2.1	21
IX	2.1	26
IX	2.3	1
IX	3.1(i)	
X	1.2(c)	103
X	1.2(c)	124
X	2.1	
X	2.1	26
X	2.3	1
X	3.1(i)	
X	21.6(a)	25
XI	1.7(c)	22
XI	2.5(f)	54
XIII	28.2(b)	
XIV	1.2(c)	92
XIV	1.3(b)	3
XIV	1.5(j)	321
XIV	1.6(d)	
XIV	1.6(f)	
XIV	1.7(d)	
XIV	1.7(i)	166
XIV	2.1	
XIV	2.2	6
XIV	2.2	8
XIV	2.3(a)	
XIV	2.3(b)	
XIV	2.3	1
XIV	2.4(a)	13
XIV	2.4(b)	21
XIV	2.4(b)	59
XIV	2.4(c)	91
XIV	2.4(c)	101
XIV	2.4(c)	107
XIV	2.4(d)	122
XIV	2.4(d)	127
XIV	2.4(e)	159
XIV	2.4(e)	168
XIV	2.5	
XIV	2.6	
XIV	2.7	
XIV	2.8(a)	25
XIV	2.8(a)	31
XIV	2.8(b)	
XIV	2.8(c)	
XIV	2.9(d)	61
XIV	2.9(d)	66
XIV	2.9(g)	159
XIV	2.9(g)	192

UNITED STATES CONSTITUTION

Amend.	Sec.	This Work Note
XIV	2.9(h)	263
XIV	2.10(b)	
XIV	2.12(a)	13
XIV	2.12(b)	
XIV	2.12(c)	
XIV	3.1(a)	
XIV	3.1(e)	
XIV	3.4(a)	
XIV	3.4(e)	93
XIV	3.4(l)	
XIV	3.5(a)	72
XIV	3.6(e)	
XIV	3.9(j)	
XIV	3.10(b)	
XIV	4.6(l)	
XIV	6.1(c)	
XIV	6.2(b)	
XIV	6.2(c)	
XIV	6.2(d)	
XIV	6.3(a)	
XIV	6.4(c)	
XIV	6.4(d)	
XIV	6.4(e)	
XIV	6.4(f)	
XIV	8.10(b)	
XIV	10.5(a)	
XIV	11.1(a)	
XIV	11.1(d)	120
XIV	11.2(a)	
XIV	11.2(f)	241
XIV	11.4(c)	56
XIV	11.7(b)	
XIV	12.2(a)	1
XIV	12.2(b)	38
XIV	12.3(c)	79
XIV	12.3(d)	105
XIV	12.3(g)	
XIV	12.4(d)	63
XIV	13.4(a)	10
XIV	13.4(d)	151
XIV	13.5(c)	
XIV	13.6(d)	
XIV	14.2(a)	
XIV	15.1(b)	14
XIV	15.1(b)	64
XIV	15.1(c)	131
XIV	15.1(c)	135
XIV	15.4(c)	
XIV	15.4(d)	116
XIV	15.4(g)	
XIV	15.5(a)	

UNITED STATES CONSTITUTION

Amend.	Sec.	This Work Note
XIV	16.1(e)	
XIV	16.3(d)	
XIV	17.2(b)	
XIV	18.1(a)	
XIV	18.5(c)	75
XIV	19.2(c)	26
XIV	19.2(e)	69
XIV	19.2(e)	70
XIV	19.3(a)	
XIV	20.4(d)	
XIV	21.2(b)	
XIV	21.3(a)	11
XIV	21.3(c)	
XIV	21.4(b)	44
XIV	22.1(a)	17
XIV	22.1(b)	
XIV	22.1(d)	76
XIV	22.2(c)	
XIV	22.2(d)	
XIV	22.2(e)	
XIV	22.3(a)	
XIV	22.3(a)	20
XIV	22.3(c)	
XIV	22.3(d)	
XIV	22.4(a)	
XIV	23.1(d)	
XIV	23.3(a)	
XIV	24.1(a)	
XIV	24.2(a)	
XIV	24.2(e)	
XIV	24.3(a)	
XIV	24.3(f)	
XIV	24.4(b)	13
XIV	24.5(a)	
XIV	24.9(b)	14
XIV	25.5(a)	
XIV	26.1(f)	
XIV	26.2(b)	
XIV	26.4(b)	
XIV	26.4(g)	
XIV	26.7(b)	
XIV	28.2(b)	26
XIV	28.2(c)	
XIV	28.3(c)	
XIV	28.3(e)	
XIV	28.4(e)	
XIV, § 1	2.3(a)	63
XIV, § 5	1.3(b)	
XIV, § 5	1.3(b)	11
XIV, § 5	2.9(h)	214
XIX	1.6(d)	

UNITED STATES CODE ANNOTATED
1 U.S.C.A.—General Provisions

	This Work	
Sec.	Sec.	Note
523(a)(7)	1.5(k)	381

5 U.S.C.A.—Government Organization and Employees

	This Work	
Sec.	Sec.	Note
552(b)(3)	8.5(b)	35

8 U.S.C.A.—Aliens and Nationality

	This Work	
Sec.	Sec.	Note
1325	6.10(c)	57
1326	1.2(d)	272
1326	16.2(c)	51
1326	21.3(e)	
1329	16.1(e)	178

12 U.S.C.A.—Banks and Banking

	This Work	
Sec.	Sec.	Note
3401 to 3422	3.2(j)	240
3401 to 3422	8.5(d)	149
3401 to 3422	8.7(b)	60
3409	8.5(d)	150
3409	8.5(d)	154
3413	8.5(d)	155
3413(i)	8.5(d)	150
3420	8.5(d)	158
3420	8.8(g)	166
3420(a)(1)	8.5(b)	33
3420(a)(3)	8.5(b)	33
3420(a)(4)	8.5(b)	33
3420(b)(1)	8.5(d)	151
3420(b)(2)	8.5(d)	151

14 U.S.C.A.—Coast Guard

	This Work	
Sec.	Sec.	Note
89(a)	3.9(g)	136

15 U.S.C.A.—Commerce and Trade

	This Work	
Sec.	Sec.	Note
1	15.1(b)	27
1	15.1(b)	38
1051	1.2(c)	94
1644	1.2(c)	129

18 U.S.C.A.—Crimes and Criminal Procedure

	This Work	
Sec.	Sec.	Note
1	1.8(c)	11

UNITED STATES CODE ANNOTATED
18 U.S.C.A.—Crimes and Criminal Procedure

	This Work	
Sec.	Sec.	Note
1	15.1(b)	75
1	15.1(d)	176
Part II	1.7(e)	
3	8.8(g)	172
4	8.8(g)	172
6	20.3(l)	228
7(1)	16.4(b)	7
7(1)	16.4(b)	10
7(3)	16.4(b)	11
7(5)	16.4(b)	7
7(5)	16.4(b)	10
7(7)	16.4(b)	30
19	1.8(c)	19
19	22.1(b)	45
36	1.2(d)	222
43	1.2(c)	114
Ch. 201 to 237	1.7(e)	63
201(c)(2)	13.2(a)	27
201(c)(2)	21.2(b)	70
Ch. 206	4.5	
228	1.2(d)	240
228(a)	1.2(c)	174
242	3.1(l)	
242	21.3(e)	280
243	1.6(d)	226
243	1.7(c)	12
323	16.1(a)	22
371	4.6(c)	52
371	16.2(g)	134
371	16.2(h)	155
401	8.3(a)	9
401	11.2(a)	24
521	1.2(d)	224
751	8.8(g)	172
752	8.8(g)	172
793(h)	26.6(d)	46
794	26.1(b)	32
801	23.1(b)	20
844	21.4(f)	174
846	21.4(f)	171
846	24.8(e)	
848	24.8(e)	
851	21.2(d)	177
853	26.6(d)	47
891 to 896	1.2(c)	153
891 to 896	1.2(d)	223
911(q)(2)(A)	1.2(c)	146
921 et seq.	1.2(d)	226
921 to 928	1.2(d)	226
922	1.2(c)	158
922(g)	1.2(d)	223

UNITED STATES CODE ANNOTATED
18 U.S.C.A.—Crimes and Criminal
Procedure

Sec.	Sec.	This Work Note
922(g)(1)	24.10(c)	41
922(h)	13.7(a)	2
922(i)	1.2(c)	147
922(j)	1.2(c)	146
922(q)	1.2(c)	147
922(q)(2)(A)	1.2(c)	187
924(c)	21.1(h)	240
924(c)	21.4(f)	171
924(c)	24.10(a)	11
924(c)(1)	13.2(a)	2
924(c)(1)	21.4(c)	
924(c)(1)	21.5(e)	
924(c)(1)	26.6(b)	29
924(c)(1)	28.9(c)	
924(d)(2)(B)	13.5(h)	167
924(e)	21.4(e)	161
924(h)	1.2(d)	270
924(k)	1.2(d)	270
931	1.2(c)	146
931	1.2(c)	147
969	16.4(b)	36
981(a)(1)(C)	8.5(b)	34
982	26.6(d)	46
982	26.6(d)	47
1001	8.3(b)	14
1001	16.2(d)	60
1001	16.2(e)	76
1014	16.2(e)	77
1030	4.6(l)	
1030	4.8(f)	
1071	8.8(g)	172
1072	8.8(g)	172
1073	1.2(c)	116
1073	16.1(e)	176
1136	16.4(b)	37
1201	1.2(c)	111
1291	27.3(b)	
1331	15.2(g)	157
1381	8.8(g)	172
1461	16.2(f)	100
1504	8.4(b)	100
1504	15.2(b)	53
1510(b)(2)	8.5(d)	151
1512(b)(3)	21.3(e)	280
1512(h)	16.2(e)	75
1542	16.2(d)	60
1546	16.4(b)	33
1621	16.2(e)	75
1622	15.5(b)	88
1623	8.3(b)	13

UNITED STATES CODE ANNOTATED
18 U.S.C.A.—Crimes and Criminal
Procedure

Sec.	Sec.	This Work Note
1623	15.5(b)	87
1623	15.7(e)	103
1702	21.4(f)	192
1863	15.2(a)	3
1864	15.2(a)	3
1867(a)	15.4(f)	144
1951	1.2(c)	129
1951	1.2(c)	131
1952	1.2(c)	114
1955	8.10(d)	103
1956(a)(1)(B)(ii)	16.2(e)	82
1956(i)	16.2(e)	83
1957	16.2(e)	82
1959(a)	16.2(h)	152
1961 to 1968	1.2(c)	129
1961 to 1968	1.2(d)	224
1961(1)	16.2(h)	149
1961(3)	16.2(h)	154
1961(4)	16.2(h)	148
1961(5)	16.2(h)	150
1962	16.2(h)	145
1962	16.2(h)	146
1962(c)	16.2(h)	147
1962(c)	16.2(h)	154
1963	16.2(h)	155
1963	26.6(d)	45
1963	26.6(d)	47
1963(d)(1)(A)	26.6(d)	66
1963(d)(1)(B)	26.6(d)	67
1963(l)	26.6(d)	72
1968	8.1(c)	45
2118	1.2(d)	222
2119	1.2(c)	146
2119	1.2(c)	147
2119	1.2(c)	148
2119	1.2(d)	221
2131(a)	4.7(e)	
2241 to 2248	19.3(b)	183
2251 to 2260	1.2(d)	223
2255	1.3(e)	43
2255	28.2(b)	29
2261	1.2(c)	114
2261	1.2(c)	172
2261(a)(1)	1.2(c)	169
2261A	1.2(c)	114
2262	1.2(c)	114
2263	12.1(f)	87
2311 to 2313	1.2(c)	110
2321	1.2(d)	223
2322	1.2(d)	223

UNITED STATES CODE ANNOTATED
18 U.S.C.A.—Crimes and Criminal Procedure

Sec.	This Work Sec.	Note
2339B	16.4(b)	37
2340	1.5(a)	15
2340A	1.5(a)	15
2381	16.4(b)	27
2421	1.2(c)	106
2510 to 2522	4.5	
2510 to 2721	1.3(b)	12
2510(1)	4.6(a)	
2510(2)	4.6(a)	
2510(4)	4.6(b)	38
2510(4)	4.6(d)	68
2510(8)	4.6(b)	
2510(8)	4.7(c)	15
2510(9)(a)	4.6(d)	68
2510(9)(b)	4.6(d)	69
2510(12)	4.6(a)	17
2510(12)	4.6(a)	23
2510(12)(c)	4.7(c)	17
2510(14)	4.8(b)	12
2510(15)	4.8(b)	9
2510(16)	4.6(l)	212
2510(17)	4.8(d)	
2510(17)(A)	4.8(b)	10
2510(17)(B)	4.8(d)	
2510(17)(B)	4.8(d)	37
2510(18)	4.6(a)	1
2511(1)	4.6(b)	24
2511(1)	4.6(o)	262
2511(1)(b)(iii)	1.2(c)	146
2511(2)	4.6(l)	
2511(2)(a)(i)	4.6(l)	
2511(2)(a)(i)	4.7(d)	
2511(2)(a)(i)	4.7(d)	28
2511(2)(a)(i)	4.8(e)	49
2511(2)(c)	4.6(a)	10
2511(2)(c)	4.6(b)	49
2511(2)(c)	4.6(l)	199
2511(2)(c)	4.7(d)	
2511(2)(c)	4.8(e)	
2511(2)(d)	4.6(b)	49
2511(2)(d)	4.7(d)	
2511(2)(d)	4.8(e)	
2511(2)(f)	4.9(b)	7
2511(2)(g)(i)	4.6(l)	211
2511(3)	4.9(a)	1
2511(3)	4.9(b)	
2511(4)(a)	4.6(o)	264
2512(1)	4.6(o)	265
2512(2)	4.6(o)	266
2514(2)(e)	4.6(c)	62

UNITED STATES CODE ANNOTATED
18 U.S.C.A.—Crimes and Criminal Procedure

Sec.	This Work Sec.	Note
2514(2)(f)	4.6(c)	62
2515	3.1(e)	127
2515	4.6(m)	215
2515	9.6(a)	14
2515	15.5(b)	86
2516(1)	4.6(c)	52
2516(1)	4.6(d)	65
2516(1)	4.6(d)	66
2516(1)	4.6(d)	67
2516(2)	1.8(b)	3
2516(2)	4.6(c)	54
2516(2)	4.6(d)	67
2517(1)	4.6(i)	154
2517(2)	4.6(i)	154
2517(5)	4.6(i)	152
2517(5)	4.6(i)	156
2517(5)	15.7(d)	80
2517(6)	4.6(i)	154
2518(1)	4.6(e)	70
2518(1)	4.6(e)	71
2518(1)(a)	4.6(e)	72
2518(1)(b)	3.4(e)	81
2518(1)(b)	4.6(e)	75
2518(1)(b)(i)	4.6(e)	76
2518(1)(b)(ii)	4.6(e)	78
2518(1)(b)(iii)	4.6(e)	81
2518(1)(c)	4.6(e)	89
2518(1)(d)	4.6(e)	103
2518(1)(d)	4.6(e)	104
2518(1)(e)	4.6(e)	107
2518(1)(f)	4.6(e)	114
2518(2)	4.6(f)	118
2518(3)	3.4(g)	134
2518(3)	4.6(c)	55
2518(3)	4.6(f)	124
2518(3)(b)	4.6(h)	146
2518(4)	4.6(c)	56
2518(4)	4.6(g)	127
2518(4)	4.6(g)	139
2518(4)(d)	4.6(g)	130
2518(4)(e)	4.6(g)	133
2518(4)(e)	4.6(g)	135
2518(5)	3.1(d)	92
2518(5)	4.6(c)	57
2518(5)	4.6(c)	58
2518(5)	4.6(e)	113
2518(5)	4.6(e)	116
2518(5)	4.6(g)	130
2518(5)	4.6(g)	134
2518(5)	4.6(g)	136

UNITED STATES CODE ANNOTATED
18 U.S.C.A.—Crimes and Criminal Procedure

Sec.	This Work Sec.	Note
2518(5)	4.6(g)	137
2518(5)	4.6(h)	144
2518(5)	4.6(i)	148
2518(5)	4.6(i)	149
2518(6)	4.6(g)	138
2518(7)	4.6(c)	60
2518(7)	4.6(c)	61
2518(7)	4.6(c)	64
2518(8)(a)	4.6(k)	171
2518(8)(a)	4.6(k)	173
2518(8)(a)	4.6(m)	238
2518(8)(d)	3.4(l)	246
2518(8)(d)	4.6(c)	63
2518(8)(d)	4.6(j)	161
2518(8)(d)	4.6(j)	164
2518(8)(d)	4.6(j)	165
2518(9)	4.6(m)	242
2518(10)	15.5(b)	100
2518(10)(a)	4.6(m)	223
2518(10)(b)	4.6(f)	126
2518(11)	3.4(e)	82
2518(11)	3.4(e)	83
2518(11)	4.6(e)	80
2518(11)	4.6(i)	149
2518(12)	4.6(e)	80
2520	4.6(n)	247
2520(d)	4.6(n)	
2520(f)	4.6(n)	254
2520(f)	4.6(n)	255
2522	4.6(g)	142
2701 to 2711	4.5	
2701 to 2711	4.8(a)	
2701 to 2711	4.9(b)	19
2701 to 2712	8.5(d)	153
2701 to 2722	4.6(b)	30
2701	4.6(l)	211
2701	4.8(b)	
2701	4.8(d)	
2701	4.8(f)	63
2702	4.8(e)	40
2702	4.8(e)	41
2702	4.9(b)	
2702(a)(1)	4.8(e)	62
2702(a)(2)	4.8(e)	61
2702(a)(3)	4.8(e)	56
2702(a)(3)	4.8(e)	60
2702(b)(1)	4.8(e)	45
2702(b)(2)	4.6(b)	30
2702(b)(2)	4.8(e)	47
2702(b)(4)	4.8(e)	46

UNITED STATES CODE ANNOTATED
18 U.S.C.A.—Crimes and Criminal Procedure

Sec.	This Work Sec.	Note
2702(b)(6)	4.6(b)	34
2702(b)(8)	4.9(b)	29
2702(c)	4.8(e)	60
2702(c)(2)	4.8(e)	48
2702(c)(3)	4.8(e)	58
2702(c)(4)	4.8(e)	59
2702(c)(4)	4.9(b)	29
2702(c)(5)	4.6(b)	34
2703	4.6(a)	8
2703	4.6(b)	
2703	4.8(c)	
2703(a)	8.5(d)	158
2703(b)	4.8(d)	28
2703(b)	4.8(d)	29
2703(b)(1)(B)(i)	8.5(d)	155
2703(c)(2)	4.8(c)	
2703(c)(2)	4.8(c)	20
2703(c)(2)	8.5(d)	155
2703(d)	4.8(c)	
2703(d)	4.8(c)	24
2705	3.4(g)	136
2705	3.4(l)	249
2705	4.8(d)	
2705	8.5(d)	154
2705	8.5(d)	155
2705(a)(2)	4.8(d)	30
2707	4.8(f)	
2707(a) to (c)	4.8(f)	64
2708	4.8(f)	68
2709	4.9(b)	
2709(a)	4.9(b)	20
2711(2)	4.8(b)	11
2711(2)	4.8(e)	41
2711(4)	4.8(e)	57
2712(a)	4.6(n)	248
2712(a)	4.8(f)	66
2712(b)	4.8(f)	67
2712(b)(1)	4.6(n)	250
2712(b)(2)	4.6(n)	251
2712(b)(3)	4.6(n)	252
2712(d)	4.6(n)	249
2712(d)	4.8(f)	68
2712(e)(1)	4.6(n)	253
2712(e)(2)	4.6(n)	253
2712(e)(3)	4.6(n)	253
3001 to 3742	1.7(e)	63
3005	1.8(e)	93
3006A	1.4(f)	130
3006A	11.2(b)	67
3006A	11.2(d)	131

UNITED STATES CODE ANNOTATED

18 U.S.C.A.—Crimes and Criminal Procedure

Sec.	This Work Sec.	Note
3006A	11.2(g)	258
3006A	13.5(h)	124
3006A	15.3(d)	63
3006A	28.12(b)	7
3006A(a)	11.2(g)	262
3006A(a)(2)(B)	28.12(b)	10
3006A(b)	26.10(b)	31
3006A(c)	11.4(b)	24
3006A(d)(1)	13.5(h)	123
3006A(e)	11.2(e)	170
3006A(e)	11.2(e)	218
3006A(e)	11.2(e)	221
3006A(f)	11.2(h)	314
3006A(g)	11.2(b)	65
3013(a)(1)(A)	27.5(b)	40
3060	14.2(b)	20
3060	14.2(b)	33
3060(d)	14.2(b)	27
3060(d)	14.2(g)	93
3060(e)	14.2(b)	27
3103a	3.4(g)	136
3103a	3.4(l)	249
3117	4.6(a)	15
3117	4.7(c)	
3121 to 3127	4.5	
3121 to 3127	4.7(a)	
3121(b)	4.7(d)	
3121(b)(1)	4.7(d)	
3121(b)(2)	4.7(d)	
3122(b)	4.7(b)	9
3124(e)	4.7(e)	32
3127(2)	4.7(b)	8
3127(3)	4.6(b)	35
3127(3)	4.7(a)	4
3127(3)	4.7(c)	12
3127(4)	4.6(b)	35
3127(4)	4.7(a)	5
3127(4)	4.7(c)	12
3127(4)	4.7(c)	23
3127(4)	4.7(c)	24
3127(5)	4.7(b)	7
3141 to 3156	1.3(e)	44
3142	12.2(a)	12
3142	12.3(b)	57
3142(b)	12.1(a)	6
3142(b)	12.3(a)	25
3142(c)	1.3(e)	44
3142(c)	12.1(a)	7
3142(c)	12.1(a)	8
3142(c)	12.1(a)	13

UNITED STATES CODE ANNOTATED

18 U.S.C.A.—Crimes and Criminal Procedure

Sec.	This Work Sec.	Note
3142(c)	12.2(b)	30
3142(c)	12.3(a)	25
3142(c)	12.4(d)	66
3142(c)(1)	12.1(f)	
3142(c)(1)(B)(xiv)	12.3(a)	21
3142(e)	12.3(a)	23
3142(e)	12.3(a)	24
3142(f)	12.3(a)	20
3142(f)(1)	12.3(f)	
3142(f)(2)	12.1(d)	50
3142(g)	12.1(a)	11
3142(h)	12.1(a)	12
3142(i)	12.2(c)	45
3142(i)	12.3(a)	23
3143(a)(1)	12.4(d)	66
3143(a)(2)(A)(i)	12.4(d)	73
3143(a)(2)(A)(ii)	12.4(d)	74
3143(a)(2)(B)	12.4(d)	72
3143(b)(1)(A)	12.4(d)	66
3143(b)(1)(B)	12.4(d)	68
3143(b)(2)	12.4(d)	75
3143(c)	12.4(e)	90
3143(c)	27.3(c)	34
3144	12.4(g)	
3144	12.4(g)	97
3144	12.4(g)	99
3144	20.2(e)	86
3145(a)	12.1(a)	15
3145(b)	12.3(a)	27
3145(c)	12.1(a)	15
3145(c)	12.3(a)	28
3145(c)	12.4(d)	68
3145(c)	12.4(d)	74
3145(c)	12.4(d)	75
3145(c)	27.3(c)	52
3146	8.8(g)	172
3146(a)	12.1(a)	19
3146(b)	12.1(a)	21
3146(c)	12.1(a)	18
3146(d)	12.1(a)	20
3146(f)	12.1(d)	50
3147	12.1(a)	12
3148(b)	12.1(a)	17
3148(b)	12.3(a)	26
3148(c)	12.1(a)	16
3149	12.4(g)	99
3154	27.3(b)	16
3154(c)	27.2(b)	15
3154(c)	27.2(c)	25
3156(a)(4)	12.3(a)	18

UNITED STATES CODE ANNOTATED

18 U.S.C.A.—Crimes and Criminal Procedure

Sec.	This Work Sec.	Note
3156(a)(4)(A)	12.4(d)	71
3156(a)(4)(B)	12.4(d)	71
3161 to 3174	1.3(e)	45
3161 to 3174	18.3(b)	2
3161(a)	22.2(e)	106
3161(b)	15.1(b)	115
3161(b)	18.3(b)	6
3161(c)(1)	18.3(b)	8
3161(c)(1)	18.3(b)	10
3161(c)(2)	18.3(b)	11
3161(d)(1)	18.3(b)	12
3161(d)(2)	18.3(b)	13
3161(e)	18.3(b)	14
3161(e)	18.3(b)	22
3161(h)	27.3(c)	33
3161(h)(1)	18.3(b)	22
3161(h)(1)	18.3(b)	28
3161(h)(1)(H)	18.3(b)	23
3161(h)(2)	18.3(b)	29
3161(h)(3)	18.3(b)	31
3161(h)(3)	18.3(b)	32
3161(h)(4)	18.3(b)	33
3161(h)(5)	18.3(b)	34
3161(h)(6)	18.3(b)	35
3161(h)(7)	18.3(b)	36
3161(h)(8)	18.3(b)	41
3161(h)(9)	18.3(b)	49
3161(j)	18.4(b)	26
3161(k)	18.3(b)	30
3162(a)(2)	18.3(b)	50
3162(a)(2)	18.3(b)	51
3162(a)(2)	18.3(b)	54
3162(a)(2)	18.4(c)	69
3162(b)	18.3(b)	60
3231	1.2(c)	44
3235	1.8(e)	86
3235	16.1(b)	81
3236	16.1(e)	177
3237	16.1(d)	148
3237	16.2(f)	95
3237(a)	16.2(f)	96
3237(b)	16.2(b)	29
3238	16.1(e)	167
3257	16.2(a)	9
3261 to 3267	16.4(b)	27
3282(b)	19.3(b)	183
3290	18.5(a)	25
3290	18.5(a)	26
3292(d)	18.3(b)	49
3301 to 3742	1.7(e)	58

UNITED STATES CODE ANNOTATED

18 U.S.C.A.—Crimes and Criminal Procedure

Sec.	This Work Sec.	Note
3322	8.5(b)	34
3322(a)	8.5(e)	204
3331 to 3334	8.1(b)	13
3331(a)	8.4(c)	116
3331(a)	15.2(a)	11
3332	8.4(b)	97
3332	15.2(b)	51
3401	1.4(g)	164
3432	1.8(e)	94
3432	20.3(h)	148
3432	22.3(b)	52
3432	22.3(b)	68
3486	8.1(c)	45
3500	10.5(e)	51
3500	20.3(i)	
3500	24.3(c)	83
3500(a)	20.3(b)	25
3500(a)	20.3(b)	26
3500(a)	20.3(i)	165
3500(b)	24.3(c)	104
3500(d)	24.3(c)	88
3500(e)	8.5(g)	217
3501	7.4(h)	126
3501(a)	6.3(b)	37
3501(a)	6.4(i)	177
3501(a)	6.5(e)	81
3501(a)	10.5(a)	6
3501(b)	6.3(b)	38
3501(b)	6.4(i)	178
3501(b)	6.5(e)	82
3501(c)	6.3(b)	36
3502	7.3(g)	123
3510	24.4(d)	53
3551 to 3673	21.1(h)	140
3551	26.1(c)	46
3553(a)	21.3(e)	283
3553(a)	21.4(d)	104
3553(a)(2)	26.9(b)	22
3553(b)	21.1(h)	
3553(b)	26.3(g)	84
3553(c)	26.3(e)	47
3553(c)(1)	26.4(d)	70
3553(c)(2)	21.1(h)	174
3553(f)	21.4(d)	102
3553(f)	26.3(c)	19
3559	26.6(b)	3
3561(a)(3)	26.1(e)	102
3561(c)	26.9(a)	11
3562(b)	26.9(c)	86
3563	26.6(c)	32

UNITED STATES CODE ANNOTATED

18 U.S.C.A.—Crimes and Criminal Procedure

Sec.	This Work Sec.	Note
3563(a)	26.9(a)	2
3563(a)(2)	26.1(e)	133
3563(a)(2)	26.9(b)	36
3563(a)(5)	26.9(b)	65
3563(b)	26.9(a)	3
3563(b)(6)	26.9(b)	43
3563(b)(19)	26.1(e)	115
3563(c)	26.9(a)	7
3563(d)	26.9(a)	4
3565	26.10(d)	90
3571(b)	26.1(f)	137
3571(b)(7)	1.8(c)	19
3571(c)(6)	22.1(b)	45
3571(d)	26.1(f)	137
3572	26.1(f)	138
3583(d)	3.9(j)	234
3591 et seq.	26.1(b)	23
3599	28.12(b)	8
3599	28.12(b)	12
3600	1.5(e)	235
3600	24.11(d)	38
3600A	1.5(e)	235
3600A	24.3(e)	137
3600A	24.11(d)	38
3621(e)(2)(B)	26.2(c)	54
3654(d)	26.9(a)	13
3661	3.1(f)	153
3661	21.2(b)	67
3661	26.5(a)	
3663	26.6(c)	33
3663(a)(1)(A)	26.6(c)	35
3663(a)(3)	21.3(e)	284
3663(b)(2)	26.6(c)	36
3663(c)(1)	26.6(c)	35
3663A	1.5(k)	379
3663A	26.6(c)	33
3664	26.1(f)	138
3664(f)(3)(B)	26.6(c)	34
3681	1.5(k)	382
3731	27.2(b)	14
3731	27.3(a)	10
3731	27.3(b)	13
3731	27.3(b)	16
3731	27.3(b)	19
3731	27.3(c)	21
3731	27.3(c)	37
3731	27.3(c)	45
3731	27.3(d)	59
3731	27.3(d)	61
3731	27.3(d)	64

UNITED STATES CODE ANNOTATED

18 U.S.C.A.—Crimes and Criminal Procedure

Sec.	This Work Sec.	Note
3731	27.3(d)	67
3742	21.2(b)	82
3742	26.3(g)	91
3742	26.3(g)	92
3742	27.3(d)	70
3742(c)	21.2(d)	202
3771 et seq.	24.4(d)	53
3771 et seq.	26.5(d)	61
3771 et seq.	27.2(b)	16
3771 to 3772	1.7(f)	76
3771	1.5(k)	337
3771	1.7(f)	77
3771	12.1(f)	70
3771	24.7(d)	36
3771(a)(1)	12.1(f)	95
3771(a)(2)	12.1(f)	80
3771(a)(2)	21.3(f)	433
3771(a)(4)	12.1(f)	72
3771(a)(4)	12.1(f)	87
3771(a)(4)	13.1(a)	17
3771(a)(4)	21.3(f)	353
3771(a)(4)	21.3(f)	363
3771(a)(4)	21.3(f)	433
3771(a)(5)	13.1(a)	15
3771(a)(5)	21.3(f)	305
3771(a)(5)	21.3(f)	350
3771(a)(5)	21.3(f)	353
3771(a)(7)	18.3(b)	39
3771(a)(8)	1.5(k)	383
3771(c)(1)	21.3(f)	380
3771(c)(1)	21.3(f)	440
3771(d)	25.1(d)	55
3771(d)	27.4(e)	61
3771(d)(1)	12.1(f)	100
3771(d)(1)	18.3(b)	40
3771(d)(1)	21.3(f)	349
3771(d)(1)	21.3(f)	434
3771(d)(1)	21.3(f)	439
3771(d)(1)	24.4(d)	67
3771(d)(2)	1.5(k)	371
3771(d)(3)	21.3(f)	351
3771(d)(3)	21.3(f)	437
3771(d)(3)	24.4(d)	66
3771(d)(5)	12.1(f)	101
3771(d)(5)	21.3(f)	352
3771(d)(5)	21.3(f)	435
3771(d)(5)	25.1(d)	74
3771(d)(5)	26.7(b)	21
3771(d)(5)(A)	21.3(f)	436
3771(d)(5)(C)	21.3(f)	432

UNITED STATES CODE ANNOTATED

18 U.S.C.A.—Crimes and Criminal Procedure

Sec.	This Work Sec.	Note
3771(d)(5)(C)	21.3(f)	441
3771(d)(6)	13.1(a)	18
3771(d)(6)	21.3(f)	358
3771(e)	1.5(k)	371
3771(e)	12.1(f)	68
3771(e)	13.1(a)	20
3771(e)	21.3(f)	301
4082(a)	21.3(b)	71
4083	15.1(b)	67
5032	13.2(a)	2
5033	6.2(c)	163
5036	18.3(b)	8
6002	8.11(a)	12
6002	15.5(b)	85
6002	15.6(b)	68
6002	15.6(b)	72
6002	15.7(d)	65
6003	8.10(c)	66
6003	8.11(a)	12
6003	8.11(d)	74
6003	15.5(b)	85
6003	15.6(b)	72
6004	8.11(a)	12
6004	8.11(d)	74
8444(i)	1.2(c)	180

18 U.S.C.A. App.—Crimes and Criminal Procedure

Sec.	This Work Sec.	Note
2.9	18.4(c)	46
2.9(1)	18.4(c)	69
3.4	20.3(l)	228
1201 to 1203	1.2(d)	226
1202(a)	13.7(a)	3

21 U.S.C.A.—Food and Drugs

Sec.	This Work Sec.	Note
801 et seq.	1.2(d)	222
801 et seq.	1.2(d)	235
841(b)	26.1(f)	137
841(b)(1)(a)	26.6(b)	3
841(c)	21.4(d)	113
848	16.2(h)	145
848	24.10(c)	43
848	28.12(b)	12
848(j)	26.5(d)	70
848(q)(4)(B)	28.8(a)	5
848(q)(4)(B)	28.12(b)	8
851	13.2(a)	2

UNITED STATES CODE ANNOTATED

21 U.S.C.A.—Food and Drugs

Sec.	This Work Sec.	Note
851(a)(1)	18.3(b)	8
851(b)	27.6(b)	20
853	26.6(d)	46
853(e)(1)(A)	26.6(d)	66
853(e)(1)(B)	26.6(d)	67
853(f)	26.6(d)	67
853(n)	26.6(d)	72
862(a)	21.4(d)	130
862a	21.4(d)	130
862b	3.9(d)	67
876(a)	8.1(c)	45
955a	16.4(b)	9
960(b)	26.1(f)	137

22 U.S.C.A.—Foreign Relations and Intercourse

Sec.	This Work Sec.	Note
1203	16.4(b)	33

26 U.S.C.A.—Internal Revenue Code

Sec.	This Work Sec.	Note
6103(h)(5)	22.3(b)	74
6103(h)(5)	22.3(b)	80
6363(b)(3)	21.4(a)	37

28 U.S.C.A.—Judiciary and Judicial Procedure

Sec.	This Work Sec.	Note
144	22.4(b)	18
144	22.4(b)	19
455	21.6(a)	35
455	22.4(b)	18
455(a)	22.4(c)	25
515(a)	15.7(c)	56
519	1.4(e)	92
530	15.6(b)	77
530B	1.7(j)	249
530B	1.7(j)	254
530B	1.7(j)	256
530B	8.8(d)	106
530B	11.8(b)	41
530B	15.7(f)	143
530B(a)	6.4(e)	91
530B(a)	8.8(d)	107
552(b)(7)	20.2(d)	77
591 to 599	13.3(f)	60
636(a)	1.4(g)	164
636(b)	1.4(g)	160
636(b)(1)	10.6(b)	10

UNITED STATES CODE ANNOTATED

28 U.S.C.A.—Judiciary and Judicial Procedure

Sec.	This Work Sec.	Note
636(b)(1)(A)	1.4(g)	161
636(b)(1)(B)	1.4(g)	162
991 to 998	21.1(h)	140
1291	27.2(a)	
1291	27.2(a)	2
1291	27.2(c)	
1291	27.3(b)	16
1291(b)	27.2(b)	
1292(a)(1)	27.2(b)	13
1292(b)	27.2(b)	13
1346(a)(2)	10.1(c)	47
1361	13.3(a)	4
1404(a)	16.3(c)	28
1442	13.5(d)	77
1442(a)(1)	27.3(b)	16
1442a	13.5(d)	78
1443	13.5(d)	83
1651	28.9(a)	
1826	8.3(a)	1
1826	8.3(a)	4
1826	8.3(a)	5
1826	8.9(b)	16
1827	24.2(g)	99
1861 to 1867	1.3(e)	46
1861 to 1869	15.4(b)	62
1861 to 1869	22.2(a)	1
1861	15.4(d)	126
1861	22.2(a)	2
1862	22.2(a)	3
1863(a)	22.2(a)	4
1863(b)	22.2(a)	6
1864	22.2(a)	7
1865(b)	22.2(a)	9
1866(c)	22.2(a)	11
1866(c)(2)	15.4(g)	151
1867	22.2(a)	13
1867(a)	15.4(b)	63
1867(f)	22.3(b)	53
1869(e)	22.2(a)	2
2071	1.7(g)	108
2072	1.7(f)	96
2072	27.2(c)	22
2111	27.6(a)	10
2241	27.4(f)	
2241	28.1(a)	
2241	28.2(b)	
2241	28.3(a)	2
2241(c)(3)	13.5(f)	105
2241(c)(3)	28.3(a)	
2244(b)(3)(E)	28.5(e)	94

UNITED STATES CODE ANNOTATED

28 U.S.C.A.—Judiciary and Judicial Procedure

Sec.	This Work Sec.	Note
2253	28.10	1
2253(b)(2)	28.2(d)	82
2254	28.1(a)	
2254	28.7(a)	2
2254(a)	1.7(c)	24
2254(a)(2)	28.2(d)	82
2254(b)	13.5(f)	106
2254(b)(1)	28.3(a)	2
2254(d)	2.11(e)	57
2254(d)	28.4(d)	49
2254(d)(1)	9.5(a)	8
2254(d)(2)	11.10(c)	135
2254(d)(2)	28.2(d)	82
2254(e)(2)	1.7(c)	24
2254(h)	28.12(b)	10
2254(i)	28.8(b)	15
2254(i)	28.12(b)	15
2255	21.4(e)	161
2255	21.5(a)	17
2255	21.5(a)	52
2255	21.5(b)	
2255	21.5(b)	66
2255	28.1(a)	
2255	28.9(a)	
2266(b)(1)(A)	28.8(b)	17
2401(a)	10.1(c)	49
2412	13.5(h)	
2412	13.5(h)	121
2412(d)(1)(B)	13.5(h)	147
2412(d)(2)(A)	13.5(h)	123
2412(d)(2)(A)	13.5(h)	195
2412(d)(2)(A)(ii)	13.5(h)	192
2412(d)(2)(B)(i)	13.5(h)	145
2412(d)(2)(B)(i)	13.5(h)	147
2515	8.9(b)	17
2680(h)	3.1(k)	276
2702(c)(6)	4.8(e)	56

29 U.S.C.A.—Labor

Sec.	This Work Sec.	Note
657(a)	3.9(c)	37

31 U.S.C.A.—Money and Finance

Sec.	This Work Sec.	Note
1102(a)	18.1(a)	2
1102(a)	18.5(b)	54
3729 to 3731	13.3(b)	28
3733	8.1(c)	45

UNITED STATES CODE ANNOTATED

33 U.S.C.A.—Navigation and Navigable Waters

Sec.	This Work Sec.	Note
1319(c)	26.1(f)	137

42 U.S.C.A.—The Public Health and Welfare

Sec.	This Work Sec.	Note
1433	1.5(e)	235
1435	1.5(e)	235
1601 et seq.	1.5(k)	374
1983	1.7(c)	22
1983	2.7(d)	256
1983	2.9(h)	261
1983	3.1(k)	
1983	13.5(a)	19
1983	14.2(a)	9
1983	18.4(c)	33
1983	21.6(a)	18
1983	26.9(c)	83
1983	28.3(b)	
2000aa	3.4(a)	21
2000aa-6	3.4(a)	21
2000aa-11	3.4(a)	21
3797k to 3797m	1.5(e)	235
10606(b)(1)	1.5(k)	383
10606(c)	1.5(k)	386
10607(c)(3)(B)	13.1(a)	16
10607(c)(3)(C)	13.1(a)	16
13032	4.6(b)	34
14132	1.5(e)	235
14132	3.5(d)	147
14135 et seq.	24.11(d)	38
14135(a)(1)	3.5(d)	147
14135a(a)(2)	3.9(j)	235
14135a(d)	3.9(j)	235
14136	1.5(e)	235
14136a to 14135e	1.5(e)	235
14136a	1.5(e)	235
14141	1.9(b)	46

46 U.S.C.A. App.—Shipping

Sec.	This Work Sec.	Note
1903	16.4(b)	31

47 U.S.C.A.—Telegraphs, Telephones, and Radiotelegraphs

Sec.	This Work Sec.	Note
605	4.5	
605	4.6(a)	18
605	4.6(b)	
605	4.6(b)	32

UNITED STATES CODE ANNOTATED

47 U.S.C.A.—Telegraphs, Telephones, and Radiotelegraphs

Sec.	This Work Sec.	Note
605	4.6(l)	
605	4.7(d)	
1001 to 1110	4.6(g)	142
1002(a)(2)	4.7(c)	
13032	4.8(e)	
13032(b)(1)	4.8(e)	51

49 U.S.C.A.—Transportation

Sec.	This Work Sec.	Note
11903	15.1(b)	27

50 U.S.C.A.—War and National Defense

Sec.	This Work Sec.	Note
1801 et seq.	3.4(g)	135
1801 to 1811	4.9(b)	
1801(f)	4.9(b)	
1801(f)(1) to (4)	4.9(b)	11
1801(n)	4.9(b)	
1803	4.9(b)	
1804(a)(7)(A)	4.9(b)	15
1804(a)(7)(B)	4.9(b)	15
1805A	4.9(b)	12
1806(e)	4.9(b)	9
1806(f)	4.9(b)	10
1821 to 1829	4.9(b)	
1821(5)	4.9(b)	27
1824(a)(3)	4.9(b)	28
1841 to 1846	4.9(b)	
1841(2)	4.9(b)	17
1842(c)(2)	4.9(b)	18
1861	3.4(a)	20
1861	4.9(b)	23
1861	8.1(c)	47
1861(a)	8.1(c)	48
1861(a)(1)	4.9(b)	25
1861(a)(3)	8.8(d)	49
1862	4.9(b)	23

UNITED STATES PUBLIC LAWS

Pub. L. No.	This Work Sec.	Note
86-256	15.1(b)	67
90-151	1.2(d)	225
90-351	4.5	5
93-415, § 223(a)(13)	1.3(b)	16
94-64	20.3(j)	203
94-64	20.3(j)	208
95-511	4.5	9

UNITED STATES PUBLIC LAWS

Pub. L. No.	This Work Sec.	Note
95-511 . . . . 4.9(b)		6
97-291 . . . . 1.5(k)		337
98-473 . . . . 1.5(k)		337
99-508 . . . . 4.5		8
101-647 . . . . 1.5(k)		337
103-322 . . . . 1.5(k)		337
103-460, § 20101 to 20102 . . . . 1.3(b)		16
104-132 . . . . 1.5(k)		337
104-132 . . . . 28.2(b)		30
105-5 . . . . 1.5(k)		337
105-119 . . . . 13.5(h)		124
105-119 . . . . 15.3(d)		63
107-56 . . . . 4.6(a)		7
107-56 . . . . 8.5(e)		205
107-56 . . . . 8.5(e)		206
108-405 . . . . 1.5(e)		235
108-405 . . . . 1.5(k)		337
110-55 . . . . 4.9(b)		12
1076, § 71 . . . . 3.9(h)		160

POPULAR NAME ACTS

ANTITERRORISM AND EFFECTIVE DEATH PENALTY ACT

Sec.	This Work Sec.	Note
440(d) . . . . 21.2(d)		

CONSUMER CREDIT PROTECTION ACT

Sec.	This Work Sec.	Note
Title II . . . . 1.2(c)		

CONTROLLED SUBSTANCES ACT

Sec.	This Work Sec.	Note
408 . . . . 28.9(b)		70

DEFENSE OF NEEDY PERSONS ACT

Sec.	This Work Sec.	Note
4(b) . . . . 11.2(g)		288

IMMIGRATION AND NATIONALITY ACT

Sec.	This Work Sec.	Note
212(c) . . . . 21.2(d)		

MODEL DEFENSE OF NEEDY PERSONS ACT

Sec.	This Work Sec.	Note
2 . . . . 11.1(d)		129

NATIONAL LABOR RELATIONS ACT

Sec.	This Work Sec.	Note
9(h) . . . . 16.2(c)		

NATIONAL SECURITY ACT OF 1947

Sec.	This Work Sec.	Note
3 . . . . 4.6(i)		154

OMNIBUS CRIME CONTROL AND SAFE STREETS ACT

Sec.	This Work Sec.	Note
Title III . . . . 8.9(b)		

RACKETEER INFLUENCED AND CORRUPT ORGINIZATIONS ACT

Sec.	This Work Sec.	Note
1962(c) . . . . 16.2(h)		

STORED COMMUNICATIONS ACT

Sec.	This Work Sec.	Note
2702 . . . . 4.8(e)		

UNIFORM JURY SELECTION AND SERVICE ACT

Sec.	This Work Sec.	Note
12 . . . . 15.4(b)		71
12 . . . . 22.2(f)		114

USA PATRIOT ACT

Sec.	This Work Sec.	Note
209 . . . . 4.6(a)		
209 . . . . 4.6(b)		
215 . . . . 4.9(b)		
216 . . . . 4.7(a)		

WIRETAP ACT

Sec.	This Work Sec.	Note
2511(2)(a) . . . . 4.6(b)		30
2517 . . . . 4.6(b)		30

CODE OF FEDERAL REGULATIONS

Tit.	This Work Sec.	Note
8, 235.1(d)(1)	6.7(b)	59
8, 2387.3	6.8(a)	16
28, 1.1 to 1.11	26.2(c)	69
28, 50.10	8.8(d)	82
28, Pt. 59	3.4(a)	21
28, 59.4(b)	3.4(a)	22
28, 77.1	1.7(j)	254
28, 77.1(b)	1.7(j)	257
28, 77.1(b)	1.7(j)	265
28, 77.4	1.7(j)	254
28, 77.4	1.7(j)	267
28, 501.3(d)	11.8(b)	43
39, 233.3	4.2(a)	
39, 233.3	4.2(c)	
39, 233.3(c)(1)	4.2(c)	18
39, 233.3(c)(2)	4.2(c)	19
39, 233.3(g)	4.2(c)	

FEDERAL RULES OF CIVIL PROCEDURE

Rule	This Work Sec.	Note
8(a)	19.1(d)	41
15(a)	28.9(b)	
15(c)(2)	28.9(b)	
26	8.6(b)	
26	8.6(b)	41
26	8.6(b)	44
26	8.6(b)	46
26	8.6(b)	51
26	8.6(b)	60
26(b)(3)	8.6(b)	42
26(b)(3)	8.6(b)	50
26(b)(3)	20.3(i)	174
26(b)(3)	20.3(j)	
26(b)(3)	20.3(j)	183
26(b)(3)	20.3(j)	190
26(c)	8.6(b)	
26(c)	8.6(b)	53
26(c)	8.6(b)	54
60(b)	28.5(d)	
60(b)	28.5(d)	91
60(b)	28.9(a)	
60(b)	28.9(b)	
60(b)	28.10	1
79(a)	13.5(h)	210

FEDERAL RULES OF CRIMINAL PROCEDURE

Rule	This Work Sec.	Note
1 to 11	19.1(d)	45
1	19.3(a)	50

FEDERAL RULES OF CRIMINAL PROCEDURE

Rule	This Work Sec.	Note
1(b)	15.1(d)	167
1.2	11.6(a)	5
1.6	22.5(b)	17
1.6(a)	11.9(c)	140
2	14.4(b)	16
2	14.4(c)	48
2	15.5(c)	108
2(4)(a)	14.2(d)	62
3	8.4(b)	78
4	15.1(g)	345
4	15.1(g)	358
4	28.9(b)	
4	28.9(b)	65
4(8)	19.5(b)	2
4(8)	19.5(b)	6
4.2	6.4(e)	91
5 to 102	22.5(c)	24
5	1.4(g)	140
5	15.1(g)	344
5	15.4(b)	26
5	15.4(b)	63
5	24.2(f)	83
5	27.5(c)	
5(5)	19.5(b)	6
5(a)	15.1(b)	115
5(a)(1)(A)	6.3(a)	11
5(c)	1.8(c)	18
5(c)	14.2(b)	
5(c)	14.2(b)	20
5(c)	14.2(b)	27
5(c)	14.2(d)	50
5(c)	15.1(b)	39
5(d)	11.5(b)	23
5.1	3.1(f)	150
5.1	14.2(b)	
5.1	14.2(b)	22
5.1	14.2(b)	25
5.1	14.2(d)	50
5.1	14.4(b)	
5.1	14.4(b)	13
5.1	14.4(b)	26
5.1	14.4(b)	31
5.1	15.1(b)	39
5.1	15.1(b)	115
5.1	15.4(b)	26
5.1(a)	14.2(b)	
5.1(c)	14.2(b)	25
5.1(d)	14.2(b)	25
5.1(d)	14.2(b)	27
5.1(e)	3.1(f)	148
5.1(e)	14.4(b)	14

FEDERAL RULES OF CRIMINAL PROCEDURE

Rule	Sec.	This Work Note
5.1(e)	14.4(c)	48
5.1(f)	24.2(f)	82
6	1.7(i)	
6	8.1(b)	
6	8.1(c)	
6	8.3(f)	30
6	8.4(c)	130
6	8.4(c)	136
6	8.5(b)	
6	8.5(b)	34
6	8.5(b)	42
6	8.5(b)	55
6	8.5(c)	115
6	8.5(g)	215
6	8.5(i)	
6	8.5(i)	305
6	15.2(g)	
6	15.2(i)	208
6	15.6(b)	
6	15.6(b)	65
6	15.6(b)	72
6	15.6(c)	94
6	15.6(e)	
6	28.7(d)	28
6	28.9(b)	71
6	28.12(b)	9
6(a)	28.9(b)	69
6(a)(1)	15.2(g)	159
6(a)(2)	15.2(g)	159
6(b)	15.4(b)	
6(b)	15.4(b)	63
6(b)	15.4(b)	64
6(b)	15.6(a)	3
6(b)	15.6(e)	154
6(b)(1)	15.4(b)	26
6(b)(1)	15.4(b)	33
6(b)(1)	15.4(b)	46
6(b)(2)	15.4(b)	26
6(b)(2)	15.4(b)	46
6(b)(2)	15.4(f)	147
6(c)	15.2(b)	25
6(c)	15.4(e)	139
6(d)	8.5(c)	79
6(d)	15.5(b)	
6(d)	15.6(b)	68
6(d)	15.6(b)	72
6(d)	15.6(e)	
6(d)	15.6(f)	
6(d)	15.6(f)	173

FEDERAL RULES OF CRIMINAL PROCEDURE

Rule	Sec.	This Work Note
6(d)	15.6(f)	175
6(d)	15.6(f)	181
6(d)	15.6(f)	187
6(d)	15.7(h)	
6(d)	15.7(h)	222
6(d)	27.6(b)	
6(e)	8.3(c)	17
6(e)	8.5(b)	
6(e)	8.5(b)	20
6(e)	8.5(b)	33
6(e)	8.5(b)	34
6(e)	8.5(b)	35
6(e)	8.5(b)	37
6(e)	8.5(b)	40
6(e)	8.5(b)	41
6(e)	8.5(b)	42
6(e)	8.5(b)	46
6(e)	8.5(b)	54
6(e)	8.5(b)	55
6(e)	8.5(c)	
6(e)	8.5(c)	70
6(e)	8.5(c)	75
6(e)	8.5(c)	76
6(e)	8.5(c)	79
6(e)	8.5(c)	85
6(e)	8.5(c)	86
6(e)	8.5(c)	90
6(e)	8.5(c)	91
6(e)	8.5(c)	92
6(e)	8.5(c)	93
6(e)	8.5(c)	95
6(e)	8.5(c)	96
6(e)	8.5(c)	97
6(e)	8.5(c)	110
6(e)	8.5(c)	115
6(e)	8.5(d)	
6(e)	8.5(d)	134
6(e)	8.5(e)	
6(e)	8.5(e)	174
6(e)	8.5(e)	182
6(e)	8.5(g)	
6(e)	8.5(h)	
6(e)	8.5(h)	291
6(e)	8.5(h)	295
6(e)	8.5(h)	299
6(e)	8.5(i)	
6(e)	8.5(i)	304
6(e)	8.5(i)	310
6(e)	8.5(i)	325
6(e)	8.5(i)	326
6(e)	8.8(e)	

FEDERAL RULES OF CRIMINAL PROCEDURE

Rule	Sec.	This Work Note
6(e)	8.8(e)	125
6(e)	8.10(c)	86
6(e)	15.2(i)	215
6(e)	15.2(j)	
6(e)	15.4(g)	181
6(e)	15.5(b)	42
6(e)	15.6(b)	
6(e)	15.6(b)	68
6(e)	15.6(b)	72
6(e)	15.6(e)	
6(e)	15.6(f)	173
6(e)	15.6(g)	
6(e)	15.7(c)	56
6(e)	23.1(d)	157
6(e)	23.1(d)	162
6(e)	27.2(c)	
6(e)	27.2(e)	
6(e)(1)	15.2(j)	233
6(e)(1)	15.2(j)	242
6(e)(2)	8.5(b)	21
6(e)(2)	8.5(c)	
6(e)(2)	8.5(c)	78
6(e)(2)	8.5(c)	90
6(e)(2)	8.5(c)	91
6(e)(2)	8.5(c)	93
6(e)(2)	8.5(c)	105
6(e)(2)	8.5(c)	106
6(e)(2)	8.5(d)	
6(e)(2)	8.5(d)	124
6(e)(2)	8.5(d)	147
6(e)(3)	8.5(b)	39
6(e)(3)	8.5(d)	
6(e)(3)	8.5(e)	
6(e)(3)	8.5(i)	310
6(e)(3)	8.8(e)	121
6(e)(3)(A) to (D)	8.5(b)	23
6(e)(3)(A)	8.5(e)	199
6(e)(3)(A)(ii)	8.5(e)	174
6(e)(3)(A)(ii)	8.5(e)	175
6(e)(3)(A)(ii)	8.5(e)	176
6(e)(3)(A)(iii)	8.5(b)	34
6(e)(3)(A)(iii)	8.5(e)	204
6(e)(3)(B)	8.5(e)	175
6(e)(3)(B)	8.5(e)	176
6(e)(3)(B)	8.5(e)	177
6(e)(3)(C)	8.5(e)	199
6(e)(3)(C)(i)	8.5(b)	39
6(e)(3)(C)(i)	8.5(c)	115
6(e)(3)(C)(i)	8.5(f)	211
6(e)(3)(C)(i)	8.5(g)	
6(e)(3)(C)(i)	8.5(h)	303

FEDERAL RULES OF CRIMINAL PROCEDURE

Rule	Sec.	This Work Note
6(e)(3)(C)(i)	8.5(i)	310
6(e)(3)(C)(i)	15.2(i)	220
6(e)(3)(C)(i)(c)	8.5(b)	38
6(e)(3)(C)(ii)	15.2(i)	
6(e)(3)(C)(ii)	15.2(i)	217
6(e)(3)(C)(ii)	15.2(i)	220
6(e)(3)(D)	8.5(e)	206
6(e)(3)(D)	8.5(h)	232
6(e)(3)(D)(ii)	8.5(e)	207
6(e)(3)(D)(iii)	8.5(e)	208
6(e)(3)(E)	8.5(e)	
6(e)(3)(E)	8.5(f)	
6(e)(3)(E)	8.5(h)	237
6(e)(3)(E)	8.5(h)	248
6(e)(3)(E)	8.5(i)	310
6(e)(3)(E)(i) to (v)	8.5(b)	22
6(e)(3)(E)(i)	8.5(c)	
6(e)(3)(E)(i)	8.5(g)	227
6(e)(3)(E)(i)	8.5(h)	
6(e)(3)(E)(i)	15.2(i)	215
6(e)(3)(E)(ii)	15.2(i)	
6(e)(3)(E)(ii)	15.2(i)	215
6(e)(3)(E)(ii)	15.2(j)	
6(e)(3)(E)(iv)	8.5(e)	200
6(e)(3)(E)(v)	8.5(e)	201
6(e)(3)(F)	8.5(b)	
6(e)(3)(F)	8.5(b)	24
6(e)(3)(F)	8.5(b)	65
6(e)(3)(F)	8.5(h)	232
6(e)(3)(F)(iii)	8.5(h)	233
6(e)(3)(G)	8.5(b)	24
6(e)(4)	8.5(b)	25
6(e)(5)	8.3(f)	30
6(e)(5)	8.5(b)	
6(e)(5)	8.5(b)	26
6(e)(5)	23.1(d)	160
6(e)(5)	23.1(d)	161
6(e)(6)	8.5(b)	27
6(e)(7)	8.5(b)	28
6(e)(iii)	8.5(e)	174
6(g)	15.2(a)	11
6(g)	15.2(g)	157
6(g)	15.4(a)	14
7	15.1(b)	
7	15.1(b)	71
7	15.1(d)	
7	15.1(d)	154
7	15.1(d)	255
7	15.1(f)	
7	15.1(f)	305
7	15.1(f)	323

FEDERAL RULES OF CRIMINAL PROCEDURE

Rule	This Work Sec.	Note
7	19.1(d)	35
7	19.1(d)	42
7	19.5(d)	75
7	28.9(b)	71
7(a)	15.1(b)	
7(a)	15.1(d)	
7(a)	15.1(d)	178
7(a)	15.1(g)	345
7(a)	19.5(d)	71
7(a)(1)	15.1(b)	32
7(a)(1)	15.1(b)	86
7(a)(1)	15.1(d)	144
7(a)(1)	15.1(f)	295
7(a)(2)	14.2(b)	22
7(a)(2)	15.1(d)	
7(b)	14.2(b)	21
7(b)	15.1(f)	286
7(b)	15.1(f)	295
7(b)	15.1(f)	317
7(b)	19.5(d)	71
7(c)	15.1(d)	
7(c)	15.1(d)	167
7(c)	15.1(d)	170
7(c)	19.1(d)	
7(c)	19.1(d)	34
7(c)	19.1(d)	40
7(c)	19.1(d)	41
7(c)	19.1(d)	42
7(c)	19.1(d)	60
7(c)	19.2(a)	
7(c)	19.2(c)	
7(c)	19.3(b)	176
7(c)(1)	19.3(b)	183
7(c)(2)	26.6(d)	52
7(c)(2)	26.6(d)	53
7(c)(3)	19.3(d)	202
7(c)(i)	19.1(d)	39
7(d)	19.5(d)	75
7(e)	19.5(b)	
7(e)	19.5(b)	2
7(e)	19.5(c)	
7(e)	19.5(d)	
7(f)	19.4(a)	1
7(f)	19.4(b)	
8	17.1(a)	7
8	17.2(a)	9
8	17.3(b)	
8(a)	16.1(f)	
8(a)	16.1(f)	225
8(a)	17.1(a)	2
8(a)	17.1(b)	18

FEDERAL RULES OF CRIMINAL PROCEDURE

Rule	This Work Sec.	Note
8(a)	17.1(b)	25
8(b)	11.9(b)	
8(b)	17.2(a)	2
8(b)	17.3(c)	
8(b)	27.6(b)	
9	27.2(b)	19
9(a)	28.5(b)	
10	16.2(f)	94
10	19.4(a)	1
10	24.2(f)	83
10(c)	21.4(a)	5
10.2(b)	22.4(d)	45
11	1.7(i)	163
11	11.6(a)	48
11	15.1(f)	
11	19.3(e)	243
11	20.3(m)	
11	21.1(h)	
11	21.2(b)	57
11	21.2(b)	83
11	21.2(c)	
11	21.2(h)	421
11	21.2(h)	435
11	21.3(c)	
11	21.3(d)	218
11	21.3(e)	266
11	21.3(e)	270
11	21.3(e)	279
11	21.3(e)	297
11	21.3(f)	432
11	21.4	
11	21.5	
11	21.6(b)	
11	21.6(b)	84
11	21.6(c)	118
11	23.1(d)	121
11	24.3(b)	
11	24.4(a)	6
11	25.1(d)	64
11	25.1(d)	65
11	26.6(d)	
11	26.10(c)	58
11	27.5(c)	53
11	27.5(d)	115
11	27.5(d)	131
11	28.9(c)	
11(a)	21.4(a)	12
11(a)	21.6(b)	
11(a)	21.6(b)	83
11(a)(2)	21.6(b)	
11(a)(2)	21.6(b)	85

FEDERAL RULES OF CRIMINAL PROCEDURE

Rule	Sec.	This Work Note
11(a)(2)	21.6(b)	96
11(a)(3)	21.4(a)	18
11(b)	21.4(a)	12
11(b)	21.4(g)	255
11(b)(1)	21.4(a)	38
11(b)(1)	21.4(b)	42
11(b)(1)	21.4(c)	66
11(b)(1)	21.4(e)	156
11(b)(1)(A)	21.2(h)	428
11(b)(1)(A)	21.5(f)	170
11(b)(1)(B) to (F)	21.4(e)	163
11(b)(1)(G)	21.5(c)	82
11(b)(1)(H)	21.4(d)	102
11(b)(1)(H)	21.4(d)	114
11(b)(1)(I)	21.4(d)	102
11(b)(1)(J)	21.4(d)	110
11(b)(1)(K)	21.4(d)	110
11(b)(1)(L)	21.4(d)	110
11(b)(1)(M)	21.4(d)	104
11(b)(1)(N)	21.2(b)	79
11(b)(1)(N)	21.4(e)	163
11(b)(3)	21.4(f)	170
11(b)(3)	21.4(f)	171
11(b)(3)	21.4(f)	176
11(b)(3)	21.4(g)	
11(c)(1)	21.2(c)	99
11(c)(1)	21.3(d)	216
11(c)(1)	21.3(d)	225
11(c)(1)	21.3(d)	228
11(c)(1)	21.4(g)	226
11(c)(1)(A)	21.1(h)	223
11(c)(1)(B)	21.1(h)	203
11(c)(1)(B)	21.2(d)	193
11(c)(1)(B)	21.2(d)	197
11(c)(1)(B)	21.3(f)	442
11(c)(1)(B)	21.4(g)	227
11(c)(1)(B)	26.4(f)	104
11(c)(1)(C)	21.1(h)	201
11(c)(1)(C)	21.2(d)	193
11(c)(1)(C)	21.2(d)	197
11(c)(1)(C)	21.2(d)	202
11(c)(1)(C)	21.2(e)	321
11(c)(1)(C)	21.4(g)	227
11(c)(2)	21.4(b)	52
11(c)(3)	21.4(b)	53
11(c)(3)	21.5(c)	
11(c)(3)(A)	21.3(f)	444
11(c)(3)(A)	21.4(g)	
11(c)(3)(A)	21.4(g)	229
11(c)(3)(B)	21.1(h)	204
11(c)(3)(B)	21.3(f)	443

FEDERAL RULES OF CRIMINAL PROCEDURE

Rule	Sec.	This Work Note
11(c)(3)(B)	21.4(g)	228
11(c)(5)	21.1(h)	202
11(c)(5)	21.3(f)	445
11(c)(5)	21.4(g)	230
11(c)(5)	21.5(a)	6
11(c)(5)	21.5(a)	18
11(c)(5)(B)	21.3(e)	282
11(c)(5)(B)	21.4(g)	
11(c)(6)	27.5(c)	56
11(d)	21.4(b)	42
11(d)	21.4(b)	50
11(d)	21.5(a)	3
11(d)(2)	21.5(a)	6
11(d)(2)	21.5(a)	18
11(d)(2)	21.5(a)	19
11(d)(2)(A)	21.5(a)	5
11(d)(2)(B)	21.5(a)	
11(d)(2)(B)	21.5(a)	34
11(e)	21.1(h)	
11(e)	21.1(h)	196
11(e)	21.5(a)	17
11(e)	21.5(a)	52
11(e)(1)	21.3(d)	218
11(e)(1)	21.5(c)	83
11(e)(1)(B)	21.2(d)	193
11(e)(1)(C)	21.1(h)	210
11(e)(1)(C)	21.2(d)	193
11(e)(1)(C)	21.5(c)	83
11(e)(2)	21.4(g)	228
11(e)(4)	21.2(d)	249
11(e)(6)	21.2(h)	418
11(e)(6)	21.2(h)	419
11(e)(6)	21.2(h)	420
11(f)	21.2(h)	420
11(f)	21.2(h)	428
11(f)	21.2(h)	434
11(f)	21.2(h)	439
11(f)	21.4(f)	171
11(f)	21.4(f)	176
11(f)	21.5(f)	170
11(f)	25.1(d)	71
11(h)	1.7(i)	167
11(h)	21.5(c)	83
11(h)	27.6(b)	19
12	11.6(a)	5
12	15.4(b)	
12	15.6(a)	3
12	19.1(d)	
12	19.1(d)	35
12	19.3(e)	243
12	20.2(e)	82

FEDERAL RULES OF CRIMINAL PROCEDURE

Rule	This Work Sec.	Note
12(2)(e)	20.5(c)	
12(b)	1.3(e)	42
12(b)	13.4(a)	27
12(b)	15.4(b)	56
12(b)	15.4(b)	64
12(b)	15.6(f)	167
12(b)	16.4(d)	143
12(b)	19.1(d)	52
12(b)	19.1(d)	54
12(b)	19.2(e)	74
12(b)	19.3(b)	147
12(b)	19.3(c)	189
12(b)	19.3(e)	213
12(b)	19.3(e)	236
12(b)	19.3(e)	241
12(b)	19.3(e)	243
12(b)	22.2(f)	118
12(b)	24.11(c)	
12(b)	28.4(d)	
12(b)(2)	19.1(d)	34
12(b)(2)	19.1(d)	52
12(b)(2)	19.1(d)	54
12(b)(2)	19.2(e)	
12(b)(2)	19.3(a)	104
12(b)(2)	19.3(e)	
12(b)(2)	19.3(e)	210
12(b)(2)	19.3(e)	236
12(b)(2)	19.3(e)	237
12(b)(2)	19.3(e)	241
12(b)(2)	19.3(e)	243
12(b)(3)	19.1(d)	54
12(b)(3)(B)	19.1(d)	54
12(b)(3)(B)	19.3(e)	
12(b)(3)(B)	19.3(e)	209
12(b)(3)(B)	19.3(e)	213
12(b)(3)(B)	19.3(e)	241
12(b)(3)(C)	10.1(a)	4
12(b)(3)(C)	20.2(d)	63
12(b)(3)(D)	17.3(d)	47
12(b)(4)	10.2(a)	10
12(b)(4)(A)	10.2(a)	10
12(b)(4)(A)	20.2(d)	63
12(b)(4)(B)	20.2(d)	63
12(c)	15.4(b)	60
12(c)	19.1(d)	54
12(d)	10.6(a)	2
12(e)	10.2(a)	8
12(e)	15.4(b)	58
12(e)	17.3(d)	47
12(e)	19.1(d)	54
12(e)	27.3(d)	66

FEDERAL RULES OF CRIMINAL PROCEDURE

Rule	This Work Sec.	Note
12(f)	10.2(a)	8
12(f)	15.4(b)	68
12(f)	15.4(b)	69
12(f)	19.1(d)	52
12(h)	8.5(b)	30
12(h)	8.5(g)	215
12(h)	10.5(e)	54
12(h)	15.2(i)	208
12(j)	27.3(d)	67
12.1	20.2(b)	14
12.1	20.5(b)	
12.1	20.5(b)	15
12.1(a)	20.5(b)	16
12.1(b)	20.5(b)	19
12.1(d)	20.6(a)	14
12.1(f)	20.4(c)	46
12.1(f)	20.5(b)	21
12.2	20.2(b)	14
12.2	20.5(c)	
12.2	20.5(c)	31
12.2	20.5(c)	43
12.2	20.5(c)	44
12.2	20.5(h)	
12.2(b)	20.5(c)	
12.2(b)	20.5(c)	40
12.3	20.2(b)	14
12.3	20.5(a)	8
12.4	20.2(b)	14
12.4	20.5(a)	8
13	11.9(b)	
13	17.3(a)	4
13(d)	8.5(a)	4
14	17.1(a)	7
14	17.1(b)	37
14	17.2(a)	2
14	17.2(d)	
14	17.3(c)	34
14	17.3(d)	48
14(a)	17.1(c)	38
15	6.4(e)	64
15	20.2(e)	
15	20.2(e)	86
15	23.1(d)	180
15(a)	20.2(e)	
15(a)	20.2(e)	86
15(a)(1)	20.2(e)	85
15(b)	28.5(b)	
15(b)	28.10	5
15(c)	28.9(b)	53
16 (a)(1)(G)	20.3(f)	114
16	8.5(b)	

FEDERAL RULES OF CRIMINAL PROCEDURE

Rule	Sec.	This Work Note
16	8.5(g)	215
16	8.6(b)	44
16	13.4(a)	25
16	13.4(b)	67
16	15.2(i)	208
16	20.1(b)	39
16	20.1(c)	44
16	20.2(b)	14
16	20.2(b)	23
16	20.2(b)	26
16	20.2(b)	28
16	20.2(b)	31
16	20.2(b)	32
16	20.2(c)	50
16	20.2(d)	63
16	20.2(d)	67
16	20.2(d)	80
16	20.2(e)	
16	20.3	
16	20.4(g)	
16	20.4(g)	100
16	20.4(g)	102
16	20.5(g)	
16	20.5(h)	98
16	20.6(a)	6
16	20.6(c)	
16	24.3(b)	49
16	24.3(b)	52
16	24.4(a)	7
16(a)	20.2(b)	26
16(a)	20.3(a)	
16(a)(1)	8.5(g)	215
16(a)(1)	15.2(i)	208
16(a)(1)	20.3(d)	93
16(a)(1)	20.3(j)	
16(a)(1)(A)	8.5(g)	221
16(a)(1)(A)	20.3(a)	5
16(a)(1)(A)	20.3(b)	55
16(a)(1)(A)	20.3(c)	67
16(a)(1)(A)	20.3(c)	83
16(a)(1)(B)	20.3(c)	67
16(a)(1)(B)(i)	20.3(a)	6
16(a)(1)(B)(i)	20.3(c)	
16(a)(1)(B)(i)	20.3(c)	73
16(a)(1)(B)(ii)	20.3(a)	5
16(a)(1)(B)(ii)	20.3(c)	81
16(a)(1)(B)(iii)	8.5(b)	29
16(a)(1)(B)(iii)	15.2(i)	208
16(a)(1)(B)(iii)	20.3(a)	5
16(a)(1)(B)(iii)	20.3(b)	61
16(a)(1)(C)	8.5(g)	215

FEDERAL RULES OF CRIMINAL PROCEDURE

Rule	Sec.	This Work Note
16(a)(1)(C)	20.3(c)	
16(a)(1)(C)	20.3(c)	67
16(a)(1)(C)	20.3(g)	120
16(a)(1)(C)	20.3(g)	121
16(a)(1)(C)	20.3(i)	163
16(a)(1)(D)	20.3(a)	6
16(a)(1)(E)	20.3(a)	6
16(a)(1)(E)	20.3(a)	7
16(a)(1)(E)	20.3(g)	121
16(a)(1)(E)	20.3(j)	
16(a)(1)(E)(i)	20.3(a)	7
16(a)(1)(E)(i)	20.3(f)	115
16(a)(1)(E)(ii)	20.3(a)	7
16(a)(1)(F)	20.3(a)	6
16(a)(1)(F)	20.3(f)	
16(a)(1)(F)	20.3(f)	100
16(a)(1)(F)	20.4(g)	
16(a)(1)(F)(iii)	20.3(f)	115
16(a)(1)(G)	20.3(f)	
16(a)(1)(G)	20.3(f)	113
16(a)(2)	20.3(i)	
16(a)(2)	20.3(j)	
16(a)(2)	20.3(j)	204
16(a)(2)	20.3(j)	205
16(a)(2)	20.3(j)	208
16(a)(2)	20.3(j)	211
16(a)(2)	24.3(b)	49
16(a)(3)	8.5(b)	29
16(a)(3)	8.5(g)	215
16(a)(3)	15.2(i)	208
16(b)	20.3(j)	207
16(b)	20.4(g)	102
16(b)(1)	20.4(g)	101
16(b)(1)	20.5(e)	69
16(b)(1)(A)	20.5(g)	89
16(b)(1)(B)	20.4(g)	
16(b)(1)(B)	20.5(h)	98
16(b)(2)	20.5(e)	69
16(b)(2)	20.5(g)	95
16(b)(2)	20.5(h)	
16(d)	20.3(l)	
16(d)	20.3(l)	232
16(d)(1)	20.3(l)	226
16(d)(2)	20.6(a)	
16(d)(2)	20.6(a)	1
17	1.7(j)	264
17	8.4(b)	
17	8.4(b)	23
17	8.4(c)	144
17	8.8(b)	
17	8.8(b)	36

FEDERAL RULES OF CRIMINAL PROCEDURE

Rule	This Work Sec.	Note
17	8.8(d)	103
17	8.8(e)	
17	8.8(e)	121
17	8.8(e)	135
17	8.8(i)	
17	20.2(d)	
17	20.2(d)	80
17	24.3(f)	
17	24.3(f)	154
17(a)	8.8(b)	36
17(a)	8.8(g)	168
17(a)	24.3(f)	138
17(b)	24.3(f)	143
17(c)	1.7(j)	
17(c)	8.7(a)	
17(c)	8.7(a)	26
17(c)	8.7(b)	34
17(c)	8.7(b)	58
17(c)	8.7(b)	62
17(c)	8.8(a)	8
17(c)	8.8(b)	
17(c)	8.8(b)	36
17(c)	8.8(c)	
17(c)	8.8(c)	45
17(c)	8.8(d)	
17(c)	8.8(d)	82
17(c)	8.8(d)	97
17(c)	8.8(e)	135
17(c)	10.5(e)	55
17(c)	20.2(d)	67
17(c)	24.3(f)	146
17.03	17.1(a)	6
18	16.1(c)	
18	16.1(c)	100
18	16.1(c)	107
18	16.1(h)	
18	16.2(h)	
18	16.3(g)	
19	23.2(h)	
20	16.1(h)	286
20(a)	16.1(f)	211
21	16.2(b)	27
21	16.2(b)	34
21	16.2(e)	
21	16.3(a)	2
21	16.3(b)	
21	16.3(b)	9
21	16.3(b)	18
21	16.3(c)	28
21(a)	16.3(c)	30
21(a)	16.3(d)	

FEDERAL RULES OF CRIMINAL PROCEDURE

Rule	This Work Sec.	Note
21(a)	16.3(g)	121
21(a)	23.2(a)	24
21(b)	16.2(b)	
21(b)	16.2(b)	29
21(b)	16.3(c)	
21(b)	16.3(c)	30
21(b)	16.3(c)	34
21(b)	16.3(g)	121
21(b)	16.4(d)	143
23	22.1(e)	88
23	22.1(h)	160
23	24.6(e)	
23	24.9(f)	103
23(a)	22.1(h)	135
23(a)	22.1(h)	150
23(b)	22.1(d)	79
23(b)	22.1(h)	157
23(b)	22.3(e)	277
23(b)	22.3(e)	287
23(b)	24.9(f)	103
23(b)	27.6(d)	142
23(c)	17.4(a)	13
23(c)	24.6(a)	11
24(a)	22.3(a)	36
24(a)	22.3(a)	37
24(b)	1.8(e)	92
24(b)	22.3(c)	157
24(b)	22.3(d)	174
24(b)	22.3(d)	176
24(c)	22.3(e)	260
24(c)	22.3(e)	262
24(c)	22.3(e)	270
24(c)	22.3(e)	271
24(c)	22.3(e)	277
24(c)	22.3(e)	279
24(c)	22.3(e)	285
24(c)	24.9(f)	102
24(c)	27.5(d)	
24(c)(1)	24.9(f)	102
24(c)(3)	22.3(e)	277
25(a)	22.4(e)	46
25(b)	22.4(e)	46
26	11.2(a)	30
26(b)	24.2(f)	85
26.2	8.5(b)	
26.2	8.5(g)	215
26.2	10.5(e)	54
26.2	15.2(i)	208
26.2	20.3(b)	26
26.2	20.3(i)	164
26.2	20.4(b)	16

FEDERAL RULES OF CRIMINAL PROCEDURE

Rule	Sec.	This Work Note
26.2	20.4(b)	20
26.2	24.3(c)	
26.2(f)	8.5(g)	217
26.2(f)	20.3(b)	26
26.2(f)(3)	8.5(b)	30
26.2(g)	8.5(b)	30
26.2(g)	14.4(c)	65
26.2(g)(1)	14.4(c)	64
29	24.6(b)	
29	24.6(b)	18
29	25.3(a)	7
29(b)	24.6(b)	26
29(b)	24.6(b)	27
29(b)	24.6(b)	33
29(c)	24.6(b)	16
29(c)	24.11(a)	1
29.1	24.7(c)	22
29.1	24.7(c)	23
29.1	24.7(i)	
30	24.8(a)	3
30	24.8(a)	14
30	24.8(b)	
30	24.8(b)	27
30	24.8(b)	35
30	24.8(f)	
31	22.1(e)	88
31	22.1(h)	160
31	24.10(d)	
31(a)	22.1(h)	160
31(b)	24.10(d)	45
31(c)	24.8(e)	
31(d)	24.9(e)	53
31(d)	24.9(e)	58
32	21.5(a)	17
32	26.4(d)	
32	26.4(d)	65
32	26.4(g)	
32	26.10(b)	32
32	28.5(b)	44
32	28.9(c)	
32(a)	28.9(c)	
32(b)(2)	26.5(b)	27
32(b)(4)(A)	26.5(b)	27
32(b)(6)	26.5(c)	46
32(c)	26.5(b)	25
32(c)	26.5(b)	26
32(c)	26.5(b)	29
32(c)(1)	26.5(b)	36
32(c)(2)	6.4(e)	107
32(c)(2)	26.4(d)	37
32(c)(2)	26.4(d)	39

FEDERAL RULES OF CRIMINAL PROCEDURE

Rule	Sec.	This Work Note
32(c)(2)	26.4(e)	83
32(c)(3)(A)	27.6(b)	20
32(c)(3)(C)	26.4(g)	138
32(d)	21.5(a)	17
32(d)	21.5(a)	34
32(d)	21.5(a)	52
32(d)	26.5(b)	30
32(d)(3)	26.5(c)	
32(d)(3)	26.5(c)	46
32(e)	21.5(c)	84
32(e)(1)	26.5(b)	31
32(e)(1)	26.5(b)	33
32(e)(2)	26.5(c)	43
32(e)(2)	26.5(c)	44
32(e)(2)	26.5(c)	51
32(h)	26.4(d)	65
32(i)	26.4(g)	
32(i)	26.4(g)	128
32(i)(3)	26.4(f)	104
32(i)(3)	26.4(g)	125
32(i)(3)(C)	26.5(c)	56
32(i)(4)(A)	26.4(g)	133
32.1	26.10(b)	10
32.1	26.10(b)	27
32.1	26.10(b)	39
32.1	26.10(c)	81
32.1(a)(2)	26.10(b)	
32.1(a)(3)(B)	26.10(b)	31
32.1(b)	26.9(a)	7
32.1(b)(2)(C)	26.10(c)	71
32.1(c)	26.8(c)	24
32.2	21.4(e)	156
32.2	26.6(d)	49
32.2(b)(4)	26.6(d)	56
32.2(b)(4)	26.6(d)	59
32.2(c)	26.6(d)	72
33	11.2(b)	52
33	12.4(d)	64
33	24.3(b)	
33	24.11(b)	
33	24.11(b)	3
33	24.11(b)	4
33	24.11(d)	
33	24.11(d)	12
33	24.11(d)	20
33	24.11(d)	34
33	24.11(d)	39
33	28.9(b)	
33	28.9(b)	41
33(b)(1)	11.7(e)	70
34	19.6(c)	46

FEDERAL RULES OF CRIMINAL PROCEDURE

Rule	This Work Sec.	Note
34	24.11(c)	
34	24.11(c)	10
35	13.5(h)	205
35	21.2(e)	317
35	26.4(e)	76
35	26.7(c)	35
35	26.9(c)	86
35	26.9(c)	93
35(a)	1.3(e)	39
35(a)	26.7(c)	35
35(a)	26.9(c)	79
35(b)	11.1(b)	39
35(b)	11.7(a)	10
35(b)	21.2(d)	
35(b)	26.4(e)	
35(b)	26.7(c)	35
35(c)	1.3(e)	39
36	26.7(c)	35
36(2)	1.7(c)	
41	1.7(f)	70
41	3.4(g)	124
41	3.4(l)	241
41	4.7(c)	
41	4.7(c)	20
41	6.7(b)	43
41	8.9(a)	10
41	27.2(d)	
41	27.2(d)	70
41	27.2(d)	72
41	27.2(d)	76
41(d)(3)	3.4(c)	40
41(e)	8.9(a)	
41(e)	10.1(c)	32
41(e)	10.1(c)	36
41(e)	10.1(c)	47
41(e)	27.2(d)	72
41(e)	27.2(d)	76
41(g)	8.9(a)	
41(g)	10.1(c)	32
41(g)	10.1(c)	36
41(g)	10.1(c)	47
41(g)	13.5(h)	203
41(g)	27.2(d)	
41(g)	27.2(d)	72
41(h)	8.9(a)	
42(b)	8.3(a)	8
42(b)	15.1(b)	86
43	24.2(a)	
43	24.2(a)	6
43	24.2(d)	
43	24.2(d)	50

FEDERAL RULES OF CRIMINAL PROCEDURE

Rule	This Work Sec.	Note
43	24.2(f)	83
43	24.2(f)	87
43	27.6(d)	84
43(a)	12.1(a)	19
43(a)	24.2(a)	8
43(b)	24.2(d)	41
43(c)	1.8(c)	37
44	11.4(c)	97
44	11.9(c)	134
44(a)	11.2(b)	79
44(c)	11.9(b)	
44(c)	11.9(b)	60
44(c)	11.9(b)	99
44(c)	11.9(c)	
44(c)	11.9(c)	116
44(c)	11.9(c)	128
44(c)	11.9(c)	129
44(c)	11.9(d)	
44(c)	27.2(c)	
44(c)(1)(B)	11.9(b)	93
44(c)(2)	11.9(b)	94
44(c)(2)	11.9(b)	95
45	4.8(c)	
45(a)	4.6(g)	136
46	8.7(e)	88
48	13.3(c)	45
48	21.3(e)	279
48	21.3(e)	297
48(a)	13.3(c)	41
48(a)	13.3(c)	44
48(a)	28.9(a)	16
48(b)	18.3(c)	110
48(b)	18.3(c)	111
51	27.5(c)	90
52	1.7(f)	70
52	18.3(b)	48
52	19.3(e)	
52	21.5(c)	
52	25.2(b)	15
52	27.5(c)	
52	27.5(d)	
52	27.5(d)	134
52	27.6(b)	
52(a)	15.6(d)	
52(a)	15.6(e)	
52(a)	15.6(f)	
52(a)	15.6(f)	175
52(a)	19.3(a)	
52(a)	27.6(a)	10
52(a)	27.6(b)	
52(a)	27.6(b)	20

FEDERAL RULES OF CRIMINAL PROCEDURE

Rule	This Work Sec.	Note
52(a)	27.6(b)	28
52(a)	27.6(b)	30
52(b)	1.7(i)	
52(b)	8.4(c)	136
52(b)	15.6(f)	
52(b)	19.2(e)	
52(b)	19.3(a)	
52(b)	19.3(e)	
52(b)	19.5(d)	
52(b)	19.6(c)	
52(b)	27.5(d)	
52(b)	27.5(d)	115
52(b)	27.5(d)	116
52(b)	27.5(d)	132
52(b)	27.6(b)	
52(b)	28.4(d)	45
53	23.3(b)	12
54	4.6(d)	
54(c)	8.5(e)	
57	1.7(g)	
57	1.7(g)	108
58	1.4(g)	140
58	1.8(c)	18
58	19.1(d)	34
58	19.1(d)	45
58	19.1(d)	
58(b) to (g)	14.2(b)	28
58(b)(1)	14.2(b)	22
58(b)(1)	15.1(d)	
58(b)(1)	15.1(d)	175
59(e)	28.10	1
177	23.1(b)	
177(3)	23.1(b)	
229	19.5(b)	14
403	17.2(e)	
410	21.5(f)	163
410	24.4(a)	6
444(d)	21.6(b)	108
606	24.9(g)	118
606	24.9(g)	122
606(b)	24.9(f)	
606(b)	24.9(g)	
606(b)	24.9(g)	126
615	24.4(d)	47
615	24.4(d)	52
615	24.4(d)	64
901	8.13(a)	14

FEDERAL RULES OF EVIDENCE

Rule	This Work Sec.	Note
2	15.5(c)	108
26	1.7(h)	152
103	24.4(a)	10
103	27.5(c)	90
103(a)(2)	24.4(a)	11
104(a)	10.5(d)	41
104(d)	10.5(c)	28
105	24.8(a)	9
401	8.13(a)	9
403	17.2(e)	128
404	26.2(b)	20
404(b)	3.1(f)	140
404(b)	5.3(a)	4
404(b)	9.6(c)	66
404(b)	16.1(f)	213
404(b)	17.1(d)	47
404(b)	20.2(d)	70
410	21.2(h)	420
410	21.2(h)	428
410	21.2(h)	434
410	21.5(f)	166
410	21.5(f)	170
606(b)	24.9(g)	
606(b)	24.9(g)	113
606(b)	24.9(g)	119
609(a)	24.5(d)	
609(a)(1)	24.5(d)	
615	24.4(d)	
615	24.4(d)	49
800(d)(2)(D)	17.2(b)	45
801(d)(2)(E)	20.3(d)	93
804(a)	14.1(d)	
804(a)	14.1(d)	50
804(b)(1)	24.3(i)	196
807	20.2(d)	69
1101(d)	14.4(b)	
1101(d)	14.4(b)	5
1101(d)	14.4(b)	6
1101(d)	14.4(b)	9
1101(d)	14.4(b)	13
1101(d)	15.2(d)	
1101(d)	15.2(d)	106
1101(d)	15.2(d)	107
1101(d)	26.5(a)	
1101(d)(3)	12.1(d)	50
1101(d)(3)	14.4(b)	13

FEDERAL RULES OF APPELLATE PROCEDURE

Rule	This Work Sec.	Note
4(a)(1)(B)	13.5(h)	199

FEDERAL RULES OF APPELLATE PROCEDURE

Rule	This Work Sec.	Note
4(a)(1)(B)	13.5(h)	209
4(b)(1)(A)	13.5(h)	198
9(b)	12.4(d)	87
22	28.10	1
22(b)(1)	28.10	2

FEDERAL REGISTER

Vol.	This Work Sec.	Note
46, 22364	3.4(a)	21
64, 19273	1.7(j)	256
64, 19273	1.7(j)	262
64, 19273	1.7(j)	267
66, 55062	11.8(b)	43
66, 55062	11.8(b)	46
66, 55064	11.8(b)	46

ALABAMA CONSTITUTION

Art.	This Work Sec.	Note
I, § 6	2.12(b)	94
I, § 6	2.12(b)	97
I, § 6	16.1(b)	92
I, § 6	16.3(a)	4
I, § 6.01	12.1(f)	69
I, § 6.01	12.1(f)	76
I, § 6.01	12.1(f)	81
I, § 6.01	12.1(f)	91
I, § 6.01	21.3(f)	302
I, § 6.01	21.3(f)	339
I, § 6.01	21.3(f)	371
I, § 6.01	21.3(f)	390
I, § 8	15.1(d)	179
I, § 8	15.1(d)	204
I, § 8	15.1(d)	205
I, § 8	15.1(d)	207
I, § 8	15.1(d)	218
I, § 8	15.1(f)	281
I, § 8	15.1(f)	284
I, § 8	15.1(f)	295
I, § 8	15.1(f)	300
I, § 16	12.3(b)	33

Amend.	This Work Sec.	Note
328, § 6.11	1.7(f)	91

ALABAMA CODE

Sec.	This Work Sec.	Note
12-1-12	22.4(b)	18
12-11-30(5)	11.2(a)	24
12-16-55	15.4(d)	101
12-16-190	8.4(c)	116
12-16-197	8.4(b)	21
12-16-200	15.2(d)	96
12-16-202	15.2(e)	128
12-16-207(a)	15.4(g)	154
12-16-209	8.4(b)	28
12-16-212	8.11(b)	20
12-16-215	8.5(d)	118
12-16-220	8.5(e)	161
13A-3-31	5.2(a)	4
13A-5-47	26.2(b)	9
13A-5-47(c)	26.2(b)	7
13A-12-250	26.1(c)	62
14-9-41(a)	26.2(c)	55
14-9-41(a)(1)	26.2(c)	56
15-1-1	1.7(e)	59
15-2-2	16.1(b)	35
15-2-2	16.1(c)	105
15-2-3	16.4(c)	80
15-2-3	16.4(c)	90
15-2-4	16.4(c)	80
15-2-4	16.4(c)	96
15-2-6	16.1(d)	150
15-2-7	16.1(e)	170
15-2-20	16.3(a)	1
15-2-24	16.3(g)	104
15-8-1	15.1(d)	247
15-8-1	15.1(d)	250
15-8-5	19.1(d)	64
15-8-33	19.1(d)	36
15-8-33	19.3(b)	135
15-8-34	19.1(d)	36
15-8-34	19.3(b)	135
15-8-35	19.3(b)	135
15-8-36	19.1(d)	36
15-8-36	19.3(b)	135
15-8-50	19.3(b)	177
15-11-1	14.2(e)	69
15-12-5	11.2(g)	299
15-12-5(b)	11.2(g)	274
15-12-5(c)	11.2(g)	310
15-12-21	11.2(a)	28
15-15-40(b)	15.4(b)	52
15-18-68	26.6(c)	35
15-22-54	26.9(a)	8
15-23-64	13.1(a)	22

ALABAMA CODE

Sec.	This Work Sec.	Note
15-23-64	21.3(f)	314
15-23-64	21.3(f)	317
15-23-71	21.3(f)	355
15-23-71	21.3(f)	410
15-23-71	21.3(f)	413
15-23-76	12.1(f)	104
15-23-76	21.3(f)	381
36-18-20	24.3(e)	137

ALABAMA RULES OF CRIMINAL PROCEDURE

Rule	This Work Sec.	Note
1	1.7(f)	71
1.2	20.2(c)	43
1.4(r)	1.8(d)	69
1.4(s)	1.8(d)	69
2.2	1.8(c)	25
3.1	12.5(a)	5
5.1	14.2(c)	36
5.1	14.2(c)	38
5.1	14.2(f)	86
5.1(b)	14.2(e)	74
5.3	14.4(b)	13
5.4	14.3(a)	2
6(b)(2)	26.5(a)	3
6.1	11.2(a)	28
6.1	11.2(a)	32
6.1	11.2(b)	81
6.1	11.2(g)	262
6.1(b)	11.3(c)	54
6.3	11.2(g)	294
8.1	18.3(c)	119
8.1	18.3(c)	120
9.1(b)(2)(I)	24.2(b)	30
12.3(c)(1)	15.1(d)	250
12.3(c)(1)	15.2(b)	20
12.3(d)	15.1(d)	250
13.3	17.1(a)	4
13.3	17.3(a)	5
13.3	17.3(d)	49
13.5	19.5(d)	68
14.3	21.3(c)	201
16	20.2(b)	16
16(a)(1)(e)	20.3(j)	204
16.1	20.3(d)	90
16.1	20.3(e)	95
16.2	20.4(g)	99
16.2(d)	20.5(g)	95
16.6	20.2(e)	85
17.6	1.8(c)	24
20.2(b)	24.6(b)	25

ALABAMA RULES OF CRIMINAL PROCEDURE

Rule	This Work Sec.	Note
26.5(a)	26.5(c)	45
27.1	26.9(a)	4
54(d)	14.3(c)	74

ALABAMA RULES OF EVIDENCE

Rule	This Work Sec.	Note
615	24.4(d)	31
615	24.4(d)	55

ALABAMA RULES OF APPELLATE PROCEDURE

Rule	This Work Sec.	Note
4	28.11(b)	34
5	28.11(b)	34

ALASKA CONSTITUTION

Art.	This Work Sec.	Note
I, § 8	15.1(d)	180
I, § 8	15.1(d)	204
I, § 8	15.1(d)	205
I, § 8	15.1(d)	209
I, § 8	15.1(f)	281
I, § 8	15.1(f)	284
I, § 8	15.1(f)	308
I, § 11	12.3(b)	33
I, § 22	2.12(b)	87
I, § 24	12.1(f)	69
I, § 24	12.1(f)	73
I, § 24	12.1(f)	81
I, § 24	12.1(f)	96
I, § 24	13.1(a)	24
I, § 24	21.3(f)	302
I, § 24	21.3(f)	306
I, § 24	21.3(f)	321
I, § 38	15.1(d)	246
IV, § 15	1.7(f)	91
IV, § 15	1.7(f)	95

ALASKA STATUTES

Sec.	This Work Sec.	Note
11.81.450	5.2(b)	24
12.05.010	1.7(e)	59
12.05.010	16.4(c)	96
12.20.010	25.5(b)	25
12.20.020	19.6(a)	6
12.25.180	1.8(c)	29

ALASKA STATUTES

Sec.	This Work Sec.	Note
12.25.180	12.5(b)	21
12.30.035	12.4(e)	88
12.40.040	15.2(b)	20
12.40.050	15.2(f)	149
12.40.070	8.4(b)	27
12.40.080	15.2(h)	191
12.47.010 to 12.47.090	20.5(c)	33
12.50.101(b)	8.11(d)	73
12.55.125	26.3(d)	22
12.55.145(a)(1)(B)	26.6(b)	26
12.55.155	26.3(d)	25
12.61.015	21.3(f)	306
18.85.170	11.2(g)	275
18.85.170(4)	11.2(g)	274
22.07.020(d)(2)	27.3(c)	32
22.10.040	16.3(a)	1
22.10.040	16.3(b)	15
22.10.040	16.3(c)	27
33.20.010	26.2(c)	55

ALASKA RULES OF CRIMINAL PROCEDURE

Rule	This Work Sec.	Note
1	1.3(e)	37
1	1.7(f)	71
1(i)(2)	1.8(c)	40
4	12.5(a)	6
4	23.1(b)	20
5(c)	11.5(b)	23
5(e)	14.2(c)	36
5(e)	14.2(e)	74
5(e)	14.2(f)	86
5(e)	14.2(f)	88
5.1	14.3(a)	1
5.1	14.4(b)	27
5.1	14.4(b)	40
5.1(d)	14.4(b)	19
5.2	12.5(b)	21
6(c)	8.3(h)	52
6(e)(1)	15.2(b)	20
6(g)	15.4(b)	45
6(i)	8.4(b)	27
6(j)	15.2(i)	213
6(j)	15.2(j)	235
6(j)	15.2(j)	243
6(l)	8.5(e)	162
6(m)	15.2(i)	209
6(m)	15.2(i)	211
6(m)	15.2(i)	213
6(p)	15.2(b)	52
6(p)	15.2(c)	62
6(q)	15.2(b)	20

ALASKA RULES OF CRIMINAL PROCEDURE

Rule	This Work Sec.	Note
6(q)	15.2(b)	29
6(r)	15.2(d)	100
6(u)	15.2(d)	104
7(a)	15.1(d)	180
7(a)	15.1(d)	210
7(a)	15.1(d)	247
7(b)	15.1(f)	286
7(b)	15.1(f)	294
7(b)	15.1(f)	308
7(b)	15.1(f)	318
7(c)	15.1(d)	248
7(c)	19.1(d)	40
7(e)	19.5(b)	2
7(e)	19.5(b)	5
7(f)	19.4(b)	11
7(o)	15.1(d)	249
8	17.1(a)	4
8	17.1(b)	23
8	17.2(a)	4
8(b)(4)	1.8(d)	69
12(b)	19.1(d)	53
12(c)	15.4(b)	61
12(e)	27.3(d)	66
13	17.3(a)	5
13.3	17.1(b)	19
13.3	17.2(a)	7
14	17.3(d)	49
16	20.2(b)	13
16	20.2(b)	16
16	20.2(b)	38
16	20.3(b)	31
16(a)	20.3(a)	2
16(b)	20.2(c)	49
16(b)	20.3(b)	41
16(b)	20.3(e)	97
16(b)	20.3(f)	117
16(b)	20.4(a)	7
16(b)(1)(A)	20.3(a)	1
16(b)(1)(A)	20.3(g)	119
16(b)(1)(A)(i)	20.3(h)	139
16(b)(1)(A)(iii)	20.3(d)	87
16(b)(1)(A)(v)	20.3(e)	97
16(b)(2)	20.2(b)	30
16(b)(7)	20.3(b)	32
16(b)(8)	20.3(j)	198
16(c)	20.4(g)	99
16(c)	20.5(h)	101
16(c)(6)	20.4(b)	30
16(d)(2)	20.5(b)	20
16(d)(6)	20.2(c)	55
16(f)	20.2(c)	57
16A	20.2(b)	13

ALASKA RULES OF CRIMINAL PROCEDURE

	This Work	
Rule	Sec.	Note
17	8.4(b)	23
22(a)	24.2(a)	23
25(b)	22.4(e)	48
25(d)	22.4(d)	32
25(d)	22.4(d)	44
29	24.6(b)	33
32.1(a)	26.5(b)	35
32.1(b)(2)	26.5(b)	31
39	11.2(a)	28
39	11.3(a)	6
39(c)	11.2(h)	316
39.1(f)	11.2(g)	266
45	18.3(c)	72
45	18.3(c)	75
45	18.3(c)	76
45	18.3(c)	78
45	18.3(c)	79
45	18.3(c)	81
45	18.3(c)	99
45	18.3(c)	100
45	18.3(c)	106
45	18.3(c)	107
45	18.3(c)	108
45	18.3(c)	119
45	18.3(c)	120

ALASKA RULES OF DISTRICT COURT

	This Work	
Rule	Sec.	Note
8	1.8(c)	30

ALASKA RULES OF APPELLATE PROCEDURE

	This Work	
Rule	Sec.	Note
402	27.2(b)	18

ALASKA RULES OF EVIDENCE

	This Work	
Rule	Sec.	Note
804	14.1(d)	50

ARIZONA CONSTITUTION

	This Work	
Art.	Sec.	Note
II, § 2.1	12.1(f)	69
II, § 2.1	12.1(f)	73
II, § 2.1	12.1(f)	82
II, § 2.1	13.1(a)	21
II, § 2.1	21.3(f)	302
II, § 2.1(A)(1)	1.5(k)	383

ARIZONA CONSTITUTION

	This Work	
Art.	Sec.	Note
II, § 8	2.12(b)	89
II, § 22	12.3(b)	37
II, § 22	12.3(b)	38
II, § 22	12.3(b)	39
II, § 22	12.3(e)	118
II, § 24	2.12(b)	95
II, § 24	27.1(a)	5
II, § 30	14.2(d)	60
II, § 30	15.1(g)	344
II, § 30	15.1(g)	345
III, § 24	2.12(b)	96
VI, § 27	24.6(e)	47

ARIZONA REVISED STATUTES ANNOTATED

	This Work	
Sec.	Sec.	Note
3-703.01.C	26.2(b)	6
3-703.01.D	26.2(b)	6
8-278	26.3(e)	30
12-2312	1.5(k)	413
13-108	16.4(c)	67
13-108	16.4(c)	76
13-108	16.4(c)	78
13-108	16.4(c)	94
13-108	16.4(c)	95
13-108	16.4(c)	102
13-108	16.4(c)	103
13-109	16.1(e)	174
13-109	16.1(e)	174
13-109	16.1(d)	151
13-109(B)(4)	16.1(e)	173
13-117	24.5(b)	21
13-206	5.2(a)	4
13-330	14.1(a)	1
13-604(P)	26.6(b)	17
13-604(W)(2)(b)	26.6(b)	24
13-702	26.3(d)	23
13-702C	26.3(d)	26
13-703(B)	26.2(b)	5
13-703(C)	26.5(c)	50
13-3801	1.7(e)	59
13-3903	1.8(c)	29
13-3903	12.5(b)	19
13-3903	12.5(b)	28
13-3925	3.1(c)	53
13-4013(B)	11.2(e)	217
13-4032	27.3(a)	10
13-4032	27.3(c)	37
13-4032	27.3(d)	61
13-4032(7)	27.3(d)	69
13-4033	27.2(a)	4

ARIZONA REVISED STATUTES ANNOTATED

Sec.	This Work Sec.	Note
13-4240	24.11(d)	46
13-4310(E)	26.6(d)	46
13-4310(E)	26.6(d)	55
13-4312(H)	26.6(d)	57
13-4419	21.3(f)	314
13-4419	21.3(f)	318
13-4419	21.3(f)	358
13-4423	21.3(f)	308
13-4423	21.3(f)	355
13-4423	21.3(f)	366
13-4423	21.3(f)	376
13-4423	21.3(f)	379
13-4423	21.3(f)	396
13-4423	21.3(f)	410
13-4428	12.1(f)	94
13-4428	12.1(f)	104
13-4428	21.3(f)	381
13-4428	21.3(f)	382
13-4428	21.3(f)	413
13-4434	1.5(k)	400
21-407(a)	8.4(b)	82
21-408	15.1(g)	359
21-408	15.2(b)	20
21-408(A)	8.4(b)	28
21-411	15.2(j)	243
21-411A	15.2(i)	209
21-412	8.14(b)	25
21-412	8.14(b)	28
21-412	15.2(b)	29
21-413	15.2(f)	148
21-421	8.1(b)	17
31-411(B)	26.2(c)	50
41-196	8.11(b)	17

ARIZONA RULES OF CRIMINAL PROCEDURE

Rule	This Work Sec.	Note
1	20.2(c)	42
1.1	1.3(e)	37
1.1	1.7(f)	71
2.1	1.8(c)	30
2.2	1.8(c)	30
3.1	12.5(a)	5
5.1	14.2(e)	67
5.1	14.2(f)	86
5.1(b)	14.2(e)	74
5.1(b)	14.2(e)	84
5.1(c)	14.2(f)	88
5.3	14.4(b)	25
5.3	14.4(c)	64

ARIZONA RULES OF CRIMINAL PROCEDURE

Rule	This Work Sec.	Note
5.3	14.4(d)	78
5.3	14.4(d)	79
5.4	14.3(a)	1
5.4	14.4(b)	19
5.4	14.4(b)	22
5.4	14.4(b)	27
5.4(c)	14.4(b)	28
5.4(c)	14.4(b)	29
6	11.2(a)	31
6.1	11.2(a)	28
6.1	11.2(a)	35
6.1	11.2(b)	81
6.1	11.3(c)	54
6.2	11.2(a)	28
6.4	11.2(g)	281
6.4	11.2(g)	294
8.1	18.3(c)	119
8.1	18.3(c)	120
8.2	18.3(c)	72
8.2	18.3(c)	117
8.4	18.3(c)	81
8.4	18.3(c)	90
8.5	18.3(c)	97
8.5	18.3(c)	104
8.5	18.3(c)	123
8.6	1.3(f)	70
8.6	18.3(c)	106
8.6	18.3(c)	112
10.2	22.4(d)	32
10.2(b)	22.4(d)	45
10.3	16.3(a)	2
10.3	16.3(d)	52
12.1(d)	15.2(e)	128
12.2	15.4(g)	154
12.2	15.4(g)	155
12.2	15.4(g)	157
12.3	15.4(g)	159
12.3(a)	15.4(f)	143
12.3(b)	15.4(b)	44
12.4(a)	15.4(a)	16
12.6	8.10(d)	101
12.8(c)	8.5(d)	133
12.9	15.6(a)	4
12.9(a)	15.5(c)	107
12.9(b)	15.4(b)	61
13.3	17.1(a)	4
13.3	17.1(b)	19
13.3	17.2(a)	7
13.3	17.3(a)	5
13.4	17.1(b)	24
13.4	17.3(d)	50

ARIZONA RULES OF CRIMINAL PROCEDURE

Rule	This Work Sec.	Note
13.5	19.5(c)	48
15	20.2(b)	16
15.1	20.2(c)	47
15.1	20.2(d)	72
15.1	20.3	262
15.1(a)	20.3(g)	119
15.1(a)(1)	20.3(h)	141
15.1(a)(2)	20.3(d)	88
15.1(b)	20.3(f)	117
15.1(b)	20.3(k)	222
15.1(b)(3)	20.3(h)	139
15.1(d)	20.3(a)	2
15.1(e)	20.2(b)	21
15.1(f)	20.4(a)	5
15.2	20.4(g)	99
15.2(b)	20.5(a)	10
15.2(b)	20.5(b)	17
15.2(b)	20.5(c)	32
15.2(b)	20.5(d)	59
15.2(b)	20.5(d)	61
15.2(b)	20.5(d)	62
15.2(c)	20.5(h)	101
15.2(c)(1)	20.5(f)	85
15.2(f)	20.5(h)	107
15.3	20.2(e)	82
15.3(a)	20.2(e)	87
15.3(a)	20.2(e)	88
15.3(a)	20.2(e)	93
15.3(a)	20.2(e)	95
15.3(d)	20.2(e)	94
15.3(e)	20.2(e)	90
15.4	20.3(j)	196
15.4(b)(1)	20.3(b)	41
15.4(b)(2)	20.3(h)	139
15.5(a)	20.3(l)	231
15.5(c)	20.3(l)	232
15.7(3)	20.6(a)	9
15.7(5)	20.6(a)	8
16.1(c)	27.3(d)	66
16.3	1.3(f)	67
16.5	20.2(d)	68
17.4	21.3(f)	333
18.4(c)	1.8(c)	35
18.6(c)	24.8(a)	2
18.6(d)	24.9(b)	18
18.6(d)	24.9(c)	20
18.6(e)	24.9(b)	13
20	24.6(b)	19
22.2	24.8(a)	16
26.4(a)	26.5(b)	37
26.14	26.8(b)	15

ARIZONA RULES OF CRIMINAL PROCEDURE

Rule	This Work Sec.	Note
27.1	26.9(a)	4
31.17	25.4(b)	19
32.2(a)(3)	28.4(b)	23

ARIZONA RULES OF EVIDENCE

Rule	This Work Sec.	Note
1101(b)	14.4(b)	19
1101(d)	15.2(d)	107

ARKANSAS CONSTITUTION

Art.	This Work Sec.	Note
II, § 8	12.3(b)	33
II, § 8	15.1(g)	358
II, § 10	16.1(b)	33
II, § 10	16.1(b)	91
II, § 10	16.3(a)	4

Amend.	This Work Sec.	Note
21, § 1	15.1(g)	345

ARKANSAS STATUTES

Sec.	This Work Sec.	Note
16-89-126(d)	24.10(a)	1
22-246	1.7(f)	96
43-918	15.2(d)	94

ARKANSAS CODE ANNOTATED

Rule	This Work Sec.	Note
1-1-101	16.2(g)	109
5-1-109(d)	24.8(f)	112
5-1-110	24.8(e)	50
5-2-209	5.2(b)	24
5-2-305	20.5(c)	33
5-4-103	26.2(b)	12
5-4-103	26.2(b)	14
5-4-301	26.1(d)	79
5-4-501(e)(3)(A)	26.6(b)	18
5-4-502	26.6(b)	17
16-10-130	18.3(c)	124
16-18-01	1.8(c)	21
16-21-106	21.3(f)	308
16-21-106	21.3(f)	317
16-21-106	21.3(f)	329
16-30-103(a)	15.2(b)	20
16-31-107	15.4(b)	51
16-32-201	15.2(a)	6

ARKANSAS CODE ANNOTATED

Rule	This Work Sec.	Note
16-33-301	15.4(b)	30
16-33-301	15.4(g)	153
16-33-301	15.4(g)	156
16-43-208	24.3(f)	144
16-43-209	24.3(f)	144
16-43-212	8.1(c)	33
16-43-212	8.1(c)	35
16-43-604	8.3(e)	26
16-68-514	15.5(c)	107
16-80-102	1.7(e)	59
16-81-106	1.8(f)	102
16-81-301	1.8(f)	102
16-81-805	1.8(f)	101
16-85-403	19.1(c)	32
16-85-405	19.1(d)	36
16-85-507	8.3(a)	1
16-85-513(a)	15.2(f)	149
16-85-514	8.5(a)	3
16-85-514(c)	8.5(a)	4
16-88-13	16.1(e)	179
16-88-101	16.1(a)	25
16-88-104	16.1(g)	240
16-88-105	16.1(a)	25
16-88-110	16.1(d)	149
16-88-201	16.3(a)	1
16-88-201	16.3(d)	50
16-88-201	16.3(f)	86
16-88-204	16.3(f)	86
16-89-103(a)(2)	24.2(b)	29
16-89-108	24.6(a)	7
16-89-116	20.2(b)	16
16-90-106(b)	26.4(g)	133
22-245	1.7(f)	86
41-103	16.4(c)	67
43-918	15.2(b)	29
43-2035	1.5(k)	413

ARKANSAS RULES OF CRIMINAL PROCEDURE

Rule	This Work Sec.	Note
1.1	1.7(f)	71
Art. II	1.3(f)	82
3(c)	27.3(c)	32
Art. V	1.3(f)	67
8.2	11.2(a)	28
8.2(b)	11.3(b)	29
9.1 to 9.6	1.7(f)	72
9.5	12.3(b)	68
9.6	12.3(b)	68
16.89-115(e)	20.3(b)	40
17.1	15.2(i)	214

ARKANSAS RULES OF CRIMINAL PROCEDURE

Rule	This Work Sec.	Note
17.1(b)(1)	15.2(i)	209
17.3(a)	20.3(a)	21
17.19	20.2(b)	16
18.2	20.5(h)	106
18.3	20.5(d)	58
18.3	20.5(d)	59
18.3	20.5(d)	62
20.3	20.2(c)	57
21.1	17.1(a)	4
21.1	17.1(b)	19
21.2	17.2(a)	6
21.3	17.4(c)	143
21.3	17.4(c)	152
21.3	17.4(c)	154
21.3	17.4(c)	155
21.3	17.4(c)	156
21.3	17.4(c)	157
21.4	16.1(f)	220
22.2	17.1(b)	22
22.2	17.3(d)	51
23.1	17.3(a)	5
23.1	17.3(a)	9
25.1	21.3(c)	202
27.1 to 30.2	1.7(f)	72
28.1	18.3(c)	72
28.1	18.3(c)	106
28.1	18.3(c)	108
28.1	18.3(c)	118
28.2	18.3(c)	72
28.2	18.3(c)	75
28.2	18.3(c)	78
28.2	18.3(c)	79
28.3	18.3(c)	81
28.3	18.3(c)	90
28.3	18.3(c)	95
28.3	18.3(c)	100
33.1	24.6(b)	32
33.3	24.8(a)	16

ARKANSAS RULES OF EVIDENCE

Rule	This Work Sec.	Note
615	24.4(d)	31
615	24.4(d)	42
616	24.4(d)	54
1101(b)	14.4(b)	5
1101(b)(2)	15.2(d)	94
1101(b)(2)	15.2(d)	107
1101(b)(3)	26.5(a)	3

CALIFORNIA CONSTITUTION

Art.	This Work Sec.	Note
I, § 1	2.12(b)	87
I, § 12	12.3(b)	37
I, § 12	12.3(b)	38
I, § 14	15.1(g)	344
I, § 14	15.1(g)	345
I, § 14.1	14.2(d)	50
I, § 14.1	14.2(d)	55
I, § 27	2.12(a)	69
I, § 28	1.5(k)	370
I, § 28	2.12(a)	69
I, § 28	12.1(f)	69
I, § 28	21.3(f)	302
VI, § 10	24.6(e)	47

CALIFORNIA PENAL CODE

Sec.	This Work Sec.	Note
27(1)	16.4(c)	87
185.5	11.2(b)	74
296	3.5(d)	148
656	25.5(b)	25
667	26.6(b)	4
667(g)	1.6(h)	472
667.9(a)	26.1(c)	62
679.02	21.3(f)	325
681	1.7(e)	59
739	14.3(d)	89
739	14.3(d)	90
777	16.1(a)	25
778	16.4(c)	80
778	16.4(c)	96
778a	16.4(c)	80
778a	16.4(c)	90
781	16.1(d)	150
785	16.1(e)	183
786	16.1(e)	179
790	16.1(e)	173
793	25.5(b)	25
805	24.8(f)	112
813	1.8(f)	101
813	12.5(a)	3
827.1	1.8(c)	29
830.1(a)	1.8(f)	102
853.6	12.5(b)	22
859b	14.2(e)	67
859b	14.2(e)	84
859b	14.2(f)	88
859b	14.2(g)	95
866	14.4(d)	78
866	14.4(d)	79
866(b)	14.1(b)	36
871	14.3(a)	1

CALIFORNIA PENAL CODE

Sec.	This Work Sec.	Note
872	14.4(b)	19
872	14.4(b)	22
872.5	14.4(b)	19
872.5	14.4(b)	20
909	15.4(b)	32
909	15.4(b)	53
910	15.4(b)	32
910	15.4(b)	51
910	15.4(b)	52
910	15.4(b)	53
913	8.4(c)	116
914	15.2(e)	128
917	8.8(a)	3
918	15.2(b)	28
934	15.2(e)	137
934	15.2(e)	140
936	8.4(b)	108
938.1(a)	15.2(i)	209
939.5	15.4(g)	148
939.5	15.4(g)	157
939.6	15.2(d)	94
939.6	15.5(c)	123
939.7	15.2(b)	29
939.7	15.7(f)	132
939.8	15.2(f)	149
939.71	15.7(f)	134
939.91	8.3(h)	37
954	17.1(a)	5
954	17.1(b)	20
954	17.1(c)	40
954	17.3(a)	5
954	17.3(d)	50
955	19.3(b)	161
960	19.1(d)	38
977(b)	24.2(a)	23
978.9	1.8(e)	94
987	11.2(a)	28
987	11.5(b)	23
987(c)	11.2(g)	303
987.8	11.2(h)	317
987.9	11.2(e)	170
995	15.5(c)	117
995(a)(2)(b)	14.3(d)	92
1004(4)	19.1(d)	55
1009	19.5(b)	42
1021	19.6(a)	6
1023	25.4(d)	45
1033	16.3(b)	15
1033	16.3(d)	50
1033(b)	16.3(f)	85
1043	24.2(a)	23
1043	24.2(b)	29
1054	20.2(b)	16

CALIFORNIA PENAL CODE

	This Work	
Sec.	Sec.	Note
1054.1	20.3(a)	10
1054.1	20.3(i)	161
1054.1	20.3	263
1054.2	20.1(c)	52
1054.2	20.3(h)	154
1054.3	20.5(f)	71
1054.3(a)	24.3(c)	92
1093(f)	24.8(a)	15
1127	24.6(e)	47
1170.12(b)(3)	26.6(b)	25
1181	24.11(d)	14
1192.7	1.6(h)	472
1192.7	21.1(g)	118
1200	26.4(g)	133
1202.4	26.6(c)	34
1202.4(a)(1)	26.6(c)	33
1203(e)	26.1(d)	79
1203.2(a)	26.1(f)	144
1203.09	26.1(d)	83
1238(a)(3)	27.3(d)	59
1238(a)(4)	27.3(d)	58
1238(a)(7)	27.3(d)	64
1238.5	1.7(f)	81
1240.1	11.7(e)	68
1247k	1.7(f)	81
1275	12.2(a)	4
1382	18.3(c)	72
1387	14.3(c)	76
1387	14.3(c)	79
1387(a)	14.3(c)	73
1405	24.11(d)	45
1473 et seq.	28.11(b)	13
1524	3.4(a)	22
1536	3.4(a)	22
1538.5(f)	14.4(b)	37
1538.5(h)	10.2(a)	8
1538.5(h)	27.3(d)	66
1538.5(i)	14.4(b)	43
1538.5(j)	14.4(b)	42
1538.5(p)	14.4(b)	42
2900.5	26.1(e)	123
2933(1)	26.2(c)	54
2933(a)	26.2(c)	55
2933(a)	26.2(c)	58
2960 to 2981	26.6(e)	80
3041.5(b)(2)	26.2(c)	50
5002	26.2(c)	54
8052	26.1(e)	98
13519.41	1.5(j)	327

CALIFORNIA RULES OF CIVIL PROCEDURE

	This Work	
Rule	Sec.	Note
170.3(a)	27.4(c)	35
170.6	22.4(d)	32

CALIFORNIA RULES OF EVIDENCE CODE ANNOTATED

	This Work	
Rule	Sec.	Note
300	14.4(b)	19
300	15.2(d)	94
300	15.5(c)	123
353	27.5(c)	91
1153	24.4(a)	6

CALIFORNIA RULES OF COURT

	This Work	
Rule	Sec.	Note
Tit. 2, § 411(a)	26.5(b)	38
4.1 et seq.	1.7(f)	74
4.421	26.3(d)	25
842	16.3(g)	106

CALIFORNIA RULES OF PROFESSIONAL CONDUCT

	This Work	
Rule	Sec.	Note
5-120	23.1(b)	11
5-120	23.1(b)	46

COLORADO CONSTITUTION

	This Work	
Art.	Sec.	Note
II, § 16	16.1(b)	92
II, § 16a	12.1(f)	69
II, § 16a	12.1(f)	75
II, § 16a	12.1(f)	88
II, § 16a	13.1(a)	25
II, § 16a	18.3(c)	123
II, § 16a	21.3(f)	302
II, § 19	12.3(b)	37
II, § 19	12.3(b)	42

COLORADO REVISED STATUTES

	This Work	
Sec.	Sec.	Note
13-2-108	1.7(f)	96
13-2-108	24.6(e)	47
13-4-108	28.11(b)	34
13.45-101	1.7(e)	69
13-71-104	15.4(d)	101
13-71-139	15.4(b)	29
13-71-139	15.4(b)	50
13-73-101 to 13-73-108	8.1(b)	16

COLORADO REVISED STATUTES

Sec.	This Work Sec.	Note
13-73-102	8.1(b)	17
13-76-106	15.4(a)	14
16-1-101	1.7(e)	59
16-2-101 et seq.	1.8(c)	18
16-2-101	1.8(c)	19
16-3-105	12.5(b)	20
16-3-308	3.1(c)	53
16-3-309	24.3(e)	126
16-5-01	11.2(a)	28
16-5-101	1.8(c)	30
16-5-204	8.3(a)	4
16-5-204	8.3(a)	5
16-5-204	8.6(a)	31
16-5-204	8.14(a)	20
16-5-204(3)(b)	15.2(b)	23
16-5-204(3)(e)	15.2(f)	148
16-5-204(4)	8.10(d)	100
16-5-204(4)	8.10(d)	101
16-5-204(4)	15.2(h)	193
16-5-204(4)(1)	15.2(c)	73
16-5-204(4)(d)	8.14(b)	24
16-5-204(4)(i)	8.8(f)	145
16-5-204(4)(j)	15.5(c)	117
16-5-204(4)(k)	15.5(c)	117
16-5-204(4)(*l*)	8.4(b)	87
16-5-204(4)(*l*)	15.2(c)	70
16-5-205	15.1(g)	344
16-5-205	15.1(g)	345
16-5-205(4)	8.3(h)	37
16-5-205(4)	8.3(h)	49
16-5-205.5	8.3(h)	49
16-5-207	12.5(a)	6
16-6-102	16.3(a)	3
16-6-103	16.3(a)	3
16-7-301	21.3(c)	202
16-8-103.5	20.5(c)	53
16-10-101	24.6(a)	7
16-10-202	19.6(b)	10
16-11-201(2)	26.1(d)	78
16-11-203	26.1(d)	86
16-12-102(1)	27.3(c)	32
16-12-102(1)	27.3(d)	59
16-12-102(2)	27.3(c)	48
16-55-501	11.2(a)	31
17-22.5-404	26.2(c)	33
17-71-101	1.7(e)	67
18-1-106	1.8(c)	16
18-1-201	16.4(c)	67
18-1-201	16.4(c)	87
18-1-201	16.4(c)	102
18-1-202(7)	16.1(f)	226
18-1-202(11)	16.1(g)	235

COLORADO REVISED STATUTES

Sec.	This Work Sec.	Note
18-1-405	18.3(c)	72
18-1-405	18.3(c)	75
18-1-405	18.3(c)	81
18-1-405	18.3(c)	95
18-1-405	18.3(c)	100
18-1-405	18.3(c)	106
18-1-405	18.3(c)	107
18-1-405	18.3(c)	108
18-1-411 to 18-1-416	24.11(d)	47
18-1-412	24.11(d)	43
18-1-709	5.2(b)	24
18-1-803	24.10(a)	11
21-1-103	11.2(a)	28
21-1-103	11.2(g)	300
24-4.1-302	12.1(f)	78
24-4.1-302	13.1(a)	25
24-4.1-302.5	12.1(f)	81
24-4.1-302.5	13.1(a)	21
24-4.1-302.5	13.1(a)	25
24-4.1-302.5	21.3(f)	366
24-4.1-303	21.3(f)	308
24-4.1-303	21.3(f)	317
24-4.1-303	21.3(f)	341
24-4.1-303	21.3(f)	347
24-4.1-303	21.3(f)	358

COLORADO RULES OF CRIMINAL PROCEDURE

Rule	This Work Sec.	Note
1	1.3(e)	37
1	1.7(f)	71
1	20.2(c)	42
4	1.8(c)	30
4.1	1.8(c)	30
5	14.4(c)	48
5(a)	14.2(e)	84
5(a)	14.3(a)	1
5(a)(4)	14.3(c)	62
5(a)(4)	14.4(b)	12
5(a)(4)(I)	14.2(f)	86
5(a)(4)(I)	14.2(f)	88
5(a)(4)(V)	14.3(c)	70
5(a)(4)(V)	14.3(c)	80
5(a)(5)	14.2(e)	66
6(b)	15.2(b)	20
6.1	8.7(e)	87
6.2(a)	8.5(c)	70
6.2(b)	8.14(b)	24
6.3	8.5(d)	118
6.5	8.4(b)	106
6.7(b)	8.3(h)	37

COLORADO RULES OF CRIMINAL PROCEDURE

Rule	This Work Sec.	Note
6.8	19.5(b)	4
6.9(b)(4)	8.5(d)	132
7(a)(2)(IV)	15.1(g)	360
7(c)(2)	14.3(c)	80
7(e)	19.5(b)	4
7(g)	19.4(b)	11
8	17.1(a)	4
8	17.1(b)	19
8	17.2(a)	5
8	17.4(c)	143
8	17.4(c)	153
8	17.4(c)	154
11(b)	1.8(c)	39
11(c)	1.8(c)	39
12(b)	19.1(d)	53
12(b)(3)	15.4(b)	61
13	17.3(a)	5
14	17.3(d)	49
15(I)(e)(1)	20.3(j)	198
16	20.2(b)	16
16, Pt. II(b)	20.5(h)	106
16(a)	20.3(a)	1
16(a)	20.3(i)	160
16(a)(1)(ii)	15.2(i)	212
16(a)(1)(vii)	20.3(h)	136
16(c)(1)	20.3(a)	21
16(e)(2)	20.3(h)	139
16(I)(a)(VII)	20.3(h)	136
16(I)(e)(2)	20.3(h)	136
16(II)(c)	20.5(e)	68
16(II)(d)	20.5(b)	15
16(II)(d)	20.5(b)	16
16(III)(d)	20.3(l)	227
16(III)(d)	20.3(l)	229
16(III)(g)	20.2(b)	19
16(III)(g)	20.6(a)	4
16(III)(g)	20.6(a)	5
16(IV)(C)	20.2(c)	57
18	16.1(c)	100
18	16.1(c)	106
18	16.1(d)	150
18	16.1(d)	153
18	16.1(f)	
18(a)(6)	16.1(f)	226
18(a)(b)	16.1(f)	225
21	16.3(a)	2
21	16.3(a)	3
21(a)	16.3(c)	27
21(b)	22.4(b)	18
32(b)	26.4(g)	133
33	24.11(d)	14

COLORADO RULES OF CRIMINAL PROCEDURE

Rule	This Work Sec.	Note
44	11.2(a)	28
44	11.2(g)	262
44(a)	11.3(b)	29
44(b)	11.9(b)	96

COLORADO RULES OF APPELLATE PROCEDURE

Rule	This Work Sec.	Note
4(b)(1)	28.11(b)	34
4.1(a)	27.3(c)	48

COLORADO RULES OF EVIDENCE

Rule	This Work Sec.	Note
804	14.1(d)	50
1101(d)	14.4(b)	5
1101(d)	14.4(b)	12
1101(d)(2)	15.2(d)	107
1101(d)(2)	15.5(c)	125

COLORADO RULES OF PROFESSIONAL CONDUCT

Rule	This Work Sec.	Note
3.8	1.7(j)	264
3.8(d)	15.7(f)	134

CONNECTICUT CONSTITUTION

Art.	This Work Sec.	Note
I, § 8	12.1(f)	69
I, § 8	12.3(b)	33
I, § 8	21.3(f)	302
I, § 8	21.3(f)	344
I, § 8	21.3(f)	365
I, § 9	2.12(a)	3

CONNECTICUT GENERAL STATUTES ANNOTATED

Sec.	This Work Sec.	Note
5-46a	14.4(b)	25
18-7a	26.2(c)	55
51-33(a)(a)	11.2(a)	24
51-296	11.2(a)	28
51-296	11.2(a)	32
51-296	11.2(b)	76
51-348	16.1(c)	99
51-352	16.1(c)	99

CONNECTICUT GENERAL STATUTES ANNOTATED

Sec.	This Work Sec.	Note
52-466 et seq. .... 28.11(b)		13
53a-15 .... 5.2(a)		4
53a-29 .... 26.1(d)		69
53a-29 .... 26.1(d)		70
53a-30(b) .... 26.9(a)		1
53a-40(g) .... 26.6(b)		23
53a-40(h) .... 26.6(b)		18
53a-61(a) .... 26.1(d)		83
54 to 96 .... 27.3(c)		56
54-1b .... 1.7(e)		59
54-46 .... 15.1(g)		344
54-46 .... 15.1(g)		345
54-46(a) .... 14.2(d)		48
54-46a .... 14.4(b)		19
54-46a .... 14.4(b)		20
54-46a .... 14.4(b)		27
54-46a .... 14.4(c)		63
54-46a .... 14.4(d)		78
54-46a .... 14.4(d)		79
54-47 .... 8.1(b)		21
54-47(a) to (h) .... 15.1(g)		346
54-47(e) .... 8.10(d)		114
54-47(f) .... 8.10(d)		101
54-47b to 54-47h .... 8.1(b)		19
54-47d .... 8.4(b)		82
54-47f(f) .... 15.7(f)		134
54-47g(f) .... 8.5(d)		132
54-57 .... 17.1(b)		20
54-60 .... 15.1(g)		345
54-82c .... 15.1(g)		345
54-82d .... 15.1(g)		345
54-82m .... 18.3(c)		72
54-82m .... 18.3(c)		106
54-82m .... 18.3(c)		109
54-84(b) .... 24.5(b)		21
54-85g .... 21.3(f)		408
54-86d .... 1.5(k)		400
54-91(a) .... 26.5(b)		37
54-91c .... 21.3(f)		368
54-91c .... 21.3(f)		381
54-91c .... 21.3(f)		389
54-91c .... 21.3(f)		409
54-91c .... 21.3(f)		410
54-102kk .... 24.11(d)		46
54-193 .... 15.1(g)		345
54-223 .... 21.3(f)		343
56-46(a) .... 14.4(b)		21
58-85a .... 24.4(d)		31
622 .... 19.1(d)		37

CONNECTICUT COURT RULES ANNOTATED

Rule	This Work Sec.	Note
Ch. 22, §§ 604 to 614 .... 15.1(g)		346

CONNECTICUT PRACTICE BOOK

Sec.	This Work Sec.	Note
Tit. 4, § 36-1 .... 1.7(f)		71
Tit. 4, § 36-13 .... 19.1(d)		40
Tit. 4, § 40-11 .... 20.3(d)		90
Tit. 4, § 40-13 .... 20.3(i)		159
Tit. 4, § 40-15 .... 20.3(b)		40
Tit. 4, § 40-26(1) .... 20.4(b)		24
Tit. 4, § 40-26(1) .... 20.5(g)		90
Tit. 4, § 41-10 .... 19.3(d)		205
Tit. 4, § 41-21 .... 19.4(b)		19
641 .... 11.2(a)		28
959 .... 11.2(a)		28
960 .... 11.2(a)		28
961 .... 11.3(b)		42
961 .... 11.5(c)		45
967 .... 24.2(e)		71

CONNECTICUT RULES OF APPELLATE PROCEDURE

Rule	This Work Sec.	Note
80-1 .... 28.11(b)		34

CONNECTICUT RULES OF CRIMINAL PROCEDURE

Rule	This Work Sec.	Note
865 .... 24.9(d)		43

CONNECTICUT SUPEREME COURT CRIMINAL RULES

Rule	This Work Sec.	Note
36-13 .... 19.1(d)		40
40-1 to 40-43 .... 20.2(b)		16
40-11 .... 20.3(d)		90
40-13 .... 20.3(i)		159
40-15 .... 20.3(b)		40
40-26 .... 20.4(b)		24
40-26 .... 20.5(g)		90
40-26(1) .... 20.5(g)		89
41-10 .... 19.3(d)		205
41-21 .... 19.4(b)		19
641 .... 11.2(a)		27

DELAWARE CONSTITUTION

Art.	This Work Sec.	Note
I, § 8	15.1(d)	181
I, § 8	15.1(d)	201
I, § 8	15.1(d)	218
I, § 8	15.1(f)	270
I, § 12	12.3(b)	33

DELAWARE CODE

Tit.	This Work Sec.	Note
10, § 4320 to 4326	8.6(b)	33
10, § 4507(c)(2)	15.4(g)	151
10, § 4508(a)	15.4(f)	144
10, § 9902(b)	27.3(c)	40
10, § 43507(c)(2)	15.4(g)	158
11, Pt. II	1.8(c)	21
11, § 232	16.1(g)	271
11, § 232	16.4(d)	131
11, § 432	5.1(c)	17
11, § 432	5.2(a)	4
11, § 905	21.3(f)	317
11, § 1509	8.1(c)	33
11, § 1509	8.1(c)	35
11, § 1701	1.7(e)	59
11, § 1907	1.8(c)	29
11, § 2701	16.1(a)	25
11, § 2732	16.1(e)	177
11, § 3102	19.1(d)	36
11, § 3103	19.1(d)	36
11, § 3104	19.1(d)	36
11, § 3105	19.1(d)	36
11, § 3106	19.1(d)	36
11, § 3506	8.11(d)	77
11, § 4209(d)	26.2(b)	7
11, § 4215(b)	26.6(b)	8
11, § 4504	24.11(d)	40
11, § 5103	11.2(a)	28
11, § 5106	21.3(f)	355
11, § 9405	13.1(a)	23
11, § 9405	21.3(f)	314
11, § 9405	21.3(f)	329
11, § 9405	21.3(f)	341
11, § 9407	1.5(k)	408
29, § 4602	11.2(a)	28

DELAWARE SUPERIOR COURT OF CIVIL RULES

Rule	This Work Sec.	Note
35(a)	1.3(e)	39

DELAWARE SUPERIOR COURT OF CRIMINAL RULES

Rule	This Work Sec.	Note
1	1.3(e)	37
1	1.7(f)	71
4	12.5(a)	4
5	14.2(c)	36
5	14.2(c)	38
5(d)	14.2(f)	86
5(d)	14.2(f)	88
5.1	14.3(a)	1
5.1	14.4(b)	13
5.2	14.4(b)	14
6(b)	15.4(f)	147
6(e)	8.5(b)	42
6(e)	15.2(i)	216
6(e)(3)(A)	8.5(e)	164
6(e)(3)(A)	8.5(e)	197
6(e)(3)(A)(ii)	8.5(e)	165
7(a)	15.1(d)	181
7(b)	15.1(f)	295
7(b)	15.1(f)	318
7(b)	15.1(f)	326
7(c)	19.1(d)	40
7(e)	19.5(b)	4
8	17.1(a)	4
8	17.1(b)	19
12(2)	19.1(d)	53
12.2	20.5(c)	31
12.2(c)	20.5(c)	48
12.2(c)	20.5(c)	49
12.2(c)	27.3(d)	66
12.2(d)	20.5(c)	34
12.2(d)	20.5(c)	38
12.2(e)	20.5(c)	51
13	17.3(a)	5
15	1.8(c)	23
15	1.8(c)	34
16	20.2(b)	16
16(a)(1)	20.3(a)	9
16(b)(2)	20.5(e)	69
16(b)(2)	20.5(g)	95
16(c)	20.4(g)	102
16(d)(1)	20.3(l)	226
16(d)(1)	20.3(l)	232
17	8.4(b)	23
17.1	20.2(d)	68
18	16.1(c)	100
18	16.1(c)	106
21	16.3(b)	15
21	16.3(g)	98
21(b)	16.3(c)	27
24	1.3(e)	40
24(b)	1.8(c)	23

DELAWARE SUPERIOR COURT OF CRIMINAL RULES

Rule	This Work Sec.	Note
25	22.4(e)	48
26.2	14.4(c)	65
29(c)	24.6(b)	16
32(c)	1.8(c)	23
32(c)	1.8(c)	40
43(b)(2)	24.2(c)	35
43(c)(2)	24.2(a)	16
44	11.2(a)	28
44(c)	11.9(b)	96
44(d)	1.3(e)	40
48	18.3(c)	69
48	18.3(c)	88

DELAWARE SUPERIOR COURT RULES OF CRIMINAL PROCEDURE

Rule	This Work Sec.	Note
6(b)	15.4(b)	28
6(b)	15.4(b)	46
7(a)	15.1(d)	247
7(b)	15.1(f)	286
8	17.2(a)	3
14	17.3(d)	49
16(a)(2)	20.3(i)	167
18	16.1(f)	225

DELAWARE RULES PROFFESSIONAL CONDUCT

Rule	This Work Sec.	Note
3.8	23.1(b)	46

DELAWARE UNIFORM RULES OF EVIDENCE

Rule	This Work Sec.	Note
1101(c)	14.4(b)	9
1101(d)(2)	15.2(d)	107

DISTRICT OF COLUMBIA CODE

Sec.	This Work Sec.	Note
11-2601	11.2(a)	28
11-2602	11.2(a)	30
22-3204(b)	26.1(d)	74
23-101	1.7(e)	59
23-106	24.3(f)	143
23-112	26.3(f)	56
23-301	15.1(d)	178
23-561	12.5(a)	3
23-561	12.5(b)	19

DISTRICT OF COLUMBIA CODE

Sec.	This Work Sec.	Note
23-1322(a)(1)	12.3(a)	10
23-1322(a)(2)	12.3(a)	15
23-1322(a)(3)	12.3(a)	16
23-1322(b)(2)(B)	12.3(a)	9
23-1322(b)(2)(C)	12.3(a)	12
23-1322(d)	12.3(a)	8
23-1323	12.3(a)	14
23-1328	26.3(f)	64
23-1331(3)	12.3(a)	11
23-1331(4)	12.3(a)	13

DISTRICT OF COLUMBIA RULES OF CRIMINAL PROCEDURE

Rule	This Work Sec.	Note
12.1	20.2(b)	16
12.2	20.2(b)	16
16	20.2(b)	16

DISTRICT OF COLUMBIA RULES OF PROFESSIONAL CONDUCT

Rule	This Work Sec.	Note
3.3(b)	24.3(d)	109

DISTRICT OF COLUMBIA SUPERIOR COURT RULES OF CRIMINAL PROCEDURE

Rule	This Work Sec.	Note
1	1.7(f)	71
7(b)	15.1(f)	286
7(b)	15.1(f)	318
23(c)	24.6(a)	11
44	11.2(a)	28
48	18.3(c)	69
48	18.3(c)	88
114	1.8(c)	15

FLORIDA CONSTITUTION

Art.	This Work Sec.	Note
I, § 12	2.12(a)	69
I, § 14	12.3(b)	37
I, § 14	12.3(b)	38
I, § 15	15.1(e)	262
I, § 15(a)	15.1(e)	258
I, § 15(a)	15.1(f)	288
I, § 16	21.3(f)	371
I, § 16	21.3(f)	388
I, § 16(b)	12.1(f)	69
I, § 16(b)	12.1(f)	76
I, § 16(b)	12.1(f)	81

FLORIDA CONSTITUTION

Art.	This Work Sec.	Note
I, § 16(b)	12.1(f)	88
I, § 16(b)	12.1(f)	91
I, § 16(b)	21.3(f)	302
I, § 16(b)	24.4(d)	55
I, § 23	2.12(b)	87
V, § 2	1.7(f)	91
V, § 2	1.7(f)	95
V, § 4 to 6	27.1(a)	5

FLORIDA STATUTES ANNOTATED

Sec.	This Work Sec.	Note
27.03	8.4(b)	28
27.04	8.1(c)	33
27.04	8.1(c)	35
27.52	11.2(g)	274
27.52	11.2(g)	299
27.52(1)(f)	11.2(g)	286
27.52(2)	11.2(g)	281
27.52(2)	11.2(g)	298
27.52(2)(b)	11.2(g)	267
27.52(3)	11.2(g)	266
34.13	1.8(c)	21
90.106	24.6(e)	47
90.404(2)(1)	20.2(d)	70
90.410	24.4(a)	6
90.804	14.1(d)	50
775.08	1.8(c)	12
775.08(1)	1.8(c)	13
775.084(1)(a)(2)	26.6(b)	24
775.084(1)(a)(4)	26.6(b)	23
775.084(3)(a)(2)	26.6(b)	8
775.089(7)	26.6(c)	38
777.201	5.2(b)	24
893.135	26.3(e)	30
900.01	1.7(e)	59
901.18	1.8(f)	102
901.25	1.8(f)	102
902.02	12.5(a)	6
905.02	15.4(b)	34
905.03	15.4(f)	143
905.04(1)(b)	15.4(g)	157
905.05	15.4(b)	27
905.05	15.4(b)	34
905.05	15.4(b)	41
905.05	15.4(b)	47
905.075	15.4(g)	155
905.16	8.4(b)	82
905.16	8.8(a)	3
905.18	15.2(e)	137
905.185	8.4(b)	19
905.19	8.4(b)	28

FLORIDA STATUTES ANNOTATED

Art.	This Work Sec.	Note
905.20	15.2(b)	20
905.27	8.5(b)	43
905.27	8.5(c)	70
905.27	8.5(e)	166
905.27(2)	8.5(b)	19
905.28(a)	8.3(h)	52
905.34	8.1(b)	18
905.34	15.2(b)	28
905.41	15.1(e)	264
910.02	16.1(e)	174
910.03	16.1(b)	35
910.03	16.1(e)	175
910.03	16.3(a)	3
910.03(2)	16.3(g)	116
910.03(3)	23.2(c)	59
910.03(3)	23.2(c)	60
910.05	16.4(c)	80
910.05	16.4(c)	87
910.10	16.1(e)	179
914.04	8.3(e)	26
914.04	8.11(d)	71
918.17	1.5(k)	413
921.141	26.2(b)	7
921.143(1)(a)	26.5(d)	69
924.051	27.5(c)	91
924.07	27.3(d)	61
924.07(1)(c)	27.3(d)	58
924.071	27.3(c)	34
924.071(2)	12.4(e)	91
924.34	25.4(b)	19
925.11	24.11(d)	41
925.11	24.11(d)	47
932.61	1.8(d)	71
938.29	11.2(h)	316
939.06	1.5(f)	248
944.275	26.2(c)	54
944.275(1)	26.2(c)	58
948.01(1)	26.1(d)	77
958.07	26.5(c)	45

FLORIDA RULES OF CRIMINAL PROCEDURE

Rule	This Work Sec.	Note
3.01	20.2(c)	42
3.010	1.7(f)	71
3.111	11.2(a)	28
3.111	11.2(a)	32
3.111	11.2(b)	81
3.111	11.2(b)	82
3.111	11.2(g)	263
3.111	11.3(b)	53

FLORIDA RULES OF CRIMINAL PROCEDURE

Rule	This Work Sec.	Note
3.111(2)	11.2(a)	35
3.111(b)(4)	11.2(g)	269
3.111(d)	11.3(b)	37
3.111(d)(5)	11.3(a)	18
3.112	1.8(e)	93
3.125	12.5(b)	21
3.131	1.7(f)	72
3.133	14.1(a)	1
3.133	14.2(d)	62
3.133	14.3(a)	1
3.133(6)	14.2(d)	47
3.140	15.1(e)	258
3.140	15.1(e)	263
3.140	15.1(e)	264
3.140	15.1(e)	267
3.140	15.1(f)	288
3.140	19.4(b)	13
3.140	19.5(c)	48
3.140	19.5(c)	50
3.140(a)(2)	15.1(e)	268
3.140(n)	19.4(b)	19
3.150	17.1(a)	4
3.150	17.1(b)	21
3.150	17.2(a)	7
3.151	17.4(c)	143
3.151	17.4(c)	152
3.151	17.4(c)	154
3.151	17.4(c)	156
3.152	17.3(d)	51
3.170	1.8(c)	37
3.170	21.3(c)	203
3.180(a)(3)	24.2(a)	23
3.190	19.1(d)	55
3.190(c)	14.2(d)	64
3.190(c)	15.4(b)	74
3.191	1.7(f)	72
3.191	1.8(c)	38
3.191	18.3(c)	72
3.191	18.3(c)	75
3.191	18.3(c)	79
3.191	18.3(c)	84
3.191	18.3(c)	91
3.191	18.3(c)	98
3.191	18.3(c)	100
3.191	18.3(c)	106
3.191	18.3(c)	107
3.191	18.3(c)	108
3.200	20.2(c)	53
3.200	20.2(c)	54
3.200	20.5(b)	15
3.200	20.5(b)	16

FLORIDA RULES OF CRIMINAL PROCEDURE

Rule	This Work Sec.	Note
3.200	20.5(b)	19
3.200	20.6(a)	14
3.200	20.6(c)	88
3.220	1.3(f)	67
3.220	1.3(f)	70
3.220	20.2(b)	13
3.220	20.2(b)	16
3.220	20.2(b)	34
3.220	20.2(c)	47
3.220	20.2(e)	87
3.220	20.3(b)	31
3.220	20.3(b)	62
3.220	20.3(g)	119
3.220	20.3(k)	222
3.220	20.4(g)	100
3.220(1)(1)	20.3(l)	227
3.220(a)	20.2(c)	50
3.220(b)	20.2(e)	103
3.220(b)	20.3(k)	222
3.220(b)(1)(A)	20.3(h)	139
3.220(b)(1)(A)(i)	20.3(h)	143
3.220(b)(1)(B)	20.3(b)	41
3.220(b)(1)(B)	20.3(k)	214
3.220(b)(1)(B)(i)	20.5(f)	71
3.220(b)(1)(C)	20.3(c)	70
3.220(b)(1)(C)	20.3(k)	214
3.220(b)(1)(E)	20.3(i)	160
3.220(b)(1)(G)	20.3(h)	139
3.220(b)(4)	20.4(g)	101
3.220(d)	20.2(b)	41
3.220(d)	20.4(g)	104
3.220(d)	20.5(g)	91
3.220(d)	20.5(h)	106
3.220(d)	24.3(c)	92
3.220(d)(1)(A)	20.5(e)	64
3.220(d)(1)(A)	20.5(e)	66
3.220(f)	20.2(b)	21
3.220(f)	20.3(b)	32
3.220(f)	20.5(h)	107
3.220(h)	20.2(e)	82
3.220(h)(1)	20.2(e)	89
3.220(h)(1)(c)	20.2(e)	92
3.220(h)(7)	20.2(e)	95
3.220(m)(1)	20.2(c)	55
3.240	16.3(a)	3
3.240	16.3(b)	8
3.240	16.3(d)	52
3.281	22.3(b)	60
3.510	24.8(f)	100
3.600	24.11(a)	1
3.800(b)	26.3(g)	95

FLORIDA RULES OF CRIMINAL PROCEDURE

	This Work	
Rule	Sec.	Note
3.985	24.8(c)	42

FLORIDA RULES OF APPELLATE PROCEDURE

	This Work	
Rule	Sec.	Note
9	27.3(c)	39
140(c)	27.3(c)	39

FLORIDA RULES OF JUDICIAL ADMINISTRATION

	This Work	
Rule	Sec.	Note
2.160	22.4(b)	18
2.170	23.3(b)	18

FLORIDA RULES OF EVIDENCE

	This Work	
Rule	Sec.	Note
99.616	24.4(d)	55

FLORIDA RULES OF PROFESSIONAL CONDUCT

	This Work	
Rule	Sec.	Note
4-3.5	24.9(g)	129
4-3.6	23.1(b)	14

GEORGIA CONSTITUTION

	This Work	
Art.	Sec.	Note
I, § 1, ¶ XVII	12.3(b)	31
VI	1.7(f)	89
VI, § 2, ¶ VIII	16.3(a)	4
VI, § 5	27.1(a)	5
IX, ¶ 1	1.7(f)	89

GEORGIA CODE ANNOTATED

	This Work	
Sec.	Sec.	Note
5	27.3(c)	21
5-5-41	24.11(d)	41
5-5-41	24.11(d)	45
5-6-34(b)	27.2(b)	17
5-7-2	27.3(c)	56
5-7-5	12.4(e)	89
13-1-8	16.4(c)	95
15-1-8	22.4(b)	18
15-8-6	15.2(e)	140
15-12-40(a)(2)	15.4(c)	95

GEORGIA CODE ANNOTATED

	This Work	
Sec.	Sec.	Note
15-12-40(b)(1)	15.4(c)	95
15-12-70	15.4(g)	155
15-18-40	1.7(j)	217
16-1-7	17.4(c)	143
16-1-7	17.4(c)	152
16-1-7	17.4(c)	153
16-1-7	17.4(c)	157
16-3-25	5.2(a)	4
16-16-5	20.2(b)	16
17	1.4(f)	124
17-1-1	1.7(e)	59
17-2-1	16.4(c)	80
17-2-2	16.1(b)	35
17-2-2	16.1(c)	105
17-2-2	16.1(e)	170
17-2-2	16.1(e)	173
17-2-2	16.1(e)	177
17-2-2(e)	16.1(e)	174
17-6-1	12.3(b)	51
17-6-4(a)(1)	20.3(c)	70
17-6-5	20.4(c)	46
17-7-20	14.1(a)	1
17-7-28	14.4(b)	6
17-7-51	15.1(d)	254
17-7-53	15.2(h)	191
17-7-53	15.2(h)	193
17-7-53	15.2(h)	194
17-7-70	15.1(f)	285
17-7-70	15.1(f)	295
17-7-70	15.1(f)	306
17-7-70	15.1(f)	326
17-7-70(a)	15.1(d)	182
17-7-71	19.1(d)	40
17-7-71(a)(1)	27.3(c)	21
17-7-150	16.3(b)	10
17-7-150	16.3(d)	50
17-7-150	16.3(f)	84
17-7-150(a)(1)	16.3(b)	18
17-7-170	18.3(c)	71
17-7-170	18.3(c)	89
17-7-170	18.3(c)	106
17-7-170	18.3(c)	108
17-8-57	27.5(d)	119
17-9-1	24.11(a)	1
17-10-1.1	21.3(f)	393
17-10-1.1	21.3(f)	394
17-10-7	26.6(b)	5
17-10-7	26.6(b)	10
17-12-2	11.2(g)	266
17-12-23	11.2(a)	28
17-12-23	11.2(a)	30
17-16-1(2)	20.3(b)	39

GEORGIA CODE ANNOTATED

Sec.	This Work Sec.	Note
17-16-1(2)	20.3(b)	40
17-16-2(a)	20.2(c)	44
17-16-4	20.2(b)	16
17-16-4	20.3(c)	68
17-16-4	20.3(f)	99
17-16-4	20.4(g)	99
17-16-4(a)	20.3(g)	119
17-16-14	20.3(c)	84
17-16-23(b)	20.3(f)	111
17-17-1	13.1(a)	23
17-17-1	21.3(f)	315
17-17-1	21.3(f)	320
24-4-6	24.6(c)	39
24-9-28	8.11(b)	17
24-9-61	24.4(d)	31
26-301	16.4(c)	67
42-9-42	26.2(c)	37

GEORGIA CODE OF PROFESSIONAL RESPONSIBILITY

Sec.	This Work Sec.	Note
DR 7-107	23.1(b)	19

GEORGIA UNIFORM SUPREME COURT RULES

Rule	This Work Sec.	Note
33.3	21.3(c)	202

HAWAII CONSTITUTION

Art.	This Work Sec.	Note
I, § 6	2.12(b)	87
I, § 10	14.2(d)	60
I, § 10	15.1(g)	344
I, § 10	15.1(g)	358
I, § 11	1.3(g)	87
I, § 11	15.2(e)	126
I, § 12	12.3(b)	31
I, § 14	16.1(b)	92

HAWAII REVISED STATUTES

Sec.	This Work Sec.	Note
28-2.5	8.1(c)	33
601-7	22.4(b)	18
603-1	16.1(c)	99
604-8	15.1(g)	358
612-23	15.4(b)	71
612-23(a)	15.4(f)	144

HAWAII REVISED STATUTES

Sec.	This Work Sec.	Note
641-13	27.3(c)	40
641-13(7)	27.3(c)	33
641-13(8)	27.3(c)	33
641-13(8)	27.3(c)	54
660	28.11(b)	13
701-106	16.4(c)	76
701-106	16.4(c)	82
701-106	16.4(c)	101
701-106	16.4(c)	111
701-106(2)	16.4(c)	81
701-109(1)	24.8(e)	77
701-109(2)	16.1(f)	220
701-109(5)	24.8(f)	120
701-114	16.1(g)	270
701-114	16.4(d)	123
701-114	16.4(d)	131
701-115	16.1(g)	270
701-115	16.4(d)	131
702-237	5.1(c)	17
702-237	5.2(b)	24
706-601(1)(a)	26.5(b)	35
706-606	26.3(f)	58
706-606.5(7)(b)	26.6(b)	26
706-620(5)	26.1(d)	83
706-624	26.9(a)	4
706-662(3)	26.6(e)	81
706-668.5	26.3(f)	58
706-670(3)(a)	26.2(c)	49
801-1	1.7(e)	59
801D-4	13.1(a)	23
801D-4	21.3(f)	310
801D-4	21.3(f)	317
802-1	11.2(a)	28
802-3	11.2(a)	28
802-4	11.2(g)	299
802-4	11.2(g)	300
802-4	11.2(g)	302
803-6	12.5(b)	20
804-3	12.3(b)	51
805-3	12.5(a)	5
806-6	15.1(g)	344
806-6	15.1(g)	345
844D-121	24.11(d)	44
844D-121	24.11(d)	47

HAWAII RULES OF CRIMINAL PROCEDURE

Rule	This Work Sec.	Note
6(c)	15.4(a)	16
6(e)	8.5(b)	42
16(b)(2)(iii)	20.3(i)	176

HAWAII RULES OF DISTRICT COURT

	This Work	
Rule	Sec.	Note
33	1.8(c)	33

HAWAII RULES OF EVIDENCE

	This Work	
Rule	Sec.	Note
1101(d)(2)	15.2(d)	107
1101(d)(2)	15.5(c)	125

HAWAII RULES OF PENAL PROCEDURE

	This Work	
Rule	Sec.	Note
1	1.3(e)	37
1	1.7(f)	71
5(b)	14.2(e)	67
5(c)	14.2(f)	86
5(c)	14.4(b)	14
5(c)(1)	14.2(d)	50
5(c)(2)	14.3(a)	5
5(c)(2)	14.3(a)	13
5(c)(4)	14.4(b)	13
5(c)(4)	14.4(c)	48
5(c)(6)	14.3(a)	1
6(b)(2)	15.4(b)	44
6(d)	15.2(j)	243
6(e)	8.5(e)	162
6(e)(2)	15.2(i)	209
6(e)(2)	15.2(i)	213
7(f)	19.5(b)	4
8	17.1(a)	4
8	17.1(b)	19
8	17.2(a)	6
8	17.4(c)	143
8	17.4(c)	156
8	17.4(c)	157
12.1	20.2(b)	16
12.1	20.4(a)	7
12.1	20.5(b)	15
12.1	20.5(b)	18
12.1(a)	20.4(c)	49
12.1(a)	20.5(b)	13
12.1(b)	20.4(a)	5
14	17.3(d)	49
16	1.8(c)	33
16	20.2(b)	16
16(a)	20.2(c)	44
16(b)	20.3(b)	40
16(b)	20.3(j)	199
16(b)(1)	20.3(a)	1
16(b)(1)	20.3(g)	121
16(b)(1)(I)	20.3(h)	141
16(b)(2)	20.3(a)	3

HAWAII RULES OF PENAL PROCEDURE

	This Work	
Rule	Sec.	Note
16(b)(2)	20.3(a)	4
16(b)(2)	20.3(a)	21
16(c)(2)	20.4(g)	99
16(c)(2)	20.5(e)	64
16(c)(2)	20.5(e)	65
16(c)(3)	20.5(d)	58
16(c)(3)	20.5(d)	59
16(d)	20.3(b)	32
16(e)(4)	20.3(l)	227
16(e)(5)(i)	20.3(j)	198
16.1	20.2(c)	44
17	8.4(b)	23
18	16.1(c)	99
18	16.1(c)	100
48	18.3(c)	72
48	18.3(c)	75
48	18.3(c)	78
48	18.3(c)	79
48	18.3(c)	81
48	18.3(c)	95
48	18.3(c)	100
48	18.3(c)	106
48	18.3(c)	112
138	17.3(a)	5

IDAHO CONSTITUTION

	This Work	
Art.	Sec.	Note
I, § 6	12.3(b)	33
I, § 8	15.1(g)	344
I, § 8	15.1(g)	345
I, § 10	15.1(g)	358
I, § 13	16.1(c)	102
I, § 17	12.3(b)	36
I, § 17	12.3(e)	118
I, § 22	12.1(f)	69
I, § 22	12.1(f)	73
I, § 22	12.1(f)	81
I, § 22	12.1(f)	92
I, § 22	13.1(a)	25
I, § 22	21.3(f)	302
I, § 22	21.3(f)	339
I, § 22	21.3(f)	342
I, § 22	21.3(f)	364
I, § 22	21.3(f)	376

IDAHO CODE

	This Work	
Sec.	Sec.	Note
1-212	1.7(f)	96
2-213	15.4(b)	71
18-111	1.8(c)	10

IDAHO CODE

Sec.	This Work Sec.	Note
18-113	1.8(c)	16
18-8004	26.2(b)	6
19-101	1.7(e)	59
19-146	19.1(d)	64
19-301	16.1(g)	239
19-301	16.1(g)	264
19-301	16.1(g)	267
19-302	16.4(c)	96
19-304	16.1(d)	150
19-304	16.1(f)	225
19-304(3)	16.1(e)	175
19-305	16.1(e)	170
19-305	16.1(e)	171
19-310	16.1(e)	183
19-310	16.1(e)	200
19-311	16.4(c)	74
19-312	16.1(e)	177
19-851	11.2(a)	28
19-852	11.2(a)	28
19-852	11.2(b)	76
19-852(a)	11.1(d)	129
19-852(c)	11.2(b)	81
19-854	11.2(g)	258
19-854	11.2(g)	299
19-854(b)	11.2(g)	295
19-857	11.3(b)	37
19-1003(e)(7)	15.4(g)	157
19-1101	8.8(a)	3
19-1101	15.1(g)	358
19-1102	15.1(g)	358
19-1105	15.2(d)	96
19-1105	15.5(c)	123
19-1106	15.2(b)	29
19-1108	8.4(b)	77
19-1108	15.2(b)	20
19-1115	8.11(d)	77
19-1433	19.3(a)	16
19-1816(a)	23.2(c)	59
19-1816(a)	23.2(c)	60
19-1816(a)	23.2(c)	61
19-2101	24.8(a)	15
19-2132(b)(1)	24.8(f)	116
19-2306	24.10(a)	1
19-2406	24.11(a)	1
19-2515	26.2(b)	5
19-2515(3)(b)	26.2(b)	6
19-2515(9)(i)	26.6(e)	77
19-3004	8.4(b)	40
19-3008	24.3(f)	144
19-3501	18.3(c)	72
19-3501	18.3(c)	95
19-4901 to 19-4911	28.11(b)	22

IDAHO CODE

Sec.	This Work Sec.	Note
19-4902	24.11(d)	40
19-4902	24.11(d)	47
19-5306	12.1(f)	68
19-5306	13.1(a)	20
19-5306	21.3(f)	301
19-5306	21.3(f)	309
19-5306	21.3(f)	327

IDAHO RULES OF CRIMINAL PROCEDURE

Rule	This Work Sec.	Note
1	1.3(e)	37
1	1.7(f)	71
2.14(a)(2)	20.3(d)	88
4	12.5(a)	6
5(f)(5)	14.2(e)	71
5.1	14.2(d)	50
5.1	14.2(e)	67
5.1	14.3(a)	37
5.1	14.4(b)	21
5.1	14.4(b)	37
5.1	14.4(d)	80
5.1(b)	14.3(a)	2
5.1(b)	14.4(b)	19
5.1(b)	14.4(b)	27
5.1(b)	14.4(b)	28
6(b)	15.4(b)	28
6(b)	15.4(b)	46
6(b)(2)	15.4(g)	165
6.1	8.10(d)	101
6.1(d)(9)	8.10(d)	114
6.1(d)(9)	8.10(d)	115
6.4	8.5(b)	43
6.4(c)	8.5(c)	70
6.4(c)	8.5(e)	166
6.6(a)	14.3(a)	37
6.6(a)	15.2(f)	149
7(b)	19.1(d)	40
7(e)	19.5(b)	5
8	17.1(a)	4
8	17.1(b)	21
10	11.2(a)	28
10(b)	11.3(b)	29
12.1	20.2(b)	16
13	17.3(a)	5
14	17.3(d)	49
15(a)	20.2(e)	84
16	1.3(e)	40
16	20.2(b)	16
16	20.2(b)	32
16	20.3(a)	2
16(a)	20.3(c)	81

IDAHO RULES OF CRIMINAL PROCEDURE

Rule	This Work Sec.	Note
16(a)	20.3	262
16(b)	20.3(i)	159
16(b)	20.3(k)	222
16(b)(1)	20.3(a)	10
16(b)(1)	20.3(c)	70
18	20.2(d)	68
21	16.3(a)	2
21(a)	16.3(d)	52
21(a)	16.3(e)	79
21(b)	16.3(c)	27
25(a)	22.4(d)	32
25(a)(1)	22.4(d)	44
25.1	22.4(e)	48
32(g)	26.5(c)	50
43(b)(2)	24.2(c)	35
44	11.2(a)	28

IDAHO RULES OF EVIDENCE

Rule	This Work Sec.	Note
1101(d)	14.4(b)	19

ILLINOIS CONSTITUTION

Art.	This Work Sec.	Note
I, § 6	2.12(b)	89
I, § 7	14.2(d)	60
I, § 8	16.1(b)	91
I, § 8	22.2(e)	103
I, § 8.1	12.1(f)	69
I, § 8.1	21.3(f)	302
I, § 8.1	21.3(f)	344
I, § 8.1	26.5(d)	62
I, § 9	12.3(b)	37
I, § 9	12.3(b)	38
I, § 9	12.3(e)	119
VI, § 6	27.1(a)	5

ILLINOIS COMPILED STATUTES

Ch.	This Work Sec.	Note
38, § 5/111-3	19.1(d)	40
38, § 5/112-6(c)	8.5(e)	164
65, § 5/1-2-1.1	1.8(d)	70
705, § 305/01	1.7(e)	67
705, § 305/19	15.1(g)	359
705, § 305/19	15.2(b)	20
720	26.6(d)	46
720, § 5/1-5	16.4(c)	95
720, § 5/1-6(c)	16.1(e)	169
720, § 5/1/b	16.1(e)	173

ILLINOIS COMPILED STATUTES

Ch.	This Work Sec.	Note
720, § 5/3-3	17.4(c)	143
720, § 5/3-3	17.4(c)	152
720, § 5/3-3	17.4(c)	153
720, § 5/3-3(b)	17.4(c)	150
720, § 5/7-12	5.2(a)	4
720, § 5/11-20.1A	26.6(d)	46
720, § 5/11-20.1A(b)(1)	26.6(d)	55
720, § 5/14-5	3.1(e)	128
720, § 5/114-1	16.1(g)	236
725	11.7(e)	68
725	27.3(d)	67
725, § 5/10-101	1.7(e)	69
725, § 5/100-1	1.7(e)	59
725, § 5/103-2.1(b)	6.8(c)	64
725, § 5/103-5	18.3(c)	72
725, § 5/103-5	18.3(c)	86
725, § 5/103-5	18.3(c)	100
725, § 5/103-5	18.3(c)	115
725, § 5/103-6	22.1(b)	57
725, § 5/107-11	12.5(a)	4
725, § 5/107-11	12.5(b)	19
725, § 5/107A-5	1.5(e)	234
725, § 5/109-3	14.2(e)	84
725, § 5/109-3.1	14.2(d)	50
725, § 5/109-3.1	14.2(f)	86
725, § 5/111-2(a)	15.1(g)	344
725, § 5/111-2(a)	15.1(g)	345
725, § 5/111-2(f)	14.3(d)	89
725, § 5/111-4	17.1(a)	4
725, § 5/111-4	17.1(b)	21
725, § 5/111-4	17.2(a)	5
725, § 5/111-5	19.5(c)	48
725, § 5/111-5	19.5(c)	50
725, § 5/111-6	19.4(b)	13
725, § 5/112-4	8.10(c)	62
725, § 5/112-4	14.3(c)	68
725, § 5/112-4	15.2(f)	148
725, § 5/112-4(a)	8.4(b)	29
725, § 5/112-4(b)	8.10(d)	101
725, § 5/112-4(d)	15.1(g)	359
725, § 5/112-5	8.4(b)	106
725, § 5/112-6(c)	8.5(c)	70
725, § 5/112-7	15.2(j)	244
725, § 5/113-3	11.2(a)	27
725, § 5/113-3	11.2(a)	28
725, § 5/113-3	11.2(e)	217
725, § 5/114	15.6(d)	108
725, § 5/114-1(a)(4)	15.4(b)	45
725, § 5/114-1(a)(4)	15.4(f)	144
725, § 5/114-3	22.2(f)	119
725, § 5/114-6	16.3(b)	17
725, § 5/114-6(c)	16.3(g)	97

ILLINOIS COMPILED STATUTES

Ch.	This Work Sec.	Note
725, § 5/114-7	17.3(a)	5
725, § 5/114-12	27.3(d)	67
725, § 5/114-13	20.2(b)	16
725, § 5/115-11	24.1(b)	25
725, § 5/116-3	24.11(d)	47
725, § 5/116-3(a)	24.11(d)	39
725, § 5/121-13	11.7(e)	68
725, § 120/4	21.3(f)	318
725, § 120/4	21.3(f)	330
725, § 120/4	21.3(f)	331
725, § 120/4.5	13.1(a)	23
725, § 215/3	8.1(b)	18
729, § 5/1-6(a)	16.1(g)	235
730, § 5/3-3-3	26.2(c)	32
730, § 5/3-6-3(a)(2)(i)	26.2(c)	55
730, § 5/5-4-1	26.4(g)	133
730, § 5/5-5-4	26.8(b)	15
730, § 5/5-6-1	26.1(d)	69
730, § 5/5-6-3	26.9(a)	2
730, § 5/5-8A-4(A)(5)	26.1(e)	121
735	1.7(e)	69
740, § 147/25	16.1(f)	225
750, § 5/1-6(r)	16.1(e)	185
750, § 5/5-5-6	26.6(c)	36
755, § 5/112-4	14.3(d)	81

ILLINOIS CODE OF CRIMINAL PROCEDURE

Sec.	This Work Sec.	Note
114-5	22.4(d)	32

ILLINOIS SUPREME COURT RULES

Rule	This Work Sec.	Note
Art. IV	27.3(c)	46
401 et seq.	1.7(f)	74
401	11.3(b)	42
401	11.3(b)	52
411	20.2(c)	44
411	20.2(c)	45
411	20.2(d)	75
412 to 415	20.2(b)	16
412	20.2(c)	47
412	20.4(a)	6
412(a)	20.3(i)	160
412(a)	20.3(i)	161
412(a)(i)	20.3(h)	136
412(a)(ii)	20.3(c)	70
412(a)(ii)	20.3(d)	87
412(a)(iii)	20.3(b)	61
412(a)(iii)	20.3(b)	62
412(g)	20.3(a)	3

ILLINOIS SUPREME COURT RULES

Rule	This Work Sec.	Note
412(g)	20.3(a)	4
412(g)	20.3(a)	21
412(j)(1)	20.3(j)	180
412(j)(1)	20.3(j)	196
413	20.4(a)	6
413	20.5(h)	104
413(c)	20.5(h)	106
413(d)	20.4(c)	49
413(d)	20.5(b)	13
413(d)	20.5(d)	58
413(d)(1)	20.5(d)	62
413(e)	20.5(h)	107
415(d)	20.3(l)	227
415(g)(ii)	20.6(a)	9
416	1.8(e)	94
416(d)	1.8(e)	93
451	24.8(c)	42
604(a)(1)	27.3(c)	46
604(a)(3)	12.4(e)	92
604(a)(3)	27.3(c)	34
607	11.2(b)	74
714	1.8(e)	93

INDIANA CONSTITUTION

Art.	This Work Sec.	Note
I, § 13	16.1(b)	91
I, § 13(b)	12.1(f)	69
I, § 13(b)	12.1(f)	74
I, § 13(b)	12.1(f)	81
I, § 13(b)	21.3(f)	302
I, § 19	22.1(g)	97
VII, § 6	27.1(a)	5

INDIANA CODE

Sec.	This Work Sec.	Note
Art. III	16.1(b)	
11-13-1-3	26.9(a)	4
11-13-3-3(i)(3)	26.2(c)	48
11-13-3-3(j)	26.2(c)	50
33-4-55-16	15.4(b)	71
33-14-1-3	8.1(c)	33
34	24.4(a)	6
35-1-15-16	8.5(b)	19
35-32-1-1	1.7(e)	59
35-32-2-1	16.1(c)	105
35-32-2-1	16.1(e)	173
35-32-2-1(h)	16.1(e)	170
35-32-2-3	16.1(e)	184
35-32-2-5	16.1(h)	304
35-32-21	16.1(e)	171

INDIANA CODE

Sec.	This Work Sec.	Note
35-33-4-1	12.5(a)	4
35-33-7-1	14.3(a)	1
35-33-7-4	14.2(d)	47
35-33-7-6	11.2(a)	28
35-34-1-1(a)	15.1(g)	344
35-34-1-1(a)	15.1(g)	345
35-34-1-2	19.3(b)	161
35-34-1-2	19.3(b)	162
35-34-1-4	19.1(d)	55
35-34-1-5	19.1(d)	37
35-34-1-5	19.5(c)	47
35-34-1-5	19.5(c)	49
35-34-1-5	19.5(c)	50
35-34-1-5	19.5(c)	51
35-34-1-7	15.4(b)	45
35-34-1-9	17.1(a)	4
35-34-1-9	17.1(b)	19
35-34-1-9	17.2(a)	6
35-34-1-9	17.3(d)	50
35-34-1-10	17.3(a)	5
35-34-1-11	17.1(b)	22
35-34-2-1	8.10(d)	115
35-34-2-3	15.2(d)	95
35-34-2-3(c)(8)	15.4(g)	157
35-34-2-3(c)(9)	15.4(g)	157
35-34-2-3(d)	8.5(d)	133
35-34-2-3(g)	15.2(b)	20
35-34-2-4	8.5(b)	43
35-34-2-4	8.5(c)	70
35-34-2-4	8.5(e)	161
35-34-2-5	8.10(c)	52
35-34-2-5	8.10(d)	114
35-34-2-5.5	8.14(b)	25
35-34-2-5.5	8.14(b)	30
35-34-2-6	8.10(c)	51
35-34-2-6	8.10(c)	52
35-34-2-8	8.11(a)	9
35-34-2-9(b)	15.2(c)	74
35-34-2-12	15.1(g)	360
35-34-2-12(d)	15.2(h)	193
35-34-2-55	8.14(d)	63
35-35-3-2	21.3(f)	378
35-35-3-5	21.3(f)	315
35-35-3-5	21.3(f)	320
35-35-3-5	21.3(f)	328
35-35-3-5	21.3(f)	355
35-35-3-5	21.3(f)	410
35-35-3-6	21.3(f)	355
35-36-2	20.2(a)	10
35-36-4	20.2(a)	10
35-37-2-1	24.8(a)	2
35-37-2-2	24.8(a)	15

INDIANA CODE

Sec.	This Work Sec.	Note
35-38-1-7.1(a)	26.3(f)	58
35-38-1-7.1(b)	26.3(f)	58
35-38-1-8.5	26.5(d)	66
35-38-1-12	26.5(c)	45
35-38-2-3	26.9(a)	8
35-38-4-2(6)	27.3(c)	57
35-38-7-8(4)	24.11(d)	46
35-38-42	27.3(a)	10
35-40-5-7	13.1(a)	21
35-40-11-1	12.1(f)	104
35-40-11-1	21.3(f)	369
35-40-11-1	21.3(f)	413
35-40-11-2	12.1(f)	94
35-40-11-2	21.3(f)	381
35-40-11-2	21.3(f)	382
35-41-1-1	16.4(c)	99
35-41-3-9	5.2(a)	4
35-50-1-2(c)	26.3(f)	58
35-50-2-8	26.6(b)	18
35-50-2-8(g)	26.6(b)	20
35-50-2-9(e)	26.2(b)	6

INDIANA RULES OF CIVIL PROCEDURE

Rule	This Work Sec.	Note
82.3	16.3(b)	14

INDIANA RULES OF CRIMINAL PROCEDURE

Rule	This Work Sec.	Note
1	1.7(f)	71
3(B)	11.2(g)	262
4	18.3(c)	72
4	18.3(c)	84
4	18.3(c)	90
4	18.3(c)	95
4	18.3(c)	106
4	18.3(c)	109
4	18.3(c)	118
12	22.4(d)	32
22	1.8(c)	36

INDIANA TRIAL RULES

Rule	This Work Sec.	Note
51	27.5(c)	91

IOWA CONSTITUTION

Art.	This Work Sec.	Note
I, § 11	15.1(g)	358

IOWA CONSTITUTION

Art.	This Work Sec.	Note
I, § 12	12.3(b)	33

IOWA CODE ANNOTATED

Sec.	This Work Sec.	Note
13B.11	11.7(e)	68
602.1602	22.4(b)	18
684.19	1.7(f)	82
801.1	1.7(e)	59
803.1	16.4(c)	80
803.1	16.4(c)	87
803.1	16.4(c)	94
803.1(2)	16.4(d)	140
803.2	16.1(g)	235
803.2	16.3(d)	52
803.3	16.1(d)	149
803.3	16.1(d)	151
805.1	12.5(b)	19
812.3	19.5(b)	6
813.2	8.4(b)	78
813.2	8.5(a)	4
813.2	8.5(d)	133
813.2	11.2(a)	28
813.2	11.2(a)	30
813.2	14.2(d)	50
813.2	14.2(d)	62
813.2	14.4(b)	16
813.2	14.4(c)	48
813.2	15.1(g)	344
813.2	15.1(g)	345
813.2	15.1(g)	358
813.2	15.2(b)	29
813.2	15.4(g)	157
813.2	19.1(c)	32
813.2	19.4(a)	1
813.2	19.5(b)	2
815.9	11.2(g)	266
815.9	11.2(g)	274
815.9	11.2(h)	311
815.10	11.2(a)	28
822.1 to 822.11	28.11(b)	22
902.1	26.1(c)	49
902.3	26.1(c)	51
903.1	1.8(c)	14
903.1	1.8(c)	20
907.3(1)	26.1(d)	78
907.3(1)	26.1(d)	83
915.13	21.3(f)	324

IOWA RULES OF CRIMINAL PROCEDURE

Rule	This Work Sec.	Note
2	14.2(d)	47
2(4)	14.2(d)	50
2.1	1.3(e)	37
2.1	1.7(f)	71
2.2	14.2(f)	86
2.2	14.3(a)	1
2.3(4)(g)	15.2(b)	29
2.6	17.2(a)	5
2.6	17.3(d)	49
2.10(1)	21.3(c)	201
2.11	19.4(b)	13
2.13	20.2(e)	82
2.13	20.2(e)	89
2.13	20.2(e)	92
2.13	20.2(e)	93
2.14	20.2(b)	16
2.14	20.3(d)	88
2.14(2)(b)	20.3(g)	121
2.19(7)(b)	22.4(e)	48
3(2)	15.4(b)	46
4	1.8(c)	20
4(6)(b)	8.5(d)	133
7	12.5(a)	4
10	16.3(b)	10
10	16.3(b)	15
10(2)(a)	15.4(b)	61
10(4)	15.4(b)	61
12	20.2(e)	103
12(a)(3)	20.2(e)	87
13	20.2(e)	103
13(2)(a)(1)	20.3(b)	61
13(2)(a)(1)	20.3(b)	62
13(2)(a)(1)	20.3(c)	79
13(2)(a)(2)	20.3(d)	90
13(6)(a)	20.3(l)	230
13(6)(a)	20.3(l)	231
13.3(a)	20.5(g)	91
18	26.6(b)	16
18(5)(f)	24.8(a)	16
23	24.11(d)	14
26	11.2(b)	79
26.1	11.1(d)	127
26.1	11.2(b)	71
26.1	11.2(b)	74
27	18.3(c)	72
27	18.3(c)	87
27	18.3(c)	106
27	18.3(c)	113
32	1.8(c)	20
Form 10	19.1(c)	32

IOWA RULES OF EVIDENCE

Rule	This Work Sec.	Note
1101(c)	14.4(b)	16
1101(c)(4)	26.5(a)	3
1101(d)(2)	15.2(d)	107

IOWA CODE OF PROFFESSIONAL RESPONSIBILITY

Sec.	This Work Sec.	Note
DR 7-107	23.1(b)	19

KANSAS CONSTITUTION

Art.	This Work Sec.	Note
XV, § 15	12.1(f)	69
XV, § 15	12.1(f)	79
XV, § 15	12.1(f)	81
XV, § 15	12.1(f)	91
XV, § 15	12.1(f)	92
XV, § 15	21.3(f)	302
XV, § 15	21.3(f)	339
XV, § 15	21.3(f)	342
XV, § 15	21.3(f)	343
XV, § 15	21.3(f)	374
XV, § 15	21.3(f)	390

KANSAS STATUTES ANNOTATED

Sec.	This Work Sec.	Note
2-3402	18.3(c)	84
19-713	8.4(b)	27
19-713	15.1(g)	359
21-3104	16.4(c)	76
21-3104	16.4(c)	102
21-3105	1.8(c)	12
21-3210	5.2(a)	4
21-3705(b)	26.1(d)	74
21-4504	26.6(b)	12
21-4601	26.1(d)	86
21-4603	1.8(c)	13
21-4608(f)	26.1(c)	46
21-4611	26.9(a)	12
21-4714(3)	26.5(d)	63
22-261	16.1(e)	173
22-2101	1.7(e)	59
22-2101	20.2(b)	37
22-2302	12.5(a)	3
22-2302	12.5(a)	4
22-2408	12.5(b)	19
22-2602	16.1(c)	105
22-2603	16.1(d)	134
22-2604	16.1(e)	171

KANSAS STATUTES ANNOTATED

Sec.	This Work Sec.	Note
22-2608	16.1(e)	174
22-2902	14.4(b)	19
22-2902	14.4(b)	21
22-2902(2)	14.2(d)	50
22-2902(3)	14.3(a)	2
22-2902(4)	14.4(d)	80
22-3001	8.1(b)	15
22-3002	15.4(b)	27
22-3002	15.4(b)	44
22-3002(2)	15.4(g)	165
22-3003	15.1(g)	359
22-3003	15.2(d)	95
22-3007(2)	8.4(b)	27
22-3009	8.10(d)	100
22-3009	8.14(a)	20
22-3009	8.14(b)	24
22-3009	8.14(b)	29
22-3009	8.14(b)	32
22-3012	8.5(b)	42
22-3012	15.2(i)	216
22-3103	8.1(c)	33
22-3103	8.1(c)	34
22-3201	1.3(e)	37
22-3201	15.1(g)	344
22-3201	15.1(g)	359
22-3201(c)	15.1(g)	345
22-3201(e)	19.5(b)	4
22-3202	17.1(a)	4
22-3202	17.1(b)	19
22-3202	17.2(a)	3
22-3211	20.2(e)	84
22-3212	20.2(b)	16
22-3212	20.3(e)	95
22-3212	20.3(g)	121
22-3212(a)	20.3(a)	8
22-3212(a)	20.3(a)	10
22-3212(b)	20.3(i)	166
22-3212(c)	20.4(g)	100
22-3212(c)	20.5(e)	69
22-3212(c)	20.5(g)	95
22-3212(c)	20.5(h)	100
22-3213	14.4(c)	64
22-3213	20.5(a)	10
22-3213(2)	20.3(i)	166
22-3216(3)	27.3(d)	66
22-3216(4)	14.4(b)	37
22-3216(4)	14.4(b)	40
22-3217	20.2(d)	68
22-3218 to 22-3220	20.2(b)	16
22-3218	24.3(c)	93
22-3219	20.5(a)	10
22-3221	24.10(a)	11

KANSAS STATUTES ANNOTATED

Sec.	This Work Sec.	Note
22-3402	18.3(c)	72
22-3402	18.3(c)	75
22-3402	18.3(c)	90
22-3402	18.3(c)	95
22-3402	18.3(c)	100
22-3402	18.3(c)	108
22-3402	18.3(c)	117
22-3404	1.8(c)	36
22-3405(2)	24.2(a)	16
22-3415	8.11(d)	70
22-3419	24.11(a)	1
22-3424(4)(c)	26.4(g)	133
22-3424(d)	26.9(b)	32
22-3602	14.3(c)	59
22-3602(b)	27.3(a)	7
22-3602(b)	27.3(c)	21
22-3602(b)	27.3(d)	59
22-3603	27.3(c)	37
22-3604(1)	12.4(e)	91
22-4503	11.2(a)	28
22-4504	11.2(g)	260
22-4504	11.2(g)	262
22-4504	11.2(g)	264
22-4504	11.2(g)	274
22-4504	11.2(g)	302
22-4504	11.2(g)	310
22-4504(b)	11.2(g)	276
22-4504(d)	11.2(h)	311
22-4505(c)	11.2(b)	70
22-4508	11.2(e)	170
22-4508	11.2(e)	219
22-4513	11.2(h)	316
43-159(e)	15.4(g)	157
43-168	22.4(e)	48
60-249	24.6(e)	47
74-7333	21.3(f)	374
74-7333	26.5(d)	66

KENTUCKY CONSTITUTION

Sec.	This Work Sec.	Note
11	16.1(b)	32
11	16.1(b)	90
11	16.3(a)	4
12	15.1(d)	183
12	15.1(d)	201
12	15.1(d)	207
12	15.1(d)	218
12	15.1(f)	270
16	12.3(b)	33
115	27.1(a)	5
116	1.7(f)	95

KENTUCKY REVISED STATUTES

Sec.	This Work Sec.	Note
29A.220	8.1(b)	19
31.100	11.2(a)	28
31.110	11.2(a)	28
31.110	11.2(b)	68
31.110	11.2(b)	73
31.110	11.2(b)	81
31.110(1)(a)	11.1(d)	129
31.110(1)(b)	11.2(e)	219
31.110(2)	11.2(b)	76
31.120	11.2(g)	258
31.120(2)	11.2(g)	295
31.120(2)	11.2(g)	298
31.120(4)	11.2(h)	313
31.120(4)	11.2(h)	314
421.500	21.3(f)	308
421.500	21.3(f)	317
421.500	21.3(f)	322
421.510	18.3(c)	124
421.520(2)	26.5(d)	66
422.285	24.11(d)	43
422.285	24.11(d)	44
431.005	1.7(e)	59
431.015	12.5(b)	20
431.200	26.6(c)	41
431.410	12.5(a)	6
452.20	16.3(g)	105
452.210	16.3(b)	19
452.210	16.3(d)	52
452.230	16.3(f)	84
452.550	16.1(d)	150
452.580	16.1(e)	179
452.620	16.1(e)	175
452.630	16.1(d)	149
500.060	16.4(c)	82
500.060	16.4(c)	99
500.060	16.4(c)	101
505.010	5.1(c)	17
505.010	5.2(a)	4
532.050	26.5(b)	35
532.055	26.2(b)	12
532.055	26.2(b)	15
532.080	26.6(b)	18
532.080(2)	26.6(b)	25
532.080(3)(c)	26.6(b)	24
533.020	26.9(a)	11
533.030	26.9(a)	4
633.010	26.1(d)	86

KENTUCKY RULES OF CIVIL PROCEDURE

Rule	This Work Sec.	Note
76.20(2)(b) .... 28.11(b)		34

KENTUCKY RULES OF CRIMINAL PROCEDURE

Rule	This Work Sec.	Note
1.02 .... 1.3(e)		37
3.05 .... 11.2(a)		28
3.05 .... 14.2(e)		70
3.07 .... 14.2(c)		38
3.10 .... 14.2(f)		86
3.10(3) .... 14.2(e)		84
3.14 .... 14.3(a)		1
3.14 .... 14.4(b)		13
3.14 .... 14.4(b)		14
3.14 .... 14.4(d)		80
3.14(2) .... 14.4(c)		48
5.02 .... 15.2(b)		20
5.02 .... 15.2(e)		128
5.06 .... 8.4(b)		21
5.08 .... 15.2(c)		62
5.10 .... 15.2(d)		106
5.10 .... 15.5(c)		107
5.14 .... 8.4(b)		28
5.14 .... 15.1(d)		251
5.16 .... 15.2(i)		214
5.16 .... 15.2(j)		235
5.16(1) .... 15.2(j)		244
5.16(3) .... 15.2(i)		209
5.16(3) .... 15.2(i)		211
5.24(1) .... 8.5(d)		119
6.02 .... 15.1(d)		183
6.02 .... 15.1(d)		247
6.02 .... 15.1(f)		286
6.02 .... 15.1(f)		294
6.02 .... 15.1(f)		326
6.06 .... 15.1(d)		251
6.16 .... 19.5(b)		5
6.18 .... 17.1(a)		4
6.18 .... 17.1(b)		19
6.18 .... 17.2(a)		3
6.22 .... 19.4(a)		1
7.10 .... 20.2(e)		84
7.24 .... 20.2(b)		16
7.24(2) .... 20.3(g)		121
7.24(2) .... 20.3(k)		222
7.24(3) .... 20.5(h)		100
7.24(3)(B) .... 20.3(l)		226
7.24(3)(B)(i) .... 20.5(c)		34
7.24(3)(B)(ii) .... 20.5(c)		48
7.24(3)(B)(ii) .... 20.5(c)		49
8.18 .... 15.4(b)		74

KENTUCKY RULES OF CRIMINAL PROCEDURE

Rule	This Work Sec.	Note
8.20 .... 15.4(b)		74
8.20 .... 19.1(d)		55
8.26 .... 16.1(h)		304
8.28(4) .... 1.8(c)		37
8.28(4) .... 24.2(a)		16
9.12 .... 17.3(a)		5
9.16 .... 17.3(d)		49
9.84 .... 26.2(b)		12
12.04(3) .... 28.11(b)		34
830 .... 11.9(b)		97
Form 15 .... 19.1(d)		47

LOUISIANA CONSTITUTION

Art.	This Work Sec.	Note
I, § 6 .... 2.12(b)		89
I, § 15 .... 15.1(e)		257
I, § 16 .... 16.1(c)		102
I, § 18 .... 12.3(b)		37
I, § 19 .... 27.1(a)		5
I, § 25 .... 12.1(f)		69
I, § 25 .... 12.1(f)		75
I, § 25 .... 12.1(f)		81
I, § 25 .... 13.1(a)		22
I, § 25 .... 21.3(f)		302
I, § 25 .... 21.3(f)		321
I, § 25 .... 21.3(f)		371
II, § 17 .... 15.1(g)		358

LOUISIANA REVISED STATUTES ANNOTATED

Sec.	This Work Sec.	Note
14:32.1(B) .... 26.3(e)		30
15:30 .... 1.7(e)		59
15:529.1 .... 26.6(b)		4
15:529.1(D) .... 26.6(b)		10
15:574.4(D) .... 26.2(c)		47
15:609 .... 3.5(d)		148
46:1842 .... 21.3(f)		373
46:1844 .... 21.3(f)		311
46:1844 .... 21.3(f)		314
46:1844 .... 21.3(f)		318
46:1844 .... 21.3(f)		410

LOUISIANA CODE OF CRIMINAL PROCEDURE

Art.	This Work Sec.	Note
1 .... 1.7(e)		59
18 .... 1.7(f)		81
18 .... 1.7(f)		84

LOUISIANA CODE OF CRIMINAL PROCEDURE

Art.	Sec.	This Work Note
66	8.1(c)	33
66	8.1(c)	34
209	12.5(a)	5
209	12.5(b)	20
211	1.8(c)	29
292	14.2(d)	49
292	14.2(e)	84
294	14.4(c)	48
296	14.3(a)	1
382	15.1(e)	257
382	15.1(e)	268
382	15.1(f)	288
382	15.1(f)	299
383	15.1(e)	267
413	15.4(a)	17
414(D)	8.4(c)	118
419	15.4(f)	142
432	15.2(e)	128
433	15.7(h)	222
434(A)	8.5(d)	118
434(A)	15.2(i)	216
436	15.2(b)	25
437	8.4(b)	78
438	15.1(e)	266
438	15.2(b)	20
438	15.2(b)	28
439	8.4(b)	21
439.1	8.11(b)	17
439.1	8.11(d)	73
442	15.2(b)	29
442	15.2(d)	95
442	15.5(c)	107
444	8.3(h)	49
465	19.1(c)	32
468	19.3(b)	162
479	19.3(a)	16
487	19.1(d)	37
487	19.6(a)	4
488	19.1(d)	57
488	19.6(a)	4
489	19.1(d)	57
493	17.1(a)	4
493	17.1(b)	19
493	17.2(a)	3
495.1	17.3(d)	49
512	11.2(a)	28
513	11.2(a)	28
517	11.9(b)	96
517	11.9(b)	97
521	15.4(b)	61
533(1)	15.4(b)	45

LOUISIANA CODE OF CRIMINAL PROCEDURE

Art.	Sec.	This Work Note
535(c)	15.4(b)	61
558	21.3(c)	203
574	24.8(f)	113
578	18.3(c)	72
579	18.3(c)	85
581	18.3(c)	106
581	18.3(c)	107
581	18.3(c)	108
612	16.1(e)	174
614	16.1(e)	170
615	16.1(g)	235
621	16.3(d)	52
622	16.3(b)	13
622	16.3(b)	21
701	1.8(c)	38
716 to 729.6	20.2(b)	16
719(A)	20.3(f)	99
723	20.3(i)	167
724	20.5(c)	31
724	20.5(g)	89
726	20.4(e)	76
726	20.5(c)	40
727(D)	20.6(a)	14
728	20.5(e)	69
728	20.5(g)	95
738	24.3(f)	144
739	24.3(f)	144
764	24.4(d)	31
768	20.2(d)	63
814	24.8(f)	100
821	25.4(b)	19
832(B)	24.2(c)	36
833(C)	24.2(c)	36
894.1(A)(1)	26.6(e)	77
920(2)	27.5(d)	118
926.1	24.11(d)	44
933(4)	1.8(d)	70
1791	24.6(e)	47
1794	24.9(b)	17

LOUISIANA RULES OF THE SUPREME COURT

Rule	Sec.	This Work Note
27	1.7(f)	74
28	1.7(f)	74

MAINE CONSTITUTION

Art.	Sec.	This Work Note
I, § 6	2.12(b)	106

MAINE CONSTITUTION

Art.	This Work Sec.	Note
I, § 6	16.1(b)	32
I, § 6	16.1(b)	90
I, § 7	15.1(d)	184
I, § 7	15.1(d)	202
I, § 7	15.1(d)	207
I, § 7	15.1(d)	209
I, § 7	15.1(d)	246
I, § 7	15.1(d)	251
I, § 7	15.1(f)	270
I, § 10	12.3(b)	34

MAINE REVISED STATUTES ANNOTATED

Tit.	This Work Sec.	Note
12, § 1214	15.4(b)	71
15, § 1	1.7(e)	59
15, § 757	26.1(c)	60
15, § 1256	8.4(b)	90
15, § 1256	15.2(c)	70
15, § 2115-A	14.3(c)	59
15, § 2115-A(1)	27.3(c)	40
15, § 2115-A(1)	27.3(c)	47
15, § 2115-A(1)	27.3(c)	57
15, § 2129	11.2(b)	76
15, § 2130	25.4(b)	19
15, § 2138	24.11(d)	41
15, § 2138	24.11(d)	44
15, § 2138	24.11(d)	45
15, § 2138	24.11(d)	47
17, § 352(5)(e)	16.1(f)	225
17-A	17.4(c)	152
17-A, § 4-A	1.8(c)	17
17-A, § 7	16.4(c)	74
17-A, § 7	16.4(c)	83
17-A, § 7	16.4(c)	101
17-A, § 7	16.4(c)	111
17-A, § 7(2)	16.4(c)	81
17-A, § 14	16.1(f)	220
17-A, § 14	17.4(c)	143
17-A, § 14	17.4(c)	152
17-A, § 14	17.4(c)	153
17-A, § 14	17.4(c)	157
17-A, § 15-A	12.5(b)	19
17-A, § 1173	21.3(f)	311
17-A, § 1173	21.3(f)	316
17-A, § 1173	21.3(f)	319
17-A, § 1173	21.3(f)	355
17-A, § 1173	21.3(f)	365
17-A, § 1173	21.3(f)	397
17-A, § 1173	21.3(f)	410
17-A, § 1173	21.3(f)	414
17-A, § 1323(1)	26.6(c)	35

MAINE REVISED STATUTES ANNOTATED

Tit.	This Work Sec.	Note
17-A, § 1323(2)	26.6(c)	34
17-A, § 1325(2)(C)	26.6(c)	37
34A, § 5801	26.1(c)	46

MAINE RULES OF CRIMINAL PROCEDURE

Rule	This Work Sec.	Note
1	1.3(e)	37
1	20.2(c)	43
4	12.5(a)	4
5(e)	14.4(d)	80
5A	14.1(a)	1
5A(e)	14.2(f)	87
6(b)	15.4(b)	28
6(b)	15.4(b)	46
6(b)(1)	15.4(g)	157
6(b)(1)	15.4(g)	158
6(d)	15.2(j)	236
6(d)	15.2(j)	245
6(e)	8.5(d)	124
7(a)	15.1(d)	184
7(a)	15.1(d)	210
7(a)	15.1(d)	247
7(a)	15.1(d)	251
7(b)	15.1(f)	286
7(b)	15.1(f)	318
7(b)	15.1(f)	326
7(c)	15.1(d)	248
7(c)	15.1(d)	251
7(e)	19.5(b)	2
8	17.1(a)	4
8	17.1(b)	19
8	17.2(a)	3
8	17.3(a)	5
8	17.3(d)	49
11A	21.3(c)	201
14	17.1(c)	39
15(a)	20.2(e)	84
16	20.2(b)	16
16(a)	20.2(c)	49
16(a)(1)	20.3	261
16(b)(2)(B)	20.3(f)	98
16(b)(2)(D)	20.3(k)	214
16(b)(3)	20.3(j)	180
16(b)(3)	20.5(b)	22
16(d)	20.2(b)	19
16.1(b)(3)	20.5(b)	16
16A(a)	20.5(c)	40
16A(b)(3)	20.2(c)	54
16A(b)(3)	20.5(b)	17
16A(b)(3)	20.5(b)	19
16A(b)(3)	20.5(e)	68

MAINE RULES OF CRIMINAL PROCEDURE

Rule	This Work Sec.	Note
21	16.1(c)	106
21(b)(2)	16.1(h)	286
21(b)(3)	16.3(c)	27
21(b)(3)	16.3(f)	88
43	24.2(a)	16
44	11.2(a)	28
44	11.2(a)	31
44	11.2(g)	259
44(a)	11.2(b)	68
44(b)	11.2(g)	281

MAINE RULES OF EVIDENCE

Rule	This Work Sec.	Note
1101(b)(3)	14.4(b)	9
1101(d)(2)	15.2(d)	107

MARYLAND CONSTITUTION

Art.	This Work Sec.	Note
IV, § 8	16.3(b)	14
IV, § 8(b)	15.1(g)	358
IV, § 41B	16.1(c)	99
XV, § 5	22.1(g)	97
XXV	12.3(b)	31

MARYLAND DECLARATION OF RIGHTS

Art.	This Work Sec.	Note
18	16.1(c)	127
47	12.1(f)	69
47	12.1(f)	74
47	12.1(f)	82
47	21.3(f)	302
47	21.3(f)	370
47	21.3(f)	376

MARYLAND ANNOTATED CODE

Art.	This Work Sec.	Note
27, § 591	18.3(c)	109
27, § 592	15.1(g)	344
27, § 645A to 645J	28.11(b)	22
27, § 776	1.5(k)	386
27A, § 1	11.2(a)	28
27A, § 2	11.2(a)	28
27A, § 2	11.2(a)	31
27A, § 2	11.2(a)	33
27A, § 4	11.2(a)	28
27A, § 7	11.2(g)	300
27A, § 7(d)	11.2(h)	317

MARYLAND CODE OF CRIMINAL PROCEDURE ANNOTATED

Sec.	This Work Sec.	Note
1-101	1.7(e)	59
4-101	12.5(b)	20
4-201	16.1(c)	99
4-201(c)	16.1(e)	169
5-202	12.3(b)	47
5-202	12.3(b)	48
5-202	12.3(b)	51
6-103	18.3(c)	72
8-201	24.11(d)	44
12-702	26.8(b)	15
36B(e)	26.1(d)	74
592(3)	15.1(g)	345

MARYLAND CODE, COURTS AND JUDICIAL PROCEEDINGS

Sec.	This Work Sec.	Note
4-26	20.3(h)	141
4-101	1.3(e)	37
4-101	1.7(f)	71
4-203	17.1(a)	4
4-203	17.1(b)	19
4-203	17.2(a)	3
4-204	19.5(c)	49
4-212	12.5(a)	4
4-214	11.2(a)	28
4-214	11.2(b)	69
4-215	11.3(c)	62
4-215(c)	11.3(c)	54
4-221	14.2(e)	66
4-221(a)	14.2(e)	84
4-241	1.8(c)	34
4-246	1.8(c)	36
4-252	16.1(g)	235
4-253	17.3(d)	49
4-254	16.3(d)	52
4-261	1.8(c)	34
4-262	1.8(c)	33
4-262	20.2(b)	16
4-262	20.2(b)	32
4-262	20.2(c)	43
4-263	1.8(c)	33
4-263	20.2(b)	16
4-263	20.3(f)	117
4-263(a)(2)	20.2(b)	30
4-263(b)	20.4(a)	5
4-263(d)	20.4(a)	7
4-263(d)	20.5(h)	101
4-301	1.8(c)	36
4-463	20.2(c)	43
4-524	16.3(b)	15

MARYLAND CODE, COURTS AND JUDICIAL PROCEEDINGS

Sec.	This Work Sec.	Note
4-642	8.5(b)	54
8-401	8.5(b)	19
8-507	8.3(f)	31
12-302(c)(3)(i)	27.3(c)	31

MASSACHUSETTS CONSTITUTION

Art.	This Work Sec.	Note
12	22.1(c)	60
26, Pt. I	12.3(b)	31

MASSACHUSETTS GENERAL LAWS ANNOTATED

Ch.	This Work Sec.	Note
58A-1/2	16.1(e)	186
58B	16.1(e)	180
211(D), § 2A	11.2(a)	30
218, § 26	16.1(a)	25
218, § 27	15.1(d)	217
233, § 20E	8.11(d)	78
263, § 4	15.1(d)	185
263, § 4A	15.1(f)	285
263, § 8	19.6(a)	6
275, § 1	1.7(e)	59
276, § 1	3.4(a)	22
276, § 24	12.5(a)	6
276, § 58	12.3(b)	48
277, § 14A	8.14(b)	31
277, § 39	19.1(d)	64
277, § 47A	16.4(d)	143
277, § 57	16.1(e)	170
277, § 57A	16.1(e)	175
277, § 58A	16.1(e)	181
278, § 16F	18.3(c)	124
279, § 1	26.1(d)	77
279, § 23	15.1(d)	217
2110, § 2A	11.2(a)	28
2110, § 5	11.2(a)	28

MASSACHUSETTS SUPREME JUDICIAL COURT RULES

Rule	This Work Sec.	Note
3:10	11.2(a)	28
3:10	11.2(g)	259
3:10	11.2(g)	301
3:10(1)(a)	11.2(g)	270
3:10(1)(e)	11.2(g)	272
3:10(3)	11.3(a)	21
3:10(9)	11.2(g)	303

MASSACHUSETTS SUPREME JUDICIAL COURT RULES

Rule	This Work Sec.	Note
3:10(b)	11.2(g)	281
3:10(b)(ii)	11.2(g)	283
3:10(b)(ii)	11.2(g)	284
3:10(f)	11.2(g)	266
3:10(h)	11.2(g)	279
3:10(ii)	11.2(g)	285

MASSACHUSETTS RULES OF CRIMINAL PROCEDURE

Rule	This Work Sec.	Note
1	1.3(e)	37
1	1.7(f)	71
3	14.2(c)	36
3	14.2(e)	66
3	15.1(d)	217
3(a)	15.1(d)	185
3(a)	15.1(d)	247
3(b)	15.1(d)	216
3(b)(1)	15.1(d)	185
3(b)(2)	15.1(f)	286
3(b)(2)	15.1(f)	295
3(b)(2)	15.1(f)	307
3(c)(1)	15.1(f)	329
3(e)	15.1(f)	310
3.8	1.7(j)	264
4(c)	15.2(d)	106
4(d)	19.5(c)	48
4(d)	19.5(c)	49
4(d)	19.5(c)	50
5(c)	8.14(b)	31
5(d)	8.5(b)	43
5(d)	8.5(e)	161
6(c)	15.2(j)	245
7.09	19.5(c)	48
8	11.2(a)	28
9	17.1(a)	4
9	17.1(b)	21
9	17.1(b)	22
9	17.2(a)	5
9	17.3(a)	5
9	17.3(d)	50
13(b)	19.4(b)	15
14	20.2(b)	16
14(1)(A)(ix)	20.3(e)	97
14(A)	20.3(i)	160
14(a)(1)	15.2(i)	214
14(a)(1)(A)(viii)	20.2(b)	30
14(a)(3)	20.5(e)	67
14(b)	15.2(i)	209
14(b)	15.2(i)	211

MASSACHUSETTS RULES OF CRIMINAL PROCEDURE

Rule	This Work Sec.	Note
14(b)(2)(B)	20.5(c)	34
14(b)(2)(B)(iv)	20.5(c)	38
14(b)(3)	20.5(d)	60
14(c)	15.2(j)	236
24(a)(2)	24.7(a)	6
25(a)	24.6(b)	19
25(b)(1)	24.6(b)	33
35	20.2(e)	85
36	18.3(c)	72
36	18.3(c)	79
36	18.3(c)	81
36	18.3(c)	99
36	18.3(c)	101
36	18.3(c)	106
36	18.3(c)	107
36	18.3(c)	109
36	18.3(c)	120
37(b)(1)	16.3(f)	86
38	22.4(e)	48

MASSACHUSETTS RULES OF PROFESSIONAL CONDUCT

Rule	This Work Sec.	Note
3.5(d)	24.9(g)	129

MASSACHUSETTS DISTRICT & SUPERIOR COURT RULES OF CRIMINAL PROCEDURE

Rule	This Work Sec.	Note
3(b)(2)	15.1(f)	297
14(b)(1)(D)	20.6(c)	88
28(d)(3)	26.5(c)	50

MICHIGAN CONSTITUTION

Art.	This Work Sec.	Note
I, § 15	12.3(b)	37
I, § 15	12.3(b)	38
I, § 15	12.3(b)	39
I, § 15	12.3(b)	40
I, § 15	12.3(b)	41
I, § 24	12.1(f)	69
I, § 24	12.1(f)	96
I, § 24	21.3(f)	302

MICHIGAN COMPILED LAWS ANNOTATED

Sec.	This Work Sec.	Note
5.288	16.1(e)	169
28.2303(a)	26.2(c)	36

MICHIGAN COMPILED LAWS ANNOTATED

Sec.	This Work Sec.	Note
28.2303(d)	26.2(c)	37
333.7409	25.5(b)	27
600.2159	24.5(b)	21
750.501	1.5(k)	371
760.1	1.7(e)	59
761.1(j)	1.8(d)	66
761.1(k)	1.8(c)	20
761.1(k)	1.8(d)	66
762.3	16.1(e)	170
762.3	16.1(e)	172
762.3	16.1(e)	175
762.7	16.3(d)	52
762.7	16.3(e)	79
762.11	16.1(e)	180
763.6	19.6(a)	6
764.1	1.5(k)	357
764.9a	1.8(c)	20
765.7	12.4(e)	92
766.7	14.2(f)	88
766.13	14.3(a)	2
766.13	14.3(a)	4
767.1	15.1(g)	344
767.1	15.1(g)	345
767.3	8.1(b)	21
767.3	8.1(c)	24
767.4	8.1(b)	20
767.4	8.1(c)	28
767.8	15.4(a)	20
767.9	8.4(b)	82
767.9	15.1(g)	360
767.13	15.4(b)	30
767.13	15.4(g)	153
767.13	15.4(g)	159
767.14	15.4(b)	52
767.19	8.3(e)	26
767.19a	8.11(d)	77
767.19c	8.3(f)	30
767.19f	8.5(b)	19
767.40a	20.2(b)	16
767.42	14.2(e)	67
767.42	14.2(e)	78
767.42(s)	14.2(e)	67
767.44	19.1(c)	25
767.44	19.1(c)	26
767.44	19.1(c)	32
767.48	19.3(a)	16
767.50	19.1(d)	36
767.54	19.1(d)	36
767.55	19.3(b)	177
767.55	19.3(b)	179
767.59	19.1(d)	36
767.61	19.1(d)	36

MICHIGAN COMPILED LAWS ANNOTATED

Sec.	This Work Sec.	Note
767.63	19.1(d)	36
767.70	19.1(d)	36
767.71	19.1(d)	36
767.71	19.3(b)	135
767.73	19.1(d)	36
767.75	19.3(c)	188
767.94a	20.2(b)	16
767A.1 to 767A.3	8.1(c)	33
768.11(1)	15.2(d)	93
768.20	20.2(b)	16
768.20	20.5(b)	16
768.20(1)	20.5(b)	17
768.20(2)	20.5(b)	19
768.20(2)	20.5(e)	68
768.20(3)	20.5(b)	20
768.21	20.2(b)	16
768.21b	20.2(b)	16
768.27a	20.2(b)	16
769.10(1)	26.6(b)	26
769.13(1)	26.6(b)	15
769.34	26.3(g)	80
770.3(2)	27.2(b)	18
770.3a(1)	11.1(b)	67
770.12	27.3(c)	56
770.16	24.11(d)	47
771.1(a)	26.1(d)	79
771.14	26.5(c)	45
775.16	11.2(a)	28
780.716	11.7(e)	68
780.752	26.5(d)	65
780.757	1.5(k)	408
780.758(1)	1.5(k)	400
780.759	18.3(c)	124
780.768(a)	1.5(k)	385
780.773	1.5(k)	386
780.816	13.1(a)	23
780.816	21.3(f)	314
780.816	21.3(f)	320
791.234(1)	26.2(c)	30
800.33(2)	26.2(c)	55

MICHIGAN COURT RULES

Rule	This Work Sec.	Note
2.003	22.4(b)	18
2.302(B)(3)(c)	20.3(b)	39
3.302	27.4(a)	2
Ch. 6	26.5(c)	50
6.001	1.7(f)	71
6.001	1.8(c)	24
6.001	1.8(c)	25
6.001(C)	20.3(j)	197

MICHIGAN COURT RULES

Rule	This Work Sec.	Note
6.004	1.8(c)	38
6.004	18.3(c)	72
6.004	18.3(c)	84
6.004	18.3(c)	86
6.004	18.3(c)	95
6.004	18.3(c)	100
6.004	18.3(c)	115
6.004	18.3(c)	119
6.004	18.3(c)	120
6.004	18.3(c)	121
6.005	11.2(a)	28
6.005	11.2(g)	259
6.005	11.2(g)	264
6.005	11.2(g)	295
6.005	11.3(b)	52
6.005	11.9(b)	97
6.005(E)	11.3(a)	18
6.103	12.5(a)	3
6.107(A)	8.5(g)	216
6.107(C)	8.14(b)	31
6.110	14.3(a)	4
6.112	19.3(b)	161
6.112(B)	8.1(b)	20
6.112(D)	19.1(c)	32
6.112(E)	19.4(b)	17
6.120	17.1(a)	6
6.120	17.1(b)	22
6.121	17.2(a)	5
6.121	17.3(d)	50
6.201	20.1(d)	61
6.201	20.2(b)	16
6.201	20.3	263
6.201(A)	20.3(k)	222
6.201(A)	20.5(e)	65
6.401	24.6(a)	7
6.403	24.6(a)	11
6.412	15.1(f)	304
6.419	24.6(b)	25
6.420(D)	24.9(e)	57
6.425(B)	26.5(c)	50
6.440(B)	22.4(e)	48
6.508(D)	28.4(b)	19
6.610	11.2(a)	31
6.1000(D)	20.3(b)	39

MICHIGAN RULES OF EVIDENCE

Rule	This Work Sec.	Note
1101(b)	15.2(d)	93

MICHIGAN RULES OF PROFESSIONAL CONDUCT

Rule	This Work Sec.	Note
3.6	23.1(b)	14

MINNESOTA CONSTITUTION

Art.	This Work Sec.	Note
I, § 6	12.3(b)	33
I, § 6	16.1(b)	92

MINNESOTA STATUTES ANNOTATED

Sec.	This Work Sec.	Note
48.0591(6)	1.7(f)	87
299C.105	3.5(d)	148
480.058	1.7(f)	87
480.059(8)	1.7(f)	87
480A.06	27.2(a)	3
590.01 to 590.06	28.11(b)	22
590.01	24.11(d)	47
609.02	1.8(c)	9
609.02	1.8(c)	19
609.02	1.8(c)	20
609.09	8.11(d)	78
609.115	26.5(c)	45
609.125	26.1(d)	70
609.135	26.1(d)	69
609.135	26.1(e)	98
609.152	26.6(e)	76
611.15	11.2(a)	28
611.18	11.2(a)	28
611.18	11.2(b)	68
611.18	11.2(b)	73
611.21	11.2(e)	170
611.21(b)	11.2(e)	219
611A.03	21.3(f)	316
611A.03	21.3(f)	365
611A.03	21.3(f)	381
611A.03	21.3(f)	397
611A.0311	1.5(k)	414
625.01	1.7(e)	59
627.15	16.1(e)	184
628.02	8.4(b)	78
631.04	24.1(b)	20

MINNESOTA RULES OF CRIMINAL PROCEDURE

Rule	This Work Sec.	Note
1.01	1.3(e)	37
1.01	1.7(f)	71
1.01	1.8(d)	66
3.01	12.5(a)	6
4.02	12.5(b)	19
5.01	11.2(b)	79
5.02	11.2(a)	28
5.02	11.2(g)	301
5.02	11.3(a)	18
5.02(1)	1.8(c)	32

MINNESOTA RULES OF CRIMINAL PROCEDURE

Rule	This Work Sec.	Note
5.02(2)	1.8(c)	32
5.02(3)	11.2(g)	263
5.04	1.8(c)	20
6.01	1.8(c)	29
7.01	20.2(d)	63
9	20.2(b)	13
9	20.2(b)	16
9.01	20.2(c)	49
9.01	20.3(b)	31
9.01	20.3(f)	117
9.01	20.3(h)	139
9.01	20.3(i)	161
9.01(I)(1)(a)	20.3(h)	136
9.01(I)(1)(a)	20.3(k)	214
9.01(I)(2)	20.3(a)	10
9.01(III)(1)	20.3(j)	180
9.02(I)(1)	20.5(g)	90
9.02(I)(3)	20.5(a)	10
9.02(I)(3)	20.5(d)	61
9.02(I)(3)	20.5(e)	64
9.02(I)(3)(b)	20.5(f)	71
9.02(I)(3)(b)	20.5(f)	72
9.02(I)(3)(b)	20.5(f)	85
9.02(I)(3)(c)	20.5(b)	18
9.03(8)	20.6(a)	2
9.03(8)	20.6(a)	3
9.03(8)	20.6(a)	4
9.03(8)	20.6(a)	9
11.10	18.3(c)	72
11.10	18.3(c)	87
11.10	18.3(c)	96
11.10	18.3(c)	105
11.10	18.3(c)	115
13.02	11.2(a)	28
15.01	1.8(c)	39
15.02	1.8(c)	39
15.07	21.3(c)	203
15.07	21.3(d)	263
17.01	15.1(e)	259
17.01	15.1(e)	268
17.01	15.1(f)	288
17.01	15.1(f)	299
17.02(2)	15.1(e)	267
17.02(4)	19.4(b)	9
17.03	17.1(a)	6
17.03	17.1(b)	22
17.03	17.2(a)	5
17.03	17.3(a)	5
17.03	17.3(d)	51
17.05	19.5(b)	5
17.06	15.6(a)	5

MINNESOTA RULES OF CRIMINAL PROCEDURE

Rule	This Work Sec.	Note
18.01	8.4(c)	116
18.02	15.4(g)	159
18.02	15.4(g)	165
18.02(1)	15.4(g)	162
18.02(2)	15.4(g)	157
18.04	8.14(b)	27
18.04	8.14(b)	32
18.05	15.2(i)	216
18.06	15.2(d)	100
18.06	15.2(f)	148
18.06(3)	15.1(e)	265
18.08	8.5(d)	124
20.01	24.3(b)	49
24.01	16.1(c)	106
24.02(2)	16.1(e)	170
24.02(2)	16.1(e)	172
24.02(4)	16.1(e)	173
24.02(11)	16.1(f)	225
24.02(12)	16.1(d)	156
24.02(12)	16.1(e)	184
24.03	16.3(b)	15
24.03	16.3(c)	27
24.03	16.3(e)	79
24.03	16.3(f)	87
24.03	16.3(f)	88
25.02	16.3(b)	15
25.02	16.3(d)	52
25.02	16.3(f)	86
26.01(2)	24.6(a)	7
27.04(2)(1)(a)	26.10(b)	31
28.02(3)	27.2(b)	18
28.04	12.4(e)	92
28.04	27.3(c)	34
28.04	27.3(c)	57

MINNESOTA GENERAL RULES OF PRACTICE FOR DISTRICT COURTS

Rule	This Work Sec.	Note
813	15.4(b)	29
813	15.4(b)	71

MINNESOTA RULES OF PROFESSIONAL CONDUCT

Rule	This Work Sec.	Note
3.6	23.1(b)	14

MISSISSIPPI CONSTITUTION

Art.	This Work Sec.	Note
III, § 26	16.1(b)	91
III, § 26A	12.1(f)	69
III, § 26A	12.1(f)	74
III, § 26A	12.1(f)	81
III, § 26A	12.1(f)	90
III, § 26A	21.3(f)	302
III, § 26A	21.3(f)	339
III, § 27	15.1(d)	186
III, § 27	15.1(d)	204
III, § 27	15.1(d)	205
III, § 27	15.1(d)	207
III, § 27	15.1(d)	218
III, § 27	15.1(f)	281
III, § 27	15.1(f)	284
III, § 27	15.1(f)	294
III, § 27	15.1(f)	329
III, § 29	12.3(b)	37
III, § 29	12.3(b)	38
III, § 29	12.3(b)	39

MISSISSIPPI CODE

Sec.	This Work Sec.	Note
9-3-40	1.7(g)	120
13-5-43	15.4(b)	52
13-5-43	15.4(f)	142
13-5-45	15.2(b)	20
13-5-47	15.2(e)	128
13-5-81	15.4(b)	52
13-5-81	15.4(f)	142
13-7-29	8.5(e)	195
13-7-35	15.2(f)	148
13-15-1	15.4(b)	51
25-31-21	8.4(b)	108
47-7-3	26.2(c)	31
47-7-33	26.1(d)	77
47-7-33	26.1(d)	78
95-15-15	11.2(a)	28
95-15-15	11.2(a)	31
97-1-25	5.2(a)	4
99-1-1	1.7(e)	59
99-7-3	19.1(d)	36
99-11-3(1)	16.1(e)	175
99-11-11	16.1(e)	180
99-11-15	16.4(c)	80
99-11-17	16.4(c)	80
99-11-17	16.4(c)	90
99-11-19	16.1(d)	150
99-11-23	16.4(c)	74
99-11-27	25.5(b)	24
99-15-35	16.3(b)	9
99-17-1	18.3(c)	72
99-17-1	18.3(c)	87

MISSISSIPPI CODE

Sec.	This Work Sec.	Note
99-17-1	18.3(c)	96
99-17-1	18.3(c)	111
99-17-27	8.11(b)	20
99-19-307	26.1(c)	62
99-43-11	13.1(a)	22
99-43-11	13.1(a)	23
99-43-11	21.3(f)	314
99-43-11	21.3(f)	317
99-43-27	21.3(f)	410
99-43-33	21.3(f)	392
99-43-37	12.1(f)	94
99-43-37	12.1(f)	104
99-43-37	21.3(f)	381
99-43-37	21.3(f)	413

MISSISSIPPI RULES OF APPELLATE PROCEDURE

Rule	This Work Sec.	Note
6	11.2(b)	68

MISSISSIPPI RULES OF EVIDENCE

Rule	This Work Sec.	Note
403	5.3(a)	4
1101(d)(2)	15.2(d)	107

MISSISSIPPI UNIFORM CRIMINAL RULE CIRCUIT & COUNTY COURT PRACTICE

Rule	This Work Sec.	Note
1.01	1.7(f)	71
6.04	14.3(a)	1
7.08	17.2(a)	7
8.04	21.3(c)	201
8.05	11.3(a)	6
8.05	11.5(c)	36
8.05	11.5(c)	45
9.04 to 9.07	20.2(b)	16
9.04(A)	20.3(a)	1
9.04(A)	20.3(i)	161
9.04(C)	20.4(g)	103
10.05	24.11(d)	12

MISSOURI CONSTITUTION

Art.	This Work Sec.	Note
I, § 17	15.1(g)	344
I, § 18(a)	16.1(b)	91
I, § 20	12.3(b)	37
I, § 32	12.1(f)	69

MISSOURI CONSTITUTION

Art.	This Work Sec.	Note
I, § 32	12.1(f)	73
I, § 32	12.1(f)	82
I, § 32	12.1(f)	92
I, § 32	12.1(f)	96
I, § 32	12.3(b)	37
I, § 32	12.3(b)	38
I, § 32	21.3(f)	302
I, § 32	21.3(f)	339
I, § 32	21.3(f)	342
I, § 32	21.3(f)	364
I, § 32	21.3(f)	376
I, § 32	26.5(d)	64
V, § 5	1.7(f)	91

MISSOURI STATUTES ANNOTATED

Sec.	This Work Sec.	Note
56.750	1.7(j)	217
217.762	26.5(d)	64
536.075	24.4(a)	7
540.021	1.7(e)	59
540.070	15.4(b)	52
540.60	15.4(b)	30
540.60	15.4(g)	153
540.60	15.4(g)	156
540.80	15.2(d)	95
540.110	8.5(d)	119
540.160	8.8(f)	145
540.200	8.3(a)	1
540.220	15.2(b)	20
541.033	16.1(d)	151
541.033(2)	16.1(e)	186
541.040	16.4(c)	74
541.060	16.1(e)	181
541.20	16.1(h)	304
544.193 to 544.197	1.7(e)	66
545.010	15.1(g)	345
545.040	15.1(g)	360
545.390	20.2(e)	82
545.400	20.2(e)	82
545.540	16.3(b)	19
545.780	18.3(c)	114
545.820	11.2(a)	28
546.080	19.6(b)	10
546.270	24.5(b)	21
547.035	24.11(d)	47
547.20	27.3(a)	10
547.200(1)	27.3(c)	55
547.200(2)	27.3(c)	55
557.021	1.8(d)	68
557.036	26.2(b)	12
557.041	21.3(f)	377

MISSOURI STATUTES ANNOTATED

Sec.	This Work Sec.	Note
557.041	21.3(f)	381
557.041	21.3(f)	389
558.026	26.3(f)	58
562.066	5.1(c)	17
562.066	5.2(a)	4
577.023(2)	26.6(b)	20
595.209	21.3(f)	321
595.209	21.3(f)	323
600.051	11.3(b)	42

MISSOURI RULES OF CRIMINAL PROCEDURE

Rule	This Work Sec.	Note
19.01	1.7(f)	71
21.03	12.5(a)	6
22.09(h)	14.3(a)	1
23.05	17.1(a)	4
23.05	17.1(b)	19
23.06	17.2(a)	3
24.06	17.3(d)	50
25	20.2(b)	16
25.03(A)	20.2(e)	103
25.03(A)	20.3(i)	161
25.03(A)(2)	20.3(c)	70
25.03(A)(2)	20.3(d)	87
25.03(A)(5)	20.3(f)	98
25.03(C)	20.3(a)	3
25.03(C)	20.3(a)	4
25.03(C)	20.3(a)	21
25.05(A)(3)	20.5(h)	104
25.05(A)(5)	20.2(c)	54
25.12	20.2(e)	82
25.12	20.2(e)	89
25.15	20.2(e)	82
25.15	20.2(e)	89
29.07(a)(1)	26.5(b)	37
31.0	11.2(a)	81
31.02	11.2(a)	28
31.02	11.2(a)	32
31.02	11.3(a)	6
31.02	11.3(b)	52

MISSOURI RULES OF EVIDENCE

Rule	This Work Sec.	Note
1101(d)(2)	15.2(d)	107

MISSOURI SUPREME COURT RULES OF CRIMINAL PROCEDURE

Rule	This Work Sec.	Note
21.06	1.8(c)	29

MONTANA CONSTITUTION

Art.	This Work Sec.	Note
II, § 10	2.12(b)	87
II, § 20(1)	15.1(g)	344
II, § 21	12.3(b)	33
II, § 24	16.1(b)	92
II, § 24	16.3(a)	4
II, § 24	16.3(d)	52

MONTANA CODE ANNOTATED

Sec.	This Work Sec.	Note
3-1-804	22.4(d)	32
25-7-301	24.8(a)	15
25-20-32(b)	24.4(a)	10
45-2-213	5.2(a)	4
46-1-101	1.3(e)	37
46-1-103	1.7(e)	59
46-2-101	16.4(c)	87
46-2-101	16.4(c)	94
46-3-112	16.1(d)	134
46-3-112	16.1(d)	150
46-6-201	12.5(a)	4
46-6-310	12.5(b)	19
46-8-101	11.2(a)	28
46-8-101	11.2(a)	35
46-8-102	11.3(a)	6
46-8-111	11.2(g)	263
46-8-111	11.2(g)	303
46-8-212	11.7(e)	68
46-10-5	14.2(d)	63
46-10-5(2)	14.2(d)	62
46-10-15	14.2(e)	67
46-10-105	14.2(d)	47
46-10-105	14.2(d)	50
46-10-203	14.3(a)	1
46-10-203	14.3(a)	37
46-10-203	14.3(c)	74
46-11-102(1)	15.1(g)	345
46-11-201	14.2(d)	63
46-11-205	19.5(c)	47
46-11-302	15.4(b)	27
46-11-302(2)	15.4(b)	44
46-11-302(2)	15.4(f)	147
46-11-304	8.4(b)	107
46-11-310	15.1(g)	360
46-11-314(2)	15.2(b)	29
46-11-316	15.2(i)	209
46-11-316	15.2(i)	214
46-11-331	14.3(a)	37
46-11-331	15.2(f)	149
46-11-404	17.1(a)	4
46-11-404	17.1(b)	19
46-11-404	17.2(a)	5

MONTANA CODE ANNOTATED

Sec.	This Work Sec.	Note
46-11-404	17.3(a)	5
46-11-404	17.3(d)	49
46-11-503	17.4(c)	143
46-11-503	17.4(c)	152
46-11-503	17.4(c)	153
46-11-504	25.5(b)	26
46-12-211	21.3(c)	201
46-13-301	10.3(c)	53
46-13-401	18.3(c)	72
46-13-401	18.3(c)	87
46-13-401	18.3(c)	95
46-13-401	18.3(c)	106
46-13-401	18.3(c)	113
46-15-103	24.3(f)	144
46-15-201(3)	1.8(c)	34
46-15-322 to 46-15-329	20.2(b)	16
46-15-323(5)	20.6(a)	11
46-15-324	20.3(h)	139
46-15-329	24.4(a)	7
46-15-329(3)	20.6(a)	9
46-15-329(5)	20.6(a)	8
46-15-331	24.3(i)	197
46-16-401(1)	24.8(a)	3
46-16-403	24.6(b)	22
46-16-702	25.4(b)	19
46-16-703	25.4(b)	19
46-18-113	26.5(c)	45
46-18-301	26.2(b)	5
46-18-404(1)	26.6(e)	76
46-18-501	26.6(b)	28
46-20-103	27.3(c)	53
46-20-104	27.2(a)	4
46-21-101 to 46-21-203	28.11(b)	22
46-21-102(2)	28.11(b)	33
46-21-110	24.11(d)	47
46-22-307	12.4(e)	88

MONTANA RULES OF EVIDENCE

Rule	This Work Sec.	Note
1101(c)(2)	15.2(d)	107

NEBRASKA CONSTITUTION

Art.	This Work Sec.	Note
I, § 9	12.3(b)	36
I, § 9	12.3(e)	118
I, § 10	15.1(g)	358
I, § 11	24.3(f)	154
I, § 23	27.1(a)	5

NEBRASKA CONSTITUTION

Art.	This Work Sec.	Note
I, § 28	12.1(f)	69
I, § 28	12.1(f)	73
I, § 28	12.1(f)	81
I, § 28	21.3(f)	302
I, § 28	21.3(f)	340

NEBRASKA REVISED STATUTES

Sec.	This Work Sec.	Note
23-1201	21.3(f)	309
23-1201	21.3(f)	317
24-739	22.4(d)	32
25-1637	15.4(b)	29
25-1637	15.4(b)	50
25-1912	27.2(a)	3
27-1101(4)(a)	15.2(d)	107
28-105.01	26.2(b)	6
28-106	1.8(c)	11
29-301	16.3(b)	19
29-422	12.5(b)	22
29-425	12.5(a)	5
29-506	14.3(a)	2
29-1205	18.3(c)	119
29-1205	18.3(c)	120
29-1207	18.3(c)	72
29-1207	18.3(c)	81
29-1207	18.3(c)	95
29-1207	18.3(c)	100
29-1208	18.3(c)	108
29-1301	16.3(b)	8
29-1306	16.1(e)	177
29-1307	16.1(e)	181
29-1401	8.1(b)	15
29-1401	8.4(b)	82
29-1401	15.2(c)	70
29-1404	15.2(b)	20
29-1409 to 29-1412.01	8.6(a)	31
29-1409	8.10(d)	100
29-1410.01	8.4(b)	87
29-1410.01	15.2(c)	73
29-1411	8.10(c)	64
29-1411	8.14(a)	20
29-1411	8.14(b)	28
29-1411	8.14(d)	61
29-1412	8.3(a)	4
29-1412	8.3(a)	5
29-1412.01(3)	8.8(h)	180
29-1416(2)	15.2(h)	193

NEBRASKA REVISED STATUTES

Sec.	This Work Sec.	Note
29-1420	8.3(h)	37
29-1501	19.1(d)	36
29-1502	19.3(d)	203
29-1601	15.1(g)	344
29-1601	15.1(g)	345
29-1912 to 29-1928	20.2(b)	16
29-1912	20.3(c)	76
29-1912	20.3(g)	118
29-1912(1)(a)	20.3(b)	39
29-1912(1)(a)	20.3(b)	40
29-1912(1)(d)	20.3(i)	173
29-1917	20.2(e)	82
29-1927	20.4(c)	49
29-1927	20.5(a)	10
29-1927	20.5(b)	13
29-1927	20.6(a)	11
29-2002	17.1(a)	4
29-2002	17.1(b)	19
29-2002	17.3(a)	5
29-2002	17.3(d)	49
29-2203	20.5(a)	10
29-2221(2)	26.6(b)	16
29-2260(2)	26.1(d)	86
29-2315.01	27.3(a)	7
29-2520	26.2(b)	5
29-2912	20.2(c)	46
29-3902	11.2(a)	28
29-3902	11.2(b)	79
29-3903	11.2(a)	28
29-3903	11.2(b)	70
29-3903	11.2(b)	73
29-3906	11.2(a)	28
29-3915	11.2(a)	28
29-3915(2)	11.2(b)	76
29-3916	11.2(a)	28
29-3916	11.2(g)	303
29-4120	24.11(d)	46
39-2315.02	27.3(a)	7
81-1848	12.1(f)	73
169.015	1.7(e)	59
172.155	15.2(f)	148

NEBRASKA RULES OF EVIDENCE

Rule	This Work Sec.	Note
1101(4)(a)	15.2(d)	107

NEBRASKA RULES OF PROFESSIONAL RESPONSIBILITY

Rule	This Work Sec.	Note
DR 7-107	23.1(b)	19

NEVADA CONSTITUTION

Art.	This Work Sec.	Note
I, § 7	12.3(b)	35
I, § 8	12.1(f)	69
I, § 8	12.1(f)	73
I, § 8	12.1(f)	82
I, § 8	15.1(g)	344
I, § 8	15.1(g)	358
I, § 9	12.3(e)	119
II, § 8	21.3(f)	302

NEVADA REVISED STATUTES

Sec.	This Work Sec.	Note
3.230	24.6(e)	47
6.130	8.1(b)	15
7.135	11.2(e)	170
7.135	11.2(e)	219
47.020	14.4(b)	6
169.05	14.3(a)	1
171.035	16.1(e)	170
171.035	16.1(e)	172
171.186	14.2(e)	70
171.1771	12.5(b)	21
171.1965	20.2(b)	16
171.1965	20.3(c)	76
171.1965	20.3(e)	95
171.1965	20.3(i)	159
172.005	15.1(g)	358
172.055	15.4(b)	40
172.055	15.4(b)	46
172.065	15.4(f)	147
172.095	15.2(e)	128
172.135	15.2(d)	95
172.135	15.5(c)	123
172.145	15.2(b)	29
172.145	15.2(c)	62
172.155	15.2(f)	148
172.155	15.5(c)	117
172.197	8.10(c)	64
172.205	8.4(b)	106
172.225(3)	15.2(i)	209
172.241	15.2(c)	74
172.267	8.3(h)	51
172.271	8.3(h)	52
172.295	8.5(d)	132
173.025	15.1(g)	345
173.035	14.2(d)	62
173.035	14.3(c)	70
173.095	19.5(b)	2
173.115	17.1(a)	4
173.115	17.1(b)	21
173.115	17.2(a)	3
174.105	16.4(d)	143

NEVADA REVISED STATUTES

Sec.	This Work Sec.	Note
174.165	17.3(d)	49
174.233 to 174.235	20.2(b)	16
174.315	8.4(b)	22
174.315	8.4(b)	40
174.455	16.3(d)	52
174.519	18.3(c)	124
175.091	22.4(e)	48
175.181	24.5(c)	39
175.554	26.2(b)	7
175.556	26.2(b)	7
176.015(3)	26.5(d)	62
176.156	26.5(c)	45
176.185	26.1(d)	78
176.185	26.1(d)	79
176.0918	24.11(d)	44
177.315 et seq.	28.11(b)	23
178.397	11.1(d)	127
178.397	11.2(a)	28
178.397	11.2(b)	79
178.556	18.3(c)	72
178.556	18.3(c)	89
178.556	18.3(c)	95
178.562(2)	14.3(c)	70
193.165	26.1(c)	60
207.010	26.6(b)	2
483.560(2)	26.1(d)	84

NEVADA RULES OF PROFESSIONAL CONDUCT

Rule	This Work Sec.	Note
177	23.1(b)	11
177	23.1(b)	14

NEW HAMPSHIRE CONSTITUTION

Pt.	This Work Sec.	Note
1	2.1	16
1, Art. 17	16.1(c)	102
1, Art. 17	16.3(a)	4
1, Art. 33	12.3(b)	31
2, Art. 88	15.1(d)	246
2, Art. 88	15.1(d)	251

NEW HAMPSHIRE REVISED STATUTES ANNOTATED

Sec.	This Work Sec.	Note
17.13	20.2(e)	82
17.13(b)	20.2(e)	90
21-M:8-k	12.1(f)	68
21-M:8-k	13.1(a)	20

NEW HAMPSHIRE REVISED STATUTES ANNOTATED

Sec.	This Work Sec.	Note
21-M:8-k	13.1(a)	23
21-M:8-k	21.3(f)	301
21-M:8-k	21.3(f)	310
21-M:8-k	21.3(f)	321
21-M:8-k	21.3(f)	339
71.020	16.4(c)	90
194.020(1)	16.4(c)	87
517.13	20.2(e)	82
517.13	20.2(e)	88
517.13(v)	20.2(e)	91
534	28.11(b)	13
592-A:1	1.7(e)	59
592-A:14	12.5(a)	4
597:1-d	12.3(b)	49
597:7-a	12.3(b)	50
600-A:1	8.1(b)	16
600-A:1	8.1(b)	18
601:1	15.1(d)	187
601:1	15.1(d)	235
601:1	15.1(d)	247
601:1	15.1(d)	251
601:2	15.1(f)	285
601:2	15.1(f)	295
601:2	15.1(f)	326
601:8	19.3(d)	205
604-A:2	11.2(a)	28
604-A:2	11.2(a)	31
604-A:2	11.2(b)	79
604-A:2(c)	11.2(g)	260
604-A:2(c)	11.2(g)	270
604-A:2(I)	11.2(g)	301
604-A:2(III)	11.2(g)	299
604-A:6	11.2(e)	219
625	16.4(c)	81
625:4	16.4(c)	76
625:4	16.4(c)	78
625:4	16.4(c)	83
625:4	16.4(c)	103
625:10	16.1(g)	270
625:10	16.4(d)	131
625:11	16.1(g)	270
625:11	16.4(d)	123
625:11	16.4(d)	131
626:5	5.2(b)	24
651:4	26.5(b)	31
651:4	26.5(c)	45
651-D:2	24.11(d)	43
651-D:2	24.11(d)	45

NEW HAMPSHIRE RULES OF EVIDENCE

Rule	This Work Sec.	Note
1101(d)(2)	15.2(d)	107
1101(d)(3)	14.4(b)	9

NEW HAMPSHIRE RULES OF SUPERIOR COURT

Rule	This Work Sec.	Note
1	1.7(f)	71
98 to 100	20.2(b)	16
98(2)	20.3(k)	222

NEW JERSEY CONSTITUTION

Art.	This Work Sec.	Note
I, ¶ 8	15.1(d)	188
I, ¶ 8	15.1(d)	207
I, ¶ 8	15.1(d)	230
I, ¶ 8	15.1(d)	246
I, ¶ 8	15.1(f)	270
I, ¶ 11	12.3(b)	33
I, ¶ 12	2.12(a)	69
I, ¶ 22	12.1(f)	69
I, ¶ 22	21.3(f)	302

NEW JERSEY STATUTES ANNOTATED

Sec.	This Work Sec.	Note
2A:81-17.2a2	8.11(d)	71
2A:81-17.3	8.11(d)	73
2A:84A-16(2)	15.2(d)	93
2A:84A-32a	24.11(d)	42
2A:84A-32a	24.11(d)	43
2A:152-1	1.7(e)	59
2A:158-14	11.2(g)	272
2A:158A-1	11.2(a)	28
2A:158A-2	11.2(a)	28
2A:158A-5	11.2(a)	28
2A:158A-14	11.2(g)	269
2A:158A-14	11.2(g)	271
2A:158A-14	11.2(g)	286
2A:158A-14	11.2(g)	296
2A:158A-14	11.2(g)	300
2A:158A-14(f)	11.2(g)	270
2A:163-5	18.3(c)	124
2A:738-1	15.2(j)	235
2B:21-3	8.4(b)	76
2B:21-9	8.3(h)	37
2B:24-1	11.2(a)	28
2B:24-1	11.2(a)	32
2B:24-1	11.2(a)	34
2B:25-11	21.3(c)	201

NEW JERSEY STATUTES ANNOTATED

Sec.	This Work Sec.	Note
2C:1-3	16.4(c)	99
2C:1-3	16.4(c)	101
2C:1-3	16.4(c)	103
2C:2-12	5.1(c)	17
2C:2-12	5.2(b)	24
2C:43-6	26.1(c)	53
2C:43-6	26.3(d)	22
2C:43-6.2	26.3(c)	19
2C:44-1	26.3(d)	25
2D:1-3	16.4(c)	111
39:5-25	12.5(b)	19
52:9M-1	8.1(c)	42
52:9M-2	8.1(c)	42

NEW JERSEY COURT RULES

Rule	This Work Sec.	Note
1:12-1	22.4(b)	18

NEW JERSEY RULES OF CRIMINAL PROCEDURE

Rule	This Work Sec.	Note
2:7-2	11.2(b)	70
3:1-1	1.7(f)	71
3:3-1	12.5(a)	6
3:5-7	10.2(a)	8
3:6-2	15.4(b)	34
3:6-2	15.4(b)	39
3:6-2	15.4(b)	40
3:6-2	15.4(b)	47
3:6-2	15.4(b)	61
3:6-6	15.2(i)	209
3:6-6	15.2(i)	211
3:6-6	15.2(j)	243
3:6-6(a)	15.7(h)	222
3:6-6(b)	8.5(d)	133
3:6-6(b)	15.2(i)	213
3:6-6-6(b)	15.2(j)	235
3:6-7	8.5(d)	125
3:6-10	8.4(c)	118
3:7-2	15.1(d)	188
3:7-2	15.1(d)	247
3:7-2	15.1(f)	295
3:7-2	15.1(f)	326
3:7-4	19.5(b)	2
3:7-4	19.5(c)	49
3:7-5	19.4(b)	13
3:7-5	19.4(b)	19
3:7-6	17.1(a)	4
3:7-6	17.1(b)	19
3:7-6	17.1(b)	21

NEW JERSEY RULES OF CRIMINAL PROCEDURE

Rule	This Work Sec.	Note
3:7-7	15.1(f)	286
3:7-7	15.1(f)	306
3:7-7	17.2(a)	3
3:10(2)	19.1(d)	55
3:12-1	20.5(d)	60
3:12-2	20.2(b)	16
3:13(e)	20.3(j)	212
3:13-3	8.5(g)	216
3:13-3	15.2(i)	209
3:13-3	15.2(i)	211
3:13-3	20.2(b)	16
3:13-3	20.2(b)	41
3:13-3	20.2(c)	45
3:13-3	20.4(g)	100
3:13-3	20.5(e)	66
3:13-3(b)	20.4(g)	104
3:13-3(c)	20.3(f)	117
3:13-3(c)	20.3(k)	222
3:13-3(c)(6)	20.3(h)	139
3:13-3(d)	20.5(h)	106
3:13-3(f)(1)	20.3(l)	230
3:13-3(f)(2)	20.3(l)	232
3:13-4	20.2(d)	75
3:15-1	17.3(a)	5
3:15-1	17.4(c)	143
3:15-1	17.4(c)	152
3:15-1(b)	16.1(f)	220
3:15-1(b)	17.4(c)	153
3:15-2	17.3(d)	49
3:24	14.3(c)	62

NEW JERSEY RULES OF APPELLATE PROCEDURE

Rule	This Work Sec.	Note
2:3-1(b)(3)	27.3(d)	69
2:3-1(b)(5)	27.3(c)	56

NEW JERSEY RULES OF EVIDENCE

Rule	This Work Sec.	Note
2	15.2(d)	93
403	26.5(d)	70

NEW MEXICO CONSTITUTION

Art.	This Work Sec.	Note
II, § 13	12.3(b)	37
II, § 13	12.3(b)	41
II, § 14	14.2(d)	60
II, § 14	15.1(g)	344

NEW MEXICO CONSTITUTION

Art.	This Work Sec.	Note
II, § 14	15.1(g)	345
II, § 14	15.1(g)	358
II, § 14	16.1(b)	92
II, § 24	12.1(f)	69
II, § 24	12.1(f)	96
II, § 24	13.1(a)	24
II, § 24	21.3(f)	302
II, § 24	21.3(f)	306
VI, § 2	27.1(a)	5

NEW MEXICO STATUTES ANNOTATED

Sec.	This Work Sec.	Note
5-501	1.8(c)	33
5-606(d)	1.8(c)	35
6-504	1.8(c)	33
6-605(c)	1.8(c)	35
29-16-6	3.5(d)	148
30-1-6	1.8(c)	11
31-1-1	1.7(e)	59
31-1-6	12.5(b)	19
31-1-6-3(b)	11.1(d)	129
31-1A-2	24.11(d)	43
31-1A-2	24.11(d)	47
31-6-1(B)	15.7(f)	134
31-6-3	15.4(b)	74
31-6-3(C)	15.4(g)	156
31-6-3(C)	15.4(g)	159
31-6-4	8.14(b)	25
31-6-4	8.14(b)	28
31-6-6	8.5(d)	125
31-6-9	15.2(e)	128
31-6-10	15.1(g)	358
31-6-10	15.2(f)	148
31-6-11	15.2(d)	96
31-6-11(B)	15.2(b)	29
31-6-11(B)	15.2(c)	74
31-6-11(B)	15.2(c)	77
31-6-11(B)	15.7(f)	149
31-6-11.1	15.2(h)	193
31-6-12	8.7(e)	87
31-6-12	8.10(c)	52
31-6-12(A)	8.4(b)	19
31-16-2 to 31-16-4	11.2(a)	28
31-16-3	11.1(d)	129
31-16-3	11.2(b)	68
31-16-3	11.2(b)	76
31-16-3	11.2(b)	81
31-16-5	11.2(g)	295
31-16-6	11.3(b)	37
31-17-1(A)(1)	26.6(c)	35
31-18-16	26.1(c)	60

NEW MEXICO STATUTES ANNOTATED

	This Work	
Sec.	Sec.	Note
31-18-19	26.6(b)	9
31-18-23	26.6(b)	25
31-21-15	26.9(a)	8
31-21-25(C)	26.2(c)	50
31-26-4	21.3(f)	306
35-3-4	1.8(c)	25
38-1-1	1.7(f)	95
38-3-3	16.3(d)	52
38-3-3(c)	16.3(b)	10
38-3-4	16.1(h)	286
38-3-7	16.3(g)	104
38-3-9	22.4(d)	32
38-3-31	16.3(b)	13
39-3-3	27.3(d)	63
57-5-20	16.2(g)	109

NEW MEXICO RULES OF EVIDENCE

	This Work	
Rule	Sec.	Note
11-1101	14.4(b)	6

NEW MEXICO RULES OF PROFESSIONAL CONDUCT

	This Work	
Rule	Sec.	Note
3.6	23.1(b)	14

NEW MEXICO DISTRICT COURT RULES OF CRIMINAL PROCEDURE

	This Work	
Rule	Sec.	Note
5-101	1.7(f)	71
5-106(F)	22.4(e)	48
5-201	19.1(d)	40
5-203	17.1(a)	4
5-203	17.1(b)	19
5-203	17.1(b)	21
5-203	17.2(a)	6
5-203	17.3(d)	49
5-204	19.5(b)	2
5-204	19.5(b)	5
5-204	19.6(a)	4
5-208	12.5(a)	4
5-301	14.2(a)	5
5-501	20.2(b)	16
5-501(A)	20.3(i)	161
5-501(A)	20.3	260
5-501(G)	20.3(b)	41
5-502	20.2(b)	16
5-503(B)	20.2(e)	85
5-506	15.2(i)	209
5-506	15.2(i)	213

NEW MEXICO DISTRICT COURT RULES OF CRIMINAL PROCEDURE

	This Work	
Rule	Sec.	Note
5-506(B)	15.2(j)	243
5-601(D)	15.4(b)	74
5-601(G)	15.4(b)	74
5-604	18.3(c)	72
5-604	18.3(c)	75
5-604	18.3(c)	76
5-604	18.3(c)	77
5-604	18.3(c)	87
5-604	18.3(c)	96
5-604	18.3(c)	105
5-604	18.3(c)	108
7-501	11.2(a)	28
7-502	21.3(c)	201

NEW YORK CONSTITUTION

	This Work	
Art.	Sec.	Note
I, § 6	15.1(d)	189
I, § 6	15.1(d)	205
I, § 6	15.1(d)	209
I, § 6	15.1(f)	279
I, § 6	15.1(f)	281
I, § 6	15.1(f)	284
I, § 6	15.1(f)	312
I, § 6	15.1(f)	326
I, § 6	15.1(f)	329
I, § 55	12.3(b)	31
XII	2.1	18
XXXIV	2.1	18
XXXV	2.1	18

NEW YORK CIVIL PRACTICE LAW

	This Work	
Sec.	Sec.	Note
10.27.140	15.2(b)	31

NEW YORK CITY CRIMINAL COURT ACT

	This Work	
Sec.	Sec.	Note
31	16.1(a)	25

NEW YORK CODE OF PROFESSIONAL RESPONSIBILITY

	This Work	
Sec.	Sec.	Note
DR 7-107	23.1(b)	11

NEW YORK CORRECTION LAW

	This Work	
Sec.	Sec.	Note
803(1)	26.2(c)	57

NEW YORK COUNTY LAW

Sec.	This Work Sec.	Note
722(c)	11.2(e)	170
722(c)	11.2(e)	219
722(c)	11.2(e)	222

NEW YORK CRIMINAL PROCEDURE LAW

Sec.	This Work Sec.	Note
1.00	1.7(e)	59
5.15	1.6(e)	325
20.30	16.4(c)	78
20.40	16.1(d)	151
20.40(2)	16.1(e)	187
20.40.4	16.1(e)	186
30.30	18.3(c)	72
30.30	18.3(c)	75
30.30	18.3(c)	76
30.30	18.3(c)	81
30.30	18.3(c)	99
30.30	18.3(c)	100
30.30	18.3(c)	106
30.30	18.3(c)	109
30.30	18.3(c)	118
40.10	16.1(f)	214
40.20	17.4(c)	143
40.20	25.5(b)	26
40.20(2)(b)	17.4(c)	151
50.10	8.11(b)	19
70.00(3)	26.2(c)	30
120.20	12.5(a)	6
140.10	1.8(f)	102
170.10	11.2(a)	28
180.10	11.2(a)	28
180.10(2)	14.2(f)	87
180.10(5)	11.3(b)	28
180.60	14.4(b)	27
180.60	14.4(d)	78
180.60(8)	14.4(b)	28
180.70	14.3(a)	1
190.05	8.4(c)	112
190.20	15.4(b)	32
190.20	15.4(b)	45
190.20(2)(b)	15.4(a)	20
190.25	8.5(b)	43
190.25	8.5(c)	70
190.25	8.5(e)	161
190.25	8.14(b)	27
190.25	15.7(h)	222
190.25(4)	8.5(h)	231
190.30	15.2(d)	100
190.30(3)	14.4(b)	28
190.30(7)	15.2(e)	140
190.35 to 190.45	8.11(b)	19

NEW YORK CRIMINAL PROCEDURE LAW

Sec.	This Work Sec.	Note
190.40 to 190.45	8.10(c)	60
190.40	8.10(c)	61
190.40	8.11(a)	9
190.40	8.11(d)	71
190.45	8.11(d)	71
190.50	8.4(b)	42
190.50	8.4(b)	44
190.50	15.2(c)	75
190.50(5)	15.2(c)	74
190.50(5)(a)	15.2(c)	77
190.50(6)	15.2(b)	52
190.52	8.14(b)	28
190.52	15.2(c)	86
190.55(2)(a)	15.3(b)	35
190.65(1)	15.2(f)	148
190.75(3)	15.2(h)	191
190.75(3)	15.2(h)	194
190.85 to 190.90	8.3(h)	54
195.10	15.1(f)	285
195.10	15.1(f)	298
195.10	15.1(f)	299
195.10(1)(b)	15.1(d)	189
195.10(1)(b)	15.1(d)	247
195.10(1)(c)	15.1(f)	312
200.20	17.1(a)	5
200.20	17.1(b)	20
200.20	17.1(b)	21
200.40	17.2(a)	7
200.50(7)	19.1(d)	40
200.70	19.5(b)	25
200.70	19.5(b)	41
200.70	19.5(b)	46
200.95	19.4(b)	16
210.20	15.6(a)	4
210.20	15.6(b)	47
210.20(1)(b)	15.5(c)	116
210.20(1)(c)	15.4(b)	45
210.30	15.5(c)	116
210.30	15.6(b)	47
210.30(2)	15.5(c)	133
210.30(b)	15.5(c)	130
210.35	15.6(a)	4
210.35	15.6(b)	47
210.35	15.6(d)	108
210.35	15.6(d)	124
210.35	15.7(d)	90
210.35(1)	15.4(b)	45
210.35(1)	15.4(f)	143
220.10	21.3(c)	203
230.20	16.3(b)	15
230.20	16.3(d)	52
240	20.2(b)	16

NEW YORK CRIMINAL PROCEDURE LAW

	This Work	
Sec.	Sec.	Note
240.20	20.3(c)	70
240.20(1)	20.3(f)	111
240.20(1)(a)	20.3(d)	88
240.45	8.5(g)	217
240.70	24.4(a)	7
240.75	20.6(b)	53
250.10	20.4(e)	76
250.10	20.5(c)	31
250.10(1)	20.5(c)	40
250.10(3)	20.5(c)	36
250.10(5)	20.5(c)	38
255.20(1)	15.4(b)	61
255.20(3)	15.4(b)	58
256	1.6(d)	279
260.30	24.8(a)	15
270.40	24.8(a)	2
275 to 295	19.1(b)	22
300.10(2)	24.8(c)	41
310.10	24.9(a)	4
310.70	24.10(d)	46
390.50	26.5(c)	45
390.50(2)(a)	26.5(c)	50
440.10	24.11(d)	14
440.30	24.11(d)	39
450.20	27.3(a)	10
450.20(8)	27.3(c)	37
450.50	27.3(c)	47
460.30	26.6(d)	54
470.05(2)	24.8(b)	32
470.15	25.4(b)	19
530.60	12.3(b)	48
552	1.6(d)	278
553	1.6(d)	278
610.25	8.8(g)	165
710.30	10.2(a)	10
710.30	20.2(d)	63

NEW YORK EXECUTIVE LAW

	This Work	
Sec.	Sec.	Note
632-a	1.5(k)	382
642	21.3(f)	314
642	21.3(f)	317
647	12.1(f)	73
647	21.3(f)	365
647	21.3(f)	375

NEW YORK JUDICIARY LAW

	This Work	
Sec.	Sec.	Note
325(1)	15.2(j)	244
325(1)	22.2(b)	16

NEW YORK PENAL LAW

	This Work	
Sec.	Sec.	Note
10.00	1.8(c)	11
11	1.6(d)	293
40.05	5.2(b)	24
70.00(2)	26.2(c)	29
70.25	26.3(f)	58
215.51	8.3(a)	10
215.70	8.5(b)	19
460.30	26.6(d)	54
460.30(2)	26.6(d)	52
460.30(2)(b)	26.6(d)	57
480.10(6)(b)	26.6(d)	57

NEW YORK UNCONSOLIDATED LAWS

	This Work	
Sec.	Sec.	Note
7502	8.1(c)	42
9803	8.1(c)	42

NORTH CAROLINA CONSTITUTION

	This Work	
Art.	Sec.	Note
I, § 22	15.1(d)	190
I, § 22	15.1(d)	200
I, § 22	15.1(d)	207
I, § 22	15.1(d)	236
I, § 22	15.1(d)	246
I, § 22	15.1(f)	279
I, § 22	15.1(f)	281
I, § 22	15.1(f)	283
I, § 24	24.6(a)	6
I, § 27	12.3(b)	31
I, § 37	12.1(f)	69
I, § 37	12.1(f)	79
I, § 37	12.1(f)	81
I, § 37	12.1(f)	92
I, § 37	12.1(f)	100
I, § 37	21.3(f)	302
I, § 37	21.3(f)	338
I, § 37	21.3(f)	339
I, § 37	21.3(f)	345

NORTH CAROLINA GENERAL STATUTES

	This Work	
Sec.	Sec.	Note
1A-450(b)	11.2(e)	220
5A-12	8.3(a)	10
7A-451	11.2(a)	28
7A-451	11.2(a)	33
7A-451	11.2(b)	81
7A-455	11.2(h)	313
7A-455	11.2(h)	316

NORTH CAROLINA GENERAL STATUTES

Sec.	This Work Sec.	Note
7AS-498.2	1.4(f)	124
8C-1	24.4(a)	6
9-1	1.7(e)	67
14-1	15.1(d)	236
14-7.1	26.6(b)	23
14-7.7 to 14-7.12	26.6(b)	4
15-6	1.7(e)	59
15-10	18.3(c)	71
15-10	18.3(c)	106
15-10	18.3(c)	115
15-173	24.6(b)	27
15-623(h)	8.4(b)	27
15A-3-3	12.5(a)	4
15A-132	16.1(d)	149
15A-132	16.1(d)	150
15A-132	16.1(f)	225
15A-133	16.1(h)	286
15A-133	16.3(g)	105
15A-134	25.5(b)	24
15A-302	12.5(b)	19
15A-304(f)	1.8(f)	101
15A-401(c)	1.8(f)	102
15A-402	1.8(f)	104
15A-603	11.2(a)	28
15A-603	11.3(a)	21
15A-603	11.3(b)	28
15A-606	14.1(a)	1
15A-606	14.2(e)	67
15A-606(a)	14.2(e)	74
15A-611	14.4(b)	37
15A-612	14.3(c)	74
15A-621	8.4(c)	112
15A-622(c)(2)	15.4(b)	32
15A-622(d)	8.4(b)	27
15A-622(e)	15.4(a)	16
15A-623(h)	15.2(j)	235
15A-626	8.4(b)	41
15A-626	8.4(b)	90
15A-626	15.2(b)	35
15A-626(a)	15.2(c)	70
15A-628	15.2(f)	148
15A-641	15.1(d)	249
15A-642	15.1(f)	285
15A-642	15.1(f)	295
15A-642	15.1(f)	329
15A-642(a)	15.1(d)	190
15A-642(a)	15.1(f)	247
15A-642(c)	15.1(f)	326
15A-832	13.1(a)	22
15A-832	13.1(a)	23
15A-832	21.3(f)	314
15A-832	21.3(f)	320

NORTH CAROLINA GENERAL STATUTES

Sec.	This Work Sec.	Note
15A-902 to 15A-910	20.2(b)	16
15A-903	20.3(f)	117
15A-903	20.3(h)	139
15A-903(3)	20.3(h)	140
15A-903(5)	20.3(b)	39
15A-903(a)(1)	20.1(c)	48
15A-903(a)(1)	20.3(i)	161
15A-905	20.5(d)	60
15A-924(a)	19.1(d)	40
15A-925(e)	19.4(a)	2
15A-926	17.1(a)	4
15A-926	17.1(b)	21
15A-926	17.2(a)	7
15A-926	17.4(c)	143
15A-926	17.4(c)	154
15A-926	17.4(c)	155
15A-926	17.4(c)	156
15A-926	17.4(c)	157
15A-927	17.3(d)	51
15A-952	15.4(b)	45
15A-952	19.1(d)	55
15A-952(c)	15.4(b)	74
15A-952(e)	15.4(b)	58
15A-957	16.3(b)	17
15A-957	16.3(g)	105
15A-0979	27.3(c)	48
15A-1053	8.11(d)	73
15A-1236	24.8(a)	3
15A-1242	11.3(b)	53
15A-1242(b)	11.5(c)	44
15A-1341(b)	26.1(d)	69
15A-1341(b)	26.1(d)	70
15A-1344	26.9(a)	12
15A-1415	24.11(d)	14
15A-1432	14.3(c)	59
17-1	1.7(e)	69
84-23	1.7(j)	245
615-173	24.6(b)	21

NORTH CAROLINA RULES OF EVIDENCE

Rule	This Work Sec.	Note
1101(b)(3)	26.5(a)	3
1101(d)(2)	15.2(d)	107

NORTH DAKOTA CONSTITUTION

Art.	This Work Sec.	Note
I, § 11	12.3(b)	33

NORTH DAKOTA CENTURY CODE

Sec.	This Work Sec.	Note
12.1-05-11	5.2(b)	24
12.1-32-09	26.6(e)	81
12.1-32-09	26.6(e)	82
12.1-34-02	26.5(d)	69
27-09.1-12	15.4(b)	71
29-01-01	1.7(e)	59
29-04-02	24.8(f)	112
29-10.1-05	15.4(b)	44
29-10.1-12	15.2(b)	20
29-10.1-26	15.2(d)	94
29-10.1-26	15.5(c)	123
29-10.1-27	15.2(b)	29
29-10.1-31	8.5(a)	4
29-10.1-38	15.2(i)	212
29-10.2-05	15.1(g)	358
29-010-13	15.1(g)	358
29-15-21	22.4(d)	32
29-15-21(4)	22.4(d)	44
29-19-02	18.3(c)	67
29-19-02	18.3(c)	121
29-28-06	27.2(a)	4
29-28-07-(5)	27.3(c)	48
29-32.1-01 to 29-32.1-14	28.11(b)	26
29-32.1-05	11.2(b)	76
29-32.1-15	24.3(e)	137
29-32.1-15	24.11(d)	47
29-101-10	15.4(b)	44

NORTH DAKOTA RULES OF CRIMINAL PROCEDURE

Rule	This Work Sec.	Note
1	1.3(e)	37
4	12.5(a)	5
5(c)	14.2(e)	74
5.1	14.3(c)	62
5.1	14.4(b)	12
7(a)	15.1(g)	344
7(a)	15.1(g)	345
7(e)	19.5(b)	4
7(f)	19.4(b)	13
7(g)	1.3(e)	40
8	17.1(a)	4
8	17.1(b)	19
8	17.2(a)	3
11	21.3(c)	201
12.1	20.2(b)	16
12.1	20.4(c)	46
12.1	20.4(e)	76
12.1(c)	20.6(a)	14
12.1(c)	20.6(c)	88

NORTH DAKOTA RULES OF CRIMINAL PROCEDURE

Rule	This Work Sec.	Note
12.1(f)	20.5(b)	22
12.2	20.2(b)	16
12.2	20.5(c)	31
12.2(c)	20.5(c)	35
12.2(c)	20.5(c)	48
12.2(e)	20.5(c)	51
13	17.3(a)	5
14	17.3(d)	49
15(a)	20.2(e)	87
15(a)(2)	20.2(e)	82
15(a)(2)	20.2(e)	88
15(a)(2)	20.2(e)	90
15(f)(1)	20.2(e)	94
16	20.2(b)	16
16(a)	20.3(c)	68
16(a)(1)	20.3(a)	8
16(a)(1)	20.3(a)	10
16(a)(1)(D)	20.3(f)	100
16(a)(1)(D)	20.3(f)	101
16(a)(2)	20.3(j)	204
16(b)(1)	20.4(g)	100
16(f)	20.3(h)	141
21	16.3(e)	79
21(b)	16.3(c)	27
25(a)	22.4(e)	48
31(e)	24.10(a)	11
32	26.5(c)	45
32(c)(1)	26.5(b)	37
35(a)	1.3(e)	39
44	11.1(d)	127
44	11.2(a)	28
44	11.2(a)	32
44	11.2(b)	68
52(a)	27.6(a)	10

NORTH DAKOTA RULES OF EVIDENCE

Rule	This Work Sec.	Note
1101	15.2(d)	94
1101	15.5(c)	123
1101(d)(2)	15.2(d)	107

NORTH DAKOTA RULES OF PROFESSIONAL CONDUCT

Rule	This Work Sec.	Note
3.6	23.1(b)	14

OHIO CONSTITUTION

Art.	This Work Sec.	Note
I, § 9	12.3(b)	37
I, § 9	12.3(b)	38
I, § 10	15.1(d)	191
I, § 10	15.1(d)	202
I, § 10	15.1(d)	207
I, § 10	15.1(d)	209
I, § 10	15.1(d)	246
I, § 10	15.1(f)	270
I, § 10	16.1(b)	91
I, § 10a	12.1(f)	69
I, § 10a	12.1(f)	100
I, § 10a	21.3(f)	302
IV, § 3	27.1(a)	5
IV, § 5(b)	1.7(f)	92

OHIO REVISED CODE

Sec.	This Work Sec.	Note
27.12(H)	16.1(f)	227
2151.35(F)	20.2(d)	69
2315.01(A)(5)	24.8(a)	14
2505.02	27.3(c)	57
2505.03	27.3(c)	57
2901.01	1.7(e)	59
2901.02	1.8(c)	11
2901.11	16.4(c)	74
2901.11	16.4(c)	99
2901.11	16.4(c)	102
2901.11	16.4(c)	103
2901.12(A)	16.1(c)	100
2901.12(A)	16.1(d)	151
2901.12(G)	16.1(e)	175
2901.12(H)	16.1(f)	225
2901.12(K)	16.3(a)	3
2901.12(K)	16.3(f)	86
2902.12(K)	16.3(c)	27
2925.42	26.6(d)	46
2925.42(B)(3)	26.6(d)	57
2929.024	11.2(e)	217
2929.04	11.2(e)	224
2929.12(D)	26.6(e)	79
2929.22(B)(1)(c)	26.6(e)	78
2930.06	21.3(f)	308
2930.06	21.3(f)	329
2935.26	12.5(b)	22
2937.11	14.4(b)	6
2937.12	14.3(a)	1
2937.13	14.3(b)	45
2939.06	15.2(b)	20
2939.07	15.2(e)	128
2939.14	8.3(a)	1
2941.021	15.1(f)	329

OHIO REVISED CODE

Sec.	This Work Sec.	Note
2941.26	19.6(b)	10
2941.28	19.3(c)	188
2941.621	15.1(f)	285
2945.1	18.3(c)	72
2945.44	8.11(b)	19
2945.50	20.2(e)	82
2945.50	20.2(e)	90
2945.67	14.3(c)	59
2945.67(a)	27.3(c)	56
2945.71	18.3(c)	89
2953.21	24.11(d)	43
2953.21	24.11(d)	46

OHIO RULES OF CRIMINAL PROCEDURE

Rule	This Work Sec.	Note
1	1.3(e)	37
1	1.7(f)	71
2	1.8(f)	99
2(c)	1.8(c)	19
2(d)	1.8(c)	18
4	12.5(a)	4
4(d)(2)	1.8(f)	101
5(a)	14.2(e)	70
5(a)(1)	20.3(a)	9
5(b)	14.2(c)	38
5(b)	14.2(f)	86
6(a)	15.2(g)	163
6(b)	15.4(b)	46
6(c)	15.1(d)	248
6(c)	15.4(a)	17
6(c)	15.4(e)	137
6(e)	8.5(b)	42
6(e)	8.5(c)	70
6(e)	8.5(d)	124
6(e)	8.5(e)	162
6(f)	15.1(d)	248
6(f)	15.2(g)	163
6(g)	15.4(a)	14
7	15.1(f)	295
7	15.1(f)	299
7(a)	1.8(c)	30
7(a)	15.1(d)	191
7(a)	15.1(d)	210
7(a)	15.1(d)	247
7(a)	15.1(f)	286
7(a)	15.1(f)	311
7(a)	15.1(f)	318
7(a)	15.1(f)	326
7(b)	15.1(d)	248
7(d)	19.5(b)	2
7(d)	19.5(b)	5
7(d)	19.6(a)	4

OHIO RULES OF CRIMINAL PROCEDURE

Rule	This Work Sec.	Note
7(e)	19.4(b)	16
7(e)	19.4(b)	19
8	17.1(a)	4
8	17.1(b)	19
8	17.2(a)	4
12(b)(1)	15.4(b)	61
12(c)	15.4(b)	61
12(g)	15.4(b)	58
12(k)	12.4(e)	91
12.1	20.2(b)	16
13	17.3(a)	5
14	17.3(d)	49
15(a)	20.2(e)	82
16	20.2(b)	16
16	20.2(b)	32
16(B)	20.3(c)	81
16(b)	20.3(f)	98
16(b)	20.3(f)	101
16(b)	20.3(i)	173
16(b)(1)	20.3(g)	121
16(b)(1)(e)	20.3(h)	154
16(b)(2)	20.3(j)	204
16(c)	20.5(e)	66
16(c)	20.5(h)	98
16(c)(1)	20.5(g)	91
16(E)	20.6(a)	5
16(E)(1)	20.3(l)	226
16(E)(3)	20.6(a)	2
16(E)(3)	20.6(a)	4
18	16.3(a)	3
18	16.3(d)	52
18	16.3(f)	87
18(B)	16.3(f)	86
21	16.3(a)	2
22	15.2(j)	235
25(a)	22.4(e)	48
30	24.8(a)	18
33	24.11(d)	14
41(A)	1.8(f)	101
44	11.2(a)	28
44(a)	11.2(b)	69
52(A)	27.6(a)	10

OHIO RULES OF APPELLATE PROCEDURE

Rule	This Work Sec.	Note
5(A)	28.4(b)	19
26(B)	28.4(b)	19

OHIO RULES OF EVIDENCE

Rule	This Work Sec.	Note
609(B)	20.2(d)	69
1101(c)(2)	15.2(d)	107

OKLAHOMA CONSTITUTION

Art.	This Work Sec.	Note
II, § 8	12.3(b)	37
II, § 8	12.3(b)	38
II, § 8	12.3(b)	42
II, § 17	15.1(g)	344
II, § 20	16.1(b)	91
II, § 27	8.11(d)	70
II, § 34	12.1(f)	69
II, § 34	21.3(f)	302
II, § 317	14.2(d)	60

OKLAHOMA STATUTES ANNOTATED

Tit.	This Work Sec.	Note
12, § 21.03	14.4(b)	6
12, § 2103	15.2(d)	93
22, § 1	1.7(e)	59
22, § 125.1	16.1(f)	225
22, § 209	12.5(b)	19
22, § 258	14.3(a)	4
22, § 258	14.4(d)	75
22, § 259	14.4(d)	84
22, § 301	15.1(g)	345
22, § 304	19.5(a)	1
22, § 315(7)	15.4(g)	157
22, § 320	15.4(b)	34
22, § 320	15.4(b)	41
22, § 320	15.4(b)	47
22, § 323	15.4(a)	17
22, § 323	15.4(e)	137
22, § 330	8.4(c)	117
22, § 333	15.2(d)	93
22, § 333	15.2(d)	96
22, § 335	15.2(b)	29
22, § 335	15.2(c)	74
22, § 336	15.2(f)	149
22, § 340	15.2(e)	142
22, § 340	15.2(i)	209
22, § 340	15.2(i)	214
22, § 340	15.2(j)	244
22, § 341	8.5(a)	3
22, § 342	8.5(a)	4
22, § 346	8.3(h)	51
22, § 401	19.1(d)	40
22, § 404	19.3(b)	177
22, § 410	19.1(d)	38

OKLAHOMA STATUTES ANNOTATED

Tit.	This Work Sec.	Note
22, § 436	17.2(a)	3
22, § 438	17.3(a)	5
22, § 439	17.3(d)	49
22, § 493	15.6(a)	5
22, § 524	14.2(d)	49
22, § 701	24.5(b)	21
22, § 705	8.4(b)	22
22, § 812.1	18.3(c)	106
22, § 812.2	18.3(c)	100
22, § 831	24.8(a)	15
22, § 991a(A)(1)	26.2(b)	16
22, § 1080 to 1089	28.11(b)	22
22, § 1082	11.2(b)	76
22, § 1355	11.2(a)	28
22, § 1355.6	11.2(a)	28
22, § 1355.6	11.2(g)	271
22, § 1355.6(F)	11.2(g)	298
22, § 2002(b)(1)	20.5(e)	65
22, § 2002(B)(1)(a)	20.5(f)	72
25, § 325	15.2(b)	52
29, § 124	16.1(d)	150
32, § 2002	20.2(b)	16
57, § 332.7(A)	26.2(c)	30
57, § 353.1	26.2(b)	12
57, § 353.1	26.2(b)	15

OKLAHOMA RULES OF PROFESSIONAL CONDUCT

Rule	This Work Sec.	Note
3.8	23.1(b)	46

OREGON CONSTITUTION

Art.	This Work Sec.	Note
I, § 11	16.1(b)	91
I, § 11	26.4(g)	134
I, § 14	12.3(b)	36
I, § 14	12.3(e)	118
I, § 41	12.1(f)	68
I, § 41	13.1(a)	20
I, § 41	21.3(f)	301
I, § 42	12.1(f)	69
I, § 42	12.1(f)	73
I, § 42	12.1(f)	82
I, § 42	13.1(a)	23
I, § 42	21.3(f)	302
I, § 42	21.3(f)	318
VII, § 5(3) to (5)	15.1(g)	344
VII, § 5(3) to (5)	15.1(g)	345

OREGON REVISED STATUTES

Sec.	This Work Sec.	Note
9.695(2)	3.4(a)	22
10.110	15.4(d)	101
14.250-70	22.4(d)	32
130.060	17.2(a)	5
131.005	1.7(e)	59
131.305	16.1(c)	100
131.305	16.1(d)	151
131.315	16.1(e)	184
131.355	16.3(b)	9
131.355	16.3(b)	18
131.355	16.3(g)	97
131.363	16.3(c)	27
131.515	17.4(c)	143
131.515	17.4(c)	152
131.515	17.4(c)	153
131.515(2)	16.1(f)	220
132.030	15.4(b)	32
132.030	15.4(b)	52
132.320	15.2(d)	100
132.320(4)	15.2(b)	29
132.340	15.1(g)	359
132.350	8.4(b)	77
132.350	15.1(g)	359
132.350	15.2(b)	20
132.350	15.2(b)	28
132.370	15.1(g)	358
132.390	14.3(a)	37
132.390	15.2(f)	149
132.440	8.3(h)	49
132.560	17.1(a)	4
132.560	17.1(b)	19
133.055	12.5(b)	19
133.110	12.5(a)	4
135.045	11.2(a)	28
135.050	11.2(a)	28
135.050	11.2(g)	281
135.050(2)	11.2(g)	294
135.055(3)	11.2(e)	219
135.055(3)	11.2(e)	223
135.070	14.2(e)	71
135.070	14.2(f)	86
135.070	14.2(f)	88
135.173	14.4(b)	19
135.173	14.4(b)	21
135.173	14.4(b)	30
135.175	14.3(a)	37
135.406	21.3(f)	310
135.406	21.3(f)	355
135.406	21.3(f)	399
135.455	20.6(a)	11
135.510	15.4(b)	51
135.510	15.5(c)	107
135.715	19.1(d)	38

OREGON REVISED STATUTES

	This Work	
Sec.	Sec.	Note
135.747	18.3(c)	88
135.753	18.3(c)	70
135.753	18.3(c)	113
135.815 to 135.835	20.2(b)	16
135.815	20.3(i)	159
135.815(1)	20.3(b)	62
135.815(1)	20.3(f)	99
135.815(2)	20.3(d)	88
135.865	20.6(a)	2
135.865	20.6(a)	3
135.865	20.6(a)	5
136.445	24.11(a)	1
136.563	8.4(b)	22
136.563	8.4(b)	40
136.617	8.11(d)	78
137.010	26.1(d)	89
137.079(2)	26.5(c)	50
137.090	26.5(a)	3
137.123	26.3(f)	58
137.530.4	1.5(k)	371
138.222	26.3(g)	88
138.510 to 138.680	28.11(b)	22
138.815(1)	20.3(i)	161
144.90(3)	26.5(d)	63
153.110	1.8(d)	68
157.020	27.3(d)	60
161.275	5.2(a)	4
161.505	1.8(d)	69
161.515	1.8(d)	69
161.725(1)	26.6(e)	81
161.735(6)	26.6(e)	82

OREGON LAWS

	This Work	
Year	Sec.	Note
2005, c. 759, § 1	24.11(d)	44
2005, c. 759, § 2	24.11(d)	44

OREGON UNIFORM TRIAL COURT RULES

	This Work	
Rule	Sec.	Note
1.010	1.7(f)	71

PENNSYLVANIA CONSTITUTION

	This Work	
Art.	Sec.	Note
I, § 9	16.1(b)	32
I, § 9	16.1(b)	90
I, § 10	15.1(g)	344
I, § 14	12.3(b)	37
I, § 14	12.3(b)	38

PENNSYLVANIA CONSTITUTION

	This Work	
Art.	Sec.	Note
IX, § 9	16.1(b)	58

PENNSYLVANIA CONSOLIDATED STATUTES

	This Work	
Tit.	Sec.	Note
4, § 8702	1.7(e)	59
18, § 11.201	13.1(a)	23
18, § 11.201	21.3(f)	312
18, § 11.201	21.3(f)	321
18, § 102	16.4(c)	78
18, § 102	16.4(c)	82
18, § 102	16.4(c)	94
18, § 102	16.4(c)	111
18, § 106	1.8(c)	16
18, § 110	17.4(c)	143
18, § 110	17.4(c)	152
18, § 110	17.4(c)	153
18, § 110(1)(ii)	16.1(f)	220
18, § 313	5.1(c)	17
18, § 313	5.2(b)	24
18, § 1106(c)(1)(I)	26.6(c)	37
18, § 1106(c)(1)(i)	26.6(c)	35
42, § 4541 to 4551	15.1(g)	346
42, § 4543	8.1(b)	19
42, § 4544	8.1(b)	18
42, § 4548	8.4(b)	82
42, § 4548	15.1(g)	358
42, § 4549	8.5(e)	160
42, § 4549	8.5(e)	195
42, § 4549(c)	8.14(b)	32
42, § 4549(c)	8.14(c)	37
42, § 4549(d)	8.5(d)	125
42, § 4551	14.2(d)	48
42, § 5552	15.1(g)	345
42, § 8702	23.2(c)	59
42, § 8702	23.2(c)	60
42, § 8931	14.2(d)	48
42, § 8931	15.1(g)	344
42, § 8931	15.1(g)	345
42, § 9543.1	24.11(d)	47
42, § 9714(b)(2)	26.6(b)	24
42, § 9714(d)	26.6(b)	12
42, § 9714(d)	26.6(b)	23
42, § 9756(b)	26.1(c)	53
42, § 9763(b)	26.1(e)	98

PENNSYLVANIA RULES OF CRIMINAL PROCEDURE

	This Work	
Rule	Sec.	Note
21	16.1(c)	100

PENNSYLVANIA RULES OF CRIMINAL PROCEDURE

Rule	This Work Sec.	Note
100	1.7(f)	71
104(A)	14.2(e)	77
110	14.2(d)	48
121	11.3(b)	53
122	11.2(a)	28
140(f)	14.2(f)	86
141 to 143	14.2(d)	48
141	14.4(d)	83
Ch. 200	15.1(g)	346
203	15.4(b)	47
203(a)	15.4(b)	34
203(a)	15.4(b)	41
229	19.5(b)	2
231(a)	14.2(d)	48
312	16.3(b)	8
316	11.2(g)	262
318	11.3(b)	42
318	11.3(b)	52
318	11.5(c)	37
318	11.5(c)	45
404 to 417	1.7(f)	72
509	12.5(a)	6
541	14.2(e)	67
541	14.2(e)	74
567 to 573	20.2(b)	16
573(13)	20.3(i)	159
573(B)	20.3(i)	161
573(B)(2)(a)(1)	20.3(h)	146
573(c)(1)(g)	20.5(b)	23
573(c)(2)(f)	20.5(c)	51
573(c)(2)(f)	20.5(e)	67
573(d)	20.6(a)	15
573(e)	20.6(a)	2
581(a)	10.1(a)	4
581(b)	10.2(a)	8
581(h)	10.3(d)	65
582	17.1(a)	5
582	17.1(b)	23
582	17.2(a)	3
583	17.3(d)	50
600	18.3(c)	72
600	18.3(c)	77
600	18.3(c)	84
600	18.3(c)	95
600	18.3(c)	118
621	22.1(h)	138
646	24.8(a)	17
1100	18.3(c)	108
1106(e)	1.8(e)	91

PENNSYLVANIA RULES OF APPELLATE PROCEDURE

Rule	This Work Sec.	Note
311(d)	27.3(c)	46

PENNSYLVANIA RULES OF PROFESSIONAL CONDUCT

Rule	This Work Sec.	Note
3.6	23.1(b)	46

RHODE ISLAND CONSTITUTION

Art.	This Work Sec.	Note
I, § 7	15.1(e)	257
I, § 7	15.1(e)	262
I, § 9	12.3(b)	37
I, § 9	12.3(b)	41
I, § 9	12.3(e)	118
I, § 9	12.3(e)	119
I, § 23	1.5(k)	383
I, § 23	12.1(f)	69
I, § 23	21.3(f)	302
I, § 37	15.1(e)	257

RHODE ISLAND GENERAL LAWS

Sec.	This Work Sec.	Note
8-6-2	1.7(f)	86
8-6-2	1.7(f)	95
10-9.1 to 10-9.1-91	28.11(b)	22
10-9.1-12	24.11(d)	46
11-34.2	16.1(e)	183
12-1-1	1.7(e)	59
12-3-4	16.1(c)	99
12-7-11	12.5(b)	19
12-12-1.1	15.1(e)	257
12-12-1.1	15.1(e)	263
12-12-1.1	15.1(f)	287
12-12-1.1	15.1(f)	295
12-12-1.1	15.1(f)	297
12-12-1.1	15.1(f)	312
12-12-1.2	15.1(e)	268
12-12-11	19.3(a)	16
12-15-8	11.2(g)	258
12-15-8	11.2(g)	276
12-15-8	11.2(g)	281
12-17-3	24.6(a)	11
12-28-3	21.3(f)	320
12-28-3	21.3(f)	392
12-28-4.1	21.3(f)	366
12-28-4.1	21.3(f)	376
21-28-5.04.1(a)	26.6(d)	52

RHODE ISLAND RULES OF EVIDENCE

Rule	This Work Sec.	Note
1101(B)(2) .... 15.2(d)		107

RHODE ISLAND DISTRICT COURT RULES OF CRIMINAL PROCEDURE

Rule	This Work Sec.	Note
44 .... 11.2(a)		28
44 .... 11.2(a)		33

RHODE ISLAND SUPERIOR COURT RULES OF CRIMINAL PROCEDURE

Rule	This Work Sec.	Note
1 .... 1.3(e)		37
1 .... 1.7(f)		71
4 .... 12.5(a)		3
6(b) .... 15.4(b)		46
6(e) .... 8.5(b)		42
6(e)(3) .... 8.5(e)		164
6(e)(3) .... 8.5(e)		165
7(c) .... 15.1(e)		267
7(e) .... 19.5(b)		2
7(e) .... 19.5(b)		4
8 .... 17.1(a)		4
8 .... 17.1(b)		19
8 .... 17.2(a)		3
12 .... 20.2(b)		16
12(b)(2) .... 15.4(b)		61
12(b)(3) .... 15.4(b)		61
13 .... 17.3(a)		5
14 .... 17.3(d)		49
14(b) .... 15.2(i)		214
15 .... 20.2(e)		85
16 .... 20.2(b)		16
16 .... 20.3(c)		76
16(a) .... 20.3(c)		68
16(a)(1) .... 20.3(i)		161
16(a)(2) .... 15.2(i)		209
16(a)(7) .... 20.3(i)		161
16(a)(8) .... 20.3(e)		97
16(b)(4) .... 20.5(f)		72
16(f) .... 20.2(e)		86
16(f) .... 20.3(l)		230
16(i) .... 20.6(a)		3
25 .... 22.4(e)		48
32 .... 26.5(c)		45
44 .... 11.2(a)		28
Forms 6 to 20 .... 19.1(d)		47

SOUTH CAROLINA CONSTITUTION

Art.	This Work Sec.	Note
I, § 10 .... 2.12(b)		89
I, § 11 .... 15.1(d)		192
I, § 11 .... 15.1(d)		201
I, § 11 .... 15.1(d)		239
I, § 11 .... 15.1(d)		246
I, § 11 .... 15.1(f)		281
I, § 15 .... 12.3(b)		35
I, § 15 .... 12.3(e)		119
I, § 22 .... 15.1(f)		283
I, § 24 .... 12.1(f)		69
I, § 24 .... 12.1(f)		73
I, § 24 .... 12.1(f)		81
I, § 24 .... 12.1(f)		94
I, § 24 .... 12.1(f)		96
I, § 24 .... 13.1(a)		21
I, § 24 .... 21.3(f)		302
I, § 24 .... 21.3(f)		321
I, § 24 .... 21.3(f)		363
V, § 4 .... 1.7(f)		92

SOUTH CAROLINA CODE ANNOTATED

Sec.	This Work Sec.	Note
14-3-310 .... 1.7(g)		119
14-7-1330 .... 24.9(d)		32
14-7-1600 to 14-7-1820 .... 8.1(b)		16
14-7-1650(A) .... 15.1(d)		251
14-7-1750 .... 15.2(f)		148
16-3-26 .... 11.2(e)		217
16-3-1505 .... 21.3(f)		308
16-3-1505 .... 21.3(f)		317
17-1-10 .... 1.7(e)		59
17-3-10 .... 11.2(a)		28
17-3-10 .... 11.2(a)		32
17-19-10 .... 15.1(d)		192
17-19-10 .... 15.1(d)		247
17-21-10 .... 16.4(c)		74
17-21-30 .... 16.4(c)		74
17-21-80 .... 16.3(d)		52
17-21-85 .... 23.2(c)		59
17-23-90 .... 18.3(c)		71
17-23-90 .... 18.3(c)		106
17-23-90 .... 18.3(c)		115
17-23-130 .... 15.1(f)		285
17-23-130 .... 15.1(f)		300
17-23-130 .... 15.1(f)		312
17-23-130 .... 15.1(f)		326
22-3-545 .... 15.1(d)		240
22-3-550 .... 15.1(d)		240
24-21-50 .... 26.2(c)		49

SOUTH CAROLINA RULES OF CRIMINAL PROCEDURE

Rule	This Work Sec.	Note
1	1.7(f)	71
2	14.2(e)	66
2(b)	14.2(f)	86
5	20.2(b)	16
5(a)	20.3(c)	84
5(a)(1)	20.3(a)	8
5(a)(1)	20.3(a)	10
5(a)(1)(D)	20.3(f)	101

SOUTH CAROLINA RULES OF PROFESSIONAL CONDUCT

Rule	This Work Sec.	Note
3.8	23.1(b)	46

SOUTH DAKOTA CONSTITUTION

Art.	This Work Sec.	Note
IV, § 7	16.1(b)	92
VI, § 8	12.3(b)	33
VI, § 10	15.1(g)	344
VI, § 10	15.1(g)	358

SOUTH DAKOTA CODIFIED LAWS

Sec.	This Work Sec.	Note
15-6-32(B)	24.4(a)	10
21-27	28.11(b)	13
22-7-11	26.6(b)	15
22-7-11	26.6(b)	21
23A-1-1 et seq.	1.7(f)	71
23A-1-1	1.3(e)	37
23A-1-1	1.7(e)	59
23A-1-1	1.8(d)	66
23A-4-3	14.2(e)	67
23A-4-3	14.2(e)	77
23A-4-3	14.2(f)	86
23A-4-6	14.4(b)	19
23A-4-6	14.4(b)	25
23A-4-7	14.3(c)	74
23A-4-30	14.2(d)	50
23A-5-3	15.4(b)	27
23A-5-3	15.4(b)	28
23A-5-3	15.4(b)	46
23A-5-11	8.14(b)	24
23A-5-11.1	15.2(j)	244
23A-5-13	8.10(d)	101
23A-5-15	15.2(b)	29
23A-5-15	15.2(d)	93
23A-5-18	15.2(f)	148

SOUTH DAKOTA CODIFIED LAWS

Sec.	This Work Sec.	Note
23A-6-1	15.1(g)	345
23A-6-3	14.2(e)	67
23A-6-23	17.1(a)	4
23A-6-23	17.1(b)	19
23A-6-24	17.2(a)	3
23A-7-8	21.3(c)	201
23A-7-8	21.3(f)	311
23A-7-8	21.3(f)	317
23A-7-9	21.3(f)	398
23A-9 to 23A-13	20.2(b)	16
23A-9	20.2(b)	15
23A-10	20.2(b)	15
23A-11-1	17.3(a)	5
23A-11-1	17.3(d)	49
23A-13	20.2(b)	15
23A-13-1	20.3(c)	84
23A-13-4	20.3(f)	100
23A-13-6 to 23A-13-11	8.5(g)	217
23A-14-11	8.1(c)	24
23A-14-29	8.11(d)	70
23A-16-8	16.1(d)	150
23A-17-6	16.3(c)	27
23A-17-15	16.3(b)	9
23A-21-3	22.4(e)	48
23A-25-3	24.10(a)	11
23A-25-13	24.10(a)	11
23A-27-7	26.5(c)	49
23A-27-7	26.5(c)	50
23A-28C-1	12.1(f)	73
23A-28C-1	12.1(f)	85
23A-28C-1	21.3(f)	314
23A-28C-1	21.3(f)	321
23A-32-7	12.4(e)	88
23A-32-7	27.3(c)	34
23A-40-6	11.2(a)	28
23A-40-6	11.2(b)	81
23A-40-6.1	11.2(a)	28
23A-40-6.1	11.2(a)	31
23A-44-5.1	18.3(c)	72
23A-44-5.1	18.3(c)	75
23A-44-5.1	18.3(c)	81
23A-44-5.1	18.3(c)	89
23A-44-5.1	18.3(c)	95
23A-44-5.1	18.3(c)	100
23A-44-5.1	18.3(c)	108
23A-B-3	20.3(c)	68
24-15-8	26.2(c)	36

SOUTH DAKOTA RULES OF CRIMINAL PROCEDURE

Rule	This Work Sec.	Note
32(c)(1)	26.5(b)	37

SOUTH DAKOTA RULES OF PROFESSIONAL CONDUCT

Rule	This Work Sec.	Note
3.8	23.1(b)	46

TENNESSEE CONSTITUTION

Art.	This Work Sec.	Note
I, § 9	16.1(b)	91
I, § 14	15.1(d)	193
I, § 14	15.1(d)	200
I, § 14	15.1(d)	207
I, § 14	15.1(d)	226
I, § 14	15.1(d)	246
I, § 14	15.1(f)	270
I, § 35	12.1(f)	69
I, § 35	12.1(f)	75
I, § 35	12.1(f)	81
I, § 35	12.1(f)	88
I, § 35	21.3(f)	302
I, § 35	21.3(f)	371
II, § 15	12.3(b)	33

TENNESSEE CODE ANNOTATED

Sec.	This Work Sec.	Note
8-7-309	1.7(j)	217
16-3-401 to 16-3-404	1.7(f)	83
16-3-406	1.7(f)	86
16-3-407	1.7(g)	119
22-2-302	22.2(b)	16
22-2-302(a)(1)	15.2(a)	6
39-11-103	16.4(c)	90
39-11-505	5.2(a)	4
40-1-104	1.7(e)	59
40-3-100	15.1(d)	254
40-3-101	15.1(d)	193
40-3-101	15.1(f)	285
40-3-101	15.1(f)	294
40-3-101	15.1(f)	329
40-3-103(2)	15.1(f)	329
40-3-103(c)(1)	15.1(f)	318
40-3-103(c)(2)	15.1(f)	326
40-7-118	12.5(b)	22
40-7-118	12.5(b)	28
40-12-104	8.4(b)	87
40-12-104(a)	15.2(c)	71
40-12-209	8.5(e)	197
40-12-215	8.11(b)	17
40-12-215	8.11(b)	19
40-12-215	8.11(d)	70
40-13-105	15.2(g)	164
40-13-202	19.1(d)	36
40-13-202	19.2(d)	46

TENNESSEE CODE ANNOTATED

Sec.	This Work Sec.	Note
40-14-101	18.3(c)	67
40-14-202	11.2(a)	28
40-14-202	11.2(g)	291
40-14-202	11.2(g)	296
40-14-202	11.2(g)	297
40-14-202	11.2(h)	311
40-14-202	11.2(h)	313
40-14-202	11.2(h)	314
40-14-202(5)	11.2(g)	274
40-14-202(b)	11.2(g)	302
40-14-202(c)(3)	11.2(g)	272
40-14-203	11.2(b)	69
40-14-207(b)	11.2(e)	170
40-18-110	24.8(f)	116
40-18-116	23.2(g)	122
40-30-303	24.11(d)	44
40-35-102	26.3(e)	37
40-35-115	26.3(f)	58
40-35-115(b)(3)	26.6(e)	77
40-35-120(i)(2)	26.6(b)	15
40-35-205(6)	26.5(b)	31
40-35-209	26.5(d)	69
40-38-114	13.1(a)	22
40-38-114	21.3(f)	314
40-38-114	21.3(f)	317
340-14-207	11.2(e)	217

TENNESSEE RULES OF CRIMINAL PROCEDURE

Rule	This Work Sec.	Note
1	1.3(e)	37
1	1.7(f)	71
4	12.5(a)	4
5(d)	14.2(e)	70
5(d)	14.2(f)	86
5.1	14.3(a)	2
5.1	14.4(b)	28
5.1	14.4(b)	37
6(a)	15.2(g)	164
6(c)(1)	15.4(g)	154
6(d)	8.8(a)	3
6(e)(2)	15.2(b)	20
6(g)	15.4(a)	17
6(g)	15.4(e)	137
6(i)	8.4(b)	19
7(c)	19.4(b)	12
8	17.1(a)	5
8	17.1(b)	19
8	17.2(a)	6
8	17.4(c)	143
8	17.4(c)	152

TENNESSEE RULES OF CRIMINAL PROCEDURE

Rule	This Work Sec.	Note
8	17.4(c)	153
12(c)	15.4(b)	60
12.1 to 12.3	20.2(b)	16
12.1	20.5(a)	10
12.2	20.5(a)	10
12.2(c)	20.5(c)	36
13	1.8(e)	93
13	17.3(a)	5
14	17.1(b)	24
14	17.3(d)	51
16	20.2(b)	16
16(a)	20.3(c)	68
16(a)(1)(A)	20.3(d)	88
16(a)(1)(D)	20.3(f)	100
16(a)(2)	20.3(j)	204
16(b)	20.4(g)	100
21	16.3(b)	15
21	16.3(g)	104
25	22.4(e)	48
26.2	14.4(c)	65
30(c)	24.8(a)	16
30.1	24.9(c)	21
32(f)	21.5(a)	21
44(c)	11.9(b)	96
52(b)	27.5(d)	116
56(e)	14.2(c)	37
57	1.7(g)	119

TENNESSEE RULES OF APPELLATE PROCEDURE

Rule	This Work Sec.	Note
9(b)	27.2(b)	17

TENNESSEE RULES OF PROFESSIONAL CONDUCT

Rule	This Work Sec.	Note
3.8	23.1(b)	46

TENNESSEE SUPREME COURT RULES

Rule	This Work Sec.	Note
13	11.2(a)	28
13(d)	11.2(b)	76
13(d)(1)	11.2(a)	30

TEXAS CONSTITUTION

Art.	This Work Sec.	Note
I, § 10	15.1(d)	194

TEXAS CONSTITUTION

Art.	This Work Sec.	Note
I, § 10	15.1(d)	202
I, § 10	15.1(d)	237
I, § 10	15.1(f)	270
I, § 11	12.3(b)	37
I, § 11a	12.3(b)	37
I, § 11a	12.3(b)	39
I, § 11a	12.3(b)	40
I, § 11a	12.3(b)	41
I, § 30	12.1(f)	69
I, § 30	12.1(f)	96
I, § 30	21.3(f)	302
I, § 30	21.3(f)	340
III, § 45	16.3(a)	4
IV, § 11(b)	26.2(c)	71
V, § 13	2.12(a)	2

TEXAS ANNOTATED CODE OF CRIMINAL PROCEDURE

Art.	This Work Sec.	Note
1.051	11.2(a)	28
1.051	11.2(a)	35
1.051	11.2(b)	71
1.051	11.3(b)	53
1.051(d)	11.2(b)	65
1.051(g)	11.3(a)	21
1.051(g)	11.5(c)	44
1.14	27.5(c)	91
1.141	15.1(d)	194
1.141	15.1(d)	247
1.141	15.1(f)	285
1.41	15.1(f)	295
1.41	15.1(f)	326
1.41	15.1(f)	329
3(a)	26.1(d)	85
5(a)(1)	28.11(b)	17
11.071	28.11(b)	17
13.17	16.1(g)	239
13.17	16.1(g)	243
13.17	16.1(g)	264
13.8	16.1(c)	100
15.03	12.5(a)	4
16.01	14.1(a)	1
16.01	14.2(f)	87
19.06	8.4(a)	13
19.06	15.2(a)	7
19.27	15.4(b)	27
19.27	15.4(b)	29
19.34	8.4(b)	82
19.31(2)	15.4(g)	159
20.06	15.2(e)	137
20.07	15.2(b)	25

TEXAS ANNOTATED CODE OF CRIMINAL PROCEDURE

Art.	This Work Sec.	Note
20.09	15.2(b)	20
20.17	8.10(d)	101
20.17	8.10(d)	114
20.17	15.2(b)	23
20.20	15.1(d)	248
20.20	15.1(d)	251
21.11	19.1(d)	40
21.11	19.2(d)	46
26.04	11.2(a)	28
26.04(b)	11.2(g)	282
26.04(b)	11.2(g)	296
26.05(a)	11.2(e)	220
26.13	21.3(f)	392
27.03(3)	15.4(b)	41
28.10	19.5(c)	47
30.01	22.4(b)	18
31.01	16.3(f)	87
31.01	16.3(g)	105
31.02	16.3(d)	52
31.03	16.3(b)	13
32A.02	18.3(c)	64
35.17	1.8(e)	91
36.04	17.3(d)	49
36.09	17.2(a)	5
37.07	26.2(b)	12
37.07	26.2(b)	14
38.05	24.6(e)	47
38.08	24.5(b)	21
38.22, § 3(a)	6.8(c)	64
38.30	24.11(d)	39
39.02	20.2(e)	82
39.02	20.2(e)	87
39.14	20.2(b)	16
39.14	20.2(c)	46
39.14(a)	20.3(c)	76
42.12	26.1(d)	85
44.01	27.3(c)	37
44.01(g)	12.4(e)	91
44.09	27.5(c)	71
48.01	26.2(c)	71
56.01	12.1(f)	68
56.01	13.1(a)	20
56.01	21.3(f)	301
56.02	21.3(f)	321
56.02(d)	1.5(k)	386
64.01	24.11(d)	43
1307	16.1(e)	173
2703	15.6(a)	5

TEXAS GOVERNMENT CODE ANNOTATED

Sec.	This Work Sec.	Note
71.051	1.4(f)	124
411.1471	3.5(d)	148
498.003(a)	26.2(c)	54
498.003(a)	26.2(c)	58
498.003(b)	26.2(c)	55

TEXAS PENAL CODE

Sec.	This Work Sec.	Note
Art. 1.04	16.4(c)	78
1.07(14)	1.8(c)	12
1.07(21)	1.8(c)	12
3.02	17.1(a)	5
3.02	17.1(b)	21
3.04	17.1(a)	5
8.06	5.2(b)	24
12.21 to 12.41	1.8(c)	13
12.42(f)	26.6(b)	25

TEXAS RULES OF APPELLATE PROCEDURE

Rule	This Work Sec.	Note
60(b)	27.5(c)	71
60(b)	27.5(c)	74
80(d)	16.1(h)	313
81(b)(2)	24.8(b)	29

TEXAS RULES OF EVIDENCE

Rule	This Work Sec.	Note
404(b)	20.2(d)	70
1101(c)(2)	15.2(d)	107

TEXAS RULES OF PROFESSIONAL CONDUCT

Rule	This Work Sec.	Note
3.07	23.1(b)	11

TEXAS ACTS

Year	This Work Sec.	Note
1881, ch. 57, p. 60, 17	19.1(b)	19

UTAH CONSTITUTION

Art.	This Work Sec.	Note
I, § 8	12.3(b)	37
I, § 8	12.3(b)	38
I, § 8	12.3(b)	39
I, § 8	12.3(b)	40
I, § 12	16.1(b)	92
I, § 12	27.1(a)	5

UTAH CONSTITUTION

Art.	This Work Sec.	Note
I, § 13	15.1(g)	344
I, § 13	15.1(g)	345
I, § 28	12.1(f)	69
I, § 28	12.1(f)	77
I, § 28	12.1(f)	82
I, § 28	21.3(f)	302
I, § 28	21.3(f)	339
I, § 28	21.3(f)	372
I, § 28	21.3(f)	421
I, § 28(1)(a)	1.5(k)	383

UTAH CODE ANNOTATED

Sec.	This Work Sec.	Note
76-1-202(2)	16.1(g)	235
76-1-202(a)	16.1(c)	100
76-1-302(c)	1.8(d)	68
76-1-305	24.8(f)	112
76-1-402	17.1(a)	4
76-1-402	17.1(b)	21
76-1-402	17.2(a)	5
76-1-402	17.4(c)	143
76-1-402	17.4(c)	152
76-1-402	17.4(c)	153
76-1-402	17.4(c)	157
76-1-501(3)	16.4(d)	130
76-2-303	5.1(c)	17
76-2-303	5.2(b)	24
76-3-203	26.1(c)	60
76-3-401	26.3(f)	58
77-1-1	1.7(e)	59
77-7-18	12.5(b)	19
77-8a-1	17.3(a)	5
77-8a-1	17.3(d)	49
77-10a-1	8.10(c)	58
77-10a-1	8.10(d)	115
77-10a-1(6)	15.2(b)	20
77-10a-13	8.10(d)	101
77-10a-13	8.14(b)	24
77-10a-13	15.7(f)	134
77-10a-13	15.7(f)	149
77-10a-13(4)(c)	8.10(d)	114
77-10a-13(5)(b)	15.2(b)	51
77-10a-13(6)(e)	8.3(a)	4
77-10a-13(7)	8.5(e)	165
77-10a-14(2)	15.2(f)	149
77-11-3(1)	15.2(d)	95
77-11-4	15.2(b)	29
77-11-9	15.2(i)	212
77-16a-8	15.4(b)	27
77-22b-1	8.11(a)	9
77-27-7	26.2(c)	47

UTAH CODE ANNOTATED

Sec.	This Work Sec.	Note
77-32-202(3)(b)(iii)	11.2(g)	277
77-32-301	11.2(a)	28
77-32-301	11.2(b)	69
77-32-301	11.2(b)	76
77-32-302	11.2(a)	28
77-38-2(9)	1.5(k)	371
77-38-4	12.1(f)	78
77-38-4	12.1(f)	94
77-38-4	21.3(f)	381
77-38-4	21.3(f)	382
77-38-4	21.3(f)	388
77-38-5	21.3(f)	373
77-38-6(1)	1.5(k)	400
77-38-7	18.3(c)	123
77-38-7(1) to (3)	1.5(k)	411
77-38-10	12.1(f)	104
77-38-10	21.3(f)	413
77-38-11	21.3(f)	416
77-100-13	8.5(d)	133
78-2-4	1.7(f)	95
78-7-6	1.7(g)	119
78-35a-301	24.11(d)	42
78-46-16(1)	15.4(b)	29
78-46-16(1)	15.4(b)	50

UTAH RULES OF CRIMINAL PROCEDURE

Rule	This Work Sec.	Note
1	1.3(e)	37
1	1.7(f)	71
4(d)	19.5(b)	5
6	12.5(a)	5
7	14.3(a)	1
7	14.4(b)	26
7(h)	14.2(e)	84
7(h)	14.4(b)	19
7(h)(2)	14.4(b)	22
8	11.2(a)	28
8	11.2(a)	32
16	20.2(b)	16
16(a)	20.3(c)	76
16(a)(5)	20.2(b)	21
16(c)(5)	20.2(b)	21
26(2)(a)	27.2(a)	4
26(2)(c)	27.2(b)	18
26(3)	27.3(c)	35
29A	22.4(d)	32

UTAH RULES OF EVIDENCE

Rule	This Work Sec.	Note
615	24.4(d)	31

UTAH RULES OF EVIDENCE

	This Work	
Rule	Sec.	Note
615	24.4(d)	55
1101(a)(5)	14.4(b)	19
1101(d)(2)	15.2(d)	107

UTAH RULES OF PROFESSIONAL CONDUCT

	This Work	
Rule	Sec.	Note
3.8	23.1(b)	46

VERMONT CONSTITUTION

	This Work	
Art.	Sec.	Note
II, § 40	12.3(b)	37
II, § 40	12.3(b)	38
II, § 40	12.3(e)	119

VERMONT STATUTES ANNOTATED

	This Work	
Tit.	Sec.	Note
3, § 2	16.4(c)	90
13, § 1	1.8(c)	16
13, § 4501	1.7(e)	59
13, § 5131	8.1(c)	24
13, § 5137	8.1(c)	27
13, § 5201	11.2(a)	28
13, § 5201	11.2(a)	33
13, § 5201	11.2(g)	263
13, § 5206	11.2(a)	28
13, § 5231	11.1(d)	129
13, § 5231	11.2(a)	28
13, § 5231	11.2(b)	81
13, § 5321	21.3(f)	317
13, § 5321	21.3(f)	332
13, § 7006	26.5(d)	62
13, § 7403	27.3(c)	48
13, § 7403	27.3(c)	57
13, § 7403(e)	12.4(e)	89
13, § 7403(e)	12.4(e)	91
13, § 7404(b)	27.3(c)	21
13, § 7553b	18.3(c)	72
13, § 7553b	18.3(c)	86
13, § 7553b	18.3(c)	115
13, § 15321	21.3(f)	309
28, § 502(b)	26.2(c)	49

VERMONT RULES OF CRIMINAL PROCEDURE

	This Work	
Rule	Sec.	Note
1	1.7(f)	71

VERMONT RULES OF CRIMINAL PROCEDURE

	This Work	
Rule	Sec.	Note
3	12.5(b)	22
3(c)	1.8(c)	29
4	12.5(a)	5
4	12.5(a)	6
6(b)	15.4(b)	45
6(d)	15.2(j)	244
6(g)	15.2(f)	149
7(a)	15.1(g)	344
7(a)	15.1(g)	345
7(d)	19.5(b)	5
8	17.1(a)	4
8	17.1(b)	19
8	17.2(a)	6
11(e)(2)	1.8(c)	39
12	14.2(d)	47
12	20.2(e)	105
12(d)	14.2(d)	64
12.1	20.2(b)	15
12.1	20.2(b)	16
12.1	20.2(c)	53
12.1(a)	20.5(a)	10
12.1(b)	20.5(b)	18
12.1(d)	20.5(b)	20
12.1(e)	20.6(a)	11
12.1(f)	20.5(b)	22
13	17.3(a)	5
13	17.4(c)	143
13	17.4(c)	152
13	17.4(c)	154
13	17.4(c)	155
13	17.4(c)	156
13	17.4(c)	157
14	17.1(b)	22
14	17.3(d)	51
15	20.2(e)	82
15(a)	20.2(e)	87
15(a)	20.2(e)	89
15(b)	20.2(e)	95
15(e)	20.2(e)	92
16	20.2(b)	16
16(2)(g)(2)	20.6(a)	9
16(a)	20.2(c)	50
16(a)	20.3(g)	121
16(a)(2)	15.2(i)	209
16(b)(1)(A)	20.3(h)	139
16(d)(1)	20.3(j)	196
16.1	20.2(b)	15
16.2(d)	20.3(l)	227
16.2(f)	20.2(c)	55
21	16.3(b)	18
21	16.3(f)	88

VERMONT RULES OF CRIMINAL PROCEDURE

Rule	This Work Sec.	Note
21	16.3(g)	98
21(b)	16.3(c)	27
21(b)	16.3(e)	79
23(c)	24.6(a)	11
25	22.4(e)	47
25	22.4(e)	50
44	11.2(a)	28

VERMONT RULES OF EVIDENCE

Rule	This Work Sec.	Note
1101(d)(2)	15.2(d)	107

VIRGINIA CONSTITUTION

Art.	This Work Sec.	Note
I, § 8	12.1(f)	100
I, § 8	16.1(b)	32
I, § 8	16.1(b)	90
I, § 8-A	12.1(f)	69
I, § 8-A	12.1(f)	81
I, § 8-A	12.1(f)	89
I, § 8-A	21.3(f)	302
I, § 8-A	21.3(f)	339
I, § 8-A	21.3(f)	346
I, § 9	12.3(b)	31
VI, § 5	1.7(f)	92

VIRGINIA CODE

Sec.	This Work Sec.	Note
15.2B	24.11(d)	45
19.2 to 24.4	16.1(c)	100
19.2-1	1.7(e)	59
19.2-11.01	12.1(f)	68
19.2-11.01	13.1(a)	20
19.2-11.01	13.1(a)	23
19.2-11.01	21.3(f)	301
19.2-11.01	21.3(f)	314
19.2-11.01	21.3(f)	318
19.2-11.01	21.3(f)	327
19.2-11.01	21.3(f)	371
19.2-74	12.5(b)	22
19.2-120	12.3(b)	51
19.2-154	22.4(e)	48
19.2-159	11.2(g)	266
19.2-159	11.2(g)	274
19.2-159	11.2(g)	282
19.2-159	11.2(g)	283
19.2-159	11.2(g)	284
19.2-159	11.2(g)	286

VIRGINIA CODE

Sec.	This Work Sec.	Note
19.2-159(2)	11.2(g)	278
19.2-159.1	11.2(g)	310
19.2-160	11.2(a)	28
19.2-160	11.3(b)	53
19.2-163.01	1.4(f)	124
19.2-183	14.2(f)	87
19.2-183	14.4(b)	6
19.2-186	14.3(a)	1
19.2-191	15.2(f)	148
19.2-194	15.2(a)	6
19.2-197	15.4(e)	137
19.2-201	8.4(b)	27
19.2-202	15.2(b)	20
19.2-203	15.4(b)	52
19.2-206	8.1(b)	19
19.2-208	8.4(b)	19
19.2-210	8.4(b)	27
19.2-212	15.2(j)	235
19.2-215.6	8.4(b)	27
19.2-217	15.1(d)	195
19.2-217	15.1(d)	238
19.2-217	15.1(d)	254
19.2-217	15.1(f)	285
19.2-217	15.1(f)	294
19.2-217	15.1(f)	326
19.2-218	14.2(c)	37
19.2-218	14.2(e)	67
19.2-231	19.5(c)	48
19.2-231	19.5(c)	49
19.2-243	18.3(c)	72
19.2-243	18.3(c)	95
19.2-243	18.3(c)	108
19.2-243	18.3(c)	117
19.2-246	16.4(c)	74
19.2-249.2	16.1(e)	186
19.2-251	16.3(b)	6
19.2-251	16.3(d)	52
19.2-270.4:1(B)	24.3(e)	137
19.2-295.1	26.2(b)	12
19.2-299.1	26.5(d)	63
19.2-310.1:1	3.5(d)	148
19.2-327.1	24.11(d)	43
19.2-390.02	1.5(e)	234
19.2-398	27.3(c)	30
50.4-3	11.2(a)	28
53.1-151(B)	26.2(c)	31
62.3-1	18.3(c)	71
62.3-21	18.3(c)	84

VIRGINIA RULES OF PROFESSIONAL CONDUCT

Rule	This Work Sec.	Note
3.6	23.1(b)	14

VIRGINIA SUPREME COURT RULES

Rule	This Work Sec.	Note
3A:1	1.7(f)	71
3A:5	8.4(b)	27
3A:6(b)(e)	15.4(b)	52
3A:6(e)	15.4(b)	45
3A:6(e)	15.4(b)	55
3A:9(c)	15.4(b)	74
3A:10	17.1(a)	4
3A:10	17.1(b)	22
3A:10	17.2(a)	5
3A:10	17.3(d)	49
3A:11	1.8(c)	33
3A:11	20.2(b)	16
3A:11	20.3(c)	70
3A:11(b)	20.3(f)	111
3A:11(b)(1)	20.3(a)	9
3A:11(b)(2)	20.3(i)	167
3A:11(c)	20.4(g)	104
7C:5	1.8(c)	33

WASHINGTON CONSTITUTION

Art.	This Work Sec.	Note
I, § 7	2.12(b)	89
I, § 20	12.3(b)	33
I, § 22	16.1(b)	91
I, § 22	27.1(a)	5
I, § 35	12.1(f)	69
I, § 35	12.1(f)	82
I, § 35	12.1(f)	100
I, § 35	21.3(f)	302
I, § 37	2.12(e)	205

WASHINGTON REVISED CODE

Sec.	This Work Sec.	Note
2.04.200	1.7(f)	86
4.12.040 to 4.12.050	22.4(d)	32
9.18.080	8.11(d)	71
9.94A.070	26.3(e)	37
9.94A.421	21.3(c)	201
9.94A.421	21.3(f)	309
9.94A.421	21.3(f)	316
9.94A.421	21.3(f)	317
9.94a.431	21.3(f)	397
9.95.013	26.2(c)	30
9A.16.070	5.2(a)	4
10.01.030	1.7(e)	59
10.25.140	23.2(c)	59
10.25.140	23.2(c)	61
10.27.020(6)	8.4(c)	112
10.27.060	15.4(a)	20

WASHINGTON REVISED CODE

Sec.	This Work Sec.	Note
10.27.060	15.4(b)	32
10.27.060(2)	15.4(g)	151
10.27.070(10)	8.4(b)	108
10.27.070(11)	15.1(g)	359
10.27.090	8.5(e)	195
10.27.090(3)	8.5(d)	119
10.27.090(5)	8.5(d)	132
10.27.090(5)	15.2(i)	212
10.27.100	15.1(g)	359
10.27.100	15.2(b)	20
10.27.120	8.14(b)	26
10.27.130	8.11(b)	19
10.27.140	8.4(b)	42
10.27.150	15.2(f)	148
10.27.170	8.1(c)	24
10.27.170	8.1(c)	27
10.28.085	15.1(g)	358
10.37.015	15.1(g)	344
10.37.015	15.1(g)	345
10.40.075	15.4(b)	47
10.52.040	24.5(b)	21
10.52.090	8.11(d)	71
10.73.150	11.2(b)	71
10.73.150(7)	11.2(b)	65
10.73.170	24.11(d)	43
10.101.010	11.2(g)	266
10.101.010	11.2(g)	267
10.101.010	11.2(g)	279
10.101.010	11.2(g)	281
10.101.010(2)	11.2(h)	311
10.101.010(4)(a)	11.2(g)	274
10.101.020(5)	11.2(h)	314
69.50.435	26.3(c)	17

WASHINGTON RULES OF EVIDENCE

Rule	This Work Sec.	Note
1101(c)	14.4(b)	11
1101(c)(3)	15.2(d)	107

WASHINGTON SUPERIOR COURT CRIMINAL RULES

Rule	This Work Sec.	Note
1.1	1.3(e)	37
1.1	1.7(f)	71
2.1	19.5(b)	2
2.2	12.5(a)	6
3.1	11.2(a)	28
3.1	11.2(b)	71
3.1	11.2(b)	73
3.1	11.2(b)	76

WASHINGTON SUPERIOR COURT CRIMINAL RULES

Rule	This Work Sec.	Note
3.1	11.2(b)	81
3.1	11.2(g)	281
3.1(d)(1)	11.2(g)	294
3.1(d)(3)	11.2(g)	303
3.3	18.3(c)	72
3.3	18.3(c)	75
3.3	18.3(c)	76
3.3	18.3(c)	78
3.3	18.3(c)	79
3.3	18.3(c)	84
3.3	18.3(c)	95
3.3	18.3(c)	103
3.3	18.3(c)	108
3.3	18.3(c)	117
3.3	18.3(c)	119
4.3	17.1(a)	4
4.3	17.1(b)	19
4.3	17.2(a)	6
4.3.1	17.4(c)	143
4.3.1	17.4(c)	153
4.3.1	17.4(c)	154
4.3.1	17.4(c)	156
4.3.1	17.4(c)	157
4.3.1A	17.4(c)	152
4.4	17.3(a)	5
4.4	17.3(d)	50
4.7	1.8(c)	23
4.7	1.8(c)	33
4.7	20.2(b)	16
4.7(a)	20.3(i)	161
4.7(a)(1)(i)	20.3(h)	136
4.7(a)(1)(vi)	20.3(e)	97
4.7(b)(1)	20.5(f)	85
4.7(f)(1)	20.3(j)	196
4.7(h)(7)	20.6(a)	2
4.7(h)(7)(i)	20.6(a)	10
5.2	16.3(d)	50
6.1	1.8(c)	23
6.4(e)	1.8(c)	23
6.4(e)	1.8(c)	35

WEST VIRGINIA CONSTITUTION

Art.	This Work Sec.	Note
I, § 4	15.1(d)	246
III, § 4	15.1(d)	196
III, § 4	15.1(d)	200
III, § 4	15.1(d)	238
III, § 4	15.1(f)	270
III, § 5	12.3(b)	31
III, § 14	16.1(c)	102

WEST VIRGINIA CONSTITUTION

Art.	This Work Sec.	Note
VIII, § 6	1.7(g)	120

WEST VIRGINIA CODE

Sec.	This Work Sec.	Note
15-2B	24.11(d)	46
15-2B-14	24.11(d)	43
28-5-27(b)	26.2(c)	57
29-21-6	11.2(g)	296
29-21-16(e)(2)	11.2(g)	275
29-21-16(e)(3)	11.2(g)	277
29-21-16(e)(4)	11.2(g)	278
29-21-16(e)(6)	11.2(g)	271
50-2-3	15.1(d)	238
52-2-2	15.2(a)	6
52-2-8	15.1(d)	253
52-2-8	15.2(b)	20
52-2-28	15.1(d)	250
53-4A-1 et seq.	28.11(b)	13
58-5-1	27.1(a)	6
58-5-9	27.1(a)	6
58-5-30	12.4(e)	91
58-5-30	27.3(c)	28
58-5-30	27.3(c)	30
61-2-6	16.4(c)	74
61-11-19	26.6(b)	18
61-11A-6	21.3(f)	317
62-1-1	1.7(e)	59
62-1-5a	12.5(b)	20
62-3-21	18.3(c)	108
62-12-13(a)(4)	26.2(c)	37
62-12-13(a)(5)	26.2(c)	36
62-12-13(d)	26.2(c)	47

WEST VIRGINIA RULES OF CRIMINAL PROCEDURE

Rule	This Work Sec.	Note
1	1.3(e)	37
1	1.7(f)	71
4	12.5(a)	4
5(c)	14.2(f)	86
5.1	14.3(a)	1
5.1	14.4(b)	14
5.1	14.4(b)	30
6	15.4(b)	27
6	15.4(b)	28
6(B)	15.4(b)	46
6(e)	8.5(b)	42
6(e)	8.5(e)	164
6(e)(i)	15.2(j)	235
7	15.1(d)	250

WEST VIRGINIA RULES OF CRIMINAL PROCEDURE

Rule	This Work Sec.	Note
7	15.1(f)	299
7	15.1(f)	329
7(a)	15.1(d)	196
7(a)	15.1(d)	238
7(a)	15.1(d)	247
7(b)	15.1(f)	286
7(b)	15.1(f)	318
7(b)	15.1(f)	326
7(c)	15.1(d)	248
7(e)	19.5(b)	4
8	17.1(a)	4
8	17.1(b)	19
8	17.2(a)	3
8	17.4(c)	143
8	17.4(c)	152
8	17.4(c)	153
8(a)	16.1(f)	220
12.1 to 12.3	20.2(b)	16
12.2(c)	20.5(c)	36
13	17.3(a)	5
14	17.3(d)	49
15(a)	20.2(e)	85
16	20.2(b)	16
16(a)	20.3(c)	68
16(a)(1)	20.3(i)	173
16(a)(1)(A)	20.3(c)	79
16(a)(1)(F)	20.3(h)	154
16(a)(2)	20.3(c)	84
16(a)(2)	20.3(i)	166
25	22.4(e)	48
26.2	20.3(i)	166
32(b)(6)(A)	26.5(c)	49
35(a)	1.3(e)	39
44	11.2(a)	28
44(c)	11.9(b)	96

WEST VIRGINIA RULES OF EVIDENCE

Rule	This Work Sec.	Note
1101(d)(2)	15.2(d)	107

WISCONSIN CONSTITUTION

Art.	This Work Sec.	Note
I, § 8	12.3(b)	37
I, § 8	12.3(b)	38
I, § 8	12.3(b)	42
I, § 8	12.3(b)	43
I, § 9m	12.1(f)	69
I, § 9m	21.3(f)	302

WISCONSIN STATUTES ANNOTATED

Sec.	This Work Sec.	Note
59.47(4)	8.4(b)	27
175.50	1.5(e)	234
751.12	1.7(f)	87
765.15	8.4(b)	27
805.13(b)(4)	24.8(a)	14
808.03(2)	27.2(b)	18
809.32	11.2(c)	99
950.04	13.1(a)	21
967.01	1.7(e)	59
967.05	15.1(g)	344
967.05	15.1(g)	345
967.06	11.2(a)	28
967.06	11.2(b)	81
967.06	11.2(b)	82
967.06	11.2(g)	300
968.04	12.5(a)	6
968.26	8.1(c)	24
968.26	8.1(c)	28
968.26	8.3(e)	26
968.40	8.4(c)	117
968.085	12.5(b)	21
970.01	14.3(d)	89
970.02	14.2(d)	49
970.03(11)	14.4(b)	28
971.04	24.2(a)	11
971.04(1)	24.2(b)	29
971.10	18.3(c)	72
971.10	18.3(c)	86
971.10	18.3(c)	91
971.10	18.3(c)	99
971.10	18.3(c)	102
971.10	18.3(c)	115
971.12	17.1(a)	4
971.12	17.1(b)	19
971.12	17.2(a)	3
971.12	17.3(a)	5
971.12	17.3(d)	49
971.19(2)	16.1(d)	134
971.20	22.4(d)	32
971.22(3)	16.3(b)	17
971.22(3)	16.3(g)	97
971.23	20.2(b)	16
971.23	20.3(g)	118
971.23	20.6(b)	39
971.23(1)(b)	20.3(c)	79
971.23(1)(d)	20.3(h)	142
971.23(7)(m)	20.6(a)	7
971.26	19.1(d)	38
971.26	19.3(d)	205
971.31	15.4(b)	56
971.31	19.1(d)	55
971.31	24.4(a)	10

WISCONSIN STATUTES ANNOTATED

Sec.	This Work Sec.	Note
971.31(2)	15.4(b)	61
971.31(5)(a)	15.4(b)	61
971.36	19.3(b)	135
971.095	21.3(f)	309
971.095	21.3(f)	314
971.095	21.3(f)	318
971.095	21.3(f)	326
971.095	21.3(f)	357
971.225	23.2(c)	59
971.225	23.2(c)	61
972.10(1)(b)	24.8(a)	3
972.081	8.3(e)	26
973.12(1)	26.6(b)	15
973.013(1)(9)	26.2(c)	29
973.20(1)	26.6(c)	34
973.20(14)(a)	26.6(c)	38
974.05(1)(a)	27.3(c)	20
974.07	24.11(d)	44
977.07	11.2(g)	275
977.07	11.2(h)	313
977.07(2)	11.2(g)	282
977.07(2)	11.2(g)	284
977.07(2)	11.2(g)	287
977.08	11.2(a)	28

WISCONSIN RULES OF EVIDENCE

Rule	This Work Sec.	Note
1101(4)(b)	15.2(d)	107

WYOMING CONSTITUTION

Art.	This Work Sec.	Note
I, § 14	12.3(b)	33

WYOMING STATUTES

Sec.	This Work Sec.	Note
1-40-203	12.1(f)	71
1-40-203	21.3(f)	370
1-40-206	24.4(d)	55
1-40-207	18.3(c)	123
5-2-113	1.7(f)	84
6-1-104(vi)	1.8(f)	100
6-1-303	16.2(g)	109
7-1-101	1.7(e)	59
7-1-106(a)	15.1(g)	344
7-1-106(a)	15.1(g)	345
7-2-103	12.5(b)	20
7-5-308	8.5(e)	194
7-6-102	11.2(a)	28

WYOMING STATUTES

Sec.	This Work Sec.	Note
7-6-102	11.2(a)	30
7-6-104	11.2(a)	28
7-6-104	11.2(b)	70
7-6-106	11.2(g)	295
7-6-106(c)	11.2(h)	313
7-13-201	26.1(c)	53
7-13-302	26.1(d)	77
26-2-124	8.11(b)	20
31-5-233	26.1(c)	60

WYOMING RULES OF CRIMINAL PROCEDURE

Rule	This Work Sec.	Note
1	1.3(e)	37
1	1.7(f)	71
1	1.8(d)	67
3	19.5(b)	4
4	12.5(a)	3
5	15.4(b)	44
5(c)	14.2(f)	86
5.1	14.3(a)	1
5.1	14.4(b)	13
6(a)(14)	8.5(c)	70
6(a)(14)	8.5(e)	165
7(a)	15.1(g)	360
7(c)	19.4(b)	11
8	17.1(a)	4
8	17.1(b)	19
8	17.2(a)	3
8	17.3(a)	5
12(d)	15.4(b)	60
12.1 to 12.3	20.2(b)	16
12.1	20.2(b)	15
12.1	20.2(c)	53
12.2	20.2(b)	15
12.3	20.2(b)	15
14	17.3(d)	49
16	20.2(b)	15
16	20.2(b)	16
16(a)(1)(A)(i)	20.2(c)	50
16(a)(2)	20.3(i)	166
16(b)(1)	20.4(g)	102
16(d)(2)	20.2(b)	19
21.1	22.4(d)	32
25	22.4(e)	48
32	1.8(c)	40
32(a)(3)(C)	26.4(f)	104
44	11.2(a)	28
44	11.2(g)	259
44	11.2(g)	264
44(b)(8)	11.1(d)	127

WYOMING RULES OF CRIMINAL PROCEDURE

Rule	This Work Sec.	Note
44(c)	11.9(b)	96
44(d)(1)	11.2(g)	270
46.1(e)	12.2(a)	12
46.1(e)	12.3(b)	57
48	18.3(c)	72
48	18.3(c)	84
48	18.3(c)	95
48	18.3(c)	103
48	18.3(c)	106
48	18.3(c)	112

WYOMING RULES OF EVIDENCE

Rule	This Work Sec.	Note
1101(b)(3)	14.4(b)	9
1101(d)(2)	15.2(d)	107

UNIFORM RULES OF CRIMINAL PROCEDURE

Rule	This Work Sec.	Note
41(e)	22.4(e)	50
211	3.5(a)	66
311	14.2(d)	65
321(b)	11.2(a)	7
342(b)	12.1(e)	62
344	14.2(d)	65
431	8.1(c)	38
432	8.1(c)	36
437	7.4(g)	115
444(a)	21.4(a)	29
444(a)	21.6(b)	108
444(d)	21.6(b)	97
444(f)	21.5(f)	173
471	17.4(c)	148
471(b)	17.4(c)	154
472	17.2(g)	144
481	14.2(d)	65
711	11.3(b)	34
731(b)	24.3(f)	144
741(c)	22.4(b)	21
741(e)	22.4(e)	50
741(e)	22.5(d)	37

ABA MODEL CODE OF PROFESSIONAL CONDUCT

Sec.	This Work Sec.	Note
1.2	11.6(a)	5
1.2	11.6(c)	103
1.2(a)	21.3(b)	79

ABA MODEL CODE OF PROFESSIONAL CONDUCT

Sec.	This Work Sec.	Note
1.7(a)	11.9(a)	35
1.7(b)	11.9(a)	36
1.8(b)	11.9(a)	39
1.8(d)	11.9(a)	38
1.8(f)	11.9(a)	37
1.8(g)	11.9(a)	39
1.9	22.5(b)	16
1.9(a)	11.9(c)	140
1.9(a)	22.5(b)	16
1.9(b)	22.5(b)	17
1.9(c)	11.9(a)	39
1.10	22.5(b)	21
1.10	22.5(d)	28
1.16(a)	11.6(a)	22
1.16(b)(3)	11.6(a)	7
3.1	11.2(c)	83
3.3	7.2(d)	59
3.3	11.10(b)	45
3.3	24.3(d)	109
3.4	24.7(d)	30
3.4(e)	24.7(e)	51
3.5(a)	22.3(b)	83
3.5(b)	21.3(b)	119
3.5(b)	22.3(b)	83
3.6	23.1(b)	
3.6	23.1(b)	10
3.6	23.1(b)	14
3.6	23.1(b)	16
3.6	23.1(b)	20
3.6	23.1(b)	21
3.6	23.1(b)	22
3.6	23.1(b)	24
3.6	23.1(b)	28
3.6	23.1(b)	30
3.6	23.1(b)	34
3.6	23.1(b)	35
3.6	23.1(b)	44
3.6	23.1(b)	46
3.6	23.1(b)	55
3.6(a)	23.1(b)	
3.6(b)	23.1(b)	
3.6(b)	23.1(b)	56
3.6(b)	23.1(b)	78
3.6(c)	23.1(b)	
3.6(c)	23.1(b)	36
3.6(c)	23.1(b)	56
3.7	1.7(j)	251
3.7	11.9(a)	23
3.7	11.9(c)	141
3.7	15.7(c)	62
3.7	22.5(c)	

ABA MODEL CODE OF PROFESSIONAL CONDUCT

Sec.	This Work Sec.	Note
3.7	22.5(c)	24
3.7(a)	7.3(e)	89
3.7(a)	11.9(a)	39
3.8	1.5(c)	133
3.8	1.7(j)	260
3.8	1.7(j)	266
3.8	8.8(d)	
3.8	8.8(d)	101
3.8	8.8(d)	103
3.8	8.8(d)	111
3.8	8.8(d)	113
3.8	8.8(d)	117
3.8	13.1(b)	33
3.8	23.1(b)	
3.8	23.1(b)	46
3.8	23.1(b)	56
3.8(f)	8.8(d)	99
3.8(f)	8.8(d)	100
3.8(g)	23.1(b)	56
4.2	1.7(j)	262
4.2	6.4(e)	91
4.2	11.8(b)	40
4.2	21.3(a)	7
4.4	22.3(b)	84
4.4	24.9(g)	128

ABA MODEL CODE OF PROFESSIONAL RESPONSIBILITY—DISCIPLINARY RULES

Sec.	This Work Sec.	Note
DR 1.2(a)	11.6(b)	66
DR 1.10(a)	11.9(a)	26
DR 3.3(b)	15.7(e)	107
DR 4-101	8.8(d)	88
DR 5-101	22.5(c)	
DR 5-101(B)	22.5(c)	24
DR 5-102	7.3(e)	89
DR 5-102	22.5(c)	
DR 5-104(A)(1)	11.8(b)	40
DR 5-105(D)	11.9(a)	26
DR 5-105(D)	22.5(b)	21
DR 5-105(D)	22.5(d)	28
DR 7-102	7.2(d)	59
DR 7-102(A)(4)	24.3(d)	109
DR 7-102(B)(1)	24.3(d)	109
DR 7-103(A)	13.1(b)	33
DR 7-103(A)	21.3(c)	
DR 7-104(A)	21.3(a)	7
DR 7-104(A)(1)	6.4(e)	91
DR 7-106(c)	7.4(g)	124
DR 7-107	23.1(b)	

ABA MODEL CODE OF PROFESSIONAL RESPONSIBILITY—DISCIPLINARY RULES

Sec.	This Work Sec.	Note
DR 7-107	23.1(b)	10
DR 7-107	23.1(b)	14
DR 7-107	23.1(b)	15
DR 7-107	23.1(b)	20
DR 7-107(B)	23.1(b)	
DR 7-107(C)	23.1(b)	36
DR 7-108(A)	22.3(b)	83
DR 7-108(E)	22.3(b)	84
DR 7-110(B)	21.3(b)	119

ABA MODEL CODE OF PROFESSIONAL RESPONSIBILITY—ETHICAL CONSIDERATIONS

Sec.	This Work Sec.	Note
EC 4-6	22.5(b)	17
EC 5-9	11.9(a)	24
EC 7-7	21.3(b)	73
EC 7-7	21.3(b)	79
EC 7-8	21.3(b)	58

ABA STANDARDS FOR CRIMINAL JUSTICE

Sec.	This Work Sec.	Note
Ch. 1	13.2(b)	47
1-1	23.1(b)	15
2.1	20.3(b)	24
2.3	11.4(a)	5
3	20.1(b)	42
3-3.1	20.3(i)	176
3.6(b)	15.7(f)	150
4-4.3(c)	20.3(i)	176
4-8.3	11.2(c)	87
4-70	21.3(b)	113
4-72	21.3(b)	114
5.2	11.6(a)	3
6.1	11.2(g)	288
6-1.7	22.4(c)	22
6-20	22.4(c)	24
6-39	11.5(a)	7
8-3.5	23.2(f)	80
8-3.5(b)	23.2(f)	94
8-3.5(b)	23.2(f)	98
8-3.6	23.1(b)	87
8-3.6(d)	23.1(e)	227
10-2.2	12.5(b)	23
10-2.3	3.5(a)	66
10-3.2	12.5(a)	11
10-3.3	12.5(a)	9
10-5.9	12.3(b)	74
10-5.9(b)(i)	12.3(g)	148

ABA STANDARDS FOR CRIMINAL JUSTICE

Sec.	This Work Sec.	Note
10-5.10	12.3(g)	161
10-5.13	12.2(c)	44
10-105	12.3(f)	126
10-105	12.3(f)	130
10-106	12.3(f)	130
10-108	12.3(d)	103
10-110	12.3(a)	4
10-114	12.2(d)	46
11-1.1	20.1(b)	19
11-6(1)(a)	20.3(j)	197
Ch. 12	18.3(c)	66
12-3.1	18.4(b)	29
13-1.2	17.1(f)	69
13-2.1	17.1(a)	17
13-2.1	17.1(b)	31
13-2.1	17.1(b)	35
13-2.1	17.1(f)	67
13-2.3	17.4(c)	147
13-2.3(d)	17.4(c)	155
13-3.1	17.1(f)	68
13-3.1	17.3(d)	51
Ch. 14	21.1(b)	31
14-3.1	21.3(c)	199
14-3.1	21.3(c)	200
14-3.1	21.3(c)	204
14-3.1	21.3(c)	205
14-3.1(d)	21.3(c)	152
14-3.3(c)	21.3(d)	224
14-12	21.4(a)	34
14-12	21.4(a)	35
14-41	21.1(e)	83
14-41	21.1(e)	99
14-49	21.1(e)	68
14-52	21.5(a)	27
14-55	21.5(a)	22
14-59	21.5(a)	53
14-62	21.5(f)	171
14-62	21.5(f)	174
14-84	21.3(d)	219
14-84	21.3(d)	251
14-90	21.2(h)	416
15-3.2(a)	24.2(e)	71
15-4.4	24.9(d)	34
15-4.4	24.9(d)	43
15-.25	22.3(c)	102
15-47	22.3(b)	51
15-59	22.3(c)	102
15-65	22.3(d)	177
15-74	22.3(e)	281
18-2.3(b)(iv)	26.9(c)	86
18-7.3(d)	26.10(d)	88
18-7.5(e)(iii)	26.10(c)	45

ABA STANDARDS FOR CRIMINAL JUSTICE

Sec.	This Work Sec.	Note
18-15	26.2(b)	13
18-81	26.1(d)	66
18-81	26.9(a)	10
18-81	26.9(a)	11
18-82	26.9(a)	11
18-193	26.3(b)	5
18-514	26.10(d)	95
18-515	26.10(d)	95
18-531	26.10(b)	30
20-67	23.1(a)	2
21-1.1 et seq.	28.11(b)	25
21.1.3(c)	21.6(b)	97
21-1.4(c)	12.4(e)	92
21-1.4(c)	27.3(c)	34
21-3.2	11.6(a)	11
58	20.3(i)	175
93-98	20.1(d)	57

ABA STANDARDS FOR CRIMINAL JUSTICE—DEFENSE FUNCTION, STANDARD

Sec.	This Work Sec.	Note
4-3.5	11.9(a)	3

ABA STANDARDS FOR CRIMINAL JUSTICE—DISCOVERY, COMMENTARY TO STANDARD

Sec.	This Work Sec.	Note
11-5.1	20.2(e)	83

ABA STANDARDS FOR CRIMINAL JUSTICE—DISCOVERY, STANDARD

Sec.	This Work Sec.	Note
1-5.2	20.2(e)	95
11-2.1	20.1(c)	49
11-2.1	20.2(b)	29
11-2.1(b)	20.2(d)	72
11-2.2	20.1(d)	60
11-2.2	20.2(b)	39

ABA STANDARDS FOR CRIMINAL JUSTICE—DISCOVERY AND TRIAL BY JURY

Sec.	This Work Sec.	Note
15-1.2	22.1(h)	134
15-1.2	22.1(h)	152
15-2.2	22.3(b)	56
15-2.3	22.2(f)	113

ABA STANDARDS FOR CRIMINAL JUSTICE—DISCOVERY AND TRIAL BY JURY

Sec.	This Work Sec.	Note
15-2.4	22.3(a)	41
15-3.2	24.2(e)	60
15-3.2.3	24.2(c)	36
123-124	22.1(b)	57

ABA STANDARDS FOR CRIMINAL JUSTICE—FAIR TRIAL AND FREE PRESS, STANDARD

Sec.	This Work Sec.	Note
8-3.2	23.1(e)	227
8-3.3	23.2(a)	50
8-3.4	23.2(e)	72
8-3.5(a)	23.2(f)	81
8-3.5(b)	23.2(f)	94
8-3.5(b)	23.2(f)	98
8-3.5(c)	23.2(f)	84
8-3.6(b)	23.2(g)	117
8-3.6(e)	23.2(g)	112

ABA STANDARDS FOR CRIMINAL JUSTICE—PLEAS OF GUILTY

Sec.	This Work Sec.	Note
14-1.3(b)	21.4(a)	3
14-1.4(a)(i)	21.4(c)	70
14-1.4(a)(ii)	21.4(d)	105
14-1.4(a)(iii)	21.4(d)	111
14-1.8(a)(i)	21.1(e)	84
14-1.8(a)(ii)	21.1(e)	88
14-1.8(a)(iii)	21.1(e)	92
14-1.8(a)(iv)	21.1(e)	95
14-1.8(b)	21.1(e)	66
14-2.1(b)(ii)	21.5(a)	50
14-2.2(b)(ii)	21.5(f)	170
14-3.1	21.3(c)	202
14-3.1(d)	21.3(c)	160
14-3.3(b)(ii)	21.3(e)	267
14-3.3(d)	21.3(d)	224
40	21.4(c)	71
42	21.4(d)	109

ABA STANDARDS FOR CRIMINAL JUSTICE—PROSECUTION FUNCTION, STANDARD

Sec.	This Work Sec.	Note
3-2.6(e)	8.10(c)	67
3-5.8(b)	24.7(e)	51
3-5.8(c)	24.7(e)	60

ABA STANDARDS FOR CRIMINAL JUSTICE—PROSECUTION FUNCTION, STANDARD

Sec.	This Work Sec.	Note
3-5.8(d)	24.7(e)	70

ABA STANDARDS FOR CRIMINAL JUSTICE—PROSECUTION FUNCTION AND DEFENSE FUNCTION

Sec.	This Work Sec.	Note
3-2.1	13.3(b)	17
3-2.5	21.3(c)	162
3-2.5(a)	13.2(f)	99
3-3.4	13.1(a)	7
3-4.1(a)	21.3(c)	159
3-5.7(c)	24.4(c)	19
4-4.1	21.3(b)	52
4-5.2(c)	21.3(b)	143
4-6.2	21.3(b)	124
4-7.6(c)	24.4(c)	19
15-5.6	24.9(e)	58
20	13.3(b)	18
20	13.3(b)	22
209	21.3(b)	125
209	21.3(b)	126

ABA STANDARDS FOR CRIMINAL JUSTICE—PROVIDING DEFENSE SERVICES, STANDARD

Sec.	This Work Sec.	Note
5-2.3	11.4(a)	5
5-5.1	11.2(a)	10
7-8	11.4(a)	7

ABA STANDARDS FOR CRIMINAL JUSTICE—SENTENCING

Sec.	This Work Sec.	Note
18-3.13	26.1(d)	68
18-5.5	26.5(b)	32
18-5.5	26.5(b)	34
18-5.6 to 18-5.7	26.5(c)	40
18-5.6 to 18-5.7	26.5(c)	48
18-5.6	26.5(c)	44
18-5.7	26.5(c)	52
18-8.3	26.3(g)	91
18-8.3	27.3(d)	70
xxiii-xxiv	26.3(b)	7
xxi-xxii	26.3(d)	22
xxi-xxv	26.3(e)	31
xxvi	26.3(e)	37

ABA STANDARDS FOR CRIMINAL JUSTICE—SPECIAL FUNCTIONS OF THE TRIAL JUDGE, STANDARD

| | This Work | |
Sec.	Sec.	Note
6-4.1	24.7(i)	97

ABA STANDARDS FOR CRIMINAL JUSTICE—THE PROSECUTION FUNCTION, STANDARD

| | This Work | |
Sec.	Sec.	Note
3-3.5(a)	15.2(e)	142
3.5	15.2(d)	114

ABA STANDARDS FOR CRIMINAL JUSTICE—TRIAL BY JURY, STANDARD

| | This Work | |
Sec.	Sec.	Note
15-1.4	16.3(g)	107
15-1.4	16.3(g)	111
15-3.4	24.7(a)	8
15-3.4	24.7(d)	30
15-3.4	24.7(e)	39
15-4.4(c)	24.8(c)	42
15-4.5	24.9(e)	53
15-5.2	24.9(c)	26
15-5.3(d)	24.8(a)	22

ALI MODEL CODE OF PRE-ARRAIGNMENT PROCEDURE

| | This Work | |
Sec.	Sec.	Note
110.2(1)(a)(i)	3.8(b)	21
110.2(1)(b)	3.8(b)	17
110.2(2)	3.8(f)	228
120.2	3.5(a)	66
120.6(1)	3.6(b)	54
120.6(1)	3.6(b)	55
132	3.4(l)	240
160.2(1)	7.4(d)	67
160.2(2)	7.4(e)	82
160.2(4)(d)	7.4(g)	115
210.3(2)	3.2(i)	226
216	13.6(d)	61
220.5(2)	3.2(i)	228
220.5(3)	3.4(k)	219
260.3(2)	3.7(c)	55
260.5	3.6(e)	131
270 to 272	3.8(b)	13
277	3.8(b)	22
278	3.8(b)	23
281 to 282	3.8(e)	226
290.4	3.3(c)	142
294 to 295	3.3(b)	72

ALI MODEL CODE OF PRE-ARRAIGNMENT PROCEDURE

| | This Work | |
Sec.	Sec.	Note
320.1	13.1(a)	30
320.3(1)	21.3(c)	194
320.9(1)	13.6(d)	62
320.9(2)	13.6(d)	63
350.3(1)	21.3(d)	208
350.4(3)	21.4(f)	184
350.6	21.5(d)	108
422	7.1(a)	2
426	7.5(c)	35
429	7.3(e)	85
429	7.3(e)	87
429	7.3(e)	91
430	7.3(e)	93
430	7.3(e)	94
431 to 432	7.3(e)	98
551 to 552	3.7(c)	56
557	10.1(a)	10
615 to 616	21.2(b)	51

MODEL PENAL CODE

| | This Work | |
Sec.	Sec.	Note
1.03	16.4(c)	67
1.03	16.4(c)	77
1.03	16.4(c)	78
1.03	16.4(c)	80
1.03	16.4(c)	87
1.03	16.4(c)	94
1.03(1)	16.4(c)	66
1.03(1)(8)	16.4(c)	94
1.03(1)(a)	16.4(c)	95
1.03(1)(b)	16.4(c)	101
1.03(1)(c)	16.4(c)	102
1.03(1)(e)	16.4(c)	103
1.03(2)	16.4(c)	81
1.03(4)	16.4(c)	99
1.03(4)	16.4(d)	139
1.07	17.4(c)	146
1.07	18.5(a)	5
1.07	18.5(a)	7
1.07(2)	16.1(f)	220
1.12	16.1(g)	244
1.12	16.4(d)	131
1.13	16.4(d)	123
1.13(9)	16.1(g)	244
1.13(a)	16.4(d)	131
1.074(c)	24.8(e)	79
1.074(c)	24.8(e)	80
2.06(2)(c)	16.2(g)	115
2.12	13.2(c)	74
2.13	5.1(c)	17

MODEL PENAL CODE

Sec.	This Work Sec.	Note
2.13	5.2(b)	22
2.13	5.2(b)	25
3.04(2)(a)	3.1(o)	303
5.03(4)	17.2(a)	18
5.03(4)(a)(ii)	17.2(a)	17
5.05	16.2(g)	134
6.02	26.1(d)	72
7.01	21.1(e)	85
7.01	26.1(d)	
19	5.2(b)	39
20	5.2(b)	34
20	5.2(c)	43
20	5.2(d)	48
21	5.3(b)	22
21	5.3(b)	24

MODEL PENAL CODE

Sec.	This Work Sec.	Note
21	5.3(d)	45
21	18.5(a)	20
22	5.3(b)	27
22	5.3(b)	29
23	5.1(c)	28
23	18.5(a)	16
24	5.1(c)	18
24	18.5(a)	34
25	18.5(a)	34
27	18.5(a)	38
28	18.5(a)	22
103(3)	16.4(c)	82
115-25	26.3(e)	50
206.13(4)	13.2(e)	92
207.4(5)	13.2(e)	92
241.3 to 241.5	8.3(b)	14

Table of Secondary Authorities

A

A Victim's Right To Be Heard Under The Victims' Rights Amendment, The Victims' Rights Act, And The Rights Of Crime Victims Act, Recent Developments In Utah Law, 2003 Utah L.Rev. 716—§ 21.3(f) n.415

A.A.L.S. & A.B.A., Report of the Joint Conference on Professional Responsibility, 44 A.B.A.J. 1159 (1958)—§ 1.5(c) n.121

ABA Committee on Professional Ethics, Formal Opinion 342, 62 A.B.A.J. 517 (1976)—§ 22.5(d) n.29

ABA Guidelines for the Appointment and Performance of Counsel in Death Penalty Cases, Guideline 10.4.A.2 (2003) [31 Hofstra L.Rev. 913 (2003)]—§§ 1.8(e) n.93; 11.6(a) n.62

Abell, Pretrial Drug Testing: Expanding Rights and Protecting Public Safety, 57 Geo.Wash.L.Rev. 943 (1989)—§ 12.1(a) n.10

Abney, Mutt and Jeff Meet the Constitution: The Propriety of Good Guy/Bad Guy Interrogation, 22 Crim.L.Bull. 118 (1986)—§ 6.2(c) n.146

Abrahamson, Criminal Law and State Constitutions: The Emergence of State Constitutional Law, 63 Tex.L.Rev. 1141 (1985)—§§ 2.12(a) n.9, 20, 53; 2.12(b) n.104; 2.12(c) n.179

Abrahamson, Redefining Roles: The Victims' Rights Movement, 1985 Utah L.Rev. 517—§§ 1.5(k) n.363 to 365, 368, 409; 1.6(h) n.470

Abramovsky, Juror Safety: The Presumption of Innocence and Meaningful Voir Dire in Federal Criminal Prosecutions—Are They an Endangered Species?, 50 Fordham L.Rev. 30 (1981)—§§ 22.3(a) n.7; 22.3(b) n.66

Abramowitz & Paget, Executive Clemency in Capital Cases, 39 N.Y.U.L.Rev. 136 (1964)—§ 26.2(c) n.69

Abramowitz & Scher, The Hyde Amendment: Congress Creates a Toehold for Curbing Wrongful Prosecution, 22 Champion 22 (Mar.1998)—§§ 13.5(h) n.124, 127, 132, 155, 167

Abrams, Conspiracy and Multi-Venue in Federal Criminal Prosecutions: The Crime Control Formula, 9 UCLA L.Rev. 751 (1962)—§§ 16.1(d) n.131, 136, 140, 144, 147, 160, 165; 16.2(c) n.42, 43; 16.2(f) n.106; 16.2(g) n.119, 124, 126, 129, 140

Abrams, Internal Policy: Guiding the Exercise of Prosecutorial Discretion, 19 UCLA L.Rev. 1 (1971)—§§ 1.7(j) n.217; 13.2(f) n.108

Abrams, Report on Jurisdiction, 1 National Commission on Reform of Federal Criminal Laws, Working Papers 33 (1970)—§ 1.2(c) n.90

Abrams, Systemic Coercion: Unconstitutional Conditions in the Criminal Law, 72 J.Crim.L. & Criminology 128 (1981)—§ 21.2(a) n.17

Abramson, The Interstate Agreement of Detainers: Narrowing Its Availability and Applications, 21 New Eng.J. on Crim. & Cir.Confinement 1 (1995)—§ 18.4(c) n.34

Acker & Walsh, Challenging the Death Penalty Under State Constitutions, 42 Vand.L.Rev. 1299 (1989)—§ 26.1(b) n.13

Acquaviva, Mental Health Courts: No Longer Experimental, 36 Set. Hall L.Rev. 971 (2006)—§ 1.6(h) n.458

Ad Hoc Committee on Federal Habeas Corpus in Capital Cases, Report on Habeas Corpus in Capital Cases, reprinted in 135 Cong.Rec. 24694 (1989)—§§ 28.8(a) n.2, 4, 8

Adams & Osborne, Gillis & Beloof, Fort, and Robinson in Symposium, Leadership Issues in Criminal Justice Policy, 33 McGeorge L.Rev. 673 (2002)—§ 1.5(k) n.362

Adelstein, Conflict of the Criminal Statute of Limitations with Lesser Offenses at Trial, 37 Wm. & Mary L.Rev. 199 (1995)—§§ 18.5(a) n.43; 24.8(f) n.88, 101

Ainsworth, In a Different Register: The Pragmatics of Powerlessness in Police Interrogation, 103 Yale L.J. 259 (1993)—§ 6.9(g) n.188

Alberts, Boyt, & Seidman, Public Defender's Conundrum: Signaling Professionalism and Quality in the Absence of Price, 39 San Diego L.R. 525 (2002)—§ 11.4(a) n.4

Albonetti, Prosecutorial Discretion: The Effects of Uncertainty, 21 Law & Soc.Rev. 291 (1987)—§ 13.1(b) n.36

Aldisert, Judicial Expansion of Federal Jurisdiction: A Federal Judge's Thoughts on Section 1983, Comity and the Federal Caseload, 1973 Law & Soc.Ord. 557—§ 28.2(c) n.48

Aldisert, Precedent: What Is It and What It Isn't; When Do We Kiss It and When Do We Kill It?, 17 Pepp.L.Rev. 605 (1990)—§ 2.9(b) n.27

Aleinikoff, Constitutional Law in the Age of Balancing, 96 Yale L.J. 943 (1987)—§§ 1.5(a) n.36, 62

Alexander, Constrained by Precedent, 63 S.Cal.L.Rev. 1 (1989)—§ 2.9(b) n.37

Alexander, Equal Protection and the Prosecution and Conviction of Crime, 2002 U.Chi.Legal F. 155— § 13.4(e) n.171

Alexander, Vicinage, Venue, and Community Cross-Section; Obstacles to a State Defendant's Right to a Trial by Representative Jury, 19 Hastings Const.L.Q. 261 (1991)—§ 16.1(b) n.30

Alfange, Jeremy Bentham and the Codification of Law, 55 Cornell L.Rev. 58 (1969)—§ 1.6(d) n.273

Alfieri, Community Prosecutors, 90 Cal.L.Rev. 1465 (2002)— §§ 1.10(e) n.219, 223

Alfini, Introductory Essay: The Misdemeanor Courts, 6 Just.Sys.J. 5 (1981)—§ 1.4(g) n.135

Alfini & Passoth, Case Processing in State Misdemeanor Courts: The Effects of Defense Attorney Presence, 6 Just.Sys.J. 100 (1981)—§ 1.4(g) n.152

Alford, Misusing International Sources To Interpret the Constitution, 98 Am.J.Int'l.L.57 (2004)—§ 2.7(c) n.181

Alito, Documents and the Privilege Against Self-Incrimination, 48 U.Pitt.L.Rev. 27 (1986)—§§ 8.12(f) n.56; 8.13(a) n.23; 8.13(c) n.78

Alldredge, Federal Habeas Corpus and Post-conviction Claims of Actual Innocence Based on DNA Evidence, 56 S.M.U.L.Rev. 1005 (2003)—§ 28.3(e) n.104

Allen, A Serendipitous Trek Through the Advance-Sheet Jungle: Criminal Justice in the Courts of Review, 70 Iowa L.Rev. 311 (1985)— §§ 24.7(i) n.90, 98

Allen, Central Problems of American Criminal Justice, 75 Mich.L.Rev. 813 (1977)—§§ 1.6(g) n.435; 1.10(c) n.41; 2.1 n.8

Allen, Federalism and the Fourth Amendment: A Requiem for Wolf, 1961 Sup.Ct.Rev. 1—§§ 1.9(e) n.121; 3.1(c) n.28, 83

Allen, Foreword—Quiescence and Ferment: The 1974 Term in the Supreme Court, 66 J.Crim.L. & Criminology 391 (1977)—§ 1.3(b) n.2

Allen, From Winship to Apprendi to Booker: Constitutional Command or Constititutional Blunder?, 58 Stan. L. Rev. 195 (2005)—§ 26.4(i) n.169

Allen, Miranda's Hollow Core, 100 Nw.U.L.Rev. 71 (2006)—§§ 6.2(b) n.47; 6.5(d) n.68

Allen, Professor Israel, The Due Process Clause and The Lessons of History, 45 St. Louis U.L.J. 467 (2001)— § 2.7(c) n.100

Allen, The Crisis of Legality in the Criminal Law? Reflections on the Rule of Law, 42 Mercer L.Rev. 811 (1991)—§ 1.5(h) n.284

Allen, The Judicial Quest for Penal Justice: The Warren Court and the Criminal Cases, 1975 U.Ill.L.F. 518—§§ 1.5(c) n.165; 1.6(f) n.386; 1.6(g) n.396; 2.1 n.8; 2.8(b) n.39, 41; 2.8(c) n.71; 2.9(g) n.185, 188; 2.11(a) n.7

Allen, The Police and Substantive Rulemaking: Reconciling Principle and Expediency, 125 U.Pa.L.Rev. 62 (1976)—§§ 1.9(d) n.97, 113

Allen, The Supreme Court and State Criminal Justice, 4 Wayne L.Rev. 191 (1958)—§§ 1.6(f) n.386, 389; 11.1(d) n.108

Allen, The Supreme Court, Federalism, and State Systems of Criminal Justice, 8 DePaul L.Rev. 213 (1959)— §§ 1.5(e) n.213; 2.5(f) n.46, 48; 2.8(c) n.61, 63

Allen & Ratnaswamy, Heath v. Alabama: A Case Study of Doctrine and Rationality in the Supreme Court, 76 J.Crim.L. & Criminology 801 (1986)—§ 25.5(c) n.30

Allen, Luttrell & Kreeger, Clarifying Entrapment, 89 J.Crim.L. & Criminology 407 (1999)—§§ 5.2(a) n.12, 19; 5.2(b) n.30

Allis, Limitations on Prosecutorial Defense Cases in Federal Courts: The Shield of Confidentiality, 50 S.Cal.L.Rev. 461 (1977)— §§ 20.4(c) n.46; 20.4(d) n.55; 20.4(e) n.80; 20.4(f) n.88; 20.5(b) n.14, 19

Alschuler, A Peculiar Privilege in Historical Perspective: The Right to Remain Silent, 94 Mich.L.Rev. 2625 (1996)—§§ 1.6(b) n.41; 1.6(d) n.254, 255, 257; 2.10(c) n.62, 65, 67, 69, 70, 76, 78, 80 to 82; 2.10(d) n.153; 6.5(b) n.33; 24.5(a) n.3; 24.5(b) n.20; 24.5(d) n.40

Alschuler, Book Review, 12 Crim.L.Bull. 629 (1976)—§ 21.1(c) n.39

Alschuler, Bright-Line Fever and the Fourth Amendment, 45 U.Pitt.L.Rev. 227 (1984)— §§ 2.9(g) n.174; 3.3(b) n.34

Alschuler, Constraint and Confession, 74 Denver U.L.Rev. 957 (1997)— §§ 6.1(b) n.16; 6.2(b) n.52

Alschuler, Courtroom Misconduct by Prosecutors and Trial Judges, 50 Tex.L.Rev. 629 (1972)—§§ 24.6(e) n.52; 24.7(d) n.29; 24.7(i) n.95

Alschuler, Implementing the Criminal Defendant's Right to Trial: Alternatives to the Plea Bargaining System, 50 U.Chi.L.Rev. 931 (1983)— §§ 1.5(c) n.172; 21.1(c) n.39; 21.1(g) n.135

Alschuler, Plea Bargaining and Its History, 79 Colum.L.Rev. 1 (1979)— §§ 1.6(a) n.23; 1.6(d) n.259; 1.6(f) n.348; 21.1(b) n.10, 13, 21 to 23

Alschuler, Racial Profiling and the Constitution, 2002 U.Chi.Legal F. 163, 223 30—§ 3.9(h) n.163

Alschuler, Racial Quotas and the Jury, 44 Duke L.J. 704 (1995)—§ 22.2(d) n.95

Alschuler, Rediscovering Blackstone, 145 U.Pa.L.Rev. 1 (1996)— §§ 1.6(b) n.27, 41; 1.6(c) n.127; 1.6(d) n.184

Alschuler, Review of Silberman, Criminal Violence, Criminal Justice, 47 U.Chi.L.Rev. 1007 (1979)—§§ 1.6(h) n.455; 26.3(b) n.11

Alschuler, Sentencing Reform and Prosecutorial Power: A Critique of Recent Proposals in "Fixed" and "Presumptive" Sentencing, 126 U.Pa.L.Rev. 550 (1978)—§ 1.9(e) n.143

Alschuler, Straining at Gnats and Swallowing Camels: The Selective Morality of Professor Bibas, 88 Cornell L. Rev. 1412 (2003)—§ 21.4(f) n.211

Alschuler, The Changing Plea Bargaining Debate, 69 Cal.L.Rev. 652 (1981)—§§ 1.10(c) n.92; 21.2(b) n.39, 40

Alschuler, The Defense Attorney's Role in Plea Bargaining, 84 Yale L.J. 1179 (1975)—§§ 1.4(f) n.100; 21.1(f) n.112; 21.2(b) n.50; 21.3(b) n.40, 81, 94, 128, 132; 21.4(f) n.211

Alschuler, The Failure of Sentencing Guidelines: A Plea for Less Aggregation, 58 U.Chi.L.Rev. 901 (1991)—§ 26.3(b) n.11

Alschuler, The Preservation of a Client's Confidences: One Value Among Many or a Categorical Imperative, 52 U.Colo.L.Rev. 343 (1981)—§ 1.5(c) n.136

Alschuler, The Prosecutor's Role in Plea Bargaining, 36 U.Chi.L.Rev. 50 (1968)—§§ 21.1(a) n.8; 21.1(b) n.36; 21.1(c) n.43; 21.1(d) n.48, 49; 21.1(e) n.105; 21.3(b) n.122; 21.3(c) n.147, 158, 164, 167, 170; 21.6(b) n.107

Alschuler, The Search For Truth Continued, The Privilege Retained: A Response to Judge Frankel, 54 U.Colo.L.Rev. 67 (1982)—§ 1.5(c) n.138

Alschuler, The Supreme Court and the Jury: Voir Dire, Peremptory Challenges and the Review of Jury Verdicts, 56 U.Chi.L.Rev. 153 (1989)—§ 22.3(d) n.187

Alschuler, The Supreme Court, the Defense Attorney, and the Guilty Plea, 47 U.Colo.L.Rev. 1 (1975)—§§ 11.10(c) n.65; 21.1(b) n.36; 21.6(a) n.15

Alschuler, The Trial Judge's Role in Plea Bargaining, Part I, 76 Colum.L.Rev. 1059 (1976)—§§ 21.1(b) n.36; 21.2(c) n.137; 21.3(d) n.208, 209, 215, 223, 232, 235, 237, 239, 241 to 243, 245, 254, 259; 21.3(e) n.294, 295

Alschuler & Deiss, A Brief History of the Criminal Jury, 61 U.Chi.L.Rev. 867 (1994)—§§ 1.6(b) n.69; 1.6(c) n.132, 143; 1.6(d) n.225, 228 to 230, 233, 237, 241

Amander, Jury Challenge in a Criminal Case: When, How, and Group Membership as a Basis Therefore, 3 Wayne L.Rev. 107 (1957)—§ 22.3(c) n.136

Amar, Double Jeopardy Law Made Simple, 106 Yale L.J. 1807 (1997)—§§ 25.1(b) n.11; 25.1(e) n.94; 25.3(b) n.11, 13, 16

Amar, Sixth Amendment First Principles, 84 Geo.L.J. 641 (1996)—§§ 24.3(f) n.157; 27.2(c) n.37; 27.6(d) n.72

Amar, The Bill of Rights and the Fourteenth Amendment, 101 Yale L.J. 1193 (1992)—§§ 2.2 n.2, 9; 2.3(a) n.12, 18, 24, 31, 35, 36, 39, 43, 50, 61, 65, 68 to 70; 2.3 n.1; 2.4(c) n.90, 102, 107; 2.4(d) n.124

Amar, The Bill of Rights as a Constitution, 100 Yale L.J. 1131 (1991)—§§ 1.5(g) n.260; 2.1 n.26; 2.3(a) n.42; 24.6(a) n.4

A. Amar & V. Amar, The New Regulation Allowing Federal Agents to Monitor Attorney-Client Conversations: Why It Threatens Fourth Amendment Values, 34 Conn.L.Rev. 1163 (2002)—§ 11.8(b) n.44

Amar & Lettow, Fifth Amendment First Principles: The Self-Incrimination Clause, 93 Mich.L.Rev. 857 (1995)—§§ 2.10(b) n.23; 2.10(d) n.119, 126; 8.11(a) n.7; 8.12(c) n.35; 24.3(i) n.183; 24.5(b) n.20

Amar & Marcus, Double Jeopardy Law after Rodney King, 95 Columb.L.Rev. 1 (1995)—§§ 25.5(a) n.5, 17

Amon, What to Do When Your Client Is a No-Show, Nat'l L.J., March 8, 1999, at A6—§ 24.2(d) n.45

Amsterdam, A Selective Survey of Supreme Court Decisions, 9 Crim.L.Bull. 389 (1973)—§ 20.3(m) n.236

Amsterdam, Criminal Prosecution Affecting Federally Guaranteed Civil Rights: Federal Removal and Habeas Corpus Jurisdiction to Abort State Court Trial, 113 U.Pa.L.Rev. 793 (1965)—§§ 13.5(d) n.75; 13.5(f) n.104

Amsterdam in The Supreme Court and The Rights of Suspects in Criminal Cases, 45 N.Y.U.L.Rev. 785 (1970)—§§ 1.6(g) n.410; 1.6(h) n.453; 2.5(a) n.9; 2.8(b) n.40; 2.8(c) n.82; 2.9(g) n.191; 6.3(b) n.31

Amsterdam, Perspectives on the Fourth Amendment, 58 Minn.L.Rev. 349 (1974)—§§ 2.5(e) n.41; 3.1(c) n.42; 3.2(a) n.17, 19, 26; 3.3(b) n.35; 3.8(e) n.223

Amsterdam, Search, Seizure, and Section 2255: A Comment, 112 U.Pa.L.Rev. 378 (1964)—§§ 9.3(b) n.13; 9.3(c) n.18

Amsterdam, Speedy Criminal Trial: Rights and Remedies, 27 Stan.L.Rev. 525 (1975)—§§ 18.1(e) n.56; 18.3(a) n.1

Amsterdam, The One-Sided Sword: Selective Prosecution in Federal Courts, 6 Rutgers-Camden L.J. 1 (1974)—§ 13.4(b) n.47

Anderson, Indigency: The Need for a Definition, 5 Tex.So.L.Rev. 45 (1978)—§ 11.2(g) n.261

Anderson, the Preliminary Hearing-Better Alternatives or More of The Same, 35 Mo.L.Rev. 281(1971)—§ 14.2(d) n.65

Anderson, Will the Punishment Fit the Victims? The Case for Pretrial Disclosure, and the Uncharted Future of Victim Impact Information In Capital Jury Sentencing, 28 Rutgers L.J. 367 (1997)—§§ 26.5(d) n.61, 73

Anderson & Woodard, Victim and Witness Assistance: New State Laws and the System's Response, 68 Judicature 221 (1985)—§ 1.5(k) n.407

Anderson, Hawley & Parsons, Challenging the Detention of a Client Who Has Been Declared a Material Witness or the Incommunicado Detention of Any Client, 27 Champion 14 (Mar.2003)—§ 12.4(g) n.101

Annot., 9 A.L.R.6th 1 (2005)—§ 6.2(c) n.173

Annot., 2 A.L.R.5th 262 (1992)—§ 26.10(d) n.98

Annot., 7 A.L.R.5th 263 (1992)—§ 26.6(b) n.28

Annot., 13 A.L.R.5th 118 (1993)—§ 27.4(f) n.65

Annot., 26 A.L.R.5th 603 (1995 & Supp.)—§ 24.8(d) n.47

Annot., 32 A.L.R.5th 149 (1995 & Supp)—§ 24.2(g) n.97

Annot., 36 A.L.R.5th 255 (1996 & Supp.)—§ 24.9(b) n.16

Annot., 40 A.L.R.5th 113 (1996 & Supp.)—§ 24.3(e) n.136

Annot., 56 A.L.R.5th 385 (1998)—§ 27.5(b) n.49

Annot., 83 A.L.R.5th 541 (2000)—§ 11.2(e) n.168

Annot., 91 A.L.R.5th 343 (2001 & Supp.)—§ 24.4(d) n.56

Annot., 101 A.L.R.5th 351 (2002)—§ 6.9(b) n.18

Annot., 117 A.L.R.5th 513 (2004)—
§ 11.10(c) n.53

Annot., 1 A.L.R.4th 382 (1980)—
§ 1.5(k) n.397

Annot., 2 A.L.R.4th 27, § 6(a) (1980)—
§§ 11.10(a) n.4, 8, 12; 11.10(b)
n.34, 46; 11.10(c) n.49

Annot., 3 A.L.R.4th 601 (1981)—
§§ 11.10(c) n.52, 57

Annot., 3 A.L.R.4th 1277 (1981)—
§ 11.4(b) n.46

Annot., 4 A.L.R.4th 617 (1981 &
Supp.)—§ 24.3(i) n.192

Annot., 4 A.L.R.4th 1274 (1981)—
§ 25.2(e) n.38

Annot., 5 A.L.R.4th 1128 (1981)—
§ 5.3(c) n.30

Annot., 6 A.L.R.4th 16 (1981)—
§ 11.10(c) n.56

Annot., 6 A.L.R.4th 802 (1981 &
Supp.)—§ 25.5(b) n.26

Annot., 6 A.L.R.4th 1208 (1981)—
§ 11.10(c) n.50

Annot., 7 A.L.R.4th 180 (1981)—
§ 11.10(c) n.55

Annot., 8 A.L.R.4th 660 (1981)—
§ 11.10(c) n.51

Annot., 8 A.L.R.4th 1160 (1981)—
§ 11.10(c) n.54

Annot., 9 A.L.R.4th 354 (1981)—
§ 11.10(c) n.55

Annot., 9 A.L.R.4th 695 (1981 &
Supp.)—§§ 22.1(h) n.129; 24.6(a)
n.6

Annot., 10 A.L.R.4th 689 (1981)—
§§ 21.2(c) n.105, 116

Annot., 11 A.L.R.4th 999 (1982)—
§ 26.10(c) n.71

Annot., 13 A.L.R.4th 533 (1982)—
§ 11.10(c) n.57

Annot., 15 A.L.R.4th 582 (1982)—
§ 11.10(c) n.57

Annot., 17 A.L.R.4th 575 (1982)—
§ 11.10(c) n.54

Annot., 19 A.L.R.4th 368 (1983 &
Supp.)—§§ 24.4(c) n.24, 27

Annot., 20 A.L.R.4th 63 (1983)—
§ 1.5(k) n.375

Annot., 22 A.L.R.4th 755 (1983)—
§ 26.10(a) n.7

Annot., 23 A.L.R.4th 397 (1983)—
§§ 15.6(d) n.118; 15.7(h) n.223,
233

Annot., 23 A.L.R.4th 799 (1983 &
Supp.)—§§ 20.4(b) n.39; 20.5(f)
n.71; 24.3(c) n.92

Annot., 23 A.L.R.4th 883 (1983)—
§ 26.10(d) n.90

Annot., 23 A.L.R.4th 1089 (1983)—
§ 7.5(a) n.7

Annot., 24 A.L.R.4th 430 (1983)—
§ 27.6(d) n.140

Annot., 24 A.L.R.4th 592 (1983)—
§ 7.2(d) n.45

Annot., 24 A.L.R.4th 789 (1983)—
§ 26.10(d) n.91

Annot., 26 A.L.R.4th 905 (1983)—
§ 26.7(c) n.34

Annot., 28 A.L.R.4th 725 (1984)—
§ 26.9(b) n.76

Annot., 28 A.L.R.4th 736 (1984 &
Supp.)—§ 26.1(d) n.91

Annot., 28 A.L.R.4th 1121 (1984)—
§ 6.3(c) n.51

Annot., 32 A.L.R.4th 990 (1984)—
§ 13.5(b) n.36

Annot., 36 A.L.R.4th 1182 (1985)—
§ 26.10(a) n.9

Annot., 38 A.L.R.4th 378 (1985)—
§ 14.1(d) n.63

Annot., 39 A.L.R.4th 597 (1985 &
Supp.)—§§ 11.2(h) n.315; 26.9(b)
n.28

Annot., 39 A.L.R.4th 800 (1985)—
§ 24.9(g) n.118

Annot., 39 A.L.R.4th 899 (1985)—
§ 18.1(c) n.30

Annot., 50 A.L.R.4th 1081 (1986 &
Supp.)—§§ 24.8(e) n.53, 78

Annot., 51 A.L.R.4th 939 (1987 &
Supp.)—§§ 26.9(c) n.87; 27.2(a)
n.5

Annot., 56 A.L.R.4th 1178 (1987)—
§ 26.10(a) n.5

Annot., 70 A.L.R.4th 664 (1989 &
Supp.)—§§ 24.7(e) n.37, 61

Annot., 71 A.L.R.4th 638 (1989)—
§ 11.2(e) n.190

Annot., 72 A.L.R.4th 874 (1989)—
§ 11.2(e) n.190

Annot., 74 A.L.R.4th 330 (1989)—
§ 11.2(e) n.189

Annot., 74 A.L.R.4th 388 (1989)—
§ 11.2(e) n.190

Annot., 74 A.L.R.4th 705 (1989 &
Supp.)—§ 24.4(d) n.57

Annot., 74 A.L.R.4th 1023 (1989)—
§§ 16.3(f) n.83, 91, 93

Annot., 76 A.L.R.4th 812 (1989 &
Supp.)—§ 24.4(c) n.21

Annot., 77 A.L.R.4th 1031 (1989 &
Supp.)—§ 24.11(d) n.25

Annot., 80 A.L.R.4th 189 (1990)—
§ 27.5(a) n.2

Annot., 81 A.L.R.4th 259 (1990)—
§ 11.2(e) n.192

Annot., 85 A.L.R.4th 19 (1991)—
§ 11.2(e) n.145

Annot., 86 A.L.R.4th 340 (1991)—
§ 18.5(c) n.75

Annot., 87 A.L.R.4th 384 (1991)—
§ 25.1(d) n.73

Annot., 88 A.L.R.4th 388 (1991 &
Supp.)—§ 24.3(h) n.176

Annot., 88 A.L.R.4th 711 (1991)—
§ 24.9(f) n.102

Annot., 1 A.L.R.3d 1251 (1965)—
§ 10.5(a) n.7

Annot., 4 A.L.R.3d 404 (1965)—
§ 13.4(a) n.22

Annot., 7 A.L.R.3d 8 at § 21 (1966)—
§§ 20.3(f) n.102; 20.3(g) n.120

Annot., 15 A.L.R.3d 968 (1967 &
Supp.)—§ 19.3(d) n.203

Annot., 33 A.L.R.3d 17 (1970)—
§§ 23.2(a) n.25 to 30, 39, 41, 44, 47,
48

Annot., 33 A.L.R.3d 589, §§ 14 to 16
(1970 & Supp.)—§ 27.4(f) n.68

Annot., 34 A.L.R.3d 16, § 17(a) (1970
& Supp.)—§ 24.3(d) n.111

Annot., 34 A.L.R.3d 470 (1970)—
§ 11.9(d) n.184

Annot., 34 A.L.R.3d 1256 (1970)—
§ 11.2(e) n.141

Annot., 34 A.L.R.3d 1313 (1970 &
Supp.)—§ 24.6(e) n.48

Annot., 37 A.L.R.3d 612 (1971)—
§ 15.2(d) n.108

Annot., 40 A.L.R.3d 681 (1971 &
Supp.)—§ 26.5(c) n.45

Annot., 44 A.L.R.3d 306 (1972 &
Supp.)—§ 26.10(b) n.31

Annot., 46 A.L.R.3d 295 (1972)—
§§ 16.3(d) n.51, 55, 74

Annot., 50 A.L.R.3d 760 (1973)—
§ 16.3(g) n.99

Annot., 51 A.L.R.3d 1108 (1973)—
§§ 11.2(g) n.261, 280, 292

Annot., 63 A.L.R.3d 586 (1975)—
§ 8.3(h) n.54

Annot., 64 A.L.R.3d 1226 (1975 &
Supp.)—§ 26.8(c) n.30

Annot., 66 A.L.R.3d 732 (1975)—
§§ 1.5(k) n.357; 13.1(a) n.6; 13.3(b)
n.15

Annot., 66 A.L.R.3d 902 (1975)—
§ 21.4(g) n.233

Annot., 66 A.L.R.3d 996, § 3 (1975)—
§ 11.4(a) n.1

Annot., 67 A.L.R.3d 988 (1975)—
§§ 16.1(g) n.239, 264, 270; 16.4(d)
n.131

Annot., 73 A.L.R.3d 907 (1976)—
§§ 16.1(d) n.138, 145; 16.2(a) n.2,
6

Annot., 79 A.L.R.3d 1025 (1977 &
Supp.)—§ 26.9(b) n.28

Annot., 80 A.L.R.3d 514 (1977)—
§ 16.1(d) n.139

Annot., 84 A.L.R.3d 29 (1978)—
§ 13.3(f) n.56

Annot., 86 A.L.R.3d 571 (1978)—
§ 22.3(b) n.85

Annot., 86 A.L.R.3d 1170 (1978)—
§ 20.3(g) n.126

Annot., 89 A.L.R.3d 263 (1979 &
Supp.)—§ 24.7(e) n.53

Annot., 89 A.L.R.3d 864 (1979)—
§ 27.5(c) n.53

Annot., 94 A.L.R.3d 1218 (1979)—
§ 26.9(b) n.55

Annot., 95 A.L.R.3d 280 (1979)—
§§ 13.4(a) n.18; 13.4(d) n.145;
13.4(e) n.164

Annot., 98 A.L.R.3d 13 (1980)—
§§ 11.5(b) n.23; 11.5(c) n.42;
11.5(d) n.72; 11.5(e) n.86, 88, 93;
11.5(f) n.102

Annot., 99 A.L.R.3d 967 (1980 &
Supp.)—§ 26.9(b) n.43

Annot., 30 A.L.R.2d 1265 (1953)—
§ 16.2(a) n.10

Annot., 38 A.L.R.2d 225 (1954)—
§ 8.10(d) n.88

Annot., 50 A.L.R.2d 176 (1956 &
Supp.)—§ 24.9(c) n.28

Annot., 59 A.L.R.2d 841 (1958)—
§ 17.3(a) n.6

Annot., 62 A.L.R.2d 432 (1958)—
§ 28.9(a) n.20

Annot., 76 A.L.R.2d 262 (1961 &
Supp.)—§ 24.3(g) n.168

Annot., 84 A.L.R.2d 1288 (1962)—
§ 22.3(e) n.259

Annot., 86 A.L.R.2d 328 (1962)—
§ 21.5(f) n.158

Annot., 89 A.L.R.2d 715 (1963)—
§ 3.5(d) n.134

Annot., 89 A.L.R.2d 1258 (1963)—
§ 8.3(b) n.13

Annot., 92 A.L.R.2d 306 (1963)—
§ 27.4(c) n.28

Annot., 93 A.L.R.2d 951 (1964 &
Supp.)—§ 24.7(a) n.2

Annot., 100 A.L.R.2d 1241 (1965 &
Supp.)—§ 22.1(c) n.64

Annot., 42 A.L.R. 272 (1926)—
§§ 16.4(c) n.62, 64

Annot., 48 A.L.R. 767 (1927 & Supp.)—
§ 22.1(h) n.128

Annot., 156 A.L.R. 862 (1945)—
§ 16.4(c) n.55

Annot., 17 A.L.R.Fed. 590 (1973)—
§ 22.2(a) n.2

Annot., 30 A.L.R.Fed. 824 (1976)—
§ 26.10(c) n.82

Annot., 37 A.L.R.Fed. 499 (1978)—
§ 28.9(a) n.18

Annot., 38 A.L.R.Fed. 617 (1978)—
§ 28.9(a) n.18

Annot., 39 A.L.R.Fed. 479 (1978)—
§ 17.1(a) n.8

Annot., 45 A.L.R.Fed 732 (1979)—
§§ 13.4(a) n.18; 13.4(d) n.144;
13.4(e) n.163

Annot., 48 A.L.R.Fed. 601 (1980)—
§ 8.5(d) n.135

Annot., 52 A.L.R.Fed. 411 (1981)—
§ 8.5(h) n.293

Annot., 52 A.L.R.Fed. 901 (1981)—
§ 16.2(e) n.79

Annot., 54 A.L.R.Fed. 805 (1981)—
§ 8.5(e) n.174

Annot., 73 A.L.R.Fed. 112 (1985)—
§ 8.5(i) n.307

Annot., 80 A.L.R.Fed. 446 (1986)—
§ 27.5(a) n.2

Annot., 91 A.L.R.Fed. 816 (1989 &
Supp.)—§ 26.5(c) n.57

Annot., 94 A.L.R.Fed. 60 (1989 &
Supp.)—§ 24.11(d) n.31

Annot., 98 A.L.R.Fed. 660 (1990)—
§ 18.3(b) n.54

Annot., 106 A.L.R.Fed 191 (1992)—
§ 13.5(h) n.181

Annot., 119 A.L.R.Fed 1 (1994)—
§ 13.5(h) n.193

Annot., 125 A.L.R.Fed 1—§ 24.3(c)
n.104

Annot., 154 A.L.R.Fed. 385 (1999)—
§ 8.5(c) n.93

Annot., 154 A.L.R.Fed. 657 (1999)—
§ 8.5(b) n.38

Annot., 158 A.L.R.Fed. 401 (1999 &
Supp.)—§ 24.3(b) n.35

Annot., 176 A.L.R.Fed. 189 (2004)—
§§ 28.3(a) n.5, 15

Annual Review of Criminal Procedure,
Prisoners' Rights: Substantive
Rights Retained by Prisoners, 35
Geo.Ann. Rev. Crim.P 958
(2006)—§ 26.2(c) n.67

Antell, The Modern Grand Jury: Benighted Supergovernment, 51 A.B.A.J. 153 (1965)—§§ 15.3(a) n.6, 12

Applegate, Prosecutorial Discretion and Discrimination in the Decision to Charge, 55 Temple L.Q. 35 (1982)—§ 13.4(b) n.50

Applegate, Witness Preparation, 68 Tex.L.Rev. 277 (1989)—§ 24.4(d) n.34

Arenella, Miranda Stories, 20 Harv.J.L. & Pub.Pol'y 375 (1997)—§ 6.5(c) n.53

Arenella, People v. Simpson: Perspectives on the Implications for the Criminal Justice System: Foreword: O.J. Lessons, 69 S.Cal.L.Rev. 1233 (1996)—§§ 22.3(b) n.64; 24.5(b) n.20

Arenella, Reforming the Federal Grand Jury and the State Preliminary Hearing to Prevent Conviction Without Adjudication, 78 Mich.L.Rev. 463 (1980)—§§ 1.5(c) n.171; 14.3(a) n.34; 15.2(d) n.111; 15.2(f) n.152; 15.3(a) n.11; 15.5(a) n.1, 2, 17, 26; 15.5(b) n.83

Arenella, Reforming the State Grand Jury System: A Model Grand Jury Act, 13 Rutgers L.J. 1 (1981)—§§ 8.6(a) n.29; 15.2(d) n.114

Arenella, Rethinking the Functions of Criminal Procedure: The Warren and Burger Courts' Competing Ideologies, 72 Geo.L.J. 185 (1983)—§§ 1.5(a) n.8, 20, 28, 30, 32; 1.5(b) n.73; 2.8(b) n.43; 2.8(c) n.85

Arenella, Schmerber and the Privilege Against Self-Incrimination: A Reappraisal, 20 Am.Crim.L.Rev. 31 (1982)—§ 7.2(a) n.6

Arenella, Televising High Profile Trials: Are We Better Off Pulling the Plug?, 37 Santa Clara L.Rev. 879 (1997)—§ 23.3(b) n.18

Arkin, Rethinking the Constitutional Right to a Criminal Appeal, 39 UCLA L.Rev. 503 (1992)—§§ 1.6(c) n.153; 27.1(a) n.3, 8, 11, 12

Arkin, Speedy Criminal Appeal: A Right Without a Remedy, 74 Minn.L.Rev. 437 (1990)—§ 18.5(c) n.84

Arkin, The Ghost at the Banquet: Slavery, Federalism, and Habeas Corpus for State Prisoners, 70 Tul.L.Rev. 1 (1995)—§§ 28.1(b) n.17, 18, 21

Arkin, The Prisoner's Dilemma: Life in the Lower Federal Courts After Teague v. Lane, 69 N.C.L.Rev. 371 (1991)—§ 28.6(c) n.17

Armacost, Organizational Culture and Police Misconduct, 72 Geo.Wash.L.Rev. 453 (2004)—§ 1.9(b) n.47

Armstrong, College Searches and Seizures: Privacy and Due Process Problems on Campus, 5 Crim.L.Bull. 537 (1969)—§ 3.9(k) n.266

Arn, Implementation of the ABA Standards for Criminal Justice: A Progress Report, 12 Am.Crim.L.Rev. 477 (1975)—§ 1.3(f) n.67

Arnella, Reforming The State Grand Jury System: A Motel Grand Jury Act, 13 Rutgers L.J. 1 (1981)—§ 15.3(a) n.11

Arnold, Law Enforcement—An Attempt at Social Dissection, 42 Yale L.J. 1 (1932)—§§ 1.9(d) n.110; 13.2(d) n.84; 13.2(f) n.97

Aroney, Formation, Representation and Amendment in Federal Constitutions, 54 Am.J.Comp.L. 277 (2006)—§ 1.2(a) n.1

Ashdown, Federalism, Federalization, and the Politics of Crime, 98 W.Va.L.Rev. 789 (1996)—§§ 1.2(c) n.156; 1.2(d) n.203, 231, 233

Ashman, Measuring the Judicial Rule-Making Power, 59 J.Am.Jud. Soc'y 215 (1975)—§ 1.7(f) n.85

Austin & Krisberg, Wider, Stronger, and Different Nets: The Dialectics of Criminal Justice Reform, 18 J.Res. in Crime & Delinq. 165 (1981)—§ 1.6(h) n.455

Avins, Fourteenth Amendment Limitations on Banning Racial Discrimination: The Original Understanding, 18 Ariz.L.Rev. 236 (1967)—§ 2.2 n.5

Avins, Incorporation of The Bill of Rights: The Crosskey—Fairman Debates, 6 Harv.J.Leg. 1 (1968)—§§ 2.3(a) n.25, 61, 67, 70

Ayer, The Fifth Amendment and the Inference of Guilt from Silence: Griffin v. California After Fifteen Years, 78 Mich.L.Rev. 841 (1980)—§§ 1.5(h) n.283; 24.5(b) n.20

Aynes, Charles Fairman, Felix Frankfurter and the Fourteenth Amendment, 70 Chi.-Kent L.Rev. 1197 (1995)—§§ 2.3(a) n.58, 61

Aynes, On Misreading John Bingham and the Fourteenth Amendment, 103 Yale L.J. 57 (1993)—§§ 2.3(a) n.23, 24, 42, 61, 66, 67, 73

Aynes, Refined Incorporation and the Fourteenth Amendment, 33 U.Rich.L.Rev. 289 (1999)—§ 2.3(a) n.61

Aynes, Unintended Consequences of the Fourteenth Amendment and What They Tell Us About Its interpretation, 39 Akron L.Rev. 289 (2006)—§ 2.3(a) n.26

B

Baade, Illegally Obtained Evidence in Criminal and Civil Cases: A Comparative Study of a Classic Mismatch, 51 Tex.L.Rev. 1325 (1973)—§ 3.1(g) n.187

Babcock, Evidence Favorable to an Accused and Effective Assistance of Counsel, 34 Stan.L.Rev. 1133 (1982)—§§ 1.5(c) n.139, 143

Babcock, Voir Dire: Preserving "Its Wonderful Power," 27 Stan.L.Rev. 545 (1975)—§§ 22.3(a) n.34; 22.3(b) n.78, 92; 22.3(c) n.137; 22.3(d) n.164, 165

Backus & Marcus, The Right to Counsel in Criminal Cases, A National Crisis, 57 Hastings L.J. 1031 (2006)—§§ 1.4(f) n.103, 106, 114, 118, 125, 129, 131; 11.8(c) n.70

Bader, Batson Meets the First Amendment: Prohibiting Peremptory Challenges That Violate a Prospective Juror's Speech and Association Rights, 24 Hofstra L.Rev.567 (1996)—§ 22.3(d) n.202

Bader and Douglas, Where to Draw the Guidelines: Factoring the Fruits of Illegal Searches into Sentencing Guidelines Calculations, 7 Touro L.Rev. 1 (1990)—§ 3.1(f) n.153

Bailey, Ake v. Oklahoma and An Indigent Defendant's "Right" To An Expert Witness: A Promise Denied or Imagined?, 10 Wm. & Mary Bill Rts.J. 401 (2002)—§§ 11.2(e) n.145, 187

Bak, Pretrial Release Behavior of Defendants Whom the U.S. Attorney Wished to Detain, 30 Am.J.Crim.L. 45 (2002)—§ 12.3(a) n.17

Baker, Conditional Federal Spending after Lopez, 95 Colum.L.Rev. 1911 (1995)—§ 1.3(b) n.16

Baker, Constitutional Theory in a Nutshell, 13 Wm. & Mary Bill Rts.J. 57 (2004)—§ 2.9(d) n.62

Baker, Nationalizing Criminal Law: Does Organized Crime Make it Necessary or Proper, 16 Rutgers L.J. 495 (1985)—§ 1.2(c) n.156

Baker, State Police Power and the Federalization of Local Crime, 72 Temple L.Rev. 673 (1999)—§ 1.2(d) n.203

Baldwin & McConville, Plea Bargaining and Plea Negotiation in England, 13 Law & Soc.Rev. 287 (1979)—§ 21.1(b) n.9

Bales, A Constitutional Defense of Qui Tam, 2001 Wis.L.Rev. 381—§ 13.3(b) n.29

Ballesteros, Don't Mess With Texas Voir Dire, 39 Houston L.Rev. 201 (2002)—§§ 22.3(b) n.61, 63, 65

Bamberger, Boosting Your Case with Your State Constitution, 72 A.B.A.J. 49 (March 1, 1986)—§ 2.12(a) n.29

Bandes, Empathy, Narrative, and Victim Impact Statements, 63 U.Chi.L.Rev. 361 (1996)—§ 26.5(d) n.73

Bandes, Patterns of Injustice: Police Brutality in the Courts, 47 Buff.L.Rev. 1275 (1999)—§§ 1.9(b) n.17, 22, 24

Bandes, Taking Rights Too Seriously: The State's Right To a Fair Trial, 60 S.Cal.L.Rev. 1019 (1987)—§§ 16.3(d) n.53, 57

Bandes, Tracing The Pattern of No Pattern: Stories of Police Brutality, 34 Loy.L.A.L.Rev. (2001)—§ 1.9(b) n.22

Bansal, The Supreme Court's Federalism Revival and Reinvigorating the Federalism Ideal, 21 St. John's J.Legal Comment 447 (2007)—§ 2.6(d) n.89

Barajas & Nelson, The Proposed Crime Victims' Federal Constitutional Amendment: Working Toward a Proper Balance, 49 Baylor L.Rev. 1 (1997)—§§ 1.5(k) n.338, 361, 362

Barber, Ohio Judicial Elections—Non-Partisan Premises with Partisan Results, 32 Ohio St.L.J. 762 (1971)—§ 1.10(e) n.203

Barber, Venue in Federal Criminal Cases: A Plea for Return to Principle, 42 Tex.L.Rev. 39 (1963)—§§ 16.2(b) n.29, 32; 16.2(c) n.43

Barkai, Lower Criminal Courts: The Perils of Procedure, 69 J.Crim.L. & Criminology 270 (1978)—§ 1.6(e) n.320

Barker & Carter, Fluffing Up the Evidence and Covering Your Ass: Some Conceptual Notes on Police Lying, 11 Deviant Behavior 61 (1990)—§ 1.9(b) n.18

Barker & Roebuck, An Empirical Topolgy of Police Corruption (1973)—§ 1.9(e) n.125

Barkow, Administering Crime, 52 UCLA L.Rev. 715 (2005)—§ 1.10(a) n.2

Barkow, Originalists, Politics, and Criminal Law on the Rehnquist Court, 74 Geo.Wash.L.Rev. 1043 (2006)—§§ 2.8(a) n.27, 28; 2.8(b) n.44, 55; 2.9(a) n.3

Barkow, Recharging the Jury: The Criminal Jury's Constitutional Role in an Era of Mandatory Sentencing, 152 U.Pa.L.Rev. 33 (2003)—§§ 22.1(g) n.105; 24.7(e) n.49

Barkow, Separation of Powers and the Criminal Law, 58 Stan.L.Rev. 989 (2006)—§§ 21.1(f) n.116, 117

Barnard, Allocution for Victims of Economic Crimes, 77 Notre Dame.L.Rev. 39 (2001)—§ 26.5(d) n.62

Barnett, Reconceiving the Ninth Amendment, 74 Cornell L.Rev. 1 (1988)—§ 2.3 n.1

Barnett, The Rational Underenforcement of Vice Laws, 54 Rutgers L.Rev. 423 (2002)—§ 13.2(a) n.18

Barr & Pease, Crime Placement, Displacement, and Deflection, in 12 Crime & Just. 277 (M. Tonry & N. Morris eds., 1990)—§ 1.5(a) n.49

Barrett, Allocution, 9 Mo.L.Rev. 115 (1944)—§ 26.4(g) n.135

Barrett, Exclusion of Evidence Obtained by Illegal Searches—A Comment on People v. Cahan, 43 Cal.L.Rev. 565 (1955)—§§ 1.5(a) n.39; 3.9(b) n.23

Barrett, Personal Rights, Property Rights, and the Fourth Amendment, 1960 Sup.Ct.Rev. 46—§§ 3.3(a) n.9; 3.3(b) n.34; 3.5(a) n.17

Barrett, The Adversary System and The Ethics of Advocacy, 37 Notre Dame L.Rev. 479 (1962)—§ 1.5(c) n.95

Barrett, The Leak and the Craft; A Hard Line Proposal to Stop Unaccountable Disclosures of Law Enforcement Information, 68 Fordham L.Rev. 613 (1999)—§ 8.5(i) n.326

Barrette, Plea Bargaining and New York's Newly Created Right of Prosecutors, 34 Syracuse L.Rev. 575 (1983)—§ 21.3(e) n.287

Bascuas, The Unconstitutionality of "Hold and Cleared": Reexamining Material Witness Detentions in the Wake of the September 11th Dragnet, 58 Vand.L.Rev. 677 (2005)—§ 12.4(g) n.101

Bates, Voir Dire Examination in Criminal Jury Trials: What is the Proper Scope of Inquiry?, 70 Fla.B.J. 64 (Jan.1996)—§ 22.3(b) n.60

Bator, Finality in Criminal Law and Federal Habeas Corpus for State Prisoners, 76 Harv.L.Rev. 441 (1963)—§§ 28.1(b) n.21; 28.2(b) n.20, 21, 28; 28.2(c) n.48, 68; 28.2(d) n.71; 28.3(b) n.40, 42, 46, 54, 57

Bator & Vorenberg, Arrest, Detention, Interrogation and the Right to Counsel, 66 Colum.L.Rev. 62 (1966)—§ 6.2(d) n.191

Baxter, Federal Discretion in the Prosecution of Local Political Corruption, 10 Pepp.L.Rev. 321 (1983)—§ 1.2(d) n.231

Bayer, Crime, Punishment, and the Decline of Liberal Optimism, 27 Crime & Delinq. 169 (1981)—§ 1.6(h) n.442

Bayley, Comparative Organization of the Police in English Speaking Countries, in Modern Policing, 15 Crime and Justice 509 (Tonry & Morris, eds., 1992)—§ 1.4(c) n.31

Bayley, Law Enforcement and the Rule of Law; Is there a Trade Off?, 2 Criminology & Pub. Pol'y 133 (2002)—§ 1.9(b) n.14

Bayley & Bittner, Learning the Skills of Policing, 47 Law & Contemp.Probs. 35 (1984)—§§ 1.9(d) n.103, 105

Bazelon, The Defective Assistance of Counsel, 42 U.Cin.L.Rev. 1 (1973)—§§ 11.10(a) n.7, 9

Bazelon, The Morality of the Criminal Law: Rights of the Accused, 72 Geo.L.J. 1143 (1981)—§§ 1.5(a) n.30, 47, 48

Bazelon, The Realities of Gideon and Argersinger, 64 Geo.L.J. 811 (1976)—§ 11.7(d) n.43

Beale, Procedural Issues Raised by Guidelines Sentencing: The Constitutional Significance of the "Elements of the Sentence," 35 Wm. & Mary L.Rev. 147 (1993)—§ 26.4(f) n.87

Beale, Reconsidering Supervisory Power in Criminal Cases: Constitutional and Statutory Limits on the Authority of the Federal Courts, 84 Colum.L.Rev. 1433 (1984)—§§ 1.7(i) n.154, 168, 170 to 173, 176, 183, 194

Beale, The Many Faces of Overcriminalization: From Morals and Mattress Tags to Over Federalization, 54 Am.U.L.Rev. 747 (2005)—§§ 1.2(d) n.203, 210

Beale, Too Many and Yet Too Few: New Principles to Define the Proper Limits For Federal Criminal Jurisdiction, 46 Hastings L.J. 979 (1995)—§§ 1.2(d) n.203, 210, 232, 235, 246

Beale, What's Law Got to Do With It? The Political, Social, Psychological and Other Non-Legal Factors Influencing The Development of (Federal) Criminal Law, 1 Buffalo Crim.L.Rev. 23 (1997)—§§ 1.6(i) n.500; 2.8(c) n.66

Beale and Felman, The Consequences of Enlisting Federal Grand Juries in the War on Terrorism: Assessing the USA Patriot Act's Changes to Grand Jury Secrecy, 26 Harv.J.L. &

Pub.Pol'y 699 (2002)—§ 8.5(e) n.208

Beck, The Administrative Law of Criminal Prosecution: The Development of Prosecutorial Policy, 27 Am.U.L.Rev. 310 (1978)— §§ 1.7(j) n.222, 223; 13.2(f) n.108

Becker, Crime and Punishment: An Economic Analysis, 76 J.Pol.Econ. 169 (1968)—§ 1.5(a) n.18

Becker, Judicial Scrutiny of Prosecutorial Discretion in the Decision Not to File a Complaint, 71 Marq.L.Rev. 749 (1988)—§ 13.2(a) n.3

Becker, Plea Bargaining and the Supreme Court, 21 Loyola L.A.L.Rev. 757 (1988)—§ 21.2(b) n.30

Becker, To Review or Not to Review: The Plain Truth About Illinois' Plain Error Rule, 37 Loyola U.Chi.L.Rev. 455 (2006)— § 27.5(d) n.137

Becker & Orenstein, The Federal Rules of Evidence After Sixteen Years— The Effect of "Plain Meaning" Jurisprudence, the Need for an Advisory Committee on the Rules of Evidence, and Suggestions for Selective Revision of the Rules, 60 Geo.Wash.L.Rev. 857 (1992)— § 26.5(a) n.13

Bedau & Radelet, Miscarriages of Justice in Potentially Capital Cases, 40 Stan.L.Rev. 21 (1987)—§ 1.5(e) n.241

Bedau, Radelet, Putnam, Convicting The Innocent In Capital Cases: Criteria, Evidence, And Inference, 52 Drake L.Rev. 587 (2004)— §§ 1.5(e) n.230; 3.1(g) n.187

Behrens & Gramling, Improving the Jury System in Kansas A Call For Jury Patriotism Legislation, 13 Kan. J.L. & Pub. Pol'y 1 (Winter 2003/ 2004)—§ 1.6(g) n.402

Beisin & Feigen, The Rule of Law at the Border: Reinventing Prosecution Policy in the Southern District of California, 12 Geo.Immigr.L.J. 285

(1998)—§ 1.2(d) n.264

Bellamy, Playing for Time: The Need for Equitable Tolling of the Habeas Corpus Statute of Limitations, 32 Am.J.Crim.L. 1 (2004)—§ 28.5(b) n.59

Bellia, Congressional Power and State Court Jurisdiction, 94 Geo.L.J. 949 (2006)—§§ 1.2(c) n.65, 80

Bellin, An Inestimable Safeguard Gives Way to Practicality: Eliminating the Juror Who "Refuses to Deliberate" Under Federal Rule of Criminal Procedure 23(b), 36 U.Memphis L.Rev. 631 (2006)—§ 24.9(f) n.104

Beloof, The Third Model of Criminal Process: The Victim Participation Model, 1999 Utah L.Rev. 289— §§ 1.5(a) n.20; 13.1(a) n.11

Beloof, The Third Wave of Crime Victims' Rights: Standing, Remedy, and Review, 2005, B.Y.U.L.Rev. 255 (2005)—§ 27.4(e) n.62

Beloof & Cassell, The Crime Victim's Right to Attend the Trial: The Reascendant National Consensus, 9 Lewis & Clark L.Rev. 481 (2005)— §§ 24.4(d) n.30, 54, 56

Belsky, The Retaliation Doctrine: Promoting Forensic Misconduct, 50 Alb.L.Rev. 763 (1986)—§ 24.7(f) n.76

Belt, John C. Morgan v. Illinois: The Right To Balance Capital Sentencing Juries As To Their Views On The Death Sentence Is Finally Granted To Defendants, 24 N.Mex.L.Rev.145 (1994)— § 22.3(c) n.152

Benner, Requiem for Miranda: The Rehnquist Court's Voluntariness Doctrine in Historical Perspective, 67 Wash.U.L.Q. 59 (1989)— § 6.2(b) n.51

Bennett, Foreword, 30 Am.Crim.L.Rev. 441 (1993)—§ 15.3(a) n.25

Bennett, From Sorrells to Jacobson: Reflections on Six Decades of Entrapment Law and Related Defenses in Federal Court, 27 Wake Forest

L.Rev. 829 (1992)—§§ 5.1(b) n.9; 5.2(a) n.1, 15

Bennett, Toward Eliminating Bargain Basement Justice: Providing Indigent Defendants With Expert Services and An Adequate Defense, 58 Law & Contemp.Probs. 95 (Winter 1995)—§§ 11.2(e) n.145, 171, 229

Berch & Berch, The Power of the Judiciary to Dismiss Criminal Charges After Several Hung Juries: A Proposed Rule to Control Judicial Discretion, 30 Loyola L.A.L.Rev. 535 (1997)—§ 25.2(e) n.38

Beres, Civil Contempt and the Rational Contemnor, 69 Ind.L.J. 723 (1994)—§ 8.3(a) n.5

Berg, The Bail Reform Act of 1984, 34 Emory L.J. 685 (1985)—§ 12.3(a) n.17

Berge, Criminal Jurisdiction and the Territorial Principle, 30 Mich.L.Rev. 238 (1932)—§§ 16.4(c) n.38, 64, 79

Berger, Incorporation of the Bill of Rights: A Response to Michael Zuckert, 26 Ga.L.Rev. 1 (1991)—§§ 2.3(a) n.61, 71

Berger, Incorporation of the Bill of Rights in the Fourteenth Amendment: A Nine Lived Cat, 42 Ohio St.L.J. 435 (1981)—§ 2.3(a) n.61

Berger, Incorporation of the Bill of Rights in the Fourteenth Amendment: A Reply to Michael Curtis, 44 Ohio St.L.J. 1 (1983)—§ 2.3(a) n.61

Berger, Law of the Land Reconsidered, 74 Nw.U.L.Rev. 1 (1979)—§§ 2.4(b) n.37, 38, 81; 28.1(b) n.8

Berger, Legislating Confession Law in Great Britain: A Statutory Approach to Police Interrogations, 24 Mich.J.L.Ref. 1 (1990)—§ 1.7(e) n.66

Berger, Rethinking the Applicability of Evidentiary Rules at Sentencing: Of Relevant Conduct and Hearsay and the Need for an Infield Fly Rule, 5 Fed.Sentencing Rep. 96 (1992)—§ 26.5(a) n.13

Berger, The Case Against Plea Bargaining, 62 A.B.A.J. 621 (1976)—§§ 21.1(c) n.42; 21.1(g) n.118

Berger, The Supreme Court and Defense Counsel: Old Roads, New Paths—A Dead End?, 86 Colum.L.Rev. 9 (1986)—§§ 11.6(c) n.112; 11.8(a) n.20; 11.10(a) n.16

Berman, The Start of the Next Revolution?: Recent State Reforms in the Sentencing of Drug Offenders, 14 Fed.Sent.Rep. 327 (2002)—§ 26.1(e) n.104

Bermann, Coercive Contempt and The Federal Grand Jury, 79 Colum.L.Rev. 735 (1979)—§ 8.3(a) n.3

Bernabe-Reifkohl, Prior Restraints on the Media and the Right to a Fair Trial: A Proposal for a New Standard, 84 Ky.L.J. 259 (1995-96)—§§ 23.1(a) n.4; 23.1(c) n.107, 108, 110 to 113

Bernhard, Exonerations Change Judicial Views on Ineffective Assistance of Counsel, 18 Crim.Just.37 (Fall 2003)—§ 11.10(c) n.152

Bernhard, Take Courage: What Courts Can Do To Improve the Delivery of Criminal Defense Services, 63 U.Pitt.L.Rev. 293 (2002)—§§ 11.8(c) n.65, 70

Berry, Spirits of the Past—Coping With Old Laws, 19 U.Fla.L.Rev. 24 (1966)—§ 13.5(c) n.61

Bertozzi, Separating Politics From the Administration of Justice: The Role of the Federal Special Prosecutor, 67 Judicature 486 (1984)—§ 13.3(f) n.60

Bester, The Birth of the Transportation Security Administration: A View From the Chief Counsel, 17 Air & Space Law. 1 (Summer 2002)—§ 3.9(h) n.161

Beytagh, Ten Years of Non-Retroactivity: A Critique and A Proposal, 61 Va.L.Rev. 1557 (1975)—§§ 2.11(a) n.6; 2.11(c) n.37

Bibas, Bargaining Outside The Shadow of Trial, 117 Harv.L.Rev. 2643 (2004)—§§ 1.5(c) n.177; 20.2(d) n.58

Bibas, Bringing Moral Values into a Flawed Plea-Bargaining System, 88 Cornell L. Rev. 1425 (2003)—§ 21.4(f) n.211

Bibas, Harmonizing Substantive-Criminal-Law Values and Criminal Procedure: The Case of Alford and Nolo Contendere Pleas, 88 Cornell L. Rev. 1361-1411 (2003)—§ 21.4(f) n.211

Bibas, Orginalism and Formalism in Criminal Procedure: The Triumph of Justice Scalia, the Unlikely Friend of Criminal Defendants, 94 Geo.L.J. 183 (2005)—§§ 2.8(b) n.55; 2.9(a) n.3; 2.9(c) n.46; 2.9(d) n.70; 21.1(h) n.245

Bibas, Plea Bargaining Outside the Shadow of Trial, 117 Harv.L.Rev. 2463 (2004)—§§ 1.5(c) n.176; 1.10(a) n.2; 21.1(d) n.44

Bibas, The Psychology of Hindsight and After-The-Fact Review of Ineffective Assistance of Counsel, 2006 Utah.L.Rev.1—§ 11.10(a) n.16

Bibas, The Rehnquist Court's Fifth Amendment Incrementalism, 74 Geo.Wash.L.Rev. 1078 (2006)—§ 2.8(b) n.44

Bibas, The Right to Remain Silent Helps Only the Guilty, 88 Iowa L.Rev. 421 (2003)—§§ 2.10(d) n.126; 6.5(c) n.56

Bibas, Transparency and Participation in Criminal Procedure, 81 N.Y.U.L.Rev. 911 (2006)—§ 1.5(j) n.325

Bickel, Judge and Jury—Inconsistent Verdicts in the Federal Courts, 63 Harv.L.Rev. 649 (1950)—§ 24.10(b) n.23

Bickel, The Supreme Court—Foreword, 75 Harv.L.Rev. 40 (1961)—§ 13.5(c) n.69

Bilionis, Criminal Justice After The Conservative Reformation, 94 Geo.L.J. 1347 (2006)—§§ 2.1 n.1; 2.8(a) n.28; 2.8(b) n.44; 2.9(c) n.47

Bilionis & Rosen, Lawyers, Arbitrariness, and the Eighth Amendment, 75 Tex.L.Rev.1301 (1997)—§ 11.10(c) n.154

Billings, Pleading Procedure and Practice: The Meaning of Due Process of Law in Seventeenth Century Virginia, 47 J. Southern Hist. 569 (1981)—§ 1.6(b) n.38

Bilonis, Conservative Reformation, Popularization, and the Lessons of Reading Criminal Justice as Constitutional Law, 52 U.C.L.A.Rev. 979 (2005)—§§ 2.8(b) n.44, 48, 52

Binder & Smith, Framed: Utilitarianism and Punishment of the Innocent, 32 Rutgers L.J.115 (2000)—§ 1.5(a) n.23

Birke, Reconciling Loss Aversion and Guilty Pleas, 1999 Utah L.Rev. 205, 248—§ 21.3(b) n.59

Birzon and Gerard, The Prospective Defendant Rule and the Privilege Against Self-Incrimination in New York, 15 Buff.L.Rev. 595 (1966)—§§ 8.10(c) n.54, 57

Bishop, Broken Bargains, 50 J.Urb.L. 231 (1972)—§ 21.5(e) n.114

Bishop, Federal Habeas Corpus in State Guilty Pleas, 71 F.R.D. 235 (1976)—§ 21.5(b) n.72

Bittner, The Police on Skid Row: A Study of Peace-Keeping, 32 Am.Soc.Rev. 699 (1967)—§ 1.9(b) n.33

Bjerk, Making the Crime Fit the Penalty: The Role of Prosecutorial Discretion Under Mandatory Minimum Sentencing, 48 J.L. & Econ. 591 (2005)—§ 26.3(c) n.18

Black, The Bill of Rights, 35 N.Y.U.L.Rev. 865 (1960)—§§ 2.2 n.9; 2.5(f) n.76; 2.8(a) n.9

Blair, Constitutional Limitations on the Lesser Included Offense Doctrine, 21 Am.Crim.L.Rev. 445 (1984)—§§ 24.8(d) n.43; 24.8(e) n.49, 59; 24.8(f) n.92, 94

Blair, Miranda and the Right to Silence in England, 11 Tulsa J.Comp. & Int'l L. 1 (2003)—§ 6.5(b) n.25

Blakesly, A Conceptual Framework For Extradition and Jurisdiction Over Extraterritorial Crimes, 1984 Utah L.Rev. 685—§§ 16.4(b) n.19, 29, 32, 36

Blakesly, The Myopia of U.S. v. Martinelli: Extraterritorial Jurisdiction in the United States in the 21st Century, 39 Geo.Wash.Int'l.Rev. 1 (2007)—§§ 16.4(b) n.20, 25

Blakey, Federal Criminal Law: The Need, Not For Revised Constitutional Theory or New Congressional States, But the Exercise of Responsible Prosecutive Discretion, 46 Hastings L.J. 1175 (1995)—§§ 1.2(c) n.102, 199; 13.2(a) n.11

Blakey, Organized Crime: Enforcement Strategies, 3 Encyclopedia of Crime and Justice 1107 (S. Kadish ed., 1983)—§ 1.2(f) n.286

Blakey, The Rule of Announcement and Unlawful Entry: Miller v. United States and Ker v. California, 112 U.Pa.L.Rev. 499 (1964)—§§ 3.4(h) n.137; 3.6(b) n.44

Blank, Plea Bargain Waivers Reconsidered: A Legal Pragmatist's Guide to Loss, Abandonment and Alienation, 68 Fordham L.Rev. 2011 (2000)—§ 21.2(b) n.60

Bloch, Gagging Bankers: Grand Jury Nondisclosure Statutes and the First Amendment, 1990 Banking L.J. 441—§ 8.5(d) n.152

Blumberg, The Practice of Law as a Confidence Game: Organizational Coaptation of a Profession, 1 Law & Soc'y Rev. 15 (1967)—

§§ 1.10(d) n.134, 139

Blume, Criminal Procedure in the Frontier, 57 Mich.L.Rev. 195 (1958)—§§ 1.6(c) n.135, 156

Blume, Ten Years of Payne: Victim Impact Evidence in Capital Cases, 88 Cornell L.Rev. 257 (2003)—§ 26.5(d) n.74

Blume, The Place of Trial of Criminal Cases: Constitutional Vicinage and Venue, 43 Mich.L.Rev. 59 (1944)—§§ 16.1(b) n.30, 38, 49, 50, 53, 58; 16.1(c) n.108, 110, 121; 16.1(d) n.146; 16.1(e) n.200; 16.1(f) n.223; 22.2(e) n.99

Blume & Garvey, Harmless Error in Federal Habeas Corpus After Brecht v. Abramson, 35 Wm. & Mary L.Rev. 163 (1993)—§ 28.6(g) n.82

Blume and Johnson, The Fourth Circuit's "Double-Edged Sword": Eviscerating The Right to Present Mitigating Evidence and Beheading The Right To The Assistance of Counsel, 58 Md.L.Rev. 1480 (1999)—§§ 11.10(a) n.16; 11.10(c) n.127

Blume & Wilkins, Death By Default: State Procedural Default Doctrine in Capital Cases, 50 S.Cal.L.Rev. 1 (1998)—§ 27.5(d) n.113

Blume, Johnson, & Paavola, Every Juror Wants a Story: Narrative Relevance, Third Party Guilt and the Right to Present A Defense, 44 Am.Crim.L.Rev. 1069 (2007)—§ 24.4(a) n.5

Blumenson, Constitutional Limitations on Prosecutorial Discovery, 18 Harv.Civ.R.-Civ.L.Rev. 122 (1983)—§ 20.4(d) n.55

Blumenthal, Reading the Text of the Confrontation Clause: "To Be" or Not "To Be," 3 U.Pa.J.Const.L. 722 (2001)—§ 2.1 n.60

Bober, The "Chemical Signature" of the Fourth Amendment: Gas Chromatography/Mass Spectrometry and the War on Drugs, 8 Seton

Hall Const.L.J. 75 (1997)—§ 3.2(b) n.54

Bodansky, The Abolition of the Party-Witness Disqualification: An Historical Survey, 70 Ky.L.J. 91 (1981-82)—§§ 1.6(d) n.252 to 254, 256

Boerner, Sentencing Guidelines and Prosecutorial Discretion, 78 Judicature 196 (Jan.-Feb. 1995)— § 26.3(b) n.11

Bogan, Slaughter-House: Five Views of the Case, 55 Hastings L.J. 333 (2003)—§§ 2.3(b) n.77, 80

Boldt, Criminal Law: Restitution, Criminal Law, and the Ideology of Individuality, 77 J.Crim.L. 969 (1986)—§§ 26.6(c) n.33, 37

Bomar, The Lindbergh Law, 1 Law & Contemp.Prob. 435 (1934)— § 1.2(c) n.112

Bond, The Maryland Practice of Trying Criminal Cases by Judges Alone, Without Juries, 11 A.B.A.J. 699 (1925)—§ 22.1(h) n.147

Bond, The Original Understanding of the Fourteenth Amendment in Illinois, Ohio, and Pennsylvania, 18 Akron L.Rev. 435 (1985)— §§ 2.3(a) n.27, 61, 68; 2.4(c) n.91

Bonfield, The Abrogation of Penal Statutes by Nonenforcement, 49 Iowa L.Rev. 389 (1964)—§§ 13.5(c) n.64, 65, 70

Borman, The Chilled Right to Appeal from a Plea Bargain Conviction: A Due Process Cure, 69 Nw.U.L.Rev. 663 (1974)—§ 21.5(e) n.128

Borman, The Hidden Right to Direct Appeal from a Federal Plea Conviction, 64 Cornell L.Rev. 319 (1979)—§ 21.5(b) n.63

Borman, The Selling of Preventive Detention 1970, 65 Nw.U.L.Rev. 879 (1971)—§§ 12.3(a) n.4, 7

Boskey & Pickering, Federal Restrictions in State Criminal Procedure, 13 U.Chi.L.Rev. 266 (1946)— § 1.6(f) n.389

Boss & Angarella, Negotiating Federal Plea Agreements Post-Booker, 21 Crim.Just. 22 (Summer 2006)— §§ 21.1(h) n.247, 248

Bottke, "Rule of Law" or "Due Process" as a Common Feature of Criminal Processes in Western Democratic Societies, 51 U.Pitt.L.Rev. 419 (1990)—§ 1.5(a) n.10

Bouza, Police Unions Paper Tigers or Roaring Lions? In Police Leadership in America, 266-79 (W. Geller, Ed. 1975)—§ 1.10(e) n.193

Bowen, Prosecutorial Inconsistency, Estoppel, and Due Process: Making the Prosecution Get Its Story Straight, 89 Cal.L.Rev. 1423 (2001)—§ 17.4(a) n.50

Bowman, Departing is Such Sweet Sorrow: A Year of Judicial Revolt on "Substantial Assistance" Departures Follows a Decade of Prosecutorial Indiscipline, 29 Stetson L.Rev. 7 (1999)—§ 21.2(d) n.260

Bowman, Fear of Law: Thoughts on Fear of Judging and the State of the Federal Sentencing Guidelines, 44 St.L.U. L.J. 299 (2000)—§ 26.2(b) n.13

Bowman, The Illinois Ten Per Cent Bail Deposit Provision, 1965 U.Ill.L.F. 35—§ 12.1(b) n.30

Bowman & Hesse, Quiet Rebellion?, Explaining Nearly a Decade of Declining Federal Drug Sentences, 86 Iowa L.Rev. 1043 (2001)—§ 1.9(b) n.31

Bracey, Truth and Legitimacy in the American Criminal Process, 90 J.Crim.L. & Criminology 691 (2000)—§§ 1.5(a) n.32; 1.5(b) n.78

Brader, Congress' Pet: Why the Clean Air Act's Favoritism of California is Unconstitutional Under the Equal Footing Doctrine, 13 Hastings W-N.W. J.Envtl.L. & Pol'y 119 (2007)—§ 1.2(b) n.8

Bradley, Criminal Procedure in the Rehnquist Court: Has the Rehnquisition Begun, 62 Ind.L.J. 273 (1987)—§ 2.8(b) n.44

Bradley, Federalism and the Federal Criminal Law, 55 Hastings L.J. 572 (2004)—§ 1.2(d) n.203

Bradley, Griffin v. California: Still Viable After All These Years, 79 Mich.L.Rev. 1290 (1981)— § 24.5(b) n.20

Bradley, Mapp Goes Abroad, 52 Case W.Res.L.Rev. 375 (2001)—§ 3.1(a) n.10

Bradley, Plea Bargaining and the Criminal Defendant's Obligation to Plead Guilty, 40 S.Tex.L.Rev. 65 (1999)—§ 21.1(e) n.79

Bradley, Racketeering and the Federalization of Crime, 22 Am.Crim.L.Rev. 213 (1984)— § 1.2(d) n.229

Bradley, The Emerging Consensus as to Criminal Procedure Rules, 14 Mich.J.Int'l L. 171 (1993)— § 1.5(a) n.10

Bradley, The "Good Faith Exception" Cases: Reasonable Exercise in Futility, 60 Ind.L.J. 287 (1985)— §§ 3.1(c) n.59, 65

Bradley, Universal Jurisdiction and U.S. law, 2001 U.Chi. Legal F.323, 330—§ 16.4(b) n.22

Bradley & Goldsmith, Treaties, Human Rights, and Conditional Consent, 149 U.Pa.L.Rev. 399 (2000)— § 1.7(c) n.18

Bradley & Hoffmann, Public Perception, Justice, and the "Search for Truth" in Criminal Cases, 69 S.Cal.L.Rev. 1267 (1996)—§§ 22.3(b) n.64; 24.5(b) n.20

Bradley, Havens, Jenkins, and Salvucci, and the Defendant's "Right" to Testify, 18 Am.Crim.L.Rev. 419 (1981)—§ 9.6(a) n.43

Brady, A Failure of Judicial Review of Racial Discrimination in Criminal Cases, 52 Syracuse L.Rev. 735 (2002)—§ 13.4(b) n.65

Braithwaite, An Analysis of The Divergence Factors: A Misguided Approach to Search and Seizure Jurisprudence Under the New Jersey Constitution, 33 Rutgers L.J. 1 (2001)—§§ 2.12(b) n.102, 103, 105

Braudes, When Constitutions Collide: A Study of Federalism in the Criminal Law Context, 18 U.Balt.L.Rev. 55 (1988)—§ 2.12(c) n.134

Braun, Ethics in Criminal Cases: A Response, 55 Geo.L.J. 1048 (1967)— §§ 13.2(d) n.86; 13.4(c) n.133; 21.3(c) n.166

Braun, Praying to False Sovereigns: The Rule Permitting Successive Prosecution in the Age of Cooperative Federalism, 20 Am.J.Crim.L. 1 (1992)—§§ 25.5(a) n.5, 11

Braun, The Grand Jury, Spirit of the Community, 15 Ariz.L.Rev. 893 (1973)—§§ 8.6(a) n.5, 14; 8.8(b) n.22; 15.1(g) n.348, 351, 352

Breitel, Controls in Criminal Law Enforcement, 27 U.Chi.L.Rev. 427 (1960)—§§ 1.9(a) n.6; 1.9(c) n.64; 13.1(c) n.39

Brennan, Constitution of the United States, Contemporary Ratification, 27 S.Tex.L.Rev. 433 (1986)— §§ 2.8(a) n.17, 19

Brennan, Constitutional Adjudication, 40 Notre Dame Lawyer 559 (1965)—§ 2.8(a) n.19

Brennan, Constitutional Adjudication and the Death Penalty: A View From the Court, 100 Harv.L.Rev. 313 (1986)—§§ 2.8(a) n.17, 21

Brennan, Construing The Constitution, 19 U.C. Davis L.Rev. 2(1985)— § 2.8(a) n.17

Brennan, Extension of the Bill of Rights to the States, 44 J.Urban L. 11 (1966)—§§ 2.2 n.9; 2.5(f) n.76, 101

Brennan, Foreword, 35 Rutgers L.Rev. 707 (1983)—§ 2.12(a) n.34

Brennan, Some Aspects of Federalism, 39 N.Y. U.L.Rev. 945 (1964)—§ 2.8(a) n.18

Brennan, State Constitutions and the Protection of Individual Rights, 90 Harv.L.Rev. 489 (1977)—§§ 2.2 n.9; 2.6(b) n.30; 2.12(a) n.20, 34; 2.12(c) n.149

Brennan, The Bill of Rights and the States, 36 N.Y.U.L.Rev. 761 (1961)—§§ 2.2 n.9; 2.5(f) n.73, 75

Brennan, The Bill of Rights and the States: The Revival of State Constitutions as Guardians of Individual Rights, 61 N.Y.U.L.Rev. 535 (1986)—§§ 2.2 n.9; 2.6(c) n.73; 2.12(a) n.34, 56

Brennan, The Criminal Prosecution: Sporting Event or Quest for Truth: A Progress Report, 68 Wash.U.L.Q. 1 (1990)—§ 20.1(c) n.54

Brennan, The Criminal Prosecution, Sporting Event or Quest or the Quest for the Truth, 1963 Wash.U.L.Q. 279—§§ 20.1(a) n.12, 13; 20.1(b) n.18, 33, 37

Brennan, The Equality Principle, A Foundation of American Law, 20 U.C. Davis L.Rev. 673 (1987)—§ 2.8(a) n.17

Brennan, The Worldwide Influence of the United States Constitution as a Charter of Human Rights, 15 Nova L.Rev. 1 (1991)—§ 2.8(a) n.19

Brennan, Why Have a Bill of Rights, 9 Oxford J.Leg.Studs. 425 (1989)—§ 2.8(a) n.17

Brenner, "Crossing-Over": The Issue-Preclusive Effects of a Civil/Criminal Adjudication Upon a Proceeding of the Opposite Character, 7 N.Ill.L.Rev. 141 (1987)—§ 17.4(a) n.62

Brenner, The Voice of the Community: A Case for Grand Jury Independence, 3 Va.J. Soc. Pol'y & L. 67 (1995)—§§ 8.4(b) n.18, 82; 15.1(g)

n.346; 15.2(a) n.1; 15.3(a) n.7, 11

Brenner & Durham, Toward Resolving Prosecutor Conflicts of Interest, 6 Geo.J.Leg. Ethics 415 (1993)—§ 22.5(a) n.2

Brereton & Casper, Does it Pay to Plead Guilty? Differential Sentencing and the Functioning of Criminal Courts, 16 Law & Soc.Rev. 45 (1981)—§ 21.1(a) n.2

Brest, The Misconceived Quest For The Original Understanding, 60 B.U.L.Rev. 204 (1980)—§ 2.9(d) n.96

Brett, Legal Decisionmaking and Bias: A Critique of an Experiment, 45 U.Colo.L.Rev. 1 (1973)—§ 1.5(c) n.120

Breyer, Active Liberty: Interpreting Our Democratic Constitution (2006), and Our Democratic Constitution, 77 N.Y.U.L.Rev. 245 (2002)—§§ 2.5(f) n.54; 2.8(a) n.9

Breyer, Federal Sentencing Guidelines Revisited, 11 Fed.Sent.Rep. 180 (1999)—§ 26.3(c) n.20

Breyer, The Federal Sentencing Guidelines and the Key Compromises Upon Which They Rest, 17 Hofstra L.Rev. 1 (1988)—§ 26.3(e) n.39

Brezner, How the Prosecuting Attorney's Office Processes Complaints, 27 Det.Law. 3 (1959)—§ 13.2(a) n.7

Brickey, Corporate Criminal Accountability; A Brief History and an Observation, 60 Wash.U.L.Q. 393 (1982)—§ 15.1(b) n.18

Brickey, Crime Control and the Commerce Clause, Life After Lopez, 46 Case Wes.Res.L.Rev. 801 (1996)—§§ 1.2(c) n.133, 157, 164; 1.2(d) n.213, 239

Brickey, Criminal Mischief: The Federalization of American Criminal Law, 46 Hastings L.J. 1135 (1995)—§§ 1.2(c) n.99; 1.2(d) n.203, 228, 233; 1.2(f) n.286

Brickey, The Commerce Clause and Federalized Crime: A Tale of Two Thieves, 543 Annals Am.Acad.Pol. & Soc.Sci. 27 (1996)—§ 1.2(c) n.112

Bridges, The Speedy Trial Act of 1974: Effect on Delays in Federal Criminal Litigation, 73 J.Crim.L. & Criminology 50 (1982)—§§ 1.6(g) n.441; 18.3(b) n.3

Brietel, Criminal Law and Equal Justice, 1966 Utah L.Rev. 1—§ 6.4(e) n.81

Briffault, Our Localism, 90 Colum.L.Rev. 1 (1990)—§ 1.4(b) n.16

Briffault, "What About the 'Ism'?": Normal and Formal Concerns in Contemporary Federalism, 47 Vand.L.Rev. 1303 (1994)—§ 2.5(f) n.59

Bright, Counsel For The Poor: The Death Sentence Not For The Worst Crime, But For the Worst Lawyer, 103 Yale L.J. 1835 (1994)—§§ 11.10(a) n.16; 11.10(c) n.154

Broderick, Why the Peremptory Challenge Should Be Abolished, 65 Temple L.Rev. 369 (1992)—§§ 1.5(j) n.332; 22.3(b) n.51; 22.3(d) n.166, 258

Broeder, Voir Dire Examinations: An Empirical Study, 38 S.Car.L.Rev. 503 (1965)—§ 22.3(a) n.3

Bronson, On the Conviction Proneness and Representativeness of the Death-Qualified Jury: An Empirical Study of Colorado Veniremen, 42 U.Colo.L.Rev. 1 (1970)—§ 22.3(c) n.158

Brooks, Fear and Fairness in the City: Criminal Enforcement and Perceptions of Fairness in Minority Communities, 73 S.Car.L.Rev. 1219 (2000)—§ 1.5(j) n.320

Brouwer, Inquisitorial and Adversary Procedures—A Comparative Analysis, 55 Australian L.J. 207 (1981)—§§ 1.5(c) n.96, 100

Browde & Occhialino, Separation of Powers and Judicial Rule-Making Power in New Mexico: The Need for Prudential Restraints, 15 N.M.L.Rev. 407 (1985)—§§ 1.7(f) n.88 to 90, 93

Brown, Criminal Procedure Entitlements, Professionalism, and Lawyering Norms, 61 Ohio St.L.J. 801 (2000)—§ 1.9(b) n.29

Brown, Frontier Justice: Wayne County, 16 Am.J. Legal Hist. 126 (1972)—§§ 1.5(g) n.279; 1.6(c) n.156

Brown, The Decline of Defense Counsel and The Rise of Accuracy in Criminal Adjudication, 93 Cal.L.Rev. 1585 (2005)—§ 1.5(e) n.236

G. Brown, Treatment of the Recidivist in the United States, 23 Can.B.Rev. 639 (1945)—§ 1.6(f) n.380

Brown & Burnell, Negotiating Justice: Prosecutorial Perspectives on Federal Plea Bargaining in the District of Columbia, 43 Am.Crim.L.Rev. 1063 (2006)—§§ 1.5(c) n.177; 20.2(d) n.58; 21.1(h) n.246, 249

Brownlee, The Revival of the Justice of the Peace in Montana, 58 Judicature 373 (1974)—§ 1.5(g) n.278

Brunk, The Problem of Voluntariness and Coercion in the Negotiated Plea, 13 Law & Soc.Rev. 527 (1979)—§ 21.2(b) n.37

Bryant, Section 3E.1 of the Federal Sentencing Guidelines: Bargaining with the Guilty, 44 Cath.U.L.Rev. 1269 (1995)—§ 26.4(c) n.26

Bubaney & Skillern, Taming the Dragon: An Administrative Law for Prosecutorial Decision Making, 13 Am.Crim.L.Rev. 473 (1976)—§ 1.7(j) n.227

Bunzel, The Probation Officer and the Federal Sentencing Guidelines, Strange Philosophical Bedfellows, 104 Yale L.J. 933 (1995)—§§ 26.5(b) n.25, 29

Burke, "Truth in Lawyering": An Essay on Lying and Deceit in the Practice of Law, 38 Ark.L.Rev. 1 (1984)— § 1.5(c) n.131

Burkoff, The Court that Devoured the Fourth Amendment: The Triumph of an Inconsistent Exclusionary Doctrine, 58 Ore.L.Rev. 151 (1979)—§ 3.1(d) n.106

Burkoff, The Pretext Search Doctrine: Now You See It, Now You Don't, 17 U.Mich.J.L.Ref. 523 (1984)— §§ 3.1(d) n.106; 3.9(g) n.142

Burnett, Of Crime, Punishment, Community and An Accused's Responsibility to Plead Guilty: A Response to Gerard Bradley, 40 S.Tex.L.Rev. 281 (1999)—§ 21.1(e) n.79

Burns, Criminal Justice: Adversary or Inquest: Did Due Process Reform the Wrong System, 2 Loyola U.Chi.L.Rev. 249 (1971)—§ 1.5(c) n.168

Burns, The Right to Effective Assistance of a Psychiatrist Under Ake v. Oklahoma, 30 Crim.L.Bull. 429 (1994)—§§ 11.2(e) n.145, 171

Buro, Joseph, Bail—Defining Sufficient Sureties: The Constitutionality Of Cash-Only Bail. State V. Biggs, 666 N.W.2d 573 (Iowa 2003), 35 Rutgers L.J. 1407 (2004)—§ 12.2(b) n.31

Burstein, Criminal Case Processing From An Organizational Perspective: Current Research Trends, 5 Just.Sys.J. 258 (1980)—§§ 1.9(e) n.143; 1.10(c) n.108; 1.10(e) n.192, 216

Burt, Forcing Protection on Children and Their Parents: The Impact of Wyman v. James, 69 Mich.L.Rev. 1259 (1971)—§§ 3.9(d) n.64, 65

Burt, Miranda and Title II: A Morganatic Marriage, 1969 Sup.Ct.Rev. 81— § 6.5(e) n.85

Busler, Quashing Witness Subpoenas Without Explicit Authority from the Federal Rules of Criminal Procedure, 25 Crim.L.Bull. 315 (July/ Aug. 1989)—§ 8.8(b) n.36

Buss, The Fourth Amendment and Searches of Students in Public Schools, 59 Iowa L.Rev. 739 (1974)—§§ 3.9(k) n.249, 250

Butler, Racially Based Jury Nullification: Black Power in the Criminal Justice System, 105 Yale L.J. 677 (1995)—§§ 1.5(j) n.322; 22.1(g) n.105

Butler, Starr is to Clinton as Regular Prosecutors are to Blacks, 40 B.C.L.Rev. 705 (1999)—§ 1.9(b) n.28

Butterfoss, Bright Line Seizures: The Need for Clarity in Determining When Fourth Amendment Activity Begins, 79 J.Crim.L. & Criminology 437 (1988)—§ 3.8(c) n.93

Butterfoss, Solving the Pretext Puzzle: The Importance of Ulterior Motives and Fabrications in the Supreme Court's Fourth Amendment Pretext Doctrine, 79 Ky. L.J. 1 (1990)— § 3.1(d) n.106

C

Cahill, Punishment and Crime: Punishment Decisions at Conviction: Recognizing the Jury as Fault-Finder, 2005 U.Chi.Legal F. 91 (2005)— § 22.1(g) n.105

Calabresi, Foreword: Antidiscrimination and Constitutional Accountability (What the Bork-Brennan Debate Ignores), 105 Harv.L.Rev. 80 (1991)—§ 2.3(a) n.51

Calabresi & Presser, Reintroducing Circuit Riding: A Timely Proposal, 90 Minn.L.Rev. 1386 (2006)—§ 1.2(c) n.77

Calabresi & Zimdahl, The Supreme Court and Foreign Sources of Law. Two Hundred Years of Practice and the Juvenile Death Penalty Decision, 47 Wm. & Mary L.Rev. 743 (2005)—§ 2.7(c) n.179

Calabresi, Lawrence, The Fourteenth Amendment, and the Supreme Court's Reliance on Foreign Constitutional Law: An Originalist Reappraisal, 65 Ohio St. L.J. 1097 (2004)—§ 2.7(c) n.181

Caldwell & Chase, The Unruly Exclusionary Rule: Heeding Justice Blackmun's Call to Examine the Rule in Light of Changing Judicial Understanding About Its Effects Outside the Courtroom, 78 Marq.U.L.Rev. 45 (1994)—§ 3.1(c) n.46

Caldwell & McDermott, A Life in the Balance: Is There a Right to Plead Guilty Even if it is to Avoid the Death Penalty?, 104 Dick.L.Rev. 409 (2000)—§ 21.4(a) n.40

Caldwell & Spiga, Crippling the Defense of an Accused: The Constitutionality of the Criminal Defendant's Right to Testify, 6 Wyo.L.Rev. 87 (2006)—§ 24.5(d) n.43

Calhoun, Waiver of the Right to Appeal, 23 Hastings Const.L.Q. 127 (1995)—§§ 21.2(b) n.76; 27.5(c) n.53, 55

Calkins, Grand Jury Secrecy, 63 Mich.L.Rev. 455 (1965)—§§ 8.5(a) n.9, 13

Callahan, Statutes of Limitations—Background, 16 Ohio St.L.J. 130 (1955)—§ 18.5(a) n.4

Callan, An Experience in Justice Without Plea Negotiations, 13 Law & Soc.Rev. 327 (1979)—§ 21.1(c) n.42

Caminker, "Appropriate" Means-Ends Constraints on Section 5 Powers, 53 Stan.L.Rev. 1127 (2001)—§ 1.2(c) n.92

Caminker, Miranda and Some Puzzles of "Prophylactic" Rules, 70 U.Cin.L.Rev. 1 (2001)—§§ 2.9(g) n.154; 2.9(h) n.212, 253, 254; 6.5(e) n.96

Camp, Out of the Quagmire After Jacobson v. United States: Toward a More Balanced Entrapment Standard, 83 J.Crim.L. & Criminology 1055 (1993)—§§ 5.2(a) n.15; 5.2(c) n.43

Campbell, Eliminate the Grand Jury, 64 J.Crim.L. & Criminology 174 (1973)—§§ 15.3(a) n.6, 12

Cannito & Becker, The Case for Limited Use of Polls in the Jury Selection Process, 7 Rutgers J.Comp., Tech. & L. 111 (1979)—§ 22.3(b) n.92

Cantrell, An Overview of the Preliminary Hearing in Oklahoma, 39 Okla.L.Rev. 457 (1986)—§ 14.4(e) n.101

Cantrell, Double Jeopardy and Multiple Punishment: An Historical and Constitutional Analysis, 24 S.Tex.L.J. 735 (1983)—§ 25.1(b) n.15

Caplan, Reflections on the Nationalization of Crime, 1973 Law & Soc.Ord. 582—§§ 1.2(d) n.252; 1.3(e) n.53; 1.6(g) n.415, 419; 1.6(h) n.447

Caplan, The Case for Rulemaking by Enforcement Agencies, 36 Law & Contemp.Probs. 500 (1971)—§§ 1.6(g) n.410; 1.7(j) n.215

Capra, Deterring the Formation of the Attorney-Client Relationship, Disclosure of Client Identity, Payment of Fees and Communications by Fiduciaries, 4 Geo.Legal Ethics J. 235 (1990)—§ 8.8(d) n.90

Cardenas, The Crime Victim in the Prosecutorial Process, 9 Harv.J.L. & Pub.Pol'y 357 (1986)—§§ 1.5(k) n.340, 345; 1.6(b) n.73, 84; 13.3(b) n.15

Cardinale & Feldman, The Federal Courts and the Right to Nondiscriminatory Administration of the Criminal Law: A Critical View, 29 Syracuse L.Rev. 659 (1978)—§§ 13.4(a) n.12; 13.4(b) n.47; 13.4(e) n.171

Carlson, Argument to the Jury: Passion, Persuasion, and Legal Controls, 33 St. Louis U.L.J. 787 (1989)—§ 24.7(d) n.27

Carlson, Bauer, Thornburg, and Wolfson in Symposium at 67 J.Crim.L. & Criminology 129-80 (1976)—§ 8.11(b) n.24

Carlson, The Act Requirement and the Foundation of the Entrapment Defense, 73 Va.L.Rev. 1011 (1987)—§§ 5.1(b) n.9; 5.2(c) n.40

Carlson, Witness Immunity in Modern Trials: Observations on the Uniform Rule of Criminal Procedure, 67 J.Crim.L. & Criminology 131 (1976)—§ 8.11(b) n.18

Carlson & Voepel, Material Witness and Material Injustice, 58 Wash.U.L.Q. 1 (1980)—§§ 12.4(g) n.98, 104 to 107

Carns & Kruse, A Re-evalution of Alaska's Plea Bargaining Ban, 8 Alaska L.Rev. 27 (1991)—§ 21.1(g) n.130

Carp, The Harris County Grand Jury—A Case Study, 12 Houst.L.Rev. 90 (1974)—§§ 8.4(a) n.9; 15.3(a) n.8; 15.3(c) n.46

Carpenter, The All-or-Nothing Doctrine in Criminal Cases: Independent Trial Strategy or Gamesmanship Gone Awry?, 26 Am.J.Crim.L. 257 (1999)—§ 24.8(f) n.120

Carrington, Federal Use of State Institutions in the Administration of Criminal Justice, 49 S. Methodist L.Rev. 557 (1996)—§ 1.2(d) n.205

Carrington, Trial by Jury, 5 Duke L.Mag. 13 (No. 1, 1987)—§ 1.5(g) n.276

Carrington & Nicholson, The Victims Movement: An Idea Where Time Has Come, 11 Pepp.L.Rev. 1 (1984)—§§ 1.5(k) n.360, 361, 369

Carter, A Beyond a Reasonable Doubt Standard in Death Penalty Proceedings: A Neglected Element of Fairness, 52 Ohio St.L.J. 195 (1991)—§§ 26.1(b) n.17; 26.4(i) n.179

Carter, Lessons From Avena; The Inadequacy of Clemency and Judicial Proceedings for Violations of the Vienna Convention in Consular Relations, 15 Duke J.Comp. & Int'l.L. 259 (2005)—§ 1.7(c) n.29

Casey, Regulating Federal Prosecutors: Why McDade Should be Repealed, 19 Ga.St.U.L.Rev. 395 (2002)—§ 6.4(e) n.91

Casper, Did You Have a Lawyer When You Went to Court? No. I Had a Public Defender, 1 Yale Rev.L. & Soc.Act. 4 (1971)—§ 21.1(f) n.107

Casper, Jonathan D., The Impact Of Criminal Justice Innovation: Feeley On Court Reform, 1983 Am.B.Found.Res.J. 959—§ 1.3(c) n.26

Casper & Zeisel, Lay Judges in the German Criminal Courts, 1 J. Legal Stud. 135 (1972)—§ 1.5(c) n.115

Cassel, The Statute That Time Forgot: 18 U.S.C.A. Section 3501 and the Overhauling of Miranda, 85 Iowa L.Rev. 175 (1999)—§ 6.5(e) n.82

Cassell, All Benefits, No Costs: The Grand Illusion of Miranda's Defenders, 90 Nw.U.L.Rev. 1084 (1996)—§§ 6.5(c) n.54; 6.5(d) n.77

Cassell, Balanced Approaches to the False Confession Problem: A Brief Comment on Ofshe, Leo & Alschuler, 74 Denver U.L.Rev. 1123 (1997)—§ 6.1(b) n.16

Cassell, Balancing the Scales of Justice; The Case for and the Effects of Utah's Victims' Rights Amendment, 1994 Utah L.Rev. 1373—§§ 1.5(k) n.361; 12.1(f) n.85; 14.3(a) n.30; 14.4(b) n.15, 26

Cassell, Barbarians at the Gates? A Reply to the Critics of the Victims' Rights Amendment, 1999 Utah L.Rev. 479 (1999)—§ 26.5(d) n.61

Cassell, Miranda's "Negligible" Effect on Law Enforcement: Some Skeptical Observations, 20 Harv.J.L. & Pub.Pol'y 325 (1997)—§ 6.5(c) n.52

Cassell, Miranda's Social Costs: An Empirical Reassessment, 90 Nw.U.L.Rev. 387 (1996)—

§§ 1.5(a) n.51; 6.5(c) n.50, 52; 6.5(d) n.77

Cassell, Recognizing Victims in the Federal Rules of Criminal Procedure: Proposed Amendments in Light of the Crime Victims' Rights Act, 2005 B.Y.U.L.Rev. 836 (2005)—§§ 1.5(k) n.362, 385, 410, 411; 24.4(d) n.53; 26.5(c) n.59

Cassell, the Costs of the Miranda Mandate: A Lesson in the Dangers of Inflexible, "Prophylactic" Supreme Court Inventions, 28 Ariz.St.L.J. 299 (1996)—§ 6.5(c) n.52

Cassell, The Guilty and the "Innocent": An Examination of Alleged Cases of Wrongful Convictions From False Confessions, 22 Harv. J. L. & Pub. Pol'y 523 (1999)—§ 1.5(e) n.229

Cassell, The Mysterious Creation of Search and Seizure Exclusionary Rules Under State Constitutions: The Utah Example, 1993 Utah L.Rev. 751—§ 2.12(e) n.217

Cassell, The Paths Not Taken: The Supreme Court's Failures in Dickerson, 99 Mich.L.Rev. 898 (2001)—§§ 2.9(h) n.253; 6.5(e) n.96

Cassell & Hayman, Police Interrogation in the 1990s: An Empirical Study of the Effects of Miranda, 43 UCLA L.Rev. 839 (1996)—§§ 6.5(c) n.35, 54

Cavallaro, Better Off Dead: Abatement, Innocence, and the Evolving Right to Appeal, 73 U.Colo.L.Rev. 943 (2003)—§§ 27.1(a) n.12; 27.5(a) n.4, 7

Cavise, The Batson Doctrine: The Supreme Court's Utter Failure to Meet the Challenge of Discrimination in Jury Selection, 1999 Wis.L.Rev. 501—§ 1.5(j) n.333

Cerruti, The Demise of the Aguilar-Spinelli Rule: A Case of Faulty Reception, 61 Denver L.J. 431 (1984)—§ 3.3(c) n.80

Cerutti, "Dancing in the Courthouse": The First Amendment Right of Access Opens a New Round, 29 U.Rich.L.Rev. 237 (1955)—§§ 23.1(d) n.122, 156, 166

Chafee, The Most Important Right in the Constitution, 32 B.U.L.Rev. 143 (1952)—§§ 28.1(b) n.9; 28.2(a) n.3

C. Chaiken & M. Chaiken, Drugs and Predatory Crime, in Drugs and Crime, 13 Crime & Just. 203 (M. Tonry & J. Wilson eds., 1990)—§ 1.5(a) n.46

Chanenson, The Civilization of the Criminal Law, 58 Vand.L.Rev. 121 (2005)—§ 26.1(c) n.46

Chanenson, The Next Era of Sentencing Reform, 54 Emory L.J. 377 (2005)—§ 26.1(c) n.46

Chao, Mirandizing Kids: Not as Simple as A-B-C, 21 Whittier L.Rev. 521 (2000)—§ 6.9(g) n.178

Charlow, Tolerating Deception and Discrimination After Batson, 50 Stan.L.Rev. 9 (1997)—§ 22.3(d) n.187

Chase, The Burger Court, The Individual, and The Criminal Process, Directions and Misdirections, 52 N.Y.U.L.Rev. 518 (1977)—§§ 2.8(b) n.43; 2.9(f) n.109; 2.9(g) n.185

Cheh, Constitutional Limits on Using Civil Remedies to Achieve Criminal Law Objectives: Understanding and Transcending the Criminal-Civil Law Distinction, 42 Hastings L.J. 1325 (1991)—§ 25.1(c) n.25

Chemerinsky, An Independent Analysis of the Los Angeles Police Department's Board of Inquiry Report on the Rampart Scandal, 34 Loy.L.A.L.Rev. 545 (2001)—§ 1.9(b) n.22

Chemerinsky, Eliminating Discrimination in Administering the Death Penalty: The Need for the Racial Justice Act, 35 Santa Clara L.Rev. 519 (1995)—§ 1.5(j) n.330

Chemerinsky, Silence is Not Golden, Protecting Lawyer Speech Under the First Amendment, 47 Emory L.J. 859 (1998)—§§ 23.1(a) n.4; 23.1(b) n.23, 25

Chevigny, The Right to Resist an Unlawful Arrest, 7 Crim.L.Bull. 189 (1971)—§ 3.1(o) n.306

Chin & Holmes, Effective Assistance of Counsel and the Consequences of Guilty Pleas, 87 Cornell L.Rev. 697 (2002)—§ 21.3(b) n.68

Chin and Wells, Can a Reasonable Doubt Have An Unreasonable Price? Limitations on Attorneys' Fees in Criminal Cases, 41 B.C.L.Rev. 1 (1999)—§ 11.1(a) n.10

Chippendale, More Harm Than Good: Assessing Federalization of Criminal Law, 79 Minn.L.Rev. 455 (1994)—§§ 1.2(d) n.203, 205

Chisum, In Defense of Modern Habeas Corpus for State Prisoners, 21 DePaul L.Rev. 682 (1972)—§ 28.2(c) n.65

J. Choper, Congressional Power to Expand Judicial Definitions of the Substantive Terms of the Civil War Amendments, 67 Minn.L.Rev. 299 (1982)—§ 1.3(b) n.11

Christian, Delay in Criminal Appeals: A Functional Analysis of One Court's Work, 23 Stan.L.Rev. 676 (1971)—§ 18.5(c) n.83

Chun, The Right to Grand Jury Indictment, 26 Am.Crim.L.Rev. 1457 (1989)—§§ 8.2(b) n.11; 8.2(c) n.32; 15.1(a) n.1; 15.1(b) n.40

Church, Examining Local Legal Culture, 1985 Am.B.Found.Res.J. 449—§§ 1.9(b) n.29; 1.10(a) n.6, 11; 1.10(c) n.108, 111; 1.10(d) n.162, 164

Church, In Defense of "Bargain Justice," 13 Law & Soc'y Rev. 509 (1979)—§§ 1.5(c) n.175, 176; 21.1(b) n.28, 32; 21.1(d) n.58; 21.1(e) n.89

Chused, Faretta and The Personal Defense: The Role of a Represented Defendant in Trial Tactics, 65 Cal.L.Rev. 636 (1977)—§§ 11.5(g) n.107, 114; 11.6(a) n.2, 9

Civiletti & Walsh, The Grand Jury Goes on Trial, 4 Litigation 37 (Summer 1978)—§§ 8.6(a) n.5, 15

Clancy, The Future of Fourth Amendment Seizure Analysis After Hodari, D. and Bostick, 28 Am.Crim.L.Rev. 799 (1991)—§ 3.8(c) n.108

Clark, Nothing to Hyde? The Flood of Wrongful Recovery Suits Has Not Materialized, 14 Crim.Just. 10 (Summer, 1999)—§§ 13.5(h) n.124, 126

Clark, The American Bar Association Standards for Criminal Justice: Prescription for an Ailing System, 47 Notre Dame L.Rev. 429 (1972)—§§ 1.3(f) n.61, 68, 70, 71

Clark, The Handmaiden of Justice, 23 Wash.U.L.Q. 297 (1938)—§ 1.5(a) n.5

Clark, The Omnibus Hearing in State and Federal Courts, 59 Cornell L.Rev. 761 (1974)—§ 20.2(c) n.57

Clark, Why the ABA Standards, 33 La.L.Rev. 541 (1973)—§§ 1.3(f) n.61, 68

Clark, Burger, Introduction in the ABA Standards for Criminal Justice, 12 Am.Crim.L.Rev. 251 (1974)—§§ 1.3(f) n.61, 68

Clarke, Plea Bargaining and Trial Penalties: When May the State Legitimately Require Criminal Defendants to Surrender Their Trial Rights, 55 Ind.L.J. 71 (1979)—§ 21.2(a) n.17

Cline, The Attorney-Client Privilege and the Federal Grand Jury, 13 Am.J.Crim.L. 67 (1985)—§ 8.8(d) n.90

Clinton, Rule 9 of the Federal Habeas Corpus Rules: A Case Study on the Need for Reform of The Rules Enabling Act, 63 Iowa L.Rev. 15

(1997)—§ 28.5(b) n.41

Clinton, The Right to Present a Defense: An Emerging Constitutional Guarantee in Criminal Trials, 9 Ind.L.Rev. 711 (1976)—§§ 20.4(d) n.55; 24.3(h) n.178; 24.4(a) n.5

Cloninger & Satoriue, Crime Rates, Clearance Rates and Enforcement Efforts: The Case of Houston, Texas, 38 Am.J.Econ. & Soc. 389 (1979)—§ 1.5(a) n.49

Clott, How to Sentence a Defendant Prosecuted Separately for Factually Unrelated Crimes: An Explanation and Defense of § 5G1.3(c), 7 Fed.Sent.Rptr. 214 (1995)—§ 26.3(f) n.62

Cloud et al., Words Without Meaning: The Constitution, Confessions, and Mentally Retarded Suspects, 69 U.Chi.L.Rev. 495 (2002)—§ 6.9(b) n.41

Cloud, Forfeiting Defense Attorney Fees; Applying an Institutional Role Theory to Define Individual Constitutional Rights, 1987 Wis.L.Rev. 1—§ 11.4(c) n.96

Cloud, Ignorance and Democracy, 39 Tex. Tech L. Rev. 1143 (Summer, 2007)—§ 6.7 n.

Cloud, Searching Through History; Searching For History, 63 U.Chi.L.Rev. 1707 (1996)—§ 2.9(d) n.58

Clymer, Compelled Statements from Police Officers and Garrity Immunity, 76 N.Y.U.L.Rev. 1309 (2001)—§§ 8.10(e) n.124; 8.11(a) n.15; 8.11(c) n.52

Clymer, Unequal Justice: The Federalization of Criminal Law, 70 S.Cal.L.Rev. 643 (1997)—§§ 1.2(d) n.203, 246

Coakley, Restrictions in the Law of Arrest, 52 Nw.L.Rev. 2 (1957)—§ 1.6(f) n.376

Cochran, "How Do You Plead, Guilty or Not Guilty?": Does the Plea Inquiry Violate the Defendant's Right to Silence?, 26 Cardozo L.Rev.

1409 (2005)—§ 21.4(a) n.10

Cohan, Torture and the Necessity Doctrine, 41 Val.U.L.Rev. 1587 (2007)—§§ 1.5(a) n.15; 6.2(c) n.61

Cohen, Can They Kill Me If I'm Gone: Trial in Absentia in Capital Cases, 36 U.Fla.L.Rev. 273 (1984)—§ 24.2(d) n.44

Cohen, Corrections Law Developments: Search and Seizure in Prison Cells—The Constitution Takes a Holiday, 21 Crim.L.Bull. 171 (1985)—§ 3.9(i) n.179

Cohen, Incapacitation As A Strategy For Crime Control: Possibilities and Pitfalls, in 5 Crime & Just. 1 (M. Tonry & N. Morris eds., 1983)—§ 1.5(a) n.49

Cohen, Wealth, Bail, and the Equal Protection of the Laws, 23 Vill.L.Rev. 977 (1978)—§ 12.2(b) n.25

Cohen & Paine: Crawford v. Washington: Confirmation Revolution, 40 Tenn.B.J. 22 (2004)—§ 2.8(b) n.55

Cohn & Sherwood, The Rise and Fall of Affirmative Action in Jury Selection, 32 U.Mich.J.L.Ref. 323 (1999)—§ 22.2(d) n.95

Colb, Innocence, Privacy, and Targeting in Fourth Amendment Jurisprudence, 96 Colum.L.Rev. 1454 (1996)—§ 2.9(f) n.111

Colb, Standing Room Only: Why Fourth Amendment Exclusion and Standing Can No Longer Logically Coexist, 28 Cardozo L.Rev. 1663 (2007)—§ 9.1(a) n.5

Colb, Stopping a Moving Target, 3 Rutgers Race & L.Rev. (No. 3) (2001)—§ 1.5(j) n.334

Colbert, Coming Soon to a Court Near You—Convicting the Unrepresented at the Bail Stage: An Autopsy of a State High Court's Sua Sponte Rejection of Indigent Defendants' Right to Counsel, 36 Seton Hall L.Rev. 653 (2006)—§ 12.1(c) n.44

Colbert, Section Endorses Appointed Counsel at Bail Hearing, 13 Crim.Just. 17 (Summer 1998)— § 12.1(c) n.40

Colbert, Thirty-Five Years After Gideon: The Illusory Right to Counsel at Bail Proceedings, 1998 U.Ill.L.Rev. 1—§§ 11.2(b) n.79; 12.1(c) n.46; 14.2(e) n.75

Colbert, Paternoster, & Bushway, Do Attorneys Really Matter? The Empirical and Legal Case for the Right to Counsel at Bail, 23 Cardozo L.Rev. 1719 (2002)—§§ 11.2(b) n.79; 12.1(c) n.46

Cole, Discretion and Discrimination Reconsidered: A Response to the New Criminal Justice Scholarship, 87 Geo.L.J. 1059 (1999)—§§ 1.5(j) n.320, 331; 1.9(e) n.129

Cole, The Fifth Amendment and Compelled Protection of Personal Documents After United States v. Hubbell-New Protection For Private Papers, 29 Am.J.Crim.L. 123 (2002)—§§ 8.13(a) n.33, 43

Cole and Zacharias, The Agony of Victory and The Ethics of Lawyer Speech, 69 S.Cal.L.Rev. 1627 (1996)—§§ 23.1(b) n.23, 29; 23.2(a) n.4

Collier, The Use and Abuse of Humanistic Theory in Law: Reexamining the Assumptions of Interdisciplinary Scholarship, 41 Duke L.J. 191 (1991)—§ 1.1(a) n.7

Collings, Habeas Corpus for Convicts— Constitutional Right or Legislative Grace?, 40 Cal.L.Rev. 335 (1952)— § 28.1(b) n.12

Collins, Article III Cases, State Court Rulings, and the Madisonian Compromise, 1995 Wis.L.Rev. 39— §§ 1.2(c) n.64, 78

Collins, Foreword, The Once "New Judicial Federalism and Its Critics," 64 Wash.L.Rev. 5 (1989)— §§ 2.12(a) n.32; 2.12(b) n.99, 113

Collins, Reliance on State Constitutions—Away From A Reactionary Approach, 9 Hastings Const.L.Q. 1 (1981)—§§ 2.12(a) n.34; 2.12(c) n.152

Collins, Reliance on State Constitutions—The Montana Disaster, 63 Tex.L.Rev. 1095 (1985)— §§ 2.12(a) n.78; 2.12(b) n.88, 104; 2.12(c) n.133

Collins, The Federal Courts, The First Congress, and the Non-Settlement of 1789, 91 Va.L.Rev. 1515 (2005)—§ 1.2(c) n.64

Collins & Galie, Cases and Commentary in State Constitutions, Nat'l L.J., Sept. 29, 1986—§ 2.12(a) n.57

Collins & Galie, Models of Post-Incorporation Judicial Review: 1985 Survey of State Constitutional Individual Rights Decisions, 55 U.Cin.L.Rev. 317 (1986)— §§ 2.12(a) n.43, 57, 77

Colquitt, Ad Hoc Plea Bargaining, 75 Tul.L.Rev. 695 (2001)—§ 21.2(b) n.60

Colquitt, Hybrid Representation: Standing the Two-Sided Coin on Its Edge, 38 Wake Forest L.Rev. 55 (2003)— §§ 11.5(g) n.110, 115

Colquitt, Judicial Use of Social Science Evidence at Trial, 30 Ariz.L.Rev. 51 (1988)—§ 23.2(a) n.43

Colquitt, Rethinking Entrapment, 41 Am.Crim.L.Rev. 1389 (2004)— § 5.1(b) n.9

Comment, 17 Akron L.Rev. 739 (1984)—§ 3.2(b) n.67

Comment, 29 Akron L.Rev. 697 (1996)—§ 5.2(a) n.6

Comment, 13 Am.Crim.L.Rev. 249 (1975)—§ 21.4(a) n.19

Comment, 20 Am.Crim.L.Rev. 507 (1983)—§ 13.7(c) n.41

Comment, 29 Am.J.Trial Advoc. 467 (2005)—§ 25.1(d) n.68

Comment, 16 Am.U.L.Rev. 403 (1967)—§ 3.1(h) n.222

Comment, 25 Am.U.L.Rev. 754 (1976)—§§ 1.5(k) n.350; 13.3(b) n.21

Comment, 45 Am.U.L.Rev. 1403 (1996)—§ 26.2(b) n.9

Comment, 50 Am.U.L.Rev. 979 (2001)—§ 18.5(a) n.32

Comment, 23 Ariz.St.L.J. 831 (1991)—§ 1.5(k) n.403

Comment, 29 Ariz.St.L.J. 1127 (1997)—§ 22.1(g) n.121

Comment, 49 Baylor L.Rev. 1107 (1997)—§ 6.7(b) n.79

Comment, 54 Brooklyn L.Rev. 171 (1988)—§ 12.3(c) n.88

Comment, 31 Buff.L.Rev. 909 (1982)—§ 13.7(c) n.66

Comment, 6 B.U.Pub.Int.L.J. 719 (1997)—§ 6.5(d) n.77

Comment, 57 Cal.L.Rev. 740 (1969)—§ 6.5(e) n.85

Comment, 62 Cal.L.Rev. 258 (1974)—§ 21.5(e) n.127

Comment, 76 Cal.L.Rev. 727 (1988)—§ 13.3(f) n.57

Comment, 77 Cal.L.Rev. 417 (1989)—§ 1.5(k) n.367

Comment, 70 Cal.L.Rev. 708 (1982)—§ 22.3(a) n.3

Comment, 78 Cal.L.Rev. 755 (1990)—§ 24.3(i) n.183

Comment, 83 Cal.L.Rev. 419 (1995)—§ 21.1(h) n.233

Comment, 82 Cal.L.Rev. 1335 (1994)—§ 27.6(e) n.162

Comment, 90 Cal.L.Rev. 2101 (2002)—§ 28.5(b) n.62

Comment, 44 Cath.U.L.Rev. 1269 (1995)—§ 21.1(h) n.212

Comment, 23 Clev.St.L.Rev. 123 (1974)—§ 3.1(m) n.288

Comment, 61 Colum.L.Rev. 1103 (1961)—§§ 13.4(a) n.6, 13, 29 to 31; 13.4(b) n.34

Comment, 65 Colum.L.Rev. 288 (1965)—§ 3.9(b) n.26

Comment, 69 Colum.L.Rev. 515 (1969)—§ 17.4(a) n.56

Comment, 59 Cornell L.Rev. 546 (1974)—§ 5.2(b) n.21

Comment, 75 Crim.L. & Criminology 1321 (1984)—§ 7.5(b) n.19

Comment, 61 Denver L.J. 579 (1984)—§ 3.8(d) n.155

Comment, 43 DePaul L.Rev. 1133 (1994)—§ 13.2(b) n.35

Comment, 48 DePaul L.Rev. 949 (1999)—§ 5.2(a) n.19

Comment, 1978 Det.Coll.L.Rev. 433 (1978)—§ 13.6(a) n.4

Comment, 47 Emory L.J. 753 (1998)—§ 21.1(g) n.121

Comment, 24 Fla.St.U.L.Rev. 659 (1997)—§ 22.1(e) n.85

Comment, 63 Geo.L.J. 241 (1974)—§ 21.3(e) n.293

Comment, 65 Geo.L.J. 1261 (1980)—§ 11.10(a) n.4

Comment, 9 Harv.Civ.Rts.-Civ.Lib.L.Rev. 372 (1974)—§§ 13.4(e) n.166, 171

Comment, 16 Harv.Civ.Rts.-Civ.Lib.L.Rev. 157 (1981)—§ 21.4(d) n.99

Comment, 9 Hous.L.Rev. 305 (1971)—§ 21.6(b) n.101

Comment, 13 Hous.L.Rev. 753 (1976)—§§ 9.4(a) n.6, 12

Comment, 17 Hous.L.Rev. 753 (1980)—§§ 21.2(f) n.375, 381, 382

Comment, 33 How.L.J. 461 (1991)—§ 24.2(a) n.5

Comment, 42 Idaho L.Rev. 471 (2006)—§ 26.1(e) n.105

Comment, 33 Idaho L.Rev. 147 (1996)—§ 5.2(a) n.6

Comment, 72 Iowa L.Rev. 359 (1987)—§ 13.4(d) n.156

Comment, 73 Iowa L.Rev. 207 (1987)—§ 6.9(b) n.37

Comment, 74 Iowa L.Rev. 1261 (1989)—§ 6.4(f) n.120

Comment, 65 J.Crim.L. & Criminology 62 (1974)—§ 13.4(b) n.47

Comment, 65 J.Crim.L. & Criminology 373 (1974)—§ 3.1(c) n.27

Comment, 69 J.Crim.L. & Criminology 197 (1978)—§ 24.3(b) n.41

Comment, 71 J.Crim.L. & Criminology 226 (1980)—§§ 13.7(a) n.7, 8, 10 to 13

Comment, 72 J.Crim.L. & Criminology 165 (1981)—§ 21.3(c) n.182

Comment, 93 J.Crim.L. & Criminology 651 (2003)—§ 9.6(a) n.48

Comment, 63 J.Crim.L.C. & P.S. 256 (1972)—§§ 3.1(c) n.41, 43

Comment, 11 J.Fam.L. 81 (1971)—§ 12.4(b) n.46

Comment, 20 J.Marshall J.Computer & Info. L. 321 (2002)—§ 3.2(j) n.266

Comment, 3 La.L.Rev. 222 (1940)—§ 16.1(d) n.145

Comment, 36 Loy.U.Chi.L.J. 285 (2004)—§ 22.3(d) n.198

Comment, 49 Marq.L.Rev. 137 (1965)—§ 24.8(a) n.12

Comment, 68 Marq.L.Rev. 57 (1984)—§ 3.2(b) n.67

Comment, 86 Marq.L.Rev. 973 (2003)—§ 5.2(a) n.6

Comment, 35 Mich.L.Rev. 456 (1937)—§ 19.1(c) n.31

Comment, 40 Miss.L.J. 257 (1969)—§ 6.5(e) n.85

Comment, 37 Mo.L.Rev. 633 (1972)—§ 5.2(b) n.21

Comment, 51 N.C.L.Rev. 630 (1973)—§ 7.3(b) n.16

Comment, 69 N.D.L.Rev. 969 (1993)—§ 5.2(b) n.24

Comment, 30 New Engl.L.Rev. 941 (1996)—§ 6.9(g) n.191

Comment, 16 N.Ill.U.L.Rev. 483 (1996)—§§ 23.1(b) n.13, 14

Comment, 69 Notre Dame L.Rev. 575 (1994)—§ 17.4(b) n.82

Comment, 79 Nw.U.L.Rev. 142 (1984)—§§ 2.3(a) n.37, 51, 61, 65

Comment, 61 Nw.U.L.Rev. 72 (1966)—§ 1.5(k) n.364

Comment, 91 Nw.U.L.Rev. 305 (1996)—§§ 5.4(c) n.29, 38

Comment, 44 N.Y.U.L.Rev. 206 (1969)—§ 3.1(h) n.219

Comment, 34 Ohio St.L.J. 928 (1973)—§ 7.3(c) n.46

Comment, 10 Okla.L.Rev. 197 (1957)—§ 13.3(a) n.14

Comment, 16 Pace L.Rev. 155 (1995)—§ 18.4(c) n.77

Comment, 9 Pac.L.J. 949 (1978)—§ 26.10(c) n.77

Comment, 28 Pac.L.J. 273 (1996)—§ 22.1(e) n.85

Comment, 47 Rutgers L.J. 247 (1994)—§ 17.4(b) n.82

Comment, 14 San Diego L.Rev. 414 (1977)—§ 3.2(j) n.240

Comment, 31 San Diego L.Rev. 729 (1994)—§ 6.2(c) n.120

Comment, 20 Santa Clara L.Rev. 491 (1980)—§ 3.4(a) n.21

Comment, 43 Santa Clara L.Rev. 213 (2002)—§§ 7.1(a) n.7; 7.5(c) n.42, 47

Comment, 42 S.Cal.L.Rev. 519 (1969)—§ 13.2(a) n.7

Comment, 24 S.D.L.Rev. 510 (1979)—§ 5.2(b) n.21

Comment, 10 St. Mary's L.J. 281 (1978)—§ 19.1(d) n.68

Comment, 26 St. Mary's L.J. 1102 (1995)—§ 1.5(k) n.365

Comment, 41 Stan.L.Rev. 121 (1988)—§ 1.5(e) n.243

Comment, 46 S.Tex.L.Rev. 661 (2005)—§ 21.2(h) n.439

Comment, 20 Temp.Envtl.L. & Tech.J. 251 (2002)—§ 3.2(j) n.266

Comment, 57 Temple L.Q. 77 (1984)—§ 3.4(f) n.120

Comment, 71 Temp.L.Rev. 347 (1998)—§ 27.5(a) n.7

Comment, 50 Tex.L.Rev. 60 (1971)—§§ 21.1(f) n.108; 21.3(b) n.122, 127

Comment, 8 Tex.Wesleyan L.Rev. 417 (2002)—§ 3.2(b) n.53

Comment, 47 Tul.L.Rev. 899 (1973)—§ 7.3(b) n.16

Comment, 76 Tul.L.Rev. 211 (2001)—
§ 3.8(b) n.52

Comment, 77 Tul.L.Rev. 767 (2003)—
§ 6.10(d) n.61

Comment, 23 U.C.Davis L.Rev. 375
(1989)—§ 24.8(d) n.47

Comment, 1998 U.Chi.Leg.F. 349—
§ 24.2(e) n.66

Comment, 24 U.Chi.L.Rev. 751
(1957)—§ 22.3(d) n.181

Comment, 25 U.Chi.L.Rev. 360
(1958)—§ 24.9(g) n.117

Comment, 28 U.Chi.L.Rev. 162
(1960)—§ 1.7(j) n.246

Comment, 28 U.Chi.L.Rev. 664
(1961)—§§ 3.3(a) n.10; 3.9(b) n.22

Comment, 28 U.Chi.L.Rev. 751
(1961)—§ 26.9(c) n.85

Comment, 32 U.Chi.L.Rev. 167
(1964)—§§ 21.3(d) n.230, 233, 253

Comment, 36 U.Chi.L.Rev. 830
(1969)—§ 7.3(f) n.121

Comment, 38 U.Chi.L.Rev. 555
(1971)—§ 3.1(h) n.208

Comment, 41 U.Chi.L.Rev. 121
(1973)—§§ 3.10(d) n.111, 120

Comment, 49 U.Chi.L.Rev. 798
(1982)—§ 27.2(e) n.82

Comment, 52 U.Chi.L.Rev. 729
(1985)—§§ 16.1(b) n.48, 59;
16.3(f) n.95; 23.2(b) n.57

Comment, 52 U.Chi.L.Rev. 751
(1985)—§ 21.2(d) n.188

Comment, 57 U.Chi.L.Rev. 873
(1990)—§§ 3.5(d) n.166, 174

Comment, 59 U.Chi.L.Rev. 719
(1992)—§ 6.6(e) n.81

Comment, 52 U.Chi.L.Rev. 729
(1985)—§ 16.3(d) n.57

Comment, 59 U.Chi.L.Rev. 1209
(1992)—§ 3.1(f) n.153

Comment, 61 U.Chi.L.Rev. 587
(1994)—§ 18.2(a) n.3

Comment, 64 U.Chi.L.Rev. 1037
(1997)—§ 18.3(b) n.43

Comment, 64 U.Chi.L.Rev. 1067
(1997)—§ 26.7(b) n.19

Comment, 64 U.Chi.L.Rev. 1331
(1997)—§ 22.3(d) n.205

Comment, 65 U.Chi.L.Rev. 285
(1998)—§ 26.7(c) n.35

Comment, 66 U.Chi.L.Rev. 1317
(1999)—§ 21.4(g) n.224

Comment, 68 U.Chi.L.Rev. 903
(2001)—§ 6.9(b) n.23

Comment, 48 U.Cin.L.Rev. 567
(1979)—§ 21.2(a) n.17

Comment, 56 U.Cin.L.Rev. 1049
(1988)—§ 6.9(b) n.37

Comment, 63 U.Cin.L.Rev. 1851
(1995)—§§ 21.1(h) n.237, 238

Comment, 66 U.Cin.L.Rev. 233
(1997)—§ 21.2(e) n.330

Comment, 19 UCLA L.Rev. 96
(1971)—§ 3.4(d) n.52

Comment, 20 UCLA L.Rev. 778
(1973)—§§ 13.3(b) n.27, 30, 32

Comment, 26 UCLA L.Rev. 360
(1978)—§§ 21.6(b) n.97, 100, 103;
21.6(c) n.113, 114

Comment, 40 UCLA L.Rev. 517
(1992)—§ 22.3(d) n.258

Comment, 43 UCLA L.Rev. 1321
(1996)—§§ 23.1(b) n.10, 17, 42, 45,
52, 56; 23.2(a) n.4

Comment, 49 UCLA L.Rev. 625
(2001)—§ 6.4(e) n.91

Comment, 52 UCLA L.Rev. 601
(2004)—§ 1.9(b) n.47

Comment, 42 U.Colo.L.Rev. 455
(1971)—§ 13.7(a) n.24

Comment, 73 U.Colo.L.Rev. 1047
(2002)—§ 22.3(e) n.289

Comment, 18 U.Haw.L.Rev. 645
(1996)—§ 27.5(e) n.163

Comment, 1968 U.Ill.L.F. 401—§ 3.7(e)
n.101

Comment, 1974 U.Ill.L.F. 648—
§§ 13.4(b) n.54, 57, 63, 71; 13.4(c)
n.132

Comment, 44 U.Kan.L.Rev. 837
(1996)—§§ 23.1(b) n.24, 52

Comment, 31 U.Miami L.Rev. 615
(1977)—§§ 9.3(c) n.25; 9.3(d) n.40;
9.3(e) n.50

Comment, 115 U.Pa.L.Rev. 399 (1967)—§§ 16.1(b) n.48, 59; 16.1(c) n.129; 16.2(f) n.100

Comment, 115 U.Pa.L.Rev. 1136 (1967)—§§ 9.3(c) n.27 to 29

Comment, 132 U.Pa.L.Rev. 327 (1984)—§ 21.1(g) n.137

Comment, 133 U.Pa.L.Rev. 1193 (1985)—§ 5.4(b) n.14

Comment, 134 U.Pa.L.Rev. 225 (1985)—§ 12.3(a) n.17

Comment, 134 U.Pa.L.Rev. 1433 (1986)—§§ 24.11(d) n.19, 32, 33, 37

Comment, 141 U.Pa.L.Rev. 283 (1992)—§ 17.4(a) n.10

Comment, 145 U.Pa.L.Rev. 1309 (1997)—§§ 13.2(g) n.125; 13.4(b) n.65

Comment, 145 U.Pa.L.Rev. 1359 (1997)—§§ 5.2(a) n.6; 26.4(b) n.23

Comment, 146 U.Pa.L.Rev. 621 (1998)—§ 22.1(d) n.70

Comment, 150 U.Pa.L.Rev. 1079 (2002)—§§ 18.5(a) n.28, 32

Comment, 28 U.Pitt.L.Rev. 643 (1967)—§ 3.9(j) n.204

Comment, 54 U.Pitt.L.Rev. 1019 (1993)—§§ 2.12(c) n.118; 2.12(e) n.199

Comment, 26 Vand.L.Rev. 1323 (1973)—§ 7.3(c) n.43

Comment, 33 Washburn L.J. 429 (1994)—§ 17.4(b) n.82

Comment, 26 Whittier L.Rev. 305 (2004)—§ 21.4(d) n.99

Comment, 1989 Wis.L.Rev. 837 (1989)—§ 26.4(d) n.54

Comment, 1993 Wis.L.Rev. 187 (1993)—§ 26.3(b) n.11

Comment, 1996 Wis.L.Rev. 295— § 13.2(f) n.108

Comment, 21 Wm. & Mary L.Rev. 521 (1979)—§ 21.2(f) n.374

Comment, 82 W.Va.L.Rev. 383 388 (1979)—§ 24.9(d) n.39

Comment, 75 Yale L.J. 262 (1965)— § 25.1(b) n.3

Comment, 65 Yale L.J. 209 (1955)— §§ 1.5(k) n.351; 13.3(b) n.15, 16

Comment, 66 Yale L.J. 204 (1956)— §§ 1.10(c) n.88; 21.1(e) n.70 to 73, 77, 78

Comment, 70 Yale L.J. 1151 (1961)— §§ 24.6(b) n.15, 30

Comment, 72 Yale L.J. 1568 (1963)— § 8.11(a) n.2

Comment, 90 Yale L.J. 1581 (1981)— §§ 21.3(c) n.187, 188, 195

Comment, 113 Yale L.J. 1991 (2004)— § 6.4(e) n.102

Conard, Macrojustice: A Systematic Approach to Conflict Resolution, 5 Ga.L.Rev. 415 (1971)—§§ 1.5(a) n.55; 2.9(i) n.271

Conaway, Mutz & Ross, Jury Nullification: A Selective Annotated Bibliography, 39 Val.U.L.Rev. 393 (2004)—§ 22.1(g) n.105

Congress Enacts Statute That Subjects Federal Prosecutors to State Law and Rules, 64 Crim.L.Rptr. 70 (Oct. 28, 1998)—§§ 6.4(e) n.91; 8.8(d) n.106

Conner, Withdrawal of Appointed Counsel from Frivolous Indigent Appeals, 49 Ind.L.J. 740 (1974)— § 11.2(c) n.93

Connick & Davis, Examining the Problem of Witness Intimidation, 66 Judicature 439 (1983)—§ 20.1(c) n.52

Connor, The Constitutional Right to a Trial by a Jury of the Vicinage, 57 U.Pa.L.Rev. 197 (1909)—§ 22.2(e) n.99

Cook, All Aboard! The Supreme Court, Guilty Pleas, and the Railroading of Criminal Defendants, 75 U.Colo.L.Rev. 863 (2004)— § 21.5(a) n.4

Cook, Black Representation in the Third Branch, 1 Black L.J. 260 (1971)— § 1.6(g) n.422

Cook, Crumbs From the Master's Table: The Supreme Court, Pro Se Defendants, and the Federal Guilty Plea Process, 81 Notre Dame L.Rev. 1895 (2006)—§ 11.3(b) n.39

Cook, The Application of the Criminal Law of a country to Acts Committed by Foreigners Outside the Jurisdiction, 40 W.Va.L.Q. 303 (1934)—§ 16.4(b) n.32

Coombs, Shared Privacy and the Fourth Amendment, or the Rights of Relationships, 75 Cal.L.Rev. 1593 (1987)—§ 9.1(b) n.91

Cooper, Crimes Aboard American Aircraft: Under what Jurisdiction are they Punishable, 37 A.B.A.J. 257 (1951)—§§ 16.4(b) n.10; 16.4(c) n.39

Cooper, Stare Decisis: Precedent and Principle in Constitutional Adjudication, 73 Cornell L.Rev. 401 (1988)—§§ 2.9(b) n.30, 31

Cope, Discretionary Review of the Decisions of Intermediate Appellate Courts: A Comparison of Florida's System with Those of the Other States and the Federal System, 45 Fla.L.Rev. 21 (1993)—§ 27.4(a) n.1

Cord, Neo-Incorporation: The Burger Court and the Due Process of the Fourteenth Amendment, 44 Fordham L.Rev. 215 (1975)—§§ 2.6(a) n.1; 2.6(c) n.80

Cord, The Incorporation Doctrine and Procedural Due Process Under the Fourteenth Amendment: An Overview, 1987 B.Y.U.L.Rev. 867—§§ 2.2 n.6, 7; 2.3(b) n.91; 2.6(a) n.1; 2.6(c) n.80, 88

Corr, Criminal Procedure and the Conflict of Laws, 73 Geo.L.J. 1217 (1985)—§ 2.12(c) n.171

Corr, State Searches, Federal Cases and Choice of Law: Just A Little Respect, 23 Pepp.L.Rev. 31 (1995)—§ 2.12(c) n.171

Corwin, The Doctrine of Due Process of Law Before the Civil War, 24 Harv.L.Rev. 366 (1971)—§§ 2.4(b) n.21, 37; 2.4(c) n.89, 92, 94, 95

Corwin, The Supreme Court's Construction of the Self-Incrimination Clause, 29 Mich.L.Rev. 191 (1930)—§ 2.10(c) n.96

Cottingham, Varieties of Retribution, 29 Phil.Q. 238 (1979)—§ 1.5(a) n.25

Cover and Aleinikoff, Dialectical Federalism: Habeas Corpus and the Court, 86 Yale L.J. 1035 (1979)—§§ 28.2(c) n.46, 64

Cowen, Federalization of State Law Questions: Upheaval Ahead, 47 Rutgers L.Rev. 137 (1995)—§ 1.2(d) n.202

Craig, Erickson, Friesen & Maxwell, Voir Dire: Criticism and Comment, 47 Denver L.J. 465 (1970)—§ 22.3(a) n.34

Cramton and Udell, State Ethics Rules and Federal Prosecutors: The Controversies Over the Anti-Contact and Subpoena Rules, 53 U.Pitt.L.Rev. 291 (1992)—§ 11.6(a) n.7

Crick, The Final Judgment as a Basis for Appeal, 41 Yale L.J. 539 (1932)—§ 27.4(b) n.4

Criminal Law—Jury Nullification—Second Circuit Holds That Juror's Intent To Nullify Is Just Cause For Dismissal—United States V. Thomas, 116 F.3d 606 (2d Cir. 1997), 111 Harv.L.Rev. 1347 (1998)—§ 22.1(g) n.109

Crocker, My Experiences as a Grand Jury Foreperson, 2 Ohio St.J.Crim.L. 289 (2004)—§ 15.3(a) n.8

Cronan, Is Any of This Making Sense? Reflecting on Guilty Pleas to Aid Criminal Juror Comprehension, 39 Am.Crim.L.Rev. 1187 (2002)—§ 24.8(c) n.42

Crosskey, Charles Fairman, "Legislative History," and the Constitutional Limitations on State Authority, 22 U.Chi.L.Rev. 1 (1954)—§§ 2.3(a) n.23, 43, 61, 67, 73

Crump, Evidence, Race, Intent and Evil: The Paradox of Purposelessness in the Constitutional Racial Discrimination Cases, 27 Hofstra L.Rev. 285 (1998)—§§ 1.5(j) n.327, 330

Crump, Lockhart v. McCree: The "Biased but Unbiased Juror," What Are the States' Legitimate Interests?, 65 Denver U.L.Rev. 1 (1988)—§ 22.3(c) n.159

D. Currie, The Constitution in the Supreme Court 276 (1985)—§ 2.4(c) n.112

Curtis, Conceived in Liberty: The Fourteenth Amendment and the Bill of Rights, 65 N.C.L.Rev. 889 (1986)—§ 2.6(c) n.86

Curtis, Congressional Powers and Federal Judicial Burdens, 46 Hastings L.J. 1019 (1995)—§ 1.2(c) n.199

Curtis, Further Adventures of the Nine-Lived Cat: A Response to Mr. Berger on Incorporation of the Bill of Rights, 43 Ohio St.L.J. 89 (1982)—§§ 2.3(a) n.36, 61

Curtis, Still Further Adventures of a Nine-Lived Cat; A Response to Mr. Berger on Incorporation of the Bill of Rights, 43 Ohio St. L.J. 89 (1982)—§ 2.3(a) n.31

Curtis, The Bill of Rights As A Limitation on State Authority: A Reply to Professor Berger, 16 Wake Forest L.Rev. 45 (1980)—§ 2.3(a) n.61

Curtis, The Effect of Federalization on the Defense Function, 543 Annals Am.Acad.Pol. & Soc.Sci. 85 (1996)—§§ 1.2(d) n.235; 1.2(f) n.293

Curtis, The Ethics of Advocacy, 4 Stan.L.Rev. 3 (1951)—§ 1.5(c) n.129

Curtis, The Fourteenth Amendment and the Bill of Rights, 14 Conn.L.Rev. 237 (1982)—§ 2.3(a) n.61

Cushman, Incorporation, Due Process, and the Bill of Rights, 51 Cornell L.Rev. 467 (1966)—§ 2.6(a) n.1

Cushman, The National Police Powers under the Commerce Clause of the Constitution, 3 Minn.L.Rev. (1919)—§ 1.2(c) n.104

D

Dalton, Taking the Right to Appeal (More or Less) Seriously, 95 Yale L.J. 62 (1985)—§§ 27.1(a) n.11, 12

Damaska, Adversary System, in 1 Encyclopedia of Crime and Justice 24 (S. Kadish ed., 1983)—§ 1.5(c) n.175

Damaska, Evidentiary Barriers to Conviction and Two Models of Criminal Procedure: A Comparative Study, 121 U.Pa.L.Rev. 506 (1973)—§§ 1.5(a) n.20; 1.5(b) n.83; 1.5(c) n.104, 105, 108, 109, 120, 157, 159, 160; 1.5(e) n.216; 27.3(a) n.9

Damaska, Presentation of Evidence and Factfinding Precision, 123 U.Pa.L.Rev. 1083 (1975)—§ 1.5(b) n.71

Damaska, Structures of Authority and Comparative Criminal Procedure, 84 Yale L.J. 480 (1975)—§§ 1.4(c) n.31; 1.5(a) n.7; 1.5(g) n.272

Dann, "Learning Lessons" and "Speaking Rights": Creating Educated and Democratic Juries, 68 Ind.L.J. 1229 (1993)—§§ 24.8(a) n.4, 23

Danzig, Toward the Creation of A Complimentary Decentralized System of Criminal Justice, 26 Stan.L.Rev. 1 (1973)—§§ 1.4(b) n.13; 1.4(c) n.51; 1.6(g) n.424, 428

Darmer, Beyond Bin Laden and Lindh: Confessions Law in an Age of Terrorism, 12 Cornell J.L. & Pub. Pol'y 319 (2003)—§ 6.10(d) n.61

Dash, The Indicting Grand Jury: A Critical Stage, 10 Am.Crim.L.Rev. 807 (1972)—§ 11.2(b) n.36

Davidow, One Justice For All: A Proposal to Establish, By Federal Constitutional Amendment, A National System of Criminal Justice, 51 N.C.L.Rev. 259 (1972)—§ 1.3(b) n.11

Davies, Do Criminal Due Process Principles Make A Difference, 1982 A.B.F.Res.J. 247—§ 1.5(a) n.12

Davies, Farther and Farther from the Original Fifth Amendment: The Recharacterization of the Right Against Self-Incrimination as a "Trial Right" in Chavez v. Martinez, 70 Tenn. L. Rev. 987 (2003)—§§ 2.10(c) n.73; 6.5(a) n.14

Davies, Recovering the Original Fourth Amendment, 98 Mich.L.Rev. 547 (1999)—§ 3.1(a) n.1

Davies, Rediscovering the Original Fourth Amendment, 98 Mich.L.Rev. 547 (1999)—§ 2.4(b) n.69

Davies, The Fictional Character of Law-and-Order Originalism: A Case Study of the Distortions and Evasions of Framing-Era Arrest Doctrine in Atwater v. Lago Vista, 37 Wake Forest L.Rev. 239 (2000)—§§ 2.4(b) n.29, 32, 43, 50

Davis, Prosecution and Race: The Power and Privilege of Discretion, 67 Fordham L.Rev. 13 (1998)—§ 1.5(j) n.325

Davis, Rodney King and the Decriminalization of Police Brutality in America: Direct and Judicial Access to the Grand Jury as Remedies for Victims of Police Brutality When the Prosecutor Declines to Prosecute, 53 Md.L.Rev. 271 (1994)—§§ 8.4(b) n.52, 86, 99

Davis, The American Prosecutor: Independence, Power, and the Threat of Tyrrany, 86 Iowa L.Rev. 393 (2001)—§§ 1.10(e) n.200; 13.2(g) n.121; 13.3(f) n.63

Davis, The Crime Victim's "Right" to a Criminal Prosecution: A Proposed Model Statute For the Governance of Private Criminal Prosecutions, 38 DePaul L.Rev. 329 (1988)—§ 13.3(b) n.16

Davis, Smith, & Davies, Effects of No-Drop Prosecution of Domestic Violence Upon Conviction Rules, 3 Justice Research and Policy 1 (Fall 2001)—§ 1.10(b) n.37

Dawson, Joint Trials of Defendants in Criminal Cases: An Analysis of Efficiencies and Prejudices, 77 Mich.L.Rev. 1379 (1979)—§§ 17.2(a) n.1; 17.2(b) n.53; 17.2(c) n.77, 85, 89, 91; 17.2(e) n.120; 17.2(f) n.134; 17.2(g) n.138 to 140, 142

Day, Appellate Court Use of the American Bar Association Standards for Criminal Justice, 12 Am.Crim.L.Rev. 415 (1975)—§ 1.3(f) n.69

Days, Race and the Federal Criminal Justice System: A Look at the Issue of Selective Prosecution, 48 Me.L.Rev. 179 (1996)—§ 13.4(a) n.12

Decker, Joinder and Severance in Federal Criminal Cases, 53 Notre Dame Law. 147 (1977)—§§ 17.1(a) n.8; 17.2(a) n.8; 17.3(b) n.24

Decker, Moriarty & Albert, The Demise of Procedural Protections in Laywitness Identifications in Federal Court: Who is the Culprit?, 9 Loy.U.L.J. 335 (1978)—§ 7.3(b) n.23

DeFeo, Entrapment as a Defense to Criminal Responsibility: Its History, Theory and Application, 1 U.S.F.L.Rev. 243 (1967)—§§ 5.1(b) n.9; 5.2(b) n.21; 5.3(b) n.19

DeFoor, Prosecutorial Misconduct in Closing Argument, 7 Nova L.J. 443 (1983)—§ 24.7(d) n.27

Dellinger, Of Rights and Remedies: The Constitution as a Sword, 85 Harv.L.Rev. 1532 (1972)—§ 3.1(c) n.45

Dempsey & Flint, Commercial Data and National Security, 72 Geo.Wash.L.Rev. 1459 (2004)— § 3.9(h) n.165

Dershowitz, Criminal Sentencing in the United States: An Historical and Conceptual Overview, 423 Annals Am.Acad.Pol. & Soc.Sci. 117 (1976)—§§ 1.6(d) n.277; 1.6(e) n.298

Dershowitz & Ely, Harris v. New York: Some Anxious Observations on the Candor and Logic of the Emerging Nixon Majority, 80 Yale L.J. 1198 (1971)—§§ 9.6(a) n.6, 17, 18

Dession, From Indictment to Information—Implications of the Shift, 42 Yale L.J. 163 (1932)—§ 15.3(b) n.36

Dession, Private Prosecution: A Remedy for District Attorney's Unwarranted Inaction, 65 Yale L.J. 209 (1955)—§ 13.2(g) n.115

Dession, The New Federal Rules of Criminal Procedure II, 56 Yale L.J. 197 (1947)—§ 8.5(d) n.129

Dession and Cohen, The Inquisitorial Functions of Grand Jury, 41 Yale L.J. 687 (1937)—§§ 8.2(c) n.33; 8.6(a) n.10; 15.1(d) n.155

Deukmajian and Thompson, All Sail and No Anchor—Judicial Review Under the California Constitution, 6 Hastings Const.L.Q. 975 (1979)— §§ 2.12(c) n.129, 177

Developments in the Law, 94 Harv.L.Rev. 1376-77 (1981)— § 11.9(a) n.7

Developments in the Law, 101 Harv.L.Rev. 1472 (1988)— § 26.4(b) n.11

Developments in the Law, Alternatives to Incarceration, 111 Harv.L.Rev. 1863 (1998)—§§ 26.1(e) n.92, 94, 107, 119, 128

Developments in the Law; Legal Responses to Domestic Violence, 106 Harv.L.Rev. 1498 (1993)— § 13.2(b) n.35

Developments in the Law—Confessions, 79 Harv.L.Rev. 938 (1966)— §§ 6.1(a) n.4; 6.1(b) n.13; 6.2(a) n.18, 21; 6.2(b) n.29; 6.3(a) n.2, 7; 6.4(c) n.35; 6.5(a) n.8

Developments in the Law—Res Judicata, 65 Harv.L.Rev. 818 (1952)— § 17.4(a) n.10

Developments in the Law—The Interpretation of State Constitutional Rights, 95 Harv.L.Rev. 1324 (1982)—§§ 2.12(a) n.37, 43; 2.12(b) n.101, 104, 108; 2.12(c) n.155; 2.12(e) n.201

Devine et al., Jury Decision Making: 45 Years of Empirical Research On Deliberating Groups, 7 Psychol.Pub.Pol'y & L. 622 (2001)—§ 22.1(d) n.71

Dewey, Logical Method and Law, 10 Cornell L.Q. 17 (1924)—§ 1.5(a) n.54

Diamond, et al., Inside the jury room: Evaluating juror discussions during trial, 87 Judicature 54 (2003)— § 24.9(f) n.63

Diamond, The Anti-Federalist Brutus, 6 Pol.Sci. Reviewer 249 (Fall 1976)—§ 1.2(c) n.18

Diamond & Zeisel, Sentencing Councils: A Study of Sentence Disparity and its Reduction, 43 U.Chi.L.Rev. 109 (1975)—§ 26.3(b) n.6

Diehm, New Federalism and Constitutional Criminal Procedure: Are We Repeating the Mistakes of the Past?, 55 Md.L.Rev. 223 (1996)— §§ 2.12(a) n.72; 2.12(c) n.171

DiFonzo, In Praise of Statutes of Limitations in Sex Offense Cases, 41 Houst.L.Rev. 1205 (2004)— § 18.5(a) n.29

Dillehay & Sandys, Life Under Wainwright v. Witt: Jury Dispositions and Death Qualifications, 20 Law &

Hum.Behavior 147 (1996)—§ 22.3(c) n.146

Dillof, Unraveling Unlawful Entrapment, 94 J.Crim.L. & Criminology 827 (2004)—§ 5.1(b) n.9

Dinh, Freedom and Security after September 11th, 25 Harv. J.L. & Pub. Pol'y 399 (2002)—§ 11.8(b) n.46

Dinh, Heyman, Stuntz, Beale & Fellman in Symposium, Law and The War on Terrorism, 25 Harv.J.L. & Pub. Poly, 399 (2001)—§ 1.5(a) n.41

Dix, Mistake, Ignorance, Expectation of Benefit, and the Modern Law of Confessions, 1975 Wash.U.L.Q. 275—§ 6.2(c) n.114

Dix, Nonarrest Investigatory Detention in Search and Seizure Law, 85 Duke L.J. 849 (1985)—§ 3.8(b) n.33

Dix, Texas Charging Instrument Law: The 1985 Revisions and Continuing Need For Reform, 38 Baylor L.Rev. 1 (1986)—§§ 19.1(d) n.69; 19.5(b) n.38

Dix, Texas Charging Instruments Law: Recent Developments and the Continuing Need for Reform, 35 Baylor L.Rev. 689 (1983)—§§ 19.1(d) n.68; 19.2(a) n.1; 19.3(e) n.242

Dix, Undercover Investigations and Police Rulemaking, 53 Tex.L.Rev. 203 (1975)—§§ 1.5(a) n.65; 5.1(b) n.6; 5.4(a) n.2, 10; 6.7(c) n.137

Dix, Waiver in Criminal Procedure: A Brief for More Careful Analysis, 55 Tex.L.Rev. 193 (1977)—§§ 6.9(b) n.45; 16.1(h) n.284, 290

Dobie, Venue in Criminal Cases in the United States District Court, 12 Va.L.Rev. 287 (1926)—§§ 16.2(c) n.37, 44

Dodson, Habeas Review of Perfunctory State Court Decisions on the Merits, 29 Am.J.Crim.L. 223 (2002)—§ 28.6(f) n.77

Doherty, Wolf! Wolf!—The Ramifications of Frivolous Appeals, 59 J. Crim.L.C. & P.S. 1 (1968)—§ 11.2(c) n.89

Doleschal, The Dangers of Criminal Justice Reform, 14 Crim.J. Abstracts 133 (1982)—§ 1.6(h) n.455

Dolinko, Is There a Rationale for the Privilege Against Self-Incrimination?, 33 UCLA L.Rev. 1063 (1986)—§§ 2.10(d) n.102, 111, 112, 128, 151, 154

Dolinko, Three Mistakes of Retributionism, 39 UCLA L.Rev. 1623 (1992)—§ 1.5(a) n.25

Donnelly, Judicial Control of Informants, Spies, Stool Pigeons and Agent Provocateurs, 60 Yale L.J. 1091 (1951)—§ 5.2(b) n.21

Doran, Jackson, & Seigel, Rethinking Adversariness in Nonjury Criminal Trials, 23 Am.J.Crim.L. 1 (1995)—§§ 1.5(c) n.100; 24.6(a) n.1

Dorf & Fagan, Problem-Solving Courts: From Innovation to Institutionalization, 40 Am.Crim.L.Rev. 1501 (2003)—§ 26.1(e) n.104

Dorf & Friedman, Shared Constitutional Interpretation, 2000 Sup.Ct.Rev. 61, 81—§ 2.9(h) n.250

Dorfman, Proving the Lie: Litigating Police Credibility, 26 Am.J.Crim.L. 455 (1999)—§ 1.9(b) n.18

Dorsen, et. al., Seventy-Fifth Anniversary Retrospective: Most Influential Articles, 75 N.Y.U.L.Rev. 1517 (2000)—§ 2.12(a) n.34

Douglas, Balancing Hearsay and Criminal Discovery, 68 Fordham L.Rev. 2097 (2000)—§§ 20.1(b) n.20; 20.3(i) n.163

Douglas, Federalism and State Constitutions, 13 Vt.L.Rev. 127 (1988)—§§ 2.12(a) n.40; 2.12(c) n.143

Douglass, Confronting Death: Sixth Amendment Rights at Capital Sentencing, 105 Colum.L.Rev. 1967 (2005)—§§ 26.1(b) n.23; 26.2(b) n.6; 26.4(f) n.108

Dowling, Escobedo and Beyond: The Need for a Fourteenth Amendment Code of Criminal Procedure, 56 J.Crim.L. & Criminology, & Police

Sci. 56 (1965)—§ 1.3(b) n.11

Doyel, The Federal Speedy Trial Act: Stampeded into Ambush, 16 J.Marshall L.Rev. 27 (1982)— § 18.3(b) n.45

Draft Report of Committee E of The American Institute of Criminal Law and Criminology, 1 J.Crim.L. & Criminology 584 (1911)—§ 1.6(e) n.323

Dressler, A Lesson in Incaution, Overwork, and Fatigue: The Judicial Miscraftsmanship of Segura v. United States, 26 Wm. & Mary L.Rev. 375 (1985)—§ 3.6(e) n.122

Dries, Sex Predators and Federal Habeas Corpus: Has the Great Writ Gone AWOL?, 39 Suffolk U.L.Rev. 673 (2006)—§ 28.3(a) n.4

Dripps, 1991 U.Ill. L.Rev. 329— § 2.10(d) n.154

Dripps, Against Police Interrogation— and the Privilege Against Self-Incrimination, 78 J.Crim.L. & Criminology 699 (1998)—§§ 2.10(d) n.123, 145; 6.5(d) n.74

Dripps, Akhil Amar on Criminal Procedure and Constitutional Law: "Here I Go Down That Wrong Road Again," 74 N.C.L.Rev. 1559 (1996)—§§ 2.3(a) n.12, 27, 40, 42, 61, 69, 74; 2.3(b) n.81; 2.4(c) n.107; 2.7(a) n.14

Dripps, Beyond the Warren Court and Its Conservative Critics: Toward A Unified Theory of Constitutional Criminal Procedure, 23 U.Mich.J.L.Rev. 591 (1990)— §§ 2.4(a) n.17; 2.7(a) n.14; 2.8(b) n.44; 2.9(f) n.109

Dripps, Constitutional Theory for Criminal Procedure: Miranda, Dickerson, and the Continuing Quest for Broad-But-Shallow, 43 Wm. & Mary L.Rev. 1 (2001)—§§ 2.9(b) n.39; 6.5(e) n.95

Dripps, Criminal Procedure, Footnote Four, and the Theory of Public Choice: Or Why Don't Legislatures Give A Damn About the Rights of the Accused, 44 Syracuse L.Rev. 1079 (1993)—§§ 1.3(b) n.14; 2.8(c) n.66

Dripps, Foreword: Against Police Interrogation—And the Privilege Against Self-Incrimination, 78 J.Crim.L. & Criminology 699 (1988)—§ 2.9(h) n.235

Dripps, Ineffective Assistance of Counsel: The Case For An Ex Ante Parity Standard, 88 J.Crim.L. & Criminology 242 (1997)—§§ 1.5(j) n.335; 11.8(c) n.65, 72, 73; 11.10(a) n.16

Dripps, Ineffective Litigation of Ineffective Assistance Claims: Some Uncomfortable Reflections in Massaro v. United States, 42 Brandeis L.J. 793 (2004)—§ 11.7(e) n.109

Dripps, Justice Harlan on Criminal Procedure: Two Cheers For The Legal Process School, 3 Ohio St. J.Crim.L. 125 (2005)—§§ 2.4(f) n.188; 2.5(e) n.38, 39; 2.5(f) n.77; 2.6(c) n.86; 2.6(e) n.108; 2.7(a) n.14; 2.9(g) n.192

Dripps, Living With Leon, 95 Yale L.J. 906 (1986)—§§ 1.10(c) n.82; 3.1(c) n.59

Dripps, On the Costs of Uniformity and the Prospects of Dualism in Constitutional Criminal Procedure, 45 St. Louis U.L.J. 433 (2001)—§ 2.6(c) n.88

Dripps, Overcriminalization, Discretion, Waiver: A Survey of Possible Exit Strategies, 109 Penn.St.L.Rev. 1155 (2005)—§ 21.1(g) n.120

Dripps, The Case for the Contingent Exclusionary Rule, 38 Am.Crim.L.Rev. 1 (2001)— § 3.1(c) n.46

Dripps, The Fourth Amendment and the Fallacy of Composition: Determinacy versus Legitimacy in A Regime of Bright-Line Rules, 74 Miss.L.J. 341 (2004)—§ 2.9(g) n.174

Drizin & Leo; The Problem of False Confessions in the Post-DNA World, 82 N.C.L.Rev. 891 (2004)— § 1.5(e) n.229

Drunk Drivers Have No Right to Jury Trial, 20 Seton Hall L.Rev. 600 (1990)—§ 22.1(b) n.40

Dubber, American Plea Bargains, German Lay Judges, and the Crisis of Criminal Procedure, 49 Stan.L.Rev. 547 (1997)—§§ 21.1(b) n.9; 21.2(b) n.46; 21.4(f) n.175

Dubber, Policing Possession: The War on Crime and the End of Criminal Law, 91 J.Crim.L. & Criminology 829 (2001)—§ 1.6(h) n.476

Dubber, Victims and the Criminal Law: American and German Perspectives, 3 Buff.Crim.L.Rev. 3 (1999)—§§ 21.3(f) n.337, 361

Dudley, Terry v. Ohio, The Warren Court and the Fourth Amendment: A Law Clerk's Perspective, 72 St. John's L.Rev. 891 (1991)—§ 2.8(a) n.28

Duke, The Right to Appointed Counsel: Argersinger and Beyond, 12 Am.Crim.L.Rev. 601 (1975)— § 11.2(g) n.261

Duker, The Right to Bail: A Historical Inquiry, 42 Alb.L.Rev. 33 (1977)— § 12.3(a) n.4

Dunahoe, Revisiting the Cost-benefit Calculus of the Misbehaving Prosecutor: Deterence Economics and transitory Prosecutors, 61 N.Y.U.Ann.Surv.Am.L.45 (2005)—§ 1.9(b) n.28

Dworkin, Fact Style Adjudication and the Fourth Amendment: The Limits of Lawyering, 48 Ind.L.J. 329 (1973)—§§ 3.1(c) n.32, 35

Dworkin, The Model of Rules, 35 U.Chi.L.Rev. 14 (1967)—§§ 1.9(a) n.2; 1.9(c) n.53, 61, 63

E

Easterbrook, Criminal Procedure as a Market System, 12 J. Legal Stud. 289 (1983)—§§ 1.5(a) n.18; 1.9(d) n.110

Easterbrook, Method, Result, and Authority: A Reply, 98 Harv.L.Rev. 622 (1985)—§ 1.5(a) n.36

Easterbrook, Plea Bargaining as Compromise, 101 Yale L.J. 1969 (1992)—§ 21.1(d) n.51

Easterbrook, Substance and Process, 1982 Sup.Ct.Rev. 85—§§ 2.4(b) n.21, 28, 33, 43, 51, 68, 70, 72, 73; 2.4(c) n.112, 116; 2.4(e) n.176

Easterbrook, Ways of Criticizing the Court, 95 Harv.L.Rev. 802 (1982)—§ 2.9(b) n.36

Edwards, Standing to Suppress Unreasonably Seized Evidence, 47 Nw.U.L.Rev. 471 (1952)—§ 9.2(c) n.24

Edwards, To Err is Human, But Not Always Harmless: When Should Legal Error Be Tolerated?, 70 N.Y.U.L.Rev. 1167 (1995)— §§ 27.6(a) n.9; 27.6(e) n.162

J. Ehrlich, Participation in Illegitimate Activities: A Theoretical and Empirical Investigation, 81 J.Pol.Econ. 521 (1973)—§ 1.5(a) n.49

Einesman, How Long is Too Long? When Pretrial Detention Violates Due Process, 60 Tenn.L.Rev. 1 (1992)—§ 12.3(d) n.97

Einesman, Vampires Among Us—Does the Grand Jury Subpoena for Blood Violate the Fourth Amendment, 22 Am.J.Crim.L. 327 (1995)— §§ 8.7(d) n.75, 80

Eisenberg & Feustel, Pretrial Identification: An Attempt to Articulate Constitutional Criteria, 58 Marq.L.Rev. 659 (1975)—§ 7.4(c) n.59

J. Eisenstein & H. Jacob, Felony Justice An Organizational Analysis of Criminal Courts, 88-89, 118, 155-56 (1977)—§ 1.4(f) n.118

Eliason, The Prosecutor's Role: A Response to Professor Davis, Amer.Univ. Criminal Law Brief 15 (Fall 2006)—§ 1.9(b) n.28

Elkins, Corporations and the Criminal Law: An Uneasy Alliance, 65 Ky.L.J. 73 (1976)—§ 15.1(b) n.18

Elson, Balancing Costs in Constitutional Construction: The Burger Court's Expansive New Approach, 17 Am.Crim.L.Rev. 160 (1979)—§§ 1.5(b) n.93; 2.8(b) n.43; 2.9(i) n.278

Elwork et al., Juridic Decisions: In Ignorance of the Law Or In Light Of It?, 1 Law & Hum.Behav. 163 (1977)—§ 24.8(a) n.4

Ely, Constitutional Interpretation: Its Allure and Impossibility, 53 Ind.L.Rev. 399 (1978)—§ 2.4(b) n.58

Emanuel, The Concurrent Sentence Doctrine Dies a Quiet Death—Or Are the Reports Greatly Exaggerated?, 16 Fla.St.U.L.Rev. 269 (1988)—§§ 27.5(b) n.34, 43, 49

Eme, Thomas J. Morgan V. Illinois: The Supreme Court Supports The Right Of A Capital Defendant To An Impartial Sentencing Jury, 24 Loy.U.Chi.L.J. 497 (1993)—§ 22.3(c) n.152

Engel, The Public's Vicinage Right: A Constitutional Argument, 75 N.Y.U.L.Rev. 1658 (2000)—§§ 16.1(b) n.30, 40, 51, 74; 16.1(c) n.125, 129; 16.3(g) n.112; 23.2(a) n.31

Enker & Elsen, Counsel for the Suspect: Massiah v. United States and Escobedo v. Illinois, 49 Minn.L.Rev. 47 (1964)—§§ 6.4(a) n.9, 10; 6.4(h) n.168; 6.5(d) n.77; 8.10(c) n.59

Enright, The Much Maligned Criminal Lawyer And/Or The State of the Profession, 46 J.St.B.Cal. 720 (1971)—§ 1.5(c) n.128

Epps, Unacceptable Collateral Damage: The Danger of Probation Conditions Restricting the Right to Have Children, 38 Creighton L.Rev. 611 (2005)—§ 26.9(b) n.55

Epstein, Advance Notice of Alibi, 55 J.Crim.L.J. Criminology 29 (1964)—§§ 20.1(d) n.55; 20.5(a) n.9; 20.5(b) n.12, 14

Erickson, Fair Trial and Free Press: The Practical Dilemma, 29 Stan.L.Rev. 485 (1977)—§ 23.2(g) n.113

Erickson, Standards of Competency for Defense Counsel in a Criminal Case, 17 Am.Crim.L.Rev. 233 (1979)—§ 11.7(d) n.44

Erickson, The Right to a Speedy Trial: Standards for its Implementation, 10 Houston L.Rev. 237 (1973)—§ 1.3(f) n.61

Erlinder & Thomas, Prohibiting Prosecutorial Vindictiveness While Protecting Prosecutorial Discretion: Toward a Principled Resolution of a Due Process Dilemma, 76 J.Crim.L. & Criminology 341 (1985)—§ 13.7(c) n.35

Ervin, Jr., The Federalization of State Crimes: Some Observations and Reflections, 90 W.Va.L.Rev. 761 (1996)—§ 1.2(d) n.202

Ervin, Preventive Detention, A Species of Lyford Law, 52 Geo.Wash.L.Rev. 113 (1983)—§ 12.3(a) n.4

Etienne, Remorse, Responsibility, and Regulating Advocacy: Making Defendants Pay for the Sins of Their Lawyers, 78 N.Y.U.L.Rev. 2103 (2003)—§ 6.4(e) n.108

Ettinger, In Search of a Reasoned Approach to the Lesser Included Offense, 50 Brook.L.Rev. 191 (1984)—§ 24.8(e) n.49

Everett, Discovery in Criminal Cases—In Search of a Standard, 1964 Duke L.J. 477—§§ 20.1(a) n.13; 20.1(c) n.50

Everett, Toward a More Effective Right to Assistance of Counsel, 58 Law & Contemp.Prob. 1 (Winter, 1995)—§ 1.4(f) n.133

Evidence: Experts, Legal Scholars Meet to Discuss Present, Future of Predicting Dangerousness, 68 Crim.L.Rptr. 95 (Nov. 1, 2000)—§ 26.6(e) n.83

Ewing, Preventive Detention and Execution: The Constitutionality of Punishing Future Crimes, 15 Law & Hum. Behavior 139 (1991)—§ 12.3(f) n.131

Ewing, Schall v. Martin: Preventive Detention and Dangerousness Through the Looking Glass, 34 Buff.L.Rev. 173 (1985)—§ 12.4(b) n.49

F

Fagan and Davies, Street Stops and Broken Windows: Terry, Race, and Disorder in New York City, 28 Ford. Urban L.J. 457 (2000)—§ 1.5(j) n.327

Fahringer, The Battle for a Bill of Particulars, 26 Crim.L.Bull. 387 (Sept.-Oct.1990)—§ 19.4(b) n.23

Fairfax, The Jurisdictional Heritage of the Grand Jury Clause, 91 Minn.L.Rev. 398 (2006)—§§ 19.2(e) n.52, 83

Fairfield, To Err is Human: The Judicial Conundrum of Curing Apprendi Error, 85 Baylor L.Rev. 889 (2003)—§ 19.2(e) n.60

Fairman, A Reply to Professor Crosskey, 22 U.Chi.L.Rev. 144 (1954)—§ 2.3(a) n.61

Fairman, Does The Fourteenth Amendment Incorporate the Bill of Rights?, 2 Stan.L.Rev. 5 (1949)—§§ 2.3(a) n.22, 27, 46, 57, 61, 66 to 69, 74

Fallon, A Constructivist Coherence Theory of Constitutional Interpretation, 100 Harv.L.Rev. 1189 (1987)—§ 2.9(c) n.49

Fallon, Judicial Legitimacy and the Unwritten Constitution: A Comment on Miranda and Dickerson, 45 N.Y.L.Sch.L.Rev. 119 (2001)—§§ 2.9(h) n.253; 6.5(e) n.95

Fallon & Meltzer, Habeas Corpus Jurisdiction, Substantive Rights, and the War on Terror, 120 Harv.L.Rev.—§ 28.2(a) n.18

Fallon & Meltzer, New Law Retroactivity, and Constitutional Remedies, 104 Harvard L.Rev. 1731 (1991)—§§ 2.11(a) n.2, 7

Farber, The Role of the Parent/Guardian in Juvenile Custodial Interrogations: Friend or Foe?, 41 Am.Crim.L.Rev. 1272 (2004)—§ 6.9(b) n.22

Farnsworth, Signatures of Ideology: The Supreme Court; Criminal Docket, 104 Mich.L.Rev. 67 (2005-06)—§ 2.8(a) n.28

Feeley, Perspectives on Plea Bargaining, 13 Law & Soc.Rev. 199 (1979)—§§ 21.1(b) n.16, 17, 19, 26; 21.1(g) n.121, 123, 125

Feeley, Two Models of the Criminal Justice System: An Organizational Perspective, 7 Law & Soc'y Rev. 407 (1973)—§ 1.10(d) n.115

Feeney and Jackson, Public Defenders, Assigned Counsel, Retained Counsel, Does the Type of Criminal Defense Counter Matter, 22 Rutgers L.J. 361 (1991)—§ 11.8(c) n.72

Feld, Criminalizing Juvenile Justice: Rules of Procedure for the Juvenile Court, 69 Minn.L.Rev. 141 (1984)—§ 12.4(b) n.49

Feldman, The Tennessee Pretrial Diversion Act: A Practitioner's Guide, 13 Memphis St.U.L.Rev. 285 (1983)—§ 13.6(c) n.48

Feldman, The Work Product Rule in Criminal Practice and Procedure, 50 U.Cinn.L.Rev. 495 (1981)—§§ 20.3(i) n.179; 20.4(f) n.88

Feldman and Abney, The Double Security of Federalism: Protecting Individual Liberty Under the Arizona Constitution, 20 Ariz.St.L.J. 115

(1988)—§ 2.12(c) n.149

Fellmeth, Civil and Criminal Sanctions in the Constitution and Courts, 94 Geo.L.J. 1 (2005)—§§ 25.1(c) n.29, 41

Felstiner, Plea Contracts in West Germany, 13 Law & Soc.Rev. 309 (1979)—§ 21.1(b) n.9

Fennell & Hall, Due Process at Sentencing: An Empirical and Legal Analysis of the Disclosure of Presentence Reports in Federal Courts, 93 Harv.L.Rev. 1613 (1980)— §§ 26.5(b) n.22; 26.5(c) n.42, 44, 48, 51, 57

Ferguson, Formulation of Enforcement Policy: An Anatomy of the Prosecutor's Discretion Prior to Accusation, 11 Rutgers L.Rev. 507 (1957)— § 13.3(a) n.1

Ferguson & Douglas, A Study of Juvenile Waiver, 7 San Diego L.Rev. 39 (1970)—§§ 6.9(b) n.21; 6.10(e) n.74

Field, Assessing the Harmlessness of Federal Constitutional Error—A Process in Need of a Rationale, 125 U.Pa.L.Rev. 15 (1976)—§§ 27.6(b) n.52, 56

Fifty States: Some Appellants' Equal Protection Is More Equal Than Others, 23 Fla.St.U.L.Rev. 625 (1996)—§ 11.2(c) n.94

Findley & Ross, Access, Accuracy and Fairness: The Federal Presentence Investigation Report Under Julian and the Sentencing Guidelines, 1989 Wis.L.Rev.837—§§ 26.4(d) n.62; 26.5(b) n.28; 26.5(c) n.48

Fine, Federal Grand Jury Investigation of Political Dissidents, 7 Harv.Civ.Rts.—Civ.Lib.L.Rev. 432 (1972)—§§ 8.2(b) n.22; 8.2(c) n.28, 30, 35 to 37; 8.5(d) n.131

Finer, Ineffective Assistance of Counsel, 58 Cornell L.Rev. 1077 (1973)— §§ 11.8(c) n.63; 11.10(b) n.32

Finkelstein, A Statistical Analysis of Guilty Plea Practices in the Federal Courts, 89 Harv.L.Rev. 293 (1975)—§ 21.1(a) n.1

Finn-DeLuca, Victim Participation at Sentencing, 30 Crim.L.Bull. 403 (1994)—§ 26.5(d) n.68

J. Fionda, Public Prosecutors and Discretion, 1995; Thaiman, Miranda in Comparative Law, 45 St. Louis U.L.J. 581 (2000)—§ 1.5(a) n.6

Fischer, Beyond Santobello—Remedies for Reneged Plea Bargains, 2 U.San Fernando Valley L.Rev. 121 (1973)—§ 21.2(e) n.283

Fisher, Categorical Requirements in Constitutional Criminal Procedure, 94 Geo.L.J. 1493 (2006)—§§ 2.6(e) n.109; 2.9(g) n.150, 151

Fisher, Judicial Suicide or Constitutional Autonomy?, A Capital Defendant's Right to Plea Guilty, 65 Alb.L.Rev. 181 (2001)—§ 21.4(a) n.11

Fisher, "Just The Facts, Ma'am": Lying and the Omission of Exculpatory Evidence in Police Reports, 28 New Eng.L.Rev. 1 (1993)—§ 24.3(c) n.94

Fisher, Plea Bargaining's Triumph, 109 Yale L.J. 857 (2000)—§§ 21.1(b) n.10; 26.1(d) n.65

Fisher, When Discretion Leads to Distortion: Recognizing Pre-Arrest Sentence-Manipulation Claims Under the Federal Sentencing Guidelines, 94 Mich.L.Rev. 2385 (1996)—§ 26.4(b) n.23

Fishman, Electronic Tracking Devices and the Fourth Amendment: Knotts, Karo, and the Questions Still Unanswered, 34 Cath.U.L.Rev. 277 (1985)—§ 3.2(j) n.251

Fishman, Interception of Communications in Exigent Circumstances, 22 Ga.L.Rev. 1 (1987)—§ 3.4(e) n.82

Fishman, Interception of Communications in Exigent Circumstances: The Fourth Amendment, Federal Legislation, and the United States Depart-

ment of Justice, 2 Ga.L.Rev. 1 (1987)—§ 4.6(e) n.80

Fiss, Dombrowski, 86 Yale L.J. 1106 (1977)—§ 13.5(e) n.95

Flaherty, Crime and Social Control in Provincial Massachusetts, 34 Hist.J. 349 (1981)—§ 1.6(b) n.94

Flaherty, History "Lite" in Modern American Constitutionalism, 95 Colum.L.Rev. 523 (1995)— § 2.9(d) n.58

Flanagan, Compelled Immunity for Defense Witnesses: Hidden Costs and Questions, 56 Notre Dame L.Rev. 447 (1981)—§ 24.3(i) n.196

Flanders, Local Rules in Federal District Courts: Usurpation, Legislation, or Information, 14 Loy.L.A.L.Rev. 213 (1981)—§§ 1.7(g) n.109, 112

Flango & McKenna, Federal Habeas Corpus Review of State Court Convictions, 31 Cal.W.L.Rev. 237 (1995)—§ 28.11(a) n.10

Fleming, Elements of the Defense Attorney's Craft: An Adoptive Expectations Model of the Preliminary Hearing Decision, 85 Law & Policy 33 (1986)—§ 14.2(e) n.83

Fleming, If You Pay the Piper, Do You Call the Tune?, 14 L. & Soc. Inquiry 393 (1989)—§ 1.4(f) n.112

Flemming, Elements of the Defense Attorney's Craft: An Adoptive Expectations Model of the Preliminary Hearing Decision, 8 Law & Policy 33 (1986)—§ 14.1(a) n.5

Flemming, If You Pay the Piper, Do You Call the Tune?, 14 Law & Soc. Inquiry 383 (1989)—§§ 1.5(c) n.177; 1.10(d) n.139

Flemming, The Political Styles and Organizational Strategies of American Prosecutors: Examples From Nine Courthouse Communities, 12 Law & Soc'y Rev. 25 (1990)—§ 1.10(a) n.7

Fletcher, Pretrial Discovery in State Criminal Cases, 12 Stan.L.Rev. 293 (1960)—§§ 20.1(a) n.5, 13; 20.1(b) n.29, 34, 36

Fletcher, Some Unwise Reflections About Discretion, 47 Law & Contemp.Probs. 270 (1984)— §§ 1.9(c) n.52, 59, 61

Fletcher, Two Kinds of Legal Rules: A Comparative Study of Burden-Of-Persuasion in Criminal Cases, 77 Yale L.J. 880 (1968)—§§ 1.5(d) n.184, 186

Foote, Safeguards in the Law of Arrest, 52 Nw.L.Rev. 16 (1957)—§§ 1.6(f) n.375, 377

Foote, The Benevolent Paternalism of Japanese Criminal Justice, 80 Cal.L.Rev. 317 (1992)—§§ 1.5(a) n.6, 13, 14

Foote, The Coming Constitutional Crisis in Bail, 113 U.Pa.L.Rev. 959 (1965)—§§ 12.2(a) n.15; 12.2(b) n.25; 12.3(a) n.4

Foote, Vagrancy-type Law and Its Administration, 104 U.Pa.L.Rev. 603 (1956)—§ 1.6(f) n.375

Forde-Mazrui, Jural Districting: Selecting Impartial Juries Through Community Representation, 52 Vand.L.Rev. 353 (1999)—§§ 1.5(j) n.333; 22.2(d) n.96

Forsythe, The Historical Origins of Broad Federal Habeas Review Reconsidered, 70 Notre Dame L.Rev. 1079 (1995)—§§ 28.1(b) n.11; 28.2(b) n.19, 20, 23, 24

Fortas, The Fifth Amendment, Nemo Tenetur Prodere Seipsum, 25 Clev.B.A.J. 91 (1954)—§§ 2.10(c) n.72; 2.10(d) n.139

Fourts, Reading the Jurors Their Rights: The Continuing Questions of Grand Jury Independence, 79 Ind.L.J. 323 (2004)—§ 15.2(g) n.179

Fowler, Gender and Jury Deliberations: The Contributions of Social Science, 12 Wm. & M. J.Women & L. 1 (2005)—§ 22.2(d) n.64

Fox, The Road Not Taken: Criminal Contempt Sanctions and Grand Jury Press Leaks, 25 U.Mich.J.L.Ref. 505 (1992)—§ 8.5(i) n.309

Foy, The Relationship Between Prosecutorial Misconduct and Wrongful Convictions, 2006 Wis.L.Rev. 399—§ 1.9(b) n.28

Frampton, Some Practical and Ethical Problems of Prosecuting Public Officials, 36 Md.L.Rev. 5 (1976)—§ 13.1(a) n.28

Francis, Failure to Advise Non-Citizens of Immigration Consequences of Criminal Convictions: Should This be Grounds to Withdraw a Guilty Plea?, 36 U. Mich.J.L.Reform 691 (2003)—§§ 21.3(b) n.68; 21.4(d) n.136

Frank, The Collection of Restitution: An Often Overlooked Service to Crime Victims, 8 St. John's J. Legal Comment. 107 (1992)—§§ 1.5(k) n.375, 380

Frankel, Lawlessness in Sentencing, 41 U.Cin.L.Rev. 1 (1972)—§§ 26.1(c) n.44; 26.3(b) n.8

Frankel, The Search for Truth: An Umpireal View, 123 U.Pa.L.Rev. 1031 (1975)—§§ 1.5(b) n.70; 1.5(c) n.117, 127, 131

Frankfurter, Judicial Review In Action, 74 U.Pa.L.Rev. 639 (1926)—§ 2.9(d) n.83

Frankfurter, Memorandum on "Incorporation" of the Bill of Rights into the Due Process Clause of the Fourteenth Amendment, 78 Harv.L.Rev. 746 (1965)—§ 2.2 n.9

Frankfurter and Corcoran, Petty Federal Offenses and the Constitutional Guaranty of Trial by Jury, 39 Harv.L.Rev. 917 (1926)—§ 2.9(d) n.72

Franklin, The Foundation and Meaning of the Slaughterhouse Cases, 18 Tulane L.Rev. 1 (1943)—§ 2.3(b) n.77

Frase, 43 U.Chi.L.Rev. 667 (1967)— § 18.3(b) n.56

Frase, Comparative Criminal Justice As a Guide to American Law Reform: How Do the French Do It, How Can We Find Out, and Why Should We Care, 78 Cal.L.Rev. 540 (1990)— §§ 1.5(a) n.6, 48; 1.5(c) n.108

Frase, Criminal Procedure in a Conservative Age: A Time to Rediscover the Critical Nonconstitutional Issues, 36 J. Legal Educ. 79 (1986)— § 1.3(b) n.1

Frase, Defining the Limits of Crime Control and Due Process, 73 Cal.L.Rev. 212 (1985)—§ 1.5(a) n.48

Frase, Excessive Prison Sentences, Punishment Goals, and the Eighth Amendment "Proportionality" Relative to What?, 89 Minn.L.Rev. 571 (2005)—§ 26.1(a) n.1

Frase, Implementing Commission-Based Sentencing Guidelines: The Lessons of the First Ten Years in Minnesota, 2 Cornell J.L. & Pub.Pol. 279 (1993)—§ 26.3(b) n.10

Frase, Is Guided Discretion Sufficient? Overview of State Sentencing Guidelines, 44 St.L.U.L.J. 425 (2000)—§ 26.3(e) n.31

Frase, Lessons of State Guideline Reforms, 8 Fed.Sent.Rep. 39 (1995)— § 26.3(e) n.33

Frase, Punishment Purposes, 58 Stan.L.Rev. 67 (2005)—§ 1.2(d) n.269

Frase, State Sentencing Guidelines: Diversity, Consensus, and Unresolved Policy Issues, 105 Colum.L.Rev. 1190 (2005)—§§ 26.3(e); 26.3(e) n.29, 30, 38

Frase, State Sentencing Guidelines: Still Going Strong, 78 Judicature 173 (Jan.-Feb. 1995)—§ 26.3(e) n.31

Frase, The Decision to File Federal Criminal Charges: A Quantitative Study of Prosecutorial Discretion, 47 U.Chi.L.Rev. 246 (1980)—

§§ 13.2(a) n.7 to 9, 11; 13.2(e) n.90; 13.2(f) n.101, 102, 104, 105, 107, 108, 110, 112; 13.2(g) n.124, 133

Frase, The Speedy Trial Act of 1974, 43 U.Chi.L.Rev. 667 (1976)— §§ 18.3(b) n.2, 15 to 17, 44, 45, 55, 57; 18.4(b) n.28

Frase & Weigend, 48 B.C.Int'l. & Comp.L.Rev. 317 (1995)— §§ 1.5(c) n.105, 109

Frase & Weigend, German Criminal Justice As A Guide to American Law Reform: Similar Problems, Better Solutions, 18 B.C. Int'l & Comp.L.Rev. 317 (1995)—§ 1.5(a) n.6

Frassler, The Italian Penal Procedure Code: An Adversarial System of Criminal Procedure in Continental Europe, 29 Colum.J. Transnat'l L. 245 (1991)—§§ 1.5(c) n.107, 109

Frederick, Jury Behavior: A Psychologist Examines Jury Selection, 5 Ohio N.U.L.Rev. 571 (1978)— § 22.3(b) n.92

Freed, Symposium: Federal Sentencing in the Wake of Guidelines: Unacceptable Limits on the Discretion of Sentencers, 101 Yale L.J. 1681 (1992)—§ 26.3(b) n.4

Freedman, et al., Severity of Penalty, Seriousness of the Charge, and Mock Jurors' Verdicts, 18 Law & Hum.Behav. 189 (1994)—§ 24.7(e) n.49

Freedman, Giarratano is a Scarecrow: The Right to Counsel in State Criminal Postconviction Proceedings, 91 Cornell L.Rev. 1079 (2006)— §§ 11.1(b) n.79; 11.2(b) n.75; 11.7(a) n.10; 28.12(a) n.3

Freedman, Judge Frankel's Search for Truth, 123 U.Pa.L.Rev. 1060 (1975)—§ 1.5(c) n.138

Freedman, Professional Discipline of Prosecutors: A Response to Professor Zacharias, 30 Hofstra L.Rev. 121 (2001)—§ 1.7(j) n.237

Freedman, The Professional Responsibility of the Prosecuting Attorney, 55 Geo.L.J. 1030 (1967)— §§ 13.2(d) n.86; 13.4(c) n.133; 21.3(c) n.166

Freeman & Earley, United States v. DiFrancesco: Government Appeal of Sentences, 18 Am.Crim.L.Rev. 91 (1980)—§ 26.3(g) n.89

Frels, Search and Seizure in the Public Schools, 11 Houston L.Rev. 876 (1974)—§ 3.9(k) n.244

Frey, Modern Police Interrogation Law: The Wrong Road Taken, 42 U.Pitt.L.Rev. 731 (1981)—§ 6.5(d) n.65

Frickey, A Further Comment On Stare Decisis and the Overruling of National League of Cities, 2 Const.Comm. 341 (1985)— §§ 2.9(b) n.16, 29, 31

Frickey, Stare Decisis in Constitutional Cases: Reconsidering National League of Cities, 2 Const.Comm. 123 (1985)—§ 2.9(b) n.15

Fried, Criminal Law: Rationalizing Criminal Forfeiture, 79 J.Crim.L. 328 (1988)—§ 26.6(d) n.46

Friedman, A Presumption of Innocence, Not of Even Odds, 52 Stan.L.Rev. 873 (2000)—§ 1.5(d) n.193

Friedman, A Tale of Two Habeas, 73 Minn.L.Rev. 247 (1988)—§ 28.2(d) n.75

Friedman, Adjusting to Crawford: High Court Decision Restors Confrontation Clause Protection, 19 Crim. J. 4 (2004)—§ 24.2(e) n.78

Friedman, Failed Enterprise, 83 Cal.L.Rev. 485 (1995)—§§ 28.3(e) n.94; 28.6(d) n.29, 37; 28.6(g) n.82

Friedman, Habeas and Hubris, 45 Vand.L.Rev. 797 (1992)— §§ 28.2(d) n.78, 80

Friedman, Legal Culture and Social Development, 4 Law & Soc'y Rev. 29 (1969)—§ 1.10(a) n.6

Friedman, Personal Responsibility in a Professional System, 27 Cath.U.L.Rev. 191 (1978)— § 11.6(a) n.9

Friedman, Plea Bargaining in Historical Perspective, 13 Law & Soc.Rev. 247 (1979)—§§ 1.6(a) n.23; 21.1(a) n.3; 21.1(b) n.10, 14; 21.1(g) n.121

Friedman, The Devil Is Not Dead, Exploring The History of Criminal Justice, 11 Ga.L.Rev. 257 (1977)— § 1.6(d) n.198

Friedman & Smith, The Sedimentary Constitution, 147 U.Pa.L.Rev. 1 (1998)—§§ 2.8(a) n.17; 2.9(d) n.54

Friendly, Is Innocence Irrelevant? Collateral Attack on Criminal Judgments, 38 U.Chi.L.Rev. 142 (1970)—§§ 28.2(d) n.84 to 86

Friendly, The Bill of Rights as a Code of Criminal Procedure, 53 Cal.L.Rev. 929 (1965)—§§ 2.1 n.3; 2.5(b) n.13; 2.6(a) n.1; 2.8(b) n.39; 6.1(a) n.7, 10; 6.7(b) n.91; 11.1(a) n.10

Friendly, The Fifth Amendment Tomorrow: The Case For Constitutional Change, 37 U.Cin.L.Rev. 671 (1968)—§ 2.10(c) n.96

Friesen, Adventures in Federalism: Some Observations on the Overlapping Spheres of State and Federal Constitutional Law, 3 Widener J.Pub.L. 25 (1993)—§§ 2.12(a) n.30, 33, 54, 68, 77; 2.12(b) n.80, 86; 2.12(c) n.118, 146; 2.12(d) n.191

Fulda, Data Mining and Privacy, 11 Alb.L.J.Sci. & Tech. 105 (2000)— § 3.2(j) n.242

Fulero & Everington, Assessing the Capacity of Persons with Mental Retardation to Waive Miranda Rights: A Jurisprudent Therapy Perspective, 28 Law & Psychol.Rev. 53 (2004)—§ 6.9(b) n.24

Fyfe, Observations on Police Deadly Force, 27 Crime & Delinq. 376 (1981)—§ 1.5(a) n.51

G

Gaba, Voir Dire of Jurors: Constitutional Limits to the Right of Inquiry Into Prejudice, 48 U.Colo.L.Rev. 525 (1977)—§ 22.3(a) n.27

Gainer, Federal Criminal Code Reform: Past and Future, 2 Buff.Criml.L.Rev. 46 (1988)— § 1.2(d) n.212

Gaines, The Newly Adopted Criminal Restitution, Statutes of South Carolina: Analysis and Recommendations for Change, 46 S.C.L.Rev. 289 (1995)—§§ 26.6(c) n.33, 37

Galie, State Supreme Courts, Judicial Federalism, and The Other Constitutions, 71 Judicature 100 (1987)— §§ 2.12(a) n.33, 37, 40; 2.12(b) n.113

Galliher et al., Abolition and Reinstatement of Capital Punishment During the Progressive Era and Early 20th Century, 83 J.Crim.L. & Criminology 538 (1992)—§ 26.1(b) n.10

Gamer & Petty, A Plea for Openness in Plea Bargaining, 16 Gonzaga L.Rev. 81 (1980)—§ 21.3(c) n.193

Gandara, Admissibility of Confessions in Federal Prosecutions, 63 Geo.L.J. 305 (1974)—§ 6.5(e) n.84

Garcia, Mental Sanity and Confessions: The Supreme Court's New Version of the Old "Voluntariness" Standard, 21 Akron L.Rev. 275 (1988)—§ 6.2(b) n.50

Garcia-Mora, Criminal Jurisdiction Over Foreigners for Treason and Offenses Against the Safety of the State Committed Upon Foreign Territory, 19 U.Pitt.L.Rev. 567 (1958)— § 16.4(b) n.32

Gardner, Sniffing for Drugs in the Classroom, 74 Nw.U.L.Rev. 803 (1980)—§ 3.2(b) n.71

Gardner, Student Privacy in the Wake of T.L.O., 22 Ga.L.Rev. 897 (1988)— § 3.9(k) n.256

Gardner, The Failed Discourse of State Constitutionalism, 90 Mich.L.Rev. 761 (1992)—§§ 2.12(a) n.11, 17, 35, 37, 45, 53, 59, 79; 2.12(c) n.122, 124; 2.12(d) n.197

Gardner, The Myth of the Impartial Psychiatric Expert—Some Comments Concerning Criminal Responsibility and the Decline of the Age of Therapy, 2 Law & Psychology Rev. 99 (1976)—§ 11.2(e) n.199

Gardner & Rifkind, 7 Crim.J. 14 (Summer 1992)—§§ 21.1(h) n.198, 219, 224, 239, 241, 242

Garoppolo, Confusion and Distortion in the Federal Sentencing Process, 27 Crim.L.Bull. 3 (1991)—§ 21.1(h) n.236

Garrett, Aggregation in Criminal Law, 95 Calif.L.Rev. 383 (2007)—§ 24.11(d) n.48

Garrett, Innocence, Harmless Error, and Federal Wrongful Conviction Law, 2005 Wis.L.Rev. 35—§ 24.11(d) n.38

Garrett, Structural Reform Prosecution, 93 Va.L.Rev. 853 (2007)—§ 13.6(a) n.14

Garvey, Aggravation and Mitigation in Capital Cases: What Do Jurors Think?, 98 Colum.L.Rev. 1538 (1998)—§ 11.10(c) n.153

Garvey, Can Shaming Punishments Educate, 65 U.Chi.L.Rev. 733 (1998)—§ 26.9(b) n.78

Gaskins, Changes in the Criminal Law in Eighteenth-Century Connecticut, 25 Am.J. Legal Hist. 309 (1981)—§§ 1.6(b) n.43, 93

Gaumer, Protecting the Innocent Victim-Witness Rights in Illinois, 83 Ill.B.J. 568 (1995)—§ 12.1(f) n.99

Geabe, Spelling Guilt Out of A Record? Harmless-Error Review of Conclusive Mandatory Presumptions and Elemental Misdescriptions, 74 B.U.L.Rev. 819 (1994)—§ 27.6(e) n.162

Geer, Representation of Multiple Criminal Defendants: Conflicts of Interest and the Professional Responsibilities of the Defense Attorney, 62 Minn.L.Rev. 119 (1978)—§ 11.9(a) n.5

Gegan & Rodriguez, Victims' Rights in the Criminal Justice System: A Fallacy of Victim Empowerment, 8 St.John's J.Legal Comment. 225 (1992)—§ 21.3(f) n.335

Geimer, A Decade of Strickland's Tin Horn: Doctrinal and Practical Undermining of the Right to Counsel, 4 Wm. & Mary Bill of Rights J. 91 (1995)—§ 11.10(a) n.16

Gelman, Liebman, West, & Kiss, A Broken System: The Persistent Pattern of Reversals in Death Sentences in the United States, 1 J. Empirical Legal Studies 209 (2004)—§ 11.10(c) n.154

Gemmil, What Is Wrong With the Administration of Our Criminal Law, 4 J.Am.Inst.Crim.L. & Criminology 698 (1913)—§ 1.6(e) n.307

Geneco, The New Adversary, 54 Brook.L.Rev. 781 (1988)—§ 1.4(f) n.102

Genego, The Future of Effective Assistance of Counsel: Performance Standards and Competent Representation, 22 Am.Crim.L.Rev. 181 (1984)—§ 11.7(c) n.36

Genego, The New Adversary, 54 Brook.L.Rev. 781 (1988)—§§ 1.5(a) n.20; 1.5(c) n.139; 11.4(c) n.97; 11.9(c) n.102

George, Extraterritorial Application of Penal Legislation, 64 Mich.L.Rev. 609 (1966)—§§ 16.4(b) n.23; 16.4(c) n.112

George, Reform of State Criminal Law and Procedure, 41 Law & Contemp.Probs. 63 (1977)—§§ 1.6(h) n.461, 477; 1.7(e) n.66

Gerhardt, A Tale of Two Textualists: A Critical Comparison of Justices Black and Scalia; 74 B.U.L.Rev. 25 (1994)—§§ 2.8(a) n.17; 2.9(c) n.46

Gerhardt, The Role of Precedent in Constitutional Decisionmaking and Theory, 60 Geo.Wash.L.Rev. 68 (1991)—§§ 2.9(b) n.14 to 17, 26, 31 to 34, 37, 38, 41

Gershman, Abscam, the Judiciary, and the Ethics of Entrapment, 91 Yale L.J. 1565 (1982)—§ 5.4(b) n.21

Gershman, Judicial Misconduct During Jury Deliberations, 27 Crim.L.Bull. 291 (1991)—§ 24.9(d) n.44

Gershman, Prosecutorial Ethics and Victims' Rights: The Prosecutor's Duty of Neutrality, 9 Lewis & Clark L.Rev. 559 (2005)—§ 13.1(a) n.10

Gershman, The Gate is Open But the Door Is Locked—Habeas Corpus and Harmless Error, 51 Wash. & Lee L.Rev. 115 (1994)—§ 28.6(g) n.82

Gershman, The New Prosecutors, 53 U.Pitt.L.Rev. 393 (1993)— § 11.4(c) n.97

Gershman, The Perjury Trap, 129 U.Pa.L.Rev. 624 (1981)—§ 8.9(b) n.22

Gershman, The Prosecutor's Duty to Truth, 14 Geo.J.Legal Ethics 309 (2001)—§ 24.3(a) n.12

Gershowitz, The Invisible Pillar of Gideon, 80 Ind. L.J.571 (2005)— §§ 11.2(g) n.261, 268

Gerstein, 80 Ethics 87 (1970)— § 2.10(d) n.151

Gerstein, The Demise of Boyd: Self-Incrimination and Private Papers in the Burger Court, 27 UCLA L.Rev. 343 (1979)—§§ 2.10(d) n.151; 8.7(a) n.2; 8.12(a) n.4

Gerstein and Robinson, Remedy for the Grand Jury: Retain But Reform, 64 A.B.A.J. 337 (1978)—§ 15.3(c) n.59

Gerstein and Robinson, Remedy for the Grand Jury: Retain But Reform, 64 A.B.A.J. 447 (1978)—§ 15.3(a) n.11

Gianelli, Criminal Discovery, Scientific Evidence, and DNA, 44 Vand.L.Rev. 767 (1991)—§ 20.3(f) n.112

Giannelli, Ake v. Oklahoma: The Right to Expert Assistance in a Post Daubert, Post-DNA World, 89 Cornell L.Rev. 1305 (2004)—§§ 11.2(e) n.145, 190

Gibbons, Waiver: Habeas Corpus Jurisdiction, 2 Seton Hall L.Rev. 291 (1971)—§ 28.4(d) n.35

Gifford, Decisions, Decisional Referents, and Administrative Justice, 37 Law & Contemp.Probs. 3 (1972)— § 1.9(c) n.55

Gifford, Equal Protection and the Prosecutor's Charging Decision: Enforcing an Ideal, 49 Geo.Wash.L.Rev. 659 (1981)—§§ 13.4(a) n.14; 13.4(b) n.41, 74, 75; 13.4(c) n.140 to 142

Gifford, Meaningful Reform of Plea Bargaining: The Control of Prosecutorial Discretion, 1983 U.Ill.L.Rev. 37, 38, 41—§ 21.1(d) n.44

Gilbert, An Ounce of Prevention: A Constitutional Prescription For Choice of Venue in Racially Sensitive Criminal Cases, 67 Tulane L.Rev. 1855 (1993)—§§ 16.3(g) n.107, 110, 123

Gilboy, Prosecutors' Discretionary Use of the Grand Jury to Initiate or Reinitiate Prosecution, 1984 A.B.F.Res.J. 1—§§ 13.1(a) n.31; 14.1(a) n.5; 14.2(c) n.45; 15.1(g) n.352

Ginsberg, Rural Criminal Justice: An Overview, 3 Am.J.Crim.L. 35 (1973)—§ 1.10(e) n.212

Girsh, The Witherspoon Question: The Social Sciences and the Evidence, 35 NLADA Briefcase 99 (1978)— § 22.3(c) n.158

Gittler, Expanding the Role of the Victim in a Criminal Action: An Overview of Issues and Problems, 11 Pepperdine L.Rev. 117 (Symposium

Issue, 1984)—§§ 1.5(k) n.340, 344, 346, 353, 365, 366; 1.6(b) n.84, 85

Givelber, The Application of Equal Protection Principles to Selective Enforcement of the Criminal Law, 1973 U.Ill.L.F. 88—§§ 13.4(b) n.50; 13.4(c) n.81, 96, 97, 114, 128, 130; 13.4(d) n.151, 152, 160, 161

Givelber, The Right to Counsel in Collateral, Post-Conviction Proceedings, 58 Md.L.Rev. 1393 (1999)—§ 11.1(b) n.83

Glazer, Thinking Strategically: How Federal Prosecutors Can Reduce Violent Crime, 26 Fordham Urb.L.J. 573 (1999)—§ 1.2(d) n.237

Glover, The Right to Privacy of Prospective Jurors During Voir Dire, 70 Cal.L.Rev. 709 (1982)—§ 22.3(a) n.7

Glueck, Principles of a Rational Penal Code, 41 Harv.L.Rev. 453 (1928)—§ 1.9(c) n.50

Gobert, In Search of the Impartial Jury, 79 J.Crim.L. & C. 269 (1988)—§ 22.2(d) n.52

Godsey, Miranda's Final Frontier-The International Arena: A Critical Analysis of United States v. Bin Laden, and a Proposal for a New Miranda Exception Abroad, 51 Duke L.J. 1703 (2002)—§ 6.10(d) n.61

Godsey, Reformulating the Miranda Warnings in Light of Contemporary Law and Understanding, 90 Minn.L.Rev. 781 (2006)—§§ 6.8(d) n.81, 82

Godsey, Rethinking the Involuntary Confession Rule: Toward a Workable Test for Identifying Compelled Self-Incrimination, 93 Cal.L.Rev. 465 (2005)—§ 6.2(b) n.27

Godsey, The New Frontier of Constitutional Confession Law-The International Arena: Exploring the Admissibility of Confessions Taken by U.S. Investigators from Non-Americans Abroad, 91 Geo.L.J. 851 (2003)—§ 6.10(d) n.61

Godsey, When Terry Met Miranda: Two Constitutional Doctrines Collide, 63 Fordham L.Rev. 715 (1994)—§ 6.6(e) n.96

Goldberg, Harmless Error: Constitutional Sneak Thief, 71 J.Crim.L. & Criminology 421 (1980)—§§ 27.6(a) n.4, 10

Goldberg, The Burger Court—1971 Term: One Step Forward, Two Steps Backwards? 63 J.Crim.L. Criminology & Pol.Sci. 463 (1972)—§ 2.8(b) n.43

Goldberg, The Extraordinary Writs and the Review of Inferior Court Judgments, 36 Cal.L.Rev. 558 (1948)—§§ 27.4(b) n.4, 7

Goldberg, Toward Expansion of Witherspoon: Capital Scruples, Jury Bias, and Use of Psychological Data to Raise Presumptions in the Law, 5 Harv.Civ.Rts.-Civ.Lib.L.Rev. 53 (1969)—§ 22.3(c) n.158

Goldfarb, When Judges Abandon Analogy: The Problem of Delay in Commencing Criminal Prosecutions, 31 Wm. & Mary L.Rev. 607 (1990)—§ 18.5(b) n.71

Goldkamp, Danger and Detention: A Second Generation of Bail Reform, 76 J.Crim.L. & Criminology 1 (1985)—§§ 1.3(e) n.44; 1.3(g) n.90 to 92; 1.6(h) n.480; 12.3(a) n.17; 12.3(b) n.29

Goldman, State Revocation of Law Enforcement Officers' Licenses and Federal Criminal Prosecution: An Opportunity For Cooperative Federalism, 22 St. Louis U.Pub.L.Rev. 121 (2003)—§ 1.9(b) n.43

Goldman & Puro, Revocation of Police Officer Certification: A Viable Remedy for Police Misconduct, 45 St. Louis U.L.J. 541 (2001)—§ 1.9(b) n.43

Goldsmith, Eavesdropping Reform: The Legality of Roving Surveillance, 1987 U.Ill.L.Rev. 401—§ 3.4(e) n.82

Goldsmith, Felony Plea Bargaining in Six Colorado Judicial Districts: A Limited Inquiry Into the Nature of the Process, 1989 Denver U.L.Rev. 243—§ 21.1(a) n.8

Goldsmith, In Vino Veritas?: Police Interrogation of Intoxicated Persons and the Requirement of Voluntariness, 4 Med. & Law 55 (1985)— § 6.2(c) n.173

Goldsmith, RICO and Enterprise Criminality: A Response to Gerard Lynch, 88 Colum.L.Rev. 774 (1988)—§ 16.2(h) n.153

Goldstein, Bar Poll Ratings as the Leading Influence on a Nonpartisan Judicial Election, 63 Judicature 377 (1980)—§ 1.10(e) n.204

Goldstein, Converging Criminal Justice Systems: Guilty Pleas and the Public Interest, 49 SMU L.Rev. 567 (1996)—§§ 21.1(b) n.9; 21.4(a) n.13; 21.4(f) n.195, 212

Goldstein, Defining the Role of the Victim in Criminal Prosecution, 52 Miss.L.J. 515 (1982)—§§ 1.5(k) n.359; 13.1(a) n.9

Goldstein, For Harold Lasswell: Some Reflections on Human Dignity, Entrapment, Informed Consent, and the Plea Bargain, 84 Yale L.J. 683 (1975)—§ 5.2(b) n.21

Goldstein, Jury Secrecy and the Media: The Problem of Postverdict Interviews, 1993 U.Ill.L.Rev. 295— § 24.9(g) n.129

Goldstein, Police Discretion Not to Invoke the Criminal Process: Low-Visibility Decisions in the Administration of Justice, 69 Yale L.J. 543 (1960)—§§ 1.9(c) n.48; 13.2(b) n.32, 39

Goldstein, Refining the Role of the Victim in Criminal Prosecution, 52 Miss.L.J. 515 (1982)—§ 26.6(c) n.33

Goldstein, Reflections on Two Models: Inquisitorial Themes in American Criminal Procedure, 26 Stan.L.Rev. 1009 (1974)—§§ 1.5(a) n.20; 1.5(c) n.95, 166; 1.5(d) n.180, 184, 205; 1.6(f) n.349; 8.2(c) n.27

Goldstein, The Krulewitch Warning, Guilt by Association, 54 Geo.L.J. 133 (1965)—§ 16.2(g) n.135

Goldstein, The Search Warrant, The Magistrate, and Judicial Review, 62 N.Y.U.L.Rev. 1173 (1987)— §§ 3.1(c) n.66; 3.4(b) n.31

Goldstein, The State and the Accused: Balance of Advantage in Criminal Procedure, 69 Yale L.J. 1149 (1960)—§§ 1.5(c) n.142; 1.5(h) n.296; 1.6(f) n.387; 15.2(d) n.95; 15.5(a) n.17; 19.3(b) n.167; 20.1(a) n.13; 20.1(b) n.23, 27, 29, 35

Goldstein & Marcus, Comments on Continental Criminal Procedure, 87 Yale L.J. 1870 (1978)—§ 1.5(c) n.106

Goldstein & Marcus, The Myth of Judicial Supervision in Three ''Inquisitorial'' Systems: France, Italy, and Germany, 87 Yale L.J. 240 (1977)—§§ 13.2(g) n.122; 21.1(b) n.9

Goldstein & Marcus, The Myth of Judicial Supervision in Three ''Inquisitorial'' Systems: France, Italy, and Germany, 87 Yale L.J. 1370 (1978)—§ 1.5(c) n.106

Goldstock and Chananie, The Use of Electronic Surveillance and Search Warrants in the Investigation and Prosecution of Attorneys Suspected of Wrongdoing, 136 U.Pa.L.Rev. 1855 (1988)—§ 3.4(a) n.22

Goldwasser, After Abscam: An Examination of Congressional Proposals to Limit Targeting Discretion in Federal Undercover Investigations, 36 Emory L.J. 75 (1987)—§ 5.4(b) n.21

Goldwasser, Vindicating the Right to Trial By Jury and the Requirement of Proof Beyond a Reasonable

Doubt: A Critique of the Conventional Wisdom About Excluding Defense Evidence, 86 Geo.L.J. 621 (1998)—§ 24.4(a) n.5

A. Golub, B. Johnson, A. Taylor, & J. Eterno, Does Quality-of-Life Policing Widen the Net?, 6 Justice Research and Policy 19 (Spring 2004) (NCJ-19896)—§ 1.10(b) n.31

Gonzalez, Ellsworth and Pembroke, Response Bias in Lineups and Show-ups, 64 J. Personality and Social Psychology 525 (1993)—§ 7.4(f) n.94

Goode, Identity, Fees, and the Attorney-Client Privilege, 59 Geo.Wash.L.Rev. 307 (1991)—§ 8.8(d) n.90

Goodpaster, On the Theory of American Adversary Criminal Trial, 78 J.Crim.L. & Criminology 118 (1987)—§§ 1.5(b) n.71; 1.5(c) n.117, 119, 149, 158, 173

Gordon, Being Tough Doesn't Work Because Being Lenient is Not the Source of the Problem, 12(5) Crim.Just.Newsl. 5 (3/2/81)—§ 1.5(a) n.48

Gordon, Review of the American Codification Movement, 36 Vand.L.Rev. 431 (1983)—§ 1.6(d) n.269

Gorelick, Pretrial Diversion: The Threat of Expanding Social Control, 10 Harv.Civ.Rts.-Civ.Lib.L.Rev. 194 (1975)—§ 13.1(d) n.48

Gorelick & Litman, Prosecutorial Discretion and the Federalization Debate, 46 Hastings L.J. 967 (1995)—§§ 1.2(d) n.204, 235; 1.2(f) n.286; 13.2(a) n.11

Gottsfield & Michkowski, Settlement Conferences Help Resolve Criminal Cases, 90 Judicature 196 (Mar.-Apr.2007)—§ 21.3(d) n.211

Gould & Mastrofski, Suspect Searches: Accessing Police Behavior Under the U.S. Constitution, 3 Criminology & Pub. Pol'y 315 (2004)—§ 1.9(b) n.17

Gould & Stern, Catastrophic Threats and the Fourth Amendment, 77 S.Cal.L.Rev. 777 (2004)—§ 3.3(b) n.37

Gowdy, Leniency Bribes: Justifying the Federal Practice of Offering Leniency for Testimony, 60 La.L.Rev. 447 (2000)—§ 21.2(b) n.71

Graham, Our "Declaratory" Fourteenth Amendment, 7 Stan.L.Rev. 3 (1954)—§ 2.3(a) n.61

Graham, What is "Custodial Interrogation?": California's Anticipatory Application of Miranda v. Arizona, 14 UCLA L.Rev. 59 (1966)—§§ 6.6(a) n.2; 6.7(b) n.92 to 94

Graham & Letwin, The Preliminary Hearing in Los Angeles: Some Field Findings and Legal Policy Observations, 18 UCLA L.Rev. 635 (1971)—§§ 14.1(a) n.5, 8, 19; 14.2(d) n.52; 14.2(e) n.83; 14.3(a) n.21, 24, 28; 14.3(b) n.47; 14.4(b) n.8; 14.4(c) n.51; 21.6(c) n.119

Grannelli, Ake v. Oklahoma: The right to Expert Assistance in a Post-Daubert, Post-DNA World, 89 Cornell L.Rev. 1305 (2004)—§ 11.2(e) n.168

Grano, Ascertaining the Truth, 77 Cornell L.Rev. 1061 (1992)—§ 1.5(b) n.70

Grano, Implementing the Objectives of Procedural Reform: The Proposed Michigan Rules of Criminal Procedure—Part I, 32 Wayne L.Rev. 1007 (1986)—§§ 1.5(a) n.5; 1.5(c) n.145 to 147; 1.5(e) n.210, 229; 2.7(c) n.202; 2.9(h) n.211; 14.2(g) n.100

Grano, Introduction—The Changed and Changing World of Constitutional Criminal Procedure: The Contribution of the Department of Justice's Office of Legal Policy, 22 U.Mich.J.L.Ref. 395 (1989)—§§ 2.8(b) n.44; 2.9(f) n.109; 6.2(d) n.204

Grano, Miranda's Constitutional Difficulties: A Reply to Professor Schulhofer, 55 U.Chi.L.Rev. 174 (1988)—§§ 2.9(g) n.155; 2.9(h) n.253

Grano, Probable Cause and Common Sense: A Reply to the Critics of Illinois v. Gates, 17 U.Mich.J.L.Ref. 465 (1984)—§§ 3.3(b) n.34, 72; 3.3(c) n.80, 85

Grano, Prophylactic Rules in Criminal Procedure: A Question of Article III Legitimacy, 80 Nw.U.L.Rev. 100 (1986)—§§ 2.9(g) n.154, 156; 2.9(h) n.211, 253

Grano, Rhode Island v. Innis: A Need to Reconsider the Constitutional Premises Underlying the Law of Confessions, 17 Am.Crim.L.Rev. 1 (1979)—§§ 6.4(h) n.169 to 171, 175

Grano, The Right to Counsel: Collateral Issues Affecting Due Process, 54 Minn.L.Rev. 1175 (1970)—§ 11.6(a) n.2

Grano, Voluntariness, Free Will, and the Law of Confessions, 65 Va.L.Rev. 859 (1979)—§§ 2.7(c) n.124, 207; 6.1(b) n.17; 6.2(b) n.32

Grano, Kirby, Biggers, and Ash: Do Any Constitutional Safeguards Remain Against the Danger of Convicting the Innocent?, 72 Mich.L.Rev. 717 (1974)—§§ 7.2(d) n.58; 7.3(b) n.16, 17, 21, 22, 28; 7.3(c) n.43; 7.3(f) n.105, 121; 7.4(e) n.79; 7.4(g) n.121; 7.5(c) n.33

Grant, Rational Choice or Wrongful Discrimination? The Law and Economics of Jury Nullification, 14 Geo.Mason U.Civ.Rts.L.J. 145 (2004)—§ 22.1(g) n.105

Grau, The Limits of Planned Change in Courts, 6 Just.Sys.J. 84 (1981)—§ 1.10(d) n.156

Gray, Do We Have an Unwritten Constitution, 27 Stan.L.Rev. 703 (1975)—§ 2.9(c) n.47

Gray, Post Trial Discovery: Disclosure of the Presentence Investigation Report, 4 U.Toledo L.Rev. 1 (1972)—§ 26.5(c) n.42

Green, Her Brother's Keeper, The Prosecutor's Responsibility When Defense Counsel Has a Potential Conflict of Interest, 16 Am.J.Crim.L. 323 (1989)—§ 11.9(c) n.102

Green, Lethal Fiction, The Meaning of "Counsel" In the Sixth Amendment, 78 Iowa L.Rev. 433 (1993)—§ 11.8(c) n.65

Green, Limits on a Prosecutor's Communications with Prospective Defense Witnesses, Crim.L.Bull. 139 (March-April 1989)—§ 24.3(h) n.176

Green, "Package" Plea Bargaining and the Prosecutor's Duty of Good Faith, 25 Crim.L.Bull. 507 (1989)—§§ 21.2(b) n.51, 59

Green, Police Encouragement and the Fourth Amendment, 20 John Marshall L.Rev. 661 (1987)—§ 5.4(b) n.14

Green, "Power, Not Reason": Justice Marshall's Valedictory and the Fourth Amendment in the Supreme Court's 1990 Term, 70 N.Car.L.Rev. 373 (1992)—§§ 3.5(a) n.49; 3.7(c) n.47; 3.10(f) n.187

Green, The Bill of Rights, The Fourteenth Amendment and the Supreme Court, 5 Mich.L.Rev. 869 (1948)—§ 2.5(e) n.40

Green, The Municipal Court of Chicago, 58 U.Pa.L.Rev. 333 (1910)—§ 1.6(e) n.317

Green, "Through A Glass Darkly": How the Court Sees Motions to Disqualify Criminal Lawyers, 89 Colum.L.Rev. 1201 (1989)—§§ 11.9(c) n.103, 105

Green & Zacharias, Prosecutorial Neutrality, 2004 Wis.L.Rev. 837, 903—§ 13.2(d) n.79

Green & Zacharias, Regulating Federal Prosecutors' Ethics, 55 Vand.L.Rev. 381 (2002)—§ 6.4(e) n.91

Greenberg, Crime, Law Enforcement, and Social Control in Colonial America, 26 Am.J. Legal Hist. 293 (1982)—§ 1.6(b) n.27

Greenberg, Probation Conditions and the First Amendment: When Reasonableness Is Not Enough, 17 Colum.J.L. & Soc.Prob. 45 (1981)—§§ 26.9(b) n.42, 49

Greenberg, The Balance of Interests Theory and the Fourth Amendment: A Selective Analysis of Supreme Court Action Since Camara and See, 61 Cal.L.Rev. 1011 (1973)—§ 3.9(c) n.60

Greenberg & Litman, The Meaning of Original Meaning, 86 Geo.L.J. 569 (1998)—§ 2.9(d) n.96

Greenberg, Kessler, & Loftin, The Effect of Police Employment on Crime, 21 Criminology 375 (1983)—§§ 1.5(a) n.50; 1.6(g) n.441

Griffin, Compelled Cooperation and the New Corporate Criminal Procedure, 82 N.Y.U.L.Rev. 311 (2007)—§ 13.6(a) n.15

Griffin, The Correction of Wrongful Convictions: A Comparative Perspective, 16 Am.U.Int'l L.Rev. 1241 (2001)—§§ 24.11(d) n.12, 13

Griffin & Katz, Sentencing Consistency: Basic Principles Instead of Numerical Grids: The Ohio Plan, 53 Case W.L.Rev. 1 (2002)—§ 26.3(b) n.10

Griffiths, Ideology in Criminal Procedure or A Third "Model" of the Criminal Process, 79 Yale L.J. 359 (1970)—§§ 1.5(a) n.20, 60; 2.8(c) n.60; 21.1(d) n.57

Griffiths & Ayres, A Postscript to the Miranda Project: Interrogation of Draft Protesters, 77 Yale L.J. 300 (1967)—§ 6.5(c) n.35

Grisso, Juveniles' Capacities to Waive Miranda Rights: An Empirical Analysis, 68 Cal.L.Rev. 1134 (1980)—§§ 6.9(b) n.21; 6.10(e) n.74

Grisso & Pomiciter, Interrogation of Juveniles: An Empirical Study of Procedures, Safeguards and Rights Waiver, 1 L. & Hum. Behav. 31 (1977)—§ 6.9(b) n.21

Groot, The Serpent Beguiled Me and I (Without Scienter) Did Eat—Denial of Crime and the Entrapment Defense, 1973 U.Ill.L.F. 254—§§ 5.3(c) n.30, 32, 33, 39

Gross, Loss of Innocence: Eyewitness Identification and Proof of Guilt, 16 J.Leg.Studies 395 (1987)—§§ 1.5(e) n.228; 7.1(a) n.1; 7.5(c) n.37, 38

Gross, The American Advantage: The Value of Inefficient Litigation, 85 Mich.L.Rev. 734 (1987)—§ 1.5(c) n.120

Gross, Update: American Public Opinion on The Death Penalty: Its Getting Personal, 83 Cornell L.Rev. 1448 (1998)—§ 11.10(c) n.153

Gross, Jacoby, Matheson, Montgomery & Patil, Exonerations in the United States, 1989 Through 2003, 95 J.Crim.L. & Criminology 523 (2005)—§§ 1.5(e) n.230, 240; 24.11(d) n.38

Grove, Suppression of Illegally Obtained Evidence: The Standing Requirement on its Last Leg, 18 Cath.U.L.Rev. 150 (1968)—§ 9.1(b) n.83

Gruben, What Is Johnny Doing In The Library? Libraries, The U.S.A. Patriot Act, And Its Amendments, 19 St. Thomas L. Rev. 297 (2006)—§ 4.9(b) n.24

Guerra, The Myth of Dual Sovereignty: Multijurisdictional Drug Law Enforcement and Double Jeopardy, 73 N.C.L.Rev.1159 (1995)—§ 25.5(a) n.18

Gurr, Historical Trends in Violent Crimes: A Critical Review of the Evidence, in 3 Crime and Justice 295 (M. Tonry & N. Morris eds., 1981)—§ 1.10(c) n.46

Gutman, The Attorney-Conducted Voir Dire of Jurors: A Constitutional Right, 39 Brooklyn L.Rev. 290 (1972)—§ 22.3(a) n.34

Gutterman, A Formulation of the Value and Means Models of the Fourth Amendment in the Age of Technologically Enhanced Surveillance, 39 Syracuse L.Rev. 647 (1988)—§ 3.2(a) n.26

H

Haddad, Retroactivity Should be Rethought: A Call For The End of The Linkletter Doctrine, 60 J.Crim.L.C. & P.S. 417 (1969)—§ 2.11(a) n.7

Hagan & Bernstein, The Sentence Bargaining of Upperworld and Underworld Crime in Ten Federal District Courts, 13 Law & Soc.Rev. 467 (1979)—§ 21.1(a) n.6

Hagel, Toward a Uniform Statutory Standard for Effective Assistance of Counsel, 17 Loy.U.Chi.L.J. 203 (1986)—§ 11.7(d) n.62

Haigh, Defining Due Process of Law: The Case of Mr. Justice Hugo Black, 17 S.D.L.Rev. 1 (1972)—§§ 2.3(b) n.90; 2.4(b) n.57

Hall, Analysis of the Criticism of the Grand Jury, 22 J.Crim.L. & Criminology 692 (1932)—§ 15.3(b) n.36

Hall et al., Independent Counsel Investigations, 36 Am.Crim.L.Rev. 809 (1997)—§ 13.3(f) n.60

Hall, Federal Anti-Theft Legislation, 1 Law & Contemp.Prob. 424 (1934)—§ 1.2(c) n.112

Hall, Legal and Social Aspects of Arrest Without a Warrant, 49 Harv.L.Rev. 566 (1936)—§ 1.6(d) n.203

Hall, Objectives of Federal Criminal Procedure Revision, 51 Yale L.J. 723 (1942)—§ 1.5(a) n.5

Hall, Subsequent Misconduct as Ground for Forfeiture of the Right to Release on Bail-A Proposal, 15 N.Y.L.F. 873 (1969)—§ 12.3(a) n.4

Hall, The Role of the Victim in the Prosecution and Disposition of a Criminal Case, 28 Vand.L.Rev. 931 (1975)—§§ 1.5(k) n.349; 13.1(a) n.9

Hall, Victim's Voices in Criminal Court: The Need for Restraint, 28 Am.Crim.L.Rev. 233 (1991)—§ 26.5(d) n.73

Haller, Plea Bargaining: The Nineteenth Century Context, 13 Law & Soc.Rev. 273 (1979)—§ 21.1(b) n.10

Halpern, Federal Habeas Corpus and the Mapp Exclusionary Rule After Stone v. Powell, 82 Colum.L.Rev. 1 (1982)—§§ 28.3(d) n.81, 86, 88

Hamilton & Work, The Prosecutor's Role in the Urban Court System: The Case for Management Consciousness, 64 J.Crim.L. & Criminology 183 (1973)—§ 1.6(g) n.433

Hampton, The Moral Education Theory of Punishment, 13 Phil. & Pub.Aff. 206 (1984)—§ 1.5(a) n.31

Hancock, The State Constitution, A Criminal Lawyer's First Line of Defense, 57 Alb.L.Rev. 271 (1993)—§§ 2.12(a) n.16, 18, 20

Hanewicz, Jacobson v. United States: The Entrapment Defense and Judicial Supervision of the Criminal Justice System, 1993 Wis.L.Rev. 1163—§§ 5.2(a) n.15; 5.2(c) n.40

Hanna, No Right to Choose: Mandated Victim Participation in Domestic Violence Prosecutions, 109 Harv.L.Rev. 1849 (1996)—§§ 1.5(k) n.409; 1.6(h) n.465; 1.8(b) n.6; 13.2(b) n.35

Hannaford, Safeguarding Juror Privacy: A New Framework for Court Policies and Procedures, 85 Judicature 28 (July-Aug.2001)—§ 22.3(a) n.7

Hannaford, Hans, & Munsterman, Permitting Jury Discussions During Trial: Impact of the Arizona Reform, 24 Law & Hum.Behavior 359 (2000)—§ 24.9(f) n.63

Hannaford-Agor & Hans, Nullification at Work? A Glimpse from the National Center for State Courts Study of Hung Juries, 78 Chi.-Kent L.Rev. 1249 (2003)—§ 22.1(g) n.99

Hans & Jehle, Avoid Bald Men and People With Green Socks? Other Ways to Improve the Voir Dire Process in Jury Selection, 78 Chi.-Kent L.Rev. 1179 (2003)—§ 22.3(a) n.1

Hansen & Reed, The Speedy Trial Act of 1974 in Constitutional Perspective, 47 Miss.L.J. 365 (1976)—§ 18.3(b) n.2

Harcourt, Unconstitutional Police Searches and Collective Responsibility, 3 Criminology & Pub. Pol'y 309 (2004)—§ 1.9(b) n.17

Harden, The Effect of Emotional Reactions Upon Retention, 3 J.Gen.Psych. 197 (1930)—§ 7.1(b) n.13

Hardin, Legal Barriers in Child Abuse Investigations: State Powers and Individual Rights, 63 Wash.L.Rev. 493 (1988)—§ 3.9(d) n.70

Hardy, The Traps of Entrapment, 3 Am.J.Crim.L. 165 (1974)—§ 5.3(a) n.1

Harley, Detroit's New Model Criminal Court, 11 J.Crim.L. & Criminology 398 (1920)—§ 1.6(e) n.317

Harno, Some Significant Developments in Criminal Law and Procedure in the Last Century, 42 J.Crim.L. & Criminology 427 (1951)—§§ 1.6(e) n.325; 1.6(f) n.335, 380

Harris, Addressing Racial Profiling in the States: A Case Study of the ''New Federalism'' in Constitutional Criminal Procedure, 3 U.Pa.J.Const.L. 367 (2001)—§ 1.5(j) n.324

Harris, Ake Revisited: Expert Psychiatric Witnesses Remain Beyond the Reach for the Indigent, 68 N.C.L.Rev. 763 (1990)—§§ 11.2(e) n.145, 184

Harris, Factors for Reasonable Suspicion: When Black and Poor Means Stopped and Frisked, 69 Ind.L.J. 659 (1994)—§ 1.5(j) n.324

Harris, Justice Rationed in the Pursuit of Efficiency: De Novo Trials in the Criminal Courts, 24 Conn.L.Rev. 381 (1992)—§§ 1.4(g) n.148, 153; 1.8(g) n.115, 117, 118; 22.1(f) n.93

Harris, Superman's X-Ray Vision and the Fourth Amendment: The New Gun Detection Technology, 69 Temple L.Rev. 1 (1996)—§§ 3.2(b) n.73, 75 to 77

Harrison, Reconstructing the Privileges and Immunities Clause, 101 Yale L.J. 1385 (1992)—§§ 2.3(a) n.14, 15, 23, 25, 49, 61

Hart, Foreword: The Time Chart of the Justices, 73 Harv.L.Rev. 84 (1959)—§ 28.3(b) n.44

Hartman, The Burger Court—1973 Term: Leaving the Sixties Behind Us, 65 J.Crim.L. & Criminology 437 (1975)—§ 2.8(b) n.43

Hartog, The Public Law of a County Court: Judicial Government in Eighteenth-Century Massachusetts, 20 Am.J. Legal Hist. 282 (1976)—§ 1.6(b) n.43

Harwood & Naylor, Recall and Recognition in Elderly and Young Subjects, 21 Aust.J.Psych. 251 (1969)—§ 7.1(b) n.17

Hashimoto, Defending the Right of Self-Representation: An Empirical Look at the Pro Se Felony Defendant, 85 N.C.L.Rev. 423 (2007)—§§ 1.11(a) n.1; 11.5(a) n.7, 14, 17; 11.5(b) n.25

Hatch, Coming Together to Resolve Police Misconduct: The Emergence of Mediation as a New Solution, 21 Ohio St. J.Disp.Resol. 447 (2006)—§ 1.4(b) n.13

Hazlett, The Nineteenth Century Origins of the Fifth Amendment Privilege Against Self-Incrimination, 42 Am.J.Legal Hist. 235 (1998)— §§ 2.10(c) n.93; 6.5(a) n.1

Heaney, The Reality of Guidelines Sentencing: No End to Disparity, 28 Am.Crim.L.Rev. 161 (1991)— § 21.1(h) n.235

Heffernan & Lovely, Evaluating the Fourth Amendment Exclusionary Rule: The Problem of Police Compliance With the Law, 24 Mich.J.L.Ref. 311 (1991)— §§ 1.9(b) n.12, 14, 26

Heidt, The Fifth Amendment Privilege and Documents—Cutting Fisher's Tangled Line, 49 Mo.L.Rev. 439 (1984)—§§ 8.12(a) n.4; 8.12(f) n.56; 8.12(g) n.68; 8.13(a) n.19

Heinz & Kerstetter, Pretrial Settlement Conference: Evaluation of a Reform in Plea Bargaining, 13 Law & Soc.Rev. 349 (1979)—§§ 21.3(d) n.211, 247, 258

Heise, Mercy by the Numbers: An Empirical Analysis of Clemency and Its Structure, 89 Va.L.Rev. 239 (2003)—§ 26.2(c) n.69

Henderson, Learning from all Fifty States: How to Apply The Fourth Amendment and Its State Analogs to Protect Third Party Information from Unreasonable Search, 55 Cath.U.L.Rev. 373 (2006)— §§ 2.12(a) n.72, 73; 8.5(d) n.156

Henderson, Revisiting Victim's Rights, 1999 Utah L.Rev. 383—§§ 12.1(f) n.83, 84, 99; 21.3(f) n.383, 385, 386

Henderson, The Wrong of Victim's Rights, 37 Stan.L.Rev. 937 (1985)—§§ 1.5(k) n.363, 368, 369; 1.6(h) n.442; 26.5(d) n.73

Henke, The Taking and Use of Video Depositions, 17 Rev.Litig. 1 (1998)—§ 20.2(e) n.81

Henkin, Infallibility Under Law: Constitutional Balancing, 78 Colum.L.Rev. 1022 (1978)— § 1.5(a) n.62

Henkin, "Selective Incorporation" in the Fourteenth Amendment, 73 Yale L.J. 74 (1964)—§§ 2.5(b) n.13; 2.5(c) n.21, 22, 25, 29; 2.5(d) n.34; 2.6(a) n.1

Henning, 69 Tenn. L.Rev 793, 820 (1996)—§ 8.12(a) n.13

Henning, Defense Discovery in White Collar Criminal Prosecutions, 15 Ga.St.L.Rev. 601 (1999)— §§ 20.2(d) n.67; 20.3(a) n.12, 18; 20.3(g) n.123

Henning, Federalism and the Federal Prosecution of State and Local Corruption, 92 Ky.L.J. 75 (2003)— § 1.2(d) n.231

Henning, Finding What Was Lost: Sorting Out the Custodian's Privilege Against Self-Incrimination from the Compelled Production of Records, 77 Neb.L.Rev. 34 (1998)— §§ 8.13(b) n.48; 8.13(d) n.92, 102, 105, 107

Henning, Misguided Federalism, 68 Mo.L.Rev. 300 (2003)—§ 1.2(c) n.175

Henning, Precedents in a Vacuum: The Supreme Court Continues to Tinker with Double Jeopardy, 31 Am.Crim.L.Rev. 1 (1993)— § 17.4(b) n.82

Henning, Prosecutorial Misconduct and Constitutional Remedies, 77 Wash.U.L.Q. 713 (1999)— §§ 13.4(a) n.14; 13.7(c) n.35; 18.5(b) n.54; 22.3(d) n.187; 24.7(i) n.98

Henning, Prosecutorial Misconduct in Grand Jury Investigations, 51 S.Car.L.Rev. 1 (1999)—§§ 1.7(j) n.253; 8.8(h) n.184; 13.5(h) n.124, 133, 144, 155, 157, 184, 196; 15.3(d) n.63; 15.7(f) n.143

Henning, Testing the Limits of Investigating and Prosecuting White Collar Crime: How Far Will the Courts Allow Prosecutors to Go, 54 U.Pitt.L.Rev. 405 (1993)— §§ 8.6(b) n.52; 8.12(c) n.41

Henning, The Conundrum of Corporate Criminal Liability: Seeking a Consistent Approach to the Constitutional Rights of Corporations in Criminal Prosecutions, 63 Tenn.L.Rev. 793 (1996)— §§ 8.12(b) n.12, 25; 15.1(b) n.21, 26

Herbert, Keeping Pace: Court Resources and Crime in Ten U.S. Cities, 66 Judicature 73 (1982)—§ 1.6(g) n.441

Herman, Death Denies Due Process, 53 DePaul L.Rev. 1777 (2004)— § 11.10(c) n.155

Herman, Frivolous Criminal Appeals, 47 N.Y.U.L.Rev. 701 (1972)— §§ 11.2(c) n.87, 89, 99

Herman, The Supreme Court and Restrictions on Police Interrogation, 25 Ohio St.L.J. 449 (1965)— § 6.5(a) n.10

Herman, The Tail that Wagged the Dog: Bifurcated Fact-Finding Under the Federal Sentencing Guidelines and the Limits of Due Process, 66 S.Cal.L.Rev. 289 (1992)—§ 26.4(a) n.2

Herman and Thompson, Scott v. Illinois and The Right to Counsel: A Decision in Search of a Doctrine?, 17 Am.Crim.L.Rev. 71 (1979)— §§ 11.2(a) n.15, 16, 18

Hess, Pretrial Detention and the 1970 District of Columbia Crime Act-The Next Step in Bail Reform, 37 Brooklyn L.Rev. 277 (1971)— § 12.3(a) n.4

Hessick, The Federalization of Airport Security: Privacy Implications, 24 Whittier L.Rev. 43 (2002)— § 3.9(h) n.162

Hessick & Saujani, Plea Bargaining and Convicting the Innocent: The Role of the Prosecutor, the Defense Counsel, and the Judge, 16 BYU J.Pub.L. 189 (2002)—§ 21.1(d) n.49

Heuer & Penrod, Increasing Juror Participation in Trials Through Note Taking and Question Asking, 79 Judicature 256 (1996)—§§ 24.9(b) n.14, 16

Heuer & Penrod, Instructing Jurors: A Field Experiment with Written and Preliminary Instructions, 13 Law & Hum.Behav. 409 (1989)—§ 24.8(a) n.4

Heuer & Penrod, Juror Notetaking and Question Asking During Trials, 18 L. & Hum.Behav. 121 (1994)— § 24.9(b) n.17

Heuer & Penrod, Some Suggestions for the Critical Appraisal of A More Active Jury, 85 Nw.U.L.Rev. 226 (1990)—§§ 24.9(b) n.12, 15

Heumann, A Note on Plea Bargaining and Case Pressure, 9 Law & Soc'y Rev. 515 (1975)—§ 1.10(c) n.110

Heumann & Cassak, Not-So-Blissful Ignorance: Informing Jurors About Punishment in Mandatory Sentencing Cases, 20 Am.Crim.L.Rev. 343 (1983)—§§ 22.1(g) n.105; 24.7(e) n.49

Heumann & Loftin, Mandatory Sentencing and the Abolition of Plea Bargaining: The Michigan Felony Firearm Statute, 13 Law & Soc.Rev. 393 (1979)—§§ 21.1(g) n.121, 124, 128

P.Heymann & M. Moore, The Federal Role In Dealing With Violent Crime: Principles, Questions, and Cautions, 543 Annals Am.Acad.Pol. & Soc.Sci. 103 (1996)—§ 1.2(d) n.236

Hickey, Preventive Detention and the Crime of Being Dangerous, 58 Geo.L.J. 287 (1969)—§ 12.3(a) n.4

Higgins, Is Capital Punishment for Killers Only?, A.B.A.J. 30 (Aug.1997)—§ 26.1(b) n.32

High Court Study, 60 Alb.L.Rev. 1871 (1997)—§ 2.12(e) n.205

Hill, Testimonial Privilege and Fair Trial, 80 Colum.L.Rev. 1173 (1980)—§ 24.3(f) n.157

Hill, The Bill of Rights and Supervisory Power, 69 Colum.L.Rev. 181 (1969)—§§ 1.7(i) n.154, 168

Hill, The Constitutional Controversy of a Juvenile's Right to Bail in Juvenile Pre-Adjudication Proceedings, 1 Hastings Const.L.Q. 215 (1974)—§ 12.4(b) n.46

Hill, The Inadequate State Ground, 65 Colum.L.Rev. 943 (1965)—§ 28.4(b) n.16

Hing, The Dark Side of Operation Gatekeeper, 7 O.C.Davis J.Int'l.L. & Pol'y 121 (2001)—§ 1.2(d) n.264

Hinkle, Peremptory Challenges Based on Religious Affiliation: Are They Constitutional, 9 Buff. Crim. L. Rev. 139 (2005)—§ 22.3(d) n.198

Hoeffel, Prosecutorial Discretion at the Core: The Good Prosecutor Meets Brady, 109 Penn.St.L.Rev. 1133 (2005)—§ 24.3(b) n.74

Hoffheimer, Requiring Jury Instructions on Eyewitness Identification Evidence at Federal Criminal Trials, 80 J.Crim.L. & C. 585 (1989)—§ 7.5(b) n.19

Hoffheimer, The Future of Constitutionally Required Lesser Included Offenses, 67 U. Pitt. L. Rev. 585 (2006)—§ 24.8(f) n.92

Hoffheimer, The Rise and Fall of Lesser Included Offenses, 36 Rutgers L.J. 351 (2005)—§§ 24.8(e) n.50, 59

Hoffman, Double Jeopardy Wars: The Case for a Civil Rights "Exception," 41 UCLA L.Rev. 649 (1994)—§ 25.5(a) n.17

Hoffman, Peremptory Challenges Should be Abolished: A Trial Judge's Perspective, 64 U.Chi.L.Rev. 809 (1997)—§§ 1.5(j) n.332; 22.3(d) n.166, 258

Hoffman, The Case for Jury Sentencing, 52 Duke L.J. 951 (2003)—§ 26.2(b) n.3

Hoffman, The Drug Court Scandal, 78 N.C.L.Rev. 1437 (2000)—§ 26.1(e) n.104

Hoffman, The Supreme Court's New Vision of Federal Habeas Corpus for State Prisoners, 1989 Sup.Ct.Rev. 165—§ 28.6(c) n.16

Hoffman, Violence and Truth, 76 Ind.L.J. 939 (2001)—§ 1.8(e) n.83

Hoffman & Stuntz, Habeas After the Revolution, 1993 Sup.Ct.Rev. 65—§ 2.8(c) n.85

Hoffman, Kahn & Fisher, Plea Bargaining in the Shadow of Death, 69 Fordham L.Rev. 2313 (2001)—§ 21.2(a) n.2

Hoffman, Rubin, and Shepherd, An Empirical Study of Defender Effectiveness: Self-Selection by the Marginally Indigent, 3 Ohio St. J.Crim.L. 223 (2005)—§§ 1.4(f) n.112; 11.8(c) n.72

Hoffmann, Protecting the Innocent: The Massachusetts Governor's Council Report, 95 J.Crim.L. & Criminology 561 (2005)—§ 27.5(e) n.159

Hoffmann & Stuntz, Habeas After the Revolution, 1993 Sup.Ct.Rev. 65—§§ 28.2(d) n.83, 86

Hoffstadt, How Congress Might Redesign A Leaner, Cleaner Writ of Habeas Corpus, 49 Duke L.J. 947 (2000)—§ 28.2(d) n.80

Hogan & Snee, The McNabb-Mallory Rule: Its Rise, Rationale, and Rescue, 47 Geo.L.J. 1 (1958)—§§ 1.7(i) n.154; 6.3(a) n.2; 6.3(b) n.26 to 28, 34

Holderman, Preindictment Prosecutorial Conduct in the Federal System, 71 J.Crim.L. & Criminology 1 (1980)—§§ 8.7(b) n.56; 8.7(e) n.88; 8.8(g) n.167, 168, 177

Holly, Ambiguous Invocation of the Right to Remain Silent: A Post-Davis Analysis and Proposal, 29 Seton Hall L.Rev. 558 (1998)—§ 6.9(g) n.161

Holman, Multiple Post-Trial Litigation in Criminal Cases, 19 DePaul L.Rev. 490 (1970)—§ 28.11(a) n.5

Holscher, The Legacy of Rock v. Arkansas: Protecting Criminal Defendants' Right to Testify on Their Own Behalf, 19 New Eng.J.Crim. & Civ.Confinement 223 (1993)—§ 24.5(d) n.58

Holtz, The "Plain Touch" Corollary: A Natural and Foreseeable Consequence of the Plain View Doctrine, 95 Dick.L.Rev. 521 (1991)—§ 3.2(b) n.89

Holtzoff, Modern Trends in Trial by Jury, 16 Wash. & Lee L.Rev. 27 (1959)—§ 24.6(e) n.48

Hong, Summation at the Border: Serious Misconduct in Final Argument in Criminal Trials, 20 Hamline L.Rev. 43 (1996)—§ 24.7(e) n.37

Hood, The Right of Appeal, 29 La.L.Rev. 498 (1969)—§ 27.1(a) n.11

Horowitz, Foreword: The State of Federal Prosecution, 43 Am.Crim.L.Rev. 1033 (2006)—§ 1.2(d) n.265

Horowitz, Unseparate but Unequal—The Emerging Fourteenth Amendment Issue in Public Education, 13 UCLA L.Rev. 1147 (1966)—§ 13.4(d) n.151

Horowitz & Lee, The Effects of Note-Taking and Trial Transcript Access on Mock Jury Decisions in a Complex Civil Trial, 25 Law & Human Behav. 373 (2001)—§ 24.9(b) n.17

Horstein, Between a Rock and a Hard Place: The Right to Testify and Impeachment by Prior Conviction, 42 Vill.L.Rev. 1 (1997)—§ 24.5(d) n.56

Horwitz, Taking the Cop Out of Copping a Plea: Eradicating Police Prosecution of Criminal Cases, 40 Ariz.L.Rev. 1305 (1998)—§ 13.1(a) n.4

Howard, Evidence in Federal Criminal Trials, 51 Yale L.J. 763 (1942)—§ 1.7(h) n.143

Howard, State Courts and Constitutional Rights in the Days of the Burger Court, 62 Va.L.Rev. 873 (1976)—§§ 2.12(b) n.104; 2.12(c) n.162

Howard, The Defunding of the Post-Conviction Defense Organizations as a Denial of the Right to Counsel, 98 W.Va.L.Rev. 863 (1996)—§ 11.8(c) n.65

Howe, Juries as Judges of the Criminal Law, 52 Harv.L.Rev. 582 (1939)—§§ 1.5(g) n.260; 1.6(b) n.67, 69; 1.6(c) n.144 to 147; 1.6(d) n.232, 233, 237, 244, 245; 22.1(g) n.121

Hudnut, State Constitutions and Individual Rights: The Case for Judicial Restraint, 63 Denv.U.L.Rev. 85 (1985)—§§ 2.12(a) n.16, 18; 2.12(c) n.124, 145, 153, 167

Hudson, The Crime Victim and the Criminal Justice System: A Time for a Change, 11 Pepp.L.Rev. 23 (1984)—§§ 1.5(k) n.363, 385

Hughes, Administrative Subpoenas and the Grand Jury: Converging the Streams of Criminal and Civil Compulsory Process, 47 Vand.L.Rev. 573 (1994)—§§ 8.1(c) n.41, 43; 8.5(a) n.13; 8.5(c) n.86, 88; 8.5(h) n.282, 288; 8.8(e) n.121, 122

Hughes, Agreements for Cooperation in Criminal Cases, 45 Vand.L.Rev. 1 (1992)—§§ 8.11(e) n.90; 13.5(b) n.36; 21.3(f) n.425

Hughes, English Criminal Justice: Is It Better Than Ours, 26 Ariz.L.Rev. 507 (1984)—§§ 1.5(a) n.39, 48

Hughes, Pleas Without Bargains, 33 Rutgers L.Rev. 753 (1981)—§ 21.2(b) n.46

Humble, Nonevidentiary Use of Compelled Testimony: Beyond the Fifth Amendment, 66 Tex.L.Rev. 351 (1987)—§ 8.11(c) n.34

Hungate, Changes in the Federal Rules of Criminal Procedure, 1975, 61 A.B.A.J. 1203 (1975)—§ 20.1(c) n.44

Hunter, The Man on the Stairs Who Wasn't There: What Does a Defendant's Pre-Arrest Silence Have to Do with Miranda, the Fifth Amendment or Due Process?, 28 Hamline L.Rev. 277 (2005)—§ 9.6(a) n.48

Hutson, The Creation of the Constitution: The Integrity of the Documentary Record, 65 Tex.L.Rev. 65 (1986)—§ 2.9(d) n.58

Hutton, Retroactivity in the States: The Impact of Teague v. Lane on State Post-conviction Remedies, 44 Ala.L.Rev. 421 (1993)—§ 28.11(b) n.15

I

Illovsky, Corporate Deferred Prosecution Agreements, 21 Crim.Just. 36 (Sum.2006)—§ 13.6(a) n.15

Imlay, Federal Jury Reformation: Saving a Democratic Institution, 6 Loyola L.Rev. 247 (1973)—§ 22.3(a) n.34

Imwinkelried, The Application of the Attorney-Client Privilege to Non Testifying Experts: Reestablishing the Boundaries Between the Attorney-Client Privilege and the Work Product Protection, 68 Wash.U.L.Q. 19 (1990)—§§ 20.5(h) n.110 to 113

Imwinkelried, The Worst Surprise of All: No Right to Pretrial Discovery of the Prosecution's Uncharged Misconduct Evidence, 56 Fordham L.Rev. 247 (1987)—§§ 20.1(b) n.40; 20.2(d) n.71; 20.3(h) n.153

Inbau, Police Interrogation—A Practical Necessity, 52 J.Crim.L.C. & P.S. 16 (1961)—§§ 6.1(a) n.2; 6.1(b) n.16

Inevitable Discovery: The Hypothetical Independent Source Exception to the Exclusionary Rule, 5 Hofstra L.Rev. 137 (1976)—§ 9.3(e) n.60

Ingber, Procedure, Ceremony, and Rhetoric: The Minimization of Ideological Conflict in Deviance Control, 56 B.U.L.Rev. 266 (1976)—§ 1.5(h) n.286

Instrument Law: The 1985 Revisions and The Continuing Need For Reform, 38 Baylor L.Rev. 1 (1986)—§ 19.3(e) n.242

Iontcheva, Jury Sentencing as Democratic Practice, 89 Va.L.Rev. 311 (2003)—§§ 26.2(b) n.3, 13

Iraola, Terrorism, Grand Juries, and the Federal Material Witness Statute, 34 St. Mary's L.J. 401 (2003)—§§ 8.7(e) n.88; 12.4(g) n.101

Isbell & Salvi, Investigators and Discrimination Testers: An Analysis of the Provisions Prohibiting Misrepresentation Under the Model Rules of Professional Conduct, 8 Geo.J.Legal Ethics 791 (1995)—§ 6.4(e) n.91

Israel, Criminal Procedure, The Burger Court, and The Legacy of The Warren Court, 75 Mich.L.Rev. 1319 (1977)—§§ 1.6(h) n.443; 2.6(c) n.73; 2.6(d) n.90; 2.8(a) n.30; 2.8(b) n.40 to 43, 56; 7.3(b) n.20, 37; 21.6(a) n.17, 69, 70; 25.2(d) n.34; 28.2(c) n.53

Israel, Excessive Criminal Justice Caseloads: Challenging the Conventional Wisdom, 48 Fla.L.Rev. 761 (1996)—§§ 1.10(c) n.63, 105

Israel, Federal Criminal Procedure as a Model for the States, 543 Annals Am.Acad.Pol. & Soc.Sci. 130 (1996)—§§ 1.3(c) n.21, 31; 1.3(e) n.42, 47

Israel, Free-Standing Due Process and Criminal Procedure: The Supreme Court's Search for Interpretive Guidelines, 45 St. Louis U.L.J. 303 (2001)—§§ 2.4(a) n.13; 2.4(b) n.23; 2.4(c) n.88, 116; 2.4(d) n.119, 122; 2.4(e) n.169; 2.4 n.6; 2.7(a) n.2, 10; 2.7(b) n.74, 83; 2.7(c) n.100

Israel, Gideon v. Wainwright, The "Art" of Overruling, 1963 Sup.Ct.Rev. 211—§§ 2.9(b) n.15, 18, 21, 30; 11.1(a) n.9, 10, 17

Israel, Legislative Regulation of Searches and Seizures: The Michigan Proposals, 73 Mich.L.Rev. 222 (1974)—§ 1.7(e) n.66

Israel, On Recognizing Variations in State Criminal Procedure, 15 Mich.J.L.Ref. 465 (1982)—§§ 1.3(e) n.41, 42

Israel, Selective Incorporation Revisited, 71 Geo.L.J. 253 (1982)—§§ 2.3(a) n.44; 2.3 n.3; 2.4(e) n.150; 2.5(a) n.9; 2.5(c) n.21, 25, 26, 29; 2.5(d) n.35; 2.5(f) n.84, 88, 90, 104; 2.6(a) n.1, 5; 2.6(c) n.83

J

Jackson, Divining Prosecutorial Motives in the Use of Peremptory Challenges: Must the Defendant in a Batson Inquiry be Allowed to Present Rebuttal Evidence?, 35 Loyola L.Rev. 189 (1989)—§ 22.3(d) n.231

Jackson, The Federal Prosecutor, 31 J.Crim.L. & Criminology 3 (1940)—§ 13.2(d) n.85

Jackson, Theories of Truthfinding in Criminal Procedure: An Evolutionary Approach, 10 Cardoza L.Rev. 475 (1988)—§§ 1.5(b) n.75; 1.5(c) n.99

Jacob, Back to Basics: Constitutional Meaning and "Tradition," Tex.Tech.L.Rev. (2007)—§ 2.9(d) n.62

Jacob, Judicial Institutions—Elections, Direct Participation, and Public Attention to the Courts in Wisconsin, 1966 Wis.L.Rev. 801—§ 1.10(e) n.202

Jacob, Keeping Pace: Court Resources and Crime in Ten U.S. Cities, 66 Judicature 73 (1982)—§ 1.10(c) n.50

Jacobson, Reducing the Impact of Juror Discrimination in Interracial Crimes: An Analysis of Turner v. Murray, 5 Law & Inequality 135 (1987)—§ 22.3(a) n.28

Jacoby, The American Prosecutor in Historical Context, 39 Prosecutor 34 (March/April 2005)—§ 1.6(b) n.84

Jaffe, Trial by Newspaper, 40 N.Y.U.L.Rev. 504 (1965)—§ 23.2(f) n.79

James, The Objective and Function of the Complaint, 14 Vand.L.Rev. 899 (1961)—§ 19.1(d) n.41

Jebson, Conditioning a Woman's Freedom on Her Using Norplant, 17 Campbell L.Rev. 301 (1995)—§ 26.9(b) n.55

Jeffries & Gleeson, The Federalization of Organized Crime: Advantages of Federal Prosecution, 46 Hastings L.J. 1135 (1995)—§ 1.2(d) n.229

Jeffries & Stephan, Defenses, Presumptions, and Burden of Proof in Criminal Law, 88 Yale L.J. 1324 (1979)—§ 2.4(a) n.19

Jeffries & Stuntz, Ineffective Assistance and Procedural Default, 57 U.Chi.L.Rev. 679 (1990)—§§ 28.2(d) n.83; 28.3(d) n.90; 28.4(a) n.2, 10; 28.4(d) n.70

Jeffries & Gleeson, The Federalization of Organized Crime: Advantages of Federal Prosecution, 46 Hastings L.J. 1095 (1995)—§§ 1.2(d) n.257; 1.2(f) n.286; 8.2(b) n.21; 8.11(b) n.23; 8.11(d) n.71, 88; 15.2(d) n.115, 117, 119

Jensen & Mosher, Adult Drug Courts: Emergence, Growth, Outcome Evaluations, and the Need for a Continuum of Care, 42 Idaho L.Rev. 443 (2006)—§ 26.1(e) n.104

Jescheck, Principles of German Criminal Procedure in Comparison With American Law, 56 Va.L.Rev. 239 (1970)—§ 1.5(c) n.115

Jessen, Multiple Representation of Criminal Defendants in White Collar Crime Cases, 137 PLI/Crim. 133 (1985)—§ 11.9(c) n.112

Joh, The Paradox of Private Policing, 95 J.Crim.L. & Criminology 49 (2004)—§ 3.1(h) n.210

Johnson, Cross-Racial Identification Errors in Criminal Cases, 69 Cornell L.Rev. 934 (1984)—§ 7.5(a) n.9

Johnson, Race and the Decision to Detain a Suspect, 93 Yale L.J. 214 (1983)—§§ 1.5(j) n.316, 320

Johnson, Racial Imagery in Criminal Cases, 67 Tulane L.Rev. 1739 (1993)—§ 24.7(e) n.61

Johnson, Retroactivity in Retrospect, 56 Calif.L.Rev. 1612 (1968)—§ 2.11(a) n.6

Johnson, The Role of Penal Quarantine in Reducing Violent Crime, 24 Crime & Delinq. 465 (1978)—§ 1.5(a) n.49

Johnson & Wiggins, Videoconferencing in Criminal Proceedings: Legal and Empirical Issues and Directions for Research, 28 Law & Policy 211 (2006)—§§ 24.2(f) n.83, 88

Johnston, The Grand Jury—Prosecutorial Abuse of the Indictment Process, 65 J.Crim.L. & Criminology 157 (1974)—§ 15.5(a) n.2

Joiner & Miller, Rules of Procedure: A Study of Judicial Rule-Making, 55 Mich.L.Rev. 623 (1957)—§ 1.7(f) n.99

Jonakait, "Witnesses" In The Confrontation Clause: Crawford v. Washington, Noah Webster and Compulsory Process, 70 Temp.L.Rev. 155 (2006)—§ 2.1 n.60

Jones, Evidence Destroyed, Innocence Lost; The Preservation of Biological Evidence Under Innocence Statutes, 42 Am.Crim.L.Rev. 1239 (2005)—§ 1.5(e) n.235

Joo, Presumed Disloyal: Executive Power, Judicial Deference, and the Construction of Race Before and After September 11, 34 Colum.Hum.Rts.L.Rev. 1 (2002)—§ 3.9(h) n.163

Joseph, Speedy Trial Rights in Application, 48 Fordham L.Rev. 611 (1980)—§§ 18.1(a) n.5; 18.1(d) n.47; 18.2(b) n.11, 27; 18.3(c) n.61, 63, 66, 92

Judges, Two Cheers for the Department of Justice's Eyewitness Evidence: A Guide for Law Enforcement, 53 Ark.L.Rev. 231 (2000)—§ 7.5(c) n.44

Junker, The Right to Counsel in Misdemeanor Cases, 43 Wash.L.Rev. 685 (1968)—§ 11.2(a) n.7

Junker, The Structure of the Fourth Amendment: The Scope of the Protection, 79 J.Crim.L. & Criminology 1105 (1989)—§§ 3.1(h) n.198; 3.2(a) n.18

Jurow, New Data on the Effect of a "Death-Qualified" Jury on the Guilt Determination Process, 84 Harv.L.Rev. 567 (1971)—§ 22.3(c) n.158

Jurow, Untimely Thoughts: A Reconsideration of the Origins of Due Process of Law, 19 Am.J. Legal Hist. 265 (1975)—§§ 2.4(b) n.25, 27, 33, 51

K

Kaczorowski, Searching for the Intent of the Framers of the Fourteenth Amendment, 5 Conn.L.Rev. 366 (1972)—§ 2.3(a) n.61

Kadish, Behind the Locked Door of An American Grand Jury: Its History, Its Secrecy, and Its Process, 24 Fla.St.U.L.Rev. 1 (1996)—§§ 8.5(a) n.2; 8.5(e) n.172, 173; 8.5(h) n.275, 288; 8.5(i) n.311

Kadish, Codifiers of the Criminal Law: Wechster's Predecessors, 78 Colum.L.Rev. 1098 (1978)—§§ 1.6(d) n.269, 270, 275

Kadish, Legal Norm and Discretion in the Police and Sentencing Processes, 75 Harv.L.Rev. 904 (1962)—§§ 1.6(d) n.270; 1.9(c) n.48; 1.9(d) n.98, 106, 107; 13.2(b) n.44, 45

Kadish, Methodology and Criteria in Due Process Adjudication—A Survey and Criticism, 66 Yale L.J. 319 (1957)—§§ 1.5(a) n.62; 1.5(h) n.282; 2.4(a) n.13; 2.4(e) n.166, 169; 2.7(c) n.152, 153

Kadish, The Folly of Over-Federalization, 46 Hastings L.J. 1247 (1995)—§ 1.2(d) n.203

Kadish, Torture, The State and The Individual, 23 Israel L.Rev. 345 (1989)—§ 1.5(a) n.15

Kadish & Kadish, On Justified Rule Departures by Officials, 59 Calif.L.Rev. 905 (1971)—§ 22.1(g) n.120

Kahan, Reciprocity, Collective Action, and Community Policing, 90 Cal.L.Rev. 1513 (2002)—§ 1.10(e) n.220

Kahan, What Do Alternative Sanctions Mean, 63 U.Chi.L.Rev. 591 (1996)—§ 26.9(b) n.78

Kahan & Meares, The Coming Crises of Criminal Procedure, 86 Geo.L.J. 1153 (1998)—§§ 1.5(j) n.320; 1.9(d) n.97; 1.9(e) n.119; 2.8(c) n.67

Kalt, Crossing Eight Mile: Juries of the Vicinage and County Line Criminal Buffer Statutes, 80 Wash.L.Rev. 277 (2005)—§§ 16.1(e) n.172, 192

Kalt, The Exclusion of Felons from Jury Service, 53 Am.U.L.Rev. 65 (2003)—§ 22.2(b) n.19

Kalven, Invoking the Fifth Amendment—Some Legal and Impractical Considerations, 9 Bull.Atomic Sci. 181—§ 2.10(d) n.104

Kamin, Harmless Error and the Right/ Remedies Split, 88 Va.L.Rev. 1 (2002)—§ 27.6(d) n.139

Kamisar, A Dissent From the Miranda Dissents: Some Comments on the "New Fifth Amendment and the Old 'Voluntariness' Test," 65 Mich.L.Rev. 59 (1966)—§ 1.6(b) n.102

Kamisar, Brewer v. Williams, Massiah, and Miranda: What is "Interrogation"? When Does it Matter?, 67 Geo.L.J. 1 (1978)—§§ 6.10(b) n.30; 7.3(b) n.24

Kamisar, "Comparative Reprehensibility" and the Fourth Amendment Exclusionary Rule, 86 Mich.L.Rev. 1 (1987)—§§ 1.5(a) n.49, 61; 3.1(c) n.85

Kamisar, Does (Did) (Should) The Exclusionary Rule Rest On A "Principled Basis" Rather Than An "Empirical Proposition," 16 Creighton L.Rev. 565 (1983)—§§ 1.5(a) n.57, 58; 3.1(b) n.26

Kamisar, Duckworth v. Eagan: A Little-Noticed Miranda Case That May Cause Much Mischief, 25 Crim.L.Bull. 550 (1989)—§ 6.8(a) n.19

Kamisar, Foreword: From Miranda to § 3501 to Dickerson to ..., 99 Mich.L.Rev. 879 (2001)—§§ 2.9(h) n.255; 6.5(e) n.95, 99

Kamisar, Gates, "Probable Cause," "Good Faith," and Beyond, 69 Iowa L.Rev. 551 (1984)— §§ 2.11(c) n.40; 3.3(c) n.80

Kamisar, Has the Court Left the Attorney General Behind? The Bazelon-Katzenbach Letters on Poverty, Equality and the Administration of Criminal Justice, 54 Ky.L.J. 464 (1966)—§ 1.5(j) n.317

Kamisar, How to Use, Abuse, and Fight Back With—Crime Statistics, 25 Okla.L.Rev. 239 (1972)—§ 1.5(a) n.44

Kamisar, Illegal Searches or Seizures and Contemporaneous Incriminating Statements: A Dialogue on a Neglected Area of Criminal Proce-

dure, 1961 U.Ill.L.F. 78, 100-01—
§ 9.5(c) n.60

Kamisar, Kauper's "Judicial Examination of the Accused": Forty Years Later—Some Comments on a Remarkable Article, 73 Mich.L.Rev. 15 (1974)—§ 1.6(f) n.364

Kamisar, Miranda Thirty-Five Years Later: A Closer Look at the Majority and Dissenting Opinions in Dickerson, 33 Ariz.St.L.J. 387 (2001)—§§ 2.9(h) n.206, 253; 6.5(e) n.95

Kamisar, On the "Fruits" of Miranda Violations, Coerced Confessions, and Compelled Testimony, 93 Mich.L.Rev. 929 (1995)—§ 2.10(b) n.23

Kamisar, On the Tactics of Police-Prosecutor Oriented Critics of the Courts, 49 Cornell L.Q. 436 (1964)—§ 1.6(g) n.415

Kamisar, Postscript: Another Look at Patane and Seibert, the 2004 "Poisoned Fruit" Cases, 2 Ohio St.J.Crim.L. 97 (2004)—§§ 9.5(b) n.48; 9.5(c) n.72

Kamisar, Public Safety v. Individual Liberties: Some "Facts" and "Theories," 53 J.Crim.L.C. & P.S. 171 (1962)—§§ 3.1(c) n.38, 39

Kamisar, Remembering the "Old World" of Criminal Procedure: A Reply to Professor Grano, 23 U.Mich.J.L.Ref. 337 (1990)—§§ 1.5(d) n.201; 1.5(h) n.296; 6.2(d) n.204

Kamisar, The Right to Counsel and The Fourteenth Amendment, 30 U.Chi.L.Rev. 1 (1962)—§§ 11.1(a) n.16, 18

Kamisar, The Warren Court and Criminal Justice: A Quarter Century Retrospective, 31 Tulsa L.J. 1 (1995)—§§ 2.8(a) n.30; 2.8(b) n.39, 44; 2.8(c) n.84; 2.9(b) n.42, 43

Kamisar, The Wiretapping-Eavesdropping Problem: A Professor's View, 44 Minn.L.Rev. 891 (1960)—§ 3.2(i) n.216

Kanner, Welcome Home Rambo: High-Minded Ethics and Low-Down Tactics In The Courts, 25 Loy.L.A.L.Rev. 81 (1991)—§§ 24.7(g) n.81; 24.7(i) n.97

Kaplan, The Limits of the Exclusionary Rule, 26 Stan.L.Rev. 1027 (1974)—§§ 1.5(a) n.53; 3.1(c) n.48, 80, 86, 88

Kaplan, The Prosecutorial Discretion—A Comment, 60 Nw.U.L.Rev. 174 (1965)—§§ 13.1(b) n.35, 36; 13.2(a) n.7

Kaplan & Greene, The Legislature's Relationship to Judicial Rulemaking, 65 Harv.L.Rev. 234 (1951)—§ 1.7(f) n.94

Kappler, Small Favors: Chapter 154 of the Antiterrorism and Effective Death Penalty Act, the States, and the Right to Counsel, 90 J.Crim.L. & Criminology 469 (2000)—§ 28.8(b) n.16

Karlan, Contingent Fees in Criminal Cases, 93 Colum.L.Rev. 595 (1993)—§ 11.9(a) n.14

Karlan, Discrete and Relational Criminal Representation: The Changing Vision of the Right to Counsel, 105 Harv.L.Rev. 670 (1992)—§§ 11.9(a) n.9, 42; 11.9(c) n.103

Karle & Sager, Are the Federal Sentencing Guidelines Meeting Congressional Goals?: An Empirical and Case Law Analysis, 40 Emory L.J. 393 (1991)—§ 26.3(b) n.7

Karmen, Who's Against Victims' Rights? The Nature of the Opposition to Pro-Victim Initiatives in Criminal Justice, 8 St. John's J. Legal Comment. 157 (1992)—§§ 1.5(k) n.360, 363, 367, 369, 385

Katkin, "Incorporation" of the Criminal Procedure Amendments: The View From the States, 84 Neb.L.Rev. 397 (2005)—§§ 2.5(f) n.91; 2.12(a) n.3

Katyal & Tribe, Waging War, Deciding Guilt: Trying the Military Tribunals, 111 Yale L.J. 1259 (2002)— § 28.2(a) n.18

Katz, In Search of the Fourth Amendment for the Twenty-First Century, 65 Ind.L.J. 549 (1990)— § 3.2(a) n.26

Katzer & Wishart, The Impact of Judicial Commentary Concerning Eyewitness Identifications on Jury Decision Making, 76 J.Crim.L. & Criminology. 733 (1985)—§ 7.5(a) n.3

Kauger, Reflections on Federalism: Protections Afforded by State Constitutions, 27 Gonz.L.Rev. 1 (1991)— § 2.12(c) n.179

Kauper, Judicial Examination of the Accused—A Remedy For the Third Degree, 30 Mich.L.Rev. 1224 (1932)—§§ 1.6(b) n.102; 1.6(c) n.155; 1.6(f) n.364

Kavanaugh, Improvement of Administration of Criminal Justice by Exercise of Judicial Power, 11 A.B.A.J. 217 (1925)—§ 27.6(a) n.6

Kay, "Originalist," Values and Constitutional Interpretation, 19 Harv.J.L. & Pub.Pol'y. 335 (1996)—§ 2.9(d) n.63

Kay, The Rulemaking Authority and the Separation of Powers in Connecticut, 8 Conn.L.Rev. 1 (1974)— § 1.7(f) n.94

Kaye, And Then There Were Twelve: Statistical Reasoning, the Supreme Court, and the Size of the Jury, 68 Calif.L.Rev. 1004 (1980)— § 22.1(d) n.77

Kaye, The Constitutionality of DNA Sampling on Arrest, 10 Cornell J.L. & Pub.Pol'y 455 (2001)—§§ 3.5(d) n.151, 152, 155, 159, 162, 163

Kaye, Two Fallacies About DNA Data Banks for Law Enforcement, 67 Brooklyn L.Rev. 179 (2001)— § 3.5(d) n.160

Kaye, Who Needs Special Needs? On the Constitutionality of Collecting DNA and Other Biometric Data From Arrestees, 34 J.L.Med. & Ethics 188 (2006)—§§ 3.5(d) n.153, 155, 163, 164

Keefe & O'Reilly, The Police and the Rape Victim in New York, 1 Victimology, An Int'l J. 272 (1976)— § 1.5(k) n.391

Keeney and Walsh, The American Bar Association's Grand Jury Principles: A Critique From A Federal Criminal Justice Perspective, 14 Idaho L.Rev. 545 (1978)—§§ 8.2(c) n.39; 8.3(d) n.23; 8.11(b) n.24; 15.2(d) n.118

Kelley, The Fourteenth Amendment Reconsidered: The Segregation Question, 54 Mich.L.Rev. 1049 (1956)—§ 2.3(a) n.71

Kelly, Have Victim Reforms Gone Too Far—Or Not Far Enough, 6 Crim.Just. 22 (1991)—§§ 1.5(k) n.337, 361, 368, 373

Kelso, Special Report on California Appellate Justice: A Report on the California Appellate System, 45 Hastings L.J. 433 (1994)— §§ 27.1(a) n.12; 27.5(e) n.172

Kemmitt, Function Over Form: Reviving the Criminal Jury's Historical Role As A Sentencing Body, 40 U.Mich.J.L.Ref. 93 (2006)— § 22.1(g) n.105

Kennedy, The State, Criminal Law, and Racial Discrimination: A Comment, 107 Harv.L.Rev. 1255 (1994)— § 1.5(j) n.320

Kennedy & Swire, State Wiretaps and Electronic Surveillance After September 11, 54 Hastings L.J. 971(2003)—§ 4.6(c) n.53

Kennelly, Multiple Representations in Grand Jury Investigations, 16 Litigation 27 (1990)—§ 8.14(d) n.40

Kerr, A User's Guide to the Stored Communications Act, and A Legislator's Guide to Amending It, 72 Geo. Wash. L. Rev. 1208 (2004)—

§§ 4.8(a) n.1; 4.8(d) n.36; 4.8(e) n.44

Kerr, Internet Surveillance After the USA PATRIOT Act: The Big Brother That Isn't, 97 Nw. U. L. Rev. 607 (2003)—§§ 4.4(a) n.1; 4.4(b) n.5; 4.7(a) n.3

Kerr, Lifting the "Fog" of Internet Surveillance: How A Suppression Remedy Would Change Computer Crime Law, 54 Hastings L.J. 805 (2003)—§ 4.8(b) n.19

Kerr, Search Warrants in an Era of Digital Evidence, 75 Miss.L.J. 85 (2005)—§ 3.4(g) n.124

Kerr, Searches and Seizures in a Digital World, 119 Harv.L.Rev. 531 (2005)—§ 3.4(j) n.202

Kerr, The Fourth Amendment in Cyberspace: Can Encryption Create a Reasonable Expectation of Privacy?, 33 Conn. L. Rev. 505 (2001)—§ 4.3(b) n.11

Kerr, The Problem of Perspective In Internet Law, 91 Geo. L.J. 357 (2003)—§ 4.4(a) n.2

Kerr, Kramer, Carroll, and Alfini, On The Effectiveness of Voir Dire In Criminal Cases With Prejudicial Publicity: An Empirical Study, 40 Am.U.L.Rev. 665 (1991)—§ 23.2(f) n.80

Kershen, Vicinage, 29 Okla.L.Rev. 801 (1976)—§§ 16.1(b) n.30, 39, 40, 42, 44 to 46, 48, 49, 51, 52, 55 to 57, 59, 63, 69, 73, 74, 76, 79, 82, 84, 86; 16.1(c) n.119, 121, 122; 16.3(g) n.112

Kershen, Vicinage, 30 Okla.L.Rev. 1 (1977)—§§ 16.1(a) n.23; 16.1(b) n.30, 82; 16.1(c) n.129; 22.2(e) n.99

Khanna, Corporate Criminal Liability: What Purpose Does it Serve?, 109 Harv.L.Rev. 1477 (1996)—§ 11.4(c) n.99

Khanna, Double Jeopardy's Asymmetric Appeal Rights: What Purpose Do They Serve, 82 B.U.L.Rev. 341 (2002)—§ 27.3(a) n.9

Khanna & Dickinson, The Corporate Monitor: The New Corporate Czar?, 105 Mich.L.Rev. 1713 (2007)—§ 13.6(a) n.12

King, Batson for the Bench? Regulating the Peremptory Challenge of Judges, 73 Chi-Kent L.Rev. 509 (1998)—§ 22.4(d) n.45

King, Book Review, 26 Colum.L.Rev. 17 (1995)—§ 23.1(a) n.4

King, et al., When Process Affects Punishment: Differences in Sentences After Guilty Plea, Bench Trial, and Jury Trial in Five Guidelines States, 105 Colum.L.Rev. 959 (2005)—§ 24.6(a) n.9

King, Judicial Oversight of Negotiated Sentences in a World of Bargained Punishment, 58 Stan.L.Rev. 293 (2005)—§ 1.9(b) n.31

King, Jury Delinquency in Criminal Trials in America, 1796-1976, 94 Mich.L.Rev. 2673 (1996)—§§ 1.6(d) n.225, 250, 261, 266; 1.6(f) n.344; 24.9(a) n.3; 24.9(c) n.19; 24.9(f) n.76, 100

King, Nameless Justice: The Case For Routine Use of Anonymous Juries in Criminal Trials, 49 Vand.L.Rev. 123 (1996)—§§ 22.3(b) n.66, 70; 23.1(c) n.103; 23.1(d) n.191; 24.9(g) n.129

King, Portioning Punishment: Constitutional Limits on Successive and Excessive Penalties, 144 U.Pa.L.Rev. 101 (1995)—§§ 25.1(c) n.29, 41

King, Postconviction Review of Jury Discrimination: Measuring the Effects of Juror Race on Jury Decisions, 92 Mich.L.Rev. 62 (1993)—§§ 15.4(i) n.204; 22.3(d) n.254

King, Priceless Process: Nonnegotiable Features of Criminal Litigation, 47 UCLA L.Rev. 113 (1999)—§§ 11.7(e) n.113; 16.1(a) n.28; 21.2(b) n.91; 27.5(c) n.52

King, Racial Jurymandering: Cancer or Cure? A Contemporary Review of Affirmative Action in Jury Selection, 68 N.Y.U.L.Rev. 707 (1993)—§§ 1.5(j) n.316, 333; 15.4(c) n.96; 16.3(g) n.107, 109, 114; 22.2(d) n.90, 93

King, Regulating Settlement: What Is Left of the Rule of Law in the Criminal Process, 88 DePaul L.Rev. 389 (2007)—§ 1.5(e) n.236

King, Silencing Jury Nullification Advocacy Inside the Jury Room and Outside the Courtroom, 65 U.Chi.L.Rev. 433 (1998)—§§ 1.6(b) n.62; 22.1(g) n.108, 112; 24.7(e) n.49; 24.9(f) n.75, 104, 106; 24.10(a) n.4; 26.3(b) n.12

King, The American Criminal Jury, 62 Law & Contemp.Prob. 41 (Spring 1999)—§ 22.3(b) n.59

King The Origins of Jury Sentencing in the United States, 78 Chi.Kent L.Rev. 937 (2003)—§§ 1.6(b) n.29; 1.6(c) n.168; 26.2(b) n.13

King, When Process Affects Punishment: Differences in Sentences After Guilty Plea, Bench Trial, and Jury Trial in Five Guideline States, 105 Column.L.Rev. 959 (2005)—§ 1.3(c) n.29

King, Why Prosecutors Are Permitted to Offer Witness Inducements: A Matter of Constitutional Authority, 29 Stetson L.Rev. 155 (1999)—§ 21.2(b) n.71

King & Klein, Apprendi and Plea Bargaining, 54 Stan.L.Rev. 289 (2001)—§ 26.4(i) n.170

King and Klein, Apres Apprendi, 14 Fed. Sentencing Reptr. 165 (2002)—§§ 19.2(e) n.60, 64, 66 to 68

King & Klein, Essential Elements, 54 Vand.L.Rev. 1467 (2001)—§§ 19.2(e) n.71; 22.1(a) n.28; 26.4(i) n.169

King & Munsterman, Stratified Jury Selection, Cross-Section by Design, 79 Judicature 273 (1996)—§ 22.2(d) n.96

King & Noble, Felony Jury Sentencing in Practice: A Three-State Study, 57 Vand.L.Rev. 885 (2004)—§§ 1.3(c) n.29; 1.10(a) n.7, 10; 24.6(a) n.6; 26.2(b) n.13, 17

King & O'Neill, Appeal Waiver and the Future of Sentencing Policy, 55 Duke L.J. 209 (2005)—§§ 11.7(e) n.112; 26.3(g) n.95; 27.5(c) n.52, 53, 59, 63, 64

King, Soule, Steen & Weidner, When Process Affects Punishment: Differences in Sentences After Guilty Plea, Bench Trial, and Jury Trial in Five Guideline States, 105 Column.L.Rev. 959 (2005)—§§ 1.10(a) n.7; 22.1(h) n.142, 143

Kingsnorth, Cummings, Lopez & Wentworth, Criminal Sentencing and the Court Probation Office: The Myth of Individualized Justice Revisited, 20 Just.Sys.J. 255 (1999)—§ 26.5(b) n.38

Kipnis, Plea Bargaining: A Critic's Rejoinder, 13 Law & Soc.Rev. 555 (1979)—§ 21.1(b) n.36

Kipperman, Inaccurate Search Warrant Affidavits as a Ground for Suppressing Evidence, 84 Harv.L.Rev. 825 (1971)—§ 3.4(d) n.57

Kirchmeier, Drink, Drugs, and Drowsiness: The Constitutional Right to Assistance of Counsel and the Strickland Prejudice Requirement, 75 Neb.L.Rev. 425 (1996)—§ 11.10(d) n.199

Kirchmeir, Drink, Drugs, and Drowsiness: The Constitutional Right to Effective Assistance of Counsel and the Strickland Prejudice Requirement, 75 Neb.L.Rev. 425 (1996)—§ 11.8(c) n.78

Kissel, Crime and Punishment—Victims Rights Movement Presses Courts, Legislatures, 70 A.B.A.J. 25 (Jan. 1984)—§ 1.5(k) n.362

Kitch, Katz v. United States: The Limits of the Fourth Amendment, 1968 Sup.Ct.Rev. 133—§§ 3.2(a) n.14, 16

Kitch, The Supreme Court's Code of Criminal Procedure 1968-69 Edition, 1969 Sup.Ct.Rev. 155—§§ 2.1 n.3; 2.9(g) n.191; 27.6(c) n.63

Klarman, An Interpretative History of Modern Equal Protection, 90 Mich.L.Rev. 213 (1991)—§ 1.5(j) n.318

Klarman, The Racial Origins of Modern Criminal Procedure, 99 Mich.L.Rev. 48 (2000)—§§ 2.4(d) n.130; 2.8(c) n.67

Klein, District Attorney's Discretion Not to Prosecute, 32 L.A.B.Bull. 323 (1957)—§ 13.2(a) n.7

Klein, Double Jeopardy's Demise, 88 Calif.L.Rev. 1001 (2000)—§ 26.3(b) n.11

Klein, Due Process Denied: Judicial Coercion and the Plea Bargaining Process, 32 Hofstra L.Rev. 1349 (2004)—§ 21.2(c) n.116

Klein, Identifying and (Re)Formulating Prophylactic Rules, Safe Harbors, and Incidental Rights in Constitutional Criminal Procedure, 99 Mich.L.Rev. 1030 (2001)—§§ 2.9(h) n.253; 6.5(e) n.96

Klein, Independent-Norm Federalism in Criminal law, 90 Cal.L.Rev. 1541 (2002)—§ 1.4(b) n.27

Klein, Miranda's Exceptions in a Post-Dickerson World, 91 J.Crim.L. & Crimin. 567 (2001)—§ 6.5(e) n.96

Klein, The Constitutionalization of Ineffective Assistance of Counsel, 58 Md.L.Rev. 1433 (1999)—§ 11.10(a) n.16

Klein, The Eleventh Commandment: Thou Shalt Not be Compelled to Render Ineffective Assistance of Counsel, 68 Ind.L.J. 363 (1993)—§ 11.8(c) n.65

Klein, The Emperor Gideon Has No Clothes: The Empty Promise of the Constitutional Right to Effective Assistance of Counsel, 13 Hast.Con.L.Q. 625 (1987)—§§ 11.7(d) n.62; 11.10(a) n.16

Klein, The Return of Federal Judicial Discretion in Criminal Sentencing, 39 Val.U.L.Rev. 693 (2005)—§ 21.1(h) n.244

Kline, Independent-Norm Federalism in Criminal Law, 90 Cal.L.Rev. 541 (2002)—§ 1.2(d) n.201

Kline, The Politicalization of Crime, 46 Hastings L.Rev. 1087 (1995)—§ 1.4(h) n.177

Knapp, Allocation of Discretion and Accountability Within Sentencing Structures, 64 U.Colo.L.Rev. 679 (1993)—§ 26.1(c) n.44

Kobil, Due Process in Death Penalty Commutations: Life, Liberty, and the Pursuit of Clemency, 27 U.Rich.L.Rev. 201 (1993)—§ 26.2(c) n.76

Kobil, The Quality of Mercy Strained: Wresting the Pardoning Power from the King, 69 Tex.L.Rev. 569 (1991)—§ 26.2(c) n.69

Koehn, A Line in the Sand: The Supreme Court and the Writ of Habeas Corpus, 32 Tulsa L.J. 389 (1997)—§ 28.2(a) n.11

Koniak, The Law Between the Bar and the State, 70 N.C.L.Rev. 1389 (1992)—§ 8.8(d) n.101

Konradi, Too Little, Too Late: Prosecutor's Pre-Court Preparation of Rape Survivors, 22 Law & Soc.Inquiry 1 (1997)—§ 24.4(d) n.34

Kousser, Expert Witnesses, Rational Choice, and the Search for Intent, 5 Const.Com. 349 (1988)—§ 2.9(d) n.58

Kozinski, That Can of Worms: The Speedy Trial Act, 62 A.B.A.J. 862 (1976)—§ 18.3(b) n.2

Kozinski & Sussman, Original Mean-[der]ings, 49 Stan. L.Rev. 1583 (1997)—§ 2.9(d) n.58

Krantz, Pretrial Discovery in Criminal Cases: A Necessity for Fair and Impartial Justice, 42 Neb.L.Rev. 12-7 (1963)—§ 20.1(b) n.20

Krasity, The Role of the Judge in Jury Trials: The Elimination of Judicial Evaluation of Fact in American State Courts From 1796-1913, 62 U.Det.L.Rev. 595 (1985)—§ 24.6(e) n.48

Krauss, An Inquiry Into the Right of Criminal Juries to Determine the Law in Colonial America, 67 J. Crim. L. & Criminology III (1998)—§ 1.6(b) n.67

Krauss, Death-Qualification After Wainwright v. Witt: The Issues in Gray v. Mississippi, 65 Wash.U.L.Q. 507 (1987)—§§ 22.3(c) n.144, 151

Kreimer, The Law of Choice and Choice of Law: Aborting the Right to Travel and Extraterritorial Regulation in American Federalism, 67 N.Y.U.L.Rev. 451 (1992)—§ 2.6(b) n.58

Kreimer & Rudousky, Double Helix, Double Bind: Factual Innocence and Postconviction DNA Testing, 151 U.Pa.L.Re. 547 (2002)—§§ 1.5(e) n.235; 28.3(e) n.104

Krent, Conditioning the President's Conditional Pardon Power, 89 Cal.L.Rev. 1665 (2001)—§ 26.2(c) n.69

Krent, Executive Control Over Criminal Law Enforcement: Some Lessons From History, 38 Am.U.L.Rev. 275 (1989)—§§ 1.2(c) n.49, 50, 53, 56

Kress, Progress and Prosecution, 403 Annals Am.Acad.Pol. & Soc.Sci. 99 (1976)—§ 1.6(b) n.78

Krey, Characteristic Features of German Criminal Proceedings—An Alternative to the Criminal Procedure Law of the United States?, 21 Loy.L.A.Int'l. & Comp.L.J. 591

(1999)—§ 1.2(a) n.1

Kruse, The Historical Meaning and Judicial Construction of the Establishment of Religion Clause of the First Amendment, 2 Washburn L.Rev. 65 (1962)—§ 2.3(a) n.30

Kuckee, The Useful, Dangerous Fiction of Grand Jury Independence, 41 Am.Crim.L.Rev. 1 (2004)—§ 8.2(c) n.30

Kuckes, Civil Due Process, Criminal Due Process, 25 Yale L. & Pol'y.Rev. 1 (2006)—§§ 2.7(a) n.10; 2.7(b) n.83; 14.2(a) n.8

Kuckes, The Democratic Prosecutor: Explaining the Constitutional Function of the Federal Grand Jury, 94 Geo.L.J. 1265 (2006)—§§ 15.2(g) n.180; 15.6(b) n.71

Kuckes, The Useful, Dangerous Fiction of Grand Jury Independence, 41 Am.Crim.L.Rev. 1 (2004)—§§ 8.2(c) n.37; 8.4(b) n.18; 15.3(d) n.73; 15.5(a) n.29

Kuh, Interrogation of Criminal Defendants—Some Views on Miranda v. Arizona, 35 Fordham L.Rev. 233 (1966)—§ 6.9(b) n.43

Kuh, Plea Bargaining: Guidelines for the Manhattan District Attorney's Office, 11 Crim.L.Bull. 48 (1975)—§ 1.7(j) n.217

Kuh, Plea Copping, 24 N.Y.Co. Bar Bull. 160 (1966-67)—§§ 21.1(f) n.109, 111

Kuh, The Grand Jury "Presentment": Foul Blow or Fair Play?, 55 Colum.L.Rev. 1103 (1955)—§ 8.3(h) n.38

Kuhns, Limiting the Criminal Contempt Power: New Rules for the Prosecutor and Grand Jury, 73 Mich.L.Rev. 483 (1975)—§ 15.1(b) n.86

Kunnert, Some Observations on the Origin and Structure of Evidence Rules Under the Common Law System and the Civil Law System of "Free Proof" in the German Code of Civil Procedure, 16 Buff.L.Rev. 122

(1966)—§ 1.5(c) n.115

Kunstler, Jury Nullification in Conscience Cases, 10 Va.J.Int'l L. 71 (1969)—§ 22.1(g) n.121

Kurki, Restorative and Community Justice in the United States, 27 Crime & Just. 135 (2000)—§ 26.1(a) n.5

Kurland, Earl Warren, The "Warren Court," and the Warren Myths, 67 Mich.L.Rev. 353 (1968)—§ 2.1 n.1

Kurland, First Principles of American Federalism and the Nature of Federal Criminal Jurisdiction, 45 Emory L.J. 1 (1966)—§§ 1.2(c) n.25, 26, 36, 38, 78

Kurland, Providing a Federal Criminal Defendant With a Unilateral Right to a Bench Trial: A Renewed Call to Amend Federal Rule of Criminal Procedure 23(a), 26 U.C.Davis L.Rev. 309 (1993)—§§ 24.6(a) n.7, 10

L

Labbe, Appellate Review of Sentences: Penology on the Judicial Doorstep, 68 J.Crim.L. & Criminology 122 (1977)—§§ 26.3(g) n.77, 81

Lacharias, Structuring The Ethics of Prosecutorial Trial Practice, 44 Vand.L.Rev. 44 (1991)—§ 24.7(i) n.98

Lacy, The Bill of Rights and the Fourteenth Amendment: The Evolution of the Absorption Doctrine, 23 Wash. & Lee L.Rev. 37 (1966)—§§ 2.5(c) n.21, 25; 2.6(a) n.1

LaFave, Alternatives to the Present Bail System, 1965 U.Ill.L.F. 8—§§ 12.5(a) n.7, 10, 12, 14

LaFave, "Case-by-Case Adjudication" Versus "Standardized Procedures": The Robinson Dilemma, 1974 S.Ct.Rev. 127—§§ 2.9(g) n.174; 3.5(b) n.81

LaFave, Constitutional Rules for Police: A Matter of Style, 41 Syracuse L.Rev. 849 (1990)—§§ 2.9(g) n.153, 157

LaFave, Controlling Discretion by Administrative Regulations: The Use, Misuse, and Nonuse of Police Rules and Policies in Fourth Amendment Adjudication, 89 Mich.L.Rev. 442 (1990)—§§ 1.7(i) n.180; 1.7(j) n.216, 234; 1.9(e) n.132, 139; 3.1(c) n.87; 3.7(e) n.105

LaFave, Fourth Amendment Vagaries (Of Improbable Cause, Imperceptible Plain View, Notorious Privacy, and Balancing Askew), 74 J.Crim.L. & Criminology 1171 (1983)—§ 1.5(a) n.41

LaFave, "Street Encounters" and the Constitution, 67 Mich.L.Rev. 39 (1968)—§§ 6.6(c) n.18, 25

LaFave, The Forgotten Motto of Obsta Principus in Fourth Amendment Jurisprudence, 28 Ariz.L.Rev. 291 (1986)—§ 2.8(a) n.10

LaFave, The Fourth Amendment in an Imperfect World: On Drawing "Bright Lines" and "Good Faith," 43 U.Pitt.L.Rev. 307 (1982)—§§ 2.9(g) n.174; 3.1(c) n.50

LaFave, Warrantless Searches and the Supreme Court: Further Ventures Into the "Quagmire," 8 Crim.L.Bull. 9 (1972)—§ 3.6(a) n.19

Lain, Accuracy Where it Matters: Brady v. Maryland in the Plea Bargaining Context, 80 Wash.U.L.Q. 1 (2002)—§ 24.3(b) n.77

Lain, Countermajoritarian Hero or Zero? Rethinking the Warren Court's Role in the Criminal Procedure Revolution, 152 U.Pa.L.Rev. 1361 (2004)—§ 2.8(b) n.39

Landers, Prosecutorial Limits on Overlapping Federal and State Jurisdiction, 543 Annals Am.Acad.Pol. & Soc.Sci. 64 (1996)—§§ 1.2(d) n.235, 237, 240

Landes & Posner, Harmless Error, 30 J.Leg.Stud. 161 (2001)—§ 27.6(d) n.139

Landis & Goodstein, When Is Justice Fair: An Integrated Approach to the Outcome v. Procedure Debate, 1986 Am.B.Found.Res.J. 675—§§ 1.5(a) n.33; 1.5(c) n.156; 1.5(i) n.302

Landsberg, Safeguarding Constitutional Rights: The Uses and Limits of Prophylactic Rules, 66 Tenn.L.Rev. 925 (1999)—§§ 2.9(h) n.212, 253

Landynski, Due Process and the Concept of Ordered Liberty, 2 Hofstra L.Rev. 1 (1974)—§§ 2.3(b) n.90; 2.5(c) n.21, 22

Lane-Reticker, Nolo Contendere in North Carolina, 34 N.C.L.Rev. 280 (1956)—§ 21.4(a) n.28

Langbein, Chancelor Kent and The History of Legal Literature, 93 Colum.L.Rev. 547 (1993)—§ 1.6(c) n.131

Langbein, Land Without Plea Bargaining: How the Germans Do It, 78 Mich.L.Rev. 204 (1979)—§ 21.1(b) n.9

Langbein, Mixed Court and Jury Court: Could the Continental Alternative Fill the American Need, 1981 Am.B.Found.Res.J. 193—§§ 1.5(c) n.115; 1.5(g) n.268, 274

Langbein, The Criminal Trial Before Lawyers, 43 U.Chi.L.Rev. 363 (1978)—§ 1.6(b) n.55

Langbein, The Historical Origins of the Privilege Against Self-Incrimination at Common Law, 92 Mich.L.Rev. 1047 (1994)—§§ 1.6(b) n.102; 24.5(a) n.3; 24.5(d) n.40

Langbein, The Jury of Presentment and the Coroner, 33 Colum.L.Rev. 3129, 1330 (1933)—§ 16.1(c) n.111

Langbein, Understanding the Short History of Plea Bargaining, 13 Law & Soc'y.Rev. 261 (1979)—§§ 1.6(a) n.23; 21.1(b) n.10, 20

Langbein & Weinreb, Continental Criminal Procedure: "Myth" and "Reality," 87 Yale L.J. 1549 (1978)—§§ 1.5(c) n.106; 13.2(g) n.123; 21.1(b) n.9

Langer, From Legal Transplants to Legal Translations: The Globalization of Plea Bargaining and the Americanization Thesis in Criminal Procedure, 45 Harv.Int'l L.J. 1 (2004)—§§ 1.5(a) n.6; 21.1(b) n.9

Langrock, Joint Trials: A Short Lesson from Little Vermont, 9 Crim.L.Bull. 612 (1973)—§ 17.2(g) n.143

Lanier & Acker, Capital Punishment, the Moratorium Movement, and Empirical Questions, 10 Psychology, Public Policy and Law 577 (2004)—§ 1.5(e) n.241

Lanni, Jury Sentencing in Noncapital Cases: An Idea Whose Time Has Come (Again)?, 108 Yale L.J. 1775 (1999)—§ 26.2(b) n.3

Lapides, Cross-Currents in Prosecutorial Discovery, 7 S.F.L.Rev. 216 (1973)—§ 20.4(d) n.55

Larson, Importing Constitutional Norms From a "Wider Civilization": Lawrence and The Rehnquist Court's Use of Foreign and International Law in Domestic Constitutional Interpretation, 65 Ohio St. L.J. 1283 (2004)—§ 2.7(c) n.181

Lassiter, The Appearance of Justice: TV or Not TV—That is the Question, 86 J.Crim.L. & Criminology 928 (1996)—§§ 23.3(b) n.13, 15 to 19; 24.4(d) n.35

Laster, Criminal Restitution: A Survey of Its Past History and an Analysis of Its Present Usefulness, 5 U.Rich.L.Rev. 71 (1970)—§ 1.5(k) n.359

Laster, Criminal Restitution, A Survey of Its Past History and An Analysis of Its Present Usefulness, 5 U.Rich.L.Rev. 71 (1990)—§§ 1.5(k) n.359, 377; 26.6(c) n.33

Latzer, A Critique of Gardner's Failed Discourse, 24 Rutgers L.J. 1009 (1993)—§ 2.12(c) n.136

Latzer, Four Half-Truths About State Constitutional Law, 63 Temp.L.Rev. 1123 (1992)—§§ 2.12(c) n.145, 150

Latzer, The New Judicial Federalism and Criminal Justice: Two Problems and A Response, 22 Rutgers L.J. 863 (1991)—§ 2.12(c) n.171

Latzer, Toward the Decentralization of Criminal Procedure: State Constitutional Law and Selective Disincorporation, 87 J.Crim.L. & Criminology 63 (1996)—§§ 2.9(g) n.191; 2.12(a) n.70 to 72

Latzer and Cauthen, Capital Appeals Revisited, 84 Judicature 64 (2000)—§ 1.8(e) n.83

Lawrence, The Id, The Ego, and Equal Protection: Reckoning with Unconscious Racism, 39 Stan.L.Rev. 317 (1987)—§ 1.5(j) n.330

Lay, Modern Administrative Proposals for Federal Habeas, 21 DePaul L.Rev. 701 (1972)—§ 28.2(c) n.42

Leading Cases, 120 Harv.L.Rev. 125 (2006)—§§ 27.6(e) n.152, 161

Lear, Contemplating the Successive Prosecution Phenomenon in the Federal System, 85 J.Crim.L. & Criminology 625 (1995)—§§ 16.1(f) n.233; 26.3(b) n.11

Lear, Is Conviction Irrelevant?, 40 UCLA L.Rev. 1179 (1993)—§§ 26.4(a) n.2; 26.4(b) n.8

Lee, From Gatekeeper to Concierge: Reigning in the Federal Prosecutor's Expanding Power Over Substantial Assistance Departures, 50 Rutgers L.Rev 199 (1997)—§ 21.2(d) n.265

Lee, Prosecutorial Discretion, Substantial Assistance, and the Federal Sentencing Guidelines, 42 UCLA L.Rev. 105 (1994)—§§ 21.2(d) n.260; 26.3(b) n.11

Lee, Section 2254(d) of the Federal Habeas Statute: Is It Beyond Reason?, 56 Hastings L.J. 283 (2004)—§ 28.6(f) n.77

Lee and Bhagwat, The McCleskey Puzzle: Remedying Discrimination Against Black Victims in Capital Sentencing, 1988 Sup.Ct.Rev. 145

(1998)—§ 1.5(j) n.330

Lefcourt, Imbalanced Funding Imperils American Rights, 22 May Champion 5 (1998)—§ 1.5(j) n.335

Lefcourt, The Blank Line-up: An Aid to the Defense, 14 Crim. L. Bull. 428 (1978)—§ 7.5(c) n.48

LeFlar, Choices of Law in Criminal Cases, 25 Case W.Res.L.Rev. 44 (1974)—§ 16.4(c) n.77

Lefstein, Incriminating Physical Evidence, The Defense Attorney's Dilemma, and the Need for Rules, 64 N.C.L.Rev. 897 (1986)—§§ 20.4(b) n.29, 30; 20.4(f) n.94

Lefstein, Plea Bargaining and the Trial Judge, the New ABA Standards, and Need to Control Judicial Discretion, 59 N.Car.L.Rev. 476 (1981)—§ 21.2(c) n.100

Lefstein, Stapleton & Tietelbaum, In Search of Juvenile Justice: Gault and Its Implementation, 3 L. & Soc'y Rev. 491 (1969)—§ 6.9(b) n.21

Leib, E-mail and the Wiretap Laws: Why Congress Should Add Electronic Communication to Title III's Statutory Exclusionary Rule and Expressly Reject A "Good Faith" Exception, 34 Harv. J. on Legis. 393 (1997)—§ 4.6(m) n.217

Leiken, Police Interrogation in Colorado: The Implementation of Miranda, 47 Denver L.J. 1 (1970)—§ 6.5(c) n.35

Leipold, Constitutionalizing Jury Selection in Criminal Cases: A Critical Evaluation, 86 Geo.L.J. 945 (1998)—§ 22.3(d) n.202

Leipold, How the Pretrial Process Contributes to Wrongful Convictions, 42 Am.Crim.L.Rev. 1123 (2005)—§ 1.5(e) n.236

Leipold, Rethinking Jury Nullification, 82 Va.L.Rev. 253 (1996)—§§ 1.6(b) n.61; 22.1(g) n.121; 24.10(a) n.4; 25.3(b) n.16; 26.3(b) n.12

Leipold, The Dangers of Race-Based Jury Nullification: A Response to Professor Butler, 44 UCLA L.Rev. 109 (1996)—§ 22.1(g) n.105

Leipold, The Problem of the Innocent, Acquitted Defendant, 94 Nw.U.L.Rev. 1297 (2000)—§§ 1.5(f) n.247; 26.10(c) n.49

Leipold, Why Are Federal Judges So Acquittal Prone?, 83 Wash.U.L.Q. 151 (2005)—§ 24.6(a) n.9

Leipold, Why Grand Juries Do Not (And Cannot) Protect The Accused, 80 Cornell L.Rev. 260 (1995)—§§ 8.2(c) n.35; 8.4(b) n.18; 15.1(a) n.5, 6; 15.2(i) n.202; 15.3(a) n.3 to 5, 11 to 15, 26, 27, 30; 15.3(b) n.31; 15.3(d) n.69; 15.5(a) n.28

Leipold & Abbasi, The Impact of Joinder and Severance on Federal Criminal Cases: An Empirical Study, 59 Vand.L.Rev. 349 (2006)—§§ 1.2(f) n.305; 17.1(f) n.72 to 74; 17.2(g) n.140

Leo, From Coercion to Deception: The Changing Nature of Police Interrogation in America, 18 Crime L. & Soc. Change 35 (1992)—§ 6.2(c) n.120

Leo, Miranda's Revenge: Police Interrogation as a Confidence Game, 30 Law & Soc.Rev. 259 (1996)—§§ 6.2(c) n.120; 6.5(c) n.45

Leo, Questioning the Relevance of Miranda in the Twenty-First Century, 99 Mich.L.Rev. 1000 (2001)—§ 6.5(d) n.80

Leo, The Impact of Miranda Revisited, 86 J.Crim.L. & Criminology 621 (1996)—§§ 6.5(c) n.45; 6.5(d) n.74

Leo & Ofshe, The Consequences of False Confessions: Deprivations of Liberty and Miscarriages of Justice in the Age of Psychological Interrogation, 88 J. Crim. L. & Criminology 429 (1998)—§ 1.5(e) n.229

Leo & White, Adapting to Miranda: Modern Interrogation Strategies for Dealing With the Obstacles Posed by Miranda, 84 Minn.L.Rev. 397

(1999)—§ 6.5(c) n.42

Lerner, The Transformation of the American Civil Trial: The Silent Judge, 42 Wm. & Mary L.Rev. 195 (2000)—§ 24.6(e) n.48

Lerner, The USA PATRIOT Act: Promoting the Cooperation of Foreign Intelligence Gathering and Law Enforcement, 11 Geo. Mason 493 (2003)—§ 8.5(e) n.208

Lessig, Translating Federalism, Lopez v. United States, 1995 Sup.Ct. Rev. 125—§ 1.2(c) n.166

Levenson, Change of Venue and the Rule of the Criminal Jury, 66 S.Cal.L.Rev. 1533 (1993)—§§ 16.3(g) n.110, 113

Levenson, Detention, Material Witnesses and the War on Terrorism, 35 Loy.L.A.L.Rev. 1217 (2002)—§ 12.4(g) n.101

Levin, Bribery or Effective Prosecution—Should Prosecutors be Legally Allowed to Give Something of Value to a Witness?, 24 S.Ill.U.L.J. 137 (1999)—§ 21.2(b) n.71

Levin, Local Rules as Experiments: A Study in the Division of Power, 139 U.Pa.L.Rev. 1567 (1991)—§ 1.7(g) n.109

Levin, Toward a More Enlightened Sentencing Procedure, 45 Neb.L.Rev. 499 (1966)—§ 26.3(b) n.8

Levine, The Impact of Sequestration on Juries, 79 Judicature 266 (1996)—§ 24.9(a) n.10

Levine & Tapp, The Psychology of Criminal Identifications: The Gap from Wade to Kirby, 121 U.Pa.L.Rev. 1079 (1973)—§§ 7.1(b) n.9, 13, 21, 22; 7.3(f) n.121

Levitt, Jurisdiction Over Crimes: The Territorial Commission Theory, 16 J. of Am.Inst.Crim.L. & Criminology 316 (1926)—§§ 16.1(c) n.110, 113, 128; 16.4(c) n.38

Levy & Lindsay, Lineup and Photo Spread Procedures, 7 Psychol.Pub.Pol'y & L. 776 (2001)—§ 7.5(c) n.39

Lewis, The Grand Jury: A Critical Evaluation, 13 Akron L.Rev. 33 (1979)—§§ 8.2(b) n.20; 8.2(c) n.35; 15.3(a) n.12, 14, 24, 25

Lewis & Trichter, The Nationalization of the Bill of Rights: History, Development and Current Status, 20 Washburn L.J. 195 (1981)—§§ 2.3(a) n.61; 2.6(a) n.1

Lichtenstein, Public Defenders: Dimensions of Cooperation, 9 Just.Sys.J. 102 (1984)—§§ 1.9(b) n.30; 1.10(d) n.137, 145, 165

Lieberman & Sales, What Social Science Teaches Us About the Instruction Process, 3 Psychol. Pub. Pol'y. & Law 589 (1997)—§ 24.8(a) n.4

Liebman, An "Effective Death Penalty"? AEDPA and Error Detection in Capital Cases, 67 Brook.L.Rev. 411 (2001)—§ 28.2(b) n.30

Liebman, Apocalypse Next Time? The Anachronistic Attack on Habeas Corpus/Direct Review Parity, 92 Colum.L.Rev. 1997 (1992)—§§ 28.1(b) n.21; 28.2(b) n.20; 28.2(d) n.75

Liebman, Capital Attrition: Error Rates in Capital Cases, 1973-95, 78 Tex.L.Rev. 1839 (2000)—§ 1.8(e) n.83

Liebman, The Overproduction of Death, 100 Colum.L.Rev. 2030 (2000)—§ 1.8(e) n.83

Liebman & Hertz, Brecht v. Abrahamson: Harmful Error in Habeas Corpus Law, 84 Crim.L. & Criminology 1109 (1994)—§ 28.6(g) n.82

Liebman, Fagan, & West, Death Matters: A Reply to Latzer and Cauthen, 84 Judicature 72 (2000)—§ 1.8(e) n.83

Lietzau, Rediscovering the Establishment Clause: Federalism and the Rollback of Incorporation, 39 De-Paul L.Rev. 1190 (1990)—§ 2.3(a) n.30

Lim, State Due Process Guarantees for Meaningful Death Penalty Clemency Proceedings, 28 Colum.J.L. & Soc.Probs. 47 (1994)—§ 26.2(c) n.76

Lind, Thibaut & Walker, Discovery and Presentation of Evidence in Adversary and Nonadversary Proceedings, 71 Mich.L.Rev. 1129 (1973)—§§ 1.5(c) n.117, 120

Linde, E Pluribus: Constitutional Theory and State Courts, 18 Ga.L.Rev. 165 (1984)—§§ 2.12(a) n.36; 2.12(c) n.133, 147

Linde, First Things First: Rediscovering the State's Bill of Rights, 9 U.Balt.L.Rev. 379 (1980)—§ 2.12(a) n.36

Linde, State Constitutions Are Not Common Law: Comments on Gardner's Failed Discourse, 24 Rutgers L.J. 927 (1993)—§§ 2.12(a) n.36; 2.12(c) n.179

Linde, Without "Due Process," 49 Or.L.Rev. 125 (1970)—§ 2.12(a) n.30

Lindo, Joy L., New Jersey Jurors Are No Longer Color-Blind Regarding Eyewitness Identification, 30 Seton Hall L.Rev. 1224 (2000)—§ 7.5(a) n.9

Linzer, The Carolene Products Footnote and the Preferred Position of Individual Rights, 12 Const. Commentary 277 (1995)—§ 2.8(c) n.64

Litman, Pretextual Prosecution, 92 Geo.L.J. 1135 (2004)—§ 13.4(c) n.133

Litman & Greenberg, 543 Annals Am.Acad.Pol. & Soc.Sci. 64 (1996)—§ 1.2(d) n.237

Little, Myths and Principles of Federalization, 46 Hastings L.J. 1029 (1995)—§§ 1.2(c) n.199; 1.2(d) n.203, 209

Littman and Greenberg, Dual Prosecutions: A Model for Concurrent Federal Jurisdiction, 543 Annals Am.Acad.Pol. & Soc.Sci. 103 (1996)—§§ 1.2(d) n.235, 237; 1.2(f) n.292

Littman & Greenberg, Federal Power and Federalism: A Theory of Commerce-Clause Based Regulation of Traditionally State Crimes, 47 Case W.Res.L.Rev. 921 (1997)—§ 1.2(c) n.157

Livingston, Disobedience and Contempt, 75 Wash.L.Rev. 345 (2000)—§ 11.2(a) n.24

Livingston, Police Discretion and The Quality of Life in Public Places: Courts, Communities, and The New Policing, 97 Colum.L.Rev. 551 (1997)—§§ 1.6(f) n.375; 1.6(g) n.428; 1.9(b) n.21; 1.9(c) n.58; 1.9(d) n.97; 1.10(b) n.31; 1.10(e) n.228; 13.2(b) n.32

Livingston, Police Patrol, Judicial Integrity, and the Limits of Judicial Control, 72 St. John's L.Rev. (1998)— § 2.8(c) n.68

Livingston, Police Reform and The Department of Justice: An Essay on Accountability, 2 Buff.Crim.L.Rev. 815 (1999)—§ 1.9(b) n.47

Loewy, Police-Obtained Evidence and the Constitution: Distinguishing Unconstitutionally Obtained Evidence from Unconstitutionally Used Evidence, 87 Mich.L.Rev. 907 (1989)—§ 1.9(b) n.34

Loewy, Protecting Citizens from Cops and Crooks: An Assessment of the Supreme Court's Interpretation of the Fourth Amendment During the 1982 Term, 62 N.C.L.Rev. 329 (1984)—§ 3.3(c) n.80

Loewy, The Fourth Amendment As a Device for Protecting the Innocent, 81 Mich.L.Rev. 1229 (1983)— §§ 2.9(f) n.111; 3.2(b) n.71

Loewy, When Jurors Lie: Differing Standards for New Trials, 22 Am.J.Crim.L. 733 (1995)— § 24.9(f) n.99

Loftin & McDowell, The Police, Crime, and Economic Theory: An Assessment, 47 Am.Soc.Rev. 393 (1982)—§ 1.5(a) n.50

Loftus & Zanni, Eyewitness Testimony: The Influence of Wording a Question, 5 Bull. Psychonomic Soc'y 86 (1975)—§ 7.1(b) n.15

Logan, The Shadow Criminal Law of Municipal Governance, 62 Ohio St.L.J. 1409 (2001)—§ 1.8(d) n.44

Lopez, Institutional Racism: Judicial Conduct and a New Theory of Racial Discrimination, 109 Yale L.J. 1717 (2000)—§ 1.5(j) n.330

Lord, Entrapment and Due Process: Moving Toward a Dual System of Defenses, 25 Fla.St.U.L.Rev. 463 (1998)—§ 5.2(a) n.4

Louisell, Criminal Discovery: Dilemma Real or Apparent?, 49 Cal.L.Rev. 56 (1961)—§§ 20.1(a) n.13; 20.1(b) n.22; 20.3(i) n.179

Love, Mandatory Sentence and Presidential Mercy: The Role of Judges in Pardon Cases, 1790-1850, 16 Fed.Sent.Rptr. 212 (2004)— § 26.2(c) n.69

Lovrich & Sheldon, Voters in Judicial Elections: An Attentive Public or an Uniformed Electorate, 9 Just.Sys.J. 23 (1984)—§§ 1.10(e) n.202, 203

Lowenthal, Evaluating the Exclusionary Rule in Search and Seizure, 49 UMKC L.Rev. 24 (1981)—§ 1.9(b) n.24

Lowenthal, Joint Representation in Criminal Cases: A Critical Appraisal, 64 Va.L.Rev. 939 (1978)— §§ 11.9(a) n.3, 5, 40, 41; 11.9(b) n.52

Lowenthal, Mandatory Sentencing Laws: Undermining the Effectiveness of Determinate Sentencing Reform, 81 Calif.L.Rev. 61 (1993)— § 26.3(c) n.18

Lowenthal, Successive Representation by Criminal Lawyers, 93 Yale L.J. 1 (1983)—§ 11.9(a) n.7

Luban, Are Criminal Defenders Different, 91 Mich.L.Rev. 1729 (1993)—§§ 1.5(c) n.128; 1.5(j) n.335; 1.10(d) n.145

Lucci, The Case for Allowing Jurors to Submit Written Questions, 89 Judicature 16 (July-August 2005)—§ 24.9(b) n.14

Luka-Hopson, The Existing Conflict Between the Defendant's Right of Confrontation and the Witness' Right to Avoid Self-Incrimination: A Constitutional Dilemma, 38 Cath.U.L.Rev. 245 (1988)—§ 24.4(c) n.18

Luna, Constitutional Road Maps, 90 J.Crim.L. & Criminology 1125 (2000)—§ 2.9(h) n.251

Luna, Sovereignty and Suspicion, 1999 Duke L.J. 789, 794—§ 3.2(a) n.18

Luna, The Models of Criminal Procedure, 2 Buffalo Crim.L.Rev. 367 (1999)—§§ 1.5(a) n.20; 1.5(h) n.282

Luna, Transparent Policing, 85 Iowa L.Rev. 1107 (2000)—§§ 1.5(j) n.325; 1.9(e) n.140

Lusky, Footnote Redux: A Carolene Products Reminiscence, 82 Colum.L.Rev. 1093 (1982)—§ 2.8(c) n.64

Lynch, Our Administrative System of Criminal Justice, 66 Ford.L.Rev. 2117 (1998)—§§ 1.5(c) n.178; 1.10(a) n.2

Lynch, RICO: The Crime of Being a Criminal, 87 Colum.L.Rev. 661 (1987)—§§ 16.2(h) n.153, 156

Lynch, Screening Versus Plea Bargaining: Exactly What Are We Trading Off?, 55 Stan.L.Rev. 1399 (2003)—§§ 1.5(c) n.177; 21.1(g) n.134

Lyon, Setting the Record Straight: A Proposal for Handling Prosecutorial Appeals to Racial, Ethnic or Gender Prejudice During Trial, 6 Mich.J.Race & L. 319 (2001)—§ 24.7(e) n.61

M

MacChesney, A Progressive Program for Procedural Reform, 3 J.Crim.L. & Criminology 528 (1913)—§§ 1.6(e) n.309, 321, 323, 327, 328, 331

Mack, The Juvenile Court, 23 Harv.L.Rev. 104 (1909)—§ 1.6(e) n.300

Maclin, "Black and Blue" Encounters—Some Preliminary Thoughts About Fourth Amendment Seizures: Should Race Matter?, 26 Val.U.L.Rev. 243 (1991)—§§ 1.5(j) n.316, 326; 3.8(c) n.79

Maclin, Is Obtaining an Arrestee's DNA a Valid Special Needs Search Under the Fourth Amendment? What Should (And Will) the Supreme Court Do?, 34 J.L.Med. & Ethics 165 (2006)—§§ 3.5(d) n.155, 163

Maclin, Let Sleeping Dogs Lie: Why the Supreme Court Should Leave Fourth Amendment History Unabridged, 82 B.U.L.Rev. 895 (2002)—§ 2.9(d) n.57

Maclin, The Decline of the Right of Locomotion: The Fourth Amendment on the Streets, 75 Cornell L.Rev. 1258 (1990)—§ 1.6(h) n.476

Maclin, What Can the Fourth Amendment Doctrine Learn From Vagueness Doctrine, 3 U.Pa.J.Const.L. 399 (2001)—§ 1.5(j) n.319

Magid, Questioning the Question-Proof Inmate: Defining Miranda Custody for Incarcerated Suspects, 58 Ohio St.L.J. 883 (1997)—§ 6.6(b) n.16

Maguire, How to Unpoison the Fruit—The Fourth Amendment and the Exclusionary Rule, 55 J.Crim.L.C. & P.S. 307 (1964)—§§ 9.3(e) n.49, 78

Mahoney, Deborah L., Constitutional Law: Capital Defendants Permitted Reverse-Witherspoon "Life Qualifying" Questions On Voir Dire [Morgan V. Illinois, 112 S. Ct. 2222 (1992)], 32 Washburn L.J.278 (1993)—§ 22.3(c) n.152

Maier, Popular Uprisings and Civil Authority in Eighteenth Century America, 27 Wm. & Mary Q. (3rd) 3 (1970)—§ 1.6(b) n.97

Maltz, False Prophet-Justice Brennan and the Theory of State Constitutional Law, 15 Hastings Const.L.Q. 429 (1988)—§§ 2.12(a) n.34; 2.12(c) n.145

Maltz, Lockstep Analysis and Concepts of Federalism, 496 Annals Am.Acad.Pol. & Soc.Sci. 98 (1988)—§§ 2.12(a) n.79; 2.12(c) n.131

Maltz, Some Thoughts on the Death of Stare Decisis in Constitutional Law, 1980 Wis.L.Rev. 467—§ 2.9(b) n.7

Maltz, The Dark Side of State Court Activism, 63 Tex.L.Rev. 995 (1985)—§§ 2.12(a) n.79; 2.12(b) n.109; 2.12(c) n.131, 132

Maltz, The Fourteenth Amendment as Political Compromise—Section One in the Joint Committee on Reconstruction, 45 Ohio St.L.J. 933 (1984)—§ 2.3(a) n.61

Manak, Constitutional Aspects of the Use of Passive Alcohol Screening Devices as Law Enforcement Tools for DWI Enforcement, 19 The Prosecutor 29 (Winter 1986)—§ 3.2(b) n.88

Mank, Post-Sentence Sentencing: Determining Probation Revocation Sanctions, 18 Cumb.L.Rev. 437 (1988)—§ 26.10(d) n.89

Mann, Punitive Civil Sanctions: The Middleground Between Criminal and Civil Law, 101 Yale L.J. 1795 (1992)—§ 25.1(c) n.29

Mannheimer, Coerced Confessions and the Fourth Amendment, 30 Hastings Const.L.Q. 57 (2002)—§ 6.2(b) n.25

Mansfield, Peremptory Challenges to Jurors Based Upon or Affecting Religion, 34 Seton Hall L.Rev. 435 (2004)—§ 22.3(d) n.198

Marano, A Reexamination of the Development of the Reasonable Doubt Rule, 55 B.U.L.Rev. 507 (1975)—§ 1.5(e) n.226

Marcus, Federal Habeas Corpus After State Default: A Definition of Cause and Prejudice, 53 Fordham L.Rev. 663 (1985)—§ 28.4(d) n.65

Marcus, Presenting Back From the (Almost) Dead, the Entrapment Defense, 47 Fla.L.Rev. 205 (1995)—§ 5.2(a) n.19

Marcus, Proving Entrapment Under the Predisposition Test, 14 Am.J.Crim.L. 53 (1987)—§ 5.2(c) n.45

Marcus, Re-evaluating Large Multiple-Defendant Criminal Prosecutions, 11 Wm. & Mary Bill Rts.J. 67 (2002)—§ 17.2(f) n.134

Marcus, State Constitutional Protection For Defendants in Criminal Prosecutions, 20 Ariz.St.L.J. 151 (1988)—§§ 2.12(a) n.41; 2.12(c) n.153

Marcus, The Development of Entrapment Law, 33 Wayne L.Rev. 5 (1986)—§ 5.1(b) n.7

Marcus, The Entrapment Defense, 30 Ohio N.U.L.Rev. 211 (2004)—§ 5.1(b) n.9

Marcus, The Revival of Fact Pleading Under the Federal Rules of Civil Procedure, 86 Colum.L.Rev. 433 (1986)—§ 19.1(d) n.41

Marcus & Waye, Australia and United States; Two Common Criminal Justice Systems Uncommonly at Odds, 12 Tul.J.Int'l. & Comp.L. 27 (2004)—§ 1.2(a) n.1

Margolin and Coliver, Pretrial Disqualification of Defense Counsel, 20 Am.Crim.L.Rev. 227 (1982)— §§ 11.9(b) n.60, 80

Margulies, Resource Deprivation and the Right to Counsel, 80 J.Crim.L. & Criminology 673 (1989)— §§ 11.8(a) n.23; 11.8(c) n.65

Markman, The Search for the Truth in Criminal Justice, 41 Rutgers L.Rev. 871 (1989)—§§ 1.5(a) n.37, 40; 2.9(f) n.109

Markman & Cassell, Protecting the Innocent: A Response to the Bedau-Radelet Study, 41 Stan.L.Rev. 121 (1988)—§ 1.5(e) n.241

Markus, Procedural Implications of Forfeiture Under RICO, the CCE, and the Comprehensive Forfeiture Act of 1984: Returning the Trial Structure, 59 Temp.L.Q. 1097 (1986)— § 26.6(d) n.58

Maroney, Emotional Competence, "Rational Understanding," and the Criminal Defendant, 43 Am.Cr.L.Rev. 1375 (2006)— § 24.2(g) n.91

Maroney, Fifty Years of Federalization of Criminal Law: Sounding the Alarm or "Crying Wolf," 50 Syracuse L.Rev. 1317 (2000)—§ 1.2(d) n.203

Marquis, The Innocent and the Shammed, 40 Prosecutor 40 (2006)—§§ 1.5(e) n.230, 240

Marquis, The Myth of Innocence, 95 J.Crim.L. & C. 501 (2005)— §§ 1.5(e) n.243, 246

Marshall, Marquis & Oskamp, Effects of Kind of Question and Atmosphere of Interrogation on Accuracy and Completeness of Testimony, 84 Harv.L.Rev. 1620 (1971)—§ 7.1(b) n.18

Martin, Policing Career Criminals: An Examination of an Innovative Crime Control Program, 77 J.Crim.L. & Criminology 1159 (1986)—§ 1.6(g) n.430

Martin & Sherman, Selective Apprehension: A Police Strategy For Career Offenders, 25 Criminology 155 (1986)—§ 1.4(d) n.61

Martin & Zerhusen, Independent Counsel—Checks and Balances, 58 Geo.Wash.L.Rev. 536 (1990)— § 13.3(f) n.60

Martinson, New Findings, New Views: A Note of Caution Regarding Sentencing Reform, 7 Hofstra L.Rev. 243 (1979)—§ 1.6(h) n.452

Martinson, What Works?—Questions and Answers About Prison Reform, 36 Public Interest 22 (1974)— § 1.6(h) n.452

Mashaw, Administrative Due Process: The Quest For a Dignitary Theory, 61 B.U.L.Rev. 885 (1981)— § 1.5(a) n.12

Mashaw, The Supreme Court's Due Process Calculus for Administrative Adjudication in Mathews v. Eldridge: Three Factors in Search of A Theory of Value, 44 U.Chi.L.Rev. 28 (1976)—§ 2.7(c) n.217

Mashburn, A Clockwork Orange Approach to Legal Ethics: A Conflicts Perspective on the Regulation of Lawyers by Federal Courts, 8 Geo.J. Legal Ethics 473 (1995)—§ 1.7(j) n.249

Massachusetts and Rhode Island provisions cited in Berger, 74 Nw.L.Rev. 1 (1971)—§ 2.4(b) n.40

Massaro, The Meanings of Shame, 3 Psych.Pub.Pol. & L. 645 (1977)— § 26.9(b) n.78

Matheny, A Bibliography on Plea Bargaining, 13 Law & Soc.Rev. 661 (1979)—§ 21.1(b) n.30

Mather, Comments on the History of Plea Bargaining, 13 Law & Soc.Rev. 281 (1979)—§§ 21.1(b) n.18, 24, 27

Matheson, The Prosecutor, The Press, and Free Speech, 58 Fordham L.Rev. 865 (1990)—§§ 23.1(b) n.21, 23

Maveal, Federal Presentence Reports: Multi-Tasking at Sentencing, 26 Seton Hall L.Rev. 544 (1996)— § 26.5(b) n.26

May, The Sound of the Gavel: Perspectives on Judicial Speech: "What do we do now?": Helping Juries Apply the Instructions, 28 Loy.L.A.L.Rev. 869 (1995)—§ 24.6(e) n.48

Mayers, The Habeas Corpus Act of 1867: The Supreme Court as Legal Historian, 33 U.Chi.L.Rev. 31 (1965)—§§ 28.2(b) n.20, 25

Mayers & Yarbrough, Bis Vexari: New Trials and Successive Prosecutions, 74 Harv.L.Rev. 1 (1960)—§ 17.4(a) n.4

McAdams, Race and Selective Prosecution: Discovering the Pitfalls of Armstrong, 73 Chi-Kent L.Rev. 605 (1998)—§ 1.5(j) n.330

McBride, The Jury is Not a Political Institution, 11 Judge's Journal 37 (April 1972)—§ 22.1(g) n.120

McCabe, Four Faces of State Constitutional Separation of Powers: Challenges to Speedy Trial and Speedy Disposition Provisions, 62 Temple L.Rev. 177 (1989)—§ 18.3(c) n.64

McCabe, State Constitutions and the "Open Fields" Doctrine: A Historical Definitional Analysis of the Scope of Protection Against Warrantless Searches of "Possessions," 13 Vt.L.Rev. 179 (1988)—§ 2.12(b) n.93

McClain, "Three Strikes and You're Out": The Solution to the Repeat Offender Problem?, 20 Seton Hall Legis.J. 97 (1996)—§ 26.6(b) n.1

McClellan, The Organized Crime Act (S.30) or its Critics: Which Threatens Civil Liberties, 46 Notre Dame Law. 55 (1970)—§ 1.2(d) n.229

McClintock, Indictments by a Grand Jury, 26 Minn.L.Rev. 153 (1941)— §§ 19.1(c) n.28, 31

McConahay, Mullin & Frederick, The Uses of Social Sciences in Trials with Political and Racial Overtones: The Trial of Joan Little, 41 Law & Contemp.Prob. 205 (Winter, 1977)—§ 22.3(b) n.92

McConnell, Active Liberty: A Progressive Alternative to Textualism and Originalism?, 119 Harv.L.Rev. 2387 (2006)—§ 2.9(d) n.102

McConnell, Federalism: Evaluating the Founder's Design, 54 U.Chi.L.Rev. 1484 (1987)—§ 2.5(f) n.61

McConnell, Tradition and Constitutionalism Before the Constitution, 1998 U.ILL.L.Rev. 173—§ 2.8(a) n.17

McConville, Protecting the Right to Effective Assistance of Capital Post Conviction Counsel: The Scope of the Constitutional Obligation to Monitor Counsel's Performance, 66 U.Pitt.L.Rev. 521 (2005)— § 11.7(a) n.19

McConville, The Right to Effective Assistance of Capital Post-conviction Counsel: Constitutional Implications of Statutory Grants of Capital Counsel, 2003 Wis.L.Rev. 31 (2003)—§§ 11.7(a) n.19; 28.12(a) n.3

McConville & Mirsky, Guilty Plea Courts; A Social Disciplinary Model of Criminal Justice, 42 Soc. Probs. 216 (1995)—§§ 1.10(d) n.118, 157

McConville and Mirsky, The Rise of Guilty Pleas in New York, 1800-1865, 22 J.L. & Soc'y 443 (1995)— § 1.6(d) n.260

McCord, Visions of Habeas, 1994 B.Y.U.L.Rev. 735 (1994)— §§ 28.2(b) n.20; 28.2(d) n.69, 70, 86

McCormick, Law of the Future: Evidence, 51 Nw.U.L.Rev. 218 (1856)—§§ 2.10(c) n.66, 67

McCormick, The Scope of Privilege in the Law of Evidence, 16 Texas L.Rev. 447 (1938)—§ 6.5(a) n.3

McCoy and Lichtenberg, Providing Effective Habeas Counsel for Indigents in Capital Cases, 21 Just.Syst.J. 81 (1999)—§ 28.8(b) n.16

McCraw, "Doubts About Our Process": Richard D. Simons and the Jurisprudence of Restraint in State Constitutional Analysis, 13 Touro L.Rev. 613 (1997)—§§ 2.12(b) n.102; 2.12(c) n.120, 148

McDonald, Towards a Bicentennial Revolution in Criminal Justice: The Return of the Victim, 13 Am.Crim.L.Rev. 649 (1976)—§§ 1.5(k) n.340; 1.6(b) n.74

McDowell & Bear, The Fourteenth Amendment: Should the Bill of Rights Apply to the States?: The Disincorporation Debate, 1987 Utah L.Rev. 951—§ 2.6(a) n.1

McGaan, Beck v. Alabama: The Right to a Lesser Included Offense Instruction in Capital Cases, Wis.L.Rev. 560 (1981)—§ 24.8(f) n.92

McGough, Good Enough for Government Work: The Constitutional Duty to Preserve Forensic Interview of Child Victims, 65 Law & Contemp.Probs. 179 (2002)—§ 24.3(e) n.122

McGowan, Constitutional Interpretation and Criminal Identification, 12 Wm. & Mary L.Rev. 235 (1970)—§§ 7.1(a) n.1; 7.3(g) n.125; 7.5(c) n.36

McGowan, Rule-Making and the Police, 70 Mich.L.Rev. 659 (1972)—§§ 1.6(g) n.410; 1.7(i) n.180

McIlwain, Due Process of Law in Magna Charta, 14 Colum.L.Rev. 27 (1914)—§§ 2.4(b) n.33, 35

McIntyre, A Study of Judicial Dominance of the Charging Process, 59 J.Crim.L.C. & P.S. 463 (1968)—§§ 1.4(g) n.158; 1.10(c) n.80; 14.1(a) n.5, 14; 14.3(a) n.44

McIntyre & Lippman, Prosecutors and Early Disposition of Felony Cases, 56 A.B.A.J. 1154 (1970)—§ 14.1(a) n.8

McKay, The Preference for Freedom, 34 N.Y.U.L.Rev. 1182 (1959)—§ 2.8(c) n.57

McKusick & Boxer, Uniform Jury Selection and Service Act, 8 Harv.J.Legis. 280 (1971)—§ 22.2(b) n.14

McLaughlin, Questions to Witnesses and Notetaking by the Jury as Aids in Understanding Complex Litigation, 18 New.Eng.L.Rev. 687 (1983)—§ 24.9(b) n.14

McLeod, An Examination of the Victim's Role at Sentencing: Results of a Survey of Probation Administrators, 71 Judicature 162 (1987)—§ 26.5(d) n.68

McMunigal, Disclosure and Accuracy in the Guilty Plea Process, 40 Hastings L.J. 957 (1989)—§ 21.3(c) n.195

McMunigal, Disclosure and Accuracy in the Guilty Plea Process, 40 Hastings L.J. 958 (1989)—§ 24.3(b) n.78

McMunigal, Prosecutorial Disclosure of Exculpatory Information During Plea Negotiations, 22 Sum.Crim.Just. 42 (2007)—§ 1.5(e) n.236

McMunigal, The Craft of Due Process, 45 St. Louis U.L.J. 477 (2000)—§§ 2.7(b) n.75; 2.7(c) n.100

McPhee, Deferred Prosecution Agreements: Ray of Hope or Guilty Plea by Another Name?, 30 Champion 12 (Oct.2006)—§§ 13.6(a) n.10, 13

McPhie, Almost Private: Pen Registers, Packet Sniffers, and Privacy at the Margin, 2005 Stan. Tech. L. Rev. 1—§ 4.7(a) n.6

Meador, Accommodating State Criminal Procedure and Federal Post Conviction Review, 50 A.B.A.J. 928 (1964)—§ 28.11(a) n.5

Meagher, Police Patrol Styles: How Pervasive is Community Variation, 12 J. Police Sci. & Admin. 36 (1985)—§§ 1.4(d) n.55; 1.10(b) n.30

Meares, Everything Old Is New Again: Fundamental Fairness And The Legitimacy Of Criminal Justice, 3 Ohio St. J.Crim.L. 105 (2005)—§§ 2.2 n.8; 2.7(a) n.14

Meares, Praying for Community Policing, 90 Cal.L.Rev. 1593 (2002)—§ 1.10(e) n.221

Meares, Rewards for Good Behavior: Influencing Prosecutorial Discretion and Conduct with Financial Incentives, 64 Fordham L.Rev. 851 (1995)—§§ 1.9(c) n.56; 24.7(i) n.94, 97, 98

Meares, Social Organizations and Drug Law Enforcement, 35 Am.Crim.L.Rev. 191 (1998)—§ 1.5(j) n.331

Meares & Harcourt, Transparent Adjudication and Social Science Research in Constitutional Criminal Procedure, 90 J.Crim.L. & Criminology 733 (2000)—§§ 1.5(a) n.55; 3.8(d) n.139

Medalie, Zeitz & Alexander, Custodial Police Interrogation in Our Nation's Capital: The Attempt to Implement Miranda, 66 Mich.L.Rev. 1347 (1968)—§§ 6.5(c) n.35, 36, 43

Media's Infatuation with Juror Interviews Tempts Court to Curtail Press Freedoms, 66 U.S.L.W. 2163 (Sept.23, 1997)—§ 24.9(g) n.130

Medwed, Daniel S., Looking Foreword: Wrongful Convictions And Systemic Reform, 42 Am.Crim.L.Rev. 1117 (2005)—§ 1.5(e) n.230

Meese, A Tribute to Justice Hugo Black, 6 St. Louis U.Pub.L.Rev. 187 (1987)—§ 2.8(a) n.17

Meese, The Jurisprudence of Clarence Thomas, 12 Regent U.L.Rev. 349 (2000)—§ 2.8(a) n.23

Melilli, Act-Of-Production Immunity, 52 Ohio St.L.J. 223 (1991)—§§ 8.13(c) n.73, 76 to 78

Melilli, Exclusion of Evidence in Federal Prosecutions on the Basis of State Law, 22 Ga.L.Rev. 667 (1988)—§§ 2.12(c) n.171 to 173

Mello, The Non-Trial of the Century: Representations of the Unabomber, 24 Vt.L.Rev. 417 (2000)—§ 11.6(a) n.26

Mello and Perkins, Ted Kaczynski's Diary, 22 Vt.L.Rev. 81 (1997)—§ 8.12(g) n.68

Mellon, Jacoby & Brewer, The Prosecutor Constrained by His Environment: A New Look at Discretionary Justice in the United States, 72 J.Crim. L. & Criminology 52 (1981)—§§ 13.2(a) n.7, 12

Meltzer, Deterring Constitutional Violations by Law Enforcement Officials: Plaintiffs and Defendants as Private Attorneys General, 88 Colum.L.Rev. 247 (1988)—§§ 3.1(b) n.24; 15.4(i) n.204

Meltzer, Harmless Error and Constitutional Remedies, 61 U.Chi.L.Rev. 1 (1994)—§§ 27.1(a) n.11; 27.6(c) n.66

Meltzer, Required Records, 18 U.Chi. L.Rev. 867 (1951)—§ 2.10(d) n.117

Meltzer, State Forfeitures of Federal Rights, 99 Harv.L.Rev. 1128 (1986)—§ 28.4(a) n.2

Mendelson, Justice Black's Fourteenth Amendment, 53 Minn.L.Rev. 711 (1969)—§ 2.3(a) n.6

Mengler, The Sad Refrain of Tough on Crime: Some Thoughts on Saving the Federal Judiciary from the Federalization of State Crime, 43 Kan.L.Rev. 503 (1995)—§§ 1.2(c) n.199; 1.2(d) n.203, 233

Mercio-Stephens, Of Federalism, Human Rights, and the Holland Caveat: Congressional Power to Implement Treaties, 25 Mich.JInt'l.L. 265 (2004)—

§§ 1.7(c) n.13, 15, 18

Merola, Modern Prosecutorial Techniques, 16 Crim.L.Bull. 232 (1980)—§§ 1.4(e) n.81, 90

Merril, Rescuing Federalism After Raich: The Case For Clear Statement Rules, 9 Lewis & Clark L.Rev. 823 (2005)—§ 1.2(c) n.136

Merrill, The Common Law Powers of Federal Courts, 52 U.Chi.L.Rev. 1 (1985)—§ 1.7(h) n.126

Merritt, Federalism as Empowerment, 47 Fla.L.Rev. 541 (1995)— §§ 2.5(f) n.60, 93

Mertens, The Fourth Amendment and the Control of Police Discretion, 17 U.Mich.J.L.Ref. 551 (1984)— § 3.8(b) n.48

Mertens & Wasserstrom, The Good Faith Exception to the Exclusionary Rule: Deregulating the Police and Derailing the Law, 70 Geo.L.J. 365 (1981)—§ 3.1(c) n.50

Metzger, Beyond the Bright Line: A Contemporary Right-To-Counsel Doctrine, 97 N.W.U.L.Rev. 1635 (2003)—§§ 6.4(e) n.108; 11.2(b) n.40; 11.7(a) n.16

Metzmeier, Preventive Detention: A Comparison of Bail Refusal Practices in the United States, England, Canada and Other Common Law Nations, 8 Pace Int'l L.Rev. 399 (1996)—§§ 12.2(b) n.33; 12.3(b) n.29

Meyer, Constitutionality of Pretrial Detention, 60 Geo.L.J. 1139 (1972)— § 12.3(a) n.4

Meyer, North Carolina's Fair Sentencing Act: An Ineffective Scarecrow, 28 Wake Forest L.Rev. 519 (1993)—§ 26.1(c) n.45

Meyer, "Nothing We Say Matters": Teague and New Rules, 61 U.Chi.L.Rev. 423 (1994)— § 28.6(d) n.37

Meyler, Toward a Common Law Originalism, 59 Stan.L.Rev. 551 (2006)—§ 2.9(d) n.54

Miccio, A House Divided: Mandatory Arrest, Domestic Violence, and the Conservatization of the Battered Women's Movement, 42 Hous.L.Rev. 237 (2005)—§ 13.2(b) n.35

Miceli, Optimal Criminal Procedure, Fairness and Deterrence, 11 Int'l Rev.L. & Econ. 3 (1991)—§ 1.5(a) n.16

Michaels, Trial Rights at Sentencing, 81 N.C.L.Rev. 1771 (2003)—§ 26.4(f) n.105

Mickenberg, Grand Jury Investigations: Multiple Representation and Conflicts of Interest in Corporate Criminality Cases, 17 Crim.L.Bull. 5 (1981)—§§ 8.14(d) n.40, 42, 45, 49

Middlekauff, What Practitioners Say About Broad Criminal Discovery, 9 Crim.Just. 14 (Spring 1994)— § 20.1(b) n.41

Mikell, The Doctrine of Entrapment in the Federal Courts, 90 U.Pa.L.Rev. 245 (1942)—§ 5.1(b) n.7

Mileski, Courtroom Encounters: An Observation Study of Lower Criminal Courts, 5 Law & Soc'y Rev. 473 (1971)—§ 1.10(d) n.130

Millar, The Reform of Criminal Pleading in Illinois, 8 J.Crim.L. & Criminology 337 (1917)—§§ 19.1(b) n.20; 19.2(d) n.44

Millar, The Statutory Notice of Alibi, 24 J.Crim.L. Criminology & Police Sci. 849 (1934)—§ 20.1(a) n.7

Millemann, Collateral Remedies in Criminal Cases in Maryland: An Assessment, 64 Md.L.Rev. 968 (2005)—§ 28.11(b) n.28

Miller, Ideology and Criminal Justice, 64 J.Crim.L. & Criminology 41 (1973)—§ 1.3(c) n.26

Miller, Information or Indictments in Felony Cases, 8 Minn.L.Rev. 379 (1924)—§ 15.3(a) n.28

Miller & Bornstein, The Use of Religion in Death Penalty Sentencing Trials, 30 L. & Hum. Behav. 675 (2006)— § 26.4(b) n.17

Miller & Guggenheim, Pretrial Detention and Punishment, 75 Minn.L.Rev. 335 (1990)—§ 12.3(a) n.4

Miller & Remington, Procedures Before Trial, 339 Annals 111 (1962)— § 13.1(e) n.52

Million, Juries, Judges, and Democracy, 18 Law & Soc. Inquiry 135 (1993)—§ 1.6(d) n.244

Mills & Bohannon, Juror Characteristics: To What Extent are They Related to Jury Verdicts, 64 Judicature 22 (1980)—§ 22.3(b) n.92

Milner, Supreme Court Effectiveness and the Police Organization, 36 Law & Contemp.Prob. 467 (1971)— § 3.1(c) n.37

Miner, Federal Courts, Federal Crimes, and Federalism, 10 Harv.J.L. & Pub.Pol. 198 (1987)—§§ 1.2(c) n.156; 1.2(d) n.202

Miner, Hearing the Danger of an Armed Felon-Allowing for a Detention Hearing under the Bail Reform Act for Those Who Unlawfully Possess Firearms, 37 U.Mich.J.L.Ref. 705 (2004)—§ 12.3(a) n.18

Minnefor, Looking For Fair Trials, in The Information Age: The Need for More Stringent Gag Orders Against Trial Participants, 30 U.S.F.L.Rev. 95 (1995)—§§ 23.1(b) n.71, 73

Mishkin, The High Court, The Great Writ, and Due Process of Time and Law, 79 Harv.L.Rev. 56 (1965)— § 2.11(a) n.1

Misner, Limiting Leon: A Mistake of Law Analogy, 77 J.Crim.L. & Criminology 507 (1986)—§ 3.1(c) n.59

Misner, Minimalism, Desuetude, and Fornication, 35 Willamette L.Rev. 1 (1999)—§ 13.5(c) n.66

Misner, Recasting Prosecutorial Discretion, 86 J.Crim.L. & Criminology 717 (1996)—§§ 13.2(a) n.7, 19

Mitchel, The Ethics of the Criminal Defense Attorney—New Answers to Old Questions, 32 Stan.L.Rev. 293 (1980)—§ 1.5(c) n.128

Mitchell, Apprendi's Domain, 2006 S.Ct.Rev. 297 (2006)—§ 22.1(a) n.28

Mitchell, Bail Reform and the Constitutionality of Pretrial Detention, 55 Va.L.Rev. 1223 (1969)—§§ 12.3(a) n.4; 12.4(a) n.13

Mitchell, Redefining The Sixth Amendment, 67 S.Cal.L.Rev. 1215 (1994)—§§ 1.4(f) n.99, 120; 11.4(a) n.4

Mitchell, Why Should the Prosecutor Get the Last Word?, 27 Am.J.Crim.L. 139 (2000)— § 24.7(c) n.25

Mnookin, Uncertain Bargains: the Rise of Plea Bargaining in America, 57 Stan.L.Rev. 1721 (2005)— § 21.1(b) n.10

Moesteller & Powell, With Disdain for the Constitutional Craft: The Proposed Victims' Rights Amendment, 78 N.C.L.Rev. 371 (2000)— § 1.5(k) n.362

Mogill, Avoiding the "Big Chill": Protecting the Attorney-Client Relationship From the Effects of Zurcher, 69 Conn.L.Rev. 293 (1989)—§ 3.4(a) n.22

Moglen, Taking the Fifth: Reconsidering the Origins of the Constitutional Privilege Against Self-Incrimination, 92 Mich.L.Rev. 1086 (1994)— §§ 1.6(b) n.103 to 105; 1.6(c) n.155; 2.10(c) n.73, 80, 83, 84; 24.5(a) n.3; 24.5(d) n.40

Moley, The Initiation of Criminal Prosecutions by Indictment or Information, 29 Mich.L.Rev. 403 (1931)— § 15.3(b) n.36

Moley, The Vanishing Jury, 2 S.Cal.L.Rev. 97 (1928)—§ 1.6(d) n.259

Monaghan, Of "Liberty" and "Property," 62 Corn.L.Rev. 405 (1977)—§ 13.6(d) n.70

Monaghan, Our Perfect Constitution, 56 N.Y.U.L.Rev. 353 (1981)—§ 2.9(d) n.83

Monaghan, Stare Decisis and Constitutional Adjudication, 88 Colum.L.Rev. 723 (1988)—§§ 2.9(b) n.7, 32, 35, 39, 45

Monaghan, Taking Supreme Court Opinions Seriously, 30 Md.L.Rev. 1 (1979)—§ 2.9(b) n.38

Monaghan, The Burger Court and "Our Federalism," 43 Law & Contemp.Probs. 39 (Summer 1980)—§ 2.6(d) n.89

Monoghan, The Supreme Court, 1974 Term—Foreword: Constitutional Common Law, 89 Harv.L.Rev. 1 (1975)—§§ 1.7(i) n.172; 6.5(e) n.85

Monohan, A Jurisprudence of Risk Assessment: Forecasting Harm Among Prisoners, Predators, and Patients, 92 Va.L.Rev. 391 (2006)—§§ 26.1(a) n,4; 26.6(e) n.80, 83

Montoya, A Theory of Compulsory Process Clause Discovery Rights, 70 Ind.L.J. 845 (1995)—§§ 24.3(a) n.2; 24.3(g) n.160

Montoya, The Future of Post-Batson Peremptory Challenge: Voir Dire by Questionnaire and the "Blind" Peremptory, 29 U.Mich.J.L. Reform 981 (1996)—§ 1.5(j) n.332

Montoya, "What's So Magic[al]; About Black Women?": Peremptory Challenges and the Intersection of Race and Gender, 3 Mich.J.Gender & L. 369 (1996)—§ 22.3(d) n.196

Moohr, Prosecutorial Power in an Adversarial System: Lessons from White Collar Cases and the Inquisitorial Model, 8 Buffalo Crim.L.Rev. 165 (2004)—§ 1.5(c) n.171

Moore, Criminal Discovery, 19 Hastings L.J. 865 (1968)—§§ 20.1(a) n.1 to 3; 20.1(b) n.22, 25

Moore, Disqualification of an Attorney Representing Multiple Witnesses Before A Grand Jury: Legal Ethics and The Stonewall Defense, 27 UCLA L.Rev. 1 (1979)—§ 8.14(d) n.40

Moore, Questioning the Autonomy of Prosecutorial Charge Decisions: Recognizing the Need to Exercise Discretion-Knowing There Will be Consequences for Crossing the Line, 60 La.L.Rev. 371 (2000)—§§ 13.2(d) n.88; 13.5(h) n.125

Moore, The Livingston Code, 19 J.Am.Inst.Crim.L. & Criminology 344 (1928)—§ 1.6(d) n.273

Moore, Torture and the Balance of Evils, 23 Israel L.Rev. 280 (1989)—§ 1.5(a) n.15

Moran, Don't Worry, I'll Be Right Back: Temporary Absences of Counsel During Criminal Trials and the Rule of Automatic Reversal, 85 Neb.L.Rev. 186 (2006)—§ 11.10(d) n.200

Moran, In Defense of the Corpus Delicti Rule, 64 Ohio St.L.J. 817 (2003)—§ 24.6(c) n.41

Moran, Traffic Stops, Littering Tickets, and Police Warnings: The Case for a Fourth Amendment Non-Custodial Arrest Doctrine, 37 Am.Crim.L.Rev. 1143 (2000)—§ 1.5(j) n.324

Morehead, When a Peremptory Challenge is No Longer Peremptory; Batson's Unfortunate Failure to Eradicate Invidious Discrimination from Jury Selection, 43 DePaul L.Rev. 625 (1994)—§ 1.5(j) n.332

Moreland, Historical Background and Implications of the Privilege Against Self-Incrimination, 44 Ky.L.J. 267 (1956)—§ 2.10(c) n.67

Morgan, A Brief History of Special Verdicts and Special Interrogatories, 32 Yale L.J. 575 (1922)—§ 24.10(a) n.1

Morgan, The Privilege Against Self-Incrimination, 34 Minn.L.Rev. 1 (1949)—§§ 2.10(c) n.59, 61, 64, 73; 6.2(a) n.2

Morrison, Choice of Law for Unlawful Searches, 41 Okla.L.Rev. 579 (1988)—§ 2.12(c) n.171

Morrison, Does the Fourteenth Amendment Incorporate the Bill of Rights?, 2 Stan.L.Rev. 140 (1949)—§§ 2.3(a) n.57, 61

Morse, A Survey of the Grand Jury System, 10 Or.L.Rev. 101 (1931)—§ 15.3(b) n.36

Morse, Blame and Danger: An Essay on Preventive Detention, 76 B.U.L.Rev. 113 (1996)—§ 26.6(e) n.83

Morse & Molsey, Crime Commissions as Aids in the Legal-Social Field, 145 Annals Am.Acad.Pol. & Soc.Sci. 68 (1929)—§ 1.6(f) n.335

Mosk, The Emerging Agenda in State Constitutional Rights Law, 496 Annals Am.Acad.Pol. & Soc.Sci. 54 (1988)—§ 2.12(a) n.40

Mosk, The Power of State Constitutions in Protecting Individual Rights, 8 N.Ill.U.L.Rev. 641 (1988)—§ 2.12(a) n.20

Moskovitz, Advising The Pro Se Defendant: The Trial Court's Duties Under Faretta, 42 Brandeis L.J. 329 (2004)—§ 11.5(c) n.32

Mosteller, Cowboy Prosecutors and Subpoenas for Incriminating Evidence: The Consequences and Correction of Excess, 58 Wash. & Lee L.Rev. 487 (2001)—§§ 8.13(a) n.33, 41, 43; 8.13(b) n.69

Mosteller, Discovery Against the Defense: Tilting the Adversarial Balance, 74 Cal.L.Rev. 1567 (1986)—§§ 20.4(c) n.46; 20.4(d) n.55, 59; 20.5(b) n.24, 25, 28, 30

Mosteller, Simplifying Subpoena Law: Taking the Fifth Amendment Seriously, 73 Va.L.Rev. 1 (1987)—§§ 8.12(b) n.24; 8.12(f) n.56; 8.13(a) n.9, 17, 19, 41; 8.13(b) n.46, 50, 68; 8.13(c) n.74, 76; 20.5(b) n.24, 25

Mosteller, Victims' Rights and the United States Constitution: An Effort to Recast the Battle on Criminal Litigation, 85 Geo.L.J. 1691 (1997)—§ 1.5(k) n.369

Moylan, The Plain View Doctrine: Unexpected Child of the Great "Search Incident" Geography Battle, 26 Mercer L.Rev. 1047 (1975)—§ 3.2(b) n.37

Mueller, Juror's Impeachment of Verdicts and Indictments in Federal Court Under Rule 606(b), 57 Neb.L.Rev. 920 (1978)—§§ 24.9(g) n.113, 119

Mueller & Le Poole, Appellate Review of Legal But Excessive Sentences: A Comparative Study, 21 Vand.L.Rev. 411 (1968)—§ 26.3(g) n.68

Muller, Solving the Batson Paradox: Harmless Error, Jury Representation, and the Sixth Amendment, 106 Yale L.J. 93 (1996)—§ 22.3(d) n.254

Muller, The Hobgoblin of Little Minds? Our Foolish Law of Inconsistent Verdicts, 111 Harv.L.Rev. 771 (1998)—§§ 24.10(b) n.27, 28, 30, 31; 24.10(d) n.47

Munster, Current Publication Abstracts, 19 J.Crim.Just. 579 (1991)—§ 2.3(a) n.63

Munsterman, A Brief History of State Jury Reform Efforts, 79 Judicature 494 (1996)—§ 1.6(g) n.402

Murchison, The Dual Sovereignty Exception to Double Jeopardy, 14 N.Y.U.Rev.L. & Soc.Change 383 (1986)—§ 25.5(a) n.5

Murphy, Jury Fact-Finding of Offense-Related Sentencing Factors, 5 Fed.Sent.Rep. 41 (1992)—§ 26.4(b) n.8

Murphy, The Narrowing of the Entitlement to Criminal Jury Trial, 1997 Wis.L.Rev. 133—§ 22.1(b) n.53

Mykkeltvedt, Justice Black and the Intentions of the Framers of the Fourteenth Amendment's First Section: The Bill of Rights and the States, 20 Mercer L.Rev. 432 (1969)—§§ 2.3(a) n.61, 74

N

Naftalis, "Queen for a Day" Agreements and the Proper Scope of Permissible Waiver of the Federal Plea-Statement Rule, 37 Colum.J.L. & Soc.Probs. 1 (2003)—§ 21.2(h) n.439

Nagareda, Compulsion "To Be A Witness" and The Resurrection of Boyd, 74 N.Y.U.L.Rev. 1575 (1999)—§§ 8.12(d) n.43; 8.12(g) n.72; 8.13(a) n.10

Nagareda, Reconceiving the Right to Present Witnesses, 97 Mich.L.Rev. 1063 (1999)—§§ 24.3(a) n.2; 24.4(a) n.5

Nagel, Discretion in the Criminal Justice System: Analyzing, Channelling, Reducing, and Controlling It, 31 Emory L.J. 601 (1982)—§ 1.9(e) n.119

Nagel, Tradeoffs in Crime Reduction Among Certainty, Severity, and Crime Benefits, 35 Rutgers L.Rev. 100 (1982)—§ 1.5(a) n.49

Nagel & Schulhofer, A Tale of Three Cities: An Empirical Study of Charging and Bargaining Practices Under the Federal Sentencing Guidelines, 66 S.Car.L.Rev. 501 (1992)—§§ 21.1(a) n.2; 21.1(h) n.240

Nakell, Criminal Discovery for the Defense and Prosecution: The Developing Constitutional Considerations, 50 N.C.L.Rev. 437 (1972)—§§ 20.2(e) n.102; 20.4(d) n.55, 59

Nakell, The Effect of Due Process On Criminal Defense Discovery, 62 Ky.L.J. 58 (1973)—§ 20.3(m) n.236

Nardulli, The Caseload Controversy and the Study of the Criminal Courts, 70 J.Crim.L. & Criminology 89 (1970)—§ 1.10(c) n.43

Nardulli, Flemming, & Eisenstein, Unraveling the Complexities of Decision-Making in Face-to-Face Groups: A Contextual Analysis of Plea-Bargaining Sentences, 78 Am.Pol.Sci.Rev. 912 (1984)—§ 1.10(d) n.126

Neef & Nagel, The Adversary Nature of the American Legal System From A Historical Perspective, 20 N.Y.L. Forum 123 (1974)—§§ 1.5(c) n.114, 153, 156

Neeley, Mr. Justice Frankfurter's Iconography of Judging, 82 Ky.L.J. 535 (1993)—§ 2.8(a) n.9

Nelson, Emerging Notions of Modern Criminal Law in the Revolutionary Era: An Historical Perspective, 42 N.Y.U.L.Rev. 450 (1967)—§§ 1.6(b) n.39; 1.6(d) n.287

Nelson, Quality Control For Indigent Defense Service Contract, 76 Cal.L.Rev. 1147 (1988)—§§ 1.4(f) n.112; 11.4(a) n.7

Nepveu, Beyond "Guilty" or "Not Guilty": Giving Special Verdicts in Criminal Jury Trials, 21 Yale L. & Pol'y.Rev. 263 (2003)—§ 24.10(a) n.9

Nervi, F.R.Crim.P. 6(e) and the Disclosure of Documents Reviewed by a Grand Jury, 57 U.Chi.L.Rev. 221 (1990)—§§ 8.5(c) n.90, 91, 93, 95, 97

Nesson & Leotta, The Fifth Amendment Privilege Against Cross-Examination, 85 Geo.L.J. 1627 (1997)—§§ 2.10(c) n.63; 24.3(i) n.194; 24.4(c) n.16, 18, 20; 24.5(a) n.3, 7; 24.5(d) n.40

Neubauer, Confessions in Prairie City, 65 J.Crim.L. & Criminology 103 (1974)—§ 6.5(c) n.35

Neuborne, "The House Was Quiet and the World Was Calm the Reader Became the Book," Reading the Bill of Rights as a Poem, 57 Vand.L.Rev. 2007 (2004)—§ 2.1 n.48

Neuborne, The Myth of Parity, 90 Harv.L.Rev. 1105 (1977)— § 28.2(c) n.46

Neuborne, The Supreme Court and Local Governmental Law (the 1989-90 Term): First Amendment, 7 Toro.L.Rev. 423 (1991)—§ 8.5(d) n.122

Neuman, Habeas Corpus, Executive Detention, and the Removal of Aliens, 98 Colum.L.Rev. 961 (1998)—§ 28.2(a) n.12

Newman, Beyond Reasonable Doubt, 68 N.Y.U.L.Rev. 979 (1993)— §§ 1.5(e) n.213, 226

Newman, Doctors, Lawyers, and the Unabomber, 60 Mont.L.Rev. 67 (1999)—§ 11.6(a) n.26

Newman, Litigation Reform and the Dangers of Growth of the Federal Judiciary, 70 Temp.L.Rev. 1125 (1997)—§ 1.2(d) n.209

Newman, The New Era of Administrative Regulation: Controlling Prosecutorial Discretion Through the Administrative Procedure Act, 3 U. Dayton L.Rev. 23 (1978)—§ 1.7(j) n.227

Newman, The 'Old Federalism': Protection of Individual Rights in an Era of Federal Courts Passivity, 15 Conn.L.Rev. 21 (1982)—§ 2.12(c) n.152

Newman, The Process of Prescribing "Due Process," 49 Calif.L.Rev. 215 (1951)—§ 2.8(c) n.73

Newman & Nemoyer, Issues of Propriety in Negotiated Justice, 47 Denver L.Rev. 367 (1970)—§§ 1.10(c) n.91; 21.4(a) n.13

Newsom, Pretrial Publicity and Individual Voir Dire, 52 Fla.L.Rev. 1039 (2000)—§ 23.2(f) n.90

Newsom, Setting Incorporation Straight: A Reinterpretation of the Slaughter-House Cases, 109 Yale L.J. 643 (2000)—§§ 2.3(a) n.61, 73; 2.3(b) n.77

Newton, Weapons, Firearms, and Federalism: Reconsidering Scarborough in Light of Lopez, 3 S.App.Prac. & Process 671 (2001)—§ 1.2(c) n.143

Nix, Boot Camp/Shock Incarceration: An Alternative to Prison for Young, Non-Violent Offenders in the United States, 28 Prosecutor 15 (Apr.1994)—§ 26.1(e) n.106

Nolan, Removing Conflicts from the Administration of Justice: Conflicts of Interest and Independent Counsels Under the Ethics in Government Act, 79 Geo.L.J. 1 (1990)— § 13.3(f) n.60

Noll, Controlling a Prosecutor's Screening Discretion Through Fuller Enforcement, 29 Syracuse L.Rev. 697 (1978)—§§ 13.2(g) n.125, 129, 139, 142

Norton, Discovery in the Criminal Process, 61 J.Crim.L. Criminology & Police Sci. 11 (1970)—§ 20.1(a) n.1

Note, 11 Am.Crim.L.Rev. 577 (1973)— § 13.3(f) n.56

Note, 12 Am.Crim.L.Rev. 231 (1974)— § 3.10(a) n.9

Note, 16 Am.Crim.L.Rev. 163 (1978)— § 21.5(d) n.97

Note, 35 Am.Crim.L.Rev. 411 (1998)— § 3.4(g) n.135

Note, 42 Am.Crim.L.Rev. 121 (2005)— § 28.3(e) n.102

Note, 21 Am.J.Crim.L. 485 (1994)— § 17.4(b) n.82

Note, 26 Am.J.Crim.L. 505 (1999)— § 21.1(b) n.36

Note, 14 Am.J.L. & Med. 431 (1989)— §§ 6.2(c) n.170; 6.9(b) n.27

Note, 21 Am.J.L. & Med. 131 (1995)— § 24.3(f) n.157

Note, 2 Am.U.J.Gender & L. 171 (1994)—§ 13.2(b) n.35

Note, 18 Am.U.L.Rev. 157 (1968)— § 6.5(e) n.85

Note, 25 Am.U.L.Rev. 897 (1976)— §§ 11.5(a) n.8; 11.5(b) n.24; 11.5(d) n.72

Note, 46 Am.U.L.Rev. 1245 (1997)— § 24.4(a) n.5

Note, 1998 Ann.Surv.Am.L. 103— § 13.4(b) n.64

Note, 10 Ariz.L.Rev. 419 (1968)— § 3.8(e) n.220

Note, 26 Ariz.L.Rev. 399 (1984)— § 7.5(b) n.19

Note, 30 Ariz.L.Rev. 551 (1988)— § 6.8(d) n.85

Note, 32 Ariz.L.Rev. 645 (1990)— § 6.8(a) n.19

Note, 38 Ariz.L.Rev. 739 (1996)— §§ 22.3(b) n.92; 22.3(d) n.246

Note, 41 Ark.L.Rev. 697 (1988)— § 12.3(c) n.88

Note, 22 B.C.L.Rev. 815 (1981)— § 21.5(c) n.81

Note, 26 B.C.L.Rev. 1277 (1985)— § 12.4(b) n.49

Note, 37 B.C.L.Rev. 743 (1996)— §§ 5.1(c) n.19, 21, 24, 33, 35

Note, 40 B.C.L.Rev. 897 (1999)— § 21.2(b) n.71

Note, 44 B.C.L.Rev. 1323 (2003)— § 6.4(g) n.159

Note, 41 Brandeis L.J. 373 (2002)— § 6.10(c) n.36

Note, 43 Brooklyn L.Rev. 91 (1976)— § 3.9(c) n.47

Note, 72 Brooklyn L.Rev. 689 (2007)— § 26.9(b) n.77

Note, 57 B.U.L.Rev. 570 (1977)— §§ 11.5(g) n.107, 108

Note, 59 B.U.L.Rev. 305 (1979)— §§ 13.6(c) n.47; 13.6(d) n.58, 73, 74

Note, 60 B.U.L.Rev. 664 (1980)— § 27.3(c) n.33

Note, 65 B.U.L.Rev. 345 (1986)— § 2.9(b) n.5

Note, 66 B.U.L.Rev. 345 (1986)— § 2.9(b) n.30

Note, 75 B.U.L.Rev. 1507 (1995)— § 26.2(c) n.76

Note, 79 B.U.L.Rev. 1067 (1999)— § 5.2(a) n.19

Note, 2007 B.Y.U. L. Rev. 201— § 22.2(d) n.75

Note, 59 Cal.L.Rev. 1479 (1971)— § 11.5(g) n.115

Note, 62 Cal.L.Rev. 408 (1974)— § 5.1(c) n.41

Note, 69 Cal.L.Rev. 1734 (1981)— §§ 6.9(f) n.122, 123

Note, 70 Cal.L.Rev. 1091 (1982)— § 21.2(e) n.306

Note, 15 Campbell L.Rev. 263 (1993)— § 21.2(d) n.251

Note, 13 Cap.Def.J. 279 (2001)— § 13.3(b) n.18

Note, 25 Cardozo L.Rev. 907 (2003)— §§ 18.5(a) n.27, 29

Note, 39 Case W.Res.L.Rev. 1371 (1989)—§ 12.3(c) n.88

Note, 40 Cath.U.L.Rev. 215 (1990)— § 26.5(d) n.63

Note, 43 Cath.U.L.Rev. 1432 (1986)— § 15.6(b) n.64

Note, 37 Chi.-Kent L.Rev. 129 (1960)— § 18.1(d) n.52

Note, 49 Clev.St.L.Rev. 17 (2001)— § 6.6(b) n.16

Note, 36 Colum.Hum.Rts.L.Rev. 755 (2005)—§ 7.4(f) n.105

Note, 6 Colum.J. Law & Soc.Prob. 345 (1970)—§ 7.5(c) n.34

Note, 35 Colum.J.Transnat'l L. 503 (1997)—§ 26.6(b) n.26

Note, 38 Colum.L.Rev. 1493 (1938)— § 15.1(d) n.162

Note, 48 Colum.L.Rev. 238 (1948)— § 26.6(b) n.14

Note, 47 Colum.L.Rev. 1214 (1947)— § 6.3(b) n.29

Note, 53 Colum.L.Rev. 829 (1953)— § 2.12(a) n.8

Note, 57 Colum.L.Rev. 846 (1957)— § 18.3(c) n.66

Note, 66 Colum.L.Rev. 400 (1966)—
§ 9.2(c) n.23

Note, 67 Colum.L.Rev. 181 (1967)—
§ 26.9(c) n.85

Note, 69 Colum.L.Rev. 1296 (1969)—
§ 7.3(e) n.84

Note, 70 Colum.L.Rev. 876 (1970)—
§§ 19.3(b) n.137; 19.4(a) n.6;
19.6(c) n.34

Note, 71 Colum.L.Rev. 1090 (1972)—
§§ 8.3(h) n.45, 46

Note, 73 Colum.L.Rev. 1476 (1973)—
§ 9.6(a) n.17

Note, 74 Colum.L.Rev. 53 (1974)—
§ 3.9(f) n.99

Note, 74 Colum.L.Rev. 88 (1974)—
§§ 9.3(e) n.46, 51, 53

Note, 74 Colum.L.Rev. 1435 (1974)—
§ 21.6(a) n.15

Note, 78 Colum.L.Rev. 1714 (1979)—
§ 26.1(b) n.32

Note, 80 Colum.L.Rev. 1053 (1980)—
§§ 11.7(d) n.38, 42

Note, 80 Colum.L.Rev. 1265 (1980)—
§ 1.3(b) n.11

Note, 82 Colum.L.Rev. 328 (1982)—
§ 12.3(c) n.87

Note, 83 Colum.L.Rev. 139 (1983)—
§ 24.3(i) n.196

Note, 84 Colum.L.Rev. 144 (1984)—
§ 13.5(a) n.13

Note, 86 Colum.L.Rev. 1697 (1986)—
§ 25.5(a) n.5

Note, 89 Colum.L.Rev. 940 (1989)—
§ 6.4(e) n.91

Note, 89 Colum.L.Rev. 1345 (1989)—
§ 26.1(b) n.26

Note, 91 Colum.L.Rev. 373 (1991)—
§§ 27.1(a) n.11, 12

Note, 93 Colum.L.Rev. 1249 (1993)—
§ 26.1(b) n.24

Note, 97 Colum.L.Rev. 781 (1997)—
§ 26.4(g) n.149

Note, 97 Colum.L.Rev. 787 (1997)—
§§ 26.2(b) n.24; 26.4(g) n.137, 147

Note, 95 Colum.L.Rev. 1232 (1995)—
§§ 22.1(g) n.105; 24.7(e) n.49

Note, 95 Colum.L.Rev. 1811 (1995)—
§§ 23.1(b) n.17, 23, 25

Note, 105 Colum.L.Rev. 1863 (2005)—
§ 13.6(a) n.15

Note, 50 Cornell L.Q. 309 (1965)—
§ 13.4(e) n.176

Note, 57 Cornell L.Rev. 794 (1972)—
§ 18.3(c) n.66

Note, 63 Cornell L.Rev. 642 (1978)—
§ 1.7(i) n.176

Note, 64 Cornell L.Rev. 538 (1979)—
§§ 27.6(b) n.14, 17, 56

Note, 65 Cornell L.Rev. 659 (1980)—
§§ 11.7(d) n.38; 11.10(a) n.4

Note, 72 Cornell L.Rev. 1075 (1987)—
§ 22.3(c) n.159

Note, 74 Cornell L.Rev. 712 (1989)—
§§ 17.2(b) n.35, 61

Note, 78 Cornell L.Rev. 336 (1993)—
§ 22.3(d) n.245

Note, 82 Cornell L.Rev. 390 (1997)—
§ 22.2(a) n.5

Note, 86 Cornell L.Rev. 437 (2001)—
§ 6.9(g) n.178

Note, 87 Cornell L.Rev. 1233 (2002)—
§ 11.8(b) n.44

Note, 90 Cornell L.Rev. 237 (2004)—
§ 13.2(a) n.8

Note, 22 DePaul L.Rev. 660 (1973)—
§ 7.3(b) n.16

Note, 38 DePaul L.Rev. 165 (1988)—
§ 12.3(c) n.88

Note, 43 DePaul L.Rev. 909 (1994)—
§ 21.2(e) n.325

Note, 82 Dick.L.Rev. 465 (1978)—
§ 7.5(b) n.19

Note, 42 Duke L.J. 382 (1992)—
§ 26.4(f) n.87

Note, 46 Duke L.J. 575 (1996)—§ 3.2(b)
n.74

Note, 48 Duke L.J. 1371 (2000)—
§ 21.2(b) n.71

Note, 50 Duke L.J. 331 (2000)—§ 1.5(j)
n.327

Note, 1978 Duke L.J. 1041—§ 18.5(b)
n.71

Note, 1986 Duke L.J. 866—§ 5.3(c)
n.30

Note, 1988 Duke L.J. 1242—§§ 15.6(f) n.184; 27.6(b) n.28

Note, 1989 Duke L.J. 1357—§ 26.9(b) n.78

Note, 18 Duq.L.Rev. 930 (1980)— § 8.1(b) n.19

Note, 35 Emory L.J. 227 (1976)— § 9.4(a) n.5

Note, 37 Emory L.Rev. 995 (1988)— § 11.2(e) n.186

Note, 15 Fed. B. J. 194(1955)— § 15.2(c) n.63

Note, 27 Fla.St.U.L.Rev. 325 (1997)— § 21.2(b) n.71

Note, 46 Fordham L.Rev. 1242 (1978)— § 21.5(f) n.172

Note, 48 Fordham L.Rev. 205 (1979)— § 22.1(b) n.39

Note, 50 Fordham L.Rev. 936 (1982)— § 26.10(c) n.63

Note, 51 Fordham L.Rev. 1091 (1983)— § 22.1(h) n.154

Note, 55 Fordham L.Rev. 1059 (1987)— § 21.2(d) n.244

Note, 58 Fordham L.Rev. 979 (1990)— § 28.1(c) n.23

Note, 62 Fordham L.Rev. 653 (1993)— §§ 20.5(c) n.54, 57

Note, 64 Fordham L.Rev. 987 (1995)— § 21.1(g) n.129

Note, 65 Fordham L.Rev. 2571 (1997)— § 13.3(e) n.49

Note, 67 Fordham L.Rev. 3005 (1999)— § 21.3(c) n.188

Note, 68 Fordham L.Rev. 1245 (2000)— § 21.2(d) n.260

Note, 73 Fordham L.Rev. 377 (2004)— § 21.2(b) n.60

Note, 73 Fordham L.Rev. 2711 (2005)— § 27.5(a) n.7

Note, 73 Fordham L.Rev. 2712 (2005)— § 26.6(c) n.42

Note, 74 Fordham L.Rev. 825 (2005)— § 24.11(d) n.24

Note, 75 Fordham L.Rev. 2193 (2007)— §§ 27.5(a) n.7, 8

Note, 10 Fordham.L.Rev. 305 (1941)— § 20.1(a) n.7

Note, 50 Fordham.L.Rev. 582 (1980)— § 8.11(d) n.86

Note, 22 Ga.L.Rev. 805 (1988)— §§ 12.3(b) n.29, 52, 54; 12.3(c) n.88; 12.3(f) n.138, 139, 141; 12.3(g) n.157

Note, 29 Ga.L.Rev. 245 (1994)— § 26.6(d) n.69

Note, 2 Geo.J.Leg.Ethics 695 (1989)— § 21.3(d) n.223

Note, 57 Geo.L.J. 438 (1968)—§§ 6.5(e) n.85; 7.3(g) n.125

Note, 64 Geo.L.J. 1187 (1976)—§ 9.1(b) n.86

Note, 67 Geo.L.J. 1455 (1979)— §§ 5.4(b) n.14; 5.4(c) n.39, 47, 48

Note, 68 Geo.L.J. 1163 (1978)— § 27.2(c) n.28

Note, 70 Geo.L.J. 315 (1981)—§ 21.2(h) n.422

Note, 77 Geo.L.J. 413 (1988)— § 11.10(d) n.167

Note, 84 Geo.L.J. 1945 (1996)—§ 5.4(c) n.38

Note, 85 Geo.L.J. 191 (1996)—§ 22.1(g) n.120

Note, 85 Geo.L.J. 455 (1996)—§ 26.9(b) n.58

Note, 49 Geo.Wash.L.Rev. 191 (1980)—§ 11.2(d) n.137

Note, 50 Geo.Wash.L.Rev. 324 (1976)—§ 13.7(c) n.40

Note, 18 Hamline J.L. & Pub.Pol'y 226 (1996)—§ 1.5(k) n.398

Note, 2 Harv. Negotiation L.Rev. 115 (1997)—§ 21.1(a) n.5

Note, 6 Harv.C.R.-C.L.L.Rev. 300 (1971)—§§ 12.3(a) n.4; 12.3(d) n.100; 12.3(f) n.129

Note, 32 Harv.C.R.-C.L.L.Rev. 249 (1997)—§ 28.2(a) n.11

Note, 42 Harv.C.R.-C.L.L.Rev. 191 (2007)—§ 11.2(h) n.315

Note, 17 Harv.J.Leg. 152 (1980)— § 3.4(a) n.21

Note, 37 Harv.L.Rev. 1121 (1924)— § 16.2(g) n.123

Note, 50 Harv.L.Rev. 677 (1937)—
§§ 1.6(e) n.298; 1.6(f) n.381

Note, 53 Harv.L.Rev. 122 (1939)—
§ 19.1(a) n.8

Note, 53 Harv.L.Rev. 126 (1939)—
§ 19.1(c) n.28

Note, 74 Harv.L.Rev. 590 (1961)—
§ 8.4(a) n.9

Note, 76 Harv.L.Rev. 1656 (1963)—
§ 1.7(i) n.154

Note, 78 Harv.L.Rev. 801 (1965)—
§§ 3.9(b) n.16, 25, 26

Note, 79 Harv.L.Rev. 1513 (1966)—
§ 3.10(d) n.123

Note, 81 Harv.L.Rev. 821 (1968)—
§ 26.4(g) n.135

Note, 82 Harv.L.Rev. 63 (1968)—
§ 27.5(a) n.30

Note, 82 Harv.L.Rev. 1392 (1969)—
§ 7.3(g) n.125

Note, 83 Harv.L.Rev. 814 (1970)—
§ 27.6(d) n.71

Note, 83 Harv.L.Rev. 1038 (1970)—
§§ 28.3(a) n.1; 28.3(b) n.44

Note, 83 Harv.L.Rev. 1387 (1970)—
§ 21.1(b) n.36

Note, 84 Harv.L.Rev. 1465 (1971)—
§§ 3.6(e) n.107, 117

Note, 85 Harv.L.Rev. 994 (1972)—
§ 20.5(a) n.2

Note, 86 Harv.L.Rev. 595 (1973)—
§§ 27.4(b) n.5; 27.4(c) n.22

Note, 89 Harv.L.Rev. 356 (1975)—
§ 26.6(b) n.14

Note, 89 Harv.L.Rev. 593 (1976)—
§ 11.7(b) n.27

Note, 90 Harv.L.Rev. 569 (1977)—
§ 21.1(a) n.1

Note, 90 Harv.L.Rev. 943 (1977)—
§ 8.12(a) n.4

Note, 90 Harv.L.Rev. 945 (1977)—
§§ 3.2(i) n.222, 225; 8.7(a) n.2

Note, 90 Harv.L.Rev. 1550 (1977)—
§ 21.6(a) n.23

Note, 91 Harv.L.Rev. 1266 (1978)—
§ 24.3(i) n.183

Note, 92 Harv.L.Rev. 1752 (1979)—
§ 8.10(e) n.120

Note, 93 Harv.L.Rev. 564 (1980)—
§ 21.6(b) n.97

Note, 93 Harv.L.Rev. 752 (1980)—
§§ 11.7(d) n.42; 11.10(a) n.6

Note, 94 Harv.L.Rev. 77 (1980)—
§ 9.6(a) n.44

Note, 94 Harv.L.Rev. 426 (1980)—
§ 12.1(e) n.67

Note, 95 Harv.L.Rev. 752 (1980)—
§ 11.7(d) n.44

Note, 95 Harv.L.Rev. 945 (1977)—
§ 8.12(a) n.5

Note, 95 Harv.L.Rev. 1122 (1982)—
§§ 5.1(c) n.32, 39

Note, 97 Harv.L.Rev. 931 (1984)—
§§ 1.5(k) n.359; 26.6(c) n.40

Note, 97 Harv.L.Rev. 1929 (1984)—
§ 26.6(d) n.45

Note, 99 Harv.L.Rev. 1004 (1986)—
§§ 21.3(c) n.173; 24.3(b) n.77

Note, 101 Harv.L.Rev. 1472 (1984)—
§ 1.5(j) n.320

Note, 101 Harv.L.Rev. 1595 (1988)—
§ 24.9(f) n.73

Note, 101 Harv.L.Rev. 1876 (1988)—
§ 17.2(b) n.61

Note, 102 Harv.L.Rev. 539 (1988)—
§ 13.5(b) n.53

Note, 105 Harv.L.Rev. 1880 (1992)—
§ 26.4(f) n.87

Note, 106 Harv.L.Rev. 705 (1993)—
§§ 16.3(g) n.99, 123

Note, 107 Harv.L.Rev. 144 (1993)—
§ 17.4(b) n.82

Note, 108 Harv.L.Rev. 665 (1995)—
§ 6.6(e) n.96

Note, 109 Harv.L.Rev. 1729 (1996)—
§ 17.4(a) n.61

Note, 111 Harv.L.Rev. 1116 (1998)—
§ 27.5(c) n.59

Note, 113 Harv.L.Rev. 2062 (2000)—
§ 1.4(f) n.129

Note, 113 Harv.L.Rev. 2080 (2000)—
§ 6.4(e) n.91

Note, 114 Harv.L.Rev. 1074 (2001)—
§ 13.7(c) n.35

Note, 114 Harv.L.Rev. 2098 (2001)—
§ 13.4(a) n.14

Note, 118 Harv.L.Rev. 1731 (2005)—
§ 11.8(c) n.65

Note, 19 Hastings Const'l L.Q. 261
(1991)—§ 22.2(e) n.112

Note, 25 Hastings L.J. 575 (1974)—
§ 3.2(e) n.169

Note, 48 Hastings L.J. 1017 (1997)—
§§ 21.1(h) n.209, 211

Note, 6 Hofstra L.Rev. 533 (1978)—
§ 17.3(b) n.24

Note, 33 Hofstra L.Rev. 1017 (2005)—
§ 3.2(g) n.200

Note, 29 Hoftsra L.Rev. 1333 (2001)—
§ 24.8(f) n.92

Note, 6 Idaho L.Rev. 131 (1969)—
§ 9.2(d) n.44

Note, 31 Ind.L.J. 486 (1956)—§§ 1.8(c)
n.50; 1.8(d) n.43, 51

Note, 34 Ind.L.J. 477 (1959)—§ 13.2(g)
n.141

Note, 50 Ind.L.J. 783 (1975)—§ 13.6(a)
n.2

Note, 62 Ind.L.J. 1061 (1987)—§ 9.5(b)
n.43

Note, 64 Ind.L.J. 375 (1989)—§ 24.7(e)
n.61

Note, 77 Ind.L.J. 341 (2002)—§ 5.2(a)
n.6

Note, 6 Ind.L.Rev. 577 (1973)—
§ 6.10(e) n.74

Note, 29 Ind.L.Rev. 379 (1995)—
§ 23.1(b) n.17

Note, 33 Ind.L.Rev. 957 (2000)—
§ 21.2(b) n.71

Note, 34 Ind.L.Rev. 1157 (2001)—
§ 13.1(a) n.12

Note, 66 Ind.L.Rev. 825 (1991)—
§ 6.8(a) n.19

Note, 56 Iowa L.Rev. 686 (1971)—
§ 5.3(c) n.30

Note, 57 Iowa L.Rev. 1354 (1972)—
§§ 15.1(g) n.348, 351

Note, 67 Iowa L.Rev. 1037 (1982)—
§§ 27.2(b) n.10, 19

Note, 72 Iowa L.Rev. 1063 (1983)—
§ 21.4(f) n.211

Note, 73 Iowa L.Rev. 743 (1988)—
§ 6.9(e) n.93

Note, 67 J.Crim.L. & Criminology 389
(1976)—§ 3.2(i) n.223

Note, 69 J.Crim.L. & Criminology 197
(1978)—§ 21.3(c) n.172

Note, 71 J.Crim.L. & Criminology 147
(1980)—§ 3.4(a) n.21

Note, 72 J.Crim.L. & Criminology 203
(1981)—§ 6.3(c) n.54

Note, 72 J.Crim.L. & Criminology 204
(1981)—§§ 6.3(c) n.51 to 53

Note, 83 J.Crim.L. & Criminology 744
(1993)—§ 21.2(d) n.251

Note, 84 J.Crim.L. & Criminology 1065
(1994)—§ 27.5(d) n.114

Note, 87 J.Crim.L. & Criminology 751
(1997)—§ 27.5(c) n.70

Note, 87 J.Crim.L. & Criminology 786
(1997)—§ 27.6(d) n.146

Note, 89 J.Crim.L. & Criminology 837
(1999)—§ 13.4(b) n.64

Note, 89 J.Crim.L. & Criminology 1007
(1999)—§ 17.4(b) n.116

Note, 93 J.Crim.L. & Criminology 1009
(2003)—§ 13.4(b) n.68

Note, 38 J.Crim.L.C. & P.S. 249
(1947)—§ 20.1(a) n.9

Note, 48 J.Crim.L.C. & P.S. 516
(1958)—§ 13.2(g) n.141

Note, 49 J.Crim.L.C. & P.S. 447
(1959)—§ 5.3(a) n.7

Note, 64 J.Crim.L.C. & P.S. 428
(1973)—§ 7.3(c) n.42

Note, 6 J.L. & Pol'y 291 (1997)—
§ 3.1(d) n.118

Note, 9 J.L. & Pol'y 835 (2001)—
§ 3.2(b) n.80

Note, 30 J.Legal Prof. 145 (2005-06)—
§ 11.2(b) n.77

Note, 29 J.Marshall L.Rev. 5499
(1996)—§ 18.4(c) n.77

Note, 80 Ky.L.J. 1037 (1992)—
§ 26.9(b) n.55

Note, 3 La.L.Rev. 222 (1940)—
§ 16.1(d) n.133

Note, 31 La.L.Rev. 601 (1971)—
§ 28.4(d) n.38

Note, 52 Law & Contemp.Probs. 325
(1989)—§ 17.1(b) n.34

Note, 7 Loyola L.A.L.Rev. 489 (1974)—
§ 3.6(g) n.158

Note, 86 Marquette L.Rev. 773 (2003)—
§ 26.4(b) n.22

Note, 6 Memphis St.U.L.Rev. 701
(1976)—§§ 19.3(b) n.175, 178

Note, 10 Memphis St.U.L.Rev. 550
(1980)—§ 21.4(a) n.19

Note, 14 Mich.J.L.Ref. 105 (1980)—
§§ 21.2(e) n.330, 331, 336, 342, 347

Note, 69 Mich.L.Rev. 762 (1971)—
§ 17.4(a) n.9

Note, 72 Mich.L.Rev. 1113 (1974)—
§§ 13.4(c) n.119, 124, 127, 131;
13.4(d) n.150, 151, 153, 154

Note, 76 Mich.L.Rev. 184 (1977)—
§ 8.7(a) n.2

Note, 76 Mich.L.Rev. 212 (1977)—
§ 8.12(a) n.4

Note, 80 Mich.L.Rev. 1695 (1982)—
§ 24.3(c) n.103

Note, 83 Mich.L.Rev. 1925 (1985)—
§ 24.11(d) n.19

Note, 84 Mich.L.Rev. 1326 (1986)—
§§ 11.2(e) n.150, 176

Note, 87 Mich.L.Rev. 1073 (1989)—
§ 6.7(a) n.9

Note, 89 Mich.L.Rev. 625 (1990)—
§ 3.1(c) n.58

Note, 89 Mich.L.Rev. 1008 (1991)—
§§ 17.2(d) n.109; 24.5(b) n.35

Note, 91 Mich.L.Rev. 2220 (1993)—
§§ 26.6(b) n.28, 29

Note, 93 Mich.L.Rev. 1139 (1995)—
§ 26.6(d) n.69

Note, 93 Mich.L.Rev. 2377 (1995)—
§ 6.7(b) n.83

Note, 94 Mich.L.Rev. 1346 (1996)—
§§ 25.2(d) n.27; 25.4(a) n.7; 25.4(c)
n.39

Note, 98 Mich.L.Rev. 2371 (2000)—
§ 5.2(a) n.19

Note, 101 Mich.L.Rev. 2525 (2003)—
§ 6.4(g) n.153

Note, 103 Mich.L.Rev. 759 (2005)—
§ 5.3(a) n.2

Note, 35 Minn.L.Rev. 774 (1971)—
§ 7.4(e) n.79

Note, 35 Minn.L.Rev. 779 (1971)—
§ 7.4(d) n.75

Note, 45 Minn.L.Rev. 1066 (1961)—
§ 17.3(c) n.40

Note, 46 Minn.L.Rev. 1119 (1962)—
§ 3.1(h) n.224

Note, 53 Minn.L.Rev. 559 (1969)—
§§ 21.5(f) n.159, 165

Note, 55 Minn.L.Rev. 779 (1971)—
§§ 7.3(f) n.108, 120; 7.4(c) n.58;
7.4(d) n.67

Note, 60 Minn.L.Rev. 597 (1976)—
§ 17.4(a) n.38

Note, 60 Minn.L.Rev. 783 (1976)—
§ 1.7(j) n.246

Note, 63 Minn.L.Rev. 457 (1979)—
§ 12.2(d) n.47

Note, 65 Minn.L.Rev. 1110 (1981)—
§ 27.4(e) n.60

Note, 68 Minn.L.Rev. 1077 (1984)—
§ 26.10(c) n.79

Note, 77 Minn.L.Rev. 983 (1993)—
§ 6.5(d) n.77

Note, 78 Minn.L.Rev. 1219 (1994)—
§ 11.9(c) n.116

Note, 78 Minn.L.Rev. 1253 (1994)—
§ 21.2(d) n.260

Note, 40 Miss.L.J. 257 (1969)—§ 7.3(g)
n.125

Note, 64 Miss.L.J. 819 (1995)—
§ 27.5(a) n.8

Note, 37 Mo.L.Rev. 633 (1972)—
§§ 5.3(a) n.7; 5.3(c) n.30

Note, 43 Mo.L.Rev. 350 (1978)—
§ 8.3(h) n.38

Note, 24 Mont.L.Rev. 137 (1963)—
§ 3.8(f) n.235

Note, 52 N.C.L.Rev. 454 (1973)—
§ 6.9(e) n.90

Note, 58 N.C.L.Rev. 599 (1980)—
§§ 21.2(f) n.368, 376, 379

Note, 66 N.C.L.Rev. 183 (1987)—
§ 22.3(c) n.159

Note, 72 N.C.L.Rev. 1721 (1994)—
§ 27.5(d) n.120

Note, 72 N.D.L.Rev. 583 (1996)—
§ 25.5(b) n.26

Note, 33 Neb.L.Rev. 428 (1954)—
§ 21.4(a) n.28

Note, 82 Neb.L.Rev. 866 (2004)—
§ 5.2(a) n.8

Note, 17 N.Eng.L.Rev. 119 (1981)—
§ 22.3(c) n.97

Note, 27 New Eng.J. on Crim. & Civ.
Confin. 253 (2001)—§ 6.5(b) n.23

Note, 50 Notre Dame L.Rev. 857
(1975)—§§ 21.5(e) n.119, 127

Note, 57 Notre Dame L.Rev. 137
(1981)—§ 22.3(e) n.286

Note, 65 Notre Dame L.Rev. 649
(1990)—§ 27.5(c) n.55

Note, 65 Notre Dame L.Rev. 853
(1990)—§ 21.2(b) n.80

Note, 66 Notre Dame L.Rev. 1075
(1991)—§ 1.5(k) n.382

Note, 81 Notre Dame L.Rev. 2101
(2006)—§ 1.2(c) n.166

Note, 2 N.Y.U.J. Int'l L. & Pol. 280
(1969)—§§ 3.1(i) n.228, 230, 233

Note, 16 N.Y.U.J.L. & Soc.Chg. 433
(1988)—§§ 6.4(g) n.160; 28.5(b)
n.62

Note, 40 N.Y.U.L.Rev. 154 (1965)—
§ 28.11(a) n.5

Note, 42 N.Y.U.L.Rev. 513 (1967)—
§ 17.3(c) n.35

Note, 43 N.Y.U.L.Rev. 578 (1968)—
§ 15.5(a) n.5

Note, 43 N.Y.U.L.Rev. 968 (1968)—
§§ 3.2(a) n.15, 23, 24

Note, 51 N.Y.U.L.Rev. 800 (1976)—
§ 3.9(j) n.226

Note, 53 N.Y.U.L.Rev. 835 (1978)—
§ 24.3(a) n.5

Note, 55 N.Y.U.L.Rev. 1266 (1980)—
§ 22.2(d) n.85

Note, 56 N.Y.U.L.Rev. 742 (1981)—
§§ 8.7(a) n.16, 25

Note, 65 N.Y.U.L.Rev. 590 (1990)—
§ 22.2(a) n.5

Note, 66 N.Y.U.L.Rev. 1077 (1991)—
§ 3.9(k) n.257

Note, 67 N.Y.U.L.Rev. 154 (1992)—
§§ 11.2(e) n.149, 170

Note, 68 N.Y.U.L.Rev. 494 (1993)—
§ 23.1(b) n.17

Note, 69 N.Y.U.L.Rev. 477 (1994)—
§ 15.5(a) n.2

Note, 69 N.Y.U.L.Rev. 563 (1994)—
§§ 8.5(a) n.13; 8.5(g) n.223; 15.6(b)
n.64; 15.7(a) n.8

Note, 70 N.Y.U.L.Rev. 166 (1995)—
§ 21.1(h) n.233

Note, 72 N.Y.U.L.Rev. 841 (1997)—
§ 21.5(e) n.149

Note, 77 N.Y.U.L.Rev. 1442 (2002)—
§ 28.6(f) n.77

Note, 34 Ohio St.L.J. 706 (1973)—
§ 9.6(a) n.8

Note, 37 Ohio St.L.J. 205 (1976)—
§ 13.5(e) n.103

Note, 53 Or.L.Rev. 411 (1974)—
§ 1.5(g) n.278

Note, 74 Or.L.Rev. 1365 (1995)—
§ 21.2(h) n.438

Note, 19 Q.L.R. 173 (2000)—§ 21.2(b)
n.71

Note, 22 Q.L.R. 569 (2004)—§ 21.4(a)
n.21

Note, 38 Rev.L&J 931 (2005)—
§§ 22.2(d) n.76; 22.3(b) n.54

Note, 10 Rutgers Camden L.J. 109
(1978)—§ 6.9(c) n.48

Note, 23 Rutgers L.Rev. 1207 (1975)—
§ 13.6(d) n.66

Note, 28 Rutgers L.Rev. 1203 (1975)—
§§ 13.6(a) n.3; 13.6(c) n.40

Note, 43 Rutgers L.Rev. 91 (1990)—
§ 6.8(a) n.19

Note, 44 S.Cal.L.Rev. 737 (1971)—
§ 21.4(a) n.19

Note, 68 S.Cal.L.Rev. 1335 (1995)—
§ 24.3(a) n.5

Note, 70 S.Cal.L.Rev. 517 (1997)—
§ 25.1(c) n.29

Note, 70 S.Cal.L.Rev. 1513 (1997)—
§ 28.5(b) n.55

Note, 71 S.Cal.L.Rev. 617 (1998)—
§ 8.4(c) n.124

Note, 49 S.Car.L.Rev. 597 (1976)—
§§ 22.3(b) n.85, 93

Note, 61 S.Car.L.Rev. 1091 (1989)—
§ 12.3(a) n.24

Note, 26 Seton Hall Legis.J. 215
(2001)—§ 12.3(a) n.18

Note, 10 Seton Hall L.Rev. 369
(1979)—§ 21.2(a) n.21

Note, 8 St. John's J.Legal Comment 225
(1992)—§ 21.3(f) n.333

Note, 8 St. John's J.Legal Comment 251
(1992)—§ 1.5(k) n.337

Note, 39 St. Louis U.L.Rev. 585
(1995)—§ 26.6(d) n.69

Note, 26 St. Mary's L.J. 1103 (1995)—
§§ 1.5(k) n.362; 26.5(d) n.61

Note, 19 Stan.L.Rev. 608 (1967)—
§ 3.1(h) n.225

Note, 20 Stan.L.Rev. 83 (1967)—
§ 27.6(c) n.62

Note, 20 Stan.L.Rev. 476 (1968)—
§ 18.3(c) n.66

Note, 24 Stan.L.Rev. 947 (1972)—
§§ 9.2(d) n.40, 41

Note, 26 Stan.L.Rev. 399 (1974)—
§§ 7.3(b) n.16; 7.3(c) n.43, 44

Note, 28 Stan.L.Rev. 1207 (1976)—
§ 14.1(a) n.23

Note, 29 Stan.L.Rev. 969 (1977)—
§§ 7.1(b) n.10, 11, 16; 7.4(c) n.61;
7.5(b) n.19, 20, 22, 31

Note, 30 Stan.L.Rev. 935 (1978)—
§ 24.4(c) n.18

Note, 34 Stan.L.Rev. 427 (1982)—
§ 1.7(i) n.170

Note, 39 Stan.L.Rev. 427 (1987)—
§ 22.3(c) n.144

Note, 45 Stan.L.Rev. 1027 (1993)—
§§ 26.5(d) n.70, 74

Note, 50 Stan.L.Rev. 1349 (1998)—
§ 26.4(b) n.9

Note, 51 Stan.L.Rev. 567 (1999)—
§§ 21.3(c) n.188; 24.3(b) n.77

Note, 52 Stan.L.Rev. 205 (1999)—
§ 13.2(b) n.35

Note, 52 Stan.L.Rev. 895 (2000)—
§ 22.3(d) n.194

Note, 25 Stetson L.Rev. 1131 (1996)—
§ 6.9(g) n.161

Note, 7 Suffolk L.Rev. 973 (1973)—
§ 22.1(h) n.154

Note, 7 Suffolk U.L.Rev. 587 (1973)—
§ 7.3(b) n.16

Note, 37 Suffolk U.L.Rev. 497 (2004)—
§ 13.3(b) n.16

Note, 38 Suffolk U.L.Rev. 169 (2004)—
§§ 18.5(a) n.27, 29

Note, 24 Temple L.Q. 445 (1951)—
§ 13.3(e) n.49

Note, 33 Temple L.Q. 78 (1959)—
§ 13.3(e) n.49

Note, 13 Temp.Pol. & Civ.Rts.L.Rev.
325 (2003)—§§ 18.5(a) n.27, 29

Note, 13 Tex.L.Rev. 101 (1935)—
§ 19.1(c) n.31

Note, 67 Tex.L.Rev. 181 (1988)—
§§ 11.2(c) n.87, 102

Note, 76 Tex.L.Rev. 1083 (1998)—
§ 3.1(d) n.118

Note, 13 Touro L.Rev. 265 (1996)—
§§ 8.12(g) n.64, 67

Note, 39 U.Chi.L.Rev. 761 (1972)—
§§ 8.4(c) n.125; 15.2(b) n.39;
15.6(g) n.215

Note, 50 U.Chi.L.Rev. 1431 (1983)—
§ 16.4(c) n.38

Note, 64 U.Chi.L.Rev. 317 (1997)—
§ 8.6(b) n.55

Note, 37 U.Cin.L.Rev. 234 (1968)—
§ 9.1(a) n.13

Note, 38 U.Cin.L.Rev. 691 (1969)—
§ 9.2(d) n.43

Note, 49 U.Cin.L.Rev. 462 (1980)—
§ 12.2(d) n.47

Note, 49 U.Cin.L.Rev. 540 (1980)—
§ 13.7(c) n.57

Note, 63 U.Cin.L.Rev. 1487 (1995)—
§ 5.2(a) n.19

Note, 15 UCLA L.Rev. 1060 (1968)—
§ 9.1(a) n.13

Note, 47 U.Colo.L.Rev. 279 (1976)—
§ 6.5(e) n.84

Note, 33 U.Det.L.J. 399 (1956)—
§ 8.1(b) n.22

Note, 40 U.Fla.L.Rev. 989 (1988)—
§ 6.7(b) n.79

Note, 37 U.How.L.Rev. 49 (1993)—
§ 15.6(b) n.64

Note, 1983 U.Ill.L.Rev. 477—
§§ 15.1(b) n.26, 39

Note, 1991 U.Ill.L.Rev. 107—§ 13.5(b)
n.36

Note, 1992 U.Ill.L.Rev. 483—§ 12.1(a)
n.15

Note, 1999 U.Ill.L.Rev. 1015—§ 9.6(a)
n.48

Note, 2001 U.Ill.L.Rev. 1207—§ 5.2(a)
n.19

Note, 2004 U.Ill.L.Rev. 501—§ 6.4(h)
n.173

Note, 49 U.Miami L.Rev. 881 (1995)—
§ 17.4(b) n.82

Note, 13 U.Mich.J.L.Ref. 571 (1980)—
§ 3.2(j) n.265

Note, 14 U.Mich.J.L.Ref. 519 (1981)—
§ 3.4(a) n.21

Note, 16 U.Mich.J.L.Ref. 561 (1983)—
§ 24.8(d) n.47

Note, 16 U.Mich.J.L.Ref. 604 (1983)—
§ 8.7(b) n.59

Note, 37 U.Mich.J.L.Ref. 1181 (2004)—
§ 21.4(b) n.64

Note, 13 U.Mich.L.J.Ref. 143 (1979)—
§ 27.5(a) n.2

Note, 85 U.Pa.L.Rev. 538 (1937)—
§ 13.3(e) n.49

Note, 99 U.Pa.L.Rev. 826 (1951)—
§ 13.3(e) n.49

Note, 102 U.Pa.L.Rev. 630 (1954)—
§§ 18.5(a) n.4, 18

Note, 103 U.Pa.L.Rev. 1057 (1955)—
§§ 13.3(c) n.38; 13.3(f) n.54

Note, 108 U.Pa.L.Rev. 265 (1959)—
§ 3.9(b) n.24

Note, 111 U.Pa.L.Rev. 955 (1963)—
§ 8.4(c) n.115

Note, 111 U.Pa.L.Rev. 1000 (1963)—
§ 15.4(g) n.185

Note, 111 U.Pa.L.Rev. 1154 (1963)—
§ 15.5(a) n.5

Note, 112 U.Pa.L.Rev. 865 (1964)—
§§ 21.1(a) n.8; 21.3(a) n.27

Note, 115 U.Pa.L.Rev. 399 (1967)—
§ 16.2(c) n.43

Note, 130 U.Pa.L.Rev. 981 (1982)—
§ 28.4(a) n.6

Note, 29 U.Pitt.L.Rev. 65 (1967)—
§§ 7.3(e) n.84; 7.5(c) n.34

Note, 45 U.Pitt.L.Rev. 741 (1984)—
§ 3.2(j) n.253

Note, 1971 Utah L.Rev. 266—§ 5.3(a)
n.7

Note, 2004 Utah.L.Rev. 827—§ 1.2(d)
n.272

Note, 11 Va.J.Soc.Pol'y & L. 89
(2003)—§ 6.5(b) n.24

Note, 23 Va.L.Rev. 824 (1936)—
§ 1.6(f) n.380

Note, 51 Va.L.Rev. 1587 (1965)—
§ 18.3(c) n.66

Note, 63 Va.L.Rev. 325 (1977)—
§ 26.3(g) n.89

Note, 63 Va.L.Rev. 451 (1977)—
§ 8.3(b) n.14

Note, 63 Va.L.Rev. 1281 (1977)—
§ 26.4(d) n.54

Note, 66 Va.L.Rev. 1169 (1980)—
§ 21.5(c) n.81

Note, 69 Va.L.Rev. 155 (1983)—
§ 9.6(a) n.37

Note, 70 Va.L.Rev. 1059 (1984)—
§ 26.6(c) n.40

Note, 70 Va.L.Rev. 1603 (1984)—
§ 3.4(c) n.39

Note, 75 Va.L.Rev. 639 (1989)—
§ 12.3(c) n.88

Note, 79 Va.L.Rev. 1381 (1993)—
§§ 25.4(b) n.25; 25.4(c) n.31

Note, 80 Va.L.Rev. 1379 (1994)—
§ 17.4(a) n.56

Note, 80 Va.L.Rev. 1699 (1994)—
§ 21.3(b) n.46

Note, 81 Va.L.Rev. 521 (1995)—
§ 27.6(d) n.146

Note, 81 Va.L.Rev. 1471 (1995)—
§ 6.2(c) n.170

Note, 26 Val.U.L.Rev. 895 (1992)—
§ 21.4(d) n.136

Note, 28 Val.U.L.Rev. 1377 (1994)—
§ 15.6(b) n.64

Note, 18 Vand.L.Rev. 754 (1965)—
§ 3.9(j) n.204

Note, 26 Vand.L.Rev. 1069 (1973)—
§ 6.9(e) n.89

Note, 39 Vand.L.Rev. 1693 (1986)—
§ 6.5(b) n.22

Note, 49 Vand.L.Rev. 197 (1996)—
§§ 26.4(b) n.22, 23

Note, 49 Vand.L.Rev. 1525 (1996)—
§ 26.9(b) n.78

Note, 50 Vand.L.Rev. 1335 (1997)—
§ 24.7(e) n.61

Note, 52 Vand.L.Rev. 1869 (1999)—
§ 5.2(a) n.19

Note, 53 Vand.L.Rev. 983 (2000)—
§ 21.6(a) n.78

Note, 53 Vand.L.Rev. 1355 (2000)—
§ 6.9(g) n.178

Note, 33 Vill.L.Rev. 895 (1988)—
§ 6.2(b) n.50

Note, 46 Vill.L.Rev. 547 (2001)—
§ 8.13(d) n.115

Note, 15 Wake Forest L.Rev. 691
(1979)—§ 21.2(f) n.374

Note, 16 Wake Forest L.Rev. 1031
(1980)—§ 11.2(e) n.141

Note, 31 Wash. & Lee L.Rev. 236
(1974)—§§ 21.4(d) n.99, 140

Note, 31 Wash. & Lee L.Rev. 399
(1974)—§ 22.2(e) n.99

Note, 45 Wash. & Lee L.Rev. 1499
(1988)—§§ 2.12(c) n.171, 173

Note, 56 Wash. & Lee L.Rev. 1079
(1999)—§ 22.3(b) n.73

Note, 59 Wash. & Lee L.Rev. 1545
(2002)—§ 26.9(b) n.55

Note, 45 Wash.L.Rev. 202 (1970)—
§ 7.3(f) n.118

Note, 67 Wash.L.Rev. 691 (1992)—
§ 24.4(c) n.21

Note, 72 Wash.L.Rev. 567 (1997)—
§ 28.6(g) n.82

Note, 52 Wash.U.J.Urb. & Contemp.L.
281 (1997)—§ 12.1(a) n.4

Note, 1963 Wash.U.L.Q. 102—
§§ 15.5(a) n.17, 22

Note, 1966 Wash.U.L.Q. 321—§ 20.3(j)
n.185

Note, 1975 Wash.U.L.Q. 423—§ 7.3(b)
n.31

Note, 59 Wash.U.L.Q. 1019, 1-24-26
(1981)—§ 11.10(c) n.120

Note, 60 Wash.U.L.Q. 1387 (1983)—
§ 7.5(a) n.7

Note, 63 Wash.U.L.Q. 523 (1985)—
§ 12.3(a) n.17

Note, 77 Wash.U.L.Q. 1343 (1999)—
§ 22.5(a) n.8

Note, 79 Wash.U.L.Q. 973 (2001)—
§ 1.8(e) n.83

Note, 34 Wayne L.Rev. 331 (1987)—
§ 6.9(c) n.61

Note, 44 Wayne L.Rev. 1519 (1998)—
§ 5.2(a) n.6

Note, 45 Wayne L.Rev. 1631 (1999)—
§ 1.7(c) n.25

Note, 47 Wayne L.Rev. 1099 (2001)—
§ 3.9(d) n.68

Note, 1990 Wis.L.Rev. 1695—§ 13.2(g)
n.125

Note, 34 Wm. & Mary L.Rev. 527
(1993)—§§ 6.4(e) n.108; 26.4(e)
n.83

Note, 40 Wm. & Mary L.Rev. 1019
(1999)—§ 21.2(b) n.86

Note, 41 Wm. & Mary L.Rev. 333
(1999)—§§ 13.5(h) n.124, 152

Note, 51 Wm. & Mary L.Rev. 333
(1999)—§ 13.5(h) n.125

Note, 12 W.New Eng.L.Rev. 245
(1990)—§ 8.5(i) n.309

Note, 17 W.New Eng.L.Rev. 303
(1995)—§ 5.2(a) n.19

Note, 22 Women's Rts.L.Rep. 169
(2001)—§ 13.2(b) n.35

Note, 1 Wyo.L.Rev. 195 (2001)—
§ 1.2(c) n.157

Note, 16 Yale J.L. & Human. 243
(2004)—§ 6.2(c) n.169

Note, 16 Yale L. & Pol'y Rev. 169
(1997)—§ 13.5(c) n.66

Note, 58 Yale L.J. 268 (1949)—§ 2.3(b)
n.91

Note, 60 Yale L.J. 559 (1951)—
§ 13.3(e) n.49

Note, 60 Yale L.J. 626 (1951)—
§§ 20.1(a) n.5, 10

Note, 65 Yale L.J. 209 (1955)—
§ 13.3(c) n.39

Note, 65 Yale L.J. 322 (1965)—
§ 22.2(c) n.34

Note, 73 Yale L.J. 1000 (1964)—
§§ 1.6(b) n.57, 58

Note, 74 Yale L.J. 170 (1964)—
§§ 1.6(b) n.67; 1.6(d) n.237

Note, 74 Yale L.J. 553 (1965)—
§§ 17.1(a) n.17; 17.1(b) n.34;
17.1(f) n.65, 66; 17.3(e) n.59, 60, 63

Note, 75 Yale L.J. 170 (1964)—
§§ 1.6(c) n.147; 1.6(d) n.238 to 240,
244

Note, 77 Yale L.J. 521 (1968)—
§§ 3.9(b) n.29, 31

Note, 77 Yale L.J. 890 (1967)—§ 7.3(e)
n.84

Note, 77 Yale L.J. 1007 (1968)—
§§ 3.9(f) n.95, 103

Note, 79 Yale L.J. 941 (1971)—
§ 12.2(d) n.47

Note, 81 Yale L.J. 1342 (1972)—
§ 20.6(c) n.70

Note, 82 Yale L.J. 286 (1972)—
§ 21.1(e) n.102

Note, 83 Yale L.J. 771 (1974)—
§ 14.3(a) n.21

Note, 83 Yale L.J. 827 (1974)—
§ 13.6(a) n.7

Note, 83 Yale L.J. 1439 (1974)—
§§ 3.2(j) n.232, 233, 239

Note, 86 Yale L.J. 1395 (1977)—
§§ 21.5(d) n.103, 106

Note, 86 Yale L.J. 1461 (1977)—§ 3.2(j)
n.267

Note, 90 Yale L.J. 889 (1981)—
§ 26.2(c) n.76

Note, 91 Yale L.J. 1641 (1982)—
§ 15.1(b) n.17

Note, 95 Yale L.J. 174 (1985)—
§ 12.4(b) n.49

Note, 97 Yale L.J. 488 (1988)—
§ 13.3(b) n.22

Note, 99 Yale L.J. 187 (1989)—
§§ 22.3(d) n.229; 24.2(a) n.5

Note, 99 Yale L.J. 885 (1990)—
§ 12.1(a) n.15

Note, 99 Yale L.J. 905 (1990)—
§§ 25.2(a) n.11; 25.3(a) n.7; 27.3(b)
n.13, 19; 27.3(d) n.67

Note, 99 Yale L.J. 1069 (1990)—
§ 1.6(b) n.84

Note, 101 Yale L.J. 2017 (1992)—
§ 26.1(f) n.135

Note, 103 Yale L.J. 1333 (1994)—
§§ 8.3(h) n.38; 15.1(d) n.159

Note, 104 Yale L.J. 933 (1995)—
§§ 26.1(d) n.65; 26.3(b) n.8

Note, 115 Yale L.J. 1450 (2006)—
§ 24.3(b) n.74

Nowak, Back to the Future Due Process
Analysis, 45 St. Louis U.L.J. 455
(2001)—§ 2.6(e) n.108

Nowak, Due Process Methodology in
the Post-Incorporation Work, 70
J.Crim.L. & Criminology 397
(1979)—§§ 2.6(e) n.108; 2.9(i)
n.271; 11.2(a) n.18

Nunn, The "Darden Dilemma": Should
African-Americans Prosecute
Crimes, 68 Fordham L.Rev. 1473
(2000)—§ 1.5(j) n.320

Nunn, The Trial as Text, Allegory, Myth
and Symbol in the Adversarial
Criminal Process—A Critique of
the Role of the Public Defender and
a Proposal for Reform, 32 Am.
Crim.L.Rev. 743 (1995)—§ 1.5(j)
n.335

Nunn, When Juries Meet the Press: Rethinking the Jury's Representative
Function in Highly Publicized
Cases, 22 Hastings Const.L.Q. 405
(1995)—§§ 16.1(b) n.39, 42

O

Oakley & Coon, The Federal Rules in
State Courts: A Survey of State
Court Systems of Civil Procedure,
61 Wash.L.Rev. 1367 (1986)—
§ 1.3(e) n.52

Oaks, Habeas Corpus in the States—
1776-1865, 32 U.Chi.L.Rev. 243
(1965)—§§ 28.1(b) n.17, 21

Oaks, Legal History in the High Court—Habeas Corpus, 64 Mich.L.Rev. 451 (1966)—§§ 28.1(b) n.12, 16; 28.2(b) n.28

Oaks, Studying the Exclusionary Rule in Search and Seizure, 37 U.Chi.L.Rev. 665 (1970)—§§ 1.5(a) n.51; 3.1(c) n.34

Oaks & Lehman, The Criminal Process of Cook County and the Indigent Defendant, 1966 U.Ill.L.F. 584—§ 13.1(a) n.5

O'Brien, Juries and Incorporation in 1971, 1971 Wash.U.L.Q. 1—§§ 2.3(a) n.61, 67; 2.6(a) n.1

O'Brien, The Fifth Amendment: Fox Hunters, Old Women, Hermits and the Burger Court, 54 Notre Dame L.Rev. 26 (1978)—§ 2.10(d) n.139

O'Connell, Pretrial Publicity, Change of Venue, Public Opinion Polls—A Theory of Procedural Justice, 65 U.Det.L.Rev. 169 (1988)—§ 23.2(a) n.43

O'Connor, Motion for Acquittal: Waiver by Introducing Evidence After the Government's Case, 6 Crim.Just.J. 1 (1982)—§§ 24.6(b) n.29, 30

O'Connor, Our Judicial Federalism, 35 Case W.Res.L.Rev. 1 (1984-985)—§ 2.12(a) n.52

O'Connor, Trends in the Relationship Between the Federal and State Courts From the Perspective of a State Court Judge, 22 Wm. & Mary L.Rev. 801 (1981)—§§ 28.2(c) n.47, 61

Office of Legal Policy, Truth in Justice Series, 22 U.Mich.J.L.Ref. 437 (1981)—§ 2.9(f) n.115

Office of Legal Policy, U.S. Department of Justice, Truth in Criminal Justice, Report No. 1 (The Law of Pretrial Interrogation), reprinted in 22 U.Mich.J.L.Ref. 451 (1989)—§ 2.9(d) n.82

Ofshe & Leo, The Decision to Confess Falsely: Rational Choice and Irrational Action, 74 Denver U.L.Rev. 979 (1997)—§ 6.1(b) n.16

Ogletree, Are Confessions Really Good for the Soul? A Proposal to Mirandize Miranda, 100 Harv.L.Rev. 1826 (1987)—§§ 6.5(d) n.74, 77

Ogletree, Arizona v. Fulminante: The Harm of Applying Harmless Error to Coerced Confessions, 105 Harv.L.Rev. 152 (1991)—§ 27.6(d) n.137

Ogletree, Beyond Justifications: Seeking Motivations to Sustain Public Defenders, 106 Harv.L.Rev. 1239 (1993)—§ 1.5(c) n.128

Ogletree, Just Say No: A Proposal to Eliminate Racially Discriminatory Uses of Peremptory Challenges, 31 Am.Crim.L.Rev. 1099 (1994)—§ 1.5(j) n.332

O'Hear, Federalism and Drug Control, 57 Vand.L.Rev. 783 (2004)—§§ 1.2(d) n.264, 269; 1.3(c) n.28

Ohm, Parallel-Effect Statutes and E-Mail "Warrants": Reframing the Internet Surveillance Debate, 72 Geo. Wash. L. Rev. 1599 (2004)—§ 4.8(d) n.27

Okun, Investigation of Jurors by Counsel: Its Impact on the Decisional Process, 56 Geo.L.J. 839 (1968)—§ 22.3(b) n.77

O'Leary and Hanrahan, Law and Practice in Parole Proceedings, 13 Crim.L.Bull. 181 (1977)—§ 11.1(a) n.33

Olsen, Judicial Proposals to Limit The Jurisdictional Scope of Federal Post-Conviction Habeas Corpus Consideration of the Claims of State Prisoners, 31 Buff.L.Rev. 301 (1982)—§§ 28.2(c) n.63; 28.3(b) n.50

O'Neill, Rethinking Miranda: Custodial Interrogation as a Fourth Amendment Search and Seizure, 37 U.C.Davis L.Rev. 1109 (2004)—§ 6.5(a) n.20

O'Neill, Understanding Federal Prosecutorial Declinations: An Emperical Analysis of Predictive Factors, 41 Am.Crim.L.Rev. 1439 (2004)—

§§ 1.2(f) n.296; 1.4(b) n.27; 1.4(d) n.65; 13.2(a) n.11

O'Neill, Vindicating the Defendant's Constitutional Right to Testify at Criminal Trial: The Need For an On-the-Record Waiver, 51 U.Pitt.L.Rev. 809 (1990)— § 24.5(d) n.58

O'Neill, When Prosecutors Don't: Trends in Federal Prosecutorial Declinations, 79 Notre Dame L.Rev. 221 (2003)—§§ 1.2(f) n.296; 1.4(e) n.94, 96; 13.2(a) n.19

O'Neill, Why Miranda Does Not Prevent Confessions: Some Lessons From Albert Camus, Arthur Miller and Oprah Winfrey, 51 Syracuse L.Rev. 863 (2001)—§ 6.5(c) n.56

Oppenheim, Waiver of Trial by Jury in Criminal Cases, 25 Mich.L.Rev. 695 (1927)—§ 24.6(a) n.2

O'Reilly, Truth-in-Sentencing: Illinois Adds Yet Another Layer of "Reform" to its Complicated Code of Corrections, 27 Loy.U.Chi.L.J. 985 (1996)—§ 26.3(c) n.17

Orfield, A Note on Joinder of Offenses, 41 Or.L.Rev. 128 (1962)— § 17.1(b) n.32

Orfield, Deterrence, Perjury, and the Heater Factor: An Exclusionary Rule in the Chicago Criminal Courts, 63 U.Colo.L.Rev. 75 (1992)—§§ 1.4(h) n.176; 1.9(b) n.12; 3.3(c) n.142

Orfield, Early Federal Criminal Procedure, 7 Wayne L.Rev. 503 (1961)— §§ 1.7(h) n.137 to 140, 144, 148

Orfield, The Defense of Entrapment in the Federal Courts, 1967 Duke L.J. 39—§ 5.4(b) n.23

Osler, This Changes Everything: A Call for a Directive, Goal Oriented Principle to Guide the Exercise of Discretion by Federal Prosecutors, 39 Val.U.L.R. 625 (2005)—§ 1.7(j) n.222

Osterhoudt, Representing a Grand Jury Witness, 16 Litig. 6 (Winter 1990)—§§ 8.7(b) n.62; 8.8(g) n.167; 8.10(a) n.25

Ostrom & Whitaker, Does Local Community Control of Police Make a Difference? Some Preliminary Findings, 17 Am.J.Pol.Sci. 48 (1973)— § 1.6(g) n.424

Ostrom, Strickland & Hannaford-Agor, Examining Trial Trends in State Courts 1976-2002, 1 J. Empirical Legal Studies 755 (2004)— §§ 1.2(d) n.263; 1.5(c) n.172; 1.5(g) n.263; 1.6(a) n.22; 1.6(h) n.496

O'Sullivan, Deadlocked Juries and the Allen Charge, 37 Me.L.Rev. 167 (1985)—§ 24.9(d) n.44

O'Sullivan, The Bakaly Debacle: The Role of the Press in High-Profile Criminal Investigations, 60 Md.L.Rev. 149 (2001)—§ 23.1(b) n.23

P

Pabst, Statistical Studies of the Costs of Six-Man Versus Twelve-Man Juries, 14 Wm. & Mary L.Rev. 327 (1972)—§ 22.1(d) n.72

Packer, Book Review, 77 Harv.L.Rev. 790 (1964)—§ 1.8(b) n.2

Packer, The Aims of the Criminal Process Revisited: A Plea for a New Look at "Substantive Due Process," 44 S.Cal.L.Rev. 490 (1971)—§ 2.4(a) n.19

Packer, The Courts, The Police, and The Rest of Us, 57 J.Crim.L., Criminology & Pol.Sci. 238 (1966)— §§ 1.6(g) n.393; 2.8(b) n.39; 2.8(c) n.67, 70

Packer, Two Models of the Criminal Process, 113 U.Pa.L.Rev. 1 (1964)—§§ 1.5(a) n.19, 22, 23, 60; 1.5(c) n.152; 1.5(e) n.206; 1.9(a) n.1, 7

Paisley, The Federal Rule on Alternate Jurors, 51 A.B.A.J. 1044 (1965)— §§ 22.3(e) n.272, 273

Palacios, Faith in Fantasy: The Supreme Court's Reliance on Commutation to Ensure Justice in Death Penalty Cases, 49 Vand.L.Rev. 311 (1996)—§ 26.2(c) n.76

Palmer & Linthicum, The Statewide Prosecutor: A New Weapon Against Organized Crime, 13 Fla.St.U.L.Rev. 653 (195)— § 1.4(e) n.71

Paris, Why It Matters, 45 St. Louis U.L.J. 495 (2001)—§ 1.5(k) n.369

Park, The Entrapment Controversy, 60 Minn.L.Rev. 163 (1976)—§§ 5.1(c) n.15; 5.2(b) n.21, 38; 5.2(d) n.47, 49, 51 to 53, 56; 5.3(a) n.10, 11; 5.3(d) n.46; 5.4(a) n.1, 4, 12; 5.4(b) n.19, 26; 5.4(c) n.40, 41

Parnas, The Police Response to the Domestic Disturbance, 1967 Wis.L.Rev. 914—§ 13.2(b) n.32

Parnas & Atkins, Abolishing Plea Bargaining: A Proposal, 14 Crim.L.Bull. 101 (1978)—§ 21.1(g) n.118

Parry & White, Interrogating Suspected Terrorists: Should Torture be an Option?, 63 U.Pitt.L.Rev. 743 (2002)—§ 6.2(c) n.61

Pascal, Habeas Corpus and the Constitution, 1970 Duke L.J. 605—§ 28.2(a) n.3

Paulsen, The Exclusionary Rule and Misconduct by the Police, 52 J.Crim.L.C. & P.C. 255 (1961)— § 3.1(c) n.44

Paulsen, The Fourteenth Amendment and the Third Degree, 6 Stan.L.Rev. 411 (1954)—§ 6.2(b) n.30

Paulsen, The Persistence of Substantive Due Process in the States, 34 Minn.L.Rev. 91 (1950)—§ 2.12(a) n.8

Peller, In Defense of Federal Habeas Corpus Relitigation, 16 Harv.Civ.Rts.-Civ.Lib.L.Rev. 579 (1982)—§§ 28.1(b) n.21; 28.2(b) n.20, 25; 28.3(b) n.39, 50

Pengilly, Never Cry Anders: The Ethical Dilemma of Counsel Appointed to Pursue a Frivolous Criminal Appeal, 9 Crim.Just. 45 (1986)— §§ 11.2(c) n.87, 97

Penrod, Eyewitness Identification Evidence, 18 Crim.Just. 36 (Spring 2003)—§ 7.5(c) n.41

Pepinsky, Better Living Through Police Discretion, 47 Law & Contemp.Probs. 248 (1984)— §§ 1.9(c) n.56, 57

Perkins, Absurdities in Criminal Procedure, 11 Iowa L.Rev. 297 (1926)— §§ 1.5(c) n.145; 19.1(b) n.23

Perkins, Parties to Crimes, 89 Pa.L.Rev. 581 (1941)—§ 16.2(g) n.111

Perkins, Short Indictments and Informations, 15 A.B.A.J. 292 (1929)— § 19.2(c) n.33

Perkins, The Law of Arrest, 25 Iowa L.Rev. 201 (1940)—§ 1.6(f) n.378

Perkins, The Territorial Principle in Criminal Law, 22 Hastings L.J. 1155 (1971)—§§ 16.4(b) n.6; 16.4(c) n.77

Petersilia, Probation in the United States, 22 Crime & Just. 149 (1997)— § 26.1(d) n.65

Petersilia, When Prisoners Return to Communities, 65 Fed. Prob. 3 (June 2001)—§ 26.1(c) n.47

Peterson, The California Grand Jury System: A Review and Suggestion For Reform, 5 Pac.L.J. 1 (1974)— § 8.4(a) n.9

Phillips, A Jury of Six in All Cases, 30 Conn.B.J. 354 (1956)—§ 22.1(h) n.155

Pindur & Lipiec, Creating Positive Police-Prosecutor Relations, 10 J.Pol.Sci. & Admin. 28 (1982)— §§ 1.10(d) n.182, 184

Pirsig & Tietjen, Court Procedure and the Separation of Powers in Minnesota, 15 Wm. Mitchell L.Rev. 141 (1989)—§§ 1.7(f) n.75, 87, 88

Pitler, Independent State Search and Seizure Constitutionalism: The New York State Court of Appeals' Quest for Principled Decisionmaking, 62 Brook.L.Rev. 1 (1996)—§§ 2.12(a) n.33, 68; 2.12(b) n.102, 103, 113; 2.12(c) n.130, 144, 180; 2.12(e) n.206, 217, 219

Pitler, "The Fruit of the Poisonous Tree" Revisited and Shepardized, 56 Cal.L.Rev. 579 (1968)—§§ 9.3(b) n.11, 12; 9.3(d) n.36; 9.3(e) n.52; 9.4(a) n.42, 45; 9.5(a) n.11

Pittman, The Colonial and Constitutional History of the Privilege Against Self-Incrimination in America, 21 Va. L.Rev. 763 (1935)—§§ 2.10(c) n.67, 78

Pizzi, Batson v. Kentucky: Curing the Disease but Killing the Patient, 1987 Sup.Ct.Rev. 97—§ 22.3(d) n.187

Pizzi, Judge Frankel and The Adversary System, 52 U.Colo.L.Rev. 357 (1981)—§ 1.5(c) n.131

Pizzi, Prosecutorial Discretion, Plea Bargaining and the Supreme Court's Opinion in Bordenkircher v. Hayes, 6 Hastings Const.L.Q. 269 (1968)—§ 21.2(b) n.36

Pizzi, Punishment and Procedure: A Different View of the American Criminal Justice System, 13 Const.Commen. 55 (1996)—§ 1.5(d) n.179

Pizzi, The Privilege Against Self-Incrimination in a Rescue Situation, 76 J.Crim.L. & C. 567 (1985)—§ 6.7(b) n.88

Pizzi, Understanding Prosecutorial Discretion in the United States: The Limits of Comparative Criminal Procedure as an Instrument of Reform, 54 Ohio St.L.J. 1325 (1993)—§§ 1.5(a) n.6; 13.2(a) n.7

Pizzi, Watts: The Decline of the Jury, 9 Fed.Sent.Rep. 303 (1997)—§ 26.4(b) n.9

Pizzi & Hoffman, Jury Selection Errors on Appeal, 38 Am.Crim.L.Rev. 1391 (2001)—§§ 22.3(c) n.157; 27.6(b) n.21

Plevan, Jury Trial Issues, in Current Developments in Federal Civil Practice, 706 PLI/Lit 443 (2004)—§ 22.3(d) n.181

Ploscowe, The Development of Present-Day Criminal Procedures in Europe and America, 48 Harv.L.Rev. 433 (1935)—§§ 1.5(c) n.104, 110, 112

Plucknett, Bonham's Case and Judicial Review, 40 Harv.L.Rev. 30 (1927)—§ 2.4(b) n.76

Podgor, Criminal Discovery of Jencks Witness Statements: Timing Makes a Difference, 15 Ga.St.U.L.Rev. 651 (1999)—§§ 20.3(i) n.168; 20.3(m) n.253

Podgor, Department of Justice Guidelines: Balancing "Discretionary Justice," 13 Cornell J.L. & Pub.Pol'y. 167 (2004)—§ 1.7(j) n.222

Podgor, Extraterritorial Criminal Jurisdiction: Replacing "Objective Territoriality" with "Defensive Territoriality," 28 Studies in Law, Politics, and Society 117 (A. Sarat & P. Ewick, eds.) (2003)—§ 16.4(b) n.20

Podgor, Form 8300: The Demise of Law as a Profession, 5 Geo.J. Legal Ethics 485 (1992)—§ 11.4(c) n.97

Podgor, International Computer Fraud: A Paradigm For Limiting National Jurisdiction, 35 U.S.Davis L.Rev. 267 (2002)—§ 16.4(b) n.20

Podgor, The Ethics and Professionalism of Prosecutors in Discretionary Decisions, 68 Fordham L.Rev. 1511 (2000)—§§ 1.9(e) n.144; 13.2(d) n.88; 15.7(f) n.144

Pollock, State Constitutions as Separate Sources of Fundamental Rights, 35 Rutgers L.Rev. 707 (1983)—§§ 2.12(a) n.20, 34

Polstein, How to "Settle" a Criminal Case, 8 Prac.Law. 35 (1962)— § 21.1(b) n.29

Pomorkski, On Multiculturalism, Concepts of Crime, and the 'De Minimis' Defense, 1997 B.Y.U.L.Rev. 51—§§ 13.2(c) n.73, 76

Ponsoldt, When Guilt Should be Irrelevant: Government Overreaching as a Bar to Reprosecution Under the Double Jeopardy Clause After Oregon v. Kennedy, 69 Cornell L.Rev. 78 (1983)—§§ 25.2(b) n.15; 25.2(d) n.27

Posner, Foreword, A Political Court, 119 Harv.L.Rev. 31 (2005)—§ 2.8(a) n.26

Posner, Rethinking the Fourth Amendment, 1981 Sup.Ct.Rev. 49, 52-53—§ 1.5(a) n.51

Posner, The Decline of Law as an Autonomous Discipline, 1962-87, 100 Harv.L.Rev. 761 (1987)—§ 1.1(a) n.7

Post, Dealing With Jurors' Expertise, Natl.L.J., Dec. 12, 2005—§ 22.3(c) n.136

Post & Seigel, Legislative Constitutionalism and Section Five Power, 112 Yale L.J. 1943 (2003)—§ 1.3(b) n.11

Post & Siegel, Originalism As A Political Practice: The Right's Living Constitution, 75 Fordham L.Rev. 545 (2006)—§ 2.9(d) n.54

Postman & Bruner, Perception Under Stress, 55 Psych.Rev. 314 (1948)— § 7.1(b) n.13

Potts, American Penal Institutions and Two Alternative Proposals for Punishment, 34 S.Tex.L.Rev. 443 (1993)—§ 26.1(e) n.95

Poulin, Criminal Justice and Videoconferencing Technology: The Remote Defendant, 78 Tulane L.Rev. 1089 (2004)—§§ 21.4(a) n.7; 24.2(f) n.83, 88

Poulin, Double Jeopardy and Judicial Accountability: When is an Acquittal Not an Acquittal, 27 Ariz.St.L.J. 953 (1995)—§ 25.1(d) n.91

Poulin, Prosecution Discretion and Selective Prosecution after United States v. Armstrong, 34 Am.Crim.L.Rev. 1071 (1997)— § 1.5(j) n.325

Poulin, Prosecutorial Inconsistency, Estoppel, and Due Process: Making the Prosecution Get Its Story Straight, 89 Cal.L.Rev. 1423 (2001)—§§ 24.3(d) n.118; 24.10(b) n.34; 26.4(f) n.111

Poulin, Supervision of the Grand Jury: Who Watches the Guardian?, 68 Wash.U.L.Q. 885 (1990)—§§ 8.5(i) n.308, 312; 15.5(a) n.2; 15.6(e) n.137

Poulin, The Limits of Double Jeopardy: A Course Into the Dark?, 39 Vill.L.Rev. 627 (1994)—§ 25.4(a) n.7

Poulin, The Role of Standby Counsel in Criminal Cases: In the Twilight Zone of the Criminal Justice System, 75 N.Y.U.L.Rev. 676 (2000)— §§ 11.4(b) n.24; 11.5(f) n.100, 106

Poulos & Coleman, Speedy Trial Slow Implementation: The ABA Standards in Search of a Statehouse, 28 Hastings L.J. 357 (1976)—§ 18.3(c) n.66

Pound, Discretion, Dispensation and Mitigation: The Problem of the Individual Special Case, 35 N.Y.U.L.Rev. 925 (1960)—§ 1.9(c) n.54

Pound, Legal Interrogation of Persons Accused or Suspected of Crime, 24 J.Crim.L.C. & P.S. 1014 (1934)— § 2.10(c) n.96

Pound, Mechanical Jurisprudence, 8 Colum.L.Rev. 605 (1908)—§ 1.5(a) n.54

Pound, Organization of Courts, 11 J.Am.Jud.Soc. 49 (1909)—§ 1.6(e) n.317

Pound, The Cannons of Procedural Reform, 12 A.B.A.J. 541 (1926)—§§ 1.5(a) n.4; 1.5(c) n.144

Pound, The Causes of Popular Dissatisfaction With The Administration of Justice, 40 Am.L.Rev. 729 (1906)—§§ 1.5(c) n.144, 145

Pound, The Rule-Making Powers of the Courts, 12 A.B.A.J. 599 (1926)—§ 1.6(e) n.333

Powell, Carolene Products Revisited, 82 Colum.L.Rev. 1087 (1982)—§ 2.8(c) n.64

Powell, Enumerated Means and Unlimited Ends, 94 Mich.L.Rev. 651 (1995)—§ 1.2(c) n.166

Powell, Jury Trial of Crimes, 23 Wash. & Lee L.Rev. 1 (1966)—§ 1.5(g) n.268

Powell, Professional Divestiture: The Cessation of Responsibility for Lawyers Discipline, 1986 Am.B.Found.Res.J. 31—§ 1.7(j) n.211

Powell, Stare Decisis and Judicial Restraint, 47 Wash. & Lee L.Rev. 281 (1990)—§§ 2.9(b) n.27, 32

Powell, The Original Understanding of Original Intent, 98 Harv. L.Rev. 98 (1985)—§ 2.9(d) n.62

Powell and Herchenov, Hostage to the Drug War: The National Purse, The Constitution, and the Black Community, 24 U.C. Davis 557 (1991)—§ 1.5(j) n.331

Prado, Process and Progress: Reviewing The Criminal Justice Act, 58 Law & Contemp.Prob. 51 (Winter, 1995)—§ 1.4(f) n.133

Prakash, The Chief Prosecutor, 73 Geo.Wash.L.R. 521 (2005)—§§ 1.2(c) n.49, 53

Prettyman, Jury Instructions—First or Last, 46 A.B.A.J. 1066 (1960)—§ 24.8(a) n.4

Preyer, Crime, Criminal Law and Reform in Post-Revolutionary Virginia, 1 Law & Hist.Rev. 53 (1983)—§§ 1.6(b) n.43, 93, 95, 100, 101, 103; 16.1(c) n.120

Preyer, Penal Measures in the American Colonies: An Overview, 26 Am.J. Legal Hist. 326 (1982)—§§ 1.6(b) n.28, 29, 34 to 36, 100

Priar & Martin, Searching and Disarming Criminals, 45 J.Crim.L.C. & P.S. 481 (1954)—§ 3.8(e) n.211

Primus, Structural Reform in Criminal Defense: Relocating Ineffective Assistance Claims, 92 Cornell L.Rev. 679 (2007)—§§ 11.7(e) n.64, 68

Project, 35 U.Chi.L.Rev. 259 (1968)—§ 18.3(c) n.93

Project, 76 Yale L.J. 1519 (1967)—§§ 6.5(c) n.35, 36, 41, 45

Project, 86 Geo.L.J. 1353 (1998)—§ 19.1(d) n.64

Project, Parole Release Decisionmaking and the Sentencing Process, 84 Yale L.J. 810 (1975)—§ 1.6(g) n.412

Project Report: Toward An Activist Role for State Bills of Rights, 8 Harv.C.R.-C.L.Rev. 271 (1973)—§ 2.12(a) n.13

Prosser, Mary, Reforming Criminal Discovery: Why Old Objections Must Yield To New Realities, 2006 Wis.L.Rev. 541—§ 1.5(e) n.230

Provine, Persistent Anomaly: The Lay Judge in the American Legal System, 6 Just.Sys.J. 28 (1981)—§ 1.5(g) n.261

Pugh & Radamaker, A Plea for Greater Judicial Control Over Sentencing and Abolition of the Present Plea Bargaining System, 42 La.L.Rev. 79 (1981)—§ 21.1(g) n.118

Pulaski, Criminal Trials: A Search For "Truth" or Something Else, 16 Crim.L.Bull. 41 (1980)—§§ 1.5(a) n.12; 1.5(b) n.71; 1.5(d) n.187

Pulaski, Extending the Disclosure Requirements of the Jencks Act to Defendants: Constitutional and Nonconstitutional Considerations, 64 Iowa L.Rev. 1 (1978)—§§ 1.5(b) n.74; 20.4(g) n.107

Purdy & Goldsmith, Better Do Your Homework: Plea Bargaining Under the New Federal Sentencing Guidelines, 3 Crim.J. 2 (Spring 1998)—§§ 21.1(h) n.198, 234

Pye, Some Views on Miranda v. Arizona, 35 Fordham L.Rev. 199 (1996)—§ 6.5(d) n.77

Pye, The Role of Counsel in the Suppression of the Truth, 1978 Duke L.J. 921, 927—§§ 1.5(c) n.128, 138, 147; 1.5(e) n.207

Pye, The Warren Court and Criminal Procedure, 67 Mich.L.Rev. 249 (1968)—§§ 1.6(g) n.396; 2.8(b) n.39; 2.8(c) n.67; 6.5(e) n.85

Q

Quackenbush, Standing to Contest a Search and Seizure, 33 Tex.B.J. 862 (1970)—§ 9.1(d) n.134

Quick, Attitudinal Aspects of Police Compliance With Procedural Due Process, 6 Am.J.Crim.L. 25 (1978)—§ 1.9(b) n.14

Quigley, Do Silver Platters Have a Place in State Federal Relations?, 20 Ariz.St.L.J. 285 (1988)—§§ 2.12(c) n.171, 173

Quinn, In the Wake of Wade: The Dimensions of the Eyewitness Identification Cases, 42 U.Colo.L.Rev. 135 (1970)—§ 7.3(f) n.121

Quinn, The Effects of Police Rulemaking on the Scope of Fourth Amendment Rights, 52 J.Urb.L. 25 (1974)—§ 1.7(j) n.216

R

Rackmill, An Analysis of Home Confinement as a Sanction, 58 Fed.Probation 45 (Mar.1994)—§§ 26.1(e) n.116 to 121

Radack, The Big Chill: Negative Effects of the McDade Amendment and the Conflict Between Federal Statutes, 14 Geo.J.Legal Ethics, 707 (2001)—§§ 1.7(j) n.263; 6.4(e) n.91

Ramirez, Affirmative Jury selection: A Proposal to Advance Both the Deliberative Ideal and Jury Diversity, 1998 U. Chi. Legal F 161 (1998)—§ 1.5(j) n.333

Ramsey, International Materials and Domestic Rights: Reflections on Atkins and Lawrence, 98 Am.J.Int'l.L. 69 (2004)—§ 2.7(c) n.181

Ramsey, The Discretionary Power of "Public" Prosecutors in Historical Perspective, 39 Am.Crim.L.Rev. 1309 (2002)—§§ 1.6(b) n.76, 83, 84; 1.6(d) n.208, 214, 260; 13.2(a) n.7

Ramseyer & Rasmusen, Why is the Japanese Conviction Rate so High, 30 J. Legal Stud. 53 (2001)—§ 1.5(a) n.6

Randall, Universal Jurisdiction Under International Law, 66 Tex.L.Rev. 785 (1988)—§ 16.4(b) n.36

Raphael & Ungvarsky, Excuses, Excuses: Neutral Explanations Under Batson v. Kentucky, 27 U.Mich.J.L.Ref. 229 (1993)—§ 22.3(d) n.226

Ray, Frivolous Appeals and the Minimum Standards Project, 24 U.Miami L.Rev. 95 (1969)—§ 11.2(c) n.97

Rayder, Comments on Child Abuse Litigation in a "Testimonial" World, 82 Ind.L.J. 1009 (2007)—§ 24.2(e) n.78

Raymond, Merits and Demerits of the Missouri System of Instructing Juries, 5 St. Louis U.L.J. 317 (1959)—§ 24.8(a) n.13

Read, Lawyers at Lineups: Constitutional Necessity or Available Extravagance, 17 UCLA L.Rev. 339 (1969)—§§ 1.7(j) n.215; 7.3(e) n.84, 96; 7.4(d) n.67; 7.5(c) n.34

Recent Case, 78 Harv.L.Rev. 884 (1965)—§ 13.4(e) n.173

Recent Case, 81 Harv.L.Rev. 707 (1968)—§ 9.1(a) n.13

Recent Case, 116 Harv.L.Rev. 697 (2002)—§ 3.8(b) n.20

Recent Decision, 51 Va.L.Rev. 499 (1965)—§ 13.4(e) n.177

Recent Developments, 11 Harv. Womens' L.J. 213 (1988)—§ 13.2(b) n.35

Recent Developments, 19 Stan.L.Rev. 1082 (1967)—§§ 21.2(c) n.115; 21.3(d) n.231, 233, 244

Recent Developments, 34 Vand.L.Rev. 431 (1981)—§§ 13.7(c) n.56, 61

Recent Developments, The USA PATRIOT Act, 39 Harv.J.Legis. 435 (2002)—§ 1.5(a) n.41

Recent Statute, 82 Harv.L.Rev. 1392 (1969)—§ 6.5(e) n.85

Redish, Revitalizing Civil Rights Removal Jurisdiction, 64 Minn.L.Rev. 523 (1980)—§§ 13.5(d) n.87, 88

Redish & Marshall, Adjudicatory Independence and the Values of Procedural Due Process, 95 Yale L.J. 455 (1986)—§§ 2.4(b) n.21, 67; 2.7(c) n.103, 110, 152

Regan, How to Think About the Federal Commerce Power and Incidentally Rewrite United States v. Lopez, 94 Mich.L.Rev. 554 (1995)—§ 1.2(c) n.163

Rehnquist, Convocation Address, Wake Forest University, 29 Wake Forest L.Rev. 1002 (1994)—§ 1.2(d) n.207

Rehnquist, Seen in a Glass Darkly: The Future of the Federal Courts, 1993 Wis.L.Rev. 1—§ 1.2(d) n.207

Rehnquist, The Notion of A Living Constitution, 54 Tex.L.Rev. 693 (1976)—§§ 2.8(a) n.9, 22

Rehnquist, Welcoming Remarks, National Conference on State-Federal Relationships, 78 Va.L.Rev. 1657 (1992)—§ 1.2(d) n.207

Reich, Mr. Justice Black and The Living Constitution, 76 Harv.L.Rev. 673 (1963)—§ 2.8(a) n.17

Reichelt, Standing Alone: Conformity, Coercion, and the Protection of the Holdout Juror, 40 U Mich.J.L.Ref. 569 (2007)—§ 24.9(f) n.104

Reidl, To What Extent May Courts Under the Rule-Making Power Prescribe Rules of Evidence, 26 A.B.A.J. 601 (1940)—§ 1.7(f) n.99

Reiss, Consequences of Compliance and Deterrence Models of Law Enforcement for the Exercise of Police Discretion, 47 Law & Contemp.Probs. 82 (1984)—§§ 1.9(d) n.105, 113

Reiss, How Serious is Serious Crime, 35 Vand.L.Rev. 541 (1982)—§§ 1.5(a) n.44; 1.6(h) n.449

Reiss, Police Brutality: Answers to Key Questions, 1968 Transactions 10-19—§ 1.9(b) n.22

Reiss, Police Organization in the Twentieth Century, in Modern Policing, 15 Crime & Just. 51 (M. Tonry & N. Morris eds., 1992)—§ 1.10(a) n.20

Reiss, Prosecutorial Intent in Constitutional Criminal Procedure, 135 U.Pa.L.Rev. 1365 (1987)—§§ 15.6(e) n.161; 24.7(a) n.15; 25.2(b) n.15

Reitz, Clients, Lawyers, and the Fifth Amendment: The Need for a Projected Privilege, 41 Duke L.J. 572 (1991)—§§ 8.13(e) n.116; 11.9(a) n.21; 20.4(b) n.30; 20.4(f) n.94

Reitz, Federal Habeas Corpus: Impact of An Abortive State Proceeding, 74 Harv.L.Rev. 1315 (1961)—§ 28.4(a) n.2

Reitz, Sentencing Facts: Travesties of Real-Offense Sentencing, 45 Stan.L.Rev. 523 (1993)—§§ 26.4(a) n.5; 26.4(b) n.8

Reitz, Sentencing Guidelines Systems and Sentence Appeals: A Comparison of Federal and State Experiences, 91 N.W.L.Rev. 1441 (1997)—§§ 26.3(e) n.33; 26.3(g) n.77, 82, 84, 88

Reitz, Testilying As a Problem of Crime Control: A Reply to Professor Slobogin, 67 U.Colo.L.Rev. 1061 (1997)—§ 1.9(b) n.24

Reitz, The Enforceability of Sentencing Guidelines, 58 Stan.L.Rev. 155 (2005)—§ 26.3(g) n.88

Reitz, The Federal Role in Sentencing Law and Policy, 543 Annals Am.Acad.Pol. & Soc.Sci. 116 (1996)—§ 1.3(b) n.16

Remington, State Prisoner Access to Post-conviction Relief—A Lessening Role for Federal Courts; An Increasingly Important Role for State Courts, 44 Ohio St.L.J. 287 (1983)—§ 28.2(c) n.62

Remington, The Changing Role of the Trial Judge in Criminal Cases—Ensuring that the Sixth Amendment Right to Assistance of Counsel is Effective, 20 U.Cal.Davis 339 (1987)—§ 11.7(d) n.62

Remington, The Law Relating to "On the Street" Detention, Questioning and Frisking of Suspected Persons and Police Arrest Privileges in General, 51 J.Crim.L.C. & P.C. 386 (1960)—§ 3.8(a) n.1

Remington & Joseph, Charging, Convicting, and Sentencing the Multiple Criminal Offender, 1961 Wis.L.Rev. 528—§ 17.1(b) n.33

Remington & Newman, The Highland Park Institute on Sentence Disparity, Fed.Probation 3 (Mar.1962)—§ 26.3(b) n.8

Remington & Rosenblum, The Criminal Law and the Legislative Process, 1960 U.Ill.L.F. 481—§§ 13.2(e) n.93; 13.4(c) n.129

Rendleman, Free Press-Fair Trial: Review of Silence Orders, 52 N.C.L.Rev. 127 (1973)—§ 27.4(e) n.60

Report to the Attorney General on Double Jeopardy and Government Appeals of Acquittals, Office of Legal Policy, reprinted in 22 U.Mich.J.L.Ref. 831 (1989)—§ 27.3(a) n.1

Restoring Confidence In The Criminal Justice System, 86 Judicature 64 (2002) Crim.Just. Spring 2003—§ 1.5(e) n.230

Rezneck, The New Federal Rules of Criminal Procedure, 54 Geo.L.J. 1276 (1966)—§§ 20.3(d) n.85; 20.3(j) n.183; 24.11(a) n.2

Rhodes, Investment of Prosecution Resources in Career Criminals, 71 J.Crim.L. & Criminology 118 (1980)—§§ 1.10(d) n.181, 184

Rice, Criminal Justice Discovery: A Prelude to Justice or an Interlude for Abuse, 45 Miss.L.J. 887 (1974)—§§ 20.3(j) n.185, 201

P. Rice & R. Katriel, Evidence Common Law and Federal Rules of Evidence § 5.03 (5th Ed. 2005)—§ 14.1(d) n.59

Rice and Saul, Is the War on Terrorism a War on Attorney-Client Privilege, 17 Criminal Justice 30 (Summer 2002)—§ 11.8(b) n.46

Richman, Cooperating Clients, 56 Ohio St.L.J. 69 (1995)—§§ 8.11(e) n.94; 11.6(a) n.7; 11.9(a) n.4

Richman, Federal Criminal Law, Congressional Delegation and Enforcement Discretion, 46 UCLA L.Rev. 772 (1999)—§§ 1.2(d) n.204, 233, 237; 1.2(f) n.296; 1.4(e) n.94

Richman, Grand Jury Secrecy: Plugging the Leaks in an Empty Bucket, 36 Am.Crim.L.Rev. 339 (1999)—§§ 8.3(f) n.32; 8.5(a) n.9; 8.5(c) n.77; 8.5(i) n.326

Richman, "Project Exile" and The Allocation of Federal Law Enforcement Authority, 43 Ariz.L.Rev. 369 (2001)—§§ 1.2(d) n.241, 244, 264; 1.2(f) n.290; 1.4(d) n.68

Richman, Prosecutors and Their Agents, Agents and Their Prosecutors, 103 Colum.L.Rev. 749 (2003)—§§ 1.4(c) n.35; 1.10(a) n.2; 1.10(d) n.115, 172; 13.2(b) n.31

Richman, The Changing Boundaries Between Federal and Local Law Enforcement, in 2 Criminal Justice 2000; Boundary Changes in Criminal Justice Organization 81 (C. Friel Ed. 2000)—§§ 1.2(c) n.104; 1.2(d) n.203, 220, 234; 1.2(f) n.298

Richman, The Past, Present, and Future of Violent Crime Federalism, 34 Crime & Justice 377 (2006)—§§ 1.2(c) n.57; 1.2(d) n.204, 220, 228, 231, 235, 264, 269

Richman & Stuntz, Al Capone's Revenge: An Essay on the Political Economy of Pretextual Prosecution, 105 Colum.L.Rev. 583 (2005)—§§ 1.2(d) n.257; 1.2(f) n.296; 13.4(c) n.133

Richter, One Hundred Years of Controversy: The Fourteenth Amendment and the Bill of Rights, 15 Loy.L.Rev. 281 (1968-69)—§ 2.3(a) n.61

Rigg, The Constitution, Compensation, and Competence: A Case Study, 27 Am.J.Crim.L. 1 (1999)—§ 11.8(c) n.65

Riley, Indiana's Problem Solving Courts Are Succeeding, 49 Res Gestae 5 (April 2006)—§ 1.6(h) n.458

Ringhand, The Rehnquist Court: A By The Numbers Retrospective 9 U.Pa.J.Const.L. 1033 (2007)—§§ 2.8(b) n.44, 46; 2.9(b) n.33, 34

Ritter, The X Files: Joint Trials, Redacted Confessions and Thirty Years of Sidestepping Bruton, 42 Vill.L.Rev. 855 (1997)—§ 17.2(b) n.28

Rizel, A Survey of 27 Victim Compensation Programs, 27 Judicature 485 (1980)—§ 1.5(k) n.360

Roberts, Race, Vagueness and Social Meaning of Order-Maintenance Policing, 89 J. Crime L. & Criminology 775 (1999)—§ 1.5(j) n.320

Robinson, Police and Prosecutor Practices and Attitudes Relating to Interrogation as Revealed by Pre-and Post-Miranda Questionnaires, 1968 Duke L.J. 425—§ 6.5(c) n.35

Robinson, Punishing Dangerousness: Cloaking Preventive Detention as Criminal Justices, 114 Harv.L.Rev. 1429 (2001)—§ 26.1(a) n.4

Robinson, The ABA Standards for Criminal Justice: What They Mean to the Criminal Defense Lawyer, 1 J.Crim.Def. 3 (1975)—§ 1.3(f) n.61

Robinson, The Decline and Potential Collapse of Federal Guideline Sentencing, 74 Wash.U.L.Q. 881 (1996)—§ 26.3(b) n.11

Rochvarg, Joint Defense Agreements and Disqualification of Co-Defendant's Counsel, 22 Am.J. Trial Advocacy 311 (1999)—§ 11.9(c) n.116

Rodgers & Rodgers, Desuetude as a Defense, 52 Iowa L.Rev. 1 (1966)—§ 13.5(c) n.71

Rodis, A Lawyer's Guide to Grand Jury Abuse, 14 Crim.L.Bull. 123 (1978)—§ 8.8(a) n.1

Rogow, Getting Immunity and Using Privileges, 16 Litig. 22 (Winter 1990)—§ 8.10(a) n.23

Roiphe, The Serpent Beguiled Me: A History of the Entrapment Defense, 33 Seton Hall L.Rev. 257 (2003)—§ 5.1(b) n.9

Roland, Progress in the Victim Reform Movement: No Longer the "Forgotten Victim," 17 Pepp.L.Rev. 35 (1989)—§§ 1.5(k) n.361, 379, 384, 385

Romero, Proxies for Loyalty in Constitutional Immigration Law: Citizenship and Race After September 11, 52 DePaul L.Rev. 871 (2003)—§ 3.9(h) n.163

Roper, Jury Size and Verdict Consistency: "A Line Has to be Drawn Somewhere," 14 Law & Soc.Rev. 977 (1980)—§ 22.1(d) n.77

Rose, Expectations of Privacy? Jurors' Views of Voir Dire Questions, 85 Judicature 10 (July-Aug.2001)—§ 22.3(a) n.7

Rose-Ackerman, Risk Taking and Re-election: Does Federalism Promote Innovation, 9 J.Legal Stud. 593 (1980)—§ 2.5(f) n.93

Rosen, Contemporary Winds and Currents in Criminal Law, with Special Reference to Constitutional Criminal Procedure: A Defense and Appreciation, 27 Md.L.Rev. 103 (1967)—§§ 2.8(b) n.39; 2.9(h) n.237

Rosen, Disciplinary Sanctions Against Prosecutors for Brady Violations: A Paper Tiger, 65 N.C.L.Rev. 693 (1987)—§ 24.7(i) n.98

Rosen, Felony Murder and the Eighth Amendment Jurisprudence of Death, 31 B.C.L.Rev. 1103 (1990)—§ 26.1(b) n.31

Rosen, Innocence and Death, 82 N.C.L.Rev. 61 (2003)—§ 1.5(e) n.207

Rosen & Goldkamp, The Constitutionality of Drug Testing at the Bail Stage, 80 J.Crim.L. & Criminology 114 (1989)—§ 12.1(a) n.10

Rosenbaum and Tokaji, Healing the Blunt Goddess: Race and Criminal Justice, 98 Mich.L.Rev. 1941 (2000)—§ 1.5(j) n.330

Rosenberg, The Federal Habeas Corpus Custody Decisions: Liberal Oasis or Conservative Prop?, 23 Am.J.Crim.L. 99 (1995)—§ 28.3(a) n.5

Rosenberg, The Future of Codefendant Confessions, 30 Seton Hall L.Rev. 516 (2000)—§ 17.2(b) n.28

Rosenberg, Winship Redux: 1970 to 1990, 69 Tex.L.Rev. 109 (1990)—§ 1.5(d) n.198

Rosenberg & Rosenberg, A Modest Proposal for the Abolition of Custodial Confessions, 68 N.Car.L.Rev. 69 (1989)—§§ 2.9(h) n.235; 6.5(d) n.78

Rosenberg & Rosenberg, Guilt: Henry Friendly Meets the Maharal of Prague, 90 Mich.L.Rev. 604 (1991)—§ 1.5(e) n.206

Rosenn, The Great Writ—A Reflection of Societal Change, 44 Ohio St.L.J. 337 (1983)—§§ 28.1(b) n.14; 28.2(b) n.19

Rosenthal, Batson Revisited in America's "New Era" of Multiracial Persons, 33 Seton Hall L.Rev. 67 (2002)—§ 22.3(d) n.218

Rosenthal, Prosecutor Misconduct, Convictions, and Double Jeopardy: Case Studies in an Emerging Jurisprudence, 71 Temple L.Rev. 887 (1998)—§ 25.4(a) n.7

Rosenzweig, Civil Liberty and the Response to Terrorism, 42 Duq.L.Rev. 663 (2004)—§ 8.8(d) n.49

Rosett, Discretion, Severity, and Legality in Criminal Justice, 46 S.Cal.L.Rev. 12 (1972)—§ 1.9(d) n.97

Rosett, The Negotiated Guilty Plea, 374 Annals 70 (1967)—§§ 1.9(d) n.99, 111; 1.9(e) n.128; 21.1(a) n.8; 21.1(d) n.44; 21.4(b) n.48

Ross, A Systems Approach to Clinical Legal Education, 13 Clinical L.Rev. 779 (2007)—§ 1.5(e) n.232

Ross, Impediments to Transnational Cooperation in Undercover Policing: A Comparative Study of the United States and Italy, 52 Am.J.Comp. Law 569 (2004)—§ 1.5(a) n.6

Ross Tradeoffs in Undercover Investigations: A Comparative Perspective, 69 U.Chi.L.Rev. 150 (2002)—§ 1.5(a) n.6

Rossman, "Were There No Appeal": The History of Review in American Criminal Courts, 81 J.Crim.L. & Criminology 518 (1990)—§§ 1.6(c) n.150, 153, 154; 27.1(a) n.3, 9, 11

Rossum, The Entrapment Defense and the Teaching of Political Responsibility, 6 Am.J.Crim.L. 287 (1978)—§§ 5.2(b) n.21; 5.2(d) n.46, 50

Rotenberg, An Essay on Consent(less) Police Searches, 69 Wash.U.L.Q. 175 (1991)—§ 3.10(a) n.10

Rotenberg, The Police Detection Practice of Encouragement: Lewis v. United States and Beyond, 4 Houston L.Rev. 609 (1967)—§ 5.4(b) n.15

Rothblatt, Police Interrogation and the Right to Counsel, Post-Escobedo v. Illinois, 17 Hastings L.J. 41 (1965)—§ 6.7(b) n.95

Rothblatt & Rothblatt, Police Interrogation: The Right to Counsel and to Prompt Arraignment, 27 Brooklyn L.Rev. 24 (1960)—§ 6.3(a) n.2

Rothman, Life After Doe: Self-incrimination and Business Documents, 56 U.Cinn.L.Rev. 387 (1987)—§§ 8.13(a) n.15, 19; 8.13(c) n.76

Rothman, Sentencing Reforms in Historical Perspective, 29 Crime & Delinq. 631 (1983)—§ 26.1(c) n.40

Rottenberg, Extraterritorial Legislative Jurisdiction and State Criminal Law, 38 Tex.L.Rev. 763 (1960)—§§ 16.4(c) n.75, 77

Rotunda, Independent Counsel and Charges of Leaking; A Brief Case Study, 68 Fordham L.Rev. 869 (1999)—§§ 8.5(c) n.75; 8.5(e) n.190; 8.5(i) n.326

Rouse, Are We in Focus on Photo Identification?, 7 U.San Fran.L.Rev. 419 (1973)—§ 7.3(c) n.43

Rowland, The Relationship between Grand Jury Composition and Performance, 60 Soc.Sc.Q. 323 (1979)—§ 15.3(c) n.45

Royster & Fausett, Fresh Pursuit Onto Native American Indian Reservations, 59 U.Colo.L.Rev. 191 (1988)—§ 3.5(a) n.27

Rubenstein & White, Plea Bargaining: Can Alaska Live Without It?, 62 Judicature 266 (1978)—§ 21.1(g) n.120

Rubin, A Statistical Study of Federal Criminal Prosecutions, 1 Law & Contemp.Prob. 494 (1934)—§ 1.2(f) n.286

Rubin & Feeley, Federalism: Some Notes on a National Neurosis, 41 UCLA L.Rev. 903 (1994)—§§ 2.5(f) n.59, 93

Rudstein, A Brief History of the Fifth Amendment Guarantee Against Double Jeopardy, 14 William & Mary Bill of Rights J. 193 (2006)—§§ 25.1(b) n.8, 15

Rudstein, Double Jeopardy and the Fraudulently Obtained Acquittal, 60 Mo.L.Rev. 607 (1995)—§§ 25.1(d) n.91, 92

Ryan, Rush to Judgment: A Constitutional Analysis of Time Limits on Judicial Decisions, 77 B.U.L.Rev. 761 (1997)—§ 28.5(e) n.92

Ryan & Alfini, Trial Judges' Participation in Plea Bargaining: An Empirical Perspective, 13 Law & Soc.Rev. 479 (1979)—§§ 21.3(d) n.209, 210, 213, 215, 222, 248, 249

S

Sager, Fair Measure: The Legal Status of Underenforced Constitutional Norms, 91 Harv.L.Rev. 1212 (1978)—§ 2.12(c) n.154

Sager, State Courts and the Strategic Space Between the Norms and Rules of Constitutional Law, 63 Tex.L.Rev. 959 (1985)—§§ 2.12(c) n.121, 123, 127

Saks, The Limits of Scientific Jury Selection: Ethical and Empirical, 17 Jurimetrics J. 3 (1976)—§ 22.3(b) n.95

Saks, The Smaller the Jury the Greater the Unpredictability, 79 Judicature 263 (1996)—§ 22.1(d) n.71

Saks & Marti, A Meta-analysis of the Effects of Jury Size, 21 Law & Hum.Behav. 451 (1997)—§ 22.1(d) n.73

Salken, Balancing Exigency and Privacy in Warrantless Searches to Prevent Destruction of Evidence: The Need for a Rule, 39 Hastings L.J. 283 (1988)—§ 3.6(e) n.108

Saltzburg, A Special Aspect of Relevance: Countering Negative Inferences Associated with the Absence of Evidence, 66 Cal.L.Rev. 1011 (1978)—§ 7.5(b) n.19

Saltzburg, Another View of Illegal Narcotics (As Illustrated by the Open Fields Doctrine), 48 U.Pitt.L.Rev. 1 (1986)—§ 1.5(a) n.41

Saltzburg, Communications Falling Within the Attorney-Client Privilege, 66 Iowa L.Rev. 811 (1981)—§§ 20.4(b) n.18, 32

Saltzburg, Foreword: The Flow and Ebb of Constitutional Criminal Procedure in the Warren and Burger Courts, 69 Geo.L.J. 151 (1980)—§§ 2.8(b) n.43; 2.9(g) n.201; 6.4(h) n.164, 165; 9.6(a) n.42

Saltzburg, Habeas Corpus: The Supreme Court and the Congress, 44 Ohio St.L.J. 367 (1983)—§§ 28.2(b) n.20, 25; 28.3(b) n.40

Saltzburg, Lawyers, Clients, and The Adversary System, 37 Mercer L.Rev. 647 (1986)—§§ 1.5(b) n.71; 1.5(c) n.150, 151, 158

Saltzburg, Pleas of Guilty and the Loss of Constitutional Rights: The Current Price of Pleading Guilty, 76 Mich.L.Rev. 1265 (1978)—§§ 21.6(a) n.53, 57, 67

Saltzburg, Privileges and Professionals: Lawyers and Psychiatrists, 66 Va.L.Rev. 597 (1980)—§§ 20.5(c) n.56, 57

Saltzburg, Standards of Proof and Preliminary Questions of Fact, 27 Stan.L.Rev. 271 (1975)—§§ 10.4(b) n.7; 10.4(c) n.22

Saltzburg, The Harm of Harmless Error, 59 Va.L.Rev. 988 (1973)—§§ 27.6(b) n.36, 50; 27.6(c) n.61

Saltzburg, The Unnecessarily Expanding Role of the American Trial Judge, 64 Va.L.Rev. 1 (1978)—§ 1.5(c) n.101

Saltzburg & Powers, Peremptory Challenges and the Clash Between Impartiality and Group Representation, 41 Md.L.Rev. 337 (1982)—§§ 22.3(b) n.56, 71

Saltzman, The Michigan Supreme Court's Abdication of Authority over Criminal Prosecutions, 80 Wake Forest L.Rev. 282 (2003)—§§ 2.12(a) n.78; 2.12(d) n.192

Sanborn, Second-Class Justice, First-Class Punishment—The Use of Juvenile Records in Sentencing Adults, 81 Judicature 206 (1998)—§§ 26.4(f) n.101; 26.6(b) n.25

Sand, A Report on Seven Experiments Conducted by the District Court Judges in the Second Circuit, 60 N.Y.U.L.Rev. 423 (1985)—§ 24.8(a) n.4

Sandalow, Constitutional Interpretation, 79 Mich.L.Rev. 1033 (1981)—§§ 2.9(i) n.271; 11.1(a) n.14

Sandalow, Henry v. Mississippi and the Adequate State Ground: Proposals for a Revised Doctrine, 1965 Sup.Ct.Rev. 187—§§ 28.4(b) n.16; 28.11(a) n.2

Sanford, Eye Witness Identification in Criminal Cases, 46 Fla.B.J. 412 (1972)—§ 7.3(e) n.84

Saphire, Specifying Due Process Values: Toward A More Responsive Approach to Procedural Protection, 127 U.Pa.L.Rev. 111 (1978)—§ 1.5(h) n.282

Sasaki, Guarding the Guardians: Police Trickery and Confessions, 40 Stan.L.Rev. 1593 (1988)—§ 6.2(c) n.120

Sauber & Waldman, Unlimited Power: Rule 29(A) and the Unreviewability of Directed Judgments of Acquittal, 44 Am.U.L.Rev. 433 (1994)—§§ 24.6(b) n.18; 25.3(c) n.22

Sax, Conscience and Anarchy: The Prosecution of War Resisters, 57 Yale Review 481 (1968)—§ 22.1(g) n.121

Saxton, How Well Do Jurors Understand Jury Instructions?, 33 Land & Water L.Rev. 59 (1998)—§ 24.8(a) n.4

Scalia, Originalism: The Lesser Evil, 57 U.Cin.L.Rev. 849 (1989)—§§ 2.8(a) n.23; 2.9(a) n.1; 2.9(d) n.62

Scalia, The Rule of Law as a Law of Rules, 56 U.Chi.L.Rev. 1175 (1989)—§§ 2.8(a) n.23; 2.9(g) n.150

Schaefer, Federalism and State Criminal Procedure, 70 Harv.L.Rev. 1 (1956)—§§ 2.4(a) n.11; 2.5(f) n.74; 2.8(c) n.59; 6.2(d) n.196; 28.2(c) n.57

Schaefer, Federalism and State Procedure, 70 Harv.L.Rev. 1 (1956)—§ 1.5(h) n.285

R. Schaefer, Law Enforcer, Peacekeeper, Service: Role Alternatives for Policemen, 6 J. Police Sci. & Admin. 324 (1978)—§ 1.6(g) n.425

Schaefer, Unresolved Issues in the Law of Double Jeopardy: Waller— § 17.4(a) n.3

Schaffer, The Defendant's Right of Access to Presentence Reports, 3 Crim.L.Bull. 674 (1967)—§ 26.5(c) n.42

Schanzenbach, Racial and Sex Disparities in Prison Sentences: The Effect of District-Level Judicial Demographics, 34 J.Legal Studies 57 (2005)—§ 22.4(d) n.45

Scheflin, Jury Nullification: The Right to Say No, 45 S.Car.L.Rev. 168 (1972)—§ 22.1(g) n.121

Scheflin & Van Dyke, Jury Nullification: The Contours of a Controversy, 43 Law & Contemp.Prob. 51 (Autumn 1980)—§§ 22.1(g) n.101, 114, 121 to 124

Scheingold & Gressett, Policy, Politics, and Criminal Courts, 1988 Am.B.Found.Res.J. 461— §§ 1.10(e) n.211, 225

Schiller & Manikas, Criminal Courts and Local Legal Culture, 36 DePaul L.Rev. 327 (1987)—§§ 1.4(f) n.100; 1.9(b) n.28, 29; 1.10(c) n.104; 1.10(e) n.211, 215

Schluhofer, Miranda and Clearance Rates, 91 Nw.U.L.Rev. 278 (1996)—§ 6.5(c) n.53

Schmolesky & Thorson, The Importance of the Presentence Investigation Report After Sentencing, 18 Crim.L.Bull. 406 (1982)—§ 26.5(c) n.54

Schneider, Discretion, Rules, and Law, Child Custody and the UMDA's Best Interest Standard, 89 Mich.L.Rev. 2215 (1991)—§ 1.9(c) n.59

Schrock, Welsh & Collins, Interrogational Rights—Reflections on Miranda v. Arizona, 52 S.Car.L.Rev. 1 (1978)—§ 6.5(e) n.85

Schroeder, Warrantless Misdemeanor Arrests and the Fourth Amendment, 58 Mo.L.Rev. 771 (1993)— § 12.5(a) n.1

Schulhofer, Bashing Miranda is Unjustified—And Harmful, 20 Harv.J.L. & Pub.Pol'y 375 (1997)—§ 6.5(c) n.53

Schulhofer, Book Review, 105 Yale L.J. 825 (1995)—§§ 21.3(f) n.336, 387

Schulhofer, Confessions and the Court, 79 Mich.L.Rev. 865 (1981)— §§ 2.9(h) n.217; 6.2(d) n.190, 193 to 195, 202, 203; 6.4(d) n.56; 6.5(d) n.60, 61, 64, 65, 67, 70, 74

Schulhofer, Criminal Justice Discretion in a Regulatory System, 17 J. Legal Stud. 43 (1988)—§§ 1.5(b) n.93; 1.9(d) n.111; 2.8(c) n.79

Schulhofer, Due Process of Sentencing, 128 U.Pa.L.Rev. 733 (1980)— §§ 26.1(a) n.2; 26.4(g) n.126

Schulhofer, Is Plea Bargaining Inevitable?, 97 Harv.L.Rev. 1037 (1984)— §§ 1.10(c) n.86; 1.10(d) n.138, 141; 21.1(g) n.133, 136

Schulhofer, Jeopardy and Mistrials, 125 U.Pa.L.Rev. 449 (1977)—§§ 25.1(d) n.46, 50; 25.2(a) n.8; 25.2(c) n.21; 25.2(d) n.25; 25.2(e) n.40

Schulhofer, Miranda, Dickerson, and the Puzzling Persistence of Fifth Amendment Exceptionalism, 99 Mich.L.Rev. 941 (2001)—§ 6.5(d) n.80

Schulhofer, Miranda's Practical Effect: Substantial Benefits and Vanishingly Small Social Costs, 90 Nw.U.L.Rev. 500 (1996)—§§ 6.5(c) n.53, 55; 6.5(d) n.77

Schulhofer, No Job Too Small; Justice Without Bargaining in The Lower Criminal Courts, 1985 Am.B.Found.Res.J. 519, 525—§ 14.1(a) n.6

Schulhofer, Plea Bargaining as a Disaster, 101 Yale L.J. 1979 (1992)—§§ 21.1(b) n.36; 21.1(d) n.44; 21.1(f) n.108

Schulhofer, Reconsidering Miranda, 54 U.Chi.L.Rev. 435 (1987)—§§ 1.5(h) n.284; 2.9(g) n.155, 156; 2.9(h) n.226, 235; 6.5(c) n.46

Schulhofer, Rethinking Mandatory Minimums, 28 Wake Forest L.Rev. 199 (1993)—§ 26.3(c) n.18

Schulhofer, Some Kind Words for the Privilege Against Self-Incrimination, 26 Val.U.L.Rev. 311 (1991)—§§ 2.10(d) n.126; 24.5(b) n.20

Schulhofer, The Constitution and the Police: Individual Rights and Law Enforcement, 66 Wash.U.L.Q. 11 (1988)—§§ 2.8(c) n.84; 2.9(g) n.185, 188, 191

Schulhofer, The Trouble With Trials: The Trouble with Us, 105 Yale L.J. 825 (1995)—§ 1.5(k) n.366

Schulhofer and Friedman, Rethinking Indigent Defense: Promoting Effective Representation Through Consumer Sovereignty and Freedom of Choice for all Criminal Defendants, 31 Am.Crim.L.Rev. 73 (1993)— §§ 1.4(f) n.112; 11.4(a) n.1, 3

Schulingkamp, Sterilization and Habitual Criminals, 5 La.L.Rev. 124 (1942)—§ 1.6(f) n.380

Schuman, A Failed Critique of State Constitutionalism, 91 Mich.L.Rev. 274 (1992)—§ 2.12(a) n.37

Schwartz, Demythologizing the Historic Myth of the Grand Jury, 10 Am.Crim.L.Rev. 701 (1972)— §§ 8.2(a) n.4; 15.3(a) n.24

Schwartz, Federal Criminal Jurisdiction and Prosecution's Discretion, 13 Law & Contemp.Prob. 64 (1948)— §§ 1.2(c) n.85, 89, 90, 98; 13.2(a) n.7

Schwartz, On Making the True Look False and the False Look True, 41 S.W.L.J. 1135 (1988)—§ 1.5(c) n.138

Schwartz, Retroactivity, Reliability, and Due Process: A Reply to Professor Mishkin, 33 U.Chi.L.Rev. 719 (1966)—§ 2.11(b) n.16

Schwartz, Stop and Frisk (A Case Study in Judicial Control of the Police), 58 J.Crim.L.C. & P.S. 433 (1967)— § 3.8(a) n.8

Schwartz, The Exercise of Supervisory Power by the Third Circuit Court of Appeals, 27 Vill.L.Rev. 506 (1982)—§ 1.7(i) n.174

Schwartz, The Legitimation of Electronic Eavesdropping: The Politics of "Law and Order," 67 Mich.L.Rev. 455 (1969)—§ 4.6(e) n.106

Schwartz, The Limits of Prosecutorial Vindictiveness, 69 Iowa L.Rev. 127 (1983)—§ 13.7(c) n.35

Schwartzer & Wheeler, On the Federalization of the Administration of Civil and Criminal Justice, 23 Stetson L.Rev. 651 (1994)—§ 1.2(d) n.202

Schwarzer, Communicating with Juries: Problems and Remedies, 69 Cal.L.Rev. 731 (1981)—§ 24.8(a) n.13

Schwarzer, Dealing with Incompetent Counsel—The Trial Judge's Role, 93 Harv.L.Rev. 633 (1980)—§ 1.5(c) n.101

Schwarzer, Reforming Jury Trials, 1990 U.Chi.Legal F. 119—§ 24.8(a) n.13

Schwatzer, Communicating with Juries: Problems and Remedies, 69 Cal.L.Rev. 731 (1981)—§ 24.9(c) n.19

Scigliano, Inquisitorial Proceedings and Separation of Functions: The Case of the Michigan One-Man Grand Jury, 38 U.Det.L.J. 82 (1960)—§ 8.1(c) n.30

Scott, Steven, Criminal Constitutional Law—Any Means To An End: Bail, The Consitution, And The Liberty Interest State v. Brooks, 604 N.W.2d 345 (Minn. 2000), 27 Wm. Mitchell L.Rev. 1273 (2000)—§ 12.2(b) n.31

Scott, Fairness in the Accusation of Crime, 41 Minn.L.Rev. 509 (1957)—§§ 19.1(a) n.6; 19.1(c) n.27; 19.2(b) n.19; 19.2(e) n.50; 19.2(f) n.99, 104; 19.3(a) n.18; 19.3(b) n.160

Scott, Jury Nullification: An Historical Perspective on a Modern Debate, 91 W.Va.L.Rev. 389 (1989)—§ 22.1(g) n.120

Scott, Pretrial Detention Under the Bail Reform Act of 1984: An Empirical Analysis, 27 Am.Crim.L.Rev. 1 (1989)—§ 12.3(a) n.17

Scott & Stuntz, Plea Bargaining as Contract, 101 Yale L.J. 1909 (1992)—§§ 21.1(c) n.40; 21.1(d) n.51; 21.2(b) n.46

Searle, The "Administrative Search" From Dewey to Burger, 16 Hastings L.J. 261 (1989)—§ 3.9(c) n.40

Sears, Principals and Accessories—Some Modern Problems, 25 Ill.L.Rev. 845 (1930)—§ 16.2(g) n.111

Seeburger & Wettick, Miranda in Pittsburgh—A Statistical Study, 29 U.Pitt.L.Rev. 1 (1967)—§ 6.5(c) n.35

Seidelson, The Right to Counsel: From Passive to Active Voice, 38 Geo.Wash.L.Rev. 849 (1970)—§§ 7.2(c) n.37, 41

Seidman, Brown and Miranda, 80 Cal.L.Rev. 673 (1992)—§§ 6.5(d) n.62, 66, 67, 72

Seidman, Factual Guilt and the Burger Court: An Examination of Continuity and Change in Criminal Procedure, 80 Colum.L.Rev. 436 (1980)—§§ 1.5(a) n.23; 2.8(b) n.43; 2.9(f) n.109, 115; 28.3(d) n.81

Seidman, Soldiers, Martyrs, and Criminals: Utilitarian Theory and the Problem of Crime Control, 94 Yale L.J. 315 (1984)—§§ 1.5(a) n.18; 1.10(c) n.69

Seidman, The Supreme Court, Entrapment, and Our Criminal Justice Dilemma, 1981 Sup.Ct.Rev. 111—§§ 5.2(c) n.40, 43

Seidman, The Trial and Execution of Bruno Richard Hauptmann: Still Another Case That "Will Not Die," 66 Geo.L.J. 1 (1977)—§ 23.2(f) n.79

Seidman & Stein, The Right To Silence Helps The Innocent: A Game-Theoretic Analysis of The Fifth Amendment Privilege, 114 Harv.L.Rev. 430 (2000)—§§ 2.10(d) n.126; 6.5(c) n.56

Seligman & Tarver, Victims' Rights in State Constitutions, 1 Emerging Issues in St.Const. Law 163 (1988)—§ 1.5(k) n.386

Semararo, A Reasoning-Process Review Model for Federal Habeas Corpus, 94 J.Crim.L. & Criminology 897 (2004)—§ 28.6(f) n.72

Semeraro, Enforcing Fourth Amendment Rights Through Federal Habeas Corpus, 58 Rutgers L.Rev. 983 (2006)—§ 28.3(c) n.79

Sepler, The Next Twenty-Five Years Facing the Criminal Justice System, 47 Am.J.Crim.L. 47 (1979)— § 1.5(a) n.43

Serr, The Federal Bail Reform Act of 1984: The First Wave of Case Law, 39 Ark.L.Rev. 169 (1985)— § 12.3(a) n.17

Serr & Maney, Racism, Peremptory Challenges, and the Democratic Jury: The Jurisprudence of a Delicate Balance, 79 J.Crim.L & C. 1 (1988)—§ 22.3(d) n.256

Seymour, Why Prosecutors Act Like Prosecutors, 11 A.B. City N.Y. Record 302 (1956)—§ 13.2(a) n.7

Shane, Money Talks: An Indigent Defendant's Right to an Ex parte Hearing for Expert Funding, 17 Cap.Def.J. 347 (2005)—§ 11.2(e) n.168

Shapiro, Should a Guilty Plea Have Preclusive Effect, 70 Iowa L.Rev. 27 (1984)—§ 21.6(a) n.3

Shapiro, The Most Cited Law Review Articles, 73 Cal.L.Rev. 1540 (1985)—§ 2.3(a) n.62

Shapiro, Using The Media to Your Advantage, 17 The Champion 6 (Jan./Feb.1993)—§ 23.2(a) n.4

Sharifi, Approaching the Bench: Trial Techniques for Defense Counsel in Criminal Bench Trials, 28 Am.J.Trial Advoc. 687 (2005)— § 24.6(a) n.1

Sharp, The Confidential Nature of Presentence Reports, 5 Cath.U.L.Rev. 127 (1955)—§ 26.5(c) n.39

Shattuck, The True Meaning of "Liberty" in Those Clauses in the Federal and State Constitutions Which Protected "Life, Liberty, and Property," 4 Harv.L.Rev. 365 (1841)— § 2.4(b) n.84

Shavell, The Appeals Process as a Means of Error Correction, 24 J.Legal Stud. 379 (1995)—§ 27.1(a) n.10

Shaw, Prosecution Appeals Taken Midtrial and Following Acquittal: Changing the Trial and Review of Criminal Cases in Ohio, 22 Ohio N.U.L.Rev. 729 (1996)—§ 27.3(a) n.7

Shellenberger, Perjury Prosecutions After Acquittals: The Evils of False Testimony Balanced Against the Sanctity of Determinations of Innocence, 71 Marq.L.Rev. 703 (1988)—§ 17.4(a) n.39

Shellenberger & Strazzella, The Lesser Included Offense Doctrine and the Constitution: The Development of Due Process and Double Jeopardy Remedies, 79 Marq.L.Rev. 1 (1995)—§§ 24.8(d) n.43, 45; 24.8(e) n.49; 24.8(f) n.92

Sherman, Experiments in Police Discretion: Scientific Boom or Dangerous Knowledge, 47 Law & Contemp.Probs. 62 (1984)— § 1.9(d) n.108

Sherry, Grand Jury Minutes, The Unreasonable Rule of Secrecy, 48 Va.L.Rev. 668 (1962)—§ 8.5(a) n.13

Sherry, The Indeterminacy of Historical Evidence, 19 Harv.J.L. & Pub.Pol'y 437 (1996)—§ 2.9(d) n.58

Shiner, Conflicts of Interest Challenges Post Mickens v. Taylor: Redefining the Defendant's Burden in Concurrent, Successive, and Personal Interests Conflicts, 60 Wash. Lee L.Rev. 965 (2003)—§ 11.9(d) n.173

Shone, Lysander Spooner, Jury Nullification, and Magna Carta, 22 QLR 651 (2004)—§ 22.1(g) n.105

Shrague, The Grand Jury in Nebraska, 33 Creighton L.Rev. 39 (1999)— § 15.1(g) n.350

Shrauger & Altrocchi, The Personality of the Perceiver as a Factor in Person Perception, 62 Psych. Bull. 289 (1964)—§ 7.1(b) n.17

Shugrue, The Grand Jury in Nebraska, 33 Creighton L.Rev. 39 (1999)— §§ 1.6(d) n.216; 8.1(b) n.19

Siegel, Spivak, and Costilo, Obtaining A Grand Jury Investigation in Pennsylvania, 35 Temp.L.Q. 73 (1961)—§§ 8.2(a) n.5; 8.2(c) n.33

Silbey, Making Sense of Lower Courts, 6 Just.Sys.J. 14 (1981)—§§ 1.4(g) n.154; 1.10(c) n.97

Silver, Equality of Arms and The Adversary Process: A New Constitutional Right, 1990 Wis.L.Rev. 1007— § 1.5(c) n.139

Silver, Truth, Justice, and the American Way: The Case Against The Client Perjury Rules, 47 Vand.L.Rev. 339 (1994)—§§ 24.3(d) n.109; 24.5(d) n.46

Silving, The Oath, 68 Yale L.J. 1329 (1959)—§ 2.10(c) n.57

Simien, The Interrelationship of the Scope of the Fourth Amendment and Standing to Object to Unreasonable Searches, 41 Ark.L.Rev. 487 (1988)—§ 9.1(b) n.32

Simma & Hoppe, From LaGrand and Avena to Medellin—A Rocky Road Toward Implementation, 14 Tol.J.Int'l. & Comp.L. 7 (2005)— § 1.7(c) n.29

Simmons, Re-Examining The Grand Jury: Is There Room For Democracy In the Criminal Justice System, 82 B.U.L.Rev. 77 (2002)— §§ 15.3(a) n.23, 24, 26; 15.3(b) n.34; 15.3(c) n.59

Simon, Fighting Back: Remedies for the Wrongfully Prosecuted?, 71 Wis.Lawyer 10 (Sept.1998)— §§ 13.5(h) n.124, 131, 134, 136, 137, 143, 179, 189, 191

Simon, Offensive Issue Preclusion in the Criminal Context: Two Steps Forward, One Step Back, 34 U.Memphis L.Rev. 753 (2004)— § 17.4(a) n.56

Simon, The Constitutionality of the Special Prosecutor Law, 16 U.Mich.J.L.Ref. 45 (1982)— § 13.3(f) n.60

Simon, The Ethics of Criminal Defense, 91 Mich.L.Rev. 1703 (1993)— § 1.10(d) n.145

Simoncelli & Steinhardt, California's Proposition 69: A Dangerous Precedent for Criminal DNA Databases, 33 J.L.Med. & Ethics 279 (2005)— § 3.5(d) n.149

Simons, Prosecutorial Discretion and Prosecutorial Guidelines: A Case Study in Controlling Federalization, 75 N.Y.U.L.Rev. 893 (2000)— §§ 1.2(d) n.203, 205, 209, 233, 240, 261; 1.4(e) n.94; 1.7(j) n.222; 13.2(f) n.103

Simson, Jury Nullification in the American System: A Skeptical View, 54 Tex.L.Rev. 488 (1976)—§ 22.1(g) n.120

Simson & Garvey, Knockin' on Heaven's Door: Rethinking the Role of Religion in Death Penalty Cases, 86 Cornell L.Rev. 1090 (2001)— § 24.7(e) n.61

Skansky, The Fourth Amendment and Common Law, 100 Colum.L.Rev. 1739 (2000)—§ 3.7(c) n.58

Skelton & Connell, The Routine Briefing Questions Exception to Miranda, 34 U.Balt.L.Rev. 55 (2004)—§ 6.7(b) n.43

Sklanksy, Quasi-Affirmative Rights in Constitutional Criminal Procedure, 88 Va.L.Rev. 1229 (2002)— § 3.1(c) n.87

Sklansky, Killer Seatbelts and Criminal Procedure, 119 Harv.L.Rev.For. 56 (2007)—§ 2.8(c) n.66

Sklansky, Not Your Father's Police Department: Making Sense of the New Demographics of Law Enforcement, 96 J.Crim.L. & Criminology 1209 (2006)—§§ 1.6(g) n.422, 440; 2.8(c) n.67

Sklansky, Police and Democracy, 103 Mich.L.Rev. 1699 (2005)—§§ 1.4(b) n.10, 11; 1.6(e) n.303; 2.8(c) n.70, 71

Sklansky, Quasi-Affirmative Rights in Constitutional Criminal Procedure, 88 Va.L.Rev. 1229 (2002)—§§ 3.4(c) n.41; 6.5(d) n.77

Sklansky, Traffic Stops, Minority Motorists, and the Future of the Fourth Amendment, 1997 Sup.Ct.Rev. 271, 326—§ 3.1(d) n.118

Skoler, An Analysis of Standards for Criminal Justice Structure and Organization, 12 Crim.L.Bull. 410 (1976)—§ 1.6(g) n.427

Skoler, Protecting the Rights of Defendants in Pretrial Intervention Programs, 10 Crim.L.Bull. 473 (1974)—§§ 1.6(g) n.437; 13.6(b) n.24; 13.6(d) n.66

Skolnick, Deception by Police, 1 Crim.Just. Ethics 40 (1982)—§ 1.9(b) n.18

Skolnick, Social Control in the Adversary System, 11 J. Conflict Resolution 52 (1967)—§§ 1.4(f) n.100; 1.10(d)n163; 1.10(d) n.163; 13.1(b) n.36

Skolnick & Leo, The Ethics of Deceptive Interrogation, 11 Crim.Just. Ethics (1992)—§ 6.2(c) n.120

Slansky, Cocaine, Race, and Equal Protection, 47 Stan.L Rev. 1283 (1995)—§ 1.5(j) n.331

Slobogin, A Jurisprudence of Dangerousness, 98 Nw.U.L.Rev. 1 (2003)—§§ 26.1(a) n.4; 26.6(e) n.80

Slobogin, An Empirically Based Comparison of American European Regulatory Approaches to Police Investigation, 22 Mich.J.Int'l. Law 423 (2001)—§ 1.5(a) n.6

Slobogin, Capacity to Contest a Search and Seizure: The Passing of Old Rules and Some Suggestions for New Ones, 18 Am.Crim.L.Rev. 387 (1981)—§ 9.1(b) n.94

Slobogin, Dangerousness and Expertise, 133 U.Pa.L.Rev. 97 (1984)—§ 26.6(e) n.83

Slobogin, Dangerousness and Expertise Redux, 56 Emory L.J. 275 (2006)—§ 26.6(e) n.83

Slobogin, Public Privacy: Camera Surveillance of Public Places and the Right to Anonymity, 72 Miss.L.J. 213 (2002)—§ 3.2(j) n.265

Slobogin, Race-Based Defenses: The Insights of Traditional Analysis, 54 Ark.L.Rev. 739 (2000)—§ 11.6(c) n.106

Slobogin, State Adoption of Federal Law: Exploring the Limits of Florida's "Forced Linkage" Amendment, 39 Fla.L.Rev. 653 (1987)—§§ 2.12(a) n.9, 69; 2.12(b) n.81; 2.12(c) n.129

Slobogin, Subpoenas and Privacy, 54 DePaul L.Rev. 805 (2005)—§§ 8.1(c) n.46; 8.7(a) n.13, 17, 19

Slobogin, Testilying: Police Perjury and What To Do About It, 67 U.Colo.L.Rev. 1037 (1997)—§ 1.9(b) n.18

Slobogin, The Civilization of the Criminal Law, 58 Vand.L.Rev. 121 (2005)—§§ 26.1(c) n.46; 26.6(e) n.80

Slobogin, The World Without A Fourth Amendment, 39 UCLA L.Rev. 1 (1991)—§ 1.5(h) n.283

Slobogin, Toward Taping, 1 Ohio St.J.Crim.L. 309 (2003)—§ 6.5(d) n.77

Slobogin and Mashburn, The Criminal Defense Lawyer's Fiduciary Duty to Clients with Mental Disability, 68 Fordham L.Rev. 1581 (2000)—§§ 11.5(c) n.59; 11.6(a) n.26

Slobogin & Schumacher, Reasonable Expectations of Privacy and Autonomy in Fourth Amendment Cases: An Empirical Look at "Understanding Recognized and Permitted by Society," 42 Duke L.J. 727 (1993)—§ 3.2(a) n.26

Slotnick, Review Essay on Judicial Recruitment and Selection, 13 Just.Sys.J. 109 (1988)—§ 1.10(e) n.205

Slusser, Hricik & Eastus, Batson, J.E.B. and Purkett: A Step-by-Step Guide to Making and Challenging Peremptory Challenges in Federal Court, 37 S.Tex.L.Rev. 127 (1995)—§ 22.3(d) n.187

Smith, Activism as Restraint, Lessons From Criminal Procedure, 80 Tex.L.Rev. 1057 (2002)—§§ 2.8(b) n.44, 48, 50; 2.9(b) n.37, 39

Smith, English Criminal Justice Administration, 1650-1850: A Historiographic Essay, 27 Law & History Review 593 (2007)—§ 1.5(c) n.111

Smith, Impact of Pretrial Instruction on Jurors' Information Processing and Decision Making, 76 J.Applied Psychol. 220 (1991)—§ 24.8(a) n.4

Smith, Reconstruction or Reaffirmation; 8 Geo.Mason L.Rev. 167 (1999)—§ 2.3(a) n.43

Smith, The Feasibility and Utility of Pretrial Instructions in the Substantive Law, 14 Law & Hum.Behav. 235 (1990)—§§ 24.8(a) n.4, 5

Smith, The Neighborhood Context of Police Behavior, 8 Crime & Just. 313 (A. Reiss & M. Tonry eds., 1986)—§ 1.10(e) n.228

Smith, The Rehnquist Court and Criminal Procedure, 73 U.Colo.L.Rev. 1337 (2002)—§ 2.8(b) n.44

Smith, The Threshold Question in Applying Miranda: What Constitutes Custodial Interrogation?, 25 S.Car.L.Rev. 699 (1974)—§ 6.6(a) n.4

Smith & Pollack, The Courts Stand Indicted in New York City, 68 J.Crim.L. & Criminology 252 (1977)—§§ 1.10(c) n.48, 54, 58, 104

Smithburn and Springman, Effective Assistance of Counsel: In Quest of A Uniform Standard of Review, 17 Wake Forest L.Rev. 497 (1981)—

§§ 11.7(d) n.42, 44, 45; 11.10(a) n.3, 4, 6, 8 to 10; 11.10(b) n.32

Smut Furor: Women's Rights v. Free Speech, 70 A.B.A.J. 42 (1984)—§ 15.2(d) n.114

Snouffer, An Article of Faith Abolishes Bail in Oregon, 53 Or.L.Rev. 273 (1974)—§ 12.2(b) n.37

Snyder, Habeas Corpus: Stoned But Not Dead, 19 Crim.L.Bull. 197 (1983)—§§ 28.3(d) n.81, 87

Sobel, Assailing the Impermissible Suggestion: Evolving Limitations on the Abuse of Pre-Trial Criminal Identification Methods, 38 Brooklyn L.Rev. 261 (1971)—§ 7.5(c) n.48

Sobel, The Exclusionary Rules in the Law of Confessions: A Legal Perspective—A Practical Perspective, N.Y.L.J., Nov. 22, 1965, at 1, col. 4—§ 6.1(a) n.3

Soifer, Protecting Civil Rights: A Critique of Raoul Berger's History, 54 N.Y.U.L.Rev. 651 (1979)—§ 2.3(a) n.64

Solomon, Causing Constitutional Harm: How Tort Law Can Help Determine Harmless Error in Criminal Trials, 99 N.W.L.Rev 1053 (2005)—§§ 27.6(a) n.2; 28.6(g) n.86

Somin, False Dawn for Federalism: Clear Statement Rules after Gonzales v. Raich, 2006 Cato Sup.Ct.Rev. 113—§ 1.2(c) n.136

Sommers & Norton, Race-Based Judgments, Race-Neutral Justifications: Experimental Examination of Peremptory Use an the Batson Challenge Procedure, 31 Law & Hum. Behav. 261 (2007)—§ 22.3(d) n.189

Soroky, Grand Jury Secrecy: Should Witnesses Have Access To Their Grand Jury Testimony As A Matter of Right?, 20 UCLA L.Rev. 804 (1973)—§ 8.5(d) n.131

Spader, Megatrends in Criminal Justice Theory, 13 Am.J.Crim.L. 157 (1986)—§ 26.1(c) n.45

Special Project, The Work Product Doctrine, 68 Cornell L.R. 760 (1983)—§ 8.6(b) n.48

Spector & Michel, The Need for a New Federalism in Criminal Justice, 462 Annals Am.Acad.Pol. & Soc.Sci. 59 (1982)—§§ 1.2(c) n.197; 1.2(d) n.228

Spiegel, The New Model Rules of Professional Conduct: Lawyer-Client Decision Making and the Role of the Rules in Structuring the Lawyer-Client Dialogue, 1980 A.B.F.Res.J. 1003—§ 11.6(c) n.103

Spindell, The Administration of Criminal Justice in North Carolina, 1720-1740, 25 Am.J. Legal Hist. 141 (1981)—§§ 1.6(b) n.43, 80, 93, 95, 103, 108, 110

Spotts, U.S. Immigration Policy on the Southwest Border From Reagan Through Clinton, 16 Geo.Immigr.L.J. 60 (2002)—§ 1.4(d) n.68

Spritzer, Criminal Waiver, Procedural Default, and the Burger Court, 126 U.Pa.L.Rev. 472 (1978)—§ 11.3(c) n.64

Stacy, The Search for Truth in Constitutional Criminal Procedure, 91 Colum.L.Rev. 1369 (1991)—§§ 1.5(b) n.78; 1.5(e) n.210; 2.8(b) n.44; 2.9(f) n.109, 111, 112, 115; 24.3(f) n.158

Stacy & Dayton, Rethinking Harmless Constitutional Error, 88 Colum.L.Rev. 79 (1988)—§§ 15.4(i) n.206; 27.6(b) n.55; 27.6(c) n.62; 27.6(d) n.110, 139; 27.6(e) n.162

Stacy & Dayton, The Under-Federalization of Crime, 6 Cornell J.L. & Pub.Pol'y 247 (1997)—§§ 1.2(c) n.199; 1.2(d) n.203

Stahl & Kuhn, Inspections and the Fourth Amendment, 11 U.Pitt.L.Rev. 256 (1950)—§§ 3.9(b) n.15, 17, 19

Stantz, The Political Constitution of Criminal Justice, 119 Harv.L.Rev. 780 (2006)—§ 1.10(c) n.53

Starkey, Trial in Absentia, 53 St.John's L.Rev. 721 (1979)—§§ 24.2(d) n.38, 42

Starr, The Court of Pragmatism and Internationalization, 94 Geo.L.J. 1565 (2006)—§ 2.8(a) n.26

State v. Jeannotte, 133 Wash.2d 847, 947 P.2d 1192 (1997)—§ 26.3(g) n.88

Stearns, Crime and Delinquency, 59 Fed.Probation 79 (Mar.1995)—§ 26.1(c) n.41

Steele, Kirby v. Illinois: Counsel at Lineups, 9 Crim.L.Bull. 49 (1973)—§ 7.4(e) n.81

Steffen, Truth as Second Fiddle: Re-evaluating the Place of Truth in the Adversarial Trial Ensemble, 1988 Utah L.Rev. 799—§§ 1.5(b) n.70; 1.5(c) n.124, 129, 136

Stegner, Why I Let Jurors Ask Questions in Criminal Trials, 40 Idaho L.Rev. 541 (2004)—§ 24.9(b) n.12

Steiker, Counter-Revolution in Constitutional Criminal Procedure, 20 Harv.J.L. & Pub.Pol'y. 435 (1997)—§ 2.8(b) n.44

Steiker, Counter-Revolution in Constitutional Criminal Procedure?: Two Audiences, Two Answers, 94 Mich.L.Rev. 2466 (1996)—§§ 2.8(b) n.44, 49, 50; 2.9(b) n.42; 2.9(f) n.113

Steiker, Incorporating the Suspension Clause: Is There a Constitutional Right to Federal Habeas Corpus for State Prisoners?, 92 Mich.L.Rev. 862 (1994)—§ 28.2(a) n.3

Steiker, Innocence and Federal Habeas, 41 UCLA L.Rev. 303 (1993)—§§ 1.5(e) n.206; 28.1(b) n.21; 28.2(d) n.83; 28.3(e) n.102, 103

Steiker, Punishment and Procedure: Punishment Theory and the Criminal-Civil Procedural Divide, 85 Geo.L.J. 775 (1997)—§§ 25.1(c) n.25, 29, 34

Steiker, Restructuring Post-Conviction Review of Federal Constitutional Claims Raised by State Prisoners: Confronting the New Face of Excessive Proceduralism, 1998 U.Chi.Leg.F. 315—§§ 28.2(d) n.75; 28.11(a) n.6

Steiker, Second Thoughts About First Principles, 107 Harv.L.Rev. 820 (1994)—§ 2.9(d) n.81

Steiker, Some Due Process Problems: A Response to Jerold Israel, 45 St. Louis U.L.J. 445 (2001)—§§ 2.7(b) n.83, 89; 2.7(c) n.100

Steiker and Steiker, Sober Second Thoughts: Reflections on Two Decades of Constitutional Regulation of Capital Punishment, 109 Harv.L.Rev. 355 (1995)—§ 26.1(b) n.13

Steinberg, From Private Prosecution to Plea Bargaining; Criminal Prosecution and the District Attorney, and American Legal History, 30 Crime & Delinq. 568 (1984)—§§ 1.6(b) n.83, 84

Steinberg, Right to Speedy Trial: The Constitutional Right and Its Applicability to the Speedy Trial Act of 1974, 66 J.Crim.L. & Criminology 229 (1975)—§ 18.3(b) n.2

Steinbock, The Fifth Amendment at Home and Abroad; A Comment on United States v. Balsys, 31 Toledo L.R. 209 (2000)—§ 8.10(b) n.46

Stephens, The Burger Court: New Dimensions in Criminal Justice, 60 Geo.L.J. 249 (1971)—§ 2.8(b) n.43

Stern, Government Appeals of Sentences: A Constitutional Response to Arbitrary and Unreasonable Sentences, 18 Am.Crim.L.Rev. 51 (1980)—§ 26.3(g) n.89

Stern, Revealing Misconduct of Public Officials Through Grand Jury Reports, 136 U.Pa.L.Rev. 73 (1987)—§ 8.3(h) n.37

Stern, The Commerce Clause and the National Economy, 1933-46, 59 Harv.L.Rev. 645 (1946)—§ 1.2(c) n.125

Stern, The Commerce Clause Revisited: The Federalization of Interstate Crime, 15 Ariz.L.Rev. 271 (1973)—§ 1.2(c) n.156

Stern, Warrants Without Probable Cause, 59 Brooklyn L.Rev. 1385 (1994)—§ 3.9(j) n.219

Stevens, Center for National Security Studies v. United States Department of Justice: Keeping the USA PATRIOT Act in Check One Material Witness at a Time, 81 N.C.L.Rev. 2157 (2003)—§ 12.4(g) n.101

Stevens, The Life Span of a Judge-Made Rule, 58 N.Y.U.L.Rev. 1 (1983)—§§ 2.9(b) n.27, 32

Stevenson, Entrapment by Numbers, 16 U.Fla.J.L. & Pub.Pol'y 1 (2005)—§ 5.3(a) n.1

Stevenson, The Politics of Fear and Death: Successive Problems in Capital Federal Habeas Corpus Cases, 77 N.Y.U.L.Rev. 699 (2002)—§ 28.5(d) n.82

Stevenson & Friedman, Deliberate Indifference: Judicial Tolerance of Racial Bias in Criminal Justice, 51 Wash. & Lee L.Rev. 509 (1994)—§ 22.3(b) n.51

Stier, Jr., Revisiting the Missing Witness Inference—Quieting the Loud Voice from the Empty Chair, 44 Md.L.Rev. 137 (1985)—§ 24.4(c) n.21

Stith, The Risk of Legal Error in Criminal Cases: Some Consequences of the Asymmetry in the Right to Appeal, 57 U.Chi.L.Rev. 1 (1990)—§§ 27.3(a) n.8, 9

Stith & Koh, The Politics of Sentencing Reform: The Legislative History of the Federal Sentencing Guidelines, 28 Wake Forest L.Rev. 223 (1993)—§ 26.3(e) n.39

Stoffelmayr & Diamond, The Conflict Between Precision and Flexibility in Explaining "Beyond a Reasonable Doubt," 6 Psych.Pub.Pol. & L. 769 (2000)—§ 24.7(e) n.49

Stone, The Miranda Doctrine in the Burger Court, 1977 Sup.Ct.Rev. 99—§§ 6.2(d) n.204; 6.5(b) n.33; 6.6(a) n.4; 6.9(f) n.105; 9.5(a) n.15

Strachan, Self-Incrimination, Immunity, and Watergate, 56 Tex.L.Rev. 791 (1978)—§ 8.11(b) n.26

Strauss, Miranda, The Constitution, and Congress, 99 Mich.L.Rev. 958 (2001)—§§ 2.9(g) n.154; 2.9(h) n.212, 214, 253; 6.5(e) n.96

Strauss, Reconstructing Consent, 92 J.Crim.L. & Criminology 211 (2001)—§ 3.10(a) n.13

Strauss, Reinterrogation, 22 Hastings Const.L.Q. 359 (1995)—§ 6.9(f) n.144

Strauss, Sequestration, 24 Am.J.Crim.L. 63 (1996)—§§ 24.9(a) n.2, 3, 8, 9; 26.1(b) n.29

Strauss, The Ubiquity of Prophylactic Rules, 55 U.Chi.L.Rev. 190 (1988)—§§ 2.9(g) n.155; 2.9(h) n.226

Strazella, The Influence of Federal Laws in the Criminal Justice System, 10 The Digest 29 (2003)—§§ 1.2(d) n.203; 1.3(e) n.47, 48

Strazzella, Ineffective Assistance of Counsel Claims: New Uses, New Problems, 19 Ariz.L.Rev. 443 (1977)—§§ 11.7(a) n.3; 11.7(b) n.27; 11.8(a) n.23; 11.10(a) n.8, 9, 11; 11.10(b) n.32; 28.4(d) n.35

Strazzella, Ineffective Identification Counsel: Cognizability Under the Exclusionary Rule, 48 Temple L.Q. 241 (1975)—§ 7.3(e) n.84

Strazzella, The Relationship of Double Jeopardy to Prosecution Appeals, 73 Notre Dame L.Rev. 1 (1997)—§§ 27.3(a) n.7; 27.3(d) n.63

Strossen, Michigan Department of State Police v. Sitz: A Roadblock to Meaningful Enforcement of Constitutional Rights, 42 Hastings L.Rev. 285 (1991)—§ 3.9(g) n.133

Strossen, The Fourth Amendment in the Balance: Accurately Setting the Scales Through the Least Intrusive Alternative Analysis, 63 N.Y.U.L.Rev. 1173 (1988)—§§ 3.8(b) n.50; 3.9(b) n.27

Studnicki & Apol, Witness Detention and Intimidation: The History and Future of Material Witness Law, 76 St. John's L.Rev. 483 (2002)—§§ 8.7(e) n.88; 12.4(g) n.97

Stuntz, Implicit Bargains, Government Power and the Fourth Amendment, 44 Stan.L.Rev. 553 (1992)—§§ 3.9(k) n.244; 3.9(l) n.268

Stuntz, Miranda's Mistake, 99 Mich.L.Rev. 975 (2001)—§ 6.5(d) n.80

Stuntz, O.J. Simpson, Bill Clinton, and the Transsubstantive Fourth Amendment, 114 Harv.L.Rev. 842 (2001)—§§ 8.7(a) n.12; 8.13(a) n.43

Stuntz, Privacy's Problem and the Law of Criminal Procedure, 93 Mich.L.Rev. 1016 (1995)—§§ 3.10(a) n.12; 8.12(b) n.13

Stuntz, Race, Class, and Drugs, 98 Colum.L.Rev. 1795 (1998)—§ 1.5(j) n.331

Stuntz, Self-Incrimination and Excuse, 88 Colum.L.Rev. 1227 (1988)—§ 2.10(d) n.155

Stuntz, Terrorism, Federalism, and Police Misconduct, 25 Harv.J.L. & Pub.Pol'y 665 (2002)—§ 1.4(b) n.7

Stuntz, The Pathological Politics of Criminal Law, 100 Mich.L.Rev. 505 (2001)—§§ 1.9(d) n.98; 13.2(a) n.13

Stuntz, The Political Constitution of Criminal Justice, 119 Harv.L.Rev. 780 (2006)—§§ 1.2(e) n.275; 1.6(h) n.494, 499; 2.8(b) n.39; 2.8(c) n.66, 85

Stuntz, The Substantive Origins of Criminal Procedure, 105 Yale L.J. 393 (1995)—§§ 2.10(c) n.52, 53

Stuntz, The Uneasy Relationship Between Criminal Procedure and Criminal Justice, 107 Yale L.J. 1 (1997)—§§ 2.8(b) n.44; 2.8(c) n.66, 74, 78; 2.9(g) n.182

Stuntz, Waiving Rights in Criminal Procedure, 75 Va.L.Rev. 761 (1989)—§§ 2.9(f) n.111; 6.9(f) n.122; 11.9(c) n.105; 16.1(h) n.284, 290

Stuntz, Steiker, and Seidman, Privacy in the Criminal Context, 67 Geo.Wash.L.Rev. 1265-1308 (1999)—§ 1.5(h) n.282

Sturm, The Development of American State Constitutions, 12 Publius 57 (1982)—§ 2.12(c) n.163

Sudnow, Normal Crimes: Sociological Features of the Penal Code in a Public Defender's Office, 12 Soc.Prob. 255 (1965)—§§ 1.5(i) n.300; 1.10(d) n.125

Suggs & Sales, Juror Self-Disclosure in the Voir Dire: A Social Science Analysis, 56 Ind.L.J. 245 (1981)—§ 22.3(b) n.92

Suggs & Sales, Using Communication Cues to Evaluate Prospective Jurors During the Voir Dire, 20 Ariz.L.Rev. 629 (1978)—§ 22.3(b) n.92

Sullivan, Electronic Recording of Custodial Interrogations: Everybody Wins, 95 J.Crim.L. & Crimin. 1127 (2005)—§§ 1.5(e) n.233; 6.5(d) n.77

Sullivan, From States' Rights to Blue States' Rights; Federalism After the Rehnquist Court, 75 Fordham L.Rev. 799 (2006)—§ 2.6(d) n.89

Sullivan, New Mexico's Summary Calendar for Disposition of Criminal Appeals: An Invitation for Inefficiency, Ineffectiveness and Injustice, 24 N.M.L.Rev. 27 (1994)—§ 27.1(a) n.12

Sullivan, Police Experiences With Recording Custodial Interrogations, 88 Judicature 132 (2004)—§ 1.5(e) n.233

Sullivan, The Capital Defendant's Right to Make a Personal Plea for Mercy, 15 N.M.L.Rev. 41 (1985)—§ 26.4(g) n.135

Sullivan and Nachtman, If It Ain't Broke, Don't Fix It: Why the Grand Jury's Accusatory Function Should Not Be Changed, 75 J.Crim.L. & Criminology 1047 (1984)—§§ 15.2(d) n.114, 115; 15.3(a) n.18; 15.5(a) n.25

Summers, Evaluating and Improving Legal Processes—A Plea for Process Values, 60 Cornell L.Rev. 1 (1974)—§§ 1.5(a) n.9, 10, 12, 62

Sundby, The Lockett Paradox: Reconciling Guided Discretion and Unguided Mitigation in Capital Sentencing, 38 UCLA L.Rev. 1147 (1991)—§ 26.1(b) n.22

Sundby, The Reasonable Doubt Rule and the Meaning of Innocence, 40 Hastings L.J. 457 (1989)—§ 1.5(e) n.227

Sundby, The Virtues of A Procedural View of Innocence—A Response to Professor Schwartz, 41 Hastings L.J. 161 (1989)—§ 1.5(e) n.227

Sunderland, The Exercise of Rule-Making Power, 12 A.B.A.J. 548 (1926)—§ 1.6(e) n.333

Sunderland, The Problem of Appellate Review, 5 Tex.L.Rev. 126 (1926)—§ 27.6(a) n.7

Suni, Intro. to the Symposium on Wrongful Convictions, 70 U.M.K.C.L. Rev. 797 (2002)—§ 1.5(e) n.230

Sunstein, Five Theories of Originalism, 19 Harv.J.L. & Pub.Pol'y. 311 (1996)—§ 2.9(d) n.63

Sutherland, Crime and Confession, 79 Harv.L.Rev. 21 (1965)—§ 6.2(b) n.49

Sutherland, The Inefficiency of the Jury System, 13 Mich.L.Rev. 302 (1914)—§§ 1.6(d) n.251; 1.7(h) n.146

Swanson, Enemy Combatants and the Writ of Habeas Corpus, 35 Ariz.St.L.J. 939 (2003)—§ 28.2(a) n.18

Swedlow, Don't Believe Everything You Read: A Review of Modern "Post-Conviction" DNA Testing Statutes, 38 Cal.W.L.Rev. 355 (2002)—§§ 24.11(d) n.39; 28.3(e) n.103

Symposium, 38 Am.U.L.Rev. 255 (1989)—§ 13.3(f) n.62

Symposium, 543 Annals Am.Acad.Pol. & Soc.Sci. 15 (1996)—§ 1.2(d) n.203

Symposium, 71 Brooklyn L.Rev. 1 (2005)—§ 2.8(b) n.55

Symposium, 31 Capital U.L.Rev. 139-241—§ 26.2(c) n.69

Symposium, 22 Const.Comm. 271 (Summer 2005)—§ 2.9(d) n.54

Symposium, 87 Geo.L.J. 2307 (1999)—§ 2.3(a) n.50

Symposium, 30 Mich.L.Rev. 1 (1931)—§ 1.6(f) n.353

Symposium, 3 Ohio St. J.Crim. Law 1 (2005)—§ 2.8(b) n.39

Symposium, 25 Ohio St.L.J. 501 (1964)—§ 10.3(b) n.26

Symposium, 17 Pepp.L.Rev. 1 (1989)—§ 1.5(k) n.366

Symposium, 24 Rutgers L.J. 927-1055 (1993)—§ 2.12(a) n.37

Symposium, 33 U.Rich.L.Rev. 289 (1999)—§ 2.3(a) n.50

Symposium, 8 Wm. & Mary Bill Rts.J. 405 (2000)—§ 2.3(a) n.50

Symposium, Congressional Power to Require DNA Testing, 29 Hofstra L.Rev. 1173 (2001)—§ 24.11(d) n.39

Symposium, Crime Victims' Rights in the Twenty-First Century, 1999 Utah L.Rev. 285—§ 1.5(k) n.362

Symposium, Criminal Discovery, 7 U.S.F.L.Rev. 203 (1973)—§ 20.1(a) n.14

Symposium, Criminal Sentencing in Transition, 68 Judicature 124 (1984)—§ 1.6(h) n.484

Symposium, Discrimination in Law Enforcement, 47 Law & Contemp.Prob. 1 (1984)—§ 13.2(b) n.32

Symposium, Federal Common Law of Crime, 4 Law & Hist.Rev. 223 (1986)—§ 1.2(c) n.35

Symposium, Federalism and the Scope of the Federal Criminal Law, 26 Am.Crim.L.Rev. 1737 (1989)—§ 1.2(d) n.203

Symposium, Free Speech is Fair Trial, 41 S.D.L.Rev. 79 (1995-96)—§ 23.1(a) n.2

Symposium, Legal Aid Work, 124 Annals Am.Acad.Pol. & Soc.Sci. 1 (1926)—§ 1.6(e) n.313

Symposium, Mandatory Arrest Laws and Policies, 3 Wm. & Mary J.Women & L. 189 (1997)—§ 13.2(b) n.35

Symposium on Norms, Law and Order in the City, 34 Law & Society Review 1 (2000)—§ 1.5(j) n.320

Symposium on the Career Criminal Program, 71 J.Crim.L. & Criminology 83-123 (1980)—§ 1.4(e) n.89

Symposium, Stranger Violence, 78 J.Crim.L. & Criminology 223 (1987)—§ 1.6(h) n.449

Symposium, The Changing Role of the Federal Prosecutor, 26 Fordham Urban L.J. 347 (1999)—§ 1.5(c) n.134

Symposium, The Cooperating Witness Conundrum: Is Justice Obtainable, 23 Cardoza L.Rev. 747 (2002)—§ 1.5(e) n.236

Symposium, The Ethics of Criminal Advocacy, 68 Fordham L.Rev. 1371 (2000)—§ 1.5(c) n.134

Symposium, The Jury's Role in Administering Justice in the United States, 21 St. Louis Pub.L.Rev. 1-121 (2002)—§ 1.5(g) n.267

Symposium, The New Data, Over-Representation of Minorities in the Criminal Justice System, 66 Law & Contemp. Probs 1-297 (2003)—§ 1.5(j) n.320

Symposium, The Role of Race-Based Jury Nullification in American Criminal Justice, 30 J.Marshall L.Rev. 907 (1997)—§ 22.1(g) n.105

Symposium, Victims: A New Rights Group Emerges, 37 Mercer L.Rev. 899 (1986)—§ 1.6(h) n.467

Symposium, Victims and Criminal Law: American and German Perspectives, 3 Buff.Crim.L.Rev. 1 (1999)—§§ 1.5(k) n.362, 370

Symposium, Victims' Rights, 8 St. John's J. Legal Comment. 1 (1992)—§ 1.6(h) n.467

Symposium, Victims' Rights, 11 Pepperdine L.Rev. (Symposium issue) (1984)—§ 1.6(h) n.467

T

Tague, An Indigent's Right to the Attorney of His Choice, 27 Stan.L.Rev. 73 (1974)—§§ 11.4(a) n.1, 2, 4

Tague, Ensuring Able Representation for Publicly-Funded Criminal Defendants, 69 U.Cin.L.Rev. 273 (2000)—§ 11.4(a) n.1

Tague, Multiple Representation and Conflicts of Interest in Criminal Cases, 67 Geo.L.J. 1075 (1979)—§§ 11.9(a) n.5; 11.9(b) n.60

Tague, Multiple Representation of Targets and Witnesses During A Grand Jury Investigation, 17 Am.Crim.L.Rev. 301 (1980)—§§ 8.14(d) n.40, 45, 46, 63

Tague, The Attempt to Improve Criminal Defense Representation, 15 Am.Crim.L.Rev. 109 (1977)—§§ 11.7(d) n.44; 11.10(a) n.6

Tague, The Fifth Amendment: If an Aid to the Guilty Defendant, an Impediment to the Innocent One, 78 Geo.L.J. 1 (1989)—§§ 24.3(i) n.183; 24.5(b) n.20

Taipale, Data Mining and Domestic Security: Connecting the Dots to Make Sense of Data, 5 Colum.Sci. & Tech.L.Rev. 2 (2003)—§ 3.2(j) n.241

Taken from Sentencing Guidelines, 35 Geo.L.J.Ann.Rev.Crim.Proc. 655 (2006)—§ 21.1(h) n.142

Tanford, Closing Argument Procedure, 10 Am.J.Tr.Advoc. 46 (1986)—§§ 24.7(b) n.19; 24.7(c) n.22

Tanford, The Law and Psychology of Jury Instructions, 69 Neb.L.Rev. 71 (1990)—§ 24.8(a) n.11

Tanigawa, The Application of the Collateral Order Doctrine to Criminal Appeals in Hawaii, 19 U.Haw.L.Rev. 73 (1997)—§ 27.2(c) n.66

Tarlow, Is There Life After Caplin and Drysdale?, 18 Champion 8 (Sept./Oct. 1989)—§ 11.4(c) n.94

Tarlow, The New Darling of the Prosecutor's Nursery, 49 Fordham L.Rev. 165 (1980)—§ 16.2(h) n.153

Tarr, The New Judicial Federalism in Perspective, 72 Notre Dame L.Rev. 1097 (1997)—§§ 2.12(a) n.6, 37

Taslitz, Eyewitness Identification, Democratic Deliberation, and the Politics of Science, 4 Cordoza Pub.L.Pol'y. & Ethics J. 271 (2006)—§ 1.5(e) n.234

Taslitz, Temporal Adversarialism, Criminal Justice and the Rehnquist Court: The Sluggish Life of Political Factfinding, 94 Geo.L.J. 1589 (2006)—§ 2.8(b) n.44

Taslitz, What Remains of Reliability: Hearsay and Freestanding Due Process After Crawford v. Washington, 20 CrimJust. 39 (Summer, 2005)—§ 2.7(a) n.10

Taube, The Rule of Sequestration in Alabama: A Proposal for Application Beyond the Courtroom, 47 Ala.L.Rev. 177 (1995)—§§ 24.4(d) n.29, 39

Taylor, A Needed Legal Specialty: The Special Prosecutor, 61 Judicature 220 (1977)—§ 13.3(f) n.57

Taylor, Leaks Sometimes Spring From Unlikely Sources, 30 National Journal no. 21 (5/23/98)—§ 8.5(i) n.320

Taylor-Thompson, Effective Assistance: Reconceiving the Role of The Chief Public Defender, 2 J.Inst.Stud. Legal Ethics 199 (1999)—§§ 1.5(c) n.139; 1.5(j) n.335

Taylor-Thompson, Institutional Actor v. Institutional Player: Alternating Visions of the Public Defender, 84 Geo.L.J. 2419 (1996)—§§ 1.4(f) n.121; 11.9(a) n.9

Teachout, Against The Stream: An Introduction to the Vermont Law Review Symposium on the Revolution in State Constitutional Law, 13 Vt.L.Rev. 13 (1988)—§§ 2.12(a) n.6, 11, 35, 77; 2.12(b) n.100; 2.12(c) n.145, 147

Teachout, Light in Ashes: The Problem of Respect For the Rule of Law in American Legal History, 53 N.Y.U.L.Rev. 241 (1978)—§ 1.6(d) n.185

Teague, Federal Habeas Corpus and Ineffective Representation of Counsel: The Supreme Court Has Work To Do, 31 Stan.L.Rev. 1 (1978)—§§ 28.4(a) n.8; 28.4(d) n.35

Thaman, Is America a Systematic Violator of Human Rights in the Administration of Criminal Justice, 44 St. Louis Univ. L.J. 999 (2000)—§ 1.7(c) n.14

Thaxton and Rodriguez-Taseff, Professionalism and Life in the Trenches: The Case of the Public Defender, 8 St. Thomas L.Rev. 185 (1995)—§ 1.5(j) n.335

The Supreme Court, 1953 Term, 68 Harv.L.Rev. 104 (1954)—§ 9.6(a) n.4

The Supreme Court, 1959 Term, 74 Harv.L.Rev. 81 (1960)—§ 17.3(c) n.39

The Supreme Court, 1970 Term, 85 Harv.L.Rev. 3 (1971)—§§ 3.4(b) n.27; 3.4(k) n.234

The Supreme Court, 1970 Term, 85 Harv.L.Rev. 38 (1971)—§ 9.6(a) n.13

The Supreme Court, 1971 Term, 86 Harv.L.Rev. 50 (1972)—§ 3.8(d) n.161

The Supreme Court, 1978 Term, 93 Harv.L.Rev. 60 (1979)—§§ 21.2(a) n.11, 20

The Supreme Court, 1986 Term Leading Cases: Confrontation Clause-Right to Discover Confidential Documents, 101 Harv.L.Rev. 119 (1987)—§ 24.3(a) n.5

Theis, Preliminary Hearings in Homicide Cases: A Hearing Delayed Is A Hearing Denied, 62 J.Crim.L.C. & P.S. 17 (1971)—§ 14.1(a) n.5

Theus, "Leaks" in Federal Grand Jury Proceedings, 10 St. Thomas L.Rev. 551 (1998)—§§ 8.3(f) n.32; 8.5(i) n.326

Thibaut, Walker & Lind, Adversary Presentation and Bias in Legal Decisionmaking, 86 Harv.L.Rev. 386 (1972)—§§ 1.5(c) n.105, 120; 1.5(i) n.302

Thomas, A Philosophical Account of Coerced Self-Incrimination, 5 Yale J.L. & Human. 79 (1993)—§ 6.5(c) n.58

Thomas, An Elegant Theory of Double Jeopardy, 1988 Ill.L.Rev. 827—§§ 25.1(b) n.13; 25.3(b) n.12; 25.4(c) n.34

Thomas, Colonial Criminal law and Procedure: The Royal Colony of New Jersey 1749-57, 1 N.Y.U.J. of Law & Lib. 671 (2005)—§§ 1.6(b) n.43, 58

Thomas, et al., Is It Ever Too Late For Innocence?, 64 U.Pitt.L.Rev. 263 (2003)—§ 28.3(e) n.100

Thomas, History's Lesson For the Right to Counsel, 2004 Illinois L.Rev. 543 (2004)—§ 11.10(a) n.16

Thomas, Improving American Justice by Looking at the World, 91 J.Crim.L. & Criminology 791 (2001)—§ 1.5(a) n.6

Thomas, Is Miranda a Real-World Failure? A Plea for More (and Better) Empirical Evidence, 43 UCLA L.Rev. 821 (1996)—§ 6.5(c) n.51

Thomas, Judges Are Not Economists and Other Reasons to be Skeptical of Contingent Suppression Orders: A Response to Professor Dripps, 38 Am.Crim.L.Rev. 47 (2001)—§ 3.1(c) n.46

Thomas, Judging, 45 U.Kan.L.Rev. 1 (1996)—§ 2.8(a) n.9

Thomas, Plain Talk About the Miranda Empirical Debate: A "Steady-State" Theory of Confessions, 43 UCLA L.Rev. 933 (1996)—§§ 6.5(c) n.56, 57

Thomas, Remapping the Criminal Procedure Universe, 82 Va.L.Rev. 1819 (1997)—§§ 2.9(f) n.111, 114

Thomas, Separated at Birth but Siblings Nonetheless: Miranda and the Due Process Notice Cases, 99 Mich.L.Rev. 1081 (2001)—§ 6.5(e) n.96

Thomas, Solving the Double Jeopardy Mistrial Riddle, 69 S.Cal.L.Rev. 1551 (1996)—§ 25.1(e) n.98

Thomas, Stories About Miranda, 102 Mich.L.Rev. 1959 (2004)—§ 6.5(c) n.43

Thomas, Symposium: Comparative Criminal Justice Issues in the United States, West Germany, England, and France: Sentencing in England, 42 Md.L.Rev. 90 (1983)—§ 26.3(g) n.68

Thomas, The Criminal Procedure Road Not Taken: Due Process and the Protection Of Innocence, 3 Ohio St. J.Crim.L. 269 (2005)—§ 2.7(a) n.14

Thomas, The Poisoned Fruit of Pretrial Detention, 61 N.Y.U.L.Rev. 413 (1986)—§ 9.4(a) n.10

Thomas, Through A Glass Darkly: Seeing the Real Warren Court Criminal Justice Legacy, 3 Ohio St. J.Crim.L. 1 (2005)—§ 2.7(a) n.12

Thomas, When Constitutional Worlds Collide: Resurrecting The Framer's Bill of Rights and Criminal Procedure, 100 Mich.L.Rev. 145 (2001)—§§ 2.2 n.8; 2.3(a) n.15, 61, 64, 67, 68, 74; 2.5(b) n.13; 2.5(f) n.91; 2.6(c) n.86, 88

Thomas & Greenbaum, Justice Story Cuts the Gordian Knot of Hung Jury Instructions, 15 Wm. & Mary Bill Rts. J. 893 (2007)—§ 24.9(d) n.32

Thompson, Death Qualification After Wainwright v. Witt and Lockhart v. McCree, 13 Law & Human Behavior 185 (1989)—§§ 22.3(c) n.144, 159

Tiersma, The Rocky Road to Legal Reform: Improving the Language of Jury Instructions, 66 Brook.L.Rev. 1081 (2001)—§ 24.8(c) n.42

Tigar, The Supreme Court 1969 Term, Foreword: Waiver of Constitutional Rights: Disquiet in the Citadel, 84 Harv.L.Rev. 1 (1970)—§ 24.2(c) n.33

Tigar, Waiver of Constitutional Rights: Disquiet in the Citadel, 84 Harv.L.Rev. 1 (1970)—§ 21.6(a) n.15

Tinkle, State Constitutional Law in Maine: At The Crossroads, 13 Vt.L.Rev. 61 (1988)—§§ 2.12(a) n.18; 2.12(c) n.134, 135, 138, 166; 2.12(d) n.182

Tobolowsky, Restitution in the Federal Criminal Justice System, 77 Judicature 90 (1993)—§ 26.6(c) n.32

Tobolowsky, Victim Participation in the Criminal Justice Process: Fifteen Years After the President's Task Force on Victims of Crime, 25 New Engl.J. on Crim. & Civ. Confinement 21 (1999)—§§ 13.1(a) n.14; 21.3(f) n.307

Tomkovicz, California v. Acevedo, The Walls Close in on the Warrant Requirement, 29 Am.Crim.L.Rev. 1103 (1992)—§§ 1.6(h) n.475; 3.5(e) n.208; 3.7(c) n.47

Tomkovicz, The Massiah Right to Exclusion: Constitutional Premises and Doctrinal Implication, 67 N.C.L.Rev. 751 (1989)—§ 2.9(h) n.217

Tomkovicz, The Truth About Massiah, 23 U.Mich.J.L.Ref. 641 (1990)—§ 2.9(h) n.217

Tomlinson, Constitutional Limits On Prosecutorial Discovery, 23 San Diego L.Rev. 923 (1986)—§§ 8.13(e) n.116; 20.4(d) n.55; 20.4(f) n.92

Tomlinson, Use of The Freedom of Information Act for Discovery Purposes, 43 Md.L.Rev. 119 (1984)—§§ 20.2(d) n.76, 80

Tone, Voir Dire, New Supreme Court Rule 24-1: How It Works, 47 Ill.B.J. 140 (1958)—§§ 22.3(a) n.34; 22.3(b) n.56

Tonry, Sentencing Guidelines and the Model Penal Code, 19 Rutgers L.J. 823 (1988)—§ 26.3(b) n.10

Tonry, The Functions of Sentencing and Sentencing Reform, 58 Stanf.L.Rev. 37 (2005)—§ 1.2(d) n.238

Tonry, Twenty Years of Sentencing Reform: Steps Forward, Steps Backward, 78 Judicature 169 (Jan.-Feb. 1995)—§ 26.1(c) n.44

Tonry & Lynch, Intermediate Sanctions, 20 Crime & Just. 99 (1996)—§ 26.1(e) n.92

Towne, The Historical Origins of Bench Trial for Serious Crime, 26 Am.J.Legal.Hist. 123 (1982)—§§ 1.6(d) n.247, 248; 24.6(a) n.2

Traynor, Ground Lost and Found in Criminal Discovery, 39 N.Y.U.L.Rev. 228 (1964)—§§ 20.1(b) n.20, 25; 20.4(d) n.54

Traynor, Mapp v. Ohio at Large in the Fifty States, 1962 Duke L.J. 319—§§ 3.1(c) n.31; 3.4(k) n.217

Traynor, The Devils of Due Process in Criminal Detection, Detention, and Trial, 33 U.Chi.L.Rev. 657 (1966)—§§ 2.10(c) n.96; 6.7(b) n.91

Tribe, An Ounce of Detention: Preventive Justice in the World of John Mitchell, 56 Va.L.Rev. 371 (1970)—§§ 12.3(a) n.4; 12.3(c) n.83, 85; 12.3(d) n.91, 101; 12.4(a) n.14

Tribe, Constitutional Calculus: Equal Justice or Economic Efficiency, 98 Harv.L.Rev. 592 (1985)—§ 1.5(a) n.36

Trotter & Cooper, State Trial Court Delay: Efforts at Reform, 31 Am.U.L.Rev. 213 (1982)—§ 18.3(c) n.66

Trowbridge, Restraining the Prosecutor: Restrictions on Threatening Prosecution for Civil Ends, 37 Me.L.Rev. 41 (1985)—§ 13.5(a) n.24

Tullis & Ludlow, Admissibility of Evidence Seized in Another Jurisdiction: Choice of Law and the Exclusionary Rule, 10 U.S.F.L.Rev. 67 (1975)—§§ 2.12(c) n.171, 173

Turner, et al., An Evaluation of the Federal Government's Violent Offender Incarceration and Truth-in-Sentencing Incentive Grants, 86 Prison J. 364 (2006)—§ 26.1(c) n.48

Turner, Nonevidentiary Use of Immunized Testimony: Twenty Years After Kastigar and the Jury Is Still Out, 20 Am.J.Crim.L. 105 (1992)—§ 8.11(c) n.34

Tushnet, Judicial Revision of the Habeas Corpus Statutes: A Note on Schneckloth v. Bustamonte, 1975 Wis.L.Rev. 484—§ 28.2(b) n.25

Tushnet, Legal Scholarship in the United States: An Overview, 50 Mod.L.Rev. 804 (1987)—§ 1.1(a) n.7

Tushnet, Observations on the New Revolution in Constitutional Criminal Procedure, 94 Geo.L.J. 1627 (2006)—§ 2.8(b) n.44

Tushnet, "The King of France with Forty Thousand Men": Felker v. Turpin and the Supreme Court's Deliberative Processes, 1996 Sup.Ct.Rev. 163—§ 28.2(a) n.11

Twist, The Crime Victims' Rights Amendment and Two Good and Perfect Things, 1999 Utah L.Rev. 369—§ 12.1(f) n.85

U

Uelman, Testing the Assumptions of Neil v. Biggers: An Experiment in Eyewitness Identification, 16 Crim.L.Bull. 358 (1980)—§ 7.4(c) n.61

Underwood, Let's Put Pleas Discussions—and Agreements—on Record, 1 Loyola L.J. 1 (1970)—§ 21.3(d) n.236

Uphoff, Convicting the Innocent: Aberration or Systemic Problem?, 2006 Wis.L.Rev. 739—§§ 1.4(f) n.113, 122

Uphoff, Who Should Control the Decision To Call A Witness: Respecting A Criminal Defendant's Tactical Choices, 68 U.Cin.L.Rev. 763 (2000)—§§ 11.6(a) n.2, 37, 60

Uphoff and Wood, The Allocation of Decisionmaking Between Defense Counsel and Defendant: An Empirical Study of Attorney-Client Decisionmaking, 47 Kan.L.Rev. 1 (1998)—§§ 11.6(a) n.2, 5, 60

Urbansky, Rachael, Seducing The Target: Sexual Intercouse As Outrageous Government Conduct, 50 Case W.Res.L.Rev. 729 (2000)—§ 5.4(c) n.29

U.S. Department of Justice, 1991 Annual Report of the United States Attorney General, 9 (1992)—§ 1.2(d) n.230

U.S. Department of Justice, Office of Legal Policy, Report to the Attorney General on the Judiciary's Use of Supervisory Power to Control Federal Law Enforcement Activity, 22 Mich.J.L.Ref. 773 (1989)—§ 1.7(i) n.154

U.S. Department of Justice, Office of Legal Policy, Truth in Criminal Justice Series, reprinted in 22 U.Mich.J.L.Ref. 437 (1989)—§ 2.9(f) n.109

Utter, State Constitutional Law: The United States Supreme Court and Democratic Accountability: Is There A Crocodile in the Bathtub?, 64 Wash.L.Rev. 19 (1989)—§§ 2.12(a) n.11; 2.12(c) n.153

Utter, Swimming in the Jaws of the Crocodile: State Court Comments on Federal Constitutional Issues When Disposing of Cases on State Constitutional Grounds, 63 Tex.L.Rev. 1025 (1985)—§§ 2.12(b) n.105; 2.12(c) n.160

Utter, The Practice of Principled Decision-Making in State Constitutionalism: Washington's Experience, 65 Temp.L.Rev. 1153 (1992)—§§ 2.12(a) n.17, 37; 2.12(b) n.103

Utter and Pitler, Presenting a State Constitutional Argument: Comment on Theory and Technique, 20 Ind.L.Rev. 635 (1987)—§§ 2.12(a) n.18; 2.12(b) n.80; 2.12(c) n.152

Uviller, Barker v. Wingo: Speedy Trial Gets a Fast Shuffle, 72 Colum.L.Rev. 1376 (1972)—§§ 18.1(b) n.17, 18; 18.2(b) n.5, 6, 8, 9; 18.2(c) n.32, 33, 35, 39

Uviller, Calling the Shots: The Allocation of Choice Between the Accused and Counsel in the Defense of a Criminal Case, 52 Rutgers L.Rev. 719 (2000)—§§ 11.6(a) n.26; 11.6(c) n.106

Uviller, Evidence from the Mind of the Criminal Suspect: A Reconsideration of the Current Rules of Access and Restraint, 87 Colum.L.Rev. 1137 (1987)—§ 3.10(c) n.83

Uviller, Foreword: Fisher Goes On the Quintessential Fishing Expedition and Hubbell Is Off the Hook, 91 J.Crim.L. & Criminology 311 (2001)—§§ 8.13(a) n.33, 42; 8.13(c) n.86

Uviller, Pleading Guilty: A Critique of Four Models, 41 Law & Contemp.Prob. 102 (1977)—§§ 1.6(h) n.461; 21.3(d) n.262; 21.4(f) n.190, 208

Uviller, The Advocate, The Truth, and Judicial Hackles: A Reaction to Judge Frankel's Idea, 123 U.Pa.L.Rev. 1067 (1975)—§§ 1.5(b) n.71, 73

Uviller, The Neutral Prosecutor: The Obligation of Dispassion in a Passionate Pursuit, 68 Fordham L.Rev. 1695 (2000)—§ 15.7(f) n.144

Uviller, The Role of the Defense Lawyer at a Lineup in Light of the Wade, Gilbert and Stovall Decisions, 4 Crim.L.Bull. 273 (1968)—§§ 7.3(e) n.84, 88, 95; 7.3(f) n.122; 7.4(g) n.108

Uviller, The Unworthy Victim: Police Discretion in the Credibility Call, 47 Law & Contemp.Probs. 15 (1984)—§§ 1.9(c) n.58, 59; 1.9(e) n.144

Uviller, The Virtuous Prosecutor in Quest of an Ethical Standard: Guidance from the A.B.A., 71 Mich.L.Rev. 1145 (1973)—§ 13.2(d) n.86

V

Vaira and Huyett, Time For A Rule Certain: A Proposal To End Multiple Representation of Grand Jury Witnesses, 85 Dick.L.Rev. 381 (1981)—§ 8.14(d) n.41

Valenti & Downing, Six Versus Twelve Member Juries; An Experimental Test of The Supreme Court Assumption of Functional Equivalence, 1 Pers. & Soc.Psychol.Bull. 273 (1974)—§ 22.1(d) n.71

Van Alstyne, Dual Sovereignty, Federalism and the National Criminal Law: Modernist Constitutional Doctrine and the Nonrole of the Supreme Court, 26 Am.Crim.L.Rev. 1740 (1986)—§§ 1.2(c) n.26; 1.2(d) n.203

Van Alstyrne, The District Attorney—A Historical Puzzle, 1952 Wis.L.Rev. 125—§ 1.6(b) n.76

Van Dam, Preliminary Hearings in a Truckload, 8 Crim.Jus.J. 195 (1986)—§§ 14.1(a) n.5; 14.4(d) n.76; 14.4(e) n.101

Van Dyke, The Grand Jury: Representative or Elite?, 28 Hastings L.J. 37 (1976)—§§ 8.4(a) n.3, 9, 15, 16

Van Kessel, Adversary Excesses in the American Criminal Trial, 67 Notre Dame L.Rev. 403 (1992)—§§ 1.5(a) n.28; 1.5(b) n.78; 1.5(c) n.106 to 108, 123, 124, 126, 129, 132, 145, 172; 1.5(d) n.179; 1.6(a) n.22; 2.9(f) n.109

Van Kessel, Prosecutorial Discovery and the Privilege Against Self-Incrimination: Accommodation or Capitulation, 4 Hast.L.Q. 855 (1977)—§§ 20.4(d) n.55, 59

Vestal, Issue Preclusion and Criminal Prosecutions, 65 Iowa L.Rev. 281 (1980)—§§ 17.4(a) n.14, 56, 57, 63

Vick, Community Based Drug Courts: Empirical Success, 52 S.D.L.Rev. 288 (2007)—§ 26.1(e) n.104

Vick, Poorhouse Justice: Underfunded Indigent Defense Services and Arbitrary Death Sentences, 43 Buff.L.Rev. 329 (1995)—§§ 11.8(c) n.65, 66

Viera, Registration, Protest and the Rationale of Wayte v. United States, 40 Ark.L.Rev. 841 (1987)—§ 13.4(d) n.156

Vitiello, 8 Notre Dame J. L., Ethics & Pub.Pol'y. 165 (1994)—§§ 2.9(b) n.17, 30

Vitiello, Three Strikes: Can We Return to Rationality?, 87 J.Crim.L. & Criminology 395 (1997)—§§ 26.6(b) n.1, 5, 6

Vitiello & Kelso, Reform of California's Grand Jury System, 35 Loy.L.A.L. Rev. 513 (2002)—§§ 8.2(b) n.23; 8.3(h) n.36; 8.14(b) n.23

Volkman-Schluch, Continental European Criminal Procedure: True or Illusive Model, 9 Am.J.Crim.L. 1 (1981)—§ 1.5(c) n.106

Volokh, Crime Severity and Constitutional Line-Drawings, 90 Va.L.Rev. 1957 (2004)—§ 1.8(c) n.8

Vorenberg, Decent Restraint of Prosecutorial Power, 94 Harv.L.Rev. 1521 (1981)—§§ 13.2(e) n.89; 13.2(f) n.103, 109, 111, 113; 13.2(g) n.127, 136, 137, 140; 13.3(a) n.10, 12; 13.4(b) n.53; 13.4(c) n.140; 13.5(a) n.13

Vorenberg, Narrowing the Discretion of Criminal Justice Officials, 1976 Duke L.J. 651—§§ 1.7(j) n.217; 1.9(d) n.95; 1.9(e) n.131; 13.2(d) n.83, 87; 13.2(e) n.96; 13.2(g) n.138

Vouin, The Role of the Prosecutor in French Criminal Trials, 18 Am.J.Comp.L. 483 (1970)—§ 1.5(c) n.109

W

Waite, Judges and the Crime Burden, 54 Mich.L.Rev. 169 (1955)—§ 1.6(f) n.379

Waite, Police Regulation by Rules of Evidence, 42 Mich.L.Rev. 679 (1944)—§ 6.3(b) n.32

Waite, Public Policy and the Arrest of Felons, 31 Mich.L.Rev. 749 (1933)—§§ 1.6(f) n.376, 378

Waite, Some Inadequacies in the Law of Arrest, 29 Mich.L.Rev. 448 (1931)—§ 1.6(f) n.375

Wald, The Unreasonable Reasonableness Test for Fourth Amendment Searches, 4 Crim.J. Ethics 2 (Spring 1985)—§ 3.3(c) n.80

Walker, Origins of the Contemporary Paradigm: The American Bar Foundation Survey, 1953-69, 9 Just.Q. 47 (1992)—§ 1.9(c) n.48

Walker, Rights and Duties of Grand Jurors, 1 Western Law J. 338 (May, 1844)—§ 1.6(d) n.224

Walker, Lind, & Thibaut, The Relationship Between Procedural and Distributive Justice, 65 Va.L.Rev. 140 (1979)—§§ 1.5(a) n.33; 1.5(i) n.302

Wallace, 8 Crim.Just. 8 (Fall 1993)—§ 1.2(d) n.228

Wallace & Carroll, The Implementation and Impact of Indigent Defense Standards, 31 Southern Univ.L.Rev. 245 (2004)—§§ 1.4(f) n.116 to 118

Waltz, Inadequacy of Trial Defense Preparation as a Ground for Post-Conviction Relief in Criminal Cases, 59 Nw.U.L.Rev. 289 (1964)—§§ 11.7(b) n.24, 26; 11.10(c) n.47

Wangerin, "Plain Error" and "Fundamental Fairness": Toward a Definition of Exceptions to the Rules of Procedural Default, 29 DePaul L.Rev. 753 (1980)—§ 27.5(c) n.92

Ward, A Kinder, Gentler System: An Examination of How Crime Victims Have Benefitted from the Women's Movement, 15 New Eng.J. on Crim. & Civ. Confinement 171 (1983)—§ 1.5(k) n.369

Ward, A Plea Best Not Taken: Why Criminal Defendants Should Avoid the Alford Plea, 68 Mo.L.Rev. 913 (2003)—§ 21.4(f) n.217

Warden, Illinois Death Penalty Reform, 95 J.Crim.L. & C. 381 (2005)—§ 1.5(e) n.239

Warner, Anders in the Fifty States: Some Appellants' Equal Protection is More Equal Than Others, 23 Fla.St.L.Rev. 625 (1996)—

§§ 11.2(c) n.90, 95, 96

Warner, Investigating the Law of Arrest, 26 A.B.A.J. 151 (1940)—§ 1.6(f) n.375

Warner, The Development of Trial By Jury, 26 Tenn.L.Rev. 459 (1959)—§§ 16.1(b) n.38, 50

Warner, The Uniform Arrest Act, 28 Va.L.Rev. 315 (1942)—§§ 1.6(f) n.376 to 378

Warner & Cabot, Changes in the Administration of Criminal Justice During the Past Fifty Years, 50 Harv.L.Rev. 583 (1937)—§§ 1.6(e) n.299, 315, 329, 332

Warren, Gina, Due Process—Prosecutorial Implications Of A Victim's Right To Be Heard: Court Upholds Victim's Right To Be Heard At Important Criminal Justice Hearings. State V. Casey, 44 P.3d 756 (Utah 2002), 34 Rutgers L.J. 1173 (2003)—§ 21.3(f) n.415

Warren, Federal Criminal Laws and the State Courts, 38 Harv.L.Rev. 545 (1925)—§§ 1.2(c) n.77, 78

Warren, New Light on the History of the Federal Judiciary Act of 1789, 37 Harv.L.Rev. 49 (1923)—§§ 16.1(b) n.68, 77

Warren, The Indigent Defendant's Toolbox: Debating the Addition of the Battered Women Syndrome Expert, 69 U.Chi.L.Rev. 1983 (2002)—§ 11.2(e) n.189

Wasserstrom, The Incredible Shrinking Fourth Amendment, 21 Am.Crim.L.Rev. 257 (1984)—§ 3.3(c) n.80

Watkins, Using The Freedom of Information Act as a Discovery Device, 1994 Ark.L.Notes, 59—§ 20.2(d) n.76

Way, The Supreme Court and State Coerced Confessions, 12 J.Pub.L. 55 (1963)—§§ 2.5(e) n.37, 38; 2.5(f) n.48

Weaver, A Change of Heart or Change of Law? Withdrawing a Guilty Plea Under Federal Rule of Criminal Procedure 32(e), 92 J.Crim.L. & Criminology 273 (2002)—§ 21.5(a) n.43

Weaver, Lopez and the Federalization of Criminal Law, 98 W.Va.L.Rev. 814 (1995)—§ 1.2(c) n.157

Webster, Building a Better Mousetrap: Reconstructing Federal Entrapment Theory From Sorrells to Mathews, 32 Ariz.L.Rev. 605 (1990)—§§ 5.1(b) n.9; 5.2(c) n.40

Wechsler, The Challenge of a Model Penal Code, 65 Harv.L.Rev. 1097 (1952)—§§ 13.1(c) n.40; 13.2(a) n.17

Weigend, Continental Cases for American Ailments: European Criminal Procedure as a Model for Law Reform, 2 Crime & Just. 381 (N. Morris & M. Tonry eds., 1980)—§ 1.5(c) n.106

Weinberg & Weinberg, The Congressional Invitation to Avoid the Preliminary Hearing: An Analysis of Section 303 of the Federal Magistrates Act of 1968, 67 Mich.L.Rev. 1361 (1969)—§§ 3.1(f) n.151; 14.2(b) n.28; 14.4(b) n.31

Weinreb, Generalities of the Fourth Amendment, 42 U.Chi.L.Rev. 47 (1974)—§§ 3.10(a) n.11; 3.10(c) n.85, 89; 3.10(d) n.113, 129; 3.10(e) n.148

Weinreb, The Adversary Process is Not an End in Itself, 2 J. Inst. For Study Legal Ethics (1999)—§§ 1.5(c) n.112, 116

Weinreb, Your Place or Mine? Privacy of Presence Under the Fourth Amendment, 1999 Sup.Ct.Rev. 253—§ 9.1(c) n.98

Weinstein, Local Responsibility for Improvement of Search and Seizure Practices, 34 Rocky Mt.L.Rev. 150 (1962)—§ 2.5(f) n.79

Weinstein, Protecting a Juror's Right to Privacy: Constitutional Constraints and Policy Options, 70 Temp.L.Rev. 1 (1997)—§ 22.3(a) n.7

Weinstein, Reform of Federal Court Rulemaking Procedure, 76 Colum.L.Rev. 905 (1976)—§ 1.7(g) n.123

Weinstein, Some Difficulties in Devising Rules for Determining Truth in Judicial Trials, 66 Colum.L.Rev. 223 (1966)—§ 20.6(c) n.84

Weisberg, Criminal Procedure Doctrine: Some Versions of the Skeptical, 76 J.Crim.L. & Criminology 832 (1985)—§§ 1.6(h) n.453; 2.8(b) n.43

Weisselberg, In the Stationhouse After Dickerson, 99 Mich.L.Rev. 1121 (2001)—§ 6.5(d) n.80

Weisselberg, Saving Miranda, 84 Cornell L.Rev. 109 (1998)—§ 6.5(c) n.42

Weissman, The Discriminatory Application of Penal Laws by State Judicial and Quasi-Judicial Officers: Playing the Shell Game of Rights and Remedies, 69 Nw.U.L.Rev. 489 (1974)—§ 13.4(d) n.149

Welling, Victim Participation in Plea Bargaining, 65 Wash.U.L.Q. 301 (1987)—§§ 1.5(k) n.367; 21.3(e) n.268

Welling, Victims in the Criminal Process: A Utilitarian Analysis of Victim Participation in the Charging Decision, 30 Ariz.L.Rev. 85 (1988)—§ 13.1(a) n.10

Wellington, Common Law Rules and Constitutional Double Standards: Some Notes on Adjudication, 83 Yale L.J. 221 (1973)—§ 2.5(f) n.74

Wells et al., Eyewitness Identification Procedures: Recommendations for Lineups and Photospreads, 22 Law. & Hum.Behav. 603 (1998)—§ 7.5(c) n.40

Wells et al., From the Lab to the Police Station: A Successful Application of Eyewitness Research, 55 Am.Psychologist 581 (2000)—§ 7.5(c) n.44

Wells, Eyewitness Identification.; Systemic Reforms, 2006 Wis.L.Rev. 615—§ 1.5(e) n.234

Wells & Cutler, The Right to Counsel at Videotaped Lineups: An Emerging Dilemma, 22 Conn.L.Rev. 373 (1990)—§ 7.3(c) n.41

Welsh, Reconsidering the Constitutional Relationship Between State and Federal Courts: A Critique of Michigan v. Long, 59 Notre Dame L.Rev. 1118 (1984)—§ 2.12(a) n.52

Welsh, Whose Federalism?—The Burger Court's Treatment of State Civil Liberties Judgments, 10 Hastings Const.L.Q. 819 (1983)—§ 2.12(a) n.21

Weninger, Criminal Discovery and Omnibus Procedure in a Federal Court: A Defense View, 49 S.Cal.L.Rev. 514 (1976)—§ 20.3(i) n.168

Weninger, The Abolition of Plea Bargaining: A Case Study of El Paso County, Texas, 35 UCLA.L.Rev. 265 (1987)—§ 21.1(g) n.129

Wermiel, Rights in the Modern Era: Applying the Bill of Rights to the States, 1 Wm. & Mary Bill of Rights J. 121 (1992)—§ 2.6(a) n.1

West, Fagan, & Liebman, Look Who's Extrapolating: A Reply to Hoffman, 76 Ind.L.J. 951 (2001)—§ 1.8(e) n.83

Westen, Away From Waiver: A Rationale for the Forfeiture of Constitutional Rights in Criminal Procedure, 75 Mich.L.Rev. 1214 (1977)—§§ 10.2(a) n.3; 11.3(c) n.64; 16.1(h) n.291; 21.6(a) n.19 to 22, 53 to 55, 57, 66, 67; 24.2(c) n.34

Westen, Compulsory Process II, 74 Mich.L.Rev. 191 (1975)—§§ 24.3(a) n.2; 24.3(f) n.144

Westen, Confrontation and Compulsory Process: A Unified Theory of Evidence for Criminal Cases, 91 Harv.L.Rev. 567 (1978)—§§ 24.3(a) n.2; 24.3(h) n.182; 24.4(b) n.13

Westen, Forfeiture by Guilty Plea—A Reply, 76 Mich.L.Rev. 1308 (1978)—§§ 21.6(a) n.24, 53, 57; 27.5(c) n.97; 28.3(b) n.59

Westen, Order of Proof: An Accused's Right to Control the Timing and Sequence of Evidence in His Defense, 66 Cal.L.Rev. 935 (1978)—§§ 11.8(a) n.10; 20.4(d) n.55, 60; 24.5(a) n.13

Westen, Reflections on Alfred Hill's "Testimonial Privilege and Fair Trial," 14 U.Mich.L.Ref. 371 (1981)—§ 24.3(f) n.157

Westen, The Compulsory Process Clause, 73 Mich.L.Rev. 71 (1974)—§§ 20.3(m) n.236; 24.3(a) n.2; 24.3(g) n.167

Westen, The Three Faces of Double Jeopardy: Reflections on Governmental Appeals of Criminal Sentences, 78 Mich.L.Rev. 1001 (1980)—§§ 25.1(b) n.5, 12; 25.3(b) n.11, 13; 25.3(c) n.20; 27.3(a) n.5

Westen & Drubel, Toward a General Theory of Double Jeopardy, 1978 Sup.Ct.Rev. 81—§§ 25.1(d) n.45, 53; 25.2(c) n.21; 25.3(b) n.11; 25.4(a) n.2

Westen & Mandell, To Talk, To Balk, or To Lie: The Emerging Fifth Amendment Doctrine of the "Preferred Response," 19 Am.Crim.L.Rev. 521 (1982)—§§ 8.10(d) n.90; 24.5(d) n.56

Westen & Ow, Reaching Agreement on When Jurors Must Agree, 10 New Crim.L.Rev. 153 (2007)—§ 24.10(c) n.44

Westen & Westin, A Constitutional Law of Remedies for Broken Plea Bargains, 66 Cal.L.Rev. 471 (1978)—§§ 21.2(e) n.284, 286 to 288, 291, 292, 296, 298, 302, 345

Wexler & Hershey, Criminal Detainers in a Nutshell, 7 Crim.L.Bull. 753 (1971)—§ 18.4(a) n.5

Whelan, Lead Us Not Into Unwarranted Temptation: A Proposal to Replace the Entrapment Defense With a Reasonable-Suspicion Requirement, 133 U.Pa.L.Rev. 1193 (1985)—§ 5.2(c) n.40

White, A Deadly Dilemma: Choices by Attorneys Representing "Innocent" Capital Defendants, 102 Mich.L.Rev. 2001 (2004)—§§ 11.6(a) n.62; 11.10(c) n.153

White, A Proposal for Reform of the Plea Bargaining Process, 119 U.Pa.L.Rev. 439 (1971)—§§ 21.1(e) n.105, 106; 21.1(f) n.107; 21.6(b) n.107

White, Confessions in Capital Cases, 2003 U.Ill.L.Rev. 979—§ 6.7(b) n.98

White, Confessions Induced by Broken Government Promises, 43 Duke L.J. 947 (1994)—§§ 6.2(c) n.94, 114

White, Death-Qualified Juries: The "Prosecution-Proneness" Argument Reexamined, 41 U.Pitt.L.Rev. 353 (1980)—§ 22.3(c) n.158

White, Evidentiary Privileges and the Defendant's Constitutional Right to Introduce Evidence, 80 J.Crim.L. & Criminology 377 (1989)—§ 24.3(f) n.157

White, Ex Proprio Vigore, 89 Mich.L.Rev. 2096 (1991)—§ 1.3(c) n.20

White, False Confessions and the Constitution: Safeguards Against Untrustworthy Confessions, 32 Harv.C.R.-C.L.L.Rev. 105 (1997)—§ 6.2(b) n.52

White, Federal Habeas Corpus: The Impact of the Failure to Assert a Constitutional Claim at Trial, 58 Va.L.Rev. 67 (1972)—§ 11.6(a) n.2

White, Improving Constitutional Criminal Procedure, 93 Mich.L.Rev. 1667 (1995)—§§ 2.8(c) n.83, 85

White, Interrogation Without Questions: Rhode Island v. Innis and United States v. Henry, 78 Mich.L.Rev. 1209 (1980)—§§ 6.4(g) n.151, 162; 6.7(a) n.13, 14, 16 to 22, 26; 6.7(b) n.31, 32, 97; 6.7(c) n.111, 117, 118

White, Miranda's Failure to Restrain Pernicious Interrogation Practices, 99 Mich.L.Rev. 1211 (2001)— § 6.5(d) n.80

White, Police Trickery in Inducing Confessions, 127 U.Pa.L.Rev. 581 (1979)—§§ 6.2(c) n.120; 6.4(h) n.166; 6.7(c) n.138; 6.9(c) n.57

White, Rhode Island v. Innis: The Significance of a Suspect's Assertion of His Right to Counsel, 17 Am.Crim.L.Rev. 53 (1979)— § 6.4(e) n.90

White, The Fourth Amendment as a Way of Talking About People: A Study of Robinson and Matlock, 1974 Sup.Ct.Rev. 165—§§ 3.10(c) n.86, 89

White, The Fourth Amendment Rights of Parolees and Probationers, 31 U.Pitt.L.Rev. 167 (1969)—§ 3.9(j) n.217

White, The Psychiatric Examination and the Fifth Amendment Privilege in Capital Cases, 74 J.Crim.L. & Crim. 943 (1983)—§ 6.7(b) n.98

White, What Is an Involuntary Confession Now?, 50 Rutgers L.Rev. 2001 (1998)—§ 6.1(b) n.16

White & Greenspan, Standing to Object to Search and Seizure, 118 U.Pa.L.Rev. 333 (1970)—§ 9.2(d) n.42

Whitebread, The Burger Court's Counter-Revolution in Criminal Procedure: The Recent Criminal Decisions of the United States Supreme Court, 24 Washburn L.J. 471 (1985)—§§ 2.8(b) n.43, 45; 2.9(f) n.109, 115

Whitebread and Conteras, Free Press v. Fair Trial: Protecting the Criminal Defendant's Rights in a Highly Publicized Trial by Applying the Sheppard-Mu'Min Remedy, 69 S.Cal.L.Rev. 1587 (1996)— §§ 23.1(b) n.81; 23.2(g) n.116

Whitman, What's Wrong With Inflicting Shame Sanctions, 107 Yale L.J. 1055 (1998)—§ 26.9(b) n.78

Whittington, The New Originalism, 2 Geo.J.L. & Pub.Pol'y. 599 (2004)— § 2.9(d) n.54

Wickersham, The Grand Jury: Weapon Against Crime and Corruption, 51 A.B.A.J. 1157 (1965)—§§ 8.2(b) n.21; 15.3(a) n.18

Wiehofen, Supreme Court Review of State Criminal Procedure, 10 Am.J. Legal Hist. 189 (1966)—§§ 2.6(a) n.1; 2.8(c) n.61

Wigmore, Criminal Procedure: "Good" Reversals and "Bad" Reversals, 4 Ill.L.Rev. 352 (1909)—§ 27.6(a) n.9

Wigmore, Nemo Tenetur Seipsum Prodere, 5 Harv.L.Rev. 71 (1891)— § 2.10(c) n.96

Wildenthal, The Lost Compromise: Reassessing the Early Understanding in Court and Congress in Incorporation of the Bill of Rights in the Fourteenth Amendment, 61 Ohio St. L.J. 1051 (2000)—§§ 2.2 n.8; 2.3(a) n.26, 61, 67, 73; 2.3(b) n.77, 82; 2.3 n.2

Wildenthal, The Road to Twining: Reassuring The Disincorporation of The Bill of Rights, 61 Ohio St. L.J. 1457 (2000)—§§ 2.3(a) n.61; 2.3(b) n.77

Wilkes, The New Federalism in Criminal Procedure Revisited, 64 Ky.L.J. 329 (1976)—§ 2.12(a) n.28

Wilkes, The New Federalism in Criminal Procedure, State Court Evasion of the Burger Court, 62 Ky.L.J. 421 (1974)—§§ 2.12(a) n.28, 32

Wilkins & Steer, Relevant Conduct: The Cornerstone of the Federal Sentencing Guidelines, 41 S.C.L.Rev. 495 (1990)—§§ 16.1(f) n.232; 26.4(b) n.7

Wilkinson, Conflicts of Interest in Texas Criminal Cases, 54 Baylor L.Rev. 171 (2002)—§ 11.9(d) n.170

Wilkinson, Justice John M. Harlan and The Values of Federalism, 57 Va.L.Rev. 1185 (1971)—§ 2.5(f) n.53

Willard, The Seventeenth Century Indictment in the Light of Modern Conditions, 24 Harv.L.Rev. 290 (1910)—§§ 19.1(a) n.10; 19.2(b) n.7, 10; 19.2(d) n.44, 47; 19.3(a) n.1

Williams, Does the ICJ's Decision in Avena Mean Anything to Mexicans on Death Row, 55 Cath.U.L.Rev. 351 (2005)—§ 1.7(c) n.29

Williams, In the Supreme Court's Shadow: Legitimacy of State Rejection of Supreme Court Reasoning and Result, 35 S.C.L.Rev. 353 (1984)—§§ 2.12(a) n.38, 78; 2.12(b) n.102, 104, 105; 2.12(c) n.143, 158

Williams, Methodology Problems in Enforcing State Constitutional Rights, 3 Ga.St.L.Rev. 143 (1986)—§ 2.12(e) n.201

Williams, Police Rulemaking Revisited: Some New Thoughts on an Old Problem, 47 Law & Contemp.Probs. 124 (1984)—§ 1.6(e) n.308

Williams, Process and Prediction: A Return to a Fuzzy Model of Pretrial Detention, 79 Minn.L.Rev. 325 (1994)—§ 12.3(f) n.134

Williams, Reinventing the Courts: The Frontiers of Judicial Activism in the State Courts, 29 Campbell L.Rev. 591 (2007)—§ 26.1(e) n.104

Williams, The Authentication of Statements to the Police, 1979 Crim.L.Rev. 1—§ 6.5(d) n.77

Williams, The Brennan Lecture: Interpreting State Constitutions As Unique Legal Documents, 27 Okla.City U.L.Rev. 189 (2002)—§ 2.12(a) n.37

Williams, The Defense of Entrapment and Related Problems in Criminal Prosecution, 28 Fordham L.Rev. 399 (1959)—§ 5.2(b) n.21

Williams, The Supreme Court and Broken Promises: The Gradual and Continual Erosion of Terry v. Ohio, 34 How.L.J. 567 (1991)—§ 1.5(j) n.324

Williams, Venue and the Ambit of Criminal Law, 81 Law Q.Rev. 276 (1965)—§§ 16.1(c) n.113, 117, 128

Wilmarth, The Original Purpose of the Bill of Rights, James Madison and The Founder's search for a Workable Balance Between Federal and State Power, 26 Am.Crim.L.Rev. 1261 (1989)—§ 2.1 n.26

Wilson, Implementation by Court Rule of Criminal Justice Standards, 12 Am.Crim.L.Rev. 323 (1974)—§§ 1.3(e) n.51; 1.3(f) n.70; 1.6(e) n.334; 1.7(f) n.71, 87, 94, 97, 99

Wilson, In Booker's Shadow: Restitution Forces a Second Debate on Honesty in Sentencing, 39 Indiana L.Rev. 369 (2006)—§ 26.6(c) n.42

Wilson, The Dawn of Criminal Jury Trials in Japan, 24 Wis.Int.L.J. 835 (2007)—§ 1.5(a) n.6

Wilson & Boland, The Effect of the Police in Crime, 12 Law & Soc'y. Rev. 367 (1978)—§§ 1.5(a) n.49; 1.10(b) n.32; 1.10(c) n.114

Wilson & Kelling, Broken Windows: The Police and Neighborhood Safety, 249 Atlantic Monthly 29 (March, 1983)—§§ 1.5(a) n.49; 1.10(b) n.31

Wing & Wolff, Defense Input into Grand Jury Proceeding, 29 Prac.Law. 35 (1983)—§§ 15.2(b) n.59; 15.2(c) n.63, 65

Winick, Forfeiture of Attorneys' Fees under RICO and CCE and The Right to Counsel of Choice, 43 U. Miami L.Rev. 763 (1989)— § 11.4(c) n.96

Winick, Presumptions and Burdens of Proof in Determining Competency to Stand Trial: An Analysis of Medina v. California and The Supreme Court's New Due Process Methodology in Criminal Cases, 47 U.Miami L.Rev. 817 (1993)— § 2.7(c) n.225

Winick, Prosecutorial Preemption, Challenge Practices in Capital Cases: An Empirical Study and a Constitutional Analysis, 81 Mich.L.Rev. 1 (1982)—§ 22.3(c) n.158

Winnick, Redefining The Role of the Criminal Defense Lawyer at Plea Bargaining and Sentencing, 5 Psychology, Public Policy, and Law, 2034 (1999)—§ 11.6(a) n.60

Winningham, The Dilemma of the Directed Acquittal, 15 Vand.L.Rev. 699 (1962)—§§ 24.6(b) n.18, 28

Winters, The Michigan One-Man Grand Jury, 24 Mich.S.B.J. 279 (1945)— § 8.1(b) n.22

Wisotsky, Use of a Master Bond Schedule: Equal Justice Under Law, 24 U.Miami L.Rev. 808 (1970)— § 12.2(a) n.7

Witt, Making the Fifth, the Constitutionalization of American Self-Incrimination Doctrine, 1791-1903, 77 Tex.L.Rev. 825 (1999)—§§ 2.10(c) n.77; 8.11(a) n.1

Witt, Non-Coercive Interrogation and the Administration of Criminal Justice, 64 J.Crim.L. & Criminology 320 (1973)—§ 6.5(c) n.35

Wofford, The Blinding Light: The Uses of History in Constitutional Interpretation, 31 U.Chi.L.Rev. 502 (1964)—§ 2.9(d) n.83

Wolchover, Should Judges Sum up on the Facts?, 1989 Crim.L.Rev. 781 (1989)—§ 24.6(e) n.46

Wollin, Policing the Police: Should Miranda Violations Bear Fruit?, 53 Ohio St. L.J. 806 (1992)—§ 9.5(b) n.39

Woods, Counterintelligence and Access to Transactional Records: A Practical History of USA Patriot Act Section 215, 1 J. Nat'l Security L. & Pol'y 37 (2005)—§ 4.9(b) n.26

Woodward and Ahrens, The Iowa Grand Jury: Before and After the New Code, 26 Drake L.Rev. 241 (1976)—§§ 15.1(g) n.352; 15.2(d) n.117, 120

Woolhandler, Demodeling Habeas, 45 Stan.L.Rev. 575 (1993)— §§ 28.1(b) n.18, 19; 28.2(b) n.20; 28.2(d) n.69

Worgan & Paulsen, The Position of a Prosecutor in a Criminal Case—A Conversation with a Prosecuting Attorney, 7 Prac.Law. 44 (Nov.1961)—§ 13.2(a) n.7

Worst Lawyer, 103 Yale L.J. 1835 (1994)—§ 11.10(c) n.132

Wray & Hur, Prosecution in a Post-Enron World: The Thompson Memo in Theory and Practice, 43 Am.Crim.L.Rev. 1095 (2006)— §§ 11.4(c) n.98, 99

Wright, How The Supreme Court Delivers Fire and Ice State Criminal Justice, 59 Wash. & Lee L.Rev. (2002)—§§ 2.12(a) n.30, 76

Wright, In Praise of State Courts, 11 Hastings Const.L.Q. 165 (1984)— § 2.12(a) n.40

Wright, Must the Criminal Go Free if the Constable Blunders?, 50 Tex.L.Rev. 736 (1972)—§ 3.1(c) n.36

Wright, Parity of Resources for Defense Counsel and the Reach of Public Choice Theory, 90 Iowa L.Rev. 219 (2004)—§ 1.5(j) n.335

Wright, Prosecutorial Guidelines and the New Terrain in New Jersey, 109 Penn.St.L.Rev. 1087 (2005)— §§ 1.7(j) n.218; 13.1(d) n.48;

13.2(f) n.106; 13.2(g) n.128; 21.1(g) n.118

Wright, Rules for Sentencing Revolutions, 108 Yale L.J. 1355 (1999)—§§ 26.2(b) n.13; 26.3(b) n.7

Wright, The Desirability of Goal Conflict Within the Criminal Justice System, 9 J.Crim.Just. 215 (1981)—§§ 1.4(c) n.40, 41; 1.6(g) n.434

Wright, The Invasion of Jury: Temperature of the War, 27 Temple L.Q. 137 (1953)—§ 24.6(e) n.48

Wright, The Political Economy of Application Fees for Indigent Criminal Defense, 47 Wm. & Mary L.Rev. 2045 (2006)—§ 11.2(h) n.315

Wright, Three Strikes Legislation and Sentencing Commission Objectives, 20 Law & Pol'y 429 (1998)—§ 26.6(b) n.1

Wright, Trial Distortion and the End of Innocence in Federal Criminal Justice, 154 U.Pa.L.Rev. 79 (2005)—§§ 1.2(d) n.209, 250; 1.2(e) n.280; 1.2(f) n.297, 298; 1.5(c) n.172; 1.6(a) n.22; 1.10(c) n.110; 21.1(b) n.13, 15, 19, 22, 25; 21.1(c) n.38; 21.1(f) n.117

Wright & Miller, Honesty and Opacity in Charge Bargains, 55 Stan.L.Rev. 1409 (2003)—§ 21.1(g) n.134

Wright & Miller, The Screening/Bargaining Tradeoff, 55 Stan.L.Rev. 29 (2002)—§§ 1.10(a) n.2, 7; 1.10(b) n.34; 14.1(a) n.7; 21.1(g) n.134

C. Wright, N. King & S. Klein, Federal Practice and Procedure-Criminal § 123 (3d Ed. 2004)—§ 19.3(a) n.13

Y

Yackle, A Primer on the New Habeas Corpus Statute, 44 Buff.L.Rev. 381 (1996)—§ 28.2(b) n.30

Yackle, The Habeas Hagioscope, 66 S.Cal.L.Rev. 2331 (1993)—§ 28.2(d) n.73

Yarborough, Justice Black and the Fourteenth Amendment and Incorporation, 30 U. Miami L.Rev. 231 (1976)—§§ 2.3(a) n.6, 61

Yellen, Probation Officers Look at Plea Bargaining and Do Not Like What They See, 8 Fed. Sentencing Rep. 339 (1996)—§ 1.9(b) n.31

Yellen, Two Cheers for a Tale of Three Cities, 66 S.Cal.L.Rev. 567 (1992)—§ 21.3(a) n.9

Yetter, Truth in Jury Instructions: Reforming the Law of Lesser Included Offenses, 9 St. Thomas L.Rev. 603 (1997)—§§ 24.8(e) n.53; 24.8(f) n.97

Yoo, Rejoinder: Treaties and Public Lawmaking: A Textual and Structural Defense of Non Self-Execution, 99 Colum.L.Rev. 2218 (1999)—§ 1.7(c) n.16

Young, Fact-Finding at Federal Sentencing: Why the Guidelines Should Meet the Rules, 79 Cornell L.Rev. 299 (1994)—§§ 26.4(a) n.4; 26.4(f) n.87, 91; 26.5(a) n.12

Young, Special Interest, Principles, and Sentencing Reform in America, 96 J.Crim.L. & Criminology 1509 (2006)—§ 1.6(h) n.494

Young, Unnecessary Evil: Police Lying in Interrogation, 28 Conn.L.Rev. 425 (1996)—§ 6.2(c) n.120

Z

Zacharias, Structuring the Ethics of Prosecutorial Trial Practice: Can Prosecutors Do Justice, 44 Vand.L.Rev. 45 (1991)—§§ 1.5(c) n.134, 141, 149

Zacharias, The Professional Discipline of Prosecutors, 79 N.C.L.Rev. 721 (2001)—§§ 1.7(j) n.237; 24.7(i) n.98

Zacharias, The Role of Prosecutors in Serving Justice After Convictions, 58 Vand.L.Rev. 171 (2005)—§ 24.11(d) n.39

Zacharias & Green, The Uniqueness of Federal Prosecutors, 88 Geo.L.J. 187 (2000)—§§ 1.2(f) n.294; 1.7(j) n.267; 8.8(d) n.108

Zacharias & Green, The Uniqueness of Federal Prosecutors, 88 Geo.L.J. 207 (2000)—§§ 1.7(j) n.253, 255; 6.4(e) n.91

Zacharis, A Critical Look at Rules Governing Grand Jury Subpoenas of Attorneys, 76 Minn.L.Rev. 917 (1992)—§ 8.8(d) n.101

Zagel & Carr, State Criminal Discovery and the New Illinois Rules, 1971 U.Ill.L.F. 557—§§ 1.5(c) n.140; 20.1(b) n.30

Zalman, The Rise and Fall of the Indeterminate Sentence, 24 Wayne L.Rev. 45 (1977)—§§ 1.6(f) n.381; 26.1(c) n.46

Zalman and Gates, Rethinking Venue in Light of the "Rodney King" Case: An Interest Analysis, 41 Clev.St.L.Rev. 215 (1993)—§§ 16.1(c) n.125; 16.3(g) n.112; 23.2(a) n.45

Zalmon & Gates, Rethinking Venue in Light of the Rodney King Case: An Interest Analysis, 41 Cleve. St.L.Rev. 215 (1993)—§ 16.1(b) n.30

Zeidman, To Plea or Not to Plead: Effective Assistance and Client-Centered Counseling, 39 B.C.L.Rev. 841 (1998)—§ 21.3(b) n.74

Zeigler, Young Adults as a Cognizable Group in Jury Selection, 76 Mich.L.Rev. 1045 (1978)— § 22.2(d) n.67

Zeisel, ... And Then There Were None: The Diminution of the Federal Jury, 38 U.Chi.L.Rev. 710 (1971)— § 22.1(d) n.73

Zeisel, Bail Revisited, 1979 Am.B.Found.Res.J. 769—§ 1.6(h) n.480

Zeisel, The Disposition of Felony Arrests, 1981 A.B.F.Rev.J. 407— § 21.1(a) n.1

Zenoff, Symposium on the ABA Criminal Justice Mental Health Standards: Controlling the Dangers of Dangerousness, the ABA Standards and Beyond, 53 Geo.Wash.L.Rev. 562 (1985)—§ 26.6(e) n.83

Zimmer, Proactive Policing Against Street-Level Drug Trafficking, 9 Am.J. of Police 43 (1990)—§ 1.4(d) n.61

Zimring, Measuring the Impact of Pretrial Diversion from the Criminal Justice System, 41 U.Chi.L.Rev. 224 (1974)—§§ 13.1(d) n.46, 47

Zimring, Penal Policy and Penal Legislation in Recent American Experience, 58 Stanf.L.Rev. 323 (2005)— § 1.6(h) n.495

Zimring & Hawkins, Toward a Principled Basis For Federal Criminal Legislation, 543 Annals Am.Acad.Pol. & Soc.Sci. 15 (1996)—§§ 1.2(c) n.197; 1.2(d) n.232

Zimring & Zuehl, Victim Injury and Death in Urban Robbery: A Chicago Study, 15 J. Leg. Studies 1 (1986)— § 1.6(h) n.449

Zipperstein, Certain Uncertainty: Appellate Review and the Sentencing Guidelines, 66 S.Cal.L.Rev. 621 (1992)—§ 26.3(g) n.68

Zorza, The Criminal Law of Misdemeanor Domestic Violence, 1970-90, 83 J.Crim.L. & Criminology 46 (1992)—§§ 1.5(j) n.320; 1.5(k) n.409; 1.6(h) n.465; 1.8(b) n.6; 1.10(e) n.217; 13.2(b) n.35

Zuckerman, Coercion and the Judicial Ascertainment of Truth, 23 Israel L.Rev. 357 (1989)—§ 1.5(a) n.14

Zuckert, Book Review, 8 Const. Commentary 149 (1991)—§ 2.3(a) n.61

Index

ABANDONED PROPERTY
Search and seizure, § 3.2(h)

ACCELERATION DOCTRINE
Discovery and disclosure, self-incrimination, § 20.4(d)

ACCUSATORY PLEADING
Pleading, Accusatory, this index

ACQUITTAL, JUDGMENT OF
General discussion, §§ 24.6(b), 24.11(a)
Double jeopardy and, §§ 25.3(b), 25.3(c)

ACT-OF-PRODUCTION DOCTRINE
Grand Jury, this index

ADMINISTRATIVE CONVENIENCE
Guilty pleas and plea bargains, § 21.1(c)

ADMINISTRATIVE AGENCIES
Investigations by subpoena, § 8.1(c)

ADMONISHMENT OF JURY
Instructions to Jury, this index
Publicity, § 23.2(g)

AFFIRMATION OR OATH
Warrants for arrest or search and seizure, § 3.4(c)

AIRPORTS
Search and seizure, § 3.9(h)

ALIBI
Discovery by prosecution, § 20.5(b)
Notice requirements, § 20.5(b)

ALLOCUTION
Sentencing, due process, § 26.4(g)

ALTERNATE JURORS
Remedy for misconduct, § 24.9(f)
Voir dire, § 22.3(e)

AMENDMENTS OF PLEADING
Pleading, Accusatory, this index

ANDERS RULES
Indigent persons, right to counsel, § 11.2(c)

INDEX

APPEAL AND REVIEW
General discussion, §§ 27.1-27.6
Collateral orders, § 27.2(c)
Concurrent sentence doctrine, scope of review, § 27.5(b)
Constitutional law
  Prosecution, appeal by, § 27.3(a)
  Right to appeal, protection of, § 27.1
Counsel on, §§ 11.1(b), 11.1(c), 11.2(c)
Defendant, appeal by
  General discussion, § 27.2
  Collateral orders, § 27.2(c)
  Final judgment, requirement of, § 27.2(a)
  Grand jury proceedings, § 27.2(e)
  Independent proceedings, § 27.2(d)
  Underlying policies and statutory exceptions, § 27.2(b)
  Writ, review by, § 27.4(c)
Final judgment, appeal by defendant, § 27.2(a)
Forfeiture of right to appeal, § 27.5(c)
Grand jury proceedings, appeal by defendant, § 27.2(e)
Habeas corpus, §§ 27.4(f), 28.10
Harmless Error, this index
Joinder and severance, claim of prejudice, § 17.3(e)
Mandamus, § 27.4(b)
Mootness, § 27.5(a)
Plain error, § 27.5(d)
Pleading, Accusatory, this index
Prohibition, § 27.4(b)
Prosecution, appeal by
  General discussion, § 27.3
  Constitutional constraints, § 27.3(a)
  Post-jeopardy rulings, § 27.3(d)
  Pretrial rulings, § 27.3(c)
  Statutory authorization, need for specific, § 27.3(b)
  Writ, review by, § 27.4(d)
Sentencing, this index
Standard of review, § 27.5(e)
Statutory authorization, appeals by prosecution, § 27.3(b)
Waiver or forfeiture of right to appeal, §§ 21.2(b), 27.5(c)
Wiretapping and electronic surveillance, § 4.6(c)
Writ, review by
  General discussion, § 27.4
  Defense, petition by, § 27.4(c)
  Extraordinary writs, generally, § 27.4(a)
  Habeas corpus, § 27.4(f)
  Prohibition and mandamus, § 27.4(b)
  Prosecution, applications by, § 27.4(d)
  Third parties, applications by, § 27.4(e)

INDEX

APPEARANCE
 First appearance, § 1.4(g)
 Identification procedures, privilege against self-incrimination, § 7.2(d)

APPOINTMENT OF COUNSEL
 Counsel, Right to, this index

APPROVAL
 Consent or Approval, this index

ARBITRARY CLASSIFICATION
 Equal protection, decision as to prosecution, § 13.4(c)
 Equality and, § 1.4(j)

ARGUMENTS OF COUNSEL
 General discussion, § 24.7
 Closing arguments, §§ 24.7(b)-24.7(i)
 Due process, § 24.7(h)
 Invited response, § 24.7(f)
 Objections, § 24.7(g)
 Opening statements, § 24.7(a)
 Order of closing arguments, § 24.7(c)
 Prohibited argument, § 24.7(e)
 Roles of prosecutor and defense counsel, § 24.7(d)
 Standard of review, § 24.7(i)

ARRAIGNMENT
 Guilty pleas, receipt of, § 21.4(a)

ARREST, SEARCH AND SEIZURE
 General discussion, §§ 3.1-3.10
 Abandoned effects, § 3.2(h)
 Airport searches, § 3.9(h)
 Border searches and related activities, § 3.9(f)
 Business premises, §§ 3.2(e), 3.9(c)
 Commercial premises, §§ 3.2(e), 3.9(c)
 Constitutional tort, § 3.1(k)
 Containers and other personal effects, §§ 3.5(e), 3.7(c)
 Descriptions, warrants for searches, §§ 3.4(e), 3.4(f)
 Deterrence objective, exclusionary rule and other remedies, § 3.1(d)
 Disciplinary proceedings, exclusionary rule and other remedies, § 3.1(*l*)
 Electronic surveillance. Wiretapping and Network Surveillance, this index
 Exclusionary rule and other remedies
  General discussion, § 3.1
  Application in criminal proceedings, § 3.1(f)
  Application in non-criminal proceedings, § 3.1(g)
  Attack on exclusionary rule, § 3.1(c)
  Burden of proof, § 10.3(b)
  Constitutional tort, § 3.1(k)
  Constitutional vs. other violations, § 3.1(e)
  Criminal prosecutions, § 3.1(*l*)

ARREST, SEARCH AND SEIZURE—Cont'd
  Exclusionary rule and other remedies—Cont'd
    Deterrence objective, § 3.1(d)
    Disciplinary proceedings, § 3.1(*l*)
    Expungement of arrest records, § 3.1(m)
    Foreign police, searches by, § 3.1(i)
    Fruits of illegally obtained confessions, § 9.5(b)
    Injunctions, § 3.1(n)
    Jurisdiction, challenge of, § 3.1(j)
    Motivation, underlying, § 3.1(d)
    Origins of exclusionary rule, § 3.1(a)
    Private or nonpolice searches, § 3.1(h)
    Purposes of exclusionary rule, § 3.1(b)
    Self-help, § 3.1(*o*)
    Standard of proof, § 10.4(c)
    Subjective matters, inquiry into, § 3.1(d)
  Expungement of arrest records, § 3.1(m)
  Fire scenes, inspections of, § 3.9(e)
  First-hand information, probable cause, § 3.3(f)
  Foreign police, searches by, § 3.1(i)
  Forthwith subpoenas, § 8.7(e)
  Grand Jury, this index
  Housing, inspections of, § 3.9(b)
  Informants, probable cause, § 3.3(c)
  Injunctions, § 3.1(n)
  Inspection and regulatory searches
    General discussion, § 3.9
    Airport searches, § 3.9(h)
    Border searches and related activities, § 3.9(f)
    Businesses, inspections of, § 3.9(c)
    Fire scenes, inspections of, § 3.9(e)
    Housing, inspections of, § 3.9(b)
    Prisoners, searches directed at, § 3.9(i)
    Probationers and parolees, searches directed at, § 3.9(j)
    Public employees, searches directed at, § 3.9(*l*)
    Students, searches directed at, § 3.9(k)
    Vehicle use regulation, § 3.9(g)
    Welfare inspections, § 3.9(d)
  Intensity of search, warrants, § 3.4(j)
  Jurisdiction, challenge of, § 3.1(j)
  Magistrate, role of, § 1.4(g)
  Mere evidence, protected areas and interests, § 3.2(i)
  Neutral and detached magistrate requirement, warrants, § 3.4(b)
  Notice, entry without, §§ 3.4(h), 3.6(b)
  Oath or affirmation, warrants, § 3.4(c)
  Open fields, § 3.2(d)
  Parolees, searches directed at, § 3.9(j)
  Personal characteristics, §§ 3.2(g), 8.7(d)

ARREST, SEARCH AND SEIZURE—Cont'd
  Persons and personal effects
    General discussion, § 3.5
    Arrest, § 3.5(a)
    Containers and other personal effects, § 3.5(e)
    Post-arrest detention, search during, § 3.5(c)
    Scene of prior arrest, search of person at, § 3.5(b)
  Plain view, smell, hearing and touch, §§ 3.2(b), 3.7(f)
  Police station, detention for interrogation at, § 3.8(g)
  Premises, entry and search of
    General discussion, § 3.6
    Arrest, search and exploration after, § 3.6(d)
    Arrest, search before and incident to, § 3.6(c)
    Basis for entry to arrest, § 3.6(a)
    Evidence, warrantless entry and search for, § 3.6(e)
    Items that may be seized, § 3.6(g)
    Notice, entry to arrest without, § 3.6(b)
    Other purposes, warrantless entry and search for, § 3.6(f)
  Prisoners, searches directed at, § 3.9(i)
  Private or nonpolice searches, § 3.1(h)
  Private papers, § 3.2(i)
  Probable cause
    General discussion, § 3.3
    First-hand information, § 3.3(f)
    Informant, information from, § 3.3(c)
    Nature, § 3.3(b)
    Police, information from or held by other, § 3.3(e)
    Special problems in search cases, § 3.3(g)
    Victim, information from, § 3.3(d)
    Warrants for searches, facially sufficient affidavit, § 3.4(d)
    Witness, information from, § 3.3(d)
  Probationers, searches directed at, § 3.9(j)
  Protected areas and interests
    General discussion, § 3.2
    Abandoned effects, § 3.2(h)
    Business premises, § 3.2(e)
    Commercial premises, § 3.2(e)
    Katz explanation of privacy test, § 3.2(a)
    Mere evidence, § 3.2(i)
    Open fields, § 3.2(d)
    Personal characteristics, § 3.2(g)
    Plain view, smell, hearing and touch, § 3.2(b)
    Private papers, § 3.2(i)
    Residential premises, § 3.2(c)
    Senses, aiding the, § 3.2(b)
    Surveillance of relationships and movements, § 3.2(j)
    Vehicles, § 3.2(f)
  Public employees, searches directed at, § 3.9(*l*)

INDEX

ARREST, SEARCH AND SEIZURE—Cont'd
  Record, warrants for searches, § 3.4(c)
  Regulatory searches. Inspection and regulatory searches, above
  Residential premises, § 3.2(c)
  Roadblocks, § 3.8(f)
  Scene of prior arrest, search of person at, § 3.5(b)
  Scope of search, warrants, § 3.4(j)
  Self-help, exclusionary rule and other remedies, § 3.1(*o*)
  Senses, aiding the, § 3.2(b)
  Stop and frisk and similar lesser intrusions
    General discussion, § 3.8
    Action short of stop, § 3.8(c)
    Brief seizure of objects, § 3.8(h)
    Dimension of permissible stop, § 3.8(b)
    Fourth Amendment theory, § 3.8(a)
    Grounds for permissible stop, § 3.8(d)
    Police station, detention for interrogation at, § 3.8(g)
    Roadblocks, § 3.8(f)
    Weapons, frisk for, § 3.8(e)
  Students, searches directed at, § 3.9(k)
  Subpoenas, Grand Jury, this index
  Subterfuge and related matters, § 3.7(f)
  Surveillance of relationships and movements, § 3.2(j)
  Time of execution of warrant for search, § 3.4(g)
  Vehicles
    General discussion, §§ 3.2(f), 3.7
    Arrest, search incident to, § 3.7(a)
    Containers, § 3.7(c)
    Evidence, search and seizure to search for, § 3.7(b)
    Force during chase, § 3.5(a)
    Inspection and regulatory searches, § 3.9(g)
    Other purposes, search and seizure for, §§ 3.7(d), 3.7(e)
    Persons within vehicles, § 3.7(c)
    Plain view and related matters, § 3.7(f)
    Protective sweep, § 3.7(e)
    Subterfuge and related matters, § 3.7(f)
  Victim, information from, § 3.3(d)
  Warrants for searches
    General discussion, § 3.4
    Description of place to be searched, § 3.4(e)
    Description of thing to be searched, § 3.4(f)
    Detention of persons, § 3.4(i)
    Intensity of search, § 3.4(j)
    Items that may be seized, § 3.4(k)
    Neutral and detached magistrate requirement, § 3.4(b)
    Notice, entry without, § 3.4(h)
    Oath or affirmation, § 3.4(c)
    Persons, detention and search of, § 3.4(i)

INDEX

ARREST, SEARCH AND SEIZURE—Cont'd
Warrants for searches—Cont'd
Probable cause: facially sufficient affidavit, § 3.4(d)
Record, § 3.4(c)
Scope of search, § 3.4(j)
Time of execution, § 3.4(g)
Weapons, frisk for, § 3.8(e)
Welfare inspections, § 3.9(d)
Wiretapping and Network Surveillance, this index
Witness, information from, § 3.3(d)

ARREST OF JUDGMENT
General discussion, § 24.11(c)

ASSOCIATION, GUILT BY
Joinder and severance, § 17.2(e)

ATTACHMENT
Double jeopardy, § 25.1(d)
Speedy trial and other prompt disposition, § 18.1(c)

ATTENUATED CONNECTION
Exclusionary rules, fruit of poisonous tree, § 9.3(c)

ATTORNEY GENERAL
Challenges to and checks upon decision not to prosecute, § 13.3(e)
Prosecutorial authority, §§ 1.4(b), 1.4(e)

ATTORNEYS
Arguments of Counsel, this index
Counsel, Right to, this index
Public Defenders, this index

AUDITA QUERELA
General discussion, § 28.9(a)

AUTOMATIC STANDING
Exclusionary rules, § 9.2(a)

BAIL
Pretrial Release, this index

BALANCING TEST
Speedy trial and other prompt disposition, § 18.2

BARE INNOCENCE CLAIMS
Post conviction review, § 28.3(e)

BIAS
Judge, § 22.4(a)-(c)
Jurors, § 22.3(c)
Prejudice, this index

INDEX

BILL OF PARTICULARS
Nature of, § 19.4(a)
Relation to discovery, § 20.2(d)
Standards of issuance, § 19.4(b)

BINDOVER DETERMINATION
Preliminary Hearings, this index

BORDER SEARCHES
General discussion, § 3.9(f)

BURDEN OF PROOF
Presumptions and Burden of Proof, this index

BUSINESS PREMISES
Arrest, search and seizure, §§ 3.2(e), 3.9(c)
Exclusionary rules, standing, § 9.1(c)

BUT FOR TEST
Exclusionary rules, fruit of poisonous tree, § 9.3(b)
Immunized evidence, § 8.11(c)

CAPITAL OFFENSES AND PUNISHMENT
Post conviction review, § 28.8
Pretrial release, § 12.4(a)
Procedural subsets, § 1.8(e)
Sentencing, § 26.1(b)

CAUSE, CHALLENGES FOR
Challenge to judge, § 22.4(b)
Challenge to prosecutor, § 22.5(a)
Jury trial, § 22.3(c)

CERTIFICATION
Post conviction review, successive petitions, § 28.5(e)

CHALLENGE TO PROSECUTOR
General discussion, § 22.5
Cause, challenge for, § 22.5(a)
Imputed disqualification, § 22.5(d)
Prior relationship with defendant, § 22.5(b)
Witness, prosecutor as, § 22.5(c)

CHALLENGES
Cause, Challenges for, this index
Judge, impartiality of, §§ 22.4(b)-22.4(d)
Jury trial, §§ 22.3(c), 22.3(d)
Peremptory Challenges, this index

CHANGE OF VENUE
Venue, this index

CHARGE, SELECTION OF
Prosecution, Decision as to, this index

INDEX

CHILLING EFFECT
Grand jury, misuse of subpoena authority, § 8.8(d)
Self-incrimination, adverse consequences, § 2.10(b)

CHOICE OF COUNSEL
Counsel, Right to, this index

CLEMENCY
General discussion, § 26.2(c)

CLOSED PROCEEDINGS
General discussion, §§ 23.1(d), 23.1(e), 24.1(b)

CLOSING ARGUMENTS
General discussion, §§ 24.7(b)-24.7(i)

COGNIZABLE CLAIMS
Post Conviction Review, this index

COLLATERAL ESTOPPEL
Joinder of related offenses, failure as to, § 17.4(a)

COLLATERAL ORDERS
Appeal by defendant, § 27.2(c)

COLLATERAL REMEDIES
Post Conviction Review, this index

COMMENT ON EVIDENCE, JUDICIAL
General discussion, § 24.6(e)

COMMERCIAL PREMISES
Business Premises, this index

COMMON LAW
General discussion, § 1.7(h)
Discovery and disclosure, §§ 20.1(a), 20.2(a)
Interrogations and confessions, voluntariness, § 6.2(a)
Pleading, accusatory, § 19.1(a)
Post conviction review, §§ 28.1(b), 28.1(c)
Supervising Authority Rulings, this index

COMMUNITY RELEASE
General discussion, § 26.1(d)

COMPETENCE OF DEFENDANT
General discussion, § 24.2(g)
Guilty pleas and plea bargains, § 21.4(b)

COMPLAINTS
Filing, § 1.3(i)

CONCURRENT SENTENCES
Discretion of court, § 26.3(f)
Review, scope of, § 27.5(b)

CONDITIONAL DISCOVERY
Constitutional limits on discovery by prosecution, § 20.4(g)

CONDITIONAL PLEAS
General discussion, § 21.6(b)

CONFESSIONS
Interrogations and Confessions, this index

CONFLICTS OF INTEREST
Counsel, Right to, this index

CONFRONTATION, RIGHT TO
Codefendant's statements, § 17.2(b)
Exclusionary rules, hearings, § 10.5(e)
Identification Procedures, this index
Probation or parole revocation, § 26.10(c)
Sentencing, § 26.4(f)
Trial, § 24.2(a)

CONFUSION OF EVIDENCE
Joinder of defendants, § 17.2(f)

CONSECUTIVE SENTENCES
Discretion of court, § 26.3(f)

CONSENT OR APPROVAL
Double jeopardy, reprosecution following mistrial, § 25.2(a)
Wiretapping and electronic surveillance, § 4.6(*l*)

CONSTITUTIONAL LAW
General discussion, §§ 1.3(b), 1.7(b), 1.7(d), 2.1-2.11
Appeal and Review, this index
Arguments of counsel, § 24.7(h)
Arrest, Search and Seizure, this index
Confrontation, Right to, this index
Counsel, Right to, this index
Discovery and Disclosure, this index
Double Jeopardy, this index
Efficiency, impact on, § 2.9(f)
Elements of constitutionalization, § 2.1
Equal Protection, this index
Evidence, access by defendant, § 24.3(a)
Exculpatory evidence, disclosure of, § 24.3(b)
Federalism, selective incorporation, §§ 2.5(f), 2.6(d)
First Amendment, this index
Fourteenth Amendment and extension of Bill of Rights guarantees to state, § 2.2
Freestanding due process. Independent content of due process, below
Fundamental fairness
General discussion, § 2.4
Application of doctrine, §§ 2.4(d), 2.4(e)
Establishment of doctrine, § 2.4(d)

CONSTITUTIONAL LAW—Cont'd
Fundamental fairness—Cont'd
Original meaning of due process, § 2.4(b)
Pre-Fourteenth Amendment cases, § 2.4(c)
Rationale, § 2.4(a)
Selective incorporation, compared, § 2.5(a)
Subjectivity, § 2.4(f)
Grand Jury, this index
Harmless error, § 27.6(c)
Historical acceptance, significance of, § 2.9(b)
Identification Procedures, this index
Independent content of due process
General discussion, § 2.7
Due process analysis, § 2.7(b)
International standards, § 2.7(b)
Procedural due process after selective incorporation, § 2.7(a)
Substantive due process, § 2.7(c)
Indictments, this index
Interpretation, guideposts for
General discussion, § 2.9
Efficiency, impact on, § 2.9(i)
Historical acceptance, significance of, § 2.9(d)
Original understanding, § 2.9(d)
Per se rules, administratively based, § 2.9(g)
Prophylactic rules, § 2.9(h)
Role of, § 2.9(a)
Stare decisis, § 2.9(b)
Truth-finding, priority for, § 2.9(f)
Interrogations and confessions, voluntariness, § 6.2(b)
Mirroring presumption, state constitutional law, §§ 2.12(b)-2.12(d)
New federalism movement, state constitutional law, § 2.12(a)
Non-retroactivity
General discussion, §§ 2.11, 28.6
Convictions not yet final, § 2.11(d)
Direct appeal, § 2.11(d)
Finalized convictions under *Teague* standards, § 2.11(e)
Habeas review, §§ 2.11(e), 28.6(a)-(e)
Linkletter, §§ 2.11(b)-2.11(e)
Rejection of *Linkletter*, §§ 2.11(d), 2.11(e)
Significance of retroactive application, § 2.11(a)
Per se rules, administratively based, § 2.9(g)
Pleading, Accusatory, this index
Post Conviction Review, this index
Preference for expansive interpretations
General discussion, § 2.8
Nature of preference, § 2.8(a)
Reasons for preference, § 2.8(c)
Shifting strength of preference, § 2.8(b)

CONSTITUTIONAL LAW—Cont'd
Preliminary hearing, right to, § **14.2(a)**
Pretrial Release, this index
Prophylactic rules, § **2.9(e)**
Search and seizure. Arrest, Search and Seizure, this index
Selective incorporation
    General discussion, §§ **2.5, 2.6**
    Application of doctrine, § **2.6**
    Due process methodology, retention of, § **2.6(e)**
    Federalism, §§ **2.5(f), 2.6(d)**
    Fundamental fairness, compared, § **2.5(a)**
    Guarantees not yet incorporated, § **2.6(b)**
    Prior precedent and absorption of individual guarantees, § **2.5(c)**
    Rationale, § **2.5(b)**
    State enforcement, facilitation of, § **2.5(e)**
    Subjectivity, avoidance of, § **2.5(d)**
Self-Incrimination, Privilege Against, this index
Sentencing, this index
Sixth Amendment, this index
Speedy Trial and Other Prompt Disposition, this index
Stare decisis, § **2.9(b)**
State constitutional law
    General discussion, § **2.12**
    Judicial acceptance or rejection of mirroring presumption, § **2.12(d)**
    Mirroring presumption, §§ **2.12(b)-2.12(d)**
    New federalism movement, § **2.12(a)**
    State specific factors, § **2.12(e)**
Subjectivity
    Court shifts, § **2.8(b)**
    Fundamental fairness, § **2.4(f)**
    Selective incorporation, § **2.5(d)**
Total incorporation, § **2.3**
Truth-finding, priority for, § **2.9(c)**
Venue, crime-committed formula, §§ **16.1(a)-(c), 16.2(b)**

CONSTITUTIONAL TORT
Arrest, search and seizure, § **3.1(k)**

CONTAINERS AND OTHER PERSONAL EFFECTS
Search and seizure, §§ **3.5(e), 3.7(c)**

CONTEMPT
Grand jury, §§ **8.3(a), 27.2(e)**
Immunized witness, § **8.11(d)**

CONTINGENT FEES
Encouragement by police and entrapment, § **5.4(a)**
Retained counsel, § **11.9(a)**

INDEX

CONTINUANCES
After *Brady* disclosure, § 24.3(b)
Publicity, § 23.2(d)

CONTINUED SURVEILLANCE
Wiretapping and electronic surveillance, § 4.6(c)

CONVENIENCE
Venue, change of, §§ 16.3(c), 16.3(e)

CORAM NOBIS
General discussion, §§ 28.1(c), 28.9(c)

CORPUS DELECTI RULE
General discussion, § 24.6(c)

COUNSEL, RIGHT TO
General discussion, §§ 11.1-11.10
Adversary system touchstone, right to effective representation, § 11.7(c)
Anders rules, indigent persons, § 11.2(c)
Appeal, § 27.1(b)
Appointed systems, § 1.4(f)
Attorney-client relationship, state invasions of, § 11.8(b)
Balancing of interests, control of counsel over strategy, § 11.6(b)
Choice of counsel
General discussion, § 11.4
Judicial discretion in selecting appointed counsel, § 11.4(a)
Pro se alternative, § 11.4(d)
Replacement of appointed counsel, § 11.4(b)
Retained counsel, § 11.4(c)
Competence of attorney, right to effective representation, § 11.10
Conditions of representation, right to effective representation, § 11.8(c)
Conflicts of interest
General discussion, § 11.9
Conviction, challenge to, § 11.9(d)
Duty of trial court to inquire, § 11.9(b)
Non-apparent actual conflicts, § 11.9(d)
Range of possible conflicts of interest, § 11.9(a)
Waiver and disqualification, § 11.9(c)
Constitutional right, generally, § 11.1
Contract counsel, § 1.4(f)
Derivative rights, § 11.1(c)
Discretion of court in selecting appointed counsel, § 11.4(a)
Disqualification, conflicts of interest, § 11.9(c)
Due process rights, § 11.1(b)
Effective representation, right to
General discussion, §§ 11.7-11.10
Adversary system touchstone, § 11.7(c)
Assistance by counsel, restrictions on, § 11.8(a)
Attorney-client relationship, state invasions of, § 11.8(b)

INDEX

COUNSEL, RIGHT TO—Cont'd
Effective representation, right to—Cont'd
  Competence of attorney, § 11.10
  Conditions of representation, § 11.8(c)
  Conflicts of interest, above
  Constitutional right to counsel as prerequisite, § 11.7(a)
  Guilty pleas and plea bargains, § 21.3(b)
  Incompetence of attorney, § 11.10
  Per se vs. actual ineffectiveness, § 11.7(d)
  Prejudice, incompetence of attorney, § 11.10(d)
  Raising claim of ineffectiveness, § 11.7(e)
  Reasonableness standard, incompetence of attorney, § 11.10(c)
  Retained vs. appointed counsel, § 11.7(b)
  Self-representation, § 11.5(e)
  State interference and other extrinsic factors, claims based on, § 11.8
Equal protection and appointed counsel, § 11.1(d)
Experts, assistance of, § 11.2(e)
Forfeiture of right, § 11.3(c)
Grand Jury, § 8.14
Guilty pleas and plea bargains, § 21.3(a)
Hybrid representation, § 11.5(g)
Identification Procedures, this index
Incompetence of attorney, right to effective representation, § 11.10
Indigent persons
  General discussion, § 11.2
  Anders rules, § 11.2(c)
  Bounds right to access, § 11.2(f)
  Experts, assistance of, § 11.2(e)
  Misdemeanor prosecutions, § 11.2(a)
  Partial contribution, § 11.2(h)
  Recoupment, § 11.2(h)
  Stages of proceeding, § 11.2(b)
  Standards of indigency, § 11.2(g)
  Transcripts, § 11.2(d)
Interference by state, effective representation, § 11.8
Interrogations and Confessions, this index
Misdemeanor prosecutions, indigent persons, § 11.2(a)
Notification, self-representation, § 11.5(b)
Partial contribution, indigent persons, § 11.2(h)
Per se vs. actual ineffectiveness of representation, § 11.7(d)
Post conviction review, § 28.12
Prejudice
  Incompetence of attorney, § 11.10(d)
  Strategy, control of counsel over, § 11.6(d)
Preliminary hearings, § 14.4(a)
Pretrial release, § 12.1(c)
Public defenders, this index
Reasonableness standard, competence of attorney, § 11.10(c)

COUNSEL, RIGHT TO—Cont'd
  Recoupment
    Expense of, where bad faith prosecution, § 13.5(h)
    From indigent persons, § 11.2(h)
  Replacement of appointed counsel, § 11.4(b)
  Retained counsel,
    Characteristics, § 1.4(f)
    Choice of, § 11.4(c)
  Self-representation
    General discussion, § 11.5
    Choice of counsel, pro se alternative, § 11.4(d)
    Denial, grounds for, § 11.5(d)
    Faretta ruling, § 11.5(a)
    Hybrid representation, § 11.5(g)
    Ineffective representation, subsequent challenge to, § 11.5(e)
    Judicial inquiry, § 11.5(c)
    Notification, § 11.5(b)
    Standby counsel, § 11.5(f)
    Warnings required, § 11.5(c)
  Sentencing, § 26.4(e)
  Sixth Amendment right, § 11.1(a)
  Standby counsel, self-representation, § 11.5(f)
  State-funded counsel, §§ 1.4(f), 11.2
  Strategy, control of counsel over
    General discussion, § 11.6
    Consultation, § 11.6(b)
    Balancing of interests, § 11.6(c)
    Prejudice, § 11.6(d)
    Strategic vs. personal decisions, § 11.6(a)
  Transcripts, indigent persons, § 11.2(d)
  Waiver
    Conflicts of interest, § 11.9(c)
    Right to counsel, § 11.3
  Warnings, self-representation, § 11.5(c)
  Withdrawal on appeal, § 11.2(c)

COVERT ENTRY
  Wiretapping and electronic surveillance, § 4.6(c)

COURTS
  Magistrates, this index
  Trial courts, § 1.4(h)

CREDIBILITY
  Preliminary hearings, bindover determination, § 14.3(b)
  Review of evidence sufficiency, § 24.6(c)

CRIME-COMMITTED FORMULA
  Venue, this index

CRIMINAL JUSTICE STATISTICS
Federal, § **1.11(d)**
Funded studies, § **1.11(e)**
National, § **1.11(b)**
Significance, § **1.11(a)**
State, § **1.11(c)**

CRIMINAL JUSTICE SYSTEM
Administrative setting
    Administrative interactions, § **1.10(d)**
    Caseload pressures, § **1.10(c)**
    Fragmentation of enforcement agencies, § **1.4(c)**
    Law variations, and, § **1.8(f)**
    Localism, § **1.4(b)**
    Policy differences, § **1.10(b)**
    Significance, § **1.10(a)**
    The influence of the local community, § **1.10(e)**
Deviance, § **1.9(b)**
Discretion
    Challenge to, § **1.9(e)**
    Deviance compared, § **1.9(b)**
    Law vs. practice, § **1.9(a)**
    Nature of, § **1.9(c)**
    Range of, § **1.9(c)**
    Reasons for, § **1.9(d)**
    Restrictions of, § **1.9(e)**
Division of authority
    Dominance of state systems, § **1.2(e)**
    Federal authority, § **1.2(c)**
    Federal/state joint projects, § **1.2(c), (e)**
    Federal/state variation, § **1.2(f)**
    Federal system expansion, § **1.2(d)**
    Federal system, significance of, § **1.2(e), (f)**
    Fifty-two jurisdictions, § **1.2(a)**
    Individualization, § **1.3(c)**
    Models, § **1.3(d)-(f)**
    Patterns in state laws, § **1.3(g)**
    State authority, § **1.2(b)**
    Uniformity, § **1.3(b)**
Goals
    Accuracy, § **1.5(b)**
    Accusatorial system, § **1.5(d)**
    Adversary system, § **1.5(c)**
    Appearance of fairness, § **1.5(i)**
    Equality, § **1.5(j)**
    Individual dignity, § **1.5(h)**
    Lay participation, § **1.5(g)**
    Minimizing burdens of accusation, § **1.5(f)**

CRIMINAL JUSTICE SYSTEM—Cont'd
Goals—Cont'd
  Minimizing erroneous convictions, § 1.5(e)
  Substantive law implementation, § 1.5(a)
  Victim concerns, § 1.5(k)
Historical development
  Colonial period, § 1.6(b)
  Core of nineteenth century, § 1.6(d)
  Era of liberal idealism, § 1.6(a)
  Future of reform, § 1.6(i)
  Introduction, § 1.6(a)
  Post-liberalism period, § 1.6(h)
  Post-revolutionary period, § 1.6(c)
  Progressive era, § 1.6(f)
  Second quarter of the twentieth century, § 1.6(f)
Laws applicable
  Common law rulings, § 1.7(h)
  Federal constitution, §§ 1.7(b), 2.1-2.7
  Federal statutes, § 1.7(c)
  General court rules, § 1.7(f)
  Internal administrative standards, § 1.7(j)
  Local court rules, § 1.7(f)
  Local ordinances, § 1.7(k)
  State constitutions, §§ 1.7(d), 2.11
  Statutes, § 1.7(e)
  Supervisory authority rulings, § 1.7(i)
  Treaties, § 1.7(c)
  Varied sources, § 1.7(a)
Offense distinctions
  Capital offenses, § 1.8(e)
  Misdemeanor/felony, § 1.8(c)
  Ordinance violation, § 1.8(e)
  Specific offenses, § 1.8(b)
Procedural subsets
  By administrating agency, § 1.8(f), (g)
  By offense, § 1.8(b)-(e)
  Lines of division, § 1.8(a)
Variations
  Agency distinctions, §§ 1.4, 1.8(f), 1.10(b)
  Discretion, and, § 1.9
  Laws, and, § 1.7
  Offense distinctions, § 1.8

CROSS-EXAMINATION
Confrontation, Right to, this index
General discussion, § 24.4(b)
Preliminary hearings, § 14.4(c)
Sentencing, § 26.4(f)

CUMULATION OF EVIDENCE
Joinder of offenses, § 17.1(e)

CUSTODIAL INTERROGATION
Self-Incrimination, Privilege Against, this index

DANGEROUS OFFENDERS
Pretrial release, § 12.3(f)
Special sentences, § 26.6(e)

DATE
Time and Date, this index

DE NOVO TRIAL
Jury trial, right to, §§ 1.4(g), 22.1(f)
Double jeopardy, § 25.1(e)

DEADLOCKED JURY
General discussion, § 24.9(d)
Mistrial, § 25.2(c)-(e)

DEATH PENALTY
Capital Offenses and Punishment, this index

DECISION TO CHARGE
General discussion, § 1.3(h)

DECLARATORY JUDGMENTS
Challenging decision to prosecute, § 13.5(e)

DELAYED PETITIONS
Post Conviction Review, this index

DEPOSITIONS
General discussion, § 20.2(e)

DERIVATIVE RIGHTS
Counsel, right to, § 11.1(c)

DERIVATIVE STANDING
Exclusionary rules, § 9.2(c)

DESCRIPTIONS
Search warrants, §§ 3.4(e), 3.4(f)
Wiretapping and electronic surveillance, Fourth Amendment, § 4.6(e)

DESUETUDE
Challenging decision to prosecute, § 13.5(c)

DETAINERS, INTERSTATE AGREEMENT ON
General discussion, § 18.4(c)

DETERRENCE
Arrest, search and seizure, exclusionary rule and other remedies, § 3.1(d)
Harmless error, § 27.6(d)

INDEX

DEVIANCE
General discussion, § 1.8(b)

DIRECTED ACQUITTAL, MOTIONS FOR
Acquittal, Judgment of, this index

DISCIPLINARY PROCEEDINGS
Exclusionary rule and other remedies, § 3.1(*l*)
Improper argument, § 24.7(i)
Internal regulations, § 1.7(j)
McDade Act, §§ 1.7(j), 8.8(d)

DISCOVERY AND DISCLOSURE
General discussion, §§ 20.1-20.6
Acceleration doctrine, self-incrimination, § 20.4(d)
Alibi defense, prosecution discovery, § 20.5(b)
Codefendant, statements of, § 20.3(d)
Common law, §§ 20.1(a), 20.2(a)
Conditional discovery, constitutional limits on discovery by prosecution,
   § 20.4(g)
Constitutional limits on discovery by prosecution
  General discussion, § 20.4
  Acceleration doctrine, self-incrimination, § 20.4(d)
  Conditional discovery, § 20.4(g) .
  Due process, § 20.4(a)
  Insanity defense, self-incrimination, § 20.4(e)
  Non-testimonial disclosures, self-incrimination, § 20.4(c)
  Self-incrimination, privilege against, §§ 20.4(b)-20.4(e)
  Sixth Amendment, § 20.4(f)
  Testimonial disclosures, self-incrimination, § 20.4(b)
Constitutional overtones, defense discovery, § 20.3(m)
Court rules, § 20.2(b)
Criminal records, defense discovery, § 20.3(e)
Defendant, statements of, § 20.3(c)
Defense discovery
  General discussion, § 20.3
  Codefendant, statements of, § 20.3(d)
  Constitutional overtones, § 20.3(m)
  Control of prosecution, § 20.3(a)
  Criminal records, § 20.3(e)
  Defendant, statements of, § 20.3(c)
  Documents, § 20.3(g)
  Exculpatory material, § 20.3(n)
  Police reports, § 20.3(k)
  Possession by prosecution, § 20.3(a)
  Protective orders, § 20.3(*l*)
  Recorded statements, § 20.3(b)
  Scientific reports, § 20.3(f)
  Tangible objects, § 20.3(g)

DISCOVERY AND DISCLOSURE—Cont'd
Defense discovery—Cont'd
  Witness, statements of, § 20.3(i)
  Witness lists, § 20.3(h)
  Work product exception, § 20.3(j)
  Written statements, § 20.3(b)
Depositions, § 20.2(e)
Discovery via alternative procedures, § 20.3(n)
Documents, §§ 20.3(g), 20.5(g)
Due process, constitutional limits on discovery by prosecution, § 20.4(a)
Exculpatory material provisions, § 20.3(n)
Expansion of discovery, § 20.1
Grand jury, § 8.5(g)
Identification of defenses, prosecution discovery, § 20.5(d)
Insanity and related defenses, §§ 20.4(e), 20.5(c)
Police reports, defense discovery, § 20.3(k)
Post conviction review, factfinding and evidentiary hearings, § 28.7(d)
Preliminary hearings, §§ 14.1(b), 20.2(d)
Presentence report, § 26.5(c)
Prosecution discovery
  General discussion, §§ 20.4, 20.5
  Alibi defense, § 20.5(b)
  Constitutional limits on discovery by prosecution, above
  Documents, § 20.5(g)
  Identification of defenses, § 20.5(d)
  Insanity and related defenses, § 20.5(c)
  Scientific reports, § 20.5(h)
  Tangible objects, § 20.5(g)
  Variations in approach, § 20.5(a)
  Witness, statements of, § 20.5(f)
  Witness lists, § 20.5(e)
Protective orders, defense discovery, § 20.3(*l*)
Recorded statements, defense discovery, § 20.3(b)
Sanctions
  General discussion, § 20.6
  Defense, violations by, § 20.6(c)
  Prosecution, violations by, § 20.6(b)
  Range, § 20.6(a)
Scientific reports, §§ 20.3(f), 20.5(h)
Self-incrimination, constitutional limits on discovery by prosecution, §§ 20.4(b)-20.4(e)
Sentencing, § 26.4(d)
Sixth Amendment, constitutional limits on discovery by prosecution, § 20.4(f)
Statutes, § 20.2(b)
Structure of discovery law
  General discussion, § 20.2
  Common law jurisdictions, § 20.2(a)
  Court rules and statutes, § 20.2(b)

DISCOVERY AND DISCLOSURE—Cont'd
Structure of discovery law—Cont'd
Depositions, § 20.2(e)
Operation of discovery provisions, § 20.2(c)
Other discovery vehicles, § 20.2(d)
Tangible objects, §§ 20.3(g), 20.5(g)
Two way street movement, § 20.1(d)
Witness, statements of, §§ 20.3(i), 20.5(f)
Witness lists, §§ 20.3(h), 20.5(e)
Work product exception, defense discovery, § 20.3(j)
Written statements, defense discovery, § 20.3(b)

DISCRETION OF COURT
Double jeopardy, reprosecution following mistrial, § 25.2(e)
Limiting discretion, § 1.9(e)
Nature and range, § 1.9(c)
Reasons, § 1.9(d)
Review of, on appeal, § 27.5(e)
Selection of appointed counsel, §§ 1.4(f), 11.4(a)
Sentencing, this index

DISCRETIONARY ENFORCEMENT
Prosecution, Decision as to, this index

DISCRIMINATORY PROSECUTION
General discussion, §§ 13.4(a), 13.7(b)

DISMISSAL
Double jeopardy, effect, §§ 25.2(f), 25.3(a)
Preliminary hearings, bindover determination, § 14.3(c)

DISORDERLY CONDUCT
Presence of defendant, § 24.2(c)

DISPARITY
Guilty pleas and plea bargains, § 21.1(e)
Sentencing, § 26.3(b)

DIVERSION
Prosecution, Decision as to, this index

DNA EVIDENCE
Exoneration by, § 7.1(a)
Inmate testing, § 3.9(i)
Parolee testing, § 3.9(j)
Post-trial testing, § 24.11(d)
Pre-conviction testing, § 3.5(d)
Preservation of, § 24.3(e)
Probationer testing, § 3.9(j)
Testing as a search, § 3.2(g)

INDEX

DOUBLE JEOPARDY
General discussion, §§ 25.1-25.5
Acquittal or dismissal, reprosecution following
    General discussion, § 25.3
    Dismissals vs. acquittals, § 25.3(a)
    Judge, acquittals by, § 25.3(c)
    Jury acquittals, § 25.3(b)
    Postconviction judgments of acquittal, § 25.3(e)
    Pre-jeopardy acquittals, § 25.3(d)
Applicability, § 25.1(c)
Attachment of jeopardy, § 25.1(d)
Consent of defendant, reprosecution following mistrial, § 25.2(a)
Conviction, reprosecution following
    General discussion, § 25.4
    Determination of sufficiency, § 25.4(c)
    Evidence insufficiency exception, § 25.4(b)
    Implied acquittal, conviction as, § 25.4(d)
Dimensions of guarantee, § 25.1
Discretion of trial court, reprosecution following mistrial, § 25.2(e)
Dismissal, reprosecution following. Acquittal or dismissal, reprosecution follow-
    ing, above
Evidence insufficiency exception, reprosecution following conviction, § 25.4(b)
Federal prosecution after state prosecution, § 25.5(a)
Goaded mistrials, reprosecution following, § 25.2(b)
History, § 25.1(b)
Implied acquittal, conviction as, § 25.4(d)
Joinder of related offenses, failure as to, § 17.4(b)
Jury acquittal, reprosecution following, § 25.3(b)
Manifest necessity standard, reprosecution following mistrial, §§ 25.2(c)-25.2(e)
Mistrial, reprosecution following
    General discussion, § 25.2
    Alternatives to mistrial, § 25.2(d)
    Consent of defendant, § 25.2(a)
    Discretion of trial court, § 25.2(e)
    Dismissals equivalent to mistrials, § 25.2(f)
    Goaded mistrials, § 25.2(b)
    Manifest necessity standard, §§ 25.2(c)-25.2(e)
Municipal-municipal, reprosecution by different sovereign, § 25.5(c)
Pleading, accusatory, § 19.2(b)
Policies, § 25.1(b)
Postconviction judgments of acquittal, reprosecution following, § 25.3(e)
Pre-jeopardy acquittal, reprosecution following, § 25.3(d)
Reprosecutions, generally, § 25.1(g)
Same offense, § 25.1(f)
Sovereign, reprosecution by different
    General discussion, § 25.5
    Federal prosecution after state, § 25.5(a)
    State prosecution after municipal, § 25.5(b)

INDEX

DOUBLE JEOPARDY—Cont'd
Sovereign, reprosecution by different—Cont'd
State-state and municipal-municipal, § 25.5(c)
State prosecution after municipal prosecution, § 25.5(b)
State-state, reprosecution by different sovereign, § 25.5(c)
Termination of jeopardy, § 25.1(e)

DRUG COURTS
General discussion, § 26.1(e)

DUE PROCESS
Constitutional Law, this index

DUPLICATIVE STATUTES
Selection of charge, § 13.7(a)

DUPLICITY
Pleading, accusatory, § 19.3(c)

EFFECTIVE REPRESENTATION
Counsel, Right to, this index

EIGHTH AMENDMENT
Capital punishment, § 26.1(b)
Pretrial release, mandatory pretrial detention, § 12.3(c)
Punishments, cumulative, § 25.1(c)

ELECTRONIC MAIL (E-MAIL)
Access to stored communications, § 4.8
Fourth Amendment, § 4.4
Wiretapping, § 4.6

ELECTRONIC SURVEILLANCE
Wiretapping and Network Surveillance, this index

EMERGENCIES
Wiretapping and electronic surveillance, Fourth Amendment, § 4.2(g)

EMULATION
General discussion, § 1.2(e)

ENCOURAGEMENT BY POLICE AND ENTRAPMENT
General discussion, §§ 5.1-5.4
Burden of proof, § 5.3(d)
Contingent fee arrangements, § 5.4(a)
Inconsistent defenses, § 5.3(c)
Inducements to those not reasonably suspected, § 5.4(b)
Jury trial or trial by court, § 5.3(b)
Overinvolvement of government in criminal enterprise, § 5.4(c)
Past conduct of defendant, admissibility of, § 5.3(a)
Procedure, § 5.3
Scope of entrapment defense, § 5.1(c)

INDEX

ENCOURAGEMENT BY POLICE AND ENTRAPMENT—Cont'd
Subjective vs. objective test for entrapment
General discussion, § 5.2
Objections to objective approach, § 5.2(d)
Objections to subjective approach, § 5.2(c)
Objective approach, § 5.2(b)
Subjective approach, § 5.2(a)

ENTERPRISE OFFENSES
Venue, crime-committed formula, § 16.2(g)

ENTRAPMENT
Encouragement by Police and Entrapment, this index

EQUAL PROTECTION
Appointed counsel, § 11.1(d)
Challenging decision to prosecute, § 13.4
Indictments, composition of grand jury, § 15.4(c)
Preliminary hearing, bypassing, § 14.2(d)
Selection of jurors, § 22.2(c)
Sentencing, § 26.4(b)

EQUITABLE TOLLING
Post Conviction Review, this index

EVIDENCE
General discussion, §§ 24.3-24.6
Access to evidence by defendant
General discussion, § 24.3
Assistance to defense in obtaining evidence, § 24.3(g)
Constitutional law, § 24.3(a)
Due process, disclosure of exculpatory evidence, § 24.3(b)
Exculpatory evidence, disclosure of, § 24.3(b)
False evidence, correction of, § 24.3(d)
Immunity of defense witness, § 24.3(i)
Interference by government, § 24.3(h)
Jencks Act, § 24.3(c)
Preservation of evidence by government, § 24.3(e)
Subpoenas, use by defense, § 24.3(f)
Witness statements, disclosure of, § 24.3(c)
Bench trials, evaluation of evidence by court, § 24.6(a)
Burden of proof. Presumptions and Burden of Proof, this index
Comment on evidence by court, § 24.6(e)
Comment on silence of defendant, § 24.5(b)
Constitutional law, access to evidence by defendant, § 24.3(a)
Cross-Examination, this index
Directed acquittal, motions for, § 24.6(b)
Double jeopardy, reprosecution following conviction, § 25.4(b)
Due process, disclosure of exculpatory evidence, § 24.3(b)

EVIDENCE—Cont'd
  Evaluation of evidence by court
    General discussion, § 24.6
    Bench trials, § 24.6(a)
    Directed acquittal, motions for, § 24.6(b)
    New trial, motion for, § 24.6(d)
    Sufficiency standard, § 24.6(c)
    Summary and comment on evidence, § 24.6(e)
  Exculpatory Evidence, this index
  False evidence, correction of, § 24.3(d)
  Immunity of defense witness, § 24.3(i)
  Indictments, § 15.5
  Instructions on silence of defendant, § 24.5(c)
  Interference by government, access to evidence by defendant, § 24.3(h)
  Jencks Act, access to evidence by defendant, § 24.3(c)
  Jurisdiction, § 16.4(d)
  New trial, motion for, § 24.6(d)
  Newly discovered, § 24.11(d)
  Post Conviction Review, this index
  Preliminary hearings, § 14.4(b)
  Presentation of evidence, § 24.4
  Preservation of evidence by government, § 24.3(e)
  Presumptions and Burden of Proof, this index
  Pretrial release, § 12.1(d)
  Privilege, forcing claim of, § 24.4(c)
  Prosecution, decision as to, §§ 13.1(b), 13.4(b)
  Right of defendant to testify, § 24.5(d)
  Rules of evidence, § 24.4(a)
  Self-incrimination, privilege against, § 6.8(c)
  Sentencing, §§ 26.4(f), 26.5(a), 26.10(c)
  Sequestration of witnesses, § 24.4(d)
  Silence of defendant
    General discussion, § 24.5
    Comment on silence, § 24.5(b)
    Instructions on silence, § 24.5(c)
    Right not to take stand, § 24.5(a)
  Subpoenas, use by defense, § 24.3(f)
  Summary of evidence by court, § 24.6(e)
  Venue, § 16.1(g)
  Witness statements, disclosure of, § 24.3(c)

EXCLUSIONARY RULES
  General discussion, §§ 9.1-9.6, 10.1-10.6
  Abolition of standing, § 9.2(d)
  Administration of exclusionary rules, §§ 10.1-10.6
  Arrest, generally. Arrest, Search and Seizure, this index
  Attenuated connection, fruit of poisonous tree, § 9.3(c)
  Automatic standing, § 9.2(a)

INDEX

EXCLUSIONARY RULES—Cont'd

Burden of proof
  General discussion, § 10.3
  Confessions, § 10.3(c)
  Identification, § 10.3(d)
  Search and seizure, § 10.3(b)
Business premises, standing, § 9.1(c)
But for test, fruit of poisonous tree, § 9.3(b)
Compulsory process, hearing on suppression, § 10.5(f)
Confessions
  Burden of proof, § 10.3(c)
  Fruit of illegal arrests and searches, § 9.4(a)
  Fruits of illegally obtained confessions, below
  Standard of proof, § 10.4(b)
Confrontation, hearing on suppression, § 10.5(e)
Derivative standing, § 9.2(c)
Evidentiary rules, hearing on suppression, § 10.5(d)
Findings, ruling and its effect, § 10.6(a)
Forfeiture of objection. Waiver or forfeiture of objection, below
Fruit of illegal arrests and searches
  General discussion, § 9.4
  Arrests, § 9.4(c)
  Confessions, § 9.4(a)
  Identification of person, § 9.4(d)
  New crime, § 9.4(f)
  Searches, § 9.4(b)
  Testimony of witness, § 9.4(e)
Fruit of poisonous tree
  General discussion, § 9.3
  Attenuated connection, § 9.3(c)
  But for test, § 9.3(b)
  Independent source, § 9.3(d)
  Inevitable discovery, § 9.3(e)
Fruits of illegally obtained confessions
  General discussion, § 9.5
  Confessions, § 9.5(c)
  New crime, § 9.5(e)
  Poisonous tree, confession as, § 9.5(a)
  Searches, § 9.5(b)
  Testimony of witness, § 9.5(d)
Grand jury proceedings, §§ 3.1(b), 8.9(a)
Guilty plea, waiver or forfeiture of objection, § 10.2(d)
Hearing on suppression
  General discussion, § 10.5
  Compulsory process, right of, § 10.5(f)
  Confrontation, right of, § 10.5(e)
  Evidentiary rules, § 10.5(d)
  Jury, presence of, § 10.5(b)

EXCLUSIONARY RULES—Cont'd
　Hearing on suppression—Cont'd
　　Testimony by defendant, § 10.5(c)
　　Trier of fact, § 10.5(a)
　Identification of person
　　Burden of proof, § 10.3(d)
　　Fruit of illegal arrests and searches, § 9.4(d)
　　Standard of proof, § 10.4(d)
　Impeachment, permissible use of illegally obtained evidence, § 9.6(a)
　Independent source, fruit of poisonous tree, § 9.3(d)
　Indictments, § 15.5
　Inevitable discovery, fruit of poisonous tree, § 9.3(e)
　Jury, presence during hearing on suppression, § 10.5(b)
　New crime
　　Fruit of illegal arrests and searches, § 9.4(f)
　　Fruits of illegally obtained confessions, § 9.5(e)
　Nolo contendere, waiver or forfeiture of objection, § 10.2(d)
　Open the door, defense tactics that, § 9.6(b)
　Perjury or other new offense, use of illegally obtained evidence in prosecution
　　for, § 9.6(c)
　Permissible use of illegally obtained evidence
　　General discussion, § 9.6
　　Defense tactics that open the door, § 9.6(b)
　　Impeachment, § 9.6(a)
　　Perjury or other new offense, prosecution for, § 9.6(c)
　Personal rights, standing, § 9.1(a)
　Preliminary hearings, § 14.4(b)
　Pretrial motion to suppress
　　General discussion, § 10.1
　　Contemporaneous objection or pretrial motion, § 10.1(a)
　　Form of motion, § 10.1(b)
　　Pre-charge motion, distinguished, § 10.1(c)
　Probation revocations, § 26.10(c)
　Recommendations, ruling and its effect, § 10.6(b)
　Reconsideration at trial, ruling and its effect, § 10.6(c)
　Residential premises, standing, § 9.1(b)
　Ruling and its effect
　　General discussion, § 10.6
　　Effect of ruling in other cases, § 10.6(d)
　　Findings, § 10.6(a)
　　Recommendations, § 10.6(b)
　　Reconsideration at trial, § 10.6(c)
　Scope of exclusionary rules, §§ 9.1-9.6
　Search and seizure, generally. Arrest, Search and Seizure, this index
　Standard of proof
　　General discussion, § 10.4
　　Confessions, § 10.4(b)
　　Identification, § 10.4(d)

EXCLUSIONARY RULES—Cont'd
Standard of proof—Cont'd
Search and seizure, § 10.4(c)
Standing
General discussion, §§ 9.1, 9.2
Abolition of standing, § 9.2(d)
Automatic standing, § 9.2(a)
Business premises, § 9.1(c)
Derivative standing, § 9.2(c)
Personal rights, § 9.1(a)
Residential premises, § 9.1(b)
Target standing, § 9.2(b)
Vehicles, § 9.1(d)
Target standing, § 9.2(b)
Testimony by defendant
Hearing on suppression, § 10.5(c)
Waiver or forfeiture of objection, § 10.2(c)
Testimony of witness
Fruit of illegal arrests and searches, § 9.4(e)
Fruits of illegally obtained confessions, § 9.5(d)
Vehicles, standing, § 9.1(d)
Waiver or forfeiture of objection
General discussion, § 10.2
Failure to make timely objection, § 10.2(a)
Failure to renew objection, § 10.2(b)
Plea of guilty or nolo contendere, § 10.2(d)
Testimony by defendant, § 10.2(c)
Wiretapping and electronic surveillance, §§ 4.6(m), 4.7(e), 4.8(f)

EXCULPATORY EVIDENCE
Disclosure, § 24.3(b)
Indictments, failure to present, § 15.7(f)

EXECUTION OF ORDER
Wiretapping and Network Surveillance, this index

EXHAUSTION OF STATE REMEDIES
Post conviction review, § 28.5(a)

EXPENSES OF LITIGATION
Recoupment of expenses, § 13.5(h)

EXPERT TESTIMONY
Assistance of experts, § 11.2(e)
Identification procedures, § 7.5(b)

EXPUNGEMENT
Arrest records, § 3.1(m)

FACTFINDING
Post Conviction Review, this index

INDEX

FAIR CROSS SECTION REQUIREMENT
Indictments, composition of grand jury, § 15.4(d)
Selection of jurors, § 22.2(d)

FAIR TRIAL
Publicity, this index
Venue, change of, §§ 16.3(b), 16.3(d)

FALSE EVIDENCE
Correction, § 24.3(d)
Sentencing, § 26.4(f)

FEDERAL AUTHORITY
General discussion, §§ 1.2(a), 1.2(b)

FEDERAL BAIL REFORM ACT
General discussion, § 12.1(a)

FEDERAL SPEEDY TRIAL ACT OF 1974
General discussion, §§ 18.3(b), 18.4(b)

FEDERALISM
Constitutional law, selective incorporation, §§ 2.5(f), 2.6(d)
Habeas corpus review, §§ 28.2(c), 28.4(a)

FELONIES
Procedural subsets, § 1.8(c)

FINAL JUDGMENTS
Appeal by defendant, § 27.2(a)

FINANCIAL SANCTIONS
Sentencing, § 26.1(f)

FIRE SCENES
Search and seizure, § 3.9(e)

FIRST AMENDMENT
Closed proceedings, publicity, §§ 23.1(d), 23.1(e)
Probation conditions, § 26.9(b)
Publicity, this index
Sentencing information, § 26.4(b)

FIRST APPEARANCE
General discussion, § 1.3(k)

FOREGONE CONCLUSION STANDARD
Grand jury, act-of-production doctrine, § 8.13(a)

FOREIGN INTELLIGENCE SURVEILLANCE ACT
Provisions of, § 4.9(b)

FOREPERSON OF GRAND JURY
Indictments, § 15.4(e)

INDEX

FORFEITURE
Appeal, right to, § 27.5(c)
Counsel, right to, §§ 11.3(c), 11.4(b)
Exclusionary Rules, this index
Guilty pleas and plea bargains, § 21.6(a)
Joinder and severance, § 17.3(d)
Sentence of, § 26.6(d)
Speedy trial and other prompt disposition, § 18.1(d)

FORMER JEOPARDY
Double Jeopardy, this index

FREE PRESS
Publicity, this index

FRUIT OF ILLEGAL ARRESTS AND SEARCHES
Exclusionary Rules, this index

FRUIT OF POISONOUS TREE
Exclusionary Rules, this index

FRUITS OF ILLEGALLY OBTAINED CONFESSIONS
Exclusionary Rules, this index

FULL AND FAIR LITIGATION
Post conviction review, § 28.3(d)

FUNCTIONAL EQUIVALENT TEST
Self-incrimination, privilege against, § 6.7(a)

FUNDAMENTAL FAIRNESS
Constitutional Law, this index

GOADED MISTRIALS
Double jeopardy, § 25.2(b)

GOOD TIME CREDIT
General discussion, § 26.2(c)

GRAND JURY
General discussion, §§ 8.1-8.15
Act-of-production doctrine, self-incrimination
General discussion, § 8.13
Agents of entity, claims by, § 8.13(d)
Documentary subpoena, below
Foregone conclusion standard, § 8.13(a)
Immunity, § 8.13(c)
Non-documentary subpoenas, § 8.13(e)
Potential incrimination, § 8.13(b)
Testimonial aspects, §§ 8.12(f), 8.13(a)
Advantages
General discussion, § 8.3
Contempt sanction, § 8.3(a)

GRAND JURY—Cont'd
  Advantages—Cont'd
    Immunity, grant of, § **8.3(e)**
    Psychological pressure, § **8.3(d)**
    Public confidence, maintenance of, § **8.3(g)**
    Reports of grand jury, § **8.3(h)**
    Secrecy, § **8.3(f)**
    Subpoena ad testificandum, § **8.3(b)**
    Subpoena authority, § **8.3(a)**
    Subpoena duces tecum, § **8.3(c)**
  Adverse consequences, privilege against self-incrimination, § **8.10(f)**
  Agents of entity, act-of-production doctrine, § **8.13(d)**
  Alternative procedures, § **8.1(c)**
  Anteroom, counsel in, § **8.15(c)**
  Appeal by defendant, § **27.2(e)**
  Calandra rule, § **8.9(a)**
  Challenge to grand jury proceeding, disclosure pursuant to, § **8.5(f)**
  Challenges to and checks upon decision not to prosecute, § **13.3(d)**
  Chilling effect, misuse of subpoena authority, § **8.8(d)**
  Civil discovery, use for, § **8.8(e)**
  Civil protective orders, § **8.6(b)**
  Compelled testimony. Immunity and compelled testimony, below
  Constitutional law
    Counsel, right to, § **8.15(a)**
    Immunity and compelled testimony, § **8.11(a)**
  Contempt sanction, § **8.3(a)**
  Counsel, right to
    General discussion, § **8.15**
    Anteroom, counsel in, § **8.15(c)**
    Constitutional requirements, § **8.15(a)**
    Grand jury room, counsel within, § **8.15(b)**
    Multiple representation, § **8.15(d)**
  Discovery rules, disclosure to defendant pursuant to, § **8.5(g)**
  Documentary subpoenas
    Act of production above
    Boyd exception, § **8.12(a), 8.12(g)**
    Required records, § **8.12(c)**
    Third party production, § **8.12(e)**
  Dual functions of traditional grand jury, § **8.1(a)**
  Electronic surveillance, inquiries based on illegal, § **8.9(b)**
  English origins, § **8.2(a)**
  Entity exception, production of documents, § **8.12(b)**
  Foregone conclusion standard, act-of-production doctrine, above
  Fourth Amendment challenges to subpoenas
    General discussion, § **8.7**
    Applicability of Fourth Amendment to subpoenas, §§ **8.7(a), 8.7(c)**
    Dionisio and *Mara* cases, § **8.7(c)**
    Forthwith subpoenas, § **8.7(e)**

GRAND JURY—Cont'd

Fourth Amendment challenges to subpoenas—Cont'd
Identification evidence, subpoenas for, § 8.7(d)
Overbreadth of documentary subpoenas, § 8.7(b)
Harassment, misuse of subpoena authority, § 8.8(h)
Historical development, § 8.2
Identification evidence, Fourth Amendment challenges to subpoenas for, § 8.7(d)
Illegally obtained evidence, inquiries based on, § 8.9
Immunity and compelled testimony
General discussion, §§ 8.3(e), 8.11
Act-of-production doctrine, § 8.13(c)
Constitutionality, § 8.11(a)
Informal grants of immunity, § 8.11(e)
Procedures for immunity, § 8.11(d)
Transactional vs. use/derivative use immunity, §§ 8.11(b), 8.11(c)
Independent investigative authority, § 8.4(b)
Indictments, this index
Investigations, generally, §§ 8.1-8.15
Judicial supervision, § 8.4(c)
Law enforcement, disclosure to further, § 8.5(e)
Legal structure of investigative grand jury
General discussion, § 8.4
Independent investigative authority, § 8.4(b)
Judicial supervision, § 8.4(c)
Representativeness of grand jurors, § 8.4(a)
Misuse of subpoena authority
General discussion, § 8.8
Chilling effect, § 8.8(d)
Civil discovery, use for, § 8.8(e)
Harassment, § 8.8(h)
Oppressiveness, § 8.8(c)
Post-indictment criminal discovery, use for, § 8.8(f)
Relevance, § 8.8(b)
Structural objections, § 8.8(i)
Subject of investigation improper, § 8.8(a)
Usurpation of subpoena power by prosecution or police, § 8.8(g)
Multiple representation, right to counsel, § 8.15(d)
Non-documentary subpoenas, act-of-production doctrine, § 8.13(e)
Oppressiveness, misuse of subpoena authority, § 8.8(c)
Overbreadth of documentary subpoenas, Fourth Amendment challenges, § 8.7(b)
Post-indictment criminal discovery, use for, § 8.8(f)
Privileges and other protections, § 8.6(b)
Psychological pressure, § 8.3(d)
Public confidence, maintenance of, § 8.3(g)
Relevance, §§ 8.2(c), 8.8(b)
Remedies, secrecy, § 8.5(i)
Reports of grand jury, § 8.3(h)
Representativeness of grand jurors, § 8.4(a)

INDEX

GRAND JURY—Cont'd

Required records exception, production of documents, § 8.12(c)

Right to every man's evidence, § 8.6

Schmerber rule, production of documents, § 8.12(d)

Secrecy

  General discussion, §§ 8.3(f), 8.5

  Challenge to grand jury proceeding, disclosure pursuant to, § 8.5(f)

  First Amendment limits, § 8.5(d)

  Discovery rules, disclosure to defendant pursuant to, § 8.5(g)

  Federal statutes, §§ 8.5(b), 8.5(d)

  Law enforcement, disclosure to further, § 8.5(e)

  Non-disclosure orders, § 8.5(d)

  Particularized need standard, § 8.5(h)

  Protected information, § 8.5(c)

  Remedies, § 8.5(i)

  Statutory structure, § 8.5(b)

  Third parties, disclosure to, § 8.5(h)

  Witness, disclosure by, § 8.5(d)

Self-incrimination, privilege against

  General discussion, §§ 8.10-8.14

  Act-of-production doctrine, above

  Adverse consequences, § 8.10(f)

  Advice as to rights, § 8.10(d)

  Another sovereign, incrimination under laws of, § 8.10(b)

  Compelled testimony. Immunity and compelled testimony, above

  Compelling target to appear, § 8.10(c)

  Documentary subpoenas, above

  Entity exception, production of documents, § 8.12(b)

  Immunity and compelled testimony, above

  Production of physical items, §§ 8.12(d), 8.13(e)

  Required records exception, production of documents, § 8.12(c)

  Schmerber rule, production of documents, § 8.12(d)

  Standard of potential incrimination, §§ 8.10(a), 8.13(b)

  Testimonial aspects of production of documents, § 8.12(f)

  Testimony before grand jury, §§ 8.10, 8.11

  Waiver by witness, § 8.10(e)

Special grand juries, § 8.1(b)

Structural objections, misuse of subpoena authority, § 8.8(i)

Subject of investigation improper, misuse of subpoena authority, § 8.8(a)

Subpoena ad testificandum, § 8.3(b)

Subpoena authority, § 8.3(a)

Subpoena duces tecum, § 8.3(c)

Testimonial character and foregone conclusion standard, act-of-production doctrine, § 8.13(a)

Third parties

  Disclosures to third parties, § 8.5(h)

  Objections by, § 8.5(h)

  Production of documents, privilege against self-incrimination, § 8.12(e)

GRAND JURY—Cont'd
Transactional vs. use/derivative use immunity, §§ **8.11(b), 8.11(c)**
Use/derivative use vs. transactional immunity, §§ **8.11(b), 8.11(c)**
Usurpation of subpoena power by prosecution or police, misuse of subpoena authority, § **8.8(g)**
Waiver of privilege against self-incrimination, § **8.10(e)**
Witness, disclosure by, § **8.5(d)**
Work product protection, § **8.6(b)**

GUILTY PLEAS AND PLEA BARGAINS
General discussion, §§ **21.1-21.6**
Accurate and fair results, § **21.1(d)**
Acting on plea bargain, § **21.4(g)**
Administrative convenience, § **21.1(c)**
Arraignment, receipt of plea, § **21.4(a)**
Broken plea bargains. Kept, broken, rejected and nonexistent plea bargains, below
Challenge of guilty plea by defendant
General discussion, § **21.5**
Admissibility of withdrawn or overturned plea and related statements, § **21.5(f)**
Compliance or noncompliance with procedures for receipt of plea, §§ **21.5(c), 21.5(d)**
Defective charging instruments, §§ **19.2(e), 19.3(3e)**
Effect of withdrawn or overturned plea, § **21.5(e)**
Record of receipt procedures missing, § **21.5(c)**
Withdrawal of plea, §§ **21.5(a), 21.5(e)**
Competence of defendant, determination of, § **21.4(b)**
Conditional pleas, effect of guilty plea, § **21.6(b)**
Consequences, understanding of, § **21.4(d)**
Counsel, right to, § **21.3(a)**
Development of plea bargaining, § **21.1(b)**
Disparity, § **21.1(e)**
Effect of guilty plea
General discussion, § **21.6**
Conditional pleas, § **21.6(b)**
Double jeopardy, § **25.1(d)**
Rights waived or forfeited, § **21.6(a)**
Stipulated facts, trial on, § **21.6(c)**
Effective assistance by defense counsel, § **21.3(b)**
Evaluation by judge of contemplated concessions, § **21.3(e)**
Exclusionary rules, waiver or forfeiture of objection, § **10.2(d)**
Factual basis of plea, § **21.4(f)**
Federal sentencing guidelines, § **21.1(h)**
Forfeiture of rights, § **21.6(a)**
Forms of plea bargaining, § **21.1(a)**
Kept, broken, rejected and nonexistent plea bargains
General discussion, § **21.2**

INDEX

GUILTY PLEAS AND PLEA BARGAINS—Cont'd
  Kept, broken, rejected and nonexistent plea bargains—Cont'd
    Admission of statements made during plea bargaining, § 21.2(h)
    Broken bargains, §§ 21.2(d), 21.2(e)
    Judge, inducements by, § 21.2(c)
    Prosecutor, inducements by, § 21.2(b)
    Remedy for broken bargain, § 21.2(e)
    Statutory inducements to plead guilty, § 21.2(a)
    Unrealized expectations, § 21.2(g)
    Withdrawn offers, § 21.2(f)
  Nonexistent plea bargains. Kept, broken, rejected and nonexistent plea bargains, above
  Pleading alternatives, § 21.4(a)
  Possible consequences, understanding of, § 21.4(d)
  Prohibition of plea bargaining, § 21.1(g)
  Receipt of plea
    General discussion, § 21.4
    Acting on plea bargain, § 21.4(g)
    Arraignment, § 21.4(a)
    Charge, understanding of, § 21.4(c)
    Competence of defendant, determination of, § 21.4(b)
    Factual basis of plea, § 21.4(f)
    Pleading alternatives, § 21.4(a)
    Possible consequences, understanding of, § 21.4(d)
    Record of missing, § 21.5(c)
    Voluntariness of plea, determination of, § 21.4(b)
    Waived rights, understanding of, § 21.4(e)
  Rejected plea bargains. Kept, broken, rejected and nonexistent plea bargains, above
  Remedy for broken bargain, § 21.2(e)
  Responsibilities of attorney and judge
    General discussion, § 21.3
    Counsel, right to, § 21.3(a)
    Effective assistance by defense counsel, § 21.3(b)
    Evaluation by judge of contemplated concessions, § 21.3(e)
    Judicial involvement, §§ 21.3(d), 21.3(e)
    Tactics of prosecutor, § 21.3(c)
  Stipulated facts, trial on, § 21.6(c)
  System for plea negotiation
    General discussion, § 21.1
    Accurate and fair results, § 21.1(d)
    Administrative convenience, § 21.1(c)
    Development of plea bargaining, § 21.1(b)
    Disparity, § 21.1(e)
    Federal sentencing guidelines, § 21.1(h)
    Forms of plea bargaining, § 21.1(a)
    Prohibition of plea bargaining, § 21.1(g)
  Tactics of prosecutor, § 21.3(c)

INDEX

GUILTY PLEAS AND PLEA BARGAINS—Cont'd
Victim's challenge of plea, § 21.3(f)
Victim's consultation re negotiations, § 21.3(f)
Voluntariness of plea, determination of, § 21.4(b)
Waiver of rights, §§ 21.4(e), 21.6(a), 27.5(c)
Withdrawal of offer or plea, §§ 21.2(f), 21.5(a), 21.5(e)

HABEAS CORPUS
Appeal and review, § 27.4(f)
Post Conviction Review, this index
Prosecution, decision as to, § 13.5(f)

HARASSMENT
Grand jury, misuse of subpoena authority, § 8.8(h)

HARMLESS ERROR
General discussion, § 27.6
Automatic reversal vs. harmless error, § 27.6(d)
Constitutional errors, § 27.6(c)
Nonconstitutional errors, § 27.6(b)
Origins of harmless error review, § 27.6(a)
Pleading errors, §§ 19.2(e), 19.3(a)
Post conviction review, § 28.3(f)
Presence of defendant, § 24.2(b)
Reasonable doubt standard for constitutional errors, § 27.6(e)

HISTORY
General discussion, § 1.5
Colonial period, § 1.5(b)
Future of reform, § 1.5(h)
Liberal idealism, era of, § 1.5(g)
Nineteenth century, core of, § 1.5(d)
Post-revolutionary period, § 1.5(c)
Progressive era, § 1.5(e)
Twentieth century, second quarter of, § 1.5(f)

HOUSING
Search and seizure, § 3.9(b)

HUNG JURY
Deadlocked Jury, this index

HYBRID REPRESENTATION
Counsel, right to, § 11.5(g)

IDENTIFICATION PROCEDURES
General discussion, §§ 7.1-7.5
Appearance, privilege against self-incrimination, § 7.2(d)
Causes of misidentification, § 7.1(b)
Change in appearance, privilege against self-incrimination, § 7.2(d)
Confrontation, right to. Counsel and confrontation, rights to, below
Cooperation, privilege against self-incrimination, § 7.2(c)

IDENTIFICATION PROCEDURES—Cont'd
  Counsel and confrontation, rights to
    General discussion, § 7.3
    Consequences of violation, § 7.3(f)
    Nature of identification procedure, § 7.3(c)
    Procedures required, § 7.3(a)
    Repeal of right, § 7.3(g)
    Role of counsel, § 7.3(e)
    Substitution of counsel, § 7.3(d)
    Time of identification, § 7.3(b)
    Waiver of counsel, § 7.3(d)
  Due process: totality of circumstances
    General discussion, § 7.4
    In-court identifications, § 7.4(g)
    Lineups, § 7.4(d)
    One-man showups, § 7.4(f)
    Pictures, use of, § 7.4(e)
    Repeal of right, § 7.4(h)
    Risk of misidentification element, § 7.4(c)
    Unnecessarily suggestive element, § 7.4(b)
  Exclusionary Rules, this index
  Expert testimony, § 7.5(b)
  Grand jury, Fourth Amendment challenges to subpoenas, § 8.7(d)
  In-court identifications, due process: totality of circumstances, § 7.4(g)
  Instructions to jury, § 7.5(a)
  Lineups, due process: totality of circumstances, § 7.4(d)
  One-man showups, due process: totality of circumstances, § 7.4(f)
  Pictures, use of, § 7.4(e)
  Police procedures, improvement in, § 7.5(c)
  Risk of misidentification element, due process: totality of circumstances, § 7.4(c)
  Role of counsel, § 7.3(e)
  Self-incrimination, privilege against
    General discussion, § 7.2
    Application to identification procedures, § 7.2(b)
    Change in appearance, § 7.2(d)
    Cooperation, lack of, § 7.2(c)
    Schmerber rule, § 7.2(a)
  Substitution of counsel, § 7.3(d)
  Time of identification, rights to counsel and confrontation, § 7.3(b)
  Unnecessarily suggestive element, due process: totality of circumstances,
    § 7.4(b)
  Waiver of counsel, § 7.3(d)

IMMUNITY
  Defense witnesses, § 24.3(i)
  Grand Jury, this index

IMPARTIALITY OF JUDGE
  General discussion, § 22.4

INDEX

IMPARTIALITY OF JUDGE—Cont'd
 Cause, challenge for, § 22.4(b)
 Peremptory challenge, § 22.4(d)
 Recusal, § 22.4(c)
 Right to impartial judge, § 22.4(a)
 Substitution of judge, § 22.4(e)

IMPEACHMENT
 Exclusionary rules, permissible use of illegally obtained evidence, § 9.6(a)

IMPLIED WAIVER
 Forfeiture, this index
 Self-incrimination, privilege against, §§ 6.9(a), 6.9(d)

INCARCERATION
 Sentencing, § 26.1(c)

INCONSISTENT DEFENSES
 Encouragement by police and entrapment, § 5.3(c)

INCONSISTENT VERDICTS OR FINDINGS
 General discussion, § 24.10(b)

IN-COURT IDENTIFICATIONS
 Due process: totality of circumstances, § 7.4(g)

INDEPENDENT SOURCE
 Exclusionary rules, fruit of poisonous tree, § 9.3(d)

INDETERMINATE SENTENCE
 Parole, this index

INDICTMENTS
 General discussion, §§ 15.1-15.7
 Assumption of other roles by prosecutor, § 15.7(c)
 Bias of grand jury, § 15.4(g)
 Challenges to indictment
  General discussion, §§ 15.4-15.7
  Composition of grand jury, below
  Costello rule, evidence, §§ 15.5(a), 15.5(b)
  Evidence, § 15.5
  Federal standard, evidence, §§ 15.5(a), 15.5(b)
  Misconduct of grand jury, below
  State standards, evidence, § 15.5(c)
 Composition of grand jury
  General discussion, §§ 15.2(a), 15.4
  Bias of jury, § 15.4(g)
  Constitutional challenges to selection of foreperson, § 15.4(e)
  Equal protection claims, § 15.4(c)
  Fair cross section requirement, § 15.4(d)
  Foreperson, selection of, § 15.4(e)
  Objections, procedures and timing, § 15.4(b)

INDICTMENTS—Cont'd
  Composition of grand jury—Cont'd
    Postconviction review, § 15.4(i)
    Publicity, preindictment, § 15.4(h)
    Selection of grand jury, procedures for, § 15.4(a)
    Statutory violations, § 15.4(f)
  Constitutional challenges to selection of foreperson of grand jury, § 15.4(e)
  Counsel, grand jury's, §§ 15.2(e), 15.7(g)
  Decision to indict, § 15.2(g)
  Defendant, testimony of prospective, § 15.2(c)
  Effectiveness of grand jury screening
    General discussion, § 15.3
    Judicial responses, § 15.3(d)
    Ongoing debate, § 15.3(a)
    Statistics, § 15.3(b)
    Variations of screening, § 15.3(c)
  Equal protection claims, composition of grand jury, § 15.4(c)
  Evidence
    Challenges to indictment, § 15.5
    Control, § 15.2(b)
    Deception in presentation, § 15.7(e)
    Exculpatory evidence, failure to present, § 15.7(f)
    Misconduct exception to *Costello*, § 15.5(b)
    Quantum of evidence, § 15.2(f)
    Rules of evidence, § 15.2(d)
  Exculpatory evidence, failure to present, § 15.7(f)
  Fair cross section requirement, composition of grand jury, § 15.4(d)
  Fifth Amendment right to prosecution by indictment, §§ 15.1(a), 15.1(b)
  Filing, § 1.3(n)
  Foreperson of grand jury, selection of, § 15.4(e)
  Fourteenth Amendment due process right to prosecution by indictment, § 15.1(c)
  Legal advice, grand jury, §§ 15.2(c), 15.7(g)
  Misconduct of grand jury
    General discussion, §§ 15.6, 15.7
    Assumption of other roles by prosecutor, § 15.7(c)
    Establishment of misconduct, § 15.6(g)
    Evidence, deception in presentation of, § 15.7(e)
    Evidence, misconduct exception to *Costello*, § 15.5(b)
    Exculpatory evidence, failure to present, § 15.7(f)
    Federal standard, § 15.6(b)
    Jury misconduct, § 15.6(c)
    Legal advice, erroneous, § 15.7(g)
    Objections, range of, § 15.7(a)
    Postconviction review, § 15.6(f)
    Prejudice, requirement of, §§ 15.6(d), 15.6(e)
    Prejudicial comments and information, § 15.7(b)
    Presence of unauthorized persons, § 15.7(h)
    Prosecutorial misconduct, §§ 15.6(a), 15.7(g)

INDICTMENTS—Cont'd
  Misconduct of grand jury—Cont'd
    Unauthorized persons, presence of, **§ 15.7(h)**
    Williams limits, **§ 15.6(b)**
    Witnesses, violation of rights of, **§ 15.7(d)**
  Objections, **§§ 15.4(b), 15.7(a)**
  Pleading, reflecting grand jury review, **§ 19.2(f)**
  Postconviction review, **§§ 15.4(i), 15.6(f)**
  Prejudice, misconduct of grand jury, **§§ 15.6(d), 15.6(e)**
  Prejudicial comments and information, misconduct of grand jury, **§ 15.7(b)**
  Presence of unauthorized persons, misconduct of grand jury, **§ 15.7(h)**
  Publicity, composition of grand jury, **§ 15.4(h)**
  Quantum of evidence, **§ 15.2(f)**
  Resubmission to grand jury, **§ 15.2(h)**
  Right to prosecution by indictment
    General discussion, **§ 15.1**
    Fifth Amendment right, **§§ 15.1(a), 15.1(b)**
    Fourteenth Amendment due process, **§ 15.1(c)**
    Indictment jurisdictions, **§§ 15.1(d), 15.1(f)**
    Information jurisdictions, **§ 15.1(g)**
    Limited indictment jurisdictions, **§§ 15.1(e), 15.1(f)**
    Waiver, **§ 15.1(f)**
  Secrecy, **§ 15.2(i)**
  Selection of grand jury, procedures for, **§ 15.4(a)**
  Statistics, effectiveness of grand jury screening, **§ 15.3(b)**
  Structure of grand jury screening, **§ 15.2**
  Testimony of prospective defendant, **§ 15.2(c)**
  Transcription, **§ 15.2(j)**
  Unauthorized persons, presence of, **§ 15.7(h)**
  Waiver of right to prosecution by indictment, **§ 15.1(f)**
  Witnesses, violation of rights of, **§ 15.7(d)**

INDIGENT PERSONS
  Counsel, Right to, this index

INEVITABLE DISCOVERY
  Exclusionary rules, fruit of poisonous tree, **§ 9.3(e)**

INFORMANTS
  Arrest, search and seizure, probable cause, **§ 3.3(c)**

INJUNCTIONS
  Arrest, search and seizure, **§ 3.1(n)**
  Challenging decision to prosecute, **§ 13.5(e)**

INNOCENCE MOVEMENT
  Exoneration studies, **§ 1.5(e)**
  Reforms, **§§ 1.5(e), 1.6(h)**

INSANITY AND RELATED DEFENSES
  Discovery and disclosure, **§§ 20.4(e), 20.5(c)**

INDEX

INSPECTIONS
Arrest, Search and Seizure, this index

INSTRUCTIONS TO JURY
General discussion, § 24.8
Content of instructions, § 24.8(c)
Defining lesser included offense, § 24.8(e)
Entitlements to lesser included offense instructions, § 24.8(f)
Identification procedures, § 7.5(a)
Lesser included offenses, §§ 24.8(d)-24.8(f)
Multiple stages for instructions, § 24.8(a)
Objections to instructions, § 24.8(b)
Requests for instructions, § 24.8(b)
Silence of defendant, § 24.5(c)

INTERMEDIATE SANCTIONS
General discussion, § 26.1(e)

INTERNAL ADMINISTRATIVE STANDARDS
General discussion, § 1.6(j)

INTERPRETATION
Constitutional Law, this index

INTERPRETERS
For trial, § 24.2(g)

INTERROGATIONS AND CONFESSIONS
General discussion, §§ 6.1-6.10
Abuse by police, extent of, § 6.1(b)
Common law, voluntariness, § 6.2(a)
Counsel, right to
    General discussion, § 6.4
    Commencement of right, § 6.4(e)
    Critique of right to counsel approach, § 6.4(h)
    Escobedo case, § 6.4(c)
    Infringement of right, § 6.4(g)
    Massiah case, §§ 6.4(b), 6.4(i)
    Pre-*Massiah* developments, § 6.4(a)
    Repeal of *Massiah* rule, § 6.4(i)
    Waiver of counsel, § 6.4(f)
    Williams case, § 6.4(d)
Due process and complex of values, voluntariness, § 6.2(b)
Escobedo case, right to counsel, § 6.4(c)
Exclusionary Rules, this index
Joinder and severance, incrimination by confession of codefendant, § 17.2(b)
Massiah case, right to counsel, §§ 6.4(b), 6.4(i)
McNabb-Mallory rule, prompt appearance, § 6.3(a)
Miranda. Self-Incrimination, Privilege Against, this index
Need for confessions, § 6.1(a)

INDEX

INTERROGATIONS AND CONFESSIONS—Cont'd
Prompt appearance
  General discussion, § 6.3
  McNabb-Mallory rule, § 6.3(a)
  Reactions to rule, § 6.3(b)
  States, prompt appearance in, § 6.3(c)
Self-Incrimination, Privilege Against, this index
Totality of circumstance, voluntariness, § 6.2(c)
Voluntariness
  General discussion, § 6.2
  Common law, § 6.2(a)
  Critique of voluntariness test, § 6.2(d)
  Due process and complex of values, § 6.2(b)
  Totality of circumstance, factors in, § 6.2(c)
Waiver of counsel, § 6.4(f)
Williams case, right to counsel, § 6.4(d)

INTERSTATE AGREEMENT ON DETAINERS
General discussion, § 18.4(c)

INVITED RESPONSE
Arguments of counsel, § 24.7(f)

***JENCKS* ACT**
Evidence, access by defendant, § 24.3(c)

JOINDER AND SEVERANCE
General discussion, §§ 17.1-17.4
Appellate review of claim of prejudice, § 17.3(e)
Association, guilt by, § 17.2(e)
Authority of court, § 17.3(a)
Collateral estoppel, failure to join related offenses, § 17.4(a)
Confession of codefendant, incrimination by, § 17.2(b)
Conflicting defenses and strategies, joinder of defendants, § 17.2(d)
Confusion of evidence, joinder of defendants, § 17.2(f)
Cumulation of evidence, joinder of offenses, § 17.1(e)
Defendants
  General discussion, § 17.2
  Association, guilt by, § 17.2(e)
  Confession of codefendant, incrimination by, § 17.2(b)
  Conflicting defenses and strategies, § 17.2(d)
  Confusion of evidence, § 17.2(f)
  Exculpatory testimony by codefendant, § 17.2(c)
  Right, severance as of, § 17.2(g)
Double jeopardy, failure to join related offenses, § 17.4(b)
Exculpatory testimony by codefendant, § 17.2(c)
Failure to join related offenses
  General discussion, § 17.4
  Collateral estoppel, § 17.4(a)
  Double jeopardy, § 17.4(b)

INDEX

JOINDER AND SEVERANCE—Cont'd
Failure to join related offenses—Cont'd
Same transaction joinder, § 17.4(c)
Failure to prove basis of joinder, § 17.3(c)
Forfeiture, § 17.3(d)
Misjoinder, § 17.3(b)
Offenses
General discussion, § 17.1
Cumulation of evidence, § 17.1(e)
Failure to join related offenses, above
Other crimes, evidence of, § 17.1(d)
Prejudice from joinder, § 17.1(f)
Related offenses, § 17.1(a)
Right, severance as of, § 17.1(f)
Separate defenses, § 17.1(c)
Similar character, offenses of, § 17.1(b)
Other crimes, evidence of, § 17.1(d)
Prejudice, appellate review of claim of, § 17.3(e)
Procedure, § 17.3
Publicity, § 23.2(e)
Related offenses, § 17.1(a)
Same transaction joinder, failure to join related offenses, § 17.4(c)
Separate defenses, joinder of offenses, § 17.1(c)
Similar character, offenses of, § 17.1(b)
Venue, § 16.1(f)
Waiver, § 17.3(d)

JURISDICTION
General discussion, § 16.4
Arrest, search and seizure, § 3.1(j)
Concept of jurisdiction, § 16.4(a)
Double jeopardy, attachment of, § 25.1(d)
Evidence, § 16.4(d)
Federal jurisdiction, § 16.4(b)
Pleading, accusatory, § 19.2(e)
State jurisdiction, § 16.4(c)
Venue, distinguished, § 16.1(a)
Waiver, § 16.4(d)

JURY TRIAL
General discussion, §§ 22.1-22.3, 24.9
Access to information, voir dire, § 22.3(b)
Alternate jurors, voir dire, § 22.3(e)
Anonymous jury, § 22.3(b)
Cause, challenges for, § 22.3(c)
Challenge to array, § 22.2(f)
De novo trial, right to jury trial, § 22.1(f)
Deadlocked jury, § 24.9(d)
Decreasing rate of jury trials, §§ 1.5(c), 1.6(h)

INDEX

JURY TRIAL—Cont'd
Encouragement by police and entrapment, § 5.3(b)
Equal protection, selection of jurors, § 22.2(c)
Exclusionary rules, presence during hearing on suppression, § 10.5(b)
Fair cross section requirement, selection of jurors, § 22.2(d)
Grand Jury, this index
Instructions to Jury, this index
Items taken to jury room, § 24.9(c)
Misconduct of jury, §§ 24.9(f), 24.9(g)
Noncriminal trials, right to jury trial, § 22.1(c)
Note taking by jury, § 24.9(b)
Nullification by jury, § 22.1(g)
Peremptory challenges, § 22.3(d)
Petty offenses, right to jury trial, § 22.1(b)
Polling of jury, § 24.9(e)
Publicity, admonishment of jury, § 23.2(g)
Questions by jury, § 24.9(b)
Right to jury trial
    General discussion, § 22.1
    De novo trial, § 22.1(f)
    Noncriminal trials, § 22.1(c)
    Nullification by jury, § 22.1(g)
    Petty offenses, § 22.1(b)
    Sentencing, § 26.2(b), 26.4(i)
    Size of jury, § 22.1(d)
    States, applicability to, § 22.1(a)
    Unanimity, § 22.1(e)
    Waiver of jury trial, § 22.1(h)
Selection of jurors
    General discussion, § 22.2
    Challenge to array, § 22.2(f)
    Equal protection, § 22.2(c)
    Fair cross section requirement, § 22.2(d)
    Federal procedures, § 22.2(a)
    Publicity, § 23.2(f)
    State procedures, § 22.2(b)
    Vicinage, § 22.2(e)
    Voir dire, below
Sentencing, §§ 26.2(b), 26.4(i)
Sequestration of Jury, this index
Size of jury, § 22.1(d)
Testimony regarding misconduct of jury, limitations on, § 24.9(g)
Unanimity, § 22.1(e)
Vicinage, selection of jurors, § 22.2(e)
Voir dire
    General discussion, § 22.3
    Access to information, § 22.3(b)
    Alternate jurors, § 22.3(e)

JURY TRIAL—Cont'd
Voir dire—Cont'd
Cause, challenges for, § 22.3(c)
Nature, § 22.3(a)
Peremptory challenges, § 22.3(d)
Publicity, generally, § 23.2(f)
Waiver of jury trial, § 22.1(h)

JUVENILE CASES
Pretrial release, § 12.4(b)
Sentencing, use in, § 26.4(i)

LAW VS. PRACTICE
General discussion, § 1.9(a)

LESSER INCLUDED OFFENSES
Double jeopardy, §§ 25.1(d), 25.4(d)
Instructions to jury, §§ 24.8(d)-24.8(f)

LINES OF DIVISION
General discussion, § 1.8(a)

LINEUPS
Due process: totality of circumstances, § 7.4(d)

LITERALISM
Venue, crime-committed formula, § 16.2(c)

LOCAL ADMINISTRATIVE SETTING
General discussion, § 1.10
Administrative interactions, § 1.10(d)
Caseload pressures, § 1.10(c)
Fragmentation of enforcement agencies, § 1.4(c)
Local community, influence of, § 1.9(g)
Localism, § 1.4(b)
Organizational policy variations, § 1.10(b)
Significance, § 1.10(a)

LOCAL ORDINANCES
General discussion, § 1.7(k)

LOCAL RULES OF COURT
General discussion, § 1.6(g)

MAGISTRATES AND MAGISTRATE COURTS
Court variations, § 1.4(g)
Courts not of record, § 1.4(g)
Federal magistrates, § 1.4(g)
Functions of, § 1.4(g)
Procedural subsets, § 1.8(g)

MANDAMUS
Appeal and review, § 27.4(b)

INDEX

MANDAMUS—Cont'd
Challenges to and checks upon decision not to prosecute, § 13.3(a)

MANIFEST NECESSITY
Double jeopardy, reprosecution following mistrial, §§ 25.2(c)-25.2(e)

MATERIAL WITNESSES
Pretrial release, § 12.4(g)

MEDIA COVERAGE
Publicity, this index

MERE EVIDENCE
Arrest, search and seizure, protected areas and interests, § 3.2(i)

MINIMIZATION
Wiretapping and electronic surveillance, execution of order, § 4.6(h)

MINIMUM SENTENCES
Discretion of court, § 26.3(c)

MIRANDA RULE
Self-Incrimination, Privilege Against, this index

MIRRORING PRESUMPTION
State constitutional law, §§ 2.12(b)-2.12(d)

MISCARRIAGE OF JUSTICE
Post conviction review, § 28.4(e)

MISCONDUCT OF GRAND JURY
Indictments, this index

MISDEMEANORS
Indigent persons, right to counsel, § 11.2(a)
Procedural subsets, § 1.8(c)

MISJOINDER
General discussion, § 17.3(b)

MISTRIALS
Double Jeopardy, this index

MOOTNESS
Appeal and review, § 27.5(a)

MOTOR VEHICLES
Arrest, Search and Seizure, this index
Exclusionary rules, standing, § 9.1(d)

MULTIPLICITY
Pleading, accusatory, § 19.3(c)

MULTI-THEORY VERDICTS
General discussion, § 24.10(c)

INDEX

MULTI-VENUE OFFENSES
General discussion, § 16.1(d)

NATIONAL SECURITY
FISA orders, § 8.1(c)
Grand jury disclosure, § 8.5(e)
Wiretapping and electronic surveillance, § 4.9

NETWORK SURVEILLANCE
Wiretapping and Network Surveillance, this index

NEUTRAL AND DETACHED MAGISTRATE REQUIREMENT
Warrants for arrest or search and seizure, § 3.4(b)

NEW CRIME
Exclusionary Rules, this index

NEW FEDERALISM MOVEMENT
State constitutional law, § 2.12(a)

NEW TRIAL
General discussion, § 24.11(b)
Delay in deciding motion for, § 18.5(c)
Evidence, § 24.6(d)

NEWLY DISCOVERED EVIDENCE
General discussion, § 24.11(d)

NOLLE PROSEQUI
Prosecution, decision as to, § 13.3(c)

NOLO CONTENDERE
Exclusionary rules, waiver or forfeiture of objection, § 10.2(d)

NOTE TAKING
Jury trial, § 24.9(b)

NOTICE
Arrest, search and seizure, §§ 3.4(h), 3.6(b)
Pleading, accusatory, § 19.2(c)
Prosecution, decision as to, § 13.5(c)
Self-representation, § 11.5(b)
Sentencing, due process, § 26.4(d)
Wiretapping and electronic surveillance, § 4.6(j), 4.8(d)

NULLIFICATION BY JURY
General discussion, § 22.1(g)

OATH OR AFFIRMATION
Warrants for arrest or search and seizure, § 3.4(c)

OBJECTIONS
Arguments of counsel, § 24.7(g)
Indictments, §§ 15.4(b), 15.7(a)
Instructions to jury, § 24.8(b)

INDEX

OBJECTIONS—Cont'd
Pleading, accusatory, § 19.3(e)
Presentence report, § 26.5(c)

OBJECTIVES OF PROCESS
General discussion, § 1.5
Accusatorial burdens, § 1.5(d)
Adversary adjudication, § 1.5(c)
Burdens of accusation and litigation, minimization of, § 1.5(f)
Dignity of individual, respect for, § 1.5(h)
Enforcement of substantive law, implementation of, § 1.5(a)
Equality in application of process, § 1.5(j)
Erroneous convictions, minimization of, § 1.5(e)
Fairness, appearance of, § 1.5(i)
Lay participation, provision of, § 1.5(g)
Truth, discovery of, § 1.5(b)
Victims, concerns of, § 1.5(k)

ONE-MAN SHOWUPS
Due process: totality of circumstances, § 7.4(f)

OPEN FIELDS
Search and seizure, § 3.2(d)

OPEN THE DOOR
Exclusionary rules, § 9.6(b)

OPENING STATEMENTS
General discussion, § 24.7(a)

OPPRESSIVENESS
Grand jury, misuse of subpoena authority, § 8.8(c)

OPT-IN REQUIREMENTS
Post conviction review, capital cases under Chapter 154 of 1996 Act, § 28.8(b)

ORDINANCES
General discussion, § 1.6(k)
Procedural subsets, § 1.7(d)

OVERBREADTH
Grand jury, Fourth Amendment challenges, § 8.7(b)

OVERLAPPING STATUTES
Selection of charge, § 13.7(a)

OVERVIEW
General discussion, §§ 1.1-1.9

PAROLE
Indeterminate sentencing, generally, § 26.1(c)
Release, § 26.2(c)
Revocation, §§ 26.2(c), 26.10
Revocation, pretrial release, § 12.4(f)

INDEX

PAROLE—Cont'd
Search and seizure of parolee, § 3.9(j)

PARTIAL VERDICTS
General discussion, § 24.10(d)

PATTERNS
State laws, § 1.2(h)

PEN REGISTER AND TRAP AND TRACE DEVISES STATUTE
Application for order, § 4.7(c)
Dialing, routing, addressing and signaling information, § 4.7(c)
Exceptions, § 4.7(d)
Remedies, § 4.7(e)

PER SE RULES
Constitutional law, § 2.9(d)

PEREMPTORY CHALLENGES
Impartiality of judge, § 22.4(d)
Jury trial, § 22.3(d)

PERJURY
Exclusionary rules, use of illegally obtained evidence in prosecution, § 9.6(c)
Government use of, §§ 24.3(b), 24.3(d)

PERMISSION
Consent or Approval, this index

PERPETUATION OF TESTIMONY
Preliminary hearings, § 14.1(d)

PETTY OFFENSES
Jury trial, right to, § 22.1(b)

PLAIN ERROR
Appeal and review, § 27.5(d)

PLAIN VIEW, SMELL, HEARING AND TOUCH
Search and seizure, §§ 3.2(b), 3.7(f)

PLEA BARGAINS
Guilty Pleas and Plea Bargains, this index

PLEADING, ACCUSATORY
Amendments
Appellate review, § 19.5(d)
Bain rule, § 19.5(d)
Form/substance distinction, § 19.5(c)
Offense charged, § 19.5(b)
Prejudice, § 19.5(b)
Varied uses, § 19.5(a)
Bill of particulars
Discovery, relation to, § 19.4

PLEADING, ACCUSATORY—Cont'd
Bill of particulars—Cont'd
Function of, § **19.4(a)**
Short-form pleadings, and, § **19.4(b)**
Standard for issuance, § **19.4(b)**
Common law rules, § **19.1(a)**
Duplicity, § **19.3(c)**
Essential element requirement
Appellate review, §§ **19.2(e), 19.3(a)**
Content, § **19.3(a)**
Grounding, § **19.2(c)-(f)**
Guilty pleas, §§ **19.2(e), 19.3(e)**
Late objections, §§ **19.2(e), 19.3(e)**
Formal defects, § **19.3(d)**
Forms, § **19.1(d)**
Functions
Analysis, § **19.2(a)**
Double jeopardy protection, § **19.2(b)**
Grand jury function, § **19.2(f)**
Judicial review function, § **19.2(d)**
Jurisdictional grounding, § **19.2(e)**
Notice, § **19.2(c)**
Liberalization, trend, §§ **19.1(b)-(e), 19.2(e), 19.3(a)**
Multiplicity, § **19.3(c)**
Notice, provided by, §§ **19.2(c), 19.3(b)**
Objections to
Timing, §§ **19.1(d), 19.3(e)**
Waiver, §§ **19.1(d), 19.2(e), 19.3(e)**
Short-form, § **19.1(a)**
Specificity requirement
Appellate review, §§ **19.2(e), 19.3(e)**
Content, § **19.3(b)**
Statutory reform, § **19.1(b),(c), (d)**
Statutory standards, § **19.1(d)**
Time and place, § **19.3(b)**
Variance
Appellate review, § **19.4(c)**
Berger standard, § **19.4(b)**
Challenges to, § **19.4(a)**
Constructive amendments, § **19.4(c)**

POLICE AGENCIES
Federal, §§ **1.4(d), 1.7(j)**
Fragmentation, § **1.4(a)**
Policies of, § **1.10(b)**
Prosecution, relation to, § **1.4(d)**
Role variations, § **1.4(d)**
State, § **1.4(d)**

POLICE AGENCIES—Cont'd
Variations generally, § 1.4(d)

POLICE REPORTS
Discovery and disclosure, § 20.3(k)

POLLING OF JURY
General discussion, § 24.9(e)

POOR PERSONS
Counsel, Right to, this index

POST CONVICTION REVIEW
General discussion, §§ 28.1-28.12
Adequate state ground standard, claims foreclosed by procedural defaults in state court, § 28.4(b)
Appellate review of district court decisions, § 28.10
Bare innocence claims, § 28.3(e)
Capital cases under Chapter 154 of 1996 Act, § 28.8
Cause and prejudice standard, claims foreclosed by procedural defaults in state court, § 28.4(d)
Certification by court of appeals, successive petitions, § 28.5(e)
Cognizable claims
General discussion, § 28.3
Bare innocence claims, § 28.3(e)
Custody requirement, § 28.3(a)
Fourth Amendment claims, § 28.3(c)
Full and fair litigation, opportunity for, § 28.3(d)
Harmless error, § 28.3(f)
Common law, §§ 28.1(b), 28.1(c)
Constitutional law
General discussion, § 28.6
Changing role of federal habeas courts, § 28.6(a)
Counsel, assistance of, § 28.12(a)
Finality of state conviction, § 28.6(c)
New rule concept, § 28.6(d)
Retroactive application of new rules of procedure, § 28.6(b)
Review of state court rulings under 2254(d), § 28.6(f)
Statute of limitations, § 28.5(b)
Teague case, §§ 28.6(b), 28.6(e)
Coram nobis, § 28.1(c)
Counsel, assistance of, § 28.12
Custody requirement, § 28.3(a)
Delayed petitions. Premature, delayed or successive petitions, below
Discovery, factfinding and evidentiary hearings, § 28.7(d)
District court decisions, appellate review of, § 28.10
Encouragement of state collateral remedies by Supreme Court, § 28.11(a)
Equitable tolling, § 28.5(b)
Evidentiary hearings. Factfinding and evidentiary hearings, below
Exhaustion of state remedies, § 28.5(a)

POST CONVICTION REVIEW—Cont'd
  Factfinding and evidentiary hearings
    General discussion, § 28.7
    Discovery, § 28.7(d)
    Evidentiary hearings, obtaining, § 28.7(c)
    Mixed determinations of law and fact vs. factfinding, § 28.7(b)
    Presumption of correctness of state court determinations of fact, § 28.7(a)
  Federal prisoners
    General discussion, § 28.9
    Nonconstitutional claims under § 2255, § 28.9(c)
    Procedural requirements under § 2255, § 28.9(b)
    Range of remedies, § 28.9(a)
  Finality of state conviction, constitutional law, § 28.6(c)
  Fourth Amendment claims, § 28.3(c)
  Full and fair litigation, opportunity for, § 28.3(d)
  Harmless error, § 28.3(f)
  Indictments, §§ 15.4(i), 15.6(f)
  Miscarriage of justice exception, claims foreclosed by procedural defaults in state court, § 28.4(e)
  Nature of collateral remedies, § 28.1(a)
  New claims, § 28.5(d)
  New rule concept, constitutional law, § 28.6(d)
  Opt-in requirements, capital cases under Chapter 154 of 1996 Act, § 28.8(b)
  Premature, delayed or successive petitions
    General discussion, § 28.5
    Certification by court of appeals, successive petitions, § 28.5(e)
    Exhaustion of state remedies, § 28.5(a)
    New claims, § 28.5(d)
    Previously advanced claims, § 28.5(c)
    Successive petitions, §§ 28.5(c)-28.5(e)
    Time limits for filing petitions, § 28.5(b)
  Presumption of correctness of state court determinations of fact, factfinding and evidentiary hearings, § 28.7(a)
  Previously advanced claims, § 28.5(c)
  Procedural defaults in state court, claims foreclosed by
    General discussion, § 28.4
    Adequate state ground standard, § 28.4(b)
    Cause and prejudice standard, § 28.4(d)
    Excusing default, §§ 28.4(c)-28.4(e)
    Miscarriage of justice exception, § 28.4(e)
    Policy debate, § 28.4(a)
    Waiver by state of procedural default defense, § 28.4(c)
  Retroactive application of new rules of procedure, constitutional law, § 28.6(b)
  State collateral remedies, § 28.11
  Statutory structure and habeas corpus
    General discussion, § 28.2
    Balancing within statutory framework, § 28.2(c)
    Constitutional right or legislative grace, § 28.2(a)

INDEX

POST CONVICTION REVIEW—Cont'd
Statutory structure and habeas corpus—Cont'd
From 1867 Act to 1966 Act, **§ 28.2(b)**
Models of habeas review, **§ 28.2(d)**
Successive petitions. Premature, delayed or successive petitions, above
Time limits for filing petitions, **§ 28.5(b)**
Waiver by state of procedural default defense, **§ 28.4(c)**

POST-VERDICT MOTIONS
General discussion, **§ 24.11**
Acquittal, judgment of, **§ 24.11(a)**
Arrest of judgment, **§ 24.11(c)**
New Trial, this index
Newly discovered evidence, **§ 24.11(d)**

POVERTY
Pretrial release, constitutional law, **§ 12.2(b)**

PREJUDICE
Amendments of pleading, **§ 19.5(b)**
Counsel, Right to, this index
Indictments, **§§ 15.4(g), 15.6(d), 15.6(e)**
Joinder and severance, appeal and review of claim, **§ 17.3(e)**
Presence of defendant, **§ 24.2(e)**
Publicity, this index
Speedy trial and other prompt disposition, balancing test, **§ 18.2(e)**

PREJUDICIAL COMMENTS AND INFORMATION
Indictments, misconduct of grand jury, **§ 15.7(b)**

PRELIMINARY HEARINGS
General discussion, **§§ 14.1-14.4**
Bindover determination
General discussion, **§ 14.3**
Bindover, consequences of, **§ 14.3(d)**
Credibility, assessment of, **§ 14.3(b)**
Dismissal, consequences of, **§ 14.3(c)**
Standard applicable, **§ 14.3(a)**
Challenges to procedural rulings, **§ 14.4(e)**
Constitutional law, right to preliminary hearing, **§ 14.2(a)**
Counsel, right to, **§ 14.4(a)**
Credibility, bindover determination, **§ 14.3(b)**
Cross-examination, right to, **§ 14.4(c)**
Demand, **§ 14.2(e)**
Discovery, **§ 14.1(b)**
Dismissal, bindover determination, **§ 14.3(c)**
Evidence, rules of, **§ 14.4(b)**
Functions, **§ 14.1**
Future impeachment, **§ 14.1(c)**
Perpetuation of testimony, **§ 14.1(d)**

INDEX

PRELIMINARY HEARINGS—Cont'd
Procedures, § 14.4
Remedies, right to preliminary hearing, § 14.2(g)
Right to preliminary hearing
General discussion, § 14.2
Demand, § 14.2(e)
Federal constitution, § 14.2(a)
Federal practice, § 14.2(b)
Indictment states, § 14.2(c)
Information states, § 14.2(d)
Remedies, § 14.2(g)
Time of hearing, § 14.2(f)
Waiver, § 14.2(e)
Screening, § 14.1(a)
Testimony, use at trial, § 14.1(c), (d)
Time of hearing, § 14.2(f)
Waiver of right to preliminary hearing, § 14.2(e)
Witnesses, right to present, § 14.4(d)

PREMATURE PETITIONS
Post Conviction Review, this index

PRESENCE OF DEFENDANT
General discussion, § 24.2
Absence of defendant, voluntary, § 24.2(d)
Conduct of defendant, forfeiture by, § 24.2(c)
Disorderly conduct by defendant, § 24.2(c)
Harmless error, § 24.2(b)
Origins and scope of right, § 24.2(a)
Prejudicial circumstances of presence, § 24.2(e)
Waiver, § 24.2(b)

PRESENTENCE REPORT
General discussion, §§ 26.5(b), 26.5(c)

PRESUMPTIONS AND BURDEN OF PROOF
Encouragement by police and entrapment, § 5.3(d)
Exclusionary Rules, this index
Mirroring presumption, state constitutional law, §§ 2.12(b)-2.12(d)
Post conviction review, factfinding and evidentiary hearings, § 28.7(a)
Sentencing, §§ 26.3(d), 26.4(h), 26.8

PRETRIAL RELEASE
General discussion, §§ 12.1-12.5
Alternatives to arrest, § 12.5
Amount of money bail, constitutional law, § 12.2(a)
Capital cases, § 12.4(a)
Citation in lieu of arrest without warrant, § 12.5(b)
Constitutional law
General discussion, §§ 12.2, 12.3

INDEX

PRETRIAL RELEASE—Cont'd
  Constitutional law—Cont'd
    Amount of money bail, **§ 12.2(a)**
    Mandatory pretrial detention, below
    Nature of pretrial custody, **§ 12.2(d)**
    Opportunity to prepare defense, **§ 12.2(c)**
    Poverty and pretrial release, **§ 12.2(b)**
  Conviction, release after, **§ 12.4(d)**
  Counsel at bail hearing, **§ 12.1(c)**
  Dangerousness, individual finding of, **§ 12.3(f)**
  Eighth Amendment ambiguity, mandatory pretrial detention, **§ 12.3(c)**
  Evidence at bail hearing, **§ 12.1(d)**
  Federal Bail Reform Act, **§ 12.1(a)**
  Interlocutory appeal, release during, **§ 12.4(e)**
  Juvenile cases, **§ 12.4(b)**
  Mandatory pretrial detention
    General discussion, **§ 12.3**
    Dangerousness, individual finding of, **§ 12.3(f)**
    Eighth Amendment ambiguity, **§ 12.3(c)**
    Federal system, **§ 12.3(a)**
    Misconduct during release, **§ 12.3(g)**
    Serious offenses, **§ 12.3(e)**
    State constitutions, **§ 12.3(b)**
  Material witnesses, **§ 12.4(g)**
  Misconduct during release, mandatory pretrial detention, **§ 12.3(g)**
  Opportunity to prepare defense, constitutional law, **§ 12.2(c)**
  Parole, revocation of, **§ 12.4(f)**
  Poverty and pretrial release, constitutional law, **§ 12.2(b)**
  Probation, revocation of, **§ 12.4(f)**
  Serious offenses, mandatory pretrial detention, **§ 12.3(e)**
  State practice, generally, **§ 12.1(b)**
  Statements by defendant, **§ 12.1(e)**
  Summons in lieu of arrest warrant, **§ 12.5(a)**
  Trial, pretrial release during, **§ 12.4(c)**
  Victim's right to be heard, **§ 12.1(f)**

PRISONERS
  Post Conviction Review, this index
  Search and seizure, **§ 3.9(i)**

PRIVATE PROSECUTIONS
  Challenges to and checks upon decision not to prosecute, **§ 13.3(b)**

PRIVILEGES AND OTHER PROTECTIONS
  Evidence, **§ 24.4(c)**
  Grand jury, **§ 8.6(b)**

PROBABLE CAUSE
  Arrest, Search and Seizure, this index

INDEX

PROBATION
Sentencing, this index

PROCEDURAL DEFAULT
Post Conviction Review, this index

PROCEDURAL SUBSETS
General discussion, § 1.8

PROHIBITION
Appeal and review, § 27.4(b)

PROMPT APPEARANCE
Interrogations and Confessions, this index

PROPHYLACTIC RULES
Constitutional law, § 2.9(h)

PROSECUTION AGENCIES
Attorney general, §§ 1.4(b), 1.4(e)
Local prosecutors, §§ 1.4(b), 1.4(e)
Municipal attorneys, § 1.4(e)
Police, relation to, § 1.4(c)
Variations, § 1.4(e)

PROSECUTION, DECISION AS TO
General discussion, §§ 13.1-13.7
Arbitrary classification, equal protection, § 13.4(c)
Attorney general, challenges to and checks upon decision not to prosecute,
     § 13.3(e)
Challenges to and checks upon decision not to prosecute
     General discussion, § 13.3
     Attorney general, § 13.3(e)
     Grand jury, § 13.3(d)
     Mandamus, § 13.3(a)
     Nolle prosequi, judicial approval of, § 13.3(c)
     Private prosecutions, § 13.3(b)
     Qui tam actions, § 13.3(b)
     Removal, § 13.3(f)
     Special prosecutor, § 13.3(f)
Challenging decision to prosecute
     General discussion, §§ 13.4, 13.5
     Arbitrary classification, equal protection, § 13.4(c)
     Civil action against prosecutor, § 13.5(g)
     Declaratory judgments in federal court, § 13.5(e)
     Desuetude, § 13.5(c)
     Discriminatory prosecution, § 13.4(a)
     Equal protection, § 13.4
     Federal relief from state prosecution, §§ 13.5(d)-13.5(f)
     Habeas corpus, federal court, § 13.5(f)
     Injunctions in federal court, § 13.5(e)

PROSECUTION, DECISION AS TO—Cont'd
  Challenging decision to prosecute—Cont'd
    Intentional or purposeful, equal protection, § **13.4(d)**
    Nonprosecution of others, equal protection, § **13.4(e)**
    Notice, lack of fair, § **13.5(c)**
    Promise, reneging on, § **13.5(b)**
    Proof, problems of, § **13.4(b)**
    Recoupment of litigation expenses, § **13.5(h)**
    Removal to federal court, § **13.5(d)**
    Vindictive prosecution, § **13.5(a)**
  Charge, selection of
    General discussion, §§ **13.1(e), 13.7**
    Discrimination, § **13.7(b)**
    Duplicative and overlapping statutes, § **13.7(a)**
    Reneging on promise, § **13.7(d)**
    Vindictiveness, § **13.7(c)**
  Civil action against prosecutor, § **13.5(g)**
  Declaratory judgments in federal court, challenging decision to prosecute,
    § **13.5(e)**
  Desuetude, challenging decision to prosecute, § **13.5(c)**
  Discretionary enforcement
    Checking discretion of prosecutor, § **13.2(g)**
    Confining discretion of prosecutor, § **13.2(e)**
    Judge and jury, discretion of, § **13.2(c)**
    Mandating discretion of prosecutor, § **13.2(h)**
    Police, discretion of, § **13.2(b)**
    Problem of discretion, § **13.2(d)**
    Prosecutor, discretion of, §§ **13.2(a), 13.2(e)-13.2(h)**
    Structuring discretion of prosecutor, § **13.2(f)**
  Discriminatory prosecution, §§ **13.4(a), 13.7(b)**
  Diversion
    General discussion, §§ **13.1(d), 13.6**
    Decision not to divert, § **13.6(c)**
    Decision to terminate by prosecute, § **13.6(d)**
    Process of diversion, § **13.6(a)**
    Statutory standards, § **13.6(b)**
  Duplicative statutes, selection of charge, § **13.7(a)**
  Equal protection, challenging decision to prosecute, § **13.4**
  Evidence, §§ **13.1(b), 13.4(b)**
  Grand jury, challenges to and checks upon decision not to prosecute, § **13.3(d)**
  Habeas corpus, federal court, § **13.5(f)**
  Injunctions in federal court, challenging decision to prosecute, § **13.5(e)**
  Intentional or purposeful, equal protection, § **13.4(d)**
  Judge and jury, discretion of, § **13.2(c)**
  Mandamus, challenges to and checks upon decision not to prosecute, § **13.3(a)**
  Mandating discretion of prosecutor, § **13.2(h)**
  Nature of decision, § **13.1**
  Nolle prosequi, judicial approval of, § **13.3(c)**

PROSECUTION, DECISION AS TO—Cont'd
Nonprosecution of others, equal protection, § 13.4(e)
Notice, lack of fair, § 13.5(c)
Overlapping statutes, selection of charge, § 13.7(a)
Police, discretion of, § 13.2(b)
Private prosecutions, challenges to and checks upon decision not to prosecute, § 13.3(b)
Promise, reneging on, § 13.5(b)
Prosecutor, discretion of, §§ 13.2(a), 13.2(e)-13.2(h)
Qui tam actions, challenges to and checks upon decision not to prosecute, § 13.3(b)
Recoupment of litigation expenses, § 13.5(h)
Removal to federal court, § 13.5(d)
Screening out cases, § 13.1(c)
Special prosecutor, challenges to and checks upon decision not to prosecute, § 13.3(f)
Victim consultation
Re charge, § 13.1(a)
Re plea negotiations, § 21.3(f)
Vindictive prosecution, §§ 13.5(a), 13.7(c)

PROTECTED AREAS AND INTERESTS
Arrest, Search and Seizure, this index

PROTECTIVE ORDERS
Discovery by defense, § 20.3(l)

PSYCHOLOGICAL PRESSURE
Grand jury, § 8.3(d)

PUBLIC DEFENDERS
Agency variations, § 1.4(f)
Counsel, right to, this index
Federal defenders, § 1.4(f)

PUBLIC EMPLOYEES
Search and seizure, § 3.9(l)

PUBLIC TRIAL
General discussion, § 24.1

PUBLICITY
General discussion, §§ 23.1-23.3
Access to proceedings, right to, § 23.1(d)
Admonishment of jury, § 23.2(g)
Broadcast coverage, § 23.3(b)
Closed proceedings, §§ 23.1(d), 23.1(e)
Continuance, § 23.2(d)
Excusal of jurors, § 23.2(h)
First Amendment, closed proceedings, §§ 23.1(d), 23.1(e)
Indictments, composition of grand jury, § 15.4(h)
Newsmen in courtroom, § 23.3(a)

INDEX

PUBLICITY—Cont'd
Photographic coverage of trial, § 23.3(b)
Prevention, § 23.1
Restriction of media, § 23.1(c)
Restriction of public statements, § 23.1(b)
Sealing of documents, § 23.1(e)
Selection of jury, § 23.2(f)
Sequestration of jury, § 23.2(g)
Severance, § 23.2(e)
Trial, conduct of, § 23.3
Venire, change of, § 23.2(c)
Venue, change of, §§ 22.2(b), 23.2(a)
Video coverage of trial, § 23.3(b)

QUI TAM ACTIONS
Challenges to and checks upon decision not to prosecute, § 13.3(b)

REASONABLE DOUBT
Harmless error, constitutional errors, § 27.6(e)

REBUTTAL EVIDENCE
Sentencing, §§ 26.4(g), 26.8(b)

RECEIPT OF PLEA
Guilty Pleas and Plea Bargains, this index

RECIDIVISTS
Sentencing, § 26.6(b)

RECORDS AND RECORDING
Transcripts, this index
Warrants for searches, § 3.4(c)
Wiretapping and electronic surveillance, § 4.6(c)

RECOUPMENT
Indigent persons, right to counsel, § 11.2(h)
Prosecution, decision as to, § 13.5(h)

RECOUPMENT OF EXPENSES
Hyde Amendment, § 13.5(h)

RECUSAL
Impartiality of judge, § 22.4(c)

REGULATORY SEARCHES
Arrest, Search and Seizure, this index

RELATED OFFENSES
Joinder and severance, § 17.1(a)

REMEDIES
Wiretapping and Network Surveillance, this index

INDEX

REMOVAL TO FEDERAL COURT
Prosecution, decision as to, § 13.5(d)

REPORTS
Grand jury, § 8.3(h)

REQUIRED RECORDS EXCEPTION
Grand jury, production of documents, § 8.12(c)

RESENTENCING
Sentencing, this index

RESTITUTION
General discussion, § 26.6(c)

RETROACTIVITY
Constitutional Law, this index
Post conviction review, § 28.6(b)-(e)

REVIEW
Appeal and Review, this index

REVOCATION
Good time, § 26.2(c)
Probation, § 26.10
Parole, § 26.10

ROADBLOCKS
Arrest, search and seizure, § 3.8(f)

RULES OF COURT
General discussion, §§ 1.7(f), 1.7(g)

SAME TRANSACTION JOINDER
Joinder of related offenses, failure as to, § 17.4(c)
Venue, § 16.1(f)

SANCTIONS
Discovery and Disclosure, this index

SCIENTIFIC REPORTS
Discovery and disclosure, §§ 20.3(f), 20.5(h)

SCOPE OF REVIEW
Appeal and Review, this index

SEALING OF DOCUMENTS
Publicity, § 23.1(e)
Wiretapping and electronic surveillance, execution of order, § 4.6(k)

SEARCH AND SEIZURE
Arrest, Search and Seizure, this index

SECRECY
Grand Jury, this index
Indictments, § 15.2(i)

INDEX

SECRET AGENTS
Wiretapping and electronic surveillance, § 4.6(*l*)

SELECTION OF JURORS
Jury Trial, this index

SELECTIVE INCORPORATION
Constitutional Law, this index

SELF-HELP
Exclusionary rule and other remedies, § 3.1(*o*)

SELF-INCRIMINATION, PRIVILEGE AGAINST
General discussion, §§ 2.10, 6.5-6.10
Act of production. Grand Jury, this index
Adverse consequences, §§ 2.10(b), 8.10(f)
Ambiguous assertion of rights as waiver, § 6.9(g)
Competence of defendant, waiver of rights, § 6.9(b)
Compulsion element, §§ 2.10(b), 6.2, 6.5
Criminal case element, § 2.10(b)
Cruel trilemma, § 2.10(b), (d)
Critique of *Miranda* approach, § 6.5(d)
Custodial interrogation
  General discussion, § 6.6
  Custody vs. focus, § 6.6(a)
  Presence at other than police station, § 6.6(d)
  Presence at police station, § 6.6(d)
  Purpose of custody, § 6.6(b)
  Subjective vs. objective approach, § 6.6(c)
Dignity rationale, § 2.10(d)
Discovery by prosecution, constitutional limits on, §§ 20.4(b)-20.4(e)
Documentary subpoena. Grand Jury, this index
Entity exception, §§ 8.12(b), 8.13(d)
Equivocal assertion of rights as waiver, § 6.9(g)
Evidence, warnings, § 6.8(c)
Experience under *Miranda*, § 6.5(c)
Follow-up questioning, interrogation, § 6.7(d)
Foreign police, questioning by, § 6.10(d)
Foreign prosecution, § 8.10(b)
Frequency of warnings, § 6.8(b)
Functional equivalent test, interrogation, § 6.7(a)
Grand Jury, this index
History of, § 2.10(c)
Identification Procedures, this index
Immunity. Grand Jury, this index
Implied waiver of rights, §§ 6.9(a), 6.9(d)
Incrimination in another jurisdiction, § 8.10(b)
Interrogation
  General discussion, § 6.7
  Functional equivalent test, § 6.7(a)

INDEX

SELF-INCRIMINATION, PRIVILEGE AGAINST—Cont'd
  Interrogation—Cont'd
    Other words or actions, § 6.7(c)
    Questioning, § 6.7(b)
    Volunteered statements and follow-up questioning, § 6.7(d)
  Limited assertion of rights, § 6.9(g)
  Limited waiver of rights, § 6.9(e)
  Minor offense, questioning about, § 6.10(a)
  Miranda rule, §§ 6.5-6.10
  Nature of offense, § 6.10(a)
  Non-police official, questioning by, § 6.10(c)
  Overview, § 2.10(b)
  Person conducting interrogation, §§ 6.10(b)-6.10(d)
  Police station, privilege in, § 6.5(a)
  Policy analysis, § 2.10(d)
  Potential incrimination requirement, §§ 2.10(b), 8.10(a), (b), 8.13(b)
  Presence at other than police station, custodial interrogation, § 6.6(d)
  Presence at police station, custodial interrogation, § 6.6(d)
  Privacy and, § 2.10(d)
  Private citizen, questioning by, § 6.10(b)
  Proceedings at which confession offered, § 6.10(e)
  Prohibited uses, §§ 2.10(b), 8.11(b), (c), 9.6(a)
  Protected persons, §§ 2.10(b), 8.10(c)
  Qualified waiver of rights, § 6.9(e)
  Range of issues, § 2.10(a)
  Repeal of *Miranda*, § 6.5(e)
  Sentencing, § 26.4(c)
  Separate sovereigns, § 8.10(b)
  Subjective vs. objective approach, custodial interrogation, § 6.6(c)
  Systemic rationales, § 2.10(d)
  Testimonial requirement, §§ 2.10(b), 7.2(a), 8.12(b)
  Time for warnings, § 6.8(b)
  Unconstitutional burdens, § 2.10(b)
  Untimely assertion of rights as waiver, § 6.9(g)
  Volunteered statements, interrogation, § 6.7(d)
  Waiver of rights
    General discussion, § 6.9
    Ambiguous assertion of rights, § 6.9(g)
    Assertion of rights, waiver after, § 6.9(f)
    Competence of defendant, § 6.9(b)
    Equivocal assertion of rights, § 6.9(g)
    Express or implied, § 6.9(a)
    Implied waiver, §§ 6.9(a), 6.9(d)
    Limited assertion of rights, § 6.9(g)
    Limited waiver, § 6.9(e)
    Partial testimony, § 8.10(e)
    Police conduct, § 6.9(c)
    Qualified waiver, § 6.9(e)

SELF-INCRIMINATION, PRIVILEGE AGAINST—Cont'd
Waiver of rights—Cont'd
Untimely assertion of rights, § 6.9(g)
Warnings required
General discussion, § 6.8
Additional admonitions, § 6.8(d)
Content, § 6.8(a)
Grand jury witness, § 8.10(d)
Manner, § 6.8(c)
Proof, § 6.8(c)
Time and frequency, § 6.8(b)
Trial witness, §§ 2.10(b), 8.10(d)

SELF-REPRESENTATION
Counsel, Right to, this index

SENTENCING
General discussion, §§ 26.1-26.10
Administrative agency decisions, § 26.2(c)
Allocation of sentencing authority, § 26.2
Allocution, due process, § 26.4(g)
Appeals
Discretion of court, § 26.3(g)
Resentencing, § 26.7(b)
Burden of proof, due process, § 26.4(h)
Capital punishment, § 26.1(b)
Community release, § 26.1(d)
Concurrent Sentences, this index
Conditions, probation, § 26.9
Consecutive sentences, discretion of court, § 26.3(f)
Constitutional law
Counsel, assistance of, § 26.4(e)
Due process, below
Probation, § 26.9(b)
Dangerous offenders, special sentences, § 26.6(e)
Disclosure of presentence report, § 26.5(c)
Discretion of court
General discussion, § 26.3
Appellate review, § 26.3(g)
Challenge to unguided discretion, § 26.3(b)
Concurrent and consecutive sentences, § 26.3(f)
Guidelines for sentencing, § 26.3(e)
Mandatory minimum sentences, § 26.3(c)
Minimum sentences, § 26.3(c)
Presumptive sentencing, § 26.3(d)
Unguided discretion, §§ 26.3(a), 26.3(b)
Double jeopardy. Resentencing, below
Due process
General discussion, § 26.4

SENTENCING—Cont'd
  Due process—Cont'd
    Allocution, § 26.4(g)
    Burden of proof, § 26.4(i)
    Counsel, assistance of, § 26.4(e)
    Exceptional enhancements, heightened protection for, § 26.4(i)
    Notice, § 26.4(d)
    Procedural rights, consideration of defendant§ s exercise of, § 26.4(c)
    Rebuttal evidence, right to offer, § 26.4(g)
    Relevant information, range of, § 26.4(b)
    Reliability of sentencing information, § 26.4(f)
    Right to be heard, § 26.4(g)
    Williams v. New York, § 26.4(a)
  Elements or sentencing factors, § 26.4(i)
  Evidence at probation revocation hearing, § 26.10(c)
  Evidentiary standards, sentencing information, § 26.5(a)
  Exceptional enhancements, heightened protection for, § 26.4(i)
  Financial sanctions, § 26.1(f)
  Forfeitures, this index
  Guidelines for sentencing, § 26.4(i)
  Guidelines for sentencing, discretion of court, § 26.3(e)
  Incarceration, § 26.1(c)
  Intermediate sanctions, § 26.1(e)
  Judicial sentencing, § 26.2(a)
  Jury sentencing, § 26.2(b)
  Legislative structuring of sentencing, §§ 26.1, 26.2
  Mandatory minimum sentences, § 26.3(c)
  Minimum sentences, discretion of court, § 26.3(c)
  Notice, due process, § 26.4(d)
  Presentence report, §§ 26.5(b), 26.5(c)
  Presumption of vindictiveness, resentencing, § 26.8
  Presumptive sentencing, discretion of court, § 26.3(d)
  Probation
    General discussion, §§ 26.9, 26.10
    Basis for revocation, § 26.10(a)
    Challenges to conditions, § 26.9(c)
    Conditions, § 26.9
    Constitutional rights and conditions, § 26.9(b)
    Decision on revocation and consequences, § 26.10(d)
    Evidence at revocation hearing, § 26.10(c)
    Process for revocation, § 26.10(b)
    Revocation, §§ 12.4(f), 26.10
    Search and seizure, § 3.9(j)
  Procedure, §§ 26.1-26.10
  Rebuttal evidence, right to offer, § 26.4(g)
  Rebuttal of presumption of vindictiveness, resentencing, § 26.8(b)
  Recidivist procedures, § 26.6(b)
  Reconviction, resentencing following, § 26.7(a)

INDEX

SENTENCING—Cont'd
Relevant information, range of, § 26.4(b)
Reliability of sentencing information, due process, § 26.4(f)
Resentencing
  General discussion, §§ 26.7, 26.8
  Appeals, § 26.7(b)
  Other criminal conduct, sentencing based on, § 26.7(d)
  Pearce ruling, presumption of vindictiveness, § 26.8
  Presumption of vindictiveness, § 26.8
  Rebuttal of presumption of vindictiveness, § 26.8(b)
  Reconviction, resentencing following, § 26.7(a)
  Trial judge, resentencing by, § 26.7(c)
  Vindictiveness, § 26.8
Restitution, § 26.6(c)
Revocation of probation, § 26.10
Right to be heard, due process, § 26.4(g)
Sentencing information
  General discussion, § 26.5
  Disclosure of presentence report, § 26.5(c)
  Evidentiary standards, § 26.5(a)
  Presentence report, §§ 26.5(b), 26.5(c)
  Victim impact statement, § 26.5(d)
Special sentences
  General discussion, § 26.6
  Dangerous offenders, § 26.6(e)
  Forfeiture, § 26.6(d)
  Recidivist procedures, § 26.6(b)
  Restitution, § 26.6(c)
Structuring of sentencing, § 26.1
Victim impact statement, § 26.5(d)
Vindictiveness, resentencing, § 26.8

SEQUESTRATION OF JURY
General discussion, § 24.9(a)
Publicity, § 23.2(g)

SEQUESTRATION OF WITNESSES
General discussion, § 24.4(d)

SEVERANCE
Joinder and Severance, this index

SHACKLES
Prejudice and, § 24.2(e)

SILENCE OF DEFENDANT
Evidence, this index

SIXTH AMENDMENT
Confrontation, Right to, this index
Counsel, right to, § 11.1(a)

SIXTH AMENDMENT—Cont'd
Discovery by prosecution, constitutional limits on, **§ 20.4(f)**
Jury, this index
Public Trial, this index

SPECIAL INTERROGATORIES
Verdicts, **§ 24.10(a)**

SPECIAL LEGISLATION
Venue, **§ 16.1(e)**

SPECIAL PROSECUTOR
Challenges to and checks upon decision not to prosecute, **§ 13.3(f)**

SPECIAL SENTENCES
Sentencing, this index

SPECIAL VERDICTS
General discussion, **§ 24.10(a)**
Jury nullification, **§ 22.1(g)**

SPECIFICITY
Pleading, accusatory, **§ 19.3(b)**

SPEECH OR DEBATE CLAUSE
Search of congressman's office, **§ 3.4(a)**

SPEEDY TRIAL AND OTHER PROMPT DISPOSITION
General discussion, **§§ 18.1-18.5**
Attachment of right, **§ 18.1(c)**
Balancing test, **§ 18.2**
Constitutional law
General discussion, **§§ 18.1, 18.2**
Assertion of right, balancing test, **§ 18.2(d)**
Attachment of right, **§ 18.1(c)**
Balancing test, **§ 18.2**
Barker case, balancing test, **§ 18.2(a)**
Imprisonment of defendant, **§ 18.4(a)**
Interests involved, **§ 18.1(b)**
Length of delay, balancing test, **§ 18.2(b)**
Pre-accusation delays, **§ 18.5(b)**
Prejudice, balancing test, **§ 18.2(e)**
Reason for delay, balancing test, **§ 18.2(c)**
Remedy for violation, **§ 18.1(e)**
Waiver or forfeiture of right, **§ 18.1(d)**
Court rules. Statutes and court rules, below
Federal Speedy Trial Act of 1974, **§§ 18.3(b), 18.4(b)**
Forfeiture of right, **§ 18.1(d)**
Imprisonment of defendant
General discussion, **§ 18.4**
Constitutional right, **§ 18.4(a)**
Federal Speedy Trial Act of 1974, **§ 18.4(b)**

INDEX

SPEEDY TRIAL AND OTHER PROMPT DISPOSITION—Cont'd
Imprisonment of defendant—Cont'd
Interstate Agreement on Detainers, § **18.4(c)**
Uniform Mandatory Disposition of Detainers Act, § **18.4(d)**
Interstate Agreement on Detainers, § **18.4(c)**
Length of delay, balancing test, § **18.2(b)**
Post-trial delays, § **18.5(c)**
Pre-accusation delays, § **18.5(b)**
Prejudice, balancing test, § **18.2(e)**
Reason for delay, balancing test, § **18.2(c)**
Remedy for violation, § **18.1(e)**
Statutes and court rules
General discussion, § **18.3**
Federal Speedy Trial Act of 1974, § **18.3(b)**
State provisions, § **18.3(c)**
Statutes of limitation, § **18.5(a)**
Uniform Mandatory Disposition of Detainers Act, § **18.4(d)**
Waiver of right, § **18.1(d)**

STANDARD OF PROOF
Exclusionary Rules, this index
Presumptions and Burdens of Proof, this index

STANDBY COUNSEL
Self-representation, § **11.5(f)**

STANDING
Exclusionary Rules, this index

STARE DECISIS
Constitutional law, § **2.9(b)**

STATE LAWS
Authority of state, § **1.2(b)**
Criminal Justice System, this index
Variations, § **1.3(b)-(g)**

STATISTICS, CRIMINAL JUSTICE
Federal statistics, § **1.11(d)**
funded statistics, § **1.11(e)**
Judicial citations, § **1.11(a)**
Grand jury statistics, § **15.3(h)**
National statistics, § **1.11(b)**
Significance, § **1.11(a)**
State system statistics, § **11.1(c)**

STATUTES
General discussion, §§ **1.6(c), 1.6(e)**

STATUTES OF LIMITATION
General discussion, § **18.5(a)**

INDEX

STOP AND FRISK AND SIMILAR LESSER INTRUSIONS
Arrest, Search and Seizure, this index

STORED COMMUNICATIONS ACT
Compelling content information, § 4.8(d)
Compelling non-content information, § 4.8(c)
Providers of service, § 4.8(b)
Remedies for violation, § 4.8(f)
Voluntary disclosure of account information, § 4.8(e)

STRATEGY
Counsel, Right to, this index

STUDENTS
Search and seizure, § 3.9(k)

SUBJECTIVITY
Constitutional Law, this index

SUBPOENAS
Administrative agencies, § 8.1(c)
Evidence, § 24.3(f)
Fourth Amendment challenges, § 8.7
Grand jury, §§ 8.3(a)-8.3(c)
Justice Department, § 8.1(c)
Prosecutor's investigation, § 8.1(c)
Types of, § 8.3(b), (c)

SUBSTANTIAL CONTACTS
Venue, crime-committed formula, § 16.2(e)

SUBSTITUTION OF COUNSEL
Identification procedures, § 7.3(d)

SUBSTITUTION OF JUDGE
Impartiality of judge, § 22.4(e)

SUBTERFUGE AND RELATED MATTERS
Arrest, search and seizure, § 3.7(f)

SUCCESSIVE PETITIONS
Post Conviction Review, this index

SUPERVISORY AUTHORITY RULINGS
General discussion, § 1.7(i)

SURVEILLANCE
Search and seizure, § 3.2(j)
Wiretapping and Network Surveillance, this index

SUSPENSION CLAUSE
General discussion, § 28.2(a)

TARGET STANDING
Exclusionary rules, § 9.2(b)

INDEX

TARGET STANDING—Cont'd
Grand jury challenges, §§ 8.5(d), 8.8(e), 8.8(h)

THIRD PARTIES
Disclosure of presentence report, § 26.5(c)
Grand Jury, this index
Victims, this index

TIME AND DATE
Preliminary hearings, § 14.2(f)
Search, execution of warrant for, § 3.4(g)
Self-incrimination, warnings regarding privilege against, § 6.8(b)

TOTALITY OF CIRCUMSTANCE
Due process analysis, §§ 2.6(e), 2.7(b), (c)
Interrogations and confessions, voluntariness, § 6.2(c)

TRANSCRIPTS
Appeals, § 27.1(b)
Indictments, § 15.2(j)
Indigent persons, right to counsel, § 11.2(d)

TRANSPORTATION OFFENSES
Venue, crime-committed formula, § 16.2(e)

TRIAL
General discussion, §§ 24.1-24.11
Arguments of Counsel, this index
Closed proceedings, § 24.1(b)
Evidence, this index
Instructions to Jury, this index
Jury Trial, this index
Post-Verdict Motions, this index
Presence of Defendant, this index
Public trial, right to, § 24.1
Verdicts, this index

TWO WAY STREET MOVEMENT
Discovery and disclosure, § 20.1(d)

UNCONSTITUTIONALITY
Constitutional Law, this index

UNIFORM MANDATORY DISPOSITION OF DETAINERS ACT
General discussion, § 18.4(d)

UNIFORMITY
General discussion, § 1.3(b)

UNNECESSARILY SUGGESTIVE ELEMENT
Due process: totality of circumstances, § 7.4(b)

VARIANCES
Pleading, Accusatory, this index

INDEX

VEHICLES
Motor Vehicles, this index

VENIRE, CHANGE OF
Publicity, § 23.2(c)

VENUE
General discussion, §§ 16.1-16.3
Change of venue
General discussion, § 16.3
Convenience, §§ 16.3(c), 16.3(e)
Court, motion of, § 16.3(f)
Fair trial, §§ 16.3(b), 16.3(d)
Selection of transfer district, § 16.3(g)
Variations, § 16.3(a)
Constitutional policy, crime-committed formula, § 16.2(b)
Convenience, change of venue, §§ 16.3(c), 16.3(e)
Crime-committed formula
General discussion, §§ 16.1(c), 16.2
Constitutional policy, § 16.2(b)
Enterprise offenses, § 16.2(h)
Literalism, § 16.2(c)
Multiple participants, § 16.2(g)
Nature of offense, §§ 16.2(d)
Recurring questions, § 16.2(a)
Substantial contacts, § 16.2(e)
Transportation offenses, § 16.2(f)
Enterprise offenses, crime-committed formula, § 16.2(h)
Evidence of venue, § 16.1(g)
Fair trial, change of venue, §§ 16.3(b), 16.3(d)
Joinder, § 16.1(f)
Jurisdiction, distinguished, § 16.1(a)
Literalism, crime-committed formula, § 16.2(c)
Multiple participants, crime-committed formula, § 16.2(f)
Multi-venue offenses, § 16.1(d)
Nature-of-offense, crime committed formula, § 16.2(d)
Publicity, change of venue, §§ 22.2(b), 23.2(a)
Special legislation, § 16.1(e)
Substantial contacts, crime-committed formula, § 16.2(e)
Transportation offenses, crime-committed formula, § 16.2(f)
Vicinage, distinguished, § 16.1(b)
Waiver, § 16.1(h)

VERDICTS
General discussion, § 24.10
Inconsistent verdicts or findings, § 24.10(b)
Multi-theory verdicts, § 24.10(c)
Partial verdicts, § 24.10(d)
Special interrogatories, § 24.10(a)

INDEX

VERDICTS—Cont'd
Special verdicts, §§ 22.1(g), 24.10(a)

VICINAGE
Selection of jurors, § 22.2(e)
Venue, distinguished, § 16.1(b)

VICTIMS
Objectives of process, § 1.5(k)
Presence at trial, § 24.4(d)
Protective rules, §§ 14.4(b), 20.2(e), 20.3(h), (i)
Sentencing, victim impact statement, § 26.5(d)

VICTIMS' RIGHTS
Consultation with prosecutor
Re charging, § 13.1(a)
Re plea negotiations, § 21.3(f)
To attend trial, § 24.4(d)
To be heard
Bail hearing, § 12.1(f)
Plea hearing, § 21.3(f)
Sentencing, § 26.5(d)
Trial, through counsel, § 24.7(d)
Venue transfer, § 16.3(g)
To review of trial court rulings, §§ 21.3(f), 25.1(d), 26.7(b), 27.4(e)
Venue transfer district, § 16.3(g)

VINDICTIVE PROSECUTION
General discussion, §§ 13.5(a), 13.7(c)
Resentencing, § 26.8

VOIR DIRE
Jury Trial, this index

VOLUNTARINESS
Guilty pleas and plea bargains, § 21.4(b)
Interrogations and Confessions, this index

WAIVER
Appeal, right to, § 27.5(c)
Counsel, Right to, this index
Exclusionary Rules, this index
Grand jury, privilege against self-incrimination, § 8.10(e)
Guilty pleas and plea bargains, §§ 21.4(e), 21.6(a)
Identification procedures, right to counsel, § 7.3(d)
Indictment, right to prosecution by, § 15.1(f)
Interrogations and confessions, right to counsel, § 6.4(f)
Joinder and severance, § 17.3(d)
Jurisdiction, § 16.4(d)
Post conviction review, procedural default defense, § 28.4(c)
Preliminary hearing, right to, § 14.2(e)

INDEX

WAIVER—Cont'd
Presence of defendant, § 24.2(b)
Self-Incrimination, Privilege Against, this index
Speedy trial and other prompt disposition, § 18.1(d)
Venue, § 16.1(h)

WARNINGS
Self-Incrimination, Privilege Against, this index

WARRANTS
Arrest, Search and Seizure, this index

WEAPONS
Arrest, search and seizure, § 3.8(e)

WELFARE
Search and seizure, § 3.9(d)

WIRETAPPING AND NETWORK SURVEILLANCE
General discussion, §§ 4.1, 4.5
Application for orders, §§ 4.6(d), 4.7(b), 4.8(c0-(d)
Basic subscriber information, § 4.8(c)
Consent, §§ 4.6(*l*), 4.7(d), 4.8(e)
Contents, §§ 4.6(c)-(d), 4.6(b), 4.8(d)
Cordless phones, § 4.3(b)
Dialing, routing, addressing, and signaling information, § 4.7(c)
Electronic Communications Privacy Act, § 4.5
Electronic communications, § 4.6(a)
E-mail, §§ 4.4(c), 4.6(b), 4.8(d)
Foreign Intelligence Surveillance Act, § 4.9(b)
Fourth Amendment, § 4.2, 4.3, 4.4, 4.9(a)
Interception, § 4.6(b)
IP addresses, § 4.4(b)
Key loggers, § 4.6(a)
Mail, see Postal Mail
Oral communications, § 4.6(a)
Pen register and trap and trace device statute, § 4.7
Postal mail, § 4.2
Provider exception, § 4.6(*l*)
Remedies, § 4.6(m)-(*o*), 4.7(e), 4.8(f)
Stored Communications Act
  Compelled disclosure, §§ 4.8(c), 4.8(d)
  Electronic communications service, § 4.8(b)
  Remedies, § 4.8(f)
  Remote computing service, § 4.8(b)
  Voluntary disclosure, § 4.8(e)
Suppression, see Remedies
Text messages, § 4.3(c)
Title III, § 4.6
Wire communications, § 4.6(a)

INDEX